Baseball Prospectus 2011

THE ESSENTIAL GUIDE TO THE 2011 BASEBALL SEASON

EDITED BY STEVEN GOLDMAN

WITH BEN LINDBERGH AND STEPH BEE

STATISTICS BY COLIN WYERS

Tommy Bennett • Clifford J. Corcoran • Ken Funck

Steven Goldman • Kevin Goldstein • Jay Jaffe

Christina Kahrl • Ben Lindbergh • Marc Normandin

Jason Parks • John Perrotto • Eric Seidman • Matt Swartz

John Wiley & Sons, Inc.

Published by John Wiley & Sons, Inc., Hoboken, New Jersey
Published simultaneously in Canada

Editorial production by *Marra*thon Production Services. www.marrathon.net

ISBN 978-0-470-62206-3

Printed in the United States of America

10 9 8 7 6 5 4 3 2 1

Contents

Foreword

Joe Posnanski

I'm writing these words on the night that Cliff Lee stunned the baseball world (and us fans of money everywhere) by signing with the Philadelphia Phillies for significantly less cash than was offered by the New York Yankees. People are e-mailing and tweeting me every few seconds, asking if I'm as shocked as everyone else. I'm mostly shocked, I guess. But more than shocked, I'm desperately ready for baseball to begin.

And for me, every year, baseball begins with the big, brilliant, beautiful book you are holding in your hands right now.

It has been like this for me for a long time—going long before 1996, the year that the first Baseball Prospectus came out. I attended high school in Charlotte, N.C., in the early 1980s, years before that city became anything even resembling major league. The city's sports heartbeat then (and, in many ways, now) was college basketball played 115 or so miles north of the city. The only baseball in town was played by the Class AA Charlotte O's in Crockett Park, a lovely old park that promoters bragged was the last wooden ballpark in America. True, they were not quite as cocky about this little factoid when the park burned down.

Our family moved from Cleveland to Charlotte the year after a rugged third baseman named Cal Ripken hit .276 with moderate power for the O's. It would depress me to no end when people around town would talk about how they saw Cal Ripken play and knew he was destined for greatness—it was like Ripken's one year in Charlotte was our one and only connection to big-time baseball. And that, among other things, made me feel about a billion miles away from big-time baseball.*

**One of my few good Charlotte baseball memories came on K-Card Day. They actually handed out cardboard K-cards to wave for a Charlotte O's pitcher named Ken Dixon. In retrospect, Dixon was not an especially great strikeout pitcher in the minor leagues and he had only a short major league career (he did strike out 170 in his one full season). But Dwight Gooden had made the K-card all the rage and, hey, Ken Dixon was our K guy. Anyway, it was at least a connection.*

The only time I felt close to big-league baseball in Charlotte was when I was at our local newsstand, which had the rather haughty name Newsstand International. The Newsstand International was not exactly the United Nations—it was a little place in the strip mall close to the apartment where we lived. I spent many, many hours at Newsstand International, most of them getting yelled at by the old woman who worked there and did have an international accent ("No read! Buy!"). It was there that my baseball imagination soared. My favorite time of year was February, when the preview magazines slowly trickled out. This was before the explosion of fantasy baseball, so the magazines all had basically the same format:

- A couple of stories in front, one usually about someone like Don Mattingly or Nolan Ryan, and the other often about some new trend in baseball like "the RBI man."
- Predictions of who would win the major awards.
- A two-page preview for every team, complete with outdated rosters.
- Basic statistics for players in the back, most of them out of line.

That was it. That was a baseball magazine in the early 1980s. Except for one, they were pretty much all the same.* They were riddled with errors—both in judgment and in grammar—and they often seemed to know significantly less about the players and teams and baseball than I did as a not-especially-bright 14- or 15-year-old boy stuck in Charlotte.

**The one magazine that was different was called* Bill Mazeroski Baseball, *and it was by far my favorite magazine. I became a sportswriter at least in part because of* Bill Mazeroski Baseball. *In retrospect, the Maz was not that different from the others. It had stories in the front, previews for each team, rosters and stats just like the rest. And I remember it had this rather odd scoring system for ranking teams that I still don't fully understand almost 30 years later. But the writing was superior, and the mistakes were few, and in the back of the issue, they had this great section where Baseball Americas Allan Simpson broke down the top prospects for every team, making every prospect sound like the next great player in baseball. Man, I loved that section. It offered the single most crucial thing February can offer: hope.*

But here's what I remember most about those baseball magazines: I loved them. I knew even then that they were terrible. I knew some of them were *worse* than terrible. But I still cannot express how much I loved them. I cannot express the thrill of seeing a new one on the stand. I cannot express the excitement I would feel when any of the magazines—even the rattiest one, with paper so thin it would rip if you looked at it too hard—predicted that my Cleveland Indians might finish fourth (or, be still my heart, *third*) in the American League East. I loved them because they were about baseball, and it was February, and these were all I had. People have always romanticized the day pitchers and catchers report. I never cared about that. I cared about the day the newest baseball magazine hit the stands.

And, happily, I can tell you that even in my 40s, I still feel precisely that same thrill when I get my Baseball Prospectus. This book you're holding? This is when baseball begins.

I can also tell you that as a kid, I would not have been able to handle all the joy that is packed into this book. It would have been too much for me, like walking out of a movie theater into brilliant sunlight. My baseball world was quite narrow then—batting averages and ERA were on the very outskirts of my landscape—and I prayed at the baseball temple of grit and heart and leadership. I was not predisposed to looking at the game in a different way. Frankly, I lacked the imagination.

Fortunately, I also did not lack curiosity. I started reading the Prospectus in 1997. I guess that's about a year after five people—Clay Davenport, Gary Huckabay, Rany Jazayerli, Christina Kahrl, and Joe Sheehan—decided they were pretty much sick and tired of the nonsense people kept sputtering about baseball. As most of you know, my friend Bill James, with his incisive thinking and great wit, changed the way many people look at baseball in the 1980s and 1990s.

And in the late 1990s throughout the 2000s , the Prospectus folks blew things up. They have no use for myths. They have no tolerance for nonsense. They are here to inform, yes . . . to entertain, yes . . . but also to challenge. Reading the old baseball preview magazines was like listening to stories from a reasonably informed uncle who once played ball. Reading the Prospectus is like being in a good bar, with good food, the music low enough to make conversation possible, and having a glorious discussion and argument about teams and players and, above all, baseball.

And now, I will give you a quick rundown of what I do when I get my Prospectus. You, of course, are welcome to read it in any order you like:

1. I read the introduction, which is always written by some amazing writer.
2. I turn to the Kansas City Royals essay to see just how bad they're going to be this year.
3. I turn to the Cleveland Indians essay to see just how bad they're going to be this year.
4. I bounce around looking to see how some of my favorite players—Brian Bannister, Raul Ibanez, Curtis Granderson, Glen Perkins, Frankie Gutierrez, Carlos Beltran, among many others—can expect to do (based on that most wonderful of statistics and acronyms, PECOTA).
5. I look at the Top 101 prospects in baseball, which might be my favorite thing to do. I *love* looking at top prospects and trying to predict, according to the paragraph written and my own intuition, who will become the next big star in baseball. My choice last year was Phillippe Aumont because there has never been a big-leaguer named Phillippe, unless you count Deacon Phillippe, a remarkable control pitcher who won 20-plus games every year from 1899 to 1903.
6. I turn *back* to the Kansas City Royals section to see if I misread anything or if they're really going to be that bad.
7. I read the essays for every manager in baseball. I'm utterly fascinated by baseball managers.
8. I read the essays for each team. I try to save this for when spring training begins.

And all the while, I'm picking through the book, looking at the predictions, trying to remember what the abbreviations mean (WXRL?), grumbling about projections that seem too high or too low, reading about the players who will make the next season great. And all the while, I'm dreaming, thinking about players whose low BABIP suggests a comeback season, considering a pitcher's *stuff* and how it might translate into success, pondering a player's percentage chance of breaking out or collapsing as the new year begins. I have to tell you, it's just as much a thrill as it was when I was 14, minus the typos and clichés.

Look: Cliff Lee is about the join Roy Halladay, Roy Oswalt, and Cole Hamels. Could this be the greatest pitching staff in baseball history? I cannot wait for my Prospectus to tell me. I wonder if it will arrive early because I wrote this introduction.

One more thing: if you are in a bookstore right now, reading this introduction, considering your buying options, I have only three words for you, words that still linger in my mind from the days when I was reading baseball magazines in the Newsstand International: No read. Buy.

Preface

The art deco lobby of the Empire State Building in New York City contains a display of the seven so-called wonders of the ancient world—the Hanging Gardens of Babylon, the Statue of Zeus at Olympia, the Hanging Gardens of Babylon, the Colossus of Rhodes, the Mausoleum of Halicarnassus, the Lighthouse of Alexandria, the Temple of Artemis at Ephesus, and the Great Pyramid. Note that with the exception of the last, none of the wonders remains. History shows that though many great enterprises are begun, only a few are completed, and fewer still survive to become institutions.

Sixteen editions into its run, the annual Baseball Prospectus book would seem worthy of being called an institution. Not just long-lived in public approbation, it is one-of-a-kind in its thorough approach and, as such, almost certainly the *last* of its kind. Our covering 30 teams and upward of 1,500 players, major league and minor league alike, at a length that would have made Proust weep with envy, all in a single winter of intensive research and writing, would surely qualify as a kind of quixotic insanity in hands less fanatical than ours. And once we pass from the scene, such a book will surely not be attempted by anyone until such time as a like-minded aggregation of highly verbal, baseball-loving obsessive-compulsives who are foolish enough to be undaunted by the task can be found.

It is a cliché to say that a project has been a labor of love, but this book has been just that. The book is also the result of a kind of compulsion on our part, one that stems from a dedication so thoroughly pervasive that we feel compelled to disclose everything we know on the subject of baseball. We have an entire organization of such writers—men and women who love the game so much that they put aside their holidays to assemble the words and statistics of which you are about to partake.

In the course of my seven annuals, I have seen the cast here at Baseball Prospectus change dramatically. Some contributors have gone on to further success with other media outlets or major-league front offices. Others have drifted on to other endeavors that have taken them out of the public eye: people change, and their goals change with them. The writing life, even the *baseball* writing life, is not a lifetime avocation for everyone. While we should never overstate the hardship of sitting at a keyboard for a living, writing, and baseball writing of the kind that we practice, requires creativity, dedication, and sacrifice, and just as Thomas Paine identified sunshine patriots, there are also sunshine pamphleteers—in every group that aspires to institution-building, there are those who are natural joiners but lack the necessary dedication.

Yet, despite our evolving lineup, the book goes on. True institutions do not survive due to the efforts of any one or two people, but because a collective of believers holds true to their animating principle, thus forming an unbroken chain from founders to inheritors. In our case, we continue to focus on cutting through baseball's homilies—stomping the dead, whenever possible, along the way—in favor of realism and hard truths. Contrast that with the cats entrusted with the Mausoleum of Halicarnassus: it fell down and they lacked the will to put it back up. After a while, someone picked up the stones and auctioned them off; I believe they're going to be used as the foundation of the Marlins' new ballpark—nothing is too good for the Marlins (as long as they aren't picking up the check).

The book you hold is one side of an argument. Within its pages, literally thousands of positions are asserted: on the value of every player, on how their careers will develop, on which teams have a sensible plan to win and which are just hoping to get by on hot dog and beer revenues. We take positions on the worth of closers compared with other positions, on the real contributions made by some celebrated starters, and on the way the mainstream is increasingly—and, we believe, errantly—evaluating defense.

The other side of the argument is provided by you, the reader. At Baseball Prospectus, we believe in a lot of things—playing for the big innings, using your best relievers in the highest-leverage situations, and that Coca-Cola produced for the Mexican market is superior to that available domestically—but one thing we emphatically do *not* believe in is groupthink. Learning is always a two-way street. The roles of teacher and student are never fixed, but alternate constantly. Thus, as much as we believe in the things that we say in this book, and can back those statements up with hard evidence if challenged, we want this to be a book you can argue with. Whether you have that argument with the guy on the next barstool or with us at our Web site (www.baseballprospectus.com) or simply mutter quietly to yourself on the subway, we hope you will push back, consider alternatives, question. We'll be waiting for you.

As I said in our previous edition, this book serves multiple purposes. It can be a fantasy guide or a season preview, but to us, more than anything else, it is a snapshot of state-of-the-art thought on the art of building a winning baseball team. Over the course of the 2011 season, we will be constantly testing the beliefs espoused here, revising and improving them, all with the goal of knowing more, of being even more informed when you crack the cover on *Baseball Prospectus 2012*. Your responses will be part of that test, one we aim to pass.

So we invite you to read on. Agree with us when you think we're right, even if we said something critical about your favorite player. Disagree when you think we've erred. Most of all, let us know, because baseball has no room for know-it-alls, only for a growing community of knowledge with which we can all fight the received wisdom of those graybeards who don't know anything more about baseball than what was on the back of a 1977 Topps card.

If we can come together in that effort and succeed in expanding the reach of rationality even to a corner of our benighted society as insignificant as baseball, that would be a wonder worthy of the name, and an accomplishment worthy of any institution, especially a baseball book now enjoying its sweet-16 season.

Steven Goldman
Editor in Chief, Baseball Prospectus
New Jersey, January 10, 2011

Statistical Introduction

Colin Wyers

Going back well over a hundred years, those passionate about baseball have been keeping detailed records of games and players through box scores, season totals, career leaderboards, encyclopedias, and more. The study of baseball statistics, dubbed *sabermetrics* by Bill James, our patron saint, owes a lot to that meticulous collection of data, but the sheer volume of information we have at our disposal can cause as many problems as it solves for those of us interested in the study of baseball. After all, it is not enough for us to look at the data—we also have to figure out what the data are telling us. That means putting things in context, examining relationships, and drawing conclusions. In short, the point of sabermetrics is to take raw data and find ways to simply and concisely express the meaning of those observations.

Any effort to affix a single number to a player's contributions is a good place to start a discussion, but a poor place to finish it. Sabermetrics provides us with a framework for talking about baseball, but not all of the answers, not yet. As a result, we have not one, but two, criteria for how good any particular metric is:

How valid the metric is: how well it measures what it purports to measure, and

How expressive the metric is: how well it communicates its meaning to the consumer.

In compiling this book, we've spent a lot of time thinking about those two criteria. One of the conclusions we came to was that we had too many stats in the book; the different ways we had of measuring certain similar things were standing between the reader and the understanding we were trying to convey. Eliminating the redundancies has brought both additional clarity and room for more commentary.

Offense

At the core of everything we do to measure offense is **True Average** (formerly Equivalent Average), or **TAv**. We've made changes under the hood to increase this measure's accuracy. We've also apportioned varying degrees of credit for the quality of a player's outs, reflecting the fact that strikeouts are a little more damaging to a team's run-scoring chances than other kinds of outs, while sacrifice bunts are a bit less damaging.

What we haven't changed is how TAv is used and interpreted. This number, which is scaled to batting average, expresses a hitter's total value, giving greater weight to extra-base hits and walks rather than the one-dimensional concept of hitting that batting average espouses. Note that I've said *hitting*. We've removed stolen bases and times caught stealing from the TAv formula because we are now making our **Baserunning Runs** (BRR) a more prominent component of our player evaluation. For the first time, a player's full baserunning runs are being incorporated into his **Wins Above Replacement Player**. BRR accounts for the value of a player's ability to steal bases, but it also accounts for his ability to go from first to third on a single or to advance on a fly ball.

Defense

We have made several, more radical changes in terms of how we measure a player's fielding value. Historically, the fielding stats we have presented improved on the concept of range factor, but shared the same underpinnings. So we calculated a player's fielding value by comparing his plays made (in terms of his putouts and assists) with those of his peers at that position (with an adjustment for the tendencies of pitchers, handedness and ground-ball rate primarily among them).

The general trend in the sabermetric community has been toward stats based on zone data, where human stringers record the type of batted ball (grounder, liner, fly ball) and its presumed landing location. The trouble is that this zone data, unlike the sorts of data that we use in the calculation of the statistics you see in this book, was never made publicly available; it was recorded by commercial data providers who kept the raw figures private, only disclosing them to a select few who paid large sums for the privilege. As additional data has come to light, we've found that the zone-based defensive metrics don't hold up especially well to outside scrutiny. Different data providers can come to very different conclusions about the same events, depending on the providers' recording practices and vantage points. Moreover, two metrics based on the same data set can suggest radically different conclusions if the starting assumptions—assumptions that haven't been tested and that are derived from methods that can't be duplicated or verified by outside analysts—are different. For example, we've seen that the quality of the fielder can bias the data. Zone-based fielding metrics will tend to attribute more expected outs to good fielders than to bad fielders, irrespective of batted-ball distribution. Scorers who work in parks with high press boxes will tend to score more line drives than scorers who work in parks with low press boxes, and so on.

Because of the secrecy surrounding the underlying data, we've barely begun to scratch the surface of quantifying these problems and their effects. Consequently, we have abandoned our efforts to produce our own zone-based metric for inclusion in this book. Simply put, no evidence shows that the inclusion of zone-based data improves defensive metrics over the short run, and much evidence shows that incorporating the data causes severe distortions over the long run.

Instead, we've revised our **Fielding Runs Above Average** (FRAA) to incorporate play-by-play data, which allows us to study defense at a much more granular level without resorting to the subjective data used in some other fielding metrics. Simply put, we count how many plays each player made, as well as the expected number of plays for the average player at each position, based upon the pitcher's estimated ground-ball tendencies and the handedness of the batter. There are also adjustments for park and the base-out situations: depending on whether there are runners on base and the number of outs, the shortstop may position himself differently, and we account for that in the average baselines.

Let's compare how a few popular defensive metrics—Defensive Runs Saved (DRS), as measured by Baseball Info Solutions; Ultimate Zone Rating (UZR), developed by Mitchel Lichtman; and Total Zone (TZ), published by Sean Smith—have viewed Yankees shortstop Derek Jeter, according to old and new FRAA:

Year	DRS	UZR	TZ	Old FRAA	New FRAA
2003	-13	-4	-14	-23	-38
2004	-12	-0.7	5	-9	-17
2005	-28	-14.9	-5	-5	5
2006	-18	-7.3	-3	-11	-30
2007	-23	-17.9	-14	-19	-27
2008	-9	-0.3	-5	-9	-33
2009	2	6.4	4	-11	-34
2010	-13	-4.7	-10	-4	-22
Total	-114	-43.4	-42	-91	-196

Because of a phenomenon called *range bias*, the "advanced" zone metrics all severely underestimate Jeter's inability to make plays on ground balls: if you simply look at the distribution of ground-ball location measured by any data provider, you can see clustering around the primary fielder positions. If we look at objectively collected data on batted-ball distribution, such as that offered by Sportvision's HITf/x system, which uses the same methods employed by the company's PITCHf/x system to track the location of the pitched ball within approximately an inch, we see a very different distribution, which is mostly smooth. This is explained by the tendency for an observer (absent better reference points) to use the location of the fielder as a guide to where the ball was hit.

That doesn't mean the distribution of batted balls is unimportant to measuring fielding value, but that a way of accurately recording that information has yet to be devised. Our new FRAA uses a great deal of situational information to estimate batted-ball distribution, but over the short run, there is still a great deal of uncertainty involved. Therefore, we have regressed the spread of FRAA values published, in order to reflect that uncertainty (and in order to put greater emphasis on things we can measure with far less uncertainty, like offense and baserunning, in the calculation of WARP).

As you can see, we've made a clean break from much of the rest of the sabermetric community on defense, in that we're not going to ask you to accept conclusions that are based on new and as-yet-untested data. Over the next few years, we expect to see exciting discoveries in fielding analysis, as new means of collecting information arise and analysts abandon (or reexamine) previously collected data. Until then, it is best to approach any purported measure of defense—including ours—with some degree of caution. In the player comments, you will see player evaluations that are based on our fielding metrics, but are not slavishly devoted to them. For now, that's the best we (or anyone else) can do.

Pitching

Of course, new findings about fielding influence how we measure pitching as well. Probably the most radical observation concerning either was made by Voros McCracken: "There is little if any difference among major-league pitchers in their ability to prevent hits on balls hit in the field of play." This was an extremely controversial finding when first published, but it has been largely validated by subsequent research. McCracken and others went forth from that finding to come up with a variety of defense-independent pitching measures, statistics that attempt to isolate the pitcher from the work of his supporting players.

The trouble is that many efforts to separate pitching from fielding have also somehow separated pitching from pitching, looking at only a handful of variables (typically, walks, strikeouts, and home runs, the "three true outcomes") in isolation from the situations in which they occurred. With our new pitching statistic, **Fair Run Average**, or **FRA** (the term *Fair RA* may seem familiar, but this is an entirely new metric), we've taken a pitcher's actual results—not just what happened, but *when* it happened as well—and adjusted them for the quality of a pitcher's defensive support, as measured by FRAA.

Now, applying FRAA to pitchers in this sense is easier than applying it to fielders. We don't have to worry about figuring out which fielder is responsible for making an out; we only need to identify the likelihood of an out's being made, so there is far less uncertainty here than there is in fielding analysis.

That's not the same as no uncertainty, of course. Again, we're right at the beginning of a renewed effort to study the impact of batted-ball distribution on fielding and in turn how pitchers can affect batted-ball distribution. We are finding that "little if any difference" does not, in fact, mean no difference, and some pitchers may have an ability to prevent hits on balls in play. We are now struggling to improve our ability to figure out who those pitchers are, given short time spans, be they a single season or even several seasons.

Fair RA means exactly that, a number scaled to a pitcher's runs allowed per game, not his earned runs allowed per game. The concept of an "earned" run seems less and less expressive as we learn how little a team's errors tell us about the kind of support a pitcher got from his fielders. In addition, looking only at earned run average (ERA) tends to overrate three kinds of pitchers over time:

Pitchers who play in parks where scorers tend to hand out more errors: the differences in error rates between parks tells us that scorers can in fact differ significantly in how likely they are to score any given play as an error.

Ground-ball pitchers: because a substantial proportion of errors occur on ground balls, ERA will tend to overrate ground-ball pitchers compared with fly-ball pitchers of equal ability.

Pitchers who aren't very good: good pitchers tend to allow fewer unearned runs than do bad pitchers, for the simple reason that good pitchers have more ways to get out of jams than bad pitchers do—a good pitcher is more likely to get a strikeout to end the inning and less likely to give up a home run.

In short, ERA (and metrics scaled to ERA) provides a distorted picture of what a pitcher actually accomplished. This is something we've long preached at Baseball Prospectus, and by starting to move away from ERA and toward FRA in our advanced pitching metrics, we hope to encourage others to adopt a more nuanced approach to pitcher evaluation.

Projection

Of course, many of you aren't turning to this book just for a look at what a player has done, but for a look at what a player is going to do: the "deadly accurate" PECOTA projections mentioned in bright yellow type on the cover.

PECOTA, initially developed by Nate Silver, consists of three parts:

Major-league equivalencies, which allow the use of minor-league stats to project how a player will perform in the majors;

Baseline forecasts, which use weighted averages and regression to the mean to produce an estimate of a player's true talent level;

A career-path adjustment, which incorporates information about how comparable players' stats changed over time.

That basic approach is still retained, but we've made a series of refinements to improve on the process. PECOTA may again someday declare the end of Ichiro, for instance, but it won't be this year—he's projected for another season of more than 200 hits.

Now that we've gone over how the book has changed from previous years, let's look at what's inside the book.

The Team Prospectus

The bulk of this book is composed of team chapters, with one for each of the 30 major-league franchises. On the first page of each chapter, you will be greeted by a box laying out some key statistics for each team.

DIAMONDBACKS PROSPECTUS

2010 W-L: 65-97, 5th in NL West

Pythag	.425	25th	**Ballpark:** Chase Field (3-yr. PF: 105). It's the elevation and dimensions that leaves pitchers all wet, not the pool
RS/G	4.4	16th	
RA/G	5.2	3rd	
TAv	.266	19th	**2010:** History's whiff-happiest lineup struggles to supply leads that baseball's worst bullpen can't preserve
BRR	-2.8	20th	
FRA	5.27	30th	
DER	1.59	15th	**2011:** Towers tries to put a pen together while hoping for more young hitters
DL	583	4th	
B-Age	26.6	2nd	
P-Age	27.9	14th	**Action Items:** Brother, can you spare a reliever, a bat that makes contact, and someone to keep the fifth-starter seat warm?
Salary	$60.7	25th	
M$/MW	$3.09	22nd	

2010 W-L is exactly as it sounds—a straight and unadjusted tally of wins and losses. **Pythag** tallies wins and losses on an adjusted basis by using the runs scored per game (RS/G) and allowed per game (RA/G) by a team in a season, running them through a refined version of Bill James' Pythagorean formula developed by David Smyth and Brandon Heipp.

A team's **runs scored** (RS) is accompanied by **True Average** (TAv)and our **Baserunning Runs (BRR)**, to provide a picture of how a team scored its runs. For run-prevention ability, we present a team's **Fair Run Average (FRA)** and **Fielding Runs Above Average,** which for the purposes of the team box, we have simplified to **Defensive Runs (DER).**

We've also incorporated several new statistics into this year's team summaries. **DL** refers to how many days a team's players logged on the disabled list over the course of the season. **B-Age** and **P-Age** tell us the average age of a team's hitters and pitchers, respectively.

Salary refers to a team's total payroll, in millions of dollars. We've supplemented that with each team's **marginal dollars per marginal win (M$/MW)**, a metric created by Doug Pappas to show how efficiently a team has been spending its money.

Position Players

After an opening essay, each chapter moves on to the player comments. Position players are listed first, in alphabetical order, and each player is listed with the major-league team with which he finished the 2010 season, meaning that free agents who eventually changed teams will be listed under their previous employer. As an example, take a gander at Albert Pujols' data at the bottom of the page.

The player-specific sections begin with biographical information before proceeding to the actual performance data. Other than cups of coffee at the various minor-league levels—trimmed out in the interest of space and in accordance with small-sample-size theory—all relevant seasons and partial seasons will be listed. The column headers begin with more standard information like **year**, **team**, **level (LVL)** (majors or minors, and which level of the minors), **age**, and the raw, untranslated tallies found on the back of a baseball card: **Plate Appearances (PA), Runs (R), Doubles (2B), Triples (3B), Home Runs (HR), Runs Batted In (RBI), Walks (BB), Strikeouts (SO), Stolen Bases (SB),** and **Caught Stealing (CS).**

Following those are the untranslated triple-slash rate statistics: **batting average (AVG), on-base percentage (OBP),** and **slugging percentage (SLG)**. Their "slash" nickname is derived from the occasional presentation of slash-delimitation, as in noting that Joey Votto hit .324/.424/.600. Each of the three statistics is flawed on its own, but put together, they describe the "shape" of a hitter's production—whether he's a slap-hitting Punch-and-Judy type, an all-or-nothing power hitter, or simply an all-around amazing hitter like Albert Pujols.

The next column is **True Average (TAv)**. As with batting average, a .350 mark is Pujolsian; a .300 mark is very good; a .260 TAv is league-average, and at around .230, you're talking about replacement-level players, waiver-wire fodder, and Quadruple-A types. This number is corrected for league offensive level and quality, as well as the parks in which each hitter played.

BABIP stands for **Batting Average on Balls in Play**. An especially low or high BABIP may mean that a hitter was especially lucky or unlucky . . . but it also may not. Line-drive hitters will tend to have especially high BABIPs from season to season, as will speedy hitters able to beat out more grounders for base hits.

Next is **Baserunning Runs (BRR)**. As described above, BRR covers all sorts of baserunning accomplishments, not just stolen bases.

The last column is **WARP**, or **Wins Above Replacement Player**. Note that here, we diverge from past volumes of the BP annual and have left out VORP, or Value Over Replacement Player, altogether. This doesn't mean that we've discarded the underpinnings of VORP; we simply determined that it wasn't necessary to have two ways of measuring the same player's contributions relative to replacement. WARP combines a player's batting runs above average (derived from a player's True Average), BRR, FRAA, an adjustment based on position played, and a credit for plate appearances. (This credit is based on the difference between the "replacement level" (derived from looking at the quality of players added to a team's roster after the start of the season) and the league average.)

Pitchers

Now let's look at how pitchers are presented.

The first line and the YEAR, TEAM, LVL, and AGE columns are the same as in the hitter's example above. The next set of columns–Wins (W), Losses (L), Saves (S), Games (G), Games

Albert Pujols **1B**

Born: **1/16/1980** Age: **31**
Bats: **R** Throws: **R** Height: **6' 3"** Weight: **210**
Breakout: **1%** Improve: **35%** Collapse: **3%**
Attrition: **5%** MLB: **99%**

Comparables:
Mark Teixeira, Lance Berkman, David Ortiz (62)

YEAR	TEAM	LVL	AGE	PA	R	2B	3B	HR	RBI	BB	SO	SB	CS	AVG/OBP/SLG	TAv	BABIP	BRR	FRAA	WARP
2008	SLN	MLB	28	641	101	44	0	37	116	104	54	7	3	.357/.462/.653	.373	.340	-1.2	1B 20, 2B 0	9.7
2009	SLN	MLB	29	700	124	45	1	47	135	115	64	16	4	.328/.443/.659	.366	.299	1.0	1B 26	10.6
2010	SLN	MLB	30	700	115	39	1	42	118	103	76	14	4	.312/.414/.596	.344	.297	2.8	1B 14	7.8
2011	*SLN*	*MLB*	*31*	*671*	*113*	*39*	*0*	*41*	*121*	*103*	*62*	*11*	*4*	*.322/.429/.618*	*.350*	*.299*	*-0.3*	*1B 19, 2B 0*	*8.1*

Roy Halladay

Born: **5/14/1977** Age: **34**
Bats: R Throws: R Height: **6′ 6″** Weight: **225**
Breakout: **18%** Improve: **48%** Collapse: **18%**
Attrition: **4%** MLB: **94%**

Comparables:
Hiroki Kuroda, Javier Vazquez, Gaylord Perry (47)

YEAR	TEAM	LVL	AGE	W	L	SV	G	GS	IP	H	HR	BB	SO	EqBB9	EqSO9	GB%	BABIP	WHIP	ERA	FRA	WARP
2008	TOR	MLB	31	20	11	0	34	33	246	220	18	39	206	1.4	7.5	54%	.284	1.10	2.78	3.29	6.4
2009	TOR	MLB	32	17	10	0	32	32	239	234	22	35	208	1.3	7.8	51%	.306	1.15	2.79	2.93	7.7
2010	PHI	MLB	33	21	10	0	33	33	250[2]	231	24	30	219	1.1	7.9	53%	.290	1.07	2.44	2.66	8.1
2011	*PHI*	*MLB*	*34*	*14*	*8*	*0*	*32*	*32*	*239*	*229*	*24*	*37*	*183*	*1.4*	*6.9*	*51%*	*.294*	*1.11*	*3.05*	*3.32*	*6.8*

Started (GS), Innings Pitched (IP), Hits (H), Home Runs (HR), Walks (BB), Strikeouts (SO), walks per nine innings (BB9), and strikeouts per nine innings (SO9)—are the actual, unadjusted, cumulative stats compiled by the pitcher during each season.

Next is GB%, which is the percentage of all batted balls that were hit on the ground, including both outs and hits. The average GB% for a major-league pitcher in 2010 was about 45%; a pitcher with a GB% anywhere north of 50% can be considered a ground-ball pitcher. As mentioned above, the classification of ground balls is based on the observations of human stringers and can be skewed by a several factors. We've included GB% as a guide, but please approach it skeptically.

BABIP is the same statistic presented for batters, but it often tells you more in the case of pitchers, since most hurlers have very little control over their Batting Average on Balls in Play. A high BABIP is most likely due to a poor defense or bad luck, rather than a pitcher's own abilities, and may be a good indicator of a potential rebound. A typical league-average BABIP hovers around .295 to .300.

WHIP and **ERA** are common to most fans, with the former measuring the number of walks and hits allowed on a per-inning basis, while the latter prorates runs allowed on a nine-inning basis. Neither is translated or adjusted in any way.

Fair Run Average (**FRA**) is the basis of **WARP** for pitchers. Significantly, incorporating play-by-play data allows us to set different replacement levels for starting pitchers and relievers. Relief pitchers have several advantages over starters. They can give their best effort on every pitch, and hitters have fewer chances to pick up on what the pitcher is doing. Consequently, it's significantly easier to find decent replacements for relief pitchers than it is for starting pitchers, and that's reflected in the replacement level for each.

We've also started crediting starters for pitching deeper into games and "saving the pen." A starting pitcher who's able to last deep into games effectively allows a manager to keep his worst relievers in the pen and bring his best relievers out to preserve a lead.

All of this means that WARP values for relief pitchers, especially closers, will be lower than what you're probably used to seeing and may conflict with traditional feelings about relief aces coming in and "saving" the game. But the save does not describe how teams win games. Saves award extra credit to the closer for what his teammates did to put him in a save spot to begin with; WARP is incapable of feeling excitement over a successful save and thus judges closers dispassionately.

PECOTA

Both pitchers and hitters have **PECOTA** projections for next season, as well as a set of biographical details that describe the performance of that player's comparable players, according to PECOTA.

The 2011 line is the PECOTA projection for the player in the upcoming season. Note that the player is projected into the league and park context as indicated by his team. All PECOTAs represent a player's projected major-league performance. The numbers beneath the player's name—Breakout, Improve, Collapse, and Attrition—are also part of PECOTA and estimate the likelihood of changes in performance relative to a player's previously established level of production, based upon the performance of the comparable players:

- **Breakout Rate** is the percent chance that a player's production will improve by at least 20 percent relative to the weighted average of his performance over his most recent seasons.
- **Improve Rate** is the percent chance that a player's production will improve at all relative to his baseline performance. A player who is expected to perform just the same as he has in the recent past will have an Improve Rate of 50 percent.
- **Collapse Rate** is the percent chance that a position player's equivalent runs produced per PA will decline by at least 25 percent relative to his baseline performance over his past three seasons.
- **Attrition Rate** operates on playing time rather than performance. Specifically, it measures the likelihood that a player's playing time will decrease by at least 50 percent relative to his established level.

Breakout Rate and Collapse Rate can sometimes be counterintuitive for players who have already experienced a radical change in their performance levels. Note also that the projected decline in a player's rate performances might not suggest an expected decline in underlying ability or skill, but rather might reflect an anticipated correction following a breakout season.

The final pieces of information, listed just to the right of the player's Attrition Rate, are his three highest-scoring comparable players as determined by PECOTA, and a similarity score from 0 to 100 describing how similar a player's comparables are to him. Occasionally, a player's top comparables will not be representative of the larger sample that PECOTA uses. Also, established major leaguers are compared to other major leaguers only, while minor-league players may be compared to major-league or minor-league players, with PECOTA strongly preferring the latter. All comparables represent a snapshot of how the listed player was performing at the same age as the current player, so if a 23-year-old hitter is compared to Sammy Sosa, he's actually being compared to a 23-year-old Sammy Sosa, not the decrepit Orioles version of Sosa, or to Sosa's career as a whole.

The Managers' Statistics

Each team chapter ends with a manager's comment and data breaking down his tactical tendencies. Though it is often difficult to isolate a manager's contributions to a team, examining aspects of his squad's performance helps to determine what a manager likes to do, even if we are still precluded from translating that information into actual wins and losses.

Following the **year**, **team**, and the actual **win-loss record (W-L)**, **Pythag +/-** shows by how many games the team under- or overperformed its Pythagenpat record. Scioscia's Angels exceeded their projected record by four games and exceeded it in the previous two seasons as well. That isn't necessarily an endorsement of Scioscia—keep in mind that Pythag +/- is a mathematical expression of team performance, not an interpretation of the manager's work, even though it has become commonplace to attribute Actual/Pythag discrepancies to the skipper.

Pitching staff usage follows, first with **Avg PC** reporting the **average pitch count** of the manager's starting pitchers with the subsequent **100+**P and 120+P offering the number of games in which the starters exceeded certain pitch thresholds. QS is the total number of quality starts—a start of at least six innings and with no more than three runs allowed—that a manager received from his starting pitchers. Blown Quality Starts (BQS), a Baseball Prospectus stat, measures games in which the starter delivered a quality start through six innings but remained in the game to allow four or more runs. A BQS, however, is not necessarily an indictment of the manager's abilities or tactics—a number of factors ranging from excellent offensive support to extremely poor bullpen support can lead a manager to leave his starter in a game after the pitcher has thrown six quality innings. Conversely, the decision by a manager to "bank" quality starts by restricting his starters to only six innings can have downsides as well, since it increases both his bullpen's workload and the opportunity for the pen to blow a game in which a starter was cruising.

Speaking of bullpen support, the next stats in the manager table tally how many pitching changes a manager made over the course of the season (**REL**) and how many times the reliever called upon didn't allow any runners, his own or inherited, to score (**REL w Zero R**). Bequeathed runners also count against REL w Zero R, meaning that relievers who exit with runners on who subsequently score prevent a manager from "padding" his tally here. Concluding the pitching section, **IBB** is simply the number of intentional walks the manager ordered during the given season, which can definitely be a mark of managerial strategy as long as outliers like Albert Pujols are accounted for.

Managers do more than manage pitchers, however; their usage of a bench can lead to added or lost performance. **Subs** lets us know the number of defensive replacements each manager employed throughout the regular season, while **PH**, **PH Avg**, and **PH HR** report the offensive statistics of pinch-hitters called upon. We then turn to the so-called small-ball tactics, starting with the running game. The manager's aggressiveness on the bases is broken down by successful steals of second and third base (**SB2, SB3**) and times caught (**CS2, CS3**). We also provide the number of sacrifices a team attempted (**SAC Att**) and its success rate (**SAC %**). Be sure to keep in mind the differences between leagues, as National League sacrifice attempts are greatly inflated by the fact that NL pitchers hit. To correct for this, we list the number of times that each manager coaxed a successful sacrifice

MANAGER: MIKE SCIOSCIA

YEAR	TEAM	W-L	Pythag +/-	Avg PC	100+ P	120+ P	QS	BQS	REL	REL w Zero R	IBB	Subs	PH	PH Avg	PH HR	SB2	CS2	SB3	CS3	SAC Att	SAC %	POS SAC	Squeeze	Swing	In Play
2008	ANA	100-62	11	99.6	85	0	87	5	383	249	32	46	74	.182	0	109	38	19	8	46	69.6%	32	3	147	113
2009	ANA	97-65	4	97.1	83	1	70	9	434	269	35	48	79	.308	2	124	57	22	5	64	67.2%	41	4	180	134
2010	ANA	80-82	1	102.4	107	3	91	7	410	267	33	33	93	.171	0	90	39	14	10	77	54.5%	41	5	157	126

from a position player (**POS SAC**), which allows for comparisons between the two leagues. We finish up with **Squeeze**, which counts the number of successful squeeze plays the team executed over the season. Finally, a couple of statistics attempt to measure the manager's hit-and-run tactics. **Swing** is the number of times a hitter swung at a pitch while the runners were in motion, while **In Play** reflects how many times a manager's hitters swung and made contact while those runners were off to the races. Granted, swings on steal attempts do not always equate to hit-and-run attempts, but managers who greatly deviate from the average can be called staunch proponents or opponents of the strategy.

Arizona Diamondbacks

Somewhere in Arizona last season, a young Diamondbacks fan with an 8:30 bedtime fell asleep after the fifth inning of every game. This fan slept soundly, since his favorite team did its best work before the sixth. Had all their games ended after a combined total of 30 outs had been recorded, the Diamondbacks would have finished 71-69. Unfortunately, their leads fell apart after our small friend went to sleep. The potentially winning record after five fell off steeply to 67-74 after six innings, 61-78 after seven, 65-81 after eight, and 60-89 after nine, with a 5-8 performance in extra innings for good measure.

The culprit behind the D'Backs' slow deaths in game after game was a historically bad bullpen that left no means of blowing a lead unexplored, up to and including a walk-off balk. Arizona's relief corps sported a collective 5.74 ERA, more than a run higher than that of the second-worst unit in the league (4.72) and nearly two full runs higher than that of the average major-league bullpen (3.94). Only one Arizona pitcher with at least five innings to his name posted an ERA under 4.26 in relief: D. J. Carrasco managed a 3.18 mark in 22 2/3 innings, but his 5.63 Fair Run Average suggests that he was fortunate to have finished with a figure that low. His comrades weren't so lucky.

DIAMONDBACKS PROSPECTUS

2010 W-L: 65-97, 5th in NL West

Pythag	.425	25th
RS/G	4.4	16th
RA/G	5.2	3rd
TAv	.266	19th
BRR	-2.8	20th
FRA	5.27	30th
DER	1.59	15th
DL	583	4th
B-Age	26.6	2nd
P-Age	27.9	14th
Salary	$60.7	25th
M$/MW	$3.09	22nd

Ballpark: Chase Field (3-yr. PF: 105). It's the elevation and dimensions that leaves pitchers all wet, not the pool

2010: History's whiff-happiest lineup struggles to supply leads that baseball's worst bullpen can't preserve

2011: Towers tries to put a pen together while hoping for more young hitters

Action Items: Brother, can you spare a reliever, a bat that makes contact, and someone to keep the fifth-starter seat warm?

Table 1. In Need of Relief: The 2010 Diamondbacks Bullpen

Reliever	IP	ERA
Aaron Heilman	72.0	4.50
Blaine Boyer	57.0	4.26
Juan Gutierrez	56.7	5.08
Esmerling Vazquez	53.7	5.20
Chad Qualls	38.0	8.29
Sam Demel	37.0	5.35
Bullpen Total	439.0	5.74

On the relatively infrequent occasions when the D'backs managed to preserve leads long enough to engender save situations, they handed the ball to one of three people. At first, they went with the experienced option in Chad Qualls, but he was stripped of his high-leverage outings (and subsequently traded to the Rays) after averaging around a run allowed per inning well into June. Aaron Heilman got the next shot and promptly blew a bevy of saves. Eventually, the baton was passed to Juan Gutierrez; he wasn't efficient, but his work constituted an improvement compared with that of his predecessors. Of course, even had Arizona identified a strong stopper, he wouldn't have been able to enter most games in time to stop the fatal hemorrhaging.

The theory behind building a bullpen has long constituted a moving target for baseball analysts. Ever since the likes of Iron Man Joe McGinnity passed from the scene and pitchers stopped completing 90 percent of their starts, the importance of good relievers has been obvious. However, given the variable nature of bullpen performance, teams that throw money at the problem often fail to assemble effective relief units; what's more, the outlay required to make the attempt deprives them of resources that could have been expended on less fungible areas, adding a substantial opportunity cost to the equation.

Evaluating bullpen performance is much easier than projecting it; with the aid of retrospective statistics, we can get a clear picture of the depths to which the Snakes' relievers sunk, even if we couldn't have seen the full extent of their demise coming. The Diamondbacks had the worst bullpen in baseball last season, but what magnified their failures was how far removed every other set of relievers was from their vicinity.

Table 2. Snakebit: Diamondbacks Bullpen Performance by WXRL

2010 Bullpen Ranking		
Rk	Team	WXRL
1	Padres	16.7
2	Rays	12.7
3	Giants	11.7
4	Rangers	10.4
5	Mets	9.4
—		
26	Brewers	4.1
27	Marlins	3.6
28	Orioles	3.1
29	Mariners	2.2
30	D'Backs	-4.4

This list contains more than one item of interest for Arizona. The best bullpen in 2010 belonged to the Padres. Though GM Kevin Towers was fired by the Friars prior to the 2009 season, he assembled the major components of their well-oiled bullpen machine during his 15-year tenure. And where is he now? Scan to the bottom of that list. His focus is now fixed squarely on the team that selected him to oversee its production of *Extreme Makeover: Bullpen Edition.*

Table 3. Bad Company: The Ten Worst Bullpens, 1954–2010

Rk	Team	Year	WXRL
1	Royals	1999	-7.7
2	Braves	1973	-6.6
3	Braves	1990	-4.8
4	D'Backs	2010	-4.4
5	Yankees	1971	-4.3
6	Astros	1967	-3.6
7	Mets	1993	-3.5
8	Mets	1978	-3.0
9	Angels	1974	-3.0
10	Cardinals	1980	-2.8
10	Cardinals	1980	-2.8

Towers has a huge challenge in front of him: repairing the fourth-worst relief unit to take the field between 1954 and 2010. Some team had to be the worst in the league, but the 6.6-win difference between the Diamondbacks and the runner-down was staggering. The 11.4-win difference between Arizona and the average team suggests that if the Diamondbacks had mustered even an average bullpen, they could have won roughly 76 or 77 games. With a few breaks, they could have pushed that to .500. Although that happy vision didn't come close to materializing, the personnel whom Towers has been handed for 2011 look less hopeless than the players who dragged the team down last season. While Gutierrez and Sam Demel are the only holdovers who seem likely to have roles in the 2011 pen, the club has several in-house relief prospects who might prove capable of offering aid. Towers can also solicit outside assistance, as he did in the December swap that sent Mark Reynolds to Baltimore in return for bullpen arms David Hernandez and Kam Mickolio, and in the signing of J. J. Putz, which should bring last season's unsuccessful closer carousel to a halt.

Even if Towers succeeds in correcting the 2010 team's most glaring weakness in the span of a single offseason, engineering a dramatic bullpen overhaul, the fact remains that 80 wins doesn't get a team to the playoffs. The bullpen wasn't the only area in which Arizona stood out in a negative sense: the new GM has also expressed understandable concern over the team's extremely high strikeout rate. The average K-rate for senior-circuit clubs rested at 19.3 percent last season, but the Snakes went down watching or whiffing 24.7 percent of the time, well above the second-most-frequent offenders, the Marlins (22.2 percent). That rate happened to be the highest in history, but it shouldn't have come as a shock: the Diamondbacks of 2008 and 2009 finished 10th and 11th all-time, respectively, and all three teams shared some of the same strikeout suspects.

Stratospheric strikeout rates are a staple of the modern game, but even after adjusting for year and league, last season's Snakes qualified for the fourth-highest rate, whiffing 28 percent more frequently than the average team. How have teams with similarly high strikeout rates fared? Pooling together all teams with a strikeout rate at least 15 percent higher than their respective leagues' yields an aggregate winning percentage of .449. The strikeouts weren't the sole cause of that shoddy play—the ERAs of those teams were a collective seven percent worse than their competition. As a result, these teams weren't going to set the world on fire regardless of their whiffing, but striking out at an excessive rate exacerbated their flaws, dooming them to losing records.

The primary source of the damage caused by a contact-challenged approach is the compounding effect that stacked strikeouts can have on a lineup. It's one thing if Reynolds repeatedly breaks his own single-season strikeout record and no one else gets in on the act, but when the majority of a lineup falls prey to empty at-bats of this sort, highly volatile run-scoring can result. The Diamondbacks scored three or more runs in an inning at virtually the same rate as the rest of the league, but managed two or fewer runs in an inning much more frequently than their NL counterparts. Their ability to mash enabled them to put up a big inning here and there, and their lack of contact saved them from a few double plays over the course of the season, but their feast-or-famine approach often prevented them from plating runners in key situations and cut down on their crooked numbers.

Sabermetric orthodoxy holds that strikeouts are essentially like any other out, so it would be easy to dismiss Towers' concerns. To do so would also be a mistake, since in this instance, the sabermetric orthodoxy obscures a larger flaw in roster construction, in that lineups that strike out as often as Arizona's haven't performed well historically. When the hitters made contact, they were dynamite—posting a .312 BABIP well above the .299 league average—but they did so at a historically low rate. In other words, the team's offense resembled that of Reynolds' writ large, which made for middling results.

So what can the Diamondbacks do to rectify their whiff-prone ways? Unfortunately, their fate and those of their strikeout-happy players appear intertwined. Much of the reason for the prevailing optimism about the club in recent years was the presence of young talent at each position. Unfortunately, most of that talent can't make contact. In addition, many of those youngsters stumbled out of the gate instead of flourishing immediately. Some have improved, whereas others have regressed, with the result being a team that hasn't hit as expected. On one hand, Stephen Drew re-emerged as a solid power threat at shortstop after a disappointing 2009. On the other, Justin Upton followed up his .532 slugging percentage from 2009 with a .442 SLG last season, negating much of the benefit from Drew's improvement. While Chris Young seemed to figure out what had turned his swing into a can-of-corn machine in 2009, Mark Reynolds dropped 24 extra-base hits and 110 points from his slugging percentage, wiping out much of the gain from Young's resurgence. Reynolds' departure is a major step toward a more contact-filled future in Arizona, although his replacement, Melvin Mora, isn't a long-term solution and barely qualifies as an acceptable stopgap.

Plenty of talent remains in the lineup, and none of the returning regulars has reached the wrong side of 30; most are under team control for at least three more years. As of this write-up, the lineup's greatest problem—apart from its systemically flawed plate approach—is a gaping hole in left field. Despite only 28 extra-base hits (just three of them homers) in 393 plate appearances, Gerardo Parra laid claim to the title of the Snakes' most frequent starting left fielder last season. The lack of production in left constitutes a concern, but the absence of other major offensive holes gives the impression that the Diamondbacks could manage to turn their team around quickly. However, as a result of the rampant strikeouts, the productivity of this current collection of players may always be limited by their proximity on the lineup card.

There is some cause for optimism other than Towers' potential to fix the broken bullpen: proactive transactions have transformed the rotation into a unit with a stronger future than it appeared to have at the dawn of 2010. A handful of trades have yielded a pitching staff even younger than the lineup, though it looks different from what most would have expected a couple of years ago. When the club traded for Dan Haren going into the 2008 season, it appeared that he and Brandon Webb would combine to lead the Snakes into the postseason; however, after both put up solid performances in 2008, Webb started only one game in the following two years, and Haren was dealt for a weak haul last season.

The current rotation offers some upside. Although Max Scherzer was sent away in a three-way trade with the Tigers and Yankees, the Diamondbacks acquired Ian Kennedy and Edwin Jackson in return. Kennedy posted an impressive 3.80 ERA as a 25-year-old, and Jackson pitched a no-hitter before being flipped to the White Sox for Daniel Hudson and minor-leaguer David Holmberg. The 23-year-old Hudson was sensational in 11 starts to close out the season, with a 1.69 ERA. The rest of the rotation is rounded out by 2007 draftee Barry Enright, who managed a 3.91 ERA in 99 innings in his rookie season, and Joe Saunders, who was acquired as part of the return for Haren last July and put together a 4.25 ERA the rest of the way.

While Saunders is only average and Enright's peripherals make him look more like a back-of-the-rotation type if not a long reliever, the Snakes do have the benefit of controlling the latter for six more years, and the former for two. The other spot in the rotation will likely be filled by a veteran on a short deal, although top prospect Jarrod Parker may stake a claim if his surgically repaired elbow gets a clean bill of health this season.

Many successful teams are built on the foundation of a couple of superstars surrounded by a supporting cast of average players; last season's Snakes had the average players, but instead of sprinkling in superstars, they tolerated holes in both their swings and their bullpen, which made them less than the sum of their parts. Still, the Diamondbacks' roster harbors more talent than the typical last-place club and remains youthful enough for a star or two to appear from within. Armed with Towers' approach to building strong bullpens, they could soon give their frustrated fans a reason to stay up past 8:30.

HITTERS

Tony Abreu INF

Born: **11/13/1984** Age: **26**
Bats: **S** Throws: **R** Height: **5' 9"** Weight: **185**
Breakout: **0%** Improve: **20%** Collapse: **3%**
Attrition: **6%** MLB: **43%**

Comparables:
Omar Quintanilla, Ray Jablonski, Brandon Phillips (74)

YEAR	TEAM	LVL	AGE	PA	R	2B	3B	HR	RBI	BB	SO	SB	CS	AVG_OBP_SLG	TAv	BABIP	BRR	FRAA	WARP
2009	CHT	AA	24	90	11	4	1	0	5	1	12	0	2	.292/.300/.360	.225	.338	-1.1	2B -1, SS 0	-0.4
2009	ABQ	AAA	24	249	38	18	4	11	49	12	42	3	1	.345/.374/.599	.318	.375	-3.7	2B 2, 3B 0	1.9
2009	LAN	MLB	24	11	0	0	0	0	1	3	2	0	1	.250/.455/.250	.316	.333	0.0	2B 0, 3B 1	0.1
2010	RNO	AAA	25	100	16	7	1	2	21	4	21	0	0	.351/.390/.511	.287	.425	0.0	SS 0, 2B 0	0.5
2010	ARI	MLB	25	201	16	11	1	1	13	4	47	2	1	.233/.244/.316	.187	.295	0.9	3B 2, SS 0	-1.0
2011	*ARI*	*MLB*	*26*	*359*	*40*	*20*	*2*	*6*	*40*	*16*	*66*	*3*	*1*	*.273/.305/.395*	*.245*	*.316*	*-0.2*	*2B -1, SS -1*	*0.3*

Abreu has had difficulty staying on the field and has done little to suggest that he can handle a full-time starting position either in sickness or in health. He hardly walks, strikes out frequently, and lacks the power or defensive prowess to make the former two characteristics acceptable. The Diamondbacks have a wide array of candidates for the utility infielder role, and it seems unlikely that Abreu will ever get the chance to be more than that in Arizona.

Brandon Allen 1B

Born: **2/12/1986** Age: **25**
Bats: **L** Throws: **R** Height: **6' 2"** Weight: **235**
Breakout: **7%** Improve: **29%** Collapse: **7%**
Attrition: **24%** MLB: **64**

Comparables:
Joey Votto, Sean Rodriguez, Alex Gordon (70)

YEAR	TEAM	LVL	AGE	PA	R	2B	3B	HR	RBI	BB	SO	SB	CS	AVG_OBP_SLG	TAv	BABIP	BRR	FRAA	WARP
2008	WNS	A+	22	362	53	26	4	15	43	41	83	13	3	.279/.376/.527	.308	.335	0.6	1B 9	3.0
2008	BIR	AA	22	184	30	6	2	14	31	20	50	3	1	.256/.342/.573	.309	.280	1.1	1B -1	1.1
2009	BIR	AA	23	272	36	12	3	7	35	30	47	1	2	.291/.375/.452	.298	.335	-2.8	1B -1	0.9
2009	CHR	AAA	23	61	6	4	0	1	8	0	13	0	0	.262/.262/.377	.213	.319	0.3	1B -1	-0.3
2009	RNO	AAA	23	165	32	8	1	12	32	20	25	6	0	.324/.418/.641	.331	.324	0.1	1B 0	1.3
2009	ARI	MLB	23	116	13	7	0	4	14	12	40	0	0	.202/.285/.385	.224	.283	-0.1	1B -3	-0.6
2010	RNO	AAA	24	459	66	18	3	25	86	83	95	0	0	.262/.414/.528	.303	.281	0.0	1B -3, LF -2	2.2
2010	ARI	MLB	24	56	5	3	0	1	6	10	20	0	0	.267/.393/.400	.285	.440	-0.1	LF 2, 1B 0	0.4
2011	*ARI*	*MLB*	*25*	*558*	*70*	*23*	*2*	*23*	*70*	*68*	*132*	*6*	*2*	*.244/.340/.448*	*.275*	*.281*	*0.0*	*1B -17, LF 0*	*-0.4*

Allen may be the most major-league-ready of the Diamondbacks' batting prospects, and the most likely replacement for Adam LaRoche at first base, but his potential is severely limited by his inability to make contact. Over his 2,978 plate appearances in the minors, Allen struck out 22 percent of the time. In 172 big-league plate appearances, that rate has soared to 35 percent. On the other hand, his walk rate has improved from a low of one every 19 plate appearances in the Sally League to once every six plate appearances in the Pacific Coast League last year, while his strikeout rate has been as low as once every 5.2 at-bats (2009). Now he just has to do it in the major leagues.

Bobby Borchering 3B

Born: **10/25/1990** Age: **20**
Bats: **B** Throws: **R** Height: **6' 3"** Weight: **200**
Breakout: **0%** Improve: **1%** Collapse: **1%**
Attrition: **1%** MLB: **2%**

Comparables:
Ron Santo, Fernando Martinez, Johnny Bench (78)

YEAR	TEAM	LVL	AGE	PA	R	2B	3B	HR	RBI	BB	SO	SB	CS	AVG_OBP_SLG	TAv	BABIP	BRR	FRAA	WARP
2009	MSO	Rk	18	120	14	12	2	4	21	5	34	0	0	.261/.300/.504	.291	.338	-0.9	3B -8	-0.1
2010	SBN	A	19	583	73	31	2	15	74	54	128	0	1	.270/.343/.423	.280	.326	-1.9	3B -18	0.5
2011	*ARI*	*MLB*	*20*	*352*	*35*	*16*	*0*	*8*	*34*	*21*	*97*	*0*	*0*	*.223/.270/.347*	*.218*	*.286*	*0.0*	*3B -8*	*-1.4*

Borchering's overall statistics belied his true hitting ability. A first-round pick two seasons ago, Borchering spent the year at South Bend and, after a slow start, showed why many considered him the country's top high-school hitter when he was drafted midway through 2009's first round. He lacked power at the beginning of the season, but found his groove in the second half, hitting .305/.385/.532 in August and September (36 games). Scouts believe that the late-season showing was a more accurate representation of his ability than what came before. However, they still have reservations about his play at third. Even if he does have to move to the more offensively demanding position, it's likely, given his age and second-half adjustments, that his bat will play in the majors.

Keon Broxton OF

Born: **5/7/1990** Age: **21**
Bats: **R** Throws: **R** Height: **6' 3"** Weight: **190**
Breakout: **0%** Improve: **0%** Collapse: **0%**
Attrition: **6%** MLB: **8%**

Comparables:
Bob Coluccio, Rick Manning, Claudell Washington (69)

YEAR	TEAM	LVL	AGE	PA	R	2B	3B	HR	RBI	BB	SO	SB	CS	AVG_OBP_SLG	TAv	BABIP	BRR	FRAA	WARP
2009	MSO	Rk	19	294	37	11	9	11	37	19	93	5	1	.246/.303/.474	.279	.328	0.1	CF -2, LF -1	1.1
2010	SBN	A	20	600	69	17	19	5	32	65	172	5	6	.228/.315/.360	.248	.324	-1.4	CF 0	0.8
2011	*ARI*	*MLB*	*21*	*447*	*39*	*15*	*4*	*6*	*36*	*31*	*153*	*1*	*0*	*.195/.250/.299*	*.196*	*.284*	*0.0*	*CF -16, LF 0*	*-3.2*

If Bud Selig were to implement a rule that pitchers could only throw fastballs, Keon Broxton would instantly become one of the most valuable prospects in baseball. Instead, he's just annoying. He has the best tools of any player in the Diamondbacks' system and has earned raves as one the best athletes in the Midwest League, but even the fringiest of breaking balls makes him look foolish. A plus-plus runner with solid defensive ability in center field, Broxton will get plenty of chances to stick at the major-league level. However, he must learn to handle secondary offerings, as developing better pitch recognition would go a long way toward separating him from those fungible Greg Golson types.

Ryan Church RF

Born: **10/14/1978** Age: **32**
Bats: L Throws: L Height: **6' 1"** Weight: **190**
Breakout: **0%** Improve: **27%** Collapse: **5%**
Attrition: **19%** MLB: **85%**

Comparables:
Jim King, Dusty Baker, Ken Henderson (80)

YEAR	TEAM	LVL	AGE	PA	R	2B	3B	HR	RBI	BB	SO	SB	CS	AVG_OBP_SLG	TAv	BABIP	BRR	FRAA	WARP
2008	NYN	MLB	29	359	54	14	1	12	49	33	83	2	3	.276/.345/.439	.274	.333	1.8	RF 0	1.3
2009	ATL	MLB	30	144	19	12	0	2	18	16	22	0	0	.260/.347/.402	.264	.301	1.0	RF 0, CF -2	0.3
2009	NYN	MLB	30	255	26	16	0	2	22	17	36	6	2	.280/.329/.375	.257	.318	-2.3	RF -2, CF -1	-0.2
2010	PIT	MLB	31	183	16	11	1	3	18	12	46	1	0	.182/.240/.312	.203	.231	-0.2	RF -3, LF 2	-0.7
2010	ARI	MLB	31	55	9	5	0	2	7	4	19	0	0	.265/.346/.490	.289	.393	0.2	LF 0, CF 1	0.5
2011	*ARI*	*MLB*	*32*	*402*	*44*	*22*	*0*	*8*	*40*	*36*	*82*	*4*	*2*	*.244/.316/.375*	*.245*	*.289*	*-0.2*	*RF -2, CF 0*	*0.0*

The prototypical fourth outfielder, Church provides security at all three outfield spots and, in most years, the ability to hit right-handers (.272/.345/.451 career). Unfortunately, this was not the case in 2010, as a wrist injury suffered on May 7 turned off Church's bat like a light bulb—from then until his trade to the D'Backs, he hit .144/.208/.234 in 120 PAs. Arizona used him primarily as a pinch-hitter, giving him just a half-dozen starts over the final two months. Ryan was more Church-like in this role, but his 55 PA total is so small as to be meaningless. Even healthy, Church has his flaws—an inability to stay healthy, field consistently, and hit same-handed pitching—but assuming he can live down his 2010 performance, he should resume having value in a reserve/platoon role.

Collin Cowgill OF

Born: **5/22/1986** Age: **25**
Bats: R Throws: L Height: **5' 9"** Weight: **195**
Breakout: **5%** Improve: **9%** Collapse: **7%**
Attrition: **13%** MLB: **25%**

Comparables:
Danny Putnam, Shin-Soo Choo, Tony Abreu (77)

YEAR	TEAM	LVL	AGE	PA	R	2B	3B	HR	RBI	BB	SO	SB	CS	AVG_OBP_SLG	TAv	BABIP	BRR	FRAA	WARP
2008	SBN	A	22	251	32	13	3	3	20	25	69	1	0	.257/.355/.381	.260	.357	-2.4	LF 4, CF -3	0.4
2008	YAK	A-	22	92	20	3	1	11	28	12	17	4	0	.304/.424/.785	.390	.250	0.8	CF 3	1.8
2009	VIS	A+	23	253	38	9	5	6	36	29	49	10	4	.277/.383/.446	.294	.325	0.4	RF 2, CF 0	1.6
2010	MOB	AA	24	587	85	34	4	16	83	58	77	25	8	.279/.360/.453	.288	.296	-2.2	RF -4, CF 1	2.5
2011	*ARI*	*MLB*	*25*	*394*	*44*	*18*	*2*	*10*	*42*	*33*	*74*	*10*	*3*	*.243/.311/.389*	*.248*	*.274*	*0.0*	*RF -3, CF -2*	*-0.1*

"The Cow" is as polished a hitter as they come, though his fire-hydrant frame often prevents him from showcasing any semblance of athleticism. He can play center field, if not necessarily well, but lacks the pop needed to stick in an outfield corner. He will make it to the majors, but only as a fourth outfielder. Think Reed Johnson without the fielding skills.

Matthew Davidson 3B

Born: **3/26/1991** Age: **20**
Bats: R Throws: R Height: **6' 3"** Weight: **225**
Breakout: **0%** Improve: **0%** Collapse: **0%**
Attrition: **1%** MLB: **1%**

Comparables:
Orlando Cepeda, Johnny Bench, Eddie Mathews (69)

YEAR	TEAM	LVL	AGE	PA	R	2B	3B	HR	RBI	BB	SO	SB	CS	AVG_OBP_SLG	TAv	BABIP	BRR	FRAA	WARP
2009	YAK	A-	18	292	29	15	0	2	28	21	75	0	2	.241/.319/.319	.234	.325	0.9	3B 8	0.9
2010	SBN	A	19	463	56	35	3	16	79	43	109	0	2	.289/.380/.504	.305	.354	0.2	3B 1	3.0
2010	VIS	A+	19	83	6	1	0	2	11	12	25	0	0	.169/.301/.268	.212	.227	-1.6	3B 1, 1B 0	-0.2
2011	*ARI*	*MLB*	*20*	*419*	*40*	*19*	*0*	*9*	*39*	*27*	*124*	*0*	*0*	*.208/.268/.333*	*.213*	*.275*	*0.0*	*3B 4, 1B 0*	*-0.6*

The 35th overall pick in the 2009 amateur draft, Davidson is a big, slow slugger who makes up for a lack of athleticism with the ability to bop the ball around and out of the yard. His position may be *listed* as third base, but realistically, he's a first baseman. The righty developed power last season at South Bend, but struggled in a small sample at High-A Visalia. The Diamondbacks lack a franchise first-sacker, but with Davidson, Allen, Borchering, Brandon Allen, and Paul Goldschmidt, they may manage to strike gold with at least one and improve elsewhere by dealing the others.

Stephen Drew SS

Born: **3/16/1983** Age: **28**
Bats: L Throws: R Height: **6' 1"** Weight: **185**
Breakout: **3%** Improve: **47%** Collapse: **2%**
Attrition: **7%** MLB: **98%**

Comparables:
Robin Yount, Brandon Phillips, Vada Pinson (66)

YEAR	TEAM	LVL	AGE	PA	R	2B	3B	HR	RBI	BB	SO	SB	CS	AVG_OBP_SLG	TAv	BABIP	BRR	FRAA	WARP
2008	ARI	MLB	25	663	91	44	11	21	67	41	109	3	3	.291/.332/.503	.282	.320	-4.3	SS -10	2.6
2009	ARI	MLB	26	595	71	29	12	12	65	49	87	5	1	.261/.318/.428	.260	.285	1.0	SS 5	2.8
2010	ARI	MLB	27	633	83	33	12	15	61	62	108	10	5	.278/.351/.458	.288	.319	1.7	SS -2	4.0
2011	*ARI*	*MLB*	*28*	*624*	*76*	*32*	*6*	*14*	*74*	*56*	*92*	*7*	*3*	*.269/.333/.427*	*.266*	*.293*	*-0.2*	*SS -3*	*2.3*

This past season was make-or-break for Drew, who had shown flashes of excellence before but remained far too inconsistent to instill confidence in his employers as his salary rose through his arbitration years. He certainly met the challenge, putting together the best season of his career on both sides of the ball. Skeptics may claim that his higher on-base percentage was an aberration, but decent defensive shortstops with true talent levels in the .270/.335/.450 range don't grow on trees. This winter, the Diamondbacks bought out Drew's remaining three arbitration years. Given how two-way shortstops have become an endangered species, it would be in the team's best interest to pursue a long-term deal. He's not going to blossom into the MVP contender we saw coming a couple years ago, but he's plenty good as it is.

Cole Gillespie **LF**

Born: **6/20/1984** Age: **27**
Bats: R Throws: R Height: **6' 1"** Weight: **205**
Breakout: **0%** Improve: **37%** Collapse: **5%**
Attrition: **19%** MLB: **70%**

Comparables:
Jeff Salazar, Carlos Beltran, Matt Carson (74)

YEAR	TEAM	LVL	AGE	PA	R	2B	3B	HR	RBI	BB	SO	SB	CS	AVG_OBP_SLG	TAv	BABIP	BRR	FRAA	WARP
2008	HUN	AA	24	544	68	38	4	14	79	75	102	15	1	.281/.388/.472	.292	.329	2.2	LF -2, RF -2	2.6
2009	BRV	A+	25	51	10	2	3	1	9	7	11	4	0	.349/.431/.605	.370	.438	2.0	LF 1, RF 0	0.9
2009	NAS	AAA	25	274	29	12	5	7	27	31	56	5	5	.242/.332/.424	.278	.278	2.6	LF 13	2.5
2009	RNO	AAA	25	168	31	6	4	5	27	27	31	8	0	.304/.423/.515	.301	.352	3.1	RF 0, LF -1	1.2
2010	RNO	AAA	26	309	53	14	6	8	49	44	49	8	5	.288/.398/.477	.280	.327	1.6	CF -6, RF 4	1.4
2010	ARI	MLB	26	113	11	8	0	2	12	7	29	1	1	.231/.283/.365	.234	.297	0.8	LF 0, RF -1	-0.4
2011	*ARI*	*MLB*	*27*	*486*	*58*	*22*	*3*	*11*	*50*	*58*	*100*	*10*	*4*	*.249/.340/.396*	*.262*	*.296*	*-0.2*	*LF -2, RF 0*	*0.5*

Gillespie possesses enough conflicting attributes to fill both a "pro" and a "con" column. On one hand, his career on-base percentage in the minors is off the charts. He can also play center field in a pinch, steal a base, and provide gap power. On the other hand, he will turn 27 this season, isn't a slugger, has minimal major-league experience, and hasn't convinced scouts of his ability to play up the middle. He stands to benefit from the club's open outfield spots, particularly in left field—if Xavier Nady is the answer, we don't want to know what the question is.

Paul Goldschmidt **1B**

Born: **9/10/1987** Age: **23**
Bats: R Throws: R Height: **6' 4"** Weight: **220**
Breakout: **1%** Improve: **23%** Collapse: **7%**
Attrition: **14%** MLB: **52%**

Comparables:
Chris Davis, Evan Longoria, Joey Votto (71)

YEAR	TEAM	LVL	AGE	PA	R	2B	3B	HR	RBI	BB	SO	SB	CS	AVG_OBP_SLG	TAv	BABIP	BRR	FRAA	WARP
2009	MSO	Rk	21	357	57	30	3	18	67	39	80	5	3	.332/.409/.620	.348	.391	-0.3	1B 3, CF 1	3.9
2010	VIS	A+	22	591	98	42	3	35	108	57	161	5	1	.314/.389/.606	.338	.385	-3.2	1B -5	4.4
2011	*ARI*	*MLB*	*23*	*474*	*58*	*24*	*0*	*23*	*67*	*38*	*143*	*0*	*0*	*.248/.309/.466*	*.265*	*.307*	*0.0*	*1B -19, CF 0*	*-1.2*

A graduate of Texas State University, 2009 eighth-rounder Goldschmidt has taken well to pro baseball, winning the California League MVP last year; he has mashed 53 home runs in 812 career at-bats. The simultaneous cause and downside of all that production is the uppercut swing and massive strength that frequently combine to launch the ball, but also result in a disconcerting number of strikeouts. More experienced pitchers in a less offense-crazy environment than the California League could use Goldschmidt's approach against him. "Massive uppercut" is also the sum of Goldschmidt's baseball skills, as he has the speed and mobility of a very firm pudding. He's the classic all-bat, no-field first baseman—probably. We're sure about the latter part, but Goldschmidt will have to survive the Double-A test before we feel secure about the former.

Kelly Johnson **2B**

Born: **2/22/1982** Age: **29**
Bats: L Throws: R Height: **6' 1"** Weight: **205**
Breakout: **0%** Improve: **49%** Collapse: **1%**
Attrition: **8%** MLB: **99%**

Comparables:
Ian Kinsler, Andre Ethier, Bernie Williams (73)

YEAR	TEAM	LVL	AGE	PA	R	2B	3B	HR	RBI	BB	SO	SB	CS	AVG_OBP_SLG	TAv	BABIP	BRR	FRAA	WARP
2008	ATL	MLB	26	614	86	39	6	12	69	52	113	11	6	.287/.344/.446	.276	.333	2.3	2B 8	3.5
2009	GWN	AAA	27	59	9	2	2	3	16	4	8	1	0	.308/.339/.596	.334	.296	-0.5	2B 1	0.7
2009	ATL	MLB	27	346	45	20	3	8	29	32	54	7	2	.224/.298/.389	.241	.241	1.8	2B 3	0.6
2010	ARI	MLB	28	671	93	36	5	26	71	79	148	13	7	.284/.368/.496	.299	.337	-1.3	2B -5	3.4
2011	*ARI*	*MLB*	*29*	*575*	*72*	*29*	*3*	*16*	*68*	*64*	*105*	*11*	*5*	*.266/.346/.435*	*.273*	*.298*	*-0.6*	*2B 0*	*2.0*

The Braves nontendered Johnson after a poor 2009, even though he'd topped three WARP in each of the two preceding seasons. The Diamondbacks wasted little time in bringing him aboard, and though his numbers last season were heavily front-loaded, thanks to a .313/.404/.750 performance with nine homers in April, he still put together the best offensive year of his career. Despite his productivity, teams are unlikely to reward him with a long-term commitment, since health questions and a lack of certainty surrounding his true abilities persist. Then again, Johnson has been worth about 12 WARP over the past four seasons, so perhaps such concerns are overstated. It would behoove the Snakes not to shed his skin, as he'll be cost-effective and better than anyone else currently in-house.

Marc Krauss **OF**

Born: **10/5/1987** Age: **23**
Bats: L Throws: R Height: **6' 3"** Weight: **235**
Breakout: **0%** Improve: **6%** Collapse: **0%**
Attrition: **6%** MLB: **12%**

Comparables:
Brandon Jones, Brandon Allen, Greg Luzinski (76)

YEAR	TEAM	LVL	AGE	PA	R	2B	3B	HR	RBI	BB	SO	SB	CS	AVG_OBP_SLG	TAv	BABIP	BRR	FRAA	WARP
2009	SBN	A	21	130	14	12	1	2	17	14	21	0	1	.304/.377/.478	.304	.355	-0.3	LF -2	0.6
2010	VIS	A+	22	592	106	27	4	25	87	57	141	1	3	.302/.373/.509	.316	.366	1.3	LF -9, 1B -1	3.6
2011	*ARI*	*MLB*	*23*	*361*	*41*	*15*	*1*	*12*	*43*	*28*	*93*	*0*	*0*	*.249/.306/.415*	*.250*	*.303*	*0.0*	*LF -10, 1B 0*	*-0.7*

Krauss has a frame similar to that of Adam Dunn, though Krauss possesses less raw power. Then again, who *does* possess Dunn's raw power? In further Big Donkey–like fashion, the lefty swinger is a poor fielder with a subpar arm, but he hits well enough to play an outfield corner. He should start the season at Double-A and will be looking to build on a monster second half of last season.

Adam LaRoche **1B**

Born: **11/6/1979** Age: **31**
Bats: L Throws: L Height: **6' 3"** Weight: **180**
Breakout: **3%** Improve: **43%** Collapse: **2%**
Attrition: **8%** MLB: **98%**

Comparables:
Alfonso Soriano, Paul Konerko, Rafael Palmeiro (68)

YEAR	TEAM	LVL	AGE	PA	R	2B	3B	HR	RBI	BB	SO	SB	CS	AVG_OBP_SLG	TAv	BABIP	BRR	FRAA	WARP
2008	PIT	MLB	28	554	66	32	3	25	85	54	122	1	1	.270/.341/.500	.289	.308	-1.8	1B 0	1.9
2009	ATL	MLB	29	242	30	11	1	12	40	28	59	0	0	.326/.401/.557	.342	.399	-2.2	1B 1	2.1
2009	BOS	MLB	29	19	2	2	0	1	3	0	2	0	0	.263/.263/.526	.258	.250	-0.2	1B 1	0.0
2009	PIT	MLB	29	368	46	25	1	12	40	41	81	2	2	.247/.329/.441	.262	.291	-1.3	1B 6	0.8
2010	ARI	MLB	30	615	75	37	2	25	100	48	172	0	1	.261/.320/.468	.271	.330	-2.8	1B 10	1.8
2011	*WAS*	*MLB*	*31*	*600*	*77*	*34*	*1*	*24*	*81*	*60*	*138*	*2*	*1*	*.263/.337/.468*	*.270*	*.308*	*-0.1*	*1B 7*	*1.6*

If LaRoche were an institution of higher learning, he'd be a safety school. Given the amount of talent at first base, replacement level at the position is particularly high. For this reason, LaRoche is the perfect example of a player whose numbers look less impressive when the appropriate context is introduced. The average major-league first baseman hit .264/.350/.452 last year, which is why the Snakes declined LaRoche's $7.5 million option for 2011. He has value, but he's always going to be someone's Plan B. He signed with Washington, the Plan B of franchises.

Miguel Montero **C**

Born: **7/9/1983** Age: **27**
Bats: L Throws: R Height: **5' 11"** Weight: **197**
Breakout: **1%** Improve: **38%** Collapse: **6%**
Attrition: **13%** MLB: **90%**

Comparables:
Ryan Doumit, J.R. House, Johnny Romano (76)

YEAR	TEAM	LVL	AGE	PA	R	2B	3B	HR	RBI	BB	SO	SB	CS	AVG_OBP_SLG	TAv	BABIP	BRR	FRAA	WARP
2008	ARI	MLB	24	207	26	16	1	5	18	19	49	0	0	.255/.329/.435	.262	.318	0.7	C 1	1.1
2009	ARI	MLB	25	470	64	30	0	16	59	38	78	1	2	.294/.353/.478	.287	.325	-0.5	C -2	2.9
2010	ARI	MLB	26	331	36	20	2	9	43	29	71	0	1	.266/.332/.438	.260	.318	-3.2	C 1	1.1
2011	*ARI*	*MLB*	*27*	*361*	*44*	*19*	*0*	*11*	*42*	*33*	*61*	*1*	*0*	*.264/.334/.425*	*.265*	*.291*	*-0.1*	*C 0*	*1.6*

One of the most promising young catchers in the game, Montero hurt his right knee in early April and returned in mid-June. His numbers took a dip in approximately half a season's worth of playing time, but remained more than acceptable by backstop standards. The Diamondbacks agreed, trading former starter Chris Snyder to the Pirates in July and solidifying Montero's status as their primary catcher in the process. As long as the injury doesn't linger, he should be even more productive this season, though it would help if he could lay off the slop out of the zone, a characteristic he had seemingly shaken during his 2009 campaign. The regression in that area could have been attributable to the bum knee, but regardless of its origins, better pitch recognition was the difference between an outstanding offensive performance by Montero and a merely good one.

Augie Ojeda **INF**

Born: **12/20/1974** Age: **36**
Bats: S Throws: R Height: **5' 8"** Weight: **165**
Breakout: **1%** Improve: **19%** Collapse: **15%**
Attrition: **25%** MLB: **64%**

Comparables:
Johnny Pesky, Keith Lockhart, Fernando Vina (69)

YEAR	TEAM	LVL	AGE	PA	R	2B	3B	HR	RBI	BB	SO	SB	CS	AVG_OBP_SLG	TAv	BABIP	BRR	FRAA	WARP
2008	ARI	MLB	33	272	27	9	2	0	17	26	24	0	0	.242/.338/.299	.230	.264	2.2	2B -1, SS 2	0.5
2009	ARI	MLB	34	310	37	17	3	1	16	32	28	3	1	.246/.332/.345	.236	.265	0.6	2B 5, SS 0	0.6
2010	ARI	MLB	35	92	6	3	0	0	5	8	8	0	1	.190/.250/.228	.183	.197	-0.5	2B -1, SS 0	-0.8
2011	*ARI*	*MLB*	*36*	*230*	*23*	*10*	*1*	*0*	*15*	*23*	*22*	*1*	*1*	*.237/.319/.298*	*.226*	*.254*	*-0.1*	*2B 1, SS 1*	*0.0*

Last year we warned that Ojeda's numbers had been historically inflated by intentional walks, a symptom of batting in front of the pitcher. This year no such warning is required, as the supposed supersub floundered with the bat without providing much utility in the field. At 36 years old, he has seen his usefulness expire, and with his nontender in December, appears to be headed for a string of minor-league deals with spring training invitations to compete for the 25th spot on a roster. Signing him might not hurt, but realistically, it won't help, either.

Chris Owings **SS**

Born: **8/12/1991** Age: **19**
Bats: R Throws: R Height: **5' 11"** Weight: **175**
Breakout: **0%** Improve: **0%** Collapse: **0%**
Attrition: **0%** MLB: **0%**

Comparables:
Adrian Beltre, Kenny Kuhn, Glenn Vaughan (77)

YEAR	TEAM	LVL	AGE	PA	R	2B	3B	HR	RBI	BB	SO	SB	CS	AVG_OBP_SLG	TAv	BABIP	BRR	FRAA	WARP
2009	MSO	Rk	17	140	28	9	3	2	15	3	31	3	0	.314/.329/.467	.299	.394	2.0	SS 0	1.3
2010	SBN	A	18	269	39	19	2	5	27	9	50	1	3	.298/.323/.447	.272	.346	0.0	SS 3	1.7
2011	*ARI*	*MLB*	*19*	*205*	*18*	*10*	*1*	*3*	*19*	*4*	*53*	*0*	*0*	*.230/.243/.324*	*.199*	*.293*	*0.0*	*SS 3*	*-0.2*

Owings is a pesky little shortstop with energy out the wazoo. As fundamentally sound as they come, he should advance quickly, though if he makes it to the major leagues, it won't be as a star. Still, there are worse everyday shortstops than Owings playing right now—at a time when there is a dearth of shortstops, adjectives like *good, solid,* and *true shortstop,* all of which have been applied to Owings, are nothing to sneeze at.

Gerardo Parra **LF**

Born: **5/6/1987** Age: **24**
Bats: L Throws: L Height: **5' 11"** Weight: **195**
Breakout: **3%** Improve: **32%** Collapse: **9%**
Attrition: **19%** MLB: **60%**

Comparables:
Chris Coghlan, Roberto Alomar, Blake DeWitt (69)

YEAR	TEAM	LVL	AGE	PA	R	2B	3B	HR	RBI	BB	SO	SB	CS	AVG_OBP_SLG	TAv	BABIP	BRR	FRAA	WARP
2008	VIS	A+	21	221	25	8	4	2	19	23	31	12	3	.301/.385/.413	.289	.346	2.4	CF -2, RF 1	1.4
2008	MOB	AA	21	297	34	14	6	4	33	24	34	15	9	.276/.343/.419	.263	.294	-0.5	CF -1, RF -1	0.7
2009	MOB	AA	22	130	23	3	1	3	12	22	13	7	4	.361/.469/.491	.343	.391	-0.1	RF 1, CF -1	1.2
2009	ARI	MLB	22	491	61	21	8	5	60	25	89	5	7	.290/.322/.404	.246	.342	1.8	LF -1, CF -3	0.0
2010	ARI	MLB	23	393	31	19	6	3	30	23	76	1	0	.261/.305/.371	.235	.318	1.1	LF 9, RF 2	0.9
2011	*ARI*	*MLB*	*24*	*524*	*58*	*24*	*4*	*6*	*51*	*37*	*83*	*11*	*5*	*.270/.321/.373*	*.245*	*.309*	*-0.7*	*CF -4, LF 2*	*0.1*

Players who make the majors sans plate discipline tend to compensate by performing well in other areas. That rule doesn't apply to Gerardo Parra. He lacks power, does not hit for average, steals very few bases, and plays mediocre defense. The only part of his résumé that might keep him employed in something greater than a bench capacity is his age, which will only be on his side for so long. He'll need to make legitimate improvements in his ability to see and hit the ball—a tall order, even in a player's age-24 season—if he wants to be more than organizational depth.

Mark Reynolds **3B**

Born: **8/3/1983** Age: **27**
Bats: R Throws: R Height: **6' 1"** Weight: **200**
Breakout: **2%** Improve: **49%** Collapse: **0%**
Attrition: **6%** MLB: **98%**

Comparables:
Duke Snider, Mike Schmidt, Al Rosen (60)

YEAR	TEAM	LVL	AGE	PA	R	2B	3B	HR	RBI	BB	SO	SB	CS	AVG_OBP_SLG	TAv	BABIP	BRR	FRAA	WARP
2008	ARI	MLB	24	613	87	28	3	28	97	64	204	11	2	.239/.320/.458	.267	.322	5.0	3B -14, 1B 0	1.4
2009	ARI	MLB	25	662	98	30	1	44	102	76	223	24	9	.260/.349/.543	.303	.338	-2.3	3B 6, 1B -5	4.4
2010	ARI	MLB	26	596	80	17	2	32	85	83	211	7	4	.198/.321/.433	.263	.257	0.3	3B 0, 1B 0	1.8
2011	*BAL*	*MLB*	*27*	*610*	*79*	*24*	*2*	*32*	*85*	*76*	*197*	*12*	*5*	*.237/.336/.475*	*.281*	*.305*	*-0.4*	*3B -3, 1B -1*	*2.5*

Pop quiz: How many players with at least 550 PAs have batted south of the Mendoza line in a season? The answer is three: Reynolds and Carlos Pena last year, and Tom Tresh in 1968. Reynolds also came close to sharing company with the select group of players whose single-season home-run totals accounted for more than a third of their hits. His high strikeout tallies don't appear to bother him, and it's easy to see why—in years past, great things happened when he did connect. Last year, that wasn't the case, as he not only made very little contact but received next to no help from that capricious BABIP fairy. Chase Field covered for a multitude of Reynolds' sins; he hit .181/.302/.341 away from home last year and now owns a career .235/.323/.461 line outside Phoenix. To paraphrase Cormac McCarthy, Reynolds may soon find that from daydreams on the road, there will be no waking after a December trade to the Orioles obliged a painful separation from his old stomping grounds. The divorce could be messy, and his ex-ballpark will likely get custody of his bat.

Ryan Roberts **UT**

Born: **9/19/1980** Age: **30**
Bats: R Throws: R Height: **5' 11"** Weight: **190**
Breakout: **1%** Improve: **26%** Collapse: **4%**
Attrition: **13%** MLB: **66%**

Comparables:
Edgar Gonzalez, John Valentin, D'Angelo Jimenez (75)

YEAR	TEAM	LVL	AGE	PA	R	2B	3B	HR	RBI	BB	SO	SB	CS	AVG_OBP_SLG	TAv	BABIP	BRR	FRAA	WARP
2008	OKL	AAA	27	560	72	28	8	12	73	70	81	15	4	.302/.393/.467	.285	.338	0.4	2B 5, 3B 5	3.8
2008	TEX	MLB	27	1	0	0	0	0	0	0	1	0	0	.000/.000/.000	.069	–	0.0	–	0.0
2009	ARI	MLB	28	351	40	17	2	7	25	40	55	7	3	.279/.365/.416	.277	.317	1.2	2B -3, 3B -1	1.1
2010	RNO	AAA	29	410	60	25	2	11	55	56	73	16	6	.265/.366/.444	.272	.300	2.2	2B 7, LF 1	2.4
2010	ARI	MLB	29	71	8	4	0	2	9	3	17	0	0	.197/.225/.349	.207	.225	-0.5	LF -1, 2B 0	-0.4
2011	*ARI*	*MLB*	*30*	*454*	*52*	*21*	*1*	*9*	*44*	*53*	*84*	*10*	*3*	*.249/.337/.378*	*.254*	*.289*	*-0.1*	*2B 2, 3B -1*	*0.8*

Roberts filled in admirably at the keystone during the 2009 season after the Diamondbacks parted ways with Felipe Lopez, but he was never viewed as anything more than a stopgap. The Snakes opted to take a flier on Kelly Johnson during the offseason and decided that Rusty Ryal was better suited for the utility infielder role, leaving Roberts off the major-league roster. When he was in the bigs, his lack of production didn't make the Arizona brass regret their decision. Roberts hit fairly well for the Reno Aces of the Pacific Coast League, but show us a 29-year-old who barely tops an 800 OPS in a Triple-A bandbox, and we'll show you a batter unlikely to contribute much with the stick in the majors. Unfortunately for Roberts, offense is the only area of his game worth noting.

Rusty Ryal UT

Born: **3/16/1983** Age: **28**
Bats: R Throws: R Height: **6' 2"** Weight: **200**
Breakout: **0%** Improve: **27%** Collapse: **7%**
Attrition: **16%** MLB: **57%**

Comparables:
Luis Terrero, Matt Carson, Lou Montanez (78)

YEAR	TEAM	LVL	AGE	PA	R	2B	3B	HR	RBI	BB	SO	SB	CS	AVG_OBP_SLG	TAv	BABIP	BRR	FRAA	WARP
2008	MOB	AA	25	500	62	22	4	16	66	35	96	4	4	.274/.340/.444	.259	.312	1.2	2B 12, 3B -1	2.3
2009	RNO	AAA	26	442	63	33	6	17	70	33	94	5	2	.290/.348/.527	.291	.336	0.1	2B 1, 3B 0	3.0
2009	ARI	MLB	26	68	11	6	2	3	9	6	21	0	0	.271/.353/.593	.304	.361	0.0	2B 0, 1B 1	0.5
2010	ARI	MLB	27	222	19	7	1	3	11	8	67	0	3	.261/.306/.348	.248	.370	-0.4	LF -1, 1B 1	0.0
2011	*ARI*	*MLB*	*28*	*411*	*47*	*19*	*2*	*11*	*48*	*26*	*98*	*3*	*1*	*.253/.306/.407*	*.250*	*.306*	*-0.2*	*2B 2, 3B -1*	*0.7*

Ryal has always displayed patience at the plate, as well as an ability to hit for power. Nevertheless Ryal was released. He signed a one-year deal with the Yomiuri Giants, so say *sayonara*. Every team needs role players, and despite his lowly TAv last season, Ryal provides depth in multiple positions at the cost of just one roster spot. Besides, anything can happen in a small sample, and it was only a year ago that his TAv topped .300.

Justin Upton RF

Born: **8/25/1987** Age: **23**
Bats: R Throws: R Height: **6' 3"** Weight: **205**
Breakout: **4%** Improve: **55%** Collapse: **3%**
Attrition: **10%** MLB: **86%**

Comparables:
Jay Bruce, Matt Kemp, Duke Snider (67)

YEAR	TEAM	LVL	AGE	PA	R	2B	3B	HR	RBI	BB	SO	SB	CS	AVG_OBP_SLG	TAv	BABIP	BRR	FRAA	WARP
2008	TUC	AAA	20	68	13	3	1	3	10	7	26	2	0	.279/.353/.508	.274	.438	0.1	RF -2	0.0
2008	ARI	MLB	20	417	52	19	6	15	42	54	121	1	4	.250/.353/.464	.277	.332	0.8	RF -7	0.7
2009	ARI	MLB	21	588	84	30	7	26	86	55	137	20	5	.300/.366/.532	.299	.359	-1.9	RF 11	4.1
2010	ARI	MLB	22	571	73	27	3	17	69	64	152	18	8	.273/.356/.442	.275	.353	0.1	RF 3	1.9
2011	*ARI*	*MLB*	*23*	*563*	*73*	*26*	*3*	*20*	*72*	*62*	*134*	*15*	*6*	*.268/.350/.456*	*.282*	*.324*	*-0.6*	*RF 1*	*2.0*

It should come as no surprise that we were particularly high on Upton over the last two seasons. His rookie year resembled Junior Griffey's, and he followed it with a .230 isolated power in his second season, a feat matched by only 13 players in history. What *did* come as a surprise was the extent of his power outage last year. In virtually the same amount of playing time, Upton traded extra-base hits for singles and struck out far more frequently, despite sustaining his solid walk rate. Unfortunately, identifying a direct cause for the decline is difficult, as his high BABIP stayed intact, his distribution of balls in play did not materially change, and he made the same amount of contact. The only noticeable difference can be found in his rate of swinging at balls around the strike zone, which dropped precipitously. Essentially, Upton was too selective, to the point that he let pitches he was accustomed to raking go by. The future is still bright, but expectations that he is going to follow in Griffey's footsteps should be tempered.

Chris Young CF

Born: **9/5/1983** Age: **27**
Bats: R Throws: R Height: **6' 2"** Weight: **180**
Breakout: **3%** Improve: **50%** Collapse: **1%**
Attrition: **12%** MLB: **98%**

Comparables:
Andruw Jones, Grady Sizemore, Chase Headley (74)

YEAR	TEAM	LVL	AGE	PA	R	2B	3B	HR	RBI	BB	SO	SB	CS	AVG_OBP_SLG	TAv	BABIP	BRR	FRAA	WARP
2008	ARI	MLB	24	699	85	42	7	22	85	62	165	14	5	.248/.312/.443	.255	.296	1.0	CF 2	1.9
2009	RNO	AAA	25	63	17	5	1	3	9	9	13	2	2	.370/.460/.667	.354	.447	-0.1	CF -4	0.4
2009	ARI	MLB	25	501	55	28	4	15	42	59	133	11	4	.213/.309/.400	.247	.266	3.1	CF -6	0.5
2010	ARI	MLB	26	664	94	33	0	27	91	74	145	28	7	.257/.340/.452	.281	.296	2.8	CF 5	3.8
2011	*ARI*	*MLB*	*27*	*617*	*75*	*31*	*2*	*22*	*76*	*66*	*132*	*20*	*6*	*.245/.327/.434*	*.266*	*.277*	*-0.1*	*CF -2*	*1.8*

From 2006 to 2009, PECOTA projected All-Star caliber production from Young, only to be terribly disappointed by the time September rolled around. Last year, the projection system effectively gave up on its problem child, forecasting a .252 TAv and one win above replacement. Naturally, Young responded with his best season, an All-Star appearance, and career highs in stolen bases and on-base percentage. Power and speed have long been his calling cards, but the majority of his improvement last season can be traced to his newly acquired patience. If Young can find a way to build on this attribute, or even sustain it, the Diamondbacks will have two of the best young players in the game in the same outfield.

PITCHERS

D. J. Carrasco

Born: **4/12/1977** Age: **34**
Bats: **R** Throws: **R** Height: **6' 1"** Weight: **215**
Breakout: **21%** Improve: **36%** Collapse: **25%**
Attrition: **12%** MLB: **80%**

Comparables:
Orlando Hernandez, Hank Aguirre, Les Walrond (75)

YEAR	TEAM	LVL	AGE	W	L	SV	G	GS	IP	H	HR	BB	SO	EqBB9	EqSO9	GB%	BABIP	WHIP	ERA	FRA	WARP
2008	CHR	AAA	31	2	1	1	8	2	25	24	0	7	24	2.5	8.6	57%	.333	1.28	2.52	4.57	0.2
2008	CHA	MLB	31	1	0	0	31	0	38^2	30	2	14	30	3.3	7.0	54%	.262	1.27	3.72	**2.82**	0.7
2009	CHA	MLB	32	5	1	0	49	1	93^1	103	5	29	62	2.8	6.0	49%	.320	1.44	3.76	3.74	1.5
2010	PIT	MLB	33	2	2	0	45	0	55^2	50	4	22	45	3.6	7.3	48%	.293	1.37	3.88	3.72	0.7
2010	ARI	MLB	33	1	0	0	18	0	22^2	18	1	12	20	4.8	7.9	51%	.266	1.37	3.18	6.13	-0.4
2011	*NYN*	*MLB*	*34*	*3*	*1*	*0*	*65*	*0*	*94*	*99*	*8*	*39*	*63*	*3.8*	*6.1*	*47%*	*.311*	*1.47*	*4.50*	*4.89*	*-0.5*

Armed with a decent sinker and a hard slider, Carrasco induces grounders with the best of them, but has stepped up his game in the strikeout department of late. Better suited for middle relief than setting up or closing, he made great strides last season again southpaws, against whom he has historically struggled. In 2009, opposite-handed hitters mashed Carrasco to the tune of a .317/.392/.463 line, but he held them to just .260/.333/.375 last year. Despite the improvement, he signed with the Mets.

Sam Demel

Born: **10/23/1985** Age: **25**
Bats: **R** Throws: **R** Height: **6' 0"** Weight: **215**
Breakout: **1%** Improve: **5%** Collapse: **2%**
Attrition: **1%** MLB: **11%**

Comparables:
Warner Madrigal, Terry Forster, Antonio Bastardo (79)

YEAR	TEAM	LVL	AGE	W	L	SV	G	GS	IP	H	HR	BB	SO	EqBB9	EqSO9	GB%	BABIP	WHIP	ERA	FRA	WARP
2008	STO	A+	22	5	3	19	60	0	74	67	5	33	96	4.0	11.7	59%	.316	1.43	3.28	4.15	0.6
2009	MID	AA	23	0	2	11	27	0	29^1	23	1	9	26	2.8	8.0	57%	.259	1.09	0.61	2.98	0.4
2009	SAC	AAA	23	2	3	3	31	0	35	30	1	21	37	5.4	9.5	49%	.299	1.49	3.09	2.84	0.8
2010	SAC	AAA	24	2	0	6	22	0	28^2	22	1	9	28	2.8	8.8	50%	.273	1.12	1.26	2.84	0.8
2010	ARI	MLB	24	2	1	2	37	0	37	42	5	12	33	2.9	8.0	53%	.325	1.49	5.35	6.64	-0.8
2011	*ARI*	*MLB*	*25*	*2*	*1*	*5*	*50*	*0*	*56*	*57*	*7*	*27*	*51*	*4.3*	*8.1*	*49%*	*.312*	*1.48*	*4.60*	*5.00*	*-0.1*

Acquired from the Athletics in the deal that sent Conor Jackson to Oakland, Demel has a rocket for an arm, but lacks an effective guidance system. Newly appointed GM Kevin Towers has a knack for building bullpens, so although Demel is not guaranteed a spot on the major-league roster to start the season, his proven ability to dial the heater up to 97 mph and miss bats with it in the bigs should help him stick out from the other candidates.

Barry Enright

Born: **3/30/1986** Age: **25**
Bats: **R** Throws: **R** Height: **6' 3"** Weight: **220**
Breakout: **9%** Improve: **19%** Collapse: **11%**
Attrition: **17%** MLB: **41%**

Comparables:
Steve Cooke, Tobi Stoner, Andrew Carpenter (69)

YEAR	TEAM	LVL	AGE	W	L	SV	G	GS	IP	H	HR	BB	SO	EqBB9	EqSO9	GB%	BABIP	WHIP	ERA	FRA	WARP
2008	VIS	A+	22	12	8	0	29	30	164^1	185	17	35	143	1.9	7.8	43%	.332	1.36	4.44	4.76	1.8
2009	MOB	AA	23	10	9	0	27	27	156	171	16	37	103	2.1	5.9	44%	.309	1.36	3.98	4.54	1.6
2010	MOB	AA	24	4	1	0	14	14	93^2	81	9	15	83	1.4	8.0	40%	.281	1.08	2.88	4.43	1.0
2010	ARI	MLB	24	6	7	0	17	18	99	97	20	29	49	2.6	4.5	37%	.248	1.28	3.91	4.73	1.0
2011	*ARI*	*MLB*	*25*	*6*	*9*	*0*	*21*	*21*	*125^2*	*149*	*22*	*39*	*74*	*2.8*	*5.3*	*41%*	*.310*	*1.51*	*5.54*	*6.02*	*0.6*

Projected as a reliever, and an iffy one at that due to middling stuff, Enright recorded a decent ERA in half a major-league season in the rotation. However, peripheral statistics expose the dubious underpinnings of his performance. He rarely struck hitters out, didn't muster Madduxian control to compensate for all the contact, and served up far too many gopher balls. In fact, although he pitched just 99 innings, his total of home runs allowed ranked among the worst 50 in the sport. Executive summary: Enright had better learn to duck, because an unkind universe is about to inflict a Charlie Brown–style counterreaction.

Matt Gorgen

Born: **1/27/1987** Age: **24**
Bats: **R** Throws: **R** Height: **6' 0"** Weight: **210**
Breakout: **1%** Improve: **4%** Collapse: **3%**
Attrition: **1%** MLB: **12%**

Comparables:
Fernando Hernandez Jr., Antonio Bastardo, Ian Kennedy (74)

YEAR	TEAM	LVL	AGE	W	L	SV	G	GS	IP	H	HR	BB	SO	EqBB9	EqSO9	GB%	BABIP	WHIP	ERA	FRA	WARP
2008	HUD	A-	21	1	1	13	22	0	23	7	2	5	35	2.0	13.7	63%	.132	0.57	2.35	4.02	1.2
2009	PCH	A+	22	4	0	15	28	0	47^2	24	1	16	59	3.0	11.1	49%	.230	0.88	0.57	2.19	1.2
2009	MNT	AA	22	3	1	4	16	0	22^2	18	2	13	18	5.2	7.1	39%	.246	1.37	2.38	2.63	0.5
2010	MNT	AA	23	3	2	22	42	0	49	34	2	21	47	3.9	8.6	33%	.248	1.18	1.65	2.05	1.5
2011	*ARI*	*MLB*	*24*	*2*	*1*	*6*	*31*	*0*	*43^1*	*39*	*5*	*21*	*40*	*4.4*	*8.4*	*43%*	*.292*	*1.39*	*4.02*	*4.37*	*0.3*

The player-to-be-named-later in the deal that sent Chad Qualls to the Rays, Gorgen is miscast as the closer, his role in the minors, given his lack of an overpowering fastball or true out pitch. That he improved his strikeout, walk, and home-run rates from their 2009 levels is a testament to his ability to shake what his momma gave him, but he has little room for error. In short, he is what he is, and if you don't expect him to do much more than pitch the sixth inning, he could help as soon as this year or until such time as he is slain by Perseus.

Juan Gutierrez

Born: **7/14/1983** Age: **27**
Bats: R Throws: R Height: **6' 3"** Weight: **200**
Breakout: **1%** Improve: **1%** Collapse: **2%**
Attrition: **4%** MLB: **5%**

Comparables:
Fernando Nieve, Marco Estrada, Shane Komine (83)

YEAR	TEAM	LVL	AGE	W	L	SV	G	GS	IP	H	HR	BB	SO	EqBB9	EqSO9	GB%	BABIP	WHIP	ERA	FRA	WARP
2008	TUC	AAA	24	5	11	0	25	25	116^{2}	152	11	44	87	3.4	6.7	48%	.362	1.72	5.86	7.60	-0.2
2009	ARI	MLB	25	4	3	9	65	0	71	67	2	30	66	3.8	8.4	41%	.316	1.41	3.93	3.77	0.9
2010	ARI	MLB	26	0	6	15	58	0	56^{2}	55	13	23	47	3.7	7.5	37%	.263	1.45	5.24	6.09	-0.9
2011	*ARI*	*MLB*	*27*	*6*	*5*	*7*	*64*	*9*	*105^{1}*	*118*	*15*	*45*	*76*	*3.8*	*6.5*	*44%*	*.317*	*1.55*	*5.26*	*5.72*	*-0.0*

Last year, we suggested that Gutierrez would take over as the Diamondbacks' closer should they move Chad Qualls. We also considered his 2.5 percent home-run-per-fly-ball rate to be completely unsustainable. Toward the end of last season, Gutierrez not only became the closer after Qualls was sent to the Rays, but also saw his HR/FB balloon to over 15 percent. To make matters worse, he also allowed a substantially higher percentage of fly balls and struck out fewer batters, neither of which is a flavorful ingredient in a recipe for success. In his favor, a HR/FB that high is unlikely to persist, and he still possesses a blistering fastball and a biting slider. Whether he'll continue to close has yet to be determined, but whatever his role, he will play a key role in the bullpen.

Aaron Heilman

Born: **11/12/1978** Age: **32**
Bats: R Throws: R Height: **6' 5"** Weight: **220**
Breakout: **14%** Improve: **31%** Collapse: **19%**
Attrition: **13%** MLB: **64%**

Comparables:
Jerry Spradlin, Scott Proctor, Bobby Seay (76)

YEAR	TEAM	LVL	AGE	W	L	SV	G	GS	IP	H	HR	BB	SO	EqBB9	EqSO9	GB%	BABIP	WHIP	ERA	FRA	WARP
2008	NYN	MLB	29	3	8	3	78	0	76	75	10	46	80	5.4	9.5	44%	.308	1.71	5.21	5.26	-0.2
2009	CHN	MLB	30	4	4	1	70	0	72^{1}	68	9	35	65	4.4	8.1	44%	.289	1.44	4.23	4.01	0.8
2010	ARI	MLB	31	5	8	6	70	0	72	73	9	26	55	3.3	6.9	37%	.290	1.44	4.38	4.69	0.0
2011	*ARI*	*MLB*	*32*	*4*	*1*	*4*	*77*	*0*	*77*	*79*	*10*	*33*	*64*	*3.8*	*7.4*	*43%*	*.302*	*1.44*	*4.60*	*5.00*	*-0.1*

Can we assume that the ship has sailed on Heilman's finding his way back into a starting rotation? It's tough to imagine that a middling reliever who hasn't excelled anywhere would somehow become a model of consistency and effectiveness with vastly increased playing time. If anything, the opposite should be expected, as he would be unable to mask any of his considerable faults in a more substantial role. Little differentiates him from a bevy of cheaper relievers, aside from name recognition.

David Holmberg

Born: **7/19/1991** Age: **19**
Bats: R Throws: L Height: **6' 4"** Weight: **220**
Breakout: **0%** Improve: **0%** Collapse: **0%**
Attrition: **0%** MLB: **0%**

Comparables:
Dick Brodowski, Joe Moeller, Rick Wise (73)

YEAR	TEAM	LVL	AGE	W	L	SV	G	GS	IP	H	HR	BB	SO	EqBB9	EqSO9	GB%	BABIP	WHIP	ERA	FRA	WARP
2009	BRI	Rk	17	2	2	0	14	8	40	40	5	18	37	4.1	8.3	50%	.307	1.50	4.72	6.10	0.1
2010	GRF	Rk	18	1	1	0	8	13	54^{2}	72	2	12	41	2.0	6.8	63%	.378	1.54	4.94	4.33	2.5
2010	MSO	Rk	18	1	4	0	7	8	37^{1}	47	2	7	47	1.7	11.3	57%	.398	1.45	3.62	4.65	2.1
2011	*ARI*	*MLB*	*19*	*2*	*6*	*0*	*11*	*11*	*60^{2}*	*81*	*10*	*37*	*28*	*5.4*	*4.2*	*48%*	*.331*	*1.94*	*7.21*	*7.84*	*-0.7*

Holmberg, who came over in the deal that sent Edwin Jackson to the White Sox, is known more for polish and acumen than raw ability, entirely appropriate for a fellow whose name is a near homonym for a formal hat with a rigidly fixed brim. The consensus seems to be that his velocity will increase as he matures and adds weight, but this projection is based on a kind of future-subjunctive dreaming that he will throw harder merely because his body type suggests that he should. If those dreams have the power of prophecy, Holmberg could blossom into a midrotation stalwart, but there is no guarantee that it will happen.

Daniel Hudson

Born: **3/9/1987** Age: **24**
Bats: R Throws: R Height: **6' 3"** Weight: **225**
Breakout: **24%** Improve: **58%** Collapse: **11%**
Attrition: **12%** MLB: **94%**

Comparables:
Max Scherzer, Yovani Gallardo, Joba Chamberlain (64)

YEAR	TEAM	LVL	AGE	W	L	SV	G	GS	IP	H	HR	BB	SO	EqBB9	EqSO9	GB%	BABIP	WHIP	ERA	FRA	WARP
2008	GRF	Rk	21	7	4	0	16	17	82^{1}	61	6	24	109	2.6	11.9	52%	.291	1.09	3.17	3.47	2.4
2009	KAN	A	22	1	2	0	4	4	22	15	0	2	30	0.8	12.3	56%	.300	0.91	1.23	2.54	0.8
2009	WNS	A+	22	4	3	0	8	8	45	31	3	13	49	2.6	9.8	53%	.252	1.02	3.40	4.14	0.9
2009	BIR	AA	22	7	0	0	9	9	56^{1}	37	1	10	63	1.6	10.1	39%	.269	0.89	1.44	2.22	2.1
2009	CHR	AAA	22	2	0	0	5	7	24	22	1	9	24	3.4	9.0	34%	.313	1.38	2.25	3.35	0.7
2009	CHA	MLB	22	1	1	0	6	2	18^{2}	16	3	9	14	4.3	6.8	34%	.236	1.39	3.38	5.13	0.1
2010	CHR	AAA	23	11	4	0	17	18	93^{1}	81	13	31	108	3.0	10.4	43%	.286	1.24	3.38	3.83	2.2
2010	CHA	MLB	23	1	1	0	3	3	15^{2}	17	1	11	14	6.3	8.0	30%	.356	1.79	6.32	5.10	0.0
2010	ARI	MLB	23	7	1	0	11	11	79^{2}	51	7	16	70	1.8	7.9	40%	.216	0.89	1.69	2.33	3.1
2011	*ARI*	*MLB*	*24*	*10*	*7*	*0*	*24*	*24*	*138*	*126*	*17*	*51*	*131*	*3.3*	*8.5*	*43%*	*.292*	*1.28*	*3.80*	*4.13*	*3.6*

The Diamondbacks turned Max Scherzer into Edwin Jackson and Ian Kennedy, then sent Jackson to the White Sox for Hudson, netting two very solid starters with six years of team control apiece. Like Kennedy, Hudson possesses above-average command and control, but, unlike his 89 mph teammate, calls upon heat in the 93-95 mph range. A 23-year-old starter producing 3.6

WARP in under 100 innings is someone to follow, but be aware that Hudson isn't known for having a plus-plus repertoire. The lack of a true out pitch and a deep arsenal stands in the way of his achieving acedom, but he is off to an auspicious start.

Ian Kennedy
Born: **12/19/1984** Age: **26**
Bats: **R** Throws: **R** Height: **6' 0"** Weight: **190**
Breakout: **21%** Improve: **57%** Collapse: **20%**
Attrition: **12%** MLB: **93%**
Comparables:
Tom Sturdivant, Mel Queen, Orel Hershiser (72)

YEAR	TEAM	LVL	AGE	W	L	SV	G	GS	IP	H	HR	BB	SO	EqBB9	EqSO9	GB%	BABIP	WHIP	ERA	FRA	WARP
2008	SWB	AAA	23	5	4	0	15	15	81	63	5	24	85	2.7	9.4	42%	.275	1.16	2.22	3.38	2.3
2008	NYA	MLB	23	0	4	0	10	9	39^{2}	50	5	26	27	5.9	6.1	43%	.333	1.94	8.17	7.94	-0.8
2009	SWB	AAA	24	1	0	0	5	5	25^{2}	18	0	7	31	2.5	10.9	40%	.290	0.97	1.40	1.67	1.3
2009	NYA	MLB	24	0	0	0	1	0	1	0	0	2	1	18.0	9.0	0%	.000	3.00	0.00	-1.34	0.1
2010	ARI	MLB	25	9	10	0	32	33	194	163	26	70	168	3.2	7.8	39%	.256	1.25	3.80	4.38	2.7
2011	*ARI*	*MLB*	*26*	*8*	*6*	*0*	*19*	*19*	100^{2}	*92*	*12*	*40*	*89*	*3.6*	*8.0*	*42%*	*.287*	*1.32*	*3.96*	*4.30*	*2.6*

Kennedy's modus operandi has long been pinpoint control, which is what made his utter lack of it with the Yankees so puzzling. The key part of the Diamondbacks' return in the deal sending Max Scherzer to the Tigers, Kennedy found his form in the senior circuit and put together a very solid season. Despite just middling stuff, he has always excelled at spotting his pitches just so, and he gets an above-average number of called strikes. Just 26 years old, Kennedy has plenty of room to improve, particularly given that he has the ability to lower his walk rate. Probably ineligible for arbitration until 2012 and under team control until 2015, Kennedy doesn't possess ace upside like Scherzer's, but he should be a very cost-effective midrotation starter for years to come.

Zach Kroenke
Born: **4/21/1984** Age: **27**
Bats: **R** Throws: **L** Height: **6' 2"** Weight: **210**
Breakout: **0%** Improve: **1%** Collapse: **1%**
Attrition: **0%** MLB: **1%**
Comparables:
Jesus Delgado, Sean Burnett, J.D. Durbin (85)

YEAR	TEAM	LVL	AGE	W	L	SV	G	GS	IP	H	HR	BB	SO	EqBB9	EqSO9	GB%	BABIP	WHIP	ERA	FRA	WARP
2008	TRN	AA	24	6	0	1	37	0	43^{2}	28	4	26	44	5.4	9.1	54%	.218	1.26	2.89	3.68	0.6
2009	SWB	AAA	25	7	1	4	40	2	78^{1}	58	4	33	60	3.8	6.9	51%	.249	1.16	1.95	3.63	1.3
2010	RNO	AAA	26	7	3	2	40	9	97^{1}	94	5	39	69	3.6	6.4	45%	.295	1.38	3.51	4.07	1.9
2010	ARI	MLB	26	1	0	0	3	1	6^{2}	9	2	4	2	5.4	2.7	50%	.292	1.95	6.75	7.03	-0.1
2011	*ARI*	*MLB*	*27*	*3*	*2*	*0*	*44*	*4*	*81*	*90*	*10*	*41*	*53*	*4.6*	*5.8*	*46%*	*.308*	*1.61*	*5.24*	*5.70*	*-0.3*

After lifting Kroenke from the Yankees in the 2009 Rule 5 draft, the Diamondbacks hoped to turn the low-velocity lefty into a southpaw specialist. Last season, he struggled mightily as a reliever at Triple-A, posting a 5.06 RA in 53 1/3 innings, but managed an impressive 2.25 RA in nine starts and 43 frames as a starter. In the majors, he continued this trend, though over a drastically reduced sample of performance. Since Kroenke has no chance of being a successful starter in the long term, it is to be hoped that the ground-ball-inclined lefty—whose name sounds like a cross between Zack Greinke and the late Crocodile Hunter Steve Irwin's catchphrase—can apply his transient success in the rotation to his work in relief.

Rodrigo Lopez
Born: **12/14/1975** Age: **35**
Bats: **R** Throws: **R** Height: **6' 1"** Weight: **180**
Breakout: **18%** Improve: **42%** Collapse: **20%**
Attrition: **15%** MLB: **84%**
Comparables:
Scott Sanderson, Ed Whitson, John Smiley (77)

YEAR	TEAM	LVL	AGE	W	L	SV	G	GS	IP	H	HR	BB	SO	EqBB9	EqSO9	GB%	BABIP	WHIP	ERA	FRA	WARP
2009	LEH	AAA	33	7	5	0	18	21	100^{1}	122	9	14	71	1.3	6.4	46%	.342	1.38	4.22	4.50	1.2
2009	PHI	MLB	33	3	1	0	7	6	30	42	3	11	19	3.3	5.7	37%	.375	1.77	6.00	5.64	0.0
2010	ARI	MLB	34	7	16	0	33	36	200	227	37	56	116	2.5	5.2	40%	.287	1.43	5.00	5.59	0.2
2011	*ARI*	*MLB*	*35*	*6*	*10*	*0*	*22*	*22*	*121*	*153*	*21*	*35*	*69*	*2.6*	*5.1*	*43%*	*.322*	*1.54*	*5.70*	*6.19*	*0.4*

Lopez had a paradoxical season, defining replacement level in terms of WARP while tallying exactly 200 innings. Generally speaking, replacement-level starters are not afforded the opportunity to make that many starts or to toe the rubber for that many frames, but desperate times in Arizona called for desperate measures. At the age of 35, Lopez is exactly who we think he is: a durable right arm with no potential or upside, who sometimes looks decent enough to merit more action.

Wade Miley

Born: **11/13/1986** Age: **24**
Bats: **L** Throws: **L** Height: **6' 2"** Weight: **190**
Breakout: **5%** Improve: **10%** Collapse: **3%**
Attrition: **6%** MLB: **15%**

Comparables:
Anthony Ortega, Aaron Laffey, Trevor Bell (77)

YEAR	TEAM	LVL	AGE	W	L	SV	G	GS	IP	H	HR	BB	SO	EqBB9	EqSO9	GB%	BABIP	WHIP	ERA	FRA	WARP
2009	SBN	A	22	5	9	0	21	23	113^{2}	127	8	29	91	2.3	7.2	58%	.342	1.41	3.96	3.57	2.6
2010	VIS	A+	23	4	5	0	14	16	80^{1}	81	1	37	50	4.1	5.6	66%	.313	1.48	3.25	3.64	1.6
2010	MOB	AA	23	5	3	0	14	17	79	64	5	28	67	3.2	7.6	61%	.276	1.18	1.82	1.83	3.6
2011	*ARI*	*MLB*	*24*	*5*	*8*	*0*	*16*	*16*	*90*	*111*	*12*	*45*	*50*	*4.5*	*5.0*	*52%*	*.323*	*1.72*	*5.91*	*6.42*	*0.1*

Upon reaching Double-A, Miley, who had been picked in the supplemental phase of 2008's first round, resumed throwing as hard as he did in college, hitting from the low 90s to 95 mph—qualities that had made him such a high draft pick in the first place and had largely disappeared when he turned pro. If the uptick was real and not a short-term fluke, Miley can be rated a very serious pitcher, the kind of hurler the Diamondbacks thought they were getting when they signed him.

Kevin Mulvey

Born: **5/26/1985** Age: **26**
Bats: **R** Throws: **R** Height: **6' 2"** Weight: **195**
Breakout: **17%** Improve: **48%** Collapse: **11%**
Attrition: **27%** MLB: **68%**

Comparables:
Mike Ekstrom, David Pauley, Marco Estrada (75)

YEAR	TEAM	LVL	AGE	W	L	SV	G	GS	IP	H	HR	BB	SO	EqBB9	EqSO9	GB%	BABIP	WHIP	ERA	FRA	WARP
2008	ROC	AAA	23	7	9	0	27	32	148	152	16	48	121	2.9	7.4	41%	.303	1.39	3.77	5.02	1.8
2009	ROC	AAA	24	5	8	0	24	26	149	153	12	54	113	3.3	6.8	52%	.308	1.44	3.81	5.19	0.8
2009	ARI	MLB	24	0	3	0	6	4	23	23	5	12	18	4.7	7.0	47%	.269	1.61	7.04	8.43	-0.5
2009	MIN	MLB	24	0	0	0	2	0	1^{1}	6	0	0	0	0.0	0.0	0%	.600	4.50	27.00	12.14	-0.1
2010	RNO	AAA	25	7	7	0	27	30	156^{2}	161	11	60	109	3.4	6.3	53%	.305	1.47	4.48	4.07	3.8
2010	ARI	MLB	25	0	0	0	2	0	3	5	2	2	1	6.0	3.0	38%	.273	2.67	6.00	5.40	0.0
2011	*ARI*	*MLB*	*26*	*7*	*9*	*0*	*22*	*22*	*127*	*142*	*16*	*52*	*83*	*3.6*	*5.9*	*47%*	*.312*	*1.52*	*5.04*	*5.48*	*1.3*

Maybe the expectations were unjustly high from the start—big things were expected, given his inclusion in 2008's Johan Santana trade—but Mulvey has shown no signs of developing into a reliable starter or reliever. His repertoire isn't deep enough to confuse hitters multiple times through the order, and the decay of his high ground-ball rate leaves him without much to offer. Rare are the pitchers who succeed strictly with command, which is about all Mulvey brings to the table these days.

Jarrod Parker

Born: **12/27/1988** Age: **22**
Bats: **R** Throws: **R** Height: **6' 1"** Weight: **180**
Breakout: **9%** Improve: **18%** Collapse: **2%**
Attrition: **5%** MLB: **22%**

Comparables:
Matt Keough, Gary Nolan, Erv Palica (75)

YEAR	TEAM	LVL	AGE	W	L	SV	G	GS	IP	H	HR	BB	SO	EqBB9	EqSO9	GB%	BABIP	WHIP	ERA	FRA	WARP
2008	SBN	A	19	13	6	0	26	28	128^{2}	121	9	37	128	2.6	9.0	46%	.304	1.28	3.29	4.06	2.2
2009	MOB	AA	20	4	6	0	16	18	78^{1}	82	2	34	74	3.9	8.5	56%	.351	1.57	3.33	3.48	2.0
2011	*ARI*	*MLB*	*22*	*7*	*9*	*0*	*22*	*22*	*106^{1}*	*119*	*13*	*51*	*79*	*4.3*	*6.7*	*46%*	*.321*	*1.59*	*5.33*	*5.79*	*1.1*

Parker, the ninth-overall pick in the 2009 draft, missed the entire season recovering from Tommy John surgery, but remains the best prospect in the system. Prior to going under the knife, he sat in the mid-90s with his fastball and could dial it up to the 97-98 mph range. He showed signs of regaining that velocity in the instructional league, so the surgery might not have damaged his chief asset. Add in a plus slider and a major-league-ready changeup, and Parker has an all-star ceiling. He will be handled very carefully this season, but could still make it to the major leagues. In light of the injury, the righty carries risk, but if his development continues without interruption, the Diamondbacks could feature a young, exciting, and team-controlled Parker-led rotation for the next five or six seasons.

Wes Roemer

Born: **10/7/1986** Age: **24**
Bats: **R** Throws: **R** Height: **6' 0"** Weight: **205**
Breakout: **15%** Improve: **19%** Collapse: **4%**
Attrition: **2%** MLB: **33%**

Comparables:
Amaury Telemaco, Billy Hoeft, Anthony Ortega (72)

YEAR	TEAM	LVL	AGE	W	L	SV	G	GS	IP	H	HR	BB	SO	EqBB9	EqSO9	GB%	BABIP	WHIP	ERA	FRA	WARP
2008	VIS	A+	21	7	12	0	28	32	162^{2}	199	25	33	122	1.8	6.8	46%	.341	1.50	4.48	5.12	1.1
2009	VIS	A+	22	3	1	0	6	6	30^{2}	33	0	13	18	3.8	5.3	55%	.327	1.53	1.76	3.59	0.6
2009	MOB	AA	22	9	9	0	22	23	134^{2}	132	13	43	98	2.9	6.5	44%	.291	1.37	4.01	462	1.2
2010	MOB	AA	23	2	1	0	8	8	52^{2}	52	5	11	43	1.9	7.3	44%	.298	1.25	2.39	3.21	1.4
2010	RNO	AAA	23	2	6	0	14	12	71^{2}	90	17	39	57	4.9	7.2	45%	.332	1.83	7.03	7.66	-0.7
2011	*ARI*	*MLB*	*24*	*4*	*9*	*0*	*18*	*18*	*108*	*137*	*21*	*46*	*66*	*3.8*	*5.4*	*44%*	*.323*	*1.68*	*6.50*	*7.07*	*-0.6*

Roemer's debut won't touch off a bidding war in fantasy auction leagues, and he's unlikely to develop into a true impact arm, but he brings enough to the table to offer hope for his future. He excels in the control department and keeps the ball on the ground. These attributes allowed him to dominate in college, but aren't enough to enable the same in the pros. Roemer is still making adjustments; the tuning is crucial, as he has no margin for error. His skill set should translate to the majors, most likely in a relief role.

Joe Saunders
Born: **6/16/1981** Age: **30**
Bats: L Throws: L Height: **6' 3"** Weight: **210**
Breakout: **11%** Improve: **39%** Collapse: **20%**
Attrition: **5%** MLB: **95%**
Comparables:
Scott Erickson, Jeremy Guthrie, Brian Bannister (73)

YEAR	TEAM	LVL	AGE	W	L	SV	G	GS	IP	H	HR	BB	SO	EqBB9	EqSO9	GB%	BABIP	WHIP	ERA	FRA	WARP
2008	ANA	MLB	27	17	7	0	31	35	198	187	21	53	103	2.4	4.7	48%	.267	1.24	3.41	4.41	2.6
2009	ANA	MLB	28	16	7	0	31	32	186	202	29	64	101	3.1	4.9	48%	.286	1.46	4.60	5.28	0.9
2010	ANA	MLB	29	6	10	0	20	22	120^{2}	135	14	45	64	3.4	4.8	44%	.304	1.50	4.62	4.93	0.3
2010	ARI	MLB	29	3	7	0	13	14	82^{2}	97	11	19	50	2.1	5.4	46%	.314	1.45	4.25	5.18	0.4
2011	*ARI*	*MLB*	*30*	*10*	*12*	*0*	*31*	*31*	*193^{2}*	*219*	*27*	*62*	*112*	*2.9*	*5.2*	*46%*	*.308*	*1.45*	*4.97*	*5.40*	*1.9*

Saunders joined the Diamondbacks as part of the Dan Haren deal and posted mediocre numbers in his new digs. One wonders what the organization saw that others didn't. Saunders does not strike out many batters, is not known for pinpoint control, and is becoming increasingly expensive as his salary rises through arbitration. He represents the type of pitcher a team lives with while under its control, not one sought to improve a rotation. Put aside who Saunders was traded for, because there is no rationalizing it; he's a decent back-of-the-rotation starter, even if—as then-GM Jerry DiPoto infamously noted—his career winning percentage is impressive.

Tyler Skaggs
Born: **7/13/1991** Age: **19**
Bats: L Throws: L Height: **6' 4"** Weight: **195**
Breakout: **0%** Improve: **0%** Collapse: **0%**
Attrition: **0%** MLB: **0%**
Comparables:
Milt Pappas, Larry Dierker, Don Drysdale (77)

YEAR	TEAM	LVL	AGE	W	L	SV	G	GS	IP	H	HR	BB	SO	EqBB9	EqSO9	GB%	BABIP	WHIP	ERA	FRA	WARP
2010	CDR	A	18	8	4	0	19	15	82^{1}	78	6	21	82	2.3	9.0	53%	.316	1.25	3.50	3.45	2.2
2011	*ARI*	*MLB*	*19*	*3*	*4*	*0*	*15*	*9*	*50^{1}*	*55*	*7*	*22*	*37*	*3.9*	*6.7*	*46%*	*.312*	*1.51*	*5.05*	*5.49*	*0.6*

The biggest prospect prize in the Haren trade, Skaggs offers plenty to dream on, but the gap between what he is and what he can be is significant. It's hard not to get excited by a skinny, long-levered lefty who can throw in the low 90s and uses a 12-to-6 curve as his out pitch, but for the trade to really pay off, he'll need to become all that was envisioned for him when he was taken by the Angels in the supplemental phase of 2009's first round. We're two years away from knowing if Skaggs is a star or back-of-the-rotation starter.

Cesar Valdez
Born: **3/17/1985** Age: **26**
Bats: R Throws: R Height: **6' 2"** Weight: **200**
Breakout: **6%** Improve: **9%** Collapse: **3%**
Attrition: **12%** MLB: **14%**
Comparables:
Mike Ekstrom, Marco Estrada, Matt Chico (81)

YEAR	TEAM	LVL	AGE	W	L	SV	G	GS	IP	H	HR	BB	SO	EqBB9	EqSO9	GB%	BABIP	WHIP	ERA	FRA	WARP
2008	VIS	A+	23	10	3	0	15	15	96	88	5	16	80	1.5	7.5	55%	.290	1.11	2.53	3.60	2.2
2008	MOB	AA	23	3	5	0	12	12	64^{1}	63	2	23	60	3.2	8.4	56%	.333	1.40	3.92	4.07	1.2
2009	RNO	AAA	24	7	6	0	19	19	96	103	16	30	60	2.8	5.6	49%	.282	1.43	4.69	5.80	0.4
2010	RNO	AAA	25	6	10	0	20	20	97^{2}	110	12	49	92	4.5	8.5	54%	.340	1.68	5.81	6.57	-0.1
2010	ARI	MLB	25	1	2	0	9	4	20	29	2	10	13	4.5	5.9	58%	.380	2.00	7.65	7.15	-0.4
2011	*PIT*	*MLB*	*26*	*7*	*10*	*0*	*22*	*22*	*115*	*135*	*16*	*50*	*69*	*3.9*	*5.4*	*49%*	*.314*	*1.60*	*5.59*	*6.08*	*0.4*

Valdez experienced early success in spite of throwing a mediocre heater, due to the difficulty younger hitters had in timing his off-speed pitches. As he progressed through the system, hitters responded more adeptly to his slurve and changeup, and the results predictably suffered. Even more concerning was his sudden loss of control, as a pitcher without a plus fastball will struggle to survive if he can't spot his offerings. Despite being sent to the Pirates as part of the Zach Duke deal, his future is still likely as that of a long reliever or swingman.

Esmerling Vasquez
Born: **11/7/1983** Age: **27**
Bats: R Throws: R Height: **6' 1"** Weight: **175**
Breakout: **3%** Improve: **7%** Collapse: **5%**
Attrition: **2%** MLB: **13%**
Comparables:
Roger Weaver, Dave Boswell, Tom Sturdivant (82)

YEAR	TEAM	LVL	AGE	W	L	SV	G	GS	IP	H	HR	BB	SO	EqBB9	EqSO9	GB%	BABIP	WHIP	ERA	FRA	WARP
2008	TUC	AAA	24	3	6	0	24	20	83	79	11	73	57	7.9	6.2	37%	.278	1.98	6.18	7.30	-0.7
2009	ARI	MLB	25	3	3	0	53	0	53	52	4	29	45	4.9	7.6	44%	.306	1.58	4.42	4.75	0.1
2010	ARI	MLB	26	1	6	0	57	0	53^{2}	46	6	38	55	6.4	9.2	33%	.296	1.68	5.37	6.13	-0.8
2011	*ARI*	*MLB*	*27*	*4*	*3*	*1*	*74*	*4*	*91*	*94*	*12*	*57*	*71*	*5.6*	*7.0*	*42%*	*.304*	*1.66*	*5.57*	*6.06*	*-0.7*

Esmerling Vasquez is another young Diamondbacks hurler who possesses the stuff to succeed, but lacks the ability to use it effectively. Unfortunately, this description could be written for umpteen other pitching prospects in the system, and little separates Vasquez from the rest. He throws hard, but without control, and does not profile as a ground-ball pitcher. Throwing 94 mph will continue to earn him shots, but he practically eliminated the slider from his repertoire in favor of a mediocre changeup last season. To be more effective, he will need to utilize both off-speed offerings to offset the velocity of his heater. However, if he can't throw the slider for strikes, this assessment is moot.

Brandon Webb

Born: **5/9/1979** Age: **32**
Bats: R Throws: R Height: **6' 2"** Weight: **228**
Breakout: **10%** Improve: **33%** Collapse: **34%**
Attrition: **11%** MLB: **92%**

Comparables:
Andy Pettitte, Don Robinson, Chris Bosio (65)

YEAR	TEAM	LVL	AGE	W	L	SV	G	GS	IP	H	HR	BB	SO	EqBB9	EqSO9	GB%	BABIP	WHIP	ERA	FRA	WARP
2008	ARI	MLB	29	22	7	0	34	37	226^{2}	206	13	65	183	2.6	7.3	65%	.288	1.25	3.30	1.93	10.6
2009	ARI	MLB	30	0	0	0	1	1	4	6	2	2	2	4.5	4.5	53%	.308	2.25	13.50	14.12	-0.2
2011	*TEX*	*MLB*	*32*	*11*	*8*	*0*	*26*	*26*	*173*	*169*	*14*	*52*	*127*	*2.7*	*6.6*	*54%*	*.298*	*1.28*	*3.63*	*3.95*	*4.2*

Easily one of the best pitchers in the game from 2003 to 2008, Webb has thrown just four innings over the past two seasons and will have to spend the next couple years reestablishing his health, never mind his pitching ability. When they exercised Webb's $8.5 million option before last season, the Diamondbacks hoped that their ace would help them contend or at least showcase enough talent to draw interest elsewhere. Unfortunately, recovery from shoulder debridement surgery did not go as planned, and he missed the entire season. Webb's is an old story, almost Shakespearean in its star-crossed dimensions: a young man with immense talent pitches his heart out and his arm off in a mostly futile effort to transcend the mediocrity of those around him, but all too soon his powers have been spent in vain. Webb may yet come back, but he will more likely have been reinvented than restored. Seneca wondered if it could be said of our beloved dead that they had not been lost, but merely gone before. In the case of a pitcher's stuff, it's often the exact opposite. The Rangers rolled the dice on a one-year contract heavy with incentives.

LINEOUTS

HITTERS

PLAYER	TEAM	LVL	AGE	PA	R	2B	3B	HR	RBI	BB	SO	SB-CS	AVG/OBP/SLG	TAv	BABIP	BRR	FRAA	WARP
INF M. Hallberg	RNO	AAA	24	451	52	24	3	1	44	51	47	5-4	.263/.344/.349	.246	.284	2.8	2B 0, 3B 0	0.8
C J. Hester	RNO	AAA	26	155	30	12	4	7	29	16	26	0-0	.372/.452/.672	.338	.415	0.0	C 1	2.0
	ARI	MLB	26	106	9	7	0	2	7	11	32	1-0	.211/.293/.347	.231	.295	-0.3	C 0	0.1
OF D. Macias*	RNO	AAA	27	329	47	11	5	6	28	51	53	0-0	.256/.395/.398	.266	.292	0.0	CF -8, RF 1	0.4
SS R. Navarro	MSO	Rk	18	312	44	13	8	3	36	20	49	2-3	.284/.327/.415	.282	.329	-0.2	SS -4	1.8
C K. Schmidt	MOB	AA	25	448	49	31	3	12	67	34	66	7-3	.314/.382/.493	.306	.345	-2.9	C 0	3.6
	ARI	MLB	25	9	0	0	0	0	0	1	0	0-0	.125/.222/.125	.159	.125	0.0	C 0	-0.1
INF R. Wheeler*	VIS	A+	21	501	60	25	2	9	57	35	98	2-1	.284/.343/.404	.280	.343	-1.8	3B -9, 1B -1	1.4
	MOB	AA	21	88	9	3	0	3	10	6	22	0-0	.220/.284/.366	.241	.263	0.2	3B -1, 1B 0	0.0

Mark Hallberg makes consistent contact, can play second and third base and even shortstop in a pinch ... in other words, he could be the next Augie Ojeda. **John Hester** is a career backup to the backup catcher, an interchangeable figure on practically every team. Nothing in his offensive or defensive skill set stands out, but his mere ability to crouch behind the plate will earn him playing time. Plus defensive skills and the ability to draw plenty of walks is going to get **Drew Macias** back to the majors at some point, albeit in a limited role. **Raul Navarro** is an 18-year-old shortstop who hit well at Missoula and has a good defensive tool set. Though extremely raw, he has an excellent base on which to build and could easily rise through the ranks over the next couple of years. **A. J. Pollock** missed the entire 2010 season with a fractured elbow. Some think he has potential as a 15-homer, 15-steal hitter with a batting average in the .280-.290 range. Others consider him a tweener, a fourth outfielder with little potential. Last year, we suggested that the reader stay tuned to Pollock's development, and in the absence of any further evidence, we'll repeat that recommendation for 2011. **Konrad Schmidt** has derived most of his minor-league success from zany BABIP figures, but when the dust settles, he could make for a decent backup catcher. He has shown a knack for being patient at the plate, comes with an adequate power supply, and has ways of making you talk, but his defense might not be up to snuff. **Ryan Wheeler** failed to build off a promising 2009 debut while also proving he's nothing more than a first baseman in an organization crowded with them.

PITCHERS

PLAYER	TEAM	LVL	AGE	W	L	SV	IP	H	HR	BB	SO	EqBB9	EqSO9	GB%	BABIP	WHIP	ERA	FRA	WARP
S. Allen	SBN	A	18	4	4	0	78	88	5	22	79	2.5	9.1	41%	.355	1.45	4.73	4.47	1.1
M. Belfiore*	SBN	A	21	3	10	0	126^{1}	139	6	42	105	3.0	7.5	48%	.334	1.44	3.99	5.05	0.9
K. Benson	RNO	AAA	35	1	2	0	22^{1}	34	5	11	14	4.4	5.6	49%	.354	2.10	8.46	8.95	-0.3
—	ARI	MLB	35	1	1	0	14	18	2	6	8	3.9	5.1	35%	.320	1.79	5.14	5.12	0.1
B. Boyer	ARI	MLB	28	3	2	0	57	59	3	29	29	4.6	4.6	65%	.296	1.56	4.26	4.29	-0.1
J. Collmenter	MOB	AA	24	8	3	0	85^{1}	67	3	23	81	2.4	8.5	44%	.277	1.07	1.69	1.89	3.7
—	RNO	AAA	24	4	3	0	57^{2}	64	8	26	39	4.1	6.1	40%	.304	1.58	5.77	5.79	0.1
M. Hampton*	ARI	MLB	37	0	0	0	41	3	0	1	3	2.1	6.2	42%	.250	0.92	0.00	-0.21	0.3
R. Mercedes	MOB	AA	23	3	4	1	54^{2}	69	5	25	45	4.1	7.4	44%	.352	1.76	4.45	3.81	0.7
J. Norberto*	RNO	AAA	23	3	0	4	291	25	2	19	38	5.8	11.7	49%	.319	1.50	3.07	3.38	0.5
—	ARI	MLB	23	0	2	0	20	16	3	22	15	9.9	6.8	40%	.241	1.90	5.85	6.70	-0.5
S. Rivera	COH	AAA	32	2	2	5	26	15	0	14	16	4.8	5.5	55%	.200	1.12	1.73	4.16	0.3
—	ARI	MLB	32	0	0	0	32	11	2	3	1	7.4	2.5	52%	.474	3.82	22.09	17.96	-0.4
R. Rodriguez	SLC	AAA	25	5	3	10	50^{1}	41	5	15	30	2.7	5.4	54%	.232	1.11	3.04	4.85	0.2
—	ANA	MLB	25	0	0	0	2	1	0	2	1	9.0	4.5	83%	.167	2.00	4.50	9.55	0.0
—	ARI	MLB	25	0	0	0	22	4	1	1	2	3.4	6.8	50%	.333	2.25	6.75	8.60	-0.1
C. Rosa	RNO	AAA	25	0	0	13	272	20	2	14	31	4.6	10.1	48%	.286	1.23	1.63	2.60	0.6
—	ARI	MLB	25	0	2	0	20	20	1	12	9	5.4	4.1	43%	.284	1.60	4.50	4.98	-0.1
L. Rosales	ARI	MLB	29	2	0	0	161	25	2	9	12	5.0	6.6	31%	.404	2.08	6.61	4.68	0.0
L. Septimo*	MOB	AA	24	2	2	4	281	16	1	23	37	7.3	11.8	46%	.259	1.45	3.81	4.68	-0.1
D. Stange	MOB	AA	24	4	1	13	33	14	1	11	20	3.0	5.5	43%	.153	0.82	1.64	3.64	0.4
—	RNO	AAA	24	4	3	2	231	29	3	10	16	3.9	6.2	53%	.338	1.67	6.17	6.75	-0.3
—	ARI	MLB	24	0	0	0	4	4	1	6	2	13.5	4.5	57%	.231	2.50	13.50	15.52	-0.3

Scottie Allen has good control for a 19-year-old, but his stuff is so unimpressive that he can get traded for a 27-year-old first baseman like Juan Miranda. ⊘ **Michael Belfiore** has been one of the most disappointing of 2009's top draftees (45th overall). His stuff is down significantly from his Boston College days, but hey, at least he's still left-handed. ⊘ This is the end of the road for **Kris Benson**, who might finally be healthy but has nothing left to offer. He will go down as one of the great disappointments in prospect history and forever serve as a glaring example of the unbearable lightness of pitching prospects. ⊘ For $725,000, **Blaine Boyer** is a cost-effective reliever. Anything more, and his salary would outweigh his contributions, which is why the Diamondbacks chose to nontender him in December. He throws hard and generates a ton of grounders, but struggles to control his sinker. ⊘ A former 15th-round pick, **Josh Collmenter** pitched at three minor-league levels last season and saw his peripherals worsen at each stop, to the point that he *might* project as a fifth starter in the big leagues ... but probably not. ⊘ **Mike Hampton** cannot stay healthy and offers next to nothing with no potential for more when actually on the mound. Considering his 38 years, spring training invitations and minor-league roster spots would be better spent on youngsters with some semblance of upside. But keep chasing that dream, Mike. ⊘ **Roque Mercedes** did not improve his walk rate and traded swings and misses for hits aplenty. It's hard to see how or where he fits right now; he could be a 10th or 11th pitcher in the big leagues. The Brewers snagged him off of waivers. ⊘ **Jordan Norberto** is one of hundreds of relievers who can miss bats but allows too many baserunners by walking hitters. About eight of them eventually figure it out. ⊘ **Saul Rivera** is a rubber-armed workhorse whose peripherals have eroded over the past two seasons. Given the fickle nature of relievers, he's worth a shot as a nonroster invitee due to his past success, but he shouldn't be penciled in as a potential rock in the bullpen. ⊘ Once the owner of a lively fastball, **Rafael Rodriguez** traded his heat for a sinker/slider combination that hasn't worked out so far. After coming over in the Dan Haren deal, he has his work cut out for him if he wants to compete for a bullpen spot. ⊘ **Carlos Rosa** is a work in progress as a starter-turned-reliever still trying to figure out how best to use his "stuff" out of the bullpen. ⊘ **Leo Rosales** is only successful when his pals Command and Control meet him on the mound. Last season, they usually refused to hang out with him. ⊘ **Leyson Septimo** is a converted outfielder who walked 29.7 percent of the batters he faced last season. Given his career walk rate of 19 percent, something tells us this conversion isn't sticking. ⊘ **Daniel Stange** is still working toward rediscovering his deadly fastball/slider combination following Tommy John surgery in 2009. Presurgery, he was a strikeout machine with solid, albeit unspectacular command. ⊘ **Clay Zavada** missed the entire 2010 season after undergoing Tommy John surgery. He and his mustache should be able to contribute sometime this season.

MANAGERS: A. J. HINCH/ KIRK GIBSON

YEAR	MGR	W-L	Pythag +/–	Avg PC	100+ P	120+ P	QS	BQS	REL	REL w Zero R	IBB	Subs	PH	PH Avg	PH HR	SB2	CS2	SB3	CS3	SAC Att	SAC %	POS SAC	Squeeze	Swing	In Play
2009	A.H.	58-75	-4	99.0	79	0	70	5	392	238	24	25	220	.185	5	68	22	13	9	74	60.8%	24	1	98	66
2010	A.H.	31-48	0	102.2	47	5	33	9	207	107	19	6	119	.213	0	42	11	3	2	21	81.0%	7	0	73	48
2010	K.G.	34-49	-3	94.5	30	1	40	3	246	157	19	20	151	.235	0	38	26	3	1	32	75.0%	9	0	48	31

After his controversial selection to serve as manager, Hinch's dismissal following a dismal start was far from shocking. The theory that players would respond to his tutelage, given his former position in player development, did not pan out, and he went 89-123 as skipper. Under his watch, relievers blew 21.4 percent of the potential quality starts they were handed, a figure that led the league by a hefty margin. But Hinch cannot be blamed for the sheer ineptitude of the bullpen—as noted elsewhere in the chapter, "reliever" was a misnomer in the vast majority of cases. Hinch was a victim of poor roster construction, as there was little he could do to prevent the batters from striking out more than any other team in history, or the bullpen from surrendering leads as though that were its the goal. On the surface, the Diamondbacks did not perform much better for Gibson than they had under his predecessor, but their 34-49 record with Gibson at the helm belied an improvement in run prevention that was reflected in their Pythagorean record. In fact, only Fredi Gonzalez's tenure with the Marlins produced a larger gap between actual and expected records. Under Gibson, the team blew just 6.9 percent of potential quality starts, and the starters averaged fewer pitches per outing than they had under Hinch, ranking among the five least-worked in the senior circuit after the former bench coach's elevation to field general. Gibson took a more active role in mixing and matching relievers and will likely pursue similar tactics during the 2011 season, since the Snakes have an ample supply of relievers with the potential to succeed, but no track record or defined roles to speak of.

Atlanta Braves

Perhaps the best that can be said of any man is that he left his corner of the world a better place than when he found it. Bobby Cox certainly did this for the Atlanta Braves, joining a team in disarray as general manager in October 1985 and leaving it, 25 years later, a perennial playoff contender. Best of all, Cox's gifts will keep on giving for some time. Unlike most older managers, who tend to avoid younger players as they themselves age, Cox did the Braves the favor of breaking in several younger players over the final years of his career, so the organization is well positioned to continue its annual push for a championship, however fruitless that pursuit has been since Cox won his sole ring in 1995.

BRAVES PROSPECTUS

2010 W-L: 91-72, 2nd in NL East

Pythag	.573	5th
RS/G	4.6	13th
RA/G	3.9	27th
TAv	.275	9th
BRR	-0.3	16th
FRA	4.11	7th
DER	14.5	5th
DL	773	18th
B-Age	28.4	11th
P-Age	29.8	26th
Salary	$84.4	15th
M$/MW	$1.76	8th

Ballpark: Turner Field (3-yr. PF: 100). Ted's front yard hosts an unfamiliar sight: a playoff sell-out

2010: Tossing Heymakers earns Bobby Cox a final post-season appearance

2011: Productive young core keeps the Braves in contention, especially if Jones is feeling Chipper

Action Items: Sorting out relief roles, searching for a center fielder, and adjusting to life after Bobby

Prior to 2010, the Braves had already committed to under-30 players such as Brian McCann, Martin Prado, Omar Infante, Tommy Hanson, Eric O'Flaherty, and Jair Jurrjens. As he went out the door, Cox made a regular of 20-year-old Jason Heyward; turned 25-year-old rookie Jonny Venters into an essential reliever (and a rare everyday lefty, something that is in its own way groundbreaking, given the current fashion in one-out southpaws); gave 24-year-old Kris Medlen a long, successful look as a starter before he was swept away by Tommy John surgery; and handed rookies Mike Minor, Craig Kimbrel, Michael Dunn, and Brandon Beachy generally successful auditions for future roles on the pitching staff. In 2011, first baseman Freddie Freeman, 21, who got some major-league time under Cox in September, is slotted to join the youth parade, simultaneously making the club younger and better.

Should the Braves not pull a Marlins and shy away from paying these players as they enter their arbitration years, the club has the foundation to compete for some time. And yet, the team remains frustratingly incomplete. For example, the last time the Braves had an outfield unit that managed at least league-average production in the aggregate was 2006. Braves outfielders last combined to be above average in 2005. It is one thing to struggle to find productive middle infielders or pitchers, another to be unable to find three competent hitters to pursue fly balls. The Braves have excelled at the former, but have failed at the latter (see Table 1).

A long, long time ago, the Braves had a great center fielder named Andruw Jones. Jones won the Gold Glove for 10 straight seasons and averaged 33 home runs per year, peaking at 51. In 2007, Jones simultaneously stopped hitting, stopped fielding, and reached free agency. The Braves quite wisely allowed him to sign with the Los Angeles Dodgers. The Braves would seem to have gotten out just in time, but they neglected a getaway car. In the ensuing three seasons, they

Table 1. Braves Infield vs. Outfield Production, 2008-2010

	OUTFIELD					INFIELD				
YEAR	AVG	OBP	SLG	TAv	TAv Rank	AVG	OBP	SLG	TAv	TAv Rank
2008	.260	.324	.367	.245	16	.290	.369	.453	.288	1
2009	.261	.328	.393	.252	16	.278	.354	.439	.272	4
2010	.250	.338	.389	.258	12	.275	.355	.426	.267	4

ran through Mark Kotsay, Gregor Blanco, Josh Anderson, Jordan Schafer, Nate McLouth, Ryan Church, Melky Cabrera, and Rick Ankiel, none of whom has performed satisfactorily (see Table 2).

Table 2. Braves Center Fielders, 2008-2010

YEAR	AVG	OBP	SLG	TAv	TAv Rank
2008	.286	.350	.397	.264	8
2009	.237	.331	.367	.248	13
2010	.232	.329	.339	.234	15

At the same time that the Braves were running through center fielders the same way that Pablo Sandoval runs through double-stuff Oreos, right fielder Jeff Francoeur was devolving from the dynamic 21-year-old of 2005 into one of the most hopeless, hapless players in baseball. In the opposite corner, Matt Diaz, who had delivered such a rich comeuppance to the Rays and Royals teams that had let him go without giving him a real look, had two subpar years in three due to injury. The successful arrival of rookie demigod Jason Heyward only partly redeemed this mess, as McLouth, who seemed the solution to the center-field mess in 2009, completely unraveled, and Cabrera, who still had a faint prospect-y sheen on him when acquired from the Yankees for Javier Vazquez, proved to be just another fourth/fifth outfielder.

Now that Heyward has been established as a major leaguer, the best Braves outfield prospect remaining in the minors is no one. Insofar as in-house solutions to the outfield problem go, the club is left with the hope that Jordan Schafer will recover from the seemingly chronic wrist problems that have all but destroyed his promise over the last two years, or for McLouth to stop being such a McDisappointment—even before suffering a concussion on June 9, he was hitting only .176/.295/.282 in 57 games. Though the former Pirate did rally from a month-long demotion to Triple-A Gwinnett to hit .273/.359/.527 in September, it is worth remembering that 2008 aside, McLouth's best has been far from exceptional.

The Braves are still paying for the decision they made in the 2008-2009 offseason to let the cup of Adam Dunn (as opposed to Adam Dunn's cup) pass from their lips. In February 2009, Dunn was without a place to play, having departed the Arizona Diamondbacks as a free agent. The previous season, Braves outfielders had hit a combined .260/.324/.367 with 27 home runs in 1,903 at-bats. Dunn had averaged .249/.382/.533 with 41 home runs over the previous five seasons. Defensive concerns aside, Dunn was exactly what they needed. When he signed with Washington for $20 million over two years, the Nationals gained a slugger they didn't need and the Braves lost a player who could have elevated their offense to a point that might have allowed them to make the playoffs in 2009 and put an earlier and longer-lasting hold on a postseason berth in 2010.

The Braves made an effort to correct this problem with the November trade of Mike Dunn and Omar Infante to the Marlins for veteran second baseman Dan Uggla. The ultimate impact that this move will have on the Braves' outfield production depends on Chipper Jones's ability to return in good form from a torn left anterior cruciate ligament at age 39 (he reaches the big *trente-neuf* in late April). Jones's spirit may be willing, but the flesh could be beyond rescue. Having hit .342/.435/.592 from 2006 to 2008, Jones was hitting .287/.407/.481 through the end of July 2009, when his bat went into cold storage. Over the final two months, he hit .225/.353/.343. He began 2010 in roughly the same place, batting .249/.376/.398 with seven home runs through his first 75 games. At about that moment in late July, the old Chipper reemerged. Over his final 20 games, Jones hit .324/.397/.529, and then, just as it seemed as if he might salvage the season, boom—no more knee.

Jones's final 2010 rates of .265/.381/.426 bear a strong resemblance to his .264/.388/.430 rates of the year before. This is not altogether bad news, as Jones's patience and remaining power mean he's still quite productive even if he is no longer a .300 hitter. Yet, in making his return, Jones will not only have to arrest his offensive decline, but also have to retain the mobility to play third. This may be expecting a bit much of a player who has never been one of the great hot-corner defenders—although, oddly, defensive metrics agree that he had an acceptable season with the glove in 2010.

Should Jones fail to return, Uggla will play second base and Prado will play third. If Jones does make it back, then Prado will move to left field. The catch is that no configuration involving Uggla, Prado, and Jones will leave the Braves with a good defense. Uggla is a notoriously poor defensive second baseman, and while Prado is less prone to errors, his inexperience in such basic matters as making the pivot on the double play renders him a decent but unexceptional defender.

Should Uggla and Prado play to expectations, the offensive benefits should outweigh any defensive disruptions—Braves right-handed hitters averaged just .260/.327/.387 last season, a prime factor behind the team's 28-27 record in games started by left-handed pitchers. Uggla is a career .253/.350/.454 hitter against portsiders, .306/.409/.575 in 2010. He's not the entire solution to the problem, but he will help, particularly since the Braves' offense wasn't far off in 2010. Even missing two outfield bats and lacking the solid hitting that shortstop Yunel Escobar had provided from 2007 to 2009, the Braves put together a True Average of .267, third in the National League and seventh in the majors. With the addition of Freeman at first base in place of Troy Glaus, Derrek Lee, and Eric Hinske, a season of greater health and consistency from Heyward, and more of the same from Brian McCann, Prado, and Uggla, Atlanta could better that mark.

Should McLouth give the Braves anything more than he did in 2010—and he will have to, if he wants to avoid immediate replacement by whatever Ankiel/Cabrera equivalent Frank Wren can find cheaply (or by the long-delayed Schafer sequel)—so much the better.

Given the uncertainty surrounding the offense, there will be great pressure on manager Fredi Gonzalez to get the most out of his pitching staff. One key to Gonzalez succeeding at that is to avoid overreaction to the departure of Billy Wagner by pulling Venters out of the long relief/set-up role in which Cox left him. The trend in recent years has been overwhelmingly toward using left-handers in spot relief ("LOOGY") rather than in all situations. Since 2000, 155 relievers have thrown 80 or more innings in a season. Only 13 of them, including Venters, were left-handers. Though the Braves employed lefty spot men in Eric O'Flaherty and Mike Dunn, who combined to make one spot reliever, assigning Venters to pitch in long relief prevented them from having to consider the pernicious alternative of having two such hurlers.

Pitchers like Randy Choate, J. C. Romero, and Trever Miller can spend an entire season on the roster and yet pitch only 40-50 innings. Consider that over the last three years, the average National League team has asked its bullpen to pitch 500 innings. Assuming a seven-man staff of relievers (alas), if the workload were split evenly, each pitcher would throw about 72 innings. However, we know that the workload is not split evenly. Ironically for pitchers who earn saves, it is closers themselves who are being saved from pitching meaningful innings. Over those same three seasons, closers—here generously defined as pitchers with 20 or more saves in a season—averaged about 64 innings as a group. Now the lefty spot-reliever's 50 innings have to be taken into account. The remaining five pitchers, or those theoretically lesser pitchers (assuming the team has picked its roster efficiently, choosing the seven best relievers in the organization to be on the team) that will be called upon to replace them in case of injury, will be asked to pitch 78 innings each. That doesn't seem like much, but consider that between both leagues, only eight relievers reached 78 innings in 2010. Your team has already reached the point where it is inevitable that in pursuit of one out at a time, it will be required to either increase the workload of its good relievers to an unsustainable point, increase the demands on its starters, or dip into the minor leagues for additional pitchers. The Braves can avoid this with judicious handling of Venters.

The great man is gone, but the good he has done will live after him. There are decisions to be made, including the final spot in the starting rotation, precise roles for the relievers, and the defensive alignment of the infield. Yet, the pieces are in place, some young but all, to a degree, tested. The real monument to Bobby Cox will be a Braves team that is competing for the NL East title long after age and Ruben Amaro Jr. have run the Phillies into the ground.

HITTERS

Rick Ankiel **CF**

Born: **7/19/1979** Age: **31**
Bats: L Throws: L Height: **6' 1"** Weight: **210**
Breakout: **0%** Improve: **31%** Collapse: **4%**
Attrition: **13%** MLB: **86%**

Comparables:
Chet Lemon, Leon Wagner, Craig Monroe (74)

YEAR	TEAM	LVL	AGE	PA	R	2B	3B	HR	RBI	BB	SO	SB	CS	AVG/OBP/SLG	TAv	BABIP	BRR	FRAA	WARP
2008	SLN	MLB	28	463	66	21	2	25	71	42	100	2	1	.264/.337/.506	.295	.289	1.5	CF -6, LF -2	2.3
2009	SLN	MLB	29	404	50	21	2	11	38	26	99	4	3	.231/.285/.387	.242	.283	1.7	CF 4, RF -5	0.8
2010	OMA	AAA	30	68	8	6	0	4	9	1	19	0	0	.254/.265/.522	.284	.296	-0.7	CF -2	0.1
2010	KCA	MLB	30	101	15	7	0	4	15	7	29	1	0	.261/.317/.467	.280	.333	-0.5	CF 0	0.4
2010	ATL	MLB	30	139	17	6	1	2	9	19	42	2	1	.210/.324/.328	.239	.307	1.4	CF -4	-0.1
2011	*WAS*	*MLB*	*31*	*446*	*53*	*21*	*1*	*19*	*58*	*36*	*108*	*4*	*2*	*.245/.309/.444*	*.260*	*.284*	*-0.2*	*CF -4, LF 1*	*0.8*

When Nate McLouth turned his last name into a synonym for "massive disappointment," the Braves made a quick deal to bring in Ankiel, who served them no better save for one dramatic post-season home run. He plays hard, maybe too hard, as it leads to injuries and too many strikeouts. Over the last two seasons, he hasn't hit well even against right-handed pitchers (.240/.308/.433), but he's a good defender with one of the better outfield arms around. Atlanta declined his $6 million option. He signed with the Nationals and will try to stake a claim in left field.

Melky Cabrera OF

Born: **8/11/1984** Age: **26**
Bats: S Throws: L Height: **5' 11"** Weight: **170**
Breakout: **1%** Improve: **56%** Collapse: **1%**
Attrition: **9%** MLB: **93%**

Comparables:
Richie Ashburn, Curt Flood, Billy Goodman (72)

YEAR	TEAM	LVL	AGE	PA	R	2B	3B	HR	RBI	BB	SO	SB	CS	AVG/OBP/SLG	TAv	BABIP	BRR	FRAA	WARP
2008	SWB	AAA	23	75	7	2	0	0	6	8	10	1	3	.308/.373/.339	.270	.351	-2.5	CF -1	0.0
2008	NYA	MLB	23	453	41	12	1	8	37	29	58	9	2	.249/.298/.341	.228	.268	-1.4	CF -2, RF 1	-0.5
2009	NYA	MLB	24	540	65	28	1	13	68	43	59	10	2	.274/.333/.417	.264	.285	0.4	CF -1, LF -1	1.2
2010	ATL	MLB	25	509	50	27	3	4	42	42	64	7	1	.256/.314/.354	.244	.284	-1.3	LF -2, CF -1	-0.3
2011	*KCA*	*MLB*	*26*	*569*	*65*	*26*	*2*	*10*	*57*	*49*	*65*	*10*	*3*	*.265/.327/.383*	*.252*	*.280*	*-0.1*	*CF -1, LF -1*	*0.7*

Yet another outfielder who failed to capitalize on the collapse of McLouth, Cabrera arrived in Atlanta as a line-drive hitter who could at least hold his own in all three outfield slots, but he got fat and became a defensive hitter. In the end, the Braves were left with a pudgy switch-hitter who can't hit lefties, doesn't walk, doesn't hit for power, and is limited to a corner. When you add that all up, you get a release at the end of the year, followed by an invitation to join the Royals' menagerie of mediocre outfielders. For the sixth year in a row, Cabrera may find himself with far more playing time than he can possibly reward.

Brooks Conrad 3B

Born: **1/16/1980** Age: **31**
Bats: S Throws: R Height: **5' 11"** Weight: **190**
Breakout: **4%** Improve: **26%** Collapse: **6%**
Attrition: **15%** MLB: **68%**

Comparables:
Justin Leone, Bobby Scales, Vern Stephens (73)

YEAR	TEAM	LVL	AGE	PA	R	2B	3B	HR	RBI	BB	SO	SB	CS	AVG/OBP/SLG	TAv	BABIP	BRR	FRAA	WARP
2008	SAC	AAA	28	544	89	30	5	31	92	45	141	4	1	.240/.307/.509	.277	.269	1.6	2B -4, SS 1	2.4
2008	OAK	MLB	28	19	0	1	0	0	2	0	9	0	0	.158/.158/.211	.105	.300	0.0	3B -1, 2B -1	-0.4
2009	GWN	AAA	29	462	64	25	0	12	64	53	108	13	1	.269/.362/.422	.273	.329	5.7	2B 1, SS 1	2.3
2009	ATL	MLB	29	58	7	1	2	2	8	3	14	0	0	.204/.259/.407	.221	.237	0.4	2B 0, 3B 0	0.0
2010	ATL	MLB	30	176	28	11	1	8	33	16	45	5	1	.252/.318/.490	.284	.293	2.0	3B -1, 2B 2	1.1
2011	*ATL*	*MLB*	*31*	*420*	*48*	*19*	*1*	*16*	*51*	*39*	*109*	*6*	*2*	*.232/.304/.419*	*.251*	*.277*	*0.0*	*2B -1, 3B -1*	*0.4*

Conrad was Atlanta's feel-good story of the year until the last 10 games the team played. With four walk-off hits, a pair of pinch-hit grand slams, and six of his eight home runs coming in the seventh inning or later, it's easy to say the Braves wouldn't have made the playoffs without him. Then he made an error in each of the last four regular-season games, and every ground ball coming his way in the postseason turned into an adventure as the defensive miscues clearly got into his head. Conrad was never meant to play every day, and defense has been a problem for him throughout his career, but the way fans reacted to Conrad's struggles—with far more sympathy than acrimony—makes one wonder if we have matured as a society or whether reality-show culture has inured us to the inept, the misplaced, and the out-of-their-depth.

Matt Diaz LF

Born: **3/3/1978** Age: **33**
Bats: R Throws: R Height: **6' 1"** Weight: **206**
Breakout: **0%** Improve: **31%** Collapse: **6%**
Attrition: **10%** MLB: **86%**

Comparables:
Marlon Anderson, Rondell White, Hank Bauer (75)

YEAR	TEAM	LVL	AGE	PA	R	2B	3B	HR	RBI	BB	SO	SB	CS	AVG/OBP/SLG	TAv	BABIP	BRR	FRAA	WARP
2008	ATL	MLB	30	140	9	2	0	2	14	3	32	4	2	.244/.264/.304	.208	.304	1.6	LF 2	-0.2
2009	ATL	MLB	31	425	56	18	4	13	58	35	90	12	5	.313/.386/.488	.305	.376	-4.6	RF -9, LF 1	1.5
2010	ATL	MLB	32	243	27	17	2	7	31	13	44	3	1	.251/.300/.440	.274	.280	0.3	LF 3	1.1
2011	*PIT*	*MLB*	*33*	*314*	*38*	*13*	*1*	*9*	*37*	*20*	*62*	*6*	*2*	*.277/.332/.426*	*.266*	*.319*	*-0.2*	*LF 3, RF -2*	*0.8*

Diaz has become the Brett Saberhagen of fourth outfielders, and next year is an odd number, so he should be good if you believe in trends you shouldn't believe in. He doesn't have power, he's a bad defensive outfielder, and he can't run. What he can do is look like an all-star when facing left-handers, against whom he boasts a career .335/.373/.533 line. As long as you know his limitations (and can read a calendar), it's easy to get value out of him. The Pirates signed him to a two-year, $4.25 million contract to (at least initially) platoon in right field with Garrett Jones. Given Jones's second-half disappearing act, there is a huge risk for Diaz to suffer from overexposure.

Freddie Freeman 1B

Born: **9/12/1989** Age: **21**
Bats: L Throws: R Height: **6' 5"** Weight: **225**
Breakout: **1%** Improve: **18%** Collapse: **0%**
Attrition: **6%** MLB: **24%**

Comparables:
Billy Butler, Orlando Cepeda, Jason Thompson (70)

YEAR	TEAM	LVL	AGE	PA	R	2B	3B	HR	RBI	BB	SO	SB	CS	AVG/OBP/SLG	TAv	BABIP	BRR	FRAA	WARP
2008	ROM	A	18	537	72	33	7	18	95	46	84	5	5	.316/.380/.521	.331	.352	-6.4	1B -4	3.2
2009	MYR	A+	19	283	40	19	0	6	33	26	41	1	4	.302/.413/.447	.298	.338	-4.0	1B 0	1.0
2009	MIS	AA	19	165	14	8	0	2	23	11	19	0	0	.248/.315/.342	.233	.263	-1.2	1B 1	-0.4
2010	GWN	AAA	20	508	72	33	2	18	84	43	84	6	2	.314/.378/.513	.297	.344	-0.3	1B -1	2.4
2010	ATL	MLB	20	24	3	1	0	1	1	0	8	0	0	.167/.167/.333	.199	.200	0.0	1B 1	-0.1
2011	*ATL*	*MLB*	*21*	*506*	*61*	*27*	*1*	*15*	*62*	*35*	*90*	*2*	*1*	*.269/.324/.432*	*.263*	*.300*	*-0.1*	*1B -17*	*-1.1*

Despite his struggles in 41 Double-A games at the end of 2009, the Braves sent the 20-year-old Freeman to Triple-A to begin 2010. What initially looked like an overaggressive assignment turned out to be just right. Freeman improved throughout the year, batting .375/.432/.595 after the All-Star break and reaching the big leagues in September.

Some scouts think Freeman is a better pure hitter than Jason Heyward, with a batting average that will make up for an average walk rate and power. Add in very good defensive skills and barring a 1-for-31 spring, Freeman will be the Opening Day first baseman and the long-term answer at a position that was a revolving door in 2010.

Troy Glaus **1B**

Born: **8/3/1976** Age: **34**
Bats: R Throws: R Height: **6' 5"** Weight: **245**
Breakout: **0%** Improve: **33%** Collapse: **3%**
Attrition: **11%** MLB: **88%**

Comparables:
Frank Thomas, Kent Hrbek, Erubiel Durazo (72)

YEAR	TEAM	LVL	AGE	PA	R	2B	3B	HR	RBI	BB	SO	SB	CS	AVG/OBP/SLG	TAv	BABIP	BRR	FRAA	WARP
2008	SLN	MLB	31	637	70	33	1	27	99	87	104	0	1	.270/.372/.484	.299	.289	-3.7	3B -5, 1B 0	3.5
2009	MEM	AAA	32	64	9	0	0	3	8	12	17	1	0	.216/.375/.392	.265	.250	-0.5	3B -3, LF 0	0.0
2009	SLN	MLB	32	32	2	2	0	0	2	3	8	0	0	.172/.250/.241	.180	.238	0.1	3B -1, 1B 0	-0.3
2010	ATL	MLB	33	483	56	18	0	16	71	63	100	0	0	.240/.344/.401	.275	.277	-0.7	1B -20, 3B 0	-0.8
2011	*ATL*	*MLB*	*34*	*476*	*60*	*19*	*0*	*18*	*55*	*64*	*94*	*1*	*0*	*.248/.352/.430*	*.276*	*.276*	*0.0*	*3B -3, 1B -6*	*0.7*

Signed to a one-year deal and given the first-base job in spring training, Glaus made the Braves look like geniuses early in the year when he all but carried the team from May to mid-June (.336/.416/.605 with 11 home runs in 41 games). Then the carriage turned into a pumpkin with bad knees, and he was all but useless after that (.181/.299/.277). Now a very old 34, Glaus is a big, sloppy player who can't move anymore, with one scout recording consistent 5.2 to 5.3 second times to first base, matching the speeds Charles Darwin recorded in the 1835 Tree Slug Games on the Galapagos Islands. Some team that remembers what it saw in May will give him a spring training invite, but that's about all he merits.

Alex Gonzalez **SS**

Born: **2/15/1977** Age: **34**
Bats: R Throws: R Height: **6' 0"** Weight: **170**
Breakout: **0%** Improve: **27%** Collapse: **7%**
Attrition: **18%** MLB: **89%**

Comparables:
Alan Trammell, Tony Batista, Jose Guillen (75)

YEAR	TEAM	LVL	AGE	PA	R	2B	3B	HR	RBI	BB	SO	SB	CS	AVG/OBP/SLG	TAv	BABIP	BRR	FRAA	WARP
2009	BOS	MLB	32	159	26	10	0	5	15	5	29	2	0	.284/.308/.453	.256	.314	0.8	SS -2	0.4
2009	CIN	MLB	32	270	16	12	0	3	26	15	36	0	1	.210/.252/.296	.194	.224	-0.4	SS -5	-1.3
2010	TOR	MLB	33	348	47	25	1	17	50	17	65	1	0	.259/.296/.497	.279	.274	0.2	SS 13	3.2
2010	ATL	MLB	33	292	28	17	2	6	38	14	53	0	2	.240/.288/.386	.235	.272	-1.5	SS 7	0.9
2011	*ATL*	*MLB*	*34*	*487*	*54*	*26*	*1*	*14*	*58*	*27*	*82*	*2*	*1*	*.246/.290/.406*	*.241*	*.264*	*-0.1*	*SS 5*	*1.3*

How many realize that Gonzalez has now managed two 23-homer seasons to go along with his plus defense at short? Unfortunately for the Braves, 17 of the 23 home runs Gonzalez hit in 2010 came in 85 games with Toronto. As a Brave, he hit just six taters while sporting an on-base percentage under .300. Still, perhaps the best thing about Gonzalez's second half was that he was not Yunel Escobar, who had at one point or another pissed off nearly every one of his teammates, because of his lackadaisical behavior and indifference to teamwork. Realistically, Gonzalez isn't going to slug around .450 again, but even so, picking up his $2.5 million option for 2011 was a no-brainer.

Jason Heyward **RF**

Born: **8/9/1989** Age: **21**
Bats: L Throws: L Height: **6' 5"** Weight: **240**
Breakout: **1%** Improve: **32%** Collapse: **0%**
Attrition: **15%** MLB: **54%**

Comparables:
Justin Upton, Billy Butler, Ken Griffey (54)

YEAR	TEAM	LVL	AGE	PA	R	2B	3B	HR	RBI	BB	SO	SB	CS	AVG/OBP/SLG	TAv	BABIP	BRR	FRAA	WARP
2008	ROM	A	18	505	88	27	6	11	52	49	74	15	3	.323/.390/.483	.326	.361	5.2	RF 11, CF 0	5.6
2008	MYR	A+	18	55	5	4	0	0	6	8	9	0	0	.196/.309/.283	.250	.237	0.6	RF -1, CF -1	-0.1
2009	MYR	A+	19	212	34	12	0	10	31	21	30	3	0	.296/.373/.519	.325	.305	1.3	RF 1, CF 1	2.1
2009	MIS	AA	19	193	31	13	4	7	30	28	19	5	1	.352/.451/.611	.376	.360	1.5	RF 7, CF 0	3.3
2010	ATL	MLB	20	623	83	29	5	18	72	91	128	11	6	.277/.393/.456	.315	.335	-1.2	RF 2	4.3
2011	*ATL*	*MLB*	*21*	*539*	*72*	*26*	*3*	*16*	*66*	*63*	*96*	*7*	*2*	*.282/.369/.457*	*.292*	*.319*	*-0.1*	*RF 4, CF 0*	*2.8*

A few players in the game draw every eye in the house when they come to the plate, and in his rookie year, Heyward added himself to that very select group. All the same, there was plenty to nitpick in his performance. While the 91 walks were wonderful, he was often *too* patient, finding himself in 0-1 and 0-2 counts by allowing pitches he could drive to go by. He still needs to improve his hitting against lefties, and his overall approach will require some adjustments now that the league has adjusted to *him*. These are minor criticisms for a season that was a remarkable achievement for a 20-year-old; Heyward should be one of the best players in the game for the next decade.

Brandon Hicks **SS**

Born: **9/14/1985** Age: **25**
Bats: R Throws: R Height: **6' 2"** Weight: **200**
Breakout: **3%** Improve: **14%** Collapse: **1%**
Attrition: **12%** MLB: **18%**

Comparables:
Elliot Johnson, Ian Desmond, Denis Menke (79)

YEAR	TEAM	LVL	AGE	PA	R	2B	3B	HR	RBI	BB	SO	SB	CS	AVG/OBP/SLG	TAv	BABIP	BRR	FRAA	WARP
2008	MYR	A+	22	426	71	23	2	20	57	49	131	13	3	.237/.340/.470	.277	.301	3.0	SS 2	2.9
2008	MIS	AA	22	63	9	3	1	1	7	7	17	0	0	.241/.333/.389	.262	.316	0.5	SS 1	0.4
2009	MIS	AA	23	529	63	25	4	10	47	53	131	17	1	.237/.318/.373	.262	.299	0.3	SS 2	2.3
2010	GWN	AAA	24	278	23	8	1	6	21	20	72	9	6	.206/.281/.315	.201	.261	1.9	SS 5	0.0
2010	ATL	MLB	24	6	0	0	0	0	0	1	2	0	0	.000/.167/.000	.101	.000	0.7	3B 1, SS 0	0.0
2011	*ATL*	*MLB*	*25*	*434*	*44*	*17*	*2*	*11*	*43*	*36*	*123*	*9*	*3*	*.215/.282/.355*	*.225*	*.275*	*0.0*	*SS 3, 3B 0*	*0.3*

A third-round pick in 2007, Hicks had a handful of stints in the big leagues as a defensive replacement at three infield positions. He's a very good defensive player with the instincts, range, actions, and arm to be an above-average big-league glove man. At the same time, his grand total of six plate appearances in his 16 games tells you everything about his bat. He can't hit, and there is no reason to think he's suddenly going to start.

Eric Hinske LF

Born: 8/5/1977 Age: 33
Bats: L Throws: R Height: 6' 2" Weight: 225
Breakout: 2% Improve: 21% Collapse: 8%
Attrition: 13% MLB: 72%

Comparables:
Walt Moryn, Jason Lane, Cliff Floyd (73)

YEAR	TEAM	LVL	AGE	PA	R	2B	3B	HR	RBI	BB	SO	SB	CS	AVG/OBP/SLG	TAv	BABIP	BRR	FRAA	WARP
2008	TBA	MLB	30	432	61	21	1	20	60	47	88	10	3	.247/.333/.465	.277	.270	0.4	RF 4, LF -5	1.2
2009	PIT	MLB	31	125	18	9	0	1	10	17	27	0	0	.248/.368/.362	.269	.325	-0.6	RF 2, 1B 0	0.4
2009	NYA	MLB	31	98	14	3	0	7	14	10	25	1	0	.226/.316/.512	.290	.222	0.0	RF -4, 3B -1	0.1
2010	ATL	MLB	32	320	42	21	1	11	51	33	75	0	0	.256/.338/.456	.282	.308	-1.4	LF 0, 1B 0	1.1
2011	*ATL*	*MLB*	*33*	*301*	*37*	*15*	*1*	*11*	*36*	*34*	*67*	*3*	*1*	*.241/.332/.429*	*.266*	*.278*	*0.0*	*LF 0, RF 0*	*0.6*

Signed to be a pinch-hitter and reserve at first base and left field, Hinske was doing just that and doing it well during the first half of the season. Then injuries and poor play by others forced him into more playing time, and things didn't go nearly as well. That's just how it is, folks; there are players who can put up impressive numbers in limited roles, but that doesn't mean they'll keep it up as everyday guys. The Braves chose to retain Hinske for at least another year because he's left-handed and an outstanding presence in the clubhouse (yup, that matters as well), but Freeman's presence at first base is going to cut into his playing time. Hinske has traditionally agitated for more time on the field, and while you can't blame him for that, both he and the Braves would be better off if he had less exposure.

Omar Infante 2B

Born: 12/26/1981 Age: 29
Bats: R Throws: R Height: 5' 9" Weight: 150
Breakout: 2% Improve: 31% Collapse: 5%
Attrition: 6% MLB: 85%

Comparables:
Bip Roberts, Esteban German, Matty Alou (67)

YEAR	TEAM	LVL	AGE	PA	R	2B	3B	HR	RBI	BB	SO	SB	CS	AVG/OBP/SLG	TAv	BABIP	BRR	FRAA	WARP
2008	ATL	MLB	26	348	45	24	3	3	40	22	44	0	1	.293/.336/.416	.271	.325	-3.4	LF -2, 3B 0	0.6
2009	ATL	MLB	27	229	23	9	1	2	27	19	28	2	0	.305/.358/.389	.265	.335	1.4	2B 0, SS -1	0.9
2010	ATL	MLB	28	506	64	15	3	8	47	29	62	7	6	.321/.356/.416	.276	.351	-0.1	2B 2, SS 6	2.9
2011	*FLO*	*MLB*	*29*	*317*	*37*	*13*	*1*	*5*	*34*	*21*	*34*	*4*	*2*	*.291/.335/.399*	*.261*	*.308*	*-0.2*	*2B 0, 3B 1*	*1.0*

With three straight good years, Infante is arguably the best utility player in the game. Certainly his unlikely selection to the All-Star team was a nod in that direction. While hardly a secondary-skills king, he's a .300 hitter who can play three infield positions and either outfield corner, while providing no worse than average defensively at any spot. Being dealt to the Marlins in the Dan Uggla deal will likely transform him into an everyday player at second base, thereby downplaying his greatest skill, versatility, and emphasizing a bat that is merely adequate if it slips below .320.

Chipper Jones 3B

Born: 4/24/1972 Age: 39
Bats: S Throws: R Height: 6' 3" Weight: 185
Breakout: 0% Improve: 14% Collapse: 7%
Attrition: 13% MLB: 86%

Comparables:
Jeff Kent, Mike Schmidt, Billy Williams (69)

YEAR	TEAM	LVL	AGE	PA	R	2B	3B	HR	RBI	BB	SO	SB	CS	AVG/OBP/SLG	TAv	BABIP	BRR	FRAA	WARP
2008	ATL	MLB	36	534	83	24	1	22	75	90	61	4	0	.365/.470/.574	.355	.383	-3.3	3B -1	6.3
2009	ATL	MLB	37	596	81	23	2	18	71	101	89	4	1	.264/.388/.430	.288	.287	-0.3	3B -10	2.4
2010	ATL	MLB	38	381	50	21	0	10	46	61	47	5	0	.265/.381/.426	.295	.281	-1.2	3B 2	2.4
2011	*ATL*	*MLB*	*39*	*519*	*71*	*24*	*1*	*17*	*61*	*81*	*68*	*4*	*1*	*.281/.392/.457*	*.299*	*.296*	*0.1*	*3B -4*	*3.0*

The extension Jones signed just prior to the 2009 season will go down as a great green albatross. He predicted a massive rebound year in 2010, but instead, he proved that 2009 was a sign of things to come. He was limited by a jammed thumb and ingrown toenail (you can't make this stuff up) during the spring, followed by a strained oblique, back and hip soreness, a groin tweak, a jammed finger, hamstring problems, and ultimately the torn ACL in August that cost him the remainder of the season. Chipper's defensive skills have degraded over the years, having never been special to begin with; that he had, by all accounts, a good year with the glove in 2010 must be considered a near-supernatural occurrence, reliant on balls magically changing direction and finding their way into his glove. Despite plenty of in-season retirement rumors, Jones has $13 million reasons to return in 2011, and the exact same number in 2012.

Mycal Jones SS

Born: **5/30/1987** Age: **24**
Bats: **R** Throws: **R** Height: **5' 10"** Weight: **165**
Breakout: **0%** Improve: **1%** Collapse: **2%**
Attrition: **7%** MLB: **9%**

Comparables:
Ramiro Pena, Donnie Murphy, Leo Cardenas (78)

YEAR	TEAM	LVL	AGE	PA	R	2B	3B	HR	RBI	BB	SO	SB	CS	AVG/OBP/SLG	TAv	BABIP	BRR	FRAA	WARP
2009	DNV	Rk	22	287	47	18	6	4	27	27	56	17	4	.255/.335/.422	.285	.300	4.1	SS 0	2.3
2010	ROM	A	23	217	26	12	0	6	33	11	48	6	3	.261/.300/.412	.259	.303	1.7	SS -4	0.6
2010	MYR	A+	23	311	50	19	1	7	22	31	66	13	4	.269/.360/.422	.284	.324	4.8	SS -10	1.4
2011	*ATL*	*MLB*	*24*	*424*	*42*	*19*	*1*	*10*	*43*	*27*	*108*	*9*	*3*	*.219/.271/.355*	*.220*	*.268*	*-0.1*	*SS -3*	*-0.4*

Jones is a difficult prospect to evaluate. Well behind the standard age/development curve, Jones was already 22 when drafted but had the baseball skills of a raw 18-year-old. He's a rough defender, especially with his throwing, and many believe a move to second base or perhaps even center field would be in his best interest. Still, he remains intriguing as one of the best athletes in the system, with good speed and well-above-average power for his position. As he is expected to begin 2011 at Double-A, we'll all know much more about his future 12 months from now.

Derrek Lee 1B

Born: **9/6/1975** Age: **35**
Bats: **R** Throws: **R** Height: **6' 5"** Weight: **205**
Breakout: **0%** Improve: **31%** Collapse: **3%**
Attrition: **12%** MLB: **92%**

Comparables:
Paul Konerko, Jermaine Dye, Torii Hunter (72)

YEAR	TEAM	LVL	AGE	PA	R	2B	3B	HR	RBI	BB	SO	SB	CS	AVG/OBP/SLG	TAv	BABIP	BRR	FRAA	WARP
2008	CHN	MLB	32	698	94	41	3	20	90	71	119	8	2	.291/.361/.462	.279	.330	-3.3	1B 15	3.0
2009	CHN	MLB	33	615	91	36	2	35	111	76	109	1	0	.306/.394/.579	.336	.327	-0.9	1B 1	5.2
2010	CHN	MLB	34	475	63	21	0	16	56	52	101	1	3	.251/.335/.416	.261	.293	-0.4	1B 7	1.0
2010	ATL	MLB	34	151	18	14	0	3	24	21	33	0	0	.287/.384/.465	.288	.362	-1.2	1B -6	-0.1
2011	*ATL*	*MLB*	*35*	*559*	*75*	*30*	*1*	*20*	*72*	*66*	*101*	*4*	*2*	*.279/.363/.467*	*.291*	*.310*	*-0.3*	*1B 3*	*2.4*

Suffering through one of his worst years as a pro, Lee exercised his 10-5 rights to void a proposed trade to the Angels, but accepted a deal to Atlanta after realizing that it would give him another shot at the postseason. He played well for the Braves despite a torn ligament in his thumb—an injury that limited his power and would have caused many players to shut it down. He's a very good defender and one of the few men in the game who truly deserves the status of role model. These attributes, combined with how well he takes care of himself, make him an excellent rebound candidate for 2011. Signed to a one-year contract with the Orioles, he could be one of the better free-agent pickups of the offseason.

Brian McCann C

Born: **2/20/1984** Age: **27**
Bats: **L** Throws: **R** Height: **6' 3"** Weight: **210**
Breakout: **1%** Improve: **52%** Collapse: **4%**
Attrition: **9%** MLB: **99%**

Comparables:
Johnny Bench, Wally Joyner, Joe Torre (73)

YEAR	TEAM	LVL	AGE	PA	R	2B	3B	HR	RBI	BB	SO	SB	CS	AVG/OBP/SLG	TAv	BABIP	BRR	FRAA	WARP
2008	ATL	MLB	24	573	68	42	1	23	87	57	64	5	0	.301/.374/.523	.310	.306	-4.4	C 6	5.5
2009	ATL	MLB	25	551	66	35	1	21	94	49	83	4	1	.281/.347/.486	.290	.295	-1.5	C 2	3.9
2010	ATL	MLB	26	566	68	25	0	21	77	74	98	5	2	.269/.375/.453	.301	.297	-3.8	C 1	4.3
2011	*ATL*	*MLB*	*27*	*551*	*75*	*32*	*0*	*22*	*75*	*59*	*74*	*4*	*1*	*.284/.364/.485*	*.296*	*.292*	*-0.1*	*C 2*	*4.3*

One of the most offensively productive catchers in the game, McCann is a career .290 hitter who hits 20-plus home runs per year. While he elevated his walk rate in 2010, that might have been the effect of often being the only hitter worth fearing in a decimated Braves lineup. A catcher who is better at the plate than behind it, McCann set a new career high in errors, handily leading the NL with 14; his fielding percentage with putouts from catching strikeouts removed was just .863, the worst of any qualifying backstop not to play for the Yankees. While his caught stealing percentage was a career best, it was also an unexceptional 30 percent. That makes David Ross all the more valuable as a backup whose skills complement the starter's deficiencies. But let's not overstate things: even with McCann's flaws, he is arguably the Braves' most valuable position player and will retain that title until Jason Heyward comes into his full maturity.

Nate McLouth CF

Born: **10/28/1981** Age: **29**
Bats: **L** Throws: **R** Height: **5' 11"** Weight: **185**
Breakout: **3%** Improve: **45%** Collapse: **0%**
Attrition: **7%** MLB: **98%**

Comparables:
Bobby Higginson, Rusty Greer, Amos Otis (77)

YEAR	TEAM	LVL	AGE	PA	R	2B	3B	HR	RBI	BB	SO	SB	CS	AVG/OBP/SLG	TAv	BABIP	BRR	FRAA	WARP
2008	PIT	MLB	26	685	113	46	4	26	94	65	93	23	3	.276/.353/.498	.291	.284	4.4	CF -8, LF -1	3.7
2009	ATL	MLB	27	396	59	20	1	11	36	47	70	12	6	.257/.351/.419	.272	.289	2.0	CF -3	1.5
2009	PIT	MLB	27	195	27	7	1	9	34	21	29	7	0	.256/.349/.470	.285	.258	0.9	CF -1	1.0
2010	GWN	AAA	28	144	17	1	0	6	18	18	20	7	0	.242/.347/.395	.266	.240	-0.4	CF 4	0.9
2010	ATL	MLB	28	287	29	12	1	6	24	33	57	7	2	.191/.293/.324	.228	.215	3.4	CF -2, LF -1	-0.1
2011	*ATL*	*MLB*	*29*	*479*	*59*	*22*	*1*	*16*	*56*	*53*	*75*	*16*	*4*	*.249/.339/.427*	*.269*	*.261*	*0.5*	*CF -3, LF 0*	*1.4*

It's easy to say the Braves made a mistake in trading for McLouth, but unfair given that saying so requires the benefit of hindsight. The outfielder looked like a valuable acquisition at the time, and not just to the Braves, but to the other teams they had to outbid to get him. His complete collapse in 2010 is one of those riddles wrapped in a mystery inside an enigma. He wasn't hurt, at least not at first (he suffered a concussion in June), he didn't make some kind of adjustment that ruined his swing, and there was no obvious off-field issue. The Braves maintain some small hope that he can return to being the nice little outfielder he was before, if only because they're stuck with him and they can't think of a good reason for him to have stopped hitting in the first place. Regardless of what he does, though, there is little chance of their being persuaded to pick up his eight-figure 2012 option.

Martin Prado 2B

Born: **10/27/1983** Age: **27**
Bats: R Throws: R Height: **6' 1"** Weight: **170**
Breakout: **1%** Improve: **47%** Collapse: **4%**
Attrition: **13%** MLB: **94%**

Comparables:
Jose Vidro, Robinson Cano, Jose Lopez (76)

YEAR	TEAM	LVL	AGE	PA	R	2B	3B	HR	RBI	BB	SO	SB	CS	AVG/OBP/SLG	TAv	BABIP	BRR	FRAA	WARP
2008	ATL	MLB	24	254	35	18	4	2	33	21	29	3	1	.320/.374/.461	.295	.353	-1.0	3B 5, 2B 2	2.0
2009	ATL	MLB	25	503	64	38	0	11	49	36	59	1	3	.307/.350/.464	.280	.322	-0.5	2B -6, 3B 3	1.5
2010	ATL	MLB	26	651	100	40	3	15	66	40	86	5	3	.307/.349/.459	.287	.333	6.7	2B -2, 3B 2	3.9
2011	*ATL*	*MLB*	*27*	*486*	*61*	*29*	*1*	*10*	*59*	*36*	*54*	*4*	*2*	*.300/.347/.440*	*.275*	*.315*	*-0.3*	*2B 0, 3B 1*	*1.8*

With Prado having batted over .300 for three consecutive seasons, his hitting can no longer be dismissed as a fluke. Hitting for average is something he can do. Unfortunately, we now have to focus on what he *can't* do, because after the trade for Dan Uggla, Prado is suddenly the team's left fielder. He doesn't profile well at the position, lacking a corner-man's traditional power. He also doesn't walk, but you don't necessarily want him to, because much of his batting average is based on bad-ball hitting. Prado's value has plummeted with the position change, but there's no reason to think he'll be anything but the player he's been for the last three years.

David Ross C

Born: **3/19/1977** Age: **34**
Bats: R Throws: R Height: **6' 2"** Weight: **205**
Breakout: **1%** Improve: **24%** Collapse: **11%**
Attrition: **24%** MLB: **76%**

Comparables:
John Wockenfuss, Ernie Whitt, Ed Bailey (75)

YEAR	TEAM	LVL	AGE	PA	R	2B	3B	HR	RBI	BB	SO	SB	CS	AVG/OBP/SLG	TAv	BABIP	BRR	FRAA	WARP
2008	BOS	MLB	31	9	1	0	0	0	0	0	3	0	0	.125/.111/.125	.204	.167	0.1	C 0	0.0
2008	CIN	MLB	31	173	19	9	0	3	13	32	36	0	1	.231/.370/.366	.266	.277	-1.4	C 1	0.8
2009	ATL	MLB	32	151	17	9	0	7	20	21	39	0	0	.273/.378/.508	.306	.337	-2.0	C 3	1.4
2010	ATL	MLB	33	145	15	13	2	2	28	20	28	0	1	.289/.386/.479	.301	.351	-1.9	C 1	1.1
2011	*ATL*	*MLB*	*34*	*245*	*30*	*11*	*1*	*8*	*28*	*32*	*57*	*1*	*0*	*.240/.336/.420*	*.264*	*.280*	*0.0*	*C 1*	*1.2*

The best backup catcher in the business, Ross is the perfect complement to McCann. He's right-handed, plays good defense, and has the kind of makeup and leadership the Braves value immensely. His statistics will always be subject to the vagaries of limited playing time, but many opposing scouts think he's worthy of an everyday job, considering the overall catching shortage. Having signed McCann to a two-year extension during the 2010 season, the Braves might only regret that they couldn't get him for longer.

Jordan Schafer CF

Born: **9/14/1986** Age: **24**
Bats: L Throws: L Height: **6' 1"** Weight: **200**
Breakout: **2%** Improve: **7%** Collapse: **0%**
Attrition: **3%** MLB: **13%**

Comparables:
Bernie Williams, Xavier Paul, Jeff Fiorentino (81)

YEAR	TEAM	LVL	AGE	PA	R	2B	3B	HR	RBI	BB	SO	SB	CS	AVG/OBP/SLG	TAv	BABIP	BRR	FRAA	WARP
2008	MIS	AA	21	383	48	22	6	11	55	50	93	13	6	.276/.376/.479	.297	.351	1.5	CF -9, RF -1	1.8
2009	ATL	MLB	22	195	18	8	0	2	8	27	63	2	1	.204/.313/.287	.218	.311	1.6	CF 2	0.1
2010	MIS	AA	23	72	7	3	0	0	5	8	12	1	1	.175/.264/.222	.221	.212	0.3	LF 1, CF -1	-0.1
2010	GWN	AAA	23	209	16	5	1	1	8	14	47	9	8	.201/.249/.254	.193	.252	-1.6	CF 6, RF 2	-0.4
2011	*ATL*	*MLB*	*24*	*307*	*31*	*12*	*1*	*5*	*27*	*30*	*77*	*9*	*4*	*.226/.299/.340*	*.228*	*.287*	*-0.6*	*CF -5, LF 0*	*-0.7*

Remember this guy? The prospect with defense, power, and speed who earned the 2009 center-field job and hit a home run on Opening Day? Two years ago, a majority of scouts would have taken Schafer over Colby Rasmus, but now Schafer is almost completely off the map. There are still plenty of tools here, but he has lost himself mechanically, while also becoming notably thinner. The latter attribute has led to speculation about the extent of his involvement with HGH, something for which he was suspended 50 games in 2008 though he denied using the substance. There's a nonzero chance that he still turns into something, but it's getting smaller by the day.

Matt Young UT

Born: **10/3/1982** Age: **28**
Bats: L Throws: R Height: **5' 8"** Weight: **175**
Breakout: **4%** Improve: **41%** Collapse: **4%**
Attrition: **15%** MLB: **87%**

Comparables:
Sam Fuld, Callix Crabbe, Jason Bourgeois (64)

YEAR	TEAM	LVL	AGE	PA	R	2B	3B	HR	RBI	BB	SO	SB	CS	AVG/OBP/SLG	TAv	BABIP	BRR	FRAA	WARP
2008	MIS	AA	25	605	75	16	11	4	53	71	67	32	13	.280/.375/.375	.279	.309	2.6	LF 16, CF -1	4.1
2009	MIS	AA	26	559	77	22	10	4	33	94	59	43	15	.289/.428/.407	.306	.321	5.4	CF -9, LF 3	3.7
2010	GWN	AAA	27	543	84	32	5	3	34	57	53	38	7	.299/.383/.405	.269	.328	7.8	LF 8, CF -3	2.8
2011	*ATL*	*MLB*	*28*	*583*	*66*	*25*	*4*	*5*	*49*	*66*	*71*	*31*	*9*	*.261/.347/.356*	*.254*	*.289*	*0.4*	*LF 5, CF -5*	*0.9*

A five-foot-eight outfielder who was undrafted out of college and turned 28 in October, Young can no longer be called a prospect, but he has spent the last three seasons at the upper levels of the Braves' system compiling an on-base percentage of near .400 with more walks than strikeouts, while stealing 112 bases. That earned him a surprise spot on the 40-man roster, along with talk that he'll get a long look this spring for a reserve outfield job. He also plays second base occasionally, which could help in the versatility department. Scouts think he's at least worth trying.

PITCHERS

Brandon Beachy

Born: **9/3/1986** Age: **24**
Bats: R Throws: R Height: **6' 3"** Weight: **215**
Breakout: **5%** Improve: **15%** Collapse: **16%**
Attrition: **14%** MLB: **45%**

Comparables:
Mark Melancon, Jordan Zimmermann, Jaime Garcia (73)

YEAR	TEAM	LVL	AGE	W	L	SV	G	GS	IP	H	HR	BB	SO	EqBB9	EqSO9	GB%	BABIP	WHIP	ERA	FRA	WARP
2009	MYR	A+	22	4	3	1	22	8	58	59	2	15	47	2.3	7.3	50%	.326	1.41	2.95	4.26	0.9
2010	MIS	AA	23	3	1	1	27	7	73^{2}	53	3	22	100	2.7	12.2	43%	.298	1.05	1.47	1.94	2.9
2010	GWN	AAA	23	2	0	1	8	7	45^{2}	40	2	6	48	1.2	9.5	45%	.295	1.05	2.17	3.58	1.2
2010	ATL	MLB	23	0	2	0	3	3	15	16	0	7	15	4.2	9.0	33%	.356	1.53	3.00	4.08	0.2
2011	*ATL*	*MLB*	*24*	*4*	*3*	*0*	*26*	*8*	*71*	*69*	*6*	*25*	*67*	*3.1*	*8.4*	*44%*	*.315*	*1.32*	*3.81*	*4.14*	*1.2*

One of the best stories in the Braves' system in 2010, Beachy went undrafted in 2008 after a college career mostly spent as a hitter at tiny Indiana Wesleyan. Braves scouts remembered being impressed by his limited mound work and gave him a chance. After pitching well enough to get to Double-A, he was called out of instructs as an emergency addition to the rotation and held his own, thanks to his ability to throw three pitches for strikes and testicles the size of bowling balls. With a fastball that gets up to 93 mph and a solid breaking ball and changeup, Beachy has big-league stuff suited for either a back-of-rotation or bullpen role. He's not going to be a star, but he's already exceeded every expectation by a nearly immeasurable margin.

Randall Delgado

Born: **2/9/1990** Age: **21**
Bats: R Throws: Height: **6' 3"** Weight: **165**
Breakout: **7%** Improve: **18%** Collapse: **3%**
Attrition: **3%** MLB: **25%**

Comparables:
Mike Witt, Steve Avery, Ken Holtzman (61)

YEAR	TEAM	LVL	AGE	W	L	SV	G	GS	IP	H	HR	BB	SO	EqBB9	EqSO9	GB%	BABIP	WHIP	ERA	FRA	WARP
2008	DNV	Rk	18	3	8	0	14	18	69	63	5	30	81	3.9	10.6	53%	.339	1.42	3.13	4.23	1.3
2009	ROM	A	19	5	10	0	25	30	124	123	9	49	141	3.6	10.2	50%	.339	1.44	4.28	4,27	1.5
2010	MYR	A+	20	4	7	0	20	21	117^{1}	89	7	32	120	2.5	9.2	54%	.271	1.09	2.45	4.02	1.8
2010	MIS	AA	20	3	5	0	8	8	43^{2}	36	2	20	42	4.1	8.7	44%	.274	1.33	4.53	5.15	0.1
2011	*ATL*	*MLB*	*21*	*7*	*8*	*0*	*21*	*21*	*109*	*114*	*14*	*59*	*89*	*4.8*	*7.3*	*46%*	*.310*	*1.58*	*5.15*	*5.60*	*0.8*

A long, skinny right-hander of Panamanian descent, Delgado doesn't have the ceiling of better-known prospects like Julio Teheran and Arodys Vizcaino, but he's probably closer to getting a big-league call-up. Using a motion that one scout likens to that of a pie thrower, Delgado sits at 93-94 mph, can touch 96, and already has a plus secondary pitch with one of the better changeups in the system. Given some improvement in his curveball and more strikes, the Braves think he can become a physically bigger version of Jair Jurrjens.

Michael Dunn

Born: **5/23/1985** Age: **26**
Bats: L Throws: L Height: **6' 1** Weight: **195**
Breakout: **11%** Improve: **14%** Collapse: **9%**
Attrition: **9%** MLB: **27%**

Comparables:
Pedro Viola, Juan Morillo, Bobby Bolin (75)

YEAR	TEAM	LVL	AGE	W	L	SV	G	GS	IP	H	HR	BB	SO	EqBB9	EqSO9	GB%	BABIP	WHIP	ERA	FRA	WARP
2008	TAM	A+	23	4	7	1	30	24	124^{2}	124	10	58	118	4.2	8.5	42%	.324	1.50	4.40	4.32	1.7
2009	TRN	AA	24	3	3	2	26	0	53^{1}	41	3	32	76	5.4	12.8	43%	.325	1.41	3.71	3.52	0.8
2009	SWB	AAA	24	1	0	0	12	0	20	17	1	14	23	6.3	10.4	42%	.314	1.60	1.80	1.65	0.9
2009	NYA	MLB	24	0	0	0	4	0	4	3	1	5	5	11.3	11.3	40%	.222	2.00	6.75	6.3	0.0
2010	GWN	AAA	25	2	0	7	38	0	47^{1}	31	1	25	64	4.8	12.2	43%	.278	1.23	1.52	1.79	1.8
2010	ATL	MLB	25	2	0	0	25	0	19	15	1	17	27	8.1	12.8	32%	.326	1.68	1.89	0.34	1.2
2011	*FLO*	*MLB*	*26*	*4*	*3*	*1*	*43*	*6*	*83*	*83*	*9*	*55*	*85*	*5.9*	*9.1*	*42%*	*.325*	*1.65*	*5.06*	*5.50*	*-0.2*

One of two players dealt to the Marlins in the Dan Uggla deal, Dunn is suddenly a candidate to close in 2011. A converted outfielder, Dunn made great strides during his second big-league stint with the Braves, giving much credit to Billy Wagner for helping him learn to trust his stuff. A pure power left-hander with two plus pitches, Dunn sits at 93-95 mph with his fastball and touches 97, and his slider can cause just as many swings-and-misses as the heater when he's throwing it for strikes. That last is the key for Dunn: like so many inexperienced arms with a ton of heat, Dunn can be a star if he can just come to grips with the strike zone. Whether he can complete the journey that Wagner started him on remains a question.

Kyle Farnsworth

Born: **4/14/1976** Age: **35**
Bats: R Throws: R Height: **6' 4"** Weight: **220**
Breakout: **11%** Improve: **23%** Collapse: **15%**
Attrition: **3%** MLB: **65%**

Comparables:
Lee Smith, Todd Worrell, Justin Speier (75)

YEAR	TEAM	LVL	AGE	W	L	SV	G	GS	IP	H	HR	BB	SO	EqBB9	EqSO9	GB%	BABIP	WHIP	ERA	FRA	WARP
2008	DET	MLB	32	1	1	0	16	0	16	27	4	5	18	2.8	10.1	26%	.469	2.00	6.75	3.92	0.2
2008	NYA	MLB	32	1	2	1	45	0	44^1	43	11	17	43	3.5	8.7	42%	.283	1.38	3.65	3.44	0.8
2009	KCA	MLB	33	1	5	0	41	0	37^1	43	3	14	42	3.4	10.1	49%	.370	1.55	4.58	4.21	0.5
2010	KCA	MLB	34	3	0	0	37	0	44^2	40	2	12	36	2.4	7.3	44%	.290	1.25	2.42	2.54	1.2
2010	ATL	MLB	34	0	2	0	23	0	20	15	2	7	25	3.2	11.3	42%	.271	1.10	5.40	5.76	-0.2
2011	*TBA*	*MLB*	*35*	*3*	*1*	*0*	*60*	*0*	*59*	*57*	*7*	*22*	*56*	*3.4*	*8.5*	*44%*	*.300*	*1.32*	*3.86*	*4.20*	*0.2*

What a difference a pennant race makes. Despite being the exact same pitcher he was in Kansas City—if not a better one, given stronger peripherals—Farnsworth's ERA more than doubled following his being dealt to Atlanta, which did nothing for his reputation as a pitcher who doesn't like pressure. Despite always throwing hard, he rarely trusts his fastball in pressure situations, which leads to his throwing his more hittable breaking ball or falling behind in the count and grooving his heater. The reliever signed a one-year with team option contract with the Rays, much to the pleasure of Yankees fans, who look forward to seeing the man they recall as "Farnsworthless" with a divisional rival.

Tommy Hanson

Born: **8/28/1986** Age: **24**
Bats: R Throws: R Height: **6' 6"** Weight: **220**
Breakout: **25%** Improve: **56%** Collapse: **17%**
Attrition: **19%** MLB: **94%**

Comparables:
Yovani Gallardo, Dan Hudson, Max Scherzer (72)

YEAR	TEAM	LVL	AGE	W	L	SV	G	GS	IP	H	HR	BB	SO	EqBB9	EqSO9	GB%	BABIP	WHIP	ERA	FRA	WARP
2008	MYR	A+	21	3	1	0	7	7	40	15	0	11	49	2.5	11.0	32%	.181	0.78	0.68	2.34	1.6
2008	MIS	AA	21	8	5	0	20	22	111	85	10	42	130	3.4	10.5	43%	.275	1.23	3.00	4.54	1.3
2009	GWN	AAA	22	3	3	0	11	11	66^1	40	5	17	90	2.3	12.2	38%	.248	0.92	1.49	2.78	2.2
2009	ATL	MLB	22	11	4	0	21	24	127^2	105	10	46	116	3.2	8.2	41%	.275	1.22	2.89	2.67	4.4
2010	ATL	MLB	23	10	11	0	34	40	202^2	182	14	56	173	2.5	7.7	43%	.286	1.24	3.33	4.46	2.1
2011	*ATL*	*MLB*	*24*	*10*	*7*	*0*	*24*	*24*	*143^1*	*124*	*13*	*53*	*134*	*3.3*	*8.4*	*42%*	*.286*	*1.23*	*3.40*	*3.70*	*3.9*

While many were disappointed that Hanson's 2010 didn't rise to the unrealistic expectations fueled by his rookie season, the 24-year-old still had a successful year, especially in terms of growth. His first-half struggles stemmed more from immaturity than mechanics, as he dealt with extended adversity for the first time as a pro. He made all the right adjustments and put up a 2.51 ERA in 16 starts after the All-Star break. This transformation resulted in just two wins thanks to brutal run support, but unless you're Murray Chass, you can't hold that against him. Hanson's breakout season is still coming, and it might arrive as early as this year.

J. J. Hoover

Born: **8/13/1987** Age: **23**
Bats: R Throws: R Height: **6' 3"** Weight: **215**
Breakout: **11%** Improve: **23%** Collapse: **4%**
Attrition: **9%** MLB: **29%**

Comparables:
Carlos Carrasco, Jaime Garcia, Derek Holland (73)

YEAR	TEAM	LVL	AGE	W	L	SV	G	GS	IP	H	HR	BB	SO	EqBB9	EqSO9	GB%	BABIP	WHIP	ERA	FRA	WARP
2009	ROM	A	21	7	6	1	25	18	134^1	135	9	25	148	1.7	9.9	47%	.341	1.24	3.08	3.39	2.9
2010	MYR	A+	22	11	6	0	24	26	132^2	126	7	35	118	2.4	8.0	43%	.299	1.26	3.12	3.59	2.8
2010	MIS	AA	22	3	1	0	4	4	20^2	15	1	15	34	6.5	14.8	27%	.350	1.45	3.48	2.63	0.8
2011	*ATL*	*MLB*	*23*	*5*	*6*	*0*	*18*	*15*	*93^2*	*102*	*11*	*40*	*72*	*3.8*	*6.9*	*42%*	*.317*	*1.51*	*4.94*	*5.37*	*0.6*

Overlooked in a system loaded with high-ceiling Latin American arms, Junior G-Man Hoover is hardly sexy, but he's much greater than the sum of his parts, and it's hard to find weaknesses in his game. He throws strikes with an average fastball, has a good breaking ball and changeup, and is one of those battlers who doesn't beat himself with too many walks or home runs. He's coming soon to the back of the rotation near you.

Tim Hudson

Born: **7/14/1975** Age: **35**
Bats: R Throws: R Height: **6' 0"** Weight: **160**
Breakout: **18%** Improve: **46%** Collapse: **26%**
Attrition: **12%** MLB: **96%**

Comparables:
Steve Rogers, Phil Niekro, Mike Cuellar (70)

YEAR	TEAM	LVL	AGE	W	L	SV	G	GS	IP	H	HR	BB	SO	EqBB9	EqSO9	GB%	BABIP	WHIP	ERA	FRA	WARP
2008	ATL	MLB	32	11	7	0	23	23	142	125	11	40	85	2.5	5.4	61%	.262	1.18	3.11	4.06	2.6
2009	ATL	MLB	33	2	1	0	7	7	42^1	49	4	13	30	2.8	6.4	61%	.338	1.46	3.61	3.08	1.2
2010	ATL	MLB	34	17	9	0	34	36	228^2	189	20	74	139	2.9	5.5	65%	.249	1.19	2.83	3.67	4.4
2011	*ATL*	*MLB*	*35*	*12*	*8*	*0*	*28*	*28*	*177*	*174*	*16*	*56*	*103*	*2.8*	*5.2*	*56%*	*.288*	*1.29*	*3.73*	*4.05*	*3.9*

The Braves saw enough of Hudson in his 2009 return from Tommy John surgery to give him a three-year extension, and he proved to be worth far more than the $9 million he was paid, turning in a season worthy of his glory years from the previous decade. Still, he's a far different pitcher from the one he was in his Oakland days. He lacks the strikeout rate one normally expects from an ace, but the results have been there thanks to a career-best, major-league-leading ground-ball rate generated by a power sinker that has gone from being just part of his arsenal to the main attraction. It will be difficult for Hudson to be consistent at such a high level while striking out only 5.5 batters per nine innings, but even if he regresses a bit, he will still be a bargain.

Jair Jurrjens

Born: **1/29/1986** Age: **25**
Bats: R Throws: R Height: **6' 1"** Weight: **160**
Breakout: **15%** Improve: **47%** Collapse: **23%**
Attrition: **5%** MLB: **99%**

Comparables:
Jack McDowell, Dennis Martinez, Ismael Valdez (70)

YEAR	TEAM	LVL	AGE	W	L	SV	G	GS	IP	H	HR	BB	SO	EqBB9	EqSO9	GB%	BABIP	WHIP	ERA	FRA	WARP
2008	ATL	MLB	22	13	10	0	31	33	188^1	188	11	70	139	3.3	6.6	52%	.301	1.39	3.68	4.20	3.2
2009	ATL	MLB	23	14	10	0	34	34	215	186	15	75	152	3.1	6.4	45%	.268	1.23	2.60	3.18	5.8
2010	ATL	MLB	24	7	6	0	20	20	116^1	120	13	42	86	3.2	6.7	43%	.300	1.41	4.64	4.76	0.9
2011	*ATL*	*MLB*	*25*	*10*	*9*	*0*	*26*	*26*	160^2	*163*	*15*	*59*	*111*	*3.3*	*6.3*	*46%*	*.301*	*1.38*	*4.15*	*4.52*	*2.7*

Following Jurrjens' season was like playing a game of "Operation." First his shoulder acted up in spring training, then his knee flared up, followed by a hamstring problem, and a foot injury was offered as the dessert course. None of the injuries was serious, and none of them is expected to be chronic, but in 2010, he had trouble staying on the mound. There's no reason he can't return to his 2008-2009 form once he gives up the Chipper Jones impression.

Kenshin Kawakami

Born: **6/22/1975** Age: **36**
Bats: R Throws: R Height: **5' 11"** Weight: **200**
Breakout: **11%** Improve: **33%** Collapse: **29%**
Attrition: **8%** MLB: **97%**

Comparables:
Bert Blyleven, Jack Morris, Dave Stewart (74)

YEAR	TEAM	LVL	AGE	W	L	SV	G	GS	IP	H	HR	BB	SO	EqBB9	EqSO9	GB%	BABIP	WHIP	ERA	FRA	WARP
2009	ATL	MLB	34	7	12	1	32	26	156^1	153	15	57	105	3.3	6.0	43%	.284	1.38	3.86	4.39	1.9
2010	ATL	MLB	35	1	10	0	18	16	87^1	98	10	32	59	3.3	6.1	42%	.305	1.50	5.15	5.49	0.0
2011	*ATL*	*MLB*	*36*	*8*	*9*	*0*	*24*	*24*	131^2	*143*	*16*	*48*	*89*	*3.3*	*6.1*	*44%*	*.308*	*1.45*	*4.73*	*5.14*	*1.5*

By the second half of the season, the Braves had clearly lost all faith in Kawakami, passing him over in favor of the unproven, rusty Brandon Beachy when they needed a fill-in for the injured Jurrjens. Without a true out pitch, Kawakami struggled in 2010, getting by (at best) with a 88-91 mph fastball and slow, looping curve that tended to get crushed in the middle innings. Still on the hook for $6.67 million in 2011, the Braves did their best to say *sayonara* by waiving Kawakami and removing him from the 40-man roster, praying all the while that Kawakami rethinks his refusal to return to Japan.

Craig Kimbrel

Born: **5/28/1988** Age: **23**
Bats: R Throws: R Height: **5' 11"** Weight: **205**
Breakout: **14%** Improve: **26%** Collapse: **16%**
Attrition: **5%** MLB: **57%**

Comparables:
Daniel Schlereth, Sam McDowell, Bob Turley (36)

YEAR	TEAM	LVL	AGE	W	L	SV	G	GS	IP	H	HR	BB	SO	EqBB9	EqSO9	GB%	BABIP	WHIP	ERA	FRA	WARP
2009	ROM	A	21	0	0	10	16	0	20	9	0	6	38	2.7	17.1	48%	.290	0.80	0.90	0.64	0.8
2009	MYR	A+	21	0	2	2	19	0	26^1	18	2	28	45	9.6	15.4	61%	.340	1.78	5.47	6.98	-0.6
2010	GWN	AAA	22	3	2	23	48	0	55^2	28	3	35	83	5.7	13.4	59%	.238	1.20	1.46	3.17	1.1
2010	ATL	MLB	22	4	0	1	21	0	20^2	9	0	16	40	7.0	17.4	28%	.281	1.21	0.44	-0.17	1.3
2011	*ATL*	*MLB*	*23*	*3*	*1*	*3*	*47*	*0*	*57*	*38*	*4*	*40*	*83*	*6.3*	*12.9*	*47%*	*.292*	*1.35*	*3.06*	*3.33*	*0.9*

After two years of doing "I'm the secret love child of Steve Dalkowski and Ricky Vaughn" shtick, Kimbrel finally began throwing strikes. When he did so, he was as unhittable as any reliever—his strikeout rate of 17.4 was the highest in history, albeit in the trivial 20-innings-and-up category. His upper-90s fastball features late sink, and his slider is nothing short of vicious. The only problem is that his career as a strike-thrower represents a grand total of one month, but if it's real, there's no reason he can't be among the best closers in the game, helping the Braves sail nimbly past Billy Wagner's premature retirement.

Derek Lowe

Born: **6/1/1973** Age: **38**
Bats: R Throws: R Height: **6' 6"** Weight: **170**
Breakout: **8%** Improve: **31%** Collapse: **20%**
Attrition: **16%** MLB: **92%**

Comparables:
Miguel Batista, Ramon Ortiz, Paul Byrd (48)

YEAR	TEAM	LVL	AGE	W	L	SV	G	GS	IP	H	HR	BB	SO	EqBB9	EqSO9	GB%	BABIP	WHIP	ERA	FRA	WARP
2008	LAN	MLB	35	14	11	0	34	38	211	194	14	45	147	1.9	6.3	61%	.280	1.14	3.24	3.85	3.8
2009	ATL	MLB	36	15	10	0	34	37	194^2	232	16	63	111	2.9	5.1	57%	.327	1.54	4.67	5.19	0.8
2010	ATL	MLB	37	16	12	0	33	34	193^2	204	18	61	136	2.8	6.3	59%	.307	1.39	4.00	4.26	2.6
2011	*ATL*	*MLB*	*38*	*13*	*11*	*0*	*34*	*34*	203^2	*218*	*18*	*62*	*126*	*2.7*	*5.6*	*55%*	*.311*	*1.38*	*4.14*	*4.50*	*3.5*

The first year of Lowe's four-year, $60 million deal was a disaster, and 2010 looked to be more of the same before a change in direction led to his becoming Atlanta's best pitcher down the stretch and into the playoffs. This wasn't just a fluke, as Lowe brought back his slider, and by the time the playoffs rolled around, it was a true out pitch. There's plenty of reason to believe that 2011 will be Lowe's best yet as a Brave, as he still gets plenty of ground balls (his ratio of ground outs to air outs was the second-highest in the majors behind Hudson), though he may end up filing suit against the Braves for creating a hostile work environment now that Dan Uggla is the team's second baseman.

Stephen Marek

Born: **9/3/1983** Age: **27**
Bats: R Throws: R Height: **6' 2"** Weight: **230**
Breakout: **0%** Improve: **0%** Collapse: **0%**
Attrition: **0%** MLB: **0%**

Comparables:
Connor Robertson, Carmen Pignatiello, Wes Littleton (85)

YEAR	TEAM	LVL	AGE	W	L	SV	G	GS	IP	H	HR	BB	SO	EqBB9	EqSO9	GB%	BABIP	WHIP	ERA	FRA	WARP
2008	ARK	AA	24	2	6	3	34	0	46^{2}	39	2	21	57	4.1	11.0	53%	.311	1.33	3.66	3.82	0.7
2008	MIS	AA	24	1	2	1	14	0	20	15	1	7	15	3.2	6.8	63%	.250	1.15	2.70	3.89	0.3
2009	MIS	AA	25	3	3	2	38	0	39^{1}	40	2	29	31	6.6	7.1	42%	.295	1.81	5.72	5.85	-0.5
2010	GWN	AAA	26	2	2	9	48	0	49^{1}	37	3	18	54	3.3	9.9	46%	.274	1.11	1.28	2.85	1.2
2011	*ATL*	*MLB*	*27*	*4*	*1*	*3*	*75*	*0*	86^{1}	*90*	*11*	*44*	*66*	*4.6*	*6.9*	*46%*	*.307*	*1.56*	*5.04*	*5.48*	*-0.9*

Based on what the Braves sent to the Rangers and received from the Angels, the Mark Teixeira deal was an unmitigated disaster on every level, but at least the Braves might get something out of it. There are plenty of organizations in which Marek would already be in the big leagues, and he'll get a shot this spring to finally earn a job. With a 91-93 mph fastball that touches 95, a plus curveball, and above-average command and control, Marek won't be a late-inning reliever in the big leagues, but he could spend the next six years delivering quality sixth and seventh innings.

Cristhian Martinez

Born: **3/6/1982** Age: **29**
Bats: R Throws: R Height: **6' 1"** Weight: **185**
Breakout: **0%** Improve: **5%** Collapse: **4%**
Attrition: **5%** MLB: **14%**

Comparables:
Willie Collazo, Levale Speigner, Hal Newhouser (81)

YEAR	TEAM	LVL	AGE	W	L	SV	G	GS	IP	H	HR	BB	SO	EqBB9	EqSO9	GB%	BABIP	WHIP	ERA	FRA	WARP
2008	GRB	A	26	4	1	0	8	10	44^{1}	44	2	9	14	1.8	2.8	54%	.264	1.26	4.26	5.98	-0.1
2008	JUP	A+	26	2	7	0	20	19	109^{1}	117	7	16	78	1.3	6.4	49%	.308	1.25	3.70	4.76	1.0
2009	JAX	AA	27	9	3	0	17	16	104	96	7	22	62	1.9	5.4	52%	.276	1.17	2.77	3.47	2.2
2009	FLO	MLB	27	1	1	0	15	0	26^{1}	27	2	8	18	2.7	6.2	56%	.298	1.33	5.13	5.90	-0.3
2010	GWN	AAA	28	5	1	0	23	2	52^{2}	45	3	8	49	1.4	8.4	49%	.282	1.01	3.08	3.46	1.1
2010	ATL	MLB	28	0	0	0	18	0	26	28	3	6	22	2.1	7.6	59%	.317	1.31	4.85	5.86	-0.3
2011	*ATL*	*MLB*	*29*	*5*	*5*	*0*	*32*	*11*	*103*	*122*	*14*	*31*	*53*	*2.7*	*4.6*	*48%*	*.308*	*1.47*	*5.08*	*5.52*	*0.0*

Often the 12th pitcher on the roster, Martinez doesn't deserve a bigger role, but he's certainly good in the one that he has. Even if he sits around for a week, you know he's not going to walk anybody when he comes in. He doesn't have much of a breaking ball, but his changeup makes him effective against left-handers, and he's sturdy enough to deliver multiple innings when needed, even as an emergency starter. You're looking at his ceiling.

Mike Minor

Born: **12/26/1987** Age: **23**
Bats: R Throws: L Height: **6' 3"** Weight: **210**
Breakout: **20%** Improve: **37%** Collapse: **11%**
Attrition: **13%** MLB: **66%**

Comparables:
Yovani Gallardo, Marc Rzepczynski, Jordan Zimmermann (70)

YEAR	TEAM	LVL	AGE	W	L	SV	G	GS	IP	H	HR	BB	SO	EqBB9	EqSO9	GB%	BABIP	WHIP	ERA	FRA	WARP
2010	MIS	AA	22	2	6	0	15	16	87	74	8	34	109	3.5	11.3	48%	.317	1.25	4.03	4.24	0.1
2010	GWN	AAA	22	4	1	0	6	6	33^{1}	19	1	12	37	3.2	10.0	47%	.234	0.93	1.89	2.84	1.2
2010	ATL	MLB	22	3	2	0	9	9	40^{2}	53	6	11	43	2.4	9.5	38%	.379	1.60	5.98	4.77	0.3
2011	*ATL*	*MLB*	*23*	*7*	*5*	*0*	*16*	*16*	*85*	*80*	*9*	*33*	*89*	*3.4*	*9.3*	*44%*	*.314*	*1.32*	*3.80*	*4.13*	*2.0*

The Braves caught some flak for using the seventh overall pick in the 2009 draft to nab Minor. Scouts agreed that he could get to the big leagues quickly, but there were questions about his upside. The former prediction certainly came true, since Minor was making big-league starts during a pennant race in his first full season, but estimates of his ceiling have risen as dramatically and unexpectedly as his velocity. What was recently an average fastball suddenly turned into a beast that touched 95 mph, and the bread and butter of his game, secondary offerings and command, were as good as ever. Clearly out of gas at the end of the year, Minor will be expected to play a bigger role for Atlanta in 2011. No one is criticizing his selection now.

Peter Moylan

Born: **12/2/1978** Age: **32**
Bats: R Throws: R Height: **6' 2"** Weight: **200**
Breakout: **19%** Improve: **45%** Collapse: **25%**
Attrition: **15%** MLB: **86%**

Comparables:
Mike Timlin, Pedro Feliciano, Juan Rincon (77)

YEAR	TEAM	LVL	AGE	W	L	SV	G	GS	IP	H	HR	BB	SO	EqBB9	EqSO9	GB%	BABIP	WHIP	ERA	FRA	WARP
2008	ATL	MLB	29	0	1	1	7	0	5^{2}	5	1	1	5	1.6	7.9	67%	.235	1.24	1.59	4.24	0.1
2009	ATL	MLB	30	6	2	0	87	0	73	65	0	35	61	4.3	7.5	64%	.308	1.40	2.84	3.57	1.1
2010	ATL	MLB	31	6	2	1	85	0	63^{2}	53	5	37	52	5.2	7.4	69%	.274	1.45	2.97	4.26	0.4
2011	*ATL*	*MLB*	*32*	*4*	*2*	*1*	*77*	*0*	61^{1}	*57*	*5*	*30*	*48*	*4.4*	*7.0*	*53%*	*.296*	*1.42*	*3.96*	*4.31*	*0.2*

It's just part of the randomness of being a ground-ball pitcher: Moylan gave up a crucial hit in Game Four of the NLDS, but if the ball had been just two feet closer to a fielder, it would have been an inning-ending double play and Moylan would be a hero. He was plenty heroic during the regular season, pitching in more than half of the team's games while generating a ridiculous ground-ball ratio of more than four to one. Bobby Cox maximized his value, understanding that he's nothing more than a right-handed specialist who keeps the ball out of the air, and as long as Fredi Gonzalez understands and expects the same, everything will be just fine.

Eric O'Flaherty

Born: **2/5/1985** Age: **26**
Bats: L Throws: L Height: **6' 2"** Weight: **195**
Breakout: **5%** Improve: **8%** Collapse: **29%**
Attrition: **6%** MLB: **45%**

Comparables:
Tim Crabtree, Warren Brusstar, Frank Smith (76)

YEAR	TEAM	LVL	AGE	W	L	SV	G	GS	IP	H	HR	BB	SO	EqBB9	EqSO9	GB%	BABIP	WHIP	ERA	FRA	WARP
2008	SEA	MLB	23	0	1	0	7	0	6^2	16	2	4	4	5.4	5.4	50%	.467	3.30	21.60	15.97	-1.1
2009	ATL	MLB	24	2	1	0	78	0	56^1	52	2	18	39	2.9	6.2	55%	.292	1.35	3.04	3.85	0.7
2010	ATL	MLB	25	3	2	0	56	0	44	37	2	18	36	3.7	7.4	58%	.282	1.27	2.45	3.48	0.7
2011	*ATL*	*MLB*	*26*	*3*	*1*	*0*	*62*	*0*	*53*	*54*	*4*	*22*	*42*	*3.6*	*7.0*	*48%*	*.310*	*1.40*	*4.10*	*4.46*	*0.1*

Through June, O'Flaherty was doing yeoman's work as a LOOGY, as he has throughout his career; those of the left-handed persuasion have hit just .225/.289/.305 against him. However, it's rare to talk about a 2010 Brave without talking about some time missed, and O'Flaherty kept things exotic with some bouts of dizziness and blurry vision that were finally diagnosed as mononucleosis. There's nothing special about his 90-92 mph fastball or slider; he's just one of those guys that for some hard-to-define reason originating in his mechanics and location, gives lefties fits. Those fits will continue in 2011.

Todd Redmond

Born: **5/17/1985** Age: **26**
Bats: R Throws: R Height: **6' 3"** Weight: **215**
Breakout: **16%** Improve: **28%** Collapse: **14%**
Attrition: **30%** MLB: **52%**

Comparables:
Daniel McCutchen, Enrique Gonzalez, Jason Vargas (74)

YEAR	TEAM	LVL	AGE	W	L	SV	G	GS	IP	H	HR	BB	SO	EqBB9	EqSO9	GB%	BABIP	WHIP	ERA	FRA	WARP
2008	MIS	AA	23	14	6	0	31	29	182	179	20	36	150	1.8	7.4	37%	.297	1.21	3.51	4.29	2.7
2009	GWN	AAA	24	9	6	0	27	30	145	152	21	47	106	2.9	6.6	33%	.289	1.42	4.34	5.18	0.7
2010	GWN	AAA	25	9	10	0	28	28	162^2	156	21	44	142	2.4	7.9	37%	.287	1.24	4.26	5.78	0.4
2011	*ATL*	*MLB*	*26*	*9*	*11*	*0*	*27*	*27*	*155*	*172*	*23*	*50*	*102*	*2.9*	*5.9*	*38%*	*.304*	*1.43*	*5.03*	*5.46*	*1.1*

Three years removed from being swapped to the Braves by the Pirates for Tyler Yates, Redmond has spent the last two seasons pitching at Triple-A Gwinnett, and he's lined up for a third tour of duty in 2011. He's a prospect inasmuch as a crafty strike-thrower who keeps his team in every game can be, the kind of guy who could pitch for numerous teams over the next decade, getting an emergency start here and there while doing nothing particularly good, but also nothing to embarrass himself. In short, there's little here to be excited about, but we thought we'd let you know about Redmond so that when his name someday shows up on a list of probable starters, you don't feel any anxiety about having missed something.

Takashi Saito

Born: **2/14/1970** Age: **41**
Bats: L Throws: R Height: **6' 1"** Weight: **202**
Breakout: **8%** Improve: **19%** Collapse: **20%**
Attrition: **6%** MLB: **51%**

Comparables:
Dan Plesac, Larry Andersen, Arthur Rhodes (61)

YEAR	TEAM	LVL	AGE	W	L	SV	G	GS	IP	H	HR	BB	SO	EqBB9	EqSO9	GB%	BABIP	WHIP	ERA	FRA	WARP
2008	LAN	MLB	38	4	4	18	45	0	47	40	1	16	60	3.1	11.5	45%	.331	1.23	2.49	2.07	1.1
2009	BOS	MLB	39	3	3	2	56	0	55^2	50	6	25	52	4.0	8.4	35%	.290	1.44	2.43	2.75	1.4
2010	ATL	MLB	40	2	3	1	56	0	54	41	4	17	69	2.8	11.5	44%	.282	1.07	2.83	2.83	1.1
2011	*ATL*	*MLB*	*41*	*3*	*1*	*8*	*59*	*0*	*58*	*48*	*5*	*21*	*65*	*3.2*	*9.9*	*44%*	*.297*	*1.19*	*2.92*	*3.17*	*1.0*

Like most Braves that were of value in the 2010 regular season, Saito was injured in September (shoulder) and unavailable for the playoffs. Despite turning 41 in February, Saito remains a highly effective reliever with a starter's arsenal, as his 90-92 mph fastball plays up thanks to deception and command, while his slider and changeup are both quality offerings. Already in his late 30s when he came to the United States, Saito was unlikely ever to achieve real free agency, so he had an interesting contract stipulation that forced the Braves to release him at the end of the year. In a world where the term *consistent reliever* approaches the level of an oxymoron, Saito is a worthwhile gamble in spite of his age. The Brewers thought so, signing him to a one-year contract.

Julio Teheran

Born: **1/27/1991** Age: **20**
Bats: R Throws: R Height: **6' 2"** Weight: **150**
Breakout: **4%** Improve: **4%** Collapse: **4%**
Attrition: **1%** MLB: **5%**

Comparables:
Ken Holtzman, Oliver Perez, Von McDaniel (70)

YEAR	TEAM	LVL	AGE	W	L	SV	G	GS	IP	H	HR	BB	SO	EqBB9	EqSO9	GB%	BABIP	WHIP	ERA	FRA	WARP
2009	ROM	A	18	1	3	0	7	7	37^2	42	2	11	28	2.6	6.7	47%	.342	1.54	3.82	4.25	0.4
2009	DNV	Rk	18	2	1	0	7	7	43^2	36	2	7	39	1.4	8.0	61%	.288	1.15	2.47	3.45	2.4
2010	ROM	A	19	2	2	0	7	7	39^1	23	1	10	45	2.3	10.3	46%	.237	0.97	1.14	2.49	1.5
2010	MYR	A+	19	4	4	0	10	10	63^1	56	6	13	76	1.8	10.8	42%	.313	1.17	2.56	3.07	1.8
2010	MIS	AA	19	3	2	0	7	7	40	29	2	17	38	3.8	8.6	38%	.260	1.18	3.38	4.74	0.4
2011	*ATL*	*MLB*	*20*	*5*	*5*	*0*	*13*	*13*	*72*	*73*	*9*	*34*	*57*	*4.2*	*7.1*	*44%*	*.301*	*1.47*	*4.80*	*5.22*	*0.8*

With Stephen Strasburg logging enough innings before his elbow went kablooey to lose his prospect status, many believe that Teheran is now the best pitching prospect in the minors. After making one of the biggest international signings in 2007, the Braves finally took the reins off the teenage Colombian in 2010, and he pitched his way across three levels while dominating every step of the way. The fact that he has a mid-90s fastball to go along with a good curve and at least average change is one thing. The fact that he has smooth arm actions and excellent control is another. The fact that he has a chance to reach the big leagues in 2011 at a time when some feel he's just beginning to scrape his potential is what's scary.

Jonny Venters

Born: **3/20/1985** Age: **26**
Bats: L Throws: L Height: **6' 3"** Weight: **195**
Breakout: **13%** Improve: **33%** Collapse: **8%**
Attrition: **21%** MLB: **54%**

Comparables:
Eulogio De La Cruz, Josh Outman, Matt Albers (74)

YEAR	TEAM	LVL	AGE	W	L	SV	G	GS	IP	H	HR	BB	SO	EqBB9	EqSO9	GB%	BABIP	WHIP	ERA	FRA	WARP
2009	MIS	AA	24	4	4	0	12	14	65^{1}	60	2	35	40	4.8	5.5	58%	.290	1.50	2.76	2.96	1.9
2009	GWN	AAA	24	4	8	0	18	20	94^{1}	111	7	44	60	4.2	5.7	51%	.333	1.67	5.82	5.72	-0.1
2010	ATL	MLB	25	4	4	1	79	0	83	61	1	39	93	4.2	10.1	69%	.289	1.30	1.95	3.42	1.3
2011	*ATL*	*MLB*	*26*	*6*	*5*	*0*	*47*	*11*	*89^{1}*	*92*	*8*	*47*	*63*	*4.7*	*6.4*	*51%*	*.308*	*1.55*	*4.77*	*5.19*	*0.5*

Easily the biggest surprise in the organization last season, Venters went from middling minor-league starter to dominating bullpen piece in the course of a year. The lefty always possessed a plus sinker as notable for its 94-95 mph velocity as its heavy sink, but pitching coach Roger McDowell helped transform his once slurvy breaking ball into a true weapon and focused him on just two pitches in short stints, and the results were immediate. Venters doesn't make it look easy with complicated and effort-filled mechanics, and he will likely always have some problems with keeping his walk totals down, but if Craig Kimbrel weren't around, Venters would be the top candidate for 2011's closing job.

Arodys Vizcaino

Born: **11/13/1990** Age: **20**
Bats: R Throws: R Height: **6' 0"** Weight: **189**
Breakout: **0%** Improve: **0%** Collapse: **0%**
Attrition: **0%** MLB: **0%**

Comparables:
Milt Pappas, Lindy McDaniel, Chris Zachary (83)

YEAR	TEAM	LVL	AGE	W	L	SV	G	GS	IP	H	HR	BB	SO	EqBB9	EqSO9	GB%	BABIP	WHIP	ERA	FRA	WARP
2008	YAN	Rk	17	3	2	0	12	6	44	38	5	13	48	2.7	9.8	39%	.277	1.18	3.48	5.05	0.5
2009	STA	A-	18	2	4	0	10	11	42^{1}	34	2	15	52	3.2	11.1	52%	.294	1.18	1.91	3.59	0.9
2010	ROM	A	19	9	4	0	14	20	71^{2}	63	1	9	68	1.1	8.5	44%	.294	1.05	2.26	2.84	2.4
2011	*ATL*	*MLB*	*20*	*4*	*5*	*0*	*11*	*11*	*53^{1}*	*59*	*7*	*24*	*37*	*4.1*	*6.2*	*43%*	*.312*	*1.56*	*5.16*	*5.61*	*0.5*

While lesser known than Melky Cabrera, Vizcaino was the key to the Javier Vazquez trade, and after the year Vazquez had in New York, it's looking even more like a historic Yankees mistake that has the potential to rise to Buhner-for-Phelps levels of infamy. Although Vizcaino was sidelined nearly half the year with a partial tear of a ligament in his pitching elbow, he was healthy at the end of the year and touching 98 mph in the instructional league. Vizcaino possesses the rare combination of mid-90s velocity and sublime control and didn't allow a run or a walk in his last five starts for Rome before getting a promotion. His curveball is already major-league quality. He has the potential to be a special arm, but he still needs to prove it over an entire season.

Billy Wagner

Born: **7/25/1971** Age: **39**
Bats: L Throws: L Height: **5' 10"** Weight: **180**
Breakout: **6%** Improve: **27%** Collapse: **23%**
Attrition: **7%** MLB: **73%**

Comparables:
Dennis Eckersley, Jesse Orosco, Larry Andersen (47)

YEAR	TEAM	LVL	AGE	W	L	SV	G	GS	IP	H	HR	BB	SO	EqBB9	EqSO9	GB%	BABIP	WHIP	ERA	FRA	WARP
2008	NYN	MLB	36	0	1	27	45	0	47	32	4	10	52	1.9	10.0	39%	.237	0.89	2.30	3.6	0.6
2009	BOS	MLB	37	1	1	0	15	0	13^{2}	8	1	7	22	4.6	14.5	31%	.280	1.17	1.98	4.36	0.1
2009	NYN	MLB	37	0	0	0	2	0	2	0	0	1	4	4.5	18.0	0%	.000	0.50	0.00	2.92	0.1
2010	ATL	MLB	38	7	2	37	71	0	69^{1}	38	5	22	104	2.9	13.5	40%	.246	0.91	1.43	1.8	1.8
2011	*ATL*	*MLB*	*39*	*3*	*2*	*14*	*57*	*0*	*56^{1}*	*41*	*5*	*19*	*73*	*3.0*	*11.6*	*42%*	*.289*	*1.06*	*2.26*	*2.45*	*1.5*

After struggling with injuries, Wagner had one of the best five seasons of his career in 2010, showing both the stuff and the ability to pitch well into the future. Nevertheless, despite getting just one out in the postseason before departing with a strained oblique, Wagner followed through on his intention to retire, returning to his small hometown in Virginia to watch his kids grow up, conduct a clinic or two at his old high school, and work with his foundation to provide tutoring and academic assistance for those in need. He's arguably the best left-handed reliever in the history of the game, finishing an 853-game career with 422 saves (two short of John Franco's lefty record), a 2.31 ERA, a WHIP under one, and just short of 12 strikeouts per nine innings. In some ways, he was the original Tim Lincecum, a short, skinny kid with upper-90s velocity that a lot of people didn't believe in, but unlike the Giants' version, this one benefited greatly from a transition to shorter stints, as he never developed a changeup and wasn't an especially efficient pitcher until his late 20s. If there weren't a bias against relievers, Wagner would be a gimme Hall of Fame selection in five years.

LINEOUTS

HITTERS

PLAYER	TEAM	LVL	AGE	PA	R	2B	3B	HR	RBI	BB	SO	SB-CS	AVG/OBP/SLG	TAv	BABIP	BRR	FRAA	WARP
C C. Bethancourt	ROM	A	18	417	30	19	2	3	34	14	62	2-0	.251/.278/.332	.235	.287	-2.4	C 0	0.1
1B B. Canizares	GWN	AAA	30	468	58	28	1	13	76	40	54	0-0	.340/.408/.502	.296	.363	0.0	1B 5	2.8
LF B. Clevlen	GWN	AAA	26	214	18	8	0	3	29	22	62	3-0	.257/.332/.346	.237	.362	-0.9	RF 1	-0.2
	ATL	MLB	26	4	1	1	0	0	0	0	1	0-0	.250/.250/.500	.190	.333	0.1	LF 1	0.1
INF E. Duncan*	MIS	AA	25	479	52	23	5	8	64	35	108	6-4	.267/.326/.396	.261	.332	0.6	2B 10, 1B 1	2.1
1B M. Gomez	MIS	AA	25	549	64	42	2	16	80	46	122	0-0	.281/.355/.471	.292	.337	0.0	1B -7	1.5
INF D. Hernandez	GWN	AAA	26	121	12	7	2	0	17	4	21	0-0	.319/.347/.414	.270	.385	0.0	SS -3, 2B 1	0.3
	ATL	MLB	26	10	1	0	0	1	1	0	4	0-0	.111/.100/.444	.173	.000	-0.1	SS -1, 2B 0	-0.2
LF C. Johnson*	MYR	A+	21	102	12	4	0	6	25	10	29	0-0	.264/.333/.506	.303	.316	0.0	LF 0	0.6
	MIS	AA	21	259	26	6	0	10	31	25	114	0-0	.189/.270/.343	.226	.309	0.0	LF 4, RF 0	0.0
SS M. Lipka	BRA	Rk	18	247	38	11	4	1	26	18	25	17-2	.294/.344/.390	.307	.325	3.5	SS 0	2.1
	BRA	Rk	18	247	38	11	4	1	26	18	25	17-2	.294/.344/.390	.307	.325	3.5	SS 0	2.1
OF W. Ramirez	ERI	AA	24	234	34	10	4	15	42	22	83	5-6	.242/.312/.540	.295	.316	0.3	CF 2, LF 0	1.7
	GWN	AAA	24	89	14	2	1	3	12	10	21	2-0	.244/.360/.410	.283	.291	-0.1	LF 1, RF 1	0.6
	TOL	AAA	24	163	14	4	2	4	14	10	60	7-2	.216/.276/.346	.212	.326	0.0	RF -1, CF 3	-0.3
SS E. Salcedo	ROM	A	18	209	22	5	4	2	16	11	56	0-0	.197/.234/.295	.206	.257	-1.0	SS 9	0.4
SS A. Simmons	DNV	Rk	20	297	36	12	1	2	30	19	14	20-5	.268/.310/.342	.297	.271	0.4	SS 17	2.7
UT J. Thurston*	GWN	AAA	30	503	50	18	4	13	66	32	64	7-7	.274/.322/.415	.251	.287	1.2	2B 12, 3B -6	1.5

Young catcher **Christian Bethancourt** is a potential defensive whiz whom people expected much more from offensively in his full-season debut. He's still young and talented, and there's plenty of time. ⊘ First baseman **Barbaro Canizares** put up huge numbers at Triple-A Gwinnett, but even with the major-league club suffering more than its share of injuries, the Braves never called. Canizares is a dreadful defender who is running out of chances now that he's 31 (and that's in Cuban years). ⊘ Former Tigers prospect **Brent Clevlen** got four big-league at-bats in 2010 and didn't deserve any of them. ⊘ Former Yankees first-round pick **Eric Duncan** got a second chance with the Braves and at second base, where the offensive expectations were far lower. He still didn't meet them. The ever-generous Rockies signed him to a minor-league contract. ⊘ **Mauro Gomez** is a fat first baseman with a good stick and doubles power, but when you're a fat first baseman, good needs to be great and doubles need to be home runs. ⊘ **Diory Hernandez** can play second base, third base, and shortstop with great aplomb, but that damn rulebook doesn't allow nonhitting designated fielders. ⊘ The Braves didn't want to add former first-round pick **Cody Johnson** to the 40-man roster, so they sent him to the Yankees for cash considerations, which is more consideration than he's worth. ⊘ The Braves' top pick in 2010 draft, **Matt Lipka** is a phenomenal athlete who would be catching passes for the Alabama Crimson Tide had he not signed for $800,000. He'll never be a power hitter, but he can run, can throw well, and showed a surprisingly advanced approach at the plate. Many Braves officials feel his name will be much better known following his full-season debut at Low-A Rome. ⊘ The Tigers gave up on toolsy outfielder **Wilkin Ramirez**, and after he spent about a month with the Braves, the Atlanta club understood why. ⊘ A big-money signee out of the Dominican Republic, shortstop **Edward Salcedo** was overmatched as an 18-year-old in Low-A, but his tools remain outstanding. ⊘ A 2010 second-round pick **Andrelton Simmons** is a defensive wizard with plenty of questions about his bat. ⊘ Versatility and great makeup keep getting **Joey Thurston** jobs—at Triple-A.

PITCHERS

PLAYER	TEAM	LVL	AGE	W	L	SV	IP	H	HR	BB	SO	EqBB9	EqSO9	GB%	BABIP	WHIP	ERA	FRA	WARP
K. Cofield	MIS	AA	23	1	3	0	55^{1}	58	4	22	38	3.6	6.2	63%	.300	1.48	4.23	5.19	0.3
E. Cordier	MIS	AA	24	11	7	0	135^{2}	116	3	69	113	4.6	7.5	51%	.291	1.40	3.58	4.03	2.2
S. Diamond*	MIS	AA	23	4	6	0	102^{1}	113	4	39	90	3.4	7.9	56%	.356	1.50	3.52	1.97	4.4
—	GWN	AAA	23	4	1	0	56^{1}	53	2	15	33	2.4	5.3	53%	.291	1.22	3.20	3.75	1.4
C. Gearrin	GWN	AAA	24	3	5	0	78^{1}	68	6	32	64	3.7	7.4	62%	.284	1.39	2.99	4.48	0.7
S. Kent*	ROM	A	21	2	0	1	39^{1}	27	1	8	54	1.8	12.4	52%	.271	0.92	0.69	0.94	2.2
K. Medlen	ATL	MLB	24	6	2	0	107^{2}	108	13	21	83	1.8	6.9	44%	.299	1.23	3.68	4.37	1.1
B. Oberholtzer*	ROM	A	20	0	2	0	23	22	1	5	19	2.0	7.4	44%	.323	1.22	1.57	2.35	0.9
—	MYR	A+	20	6	6	2	112^{2}	123	7	18	107	1.4	8.5	50%	.344	1.29	3.91	3.99	1.7
C. Perez*	DNV	Rk	18	2	0	0	42	27	0	22	35	4.7	7.5	61%	.255	1.17	1.07	2.29	5.2
S. Proctor	GWN	AAA	33	3	3	0	33^{1}	43	6	15	28	4.1	7.6	43%	.346	1.77	7.29	7.17	-0.7
—	ATL	MLB	33	0	0	0	5^{2}	4	1	4	6	6.4	9.5	21%	.231	1.41	6.35	7.85	-0.2

Acquired from the Braves in the Scott Linebrink deal, right-hander **Kyle Cofield** has a plus sinker and a good breaking ball, but he also has a history of elbow problems and control issues. ⚾ Big righty **Erik Cordier** isn't the same power arm he was prior to Tommy John surgery, but he could still end up a nice middle reliever. ⚾ **Scott Diamond** is one of those upper-level strike throwers who isn't nearly as good as his stats might suggest, but he is durable and left-handed; said qualities got him a shot to make the Twins as a Rule 5 draft selection. ⚾ Right-hander **Cory Gearrin** is a side-armer with the corresponding huge ground-ball rate, but the Braves already have a better version in Peter Moylan. ⚾ Little Australian lefty **Steven Kent** has decent velocity, tons of deception, and dominant numbers at Low-A; for now, he's just worth keeping an eye on. ⚾ An undersized righty who gets the most out of his ability, **Kris Medlen** was valued for his versatility, performing well in both starting and relief roles before his elbow went pop in August. He'll miss the majority of the 2011 season, but the Braves think he can return to form quickly, using his solid fastball and outstanding changeup to get outs in a variety of roles once again. ⚾ Southpaw **Brett Oberholtzer** doesn't walk anybody, but he doesn't exactly miss a lot of bats, either. ⚾ The Braves already have a highly regarded trio of Latin American pitchers in Delgado, Julio Teheran, and Arodys Vizcaino, and many scouts believe **Carlos Perez** is close to making it a quartet. A 19-year-old Dominican, Perez already has low-90s heat and a very advanced changeup for his age, along with the kind of frame and mechanics that just ooze projection. For now, he's simply something to dream on, but it's the kind of really intense crazy dream you get when you have the flu or are on prescription medicine. ⚾ **Scott Proctor** barely pitched while recovering from Tommy John surgery, and the Braves will give him another shot in 2011. Unless Joe Torre comes out of retirement, it's hard to see him getting many chances.

MANAGER: BOBBY COX

YEAR	TEAM	W-L	Pythag +/-	Avg PC	100+ P	120+ P	QS	BQS	REL	REL w Zero R	IBB	Subs	PH	PH Avg	PH HR	SB2	CS2	SB3	CS3	SAC Att	SAC %	POS SAC	Squeeze	Swing	In Play
2009	ATL	86-76	-6	95.3	66	2	94	3	488	334	59	49	249	.243	3	56	24	2	2	136	69.9%	44	0	96	78
2010	ATL	91-71	-3	94.3	59	1	82	8	490	347	64	74	258	.250	10	55	25	7	3	105	65.7%	34	3	141	100

At a certain point, some major-league managers seem to ossify, inflicting the narrowing and hardening of their own arteries on the pipelines that bring the lifeblood of young talent to their rosters. Although Cox could have been forgiven for growing a little veteran-happy in his twilight years, he never succumbed to the same fetish for established players that plagued Joe Torre, another future Hall of Fame manager whose swan song was sung last season. In his final year at the helm, Cox welcomed a wave of rookie recruits, most notably by championing right fielder Jason Heyward's inclusion on the Opening Day roster, and earned a final playoff appearance as a result. It falls to new hire Fredi Gonzalez to shepherd the last crop of Cox appointees to maturity, and the longest-tenured manager in Marlins history makes a logical choice. A close confidant of Cox, Gonzalez served under the outgoing manager for four seasons as third-base coach and shares his predecessor's affection for the intentional walk (though he seemed to temper that tendency last season). He continued to make his off-season home in the Atlanta area during the last few years. Gonzalez was dismissed in late June by a fickle group of Marlins decision makers who made eyes at

Bobby Valentine while harboring unreasonable expectations for their club. Before his ouster, Gonzalez's season was defined by his success in taking the high road and retaining the respect of his players during a well-publicized spat with Hanley Ramirez—the team's highest-paid and most marketable star—whom he had benched for lack of hustle. Given the realities of managing under misers in Miami, where on-field triumphs guarantee an early ticket out of town, Gonzalez has become well-versed in nurturing young talent, and thanks to his prior Atlanta experience, the laid-back manager's fresh perspective won't preclude a sense of continuity with Cox.

Baltimore Orioles

The Orioles haven't been a factor in the AL East since 1997, but for several years prior to 2010, they could at least be relied upon to raise their fans' hopes for a spell early on before succumbing to an inevitable second-half demise. Each iteration of the O's from 2005 to 2009 could be described as a "first-half team," if only in a relative sense; none of those clubs finished any higher than fourth, but they managed a combined .474 winning percentage before the All-Star breaks of their respective seasons, compared to a dismal .367 figure thereafter.

In 2010, that trend came to an end, and its reversal cost Dave Trembley his job. En route to the organization's third consecutive fifth-place finish, Baltimore turned in a miserable 29-59 performance before the break, and stumbled to a 3-14 start out of the gate in the second half. Trembley, a players' manager who had shepherded the Orioles' previous two descents into the cellar, lasted only 54 games into his third season at the helm before being forced to walk the plank with the weight of his team's 15-39 record chained to his leg. Third-base coach Juan Samuel took over on an interim basis in time for a dead-cat bounce, though the 17-34 mark that the club put together on his watch wouldn't register as an acceptable improvement for any unit since the 2003 Tigers.

When he dismissed Trembley, GM Andy MacPhail told reporters, "Nobody believes the reason we have the record we do is somehow Dave Trembley's fault, or that making a change will magically change everything." He was right about that. However, MacPhail's second managerial move of the season did appear to yield miraculous results, at least on the surface.

In the time-honored tradition of filling a managerial vacancy with a Bizarro version of the outgoing skipper, the Orioles hired strong-willed disciplinarian Buck Showalter to succeed the easygoing Trembley. Showalter, who had last occupied a manager's office with the 2006 Rangers, boasted a .514 lifetime record at the time of his hiring, which qualifies as a successful track record by the standards of experienced skippers, few of whom manage to keep their noses far above .500. However, his previous 11 years of managerial experience had primarily distinguished him as the perpetual bridesmaid of MLB managers: in both New York and Arizona, Showalter had helped transform franchises, but had been dismissed just prior to their receipt of October rewards. Fed up with their long-standing status as competitive nonentities, the Orioles hired Uncle Buck to reprise his past performances and take them to the verge of contention, if not beyond, but they didn't expect results overnight—which is exactly what their fresh field general delivered.

ORIOLES PROSPECTUS

2010 W-L: 66-96, 5th in AL East

Pythag	.387	28th
RS/G	3.8	27th
RA/G	4.8	5th
TAv	.256	27th
BRR	-0.5	17th
FRA	4.99	27th
DER	5.74	10th
DL	651	10th
B-Age	28.7	13th
P-Age	28.2	18th
Salary	$81.6	17th
M$/MW	$4.12	27th

Ballpark: Camden Yards (3-yr. PF: 101). Retro park remains picturesque, if sparsely populated, but Boog's value over replacement BBQ stand has been greatly exaggerated

2010: Young Orioles tumble from the nest under Trembley, but take flight when the Buck stops in Baltimore

2011: If in-house hitters can't keep pace with the hurler harvest, the O's will stay cool in the cellar

Action Items: Sustaining second-half gains

Presiding over a collection of players that had been winning at a .305 clip, Showalter beat the Angels on his first night on the job. The O's won three more before they lost again, and followed that defeat with another four consecutive tallies in the win column. The team reeled off three more four-game winning streaks before the schedule said "time up," finishing 34-23 under the new skipper—a pace that would have won them the division had it been sustained all season. To make matters even more impressive, the Orioles elevated their level of play during a stretch that pitted them against their most formidable opponents, and they even held their own in matchups with intradivision rivals, against whom they went 14-13.

As research by *Baseball Prospectus* author Steven Goldman has shown, of the 16 teams in history that have finished with a losing record, made a managerial change at a similarly late point in the season, and played above-.500

baseball under the new skipper, the Orioles' improvement under Showalter was easily the most dramatic. In fact, among teams with overall winning percentages as poor as the Orioles' .407, their blistering post-Samuel stretch was almost unprecedented, new manager or not.

Table 1. The Buck Starts Here: Fast Finishes by Poor Teams

Year	Team	Overall WP	Last-57 WP	Difference	Following Year WP
1907	SLN	.340	.545	.206	.318
2010	BAL	.407	.596	.189	?
1929	BOS	.377	.518	.141	.338
1923	BOS	.351	.482	.132	.309
1904	PHI	.342	.473	.131	.546
1955	BAL	.370	.500	.130	.448
1911	BSN	.291	.415	.124	.340
1912	BSN	.340	.455	.115	.457
1981	CHN	.369	.482	.113	.451
2001	TBA	.383	.491	.109	.342

As the inclusion of both the 1911 and 1912 Boston Braves in Table 1 should make clear, a strong finish doesn't always carry over to the following season. The Orioles posted the second-most drastic improvement over their final 57 contests of any team to finish with a winning percentage of .407 or below, but the only team that ranked above them actually went backward in the year after its season-concluding sprint. Of the other eight, only five improved at all, let alone by leaps and bounds. However, a list of the .407-or-under teams with the hottest stretches of at least 50 games over any part of their seasons offers more reason for optimism (Table 2).

Table 2. Flash in the Pan? Hot Streaks by Cold Teams

Year	Team	Overall WP	Hot-Streak WP	Games	Following Year YP
1914	CIN	.390	.612	50	.461
2010	BAL	.407	.607	56	?
1987	SDN	.401	.596	52	.516
1926	SLA	.403	.582	55	.386
1907	BOS	.396	.571	50	.487
1956	CHN	.390	.569	51	.403
1907	SLN	.340	.560	52	.318
1949	WS1	.325	.560	50	.435
2000	PHI	.401	.560	50	.531
1950	CHA	.390	.560	50	.526

Here, too, last year's Orioles rank second-best, but their company is a little more encouraging. All but two of these teams improved in the seasons following their transient torrid performances (in most cases by wide margins), as if those fledgling stretches of unaccustomed performance, like the first crack in an adolescent's voice, prefigured a more lasting maturation to come.

Before we lament the fact that Showalter wasn't hired early enough to make an Orioles fan's dream of a 97-win pace sustained over six months come true, we should attempt to determine how much—if anything—he had to do with the turnaround. It's easy enough to establish that the Orioles' improved record wasn't simply a fluky affront to Pythagoras. Although Showalter's arrival didn't coincide with any miraculous performance boost from the offense, which managed a .254 TAv prior to his hiring and a .252 TAv with him at the helm, the cellar dwellers actually played much better baseball after casting off their original managerial reins (Table 3).

Table 3. Bucking the Trend: On-Field Improvements After Hiring Showalter

Statistic	Pre-Buck	With-Buck	Pre-Buck Rank	With-Buck Rank
DE	.679	.723	27	1
PADE	-2.22	5.67	21	1
ERA	5.18	3.54	29	7
SIERA	4.72	4.16	30	16

Some degree of common sense should enter the equation here. With our accumulated knowledge of baseball, we'd be hard put to construct a scenario in which a man who never hits, fields, or throws a ball in anger could turn an assortment of sad-sack losers into a team that plays like a pennant contender; even Morris Buttermaker would have been hard-pressed to engineer a happy ending without Whurlitzer and Leak. What's more, the manager whom Buck replaced was hired both for his way with youngsters and his ability to inculcate an appreciation for the fundamentals, so it seems unlikely that he could have utterly failed where Showalter spectacularly succeeded in unlocking a deep reservoir of latent talent within the Orioles roster.

In addition, one struggles to ascribe any moves of managerial genius to the new man on the job. It's not as if Showalter showed up with a bulging playbook under his arm, scrawled a series of X's and O's on a clubhouse chalkboard, and oversaw a military-style training camp; MLB managers have fewer levers and dials at their disposal than do coaches in less probabilistic sports. For the most part, the benighted Birds who lost under Trembley and Samuel were composed of the same players, stationed at the same positions, as the team that took flight under Showalter's wing.

Consider the team's fielding performance, which experienced the most notable renaissance under the new manager. Whatever Showalter's abilities to improve that aspect of his roster's performance might be, the two nonexpansion clubs for which he'd previously assumed responsibility didn't experience any dramatic turnarounds in the defense department: the 1992 Yankees converted a few more balls in play into outs than the 1991 club, but the 2003 Rangers saw their gloves go south. Perhaps Showalter's best move was having the good sense to swoop in as the defensive cavalry arrived. Just prior to his hiring, two defensive dominoes fell: second baseman Brian Roberts returned after a 3½-month absence, which displaced the faux-leather collection of Ty Wigginton, Julio Lugo, and Scott Moore, and third baseman Miguel Tejada headed for the sunny climes of Southern California, which made way for Josh Bell's capable glove work.

Whether the Orioles' glovely showing late in the season stemmed from personnel changes or a convincing Svengali act from Showalter, it can't explain the entirety of the run-prevention improvement by a team that allowed an average of 5.5 runs per game before his hiring, and just 3.7 runs per game thereafter. As their end-of-season reduction in SIERA suggested, Orioles pitchers made some defense-independent advances of their own, improving in each of the Three True Outcomes (Table 4).

Table 4. Peripheral Improvements: Defense-Independent Pitching Gains Under Showalter

Statistic	Pre-Buck	With-Buck
K/9	6.1	6.7
BB/9	3.6	2.7
HR/9	1.2	1.1

Unless a stint as a talking head on ESPN's *Baseball Tonight* taught Showalter the secret to baseball alchemy, enabling him to turn Baltimore's diluted and watery roster into wine—which would seem unlikely, considering the intellectual and analytical powers of his cohosts—we should probably attribute the bulk of the transformation that took place on his watch to other factors. Buck did his part, but that 34-23 finish probably represented some combination of regression to the mean, minor roster improvements, and, perhaps, the first stirrings of a club beginning to come into its own.

Prior to Opening Day, MacPhail inaugurated "Phase Two" of the team's rebuilding plan, which put the onus on his major-league staff to deliver results. Unfortunately, the meager two-game boost that followed his pronouncement made it appear as if the GM had in fact set his phasers to "stun" and trained them on his roster. In retrospect, declaring the completion of "Phase One" before yet another fifth-place finish might strike a jaded victim of the Angelos' administration as Bush 43's "Mission Accomplished" stunt writ small, but it's easy to see what MacPhail meant. Whereas the early stages of the rebuilding movement were devoted to filling the prospect pipeline with young talent, 2010 was to be the proud moment when the by-products pooled and congealed at the major-league level to form something vaguely recognizable as the next title contender's core.

Although it's tempting to think that the process of tearing down a teetering team and replacing it with a cost-controlled collection of competitors has a simple recipe—add scouts to a stock of progressive front office; season with smart spending, adept trading, and a dash of high draft picks; let sit; and stir occasionally for three to five years before serving—rebuilding movements aren't guaranteed to result in contenders. The Orioles' effort remains in little danger of being declared DOA, but given their lack of forward progress last season, as well as the strip-mined system left behind by a recent rash of promotions, it runs a severe risk of stalling.

What appeared in spring training to be the offensive foundation of a winning Orioles team was tarnished over a season's worth of exposure to the elements. Nick Markakis failed to improve upon 2009's down year and apparently has settled in as three-win player, rather than the budding seven-win superstar he seemed to be in 2008. Adam Jones and Matt Wieters treaded water even by the kindest interpretation of their production. By mid-May, Nolan Reimold had slumped his way back to Norfolk, and Bell's flaws were exposed at the major-league level.

On the pitching side of the equation, 2010 yielded rosier returns. If they so choose, the O's could field a competent 25-or-under rotation behind nominal ace Jeremy Guthrie this season, since Brian Matusz, Brad Bergesen, Jake Arrieta, and Chris Tillman staked claims to major-league roster spots last year, while top prospect Zach Britton knocked loudly on the door from Norfolk. None of those pitchers has proven himself above average at the highest level, but collectively, they offer enough promise to suggest that the team is doing something right in developing hurlers. However, if the organization doesn't address the imbalance between their pitching potential and mediocre offensive outlook, they could find themselves with a unequal distribution of talent, thanks to a dearth of quality position players on the farm. Given the strength of the team's AL East rivals, only overlapping waves of pitcher- and position-player talent cresting in the Inner Harbor could manage to unbeach Baltimore. Andy MacPhail took a step toward leveling his lopsided roster by sending two relievers apiece to the Diamondbacks and Brewers for Mark Reynolds and J. J. Hardy, respectively, in December. Although Reynolds' unsightly career stats away from Arizona call the wisdom of the first move into question, the latter acquisition gives the Orioles a potentially league-average (or better) bat at shortstop. Finally, even an age-diminished Derrek Lee should easily surpass the .226/.289/.336 put up by last year's first basemen.

Last year, Baltimore proved oddly resistant to shedding veterans; although MacPhail insisted that "no one [was] untouchable," only Tejada and Will Ohman ended up being touched by other teams. The Orioles passed up opportunities to trade Luke Scott, Wigginton (who signed with the Rockies in December), and, before his injury issues, Roberts. Any of these players could have offered some aid to a system that boasts only one five-star position player (18-year-old shortstop Manny Machado), as adjudged by *Baseball Prospectus* prospect authority Kevin Goldstein. A more aggressive approach to restocking the system might bolster the sagging underpinnings of the Oriole edifice before the entire structure ends up condemned.

This winter, the Orioles' official Web site greeted potential season-ticket buyers with a textual plea to "Join Buck's Birds for 2011," accompanied by an image of the stoic skipper gazing into an uncertain but orange-tinged future. Pinning a franchise's future to a manager in that manner seems like an admission of a shortage of marketable stars, since a skipper only succeeds to the extent that his roster makes possible. Even if the Orioles believe that Showalter exerted an appreciable effect on their fortunes last season, they shouldn't count on him to complete their regrowth; complacency can kill a roster as quickly as age or attrition, and even a budding rebuilding movement requires careful cultivation to come to full bloom. Without continued development from the Orioles' young core and an influx of additional cost-controlled talent, the 2010 club's .596 finish may prove to be for the birds.

HITTERS

Ryan Adams **INF**

Born: **4/21/1987** Age: **24**
Bats: R Throws: R Height: **5' 11"** Weight: **195**
Breakout: **0%** Improve: **3%** Collapse: **6%**
Attrition: **15%** MLB: **21%**

Comparables:
Travis Denker, Brad Harman, Luis Valbuena (76)

YEAR	TEAM	LVL	AGE	PA	R	2B	3B	HR	RBI	BB	SO	SB	CS	AVG_OBP_SLG	TAv	BABIP	BRR	FRAA	WARP
2008	DEL	A	21	491	67	26	5	11	57	36	109	12	5	.308/.367/.462	.310	.379	1.4	2B 4, SS 0	4.1
2009	FRD	A+	22	234	26	14	0	2	25	19	41	2	4	.288/.350/.381	.275	.349	0.2	2B -3	0.6
2010	BOW	AA	23	579	80	43	0	15	68	45	120	2	2	.299/.371/.465	.286	.358	-1.3	2B 9, 3B -2	3.5
2011	*BAL*	*MLB*	*24*	*435*	*48*	*24*	*1*	*9*	*47*	*26*	*104*	*2*	*1*	*.255/.302/.386*	*.241*	*.316*	*-0.1*	*2B 7, 3B -1*	*0.8*

Adams can hit, but questions about his hands at second base are rapidly solidifying into unpleasant answers, as suggested by his career fielding percentage of .936. This isn't necessarily a disaster, since Brian Roberts isn't going anywhere and neither Mark Reynolds nor Josh Bell inspires confidence, given the former's weak hitting record away from Chase Field and mediocre glove and the latter's weak conception of the strike zone. Adams' ability to hold down another position should not be taken for granted, but his future may depend on his having the hands to play third. If not, he will fall into that neither-fish-nor-fowl category that largely precludes regular playing time.

Robert Andino **INF**

Born: **4/25/1984** Age: **27**
Bats: R Throws: R Height: **6' 0"** Weight: **170**
Breakout: **6%** Improve: **30%** Collapse: **6%**
Attrition: **16%** MLB: **56%**

Comparables:
Ronny Cedeno, Brian Barden, Eric Patterson (78)

YEAR	TEAM	LVL	AGE	PA	R	2B	3B	HR	RBI	BB	SO	SB	CS	AVG_OBP_SLG	TAv	BABIP	BRR	FRAA	WARP
2008	ABQ	AAA	24	202	28	14	3	6	26	18	31	9	5	.287/.356/.497	.268	.313	-0.4	SS 5, 2B 0	1.5
2008	FLO	MLB	24	68	6	2	0	2	9	4	23	0	0	.206/.250/.333	.204	.282	3.1	2B 3, CF 0	0.4
2009	BAL	MLB	25	215	27	7	0	2	10	15	47	3	3	.222/.274/.288	.222	.278	0.3	SS 3, 2B -2	0.1
2010	NOR	AAA	26	584	71	30	4	13	76	29	110	16	3	.264/.303/.405	.246	.303	-1.2	SS 9, 2B -1	2.1
2010	BAL	MLB	26	66	6	4	0	2	6	3	13	1	1	.295/.333/.459	.262	.340	-0.3	3B -2, 2B -1	-0.1
2011	*BAL*	*MLB*	*27*	*473*	*50*	*21*	*3*	*9*	*49*	*28*	*99*	*11*	*4*	*.248/.293/.370*	*.235*	*.295*	*-0.5*	*SS 3, 2B 0*	*0.6*

Though he still can't get on base to save his life, over the last few years, Andino has wrung a bit of power out of his swing at Triple-A. In September, he flashed that power in the majors, homering off of A. J. Burnett and CC Sabathia in consecutive games. Let's hope he got the balls for his mantelpiece, because it was a fluke.

Xavier Avery **CF**

Born: **1/1/1990** Age: **21**
Bats: L Throws: L Height: **5' 11"** Weight: **180**
Breakout: **0%** Improve: **2%** Collapse: **0%**
Attrition: **1%** MLB: **2%**

Comparables:
Rick Manning, Joe Lovitto, Rod Carew (79)

YEAR	TEAM	LVL	AGE	PA	R	2B	3B	HR	RBI	BB	SO	SB	CS	AVG_OBP_SLG	TAv	BABIP	BRR	FRAA	WARP
2008	ORI	Rk	18	188	27	8	1	0	7	10	51	11	3	.280/.335/.337	.246	.386	0.2	CF -3	0.0
2009	DEL	A	19	505	50	15	8	2	36	27	111	30	10	.262/.307/.340	.248	.334	2.6	CF -6	0.5
2010	FRD	A+	20	509	72	25	6	4	47	44	100	28	14	.271/.346/.377	.262	.335	3.1	CF -7, LF -4	0.6
2010	BOW	AA	20	118	9	6	0	3	18	7	34	8	0	.234/.288/.374	.239	.297	0.8	CF 2	0.3
2011	*BAL*	*MLB*	*21*	*440*	*41*	*17*	*3*	*4*	*37*	*22*	*116*	*16*	*5*	*.225/.265/.313*	*.206*	*.297*	*-0.2*	*CF -15, LF -2*	*-2.8*

Sometimes, when you ask why a particular player is considered a top prospect despite mediocre results, the scouty types will answer with a question: "Have you ever seen him naked?" This is their clever way of indicating that the player in question has incredible physical gifts that make him worth waiting for. They also may be propositioning you, but put that aside. Avery is a "seen him naked" guy, a toolsy athlete who would have been playing college football had the Orioles not shown him the green in 2008. The results have been equivocal: Avery made it to Double-A at 20, and although he began to look more like a ballplayer than a tourist in 2010, there is still a way to go. He has plus speed, but its application is unrefined, and most important of all, he just hasn't hit yet. Avery's tools remain blunt objects awaiting refinement into precision instruments. Sometimes, players with this skill set eventually blossom into regulars; more often, they fill out the ranks of America's proud fourth and fifth outfielders.

Josh Bell **3B**

Born: **11/13/1986** Age: **24**
Bats: S Throws: R Height: **6' 3"** Weight: **220**
Breakout: **4%** Improve: **13%** Collapse: **6%**
Attrition: **26%** MLB: **42%**

Comparables:
Matt Tuiasosopo, Travis Metcalf, Evan Longoria (78)

YEAR	TEAM	LVL	AGE	PA	R	2B	3B	HR	RBI	BB	SO	SB	CS	AVG_OBP_SLG	TAv	BABIP	BRR	FRAA	WARP
2008	SBR	A+	21	223	34	12	2	6	21	31	56	4	2	.273/.368/.455	.298	.354	-0.8	3B -6	0.7
2009	BOW	AA	22	128	18	5	0	9	24	11	28	0	0	.290/.344/.570	.327	.304	-0.3	3B -4	0.7
2009	CHT	AA	22	389	48	30	2	11	52	50	70	3	5	.296/.388/.497	.304	.341	-3.3	3B 0	2.6
2010	NOR	AAA	23	343	43	25	0	13	49	23	78	0	0	.279/.329/.481	.272	.329	0.0	3B -2	1.3
2010	BAL	MLB	23	161	15	5	0	3	12	2	53	0	1	.214/.224/.302	.208	.301	0.9	3B 2	-0.1
2011	*BAL*	*MLB*	*24*	*413*	*48*	*22*	*1*	*13*	*50*	*33*	*103*	*2*	*1*	*.253/.311/.419*	*.255*	*.309*	*-0.2*	*3B -5*	*0.3*

Acquired from the Dodgers at the 2009 trading deadline for George Sherrill, Bell had a strong year in the Orioles system, earning a shot at the major-league hot-corner job when Miguel Tejada was traded. Bell got credit for improved defense after an apparent case of stage fright early on, but his hitting was disastrous. The average AL hitter walked in 8.5 percent of his plate appearances; Bell walked in 1.2 percent of his. Had he qualified, his walk percentage would have trailed the league by a considerable margin. This is an existential-level problem for Bell; it is impossible to hit for an average sufficient to stick in the big leagues if you are behind in the count this often. In addition, Bell has always been a reluctant switch-hitter, with results to match. Hitting .250/.315/.400 against Triple-A southpaws was a major triumph given sub-Mendoza results in the past. He hit all three of his major-league home runs against lefties, but averaged only .217 and drew not a single walk (46 PAs). Bell has real power and has been more selective in the minors, but if his hackery wasn't an extreme case of rookie jitters, he's going to join Leo Gomez and Ryan Minor on history's discard pile of Orioles third-base pretenders. In the wake of Mark Reynolds' arrival, he'll have plenty of time to work out the kinks (or try another position) at Triple-A.

Jake Fox **UT**

Born: **7/20/1982** Age: **28**
Bats: R Throws: R Height: **6' 0"** Weight: **210**
Breakout: **1%** Improve: **35%** Collapse: **2%**
Attrition: **10%** MLB: **75%**

Comparables:
Mike Napoli, Matthew Brown, Rick Ankiel (69)

YEAR	TEAM	LVL	AGE	PA	R	2B	3B	HR	RBI	BB	SO	SB	CS	AVG_OBP_SLG	TAv	BABIP	BRR	FRAA	WARP
2008	TEN	AA	25	442	71	29	1	25	78	46	73	4	2	.307/.412/.580	.318	.315	-3.9	1B 0, LF -2	2.8
2008	IOW	AAA	25	137	18	11	1	6	26	5	37	3	0	.220/.256/.455	.241	.258	0.8	1B -1, LF 0	-0.3
2009	IOW	AAA	26	186	41	14	3	17	53	21	31	2	1	.409/.516/.842	.421	.427	-2.3	1B 1, RF -2	3.0
2009	CHN	MLB	26	241	23	12	0	11	44	14	47	0	0	.259/.311/.468	.262	.274	-2.9	3B 0, LF 3	0.4
2010	OAK	MLB	27	106	11	5	0	2	12	5	26	0	0	.214/.264/.327	.211	.268	-0.5	C 0, LF 0	-0.3
2010	BAL	MLB	27	105	11	5	1	5	10	3	23	0	0	.220/.257/.440	.276	.236	0.6	1B 0, C 1	0.5
2011	*BAL*	*MLB*	*28*	*430*	*56*	*23*	*1*	*21*	*64*	*29*	*91*	*2*	*1*	*.261/.323/.491*	*.281*	*.285*	*0.0*	*1B -5, LF 0*	*1.0*

Long a man without a position, Fox enjoys a career .293/.357/.528 minor-league line that inspired fantasies of exemplary offense from an everyday sub who could play all four corners *and* catch—if only his defensive shortcomings could be tolerated. Two years ago, the Cubs saw the dream realized, but only for a moment—after taking the league by storm for two months, Fox slumped in August 2009 and hasn't hit since, batting .215/.268/.373 in 75 games and drifting through three teams in the process. Much of the problem has been the selfish hitting that has plagued so many Crowley-coached Birds. Fox came equipped with OBP issues, but upon his reaching the Orioles, a pitcher had to throw four into the parking lot to pass him. As to his much-maligned catching, give him this much credit: he had no passed balls and just four wild pitches, about the same rate as Wieters' and much better than Tatum's.

LJ Hoes **2B**

Born: **3/5/1990** Age: **21**
Bats: R Throws: R Height: **6' 1"** Weight: **181**
Breakout: **0%** Improve: **1%** Collapse: **0%**
Attrition: **0%** MLB: **1%**

Comparables:
Asdrubal Cabrera, Bill Mazeroski, Wil Cordero (78)

YEAR	TEAM	LVL	AGE	PA	R	2B	3B	HR	RBI	BB	SO	SB	CS	AVG_OBP_SLG	TAv	BABIP	BRR	FRAA	WARP
2008	ORI	Rk	18	191	33	4	3	1	18	30	22	10	0	.308/.414/.390	.313	.348	2.0	2B -3, 3B 0	1.5
2009	DEL	A	19	462	41	19	0	2	47	23	80	19	5	.260/.299/.318	.236	.308	-2.5	2B -9	-1.2
2010	FRD	A+	20	428	53	21	2	3	46	54	71	10	8	.284/.379/.376	.278	.340	-0.5	2B -1	1.5
2011	*BAL*	*MLB*	*21*	*373*	*38*	*16*	*1*	*3*	*31*	*28*	*76*	*6*	*2*	*.245/.300/.329*	*.228*	*.299*	*-0.1*	*2B -2, 3B 0*	*-0.6*

The game is starved for talented tyros at short—the Orioles have one of the few in Manny Machado—but systems are crawling with second-base prospects. The majors are thick with capable keystoners as well, which leads to situations like that of the Orioles, who have both Ryan Adams and Hoes stacked up behind Brian Roberts. Given Adams' age and defensive problems, Hoes is the better bet to push Roberts at some point. Prior to running down due to the debilitating effects of the mononucleosis virus, Hoes made great strides in improving his selectivity at the plate and cutting his errors in the field. Unfortunately, like a 300-pound man who has just shed his first 40, Hoes still has a few more errors to trim, and he's not exactly fluid on the double play. The one knock on his offensive game is that his ground-ball-oriented approach isn't going to produce much power. Just 21, he has time to make refinements.

Cesar Izturis SS

Born: **2/10/1980** Age: **31**
Bats: S Throws: R Height: **5' 9"** Weight: **155**
Breakout: **3%** Improve: **31%** Collapse: **9%**
Attrition: **23%** MLB: **89%**

Comparables:
Luis Aparicio, Omar Vizquel, Jerry Remy (75)

YEAR	TEAM	LVL	AGE	PA	R	2B	3B	HR	RBI	BB	SO	SB	CS	AVG_OBP_SLG	TAv	BABIP	BRR	FRAA	WARP
2008	SLN	MLB	28	454	49	10	3	1	24	29	26	24	6	.263/.317/.309	.232	.276	2.3	SS 9, 3B 0	1.5
2009	BAL	MLB	29	412	33	14	4	2	30	18	38	12	4	.256/.291/.328	.219	.276	-5.0	SS 11	0.4
2010	BAL	MLB	30	513	40	13	1	1	28	25	53	11	5	.230/.273/.269	.203	.252	1.0	SS -7	-1.5
2011	*BAL*	*MLB*	*31*	*400*	*39*	*14*	*2*	*2*	*31*	*24*	*36*	*11*	*4*	*.248/.294/.312*	*.220*	*.263*	*-0.3*	*SS 1, 3B 0*	*-0.1*

It is tempting to write that Izturis gave the Orioles a season out of the Mark Belanger catalog, but that would be inaccurate—Belanger was actually a better hitter. As measured by True Average, Izturis turned in the worst offensive performance of anyone to get 400 plate appearances in the majors last year. He's usually a little better than that, but not so much better that he's more than a replacement-level player. Never mind Cal Ripken; Izturis is enough to make one long for the glory days of Mike Bordick. Unfortunately, the shortstop development biz is going through a dry period like the one that afflicted catching prospects in the late 1980s, and solid major leaguers and exciting prospects are in short supply, prompting folks to wonder if there will ever be another A-Rod or Tulo. This imbalance of supply and demand is cyclical, but in a world in which Jamey Carroll is a highly productive hitter for the position, bringing back Izturis—who is, at least, a superior fielder—wouldn't have been a surrender to anything but reality. After replacing Izturis's anemic bat with the more potent one wielded by J. J. Hardy, the Orioles acknowledged this by retaining Izturis as a utility player.

Adam Jones CF

Born: **8/1/1985** Age: **25**
Bats: R Throws: R Height: **6' 2"** Weight: **200**
Breakout: **7%** Improve: **56%** Collapse: **3%**
Attrition: **18%** MLB: **95%**

Comparables:
Ellis Burks, Carlos Gonzalez, Duke Snider (78)

YEAR	TEAM	LVL	AGE	PA	R	2B	3B	HR	RBI	BB	SO	SB	CS	AVG_OBP_SLG	TAv	BABIP	BRR	FRAA	WARP
2008	BAL	MLB	22	514	59	21	7	9	57	23	108	10	3	.270/.309/.400	.250	.327	1.7	CF -3	0.8
2009	BAL	MLB	23	519	83	22	3	19	70	36	93	10	4	.277/.335/.457	.275	.308	-0.5	CF 15	3.7
2010	BAL	MLB	24	621	76	25	5	19	69	23	119	7	7	.284/.324/.442	.277	.327	2.9	CF 6	3.5
2011	*BAL*	*MLB*	*25*	*534*	*65*	*24*	*4*	*17*	*68*	*31*	*108*	*9*	*4*	*.272/.323/.443*	*.269*	*.312*	*-0.6*	*CF 3*	*2.2*

In 2009, Jones followed up a brilliant start with a series of injury-inspired slumps that saw him hit .234/.296/.362 from June 1 on, before missing the month of September. He began 2010 where he'd left off the previous season, hitting .251/.274/.382 through the end of May and drawing just five walks in 215 plate appearances. To that point, his walks and home runs combined (10) barely outnumbered his double plays (seven). Jones woke up after that, hitting .302/.351/.476 the rest of the way. Yet, his problems with patience hadn't really gone away, nor had his habit—unusual for a right-handed hitter—of struggling with southpaws; he has hit .256/.307/.369 in 535 career plate appearances against them, versus .281/.324/.451 in 1266 PAs against right-handers. Still only 25 and an exemplary defensive outfielder, he retains a chance at stardom if he can rein in his overeager approach. If not, his glove will keep him in big-league meal money, but right now, his career arc is precariously balanced between those of Torii Hunter and his Orioles teammate, Corey Patterson.

Caleb Joseph C

Born: **6/18/1986** Age: **25**
Bats: R Throws: R Height: **6' 3"** Weight: **180**
Breakout: **2%** Improve: **5%** Collapse: **0%**
Attrition: **8%** MLB: **10%**

Comparables:
Jose Lobaton, Jesus Flores, Andy Marte (76)

YEAR	TEAM	LVL	AGE	PA	R	2B	3B	HR	RBI	BB	SO	SB	CS	AVG_OBP_SLG	TAv	BABIP	BRR	FRAA	WARP
2008	ABE	A-	22	261	33	19	0	8	34	15	56	2	0	.261/.303/.441	.263	.297	0.1	C -1, 1B 0	0.7
2009	FRD	A+	23	407	46	23	2	12	60	26	64	2	1	.284/.342/.450	.286	.315	-2.3	C 2	2.8
2010	BOW	AA	24	415	41	15	1	11	51	33	63	1	6	.236/.301/.369	.248	.253	-3.3	C -1, LF 0	0.7
2011	*BAL*	*MLB*	*25*	*361*	*38*	*16*	*1*	*10*	*39*	*20*	*73*	*1*	*1*	*.237/.278/.377*	*.229*	*.270*	*-0.1*	*C 0, 1B 0*	*0.2*

Even backup catchers make good money, and that's because they're important. Assuming perfect health for the first-string backstop, the understudy can still expect to start 20-30 games, more if the main guy has any kind of injury. Over the last two seasons, starting catchers (defined as the catcher who got the most plate appearances for his team) averaged only 61 percent of total catcher PAs; out of every 650 PAs, the ostensible starter received roughly 400. The balance constitutes a lot of potential offense to blow on a catch-and-throw backup. Joseph, a 2008 seventh-rounder, has a bit of power and makes good contact, but getting on base has been a problem, as hitting consistency has eluded him. Despite so-so throwing, Joseph has the catching skills to have a career, but even if he didn't have Wieters in front of him, his bat would preclude a starting role.

Julio Lugo **2B**

Born: **11/16/1975** Age: **35**
Bats: R Throws: R Height: **5' 10"** Weight: **165**
Breakout: **0%** Improve: **32%** Collapse: **10%**
Attrition: **25%** MLB: **83%**

Comparables:
Jamey Carroll, Kazuo Matsui, Tony Taylor (74)

YEAR	TEAM	LVL	AGE	PA	R	2B	3B	HR	RBI	BB	SO	SB	CS	AVG_OBP_SLG	TAv	BABIP	BRR	FRAA	WARP
2008	BOS	MLB	32	307	27	13	0	1	22	34	51	12	4	.268/.352/.330	.244	.318	-0.6	SS -6, LF 0	0.0
2009	BOS	MLB	33	123	16	4	1	1	8	12	18	3	0	.284/.350/.367	.270	.326	-1.7	SS -10	-0.5
2009	SLN	MLB	33	170	24	9	4	2	13	17	27	6	0	.277/.347/.432	.288	.317	1.9	SS -1, 2B 0	1.0
2010	BAL	MLB	34	264	21	4	2	0	20	15	50	5	7	.249/.292/.282	.217	.305	0.8	2B 0, SS 2	-0.3
2011	*BAL*	*MLB*	*35*	*400*	*41*	*16*	*2*	*3*	*32*	*36*	*68*	*14*	*5*	*.246/.310/.329*	*.233*	*.286*	*-0.4*	*SS -4, 2B 0*	*-0.2*

As recently as 2009, Lugo provided the Orioles and Red Sox with something of a lively bat for a utility infielder, even if his defense had severely decayed over time. Pardon the qualifier; as a generous interpretation is necessary to say that Lugo cleared even that low bar. No similar act of charity is possible for 2010, as Lugo's bat shriveled, leaving him lacking even the moderate patience and occasional power he had flashed in the past. Though his batting average recovered after a 3-for-28 April, the .268 he hit thereafter was emptier than a politician's promise. Lugo has finally run through the ill-considered four-year, $36 million contract the Red Sox gave him in December 2006; his next deal is likely to come as a rude awakening.

Joe Mahoney **1B**

Born: **2/1/1987** Age: **24**
Bats: L Throws: L Height: **6' 7"** Weight: **255**
Breakout: **0%** Improve: **4%** Collapse: **1%**
Attrition: **3%** MLB: **7%**

Comparables:
Joel Guzman, Kyle Blanks, Dave Winfield (74)

YEAR	TEAM	LVL	AGE	PA	R	2B	3B	HR	RBI	BB	SO	SB	CS	AVG_OBP_SLG	TAv	BABIP	BRR	FRAA	WARP
2008	DEL	A	21	383	38	22	1	7	61	24	96	2	0	.222/.277/.349	.236	.277	-1.0	1B -2, LF -2	-1.1
2009	DEL	A	22	430	59	16	7	7	53	30	93	28	1	.279/.333/.408	.279	.345	4.3	1B 3, LF 0	1.8
2010	FRD	A+	23	296	37	18	0	9	49	22	56	5	3	.299/.362/.465	.307	.346	-2.5	1B 0, LF 0	1.3
2010	BOW	AA	23	208	30	12	2	9	29	17	39	8	1	.319/.380/.545	.334	.364	-2.9	1B 3, LF 1	1.9
2011	*BAL*	*MLB*	*24*	*449*	*48*	*21*	*2*	*11*	*50*	*24*	*113*	*7*	*2*	*.244/.283/.386*	*.235*	*.302*	*0.2*	*1B -10, LF 0*	*-1.7*

Upon observing the gigantic Frank Howard tap a weak grounder, Casey Stengel asked, "How can a guy who's so big and strong hit the ball so near?" The same could be said of the massive Mahoney. Three seasons into his pro career, the 2007 sixth-rounder wasn't much of a prospect, non-hitting first basemen being the baseball equivalent of an anorexic sumo wrestler. Mahoney changed all of that in year four, putting together the batting average and power that had previously eluded him. To convince the skeptics, he will need to keep it up and perhaps do more: because of his contact-oriented approach, it's hit his way on base or bust.

Nick Markakis **RF**

Born: **11/17/1983** Age: **27**
Bats: L Throws: L Height: **6' 2"** Weight: **195**
Breakout: **2%** Improve: **58%** Collapse: **1%**
Attrition: **11%** MLB: **100%**

Comparables:
Al Kaline, Tony Oliva, Andre Ethier (71)

YEAR	TEAM	LVL	AGE	PA	R	2B	3B	HR	RBI	BB	SO	SB	CS	AVG_OBP_SLG	TAv	BABIP	BRR	FRAA	WARP
2008	BAL	MLB	24	697	106	48	1	20	87	99	113	10	7	.306/.406/.491	.320	.350	3.9	RF -5	5.2
2009	BAL	MLB	25	711	94	45	2	18	101	56	98	6	2	.293/.347/.453	.285	.317	4.6	RF -17	1.7
2010	BAL	MLB	26	709	79	45	3	12	60	73	93	7	2	.297/.370/.436	.289	.331	-1.4	RF -2	2.7
2011	*BAL*	*MLB*	*27*	*674*	*88*	*41*	*2*	*17*	*81*	*72*	*97*	*8*	*3*	*.287/.363/.446*	*.285*	*.316*	*-0.3*	*RF -7*	*1.9*

Markakis joined Hall of Famers Tris Speaker and Ducky Medwick as the only players to hit 40-plus doubles in four straight seasons, which is nice, but his home-run total dropped for the third straight season, which isn't. Markakis has increasingly stopped pulling the ball; instead, the vast majority of his swings are directed toward center field. This is a tough way to make a living as a power hitter, given that straightaway center is the deepest part of every ballpark. When Markakis does pull the ball, he still hits home runs, but he has either misplaced or lost the ability to do that on a regular basis. He remains a valuable hitter and fielder, but unless he stops trying to hit 'em where they have acres of grass, his run production won't return to its levels of 2007-2008.

Greg Miclat **SS**

Born: **7/23/1987** Age: **23**
Bats: S Throws: R Height: **5' 9"** Weight: **180**
Breakout: **1%** Improve: **1%** Collapse: **2%**
Attrition: **5%** MLB: **5%**

Comparables:
Brian Bocock, Ramiro Pena, Gregorio Petit (82)

YEAR	TEAM	LVL	AGE	PA	R	2B	3B	HR	RBI	BB	SO	SB	CS	AVG_OBP_SLG	TAv	BABIP	BRR	FRAA	WARP
2008	ABE	A-	20	67	8	2	0	0	6	8	13	3	2	.291/.373/.327	.301	.348	0.5	SS 6, 2B 1	1.1
2009	DEL	A	21	454	47	14	2	0	22	42	79	25	6	.228/.293/.273	.237	.273	1.6	SS -5	0.3
2010	FRD	A+	22	188	25	12	0	1	19	20	27	8	2	.311/.410/.402	.286	.357	1.3	SS 4	1.8
2010	BOW	AA	22	255	35	9	2	1	16	24	52	4	6	.246/.314/.316	.247	.309	-1.8	SS -3	0.1
2011	*BAL*	*MLB*	*23*	*332*	*31*	*13*	*1*	*2*	*24*	*26*	*70*	*8*	*3*	*.231/.289/.300*	*.215*	*.286*	*-0.2*	*SS 2, 2B 0*	*-0.1*

Miclat wouldn't be rated much of a chance in most other organizations, but as a shortstop in one that will have to convince J. J. Hardy to forego departure via free agency, he has a chance to rise to the surface, drawn there by the vacuum at the major-league position. Defense is Miclat's calling card, though like most young shortstops, he's prone to errors. He will need to rid himself of that tendency, because he has very little going with the stick. The most you can say is that he showed some patience, which connotes intelligence: many hitters of his skills not only fail to hit, but also hack, thereby costing themselves millions.

Corey Patterson **LF**

Born: **8/13/1979** Age: **31**
Bats: L Throws: R Height: **5' 9"** Weight: **180**
Breakout: **3%** Improve: **39%** Collapse: **9%**
Attrition: **22%** MLB: **94%**

Comparables:
Reed Johnson, Dan Gladden, Tony Gonzalez (78)

YEAR	TEAM	LVL	AGE	PA	R	2B	3B	HR	RBI	BB	SO	SB	CS	AVG_OBP_SLG	TAv	BABIP	BRR	FRAA	WARP
2008	CIN	MLB	28	392	44	17	2	10	34	16	57	14	9	.205/.235/.344	.209	.211	0.7	CF 4	-0.5
2009	NAS	AAA	29	135	24	12	3	5	22	8	25	7	3	.331/.363/.597	.325	.371	0.5	CF -1, RF 0	1.3
2009	SYR	AAA	29	280	28	16	1	7	40	13	66	14	4	.273/.318/.421	.250	.335	1.6	CF 0, LF 2	0.6
2009	MIL	MLB	29	15	0	0	0	0	0	0	7	0	1	.071/.067/.071	.037	.125	0.0	CF -1	-0.4
2009	WAS	MLB	29	15	0	0	0	0	0	0	6	2	0	.133/.133/.133	.105	.222	0.0	CF -1, RF 0	-0.3
2010	NOR	AAA	30	62	6	5	1	0	2	5	8	3	3	.368/.419/.491	.311	.429	-2.3	CF -1, RF 3	0.4
2010	BAL	MLB	30	341	41	16	1	8	32	20	75	21	4	.270/.305/.406	.253	.318	3.3	LF 4, CF 1	1.1
2011	*TOR*	*MLB*	*31*	*453*	*49*	*22*	*2*	*8*	*48*	*25*	*89*	*25*	*9*	*.256/.294/.378*	*.235*	*.295*	*-0.3*	*CF -2, LF 2*	*-0.1*

When Nolan Reimold imploded, the O's turned to an old pal, Dusty Baker's favorite outfielder. Conveniently, Patterson was found slumming it in Norfolk, having been signed after failing to beat out Eric Byrnes for a spot with the Mariners. This is a bit like losing an election to a dead man, but the Orioles have long had a policy of not discriminating on the basis of talent. After 11 seasons, Patterson's story remains unchanged: he's a fine outfielder and baserunner with a bit of pop in his bat, but his complete inability to control the strike zone makes him an out machine. His brief bout of early success—by his standards (.289/.335/.423 before the break)—was based on good luck on balls in play and quickly evaporated. Almost 13 years removed from having been the third overall pick in the amateur draft, he remains a fifth outfielder at best.

Felix Pie **LF**

Born: **2/8/1985** Age: **26**
Bats: L Throws: L Height: **6' 2"** Weight: **170**
Breakout: **2%** Improve: **50%** Collapse: **1%**
Attrition: **11%** MLB: **74%**

Comparables:
Billy Williams, Angel Pagan, Trent Oeltjen (74)

YEAR	TEAM	LVL	AGE	PA	R	2B	3B	HR	RBI	BB	SO	SB	CS	AVG_OBP_SLG	TAv	BABIP	BRR	FRAA	WARP
2008	IOW	AAA	23	382	57	21	6	9	56	23	55	12	6	.285/.333/.456	.266	.309	2.4	CF 6	2.2
2008	CHN	MLB	23	93	8	2	1	1	10	7	29	3	0	.241/.312/.325	.221	.352	-1.2	CF 2, LF 0	-0.1
2009	BAL	MLB	24	281	35	10	3	9	29	24	58	1	3	.266/.324/.437	.259	.305	-0.2	CF 5, LF 7	1.8
2010	BAL	MLB	25	308	38	15	5	5	31	13	52	5	2	.274/.302/.413	.257	.312	3.9	LF 6, CF -2	1.3
2011	*BAL*	*MLB*	*26*	*392*	*45*	*18*	*4*	*9*	*45*	*27*	*75*	*8*	*3*	*.263/.313/.406*	*.252*	*.304*	*-0.4*	*CF 0, LF 4*	*0.9*

Like Patterson, Pie makes up half of Baltimore's bookend set of failed Cubs outfielders. Well positioned to grab the starting left-field job because of his strong 2009 finish, he was almost instantly sidelined by a severe shoulder injury and disappeared for the next 2½ months. Pie returned in early July and hit .265/.293/.396 the rest of the way. A hitting coach is limited by the talent he is given, but one of the biggest indictments of deposed instructor Terry Crowley is that he had so many young hitters—including Bell, Jones, and Pie—who not only refused to draw ball four, but went backward from 2009. Pie's post-injury walk rate would have been the fourth-lowest in the league, had he qualified. Though a fine defensive outfielder, Pie is now in his arbitration years and far removed from his days as a hot prospect. In a deeper organization, he would have already been consigned to fourth-outfielder purgatory.

Nolan Reimold **LF**

Born: **10/12/1983** Age: **27**
Bats: R Throws: R Height: **6' 4"** Weight: **205**
Breakout: **2%** Improve: **32%** Collapse: **6%**
Attrition: **23%** MLB: **65%**

Comparables:
Ben Francisco, Gary Matthews, Jeremy Hermida (72)

YEAR	TEAM	LVL	AGE	PA	R	2B	3B	HR	RBI	BB	SO	SB	CS	AVG_OBP_SLG	TAv	BABIP	BRR	FRAA	WARP
2008	BOW	AA	24	596	88	30	3	29	94	63	83	7	3	.288/.374/.523	.309	.290	-1.6	RF -5, LF 0	3.3
2009	NOR	AAA	25	128	21	11	0	9	27	18	25	5	1	.395/.492/.743	.411	.447	-0.1	LF -2	2.0
2009	BAL	MLB	25	411	50	18	2	15	45	47	77	8	2	.279/.365/.467	.294	.316	-0.4	LF 0, RF 0	2.1
2010	NOR	AAA	26	393	50	12	0	10	37	54	61	0	0	.249/.372/.374	.257	.276	0.0	LF 1, 1B -1	0.4
2010	BAL	MLB	26	131	9	5	0	3	14	12	26	0	0	.207/.282/.328	.218	.236	-1.0	LF 0, RF 0	-0.4
2011	*BAL*	*MLB*	*27*	*553*	*69*	*24*	*1*	*19*	*65*	*63*	*101*	*6*	*2*	*.254/.344/.431*	*.275*	*.279*	*-0.1*	*LF -1, RF -3*	*1.1*

Reimold's season was a disaster picture that would rank with any film in the Irwin Allen oeuvre. Still suffering the effects of the Achilles tear that ended his 2009 season, he had all the outfield mobility of a dump truck with three flat tires. Given that defense was never his strong suit, he might have survived this had his bat not decided to jump into the dump truck as well. After he was demoted in May, three months of nonhitting followed. Reimold finally heated up in August, albeit without his customary power (.320/.460/.443, two home runs in 97 at-bats). Recalled when rosters expanded, he was mostly ignored by Showalter, logging just 35 plate appearances. To say his major-league career is at a crossroads would be an understatement.

Brian Roberts **2B**

Born: **10/9/1977** Age: **33**
Bats: S Throws: R Height: **5' 9"** Weight: **170**
Breakout: **0%** Improve: **35%** Collapse: **2%**
Attrition: **8%** MLB: **95%**

Comparables:
Ronnie Belliard, Tadahito Iguchi, Mark Ellis (72)

YEAR	TEAM	LVL	AGE	PA	R	2B	3B	HR	RBI	BB	SO	SB	CS	AVG_OBP_SLG	TAv	BABIP	BRR	FRAA	WARP
2008	BAL	MLB	30	704	108	51	8	9	57	82	104	40	10	.296/.376/.450	.295	.339	3.2	2B 2	4.8
2009	BAL	MLB	31	717	110	56	1	16	79	74	112	30	7	.283/.356/.451	.284	.318	2.2	2B -12	2.6
2010	BAL	MLB	32	261	28	14	0	4	15	26	40	12	2	.278/.353/.391	.271	.318	0.3	2B -6	0.4
2011	*BAL*	*MLB*	*33*	*613*	*75*	*38*	*2*	*10*	*65*	*68*	*95*	*30*	*7*	*.274/.353/.408*	*.269*	*.312*	*0.8*	*2B -5*	*1.5*

Showalter got all the credit for reinvigorating the Orioles, but a good share of the applause should have gone to Roberts for handling the practical, as opposed to the motivational, side of things. Having missed all but four games with a herniated disk, as well as a connoisseur's collection of other injuries, Roberts' late-July return pushed the defensively ineffective Ty Wigginton and Julio Lugo off second base; Roberts isn't Frank White with the glove, but he's an all-time great compared with that pair of keystone impostors. The impact on the pitching staff was hard to overstate. However, even after returning, Roberts missed time due to a bruised shin, a hip strain, a sore knee, and "concussion-like symptoms," the last apparently the result of his knocking himself in the helmet with his bat. Signed through 2013, the question now is whether Roberts can return to the .290/.370/.444 form of 2007-2009 and stay intact long enough to reward the Orioles for the $30 million still headed his way.

Luke Scott **DH**

Born: **6/25/1978** Age: **33**
Bats: L Throws: R Height: **6' 0"** Weight: **210**
Breakout: **0%** Improve: **31%** Collapse: **4%**
Attrition: **7%** MLB: **94%**

Comparables:
Roy Sievers, Lance Berkman, Geoff Jenkins (75)

YEAR	TEAM	LVL	AGE	PA	R	2B	3B	HR	RBI	BB	SO	SB	CS	AVG_OBP_SLG	TAv	BABIP	BRR	FRAA	WARP
2008	BAL	MLB	30	536	72	29	2	23	65	53	102	2	2	.257/.336/.472	.289	.281	-1.1	LF 2	2.6
2009	BAL	MLB	31	506	64	26	1	25	77	55	104	0	0	.258/.340/.488	.292	.284	-1.2	LF 1, 1B -1	2.1
2010	BAL	MLB	32	517	70	29	1	27	72	59	98	2	0	.284/.368/.535	.324	.304	-6.9	1B 0, LF 0	3.0
2011	*BAL*	*MLB*	*33*	*526*	*70*	*27*	*1*	*23*	*73*	*61*	*107*	*2*	*1*	*.262/.349/.481*	*.287*	*.289*	*0.0*	*LF 1, 1B 0*	*2.1*

Aside from Jim Thome, Scott was the league's most productive DH. As such, one of the great mysteries of the ages is why he remained an Oriole through the end of the 2009 season, let alone the 2010 season. As a defensively limited, thirtysomething player whose salary is increasing through arbitration, the benefit his hitting prowess provides to Baltimore is dwarfed by his short shelf life and the possibility that he could bring a farm system chronically short of talented position players even one warm body who might someday contribute to the next winning Orioles team. Scott's main skill, the ability to launch the ball in Camden Yards (as an Oriole, he has hit .294/.382/.576 with a home run every 14.4 at-bats at home versus .238/.311/.418 with a home run every 25.2 at-bats on the road), might thrill the hometown fans (those who still bother to show up). But if a trade is fruitful, the long-term gain will outweigh the short-term pain to those who march under the banner of the "Orange Carpet," as this year's season ticket come-on rather desperately inveigles us to do.

Brandon Snyder **1B**

Born: **11/23/1986** Age: **24**
Bats: R Throws: R Height: **6' 2"** Weight: **215**
Breakout: **6%** Improve: **8%** Collapse: **3%**
Attrition: **22%** MLB: **25%**

Comparables:
Mike Carp, Wes Bankston, Jake Fox (83)

YEAR	TEAM	LVL	AGE	PA	R	2B	3B	HR	RBI	BB	SO	SB	CS	AVG_OBP_SLG	TAv	BABIP	BRR	FRAA	WARP
2008	FRD	A+	21	472	67	33	2	13	80	29	83	3	2	.315/.360/.490	.289	.357	-4.5	1B 1, 3B -1	1.5
2009	BOW	AA	22	231	24	19	1	10	45	27	45	0	1	.343/.424/.597	.350	.396	-1.9	1B -1	2.0
2009	NOR	AAA	22	292	34	18	2	2	43	24	64	3	1	.248/.322/.355	.241	.312	-0.7	1B -3, 3B 3	-0.3
2010	NOR	AAA	23	369	35	22	1	9	42	28	101	3	1	.257/.331/.407	.253	.338	3.0	1B 1, 3B -2	0.3
2010	BAL	MLB	23	20	1	2	0	0	3	0	3	0	1	.300/.300/.400	.256	.353	-0.6	1B 2	0.1
2011	*BAL*	*MLB*	*24*	*466*	*52*	*26*	*1*	*11*	*51*	*33*	*114*	*2*	*1*	*.251/.307/.393*	*.245*	*.312*	*-0.1*	*1B -12, 3B 0*	*-1.4*

Make a list of current major-league first basemen: Mark Teixeira. Kevin Youkilis. Justin Morneau. Paul Konerko. We'll stop there, not even having gotten around to Albert Pujols and Joey Votto. The offensive bar at first base is incredibly high, and Snyder isn't rising above it so much as treating it like a limbo stick. Part of the problem with his disappointing season may have been the back injury that kept him shelved for five weeks (making the limbo that much harder), but that doesn't excuse his lack of power and patience. Barring a major change in Snyder's offensive profile—theoretically possible given his age, but unlikely—there just isn't enough here to project him as a regular.

Tyler Townsend 1B

Born: **5/14/1988** Age: **23**
Bats: L Throws: R Height: **6' 3"** Weight: **215**
Breakout: **0%** Improve: **2%** Collapse: **0%**
Attrition: **0%** MLB: **2%**

Comparables:
Greg Walker, Ryan Klesko, Paul Konerko (84)

YEAR	TEAM	LVL	AGE	PA	R	2B	3B	HR	RBI	BB	SO	SB	CS	AVG_OBP_SLG	TAv	BABIP	BRR	FRAA	WARP
2009	ABE	A-	21	130	10	7	0	4	16	10	39	1	1	.143/.231/.303	.196	.169	-0.9	1B 3	-0.6
2010	DEL	A	22	126	15	12	2	3	26	9	18	0	0	.342/.405/.556	.363	.385	-0.4	1B 0	1.4
2010	FRD	A+	22	88	6	6	2	3	16	10	19	1	0	.282/.386/.526	.305	.339	-2.3	1B 1	0.4
2011	*BAL*	*MLB*	*23*	*186*	*20*	*10*	*1*	*5*	*21*	*13*	*48*	*0*	*0*	*.233/.291/.388*	*.238*	*.291*	*0.0*	*1B -5*	*-0.7*

Not one of the myriad Townsends to play in organized baseball over the years has had the decency to spell his name with an "H" like The Who's Pete Townshend. Perhaps none had the chops. Tyler might, actually, but first he has to stay on the field long enough to prove it. A thumb injury held him back in 2009, and a bad hamstring crippled him in 2010, but not so much that he didn't hit the tar out of the ball when he was around. Even his winter-league activities were aborted due to a cyst in his hand that required surgery. As a college player, Townsend excelled at hitting for average, but the usual caveats for aspiring sluggers apply: you have to hit .300, hit with power, or do both to make it in the first-base biz. Townsend hit a boatload of doubles in his limited time on the field, so there are reasons to be intrigued, but until he has a healthy season, he's just Mychal Givens with a higher hurdle on his path to the majors.

Brandon Waring 3B

Born: **1/2/1986** Age: **25**
Bats: R Throws: R Height: **6' 4"** Weight: **195**
Breakout: **2%** Improve: **13%** Collapse: **9%**
Attrition: **31%** MLB: **49%**

Comparables:
Scott Moore, Brandon Wood, Jeff Larish (72)

YEAR	TEAM	LVL	AGE	PA	R	2B	3B	HR	RBI	BB	SO	SB	CS	AVG_OBP_SLG	TAv	BABIP	BRR	FRAA	WARP
2008	DYT	A	22	508	63	24	2	21	71	43	162	1	0	.273/.354/.472	.291	.369	1.2	3B -2, 1B 0	2.7
2009	FRD	A+	23	531	69	35	2	26	90	51	121	5	3	.273/.362/.520	.297	.309	-0.5	1B 0, 3B -7	2.3
2010	BOW	AA	24	533	67	32	2	22	70	59	177	0	1	.243/.345/.460	.281	.335	-2.6	3B -5, 1B 0	1.7
2011	*BAL*	*MLB*	*25*	*533*	*59*	*25*	*1*	*21*	*65*	*44*	*176*	*0*	*0*	*.218/.289/.411*	*.242*	*.287*	*0.0*	*3B -4, 1B -4*	*-0.5*

Waring is the last remaining player from the 2008 Ramon Hernandez deal with the Reds, and his chances of having any kind of significant impact are declining. When he makes contact, the ball often goes far, but he doesn't make contact all that often. As he is by no means a top defender at third, the Orioles have also had Waring play first base and left field. In attempting to expand his positional repertoire, they are on the right track; given that Waring would struggle to hit .250 in the majors, his best chance at a career would be in a four-corner reserve/platoon role.

Matt Wieters C

Born: **5/21/1986** Age: **25**
Bats: S Throws: R Height: **6' 5"** Weight: **225**
Breakout: **1%** Improve: **30%** Collapse: **5%**
Attrition: **17%** MLB: **58%**

Comparables:
Adam Moore, Jason Thompson, Joey Votto (73)

YEAR	TEAM	LVL	AGE	PA	R	2B	3B	HR	RBI	BB	SO	SB	CS	AVG_OBP_SLG	TAv	BABIP	BRR	FRAA	WARP
2008	FRD	A+	22	278	44	8	0	15	40	44	47	1	2	.345/.450/.576	.340	.372	-3.4	C -1	2.9
2008	BOW	AA	22	268	42	14	2	12	52	42	33	1	0	.350/.452/.592	.343	.365	0.2	C 0	3.3
2009	NOR	AAA	23	163	26	9	2	5	30	20	30	0	0	.305/.387/.504	.307	.352	-0.2	C 0	1.3
2009	BAL	MLB	23	385	38	15	1	9	43	28	86	0	0	.288/.340/.412	.262	.356	-6.4	C 0	0.9
2010	BAL	MLB	24	502	42	22	1	11	55	47	94	0	1	.249/.319/.377	.254	.287	0.2	C -1	1.6
2011	*BAL*	*MLB*	*25*	*532*	*66*	*23*	*2*	*16*	*61*	*56*	*105*	*0*	*0*	*.268/.345/.425*	*.270*	*.309*	*0.0*	*C -1*	*2.3*

In terms of pitches seen per plate appearance, Wieters was one of the 25 most-selective hitters in the AL. Alas, given that the names ahead of him on the list included Franklin Gutierrez, Chone Figgins, and Brandon Inge, working the pitcher is only half the battle—you also have to hit those cripple pitches you're working up to for the occasional safety. Wieters, his swing mechanics snarled, largely failed to do that. He managed a couple of small hot streaks, one following his brief disabled-list stay in July and another in early September, but they quickly evaporated in a flurry of weak contact. Another of the Orioles' not-quite switch-hitters, the catcher hit .210/.236/.328 against left-handers after hitting just .248/.313/.358 against them in 2009. Wieters has been the subject of great expectations, from our first PECOTA forecast to a *Sports Illustrated* cover. He turns 25 in May, and unless he can quickly rediscover the swing that fueled those MVP dreams, it's possible that they will remain just that, making Wieters' calling card above-average defense instead of top-of-the-line hitting.

Ty Wigginton 1B

Born: **10/11/1977** Age: **33**
Bats: R Throws: R Height: **6' 0"** Weight: **200**
Breakout: **1%** Improve: **36%** Collapse: **4%**
Attrition: **8%** MLB: **96%**

Comparables:
Carl Furillo, Don Money, Cecil Cooper (78)

YEAR	TEAM	LVL	AGE	PA	R	2B	3B	HR	RBI	BB	SO	SB	CS	AVG_OBP_SLG	TAv	BABIP	BRR	FRAA	WARP
2008	HOU	MLB	30	429	51	22	1	23	58	32	69	4	6	.285/.350/.526	.296	.293	-2.2	3B -1, LF -1	2.3
2009	BAL	MLB	31	436	44	19	0	11	41	23	57	1	2	.273/.314/.400	.247	.295	-4.2	1B -5, 3B -8	-1.4
2010	BAL	MLB	32	649	67	29	1	22	76	50	116	0	1	.248/.311/.415	.265	.269	-1.5	1B 3, 2B 0	1.3
2011	*COL*	*MLB*	*33*	*525*	*59*	*22*	*0*	*17*	*58*	*40*	*92*	*3*	*2*	*.245/.309/.397*	*.250*	*.268*	*-0.4*	*3B -2, 1B -1*	*0.1*

Wigginton became *the* hot subject of trade rumors early in the 2010 season by hitting .288/.369/.565 with 13 home runs in the first two months. Any number of potential buyers got the last laugh on the rumormongers when Wigginton pulled one of the game's great disappearing acts, leaving not even a

Cheshire cat grin behind to mark his passing. From June 1 through the end of the season, he hit .231/.287/.353 with nine home runs in 453 plate appearances. The thickset Wigginton was a valuable multiposition sub in his years before coming to Baltimore, but after two years of his poor hitting, particularly against the southpaws he was expected to dominate (.244/.320/.344), it is unclear whether deploying this everyday utilityman is actually a utilitarian act. Nonetheless, he landed a two-year deal with Colorado in December and will attempt to recapture his bat's first-half magic in the favorable offensive environment of Coors Field.

PITCHERS

Matt Albers

Born: **1/20/1983** Age: **28**
Bats: L Throws: R Height: **6′ 0″** Weight: **205**
Breakout: **18%** Improve: **43%** Collapse: **14%**
Attrition: **8%** MLB: **72%**

Comparables:
Mark Eichhorn, Steve Busby, Joe Gibbon (78)

YEAR	TEAM	LVL	AGE	W	L	SV	G	GS	IP	H	HR	BB	SO	EqBB9	EqSO9	GB%	BABIP	WHIP	ERA	FRA	WARP
2008	BAL	MLB	25	3	3	0	28	3	49	43	4	22	26	4.0	4.8	54%	.255	1.37	3.49	4.68	0.4
2009	BAL	MLB	26	3	6	0	56	0	67	80	3	36	49	4.8	6.6	51%	.352	1.76	5.64	5.44	-0.2
2010	BAL	MLB	27	5	3	0	62	0	75^2	78	6	34	49	4.0	5.8	58%	.303	1.51	4.64	5.23	-0.4
2011	*BOS*	*MLB*	*28*	*4*	*1*	*0*	*83*	*0*	*105^2*	*115*	*10*	*51*	*70*	*4.3*	*5.9*	*49%*	*.312*	*1.57*	*4.98*	*5.42*	*-0.8*

With a groundward tilt to his pitches, Albers has been good at keeping batters from piling up extra-base hits, but that hasn't stopped them from singling and walking him to death. Given a full season in front of a terrific defense, he might show superficial improvement, but that possibility aside, there is no reason to think he's well suited for any job other than the lowest of low-leverage relief work, which is likely how the Red Sox will use him.

Jake Arrieta

Born: **3/6/1986** Age: **25**
Bats: R Throws: R Height: **6′ 4″** Weight: **225**
Breakout: **20%** Improve: **50%** Collapse: **13%**
Attrition: **27%** MLB: **87%**

Comparables:
Billy Buckner, Homer Bailey, CC Sabathia (68)

YEAR	TEAM	LVL	AGE	W	L	SV	G	GS	IP	H	HR	BB	SO	EqBB9	EqSO9	GB%	BABIP	WHIP	ERA	FRA	WARP
2008	FRD	A+	22	6	5	0	20	23	113	80	7	51	120	4.1	9.6	50%	.262	1.21	2.71	2.48	4.6
2009	BOW	AA	23	6	3	0	11	12	59	45	4	23	70	3.5	10.7	38%	.287	1.22	2.44	2.77	1.9
2009	NOR	AAA	23	5	8	0	17	20	91^2	97	9	33	78	3.2	7.7	43%	.324	1.52	3.83	4.06	1.6
2010	NOR	AAA	24	6	2	0	12	11	73	48	3	34	64	4.2	7.9	52%	.237	1.15	1.73	3.23	2.1
2010	BAL	MLB	24	6	6	0	18	19	100^1	106	9	48	52	4.3	4.7	44%	.289	1.57	4.66	4.82	0.8
2011	*BAL*	*MLB*	*25*	*9*	*9*	*0*	*25*	*25*	*139*	*137*	*15*	*67*	*104*	*4.3*	*6.7*	*45%*	*.292*	*1.45*	*4.43*	*4.82*	*2.1*

What we have here is a work in progress: Arrieta's pitching isn't quite as mature as his mustache makes him out to be. He has a terrific fastball that sits around 93, but he doesn't command it well, and his off-speed pitches don't do much for him. The result was difficulty in getting batters to swing and miss, and as a result, his walks outnumbered his strikeouts through August. Before being shut down in mid-September with a bone spur in his right elbow (he opted not to have surgery and should be ready to go in spring training), he caught the same transformative wave that benefited the rest of the staff—it was as if the whole group simultaneously leveled up in some cosmic baseball role-playing game—and he walked just two batters in his final three starts. His long-term future is going to depend on the progress he makes with those secondary offerings; he kept the righties down (.213/.304/.290), but left-handers hit him hard (.315/.394/.505).

Brad Bergesen

Born: **9/25/1985** Age: **25**
Bats: L Throws: R Height: **6′ 2″** Weight: **210**
Breakout: **17%** Improve: **40%** Collapse: **12%**
Attrition: **9%** MLB: **66%**

Comparables:
Bobby J. Jones, Stan Bahnsen, Bill Wegman (71)

YEAR	TEAM	LVL	AGE	W	L	SV	G	GS	IP	H	HR	BB	SO	EqBB9	EqSO9	GB%	BABIP	WHIP	ERA	FRA	WARP
2008	BOW	AA	22	16	6	0	25	24	156	147	12	28	78	1.6	4.5	54%	.265	1.14	3.17	3.46	3.8
2009	BAL	MLB	23	7	5	0	19	20	123^1	126	11	32	65	2.3	4.7	51%	.283	1.32	3.43	4.19	2.3
2010	BAL	MLB	24	8	12	0	30	29	170	193	26	51	81	2.7	4.3	50%	.287	1.48	4.98	5.49	0.0
2011	*BAL*	*MLB*	*25*	*8*	*9*	*0*	*24*	*24*	*143*	*164*	*20*	*41*	*64*	*2.6*	*4.0*	*49%*	*.295*	*1.43*	*4.96*	*5.39*	*1.1*

Bergesen's season conformed to a pattern that you will see repeatedly throughout these comments: he started poorly, then came on after Showalter arrived and the Orioles made changes to their defense. His ERA through July 26 was 6.95; in 12 starts thereafter, it was 2.85. His strikeout rate rose, his walk rate decreased, and his home-run rate fell as well. Given that what happened to the Orioles was unprecedented, it is difficult to discern what is real progress from what may be one of Divine Providence's cruelest jokes, having the Orioles experience success only to yank them back hard. For Bergesen, success clearly depends on his using a sinking fastball and slider to induce weak contact; of AL pitchers who threw 100 or more innings, his swinging-strike percentage ranked 70th out of 72. So far, not missing bats has been a break-even proposition for him, with a quality start rate of around 50 percent. As good as he was down the stretch, that might be his limit; as an extreme pitch-to-contact type, he is always going to be excessively vulnerable to variable results on balls in play.

Jason Berken
Born: **11/27/1983** Age: **27**
Bats: R Throws: R Height: **6' 0"** Weight: **205**
Breakout: **13%** Improve: **32%** Collapse: **9%**
Attrition: **12%** MLB: **51%**
Comparables:
Eric Rasmussen, Donovan Osborne, Rick Aguilera (76)

YEAR	TEAM	LVL	AGE	W	L	SV	G	GS	IP	H	HR	BB	SO	EqBB9	EqSO9	GB%	BABIP	WHIP	ERA	FRA	WARP
2008	BOW	AA	24	12	4	0	27	28	151^{2}	147	11	40	131	2.4	7.8	48%	.304	1.29	3.50	4.13	2.6
2009	NOR	AAA	25	2	0	0	5	5	25^{2}	19	1	6	16	2.1	5.6	47%	.240	0.97	1.05	3.29	0.7
2009	BAL	MLB	25	6	12	0	24	25	119^{2}	164	19	44	66	3.3	5.0	41%	.341	1.79	6.54	6.13	-0.1
2010	BAL	MLB	26	3	3	0	41	0	62^{1}	64	5	19	45	2.7	6.5	49%	.307	1.33	3.03	3.58	1.0
2011	*BAL*	*MLB*	*27*	*6*	*7*	*0*	*29*	*17*	*108*	*126*	*14*	*39*	*67*	*3.3*	*5.5*	*45%*	*.314*	*1.52*	*5.13*	*5.58*	*0.5*

Berken shifted to the bullpen after a less-than-promising attempt at starting in 2009; his stuff hadn't portended advancement beyond the back of the rotation, anyway. The change was instantly successful, but perhaps because Berken was one of the few Orioles pitchers with reliable results, Dave Trembley and Juan Samuel worked him hard, asking him to make 12 appearances of between two and five innings. By the All-Star break, Berken had already pitched 50 2/3 innings with a 1.95 ERA, and he lasted just nine more games, getting hit hard before being diagnosed with a frayed rotator cuff and a slightly torn labrum. Surgery was not indicated, and the right-hander is expected to be ready for spring training. Showalter never got a chance to establish his own role for Berken, so the pitcher's 2011 outlook depends on both his health and how the manager utilizes him.

Zach Britton
Born: **12/22/1987** Age: **23**
Bats: L Throws: L Height: **6' 3"** Weight: **195**
Breakout: **7%** Improve: **13%** Collapse: **13%**
Attrition: **1%** MLB: **14%**
Comparables:
Aaron Laffey, Nick Adenhart, Joe Coleman (71)

YEAR	TEAM	LVL	AGE	W	L	SV	G	GS	IP	H	HR	BB	SO	EqBB9	EqSO9	GB%	BABIP	WHIP	ERA	FRA	WARP
2008	DEL	A	20	12	7	0	27	28	147^{1}	118	9	49	114	3.0	7.0	66%	.255	1.17	2.99	3.62	2.8
2009	FRD	A+	21	9	6	0	25	26	140	123	6	55	131	3.5	8.4	68%	.294	1.34	2.57	3.03	4.3
2010	BOW	AA	22	7	3	0	15	14	86^{2}	76	4	26	68	2.7	7.1	65%	.278	1.21	2.39	2.88	2.7
2010	NOR	AAA	22	3	4	0	12	12	66^{1}	63	3	23	56	3.1	7.6	64%	.303	1.31	2.98	3.4	1.8
2011	*BAL*	*MLB*	*23*	*6*	*7*	*0*	*18*	*18*	*100*	*109*	*11*	*47*	*60*	*4.2*	*5.3*	*57%*	*.301*	*1.56*	*4.98*	*5.41*	*0.8*

If you were to order up the perfect pitcher from the factory, you could do no better than to insist that he be a ground-ball machine that can also get strikeouts. In Britton, the Orioles have a pitcher who answers to that description. The lefty induced 2.5 ground outs for each fly out with his sinking, low- to mid-90s fastball while employing his plus slider to whiff 7.3 batters per nine innings. His control is evolving, but has already reached a good place for a young, hard-throwing lefty. Note the 61 wild pitches he has delivered in 538 1/3 professional innings, or about one per nine innings pitched; the average 2010 major-league pitcher threw one every three games. That's not a function of wildness, but of minor-league catchers missing Britton's diving stuff; it will be interesting to see if Britton gets as many by Wieters (as well as by big-league batters) when he makes the jump to the majors this year.

Mike Gonzalez
Born: **5/23/1978** Age: **33**
Bats: R Throws: L Height: **6' 2"** Weight: **213**
Breakout: **30%** Improve: **47%** Collapse: **22%**
Attrition: **6%** MLB: **84%**
Comparables:
Lee Smith, Duane Ward, Eric Plunk (76)

YEAR	TEAM	LVL	AGE	W	L	SV	G	GS	IP	H	HR	BB	SO	EqBB9	EqSO9	GB%	BABIP	WHIP	ERA	FRA	WARP
2008	ATL	MLB	30	0	3	14	36	0	33^{2}	26	6	14	44	3.7	11.8	33%	.260	1.22	4.28	5.43	-0.1
2009	ATL	MLB	31	5	4	10	80	0	74^{1}	56	7	33	90	4.0	10.9	41%	.275	1.29	2.42	3.20	1.3
2010	BAL	MLB	32	1	3	1	29	0	24^{2}	18	1	14	31	5.1	11.3	36%	.283	1.30	4.01	4.31	0.2
2011	*BAL*	*MLB*	*33*	*3*	*1*	*4*	*49*	*0*	*45*	*40*	*5*	*20*	*50*	*4.0*	*9.9*	*42%*	*.302*	*1.32*	*3.66*	*3.98*	*0.4*

In *The Magnificent Seven*, Steve McQueen posits a number of ill-conceived ideas, such as stripping naked and jumping into "a mess of cactus." Asked for an explanation, he always gives the same answer: "It seemed to be a good idea at the time." Having dealt George Sherrill and been unimpressed by Jim Johnson's work in the closer role, the Orioles signed Gonzalez to a two-year deal to take on the job. It *was* a good idea at the time, as (A) Gonzalez's fastball-slider combination has been pure hell on all batters, not just same-side hitters, and (B) he was well removed from his 2008 Tommy John surgery, so it was easy to believe that he had fulfilled his injury quota. Alas, this was true of the elbow, but not the shoulder. He blew two saves in the Orioles' first four games and vanished until late July. Gonzalez pitched as well as ever upon his return and could eventually. Whatever his role, he should make for an intriguing trade chip come July.

Jeremy Guthrie

Born: **4/8/1979** Age: **32**
Bats: R Throws: R Height: **6' 1"** Weight: **200**
Breakout: **10%** Improve: **38%** Collapse: **28%**
Attrition: **5%** MLB: **98%**

Comparables:
Gaylord Perry, Dave Goltz, Frank Viola (71)

YEAR	TEAM	LVL	AGE	W	L	SV	G	GS	IP	H	HR	BB	SO	EqBB9	EqSO9	GB%	BABIP	WHIP	ERA	FRA	WARP
2008	BAL	MLB	29	10	12	0	30	31	190^2	176	24	58	120	2.7	5.7	45%	.259	1.26	3.63	4.75	2.0
2009	BAL	MLB	30	10	17	0	33	34	200	224	35	60	110	2.7	5.0	37%	.286	1.47	5.04	6.20	-0.3
2010	BAL	MLB	31	11	14	0	32	32	209^1	193	25	50	119	2.1	5.1	43%	.254	1.24	3.83	4.57	2.0
2011	*BAL*	*MLB*	*32*	*11*	*10*	*0*	*29*	*29*	*183*	*187*	*26*	*51*	*103*	*2.5*	*5.1*	*42%*	*.277*	*1.30*	*4.30*	*4.68*	*2.7*

Between shoulder problems and the hellish environment that the Orioles had constructed for a pitcher in need of heavy defensive support, Guthrie seemed to have gone from the team's nominal ace to AL punching bag. In 2009, he led the league in losses and home runs allowed and spent much of last season's first half in the same mode; he was 3-10 with a 4.77 ERA at the break. As the Orioles began to crawl into the light, he found consistency, posting a 2.76 ERA after the break. It wasn't just having a real second baseman that did the trick; he also showed better control, dropping his walk rate to 1.5 per nine innings and adding a strikeout per game. Despite the turnaround, Guthrie has a very small margin for error, given his low strikeout rate and middling ground-ball tendencies. He and the Orioles are entering a dangerous place, where the confluence of age, increasing salary, and tenuous skills makes him a ticking time bomb.

Mark Hendrickson

Born: **6/23/1974** Age: **37**
Bats: L Throws: L Height: **6' 9"** Weight: **230**
Breakout: **15%** Improve: **18%** Collapse: **10%**
Attrition: **16%** MLB: **36%**

Comparables:
Jason Johnson, Brett Tomko, Mark Redman (66)

YEAR	TEAM	LVL	AGE	W	L	SV	G	GS	IP	H	HR	BB	SO	EqBB9	EqSO9	GB%	BABIP	WHIP	ERA	FRA	WARP
2008	FLO	MLB	34	7	8	0	36	19	133^2	148	17	48	81	3.2	5.5	46%	.298	1.50	5.45	5.78	0.0
2009	BAL	MLB	35	6	5	1	53	12	105	116	16	33	61	2.8	5.2	47%	.290	1.44	4.46	5.44	0.4
2010	BAL	MLB	36	1	6	0	52	1	75^1	97	9	20	55	2.4	6.6	45%	.349	1.59	5.14	4.44	0.4
2011	*BAL*	*MLB*	*37*	*6*	*5*	*0*	*54*	*12*	*120*	*140*	*16*	*38*	*73*	*2.9*	*5.4*	*45%*	*.312*	*1.48*	*4.93*	*5.36*	*0.2*

Hendrickson has rarely been good, but because he's left-handed, he has made approximately $10 million in his major-league career. This truly is the land of opportunity. Righties hit him hard. Lefties hit him hard. Even late in the season, when some kind of holy light was shining down on nearly every Oriole pitcher, he was hit hard. A bellwether of bad teams, Hendrickson has pitched for five clubs that lost between 91 and 105 games in a nine-season career. In fairness to Hendrickson, he pitched a bit better than his ERA suggests, but even granting that, there is simply no upside here.

David Hernandez

Born: **5/13/1985** Age: **26**
Bats: R Throws: R Height: **6' 2"** Weight: **230**
Breakout: **12%** Improve: **29%** Collapse: **12%**
Attrition: **13%** MLB: **58%**

Comparables:
Bud Norris, Ralph Branca, Dennis Rasmussen (68)

YEAR	TEAM	LVL	AGE	W	L	SV	G	GS	IP	H	HR	BB	SO	EqBB9	EqSO9	GB%	BABIP	WHIP	ERA	FRA	WARP
2008	BOW	AA	23	10	5	0	28	29	143	117	11	74	167	4.7	10.5	37%	.300	1.39	2.90	3.50	3.7
2009	NOR	AAA	24	3	2	0	11	12	57^1	42	5	18	79	2.8	12.4	40%	.289	1.08	3.30	4.05	1.0
2009	BAL	MLB	24	4	10	0	20	19	101^1	118	27	46	68	4.1	6.0	31%	.284	1.63	5.33	6.56	-0.6
2010	BAL	MLB	25	8	8	2	41	8	79^1	72	9	41	72	4.7	8.2	29%	.285	1.47	4.31	5.54	-0.1
2011	*ARI*	*MLB*	*26*	*8*	*9*	*1*	*41*	*21*	*132*	*136*	*22*	*66*	*123*	*4.4*	*8.4*	*38%*	*.308*	*1.52*	*5.14*	*5.58*	*1.1*

Despite, as we said here last year, "handing out home runs like they were business cards," Hernandez won the fifth starter's job in spring training, beating out Chris Tillman. Eight starts later, he was sent to the bullpen with a 5.31 ERA and sub-one strikeout-to-walk ratio. He took a brief stab at closing before giving over to Alfredo Simon and thereafter remained in the pen, pitching in the seventh and eighth innings. Hernandez seems to have found a home there; his ERA was 3.16 as a reliever and his strikeout rate jumped from 5.7 per nine innings to 10.9. As Ray Davies sang in 1967, "This is where I belong." Hernandez will remain in relief after being targeted by bullpen-builder extraordinaire Kevin Towers in the December trade that sent him to Arizona.

Jim Johnson

Born: **6/27/1983** Age: **28**
Bats: R Throws: R Height: **6' 5"** Weight: **224**
Breakout: **2%** Improve: **8%** Collapse: **5%**
Attrition: **7%** MLB: **15%**

Comparables:
Jeff Gray, Jae Kuk Ryu, Darrell Rasner (83)

YEAR	TEAM	LVL	AGE	W	L	SV	G	GS	IP	H	HR	BB	SO	EqBB9	EqSO9	GB%	BABIP	WHIP	ERA	FRA	WARP
2008	BAL	MLB	25	2	4	1	54	0	68^2	54	0	28	38	3.7	5.0	59%	.255	1.24	2.23	3.10	1.4
2009	BAL	MLB	26	4	6	10	64	0	70	73	8	23	49	3.0	6.3	54%	.300	1.41	4.11	4.46	10.5
2010	BAL	MLB	27	1	1	1	26	0	26^1	32	2	5	22	1.7	7.5	51%	.345	1.44	3.42	4.15	0.2
2011	*BAL*	*MLB*	*28*	*4*	*1*	*3*	*85*	*0*	*95*	*106*	*11*	*34*	*59*	*3.2*	*5.6*	*49%*	*.308*	*1.46*	*4.71*	*5.11*	*-0.4*

Johnson, who had finished out 2009 closing (badly), pitched poorly in April and then was found to be suffering from a small tear in his pitching elbow. Though he was able to avoid surgery, he still lost nearly four months to rest and rehabilitation. He pitched well upon his return, allowing just four runs in 16 2/3 innings, striking out 13 and walking one while pitching the eighth inning for Koji Uehara. With Kevin Gregg on the team and Mike Gonzalez healthy, Johnson will likely see more time in lower leverage situations.

Brian Matusz

Born: **2/11/1987** Age: **24**
Bats: **L** Throws: **L** Height: **6' 4"** Weight: **190**
Breakout: **27%** Improve: **54%** Collapse: **12%**
Attrition: **8%** MLB: **89%**

Comparables:
Junichi Tazawa, Matt Young, Dontrelle Willis (59)

YEAR	TEAM	LVL	AGE	W	L	SV	G	GS	IP	H	HR	BB	SO	EqBB9	EqSO9	GB%	BABIP	WHIP	ERA	FRA	WARP
2009	FRD	A+	22	4	2	0	11	13	66^2	56	5	21	75	2.8	10.1	52%	.293	1.17	2.16	2.41	2.5
2009	BOW	AA	22	7	0	0	8	8	46^1	31	2	11	46	2.1	8.9	47%	.250	0.93	1.36	1.64	2.2
2009	BAL	MLB	22	5	2	0	8	9	44^2	52	6	14	38	2.8	7.7	31%	.333	1.48	4.63	4.09	0.9
2010	BAL	MLB	23	10	12	0	32	33	175^2	173	19	63	143	3.2	7.3	37%	.292	1.38	4.30	4.40	2.3
2011	*BAL*	*MLB*	*24*	*11*	*9*	*0*	*29*	*29*	*165*	*164*	*19*	*58*	*136*	*3.2*	*7.4*	*42%*	*.299*	*1.34*	*4.06*	*4.41*	*3.3*

Another beneficiary of the Orioles' defensive renaissance, Matusz ended July with a 5.46 ERA, having mixed solid starts with thrashings in about equal measure. Back in 1991, many mocked John Schuerholz for bringing the relatively light hitters Sid Bream and Terry Pendleton to Atlanta, but the defensive difference—the Braves went from last to first in defensive efficiency—really paid off for the likes of Tom Glavine and Steve Avery, just as the changeover from Wigginton and Tejada to Roberts and Bell seemed to help Matusz. That's not to deprive the pitcher of his due—like so many Orioles pitchers, he discovered his command when Showalter arrived. In his final eight starts, all against tough opponents, his ERA was 1.57, as he allowed just 29 hits and struck out 43 in 46 innings. Unlike the older pitchers on the staff who had strong finishes, Matusz enjoyed late-season dominance that could easily be considered a turning point rather than a fluke. He has the tools to be a terrific pitcher and has begun to use them. Only caveat: as an extreme fly-ball pitcher, he will always be in jeopardy of having his mistakes become souvenirs, but that's in no way a fatal flaw given his ability to get batters to swing and miss.

Kam Mickolio

Born: **5/10/1984** Age: **27**
Bats: **R** Throws: **R** Height: **6' 9"** Weight: **255**
Breakout: **3%** Improve: **3%** Collapse: **5%**
Attrition: **3%** MLB: **6%**

Comparables:
Cory Doyne, Connor Robertson, Jermaine Van Buren (80)

YEAR	TEAM	LVL	AGE	W	L	SV	G	GS	IP	H	HR	BB	SO	EqBB9	EqSO9	GB%	BABIP	WHIP	ERA	FRA	WARP
2008	BOW	AA	24	2	1	1	28	0	38^1	39	2	22	40	5.2	9.4	58%	.333	1.67	4.23	4.30	0.3
2008	NOR	AAA	24	1	0	2	17	0	20	13	0	9	23	4.1	10.4	61%	.245	1.20	1.80	3.20	0.5
2008	BAL	MLB	24	0	1	0	9	0	7^2	8	0	4	8	4.7	9.4	38%	.333	1.57	5.87	5.59	0.0
2009	NOR	AAA	25	3	3	0	35	0	43^2	32	4	16	52	3.3	10.7	31%	.267	1.10	3.50	5.45	-0.3
2009	BAL	MLB	25	0	2	0	11	0	13^2	11	0	7	14	4.6	9.2	39%	.290	1.32	2.63	3.95	0.2
2010	NOR	AAA	26	4	3	0	30	0	35^1	44	4	17	48	4.3	12.2	48%	.400	1.73	6.37	4.19	0.5
2010	BAL	MLB	26	0	0	0	3	0	3^2	5	1	3	4	7.4	9.8	17%	.364	2.18	7.36	2.94	0.1
2011	*ARI*	*MLB*	*27*	*2*	*1*	*0*	*41*	*0*	*50*	*49*	*6*	*24*	*50*	*4.4*	*9.0*	*45%*	*.319*	*1.48*	*4.57*	*4.96*	*-0.0*

At 6-foot-9 and 255 pounds, Mickolio seems as likely to grab Fay Wray and climb the Empire State Building as he is to establish himself as a big-league reliever, but this gift of the Erik Bedard trade throws hard enough to be something special if he could get over his lack of command and recent tendency toward injury. A stint in the Arizona Fall League this winter offered hints that fixing the former problem might lie within the realm of possibility, and Mickolio will get to see whether the dry air of Arizona continues to suit him after being traded to the Diamondbacks in December.

Kevin Millwood

Born: **12/24/1974** Age: **36**
Bats: **R** Throws: **R** Height: **6' 4"** Weight: **205**
Breakout: **13%** Improve: **35%** Collapse: **23%**
Attrition: **11%** MLB: **93%**

Comparables:
Jeff Suppan, Mike Krukow, Bert Blyleven (66)

YEAR	TEAM	LVL	AGE	W	L	SV	G	GS	IP	H	HR	BB	SO	EqBB9	EqSO9	GB%	BABIP	WHIP	ERA	FRA	WARP
2008	TEX	MLB	33	9	10	0	29	32	168^2	220	18	48	125	2.6	6.7	42%	.355	1.62	5.07	4.31	3.2
2009	TEX	MLB	34	13	10	0	31	31	198^2	195	26	71	123	3.2	5.6	44%	.273	1.39	3.67	4.18	3.9
2010	BAL	MLB	35	4	16	0	31	32	190^2	223	30	65	132	3.1	6.2	39%	.317	1.54	5.10	5.15	0.58
2011	*BAL*	*MLB*	*36*	*10*	*12*	*0*	*31*	*31*	*191*	*220*	*26*	*63*	*125*	*3.0*	*5.9*	*43%*	*.316*	*1.48*	*4.98*	*5.42*	*1.3*

Millwood's seasonal ERA was shaped like a bell curve. Due to poor run support, he couldn't buy a win early on, despite pitching well enough to earn wins, putting up a 3.89 ERA in 11 starts in April and May. Then fatigue, frustration, or injury set in, and he posted an unsightly 9.89 ERA over his next seven starts before hitting the disabled list with a forearm strain—which he insisted was caused by his poor pitching, and not the other way around—in early July. As an imminent free agent with no apparent trade value, he could simply have been released by the Orioles. Instead, they watched him turn things around. Millwood managed seven quality starts in his final 10 attempts, putting up a 3.29 ERA over that span. Despite the happy ending, the end is nigh: Millwood's velocity is down, and though his peripherals were slightly improved from 2009, they still aren't in a happy place. Given his age, they aren't likely to escape the undiscovered country from whose bourn no pitching arm returns.

Wynn Pelzer

Born: 6/23/1986 **Age:** 25
Bats: R Throws: R Height: 6' 1" Weight: 205
Breakout: 9% Improve: 29% Collapse: 9%
Attrition: 12% MLB: 60%
Comparables:
Bob Walk, Ron Schueler, Matt Young (71)

YEAR	TEAM	LVL	AGE	W	L	SV	G	GS	IP	H	HR	BB	SO	EqBB9	EqSO9	GB%	BABIP	WHIP	ERA	FRA	WARP
2008	FTW	A	22	9	6	0	29	26	118^{1}	114	9	32	100	2.4	7.6	58%	.293	1.36	2.97	4.70	1.4
2009	LEL	A+	23	11	8	0	28	30	157^{2}	137	6	62	154	3.5	8.8	59%	.312	1.38	3.54	4.6	1.1
2010	BOW	AA	24	1	0	0	10	1	20	24	2	7	20	3.2	9.0	47%	.367	1.60	4.50	3.24	0.4
2010	SAN	AA	24	6	9	0	22	18	94^{1}	102	9	56	83	5.3	7.9	47%	.328	1.76	4.10	4.87	0.4
2011	*BAL*	*MLB*	*25*	*7*	*10*	*0*	*30*	*22*	*123*	*137*	*16*	*67*	*82*	*4.9*	*6.0*	*49%*	*.309*	*1.66*	*5.73*	*6.22*	*-0.0*

Pelzer had a tough year. He struggled with mechanics and control at Double-A, then found out he wasn't going to rise to Petco's pitcher heaven but instead was heading east to Hieronymus Bosch's Very Own Division in exchange for Miguel Tejada. He remains an interesting prospect, due to a fastball that sits 91-93 (touching 95) and a good slider, though his command of both comes and goes. Note there is no mention of a third pitch in the foregoing; because Pelzer's tertiary offerings are still in the R&D phase and aren't expected to be finished, well, ever, he made what should be a permanent shift to the bullpen upon donning the orange and black. Advancement will await consistency.

Alfredo Simon

Born: 5/8/1981 **Age:** 30
Bats: R Throws: R Height: 6' 4" Weight: 230
Breakout: 0% Improve: 0% Collapse: 0%
Attrition: 0% MLB: 0%
Comparables:
Jon Leicester, Gary Majewski, Andrew Good (81)

YEAR	TEAM	LVL	AGE	W	L	SV	G	GS	IP	H	HR	BB	SO	EqBB9	EqSO9	GB%	BABIP	WHIP	ERA	FRA	WARP
2008	MTR	MEX	27	0	0	0	20	15	106^{2}	100	11	27	78	2.3	6.6	47%	.273	1.23	3.80	4.22	1.8
2008	BAL	MLB	27	0	0	0	4	1	13	16	4	2	8	1.4	5.5	62%	.279	1.54	6.23	7.05	-0.3
2009	BAL	MLB	28	0	1	0	2	3	6^{1}	8	5	2	3	2.8	4.3	22%	.167	1.58	9.95	12.32	-0.3
2010	BAL	MLB	29	4	2	17	49	0	49^{1}	54	10	22	37	4.0	6.8	48%	.291	1.58	4.93	5.82	-0.5
2011	*BAL*	*MLB*	*30*	*2*	*3*	*2*	*24*	*6*	*59^{2}*	*72*	*11*	*25*	*36*	*3.7*	*5.4*	*45%*	*.312*	*1.63*	*6.11*	*6.64*	*-0.6*

Hardcore sabermetric types sometimes like to claim, "Anyone can close," but cripes, they weren't talking about Alfredo Simon. When Mike Gonzalez went down with a shoulder strain, the O's cast about for a fireman and found the beefy journeyman. Simon is ludicrously prone to the home run—in his brief career, opponents have slugged .538 against him. His 1.8 home runs per nine innings was the highest of any AL pitcher with more than 10 saves, and doubled or tripled that of almost every other pitcher on the list. Although he has decent stuff, Simon lacks the command to close and perhaps to protect a lead at any point in the game. That he converted 17 of 21 save opportunities in spite of his shortcomings suggests that those hardcore sabermetricians might have had a point after all. Alas, sabermetricians are not criminologists, so there was no foreseeing that Simon would be accused of murder during the offseason. As such, he will almost certainly spend the spring fighting for his life instead of a roster spot.

Chris Tillman

Born: 4/15/1988 **Age:** 23
Bats: R Throws: R Height: 6' 5" Weight: 200
Breakout: 10% Improve: 24% Collapse: 5%
Attrition: 11% MLB: 33%
Comparables:
Johnny Cueto, Eric Hurley, Daryl Thompson (78)

YEAR	TEAM	LVL	AGE	W	L	SV	G	GS	IP	H	HR	BB	SO	EqBB9	EqSO9	GB%	BABIP	WHIP	ERA	FRA	WARP
2008	BOW	AA	20	11	5	0	29	31	138	118	11	67	156	4.4	10.2	40%	.302	1.37	3.20	3.64	3.5
2009	NOR	AAA	21	8	6	0	18	20	96^{2}	85	5	26	99	2.4	9.2	41%	.302	1.19	2.70	3.70	2.1
2009	BAL	MLB	21	2	5	0	12	13	65	77	15	24	39	3.3	5.4	39%	.302	1.58	5.40	5.87	0.1
2010	NOR	AAA	22	11	7	0	21	24	121^{1}	120	10	30	94	2.2	7.0	39%	.301	1.25	3.26	4.77	1.4
2010	BAL	MLB	22	2	5	0	11	11	53^{2}	51	9	31	31	5.2	5.2	42%	.256	1.55	5.87	7.04	-0.6
2011	*BAL*	*MLB*	*23*	*8*	*9*	*0*	*24*	*24*	*126*	*132*	*17*	*53*	*95*	*3.8*	*6.8*	*41%*	*.304*	*1.47*	*4.74*	*5.15*	*1.6*

It was something of a surprise when Tillman was demoted out of spring training. An April no-hitter against Gwinnett was merely an interesting sidelight along the way to adding a cutter and, at least theoretically, improved command. That command was nowhere in evidence when Tillman was called up in late May, and he was hustled back to Triple-A with an ERA of 8.40. Another call-up in July, not long after a complete-game one-hitter against Norfolk, resulted in a split decision, with Tillman taking a no-hitter into the eighth inning against the Rangers before receiving a pounding by the Rays, followed by another quick demotion. Finally plugged into the rotation for good when rosters expanded, he held opposing hitters to a .172 average in 28 2/3 innings, but walked 18 and was frighteningly easy to take deep. As Tillman's occasional moments of dominance suggest, the makings of a successful pitcher remain inside him, but will require a lot of work to unearth. Still just 23, he has ample time left for digging.

Koji Uehara

Born: **4/3/1975** Age: **36**
Bats: R Throws: R Height: **6' 1"** Weight: **190**
Breakout: **25%** Improve: **44%** Collapse: **22%**
Attrition: **14%** MLB: **85%**

Comparables:
Rollie Fingers, Doug Jones, John Smoltz (73)

YEAR	TEAM	LVL	AGE	W	L	SV	G	GS	IP	H	HR	BB	SO	EqBB9	EqSO9	GB%	BABIP	WHIP	ERA	FRA	WARP
2009	BAL	MLB	34	2	4	0	12	12	66^{2}	71	7	12	48	1.6	6.5	32%	.302	1.25	4.05	3.73	1.8
2010	BAL	MLB	35	1	2	13	43	0	44	37	5	6	55	1.2	11.3	24%	.294	0.98	2.86	3.03	1.0
2011	*BAL*	*MLB*	*36*	*4*	*2*	*4*	*37*	*6*	*57^{1}*	*56*	*7*	*12*	*50*	*1.9*	*7.9*	*40%*	*.304*	*1.20*	*3.44*	*3.73*	*1.2*

Part of the Orioles' surprising flight from 100-plus losses was the decision to let Uehara close, something he had done very successfully in Japan. This stood in marked contrast to Simon, who not only had never closed successfully, but had never pitched successfully. The O's might have come to this realization sooner had Uehara been more available. He missed the first month of the season with hamstring problems, then lost another six weeks to a strained elbow. Uehara's fastball doesn't escape the mid- to upper 80s, but his outstanding control plays up in the late innings, pressuring batters not to fall behind. From his second DL return on, he walked just three batters in 39 innings. Over his final 25 games, comprising 26 1/3 innings, he walked no one while striking out 35. He was particularly baffling to right-handed hitters, holding them to a .185/.202/.272 line on the season. There are three knocks against Uehara: his age, his injury history, and the danger that as a fly-ball pitcher who is always around the plate, he will watch his mistakes get launched. The first two make Uehara a risk, but the potential upside of a short-term contract and a late-inning role make the gamble worthwhile.

Rick VandenHurk

Born: **5/22/1985** Age: **26**
Bats: R Throws: R Height: **6' 5"** Weight: **195**
Breakout: **16%** Improve: **33%** Collapse: **11%**
Attrition: **31%** MLB: **55%**

Comparables:
Carlos Torres, Radhames Liz, Jensen Lewis (78)

YEAR	TEAM	LVL	AGE	W	L	SV	G	GS	IP	H	HR	BB	SO	EqBB9	EqSO9	GB%	BABIP	WHIP	ERA	FRA	WARP
2008	CAR	AA	23	3	3	0	10	10	55^{1}	49	8	19	55	3.1	8.9	41%	.279	1.27	4.07	5.71	0.1
2008	FLO	MLB	23	1	1	0	4	4	14	20	1	10	20	6.4	12.9	38%	.463	2.29	7.71	5.18	0.2
2009	NWO	AAA	24	5	2	0	11	11	59^{2}	43	3	16	51	2.4	7.7	37%	.237	1.02	2.87	4.05	1.0
2009	FLO	MLB	24	3	2	0	11	11	58^{2}	57	11	21	49	3.2	7.5	29%	.269	1.40	4.30	4.50	0.8
2010	NOR	AAA	25	1	1	0	3	3	20^{2}	15	0	4	7	1.7	3.0	35%	.221	0.97	1.74	3.56	0.5
2010	NWO	AAA	25	8	4	0	19	20	98	100	11	40	87	3.7	8.0	34%	.306	1.49	4.59	4.39	1.5
2010	FLO	MLB	25	0	0	0	2	0	1^{1}	3	0	1	1	6.8	6.8	43%	.429	3.00	6.75	11.04	0.0
2010	BAL	MLB	25	0	1	0	7	2	16^{1}	13	2	7	17	3.9	9.4	33%	.282	1.35	4.96	6.24	-0.2
2011	*BAL*	*MLB*	*26*	*7*	*7*	*0*	*19*	*19*	*101*	*101*	*14*	*43*	*84*	*3.8*	*7.4*	*39%*	*.296*	*1.42*	*4.58*	*4.98*	*1.5*

The Orioles got a shot at a high-upside project when they liberated VandenHurk from the Marlins in return for Will Ohman. The Dutch Dilemma has a fine fastball, but his durability, off-speed pitches, command, and powerful aversion to grounders have held him back. The Marlins grudgingly gave him parts of four years before giving up—dealing a 25-year-old starter for a 32-year-old situational lefty is tantamount to waving the white flag. In actuality, they had given up even before that, handing his rotation spot to Nate Robertson, a 32-year-old, soft-tossing lefty who had an ERA of 5.52 over the previous three seasons. As presently constituted, VandenHurk is singularly ill suited to pitch in the AL East given its combination of stacked lineups and hitter-friendly parks—his predilection for fly balls just isn't going to play well in Fenway Park, Yankee Stadium, or, for that matter, Camden Yards. If Orioles coaches can help VandenHurk in ways the Marlins could not, he has the stuff to become something more than merely the greatest Hurk ever to pitch in the major leagues, but that's a big if.

LINEOUTS

HITTERS

PLAYER	TEAM	LVL	AGE	PA	R	2B	3B	HR	RBI	BB	SO	SB-CS	AVG/OBP/SLG	TAv	BABIP	BRR	FRAA	WARP
OF M. Angle*	BOW	AA	24	69	10	2	0	1	9	6	5	5-2	.373/.406/.458	.311	.368	-1.1	CF 2	0.6
	NOR	AAA	24	399	55	4	4	1	24	41	54	24-4	.260/.333/.303	.247	.298	4.7	CF 2, LF -1	1.2
1B G. Atkins	BAL	MLB	30	152	5	7	0	1	9	12	30	0-0	.214/.276/.286	.206	.266	-1.1	1B -1	-0.9
SS P. Florimon Jr.#	FRD	A+	23	261	31	10	4	4	33	20	56	7-4	.294/.372/.420	.269	.365	1.6	SS 4	1.8
	BOW	AA	23	134	16	3	0	1	12	11	31	4-1	.183/.246/.233	.210	.231	1.4	SS -4	-0.4
OF J. Gathright*	NOR	AAA	28	244	25	4	2	0	7	21	40	12-6	.185/.250/.222	.187	.219	-0.2	CF -2, LF 1	-1.3
1B R. Hughes*	NOR	AAA	26	421	42	25	2	10	39	29	121	0-0	.258/.316/.410	.251	.345	0.0	RF 1, 1B 0	0.2
	BAL	MLB	26	51	3	2	0	0	4	4	19	0-0	.213/.275/.255	.225	.357	0.4	1B 0	-0.1
LF L. Montanez	NOR	AAA	28	101	14	5	2	2	20	4	12	2-1	.289/.317/.443	.269	.313	-0.8	RF -1, LF 2	0.3
	BAL	MLB	28	58	2	0	0	0	3	1	9	1-0	.140/.155/.140	.097	.167	0.0	LF 1, RF -1	-0.8
INF S. Moore*	NOR	AAA	26	250	34	9	1	11	44	21	47	2-3	.280/.348/.476	.283	.304	-2.0	3B -6, 2B -1	0.2
	BAL	MLB	26	96	7	2	0	3	10	8	19	3-0	.209/.271/.337	.227	.227	0.1	2B -1, 1B 1	-0.1
SS J. Schoop	BLU	Rk	18	148	16	11	1	2	16	12	14	1-1	.316/.365/.459	.312	.333	-4.5	SS 1	0.9
	ORI	Rk	18	104	17	6	0	5	25	10	10	0-0	.253/.317/.484	.318	.228	-0.3	SS -8	0.7
C C. Tatum	BAL	MLB	27	126	10	4	0	0	9	12	21	1-0	.281/.349/.316	.238	.344	-1.3	C 2	0.3
RF R. Welty	FRD	A+	22	574	84	32	3	19	83	48	165	12-4	.280/.352/.463	.285	.371	2.4	RF 5	3.0

Matt Angle hopes to become the poor man's Brett Gardner. He has good speed, plays excellent defense, and has no power to speak of. His 2010 performance was hampered by a broken hamate bone, so he might have *a little* more to give than he showed last year. From 2009 to 2010, **Garrett Atkins** hit .223/.299/.326 in 494 PAs. The Orioles signed him to suggest to their fans that they were doing something. They were—giving $4.5 million to a player who was a mediocrity even as a denizen of Coors Field. In an act of pathological optimism, the Orioles placed **Pedro Florimon Jr**. on their 40-man roster and kept him there all year. A supposed defensive whiz despite a .937 fielding percentage in nearly 500 career games, Florimon is as likely to hit enough to stick in the major leagues as an elephant is to mate with your tabby and produce a bewhiskered pachycat that sports a trunk and answers to the name "Mr. Jumbo Muffin-Paws." **Joey Gathright** was a career .317 minor-league hitter entering 2010, but he hit 132 points less than that and drew his release in July. He failed to catch on with another team and may now be restricted to using his excellent speed to make really fast trips for Chinese takeout. No matter how great a prospect you are, you actually have to play to fulfill your promise. Drafted in 2009's second round, **Mychal Givens** signed too late to play in 2009, then ruptured a tendon in his thumb making the ever-brilliant slide into first base just after being sprung from extended spring training (where he excelled). As a result, Givens has punted two years of development, and while it seems as if the Orioles might get a solid infielder out of their 2009 second-rounder, we're still waiting for him to get started. A desperate attempt at patching Garrett Atkins' failure, **Rhyne Hughes** was quickly dispatched back to Norfolk, where his poor production would be the death knell for any first-base prospect, let alone one who is already 27 years old. One of the consensus top talents in the 2010 draft, **Manny Machado** seemed to reward the Orioles for making him the third-overall pick in his professional debut. He has the makings of a strong hitter for both average and power, and unlike the defense of most shortstop prospects, his is good enough that no one is talking about moving him to second, third, or center. Despite winning the Eastern League triple crown in 2008, **Lou Montanez** lacks the offensive chops to get by as a graceless corner outfielder. **Scott Moore** has decent pop for a would-be utility infielder, but can't stick, because of injury problems and inadequate defense. He moved on to the Cubs on a minor-league deal. **Jonathan Schoop** is someone to be aware of not for 2011, but for the future. A teenager with a strong bat, good fielding instincts, and a last name out of a Betty Everett song, he gives the Orioles either a second good shortstop prospect or a mediocre third-base prospect, depending on how his body fills out. As a member of the International Brotherhood of Catch 'n' Throw reserves, **Craig Tatum** is required to pay his dues on time, never show any power, and play solid defense. He got the first two but failed the last, catching just seven percent of attempted basestealers, tying with the now-retired Mike Redmond for the lowest caught-stealing percentage of any backstop with over 100 innings. Worse, his ability to hit for average was overstated. **Ron Welty**, a 20th-rounder in 2008, has a good handle on hitting for average and can catch and throw in right field, but his good-not-great power might not be enough to carry his position.

PITCHERS

PLAYER	TEAM	LVL	AGE	W	L	SV	IP	H	HR	BB	SO	EqBB9	EqSO9	GB%	BABIP	WHIP	ERA	FRA	WARP
P. Beato	BOW	AA	23	2	0	13	56^2	48	4	18	47	2.9	7.5	45%	.277	1.22	2.22	2.20	1.6
R. Berry	DEL	A	21	0	3	0	46^1	49	4	11	43	2.1	8.4	55%	.326	1.32	3.50	4.57	0.6
—	FRD	A+	21	2	2	2	71	57	5	25	63	3.2	8.0	56%	.264	1.27	2.92	4.64	0.8
R. Bundy	DEL	A	20	4	6	0	116	100	12	42	91	3.3	7.1	48%	.272	1.29	3.34	4.98	0.5
A. Castillo*	NOR	AAA	34	1	2	4	39^2	46	4	15	43	3.4	9.8	44%	.359	1.71	3.86	2.76	1.1
—	BAL	MLB	34	1	0	0	10^2	16	5	6	11	5.1	9.3	41%	.379	2.06	10.13	9.58	-0.6
P. Egan	BOW	AA	25	4	0	5	46^2	29	1	7	25	1.4	4.8	64%	.199	0.81	2.12	4.87	0.0
—	NOR	AAA	25	1	1	0	37	54	2	9	17	2.2	4.1	61%	.382	1.73	5.11	5.99	-0.3
B. Erbe	NOR	AAA	22	0	10	0	70^2	86	11	22	50	2.8	6.4	36%	.318	1.58	5.48	5.66	0.3
A. Gabino	NOR	AAA	26	7	0	2	83^2	62	7	24	75	2.6	8.1	40%	.244	1.08	2.26	3.89	1.7
—	BAL	MLB	26	0	0	0	4^2	9	3	3	2	5.8	3.9	43%	.333	2.57	13.50	9.96	-0.3
M. Hobgood	DEL	A	19	3	7	0	94	90	6	38	59	3.6	5.6	59%	.288	1.46	4.12	5.46	0.3
J. Hoey	BOW	AA	27	2	0	0	31^1	26	1	17	38	4.9	10.9	46%	.313	1.37	2.87	2.43	0.9
—	NOR	AAA	27	4	0	0	21^1	11	0	17	32	7.2	13.5	43%	.262	1.45	2.95	3.00	0.5
B. Jacobson	FRD	A+	23	8	1	1	74	68	7	26	68	3.2	8.3	55%	.288	1.36	2.55	4.73	0.1
S. Johnson	BOW	AA	22	6	6	0	145	144	24	78	128	4.8	7.9	28%	.292	1.61	4.84	5.37	0.5
F. Mata	NOR	AAA	26	5	3	8	42^2	34	2	20	30	4.2	6.3	58%	.254	1.31	3.16	4.01	0.6
—	BAL	MLB	26	0	0	0	17^1	24	2	8	9	4.2	4.7	56%	.344	1.96	7.79	8.51	-0.6
C. Meredith	NOR	AAA	27	1	2	0	27	32	2	12	17	4.0	5.7	58%	.316	1.70	6.00	6.82	-0.5
—	BAL	MLB	27	0	2	1	15	18	4	4	7	2.4	4.2	55%	.275	1.53	5.40	6.89	-0.4
T. Patton*	NOR	AAA	24	8	11	0	136	144	15	43	89	2.8	5.9	41%	.295	1.43	4.24	4.83	1.6
—	BAL	MLB	24	0	0	0	0^2	1	0	1	1	13.5	13.5	50%	.500	3.00	0.00	-2.61	0.0
C. Spoone	BOW	AA	24	5	5	0	132	132	12	79	88	5.4	6.0	54%	.296	1.70	3.75	5.01	0.8
W. Startup*	ABE	A-	25	1	0	0	25^1	16	2	5	21	1.8	7.5	37%	.212	0.87	2.13	4.31	0.1
P. Viola*	BOW	AA	27	3	2	0	62^2	61	2	19	64	2.7	9.2	39%	.335	1.32	3.59	2.88	1.8
—	BAL	MLB	27	0	0	0	11	1	1	1	3	6.8	20.3	0%	.000	1.50	13.50	15.53	-0.1

Pedro Beato last appeared in the 2008 edition of this book. It took the last three seasons for the O's to give up on the idea of their 2006 supplemental first-rounder as a starter. The overdue move to the bullpen, based on the simple fact that Beato's breaking stuff has always lagged behind his fastball, paid immediate dividends. The Mets will give him a chance to stick in a wide-open bullpen after selecting him in the Rule 5 draft. ⚾ In **Ryan Berry**'s official team photo, he bears a passing resemblance to Weird Al Yankovic circa 1984. Fortunately, his pitching is more inclined toward sinkers than song parodies, which is good, given that today's Top 40 is beyond mockery. Berry has good control and will have to keep it, because his fastball sits in the high 80s. ⚾ **Robert Bundy**'s fastball sits in the low 90s with a bit of sink, but the youthful righty's mechanics and secondary stuff aren't yet in the same league. ⚾ Situational southpaw **Alberto Castillo** allowed left-handed hitters to bat .391/.417/.957 against him, which made him about as useful as a gelding at a stud farm. ⚾ Two-time Orioles draftee **Pat Egan** struck out only 42 batters in 82 2/3 innings split between Double- and Triple-A last season, which didn't deter the Brewers from selecting the towering ground-baller in the Rule 5 draft. ⚾ **Brandon Erbe** paid the ultimate price for his helter-skelter mechanics when he underwent surgery to repair a torn labrum in August. Despite a good fastball, Erbe was always a long shot due to a delivery conceived by Picasso. Postsurgery, his chance has gone from a "Hail Mary" to that of a snowball in hell. ⚾ **Armando Gabino** is an anagram for "Airbag and Mono." His major-league pitching has been a bit like that, involving jarring crashes with the potential to induce crippling illness. He can be better than that, but not enough that he'd be suited for anything but a back-end role. ⚾ Sadly, the name **Matthew Hobgood** has become synonymous with "chunky overdraft." The stuff the Orioles thought they saw when they made him the fifth-overall pick of the 2009 draft just isn't there. ⚾ Prior to shoulder surgery, **Jim Hoey** was an intriguing prospect due to a fastball that could touch 100 mph. He's still getting the strikeouts, but his command has yet to return. The Twins will attempt to lure it out of hiding after acquiring him in the J. J. Hardy trade. ⚾ Big right-hander **Brett Jacobson** throws hard, but for a 24-year-old who hasn't thrown a pitch above High-A, his relief for Fredericksburg last season seems less impressive. The 2008 fourth-rounder is now the property of the Twins, after changing hands in the J. J. Hardy trade. ⚾ The son of former Orioles pitcher Dave Johnson, **Steve Johnson** survived a Rule 5 kidnapping to stick with the Birds. He has always struck out more batters than his just-decent arsenal suggests he should, but his command comes and goes, and his results have been mixed. He needs to be tried in middle relief. ⚾ The Orioles drafted UCLA closer **Dan Klein** in the 2010 third round. He has the repertoire of pitches to start, so the Orioles may try him there first, but past shoulder problems could make them think twice. If Baltimore opts for the bullpen, Klein and his low-90s fastball/change combo could rise quickly. **Luis Lebron** didn't pitch in 2010, because of Tommy John surgery; his calling card before going under the knife was a high-90s fastball and a good deal of wildness. If he's more or less intact, he could eventually claim a back-end bullpen role. Signed as a minor-league free agent, **Frank Mata** is a career reliever who lacks the stuff or results to distinguish him from any of 50 other standard minor-league righties. He was pulled off the 40-man in November. **Cla Meredith** used to be somebody; now he's just another reliever without enough letters in his name. **Troy Patton** has been working for two years to get back to the bigs after labrum surgery. That he made it, however briefly, was a triumph, but it remains doubtful that he can get back to where he was headed a few years ago (no place special). Remember back in the 1980s, when people used to say, "Gag me with a spoon"? Little known fact: "**Chorye Spoone**" is the sound that one's throat makes when actually gagged by said utensil. Having lost most of 2009 to labrum surgery, Spoone retains his trademark sink but spent last year trying to recover command he never had. Ironically named reliever **Will Startup** missed most of two seasons due to Tommy John surgery and spent 2010 rebuilding his career from the ground up, starting in A-ball. He showed better command than he did before his injury and could get noticed quickly. The Orioles claimed lefty **Pedro Viola** off waivers last April and sent him to Norfolk, where he was again treated roughly due to vanishing control—a disease that apparently afflicts Viola whenever he's promoted to Triple-A. His solid strikeout rate may earn him another chance.

MANAGER: BUCK SHOWALTER

YEAR	TEAM	W-L	Pythag +/-	Avg PC	100+ P	120+ P	QS	BQS	REL	REL w Zero R	IBB	Subs	PH	PH Avg	PH HR	SB2	CS2	SB3	CS3	SAC Att	SAC %	POS SAC	Squeeze	Swing	In Play
2010	BAL	33-23	3	99.1	31	0	35	3	142	88	10	14	20	.118	0	24	9	4	0	14	78.6%	11	2	35	26

Whether we should infer a causal relationship from that sequence of events is unclear, but after GM Andy MacPhail expressed his hope to "ignite a spark" by switching skippers, he got an inferno: following an unremarkable stretch under interim manager Juan Samuel, the team began winning at a torrid pace under "permanent" hire Buck Showalter. The immediate on-field turnaround—detailed elsewhere in this chapter—that followed his installation appears to have been divorced from any in-game decisions Showalter may have made, since the new skipper was tactically inert, pulling relatively few strings as he familiarized himself with his roster. The passage of time might not give rise to increased in-game activity, given that Showalter's Rangers ranked at or near the bottom of the league in intentional passes and sac bunts in his last two seasons at the helm. But the Rangers also led the league in relievers used (which was as much a function of their poor pitching as a quick hook on the manager's part). After inheriting the Orioles, Showalter's work in the clubhouse drew rave reviews, as players and observers alike responded to a newfound culture of discipline, accountability, and attention to detail, tinged with an undercurrent of anxiety emitted by a passel of young players anxious to prove their worth to the arbiter of their playing time. If history is any guide, Showalter will wear out his welcome a few years down the road, but he has a chance to make something of a pliable young team before his approach loses its luster. His success will hinge on the work of new pitching coach Mark Connor, who has served as Buck's sidekick in each of his three stints as skipper. Connor has a reputation for a hands-off approach with veterans, but he'll have to take an active role as he attempts to cajole some consistency out of the Orioles' young staff.

Boston Red Sox

The 2010 season can be interpreted as having had a variety of meanings for the Boston Red Sox. To some, the team's failure to reach the postseason was an unforgivable letdown. To others, the Red Sox's near replication of the success of 2009, despite facing more injury hurdles than any other club, says more about the quality of the on-field product and the front-office team that assembled it than does its place in the standings.

The first point of view ignores process in favor of results, an approach that, if followed, leads to rash decision-making of the vintage Steinbrennerian sort, loading up on free agents no matter the cost or fit because your injury-riddled team fell a few games short of the playoffs. The second recognizes that the 2010 Red Sox were built on a strong foundation and that despite making more trips to the disabled list than any other team, losing more than 1,100 days to the DL in the process, they just missed extending their October thanks to a bevy of quality replacements and a core strong enough to withstand losing most of its major components.

RED SOX PROSPECTUS

2010 W-L: 89-73, 3rd in AL East

Pythag	.545	11th	**Ballpark:** Fenway Park (3-yr. PF: 101). Despite annual facelifts, baseball's oldest park is aging gracefully
RS/G	5.0	2nd	
RA/G	4.6	8th	
TAv	.285	1st	**2010:** The offense is willing, but the flesh and bullpen are weak
BRR	-10.4	28th	
FRA	4.67	23rd	**2011:** Off-season deals and fewer DL days make a MASH unit into a mash unit
DER	5.53	11th	
DL	1,112	28th	
B-Age	31.0	29th	**Action Items:** Balancing backstops, laughing at other teams' lineup cards
P-Age	29.8	27th	
Salary	$162.4	2nd	
M$/MW	$3.77	25th	

There is a third perception that may miss the importance of process over results by an even wider mark than the "I don't care, just win" crowd. It originated with members of the local media, who proceeded from the front office's claim that pitching and defense were integral to winning. Boston scribes regarded the ability to pitch and field as precluding the ability to produce at the plate, a doubly strange notion in light of the Red Sox's signing of quality defenders who were also above-average offensive contributors over the winter. These same writers decided that Boston's failure to make the playoffs (and before that, its slow start) was attributable to its decision to let the offensive-minded Jason Bay depart for the Mets, which—allegedly—left the lineup "thin."

To the extent that any aspect of the 2010 team was thin, it wasn't because Bay left town to be replaced by Mike Cameron (who hit 4 homers to Bay's 6): the roster suffered because of all the time missed by three of the most productive hitters at their respective positions. Due to various maladies, Victor Martinez, Kevin Youkilis, and Dustin Pedroia were absent for a combined 163 games, many of them overlapping. These were compounded by injuries to the pitching staff, and inning after inning in which inferior players filled in for disabled defensive standouts.

Even when all of the supposed holes left in the lineup are accounted for, the 2010 Red Sox were as potent at the plate as their 2009 counterparts: the 2010 club had a collective True Average of .273, which ranked first in the American League, while the 2009 model posted a .277 TAv, good for second in the AL. The slight difference in results is astonishing when you consider some of the replacements for players like Youkilis, Pedroia, and Martinez: Sox first basemen hit .272/.338/.396 for the final two months of the season, second basemen hit .244/.302/.383 from June 25 onward, and Kevin Cash and The Cashettes combined for a line of .169/.221/.169 in the month Martinez missed. Throw in a combined outfield line of .245/.314/.412, rather than the .282/.361/.471 projected by PECOTA in the spring of 2010 for the starting three plus fourth outfielder Jeremy Hermida, and the team's success in spite of its injury-related obstacles almost defies belief.

The keystone production post-Pedroia would have been better, but the team's second and third options at the position, Bill Hall and Eric Patterson, had to spend time covering in the outfield, where the absence of Jacoby Ellsbury and Cameron was causing all sorts of defensive issues. Boston's 736 OPS in the month when neither Pedroia nor Martinez were in the lineup had nothing to do with a failure of pitching and defense to carry the club, and everything to do with the Red Sox's using replacements for the replacements at a rate that most teams in recent memory, outside of the injury-ravaged 2009 Mets, can hardly imagine. And unlike the Mets team that finished the year with 92 losses, Boston made the playoff race interesting until the final week of the season.

Singling out the hitters isn't to absolve the team's pitching of blame, for the hurlers had their own share of concerns. Josh Beckett was either injured, terrible, or both, thanks to a bad back that disrupted his command. Daisuke Matsuzaka again missed a large chunk of time that kept him from nearing the 200-innings mark. Clay Buchholz was healthier than those two, but still spent some time on the disabled list, though he was highly successful when he took the mound. John Lackey and Jon Lester remained in the rotation all season, with very different results. Spoiler alert: the high-priced one was a disappointment, though his second half gives the Sox reason to be more optimistic about their starting five this coming season.

The bullpen was a disaster that ranked 25th in the majors in WXRL—of the team total of 5.6 wins added, Daniel Bard accounted for 4.7. The pen problem made itself felt most forcefully after the trade deadline, when Boston decided not to pick up any bullpen help, due to the injuries elsewhere: from the start of the season through the deadline, the team's WXRL was 5.2 (13th overall), but from August 1 onward, it was a wretched 0.4, 29th in the majors. This touched off a domino effect, as the lack of a reliable third option in the pen caused Bard and Jonathan Papelbon to tire over the final two months. While not as culpable as the injuries, the bullpen meltdown qualifies as another reason for the lack of a Boston delegation in the playoffs.

Boston is fortunate to have bullpen holes at a time when dependable relievers were available via free agency; the Sox signed defrocked White Sox closer Bobby Jenks, veteran Rays set-up man Dan Wheeler, and failed Orioles project Matt Albers to provide the depth that was missing in 2010. A full season of Felix Doubront will also go a long way—though he is the team's most advanced starting pitching prospect, he was sent to the bullpen before being shut down with a pectoral injury. Boston plans to use him as a reliever in spring training and may keep him in the pen all year as a set-up man. Combine this with all of the addition-by-subtraction from the summer of 2010 (Manny Delcarmen and Ramon Ramirez were jettisoned), and while the Sox may not field the most dominant pen, the future looks brighter than the immediate past.

Although an offensive shortfall turned out to be a baseless fear heading into 2010, there was legitimate worry that 2011 might be a problem, with Martinez gone to Detroit and Adrian Beltre gone as well. While the current personnel constitute a downgrade from 2010's backstop situation, which was anchored by Martinez, the Sox still find themselves in a better place behind the plate than many other clubs. The acquisition of Adrian Gonzalez gives the Red Sox the replacement they needed for Beltre's 2010 production, as a healthy Gonzalez is capable of replicating the third baseman's value in 2011. Gonzalez is one of the top hitters in all of baseball, and he is one that general manager Theo Epstein has coveted since Epstein worked for the Padres and Gonzalez was still in high school. Youkilis's glove won't win him any hardware after he shifts to the hot corner the way it has at first base, but as he is shifting to a position at which his bat will stand out even more than it has at first, he will still be as invaluable as he has been in the past. The cost of top prospects Casey Kelly and Anthony Rizzo, along with Reymond Fuentes, was a high one and out of character for Boston—it is the most the club has given up since the trade that sent Hanley Ramirez and Anibal Sanchez to Florida for Josh Beckett and Mike Lowell—but that is the cost of business when it comes to acquiring a player with Gonzalez's impact.

While Boston did not have an outfield void for 2011, J. D. Drew's departure following the season would have opened one. That is why the Red Sox signed Carl Crawford in another uncharacteristic move, one that saw him get a seven-year, $142 million contract. Crawford may miss the turf of Tropicana, as he has always been a superior hitter on the fake surface, but his batted-ball data suggests that Fenway is going to be his new best friend. Crawford is not a pull hitter, and his liners and fly balls will target Fenway's new and improved power alley in right field, as well as the triangle in right center. What he loses in ground-ball singles and legged-out ground-ball doubles will be made up for in triangle triples, wall balls, and additional home-run power.

The rotation didn't change, but that's a state of affairs that Boston fans need to get used to—Matsuzaka is a free agent after 2012, but the other four pitchers are locked in through 2014. As disappointing as the rotation was in 2010, it has all the makings of a dominant one—teams have made it out of the AL East with less, as the 2010 Yankees will attest.

Perhaps the most talked-about change heading into 2011 wasn't a player being moved, but the fences—a move that didn't actually happen, as the Red Sox withdrew their request to redraw the right field boundary. Fenway Park has long been a hitter's paradise, but a common misconception is that baseball's oldest stadium makes hitting home runs easy. The shallow wall in left field, famously dubbed the "Green Monster," helps some fly balls become homers, but as the saying goes, "the wall giveth, and the wall taketh away." By virtue of standing over 37 feet high, that fence has taken away its share of line-drive shots that would have cleared a normal wall, as well as gifted many hitters with round-trippers on balls nearly indistinguishable from pop-ups. That is just one side of the field, though. Center field not only sports what would be considered a tall fence were it not next to the one with a nickname, but also stands around 390 feet from the plate in dead center and 420 feet at its deepest point. Right-center isn't close, either, as it is situated 383 feet away from the plate where it meets the bullpen, and loses only a few feet of depth along the bullpen wall before meeting right field at a distance of 380 feet.

Those deep dimensions make Fenway a favorable park for doubles, almost all of which come at the expense of the long ball. The fences are especially tough on left-handers—outside of the occasional 302-foot dinger down the foul line and around the Pesky Pole, right field is anywhere from slightly above average in terms of homers to far below the league average in right-center.

The Red Sox had planned to move in the fences in front of the bullpens in right by nine feet for the upcoming season. The stated reason for the alteration was that the bullpens are not designed with modern standards in mind—lopping nine feet off the playing field would have given the relievers more space between pitching rubbers. If you have ever seen two pitchers in Boston's pen warm up simultaneously in cramped conditions, you will know how necessary that extra space is.

The announcement provoked an expected outcry: the *Boston Herald*'s editorial staff penned a piece whose main message was, "Stop trying to improve the offense with cheap tactics like stadium renovation"—a specious point given how good Boston's offense actually was.

Despite this, at least one member of the team cheered the move. Left-handed slugger David Ortiz claimed in conversation with WEEI.com's Rob Bradford that the right-field wall has cost him "around 100" homers over the years, as he has "hit a lot of balls in front of that fence, or off that fence. A lot!" While we appreciate Ortiz's enthusiasm in regard to applying park factors to his career totals, he's way off the mark in terms of how many homers Fenway's fence has stolen from him.

In the illustration, prepared by Greg Rybarczyk of Hit Tracker (hittrackeronline.com), the thick dotted line is the

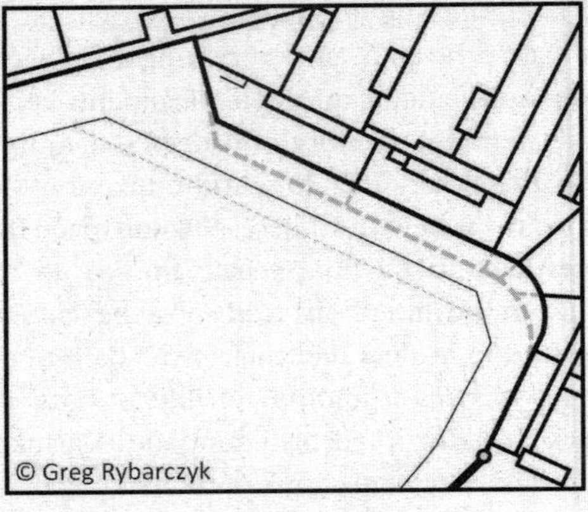

new fence, and the solid black line is the old fence. The thin dotted line further out on the field is where the warning track will now begin. Directly behind the thin dotted line is the old warning track. While the walls in front of the bullpen are being moved in nine feet, the angle on the left side of the pen and the curve closer to the foul line demands that they actually be moved in by anywhere from one foot to 10 feet, depending on the location.

We collected all of Papi's non-home-run fly balls and line drives that were hit to deep right and deep right-center, and then viewed them in the MLB.tv archives. This gave us five years' worth of data to work with (2006-2010). If the right-field fences had been in the proposed new positions during this period, Ortiz would have ended up with somewhere in the vicinity of 10 additional home runs. Not 10 per season, which would still fall short of his estimate, but 10 total, meaning that Ortiz lost an average of two bombs per season.

Park factors suggest that it has been difficult for left-handers like Ortiz to go deep in right-center, and while moving the fences might have changed that slightly, it's not as if a difference of a few feet would have altered the course of many games. Rybarczyk's work and the numbers compiled for Ortiz suggest that the effect of the moved-in fences would not have been that dramatic—we're talking roughly 10 homers total, per year, between the Red Sox and visiting players. That hardly sounds like the makings of a manufactured hitter's paradise.

HITTERS

Lars Anderson **1B**

Born: **9/25/1987** Age: **23**
Bats: **L** Throws: **L** Height: **6' 4"** Weight: **215**
Breakout: **4%** Improve: **27%** Collapse: **3%**
Attrition: **24%** MLB: **47%**

Comparables:
Mike Carp, Nick Evans, Matt Tuiasosopo (75)

YEAR	TEAM	LVL	AGE	PA	R	2B	3B	HR	RBI	BB	SO	SB	CS	AVG/OBP/SLG	TAv	BABIP	BRR	FRAA	WARP
2008	LNC	A+	20	355	58	19	1	13	50	46	64	0	0	.317/.411/.513	.319	.362	-0.7	1B 6	3.0
2008	PME	AA	20	175	28	13	0	6	31	30	47	1	0	.306/.423/.521	.312	.413	-1.8	1B -2	0.7
2009	PME	AA	21	511	51	23	0	9	51	63	114	2	0	.233/.329/.345	.248	.292	-0.3	1B -1	-0.4
2010	PME	AA	22	71	14	5	0	5	16	7	16	1	1	.355/.409/.677	.369	.395	-0.1	1B -3	0.5
2010	PAW	AAA	22	456	48	32	3	10	53	44	109	2	2	.262/.344/.428	.259	.331	-5.5	1B -4	-0.6
2010	BOS	MLB	22	43	4	1	0	0	4	7	8	0	0	.200/.326/.229	.211	.250	0.5	1B -1	-0.2
2011	*BOS*	*MLB*	*23*	*537*	*62*	*24*	*1*	*14*	*56*	*54*	*131*	*1*	*1*	*.246/.324/.392*	*.254*	*.305*	*-0.1*	*1B -17*	*-1.6*

In his first full season at Triple-A, Anderson hit an offensive wall much like the one he'd encountered in his first full campaign at Double-A, posting an un-first-baseman-like line and barely cracking double digits in homers. Lefty-friendly Pawtucket didn't warm up to the would-be southpaw slugger, who did most of his damage on the road, and portsiders put him on ice (.215/.261/.299 in 107 at-bats). Still just 23, Anderson continued to display advanced patience at the plate, even in his September stint with Boston, but his power potential remains in question. He'll need to mash to become a mainstay in the majors, and since his lone season with an ISO of at least .200 and a slugging percentage above .500 owed much to the high-octane environs of Lancaster, his prospect status doesn't weather park adjustments any better than his stats.

Adrian Beltre **3B**

Born: **4/7/1979** Age: **32**
Bats: **R** Throws: **R** Height: **5' 11"** Weight: **170**
Breakout: **1%** Improve: **23%** Collapse: **6%**
Attrition: **10%** MLB: **96%**

Comparables:
Vinny Castilla, Jose Guillen, Miguel Tejada (72)

YEAR	TEAM	LVL	AGE	PA	R	2B	3B	HR	RBI	BB	SO	SB	CS	AVG/OBP/SLG	TAv	BABIP	BRR	FRAA	WARP
2008	SEA	MLB	29	612	74	29	1	25	77	50	90	8	2	.266/.327/.457	.282	.276	-3.2	3B 3	3.1
2009	SEA	MLB	30	477	54	27	0	8	44	19	74	13	2	.265/.304/.379	.253	.301	4.1	3B 9	2.3
2010	BOS	MLB	31	641	84	49	2	28	102	40	82	2	1	.321/.365/.554	.316	.331	2.0	3B 15	6.9
2011	*BOS*	*MLB*	*32*	*610*	*76*	*32*	*1*	*22*	*81*	*38*	*92*	*8*	*2*	*.275/.324/.456*	*.271*	*.291*	*0.0*	*3B 8*	*3.1*

Beltre's decline following his departure from the Dodgers was a Safeco-spawned myth, which both the Red Sox and superagent Scott Boras knew could be remedied by a furlough in Fenway. Although a change in home field was just what the Dominican needed, Beltre's *road* numbers helped him build a case for the American League MVP: the third baseman posted a 953 OPS on the road, 73 points above his Fenway figure, and backed up his offensive exploits with some of the slickest fielding available at his position. The righty's pronounced platoon splits from his latter days in Seattle (710 OPS vs. RHP, 917 OPS vs. LHP from 2007 to 2009) didn't make the cross-country trip, but even if they reappear, his new employer can take solace in the combined .297/.341/.513 line he's mustered away from home over the past four years.

Mike Cameron **CF**

Born: **1/8/1973** Age: **38**
Bats: **R** Throws: **R** Height: **6' 1"** Weight: **170**
Breakout: **0%** Improve: **21%** Collapse: **6%**
Attrition: **16%** MLB: **92%**

Comparables:
Jim Edmonds, Willie Mays, Jeff Kent (64)

YEAR	TEAM	LVL	AGE	PA	R	2B	3B	HR	RBI	BB	SO	SB	CS	AVG/OBP/SLG	TAv	BABIP	BRR	FRAA	WARP
2008	MIL	MLB	35	508	69	25	2	25	70	54	142	17	5	.243/.331/.478	.278	.295	0.7	CF 0	2.4
2009	MIL	MLB	36	628	79	32	3	24	70	75	156	7	3	.250/.342/.452	.274	.304	-0.9	CF 10	3.5
2010	BOS	MLB	37	180	24	11	0	4	15	14	44	0	1	.259/.328/.401	.272	.330	-0.4	CF 0	0.6
2011	*BOS*	*MLB*	*38*	*532*	*64*	*23*	*2*	*19*	*63*	*58*	*134*	*10*	*4*	*.238/.325/.422*	*.263*	*.288*	*-0.3*	*CF 1, LF 0*	*1.6*

At one point in the season, the Red Sox had enough outfield injuries that the best replacement for an injured Mike Cameron was an injured Mike Cameron. Although he tried to stay on the field long enough for Jacoby Ellsbury to replace him, Cameron wasn't of much use in center with a torn abdominal muscle that ultimately required a 4½-hour surgery to fix. He still had good reads on balls hit to the outfield, but his normally excellent jumps and range were diminished. Cameron will patrol left field for Boston in 2011, as Ellsbury is being viewed as the everyday center fielder once again. The shift to a less demanding defensive position could keep Cameron healthy—the last time he played through injury and struggled for an extended period was 2007, and while he bounced back fine, he wasn't 38 in 2008.

J. D. Drew **RF**

Born: **11/20/1975** Age: **35**
Bats: **L** Throws: **R** Height: **6' 1"** Weight: **195**
Breakout: **0%** Improve: **36%** Collapse: **5%**
Attrition: **7%** MLB: **96%**

Comparables:
Frank Robinson, Geoff Jenkins, Bobby Abreu (75)

YEAR	TEAM	LVL	AGE	PA	R	2B	3B	HR	RBI	BB	SO	SB	CS	AVG/OBP/SLG	TAv	BABIP	BRR	FRAA	WARP
2008	BOS	MLB	32	456	80	23	4	19	64	79	80	4	1	.280/.408/.519	.321	.307	1.7	RF -2, CF -1	3.4
2009	BOS	MLB	33	539	85	30	4	24	68	82	109	2	6	.279/.392/.522	.316	.318	-0.7	RF 3	4.1
2010	BOS	MLB	34	546	70	24	2	22	68	60	105	3	1	.255/.341/.452	.287	.282	0.1	RF 4	2.6
2011	*BOS*	*MLB*	*35*	*537*	*70*	*23*	*2*	*20*	*65*	*75*	*104*	*4*	*2*	*.256/.361/.449*	*.284*	*.287*	*-0.3*	*RF 2, CF 0*	*2.2*

Following two consecutive seasons as one of the most productive outfielders in the game, Drew saw his offense slip in 2010. Righties presented no problem (.277/.358/.517), but left-handers tore him to pieces (.208/.302/.309); he has shown pronounced splits throughout his time in Boston, though he hadn't to that degree since 2007. Drew had not walked in fewer than 14.3 percent of his plate appearances since 2003, when free passes came 11 percent of the time, but he turned his walk rate to 11 again last season. Part of the problem was his own patience: opponents took advantage of his passive approach by throwing more first-pitch strikes. His flailing after falling behind led to twice as many double plays, a drop in his fly-ball production, and a failure to hit liners at his normal rates. Drew is in the last year of his deal; Boston is hoping he adjusts or holds steady one more time.

Jacoby Ellsbury **LF**

Born: **9/11/1983** Age: **27**
Bats: **L** Throws: **L** Height: **6' 1"** Weight: **185**
Breakout: **3%** Improve: **45%** Collapse: **3%**
Attrition: **14%** MLB: **81%**

Comparables:
Kenny Lofton, Johnny Damon, Tony Gwynn (75)

YEAR	TEAM	LVL	AGE	PA	R	2B	3B	HR	RBI	BB	SO	SB	CS	AVG/OBP/SLG	TAv	BABIP	BRR	FRAA	WARP
2008	BOS	MLB	24	609	95	22	7	9	47	41	80	50	11	.280/.333/.394	.259	.309	7.8	CF 7, LF 8	4.1
2009	BOS	MLB	25	693	95	27	10	8	60	49	74	70	12	.301/.351/.415	.272	.325	8.2	CF -7	2.8
2010	BOS	MLB	26	84	10	4	0	0	5	4	9	7	1	.192/.238/.244	.192	.217	0.9	CF 1, LF 0	-0.1
2011	*BOS*	*MLB*	*27*	*506*	*59*	*20*	*4*	*7*	*52*	*36*	*58*	*42*	*9*	*.283/.336/.391*	*.260*	*.304*	*1.6*	*CF -1, LF 2*	*1.6*

It was a strange year for Ellsbury, as the outfielder and the Red Sox training staff could not agree on when and how he broke his ribs: when Adrian Beltre violently staked a claim on a pop fly or when Ellsbury made an outfield dive six weeks later. While attempting to compensate for the pain of the five broken ribs, Ellsbury added a strained lat to his medical troubles. When he returned from his rehab—not soon enough for either Kevin Youkilis or the media, both of whom suggested Ellsbury was soft—he reinjured the ribs and was shut down for the season. If he is finally equipped with a full rib cage, there is no reason to think that Ellsbury will be anything other than the above-average outfielder whom the Red Sox hoped to see in 2010.

Bill Hall **UT**

Born: **12/28/1979** Age: **31**
Bats: **R** Throws: **R** Height: **6' 0"** Weight: **175**
Breakout: **5%** Improve: **40%** Collapse: **6%**
Attrition: **11%** MLB: **89%**

Comparables:
Jeff Kent, Howard Johnson, Rico Petrocelli (71)

YEAR	TEAM	LVL	AGE	PA	R	2B	3B	HR	RBI	BB	SO	SB	CS	AVG/OBP/SLG	TAv	BABIP	BRR	FRAA	WARP
2008	MIL	MLB	28	448	50	22	1	15	55	37	124	5	6	.225/.292/.396	.243	.283	-3.4	3B -5, 2B 2	-0.1
2009	MIL	MLB	29	234	22	12	0	6	24	19	72	1	0	.201/.265/.341	.206	.270	0.1	3B 13, RF 1	0.8
2009	SEA	MLB	29	131	10	8	1	2	12	8	48	1	2	.200/.244/.333	.213	.301	0.4	LF 0, RF 2	-0.2
2010	BOS	MLB	30	382	44	16	1	18	46	34	104	9	1	.247/.314/.456	.282	.298	-0.6	2B -3, LF 3	1.6
2011	*HOU*	*MLB*	*31*	*466*	*53*	*23*	*0*	*17*	*56*	*42*	*128*	*7*	*3*	*.236/.304/.414*	*.250*	*.292*	*-0.5*	*3B 4, LF 1*	*1.0*

The Sox acquired Hall in exchange for Casey Kotchman, which was a sensible move even without the benefit of hindsight—shoring up the infield depth was important, since Boston's equivalent of Patient Zero, Jed Lowrie, couldn't be relied on to back up anyone but the overworked training staff. Although a platoon split that leaves Hall vulnerable to right-handers prevents him from assuming a full-time role—he actually had a fluke .283/.346/.495 against right-handers in 2010, but from 2007 to 2009, he hit .207/.273/.356 against them—he boasts an above-average glove at multiple positions and wields a stick that makes him valuable in the infield and serviceable in the outfield. Also noteworthy, in just 336 at-bats, Hall out-homered every member of his previous team.

Jose Iglesias **SS**

Born: **1/5/1990** Age: **21**
Bats: **R** Throws: **R** Height: **5' 11"** Weight: **175**
Breakout: **2%** Improve: **3%** Collapse: **2%**
Attrition: **3%** MLB: **5%**

Comparables:
Rance Mulliniks, Asdrubal Cabrera, Jeff Blauser (83)

YEAR	TEAM	LVL	AGE	PA	R	2B	3B	HR	RBI	BB	SO	SB	CS	AVG/OBP/SLG	TAv	BABIP	BRR	FRAA	WARP
2010	PME	AA	20	232	28	10	3	0	13	8	48	5	2	.286/.319/.359	.240	.358	4.4	SS -10	-0.2
2011	*BOS*	*MLB*	*21*	*279*	*27*	*12*	*2*	*3*	*25*	*12*	*63*	*4*	*2*	*.244/.282/.333*	*.220*	*.305*	*-0.1*	*SS -4*	*-0.6*

Iglesias's defense at short is unsurpassed in the minors. The Cuban defector's movement is fluid and effortless, with range to spare in all directions. His glove would play in the majors right now, and while he hasn't shown much at the plate, he wasn't helped by a broken index finger that cost him all but 57 games at Portland. Given his advanced glove work, the 21-year-old can be forgiven for failing to produce in his pro debut, though the Sox are enthused by what he did in light of the level and his lack of professional experience. Iglesias needs to work on his plate discipline, as the finger injury wasn't responsible for his 3.4 percent walk rate, but Boston is optimistic that he can contribute in the majors as early as 2012, whether he brings a bat or not.

Ryan Kalish **CF**

Born: **3/28/1988** Age: **23**
Bats: L Throws: L Height: **6' 1"** Weight: **205**
Breakout: **6%** Improve: **36%** Collapse: **3%**
Attrition: **18%** MLB: **57%**

Comparables:
Carlos Gonzalez, Colby Rasmus, Jordan Schafer (76)

YEAR	TEAM	LVL	AGE	PA	R	2B	3B	HR	RBI	BB	SO	SB	CS	AVG/OBP/SLG	TAv	BABIP	BRR	FRAA	WARP
2008	GRN	A	20	416	48	16	1	3	32	53	76	18	4	.281/.380/.356	.278	.345	-0.3	RF -6, CF 8	1.8
2008	LNC	A+	20	88	6	6	0	2	15	9	24	1	0	.218/.296/.372	.243	.283	-0.5	RF -1	-0.2
2009	SLM	A+	21	142	21	5	2	5	21	26	20	7	3	.304/.437/.513	.342	.330	0.8	RF 6, CF 0	2.0
2009	PME	AA	21	436	62	19	4	13	56	42	87	14	3	.271/.342/.440	.275	.316	4.0	CF 3, LF 9	3.2
2010	PME	AA	22	181	33	9	1	8	29	28	21	12	1	.293/.409/.527	.329	.290	0.6	RF 0, LF 2	1.6
2010	PAW	AAA	22	159	22	9	1	5	18	14	32	13	2	.294/.359/.476	.279	.343	2.6	CF 8, LF 2	1.9
2010	BOS	MLB	22	179	26	11	1	4	24	12	38	10	1	.252/.302/.405	.260	.298	1.8	CF 3, LF 1	0.9
2011	*BOS*	*MLB*	*23*	*534*	*62*	*21*	*3*	*15*	*59*	*51*	*110*	*18*	*4*	*.255/.325/.405*	*.257*	*.297*	*0.7*	*CF 2, RF -2*	*1.2*

Kalish's bat progressed enough at the upper levels of the minors to dispel the "tweener" tag that had dogged him heading into the year. Defensively, he has the range to play anywhere and an arm strong enough for center and left, skills he showed off when he was called to the majors during the big club's all-hands-on-deck injury emergency. The 23-year-old will start 2011 at Triple-A, since the Red Sox outfield should be whole and he needs to work on his strike-zone recognition and patience. When not chasing pitches, Kalish shows flashes of the offensive talent that could make him an all-star in center, and the Sox are hoping for more sustained barrages by the time they're ready to offer him a full-time gig.

Ryan Lavarnway **C**

Born: **8/7/1987** Age: **23**
Bats: R Throws: R Height: **6' 4"** Weight: **225**
Breakout: **2%** Improve: **14%** Collapse: **1%**
Attrition: **13%** MLB: **38%**

Comparables:
Earl Williams, Mike Carp, John Olerud (72)

YEAR	TEAM	LVL	AGE	PA	R	2B	3B	HR	RBI	BB	SO	SB	CS	AVG/OBP/SLG	TAv	BABIP	BRR	FRAA	WARP
2008	LOW	A-	20	92	10	5	0	2	12	11	22	0	1	.200/.326/.338	.256	.246	-1.9	C 0	0.0
2009	GRN	A	21	485	61	36	2	22	89	52	118	1	2	.286/.371/.534	.313	.341	-2.5	C -1	3.7
2010	SLM	A+	22	351	63	18	0	14	63	44	62	1	0	.290/.402/.487	.314	.320	-0.3	C 0	2.7
2010	PME	AA	22	185	25	9	0	8	37	26	42	0	0	.280/.400/.490	.299	.330	0.9	C 0	1.2
2011	*BOS*	*MLB*	*23*	*371*	*45*	*16*	*0*	*15*	*46*	*35*	*94*	*0*	*0*	*.243/.320/.434*	*.263*	*.286*	*0.0*	*C -1*	*0.9*

Drafted out of Yale in 2008 as a third baseman with a philosophy background ("The utilitarian imperative is the quintessence of the social being; now excuse me while I field this grounder"), Lavarnway has made Boston look good for going over slot in the sixth round, and he has done it as a backstop. Building on his 2009 breakout, the 22-year-old mashed at both High-A and Double-A and now has 43 homers under his belt in two full minor-league seasons. His defense isn't on the level of his bat, but it's good enough to allow him to stick behind the plate. With Jarrod Saltalamacchia and Jason Varitek in front of him, Lavarnway's path to the bigs will be clear for 2012 if he can conquer Triple-A; the players in front of him are more experienced, but less promising.

Che-Hsuan Lin **CF**

Born: **9/21/1988** Age: **22**
Bats: R Throws: R Height: **6' 0"** Weight: **180**
Breakout: **3%** Improve: **13%** Collapse: **0%**
Attrition: **4%** MLB: **20%**

Comparables:
Melky Cabrera, Andrew McCutchen, Roberto Alomar (75)

YEAR	TEAM	LVL	AGE	PA	R	2B	3B	HR	RBI	BB	SO	SB	CS	AVG/OBP/SLG	TAv	BABIP	BRR	FRAA	WARP
2008	GRN	A	19	406	60	13	6	5	37	43	62	32	7	.249/.350/.359	.277	.287	0.6	CF 6, RF 0	2.4
2009	SLM	A+	20	586	79	23	2	8	56	69	76	27	11	.261/.352/.362	.268	.286	0.8	CF 2	2.4
2010	PME	AA	21	528	83	17	4	2	34	71	62	25	11	.275/.392/.343	.278	.313	1.8	CF 16, RF 2	4.3
2011	*BOS*	*MLB*	*22*	*507*	*53*	*16*	*3*	*6*	*40*	*50*	*81*	*18*	*6*	*.244/.320/.332*	*.240*	*.280*	*-0.1*	*CF -4, RF 0*	*-0.1*

Taiwanese outfielder Lin's bat is evolving at a Darwinian pace, but at least his strongest traits are advantageous to his survival. His walk rates have increased every year, while his strikeouts have decreased, and the 21-year-old just completed his first campaign with more free passes than whiffs. Lin has shown no aptitude for power, though the lack of thump is offset by his standing as one of the minors' best defenders in center. Lin's glove will take him to the majors someday, but it's his speed and patience that will make him more than just a defensive replacement.

Felipe Lopez **3B**

Born: **5/12/1980** Age: **31**
Bats: S Throws: R Height: **6' 1"** Weight: **175**
Breakout: **2%** Improve: **36%** Collapse: **2%**
Attrition: **3%** MLB: **96%**

Comparables:
Pedro Feliz, Buddy Bell, Jeff Cirillo (78)

YEAR	TEAM	LVL	AGE	PA	R	2B	3B	HR	RBI	BB	SO	SB	CS	AVG/OBP/SLG	TAv	BABIP	BRR	FRAA	WARP
2008	SLN	MLB	28	169	30	8	2	4	21	11	28	4	3	.385/.426/.539	.333	.448	0.1	2B 1, 3B 1	1.6
2008	WAS	MLB	28	363	33	20	0	2	25	32	54	4	5	.234/.303/.314	.219	.271	-2.5	2B 0, SS 2	-0.8
2009	ARI	MLB	29	383	44	18	1	6	25	34	59	6	3	.301/.363/.412	.272	.346	0.0	2B 7	2.0
2009	MIL	MLB	29	297	44	20	2	3	32	37	41	0	3	.321/.407/.448	.300	.372	-4.6	2B -1	1.4
2010	BOS	MLB	30	16	2	0	0	1	1	1	4	0	0	.267/.313/.467	.275	.300	0.2	2B 0, 3B -1	0.0
2010	SLN	MLB	30	425	50	18	1	7	36	43	77	8	2	.231/.308/.340	.244	.269	-1.1	3B -4, SS -6	-0.6
2011	*BOS*	*MLB*	*31*	*608*	*70*	*26*	*2*	*10*	*59*	*59*	*96*	*13*	*6*	*.267/.337/.380*	*.256*	*.302*	*-0.8*	*2B 1, 3B -1*	*1.0*

In four of the past five seasons, Lopez has failed to make it through a full schedule without switching teams, a trend that continued when he was cut by the Cardinals and picked up by the Red Sox last September. While with St. Louis, he was of little use either at the plate or in the field, but his bat and glove weren't the only things missing: Lopez himself was cut for "repeated tardiness" on game days, which was doubly annoying because his swing-and-miss on off-speed pitches kept showing up early. If his 2011 is anything like his 2010, his greatest contribution will be the sandwich-round pick Boston smartly nabbed by scooping him up.

Jed Lowrie **INF**

Born: **4/17/1984** Age: **27**
Bats: S Throws: R Height: **6' 0"** Weight: **180**
Breakout: **1%** Improve: **39%** Collapse: **2%**
Attrition: **6%** MLB: **80%**

Comparables:
Tim Teufel, John Valentin, Graig Nettles (75)

YEAR	TEAM	LVL	AGE	PA	R	2B	3B	HR	RBI	BB	SO	SB	CS	AVG/OBP/SLG	TAv	BABIP	BRR	FRAA	WARP
2008	PAW	AAA	24	234	35	14	2	5	32	31	43	1	0	.268/.359/.434	.284	.310	-0.4	SS -2, 3B -1	1.4
2008	BOS	MLB	24	306	34	25	3	2	46	35	68	1	0	.258/.337/.400	.255	.325	0.0	SS -2, 3B 4	1.0
2009	PAW	AAA	25	82	9	3	0	3	8	13	13	0	0	.177/.317/.353	.245	.170	0.1	SS -1	0.1
2009	BOS	MLB	25	76	4	2	0	2	11	6	20	0	0	.147/.211/.265	.181	.167	0.4	SS 0, 3B 1	-0.3
2010	BOS	MLB	26	197	35	14	0	9	24	25	25	1	1	.287/.381/.526	.331	.292	-0.5	2B 3, SS -3	1.8
2011	*BOS*	*MLB*	*27*	*317*	*38*	*16*	*1*	*9*	*35*	*38*	*59*	*1*	*0*	*.247/.338/.411*	*.264*	*.279*	*0.0*	*SS -2, 3B 1*	*1.0*

A bout of mono kept Lowrie out until July, but upon his return, the infielder made strides toward proving he belongs in the majors. A .240 isolated power (ISO) mark suggests that Lowrie's long-suffering wrist has finally healed. Strikeouts in fewer than 13 percent of his plate appearances indicate that he is making the contact he could not during his first two fractional seasons in the majors. While Lowrie's injury history is almost entirely attributable to his wrist, the fact it bothered him for as long as it did raises concerns about his ability to bounce back from the daily wear and tear of a starting gig. His defense remains a work in progress—at second, Lowrie looks as if he attended Todd Walker University and graduated *magna non range*. Scouts don't see him at third, but the Sox believe Lowrie's bat will carry him anywhere, including shortstop. The bar for middle infielders is set so low that the Sox may be onto something, and with Marco Scutaro heading into his age-35 season after playing through assorted aches and pains in 2010, Lowrie represents insurance that 29 other teams wish they had.

Victor Martinez **C**

Born: **12/23/1978** Age: **32**
Bats: S Throws: R Height: **6' 2"** Weight: **170**
Breakout: **4%** Improve: **37%** Collapse: **0%**
Attrition: **6%** MLB: **99%**

Comparables:
Rafael Palmeiro, Mike Sweeney, Carlos Ruiz (64)

YEAR	TEAM	LVL	AGE	PA	R	2B	3B	HR	RBI	BB	SO	SB	CS	AVG/OBP/SLG	TAv	BABIP	BRR	FRAA	WARP
2008	CLE	MLB	29	294	31	17	0	2	35	24	32	0	0	.278/.337/.365	.248	.306	-1.5	C -2, 1B -1	0.3
2009	BOS	MLB	30	237	32	12	0	8	41	24	23	1	0	.337/.405/.507	.323	.348	-2.5	C 0, 1B -1	1.8
2009	CLE	MLB	30	435	56	21	1	15	67	51	51	0	0	.284/.368/.464	.294	.291	-2.8	C -1, 1B -3	2.0
2010	BOS	MLB	31	538	66	32	1	20	79	40	52	1	0	.302/.351/.493	.303	.303	-5.7	C -1, 1B 4	3.9
2011	*DET*	*MLB*	*32*	*567*	*74*	*31*	*0*	*19*	*72*	*55*	*66*	*1*	*0*	*.287/.357/.458*	*.285*	*.296*	*0.0*	*C -2, 1B 0*	*2.9*

Martinez racked up 537 plate appearances and finished third in True Runs among catchers, despite some health snags. While it took time for his power to return after he suffered a broken thumb in late June—Martinez hit just .263/.299/.347 with a single homer in the month afterward—he reminded everyone that he was still Victor Martinez as September neared, posting a .651 SLG and 10 homers over a 129 at-bat stretch. That feat of strength helped convince the Tigers to swoop in and ink Martinez this offseason, but not to plug their gaping backstop hole—instead, he'll spend much of his time at DH. That or first base was always going to be the final destination for the defensively challenged Martinez, and while his bat won't be the asset it was behind the plate, it will still pose a threat to opposing pitchers this season.

Darnell McDonald OF

Born: 11/17/1978 Age: 32
Bats: R Throws: R Height: 5' 11" Weight: 210
Breakout: 0% Improve: 32% Collapse: 2%
Attrition: 7% MLB: 91%

Comparables:
Marlon Byrd, Ken Griffey, Chuck Hinton (71)

YEAR	TEAM	LVL	AGE	PA	R	2B	3B	HR	RBI	BB	SO	SB	CS	AVG/OBP/SLG	TAv	BABIP	BRR	FRAA	WARP
2008	ROC	AAA	29	398	53	25	4	11	56	34	79	18	3	.269/.334/.452	.274	.314	-1.6	LF -5, RF 1	0.8
2009	LOU	AAA	30	303	41	22	7	9	40	16	56	7	3	.314/.347/.539	.306	.356	-1.1	RF 6, CF 2	2.5
2009	CIN	MLB	30	111	12	6	1	2	10	5	31	1	0	.267/.306/.400	.231	.361	-1.3	LF -1, RF 3	0.0
2010	BOS	MLB	31	363	38	18	3	9	34	30	85	9	1	.270/.325/.430	.274	.325	-4.1	CF -5, RF 0	0.7
2011	*BOS*	*MLB*	*32*	*445*	*51*	*22*	*3*	*10*	*52*	*32*	*99*	*12*	*3*	*.261/.312/.410*	*.254*	*.311*	*0.3*	*RF 1, LF -1*	*0.5*

McDonald was a key to the Red Sox's remaining in the race into late September, filling in for Ellsbury and Cameron during their injury-related absences. Like Daniel Nava, he made contributions that were a credit to Boston's front office and scouting department, as his acquisition through minor-league free agency supplied depth that the team would need to draw upon more than once during 2010. While McDonald is stretched on defense in center field thanks to iffy range, he is more than capable of holding down a spot in left on both sides of the ball—his bat adequately replaced Ellsbury's despite a season-long UCL injury in his thumb. It's a shame that the 32-year-old's peak years went to waste (an ill-timed labrum injury on the cusp of the majors had much to do with that), but he can still contribute in the majors in the right role.

Will Middlebrooks 3B

Born: 9/9/1988 Age: 22
Bats: R Throws: R Height: 6' 4" Weight: 200
Breakout: 1% Improve: 4% Collapse: 2%
Attrition: 5% MLB: 7%

Comparables:
Ian Stewart, Matt Tuiasosopo, Hank Blalock (76)

YEAR	TEAM	LVL	AGE	PA	R	2B	3B	HR	RBI	BB	SO	SB	CS	AVG/OBP/SLG	TAv	BABIP	BRR	FRAA	WARP
2008	LOW	A-	19	238	23	17	3	2	23	14	76	10	0	.267/.315/.398	.255	.390	1.2	3B -5	0.2
2009	GRN	A	20	446	55	26	3	8	59	52	130	6	4	.261/.350/.404	.278	.367	0.4	3B -8	1.3
2010	SLM	A+	21	477	67	31	2	12	70	35	121	5	3	.276/.333/.439	.279	.350	-0.4	3B 13	3.5
2011	*BOS*	*MLB*	*22*	*387*	*39*	*18*	*1*	*8*	*39*	*24*	*122*	*2*	*1*	*.231/.277/.356*	*.223*	*.319*	*0.0*	*3B 4*	*0.0*

After a promotion to High-A, Middlebrooks' numbers progressed once again. His isolated power climbed to .163 on the strength of hard-hit doubles, and he posted a 25.2 percent strikeout rate (after entering the season with a career rate of 30.0 percent) thanks to excellent plate coverage. The third baseman is one of the top defenders at his position in the minors, but he's not without his worrisome traits, as he drew just 13 walks in his final 69 games after strolling to first 22 times in his first 45 contests. The development (or stagnation) of the 21-year-old free swinger's plate discipline at his next gig in Double-A could go a long way toward determining his career arc.

Daniel Nava LF

Born: 2/22/1983 Age: 28
Bats: S Throws: L Height: 5' 10" Weight: 200
Breakout: 1% Improve: 23% Collapse: 4%
Attrition: 10% MLB: 53%

Comparables:
Danny Putnam, Paul McAnulty, John Milner (76)

YEAR	TEAM	LVL	AGE	PA	R	2B	3B	HR	RBI	BB	SO	SB	CS	AVG/OBP/SLG	TAv	BABIP	BRR	FRAA	WARP
2008	LNC	A+	25	414	59	29	1	10	64	49	77	3	2	.332/.423/.503	.312	.392	2.4	RF -3, LF 4	3.2
2009	SLM	A+	26	129	16	12	1	1	13	18	21	0	2	.339/.434/.495	.317	.405	0.6	RF -2	0.8
2009	PME	AA	26	143	24	10	1	4	23	25	12	0	0	.364/.483/.568	.363	.382	-0.4	LF -2, RF 0	1.5
2010	PAW	AAA	27	314	38	16	1	10	47	28	64	4	2	.289/.385/.458	.283	.340	1.0	RF 3, LF 8	2.4
2010	BOS	MLB	27	188	25	14	1	1	26	19	46	1	1	.242/.351/.360	.268	.333	-0.3	LF -5	0.0
2011	*BOS*	*MLB*	*28*	*396*	*47*	*19*	*1*	*9*	*41*	*40*	*83*	*2*	*1*	*.259/.343/.400*	*.263*	*.310*	*-0.1*	*RF -2, LF 0*	*0.5*

Nava's story makes him easy to root for. He failed as a walk-on player at Santa Clara University and became the equipment manager before leaving, but worked his way to Junior-College-All-American status at San Mateo (after which a sheepish Santa Clara offered him a full scholarship). Undrafted, Nava went to the indie leagues and got cut once even there, though when he did stick, he was named the top indie-league prospect by *Baseball America*. After assistant director of pro scouting Jared Porter recommended that he be signed, Nava tore his way through the Red Sox system starting in 2008; the only thing he couldn't do was get ESPN reporter Erin Andrews to attend one of his games, despite routinely leaving tickets in her name. Nava displayed some patience after making the majors, but he struck out at an alarming rate relative to his minor-league numbers and displayed little of the thump he was known for. On defense, Nava is lost: if his first instinct were to fall down and then run after the ball, it would look about the same as his current outfield strategy.

Yamaico Navarro **SS**

Born: **10/31/1987** Age: **23**
Bats: **R** Throws: **R** Height: **5' 11"** Weight: **170**
Breakout: **3%** Improve: **10%** Collapse: **1%**
Attrition: **14%** MLB: **25%**

Comparables:
Asdrubal Cabrera, Blake DeWitt, Danny Richar (80)

YEAR	TEAM	LVL	AGE	PA	R	2B	3B	HR	RBI	BB	SO	SB	CS	AVG/OBP/SLG	TAv	BABIP	BRR	FRAA	WARP
2008	GRN	A	20	358	45	14	4	7	53	29	73	3	2	.280/.344/.412	.265	.337	-1.2	SS -5, 3B 2	1.1
2008	LNC	A+	20	236	42	14	2	4	27	18	39	3	2	.343/.398/.482	.307	.400	1.1	SS -11	1.2
2009	SLM	A+	21	100	10	9	0	4	17	6	12	2	2	.319/.380/.543	.314	.333	-0.4	SS -5	0.4
2009	PME	AA	21	150	15	6	2	2	11	14	28	5	0	.185/.273/.304	.206	.217	0.1	SS 1	-0.2
2010	PME	AA	22	376	48	19	3	8	55	42	54	16	5	.273/.359/.421	.279	.302	-1.9	SS -8, 3B 2	1.3
2010	PAW	AAA	22	59	8	4	0	3	6	5	6	2	1	.283/.339/.528	.300	.267	1.0	SS -2, 3B -1	0.3
2010	BOS	MLB	22	46	2	0	0	0	5	2	17	0	0	.143/.174/.143	.115	.222	0.2	SS -1, 3B 1	-0.6
2011	*BOS*	*MLB*	*23*	*449*	*49*	*18*	*2*	*10*	*47*	*31*	*88*	*8*	*3*	*.248/.301/.377*	*.240*	*.287*	*-0.2*	*SS -6, 3B 0*	*0.1*

Navarro is the kind of player you expect to see on a major-league roster come September, but with Eric Patterson on the disabled list and Dustin Pedroia unable to return, he made it to Boston in mid-August. Greener than a yuppie in a hybrid, Navarro did little to curb to the lack of production from second base to close out the year. The 22-year-old mustered a 772 OPS at Double-A Portland and even smashed three homers in 58 at-bats in Pawtucket, but as a result of sharing a system with stud prospect Jose Iglesias, Navarro may already be on the utility-infielder career path.

David Ortiz **DH**

Born: **11/18/1975** Age: **35**
Bats: **L** Throws: **L** Height: **6' 4"** Weight: **230**
Breakout: **0%** Improve: **30%** Collapse: **5%**
Attrition: **9%** MLB: **93%**

Comparables:
Carlos Delgado, Lance Berkman, Derrek Lee (65)

YEAR	TEAM	LVL	AGE	PA	R	2B	3B	HR	RBI	BB	SO	SB	CS	AVG/OBP/SLG	TAv	BABIP	BRR	FRAA	WARP
2008	BOS	MLB	32	491	76	30	1	23	89	70	74	1	0	.264/.369/.507	.302	.269	-0.3	—	2.4
2009	BOS	MLB	33	627	80	35	1	28	99	74	134	0	2	.238/.332/.462	.280	.262	-5.2	1B 2	1.4
2010	BOS	MLB	34	606	87	36	1	32	102	82	145	0	1	.270/.370/.529	.314	.313	-3.5	1B -1	3.2
2011	*BOS*	*MLB*	*35*	*620*	*85*	*31*	*1*	*31*	*88*	*86*	*127*	*1*	*1*	*.256/.360/.494*	*.294*	*.276*	*-0.1*	*1B 0*	*2.5*

Ortiz's 2010 began much like his 2009—with a worrisome slump. Unlike the year prior, in May Ortiz stopped chasing pitches out of the strike zone as often, and pitchers who dared throw him something hittable paid for it to the tune of a .286/.385/.558 line from that point forward. Boston has faith that Ortiz can replicate that production, as they picked up his $12.5 million, above-market-rate option for 2011. The fact that the Sox didn't sign Ortiz to the multiyear extension he sought reveals their commitment to limiting their exposure to risk—i.e., Ortiz's mid-30s decline—even at the expense of appeasing the fan base, which has been an occasional knock against the organization.

Eric Patterson **LF**

Born: **4/8/1983** Age: **28**
Bats: **L** Throws: **R** Height: **5' 11"** Weight: **170**
Breakout: **1%** Improve: **34%** Collapse: **6%**
Attrition: **13%** MLB: **77%**

Comparables:
Jeff Salazar, Wally Moon, Johnny Callison (71)

YEAR	TEAM	LVL	AGE	PA	R	2B	3B	HR	RBI	BB	SO	SB	CS	AVG/OBP/SLG	TAv	BABIP	BRR	FRAA	WARP
2008	IOW	AAA	25	219	33	16	3	6	28	12	45	11	0	.320/.356/.517	.304	.378	-0.4	2B 6, CF -2	2.0
2008	SAC	AAA	25	123	17	8	2	4	19	9	28	7	2	.330/.374/.551	.312	.390	2.1	2B -4, CF 1	1.0
2008	CHN	MLB	25	44	5	1	0	1	7	5	12	2	1	.237/.318/.342	.232	.308	0.3	LF -1, 2B -1	-0.1
2008	OAK	MLB	25	104	11	3	0	0	8	12	24	8	0	.174/.269/.207	.190	.235	0.9	2B -1, LF 0	-0.5
2009	SAC	AAA	26	528	90	29	11	12	56	52	81	41	6	.307/.373/.494	.316	.342	7.6	2B 4, CF -6	4.5
2009	OAK	MLB	26	110	11	5	1	1	11	14	25	6	1	.287/.373/.394	.302	.371	0.7	LF -2, CF -1	0.5
2010	OAK	MLB	27	111	10	5	2	4	9	7	31	6	0	.204/.252/.408	.248	.246	-3.2	LF 3, CF 1	0.1
2010	BOS	MLB	27	93	10	3	3	2	7	7	31	5	1	.226/.290/.405	.252	.327	-1.1	LF 1, CF -3	-0.2
2011	*SDN*	*MLB*	*28*	*492*	*60*	*25*	*5*	*12*	*59*	*41*	*101*	*25*	*5*	*.271/.331/.430*	*.266*	*.319*	*1.0*	*2B -1, LF 0*	*1.2*

Acquired after the Dustin Pedroia injury, Patterson provided the Red Sox with more of the depth they required in both the infield and the outfield. He has more pop and patience than brother Corey (which isn't saying much), but he can't make contact anywhere near often enough for a starting role. Thanks to a game-winning single that kept the Yankees from winning the AL East in the last weekend of regular-season play, the final memory Boston fans have of Patterson's 2010 won't be the gaffe in center field that broke up a Jon Lester perfect-game bid. The Padres chose him as the PTBNL in the Adrian Gonzalez contract, and while Petco won't help his batting-average problems, his walk rate and multiple positions will make him a useful commodity.

Dustin Pedroia 2B

Born: **8/17/1983** Age: **27**
Bats: **R** Throws: **R** Height: **5' 9"** Weight: **180**
Breakout: **0%** Improve: **50%** Collapse: **3%**
Attrition: **8%** MLB: **99%**

Comparables:
Edgardo Alfonzo, Gregg Jefferies, Jose Vidro (68)

YEAR	TEAM	LVL	AGE	PA	R	2B	3B	HR	RBI	BB	SO	SB	CS	AVG/OBP/SLG	TAv	BABIP	BRR	FRAA	WARP
2008	BOS	MLB	24	726	118	54	2	17	83	50	52	20	1	.326/.372/.493	.303	.327	3.4	2B 5	5.7
2009	BOS	MLB	25	714	115	48	1	15	72	74	45	20	8	.296/.370/.447	.293	.296	3.4	2B -3	4.1
2010	BOS	MLB	26	351	53	24	1	12	41	37	38	9	1	.288/.365/.493	.305	.289	0.8	2B -9	1.5
2011	*BOS*	*MLB*	*27*	*592*	*78*	*35*	*1*	*15*	*73*	*55*	*45*	*13*	*4*	*.297/.363/.454*	*.288*	*.296*	*0.1*	*2B -4*	*2.6*

Before succumbing to a broken foot that would later end his season, Pedroia was hitting .292/.370/.502 and was one game removed from a three-homer, five-hit performance against the Rockies. The Red Sox were just two games out of first place and tied for the wild card at the time of his demise, and while losing their diminutive second baseman didn't doom their playoff pursuit to failure, it played as large a role as any other injury. Pedroia and the Red Sox chose surgery, and a screw was inserted into his foot to aid the recovery process. Now entering his age-27 campaign, he's looking at the potential for a monster year here.

Josh Reddick OF

Born: **2/19/1987** Age: **24**
Bats: **L** Throws: **R** Height: **6' 2"** Weight: **180**
Breakout: **6%** Improve: **32%** Collapse: **6%**
Attrition: **23%** MLB: **55%**

Comparables:
John Bowker, Brett Carroll, Adam Jones (73)

YEAR	TEAM	LVL	AGE	PA	R	2B	3B	HR	RBI	BB	SO	SB	CS	AVG/OBP/SLG	TAv	BABIP	BRR	FRAA	WARP
2008	GRN	A	21	58	7	4	2	0	9	5	8	2	1	.340/.397/.491	.324	.400	-0.3	RF -2	0.3
2008	LNC	A+	21	331	60	11	8	17	57	17	49	9	1	.343/.375/.593	.331	.363	1.9	RF 0, CF -2	3.0
2008	PME	AA	21	142	23	4	2	6	26	13	29	3	1	.205/.282/.409	.243	.213	0.1	CF -4, RF 0	-0.2
2009	PME	AA	22	287	47	17	3	13	29	30	62	5	5	.277/.352/.520	.307	.319	3.6	CF -4, LF 0	2.1
2009	PAW	AAA	22	79	1	0	2	0	6	6	13	0	1	.127/.190/.183	.153	.150	-0.8	CF 2, RF 3	-0.3
2009	BOS	MLB	22	62	5	4	0	2	4	2	17	0	0	.170/.210/.339	.206	.200	-0.2	LF 1, RF 1	-0.1
2010	PAW	AAA	23	481	59	28	4	18	65	25	73	4	7	.266/.302/.466	.266	.280	0.7	CF -3, RF -1	1.6
2010	BOS	MLB	23	63	4	3	1	1	5	1	15	1	0	.194/.206/.323	.211	.239	0.3	RF 0, CF 1	0.0
2011	*BOS*	*MLB*	*24*	*501*	*58*	*21*	*4*	*18*	*65*	*27*	*98*	*6*	*3*	*.254/.293/.433*	*.251*	*.280*	*-0.5*	*CF -6, RF -1*	*0.1*

Reddick is a gifted, toolsy outfielder, but if you saw him in the first half, you never would have known it. He turned things on after the All-Star break to finish the season strong (.351/.372/.627 over 185 at-bats), which helped earn him a September call-up and save what had begun to look like a lost season. Despite his pirate-inspired facial hair, he again failed to impress with the Sox. Reddick's strike zone is the size of Prince Fielder's pregame spread—it's been expanding ever since he was first called up to the majors in 2009, and he didn't have much patience to give away in the first place. Unless he can shrink his zone to its former size, cracking Boston's outfield corps will be a challenge. The Sox have attempted to make Reddick lay off bad pitches for years now, so their patience may run out before he acquires any.

Anthony Rizzo 1B

Born: **8/8/1989** Age: **21**
Bats: **L** Throws: **L** Height: **6' 3"** Weight: **220**
Breakout: **0%** Improve: **6%** Collapse: **0%**
Attrition: **3%** MLB: **8%**

Comparables:
Jason Thompson, Orlando Cepeda, Billy Butler (76)

YEAR	TEAM	LVL	AGE	PA	R	2B	3B	HR	RBI	BB	SO	SB	CS	AVG/OBP/SLG	TAv	BABIP	BRR	FRAA	WARP
2008	GRN	A	18	86	9	6	0	0	11	3	15	0	0	.374/.407/.446	.338	.456	0.2	1B -2	0.5
2009	GRN	A	19	273	40	21	0	9	42	25	60	2	1	.298/.366/.494	.311	.360	-1.9	1B 2	1.6
2009	SLM	A+	19	258	25	19	0	3	26	26	47	2	0	.297/.368/.419	.288	.357	-2.7	1B 2	0.9
2010	SLM	A+	20	135	26	12	0	5	20	16	32	3	0	.248/.333/.479	.281	.293	1.6	1B 0	0.5
2010	PME	AA	20	464	63	30	0	20	80	45	100	7	1	.264/.336/.482	.288	.298	-1.6	1B 8	2.3
2011	*BOS*	*MLB*	*21*	*405*	*47*	*19*	*2*	*13*	*50*	*29*	*98*	*2*	*1*	*.253/.306/.427*	*.253*	*.303*	*0.0*	*1B -10*	*-1.0*

Rizzo's projected power has been replaced by realized power, and though his former high batting averages went missing, nothing in his approach suggests they are lost forever—punching out in 21 percent of plate appearances is not a rate to fret about, and Rizzo has the skill set to recover those hits. He is now in line to become the first baseman of the future in San Diego rather than Boston, thanks to the Adrian Gonzalez trade. His first taste of Triple-A should give him a chance to get back on the .300 average, 20-25 homer track, though lefty-hating Petco Park will not be as friendly to Rizzo as Fenway would have been once he makes it to the bigs.

Jarrod Saltalamacchia C

Born: **5/2/1985** Age: **26**
Bats: **S** Throws: **R** Height: **6' 4"** Weight: **195**
Breakout: **0%** Improve: **20%** Collapse: **4%**
Attrition: **17%** MLB: **61%**

Comparables:
John Buck, Nick Hundley, Luke Montz (75)

YEAR	TEAM	LVL	AGE	PA	R	2B	3B	HR	RBI	BB	SO	SB	CS	AVG/OBP/SLG	TAv	BABIP	BRR	FRAA	WARP
2008	OKL	AAA	23	62	9	3	1	2	13	7	15	0	0	.291/.403/.491	.282	.368	-0.5	C 0	0.4
2008	TEX	MLB	23	229	27	13	0	3	26	31	73	0	2	.254/.354/.366	.268	.385	-1.4	C 0	1.0
2009	TEX	MLB	24	310	34	12	0	9	34	22	97	0	2	.233/.287/.371	.225	.315	-2.2	C -1	-0.1
2010	OKL	AAA	25	265	37	11	2	11	33	25	60	0	0	.244/.332/.445	.257	.278	0.0	C 0	1.0
2010	TEX	MLB	25	5	0	0	0	0	1	0	1	0	0	.200/.200/.200	.154	.250	0.0	C 0	0.0
2010	BOS	MLB	25	25	2	3	0	0	1	6	4	0	0	.158/.360/.316	.269	.200	0.3	C 0, 1B 0	0.1
2011	*BOS*	*MLB*	*26*	*341*	*38*	*14*	*1*	*11*	*38*	*31*	*90*	*1*	*1*	*.237/.309/.396*	*.247*	*.294*	*-0.1*	*C -1, 1B 0*	*0.8*

A case of the yips set the tone for Saltalamacchia's 2010: he lost the starting job in Texas and was sent packing to Boston as part Victor Martinez insurance, part "Please, anything but more Kevin Cash." The upside grab didn't get the chance to do much besides impress in a limited sample with his plate patience and go through the initiation process required of the 2010 Red Sox by hitting the DL and undergoing surgery to repair the UCL in his thumb. With Martinez signing in Motown, Saltalamacchia should get another extended shot at playing time, though at-bats will have to be divvied up with Jason Varitek. Salty is capable of average offense and defense, a far cry from what was expected when he was the perceived centerpiece in the Mark Teixeira deal, but enough for Boston to get by on, assuming he follows through.

Marco Scutaro SS

Born: **10/30/1975** Age: **35**
Bats: **R** Throws: **R** Height: **5' 10"** Weight: **170**
Breakout: **0%** Improve: **14%** Collapse: **11%**
Attrition: **24%** MLB: **88%**

Comparables:
Alan Trammell, Orlando Cabrera, Miguel Tejada (74)

YEAR	TEAM	LVL	AGE	PA	R	2B	3B	HR	RBI	BB	SO	SB	CS	AVG/OBP/SLG	TAv	BABIP	BRR	FRAA	WARP
2008	TOR	MLB	32	592	75	23	1	7	60	57	65	7	2	.267/.338/.356	.260	.286	3.1	SS 9, 2B 2	3.9
2009	TOR	MLB	33	680	101	35	1	12	60	90	75	14	5	.282/.377/.409	.283	.301	-0.1	SS -1, 2B 1	4.1
2010	BOS	MLB	34	695	92	38	0	11	56	53	71	5	4	.275/.331/.388	.264	.293	0.9	SS 0, 2B 1	3.0
2011	*BOS*	*MLB*	*35*	*554*	*63*	*23*	*1*	*9*	*51*	*56*	*64*	*7*	*3*	*.262/.334/.366*	*.252*	*.279*	*-0.3*	*SS 0, 2B 1*	*1.6*

Scutaro (or Scooter Rowe, if one believes NESN's closed captioning) dropped to his previous offensive levels, but there was more to his season than the stat line. Scutaro played with a pinched nerve and subsequently a rotator-cuff injury for most of the second half. He shifted to second base once an MRI revealed the tears, which allowed him to use his wrist rather than his arm for throws. Maladies aside, Scutaro was right there with the AL's premier shortstops and plugged a half-decade-long hole for Boston, nearly matching the combined WARP output of the starters in those years in a single season. The Venezuelan product had an isolated power of .131 with the use of one arm, as opposed to his .105 ISO with two working appendages, but despite his shorthanded success, Boston's front office is not convinced that missing limbs are the new market inefficiency.

Jason Varitek C

Born: **4/11/1972** Age: **39**
Bats: **S** Throws: **R** Height: **6' 2"** Weight: **210**
Breakout: **2%** Improve: **13%** Collapse: **23%**
Attrition: **34%** MLB: **72%**

Comparables:
Fred McGriff, Carlton Fisk, Damian Miller (75)

YEAR	TEAM	LVL	AGE	PA	R	2B	3B	HR	RBI	BB	SO	SB	CS	AVG/OBP/SLG	TAv	BABIP	BRR	FRAA	WARP
2008	BOS	MLB	36	483	37	20	0	13	43	52	122	0	1	.220/.313/.359	.239	.276	-6.1	C -1	0.3
2009	BOS	MLB	37	425	43	24	0	14	51	54	90	0	0	.209/.313/.390	.253	.235	-2.0	C -1	1.1
2010	BOS	MLB	38	123	18	6	0	7	16	10	35	0	0	.232/.293/.473	.261	.268	-0.3	C -1	0.4
2011	*BOS*	*MLB*	*39*	*396*	*43*	*15*	*1*	*12*	*38*	*45*	*96*	*1*	*0*	*.213/.307/.365*	*.239*	*.255*	*-0.1*	*C -2*	*0.6*

Boston's captain alternated between awful and awesome, striking out 35 times in 123 plate appearances with a sub-.300 OBP while also knocking seven balls over the fence. Like every other Sox starting catcher, Varitek got hurt and didn't return until Victor Martinez was already back and the Sox were all but mathematically eliminated. Considering that Varitek has hit .187/.259/.354 since Boston acquired Martinez and has thrown out fewer than 19 percent of potential base thieves in the past two years, don't expect him to have much impact outside of a mentoring or clubhouse role.

Kolbrin Vitek 3B

Born: **4/1/1989** Age: **22**
Bats: **R** Throws: **R** Height: **6' 2"** Weight: **195**
Breakout: **0%** Improve: **1%** Collapse: **1%**
Attrition: **1%** MLB: **2%**

Comparables:
Mark Bellhorn, Andy Van Slyke, Roy Howell (82)

YEAR	TEAM	LVL	AGE	PA	R	2B	3B	HR	RBI	BB	SO	SB	CS	AVG/OBP/SLG	TAv	BABIP	BRR	FRAA	WARP
2010	GRN	A	21	71	8	3	1	0	5	9	26	0	0	.242/.338/.323	.244	.417	0.0	3B -1	-0.1
2010	LOW	A-	21	234	28	13	3	4	30	26	61	0	0	.270/.368/.422	.277	.357	0.0	3B -3	0.5
2011	*BOS*	*MLB*	*22*	*305*	*29*	*11*	*1*	*5*	*24*	*27*	*101*	*0*	*0*	*.204/.277/.308*	*.211*	*.297*	*0.0*	*3B -1*	*-1.1*

Vitek was Boston's first choice in the 2010 draft, and while he could be considered a steal as the 20th overall selection—San Diego considered taking him with the ninth pick—it's unclear just what he is supposed to become. He has no true defensive home, so his bat is going to have to carry him wherever he plays. He can drive the ball, as evidenced by his 24 extra-base hits in 244 at-bats, and he has loads of patience despite his youth. Vitek will need to cut down on his punchouts to keep his average up, but if he does, Boston won't be too worried about his glove.

Mark Wagner C

Born: **6/11/1984** Age: **27**
Bats: **R** Throws: **R** Height: **6' 1"** Weight: **205**
Breakout: **6%** Improve: **21%** Collapse: **6%**
Attrition: **20%** MLB: **38%**

Comparables:
Guillermo Quiroz, Ed Herrmann, Alvin Colina (78)

YEAR	TEAM	LVL	AGE	PA	R	2B	3B	HR	RBI	BB	SO	SB	CS	AVG/OBP/SLG	TAv	BABIP	BRR	FRAA	WARP
2008	PME	AA	24	398	41	20	0	10	47	38	81	0	0	.215/.304/.357	.225	.245	-1.1	C 0	-0.1
2009	PME	AA	25	185	20	18	0	3	23	28	26	1	0	.301/.416/.477	.306	.336	-1.2	C -1	1.4
2009	PAW	AAA	25	167	11	12	0	3	20	11	29	0	0	.214/.270/.351	.218	.242	-0.3	C 0	-0.2
2010	PAW	AAA	26	143	11	5	0	3	16	10	25	0	0	.205/.252/.315	.203	.219	0.0	C 0	-0.3
2011	*BOS*	*MLB*	*27*	*302*	*30*	*14*	*0*	*6*	*27*	*27*	*61*	*0*	*0*	*.216/.289/.341*	*.223*	*.250*	*0.0*	*C -1*	*-0.1*

Wagner has had bright spots in the minors—most notably his 2007 in High-A and his 2009 in Double-A—but he has always been old for his level and unable to replicate those finer flashes at Triple-A. Wagner doesn't necessarily need to hit, since he has a future as a defensive-minded backup catcher. He may not latch on with the Sox, as Boston is so loaded with backstops that Wagner had to DH in Pawtucket, but in a world where Brad Ausmus retired before he ran out of job opportunities, Wagner will find work someday.

Ryan Westmoreland 3B

Born: **4/27/1990** Age: **21**
Bats: **L** Throws: **R** Height: **6' 2"** Weight: **195**
Breakout: **-%** Improve: **-%** Collapse: **-%**
Attrition: **-%** MLB: **-%**

Comparables:

YEAR	TEAM	LVL	AGE	PA	R	2B	3B	HR	RBI	BB	SO	SB	CS	AVG/OBP/SLG	TAv	BABIP	BRR	FRAA	WARP
2009	LOW	A-	19	264	37	15	3	7	35	38	49	19	0	.296/.405/.484	.327	.347	1.4	LF 1	2.3
2011	*BOS*	*MLB*	*21*	—	—	—	—	—	—	—	—	—	—	—	—	—	—	—	—

Westmoreland did not appear in a game last season, thanks to a vascular abnormality that required brain surgery. What this means for his career is unclear at this stage—doctors were not even sure if Westmoreland would be able to walk or talk after the surgery—but prior to the procedure, he was a five-tool player who already gleamed with polish despite his youth. A smart and quick baserunner, Westmoreland boasted a powerful swing with projection for more pop and advanced strike-zone recognition that belied his lack of pro experience. On raw ability alone, Westmoreland was the finest player Boston's farm system had to offer, but no one knows what he will now become or if he will even be able to play again.

Kevin Youkilis 1B

Born: **3/15/1979** Age: **32**
Bats: **R** Throws: **R** Height: **6' 1"** Weight: **220**
Breakout: **0%** Improve: **29%** Collapse: **5%**
Attrition: **8%** MLB: **98%**

Comparables:
Lance Berkman, Gil Hodges, Fred McGriff (69)

YEAR	TEAM	LVL	AGE	PA	R	2B	3B	HR	RBI	BB	SO	SB	CS	AVG/OBP/SLG	TAv	BABIP	BRR	FRAA	WARP
2008	BOS	MLB	29	621	91	43	4	29	115	62	108	3	5	.312/.390/.569	.334	.339	0.9	1B 1, 3B 7	6.3
2009	BOS	MLB	30	588	100	36	1	27	94	77	125	7	2	.306/.413/.548	.338	.359	3.2	1B 1, 3B 3	6.3
2010	BOS	MLB	31	435	77	26	5	19	62	58	67	4	1	.307/.412/.564	.355	.327	1.8	1B -2, 3B 1	4.4
2011	*BOS*	*MLB*	*32*	*591*	*84*	*31*	*2*	*23*	*81*	*73*	*108*	*5*	*2*	*.286/.386/.498*	*.309*	*.319*	*-0.2*	*1B 1, 3B 3*	*3.9*

Youkilis was in the midst of his third straight exceptional season when he was forced to cut things short due to a muscle tear in his right thumb. The Sox medical staff discovered the injury a few weeks after it occurred, when Youk was hit on the hand by a pitch. An MRI revealed the older hurt—something Youkilis had been hiding from Boston and one that could have had career-altering implications, had the muscle torn from the bone. This shouldn't be a surprise given his public displeasure with Ellsbury's absence and his pro-playing stance for other injured parties, but the Sox, and Youkilis himself, could have paid for this in 2011 and beyond had the tear remained undiscovered. Just because you can play through the pain—and Youkilis did, hitting .340/.407/.554 the month before he was shut down—does not mean you should.

PITCHERS

Scott Atchison

Born: **3/29/1976** Age: **35**
Bats: R Throws: R Height: **6' 2"** Weight: **180**
Breakout: **21%** Improve: **25%** Collapse: **12%**
Attrition: **2%** MLB: **45%**

Comparables:
Joel Peralta, Randy Flores, Jason Childers (77)

YEAR	TEAM	LVL	AGE	W	L	SV	G	GS	IP	H	HR	BB	SO	EqBB9	EqSO9	GB%	BABIP	WHIP	ERA	FRA	WARP
2010	BOS	MLB	34	2	3	0	43	1	60	58	9	19	41	2.9	6.2	48%	.268	1.30	4.35	5.81	-0.6
2011	*BOS*	*MLB*	*35*	*3*	*1*	*0*	*51*	*0*	*67*	*70*	*8*	*23*	*51*	*3.1*	*6.7*	*46%*	*.305*	*1.38*	*4.31*	*4.69*	*0.1*

The pitcher that defined the Red Sox bullpen best in 2010 was Atchison, who performed nearly as close to replacement level as you can get. He made 43 appearances and logged 60 innings, only because no one else who could avoid regular embarrassment on the mound was around to take them. The right-hander works with a fastball/slider combo and below-average strikeout rates, but he can get his pitches over the plate on a consistent basis. Atchison's home-run rates suggest that his control isn't always a positive, but Boston picked up his 2011 option anyway.

Chris Balcom-Miller

Born: **3/3/1989** Age: **22**
Bats: R Throws: R Height: **6' 2"** Weight: **210**
Breakout: **9%** Improve: **25%** Collapse: **4%**
Attrition: **7%** MLB: **35%**

Comparables:
Jaime Garcia, Storm Davis, Johnny Cueto (65)

YEAR	TEAM	LVL	AGE	W	L	SV	G	GS	IP	H	HR	BB	SO	EqBB9	EqSO9	GB%	BABIP	WHIP	ERA	FRA	WARP
2009	CAS	Rk	20	4	0	0	11	12	57	37	3	10	60	1.6	9.5	68%	.239	0.89	1.42	2.84	4.4
2010	ASH	A	21	6	7	0	19	23	108^2	86	3	19	117	1.6	9.7	61%	.291	1.09	2.82	3.64	52.9
2011	*BOS*	*MLB*	*22*	*6*	*5*	*0*	*15*	*15*	*81^2*	*79*	*9*	*34*	*63*	*3.8*	*7.0*	*51%*	*.294*	*1.40*	*4.35*	*4.73*	*1.3*

Balcom-Miller was a sleeper in the Colorado system when 2010 began, but the 21-year-old starter used his plus fastball along with a slider/changeup combo to become one of the top arms in the system. The Rox then gave him up for perpetual headache Manny Delcarmen in August, which—while not Bagwellian in nature—is sure to elicit future giggles if the ground-balling righty turns into a useful back-of-the rotation type. His fastball will be tested when he hits the upper minors—a pitcher with one dominating offering in the low minors can appear far more promising than his actual talent dictates—but his ground-ball tendencies and fantastic command should offset a dip in whiffs.

Daniel Bard

Born: **6/25/1985** Age: **26**
Bats: R Throws: R Height: **6' 4"** Weight: **200**
Breakout: **16%** Improve: **30%** Collapse: **16%**
Attrition: **16%** MLB: **57%**

Comparables:
Clay Zavada, Tony Sipp, Billy Sadler (73)

YEAR	TEAM	LVL	AGE	W	L	SV	G	GS	IP	H	HR	BB	SO	EqBB9	EqSO9	GB%	BABIP	WHIP	ERA	FRA	WARP
2008	GRN	A	23	1	0	0	15	0	28	12	1	4	43	1.3	13.8	66%	.225	0.68	0.64	1.41	1.0
2008	PME	AA	23	4	1	7	31	0	49^2	30	3	26	64	4.7	11.6	60%	.252	1.19	1.81	3.23	0.9
2009	BOS	MLB	24	2	2	1	49	0	49^1	41	5	22	63	4.0	11.5	48%	.303	1.34	3.65	3.71	0.7
2010	BOS	MLB	25	1	2	3	73	0	74^2	45	6	30	76	3.6	9.2	47%	.216	1.03	1.93	2.84	1.4
2011	*BOS*	*MLB*	*26*	*3*	*1*	*1*	*56*	*0*	*71*	*59*	*7*	*40*	*76*	*5.1*	*9.6*	*48%*	*.287*	*1.38*	*3.85*	*4.18*	*0.5*

Bard was on Boston's short list of untouchables, and he showed why in his first full major-league campaign until the lack of a dependable third option in the pen wore him down by the final two months. His combined K/PA in August and September dropped four percentage points while his BB/PA climbed by an equal margin, and he stopped inducing as many misses with his four-seamer and normally devastating slider. Fatigue hurt Bard's peripherals, but a deeper and more effective bullpen should keep him rested and have him pitching in top form once again.

Josh Beckett

Born: **5/15/1980** Age: **31**
Bats: R Throws: R Height: **6' 4"** Weight: **190**
Breakout: **15%** Improve: **53%** Collapse: **20%**
Attrition: **8%** MLB: **96%**

Comparables:
Sonny Siebert, Johan Santana, Bert Blyleven (67)

YEAR	TEAM	LVL	AGE	W	L	SV	G	GS	IP	H	HR	BB	SO	EqBB9	EqSO9	GB%	BABIP	WHIP	ERA	FRA	WARP
2008	BOS	MLB	28	12	10	0	27	29	174^1	173	18	34	172	1.8	8.9	43%	.315	1.24	4.03	4.02	3.5
2009	BOS	MLB	29	17	6	0	32	34	212^1	198	25	55	199	2.3	8.4	48%	.290	1.22	3.86	4.35	3.7
2010	BOS	MLB	30	6	6	0	21	21	127^2	151	20	45	116	3.2	8.2	47%	.338	1.60	5.78	6.03	-0.6
2011	*BOS*	*MLB*	*31*	*12*	*9*	*0*	*29*	*29*	*187*	*186*	*22*	*52*	*167*	*2.5*	*8.0*	*46%*	*.308*	*1.27*	*3.95*	*4.30*	*3.6*

Beckett dealt with an on-and-off back injury that kept him from commanding his breaking ball. He stopped throwing as many benders, which made sitting on his fastballs easier, and the result was a mere five fewer homers than he'd allowed in 2009, but in 85 1/3 fewer innings pitched. His peripherals suggest better results than he got, but if he can't locate his pitches and if hitters know what to expect, then his home-run rate won't regress. After signing the potentially dominant righty to a four-year, $68 million extension, the Sox will need an able-bodied Beckett to get their money's worth.

Michael Bowden

Born: **9/9/1986** Age: **24**
Bats: R Throws: R Height: **6' 3"** Weight: **215**
Breakout: **9%** Improve: **19%** Collapse: **11%**
Attrition: **12%** MLB: **49%**

Comparables:
David Huff, Larry Dierker, Scott Lewis (69)

YEAR	TEAM	LVL	AGE	W	L	SV	G	GS	IP	H	HR	BB	SO	EqBB9	EqSO9	GB%	BABIP	WHIP	ERA	FRA	WARP
2008	PME	AA	21	9	4	0	19	20	104^1	72	5	24	101	2.1	8.7	43%	.245	0.92	2.33	2.7	3.9
2008	PAW	AAA	21	0	3	0	8	8	41^2	42	5	6	30	1.3	6.5	38%	.289	1.15	3.24	3.39	1.1
2008	BOS	MLB	21	1	0	0	1	1	5	7	0	1	3	1.8	5.4	17%	.389	1.60	3.60	3.16	0.2
2009	PAW	AAA	22	4	6	0	24	26	126^1	106	11	47	88	3.3	6.3	32%	.257	1.22	2.99	4.50	1.4
2009	BOS	MLB	22	1	1	0	8	1	16	23	3	6	12	3.4	6.8	42%	.370	1.81	9.56	8.42	-0.3
2010	PAW	AAA	23	6	4	1	31	20	105^2	84	13	37	77	3.2	6.6	25%	.238	1.16	3.58	3.80	2.1
2010	BOS	MLB	23	0	1	0	14	0	15^1	20	2	4	13	2.3	7.6	27%	.383	1.57	5.28	5.50	-0.1
2011	*BOS*	*MLB*	*24*	*8*	*7*	*0*	*36*	*20*	129^1	*132*	*16*	*50*	*89*	*3.5*	*6.2*	*37%*	*.293*	*1.41*	*4.46*	*4.84*	*1.7*

The strikeouts Bowden lost in his 2008 Triple-A debut seem gone forever, and as an extreme fly-ball pitcher lacking a true out pitch, Bowden has debatable viability as a starter. If you squint, the 23-year-old right-hander seems salvageable as a reliever: a 7.6 K/9 with Boston is encouraging and a step up from his previous stints, but given the low quality of his stuff—his curve, once a plus pitch, is now slow and flat—and the fact he's hit been hard in the majors (.377 BABIP in 36 1/3 innings), you have to wonder if he's a few homers away from buying a condo in Rhode Island.

Clay Buchholz

Born: **8/14/1984** Age: **26**
Bats: L Throws: R Height: **6' 3"** Weight: **190**
Breakout: **8%** Improve: **42%** Collapse: **32%**
Attrition: **13%** MLB: **95%**

Comparables:
Mike Witt, Kevin Millwood, Erik Hanson (72)

YEAR	TEAM	LVL	AGE	W	L	SV	G	GS	IP	H	HR	BB	SO	EqBB9	EqSO9	GB%	BABIP	WHIP	ERA	FRA	WARP
2008	PME	AA	23	1	0	0	3	3	21	13	1	2	27	0.9	11.6	53%	.250	0.71	2.57	3.50	0.5
2008	PAW	AAA	23	4	2	0	9	11	43^2	36	3	17	43	3.5	8.9	42%	.295	1.26	2.47	2.42	1.8
2008	BOS	MLB	23	2	9	0	16	17	76	93	11	41	72	4.9	8.5	49%	.355	1.79	6.75	6.58	-0.4
2009	PAW	AAA	24	7	2	0	17	16	99	67	7	30	89	2.7	8.1	54%	.230	0.98	2.36	3.08	2.8
2009	BOS	MLB	24	7	4	0	16	17	92	91	13	36	68	3.5	6.7	54%	.279	1.40	4.21	4.82	1.3
2010	BOS	MLB	25	17	7	0	28	30	173^2	142	9	67	120	3.5	6.2	52%	.261	1.23	2.33	3.21	4.6
2011	*BOS*	*MLB*	*26*	*11*	*8*	*0*	*27*	*27*	*152*	*139*	*14*	*61*	*126*	*3.6*	*7.5*	*49%*	*.289*	*1.31*	*3.65*	*3.97*	*3.8*

Pitchers *can* have fantastic stuff without racking up strikeouts, and Buchholz is Exhibit A. The young right-hander *should* punch out more batters with his mid-90s heater, a 90-mph slider, and his finest pitch, a vanishing changeup, and those strikeouts are coming. His fastballs and sliders were fouled off at a 20 percent clip, which suggests that once he grows into his stuff, the whiffs will pile up. Normally, it would be odd to talk about a 26-year-old growing into anything, but his 30s, but the velocity is new to Buchholz, whose slider averaged 81 mph two years ago. The added giddyup resulted from a change to his grip, which now resembles that used for a cutter, and the slider now functions as a fastball variant with a break he can command. Even without the extra strikeouts, the 25-year-old induced weak contact and grounders aplenty. Buchholz may never post a 2.33 ERA again, but he does have ace potential.

Cesar Cabral

Born: **2/11/1989** Age: **22**
Bats: L Throws: L Height: **6' 3"** Weight: **175**
Breakout: **0%** Improve: **1%** Collapse: **1%**
Attrition: **1%** MLB: **1%**

Comparables:
Nick Adenhart, Steve Trout, John Denny (84)

YEAR	TEAM	LVL	AGE	W	L	SV	G	GS	IP	H	HR	BB	SO	EqBB9	EqSO9	GB%	BABIP	WHIP	ERA	FRA	WARP
2008	RSX	Rk	19	2	5	0	11	12	48^1	55	3	15	51	2.8	9.5	56%	.359	1.57	4.84	5.31	0.6
2009	LOW	A-	20	1	6	4	16	10	61^1	67	2	18	48	2.6	7.0	57%	.316	1.43	3.96	4.16	0.7
2010	GRN	A	21	2	0	5	17	0	31^1	16	0	7	35	2.0	10.1	70%	.232	0.83	0.29	1.39	1.2
2010	SLM	A+	21	2	0	4	28	0	48	60	1	14	45	2.6	8.4	53%	.396	1.58	6.00	4.51	0.2
2011	*TBA*	*MLB*	*22*	*2*	*2*	*1*	*23*	*4*	*53*	*61*	*6*	*27*	*32*	*4.5*	*5.3*	*48%*	*.313*	*1.64*	*5.47*	*5.95*	*-0.6*

Cabral looked great at relief in Single-A, punching out five times as many hitters as he walked with his above-average heater and mix of secondary stuff. His ERA ballooned with a promotion to High-A, but he still missed plenty of bats and maintained his excellent control. The Rays scooped him up in the Rule 5 draft, and the lefty may work as a LOOGY out of the pen.

Robert Coello

Born: **11/23/1984** Age: **26**
Bats: R Throws: R Height: **6' 5"** Weight: **250**
Breakout: **14%** Improve: **16%** Collapse: **7%**
Attrition: **16%** MLB: **25%**

Comparables:
Brad Kilby, Andrew Bailey, John Meloan (66)

YEAR	TEAM	LVL	AGE	W	L	SV	G	GS	IP	H	HR	BB	SO	EqBB9	EqSO9	GB%	BABIP	WHIP	ERA	FRA	WARP
2009	SLM	A+	24	5	3	2	36	0	72	40	4	35	89	4.4	11.1	39%	.225	1.17	1.50	2.37	2.2
2010	PME	AA	25	4	1	1	14	4	43^1	38	4	14	51	2.9	10.6	28%	.309	1.22	3.12	2.99	1.2
2010	PAW	AAA	25	3	5	0	18	12	64	44	10	30	79	4.2	11.1	25%	.236	1.25	3.94	4.76	0.8
2010	BOS	MLB	25	0	0	0	6	0	5^2	4	0	5	5	7.9	7.9	13%	.250	1.59	4.76	2.25	0.1
2011	*BOS*	*MLB*	*26*	*3*	*2*	*0*	*26*	*5*	67^2	*57*	*8*	*35*	*69*	*4.7*	*9.2*	*38%*	*.284*	*1.37*	*4.01*	*4.36*	*0.8*

Coello is a one-pitch pitcher, and the only time this pitch cracks well over 90 mph is when it breaks the sound barrier heading back toward the stands. Despite the auditory explosion emanating from a well-struck Coello offering, a .251 BABIP kept his ERA out of unsightly territory for the PawSox and allowed him to preserve his warm-body standing and Boston-bullpen eligibility. Without a second pitch, the right-hander may not even earn "organizational soldier" status.

Felix Doubront

Born: **10/23/1987** Age: **23**
Bats: **L** Throws: **L** Height: **6' 2"** Weight: **165**
Breakout: **2%** Improve: **7%** Collapse: **8%**
Attrition: **4%** MLB: **8%**

Comparables:
Melido Perez, Ken Holtzman, Rick Baldwin (79)

YEAR	TEAM	LVL	AGE	W	L	SV	G	GS	IP	H	HR	BB	SO	EqBB9	EqSO9	GB%	BABIP	WHIP	ERA	FRA	WARP
2008	GRN	A	20	12	8	0	23	24	115^{1}	115	9	24	118	1.9	9.2	46%	.331	1.24	3.43	3.13	3.5
2008	LNC	A+	20	1	1	0	5	5	24	26	1	8	26	3.0	9.8	41%	.368	1.46	3.75	2.35	1.0
2009	PME	AA	21	8	6	0	26	28	121	119	8	52	101	3.9	7.5	47%	.304	1.49	3.05	3.22	3.7
2010	PME	AA	22	4	0	0	8	8	43	39	0	17	38	3.6	8.0	44%	.325	1.35	2.30	1.93	2.0
2010	PAW	AAA	22	4	3	0	9	8	37	36	1	16	34	3.9	8.3	56%	.340	1.51	2.92	2.53	1.5
2010	BOS	MLB	22	2	2	2	12	3	25	27	3	10	23	3.6	8.3	46%	.316	1.52	4.32	4.90	0.1
2011	*BOS*	*MLB*	*23*	*6*	*9*	*0*	*20*	*20*	*95*	*111*	*12*	*48*	*64*	*4.5*	*6.0*	*44%*	*.322*	*1.65*	*5.69*	*6.18*	*0.3*

Doubront was a starting pitching prospect with stuff that surpassed his results to begin the year and exited it as a reliever at the major-league level. After making the jump to Triple-A, Doubront survived a pair of spot starts and earned a bullpen gig, punching out 12.1 per nine in that role before a strained pectoral ended his season. The Venezuelan southpaw has above-average velocity, and all of his pitches—four- and two-seam fastballs, change, and curve—can miss bats if his command is present. Just 23 years old, Doubront could have a future in the middle of a rotation, but he will serve primarily as a reliever for at least the 2011 season.

Rich Hill

Born: **3/11/1980** Age: **31**
Bats: **L** Throws: **L** Height: **6' 5"** Weight: **205**
Breakout: **15%** Improve: **24%** Collapse: **13%**
Attrition: **16%** MLB: **52%**

Comparables:
Jorge Julio, Charlie Manning, John Parrish (64)

YEAR	TEAM	LVL	AGE	W	L	SV	G	GS	IP	H	HR	BB	SO	EqBB9	EqSO9	GB%	BABIP	WHIP	ERA	FRA	WARP
2008	IOW	AAA	28	2	4	0	7	7	26	22	4	28	32	9.7	11.1	42%	.295	2.00	5.54	6.08	0.0
2008	CHN	MLB	28	1	0	0	5	6	19^{2}	13	2	18	15	8.2	6.9	36%	.208	1.63	4.12	5.70	0.2
2009	BAL	MLB	29	3	3	0	14	14	57^{2}	68	7	40	46	6.2	7.2	35%	.337	1.89	7.65	7.73	-0.8
2010	MEM	AAA	30	4	3	0	23	4	46	35	5	30	47	5.9	9.2	45%	.266	1.59	3.72	4.16	0.8
2010	PAW	AAA	30	3	1	0	19	6	53	45	3	29	55	4.9	9.3	49%	.307	1.57	3.40	3.06	1.5
2010	BOS	MLB	30	1	0	0	6	0	4	5	0	1	3	2.3	6.8	57%	.357	1.50	0.00	-1.73	0.3
2011	*BOS*	*MLB*	*31*	*8*	*7*	*0*	*49*	*18*	*121^{2}*	*110*	*13*	*71*	*112*	*5.3*	*8.2*	*44%*	*.290*	*1.49*	*4.55*	*4.95*	*1.4*

Hill started 10 games in the minors while splitting time in the Cardinals' and Red Sox's systems, but most of his innings came in relief. The southpaw had 102 punchouts against 58 unintentional walks in 99 minor-league innings, but Boston tried every fungible Triple-A reliever it had before it got to Hill. He's a long shot to contribute, but the southpaw has a year as an above-average starter on his résumé and, despite his wildness, still regularly blows the ball by hitters. He's trying a new sidearm delivery, and if he can keep his walks down, a low-stakes gamble on the vet could pay off.

Casey Kelly

Born: **10/4/1989** Age: **21**
Bats: **R** Throws: **R** Height: **6' 3"** Weight: **195**
Breakout: **5%** Improve: **6%** Collapse: **6%**
Attrition: **2%** MLB: **8%**

Comparables:
Don Kaiser, Joe Moeller, Lindy McDaniel (76)

YEAR	TEAM	LVL	AGE	W	L	SV	G	GS	IP	H	HR	BB	SO	EqBB9	EqSO9	GB%	BABIP	WHIP	ERA	FRA	WARP
2009	GRN	A	19	6	1	0	9	9	48^{1}	32	0	9	39	1.7	7.3	54%	.237	0.85	1.12	3.34	1.2
2009	SLM	A+	19	1	4	0	8	8	46^{2}	33	4	7	35	1.4	6.8	53%	.221	0.88	3.09	5.06	0.2
2010	PME	AA	20	3	5	0	21	23	95	118	10	35	81	3.3	7.7	47%	.361	1.63	5.21	4.67	1.3
2011	*BOS*	*MLB*	*21*	*6*	*7*	*0*	*18*	*18*	*88*	*101*	*11*	*36*	*57*	*3.7*	*5.7*	*46%*	*.314*	*1.54*	*5.23*	*5.69*	*0.7*

Kelly was Boston's first-rounder back in 2008, and the former two-way talent is now a full-time starting pitcher. It was expected that he would repeat High-A given his lack of pro experience on the mound, so his struggles as a 20-year-old in the upper minors are not a surprise, though the cracked fingernail he had on his middle finger didn't help things either. The righty sits 90-94 with his heater and has a plus curve in addition to an off-speed pitch that may evolve into a plus offering. Kelly's delivery is surprisingly clean and repeatable for someone who was spending much of his time at shortstop until recently, and he projects to be an above-average starter once he figures out pitch sequencing and command. Kelly will repeat Double-A in 2011, but this time as a member of the Padres—he was the key of the Adrian Gonzalez trade and may slot in behind Mat Latos in the rotation as early as 2012.

John Lackey

Born: **10/23/1978** Age: **32**
Bats: R Throws: R Height: **6' 6"** Weight: **205**
Breakout: **14%** Improve: **51%** Collapse: **22%**
Attrition: **15%** MLB: **95%**

Comparables:
Gil Meche, Ted Lilly, Brad Penny (73)

YEAR	TEAM	LVL	AGE	W	L	SV	G	GS	IP	H	HR	BB	SO	EqBB9	EqSO9	GB%	BABIP	WHIP	ERA	FRA	WARP
2008	ANA	MLB	29	12	5	0	24	24	163^1	161	26	40	130	2.2	7.2	45%	.288	1.29	3.75	4.12	2.7
2009	ANA	MLB	30	11	8	0	27	27	176^1	177	17	47	139	2.4	7.1	46%	.299	1.32	3.83	4.24	2.9
2010	BOS	MLB	31	14	11	0	33	33	215	233	18	72	156	3.0	6.5	46%	.319	1.46	4.40	4.03	3.5
2011	*BOS*	*MLB*	*32*	*12*	*10*	*0*	*32*	*32*	*203*	*209*	*20*	*61*	*152*	*2.7*	*6.8*	*46%*	*.310*	*1.33*	*4.13*	*4.49*	*3.4*

The Red Sox signed Lackey to a five-year, $82.5 million contract, making him their highest-paid player in 2010. His first-half performance made the signing look like a miscalculation—the righty struck out just 5.4 hitters per nine innings while allowing an OPS of 816, and he posted a 1.5 strikeout-to-walk ratio due to pitiable command of his secondary pitches. His second half salvaged the season, featuring 7.8 strikeouts per nine innings, a much more Lackey-like 3.4 K/BB, and a 705 OPS against. Feasting on the punchless Mariners, Indians, and Athletics helped, but Lackey's command was improved—repeating that second act is the key to a successful 2011 for the Texan.

Jon Lester

Born: **1/7/1984** Age: **27**
Bats: L Throws: L Height: **6' 2"** Weight: **190**
Breakout: **9%** Improve: **39%** Collapse: **37%**
Attrition: **7%** MLB: **99%**

Comparables:
Bert Blyleven, Scott Kazmir, Erik Hanson (67)

YEAR	TEAM	LVL	AGE	W	L	SV	G	GS	IP	H	HR	BB	SO	EqBB9	EqSO9	GB%	BABIP	WHIP	ERA	FRA	WARP
2008	BOS	MLB	24	16	6	0	33	34	210^1	202	14	66	152	2.8	6.5	50%	.298	1.32	3.21	3.53	5.5
2009	BOS	MLB	25	15	8	0	32	35	203^1	186	20	64	225	2.8	10.0	49%	.313	1.24	3.41	3.62	5.3
2010	BOS	MLB	26	19	9	0	32	36	208	167	14	83	225	3.6	9.7	54%	.289	1.25	3.25	3.79	4.0
2011	*BOS*	*MLB*	*27*	*12*	*8*	*0*	*29*	*29*	*182^2*	*166*	*15*	*70*	*173*	*3.4*	*8.5*	*49%*	*.304*	*1.29*	*3.48*	*3.78*	*4.6*

Lester's 3.89 second-half ERA, more than a run higher than that of the first half, was a source of concern to Bostonians after the break, but the cause lay not with the pitcher, but in his defense—as the team's injuries mounted, Lester did his hurling in front of a cast of understudies, sand-lotters, and old Muppets the late Jim Henson had rejected as being too disturbing for *Sesame Street*. The bloated ERA belied Lester's peripherals, which improved throughout the season; he whiffed 10.2 per nine from July onward while allowing only 3.3 walks per nine. Lester's SIERA, a measure of defense-independent pitching, was 3.14 after the break, one-tenth of a run *better* than his first-half mark. That is something to keep in mind when making your Cy Young predictions for 2011.

Robert Manuel

Born: **7/9/1983** Age: **27**
Bats: R Throws: R Height: **6' 3"** Weight: **205**
Breakout: **2%** Improve: **8%** Collapse: **9%**
Attrition: **11%** MLB: **21%**

Comparables:
Scott Lewis, Guillermo Moscoso, Alfredo Aceves (69)

YEAR	TEAM	LVL	AGE	W	L	SV	G	GS	IP	H	HR	BB	SO	EqBB9	EqSO9	GB%	BABIP	WHIP	ERA	FRA	WARP
2008	CHT	AA	24	5	3	3	47	0	77	47	2	16	92	1.9	10.8	39%	.239	0.86	1.40	2.52	2.1
2009	LOU	AAA	25	3	4	10	36	0	46^2	37	2	10	38	1.9	7.3	29%	.257	1.05	2.51	4.35	0.3
2009	TAC	AAA	25	1	1	4	16	0	20	17	5	7	11	3.2	5.0	31%	.200	1.20	5.40	7.46	-0.5
2009	CIN	MLB	25	0	0	0	3	0	4^1	5	0	1	2	2.1	4.2	33%	.333	1.38	0.00	0.12	0.2
2010	PAW	AAA	26	8	2	13	45	0	64^1	46	4	13	48	1.8	6.7	23%	.231	0.93	1.68	3.75	1.1
2010	BOS	MLB	26	1	0	0	10	0	12^2	10	5	7	5	5.0	3.6	19%	.135	1.34	4.26	6.73	-0.3
2011	*BOS*	*MLB*	*27*	*3*	*1*	*2*	*52*	*0*	*75*	*74*	*9*	*25*	*53*	*3.0*	*6.3*	*38%*	*.285*	*1.31*	*3.92*	*4.26*	*0.5*

Manuel's reliance on deception caught up to him when he reached Triple-A, and the righty who twirled a 6.1 strikeout-to-walk ratio at Double-A three years ago barely managed a *strikeout rate* higher than that between Pawtucket and Boston. Manuel's arsenal includes a mid-80s fastball paired with a slow slider that just avoids being slapped with a "disco" designation because it's stuck in the 70s. That pitch will never cross over from white polyester pants to New Wave, making Manuel a replacement-level reliever, something Boston required more often than is healthy in 2010.

Daisuke Matsuzaka

Born: **9/13/1980** Age: **30**
Bats: R Throws: R Height: **6' 0"** Weight: **185**
Breakout: **15%** Improve: **48%** Collapse: **24%**
Attrition: **14%** MLB: **100%**

Comparables:
Mark Langston, Bob Gibson, Sonny Siebert (75)

YEAR	TEAM	LVL	AGE	W	L	SV	G	GS	IP	H	HR	BB	SO	EqBB9	EqSO9	GB%	BABIP	WHIP	ERA	FRA	WARP
2008	BOS	MLB	27	18	3	0	29	29	167^2	128	12	94	154	5.0	8.3	39%	.258	1.37	2.90	3.46	4.7
2009	BOS	MLB	28	4	6	0	12	12	59^1	81	10	30	54	4.6	8.2	35%	.380	1.90	5.76	4.4	1.2
2010	BOS	MLB	29	9	6	0	25	25	153^2	137	13	74	133	4.3	7.8	35%	.284	1.43	4.69	5.51	0.0
2011	*BOS*	*MLB*	*30*	*11*	*9*	*0*	*28*	*28*	*157^1*	*147*	*16*	*75*	*140*	*4.3*	*8.0*	*40%*	*.297*	*1.41*	*4.22*	*4.58*	*2.8*

Matsuzaka has thrown 200 innings only once in his major-league career and has managed just 37 starts over the past two seasons. Inefficiency contributes to his low innings totals, with Matsuzaka averaging 4.0 pitches per plate appearance for his career, granting every hitter that faces him the patience of Wade Boggs. The Sox were encouraged by an uptick in four-seamer and slider velocity over the last two months of 2010, a period during which Dice-K also averaged over 6.1 innings per start. On the surface, he appeared more efficient, lowering his rate to

3.8 P/PA, but that deceptive improvement was due to his being hit harder earlier in the count: Dice-K had a 5.34 ERA (and 4.45 SIERA) over those 64 innings, so maybe the team's expectations should be as low as his K/BB ratio.

Hideki Okajima

Born: **12/25/1975** Age: **35**
Bats: L Throws: L Height: **6' 1"** Weight: **194**
Breakout: **29%** Improve: **49%** Collapse: **19%**
Attrition: **6%** MLB: **82%**

Comparables:
Rollie Fingers, Barney Schultz, Jay Howell (79)

YEAR	TEAM	LVL	AGE	W	L	SV	G	GS	IP	H	HR	BB	SO	EqBB9	EqSO9	GB%	BABIP	WHIP	ERA	FRA	WARP
2008	BOS	MLB	32	3	2	1	64	0	62	49	6	23	60	3.3	8.7	35%	.256	1.18	2.61	2.34	2.0
2009	BOS	MLB	33	6	0	0	68	0	61	56	8	21	53	3.1	7.8	34%	.276	1.30	3.39	3.00	1.3
2010	BOS	MLB	34	4	4	0	56	0	46	59	6	20	33	3.9	6.5	40%	.344	1.72	4.50	3.01	0.9
2011	*BOS*	*MLB*	*35*	*3*	*1*	*0*	*68*	*0*	*59*	*60*	*7*	*22*	*48*	*3.3*	*7.3*	*41%*	*.302*	*1.37*	*4.11*	*4.46*	*0.2*

The slide continued for Okajima, whose K/BB ratio and ERA continued to head in the wrong directions for the third straight year. Initially the third option out of the pen, the Japanese lefty caused more damage than any other Sox reliever thanks to the aging of his "Oki Doke," a splitter/change hybrid that has picked up fewer whiffs with each passing year. Even a livelier rainbow curve couldn't bring his strikeout rate up to league average. After returning from a hamstring-related DL stint, Okajima posted a 1.32 ERA, giving false hope to those who failed to notice his relentlessly Okajima-esque peripherals.

Jonathan Papelbon

Born: **11/23/1980** Age: **30**
Bats: R Throws: R Height: **6' 4"** Weight: **230**
Breakout: **15%** Improve: **29%** Collapse: **27%**
Attrition: **12%** MLB: **79%**

Comparables:
Lee Smith, Jeff Nelson, Michael Wuertz (60)

YEAR	TEAM	LVL	AGE	W	L	SV	G	GS	IP	H	HR	BB	SO	EqBB9	EqSO9	GB%	BABIP	WHIP	ERA	FRA	WARP
2008	BOS	MLB	27	5	4	41	67	0	69^{1}	58	4	8	77	1.0	10.0	51%	.294	0.95	2.34	3.00	1.13
2009	BOS	MLB	28	1	1	38	66	0	68	54	5	24	76	3.2	10.1	28%	.278	1.21	1.85	1.61	2.0
2010	BOS	MLB	29	5	7	37	65	0	67	57	7	28	76	3.8	10.2	40%	.287	1.30	3.90	4.76	0.0
2011	*BOS*	*MLB*	*30*	*3*	*2*	*29*	*63*	*0*	64^{2}	*53*	*5*	*21*	*73*	*3.0*	*10.1*	*43%*	*.294*	*1.16*	*2.79*	*3.04*	*1.3*

Those unfamiliar with the ins and outs of Papelbon's 2010 may wonder what all the fuss was about. His 3.90 ERA was high but not hideous, and he struck out over 10 batters per nine. However, a peek at his individual performances tells a darker tale: when Papelbon could not command his splitter, he threw heater after heater, and the opposition teed off. His control didn't recover from its previous decline, and after posting a 6.6 strikeout-to-walk ratio from 2006 to 2008, Papelbon has managed only a 2.9 ratio over his last 135 innings. Despite his performance problems, calls to remove him from the closer's role are misguided—Boston would be better served by letting Daniel Bard act as a "relief ace" in the highest-leverage situations while confining Papelbon to the relative safety of the ninth, where he can remember his impending free agency before he decides to throw another predictable fastball.

Dustin Richardson

Born: **1/9/1984** Age: **27**
Bats: L Throws: L Height: **6' 6"** Weight: **220**
Breakout: **1%** Improve: **1%** Collapse: **5%**
Attrition: **6%** MLB: **9%**

Comparables:
Joe Bisenius, Emiliano Fruto, Brent Leach (77)

YEAR	TEAM	LVL	AGE	W	L	SV	G	GS	IP	H	HR	BB	SO	EqBB9	EqSO9	GB%	BABIP	WHIP	ERA	FRA	WARP
2008	PME	AA	24	7	10	0	22	22	106^{2}	108	17	51	114	4.3	9.6	39%	.323	1.54	6.16	5.46	0.7
2009	PME	AA	25	2	2	4	38	0	63^{1}	42	2	40	80	5.7	11.4	38%	.274	1.34	2.70	2.76	1.6
2009	BOS	MLB	25	0	0	0	3	0	3^{1}	3	0	1	0	2.7	0.0	38%	.231	1.20	0.00	3.36	0.0
2010	PAW	AAA	26	3	0	2	32	0	44	27	4	31	56	6.3	11.5	48%	.258	1.32	2.86	4.02	0.7
2010	BOS	MLB	26	0	0	0	26	0	13	15	2	14	12	9.7	8.3	48%	.342	2.31	4.15	2.70	0.3
2011	*FLO*	*MLB*	*27*	*3*	*2*	*0*	*48*	*4*	*76*	*74*	*10*	*51*	*78*	*6.0*	*9.1*	*42%*	*.314*	*1.63*	*5.18*	*5.63*	*-0.4*

Ever since William James coined the term *multiverse* in 1895, the idea of parallel universes has permeated scientific thought as well as the arenas of cinema and fiction. These theoretical realms can house entire worlds and laws of physics we cannot comprehend, and can even act as alternate, mirrored dimensions of our own, where good is bad and Lindsay Lohan is sober. It's times like these when scientific theory is comforting, as somewhere out there is a universe where Dustin Richardson can throw pitches in the strike zone without watching them end up in the bleachers.

Tim Wakefield

Born: **8/2/1966** Age: **44**
Bats: R Throws: R Height: **6' 2"** Weight: **204**
Breakout: **5%** Improve: **11%** Collapse: **5%**
Attrition: **7%** MLB: **26%**

Comparables:
Kenny Rogers, Woody Williams, Tom Glavine (61)

YEAR	TEAM	LVL	AGE	W	L	SV	G	GS	IP	H	HR	BB	SO	EqBB9	EqSO9	GB%	BABIP	WHIP	ERA	FRA	WARP
2008	BOS	MLB	41	10	11	0	30	33	181	154	25	60	117	3.0	5.8	36%	.239	1.25	4.13	6.1	-0.3
2009	BOS	MLB	42	11	5	0	21	22	129^{2}	137	12	50	72	3.5	5.0	38%	.292	1.52	4.58	4.40	2.2
2010	BOS	MLB	43	4	10	0	32	19	140	153	19	36	84	2.3	5.4	39%	.288	1.39	5.34	6.17	-1.1
2011	*BOS*	*MLB*	*44*	*9*	*10*	*0*	*26*	*26*	*154*	*171*	*20*	*53*	*90*	*3.1*	*5.3*	*40%*	*.300*	*1.45*	*4.92*	*5.34*	*1.3*

In his penultimate campaign, Wakefield took over the top spots on Boston's all-time leaderboards for innings and games pitched. The knuckler isn't about to erase Roger Clemens from Boston's history, but when he retires, he will leave Red Sox Nation with far fuzzier memories, thanks to his 17 seasons in town. Wake had a part-time seat in the bullpen, but also made 19 starts when injuries to starters struck. His ERA was its highest relative to the league average since 1993, since his knuckler doesn't knuckle like it used to as a result of a recurring back injury. With R. A. Dickey taking up the knuckleball mantle, Wakefield can rest easy when his retirement begins this fall.

LINEOUTS

HITTERS

PLAYER	TEAM	LVL	AGE	PA	R	2B	3B	HR	RBI	BB	SO	SB-CS	AVG/OBP/SLG	TAv	BABIP	BRR	FRAA	WARP
OF B. Brentz	LOW	A-	21	285	27	14	4	5	39	21	76	0-0	.199/.260/.340	.233	.257	0.0	RF 1, CF 0	0.1
C D. Brown	PAW	AAA	28	268	31	19	0	7	28	27	66	1-0	.219/.306/.387	.241	.268	1.8	C 0, LF 0	0.7
	BOS	MLB	28	12	0	1	0	0	2	0	2	0-0	.250/.250/.333	.175	.300	0.0	C 0	-0.1
C K. Cash	BOS	MLB	32	68	1	1	0	0	1	6	16	0-0	.133/.221/.150	.147	.178	0.2	C 1	-0.3
	HOU	MLB	32	61	3	1	0	2	4	5	13	0-0	.204/.262/.333	.204	.220	0.3	C 0, P 0	0.0
C L. Exposito	PME	AA	23	538	64	39	1	11	92	55	92	0-0	.260/.342/.417	.264	.296	0.0	C 0	1.9
CF R. Fuentes*	GRN	A	19	429	54	15	5	5	44	27	93	27-1	.261/.322/.363	.249	.322	0.8	CF 1	0.9
3B J. Hannahan*	PAW	AAA	30	128	15	8	0	4	12	17	27	2-0	.255/.359/.436	.266	.304	0.6	3B 13, 2B 0	1.8
	TAC	AAA	30	262	31	9	1	5	32	34	55	1-0	.228/.332/.344	.245	.274	-1.4	2B 3, 3B 8	1.0
OF J. Hazelbaker*	GRN	A	22	523	80	29	10	13	64	62	140	37-10	.265/.363/.457	.297	.354	0.3	RF 0, CF -3	2.7
1B M. Lowell	BOS	MLB	36	244	23	13	0	5	26	23	34	0-0	.239/.307/.367	.245	.258	-2.5	1B 1, 3B 0	-0.3
C G. Molina	PAW	AAA	28	119	12	5	0	8	18	7	23	0-0	.241/.286/.500	.262	.235	-0.9	C -1	0.3
	BOS	MLB	28	7	1	0	0	0	0	0	2	0-0	.143/.143/.143	.125	.200	-0.1	C 0	0.0
INF N. Romero#	PAW	AAA	25	390	38	14	0	3	20	32	57	13-6	.246/.310/.311	.226	.279	-1.4	2B -4, SS 4	-0.2
	BOS	MLB	25	4	0	0	0	0	0	0	0	0-0	.000/.000/.000	-0.020	.000	0.0	1B 0, 2B 0	-0.1
1B R. Shealy	DUR	AAA	30	203	26	15	1	10	38	29	48	0-0	.238/.360/.512	.297	.267	-2.8	1B -1	0.6
	PAW	AAA	30	131	14	7	0	5	17	17	34	0-0	.219/.336/.412	.258	.267	0.8	1B 1	0.3
	BOS	MLB	30	7	0	0	0	0	0	0	2	0-0	.000/.000/.000	.013	.000	0.0	1B 0	-0.1
2B O. Tejeda	SLM	A+	20	550	76	32	5	11	69	32	96	17-7	.307/.346/.455	.290	.353	2.7	2B -4	2.9

Bryce Brentz put up massive numbers in college, but there are concerns that the 21-year-old doesn't have the body to hit for power professionally and needs aluminum to thrive. The Red Sox have cornered the market on backup catchers who make contact as often as SETI, but at least 28-year-old **Dusty Brown** has a strong defensive reputation and an even stronger throwing arm to make up for his misses. It took a hit-by-pitch with the bases loaded for **Kevin Cash** to pick up his lone RBI with the Sox. Cash is the epitome of defense-first catchers, but if he hangs around long enough, he can still finish with more career homers than Juan Pierre—Pierre is up by two in 5,543 more at-bats. **Carlos Delgado** missed most of the season with problems in his *non*-surgically repaired hip and was unable to help the Sox fill their first-base needs. **Luis Exposito** lacks the bat to catch every day or the glove to be a backup, and he's so nondescript that you couldn't pick him out of a lineup of one. **Reymond Fuentes** is still more tools than numbers. Just 19, the gifted athlete boasts plus-plus speed, a strong arm, and quality defense in center. He profiles as an old-school leadoff type whose batting average and defense would carry the day, though he may still develop slight power thanks to strong, quick wrists. The Padres should be happy with his amalgam of skills whether he develops the power or not. **Jack Hannahan** is 30 and has more organizations than years of major-league service behind him. Despite his ability to draw a walk, his bat is below average even by minor-league standards, but he can play plus defense at third for a team in a bind. **Jeremy Hazelbaker**'s numbers tell you everything you need to know—he's a low-average hitter with some power who could lead the world in strikeouts with enough playing time. Trade rumors swirled from spring through August, but **Mike Lowell** finished his career with Boston. Hip and thumb injuries encouraged an early exit for the 36-year-old, but Lowell racked up two World Series rings, four All-Star appearances, a Gold Glove reputation, and nearly 40 WARP over his 13 years in the majors. He's not one of *the* Molinas, though confusion over his genealogy may keep **Gustavo Molina** employed for at least a few more years. He does have the more familiar Molinas' defensive skills and strong arm, so it could be that those tools are tied to the name itself rather than the genetics. **Niuman Romero** has never hit in the minors—even by the low offensive standards of the shortstop position—but he can pick it anywhere in the infield. Assuming the Red Sox remain healthier than they were in 2010, they may never break the glass on Romero's case again. **Ryan Shealy**'s numbers in Triple-A with both Tampa Bay and Boston were unimpressive for a 30-year-old with 3,000-plus minor-league plate appearances. Boston cut him loose in August despite Kevin Youkilis's bad thumb and Mike Lowell's balky hip, which may mean the end of his major-league chances. Former shortstop **Oscar Tejeda** moved to second base, where he is a better defensive fit. At the plate, he acted more like a second baseman rather than the power hitter he isn't, which resulted in his top campaign to date, but he needs to whiff less or walk more to keep it up.

PITCHERS

PLAYER	TEAM	LVL	AGE	W	L	SV	IP	H	HR	BB	SO	EqBB9	EqSO9	GB%	BABIP	WHIP	ERA	FRA	WARP
D. Britton*	GRN	A	21	4	3	0	90^{1}	78	5	30	91	3.0	9.1	50%	.296	1.23	2.89	3.88	2.2
F. Cabrera	PAW	AAA	28	2	5	22	60^{2}	64	5	24	76	3.6	11.3	35%	.383	1.47	3.86	3.54	1.2
—	BOS	MLB	28	0	0	0	1^{1}	2	1	2	0	13.5	0.0	80%	.250	3.00	20.25	23.56	-0.2
M. Fox	ROC	AAA	27	6	9	0	122^{2}	124	17	50	104	3.7	7.6	35%	.304	1.43	3.96	4.60	1.8
—	BOS	MLB	27	0	0	0	1^{2}	4	0	1	0	5.4	0.0	22%	.444	3.00	10.80	5.59	0.0
—	MIN	MLB	27	0	0	0	5^{2}	4	0	1	0	1.6	0.0	40%	.200	0.88	3.18	5.01	0.0
J. Rice	PME	AA	24	2	2	12	58	44	6	29	69	4.5	10.7	37%	.282	1.36	2.48	2.77	1.3
S. Schoeneweis*	BOS	MLB	36	1	0	0	13^{2}	19	2	10	13	6.6	8.6	40%	.395	2.12	7.90	6.71	-0.3
D. Turpen	RIC	AA	23	0	0	0	50^{2}	55	4	19	42	3.4	7.5	59%	.323	1.48	4.09	4.32	0.4

Drake Britton missed most of 2009 thanks to Tommy John surgery, but displayed command and control at Single-A. Southpaws who can hit 95-96 are rare, and Boston is excited to see what Britton can do on a less restrictive pitch count another year removed from the procedure. If a pitching coach could halt **Fernando Cabrera**'s homeritis, his team would have a shutdown righty reliever in spite of ongoing control problems. **Matt Fox** made one emergency spot start before the Twins designated him for assignment. The Red Sox picked him up to reinforce their September relief corps, but that says more about their needs than Fox's upside. With his fringy stuff, his strikeout-to-walk rate won't cut it, as Boston learned during the season's final month. Short and stocky right-hander **Jason Rice** is a sleeper. He boasts above-average fastball velocity and command to go along with an aggressive approach, but he needs a better breaking ball to complement his primary offering. The long-ball problems that have plagued **Scott Schoeneweis**'s last four campaigns followed him to Boston, and the lefty no longer looks like even a passable LOOGY thanks to nearly as many free passes as punchouts over his last two seasons. Tommy John surgery ended **Junichi Tazawa**'s season before it began, and he may not return until mid-2011. At this point, Tazawa's future in Boston lies in middle relief, since the alternative is a back-end starter with an underwhelming fastball. The Red Sox dealt Ramon Ramirez for **Daniel Turpen**, who's also bound for the pen if he can survive the high minors. The righty sits 90-92 with sink on his fastball, and his changeup is more effective than his slider. His high BABIP allowed should drop with better defenses behind him, and he'll need that boost as a Rule 5 pick of the Yankees.

MANAGER: TERRY FRANCONA

YEAR	TEAM	W-L	Pythag +/-	Avg PC	100+ P	120+ P	QS	BQS	REL	REL w Zero R	IBB	Subs	PH	PH Avg	PH HR	SB2	CS2	SB3	CS3	SAC Att	SAC %	POS SAC	Squeeze	Swing	In Play
2009	BOS	95-67	0	99.1	80	3	80	3	463	309	24	41	84	.205	0	106	35	19	4	32	59.4%	17	0	131	97
2010	BOS	89-73	0	103.1	113	4	82	8	443	271	30	71	124	.265	2	56	14	11	2	38	76.3%	24	0	138	108

Francona's strength is his ability to stay engaged as a manager without simultaneously disrupting his players' performance. Boston's injury tsunami placed unaccustomed demands on the Red Sox skipper, and Francona found himself playing offensive and defensive matchups more often than he'd had to in the past; an elevated substitutions total reveals that he didn't stop pulling strings once the games had begun. A Sox club that should have been devastated by injuries won 89 games, thanks to Francona's willingness to utilize a large number of players he had never seen outside of spring training—not that his depleted roster left him much of a choice—and though there were situations in which he should have stuck with Darnell McDonald over Daniel Nava, or let Jed Lowrie pick up more at-bats rather than give them to Yamaico Navarro, it's hard to find a fault worth getting worked up over. No manager in today's game—or history—could have made Boston's bullpen any more effective than it was, though he could have eased up on the Daniel Bard pedal a little earlier than he did.

Chicago Cubs

For many teams, success and failure operate in tandem, as a cycle where teams swing from winning to rebuilding and back again. Now that the Piniella years are over, and the Cubs still haven't won a pennant in decades, it's fair to ask, Have the Cubs been moving through that rebuilding cycle quickly or slowly?

The organization has given the Wrigleyville faithful four pennant winners: the 1998 team that represented the pinnacle of the Lynch/MacPhail era, followed by the 2003 team, and then the 2007 and 2008 teams that have Jim Hendry's stamp on them. These broad strokes understate the measure of the club's competitiveness: in both 2001 and 2004, the Cubs came into September with clear opportunities to win the wild card, only to come up empty. To paint these as four- or five-year cycles would overstate the breadth of the swings. The last 13 seasons have involved a relatively quick series of short-term bids, quick tear-downs, and equally quick recoveries.

CUBS PROSPECTUS

2010 W-L: 75-87, 5th in NL Central

Pythag	.447	22nd	**Ballpark:** Wrigley Field (3-yr. PF: 105). Why watch from a rooftop when you can enjoy an obstructed view from inside?
RS/G	4.2	18th	
RA/G	4.7	6th	
TAv	.262	23rd	**2010:** Cubs complete two-year first-to-worst reversal as tumbleweeds round the basepaths
BRR	1.0	13th	
FRA	4.67	24th	
DER	-11.0	23rd	**2011:** Pieces of past and future Cubs clubs combine to form a potential present contender
DL	282	1st	
B-Age	29.4	21st	
P-Age	28.6	21st	**Action Items:** Bidding farewell to Fukudome, reordering a Rubik's Cube roster, fertilizing the farm
Salary	$146.6	3rd	
M$/MW	$5.17	29th	

So, before the Wrigleyville faithful despair of another half decade of rebuilding, keep in mind that today's Cubs are not the hapless and hopeless—or flat-out dull—Cubbie clubs of much of the 1970s or 1990s, or most of the 20th century when you get right down to it. They are instead very much creatures of today's competitive environment, building up their own opportunities, trying and failing, and quickly gearing up to take another chance.

If you take a gander at Table 1, you'll see what we're talking about, in that as frustratingly up-and-down as things have been, it hasn't been an utterly hopeless exercise. (For that, skip ahead to the Pirates chapter.) If the peaks of the Cubs' successes have generally been low, the troughs of their failures have been fairly brief.

That's not to say Cubs fans should be grateful for what they've gotten. Generally speaking, in each cycle, their latest collection of veterans makes its play, crashes, and is promptly replaced. You can note that the 2003-2004 team had one thing that set it apart, in that it boasted a tremendous trio of young pitchers with the sort of talent that could conjure up comparisons to the Braves of the 1990s. Well, at least Carlos Zambrano is still here.

However, where the 1990s were understandably rife with concerns that the organization was cynically exploiting willing ticket-buyers without making a full-faith effort, the recent past has supplied less cause for suspicion. Instead, the near future offers a shift from high-priced veterans to a strong farm system that speaks to the collective efforts of Hendry, scouting director Tim Wilken, farm director Oneri Fleita, and the rest of the player-development gang.

The two best things the Cubs' farm has going for it are the two things everyone wants: up-the-middle talent and power arms. Up the middle, their shortstop of the future just arrived, having rocketed through the system faster than anyone might have foreseen. Starlin Castro won't exactly make people forget Shawon Dunston—nobody's sighted a Starlin-O-Meter yet—but the comparisons to a young Edgar Renteria aren't unfair, because Castro may be the better all-around hitter while providing brilliant defense once he settles in.

But they also have a blue-chip center fielder to match in Brett Jackson, their top pick in 2009. In his full-season debut, Jackson thumped almost 60 extra-base hits, stole 30 bags, drew 70 walks, and played an excellent center. He reached Double-A, which means they can reasonably anticipate his arrival during the 2011 season. Adding Jackson to an outfield that features another Hendry pick, Tyler Colvin, who enjoyed

Table 1. Taking Turns: NL Competitive Ecology, 1998-2010

Team	50 wins	60 wins	70 wins	80 wins	90 wins	100 wins	Playoffs
Braves	-	-	2	3	4	4	9
Dodgers	-	-	2	8	3	-	4
Cardinals	-	-	2	5	4	2	7
Phillies	-	1	2	7	3	-	4
Astros	-	-	4	5	3	1	5
Giants	-	-	4	3	5	1	4
Mets	-	1	4	5	3	-	3
D'backs	1	2	3	3	3	1	4
Cubs	-	4	2	5	2	-	4
Marlins	1	1	5	5	1	-	1
Padres	-	3	4	4	2	-	3
Reds	-	2	7	2	2	-	1
Rockies	-	2	7	2	2	-	2
Brewers	1	3	5	3	1	-	1
ExNats	2	6	2	3	-	-	-
Pirates	1	8	4	-	-	-	-

his own breakout in 2010, seems like reasonable cause for pride, not to mention the basis of a contending lineup if Colvin's power wasn't just a rookie fluke.

On the mound, their bluest of blue-chippers also just arrived, and while Andrew Cashner's eventual role might not yet be set, his immediate value in a pen that leaned heavily on a late-game dynamic duo should be significant in 2011. But coming up behind Cashner are quality hurlers like Chris Archer, "Not the" Chris Carpenter, Trey McNutt, and Rafael Dolis, any one of whom would stand atop another organization's prospect wedding cake. They won't all wind up relieving, but together, they constitute the wave of guys who will be squeezing the Diamonds, Schlitters, or even the odd Samardzija out of the picture.

More broadly, there's depth beyond the causes for excitement at the top of the heap. The organization has the fruits of its Far East scouting effort to look forward to, especially shortstop Hak-Ju Lee, but its scouts mine Latin America effectively as well. The Cubs have in the system a gaggle of catchers who can throw and hit. The club also has a stack of infielders, several of whom might be its future answers at second or third base. The Cubs even get the benefit of the occasional surprise like outfielder Brandon Guyer, whose breakout at the plate might put him into the 2011 picture at some point as well. It is, in short, the kind of deep, multisourced farm system on which a successful, winning organization is built.

This might sound strange, especially when talking about the Cubs. In recent years, the more predictable theme has been one of money ill-spent at the major-league level; talking about the minors often began and ended with bringing up the expense to buy Jeff Samardzija away from football as a laugh line. That's because it fits in with a wider, well-rehearsed argument: if there's a dead horse that has been beaten beyond the point the bones were ground to powder, it's the monumental financial commitments that Hendry made in the Aughties, and how this potentially cripples the team's freedom of action.

That Hendry has spent an awful lot of other people's money is true. What's more, the expense has not guaranteed victory, but then the Yankees or Red Sox would give the man an "amen" to that bit of obviousness. The expense also hampers the team's freedom of action, but as the Cubs increasingly devote themselves to improving their farm, this limitation will have less and less impact. That's not to say that the expenses aren't daunting. Even disregarding the financial aid from the Mariners in helping to defray the expense of employing Carlos Silva, the eight-figure salaries of a half dozen Cubs make it hard to add a major player. And in delegating close to $20 million to players like Carlos Zambrano and Alfonso Soriano, the Cubs are paying for stars who cast neither heat nor light.

But this is to some extent a transient problem. After 2011, Kosuke Fukudome and Silva both go away, and the Cubs may well elect to buy out Aramis Ramirez's 2012 option if he doesn't produce his first good season since 2008. Ryan Dempster's 2012 option is his call, while Carlos Zambrano's 2013 option vests only if he gets Cy Young consideration—even with his stretch-run comeback, that's a stretch. The expensive legacies of the Piniella teams effectively go away within any four- or five-year cycle. If the Cubs are heading into another valley, it's going to be brief before giving way to the good stuff on the horizon.

One problem is whether Hendry has the freedom to convert any of these commitments, but to his credit, he's been creative in the past. Flipping Milton Bradley for Silva provided a remarkable return, but it also opened space and payroll flexibility to sign Marlon Byrd, another move to Hendry's credit, not so much because of Byrd's limited value in the heart of the order, but because he gave the Cubs a major-league center fielder. Lament the difficulty of stashing Fukudome or Zambrano on somebody else's roster, but in the past, Hendry has found a way to dig his way back out of the holes he's dug.

In the meantime, there's the less happy matter of sorting out who to keep and play. Consider the Cubs' four-headed outfield puzzle box. Byrd and Colvin can field, but Soriano and Fukudome not so much, and Byrd is the only one who can handle center. Colvin and Soriano provide power; Fukudome and Byrd do not. Only Fukudome gets on base reliably well, but he's the one of the four who can't run. You could derive some platoon benefits by sitting Byrd against righties and Fukudome against lefties, but then there is the problem of not really having somebody else who can play center. In the not-so-distant future, Jackson and perhaps Guyer will arrive, the former pushing Byrd out of center.

The ugly contretemps with the rotation is this: given the understandable reluctance anyone might have about what Silva or the Big Z might or might not deliver, the one starter Hendry might be able to extract value for by trading is the popular Ryan Dempster. Signed through 2011 with a $14 million player option for 2012, Dempster may represent more of a sure thing, especially after posting a career-best strikeout rate. But dealing the Cubs' most reliable starter could also be taken as a more personal betrayal; Dempster's comfort with the organization is reflected in his willingness to defer $3 million from his 2010 compensation.

Rather than think in those terms, Hendry instead went for one more throw of the dice, trading five prospects to the Rays in January for Matt Garza's next three seasons. Moving away from the AL East might serve the young right-hander especially well: his RA/9 last season against everyone but Boston and New York was 3.35 while notching 6.9 K/9. But facing the Yankee and Red Sox league-best lineups a third of the time, his RA/9 was 6.53. The Cubs can avoid worrying about that until they reach the World Series, but in the meantime, considering the package of kids dealt, Hendry did not seriously harm the future while finding a quality starter in a market short of them. As win-now moves go, it ranks among the winter's best.

Wait: win-now moves? The Cubs? It's not quite as improbable as it sounds, given the talent on the roster and on the way up, but it's also quite tangible when you're talking about the National League and particularly the NL Central, where nobody looks like a lock to win 90 games in any given season, let alone this one. Which would make this the shallowest trough yet, with a comeback balanced on the last, expensive remnants of the Piniella push, plus the front edge of the wave Hendry has patiently assembled on the farm. It's the sort of speedy turnaround that represents a better platform from which to project lasting success and an end to the cycling.

HITTERS

Jeff Baker **UT**

Born: **6/21/1981** Age: **30**
Bats: R Throws: R Height: **6' 2"** Weight: **210**
Breakout: **0%** Improve: **28%** Collapse: **12%**
Attrition: **7%** MLB: **78%**
Comparables:
Luis Terrero, Sean Berry, Dave Hollins (73)

YEAR	TEAM	LVL	AGE	PA	R	2B	3B	HR	RBI	BB	SO	SB	CS	AVG/OBP/SLG	TAv	BABIP	BRR	FRAA	WARP
2008	COL	MLB	27	333	55	22	1	12	48	26	85	4	0	.268/.321/.468	.256	.325	-0.1	2B 1, 1B 1	0.8
2009	CHN	MLB	28	224	27	15	1	4	21	17	46	0	0	.305/.362/.448	.285	.374	-1.6	2B 4, 3B 1	1.5
2009	COL	MLB	28	24	0	0	1	0	3	1	7	1	0	.130/.167/.217	.098	.188	0.0	2B 0, 3B 0	-0.3
2010	CHN	MLB	29	224	29	13	2	4	21	16	50	1	0	.272/.326/.413	.262	.340	-0.4	3B 4, 2B -1	0.8
2011	*CHN*	*MLB*	*30*	*321*	*38*	*17*	*1*	*8*	*37*	*26*	*71*	*2*	*0*	*.258/.319/.413*	*.257*	*.309*	*0.0*	*2B 1, 3B 1*	*0.8*

The somewhat simplistic argument that platoon value is flat across the broad population of ballplayers doesn't do very well when it comes to describing the outsized platoon performance of a guy like Baker, who mashed lefties at a .350/.395/.550 clip last year. That's not much different from his .308/.363/.545 career mark, numbers accumulated during his age-27-29 seasons—or the tail end of a normal peak stretch, for a player with what might be the extreme form of a particular virtue. With value at all four corners plus second base, Baker is a better real-world asset than a bauble for your fantasy team: an extremely useful bench player, especially platooning with Fukudome or Colvin in right, DeWitt at second, or first baseman Carlos Pena.

Darwin Barney **INF**

Born: **11/8/1985** Age: **25**
Bats: R Throws: R Height: **5' 10"** Weight: **180**
Breakout: **4%** Improve: **15%** Collapse: **9%**
Attrition: **23%** MLB: **35%**
Comparables:
Gregorio Petit, Chin-lung Hu, Omar Quintanilla (78)

YEAR	TEAM	LVL	AGE	PA	R	2B	3B	HR	RBI	BB	SO	SB	CS	AVG/OBP/SLG	TAv	BABIP	BRR	FRAA	WARP
2008	DAY	A+	22	484	52	25	4	3	54	39	59	7	3	.271/.331/.367	.256	.300	-0.2	SS 13	2.9
2009	TEN	AA	23	283	30	12	0	3	32	23	33	5	1	.319/.364/.402	.270	.344	-0.8	SS 1, 2B 0	1.4
2009	IOW	AAA	23	230	25	12	1	0	17	13	32	4	1	.264/.300/.330	.234	.304	1.7	SS 5, 2B -3	0.5
2010	IOW	AAA	24	511	69	24	4	2	49	23	52	11	3	.299/.331/.378	.251	.328	-2.4	SS 1, 2B -1	1.3
2010	CHN	MLB	24	85	11	4	0	0	2	6	12	0	0	.241/.294/.291	.221	.284	2.5	SS 1, 2B 0	0.4
2011	*CHN*	*MLB*	*25*	*529*	*53*	*23*	*2*	*3*	*44*	*28*	*75*	*5*	*2*	*.259/.295/.329*	*.222*	*.292*	*0.0*	*SS 4, 2B -1*	*0.3*

If this were the 1970s and not the Aughties, folks might look at Barney and see what he'd have been back then: a decent prospect at shortstop, a good chip off the Tommy Veryzer block. But look beyond the defense, and you have a hitter with no power or patience and merely modest contact skills. He could wind up starting for a bad team or be carried as a starter on a club with seven or eight good players, but there's no time like the present, and his Cubs future is stillborn with Castro already in place.

Marlon Byrd **CF**

Born: **8/30/1977** Age: **33**
Bats: R Throws: R Height: **6' 0"** Weight: **225**
Breakout: **0%** Improve: **32%** Collapse: **5%**
Attrition: **4%** MLB: **96%**

Comparables:
Felipe Alou, Jackie Robinson, Gary Matthews (68)

YEAR	TEAM	LVL	AGE	PA	R	2B	3B	HR	RBI	BB	SO	SB	CS	AVG/OBP/SLG	TAv	BABIP	BRR	FRAA	WARP
2008	TEX	MLB	30	462	70	28	4	10	53	46	62	7	2	.298/.379/.462	.298	.328	-2.9	CF 4, RF 0	2.9
2009	TEX	MLB	31	599	66	43	2	20	89	32	98	8	4	.283/.329/.479	.282	.308	-5.9	CF -11, LF 0	1.4
2010	CHN	MLB	32	630	84	39	2	12	66	31	98	5	1	.293/.346/.429	.280	.335	-4.2	CF 6	3.1
2011	*CHN*	*MLB*	*33*	*549*	*66*	*31*	*2*	*13*	*64*	*37*	*89*	*6*	*2*	*.275/.334/.421*	*.268*	*.308*	*-0.3*	*CF -2, LF 1*	*1.6*

In the broad strokes, you might figure that Byrd lost much of his value when he left Texas—and his .200 career isolated power (ISO) in Arlington—behind. To his credit, he didn't try to be the same hitter in Chicago, cutting down his stroke, delivering more contact but less power, putting more balls on the ground, and winding up roughly as valuable at the plate while playing a competent center. Unfortunately, there are problems. First, he didn't slug .400 against right-handers, and that makes for a tough everyday choice for the heart of a big-league lineup. He also hit just .275/.340/.369 after June, which suggests that the new approach only went so far before the league caught up to him. Now that he's past 33 and heading into the more expensive portion of his back-loaded contract ($12 million over the next two years), it isn't hard to anticipate this deal going from looking good after one year to bad on the back end.

Welington Castillo **C**

Born: **4/24/1987** Age: **24**
Bats: R Throws: R Height: **5' 10"** Weight: **200**
Breakout: **1%** Improve: **5%** Collapse: **6%**
Attrition: **10%** MLB: **21%**

Comparables:
Alex Avila, Jose Lobaton, Angel Salome (78)

YEAR	TEAM	LVL	AGE	PA	R	2B	3B	HR	RBI	BB	SO	SB	CS	AVG/OBP/SLG	TAv	BABIP	BRR	FRAA	WARP
2008	DAY	A+	21	126	15	8	0	0	12	4	23	1	0	.273/.302/.339	.222	.333	-0.9	C -1	-0.2
2008	TEN	AA	21	214	23	11	0	4	24	14	50	0	0	.298/.369/.414	.260	.377	-2.6	C 0	0.6
2009	TEN	AA	22	355	27	18	0	11	42	17	79	1	0	.241/.287/.393	.229	.282	-4.4	C 2	0.1
2010	IOW	AAA	23	266	35	17	1	13	58	19	58	0	0	.255/.323/.498	.261	.273	0.0	C -2	1.1
2010	CHN	MLB	23	21	3	4	0	1	5	1	7	0	0	.300/.333/.650	.346	.417	-0.2	C 0	0.3
2011	*CHN*	*MLB*	*24*	*330*	*34*	*16*	*0*	*10*	*37*	*15*	*80*	*0*	*0*	*.230/.270/.383*	*.225*	*.272*	*0.0*	*C -1*	*0.1*

If the Cubs shop Soto, Castillo is first in line to take his place, but only just; as his 2009 line reveals, his career has not been one of inexorable progress. Castillo's strengths are straightforward enough: he's young, he has bopped a bit, and he's strong-armed, thwarting 39 percent of opposing stolen-base attempts at Iowa. There are negatives, though, like his sloppy receiving skills and his struggle to hit quality breaking stuff. What's more, last year's improvements didn't come in prospect-laden Double-A, but against the older dead-enders that hold on at Triple-A. Still, we're talking about a young catcher with some power and a strong arm, so a Miguel Olivo–like upside isn't unrealistic.

Starlin Castro **SS**

Born: **3/24/1990** Age: **21**
Bats: R Throws: R Height: **6' 0"** Weight: **190**
Breakout: **5%** Improve: **28%** Collapse: **2%**
Attrition: **11%** MLB: **42%**

Comparables:
Elvis Andrus, Alcides Escobar, Roberto Alomar (70)

YEAR	TEAM	LVL	AGE	PA	R	2B	3B	HR	RBI	BB	SO	SB	CS	AVG/OBP/SLG	TAv	BABIP	BRR	FRAA	WARP
2008	CUB	Rk	18	212	32	11	5	3	22	14	33	5	4	.311/.368/.464	.293	.358	1.5	SS 8, 2B 8	3.2
2009	DAY	A+	19	384	44	17	3	3	35	19	41	22	11	.302/.339/.391	.273	.327	0.8	SS 14	3.4
2009	TEN	AA	19	157	10	6	3	0	17	11	18	6	0	.292/.338/.375	.264	.328	-1.5	SS 3	0.8
2010	TEN	AA	20	120	19	8	5	1	20	9	11	4	5	.376/.425/.569	.331	.404	-0.8	SS 0	1.2
2010	CHN	MLB	20	506	53	31	5	3	41	29	71	10	8	.300/.344/.408	.261	.343	1.1	SS -2	1.8
2011	*CHN*	*MLB*	*21*	*460*	*51*	*24*	*4*	*4*	*47*	*23*	*65*	*12*	*6*	*.278/.314/.379*	*.245*	*.312*	*-0.9*	*SS 6, 2B 1*	*1.5*

Credit the Cubs for their aggressive handling, because if Triple-A is where organizational soldiers go gray, the best prospects observe and deserve their own timetables. In 2009 Castro skipped both short- and full-season Low-A, earned a late-season spin at Double-A, and in 2010 logged a second month there to demonstrate that he had nothing left to prove. He's not a mere slapper, so skip the mournful, perfunctory "his BABIP is too high" bleating, because he has the contact ability and plate coverage to keep hitting for good averages. Whether the walks ever come, or how much power he'll add (especially against righties after a .086 ISO last year), makes for happy possibilities, not outright probabilities; still, the growth potential for a 21-year-old sophomore is extraordinary. Two particular areas to follow will be his growth as a fielder and as a baserunner; the arm and range are both there for him to become a premium defender, and he has the foot speed to steal 20 bases per year. It's all a matter of reps and aptitude, and Castro is credited with an excellent reputation for his work ethic. Expect greatness.

Robinson Chirinos C

Born: 6/5/1984 Age: 27
Bats: R Throws: R Height: 6' 1" Weight: 195
Breakout: 1% Improve: 30% Collapse: 9%
Attrition: 20% MLB: 69%

Comparables:
Chris Iannetta, Ryan Doumit, Scott Hairston (71)

YEAR	TEAM	LVL	AGE	PA	R	2B	3B	HR	RBI	BB	SO	SB	CS	AVG/OBP/SLG	TAv	BABIP	BRR	FRAA	WARP
2008	DAY	A+	24	150	20	4	2	5	18	26	21	2	1	.283/.440/.475	.311	.296	-0.1	C 0, 2B 4	1.6
2008	TEN	AA	24	117	12	7	3	0	8	10	18	0	0	.243/.299/.369	.249	.281	0.7	3B -4, SS 0	-0.1
2009	DAY	A+	25	265	39	13	5	11	47	35	40	2	2	.300/.408/.546	.335	.318	-0.8	C 0, 1B 0	3.0
2010	TEN	AA	26	332	58	25	0	17	68	44	39	2	5	.327/.428/.598	.342	.323	-1.5	C 1	4.0
2010	IOW	AAA	26	57	9	4	0	3	10	2	8	0	0	.364/.474/.600	.318	.386	0.2	C 1	0.7
2011	*CHN*	*MLB*	*27*	*330*	*43*	*16*	*2*	*12*	*43*	*36*	*53*	*1*	*1*	*.267/.353/.463*	*.284*	*.282*	*-0.1*	*C 0, 3B -1*	*1.9*

The Venezuelan infielder was eight years into his gig as an organizational soldier when the Cubs decided to move him behind the plate in 2008, giving him a career path that might now land him in the bigs. (They did likewise with Steve Clevenger, his catching partner at Double-A, and received a pair of interesting backstops for their efforts.) Chirinos has made progress in mastering the finer points of receiving and last year gunned down 32 percent of stolen-base attempts. Good-hit backups are a rare enough commodity behind the plate, so pegging his future as that of a second-stringer sells him short. But keep in mind that he has spent parts of the last four years at Double-A—take last season's bopping with a few grains of salt as he moves to the Rays in the Garza deal.

Tyler Colvin OF

Born: 9/5/1985 Age: 25
Bats: L Throws: L Height: 6' 3" Weight: 210
Breakout: 7% Improve: 32% Collapse: 4%
Attrition: 21% MLB: 60%

Comparables:
Mark Teahen, Nate Schierholtz, Bronson Sardinha (73)

YEAR	TEAM	LVL	AGE	PA	R	2B	3B	HR	RBI	BB	SO	SB	CS	AVG/OBP/SLG	TAv	BABIP	BRR	FRAA	WARP
2008	TEN	AA	22	598	67	27	11	14	80	44	101	7	4	.256/.311/.424	.260	.283	5.3	LF 5, CF 3	2.3
2009	DAY	A+	23	128	18	5	2	1	10	13	27	1	1	.250/.328/.357	.245	.310	2.1	LF 0, CF 0	0.1
2009	TEN	AA	23	362	55	15	7	15	54	18	64	5	1	.289/.323/.509	.287	.311	2.5	RF -3, LF -2	1.4
2009	CHN	MLB	23	20	1	0	0	0	2	2	5	0	0	.177/.250/.177	.175	.231	0.3	CF 2	0.1
2010	CHN	MLB	24	395	59	18	5	20	56	30	100	6	1	.254/.314/.500	.279	.295	1.0	RF 2, LF -1	1.4
2011	*CHN*	*MLB*	*25*	*500*	*57*	*22*	*4*	*17*	*63*	*31*	*107*	*4*	*1*	*.245/.292/.424*	*.246*	*.276*	*-0.1*	*RF -2, LF -1*	*-0.1*

Is Colvin baseball's answer to the fish taco? In his way, he's an interesting collection of unlikely elements that make for a surprising treat in concert. He's too athletic to be a mere slug, providing good speed on the bases and a fly-ball stroke that limits GIDPs, the arm for right field if not the range for center, and less patience than you'd like but more than he used to have. Whether he's an interesting oddity or a burgeoning star will depend on his ability to keep delivering homers at a steep clip; his home run/fly ball rate was up in the same stratosphere as those for guys named Pujols, Konerko, and Papi. If he can do that and play a great right field, he'll deserve an everyday gig, even while exacerbating the team's OBP problem. The near tragedy of his being speared by the barrel of Welington Castillo's shattered maple bat shouldn't be an issue for him in camp.

Blake DeWitt 2B

Born: 8/20/1985 Age: 25
Bats: L Throws: R Height: 5' 11" Weight: 175
Breakout: 5% Improve: 42% Collapse: 4%
Attrition: 21% MLB: 84%

Comparables:
Roberto Alomar, Jim Gilliam, Warren Morris (76)

YEAR	TEAM	LVL	AGE	PA	R	2B	3B	HR	RBI	BB	SO	SB	CS	AVG/OBP/SLG	TAv	BABIP	BRR	FRAA	WARP
2008	LVG	AAA	22	123	14	4	2	4	18	10	14	1	0	.306/.366/.487	.282	.316	-1.8	2B -4, 3B 1	0.1
2008	LAN	MLB	22	421	43	13	2	9	52	45	68	3	0	.264/.344/.383	.266	.297	3.2	3B 13, 2B -3	2.7
2009	ABQ	AAA	23	415	65	22	9	7	47	48	47	2	2	.258/.352/.426	.253	.278	2.1	3B -6, 2B -4	0.0
2009	LAN	MLB	23	53	4	3	0	2	4	3	7	0	0	.204/.245/.388	.227	.195	-0.1	3B 0, SS 0	-0.1
2010	LAN	MLB	24	292	29	15	4	1	30	30	49	2	2	.270/.349/.371	.266	.325	-0.9	2B -2	0.6
2010	CHN	MLB	24	204	18	9	1	4	22	17	37	1	0	.250/.314/.375	.243	.290	0.7	2B 0, 3B 0	0.2
2011	*CHN*	*MLB*	*25*	*503*	*58*	*22*	*4*	*9*	*50*	*51*	*74*	*3*	*1*	*.253/.330/.383*	*.252*	*.280*	*-0.1*	*2B -3, 3B 1*	*0.7*

Picked up in the Theriot trade, DeWitt faces a future no more certain with the Cubs than it was with the Dodgers. Though young he is enough to have a career and is sufficiently adaptable to give the keystone a shot, his work at second remains rough. It's nice that he's walking roughly 10 percent of the time, but for his defense to make him a genuine asset, some of the power he delivered as a 20- and 21-year-old prospect in the minors really does need to show up at some point. In the meantime, he provides a left-handed break from the wall of right-handed hitters in the lineup, but he will need to show some early progress at the plate and in the field in 2011 to hold off a cresting wave of organizational infielders.

Ryan Flaherty INF

Born: 7/27/1986 Age: 24
Bats: L Throws: R Height: 6' 3" Weight: 220
Breakout: 5% Improve: 11% Collapse: 4%
Attrition: 16% MLB: 24%

Comparables:
Chris Johnson, Neil Walker, Daniel Murphy (76)

YEAR	TEAM	LVL	AGE	PA	R	2B	3B	HR	RBI	BB	SO	SB	CS	AVG/OBP/SLG	TAv	BABIP	BRR	FRAA	WARP
2008	BOI	A-	21	244	38	19	2	8	26	24	51	4	2	.297/.369/.511	.312	.354	1.7	SS 1	2.5
2009	PEO	A	22	551	83	24	5	20	81	52	100	7	6	.274/.343/.465	.295	.303	-6.0	2B 8, SS 0	3.5
2010	DAY	A+	23	468	65	34	3	9	63	41	73	6	3	.288/.350/.448	.295	.322	2.0	3B 1, 2B 4	3.6
2010	TEN	AA	23	83	9	2	0	1	8	10	12	1	0	.183/.289/.254	.209	.200	-0.9	2B -3, 3B -1	-0.7
2011	*CHN*	*MLB*	*24*	*449*	*48*	*21*	*1*	*12*	*49*	*31*	*94*	*1*	*1*	*.240/.291/.385*	*.235*	*.278*	*-0.1*	*2B 3, SS 1*	*0.5*

Pushing Flaherty up to Double-A in his second full season as a pro made sense, given his Vanderbilt college-ball pedigree and his age. Unfortunately, his ride on the fast train shot right off the rails, as a bad first month got him demoted to Daytona, where he took turns with D. J. LeMahieu manning second and third. The power that is supposed to be his calling card wasn't as evident when he was no longer beating up on less advanced players in Low-A, and he didn't shine in the Arizona Fall League. A 2011 breakthrough is a must if he's going to challenge DeWitt for the second-base job rather than join him in a pileup of Fontenot wannabes. If there's solace to be taken, it's that Brandon Guyer rode this same roller coaster in 2009 and rebounded to shine in Tennessee in 2010.

Kosuke Fukudome **RF**

Born: **4/26/1977** Age: **34**
Bats: L Throws: R Height: **6' 0"** Weight: **190**
Breakout: **1%** Improve: **31%** Collapse: **8%**
Attrition: **18%** MLB: **97%**

Comparables:
Bobby Murcer, Chet Lemon, Andy Pafko (79)

YEAR	TEAM	LVL	AGE	PA	R	2B	3B	HR	RBI	BB	SO	SB	CS	AVG/OBP/SLG	TAv	BABIP	BRR	FRAA	WARP
2008	CHN	MLB	31	590	78	25	3	10	58	81	104	12	4	.258/.358/.379	.264	.302	2.7	RF 2, CF -2	1.4
2009	CHN	MLB	32	603	79	38	5	11	54	93	112	6	10	.259/.373/.421	.277	.307	0.2	CF -9, RF 10	2.7
2010	CHN	MLB	33	429	45	20	2	13	44	64	67	7	8	.263/.368/.439	.283	.284	-0.1	RF 1	1.7
2011	*CHN*	*MLB*	*34*	*541*	*65*	*25*	*2*	*11*	*52*	*80*	*92*	*10*	*6*	*.248/.356/.387*	*.266*	*.280*	*-1.2*	*RF 4, CF -3*	*1.3*

In an outfield overstocked with players equipped with a mismatched jumble of things they do and don't do, Fukudome is the one with the fewest virtues, but his one real strength, a willingness to take a free pass, makes him virtually unique on the roster. You might think that this would make him an indispensable cog in a lineup that ranked 14th in the league in TAv and walk rate, but a slow, low-powered corner-pasture-prowler with little defensive value has a way of getting singled out for the skills he lacks. Add his $13.5 million salary and no-trade protection, season with one dash of bitters and a squeeze of regret; serve cold.

Sam Fuld **CF**

Born: **11/20/1981** Age: **29**
Bats: L Throws: L Height: **5' 10"** Weight: **185**
Breakout: **0%** Improve: **39%** Collapse: **5%**
Attrition: **12%** MLB: **76%**

Comparables:
David DeJesus, Skip Schumaker, Joe Inglett (67)

YEAR	TEAM	LVL	AGE	PA	R	2B	3B	HR	RBI	BB	SO	SB	CS	AVG/OBP/SLG	TAv	BABIP	BRR	FRAA	WARP
2008	TEN	AA	26	394	47	16	3	5	48	50	40	7	8	.271/.368/.381	.260	.291	-0.8	CF -3, RF 0	0.8
2008	IOW	AAA	26	84	13	5	0	1	4	8	12	3	2	.246/.298/.362	.249	.262	0.3	CF -1, RF 1	0.1
2009	IOW	AAA	27	368	59	17	10	2	33	38	24	22	5	.281/.356/.413	.271	.296	4.4	CF 3	2.1
2009	CHN	MLB	27	115	16	6	1	1	2	17	10	2	1	.299/.409/.412	.303	.326	1.3	CF -2, LF 4	1.1
2010	IOW	AAA	28	438	69	15	9	4	27	66	37	0	0	.272/.384/.394	.280	.290	0.0	CF 14	3.6
2010	CHN	MLB	28	31	3	1	0	0	3	3	5	0	0	.143/.226/.179	.140	.174	-0.1	CF 3, LF 0	0.0
2011	*CHN*	*MLB*	*29*	*471*	*52*	*20*	*4*	*3*	*38*	*55*	*52*	*13*	*5*	*.251/.338/.345*	*.246*	*.274*	*-0.4*	*CF 2, LF 0*	*0.8*

If Colvin's breakthrough put a big dent in Nady's utility to the Cubs' outfield, it slammed shut Fuld's already narrow window of opportunity to stick around as the last man on the bench. Now heading into his age-29 season, Fuld is a fifth outfielder candidate playing in a competitive environment where few clubs make room for one. If there is anything to the suggestion that teams are favoring defense in their lineups and their outfields, that would eliminate a lot of need to carry a pinch-runner and defensive replacement. Even so, there ought to be something for a guy who walks 15 percent of the time, runs, and plays center, and perhaps Fuld will find it in Tampa, a team that appreciates versatile reserves.

Brandon Guyer **OF**

Born: **1/28/1986** Age: **25**
Bats: R Throws: R Height: **6' 1"** Weight: **210**
Breakout: **1%** Improve: **21%** Collapse: **10%**
Attrition: **22%** MLB: **47%**

Comparables:
Chris Pettit, Tommy Davis, Ben Francisco (74)

YEAR	TEAM	LVL	AGE	PA	R	2B	3B	HR	RBI	BB	SO	SB	CS	AVG/OBP/SLG	TAv	BABIP	BRR	FRAA	WARP
2008	PEO	A	22	350	51	27	3	14	38	19	63	20	7	.269/.343/.499	.294	.291	2.2	LF 5, CF -1	2.4
2009	DAY	A+	23	297	39	16	3	2	32	24	34	22	2	.347/.418/.453	.318	.380	-0.4	RF -4, CF -2	1.7
2009	TEN	AA	23	210	24	12	2	1	14	11	34	8	5	.191/.238/.289	.216	.220	-5.0	CF -5, LF 2	-1.2
2010	TEN	AA	24	436	74	40	6	15	61	28	53	27	4	.333/.392/.575	.331	.347	0.9	LF 13, RF -1	5.3
2011	*CHN*	*MLB*	*25*	*431*	*49*	*26*	*2*	*10*	*51*	*21*	*71*	*17*	*4*	*.259/.300/.412*	*.250*	*.285*	*0.5*	*CF -4, LF 3*	*0.1*

Guyer earned recognition as the minor-league system's player of the year after overcoming an early shoulder injury to help the Smokies win a franchise-record 86 games while leading the Southern League in slugging percentage. He can thank an especially blistering second half in which he hit .424/.459/.724, which—cast against early-career struggles with shoulder and elbow problems and a return engagement at Double-A—makes one wonder if this was a true breakout or an older player beating up on familiar competition. Some torrid hitting in winter ball argues for "breakout." His past injuries are the downside of an aggressive mentality that reflects his past gridiron experience, and they contribute to the concern that he'll always be limited to a corner. There's no arguing with the other tools: quick hands, excellent plate coverage and pitch recognition, and speed on the bases. The truth will out in the Rays organization, which may have an open corner spot in Tampa to start the season.

Koyie Hill C

Born: **3/9/1979** Age: **32**
Bats: **S** Throws: **R** Height: **6' 0"** Weight: **190**
Breakout: **4%** Improve: **37%** Collapse: **14%**
Attrition: **32%** MLB: **85%**

Comparables:
Don Slaught, Joe Nolan, Robby Hammock (83)

YEAR	TEAM	LVL	AGE	PA	R	2B	3B	HR	RBI	BB	SO	SB	CS	AVG/OBP/SLG	TAv	BABIP	BRR	FRAA	WARP
2008	IOW	AAA	29	405	54	24	2	17	64	40	74	3	2	.278/.353/.497	.284	.303	0.3	C -1, 1B -1	2.6
2008	CHN	MLB	29	22	0	1	0	0	1	0	12	0	0	.095/.091/.143	.085	.200	-0.1	C 0	-0.3
2009	CHN	MLB	30	284	26	12	2	2	24	27	78	0	0	.237/.310/.324	.228	.330	0.1	C -1, 3B 0	0.1
2010	CHN	MLB	31	231	18	13	1	1	17	12	61	1	0	.214/.251/.298	.205	.287	2.7	C 1, 3B 0	0.1
2011	*CHN*	*MLB*	*32*	*302*	*30*	*14*	*1*	*5*	*28*	*24*	*72*	*1*	*0*	*.229/.288/.342*	*.222*	*.284*	*0.0*	*C 0, 1B 0*	*0.0*

On the list of offensive seasons delivered by a switch-hitting catcher, Hill's 2010 was the sixth-worst in the Retrosheet-era database among those with 200 PAs in a season, behind Alan Ashby's 1979, Buck Rodgers' 1968, Rick Sweet's 1983, and Matt Walbeck's 1994 and 1996 campaigns. Sweet and Rodgers were done, but Ashby and Walbeck had long years ahead of them, so not even this level of failure guarantees future flailing. In the end, if a dude can catch, people will call, and Hill can catch. In a perfect world, he'd be paired up with someone who can handle 120 starts, but Soto hasn't gotten there in either of the last two seasons.

Brett Jackson OF

Born: **8/2/1988** Age: **22**
Bats: **L** Throws: **R** Height: **6' 2"** Weight: **210**
Breakout: **0%** Improve: **20%** Collapse: **3%**
Attrition: **18%** MLB: **43%**

Comparables:
Jordan Schafer, Adam Jones, Justin Upton (76)

YEAR	TEAM	LVL	AGE	PA	R	2B	3B	HR	RBI	BB	SO	SB	CS	AVG/OBP/SLG	TAv	BABIP	BRR	FRAA	WARP
2009	PEO	A	20	123	28	5	1	7	17	11	32	11	1	.295/.398/.545	.325	.356	0.9	CF 4	1.6
2009	BOI	A-	20	105	13	1	1	1	15	17	20	2	1	.330/.448/.398	.330	.418	0.5	CF -6	0.5
2010	DAY	A+	21	306	56	19	8	6	38	42	63	12	6	.316/.425/.517	.336	.395	5.2	CF 5	4.2
2010	TEN	AA	21	300	49	17	6	7	30	36	73	17	4	.269/.363/.463	.286	.339	1.9	RF -4, CF 2	1.0
2011	*CHN*	*MLB*	*22*	*423*	*49*	*19*	*3*	*10*	*45*	*44*	*108*	*13*	*4*	*.246/.327/.398*	*.256*	*.311*	*0.0*	*CF -5, RF -1*	*0.1*

A tasty selection out of Cal at the end of the first round in 2009, Jackson is the complete package, matching tremendous production with drool-worthy tools. He's a true center fielder who can cover the gaps, uncork laser-like throws, run, hit for power, draw walks, hammer breaking stuff . . . basically, he's one of those prospects who might finally knock sliced bread off that top berth for best thing. He's also the one Cubs outfield prospect moving up fast without stumbling, earning a promotion to Double-A at the end of June in his first pro season. Concerns about his strikeout rate aren't entirely unfounded, but whiffing at a 24 percent clip in Double-A isn't deadly. The conservative evaluation is that Jackson will be knocking at the door for the job in center by 2012, but his fast-rising trajectory doesn't seem to be losing any helium.

Hak-Ju Lee SS

Born: **11/4/1990** Age: **20**
Bats: **L** Throws: **R** Height: **6' 2"** Weight: **170**
Breakout: **2%** Improve: **5%** Collapse: **0%**
Attrition: **2%** MLB: **6%**

Comparables:
Edgar Renteria, Elvis Andrus, Roberto Alomar (73)

YEAR	TEAM	LVL	AGE	PA	R	2B	3B	HR	RBI	BB	SO	SB	CS	AVG/OBP/SLG	TAv	BABIP	BRR	FRAA	WARP
2009	BOI	A-	18	303	55	14	2	2	33	31	50	25	8	.330/.393/.421	.302	.386	2.9	SS 12	3.8
2010	PEO	A	19	546	82	22	4	1	39	49	86	22	4	.283/.350/.351	.265	.332	2.7	SS 9	3.4
2011	*CHN*	*MLB*	*20*	*425*	*40*	*17*	*2*	*2*	*33*	*27*	*88*	*11*	*3*	*.240/.284/.307*	*.212*	*.295*	*0.0*	*SS 11*	*0.6*

Signed in June 2008 as yet another quality product of the Cubs' aggressive Pacific push in player development, the Korean teen fulfilled expectations in his full-season debut. Lee is a flashy defender in that he has both the range and the shoulder-mounted cannon you would expect from budding greatness, but he still needs reps to become a truly brilliant defender. He's likely the keeper in the Rays' take for Garza. Factor in his plus speed and aptitude for stealing bases, a decent batting eye, and good plate coverage, and he's one to patiently wait for as he moves slowly up the chain.

D. J. LeMahieu 2B

Born: **7/13/1988** Age: **22**
Bats: **R** Throws: **R** Height: **6' 4"** Weight: **185**
Breakout: **0%** Improve: **0%** Collapse: **0%**
Attrition: **1%** MLB: **2%**

Comparables:
Dalton Jones, Harvey Kuenn, Sean Burroughs (74)

YEAR	TEAM	LVL	AGE	PA	R	2B	3B	HR	RBI	BB	SO	SB	CS	AVG/OBP/SLG	TAv	BABIP	BRR	FRAA	WARP
2009	PEO	A	20	175	19	4	2	0	31	13	23	2	2	.313/.371/.363	.260	.360	0.2	SS 2, 2B -2	0.5
2010	DAY	A+	21	595	62	24	5	2	72	29	61	15	7	.315/.341/.387	.266	.340	-1.1	2B 4, 3B 4	2.4
2011	*CHN*	*MLB*	*22*	*394*	*40*	*15*	*2*	*2*	*35*	*15*	*58*	*4*	*2*	*.267/.291/.340*	*.223*	*.302*	*-0.1*	*2B 1, SS 0*	*-0.1*

The Cubs' latest Cajun infielder out of LSU, LeMahieu has fine contact-hitting skills, but he struggled to do much beyond thwacking singles, keeping his ceiling low. Admittedly, his campaign at Daytona was his full-season debut, but balanced against the hope that he might deliver more power is the concern over what he'll do hitting toward better infielders at higher levels. He's already a double-play risk and not gifted with much speed, and absent any patience, his bat will only profile at second. His poor range at short is already pushing him in that direction.

Xavier Nady **OF**

Born: **11/14/1978** Age: **32**
Bats: **R** Throws: **R** Height: **6' 0"** Weight: **180**
Breakout: **2%** Improve: **35%** Collapse: **5%**
Attrition: **13%** MLB: **86%**

Comparables:
Phil Nevin, Don Money, Felix Mantilla (74)

YEAR	TEAM	LVL	AGE	PA	R	2B	3B	HR	RBI	BB	SO	SB	CS	AVG/OBP/SLG	TAv	BABIP	BRR	FRAA	WARP
2008	NYA	MLB	29	247	27	11	0	12	40	14	48	1	1	.268/.320/.474	.274	.290	-0.1	LF -2, RF -1	0.6
2008	PIT	MLB	29	360	50	26	1	13	57	25	55	1	0	.330/.383/.535	.308	.363	-0.7	RF 0	2.3
2009	NYA	MLB	30	29	4	4	0	0	2	1	6	0	0	.286/.310/.429	.238	.364	0.5	RF 0	0.0
2010	CHN	MLB	31	347	33	13	0	6	33	17	85	0	0	.256/.306/.353	.231	.325	1.6	1B 0, RF -5	-0.9
2011	*ARI*	*MLB*	*32*	*397*	*46*	*19*	*0*	*11*	*45*	*25*	*77*	*1*	*1*	*.263/.319/.411*	*.256*	*.301*	*-0.1*	*RF -3, LF -1*	*0.1*

The Cubs already boasted the most right-handed lineup in baseball, but signing a bum-winged right-handed outfielder for $3.3 million nonetheless found a prominent place on their list of off-season must-dos. Why? They had already faced the fewest lefties in the majors in 2009. Sure, maybe there's a threat of left-handed Lectroids from the eighth dimension that we don't know about, and Buckaroo Jim Hendry is protecting us all from such threats. No price is too high to pay for eternal vigilance, right? As an expensive bit of overcompensation for the vagaries of employing Soriano, or Fukudome's limitations, Nady's acquisition left the Cubs with a player they didn't need and who flopped in a part-time role after a year lost to elbow surgery. Plugged in at first after Lee was traded away, he at least fielded the position creditably. He'll need that lone positive to make himself useful as a Diamondbacks reserve.

Aramis Ramirez **3B**

Born: **6/25/1978** Age: **33**
Bats: **R** Throws: **R** Height: **6' 1"** Weight: **219**
Breakout: **1%** Improve: **37%** Collapse: **4%**
Attrition: **9%** MLB: **95%**

Comparables:
George Brett, Morgan Ensberg, Ken Caminiti (73)

YEAR	TEAM	LVL	AGE	PA	R	2B	3B	HR	RBI	BB	SO	SB	CS	AVG/OBP/SLG	TAv	BABIP	BRR	FRAA	WARP
2008	CHN	MLB	30	645	97	44	1	27	111	74	94	2	2	.289/.380/.518	.303	.303	-1.7	3B -14	3.2
2009	CHN	MLB	31	342	46	14	1	15	65	28	43	2	1	.317/.389/.516	.312	.331	-0.7	3B -3	2.4
2010	CHN	MLB	32	507	62	21	1	25	83	34	90	0	0	.241/.294/.452	.260	.245	-1.2	3B -9	0.5
2011	*CHN*	*MLB*	*33*	*546*	*71*	*27*	*1*	*24*	*76*	*49*	*77*	*1*	*1*	*.271/.342/.479*	*.284*	*.274*	*-0.1*	*3B -7*	*2.1*

Between a bum thumb and whatever else, Ramirez was horrific in the first two months, hitting .168/.232/.285 before landing on the DL in early June. Once he came back, he was the A-Ram of old, bopping at a .287/.333/.557 clip. After the season, he said there was more than the thumb holding him back, and he played through a few nagging hurts at the end to boot. All of which brings home the nagging fear that as he moves deeper into his 30s, he is not the four- or five-win player he was in his prime and never will be again. His strikeout and walk rates hit low points not seen since his days as a young Pirate, and more disconcerting still has been the near-total disappearance of his range—like watching a mime, you can stare at him for hours and still not be sure if he moved. His 2012 option is riding on a comeback, but if he simply manages a healthy season, the counting stats will prop up the reputation he earned in the Aughties.

Marquez Smith **3B**

Born: **3/20/1985** Age: **26**
Bats: **R** Throws: **R** Height: **5' 10"** Weight: **210**
Breakout: **3%** Improve: **17%** Collapse: **10%**
Attrition: **28%** MLB: **48%**

Comparables:
Delwyn Young, Matthew Brown, Steve Pearce (73)

YEAR	TEAM	LVL	AGE	PA	R	2B	3B	HR	RBI	BB	SO	SB	CS	AVG/OBP/SLG	TAv	BABIP	BRR	FRAA	WARP
2008	PEO	A	23	355	52	17	4	14	49	35	65	1	3	.295/.375/.508	.315	.328	1.1	3B -1, 2B 2	3.1
2008	DAY	A+	23	152	18	10	1	3	19	12	32	0	0	.236/.316/.386	.245	.286	-0.5	3B 2	0.2
2009	DAY	A+	24	55	9	1	0	5	18	5	13	1	1	.260/.327/.580	.293	.250	-0.6	3B 1, 2B 0	0.4
2009	TEN	AA	24	479	60	38	1	10	51	36	90	3	0	.282/.342/.441	.276	.332	-0.6	3B 13, SS 0	3.4
2010	IOW	AAA	25	337	56	26	1	17	53	31	70	0	0	.314/.389/.574	.312	.356	0.0	3B -2, 2B 0	2.7
2011	*CHN*	*MLB*	*26*	*476*	*56*	*26*	*1*	*16*	*60*	*34*	*108*	*1*	*0*	*.250/.305/.428*	*.255*	*.290*	*0.0*	*3B 1, 2B 0*	*1.1*

With all that ails A-Ram, Smith might have made himself into a stealthy interim solution, especially while Josh Vitters continues to stumble. A teammate of Colvin's at Clemson, Smith plays an excellent, strong-armed third that might conjure up memories of what could have been had the Cubs held on to Casey McGehee. Although he was interrupted by a demotion to Double-A to make room for Chad Tracy, Smith's work with hitting coach Von Joshua at Iowa helped him adapt to the amount of junk one sees in the PCL. In August, he unloaded on the circuit, bopping 12 homers. With A-Ram's defense at the hot corner turning ugly, Smith might already have value as a substitute since he can play a workmanlike second and either outfield corner. If Ramirez were to get hurt or move to first base, even for short stints, Smith is the best upper-level option in the organization.

Brad Snyder **RF**

Born: **5/25/1982** Age: **29**
Bats: L Throws: L Height: **6' 3"** Weight: **200**
Breakout: **3%** Improve: **31%** Collapse: **2%**
Attrition: **12%** MLB: **50%**
Comparables:
Ray Sadler, Jason Perry, Todd Linden (75)

YEAR	TEAM	LVL	AGE	PA	R	2B	3B	HR	RBI	BB	SO	SB	CS	AVG/OBP/SLG	TAv	BABIP	BRR	FRAA	WARP
2008	BUF	AAA	26	443	51	28	5	12	61	27	124	7	3	.245/.298/.425	.238	.318	-1.1	CF -1, RF 1	0.1
2009	IOW	AAA	27	259	37	16	3	14	44	20	68	10	4	.279/.336/.549	.298	.331	-1.9	RF 5, CF -1	1.7
2010	IOW	AAA	28	539	95	37	6	25	105	56	125	18	4	.308/.384/.568	.318	.366	2.3	RF -14, CF 0	3.1
2010	CHN	MLB	28	28	1	1	0	0	5	1	12	0	0	.185/.214/.222	.189	.333	0.0	RF 1, LF 0	-0.1
2011	*CHN*	*MLB*	*29*	*429*	*51*	*22*	*2*	*16*	*55*	*35*	*119*	*10*	*3*	*.244/.305/.435*	*.254*	*.304*	*-0.1*	*RF -4, CF -3*	*-0.1*

Credit Hendry's scouting instincts for seeing something still there in Snyder after the former 18th overall pick from the 2003 draft washed out of the outfielder-hungry Indians organization. He has the arm for right, where he can still cover ground; he's fast on the bases; and power was never really a problem. Staying healthy and making contact had been, but last year Snyder got his strikeout rate below 25 percent for the first time as a pro, while also staying healthy.

Alfonso Soriano **LF**

Born: **1/7/1978** Age: **33**
Bats: R Throws: R Height: **6' 1"** Weight: **180**
Breakout: **0%** Improve: **37%** Collapse: **2%**
Attrition: **7%** MLB: **96%**
Comparables:
Andruw Jones, Geoff Jenkins, Ben Oglivie (71)

YEAR	TEAM	LVL	AGE	PA	R	2B	3B	HR	RBI	BB	SO	SB	CS	AVG/OBP/SLG	TAv	BABIP	BRR	FRAA	WARP
2008	CHN	MLB	30	503	77	27	0	29	75	43	103	19	3	.280/.344/.532	.288	.302	5.0	LF 2, 2B 1	3.1
2009	CHN	MLB	31	522	64	25	1	20	55	40	118	9	2	.241/.303/.424	.252	.279	-0.3	LF 0, 2B 0	0.5
2010	CHN	MLB	32	548	67	40	3	24	79	45	123	5	1	.258/.321/.496	.285	.295	1.8	LF -7	1.8
2011	*CHN*	*MLB*	*33*	*585*	*74*	*32*	*1*	*27*	*83*	*48*	*125*	*13*	*4*	*.257/.319/.474*	*.272*	*.283*	*0.1*	*LF 1*	*1.8*

In his fourth season on the team, Soriano set his single-season high for games played as a Cub. He has managed, in that time, to become perhaps the ultimate example of Cubbiedom. When initially introduced, he was reputed to be able to do all sorts of things, like run or play center and be a superstar. Now he's reduced to scaring people when he tries anything on the bases or afield, and his brand of walkless power boils down to very pedestrian production for a left fielder. His OBP against right-handers has slipped every year in his Cubs stint, dipping below .300 last season. His fielding sums him up: he's not awful as much as frustrating, making mistakes and scrambling to repair the damage. Considering he has four years to go, you might wonder if the voters shouldn't have asked for an initiative to recall left fielders as well as governors last November.

Geovany Soto **C**

Born: **1/20/1983** Age: **28**
Bats: R Throws: R Height: **6' 1"** Weight: **230**
Breakout: **3%** Improve: **43%** Collapse: **1%**
Attrition: **13%** MLB: **87%**
Comparables:
Joe Torre, Johnny Bench, Josh Whitesell (73)

YEAR	TEAM	LVL	AGE	PA	R	2B	3B	HR	RBI	BB	SO	SB	CS	AVG/OBP/SLG	TAv	BABIP	BRR	FRAA	WARP
2008	CHN	MLB	25	563	68	35	2	23	86	62	121	0	1	.285/.364/.504	.296	.332	-3.9	C -2	3.8
2009	CHN	MLB	26	389	27	19	1	11	47	50	77	1	0	.218/.321/.381	.239	.246	-0.9	C 1	0.8
2010	CHN	MLB	27	387	49	19	0	17	53	62	83	0	1	.280/.393/.497	.312	.324	-0.8	C -2	3.2
2011	*CHN*	*MLB*	*28*	*455*	*61*	*23*	*0*	*18*	*59*	*59*	*93*	*1*	*0*	*.267/.362/.469*	*.288*	*.301*	*0.0*	*C -1*	*2.9*

Yes, it might seem as if Soto just got here, but he's already entering his age-28 season. Frustratingly enough, Soto—the franchise's best catcher since Gabby Hartnett—lost time to injuries again, this time a knee and his throwing shoulder; off-season surgery on the latter should leave him squared away in plenty of time for camp. Despite generally getting marooned toward the end of the order, he's become even more patient while hitting for the same kind of power he delivered in his rookie season. Useless info: Soto led all catchers in outs made on the bases trying to advance, getting killed on six nonsteal plays. Now, somebody has to earn that unhappy label, but Soto? And not, say, Russell Martin? Shouldn't somebody notify the third-base coach or something? Wait, that guy is now the manager?

Tony Thomas **2B**

Born: **7/10/1986** Age: **24**
Bats: R Throws: R Height: **5' 10"** Weight: **180**
Breakout: **4%** Improve: **7%** Collapse: **8%**
Attrition: **24%** MLB: **35%**
Comparables:
Elliot Johnson, Danny Richar, Eric Patterson (76)

YEAR	TEAM	LVL	AGE	PA	R	2B	3B	HR	RBI	BB	SO	SB	CS	AVG/OBP/SLG	TAv	BABIP	BRR	FRAA	WARP
2008	DAY	A+	21	526	67	31	5	8	51	37	117	22	10	.280/.327/.417	.269	.343	-0.9	2B 14	2.9
2009	TEN	AA	22	497	62	25	1	11	43	50	107	12	12	.245/.338/.382	.251	.293	-2.9	2B -12	-0.6
2010	TEN	AA	23	474	68	30	11	12	75	33	103	15	2	.278/.340/.482	.286	.332	3.8	2B -2, RF 1	2.7
2011	*CHN*	*MLB*	*24*	*498*	*52*	*25*	*3*	*10*	*52*	*31*	*119*	*11*	*4*	*.236/.286/.373*	*.231*	*.289*	*-0.4*	*2B 2, RF 0*	*-0.2*

Higher ambitions keep getting attached to other names, while Thomas, the organizational soldier and former Florida State star, just endures. Marking time in a necessary repeat of Double-A, he was in danger of watching Flaherty pass him by, but a month into the season, Flaherty had flopped and the keystone was all his again. Thomas's baserunning, power production, and performance against righties all improved, and if he lacks a clean shot at a big-league future, he has the benefit of playing in an organization with no star above him and no great prospect overtaking him.

Josh Vitters 3B

Born: **8/27/1989** Age: **21**
Bats: **R** Throws: **R** Height: **6' 2"** Weight: **200**
Breakout: **1%** Improve: **7%** Collapse: **1%**
Attrition: **6%** MLB: **10%**

Comparables:
Ron Santo, Fernando Martinez, David Wright (76)

YEAR	TEAM	LVL	AGE	PA	R	2B	3B	HR	RBI	BB	SO	SB	CS	AVG/OBP/SLG	TAv	BABIP	BRR	FRAA	WARP
2008	BOI	A-	18	274	37	25	2	5	36	13	45	1	3	.328/.369/.498	.308	.379	-0.9	3B -2	1.9
2009	PEO	A	19	279	40	12	1	15	46	7	42	4	0	.316/.362/.535	.311	.326	-2.1	3B -5	1.5
2009	DAY	A+	19	195	20	7	2	3	22	5	23	2	1	.238/.262/.344	.233	.256	0.6	3B 0	0.0
2010	DAY	A+	20	118	14	8	0	3	13	8	22	4	1	.291/.356/.446	.311	.341	0.1	3B -5	0.4
2010	TEN	AA	20	221	24	12	0	7	26	13	41	1	0	.223/.299/.384	.225	.244	-0.6	3B -5	-0.6
2011	*CHN*	*MLB*	*21*	*367*	*39*	*18*	*1*	*11*	*43*	*10*	*73*	*1*	*0*	*.245/.270/.394*	*.231*	*.275*	*0.0*	*3B -5*	*-0.6*

After an okay first month in Daytona, the Cubs exchanged their top prospect with a rushed Ryan Flaherty at Double-A, doing him no favor with the premature assignment. Against much older and much more advanced competition, Vitters showed poor strike-zone judgment and sloppy play at third before a broken finger squelched any shot at regular-season redemption. He disappointed again in the AFL, delivering tepid results at the plate while making a few appearances at first base. Vitters' youth only excuses so much; at some point, the sweet swing he's been expected to show off ever since he was the third overall pick in 2007 has to start showing up in games.

PITCHERS

Chris Archer

Born: **9/26/1988** Age: **22**
Bats: **R** Throws: **R** Height: **6' 3"** Weight: **180**
Breakout: **1%** Improve: **4%** Collapse: **4%**
Attrition: **1%** MLB: **4%**

Comparables:
Fabio Castro, Pete Schourek, Nick Adenhart (70)

YEAR	TEAM	LVL	AGE	W	L	SV	G	GS	IP	H	HR	BB	SO	EqBB9	EqSO9	GB%	BABIP	WHIP	ERA	FRA	WARP
2008	LKC	A	19	4	9	0	28	30	117	99	9	87	106	6.7	8.2	55%	.279	1.68	4.54	5.92	-0.3
2009	PEO	A	20	6	4	0	27	30	109	78	0	66	119	5.4	9.8	56%	.288	1.39	2.64	3.49	2.6
2010	DAY	A+	21	7	1	0	15	14	72^1	54	4	26	82	3.2	10.2	49%	.272	1.15	2.74	4.25	1.2
2010	TEN	AA	21	9	3	0	15	18	79	60	4	43	78	4.9	8.9	56%	.275	1.33	2.28	3.39	2.2
2011	*CHN*	*MLB*	*22*	*5*	*8*	*0*	*19*	*19*	*84*	*86*	*10*	*62*	*65*	*6.6*	*7.0*	*48%*	*.305*	*1.76*	*5.68*	*6.18*	*0.7*

In his second season in the organization since coming over from the Tribe in the DeRosa deal, Archer provided a reminder that sometimes it's the throw-ins who make a trade worthwhile. The lanky North Carolinian was one of last year's massive breakout performers, handily winning the system's pitcher of the year award by exploiting and improving his talent. Already the owner of a plus sinker, he added velocity (reliably touching 96-97) and mastered his plus slider, propelling himself from wild and interesting to purely overpowering. Despite clean mechanics, command is still an area for improvement, but he's shown fine aptitude, ending talk of an eventual move to the bullpen. The Rays added him to their deep pile of pitching in the Garza deal, though Archer will likely be better served in that organization.

Esmailin Caridad

Born: **10/28/1985** Age: **25**
Bats: **R** Throws: **R** Height: **5' 10"** Weight: **195**
Breakout: **8%** Improve: **19%** Collapse: **8%**
Attrition: **2%** MLB: **46%**

Comparables:
Brian Kingman, Fabio Castro, Bob Moose (74)

YEAR	TEAM	LVL	AGE	W	L	SV	G	GS	IP	H	HR	BB	SO	EqBB9	EqSO9	GB%	BABIP	WHIP	ERA	FRA	WARP
2008	DAY	A+	22	6	4	0	14	16	69^1	64	3	17	38	2.2	4.9	45%	.279	1.20	4.15	5.85	0.1
2008	TEN	AA	22	7	3	0	14	14	82^2	67	15	21	50	2.3	5.4	47%	.209	1.09	3.16	4.60	1.2
2009	IOW	AAA	23	5	10	0	25	27	131^2	139	17	46	114	3.1	7.8	38%	.307	1.43	4.03	4.48	1.8
2009	CHN	MLB	23	1	0	0	14	0	19^1	15	0	3	17	1.4	7.9	37%	.294	1.09	1.40	1.65	0.5
2010	CHN	MLB	24	0	1	0	8	0	4	4	1	5	4	11.3	9.0	50%	.231	2.25	11.25	12.96	-0.4
2011	*CHN*	*MLB*	*25*	*6*	*7*	*0*	*37*	*16*	*102^1*	*117*	*15*	*38*	*65*	*3.4*	*5.7*	*43%*	*.309*	*1.52*	*5.32*	*5.78*	*0.6*

When you're one of the organization's middling pitching talents, the wage paid for time lost is uncertainty, because it's easy to get lost in the shuffle. Caridad came into the season set to pitch in the big-league bullpen, but a strained forearm in April resolved into an elbow injury that kept him shelved until August. If he's healthy come spring, he has the same virtues as before: low-90s heat, but not a lot of deception, especially with a pedestrian off-speed assortment. He can be part of a good pen, but he's also eminently replaceable middle-relief fodder.

Chris Carpenter

Born: **12/26/1985** Age: **25**
Bats: R Throws: R Height: **6' 4"** Weight: **215**
Breakout: **15%** Improve: **25%** Collapse: **11%**
Attrition: **29%** MLB: **49%**

Comparables:
Enrique Gonzalez, Charlie Haeger, Matt Albers (77)

YEAR	TEAM	LVL	AGE	W	L	SV	G	GS	IP	H	HR	BB	SO	EqBB9	EqSO9	GB%	BABIP	WHIP	ERA	FRA	WARP
2008	BOI	A-	22	4	2	0	10	6	.32	32	2	22	24	6.2	6.8	62%	.300	1.75	4.22	6.02	-0.1
2009	PEO	A	23	4	3	0	15	15	73^{2}	55	4	33	60	4.0	7.3	57%	.251	1.21	2.44	3.77	1.5
2009	DAY	A+	23	2	1	0	5	5	25	15	1	8	33	2.9	11.9	61%	.241	0.96	1.44	3.43	0.7
2009	TEN	AA	23	0	3	0	8	8	36^{1}	34	0	15	30	3.7	7.4	53%	.312	1.46	3.96	4.76	0.4
2010	TEN	AA	24	9	6	0	25	27	129^{1}	129	5	52	112	3.6	7.8	56%	.322	1.46	3.20	4.45	2.2
2011	*CHN*	*MLB*	*25*	*6*	*9*	*0*	*21*	*21*	*97*	*109*	*11*	*53*	*66*	*4.9*	*6.0*	*50%*	*.316*	*1.66*	*5.48*	*5.96*	*0.9*

Two elbow surgeries in college had already helped drop "The Other" Carpenter to the third round of the 2008 draft, but last year, the Kent State product had to be disabled after shoulder soreness in spring training created new concerns. Once he returned to action, much of last year's work involved improving his changeup to give him something beyond his slurvy curve to mix in with a plus four-seamer and a big-sinking two-seam fastball. Before his promotion to Iowa, he got stronger as the season progressed, with his ground-ball rate almost doubling in the second half. His lively assortment creates command problems, and he's probably always going to be a tough assignment for catchers, a combination that—coupled with his injury history—might push him to the pen. Even so, it might also get him fast-tracked to the majors.

Andrew Cashner

Born: **9/11/1986** Age: **24**
Bats: R Throws: R Height: **6' 6"** Weight: **210**
Breakout: **11%** Improve: **17%** Collapse: **7%**
Attrition: **16%** MLB: **32%**

Comparables:
Fernando Hernandez Jr., Jaime Garcia, Josh Outman (76)

YEAR	TEAM	LVL	AGE	W	L	SV	G	GS	IP	H	HR	BB	SO	EqBB9	EqSO9	GB%	BABIP	WHIP	ERA	FRA	WARP
2009	DAY	A+	22	0	0	0	12	12	42	31	1	15	34	3.2	7.3	50%	.250	1.17	1.29	2.59	1.7
2009	TEN	AA	22	3	5	0	14	16	66^{1}	53	1	31	43	4.2	5.8	49%	.254	1.30	3.53	5.40	0.3
2010	TEN	AA	23	3	1	0	6	6	36	22	1	13	42	3.3	10.5	54%	.253	0.97	2.75	3.40	1.0
2010	IOW	AAA	23	3	0	0	5	3	21	17	0	2	17	0.9	7.3	60%	.283	0.95	0.86	1.65	1.2
2010	CHN	MLB	23	2	6	0	53	0	54^{1}	55	8	30	50	5.0	8.3	52%	.301	1.64	4.80	5.19	-0.3
2011	*CHN*	*MLB*	*24*	*5*	*5*	*0*	*36*	*11*	*78*	*80*	*8*	*41*	*60*	*4.7*	*6.8*	*47%*	*.304*	*1.53*	*4.75*	*5.17*	*0.9*

Having drafted the college closer as a 2008 first-rounder, the Cubs successfully steered Cashner toward a career in the rotation, but his readiness to pitch plus the team's need for immediate relief puts them on the cusp of a tough decision about his future role. He could certainly stick around as a quality set-up man from here on out, especially as questions about his mechanics and delivery contributed to the decision to move him back to the pen, even with his quality three-pitch assortment. In a relief role, his heat reliably stays in the high 90s; if he heads back into the rotation, it will come back down below 95. Given his youth and the veteran rotation, a year in the pen would be sensible enough, but leaving him there to stay would be a waste of his upside as a starter.

Casey Coleman

Born: **7/3/1987** Age: **23**
Bats: L Throws: R Height: **6' 0"** Weight: **180**
Breakout: **8%** Improve: **34%** Collapse: **11%**
Attrition: **9%** MLB: **72%**

Comparables:
Dave Fleming, Mel Stottlemyre, Tom Murphy (66)

YEAR	TEAM	LVL	AGE	W	L	SV	G	GS	IP	H	HR	BB	SO	EqBB9	EqSO9	GB%	BABIP	WHIP	ERA	FRA	WARP
2008	PEO	A	20	2	2	0	5	5	23^{1}	25	1	4	18	1.5	6.9	56%	.329	1.24	2.70	4.45	0.3
2008	BOI	A-	20	1	1	0	7	4	26^{2}	27	4	7	24	2.4	8.1	65%	.291	1.31	4.05	4.88	0.4
2009	TEN	AA	21	15	6	0	29	30	160^{2}	151	9	61	89	3.4	5.0	51%	.276	1.35	3.64	3.33	4.3
2010	IOW	AAA	22	10	7	0	20	20	117^{1}	106	10	35	59	2.7	4.5	57%	.256	1.22	3.99	3.07	3.6
2010	CHN	MLB	22	4	2	0	12	9	57	56	3	25	27	3.9	4.3	48%	.278	1.46	4.11	4.65	0.7
2011	*CHN*	*MLB*	*23*	*7*	*9*	*0*	*22*	*22*	*124*	*142*	*14*	*52*	*55*	*3.8*	*4.0*	*49%*	*.301*	*1.56*	*5.21*	*5.66*	*1.1*

Casey, son of Joe, son of Joe, is every bit the craftsman you might expect from the son and grandson of All-Star pitchers. He has sharp command of a sinker and changeup, an excellent move to first base, and a perfectionism that belies his youth. Nevertheless, he's not a flashy prospect as much as a fine-tuned organizational arm, a guy who knows what he's doing and gets the most out of what he has. There is room for improvement with his breaking stuff, but his ceiling is low, in that he might "just" be an employable back-end rotation starter instead of the third generation of Coleman All-Stars. A better real-world asset than a fantasy pick, he's probably the best near-term placeholder for the rotation if one of the veterans breaks down.

Ryan Dempster

Born: **5/3/1977** Age: **34**
Bats: R Throws: R Height: **6' 1"** Weight: **201**
Breakout: **24%** Improve: **55%** Collapse: **26%**
Attrition: **5%** MLB: **99%**

Comparables:
Steve Carlton, Vic Raschi, Jim Bunning (78)

YEAR	TEAM	LVL	AGE	W	L	SV	G	GS	IP	H	HR	BB	SO	EqBB9	EqSO9	GB%	BABIP	WHIP	ERA	FRA	WARP
2008	CHN	MLB	31	17	6	0	33	34	206^{2}	174	14	76	187	3.3	8.1	49%	.280	1.24	2.96	3.56	5.5
2009	CHN	MLB	32	11	9	0	31	32	200	196	22	65	172	2.9	7.7	49%	.302	1.34	3.65	4.26	3.1
2010	CHN	MLB	33	15	12	0	34	35	215^{1}	198	25	86	208	3.6	8.7	50%	.294	1.37	3.85	4.70	2.2
2011	*CHN*	*MLB*	*34*	*9*	*8*	*0*	*24*	*24*	*153*	*150*	*17*	*59*	*132*	*3.4*	*7.7*	*48%*	*.305*	*1.36*	*4.10*	*4.46*	*3.1*

Dempster's transmogrification from former blue-chip Marlin to damaged goods to expensive closer to beloved Cub workhorse ought to be enough of a roller coaster to challenge the notion that American lives have no third act. The late-career addition of a fluttering glove flip when he's pitching from a full windup gives a new generation of Cubs fans one of those lovely idiosyncrasies to forever retain in their mind's eye, like Rick Sutcliffe's big, rolling wrist snap or Lee Smith's saunter or Turk Wendell's endless rituals. At this stage, there's little you don't already know about Dempster. Although he posted a career-best strikeout rate, his season can come across as somewhat mediocre, right down to a .500 support-neutral winning percentage. However, he was undercut by some of the bullpen's issues, as he suffered three blown quality starts after the first six innings; using three runs and six frames as the standard, he delivered a winnable ballgame in 23 of 34 turns.

Thomas Diamond

Born: **4/6/1983** Age: **28**
Bats: R Throws: R Height: **6' 3"** Weight: **240**
Breakout: **7%** Improve: **9%** Collapse: **10%**
Attrition: **5%** MLB: **12%**

Comparables:
Bill Murphy, Neal Musser, Taylor Tankersley (75)

YEAR	TEAM	LVL	AGE	W	L	SV	G	GS	IP	H	HR	BB	SO	EqBB9	EqSO9	GB%	BABIP	WHIP	ERA	FRA	WARP
2008	FRI	AA	25	3	3	0	12	12	53^{2}	54	3	37	47	6.2	7.9	37%	.323	1.81	5.70	6.48	-0.4
2009	FRI	AA	26	1	3	1	32	0	44^{2}	43	3	37	50	7.5	10.1	39%	.336	1.86	3.43	4.03	0.4
2010	IOW	AAA	27	5	4	0	21	22	108^{1}	86	9	46	104	3.8	8.6	35%	.266	1.24	3.16	3.10	3.5
2010	CHN	MLB	27	1	3	0	16	3	29	33	5	18	36	5.6	11.2	32%	.368	1.83	6.83	6.10	-0.2
2011	*CHN*	*MLB*	*28*	*5*	*5*	*0*	*38*	*11*	*91^{2}*	*92*	*11*	*56*	*84*	*5.5*	*8.3*	*40%*	*.314*	*1.62*	*5.13*	*5.57*	*0.4*

Old prospects don't have to die or fade away; nor do they have to wind up on a former first-rounders' season of *Big Brother*, regaling the world about what might have been. The missing third man of the Rangers' once-vaunted DVD trio joined John Danks and Edinson Volquez in "The Show" as the result of a salvage op inspired by assistant GM Randy Bush's suggestion that Diamond—his former ace at the University of New Orleans—might be a nice pickup. Having gotten here, Diamond will have to settle for utility pitcher work; since injuring his elbow and shoulder, his fastball has topped out at around 90, and he has never come up with a reliable breaking pitch. His extreme fly-ball-generating tendencies and lack of deception might make him suitable for pitching only in the biggest ballparks.

Rafael Dolis

Born: **1/10/1988** Age: **23**
Bats: R Throws: R Height: **6' 4"** Weight: **215**
Breakout: **0%** Improve: **0%** Collapse: **0%**
Attrition: **0%** MLB: **0%**

Comparables:
Ryan Tucker, Nick Adenhart, Jhoulys Chacin (83)

YEAR	TEAM	LVL	AGE	W	L	SV	G	GS	IP	H	HR	BB	SO	EqBB9	EqSO9	GB%	BABIP	WHIP	ERA	FRA	WARP
2009	DAY	A+	21	3	9	0	27	26	99^{2}	78	4	53	75	4.8	6.8	55%	.263	1.38	3.43	4.77	1.1
2010	DAY	A+	22	4	5	0	14	15	71	63	3	30	48	3.8	6.1	63%	.278	1.34	2.79	4.89	0.6
2010	TEN	AA	22	5	4	0	12	13	55^{1}	65	3	27	45	4.4	7.3	56%	.354	1.68	4.07	5.21	0.5
2011	*CHN*	*MLB*	*23*	*4*	*7*	*0*	*15*	*15*	*64*	*75*	*7*	*41*	*37*	*5.7*	*5.1*	*50%*	*.317*	*1.79*	*5.96*	*6.48*	*0.4*

The big Dominican has a tremendous sinker that generated twice as many ground-ball outs as flies; the difficulty of generating much lift against him is illustrated by his having allowed just 25 extra-base hits all year. Dolis can also touch triple digits when he really lets it fly. Beyond the dominating hard stuff, the expectation that a move to the pen could accelerate his timetable seems reasonable: he wore down and got hittable after the third inning in both High-A and Double-A, and his command of a potentially excellent slider comes and goes. He also has a good move to the bag, one of those finer points you might not get so quickly from a converted position player. A former shortstop, Dolis is still mastering his craft; losing 2008 to Tommy John surgery didn't help him get the reps he needs, but it did feed the thought that there's potential as a starter yet untapped if the Cubs can afford him the development time.

Tom Gorzelanny

Born: **7/12/1982** Age: **28**
Bats: L Throws: L Height: **6' 2"** Weight: **207**
Breakout: **19%** Improve: **52%** Collapse: **22%**
Attrition: **12%** MLB: **96%**

Comparables:
Chuck Finley, Bob Rush, Dwight Gooden (81)

YEAR	TEAM	LVL	AGE	W	L	SV	G	GS	IP	H	HR	BB	SO	EqBB9	EqSO9	GB%	BABIP	WHIP	ERA	FRA	WARP
2008	IND	AAA	25	3	1	0	7	8	35	28	1	4	33	1.0	8.5	46%	.281	0.94	2.06	2.84	1.3
2008	PIT	MLB	25	6	9	0	21	22	105^{1}	120	20	70	67	6.0	5.7	42%	.301	1.81	6.66	6.86	-0.9
2009	IND	AAA	26	4	3	0	15	18	87	73	3	30	85	3.1	8.8	42%	.297	1.23	2.28	2.60	3.2
2009	CHN	MLB	26	4	2	0	13	8	38^{1}	39	6	13	40	3.1	9.4	41%	.306	1.38	5.63	5.90	0.0
2009	PIT	MLB	26	3	1	0	9	0	8^{2}	6	0	4	7	4.2	7.3	48%	.240	1.15	5.19	6.64	-0.1
2010	CHN	MLB	27	7	9	1	29	27	136^{1}	136	11	68	119	4.5	7.9	43%	.309	1.51	4.09	4.50	1.9
2011	*CHN*	*MLB*	*28*	*10*	*11*	*0*	*28*	*28*	*151*	*158*	*16*	*68*	*117*	*4.0*	*6.9*	*43%*	*.313*	*1.50*	*4.73*	*5.15*	*2.3*

Another brag-worthy Hendry salvage project rescued from Pittsburgh, Gorzo the Magnificent can't help but tantalize people with the possibilities of what he could be: after all, he's a power lefty two years removed from free agency. Still, there's a bit of Rusch'n roulette about him, where you can see too much—stare at the strikeouts long enough, and you start thinking he's about to become Ted Lilly, not unlike former sabermetric fave Glendon Rusch during his Brewer and Met incarnations as a rotation regular. But like Rusch, Gorzelanny may have no corner to turn and may be just a guy who can strike out around 19 percent of batters without being able to translate that into frequent quality starts or anything more than utility value. Gorzo was bounced from the rotation in favor of Carlos Zambrano for most of June and lost time to a broken finger in September, but he did so without drama. Nonetheless, he was declared surplus after the Garza deal and shipped off to Washington.

John Grabow

Born: **11/4/1978** Age: **32**
Bats: **L** Throws: **L** Height: **6' 2"** Weight: **185**
Breakout: **15%** Improve: **41%** Collapse: **24%**
Attrition: **15%** MLB: **89%**

Comparables:
Dave Righetti, Roy Thomas, Mike Henneman (82)

YEAR	TEAM	LVL	AGE	W	L	SV	G	GS	IP	H	HR	BB	SO	EqBB9	EqSO9	GB%	BABIP	WHIP	ERA	FRA	WARP
2008	PIT	MLB	29	6	3	4	74	0	76	60	9	37	62	4.4	7.3	43%	.239	1.29	2.84	3.52	1.3
2009	CHN	MLB	30	0	0	0	30	0	25	19	1	13	16	4.7	5.8	50%	.240	1.32	3.24	4.66	0.1
2009	PIT	MLB	30	3	0	0	45	0	47^{1}	43	4	28	41	5.3	7.8	43%	.291	1.54	3.42	3.81	0.5
2010	CHN	MLB	31	1	3	0	28	0	25^{2}	35	5	13	20	4.6	7.0	45%	.345	1.91	7.36	6.52	-0.6
2011	*CHN*	*MLB*	*32*	*3*	*1*	*1*	*62*	*0*	*60^{1}*	*63*	*7*	*30*	*45*	*4.5*	*6.8*	*45%*	*.306*	*1.54*	*4.92*	*5.35*	*-0.3*

If there are so many other reasons to feel good about Cubs pitching, there's also the latest instance of Hendry's failure to properly assess market value for middling relief help. Paying John Grabow $7.5 million for two years was a bad idea, regardless of whether he subsequently got hurt. That he blew out the MCL in his left (push) knee last year just provides an excuse for a bad year before he broke down, but he wasn't being used situationally, and with a career OPS north of 700 against lefties, it isn't like he'd even be that valuable in a LOOGY role. Moving to sign Grabow to that extension in mid-November of 2009 reflected a failure to appreciate where the market for filler talent had long since moved. Here's hoping the Cubs can chalk it up as a lesson learned, and count on Grabow as nothing more than an expensive second lefty before he gets kicked to the curb.

Jay Jackson

Born: **10/27/1987** Age: **23**
Bats: **R** Throws: **R** Height: **6' 1"** Weight: **195**
Breakout: **19%** Improve: **41%** Collapse: **8%**
Attrition: **9%** MLB: **62%**

Comparables:
Johnny Cueto, Fabio Castro, Kevin Millwood (71)

YEAR	TEAM	LVL	AGE	W	L	SV	G	GS	IP	H	HR	BB	SO	EqBB9	EqSO9	GB%	BABIP	WHIP	ERA	FRA	WARP
2008	PEO	A	20	2	2	0	6	1	24	22	3	5	37	1.9	13.9	38%	.388	1.17	3.00	3.24	0.5
2008	DAY	A+	20	3	0	0	5	6	22^{2}	15	0	7	26	2.8	10.3	32%	.268	0.97	1.19	0.69	1.0
2009	DAY	A+	21	2	2	0	7	7	38^{1}	31	3	4	46	0.9	10.8	50%	.295	0.97	1.41	2.73	1.3
2009	TEN	AA	21	5	4	0	15	15	78^{2}	66	6	37	73	4.2	8.4	40%	.277	1.32	2.97	3.51	2.0
2010	IOW	AAA	22	11	8	0	32	26	157^{1}	153	20	48	119	2.7	6.8	37%	.278	1.36	4.35	4.95	1.4
2011	*CHN*	*MLB*	*23*	*6*	*6*	*0*	*23*	*16*	*107^{1}*	*110*	*14*	*41*	*85*	*3.5*	*7.1*	*41%*	*.302*	*1.41*	*4.62*	*5.02*	*1.4*

The most advanced of the Cubs' rotation prospects, Jackson had to live with the repercussions of top-down uncertainty in the big-league bullpen in-season. The Cubs bumped him to the Iowa pen for most of May for reasons that defy easy defense before getting him back into the rotation once they decided Cashner was the guy who would wind up in the pen in the majors. The chunky right-hander from Furman throws four pitches for strikes, mixing curves and sliders with a mid-90s fastball and a solid changeup. His lack of tilt, a function of his stature, means he ends up giving up a lot of flies and long drives, and trying to back people off the plate and keep the inside corner led to 13 hit batsmen last year. Add in how often he misses against lefties, leading to a strikeout and walk rate almost half of his levels against righties, and there's obviously still work to be done. Just keep in mind that the stuff is there—Jackson made it to Triple-A in his second full season as a pro because the future is still bright.

Scott Maine

Born: **2/2/1985** Age: **26**
Bats: **L** Throws: **L** Height: **6' 3"** Weight: **210**
Breakout: **6%** Improve: **2%** Collapse: **2%**
Attrition: **5%** MLB: **7%**

Comparables:
Warner Madrigal, David Davidson, Carlos Guevara (83)

YEAR	TEAM	LVL	AGE	W	L	SV	G	GS	IP	H	HR	BB	SO	EqBB9	EqSO9	GB%	BABIP	WHIP	ERA	FRA	WARP
2008	VIS	A+	23	3	2	5	32	0	48	48	4	21	53	3.9	9.9	48%	.341	1.52	3.19	3.40	0.9
2009	MOB	AA	24	3	3	5	36	0	47^{1}	56	2	15	46	2.9	8.7	44%	.383	1.54	2.47	0.56	2.6
2010	IOW	AAA	25	3	1	5	33	0	41	33	4	21	47	4.6	10.3	48%	.274	1.37	3.51	3.39	0.7
2010	CHN	MLB	25	0	0	0	13	0	13	9	1	5	11	3.5	7.6	55%	.216	1.08	2.08	3.76	0.1
2011	*CHN*	*MLB*	*26*	*2*	*1*	*2*	*37*	*0*	*46*	*48*	*5*	*23*	*41*	*4.3*	*8.0*	*45%*	*.317*	*1.50*	*4.67*	*5.08*	*-0.1*

If you are searching for a reason why the Grabows of the world don't have to cost you $7.5 million, consider how easily the Cubs found a fully functional alternative in Maine: by ditching Aaron Heilman on Arizona, straight up. Maine doesn't throw especially hard, touching the low 90s with a fastball he uses effectively to set up a slider and change. He can get a bit cute against lefties, losing them on walks more than you'd like, but he can fool enough people often enough to be a useful second southpaw in a big-league bullpen.

Carlos Marmol

Born: **10/14/1982** Age: **28**
Bats: **R** Throws: **R** Height: **6' 2"** Weight: **180**
Breakout: **21%** Improve: **40%** Collapse: **35%**
Attrition: **15%** MLB: **94%**

Comparables:
Armando Benitez, Brad Lidge, Francisco Rodriguez (57)

YEAR	TEAM	LVL	AGE	W	L	SV	G	GS	IP	H	HR	BB	SO	EqBB9	EqSO9	GB%	BABIP	WHIP	ERA	FRA	WARP
2008	CHN	MLB	25	2	4	7	82	0	87^{1}	40	10	41	114	4.2	11.7	36%	.170	1.00	2.68	3.82	0.8
2009	CHN	MLB	26	2	4	15	79	0	74	43	2	65	93	7.9	11.3	41%	.252	1.62	3.41	3.57	1.1
2010	CHN	MLB	27	2	3	38	77	0	77^{2}	40	1	52	138	6.0	16.0	33%	.293	1.29	2.55	2.17	1.7
2011	*CHN*	*MLB*	*28*	*5*	*2*	*17*	*96*	*0*	*96^{1}*	*65*	*7*	*61*	*129*	*5.7*	*12.0*	*41%*	*.281*	*1.31*	*3.20*	*3.48*	*1.6*

Using 40 innings pitched as a cutoff, Marmol struck out a major-league-leading 42 percent of all batters; he also walked 14 percent of his opponents. The other seven pitchers who walked that many lost their jobs or won their walking papers, but they didn't have Marmol's K-rate (the fourth-highest all-time) going for them. The only three seasons ahead of Marmol were Eric Gagne's enhanced 2003 (44.8 percent), Billy Wagner's 1999 (43.4 percent), and Brad Lidge's 2004 (42.6 percent). If Crash Davis is right about strikeouts, then fascism is on the rise and Marmol is the reigning Duce. By expected wins added, his 2010 season constitutes the third-best Cubs relief season ever, behind Bruce Sutter's 1977 and Lee Smith's 1983. What is particularly remarkable is that more than anyone else, Marmol was the reliever being used in a real fireman's role, pitching with 40 inherited baserunners, more than twice as many as most of the game's other 30-save guys, 10 times as many as David Aardsma or Francisco Cordero and 10 more than Brian Wilson. We shall see if this inspires more managers to reach for their closers earlier than the ninth, but Marmol's utter dominance lost nothing to being asked to come into the eighth or pitch from the stretch from the outset. His control issues sound terrible, but they boil down to giving the man a clean slate against someone who might be even more hard-pressed to make contact. Marmol doesn't give in to batters—he can afford to give up and smoke the next guy.

Sean Marshall

Born: **8/30/1982** Age: **28**
Bats: **L** Throws: **L** Height: **6' 7"** Weight: **205**
Breakout: **17%** Improve: **36%** Collapse: **23%**
Attrition: **22%** MLB: **68%**

Comparables:
Manny Delcarmen, Duaner Sanchez, Jeremy Accardo (74)

YEAR	TEAM	LVL	AGE	W	L	SV	G	GS	IP	H	HR	BB	SO	EqBB9	EqSO9	GB%	BABIP	WHIP	ERA	FRA	WARP
2008	IOW	AAA	25	1	1	0	7	7	31^{2}	26	2	6	25	1.7	7.1	52%	.261	1.04	3.41	2.38	1.3
2008	CHN	MLB	25	3	5	1	34	7	65^{1}	60	9	23	58	3.2	8.0	43%	.276	1.33	3.99	3.99	1.1
2009	CHN	MLB	26	3	7	0	55	9	85^{1}	91	10	32	68	3.4	7.2	52%	.309	1.45	4.32	4.81	0.6
2010	CHN	MLB	27	7	5	1	80	0	74^{2}	58	3	25	90	3.0	10.8	53%	.294	1.14	2.65	3.10	1.5
2011	*CHN*	*MLB*	*28*	*7*	*4*	*0*	*74*	*10*	*108^{2}*	*108*	*12*	*40*	*89*	*3.4*	*7.4*	*47%*	*.305*	*1.38*	*4.18*	*4.54*	*1.4*

The Cubs' other effective reliever, Marshall joined Marmol to give the team a pair of pitchers on the leaderboard for appearances (a distinction they shared with the Braves' Peter Moylan and Jonny Venters). Left alone in a relief role that didn't limit him to situational nonsense because of his left-handedness, Marshall adapted handily, adding a few notches to his heat to get it up around 90 without running out of gas at any point of the season. In light of his great ground-ball rate and C. J. Wilson's successful conversion to starting in Texas, it's easy to wonder whether Marshall might be the sort of guy who deserves to be converted back to rotation work. However, the Cubs aren't short of starting alternatives, and they have few reliable answers in the pen; there's nothing wrong with letting the left-handed analogue to Jon Rauch be, now that they've found him.

Marcos Mateo

Born: **4/18/1984** Age: **27**
Bats: **R** Throws: **R** Height: **6' 1"** Weight: **160**
Breakout: **0%** Improve: **0%** Collapse: **0%**
Attrition: **0%** MLB: **0%**

Comparables:
Alberto Arias, Arturo Lopez, Davis Romero (88)

YEAR	TEAM	LVL	AGE	W	L	SV	G	GS	IP	H	HR	BB	SO	EqBB9	EqSO9	GB%	BABIP	WHIP	ERA	FRA	WARP
2008	DAY	A+	24	4	4	0	27	21	96	98	7	32	70	3.0	6.6	42%	.303	1.43	3.47	4.91	1.0
2009	TEN	AA	25	5	7	0	38	15	104	101	10	45	77	3.9	6.7	45%	.284	1.51	3.63	4.04	1.6
2010	TEN	AA	26	0	0	4	17	1	20^{2}	23	2	3	29	1.3	12.6	53%	.362	1.26	2.18	2.25	0.6
2010	CHN	MLB	26	0	1	0	21	0	21^{2}	20	6	9	26	3.7	10.8	39%	.275	1.38	5.82	6.98	-0.5
2011	*CHN*	*MLB*	*27*	*4*	*4*	*0*	*40*	*8*	*74*	*85*	*11*	*36*	*50*	*4.3*	*6.1*	*44%*	*.315*	*1.62*	*5.70*	*6.19*	*-0.3*

If pitching were like figure skating and had judges instead of umps and batters, Mateo might be an instant star, because in the abstract, the stuff is there: a high-90s heater and a high-80s slider sounds awesome, right? Unfortunately, everyone's a critic, especially in the majors, where players take a good look at purportedly nuclear offerings and figure out ways to turn them into souvenirs. Despite making his big-league debut, Mateo had an uneven season, losing six weeks to a knee injury, but his performance after his August call-up didn't secure him anything going forward. He will keep getting looks as a reliever, but without translating performance into results, he's just going to be the guy they got from the Reds for Buck Coats, a deal neither team has yet had cause to regret.

Trey McNutt
Born: **8/2/1989** Age: **21**
Bats: R Throws: R Height: **6' 4"** Weight: **205**
Breakout: **2%** Improve: **1%** Collapse: **2%**
Attrition: **1%** MLB: **3%**
Comparables:
Chris Tillman, Jaime Garcia, Trevor Cahill (72)

YEAR	TEAM	LVL	AGE	W	L	SV	G	GS	IP	H	HR	BB	SO	EqBB9	EqSO9	GB%	BABIP	WHIP	ERA	FRA	WARP
2009	BOI	A-	19	3	0	0	7	2	20^{1}	9	1	12	21	5.3	9.3	51%	.174	1.18	1.33	5.25	-0.1
2010	PEO	A	20	6	0	0	13	14	59^{2}	43	0	24	70	3.6	10.6	47%	.293	1.16	1.36	1.90	2.7
2010	DAY	A+	20	4	0	0	9	10	41	29	3	9	49	2.0	10.8	41%	.255	0.98	2.63	3.04	1.3
2010	TEN	AA	20	1	2	0	5	7	26^{2}	30	3	8	25	2.7	8.4	47%	.346	1.43	4.39	4.91	0.2
2011	*CHN*	*MLB*	*21*	*6*	*6*	*0*	*21*	*15*	*72*	*71*	*8*	*36*	*62*	*4.5*	*7.7*	*44%*	*.306*	*1.49*	*4.59*	*4.99*	*1.4*

Sometimes it pays to be lucky as well as good, because happy accident led the Cubs to draft McNutt after they belatedly came across him at the College World Series in 2009. A weak season had harmed his draft status in other organization's eyes, but on that day, he showed better velocity (despite getting knocked around), good enough to get him six figures as a 32nd-rounder. He's only improved since, dialing it up to the mid-90s while mixing in a plus breaking pitch. That stuff earned him a rapid series of promotions in his full-season debut, as he tallied 132 strikeouts across three levels in 116 1/3 innings pitched. If not for Chris Archer's even bigger breakout, McNutt might have garnered more headlines, but flying under the radar has served him well so far; this last dose won't hurt him any, because he'll never be overlooked again.

Dae-Eun Rhee
Born: **3/23/1989** Age: **22**
Bats: L Throws: R Height: **6' 2"** Weight: **190**
Breakout: **0%** Improve: **0%** Collapse: **0%**
Attrition: **0%** MLB: **0%**
Comparables:
Joel Davis, Dick Brodowski, Alan Wirth (88)

YEAR	TEAM	LVL	AGE	W	L	SV	G	GS	IP	H	HR	BB	SO	EqBB9	EqSO9	GB%	BABIP	WHIP	ERA	FRA	WARP
2008	PEO	A	19	4	1	0	10	11	40	28	0	16	33	3.6	7.4	62%	.250	1.10	1.80	5.25	1.2
2010	DAY	A+	21	5	12	0	26	25	114^{1}	125	11	40	70	3.1	5.5	52%	.304	1.50	5.12	5.37	0.4
2011	*CHN*	*MLB*	*22*	*3*	*6*	*0*	*12*	*12*	*50^{1}*	*63*	*8*	*27*	*22*	*4.8*	*3.9*	*47%*	*.317*	*1.79*	*6.58*	*7.15*	*0.1*

A much-lauded Korean teen phenom when he signed in 2007, Rhee was delayed in his long-anticipated first full season by his comeback from Tommy John surgery. In the aggregate, it may not look as if he was worth the wait, but remember that the Cubs placed him in High-A in his return from injury with less than 60 pro innings to his credit. His overall numbers look worse as a result of his running out of gas at the end of July, as he gave up 23 of his total 74 runs allowed in his last five starts (and in just 15 1/3 innings pitched). Perhaps a larger item of concern, his velocity only sat around 90, and his off-speed stuff didn't provide much in the way of swing-and-miss happiness. Even so, keep in mind that he was just 21 and that the Cubs can afford to grant him the time to develop.

Jim Russell
Born: **1/8/1986** Age: **25**
Bats: L Throws: L Height: **6' 4"** Weight: **205**
Breakout: **4%** Improve: **1%** Collapse: **5%**
Attrition: **3%** MLB: **6%**
Comparables:
Matt Chico, Jason Miller, Bill Greif (80)

YEAR	TEAM	LVL	AGE	W	L	SV	G	GS	IP	H	HR	BB	SO	EqBB9	EqSO9	GB%	BABIP	WHIP	ERA	FRA	WARP
2008	DAY	A+	22	2	3	0	10	10	51^{2}	50	6	14	32	2.4	5.6	41%	.282	1.24	4.18	4.32	0.8
2008	TEN	AA	22	4	8	0	18	19	86^{1}	111	18	25	62	2.6	6.5	37%	.333	1.64	6.25	5.83	0.2
2009	TEN	AA	23	2	3	0	11	5	37	45	5	9	26	2.2	6.3	34%	.336	1.49	5.11	4.18	0.6
2009	IOW	AAA	23	3	3	0	26	7	65^{2}	71	6	19	46	2.6	6.3	38%	.301	1.37	3.43	2.75	2.1
2010	CHN	MLB	24	1	1	0	57	0	49	55	11	11	42	2.0	7.7	32%	.291	1.43	4.96	6.66	-1.1
2011	*CHN*	*MLB*	*25*	*3*	*4*	*0*	*36*	*8*	*74*	*92*	*14*	*26*	*46*	*3.1*	*5.5*	*40%*	*.318*	*1.58*	*6.04*	*6.56*	*-0.5*

Another legacy, Russell didn't exactly live up to papa Jeff's legacy for relief effectiveness in his rookie season. Still, his being here represented a modest surprise in the first place. He's more of an organizational arm, but a good showing in camp while others struggled or got hurt earned him an Opening Day slot as a third lefty, at least until June, when he had pitched his way off the roster, only to be called back when Grabow's knee gave out. Russell's mastery of a fairly pedestrian fastball/slider mix leads to a lot of fly balls and more than a few homers. Better execution against lefties might earn him a situational role, but five of his 11 taters were surrendered to the same-handed.

Jeff Samardzija
Born: **1/23/1985** Age: **26**
Bats: R Throws: R Height: **6' 5"** Weight: **220**
Breakout: **10%** Improve: **12%** Collapse: **14%**
Attrition: **15%** MLB: **19%**
Comparables:
J.D. Durbin, Travis Chick, Fernando Rodriguez (83)

YEAR	TEAM	LVL	AGE	W	L	SV	G	GS	IP	H	HR	BB	SO	EqBB9	EqSO9	GB%	BABIP	WHIP	ERA	FRA	WARP
2008	TEN	AA	23	3	5	0	16	15	76	71	6	42	44	5.0	5.2	41%	.273	1.51	4.74	5.07	0.8
2008	IOW	AAA	23	4	1	0	6	8	37^{1}	32	5	16	40	3.9	9.6	47%	.300	1.31	3.13	4.35	0.8
2008	CHN	MLB	23	1	0	1	26	0	27^{2}	24	0	15	25	4.9	8.1	47%	.289	1.45	2.28	3.52	0.4
2009	IOW	AAA	24	6	6	0	18	17	89	98	12	27	71	2.7	7.2	42%	.317	1.44	4.25	4.62	1.0
2009	CHN	MLB	24	1	3	0	20	2	34^{2}	46	7	15	21	3.9	5.5	44%	.333	1.79	7.53	6.92	-0.5
2010	IOW	AAA	25	11	3	0	35	16	111^{1}	86	9	67	102	5.4	8.2	38%	.255	1.39	4.20	6.15	-0.6
2010	CHN	MLB	25	2	2	0	7	3	19^{1}	21	4	20	9	9.3	4.2	30%	.262	2.22	8.38	10.45	-0.8
2011	*CHN*	*MLB*	*26*	*5*	*7*	*0*	*35*	*16*	*109^{2}*	*125*	*16*	*59*	*69*	*4.9*	*5.7*	*42%*	*.310*	*1.69*	*5.78*	*6.28*	*-0.1*

After Angel Guzman's shoulder exploded, the Cubs needed a live-armed righty in the worst way. No problem—they had their expensive wonderboy, Samardzija, so here at last would be his big opportunity. Three bad April ballgames later, whatever lukewarm enthusiasm there was for keeping him had curdled into disgust and a return trip to Iowa. By June, the Cubs had come to the desultory decision to put him back in the rotation to see if increased innings would lead to good things, but even the addition of a new cutter didn't produce consistent success. As hard as Samardzija has worked to improve his breaking stuff, it just hasn't been enough to make his fastball any less fast, fat, and flat. Armed with nothing he can reliably fire for a quality strike, he's a latter-day Todd Van Poppel, not really a reliable asset as a set-up man or a starter, but one who might be able to help out in the middle innings. There's no point in bitching about the money long since spent to buy him away from football; that mistake has been made. He's out of options and has no-trade protection, so he'll have to make the team or disappear on waivers, where he's almost sure to get snagged. Here's hoping the Cubs don't make the mistake Oakland made with Van Poppel and simply discard him, because if they can set aside the regret and the frustration, he might have value as a middle man.

Carlos Silva

Born: **4/23/1979** Age: **32**
Bats: R Throws: R Height: **6' 4"** Weight: **225**
Breakout: **15%** Improve: **32%** Collapse: **26%**
Attrition: **17%** MLB: **76%**
Comparables:
Jae Seo, Ron Reed, Paul Minner (74)

YEAR	TEAM	LVL	AGE	W	L	SV	G	GS	IP	H	HR	BB	SO	EqBB9	EqSO9	GB%	BABIP	WHIP	ERA	FRA	WARP
2008	SEA	MLB	29	4	15	0	28	29	153^{1}	213	20	32	69	1.9	4.1	45%	.342	1.62	6.46	5.49	0.2
2009	SEA	MLB	30	1	3	0	8	6	30^{1}	41	5	11	10	3.3	3.0	47%	.319	1.81	8.60	8.07	-0.7
2010	CHN	MLB	31	10	6	0	21	21	113	120	11	24	80	1.9	6.4	50%	.305	1.34	4.22	4.43	1.8
2011	*CHN*	*MLB*	*32*	*9*	*12*	*0*	*28*	*28*	*139^{1}*	*175*	*18*	*32*	*68*	*2.1*	*4.4*	*46%*	*.325*	*1.49*	*5.31*	*5.78*	*1.4*

To some extent, all Silva had to do was deliver a better-seeming season than Milton Bradley did, but the combination of Bradley's latest meltdown (performance-wise, for a change) and Silva's rattling off 13 quality starts in his first 16 turns made Hendry's off-season exchange of disappointments seem inspired. Things fell apart fast after that, though, as the beefy Silva got bombed while struggling with calf problems in July. Then he came out of his start on August 1 unable to catch his breath; he ended up needing "minor" surgery to correct heart arrhythmia. In September, he returned to make a single start before being shut down with elbow tendinitis. Before this litany of new setbacks, the finesse righty was pitching as if the years since his Twins heyday hadn't happened, firing strikes with his slow heat/slider mix en route to setting a career-high strikeout rate. Given the breadth of concerns that cropped up, it will be hard to count on him, but he has already rewarded the faith that there was still something there.

Randy Wells

Born: **8/28/1982** Age: **28**
Bats: R Throws: R Height: **6' 3"** Weight: **230**
Breakout: **16%** Improve: **45%** Collapse: **16%**
Attrition: **7%** MLB: **85%**
Comparables:
Don Newcombe, Paul Maholm, Frank Sullivan (73)

YEAR	TEAM	LVL	AGE	W	L	SV	G	GS	IP	H	HR	BB	SO	EqBB9	EqSO9	GB%	BABIP	WHIP	ERA	FRA	WARP
2008	IOW	AAA	25	11	5	0	29	23	129^{2}	136	18	38	113	2.6	7.8	47%	.305	1.36	4.10	4.96	1.3
2008	CHN	MLB	25	0	0	0	3	0	4^{1}	0	0	2	1	4.2	2.1	64%	.000	0.46	0.00	7.78	-0.2
2008	TOR	MLB	25	0	0	0	1	0	1	0	0	1	0	9.0	0.0	67%	.000	1.00	0.00	9.21	0.0
2009	IOW	AAA	26	3	0	0	5	5	26	19	1	7	21	2.4	7.3	56%	.250	1.00	2.77	3.44	0.6
2009	CHN	MLB	26	12	10	0	27	32	165^{1}	165	14	46	104	2.5	5.7	49%	.288	1.31	3.05	3.71	3.8
2010	CHN	MLB	27	8	14	0	32	32	194^{1}	209	19	63	144	2.9	6.7	49%	.311	1.43	4.26	4.56	2.3
2011	*CHN*	*MLB*	*28*	*9*	*10*	*0*	*26*	*26*	*147*	*163*	*17*	*50*	*102*	*3.1*	*6.2*	*47%*	*.315*	*1.45*	*4.71*	*5.12*	*2.2*

While MiniDempster might be counted among the disappointments of 2010, in the broad strokes he produced a season much like his rookie campaign, with relatively minor variations. Both his strikeout and walk rates went up slightly, his BABIP moved to the dark side of league average, and his rate of homers per fly ball got a little worse. All no big deal, just normal performance variation, right? The big difference was that last year, he was getting hit hard by right-handed people, with his ISO allowed against them more than doubling after 2009, from .081 to .172. That's the symptom of a guy whose bag of tricks isn't as deep as you'd like. You can get into cause-and-effect dickering over whether he had special first-inning problems, lost his confidence, or suffered from some other complaint, but if right-handers keep banging away at that clip, he's a fourth starter at best and not somebody you reward with unlimited job security.

Carlos Zambrano

Born: **6/1/1981** Age: **30**
Bats: S Throws: R Height: **6' 5"** Weight: **250**
Breakout: **10%** Improve: **34%** Collapse: **24%**
Attrition: **16%** MLB: **87%**
Comparables:
Andy Benes, Victor Marte, Brandon Webb (57)

YEAR	TEAM	LVL	AGE	W	L	SV	G	GS	IP	H	HR	BB	SO	EqBB9	EqSO9	GB%	BABIP	WHIP	ERA	FRA	WARP
2008	CHN	MLB	27	14	6	0	30	31	188^{2}	172	18	72	130	3.4	6.2	48%	.270	1.33	3.91	4.15	3.5
2009	CHN	MLB	28	9	7	0	28	30	169^{1}	155	10	78	152	4.1	8.1	46%	.300	1.43	3.77	4.22	2.8
2010	CHN	MLB	29	11	6	0	36	20	129^{2}	119	7	69	117	4.8	8.1	45%	.301	1.50	3.33	3.53	2.9
2011	*CHN*	*MLB*	*30*	*12*	*11*	*0*	*31*	*31*	*184*	*180*	*16*	*88*	*148*	*4.3*	*7.3*	*46%*	*.303*	*1.45*	*4.32*	*4.69*	*3.5*

If ever you wanted an example of the increasing insanity of relief-related obsessions, consider the Cubs' lurch into hauling Zambrano out of the rotation four spins through. As a win-now move, would you really pull Zambrano and leave your starting staff with a converted catcher, a Pirates castoff, and a broken-down tubbo who had allowed seven runs per nine over the last two years? After a month of that nonsense had done little to advance the Cubs' cause in any particular direction and they moved Z back into the rotation, could you blame him when he subsequently blew his stack an inning into a bad start? The entire situation was ludicrous, and Zambrano's outrage might have been the closest thing to reason involved. For this, he was suspended for a month, an overreaction almost as petty as the Milton Bradley suspension the year before. Once Zambrano finally entered the rotation to stay in August, he delivered eight quality starts in 11—you know, the stuff he's paid to do—at which point the Cubs magically remembered that this guy was still their best starter. There are a few ways to handle a staff ace—perhaps especially a temperamental one—but the Cubs' method ranks somewhere very low on the list.

LINEOUTS

HITTERS

PLAYER	TEAM	LVL	AGE	PA	R	2B	3B	HR	RBI	BB	SO	SB-CS	AVG/OBP/SLG	TAv	BABIP	BRR	FRAA	WARP
CF T. Campana*	TEN	AA	24	583	77	23	5	1	44	47	83	47-22	.317/.374/.386	.273	.365	-0.2	CF 2, LF 0	2.5
INF M. Cerda*	PEO	A	20	529	76	21	6	5	80	68	68	2-1	.271/.365/.377	.293	.302	2.9	3B -4, 2B -2	2.9
C S. Clevenger*	TEN	AA	24	305	40	24	0	6	48	22	29	0-6	.312/.367/.461	.281	.331	-1.5	C -1, 3B 0	1.6
OF J. Dubois	IOW	AAA	31	253	48	12	1	20	59	28	62	0-0	.300/.391/.632	.338	.329	-0.6	LF -3, 1B 0	2.2
OF J. Ha	PEO	A	19	309	36	15	4	7	46	10	45	7-2	.317/.333/.468	.304	.348	-1.9	RF -7, CF -1	1.0
1B M. Hoffpauir*	IOW	AAA	30	489	80	35	2	22	95	56	74	1-0	.283/.372/.529	.306	.294	-1.0	1B 1, RF -1	2.8
	CHN	MLB	30	57	5	3	0	0	5	5	15	0-0	.173/.246/.231	.158	.243	0.0	1B 0, LF 0	-0.5
1B B. LaHair*	IOW	AAA	27	475	71	30	0	25	81	51	94	0-0	.308/.387/.557	.314	.344	0.0	1B 2, LF -3	3.3
SS J. Lake	DAY	A+	20	439	55	18	4	9	46	35	99	13-7	.265/.333/.400	.265	.321	-1.8	SS 8, 3B 0	2.5
UT B. Scales#	IOW	AAA	32	452	65	33	3	10	53	72	77	5-2	.268/.403/.453	.292	.307	0.3	2B -10, 3B 2	2.0
	CHN	MLB	32	20	4	0	0	0	2	7	5	1-0	.308/.550/.308	.336	.500	-0.2	3B -1	0.1
OF M. Szczur	BOI	A-	20	81	16	9	0	0	8	6	11	0-0	.397/.444/.521	.326	.453	0.0	CF 0, LF -1	0.6
2B L. Watkins*	PEO	A	20	517	68	15	8	1	30	58	97	10-5	.261/.340/.339	.266	.316	1.8	2B -2, CF -5	1.1
OF T. Wright	TEN	AA	25	306	48	21	0	10	49	14	35	4-2	.298/.343/.474	.280	.308	2.5	LF 2, CF -1	1.6
	IOW	AAA	25	186	20	7	1	1	16	7	24	3-0	.240/.290/.309	.211	.266	1.0	LF -1, RF 3	-0.4

The latest variation on the theme of a man in Fuld, **Tony Campana** is a diminutive bunt, slap, and tickle speedster out of the University of Cincinnati. ⚾ The organization is crowded with infield prospects, but add **Matt Cerda** to the list of Fontenotesque aspirants at second after he hit .290/.386/.404 against right-handers in his full-season debut. ⚾ Paired up with Chirinos behind the plate, former infielder **Steve Clevenger** walloped right-handed pitching (958 OPS) with line-drive sock while throwing out 30 percent of stolen-base attempts; in the Cubs' catching crowd, he might be the one who becomes a deluxe caddy. ⚾ Triple-A is chock-a-block with thirtysomethings, so you can't say **Jason Dubois** was a man among boys, just that he provided another reminder that he probably shouldn't be there. ⚾ A 2010 second-rounder, **Reggie Golden** becomes the latest toolsy center-field option in the system, matching 20-homer potential with decent speed. ⚾ Further proof that the Cubs are hunting high and low for talent, **Jae-Hoon "A" Ha** gave the Chiefs a second Korean teen, this one gifted with good range in right and an interesting contact-oriented bat. ⚾ Cornfield notoriety after playing parts of the last seven seasons for Iowa got **Micah Hoffpauir** a one-year contract with the Nippon Ham Fighters. ⚾ Having re-signed journeyman **Bryan LaHair** to a minor-league deal early, the Cubs happily turned him into Triple-A depth with the Carlos Pena signing. ⚾ Young Dominican **Junior Lake** boasts a tremendous throwing arm and made big strides with his approach at the plate, but he's error-prone and might outgrow short, and he needs to keep developing at the plate to profile well at third. ⚾ **Bobby Scales** notched an eighth Triple-A campaign, but utilitymen who don't play short tend to get the short shrift, no matter how well they hit. ⚾ Villanova product **Matt Szczur** came to the Cubs in the fifth round, bringing blazing speed and a Chicago-friendly consonant-heavy surname (it's pronounced "caesar"), but his preference for football may put him out of the picture no sooner than he appeared in it. ⚾ Toolsy **Logan Watkins** has the athleticism to man second or center, and they've tried him at short, but he needs to deliver more than the odd walk to become a really interesting prospect. ⚾ **Ty Wright** had a nice power spike while repeating Double-A, but it wasn't *that* high, and his age and limitation to a corner count against him.

PITCHERS

PLAYER	TEAM	LVL	AGE	W	L	SV	IP	H	HR	BB	SO	EqBB9	EqSO9	GB%	BABIP	WHIP	ERA	FRA	WARP
M. Atkins	IOW	AAA	24	8	3	1	106^{2}	98	14	42	76	3.5	6.4	37%	.263	1.34	3.63	2.63	1.5
—	CHN	MLB	24	0	0	0	10	12	2	6	10	5.4	9.0	34%	.333	1.90	6.30	5.12	0.0
J. Beliveau*	DAY	A+	23	4	1	2	53	41	4	23	74	3.9	12.6	43%	.303	1.25	2.72	2.63	1.5
J. Berg	IOW	AAA	26	4	1	0	29^{2}	24	2	12	16	3.6	4.9	72%	.239	1.28	3.34	5.18	0.0
—	CHN	MLB	26	0	1	0	40	45	3	20	14	4.5	3.2	54%	.286	1.70	5.18	6.09	-0.6
A. Bibens-Dirkx	TEN	AA	25	5	3	0	85^{1}	59	6	27	68	2.8	7.2	41%	.227	1.03	3.16	4.86	1.0
—	IOW	AAA	25	5	4	0	52^{2}	55	9	21	34	3.6	5.8	38%	.275	1.46	4.61	6.05	-0.1
J. Gaub*	IOW	AAA	25	3	4	3	29	27	1	25	38	7.8	11.8	35%	.356	1.86	5.90	5.50	-0.1
J. Gray	IOW	AAA	28	3	1	1	35	45	2	15	25	3.9	6.4	55%	.361	1.83	5.40	5.55	-0.1
—	CHN	MLB	28	1	0	0	9^{1}	12	1	5	4	4.8	3.9	66%	.324	1.93	6.75	8.76	-0.4
T. Harris	MYR	A+	23	1	2	1	26^{2}	23	0	12	37	4.1	12.5	64%	.349	1.39	3.71	3.83	0.3
B. Howry	ARI	MLB	36	1	0	0	14^{1}	18	6	6	6	3.8	3.8	25%	.245	1.67	10.67	7.03	-0.5
—	CHN	MLB	36	0	3	0	20^{2}	29	2	7	8	3.0	3.5	41%	.321	1.74	5.66	12.06	-1.0
B. Raley*	DAY	A+	22	8	6	0	136^{1}	151	9	43	97	2.8	6.4	45%	.330	1.45	3.43	3.09	4.2
B. Schlitter	IOW	AAA	24	2	1	13	45^{2}	44	3	21	42	4.1	8.3	47%	.308	1.45	2.96	3.11	0.9
—	CHN	MLB	24	0	1	0	8	18	2	5	7	5.6	7.9	34%	.485	3.00	12.38	6.72	-0.2
H. Simpson	DNP	—	22	—	—	—	—	—	—	—	—	—	—	—	—	—	—	—	—
K. Smit	SBR	A+	22	5	3	6	50^{2}	51	4	10	46	1.8	8.2	58%	.313	1.26	2.49	3.21	1.3
—	TEN	AA	22	5	1	1	24	29	1	5	20	1.9	7.5	42%	.364	1.46	1.88	2.17	0.8
J. Stevens	IOW	AAA	26	0	2	10	42^{2}	31	3	26	43	5.5	9.1	44%	.246	1.34	3.16	3.68	0.7
—	CHN	MLB	26	0	0	0	17^{2}	21	4	10	15	5.1	7.6	41%	.309	1.75	6.11	7.80	-0.7
B. Wallach	GRL	A	21	6	0	0	84^{2}	73	7	43	92	4.6	9.8	40%	.300	1.44	3.40	3.87	1.7
—	PEO	A	21	0	4	0	29^{2}	28	2	18	24	5.5	7.3	42%	.280	1.65	5.16	7.03	-0.4

As desperate as the Cubs were for right-handed pitching help, they couldn't trust **Mitch Atkins**' weak stuff, outrighting him from the 40-man in September; he was signed by the O's to a minor-league deal. ⊘ Never trust a big butt and smile, but **Jeff Beliveau** is only poison to lefty batters, striking out 38 percent of them at Daytona. ⊘ Repeated attempts to reap the benefit of **Justin Berg**'s extreme ground-ball tendencies ran up against his inability to get big-league hitters to cooperatively tap them into play. ⊘ Retreaded from the indie leagues after getting discarded by the Mariners, **Austin Bibens-Dirkx** mixes things up, changing arm slots to get the most out of a modest assortment. ⊘ Once seen as a key part of the DeRosa deal, **John Gaub** was felled by Steve Blass disease in July, losing all sense of the strike zone and landing on the inactive list, with no suggestion as to when or if he'll be back. ⊘ **Jeff Gray** can pump flat gas at high velocity, but an early injury struggle and subsequent ones got him outrighted from the 40-man. ⊘ Slow-developing **Ty'Relle Harris** came over in the Derrek Lee deal and might have a future as a big (6'4", approximately 235 pounds) reliever. ⊘ Hendry snagged **Bob Howry** after he'd been cut from the worst bullpen in baseball history, only to learn why. ⊘ **Brooks Raley** might be more of an organizational arm, but the big lefty had a strong second half in his full-season debut, and he can touch 94 with his fastball. ⊘ The Iowa shuttle briefly deposited **Brian Schlitter** in Wrigleyville, but after putting half of the batters he faced on base, it promptly took the big guy back to corn country. The Yankees claimed him off of waivers. ⊘ Hard-throwing 2010 first-rounder **Hayden Simpson** was seen as a reach pick, but after he contracted mono, seeing him in action had to wait 'til 2011. ⊘ The low-upside guy from the Lilly deal, **Kyle Smit** has a nice sinker/slider combo that he might parlay into a middle relief job; he was added to the 40-man in November. ⊘ **Jeff Stevens** should have been among the club's better answers for its right-handed relief needs, but inconsistent use during his stint in "The Show" led to inconsistent results. ⊘ Received from the Dodgers in the Lilly deal, **Brett Wallach** is big, with a fastball that sits in the low 90s and decent off-speed stuff, but he needs to achieve consistency to pan out.

MANAGER: LOU PINIELLA/MIKE QUADE

YEAR	MGR	W-L	Pythag +/-	Avg PC	100+ P	120+ P	QS	BQS	REL	REL w Zero R	IBB	Subs	PH	PH Avg	PH HR	SB2	CS2	SB3	CS3	SAC Att	SAC %	POS SAC	Squeeze	Swing	In Play
2009	L.P.	83-78	-2	96.6	69	2	91	6	480	314	46	72	272	.222	5	49	30	7	2	95	68.4%	33	2	143	106
2010	L.P.	51-74	-1	97.2	67	8	69	6	371	213	33	40	188	.222	7	38	20	5	3	69	69.6%	14	3	109	86
2010	M.Q.	24-13	4	96.7	18	2	22	0	111	81	9	18	43	.179	0	9	6	2	1	17	70.6%	2	0	18	14

Taking the interim tag off Quade reflected a reluctance to chain the future to Ryne Sandberg's fame, but managerial jobs aren't entitlements—if Ryno had put in four years in the minors at the organization's request, swell, but Quade was a two-time manager of the year with 17 years' experience skippering in the minors, and once put into Piniella's cleats, he was ready to roll with pregame prep and operational planning. During a transitional period where the next skipper might very well be the scapegoat of 2012 or 2013, do you think that the new owners relished the risk of firing the franchise's single most recognizable person within their first five years of acquiring the team? Three years of coaching with the A's during the *Moneyball* days of the early Aughties, plus his lengthy tenure in the Cubs' minor-league system, gives Quade a lot of experience with players in the organization, as well as interesting references. However, most of Quade's time skippering the club came during September—with expanded rosters—so there aren't many conclusions to draw about whether he will be a significantly different tactician than Piniella was.

Chicago White Sox

As with all forms of life everywhere, baseball teams evolve and change over time, trying to adapt to their competitive environment. That isn't to say that they all do it well—the Pirates' standard for failure beggars description, of course, unless you want to reach for other living metaphors for unintelligent design, like the hapless panda bear.

A key element of what BP alum Keith Woolner referred to as the "competitive ecology" of baseball is that the standards for success vary according to time and place. Teams are generally striving to achieve the same end (or niche): winning ballgames, getting to the postseason, collecting extra cash—rinse, repeat. Considering the geographic distribution of the various divisions, you can forgive general managers in the divisions that aren't the AL East if they focus on keeping up with the Joneses instead of wondering about what the Steinbrenners are up to, and thereby end up scrabbling for and achieving that measure of fairly limited success. The problem is that if you only build to win last year's division race or address just the failings of last year's ballclub, you risk losing sight of the big picture. Worse yet, you might just run into a team actually built to last, to win and keep winning.

WHITE SOX PROSPECTUS

2010 W-L: 88-74, 2nd in AL Central

Pythag	.531	13th	**Ballpark:** U.S. Cellular Field (3-yr. PF: 103). Juan Pierre was held homerless, but Andruw Jones can testify to the Cell's launching-pad properties.
RS/G	4.6	10th	
RA/G	4.3	15th	
TAv	.268	16th	
BRR	8.6	6th	**2010:** Manny and Edwin arrive too late to quiet the team's Thome ache
FRA	4.20	10th	
DER	-14.6	27th	
DL	595	5th	**2011:** Swapping Kotsay for Dunn may be all it takes to trade places with Twins
B-Age	30.7	28th	
P-Age	28.9	22nd	**Action Items:** A healthy Peavy, a productive Quentin, a third baseman, and good Gordon Beckham from the start
Salary	$105.5	7th	
M$/MW	$2.42	13th	

Naturally, incidents of this type have happened in baseball history already. At the start of the 1980s, the game's previous era of fairly dynamic competitive parity, winning the old seven-team AL West generally involved a lower threshold for success than did winning the AL East. The Royals had been miraculous world champs of 1985, disappointments in 1986, and a near miss in 1987, as GM John Schuerholz traded aggressively to try to get back on top right away—acquiring a shortstop by swapping Danny Jackson for Kurt Stillwell, adding pop in the outfield by liberating Danny Tartabull from the Mariners, and trading four young pitchers for an established rotation workhorse in Floyd Bannister.

However, doing all that ignored two very real problems. First, Schuerholz didn't really come to terms with the fact that stars like Frank White and Willie Wilson were getting old, and a weak offense wasn't going to get that much better carrying them, let alone with somebody like Pat Tabler at DH. As long as the old standards for what could win the division held, maybe this would have worked in one year or another, but one of the Royals' division rivals was gearing up to set a higher standard, taking things up from a 90- to a 100-win target. The A's of Sandy Alderson and Tony La Russa (with the help of sabermetrician Eric Walker), armed with the Bash Brothers and Eck and Dave Stewart, were that team, and they decisively consigned the last three Schuerholz-era ballclubs in Kansas City to history's dustbin. The Royals haven't mattered since, not in any divisional configuration.

The question that is relevant to Bridgeport's ballclub is whether we can look at these White Sox as something like the Royals of the late 1980s—adapted for a competitive environment that may no longer exist. That's because Kenny Williams and Ozzie Guillen may have adapted as far as they could within the limits of their aspirations (and their budget), only to find that their concept of what it takes to contend in their division no longer lives up to the higher standard the Twins seem ready to set and live up to. After the 2010 breakouts of Delmon Young and Francisco Liriano, Minnesota may no longer be just the M&M boys, going only as far as Joe Mauer and Justin Morneau can carry them. Thanks to a 9-3 Sox finish while the Twins geared up for the playoffs, the final standings convey a prettier picture than one taken two weeks earlier would have presented, with the White Sox already a dozen games out and no more relevant to the post-season picture than, say, the 1989 Royals and their 92 wins had been.

Dropping into also-ran status is a problem for a Chicago team that, in isolation, has made its share of individually clever moves and spent plenty in terms of money and talent to keep up with the Twins and Tigers of the last couple seasons. As we discussed last year in this space, Kenny Williams is nothing if not active, and—like Schuerholz before he left KC for Atlanta—he has successes he can brag about, up to and including a title. From Williams' recent curriculum vitae: big-ticket pick-ups of Alex Rios and Jake Peavy had their merits and didn't cost the club much more than money it could spend and replaceable talent. Taking a less expensive chance on Edwin Jackson's shot at fulfilling the potential seen in him for a decade was a similar type of transaction, in that Williams picked up a talent people drool over, but one that keeps leaving people thinking there's some higher level of performance not yet tapped. If Jackson blossoms in 2011 after a full camp with pitching coach Don Cooper, his acquisition would be a scouting coup that would trump the club's turnaround of an underperforming Jose Contreras. The same basic idea of getting potentially premium talent at a discount guided Williams' inspired additions of talent ranging from John Danks and Gavin Floyd in the rotation to Carlos Quentin in the outfield, and even as far as Bobby Jenks and Matt Thornton in the pen.

The problem when we get into elective decision-making for the White Sox isn't one of clever moves in isolation, though. It's the big-picture solutions they're coming up with, and whether these are the moves they should be making to win. Not every instance of Williams' acquisitiveness worked, not that anyone's acquisitions always do; in 2010, Mark Teahen and Mark Kotsay wound up being disappointments, later to be joined by Manny Ramirez. Leaning on Kotsay to help cover the club's DH slot at the outset reflected a weakness of design: the indulging of Ozzie Guillen's stated desire to change from a homer-driven offense to one with more speed and contact hitting. Ditching station-to-station slugger Jim Thome to add a Kotsay/Andruw Jones platoon at DH produced a classic case of more is less, with the added indignity of freeing Thome to put on a Twins uni and help secure their decisive offensive advantage over the Sox.

Unfortunately, this wasn't Williams' only indulgence of his outspoken skipper's desire to get that old Podzilla feeling back, and unfortunately enough, pursuing speed or manufactured runs or oxymoronic "productive outs" creates perverse incentives. Choosing to live hand-to-mouth on offense might sound aggressive and tough, because it demands action, puts tactical pressure on defenses, and creates diversity in your offensive options. In reality, though, it's self-limiting—which brings us to the selection of Juan Pierre as the team's leadoff man and left fielder. Thinking along with the Sox, you can almost understand where Ozzie and Kenny were coming from. In terms of their own experiences, when the team had been a better baserunning ballclub, success in the standings seemed to follow. In their division-winning 2005 and 2008 campaigns, the White Sox had finished in the top half of the majors in Baserunning Runs, while finishing in the bottom third in 2006-2007 and 2009. Getting Pierre was a matter of associating an effect with a perceived cause and trying to replicate it. In this, the Sox were successful, at least in terms of returning to the top half of the majors in BRR, as Guillen turned his team loose and pushed his baserunners hard.

Still, aggression didn't really pay for itself—not that it could. Maybe it should be taken as a hint when somebody else wants to pay you $10.5 million to put one of their players in your uniform. Remember, the choice to employ Pierre as the team's left fielder involves an opportunity cost, namely, all those at-bats you might have given to somebody who hit more like a left fielder or, better still, somebody who hit more like a good left fielder, which this team needed. Pierre's production, counting baserunning, was still well below the standard for big-league left fielders. To go back to the Royals comparison, picking Pierre was like Schuerholz's decision to employ guys like Tabler or Gerald Perry at DH, instead of people who could hit—Tabler and Perry were the kind of hitters the Royals thought they could win with at DH, because these players vaguely resembled Hal McRae and, as contact hitters, were interpreted as guys who would do damage on turf. The Sox didn't even have to shell out top dollar during the winter to get better ballplayers like Hideki Matsui or Johnny Damon—guys like Fred Lewis or Pat Burrell were there for the taking during the course of the season. Only at the end, when the Sox took on Manny's salary as their opportunity to keep up with the Twins slipped away, did the problem with employing bad bats like Pierre or Kotsay in boppers' spots get addressed.

The misfortune is that the Sox were handing back gains they had made with their willingness to risk a positional reach or two. Williams and Guillen had sensibly identified that Alex Rios could play center and that Alexei Ramirez could play short, and accrued offensive benefits at positions where good-hitting help is hard to find. Employing Pierre and Kotsay in sluggers' slots eroded the advantage Rios and Ramirez conferred. That's affordable if you're getting offense all over the rest of the lineup, but with insufficient answers at third, Gordon Beckham's terrible sophomore season, Quentin's regression into adequacy, and A. J. Pierzynski's bad year, this just wasn't that kind of offense. Finishing even ninth in the league in True Average owed much more to Paul Konerko's career-best offensive performance than Pierre's "successful" season.

You can hope there's a lesson learned. The problem now is that the Sox are confronted with a future where their key players have little unrealized upside. Bringing back Paul

Konerko and signing Adam Dunn will neatly resolve the club's needs at first base and DH, but the Sox are not likely to get a season as good as Konerko's 2010 from either, and Dunn did just set his career low in walk rate—is that supposed to get better in the AL? Quentin has turned in consecutive seasons without coming close to his 2008 breakout. Even if Beckham builds on his second-half bounce-back, and even if Brent Morel establishes himself at the hot corner, it's an attack in danger of losing ground as a relentless function of age in 2011, something that having Juan Pierre get 650 plate appearances won't help.

Can the Sox nevertheless stay in the increasingly difficult Central race on the strength of their pitching? That has to be the hope, but consider what that hope rests upon. First, that Danks and Floyd log quality campaigns closer to the higher end of their possibilities. Second, that Mark Buehrle doesn't lose more ground to Father Time. Third, that Jackson blossoms in his walk year. And all of that on top of getting a miracle from Herm Schneider's outstanding training staff so that Peavy comes back from an unusual injury earlier rather than later. Those are a lot of maybes and involve working with narrow margins. While Sox player development may not produce depth, it can take credit for making a number of its more expensive recent investments pay off. Last year's first-rounder, power lefty Chris Sale, raced to the majors ready for a relief role. If Peavy isn't ready by April, Sale might be the Sox's only real alternative with the kind of upside they can try to win with.

Unfortunately, there are also the Twins' actions to consider, because Minnesota is a moving target that has already raised the standard for what it takes to win the division. The Twins are the team with three million fannies in the seats in a new stadium, paying to see a roster already peopled with some of the game's best ballplayers, and the franchise is set up to bring in additional big-ticket help if it wants to secure its advantage. Williams' willingness to gamble and to go for it, admirable as it has been, might have shot its bolt if the Sox can't get serious about simply scoring runs, instead of fidgeting over how they score them.

HITTERS

Gordon Beckham **2B**

Born: **9/16/1986** Age: **24**
Bats: R Throws: R Height: **6' 0"** Weight: **185**
Breakout: **1%** Improve: **30%** Collapse: **7%**
Attrition: **15%** MLB: **72%**

Comparables:
J.J. Hardy, Carlos Baerga, Jim Lefebvre (71)

YEAR	TEAM	LVL	AGE	PA	R	2B	3B	HR	RBI	BB	SO	SB	CS	AVG/OBP/SLG	TAv	BABIP	BRR	FRAA	WARP
2008	KAN	A	21	63	11	2	0	3	8	5	7	0	1	.310/.365/.500	.295	.313	-0.7	SS 4	0.8
2009	BIR	AA	22	164	22	17	0	4	22	14	24	1	0	.299/.366/.497	.298	.328	0.6	SS 3, 2B 0	1.6
2009	CHA	MLB	22	430	57	28	1	14	63	41	65	7	4	.270/.347/.460	.281	.290	4.0	3B 1	2.7
2010	CHA	MLB	23	498	57	25	2	9	49	37	92	4	6	.252/.313/.378	.255	.292	-0.7	2B -1	0.7
2011	*CHA*	*MLB*	*24*	*395*	*47*	*23*	*1*	*9*	*44*	*31*	*65*	*5*	*3*	*.266/.327/.410*	*.260*	*.297*	*-0.4*	*2B 0, 3B 1*	*1.2*

If Becks had delivered his second-half rates over a full season, he'd have fulfilled expectations and then some, given that he hit .285/.336/.459 after June. Unfortunately, there were those first three months, not all of which you can blame on the distractions of batting second after Juan Pierre—a month into the season, Becks been banished to the ninth slot. Happily, he rallied before his season was effectively ended early after getting struck on the hand with a pitch: his walk rate and ISO both returned to their rookie-season standards. If you can look past the half-season hiccup, he should be fine. Another year should provide good news at the plate as well as afield; last year, Beckham showed off excellent footwork around the bag on the deuce, feeding the expectation that like Alexei Ramirez, he would find a second season at the same position a big step forward. If not, the huge number of Beckham jerseys you see in the stands will require some explanation to the uninitiated.

Ramon Castro **C**

Born: **3/1/1976** Age: **35**
Bats: R Throws: R Height: **6' 3"** Weight: **225**
Breakout: **1%** Improve: **16%** Collapse: **12%**
Attrition: **20%** MLB: **68%**

Comparables:
Sal Fasano, Daryle Ward, Mark Parent (66)

YEAR	TEAM	LVL	AGE	PA	R	2B	3B	HR	RBI	BB	SO	SB	CS	AVG/OBP/SLG	TAv	BABIP	BRR	FRAA	WARP
2008	NYN	MLB	32	157	15	7	0	7	24	13	34	0	0	.245/.312/.441	.263	.275	-3.4	C 0	0.4
2009	CHA	MLB	33	84	8	3	0	4	12	8	23	0	0	.184/.262/.382	.231	.204	-0.7	C -1	-0.1
2009	NYN	MLB	33	87	6	5	0	3	13	8	16	0	0	.253/.322/.430	.253	.283	0.3	C -1	0.2
2010	CHA	MLB	34	128	18	2	0	8	21	9	26	1	0	.278/.320/.504	.286	.282	-0.2	C 0	0.8
2011	*CHA*	*MLB*	*35*	*163*	*19*	*6*	*0*	*7*	*21*	*14*	*37*	*0*	*0*	*.244/.308/.432*	*.256*	*.272*	*0.0*	*C -1*	*0.5*

When you want to talk about practically perfect backup catchers, you can get hung up on certain features, like whether a guy walks, or bats lefty or switch, or is a particularly pleasant batterymate preferred by some high-strung hurler. Chucking all of that, Castro provides the no-nonsense basics: power that plays in any park and an arm strong enough to keep the running game in check when he plays. You might figure that this would make Castro a starter, given lower standards for what plays behind the plate, but concerns over his long stroke, his getting overpowered by some right-handers, and his bulk have combined to keep him pigeonholed as a high-end reserve. That won't change in 2011, as the Sox picked up his option and then re-signed Pierzynski.

Nick Ciolli CF

Born: **12/6/1987** Age: **23**
Bats: **L** Throws: **R** Height: **6' 2"** Weight: **215**
Breakout: **1%** Improve: **3%** Collapse: **0%**
Attrition: **4%** MLB: **6%**

Comparables:
Ian Desmond, Jai Miller, Ron Swoboda (76)

YEAR	TEAM	LVL	AGE	PA	R	2B	3B	HR	RBI	BB	SO	SB	CS	AVG/OBP/SLG	TAv	BABIP	BRR	FRAA	WARP
2009	GRF	Rk	21	281	45	17	1	7	36	26	54	25	4	.315/.388/.472	.338	.376	1.0	LF 2, CF -1	3.0
2010	KAN	A	22	465	57	22	5	12	73	17	123	8	6	.296/.320/.451	.278	.377	1.7	RF 1, CF -3	1.7
2011	*CHA*	*MLB*	*23*	*396*	*40*	*17*	*2*	*8*	*42*	*14*	*116*	*7*	*2*	*.241/.268/.364*	*.221*	*.318*	*-0.1*	*RF 0, LF -3*	*-1.3*

In Ciolli's first full season, the 2009 10th-rounder out of Indiana State gave plenty of indication that he might be that program's best hitter since Clint Barmes . . . by being a hitter a lot like Clint Barmes. He's caught in the quandary of being seen as something of a toolsy tweener, but you can see that the issues in his stats above combine to make him something of a tweener in all things, not just the doubt over whether he can play center regularly: he's a hacker without any power payoff, a speed guy without all that much speed, and whiffable without walking. In most systems, he wouldn't merit more than a lineout at this point, but the Sox have so few commendable hitters that we figure you Sox fans will want to see something on somebody.

Jordan Danks CF

Born: **8/7/1986** Age: **24**
Bats: **L** Throws: **R** Height: **6' 4"** Weight: **210**
Breakout: **3%** Improve: **3%** Collapse: **2%**
Attrition: **4%** MLB: **5%**

Comparables:
Jordan Schafer, Chili Davis, Bernie Williams (80)

YEAR	TEAM	LVL	AGE	PA	R	2B	3B	HR	RBI	BB	SO	SB	CS	AVG/OBP/SLG	TAv	BABIP	BRR	FRAA	WARP
2009	WNS	A+	22	138	25	11	2	3	21	18	32	5	1	.322/.406/.525	.322	.412	-1.8	CF -4	0.7
2009	BIR	AA	22	340	44	12	1	6	20	39	77	6	3	.233/.329/.341	.253	.289	2.3	CF 1, LF 1	1.0
2010	CHR	AAA	23	498	60	27	3	8	42	41	151	15	6	.245/.309/.373	.236	.339	3.9	CF -10, LF 2	-0.4
2011	*CHA*	*MLB*	*24*	*340*	*34*	*15*	*1*	*5*	*30*	*28*	*97*	*7*	*2*	*.227/.291/.337*	*.223*	*.306*	*-0.2*	*CF -7, LF 0*	*-1.1*

The organization had its share of colossal disappointments on the farm front in 2010, but few cratered more deeply than Danks did. Exposed to older pitchers with better breaking stuff at Triple-A, the younger brother of the staff ace got carved up as if it were exam day at teppanyaki school; worse yet, he showed no progress in-season. He has essentially failed to live up to expectations, both at college and for most of his pro career, which leads to questions about whether we should still harbor any hope for his future. Given that Danks has little else in terms of signal virtues beyond a good glove, he's now in a position where he *has* to make progress this season, especially in the power department, because it's either that or hope to get voted into the Nix family as an honorary sibling.

Eduardo Escobar SS

Born: **1/5/1989** Age: **22**
Bats: Throws: Height: **5' 10"** Weight: **150**
Breakout: **4%** Improve: **12%** Collapse: **0%**
Attrition: **9%** MLB: **22%**

Comparables:
Alcides Escobar, Everth Cabrera, Joaquin Arias (72)

YEAR	TEAM	LVL	AGE	PA	R	2B	3B	HR	RBI	BB	SO	SB	CS	AVG/OBP/SLG	TAv	BABIP	BRR	FRAA	WARP
2008	KAN	A	19	266	37	6	1	0	22	13	65	4	3	.268/.293/.300	.229	.346	0.6	SS 4, 2B -2	0.4
2009	KAN	A	20	516	62	11	7	3	40	30	92	20	6	.256/.293/.329	.265	.299	2.4	SS 4, 2B -3	2.5
2010	WNS	A+	21	406	58	18	8	3	38	23	76	0	0	.285/.320/.402	.257	.336	0.0	SS 5	1.9
2010	BIR	AA	21	216	22	8	3	3	22	9	35	0	0	.262/.287/.376	.256	.296	0.0	SS 5	1.2
2011	*CHA*	*MLB*	*22*	*477*	*44*	*17*	*4*	*2*	*41*	*15*	*103*	*6*	*2*	*.244/.262/.315*	*.206*	*.299*	*-0.2*	*SS 9, 2B -1*	*0.0*

If Sox prospects are few and far between, there is at least the satisfaction that the happy few really deserve the label. Escobar is a Venezuelan shortstop who was always gifted with the sort of special fielding skill that was going to get him taken seriously, especially with a plus-plus arm. But last year, he started showing off a line-drive stroke that made him something more than a fruit from the glove bush, earning a promotion to Double-A that he took in stride. This, in turn, got him an invite to the AFL, where he crushed triples like a latter-day Chief Wilson. Put all of that together, and you have a genuine shortstop prospect with some offensive upside and a smattering of upper-level experience, and he has only just turned 22. With Alexei Ramirez's development as a defender, the Sox can afford to wait and see, but if Kenny Williams decides to go shopping, in Escobar he has what folks in Illinois refer to as a frickin' valuable thing.

Tyler Flowers **C**

Born: **1/24/1986** Age: **25**
Bats: R Throws: R Height: **6' 4"** Weight: **245**
Breakout: **4%** Improve: **26%** Collapse: **7%**
Attrition: **22%** MLB: **57%**

Comparables:
Scott Rolen, Aaron Bates, Geovany Soto (65)

YEAR	TEAM	LVL	AGE	PA	R	2B	3B	HR	RBI	BB	SO	SB	CS	AVG/OBP/SLG	TAv	BABIP	BRR	FRAA	WARP
2008	MYR	A+	22	550	75	35	1	19	93	103	112	8	7	.294/.435/.506	.348	.351	-9.2	C 3, 1B 0	6.4
2009	BIR	AA	23	308	52	18	2	13	42	57	76	3	0	.302/.458/.548	.353	.383	1.1	C 0	4.1
2009	CHR	AAA	23	116	13	10	0	2	12	10	32	0	0	.286/.371/.438	.265	.389	0.3	C 0	0.6
2009	CHA	MLB	23	20	3	1	0	0	0	3	8	0	0	.188/.350/.250	.232	.375	-0.1	C 0	0.0
2010	CHR	AAA	24	406	43	22	2	16	53	55	121	0	0	.220/.337/.434	.263	.280	0.0	C 0	1.8
2010	CHA	MLB	24	15	2	0	0	0	0	4	5	0	0	.091/.333/.091	.210	.167	0.4	C 0	0.0
2011	*CHA*	*MLB*	*25*	*472*	*58*	*22*	*1*	*14*	*51*	*66*	*131*	*1*	*0*	*.237/.350/.410*	*.271*	*.308*	*-0.1*	*C 0, 1B 0*	*2.1*

Like Danks, Flowers wilted at Charlotte, putting up a season that did little to recommend him now or in the future. His problems making contact undermined his ability to deliver any power, and things don't get easier in the majors. To put it charitably, he's still settling in as a receiver, and some scouts feel that he's losing ground (evidenced by his caught-stealing rate, which dropped to 26 percent). Put that together, and you resurrect concerns that he may not be an effective everyday catcher—not unless he hits, which he didn't. Rather than risk Flowers' complete failure by trusting in him in 2011, the Sox re-signed both Pierzynski and Castro, leaving the flickering hope that Flowers might be a late bloomer.

Stefan Gartrell **OF**

Born: **1/14/1984** Age: **27**
Bats: R Throws: R Height: **6' 3"** Weight: **230**
Breakout: **4%** Improve: **21%** Collapse: **2%**
Attrition: **15%** MLB: **37%**

Comparables:
David Freese, John Mayberry, Terry Evans (74)

YEAR	TEAM	LVL	AGE	PA	R	2B	3B	HR	RBI	BB	SO	SB	CS	AVG/OBP/SLG	TAv	BABIP	BRR	FRAA	WARP
2008	BIR	AA	24	470	50	23	2	14	52	45	107	6	1	.251/.334/.415	.266	.299	0.3	RF 1, LF 3	1.4
2009	BIR	AA	25	408	71	20	4	19	70	46	99	6	0	.285/.375/.521	.329	.344	-1.1	RF -13, LF 1	2.2
2009	CHR	AAA	25	120	14	11	1	4	19	7	29	0	2	.266/.317/.487	.297	.325	2.4	RF -4, LF 0	0.4
2010	CHR	AAA	26	577	72	20	1	27	80	40	151	4	2	.254/.317/.448	.256	.301	2.9	RF -2, LF -3	0.4
2011	*CHA*	*MLB*	*27*	*525*	*60*	*21*	*2*	*19*	*63*	*38*	*139*	*3*	*1*	*.243/.300/.416*	*.250*	*.296*	*-0.1*	*RF -7, LF -1*	*-0.5*

The 2010 season represented Gartrell's latest success in the face of nonexistent expectations for the big former 31st-rounder. He's not an especially mobile corner outfielder, and with 110 strikeouts versus 19 walks in 410 PAs against right-handers last year, he's not going to blossom into a major-league regular. It's safe to say he's just an organizational player coming off a good season, but give the guy props for getting this far.

Andruw Jones **OF**

Born: **4/23/1977** Age: **34**
Bats: R Throws: R Height: **6' 1"** Weight: **170**
Breakout: **0%** Improve: **25%** Collapse: **8%**
Attrition: **12%** MLB: **95%**

Comparables:
Fred Lynn, Ben Oglivie, Fernando Tatis (70)

YEAR	TEAM	LVL	AGE	PA	R	2B	3B	HR	RBI	BB	SO	SB	CS	AVG/OBP/SLG	TAv	BABIP	BRR	FRAA	WARP
2008	LAN	MLB	31	238	21	8	1	3	14	27	76	0	1	.158/.256/.249	.198	.229	1.1	CF 0	-0.7
2009	TEX	MLB	32	331	46	18	0	17	43	45	72	5	1	.214/.323/.459	.279	.221	-1.7	LF 1, RF -2	0.6
2010	CHA	MLB	33	328	41	12	1	19	48	45	73	9	2	.230/.342/.486	.287	.239	0.3	RF -2, CF -1	1.0
2011	*CHA*	*MLB*	*34*	*455*	*54*	*17*	*1*	*19*	*54*	*56*	*102*	*7*	*2*	*.224/.325/.423*	*.264*	*.249*	*-0.1*	*CF 0, RF -1*	*0.8*

After his wipeout with the Dodgers, you can credit Jones for being sensible about where he has gone to keep having a career. Signing first with Texas and then the Sox put him in a pair of parks that reward right-handed power; slugging .507 in Arlington and then .558 on the South Side is the sort of thing that helps keep him in cleats. Add in that he's playable in either outfield corner, with an arm that still has some deterrent value, and he's a handy ex-famous dude. That isn't to say he's perfect or someone who might be worth starting every day again. Even setting aside irksome things like his grounding into double plays at a team-leading 22 percent clip last year, there's the more practical problem of keeping Jones in working order, as well as the doubt over whether his production would hold up over a full season facing the best right-handed pitching in either league. If he's happy to keep contributing in this kind of role, he's worth carving out space for on most rosters.

Paul Konerko **1B**

Born: **3/5/1976** Age: **35**
Bats: R Throws: R Height: **6' 3"** Weight: **205**
Breakout: **0%** Improve: **34%** Collapse: **0%**
Attrition: **7%** MLB: **93%**

Comparables:
Lance Berkman, Carlos Delgado, Roy Sievers (74)

YEAR	TEAM	LVL	AGE	PA	R	2B	3B	HR	RBI	BB	SO	SB	CS	AVG/OBP/SLG	TAv	BABIP	BRR	FRAA	WARP
2008	CHA	MLB	32	514	62	19	1	22	62	65	80	2	0	.240/.344/.438	.272	.244	-5.8	1B -3	0.2
2009	CHA	MLB	33	621	78	30	1	28	88	58	89	1	0	.277/.353/.489	.292	.282	-3.1	1B 3	2.5
2010	CHA	MLB	34	631	91	30	1	39	111	72	110	0	1	.312/.393/.584	.344	.326	-3.7	1B -6	4.7
2011	*CHA*	*MLB*	*35*	*613*	*82*	*27*	*1*	*28*	*84*	*68*	*99*	*1*	*0*	*.272/.358/.481*	*.292*	*.284*	*0.0*	*1B -2*	*2.1*

Last year's comment that Konerko "isn't going to get any better as he ages" could not have been more decisively disproved: he set career highs in OBP, SLG, and TAv. He even tied his career-low in GIDPs, although a major factor for that was a career-low number of opportunities, a positive product of the conscious effort to play actual Ozzieball instead of just talking about it. It's fairly well established within the sabermetric community that RBI should not count for anything, but if you haven't gotten the news, consider the uneven distribution of opportunities: Konerko drove in a slightly higher percentage of his men on base than did Miguel Cabrera (18.5 percent to 18.4). But with almost 50 fewer at-bats and 90 fewer baserunners, it was utterly unsurprising that he wound up behind the league leader despite smacking one more homer. The name of the game is opportunities, and it always has been. Paulie remains the most popular Sock bar none, in part because he tends to please the home fans—see his career .260 ISO at the Cell. Perhaps this three-way relationship between player, park, and patrons was on his mind when he agreed to a three-year, $37.5 million deal to continue bashing on the South Side as he heads toward the back half of his 30s.

Mark Kotsay **OF**

Born: **12/2/1975** Age: **35**
Bats: L Throws: L Height: **6' 0"** Weight: **180**
Breakout: **0%** Improve: **21%** Collapse: **14%**
Attrition: **33%** MLB: **65%**

Comparables:
Todd Walker, Kevin Seitzer, Denny Walling (77)

YEAR	TEAM	LVL	AGE	PA	R	2B	3B	HR	RBI	BB	SO	SB	CS	AVG/OBP/SLG	TAv	BABIP	BRR	FRAA	WARP
2008	ATL	MLB	32	345	39	17	3	6	37	25	34	2	3	.289/.339/.418	.262	.307	0.9	CF -9	0.3
2008	BOS	MLB	32	91	6	8	1	0	12	7	11	0	1	.226/.286/.345	.233	.260	0.3	RF 0, 1B -1	-0.2
2009	BOS	MLB	33	79	5	2	0	1	5	4	12	2	1	.257/.291/.324	.227	.290	-0.5	1B 1, CF -1	-0.3
2009	CHA	MLB	33	127	12	7	0	3	18	11	9	1	1	.292/.347/.434	.278	.289	1.3	1B -2, RF 0	0.3
2010	CHA	MLB	34	359	36	17	2	8	31	32	36	1	3	.239/.306/.376	.248	.247	-1.9	1B -2, RF -2	-0.6
2011	*CHA*	*MLB*	*35*	*376*	*40*	*18*	*1*	*4*	*34*	*30*	*39*	*4*	*2*	*.250/.308/.350*	*.234*	*.267*	*-0.4*	*CF -3, 1B -1*	*-0.9*

When it comes to one crummy lefty bat versus another, there's a difference between getting Mark Teahen to play third and finding him unavailable or inadequate on the one hand and starting Kotsay 86 times as a matter of design on the other. Most of that playing time came at first base and DH, but Kotsay isn't a good glove at first and his bat won't cover either slot. This was not a new development, just more of the same. Add in that he and Andruw Jones were on the roster to replace Jim Thome, taking up twice as much roster space without delivering the value Thome had, and the whole thing winds up as one of the season's major miscalculations. Given Kotsay's limited value at any position or at the plate, you can reasonably wonder where he'll wash up, but places like Houston and Pittsburgh might suit him.

Brent Lillibridge **INF**

Born: **9/18/1983** Age: **27**
Bats: R Throws: R Height: **5' 11"** Weight: **190**
Breakout: **0%** Improve: **12%** Collapse: **3%**
Attrition: **7%** MLB: **27%**

Comparables:
Drew Meyer, Ivan Ochoa, Ivan DeJesus (78)

YEAR	TEAM	LVL	AGE	PA	R	2B	3B	HR	RBI	BB	SO	SB	CS	AVG/OBP/SLG	TAv	BABIP	BRR	FRAA	WARP
2008	RIC	AAA	24	392	44	18	7	4	39	33	88	21	7	.220/.296/.346	.224	.273	1.6	SS 1	0.3
2008	ATL	MLB	24	85	7	6	1	1	8	3	23	2	0	.200/.235/.338	.212	.263	0.8	SS -1, 3B 0	-0.1
2009	CHR	AAA	25	279	32	9	4	3	23	29	57	15	1	.252/.341/.358	.249	.311	3.0	SS -1, CF 2	1.1
2009	CHA	MLB	25	112	7	2	0	0	3	14	26	6	3	.158/.268/.179	.180	.211	1.5	2B 0, CF -4	-0.9
2010	CHR	AAA	26	205	26	8	0	4	16	17	46	0	0	.270/.332/.378	.253	.333	0.0	SS 1, 2B 2	0.9
2010	CHA	MLB	26	101	8	5	2	2	16	3	36	5	3	.225/.248/.378	.219	.333	0.1	2B 1, CF -1	-0.2
2011	*CHA*	*MLB*	*27*	*391*	*38*	*15*	*3*	*4*	*31*	*31*	*96*	*17*	*6*	*.222/.287/.316*	*.217*	*.285*	*-0.1*	*SS 0, 2B 0*	*-0.4*

We're Here Because We're Here is an album by the British death metal group Anathema, which seems an appropriate explanation for why we have to write a full-length player comment on Brent Lillibridge. The thinking mind rebels, but hey, this guy does . . . well, *stuff*, right? He plays all sorts of positions, hits something against major-league pitching, and maybe even solves crimes after hours. What his listing is actually meant for on a big-league roster defies easy explanation. Third-string shortstop? Pinch-runner for designated narcoleptics? Roster yo-yo until he runs out of options and winds up on the Royals someday? Oh, wait, that last one sounds good! He even has that honeyed former association with the Braves that is ambrosia to Dayton Moore.

Jared Mitchell **OF**

Born: **10/13/1988** Age: **22**
Bats: L Throws: L Height: **6' 0"** Weight: **205**
Breakout: –% Improve: –% Collapse: –%
Attrition: –% MLB: –%

Comparables:

YEAR	TEAM	LVL	AGE	PA	R	2B	3B	HR	RBI	BB	SO	SB	CS	AVG/OBP/SLG	TAv	BABIP	BRR	FRAA	WARP
2009	KAN	A	20	133	11	11	2	0	10	22	39	5	3	.288/.414/.423	.325	.444	-4.7	CF 0	0.8
2011	*CHA*	*MLB*	*22*	—	—	—	—	—	—	—	—	—	—	—	—	—	—	—	—

High expectations have had to be put on hold for the 2009 first-round pick out of LSU. That's because Mitchell effectively missed the entire season after hitting a wall making a catch in spring training and damaging a tendon in his ankle, which required surgery to repair. After he got a clean bill of health, the first action he saw came in the Arizona Fall League, where he struggled, striking out 30 percent of the time without doing much damage in a hitter's circuit. Even so, don't get too hung up on the poor performance: Mitchell is as toolsy as they come, but was also very raw from the day he was drafted. He needs reps he hasn't gotten yet, so it's too soon to get too down or up on a guy who only just turned 22.

Brent Morel **3B**

Born: **4/21/1987** Age: **24**
Bats: R Throws: R Height: **6' 2"** Weight: **220**
Breakout: **6%** Improve: **25%** Collapse: **7%**
Attrition: **19%** MLB: **37%**

Comparables:
Ian Desmond, Ian Stewart, Chris Johnson (77)

YEAR	TEAM	LVL	AGE	PA	R	2B	3B	HR	RBI	BB	SO	SB	CS	AVG/OBP/SLG	TAv	BABIP	BRR	FRAA	WARP
2008	KAN	A	21	190	26	6	2	6	24	16	28	5	2	.297/.363/.459	.297	.321	1.6	3B 1	1.5
2008	GRF	Rk	21	70	11	0	2	0	3	6	7	7	0	.375/.443/.438	.334	.421	1.3	3B -1	0.8
2009	WNS	A+	22	536	79	33	1	16	83	38	69	25	9	.284/.340/.452	.287	.300	2.3	3B 6	3.8
2010	BIR	AA	23	201	25	13	1	2	30	14	36	5	5	.326/.378/.440	.303	.389	-0.7	3B 1	1.4
2010	CHR	AAA	23	324	40	24	4	8	34	13	50	3	0	.320/.343/.503	.296	.356	1.5	3B 2, SS -1	2.6
2010	CHA	MLB	23	70	9	3	0	3	7	4	17	2	0	.231/.271/.415	.244	.261	0.4	3B -1	0.0
2011	*CHA*	*MLB*	*24*	*464*	*53*	*24*	*2*	*10*	*54*	*22*	*81*	*10*	*3*	*.276/.308/.409*	*.252*	*.313*	*-0.1*	*3B 0, SS 0*	*0.9*

The word *aggressive* describes Morel's virtues both at the plate and in the field. As a batsman, he's a hacker with excellent plate coverage. While projected as more of a doubles and line-drive power guy, you could see the light go off in his head during his September debut: pulling pitches in the Cell leads to favorable outcomes for right-handed batters. Initial expectations put his homer output as a regular in the teens, but a peak in the 20s wouldn't be a reach. As a glove, he's nothing short of excellent, an all-out acrobat with a gun for an arm. And for all that, he also made it up playing through a torn labrum in his left shoulder, toughing out his promotions and seemingly losing little in terms of performance. With Dayan Viciedo's move across the diamond, Morel's path to the job at the hot corner is relatively clear—he might initially get spotted for by Teahen in obvious platoon-worthy situations, but given that his OBP against right-handers won't have many walks going for it, that's not a bad idea.

Juan Pierre **OF**

Born: **8/14/1977** Age: **33**
Bats: L Throws: L Height: **6' 0"** Weight: **180**
Breakout: **0%** Improve: **28%** Collapse: **4%**
Attrition: **10%** MLB: **94%**

Comparables:
Jason Tyner, Richie Ashburn, Scott Podsednik (60)

YEAR	TEAM	LVL	AGE	PA	R	2B	3B	HR	RBI	BB	SO	SB	CS	AVG/OBP/SLG	TAv	BABIP	BRR	FRAA	WARP
2008	LAN	MLB	30	406	44	10	2	1	28	22	24	40	12	.283/.323/.328	.239	.295	2.9	LF 2, CF 0	0.4
2009	LAN	MLB	31	425	55	16	8	0	31	27	27	30	12	.308/.358/.392	.268	.322	3.0	LF 2, CF 0	1.7
2010	CHA	MLB	32	734	96	18	3	1	47	45	47	68	18	.275/.334/.316	.242	.287	8.1	LF 6	1.3
2011	*CHA*	*MLB*	*33*	*610*	*65*	*20*	*4*	*0*	*49*	*36*	*38*	*51*	*15*	*.280/.323/.333*	*.237*	*.286*	*0.0*	*LF 4, CF 0*	*0.2*

Picked up for little more than 40 percent of the value of his contract to indulge Chicago's hankering for an actual Ozzieball talent, Pierre was turned loose and given everyday play. To his credit, he was a considerable asset on the bases, while helping his OBP with a career-high 21 HBPs. En route to winning the stolen-base title, he tallied just less than a full win's worth of difference with his wheels. That's the upside for employing a bat that was a win's worth of value below the average left fielder—*counting the baserunning*. While there was some hope that having a former center fielder in left would save runs, the panoply of fielding metrics wasn't overly kind, generally describing the results as adequate to good. Still, as long as they were stuck with him, the Sox were right to put him in left; if you're going to employ him at all, you don't play him in center, where his bat profiles best in the abstract, but where his raggedy arm does the least harm. Within his own lights and relative to the expectations the Sox entertained for him going in, he was an unqualified success, the best Juan Pierre he could be, but the problem with employing him as a matter of preference was that it didn't really advance the Sox's cause in any particular direction.

A. J. Pierzynski **C**

Born: **12/30/1976** Age: **34**
Bats: L Throws: R Height: **6' 3"** Weight: **220**
Breakout: **0%** Improve: **36%** Collapse: **12%**
Attrition: **18%** MLB: **94%**

Comparables:
Gary Carter, Bengie Molina, Ramon Hernandez (73)

YEAR	TEAM	LVL	AGE	PA	R	2B	3B	HR	RBI	BB	SO	SB	CS	AVG/OBP/SLG	TAv	BABIP	BRR	FRAA	WARP
2008	CHA	MLB	31	570	66	31	1	13	60	19	71	1	0	.281/.311/.416	.250	.299	-2.9	C -3	1.3
2009	CHA	MLB	32	535	58	22	1	13	49	24	52	1	1	.300/.329/.425	.263	.310	-4.3	C -3	1.7
2010	CHA	MLB	33	503	43	29	0	9	56	15	39	3	4	.270/.296/.388	.235	.274	-0.3	C -2	0.6
2011	*CHA*	*MLB*	*34*	*532*	*58*	*25*	*1*	*9*	*56*	*21*	*58*	*2*	*1*	*.268/.299/.378*	*.236*	*.281*	*-0.2*	*C -2*	*0.7*

The catcher whom 29 teams love to hate couldn't have chosen a worse time to have his worst season at the plate, because the winter market was awash in mediocre catchers. While part of the problem was a stone-cold start that not even a geologist could get into, Pierzynski is an older contact hitter with little else to add beyond batting left. Although he isn't one of the best throwers, having Danks and Buehrle around helps nuke opposing running games. Instead, AJP's value is tied to his durability as a receiver, because guys who can start 120 games a year aren't omnipresent. In light of Flowers' flop, a short-term return to the South Side for two years and $8 million wasn't the worst outcome—the Sox are familiar with his charms, and if he loses a few more at-bats to Castro at home, maybe everyone comes out feeling good.

Carlos Quentin **RF**

Born: **8/28/1982** Age: **28**
Bats: R Throws: R Height: **6' 1"** Weight: **225**
Breakout: **0%** Improve: **39%** Collapse: **5%**
Attrition: **14%** MLB: **95%**

Comparables:
Roger Maris, Andre Ethier, Austin Kearns (74)

YEAR	TEAM	LVL	AGE	PA	R	2B	3B	HR	RBI	BB	SO	SB	CS	AVG/OBP/SLG	TAv	BABIP	BRR	FRAA	WARP
2008	CHA	MLB	25	569	96	26	1	36	100	66	80	7	3	.288/.394/.571	.335	.278	-0.2	LF 2	5.7
2009	CHA	MLB	26	399	48	14	0	21	56	31	52	3	0	.237/.323/.456	.273	.221	-2.6	LF -2	0.8
2010	CHA	MLB	27	527	79	25	2	26	87	50	83	2	2	.243/.342/.479	.291	.241	1.2	RF -10	1.4
2011	*CHA*	*MLB*	*28*	*496*	*66*	*23*	*1*	*22*	*67*	*48*	*72*	*3*	*1*	*.256/.352/.474*	*.289*	*.257*	*-0.2*	*LF 1, RF -2*	*2.1*

When Quentin arrived, he was a tout-worthy find, a rescued talent, a wonderful slugger who inspired confidence for what the future might bring, not unlike Ron Kittle back in 1983. And then, as the subsequent seasons unfolded, Quentin was revealed as a guy who struggled to make solid contact, deliver the same kind of power, play the field effectively, and stay healthy . . . not unlike Ron Kittle. Quentin's power is very much a product of the Cell's friendly left-field target—19 of last season's shots came at home. The question is whether aiming for that target has undermined his approach and made him less effective going to other fields, and he hit just .214/.299/.391 on the road. His walk rate has also dropped below 10 percent in each of the last two seasons, but his OBP gets floated by his reliable willingness to crowd the plate and take one for the team, with another 20 HBPs last year. Quentin is already 28, so if these were his peak seasons, he's losing a lot of ground as he heads toward 30. Health and a better approach might produce another 2008, but if not, he's already a mediocre regular in a corner, and if his fielding gets any worse, he'll be a mediocre DH. A lot like Ron Kittle, come to think of it.

Alexei Ramirez **SS**

Born: **9/22/1981** Age: **29**
Bats: R Throws: R Height: **6' 3"** Weight: **185**
Breakout: **3%** Improve: **52%** Collapse: **3%**
Attrition: **6%** MLB: **96%**

Comparables:
Buddy Bell, Felipe Lopez, Jeff Cirillo (71)

YEAR	TEAM	LVL	AGE	PA	R	2B	3B	HR	RBI	BB	SO	SB	CS	AVG/OBP/SLG	TAv	BABIP	BRR	FRAA	WARP
2008	CHA	MLB	26	509	64	22	2	21	77	18	61	13	9	.290/.314/.475	.281	.291	-0.6	2B -1, CF 0	2.2
2009	CHA	MLB	27	606	72	14	1	15	68	49	66	14	5	.277/.330/.389	.258	.284	0.3	SS -7	1.6
2010	CHA	MLB	28	626	83	29	2	18	70	27	82	13	8	.282/.310/.431	.267	.296	6.0	SS 21	5.3
2011	*CHA*	*MLB*	*29*	*580*	*68*	*24*	*2*	*15*	*68*	*33*	*69*	*13*	*6*	*.277/.316/.415*	*.258*	*.287*	*-0.9*	*SS 4, 2B 0*	*2.1*

The Cuban Missile's trajectory has been generally unpredictable, but three years into its Midwestern deployment, you can still convincingly describe it as "up." He's tremendously adaptable as well as athletic, which leads to turnarounds as dramatic as his development last season into one of the top shortstop gloves in the game today. While his walk rate and his power seem to be on poor terms, refusing to show up at the same parties, if Ramirez can turn himself into a premium defender, why not hold out hope that he can put it all together at the plate in a season? Even if he doesn't, between the defense and his ability to exploit the cozier corners of the Cell at the plate, he's an outstanding contributor, another find from a front office that doesn't seem to get a ton of acclaim for its focus on landing high-end contributors instead of mere organizational depth.

Manny Ramirez **LF**

Born: **5/30/1972** Age: **39**
Bats: R Throws: R Height: **6' 0"** Weight: **190**
Breakout: **0%** Improve: **14%** Collapse: **6%**
Attrition: **15%** MLB: **85%**

Comparables:
Hank Aaron, Frank Robinson, Jim Edmonds (70)

YEAR	TEAM	LVL	AGE	PA	R	2B	3B	HR	RBI	BB	SO	SB	CS	AVG/OBP/SLG	TAv	BABIP	BRR	FRAA	WARP
2008	BOS	MLB	36	425	68	22	1	20	68	52	86	1	0	.299/.398/.529	.322	.344	-2.4	LF -4	2.8
2008	LAN	MLB	36	229	36	14	0	17	53	35	38	2	0	.396/.489/.743	.418	.419	-3.6	LF 2	4.0
2009	LAN	MLB	37	431	64	24	2	19	63	71	81	0	1	.290/.418/.531	.334	.328	-2.0	LF -5	3.4
2010	CHA	MLB	38	88	9	1	0	1	2	14	23	0	0	.261/.421/.319	.283	.378	-0.3	—	0.2
2010	LAN	MLB	38	232	33	15	0	8	40	32	38	1	1	.311/.405/.510	.325	.346	-0.9	LF 1	1.9
2011	*CHA*	*MLB*	*39*	*513*	*71*	*24*	*1*	*19*	*64*	*72*	*98*	*1*	*1*	*.278/.387/.469*	*.298*	*.316*	*-0.1*	*LF -3*	*2.4*

If you were wondering when "Manny being Manny" was going to be reduced to a reality TV parody of itself, his Mannyness's 2010 season could certainly get you thinking. He delivered career-low isolated power and home run/fly ball marks despite getting to spend a good chunk of the season in one of the most righty-friendly parks on the planet. Even so, he was also less than 100 percent all year, so it's hard to say the Sox got the contents listed on the packaging: Manny dealt with calf and hamstring problems for most of the year before requiring an off-season hernia repair. Speculating over whether he can go back to being a bopper and less a figure of sports infotainment depends on the assumptions that he will be healthy and go someplace where he'll feel excited about playing. Both are possible, and his fielding isn't quite so awful that he should only DH from here on out; there's just the question of whether the 39-year-old risks injury doing anything more than what he's always done best: putting runs on the board.

Alex Rios **CF**

Born: **2/18/1981** Age: **30**
Bats: **R** Throws: **R** Height: **6' 5"** Weight: **194**
Breakout: **3%** Improve: **34%** Collapse: **2%**
Attrition: **6%** MLB: **98%**

Comparables:
Vernon Wells, Tony Oliva, Shawn Green (70)

YEAR	TEAM	LVL	AGE	PA	R	2B	3B	HR	RBI	BB	SO	SB	CS	AVG/OBP/SLG	TAv	BABIP	BRR	FRAA	WARP
2008	TOR	MLB	27	687	91	47	8	15	79	44	112	32	8	.291/.336/.461	.286	.331	3.5	RF 3, CF 7	4.4
2009	CHA	MLB	28	154	11	6	0	3	9	6	29	5	2	.199/.227/.301	.191	.224	-1.1	CF 0, RF -2	-0.9
2009	TOR	MLB	28	479	52	25	2	14	62	31	78	19	3	.264/.317/.427	.268	.289	0.3	RF 6, CF 2	1.9
2010	CHA	MLB	29	617	89	29	3	21	88	38	93	34	14	.284/.334/.457	.275	.306	-1.5	CF 4, LF 1	2.8
2011	*CHA*	*MLB*	*30*	*631*	*75*	*34*	*3*	*16*	*76*	*42*	*100*	*26*	*9*	*.271/.322/.426*	*.263*	*.299*	*-0.3*	*CF 3, RF 1*	*1.8*

After sleepwalking through his initial introduction to Sox-dom in 2009, Kenny Williams' huge waiver-claim gamble paid off in Rios' first full season as a Sock. He was perhaps the closest synthesis of what an idealized White Sox hitter is supposed to be, providing both useful baserunning and power and, on a situational level, even finished among the better RBI men in the league by ranking 12th in the percentage of his baserunners driven in. Additionally, he did exactly what was intended in terms of moving into the middle pasture and playing an outstanding center. With four years and $50 million left to go (taking him through his age-34 season), Williams' grab looks more obviously like the inspired snag that it was, especially given the shortage of quality everyday center fielders floating around on the market.

Mark Teahen **3B**

Born: **9/6/1981** Age: **29**
Bats: **L** Throws: **R** Height: **6' 3"** Weight: **210**
Breakout: **0%** Improve: **44%** Collapse: **7%**
Attrition: **9%** MLB: **99%**

Comparables:
Ken McMullen, Puddin Head Jones, Tim Wallach (80)

YEAR	TEAM	LVL	AGE	PA	R	2B	3B	HR	RBI	BB	SO	SB	CS	AVG/OBP/SLG	TAv	BABIP	BRR	FRAA	WARP
2008	KCA	MLB	26	623	65	31	4	15	59	46	131	4	3	.255/.313/.402	.255	.306	-1.2	RF 4, LF 6	0.9
2009	KCA	MLB	27	571	69	34	1	12	50	37	123	8	1	.271/.324/.408	.262	.331	0.5	3B -6, RF -6	0.5
2010	CHA	MLB	28	262	31	13	2	4	25	25	61	3	5	.258/.324/.382	.246	.326	-0.2	3B 0, RF -2	0.0
2011	*CHA*	*MLB*	*29*	*528*	*60*	*27*	*3*	*9*	*54*	*45*	*110*	*7*	*3*	*.261/.326/.388*	*.252*	*.316*	*-0.4*	*3B -3, RF 0*	*0.4*

Say this for Kenny Williams: when he makes a deal, he doesn't just go in; he goes all in. Ditching organizational depth to add a lefty bat might have seemed sensible enough in the abstract, but betting on Teahen's age-28 season was dodgy enough without then signing him to a three-year, $14 million extension. That's about as unqualified an endorsement of a man with one genuinely good season in five as you might give; since slugging .517 in 2006, Teahen has never topped .410. In 2010, Teahen made it one good year in six, and he played an especially brutal third base. On top of his other woes, he missed half the season with a broken finger. With Morel's arrival, Teahen is now an expensive corner utilityman, essentially moving into the roster spot that had been Kotsay's, with the danger that he too could be sucked into way too much playing time.

Dayan Viciedo **3B**

Born: **3/10/1989** Age: **22**
Bats: Throws: Height: **5' 11"** Weight: **240**
Breakout: **4%** Improve: **26%** Collapse: **0%**
Attrition: **13%** MLB: **37%**

Comparables:
Billy Butler, Pablo Sandoval, Johnny Bench (60)

YEAR	TEAM	LVL	AGE	PA	R	2B	3B	HR	RBI	BB	SO	SB	CS	AVG/OBP/SLG	TAv	BABIP	BRR	FRAA	WARP
2009	BIR	AA	20	545	72	20	0	12	77	24	93	5	2	.280/.321/.388	.255	.317	1.5	3B -2, 1B 0	1.1
2010	CHR	AAA	21	357	41	15	0	20	47	11	78	1	1	.274/.311/.493	.248	.298	-1.4	1B 0, 3B 1	0.1
2010	CHA	MLB	21	106	17	7	0	5	13	2	25	1	0	.308/.321/.519	.305	.365	-0.1	3B -3, 1B -1	0.3
2011	*CHA*	*MLB*	*22*	*504*	*56*	*22*	*0*	*17*	*63*	*13*	*106*	*2*	*1*	*.264/.286/.417*	*.245*	*.300*	*-0.1*	*3B -4, 1B -4*	*-0.5*

The other, younger Cuban beyond Alexei Ramirez whom the Sox made a point of signing for major money, Viciedo is still young enough that you can't be sure how well he will turn out. But that's as nice a lip gloss as you can put on that pig of a proposition, because he's turning 22 this spring and outgrowing third base. That means he'll be moving across the diamond, at the same time that he has failed to hit right-handed pitching well enough or walk enough to stick as a quality option at a bopper's spot like first base. There's still cause for hope: a pull hitter, he mashed four of his five big-league taters in the Cell, albeit all of them in games the Sox already handily led. If he likes the park, that's one source of help toward his having a career, but Viciedo is going to have to take a big developmental step forward before he can be considered a legitimate prospect at first base.

Omar Vizquel **INF**

Born: **4/24/1967** Age: **44**
Bats: **S** Throws: **R** Height: **5' 9"** Weight: **165**
Breakout: **2%** Improve: **10%** Collapse: **11%**
Attrition: **15%** MLB: **39%**

Comparables:
Davey Lopes, Steve Finley, Graig Nettles (45)

YEAR	TEAM	LVL	AGE	PA	R	2B	3B	HR	RBI	BB	SO	SB	CS	AVG/OBP/SLG	TAv	BABIP	BRR	FRAA	WARP
2008	SFN	MLB	41	300	25	10	1	0	23	24	29	5	4	.222/.277/.267	.192	.239	1.2	SS -2	-1.1
2009	TEX	MLB	42	195	17	7	2	1	14	13	27	4	0	.266/.308/.345	.236	.299	-0.6	SS 3, 2B 4	0.8
2010	CHA	MLB	43	391	35	11	1	2	30	34	45	11	7	.276/.335/.331	.244	.302	0.5	3B -6, 2B -3	-0.6
2011	*CHA*	*MLB*	*44*	*427*	*40*	*13*	*2*	*1*	*28*	*34*	*49*	*10*	*5*	*.240/.295/.288*	*.213*	*.262*	*-0.6*	*SS 1, 3B -2*	*-0.8*

Vizquel was signed (and has already been re-signed) as part of a Sox bench that put *The Hollywood Squares* to shame for its star-studded collection of the formerly famous. But, like Andruw Jones and (less happily) Mark Kotsay, he got a lot more playing time than a mere benchie might expect, slotting into the everyday lineup at third base from June through August, a stretch during which the team went 42-25 as Little O brought some BABIP-driven OBP for the baserunner-starved White Sox (the team's OBP was .315 at the end of May). His next hit will be his 2,800th, which obviously can get you to thinking about his shot at 3,000 and additional immortality, but keep in mind he hasn't had a 100-hit season since 2007, and a utility role would basically make the feat a three-year campaign. He's said he's taking his career year-by-year, but as long as he's chipping in as an infield mentor who happens to switch-hit and draw a few more walks than most utility guys, he's worth the roster spot.

PITCHERS

Mark Buehrle

Born: **3/23/1979** Age: **32**
Bats: **L** Throws: **L** Height: **6' 2"** Weight: **200**
Breakout: **12%** Improve: **40%** Collapse: **29%**
Attrition: **12%** MLB: **97%**

Comparables:
Joel Pineiro, Frank Viola, Gaylord Perry (66)

YEAR	TEAM	LVL	AGE	W	L	SV	G	GS	IP	H	HR	BB	SO	EqBB9	EqSO9	GB%	BABIP	WHIP	ERA	FRA	WARP
2008	CHA	MLB	29	15	12	0	34	34	218^{2}	240	22	52	140	2.1	5.8	51%	.312	1.36	3.79	4.29	3.5
2009	CHA	MLB	30	13	10	0	33	33	213^{1}	222	27	45	105	1.9	4.4	47%	.282	1.27	3.80	4.39	3.5
2010	CHA	MLB	31	13	13	0	33	34	210^{1}	246	17	49	99	2.1	4.2	47%	.313	1.41	4.28	4.34	3.0
2011	*CHA*	*MLB*	*32*	*12*	*12*	*0*	*33*	*33*	*209*	*235*	*27*	*52*	*109*	*2.2*	*4.7*	*47%*	*.303*	*1.37*	*4.51*	*4.91*	*2.8*

While Buehrle logged his 10th consecutive 30-start/200-IP campaign and won (and deserved) his second Gold Glove, his quick-fire stylings delivered mixed results, creating concern for what the future will bring. The narrow margin between success and failure for a command-and-control guy is fairly easy to cross; always hittable, Buehrle suffered through career lows in double plays induced (by rate and simple tally) while also posting a career-low strikeout rate. Becoming that much more hittable while already getting pulled for power more frequently by right-handers during the last couple of seasons just exacerbated the damage that can be done against him. Swapping out Teahen for Morel at third might help him a little, but the basic problem is that Buehrle is fooling fewer people than ever before. If he's running out of tricks and remains that much more dependent on his defense, his days as a rotational front man are over. Even so, as he heads into the walk year of his four-season deal, he's an asset at the back end, given his durability, his fielding, and his throttling of the running game.

Anthony Carter

Born: **4/4/1986** Age: **25**
Bats: **L** Throws: **R** Height: **6' 3"** Weight: **180**
Breakout: **2%** Improve: **3%** Collapse: **3%**
Attrition: **2%** MLB: **4%**

Comparables:
Daryl Thompson, Alfredo Figaro, Rafael Rodriguez (77)

YEAR	TEAM	LVL	AGE	W	L	SV	G	GS	IP	H	HR	BB	SO	EqBB9	EqSO9	GB%	BABIP	WHIP	ERA	FRA	WARP
2008	KAN	A	22	5	2	0	11	12	61^{2}	47	5	11	66	1.6	9.6	43%	.273	0.96	2.77	3.29	1.6
2008	WNS	A+	22	6	5	0	17	19	82^{2}	91	11	30	41	3.3	4.5	39%	.287	1.50	4.68	4.96	0.9
2009	WNS	A+	23	11	7	0	28	33	159^{2}	156	23	43	123	2.4	6.9	41%	.284	1.30	4.17	3.86	3.5
2010	BIR	AA	24	1	4	22	46	3	57^{1}	47	6	22	58	3.5	9.1	35%	.272	1.22	3.77	4,27	0.7
2011	*CHA*	*MLB*	*25*	*4*	*7*	*3*	*26*	*15*	92^{2}	*111*	*19*	*44*	*51*	*4.3*	*5.0*	*40%*	*.304*	*1.68*	*6.37*	*6.92*	*-0.6*

Mild sleeper alert! OK, that sounds slightly nonsensical, like rating a threat level "Orange Julius," but the point here is that Carter's is a name to know, and for more than you few USFL fans missing the Michigan Panthers' great wideout. Carter is pure power, throwing his fastball up to 98 mph, but the Sox belatedly came around to the idea of relegating him to relief work last May, after initially hoping to harness that power in a starting role. But after 10 runs allowed (40 percent of his final tally) in two starts totaling five innings, they shunted him to closing, where he slammed doors shut, striking out 55 in 52 1/3 innings pitched while allowing just 53 baserunners. He followed up his regular-season success by sizzling in the AFL, striking out 16 in 10 innings without giving up a walk. Added to the 40-man, he'll have a shot at pitching his way into the back end of the bullpen.

John Danks

Born: **4/15/1985** Age: **26**
Bats: **L** Throws: **L** Height: **6' 1"** Weight: **200**
Breakout: **7%** Improve: **35%** Collapse: **32%**
Attrition: **9%** MLB: **100%**

Comparables:
Steve Busby, Kevin Millwood, Jon Matlack (76)

YEAR	TEAM	LVL	AGE	W	L	SV	G	GS	IP	H	HR	BB	SO	EqBB9	EqSO9	GB%	BABIP	WHIP	ERA	FRA	WARP
2008	CHA	MLB	23	12	9	0	33	36	195	182	15	57	159	2.6	7.3	44%	.294	1.25	3.28	3.51	5.2
2009	CHA	MLB	24	13	11	0	32	34	200^{1}	184	28	73	149	3.3	6.7	46%	.267	1.31	3.77	4.27	3.5
2010	CHA	MLB	25	15	11	0	32	32	213	189	18	70	162	3.0	6.8	46%	.274	1.23	3.72	4.14	3.4
2011	*CHA*	*MLB*	*26*	*11*	*9*	*0*	*29*	*29*	*179*	*172*	*23*	*64*	*140*	*3.2*	*7.0*	*45%*	*.289*	*1.31*	*4.01*	*4.35*	*3.6*

Danks has managed roughly equivalent seasons the last two years in terms of gross-scale outcomes, with nearly identical support-neutral marks (.552 followed by .548), but his walk and strikeout rates improved as he took on a larger workload. He's on the cusp of better things if he can keep whittling down opponents' power production, after getting it down to a .118 ISO allowed last year. Throw in his picking up Buehrle's gift for killing the running game (matching him with a 6-for-12 figure in stolen-base attempts), and you've got a young and improving power lefty. If he ever escaped the Cell, he'd blossom even more quickly, but as a fly-ball pitcher, he's always going to have to work with that particular problem.

Gavin Floyd

Born: **1/27/1983** Age: **28**
Bats: **R** Throws: **R** Height: **6' 4"** Weight: **212**
Breakout: **15%** Improve: **43%** Collapse: **22%**
Attrition: **8%** MLB: **95%**

Comparables:
Don Drysdale, Steve Carlton, Tom Gorzelanny (74)

YEAR	TEAM	LVL	AGE	W	L	SV	G	GS	IP	H	HR	BB	SO	EqBB9	EqSO9	GB%	BABIP	WHIP	ERA	FRA	WARP
2008	CHA	MLB	25	17	8	0	33	37	206^1	190	30	70	145	3.1	6.3	42%	.256	1.30	3.84	4.69	2.5
2009	CHA	MLB	26	11	11	0	30	30	193	178	21	59	163	2.8	7.6	46%	.284	1.24	4.06	4.50	2.8
2010	CHA	MLB	27	10	13	0	30	30	187^1	199	14	58	151	2.8	7.3	50%	.325	1.40	4.08	4.28	2.8
2011	*CHA*	*MLB*	*28*	*11*	*10*	*0*	*30*	*30*	*190^2*	*191*	*25*	*65*	*146*	*3.1*	*6.9*	*46%*	*.299*	*1.34*	*4.24*	*4.61*	*3.3*

Like Danks, Floyd has shown a capacity to improve with experience—once utterly helpless when it came to keeping runners close, Floyd has radically improved his move to the bag, holding opponents to just 11 attempts. After he logged 21 quality starts (through the first six innings) in his first 28 turns, a tired shoulder earned him an early shutdown. The injury was diagnosed as nothing more serious than wear and tear, but an off-season conditioning program is supposed to armor him against its recurrence. Between Floyd's shoulder and Jake Peavy's uncertain timetable, the Sox may not have the depth to shop the former's middling contract (two years for $12 million, with a 2013 club option for $9.5 million).

Freddy Garcia

Born: **6/10/1976** Age: **35**
Bats: **R** Throws: **R** Height: **6' 4"** Weight: **235**
Breakout: **18%** Improve: **35%** Collapse: **14%**
Attrition: **11%** MLB: **63%**

Comparables:
John Candelaria, Eric Milton, Turk Farrell (70)

YEAR	TEAM	LVL	AGE	W	L	SV	G	GS	IP	H	HR	BB	SO	EqBB9	EqSO9	GB%	BABIP	WHIP	ERA	FRA	WARP
2008	DET	MLB	32	1	1	0	3	3	15	11	3	6	12	3.6	7.2	43%	.205	1.20	4.20	6.36	0.0
2009	CHA	MLB	33	3	4	0	9	11	56	56	4	12	37	1.9	5.9	46%	.296	1.21	4.34	4.27	1.0
2010	CHA	MLB	34	12	6	0	28	30	157	171	23	45	89	2.6	5.1	42%	.290	1.39	4.64	4.80	1.5
2011	*CHA*	*MLB*	*35*	*7*	*7*	*0*	*20*	*20*	*109*	*119*	*17*	*33*	*68*	*2.7*	*5.6*	*44%*	*.300*	*1.40*	*4.81*	*5.23*	*1.3*

Whether or not it's oxymoronic to refer to someone as one of the best fifth starters in the league, you can give the right-handed Garcia this sort of left-handed compliment. Perhaps it's even appropriate, because "crafty righty" isn't exactly in common usage. Despite throwing with less velocity than before he'd torn up his shoulder, in his first full campaign back in action Garcia was good for 19 quality starts (through the first six innings). He's a fly-baller with home-run issues, but U.S. Cellular Field made matters worse for him; he allowed 1.6 homers per nine innings there, against 1.0 on the road. As Garcia heads into low-cost free agency, he could be a nice fit as back-end rotation filler in the right (big) ballpark.

Lucas Harrell

Born: **6/3/1985** Age: **26**
Bats: **S** Throws: **R** Height: **6' 2"** Weight: **200**
Breakout: **9%** Improve: **23%** Collapse: **9%**
Attrition: **11%** MLB: **35%**

Comparables:
Aaron Laffey, Mike Ekstrom, Brian Duensing (75)

YEAR	TEAM	LVL	AGE	W	L	SV	G	GS	IP	H	HR	BB	SO	EqBB9	EqSO9	GB%	BABIP	WHIP	ERA	FRA	WARP
2008	BIR	AA	23	3	4	0	12	13	61^2	62	3	20	41	2.9	6.0	56%	.307	1.36	3.21	4.16	1.0
2009	BIR	AA	24	8	3	0	14	15	80^1	78	4	32	51	3.6	5.7	60%	.302	1.39	3.25	1.66	3.8
2009	CHR	AAA	24	4	1	0	11	12	65^2	58	3	37	42	5.1	5.8	58%	.284	1.49	3.29	3.47	1.6
2010	CHR	AAA	25	10	9	0	25	27	132	134	10	57	81	3.9	5.5	51%	.294	1.48	4.36	5.19	1.2
2011	*CHA*	*MLB*	*26*	*6*	*9*	*0*	*21*	*21*	*113*	*126*	*14*	*60*	*61*	*4.8*	*4.8*	*51%*	*.305*	*1.65*	*5.44*	*5.92*	*0.6*

A 2004 fourth-round pick, Harrell delivered his second healthy season after missing all or some of the previous three with shoulder injuries (and surgery), earning his first shot at "The Show." Health only reconfirmed the expectation that a future in relief beckons, because he's still working without a reliably effective breaking pitch. Currently, he alternates sinkers, low-90s heat, and a good changeup, a mix that didn't often get him past the fifth inning in Triple-A. Coming out of the pen, he ought to get the usual benefits in terms of slightly better strikeout and home-run rates, but to stick around in a relief role, he's going to have to master throwing from the stretch, as his strikeout rate dropped from 16.9 to 10.5 percent with men on base.

Gregory Infante

Born: **7/10/1987** Age: **23**
Bats: R Throws: R Height: **6' 2"** Weight: **185**
Breakout: **0%** Improve: **0%** Collapse: **0%**
Attrition: **0%** MLB: **0%**

Comparables:
A.J. Burnett, Ryan Tucker, Jason Schmidt (84)

YEAR	TEAM	LVL	AGE	W	L	SV	G	GS	IP	H	HR	BB	SO	EqBB9	EqSO9	GB%	BABIP	WHIP	ERA	FRA	WARP
2008	BRI	Rk	20	4	3	0	13	13	74^{1}	63	4	19	57	2.3	6.9	56%	.274	1.21	2.30	3.93	1.6
2009	KAN	A	21	3	5	0	15	17	88^{1}	76	4	37	75	3.8	7.6	52%	.293	1.38	2.95	3.98	1.5
2009	WNS	A+	21	1	2	0	6	6	20^{2}	18	3	23	10	10.0	4.4	44%	.238	2.23	6.10	7.49	-0.2
2010	WNS	A+	22	1	2	9	31	0	33^{2}	32	0	15	35	4.0	9.4	61%	.337	1.46	3.48	2.69	0.6
2010	BIR	AA	22	2	2	3	24	0	26^{1}	23	0	12	34	4.1	11.6	47%	.349	1.37	3.08	2.53	0.6
2010	CHA	MLB	22	0	0	0	5	0	4^{2}	2	0	4	5	7.7	9.6	40%	.200	1.29	0.00	1.74	0.1
2011	*CHA*	*MLB*	*23*	*2*	*3*	*1*	*28*	*6*	57^{2}	*63*	*8*	*42*	*35*	*6.5*	*5.5*	*47%*	*.302*	*1.82*	*6.33*	*6.88*	*-0.7*

The Sox don't get a ton of credit for having a system well-stocked in arms with good gun readings, but then with pitchers like Infante, you get reminders about how quickly a guy's prospects improve if he's put in the pen and assigned the straightforward task of throwing as hard as he can for an inning. Converted to relief work, the young Venezuelan pumped gas in the 95-97 range, the sort of thing that punches a ticket to the majors with matching alacrity. The question is whether he'll adapt and adjust as hitters learn to sit dead-red, but if he does, he'll be sticking around in a bullpen for years to come.

Edwin Jackson

Born: **9/9/1983** Age: **27**
Bats: R Throws: R Height: **6' 3"** Weight: **190**
Breakout: **12%** Improve: **39%** Collapse: **30%**
Attrition: **12%** MLB: **96%**

Comparables:
Mike Witt, John Lackey, Ian Snell (73)

YEAR	TEAM	LVL	AGE	W	L	SV	G	GS	IP	H	HR	BB	SO	EqBB9	EqSO9	GB%	BABIP	WHIP	ERA	FRA	WARP
2008	TBA	MLB	24	14	11	0	32	31	183^{1}	199	23	77	108	3.8	5.3	40%	.302	1.52	4.42	4.34	2.9
2009	DET	MLB	25	13	9	0	33	34	214	200	27	70	161	2.9	6.8	41%	.276	1.29	3.57	3.70	4.9
2010	ARI	MLB	26	6	10	0	21	23	134^{1}	141	13	60	104	4.0	7.0	52%	.316	1.53	5.16	5.16	0.6
2010	CHA	MLB	26	4	2	0	11	11	75	73	8	18	77	2.2	9.2	48%	.308	1.23	3.24	3.60	1.7
2011	*CHA*	*MLB*	*27*	*10*	*10*	*0*	*28*	*28*	*179*	*186*	*23*	*73*	*136*	*3.7*	*6.8*	*44%*	*.305*	*1.45*	*4.63*	*5.03*	*2.2*

Oh, no, he did it again? As noted in the essay, grabbing Jackson is another instance of Kenny Williams' favoring tools and upside where others have given up on an increasingly expensive brand of frustration. Whatever the cost, Jackson returned to the AL in style, managing eight quality starts (through the first six innings pitched) in his 11 Sox spins, while also allaying concerns that his second-half fade in 2009 was a symptom of coming trouble. At this point, Jackson's inconsistency is his sphinxy riddle, leaving open the question of who gets to be Oedipus: the pitcher himself? Ozzie? Pitching coach Don Cooper? Jackson has been tantalizing the talent hounds with plus stuff for almost a decade now, and he keeps darting around the expectation that *this* will be the year he turns into a truly dominating pitcher. With a year to go before he reaches free agency, the Sox are betting that this year will be it, and you can see why. After ratcheting up his strikeout rate to a full-season career high thanks to striking out almost a quarter of all batters in his Sox intro, in addition to lowering his walk rate below six percent while with them, Jackson might join Jose Contreras on the organization's list of massive midcareer turnarounds.

Bobby Jenks

Born: **3/14/1981** Age: **30**
Bats: R Throws: R Height: **6' 3"** Weight: **270**
Breakout: **6%** Improve: **4%** Collapse: **6%**
Attrition: **0%** MLB: **7%**

Comparables:
Tim Stoddard, Heath Bell, Jose Valverde (62)

YEAR	TEAM	LVL	AGE	W	L	SV	G	GS	IP	H	HR	BB	SO	EqBB9	EqSO9	GB%	BABIP	WHIP	ERA	FRA	WARP
2008	CHA	MLB	27	3	1	30	57	0	61^{2}	51	3	17	38	2.5	5.5	59%	.261	1.12	2.63	3.30	0.9
2009	CHA	MLB	28	3	4	29	52	0	53^{1}	52	9	16	49	2.7	8.3	48%	.283	1.31	3.71	4.32	0.4
2010	CHA	MLB	29	1	3	27	55	0	52^{2}	54	3	18	61	3.1	10.4	60%	.345	1.39	4.44	3.18	0.8
2011	*BOS*	*MLB*	*30*	*3*	*1*	*27*	*60*	*0*	*60*	*57*	*5*	*20*	*55*	*2.9*	*8.2*	*49%*	*.304*	*1.26*	*3.43*	*3.73*	*0.8*

There comes a point where a high-maintenance relationship is no longer worth the time required to keep it going. Jenks has slowly become that kind of guy, especially after a 2010 season in which he struggled with calf, back, and forearm injuries, the last ending his season a month early and scotching a bid for 30 saves. The main positives are that he still throws hard and that he got his strikeout and ground-ball rates back up where they'd been during his early-career glory years. If you want to believe that the BABIP fairy will smile on him while he keeps his strikeout rate up, you're probably also willing to keep waiting for that initial magic to come back, too. Having spent as much time as they have waiting for it, the Sox could be forgiven their decision to nontender Jenks a year before free agency.

Scott Linebrink

Born: **8/4/1976** Age: **34**
Bats: R Throws: R Height: **6' 3"** Weight: **185**
Breakout: **23%** Improve: **43%** Collapse: **15%**
Attrition: **13%** MLB: **72%**

Comparables:
Rick Aguilera, Joel Peralta, Randy Flores (76)

YEAR	TEAM	LVL	AGE	W	L	SV	G	GS	IP	H	HR	BB	SO	EqBB9	EqSO9	GB%	BABIP	WHIP	ERA	FRA	WARP
2008	CHA	MLB	31	2	2	1	50	0	46^{1}	41	8	9	40	1.7	7.8	40%	.256	1.08	3.69	3.75	0.6
2009	CHA	MLB	32	3	7	2	57	0	56	70	9	23	55	3.7	8.8	39%	.361	1.71	4.66	4.63	0.3
2010	CHA	MLB	33	3	2	0	52	0	57^{1}	59	11	17	52	2.7	8.2	34%	.289	1.38	4.40	4.45	0.2
2011	*ATL*	*MLB*	*34*	*3*	*1*	*1*	*61*	*0*	61^{2}	*63*	*9*	*20*	*53*	*3.0*	*7.8*	*42%*	*.306*	*1.36*	*4.45*	*4.84*	*-0.2*

Obviously, Kenny Williams does not have the Midas touch with every one of his moves: three seasons into his four-year, $19 million contract, Linebrink's WXRL tally as a White Sock is effectively zero, making for very expensive replacement-level pitching. Familiar with disappointment, Guillen punted his pricey charge to the near irrelevancy of late-game work in losing causes, only trusting Linebrink with five run-width leads at any point of a ballgame (and Linebrink blew one anyway). Last year's massive platoon split and problems with lefties don't exactly suggest a situational role for the last season of his deal, given that he's been tateriffic against right-handers in seasons spent in more relevant situations; like his strikeout rate, it's work accumulated in near-meaningless opportunities, not a predictor of unrecognized utility. Dumping him on the Braves (for Kyle Cofield) was probably the nicest thing Williams could have done under the circumstances, since a change of scenery and a move to the weaker league should help Linebrink's shot at bouncing back.

Jake Peavy

Born: **5/31/1981** Age: **30**
Bats: R Throws: R Height: **6' 1"** Weight: **180**
Breakout: **6%** Improve: **42%** Collapse: **24%**
Attrition: **9%** MLB: **95%**

Comparables:
Jason Schmidt, Kevin Appier, Sonny Siebert (68)

YEAR	TEAM	LVL	AGE	W	L	SV	G	GS	IP	H	HR	BB	SO	EqBB9	EqSO9	GB%	BABIP	WHIP	ERA	FRA	WARP
2008	SDN	MLB	27	10	11	0	27	28	173^{2}	146	17	59	166	3.1	8.6	43%	.279	1.21	2.85	2.89	5.1
2009	CHA	MLB	28	3	0	0	3	3	20	11	1	6	18	2.7	8.1	51%	.200	0.85	1.35	1.75	1.0
2009	SDN	MLB	28	6	6	0	13	13	81^{2}	69	7	28	92	3.1	10.1	44%	.300	1.20	3.97	4.11	0.9
2010	CHA	MLB	29	7	6	0	17	17	107	98	13	33	93	2.8	7.8	43%	.279	1.27	4.63	4.63	1.2
2011	*CHA*	*MLB*	*30*	*12*	*7*	*0*	*26*	*26*	*164*	*144*	*18*	*56*	*159*	*3.1*	*8.7*	*44%*	*.288*	*1.21*	*3.24*	*3.53*	*5.0*

With two years and $33 million to go before a club option that will cost $4 million to buy out or $22 million to employ, there is probably an element of regret attached to acquiring Peavy. But as things stand, it's a trade that might only wind up being Peavy and the cost of employing him for Clayton Richard and a whole lot of daydreams, and the Sox play for high stakes. But after an unenchanted April, Peavy became the staff ace he had been acquired to be, striking out 71 against 13 walks in 78 1/3 innings across 12 turns, while allowing 30 runs. Then came his freak shoulder injury, a detached latissimus dorsi in the second inning of a start against the Angels. The injury required surgery and was sufficiently unusual to create questions about a timetable for his return. Whether it's April or June, Peavy will be working with the benefit of one of baseball's best training staffs, and in his brief stints in action, he's given indications that he can be what the Sox are paying for. The problem is that, at best, they'll get one season without an injury before they have to decide on 2013, and that's if you assume no additional setbacks—at this point, far from a safe bet.

Tony Pena

Born: **1/9/1982** Age: **29**
Bats: R Throws: R Height: **6' 1"** Weight: **219**
Breakout: **9%** Improve: **38%** Collapse: **21%**
Attrition: **15%** MLB: **79%**

Comparables:
Joe Gibbon, Larry Christenson, Jose Mesa (78)

YEAR	TEAM	LVL	AGE	W	L	SV	G	GS	IP	H	HR	BB	SO	EqBB9	EqSO9	GB%	BABIP	WHIP	ERA	FRA	WARP
2008	ARI	MLB	26	3	2	3	72	0	72^{2}	80	5	17	52	2.1	6.4	50%	.318	1.38	4.33	4.57	0.4
2009	ARI	MLB	27	5	3	1	37	0	34	41	3	11	26	2.9	6.9	47%	.339	1.56	4.24	3.97	0.5
2009	CHA	MLB	27	1	2	1	35	0	36	40	4	9	29	2.3	7.3	46%	.310	1.39	4.00	4.91	0.0
2010	CHA	MLB	28	5	3	0	52	4	100^{2}	108	10	46	56	4.1	5.0	50%	.295	1.54	5.01	5.44	-0.6
2011	*CHA*	*MLB*	*29*	*4*	*1*	*1*	*72*	*0*	80^{2}	*85*	*10*	*30*	*53*	*3.4*	*5.9*	*47%*	*.301*	*1.44*	*4.56*	*4.96*	*-0.0*

Sometimes being employed as a utility pitcher implies the lack of a useful role more than potential usefulness. Despite possession of heat that gets into the mid-90s, an occasionally excellent slider, and a record for doing solid work in higher-leverage situations with the Snakes, Pena was generally relegated to mop-up duty in his first full season with the Sox, making more than half of his relief appearances with the team four or more runs up or down. The club has been willing to stow talented, frustrating righties on the roster and see if it can sort out what to do with them as it goes along, as it did with Nick Masset and Brandon McCarthy, but it also flipped McCarthy and Masset as soon as it identified something more tangibly important than mere promise. Pena is roster ballast until he proves otherwise and is just the latest bargaining chip to convert if he doesn't wind up in the fifth-starter's-slot picture during Peavy's absence.

J. J. Putz

Born: **2/22/1977** Age: **34**
Bats: R Throws: R Height: **6' 5"** Weight: **250**
Breakout: **13%** Improve: **29%** Collapse: **13%**
Attrition: **2%** MLB: **57%**

Comparables:
Brian Fuentes, Kerry Wood, B.J. Ryan (62)

YEAR	TEAM	LVL	AGE	W	L	SV	G	GS	IP	H	HR	BB	SO	EqBB9	EqSO9	GB%	BABIP	WHIP	ERA	FRA	WARP
2008	SEA	MLB	31	6	5	15	47	0	46^1	46	4	28	56	5.4	10.9	40%	.347	1.64	3.88	3.30	0.9
2009	NYN	MLB	32	1	4	2	29	0	29^1	29	1	19	19	5.8	5.8	46%	.292	1.64	5.22	5.61	-0.2
2010	CHA	MLB	33	7	5	3	59	0	54	41	4	15	65	2.5	10.8	49%	.276	1.06	2.83	3.33	0.9
2011	*ARI*	*MLB*	*34*	*3*	*1*	*10*	*58*	*0*	*55^1*	*48*	*5*	*21*	*60*	*3.3*	*9.8*	*45%*	*.303*	*1.24*	*3.25*	*3.53*	*0.9*

Putz's ERA and strikeout rate oversell his success coming back from elbow problems; while it's hard to regard his contributions as disappointing in light of the injuries and ineffectiveness that had plagued his previous two seasons, he proved to be another expensive, unreliable addition, compounding the pen's other hi-Jenks. In addition to his tendency to turn in his best work in low-leverage situations, a big part of the problem was that Putz had to be treated delicately. This worked out well initially, but as problems in the pen crested in August, Putz exacerbated them by breaking down when need drove Guillen to use him without rest between outings in three straight games. Handled with care, Putz can still be a useful part in a deep pen, but questions about his durability make him a poor choice as a pen's save accumulator or lone set-up asset. After signing him to fill their closer void in December, the bullpen-challenged Diamondbacks will attempt to harness his value with kid gloves.

Chris Sale

Born: **3/30/1989** Age: **22**
Bats: L Throws: L Height: **6' 5"** Weight: **170**
Breakout: **2%** Improve: **7%** Collapse: **7%**
Attrition: **4%** MLB: **16%**

Comparables:
Balor Moore, Masanori Murakami, Dave Righetti (60)

YEAR	TEAM	LVL	AGE	W	L	SV	G	GS	IP	H	HR	BB	SO	EqBB9	EqSO9	GB%	BABIP	WHIP	ERA	FRA	WARP
2010	CHA	MLB	21	2	1	4	21	0	23^1	15	2	10	32	3.9	12.3	52%	.271	1.07	1.93	2.17	0.7
2011	*CHA*	*MLB*	*22*	*2*	*1*	*1*	*30*	*0*	*32^1*	*25*	*3*	*15*	*40*	*4.1*	*11.4*	*46%*	*.300*	*1.22*	*3.05*	*3.31*	*0.6*

Sale was seen in some quarters as the top college arm available last June, so the Sox were understandably delighted that the big power lefty fell to them with the 13th overall pick. With a fastball that sits in the mid-90s and tops out at 98, and supplemented with a polished change, he didn't have much to prove in the minors if only tasked with relief work, which put him in the majors less than two months after being drafted. The question now is whether the pen was just a workload-minded vehicle for Sale's fast-track adaptation to the pro game, or if he might get moved back to starting. Questions about Peavy's availability early in the season will define what is immediately possible, but the chance for Sale's total innings count to be managed via pitching in the skippable fifth slot and then limited by a return to the pen upon Peavy's return would be a great way to make sure the lanky lefty gets employed to good effect.

Sergio Santos

Born: **7/4/1983** Age: **27**
Bats: R Throws: R Height: **6' 3"** Weight: **240**
Breakout: **13%** Improve: **16%** Collapse: **13%**
Attrition: **10%** MLB: **37%**

Comparables:
Bob James, Royce Ring, Taylor Tankersley (68)

YEAR	TEAM	LVL	AGE	W	L	SV	G	GS	IP	H	HR	BB	SO	EqBB9	EqSO9	GB%	BABIP	WHIP	ERA	FRA	WARP
2010	CHA	MLB	26	2	2	1	56	0	51^2	53	2	26	56	4.5	9.8	45%	.345	1.59	2.96	2.62	1.3
2011	*CHA*	*MLB*	*27*	*2*	*1*	*0*	*40*	*0*	*42*	*41*	*5*	*22*	*40*	*4.7*	*8.5*	*45%*	*.313*	*1.50*	*4.52*	*4.91*	*-0.0*

The latest position-playing prospect whose struggles at the plate suggested a move to the mound, Santos proved a quick study thanks to a mid-90s fastball that touched 98. He turned heads with a good AFL campaign and provided an encore with a commendable Cactus League to rocket his way onto the active roster. Starting out in a garbage-time role, Santos earned a greater measure of trust during the season, but delivered increasingly mixed results. Still finding his way with his slider and change (no surprise, given his limited experience), he can become a predictable hothouse flower, turning up the heat, only to get burned by it. There was a lot to like about his pitching debut, but since Santos' days as an infielder burned up his options, he'll have to learn and adapt at the major-league level or risk getting lost on waiver claims sure to be made.

Matt Thornton

Born: **9/15/1976** Age: **34**
Bats: L Throws: L Height: **6' 6"** Weight: **220**
Breakout: **10%** Improve: **29%** Collapse: **16%**
Attrition: **6%** MLB: **64%**

Comparables:
J.R. Richard, Brian Fuentes, Lee Smith (73)

YEAR	TEAM	LVL	AGE	W	L	SV	G	GS	IP	H	HR	BB	SO	EqBB9	EqSO9	GB%	BABIP	WHIP	ERA	FRA	WARP
2008	CHA	MLB	31	5	3	1	74	0	67^1	48	5	19	77	2.5	10.3	54%	.261	1.02	2.67	3.00	1.4
2009	CHA	MLB	32	6	3	4	70	0	72^1	58	5	20	87	2.5	10.8	47%	.298	1.09	2.74	2.57	2.0
2010	CHA	MLB	33	5	4	8	61	0	60^2	41	3	20	81	3.0	12.0	41%	.286	1.04	2.67	2.82	1.2
2011	*CHA*	*MLB*	*34*	*4*	*2*	*2*	*64*	*0*	*62*	*51*	*6*	*22*	*72*	*3.1*	*10.3*	*46%*	*.297*	*1.16*	*2.82*	*3.07*	*1.3*

Despite a late-season stint on the DL as well as his not being a closer, Thornton nevertheless finished 10th in the majors in WXRL. After witnessing Jenks's failures and the Sox's Putz-ing around with an alternative, the power lefty has made it clear that he feels it's high time that he graduated to full-time closing.

And depending on your conception of the job, he does have an argument: he was 8-for-8 in ninth-inning save opportunities last season. The timing couldn't be any better for him if he does replace the Human Barrel in 2011, since Thornton is entering the last option year of an arbitration-avoiding agreement that ran five years for just $8 million, total. The Sox can keep affording big-ticket pickups because commitments such as that have helped to pave the way.

Carlos Torres

Born: **10/22/1982** Age: **28**
Bats: R Throws: R Height: **6' 1"** Weight: **190**
Breakout: **14%** Improve: **40%** Collapse: **12%**
Attrition: **7%** MLB: **73%**

Comparables:
Dusty Hughes, Chad Gaudin, Don Wilson (70)

YEAR	TEAM	LVL	AGE	W	L	SV	G	GS	IP	H	HR	BB	SO	EqBB9	EqSO9	GB%	BABIP	WHIP	ERA	FRA	WARP
2008	BIR	AA	25	9	5	0	21	19	101^{1}	86	4	29	93	2.6	8.3	47%	.297	1.18	2.93	3.85	2.0
2009	CHR	AAA	26	10	4	1	23	21	128	96	4	56	130	3.9	9.1	49%	.275	1.22	2.25	3.19	3.6
2009	CHA	MLB	26	1	2	0	8	5	28^{1}	30	5	17	22	5.4	7.0	39%	.298	1.73	6.04	7.42	-0.3
2010	CHR	AAA	27	9	9	0	27	27	160^{1}	125	13	71	140	4.0	7.9	48%	.258	1.24	3.31	4.80	1.8
2010	CHA	MLB	27	0	1	0	5	1	13^{2}	23	2	9	13	5.9	8.6	31%	.447	2.34	8.56	7.21	-0.3
2011	*CHA*	*MLB*	*28*	*7*	*7*	*0*	*25*	*19*	*123*	*121*	*14*	*61*	*100*	*4.5*	*7.3*	*46%*	*.300*	*1.48*	*4.50*	*4.89*	*1.7*

A durable battler, Torres is something of a finesse righty who survives on upsetting timing by taking something off heat that only touches the low 90s and mixing in mediocre off-speed stuff for effect. There's not a lot of upside here, but as a 15th-rounder selected in 2004, he'll be fighting against that year's fourth-round pick, Lucas Harrell, for the last-man slot on the staff. Torres' clean mechanics have the additional benefit of translating well to pitching from the stretch. Put all of that together, and you get a guy who could be the new D. J. Carrasco, not exactly the stuff of fairy tales, but not too shabby as a happy ending for an organizational arm.

LINEOUTS

HITTERS

PLAYER	TEAM	LVL	AGE	PA	R	2B	3B	HR	RBI	BB	SO	SB-CS	AVG/OBP/SLG	TAv	BABIP	BRR	FRAA	WARP
C C. Armstrong*	BIR	AA	26	368	34	16	0	8	43	49	56	0-0	.276/.370/.403	.277	.310	0.0	C -1	2.0
C M. Blanke	GRF	Rk	21	311	39	21	1	7	45	25	44	0-0	.324/.376/.479	.330	.362	-4.4	C -2	2.9
OF A. De Aza*	CHR	AAA	26	348	51	20	4	5	48	29	60	0-0	.300/.368/.438	.280	.350	0.0	LF 0, CF -1	1.4
	CHA	MLB	26	32	4	3	0	0	2	1	4	2-1	.300/.313/.400	.258	.333	0.1	CF -2, RF 1	0.0
3B J. Gilmore	WNS	A+	21	640	82	26	4	5	81	40	94	1-2	.307/.350/.390	.269	.353	-2.8	3B -8	1.4
CF J. Greene	WNS	A+	24	285	48	15	9	10	44	28	73	15-7	.309/.390/.562	.327	.385	-3.4	CF -9, RF 0	1.6
	BIR	AA	24	178	20	7	3	3	22	8	54	6-4	.232/.270/.363	.226	.319	0.7	CF -5, RF -1	-0.7
1B S. Loman#	WNS	A+	24	586	82	34	3	26	93	43	133	0-0	.293/.398/.511	.296	.346	0.0	1B -10	1.7
C J. Phegley	WNS	A+	22	99	15	3	0	3	12	7	22	0-0	.292/.333/.427	.268	.343	0.6	C 0	0.5
	BIR	AA	22	78	6	4	0	2	13	2	22	0-0	.292/.308/.431	.242	.365	0.6	C 0	0.2
INF L. Rodriguez#	CHR	AAA	30	395	50	17	2	16	55	42	34	3-5	.293/.362/.496	.298	.277	-4.0	SS -2, 2B 4	3.0
SS T. Saladino	KAN	A	20	194	38	14	1	2	18	22	44	0-0	.309/.397/.442	.294	.389	0.0	SS -3	1.2
	BRI	Rk	20	81	8	3	0	1	10	6	16	1-0	.254/.296/.338	.264	.293	-0.9	SS -2	0.0
OF B. Short	WNS	A+	21	553	72	31	5	16	81	29	113	6-11	.314/.371/.487	.286	.367	2.8	RF 0, CF -9	2.0
OF T. Thompson	KAN	A	19	234	26	13	3	8	31	21	69	3-4	.229/.303/.433	.270	.296	1.3	CF 3	1.3

Outrighted and bumped down a level, **Cole Armstrong** ought to move on as a minor-league free agent, because a cheap lefty bat who throws well from behind the plate has value. ⚾ Catcher **Michael Blanke** had an outstanding pro debut after getting picked in the 14th round of the draft, flashing pop and good receiving skills. ⚾ Consistent in all things, the well-traveled **Alejandro De Aza** lost another six weeks to injury, and raked and ran well when he was healthy; he's still hoping to get the kind of opportunity that went to Endy Chavez and Timo Perez. ⚾ After passing his High-A audition, **Jon Gilmore** will have to deliver more power with his line-drive swing in his age-22 season. ⚾ Toolsy speedster **Justin Greene** has the athleticism to play a good center field, but beating on younger pitching in A-ball and struggling when he leveled up is hardly the hallmark of a big future. ⚾ Bouncing from the Angels to the indie leagues to the Sox, **Seth Loman** is an old man marking time in A-ball, just trying to stay one step ahead of the Arthur Miller gags. ⚾ After he missed most of 2010 upon diagnosis of a rare blood disorder (ITP), catching prospect **Josh Phegley**'s career is in doubt, but he'll give it another shot in 2011. ⚾ **Luis Rodriguez** proved you don't have to be at a corner to be a Quad-A guy just biding time until his next shot; he'll be in the Mariners' camp as an NRI. ⚾ Seventh-rounder **Tyler Saladino** arrived with a good-glove rep last summer, but he enhanced his prospect status by answering questions about his bat. ⊘ **Brandon Short** put up an early 26-game hitting streak and earned Carolina League all-star honors, but his glove profiles in a corner, meaning he'd better sock lest his Sox prospects pop. ⊘ **Trayce Thompson** missed 2½ months with a broken thumb, but showed excellent power in his full-season debut and remains a prospect to follow.

PITCHERS

PLAYER	TEAM	LVL	AGE	W	L	SV	IP	H	HR	BB	SO	EqBB9	EqSO9	GB%	BABIP	WHIP	ERA	FRA	WARP
K. Bellamy	WNS	A+	22	5	0	5	47^1	38	1	14	59	2.7	11.2	55%	.308	1.16	1.33	2.942	1.2
—	BIR	AA	22	2	2	0	25^2	31	1	22	19	7.7	6.7	60%	.357	2.14	6.31	6.06	-0.4
J. Collop	KAN	A	22	9	12	0	154^1	170	10	31	130	1.8	7.6	50%	.341	1.37	4.02	4.70	1.5
D. Heath	BIR	AA	24	2	4	2	57^2	49	4	32	84	5.0	13.1	43%	.357	1.47	2.97	2.57	1.7
M. Heidenreich	BRI	Rk	19	6	2	0	85^1	87	4	13	66	1.4	7.0	62%	.322	1.17	2.95	3.17	7.2
B. Hynick	BIR	AA	25	3	1	0	53^1	51	3	13	37	2.2	6.2	48%	.291	1.24	2.36	3.20	1.5
—	CHR	AAA	25	1	4	0	59^1	79	13	21	44	3.2	6.7	33%	.337	1.72	6.07	5.71	0.2
N. Jones	WNS	A+	24	11	7	0	162	181	10	67	117	3.7	6.5	47%	.335	1.60	3.61	4.17	2.9
C. Leesman*	WNS	A+	23	9	4	0	84^2	98	6	44	39	4.7	4.1	55%	.314	1.81	4.57	4.31	1.5
—	BIR	AA	23	5	2	0	63^2	47	1	20	51	2.8	7.2	56%	.261	1.10	2.54	3.09	1.8
J. Marquez	CHR	AAA	25	8	9	0	144^2	160	14	49	89	3.0	5.5	46%	.312	1.47	4.42	15.35	0.0
—	CHA	MLB	25	0	0	0	1	2	1	0	0	0.0	0.0	40%	.250	2.00	18.00	20.65	-0.0
J. Nunez	BIR	AA	24	1	4	0	51	53	3	17	38	3.0	6.7	46%	.313	1.37	3.71	4.35	0.7
—	CHR	AAA	24	5	2	1	44^1	46	6	19	45	3.9	9.1	33%	.318	1.51	5.28	6.08	-0.4
J. Petricka	BRI	Rk	22	2	4	0	43^2	30	1	7	48	1.4	9.9	62%	.266	0.85	2.68	3.86	3.0
D. Remenowsky	WNS	A+	24	2	1	5	39^1	34	3	13	60	3.0	13.7	52%	.369	1.25	2.29	2.21	1.0
A. Rienzo	KAN	A	22	8	4	0	101	95	5	32	125	2.9	11.1	48%	.336	1.28	3.56	4.00	2.0
C. Santeliz	CHR	AAA	23	1	4	2	54	40	9	34	50	5.7	8.3	41%	.235	1.43	4.50	5.84	-0.4
E. Threets*	CHR	AAA	28	1	0	2	21	12	0	5	10	2.1	4.3	57%	.191	0.81	0.86	2.41	0.8
—	CHA	MLB	28	0	0	0	12^1	9	0	3	6	2.2	4.4	56%	.250	0.97	0.73	2.21	1.0

Sidearmer **Kyle Bellamy** might have a future as a situational right-hander, thanks to his delivery and a nasty high-80s sinker. ⊘ **Justin Collop** had a decent full-season debut, improving significantly in the second half while flashing a low-90s fastball and inducing lots of DP grounders. ⊘ Ditched by the Braves after a solicitation arrest in spring training, **Deunte Heath** bounced back in the Sox system to notch a stack of strikeouts, but command is a problem. ⊘ **Matt Heidenreich** was a fourth-round high school pick in 2009, and with a big frame and heat that sits in the low 90s, he's worth waiting on, if a long way off. ⊘ The return for trading Jose Contreras to the Rockies, **Brandon Hynick** only solidified his org-soldier status. ⊘ Moving **Nathan Jones** into the rotation gave him the reps to try to add a consistent breaking pitch to his menu of heat that tops out just shy of triple-digits. ⊘ If **Charles Leesman** can find a reliable off-speed pitch to go with a low-90s sinker, he'll stop doing things like finishing his Double-A year with six straight quality starts, then giving up more than three baserunners per inning in an awful AFL campaign. ⊘ **Jeff Marquez** has struggled to generate ground-ball outs, get lefties out, or pitch effectively a second or third time through an order, which suggests a future in the bullpen. Or elsewhere. ⊘ An early-season experiment with starting **Jhonny Nunez** went well, but his mix of mid-90s heat and an inconsistent slider flopped against lefties in both roles at two levels. ⊘ Selecting tall, lanky **Jacob Petricka** out of Indiana State in the second round of last summer's draft was an endorsement of a fastball that touches 95; though he's raw, a future in the pen awaits. ⊘ **Dan Remenowsky**'s June knee injury ended his second promising season early, but the former indie leaguer is worth watching for a big leg kick, deceptive delivery, and excellent command of a low-velo mix. ⊘ A rare Brazilian import, **Andre Rienzo** throws mid-90s heat and took a big step forward in the second half, striking out 31 percent of opposing batters. ⊘ While **Clevelan Santeliz** has dialed his heat into the mid-90s, his bulk, lack of durability, command issues, and time lost to shoulder woes got him taken off the 40-man. ⊘ A big former Giants prospect, **Erick Threets** looked as if he might be a quality second lefty before blowing out his elbow; he'll miss most or all of 2011, so the White Sox nontendered him.

MANAGER: OZZIE GUILLEN

YEAR	TEAM	W-L	Pythag +/-	Avg PC	100+ P	120+ P	QS	BQS	REL	REL w Zero R	IBB	Subs	PH	PH Avg	PH HR	SB2	CS2	SB3	CS3	SAC Att	SAC %	POS SAC	Squeeze	Swing	In Play
2009	CHA	79-83	-1	95.1	62	0	85	9	415	246	41	35	105	.106	2	105	45	6	3	49	69.4%	30	1	139	113
2010	CHA	88-74	2	99.5	89	3	89	11	406	265	41	49	85	.263	3	134	68	24	4	69	72.5%	48	4	179	146

As skippers go, Ozzie is a throwback to the 1970s and 1980s, not in terms of any one legacy, but in terms of all of them. He likes to run and to manufacture runs, and he finally had a roster he could really do it with. His club nevertheless also ranked seventh-highest in MLB with its "Guillen number," the percentage of runs scored on homers. In an era of well-worn tracks between the dugout and the mound, he's the least likely manager to go to the pen or use a specific reliever on consecutive days. He tends to give his starters a reasonably long leash and seems to have escaped getting much credit for the development of Danks or Floyd. If there's a source of frustration in watching one of the game's most entertaining managers work, it's his willingness to order up intentional walks, which burns him with a regularity that would crush lesser men.

Cincinnati Reds

The Reds entered 2010 as something of a post-hype sleeper. Heading into 2009, they'd been a popular preseason pick to make some noise in the NL Central, thanks to a coalescing core of talented youngsters, a new GM with a successful track record, and the addition of a few promising plugs to the glaring holes that had plagued the previous year's team. However, despite the hype, Cincinnati added only four wins to its meager 2008 total, as a rash of injuries and widespread underperformance by its up-and-comers resulted in a disappointing fourth-place finish.

Still, latent talent lingered, primed to be unlocked by additional seasoning and a reduction in DL days. With the aid of better health and another year of experience under the belts of the organization's emerging stars, the Reds added 18 wins to their 2009 tally, qualifying for the playoffs for the first time since 1995. After sticking close to the Cardinals for the first four months of the season, the Reds leapfrogged St. Louis on the ides of a 19-8 August and never looked back. Their forward progress was finally halted in the NLDS, from which they were dispatched in short order by the combined might of the Phillies' tripartite top of the rotation, but their ignoble end shouldn't put a damper on a successful first six months.

Despite its aborted playoff aspirations, the 2009 transition team distinguished itself as one of baseball's best defensive units following several seasons of fielding folly in the Queen City, furnishing its successor with a firmer foundation on which to build. After the 2009 club got religion on defense, the 2010 team managed to stay devout (Table 1).

As impressive as their turnaround was, the 2009 Reds' improved defensive play had come at the expense of their bats, whose .252 True Average (TAv) ranked 24th in the majors. In recent years, Cincinnati's offensive attack has tended to sputter at the top before heating up to varying degrees lower in the order. Only once since 2001—in a 2007 performance buoyed by 121 plate appearances from unlikely leadoff contributor Josh Hamilton—have Cincy's leadoff efforts earned a place among the top half of major-league teams (Table 2).

Although Dusty Baker again failed to settle on a sublime solution at the top of the order (if not to the disastrous extent that he had during the Willy Taveras era), the Reds managed to overcome the poor first impressions they made on opposing pitchers. Without sacrificing a smidgen of the 2009 team's glove work, last year's model underwent an offensive makeover that rivaled the most drastic ever achieved (Table 3).

REDS PROSPECTUS

2010 W-L: 91-71, 1st in NL Central

Pythag	.567	7th
RS/G	4.9	4th
RA/G	4.2	21st
TAv	.283	3rd
BRR	11.7	4th
FRA	4.51	17th
DER	21.3	2nd
DL	731	15th
B-Age	29.1	17th
P-Age	27.6	11th
Salary	$71.8	20th
M$/MW	$1.46	6th

Ballpark: Great American Ball Park (3-yr. PF: 101). The name sounds patriotic, but it's trying to sell you insurance

2010: Continued good glove work and offensive improvements give young Reds green light for October

2011: A full season of Chapmania highlights homegrown playoff-caliber core

Action Items: A left fielder who provokes fewer groans than Gomes

Table 1. North of the Bor-DER: Reds Team Defense, 2008-2010

Year	DE	DE Rank	PADE	PADE Rank
2010	.704	7	1.13	5
2010	.705	4	0.64	6
2008	.673	29	-3.83	30

Table 2. Slow Starters: Performance by Reds Leadoff Batters, 2001-2010

Year	Primary Leadoff Batter	Cumulative Leadoff TAv	Rank
2001	Todd Walker	0.255	14
2002	Todd Walker	0.232	27
2003	Felipe Lopez	0.247	21
2004	Ryan Freel	0.241	25
2005	Ryan Freel	0.255	22
2006	Ryan Freel	0.258	17
2007	Ryan Freel	0.281	8
2008	Jerry Hairston	0.257	20
2009	Willy Taveras	0.236	30
2010	Brandon Phillips	0.247	22

Table 3. Getting Offensive: Highest Single-Season TAv Turnarounds

Year 1	Year 2	Team	TAv1	TAv2	Differential
1971	1972	HOU	0.255	0.290	0.036
1977	1978	MIL	0.252	0.285	0.033
2003	2004	DET	0.238	0.271	0.033
1964	1965	CIN	0.262	0.293	0.031
1999	2000	ANA	0.242	0.272	0.030
2009	**2010**	**CIN**	**0.252**	**0.280**	**0.028**
1966	1967	SLN	0.257	0.285	0.028
1971	1972	CIN	0.261	0.288	0.028
1992	1993	SFN	0.253	0.280	0.027
1969	1970	SDN	0.240	0.266	0.026

Table 4. First-Round Flops? Reds Number-One Picks Since Barry Larkin

Year	Pick	Name	Career WARP
2010	12	Yasmani Grandal	N/A
2009	8	Mike Leake	1.6
2008	7	Yonder Alonso	-0.2
2007	15	Devin Mesoraco	N/A
2006	8	Drew Stubbs	7.2
2005	12	Jay Bruce	9.0
2004	7	Homer Bailey	0.6
2003	14	Ryan Wagner	0.2
2002	3	Chris Gruler	N/A
2001	20	Jeremy Sowers	2.1
2000	23	David Espinosa	N/A
1999	14	Ty Howington	N/A
1998	7	Austin Kearns	19.6
1997	14	Brandon Larson	-0.8
1996	25	John Oliver	N/A
1994	9	C.J. Nitkowski	1.3
1992	5	Chad Mottola	-0.7
1991	20	Pokey Reese	11.1
1990	7	Daniel Wilson	N/A
1989	20	Scott Bryant	N/A
1987	18	Jack Armstrong	0.7
1986	17	Scott Scudder	-1.6

An improvement of that magnitude might lead you to believe that the Reds went wild on the free-agent market, enlisting the services of every available slugger, but most bears had busier winters than Walt Jocketty. Aside from making a splash in landing Aroldis Chapman—who, despite the attention generated by his triple-digit heat, contributed a grand total of 15 innings to the Reds' cause and did nothing to improve their formerly feeble offense—Cincinnati played it safe with outside acquisitions. The team's highest-profile additions on the offensive side were Miguel Cairo and Orlando Cabrera, neither of whom was intended as an antidote to anemic run creation.

Aside from a few examples of addition by subtraction, most notably in the case of Taveras, Cincinnati's greatest gains at the plate came from players already under contract. Although resurgent seasons from veterans Scott Rolen (whose 2009 acquisition had been roundly criticized) and Ramon Hernandez played a role, homegrown players supplied the biggest boosts. The Reds received more plate appearances at elevated rates of production from Joey Votto, Jay Bruce, and Drew Stubbs, as well as a valuable small-sample performance from the league's most overqualified backup catcher, Ryan Hanigan. Thanks to the contributions of Votto, Rolen, Hernandez, and Hanigan, among others, the Reds' infield amassed the highest VORP of any in baseball, though Bruce and Stubbs ensured that their outfield was no slouch with the stick, either.

Offense wasn't the only area in which the Reds' farm yielded a strong crop last season, as a host of homegrown hurlers got in on the act. Four of the six starters who saw the most action for Cincinnati last season were either drafted or signed as amateur free agents by the Reds. That kind of support from the system simply hadn't been forthcoming in recent years, in large part because the organization had gotten almost nothing out of its first-round picks for the better part of two decades (Table 4).

With their 1985 first-round pick, the Reds snagged Barry Larkin, who went on to spend the entirety of a Cooperstown-caliber career in Cincinnati. But from 1986 through 2003, the best the Reds could muster with their highest picks was Austin Kearns, a useful complementary piece, but hardly the best-case return a team would hope to acquire with any one of its first-round selections, let alone a string of 15. The only other Reds first-rounder who managed to poke his head above replacement level by a significant margin during this fallow period of Reds first rounds was Pokey Reese, a defense-oriented shortstop who clung to a major-league roster spot for several years. The rest of the field was rounded out by marginal talents who made little impact in the majors, if they made the majors at all.

Contrast that woeful track record with the first-round finds of the post-2003 era. Despite the recency of the draft classes involved, five of the organization's last seven selections have already made the majors, with a sixth (Mesoraco) on the verge, and a seventh (Grandal) sitting pretty in the low minors following his 2010 professional debut. Each of those five spent time on the Reds' active roster last season, with all but Alonso seeing significant action.

The blame for the team's first-round failures from 1986 through 2003 must be distributed among the six scouting directors who spearheaded the team's selections over that span, but the bulk of the credit for the successes of the past several years belongs to two men: Terry Reynolds and Chris Buckley. Reynolds served as scouting director in 2004 and 2005 before moving to the farm-director role he's held ever since, while Buckley has overseen the team's last five drafts. The latter seems to skew toward safer college selections, with frequent exceptions for high-upside high schoolers, a pattern that has served him well since his days running Toronto's drafts from 2001 to 2003. Together, the two have restocked the Reds' system and packed the major-league roster with players who have known no organization but Cincinnati.

Of course, effective drafting depends not only on the quality of a team's scouting, but also on the depth of its owner's pockets and their willingness to dig therein, and the Reds have gradually increased their spending on signing bonuses in recent seasons (Table 5).

Table 5. In the Red: Cincinnati Draft Spending, 2003-2010

Year	Spending	MLB Rank
2010	5.7	16
2009	5.9	16
2008	4.8	21
2007	4.4	12
2006	3.9	19
2005	3.8*	20
2004	4.7*	14
2003	3.1*	24

*First 10 rounds only

While the Reds have yet to reach the upper tier in draft spending, membership in the middle of the pack constitutes an improvement over the dark days of 2003. The organization has historically adhered to MLB slot recommendations, but spent 122 percent over slot on its first 10 picks last year, receiving 10 fresh signatures as a reward. In addition, ownership has loosened its purse strings in South America, making the Reds one of the most aggressive teams in international affairs after years of sitting on the sidelines. As a result, the lower levels of the Cincinnati system are littered with high-ceiling talents who should soon begin to make their presence felt, if they haven't already.

Using a method developed by *Baseball Prospectus* author Matt Swartz, we can see exactly how much major-league talent the Reds' system has generated over the past few seasons, without restricting our inquiries to the Cincinnati roster alone. By artificially assigning every player who spent time in the majors from 2007 to 2009 to the team that first signed him to a contract—either as a draft pick, an undrafted player, or an international free agent—and then crediting each organization with the WARP that its scattered progeny contributed to their *actual* teams, we can arrive at a hypothetical win total for every organization in a world in which none of the players had departed their original baseball homes. For Cincinnati, life in a no-turnover world looked bleak from 2007 to 2009 (Table 6).

In both 2007 and 2008, the Reds were responsible for discovering less of the talent on display across the league than any other organization, and a modest improvement in 2009 barely budged their MLB rank. However, after the great leaps forward enjoyed by a number of Reds-developed players in 2010, the picture began to look far rosier (Table 7).

Table 6. Turn-Down Service: Reds "No Turnover" Records, 2007-2009

Year	Record	MLB Rank	Wins Below Average
2007	47-113	30	32
2008	51-111	30	30
2009	64-98	29	17

Table 7. Going to WARP Speed: Win Value of Reds Amateur Draftees/Signees

Year	MLB-wide WARP	CIN WARP
2007	10.8	4.9
2008	10.9	3.9
2009	25.1	15.2
2010	41.4	33.8

Table 7 paints a portrait of a team coming into its own, as a combination of adept scouting and increased amateur spending has translated to substantial gains at the big-league level. Most of the youthful major-league talent unearthed by the Reds in recent years has stayed within the organization rather than migrate elsewhere in return for well-cured veteran meat. The Reds have more talent flowing swiftly through their pipeline, but now that Jocketty has established a base, he needn't be afraid to use his excess talent to make a few final trades and signings to put his team over the top. The restraint he exhibited last winter as he waited for his homegrown charges to cohere will serve him well, as a roster enviably free of long-term commitments awaits his finishing touches in a wide-open division.

This offseason, Jocketty passed up an opportunity to hand another starting gig to a homegrown Red, signing Edgar Renteria to start over 2004 draftee and perpetual understudy Paul Janish at short. Still, the position won't long be held by an out-of-towner, since Cincinnati's system features a ready replacement in Zack Cozart. Although Jonny Gomes' lease on major-league life was renewed when the Reds exercised his option for 2011, the team boasts an array of outfield talent capable of bettering Gomes' dubious production in left as soon as this season. With the departure of the team's longest-tenured player, Aaron Harang, every candidate for the rotation, excluding Bronson Arroyo and Edinson Volquez, has worn a Reds uniform to the exclusion of all others, putting the team in the unfamiliar position of possessing enough pitching depth to make the arbitration-eligible Volquez expendable for the right return.

Enough grist remains in the talent mill to assemble, if not quite an equivalent powerhouse, at least a spiritual successor to the Reds mid-1970s dynasty, a unit that should remain competitive for years to come while perhaps falling short of inducing the same reverent tones in future generations. Still, the team's wave of talent is cresting at just the right time: in today's NL Central, even a Medium Red Machine could prove unbeatable.

HITTERS

Yonder Alonso 1B
Born: 4/8/1987 Age: 24
Bats: L Throws: R Height: 6' 2" Weight: 210
Breakout: 3% Improve: 7% Collapse: 1%
Attrition: 10% MLB: 19%
Comparables:
Wes Bankston, Jeff Clement, Kendry Morales (76)

YEAR	TEAM	LVL	AGE	PA	R	2B	3B	HR	RBI	BB	SO	SB	CS	AVG_OBP_SLG	TAv	BABIP	BRR	FRAA	WARP
2009	SAR	A+	22	201	21	13	0	7	38	24	30	0	1	.303/.383/.497	.314	.329	-0.7	1B 1	1.3
2009	CAR	AA	22	121	12	11	0	2	14	14	15	1	0	.295/.372/.457	.306	.322	0.9	1B 4	1.1
2010	CAR	AA	23	120	19	5	0	3	13	19	16	4	2	.267/.392/.406	.280	.293	-0.9	LF -2, 1B 0	0.2
2010	LOU	AAA	23	439	48	30	2	12	56	37	74	9	1	.297/.358/.471	.277	.339	-2.0	1B 0, LF -3	0.8
2010	CIN	MLB	23	29	2	2	0	0	3	0	10	0	0	.207/.207/.276	.163	.316	-0.2	1B 2	0.0
2011	*CIN*	*MLB*	*24*	*325*	*38*	*17*	*0*	*7*	*35*	*30*	*57*	*4*	*1*	*.261/.327/.401*	*.255*	*.295*	*0.0*	*1B -6, LF -1*	*-0.6*

In his age-23 season, Joey Votto hit 22 homers in Triple-A and posted a .227 isolated power in his first taste of the majors. At the same age, Alonso managed just 12 long balls for Louisville and looked outmatched in an even briefer major-league cameo. Given that Votto has blossomed into the NL's best hitter, a failure to match the Canadian's early offensive output hardly qualifies as a kiss of death. Still, when you share both a position and a team with a superstar, it's best not to fall too far behind. Alonso hit much better during the second half of the minor-league season, but the southpaw has yet to exhibit the kind of power expected of a first-round first baseman. The 30 games he spent in left last year were likely just a taste of what's to come, since last season's closest thing to a Triple Crown winner isn't about to be dislodged by a player who hasn't managed a .500 slugging percentage at any level.

Willie Bloomquist OF
Born: 11/27/1977 Age: 33
Bats: R Throws: R Height: 5' 11" Weight: 180
Breakout: 0% Improve: 18% Collapse: 18%
Attrition: 22% MLB: 79%
Comparables:
Danny Bautista, Marvin Benard, Dave Martinez (75)

YEAR	TEAM	LVL	AGE	PA	R	2B	3B	HR	RBI	BB	SO	SB	CS	AVG_OBP_SLG	TAv	BABIP	BRR	FRAA	WARP
2008	SEA	MLB	30	192	30	1	0	0	9	25	29	14	3	.279/.375/.285	.278	.336	2.8	CF 2, SS -4	0.8
2009	KCA	MLB	31	468	52	11	8	4	29	27	73	25	6	.265/.306/.355	.242	.306	3.4	RF 2, SS 1	0.7
2010	CIN	MLB	32	18	0	0	0	0	0	1	3	0	0	.294/.333/.294	.237	.357	-0.1	RF 0, LF 0	-0.1
2010	KCA	MLB	32	181	19	10	1	3	17	8	25	8	5	.265/.293/.388	.245	.290	-0.4	RF -2, 3B 1	-0.1
2011	*CIN*	*MLB*	*33*	*266*	*28*	*9*	*1*	*3*	*23*	*19*	*41*	*13*	*4*	*.258/.309/.340*	*.234*	*.293*	*-0.2*	*RF 0, CF -1*	*-0.2*

In need of some September depth, the Reds turned to the quintessential replacement player, who delivered a predictably replacement-level performance in his brief time with the team. Since the danger posed by Bloomquist manifests mainly through extended exposure, Walt Jocketty prudently refrained from pulling the trigger until he knew that the ex-Royal would be ineligible for the playoff roster. In his 11 games with Cincinnati, Bloomquist showcased his usual versatility, appearing at three positions, but he also failed to post a slugging percentage higher than his OBP, which we could dismiss as a small-sample-size fluke if he hadn't sustained similarly lopsided lines in two prior seasons. The righty did manage to post a triple-digit seasonal ISO for the first time, but solidified his status as an offensive offender by walking even less frequently than usual. He's not a bad Band-Aid, but can become an uncomfortable cast very quickly if the underlying ailment is left untreated.

Jay Bruce RF
Born: 4/3/1987 Age: 24
Bats: L Throws: L Height: 6' 3" Weight: 205
Breakout: 3% Improve: 53% Collapse: 2%
Attrition: 10% MLB: 91%
Comparables:
Grady Sizemore, Frank Robinson, Tony Conigliaro (71)

YEAR	TEAM	LVL	AGE	PA	R	2B	3B	HR	RBI	BB	SO	SB	CS	AVG_OBP_SLG	TAv	BABIP	BRR	FRAA	WARP
2008	LOU	AAA	21	201	34	9	5	10	37	12	45	8	1	.364/.393/.630	.338	.425	-2.0	CF 0, RF 2	2.4
2008	CIN	MLB	21	452	62	17	1	21	52	33	110	4	6	.254/.314/.453	.264	.296	-0.7	RF 2, CF -2	0.8
2009	CIN	MLB	22	387	47	15	2	22	58	38	75	3	3	.223/.302/.470	.266	.220	-0.4	RF 5	1.2
2010	CIN	MLB	23	573	80	23	5	25	70	58	136	5	4	.281/.353/.493	.297	.334	0.5	RF 25	5.3
2011	*CIN*	*MLB*	*24*	*550*	*72*	*22*	*3*	*25*	*78*	*53*	*116*	*8*	*4*	*.269/.339/.482*	*.284*	*.299*	*-0.5*	*RF 10, CF -1*	*3.0*

You wouldn't know it from watching Joey Votto, but even top prospects don't often spring forth from the minor-league womb as fully formed stars. After leaping out of the gate in 2008, Bruce looked lost for the remainder of his rookie campaign and followed that up with an equally underwhelming sophomore effort. Last season, he made great strides toward harnessing the abilities that made him such a highly touted talent. Much of his improvement can be attributed to a hundred-plus-point rise in BABIP, but that boost came from hitting the ball with greater authority, as evidenced by a nearly 50 percent climb in his line-drive rate. After struggling to hit lefties at all in his first two seasons, he punished them even more than he did righties in 2010, quieting any incipient platoon talk, though he has shown a dramatic home/road split in favor of Cincinnati over the course of his career. The southpaw has blossomed into a superior defender, as evidenced by his MLB-leading FRAA, and sports one of the best outfield arms in baseball. As he enters his age-24 season, it's become quite clear that there's little the Super-Two can't do; a six-year extension (with a club option for a seven season) signed in December will ensure that he doesn't do it in another uniform.

Orlando Cabrera SS

Born: **11/2/1974** Age: **36**
Bats: **R** Throws: **R** Height: **5' 11"** Weight: **165**
Breakout: **1%** Improve: **14%** Collapse: **14%**
Attrition: **25%** MLB: **93%**

Comparables:
Miguel Tejada, Mark Loretta, Luis Aparicio (68)

YEAR	TEAM	LVL	AGE	PA	R	2B	3B	HR	RBI	BB	SO	SB	CS	AVG_OBP_SLG	TAv	BABIP	BRR	FRAA	WARP
2008	CHA	MLB	33	730	94	33	1	8	57	56	71	19	6	.281/.333/.371	.253	.300	4.5	SS 0	2.7
2009	MIN	MLB	34	260	42	13	3	5	36	11	32	2	0	.289/.312/.430	.258	.307	4.2	SS -1	1.3
2009	OAK	MLB	34	448	41	23	0	4	41	25	39	11	4	.280/.315/.365	.243	.295	1.9	SS -11	0.0
2010	CIN	MLB	35	537	64	33	0	4	42	28	53	11	4	.263/.300/.354	.239	.281	2.3	SS -7	0.4
2011	*CIN*	*MLB*	*36*	*671*	*71*	*34*	*1*	*5*	*60*	*44*	*64*	*15*	*5*	*.266/.311/.349*	*.238*	*.282*	*0.0*	*SS -8*	*0.2*

For several years, the party line on Cabrera was that while his offensive production may not have been impressive, his employers could at least count on its being unimpressive in a durable and consistent way. That changed in 2010, as the shortstop not only sank to lows with the lumber unseen since his early days with Montreal, but also failed to play at least 140 games for the first time since 2000, suffering from a slow-healing oblique injury that continued to hamper him in the playoffs. Perhaps even more damning, the Colombian's glove no longer resembled the Grade-A leather that used to make his subpar stick work acceptable. The current Cabrera package doesn't add up to a starter, and the Reds accordingly declined their $4 million 2011 option for his services.

Miguel Cairo 3B

Born: **5/4/1974** Age: **37**
Bats: **R** Throws: **R** Height: **6' 0"** Weight: **160**
Breakout: **0%** Improve: **18%** Collapse: **17%**
Attrition: **25%** MLB: **66%**

Comparables:
Tony Graffanino, Billy Goodman, Juan Beniquez (74)

YEAR	TEAM	LVL	AGE	PA	R	2B	3B	HR	RBI	BB	SO	SB	CS	AVG_OBP_SLG	TAv	BABIP	BRR	FRAA	WARP
2008	SEA	MLB	34	250	27	14	2	0	23	18	32	5	2	.249/.308/.330	.237	.281	3.6	1B -3, 3B 0	-0.2
2009	LEH	AAA	35	313	43	12	2	5	33	15	40	8	1	.287/.326/.392	.248	.316	-2.9	SS -7, 2B -1	-0.2
2009	PHI	MLB	35	47	5	2	1	1	2	0	4	0	0	.267/.277/.422	.246	.268	0.4	2B -1, SS 0	0.0
2010	CIN	MLB	36	226	30	12	0	4	28	17	30	4	0	.290/.350/.410	.279	.316	-0.2	3B -8, 1B -1	0.1
2011	*CIN*	*MLB*	*37*	*262*	*27*	*12*	*1*	*2*	*23*	*17*	*36*	*5*	*1*	*.252/.303/.338*	*.231*	*.280*	*0.1*	*SS -1, 1B -1*	*-0.4*

The Reds signed up for Cairo's age-36 season in hopes of receiving the same acceptable glove work at a plethora of positions that he'd long since proven himself capable of providing. What they got in addition to that were his best offensive rates ever. The added benefit came by virtue of a .320 BABIP, a mark identical to the one he sported during his last above-average season with the bat in 2004, but he also showed a greater-than-normal willingness to take a walk this time around. Despite playing on the same team as Joey Votto, the slap-hitting utilityman began 10 games at first base, bringing his career total of starts at the game's premier offensive position to an inexplicable 78. In a season that saw him wear his ninth major-league uniform, the veteran Venezuelan also sported his ninth unique uniform number. Either Cairo is not a sentimental man, or he has decided that having a vanity number on his back isn't worth the costs he'd incur in Rolex bribes due to playing musical chairs every offseason.

Zack Cozart SS

Born: **8/12/1985** Age: **25**
Bats: **R** Throws: **R** Height: **6' 0"** Weight: **195**
Breakout: **4%** Improve: **13%** Collapse: **17%**
Attrition: **32%** MLB: **48%**

Comparables:
Chin-lung Hu, Gregorio Petit, Luis Valbuena (79)

YEAR	TEAM	LVL	AGE	PA	R	2B	3B	HR	RBI	BB	SO	SB	CS	AVG_OBP_SLG	TAv	BABIP	BRR	FRAA	WARP
2008	DYT	A	22	471	56	20	6	15	51	24	80	3	3	.276/.327/.453	.278	.298	1.2	SS -4, 2B 1	2.4
2009	CAR	AA	23	531	67	29	2	10	58	63	87	10	2	.262/.365/.398	.271	.299	2.7	SS 2	2.9
2010	LOU	AAA	24	622	90	30	4	17	67	40	113	30	4	.250/.304/.406	.243	.279	3.6	SS 6	2.3
2011	*CIN*	*MLB*	*25*	*541*	*57*	*24*	*2*	*12*	*55*	*37*	*103*	*11*	*3*	*.237/.291/.368*	*.233*	*.269*	*0.2*	*SS 1, 2B 0*	*0.6*

Just when it seemed safe to declare Cozart's 2008 power surge dead, he set a career high in homers. The additional power came at the cost of some plate discipline, so the overall package wasn't more productive than the 2009 model, but the righty held his own despite climbing to the minor-league ladder's highest rung. As one of the best defensive shortstops in any team's system, Cozart doesn't have to excel with the stick to get the call, but he's done plenty to dispel his former all-glove reputation, and might well have surpassed Orlando Cabrera at the plate last season had he gotten the chance. Edgar Renteria should take plenty of pictures of his first season as the Reds' starting shortstop, because he likely won't get another.

Juan Francisco 3B

Born: 6/24/1987 Age: 24
Bats: S Throws: R Height: 6' 2" Weight: 180
Breakout: 2% Improve: 18% Collapse: 10%
Attrition: 33% MLB: 58%

Comparables:
Brandon Wood, Scott Moore, Mat Gamel (71)

YEAR	TEAM	LVL	AGE	PA	R	2B	3B	HR	RBI	BB	SO	SB	CS	AVG_OBP_SLG	TAv	BABIP	BRR	FRAA	WARP
2008	SAR	A+	21	539	71	34	5	23	91	19	123	1	2	.277/.304/.496	.276	.321	-0.6	3B -3, LF 0	2.1
2009	CAR	AA	22	460	64	26	2	22	73	20	91	6	2	.282/.320/.501	.283	.309	-2.3	3B -3	1.8
2009	LOU	AAA	22	120	21	6	1	7	24	4	27	0	0	.351/.375/.605	.336	.402	-3.7	3B 3, LF 1	1.3
2009	CIN	MLB	22	25	4	1	0	1	7	3	7	0	0	.429/.520/.619	.400	.615	0.4	3B 1	0.6
2010	LOU	AAA	23	322	44	24	4	17	58	16	81	0	0	.286/.326/.559	.295	.337	0.0	3B -7, LF 1	1.4
2010	CIN	MLB	23	59	3	3	0	1	7	4	20	0	1	.273/.322/.382	.243	.412	-0.4	3B -2	-0.2
2011	*CIN*	*MLB*	*24*	*508*	*61*	*27*	*2*	*21*	*73*	*18*	*125*	*2*	*1*	*.265/.290/.465*	*.257*	*.307*	*-0.1*	*3B -6, LF 0*	*0.5*

The Reds were bewitched enough by Francisco's power to give the young lefty an extended, if sporadic look over the last two months of the season, but he left his extra-base hits in Louisville. After three consecutive seasons of improvement, Francisco's strikeout-to-walk ratio plateaued in the vicinity of five at Triple-A, though he managed to narrow that margin to a slightly more respectable four in his intermittent postpromotion plate appearances. Despite his contact problems, the Dominican has managed to maintain respectable batting averages on the strength of his perennially high BABIPs, which stand as a testament to how hard he hits the ball. He'll have to start hitting it even harder, since the handful of games he spent at first and in left may signal the beginning of a slide down the defensive spectrum.

Todd Frazier LF

Born: 2/12/1986 Age: 25
Bats: R Throws: R Height: 6' 3" Weight: 220
Breakout: 3% Improve: 14% Collapse: 11%
Attrition: 28% MLB: 40%

Comparables:
Brandon Jones, Seth Smith, Adam Moore (79)

YEAR	TEAM	LVL	AGE	PA	R	2B	3B	HR	RBI	BB	SO	SB	CS	AVG_OBP_SLG	TAv	BABIP	BRR	FRAA	WARP
2008	DYT	A	22	127	24	10	0	7	20	15	28	4	2	.321/.402/.598	.369	.377	-0.4	SS 3, 1B 2	2.1
2008	SAR	A+	22	410	62	20	3	12	54	41	84	8	4	.281/.361/.451	.286	.333	1.9	SS 1, 1B 2	2.9
2009	CAR	AA	23	498	59	40	2	14	68	42	67	7	8	.291/.351/.481	.292	.312	-0.6	LF 2, 2B -3	2.3
2009	LOU	AAA	23	92	12	5	0	2	11	9	16	2	0	.301/.370/.434	.281	.354	-0.1	2B 2, LF 0	0.6
2010	LOU	AAA	24	543	73	31	4	19	70	48	129	0	0	.258/.341/.453	.265	.311	0.0	LF 7, 3B 0	2.1
2011	*CIN*	*MLB*	*25*	*557*	*65*	*30*	*2*	*16*	*66*	*44*	*118*	*7*	*3*	*.254/.315/.417*	*.256*	*.295*	*-0.4*	*LF 1, SS 1*	*1.0*

Frazier's frenzied game of musical positions didn't miss a beat in his fourth professional season, but his bat finally got lost in all the excitement. The righty had never been regarded as a fit for a premium defensive position, but he appeared to offer enough offense to carry second or third. That rosy vision of the future wavered in his first full season at Triple-A, where he spent the majority of his time as a left fielder, but hit more like a utilityman thanks to a dramatically inflated strikeout rate. His patience and power survived the promotion, so if his contact talents return with additional seasoning, he could still make his way to the majors at the end of Jonny Gomes' tenure, if not sooner. A 947 OPS in 144 August and September at-bats bodes well.

Jonny Gomes LF

Born: 11/22/1980 Age: 30
Bats: R Throws: R Height: 6' 1" Weight: 205
Breakout: 1% Improve: 35% Collapse: 2%
Attrition: 7% MLB: 89%

Comparables:
Josh Willingham, Jason Bay, Ron Gant (76)

YEAR	TEAM	LVL	AGE	PA	R	2B	3B	HR	RBI	BB	SO	SB	CS	AVG_OBP_SLG	TAv	BABIP	BRR	FRAA	WARP
2008	DUR	AAA	27	151	23	11	0	4	19	15	40	0	1	.252/.364/.422	.265	.326	1.3	LF 0, RF 0	0.4
2008	TBA	MLB	27	177	22	5	1	8	21	15	46	8	1	.182/.283/.383	.247	.198	1.2	RF -1, LF 2	0.1
2009	LOU	AAA	28	143	18	10	1	9	27	12	36	4	1	.282/.371/.580	.304	.326	-1.4	LF 2, RF -3	0.7
2009	CIN	MLB	28	314	40	17	0	20	51	26	85	3	1	.267/.338/.541	.295	.309	0.4	LF -6, RF -2	0.9
2010	CIN	MLB	29	571	77	24	3	18	86	39	123	5	3	.266/.328/.431	.279	.311	3.0	LF -9	1.5
2011	*CIN*	*MLB*	*30*	*453*	*56*	*21*	*1*	*18*	*57*	*40*	*110*	*7*	*3*	*.248/.327/.443*	*.270*	*.291*	*-0.2*	*LF -4, RF -1*	*0.6*

Gomes improbably led the NL in infield-hit percentage and ranked second in the majors to Ichiro Suzuki. The ability to beat out slow rollers has never been a particular talent of the stocky outfielder/DH and isn't likely to stay one going forward, but as flukes go, this one was well timed. Gomes posted his lowest ISO yet and coupled his power outage with a career-worst walk rate, so he needed all the excuse-me singles he could get. FRAA was kinder to his fielding than the other advanced defensive metrics, which judged his glove work so harshly as to cast his overall contribution as subreplacement in nature. If Gomes' decline continues as he hits the wrong side of 30, the number of major-league seasons left in the righty's career could be counted on the pitching hand of Three Finger Brown.

Yasmani Grandal C

Born: **11/8/1988** Age: **22**
Bats: **S** Throws: **R** Height: **6' 2"** Weight: **215**
Breakout: **0%** Improve: **0%** Collapse: **1%**
Attrition: **1%** MLB: **1%**
Comparables:

YEAR	TEAM	LVL	AGE	PA	R	2B	3B	HR	RBI	BB	SO	SB	CS	AVG_OBP_SLG	TAv	BABIP	BRR	FRAA	WARP
2011	*CIN*	*MLB*	*22*	—	—	—	—	—	—	—	—	—	—	—	—	—	—	—	—

For the second time in four drafts, the Reds used their first-round pick on a catcher, selecting Grandal 12th overall. The switch-hitter showed plenty of patience at the expense of little power during his brief professional debut, but both are expected to qualify as strengths going forward. An accomplished salsa dancer, Grandal still needs to work on his footwork behind the plate, but he boasts a strong arm and capable receiving skills. The greatest obstacles in the Cuban's path are Devin Mesoraco, who's only six months older, but significantly closer to the majors, and taking a sword in the gut from a misdirected Beowulf.

Ryan Hanigan C

Born: **8/16/1980** Age: **30**
Bats: **R** Throws: **R** Height: **6' 0"** Weight: **195**
Breakout: **0%** Improve: **31%** Collapse: **9%**
Attrition: **13%** MLB: **80%**
Comparables:
John Stearns, Gerald Perry, Del Crandall (73)

YEAR	TEAM	LVL	AGE	PA	R	2B	3B	HR	RBI	BB	SO	SB	CS	AVG_OBP_SLG	TAv	BABIP	BRR	FRAA	WARP
2008	LOU	AAA	27	303	35	14	0	4	34	25	39	1	0	.324/.399/.419	.260	.357	-2.2	C -1, 1B 0	1.0
2008	CIN	MLB	27	98	9	2	0	2	9	10	9	0	0	.271/.367/.365	.252	.284	-0.2	C 1	0.4
2009	CIN	MLB	28	293	22	6	1	3	11	37	31	0	0	.263/.358/.331	.252	.286	-0.3	C 3	1.2
2010	CIN	MLB	29	243	27	11	0	5	40	33	21	0	0	.301/.403/.429	.301	.311	-0.6	C -1	1.8
2011	*CIN*	*MLB*	*30*	*352*	*41*	*15*	*0*	*4*	*30*	*41*	*38*	*0*	*0*	*.271/.361/.366*	*.263*	*.291*	*0.0*	*C 0*	*1.5*

It's hard to blame the Reds for restricting Hanigan's appearances, given that veteran co-catcher Ramon Hernandez was no slouch on either side of the ball, but Hanigan deserves to be starting somewhere. A fractured left thumb kept him out of action at least as much as Dusty Baker did, but when the catcher was healthy and in the lineup, his value rivaled that of any backstop in the league. Catcher defense is notoriously difficult to assess, but the body of evidence suggests that Hanigan has few equals when it comes to receiving pitches or limiting the running game and his increasing selectivity coupled with crack contact skills have made him an asset at the plate. Catchers get old faster than pop-culture references, and Hanigan will hit 30 in August, so the Reds should leverage their competitive advantage behind the plate before it's too late. Unfortunately, their decision to re-sign the older, more expensive Hernandez will probably make Hanigan more benched than Bench in 2011, and the Reds' system is rich in catching talent.

Chris Heisey OF

Born: **12/14/1984** Age: **26**
Bats: **R** Throws: **R** Height: **6' 0"** Weight: **215**
Breakout: **3%** Improve: **21%** Collapse: **9%**
Attrition: **25%** MLB: **55%**
Comparables:
Matt Murton, Clete Thomas, Nick Stavinoha (75)

YEAR	TEAM	LVL	AGE	PA	R	2B	3B	HR	RBI	BB	SO	SB	CS	AVG_OBP_SLG	TAv	BABIP	BRR	FRAA	WARP
2008	SAR	A+	23	504	73	31	7	7	50	57	69	25	2	.287/.383/.438	.301	.318	6.8	RF 14, CF 4	5.5
2008	CHT	AA	23	82	11	6	1	2	10	3	15	5	0	.317/.342/.494	.265	.371	1.4	CF 0	0.4
2009	CAR	AA	24	309	51	18	2	13	40	34	34	12	1	.347/.430/.572	.351	.355	3.0	CF -3	3.7
2009	LOU	AAA	24	289	36	19	1	9	39	18	50	7	2	.277/.336/.458	.272	.302	-0.1	CF 1, LF 1	1.0
2010	LOU	AAA	25	88	6	3	0	4	13	7	23	2	0	.241/.307/.430	.243	.278	0.0	CF -2, RF -2	-0.2
2010	CIN	MLB	25	226	32	10	1	8	21	16	57	1	2	.254/.323/.433	.270	.309	2.0	RF 0, CF 0	0.9
2011	*CIN*	*MLB*	*26*	*499*	*60*	*25*	*2*	*14*	*59*	*40*	*93*	*10*	*2*	*.260/.326/.421*	*.263*	*.292*	*0.3*	*CF -3, RF 0*	*0.9*

Heisey is essentially what teams are looking for in a fourth outfielder: he's capable of playing adequate defense in all three pastures, with plus potential in the corners, and his bat isn't bad enough to qualify as a serious handicap, especially if he's started selectively as the short half of a platoon—the reverse split he showed last season was anomalous and is unlikely to reappear. In spring training of 2009, Heisey narrowed his stance and shortened his stride to improve his timing. He briefly upped his Double-A power output to exciting levels soon after, but his ISOs have subsequently settled back into their usual, unremarkable range. He won't be a star, but he should merit a major-league roster spot for the next several years, more than most 17th-rounders can say.

Ramon Hernandez C

Born: **5/20/1976** Age: **35**
Bats: **R** Throws: **R** Height: **6' 0"** Weight: **227**
Breakout: **0%** Improve: **29%** Collapse: **10%**
Attrition: **18%** MLB: **89%**
Comparables:
Gary Carter, Ted Simmons, Jeff Conine (74)

YEAR	TEAM	LVL	AGE	PA	R	2B	3B	HR	RBI	BB	SO	SB	CS	AVG_OBP_SLG	TAv	BABIP	BRR	FRAA	WARP
2008	BAL	MLB	32	507	50	22	1	15	65	32	62	0	0	.257/.308/.406	.255	.265	-2.6	C 1, 1B 0	1.7
2009	CIN	MLB	33	331	27	13	1	5	37	33	34	1	0	.258/.332/.362	.239	.270	-1.1	C 1, 1B 2	0.5
2010	CIN	MLB	34	352	34	18	1	7	48	29	49	0	0	.297/.361/.428	.282	.328	-0.9	C 4, 1B -1	2.3
2011	*CIN*	*MLB*	*35*	*435*	*50*	*19*	*1*	*9*	*44*	*38*	*55*	*1*	*0*	*.260/.329/.383*	*.253*	*.277*	*0.0*	*C 1, 1B 0*	*1.5*

Hernandez had a valuable offensive peak, especially by the standards of his position, but from 2007 to 2009, he settled for production that fell well below league average, with a combined .258/.324/.387 line. Last season, he rebounded to post numbers that wouldn't have seemed out of place during his heyday, but his apparent resurgence rested on a BABIP well above his lifetime average despite a line-drive percentage that hovered just below his career rate. When healthy, Hernandez continued to excel at throwing out runners, but he spent time on the DL with knee soreness a year after undergoing surgery on the same joint. The Reds re-upped him on a one-year basis, but he's in line for decline and best suited for a subordinate role.

Paul Janish **SS**

Born: **10/12/1982** Age: **28**
Bats: R Throws: R Height: **6' 2"** Weight: **190**
Breakout: **1%** Improve: **39%** Collapse: **10%**
Attrition: **14%** MLB: **73%**

Comparables:
Bobby Crosby, Ken Aspromonte, Edwin Maysonet (73)

YEAR	TEAM	LVL	AGE	PA	R	2B	3B	HR	RBI	BB	SO	SB	CS	AVG_OBP_SLG	TAv	BABIP	BRR	FRAA	WARP
2008	LOU	AAA	25	372	47	21	1	8	46	27	74	2	0	.256/.325/.398	.236	.293	0.8	SS -3, 2B 0	0.3
2008	CIN	MLB	25	89	4	2	0	1	6	7	18	0	0	.188/.270/.250	.198	.230	-1.5	SS 4	0.0
2009	CIN	MLB	26	291	35	21	0	1	16	26	39	2	0	.212/.292/.306	.213	.241	1.9	SS 10, 3B 1	0.9
2010	CIN	MLB	27	228	22	10	0	5	25	22	30	1	3	.260/.333/.385	.263	.278	-1.9	SS -4, 3B 0	0.2
2011	*CIN*	*MLB*	*28*	*327*	*35*	*17*	*0*	*5*	*29*	*29*	*50*	*2*	*1*	*.240/.313/.351*	*.237*	*.265*	*-0.1*	*SS 2, 3B 0*	*0.6*

For the second consecutive season, serving as the understudy to a rickety veteran shortstop worked in Janish's favor, as the nominal backup enjoyed another extended taste of starting. This time, he did it with a positive VORP, though his age and minor-league performance suggest that he's already bumped up against his low offensive ceiling. As long as his bat doesn't stray back below replacement level, his defensive chops should ensure at least an average performance at the position. The Reds' decision to decline Orlando Cabrera's option briefly handed Janish a full-time job, but Edgar Renteria's arrival snatched it away again, dooming Janish to a third straight season of coming off the bench despite being better than the first-stringer.

Devin Mesoraco **C**

Born: **6/19/1988** Age: **23**
Bats: R Throws: R Height: **6' 1"** Weight: **220**
Breakout: **0%** Improve: **8%** Collapse: **3%**
Attrition: **13%** MLB: **20%**

Comparables:
Buster Posey, Nick Evans, Joe Torre (77)

YEAR	TEAM	LVL	AGE	PA	R	2B	3B	HR	RBI	BB	SO	SB	CS	AVG_OBP_SLG	TAv	BABIP	BRR	FRAA	WARP
2008	DYT	A	20	345	32	15	1	9	42	23	70	2	2	.264/.322/.403	.270	.309	-3.1	C -1	1.3
2009	SAR	A+	21	353	32	22	1	8	36	35	76	0	1	.228/.312/.381	.251	.269	0.6	C -2	0.8
2010	LYN	A+	22	178	24	11	2	10	31	19	29	2	2	.335/.421/.620	.360	.358	-0.9	C 1	2.4
2010	CAR	AA	22	208	42	11	3	13	31	18	37	1	0	.294/.370/.594	.331	.300	-0.8	C 0	2.3
2010	LOU	AAA	22	71	7	5	0	3	15	8	18	0	1	.258/.338/.484	.294	.310	0.3	C 1	0.6
2011	*CIN*	*MLB*	*23*	*385*	*46*	*19*	*2*	*14*	*49*	*29*	*86*	*1*	*0*	*.253/.311/.436*	*.261*	*.291*	*0.0*	*C -1*	*1.3*

It's easy to dismiss the news that a player has reported to camp in "the best shape of his life," since so many of those makeovers fail to produce a perceptible improvement. But once in a while, it means something, though it's difficult to identify the players who stand to benefit the most from a *Rocky*-style training montage in advance. Before last season, the impressive tools that prompted the Reds to select Mesoraco with the 15th overall pick in the 2007 draft had become buried under years of poor conditioning, and his on-field struggles invited frequent applications of the "bust" label. Last season, a physical reinvention helped the righty tighten his swing in addition to his belt buckle; after entering 2010 with a .240/.311/.368 professional line, he exploded for a .302/.377/.587 performance across three levels, easily besting his home-run total from the previous three seasons combined. Although he continues to struggle with passed balls, the catcher made strides not only while standing at the plate, but also while squatting behind it, where he thwarted 41 percent of attempted steals. His stroke remains a bit long, but the new force behind it has propelled him to the brink of the big leagues.

Kris Negron **SS**

Born: **2/1/1986** Age: **25**
Bats: R Throws: R Height: **6' 0"** Weight: **180**
Breakout: **7%** Improve: **29%** Collapse: **10%**
Attrition: **43%** MLB: **61%**

Comparables:
Brent Lillibridge, Eric Young, Emilio Bonifacio (78)

YEAR	TEAM	LVL	AGE	PA	R	2B	3B	HR	RBI	BB	SO	SB	CS	AVG_OBP_SLG	TAv	BABIP	BRR	FRAA	WARP
2008	GRN	A	22	352	48	15	5	1	27	31	48	22	5	.244/.332/.334	.252	.276	6.5	2B -2, 3B 2	1.4
2008	LNC	A+	22	166	23	9	4	9	26	5	35	6	1	.310/.380/.594	.314	.333	0.1	2B 9, CF 6	2.8
2009	SLM	A+	23	456	66	17	4	3	33	39	83	17	3	.264/.340/.347	.260	.317	4.1	SS -15, 2B 4	0.9
2009	CAR	AA	23	63	9	2	0	2	5	8	7	3	1	.241/.397/.389	.269	.239	0.9	2B 1, CF 1	0.4
2010	CAR	AA	24	531	73	19	6	11	41	51	97	30	9	.272/.367/.409	.274	.315	5.2	SS 5	3.7
2011	*CIN*	*MLB*	*25*	*546*	*54*	*20*	*4*	*8*	*47*	*39*	*110*	*17*	*4*	*.224/.288/.331*	*.225*	*.264*	*0.4*	*SS 0, 2B 5*	*0.4*

Negron was known for his glove before coming to the Reds' organization in the Alex Gonzalez trade, but his bat has perked up after the swap. The natural shortstop has spent time at every position but first, catcher, and pitcher, and his speed has served him well on the basepaths, where he boasts a career 83.2 percent stolen-base success rate. After posting a 952 OPS in the Arizona Fall League, he's on the verge of major-league utilitymanhood.

Laynce Nix **LF**

Born: **10/30/1980** Age: **30**
Bats: L Throws: L Height: **6' 0"** Weight: **190**
Breakout: **4%** Improve: **35%** Collapse: **4%**
Attrition: **8%** MLB: **75%**

Comparables:
Ryan Raburn, Ryan Church, Scott Hairston (76)

YEAR	TEAM	LVL	AGE	PA	R	2B	3B	HR	RBI	BB	SO	SB	CS	AVG_OBP_SLG	TAv	BABIP	BRR	FRAA	WARP
2008	NAS	AAA	27	418	62	22	3	23	60	36	88	5	3	.284/.349/.540	.293	.314	-0.7	RF 0, CF -4	2.1
2008	MIL	MLB	27	13	1	0	0	0	0	1	3	0	0	.083/.154/.083	.076	.111	0.0	LF 0	-0.2
2009	CIN	MLB	28	337	42	26	1	15	46	22	81	0	1	.240/.291/.476	.264	.272	2.0	LF -4, RF -1	0.5
2010	CIN	MLB	29	182	16	11	2	4	18	15	39	0	1	.291/.346/.455	.284	.355	-0.9	LF -1, RF 0	0.6
2011	*CIN*	*MLB*	*30*	*362*	*44*	*19*	*1*	*15*	*49*	*27*	*86*	*2*	*1*	*.253/.310/.453*	*.262*	*.292*	*-0.1*	*LF -1, RF 0*	*0.4*

Nix should never be allowed to attempt to hit left-handed pitching. Like most of his previous employers, the Reds received that memo and weren't tempted to dismiss it despite the outfielder's small-sample 5-for-16 "breakout" against southpaws last season. Overall, his offensive production can't be described as much more than adequate for a corner bat, given that NL left fielders batted .267/.337/.434 as a group and most of them didn't get to hit in Great American Ball Park or hog a roster spot in exchange for under 200 platoon-advantaged plate appearances. Nix is a major defensive asset in left, which helped the Reds reduce the fallout from Jonny Gomes' radioactive glove. In fact, that Gomes was ever allowed to start over Nix against a righty makes about as much sense as a Charlie Kaufman screenplay.

Brandon Phillips **2B**

Born: **6/28/1981** Age: **30**
Bats: R Throws: R Height: **5' 11"** Weight: **185**
Breakout: **1%** Improve: **44%** Collapse: **0%**
Attrition: **1%** MLB: **99%**

Comparables:
Orlando Hudson, Mark Ellis, Roberto Alomar (75)

YEAR	TEAM	LVL	AGE	PA	R	2B	3B	HR	RBI	BB	SO	SB	CS	AVG_OBP_SLG	TAv	BABIP	BRR	FRAA	WARP
2008	CIN	MLB	27	609	80	24	7	21	78	39	93	23	10	.261/.312/.442	.263	.277	0.8	2B 2	1.9
2009	CIN	MLB	28	644	79	30	5	20	98	44	75	25	9	.276/.328/.447	.262	.283	5.7	2B -4	1.8
2010	CIN	MLB	29	687	97	33	5	18	59	46	83	16	12	.275/.329/.430	.270	.290	5.1	2B 6	3.3
2011	*CIN*	*MLB*	*30*	*646*	*79*	*29*	*4*	*19*	*80*	*46*	*78*	*23*	*9*	*.274/.329/.439*	*.269*	*.282*	*-1.0*	*2B -1*	*1.9*

Phillips' age-26 power explosion may have created unrealistic expectations for his offensive production: the second baseman is little better than league average at the plate. His work on the basepaths generally ranks among the best on the Reds, contributing a few additional runs per year despite his tendency to get caught stealing. Although he held on to most of his 2009 reduction in strikeout rate last season, the righty still doesn't walk without putting up a fight, so he's hardly Morgan-esque in the OBP department. Despite his shortcomings, Phillips' defensive skills make him a safe bet to furnish the Reds with three to four wins this season.

Scott Rolen **3B**

Born: **4/4/1975** Age: **36**
Bats: R Throws: R Height: **6' 4"** Weight: **240**
Breakout: **0%** Improve: **25%** Collapse: **8%**
Attrition: **16%** MLB: **89%**

Comparables:
Vladimir Guerrero, Cliff Floyd, Bobby Bonilla (68)

YEAR	TEAM	LVL	AGE	PA	R	2B	3B	HR	RBI	BB	SO	SB	CS	AVG_OBP_SLG	TAv	BABIP	BRR	FRAA	WARP
2008	TOR	MLB	33	467	58	30	3	11	50	46	71	5	0	.262/.349/.431	.284	.292	1.2	3B 5	3.0
2009	CIN	MLB	34	162	25	7	1	3	24	19	20	1	2	.270/.364/.402	.271	.291	1.5	3B -1	0.7
2009	TOR	MLB	34	373	52	29	0	8	43	26	42	4	2	.320/.370/.476	.304	.341	1.0	3B -2	2.7
2010	CIN	MLB	35	537	66	34	3	20	83	50	82	1	2	.285/.358/.497	.298	.302	-2.1	3B 12	4.4
2011	*CIN*	*MLB*	*36*	*518*	*64*	*31*	*1*	*12*	*59*	*49*	*69*	*4*	*2*	*.269/.345/.423*	*.272*	*.289*	*-0.3*	*3B 5*	*2.5*

Rolen bounced back from a series of injury-diminished campaigns with a six-win season, his most productive performance (and his first without a DL stint) since 2006. If his fielding has slipped, it certainly hasn't fallen, as FRAA continues to deem him one of the best the hot corner has to offer. Although he was never rendered officially inactive, Rolen did miss time with back complaints in April, July, and September, so it's not as if he's found the fountain of youth; he'll turn 36 in April, and his current contract (which runs through 2012) may well be his last. He has already done enough to earn enshrinement in Cooperstown, where third basemen remain underrepresented, but the Reds hope he'll remain healthy enough to continue to pad his case.

Dave Sappelt **OF**

Born: **1/2/1987** Age: **24**
Bats: R Throws: R Height: **5' 9"** Weight: **193**
Breakout: **6%** Improve: **21%** Collapse: **8%**
Attrition: **25%** MLB: **46%**

Comparables:
Gerardo Parra, Tony Gwynn, Chin-lung Hu (71)

YEAR	TEAM	LVL	AGE	PA	R	2B	3B	HR	RBI	BB	SO	SB	CS	AVG_OBP_SLG	TAv	BABIP	BRR	FRAA	WARP
2008	BIL	Rk	21	286	50	21	5	7	36	21	47	6	3	.298/.350/.496	.303	.337	0.4	CF 0, LF 1	2.3
2009	DYT	A	22	329	44	14	7	3	25	23	46	26	10	.269/.322/.392	.275	.304	2.4	CF 10, LF 4	2.9
2009	SAR	A+	22	265	26	9	3	4	21	13	28	19	10	.292/.328/.401	.284	.309	0.3	CF 8	2.2
2010	LYN	A+	23	76	7	5	0	0	4	5	15	6	4	.282/.342/.352	.268	.357	-0.4	CF -1	0.2
2010	CAR	AA	23	369	52	19	8	9	62	31	46	14	11	.361/.415/.549	.345	.389	-3.8	CF 5, LF 0	4.3
2010	LOU	AAA	23	135	11	9	3	1	10	6	19	3	1	.297/.333/.438	.265	.339	-1.9	CF 3	0.5
2011	*CIN*	*MLB*	*24*	*487*	*54*	*23*	*4*	*6*	*52*	*25*	*80*	*18*	*8*	*.274/.308/.389*	*.247*	*.311*	*-1.0*	*CF -4, LF 0*	*0.2*

Dave Sappelt is an odd prospect, short and stocky, but with the range to play center field. Although he's built like Hack Wilson, in 2010 Sappelt benefited from realizing that he lacks Hack Wilson's power. Casey Stengel once said not to *try* to hit, "just tra-la-la." Sappelt tra-la-la'd his way to Southern League MVP honors by going with pitches instead of trying to hit them to the moon. Despite the strong season, the little guy does have some defects, including a popgun arm and a stolen-base record that is quite poor for a player with his 60-rated speed. Sappelt might get a chance to start on some teams, but with the Reds, he will be hard-pressed to push Drew Stubbs and will begin major-league life as a fourth outfielder.

Drew Stubbs **CF**

Born: **10/4/1984** Age: **26**
Bats: **R** Throws: **R** Height: **6' 4"** Weight: **205**
Breakout: **3%** Improve: **43%** Collapse: **3%**
Attrition: **24%** MLB: **72%**

Comparables:
Will Venable, Ellis Burks, Hunter Pence (71)

YEAR	TEAM	LVL	AGE	PA	R	2B	3B	HR	RBI	BB	SO	SB	CS	AVG_OBP_SLG	TAv	BABIP	BRR	FRAA	WARP
2008	SAR	A+	23	356	48	21	4	5	38	50	82	27	8	.261/.368/.406	.277	.338	1.7	CF -11	0.8
2008	CHT	AA	23	104	12	8	0	0	9	11	21	3	1	.315/.404/.402	.285	.403	1.1	CF 4	1.1
2008	LOU	AAA	23	101	16	4	2	2	13	7	28	3	0	.261/.327/.413	.230	.344	0.0	CF 2	0.1
2009	LOU	AAA	24	468	56	25	2	3	39	51	104	41	8	.268/.353/.360	.263	.345	4.4	CF 13, LF -1	2.9
2009	CIN	MLB	24	196	27	5	1	8	17	15	49	10	4	.267/.321/.439	.272	.323	1.0	CF 1	0.9
2010	CIN	MLB	25	583	91	19	6	22	77	55	168	30	6	.255/.328/.444	.275	.327	9.3	CF 6	3.9
2011	*CIN*	*MLB*	*26*	*603*	*69*	*25*	*3*	*14*	*62*	*61*	*152*	*32*	*8*	*.247/.324/.385*	*.253*	*.312*	*0.6*	*CF -1, LF 0*	*1.1*

Stubbs averaged one home run every 57 at-bats in the minors and made few strides in the power department with age and experience, going deep just once every 97 at-bats at Triple-A. However, upon making it to the majors in mid-August 2009, he immediately became far more adept at yard-work, and after sustaining his gains last season, has now averaged a big fly every 23 at-bats in the bigs. Most of his homers have come at Great American, whose homer-friendly dimensions can be credited with some of Stubbs' empowerment, but scouts always foresaw healthy home-run totals in the six-foot-four righty's future. The 2006 first-rounder strikes out too often to post Votto-esque OBPs, but he plays a mean center field and demonstrates the capacity to be both a prolific and a high-percentage basestealer, so the increased power makes for quite an attractive package.

Chris Valaika **2B**

Born: **8/14/1985** Age: **25**
Bats: **R** Throws: **R** Height: **6' 0"** Weight: **215**
Breakout: **1%** Improve: **3%** Collapse: **8%**
Attrition: **13%** MLB: **18%**

Comparables:
Justin Turner, Travis Denker, Angel Chavez (75)

YEAR	TEAM	LVL	AGE	PA	R	2B	3B	HR	RBI	BB	SO	SB	CS	AVG_OBP_SLG	TAv	BABIP	BRR	FRAA	WARP
2008	SAR	A+	22	144	19	9	0	7	31	7	28	1	0	.363/.396/.585	.340	.412	2.2	SS 5	2.4
2008	CHT	AA	22	414	57	19	1	11	50	28	74	7	4	.301/.350/.443	.274	.342	-3.7	SS -2	1.7
2009	LOU	AAA	23	409	35	21	1	6	38	18	83	1	0	.234/.274/.340	.214	.278	2.7	SS 0, 2B 2	-0.1
2010	LOU	AAA	24	453	48	27	2	4	51	19	72	0	0	.302/.327/.405	.250	.344	0.0	2B -3, SS 0	0.4
2010	CIN	MLB	24	40	3	1	0	1	2	1	9	0	0	.263/.275/.368	.207	.310	-1.7	2B 0, SS 0	-0.2
2011	*CIN*	*MLB*	*25*	*487*	*51*	*23*	*1*	*7*	*48*	*21*	*94*	*2*	*1*	*.258/.290/.362*	*.229*	*.302*	*-0.1*	*SS 1, 2B -1*	*0.1*

A BABIP boost rendered Valaika's Triple-A take two less disastrous than his rough cut from 2009, but the power he flashed in 2008 has evaporated at higher levels. Since he doesn't walk, his offensive value hinges almost completely on his batting average, which has rarely reached impressive heights. Worse still, the righty's long-foretold move from shortstop to second base finally came to pass in 2010, raising the offensive bar high enough for Valaika to pass beneath while perched on Danny Herrera's shoulders. If a late-night visit from the Ghost of Infields Yet to Come shows Valaika a vision of a futilityman future, he should consider himself lucky.

Joey Votto **1B**

Born: **9/10/1983** Age: **27**
Bats: **L** Throws: **R** Height: **6' 3"** Weight: **220**
Breakout: **1%** Improve: **57%** Collapse: **3%**
Attrition: **12%** MLB: **95%**

Comparables:
Mark Teixeira, Adrian Gonzalez, Eddie Murray (73)

YEAR	TEAM	LVL	AGE	PA	R	2B	3B	HR	RBI	BB	SO	SB	CS	AVG_OBP_SLG	TAv	BABIP	BRR	FRAA	WARP
2008	CIN	MLB	24	589	69	32	3	24	84	59	102	7	5	.297/.368/.506	.302	.328	-7.6	1B 14	3.5
2009	CIN	MLB	25	544	82	38	1	25	84	70	106	4	1	.322/.414/.567	.334	.372	-3.4	1B 3	4.4
2010	CIN	MLB	26	648	106	36	2	37	113	91	125	16	5	.324/.424/.600	.357	.361	-2.8	1B 2	6.5
2011	*CIN*	*MLB*	*27*	*615*	*92*	*33*	*1*	*29*	*93*	*79*	*109*	*11*	*4*	*.302/.394/.534*	*.319*	*.329*	*-0.3*	*1B 3*	*4.2*

Votto famously did not hit an infield fly ball all season, according to Baseball Info Solutions stringers. All that really means is that the Canadian slugger's popups all happened to travel as far as the outfield grass before settling into a fielder's glove, but the implied conclusion—that Votto never fails to hit the ball a long way—has a compelling quality to it, given how well the first baseman performed last season. En route to taking home MVP hardware, he finished no worse than third in the NL in each of the traditional Triple Crown categories and nearly took home the so-called Sabermetric Triple Crown, missing out on sweeping the slash stats by 12 points of batting average. Votto certainly picked the right park to call home, but he's far from a creation of Great American Ball Park, where he has actually hit worse than he has on the road. Last season, he added to his value by living up to his "Vottomatic" billing with runners in scoring position, hitting .369/.491/.638 in those situations. Have we mentioned that he can field and won't turn 27 till September? The Reds bought out his extension years with a three-year, $38-million deal in January.

PITCHERS

Bronson Arroyo

Born: **2/24/1977** Age: **34**
Bats: **R** Throws: **R** Height: **6' 5"** Weight: **180**
Breakout: **22%** Improve: **49%** Collapse: **22%**
Attrition: **14%** MLB: **91%**

Comparables:
Jarrod Washburn, Hiroki Kuroda, Tim Hudson (61)

YEAR	TEAM	LVL	AGE	W	L	SV	G	GS	IP	H	HR	BB	SO	EqBB9	EqSO9	GB%	BABIP	WHIP	ERA	FRA	WARP
2008	CIN	MLB	31	15	11	0	34	35	200	219	29	68	163	3.1	7.3	44%	.314	1.47	4.77	4.82	2.1
2009	CIN	MLB	32	15	13	0	33	34	220^1	214	31	65	127	2.7	5.2	46%	.265	1.31	3.84	4.37	2.8
2010	CIN	MLB	33	17	10	0	33	33	215^2	188	29	59	121	2.5	5.0	44%	.239	1.17	3.88	5.21	0.4
2011	*CIN*	*MLB*	*34*	*13*	*12*	*0*	*34*	*34*	*218^1*	*224*	*32*	*65*	*136*	*2.7*	*5.6*	*45%*	*.283*	*1.33*	*4.31*	*4.69*	*4.3*

If ever we wanted to reprint a comment from one of our previous annual publications, this could be our chance, since Arroyo produced an almost exact replica of his 2009 campaign last season. The righty embraced the League-Average Innings Muncher lifestyle in the process of securing his sixth consecutive 200-plus-inning season, a streak equaled or surpassed among active pitchers by only Dan Haren and Mark Buehrle; the chemical cocktail that Arroyo admitted to using two seasons ago seems to be doing the trick. The odd variations in movement of his pitches flummox classification algorithms, but major-league batters haven't had much better luck—and we mean that literally, as a glance at his recent BABIPs should reveal. The Reds chose to exercise Arroyo's $11 million option and then tack two additional years on top of that rather than accept the uncertain returns of a youngster, though it wouldn't come as a shock if the innings he munches don't live up to league average this season.

Homer Bailey

Born: **5/3/1986** Age: **25**
Bats: **R** Throws: **R** Height: **6' 4"** Weight: **205**
Breakout: **19%** Improve: **54%** Collapse: **11%**
Attrition: **24%** MLB: **87%**

Comparables:
Garrett Olson, Mitch Talbot, John Danks (79)

YEAR	TEAM	LVL	AGE	W	L	SV	G	GS	IP	H	HR	BB	SO	EqBB9	EqSO9	GB%	BABIP	WHIP	ERA	FRA	WARP
2008	LOU	AAA	22	5	7	0	20	22	117^1	120	10	47	104	3.6	8.0	47%	.326	1.45	4.45	4.64	1.8
2008	CIN	MLB	22	0	6	0	8	10	36^1	59	8	17	18	4.2	4.5	46%	.372	2.09	7.93	6.59	-0.2
2009	LOU	AAA	23	8	5	0	14	17	89^2	87	10	27	82	2.7	8.2	46%	.301	1.32	2.61	3.68	2.0
2009	CIN	MLB	23	8	5	0	20	21	113^1	115	12	52	86	4.1	6.8	43%	.300	1.50	4.53	4.79	1.1
2010	CIN	MLB	24	4	3	0	19	19	109	109	11	40	100	3.3	8.3	44%	.315	1.39	4.46	4.31	1.4
2011	*CIN*	*MLB*	*25*	*9*	*9*	*0*	*26*	*26*	*147*	*155*	*18*	*63*	*117*	*3.8*	*7.1*	*45%*	*.310*	*1.48*	*4.64*	*5.04*	*2.6*

As it turns out, Bailey's electric end to 2009 didn't augur a dominant 2010, but the faded phenom made strides toward capturing some of his promise by cutting his walk rate and upping his strikeout rate. The improvement in his peripherals hardly moved the needle in the ERA department, but SIERA was far more sanguine about his chances of posting at least a league-average figure going forward. After a velocity spike in 2009, the righty's average fastball velocity fell back into the low 90s, though he didn't seem to show any adverse effects following an extended battle with shoulder inflammation that kept him out of action from late-May to mid-August.

Bill Bray

Born: **6/5/1983** Age: **28**
Bats: **L** Throws: **L** Height: **6' 3"** Weight: **215**
Breakout: **20%** Improve: **38%** Collapse: **23%**
Attrition: **13%** MLB: **72%**

Comparables:
Dan Plesac, Tom Henke, Lee Smith (77)

YEAR	TEAM	LVL	AGE	W	L	SV	G	GS	IP	H	HR	BB	SO	EqBB9	EqSO9	GB%	BABIP	WHIP	ERA	FRA	WARP
2008	CIN	MLB	25	2	2	0	63	0	47	50	4	24	54	4.6	10.3	39%	.349	1.60	2.87	2.01	1.8
2010	CIN	MLB	27	0	2	0	35	0	28^1	21	4	10	30	3.2	9.5	39%	.233	1.09	4.13	4.73	0.0
2011	*CIN*	*MLB*	*28*	*3*	*1*	*0*	*53*	*0*	*44^2*	*40*	*5*	*18*	*48*	*3.6*	*9.8*	*44%*	*.306*	*1.31*	*3.63*	*3.94*	*0.6*

Injuries have limited Bray to only 117 1/3 innings in his 4½ seasons with Cincinnati. In his midseason comeback from Tommy John surgery, the lefty held the opposition scoreless in 10 1/3 minor-league innings before returning to the majors, where he showed that he could still rack up strikeouts despite having lost some of his previously impressive velocity. The perennially promising first-rounder won't turn 28 until June, and while his spotty control will always hold him back, this could be the season that reveals the player for whom the Reds traded—as Emily Dickinson said, hope is the thing with feathers and/or a lefty reliever with a bad arm.

Jared Burton

Born: **6/2/1981** Age: **30**
Bats: **R** Throws: **R** Height: **6' 5"** Weight: **225**
Breakout: **2%** Improve: **11%** Collapse: **6%**
Attrition: **5%** MLB: **20%**

Comparables:
Matt Lindstrom, Ryan Braun, Royce Ring (77)

YEAR	TEAM	LVL	AGE	W	L	SV	G	GS	IP	H	HR	BB	SO	EqBB9	EqSO9	GB%	BABIP	WHIP	ERA	FRA	WARP
2008	CIN	MLB	27	5	1	0	54	0	58^2	56	6	25	58	3.8	8.9	51%	.301	1.41	3.22	3.22	1.4
2009	CIN	MLB	28	1	0	0	53	0	59^1	61	5	23	45	3.5	6.8	44%	.298	1.48	4.40	4.71	0.1
2010	LOU	AAA	29	3	2	5	35	0	40^1	29	4	18	38	4.0	8.5	42%	.234	1.19	2.45	2.92	0.7
2010	CIN	MLB	29	0	0	0	4	0	3^1	0	0	0	1	0.0	2.7	44%	.000	0.00	0.00	5.19	0.0
2011	*CIN*	*MLB*	*30*	*3*	*1*	*0*	*56*	*0*	*61*	*60*	*7*	*27*	*50*	*3.9*	*7.3*	*45%*	*.298*	*1.41*	*4.21*	*4.58*	*0.4*

Last season was something of a lost one for Burton, since the righty was too tired to make his season debut until late May. We don't mean to sound flippant—it's not as though Burton was lying in bed, hitting the snooze button and asking Walt Jocketty for "five more minutes"—but it's impossible to be more specific, since multiple visits to specialists and a battery of tests failed to identify the cause of his debilitating fatigue and lack of strength. Once he managed to make it onto a mound, Burton didn't look particularly lethargic, pitching to his career Triple-A averages in just under 40 innings with Louisville. He returned to the majors in time to make four scoreless late-September appearances and should be a useful middle-inning arm this season, barring a recurrence of his unexplained ailment.

Aroldis Chapman

Born: **2/28/1988** Age: **23**
Bats: **L** Throws: **L** Height: **6' 4"** Weight: **185**
Breakout: **19%** Improve: **33%** Collapse: **19%**
Attrition: **11%** MLB: **74%**

Comparables:
David Robertson, Gio Gonzalez, Kerry Wood (53)

YEAR	TEAM	LVL	AGE	W	L	SV	G	GS	IP	H	HR	BB	SO	EqBB9	EqSO9	GB%	BABIP	WHIP	ERA	FRA	WARP
2010	LOU	AAA	22	9	6	8	39	14	95^{2}	77	7	52	125	4.9	11.8	47%	.314	1.40	3.39	3.35	2.4
2010	CIN	MLB	22	2	2	0	15	0	13^{1}	9	0	5	19	3.4	12.8	70%	.333	1.05	2.03	3.14	0.3
2011	*CIN*	*MLB*	*23*	*8*	*4*	*2*	*54*	*13*	*108*	*89*	*10*	*54*	*129*	*4.5*	*10.7*	*46%*	*.303*	*1.32*	*3.44*	*3.74*	*2.9*

After making a June conversion to the bullpen and a late-August ascent to "The Show," Chapman let fly a host of the hardest heaters ever recorded, which routinely maxed out Twitter's capacity on their brief trips from his left hand to home plate. Given that his average fastball velocity approached three digits, it's not surprising that Chapman chose to throw the pitch nearly 80 percent of the time, though his slider also represents a formidable weapon. In a late-October interview, Dusty Baker cited Chapman's promising secondary pitches and ability to retire batters of either handedness as reasons to keep him in the back end of the bullpen. Eventually, it might occur to the skipper that those qualities make the expensive Cuban import even better suited for a starting role, though his control issues might prove difficult to correct without a remedial trip to the minors.

Francisco Cordero

Born: **5/11/1975** Age: **36**
Bats: **R** Throws: **R** Height: **6' 2"** Weight: **200**
Breakout: **18%** Improve: **36%** Collapse: **17%**
Attrition: **10%** MLB: **77%**

Comparables:
Kazuhiro Sasaki, Jay Howell, Dan Plesac (73)

YEAR	TEAM	LVL	AGE	W	L	SV	G	GS	IP	H	HR	BB	SO	EqBB9	EqSO9	GB%	BABIP	WHIP	ERA	FRA	WARP
2008	CIN	MLB	33	5	4	34	72	0	70^{1}	61	6	38	78	4.9	10.0	43%	.302	1.45	3.33	3.29	1.2
2009	CIN	MLB	34	2	6	39	68	0	66^{2}	58	2	30	58	4.1	7.8	42%	.301	1.32	2.16	3.00	1.3
2010	CIN	MLB	35	6	5	40	75	0	72^{2}	68	5	36	59	4.5	7.3	44%	.294	1.46	3.84	3.89	0.5
2011	*CIN*	*MLB*	*36*	*4*	*1*	*33*	*71*	*0*	69^{2}	*65*	*6*	*32*	*65*	*4.2*	*8.4*	*44%*	*.307*	*1.40*	*3.87*	*4.20*	*0.7*

Cordero's SIERA rose for the third consecutive season, as further erosion in his skills left him dependent on a continued ability to suppress home runs on fly balls to maintain any semblance of value. The Dominican hasn't lost any velocity since his heyday, but his plummeting strikeout rate has made him much more contact-oriented. Since that elevated contact rate hasn't been accompanied by an increased incidence of ground balls, the current Cordero is more likely to get himself into trouble and less likely to get himself out of it. He is no longer what you would look for in a closer, but since he's still being paid like one, he'll continue to hold the job. The Reds are only on the hook for one more season, after which they'll consider a $1 million buyout a bargain to rid themselves of a rapidly depreciating asset.

Johnny Cueto

Born: **2/15/1986** Age: **25**
Bats: **R** Throws: **R** Height: **5' 10"** Weight: **185**
Breakout: **19%** Improve: **60%** Collapse: **12%**
Attrition: **6%** MLB: **99%**

Comparables:
Randy Wolf, Javier Vazquez, Catfish Hunter (77)

YEAR	TEAM	LVL	AGE	W	L	SV	G	GS	IP	H	HR	BB	SO	EqBB9	EqSO9	GB%	BABIP	WHIP	ERA	FRA	WARP
2008	CIN	MLB	22	9	14	0	31	33	174	178	29	68	158	3.5	8.2	40%	.298	1.49	4.81	5.16	1.4
2009	CIN	MLB	23	11	11	0	30	32	171^{1}	172	24	61	132	3.2	6.9	43%	.291	1.44	4.41	4.73	1.8
2010	CIN	MLB	24	12	7	0	31	31	185^{2}	181	19	56	138	2.7	6.7	44%	.290	1.33	3.64	4.08	2.9
2011	*CIN*	*MLB*	*25*	*10*	*10*	*0*	*28*	*28*	*163*	*165*	*22*	*55*	*128*	*3.1*	*7.1*	*43%*	*.297*	*1.35*	*4.43*	*4.82*	*3.3*

Cueto had his best season yet, but no longer misses enough bats to develop into the up-and-coming ace he appeared to be during his accelerated ascent through the minors. He strikes out fewer batters than he did as a rookie—despite throwing just as hard—primarily because he's surrendered some movement on his slider, which no longer induces whiffs at an above-average rate. However, improved fastball command has allowed him to limit both his walks and his long balls, which plagued him in his initial exposure to the majors. The Dominican managed his first season free of arm problems, but his build doesn't inspire the greatest confidence in a pain-free future.

Carlos Fisher

Born: **2/22/1983** Age: **28**
Bats: R Throws: R Height: **6' 4"** Weight: **225**
Breakout: **9%** Improve: **7%** Collapse: **7%**
Attrition: **6%** MLB: **10%**

Comparables:
Edwin Moreno, Wes Littleton, Connor Robertson (81)

YEAR	TEAM	LVL	AGE	W	L	SV	G	GS	IP	H	HR	BB	SO	EqBB9	EqSO9	GB%	BABIP	WHIP	ERA	FRA	WARP
2008	CHT	AA	25	1	5	8	36	0	50^{2}	52	3	20	46	3.6	8.2	60%	.314	1.44	3.55	4.48	0.3
2009	CIN	MLB	26	1	1	0	39	0	52^{1}	50	4	31	48	5.3	8.3	45%	.324	1.57	4.30	3.95	0.6
2010	LOU	AAA	27	1	1	4	30	0	36^{1}	23	4	8	38	2.0	9.4	42%	.216	0.88	2.23	3.53	0.8
2010	CIN	MLB	27	1	1	0	18	0	22^{1}	22	1	13	21	5.2	8.5	43%	.328	1.61	5.64	4.41	0.1
2011	*CIN*	*MLB*	*28*	*4*	*1*	*1*	*73*	*0*	*96^{2}*	*101*	*11*	*43*	*77*	*4.0*	*7.2*	*46%*	*.313*	*1.50*	*4.68*	*5.09*	*0.0*

After nearly 75 major-league innings, Fisher's ERA rests at 4.82, a rather unsightly mark for a full-time reliever, even one who gets little high-leverage work. He has managed to earn his fair share of strikeouts, so it's clear that the main culprit is a walk rate upward of five batters per nine; the Californian doesn't possess the strikeout stuff or the ground-ball-induction abilities to pitch around that profusion of free passes. Fisher's control has been far better at Triple-A, where he has excelled in parts of three seasons, so it's possible that his relative success on the farm could begin to carry over. Perhaps he simply doesn't trust his assortment of sinkers and cutters sufficiently, but then again, he might be right not to.

Aaron Harang

Born: **5/9/1978** Age: **33**
Bats: R Throws: R Height: **6' 7"** Weight: **240**
Breakout: **22%** Improve: **43%** Collapse: **17%**
Attrition: **18%** MLB: **76%**

Comparables:
Nate Robertson, Gene Conley, Kevin Millwood (56)

YEAR	TEAM	LVL	AGE	W	L	SV	G	GS	IP	H	HR	BB	SO	EqBB9	EqSO9	GB%	BABIP	WHIP	ERA	FRA	WARP
2008	CIN	MLB	30	6	17	0	30	30	184^{1}	205	35	50	153	2.4	7.5	36%	.307	1.39	4.78	5.16	1.2
2009	CIN	MLB	31	6	14	0	26	29	162^{1}	186	24	43	142	2.4	7.9	37%	.331	1.44	4.16	3.85	3.1
2010	CIN	MLB	32	6	7	0	22	22	111^{2}	139	16	38	82	3.1	6.6	38%	.338	1.62	5.32	5.45	0.1
2011	*SDN*	*MLB*	*33*	*12*	*11*	*0*	*31*	*31*	*189*	*200*	*26*	*56*	*156*	*2.7*	*7.4*	*40%*	*.311*	*1.36*	*4.34*	*4.71*	*2.0*

Pitchers have limited shelf lives, and the problem with talking up an underappreciated one is that he's liable to be a lot less special by the time people come around. Such has been the case with Harang, who labored in virtual obscurity as the Reds' durable, late-blooming ace from 2005 to 2007, but who seems to have buckled under the combined strains of advancing age and heavy workloads in the seasons since. Last year, the big righty posted his lowest innings total and strikeout rate since 2003 and walked batters at a career-high clip. He isn't throwing any softer than he did in his prime (not that he ever threw hard), but he's getting less movement on his pitches and coming up lame with a myriad of physical complaints. Harang's season ended on a low note, as batters teed off on his offerings to the tune of a .396/.492/.585 line following his return from a back injury at the end of August. Harang signed in his native San Diego in December—he will attempt to resuscitate his career in a park built for just that purpose.

Daniel Herrera

Born: **10/21/1984** Age: **26**
Bats: L Throws: L Height: **5' 7"** Weight: **145**
Breakout: **1%** Improve: **1%** Collapse: **1%**
Attrition: **0%** MLB: **1%**

Comparables:
Mike Boddicker, Orlando Pena, Mike Koplove (78)

YEAR	TEAM	LVL	AGE	W	L	SV	G	GS	IP	H	HR	BB	SO	EqBB9	EqSO9	GB%	BABIP	WHIP	ERA	FRA	WARP
2008	LOU	AAA	23	4	4	6	49	0	55^{2}	47	4	10	51	1.6	8.2	53%	.272	1.02	2.75	3.26	1.2
2008	CIN	MLB	23	0	0	0	7	0	7^{1}	10	1	3	8	3.7	9.8	67%	.391	2.05	7.36	8.02	-0.2
2009	CIN	MLB	24	4	4	0	70	0	61^{2}	63	5	24	44	3.5	6.4	52%	.310	1.44	3.21	4.86	0.0
2010	LOU	AAA	25	2	2	5	28	2	39	34	2	6	34	1.4	7.8	55%	.291	1.15	3.69	4.12	0.5
2010	CIN	MLB	25	1	3	0	36	0	23	31	2	6	14	2.3	5.5	42%	.354	1.61	3.91	4.04	0.2
2011	*CIN*	*MLB*	*26*	*3*	*1*	*1*	*60*	*0*	*63*	*65*	*7*	*21*	*49*	*3.0*	*6.9*	*48%*	*.310*	*1.36*	*4.20*	*4.56*	*0.4*

For the second season in a row, Herrera faced more righties than lefties, which seems like managerial malpractice, considering that he isn't about to wake up one of these days and discover that he's not a LOOGY. The diminutive southpaw pitched almost exactly as well as he had in 2009, but his BABIP went against him in his second go-around, and the return of Bill Bray rendered his services inessential. The perils of being five-foot-seven, a screwballer with a low-80s fastball, and a pitcher suitable for duty only against same-handed batters will continue to impair Herrera's efforts to secure a roster spot, but a skipper who puts him in a position to succeed would be rewarded with serviceable relief.

Donnie Joseph

Born: **11/1/1987** Age: **23**
Bats: L Throws: L Height: **6' 3"** Weight: **180**
Breakout: **2%** Improve: **6%** Collapse: **5%**
Attrition: **5%** MLB: **14%**

Comparables:
David Robertson, Jim York, Balor Moore (73)

YEAR	TEAM	LVL	AGE	W	L	SV	G	GS	IP	H	HR	BB	SO	EqBB9	EqSO9	GB%	BABIP	WHIP	ERA	FRA	WARP
2009	DYT	A	21	2	2	4	16	0	20^{2}	13	0	10	31	4.4	13.5	42%	.289	1.16	3.92	3.85	0.2
2010	DYT	A	22	2	1	6	19	0	23	13	0	7	40	2.7	15.7	46%	.317	0.87	0.78	1.47	0.9
2010	LYN	A+	22	0	4	17	31	0	35	23	2	16	56	4.1	14.4	63%	.296	1.14	2.31	2.17	1.1
2011	*CIN*	*MLB*	*23*	*2*	*1*	*3*	*40*	*0*	*46*	*39*	*4*	*24*	*55*	*4.5*	*10.5*	*46%*	*.307*	*1.34*	*3.57*	*3.88*	*0.6*

If the Reds need another reason to banish Aroldis Chapman from the bullpen, they need look no further than another young lefty on the fast track to Cincy. After BP picked The Man with Two First Names as a preseason sleeper, Joseph proceeded to wake up plenty of observers. Expending an early pick on a college reliever, as the Reds did when they selected Joseph in the third round of the 2009 draft, smacks of low standards. Even with a best-case outcome, you're left with a pitcher who's hard-pressed to give you 70 innings in a season. On the plus side, such players are often capable of advancing quickly, as the strikeout victims scattered in the wake of Joseph's rapid ascent to Double-A can attest. Armed with a fastball that touches 95, Joseph packs plenty of heat for a southpaw, but his refined slider made the biggest waves last season.

Mike Leake

Born: **11/12/1987** Age: **23**
Bats: R Throws: R Height: **6' 1"** Weight: **190**
Breakout: **26%** Improve: **57%** Collapse: **13%**
Attrition: **12%** MLB: **95%**

Comparables:
Jeff Weaver, Dontrelle Willis, Mark Mulder (74)

YEAR	TEAM	LVL	AGE	W	L	SV	G	GS	IP	H	HR	BB	SO	EqBB9	EqSO9	GB%	BABIP	WHIP	ERA	FRA	WARP
2010	CIN	MLB	22	8	4	0	24	23	138^1	158	19	49	91	3.2	5.9	51%	.315	1.52	4.23	5.13	0.5
2011	*CIN*	*MLB*	*23*	*8*	*9*	*0*	*23*	*23*	*140^1*	*155*	*19*	*50*	*92*	*3.2*	*5.9*	*47%*	*.310*	*1.46*	*4.88*	*5.31*	*1.9*

In most cases, we have recourse to minor-league statistics when attempting to determine whether a rookie pitcher's performance accurately reflects his underlying abilities. Leake is a little different. Last year, we wrote that the righty out of Arizona State "could move quickly through the system," which turned out to be an understatement: Leake leapfrogged the system entirely, becoming the first player in a decade (and the first pitcher in 15 years) to make the majors without passing Go at any minor-league level (though he did collect considerably more than $200). Cincinnati had the right idea: at 22, Leake was more or less a finished product, prepolished to a shine by hundreds of innings of collegiate elbow grease. Rather than waste his bullets against minor-league batters, the Reds recognized a midrotation ground-ball machine when they saw one, and they received a roughly league-average performance in return, though they appeared to be in line for better before mounting fatigue reduced Leake's effectiveness and ended his season in late August. The career .299/.402/.485 college hitter even helped his cause at the plate with a .289 TAv, second only to Yovani Gallardo among pitchers with a minimum of 60 plate appearances.

Sam LeCure

Born: **5/4/1984** Age: **27**
Bats: R Throws: R Height: **6' 1"** Weight: **205**
Breakout: **15%** Improve: **30%** Collapse: **14%**
Attrition: **19%** MLB: **54%**

Comparables:
Dusty Hughes, Garrett Olson, Enrique Gonzalez (76)

YEAR	TEAM	LVL	AGE	W	L	SV	G	GS	IP	H	HR	BB	SO	EqBB9	EqSO9	GB%	BABIP	WHIP	ERA	FRA	WARP
2008	CHT	AA	24	9	7	0	27	27	155^1	147	12	57	128	3.3	7.4	41%	.297	1.36	3.30	3.78	3.8
2009	LOU	AAA	25	10	9	0	26	27	149^1	149	17	47	127	2.8	7.7	40%	.305	1.36	4.52	5.49	0.4
2010	LOU	AAA	26	8	3	0	15	16	98	98	8	23	87	2.1	8.0	54%	.323	1.30	3.40	3.64	2.5
2010	CIN	MLB	26	2	5	0	15	6	48	50	6	25	37	4.7	6.9	46%	.306	1.67	4.50	4.53	0.4
2011	*CIN*	*MLB*	*27*	*8*	*9*	*0*	*23*	*23*	*135*	*147*	*19*	*53*	*100*	*3.5*	*6.6*	*44%*	*.310*	*1.48*	*4.86*	*5.28*	*2.0*

Low-velocity LeCure packs a four-pitch arsenal, but you would be hard-pressed to describe any of his standard-issue offerings as "plus," at least while keeping a straight face. The 2005 fourth-rounder has better control than he showed in his MLB debut, but the rest of the package doesn't stand to get much better. Formerly an extreme fly-ball pitcher, LeCure induced grounders at a higher rate last season, a trend that will have to continue for him to succeed while calling Great American Ball Park home. As a starter, his potential probably surpasses replacement level, which makes him an adequate short-term substitute for, say, an injured Homer Bailey, but not the kind of arm on which a team would want to rely for long. LeCure was far more effective in a small-sample taste of relief, which should provide the Reds with food for thought about his future.

Matt Maloney

Born: **1/16/1984** Age: **27**
Bats: L Throws: L Height: **6' 4"** Weight: **220**
Breakout: **15%** Improve: **43%** Collapse: **19%**
Attrition: **22%** MLB: **83%**

Comparables:
Mitch Talbot, Daniel McCutchen, Jack Egbert (73)

YEAR	TEAM	LVL	AGE	W	L	SV	G	GS	IP	H	HR	BB	SO	EqBB9	EqSO9	GB%	BABIP	WHIP	ERA	FRA	WARP
2008	LOU	AAA	24	11	6	0	26	28	146^1	147	21	41	136	2.5	8.4	41%	.301	1.33	4.49	4.34	2.8
2009	LOU	AAA	25	9	9	0	22	22	143	143	11	24	125	1.5	7.9	43%	.311	1.22	3.02	2.82	4.7
2009	CIN	MLB	25	2	4	0	7	7	40^2	43	9	8	28	1.8	6.2	36%	.279	1.33	4.87	5.07	0.3
2010	LOU	AAA	26	10	7	0	24	25	134^2	132	9	28	104	1.9	7.0	46%	.300	1.26	3.14	3.93	3.1
2010	CIN	MLB	26	2	2	0	7	2	20^2	20	2	5	13	2.2	5.7	37%	.277	1.26	3.05	3.49	0.3
2011	*CIN*	*MLB*	*27*	*11*	*10*	*0*	*29*	*29*	*166*	*171*	*22*	*49*	*125*	*2.6*	*6.7*	*43%*	*.297*	*1.32*	*4.26*	*4.63*	*3.7*

Control is the name of Maloney's game. Although his slow changeups and sliders possessed the power to mystify minor-league mashers, he doesn't appear to have the stuff to punch out big-league batters, who salivate at the sight of his mid- to high-80s heaters and even more belated breaking balls. If anything, the strapping lefty could stand to slow his supplementary pitches even further, since he employs relatively little velocity separation for a finesse type who relies on changing speeds. As befits a player with the profile of a less gifted Glen Perkins, Maloney's approach would play better in a more spacious park, but until he finds somewhere more fly-ball-friendly to call home, he'll have to minimize the damage by forcing any batters intent on reaching base to hit their way on.

Nick Masset

Born: **5/17/1982** Age: **29**
Bats: R Throws: R Height: **6' 4"** Weight: **190**
Breakout: **18%** Improve: **31%** Collapse: **13%**
Attrition: **11%** MLB: **51%**

Comparables:
Craig Breslow, Ramon Ramirez, Juan Rincon (78)

YEAR	TEAM	LVL	AGE	W	L	SV	G	GS	IP	H	HR	BB	SO	EqBB9	EqSO9	GB%	BABIP	WHIP	ERA	FRA	WARP
2008	CHA	MLB	26	1	0	1	32	2	44^{2}	55	4	21	32	4.2	6.4	58%	.354	1.75	4.84	5.76	-0.2
2008	CIN	MLB	26	1	0	0	10	0	17^{1}	16	3	5	11	2.6	5.7	47%	.265	1.21	2.08	4.23	0.2
2009	CIN	MLB	27	5	1	0	74	0	76	54	6	24	70	2.8	8.3	55%	.250	1.03	2.37	3.82	1.6
2010	CIN	MLB	28	4	4	2	82	0	76^{2}	64	7	33	85	3.9	10.0	47%	.291	1.28	3.40	3.46	1.1
2011	*CIN*	*MLB*	*29*	*4*	*1*	*1*	*74*	*0*	*83*	*82*	*9*	*34*	*72*	*3.7*	*7.7*	*48%*	*.307*	*1.39*	*4.09*	*4.45*	*0.6*

The 2008 trade that sent Ken Griffey Jr. to the White Sox may have mostly been about salary relief, but thanks to Masset, the Reds have seen substantial on-field returns from the swap. The durable right-handed reliever has accounted for a combined 150-plus innings over the past two seasons, while showing no platoon split to speak of. Last season, balls in play didn't fall his way as often they had in 2009, but his defense-independent performance was a dead ringer for that of previous campaigns. The sinkerballer's strikeout rate has increased in each of his major-league seasons and reached heights it had never before attained in 2010, handing him the keys to a potent mixture of punchouts and grounders that allowed him to work around walks with few ill effects. Masset's sustained success was rewarded with the highest-leverage innings in the Reds' pen outside of anyone but closer Francisco Cordero, pricey rookie sensation Aroldis Chapman, and ageless lefty Arthur Rhodes.

Logan Ondrusek

Born: **2/13/1985** Age: **26**
Bats: R Throws: R Height: **6' 8"** Weight: **225**
Breakout: **4%** Improve: **6%** Collapse: **6%**
Attrition: **6%** MLB: **7%**

Comparables:
Jim Johnson, Jeff Gray, Burke Badenhop (85)

YEAR	TEAM	LVL	AGE	W	L	SV	G	GS	IP	H	HR	BB	SO	EqBB9	EqSO9	GB%	BABIP	WHIP	ERA	FRA	WARP
2008	SAR	A+	23	1	6	1	40	3	79^{2}	93	5	32	58	3.6	6.6	47%	.331	1.64	4.74	5.20	0.0
2009	CAR	AA	24	2	1	7	24	0	32^{2}	21	0	12	24	3.3	6.6	53%	.228	1.01	1.65	2.04	1.0
2009	LOU	AAA	24	0	0	14	22	0	24^{1}	16	1	2	15	0.7	5.5	59%	.214	0.78	1.48	3.49	0.3
2010	CIN	MLB	25	5	0	0	60	0	58^{2}	49	7	20	39	3.1	6.0	50%	.241	1.18	3.68	4.74	0.0
2011	*CIN*	*MLB*	*26*	*3*	*1*	*2*	*62*	*0*	*79*	*86*	*9*	*35*	*45*	*3.9*	*5.1*	*47%*	*.299*	*1.52*	*4.95*	*5.38*	*-0.2*

On the surface, Ondrusek's rookie season looked like a rousing success punctuated by a 22-inning scoreless streak, but storm clouds could be seen gathering on the horizon. The towering righty put himself on the prospect map with a BABIP-aided 2009, and his luck held upon earning a major-league gig. The Texan relies on a low-90s sinker/cutter combo that garners a healthy helping of grounders, but doesn't miss many bats. If Ondrusek possesses any intrinsic ability to prevent hits on balls in play, he didn't begin to tap into it until his fifth professional season, but in some cases, a few fortunate and well-timed bounces are all it takes to carve out a major-league career.

Micah Owings

Born: **9/28/1982** Age: **28**
Bats: R Throws: R Height: **6' 5"** Weight: **225**
Breakout: **9%** Improve: **35%** Collapse: **16%**
Attrition: **11%** MLB: **59%**

Comparables:
Dennis Rasmussen, Jim Beattie, Mark McLemore (75)

YEAR	TEAM	LVL	AGE	W	L	SV	G	GS	IP	H	HR	BB	SO	EqBB9	EqSO9	GB%	BABIP	WHIP	ERA	FRA	WARP
2008	ARI	MLB	25	6	9	0	22	20	104^{2}	104	14	41	87	3.5	7.5	35%	.289	1.50	5.93	2.87	-0.1
2009	CIN	MLB	26	7	12	1	26	19	119^{2}	126	18	64	68	4.8	5.1	38%	.280	1.64	5.34	5.35	0.7
2010	LOU	AAA	27	0	1	0	10	5	23	23	2	11	14	4.3	5.5	36%	.288	1.74	2.35	1.58	1.2
2010	CIN	MLB	27	3	2	0	22	0	33^{1}	28	3	25	35	6.8	9.5	32%	.287	1.68	5.40	4.29	0.2
2011	*CIN*	*MLB*	*28*	*7*	*7*	*0*	*40*	*18*	*123^{1}*	*126*	*17*	*59*	*86*	*4.3*	*6.2*	*40%*	*.289*	*1.49*	*4.98*	*5.41*	*1.3*

The Reds tried chaining Owings to the bullpen, which resulted in a slight uptick in velocity—though not to anywhere near the mid-90s heat he used to possess—and a sizable increase in strikeout rate, but any potential benefits were undone by a walk rate that ballooned to "precautionary MRI" levels, and he saw no major-league action after July. Despite not making a start, he did get 14 plate appearances, seven of them coming as a pinch-hitter, and added another home run to his tally, bringing career batting line to .293/.323/.538 in 198 plate appearances. With each passing year, it becomes more apparent that Owings' only chance at extended playing time is a change of position.

Arthur Rhodes

Born: **10/24/1969** Age: **41**
Bats: L Throws: L Height: **6' 2"** Weight: **206**
Breakout: **5%** Improve: **14%** Collapse: **16%**
Attrition: **6%** MLB: **39%**

Comparables:
Rudy Seanez, Trevor Hoffman, Tom Gordon (69)

YEAR	TEAM	LVL	AGE	W	L	SV	G	GS	IP	H	HR	BB	SO	EqBB9	EqSO9	GB%	BABIP	WHIP	ERA	FRA	WARP
2008	FLO	MLB	38	2	0	1	25	0	13^{1}	11	0	3	14	2.0	9.5	27%	.297	1.05	0.68	2.87	0.6
2008	SEA	MLB	38	2	1	1	36	0	22	17	0	13	26	5.3	10.6	32%	.321	1.36	2.86	-0.41	0.7
2009	CIN	MLB	39	1	1	0	66	0	53^{1}	37	3	20	48	3.4	8.1	44%	.238	1.09	2.53	3.17	1.2
2010	CIN	MLB	40	4	4	0	69	0	55	38	4	18	50	2.9	8.2	39%	.236	1.04	2.29	3.10	1.0
2011	*TEX*	*MLB*	*41*	*3*	*1*	*1*	*67*	*0*	*46*	*43*	*4*	*20*	*41*	*3.9*	*7.9*	*43%*	*.290*	*1.35*	*3.69*	*4.01*	*0.5*

Rhodes has posted a 2.32 ERA in 142 2/3 innings stretched across his age-38 through age-40 seasons, an impressive accomplishment for a man whose career mark still surpasses four. En route to becoming the fifth 40-

plus first-time All-Star in major-league history, he tied a major-league record by making 33 consecutive scoreless appearances, which translated to a total of 30 straight scoreless frames. The ancient lefty suffered from a sore foot and was used sparingly; since he's never been completely helpless against batters of opposite handedness, he faced more righties than lefties and actually held them to .189/.289/.245 last season, a better line than he had against left-handers (.214/.230/.393). Platoon stats vary from year to year due to small samples, so don't expect that to last; Rhodes doesn't throw as hard or secure as many strikeouts as he once did, and his late-career renaissance owes a sizable debt to good fortune on balls in play. Things could turn ugly at any time.

Jordan Smith

Born: **2/4/1986** Age: **25**
Bats: R Throws: R Height: **6' 4"** Weight: **220**
Breakout: **1%** Improve: **0%** Collapse: **0%**
Attrition: **1%** MLB: **1%**

Comparables:
Cesar Ramos, Ed Halicki, Larry Christenson (85)

YEAR	TEAM	LVL	AGE	W	L	SV	G	GS	IP	H	HR	BB	SO	EqBB9	EqSO9	GB%	BABIP	WHIP	ERA	FRA	WARP
2008	SAR	A+	22	7	2	0	10	10	67	61	2	7	44	0.9	5.9	56%	.278	1.06	2.55	3.82	1.3
2008	CHT	AA	22	2	6	0	11	11	55	72	6	17	42	2.8	6.9	56%	.355	1.69	4.91	5.50	0.4
2009	CAR	AA	23	5	3	0	13	15	73^{1}	77	4	21	39	2.6	4.8	52%	.299	1.36	3.19	3.94	1.4
2010	CAR	AA	24	1	3	9	27	0	28^{1}	38	3	8	14	2.5	4.4	54%	.343	1.66	5.08	6.26	-0.4
2010	CIN	MLB	24	3	2	1	37	0	42	45	7	11	26	2.4	5.6	51%	.286	1.38	3.86	3.94	0.4
2011	*CIN*	*MLB*	*25*	*4*	*4*	*2*	*50*	*7*	*88*	*111*	*13*	*33*	*39*	*3.4*	*3.9*	*49%*	*.313*	*1.63*	*5.93*	*6.44*	*-0.5*

A severely slipping strikeout rate convinced the Reds to stick Smith in the Double-A bullpen, but that didn't halt the decline. The Reds deemed him major-league material anyway and summoned him to Cincinnati in mid-June without an intermediate stop in Triple-A. The promotion breathed a modicum of life into his strikeout rate, but he survived on the strength of his ability to keep the ball on the ground and in the zone (though the latter quality made him easy fodder for home-run hitters). Among Reds hurlers with a minimum of 20 innings pitched, Smith trailed only Edinson Volquez and Mike Leake in ground-ball percentage. Since his heavy sinker doesn't miss many bats, his success will always depend on the infield defense behind him.

Philippe Valiquette

Born: **2/14/1987** Age: **24**
Bats: L Throws: L Height: **6' 1"** Weight: **205**
Breakout: **1%** Improve: **2%** Collapse: **2%**
Attrition: **1%** MLB: **3%**

Comparables:
Sergio Escalona, Justin Thompson, Sean Runyan (77)

YEAR	TEAM	LVL	AGE	W	L	SV	G	GS	IP	H	HR	BB	SO	EqBB9	EqSO9	GB%	BABIP	WHIP	ERA	FRA	WARP
2008	DYT	A	21	0	1	1	16	0	26	25	2	10	32	3.5	11.1	47%	.333	1.38	3.12	2.6	0.6
2008	SAR	A+	21	2	2	2	31	0	39	45	4	18	33	4.2	7.6	44%	.345	1.64	3.92	3.58	0.8
2009	CAR	AA	22	1	1	3	27	0	32^{2}	25	2	20	27	5.5	7.4	50%	.258	1.44	2.76	3.88	0.3
2010	CAR	AA	23	2	0	4	25	0	29^{1}	34	0	16	21	4.9	6.4	56%	.366	1.70	3.99	3.30	0.3
2010	LOU	AAA	23	3	1	1	30	0	35	33	2	14	33	3.6	8.5	56%	.310	1.34	4.37	5.15	0.0
2011	*CIN*	*MLB*	*24*	*2*	*1*	*2*	*41*	*0*	*51^{1}*	*59*	*7*	*29*	*33*	*5.2*	*5.9*	*46%*	*.320*	*1.73*	*5.76*	*6.26*	*-0.6*

In his sixth professional season, Valiquette's Sisyphean climb to the top of the minor-league ladder finally resulted in a stint at Triple-A. It's not clear what part of the lefty's 1.3 strikeout-to-walk ratio in the Southern League convinced the Reds that he was Louisville material, but to his credit, the French Canadian did a creditable job of dispatching International League hitters. The southpaw can pump his fastball in the mid- to high 90s and induce grounders at an impressive rate, but his poor control and shortage of quality secondary stuff prevents him from racking up the high strikeout totals one might expect from a pitcher with that kind of velocity. The Reds aren't lacking lefties in relief, so it might take a trade to earn Valiquette an extended major-league look. A poor showing in the Arizona Fall League didn't help his case.

Edinson Volquez

Born: **7/3/1983** Age: **27**
Bats: R Throws: R Height: **6' 1"** Weight: **190**
Breakout: **25%** Improve: **49%** Collapse: **21%**
Attrition: **13%** MLB: **94%**

Comparables:
Steve Bedrosian, Jack Harshman, Dennis Higgins (74)

YEAR	TEAM	LVL	AGE	W	L	SV	G	GS	IP	H	HR	BB	SO	EqBB9	EqSO9	GB%	BABIP	WHIP	ERA	FRA	WARP
2008	CIN	MLB	24	17	6	0	33	35	196	167	14	93	206	4.3	9.5	47%	.299	1.40	3.21	3.61	4.9
2009	CIN	MLB	25	4	2	0	9	9	49^{2}	34	6	32	47	5.8	8.5	47%	.219	1.43	4.35	5.48	0.1
2010	LOU	AAA	26	3	0	0	4	4	23	11	1	8	21	3.1	8.2	41%	.175	0.87	1.96	4.59	0.4
2010	CIN	MLB	26	4	3	0	12	13	62^{2}	59	6	35	67	5.0	9.6	57%	.323	1.55	4.31	4.85	0.6
2011	*CIN*	*MLB*	*27*	*9*	*7*	*0*	*23*	*23*	*133*	*117*	*15*	*67*	*130*	*4.5*	*8.8*	*47%*	*.289*	*1.38*	*4.03*	*4.38*	*3.4*

Just 13½ months after throwing his final pitch with his old UCL, Volquez returned to a major-league mound looking none the worse for his new one. Then, 3½ months after *that*, he found himself starting Game One of the NLDS, his return to the top of the Reds' rotation complete. Another Tommy John success story in the making, the Dominican came back throwing at least as hard as he had before the surgery (and a subsequent PED-related suspension, which he served while on the DL), and his strikeout and ground-ball rates topped anything he'd managed in the majors with his original anatomy intact. Control is often the last talent to return after an elbow injury, and the undersized righty did weather some initial struggles in that department, but he improved to issue only 2.6 free passes per nine in September. This bodes well for his chances of a command performance this season.

Travis Wood

Born: 2/6/1987 Age: 24
Bats: R Throws: L Height: 5' 11" Weight: 165
Breakout: 20% Improve: 53% Collapse: 17%
Attrition: 6% MLB: 93%

Comparables:
Ramon Martinez, Sammy Ellis, Joel Pineiro (67)

YEAR	TEAM	LVL	AGE	W	L	SV	G	GS	IP	H	HR	BB	SO	EqBB9	EqSO9	GB%	BABIP	WHIP	ERA	FRA	WARP
2008	SAR	A+	21	3	4	0	9	10	46^{2}	39	2	21	41	4.1	7.9	48%	.278	1.33	2.51	3.46	1.2
2008	CHT	AA	21	4	9	0	17	17	80	91	9	48	58	5.4	6.5	38%	.323	1.88	6.64	7.00	-0.7
2009	CAR	AA	22	9	3	0	19	20	119	78	2	37	103	2.8	7.8	43%	.244	1.01	1.13	2.20	4.9
2009	LOU	AAA	22	4	2	0	9	9	53^{2}	49	4	19	37	3.2	6.2	46%	.280	1.30	3.02	3.72	1.2
2010	LOU	AAA	23	5	6	0	16	17	100	86	9	24	99	2.2	8.9	45%	.287	1.14	3.06	3.87	2.1
2010	CIN	MLB	23	5	4	0	17	17	102^{2}	85	9	26	86	2.3	7.5	32%	.259	1.12	3.51	4.17	1.5
2011	*CIN*	*MLB*	*24*	*9*	*8*	*0*	*23*	*23*	*133^{2}*	*130*	*16*	*53*	*101*	*3.6*	*6.9*	*42%*	*.290*	*1.37*	*4.16*	*4.52*	*3.1*

Wood belongs a cut above the Sam LeCures and Matt Maloneys of the world, so it didn't come as a shock that he managed to stick around well into October after being summoned to reinforce an injury-ravaged rotation in early July. A near-perfect performance in his third outing may have generated unfair expectations, but he hardly disappointed the rest of the way. Although the mid-90s heat that he flashed in high school didn't accompany him to the professional ranks, the southpaw has plenty of weapons at his disposal, complementing a 90-mph sinker with a plus changeup and a quality cutter that he picked up in 2009. His sub-four ERA shows signs of having benefited from a well-received sacrifice at the altar of the BABIP gods, but history suggests that he'll keep the ball on the ground more often in the future, which should help him counter any correction on balls in play.

LINEOUTS

HITTERS

PLAYER	TEAM	LVL	AGE	PA	R	2B	3B	HR	RBI	BB	SO	SB-CS	AVG/OBP/SLG	TAv	BABIP	BRR	FRAA	WARP
SS J. Arias	CIN	Rk	18	241	52	14	7	6	26	12	63	1-2	.303/.336/.504	.295	.394	1.0	SS -5	1.6
OF W. Balentien	LOU	AAA	25	461	69	23	2	24	77	39	86	12-1	.278/.336/.520	.284	.289	0.6	RF 2, CF 0	2.1
C T. Barnhart	BIL	Rk	19	152	17	9	0	0	12	20	31	4-1	.296/.388/.364	.318	.386	-1.1	C 2	1.6
CF J. Edmonds*	CIN	MLB	40	32	6	2	0	3	3	3	7	0-0	.207/.281/.586	.300	.158	0.2	CF 0, 1B -1	0.0
	MIL	MLB	40	240	39	21	0	8	20	21	53	2-0	.286/.350/.493	.299	.344	-0.7	CF 6, RF 0	2.0
SS B. Hamilton	BIL	Rk	19	357	68	16	11	2	26	32	67	45-7	.311/.370/.447	.330	.383	8.3	2B 19, SS -1	5.4
OF R. LaMarre	DYT	A	21	251	38	11	0	5	29	21	53	11-1	.282/.387/.397	.269	.343	1.3	CF 1, RF 3	1.3
CF G. Matthews#	LOU	AAA	35	108	16	7	1	3	6	7	26	3-2	.317/.361/.495	.290	.403	-1.4	CF -2	0.4
	NYN	MLB	35	65	9	3	0	0	1	6	24	1-0	.190/.262/.241	.189	.314	0.7	CF 2, RF -1	-0.1
C C. Miller	LOU	AAA	34	205	27	13	0	6	35	19	31	0-1	.276/.361/.448	.272	.297	-0.9	C 4	1.5
	CIN	MLB	34	79	5	5	0	2	9	2	16	0-0	.243/.279/.392	.231	.281	-0.3	C 0	0.0
2B H. Rodriguez#	DYT	A	20	543	73	37	3	14	78	22	70	14-5	.307/.339/.473	.294	.330	-0.8	2B -6, SS 0	2.6
OF Y. Rodriguez	BIL	Rk	17	225	30	9	4	3	53	8	38	11-2	.346/.360/.469	.349	.398	1.9	RF -2, CF 0	2.5
1B N. Soto	LYN	A+	21	557	70	33	2	21	73	32	105	0-0	.268/.323/.460	.274	.298	-4.6	1B -5, C 0	0.5
3B D. Vidal	BIL	Rk	20	54	2	0	0	0	0	3	6	0-1	.188/.222/.188	.167	.200	0.1	3B -4, 2B -1	-0.8
	CIN	Rk	20	153	26	13	2	6	32	12	26	0-0	.290/.340/.544	.320	.312	-1.6	3B 2	1.3

The first season stateside went well for **Junior Arias**, a line-drive-hitting Dominican signed at 16 in 2008. The Reds will leave him in the oven for a few more years and hope he comes out looking like a major-league shortstop, though their system should offer plenty of tasty alternatives by then. ⊘ The Reds thought little enough of his work in the second half of 2009 to banish **Wladimir Balentien** to Louisville for the entirety of 2010, where the athletic righty turned in the best minor-league performance of his career. Rather than spend another season wondering what the big club sees in Jonny Gomes, he took his act to Japan in exchange for some bigger numbers, both on the field and in his bank account. ⊘ Evidently, no one told **Tucker Barnhart** that the Reds already had enough talented young backstops. The compact catcher threw out over half of attempted basestealers while exhibiting Hanigan-caliber plate discipline in the Pioneer League, though he has yet to develop much power. ⊘ Taking 2009 off didn't seem to hurt **Jim Edmonds** any. The 40-year-old outfielder padded an already-persuasive Hall of Fame case with a better bat and glove than he showed during 2008's false ending, though Achilles tendonitis and oblique issues restricted him to an even more limited role than his managers had in mind. He has apparently decided to hang up his bat with something left in the tank. ⊘ After an underwhelming professional debut, **Billy Hamilton** used his impressive array of tools to build a spectacular 2010 season in the Pioneer League. Much like his turn-of-last-century spiritual predecessor, "Sliding Billy" Hamilton, the 2009 second-rounder possesses plus speed and base-swiping ability, though that may not be enough to keep him at short, where his bat could be special. Toolsy 2010 second-rounder **Ryan LaMarre** can reach the gaps and run the bases well, but is likely to embody the term *tweener*, since he lacks the range for center and the pop for the corners. After washing out with the Mets, **Gary Matthews Jr.** passed through Louisville on his way to the breadline. **Corky Miller** has managed to spend parts of 10 seasons in the majors despite a .188 career average, which goes to show both that a good defensive catcher never goes hungry and that everyone likes the name Corky. Many a young Dominican has seen his development stunted by the belief that "you can't walk off the island." Thanks to Panama, among other countries, one *can* walk off Venezuela, but **Henry Rodriguez** didn't get the memo. Fortunately, the capable second baseman boasts a potent power-speed combo that eases the pain of his impatience considerably. **Yorman Rodriguez** cost the Reds $2.5 million in 2008—a record for a Venezuelan import—but their investment began to pay off in a walk-deprived, but otherwise impressive age-17 performance in the Pioneer League. Reputed to be a four-tool player after signing at 16, the outfielder sported a .339 mark that suggests that he might possess the ability to hit for average after all. **Neftali Soto**'s second offensive attempt at High-A was more successful, but a defensive migration across the diamond raised the bar for his bat. Although he spent most of his time at first base, the 2007 third-rounder did try his hand at 10 games behind the plate, where he could prove to be very valuable. *Baseball America* rated **David Vidal** the best pure hitter in Cincinnati's 2010 draft class, and following a slow start, the eighth-rounder lived up to his billing, breaking out of his slump with a three-homer game in Arizona. The undersized righty has the arm for third, but hands best suited for the outfield, so his defensive home of the future remains hazy.

PITCHERS

PLAYER	TEAM	LVL	AGE	W	L	SV	IP	H	HR	BB	SO	EqBB9	EqSO9	GB%	BABIP	WHIP	ERA	FRA	WARP
B. Boxberger	LYN	A+	22	4	6	0	62	57	3	20	70	2.9	10.2	52%	.335	1.32	2.90	4.03	1.2
—	CAR	AA	22	1	4	0	29^2	35	4	22	40	6.7	12.1	45%	.392	2.02	8.19	6.27	-0.5
I. Guillon*	CIN	Rk	18	0	0	0	70^2	49	1	28	90	3.6	11.5	42%	.296	1.09	3.06	3.89	2.5
J. Horst*	CAR	AA	24	3	2	0	43	35	1	9	46	1.9	9.6	48%	.291	1.02	2.09	1.83	0.7
M. Lincoln	CIN	MLB	35	1	0	0	19^2	25	1	10	12	4.6	5.5	51%	.348	1.88	7.32	7.31	-0.5
K. Lotzkar	BIL	Rk	20	2	0	0	20	8	1	2	33	0.9	14.9	50%	.212	0.50	0.45	1.18	3.4
—	CIN	Rk	20	0	0	0	29^1	27	2	13	31	4.0	9.5	58%	.325	1.36	3.99	3.73	1.2
R. Springer	CIN	MLB	41	0	0	0	1^2	2	0	0	1	0.0	5.4	17%	.333	1.20	5.40	3.18	0.0
D. Thompson	CAR	AA	24	0	5	0	51	38	3	11	52	1.9	9.2	33%	.273	0.98	3.71	3.91	1.2

Jose Arredondo underwent Tommy John surgery last February, so he should be ready to return at or near the start of the season. The Reds hope his comeback tour will summon memories of his dreamy 2008 and not his nightmarish 2009, though SIERA didn't see much difference between the two. The Reds moved 2009 first-rounder **Brad Boxberger** to the bullpen after a promotion to Double-A, where his strikeout rate grew even more impressive, but a combination of walks and a high BABIP did him in. The conversion was presented as a means of limiting the righty's innings, but once ensconced within its walls, a pitcher with his inconsistent mechanics might find the bullpen about as easy to escape as the Hotel California. Signed out of Venezuela for a sizable bonus as a 16-year-old in late 2008, **Ismael Guillon** got to strut his stuff in Arizona last summer, with impressive results. The hard-throwing lefty gave both scouts and stat geeks plenty to get giddy about, thanks to an intoxicating mix of projection and polish. **Jeremy Horst** was old for his level when the season started, but considerably less so by the time it came to an end, thanks to a pair of well-deserved promotions. The lefty has been moved into and out of the rotation more frequently than *Futurama*, but it's clear that his best work comes in short bursts. **Mike Lincoln** had already suffered through two Tommy John surgeries and three full seasons of rehab before finding his way to Cincinnati, so his perseverance in the face of prolonged pain merits admiration. Still, at some point, someone will have to wait until the kids are at school, carry him to the car, tell him he's going to the ballpark, and have him put out of his misery. Former supplemental first-rounder **Kyle Lotzkar** pitched well in his first taste of action since 2008, but he probably hadn't envisioned spending his age-20 season with the same rookie-ball affiliate he pitched for at 17. Maybe next time, he'll think twice about fracturing his elbow and undergoing a subsequent Tommy John surgery. **Russ Springer** added a 10th major-league team to his résumé when he signed with Louisville in July and tossed a couple innings for the big club in August. He underwent season-ending hip surgery later that month and set sail for bullpen Valhalla shortly after the anesthesia wore off. After spending most of 2009 suffering from elbow inflammation and a frayed labrum, **Daryl Thompson** succumbed to another succession of injuries last season, but pitched well when healthy. An additional 18 innings of work in the AFL convinced the Reds to give him a spot on the 40-man, but only one of the fragile righty's Arizona outings came in the bullpen, where the Reds should consider keeping him.

MANAGER: DUSTY BAKER

YEAR	TEAM	W-L	Pythag +/-	Avg PC	100+ P	120+ P	QS	BQS	REL	REL w Zero R	IBB	Subs	PH	PH Avg	PH HR	SB2	CS2	SB3	CS3	SAC Att	SAC %	POS SAC	Squeeze	Swing	In Play
2009	CIN	78-84	3	98.7	89	2	77	3	477	320	36	43	251	.227	4	80	35	15	4	137	73.0%	47	4	122	98
2010	CIN	91-71	-1	97.9	81	4	87	6	501	345	32	72	256	.236	10	79	36	14	5	106	62.3%	28	6	136	100

Baker may never shed his reputation as a destroyer of arms, but while confirmation bias ensures that any hint of a long outing by one of his pitchers still elicits a knowing smirk or eye roll from fans with memories long enough to encompass his days in Chicago, the veteran manager did little to justify continued reprobation last season. While he didn't coddle his young arms, he didn't endanger them, either, coming in only moderately above average in the pitch-count department. On the tactical side, Baker demonstrated an admirable unwillingness to indulge in the four-ball bonanzas that stir up sabermetricians, calling for the fewest free passes among full-season NL managers, or roughly the number that Joe Girardi handed out in the ALCS alone. Although the Reds' roster was deep enough to succeed despite any suboptimal decisions on the margins, Baker's lineup choices occasionally took on a questionable tinge. The skipper evinced a baffling fondness for starting Jonny Gomes despite possessing superior left-field options, and although the absence of a base unclogger on the level of Corey Patterson or Willy Taveras limited his ability to hamstring an otherwise-potent lineup, he proved unable to supply a happy ending to the Reds' long-running production of *Leadoff Idol*. Only the Nats' Nyjer Morgan–depressed performance elicited a mark worse than Cincinnati's .306 OBP from the leadoff spot, and while Baker's roster lacked a true top-of-the-lineup talent, his decision to bat Orlando Cabrera first or second on 110 occasions made the worst of a bad situation. To paraphrase Benjamin Franklin, those who would give up essential on-base percentage to purchase a little temporary bat control deserve neither.

Cleveland Indians

The Indians got within one win of the American League pennant in 2007, but in July 2008, they were languishing in last place in the AL Central, more than 10 games under .500 and a similar distance out of first place. With ace CC Sabathia due to become a free agent at the end of the year, general manager Mark Shapiro chose that moment to throw in the towel, trading Sabathia to the Brewers for a package built around minor-league hitting stud Matt LaPorta. With that trade, Shapiro initiated a rebuilding process, the first stage of which finally concluded in 2010 with the deadline trades of Jhonny Peralta, Jake Westbrook, and Kerry Wood. All totaled, in just over two calendar years, the Indians traded 17 players, all of them major leaguers, most of them veterans, and received 29 players in return, most of them minor leaguers, but not all of them prospects (see Table 1).

INDIANS PROSPECTUS

2010 W-L: 69-93, 4th in AL Central

Pythag	.430	24th	**Ballpark:** Progressive Field (3-yr. PF: 99). The drum still beats, but fannies no longer fill the seats
RS/G	4.0	26th	
RA/G	4.6	7th	
TAv	.261	26th	**2010:** Beating the Royals is all Chief Wahoo has to hang his headband on
BRR	1.0	14th	
FRA	4.62	21st	**2011:** Young team in transition experiences little standings success
DER	-7.87	21st	
DL	465	2nd	
B-Age	27.2	4th	**Action Items:** Some reinforcements for a rotation of non-starters, a healthy Hafner, and LaPower from LaPorta or bust
P-Age	26.2	2nd	
Salary	$61.2	24th	
M$/MW	$2.51	15th	

Entering the 2011 season, the Indians' 40-man roster includes just two players born prior to 1982: designated hitter Travis Hafner, who will be 34 in June but whose contract, which entitles him to $26 million over the next two seasons plus a $2.75 million buyout for 2013, has rendered him untradable, and 31-year-old outfielder Shelley Duncan, who has just 422 major-league plate appearances to his name. Other than Hafner, just two men on the roster are signed to multiyear deals: center fielder Grady Sizemore, who is entering the final year of a six-year contract that also includes a team option for 2012, and right-handed starter Fausto Carmona, who is also entering the final guaranteed year of his four-year contract, but who has club options for each of the next three seasons through 2014. Given Carmona's struggles in 2008 and 2009 and Sizemore's recent injury problems, neither is a sure bet to have his 2012 option picked up.

With the major-league roster effectively stripped bare and the farm system thoroughly restocked via those 16 trades and three strong drafts, Shapiro handed the GM reins over to his longtime assistant, Chris Antonetti, in October. The chain of command remains the same, with Shapiro ascending to team president and continuing to be Antonetti's boss, and former director of baseball operations Mike Chernoff moving up to become Antonetti's right-hand man in his boss's former role of assistant general manager. The primary difference is that now, Antonetti will have to sort through the amassed talent and turn it into a functioning, and ideally winning, baseball team.

So what does Antonetti have to work with? Sizemore and Carmona were supposed to be the anchors of the rebuilt Indians lineup and rotation, respectively, but both have seen their stock plummet since the rebuild began. It's easy to forget that it was Carmona, not Cliff Lee, who was seen as the dominant second starter behind Sabathia coming out of that deep October run in 2007. Carmona's performance that year earned him his current contract, but he has failed to live up to it. He did finally seem to harness the wildness that plagued him in 2008 and 2009 last year, but his ground-ball rate continued to decline, a particularly problematic trend given his below-average strikeout rates. Sizemore's last two seasons were each ruined by injury and ended early due to surgery (to his left elbow and abdomen in 2009 and microfracture surgery on his left knee last year), the more recent of which could keep him out past Opening Day. Beyond concerns about his health, those injuries cost the now-28-year-old Sizemore two crucial years of maturation as a hitter, and the knee surgery could force him out of center field.

Right fielder Shin-Soo Choo, stolen from the Mariners for Ben Broussard prior to the 2006 trade deadline, has risen to take Sizemore's place as a five-tool centerpiece and one of the best players in baseball, and catcher Carlos Santana, similarly stolen from the Dodgers for Casey Blake exactly two

Table 1. The Take: The Final Accounting of the Indians' 2008-2010 Fire Sale

Major leaguers traded (in chronological order):

CC Sabathia (LHP), Casey Blake (3B), Paul Byrd (RHP), Franklin Gutierrez (CF), Mark DeRosa (UT), Cliff Lee (LHP), Ben Francisco (OF), Rafael Betancourt (RHP), Ryan Garko (1B), Victor Martinez (C), Carl Pavano (RHP), Kelly Shoppach (C), Russell Branyan (1B), Jhonny Peralta (SS/3B), Austin Kearns (OF), Jake Westbrook (RHP), Kerry Wood (RHP)

Players acquired (by position):

1B/OF – Matt LaPorta (from Brewers for Sabathia)
2B – Luis Valbuena (from Mariners for Gutierrez)
2B/SS – Jason Donald (from Phillies for Lee)
SS – Juan Diaz (from Mariners for Branyan)
2B/3B – Matt Cusick (from Yankees for Wood)
C – Carlos Santana (from Dodgers for Blake)
C – Lou Marson (also for Lee)
OF – Michael Brantley (also for Sabathia)
OF – Ezequiel Carrera (also for Branyan)
OF – Mickey Hall (from Red Sox for Byrd)
RHP – Justin Masterson (from Red Sox for Martinez)
RHP – Mitch Talbot (from Rays for Shoppach)
RHP – Carlos Carrasco (also for Lee)
RHP – Chris Perez (from Cardinals for DeRosa)
RHP – Joe Smith (from Mets in the Gutierrez deal)
RHP – Jess Todd (also for DeRosa)
RHP – Nick Hagadone (also for Martinez)
RHP – Zach McAllister (from Yankees for Kearns)
RHP – Corey Kluber (from Padres for Westbrook)
RHP – Jason Knapp (also for Lee)
LHP – Giovanni Soto (from Tigers for Peralta)
LHP – Scott Barnes (from Giants for Garko)
RHP – Bryan Price (also for Martinez)
RHP – Rob Bryson (also for Sabathia)
RHP – Connor Graham (from Rockies for Betancourt)
RHP – Andrew Shive (also for Wood)
RHP – Yohan Pino (from Twins for Pavano)
LHP – Zach Jackson (also for Sabathia)
RHP – Jon Meloan (also for Blake)

years later, showed in his brief major-league stint last year that he's ready to join Choo as a monster bat in the heart of the order. The rotation, however, lacks such marquee talent.

That Shapiro managed to acquire 19 young pitchers in those 16 roster-clearing trades without acquiring one who projects as a rotation anchor is particularly disappointing. Carlos Carrasco, acquired from the Phillies in the Cliff Lee deal at the 2009 deadline, should spend his first full season in the rotation this year, but he's likely to be a third starter at best and more likely a fourth starter, which seems to be the limit for even the best pitchers Shapiro acquired. Joining Carrasco in the front five will be side-arming righty Justin Masterson, acquired from the Red Sox in the Victor Martinez deal two days later. Although he will be unencumbered by an innings limit this year, he still seems better suited for the bullpen. Mitch Talbot, acquired from the Rays for backup catcher Kelly Shoppach last winter, is the other incumbent, but as a 27-year-old sophomore, seems like little more than a placeholder.

Fortunately, the Indians have had much more success in landing pitching talent through the draft. The Tribe had a somewhat disastrous draft in 2007, when they lost their second- and third-round picks as compensation for signing reliever Roberto Hernandez (who posted 6.23 ERA in 26 innings for the Indians before being released in July) and outfielder David Dellucci (who hit .238/.308/.394 in two-plus injury-plagued seasons in Cleveland). Their first-round pick that year was slugging college first baseman Beau Mills, who left it all on campus, hitting .241/.312/.377 in a repeat of Double-A last year. The only player drafted by the Indians that year to merit a player comment in this chapter was right-handed reliever Josh Judy, who was taken in the 34th round.

Since then, however, the Indians have drafted well despite having traded all of their impending Type-A and Type-B free agents and thus not having had a compensation pick since 2006. According to Kevin Goldstein's list of the organization's top 11 prospects published on our Web site in November, the Indians' top five prospects, six of their top seven, and eight of their top 10 have come out of the first three rounds of the last three drafts, and the ninth man from those rounds ranked 16th. Three of those top seven prospects are pitchers, including a pair of four-star first-rounders, 2009 pick Alex White and 2010 fifth-overall pick lefty Drew Pomeranz.

Of those two, Pomeranz, who signed out of Ole Miss for $2.65 million, is the pitcher the Indians hope will be their homegrown rotation anchor, though he may not arrive until 2013. White, a righty who projects as more of a ground-balling innings eater, should arrive much sooner. Drafted out of the University of North Carolina, White made his professional debut in High-A last year and spent the bulk of the season in Double-A, where he posted a 2.28 ERA. He could crack the major-league rotation in the second half of the coming season and be a full-timer in 2012.

In fact, 2012 is when much of the Indians' crop is expected to start bearing fruit. Top position prospects Jason Kipnis and Lonnie Chisenhall could take over the starting second- and third-base jobs at some point this season, while left fielder Nick Weglarz, a 2005 pick out of high school who hits like a left fielder should, is on a similar pace to fill that position. With the return of Sizemore; a full season of Santana, who is also returning from knee surgery following a gruesome but ultimately not-that-catastrophic home-plate collision in August; and Choo, who was recently excused from military duty in his native South Korea after helping the South Korean team win gold in the Asian Games, the Indians' lineup looks ready to begin coalescing this year with an eye toward a coming-out party in 2012. If someone in the organization can figure out what's wrong with LaPorta, the Indians have the potential to be downright dangerous at the plate in 2012. That is an awful lot of "if" "ifs" for one team.

However the offense develops, the pitching staff will certainly lag. White might come up this year, and Masterson might show some growth after a full season in the rotation in 2010, but 2009 third-round pick Joe Gardner is merely a lesser version of White and a year off the pace. Pomeranz is still far away, and the system is thin after these players. Chris Perez, obtained from the Cardinals for Mark DeRosa two days before the Cliff Lee trade, has emerged as a shutdown closer, but he's like a bullet-proof lock on a door rotting off its hinges. Perhaps if that budget-price lineup does coalesce, Antonetti can convince ownership to make a big free-agent splash for rotation help. If so, the Indians could make waves in the Central Division in the coming seasons, but there, again, are more ifs.

One thing is for certain: the 2011 Indians will not be a winning team. Cleveland fans will have, at minimum, one more year of filler and rebuilding to endure, and if the Indians do start to rise in 2012, they could very well have a similarly ascendant Royals team to contend with. A lot can go wrong on that road to glory, but there is hope and a plan in place. What the team and its fans need most now is patience.

HITTERS

Michael Brantley CF

Born: **5/15/1987** Age: **24**
Bats: L Throws: L Height: **6' 2"** Weight: **200**
Breakout: **2%** Improve: **33%** Collapse: **7%**
Attrition: **23%** MLB: **72%**

Comparables:
Ryan Sweeney, Terry Puhl, Chris Coghlan (70)

YEAR	TEAM	LVL	AGE	PA	R	2B	3B	HR	RBI	BB	SO	SB	CS	AVG_OBP_SLG	TAv	BABIP	BRR	FRAA	WARP
2008	HUN	AA	21	475	79	17	2	4	40	50	27	28	8	.319/.396/.398	.284	.330	2.8	CF 4, 1B 2	3.2
2009	COH	AAA	22	527	79	21	2	6	37	59	48	46	5	.267/.345/.361	.252	.280	1.8	CF -2, LF 2	1.2
2009	CLE	MLB	22	121	10	4	0	0	11	8	19	4	4	.313/.355/.348	.253	.372	0.2	CF -2, LF 0	0.0
2010	COH	AAA	23	314	53	13	2	4	29	34	28	13	5	.319/.392/.425	.277	.335	4.1	CF 6, LF 2	2.5
2010	CLE	MLB	23	325	38	9	3	3	22	22	38	10	2	.246/.292/.327	.226	.267	5.2	CF -2, LF -3	-0.2
2011	*CLE*	*MLB*	*24*	*587*	*67*	*21*	*2*	*7*	*54*	*53*	*63*	*28*	*7*	*.279/.341/.370*	*.255*	*.297*	*0.5*	*CF -2, LF -1*	*0.9*

Brantley's numbers were brought down by a brutal showing during an early-season call-up, but even when he was hitting for average (.288 after August 1), there wasn't much offensive value there. His minor-league abilities revolved around slashing line drives, drawing some walks, and running, but all he has really done in the majors is hit a little bit, as the walk rate has been down from his minor-league days and he'll never have power. He's not a failure so much as a nice fourth outfielder being asked to do too much by playing every day.

Jordan Brown UT

Born: **12/18/1983** Age: **27**
Bats: L Throws: L Height: **6' 0"** Weight: **205**
Breakout: **1%** Improve: **19%** Collapse: **8%**
Attrition: **19%** MLB: **38%**

Comparables:
Michael Aubrey, Brian Buscher, Brandon Jones (76)

YEAR	TEAM	LVL	AGE	PA	R	2B	3B	HR	RBI	BB	SO	SB	CS	AVG_OBP_SLG	TAv	BABIP	BRR	FRAA	WARP
2008	BUF	AAA	24	458	51	30	3	7	51	35	67	2	3	.281/.338/.417	.263	.318	-5.3	1B -3	-0.3
2009	COH	AAA	25	453	63	35	1	15	67	30	64	2	4	.336/.380/.532	.304	.363	-3.0	LF 5, RF -6	2.0
2010	COH	AAA	26	352	33	28	1	8	67	21	48	2	0	.298/.344/.463	.257	.324	-3.9	LF 1, RF -1	-0.1
2010	CLE	MLB	26	92	10	7	0	0	2	4	10	0	0	.230/.272/.310	.217	.260	-0.2	1B 1, LF 1	-0.2
2011	*CLE*	*MLB*	*27*	*452*	*54*	*27*	*1*	*10*	*53*	*29*	*69*	*2*	*1*	*.278/.324/.421*	*.259*	*.306*	*-0.1*	*1B -8, LF 0*	*-0.4*

A career .306/.369/.463 hitter in the minors with a pair of league MVP awards on his mantle, Brown isn't nearly the prospect his résumé might suggest. Limited to first base or occasional play in an outfield corner, Brown can certainly hit, but he doesn't have the power needed for the position; nor does he have much patience. He's one of those guys who could spend the next five years bouncing between Triple-A and the majors or head to find stardom in Japan.

Asdrubal Cabrera SS

Born: **11/13/1985** Age: **25**
Bats: S Throws: R Height: **6' 0"** Weight: **170**
Breakout: **6%** Improve: **54%** Collapse: **5%**
Attrition: **15%** MLB: **88%**

Comparables:
Alan Trammell, Robinson Cano, Edgardo Alfonzo (74)

YEAR	TEAM	LVL	AGE	PA	R	2B	3B	HR	RBI	BB	SO	SB	CS	AVG_OBP_SLG	TAv	BABIP	BRR	FRAA	WARP
2008	BUF	AAA	22	148	24	7	1	4	13	7	25	2	2	.326/.385/.475	.281	.375	1.0	SS -5, 2B 0	0.5
2008	CLE	MLB	22	418	47	20	0	6	47	46	77	4	4	.259/.337/.367	.261	.298	1.4	2B 12, SS -1	2.4
2009	CLE	MLB	23	581	81	42	4	6	68	44	89	17	4	.308/.355/.438	.290	.352	2.5	SS -3, 2B -2	3.5
2010	CLE	MLB	24	425	39	16	1	3	29	25	60	6	4	.276/.318/.347	.247	.307	0.7	SS -3	0.8
2011	*CLE*	*MLB*	*25*	*565*	*68*	*28*	*2*	*9*	*60*	*46*	*86*	*13*	*5*	*.286/.341/.403*	*.263*	*.318*	*-0.3*	*SS -4, 2B 2*	*1.7*

Having been one of the brighter spots on the team in 2009, Cabrera had the potential for a breakout year in 2010, but instead, his season was defined by a broken arm at the end of May—an injury that required surgery and cost him more than two months of play. What you see is what you get with Cabrera. When he hits .300, as he did in 2009, he's of tremendous value once you weigh in his defensive skills. When he hits .276, as he did in 2010, his value is diminished by a lack of power and walks. He'll always be susceptible to the vagaries of batting average, but he's also years away from peaking, which makes him a valuable commodity.

Lonnie Chisenhall 3B

Born: **10/4/1988** Age: **22**
Bats: **L** Throws: **R** Height: **6' 1"** Weight: **200**
Breakout: **5%** Improve: **17%** Collapse: **3%**
Attrition: **20%** MLB: **30%**

Comparables:
Mat Gamel, Carlos Gonzalez, Nick Evans (78)

YEAR	TEAM	LVL	AGE	PA	R	2B	3B	HR	RBI	BB	SO	SB	CS	AVG_OBP_SLG	TAv	BABIP	BRR	FRAA	WARP
2008	MHV	A-	19	301	35	20	3	5	45	24	32	7	2	.290/.359/.438	.310	.313	0.8	SS 1	2.7
2009	KIN	A+	20	427	56	26	2	18	78	37	80	2	1	.276/.349/.492	.303	.305	1.3	3B -4	2.7
2009	AKR	AA	20	134	20	7	1	4	15	9	18	1	1	.252/.299/.423	.280	.262	0.4	3B -1	0.6
2010	AKR	AA	21	514	74	22	3	17	84	46	77	2	0	.278/.358/.450	.296	.297	-0.5	3B -4	2.8
2011	*CLE*	*MLB*	*22*	*459*	*54*	*21*	*2*	*15*	*57*	*30*	*84*	*1*	*0*	*.262/.313/.430*	*.258*	*.289*	*0.0*	*3B -4, SS 1*	*0.8*

Chisenhall's numbers at Double-A in 2010 fall into the "pretty good" category, but he's much better than that, as he spent much of the first half playing through a shoulder problem. While it's a cliché and in no way a guarantee of stardom, Chisenhall really does have one of the prettiest swings in the minors, as well as solid power and defensive skills at third base. He doesn't have the ceiling of most top prospects, but he has one of the higher floors; it's impossible to find a scout who doesn't think he'll be an above-average everyday player at a position the Indians desperately need to fill.

Shin-Soo Choo RF

Born: **7/13/1982** Age: **28**
Bats: **L** Throws: **L** Height: **5' 11"** Weight: **178**
Breakout: **2%** Improve: **43%** Collapse: **0%**
Attrition: **6%** MLB: **96%**

Comparables:
Billy Williams, Sixto Lezcano, Manny Ramirez (75)

YEAR	TEAM	LVL	AGE	PA	R	2B	3B	HR	RBI	BB	SO	SB	CS	AVG_OBP_SLG	TAv	BABIP	BRR	FRAA	WARP
2008	CLE	MLB	25	369	68	28	3	14	66	44	78	4	3	.310/.398/.551	.335	.368	4.2	RF -4, LF -5	2.9
2009	CLE	MLB	26	685	87	38	6	20	86	78	151	21	2	.300/.394/.489	.319	.370	4.5	RF 5, LF -1	5.9
2010	CLE	MLB	27	646	81	31	2	22	90	83	118	22	7	.300/.401/.484	.324	.347	-1.1	RF -5	4.4
2011	*CLE*	*MLB*	*28*	*522*	*71*	*26*	*2*	*16*	*64*	*62*	*105*	*15*	*5*	*.285/.379/.462*	*.295*	*.335*	*0.0*	*RF -2, LF -2*	*2.2*

Choo is truly a wonderful player. He will never win a batting title, but has hit at least .300 in each of the last three seasons. He will never be a classic slugger, but he's going to give you 20-25 home runs every year. He will also draw his share of walks, steal 20 bases, and play a good right field with a cannon for an arm. Great at few things but good at everything, Choo is flying under the radar as one of the better outfielders in baseball, and he won't get too expensive for three more years. His finest achievement in 2010 actually occurred after the season, when he led his home country's team to a tournament win in the Asian Games, with the prize being a waiver from two years of mandatory service in the South Korean military.

Trevor Crowe CF

Born: **11/17/1983** Age: **27**
Bats: **S** Throws: **R** Height: **6' 0"** Weight: **190**
Breakout: **2%** Improve: **24%** Collapse: **6%**
Attrition: **15%** MLB: **74%**

Comparables:
Mark Kotsay, Jeremy Reed, Johnny Groth (81)

YEAR	TEAM	LVL	AGE	PA	R	2B	3B	HR	RBI	BB	SO	SB	CS	AVG_OBP_SLG	TAv	BABIP	BRR	FRAA	WARP
2008	AKR	AA	24	228	44	16	2	4	28	27	29	13	5	.323/.404/.485	.318	.357	5.2	LF 3, CF 2	2.9
2008	BUF	AAA	24	162	24	12	2	5	13	15	43	4	2	.274/.352/.486	.272	.354	0.7	LF -2, CF -2	0.2
2009	COH	AAA	25	217	27	11	1	2	20	30	31	14	7	.297/.401/.400	.271	.344	0.1	RF 0, CF 2	1.1
2009	CLE	MLB	25	202	21	9	3	1	17	11	39	6	0	.235/.272/.333	.224	.280	-1.4	LF -3, CF 4	-0.1
2010	COH	AAA	26	128	21	4	1	1	13	7	19	0	0	.244/.281/.319	.218	.277	0.0	RF 0, LF 2	0.2
2010	CLE	MLB	26	479	47	24	3	2	36	29	73	20	7	.251/.299/.333	.233	.293	0.0	CF 1, LF 5	0.4
2011	*CLE*	*MLB*	*27*	*472*	*52*	*22*	*2*	*6*	*45*	*37*	*80*	*19*	*7*	*.258/.316/.364*	*.241*	*.297*	*-0.4*	*CF 1, LF 2*	*0.4*

Crowe has an impressive minor-league track record, at least for hitting line drives, drawing some walks, and running well, but the bat just hasn't translated to the big leagues, a direct result of his dissipating patience. At 27, he's not going to get better skills-wise, but he could get smarter and turn into a decent bench outfielder. After last season, it will be tough for him to get another opportunity as an everyday player.

Jason Donald INF

Born: **9/4/1984** Age: **26**
Bats: **R** Throws: **R** Height: **6' 1"** Weight: **195**
Breakout: **1%** Improve: **21%** Collapse: **5%**
Attrition: **18%** MLB: **45%**

Comparables:
Matt Antonelli, Elliot Johnson, Xavier Paul (77)

YEAR	TEAM	LVL	AGE	PA	R	2B	3B	HR	RBI	BB	SO	SB	CS	AVG_OBP_SLG	TAv	BABIP	BRR	FRAA	WARP
2008	REA	AA	23	410	55	19	4	14	53	47	86	10	2	.307/.395/.497	.302	.369	-2.4	SS -20	1.3
2009	LEH	AAA	24	225	23	15	1	1	16	14	53	6	0	.236/.302/.332	.224	.306	0.1	SS 6, 3B -1	0.5
2010	COH	AAA	25	159	25	10	2	2	17	21	33	0	0	.277/.409/.423	.263	.350	0.0	2B 2, SS 1	0.8
2010	CLE	MLB	25	325	39	19	3	4	24	22	70	5	1	.253/.308/.378	.260	.314	2.9	SS -1, 2B -1	1.1
2011	*CLE*	*MLB*	*26*	*394*	*43*	*19*	*2*	*7*	*39*	*33*	*91*	*6*	*2*	*.245/.314/.373*	*.245*	*.304*	*0.1*	*SS -2, 2B 0*	*0.5*

When Luis Valbuena did unspeakable things at second base last year, the Indians called on

Donald to fill the gap, and he did, at least in the sense that he wore a glove and sometimes stood between first and second. Acquired from the Phillies in the 2009 Cliff Lee deal, Donald had a fine season at Double-A Reading in 2008, but has done little since, hitting just .253/.339/.371 in two years at Triple-A before getting the call. He's the incumbent second baseman, but he's hardly a solution.

Shelley Duncan LF

Born: **9/29/1979** Age: **31**
Bats: R Throws: R Height: **6' 5"** Weight: **215**
Breakout: **2%** Improve: **25%** Collapse: **5%**
Attrition: **12%** MLB: **67%**
Comparables:
Jason Dubois, Rico Carty, Micah Hoffpauir (69)

YEAR	TEAM	LVL	AGE	PA	R	2B	3B	HR	RBI	BB	SO	SB	CS	AVG_OBP_SLG	TAv	BABIP	BRR	FRAA	WARP
2008	SWB	AAA	28	286	42	16	0	13	48	45	64	6	1	.228/.353/.460	.282	.250	-0.1	RF 2, 1B 2	1.4
2008	NYA	MLB	28	65	7	3	0	1	6	7	13	0	0	.175/.262/.281	.231	.205	0.3	1B 0, RF 0	-0.2
2009	SWB	AAA	29	521	83	30	1	30	99	64	94	2	0	.277/.374/.547	.320	.285	-2.8	RF -8, 1B 1	2.9
2009	NYA	MLB	29	15	1	0	0	0	1	0	5	0	0	.200/.200/.200	.115	.300	-0.3	RF 0	-0.2
2010	COH	AAA	30	164	21	11	0	6	33	17	28	0	0	.301/.384/.500	.279	.336	1.2	RF -4, 1B 0	0.3
2010	CLE	MLB	30	259	29	10	0	11	36	26	76	1	0	.231/.317/.419	.273	.294	-0.5	LF -3, RF -1	0.3
2011	*CLE*	*MLB*	*31*	*447*	*56*	*19*	*0*	*21*	*59*	*50*	*104*	*1*	*0*	*.245/.334/.457*	*.274*	*.275*	*0.0*	*RF -3, LF -1*	*0.6*

Duncan brought his Triple-A slugging services to Cleveland in 2010, and they actually ended up being needed due to injuries and other players stinking up the field. Despite playing just 85 games for the Indians, he finished fifth on the team in home runs. Duncan certainly has power and is a big-league-worthy player against left-handers—his career split is now .198/.283/.357 against right-handers and .263/.335/.488 against left-handers—but he's still a 31-year-old Quad-A type who will never hit for average and offers zero in terms of speed or defense. The Tribe kept him on the 40-man roster, and he'll have a role on the 2011 team. If the Indians have done their winter's work well, it will be in a more limited capacity.

Chris Gimenez C

Born: **12/27/1982** Age: **28**
Bats: R Throws: R Height: **6' 2"** Weight: **215**
Breakout: **2%** Improve: **23%** Collapse: **1%**
Attrition: **9%** MLB: **56%**
Comparables:
John Baker, John Buck, Chris Snyder (79)

YEAR	TEAM	LVL	AGE	PA	R	2B	3B	HR	RBI	BB	SO	SB	CS	AVG_OBP_SLG	TAv	BABIP	BRR	FRAA	WARP
2008	AKR	AA	25	232	47	15	1	6	26	52	33	0	1	.339/.487/.537	.369	.383	0.6	C 1, 1B 1	3.8
2008	BUF	AAA	25	225	22	9	1	3	19	23	60	2	1	.272/.356/.374	.247	.360	-1.0	C 1, 3B 0	0.7
2009	COH	AAA	26	154	20	8	0	6	15	15	40	0	0	.235/.325/.427	.249	.280	-0.9	C 0, LF -3	-0.1
2009	CLE	MLB	26	130	12	2	0	3	7	17	36	1	1	.144/.254/.243	.185	.176	-0.4	1B 0, LF 0	-0.8
2010	COH	AAA	27	219	33	10	0	9	32	20	38	0	0	.276/.338/.464	.261	.296	0.0	RF -3, C 0	0.4
2010	CLE	MLB	27	67	6	5	0	1	8	8	22	0	0	.190/.284/.328	.229	.278	-0.7	C 0, LF 0	0.0
2011	*SEA*	*MLB*	*28*	*342*	*41*	*15*	*0*	*10*	*37*	*40*	*79*	*1*	*0*	*.248/.337/.409*	*.263*	*.296*	*-0.1*	*C 0, RF -1*	*1.0*

While he played 28 big-league games in 2010, Gimenez's opportunity was more an act of desperation than an endorsement of his abilities; once Carlos Santana's knee went kablooey, the club turned to anyone who knew how to wear a catcher's mask. While you could envision Gimenez as an Eli Marrero type, a player who could catch and play both the infield and the outfield corners, he just isn't a good enough hitter to justify actually playing him at those positions. Removed from the 40-man after the season, he'll ply his trade elsewhere in 2011, since just as Ben Geisler in *Barton Fink* always needs Indians, baseball always needs catchers.

Travis Hafner DH

Born: **6/3/1977** Age: **34**
Bats: L Throws: R Height: **6' 3"** Weight: **240**
Breakout: **2%** Improve: **34%** Collapse: **4%**
Attrition: **7%** MLB: **76%**
Comparables:
Erubiel Durazo, Cliff Floyd, Kevin Millar (75)

YEAR	TEAM	LVL	AGE	PA	R	2B	3B	HR	RBI	BB	SO	SB	CS	AVG_OBP_SLG	TAv	BABIP	BRR	FRAA	WARP
2008	CLE	MLB	31	234	22	10	0	5	24	27	55	1	1	.197/.303/.323	.228	.241	-0.6	—	-0.6
2009	CLE	MLB	32	383	46	19	0	16	49	41	67	0	0	.272/.355/.470	.299	.297	-3.5	—	1.5
2010	CLE	MLB	33	462	48	29	0	13	50	51	94	2	1	.278/.375/.450	.308	.332	-0.7	—	2.4
2011	*CLE*	*MLB*	*34*	*476*	*62*	*22*	*0*	*16*	*56*	*60*	*92*	*1*	*1*	*.262/.364/.440*	*.278*	*.298*	*-0.1*	—	*1.2*

Hafner had a bounce-back year in 2010, enjoying his best season since his last really good one in 2006. It's easy to focus on what he can't do: he's powerless against left-handers, and he can't stay healthy, due to the kind of ailments (back, shoulder) that tend to affect hulking sluggers in their 30s. However, he is very good against righties and had an excellent second half once fully healthy. Hafner isn't worth the $26 million he'll be paid over the next two years, not to mention the $2.75 million buyout afterward, but Cleveland is stuck with him, and there's some optimism that he won't be a total bust.

Jason Kipnis 2B

Born: **4/3/1987** Age: **24**
Bats: **L** Throws: **R** Height: **5' 10"** Weight: **175**
Breakout: **1%** Improve: **5%** Collapse: **3%**
Attrition: **8%** MLB: **19%**

Comparables:
Tony Abreu, Danny Richar, Shin-Soo Choo (77)

YEAR	TEAM	LVL	AGE	PA	R	2B	3B	HR	RBI	BB	SO	SB	CS	AVG/OBP/SLG	TAv	BABIP	BRR	FRAA	WARP
2009	MHV	A-	22	149	21	8	3	3	22	19	24	4	3	.297/.389/.477	.327	.340	-1.8	LF 8, CF -2	1.6
2010	KIN	A+	23	227	30	12	3	5	30	23	44	2	3	.300/.392/.465	.303	.355	1.4	2B -3	1.3
2010	AKR	AA	23	348	60	20	5	10	43	31	61	7	1	.311/.391/.502	.313	.358	2.0	2B 4	3.3
2011	*CLE*	*MLB*	*24*	*372*	*44*	*17*	*3*	*10*	*43*	*29*	*77*	*3*	*1*	*.263/.325/.419*	*.260*	*.309*	*-0.1*	*2B 2, LF 1*	*1.1*

When Kipnis was at playing at a suburban Chicago high school, a pitching teammate of his was the better draft prospect. When that pitcher's arm got hurt, scouts avoided the school. After Kipnis put up big numbers at Kentucky and even bigger ones at Arizona State, he was still seen as a little small and lacking in star-level tools, which dropped him to the second round of the 2009 draft. Now, after Kipnis's full-season debut, it's hard to count the number of scouts who are kicking themselves, as he continued to put up big numbers as a pro and is on the verge of the big leagues. A compact athlete who works the count and consistently barrels up balls with enough power for 15-20 home runs annually in the big leagues, Kipnis saw his value skyrocket not only with his hitting skills, but also with a successful conversion from outfielder to second baseman. Scouts think he can be average at the keystone, with a bat that is well above that.

Matt LaPorta 1B

Born: **1/8/1985** Age: **26**
Bats: **R** Throws: **R** Height: **6' 2"** Weight: **210**
Breakout: **3%** Improve: **38%** Collapse: **5%**
Attrition: **23%** MLB: **67%**

Comparables:
Ryan Garko, Jeff Clement, Joey Votto (82)

YEAR	TEAM	LVL	AGE	PA	R	2B	3B	HR	RBI	BB	SO	SB	CS	AVG_OBP_SLG	TAv	BABIP	BRR	FRAA	WARP
2008	AKR	AA	23	97	13	2	0	5	14	11	17	0	0	.259/.381/.459	.288	.266	-0.4	LF 5	0.9
2008	HUN	AA	23	351	53	23	2	20	65	45	63	2	1	.288/.419/.576	.307	.300	-0.6	RF -2, LF 0	2.0
2009	COH	AAA	24	385	61	23	2	17	59	42	56	1	2	.299/.395/.530	.298	.312	-1.4	1B -5, LF -1	1.1
2009	CLE	MLB	24	198	28	13	0	7	21	12	37	2	0	.254/.308/.442	.267	.281	1.1	LF -1, RF 2	0.6
2010	COH	AAA	25	81	7	4	0	5	16	12	10	0	1	.362/.457/.638	.342	.370	-1.4	LF -2, 1B 0	0.6
2010	CLE	MLB	25	425	43	15	1	12	41	46	82	0	0	.221/.306/.362	.246	.250	-2.5	1B -15, LF -3	-2.3
2011	*CLE*	*MLB*	*26*	*512*	*65*	*23*	*1*	*21*	*66*	*53*	*93*	*1*	*0*	*.257/.341/.455*	*.278*	*.275*	*0.0*	*1B -7, LF -2*	*0.5*

LaPorta has now played 162 games in the major leagues, while offering little evidence that he will live up to being the big prize in the CC Sabathia deal of 2008. Exactly why he's not producing is a mystery surrounded by an enigma wrapped in a 694 career OPS sandwich. Time after time, he goes down to Triple-A and bashes (he has hit .310/.400/.548 at Columbus), encouraging the team to think he's figured something out, only to head 150 miles north on I-71 and revert to his previous futile form. LaPorta's résumé and tools are not those of a Quad-A hitter, but he's starting to look like one, and while it's dumb to call a 26-year-old player done, good major-league players have established themselves by now. This is a make-or-break season for LaPorta, and the smart money is on the bad side of the ledger.

Lou Marson C

Born: **6/26/1986** Age: **25**
Bats: **R** Throws: **R** Height: **6' 1"** Weight: **200**
Breakout: **2%** Improve: **19%** Collapse: **7%**
Attrition: **13%** MLB: **43%**

Comparables:
Kurt Suzuki, Rob Johnson, Bill Freehan (81)

YEAR	TEAM	LVL	AGE	PA	R	2B	3B	HR	RBI	BB	SO	SB	CS	AVG_OBP_SLG	TAv	BABIP	BRR	FRAA	WARP
2008	REA	AA	22	393	54	18	0	5	46	68	70	3	3	.314/.435/.416	.299	.384	1.5	C -1	3.3
2008	PHI	MLB	22	4	2	0	0	1	2	0	2	0	0	.500/.500/1.250	.575	1.000	-0.1	C 0	0.1
2009	COH	AAA	23	114	9	5	1	1	9	10	19	1	0	.243/.325/.340	.219	.286	-0.8	C 0	-0.1
2009	LEH	AAA	23	241	29	13	0	1	24	30	40	3	1	.294/.382/.370	.261	.359	-3.1	C 0	0.7
2009	CLE	MLB	23	52	6	6	0	0	4	7	14	0	0	.250/.346/.386	.246	.355	-0.3	C 0	0.1
2009	PHI	MLB	23	20	3	1	0	0	0	3	7	0	0	.235/.350/.294	.221	.400	0.5	C 1	0.1
2010	COH	AAA	24	146	19	7	1	4	14	22	24	0	0	.202/.329/.371	.248	.219	0.0	C 0	0.5
2010	CLE	MLB	24	294	29	15	0	3	22	26	55	8	1	.195/.272/.286	.220	.232	0.5	C -1	0.0
2011	*CLE*	*MLB*	*25*	*421*	*47*	*19*	*1*	*6*	*36*	*50*	*82*	*4*	*1*	*.246/.337/.353*	*.250*	*.295*	*-0.1*	*C -1*	*1.2*

Part of the package received from the Phillies in return for Cliff Lee, Marson began the year as the starting catcher in the big leagues, and the Indians hoped that he'd be what he was in the minors: an athletic yet powerless backstop who could get on base thanks to a line-drive bat and good eye at the plate. Both he and the Tribe knew that it was a temporary gig until Carlos Santana relegated him to a backup role, but now it's not even clear if he can handle that. Marson didn't hit at all (as you can see) and wasn't any better after going down to Triple-A, nor after Santana's knee gave him a second chance. He is young and cheap and still has some potential, so he'll get a third shot in 2011, but a backup role is his ceiling for now.

Andy Marte **3B**

Born: **10/21/1983** Age: **27**
Bats: **R** Throws: **R** Height: **6' 1"** Weight: **185**
Breakout: **1%** Improve: **33%** Collapse: **1%**
Attrition: **9%** MLB: **66%**

Comparables:
Jose Bautista, Jorge Cantu, Casey McGehee (76)

YEAR	TEAM	LVL	AGE	PA	R	2B	3B	HR	RBI	BB	SO	SB	CS	AVG/OBP/SLG	TAv	BABIP	BRR	FRAA	WARP
2008	CLE	MLB	24	257	22	11	1	3	17	14	52	1	2	.221/.261/.315	.210	.262	1.2	3B 7, 1B 0	0.3
2009	COH	AAA	25	326	48	24	1	18	66	22	50	3	0	.327/.368/.593	.325	.339	0.4	3B 10, 1B -1	3.9
2009	CLE	MLB	25	175	20	6	1	6	25	14	30	0	0	.232/.291/.400	.235	.242	-0.3	1B -1	-0.5
2010	CLE	MLB	26	188	18	7	2	5	19	17	35	0	3	.229/.298/.382	.264	.260	0.9	3B 1, 1B 1	0.7
2011	*PIT*	*MLB*	*27*	*391*	*46*	*17*	*1*	*14*	*49*	*29*	*73*	*2*	*1*	*.256/.310/.432*	*.257*	*.280*	*-0.1*	*3B 5, 1B 0*	*1.2*

Once among the top offensive prospects in baseball, Marte was given five years to prove everyone was right about him when he was in the minors, but he's gained far more weight than he has fans in the scouting community. Now slow and stiff, Marte wields a bat too slow to catch up to better fastballs, and he's no longer an adequate third baseman. Released at the end of the year, Marte hooked on with the Pirates early in the free-agency period, the perfect marriage of thwarted hopes and low expectations.

Jayson Nix **INF**

Born: **8/26/1982** Age: **28**
Bats: **R** Throws: **R** Height: **5' 11"** Weight: **185**
Breakout: **0%** Improve: **36%** Collapse: **4%**
Attrition: **9%** MLB: **82%**

Comparables:
Ron Cey, Howard Johnson, Jim Ray Hart (72)

YEAR	TEAM	LVL	AGE	PA	R	2B	3B	HR	RBI	BB	SO	SB	CS	AVG_OBP_SLG	TAv	BABIP	BRR	FRAA	WARP
2008	CSP	AAA	25	298	61	21	2	17	50	27	64	11	5	.303/.376/.591	.312	.332	0.9	2B -2, 3B 0	2.4
2008	COL	MLB	25	65	2	2	0	0	2	7	17	1	0	.125/.231/.161	.163	.175	0.7	2B 3	-0.1
2009	CHA	MLB	26	290	35	11	0	12	32	28	64	10	2	.224/.307/.408	.258	.247	2.4	2B 4, SS -1	1.3
2010	CHA	MLB	27	57	2	1	0	1	5	7	12	0	0	.163/.263/.245	.186	.189	0.1	3B -2, 2B 0	-0.4
2010	CLE	MLB	27	306	29	14	0	13	29	13	75	1	2	.234/.281/.422	.261	.268	0.8	3B 1, 2B -1	0.7
2011	*CLE*	*MLB*	*28*	*351*	*42*	*15*	*0*	*14*	*44*	*29*	*78*	*7*	*3*	*.248/.316/.432*	*.262*	*.280*	*-0.2*	*2B 3, 3B 0*	*1.1*

Hitting just .163 when the White Sox released him in June, Nix caught on with the Indians, who just didn't have enough unproductive infielders at the time, and filled in at second and third base while somehow tying for second on the team with 13 home runs in just 78 games. Nix has always been a solid defender, but those home runs are really the only kind thing to say about him offensively. Having average power but otherwise being a pure out machine just doesn't work in a full-time role. Nix will get a shot at the everyday third-base job in spite of his limitations, holding down the fort until Lonnie Chisenhall is deemed ready.

Cord Phelps **INF**

Born: **1/23/1987** Age: **24**
Bats: **S** Throws: **R** Height: **6' 2"** Weight: **200**
Breakout: **2%** Improve: **10%** Collapse: **4%**
Attrition: **19%** MLB: **27%**

Comparables:
Matt Antonelli, Luis Valbuena, Jeff Fiorentino (78)

YEAR	TEAM	LVL	AGE	PA	R	2B	3B	HR	RBI	BB	SO	SB	CS	AVG_OBP_SLG	TAv	BABIP	BRR	FRAA	WARP
2008	MHV	A-	21	157	24	10	2	2	21	15	22	4	3	.312/.376/.454	.313	.356	0.6	2B -7	0.6
2009	KIN	A+	22	576	72	27	5	4	52	93	97	15	13	.261/.389/.363	.288	.317	-1.3	2B 1	2.9
2010	AKR	AA	23	217	23	8	3	2	23	15	29	1	4	.297/.346/.397	.278	.333	-1.9	2B -7	0.1
2010	COH	AAA	23	308	43	23	4	7	36	31	43	5	2	.316/.396/.506	.302	.352	-3.0	2B -3	1.6
2011	*CLE*	*MLB*	*24*	*421*	*49*	*19*	*3*	*6*	*40*	*42*	*75*	*6*	*3*	*.266/.340/.380*	*.258*	*.312*	*-0.6*	*2B -2*	*0.6*

Selected in the third round of the 2008 draft as one of those polished college types with a low ceiling but some certainty, Phelps became surprisingly uncertain after an uninspiring 2009 season but put it all together last year, splitting time between Double-A and Triple-A and producing at both levels. A line-drive hitter with doubles power and a decent eye, Phelps lacks the pop and athleticism that would make him a star, and the team put even more pressure on his bat by moving him from second base to the hot corner in the Arizona Fall League. He's an upgrade at either position on the big-league incumbents, but not an irreplaceable option himself.

Josh Rodriguez **MI**

Born: **12/18/1984** Age: **26**
Bats: **R** Throws: **R** Height: **6' 0"** Weight: **185**
Breakout: **6%** Improve: **32%** Collapse: **8%**
Attrition: **27%** MLB: **57%**

Comparables:
Craig Stansberry, Shin-Soo Choo, Brian Barden (80)

YEAR	TEAM	LVL	AGE	PA	R	2B	3B	HR	RBI	BB	SO	SB	CS	AVG/OBP/SLG	TAv	BABIP	BRR	FRAA	WARP
2008	AKR	AA	23	656	82	23	12	7	50	81	127	12	6	.242/.331/.362	.263	.293	2.5	SS -3, 2B 5	2.7
2009	AKR	AA	24	164	23	8	0	1	20	25	35	4	3	.314/.427/.394	.319	.408	1.0	2B 7	2.1
2010	AKR	AA	25	78	11	7	0	1	11	11	10	0	0	.318/.410/.476	.307	.339	0.0	3B 0, SS 0	0.4
2010	COH	AAA	25	395	51	26	1	13	54	42	83	0	0	.291/.365/.484	.269	.342	0.0	SS 12, 2B 0	2.9
2011	*PIT*	*MLB*	*26*	*431*	*50*	*19*	*2*	*9*	*43*	*46*	*95*	*6*	*2*	*.254/.332/.383*	*.254*	*.309*	*-0.3*	*SS 3, 2B 2*	*1.4*

A second-round pick in 2006, Rodriguez has had an up-and-down career in terms of both performance and health, but his 2010 campaign represented a career year. Drafted as a shortstop, Rodriguez spent time at six positions. His bat may play best at short, but his holding a job there will take some unlikely defensive improvement, as he's not athletically gifted enough to play the position regularly. Rodriguez was not protected from the Rule 5 draft, and the Pirates took advantage, making him the first overall pick. He will have a good chance of sticking on the bench, given the team's lack of second-line players.

Carlos Santana **C**

Born: **4/8/1986** Age: **25**
Bats: **S** Throws: **R** Height: **5' 11"** Weight: **190**
Breakout: **4%** Improve: **37%** Collapse: **6%**
Attrition: **23%** MLB: **80%**

Comparables:
Jeff Clement, Matthew Brown, Alvin Davis (65)

YEAR	TEAM	LVL	AGE	PA	R	2B	3B	HR	RBI	BB	SO	SB	CS	AVG_OBP_SLG	TAv	BABIP	BRR	FRAA	WARP
2008	KIN	A+	22	126	33	5	1	6	19	20	24	3	0	.352/.452/.591	.360	.408	1.0	C 0	1.9
2008	SBR	A+	22	430	86	34	4	14	96	69	59	7	4	.323/.433/.563	.348	.344	2.4	C 1, RF 0	6.0
2009	AKR	AA	23	560	97	30	2	26	101	95	87	2	1	.290/.420/.536	.329	.301	4.2	C 2	6.3
2010	COH	AAA	24	243	37	14	1	13	51	45	39	6	0	.316/.453/.597	.336	.336	1.8	C 1	3.2
2010	CLE	MLB	24	192	23	13	0	6	22	37	29	3	0	.260/.401/.467	.316	.277	0.6	C 1	1.9
2011	*CLE*	*MLB*	*25*	*522*	*74*	*26*	*1*	*22*	*70*	*81*	*90*	*3*	*1*	*.274/.389/.494*	*.306*	*.295*	*0.0*	*C 0, RF 0*	*4.1*

Santana pulled off a rare double play by successively representing the most exciting and agonizing parts of the Indians' 2010 season. After spending two months proving to the big-league brass that the minor leagues were a complete waste of his time, Santana spent the first month of his Cleveland career looking as if he were also too good for the major-league level before the league caught up to him with a steadier stream of breaking balls. Still, he looked like an excellent Rookie of the Year candidate before August 2, when Red Sox outfielder Ryan Kalish didn't so much collide with Santana as direct a 205-pound guided missile at the young catcher's knee. Obviously, speed was never part of Santana's game, so the team expects a full recovery in time for 2011. It won't be long before he's considered one of the best offensive catchers in the game.

Grady Sizemore **CF**

Born: **8/2/1982** Age: **28**
Bats: **L** Throws: **L** Height: **6' 2"** Weight: **200**
Breakout: **2%** Improve: **55%** Collapse: **0%**
Attrition: **6%** MLB: **100%**

Comparables:
Bernie Williams, Andre Ethier, Reggie Smith (75)

YEAR	TEAM	LVL	AGE	PA	R	2B	3B	HR	RBI	BB	SO	SB	CS	AVG_OBP_SLG	TAv	BABIP	BRR	FRAA	WARP
2008	CLE	MLB	25	745	101	39	5	33	90	98	130	38	5	.268/.375/.502	.310	.290	0.3	CF -6	5.3
2009	CLE	MLB	26	503	73	20	6	18	64	60	92	13	8	.248/.342/.445	.291	.274	-0.2	CF 4	3.2
2010	CLE	MLB	27	140	14	6	2	0	13	9	35	4	2	.211/.271/.289	.211	.287	1.9	CF -6	-0.7
2011	*CLE*	*MLB*	*28*	*577*	*76*	*26*	*4*	*21*	*72*	*71*	*109*	*22*	*7*	*.262/.360/.457*	*.286*	*.294*	*-0.2*	*CF -5*	*2.4*

Once one of the best young players in the game—a player with true face-of-the-franchise potential—Sizemore ended the 2010 season by being most notable for some naked photos that ended up on the Internet. (For the record, our girlfriends were impressed. Also for the record: we have girlfriends.) His miserable 2010 began with a sore back and a swing that looked hampered by 2009's elbow woes. The season came to an early end following a knee injury that was initially labeled a contusion and ended with microfracture surgery, a newer procedure with a limited track record of success. Even as late as November, statements by team brass were extremely cautious, and a 2012 team option for $8.5 million that looked like the bargain of the century two years ago is now up in the air.

Luis Valbuena **2B**

Born: **11/30/1985** Age: **25**
Bats: **L** Throws: **R** Height: **5' 10"** Weight: **200**
Breakout: **6%** Improve: **34%** Collapse: **6%**
Attrition: **20%** MLB: **63%**

Comparables:
Jim Lefebvre, Ian Kinsler, Edgardo Alfonzo (76)

YEAR	TEAM	LVL	AGE	PA	R	2B	3B	HR	RBI	BB	SO	SB	CS	AVG_OBP_SLG	TAv	BABIP	BRR	FRAA	WARP
2008	WTN	AA	22	277	42	12	2	9	40	31	37	8	4	.304/.376/.483	.296	.320	1.1	2B 10, 3B 0	2.7
2008	TAC	AAA	22	246	41	9	0	2	20	28	32	10	4	.302/.374/.373	.285	.337	1.0	2B 0, 3B -1	1.3
2008	SEA	MLB	22	54	6	5	0	0	1	4	11	0	0	.245/.315/.347	.248	.316	1.0	2B -2, SS 0	0.0
2009	COH	AAA	23	95	14	4	2	3	13	16	13	3	3	.321/.432/.539	.330	.349	-2.0	2B -2, SS -1	0.6
2009	CLE	MLB	23	398	52	25	3	10	31	26	83	2	3	.250/.297/.416	.258	.294	0.6	2B -1, SS 2	1.3
2010	COH	AAA	24	118	23	8	1	6	20	19	21	0	0	.313/.424/.604	.338	.333	0.0	SS 1, 3B -2	1.2
2010	CLE	MLB	24	310	20	12	0	2	24	28	61	1	2	.193/.271/.258	.204	.236	-1.2	2B 3, 3B -1	-0.8
2011	*CLE*	*MLB*	*25*	*499*	*58*	*23*	*2*	*11*	*53*	*49*	*91*	*8*	*4*	*.258/.330/.398*	*.258*	*.293*	*-0.6*	*2B 1, SS 0*	*1.2*

In 2009, Valbuena showed some surprising power for second base (though little else), which was enough to give the young player an Opening Day job last season. His response? One of the worst offensive seasons imaginable, and that's only because he finished strong. A 3-for-46 slump in May dropped his average to a bad-hitting-pitcher-esque .134, but the trade of Jhonny Peralta gave him a second chance after a good minor-league stint, and he hit .254 in September. Valbuena is young and has always hit in the minors. It's either him or Jason Donald at the keystone in 2011, a Hobson's choice that will only resolve itself once Jason Kipnis is ready.

Nick Weglarz LF

Born: **12/16/1987** Age: **23**
Bats: L Throws: L Height: **6' 3"** Weight: **240**
Breakout: **2%** Improve: **16%** Collapse: **1%**
Attrition: **13%** MLB: **32%**

Comparables:
Carmelo Martinez, Mike Carp, Billy Butler (70)

YEAR	TEAM	LVL	AGE	PA	R	2B	3B	HR	RBI	BB	SO	SB	CS	AVG_OBP_SLG	TAv	BABIP	BRR	FRAA	WARP
2008	KIN	A+	20	447	65	20	5	10	40	71	78	8	5	.272/.403/.432	.295	.319	2.3	LF 1, RF 0	2.6
2009	AKR	AA	21	418	68	17	2	16	65	75	78	1	3	.227/.385/.431	.303	.245	-0.9	LF 0, RF 0	2.4
2010	AKR	AA	22	161	20	10	0	7	27	22	26	1	0	.285/.391/.511	.321	.302	-0.2	LF 4	1.6
2010	COH	AAA	22	205	29	17	1	6	20	28	43	2	2	.286/.400/.497	.287	.344	-2.2	LF -3, RF 0	0.5
2011	*CLE*	*MLB*	*23*	*410*	*52*	*19*	*1*	*13*	*46*	*56*	*85*	*2*	*1*	*.246/.355/.426*	*.275*	*.282*	*-0.1*	*LF -4, RF 0*	*0.8*

Always a walk machine, Weglarz slugged a career-high .503 in 2010, but he still leaves scouts wanting more. The value of this massive slug of a human being who plays a laughable left field lies entirely in his bat, and while he has plus-plus raw power, he also has just 39 home runs over 1,026 at-bats in the last three years. The low number of at-bats shows that he hasn't been healthy, either, having yet to play more than 106 games in any of those three years. Weglarz still projects as a productive everyday hitter, the kind of guy who fits in the fifth spot in a good lineup, but it's a little disappointing that he's still more projection than reality.

PITCHERS

Fausto Carmona

Born: **12/7/1983** Age: **27**
Bats: R Throws: R Height: **6' 4"** Weight: **190**
Breakout: **10%** Improve: **43%** Collapse: **30%**
Attrition: **10%** MLB: **95%**

Comparables:
Mark Mulder, Jeff Weaver, Gary Lucas (77)

YEAR	TEAM	LVL	AGE	W	L	SV	G	GS	IP	H	HR	BB	SO	EqBB9	EqSO9	GB%	BABIP	WHIP	ERA	FRA	WARP
2008	CLE	MLB	24	8	7	0	22	23	120^{2}	126	7	70	58	5.2	4.3	65%	.294	1.70	5.44	6.02	-0.2
2009	COH	AAA	25	1	3	0	5	5	33	32	5	6	27	1.6	7.4	61%	.273	1.24	3.27	4.47	0.5
2009	CLE	MLB	25	5	12	0	24	24	125^{1}	151	16	70	79	5.0	5.7	56%	.319	1.83	6.25	6.96	-1.3
2010	CLE	MLB	26	13	14	0	33	38	210^{1}	203	17	72	124	3.1	5.3	56%	.283	1.35	3.77	4.32	2.3
2011	*CLE*	*MLB*	*27*	*11*	*10*	*0*	*29*	*29*	*167^{1}*	*170*	*15*	*66*	*101*	*3.6*	*5.4*	*54%*	*.295*	*1.41*	*4.36*	*4.74*	*2.3*

Carmona pitched way over his head in 2007, when he was one of the league's top arms; that kind of level is hard to sustain when you strike out fewer than six batters per nine innings. After struggling with health and control for a two-year period, Carmona may have finally found his level in 2010 as a solid but unspectacular ground-balling innings eater. His velocity is a tick below that of his heyday, but he still gets plenty of sink on the ball, and he has found a more consistent secondary pitch in his slider. He just turned 27, so he can look forward to a performance similar to last year's.

Carlos Carrasco

Born: **3/21/1987** Age: **24**
Bats: R Throws: R Height: **6' 3"** Weight: **220**
Breakout: **14%** Improve: **38%** Collapse: **8%**
Attrition: **16%** MLB: **63%**

Comparables:
Ricky Romero, Derek Holland, Johnny Cueto (72)

YEAR	TEAM	LVL	AGE	W	L	SV	G	GS	IP	H	HR	BB	SO	EqBB9	EqSO9	GB%	BABIP	WHIP	ERA	FRA	WARP
2008	REA	AA	21	7	7	0	20	20	114^{2}	109	13	45	109	3.5	8.6	47%	.308	1.40	4.16	4.66	1.6
2008	LEH	AAA	21	2	2	0	6	6	36^{2}	37	1	13	46	3.2	11.3	49%	.353	1.39	1.72	2.89	1.2
2009	COH	AAA	22	5	1	0	6	7	42^{1}	31	3	7	36	1.5	7.7	40%	.233	0.90	3.19	5.22	0.1
2009	LEH	AAA	22	6	9	0	20	22	114^{2}	118	14	38	112	3.0	8.8	43%	.315	1.42	5.10	5.49	0.1
2009	CLE	MLB	22	0	4	0	5	6	22^{1}	40	6	11	11	4.4	4.4	48%	.405	2.28	8.87	8.79	-0.6
2010	COH	AAA	23	10	6	0	25	31	150^{1}	139	16	46	133	2.8	8.0	49%	.292	1.28	3.47	4.36	3.2
2010	CLE	MLB	23	2	2	0	7	7	44^{2}	47	6	14	38	2.8	7.7	57%	.318	1.39	3.83	4.02	0.7
2011	*CLE*	*MLB*	*24*	*10*	*10*	*0*	*27*	*27*	*161*	*165*	*21*	*66*	*125*	*3.7*	*7.0*	*46%*	*.300*	*1.43*	*4.69*	*5.10*	*1.5*

It's hard to know exactly what happened here. Maybe he saw a hypnotist, maybe he got kicked in the head by a horse, or maybe someone just sat Carrasco down and explained to him that he has all the ability in the world to be a good major-league starter and it sure pays pretty damn well. Or maybe none of that happened and Carrasco somehow figured out how to knuckle down with runners on base, which had been the frustrating bugaboo that defined his career. After a great second-half stretch at Triple-A Columbus, he went 6-for-7 in the quality-start department for the big-league club, and he'll open the year with a rotation spot all but guaranteed. Considering his 92-94 mph fastball, decent breaking ball, and good changeup, there's no reason this can't continue, other than his inability to succeed with the same combination for a while. Guarded optimism would be the best way to approach things.

Joseph Gardner

Born: **3/18/1988** Age: **23**
Bats: **R** Throws: **R** Height: **6' 4"** Weight: **220**
Breakout: **19%** Improve: **51%** Collapse: **9%**
Attrition: **13%** MLB: **77%**

Comparables:
CC Sabathia, Freddy Garcia, Homer Bailey (57)

YEAR	TEAM	LVL	AGE	W	L	SV	G	GS	IP	H	HR	BB	SO	EqBB9	EqSO9	GB%	BABIP	WHIP	ERA	FRA	WARP
2010	LKC	A	22	1	0	0	6	7	25	17	2	11	38	4.0	13.7	72%	.289	1.16	2.88	4.26	0.4
2010	KIN	A+	22	12	6	0	23	30	127^1	90	5	55	107	3.9	7.6	67%	.250	1.29	2.47	4.32	1.7
2011	*CLE*	*MLB*	*23*	*10*	*9*	*0*	*27*	*27*	*139^2*	*125*	*14*	*78*	*107*	*5.0*	*6.9*	*52%*	*.276*	*1.45*	*4.35*	*4.73*	*2.1*

A third-round pick in 2009, Gardner went from being a nice arm to one of the better starting prospects in the system during his pro debut. Gardner's 90-93 mph heavy fastball (one scout called it "a bowling ball") distinguished itself as one of the best sinkers in the minors, generating a ridiculous 6.4-to-1 ground-ball ratio in six starts for Low-A Lake County, and his final total across three levels surpassed three. His slider needs work, as does his control, but he has that one special pitch that could be the ticket to the big leagues on its own.

Justin Germano

Born: **8/6/1982** Age: **28**
Bats: **R** Throws: **R** Height: **6' 1"** Weight: **190**
Breakout: **2%** Improve: **33%** Collapse: **14%**
Attrition: **6%** MLB: **64%**

Comparables:
John Smiley, Willie Collazo, Glen Perkins (75)

YEAR	TEAM	LVL	AGE	W	L	SV	G	GS	IP	H	HR	BB	SO	EqBB9	EqSO9	GB%	BABIP	WHIP	ERA	FRA	WARP
2008	POR	AAA	25	2	9	0	17	17	98	119	12	25	67	2.3	6.2	51%	.323	1.49	5.42	5.61	-0.2
2008	SDN	MLB	25	0	3	0	12	7	43^2	54	8	13	17	2.7	3.5	49%	.297	1.56	5.98	5.90	-0.3
2010	COH	AAA	27	3	2	1	17	6	53^1	49	8	10	37	1.7	6.2	52%	.255	1.13	3.38	5.32	0.4
2010	CLE	MLB	27	0	3	0	23	1	35^1	27	6	8	29	2.0	7.4	42%	.217	1.16	3.31	4.82	0.1
2011	*CLE*	*MLB*	*28*	*7*	*6*	*0*	*47*	*16*	*144*	*154*	*18*	*39*	*82*	*2.4*	*5.1*	*47%*	*.293*	*1.34*	*4.41*	*4.80*	*1.1*

Signed prior to the 2010 season as a journeyman who tried to resurrect his career with a season in Japan, Germano got back to the majors in late July, but the fact that his big-league line was better than his numbers at either Double-A or Triple-A should be a cause for concern. Nevertheless, the Indians kept the faith by allowing him to remain on the 40-man roster after the season. A pure strike thrower, Germano doesn't walk anyone, but in light of his upper-80s fastball and his history of getting hit hard, it's tough to see his strikeout rate as anything but fluky. He's not a sexy-enough name to be picked as a target for 2011 regression, but we'll say it anyway.

Jeanmar Gomez

Born: **10/2/1988** Age: **22**
Bats: **R** Throws: **R** Height: **6' 3"** Weight: **170**
Breakout: **6%** Improve: **10%** Collapse: **1%**
Attrition: **4%** MLB: **13%**

Comparables:
Shairon Martis, Trevor Bell, Rick Jones (71)

YEAR	TEAM	LVL	AGE	W	L	SV	G	GS	IP	H	HR	BB	SO	EqBB9	EqSO9	GB%	BABIP	WHIP	ERA	FRA	WARP
2008	KIN	A+	19	5	9	0	27	29	138^1	154	14	46	110	3.0	7.2	47%	.328	1.53	4.29	4.73	1.5
2009	KIN	A+	20	2	2	0	4	4	24	17	2	5	15	1.9	5.6	63%	.217	0.96	2.63	5.38	0.0
2009	AKR	AA	20	11	4	0	24	25	134^1	129	12	44	117	2.9	7.8	48%	.298	1.31	3.28	4.36	1.6
2010	COH	AAA	21	8	8	0	20	20	116	129	16	42	78	3.3	6.1	45%	.308	1.48	5.12	5.94	0.6
2010	CLE	MLB	21	4	5	0	11	11	57^2	73	7	22	34	3.4	5.3	47%	.330	1.68	4.68	5.38	0.0
2011	*CLE*	*MLB*	*22*	*7*	*10*	*0*	*23*	*23*	*126*	*148*	*19*	*55*	*71*	*3.9*	*5.0*	*46%*	*.311*	*1.61*	*5.69*	*6.18*	*-0.1*

Gomez is better than his numbers, but he was rushed to the big leagues, getting called up when he was the hottest pitcher at Triple-A and a need arose. He'll never be a star, as he's the type of arm whose 90-92 mph fastball and two solid secondary offerings play up thanks to an ability to hit his spots. All he needs to do now is learn how to use those strengths and weaknesses at the upper levels. Gomez can be a back-end starter, but will have to fight for a job this spring. More time at Triple-A might not be the worst thing for him.

Nick Hagadone

Born: **1/1/1986** Age: **25**
Bats: **L** Throws: **L** Height: **6' 5"** Weight: **230**
Breakout: **0%** Improve: **5%** Collapse: **5%**
Attrition: **3%** MLB: **5%**

Comparables:
Victor Garate, Emiliano Fruto, Jose Mijares (82)

YEAR	TEAM	LVL	AGE	W	L	SV	G	GS	IP	H	HR	BB	SO	EqBB9	EqSO9	GB%	BABIP	WHIP	ERA	FRA	WARP
2009	GRN	A	23	0	2	0	10	12	25	13	0	14	32	5.0	11.5	69%	.236	1.24	2.16	3.69	0.9
2010	KIN	A+	24	1	3	0	10	13	37^2	28	2	29	45	6.9	10.8	49%	.286	1.51	2.39	2.46	1.5
2010	AKR	AA	24	2	2	1	19	7	48	44	5	34	44	6.4	8.3	43%	.291	1.65	4.31	5.10	0.2
2011	*CLE*	*MLB*	*25*	*4*	*4*	*0*	*13*	*10*	*38*	*36*	*4*	*28*	*35*	*6.6*	*8.2*	*46%*	*.297*	*1.65*	*4.91*	*5.34*	*0.5*

Hagadone was coming off Tommy John surgery when he headed to Cleveland in the Victor Martinez trade, but as a six-foot-five left-hander with upper-90s heat, Cleveland was willing to assume the risk. In his first full season after the procedure, his velocity went from plus-plus to merely plus, and his control completely disintegrated. Unfortunately, this is what happens when one assumes risk. He has the pure arm strength for a bright future, but 2010 was a major step in the wrong direction.

Frank Herrmann

Born: **5/30/1984** Age: **27**
Bats: L Throws: R Height: **6' 4"** Weight: **220**
Breakout: **4%** Improve: **10%** Collapse: **5%**
Attrition: **7%** MLB: **18%**

Comparables:
Tim Stauffer, Edgar Gonzalez, Doug Mathis (79)

YEAR	TEAM	LVL	AGE	W	L	SV	G	GS	IP	H	HR	BB	SO	EqBB9	EqSO9	GB%	BABIP	WHIP	ERA	FRA	WARP
2008	AKR	AA	24	12	7	0	25	26	144	149	9	37	89	2.3	5.6	34%	.299	1.32	3.81	3.79	3.1
2009	AKR	AA	25	2	1	0	5	5	30^2	27	4	5	12	1.5	3.5	50%	.235	1.04	2.93	3.58	0.6
2009	COH	AAA	25	2	3	2	44	0	76	83	3	13	50	1.5	5.9	37%	.319	1.29	2.96	3.03	1.6
2010	COH	AAA	26	3	0	2	19	0	28^2	15	0	8	22	2.5	6.9	47%	.200	0.80	0.31	2.78	0.6
2010	CLE	MLB	26	0	1	1	40	0	44^2	48	6	9	24	1.8	4.8	37%	.286	1.32	4.03	4.81	0.0
2011	*CLE*	*MLB*	*27*	*5*	*4*	*1*	*55*	*9*	*118^1*	*134*	*14*	*37*	*57*	*2.8*	*4.3*	*40%*	*.300*	*1.45*	*4.81*	*5.22*	*0.0*

After pitching 40 games in 2010, Herrmann now ranks third in big-league appearances among Harvard men—not that it's an impressive list. To move up the list (Walter Clarkson is next, with 78), he's going to have to figure out how to miss more bats. A mid-90s fastball was enough to achieve that goal in the minors, but if he doesn't develop a consistent breaking ball to back it up, big-league hitters could sit on the pitch and torch him. The good news is that if this whole baseball thing doesn't work out, he can, with an economics degree from Harvard, probably get a Wall Street job that pays more than major-league minimum.

David Huff

Born: **8/22/1984** Age: **26**
Bats: L Throws: L Height: **6' 2"** Weight: **215**
Breakout: **19%** Improve: **39%** Collapse: **17%**
Attrition: **22%** MLB: **73%**

Comparables:
Glen Perkins, Larry Dierker, Jason Vargas (77)

YEAR	TEAM	LVL	AGE	W	L	SV	G	GS	IP	H	HR	BB	SO	EqBB9	EqSO9	GB%	BABIP	WHIP	ERA	FRA	WARP
2008	AKR	AA	23	5	1	0	11	10	65^2	44	5	14	62	1.9	8.5	51%	.228	0.90	1.92	2.99	1.9
2008	BUF	AAA	23	6	4	0	16	16	80^2	68	8	15	81	1.7	9.0	53%	.278	1.07	3.01	2.91	3.0
2009	COH	AAA	24	5	1	0	7	7	39^1	35	5	16	32	3.7	7.3	34%	.273	1.30	4.35	4.14	0.8
2009	CLE	MLB	24	11	8	0	23	24	128^1	159	16	41	65	2.9	4.6	39%	.317	1.57	5.61	5.30	0.7
2010	COH	AAA	25	9	2	0	14	14	88^1	94	9	23	62	2.3	6.3	42%	.310	1.35	3.77	3.82	2.5
2010	CLE	MLB	25	2	11	0	15	15	79^2	101	14	34	37	3.8	4.2	38%	.310	1.73	6.21	6.51	-0.9
2011	*CLE*	*MLB*	*26*	*7*	*7*	*0*	*19*	*19*	*108*	*120*	*14*	*37*	*65*	*3.1*	*5.4*	*43%*	*.304*	*1.45*	*4.87*	*5.30*	*0.8*

A Google search comes up with nearly 5,000 pages that feature the name David Huff and the word *crafty*, which is a nice baseball euphemism for guys who can throw strikes from the left side but don't have an out pitch. With an average fastball and no real breaking pitch (his best offering is a changeup), Huff is just that. Between Jeremy Sowers and Huff (a supplemental first-rounder in 2006), the Indians have spent some high draft picks on these types of pitchers, and the team's fans hope the front office has learned its lesson by now.

Corey Kluber

Born: **4/10/1986** Age: **25**
Bats: R Throws: R Height: **6' 4"** Weight: **215**
Breakout: **12%** Improve: **30%** Collapse: **5%**
Attrition: **20%** MLB: **46%**

Comparables:
Billy Buckner, Ricky Romero, P.J. Walters (73)

YEAR	TEAM	LVL	AGE	W	L	SV	G	GS	IP	H	HR	BB	SO	EqBB9	EqSO9	GB%	BABIP	WHIP	ERA	FRA	WARP
2008	FTW	A	22	4	3	0	10	10	56	49	8	13	72	2.1	11.6	38%	.304	1.21	2.89	3.53	1.4
2008	LEL	A+	22	2	5	0	19	17	85^1	93	9	34	75	3.6	7.9	45%	.327	1.51	5.91	6.33	-0.6
2009	LEL	A+	23	7	9	0	19	21	109	110	9	36	124	3.0	10.2	49%	.344	1.39	4.54	5.10	0.1
2009	SAN	AA	23	2	5	0	10	11	48^2	52	6	36	40	6.7	7.4	34%	.317	1.85	5.18	5.46	-0.1
2010	AKR	AA	24	2	2	0	5	5	26^1	38	0	10	21	3.4	7.2	41%	.418	1.90	3.42	1.64	1.2
2010	SAN	AA	24	6	6	0	22	23	122^2	121	7	40	136	2.9	10.0	43%	.342	1.39	3.30	3.64	2.3
2011	*CLE*	*MLB*	*25*	*6*	*9*	*0*	*22*	*22*	*118^2*	*132*	*15*	*59*	*96*	*4.5*	*7.3*	*42%*	*.326*	*1.62*	*5.54*	*6.02*	*0.1*

Received from San Diego in a three-team exchange that sent Jake Westbrook to St. Louis, Kluber allowed 58 baserunners during his first 37 1/3 innings as part of the Cleveland organization, so "got off to a good start" is not exactly the phrase that comes to mind. He's a big, physical left-hander with a low-90s fastball that he uses to set up a decent slider/changeup combination. While that kind of arsenal should lead to some limited big-league value, it's not going to come until he cuts down on the walks.

Jason Knapp

Born: **8/31/1990** Age: **20**
Bats: R Throws: R Height: **6' 5"** Weight: **235**
Breakout: **1%** Improve: **1%** Collapse: **2%**
Attrition: **1%** MLB: **2%**

Comparables:
Edwin Nunez, Clayton Kershaw, Terry Forster (70)

YEAR	TEAM	LVL	AGE	W	L	SV	G	GS	IP	H	HR	BB	SO	EqBB9	EqSO9	GB%	BABIP	WHIP	ERA	FRA	WARP
2008	PHL	Rk	17	3	1	0	7	8	31	26	1	12	38	3.5	11.0	40%	.329	1.32	2.61	3.50	1.3
2009	LWD	A	18	2	7	0	17	21	85^1	63	3	39	111	4.1	11.7	43%	.309	1.34	3.90	4.59	0.6
2010	LKC	A	19	2	0	0	6	6	24^1	16	0	9	41	3.3	15.2	54%	.348	1.11	2.22	2.39	1.0
2011	*CLE*	*MLB*	*20*	*4*	*4*	*0*	*11*	*11*	*50*	*43*	*5*	*32*	*52*	*5.7*	*9.3*	*43%*	*.295*	*1.49*	*4.28*	*4.65*	*1.0*

Knapp was acquired from the Phillies in the Cliff Lee trade, but shoulder problems delayed his 2010 debut much longer than originally expected. The good news is that he was nearly unhittable upon his return, striking out 47 over just 28 1/3 innings. He's similar to Nick Hagadone (but from the right side) and has the strongest arm in the system, sitting in the mid-90s while touching as high as 99 mph. That's about the sum of

Knapp's skills, as he's still far more a thrower than a pitcher. Even though he is only 20 years old with just over 150 innings of pro experience, many scouts have already pegged him as a future reliever. That's not an insult, as he could be closer-worthy.

Aaron Laffey

Born: **4/15/1985** Age: **26**
Bats: **L** Throws: **L** Height: **6' 0"** Weight: **185**
Breakout: **14%** Improve: **46%** Collapse: **19%**
Attrition: **5%** MLB: **90%**
Comparables:
Bob Sadowski, Todd Burns, Pedro Astacio (74)

YEAR	TEAM	LVL	AGE	W	L	SV	G	GS	IP	H	HR	BB	SO	EqBB9	EqSO9	GB%	BABIP	WHIP	ERA	FRA	WARP
2008	BUF	AAA	23	6	2	0	11	12	61^2	72	2	18	47	2.6	6.9	55%	.348	1.49	4.38	4.01	1.3
2008	CLE	MLB	23	5	7	0	16	16	93^2	103	10	31	43	3.0	4.1	52%	.294	1.53	4.23	5.17	0.6
2009	CLE	MLB	24	7	9	1	25	21	121^2	140	9	57	59	4.2	4.4	50%	.318	1.64	4.44	4.73	1.2
2010	COH	AAA	25	0	1	0	13	4	30^1	35	2	18	13	5.3	3.9	46%	.306	1.75	4.45	5.02	0.3
2010	CLE	MLB	25	2	3	0	29	5	55^2	62	1	28	28	4.5	4.5	52%	.316	1.65	4.53	4.87	0.2
2011	*CLE*	*MLB*	*26*	*8*	*8*	*0*	*52*	*20*	*142*	*160*	*12*	*59*	*70*	*3.7*	*4.4*	*49%*	*.310*	*1.54*	*4.91*	*5.33*	*0.6*

The Indians tried Laffey as both a starter and reliever again in 2010, which afforded them another opportunity to confirm that he's not especially good at either. Shoulder problems certainly didn't help his cause. At this point, he's received more chances than he's deserved, as radar-gun readings above 90 are a rarity for him—he tries to survive on a plus slider and changing speeds. Without LOOGY-esque splits, he doesn't have a future in a situational role, either, and he'll be fighting for a job in the spring.

Jensen Lewis

Born: **5/16/1984** Age: **27**
Bats: **R** Throws: **R** Height: **6' 3"** Weight: **195**
Breakout: **13%** Improve: **32%** Collapse: **14%**
Attrition: **20%** MLB: **58%**
Comparables:
Ramon Ramirez, Anibal Sanchez, Guillermo Moscoso (76)

YEAR	TEAM	LVL	AGE	W	L	SV	G	GS	IP	H	HR	BB	SO	EqBB9	EqSO9	GB%	BABIP	WHIP	ERA	FRA	WARP
2008	BUF	AAA	24	1	2	1	11	0	20	16	2	8	18	3.6	8.1	42%	.241	1.25	3.60	5.39	0.0
2008	CLE	MLB	24	0	4	13	51	0	66	68	8	27	52	3.7	7.1	37%	.300	1.52	3.82	3.94	0.7
2009	CLE	MLB	25	2	4	1	47	0	66^1	62	13	29	62	3.9	8.4	39%	.274	1.40	4.75	5.44	-0.2
2010	COH	AAA	26	2	1	2	24	0	30^1	29	2	8	30	2.4	8.9	29%	.321	1.25	2.67	2.63	0.8
2010	CLE	MLB	26	4	2	0	36	0	36^1	28	1	19	29	4.7	7.2	32%	.260	1.29	2.97	3.68	0.5
2011	*CLE*	*MLB*	*27*	*4*	*1*	*2*	*72*	*0*	*94^1*	*88*	*10*	*39*	*83*	*3.7*	*8.0*	*41%*	*.296*	*1.36*	*3.99*	*4.34*	*0.3*

Lewis had some control problems early in the year and then became that guy who is always the lesser name on the transaction sheets. He got called back up when Kerry Wood was dealt to the Yankees, went back down when Asdrubal Cabrera returned, and then got another shot when Mitch Talbot hit the disabled list. He's primarily a fastball/changeup pitcher without a breaking ball, and that's a tough combination unless one of the pitches is really special. If the late Lloyd Bentsen were still around and an Indians fan, he'd tell Lewis, "I knew Trevor Hoffman, and you, sir, are no Trevor Hoffman."

Justin Masterson

Born: **3/22/1985** Age: **26**
Bats: **R** Throws: **R** Height: **6' 6"** Weight: **250**
Breakout: **13%** Improve: **39%** Collapse: **18%**
Attrition: **28%** MLB: **80%**
Comparables:
Dana Eveland, Randy Wells, Garrett Mock (67)

YEAR	TEAM	LVL	AGE	W	L	SV	G	GS	IP	H	HR	BB	SO	EqBB9	EqSO9	GB%	BABIP	WHIP	ERA	FRA	WARP
2008	PME	AA	23	1	3	0	8	9	38^1	37	0	16	37	3.8	8.7	68%	.327	1.46	4.23	4.31	0.7
2008	BOS	MLB	23	6	5	0	36	9	88^1	68	10	40	68	4.1	6.9	55%	.243	1.31	3.16	4.26	1.4
2009	BOS	MLB	24	3	3	0	31	6	72	72	7	25	67	3.1	8.4	53%	.314	1.43	4.25	5.10	0.6
2009	CLE	MLB	24	1	7	0	11	10	57^1	56	5	35	52	5.5	8.2	59%	.315	1.62	4.55	5.10	0.6
2010	CLE	MLB	25	6	13	0	34	32	180	197	14	73	140	3.7	7.0	60%	.325	1.56	4.70	3.71	3.5
2011	*CLE*	*MLB*	*26*	*8*	*6*	*0*	*38*	*17*	*126^2*	*126*	*11*	*53*	*97*	*3.7*	*6.9*	*53%*	*.304*	*1.41*	*4.26*	*4.63*	*1.5*

The Indians hoped that Masterson, one of the keys to the deal that sent Victor Martinez to Boston, would be a quality major-league starter by now, but he lacks that first adjective. Yes, he gets plenty of ground balls, but ground balls alone don't make a pitcher good by default—especially when you play with a team as soft on defense up the middle as Cleveland was last year—just as walks don't automatically make a hitter good. Speaking of walks, Masterson made some progress in that department during the second half of the year, so there's still some hope for his future.

Chris Perez

Born: **7/1/1985** Age: **25**
Bats: **R** Throws: **R** Height: **6' 4"** Weight: **225**
Breakout: **14%** Improve: **22%** Collapse: **11%**
Attrition: **5%** MLB: **43%**
Comparables:
B.J. Ryan, Joel Zumaya, John Rocker (70)

YEAR	TEAM	LVL	AGE	W	L	SV	G	GS	IP	H	HR	BB	SO	EqBB9	EqSO9	GB%	BABIP	WHIP	ERA	FRA	WARP
2008	MEM	AAA	22	1	1	11	25	0	24^1	17	3	12	36	4.4	13.3	48%	.286	1.23	2.96	3.88	0.3
2008	SLN	MLB	22	3	3	7	41	0	41^2	34	5	22	42	4.8	9.1	39%	.271	1.37	3.46	4.08	0.4
2009	CLE	MLB	23	0	1	1	32	0	33^1	24	5	12	38	3.2	10.3	35%	.253	1.17	4.32	5.05	0.1
2009	SLN	MLB	23	1	1	1	29	0	23^2	17	3	15	30	5.7	11.4	37%	.255	1.48	4.18	4.31	0.2
2010	CLE	MLB	24	2	2	23	63	0	63	40	4	28	61	4.0	8.7	37%	.222	1.16	1.71	2.83	1.2
2011	*CLE*	*MLB*	*25*	*3*	*1*	*5*	*55*	*0*	*54^2*	*41*	*5*	*29*	*59*	*4.8*	*9.8*	*42%*	*.274*	*1.29*	*3.46*	*3.76*	*0.6*

One of the few positive developments of the 2010 season was that the Indians' search for a closer of the future culminated in the ascendance of Perez, who allowed just two runs over 27 appearances after the All-Star break while limiting opposing hitters to a .158 batting average. Armed with a darting 94-97 mph fastball and good slider, he has the stuff to continue earning saves, but the next step to star level will come only if he can throw more strikes. It takes considerable effort to generate the stuff he does, and he's not always able to control it. Still, on a team loaded with mediocre fastballs, Perez stands out in a good way.

Rafael Perez
Born: **5/15/1982** Age: **29**
Bats: L Throws: L Height: **6' 3"** Weight: **185**
Breakout: **15%** Improve: **37%** Collapse: **17%**
Attrition: **10%** MLB: **63%**
Comparables:
Ehren Wassermann, Lindy McDaniel, Jeff Robinson (74)

YEAR	TEAM	LVL	AGE	W	L	SV	G	GS	IP	H	HR	BB	SO	EqBB9	EqSO9	GB%	BABIP	WHIP	ERA	FRA	WARP
2008	CLE	MLB	26	4	4	2	73	0	76^{1}	67	8	23	86	2.7	10.1	58%	.304	1.21	3.42	3.66	1.2
2009	COH	AAA	27	1	0	3	16	0	21^{2}	23	0	5	23	2.1	9.6	56%	.371	1.34	0.83	0.78	1.1
2009	CLE	MLB	27	4	3	0	54	0	48	66	5	25	32	4.7	6.0	51%	.368	1.94	7.13	5.56	-0.2
2010	CLE	MLB	28	6	1	0	70	0	61	72	3	26	36	3.8	5.3	59%	.332	1.61	3.25	3.33	1.1
2011	*CLE*	*MLB*	*29*	*4*	*2*	*1*	*85*	*0*	*83*	*85*	*7*	*31*	*65*	*3.4*	*7.0*	*50%*	*.314*	*1.40*	*4.09*	*4.44*	*0.2*

In 2008, Perez struck out 10.1 batters per nine innings; by 2010, that mark had dropped to 5.3. Stuff is down, right? Wrong. His average fastball was actually half a tick *faster* than it was in 2008, as was his plus slider. The problem may be an overreliance on that slider: two years ago, fastballs constituted half his pitches, whereas in 2010, they accounted for just over one-third. He leaned on his breaking pitch so much last year that hitters knew it was coming. The worst aspect of Perez's struggles is that he's not even able to retire same-side hitters: over the last two years, left-handers have hit .352/.413/.474. Right-handers have hit .286/.365/.394, which isn't helpful, either. Given those splits, it's hard to think of a good reason to bring Perez into a game unless it's to carry the white flag in from the bullpen.

Zach Putnam
Born: **7/3/1987** Age: **23**
Bats: R Throws: R Height: **6' 2"** Weight: **225**
Breakout: **7%** Improve: **4%** Collapse: **8%**
Attrition: **2%** MLB: **9%**
Comparables:
Britt Burns, Michael Bowden, Steve Woodard (71)

YEAR	TEAM	LVL	AGE	W	L	SV	G	GS	IP	H	HR	BB	SO	EqBB9	EqSO9	GB%	BABIP	WHIP	ERA	FRA	WARP
2009	KIN	A+	21	2	0	0	5	5	24	22	1	5	23	1.9	8.6	54%	.313	1.13	4.13	5.57	0.0
2009	AKR	AA	21	5	2	2	36	0	61	61	2	18	60	2.7	8.9	57%	.332	1.31	3.84	4.42	0.2
2010	AKR	AA	22	3	1	3	20	8	51^{1}	58	2	9	41	1.6	7.2	46%	.339	1.31	3.86	3.88	0.8
2010	COH	AAA	22	1	1	0	21	0	28^{1}	21	2	7	29	2.2	9.2	46%	.257	0.99	2.86	4.58	0.2
2011	*CLE*	*MLB*	*23*	*3*	*2*	*0*	*28*	*5*	*56*	*60*	*5*	*19*	*42*	*3.0*	*6.7*	*47%*	*.314*	*1.39*	*4.19*	*4.55*	*0.5*

When Putnam was a high-school star in Michigan, he was generally seen as one of the top players in the country. His stock slipped after three years at his home state's university, and while he'll never be a star, he should at least provide some relief help. His 92-94 mph fastball played better out of the pen, and he pounds the strike zone with it before throwing hitters off-balance with an average slider and an impressive split/change that produces some ugly swings. Putnam's ceiling is that of a seventh- or eighth-inning arm, but he's close to being ready.

Tony Sipp
Born: **7/12/1983** Age: **27**
Bats: L Throws: L Height: **6' 0"** Weight: **190**
Breakout: **19%** Improve: **38%** Collapse: **19%**
Attrition: **7%** MLB: **74%**
Comparables:
John Wetteland, Bill Caudill, Don Carman (70)

YEAR	TEAM	LVL	AGE	W	L	SV	G	GS	IP	H	HR	BB	SO	EqBB9	EqSO9	GB%	BABIP	WHIP	ERA	FRA	WARP
2008	AKR	AA	24	0	3	1	20	0	26	24	4	9	37	3.1	12.8	43%	.339	1.27	3.46	3.20	0.6
2009	CLE	MLB	25	2	0	0	46	0	40	27	5	25	48	5.6	10.8	38%	.244	1.30	2.93	3.91	0.6
2010	CLE	MLB	26	2	2	1	70	0	63	48	12	39	69	5.6	9.9	33%	.250	1.41	4.14	5.41	-0.5
2011	*CLE*	*MLB*	*27*	*3*	*1*	*0*	*51*	*0*	*54*	*46*	*7*	*30*	*62*	*4.8*	*10.2*	*42%*	*.295*	*1.38*	*3.98*	*4.33*	*0.2*

Now well removed from Tommy John surgery, Sipp settled into the role of power southpaw reliever and got better as the season wore on, posting a 2.81 ERA after the All-Star break with greatly reduced hit and walk rates. Equipped with a 91-94 mph fastball, Sipp has above-average velocity for a lefty, as well as a sharp slider, and if he can stay healthy and find a way to cope with the fly-ball tendencies that led to 12 home runs in 63 innings last year, he could last another decade or more.

Joe Smith
Born: **3/22/1984** Age: **27**
Bats: R Throws: R Height: **6' 2"** Weight: **205**
Breakout: **15%** Improve: **31%** Collapse: **31%**
Attrition: **10%** MLB: **73%**
Comparables:
Bob Howry, Gregg Olson, Doug Henry (77)

YEAR	TEAM	LVL	AGE	W	L	SV	G	GS	IP	H	HR	BB	SO	EqBB9	EqSO9	GB%	BABIP	WHIP	ERA	FRA	WARP
2008	NYN	MLB	24	6	3	0	82	0	63^{1}	51	4	31	52	4.4	7.4	64%	.261	1.36	3.55	4.76	0.2
2009	CLE	MLB	25	0	0	0	37	0	34	30	4	13	30	3.4	7.9	56%	.274	1.26	3.44	5.10	0.0
2010	COH	AAA	26	2	1	2	20	0	23	17	0	10	19	3.9	7.4	64%	.266	1.17	1.96	4.79	0.1
2010	CLE	MLB	26	2	2	0	53	0	40	30	4	24	32	5.4	7.2	56%	.239	1.38	3.83	4.99	-0.1
2011	*CLE*	*MLB*	*27*	*3*	*1*	*0*	*59*	*0*	*50^{2}*	*46*	*4*	*25*	*42*	*4.4*	*7.4*	*51%*	*.290*	*1.40*	*3.93*	*4.27*	*0.2*

If you are going to have a lot of mediocre fastballs in your bullpen, you might as well have one that's thrown side-arm. That's Joe Smith in a nutshell, but unlike many sidewinders, Smith has control problems, with a career walk rate of just under one for every two innings pitched. Even when he's struggling to throw strikes, right-handers can't touch him—they posted a .160/.264/.274 line against him in 2010—so if you pick his spots right, he's usable.

Bryce Stowell

Born: **9/23/1986** Age: **24**
Bats: R Throws: R Height: **6' 2"** Weight: **205**
Breakout: **9%** Improve: **19%** Collapse: **8%**
Attrition: **11%** MLB: **37%**

Comparables:
Scott Elbert, Antonio Bastardo, Daniel Bard (68)

YEAR	TEAM	LVL	AGE	W	L	SV	G	GS	IP	H	HR	BB	SO	EqBB9	EqSO9	GB%	BABIP	WHIP	ERA	FRA	WARP
2009	KIN	A+	22	4	6	0	19	8	61	64	6	34	62	5.0	9.1	40%	.337	1.66	5.02	5.09	0.1
2010	KIN	A+	23	1	0	0	11	0	25^{1}	16	2	8	41	2.8	14.6	49%	.326	0.95	1.42	2.07	0.8
2010	AKR	AA	23	0	0	6	14	1	22^{1}	15	0	11	33	4.4	13.3	48%	.313	1.21	0.00	-0.53	1.4
2011	*CLE*	*MLB*	*24*	*3*	*2*	*0*	*33*	*3*	*66^{1}*	*57*	*7*	*40*	*73*	*5.4*	*9.9*	*44%*	*.304*	*1.47*	*4.21*	*4.57*	*0.3*

A nondescript 22nd-round pick in 2009, Stowell suddenly put himself on the map by pitching across three levels and striking out nearly 14 per nine in the process. Working solely as a reliever led to a velocity jump; his 94-97 mph fastball is a big-time offering, and his above-average slider gives him a second plus pitch. Strangely, left-handed hitters can't touch Stowell, going 16-for-107 (.150) with 52 strikeouts against him, which makes him more valuable. He's more than just a sleeper and could make an impact by midseason.

Mitch Talbot

Born: **10/17/1983** Age: **27**
Bats: R Throws: R Height: **6' 2"** Weight: **200**
Breakout: **22%** Improve: **51%** Collapse: **12%**
Attrition: **22%** MLB: **74%**

Comparables:
Mike Ekstrom, Dusty Hughes, Matt Albers (75)

YEAR	TEAM	LVL	AGE	W	L	SV	G	GS	IP	H	HR	BB	SO	EqBB9	EqSO9	GB%	BABIP	WHIP	ERA	FRA	WARP
2008	DUR	AAA	24	13	10	0	30	31	171	177	9	39	154	2.1	8.1	55%	.326	1.33	3.79	4.41	3.3
2008	TBA	MLB	24	0	0	0	3	1	9^{2}	16	3	11	5	10.2	4.7	38%	.382	2.90	11.17	9.49	-0.3
2009	DUR	AAA	25	4	5	0	12	15	60^{2}	76	3	22	45	3.3	6.7	49%	.365	1.65	4.15	4.19	1.1
2010	CLE	MLB	26	10	13	0	28	31	159^{1}	169	13	68	88	3.8	5.0	49%	.301	1.54	4.41	4.88	1.0
2011	*CLE*	*MLB*	*27*	*10*	*10*	*0*	*27*	*27*	*146*	*159*	*13*	*58*	*98*	*3.5*	*6.1*	*48%*	*.314*	*1.48*	*4.68*	*5.09*	*1.6*

Acquired from the Rays for Kelly Shoppach, Talbot is, in many ways, the ultimate generic right-hander. He has a 90-92 mph fastball that he can sink or cut, average secondary pitches in a slider and changeup, and average command and control. The problem is that when he needs that one pitch to retire a hitter, it's just not in him. With these types of pitchers, you hope for a quality start that can keep you in the game, but Talbot delivered that just 11 times in 28 attempts last year. He's likely to be the fourth starter to open the season, but only because the Indians don't necessarily have a better option at this time.

Jess Todd

Born: **4/20/1986** Age: **25**
Bats: R Throws: R Height: **5' 11"** Weight: **210**
Breakout: **5%** Improve: **18%** Collapse: **10%**
Attrition: **10%** MLB: **38%**

Comparables:
Kris Medlen, Antonio Bastardo, Danys Baez (64)

YEAR	TEAM	LVL	AGE	W	L	SV	G	GS	IP	H	HR	BB	SO	EqBB9	EqSO9	GB%	BABIP	WHIP	ERA	FRA	WARP
2008	PMB	A+	22	3	0	1	7	6	27^{1}	18	0	7	35	2.3	11.5	52%	.277	0.95	1.65	1.71	1.2
2008	SFD	AA	22	4	5	0	17	20	103	79	12	24	81	2.1	7.1	53%	.244	1.13	2.97	4.75	1.1
2008	MEM	AAA	22	1	1	0	4	4	22^{2}	19	4	11	20	4.4	7.9	45%	.250	1.37	3.97	5.43	0.2
2009	MEM	AAA	23	4	2	24	41	0	49	39	3	13	59	2.4	10.8	46%	.290	1.06	2.20	2.09	1.4
2009	CLE	MLB	23	0	1	0	19	0	20^{2}	31	3	7	18	3.0	7.8	34%	.394	1.84	7.40	5.46	-0.1
2009	SLN	MLB	23	0	0	0	1	0	1^{2}	3	1	2	2	10.8	10.8	67%	.400	3.00	10.80	6.75	0.0
2010	COH	AAA	24	4	2	4	46	0	51	48	6	18	56	3.2	9.9	44%	.304	1.35	3.00	3.29	1.0
2010	CLE	MLB	24	0	0	0	5	0	6	9	0	3	9	4.5	13.5	39%	.500	2.00	7.50	4.46	0.0
2011	*CLE*	*MLB*	*25*	*4*	*3*	*2*	*47*	*5*	*82^{1}*	*79*	*10*	*30*	*74*	*3.3*	*8.1*	*46%*	*.300*	*1.33*	*4.04*	*4.39*	*0.7*

Todd was packaged with Chris Perez in the 2009 Mark DeRosa deal and was expected to be used in the big leagues as much as his trade companion. Instead, he spent the entire year at Triple-A with the exception of a 10-day big-league stint in July. While his final tally for Columbus looks good, it's the result of consistent inconsistency. Case in point: he had a 0.00 ERA in July followed by a 6.75 mark in August. The fastball of this short and stocky hurler is solid-average, but his slider is a true out pitch—when he can control it. He'll compete for a bullpen job in the spring, and let's face it, the competition for the last few spots isn't exactly fierce.

Josh Tomlin

Born: **10/19/1984** Age: **26**
Bats: R Throws: R Height: **6' 1"** Weight: **195**
Breakout: **12%** Improve: **36%** Collapse: **10%**
Attrition: **16%** MLB: **71%**

Comparables:
Glen Perkins, Carlos Rosa, Bill Gullickson (66)

YEAR	TEAM	LVL	AGE	W	L	SV	G	GS	IP	H	HR	BB	SO	EqBB9	EqSO9	GB%	BABIP	WHIP	ERA	FRA	WARP
2008	KIN	A+	23	9	5	3	40	10	102^{2}	82	10	16	109	1.4	9.6	43%	.280	1.02	2.72	3.29	2.4
2009	AKR	AA	24	16	9	0	28	29	159	157	22	27	140	1.5	7.9	38%	.297	1.20	3.85	4.71	1.1
2010	COH	AAA	25	8	4	0	20	17	107^{1}	83	11	33	80	2.8	6.7	39%	.238	1.10	2.68	3.42	3.5
2010	CLE	MLB	25	6	4	0	12	12	73	72	10	19	43	2.3	5.3	32%	.274	1.29	4.56	4.80	0.4
2011	*CLE*	*MLB*	*26*	*7*	*7*	*1*	*28*	*18*	*124*	*128*	*19*	*39*	*82*	*2.8*	*5.9*	*40%*	*.286*	*1.34*	*4.47*	*4.86*	*1.3*

Called up in late July, Tomlin out-dueled CC Sabathia in his pro debut by allowing just one run over seven innings, and he threw a complete-game four-hitter at the end of the season against the Royals. In between those two highlights was a ton of mediocrity. With three average pitches, he's a younger version of Mitch Talbot with better control, so that's a minor upgrade. Rotations can't be filled with impact arms, and teams need guys like Tomlin, but they don't want to depend on them.

Alex White

Born: **8/29/1988** Age: **22**
Bats: R Throws: R Height: **6' 3"** Weight: **200**
Breakout: **16%** Improve: **40%** Collapse: **8%**
Attrition: **9%** MLB: **65%**

Comparables:
Dontrelle Willis, Bill Parsons, Matt Morris (60)

YEAR	TEAM	LVL	AGE	W	L	SV	G	GS	IP	H	HR	BB	SO	EqBB9	EqSO9	GB%	BABIP	WHIP	ERA	FRA	WARP
2010	KIN	A+	21	2	3	0	8	10	44	32	4	19	41	3.9	8.4	56%	.237	1.16	2.86	4.73	0.4
2010	AKR	AA	21	7	7	0	18	17	106^{2}	91	8	27	76	2.3	6.4	58%	.255	1.13	2.28	4.69	0.8
2011	*CLE*	*MLB*	*22*	*9*	*9*	*0*	*25*	*25*	*143*	*149*	*17*	*57*	*90*	*3.6*	*5.6*	*49%*	*.292*	*1.43*	*4.51*	*4.90*	*1.7*

The Indians' top pick in 2009, White reached Double-A in his full-season debut and pitched well there, but scouts' opinions are still mixed as to his upside and his future role. White is a unique pitcher who primarily throws a fastball and a split-fingered fastball. Both are plus pitches, with the pure heater scraping 94 mph and the split adding plenty of confusing tumble, but with no dependable third pitch (he's working on a slider) and no horizontal aspect to his game, he may find his role as a future late-inning reliever as opposed to a successful starter. White will remain in the rotation until the results say otherwise, and he could even reach the big leagues late this year.

LINEOUTS

HITTERS

PLAYER	TEAM	LVL	AGE	PA	R	2B	3B	HR	RBI	BB	SO	SB-CS	AVG/OBP/SLG	TAv	BABIP	BRR	FRAA	WARP
C L. Carlin#	COH	AAA	29	73	14	5	0	4	11	12	17	0-0	.271/.384/.559	.305	.300	-0.2	C 0	0.6
	IND	AAA	29	230	23	8	1	2	23	27	49	5-2	.239/.335/.318	.220	.303	-1.0	C -1, RF 0	-0.1
	CLE	MLB	29	16	4	0	0	2	3	2	5	0-0	.357/.438/.786	.434	.429	0.2	C 0	0.4
OF E. Carrera*	COH	AAA	23	222	24	8	4	2	20	18	37	14-3	.287/.333/.401	.254	.321	-3.2	CF 10	1.2
	TAC	AAA	23	240	20	6	2	0	18	20	32	9-5	.268/.333/.315	.236	.303	-1.9	CF 2, LF -1	-0.1
C C. Chen	LKC	A	21	237	28	21	3	6	39	17	38	1-1	.312/.371/.518	.328	.352	-1.0	C 0	2.1
	KIN	A+	21	229	31	18	1	6	32	41	41	4-1	.315/.445/.522	.334	.369	1.6	C -1	2.6
OF D. Cid	LKC	A	20	613	80	16	2	3	39	37	148	38-7	.247/.305/.298	.227	.320	0.3	CF 0, LF 2	-0.2
OF J. Constanza#	COH	AAA	26	489	72	12	8	1	35	38	59	0-0	.316/.362/.386	.255	.353	0.0	RF -4, CF -4	0.1
3B J. Goedert	AKR	AA	25	184	26	14	0	7	32	16	35	0-0	.325/.386/.540	.333	.365	0.0	3B 1, LF -1	1.7
	COH	AAA	25	395	59	26	1	22	56	40	79	0-0	.269/.354/.535	.276	.287	0.0	3B 3	2.1
2B M. Grudzielanek	CLE	MLB	40	119	10	0	0	0	11	8	10	2-0	.273/.328/.273	.232	.300	-0.4	2B 0	-0.1
OF J. Henry*	KIN	A+	22	189	31	4	0	0	13	30	26	14-2	.342/.444/.367	.318	.406	5.2	CF -3	1.9
	AKR	AA	22	337	45	8	4	0	16	46	59	15-4	.300/.392/.355	.283	.371	0.5	CF -1	1.7
INF W. Hodges	COH	AAA	25	567	71	29	3	18	70	33	105	2-0	.272/.312/.442	.244	.304	-2.2	1B -2	-0.9
1B M. McBride	AKR	AA	25	400	53	25	1	17	63	30	62	0-2	.283/.350/.499	.299	.296	1.5	RF 3, 1B 1	2.5
	COH	AAA	25	130	17	6	0	4	11	5	19	0-0	.262/.285/.410	.238	.275	-1.5	1B 0, LF 4	0.1
1B B. Mills*	AKR	AA	23	473	55	26	1	10	72	42	71	0-0	.241/.315/.377	.254	.266	0.0	1B -1	0.0
C M. Redmond	CLE	MLB	39	68	7	4	0	0	5	2	10	0-0	.206/.235/.270	.189	.236	0.3	C 0	-0.2
SS D. Sutton#	COH	AAA	27	137	11	9	0	2	18	19	26	4-0	.307/.402/.439	.280	.367	-0.5	LF 2, 2B -1	0.4
	LOU	AAA	27	311	34	16	1	3	27	41	70	4-3	.265/.363/.369	.271	.335	0.1	1B 0, LF -2	0.5
	CIN	MLB	27	3	1	0	0	1	4	0	1	0-0	.667/.667/1.667	.770	1.000	0.0	SS 0, 2B 0	0.2
	CLE	MLB	27	39	4	1	0	1	4	3	12	0-0	.222/.282/.333	.213	.304	0.1	SS 0, 2B 2	0.2

Proving that the ability to catch can keep you around for a long time, **Luke Carlin** got into six big-league games in 2010 and was quickly re-signed to handle the staff at Columbus. Outfielder **Ezequiel Carrera** has speed and some hitting ability, but doesn't walk, doesn't hit for power, and . . . bah, you know the type. Taiwanese import **Chun-Hsiu Chen** showed impressive hitting skills during his full-season debut, but scouts question his ability to stay behind the plate. Outfielder **Delvi Cid** was caught stealing 16 times in 2009, and swiped only 33 bags. Last season, he was again caught stealing 16 times, but led the minor leagues with 71 successful attempts, so he seems to be getting the hang of that baserunning thing. With that, we're done saying nice things about him. ⚾ **Constanza, Jose**: See *Carrera, Ezequiel.* ⚾ An unathletic third baseman who makes up for his defense by providing power and patience, **Jared Goedert** might have a limited big-league career that would allow him to become one of the best all-time players whose last name almost rhymes with "yogurt." ⚾ Infielder **Mark Grudzielanek**'s comeback lasted 110 at-bats without an extra-base hit before he injured a hamstring and got released. ⚾ **Jordan Henry** has impact speed, some on-base abilities, and as much power as New York City (during the great blackout of 1979). ⚾ A second-round pick in 2006, **Wes Hodges** can hit a little bit, but a little bit isn't enough when you are a sloppy-bodied first baseman. ⚾ When **Matt McBride** was an offense-oriented catcher, he was an interesting prospect. As a first baseman, not so much. ⚾ Former first-round pick **Beau Mills** put up Babe Ruth-ian numbers at Lewis and Clark College, but he can't find the Sacagawea he needs to guide him to the big leagues and interpret breaking balls. ⚾ Catcher **Mike Redmond** did nothing of note in his 22 major-league games. The Blue Jays signed him after the season—not to play, but to be their manager at Low-A Lansing. ⚾ Infielder **Drew Sutton** is a nice little utilityman who can play every position, but he can't hit. He'll try to hook on with Boston this spring. ⚾ A late first-round pick in 2009 who didn't come to terms with the Rays, **LeVon Washington** hoped that a year in junior college would increase his draft value after being hurt during his senior year at high school; the gamble paid off in first-round money despite his being a second-round pick. Washington has plus-plus speed, the ability to stay in center, and some power potential, but he's rarely played up to his ability. He could be the top prospect in the system a year from now, or we could be writing about what a disaster his full-season debut was. ⚾ Cleveland's 2010 third-round pick, **Tony Wolters**, is one of those players who won't impress with his size or athleticism, but scouts love his bat and defensive fundamentals.

PITCHERS

PLAYER	TEAM	LVL	AGE	W	L	SV	IP	H	HR	BB	SO	EqBB9	EqSO9	GB%	BABIP	WHIP	ERA	FRA	WARP
H. Ambriz	CLE	MLB	26	0	2	0	48^{1}	68	10	17	37	3.2	6.9	43%	.365	1.78	5.59	5.01	-0.1
J. Flores	LKC	A	21	1	2	6	49^{1}	40	1	11	63	2.0	11.5	41%	.328	1.03	2.55	2.45	1.3
J. Judy	COH	AAA	24	3	1	2	49^{2}	50	5	16	57	2.9	10.3	32%	.338	1.33	2.72	3.25	0.8
Z. McAllister	COH	AAA	22	2	2	0	29^{2}	31	4	8	20	2.4	6.1	36%	.287	1.35	3.94	5.41	0.6
—	SWB	AAA	22	8	10	0	132^{2}	165	20	38	88	2.6	6.0	40%	.331	1.58	4.88	6.34	0.1
V. Pestano	COH	AAA	25	1	2	15	50^{1}	37	2	15	67	2.7	12.0	54%	.297	1.05	1.61	3.02	1.1
—	CLE	MLB	25	0	0	1	5	4	0	5	8	9.0	14.4	30%	.400	1.80	3.60	2.39	0.1
D. Pomeranz	TUL	AA	25	1	6	18	49	57	5	20	53	3.7	9.7	46%	.361	1.59	3.67	3.73	0.6
H. Rondon	COH	AAA	22	1	3	0	31^{2}	48	12	10	33	2.8	9.4	36%	.379	1.89	8.53	8.42	-0.5
G. Soto*	LKC	A	19	3	3	0	42^{2}	29	6	20	48	4.2	10.1	51%	.242	1.24	3.59	5.20	0.2
—	WMI	A	19	6	6	0	82^{2}	75	2	25	76	2.7	8.3	61%	.316	1.28	2.50	2.86	2.7
J. Sowers*	COH	AAA	27	2	6	0	52^{1}	55	2	18	29	3.1	5.0	52%	.293	1.41	5.85	5.82	-0.1

Hector Ambriz was drafted out of college as one of those low-ceiling/high-reliability control pitchers. Rule 5'd to the Indians, he gave up an obscene number of home runs in middle relief, then went down for Tommy John surgery in September. ⚾ The Mariners lifted Low-A reliever **Jose Flores** from the Indians in the Rule 5 draft; given that he's one of four prospects with that name currently making their way through the minors, it's entirely possible that Seattle was looking for a different guy. This one has above-average velocity and command, but no secondary stuff to speak of. ⚾ Another part of a crowded bullpen picture, **Josh Judy** has a plus fastball/breaking-ball combination and is one of any number of relievers who are nearly big-league ready. ⚾ A former Yankee who came over in the Austin Kearns deal, **Zach McAllister** always makes scouts wonder where and when his lack of stuff would catch up with him. The answers are Triple-A and 2010, respectively. ⚾ Righty reliever **Vinny Pestano** has above-average velocity and command, and he could get back to the big leagues in 2011. ⚾ With the fifth overall pick in a 2010 draft, the Indians took **Drew Pomeranz**, who was considered the best college pitcher in the draft—a six-foot-five, 240-pound frame with mid-90s heat and a plus power curveball are unusual qualities in a lefty. Caveats: Pomeranz walked nine over three innings in his biggest game of the spring; two years from now, he could still be struggling to find the plate at Double-A. ⚾ Once one of the brighter young arms in the system, **Hector Rondon** suffered through an ineffective and injury-plagued 2010. ⚾ A southpaw who arrived from Detroit in the Jhonny Peralta trade, **Giovanni Soto** is a six-foot-three, 155-pound stick figure with good control and a breaking ball who could become a prospect if he adds weight and the corresponding velocity. ⚾ A perpetual disappointment since being the sixth overall pick in the 2004 draft, **Jeremy Sowers** converted to the bullpen in 2010, but he never got a big-league call—and never deserved one, either.

MANAGER: MANNY ACTA

YEAR	TEAM	W-L	Pythag +/-	Avg PC	100+ P	120+ P	QS	BQS	REL	REL w Zero R	IBB	Subs	PH	PH Avg	PH HR	SB2	CS2	SB3	CS3	SAC Att	SAC %	POS SAC	Squeeze	Swing	In Play
2009	WAS	26-61	-7	93.3	21	0	32	3	280	152	26	29	145	.215	2	31	15	5	2	48	64.6%	10	0	78	65
2010	CLE	69-93	0	96.8	77	0	69	4	468	305	36	47	79	.171	1	80	29	11	4	50	72.0%	34	3	136	107

You have to feel for Manny Acta, still having to slum it in the second division four years into his career. Still, better to reign in Cleveland than serve in Washington; the former is at least perceptibly building, while feckless ownership—the special curse of Washington teams—may doom the latter to perennial status as an also-ran. Acta is a quiet strategist; the only notable black ink on his record results from his having led two leagues in losses, making him a kind of Anti–Sparky Anderson. The major change in his tactics upon reaching Cleveland was an embrace of the hit and run, which had been largely absent in the District. What we don't know, and may never know, is if Acta will be more of an activist once he has better tools at his disposal, or if he will remain content to sit back and let 'em play.

Colorado Rockies

The next several seasons represent a crossroads for the Colorado Rockies. With three young potential superstars entering their primes together, the Rockies have an opportunity to become a perennial contender in the National League for the first time in franchise history. However, to realize that potential, they need to be diligent. That means avoiding replacement-level players throughout their lineup and seizing every opportunity to upgrade at positions that are flagging relative to league-wide standards. Because they are a midmarket team, the Rockies need to do that while also staying within budget and allowing in-house prospects to develop and earn major-league opportunities.

These challenges are not unique to Colorado, but the opportunity is unique in its history. The Rockies have had great hitters before, and they've had effective pitchers before, but never have they had a dominant ace in his prime, never mind at the same time they possessed two of the games' top position players, each of whom is younger than the pitcher in question. Ubaldo Jimenez has spent just three full seasons in the major leagues, and each season ranks in the top eight pitching seasons in Rockies history according to Support Neutral Lineup-adjusted Value Above Replacement (SNLVAR), with the last two topping the list. As you can see in Table 1, no other pitcher has placed even two seasons in the top nine.

With Jimenez leading the way, the overall performance of the Rockies' pitching staff has followed suit. Beginning five seasons ago, the Rockies began to make unprecedented strides in run prevention. The only seasons in Rockies history in which they have allowed fewer than five runs per game and/or ranked higher than 12th in the league in run prevention have been 2007, 2009, and 2010. Those last two seasons, Jimenez's best, rank as the Rockies' best teamwide pitching seasons as well. With Jimenez as their ace, the Rockies have allowed nearly identical totals of 715 and 717 runs, which works out to 4.42 runs per game over the two seasons. In 2009, that made the Rockies something they could only hope to be for the first decade and a half of their existence: league-average run preventers. With run scoring down a tenth of a run per game in the National League, the Rockies finished just a tad below average in run prevention in 2010, despite their home park, and their team peripherals were in many cases superior to those of 2009.

ROCKIES PROSPECTUS

2010 W-L: 83-79, 3rd in NL West

Pythag	.534	12th
RS/G	4.8	8th
RA/G	4.4	13th
TAv	.269	15th
BRR	16.5	1st
FRA	4.53	19th
DER	5.25	12th
DL	996	26th
B-Age	28.8	14th
P-Age	27.6	12th
Salary	$84.2	16th
M$/MW	$2.16	11th

Ballpark: Coors Field (3-yr. PF: 111). Rockies hitters still hate leaving Coors, but their pitchers now find it humidorable

2010: A 10-game September winning streak makes things interesting, but mile-high magic ends there

2011: With little high-caliber help on the way, the Rockies aim to win now

Action Items: Contact for Chris Iannetta, a retirement home for Helton

As a result of that improvement on the mound, the Rockies have already become something of a perennial contender. They were the surprise pennant winners in 2007, returned to the playoffs in 2009, and weren't eliminated until the final week of the 2010 season. However, the Rockies have yet to win their division, have won just one post-season game since reaching the 2007 World Series and—though they hung with the Giants and Padres for most of 2010—fell out of first place for good on the second day of the season, finishing with just 83 wins after having ranked no higher than third after July 18.

That 2010 performance was especially disappointing, given that their three young stars—Jimenez, shortstop Troy Tulowitzki, and outfielder Carlos Gonzalez—each took superstar turns at one point or another during the season. Jimenez started his age-26 season by going 13-1 with a 1.15 ERA through his first 14 starts, the third of which was a no-hitter. Tulowitzki, 25, hit 14 home runs in 15 games in September, the greatest September homer outburst in the game's history. Gonzalez, 24, hit .369/.419/.699 with 22 homers, 71 RBI, and 15 stolen bases in 19 attempts over the season's final three months. He threatened to win the Triple Crown and settled for the batting title and a third-place

Table 1. Taming the Beast: The Top 10 Pitching Seasons in Rockies History, by SNLVAR

Rk	Pitcher	Year	SNLVAR
1.	Ubaldo Jimenez	2010	7.5
2.	Ubaldo Jimenez	2009	6.0
3.	Jason Jennings	2006	5.7
4.	Jeff Francis	2007	5.3
5.	Aaron Cook	2006	4.6
6.	Joe Kennedy	2004	4.5
7.	Jason Marquis	2009	4.4
8.	Ubaldo Jimenez	2008	4.4
9.	Jorge De La Rosa	2009	4.2
10.	Jeff Francis	2006	4.2

finish in the MVP voting. The inability of a team that made the postseason the year to convert those performances into more than 83 wins is fairly convincing evidence that work remains to be done on this roster.

For one thing, while the Rockies' fielding had gotten a lot of credit for the team's improvement in run prevention over the past several seasons, in part because of Tulowitzki's outstanding play at shortstop, it was really only in 2007 that team defense gave Colorado a meaningful edge. That year, when the Rockies stunned everyone by winning 21 of 22 games on their way to the pennant, they did indeed have the best fielding season in team history according to Park Adjusted Defensive Efficiency (PADE), ranking second in the majors in that category to the team that beat them in the World Series, the Red Sox. Since then, however, the Rockies' fielding has been ordinary to poor, and they have posted a positive PADE just once in the last three years.

More significantly, the offense has been inconsistent. In 2008, the Rockies scored the second-fewest runs per game in team history and finished below fifth in the league in that category for the only time in their existence. The bats perked up in 2009, but despite Gonzalez's breakout and Tulowitzki's outburst, the Rockies again saw their production drop off in 2010. What's most troubling about that 2010 performance is that the Rockies scored fewer total runs than they had in 2007 and 2009, despite scoring more runs at home than in any season since 2004. That's because they failed to score 300 runs on the road for the first time since 2005. The result was the team's largest gap in runs scored at home versus on the road since 2002, the year the humidor was introduced at Coors Field.

The alarming split has called attention to the Rockies' best-kept secret. It turns out that the concern over pitching at altitude was just a red herring. The real challenge created by playing half of your games a mile above sea level is the effect it has on your hitters on the road. Looking at the Rockies' annual team home/road splits for runs scored and runs allowed, the gap between the Rockies' runs scored at home versus on the road has been larger than their gap in runs allowed at home and on the road, both in raw numbers and as a percentage of total runs scored or allowed, in 16 of their 18 seasons and in each year dating back to 1996. In fact, over the entire 18-year history of the franchise, the gap between runs scored at home and away has been roughly twice as large (again both in raw numbers and as a percentage) as the gap between runs allowed at home and on the road.

As one might suspect, both gaps have closed considerably since the introduction of the humidor, but that has only thrown the team's hitting splits into greater relief. Over the past six years, the pitching staff's home/road split for runs allowed has closed to such a degree that it's almost negligible. The Rockies have averaged just 30 fewer runs allowed on the road per season over the last six years, a difference equivalent to just four percent of the team's total runs allowed. By comparison, the offense has averaged 124 fewer runs on the road than at home over the past six years, a total equal to 16 percent of their total runs scored. In other words, the home/road runs gap of the Rockies' offense has been four times as large as that of the pitching staff over the last six seasons.

To be fair, not all of that is due to problems hitting on the road. It seems the Rockies also derive a greater benefit from hitting at Coors Field than their opponents do. Some have speculated that that is a by-product of having a fly-ball-hitting lineup, but the Rockies were solidly middle-of-the-pack in fly-ball percentages in 2010 and 2008 and toward the bottom of the league in fly balls in 2007. Instead, it seems the exaggerated difference between the Rockies' offensive performance at home and on the road has more to do with how the ball behaves coming toward the plate than heading away from it.

Bojan Koprivica of the SB-Nation blog *Athletics Nation* did some excellent work on the subject in a piece published on that site on August 8, 2010, revealing in graphical form how the thin air affects seven types of pitches. Contrary to prior beliefs about curveballs not curving at altitude, Koprivica's research showed that curves, sliders, and cutters move just fine at Coors Field, largely replicating their behavior at sea level. Rather, the pitches most altered by the thin air are the straighter ones, specifically, four- and two-seam fastballs and sinkers and, ironically, given the Great Changeup Experiment of 2001, changeups. Four-seam fastballs lose their rise almost completely, while all three types of fastball lose their inside action, and all four pitch types, if intended to break inside to a same-handed batter, are more likely to sit in the hitting area down and over the plate at Coors than elsewhere.

While Koprivica also showed that pitches lose less velocity on the way to the plate in the thin air, it's a baseball truism that movement and location are more important than speed, and if pitchers at Coors Field are throwing straight fastballs that aren't rising or jamming hitters, an extra mile per hour on the gun isn't going to stop those pitches from being hit hard. Pitcher behavior supports Koprivica's findings, as Rockies pitchers threw significantly fewer four- and two-seam fastballs at home relative to on the road in 2010, while throwing curves and sliders at the same rate in both locations.

Exactly how that translates to struggles on the road is the part of the riddle that remains uncracked. The prevailing assumption remains that if a hitter isn't seeing a strong break on a certain pitch at home, then he will struggle against that break on the road. That certainly seemed to be the case for Carlos Gonzalez, who, as Koprivica's research showed, struggled mightily against fastballs on the road in 2010. But what separates a hitter like Gonzalez from someone like Ian Stewart, a lifetime Rockie who has historically hit better on the road than at home, as he did again in 2010?

Koprivica theorizes that Coors aids free swingers like Gonzalez with pitch recognition by taking some of the mystery out of where a pitch is going to end up, while hitters with superior batting eyes are better at anticipating a pitch's path and thus suffer less when they see real fastball movement at sea level. Looking at the home/road OPS splits of the Rockies' nine most frequent batters in 2010 (Table 2), we see this is an imperfect answer. Dexter Fowler, among the most patient men on the team, had the second-most-severe home/road split in 2010, while the hacktastic Clint Barmes seemed to reap little benefit from seeing straighter pitches at home. Perhaps you could chalk that up to Fowler's inexperience against major-league pitching and Barmes' ability to stink just about anywhere, but for now the jury is still out.

Table 2. They Say That the Road Ain't No Place to Start a Family: Home/Road OPS Splits of the Rockies' 2010 Regulars

Player	Home	Road	Difference
Gonzalez	1161	775	-386
Fowler	932	595	-337
Olivo	905	598	-307
Smith	937	634	-303
Spilborghs	903	694	-209
Tulowitzki	1034	863	-171
Helton	770	668	-102
Barmes	675	639	-36
Stewart	757	802	+45

It's never a bad idea to stock your lineup with patient hitters, but that speaks to the observation that the best solution for the Rockies, as has proved to be the case in the rotation, probably has less to do with the type of hitters they employ than the quality of hitters they employ. Unfortunately, the Rockies' midsized payroll has locked them into a certain level of mediocrity at the plate. Their offense was middling in 2010 because of its struggles on the road, but taking all 162 games together, Colorado was only significantly below average at the plate at one position: second base. That limits the team's opportunities for improvement.

Because of the potential cost benefit, the Rockies owe it to themselves to give moderately productive young players such as Fowler and Stewart a chance to improve. Indeed, their two best hitters, Tulowitzki and Gonzalez, are team-controlled players of similar ages (Stewart and Tulowitzki will be 26 this season; Fowler and Gonzalez, 25). Cost benefit also makes a productive and defensively adept left-handed platoon player like Seth Smith, 28, a viable solution in the outfield corner not occupied by Gonzalez, but suddenly you have three positions dedicated to players who aren't meaningfully above average. You can make it four when you consider that the Rockies' catching options are effectively a repeat of what Miguel Olivo gave them in 2010 via a multimillion-dollar (and, given John Bucks' Marlins contract, multiyear) free-agent investment, or one last chance for disappointing and aging prospect Chris Iannetta, who will also be 28 this season. That brings us back to second base, where the Rockies acquired the Mariners' nontender candidate Jose Lopez in early December. Lopez has good power for a middle infielder, but is terribly inconsistent and impatient—two years ago, he had more home runs than walks. A career .266/.297/.400 hitter, Lopez has hit .280/.312/.413 away from Safeco's pitcher's haven, not enough to encourage thoughts of a Colorado breakout.

The lack of opportunity for a big upgrade elsewhere makes the Rockies' continued association with Todd Helton all the more crippling. Relative to the offensive standards of the position, Colorado's second-worst position in 2010 was first base, where a flare-up of Helton's chronic back problems resulted in his worst-ever season at age 36. That came after the Rockies reacted to Helton's strong 2009 showing by reworking the final year of his contract in March, deferring $13.1 million of his 2011 salary while adding two years for a total of $9.9 million. That gave the Rockies the financial flexibility to re-sign Jorge De La Rosa, but at the cost of being stuck with Helton for two more years when his nine-year albatross of a contract was finally set to expire. If Helton's reduced pay is used to rationalize a reduced role, perhaps that extension will be justified. But if, as the team has suggested thus far, they really are looking at Helton, bad back and all, to be their starting first baseman through age 39, they are punting the one position where a significant upgrade could easily be obtained.

Amazingly, the Rockies not only extended Helton with the end of his contract finally in sight, but also then turned around and inked both Tulowitzki and Gonzalez to even larger deals. The seven-year, $134 million extension the Rockies gave Tulowitzki in November results in a 10-year,

$157.75 million commitment to the fragile shortstop—a deal that will take him through his age-35 season. Tulowitzki is a monster talent at a key position, but he'll be making an average of nearly $20 million dollars over the final seven years of his contract, an amount equal to a quarter of the Rockies' payroll in recent years. That means that even if Tulowitzki stays healthy and plays to his abilities over the next decade, his contract could prevent the Rockies from making a significant investment anywhere else on their roster, which is likely to mean an inability to retain Jimenez or Gonzalez beyond his arbitration years. That's the best-case scenario. The worst-case is Eric Chavez times two.

Tulo's rapidly increasing salary (he will make just $5.5 million in 2011) is yet another reason that the future is now in Denver. Heading into 2011, the Rockies stand to enjoy some improvement via the continued maturation of their mid-20s stars and starters; the possibility of fully healthy seasons from Tulowitzki, De La Rosa, and closer Huston Street; some positive correction and increased stamina for Jason Hammel and a full season of Jhoulys Chacin in the rotation. In the bigger picture, however, there are no stud prospects on the way (lefties Christian Friedrich and Tyler Matzek made no meaningful progress toward the majors in 2010). And with Helton's departure no longer imminent and Tulowitzki's contract hanging like the sword of Damocles over the team's financial future, there's nothing to wait for. The future is now. The only question is whether the Rockies are ready for it.

HITTERS

Nolan Arenado **3B**

Born: **4/16/1991** Age: **20**
Bats: **R** Throws: **R** Height: **6' 1"** Weight: **205**
Breakout: **0%** Improve: **0%** Collapse: **0%**
Attrition: **0%** MLB: **0%**

Comparables:
Conor Gillaspie, Dalton Jones, Rusty Staub (70)

YEAR	TEAM	LVL	AGE	PA	R	2B	3B	HR	RBI	BB	SO	SB	CS	AVG/OBP/SLG	TAv	BABIP	BRR	FRAA	WARP
2009	CAS	Rk	18	225	28	15	0	2	22	16	18	5	2	.300/.351/.404	.276	.316	0.9	3B -8	0.4
2010	ASH	A	19	402	45	41	1	12	65	19	52	1	3	.308/.338/.520	.291	.326	-1.3	3B -7	1.6
2011	*COL*	*MLB*	*20*	*311*	*31*	*17*	*1*	*6*	*32*	*13*	*57*	*0*	*0*	*.232/.263/.357*	*.214*	*.264*	*0.0*	*3B -3*	*-0.9*

The Rockies' second-round pick in 2009, Arenado spent April in extended spring training recuperating from minor surgery and made his Sally League debut in May. Breaking into a full-season league as a teenager, he exceeded expectations, particularly in the power department, where he more than doubled his isolated power from 2009, thanks to his 41 doubles in just 400 plate appearances. The Rockies have visions that a good portion of those doubles will turn into home runs as both his skills and his body mature. Mix in solid play at the hot corner from the former high school shortstop, and the Rockies think they have their Third Baseman of the Future, but there's a lot of optimism built into that projection.

Clint Barmes **INF**

Born: **3/6/1979** Age: **32**
Bats: **R** Throws: **R** Height: **6' 0"** Weight: **175**
Breakout: **0%** Improve: **33%** Collapse: **3%**
Attrition: **11%** MLB: **97%**

Comparables:
Mark Ellis, Bobby Doerr, Roberto Alomar (83)

YEAR	TEAM	LVL	AGE	PA	R	2B	3B	HR	RBI	BB	SO	SB	CS	AVG/OBP/SLG	TAv	BABIP	BRR	FRAA	WARP
2008	COL	MLB	29	417	46	25	6	11	44	17	69	13	4	.290/.319/.468	.259	.324	1.3	2B 4, SS 3	2.0
2009	COL	MLB	30	604	69	32	3	23	76	31	121	12	10	.246/.291/.440	.243	.267	-2.1	2B 9, SS 6	1.7
2010	COL	MLB	31	432	42	21	0	8	50	35	66	3	2	.235/.303/.351	.233	.261	2.0	2B -1, SS 6	0.8
2011	*HOU*	*MLB*	*32*	*501*	*57*	*25*	*2*	*13*	*57*	*31*	*79*	*8*	*4*	*.254/.306/.404*	*.248*	*.274*	*-0.7*	*2B 2, SS 3*	*1.2*

Barmes opened 2010 as the Rockies' starting second baseman, but spent more than a month at shortstop in place of the injured Troy Tulowitzki, hitting .284/.358/.385 in 32 starts. That was the only hitting Barmes did all season, however, as he batted .216/.282/.338 the rest of the time. Not long after Tulo's return, Barmes' hold on the keystone began to slip as the Rockies opted to give Eric Young Jr. a look in late August, even as the pennant race heated up. Arbitration-eligible again after making $3.324 million in 2010, Barnes was dealt to the Astros for pitcher Felipe Paulino. The Astros' middle infield is wide open, and Barmes could find himself playing second, short, or both. An excellent defensive shortstop who has hit .285/.333/.487 against lefties in his career, Barmes is best suited for a utility role, but the Astros aren't in a position to use him to best advantage.

Charles Blackmon **CF**

Born: **7/1/1986** Age: **24**
Bats: **L** Throws: **L** Height: **6' 3"** Weight: **200**
Breakout: **8%** Improve: **28%** Collapse: **10%**
Attrition: **29%** MLB: **50%**

Comparables:
Ryan Sweeney, Xavier Paul, Julio Borbon (77)

YEAR	TEAM	LVL	AGE	PA	R	2B	3B	HR	RBI	BB	SO	SB	CS	AVG/OBP/SLG	TAv	BABIP	BRR	FRAA	WARP
2008	TRI	A-	21	321	42	21	5	2	33	16	37	13	7	.338/.386/.466	.314	.375	-1.9	CF 0, RF 1	2.4
2009	MOD	A+	22	616	87	34	7	7	69	39	83	30	13	.307/.369/.433	.288	.346	-0.9	CF -5	2.7
2010	TUL	AA	23	381	53	22	4	11	55	32	43	19	7	.297/.360/.484	.312	.306	0.0	CF -6, LF 1	2.5
2011	*COL*	*MLB*	*24*	*433*	*46*	*22*	*2*	*7*	*45*	*23*	*69*	*11*	*5*	*.254/.299/.374*	*.238*	*.284*	*-0.5*	*CF -11, LF 0*	*-1.0*

The Rockies' second-round pick in 2008 out of Georgia Tech, Blackmon missed two months due to a pair of left hamstring strains before making his Double-A debut at the end of May. He showed no ill effects, building on his 2009 campaign with added power (.187 ISO, up from an average of .127 in his first two pro seasons) and walks (an unintentional pass every 12.7 plate appearances compared with one every 16.2 in 2009), while cutting his strikeout rate to its 2008 level. He followed that up by showing excellent strike-zone command in the Arizona Fall League and now looks as though he has the makings of a legitimate major-league starting center fielder.

Dexter Fowler **CF**

Born: **3/22/1986** Age: **25**
Bats: **R** Throws: **R** Height: **6' 4"** Weight: **175**
Breakout: **4%** Improve: **50%** Collapse: **1%**
Attrition: **11%** MLB: **73%**
Comparables:
Felix Pie, Derek Jeter, Gene Richards (65)

YEAR	TEAM	LVL	AGE	PA	R	2B	3B	HR	RBI	BB	SO	SB	CS	AVG/OBP/SLG	TAv	BABIP	BRR	FRAA	WARP
2008	TUL	AA	22	505	92	31	9	9	64	65	89	20	8	.335/.424/.515	.334	.395	4.3	CF 3	6.0
2008	COL	MLB	22	27	3	0	0	0	0	0	5	0	1	.154/.185/.154	.137	.191	0.2	CF 0, RF 0	-0.3
2009	COL	MLB	23	518	72	29	10	4	34	67	116	27	10	.266/.353/.407	.260	.336	8.1	CF -3	1.9
2010	CSP	AAA	24	124	23	10	4	2	13	17	27	1	0	.340/.435/.566	.301	.442	0.0	CF 2	1.1
2010	COL	MLB	24	505	73	20	14	6	36	57	104	13	8	.260/.343/.410	.263	.321	4.6	CF -1	1.8
2011	*COL*	*MLB*	*25*	*561*	*66*	*28*	*6*	*6*	*54*	*69*	*117*	*20*	*8*	*.257/.345/.381*	*.259*	*.316*	*-0.9*	*CF -4*	*0.9*

After hitting .216/.327/.317 over the first two months of the 2010 season, Fowler was optioned to Triple-A Colorado Springs, where he caught fire, hit for the cycle, and earned his return just a month later. Reinstalled in center field, he hit .288/.362/.466 from July 1 on, a performance that, combined with his improvement in the field, bodes well for his continued growth. That growth will have to keep coming. Even after his return, he didn't hit lefties (.239/.341/.339) or on the road (.226/.303/.328), and the stolen base seems to have fallen out of his bag of tricks (he stole just one bag in his month in the minors and was successful in just 64 percent of his attempts over the final three months). With arbitration due after the coming season and Blackmon rising, Fowler will have to prove he is worth the Rockies' continued investment.

Cole Garner **OF**

Born: **12/15/1984** Age: **26**
Bats: **R** Throws: **R** Height: **6' 2"** Weight: **210**
Breakout: **6%** Improve: **19%** Collapse: **2%**
Attrition: **27%** MLB: **48%**
Comparables:
Travis Buck, Jeff Baker, Nate Schierholtz (78)

YEAR	TEAM	LVL	AGE	PA	R	2B	3B	HR	RBI	BB	SO	SB	CS	AVG/OBP/SLG	TAv	BABIP	BRR	FRAA	WARP
2008	MOD	A+	23	206	27	14	2	2	17	9	51	7	5	.318/.359/.443	.291	.421	1.5	LF 4	1.5
2009	TUL	AA	24	440	65	25	4	16	64	23	78	13	5	.288/.339/.492	.293	.315	-0.3	LF -4, CF -2	1.8
2010	CSP	AAA	25	469	81	31	10	13	61	39	89	8	5	.304/.374/.520	.287	.353	0.0	LF 5, CF -5	2.3
2011	*COL*	*MLB*	*26*	*364*	*40*	*18*	*2*	*9*	*41*	*22*	*84*	*7*	*3*	*.248/.300/.397*	*.244*	*.298*	*-0.2*	*LF -2, CF -2*	*-0.2*

A late-round pick and a late bloomer, Garner had something of a breakout season upon making the leap to Double-A at age 24 in 2009 and trumped that in 2010 by having his best professional season in his Triple-A debut. Garner doesn't do anything particularly well. He's not a basestealer, he's not a home-run hitter, he's not going to draw a lot of walks, and he's really only viable in left field. But when you combine the speed, power, and patience he does have with a solid batting average (he has hit exactly .300 over the last three seasons combined), consistent production throughout his platoon, home/road and monthly splits, and the major-league minimum salary, you get a compelling ballplayer worth a major-league look.

Jason Giambi **1B**

Born: **1/8/1971** Age: **40**
Bats: **L** Throws: **R** Height: **6' 2"** Weight: **200**
Breakout: **0%** Improve: **18%** Collapse: **7%**
Attrition: **22%** MLB: **72%**
Comparables:
Frank Robinson, Darrell Evans, Norm Cash (76)

YEAR	TEAM	LVL	AGE	PA	R	2B	3B	HR	RBI	BB	SO	SB	CS	AVG/OBP/SLG	TAv	BABIP	BRR	FRAA	WARP
2008	NYA	MLB	37	565	70	19	1	32	96	76	111	2	1	.247/.374/.502	.306	.250	-0.9	1B -8	2.3
2009	COL	MLB	38	31	5	1	0	2	11	7	8	0	0	.292/.452/.583	.348	.357	-0.1	1B 0	0.3
2009	OAK	MLB	38	328	43	13	0	11	40	50	72	0	0	.193/.332/.364	.273	.218	1.2	1B -3	0.5
2010	COL	MLB	39	222	20	9	0	6	35	35	47	2	0	.244/.378/.398	.268	.289	-0.8	1B -1	0.2
2011	*COL*	*MLB*	*40*	*417*	*50*	*13*	*0*	*16*	*42*	*64*	*89*	*2*	*1*	*.214/.353/.395*	*.268*	*.238*	*-0.1*	*1B -4*	*0.3*

Nearly a decade and a half after Giambi and Matt Stairs made the A's look like a beer-league softball team, those don't-spill-my-beer skills continue to pay off for both men. Though running, fielding, and hitting for average have long since ceased being aspects of his game (if the first two ever were), Giambi can still work the count and crush the odd pitch. Curiously, he's been more effective doing the latter against lefties over the last two years, with nine of his 19 taters coming in the mere 29 percent of his at-bats that have come against southpaws. That makes him a nifty trap as a pinch-hitter for a manager aware enough to lure his opponent into a lefty-on-lefty matchup, but at 40, that may be the last trick this old dog can do. Nonetheless, the Rockies re-signed him for another campaign.

Carlos Gonzalez **OF**

Born: 10/17/1985 Age: 25
Bats: L Throws: L Height: 6' 1" Weight: 200
Breakout: 1% Improve: 55% Collapse: 0%
Attrition: 7% MLB: 95%

Comparables:
Ryan Braun, Grady Sizemore, Duke Snider (67)

YEAR	TEAM	LVL	AGE	PA	R	2B	3B	HR	RBI	BB	SO	SB	CS	AVG/OBP/SLG	TAv	BABIP	BRR	FRAA	WARP
2008	SAC	AAA	22	189	23	9	1	4	28	16	35	1	1	.283/.344/.416	.288	.336	-0.1	CF -3, RF 0	0.9
2008	OAK	MLB	22	316	31	22	1	4	26	13	81	4	1	.242/.272/.361	.226	.317	1.9	CF 7, RF 2	0.7
2009	CSP	AAA	23	223	43	12	7	10	59	22	32	6	3	.339/.413/.630	.325	.357	1.3	CF -1, RF -1	2.0
2009	COL	MLB	23	317	53	14	7	13	29	28	70	16	4	.284/.347/.525	.280	.325	3.7	LF 5, CF 4	2.5
2010	COL	MLB	24	636	111	34	9	34	117	40	135	26	8	.336/.376/.598	.323	.384	2.4	LF -4, CF 4	5.3
2011	*COL*	*MLB*	*25*	*570*	*75*	*28*	*5*	*22*	*81*	*44*	*117*	*17*	*6*	*.283/.338/.485*	*.284*	*.320*	*-0.3*	*CF 2, LF 0*	*2.7*

If Gonzalez finally started to flower down the stretch in 2009, he was in full bloom over the final three months of 2010. Opening July with five home runs in nine games (and closing it with homers in four straight contests), Gonzalez enjoyed a boiling hot streak from July 1 through October 1, rivaling what Josh Hamilton did in the other league from June through August. In fact, the similarities between the two 2010 batting champions are considerable. Both are left-handed outfielders who can play center but are better off in a corner, both are five-tool studs who lack only the willingness to take a walk, and both benefited greatly from their hitter-friendly home ballparks in 2010. Gonzalez did most of his hitting at Coors (.380/.425/.737 versus .289/.322/.453 on the road), but we needn't necessarily downplay the value of his performance as a result of its reliance on rarefied air, since the ability to take advantage of one's home park is a skill that doesn't depreciate without a change in venue. Although Gonzalez was dogged by allegations of a lack of effort in Oakland, a third-place MVP finish in one's age-24 season has a way of dispelling such concerns, and the Rockies rewarded his efforts with a seven-year, $80 million deal.

Todd Helton **1B**

Born: 8/20/1973 Age: 37
Bats: L Throws: L Height: 6' 2" Weight: 195
Breakout: 0% Improve: 28% Collapse: 5%
Attrition: 12% MLB: 97%

Comparables:
Eddie Murray, Rafael Palmeiro, Kevin Millar (80)

YEAR	TEAM	LVL	AGE	PA	R	2B	3B	HR	RBI	BB	SO	SB	CS	AVG/OBP/SLG	TAv	BABIP	BRR	FRAA	WARP
2008	COL	MLB	34	361	39	16	0	7	29	61	50	0	0	.264/.391/.388	.270	.298	-2.1	1B 0	0.5
2009	COL	MLB	35	645	80	38	3	15	86	89	73	0	1	.325/.416/.489	.300	.348	-5.7	1B -9	1.7
2010	COL	MLB	36	473	49	18	1	8	37	67	90	0	0	.256/.362/.367	.257	.307	-3.0	1B -2	-0.3
2011	*COL*	*MLB*	*37*	*566*	*69*	*26*	*0*	*9*	*50*	*85*	*79*	*1*	*0*	*.265/.376/.380*	*.272*	*.296*	*0.0*	*1B -3*	*0.8*

Helton didn't hit a lick for the first three months of 2010 before finally landing on the disabled list with more of the lower-back problems that have plagued him for much of the last decade and required surgery in late 2008. He returned relatively rejuvenated, hitting .273/.401/.460 over the season's final two months. Helton's patience and glove work remain assets, but the latter suffers along with his bat when his back acts up. Mercifully, Helton agreed to rework the final two years of his contract prior to the 2010 season, deferring $13.1 million of his 2011 salary. Regrettably, the price the Rockies had to pay for that salary relief was a two-year, $9.9 million extension. Yes, Helton is finally making a tradable salary, but his back and his full no-trade clause could now keep him in purple and black through 2013.

Jonathan Herrera **INF**

Born: 11/3/1984 Age: 26
Bats: S Throws: R Height: 5' 9" Weight: 150
Breakout: 2% Improve: 26% Collapse: 4%
Attrition: 11% MLB: 46%

Comparables:
Alexi Casilla, Eider Torres, Luis Castillo (76)

YEAR	TEAM	LVL	AGE	PA	R	2B	3B	HR	RBI	BB	SO	SB	CS	AVG/OBP/SLG	TAv	BABIP	BRR	FRAA	WARP
2008	CSP	AAA	23	250	40	7	0	3	31	19	30	15	2	.310/.364/.381	.252	.342	3.2	SS 0, 2B -2	0.7
2008	COL	MLB	23	66	5	1	1	0	3	4	10	1	1	.230/.273/.279	.216	.269	0.1	2B 0, SS 0	-0.1
2009	CSP	AAA	24	450	63	11	5	2	33	49	51	16	5	.268/.342/.339	.251	.290	6.3	SS 1, 2B 0	1.9
2010	CSP	AAA	25	260	30	6	1	2	17	27	29	3	3	.261/.340/.324	.235	.279	0.0	SS 11, 2B -3	1.1
2010	COL	MLB	25	257	34	6	2	1	21	25	36	2	2	.284/.342/.342	.242	.318	1.8	2B 8, 3B -2	0.7
2011	*COL*	*MLB*	*26*	*425*	*43*	*12*	*2*	*2*	*29*	*42*	*58*	*10*	*3*	*.250/.321/.308*	*.230*	*.280*	*-0.1*	*SS 3, 2B 1*	*0.5*

What the Rockies got from Herrera in 2010 is more or less the player he is. He's a strong fielder with no power at the plate who can hit .280 (his minor-league career average) and draw enough walks to avoid killing the offense in the eight-hole. That's better than they got from Barmes in 2010 and more than they have seen from Eric Young Jr., who is just six months Herrera's junior, at the major-league level. It's also the profile of a stopgap player best suited for a utility role.

Chris Iannetta **C**

Born: 4/8/1983 Age: 28
Bats: R Throws: R Height: 5' 11" Weight: 195
Breakout: 0% Improve: 39% Collapse: 3%
Attrition: 10% MLB: 93%

Comparables:
Ryan Doumit, Todd Hundley, Gary Sheffield (72)

YEAR	TEAM	LVL	AGE	PA	R	2B	3B	HR	RBI	BB	SO	SB	CS	AVG/OBP/SLG	TAv	BABIP	BRR	FRAA	WARP
2008	COL	MLB	25	407	54	22	2	18	65	56	92	0	0	.264/.388/.505	.302	.308	-1.4	C 1, 3B 0	3.4
2009	COL	MLB	26	350	41	15	2	16	52	43	75	0	1	.228/.343/.460	.268	.244	0.3	C 3	2.1
2010	CSP	AAA	27	76	17	7	0	5	21	10	10	0	0	.349/.447/.698	.338	.347	0.0	C 0, 1B 0	0.9
2010	COL	MLB	27	223	20	6	1	9	27	30	48	1	0	.197/.318/.383	.243	.212	-1.6	C 1, 1B 0	0.4
2011	*COL*	*MLB*	*28*	*363*	*45*	*15*	*1*	*14*	*42*	*48*	*76*	*1*	*0*	*.234/.351/.429*	*.275*	*.261*	*0.0*	*C 1, 1B 0*	*2.1*

The Rockies bought out Iannetta's arbitration years with a three-year, $8.35 million extension prior to the 2010 season. Then, before the end of April, having given him just eight starts behind the plate, they sent him down to Triple-A. Though he returned to the majors a month later after again demolishing Triple-A pitching, Iannetta never broke free of the backup catcher role in 2010. After starting the first two games of the season, he didn't start consecutive games again until late July and never started three in a row all season. Blame the Rockies if you want, but they let him hit his way into the starting job in 2008, and he hit his way out of it in 2009. Now that they're a perennial contender, there's only so much patience the team can show an aging prospect who keeps flirting with the Mendoza line. It might take a change of scenery for the soon-to-be 28-year-old Iannetta to avoid having four scarlet A's hung on his chest.

Michael McKenry **C**

Born: **3/4/1985** Age: **26**
Bats: R Throws: R Height: **5' 10"** Weight: **200**
Breakout: **2%** Improve: **16%** Collapse: **9%**
Attrition: **19%** MLB: **33%**

Comparables:
Nick Hundley, Miguel Montero, George Kottaras (76)

YEAR	TEAM	LVL	AGE	PA	R	2B	3B	HR	RBI	BB	SO	SB	CS	AVG/OBP/SLG	TAv	BABIP	BRR	FRAA	WARP
2008	MOD	A+	23	472	59	28	1	18	75	55	101	2	4	.258/.356/.468	.291	.295	-2.7	C -1	3.0
2009	TUL	AA	24	417	52	25	1	12	50	54	69	2	2	.279/.374/.455	.295	.314	-2.5	C 0	3.0
2010	CSP	AAA	25	384	44	23	1	10	49	32	77	1	1	.265/.328/.424	.248	.312	-6.0	C 1	0.7
2010	COL	MLB	25	9	0	0	0	0	0	1	5	0	0	.000/.111/.000	.056	.000	-0.1	C 0	-0.2
2011	*COL*	*MLB*	*26*	*427*	*46*	*20*	*0*	*11*	*42*	*41*	*99*	*1*	*0*	*.229/.305/.368*	*.238*	*.274*	*0.0*	*C -1*	*0.6*

Unfortunately for the Rockies, an in-house solution to their frustrations with Iannetta is further away than McKenry, a strong defensive backstop whose Triple-A debut at hitter-friendly Colorado Springs in 2010 resulted in his worst full pro season at the plate. Every aspect of McKenry's offensive game took a step backward in 2010, which, entering his age-26 season, makes him look more than ever like a future backup at best.

Melvin Mora **UT**

Born: **2/2/1972** Age: **39**
Bats: R Throws: R Height: **5' 11"** Weight: **180**
Breakout: **0%** Improve: **20%** Collapse: **17%**
Attrition: **13%** MLB: **78%**

Comparables:
Mark Grudzielanek, Jose Cruz, Graig Nettles (70)

YEAR	TEAM	LVL	AGE	PA	R	2B	3B	HR	RBI	BB	SO	SB	CS	AVG/OBP/SLG	TAv	BABIP	BRR	FRAA	WARP
2008	BAL	MLB	36	569	77	29	2	23	104	37	69	3	7	.285/.341/.484	.287	.287	0.5	3B 7, SS 0	3.9
2009	BAL	MLB	37	496	44	20	0	8	48	34	60	3	3	.260/.321/.358	.239	.282	-4.0	3B 12	1.2
2010	COL	MLB	38	353	38	11	5	7	44	31	53	2	1	.283/.354/.416	.266	.319	0.2	3B -6, 1B 2	1.0
2011	*ARI*	*MLB*	*39*	*532*	*58*	*20*	*1*	*10*	*50*	*41*	*73*	*5*	*3*	*.251/.316/.364*	*.243*	*.271*	*-0.5*	*3B 4, 1B 0*	*0.9*

Mora was hitting .267/.353/.376 on August 25 when an injury to Ian Stewart handed him the third-base job for a month. Mora seized the opportunity, hitting .326/.379/.505 in Stewart's stead, but it is the light-hitting utilityman from the season's first five months that his new team can expect to show up for 2011. At 39, Mora will still get on base more often than the Miguel Cairos of the world, but he has played just two innings of shortstop in the last seven years and is a below-average fielder everywhere else. Even though the end is near, the Diamondbacks inked him to a two-year deal.

Chris Nelson **INF**

Born: **9/3/1985** Age: **25**
Bats: R Throws: R Height: **5' 11"** Weight: **175**
Breakout: **3%** Improve: **12%** Collapse: **1%**
Attrition: **10%** MLB: **20%**

Comparables:
Donnie Murphy, Jeff Blauser, Ronny Cedeno (76)

YEAR	TEAM	LVL	AGE	PA	R	2B	3B	HR	RBI	BB	SO	SB	CS	AVG/OBP/SLG	TAv	BABIP	BRR	FRAA	WARP
2008	TUL	AA	22	329	38	18	2	3	42	35	69	6	1	.237/.322/.346	.217	.294	1.3	SS -4	-0.5
2009	TUL	AA	23	122	21	5	2	4	17	12	21	5	2	.280/.352/.477	.337	.310	1.5	SS -3, 2B 0	1.2
2010	CSP	AAA	24	356	60	15	3	12	55	29	53	7	3	.313/.376/.492	.283	.341	-0.8	SS -3, 2B -3	1.3
2010	COL	MLB	24	27	6	1	0	0	0	1	4	1	0	.280/.296/.320	.204	.318	1.4	2B 0, 3B 0	0.0
2011	*COL*	*MLB*	*25*	*284*	*31*	*12*	*1*	*6*	*28*	*23*	*58*	*5*	*2*	*.247/.309/.372*	*.243*	*.290*	*-0.1*	*SS -4, 2B 0*	*0.0*

The ninth overall pick way back in 2004, Nelson had his best plate performance since rookie ball in his Triple-A debut last year. Of course, the oft-injured shortstop missed a month with an oblique strain before he actually made that debut. He also did most of his hitting in a two-month span across June and July and hit just .283/.337/.428 away from Colorado Springs. Still, after getting his first taste of the majors in 2010 and making three starts at the keystone in the season's final week, Nelson has at long last thrust himself into a battle for a big-league job. His odds of winning it grew longer after the acquisition of Jose Lopez.

Miguel Olivo **C**

Born: **7/15/1978** Age: **32**
Bats: R Throws: R Height: **6' 0"** Weight: **180**
Breakout: **1%** Improve: **34%** Collapse: **5%**
Attrition: **11%** MLB: **98%**

Comparables:
Brandon Inge, Claudell Washington, Benito Santiago (66)

YEAR	TEAM	LVL	AGE	PA	R	2B	3B	HR	RBI	BB	SO	SB	CS	AVG/OBP/SLG	TAv	BABIP	BRR	FRAA	WARP
2008	KCA	MLB	29	317	30	22	0	12	41	7	82	7	0	.255/.278/.444	.251	.310	0.5	C 1	0.9
2009	KCA	MLB	30	416	52	15	5	23	65	19	126	5	2	.249/.291/.490	.267	.305	0.1	C -3	1.7
2010	COL	MLB	31	427	55	17	6	14	58	27	117	7	4	.269/.314/.449	.259	.343	2.3	C 0	1.9
2011	*TOR*	*MLB*	*32*	*416*	*47*	*18*	*3*	*14*	*52*	*22*	*111*	*6*	*2*	*.248/.290/.420*	*.245*	*.305*	*-0.2*	*C 0*	*0.9*

For a player who once drew five unintentional walks in 448 plate appearances, Olivo's career-high 22 unintentional passes in 2010 represented something of a breakthrough. Those walks, combined with a personal best in batting average, pushed Olivo's on-base percentage above the Pedro Feliz line for the first time in his nine-year major-league career. A .315 OBP is still dismal by most standards, but major-league catchers as a group only got on base 32 percent of the time in 2010, and when you mix in Olivo's 15-homer power and outstanding throwing arm (he nailed 42 percent of attempting basestealers in 2010, matching a career best he set in 2008), he's clearly a deserving starter if he can hold on to those walks. The only catch, or should we say "miss," is that he has led his league in passed balls in four of the last five seasons and the majors in three of the last four.

Jordan Pacheco **C**

Born: **1/30/1986** Age: **25**
Bats: **R** Throws: **R** Height: **6' 1"** Weight: **190**
Breakout: **1%** Improve: **16%** Collapse: **10%**
Attrition: **21%** MLB: **40%**

Comparables:
John Jaso, Jose Morales, Brian Horwitz (76)

YEAR	TEAM	LVL	AGE	PA	R	2B	3B	HR	RBI	BB	SO	SB	CS	AVG/OBP/SLG	TAv	BABIP	BRR	FRAA	WARP
2008	TRI	A-	22	251	25	8	3	1	35	26	20	3	3	.280/.367/.360	.266	.298	-1.5	C 0	0.9
2009	ASH	A	23	507	67	30	4	13	79	38	44	12	2	.322/.377/.492	.292	.327	1.7	C -1	3.1
2010	MOD	A+	24	460	59	27	3	5	70	54	36	5	6	.321/.407/.444	.313	.336	0.9	C -1	3.9
2010	TUL	AA	24	91	11	5	0	1	19	6	6	1	1	.333/.396/.436	.284	.338	0.5	C 1	0.7
2011	*COL*	*MLB*	*25*	*431*	*46*	*19*	*1*	*6*	*39*	*34*	*55*	*1*	*1*	*.251/.312/.352*	*.236*	*.273*	*-0.1*	*C -1*	*0.2*

Drafted as an infielder out of the University of New Mexico in 2007, Pacheco was moved behind the plate in 2008 at age 22. Though he has caught exclusively since, he is still learning his position. Fortunately, he has the hitting thing down. Pacecho has batted .322 with doubles power over the past two seasons and walked more than he struck out in two of his last three minor-league seasons. If he can master a certain level of competence behind the dish, he'll be a valuable offense-first catcher.

Kyle Parker **RF**

Born: **9/30/1989** Age: **21**
Bats: **R** Throws: **R** Height: **6' 0"** Weight: **100**
Breakout: **–%** Improve: **–%** Collapse: **–%**
Attrition: **–%** MLB: **–%**

Comparables:

YEAR	TEAM	LVL	AGE	PA	R	2B	3B	HR	RBI	BB	SO	SB	CS	AVG/OBP/SLG	TAv	BABIP	BRR	FRAA	WARP
2010	DNP	—	21	—	—	—	—	—	—	—	—	—	—	—	—	—	—	—	—
2011	*COL*	*MLB*	*21*	—	—	—	—	—	—	—	—	—	—	—	—	—	—	—	—

The Rockies have a fetish for quarterbacks, due to the combination of leadership and athleticism the position demands. Todd Helton (first round, 1995) backed up Peyton Manning at Tennessee, Seth Smith (second, 2004) held the clipboard for Manning's younger brother, Eli, at Mississippi, and Matt Holliday (seventh, 1998) was one of the top high school quarterbacks in the nation (it took a nearly-seven-figure bonus to prevent him from taking snaps at Oklahoma State). The Rockies even drafted Michael Vick out of Virginia Tech in the 30th round of the 2000 draft despite the fact that he hadn't played baseball since high school. Colorado continued the trend in 2010 by taking North Carolina State signal-caller Russell Wilson in the fourth round and Clemson freshman Parker in the first. Parker wasn't ready to give up football, but ultimately signed for $1.4 million with a stipulation that he could return to school for his sophomore year. During the spring, he was one of the best power hitters in college baseball, slugging 20 home runs in 247 at-bats while also leading the Clemson Tigers in walks. That's a classic corner-outfield profile, but ironically, his average throwing arm could limit him to left field, at least until he stops throwing the baseball like it's a football.

Wilin Rosario **C**

Born: **2/23/1989** Age: **22**
Bats: **R** Throws: **R** Height: **5' 11"** Weight: **190**
Breakout: **0%** Improve: **1%** Collapse: **0%**
Attrition: **1%** MLB: **2%**

Comparables:
Jesus Flores, David Wright, Raul Mondesi (74)

YEAR	TEAM	LVL	AGE	PA	R	2B	3B	HR	RBI	BB	SO	SB	CS	AVG/OBP/SLG	TAv	BABIP	BRR	FRAA	WARP
2008	CAS	Rk	19	291	48	15	3	12	49	24	57	4	3	.316/.371/.532	.308	.360	1.8	C -1	2.7
2009	MOD	A+	20	222	17	12	2	4	33	10	55	2	1	.266/.293/.404	.253	.329	-1.0	C -1	0.5
2010	TUL	AA	21	297	42	13	1	19	52	21	57	1	0	.285/.342/.552	.307	.294	-1.3	C -1	2.3
2011	*COL*	*MLB*	*22*	*267*	*29*	*11*	*1*	*10*	*34*	*14*	*66*	*0*	*0*	*.241/.279/.416*	*.240*	*.279*	*0.0*	*C -1*	*0.3*

This is the Rockies' Catcher of the Future. The Dominican Rosario slugged .552 in Double-A at age 21 last year and threw out 41 percent of attempted basestealers. He's still a bit clumsy behind the plate, as he allowed 11 passed balls and committed 11 other errors last year, but he has a compact catcher's build that bodes well for his ability to learn the finer points of the position, and his bat and arm should win out even if he doesn't. A ruptured anterior cruciate ligament in his right knee suffered during a rundown in early August will keep him out through spring training, but he's expected to be back at full strength and behind the plate by mid-April.

Seth Smith LF

Born: **9/30/1982** Age: **28**
Bats: L Throws: L Height: **6' 3"** Weight: **215**
Breakout: **2%** Improve: **40%** Collapse: **6%**
Attrition: **7%** MLB: **87%**

Comparables:
Bob Watson, Jon Knott, Andre Ethier (72)

YEAR	TEAM	LVL	AGE	PA	R	2B	3B	HR	RBI	BB	SO	SB	CS	AVG/OBP/SLG	TAv	BABIP	BRR	FRAA	WARP
2008	CSP	AAA	25	303	55	16	2	10	53	46	46	11	0	.323/.426/.524	.315	.354	2.3	LF 2, RF -2	2.6
2008	COL	MLB	25	123	13	7	0	4	15	15	23	1	0	.259/.350/.435	.274	.296	-0.8	RF -1, CF 3	0.6
2009	COL	MLB	26	387	61	20	4	15	55	46	67	4	1	.293/.377/.510	.290	.323	3.3	LF 8	3.0
2010	COL	MLB	27	398	55	19	5	17	52	35	67	2	1	.246/.314/.469	.270	.256	0.4	LF 6, RF 1	1.8
2011	*COL*	*MLB*	*28*	*428*	*54*	*20*	*2*	*15*	*53*	*47*	*72*	*4*	*1*	*.261/.345/.445*	*.277*	*.283*	*0.0*	*LF 6, RF -1*	*1.9*

Smith was hitting .287/.344/.543 on July 30 of last year when his bat went cold. An 0-for-21 slump touched off a .153/.248/.306 finish that seemed to be as much bad luck as anything else. Smith hit just .182 on balls in play over those final 111 at-bats, which was reflected in his .256 season mark, but there were no meaningful changes in his batted-ball types on the season. Thus, it seems safe to assume that Smith's .290/.364/.524 line over the 10 months of regular-season play from April 2009 to July 2010 represents his true performance level, provided you keep him away from left-handed pitching, which the Rockies have been careful to do.

Ryan Spilborghs OF

Born: **9/5/1979** Age: **31**
Bats: R Throws: R Height: **6' 1"** Weight: **190**
Breakout: **2%** Improve: **34%** Collapse: **5%**
Attrition: **8%** MLB: **94%**

Comparables:
Moises Alou, Ryan Church, Scott Hairston (78)

YEAR	TEAM	LVL	AGE	PA	R	2B	3B	HR	RBI	BB	SO	SB	CS	AVG/OBP/SLG	TAv	BABIP	BRR	FRAA	WARP
2008	COL	MLB	28	275	39	14	2	6	36	38	41	7	4	.313/.407/.468	.295	.355	-3.0	LF -1, RF 1	1.2
2009	COL	MLB	29	393	55	24	3	8	48	34	79	9	5	.242/.308/.395	.244	.285	2.1	LF -1, RF 0	0.3
2010	COL	MLB	30	387	41	20	2	10	39	39	83	4	5	.279/.359/.438	.275	.340	2.3	RF 0, LF -3	0.9
2011	*COL*	*MLB*	*31*	*405*	*48*	*19*	*1*	*9*	*42*	*43*	*75*	*8*	*4*	*.259/.340/.395*	*.262*	*.300*	*-0.7*	*LF -1, RF 0*	*0.5*

With a fairly convincing recovery in 2010, Spilborghs revealed his poor 2009 season to be an off year. Indeed, a peek behind the curtain shows that his line-drive percentage dipped by six percentage points in 2009, then rebounded by seven points last year. Curiously, despite otherwise appearing to return to his old form, Spilborghs posted a reverse split in 2010. Then again, he was never a perfect fit for the role of lefty-killer. As a fourth outfielder capable of filling in at all three positions and as Smith's platoon partner, however, he's an asset.

Ian Stewart 3B

Born: **4/5/1985** Age: **26**
Bats: L Throws: R Height: **6' 3"** Weight: **205**
Breakout: **1%** Improve: **45%** Collapse: **6%**
Attrition: **23%** MLB: **90%**

Comparables:
Mark Reynolds, Josh Fields, Eddie Mathews (73)

YEAR	TEAM	LVL	AGE	PA	R	2B	3B	HR	RBI	BB	SO	SB	CS	AVG/OBP/SLG	TAv	BABIP	BRR	FRAA	WARP
2008	CSP	AAA	23	298	65	15	6	19	57	34	66	7	2	.280/.372/.607	.308	.305	0.6	3B 3, 2B -1	2.7
2008	COL	MLB	23	304	33	18	2	10	41	30	94	1	1	.259/.349/.455	.271	.362	0.7	3B 2, 2B 3	1.7
2009	COL	MLB	24	491	74	19	3	25	70	56	138	7	4	.228/.322/.464	.262	.270	0.4	3B -4, 2B -4	0.6
2010	COL	MLB	25	441	54	14	2	18	61	45	110	5	2	.257/.338/.443	.270	.308	1.8	3B 3	2.2
2011	*COL*	*MLB*	*26*	*512*	*63*	*20*	*2*	*21*	*63*	*56*	*130*	*6*	*2*	*.244/.332/.439*	*.269*	*.291*	*-0.2*	*3B 1, 2B 0*	*1.9*

Stewart doesn't really do anything poorly. He isn't useless against left-handed pitching; at the very least, he can work southpaws for walks as well as he can the normal-handed. He's the rare Rockie who hits for more power on the road than at home (29 career homers and a .215 isolated power on the road, versus 25 and .197 at home). He's an average fielder. He draws just enough walks to survive his generally poor but not disastrous batting averages and strikes out a lot, but not enough to put him among the league leaders. He also has more power than the average third baseman. All that at arbitration prices makes Stewart something of an asset, but one whom it's difficult to get excited about, particularly given that he was the 10th overall pick back in 2003. Unless he shows some growth in one of those elements, he'll be easy to discard once free agency threatens to drive up his price.

Troy Tulowitzki SS

Born: **10/10/1984** Age: **26**
Bats: R Throws: R Height: **6' 3"** Weight: **205**
Breakout: **1%** Improve: **54%** Collapse: **2%**
Attrition: **9%** MLB: **98%**

Comparables:
Hanley Ramirez, Ryan Zimmerman, Cesar Cedeno (70)

YEAR	TEAM	LVL	AGE	PA	R	2B	3B	HR	RBI	BB	SO	SB	CS	AVG/OBP/SLG	TAv	BABIP	BRR	FRAA	WARP
2008	COL	MLB	23	421	48	24	2	8	46	38	56	1	6	.263/.330/.401	.247	.287	-1.2	SS 1	1.1
2009	COL	MLB	24	628	102	25	9	32	92	73	112	20	11	.297/.377/.553	.303	.316	0.4	SS -1	5.1
2010	COL	MLB	25	529	89	32	3	27	95	48	78	11	2	.315/.380/.568	.311	.326	0.8	SS 6	5.1
2011	*COL*	*MLB*	*26*	*581*	*78*	*28*	*3*	*23*	*79*	*60*	*91*	*11*	*5*	*.279/.356/.479*	*.291*	*.296*	*-0.8*	*SS 4*	*4.2*

One of these years, Tulowitzki is going to stay healthy and hit consistently for a full season, and when he does, he's probably going to be the NL MVP. Last year, an errant Alex Burnett pitch that broke his left wrist and kept him out for more than a month was what suppressed his numbers. Tulo did his best to make up for lost time with the greatest September home-run binge in the game's history, hitting 14 home runs over a 15-game span from September 3 to September 18, besting Hank Greenberg's 13 dingers in 16 contests in September 1940. Neither the wrist injury nor the September outburst altered his hitting in a huge way, however. He was hitting .306/.375/.502 when he was struck by the pitch; he hit .344/.407/.492 in 32 games after returning and before the first of those 14 homers and hit "just" .301 with a .363 on-base percentage from the date of the first homer through the end of the season, albeit with a .788 slugging percentage. So the consistency is there, and he finally got his overdue Gold Glove. It could be that Tulo is even closer to that MVP than we thought.

Eric Young Jr. **2B**
Born: **5/25/1985** Age: **26**
Bats: S Throws: R Height: **5' 10"** Weight: **180**
Breakout: **6%** Improve: **29%** Collapse: **4%**
Attrition: **26%** MLB: **54%**
Comparables:
Chris Getz, Alexi Casilla, Eric Patterson (74)

YEAR	TEAM	LVL	AGE	PA	R	2B	3B	HR	RBI	BB	SO	SB	CS	AVG/OBP/SLG	TAv	BABIP	BRR	FRAA	WARP
2008	TUL	AA	23	476	74	24	4	3	33	61	77	46	16	.290/.387/.392	.284	.347	5.9	2B 4, CF -2	3.2
2009	CSP	AAA	24	552	118	21	10	7	43	56	79	58	14	.299/.379/.430	.282	.337	13.1	2B 19, CF 3	5.8
2009	COL	MLB	24	61	7	1	0	1	1	4	12	4	4	.246/.295/.316	.221	.296	1.1	2B -1, CF -2	-0.3
2010	CSP	AAA	25	142	20	5	1	1	9	15	32	10	0	.252/.340/.333	.242	.326	1.8	2B 1, CF -1	0.2
2010	COL	MLB	25	189	26	5	1	0	8	17	32	17	6	.244/.312/.285	.227	.300	2.3	2B 7, LF 0	0.7
2011	*COL*	*MLB*	*26*	*470*	*49*	*17*	*2*	*3*	*35*	*48*	*88*	*34*	*10*	*.242/.322/.320*	*.236*	*.292*	*0.0*	*2B 8, CF 0*	*0.7*

It's hard to glean much from Young's 2010 season. Called up after 15 games in April, he suffered a stress fracture of his right tibia while running the bases after just 13 major-league games, missed three months, played four rehab games in Double-A, played 18 games in Triple-A, then was called back to "The Show" in mid-August. Installed at second base on August 22, he hit just .234/.292/.261 in 31 games—28 of them starts—before pain in the leg ended his season a few days early. Young, who is expected to heal fully over the winter, did steal 20 bases in 25 attempts after returning from the disabled list, so the injury isn't much of a concern—but his bat is. Young's game is hitting .290 with a healthy supply of walks and a ton of stolen bases, something he did reliably in the minors over the previous five seasons, but he will be 26 in May, has yet to bring the first two of those skills to the majors, and isn't a particularly strong fielder. His minor-league track record and familiar name might have given him the inside track to a second-base job, but he now has December import Jose Lopez to contend with.

PITCHERS

Joe Beimel
Born: **4/19/1977** Age: **34**
Bats: L Throws: L Height: **6' 2"** Weight: **201**
Breakout: **13%** Improve: **32%** Collapse: **30%**
Attrition: **16%** MLB: **73%**
Comparables:
Mark Eichhorn, Rick White, Tim Burke (80)

YEAR	TEAM	LVL	AGE	W	L	SV	G	GS	IP	H	HR	BB	SO	EqBB9	EqSO9	GB%	BABIP	WHIP	ERA	FRA	WARP
2008	LAN	MLB	31	5	1	0	71	0	49	50	0	21	32	3.9	5.9	48%	.317	1.51	2.02	2.09	1.8
2009	COL	MLB	32	0	1	0	26	0	15^{2}	19	2	4	11	2.3	6.3	43%	.333	1.47	4.02	4.04	0.2
2009	WAS	MLB	32	1	5	1	45	0	39^{2}	38	3	15	24	3.4	5.4	40%	.271	1.36	3.40	3.69	0.4
2010	COL	MLB	33	1	2	0	71	0	45	46	5	15	21	3.0	4.2	44%	.279	1.36	3.40	3.60	0.6
2011	*COL*	*MLB*	*34*	*4*	*1*	*1*	*81*	*0*	*57*	*68*	*6*	*21*	*30*	*3.3*	*4.6*	*45%*	*.314*	*1.54*	*5.13*	*5.58*	*-0.2*

Though he hasn't averaged more than an inning per appearance since 2006, Beimel didn't have an extreme platoon split in the four years leading up to 2010. From 2006 to 2009, lefties hit .263/.325/.377 against him, and righties hit .280/.350/.396. Last year, however, he pitched like a textbook LOOGY, holding southpaws to a .221/.275/.379 line while being crushed by righties (.329/.388/.474). We'd blame that on his abandoning his slider in favor of an increasing reliance on his curveball, a pitch he threw nearly a quarter of the time in 2010, if it weren't for the fact that he made that change in 2009 without a similar widening of his platoon gap. Perhaps the 2010 split was a fluke, but given that his strikeout rates are weak, his control is pedestrian, he doesn't get an excess of ground balls, and his fastball sits in the upper 80s, there's little reason to expect more than matchup work from him going forward.

Matt Belisle
Born: **6/6/1980** Age: **31**
Bats: R Throws: R Height: **6' 3"** Weight: **195**
Breakout: **10%** Improve: **34%** Collapse: **14%**
Attrition: **8%** MLB: **67%**
Comparables:
Dick Hall, Scott Sanderson, Jorge Campillo (73)

YEAR	TEAM	LVL	AGE	W	L	SV	G	GS	IP	H	HR	BB	SO	EqBB9	EqSO9	GB%	BABIP	WHIP	ERA	FRA	WARP
2008	LOU	AAA	28	5	1	4	26	1	38	43	1	11	27	2.6	6.4	62%	.331	1.53	4.26	4.77	0.3
2008	CIN	MLB	28	1	4	0	6	6	29^{2}	47	4	6	14	1.8	4.2	52%	.364	1.79	7.28	7.97	-0.6
2009	CSP	AAA	29	1	1	9	33	4	58^{1}	58	2	15	47	2.3	7.3	56%	.324	1.25	3.09	3.59	1.0
2009	COL	MLB	29	3	1	0	24	0	31	35	6	5	22	1.5	6.4	42%	.293	1.32	5.23	5.78	-0.3
2010	COL	MLB	30	7	5	1	76	0	92	84	7	16	91	1.6	8.9	49%	.309	1.11	2.84	3.30	1.6
2011	*COL*	*MLB*	*31*	*4*	*3*	*2*	*63*	*5*	*100^{2}*	*117*	*13*	*25*	*69*	*2.2*	*6.2*	*48%*	*.327*	*1.41*	*4.76*	*5.17*	*0.5*

After scuffling through his 20s, Belisle had a breakout season at age 30 in 2010, posting a career-best strikeout rate of effectively one per inning and maintaining the immaculate control he has shown in recent seasons to produce a splendid 5.69 strikeout-to-walk ratio. That he did this after a strong showing in September 2009 suggests that it was more than just a fluke. The key to Belisle's success seems to have been abandoning his changeup in favor of more sliders and curves and establishing a simple pattern of getting ahead with his low-90s fastball, then using his breaking stuff to put hitters away when ahead in the count. That sounds simple, but it's one thing to have a plan and another to be able to execute it with confidence and command, which is what Belisle is finally doing. Jim Tracy rode Belisle hard, using him for a major-league-leading number of relief innings, including 29 appearances of over an inning pitched. We shall see if the workload produces any kind of hangover.

Rafael Betancourt

Born: 4/29/1975 Age: 36
Bats: R Throws: R Height: 6' 2" Weight: 176
Breakout: 18% Improve: 36% Collapse: 17%
Attrition: 17% MLB: 79%

Comparables:
Robb Nen, Rollie Fingers, Damaso Marte (66)

YEAR	TEAM	LVL	AGE	W	L	SV	G	GS	IP	H	HR	BB	SO	EqBB9	EqSO9	GB%	BABIP	WHIP	ERA	FRA	WARP
2008	CLE	MLB	33	3	4	4	69	0	71	76	11	25	64	3.2	8.1	31%	.311	1.42	5.20	5.41	-0.2
2009	CLE	MLB	34	1	2	1	28	0	30^{2}	25	3	15	32	4.4	9.4	34%	.279	1.30	3.82	4.96	0.1
2009	COL	MLB	34	3	1	1	32	0	25^{1}	17	1	5	29	1.8	10.3	30%	.254	0.87	1.78	2.07	0.7
2010	COL	MLB	35	5	1	1	72	0	62^{1}	52	9	8	89	1.2	12.9	28%	.303	0.96	3.61	4.17	0.4
2011	*COL*	*MLB*	*36*	*4*	*2*	*2*	*68*	*0*	*64*	*60*	*8*	*16*	*69*	*2.3*	*9.6*	*39%*	*.307*	*1.18*	*3.33*	*3.62*	*1.1*

Four of the top eight strikeout-to-walk ratios in baseball history by pitchers with 60 or more innings pitched were recorded in 2010. Betancourt's 11.13 ratio ranked second in that quartet and fourth all-time. That dominance in the zone was important, because Betancourt's line-drive and home-run rates spiked. The latter seemed a given for such an extreme fly-ball pitcher in Coors Field, and indeed all but two of the home runs he allowed in 2010 came at home. More curiously, Betancourt has devolved into a ROOGY over the last two years, averaging less than an inning per outing and holding righties to a .179/206/.284 line, while lefties have hit a respectable .272/.339/.473 against him. Although these things would seem to limit his value, he was still the Rockies' top reliever in 2010, according to expected wins added, and should continue to rank among the top set-up men in the game in 2011.

Rex Brothers

Born: 12/18/1987 Age: 23
Bats: L Throws: L Height: 6' 0" Weight: 205
Breakout: 2% Improve: 3% Collapse: 5%
Attrition: 3% MLB: 9%

Comparables:
Antonio Bastardo, John Rocker, Rich Gossage (76)

YEAR	TEAM	LVL	AGE	W	L	SV	G	GS	IP	H	HR	BB	SO	EqBB9	EqSO9	GB%	BABIP	WHIP	ERA	FRA	WARP
2010	MOD	A+	22	0	2	3	33	0	37	20	0	19	43	4.6	10.5	56%	.235	1.05	2.92	4.96	0.0
2010	TUL	AA	22	2	1	4	24	0	23	14	2	18	27	7.0	10.6	56%	.226	1.43	3.91	4.53	-0.1
2011	*COL*	*MLB*	*23*	*2*	*1*	*1*	*35*	*0*	*38^{1}*	*35*	*4*	*23*	*38*	*5.5*	*8.9*	*47%*	*.306*	*1.54*	*4.70*	*5.11*	*0.0*

Not to be confused with classical musicians Charles and Christopher Rex, this Rex Brothers was a supplemental pick out of Lipscomb University in 2009 and features a phenomenal fastball that sits in the mid-90s with cutting and sinking action low in the strike zone. It's a monster pitch that he complements with a sharp slider, a remarkable combo coming from a left-hander, but he has thus far struggled to control both. If he can reduce his walks upon returning to Double-A, he could be in the majors by year's end, if not sooner, and could be a closer candidate further down the road in the organization that introduced fellow lefty Brian Fuentes to that role.

Jhoulys Chacin

Born: 1/7/1988 Age: 23
Bats: R Throws: R Height: 6' 3" Weight: 215
Breakout: 14% Improve: 28% Collapse: 7%
Attrition: 13% MLB: 49%

Comparables:
Marc Rzepczynski, Sean Gallagher, Dennis Bennett (75)

YEAR	TEAM	LVL	AGE	W	L	SV	G	GS	IP	H	HR	BB	SO	EqBB9	EqSO9	GB%	BABIP	WHIP	ERA	FRA	WARP
2008	ASH	A	20	10	1	0	16	16	111^{1}	82	3	30	98	2.4	7.9	66%	.260	1.11	1.86	3.32	3.2
2008	MOD	A+	20	8	2	0	12	12	66^{1}	61	3	12	62	1.6	8.4	57%	.317	1.16	2.31	3.24	2.0
2009	TUL	AA	21	8	6	0	18	18	103^{1}	87	10	35	86	3.0	7.5	57%	.263	1.25	3.14	4.14	1.2
2009	COL	MLB	21	0	1	0	9	1	11	6	1	11	13	9.0	10.6	50%	.217	1.55	4.91	6.44	0.0
2010	CSP	AAA	22	3	2	0	7	7	35^{2}	27	1	17	34	4.3	8.7	70%	.283	1.31	1.51	2.95	1.4
2010	COL	MLB	22	9	11	0	28	21	137^{1}	114	10	61	138	4.0	9.0	47%	.285	1.34	3.28	4.32	2.4
2011	*COL*	*MLB*	*23*	*7*	*8*	*0*	*20*	*20*	*119*	*124*	*15*	*56*	*89*	*4.2*	*6.7*	*52%*	*.305*	*1.51*	*4.93*	*5.36*	*1.8*

Simultaneous injuries to Jason Hammel and Jorge De La Rosa handed Chacin a rotation spot at the end of April, but despite his excellent performance in 12 starts (3.64 ERA, 74 strikeouts in 71 2/3 innings), their returns pushed him to the bullpen in July, where he struggled, earning a demotion to Triple-A. Jeff Francis's shoulder problems cleared the way for his return in late August, and after a lone dud start, he posted a 1.44 ERA over his final eight games. The net result was a 2.98 ERA in 21 starts, which made him the Rockies' second-best starter on the year. Chacin still has to work on his control, but as a 23-year-old with five pitches who gets a Coors-friendly combination of strikeouts and ground balls, he should be an asset in the rotation for years to come.

Aaron Cook

Born: **2/8/1979** Age: **32**
Bats: R Throws: R Height: **6' 3"** Weight: **175**
Breakout: **18%** Improve: **47%** Collapse: **28%**
Attrition: **18%** MLB: **97%**

Comparables:
Lew Burdette, Larry Jackson, Charlie Leibrandt (70)

YEAR	TEAM	LVL	AGE	W	L	SV	G	GS	IP	H	HR	BB	SO	EqBB9	EqSO9	GB%	BABIP	WHIP	ERA	FRA	WARP
2008	COL	MLB	29	16	9	0	32	32	211^1	236	13	48	96	2.0	4.1	57%	.308	1.36	3.96	4.45	3.7
2009	COL	MLB	30	11	6	0	27	27	158	175	19	47	78	2.7	4.4	58%	.295	1.42	4.16	4.43	2.7
2010	COL	MLB	31	6	8	0	23	23	127^2	147	11	52	62	3.7	4.4	59%	.307	1.59	5.08	5.57	0.5
2011	*COL*	*MLB*	*32*	*9*	*12*	*0*	*29*	*29*	*174*	*215*	*20*	*53*	*70*	*2.7*	*3.6*	*54%*	*.319*	*1.54*	*5.32*	*5.78*	*1.8*

One of the requirements of succeeding as a pitch-to-contact ground-baller like Cook is actually making batters swing, but in 2010, Cook's walk rate crept perilously close to his strikeout rate, and his ERA scooted up as a result. That relative wildness was unrelated to the sprained right big toe that contributed to his 8.31 ERA from July 7 to August 3 and landed him on the disabled list for a month thereafter: Cook had 39 walks against 43 strikeouts before that skid. Two starts into his return from the toe injury, a comebacker off the bat of Joey Votto fractured his fibula, ending his season. The oft-injured righty should be healed by spring training.

Matt Daley

Born: **6/23/1982** Age: **29**
Bats: R Throws: R Height: **6' 2"** Weight: **180**
Breakout: **3%** Improve: **3%** Collapse: **0%**
Attrition: **1%** MLB: **4%**

Comparables:
Brett Campbell, Santiago Casilla, Eric Hull (81)

YEAR	TEAM	LVL	AGE	W	L	SV	G	GS	IP	H	HR	BB	SO	EqBB9	EqSO9	GB%	BABIP	WHIP	ERA	FRA	WARP
2008	CSP	AAA	26	4	6	1	60	0	62^1	56	6	33	61	4.8	8.8	37%	.289	1.51	3.76	4.61	0.4
2009	COL	MLB	27	1	1	0	57	0	51	43	6	18	55	3.2	9.7	35%	.285	1.24	4.24	3.86	0.2
2010	COL	MLB	28	0	1	0	28	0	23^1	27	2	10	18	3.9	6.9	40%	.333	1.71	4.24	3.15	-0.3
2011	*COL*	*MLB*	*29*	*3*	*1*	*0*	*66*	*0*	*63^2*	*69*	*9*	*25*	*54*	*3.5*	*7.7*	*42%*	*.320*	*1.48*	*5.14*	*5.58*	*-0.3*

Daley is a middling middle reliever whose sophomore season was most notable for the three months of it he spent on the disabled list with shoulder inflammation. Prior to the injury, most of his peripherals were headed in the wrong direction (line-drive rate up, walks up, strikeouts way down), but given that he made just two appearances 18 days apart after returning from the DL, it's nearly impossible to say how much of that was a sign of the coming shoulder problems and how much was just a 28-year-old pitcher with unimpressive stuff finding his level in the majors.

Jorge De La Rosa

Born: **4/5/1981** Age: **30**
Bats: L Throws: L Height: **6' 1"** Weight: **190**
Breakout: **16%** Improve: **47%** Collapse: **19%**
Attrition: **11%** MLB: **96%**

Comparables:
Hideo Nomo, Bert Blyleven, Matt Clement (74)

YEAR	TEAM	LVL	AGE	W	L	SV	G	GS	IP	H	HR	BB	SO	EqBB9	EqSO9	GB%	BABIP	WHIP	ERA	FRA	WARP
2008	OMA	AAA	27	3	0	0	4	4	22	18	0	7	23	2.9	9.4	55%	.300	1.14	1.64	1.81	1.0
2008	COL	MLB	27	10	8	0	28	23	130	128	13	62	128	4.3	8.9	47%	.319	1.52	4.92	4.83	2.0
2009	COL	MLB	28	16	9	0	33	32	185	172	20	83	193	4.0	9.4	46%	.308	1.43	4.38	4.77	2.7
2010	COL	MLB	29	8	7	0	20	20	121^2	105	15	55	113	4.1	8.4	53%	.278	1.36	4.14	4.87	1.4
2011	*COL*	*MLB*	*30*	*8*	*10*	*0*	*25*	*25*	*143*	*152*	*19*	*64*	*125*	*4.0*	*7.8*	*47%*	*.322*	*1.51*	*5.09*	*5.53*	*2.0*

A torn flexor band on his left middle finger cost De La Rosa May and June, but otherwise, he did a fine job of following up his 2009 breakout campaign, posting a 3.56 ERA over his last 14 starts and increasing his ground-ball rate. The secret to his success in Colorado has been his backing off the curveball in favor of more sliders and changeups. His slider is roughly 10 mph slower than his mid-90s heater (he was just one of five left-handed starters to average more than 93 mph with his fastball in 2010), and both his slider and his changeup result in his helpful mix of strikeouts and grounders. The wishful-thinking department would have De La Rosa reduce his walk rate (an average of 4.0 per nine innings over the last four seasons) and would ask for health—his new contract represents a considerable gamble, given that only once in the majors has he made more than 23 starts in a season or thrown more than 130 innings.

Manny Delcarmen

Born: **2/16/1982** Age: **29**
Bats: R Throws: R Height: **6' 3"** Weight: **195**
Breakout: **22%** Improve: **37%** Collapse: **25%**
Attrition: **13%** MLB: **79%**

Comparables:
Ramon Ramirez, Doug Henry, Brandon Medders (80)

YEAR	TEAM	LVL	AGE	W	L	SV	G	GS	IP	H	HR	BB	SO	EqBB9	EqSO9	GB%	BABIP	WHIP	ERA	FRA	WARP
2008	BOS	MLB	26	1	2	2	73	0	74^1	55	5	28	72	3.4	8.7	53%	.251	1.16	3.27	4.18	0.6
2009	BOS	MLB	27	5	2	0	64	0	59^2	64	5	34	44	5.1	6.6	43%	.309	1.71	4.83	5.15	0.0
2010	BOS	MLB	28	3	2	0	48	0	44	33	7	28	32	5.7	6.5	47%	.208	1.41	4.70	6.81	-1.0
2010	COL	MLB	28	0	2	0	9	0	8^1	12	1	4	6	4.3	6.5	42%	.367	1.92	6.48	4.61	0.0
2011	*COL*	*MLB*	*29*	*3*	*1*	*0*	*68*	*0*	*64^2*	*66*	*8*	*32*	*53*	*4.4*	*7.3*	*46%*	*.303*	*1.51*	*4.77*	*5.18*	*0.0*

Delcarmen's late 2009 bout of wildness proved not to be a fluke in 2010, as his falling strikeout rate and climbing walk rate threatened to meet in the middle. Surely, lingering back pain from his October 2009 car accident didn't help; nor did the forearm strain that briefly disabled him in early July. Whatever the specific physical cause, Delcarmen's average fastball was more than two mph slower in 2010 than it had been in 2008, and while he was still averaging 93, those missing ticks helped opposing batters make better contact more often, something that luck on balls in play masked early in the season (.165 BABIP through his first 30 appearances). Once his luck ran out, things got ugly (.333 BABIP, 9.45 ERA, 2.05 WHIP, 42 percent of inherited runners scoring over his final 27 appearances), and he was flipped to the Rockies for Sally League starter Chris Balcom-Miller on the final day of August. His tenure in the Rocky Mountains proved short, as Colorado nontendered him.

Octavio Dotel

Born: 11/25/1973 **Age:** 37
Bats: R **Throws:** R **Height:** 6' 0" **Weight:** 175
Breakout: 16% **Improve:** 28% **Collapse:** 22%
Attrition: 11% **MLB:** 71%

Comparables:
Jesse Orosco, Dennis Cook, Mike Remlinger (63)

YEAR	TEAM	LVL	AGE	W	L	SV	G	GS	IP	H	HR	BB	SO	EqBB9	EqSO9	GB%	BABIP	WHIP	ERA	FRA	WARP
2008	CHA	MLB	34	4	4	1	72	0	67	52	12	29	92	3.9	12.4	40%	.267	1.28	3.90	4.30	0.6
2009	CHA	MLB	35	3	3	0	62	0	62^{1}	54	7	36	75	5.2	10.8	32%	.313	1.44	3.32	3.09	1.5
2010	PIT	MLB	36	2	2	21	41	0	40	35	5	17	48	3.8	10.8	32%	.300	1.38	4.28	4.76	0.0
2010	LAN	MLB	36	1	1	1	19	0	18^{2}	11	3	11	21	5.3	10.1	35%	.186	1.18	3.38	4.93	-0.1
2010	COL	MLB	36	0	1	0	8	0	5^{1}	6	1	4	6	6.8	10.1	28%	.294	1.88	5.06	4.41	0.0
2011	*TOR*	*MLB*	*37*	*3*	*1*	*4*	*54*	*0*	*51^{1}*	*45*	*7*	*24*	*59*	*4.3*	*10.4*	*41%*	*.298*	*1.35*	*4.05*	*4.40*	*0.3*

Dotel's 2010 season was roughly a repeat of his 2007. A long-suffering team in no real need of a multimillion-dollar closer signed him, let him close for four months, then flipped him to a contender that overpaid for him at the deadline (the Dodgers gave the Pirates righty James McDonald and minor-league outfielder Andrew Lambo), after which Dotel made very little impact as a set-up man for his new club. The wrinkle last year was that the Dodgers went from buyers to sellers with alarming speed and flipped Dotel to the Rockies, who ultimately gave up speedy, slap-hitting 26-year-old Double-A utilityman Anthony Jackson for 5 1/3 innings of work, all but one of which came in a Colorado loss. Dotel, meanwhile, has shown very little fluctuation in his performance since returning from Tommy John surgery four years ago, despite losing another tick off his fastball last year. Strikeouts, walks, and homers abound, but there are enough of the first to stave off disaster in the Blue Jays' bullpen this season.

Edgmer Escalona

Born: 10/6/1986 **Age:** 24
Bats: R **Throws:** R **Height:** 6' 4" **Weight:** 215
Breakout: 1% **Improve:** 1% **Collapse:** 0%
Attrition: 1% **MLB:** 1%

Comparables:
Jhonny Nunez, Sergio Escalona, Warner Madrigal (84)

YEAR	TEAM	LVL	AGE	W	L	SV	G	GS	IP	H	HR	BB	SO	EqBB9	EqSO9	GB%	BABIP	WHIP	ERA	FRA	WARP
2008	ASH	A	21	6	2	1	44	0	78^{1}	71	9	18	79	2.1	9.1	51%	.298	1.21	3.22	3.02	1.3
2009	MOD	A+	22	2	0	0	28	0	32^{2}	25	3	7	34	1.9	9.4	40%	.262	1.04	2.48	2.42	0.9
2009	TUL	AA	22	1	2	4	31	0	36^{2}	33	5	11	32	2.7	7.8	40%	.262	1.28	2.45	3.37	0.6
2010	CSP	AAA	23	3	5	1	57	0	69	66	17	32	74	4.2	9.7	37%	.274	1.48	5.87	6.59	-0.9
2010	COL	MLB	23	0	0	0	5	0	6	4	0	4	2	6.0	3.0	30%	.200	1.33	1.50	0.91	0.2
2011	*COL*	*MLB*	*24*	*2*	*1*	*1*	*39*	*0*	*50*	*56*	*10*	*24*	*39*	*4.2*	*6.9*	*43%*	*.307*	*1.58*	*5.83*	*6.34*	*-0.6*

Things got ugly at Triple-A Colorado Springs for Venezuelan righty reliever Escalona. Despite an encouraging increase in his strikeout rate, his high strikes often turned into either home runs or walks, given better batters and thinner air. He still got a cup of coffee in "The Show" in September, but he'll have to prove he can keep the ball both in the zone and then in the park if he wants a return engagement.

Jeff Francis

Born: 1/8/1981 **Age:** 30
Bats: L **Throws:** L **Height:** 6' 5" **Weight:** 200
Breakout: 16% **Improve:** 30% **Collapse:** 25%
Attrition: 13% **MLB:** 85%

Comparables:
Kyle Lohse, Brian Bannister, Kevin Correia (77)

YEAR	TEAM	LVL	AGE	W	L	SV	G	GS	IP	H	HR	BB	SO	EqBB9	EqSO9	GB%	BABIP	WHIP	ERA	FRA	WARP
2008	COL	MLB	27	4	10	0	24	24	143^{2}	164	21	49	94	3.1	5.9	45%	.305	1.50	5.01	5.28	1.3
2010	COL	MLB	29	4	6	0	20	19	104^{1}	119	11	23	67	2.0	5.8	49%	.320	1.38	5.00	5.40	0.6
2011	*KCA*	*MLB*	*30*	*11*	*11*	*0*	*31*	*31*	*172*	*195*	*20*	*49*	*109*	*2.6*	*5.7*	*46%*	*.315*	*1.41*	*4.65*	*5.05*	*2.2*

February 2009 surgery to repair a torn labrum and damaged rotator cuff in his pitching shoulder cost Francis all of the 2009 season and the first 1½ months of 2010, while lingering soreness in the shoulder put him back on the DL for a month down the stretch and probably limited his effectiveness the rest of the year. The good news is that the individual elements of his performance in 2010 weren't far off his career marks and his walk and ground-ball rates were personal bests, which offers hope that after having another offseason to rest his tender wing, Francis can make a positive contribution at a lower altitude for the Royals in 2011. He'll probably never be a front-line starter again, but he was overextended in that role to begin with.

Christian Friedrich

Born: **7/8/1987** Age: **23**
Bats: **R** Throws: **L** Height: **6' 4"** Weight: **215**
Breakout: **8%** Improve: **12%** Collapse: **5%**
Attrition: **12%** MLB: **24%**

Comparables:
Jhonny Nunez, Jordan Zimmermann, Marc Rzepczynski (78)

YEAR	TEAM	LVL	AGE	W	L	SV	G	GS	IP	H	HR	BB	SO	EqBB9	EqSO9	GB%	BABIP	WHIP	ERA	FRA	WARP
2008	TRI	A-	20	2	1	0	8	8	36	31	2	8	50	2.0	12.5	51%	.337	1.11	3.00	3.39	0.9
2009	ASH	A	21	3	3	0	8	8	45^{1}	35	2	15	66	3.0	13.1	61%	.340	1.13	2.18	2.96	1.6
2009	MOD	A+	21	3	2	0	15	16	79^{1}	65	5	30	103	3.4	11.7	41%	.313	1.26	2.61	3.11	2.1
2010	TUL	AA	22	3	6	0	18	18	87^{1}	100	10	35	78	3.6	8.1	46%	.342	1.58	5.05	4.98	0.7
2011	*COL*	*MLB*	*23*	*5*	*7*	*0*	*16*	*16*	*81^{2}*	*91*	*12*	*39*	*73*	*4.3*	*8.1*	*45%*	*.332*	*1.60*	*5.46*	*5.93*	*1.0*

The Double-A debut of the Rockies' top prospect was hampered by more of the elbow soreness that sidelined him for a month in 2009, something that wasn't helped when a comebacker hit Friedrich in the offending joint during a mid-July start. The result was an aggravating inconsistency that sent all of his rates in the wrong direction and slowed his progress toward the majors. When healthy, he features a killer curve and a low-90s fastball. He occasionally flashed the stuff that made him a breakout player in 2009, but 2010 created more questions than answers.

Jason Hammel

Born: **9/2/1982** Age: **28**
Bats: **R** Throws: **R** Height: **6' 6"** Weight: **200**
Breakout: **12%** Improve: **38%** Collapse: **18%**
Attrition: **20%** MLB: **82%**

Comparables:
Erik Hanson, Brian Bannister, Kevin Correia (73)

YEAR	TEAM	LVL	AGE	W	L	SV	G	GS	IP	H	HR	BB	SO	EqBB9	EqSO9	GB%	BABIP	WHIP	ERA	FRA	WARP
2008	TBA	MLB	25	4	4	2	40	5	78^{1}	83	11	35	44	4.0	5.1	47%	.284	1.53	4.60	5.58	-0.2
2009	COL	MLB	26	10	8	0	34	30	176^{2}	203	17	42	133	2.1	6.8	48%	.326	1.44	4.33	4.66	2.6
2010	COL	MLB	27	10	9	0	30	30	177^{2}	201	18	47	141	2.4	7.1	48%	.328	1.43	4.81	4.78	2.2
2011	*COL*	*MLB*	*28*	*8*	*10*	*1*	*37*	*23*	*153^{2}*	*182*	*20*	*47*	*107*	*2.8*	*6.3*	*47%*	*.331*	*1.49*	*5.15*	*5.59*	*1.6*

Hammel's second year in Colorado was a near carbon copy of the first, with one bizarre exception. Whereas in 2009 he posted a 3.13 ERA on the road against a 5.73 mark at home, those numbers almost perfectly reversed themselves in 2010, with Hammel posting a 5.71 ERA on the road and a 4.07 mark at home. It seems as much a fluke as anything else, as his peripherals were fairly consistent both home and away in 2010 as opposed to 2009, when he simply got smacked around at Coors. That bodes well for his chances of evening out that split and delivering a more consistent performance in 2011, provided the shoulder fatigue that plagued him in September was nothing more than a bit of late-season dead-arm experienced by a pitcher unaccustomed to a starter's full-season workload.

Ubaldo Jimenez

Born: **1/22/1984** Age: **27**
Bats: **R** Throws: **R** Height: **6' 4"** Weight: **200**
Breakout: **10%** Improve: **44%** Collapse: **33%**
Attrition: **14%** MLB: **98%**

Comparables:
Jon Lester, John Smoltz, Steve Carlton (63)

YEAR	TEAM	LVL	AGE	W	L	SV	G	GS	IP	H	HR	BB	SO	EqBB9	EqSO9	GB%	BABIP	WHIP	ERA	FRA	WARP
2008	COL	MLB	24	12	12	0	34	34	198^{2}	182	11	103	172	4.7	7.8	56%	.299	1.48	3.99	4.48	3.5
2009	COL	MLB	25	15	12	0	33	33	218	183	13	85	198	3.5	8.2	55%	.280	1.28	3.47	3.96	4.7
2010	COL	MLB	26	19	8	0	33	33	221^{2}	164	10	92	214	3.7	8.7	50%	.271	1.20	2.88	3.26	6.4
2011	*COL*	*MLB*	*27*	*12*	*10*	*0*	*31*	*31*	*195*	*184*	*17*	*88*	*167*	*4.0*	*7.7*	*51%*	*.302*	*1.39*	*4.02*	*4.37*	*4.7*

Nothing stoked the Year of the Pitcher talk in early 2010 like Jimenez's first dozen starts. Jimenez no-hit the Braves in his third start of the year, twice made three starts in a row without allowing a run, allowed no more than two runs in any of those first dozen outings, and woke up on the morning of June 7 with an 11-1 record and a shocking 0.93 ERA. Visions of Bob Gibson and Denny McLain vanished when lazy mechanics and a change in luck resulted in a 7.64 ERA across six midseason starts, but Jimenez rallied for a strong finish (3.09 ERA over his final 13 starts with more than a strikeout per inning and just three home runs allowed), though curiously his ground-ball rate plunged and his line-drive percentage spiked during those final 13 outings. The result was a season not terribly dissimilar to his 2009 campaign, which is to say that while Jimenez isn't Bob Gibson in 1968, he should be a Cy Young contender for years to come.

Tyler Matzek

Born: **10/19/1990** Age: **20**
Bats: **L** Throws: **L** Height: **6' 3"** Weight: **210**
Breakout: **2%** Improve: **6%** Collapse: **1%**
Attrition: **2%** MLB: **9%**

Comparables:
Rudy May, Jim Palmer, Jim Maloney (47)

YEAR	TEAM	LVL	AGE	W	L	SV	G	GS	IP	H	HR	BB	SO	EqBB9	EqSO9	GB%	BABIP	WHIP	ERA	FRA	WARP
2010	ASH	A	19	5	1	0	18	18	89^{1}	62	6	62	88	6.3	8.9	40%	.259	1.44	2.92	3.86	2.2
2011	*COL*	*MLB*	*20*	*4*	*7*	*0*	*16*	*16*	*79*	*79*	*11*	*65*	*61*	*7.3*	*6.9*	*42%*	*.294*	*1.80*	*5.87*	*6.38*	*0.6*

The 11th overall pick in the 2009 draft, Matzek made his pro debut as a 19-year-old in the Sally League in 2010 and generally acquitted himself well save for an uncharacteristic bout of wildness. Luck on balls in play prevented those walks from doing major damage to his overall line, but even more problematic was his inconsistent stuff. For now we can chalk that up to youth, inexperience, and physical (if not mental) immaturity. When he's on, Matzek complements the sort of mid-90s heat that could put him in that elite group of flame-throwing lefty starters with a heavy slider and a curve. He remains one of the team's top prospects.

Franklin Morales

Born: **1/24/1986** Age: **25**
Bats: L Throws: L Height: **6' 0"** Weight: **170**
Breakout: **10%** Improve: **21%** Collapse: **10%**
Attrition: **10%** MLB: **38%**

Comparables:
Dave Boswell, Jason Bere, Pete Richert (76)

YEAR	TEAM	LVL	AGE	W	L	SV	G	GS	IP	H	HR	BB	SO	EqBB9	EqSO9	GB%	BABIP	WHIP	ERA	FRA	WARP
2008	CSP	AAA	22	10	5	0	21	21	110^{1}	108	14	82	83	6.7	6.8	45%	.298	1.78	5.47	5.65	0.9
2008	COL	MLB	22	1	2	0	5	5	25^{1}	28	2	17	9	6.0	3.2	41%	.286	1.82	6.39	7.30	-0.2
2009	CSP	AAA	23	2	2	0	8	8	41^{1}	39	4	19	37	4.1	8.1	45%	.304	1.48	3.49	3.18	1.5
2009	COL	MLB	23	3	2	7	40	2	40	38	4	23	41	5.2	9.2	31%	.309	1.55	4.50	4.93	0.2
2010	CSP	AAA	24	3	0	1	24	0	30^{1}	20	3	19	34	5.7	10.2	40%	.239	1.36	2.67	3.63	0.6
2010	COL	MLB	24	0	4	3	35	0	28^{2}	28	5	24	27	7.5	8.5	40%	.284	1.92	6.59	7.52	-0.8
2011	*COL*	*MLB*	*25*	*6*	*6*	*3*	*63*	*12*	*109*	*116*	*15*	*72*	*85*	*5.9*	*7.0*	*43%*	*.309*	*1.71*	*5.78*	*6.28*	*-0.1*

Morales seemed to find something with his late-2009 move to the bullpen, but it was gone again in 2010. With Huston Street on the DL to start the season, Morales opened 2010 as the Rockies' closer, but struggled in that role in April, hit the DL himself with shoulder inflammation in May, and, after pitching his way out of a set-up role in June, found himself back in Triple-A in July. Morales steadied himself in Colorado Springs with the aid of some luck on balls in play and used his two months in the minors to continue developing the slider that pitching coach Bob Apodaca had introduced him to in spring training. But things were only marginally better upon his return to the bigs at the end of August, and his walk and fly-ball rates remain significant concerns.

Juan Nicasio

Born: **8/31/1986** Age: **24**
Bats: R Throws: R Height: **6' 3"** Weight: **200**
Breakout: **20%** Improve: **51%** Collapse: **9%**
Attrition: **13%** MLB: **80%**

Comparables:
Arnie Portocarrero, Junichi Tazawa, Matt Morris (49)

YEAR	TEAM	LVL	AGE	W	L	SV	G	GS	IP	H	HR	BB	SO	EqBB9	EqSO9	GB%	BABIP	WHIP	ERA	FRA	WARP
2010	MOD	A+	23	12	10	0	28	28	177^{1}	186	14	31	171	1.6	8.7	45%	.328	1.25	3.91	4.49	1.8
2011	*COL*	*MLB*	*24*	*9*	*11*	*0*	*27*	*27*	*173*	*208*	*25*	*53*	*124*	*2.8*	*6.4*	*44%*	*.330*	*1.51*	*5.27*	*5.73*	*1.7*

Nicasio has posted a 5.30 strikeout-to-walk ratio over the past two seasons, thanks to strong strikeout rates and outstanding control. As impressive as that has been, he remained old for his league as a 23-year-old in High-A in 2010, and his dominance didn't extend beyond his command of the strike zone. His big test will come this season with the jump to Double-A, but he's likely to be no more than a back-end starter at the major-league level.

Matthew Reynolds

Born: **10/2/1984** Age: **26**
Bats: L Throws: L Height: **6' 5"** Weight: **240**
Breakout: **9%** Improve: **16%** Collapse: **8%**
Attrition: **14%** MLB: **24%**

Comparables:
Shawn Kelley, Jose Mijares, Connor Robertson (78)

YEAR	TEAM	LVL	AGE	W	L	SV	G	GS	IP	H	HR	BB	SO	EqBB9	EqSO9	GB%	BABIP	WHIP	ERA	FRA	WARP
2008	ASH	A	23	6	2	2	42	0	57	49	4	14	53	2.2	8.4	56%	.273	1.12	2.53	2.67	1.4
2009	MOD	A+	24	5	3	3	39	0	49	32	2	8	58	1.5	10.7	51%	.273	0.82	1.47	1.84	1.6
2009	TUL	AA	24	1	2	1	21	0	25^{2}	23	3	9	29	3.2	10.2	42%	.303	1.28	4.20	3.05	0.5
2010	CSP	AAA	25	1	3	7	50	0	55	49	2	16	67	2.6	11.0	48%	.333	1.20	2.45	2.55	1.5
2010	COL	MLB	25	1	0	0	21	0	18	10	2	5	17	2.5	8.5	43%	.182	0.94	2.00	4.36	0.1
2011	*COL*	*MLB*	*26*	*2*	*1*	*1*	*49*	*0*	*56*	*60*	*7*	*20*	*49*	*3.2*	*7.8*	*46%*	*.319*	*1.41*	*4.57*	*4.97*	*0.1*

Lefty reliever Matt Reynolds, a late-round pick out of Tennessee's Austin Peay State in 2007, didn't get out of A-Ball until age 24, but came on strong in his Triple-A debut last year, dominating the strike zone and earning an August call-up to "The Show." A big fella with a three-quarter delivery, excellent control, and an effective slider/splitter combo, Reynolds dominates lefties, hangs in against righties, and will give the Rockies a solid, full-inning option from the left side for 2011.

Chaz Roe

Born: **10/9/1986** Age: **24**
Bats: R Throws: R Height: **6' 5"** Weight: **190**
Breakout: **3%** Improve: **5%** Collapse: **3%**
Attrition: **7%** MLB: **12%**

Comparables:
Esmil Rogers, Ryan Feierabend, Trevor Bell (83)

YEAR	TEAM	LVL	AGE	W	L	SV	G	GS	IP	H	HR	BB	SO	EqBB9	EqSO9	GB%	BABIP	WHIP	ERA	FRA	WARP
2008	TUL	AA	21	5	4	0	16	16	105^{1}	98	15	34	70	2.9	6.0	50%	.259	1.34	4.27	5.22	0.4
2009	TUL	AA	22	7	3	0	20	20	117	105	7	43	77	3.3	5.9	48%	.274	1.32	3.15	4.28	1.4
2010	CSP	AAA	23	9	13	0	27	27	158	210	18	53	115	3.0	6.6	50%	.361	1.71	5.98	6.46	0.2
2011	*SEA*	*MLB*	*24*	*7*	*9*	*0*	*21*	*21*	*128*	*144*	*16*	*56*	*77*	*3.9*	*5.4*	*47%*	*.308*	*1.55*	*5.14*	*5.59*	*-0.1*

A supplemental pick out of an Ohio high school in 2005, tall, lean righty starter Roe failed to impress in his Triple-A debut in 2010. Bad luck on balls in play played a large role in that, but Roe's pedestrian peripherals fail to inspire much confidence. He looks like little more than an organizational arm at the moment, but he won't serve in that capacity in Colorado, since the Rockies dealt Roe to the Mariners in December for Jose Lopez.

Esmil Rogers

Born: **8/14/1985** Age: **25**
Bats: R Throws: R Height: **6' 1"** Weight: **190**
Breakout: **7%** Improve: **17%** Collapse: **8%**
Attrition: **7%** MLB: **38%**

Comparables:
Marco Estrada, Gil Meche, James Baldwin (76)

YEAR	TEAM	LVL	AGE	W	L	SV	G	GS	IP	H	HR	BB	SO	EqBB9	EqSO9	GB%	BABIP	WHIP	ERA	FRA	WARP
2008	MOD	A+	22	9	7	0	25	25	143^{2}	146	9	45	116	2.8	7.3	43%	.315	1.36	3.95	4.51	1.7
2009	TUL	AA	23	8	2	0	15	15	94^{1}	87	2	19	83	1.8	7.9	46%	.310	1.19	2.48	3.02	2.6
2009	CSP	AAA	23	3	5	0	12	11	60^{2}	77	9	35	46	5.2	6.8	48%	.351	1.90	7.12	7.48	-0.6
2009	COL	MLB	23	0	0	0	1	1	4	3	0	2	3	4.5	6.8	55%	.273	1.25	4.50	6.76	-0.1
2010	CSP	AAA	24	3	3	0	12	11	61	62	6	19	53	2.8	7.8	52%	.308	1.39	5.75	5.81	0.4
2010	COL	MLB	24	2	3	0	28	8	72	94	5	26	66	3.3	8.3	51%	.385	1.74	6.13	6.03	-0.5
2011	*COL*	*MLB*	*25*	*5*	*9*	*0*	*27*	*19*	*117*	*149*	*16*	*50*	*77*	*3.8*	*5.9*	*45%*	*.340*	*1.69*	*6.18*	*6.71*	*0.0*

A lanky righty converted from shortstop upon signing out of the Dominican, Rogers was shuffled between the major-league bullpen, rotation, and Triple-A throughout 2010, never spending more than a month in one place, so it's no wonder that he never seemed to settle down. Bad luck on balls in play as well as struggles in his hitter-friendly home ballparks and against left-handed batters contributed to his poor showing. He's still an option at the back of the major-league rotation, but it would be to his benefit to be left alone to work things out as a Triple-A starter before the team starts jerking him around again. His ultimate destiny could be the role of a Ramiro Mendoza–like utility pitcher.

Huston Street

Born: **8/2/1983** Age: **27**
Bats: R Throws: R Height: **6' 0"** Weight: **185**
Breakout: **26%** Improve: **47%** Collapse: **23%**
Attrition: **3%** MLB: **92%**

Comparables:
Rollie Fingers, Joe Sambito, Robb Nen (73)

YEAR	TEAM	LVL	AGE	W	L	SV	G	GS	IP	H	HR	BB	SO	EqBB9	EqSO9	GB%	BABIP	WHIP	ERA	FRA	WARP
2008	OAK	MLB	24	7	5	18	63	0	70	58	6	27	69	3.5	8.9	38%	.283	1.23	3.73	4.34	0.5
2009	COL	MLB	25	4	1	35	64	0	61^{2}	43	7	13	70	1.9	10.2	41%	.240	0.91	3.06	3.63	0.7
2010	COL	MLB	26	4	4	20	44	0	47^{1}	39	5	11	45	2.1	8.6	38%	.274	1.10	3.61	4.77	0.0
2011	*COL*	*MLB*	*27*	*3*	*1*	*14*	*58*	*0*	*61*	*57*	*7*	*17*	*61*	*2.5*	*9.0*	*42%*	*.305*	*1.21*	*3.41*	*3.70*	*1.0*

After opening the season on the disabled list due to shoulder inflammation, Street suffered a groin injury during a rehab outing in mid-May and didn't get into a major-league game until June 23. A month later, he was hit in the abdomen by a line drive during batting practice and was out of action for four days after being rushed to the hospital. A few weeks later, he began to experience discomfort on his right side as a result of some combination of an oblique strain and a rib injury that persisted into the offseason. He pitched through that, and when he was on the mound, it was business as usual, save for a minor mid-August hiccup probably connected to the discomfort in his side. Street was nails in September despite the pain and should be at full strength by spring training.

LINEOUTS

HITTERS

PLAYER	TEAM	LVL	AGE	PA	R	2B	3B	HR	RBI	BB	SO	SB-CS	AVG/OBP/SLG	TAv	BABIP	BRR	FRAA	WARP
OF S. Beerer	TUL	AA	27	425	40	10	0	4	40	20	63	5-4	.258/.295/.315	.233	.290	-1.2	LF 2, RF 1	-0.5
SS T. Field	SCO		23	74	9	3	0	1	5	5	22	2-0	.209/.260/.299		.289	0.0		0.0
	MOD	A+	23	544	84	21	7	15	72	66	114	16-5	.284/.397/.466	.303	.336	0.5	SS -2	4.2
SS H. Gomez	TRI	A-	22	75	8	2	1	2	7	5	15	0-0	.246/.293/.391	.304	.283	0.0	SS 3	0.8
OF R. Ortega*	LAG		19	62	7	0	2	0	6	8	13	5-3	.212/.317/.288		.268	0.0		0.0
	CAS	Rk	19	322	69	17	3	7	45	28	42	23-9	.358/.416/.510	.333	.395	3.1	CF 7	4.5
1B B. Paulsen*	MOD	A+	22	541	65	29	8	12	83	33	113	5-4	.311/.353/.474	.302	.376	0.2	1B 0, 3B 0	3.0
LF J. Payton	CSP	AAA	37	470	62	36	5	6	74	25	47	13-3	.323/.365/.469	.265	.351	3.3	LF -6, CF 0	0.9
	COL	MLB	37	36	3	4	1	0	1	1	4	1-0	.343/.361/.514	.289	.387	-1.9	LF 0, CF 0	0.0
C W. Swanner	CAS	Rk	18	78	14	4	0	7	13	0	33	0-1	.303/.321/.632	.325	.444	-0.5	C 0	0.6
CF T. Wheeler*	MOD	A+	22	592	88	21	6	12	63	60	114	22-8	.249/.341/.384	.261	.293	3.5	CF 4, RF 0	2.3

His pitching career ruined by labrum surgery, **Scott Beerer** retired at 24, then returned as an outfielder in 2009, tearing through A-ball before running aground in Double-A last year in his age-27 season. A middle infielder with modest amounts of speed, patience, and power with a glove to match, **Thomas Field** has been a bit old for his leagues since coming out of college. The Rockies should get a better feel for whether there's anything here after he makes the jump to Double-A this year. **Hector Gomez** is an intriguing shortstop project, or would be if he could stay healthy. Back problems limited him to 27 games in 2010, but he'll look to pick up where he left off at Double-A this year. Venezuelan center fielder **Rafael**

Ortega raked in his first season in the States as a 19-year-old. He is a talent well worth tracking. ⚾ A third-round pick out of Clemson in 2009, big first baseman **Ben Paulsen** hit well in High-A in 2010, but his power and patience are lacking for his position, and he has yet to face the big test at Double-A. ⚾ An ill-timed workout injury kept veteran outfielder **Jay Payton** out of action in 2009, but the year off seemed to do him nothing but good as he tore through the Pacific Coast League and his September call-up in 2010. ⚾ The Rockies' catching prospects just keep coming. The team gave 2010 15th-round pick **Will Swanner** second-round money not to follow his older brother to Pepperdine. He has a lot of work do to behind the plate, but as his seven homers in 18 games in his pro debut suggest, he can hit. ⚾ The final first-round pick of 2009, former Sacramento State center fielder **Tim Wheeler** was just okay at High-A last year, which is problematic for a player who does a little bit of everything well but has not one remarkable skill.

PITCHERS

PLAYER	TEAM	LVL	AGE	W	L	SV	IP	H	HR	BB	SO	EqBB9	EqSO9	GB%	BABIP	WHIP	ERA	FRA	WARP
B. Billings	TUL	AA	24	11	6	1	109^{2}	86	6	44	101	3.6	8.3	47%	.270	1.25	3.28	3.22	2.6
A. Campos	CAS	Rk	19	4	4	0	88	80	5	17	68	1.7	7.0	53%	.292	1.14	2.05	4.75	4.4
M. Corpas	COL	MLB	27	3	5	10	62^{1}	66	7	22	47	3.2	6.8	44%	.301	1.44	4.62	4.44	0.3
S. Deduno	CSP	AAA	26	3	1	0	30^{2}	20	3	18	29	5.4	8.6	64%	.218	1.42	2.93	5.24	0.4
—	COL	MLB	26	0	0	0	2^{2}	3	1	1	3	3.4	10.1	38%	.286	1.50	3.38	3.24	0.0
E. Hollingsworth	MOD	A+	23	12	8	0	160^{1}	161	14	34	153	1.9	8.6	48%	.319	1.30	3.31	4.32	1.7
A. Jorgenson	MOD	A+	24	0	2	24	39^{1}	31	1	13	47	3.0	10.8	40%	.297	1.18	1.60	2.06	1.0
G. Reynolds	TUL	AA	24	7	6	0	89^{2}	105	10	15	45	1.5	4.5	44%	.306	1.39	5.22	5.53	0.1
C. Riordan	TUL	AA	24	8	5	0	161^{2}	168	20	38	135	2.1	7.5	38%	.310	1.31	4.01	4.24	2.1
P. Tago	DNP	—	18	—	—	—	—	—	—	—	—	—	—	—	—	—	—	—	—
C. Weathers	MOD	A+	25	0	2	4	20	21	2	17	26	7.7	11.7	42%	.373	1.95	5.85	6.42	-0.3

A late-round pick out of San Diego State in 2007, 25-year-old righty **Bruce Billings** was moved to the bullpen in Double-A last year. His low-90s fastball and solid slider proved effective in his new role and in the Arizona Fall League, prompting his addition to the 40-man roster in November. ⚾ Big Venezuelan righty **Albert Campos** made a strong stateside debut in the Pioneer League at age 19 in 2010, displaying excellent control of his sinking fastball and plus curve. ⚾ Righty reliever **Manuel Corpas** enjoyed an expected BABIP recovery in 2010, but that was undermined by a spike in his walk rate, a dip in his ground-ball rate, and ultimately season-ending Tommy John surgery, which should keep him out until rosters expand, if not for all of 2011. The Rockies released him in November. ⚾ Lanky Dominican righty **Samuel Deduno** made just four Triple-A starts in 2010 before elbow inflammation shut him down for three months. He got a major-league cup of coffee in September, but lost another year of development time and will be 28 in July. He's destined for the bullpen. ⚾ A fourth-round pick out of Western Michigan University in 2008, righty **Ethan Hollingsworth** is a command-and-deception starter who will face a big challenge with a leap to Double-A in 2011. ⚾ A late-round pick out of Cal State Fullerton in 2008, righty reliever **Adam Jorgenson** has put up some outstanding strikeout rates but is such an extreme fly-ball pitcher that he seems headed for certain disaster in this organization. He might want to compare notes with Rafael Betancourt. ⚾ The second overall pick in 2006, **Greg Reynolds** returned from yet another shoulder surgery in 2010 only to stall at Double-A, where he showed excellent control but struck out batters at a lower rate than ever before. Reynolds was drafted out of college as a low-risk, low-reward, midrotation solution, but it now looks as if he'll fail even to turn into that. ⚾ A finesse righty drafted out of Fordham in 2007, **Cory Riordan** survived the jump to Double-A last year at age 24 with his strong peripherals intact, earning a spot on the 40-man roster despite his lack of upside. ⚾ Longtime Dodgers property **Eric Stults** is a 31-year-old lefty starter who doesn't fare all that well against his fellow lefties, which makes him a poor relief option, and he gives up a lot of fly balls, which makes him a poor fit for the Rockies, who brought him back from Japan via a minor-league deal. ⚾ The supplemental-round pick the Rockies received when Jason Marquis signed with the Nationals, Southern California high school right-hander **Peter Tago** is athletic, with good stuff and a bright future. He'll begin his climb toward the Rockies' rotation with his professional debut this year. ⚾ The eighth overall pick in 2007 out of Vanderbilt, righty reliever **Casey Weathers** was behind the development curve *before* his 2009 Tommy John surgery, due to spending four years in college, being a converted outfielder, and struggling with his control. Returning from the surgery last year, he got his velocity and slider back, but his control was worse than ever, and he didn't get back to High-A until after the All-Star break, a particularly troubling pace for a pitcher who will turn 26 in June.

MANAGER: JIM TRACY

YEAR	TEAM	W-L	Pythag +/-	Avg PC	100+ P	120+ P	QS	BQS	REL	REL w Zero R	IBB	Subs	PH	PH Avg	PH HR	SB2	CS2	SB3	CS3	SAC Att	SAC %	POS SAC	Squeeze	Swing	In Play
2009	COL	73-42	4	95.9	55	5	66	6	347	225	39	50	182	.281	3	66	36	9	2	85	64.7%	30	3	102	75
2010	COL	83-79	-4	96.0	65	9	80	5	512	336	52	69	256	.236	6	88	36	10	6	87	64.4%	24	2	145	110

Jim Tracy's hands-off approach was a welcome and effective alternative to Clint Hurdle's overmanaging in 2009, but at times in 2010, it seemed as though Tracy was asleep at the wheel. Most problematically, he kept running out struggling veterans such as Brad Hawpe, Todd Helton, and Clint Barmes to the detriment of the team while simultaneously showing little patience with younger players like Dexter Fowler and Chris Iannetta, both of whom received early-season demotions. Fowler established himself in center field after his return, but after a year and a half under Tracy, Iannetta's career seems to be at a crossroads not unlike that at which Hee Seop Choi found himself under Tracy in Los Angeles. A similar pattern established itself in the rotation when a thriving Jhoulys Chacin was bounced to the bullpen midseason and later lingered in the minors well past the point at which the team required his return. Meanwhile, Tracy's push-button bullpen management resulted in Matt Belisle's leading the majors with 92 relief innings. On one particularly perplexing occasion, Belisle, despite being just the third man out of the Rockies' pen that night, was allowed to lose an extra-inning game in his third inning of work, while pitching for the third consecutive day, without so much as another man warming up behind him. In a similar case of Tracy's possible overreliance on a single pitcher, all nine of the 120-plus-pitch starts listed above were made by Ubaldo Jimenez, who topped out at 128 pitches in his no-hitter and matched that total in his other shutout.

Detroit Tigers

The Detroit Tigers enter the 2011 season fresh off one of the more impressive 81-81 seasons you're likely to see. Although they didn't win the AL Central last year, they did manage to hang with the Twins and White Sox until late July. They didn't improve their record, losing five more games than the year before, but they did avoid losing more than they won. Nor did they break in a fresh crop of impressive homegrown talent, though theay did field a Rookie of the Year candidate. No, the most impressive feats they accomplished were to be found in the front office, where general manager Dave Dombrowski pushed the reset button on a team that was burdened with bloated contracts for aging, injured, and ineffective players while maintaining a competitive team on the field. While certainly not the most important restructuring effort going on in the city last year, Dombrowski's reworking of the Detroit roster has the Tigers well positioned to roar back into contention and forms a timely example of how even the most hopeless-looking financial mess can be turned around with a few bold strokes.

TIGERS PROSPECTUS

2010 W-L: 81-81, 3rd in AL Central

Pythag	.505	16th
RS/G	4.6	11th
RA/G	4.6	9th
TAv	.277	7th
BRR	-1.1	18th
FRA	4.64	22nd
DER	.595	16th
DL	735	16th
B-Age	29.0	16th
P-Age	26.2	3rd
Salary	$122.9	6th
M$/MW	$3.48	24th

Ballpark: Comerica Park (3-yr. PF: 100). The carousel and ferris wheel are nice, but a playoff team would make this a real amusement park

2010: Pre-season swaps pan out for an all-around average club with a cast of fresh faces

2011: Product of a quickie rebuilding rides power-pitching pedigree to contention

Action Items: Enough O from Avila to leave Victor's arm at DH

Detroit's payroll had grown well above nine figures, with a total of $42.5 million owed last year to Magglio Ordonez, Jeremy Bonderman, and Dontrelle Willis, a trio with enough questions about their health and future effectiveness to fill out the card set of *Trivial Pursuit: Immovable Contracts Edition*. Dombrowski didn't just throw up his hands at the situation and muddle along until all that regrettable paper expired at the end of the season. Nor did he ask pizza mogul Mike Ilitch to buy his way out of purgatory. Instead, the Tigers' GM swallowed hard and cast his eyes a little further down the contract list and lit upon center fielder Curtis Granderson and starter Edwin Jackson, two members of baseball's financial middle class certain to be coveted by other teams. Trading two such young veterans working under favorable contracts certainly cuts against the grain, but that's exactly what the Tigers did—accompanied by much wailing and gnashing of teeth in certain corners of the media, as both players were coming off All-Star Game appearances and Granderson had become the well-spoken face of the franchise. It was a bold and controversial move that wound up paying off in spades.

In return, the Tigers received top center-field prospect Austin Jackson and pitcher Phil Coke from the Yankees, and two power arms in starter Max Scherzer and reliever Daniel Schlereth from the Diamondbacks. Each player was considerably cheaper, and all but Coke are younger, than the men they replaced. Financially, the trade reduced the payroll by roughly $7 million in 2010 and somewhere between $8 million and $15 million each year after through 2013, while adding four major leaguers under team control for a total of 26 player-seasons (see Table 1). Since cheap talent is the lifeblood of a winning organization, all those future inexpensive seasons would be worth their weight in gold if the players in question panned out.

Instead of merely waiting for the dead-limb contracts of Ordonez, Willis, and Bonderman to expire before getting to work, in one stroke Dombrowski pruned the payroll elsewhere and grafted on new branches that have already started to bud: surprisingly, the new Tigers outproduced the stars they replaced. A-Jax took over as Detroit's center fielder and leadoff man and performed like a Rookie of the Year, hitting for average, stealing bases, and showing a plus glove. Scherzer overcame early struggles to pitch like an ace down the stretch. Coke was effective all year in the pen, and Schlereth showed that he has closer-level stuff if he can cut down on his walks. Together, the new blood contributed 8.9 Wins Above Replacement Player (WARP), compared with a combined 5.9 WARP posted by Granderson and Jackson in their new cities.

Table 1. Fast, Cheap, and Under Control

Tigers	Age	2010 Salary	2010 WARP	Free Agency
Max Scherzer	25	$1,500,000	3.8	2015
Austin Jackson	23	$400,000	3.6	2016
Phil Coke	27	$425,000	1.0	2015
Daniel Schlereth	24	$400,000	0.5	2016
Ex-Tigers	**Age**	**2010 Salary**	**2010 WARP**	**Free Agency**
Edwin Jackson	26	$4,200,000	2.3	2012
Curtis Granderson	29	$5,500,000	3.6	2013
		2010 Salary	**2010 WARP**	**Seasons Controlled**
Tigers		$2,725,000	8.9	26
Ex-Tigers		$9,700,000	5.9	7
Difference		($6,975,000)	3.0	17

It's reasonable to say that the Tigers won three more games last year with the players they acquired than they would have had they stood pat. That doesn't mean the Yankees or Diamondbacks should regret the trade—on the contrary, there are good reasons for the Bombers and Snakes to be happy with their respective returns—but from Detroit's perspective, it couldn't have worked out any better so far.

Last year's Tigers earned their .500 record by being average in most phases of the game. Offensively, they were led by MVP candidate Miguel Cabrera, who bounced back from a difficult offseason to etch his name near the top of most offensive categories. A healthy Ordonez contributed a terrific bounce-back season before an ugly midseason ankle injury put him on the shelf, while rookie outfielders Jackson and Brennan Boesch were superb early on before fading or, in Boesch's case, plummeting. Utility outfielder Ryan Raburn built a case for an expanded role with a powerful second half, and rookie catcher Alex Avila was solid behind the dish while struggling at the plate.

All of this was only partly able to overcome a series of lineup disasters in the middle infield. Incumbent shortstop Adam Everett hit his way out of Detroit, though not out of a wet paper bag, and rookie second baseman Scott Sizemore was unable to fill the shoes of the departed Placido Polanco and was demoted in favor of lefty popgun Will Rhymes. Jhonny Peralta, former Indian and former shortstop, was brought in to add punch to the left side of the infield, but was only an asset when compared with the Lilliputian production the Tigers had been receiving there. At DH, East Coast sophisticate Johnny Damon was invited to the Upper Midwest on a one-year deal, but brought neither his power bat nor a dish to pass and hasn't been invited back. Taken together, there were too many easy outs and not enough power to help the offense rise from the middle of the pack.

The pitching staff last year displayed a similar collection of highs and lows. Dombrowski used some of the payroll flexibility he earned to ink starter Justin Verlander to a long-term deal, and the ace right-hander responded with another terrific season. Scherzer was dominant down the stretch, causing more than a few fans to breathlessly declare him Verlander's equal, while struggling tyro Rick Porcello pitched well enough after a midseason demotion to coax some (but not all) analysts back onto his Cy Very Young bandwagon. All this good work was significantly undermined by Porcello's execrable first half, the sad final act of Bonderman's injury-marred Detroit career, and too many mediocre innings from Armando Galarraga, who apparently used up most of his quota of good ones on a single night in June. In the pen, new closer Jose Valverde was lights-out early and lit up late, while a cast of promising young power arms was better at wearing down radar guns than opposing hitters.

Though the 2010 Tigers weren't world beaters, you didn't need to squint to see a core of young players who could form the base of a championship team, and with Ilitch ever willing to plow money back into the franchise in quest of a ring, the removal of all that bad paper at season's end gave Dombrowski a big pen going into the offseason. Thankfully, due to scouting director David Chadd's power-arm fetish, much of that core is pitching talent—the most difficult and expensive thing to acquire on the open market.

Verlander and Scherzer give the Tigers' rotation a lethal one-two punch, with Porcello's backers insisting he'll soon make it a trio. If not, top prospect Jacob Turner has the stuff and pedigree to match any of them, and given the organization's willingness to throw young power arms into the breach, he may be pitching in Comerica before he can order an Atwater Michigan Lager there. Detroit also plans to move Coke into the rotation, a job his solid three-pitch arsenal can support, leaving new arrival Brad Penny holding the final rotation spot, with lefty Andy Oliver as insurance. Valverde is on hand for one more year, and Dombrowski wasted little time signing Joaquin Benoit, the best middle reliever on the market, to take over set-up chores, giving the Tigers more time to groom Schlereth or rocket-armed Ryan Perry for ninth-inning duties. Add in triple-digit reliever Joel Zumaya, who's attempting to come back from a gruesome elbow fracture, and few teams can match the Tigers' combination of talented power arms at bargain-basement prices, with only Verlander set to earn anything like a big paycheck over the next few years.

With little need to spend big bucks on pitching, the first thing the Tigers did with their long-awaited windfall was re-up the left side of the infield. Both Peralta and third baseman Brandon Inge were signed to contracts that are virtual matches in length (two years), dollars (around $11 million), and questionability (lots). Although making this the first order of business must have felt like using lottery winnings to pay the water bill, Dombrowski clearly believed there weren't better options available than an OBP-challenged thirty-something at the hot corner and an OBP-challenged defensive liability at shortstop. Sadly, he may have been right, and Peralta has promised better conditioning and improved flexibility to improve his defense at short, but that's still a lot of money for so little production.

The Tigers are devoid of high-ceiling hitting prospects in the upper minors—2010 first-rounder Nick Castellanos is their most talented future bat but remains years away—so the Tigers are using their cash on hand to sign free-agent hitters in hopes of building a first-rate lineup around Cabrera. Since a lefty bat or two is the biggest need, switch-thumper Victor Martinez was designated to hit and provide catching depth. With Avila's bat unproven, it makes sense to bring in an insurance policy (preferably one with a lower co-pay than December acquisition Omir Santos), though given V-Mart's defensive shortcomings, the Tigers would rather not have to make a claim. More disquieting, however, is that Martinez hasn't exactly pounded right-handed pitching lately, posting a .283/.346/.410 line against northpaws over the last three seasons, which leaves the team a little short in the lefty power department. Another bat would be useful, especially one that could upgrade Detroit's shaky outfield defense, and plenty of options exist to sign another hitter who could instantly boost the Tigers' offense into the junior circuit's upper echelons.

With a roster suddenly bursting with talented, low-cost pitchers and an ability to purchase run producers off the rack, the Tigers have managed to retool on the fly. There are still lineup holes at shortstop and third base, but a lot has been added to a team that wasn't too shabby to begin with. There's no reason the Tigers shouldn't have as good a shot at winning the Central as anyone, and once your playoff ticket has been punched, anything can happen. Fans in Detroit shouldn't be blamed if they mentally compare their pitching to that of San Francisco and remember that they have Miguel Cabrera and the Giants didn't, and ask themselves, "Why not us?"

HITTERS

Alex Avila C

Born: **1/29/1987** Age: **24**
Bats: L Throws: R Height: **5' 11"** Weight: **210**
Breakout: **3%** Improve: **12%** Collapse: **8%**
Attrition: **14%** MLB: **32%**

Comparables:
Miguel Montero, Nick Hundley, Jose Lobaton (78)

YEAR	TEAM	LVL	AGE	PA	R	2B	3B	HR	RBI	BB	SO	SB	CS	AVG/OBP/SLG	TAv	BABIP	BRR	FRAA	WARP
2008	WMI	A	21	244	21	14	0	1	22	27	41	0	1	.305/.381/.385	.279	.368	-3.4	C 0	1.0
2009	ERI	AA	22	387	52	23	1	12	55	52	77	2	1	.264/.362/.450	.293	.306	-2.0	C 0, 1B 0	2.5
2009	DET	MLB	22	72	9	4	0	5	14	10	18	0	0	.279/.375/.590	.338	.308	-1.1	C 0	0.7
2011	*DET*	*MLB*	*24*	*349*	*40*	*16*	*0*	*9*	*36*	*38*	*76*	*1*	*1*	*.246/.328/.391*	*.254*	*.292*	*-0.1*	*C -1, 1B 0*	*0.9*

While Avila's rookie season may not have matched the jaw-dropping backstop debuts of Buster Posey and Carlos Santana, in its own way it was more surprising. An unheralded fifth-round pick just two years ago, Avila has already established himself as the Tigers' backstop of the present and near future. The organization was pleased with his steady improvement behind the dish as he gradually eclipsed Gerald Laird to become the everyday catcher, and while Avila's offensive numbers were nothing special, his lefty bat and patient approach make him a reasonable bet to provide league-average production. He will never be a star, but the money Detroit stood to save with him behind the plate allowed the club to sign catcher/DH Victor Martinez to spot for Avila, or to replace him, should his bat continue to slump.

Brennan Boesch RF

Born: **4/12/1985** Age: **26**
Bats: L Throws: L Height: **6' 4"** Weight: **235**
Breakout: **3%** Improve: **33%** Collapse: **0%**
Attrition: **10%** MLB: **51%**

Comparables:
Daniel Ortmeier, Jamie Hoffmann, Nate Schierholtz (73)

YEAR	TEAM	LVL	AGE	PA	R	2B	3B	HR	RBI	BB	SO	SB	CS	AVG/OBP/SLG	TAv	BABIP	BRR	FRAA	WARP
2008	LAK	A+	23	461	46	17	8	7	64	36	90	3	5	.249/.310/.379	.240	.298	-4.0	RF -8	-1.4
2009	ERI	AA	24	571	89	26	7	28	93	33	127	11	2	.275/.317/.510	.284	.308	1.4	RF -2	2.1
2010	TOL	AAA	25	66	6	3	1	3	17	4	17	2	1	.379/.455/.621	.349	.500	0.0	RF -1, CF 0	0.6
2010	DET	MLB	25	512	49	26	3	14	67	40	99	7	1	.256/.320/.416	.275	.297	-0.7	RF 0, LF 2	1.7
2011	*DET*	*MLB*	*26*	*533*	*62*	*24*	*3*	*18*	*66*	*35*	*121*	*5*	*2*	*.250/.302/.424*	*.252*	*.291*	*-0.1*	*RF -5, LF 0*	*-0.1*

Detroit's Bunyanesque rookie outfielder posted a monster first half, with a .342/.397/.593 line that kept company with folk heroes like Pujols, Cabrera, and Hamilton, not to mention dwarfing the output of mere mortals like . . . Brennan Boesch, whose .163/.237/.222 line after the All-Star break was the worst half-season by a regular during the 21st century. Pitchers soon learned how to exploit his long swing, large strike zone, and hacktastic approach—A. J. Pierzynski offered at fewer pitches—and Boesch was never able to adjust. Already 26 and with his bat his only tool, he has not been guaranteed a roster spot, so unless Boesch sorts things out quickly at the plate, he won't even stick as an outfield reserve.

Miguel Cabrera 1B

Born: **4/18/1983** Age: **28**
Bats: **R** Throws: **R** Height: **6' 2"** Weight: **185**
Breakout: **1%** Improve: **61%** Collapse: **2%**
Attrition: **3%** MLB: **100%**

Comparables:
Mark Teixeira, Todd Helton, Albert Pujols (65)

YEAR	TEAM	LVL	AGE	PA	R	2B	3B	HR	RBI	BB	SO	SB	CS	AVG/OBP/SLG	TAv	BABIP	BRR	FRAA	WARP
2008	DET	MLB	25	684	86	36	2	37	127	56	126	1	0	.292/.349/.537	.304	.310	-2.7	1B -10, 3B 0	2.5
2009	DET	MLB	26	684	97	34	0	34	103	68	106	6	2	.325/.396/.548	.328	.348	-3.6	1B -5	4.4
2010	DET	MLB	27	648	112	45	1	38	126	89	95	3	3	.329/.420/.622	.365	.336	-1.8	1B -5	6.4
2011	*DET*	*MLB*	*28*	*674*	*102*	*39*	*0*	*36*	*110*	*78*	*111*	*4*	*2*	*.308/.390/.558*	*.323*	*.324*	*-0.2*	*1B -5, 3B 0*	*4.2*

After an offseason featuring alcohol counseling and questions about his commitment, Cabrera let his bat do the talking and put to rest any doubt that he can become one of the game's all-time greats. Cabrera produced an MVP-caliber season, hitting for power and average, leading the league in on-base percentage and RBI, and setting career highs in home runs, slugging percentage, TAv, and WARP. Perhaps most importantly for his future, Cabrera improved both his walk and strikeout rates and has become a reliable glove at first base. Still years shy of his 30th birthday, given continued good health, Cabrera is likely to get top billing in pitchers' nightmares for the foreseeable future. Only two questions remain: How far will he climb up baseball's career leaderboards, and how much gaudier might his statistics be if he spent more time in hitter-friendly ballparks?

Nick Castellanos 3B

Born: **3/4/1992** Age: **19**
Bats: **R** Throws: **R** Height: **6' 4"** Weight: **195**
Breakout: **0%** Improve: **0%** Collapse: **0%**
Attrition: **0%** MLB: **0%**

Comparables:
Walt Streuli, Jack Clark, Al Kaline (87)

YEAR	TEAM	LVL	AGE	PA	R	2B	3B	HR	RBI	BB	SO	SB	CS	AVG/OBP/SLG	TAv	BABIP	BRR	FRAA	WARP
2011	*DET*	*MLB*	*19*	—	—	—	—	—	—	—	—	—	—	—	—	—	—	—	—

Widely viewed as one of the top high-school bats in last year's draft, signability concerns caused Castellanos to slip into the supplemental round. The Tigers scooped him up and eventually hammered out a $3.45 million contract, the largest ever awarded to a non-first-rounder. Although he was drafted as a shortstop, Detroit believes his future lies at third base, where his power potential and pure hitting skills will play nicely. Castellanos' long-term value will depend heavily on where he eventually lands on the defensive spectrum, but in a system desperately short on young impact bats, he's already at the top of the organizational heap.

Johnny Damon OF

Born: **11/5/1973** Age: **37**
Bats: **L** Throws: **L** Height: **6' 2"** Weight: **175**
Breakout: **0%** Improve: **29%** Collapse: **5%**
Attrition: **8%** MLB: **98%**

Comparables:
Billy Williams, Jose Cruz, Minnie Minoso (71)

YEAR	TEAM	LVL	AGE	PA	R	2B	3B	HR	RBI	BB	SO	SB	CS	AVG/OBP/SLG	TAv	BABIP	BRR	FRAA	WARP
2008	NYA	MLB	34	623	94	27	5	17	71	64	82	29	8	.303/.374/.461	.296	.329	-0.4	LF 5, CF -4	3.5
2009	NYA	MLB	35	626	109	36	3	24	82	71	98	12	0	.282/.364/.489	.308	.304	3.4	LF -6	4.0
2010	DET	MLB	36	613	81	36	5	8	51	69	90	11	1	.271/.354/.401	.289	.311	1.4	LF -1, CF -1	2.3
2011	*DET*	*MLB*	*37*	*628*	*77*	*32*	*2*	*15*	*69*	*70*	*96*	*17*	*4*	*.265/.346/.414*	*.272*	*.292*	*0.6*	*LF 1, CF -1*	*1.8*

While Damon's wife and family apparently enjoyed their summer in the Motor City more than was initially anticipated, it was his bat that most loudly disapproved of the move. Damon's home-run tally plummeted, and he lost 70 points of isolated power. And though the switch from Yankee Stadium's short porch to Comerica's spacious pastures certainly had some impact, his road line of .249/.351/.364 with just one bomb shows there's more going on here than mere geography. Home-run rates can fluctuate, but at Damon's age, a sudden lack of punch is more often the result of deteriorating skill than random chance. He can still get on base, but declining speed and a popgun throwing arm make him best suited to DH, a position where his bat now lacks the requisite juice.

Andy Dirks OF

Born: **1/24/1986** Age: **25**
Bats: **L** Throws: **L** Height: **6' 0"** Weight: **195**
Breakout: **1%** Improve: **10%** Collapse: **3%**
Attrition: **12%** MLB: **23%**

Comparables:
Chris Pettit, Brian Horwitz, Lastings Milledge (83)

YEAR	TEAM	LVL	AGE	PA	R	2B	3B	HR	RBI	BB	SO	SB	CS	AVG/OBP/SLG	TAv	BABIP	BRR	FRAA	WARP
2009	LAK	A+	23	117	11	5	0	0	18	13	11	10	2	.330/.410/.379	.286	.370	0.6	LF 1	0.7
2009	ERI	AA	23	408	46	14	1	6	44	36	61	11	5	.255/.321/.349	.240	.285	2.5	LF 6, CF -1	0.5
2010	TDE	—	24	128	18	5	5	3	18	8	22	9	1	.292/.336/.492	—	.337	0.0	—	—
2010	ERI	AA	24	434	64	20	2	11	46	35	59	19	4	.278/.342/.425	.283	.299	0.1	LF -3, CF -2	1.4
2010	TOL	AAA	24	93	14	10	1	4	17	3	12	3	0	.375/.398/.648	.349	.397	0.3	LF 6, CF 1	1.8
2011	*DET*	*MLB*	*25*	*363*	*41*	*17*	*1*	*8*	*39*	*25*	*61*	*10*	*3*	*.262/.313/.393*	*.250*	*.293*	*0.2*	*LF 1, CF -1*	*0.3*

Dirks is a gamer who worked his way up to Triple-A and profiles as a likable fourth outfielder. With good speed and enough range to play a passable center field, he works the count, hangs in well against lefties, and can punish a pitcher's mistakes. The Tigers are already drowning in backup outfielders, but Dirks has the type of game you can easily see Leyland falling for.

Daniel Fields CF

Born: **1/23/1991** Age: **20**
Bats: L Throws: R Height: **6' 1"** Weight: **201**
Breakout: **1%** Improve: **4%** Collapse: **1%**
Attrition: **5%** MLB: **10%**

Comparables:
Justin Upton, Fernando Martinez, Willie Mays (74)

YEAR	TEAM	LVL	AGE	PA	R	2B	3B	HR	RBI	BB	SO	SB	CS	AVG/OBP/SLG	TAv	BABIP	BRR	FRAA	WARP
2010	LAK	A+	19	438	33	13	6	8	47	55	119	8	9	.240/.343/.371	.271	.327	-3.1	CF -5	0.9
2011	*DET*	*MLB*	*20*	*430*	*44*	*16*	*2*	*9*	*38*	*43*	*130*	*5*	*3*	*.216/.297/.340*	*.229*	*.296*	*-0.4*	*CF -13*	*-1.4*

The numbers above might not look very sexy, but context is like lingerie: a little goes a long way. Few high-school draftees starting their first professional season have faced as big a challenge as does Fields; he was asked to change position from shortstop to center and take on an assignment to High-A. A raw athlete, Fields has a lot to learn but impressed the organization with his arm, greyhound speed, and power potential. At the plate, Fields struck out in almost a third of his plate appearances, but surprisingly drew enough walks to keep his OBP afloat. He'll need to take better advantage of his speed in the field and on the basepaths, and cutting down on strikeouts will be atop the priorities list, but for a teenager in the Florida State League, this was an impressive year.

Carlos Guillen 2B

Born: **9/30/1975** Age: **35**
Bats: S Throws: R Height: **6' 1"** Weight: **180**
Breakout: **0%** Improve: **23%** Collapse: **8%**
Attrition: **15%** MLB: **87%**

Comparables:
Bobby Doerr, Mark DeRosa, Jeff Kent (80)

YEAR	TEAM	LVL	AGE	PA	R	2B	3B	HR	RBI	BB	SO	SB	CS	AVG/OBP/SLG	TAv	BABIP	BRR	FRAA	WARP
2008	DET	MLB	32	489	68	29	2	10	54	60	67	9	3	.286/.374/.436	.293	.315	-0.1	3B 11, 1B -1	3.9
2009	DET	MLB	33	322	38	10	3	11	41	39	56	1	3	.242/.339/.419	.277	.263	0.0	LF 2, 1B -1	1.1
2010	DET	MLB	34	275	26	17	1	6	34	21	41	1	2	.273/.327/.419	.268	.304	-2.9	2B 3, LF 0	0.7
2011	*DET*	*MLB*	*35*	*478*	*59*	*25*	*2*	*13*	*55*	*52*	*77*	*7*	*4*	*.265/.346/.425*	*.272*	*.294*	*-0.7*	*3B 3, 2B 0*	*1.9*

After several years of disconcerting wobble, the wheels appear to have finally fallen off Guillen's career—literally, as a litany of hamstring, calf, and knee woes culminating in microfracture surgery at season's end have left his future in doubt. Guillen was once a tremendously productive and valuable switch-hitting shortstop, but over the last three seasons, he has missed more than 200 games, and his .269/.352/.426 batting line has been subpar for the corner infielder/outfielder/DH he's become. The Tigers hope Guillen will be healthy in time to compete with Sizemore and Rhymes for the second-base job in spring training, making good on the final year of his four-year, $48 million contract; in related news, they hope to capture and train a unicorn this spring. The likelihood of Guillen's staying upright in the middle infield is supermodel slim, while his declining bat keeps him from being an asset anywhere else he might play.

Brandon Inge 3B

Born: **5/19/1977** Age: **34**
Bats: R Throws: R Height: **5' 11"** Weight: **185**
Breakout: **0%** Improve: **31%** Collapse: **7%**
Attrition: **10%** MLB: **93%**

Comparables:
Howard Johnson, Al Smith, Bob Elliott (77)

YEAR	TEAM	LVL	AGE	PA	R	2B	3B	HR	RBI	BB	SO	SB	CS	AVG/OBP/SLG	TAv	BABIP	BRR	FRAA	WARP
2008	DET	MLB	31	407	41	16	4	11	51	43	94	4	3	.205/.300/.369	.238	.239	-3.2	C 0, 3B 5	0.6
2009	DET	MLB	32	637	73	16	1	27	84	54	170	2	5	.230/.314/.406	.268	.276	-1.2	3B 4	2.6
2010	DET	MLB	33	580	47	28	5	13	70	54	134	4	3	.247/.321/.397	.265	.305	-5.4	3B 9	2.3
2011	*DET*	*MLB*	*34*	*564*	*63*	*22*	*2*	*17*	*59*	*52*	*142*	*5*	*3*	*.228/.309/.385*	*.246*	*.277*	*-0.5*	*3B 7, C 0*	*1.5*

A former catcher converted to third base, Inge possesses a terrific glove, a strong arm, occasional power, an infectious enthusiasm for the game, and an admirable civic-mindedness culminating in his recent Marvin Miller Man of the Year award. What he doesn't possess is enough skill at avoiding outs to be worth his newly minted two-year, $11.5 million contract. Over the life of his previous four-year, $24 million deal, Inge hit .231/.314/.389, so why would Detroit agree to again pay for two more years of woeful offensive production from a player entering his mid-30s? Because a thin free-agent crop didn't look much better to the Tigers, that's why. Marvin Miller should be the front-runner for this year's Brandon Inge Man of the Year award.

Austin Jackson CF

Born: **2/1/1987** Age: **24**
Bats: R Throws: R Height: **6' 1"** Weight: **185**
Breakout: **8%** Improve: **41%** Collapse: **9%**
Attrition: **26%** MLB: **71%**

Comparables:
Roger Bernadina, Felix Pie, Andrew McCutchen (75)

YEAR	TEAM	LVL	AGE	PA	R	2B	3B	HR	RBI	BB	SO	SB	CS	AVG/OBP/SLG	TAv	BABIP	BRR	FRAA	WARP
2008	TRN	AA	21	584	75	33	5	9	69	56	113	19	6	.285/.353/.419	.291	.344	0.6	CF -10, LF 0	2.8
2009	SWB	AAA	22	557	67	23	9	4	65	40	123	24	4	.300/.354/.405	.274	.383	6.1	CF -9, LF -1	1.7
2010	DET	MLB	23	675	103	34	10	4	41	47	170	27	6	.293/.344/.400	.277	.393	4.6	CF 3	3.6
2011	*DET*	*MLB*	*24*	*624*	*71*	*30*	*5*	*8*	*62*	*48*	*152*	*19*	*5*	*.268/.325/.381*	*.251*	*.346*	*0.3*	*CF -8, LF 0*	*0.2*

Expectations were high for Jackson when he came over from the Yankees to replace popular fixture Curtis Granderson, and the Rookie of the Year runner-up clearly exceeded them. A-Jax oozes athleticism, displaying smooth actions and excellent range in center field, speed on the base paths, and gap power, but his plate approach could become his Achilles' heel. His future value depends on his ability to reach base, and a pedestrian walk rate means he'll need to hit his way on, a tough task if he doesn't reduce his strikeouts. Jackson's BABIP was the highest in baseball last year, and while his speed, low fly-ball rate, and penchant for hard contact certainly help, hitting close to .400 on balls in play is just not sustainable. A few more at-'em balls will set off the klaxons on Jackson's OBP monitor, and unless a change in approach leads to more walks, fewer strikeouts, or more home-run clout, his value will plummet.

Don Kelly **OF**

Born: **2/15/1980** Age: **31**
Bats: **L** Throws: **R** Height: **6' 4"** Weight: **190**
Breakout: **0%** Improve: **20%** Collapse: **10%**
Attrition: **18%** MLB: **65%**

Comparables:
Lee Maye, Terry Puhl, Joe Orsulak (70)

YEAR	TEAM	LVL	AGE	PA	R	2B	3B	HR	RBI	BB	SO	SB	CS	AVG/OBP/SLG	TAv	BABIP	BRR	FRAA	WARP
2008	TUC	AAA	28	479	61	24	5	8	55	32	44	2	1	.275/.322/.408	.253	.285	1.1	2B 2, SS -10	0.5
2009	TOL	AAA	29	420	57	20	6	6	40	43	51	27	4	.331/.402/.465	.297	.369	1.6	CF 0, 1B 1	3.1
2009	DET	MLB	29	62	8	3	1	0	3	4	10	1	0	.250/.306/.339	.244	.298	0.5	LF 1, RF 1	0.3
2010	DET	MLB	30	251	30	4	0	9	27	8	42	3	0	.244/.271/.374	.245	.258	1.0	LF 1, 1B 1	1.0
2011	*DET*	*MLB*	*31*	*353*	*39*	*14*	*2*	*7*	*36*	*26*	*52*	*8*	*2*	*.261/.316/.380*	*.246*	*.287*	*0.1*	*CF 0, 2B 0*	*0.5*

Versatility is Kelly's stock in trade, as the longtime minor leaguer flitted around the field like an overcaffeinated bat, acquitting himself well in center and at all four corners. His own bat, however, continued its career-long slumber, allowing younger talents like Boesch and Casper Wells to tiptoe past him on the depth chart. If he could play shortstop, Kelly might have found a career as Leyland's Bloomquistian security blanket; instead, he's probably Toledo bound.

Gerald Laird **C**

Born: **11/13/1979** Age: **31**
Bats: **R** Throws: **R** Height: **6' 2"** Weight: **195**
Breakout: **1%** Improve: **33%** Collapse: **9%**
Attrition: **16%** MLB: **89%**

Comparables:
Bob Boone, John Stearns, Yorvit Torrealba (77)

YEAR	TEAM	LVL	AGE	PA	R	2B	3B	HR	RBI	BB	SO	SB	CS	AVG/OBP/SLG	TAv	BABIP	BRR	FRAA	WARP
2008	TEX	MLB	28	381	54	24	0	6	41	23	63	2	4	.276/.326/.398	.260	.315	-0.6	C -1, 3B 0	1.4
2009	DET	MLB	29	477	49	23	2	4	33	40	68	5	0	.225/.300/.320	.229	.251	-0.9	C 0, 1B 0	0.4
2010	DET	MLB	30	299	21	11	0	5	25	18	57	3	1	.207/.258/.304	.203	.236	-1.4	C 2	-0.4
2011	*SLN*	*MLB*	*31*	*376*	*39*	*18*	*1*	*7*	*36*	*27*	*68*	*4*	*1*	*.234/.293/.352*	*.230*	*.265*	*-0.1*	*C 0, 3B 0*	*0.4*

On the surface, Laird's offensive numbers may appear dreadful, but after digging a little deeper, it becomes clear that they are, in fact, dreadful. The arrival of Alex Avila's more promising lefty bat meant the end of Laird's stay in Detroit despite his terrific defensive reputation. The only plausible explanations for giving Laird more than 200 plate appearances in a future season would be injury, penury, or apathy. Fortunately, the Cardinals, who signed Laird to back up Yadier Molina, required only 135 plate appearances from their reserve backstops last season.

Magglio Ordonez **RF**

Born: **1/28/1974** Age: **37**
Bats: **R** Throws: **R** Height: **5' 11"** Weight: **170**
Breakout: **0%** Improve: **33%** Collapse: **9%**
Attrition: **12%** MLB: **93%**

Comparables:
Minnie Minoso, Melvin Mora, Hal McRae (69)

YEAR	TEAM	LVL	AGE	PA	R	2B	3B	HR	RBI	BB	SO	SB	CS	AVG/OBP/SLG	TAv	BABIP	BRR	FRAA	WARP
2008	DET	MLB	34	623	73	32	2	21	103	53	76	1	5	.317/.376/.494	.294	.334	-0.3	RF -23	0.9
2009	DET	MLB	35	518	58	24	2	9	50	51	65	3	1	.310/.376/.428	.284	.344	-2.1	RF -10	0.8
2010	DET	MLB	36	365	57	17	1	12	59	40	38	1	0	.303/.378/.474	.312	.313	2.5	RF -3	2.3
2011	*DET*	*MLB*	*37*	*567*	*74*	*29*	*0*	*17*	*69*	*57*	*73*	*3*	*1*	*.293/.363/.451*	*.287*	*.312*	*-0.2*	*RF -12*	*1.1*

Ordonez missed the season's second half after breaking his ankle sliding into home, cutting short what had been a tremendous bounce-back season. It was an ugly injury, but it helped avoid an even uglier situation later in the year, when the Tigers might have had to consider sitting Ordonez to avoid triggering his expensive 2011 option, forcing owner Mike Ilitch to intone "269 starts are not 270, Magglio." With his play so often overshadowed by his contract, it's easy to forget that a healthy Mags is still one of the league's best pure hitters, lacking perhaps the power of his youth but retaining a preternatural ability to square up a round bat on a round ball. Last season's .304 TAv was the third-best of his career, and he walked more than he whiffed. Though age and injuries have made him a liability in the field, Ordonez is still a good bet to continue lashing line drives for several more years. Having ducked his $15 million option, the Tigers brought him back for $10 million. The only negative is that Victor Martinez's presence will keep Ordonez in the field.

Jhonny Peralta **SS**

Born: **5/28/1982** Age: **29**
Bats: **R** Throws: **R** Height: **6' 1"** Weight: **180**
Breakout: **2%** Improve: **52%** Collapse: **1%**
Attrition: **5%** MLB: **99%**

Comparables:
Adrian Beltre, Todd Zeile, Brooks Robinson (75)

YEAR	TEAM	LVL	AGE	PA	R	2B	3B	HR	RBI	BB	SO	SB	CS	AVG/OBP/SLG	TAv	BABIP	BRR	FRAA	WARP
2008	CLE	MLB	26	664	105	42	4	23	89	48	126	3	1	.276/.330/.473	.281	.311	2.8	SS -3, 3B 0	3.9
2009	CLE	MLB	27	645	58	35	1	11	83	51	134	0	2	.254/.315/.375	.250	.308	-6.4	3B -1, SS 1	0.7
2010	CLE	MLB	28	373	37	23	2	7	43	32	69	1	0	.246/.308/.389	.262	.284	-5.3	3B 5	1.1
2010	DET	MLB	28	242	23	7	0	8	38	21	34	0	0	.254/.314/.396	.266	.263	-0.7	SS 1, 3B -2	0.9
2011	*DET*	*MLB*	*29*	*641*	*75*	*33*	*1*	*17*	*72*	*57*	*127*	*2*	*1*	*.256/.323/.408*	*.258*	*.296*	*-0.1*	*SS 0, 3B 1*	*1.9*

The Tigers traded for Peralta at midseason to help shore up the left side of their infield, and the former Indians third baseman impressed his new employers enough to wrangle a new two-year deal at shortstop. What made Peralta special earlier in his career, other than his unique taste in consonant placement, was an ability to provide punch at shortstop, but there's little in his recent history to suggest that he remains either an offensive force or a shortstop. Sure, he launched a few more bombs last year, but Peralta's single-minded quest to renew his slugger's license caused his ground-ball rate to fall an astonishing 16 percent, further eroding an already subpar batting average and OBP. While his bat plays better at shortstop, his glove certainly doesn't—there's a reason the Tribe exiled him to the hot corner—making this a regretful decision on several levels.

Ryan Raburn UT

Born: **4/17/1981** Age: **30**
Bats: **R** Throws: **R** Height: **6' 0"** Weight: **185**
Breakout: **3%** Improve: **40%** Collapse: **3%**
Attrition: **7%** MLB: **87%**
Comparables:
Scott Hairston, Milton Bradley, Ryan Church (77)

YEAR	TEAM	LVL	AGE	PA	R	2B	3B	HR	RBI	BB	SO	SB	CS	AVG/OBP/SLG	TAv	BABIP	BRR	FRAA	WARP
2008	DET	MLB	27	199	26	10	1	4	20	16	49	3	1	.236/.296/.368	.247	.300	2.4	LF 1, 2B -2	0.4
2009	TOL	AAA	28	56	11	3	0	5	9	7	13	2	1	.255/.357/.638	.318	.233	0.5	CF 1	0.6
2009	DET	MLB	28	292	44	11	2	16	45	26	61	5	4	.290/.356/.530	.310	.321	0.3	LF 5, RF 1	2.8
2010	DET	MLB	29	409	54	25	1	15	62	27	91	2	2	.281/.340/.476	.297	.332	2.7	LF 1, 2B -1	2.3
2011	*DET*	*MLB*	*30*	*381*	*49*	*20*	*1*	*15*	*52*	*34*	*85*	*6*	*3*	*.266/.337/.469*	*.280*	*.307*	*-0.3*	*LF 2, CF 1*	*1.6*

Over the years, Raburn's role has slowly grown from utility fill-in to job-share participant to lineup regular. The Tigers plan to install him as a starting corner outfielder this spring, his scorching-hot stretch run (.333/.382/.586 with 13 bombs after August 1) still fresh in their minds, but they'd be wise to remember his moribund .211/.287/.329 batting line up to that point. Too much playing time is likely to overexpose him, as he has spent his career beating up on lefties—his career OPS is an uninspiring 752 against same-side pitching—and is already facing the downslope of the aging curve. Raburn owns a leather multitool that allows him to help out at six defensive positions in a pinch, making his ideal role that of a platoon partner and supersub, not a middle-of-the-order outfield thumper.

Will Rhymes 2B

Born: **4/1/1983** Age: **28**
Bats: **L** Throws: **R** Height: **5' 9"** Weight: **155**
Breakout: **3%** Improve: **36%** Collapse: **1%**
Attrition: **11%** MLB: **73%**
Comparables:
Anderson Hernandez, Ichiro Suzuki, Melvin Dorta (70)

YEAR	TEAM	LVL	AGE	PA	R	2B	3B	HR	RBI	BB	SO	SB	CS	AVG/OBP/SLG	TAv	BABIP	BRR	FRAA	WARP
2008	ERI	AA	25	576	76	21	7	3	60	44	66	17	6	.306/.356/.391	.273	.337	0.4	2B -4, SS -4	1.6
2009	TOL	AAA	26	455	48	17	6	3	41	36	58	20	8	.260/.316/.354	.240	.287	-0.8	2B -5, 3B 3	-0.1
2010	TOL	AAA	27	421	59	20	7	2	35	36	35	22	5	.305/.370/.415	.274	.317	0.0	2B 0, 3B -2	1.1
2010	DET	MLB	27	213	30	12	3	1	19	14	16	0	3	.304/.338/.414	.281	.313	-1.1	2B 3	1.1
2011	*DET*	*MLB*	*28*	*559*	*61*	*25*	*4*	*4*	*51*	*41*	*71*	*13*	*5*	*.267/.318/.357*	*.240*	*.294*	*-0.6*	*2B -3, SS -1*	*-0.2*

Diminutive stature? Grinder approach? Entertainingly hirsute? Pun-friendly name? Check, check, check, and check. It may have taken a string of infield disasters to bring Rhymes to Comerica, but once there, he evinced a style of play sure to win admirers, if not a solid grip on the starting job. Rhymes plays solid defense, works the count, takes his walks, lashes the occasional gapper, and, most importantly, looks like he belongs. He doesn't have Sizemore's ceiling, but his broad-based skill set and patient lefty bat mean he'll probably have a career.

Ramon Santiago SS

Born: **8/31/1979** Age: **31**
Bats: **S** Throws: **R** Height: **5' 11"** Weight: **150**
Breakout: **1%** Improve: **22%** Collapse: **8%**
Attrition: **17%** MLB: **76%**
Comparables:
Adam Everett, Abraham Nunez, Wilson Valdez (73)

YEAR	TEAM	LVL	AGE	PA	R	2B	3B	HR	RBI	BB	SO	SB	CS	AVG/OBP/SLG	TAv	BABIP	BRR	FRAA	WARP
2008	DET	MLB	28	155	28	6	2	4	18	21	17	1	0	.282/.394/.460	.310	.287	0.4	SS 0, 2B -1	1.2
2009	DET	MLB	29	296	29	6	2	7	35	17	57	1	2	.267/.307/.386	.245	.299	-1.1	SS 1, 2B -1	0.4
2010	DET	MLB	30	367	38	9	1	3	22	30	56	2	2	.263/.330/.325	.252	.299	0.7	SS 7, 2B 0	1.7
2011	*DET*	*MLB*	*31*	*299*	*32*	*11*	*1*	*5*	*28*	*22*	*51*	*3*	*1*	*.252/.312/.358*	*.239*	*.281*	*-0.2*	*SS 3, 2B 0*	*0.6*

Santiago, a weak hitter with a nifty glove, was born to caddy for a more complete shortstop, but the Tigers haven't had one of those for some time now. This year's starter is Jhonny Peralta, who will certainly need the defensive support but whose recent work at the plate has hardly been more impressive than Santiago's. Expect Santiago to once again play more than he should in an ideal world and less than he should in this one.

Scott Sizemore 2B

Born: **1/4/1985** Age: **26**
Bats: **R** Throws: **R** Height: **6' 0"** Weight: **185**
Breakout: **4%** Improve: **26%** Collapse: **7%**
Attrition: **18%** MLB: **51%**
Comparables:
Jayson Nix, Brandon Phillips, Kevin Melillo (78)

YEAR	TEAM	LVL	AGE	PA	R	2B	3B	HR	RBI	BB	SO	SB	CS	AVG/OBP/SLG	TAv	BABIP	BRR	FRAA	WARP
2008	LAK	A+	23	234	32	11	1	4	20	24	44	14	3	.286/.363/.409	.287	.340	-0.1	2B 12	2.4
2009	ERI	AA	24	269	39	17	4	9	33	35	46	7	3	.307/.398/.535	.331	.345	-1.4	2B -3	2.1
2009	TOL	AAA	24	330	49	22	1	8	33	29	49	14	1	.308/.373/.473	.281	.342	-1.3	2B -3, SS 0	1.1
2010	TOL	AAA	25	342	49	23	1	9	37	31	77	2	2	.298/.378/.472	.286	.370	-0.8	2B -1, 3B 1	1.5
2010	DET	MLB	25	163	19	7	0	3	14	15	40	0	0	.224/.288/.336	.224	.276	1.4	2B -2, 3B 0	-0.3
2011	*DET*	*MLB*	*26*	*440*	*52*	*23*	*1*	*11*	*49*	*41*	*96*	*7*	*2*	*.259/.332/.412*	*.262*	*.308*	*0.0*	*2B -1, 3B 0*	*1.0*

An advanced hitter with an iffy glove but impressive power for a middle infielder, Sizemore was handed the keys to the keystone out of spring training and promptly backed over the rose bushes, clipped the mailbox, and plowed into a UPS truck. He may have still been recovering from fall ankle surgery, but Sizemore simply had trouble making hard contact, batting .206/.297/.289 through mid-May before being sent down to rediscover his stroke. Sizemore duplicated his impressive 2009 numbers in Toledo, but was never able to reestablish himself in Detroit. The organization believes in his bat and his makeup, however, and he'll compete with grinder Will Rhymes and fragile Carlos Guillen for the starting job this spring—a competition the club clearly hopes he'll win.

Ryan Strieby LF

Born: **8/9/1985** Age: **25**
Bats: **R** Throws: **R** Height: **6′ 5″** Weight: **235**
Breakout: **3%** Improve: **12%** Collapse: **2%**
Attrition: **15%** MLB: **36%**

Comparables:
Joe Koshansky, John Mayberry, Matt LaPorta (70)

YEAR	TEAM	LVL	AGE	PA	R	2B	3B	HR	RBI	BB	SO	SB	CS	AVG/OBP/SLG	TAv	BABIP	BRR	FRAA	WARP
2008	LAK	A+	22	478	65	19	7	29	94	46	101	0	1	.278/.351/.563	.298	.296	-0.3	1B 3	2.5
2009	ERI	AA	23	362	64	18	1	19	58	57	80	2	0	.303/.425/.565	.343	.354	-0.9	1B 1, LF -1	3.3
2010	TOL	AAA	24	325	29	15	0	10	49	33	85	1	1	.245/.323/.400	.248	.311	0.0	LF -8, 1B 3	-0.4
2011	*DET*	*MLB*	*25*	*384*	*48*	*16*	*1*	*17*	*51*	*40*	*100*	*0*	*0*	*.247/.330/.457*	*.273*	*.292*	*0.0*	*1B -6, LF -3*	*0.0*

Strieby combines a patient approach with light-tower power, and the Tigers thought enough of his bat to have converted him to left field, removing him from Miguel Cabrera's shadow. He suffers from recurring wrist problems, however, which last year drained the juice from his bat and eventually cost him half a season. Strieby is not particularly young and will never be an asset in the field, but if he can get healthy, he's a better hitter than any number of reserve corner-men and lefty-mashers cluttering up major-league rosters.

Casper Wells RF

Born: **11/23/1984** Age: **26**
Bats: **R** Throws: **R** Height: **6′ 2″** Weight: **210**
Breakout: **1%** Improve: **26%** Collapse: **2%**
Attrition: **31%** MLB: **61%**

Comparables:
Justin Ruggiano, Ray Sadler, Sean Rodriguez (71)

YEAR	TEAM	LVL	AGE	PA	R	2B	3B	HR	RBI	BB	SO	SB	CS	AVG/OBP/SLG	TAv	BABIP	BRR	FRAA	WARP
2008	WMI	A	23	211	30	7	0	10	26	22	39	17	5	.240/.351/.447	.288	.252	0.6	RF 4, CF 0	1.3
2008	ERI	AA	23	313	60	18	6	17	53	30	66	8	3	.289/.374/.589	.316	.319	0.9	CF -4, RF 0	2.2
2009	ERI	AA	24	367	52	18	4	15	41	43	103	8	8	.260/.368/.489	.298	.338	1.3	CF 0	2.4
2010	TOL	AAA	25	430	56	22	6	21	46	34	111	7	8	.233/.309/.483	.262	.271	-0.1	CF 1, RF 0	1.2
2010	DET	MLB	25	99	14	6	1	4	17	6	19	0	1	.323/.364/.538	.336	.371	0.7	RF -4, LF -1	0.5
2011	*DET*	*MLB*	*26*	*461*	*56*	*21*	*3*	*21*	*62*	*40*	*125*	*8*	*4*	*.233/.310/.454*	*.266*	*.275*	*-0.6*	*CF -4, RF -2*	*0.6*

Yet another not-so-young Tigers outfield prospect, Wells boasts tools that help separate him from the madding crowd. A talented outfielder with range to cover center in a pinch, Wells has a cannon arm and enough thunder in his bat to support a future in right field, and he turned a few organizational heads during his late-season cameo. His plate approach is a work in progress, and his long swing leads to enough strikeouts to ensure that he'll never hit for much of an average over a full season. Right now, he's behind Raburn on the depth charts, but Wells has yet to prove that he can't support a bigger role, so the Tigers would be wise to put him on the roster and let his production show them what he can be.

Danny Worth SS

Born: **9/30/1985** Age: **25**
Bats: **R** Throws: **R** Height: **6′ 1″** Weight: **185**
Breakout: **0%** Improve: **0%** Collapse: **6%**
Attrition: **9%** MLB: **9%**

Comparables:
Niuman Romero, Ramiro Pena, Brian Bocock (87)

YEAR	TEAM	LVL	AGE	PA	R	2B	3B	HR	RBI	BB	SO	SB	CS	AVG/OBP/SLG	TAv	BABIP	BRR	FRAA	WARP
2008	ERI	AA	22	330	41	18	3	5	33	32	58	8	0	.253/.330/.387	.254	.294	0.9	SS -9	0.3
2009	ERI	AA	23	315	30	17	3	0	23	26	74	4	5	.239/.308/.319	.238	.316	0.6	2B -3, SS -1	-0.2
2009	TOL	AAA	23	162	9	4	1	0	4	11	40	3	1	.212/.265/.252	.188	.288	-1.0	2B -8, 3B 3	-1.4
2010	TOL	AAA	24	175	17	5	0	2	18	10	29	12	2	.287/.337/.354	.245	.336	0.3	3B 3, SS -3	0.4
2010	DET	MLB	24	115	9	5	0	2	8	6	13	1	2	.255/.287/.359	.250	.266	0.7	SS -5, 2B 3	0.2
2011	*DET*	*MLB*	*25*	*366*	*36*	*16*	*1*	*4*	*31*	*25*	*78*	*8*	*3*	*.238/.291/.331*	*.223*	*.291*	*-0.2*	*SS -3, 2B -2*	*-0.6*

A former second-round pick out of Pepperdine, Worth earned his first stint with the big club last year and cemented the opinion that he possesses a world-class glove and a bat unlikely to meet even the modest offensive ambitions of a modern-day starting shortstop. If that reminds you of Ramon Santiago, it should, as Worth stands a good chance of inheriting the same "utility/desperation starter" role when Santiago's contract expires this fall.

PITCHERS

Jeremy Bonderman

Born: **10/28/1982** Age: **28**
Bats: R Throws: R Height: **6' 2"** Weight: **210**
Breakout: **22%** Improve: **58%** Collapse: **19%**
Attrition: **16%** MLB: **95%**
Comparables:
Mark Gubicza, Larry Christenson, Bob Rush (83)

YEAR	TEAM	LVL	AGE	W	L	SV	G	GS	IP	H	HR	BB	SO	EqBB9	EqSO9	GB%	BABIP	WHIP	ERA	FRA	WARP
2008	DET	MLB	25	3	4	0	12	12	71^{1}	75	9	36	44	4.5	5.6	48%	.291	1.60	4.16	4.92	0.7
2009	TOL	AAA	26	1	4	1	14	4	34	40	4	7	26	1.9	6.9	42%	.330	1.41	4.24	4.68	0.3
2009	DET	MLB	26	0	1	0	8	1	10^{1}	16	4	8	5	7.0	4.4	33%	.343	2.42	8.71	7.58	-0.1
2010	DET	MLB	27	8	10	0	30	29	171	187	25	60	112	3.2	5.9	46%	.296	1.50	5.47	5.79	-0.6
2011	*DET*	*MLB*	*28*	*8*	*8*	*0*	*35*	*20*	136^{2}	*151*	*18*	*47*	*92*	*3.1*	*6.1*	*45%*	*.310*	*1.45*	*4.79*	*5.21*	*1.0*

It's hard to believe that Bonderman is still only 28, given the popular conception of his epic fall from the pinnacle of success. His last year in Detroit demonstrated that he was healthy enough to pitch, but not that he could still pitch effectively—his fastball struggled to break 90, and his strikeout rate sagged. While injuries may have left him a shadow of the pitcher he once was, it's fair to wonder whether he was ever truly that special. Pitchers who can show major-league success before they can legally order a vodka tonic are rare and often special, so Bonderman's early arrival, strikeout rate, and darting slider led to numerous forecasts of future Cy Young awards. Yet he was most notable for continually underperforming his peripherals—only once did the pre-injury Bonderman post an ERA below 4.50, despite SIERAs that were frequently more than a full run lower. His career has been a putt that analysts have continually misread, so if there's any consolation to be had as he starts his second act amid dire predictions, it's that his performance has routinely defied expectation.

Eddie Bonine

Born: **6/6/1981** Age: **30**
Bats: R Throws: R Height: **6' 5"** Weight: **220**
Breakout: **2%** Improve: **8%** Collapse: **3%**
Attrition: **2%** MLB: **17%**
Comparables:
Shane Loux, Paul Minner, Matt Ginter (79)

YEAR	TEAM	LVL	AGE	W	L	SV	G	GS	IP	H	HR	BB	SO	EqBB9	EqSO9	GB%	BABIP	WHIP	ERA	FRA	WARP
2008	TOL	AAA	27	12	4	0	17	17	106^{1}	107	10	18	69	1.5	5.8	57%	.287	1.22	4.15	5.31	0.8
2008	DET	MLB	27	2	1	0	5	5	26^{2}	36	3	5	9	1.7	3.0	50%	.337	1.61	5.40	5.65	0.0
2009	TOL	AAA	28	4	5	0	17	17	102	112	9	16	51	1.4	4.5	53%	.300	1.29	4.41	5.33	0.5
2009	DET	MLB	28	1	1	0	10	4	34^{1}	40	7	12	19	3.1	5.0	58%	.311	1.54	4.46	4.03	0.6
2010	DET	MLB	29	4	1	0	47	1	68	84	7	22	26	2.9	3.4	50%	.314	1.60	4.63	4.77	0.1
2011	*PHI*	*MLB*	*30*	*6*	*7*	*0*	*34*	*16*	119^{2}	*142*	*17*	*32*	*47*	*2.4*	*3.5*	*50%*	*.301*	*1.46*	*5.18*	*5.63*	*0.2*

Not so much a knuckleball artist as a knuckleball tourist, Bonine spent the year tossing the occasional flutterball alongside a more mundane assortment of junk, with diminishing returns—opposing bats managed a .237/.310/.378 line before the All-Star break, compared with a .395/.426/.563 performance thereafter. Released at season's end to free up roster space, Bonine employs a slow-and-slower routine that is more effective at fooling lefties. The Phillies are set to give him a spin for some bullpen bassackwardness.

Phil Coke

Born: **7/19/1982** Age: **28**
Bats: L Throws: L Height: **6' 1"** Weight: **210**
Breakout: **7%** Improve: **17%** Collapse: **13%**
Attrition: **9%** MLB: **37%**
Comparables:
Fernando Nieve, Dale Thayer, Greg McMichael (75)

YEAR	TEAM	LVL	AGE	W	L	SV	G	GS	IP	H	HR	BB	SO	EqBB9	EqSO9	GB%	BABIP	WHIP	ERA	FRA	WARP
2008	TRN	AA	25	9	4	0	23	20	118^{1}	105	7	39	115	3.0	8.7	50%	.303	1.22	2.51	2.33	4.6
2008	NYA	MLB	25	1	0	0	12	0	14^{2}	8	0	2	14	1.2	8.6	50%	.222	0.68	0.61	2.2	0.4
2009	NYA	MLB	26	4	3	2	72	0	60	44	10	20	49	3.0	7.4	39%	.215	1.08	4.65	6.58	-0.9
2010	DET	MLB	27	7	5	2	74	1	64^{2}	67	2	26	53	3.6	7.4	38%	.335	1.50	3.62	3.34	1.0
2011	*DET*	*MLB*	*28*	*6*	*4*	*1*	*49*	*11*	96^{1}	*99*	*9*	*38*	*72*	*3.6*	*6.7*	*44%*	*.310*	*1.44*	*4.25*	*4.62*	*1.0*

Moving from the Yankees to Detroit means pitching on a smaller stage metaphorically, but a larger one physically, and for a fly-ball pitcher like Coke, the latter is more important. His Bronx sojourn featured great success at limiting hits, but lots of home runs; this year, Coke allowed more hits, though he kept all but two of them in the yard. An improved changeup helped him better handle right-handed hitters, a development that explains the Tigers' plan to move him to the rotation. The success of C. J. Wilson in escaping the bullpen will surely prompt a slew of copycat conversions, some better considered than others, but Coke's stuff makes him an excellent candidate for a transition to starting. He'll be likely to give up a few more bombs and inspire a gazillion lazy soda-pop references, but there's good reason to believe that he can provide solid results at a bargain price.

Charles Furbush

Born: **4/11/1986** Age: **25**
Bats: L Throws: L Height: **6' 5"** Weight: **215**
Breakout: **15%** Improve: **32%** Collapse: **6%**
Attrition: **30%** MLB: **56%**

Comparables:
P.J. Walters, Eric Hurley, Wade LeBlanc (72)

YEAR	TEAM	LVL	AGE	W	L	SV	G	GS	IP	H	HR	BB	SO	EqBB9	EqSO9	GB%	BABIP	WHIP	ERA	FRA	WARP
2009	LAK	A+	23	6	7	0	24	23	111^{1}	111	10	32	93	2.6	7.5	44%	.303	1.34	3.96	4.07	2.1
2010	LAK	A+	24	4	5	0	13	13	77	68	7	14	109	1.6	12.7	43%	.330	1.09	3.39	3.30	2.0
2010	ERI	AA	24	1	0	0	5	5	33^{1}	31	5	10	37	2.7	10.1	38%	.306	1.27	3.24	2.63	1.2
2010	TOL	AAA	24	3	4	0	9	9	48^{2}	59	9	16	37	3.0	6.9	44%	.333	1.56	6.29	6.24	-0.1
2011	*DET*	*MLB*	*25*	*7*	*8*	*0*	*20*	*20*	*107^{1}*	*119*	*16*	*41*	*86*	*3.4*	*7.2*	*42%*	*.318*	*1.49*	*5.02*	*5.46*	*0.8*

Last spring, Furbush was an anonymous 24-year-old starter in the Florida State League, but 189 strikeouts and two leagues later, he's gotten the organization's attention. A fourth-round pick who missed all of 2008 after elbow surgery, the big lefty works the corners with his low-90s heater, mixes in a slow curve and an unremarkable changeup, and relies more on a deceptive delivery and excellent command than raw stuff to keep hitters off balance. Punchouts were harder to come by in Triple-A, however, so there's a very real chance that Furbush's version of Three Pitch Monty won't fool hitters more advanced. The Tigers will nevertheless give him every opportunity to try.

Armando Galarraga

Born: **1/15/1982** Age: **29**
Bats: R Throws: R Height: **6' 4"** Weight: **180**
Breakout: **11%** Improve: **35%** Collapse: **20%**
Attrition: **13%** MLB: **85%**

Comparables:
Mike Witt, Ian Snell, Jeff Weaver (74)

YEAR	TEAM	LVL	AGE	W	L	SV	G	GS	IP	H	HR	BB	SO	EqBB9	EqSO9	GB%	BABIP	WHIP	ERA	FRA	WARP
2009	DET	MLB	27	6	10	0	29	25	143^{2}	158	24	67	95	4.2	6.0	41%	.298	1.61	5.58	5.73	0.2
2009	DET	MLB	27	6	10	0	29	26	143^{2}	158	24	67	95	4.2	6.0	41%	.298	1.61	5.58	5.73	0.2
2010	TOL	AAA	28	4	2	0	8	7	44^{1}	40	4	14	40	2.9	8.2	45%	.283	1.27	3.65	4.52	0.7
2010	DET	MLB	28	4	9	0	25	24	144^{1}	143	21	51	74	3.2	4.6	39%	.261	1.37	4.49	5.71	-0.4
2011	*DET*	*MLB*	*29*	*9*	*9*	*0*	*25*	*25*	*149*	*155*	*21*	*58*	*93*	*3.5*	*5.6*	*43%*	*.286*	*1.42*	*4.69*	*5.09*	*1.5*

In some ways, it was better that several flavors of shortsightedness conspired to deprive Galarraga of his well-deserved perfect game, if only to witness the man's dignified acceptance of his fate and forgiveness of umpire Jim Joyce. Galarraga's response transcended the game and earned him enduring respect and a "Medal of Reasonableness" from Jon Stewart—even Roy Halladay doesn't have one of those. If only the rest of his season had been quite so admirable. Galarraga lowered his ERA, but still managed to pitch his way out of Detroit's good graces, relying on a fastball/slider combination that no longer misses bats. His strikeout rate plummeted to Suppan-esque levels, and only Scott Kazmir pitched more innings last year with a higher SIERA than Galarraga's 5.23. Galarraga's Q-Rating will doubtless earn him more chances despite being DFA'd by Detroit in January, but to succeed, he'll need to find a way to retire more batters on his own, something he should know all too well.

Enrique Gonzalez

Born: **7/14/1982** Age: **28**
Bats: R Throws: R Height: **5' 10"** Weight: **210**
Breakout: **3%** Improve: **7%** Collapse: **2%**
Attrition: **5%** MLB: **11%**

Comparables:
Donovan Osborne, Rick Helling, Luis Leal (81)

YEAR	TEAM	LVL	AGE	W	L	SV	G	GS	IP	H	HR	BB	SO	EqBB9	EqSO9	GB%	BABIP	WHIP	ERA	FRA	WARP
2008	POR	AAA	25	7	5	0	35	13	99^{1}	106	10	50	82	4.5	7.4	40%	.315	1.58	4.44	4.97	0.8
2008	SDN	MLB	25	1	0	0	4	0	3^{1}	4	0	2	1	5.4	2.7	50%	.333	1.80	10.80	10.46	-0.2
2009	PAW	AAA	26	8	11	0	26	23	139	159	20	53	99	3.4	6.4	37%	.312	1.53	5.12	5.48	-0.1
2009	BOS	MLB	26	0	0	0	2	0	3^{2}	5	1	2	1	4.9	2.5	33%	.286	1.91	4.91	6.51	0.0
2010	TOL	AAA	27	4	5	0	12	11	66	69	9	16	54	2.2	7.4	39%	.299	1.32	3.41	3.93	1.45
2010	DET	MLB	27	0	1	0	18	0	26	21	4	17	13	5.9	4.5	47%	.233	1.46	3.81	5.38	-0.1
2011	*DET*	*MLB*	*28*	*6*	*8*	*0*	*37*	*18*	*129^{2}*	*153*	*17*	*56*	*77*	*3.9*	*5.3*	*41%*	*.318*	*1.62*	*5.59*	*6.08*	*-0.4*

A former Diamondbacks prospect who landed in Detroit after floating through three organizations, Gonzalez has a build best described as "stocky" and stuff best described as "borderline." When he can get batters to swing at his wide assortment of off-speed pitches, he can be an asset; when batters don't, he hands out walks like college band flyers. Back on the street this offseason, Gonzalez is just about due for one of those random, fleeting stretches of bullpen effectiveness that most fringe relievers stumble upon at least once.

Zach Miner

Born: **3/12/1982** Age: **29**
Bats: R Throws: R Height: **6' 3"** Weight: **200**
Breakout: **20%** Improve: **42%** Collapse: **19%**
Attrition: **13%** MLB: **74%**

Comparables:
Pete Schourek, Joe Gibbon, Lance Cormier (81)

YEAR	TEAM	LVL	AGE	W	L	SV	G	GS	IP	H	HR	BB	SO	EqBB9	EqSO9	GB%	BABIP	WHIP	ERA	FRA	WARP
2008	DET	MLB	26	8	5	0	45	13	118	118	10	46	62	3.5	4.7	47%	.281	1.44	4.35	5.25	0.5
2009	DET	MLB	27	7	5	1	51	5	92^{1}	101	11	45	62	4.4	6.0	47%	.311	1.60	4.29	4.68	0.9
2011	*KCA*	*MLB*	*29*	*6*	*5*	*0*	*49*	*12*	*115*	*126*	*12*	*49*	*71*	*3.8*	*5.5*	*46%*	*.309*	*1.51*	*4.81*	*5.23*	*0.4*

Miner showed up at camp last spring with a sore elbow and tried to pitch through it, a plan that sometimes wins you some old-school respect but more often earns you a visit to Dr. Yocum. Currently rehabbing from last May's ligament surgery, Miner hopes to be back on track and sponging up his usual assortment of low-leverage relief innings and spot starts by Memorial Day, though Bastille Day may be a more realistic goal. The Tigers weren't willing to wait for results and designated the northpaw for assignment in November after which he signed with Kansas City.

Fu-Te Ni

Born: **11/14/1982** Age: **28**
Bats: **L** Throws: **L** Height: **6' 0"** Weight: **170**
Breakout: **14%** Improve: **25%** Collapse: **19%**
Attrition: **11%** MLB: **56%**

Comparables:
Xavier Hernandez, Stan Belinda, Allan Simpson (78)

YEAR	TEAM	LVL	AGE	W	L	SV	G	GS	IP	H	HR	BB	SO	EqBB9	EqSO9	GB%	BABIP	WHIP	ERA	FRA	WARP
2009	TOL	AAA	26	3	0	0	24	0	34^{2}	31	4	9	32	2.3	8.3	39%	.287	1.15	2.59	2.66	1.0
2009	DET	MLB	26	0	0	0	36	0	31	20	3	11	21	3.2	6.1	33%	.200	1.03	2.61	2.63	0.9
2010	DET	MLB	27	0	1	0	22	0	23	27	2	19	22	7.4	8.6	34%	.352	2.09	6.65	9.5.21	-0.1
2011	*DET*	*MLB*	*28*	*2*	*1*	*0*	*46*	*0*	*49*	*51*	*6*	*23*	*41*	*4.3*	*7.5*	*42%*	*.308*	*1.50*	*4.66*	*5.06*	*-0.2*

What do you get when you cross a soft-tossing southpaw with a sudden inability to retire lefty hitters? A bus ticket to Toledo, that's what. Ni started the year with a chance to work his way up the bullpen pecking order, but had trouble consistently throwing his off-speed pitches over the plate and saw his walk rate double, earning a midseason demotion. Passed on the depth charts by Daniel Schlereth, Ni is staring at a more and more situational future. Though he still threw 12 strikeouts per nine against lefties even in a down year, the Tigers won't be able to say "Ni" unless they place him back on the 40-man roster—he was outrighted in November.

Andy Oliver

Born: **12/3/1987** Age: **23**
Bats: **L** Throws: **L** Height: **6' 3"** Weight: **210**
Breakout: **20%** Improve: **54%** Collapse: **5%**
Attrition: **7%** MLB: **76%**

Comparables:
Freddy Garcia, Brian Matusz, Junichi Tazawa (60)

YEAR	TEAM	LVL	AGE	W	L	SV	G	GS	IP	H	HR	BB	SO	EqBB9	EqSO9	GB%	BABIP	WHIP	ERA	FRA	WARP
2010	ERI	AA	22	6	4	0	14	14	77^{1}	74	7	25	70	2.9	8.2	42%	.306	1.30	3.61	3.22	2.2
2010	TOL	AAA	22	3	4	0	9	9	53	43	6	25	49	4.2	8.3	41%	.266	1.30	3.23	3.74	1.3
2010	DET	MLB	22	0	4	0	5	5	22	26	3	13	18	5.3	7.4	43%	.349	1.86	7.36	8.27	-0.5
2011	*DET*	*MLB*	*23*	*10*	*10*	*0*	*27*	*27*	*146*	*153*	*17*	*65*	*115*	*4.0*	*7.1*	*43%*	*.308*	*1.48*	*4.67*	*5.07*	*1.7*

A lanky power lefty with a fastball that sits comfortably in the mid-90s, Oliver was called on to make five big-league starts barely more than a year after the Tigers drafted him in the second round, with predictable results. Oliver had problems locating his fastball, continually fell behind hitters, and took his lumps, though his solid strikeout rate spoke volumes about his top-notch stuff. His work in the upper minors both before and after his big-league stint was even more impressive, given his inexperience. Most scouts had long been sold on his fastball and changeup, but Oliver made enough progress with his slider to end any speculation that he'd be moved to the pen. He'll start the year in Toledo, but with the always-aggressive Tigers, you never know where he'll end it.

Ryan Perry

Born: **2/13/1987** Age: **24**
Bats: **R** Throws: **R** Height: **6' 4"** Weight: **200**
Breakout: **9%** Improve: **24%** Collapse: **11%**
Attrition: **7%** MLB: **44%**

Comparables:
Ray Burris, Fabio Castro, Kevin McGlinchy (77)

YEAR	TEAM	LVL	AGE	W	L	SV	G	GS	IP	H	HR	BB	SO	EqBB9	EqSO9	GB%	BABIP	WHIP	ERA	FRA	WARP
2009	DET	MLB	22	0	1	0	53	0	61^{2}	56	7	38	60	5.5	8.8	43%	.293	1.54	3.79	4.24	0.7
2010	DET	MLB	23	3	5	2	60	0	62^{2}	55	6	23	45	3.3	6.5	46%	.269	1.32	3.59	4.39	0.3
2011	*DET*	*MLB*	*24*	*2*	*1*	*1*	*46*	*0*	*51*	*50*	*5*	*25*	*42*	*4.3*	*7.4*	*45%*	*.300*	*1.45*	*4.29*	*4.67*	*0.0*

Perry spent his second season in the Detroit pen trying to make the most of his big fastball, with mixed results. His heater can reach triple digits, but is Jimmy Stewart straight, and most major-league hitters can turn that around if they know where and when to find it. To keep them off-balance, Perry mixed in more sliders and changeups, which helped feed a great leap forward against lefty bats. His walk rate also improved dramatically, though he whiffed fewer than his stuff would suggest. If Perry wants to take over ninth-inning chores from Jose Valverde in 2012, he'll need to amp up the strikeouts to Daniel Schlereth's level while keeping his walks in check.

Rick Porcello

Born: **12/27/1988** Age: **22**
Bats: **R** Throws: **R** Height: **6' 5"** Weight: **200**
Breakout: **15%** Improve: **35%** Collapse: **9%**
Attrition: **8%** MLB: **62%**

Comparables:
Mike Witt, Bill Parsons, Dave Rozema (56)

YEAR	TEAM	LVL	AGE	W	L	SV	G	GS	IP	H	HR	BB	SO	EqBB9	EqSO9	GB%	BABIP	WHIP	ERA	FRA	WARP
2008	LAK	A+	19	8	6	0	24	24	125	116	7	33	72	2.4	5.2	66%	.270	1.28	2.66	4.49	2.0
2009	DET	MLB	20	14	9	0	31	31	170^{2}	176	23	52	89	2.7	4.7	55%	.277	1.35	3.90	4.53	2.5
2010	TOL	AAA	21	1	2	0	4	4	28	24	0	10	19	3.2	6.1	65%	.296	1.25	3.21	4.90	0.2
2010	DET	MLB	21	10	12	0	27	27	162^{2}	188	18	38	84	2.1	4.6	51%	.307	1.43	4.92	5.30	0.3
2011	*DET*	*MLB*	*22*	*10*	*10*	*0*	*28*	*28*	*160*	*175*	*18*	*49*	*78*	*2.7*	*4.4*	*52%*	*.296*	*1.39*	*4.40*	*4.78*	*2.3*

Youth provides the opportunity for growth, not a guarantee of it, and as he enters his third year in the Tigers' rotation, it's hard to measure much growth in Porcello. When he was drafted, the dream was that he might become Justin Verlander, overpowering batters with an upper-90s fastball. When he proved to be more of a worm-killer in the minors, the ideal became Brandon Webb. Now, after two full seasons with a subpar strikeout rate, is he really just Jon Garland?

Porcello induced the same number of swinging strikes last year as Aaron Cook, and while many point to improvement after his brief midseason demotion, upping his strikeout rate from 4.22 to 4.97 per nine innings had better be the first step of a journey, not the destination. Ground balls may be more democratic, but Porcello needs to act more like a dictator on the mound or he'll become just another midrotation journeyman.

Max Scherzer

Born: **7/27/1984** Age: **26**
Bats: **R** Throws: **R** Height: **6' 3"** Weight: **215**
Breakout: **13%** Improve: **47%** Collapse: **23%**
Attrition: **7%** MLB: **96%**

Comparables:
Roger Clemens, Zack Greinke, Len Barker (66)

YEAR	TEAM	LVL	AGE	W	L	SV	G	GS	IP	H	HR	BB	SO	EqBB9	EqSO9	GB%	BABIP	WHIP	ERA	FRA	WARP
2008	TUC	AAA	23	1	1	0	13	10	53	35	2	22	79	3.7	13.4	53%	.289	1.11	2.72	3.67	1.6
2008	ARI	MLB	23	0	4	0	16	7	56	48	5	21	66	3.4	10.6	43%	.307	1.32	3.05	3.48	1.4
2009	ARI	MLB	24	9	11	0	30	30	170^{1}	166	20	63	174	3.3	9.2	43%	.308	1.40	4.12	4.78	2.1
2010	DET	MLB	25	12	11	0	31	31	195^{2}	174	20	70	184	3.2	8.5	42%	.297	1.28	3.50	3.73	3.8
2011	*DET*	*MLB*	*26*	*11*	*7*	*0*	*26*	*26*	*145*	*132*	*14*	*55*	*143*	*3.4*	*8.8*	*44%*	*.302*	*1.29*	*3.61*	*3.93*	*3.6*

Scherzer struggled out of the gate last year, posting a 7.29 ERA through his first eight starts before being sent down to Toledo to fix his mechanics. It didn't take long to find the problem (a matter of arm positioning to stay on top of the ball), and when Scherzer returned, he was lights-out. From May 30 forward, he posted a 2.46 ERA, held opponents to a .220/.293/.328 batting line, and struck out more than a batter per inning—extrapolate those numbers to a full season, and you have a Cy Young candidate. Scherzer is known for his heavy, moving, low-90s fastball, but it's the continued improvement of his slider and changeup that has toggled his ace descriptor from "future" to "current."

Daniel Schlereth

Born: **5/9/1986** Age: **25**
Bats: **L** Throws: **L** Height: **6' 0"** Weight: **210**
Breakout: **20%** Improve: **32%** Collapse: **21%**
Attrition: **5%** MLB: **67%**

Comparables:
Steve Bedrosian, Gregg Olson, Ken Howell (51)

YEAR	TEAM	LVL	AGE	W	L	SV	G	GS	IP	H	HR	BB	SO	EqBB9	EqSO9	GB%	BABIP	WHIP	ERA	FRA	WARP
2009	MOB	AA	23	0	0	4	21	0	26^{2}	14	1	16	39	5.4	13.2	51%	.250	1.16	1.01	0.91	1.2
2009	ARI	MLB	23	1	4	0	21	0	18^{1}	15	1	15	22	7.4	10.8	60%	.298	1.69	5.89	6.70	-0.4
2010	TOL	AAA	24	1	3	0	38	0	49^{1}	40	0	34	60	6.2	11.0	52%	.323	1.55	2.37	2.40	1.7
2010	DET	MLB	24	2	0	1	18	0	18^{2}	20	2	10	19	4.8	9.2	49%	.327	1.66	2.89	2.35	0.5
2011	*DET*	*MLB*	*25*	*2*	*1*	*0*	*38*	*0*	43^{1}	*37*	*3*	*26*	*47*	*5.4*	*9.8*	*47%*	*.304*	*1.45*	*3.76*	*4.08*	*0.3*

When you watch Schlereth overpower hitters with his plus fastball and baffling curve, it's easy to envision him as a late-inning beast. There is still work to be done, as the continued reduction of his once-stratospheric walk rate will determine whether he becomes a premium closer or something less, but as long as he continues to pile up the strikeouts, he'll be working high-leverage situations. With Jose Valverde again on hand to work the ninth, Schlereth and Ryan Perry will spend the year jockeying to be his inevitable replacement.

Brad Thomas

Born: **10/22/1977** Age: **33**
Bats: **L** Throws: **L** Height: **6' 3"** Weight: **204**
Breakout: **7%** Improve: **23%** Collapse: **19%**
Attrition: **12%** MLB: **54%**

Comparables:
Jason Stanford, Mike Smith, Jim Perry (78)

YEAR	TEAM	LVL	AGE	W	L	SV	G	GS	IP	H	HR	BB	SO	EqBB9	EqSO9	GB%	BABIP	WHIP	ERA	FRA	WARP
2010	DET	MLB	32	6	2	0	49	2	69^{1}	77	4	29	30	3.8	3.9	52%	.304	1.59	3.89	4.10	0.7
2011	*DET*	*MLB*	*33*	*3*	*1*	*0*	*69*	*0*	*92*	*107*	*9*	*38*	*48*	*3.7*	*4.7*	*47%*	*.314*	*1.57*	*5.06*	*5.50*	*-0.9*

hA former top prospect in the Twins organization, Thomas is a lefty reliever who spent the last decade earning massive frequent-flyer miles. Among stints with the Red Sox and Mariners organizations, Thomas spent time in both Japan and Korea and pitched for the national team in his native Australia before signing with the Tigers. He shouldn't have been allowed to see so many righties—they torched him to the tune of .322/.389/.497, with more than twice as many walks as strikeouts—but he might hang on for a few years as a LOOGY. Most likely, however, his best contributions will involve keeping his more talented bullpen-mates loose with tales of kimchee, fugu, funnel-web spiders, and toilets that flush counterclockwise.

Jacob Turner

Born: **5/21/1991** Age: **20**
Bats: **R** Throws: **R** Height: **6' 5"** Weight: **210**
Breakout: **7%** Improve: **13%** Collapse: **1%**
Attrition: **2%** MLB: **17%**

Comparables:
Madison Bumgarner, Don Drysdale, Rick Porcello (62)

YEAR	TEAM	LVL	AGE	W	L	SV	G	GS	IP	H	HR	BB	SO	EqBB9	EqSO9	GB%	BABIP	WHIP	ERA	FRA	WARP
2010	WMI	A	19	2	3	0	11	10	54	53	4	9	51	1.5	8.5	44%	.301	1.17	3.67	4.72	0.6
2010	LAK	A+	19	4	2	0	13	13	61^{1}	53	3	14	51	2.1	7.5	48%	.282	1.21	2.93	3.02	1.9
2011	*DET*	*MLB*	*20*	*8*	*8*	*0*	*23*	*23*	*108*	*117*	*13*	*40*	*66*	*3.3*	*5.5*	*44%*	*.298*	*1.43*	*4.59*	*4.99*	*1.7*

Teenage starters in the Florida State League generally fall into one of two categories: five-star prospect, or Tigers prospect. Turner is both, the jewel of a Detroit system never afraid to challenge its best young arms with difficult assignments. The consensus top high-school pitcher in the 2009 draft, Turner is a classic power starter with a heavy, mid-90s fastball, solid curveball, and improving changeup. Unlike most debuting young flamethrowers, he avoided walks with aplomb and commanded his fastball exceptionally well, while scouts think his curve could eventually rival anyone's. In short, he could be a behemoth, and if he's successful in the upper minors as a 20-year-old, it's not crazy to think he could help the Tigers' bullpen down the stretch.

Jose Valverde

Born: **7/24/1979** Age: **31**
Bats: R Throws: R Height: **6' 4"** Weight: **254**
Breakout: **14%** Improve: **24%** Collapse: **12%**
Attrition: **6%** MLB: **51%**

Comparables:
Heath Bell, Jeff Nelson, Henry Owens (64)

YEAR	TEAM	LVL	AGE	W	L	SV	G	GS	IP	H	HR	BB	SO	EqBB9	EqSO9	GB%	BABIP	WHIP	ERA	FRA	WARP
2008	HOU	MLB	28	6	3	44	74	0	72	62	10	23	83	2.9	10.4	39%	.281	1.21	3.38	397	0.7
2009	HOU	MLB	29	4	2	25	52	0	54	40	5	21	56	3.5	9.3	41%	.259	1.17	2.33	2.90	1.1
2010	DET	MLB	30	2	4	26	60	0	63	41	5	32	63	4.6	9.0	54%	.231	1.21	3.00	4.27	0.3
2011	*DET*	*MLB*	*31*	*3*	*1*	*20*	*64*	*0*	*64*	*54*	*6*	*28*	*67*	*3.9*	*9.3*	*45%*	*.287*	*1.27*	*3.37*	*3.67*	*0.8*

Papa Grande was unhittable early and unspeakable late, with opponents batting .125/.226/.172 before the All-Star break and .263/.381/.453 afterward. Elbow tendinitis that eventually caused him to miss some time in September probably had something to do with his ineffectiveness, but health will always be an issue for Valverde. The overall results were similar to his 2009 numbers, with more walks and a smidge fewer strikeouts, but the ways in which he achieved them were quite different. Valverde threw his legendary splitter twice as often as usual, relying on his mid-90s fastball less than half the time, and as a result, he morphed into a certifiable ground-ball machine. The Tigers don't care how he gets it done, as long as he's healthy and keeps runs off the board, both of which are open questions going into his final guaranteed year.

Justin Verlander

Born: **2/20/1983** Age: **28**
Bats: R Throws: R Height: **6' 5"** Weight: **200**
Breakout: **6%** Improve: **36%** Collapse: **28%**
Attrition: **10%** MLB: **97%**

Comparables:
Daisuke Matsuzaka, Jake Peavy, Don Drysdale (62)

YEAR	TEAM	LVL	AGE	W	L	SV	G	GS	IP	H	HR	BB	SO	EqBB9	EqSO9	GB%	BABIP	WHIP	ERA	FRA	WARP
2008	DET	MLB	25	11	17	0	33	33	201	195	18	87	163	3.9	7.3	41%	.296	1.47	4.84	5.37	0.9
2009	DET	MLB	26	19	9	0	35	35	240	219	20	63	269	2.4	10.1	37%	.319	1.20	3.45	4.11	4.3
2010	DET	MLB	27	18	9	0	33	33	224^1	190	14	71	219	2.8	8.8	42%	.286	1.19	3.37	3.51	4.7
2011	*DET*	*MLB*	*28*	*14*	*8*	*0*	*32*	*32*	212^2	*197*	*17*	*68*	*198*	*2.9*	*8.4*	*41%*	*.303*	*1.25*	*3.32*	*3.61*	*5.5*

The worst thing you can say about Verlander's 2010 campaign is that it didn't surpass his 2009 campaign, which is rather like complaining that *Let It Bleed* isn't any better than *Beggars Banquet*. While baseball's prototypical power pitcher was unable to again strike out more than a batter per inning and never gained traction in the Cy Young debate, Verlander lowered his ERA and established a peak level of performance significantly above that of his early career. His fastball is still explosive, his curveball down the stretch was especially filthy, and he tossed in a few more sliders just for grins. The main concern now is durability, as Verlander again threw more pitches than any other AL starter. So far, he's been a horse, but with the Tigers on the hook for $72.75 million through 2014, they may want to pull back a little on the reins.

Brayan Villarreal

Born: **5/10/1987** Age: **24**
Bats: R Throws: R Height: **6' 0"** Weight: **170**
Breakout: **3%** Improve: **3%** Collapse: **1%**
Attrition: **1%** MLB: **4%**

Comparables:
Jose Ascanio, Don Demola, Ugueth Urbina (75)

YEAR	TEAM	LVL	AGE	W	L	SV	G	GS	IP	H	HR	BB	SO	EqBB9	EqSO9	GB%	BABIP	WHIP	ERA	FRA	WARP
2008	TGR	Rk	21	1	5	0	11	7	37	26	0	11	37	2.7	9.0	60%	.263	1.14	3.16	5.77	0.1
2009	WMI	A	22	5	5	2	26	18	103^1	85	5	34	118	3.0	10.3	45%	.310	1.28	2.61	3.34	2.4
2010	LAK	A+	23	7	4	0	16	16	85^2	73	8	23	90	2.4	9.5	40%	.291	1.20	3.47	4.02	1.4
2010	ERI	AA	23	0	4	0	8	8	43^2	37	6	16	46	3.3	9.6	36%	.277	1.32	3.71	4.73	0.6
2011	*DET*	*MLB*	*24*	*4*	*4*	*0*	*13*	*10*	58^2	*59*	*8*	*28*	*46*	*4.3*	*7.1*	*42%*	*.299*	*1.49*	*4.89*	*5.32*	*0.5*

Villarreal continued his steady climb up Detroit's minor-league ladder, blowing through High-A and into the high minors while continuing to whiff more than a man per inning and keep his walks in check. His fastball can reach the mid-90s, and his slider has become such a wipeout pitch that minor-league batters often hear The Surfaris as they mutter their way back to the dugout. His changeup is a work in progress, however, and since he lacks ideal size, many think his future lies in the bullpen—an especially bright future, if his stuff becomes even filthier in shorter appearances.

Robert Weinhardt

Born: **12/8/1985** Age: **25**
Bats: R Throws: R Height: **6' 2"** Weight: **205**
Breakout: **2%** Improve: **8%** Collapse: **8%**
Attrition: **7%** MLB: **22%**

Comparables:
Fernando Hernandez Jr., Warner Madrigal, Osiris Matos (79)

YEAR	TEAM	LVL	AGE	W	L	SV	G	GS	IP	H	HR	BB	SO	EqBB9	EqSO9	GB%	BABIP	WHIP	ERA	FRA	WARP
2008	LAK	A+	22	3	1	4	21	0	35^1	19	1	11	44	2.8	11.2	45%	.222	0.91	2.04	3.65	0.6
2009	LAK	A+	23	1	1	3	22	0	31^2	24	2	10	40	2.8	11.4	56%	.282	1.11	0.85	1.25	1.4
2009	ERI	AA	23	0	1	2	20	0	31^1	28	0	16	32	4.6	9.2	47%	.315	1.53	2.30	1.37	1.1
2010	TOL	AAA	24	1	1	1	24	0	34^1	26	0	7	25	1.8	6.6	63%	.265	1.00	1.57	3.20	0.8
2010	DET	MLB	24	2	2	0	28	0	29^1	40	2	8	21	2.5	6.4	55%	.376	1.74	6.14	5.59	-0.3
2011	*DET*	*MLB*	*25*	*2*	*1*	*1*	*40*	*0*	55^2	*55*	*5*	*22*	*44*	*3.6*	*7.1*	*48%*	*.305*	*1.39*	*4.02*	*4.37*	*0.2*

Weinhardt's sinker/slider repertoire doesn't cause jaws to drop, but it generates copious grounders, keeps the ball in the park, and more often than not puts zeros on the scoreboard—at least in the minors, where Weinhardt owns a career 1.64 ERA and has struck out more than a man per inning. His big-league debut was far less impressive, but the organization saw enough in Weinhardt to pencil him into this year's bullpen, where his sinker will come in handy when the Tigers need a double play.

Adam Wilk

Born: **12/9/1987** Age: **23**
Bats: **L** Throws: **L** Height: **6' 2"** Weight: **175**
Breakout: **9%** Improve: **27%** Collapse: **14%**
Attrition: **10%** MLB: **60%**

Comparables:
Dave Rozema, Shairon Martis, Junichi Tazawa (58)

YEAR	TEAM	LVL	AGE	W	L	SV	G	GS	IP	H	HR	BB	SO	EqBB9	EqSO9	GB%	BABIP	WHIP	ERA	FRA	WARP
2009	WMI	A	21	2	1	0	7	7	36^1	30	2	2	33	0.5	8.2	43%	.280	0.91	1.49	2.08	1.8
2009	ONE	A-	21	2	0	0	7	7	37^1	23	0	5	34	1.2	8.2	43%	.230	0.78	1.45	2.04	1.6
2010	LAK	A+	22	9	5	0	24	24	143^2	139	8	19	100	1.2	6.3	40%	.287	1.13	3.01	3.25	3.8
2010	ERI	AA	22	2	0	0	3	3	23^2	10	1	5	14	1.9	5.4	34%	.143	0.69	1.14	4.06	0.4
2011	*DET*	*MLB*	*23*	*7*	*7*	*0*	*19*	*19*	*111*	*124*	*13*	*32*	*56*	*2.6*	*4.5*	*41%*	*.295*	*1.40*	*4.47*	*4.86*	*1.5*

The Tigers are known for their unabashed man-crushes on power arms, yet Wilk continues to work his off-speed assortment up the organizational ladder. Command and deception are his calling cards, as he walked less than a batter per start, mixing in curveballs, changeups, and an upper-80s fastball to keep batters guessing and induce weak contact. He'll start the year at Double-A, where the organization will be watching to learn whether more-advanced batters can see the magician's hand.

Joel Zumaya

Born: **11/9/1984** Age: **26**
Bats: **R** Throws: **R** Height: **6' 3"** Weight: **210**
Breakout: **14%** Improve: **31%** Collapse: **18%**
Attrition: **8%** MLB: **64%**

Comparables:
Joe Smith, Ray Newman, Bob Howry (79)

YEAR	TEAM	LVL	AGE	W	L	SV	G	GS	IP	H	HR	BB	SO	EqBB9	EqSO9	GB%	BABIP	WHIP	ERA	FRA	WARP
2008	DET	MLB	23	0	2	1	21	0	23^1	24	3	22	22	8.5	8.5	40%	.313	1.97	3.47	4.51	0.1
2009	DET	MLB	24	3	3	1	28	0	31	34	5	21	30	6.1	8.7	35%	.319	1.81	4.94	4.65	0.2
2010	DET	MLB	25	2	1	1	31	0	38^1	32	1	11	34	2.6	8.0	41%	.282	1.12	2.82	3.43	0.6
2011	*DET*	*MLB*	*26*	*2*	*1*	*0*	*40*	*0*	*45^1*	*42*	*4*	*23*	*41*	*4.7*	*8.1*	*43%*	*.300*	*1.45*	*4.12*	*4.48*	*0.1*

Throwing a 99 mph fastball is an unnatural act, an observation brought home last June by the sight of Zumaya crumpled on the ground in agony after suffering a fracture in his elbow. This ended the latest of approximately 116 injury comebacks for the hard-throwing righty since his triumphant rookie season and was especially disappointing, as Zumaya was looking better than he had in years, commanding his overpowering heater and avoiding the walks that have traditionally plagued him. Still just 26 years old, Zumaya and the surgically implanted screw in his arm may be ready by spring training to try once again to defy the cloud of bad fortune that has so often enveloped him. It would be wonderful to see him take his rightful place in the bullpen alongside fellow fire-breathers Ryan Perry and Daniel Schlereth, but given his history, who's willing to bet on it? Zumaya rides his fastball like Evel Knievel, and fans, teammates, and family members should be excused if they peek through their fingers every time he lets one fly.

LINEOUTS

HITTERS

PLAYER	TEAM	LVL	AGE	PA	R	2B	3B	HR	RBI	BB	SO	SB-CS	AVG/OBP/SLG	TAv	BABIP	BRR	FRAA	WARP
3B A. Ciriaco	ERI	AA	23	251	28	8	4	9	36	8	49	0-0	.241/.263/.419	.235	.265	0.0	3B 3, SS -1	0.3
SS B. Dlugach	TOL	AAA	27	484	52	22	3	6	41	25	149	12-4	.258/.303/.360	.234	.368	0.0	SS -2, 3B 1	0.2
SS A. Everett	DET	MLB	33	89	6	5	0	0	4	4	18	2-1	.185/.214/.247	.168	.224	-0.4	SS -3	-0.8
4C J. Frazier	TOL	AAA	27	516	72	34	2	25	73	32	89	7-1	.256/.306/.493	.268	.265	0.0	LF 11, 1B 1	2.3
	DET	MLB	27	24	3	1	0	0	1	1	6	0-0	.217/.250/.261	.162	.294	0.5	LF 2, RF 0	0.0
OF A. Garcia	WMI	A	19	524	58	17	4	4	63	20	113	20-4	.281/.313/.356	.247	.353	-2.0	RF 3	0.2
3B W. Gaynor	WMI	A	22	574	91	39	4	10	80	46	111	13-5	.286/.354/.436	.291	.345	-1.4	3B 1	3.5
SS C. Iorg	ERI	AA	24	454	50	22	1	10	33	17	139	12-5	.211/.248/.337	.203	.282	3.9	SS -2	-0.7
	TOL	AAA	24	70	7	6	1	1	9	2	20	0-1	.242/.271/.409	.219	.326	-0.2	SS 2	0.2
SS G. Nunez#	LAK	A+	22	572	66	13	6	2	33	21	93	33-8	.222/.263/.281	.205	.255	4.5	SS 8	0.1
C M. St. Pierre	ERI	AA	30	74	13	0	1	5	14	11	5	2-0	.217/.347/.500	.289	.154	-0.2	C 1	0.6
	ERI	AA	30	74	13	0	1	5	14	11	5	2-0	.217/.347/.500	.289	.154	-0.2	C 1	0.6
	TOL	AAA	30	147	16	7	0	5	22	11	21	1-1	.300/.356/.469	.275	.315	1.0	C -2	0.8
	TOL	AAA	30	147	16	7	0	5	22	11	21	1-1	.300/.356/.469	.275	.315	1.0	C -2	0.8
	DET	MLB	30	9	1	1	0	0	0	0	2	0-0	.222/.222/.333	.195	.286	-0.4	C 0	-0.1
	DET	MLB	30	9	1	1	0	0	0	0	2	0-0	.222/.222/.333	.195	.286	-0.4	C 0	-0.1
OF C. Thomas*	TOL	AAA	26	86	14	2	1	4	13	12	32	9-0	.183/.318/.408	.263	.250	1.0	CF 4, LF -1	0.8

The Tigers keep hoping toolsy former shortstop **Audy Ciriaco** can find the formula that makes power potential plus athleticism equal production, but since the best-fit equation for his career arc is E = HR + BB, it's obvious that there's still a lot of work to do. The Tigers tired of watching glove doctor **Brent Dlugach** flail away helplessly at the plate, so they shipped him to the Red Sox; he'll spend the summer stabilizing the Pawtucket infield and confounding International League public address announcers. Veteran glove man **Adam Everett** might still play a creditable shortstop, but his bat hasn't been seen since 2004 and will soon be declared dead. **Jeff Frazier** slugged his way through the International League and earned a brief call-up, but 27-year-old corner-men are expected to do that; removed from the 40-man roster, he may be destined for Quad-A purgatory with his new team, the Nationals. Venezuelan teenager **Avisail Garcia** has speed, a strong arm, and absolutely no sense of the strike zone; the Tigers felt that he improved his approach as the season progressed, and since it's hard to conceive of its getting worse, they're probably right. His broad but shallow skill set—a little speed, a little pop—might be good enough at third base, but if, as feared, he has to move down the defensive spectrum, **Wade Gaynor** will have to bulk up his power stats and fatten his OBP in order to have a career. Wags may soon be calling shortstop **Cale Iorg** "K-Large," as striking out nearly once every three at-bats completely overshadows his flashy glove work and occasional power. Pint-sized shortstop **Gustavo Nunez** can fly around the bases and is Teflon slick afield, but he might as well bring his glove to the plate for all the good his bat does him; until he learns to make more contact and draw a few walks, his ceiling lies somewhere between those of Juan Castro and a floor lamp. After 14 years spent bouncing through the bus leagues, **Max St. Pierre** finally made his big-league debut at age 30. The Quebecois catcher has overcome enough adversity to fill several Afternoon Specials—difficulty learning English, isolation, homesickness, struggles with alcohol abuse, and a brief, ill-fated conversion to pitcher—but the career .251/.319/.361 hitter somehow put together a solid year with the bat and earned a late-season call-up. **Clete Thomas** didn't make the Opening Day roster, then tore up his knee in Toledo, making it even harder for Jim Leyland to pick him out of a reserve outfielder lineup alongside Boesch, Wells, Kelly, Strieby, McManus, Keaton, Fenster, Hockney, and Kevin Spacey as "Verbal."

PITCHERS

PLAYER	TEAM	LVL	AGE	W	L	SV	IP	H	HR	BB	SO	EqBB9	EqSO9	GB%	BABIP	WHIP	ERA	FRA	WARP
D. Below*	ERI	AA	24	7	12	0	126	137	17	37	103	2.6	7.4	45%	.313	1.40	4.93	4.75	1.6
C. Crosby*	TGR	Rk	21	0	1	0	21^1	33	1	6	18	2.5	7.6	53%	.444	1.83	7.17	7.28	0.1
C. Fien	TOL	AAA	26	3	3	8	62^1	54	8	13	44	1.9	6.4	41%	.256	1.10	2.60	4.17	0.7
—	DET	MLB	26	0	0	0	2^2	4	2	0	0	0.0	0.0	42%	.200	1.50	10.13	14.99	-0.3
A. Figaro	TOL	AAA	25	10	6	0	124	142	11	39	112	2.8	8.1	44%	.349	1.50	4.14	3.23	3.8
—	DET	MLB	25	0	2	0	14^2	18	1	8	5	4.9	3.1	39%	.309	1.77	7.36	6.40	-0.2
L. Oliveros	ERI	AA	22	1	2	14	25^1	20	3	21	36	7.5	12.9	47%	.309	1.71	4.97	4.58	0.1
J. Ortega	WMI	A	21	0	3	1	25^2	28	1	17	22	6.1	7.9	52%	.338	1.79	4.56	4.67	0.1
—	ERI	AA	21	1	0	0	23^2	22	2	7	19	2.7	7.4	41%	.282	1.29	3.04	3.07	0.5
B. Rondon	TGR	Rk	19	0	0	15	25^2	11	1	14	26	5.0	9.3	53%	.169	1.19	0.70	2.45	2.2
J. Sborz	TOL	AAA	25	1	6	19	43^2	38	8	24	42	5.0	8.8	45%	.256	1.55	4.74	5.29	-0.0
—	DET	MLB	25	0	0	0	0^2	3	0	0	1	0.0	13.5	20%	.750	7.50	67.50	52.70	-0.4
D. Smyly*	DNP	—	22	—	—	—	—	—	—	—	—	—	—	—	—	—	—	—	—

Duane Below made a surprisingly quick recovery from Tommy John surgery and found enough of his power-lefty mojo in Double-A for the team to stash him on the 40-man. Light workloads didn't keep elbow problems from again shelving ultratalented power lefty **Casey Crosby**; if he can't stay healthy when starting, he might still become a dominant bullpen force. In his Triple-A career, **Casey Fien** has posted a four-to-one strikeout-to-walk ratio with nearly a whiff per inning; released by the Tigers and signed by Houston, his fastball/slider/cutter arsenal could conceivably find success in the Astros' pen. **Alfredo Figaro** can be Figaro Alfredo, which is to say that he doesn't lack cheese; the slight Dominican whips a low-90s fastball and darting slider that would probably play up in shorter appearances. His dodgy changeup will determine whether he'll be trusted to face big-league lefties. In the short term, the Tigers didn't trust him to face big-league anyone, selling his contract to the Orix Buffaloes. **Lester Oliveros** is your standard-issue minor-league relief suspect with a live arm, swing-and-miss stuff, and too many walks; if he can fix that last bit, his fastball/slider combination may be coming to a bullpen near you. Wiry reliever **Jose Ortega** has the sort of heat that makes the Tigers drool, though there's little in his repertoire to supplement his upper-90s fastball; if he can develop a little somethin' somethin' to keep hitters from sitting on his primary pitch, he'll become a bullpen asset. Single young right-hander seeks better command of heavy mid-90s fastball and slider to reduce walk rate and complete transformation from sleeper prospect to bullpen beast. Long-term relationship desired. Send all inquiries to **Bruce Rondon**, care of the Lakeland Flying Tigers. Former Longhorns closer and supplemental first rounder **Chance Ruffin** showed off his live fastball and plus slider closing in the Arizona Fall League and has the late-inning stuff and pedigree to move fast. After losing a season to shoulder woes, top-flight relief prospect **Cody Satterwhite** needs to prove that he can still unleash his mid-90s heat and sharp-breaking slider. The Tigers are positively awash with power arms, so effective minor-league closer **Jay Sborz** was lost in the shuffle and outrighted, which made him exactly the sort of bargain a savvy GM—in this case the Braves' Frank Wren—aims to skim out of the free-talent pool. Veteran lefty reliever **Bobby Seay** spent the year on the DL before opting for shoulder surgery; he's now a free agent and unlikely to pitch in 2011. The Tigers were happy to nab college starter **Drew Smyly** in the second round, hoping he can refine his four-pitch lefty arsenal enough to soon fulfill their midrotation dreams.

MANAGER: JIM LEYLAND

YEAR	TEAM	W-L	Pythag +/-	Avg PC	100+ P	120+ P	QS	BQS	REL	REL w Zero R	IBB	Subs	PH	PH Avg	PH HR	SB2	CS2	SB3	CS3	SAC Att	SAC %	POS SAC	Squeeze	Swing	In Play
2008	DET	74-88	-4	94.9	68	2	63	12	440	237	63	66	66	.254	2	58	24	5	5	42	71.4%	27	0	148	122
2009	DET	86-77	5	97.1	72	13	68	5	437	266	42	78	122	.221	3	63	29	8	2	71	74.6%	51	4	158	126
2010	DET	81-81	-1	99.8	87	12	75	4	416	242	29	65	126	.222	2	68	22	1	8	62	66.1%	39	2	149	109

Watching Leyland work interleague games cements the impression that he's happiest when negotiating the maze of double-switches, pinch-hits, and sacrifice bunts that characterized his younger days in the senior circuit, but to his credit, he has always adapted his tactics to the talent he's been given. Give him Adam Everett at shortstop, and Leyland is content to take the bat out of his hands; give him Jhonny Peralta, and he'll let the infielder swing. Leyland is happy enough to pencil rookies into the lineup, and he lets his pitchers pitch without rifling through every situational option—last year, Tigers relievers were near the bottom in appearances and near the top in multi-inning outings, and Tigers starters led the majors in outings of 120 pitches or more, doubling the total of every other AL Central team combined. Couple his adaptability with a reputation for getting the most out of his players—something far more important over the course of a season than tactical wizardry—and Old Smokey remains one of the league's better skippers, worth his seat in the clubhouse for as long as the game still engages him.

Florida Marlins

As far as Miami baseball was concerned, the biggest story of 2010 did not come as the result of on-field feats in any game or games. Nor was it a trade consummated or a contract negotiated or an overriding change in operating principles. Instead, it was a truth revealed: the Marlins are a profitable enterprise, more than honest avarice dared admit, and thanks to internal documents leaked by Deadspin.com on August 23, we know how profitable—very.

MARLINS PROSPECTUS

2010 W-L: 80-82, 3rd in NL East

Pythag	.501	18th	**Ballpark:** Land Shark Stadium (3-yr. PF: 102). Six names later, Joe Robbie-that-was remains a football stadium first
RS/G	4.4	15th	
RA/G	4.4	13th	
TAv	.270	14th	**2010:** The Fish swim against the financial current, but don't go belly-up
BRR	15.1	3rd	
FRA	4.38	15th	
DER	-8.63	22nd	**2011:** After replenishing their roster with farm-raised stock, the Fish swim in more competitive streams
DL	614	6th	
B-Age	26.8	3rd	
P-Age	26.7	4th	**Action Items:** Defense, infield alignment, and Chris Coghlan's final destination
Salary	$57.0	26th	
M$/MW	$1.50	7th	

There is little secret to how the Marlins have managed to turn a profit. In 2008-2009, they received almost $92 million in revenue-sharing monies from their rivals and peers, more than $20 million over what they paid out in salaries. That allowed all other sources of income—ticket sales, local media deals, munchies, souvenirs, parking, and the like—to flow into the club's coffers or directly into the hands of Jeffrey Loria and his collection of carpetbaggers, who paid themselves $5.4 million via their related-partner management company, Double Play. Given the extent of their own profitability, you can understand a willingness to compensate themselves—off the field, they were in the business of successfully acquiring a $634 million stadium complex but contributing just a quarter of the price, while on the field they were operating a competitive ballclub on a shoestring budget. Call it an echo of the Age of Madoff if you wish, but paying yourself handsomely for this kind of success is consistent with what bigger operators do in larger industries, often with less cause.

None of this should have been overly surprising. The more fundamental question, whether the Marlins were somehow engaged in a morally questionable practice, brings us into a broader debate about public policy, community business ethics, and whether sports franchises are public trusts or the province of latter-day robber barons. However fishy the stadium deal, the Fish were simply looking out for number one. They got their stadium from a group of elected officials who abdicated their responsibilities to acquire the best deal possible for their constituents after identifying the Marlins as a local business worth subsidizing. Although the officials pressured the Lorians to open their books, these public servants caved when the owners refused to do so as part of the process.

In some ways, the Marlins' use of their revenue-sharing cash has been a matter of adapting to the idiosyncrasies of the baseball industry. The Fish face a large line item in the form of a $155 million contribution to the construction of Marlins Stadium on the Orange Bowl site in Little Havana, and they have elected to put portions of their revenue-sharing proceeds toward paying for their new home.

If Commissioner Bud Selig or his lot wanted to complain about this exploitation of the revenue-sharing system, they would no doubt have had to remember Loria's role and their own in the franchise switcheroo of 2002. Selig's handpicked selections to own the Red Sox and Marlins agreeably participated in a scheme to enrich themselves and the other owners by stripping Montreal of the Expos and reducing the newborn Nats to a ward of the industry, to be sold profitably for their own enrichment after the Nationals' talent had been pillaged and a stadium extorted from another city desperate to please. Instead, it was left to the union to belatedly complain last spring, noting that revenue-sharing money is supposed to be used to improve a club's performance on the field. This left unanswered the big-picture question of whether socking away cash to help finance a stadium intended to improve their financial performance might be an indirect way of reaching that goal.

If there is a legitimate cause for complaint to aim at the Lorians, it's that they poor-mouthed their SoFla situation, crying poverty when their local revenue streams and expenses seemed rather neatly balanced. They did so out of self-interest, on the theory that such a lie would help them with their bottom line and that they'd get their stadium while telling it. They were right. Wags might comment on the honor between thieves, but the Lorians and the contractors working on their new ballpark have contributed cash to help Miami-Dade County Mayor Carlos Alvarez in the face of a recall campaign. If he loses, he won't be the first or last local politician consumed by citizens angry over this kind of corporate/sports industry collusion, but that's hardly the Marlins' problem, as long as they get their park.

Where this leaves the Marlins in the long term is unknown. For these successfully selfish bad actors on the public stage, there is still the nagging problem of whether the new park is supposed to magically produce better revenues from a market that has generally shrugged them off. Miamians have found other ways to spend their leisure time since the team's inaugural season and the subsequent strike-strangled 1994 season. In 1993, the Marlins drew over three million, and in 1997—the year of their first World Series win—they topped two million. They have never topped two million in any other season. Going back 12 years, they have ranked last or next-to-last in every year save one, 2004, the year after their second title, when they drew enough customers to rank a desultory 14th in the National League. Most franchises reap a big year-after attendance boost after a title, but in both 1998 and 2004, the year-after effect was killed in its crib by the club's aggressive teardowns.

Last year, paid attendance went up by a few hundred, but the Marlins still ranked last in the league for the fifth consecutive season. They drew a thousand fewer fans per game than did both the Royals and the Pirates, the game's ultimate examples of hapless, hopeless participation. If folks won't spend to see a club that has won at least 80 games in each of the last three years or to view one of the game's best position players (Hanley Ramirez) or pitchers (Josh Johnson), will they come out to see anyone or anything?

There are two larger contributing factors to why local revenues are awful—one hard, one soft. The hard fact is that their home park, under any of the seven names it has worn since its opening in 1987, is a charmless facility for baseball, handicapped by sightlines designed for its primary function as a football stadium. The act of going to a game, whatever the elaborate concerns about Miami's weather, is an act of endurance as much as love, one that fans have effectively been avoiding forever, at least as far as Marlins history is concerned. The soft factor is the matter of perception. This goes beyond any distaste for the latest carpetbagger owner-operator, or the post-title teardowns, or the furor over the Marlins' finances after Deadspin's revelations. This proceeds from the team's obvious, demoralizing cheapness, which gives rise to an environment where every roster move is cynically evaluated not in terms of its baseball savvy, but rather by how much money the Marlins are saving.

The conundrum is that by successfully resolving the hard problem of achieving a better venue, the Marlins have risked permanently poisoning their brand. Having been publicly caught in a lie about their own financial position and bullied their way through the process of getting their new stadium financed, the franchise now faces the question of whether those same angry voters will ever become satisfied Marlins customers.

To help combat the perception problem, the Fish are doing all sorts of things right when it comes to the baseball side of franchise operations. First, the Marlins haven't been shy about spending money on player development, ranking as the industry leader according to some sources. The fruits of that investment were on display last season, with Mike Stanton, Gaby Sanchez, and Logan Morrison arriving to stock three of the four corners, thereby allowing the club to graduate from using veteran place-holding temps like Jorge Cantu and Ross Gload, not to mention failed former prospects like Jeremy Hermida. The system will have even more to offer in the near future, with a decent crop of power arms to stock the pen, strike-throwing alternatives for the back end of a rotation already armed with high-upside talents, and—potentially—a new left side of the infield, since both third baseman Matt Dominguez and shortstop Osvaldo Martinez are nearing readiness.

However cheap it has been in dealing with replaceable veterans and easily regenerated relief arms, the front office hasn't been shy about spending money where it makes the most difference. The Marlins have already retained their best young players, having inked both Ramirez and Johnson to long-term deals. That both contracts call for less cash than what either player would have received on the open market is an obvious exploitation of the mechanisms of pre-free-agency player control, but in cases like this, both owners and players work the system to mutual advantage. Ramirez and Johnson acquire certainty in their wealth, the Marlins certainty in their talent, and everyone gets to avoid the noisome squabbling of arbitration.

The Marlins also made an effort to sign Dan Uggla to a four-year, $48 million deal after last season, but when the 31-year-old veteran refused, they promptly dealt him, giving up their last year of control. In return, they received utility star Omar Infante and power lefty reliever Michael Dunn from the Braves. Considering their lack of leverage and Uggla's age—and likely future playing a corner, where the Marlins are already almost fully stocked—you can respect the decision to cut ties with Uggla, one of the most successful Rule 5 selections in history. They were similarly willing to dole out dollars in other ways, inking Jays catcher John Buck to a three-year, $18 million deal, and fallen ace Javier Vazquez to a one-year, $7 million contract. Whatever the merits of those players, if you wanted evidence of a willingness to start spending, the Marlins are trying to provide it.

Acquiring Infante was not a casual choice. The Marlins' lack of firm answers in center field and at second and third base creates three different, overlapping opportunities for them to apply one of the game's best moving parts. If 2009 Rookie of the Year Chris Coghlan can move to center or, failing that, back into the infield, they may have a question mark at only one slot in a good lineup. Worries over infield defense in particular might be less pronounced with Uggla's departure, but bringing back 2002-2006 infield coach Perry Hill, renowned for his ability to improve his fielders' performances, might help with Hanley Ramirez's inconsistency, and the likely arrival of the slick-fielding Dominguez at the hot corner would go far toward killing off this complaint. If he can rebound from another lost year in New York, the addition of Vazquez to the rotation may well erase any questions there, again leaving the bullpen to be stocked by a combination of homegrown assets and cannily identified journeymen. If the Marlins have been able to win 80 games or more with worse in the recent past, this club offers the possibility of an even better bid for the postseason, one armed with the talent to sustain that bid beyond 2011.

This leaves the question of whether anyone is left to care about the team's fortunes. In light of the means used to achieve the end of a new stadium, that end may in itself prove a sterile success if understandably sullen fans continue to stay away from Marlins-brand baseball in droves. If the new ballpark fails to pump up local revenues, the organization will finally become dependent on revenue-sharing to finance its payroll as the young roster acquires service time and arbitration eligibility and reaches free agency. There is an inescapable bit of irony in that.

Lest we judge the Marlins too harshly, consider an alternative scenario: What if they had spent that revenue-sharing money on big-league talent in years past? They might have won more and they might have more convincingly contended; they also might not have done so, since the game's recent past is littered with the bloody bottom lines of clubs with outsized short-term ambitions. (Consider the Mets.) If they had spent that money then, would they have been able to afford their current $155 million contribution to the new ballpark's funding? Would they have been more popular yet poorer and left asking for an even larger share of financing from local leaders? The choices made produced a ballpark and a club capable of contending. However many feelings were hurt, politicians ruined, and local governments bankrupted, there are probably many baseball fans who couldn't care less, given the club's having achieved those two goals—at least, that's what Loria is hoping.

HITTERS

Chase Austin 3B

Born: **12/4/1987** Age: **23**
Bats: R Throws: R Height: **6' 2"** Weight: **185**
Breakout: **0%** Improve: **2%** Collapse: **1%**
Attrition: **1%** MLB: **6%**

Comparables:
Hank Blalock, Bob Bailey, Wil Cordero (79)

YEAR	TEAM	LVL	AGE	PA	R	2B	3B	HR	RBI	BB	SO	SB	CS	AVG/OBP/SLG	TAv	BABIP	BRR	FRAA	WARP
2009	JAM	A-	21	270	34	10	3	3	26	18	45	7	1	.252/.300/.354	.257	.291	1.9	3B 1, SS 0	1.0
2010	GRB	A	22	439	55	25	0	14	52	42	74	8	6	.268/.350/.445	.279	.292	-0.7	3B 7	2.7
2011	*FLO*	*MLB*	*23*	*350*	*36*	*14*	*1*	*9*	*37*	*22*	*72*	*2*	*1*	*.235/.282/.371*	*.230*	*.265*	*-0.1*	*3B 5, SS 0*	*0.3*

An athletic college shortstop for the Elon Fightin' Christians (yes, really), Austin was snagged in the fifth round of the 2009 draft and shifted to third despite predictions that he would move to second as a pro. Initially stiff and error-prone at the hot corner, he showed better range in the second half, but remains a defensive work in progress. Austin also got more comfortable at the plate after the break, producing a .198 isolated power that justified high expectations for his power potential. He will need to build on that second half to move up quickly, but so far, he looks as if he might be more than an organizational player.

Emilio Bonifacio UT

Born: **4/23/1985** Age: **26**
Bats: S Throws: R Height: **5' 11"** Weight: **180**
Breakout: **2%** Improve: **35%** Collapse: **3%**
Attrition: **21%** MLB: **64%**

Comparables:
Michael Bourn, Brett Gardner, Gene Richards (74)

YEAR	TEAM	LVL	AGE	PA	R	2B	3B	HR	RBI	BB	SO	SB	CS	AVG/OBP/SLG	TAv	BABIP	BRR	FRAA	WARP
2008	TUC	AAA	23	402	49	18	5	1	29	27	64	17	8	.303/.343/.387	.255	.355	-0.7	2B 3, LF 0	0.9
2008	ARI	MLB	23	12	2	1	0	0	2	0	5	1	0	.167/.167/.250	.140	.286	0.5	RF -1, LF 0	-0.2
2008	WAS	MLB	23	174	26	5	5	0	12	14	41	6	4	.248/.305/.344	.229	.328	3.7	2B -7	-0.5
2009	FLO	MLB	24	509	69	11	6	1	27	34	95	21	9	.252/.299/.308	.222	.305	4.2	3B 3, SS -2	0.2
2010	NWO	AAA	25	182	19	8	3	0	11	16	33	8	4	.274/.335/.360	.258	.338	-0.9	CF -6, 2B -5	-1.1
2010	FLO	MLB	25	201	27	6	3	0	10	17	42	12	0	.261/.318/.328	.234	.331	5.4	CF 0, SS -3	0.4
2011	*FLO*	*MLB*	*26*	*535*	*55*	*19*	*4*	*3*	*45*	*36*	*93*	*23*	*8*	*.260/.306/.334*	*.231*	*.306*	*-0.4*	*2B -1, 3B 1*	*-0.5*

After making the big mistake of employing Bonifacio as an everyday player in 2009, the Marlins kicked him back onto the Big

Easy shuttle and into utility work last season. Even so, it might seem as if Florida exceeded its recommended daily allowance of vitamin Bonifacio, but keep in mind that 20 of his 37 big-league starts came in September, after the Marlins were already out of it. As choices for the last man on a bench go, you could do worse; he can plausibly play six different positions and has value as a pinch-runner and early-inning pinch-hitter. He'd fit right in were he to get in the Wayback Machine and take the place of Matt Alexander or Larry Lintz.

Chris Coghlan **LF**

Born: **6/18/1985** Age: **26**
Bats: **L** Throws: **R** Height: **6' 0"** Weight: **205**
Breakout: **5%** Improve: **45%** Collapse: **4%**
Attrition: **17%** MLB: **81%**
Comparables:
Mike Hargrove, Andre Ethier, Brandon Jones (75)

YEAR	TEAM	LVL	AGE	PA	R	2B	3B	HR	RBI	BB	SO	SB	CS	AVG/OBP/SLG	TAv	BABIP	BRR	FRAA	WARP
2008	CAR	AA	23	565	83	32	5	7	74	67	65	34	10	.298/.395/.429	.278	.331	5.6	2B -1, 3B 2	3.2
2009	NWO	AAA	24	110	21	9	1	3	22	12	10	9	1	.344/.418/.552	.344	.357	1.9	2B -3, 3B 0	1.0
2009	FLO	MLB	24	565	84	31	6	9	47	53	77	8	5	.321/.388/.460	.295	.363	2.1	LF -4, 2B -1	2.8
2010	FLO	MLB	25	400	60	20	3	5	28	33	84	10	3	.268/.332/.383	.264	.332	4.6	LF -2	1.1
2011	*FLO*	*MLB*	*26*	*554*	*68*	*28*	*3*	*10*	*60*	*52*	*77*	*16*	*5*	*.283/.351/.413*	*.270*	*.312*	*-0.1*	*LF -1, 2B -1*	*1.5*

The 2009 Rookie of the Year took a major tumble at the plate before tearing the meniscus in his left knee and missing the last 10 weeks of the year, but the knee was just the coup de grâce in a season-long litany of hurts. While a torrid June (.477/.463/.642, with 20 extra-base hits) provided a quick reminder of his capabilities, time may not heal all that ails him. Beyond the possibility that the knee could hamper his stated desire to bring his minor-league aggression on the basepaths to his big-league game, the other major red flag is the big spike in his strikeout rate, because if Coghlan keeps whiffing 20 percent of the time, what does that leave? Not a lot of power and a walk rate below 10 percent, and it's hard to expect him to repeat his rookie .368 batting average on balls in play on demand. In the wake of the Cameron Maybin trade, the Marlins are now pondering a camp tryout in center; set your expectations low, and if Matt Dominguez doesn't claim third base for himself, don't be surprised if that shift reappears on the options menu for Coghlan.

Scott Cousins **OF**

Born: **1/22/1985** Age: **26**
Bats: **L** Throws: **L** Height: **6' 1"** Weight: **195**
Breakout: **7%** Improve: **37%** Collapse: **3%**
Attrition: **37%** MLB: **65%**
Comparables:
Xavier Paul, Jeff Salazar, Ray Sadler (77)

YEAR	TEAM	LVL	AGE	PA	R	2B	3B	HR	RBI	BB	SO	SB	CS	AVG/OBP/SLG	TAv	BABIP	BRR	FRAA	WARP
2008	JUP	A+	23	211	35	9	2	9	29	20	47	11	3	.304/.370/.513	.325	.363	1.8	RF 2, CF -2	2.0
2008	CAR	AA	23	103	15	7	1	1	9	10	28	4	1	.264/.350/.396	.298	.371	-1.6	RF -2, CF -2	0.3
2009	JAX	AA	24	533	60	31	11	12	74	42	107	27	9	.263/.323/.448	.286	.312	-0.4	CF -9, RF -2	1.8
2010	NWO	AAA	25	451	74	20	5	14	49	32	78	12	4	.285/.336/.461	.281	.317	-3.5	CF -7, RF 6	1.6
2010	FLO	MLB	25	38	2	2	2	0	2	1	13	0	0	.297/.316/.460	.272	.458	-0.9	CF 2, RF 0	0.2
2011	*FLO*	*MLB*	*26*	*468*	*54*	*21*	*4*	*13*	*56*	*30*	*99*	*14*	*4*	*.259/.305/.414*	*.251*	*.301*	*0.0*	*CF -7, RF 0*	*-0.1*

Most of the time, tweeners have to settle for their lot, aspiring to job security as a fourth outfielder, or maybe lucking out and getting sucked into an opening created by some sort of mishap. They lurch between gigs that get them a couple hundred at-bats. Every once in a while, a guy like Todd Hollandsworth gets every possible break and winds up with a career. Cousins has a shot at being the next Hollandsworth, in that he has a broad base of skills. He has the arm for right, enough athleticism to cover the middle pasture, and a bat that profiles as useful, as long as he's not asked to man a corner every day. He might also have an opportunity, at least as long as the plan for center calls for giving Coghlan first crack.

Brad Davis **C**

Born: **12/29/1982** Age: **28**
Bats: **R** Throws: **R** Height: **6' 1"** Weight: **190**
Breakout: **5%** Improve: **14%** Collapse: **5%**
Attrition: **18%** MLB: **41%**
Comparables:
Dusty Brown, Jeff Mathis, John Baker (78)

YEAR	TEAM	LVL	AGE	PA	R	2B	3B	HR	RBI	BB	SO	SB	CS	AVG/OBP/SLG	TAv	BABIP	BRR	FRAA	WARP
2008	CAR	AA	25	296	30	15	1	6	28	35	57	0	2	.205/.301/.345	.243	.231	-1.0	C 0	0.7
2009	JAX	AA	26	314	36	23	0	10	43	28	62	0	0	.236/.309/.425	.259	.265	-0.2	C 1	1.4
2010	NWO	AAA	27	275	35	14	0	9	34	24	53	1	2	.287/.354/.455	.280	.332	0.0	C 0, 1B 0	1.8
2010	FLO	MLB	27	123	8	7	1	3	16	9	37	2	0	.211/.268/.376	.239	.274	-0.7	C 2	0.3
2011	*FLO*	*MLB*	*28*	*365*	*39*	*17*	*0*	*10*	*40*	*27*	*80*	*1*	*1*	*.229/.287/.381*	*.234*	*.262*	*0.0*	*C 0*	*0.6*

An organizational soldier with seven seasons in the system, Davis finally got the call when the Marlins needed to replace Ronny Paulino after the latter's PED suspension in August. The main rationale for keeping their choices for John Buck's backup limited to Davis or Brett Hayes would be the familiarity either has with the stack of farmhands likely to get looks in "The Show." That's a nice-enough reason as these things go, but don't count on much offense in the 40-50 games that Buck isn't behind the plate. The argument for Davis over Hayes is a slightly better bat, but that's a choice between "dead" and "mostly lifeless."

Matt Dominguez 3B

Born: **8/28/1989** Age: **21**
Bats: R Throws: R Height: **6' 1"** Weight: **205**
Breakout: **3%** Improve: **11%** Collapse: **1%**
Attrition: **11%** MLB: **20%**

Comparables:
Ron Santo, Conor Gillaspie, Butch Wynegar (73)

YEAR	TEAM	LVL	AGE	PA	R	2B	3B	HR	RBI	BB	SO	SB	CS	AVG/OBP/SLG	TAv	BABIP	BRR	FRAA	WARP
2008	GRB	A	18	381	59	16	0	18	70	28	68	0	1	.296/.354/.499	.293	.321	0.5	3B -8	1.6
2009	JUP	A+	19	429	49	25	1	11	53	38	68	1	0	.262/.333/.420	.279	.290	0.4	3B 9, 1B 0	2.9
2009	JAX	AA	19	114	10	7	0	2	9	14	24	0	0	.186/.289/.320	.217	.219	-1.6	3B 0	-0.3
2010	JAX	AA	20	577	61	34	2	14	81	56	96	0	2	.252/.333/.411	.285	.281	0.4	3B 6	3.9
2011	*FLO*	*MLB*	*21*	*514*	*57*	*25*	*1*	*16*	*60*	*37*	*94*	*0*	*0*	*.243/.298/.403*	*.245*	*.266*	*0.0*	*3B 1, 1B 0*	*0.8*

Maybe coaching will be the critical factor in tightening up the infield defense, but if Dominguez wins the job at third, Perry Hill's task will be that much easier. An electric defender gifted with ample range and a shoulder-mounted rocket-launcher at the hot corner, Dominguez started 30 double plays last year. At the plate, he's a work in progress without superior patience or power, but he's been so much younger than his leagues that we will have to wait to see if he consolidates lessons about laying off breaking stuff out of the zone. He did finish hot at the plate, capping a final flurry with three bombs in the Southern League playoffs. While Dominguez could conceivably win the Opening Day assignment at third with a good camp, if he's sent back down for a multimonth tune-up, the short-term danger for his future is that Coghlan could flop as a center fielder and need to move to third, or that nonroster invitee Ruben Gotay could catch on and hit early.

Brett Hayes C

Born: **2/13/1984** Age: **27**
Bats: R Throws: R Height: **6' 1"** Weight: **205**
Breakout: **1%** Improve: **7%** Collapse: **1%**
Attrition: **6%** MLB: **18%**

Comparables:
Mike Rabelo, Donny Lucy, Justin Knoedler (82)

YEAR	TEAM	LVL	AGE	PA	R	2B	3B	HR	RBI	BB	SO	SB	CS	AVG/OBP/SLG	TAv	BABIP	BRR	FRAA	WARP
2008	CAR	AA	24	194	19	8	0	6	18	10	43	1	4	.232/.273/.376	.224	.269	-0.1	C 0, 1B 0	0.0
2008	ABQ	AAA	24	126	21	3	1	5	17	4	23	1	1	.293/.325/.466	.246	.319	1.1	C 0	0.5
2009	NWO	AAA	25	353	27	15	0	4	37	20	66	2	0	.240/.278/.324	.215	.279	0.4	C -1, 2B 0	-0.2
2009	FLO	MLB	25	11	5	1	0	1	2	0	3	0	0	.300/.364/.700	.318	.333	0.3	1B 0	0.1
2010	NWO	AAA	26	63	7	3	0	1	5	2	9	0	0	.220/.254/.322	.213	.240	0.0	C 1	0.0
2010	FLO	MLB	26	83	6	6	1	2	6	6	26	0	0	.208/.265/.390	.224	.286	-1.2	C 1	0.0
2011	*FLO*	*MLB*	*27*	*283*	*28*	*11*	*1*	*7*	*29*	*14*	*61*	*1*	*1*	*.229/.268/.356*	*.218*	*.264*	*-0.1*	*C 0, 1B 0*	*0.0*

The 79th overall selection in the 2005 draft, Hayes was taken with the compensation pick received for Mike Redmond's defection via free agency. His draft class yielded an awful crop of catchers: Jeff Clement went in the first round, and Nick Hundley, Taylor Teagarden, and Bryan Anderson were the other noteworthy early-round selections; the best of the lot will turn out to be the Mets' 13th-round selection of Josh Thole. Consider Hayes representative of his cadre; he will never hit well enough to replace Redmond, but he's a nimble receiver with an accurate arm, and he gets good marks for how he handles pitchers. That might be enough to get him sufficient service time to earn full-fledged membership in the Miami local of the International Brotherhood of Backup Backstops.

Wes Helms 3B

Born: **5/12/1976** Age: **35**
Bats: R Throws: R Height: **6' 4"** Weight: **230**
Breakout: **3%** Improve: **25%** Collapse: **9%**
Attrition: **21%** MLB: **68%**

Comparables:
Ken McMullen, Walker Cooper, Ed Sprague (69)

YEAR	TEAM	LVL	AGE	PA	R	2B	3B	HR	RBI	BB	SO	SB	CS	AVG/OBP/SLG	TAv	BABIP	BRR	FRAA	WARP
2008	FLO	MLB	32	278	27	11	0	5	31	17	65	0	0	.243/.299/.347	.236	.301	-2.7	3B 0, 1B 1	-0.3
2009	FLO	MLB	33	234	19	11	0	3	33	13	54	1	1	.271/.316/.365	.234	.342	-2.1	3B -1, 1B 3	0.0
2010	FLO	MLB	34	287	27	12	4	4	39	26	76	0	2	.221/.300/.347	.238	.294	0.0	3B 1, 1B 0	0.2
2011	*FLO*	*MLB*	*35*	*277*	*29*	*12*	*1*	*5*	*26*	*21*	*61*	*1*	*1*	*.236/.299/.350*	*.232*	*.288*	*-0.1*	*3B 0, 1B 0*	*-0.1*

After cranking out quality seasons as a pinch-hitter in four of the last five years, Helms had a terrible 2010. Small-sample theater that such things represent, it was symptomatic of a career-wide implosion. His career-high rate of pitches per plate appearance—and his rising walk and strikeout rates—reflect a hitter with slowing reflexes, while his defensive game, never a strong suit, has also withered with age. All you're left with is the familiarity and professionalism that, year after year, seem to recommend Helms to the Marlins, who already re-upped him for 2011 back in August. If he earns another contract in 2012, just think, he could earn his 10-and-5 rights, improbable as that might seem—not that he's likely to turn up in anyone else's uni.

Osvaldo Martinez SS

Born: **5/7/1988** Age: **23**
Bats: R Throws: R Height: **5' 10"** Weight: **190**
Breakout: **3%** Improve: **17%** Collapse: **2%**
Attrition: **14%** MLB: **36%**

Comparables:
Chin-lung Hu, Gregorio Petit, Steve Sax (73)

YEAR	TEAM	LVL	AGE	PA	R	2B	3B	HR	RBI	BB	SO	SB	CS	AVG/OBP/SLG	TAv	BABIP	BRR	FRAA	WARP
2008	GRB	A	20	331	44	11	3	6	29	13	46	5	5	.296/.323/.411	.263	.321	3.2	SS 11, 1B 0	2.6
2009	JUP	A+	21	485	54	16	5	1	45	41	51	16	4	.254/.320/.321	.247	.281	4.6	SS 7	2.3
2010	JAX	AA	22	587	90	28	4	5	54	49	64	13	9	.302/.372/.401	.278	.328	4.3	SS -2	3.7
2010	FLO	MLB	22	48	8	4	1	0	2	4	6	1	0	.326/.375/.465	.301	.368	1.2	SS -1	0.4
2011	*FLO*	*MLB*	*23*	*489*	*51*	*19*	*3*	*5*	*45*	*27*	*61*	*7*	*3*	*.260/.298/.348*	*.231*	*.281*	*-0.3*	*SS 4, 1B 0*	*0.8*

Martinez's season capped a comeback from an incident that nearly killed more than a career: he was shot three times in a mistaken-identity drive-by shooting in Puerto Rico in September 2009. If there's a wild-card scenario where HanRam moves to center or third sometime soon, it will be because Martinez is a legit prospect. He may not have ideal range, but he's strong-armed and coachable. Despite his youth, Martinez's batting has improved markedly the last two years as he's advanced; he has improved his strike-zone recognition, better understands what he can and can't do with breaking stuff, and possesses enough line-drive power to exploit a quick swing. He won't push Ramirez—not right away—but he might outshine Dominguez (and Coghlan, too) sufficiently to make the club. And from there, the contrast to HanRam will be increasingly obvious.

Cameron Maybin CF

Born: **4/4/1987** Age: **24**
Bats: R Throws: R Height: **6' 4"** Weight: **205**
Breakout: **8%** Improve: **50%** Collapse: **3%**
Attrition: **22%** MLB: **69%**
Comparables:
Michael Saunders, Wilkin Ramirez, Ellis Burks (67)

YEAR	TEAM	LVL	AGE	PA	R	2B	3B	HR	RBI	BB	SO	SB	CS	AVG/OBP/SLG	TAv	BABIP	BRR	FRAA	WARP
2008	CAR	AA	21	459	73	15	8	13	49	60	124	21	7	.277/.373/.456	.284	.367	-0.7	CF 10	3.5
2008	FLO	MLB	21	36	9	2	0	0	2	3	8	4	0	.500/.528/.562	.369	.640	1.4	CF 3	0.9
2009	NWO	AAA	22	343	44	18	8	3	39	38	58	8	2	.319/.397/.463	.310	.382	2.4	CF 10, LF 0	3.9
2009	FLO	MLB	22	199	30	12	2	4	13	17	51	1	3	.250/.312/.409	.262	.318	-0.1	CF 3	0.9
2010	NWO	AAA	23	148	21	6	2	4	23	13	24	5	1	.338/.407/.508	.308	.385	0.0	CF 5	1.6
2010	FLO	MLB	23	321	46	7	3	8	28	24	91	9	2	.234/.302/.362	.244	.311	2.2	CF 9	1.4
2011	*SDN*	*MLB*	*24*	*496*	*61*	*22*	*4*	*12*	*57*	*46*	*119*	*14*	*4*	*.271/.341/.425*	*.272*	*.338*	*0.1*	*CF 6, LF 0*	*2.4*

Before earning an early June demotion, Maybin was striking out 28 percent of the time; when the Marlins called him back up, little had changed. Exasperated, the Fish ditched Tool Time on the Padres to land Edward Mujica and Ryan Webb. The huge difference between Maybin's major- and minor-league strikeout rates isn't a product of mean umps hating on a kid—Maybin swings and misses a third again as often as your average major leaguer. You can hope that's correctable, but Petco doesn't seem a likely spot. However, at the very least, he should get as much as three consecutive months to show his new team something, a luxury the Marlins never afforded him, despite their lack of an obvious alternative in center. There is a glass-half-full comparison that can be made to Devon White's career. Both he and Maybin had a similar breadth of tools and problems controlling the strike zone. Devo didn't really break out until his age-28 season, but he got his first clean shot at everyday play at 24 and held his own when left alone.

Logan Morrison LF

Born: **8/25/1987** Age: **23**
Bats: L Throws: L Height: **6' 3"** Weight: **235**
Breakout: **3%** Improve: **37%** Collapse: **3%**
Attrition: **17%** MLB: **62%**
Comparables:
Barry Bonds, Daric Barton, James Loney (64)

YEAR	TEAM	LVL	AGE	PA	R	2B	3B	HR	RBI	BB	SO	SB	CS	AVG/OBP/SLG	TAv	BABIP	BRR	FRAA	WARP
2008	JUP	A+	20	555	71	38	1	13	74	57	80	9	3	.332/.402/.494	.322	.372	-1.8	1B -2	3.7
2009	JAX	AA	21	343	48	18	2	8	47	63	46	9	4	.277/.411/.442	.327	.307	0.5	1B 8, LF -1	3.6
2010	NWO	AAA	22	293	36	17	4	6	45	48	35	1	2	.307/.427/.487	.317	.335	0.0	1B 0, LF 2	2.3
2010	FLO	MLB	22	287	43	20	7	2	18	41	51	0	1	.283/.390/.447	.307	.351	2.2	LF -2	1.8
2011	*FLO*	*MLB*	*23*	*512*	*66*	*28*	*4*	*10*	*56*	*65*	*75*	*4*	*2*	*.279/.370/.427*	*.282*	*.311*	*-0.2*	*1B -13, LF -1*	*0.3*

Morrison got banged up early on, missing a month at New Orleans after a collision at first. After Coghlan's breakdown, the Marlins slotted Morrison directly into the everyday lineup as an outfielder. The batsmanship is there: between tremendous plate coverage and pitch identification, Morrison will be an OBP force. The problem is that he hasn't delivered power since a Sally League stint in 2007, his last season with an isolated power above .200. As long as Morrison is reaching base around 40 percent of the time, his clubs can afford to let him stomp around a corner, but showing some kind of pop would make a huge difference in terms of his being either a Dave Magadan–like curiosity or a bona fide star.

Marcell Ozuna OF

Born: **11/12/1990** Age: **20**
Bats: R Throws: R Height: **6' 2"** Weight: **190**
Breakout: **0%** Improve: **2%** Collapse: **0%**
Attrition: **0%** MLB: **5%**
Comparables:
Tony Conigliaro, Andruw Jones, Alex Rodriguez (70)

YEAR	TEAM	LVL	AGE	PA	R	2B	3B	HR	RBI	BB	SO	SB	CS	AVG/OBP/SLG	TAv	BABIP	BRR	FRAA	WARP
2008	dml	Rk	17	263	33	14	0	6	43	23	61	8	1	.279/.335/.416	—	.341	0.0	—	—
2009	MRL	Rk	18	244	32	22	0	5	39	22	52	4	2	.313/.377/.486	.326	.383	1.1	RF 3, LF 0	2.6
2010	JAM	A-	19	293	53	11	2	21	60	17	94	3	1	.267/.314/.556	.298	.323	0.0	RF 5, CF 1	2.2
2011	*FLO*	*MLB*	*20*	*293*	*30*	*12*	*1*	*12*	*37*	*13*	*100*	*0*	*0*	*.220/.256/.405*	*.227*	*.286*	*0.0*	*RF -3, CF 0*	*-0.8*

After an early-season injury short-circuited an attempt to get Ozuna some full-season exposure, he settled for coming back for a short-season assignment and set the Jamestown record for bombs as a result. The Dominican is an athletic outfielder with the arm for right field and is young enough that losing the first half won't dent his development. Ozuna's strength and quick wrists make for pure power, but he's still missing on quality breaking stuff with alarming regularity, contributing to a slight bassackward split. As (or if) he learns, he'll iron that out and fulfill his destiny, that of Mike Stanton's successor as the system's best slugging prospect.

Ronny Paulino **C**

Born: **4/21/1981** Age: **30**
Bats: **R** Throws: **R** Height: **6' 3"** Weight: **235**
Breakout: **0%** Improve: **21%** Collapse: **17%**
Attrition: **9%** MLB: **88%**

Comparables:
Javy Lopez, Lamar Johnson, Dave Nilsson (77)

YEAR	TEAM	LVL	AGE	PA	R	2B	3B	HR	RBI	BB	SO	SB	CS	AVG/OBP/SLG	TAv	BABIP	BRR	FRAA	WARP
2008	IND	AAA	27	126	16	13	1	4	18	13	31	0	2	.306/.373/.550	.293	.385	-1.4	C 0	0.8
2008	PIT	MLB	27	130	8	5	0	2	18	11	24	0	0	.212/.277/.305	.217	.247	0.0	C 0	-0.1
2009	FLO	MLB	28	266	25	10	1	8	27	25	48	1	0	.272/.338/.423	.267	.308	-2.2	C 1	1.1
2010	FLO	MLB	29	344	32	18	0	4	37	25	51	1	0	.260/.311/.354	.245	.296	2.3	C 1	1.1
2011	*NYN*	*MLB*	*30*	*381*	*45*	*19*	*0*	*9*	*42*	*30*	*65*	*1*	*1*	*.270/.326/.404*	*.257*	*.304*	*-0.1*	*C 0*	*1.4*

Sucked into everyday action after John Baker's breakdown, Paulino flaunted all of the defining characteristics of his career, struggling to top a .300 on-base or slugging percentage against righties, mashing against southpaws (.338/.390/.491 in 531 career PAs), and providing a durable target with solid receiving skills and a strong arm behind the plate. Added up, that's useful enough as backup catchers go, but Paulino simply gets overexposed trying to cut it as an everyday player. It isn't his fault the organization lacked an alternative, but he may find himself in a similar situation after inking a one-year deal to serve as the Mets' backup backstop this season. Regardless, he'll have to miss the first eight games of the regular season to complete his late-August 50-game suspension for testing PED-positive.

Bryan Petersen **OF**

Born: **4/9/1986** Age: **25**
Bats: **L** Throws: **R** Height: **6' 0"** Weight: **205**
Breakout: **6%** Improve: **16%** Collapse: **4%**
Attrition: **19%** MLB: **33%**

Comparables:
Brandon Jones, Will Venable, Chris Pettit (78)

YEAR	TEAM	LVL	AGE	PA	R	2B	3B	HR	RBI	BB	SO	SB	CS	AVG/OBP/SLG	TAv	BABIP	BRR	FRAA	WARP
2008	GRB	A	22	345	60	10	2	19	58	38	74	15	6	.301/.380/.541	.318	.333	0.9	CF -4, RF 0	2.6
2008	JUP	A+	22	175	23	5	0	3	12	15	29	7	1	.265/.337/.355	.261	.304	2.8	RF 1, CF -2	0.5
2009	JAX	AA	23	494	64	15	7	7	49	50	66	13	12	.297/.368/.413	.288	.330	-2.8	LF -8, CF 2	1.4
2010	NWO	AAA	24	369	47	13	2	5	27	34	63	5	4	.255/.332/.354	.249	.295	-0.2	LF 1, RF 8	1.1
2010	FLO	MLB	24	25	1	0	0	0	2	1	6	0	0	.083/.120/.083	.094	.111	0.2	LF 0, RF 0	-0.4
2011	*FLO*	*MLB*	*25*	*489*	*54*	*16*	*2*	*11*	*49*	*38*	*87*	*9*	*4*	*.252/.310/.375*	*.242*	*.283*	*-0.5*	*LF -3, CF -6*	*-0.7*

Petersen is an upper-round product of UC Irvine's reborn baseball program and a veteran of the 2007 team that nearly achieved an upset win in the College World Series. His absence of outright failure as a pro so far has kept his name on some prospect lists. He has only really hit in two places, though: his intro to full-season ball in Low-A (lower than a Big West star should have been) and the Arizona Fall League, where even the zombies swing live bats. Petersen is an athletic, scrappy tweener with a swing holey enough that not even a platoon of Dutch boys might plug it up, leaving you with a guy worth mentioning mostly because the Marlins are cheap and don't have an automatic answer for who next year's center fielder might be.

Hanley Ramirez **SS**

Born: **12/23/1983** Age: **27**
Bats: **R** Throws: **R** Height: **6' 3"** Weight: **195**
Breakout: **2%** Improve: **57%** Collapse: **4%**
Attrition: **7%** MLB: **100%**

Comparables:
David Wright, Alex Rodriguez, Ryan Braun (63)

YEAR	TEAM	LVL	AGE	PA	R	2B	3B	HR	RBI	BB	SO	SB	CS	AVG/OBP/SLG	TAv	BABIP	BRR	FRAA	WARP
2008	FLO	MLB	24	693	125	34	4	33	67	92	122	35	12	.301/.400/.540	.324	.329	0.8	SS 2	7.4
2009	FLO	MLB	25	651	102	42	1	24	106	60	101	27	8	.342/.409/.543	.325	.379	3.3	SS -10	6.2
2010	FLO	MLB	26	619	93	28	2	21	76	64	93	32	10	.300/.378/.475	.305	.327	1.3	SS -10	4.2
2011	*FLO*	*MLB*	*27*	*674*	*97*	*35*	*2*	*27*	*98*	*69*	*91*	*35*	*11*	*.310/.384/.516*	*.312*	*.323*	*-0.2*	*SS -9*	*5.0*

Arguments over HanRam's long-term future at short are basically the off-off-Broadway rendition of the same song that has been part of Derek Jeter's soundtrack over the course of the Captain's career: when a hitter contributes this much value offensively *and* plays a useful-enough brand of short, you have an incredibly valuable asset. At the very least, various statistical evaluations of Ramirez's fielding are not quite so consistently damning as Jeter's. However, Ramirez's season was an ugly slide back toward his terrible 2007, which had coincided with Perry Hill's departure as the club's infield coach. Now that Hill is back, we'll see what that means for HanRam's play at short, but after last year's showdown with Fredi Gonzalez over a perceived lack of hustle, his worst year at the plate since his rookie season in 2006, plus a bum left elbow that effectively ended his year two weeks early, you can bet 2010 was a campaign Ramirez would rather forget.

Gaby Sanchez **1B**

Born: **9/2/1983** Age: **27**
Bats: **R** Throws: **R** Height: **6' 2"** Weight: **225**
Breakout: **4%** Improve: **36%** Collapse: **8%**
Attrition: **19%** MLB: **76%**

Comparables:
Ryan Garko, Conor Jackson, Kendry Morales (79)

YEAR	TEAM	LVL	AGE	PA	R	2B	3B	HR	RBI	BB	SO	SB	CS	AVG/OBP/SLG	TAv	BABIP	BRR	FRAA	WARP
2008	CAR	AA	24	557	70	42	1	17	92	69	70	17	8	.314/.404/.513	.313	.337	-5.7	1B 5, 3B 5	4.7
2008	FLO	MLB	24	8	0	2	0	0	1	0	2	0	0	.375/.375/.625	.357	.500	0.0	1B 0	0.0
2009	NWO	AAA	25	370	55	11	0	16	56	41	44	5	0	.289/.373/.475	.296	.288	2.3	1B -3, 3B -5	1.5
2009	FLO	MLB	25	23	2	0	0	2	3	2	3	0	0	.238/.304/.524	.266	.188	-0.2	1B 0	0.0
2010	FLO	MLB	26	643	72	37	3	19	85	57	101	5	0	.273/.339/.448	.279	.297	-1.3	1B -5	1.1
2011	*FLO*	*MLB*	*27*	*541*	*69*	*27*	*1*	*19*	*69*	*51*	*73*	*6*	*2*	*.275/.345/.456*	*.279*	*.284*	*0.0*	*1B -8, 3B -1*	*0.8*

Sanchez is as fine an example of an organizational player made good as you might like to find. He's not really a great option for everyday play at first base, not when he hit just .256/.324/.419 against right-handed pitching, and his moves back and forth across the diamond as he made his way to the majors seem to have bred a fairly passive brand of first-base D, so reports of a strong arm are more rumor than evidenced by in-game action. His defense might improve now that he has dibs on the job—at least until the Marlins have cause to move Logan Morrison back to first—and he mashes lefties and makes a goodly amount of contact. Despite his real-world limits, fantheads in RBI leagues should watch for his lineup position, because if he bats behind Hanley Ramirez and Logan Morrison for a full season, he should easily repeat last season's top-20 finish in terms of total baserunners aboard when he bats, and opportunities define possibilities where such things are concerned.

Kyle Skipworth **C**

Born: **3/1/1990** Age: **21**
Bats: L Throws: R Height: **6' 4"** Weight: **205**
Breakout: **0%** Improve: **0%** Collapse: **0%**
Attrition: **0%** MLB: **0%**

Comparables:
Clint Hurdle, Bill Freehan, Ken Harrelson (75)

YEAR	TEAM	LVL	AGE	PA	R	2B	3B	HR	RBI	BB	SO	SB	CS	AVG/OBP/SLG	TAv	BABIP	BRR	FRAA	WARP
2008	MRL	Rk	18	176	22	6	0	5	21	13	46	2	2	.208/.261/.340	.231	.250	-1.1	C -1	-0.1
2009	GRB	A	19	286	28	14	1	7	37	18	91	1	2	.208/.262/.348	.221	.286	-3.8	C 1	-0.3
2010	PDD	—	20	66	8	4	0	3	12	5	15	0	0	.267/.333/.483	—	.310	0.0	—	—
2010	GRB	A	20	436	55	17	1	17	59	32	132	1	2	.249/.312/.426	.261	.328	1.0	C 2	1.8
2011	*FLO*	*MLB*	*21*	*300*	*28*	*10*	*0*	*10*	*32*	*14*	*101*	*0*	*0*	*.205/.241/.352*	*.205*	*.272*	*0.0*	*C 0*	*-0.5*

The sixth overall selection from 2008 hasn't lived up to his billing, but the power-hitting catcher people hoped for finally became recognizable in the results. Repeating at Low-A in a hitter's park produced happier results than Skipworth's first go-round, but his strike-zone judgment remains almost laughably bad. Happily, he demonstrated much-improved throwing, overcoming some elbow issues from the year before to log a 35 percent kill rate on stolen-base attempts. Skipworth's receiving skills and footwork were never in doubt, so at 21, he still has plenty of time to sort out what he shouldn't wave at. With John Buck inked to a three-year deal, the Fish can afford to wait.

Mike Stanton **RF**

Born: **11/8/1989** Age: **21**
Bats: R Throws: R Height: **6' 5"** Weight: **235**
Breakout: **4%** Improve: **37%** Collapse: **2%**
Attrition: **6%** MLB: **60%**

Comparables:
Jay Bruce, Travis Snider, Justin Upton (50)

YEAR	TEAM	LVL	AGE	PA	R	2B	3B	HR	RBI	BB	SO	SB	CS	AVG/OBP/SLG	TAv	BABIP	BRR	FRAA	WARP
2008	GRB	A	18	540	89	26	3	39	97	58	153	4	2	.293/.381/.611	.332	.351	-2.8	RF -1, CF 7	5.2
2009	JUP	A+	19	210	27	9	3	12	39	28	45	2	2	.294/.390/.578	.340	.331	-2.3	RF -1, CF -1	1.6
2009	JAX	AA	19	341	49	15	2	16	53	31	99	1	1	.231/.311/.455	.274	.280	0.6	RF 12	2.3
2010	JAX	AA	20	240	42	13	2	21	52	44	53	1	0	.313/.442/.729	.395	.325	-0.5	RF 5, LF 1	4.1
2010	FLO	MLB	20	397	45	21	1	22	59	34	124	5	2	.258/.325/.506	.291	.330	-1.4	RF 11	2.7
2011	*FLO*	*MLB*	*21*	*580*	*79*	*24*	*2*	*36*	*94*	*56*	*162*	*2*	*1*	*.256/.330/.527*	*.291*	*.293*	*-0.1*	*RF 5, CF -1*	*3.1*

His first name is actually Giancarlo, which would be a lot cooler to see deployed than yet another Mike Stanton in the history books, but while the other two were pitchers, this one is devoted to their destruction. Comments on BP.com about his being ready to slug .500 last year weren't just glib endorsements, as he promptly demonstrated after his call-up two months into the season: the power isn't just real; it's extraordinary. The change in his strikeout rate in-season after his call-up reflects how much growth potential there still is: after whiffing at an epic 40 percent clip in his first 100 PAs or so, he got his ratio down below 30 percent in the second half. And all of this was without his cutting loose against major-league lefties, which suggests that he'll be a monster once he fully adapts. Stanton's full range of skills transcend just monster slugging feats to come, though; third-base coaches learned that his arm is a gun to respect, and his range in right is excellent. Comparisons to Jermaine Dye sell Stanton short—Dye never led his league in homers, but at some point, Stanton will.

Dan Uggla **2B**

Born: **3/11/1980** Age: **31**
Bats: R Throws: R Height: **5' 11"** Weight: **200**
Breakout: **1%** Improve: **52%** Collapse: **0%**
Attrition: **2%** MLB: **100%**

Comparables:
Al Rosen, Jason Bay, Ron Santo (64)

YEAR	TEAM	LVL	AGE	PA	R	2B	3B	HR	RBI	BB	SO	SB	CS	AVG/OBP/SLG	TAv	BABIP	BRR	FRAA	WARP
2008	FLO	MLB	28	619	97	37	1	32	92	77	171	5	5	.260/.360/.514	.302	.320	2.7	2B 1	4.6
2009	FLO	MLB	29	668	84	27	1	31	90	92	150	2	1	.243/.353/.459	.280	.273	-0.6	2B -2	2.7
2010	FLO	MLB	30	674	100	31	0	33	105	78	149	4	1	.287/.369/.508	.312	.330	-0.6	2B -6	4.3
2011	*ATL*	*MLB*	*31*	*674*	*90*	*32*	*1*	*31*	*93*	*82*	*149*	*4*	*2*	*.261/.354/.482*	*.291*	*.293*	*-0.3*	*2B -4*	*3.2*

Five years into his career and with four straight 30-homer seasons under his belt, Uggla has been one of the most reliable commodities around, all without achieving stardom. Some of that is tied to being a Marlin, but there's also the All-Star Game infamy that highlighted his iron glove. To Uggla's credit, his patience has improved and his power has been stable. Offered a four-year, $48 million deal to stick around, Uggla rejected that out of hand, triggering the Marlins' quick swap with the Braves and reuniting Uggla and Fredi Gonzalez. Given that he came up late, is already 31, yet is also one more year removed from free agency, a four-year deal is about as far as anyone should go.

PITCHERS

Burke Badenhop

Born: **2/8/1983** Age: **28**
Bats: R Throws: R Height: **6' 5"** Weight: **220**
Breakout: **9%** Improve: **21%** Collapse: **9%**
Attrition: **18%** MLB: **37%**

Comparables:
Darrell Rasner, Jeff Gray, Justin Hampson (78)

YEAR	TEAM	LVL	AGE	W	L	SV	G	GS	IP	H	HR	BB	SO	EqBB9	EqSO9	GB%	BABIP	WHIP	ERA	FRA	WARP
2008	FLO	MLB	25	2	3	0	13	8	47^1	55	7	21	35	4.0	6.7	55%	.316	1.67	6.08	6.65	-0.3
2009	FLO	MLB	26	7	4	0	35	2	72	71	5	24	57	3.0	7.1	56%	.306	1.33	3.88	4.45	0.5
2010	FLO	MLB	27	2	5	1	53	0	67^2	62	5	21	47	2.8	6.3	59%	.277	1.26	3.99	5.45	-0.5
2011	*FLO*	*MLB*	*28*	*5*	*4*	*0*	*64*	*7*	*109*	*117*	*10*	*42*	*69*	*3.5*	*5.7*	*50%*	*.308*	*1.46*	*4.59*	*4.99*	*0.3*

Marlins fans worried that their club's only concern is cash can rest assured that Florida did not just achieve cost savings from dumping Miguel Cabrera and Dontrelle Willis—it also got Burke Badenhop. As the last functioning part of the package received still in teal, Badenhop offers thin solace in his utility as a sinker-balling middle-relief asset. And before you ask, no, you generally don't have to trade a couple of All-Stars to have one.

Jose Ceda

Born: **1/28/1987** Age: **24**
Bats: R Throws: R Height: **6' 4"** Weight: **275**
Breakout: **0%** Improve: **0%** Collapse: **0%**
Attrition: **1%** MLB: **1%**

Comparables:
Jose Mijares, Emiliano Fruto, Ambiorix Burgos (69)

YEAR	TEAM	LVL	AGE	W	L	SV	G	GS	IP	H	HR	BB	SO	EqBB9	EqSO9	GB%	BABIP	WHIP	ERA	FRA	WARP
2008	DAY	A+	21	2	2	0	15	12	54^1	41	4	28	53	4.6	8.8	38%	.264	1.34	4.81	5.59	0.2
2008	TEN	AA	21	2	1	9	22	0	30^1	26	2	14	42	4.2	12.5	36%	.343	1.35	2.08	1.17	1.1
2010	JAX	AA	23	4	1	6	27	0	32^1	18	2	20	45	5.6	12.6	39%	.250	1.28	1.39	1.71	1.0
2010	FLO	MLB	23	0	0	0	8	0	8^2	8	1	11	9	11.4	9.3	29%	.304	2.31	5.19	6.17	-0.1
2011	*FLO*	*MLB*	*24*	*3*	*2*	*1*	*34*	*4*	*53^2*	*46*	*6*	*37*	*57*	*6.3*	*9.6*	*41%*	*.297*	*1.57*	*4.64*	*5.05*	*0.2*

After a year lost to labrum surgery, the prize received for putting Kevin Gregg in Wrigleyville finally pitched for the Marlins. The huge Dominican was understandably rusty when he showed up in camp, so the team put Ceda back into action slowly, only getting him into games in June. Happily, he didn't leave his plus fastball on the surgeon's table, as he was reliably throwing into the mid-90s in September. Command of an occasionally plus slider is still an issue, which is going to hamper any ongoing propositions that he may yet become a relief ace, but there is plenty of cause for the Cubs to yet rue the day they rushed to get the arb-eligible Gregg.

Steven Cishek

Born: **6/18/1986** Age: **25**
Bats: R Throws: R Height: **6' 6"** Weight: **200**
Breakout: **2%** Improve: **6%** Collapse: **1%**
Attrition: **5%** MLB: **9%**

Comparables:
Fernando Hernandez Jr., David Davidson, Travis Schlichting (83)

YEAR	TEAM	LVL	AGE	W	L	SV	G	GS	IP	H	HR	BB	SO	EqBB9	EqSO9	GB%	BABIP	WHIP	ERA	FRA	WARP
2008	GRB	A	22	3	5	2	50	0	75^1	69	8	34	75	4.1	9.0	46%	.302	1.50	4.66	4.88	-0.1
2009	JUP	A+	23	3	4	2	37	0	57	36	2	16	45	2.5	7.1	59%	.215	1.07	2.21	4.69	0.1
2010	JUP	A+	24	0	5	3	26	0	35	29	0	19	28	4.9	7.2	52%	.279	1.54	2.57	3.42	0.7
2010	JAX	AA	24	3	1	2	22	0	31^1	30	0	10	34	2.9	9.8	41%	.349	1.45	4.31	2.46	0.9
2010	FLO	MLB	24	0	0	0	3	0	4^1	1	0	1	3	2.1	6.2	45%	.091	0.46	0.00	0.93	0.1
2011	*FLO*	*MLB*	*25*	*2*	*1*	*1*	*38*	*0*	*54^1*	*54*	*5*	*31*	*41*	*5.1*	*6.8*	*46%*	*.298*	*1.57*	*5.03*	*5.47*	*-0.5*

Cishek's season was an in-season roster roller-coaster ride, with two promotions to Double-A (he got sent back down in June after a rough two weeks), redemption and contributions to the Suns' second consecutive Southern League championship the second time around, and then a surprise call to the majors at season's end. To cap it off, he made a nice impression in the AFL, striking out 18 against four walks in 13.1 innings pitched. Cishek was the Marlins' fifth-round pick in 2007, coming after they'd picked Dominguez, Stanton, a high-school catcher going nowhere by the name of Jameson Smith, and Bryan Petersen, which makes four guys from one crop who might make the 2011 team. Even so, Cishek isn't a massive prospect, but he is a tall dude with a low-90s sinker/slider mix who should stick around in the pen.

Brad Hand

Born: **3/20/1990** Age: **21**
Bats: L Throws: L Height: **6' 2"** Weight: **185**
Breakout: **8%** Improve: **13%** Collapse: **2%**
Attrition: **4%** MLB: **19%**

Comparables:
Steve Avery, Rich Hand, Mike Witt (66)

YEAR	TEAM	LVL	AGE	W	L	SV	G	GS	IP	H	HR	BB	SO	EqBB9	EqSO9	GB%	BABIP	WHIP	ERA	FRA	WARP
2008	MRL	Rk	18	2	0	0	9	7	32^2	25	0	11	34	3.0	9.4	71%	.294	1.16	2.48	3.56	0.9
2009	GRB	A	19	7	13	0	26	26	127^2	130	12	66	122	4.7	8.6	52%	.324	1.59	4.86	4.77	1.5
2010	JUP	A+	20	8	8	0	26	26	140^2	153	10	49	134	3.1	8.6	48%	.349	1.48	3.33	3.55	3.0
2011	*FLO*	*MLB*	*21*	*5*	*10*	*0*	*20*	*20*	*102*	*118*	*13*	*64*	*75*	*5.6*	*6.6*	*47%*	*.327*	*1.77*	*6.07*	*6.60*	*-0.1*

Survival and stuff are usually the two elements that define whether a pitching prospect can live up to the label, and Hand has both going for him so far. The 2008 second-rounder sometimes gets a tick or two beyond average lefty velocity to set up a lovely curve and managed to show improved control while taking on an expanded workload. He even chipped in a pair of complete-game shutouts in June and a pair of playoff wins for the Suns to cap his late-season promotion to Double-A. Considering that he was fairly hittable while essentially giving up a run every other frame in the Florida State League, we'll see how much he profits from better infielders at higher levels. But so far, so good.

Clay Hensley

Born: **8/31/1979** Age: **31**
Bats: R Throws: R Height: **5' 11"** Weight: **190**
Breakout: **18%** Improve: **42%** Collapse: **23%**
Attrition: **15%** MLB: **89%**

Comparables:
Terry Adams, Kevin Appier, Dave Stewart (78)

YEAR	TEAM	LVL	AGE	W	L	SV	G	GS	IP	H	HR	BB	SO	EqBB9	EqSO9	GB%	BABIP	WHIP	ERA	FRA	WARP
2008	POR	AAA	28	1	1	0	16	10	48	46	7	16	34	3.0	6.4	43%	.271	1.35	3.94	4.72	0.5
2008	SDN	MLB	28	1	2	0	32	1	39	36	2	25	26	5.8	6.0	51%	.286	1.59	5.31	6.51	-0.4
2009	NWO	AAA	29	8	4	0	19	19	114	105	8	38	82	3.0	6.5	51%	.283	1.27	3.24	3.83	2.1
2010	FLO	MLB	30	3	4	7	68	0	75	54	3	29	77	3.5	9.2	55%	.263	1.16	2.16	2.88	1.4
2011	*FLO*	*MLB*	*31*	*7*	*5*	*1*	*67*	*11*	*117^{1}*	*122*	*11*	*56*	*88*	*4.3*	*6.8*	*48%*	*.311*	*1.52*	*4.67*	*5.08*	*0.6*

Earlier in his career, the short right-hander looked as though he might beat the biases against his type of pitcher and give the Padres a solid midrotation starter. Four years, a couple of shoulder injuries, and two organizations later, Hensley had to settle for breaking back in as an unlikely late-game relief asset. With his mix of sinkers and breaking stuff and a nifty change, he's not really anyone's idea of closer material, but a 7-for-7 success rate in actual save opportunities in the last month—as opposed to getting handed a blown save earlier in games—ought to remind people that overpowering stuff isn't the only qualification for a fireman. Even so, you can take that last month as a reflection of Hensley's real role: utility reliever, capable of going long, setting up, or closing, as needed.

Chad James

Born: **1/23/1991** Age: **20**
Bats: L Throws: L Height: **6' 3"** Weight: **185**
Breakout: **6%** Improve: **13%** Collapse: **2%**
Attrition: **2%** MLB: **19%**

Comparables:
Jim Palmer, Mike Witt, Dave Morehead (60)

YEAR	TEAM	LVL	AGE	W	L	SV	G	GS	IP	H	HR	BB	SO	EqBB9	EqSO9	GB%	BABIP	WHIP	ERA	FRA	WARP
2010	GRB	A	19	5	10	0	24	24	114^{1}	116	3	65	105	5.1	8.3	51%	.339	1.63	5.12	5.04	1.2
2011	*FLO*	*MLB*	*20*	*6*	*11*	*0*	*22*	*22*	*106*	*119*	*11*	*79*	*76*	*6.7*	*6.4*	*45%*	*.322*	*1.86*	*6.09*	*6.62*	*-0.0*

The highly regarded high-school lefty was taken 12th overall in the first round of 2009, but James signed late and wound up making his pro debut last year. He struggled with just about everything: consistency, command, and hitters, even hitting his catcher (throwing 18 wild pitches). Despite all that, the stuff that got him drafted so high showed up, as he would occasionally touch 95 with a fastball that sat in the low 90s, while mixing in a nice change and curve. Several scouts have sounded alarm bells over his mechanics and high-effort delivery, which, combined with the wildness, suggests a slow path toward "The Show."

Daniel Jennings

Born: **4/17/1987** Age: **24**
Bats: L Throws: L Height: **6' 3"** Weight: **190**
Breakout: **1%** Improve: **2%** Collapse: **0%**
Attrition: **1%** MLB: **2%**

Comparables:
Cesar Jimenez, Josh Outman, Nick Adenhart (83)

YEAR	TEAM	LVL	AGE	W	L	SV	G	GS	IP	H	HR	BB	SO	EqBB9	EqSO9	GB%	BABIP	WHIP	ERA	FRA	WARP
2008	JAM	A-	21	1	4	0	13	13	58^{2}	79	2	18	62	2.8	9.5	57%	.418	1.67	3.53	1.60	3.5
2009	GRB	A	22	1	2	0	34	0	49^{1}	42	1	21	54	3.8	9.9	60%	.315	1.28	2.74	3.59	0.6
2010	JAX	AA	23	4	2	0	37	0	52^{2}	49	0	26	44	4.5	7.6	62%	.320	1.44	2.56	2.72	1.2
2011	*FLO*	*MLB*	*24*	*2*	*2*	*1*	*37*	*3*	*57*	*66*	*6*	*33*	*45*	*5.2*	*6.9*	*49%*	*.335*	*1.71*	*5.50*	*5.98*	*-0.6*

Credit the organization for not pigeonholing a guy just because he's left-handed and a reliever. The obvious temptation is to make Jennings into a situational specialist, but why cut to that particular chase when you can sort out whether his improving slider and low-90s heat works against everybody, producing tons of ground-ball outs? It seemed to be working for Jennings, up until a late-July suspension for 50 games after testing positive for methylhexaneamine, a banned stimulant. Having already served most of that, he'll be back in action in April with a great shot at erasing that mistake from most memories.

Josh Johnson

Born: **1/31/1984** Age: **27**
Bats: L Throws: R Height: **6' 7"** Weight: **240**
Breakout: **16%** Improve: **40%** Collapse: **19%**
Attrition: **19%** MLB: **85%**

Comparables:
Dustin McGowan, Jeremy Bonderman, Ricky Nolasco (60)

YEAR	TEAM	LVL	AGE	W	L	SV	G	GS	IP	H	HR	BB	SO	EqBB9	EqSO9	GB%	BABIP	WHIP	ERA	FRA	WARP
2008	FLO	MLB	24	7	1	0	14	14	87^{1}	91	7	27	77	2.8	7.9	50%	.332	1.36	3.61	2.94	2.8
2009	FLO	MLB	25	15	5	0	33	33	209	184	14	58	191	2.5	8.2	51%	.290	1.19	3.23	3.56	5.0
2010	FLO	MLB	26	11	6	0	28	28	183^{2}	155	7	48	186	2.4	9.1	48%	.298	1.13	2.30	2.55	6.4
2011	*FLO*	*MLB*	*27*	*10*	*6*	*0*	*22*	*22*	*140^{1}*	*132*	*9*	*46*	*135*	*2.9*	*8.7*	*48%*	*.315*	*1.27*	*3.28*	*3.57*	*4.0*

Johnson was signed to a four-year, $39 million contract before 2010, which proved that while the Marlins might be cheap, they're not suicidal—pitching this good costs much more than that on the open market. The statistical superlatives pile up for the league's ERA titleist, even allowing for his being shut down a month early with back trouble—there was nothing at stake but walk-up sales on a few dates, so why bother? Naturally, you'll still find workload nellies fretting over the doubling of Johnson's ERA before and after the All-Star break: 1.70 before, 3.50 after, with a walk rate that jumped by 0.7 (to 2.7), but with the same strikeout rate. Try to dial all that fear-mongering back and just keep in mind that Johnson has really only suffered the one elbow injury as far as significant, potentially career-altering hurts. Instead, focus on the good stuff, like his possession of an uncomplicated mix: one of the best fastballs in the game, reliably in the mid-90s, supplemented with a plus slider. His actual .672 winning percentage—achieved on the Marlins, mind you—is tops among starters with 50 or more decisions. Only two pitchers in the NL with 10 or more starts managed better Support-Neutral Winning Percentages than Johnson's .635: the Snakes' Dan Hudson (.654) and some guy named Roy Halladay (.646). Johnson was one of six starters who managed to strike out a quarter of all batters faced, and from among them, only Jered Weaver had a lower walk rate. Add in the care with which he's been handled since Joe Girardi's black day, and you have the best starter in the league, likely to stay that way for years to come.

Tom Koehler

Born: **6/29/1986** Age: **25**
Bats: R Throws: R Height: **6' 3"** Weight: **235**
Breakout: **14%** Improve: **24%** Collapse: **14%**
Attrition: **28%** MLB: **50%**

Comparables:
Enrique Gonzalez, Billy Buckner, Andrew Carpenter (75)

YEAR	TEAM	LVL	AGE	W	L	SV	G	GS	IP	H	HR	BB	SO	EqBB9	EqSO9	GB%	BABIP	WHIP	ERA	FRA	WARP
2008	JAM	A-	22	5	5	0	15	13	66	66	0	29	58	4.0	7.9	49%	.330	1.59	3.68	4.16	1.3
2009	GRB	A	23	5	5	0	18	18	98^{1}	88	9	39	82	3.6	7.5	49%	.280	1.40	3.20	3.73	2.2
2009	JUP	A+	23	4	1	0	6	6	34^{2}	35	0	9	25	2.3	6.5	46%	.333	1.33	3.37	3.32	0.8
2010	JAX	AA	24	16	2	0	28	28	158^{2}	140	11	46	145	2.6	8.2	42%	.293	1.23	2.61	3.20	4.6
2011	*FLO*	*MLB*	*25*	*7*	*9*	*0*	*21*	*21*	*115*	*126*	*14*	*55*	*83*	*4.3*	*6.5*	*43%*	*.311*	*1.57*	*5.26*	*5.72*	*0.7*

If you're a bulky right-hander without any one great pitch, you already have several big strikes against you in most prospect-mongers' eyes. That's what Koehler is up against as more of a "performance" prospect: after tying for the minor-league lead in wins last season; he can hope to avoid becoming a Quad-A fixture, but unless he starts using Flubber as a latter-day cross of Fred MacMurray and Gaylord Perry, he's not the sort of young pitcher who will get an unlimited number of cracks at avoiding a journeyman's fate. Still, Koehler has put himself on the radar for back-end rotation-slot consideration, which is important, given that he'll turn 25 in June. He sets up a fine changeup with a useful slider and average heat (89-92 mph), but he spiced things up a bit in 2010, working hard on a cutter to help him against lefties.

Jhan Marinez

Born: **8/12/1988** Age: **22**
Bats: R Throws: R Height: **6' 1"** Weight: **165**
Breakout: **0%** Improve: **0%** Collapse: **0%**
Attrition: **0%** MLB: **0%**

Comparables:
Jimmy Haynes, Armando Benitez, Santiago Guzman (85)

YEAR	TEAM	LVL	AGE	W	L	SV	G	GS	IP	H	HR	BB	SO	EqBB9	EqSO9	GB%	BABIP	WHIP	ERA	FRA	WARP
2009	JUP	A+	20	1	1	1	29	0	43	28	4	20	42	4.2	8.8	40%	.220	1.21	3.14	4.94	0.0
2010	JUP	A+	21	0	1	4	21	1	25^{1}	12	1	14	44	5.0	15.8	37%	.282	1.08	1.42	1.45	1.2
2010	FLO	MLB	21	1	1	0	4	0	2^{2}	3	1	3	3	10.1	10.1	38%	.286	2.25	6.75	8.83	-0.1
2011	*FLO*	*MLB*	*22*	*1*	*0*	*1*	*23*	*0*	*27*	*25*	*3*	*20*	*28*	*6.4*	*9.3*	*43%*	*.307*	*1.63*	*4.93*	*5.36*	*-0.2*

Relief prospect isn't an oxymoron, with Marinez providing a great example of why not. Armed with a fastball he can dial up to 98 and an explosive late-breaking slider, he has the weapons for a quality penster. That's the stuff that gets a guy from High-A to the majors in little more than three months. The handicaps are equally straightforward: because he has made only 109 appearances in five years as a pro, it isn't surprising that Marinez is plagued with inconsistent mechanics, let alone far from finished when it comes to mastering little things, like holding baserunners or fielding. His first shot at "The Show" ended quickly when elbow problems put him on the DL, but he recovered in time to make a pair of late-season minor-league appearances to demonstrate health. He'll come into camp with a shot at sticking, and the talent is there to make him a long-term stalking horse for the closer's role.

Adalberto Mendez

Born: **2/22/1982** Age: **29**
Bats: R Throws: R Height: **6' 2"** Weight: **160**
Breakout: **0%** Improve: **0%** Collapse: **0%**
Attrition: **0%** MLB: **0%**

Comparables:
Arnie Munoz, Brett Campbell, Ezequiel Astacio (85)

YEAR	TEAM	LVL	AGE	W	L	SV	G	GS	IP	H	HR	BB	SO	EqBB9	EqSO9	GB%	BABIP	WHIP	ERA	FRA	WARP
2008	JUP	A+	26	3	7	29	57	0	57	46	3	24	59	3.8	9.3	35%	.276	1.26	3.32	3.13	0.9
2009	JAX	AA	27	2	4	0	27	0	36	29	2	16	32	4.0	8.0	37%	.276	1.25	3.50	4.68	0.0
2010	NWO	AAA	28	5	4	1	28	9	71^{2}	64	7	29	73	3.7	9.2	31%	.292	1.35	4.14	3.75	1.7
2010	FLO	MLB	28	1	3	0	5	5	24^{2}	28	7	12	11	4.4	4.0	30%	.273	1.70	5.11	5.30	0.1
2011	*FLO*	*MLB*	*29*	*3*	*3*	*5*	*38*	*6*	*69*	*72*	*9*	*38*	*56*	*5.0*	*7.3*	*39%*	*.308*	*1.60*	*5.27*	*5.73*	*-0.2*

A Cubs farmhand once upon a time, Mendez was snagged by the Marlins in the minor-league portion of the Rule 5 draft after 2007. The Fish have subsequently used him as a utility arm in the organization, letting him beat up on kids as a closer in 2008, moving him to rotation work last year, and slotting him into the big-league starting five after rosters expanded (and after they had shut down Johnson and Ricky Nolasco). The stringy Dominican isn't a prospect—how many 28-year-old rookies could be?—but he's an efficient strike-thrower with a low-90s fastball and a decent slider, and he'll be a long shot in the mix for the fifth starter's job.

Andrew Miller

Born: **5/21/1985** Age: **26**
Bats: R Throws: L Height: **6' 6"** Weight: **210**
Breakout: **12%** Improve: **24%** Collapse: **5%**
Attrition: **16%** MLB: **37%**

Comparables:
Randy Johnson, Bobby Parnell, Evan Meek (73)

YEAR	TEAM	LVL	AGE	W	L	SV	G	GS	IP	H	HR	BB	SO	EqBB9	EqSO9	GB%	BABIP	WHIP	ERA	FRA	WARP
2008	FLO	MLB	23	6	10	0	29	20	107^{1}	120	7	56	89	4.7	7.5	48%	.336	1.68	5.87	5.63	0.3
2009	FLO	MLB	24	3	5	0	20	14	80	85	7	43	59	4.8	6.6	50%	.306	1.63	4.84	5.87	-0.0
2010	JAX	AA	25	1	8	0	18	18	85^{1}	98	6	61	66	6.5	7.0	49%	.338	1.93	6.01	6.52	-0.8
2010	FLO	MLB	25	1	5	0	9	7	32^{2}	51	6	26	28	7.2	7.7	42%	.409	2.39	8.54	7.20	-0.4
2011	*BOS*	*MLB*	*26*	*6*	*10*	*0*	*21*	*21*	*103*	*115*	*10*	*68*	*77*	*5.9*	*6.8*	*46%*	*.328*	*1.77*	*5.84*	*6.35*	*0.2*

Along with Cameron Maybin, Miller was a key part of the Miguel Cabrera/Dontrelle Willis dump deal with the Tigers, and the pair succeeded so well as Marlins that Ben & Jerry's should name a teal-colored flavor after them: "Blue-Chip Disappointment." Nobody questions Miller's stuff, because lefties with plus velocity get taken seriously; the problem is the unending litany of setbacks, an accumulation of little hurts, and the too-frequent disassociation with strikes that finally drove the Marlins beyond despair, all the way to disgust. Dealt to the Red Sox after the season for lefty Dustin Richardson, Miller will become a project for new pitching coach Curt Young, free of the expectations that come with being a high draft pick and a major trade acquisition.

Ricky Nolasco

Born: **12/13/1982** Age: **28**
Bats: R Throws: R Height: **6' 2"** Weight: **220**
Breakout: **18%** Improve: **47%** Collapse: **26%**
Attrition: **9%** MLB: **96%**

Comparables:
Fergie Jenkins, Don Drysdale, Gaylord Perry (70)

YEAR	TEAM	LVL	AGE	W	L	SV	G	GS	IP	H	HR	BB	SO	EqBB9	EqSO9	GB%	BABIP	WHIP	ERA	FRA	WARP
2008	FLO	MLB	25	15	8	0	34	32	212^{1}	192	28	42	186	1.8	7.9	40%	.271	1.13	3.52	4.02	3.8
2010	FLO	MLB	27	14	9	0	26	26	157^{2}	169	24	33	147	1.9	8.4	42%	.316	1.29	4.51	4.37	2.0
2010	FLO	MLB	27	14	9	0	26	29	157^{2}	169	24	33	147	1.9	8.4	42%	.316	1.29	4.51	4.37	2.0
2011	*FLO*	*MLB*	*28*	*10*	*8*	*0*	*25*	*25*	*154*	*158*	*20*	*40*	*146*	*2.3*	*8.5*	*42%*	*.315*	*1.28*	*4.00*	*4.35*	*3.0*

The Nolasco Kid might very well be the perfect Marlin, since he's either the poor man's Dan Haren or the Marlins' answer to James Shields. Generally, guys who strike out 20 percent of their opponents and walk less than five percent are supposed to be league-leading hurlers, but Nolasco has found a way to avoid it. That's because of his ongoing problem with homers allowed, as his tendency to leave something over the plate early in the count led to an incredible 17 homers on his first or second pitch to a batter. While he's a fly-ball/strikeout pitcher, and the high home-run rate is a function of that, last year marked Nolasco's highest rate of homers per fly ball. If he can come back from approaching 10 percent to something closer to the league-average 7.6 percent clip, he'll be the sort of midrotation asset who can help a team in a big ballpark get to the postseason.

Leo Nunez

Born: **8/14/1983** Age: **27**
Bats: R Throws: R Height: **6' 1"** Weight: **160**
Breakout: **10%** Improve: **18%** Collapse: **16%**
Attrition: **9%** MLB: **44%**

Comparables:
Doug Bird, Jose Melendez, Rawly Eastwick (74)

YEAR	TEAM	LVL	AGE	W	L	SV	G	GS	IP	H	HR	BB	SO	EqBB9	EqSO9	GB%	BABIP	WHIP	ERA	FRA	WARP
2008	KCA	MLB	24	4	1	0	45	0	48^{1}	45	2	15	26	2.8	4.8	42%	.272	1.32	2.98	2.94	1.5
2009	FLO	MLB	25	4	6	26	75	0	68^{2}	59	13	27	60	3.5	7.9	42%	.243	1.31	4.06	5.21	-0.2
2010	FLO	MLB	26	4	3	30	68	0	65	62	5	21	71	2.9	9.8	54%	.330	1.28	3.46	2.89	1.1
2011	*FLO*	*MLB*	*27*	*3*	*1*	*14*	*69*	*0*	*67*	*66*	*8*	*25*	*61*	*3.4*	*8.1*	*45%*	*.304*	*1.35*	*4.12*	*4.47*	*0.2*

If you need an exhibit on the fungibility of save-generating dudes, the Marlins are perhaps the franchise best equipped to give it to you. Nunez's campaign was the ninth 30-save season in franchise history, joining such luminaries as Kevin Gregg, Antonio Alfonseca, and Joe Borowski. Getting them took little or nothing in terms of talent or money, employing them has rarely taken the Fish out of the low seven figures, and moving them has helped bring back goodies like Dontrelle Willis and Jose Ceda. Nunez logged 30 saves *despite losing his job with a month to go* and in the face of season-long complaints that he was becoming overreliant on his changeup without adequately setting up a flat fastball that sits around 94. He could iron out this kink and start setting up his pitches more effectively, but restricted to the Eck-style ninth-inning role, it isn't as if he's free to experiment. If Nunez is bumped from closing, it might actually help his long-term development, because pitching in an old-man's usage pattern isn't doing him any favors—beyond generating saves in an unremarkable four out of every five opportunities.

Will Ohman

Born: **8/13/1977** Age: **33**
Bats: L Throws: L Height: **6' 2"** Weight: **195**
Breakout: **24%** Improve: **45%** Collapse: **21%**
Attrition: **11%** MLB: **80%**

Comparables:
Paul Assenmacher, Jay Howell, Moe Drabowsky (78)

YEAR	TEAM	LVL	AGE	W	L	SV	G	GS	IP	H	HR	BB	SO	EqBB9	EqSO9	GB%	BABIP	WHIP	ERA	FRA	WARP
2008	ATL	MLB	30	4	1	1	83	0	58^{2}	51	3	22	53	3.4	8.1	38%	.284	1.26	3.68	4.14	0.6
2009	LAN	MLB	31	1	0	1	21	0	12^{1}	12	4	8	7	5.8	5.1	26%	.229	1.62	5.84	4.09	0.1
2010	BAL	MLB	32	0	0	0	51	0	30	30	3	18	29	5.4	8.7	53%	.321	1.63	3.30	5.42	-0.1
2010	FLO	MLB	32	0	2	0	17	0	12	10	1	5	14	3.8	10.5	34%	.290	1.25	3.00	3.42	0.6
2011	*CHA*	*MLB*	*33*	*4*	*1*	*1*	*71*	*0*	*46*	*45*	*6*	*23*	*42*	*4.5*	*8.1*	*44%*	*.301*	*1.47*	*4.43*	*4.81*	*0.0*

Situational relief, like situational comedy, gets a bit formulaic. You know what Will Ohman is good for and what he'll be asked to do, sort of like the brain cells you've committed to the existence of Jason Alexander. You can be reasonably certain he's not going to be asked to do something he can't, like start, close, or play Heathcliff in a modern interpretation of *Wuthering Heights*. The nicest thing you can say is that the Marlins traded for him at the deadline as a concession to their being just a half-dozen games out, only to find out that Ohman still needs to be handled with care, as his elbow wore out in September. He'll entrust it to the capable hands of White Sox trainer Herm Schneider after reaching a two-year agreement withthe Pale Hose in January.

Evan Reed

Born: **12/31/1985** Age: **25**
Bats: R Throws: R Height: **6' 4"** Weight: **225**
Breakout: **0%** Improve: **0%** Collapse: **0%**
Attrition: **2%** MLB: **2%**

Comparables:
Sergio Escalona, Jesus Delgado, Jhonny Nunez (87)

YEAR	TEAM	LVL	AGE	W	L	SV	G	GS	IP	H	HR	BB	SO	EqBB9	EqSO9	GB%	BABIP	WHIP	ERA	FRA	WARP
2008	BAK	A+	22	7	10	0	23	23	121	130	14	55	89	4.1	6.6	42%	.302	1.58	6.17	6.56	-0.8
2009	BAK	A+	23	2	2	25	44	0	48^{2}	44	1	28	65	5.2	12.0	57%	.364	1.50	2.96	2.48	1.1
2010	FRI	AA	24	1	1	5	30	0	39	35	0	14	34	3.2	7.8	50%	.310	1.26	1.62	1.71	1.4
2011	*FLO*	*MLB*	*25*	*3*	*3*	*4*	*34*	*5*	*63*	*71*	*7*	*37*	*47*	*5.3*	*6.7*	*45%*	*.321*	*1.70*	*5.59*	*6.08*	*-0.5*

The other arm received from the Rangers for Cantu, Reed had been a reliever at Cal Poly San Luis Obispo, the program that has cranked out Garrett Olson, Bud Norris, and Brent Morel. The Rangers nabbed Reed in the third round of 2007 and, seeing a big guy who could throw mid-90s heat, gave him a spin as a starter in 2008. That was a disaster, but moving him back to the bullpen produced predictably happy results in the lower minors. Less happily, Reed hurt his elbow in his Marlins debut, never to appear again, and the absence of a quality off-speed pitch limits his upside in anything more than a supporting relief role.

Sandy Rosario

Born: **8/22/1985** Age: **25**
Bats: R Throws: R Height: **6' 1"** Weight: **170**
Breakout: **0%** Improve: **0%** Collapse: **0%**
Attrition: **0%** MLB: **0%**

Comparables:
Frank Bork, Jose Garcia, John Curtis (77)

YEAR	TEAM	LVL	AGE	W	L	SV	G	GS	IP	H	HR	BB	SO	EqBB9	EqSO9	GB%	BABIP	WHIP	ERA	FRA	WARP
2009	GRB	A	23	3	2	0	7	7	40^{1}	57	4	6	36	1.3	8.0	46%	.384	1.59	5.14	4.65	0.6
2009	JAM	A-	23	4	2	0	9	9	42^{1}	48	1	8	41	1.7	8.7	50%	.359	1.44	1.70	2.19	1.8
2010	GRB	A	24	7	2	3	43	0	90	92	9	17	122	1.7	12.2	50%	.367	1.24	3.60	3.85	1.1
2010	FLO	MLB	24	0	0	0	2	0	1	9	2	1	0	9.0	0.0	45%	.778	10.00	54.00	31.60	-0.2
2011	*FLO*	*MLB*	*25*	*1*	*1*	*0*	*20*	*2*	*44^{2}*	*53*	*6*	*18*	*36*	*3.7*	*7.4*	*45%*	*.343*	*1.62*	*5.73*	*6.23*	*-0.6*

Part of the system's bevy of Latin talent, Rosario is a Dominican who has spent portions of the last four years at Greensboro. Although he was an old man for the Sally League, moving to the pen finally allowed him to open up and throw (although he continued to average over two innings per appearance), using a solid mix of sliders and a mid-90s fastball. Since he was going to have to be exposed to the Rule 5 draft or get added to the 40-man after the season anyway, the Marlins promoted him to the majors, a fairly extraordinary move, given that the guy was pitching in Low-A in September. He promptly got into the history books by giving up homers to his first two big-league batters. Nevertheless, the results are less important than Rosario's possession of a live arm, and he'll have a shot at bullpen work in 2011.

Alejandro Sanabia

Born: **9/8/1988** Age: **22**
Bats: R Throws: R Height: **6' 2"** Weight: **165**
Breakout: **7%** Improve: **11%** Collapse: **6%**
Attrition: **4%** MLB: **21%**

Comparables:
Rich Nye, Leo Kiely, Mike Mussina (72)

YEAR	TEAM	LVL	AGE	W	L	SV	G	GS	IP	H	HR	BB	SO	EqBB9	EqSO9	GB%	BABIP	WHIP	ERA	FRA	WARP
2008	GRB	A	19	5	5	0	19	19	96^{2}	106	11	25	75	2.3	7.0	48%	.309	1.38	4.93	5.95	-0.0
2009	JUP	A+	20	9	5	0	19	18	104^{1}	89	6	36	68	3.1	5.9	41%	.262	1.27	3.45	4.68	0.7
2010	JAX	AA	21	5	1	0	14	14	84^{1}	59	2	16	65	1.7	7.0	48%	.238	0.93	2.03	2.51	3.0
2010	FLO	MLB	21	5	3	0	15	12	72^{1}	74	6	16	47	2.0	5.8	39%	.289	1.29	3.73	3.57	1.5
2011	*FLO*	*MLB*	*22*	*5*	*6*	*0*	*16*	*16*	*85^{2}*	*93*	*9*	*34*	*52*	*3.6*	*5.4*	*43%*	*.302*	*1.49*	*4.84*	*5.26*	*0.9*

A 32nd-round pick in 2006 at the tender age of 17, Sanabia has simply made his way up through the system with moxie and surprising inexorability, showing fine command of a sinking fastball and touch on a slider. His changeup could use work, but for an utterly untouted 21-year-old to make the majors and not get eaten alive says something nice about the system's underrated depth. For now, the lanky control fiend will be in the mix for the fifth slot, with some hoping that he'll add velocity and better fade on his change as he fills out and matures.

Brian Sanches

Born: **8/8/1978** Age: **32**
Bats: R Throws: R Height: **6' 0"** Weight: **190**
Breakout: **25%** Improve: **46%** Collapse: **15%**
Attrition: **8%** MLB: **84%**

Comparables:
Rick Aguilera, Rollie Fingers, Moe Drabowsky (74)

YEAR	TEAM	LVL	AGE	W	L	SV	G	GS	IP	H	HR	BB	SO	EqBB9	EqSO9	GB%	BABIP	WHIP	ERA	FRA	WARP
2008	COH	AAA	29	2	1	13	32	0	33^{2}	24	2	9	45	2.4	12.0	28%	.289	1.01	2.40	2.88	1.0
2008	WAS	MLB	29	2	0	0	12	0	11	16	2	5	10	4.1	8.2	42%	.389	2.00	7.36	6.49	-0.2
2009	FLO	MLB	30	4	2	0	47	0	56^{1}	50	5	26	51	4.2	8.1	35%	.281	1.46	2.56	3.65	0.8
2010	FLO	MLB	31	2	2	0	61	0	63^{2}	43	7	27	54	3.8	7.6	34%	.218	1.12	2.40	4.80	0.0
2011	*FLO*	*MLB*	*32*	*3*	*1*	*2*	*56*	*0*	*60*	*56*	*7*	*26*	*59*	*3.9*	*8.8*	*40%*	*.301*	*1.35*	*3.90*	*4.24*	*0.3*

The pen's other veteran junkballer, Sanches was generally the guy coming into tight games in front of Hensley and another example of the Marlins' ability (or willingness) to scrape useful relievers out of the discard pile and put them to use. He'll top 90 on the gun barely and rarely, using his tepid heater to help sell a changeup in the 70s. If this sounds an awful lot like Joe Nelson, whom the Fish nontendered after 2008 once the thirtysomething soft-tosser became seven-figures expensive due to arb eligibility, you'd be exactly right. And given how easily they found a one-to-one replacement, you can understand why they were right to do so. Sanches has another year to go before he achieves his first hookup with the panel, which very well might coincide with the end of his Marlins career if the team stays true to form.

Anibal Sanchez

Born: **2/27/1984** Age: **27**
Bats: R Throws: R Height: **6' 0"** Weight: **180**
Breakout: **17%** Improve: **45%** Collapse: **23%**
Attrition: **3%** MLB: **97%**

Comparables:
Bob Welch, Bob Grim, Dustin Hermanson (81)

YEAR	TEAM	LVL	AGE	W	L	SV	G	GS	IP	H	HR	BB	SO	EqBB9	EqSO9	GB%	BABIP	WHIP	ERA	FRA	WARP
2008	FLO	MLB	24	2	5	0	10	10	51^{2}	54	7	26	50	4.5	8.7	42%	.311	1.66	5.57	5.48	0.3
2009	FLO	MLB	25	4	8	0	16	16	86	84	10	46	71	4.8	7.4	44%	.290	1.52	3.87	4.14	1.6
2010	FLO	MLB	26	13	12	0	32	32	195	192	10	70	157	3.2	7.2	47%	.305	1.38	3.55	3.83	3.6
2011	*FLO*	*MLB*	*27*	*8*	*7*	*0*	*22*	*22*	*122*	*123*	*10*	*54*	*100*	*4.0*	*7.4*	*45%*	*.312*	*1.45*	*4.26*	*4.63*	*2.2*

It was a long time coming, but the Marlins finally got a full season out of Sanchez. He didn't disappoint, delivering 20 quality starts. For all the hoopla left over from the 2006 no-hitter, he has become a much more mature pitcher in the intervening time, learning how to cut and take something off his fastball, usually sitting in the low 90s but sometimes cranking it up to 95 or so, sinking it, setting up a nifty change, and slathering the lot with a heaping helping of sliders. It makes for a balanced blend and a more polished pitcher, and while last year's 3.6 percent ratio of homers per fly ball was less than half the major-league rate, his broad assortment proved hard to hit for any kind of power by anybody in any park. Couple that with better defensive support, and Sanchez will take things up another notch in 2011.

Jose Veras

Born: **10/20/1980** Age: **30**
Bats: R Throws: R Height: **6' 5"** Weight: **230**
Breakout: **9%** Improve: **20%** Collapse: **14%**
Attrition: **11%** MLB: **51%**

Comparables:
Jeff Nelson, Chris Schroder, Lee Smith (76)

YEAR	TEAM	LVL	AGE	W	L	SV	G	GS	IP	H	HR	BB	SO	EqBB9	EqSO9	GB%	BABIP	WHIP	ERA	FRA	WARP
2008	NYA	MLB	27	5	3	0	60	0	57^{2}	52	7	29	63	4.5	9.8	42%	.298	1.46	3.59	3.81	0.8
2009	CLE	MLB	28	1	2	0	22	0	24^{2}	19	3	14	22	5.1	8.0	42%	.242	1.42	4.38	6.83	-0.5
2009	NYA	MLB	28	3	1	0	25	0	25^{2}	23	5	14	18	4.9	6.3	35%	.234	1.60	5.96	6.05	-0.2
2010	NWO	AAA	29	1	1	2	24	0	29^{1}	34	2	15	37	4.6	11.4	42%	.395	1.68	4.60	2.22	1.0
2010	FLO	MLB	29	3	3	0	48	0	48	32	5	29	54	5.4	10.1	42%	.241	1.29	3.75	5.05	0.9
2011	*FLO*	*MLB*	*30*	*3*	*1*	*1*	*58*	*0*	*59*	*53*	*6*	*33*	*64*	*4.9*	*9.7*	*43%*	*.303*	*1.43*	*4.13*	*4.49*	*0.1*

Last spring's veteran nonroster invitee who was seemingly guaranteed an Opening Day roster spot to provide bracing veteranosity or an ex-Yankee contact high, Veras bollixed that proposition by giving up runs every time out in April, playing his way back off the roster and earning a one-way ticket to the Big Easy. Veras returned in June and earned his keep with his still-exciting blend of mid-90s heat and a nice, slow curve. He's far too wild to rely on, but even though he was nontendered in December, you can count on another nonroster invite at the very least.

Elih Villanueva

Born: **7/26/1986** Age: **24**
Bats: R Throws: R Height: **6' 2"** Weight: **235**
Breakout: **11%** Improve: **25%** Collapse: **10%**
Attrition: **16%** MLB: **58%**

Comparables:
Tobi Stoner, Jim Nash, Esmailin Caridad (49)

YEAR	TEAM	LVL	AGE	W	L	SV	G	GS	IP	H	HR	BB	SO	EqBB9	EqSO9	GB%	BABIP	WHIP	ERA	FRA	WARP
2008	JAM	A-	21	3	1	0	6	2	25	19	2	6	30	2.2	10.8	54%	.270	1.00	1.44	3.01	0.7
2009	JUP	A+	22	9	12	0	26	25	158	159	10	18	110	1.0	6.3	41%	.296	1.19	3.08	5.04	0.4
2010	JAX	AA	23	14	4	0	28	28	179	137	15	34	115	1.7	5.8	39%	.227	1.00	2.26	4.98	0.7
2011	*FLO*	*MLB*	*24*	*7*	*6*	*0*	*24*	*19*	*127*	*135*	*16*	*38*	*74*	*2.7*	*5.2*	*40%*	*.289*	*1.35*	*4.32*	*4.70*	*1.8*

A chunky, durable control artist, Villanueva won the organization's pitcher-of-the-year award. The former Florida State star spun a trio of complete-game shutouts while winning the Southern League ERA title. However, exceptional command of a mediocre assortment and slow fastballs generally doesn't get you listed on top-prospect lists, so like his fellow underregarded teammate, Tom Koehler, Villanueva is stuck in the "show me" pile for the time being. Given the crowd ahead of him for the fifth slot in the rotation, he will have to take a number and wait for a back-end rotation opportunity.

Chris Volstad

Born: **9/23/1986** Age: **24**
Bats: **R** Throws: **R** Height: **6' 7"** Weight: **190**
Breakout: **8%** Improve: **20%** Collapse: **8%**
Attrition: **20%** MLB: **38%**
Comparables:
Clayton Mortensen, Troy Patton, Mike Ekstrom (74)

YEAR	TEAM	LVL	AGE	W	L	SV	G	GS	IP	H	HR	BB	SO	EqBB9	EqSO9	GB%	BABIP	WHIP	ERA	FRA	WARP
2008	CAR	AA	21	4	4	0	15	15	91	86	0	30	56	3.0	5.5	60%	.292	1.30	3.26	4.06	1.8
2008	FLO	MLB	21	6	4	0	15	14	84^1	76	3	36	52	3.8	5.5	56%	.271	1.39	2.88	3.82	1.9
2009	FLO	MLB	22	9	13	0	29	29	159	169	29	59	107	3.3	6.1	52%	.289	1.45	5.21	5.74	0.1
2010	FLO	MLB	23	12	9	0	30	30	175	187	17	60	102	3.1	5.2	49%	.298	1.46	4.58	5.05	0.9
2011	*FLO*	*MLB*	*24*	*9*	*11*	*0*	*29*	*29*	*164*	*184*	*19*	*68*	*104*	*3.7*	*5.7*	*50%*	*.312*	*1.53*	*5.03*	*5.47*	*1.3*

Repeated opportunities aren't doing Volstad much good. The gentle giant used to be seen as a worm-killing workhorse, a big man who kept everything in the infield instead of overpowering people, but his sinker isn't generating ground balls, let alone all that many outs. One of the key propositions for a ground-baller is to keep the double-play in order, yet Volstad was party to 29 successful stolen bases in 33 attempts. While that sort of unhappy indifference was irritating, he did at least improve his home-run rate, but his breaking stuff isn't fooling lefties, leaving you with . . . what? A gentle workhorse? A wormy infield? A guy hard-pressed to hold the last slot in the rotation now that Javier Vazquez has been signed? You'd think so, but his 8-1 record after the break will help win hearts and minds, if not ballgames.

Sean West

Born: **6/15/1986** Age: **25**
Bats: **L** Throws: **L** Height: **6' 8"** Weight: **260**
Breakout: **8%** Improve: **10%** Collapse: **2%**
Attrition: **5%** MLB: **17%**
Comparables:
Garrett Mock, Felipe Paulino, Randy Wells (75)

YEAR	TEAM	LVL	AGE	W	L	SV	G	GS	IP	H	HR	BB	SO	EqBB9	EqSO9	GB%	BABIP	WHIP	ERA	FRA	WARP
2008	JUP	A+	22	6	5	0	21	20	100^2	79	3	60	92	5.4	8.2	51%	.287	1.44	2.41	2.98	3.3
2009	JAX	AA	23	7	3	0	12	11	64	68	12	28	65	3.9	9.1	39%	.311	1.53	4.64	4.13	0.9
2009	FLO	MLB	23	8	6	0	20	20	103^1	115	11	44	70	3.8	6.1	42%	.307	1.57	4.70	4.97	1.0
2010	NWO	AAA	24	4	3	0	11	11	57^2	60	4	19	46	3.0	7.2	45%	.311	1.38	3.12	3.36	1.6
2010	FLO	MLB	24	0	2	0	2	2	9^1	15	2	4	8	3.9	7.7	46%	.394	2.04	7.71	3.82	0.2
2011	*FLO*	*MLB*	*25*	*7*	*9*	*0*	*21*	*21*	*108*	*119*	*13*	*56*	*84*	*4.6*	*6.9*	*44%*	*.317*	*1.61*	*5.31*	*5.77*	*0.8*

In the mounting tension between the so-called talented prospects and the effective ones, West is found in the first pile, but that's in no small part because repeated injuries have kept the hard-throwing lefty from earning a spot in the second. The big man was hampered by back and knee trouble during the year and then had to bail out on an AFL assignment because his elbow started aching, but when he did pitch, he continued to have difficulties with right-handed batters while owning lefties. While the size and the power potential in his arm remain remarkable, he's now several spins into his own ride on the honorary "No Anibal Sanchez Yet Extended Anticipation Tour" (or NASYEAT), a merry-go-round with which the Marlins are only too familiar.

LINEOUTS

HITTERS

PLAYER	TEAM	LVL	AGE	PA	R	2B	3B	HR	RBI	BB	SO	SB-CS	AVG/OBP/SLG	TAv	BABIP	BRR	FRAA	WARP
C J. Baker*	FLO	MLB	29	88	7	3	1	0	6	9	18	0-0	.218/.307/.282	.219	.283	1.2	C -1	0.0
INF B. Barden	NWO	AAA	29	204	30	14	1	3	23	18	38	3-3	.353/.407/.489	.314	.428	0.2	3B -2, SS -1	1.4
	FLO	MLB	29	32	2	0	0	0	3	3	12	0-2	.179/.281/.179	.194	.312	-0.5	SS -1, 3B 2	0.1
RF B. Carroll	NWO	AAA	27	277	32	16	0	8	30	22	54	4-2	.221/.299/.385	.235	.246	0.0	RF -1, CF -2	-0.6
	FLO	MLB	27	90	13	4	0	2	7	6	29	2-1	.197/.311/.329	.246	.283	0.6	RF -2, LF 0	-0.1
CF I. Galloway	JUP	A+	20	108	9	3	3	0	6	5	21	4-3	.200/.259/.290	.219	.253	-0.4	RF 3, CF 2	0.1
C C. Hatcher#	JAX	AA	25	293	23	9	1	3	26	20	92	1-2	.202/.261/.277	.203	.290	-0.7	C 2, P 0	-0.4
	NWO	AAA	25	61	10	1	0	2	10	9	19	0-0	.167/.333/.313	.222	.214	0.5	C 0	0.1
	FLO	MLB	25	8	0	0	0	0	0	2	5	0-0	.000/.250/.000	.129	.000	0.0	C 0	0.0
OF B. Keys*	JAM	A-	19	261	39	8	1	0	25	31	36	11-4	.267/.360/.313	.268	.302	0.0	CF -10, LF 1	0.0
INF H. Luna	NWO	AAA	30	411	55	17	0	16	71	42	64	7-1	.294/.367/.477	.301	.310	0.5	3B -5, 1B 0	2.5
	FLO	MLB	30	30	2	1	0	2	4	0	13	0-1	.138/.133/.379	.174	.133	-0.1	3B 0, 2B 0	-0.2
INF D. Murphy	NWO	AAA	27	224	31	12	1	12	35	16	41	0-0	.277/.335/.519	.294	.294	0.7	SS 2	1.9
	FLO	MLB	27	47	9	6	1	3	16	2	19	0-0	.318/.340/.704	.353	.478	-0.1	3B 0, SS 0	0.6
OF J. Raynor	NWO	AAA	26	151	21	6	0	2	13	13	27	3-0	.284/.349/.373	.255	.333	0.0	LF 2, CF 1	0.5
	PIT	MLB	26	11	1	0	0	0	0	1	3	0-0	.200/.273/.200	.183	.286	0.0	RF 0, CF 0	0.0
3B J. Smolinski	JUP	A+	21	443	45	27	3	5	51	31	62	8-5	.264/.318/.383	.268	.298	-0.1	3B -6, LF -2	0.7
3B C. Tracy*	IOW	AAA	30	96	21	8	0	5	18	5	9	0-1	.396/.427/.648	.379	.403	1.3	3B 3	1.9
	SWB	AAA	30	73	14	5	0	6	18	4	6	0-0	.324/.356/.662	.330	.281	0.0	3B 0, 1B 0	0.7
	CHN	MLB	30	49	6	2	0	0	5	5	15	0-0	.250/.327/.296	.234	.379	0.2	3B -2, 1B 0	-0.2
	FLO	MLB	30	111	5	6	0	1	10	6	21	0-0	.245/.297/.333	.222	.296	0.2	3B 1, 1B 0	0.0

John Baker lost most of the season to a sore forearm that finally resolved into a need for Tommy John surgery, which should keep him shelved for most of 2011. Initially kept around as a utilityman, **Brian Barden** went stale with disuse, earning a demotion midway through the season; he'll be a Rangers nonroster invitee this spring. **Brett Carroll**'s basic skills—an arm good enough for right, a modest threat to lefties—weren't enough to make him a viable reserve, but he'll give it another shot with the Royals. Toolsy **Isaac Galloway** lost most of his season to kidney damage after an outfield collision, further stalling his development after an 2009 hampered by a bum wrist. Rare flashes of power from a switch-hitting stroke plus an excellent arm might get **Chris Hatcher** a shot at Koyie Hill's career. The Marlins like slappy speed guys, and **Brent Keys** is the latest of the more successful ones in a system littered with more than a few failures. Although **Hector Luna** outgrew the middle infield long ago, he might provide pop and contact in a utility role for Boston this season afer the inevitable Jed Lowrie breakdown before the period. After bopping as Edwin Rodriguez's shortstop in New Orleans, journeyman **Donnie Murphy** got hauled up by his skipper to provide bench power, doing well before dislocating his wrist. He's sure to get another shot somewhere. Speedy **John Raynor** spent last spring with the Pirates as a Rule 5 pick before getting returned in May, only to lose six weeks to a hamstring injury. Expectations that **Jake Smolinski**'s line-drive stroke would start producing power haven't panned out, and a late-season move to left field bodes even worse. **Chad Tracy** used the system to good advantage last year, drifting through three organizations to reach 111 PAs with a Marlins team desperate for a reserve that wasn't Mike Lamb; he will drift on to the Hiroshima Carp for 2011. A pretty swing always turns a few heads, but few expected that **Christian Yelich**'s stroke was enough of a looker to get him picked 23rd overall by the Marlins last June. He's big enough to inspire hope, and if the pop comes and he can handle left, the Marlins will find plenty of people to share their enthusiasm for his upside.

PITCHERS

PLAYER	TEAM	LVL	AGE	W	L	SV	IP	H	HR	BB	SO	EqBB9	EqSO9	GB%	BABIP	WHIP	ERA	FRA	WARP
J. Allison	JAX	AA	25	6	11	0	110^{2}	132	16	33	56	2.7	4.6	40%	.311	1.56	5.04	5.59	-0.1
J. Alvarez*	GRB	A	21	10	3	0	108	114	9	32	113	2.7	9.4	47%	.350	1.38	3.58	3.38	2.7
P. Andrelczyk	JUP	A+	24	3	4	2	68	48	4	30	72	4.0	9.5	54%	.257	1.22	3.04	4.56	0.3
J. Buente	NWO	AAA	26	0	1	0	30^{1}	22	3	18	38	5.4	11.4	56%	.268	1.33	2.67	4.54	0.2
—	FLO	MLB	26	0	0	0	11	16	0	11	9	9.0	7.4	54%	.410	2.45	6.55	5.33	-0.1
A. Caminero	GRB	A	23	5	2	3	74^{2}	55	4	34	97	4.1	11.8	51%	.283	1.29	3.01	4.27	0.6
D. Meyer*	NWO	AAA	28	1	2	2	40	32	4	16	27	3.6	6.1	42%	.233	1.25	2.93	4.73	0.2
—	FLO	MLB	28	0	1	0	9^{1}	15	1	12	4	11.6	3.9	42%	.378	3.00	9.64	6.90	-0.2
E. Olmos*	GRB	A	20	3	9	0	117^{1}	122	9	59	108	4.5	8.3	47%	.331	1.68	4.37	4.14	2.4
A. Ramos	GRB	A	23	3	7	28	58^{1}	40	3	32	78	5.0	12.1	52%	.291	1.33	3.70	4.57	0.2
J. Rosario	JAX	AA	24	5	4	0	83^{1}	79	7	38	68	4.1	7.4	40%	.288	1.42	3.24	3.20	2.5
J. Sosa	NWO	AAA	33	5	4	1	59	74	5	15	45	2.3	6.9	44%	.359	1.53	4.73	4.51	0.7
—	FLO	MLB	33	2	3	0	36^{2}	39	4	18	19	4.4	4.7	41%	.282	1.55	4.66	4.88	0.0
T. Tankersley*	NWO	AAA	27	4	2	1	26^{1}	20	3	8	22	2.8	7.6	36%	.233	1.07	3.42	3.90	0.4
—	FLO	MLB	27	0	0	0	12	12	4	7	7	5.3	5.3	33%	.211	1.67	6.75	7.37	-0.4
T. Wood	FLO	MLB	27	0	1	1	27^{2}	33	2	15	10	4.9	3.3	42%	.304	1.73	5.53	5.23	-0.2

As inspiring as **Jeff Allison**'s comeback from substance abuse might be, Double-A beat him like a drum as the season wore on, making his story closer to an after-school special than Josh Hamilton's ticket to the marquee. Little lefty **Jose Alvarez** is the prize from the Hermida trade, but presents a difficulty as far as figuring out what matters most: his .173/.295/.210 line against lefties, or his 6.46 ERA when relieving. Like Steve Cishek, **Pete Andrelczyk** is a right-handed sinker/slider guy who made a splash in the AFL, but Andrelczyk is older and slightly further behind. Despite having a fastball that touches 95 and a nice splitter, **Jay Buente** isn't anything more than an organizational arm, getting outrighted from the 40-man after being too cute in his brief opportunities. When a player shares a name with a great inventor and mathematician of ancient Greece, as does **Arquimedes Caminero**, one might expect a stat-head fave, but scouts sign on for the high-90s heat that got him added to the roster. Proof that you shouldn't get too excited about filler, **Dan Meyer** washed out with the Fish, but he'll try to catch on with the Phillies in camp. After missing most of 2009 with shoulder surgery, **Edgar Olmos** finally got to stand and deliver a broad assortment of off-speed offerings, but with mixed results. Although **Omar Poveda** missed all of 2010 recovering from Tommy John surgery in March, he's arguably the best pitcher received from the Rangers in the Jorge Cantu deal. Assuming he comes back without any post-op problems—not all do—what the Fish should find is a big-bodied Venezuelan with good command of a fastball that sits in the low 90s, a plus changeup, and no reliable, outstanding breaking pitch. Short righty **Alejandro Ramos** mowed down Sally Leaguers with low-90s heat, but as a former Texas Tech pitcher, he was a bit old and advanced for the circuit. Slender southpaw **Rob Rasmussen** was last summer's second-round pick out of UCLA. Not surprising for a top-program pick, Rasmussen is a finished product, mixing sharp curves with above-average velocity for a lefty (89-93 mph) and excellent command. The Marlins could let him start and bring him along slowly, but the stuff, command, and concerns about his frame might lead to a permanent move to the pen. If that happens, he could clamber up the ladder at an accelerated pace. Wait, another Rosario? **Jose Rosario**? The Marlins really are trying to confuse you about who's who, but this one was Organizational Pitcher of the Year in 2009, and he's one of the slender strike-throwers instead of one of the hard-throwing monsters. When you're trawling for relief help in Davy Jones's locker, some of the strangest things get netted, including **Jorge Sosa** for two different stretches. No, he still couldn't get lefties out, so back in the drink he went. Former first-rounder **Taylor Tankersley** was officially judged a Fishy flop and kicked out of the tank after the season. Appropriately, given the fate of most discarded fish, he landed in Flushing. Multiple passes at a bullpen job didn't win hard-throwing **Tim Wood** the job security he sought, but he'll be in the Nats' NRI mash-up come spring training.

MANAGER: FREDI GONZALEZ /EDWIN RODRIGUEZ

YEAR	MGR	W-L	Pythag +/–	Avg PC	100+ P	120+ P	QS	BQS	REL	REL w Zero R	IBB	Subs	PH	PH Avg	PH HR	SB2	CS2	SB3	CS3	SAC Att	SAC %	POS SAC	Squeeze	Swing	In Play
2008	F.G.	84-77	3	93.6	46	2	70	5	510	337	66	80	248	.211	7	69	25	7	2	80	61.3%	15	4	122	89
2009	F.G.	87-75	5	92.6	44	1	72	3	529	346	60	74	278	.280	8	66	28	9	6	106	66.0%	26	3	127	92
2010	F.G.	35-36	-4	96.2	30	1	41	1	196	114	18	25	102	.208	1	41	9	3	2	37	59.5%	4	1	57	47
2010	E.R.	-46	3	93.4	32	1	41	1	313	219	24	105	151	.181	3	46	12	1	1	43	67.4%	7	1	71	41

Stepping in for Fredi Gonzalez and then left in place after the Marlins' extended flirtations with either conjuring up Ozzie Guillen or getting Bobby Valentine to come out of the booth came up empty, Rodriguez didn't rock the boat all that much. He presided over Logan Morrison's assignment to left field after Chris Coghlan broke down, but there wasn't a ton of elective decision-making on offense to distinguish his guidance from Gonzalez's as he got a read on his new charges. He did use his pen a bit more aggressively and to better effect, relying on a core quintet while refusing to settle for Leo Nunez's inconsistency in the closer's slot. After eight years in the organization as a manager and hitting coach, the first skipper of Puerto Rican extraction is familiar with a lot of what's on hand and on the way up through the pipeline, which should serve him well as the organization starts integrating more of its own and relies less on the drifters of the recent past.

Houston Astros

The Astros will assemble in Kissimmee for the first day of spring training with one unified thought—mimicking the 2010 Padres. That was already the talk around the clubhouse during the final weeks of 2010, and it carried on throughout the winter months. The Padres came from the proverbial nowhere last year to lead the National League West for most of the season, losing a showdown with the Giants for the division title in the final game of the regular-season schedule. The Astros believe they can tread the same path in a division that does not have a prohibitive favorite.

The Astros somewhat understandably feel that they can follow in the Padres' footsteps. Like the Padres in 2009, the Astros had an awful start in 2010 before finishing strong; they lost their first eight games under new manager Brad Mills and were 17-34 at the end of April. However, they went 60-52 the rest of the way, including a 36-26 record from July 27 until the end of the season, which was the third-best mark in the NL during that span, behind those of only the Phillies (43-19) and the Reds (35-25). At the risk of spoiling the upbeat mood, however, it must be noted that the comparison between the Astros and Padres breaks down under closer scrutiny. The Astros organization believes pitching can carry it this season, much as pitching supported the Padres on their journey to 90 wins last season. But the Astros' pitching staff wasn't close to being among baseball's elite last season, especially following the July trade of ace Roy Oswalt to the Phillies.

ASTROS PROSPECTUS

2010 W-L: 76-86, 4th in NL Central

Pythag	.420	26th
RS/G	3.77	28th
RA/G	4.50	11th
TAv	.248	29th
BRR	15.8	2nd
FRA	4.38	14th
DER	-14.4	26th
DL	812	20th
B-Age	29.4	22nd
P-Age	29.5	25th
Salary	$92.4	13th
M$/MW	$3.01	20th

Ballpark: Minute Maid Park (3-yr. PF: 96). A physical connection to Union Station makes it easy to leave early

2010: A hot second half and Pythagorean overperformance rescue Houston from embarrassment

2011: Nothing rescues Houston from embarrassment

Action Items: A productive farm system, a player better than Hunter Pence, Ex-Lax for Carlos Lee

The Astros allowed 4.50 runs per game, which ranked 11th in the NL and 20th overall. Furthermore, the Astros did not have the type of strong fielding club needed to win games with a strategy based on run prevention, as they managed only a .680 Defensive Efficiency, finishing 13th in the NL and 26th in the majors. While Astros starters were second in the NL with quality starts in 59 percent of opportunities, which trailed only the Cubs, as measured by expected wins added (WXRL), the bullpen placed only eighth.

That's not to say that the Astros' staff is completely unsalvageable. Brett Myers enjoyed a rebound season last year after general manager Ed Wade took a gamble on the free agent. Left-hander Wandy Rodriguez recovered from a miserable start to post a 2.11 ERA in 14 second-half starts, while lefty J. A. Happ and righty Bud Norris showed some upside. Right-hander Jordan Lyles, who reached Triple-A at age 19 late in the minor-league season, stands out as the best prospect in an otherwise thin farm system.

The Astros could boast about having the only duo of relievers to notch 20 saves in a season in the NL; Brandon Lyon and Matt Lindstrom were the first since Norm Charlton and Rob Dibble of the 1992 Reds to pull off that feat. However, the Astros had dual 20-save closers out of necessity rather than design. Lindstrom's production again failed to live up to his promise, as his high-90s fastball translated into nothing more than replacement-level production. Conversely, Lyon had 5.3 WXRL and helped fuel the Astros' late-season run. Yet right-hander Wilton Lopez, who became the king of stranding inherited runners in his rookie season (he prevented 6.4 runs' worth of inherited baserunners from scoring, second-best in the NL after the Giants' Santiago Casilla), was the only other reliever to add as much as one win over replacement.

The pitching will have to be better for the Astros to have any chance of being a surprise contender, because the hitting was awful last season and should remain awful. The Astros' .247/.303/.362 triple-slash line was markedly below the NL average of .255/.324/.399; both their on-base and slugging percentages were the second-lowest in the majors.

There is little hope that the offense will pick up substantially this season, as even in an injury-plagued season during the decline phase of his career, first baseman Lance Berkman led the team with a .297 True Average before being dealt to the Yankees at the trade deadline. Once he was gone, little real production was left behind. Rookie third baseman Chris Johnson (.296), right fielder Hunter Pence (.284), and second baseman Jeff Keppinger (.280) all mustered TAvs of .280 or higher. Unfortunately, Johnson's minor-league statistics do not suggest that he will be anything more than an average big-leaguer, Pence is a solid contributor but not a star, and Keppinger can hit for average but has no pop. The Astros' lineup was so weak last season that it was better than the NL average in TAv at only one of the eight positions (Table 1).

Table 1. The Truth Hurts: True Averages of the Astros' Lineup in 2010

Position	Astros	NL average
Catcher	.212	.254
First base	.276	.286
Second base	.259	.265
Third base	.254	.264
Shortstop	.218	.253
Left field	.254	.273
Center field	.272	.270
Right field	.284	.284

Left fielder Carlos Lee gives the noble albatross a bad name, as he is eating up a large chunk of the payroll and the Houston-area food supply while barely producing at replacement level. Last season, he contributed 1.3 VORP and had a .258 TAv. To understand how little Lee contributed to the offense, consider that four Astros pitchers had higher offensive VORP figures than the 34-year-old who is owed $37 million over the final two seasons of a six-year, $100 million contract that can't expire quickly enough for the Astros, since it severely limits their payroll flexibility.

Making the situation more difficult for the team is a paucity of prospects capable of helping them in the next few years. The system has been left fallow by owner Drayton McLane's longtime willingness to go along with the draft slotting system of the commissioner's office until finally breaking ranks last year. Lyles is the only prospect who could make an impact this season, and though his progress has been impressive, his upside is considered no higher than that of a third starter.

The Astros also have high hopes for two other young players in catcher Jason Castro and first baseman Brett Wallace, who made their major-league debuts last season. However, there are questions about the offensive ceilings of both. Castro's rookie TAv was just .216 in 217 plate appearances, and Wallace had a .229 mark in 157 PAs after being acquired from the Blue Jays in late July. The Astros blame Castro's inexperience for his struggles, citing the fact that he had less than 1,000 professional plate appearances before reaching the majors. They also believe that settling into one organization and one position will benefit Wallace, who was the Cardinals' first-round draft pick in 2008 as a third baseman and has since switched organizations three times, going from the Athletics to the Blue Jays to the Astros.

While it is heartening that McLane finally found religion when it came to the draft and player development, the downside is that it took him too long to realize that his organization needed an overhaul. After getting to the World Series for the only time in franchise history in 2005, McLane tried desperately to get back without an extended dry spell. However, Jeff Bagwell retired after that season and fellow franchise icon Craig Biggio followed suit in 2007 (and none too soon). The Astros finished second in the NL Central in 2006, but haven't come close since, despite hoping that the combination of Berkman and Oswalt could lead them to another pennant.

In light of that protracted period of denial, the trades of Oswalt and Berkman constituted a watershed moment in McLane's 19 seasons as owner. As first-year manager Brad Mills so tactfully put it after the duo was traded, "Roy and Lance had been here a long time and were used to doing things a certain way, and now we're doing things a little differently." You don't have to read very deep between the lines to understand that management felt that both veterans were becoming disgruntled and risked poisoning the younger players' attitudes. Those around the Astros fear the same thing might happen with Lee.

Wade has taken his share of heat since replacing Tim Purpura as general manager late in the 2007 season. He's not a favorite of the analytical set, because he makes no secret that he weighs the advice of his scouts more heavily than he does statistics. However, most of his shortsighted moves prior to last season were spawned from McLane's refusal to give in to the idea that the Astros needed to revamp their roster. As the owner famously liked to say, "Rebuilding is not in my vocabulary."

Keep in mind, however, that Wade laid much of the groundwork that has enabled the Phillies to win the last four NL East championships when he was the GM in Philadelphia from 1998 to 2005. He oversaw Mike Arbuckle's selections of Ryan Howard, Chase Utley, Jimmy Rollins, and Cole Hamels, and he always preached the importance of building a core from within. Furthermore, it was Wade who brought highly regarded scouting director Bobby Heck to the Astros from the Brewers, a move that was lauded throughout the industry. Now that he's finally been given the resources to do his job properly, Heck's impact is already being felt in the lower levels of the minor leagues with such prospects as right-handers Mike Foltynewicz and Vincent Velasquez, second baseman Delino DeShields Jr., third baseman Mike Kvasnicka, and outfielder J. D. Martinez.

It was also Wade who hired Mills as manager during the 2009-2010 offseason. Those who know Mills insist that he was long overdue to get a crack at managing after spending the previous six seasons as Terry Francona's bench coach with the Red Sox. He was certainly an upgrade over Cecil Cooper, who was aloof and distant with his players while making frequent tactical mistakes during his two years on the job. And before Wade gets any demerits for hiring Cooper, it's only fair to point out that McLane made the call on that move after Commissioner Bud Selig called and strongly recommended Cooper, who had played for the Brewers when baseball's current czar owned the Milwaukee club.

Mills appears to represent an improvement, although McLane's dubbing him the franchise's "greatest asset" only serves to highlight the talent-starved nature of the team's player pool. Last season, the Astros finished 7.9 wins above their Pythagenport record, the highest total in the major leagues, and 10 wins above their third-order standings record of 66-96. While a little luck is involved in a team's outplaying its run differential to that degree, it could also be seen as a sign that Mills squeezed what he could out of the mostly unappealing options as his disposal.

The downside to a team's playing so far above its run differential and component statistics is that the team is almost always due for regression the next season. In light of the extent to which last season's total of 76 wins may have been misleading, it's difficult to imagine that the Astros will even repeat that level of success, let alone qualify as a Padres-like surprise.

McLane was once willing to throw as much money as possible at free agents to stay competitive. However, he closed his checkbook in recent years and put the team up for sale in November. The Astros should get a bump in revenue in 2012 when their regional cable sports network begins operating in conjunction with Comcast and the NBA's Houston Rockets. Barring a new, deep-pocketed owner willing to spend massive amounts of money, the Astros will have to continue to try to build from within and make the draft a top priority in an effort to upgrade the organization's talent base. As a result, it would be more realistic for the 2016 Astros to set a goal of mimicking the 2010 Padres than the 2011 club.

HITTERS

Jose Altuve — 2B

Born: **5/6/1990** Age: **21**
Bats: **R** Throws: **R** Height: **5' 5"** Weight: **148**
Breakout: **0%** Improve: **0%** Collapse: **0%**
Attrition: **0%** MLB: **0%**

Comparables:
Harry Chappas, Wally Backman, Joe Morgan (72)

YEAR	TEAM	LVL	AGE	PA	R	2B	3B	HR	RBI	BB	SO	SB	CS	AVG/OBP/SLG	TAv	BABIP	BRR	FRAA	WARP
2008	GRV	Rk	18	152	26	9	3	2	21	8	26	8	2	.284/.316/.433	.271	.328	1.7	2B 1, 3B 0	0.8
2009	TCV	A-	19	87	13	5	0	0	7	8	10	7	2	.250/.333/.316	.264	.284	3.4	2B 3	0.9
2009	GRV	Rk	19	208	45	20	2	3	18	26	16	21	4	.324/.404/.508	.332	.337	1.0	2B 5	2.7
2010	MAG	—	20	81	8	5	1	0	6	3	12	4	2	.329/.364/.425	—	.369	0.0	—	—
2010	LEX	A	20	434	75	15	3	11	45	33	49	39	14	.308/.364/.445	.314	.324	3.2	2B -4, 3B 0	3.3
2010	LNC	A+	20	127	18	5	2	4	22	9	17	3	4	.276/.333/.457	.259	.292	1.5	2B 0, 3B 0	0.4
2011	*HOU*	*MLB*	*21*	*333*	*37*	*15*	*1*	*7*	*36*	*21*	*55*	*13*	*5*	*.266/.311/.393*	*.251*	*.297*	*-0.3*	*2B 2, 3B 0*	*0.6*

After tearing through the Appalachian League in 2009, Altuve had an equally impressive full-season debut. Just 20, he spent the last quarter of the season at High-A and more than held his own with the bat—the results above speak for themselves—while showing tremendous defensive fundamentals. That certainly sounds like one helluva prospect, but you won't find Altuve on any Top 100, and many Astros-specific lists will barely mention him, either. The problem is that he's listed at five-foot-five, and that's generous—his NBA height, if you will. Because of that, scouts understandably have a difficult time wrapping their heads around him. He's certainly adorable, like an athletic teddy bear, but there is no modern precedent for a player of his stature. All he can do is keep performing, which shouldn't be too hard at High-A Lancaster in 2011. We're two years away from knowing if he's truly some kind of mold-breaker.

Geoff Blum — INF

Born: **4/26/1973** Age: **38**
Bats: **S** Throws: **R** Height: **6' 3"** Weight: **195**
Breakout: **0%** Improve: **17%** Collapse: **13%**
Attrition: **23%** MLB: **66%**

Comparables:
Aaron Boone, Carl Furillo, Buddy Bell (71)

YEAR	TEAM	LVL	AGE	PA	R	2B	3B	HR	RBI	BB	SO	SB	CS	AVG/OBP/SLG	TAv	BABIP	BRR	FRAA	WARP
2008	HOU	MLB	35	356	36	14	1	14	53	21	54	1	2	.240/.287/.419	.246	.242	-1.8	3B 7, 2B 1	1.0
2009	HOU	MLB	36	427	34	14	1	10	49	33	61	0	1	.247/.314/.368	.243	.266	-0.2	3B -11, 1B 0	-0.6
2010	HOU	MLB	37	218	24	10	1	2	22	15	33	0	0	.267/.321/.356	.253	.311	2.1	SS -1, 3B 2	0.6
2011	*ARI*	*MLB*	*38*	*337*	*34*	*14*	*0*	*6*	*29*	*25*	*49*	*1*	*0*	*.233/.294/.336*	*.225*	*.256*	*-0.1*	*3B -1, SS 0*	*-0.4*

Blum hasn't had a True Average of .260 or contributed more than 1.8 WARP since 2002, yet he was the first free agent signed by new Diamondbacks general manager Kevin Towers, receiving a two-year, $2.7 million contract for his age-38 and age-39 seasons. Versatility apparently has value, as Blum is a switch-hitter who can play all four infield positions and both outfield corners, which makes him an ideal double-switch player in every respect but his underwhelming production. Perhaps the most memorable aspect of his 2010 was the month he missed recuperating from arthroscopic surgery to remove loose bodies from his right elbow joint after feeling a postgame pop while buttoning his shirt.

Brian Bogusevic OF

Born: **2/18/1984** Age: **27**
Bats: **L** Throws: **L** Height: **6' 3"** Weight: **210**
Breakout: **2%** Improve: **14%** Collapse: **6%**
Attrition: **23%** MLB: **34%**

Comparables:
Drew T Anderson, T.J. Bohn, Lou Montanez (76)

YEAR	TEAM	LVL	AGE	PA	R	2B	3B	HR	RBI	BB	SO	SB	CS	AVG/OBP/SLG	TAv	BABIP	BRR	FRAA	WARP
2008	CCH	AA	24	145	21	10	2	3	20	16	24	8	1	.371/.434/.556	.352	.426	-0.8	CF -2, RF 0	1.1
2009	ROU	AAA	25	581	68	25	3	6	53	53	118	22	3	.271/.339/.365	.248	.337	2.2	LF 8, CF -11	0.5
2010	ROU	AAA	26	575	91	26	2	13	57	67	108	23	1	.277/.364/.414	.273	.328	5.5	LF 1, 1B -6	2.5
2010	HOU	MLB	26	32	5	3	0	0	3	3	12	1	1	.179/.250/.286	.183	.312	0.8	LF 2, CF 0	0.1
2011	*HOU*	*MLB*	*27*	*445*	*50*	*20*	*1*	*7*	*42*	*45*	*96*	*13*	*3*	*.256/.330/.369*	*.250*	*.313*	*0.5*	*LF 1, CF -3*	*0.1*

A little less than three years after the 2005 first-round draft pick from Tulane converted from pitcher to position player, Bogusevic made his major-league debut as a September call-up. It's too easy to point out that the first syllable of Bogusevic is "bogus" and let things stand there; he has value as a player who has the versatility to play all three outfields and first base while swinging a lefty line-drive bat, showing a good eye, and stealing bases at low volume but with a high rate of success. A .274/.353/.389 hitter at Triple-A and already at an age where most players would be unlikely to develop further (he may have a little more room to grow than a player of the same age, given his late conversion), Bogusevic can be a fine fourth outfielder, better than nothing after washing out on the mound.

Jason Bourgeois OF

Born: **1/4/1982** Age: **29**
Bats: **R** Throws: **R** Height: **5' 9"** Weight: **190**
Breakout: **1%** Improve: **30%** Collapse: **10%**
Attrition: **14%** MLB: **65%**

Comparables:
Rajai Davis, Chris Duffy, Norris Hopper (73)

YEAR	TEAM	LVL	AGE	PA	R	2B	3B	HR	RBI	BB	SO	SB	CS	AVG/OBP/SLG	TAv	BABIP	BRR	FRAA	WARP
2008	CHR	AAA	26	559	83	23	5	9	48	33	65	30	11	.286/.329/.404	.253	.306	7.3	LF -1, CF -7	0.8
2008	CHA	MLB	26	3	0	1	0	0	0	0	0	0	0	.333/.333/.667	.322	.333	0.0	2B 0	0.0
2009	NAS	AAA	27	454	61	18	6	2	41	22	40	36	7	.316/.352/.401	.270	.342	8.6	CF -4, LF -1	1.8
2009	MIL	MLB	27	40	6	0	0	1	3	3	7	3	0	.189/.250/.270	.202	.207	0.6	RF 1, LF 0	0.0
2010	MOC	—	28	75	12	4	1	1	13	8	7	4	1	.323/.400/.462	—	.345	0.0	—	—
2010	ROU	AAA	28	261	37	10	3	5	28	21	28	18	6	.345/.405/.477	.301	.373	-1.0	CF -7	1.1
2010	HOU	MLB	28	136	16	4	1	0	3	13	16	12	4	.220/.294/.268	.206	.252	0.0	CF 1, LF 0	-0.3
2011	*HOU*	*MLB*	*29*	*480*	*54*	*19*	*3*	*6*	*47*	*32*	*59*	*28*	*8*	*.280/.327/.375*	*.251*	*.305*	*0.1*	*CF -6, LF -1*	*0.1*

After signing Bourgeois as a minor-league free agent, the Astros gave him his first extended look at the major leagues last season. His hometown organization was the sixth to give him a shot, but won't be his last; though he's Bourgeois, Jason just doesn't control the means of production. Outside of showing good plate discipline, the speedy slap-hitter did little to distinguish himself. He began his professional career as a middle infielder, but now plays strictly in the pastures, which hurts his value as a potential 25th man. Undaunted, the Astros kept him on the 40-man roster after 2010 and think he can help as a fourth or fifth outfielder. Fun fact: Houston natives Carl Crawford and Michael Bourn were on his Little League team, which may have given Houston's current farm system a run for its money in terms of future major-league talent.

Michael Bourn CF

Born: **12/27/1982** Age: **28**
Bats: **L** Throws: **R** Height: **5' 11"** Weight: **180**
Breakout: **2%** Improve: **40%** Collapse: **2%**
Attrition: **14%** MLB: **77%**

Comparables:
Gene Richards, Kenny Lofton, Chris Duffy (73)

YEAR	TEAM	LVL	AGE	PA	R	2B	3B	HR	RBI	BB	SO	SB	CS	AVG/OBP/SLG	TAv	BABIP	BRR	FRAA	WARP
2008	HOU	MLB	25	514	57	10	4	5	29	37	111	41	10	.229/.284/.300	.213	.284	2.4	CF 0	-0.8
2009	HOU	MLB	26	678	96	27	12	3	35	63	140	61	12	.286/.351/.385	.265	.362	12.4	CF 3	3.7
2010	HOU	MLB	27	605	84	25	6	2	38	59	109	52	12	.265/.337/.346	.253	.324	10.2	CF 7	2.9
2011	*HOU*	*MLB*	*28*	*495*	*55*	*19*	*4*	*4*	*43*	*48*	*90*	*41*	*9*	*.265/.332/.355*	*.248*	*.315*	*1.3*	*CF 2*	*1.1*

A smart guy and a hard worker, Bourn made his first All-Star team last season and won another well-deserved Gold Glove as he continued to establish himself as a front-line center fielder in the major leagues. Bourn has grown since his tough rookie season in 2008—he is more patient at the plate, has become adept at hitting the ball on the ground to take advantage of his own speed (although that didn't work out as well in 2010 as it did the year before), and has also learned to read balls better off the bat. The 13-point drop in his OBP last season was cause for some concern, but Bourn remained a high-percentage basestealer despite being bothered by a strained quad late in the year.

Jason Castro **C**

Born: **6/18/1987** Age: **24**
Bats: L Throws: R Height: **6' 3"** Weight: **210**
Breakout: **3%** Improve: **16%** Collapse: **4%**
Attrition: **11%** MLB: **26%**

Comparables:
John Jaso, Bill Freehan, Daniel Murphy (79)

YEAR	TEAM	LVL	AGE	PA	R	2B	3B	HR	RBI	BB	SO	SB	CS	AVG/OBP/SLG	TAv	BABIP	BRR	FRAA	WARP
2008	TCV	A-	21	162	10	9	0	2	12	22	32	0	2	.275/.383/.384	.279	.346	-1.4	C 0	0.7
2009	LNC	A+	22	243	27	20	1	7	44	30	41	1	1	.309/.399/.517	.312	.352	-3.5	C -1	1.7
2009	CCH	AA	22	268	38	11	1	3	29	25	35	2	1	.293/.362/.385	.282	.330	-2.9	C -1	1.3
2010	ROU	AAA	23	244	31	7	0	4	26	32	34	1	1	.265/.365/.355	.254	.301	-0.5	C 0	0.8
2010	HOU	MLB	23	217	26	8	1	2	8	22	41	0	0	.205/.286/.287	.221	.250	-0.3	C 0	0.0
2011	*HOU*	*MLB*	*24*	*375*	*42*	*17*	*1*	*6*	*35*	*39*	*66*	*1*	*0*	*.256/.333/.369*	*.251*	*.297*	*0.0*	*C -1*	*0.9*

There is little doubt that Castro has a chance to be an above-average defensive catcher. He threw out 37 percent of attempted basestealers as a rookie last season and is a student of the game who works well with a pitching staff. The big question is whether Castro—the Astros' first-round draft pick in 2008—will ever contribute anything with the stick, since he lacks both bat speed and strength. He returned to Stanford at the end of the 2010 campaign to complete his sociology degree, and the credits might come in handy if he flunks his final on major-league hitting.

Koby Clemens **1B**

Born: **12/4/1986** Age: **24**
Bats: R Throws: R Height: **5' 11"** Weight: **193**
Breakout: **5%** Improve: **24%** Collapse: **5%**
Attrition: **27%** MLB: **55%**

Comparables:
Brandon Moss, Steve Pearce, Brett Carroll (74)

YEAR	TEAM	LVL	AGE	PA	R	2B	3B	HR	RBI	BB	SO	SB	CS	AVG/OBP/SLG	TAv	BABIP	BRR	FRAA	WARP
2008	SLM	A+	21	458	54	29	5	7	52	61	99	1	4	.268/.369/.423	.285	.338	-3.9	C -1, 3B 0	2.3
2009	LNC	A+	22	492	74	45	6	22	121	51	109	4	1	.345/.419/.636	.354	.412	-2.3	C -2, LF -2	5.5
2010	PEJ	—	23	86	17	6	1	2	13	6	23	1	0	.288/.337/.463	—	.382	0.0	—	—
2010	CCH	AA	23	535	75	22	3	26	85	69	143	9	3	.241/.350/.476	.291	.288	3.2	1B -8, 3B 0	1.6
2011	*HOU*	*MLB*	*24*	*495*	*62*	*26*	*2*	*19*	*64*	*52*	*130*	*2*	*1*	*.252/.332/.453*	*.272*	*.309*	*-0.1*	*C -1, 1B -7*	*0.9*

Best known for being the oldest of the four sons of 300-game winner Roger Clemens, Koby Clemens has shown the ability to hit the ball out of the park in the minor leagues. However, his aggressiveness at the plate was exploited by more experienced pitchers last season, which resulted in a 31.6 percent whiff rate. Clemens has also switched positions three times in his six-year career, bouncing from third base to catcher to left field to first base. The next position on the defensive spectrum is designated hitter, which doesn't bode well for any prospect.

Collin DeLome **LF**

Born: **12/18/1985** Age: **25**
Bats: L Throws: R Height: **6' 2"** Weight: **195**
Breakout: **8%** Improve: **21%** Collapse: **3%**
Attrition: **24%** MLB: **40%**

Comparables:
Brent Clevlen, Carlos Gonzalez, Brandon Jones (72)

YEAR	TEAM	LVL	AGE	PA	R	2B	3B	HR	RBI	BB	SO	SB	CS	AVG/OBP/SLG	TAv	BABIP	BRR	FRAA	WARP
2008	LEX	A	22	252	41	9	6	12	36	18	71	7	2	.261/.329/.513	.297	.324	0.8	LF 0, CF 1	1.6
2008	SLM	A+	22	267	40	14	3	10	35	17	57	7	2	.232/.303/.443	.254	.259	2.0	LF -6, RF 0	-0.1
2009	CCH	AA	23	522	79	18	10	20	61	37	141	15	8	.255/.320/.465	.282	.316	1.5	LF 8, CF -9	2.3
2010	ROU	AAA	24	368	49	15	6	17	56	17	113	11	3	.224/.270/.452	.243	.278	1.6	LF -4, CF 1	0.0
2011	*HOU*	*MLB*	*25*	*469*	*50*	*19*	*4*	*18*	*59*	*24*	*144*	*8*	*3*	*.221/.268/.409*	*.233*	*.277*	*-0.3*	*LF -4, CF -3*	*-1.0*

DeLome was considered a five-tool player when the Astros plucked him out of Lamar University in the fifth round of the 2007 draft. However, he has not been able to convert his raw ability into consistent production. He hits some home runs and steals some bases, but a total lack of plate discipline has undercut his chances to become a real prospect. DeLome has plenty of range and a strong arm in the outfield, but suffers from the occasional lapse in concentration that causes him to drop a routine fly ball. His ability is something to dream on, but that's all it will be until he does something about that hideous strikeout-to-walk ratio.

Matt Downs **2B**

Born: **3/19/1984** Age: **27**
Bats: R Throws: R Height: **6' 2"** Weight: **190**
Breakout: **4%** Improve: **29%** Collapse: **5%**
Attrition: **20%** MLB: **45%**

Comparables:
Angel Chavez, Casey McGehee, Ian Kinsler (78)

YEAR	TEAM	LVL	AGE	PA	R	2B	3B	HR	RBI	BB	SO	SB	CS	AVG/OBP/SLG	TAv	BABIP	BRR	FRAA	WARP
2008	SJO	A+	24	489	74	30	1	17	75	34	57	24	13	.304/.352/.494	.297	.309	1.2	2B -1, 3B -1	3.4
2008	FRE	AAA	24	94	10	5	0	3	7	4	10	1	0	.244/.298/.407	.212	.243	-0.3	2B -5, LF -1	-0.9
2009	FRE	AAA	25	467	68	33	3	14	74	25	58	8	2	.300/.340/.491	.293	.311	-1.3	2B -5, 3B -4	1.6
2009	SFN	MLB	25	60	6	2	0	1	2	6	13	1	0	.170/.250/.264	.193	.200	1.5	2B 1	0.0
2010	FRE	AAA	26	228	37	9	1	7	28	25	35	3	4	.254/.348/.416	.265	.274	0.0	3B -4, 2B 1	0.7
2010	SFN	MLB	26	88	6	7	0	1	7	8	18	0	0	.244/.318/.372	.261	.300	-0.7	2B 1	0.2
2010	HOU	MLB	26	21	2	0	0	0	0	1	2	0	0	.105/.190/.105	.166	.118	-0.2	3B 0, 2B -1	-0.3
2011	*HOU*	*MLB*	*27*	*492*	*57*	*26*	*1*	*13*	*57*	*35*	*76*	*9*	*4*	*.258/.313/.411*	*.254*	*.277*	*-0.3*	*2B -4, 3B -2*	*0.3*

The Astros claimed Downs off waivers from the Giants late last August, but he played only sporadically down the stretch. Armed with a short right-handed stroke, he has always been able to hit, especially for average—in the lower levels of the minors, anyway. He has a strong arm, but limited range keeps him from playing shortstop and tarnishes his value as a utility infielder. The Astros already have a similar player in front of him in second baseman Jeff Keppinger, meaning that Downs' best chance to make the club may come as a pinch-hitter.

Jonathan Gaston OF

Born: **11/13/1986** Age: **24**
Bats: L Throws: R Height: **6' 0"** Weight: **210**
Breakout: **4%** Improve: **17%** Collapse: **1%**
Attrition: **14%** MLB: **29%**

Comparables:
Brandon Jones, Mat Gamel, Bronson Sardinha (63)

YEAR	TEAM	LVL	AGE	PA	R	2B	3B	HR	RBI	BB	SO	SB	CS	AVG/OBP/SLG	TAv	BABIP	BRR	FRAA	WARP
2008	TCV	A-	21	236	18	11	1	2	25	25	65	0	2	.193/.292/.285	.216	.271	-0.2	RF 4, CF 3	-0.1
2009	LNC	A+	22	607	119	31	15	35	100	71	164	14	4	.278/.367/.598	.328	.331	1.0	LF -3, RF -8	4.2
2010	CCH	AA	23	520	64	16	8	13	51	47	105	13	5	.245/.320/.399	.265	.287	1.7	RF 11, CF -2	2.3
2011	*HOU*	*MLB*	*24*	*448*	*51*	*19*	*4*	*16*	*55*	*39*	*118*	*6*	*2*	*.232/.298/.417*	*.247*	*.280*	*-0.1*	*RF -1, LF -2*	*-0.2*

Gaston's numbers came back to earth last season following a year in which he led the minor leagues in home runs at Lancaster, the most generous hitting environment in professional baseball. What was left once the park effects were taken away was not good, certainly not enough to carry a key offensive position in the big leagues, and that's what Gaston will have to do to have a career, because his range is comparable to Tom Waits with a bad cold. Thus, he's bound for first base without the ability to hit like a first baseman. In short, he's doomed.

Chris Johnson 3B

Born: **10/1/1984** Age: **26**
Bats: R Throws: R Height: **6' 3"** Weight: **220**
Breakout: **2%** Improve: **24%** Collapse: **5%**
Attrition: **21%** MLB: **54%**

Comparables:
David Freese, James D'Antona, Jeff Baisley (76)

YEAR	TEAM	LVL	AGE	PA	R	2B	3B	HR	RBI	BB	SO	SB	CS	AVG/OBP/SLG	TAv	BABIP	BRR	FRAA	WARP
2008	CCH	AA	23	358	43	24	0	12	58	20	61	5	0	.324/.363/.506	.288	.363	-4.8	3B 8	2.4
2008	ROU	AAA	23	107	10	2	1	1	9	5	25	0	0	.218/.252/.287	.195	.276	-1.2	3B 1	-0.5
2009	ROU	AAA	24	412	48	20	5	13	42	21	90	2	1	.281/.323/.461	.266	.335	-0.5	3B -1	1.3
2009	HOU	MLB	24	23	1	0	0	0	1	1	6	0	0	.091/.130/.091	.094	.125	0.1	3B -2	-0.5
2010	ROU	AAA	25	163	26	10	1	8	33	9	23	0	0	.329/.362/.570	.325	.336	0.0	3B -2	1.4
2010	HOU	MLB	25	362	40	22	2	11	52	15	91	3	0	.308/.337/.481	.288	.387	0.2	3B -13	0.7
2011	*HOU*	*MLB*	*26*	*477*	*58*	*25*	*2*	*15*	*62*	*24*	*103*	*2*	*1*	*.280/.316/.446*	*.263*	*.327*	*0.0*	*3B -5*	*0.9*

Johnson was a pleasant surprise last season, taking over as the starting third baseman in mid-June after the Astros finally figured out that Pedro Feliz couldn't hit and wasn't exactly Brooks Robinson in the field, despite his reputation. Johnson showed good power, boasting more pop than he had in his three previous full minor-league seasons. However, he struck out six times as often as he walked, a major red flag and an indicator that pitchers stand a good chance of figuring him out this season, when he probably won't be able to reenlist the aid of a .387 BABIP. When that happens, the Astros will be back where they started, because Johnson's glove *is* like Brooks Robinson's. The problem is, Robinson is 73 years old.

Jeff Keppinger 2B

Born: **4/21/1980** Age: **31**
Bats: R Throws: R Height: **6' 0"** Weight: **180**
Breakout: **0%** Improve: **34%** Collapse: **1%**
Attrition: **2%** MLB: **98%**

Comparables:
Johnny Ray, Roberto Alomar, Tom Herr (77)

YEAR	TEAM	LVL	AGE	PA	R	2B	3B	HR	RBI	BB	SO	SB	CS	AVG/OBP/SLG	TAv	BABIP	BRR	FRAA	WARP
2008	CIN	MLB	28	502	45	24	2	3	43	30	24	3	1	.266/.307/.346	.223	.269	2.8	SS -10, 3B 1	-0.8
2009	HOU	MLB	29	344	35	13	3	7	29	27	33	0	2	.256/.314/.387	.243	.259	-1.9	3B -3, 2B 0	-0.1
2010	HOU	MLB	30	575	63	34	1	6	59	51	36	4	1	.288/.348/.393	.269	.295	-1.9	2B 12, SS -4	2.5
2011	*HOU*	*MLB*	*31*	*515*	*61*	*27*	*1*	*6*	*53*	*44*	*31*	*3*	*1*	*.290/.346/.396*	*.262*	*.290*	*-0.2*	*2B 4, SS -4*	*1.4*

It's tempting to talk about what Keppinger can't do, how he lacks power on offense and range on defense. However, few players in the major leagues can put the bat on the ball as consistently as he can. Keppinger sprayed line drives all over the field and finished with the lowest strikeout rate in the major leagues last season. He also has an outstanding eye, walking more often than he succumbs to the K. A vastly superior hitter against left-handers (.331/.385/.480, versus .260/.319/.352 against righties), he batted second for most of the season, but really shouldn't be in the top half of the order except when a southpaw is on the mound. That's not a knock on Keppinger; the Astros had no better option.

Carlos Lee LF

Born: **6/20/1976** Age: **35**
Bats: R Throws: R Height: **6' 2"** Weight: **235**
Breakout: **0%** Improve: **25%** Collapse: **4%**
Attrition: **10%** MLB: **96%**

Comparables:
Vladimir Guerrero, Hideki Matsui, Albert Belle (62)

YEAR	TEAM	LVL	AGE	PA	R	2B	3B	HR	RBI	BB	SO	SB	CS	AVG/OBP/SLG	TAv	BABIP	BRR	FRAA	WARP
2008	HOU	MLB	32	481	62	27	0	28	100	37	49	4	1	.314/.368/.569	.318	.300	-2.4	LF -6	3.0
2009	HOU	MLB	33	662	68	35	1	26	102	41	51	5	3	.300/.343/.489	.287	.290	-5.2	LF -19, 1B 0	0.7
2010	HOU	MLB	34	649	68	29	1	24	89	37	59	3	3	.246/.291/.417	.250	.238	-0.4	LF -15, 1B -1	-1.1
2011	*HOU*	*MLB*	*35*	*637*	*82*	*32*	*0*	*26*	*88*	*46*	*53*	*6*	*3*	*.282/.333/.473*	*.279*	*.269*	*-0.3*	*LF -13, 1B 0*	*1.1*

Lee's OPS has nosedived from its high-water mark of 937 in 2008, declining to 831 in 2009 and 708 last season while his weight headed in the opposite direction. The added pounds have robbed him of his once-considerable athletic ability; his bat and foot speed have slowed, and his range in left field has become so deficient that the Astros are toying with the idea of moving him to first base. Lee has two years and $37 million left on his six-year, $100 million contract, and the Astros are stuck with him. No team would be willing to take on that much salary, and Lee would probably invoke his no-trade rights even if the Astros were to find a taker, because he'd prefer to stay close to his Brahma bull ranch in Boling, Texas. By the time his deal expires, he may be fit for entry in a livestock show himself.

Andrew Locke RF

Born: **2/28/1983** Age: **28**
Bats: R Throws: R Height: **6′ 1″** Weight: **205**
Breakout: **1%** Improve: **28%** Collapse: **5%**
Attrition: **16%** MLB: **51%**

Comparables:
Lou Montanez, Ben Francisco, Matt Murton (73)

YEAR	TEAM	LVL	AGE	PA	R	2B	3B	HR	RBI	BB	SO	SB	CS	AVG/OBP/SLG	TAv	BABIP	BRR	FRAA	WARP
2008	SBR	A+	25	522	81	37	4	11	85	42	86	5	2	.311/.364/.477	.307	.354	0.1	1B 5, RF -2	3.3
2009	CCH	AA	26	558	81	31	3	20	109	46	84	2	2	.338/.389/.531	.326	.369	0.4	RF -5, LF -6	3.6
2010	ZUL	—	27	62	4	2	1	1	9	5	9	1	0	.246/.306/.368	—	.277	0.0	—	—
2010	ROU	AAA	27	524	71	36	4	17	74	43	92	6	1	.279/.338/.478	.280	.313	-0.4	RF 4, 1B 2	2.5
2011	*HOU*	*MLB*	*28*	*536*	*66*	*30*	*1*	*15*	*68*	*38*	*103*	*2*	*1*	*.284/.331/.444*	*.271*	*.325*	*0.0*	*RF -3, 1B -3*	*0.5*

Enlightenment philosopher John Locke believed that we were born as blank slates for experience to write upon. Andrew Locke knows this from experience, having spent six seasons in the minors, and not only is his slate no longer blank, but experience has had to turn it over and write on the back. Among the notes are "Locke's 2010 season doesn't speak too highly of a 27-year-old in Triple-A," and "Don't overrate a player on the basis of high averages compiled in the California and Texas Leagues," as well as "Locke's right-handed power could play well at Minute Maid Park, but since defensively he's restricted to a corner, it won't be easy to get and hold a roster spot." Experience then got bored and started doodling in the margins.

Tommy Manzella SS

Born: **4/16/1983** Age: **28**
Bats: R Throws: R Height: **6′ 2″** Weight: **200**
Breakout: **2%** Improve: **18%** Collapse: **2%**
Attrition: **4%** MLB: **36%**

Comparables:
Alvin Dark, Hubie Brooks, Brendan Harris (78)

YEAR	TEAM	LVL	AGE	PA	R	2B	3B	HR	RBI	BB	SO	SB	CS	AVG/OBP/SLG	TAv	BABIP	BRR	FRAA	WARP
2008	CCH	AA	25	249	27	11	5	4	34	17	35	4	4	.299/.341/.446	.269	.328	-1.1	SS -3	0.8
2008	ROU	AAA	25	247	19	15	1	0	15	17	39	0	4	.219/.271/.294	.204	.262	-2.9	SS 6	-0.2
2009	ROU	AAA	26	580	68	31	5	9	56	40	99	12	3	.289/.334/.417	.267	.334	-3.9	SS -1	2.1
2009	HOU	MLB	26	5	0	0	0	0	0	0	4	0	0	.200/.200/.200	.139	1.000	0.0	SS 0	0.0
2010	HOU	MLB	27	282	17	7	0	1	21	13	71	0	1	.225/.262/.264	.191	.294	2.9	SS -1	-0.7
2011	*HOU*	*MLB*	*28*	*467*	*49*	*21*	*2*	*6*	*44*	*29*	*92*	*5*	*2*	*.259/.303/.356*	*.234*	*.308*	*-0.3*	*SS -1*	*0.4*

A broken right pinky finger interrupted Manzella's rookie season in late June, landing him on the disabled list for two months. He regained his starting job upon his return, but did little to suggest that he's a long-term answer at shortstop. Manzella is a slick fielder with good footwork and a strong arm, but his lack of hitting ability may preclude a career as a regular. Evidently reaching the same conclusion, the Astros dealt for the Rockies' Clint Barmes in November, a move likely to push Manzella into a utility role for which he is better suited, if not back to Triple-A.

J. D. Martinez OF

Born: **8/21/1987** Age: **23**
Bats: R Throws: R Height: **6′ 3″** Weight: **175**
Breakout: **4%** Improve: **22%** Collapse: **4%**
Attrition: **18%** MLB: **40%**

Comparables:
Matt Joyce, Andy Marte, Adam Lind (72)

YEAR	TEAM	LVL	AGE	PA	R	2B	3B	HR	RBI	BB	SO	SB	CS	AVG/OBP/SLG	TAv	BABIP	BRR	FRAA	WARP
2009	TCV	A-	21	208	25	15	2	7	33	15	30	1	0	.326/.380/.540	.327	.353	-2.3	LF 4, 1B 0	1.8
2009	GRV	Rk	21	83	17	9	1	5	23	5	14	0	0	.403/.446/.740	.399	.448	1.3	LF 0, 1B 0	1.4
2010	LEX	A	22	393	83	31	3	15	64	33	55	3	0	.362/.433/.598	.356	.398	-2.1	RF 1	4.1
2010	CCH	AA	22	208	24	9	1	3	25	15	42	2	2	.302/.357/.407	.271	.372	-2.4	RF -5, LF 2	0.1
2011	*HOU*	*MLB*	*23*	*435*	*54*	*24*	*1*	*13*	*56*	*26*	*89*	*1*	*0*	*.278/.326/.447*	*.267*	*.320*	*0.0*	*RF -4, LF 1*	*0.5*

Martinez has accomplished quite a lot since becoming the Astros' 20th-round draft pick out of Division-II Nova Southeastern University in 2009. He won the short-season New York-Penn League batting title in his professional debut, then took home the Sally League MVP award last year, earning a promotion to Double-A. Questions still surround Martinez, most of them concerning whether he will develop enough power to play a corner outfield spot in the major leagues (you can dismiss all those home runs at Lexington). He'll have to do so, because he lacks the range to play center. He will try to take another step toward answering that question in the affirmative as he returns to Corpus Christi to start this season, but it's hard not to like what he's done to this point.

Jason Michaels OF

Born: **5/4/1976** Age: **35**
Bats: **R** Throws: **R** Height: **6' 0"** Weight: **204**
Breakout: **0%** Improve: **16%** Collapse: **22%**
Attrition: **39%** MLB: **70%**

Comparables:
Bob Elliott, Raul Mondesi, Kevin McReynolds (75)

YEAR	TEAM	LVL	AGE	PA	R	2B	3B	HR	RBI	BB	SO	SB	CS	AVG/OBP/SLG	TAv	BABIP	BRR	FRAA	WARP
2008	CLE	MLB	32	67	2	4	0	0	9	4	13	1	1	.207/.254/.276	.196	.245	0.1	LF 1, RF 2	0.0
2008	PIT	MLB	32	254	25	9	1	8	44	23	52	1	0	.228/.299/.382	.237	.259	-0.5	RF 4, LF 0	0.5
2009	HOU	MLB	33	152	17	12	1	4	16	16	38	1	2	.237/.322/.430	.261	.301	-1.7	CF 1, LF 0	0.3
2010	HOU	MLB	34	203	23	14	1	8	26	12	29	0	0	.253/.310/.468	.276	.260	0.7	LF -3, CF -2	0.2
2011	*HOU*	*MLB*	*35*	*305*	*35*	*16*	*1*	*8*	*33*	*26*	*55*	*3*	*1*	*.245/.312/.396*	*.249*	*.275*	*-0.3*	*LF -1, RF 1*	*0.3*

Just when it looked as if he was ready to fade away, Michaels bounced back with a solid season as the Astros' fourth outfielder and primary pinch-hitter in 2010. He is a favorite of general manager Ed Wade, who oversaw his selection in the 1998 draft while Michaels was with the Phillies. Thus, it came as no surprise that the Astros exercised Michaels' $900,000 club option for this year the day after the 2010 season ended. As long as he can keep mashing left-handers (against whom he slugged .549 last season), he has value.

Hunter Pence RF

Born: **4/13/1983** Age: **28**
Bats: **R** Throws: **R** Height: **6' 4"** Weight: **220**
Breakout: **1%** Improve: **43%** Collapse: **3%**
Attrition: **7%** MLB: **90%**

Comparables:
Andre Dawson, Ken Boyer, Corey Hart (62)

YEAR	TEAM	LVL	AGE	PA	R	2B	3B	HR	RBI	BB	SO	SB	CS	AVG/OBP/SLG	TAv	BABIP	BRR	FRAA	WARP
2008	HOU	MLB	25	642	78	34	4	25	83	40	124	11	10	.269/.318/.466	.270	.301	-0.9	RF 11	2.6
2009	HOU	MLB	26	647	76	26	5	25	72	58	109	14	11	.282/.346/.472	.274	.308	3.3	RF 7	2.9
2010	HOU	MLB	27	658	93	29	3	25	91	41	105	18	9	.282/.325/.461	.288	.304	3.2	RF 10	4.0
2011	*HOU*	*MLB*	*28*	*634*	*83*	*31*	*3*	*24*	*88*	*49*	*101*	*16*	*8*	*.285/.339/.477*	*.286*	*.305*	*-1.4*	*RF 7*	*3.0*

In the context of the Astros' lineup, Pence is an offensive standout. In the context of National League right fielders, he's no better than average. That's an important distinction to make, as the inferior quality of his Houston teammates often results in Pence's being referred to as the Astros' "star right fielder." Nevertheless, he's certainly a useful player; Pence has hit exactly 25 home runs in three consecutive seasons, can steal a base (albeit not without getting gunned down with disturbing regularity), and has one of the more accurate outfield arms in the game despite some funky throwing mechanics. Pence is reaching the point of his career at which he is going to start becoming very expensive, and after this season, the Astros will be forced to decide whether they want to commit long term or trade him for younger pieces with potentially more impact.

Humberto Quintero C

Born: **8/2/1979** Age: **31**
Bats: **R** Throws: **R** Height: **5' 9"** Weight: **215**
Breakout: **1%** Improve: **24%** Collapse: **8%**
Attrition: **14%** MLB: **57%**

Comparables:
Matt Batts, Duane Josephson, Carlos Hernandez (73)

YEAR	TEAM	LVL	AGE	PA	R	2B	3B	HR	RBI	BB	SO	SB	CS	AVG/OBP/SLG	TAv	BABIP	BRR	FRAA	WARP
2008	ROU	AAA	28	124	13	2	2	3	18	5	15	0	2	.237/.274/.364	.229	.250	1.6	C 2, 1B 0	0.5
2008	HOU	MLB	28	183	16	6	0	2	12	6	34	0	0	.226/.262/.298	.204	.263	1.1	C 1	-0.1
2009	HOU	MLB	29	168	11	8	1	4	14	7	41	0	0	.236/.286/.376	.220	.295	-0.8	C 1	0.1
2010	HOU	MLB	30	276	13	10	0	4	20	8	59	0	0	.234/.261/.317	.211	.286	-0.7	C 1	-0.1
2011	*HOU*	*MLB*	*31*	*270*	*28*	*12*	*1*	*5*	*27*	*12*	*51*	*0*	*0*	*.248/.286/.356*	*.227*	*.287*	*0.0*	*C 1, 1B 0*	*0.3*

Quintero is one of the best defensive catchers in the game. If he weren't, he wouldn't have lasted as long as he has in the majors, because he contributes almost nothing offensively. Quintero can handle pitchers and possesses a strong arm and impressive mobility in blocking balls. The problem is that the Astros' starting catcher, Jason Castro, has the same profile. Two backup catchers don't add up to a starter. An entire decade has come and gone since Mitch Meluskey gave the Astros their last offensively useful season from a backstop. "Then I said, Lord, how long?" (Isaiah 6:11)

Angel Sanchez SS

Born: **9/20/1983** Age: **27**
Bats: **R** Throws: **R** Height: **6' 2"** Weight: **185**
Breakout: **0%** Improve: **20%** Collapse: **4%**
Attrition: **13%** MLB: **50%**

Comparables:
Tommy Manzella, Cliff Pennington, Fernando Cortez (77)

YEAR	TEAM	LVL	AGE	PA	R	2B	3B	HR	RBI	BB	SO	SB	CS	AVG/OBP/SLG	TAv	BABIP	BRR	FRAA	WARP
2008	NWA	AA	24	277	28	7	2	1	23	28	40	4	4	.261/.332/.320	.249	.300	0.4	SS 16	2.3
2008	OMA	AAA	24	145	13	7	1	1	13	9	20	1	1	.221/.262/.313	.201	.243	0.2	SS -2	-0.5
2009	LVG	AAA	25	506	67	29	4	6	60	39	67	1	2	.305/.356/.428	.267	.336	-0.5	SS 10, 2B 4	3.5
2010	MAY	—	26	65	2	0	0	0	2	8	7	1	0	.204/.313/.204	—	.224	0.0	—	—
2010	PAW	AAA	26	252	26	10	1	0	17	24	30	6	1	.274/.348/.327	.242	.311	1.1	SS -9, 2B -2	-0.6
2010	BOS	MLB	26	3	0	0	0	0	0	0	0	0	0	.000/.000/.000	-.004	.000	0.0	SS 1	0.0
2010	HOU	MLB	26	269	30	9	4	0	25	11	45	0	1	.280/.309/.348	.235	.332	0.9	SS -11, 2B -1	-0.7
2011	*HOU*	*MLB*	*27*	*528*	*56*	*22*	*3*	*4*	*46*	*37*	*78*	*3*	*2*	*.268/.316/.349*	*.237*	*.303*	*-0.2*	*SS -1, 2B 0*	*0.5*

Sanchez hit .280 in 269 plate appearances for the Astros last season, which proves only one thing: sabermetricians are correct when they claim that batting average is one of the most meaningless statistics in baseball. You don't need to be of that religion or a devotee of advanced metrics to understand that in spite of his veneer of competency, Sanchez is merely a journeyman who barely kept his head above replacement level. Sanchez got a chance to start for two months when Tommy Manzella broke a finger, but he is likely to find himself in a utility role or back at Triple-A this season, as Clint Barmes has the inside track on the shortstop job after being acquired from the Rockies in a November trade.

J. B. Shuck — OF

Born: **6/18/1987** Age: **24**
Bats: L Throws: L Height: **5' 11"** Weight: **185**
Breakout: **4%** Improve: **29%** Collapse: **4%**
Attrition: **27%** MLB: **59%**

Comparables:
Tony Gwynn, Jacoby Ellsbury, Julio Borbon (77)

YEAR	TEAM	LVL	AGE	PA	R	2B	3B	HR	RBI	BB	SO	SB	CS	AVG/OBP/SLG	TAv	BABIP	BRR	FRAA	WARP
2008	TCV	A-	21	303	51	12	5	4	24	35	34	8	6	.300/.383/.430	.312	.329	1.5	CF -4, LF -3	1.9
2009	LNC	A+	22	628	98	30	11	1	36	64	55	18	9	.315/.387/.414	.288	.345	2.2	CF -7, RF -1	2.5
2010	CCH	AA	23	435	52	14	2	2	28	46	56	9	9	.298/.372/.360	.283	.344	-0.7	LF -5, CF -6	0.8
2010	ROU	AAA	23	156	15	2	2	0	7	16	15	7	3	.273/.348/.317	.255	.304	-2.0	CF -11	-0.8
2011	*HOU*	*MLB*	*24*	*505*	*57*	*20*	*3*	*3*	*44*	*44*	*64*	*9*	*5*	*.282/.342/.360*	*.254*	*.316*	*-0.7*	*CF -13, LF -4*	*-1.0*

Shuck is a tweener in more ways than one. He boasts the on-base skills of a leadoff hitter, but lacks the speed managers usually prefer at the top of the lineup. In addition, he can't cover enough ground to play a good center field, and finding playing time at a corner outfield spot will be difficult due to an absence of power. While having a good OBP is always a plus, it's hard to leverage that ability into a big-league job without some ancillary skills.

J. R. Towles — C

Born: **2/11/1984** Age: **27**
Bats: R Throws: R Height: **6' 2"** Weight: **175**
Breakout: **3%** Improve: **14%** Collapse: **6%**
Attrition: **12%** MLB: **29%**

Comparables:
Dusty Brown, Jeff Fiorentino, Terry Steinbach (76)

YEAR	TEAM	LVL	AGE	PA	R	2B	3B	HR	RBI	BB	SO	SB	CS	AVG/OBP/SLG	TAv	BABIP	BRR	FRAA	WARP
2008	ROU	AAA	24	192	28	8	2	7	28	13	31	4	3	.304/.365/.500	.281	.326	2.6	C 0	1.5
2008	HOU	MLB	24	171	10	5	0	4	16	16	40	0	0	.137/.246/.253	.194	.152	-0.9	C 0	-0.5
2009	ROU	AAA	25	178	23	12	1	4	22	22	27	3	0	.276/.382/.455	.307	.303	0.4	C 0	1.6
2009	HOU	MLB	25	53	7	2	0	2	3	3	16	0	0	.188/.245/.354	.214	.226	-0.1	C 0	0.0
2010	HOU	MLB	26	51	3	3	0	1	8	2	12	0	0	.192/.235/.319	.196	.229	0.1	C 0	-0.1
2011	*HOU*	*MLB*	*27*	*273*	*31*	*12*	*1*	*7*	*28*	*25*	*52*	*3*	*2*	*.237/.325/.390*	*.255*	*.266*	*-0.2*	*C 0*	*0.9*

It seems as if Towles has been the Astros' catcher of the future since Alan Ashby was the regular behind the plate. It also seems as if the future has passed him by, now that Jason Castro has laid a claim (however precarious) to the starting job. Whether 319 plate appearances stretched over the last four seasons constituted a fair opportunity for Towles is open to debate. What isn't debatable, though, is that the catcher has done nothing offensively in his various major-league auditions, producing -0.7 WARP and a .216 TAv. He wound up all the way back at Double-A in 2010 before undergoing surgery in July to repair torn tendons in his thumb.

Brett Wallace — 1B

Born: **8/26/1986** Age: **24**
Bats: L Throws: R Height: **6' 2"** Weight: **205**
Breakout: **4%** Improve: **20%** Collapse: **6%**
Attrition: **27%** MLB: **45%**

Comparables:
Jake Fox, Nick Evans, Mike Carp (80)

YEAR	TEAM	LVL	AGE	PA	R	2B	3B	HR	RBI	BB	SO	SB	CS	AVG/OBP/SLG	TAv	BABIP	BRR	FRAA	WARP
2008	QUD	A	21	177	28	8	1	5	25	17	32	0	0	.327/.418/.490	.333	.388	-1.3	3B -2	1.4
2008	SFD	AA	21	57	13	5	0	3	11	2	7	0	0	.367/.456/.653	.364	.385	0.2	3B 0	0.7
2009	SFD	AA	22	154	22	5	0	5	16	18	34	0	0	.281/.403/.438	.281	.348	-1.9	3B 0	0.5
2009	MEM	AAA	22	243	22	11	0	6	19	15	42	0	1	.293/.346/.423	.265	.335	-1.5	3B 1, 1B 1	0.8
2009	SAC	AAA	22	203	32	10	0	9	28	14	40	1	1	.302/.365/.505	.301	.341	-0.6	3B -7, 1B 0	0.8
2010	LVG	AAA	23	423	64	24	1	18	61	27	83	1	1	.301/.359/.509	.268	.343	-0.4	1B -1	0.6
2010	HOU	MLB	23	159	14	6	1	2	13	8	50	0	0	.222/.296/.319	.241	.326	0.5	1B 2	0.1
2011	*HOU*	*MLB*	*24*	*469*	*56*	*21*	*1*	*16*	*56*	*31*	*106*	*0*	*0*	*.262/.325/.427*	*.263*	*.308*	*0.0*	*3B -4, 1B -4*	*0.3*

Few prospects have bounced around like Wallace has since his selection by the Cardinals in the first round of the 2008 draft, as a series of organizations have acquired him with high hopes only to sour on his future after observing him over an extended period. The Astros became the fourth organization he's fooled last July after trading outfielder Anthony Gose—whom they had acquired from the Phillies in the Roy Oswalt deal just minutes earlier—to the Blue Jays for Wallace, who was in the midst of a middling PCL performance. The portly southpaw showed almost nothing at the plate in his major-league debut, which didn't come as a complete shock, given his merely adequate minor-league performances in recent seasons. As a bat-only prospect at a premium offensive position, Wallace has to mash to fulfill his potential, but his ceiling now appears to be that of a gap hitter with little foot speed and a reputation for selectivity that is wholly imaginary, an unimpressive profile that already has his new team pondering the possibility of trying left fielder Carlos Lee at first this spring. The best-case scenario is that the man they call "The Walrus" turns out to be the next Kevin Youkilis, but that's about as likely as the Walrus having actually been Paul.

PITCHERS

Fernando Abad

Born: **12/17/1985** Age: **25**
Bats: L Throws: L Height: **6' 2"** Weight: **205**
Breakout: **0%** Improve: **1%** Collapse: **1%**
Attrition: **1%** MLB: **2%**

Comparables:
Scott Lewis, Eric Rasmussen, Osiris Matos (79)

YEAR	TEAM	LVL	AGE	W	L	SV	G	GS	IP	H	HR	BB	SO	EqBB9	EqSO9	GB%	BABIP	WHIP	ERA	FRA	WARP
2008	LEX	A	22	2	7	3	45	0	76^{1}	78	9	13	94	1.5	11.1	38%	.337	1.25	3.30	2.82	1.7
2009	LNC	A+	23	4	6	6	41	0	82^{2}	78	8	8	79	0.9	8.6	37%	.304	1.10	4.14	3.72	1.0
2010	CCH	AA	24	4	3	0	14	4	39^{2}	48	3	6	33	1.4	7.6	43%	.360	1.38	2.50	2.86	1.3
2010	HOU	MLB	24	0	1	0	22	0	19	14	3	5	12	2.4	5.7	32%	.196	1.00	2.84	4.60	0.0
2011	*HOU*	*MLB*	*25*	*3*	*2*	*0*	*38*	*3*	*66^{1}*	*74*	*10*	*20*	*48*	*2.8*	*6.5*	*40%*	*.310*	*1.43*	*4.89*	*5.32*	*-0.4*

Abad paid his dues before finally making his major-league debut last season. It took him four years just to get out of the Dominican Summer League before making his stateside debut in 2007. Left-handers who throw 90 mph always get more opportunities, and in this case, it paid off. Abad's second-best pitch is a changeup that has good run. He can be hittable at times, but he throws strikes, and left-handed hitters have a hard time picking up his across-the-body delivery.

Alberto Arias

Born: **10/14/1983** Age: **27**
Bats: R Throws: R Height: **5' 11"** Weight: **155**
Breakout: **0%** Improve: **1%** Collapse: **0%**
Attrition: **0%** MLB: **1%**

Comparables:
Omar Daal, Dooley Womack, Al Corwin (84)

YEAR	TEAM	LVL	AGE	W	L	SV	G	GS	IP	H	HR	BB	SO	EqBB9	EqSO9	GB%	BABIP	WHIP	ERA	FRA	WARP
2008	CSP	AAA	24	3	4	0	30	0	45^{2}	50	3	16	41	3.2	8.1	58%	.346	1.53	4.73	4.53	0.3
2008	ROU	AAA	24	1	0	1	8	3	23^{2}	21	0	5	15	1.9	5.7	72%	.284	1.14	1.52	3.46	0.6
2008	COL	MLB	24	0	0	0	12	0	13^{2}	12	1	4	5	2.6	3.3	67%	.244	1.24	2.63	4.03	0.1
2008	HOU	MLB	24	1	1	0	3	2	8	11	0	6	8	6.8	9.0	71%	.458	2.25	6.75	4.64	0.4
2009	HOU	MLB	25	2	1	0	42	0	45^{2}	49	1	19	39	3.7	7.7	63%	.333	1.62	3.15	2.64	1.2
2011	*HOU*	*MLB*	*27*	*3*	*2*	*0*	*46*	*4*	*73^{1}*	*77*	*7*	*31*	*51*	*3.9*	*6.2*	*51%*	*.309*	*1.48*	*4.63*	*5.03*	*-0.1*

Arias missed the 2010 season because of shoulder problems that began in spring training and required surgery on April 22 to repair the rotator cuff and remove calcium deposits. That came on the heels of his missing the final five weeks of the 2009 season after having arthroscopic surgery on his right knee. When healthy, Arias obtains success from a big-breaking curveball, though it is easy to wonder if that pitch will have the same bite after the surgery.

Tim Byrdak

Born: **10/31/1973** Age: **37**
Bats: L Throws: L Height: **5' 11"** Weight: **190**
Breakout: **16%** Improve: **28%** Collapse: **12%**
Attrition: **10%** MLB: **58%**

Comparables:
Moe Drabowsky, Dennis Cook, Randy Myers (77)

YEAR	TEAM	LVL	AGE	W	L	SV	G	GS	IP	H	HR	BB	SO	EqBB9	EqSO9	GB%	BABIP	WHIP	ERA	FRA	WARP
2008	HOU	MLB	34	2	1	0	59	0	55^{1}	45	10	29	47	4.7	7.6	44%	.235	1.37	3.90	4.88	0.1
2009	HOU	MLB	35	1	2	0	76	0	61^{1}	39	10	36	58	5.3	8.5	43%	.188	1.27	3.52	5.26	-0.3
2010	HOU	MLB	36	2	2	0	64	0	38^{2}	40	4	20	29	4.7	6.8	31%	.308	1.55	3.72	3.64	0.5
2011	*HOU*	*MLB*	*37*	*3*	*1*	*0*	*63*	*0*	*49*	*46*	*6*	*26*	*43*	*4.7*	*7.8*	*43%*	*.287*	*1.46*	*4.52*	*4.91*	*-0.2*

Only one quality keeps Byrdak in major-league meal money: his ability to retire left-handed hitters. The Astros have been careful to keep Byrdak away from righties, as he has averaged less than an inning per outing during each of his three seasons in Houston. He isn't a hard thrower, as his fastball averages 89 mph, but his 82-mph slider gives left-handers fits. It took him some time to get there, but Byrdak has reached the point in his career where he could become expensive through arbitration, so the Astros released him last November. If he doesn't price himself out of the market, he could still have a few good years of major-league LOOGY-dom ahead of him.

Cesar Carrillo

Born: **4/29/1984** Age: **27**
Bats: R Throws: R Height: **6' 3"** Weight: **170**
Breakout: **0%** Improve: **1%** Collapse: **0%**
Attrition: **1%** MLB: **1%**

Comparables:
Mike Hinckley, Jerome Williams, Levale Speigner (87)

YEAR	TEAM	LVL	AGE	W	L	SV	G	GS	IP	H	HR	BB	SO	EqBB9	EqSO9	GB%	BABIP	WHIP	ERA	FRA	WARP
2008	LEL	A+	24	3	5	0	15	14	57^{1}	69	6	33	32	5.2	5.0	54%	.318	1.83	5.97	6.77	-0.5
2009	SAN	AA	25	8	4	0	20	20	121	115	10	37	57	2.8	4.2	55%	.271	1.33	4.24	5.04	0.2
2009	POR	AAA	25	0	3	0	5	5	29^{1}	37	2	9	26	2.8	8.0	53%	.376	1.60	5.53	4.15	0.5
2009	SDN	MLB	25	1	2	0	3	3	10^{1}	16	4	11	4	9.6	3.5	40%	.316	2.81	13.06	11.24	-0.5
2010	POR	AAA	26	5	14	0	27	27	151	167	20	57	95	3.4	5.7	48%	.298	1.50	5.60	5.89	-0.7
2011	*HOU*	*MLB*	*27*	*4*	*7*	*0*	*16*	*16*	*85*	*101*	*13*	*39*	*43*	*4.1*	*4.5*	*48%*	*.306*	*1.64*	*5.86*	*6.37*	*-0.2*

Carrillo's name seemingly showed up in the transactions every day last September. The Padres designated him for assignment, after which he was claimed off waivers by the Phillies. Then the Phillies DFA'd him and the Padres reclaimed him. When the Padres waived him a second time, the Astros nabbed him in hopes of resurrecting his flagging career this season. Carrillo was the Padres' first-round draft pick in 2005 after starring at the University of Miami, where the

Hurricanes went a remarkable 34-0 in his starts. However, he lost more than just his original UCL in his 2007 Tommy John surgery and hasn't been quite the same since.

Gustavo Chacin

Born: **12/4/1980** Age: **30**
Bats: L Throws: L Height: **5' 11"** Weight: **193**
Breakout: **8%** Improve: **15%** Collapse: **12%**
Attrition: **6%** MLB: **31%**

Comparables:
Billy Muffett, Jeff Shaw, Ray Washburn (80)

YEAR	TEAM	LVL	AGE	W	L	SV	G	GS	IP	H	HR	BB	SO	EqBB9	EqSO9	GB%	BABIP	WHIP	ERA	FRA	WARP
2008	DUN	A+	27	1	7	0	11	11	45^{2}	72	9	12	22	2.4	4.3	32%	.375	1.88	7.88	6.75	-0.2
2009	LEH	AAA	28	8	4	0	18	18	106^{2}	105	9	41	62	3.5	5.2	40%	.287	1.40	3.21	3.40	2.6
2010	ROU	AAA	29	1	1	0	6	5	25	24	5	6	14	2.2	5.0	43%	.250	1.20	3.60	3.78	0.7
2010	HOU	MLB	29	2	2	1	44	0	38^{1}	51	3	21	31	4.9	7.3	38%	.364	1.88	4.70	3.66	0.5
2011	*HOU*	*MLB*	*30*	*4*	*5*	*0*	*33*	*10*	71^{2}	*85*	*11*	*30*	*36*	*3.8*	*4.6*	*41%*	*.307*	*1.61*	*5.66*	*6.15*	*-0.4*

As a starter for the Blue Jays, Chacin was once so popular in Toronto that a local cosmetics company named a cologne after him in 2006. However, the fragrance soon wore off, and Chacin spent all of 2008 and 2009 in the minor leagues before reemerging in the majors in 2010 as a lefty specialist in the Astros' bullpen. He lacks the stuff to be a starter, as his fastball now tops out at 87 mph. However, his stutter-step delivery and cutter make him tough on left-handed batters, giving him a new lease on a relief career. That career will continue in Houston, where enlisted for another tour of duty in December.

Enerio Del Rosario

Born: **10/16/1985** Age: **25**
Bats: R Throws: R Height: **6' 2"** Weight: **165**
Breakout: **0%** Improve: **0%** Collapse: **0%**
Attrition: **0%** MLB: **0%**

Comparables:
Mike Thurman, Larry McWilliams, Rafael Rodriguez (81)

YEAR	TEAM	LVL	AGE	W	L	SV	G	GS	IP	H	HR	BB	SO	EqBB9	EqSO9	GB%	BABIP	WHIP	ERA	FRA	WARP
2008	DYT	A	22	6	2	5	20	10	77	60	3	14	55	1.6	6.4	56%	.252	0.96	1.17	3.36	1.8
2008	SAR	A+	22	1	4	0	13	6	44^{1}	57	2	23	32	4.7	6.5	46%	.374	1.83	5.89	5.09	0.3
2009	SAR	A+	23	2	1	7	31	0	50	40	2	6	33	1.1	5.9	67%	.247	1.02	1.98	3.57	0.8
2009	LOU	AAA	23	1	0	4	18	0	29^{2}	26	1	7	12	2.1	3.6	74%	.263	1.11	0.91	3.67	0.3
2010	LOU	AAA	24	4	4	4	50	0	64	61	7	17	34	2.4	4.8	61%	.266	1.27	3.09	4.75	0.4
2010	CIN	MLB	24	1	1	0	9	0	8^{2}	13	0	4	3	4.2	3.1	57%	.371	1.96	2.08	2.46	0.2
2010	HOU	MLB	24	0	0	0	2	0	1^{1}	4	0	0	1	0.0	6.8	71%	.571	3.75	20.25	13.51	-0.1
2011	*HOU*	*MLB*	*25*	*3*	*2*	*1*	*44*	*3*	78^{2}	*90*	*10*	*32*	*32*	*3.6*	*3.7*	*51%*	*.298*	*1.55*	*5.24*	*5.69*	*-0.8*

The Astros acquired the side-arming Del Rosario from the Reds in a cash deal last September after the righty had been designated for assignment. Del Rosario throws a power sinker in the 90-92 mph range that breaks bats with the aid of outstanding movement. His slider also has a sharp break, but as Yoda advised Luke Skywalker in *The Empire Strikes Back*, "control, control, you must learn control." Del Rosario has a good shot to make the Astros' bullpen this spring, where his sinker should make him an effective weapon to deploy in situations where a double play is needed.

Nelson Figueroa

Born: **5/18/1974** Age: **37**
Bats: R Throws: R Height: **6' 1"** Weight: **155**
Breakout: **10%** Improve: **31%** Collapse: **21%**
Attrition: **13%** MLB: **78%**

Comparables:
Danny Darwin, Mark Langston, Don Sutton (61)

YEAR	TEAM	LVL	AGE	W	L	SV	G	GS	IP	H	HR	BB	SO	EqBB9	EqSO9	GB%	BABIP	WHIP	ERA	FRA	WARP
2008	NWO	AAA	34	4	7	0	20	16	113^{2}	120	15	33	97	2.6	7.7	42%	.314	1.38	4.43	5.16	0.7
2008	NYN	MLB	34	3	3	0	16	6	45^{1}	48	3	26	36	5.2	7.1	43%	.313	1.68	4.57	4.44	0.5
2009	BUF	AAA	35	7	5	0	17	17	112	91	5	24	94	1.9	7.6	39%	.275	1.04	2.25	3.03	3.4
2009	NYN	MLB	35	3	8	0	16	10	70^{1}	80	8	24	59	3.1	7.5	39%	.327	1.61	4.09	4.00	1.0
2010	PHI	MLB	36	2	1	1	13	1	26	20	1	9	15	3.1	5.2	45%	.241	1.12	3.46	4.86	0.0
2010	HOU	MLB	36	5	3	0	18	10	67	64	9	25	58	3.4	7.8	44%	.287	1.36	3.22	3.84	1.1
2011	*HOU*	*MLB*	*37*	*6*	*5*	*0*	*25*	*14*	105^{1}	*105*	*12*	*36*	*78*	*3.1*	*6.7*	*42%*	*.295*	*1.34*	*4.00*	*4.35*	*1.5*

Much like crabgrass, Figueroa is very difficult to eradicate. Every time that it seems he is ready to wash out of the major leagues—for instance, in 2007, when he pitched in Mexico and Taiwan—he finds a way to get more mileage out of his arm, and he has now pitched for seven teams since 2000. He was twice claimed off waivers last season, the Phillies first getting him from the Mets in April and the Astros grabbing him in July. An extremely intelligent player who relies more on guile than stuff (his fastball rarely touches 90 mph), Figueroa mixes in a slider, curveball, and changeup. He is a viable candidate for the fifth starter's job this spring.

Michael Foltynewicz

Born: **10/7/1991** Age: **19**
Bats: R Throws: R Height: **6' 4"** Weight: **200**
Breakout: **0%** Improve: **0%** Collapse: **0%**
Attrition: **0%** MLB: **0%**

Comparables:
Dick Brodowski, Rick Wise, Milt Pappas (85)

YEAR	TEAM	LVL	AGE	W	L	SV	G	GS	IP	H	HR	BB	SO	EqBB9	EqSO9	GB%	BABIP	WHIP	ERA	FRA	WARP
2010	GRV	Rk	18	0	3	0	12	12	44^2	46	3	15	39	3.1	7.9	55%	.328	1.52	4.03	4.15	3.5
2011	*HOU*	*MLB*	*19*	*3*	*5*	*0*	*11*	*11*	*43^1*	*50*	*6*	*25*	*22*	*5.2*	*4.6*	*46%*	*.305*	*1.74*	*5.97*	*6.49*	*0.1*

The second of the Astros' two first-round draft choices last year, Foltynewicz signed quickly for $1.3 million following his senior year at Minooka (Ill.) Community High School, passing up the chance to pitch at the University of Texas. Foltynewicz might give proofreaders and headline writers nightmares now, but the Astros expect him to be equally hard on major-league hitters in the future. He has a good feel for pitching, as he can sink his fastball (which sits at 91-93 mph and touches 96) and has advanced command of his changeup, although the Astros would like to see him further refine his curveball.

Jeff Fulchino

Born: **11/26/1979** Age: **31**
Bats: R Throws: R Height: **6' 5"** Weight: **252**
Breakout: **0%** Improve: **0%** Collapse: **0%**
Attrition: **0%** MLB: **0%**

Comparables:
Alay Soler, Kevin Barry, Jason Jennings (81)

YEAR	TEAM	LVL	AGE	W	L	SV	G	GS	IP	H	HR	BB	SO	EqBB9	EqSO9	GB%	BABIP	WHIP	ERA	FRA	WARP
2008	OMA	AAA	28	3	4	5	25	5	61^1	71	2	27	53	4.0	7.8	47%	.361	1.60	4.85	4.98	0.5
2008	KCA	MLB	28	0	1	0	12	0	14	21	2	8	12	5.1	7.7	49%	.388	2.14	9.00	7.44	-0.3
2009	HOU	MLB	29	6	4	0	61	0	82	70	7	27	71	3.0	7.8	50%	.276	1.22	3.40	3.90	1.0
2010	HOU	MLB	30	2	1	0	50	0	47^1	53	7	22	46	4.2	8.7	42%	.331	1.65	5.51	5.45	-0.4
2011	*HOU*	*MLB*	*31*	*4*	*2*	*0*	*61*	*3*	*88^2*	*95*	*10*	*38*	*67*	*3.9*	*6.7*	*46%*	*.313*	*1.50*	*4.82*	*5.24*	*-0.5*

Last season was Fulchino's 10th as a professional, but his first spent entirely in the majors, save for a brief injury rehabilitation assignment (elbow) at Triple-A. Fulchino is a big guy who is all about the hard stuff, as his fastball averages 94 mph and his slider sits at 85. A lack of command keeps him from being entrusted with late-inning duty, though an abnormally high BABIP (.345) and line-drive rate inflated his ERA last season. Fulchino had arthroscopic elbow surgery last October to remove bone chips, but is expected to be ready for Opening Day.

Samuel Gervacio

Born: **1/10/1985** Age: **26**
Bats: R Throws: R Height: **6' 0"** Weight: **175**
Breakout: **5%** Improve: **11%** Collapse: **7%**
Attrition: **5%** MLB: **29%**

Comparables:
Luis Perdomo, Wesley Wright, John Wetteland (74)

YEAR	TEAM	LVL	AGE	W	L	SV	G	GS	IP	H	HR	BB	SO	EqBB9	EqSO9	GB%	BABIP	WHIP	ERA	FRA	WARP
2008	CCH	AA	23	2	5	5	47	0	65^1	69	8	26	82	3.6	11.3	42%	.365	1.50	4.13	4.08	0.7
2009	ROU	AAA	24	2	2	0	39	0	52^1	43	5	21	58	3.6	10.0	45%	.277	1.28	4.82	5.06	-0.1
2009	HOU	MLB	24	1	1	0	29	0	21	16	1	8	25	3.4	10.7	57%	.313	1.19	2.14	2.94	0.5
2010	HOU	MLB	25	0	1	0	6	0	3^2	4	1	5	3	12.3	7.4	46%	.250	2.45	9.82	13.28	-0.4
2011	*HOU*	*MLB*	*26*	*3*	*1*	*1*	*51*	*0*	*62*	*56*	*7*	*29*	*64*	*4.2*	*9.3*	*45%*	*.304*	*1.37*	*4.03*	*4.38*	*0.1*

Shoulder inflammation wiped out most of Gervacio's 2010, which robbed the Houston faithful of some good theater in addition to potentially effective relief. The righty is best known for his unorthodox mound routine, which involves holding the ball in front of him before every pitch, staring at it, glaring at the hitter, and uncorking an exaggerated leg kick before delivering the ball with a crossfire motion from what he calls a "five-eighths" angle, something midway between sidearm and three-quarters. Histrionics always work better if a pitcher can get people out, and despite all that staring, Gervacio doesn't always foresee where the ball will end up. Still, his 95-mph fastball and plus slider make up for a lot of misrouted deliveries. The Astros signed Gervacio to a minor-league deal in December, and he should be ready to resume high kicking by spring training.

J. A. Happ

Born: **10/19/1982** Age: **28**
Bats: L Throws: L Height: **6' 6"** Weight: **200**
Breakout: **7%** Improve: **29%** Collapse: **13%**
Attrition: **15%** MLB: **59%**

Comparables:
John Maine, Jason Bergmann, Carlos Torres (75)

YEAR	TEAM	LVL	AGE	W	L	SV	G	GS	IP	H	HR	BB	SO	EqBB9	EqSO9	GB%	BABIP	WHIP	ERA	FRA	WARP
2008	LEH	AAA	25	8	7	0	24	23	135	116	14	48	151	3.2	10.1	44%	.302	1.22	3.60	3.47	3.7
2008	PHI	MLB	25	1	0	0	8	4	31^2	28	3	14	26	4.0	7.4	35%	.266	1.36	3.69	3.74	0.7
2009	PHI	MLB	26	12	4	0	35	24	166	149	20	56	119	3.0	6.5	40%	.267	1.27	2.93	3.07	4.7
2010	LEH	AAA	27	0	1	0	5	4	22^1	26	3	15	22	6.1	9.0	50%	.348	1.86	4.84	4.72	0.3
2010	PHI	MLB	27	1	0	0	3	3	15^1	13	1	12	9	7.0	5.3	37%	.250	1.63	1.76	0.22	1.1
2010	HOU	MLB	27	5	4	0	13	13	72	60	7	35	61	4.4	7.6	41%	.265	1.33	3.75	4.98	0.3
2011	*HOU*	*MLB*	*28*	*10*	*9*	*0*	*26*	*26*	*144*	*141*	*18*	*65*	*116*	*4.0*	*7.2*	*42%*	*.293*	*1.42*	*4.35*	*4.72*	*2.1*

After perusing his peripherals and considering the two ballparks he has called home in his brief major-league career, you can immediately see that Happ has led a charmed on-field existence. He's far from dominant, recording 6.8 strikeouts, 3.8 walks, and 1.1 home runs per nine innings, and as a fly-ball pitcher with just two pitches (fastball/changeup) who has called two hitters' parks (Citizens Bank and Minute Maid) home, he has no right to a career ERA in the low 3.00s. Unfazed by the facts, Happ continued to be quite effective last season after missing most of the first half with a strained forearm. The Phillies dealt the southpaw to the Astros in the Roy Oswalt deal, which will put Houston on the hook when the law of averages catches up to Happ and his .273 career BABIP.

Matt Lindstrom

Born: **2/11/1980** Age: **31**
Bats: **R** Throws: **R** Height: **6' 4"** Weight: **210**
Breakout: **8%** Improve: **19%** Collapse: **12%**
Attrition: **8%** MLB: **37%**

Comparables:
Vinnie Chulk, Jerry Spradlin, Duaner Sanchez (79)

YEAR	TEAM	LVL	AGE	W	L	SV	G	GS	IP	H	HR	BB	SO	EqBB9	EqSO9	GB%	BABIP	WHIP	ERA	FRA	WARP
2008	FLO	MLB	28	3	3	5	66	0	57^{1}	57	1	26	43	4.1	6.8	49%	.322	1.47	3.14	3.04	1.3
2009	FLO	MLB	29	2	1	15	54	0	47^{1}	54	5	24	39	4.6	7.4	46%	.329	1.69	5.89	6.41	-0.7
2010	HOU	MLB	30	2	5	23	58	0	53^{1}	68	5	20	43	3.4	7.3	50%	.358	1.65	4.39	3.45	0.6
2011	*COL*	*MLB*	*31*	*3*	*1*	*8*	*64*	*0*	57^{1}	*66*	*6*	*23*	*44*	*3.7*	*6.9*	*46%*	*.334*	*1.56*	*5.10*	*5.54*	*-0.2*

Lindstrom may no longer be able to throw a strawberry through a locomotive as he could when he was younger and hitting 101 mph, but his heater still averages 95. So why hasn't he become a dominant late-inning reliever? Some theorize that he's soft, while others point to his inability to master his second pitch, a slider. BABIP has become the go-to stat to explain any pitcher's woes, and while such reductionism often smacks of oversimplification, there may be something to it in Lindstrom's case: a .341 career BABIP (including a Cobb-like .370 last season) suggests that he's been either incredibly unlucky or incredibly easy to hit. Lindstrom may have lost his last chance at regular save opportunities when he surrendered the closer's role to Brandon Lyon last August, but he'll continue his pursuit of a late-inning gig with the Rockies after being traded in December and agreeing to a two-year deal in January. He'd have an easier time of it if a few more of his batted balls passed within range of his fielders' leather.

Wilton Lopez

Born: **7/19/1983** Age: **27**
Bats: **R** Throws: **R** Height: **6' 0"** Weight: **190**
Breakout: **11%** Improve: **29%** Collapse: **9%**
Attrition: **10%** MLB: **52%**

Comparables:
Wally Whitehurst, Scott Sanderson, Reggie Cleveland (68)

YEAR	TEAM	LVL	AGE	W	L	SV	G	GS	IP	H	HR	BB	SO	EqBB9	EqSO9	GB%	BABIP	WHIP	ERA	FRA	WARP
2008	LEL	A+	24	2	1	12	30	0	30^{2}	34	0	4	26	1.2	7.6	60%	.358	1.27	2.64	4.32	0.2
2008	SAN	AA	24	0	2	0	27	0	38^{1}	41	2	9	24	2.1	5.6	64%	.310	1.33	4.93	5.04	0.0
2009	CCH	AA	25	4	5	0	29	15	110^{1}	133	8	13	69	1.1	5.6	56%	.331	1.33	4.73	4.09	1.5
2009	HOU	MLB	25	0	2	0	8	2	19^{1}	32	4	8	9	3.7	4.2	59%	.373	2.12	8.38	10.04	-0.8
2010	HOU	MLB	26	5	2	1	68	0	67	66	4	5	50	0.7	6.7	57%	.305	1.06	2.82	2.74	1.7
2011	*HOU*	*MLB*	*27*	*4*	*3*	*1*	*52*	*4*	82^{1}	*101*	*10*	*18*	*45*	*2.0*	*4.9*	*51%*	*.327*	*1.45*	*4.96*	*5.39*	*-0.4*

Released from the Yankees organization in 2007 and then claimed off waivers by the Astros from the Padres in 2009, Lopez rode a whirlwind journey of perseverance to a full-time gig in a major-league bullpen last year. It's safe to say that Lopez earned the trust of his fellow Astros pitchers in his rookie campaign, since he refused to give up his teammates' runs: only one of the 33 runners he inherited scored. He will never be a dominant late-inning reliever, but he can be useful as a seventh-inning guy with his sinker/slider combination, as he doesn't walk batters and he keeps the ball in the park.

Jordan Lyles

Born: **10/19/1990** Age: **20**
Bats: **R** Throws: **R** Height: **6' 4"** Weight: **185**
Breakout: **5%** Improve: **9%** Collapse: **1%**
Attrition: **1%** MLB: **12%**

Comparables:
Mike Witt, Frank Tanana, Bert Blyleven (68)

YEAR	TEAM	LVL	AGE	W	L	SV	G	GS	IP	H	HR	BB	SO	EqBB9	EqSO9	GB%	BABIP	WHIP	ERA	FRA	WARP
2008	GRV	Rk	17	3	3	0	13	13	49^{2}	44	4	10	64	1.8	11.6	49%	.315	1.15	3.98	4.03	1.4
2009	LEX	A	18	7	11	0	26	26	144^{2}	134	5	38	167	2.4	10.4	45%	.342	1.29	3.23	2.70	4.5
2010	CCH	AA	19	7	9	0	21	20	127	133	10	35	115	2.5	8.1	45%	.327	1.36	2.98	3.54	2.8
2010	ROU	AAA	19	0	3	0	6	6	31^{2}	48	2	11	22	3.2	6.3	52%	.397	1.96	5.40	4.65	0.4
2011	*HOU*	*MLB*	*20*	*7*	*9*	*0*	*22*	*22*	*114*	*125*	*14*	*48*	*89*	*3.8*	*7.0*	*44%*	*.321*	*1.51*	*4.99*	*5.42*	*0.9*

Lyles reached Triple-A as a 19-year-old barely two years after he was selected by the Astros in the supplemental first round of the 2008 draft and signed for $930,000, thereby foregoing the opportunity to take snaps on scholarship as a wide receiver at the University of South Carolina. Lyles draws rave reviews for his maturity and mound presence, with some scouts saying that he pitches with the savvy of a 30-year-old. His stuff is not dominant, but plays up because of his approach and ability to keep things unpredictable, mixing a 90-92 mph fastball with late life, a big-breaking curveball, a slider capable of snapping lumber, and a changeup that's already a swing-and-miss offering. Lyles is already close to his ceiling, but the Astros figure to have their top prospect start the season back at Triple-A, if for no other reason than to keep his service-time clock from ticking.

Brandon Lyon

Born: **8/10/1979** Age: **31**
Bats: **R** Throws: **R** Height: **6' 1"** Weight: **170**
Breakout: **14%** Improve: **42%** Collapse: **28%**
Attrition: **12%** MLB: **92%**

Comparables:
Steve Gromek, Bill Henry, Mike Henneman (73)

YEAR	TEAM	LVL	AGE	W	L	SV	G	GS	IP	H	HR	BB	SO	EqBB9	EqSO9	GB%	BABIP	WHIP	ERA	FRA	WARP
2008	ARI	MLB	28	3	5	26	61	0	59^{1}	75	7	13	44	2.0	6.7	41%	.338	1.48	4.70	4.44	0.3
2009	DET	MLB	29	6	5	3	65	0	78^{2}	56	7	31	57	3.5	6.5	49%	.226	1.13	2.97	4.08	0.9
2010	HOU	MLB	30	6	6	20	79	0	78	68	2	31	54	3.6	6.2	42%	.272	1.31	3.12	2.98	1.7
2011	*HOU*	*MLB*	*31*	*4*	*1*	*15*	*68*	*0*	71^{2}	*70*	*6*	*25*	*48*	*3.2*	*6.0*	*45%*	*.287*	*1.33*	*3.68*	*4.00*	*0.4*

Lyon stepped into the closer's role at the beginning of August, when Lindstrom went on the disabled list with a back strain, and he filled in quite capably. The rare late-game reliever who throws four pitches, Lyon has started to rely more on a hard slider as he has aged. The pitch averaged 89 mph last season, and he mixes it with a 92-mph fastball, a curveball, and an occasional changeup. Beyond the slider, Lyon's stuff is ordinary, but he will brush hitters back and effectively use both sides of the plate. Entering the second year of his bloated three-year, $15 million deal, Lyon is poised to keep the closer's job.

Mark Melancon

Born: **3/28/1985** Age: **26**
Bats: **R** Throws: **R** Height: **6' 2"** Weight: **215**
Breakout: **6%** Improve: **14%** Collapse: **5%**
Attrition: **5%** MLB: **26%**

Comparables:
Warner Madrigal, Fernando Hernandez Jr., Bob Howry (77)

YEAR	TEAM	LVL	AGE	W	L	SV	G	GS	IP	H	HR	BB	SO	EqBB9	EqSO9	GB%	BABIP	WHIP	ERA	FRA	WARP
2008	TAM	A+	23	1	0	0	13	0	25^1	26	2	6	20	2.1	7.1	44%	.308	1.30	2.85	2.96	0.8
2008	TRN	AA	23	6	0	2	19	0	49^2	32	3	12	47	2.2	8.5	64%	.227	0.89	1.81	3.46	0.9
2008	SWB	AAA	23	1	1	1	12	0	20	11	1	4	22	1.8	9.9	53%	.213	0.80	2.70	4.61	0.1
2009	SWB	AAA	24	4	0	3	32	0	53	37	3	11	54	1.9	9.2	59%	.254	1.02	2.55	4.17	0.5
2009	NYA	MLB	24	0	1	0	13	0	16^1	13	0	10	10	5.5	5.5	60%	.260	1.65	3.86	4.79	0.1
2010	SWB	AAA	25	6	1	6	40	0	56^1	63	5	31	58	5.0	9.3	55%	.360	1.73	3.67	2.05	2.1
2010	NYA	MLB	25	0	0	0	2	0	4	7	1	0	3	0.0	6.8	44%	.400	1.75	9.00	9.59	-0.1
2010	HOU	MLB	25	2	0	0	20	0	17^1	12	1	8	19	4.2	9.9	47%	.262	1.21	3.12	4.22	0.1
2011	*HOU*	*MLB*	*26*	*2*	*1*	*0*	*40*	*0*	63^2	*59*	*6*	*25*	*54*	*3.6*	*7.7*	*50%*	*.296*	*1.32*	*3.88*	*4.22*	*0.2*

The Astros received some heat for not acquiring someone better than Melancon as the key component in the trade that fitted Lance Berkman for pinstripes. Over three years removed from Tommy John surgery, the formerly dependable righty had posted an uncharacteristically high 3.67 ERA for the Scranton/Wilkes-Barre Yankees prior to the trade, largely due to a huge spike in his walk rate. A change of scenery seems to have helped, and pitching coach Brad Arnsberg is convinced that Melancon could eventually close in the major leagues on the strength of his mound presence and fearlessness (he enjoyed skydiving while at the University of Arizona). With only Brandon Lyon ahead of him, he may get his chance before long. Melancon has the type of nasty stuff typically associated with closers, featuring a fastball that sits at 92-94 mph and can reach 96, and he complements his heater with a big 12-to-6 curveball capable of getting hitters to chase in the dirt.

Danny Meszaros

Born: **9/6/1985** Age: **25**
Bats: **R** Throws: **R** Height: **6' 0"** Weight: **170**
Breakout: **0%** Improve: **0%** Collapse: **3%**
Attrition: **2%** MLB: **3%**

Comparables:
Jose Ascanio, Luis Perdomo, Jose Arredondo (79)

YEAR	TEAM	LVL	AGE	W	L	SV	G	GS	IP	H	HR	BB	SO	EqBB9	EqSO9	GB%	BABIP	WHIP	ERA	FRA	WARP
2008	TCV	A-	22	1	3	1	12	0	26^1	21	2	8	46	2.7	15.7	29%	.352	1.25	4.45	3.33	0.5
2009	CCH	AA	23	3	3	1	37	0	61^2	63	7	17	48	2.5	7.0	40%	.299	1.33	3.35	3.97	0.6
2010	CCH	AA	24	3	1	10	26	0	32	28	1	16	42	4.5	11.8	41%	.342	1.41	3.09	3.72	0.4
2011	*HOU*	*MLB*	*25*	*2*	*1*	*2*	*32*	*0*	*46*	*44*	*5*	*20*	*42*	*3.9*	*8.2*	*42%*	*.306*	*1.40*	*4.18*	*4.55*	*-0.0*

Meszaros has proven to be a real steal since the Astros selected him in the 48th round of the 2008 draft from the University of Charleston, where he had posted a 9.63 ERA in seven start after undergoing shoulder surgery in 2007. He goes right after hitters with a fastball in the 90-92 mph range and a sharp curveball. That approach has resulted in lofty strikeout rates in the minors, but he'll begin his 2011 campaign by serving out the remainder of a 50-game suspension he received last August for violating the minor-league drug prevention and treatment policy by testing positive for methylhexaneamine, a nasal decongestant that reportedly gives users an adrenaline rush. Unfortunately, he had little choice; baseball has also banned aloe-impregnated paper tissues.

Brian Moehler

Born: **12/31/1971** Age: **39**
Bats: **R** Throws: **R** Height: **6' 3"** Weight: **195**
Breakout: **5%** Improve: **11%** Collapse: **9%**
Attrition: **10%** MLB: **37%**

Comparables:
Mike Krukow, Sonny Siebert, Ed Whitson (71)

YEAR	TEAM	LVL	AGE	W	L	SV	G	GS	IP	H	HR	BB	SO	EqBB9	EqSO9	GB%	BABIP	WHIP	ERA	FRA	WARP
2008	HOU	MLB	36	11	8	0	31	26	150	166	20	36	82	2.2	4.9	45%	.287	1.37	4.56	4.72	1.7
2009	HOU	MLB	37	8	12	0	29	29	154^2	187	21	51	91	3.0	5.3	46%	.315	1.56	5.41	5.76	-0.2
2010	HOU	MLB	38	1	4	0	20	8	56^2	66	5	26	28	4.1	4.4	44%	.323	1.64	5.08	4.71	0.4
2011	*HOU*	*MLB*	*39*	*7*	*9*	*0*	*22*	*22*	*113*	*134*	*15*	*37*	*56*	*3.0*	*4.5*	*45%*	*.310*	*1.51*	*5.17*	*5.62*	*0.6*

How long has Moehler been around? He was once suspended by American League president Gene Budig. Remember league presidents? That was back in 1999, when Moehler was pitching for the Tigers and umpires found sandpaper taped to his thumb. Many years have passed since, and even without the aid of foreign substances (presumably), Moehler has quietly pieced together a long career as a journeyman. However, he might be nearing the end of the line after tearing a tendon off a bone in his groin area last August, an injury that required reattachment surgery (and made men everywhere cringe). The Astros decided not to re-sign Moehler as a free agent, and as a 39-year-old coming off surgery, he faces an uphill climb back to the majors.

Brett Myers

Born: **8/17/1980** Age: **30**
Bats: R Throws: R Height: **6' 4"** Weight: **215**
Breakout: **10%** Improve: **43%** Collapse: **24%**
Attrition: **11%** MLB: **98%**

Comparables:
Gaylord Perry, Gil Meche, Dave Bush (74)

YEAR	TEAM	LVL	AGE	W	L	SV	G	GS	IP	H	HR	BB	SO	EqBB9	EqSO9	GB%	BABIP	WHIP	ERA	FRA	WARP
2008	PHI	MLB	27	10	13	0	30	30	190	197	29	65	163	3.1	7.7	48%	.303	1.41	4.50	4.79	2.0
2009	PHI	MLB	28	4	3	0	18	10	70^{2}	74	18	23	50	2.9	6.4	48%	.268	1.43	4.84	5.26	0.3
2010	HOU	MLB	29	14	8	0	33	33	223^{2}	212	20	66	180	2.7	7.2	50%	.288	1.26	3.14	3.54	4.4
2011	*HOU*	*MLB*	*30*	*10*	*8*	*0*	*26*	*26*	*159*	*156*	*20*	*51*	*130*	*2.9*	*7.4*	*47%*	*.293*	*1.30*	*3.99*	*4.34*	*2.7*

The Astros seemed to be taking a big gamble when they guaranteed Myers $5 million after a season in which he was limited to 70 2/3 innings for the Phillies following hip surgery. However, the pact turned into a massive bargain for Houston, as Myers proved to be a workhorse, pitching at least six innings in all but one start last season (he bowed out after 5 2/3 frames in the last of his 33 outings). The righty began relying on his slider more in 2010 because his fastball lacked the velocity it had boasted before surgery, averaging only 89 mph. The speed reduction didn't seem to hurt him any; for the first time since 2003, he coughed up less than one home run per nine innings. Although he didn't allow fewer fly balls, a vastly reduced percentage of them left the park, a development that—given Myers' track record in that respect—isn't likely to last. Nevertheless, the Astros were impressed enough to re-sign him to a two-year pact worth $21 million, with a club option for 2013.

Matt Nevarez

Born: **2/26/1987** Age: **24**
Bats: R Throws: R Height: **6' 4"** Weight: **220**
Breakout: **1%** Improve: **1%** Collapse: **0%**
Attrition: **1%** MLB: **2%**

Comparables:
Victor Garate, J.R. Richard, Gary Kroll (83)

YEAR	TEAM	LVL	AGE	W	L	SV	G	GS	IP	H	HR	BB	SO	EqBB9	EqSO9	GB%	BABIP	WHIP	ERA	FRA	WARP
2008	SPO	A-	21	4	2	0	16	7	43^{1}	39	3	43	50	8.9	10.4	49%	.321	1.94	4.36	4.46	0.4
2009	HIC	A	22	1	4	9	34	0	35	22	1	15	50	3.9	12.9	48%	.269	1.17	2.57	4.09	0.2
2010	CCH	AA	23	2	1	1	36	0	38^{1}	30	1	46	41	10.9	9.7	47%	.309	1.99	3.76	4.34	0.2
2011	*HOU*	*MLB*	*24*	*1*	*1*	*2*	*24*	*1*	*30*	*28*	*3*	*26*	*29*	*7.7*	*8.7*	*45%*	*.301*	*1.77*	*5.29*	*5.75*	*-0.3*

Nevarez, whom the Astros acquired from the Rangers in the Ivan Rodriguez trade during the 2009 season, struggled in the midst of making the two-level jump from Low-A to Double-A last year, walking more than a hitter per inning. His stuff is beyond reproach, which he showed by striking out better than one batter per inning with a hard slider and a fastball that hit 95. However, more than five years after being drafted, he still has little idea of where the ball is going. Predicting Nevarez's future is simple: if he learns to throw strikes, he'll be a short reliever in the major leagues; if he doesn't, he won't. Houston didn't like the chances of his discovering the strike zone's secret hideout and removed him from the 40-man roster last November.

Bud Norris

Born: **3/2/1985** Age: **26**
Bats: R Throws: R Height: **6' 0"** Weight: **225**
Breakout: **13%** Improve: **41%** Collapse: **12%**
Attrition: **9%** MLB: **72%**

Comparables:
Scott Sanders, Vinegar Bend Mizell, Britt Burns (68)

YEAR	TEAM	LVL	AGE	W	L	SV	G	GS	IP	H	HR	BB	SO	EqBB9	EqSO9	GB%	BABIP	WHIP	ERA	FRA	WARP
2008	CCH	AA	23	3	8	0	19	19	80	89	8	31	84	3.5	9.5	50%	.365	1.59	4.05	4.02	1.7
2009	ROU	AAA	24	4	9	0	19	19	120	104	6	53	112	4.0	8.4	50%	.293	1.34	2.63	3.66	2.4
2009	HOU	MLB	24	6	3	0	11	10	55^{2}	59	9	25	54	4.0	8.7	41%	.317	1.56	4.53	4.13	0.7
2010	HOU	MLB	25	9	10	0	27	27	153^{2}	151	18	77	158	4.5	9.3	45%	.314	1.52	4.92	4.89	0.5
2011	*HOU*	*MLB*	*26*	*7*	*8*	*0*	*21*	*21*	112^{1}	*113*	*13*	*54*	*103*	*4.4*	*8.2*	*46%*	*.314*	*1.49*	*4.63*	*5.03*	*1.3*

David Norris became known as Bud at the age of three, after mimicking the rest of the adult males at a restaurant table by ordering Anheuser-Busch's best-known beverage. The Astros are banking on his becoming a Clydesdale in their rotation, but his walk rate is closer to a canter than a trot. Norris flashes the potential to be a dominant top-of-the-rotation starter and finished the season with 9.25 punchouts per nine innings, the fifth-highest strikeout rate recorded by an NL hurler with a minimum of 150 innings pitched. A power pitcher with a fastball that sits at 94 mph and a slider that reaches 88, Norris tends to telegraph and overthrow his curveball. He has trouble with control and suffers from the misfortune of being a fly-ball pitcher working in a park that punishes pitchers for allowing balls in the air.

Felipe Paulino

Born: **10/5/1983** Age: **27**
Bats: R Throws: R Height: **6' 3"** Weight: **245**
Breakout: **1%** Improve: **6%** Collapse: **2%**
Attrition: **3%** MLB: **13%**

Comparables:
Ronald Belisario, Gene Brabender, Ron Robinson (77)

YEAR	TEAM	LVL	AGE	W	L	SV	G	GS	IP	H	HR	BB	SO	EqBB9	EqSO9	GB%	BABIP	WHIP	ERA	FRA	WARP
2009	ROU	AAA	25	2	1	0	7	7	34^{2}	30	1	23	29	6.0	7.5	59%	.282	1.59	3.11	4.03	0.7
2009	HOU	MLB	25	3	11	0	23	17	97^{2}	126	20	37	93	3.4	8.6	45%	.361	1.71	6.17	6.05	-0.4
2010	HOU	MLB	26	1	9	0	19	14	91^{2}	95	4	46	83	4.5	8.1	45%	.332	1.57	5.11	5.80	-0.5
2011	*COL*	*MLB*	*27*	*5*	*8*	*0*	*17*	*17*	*93*	*108*	*12*	*45*	*74*	*4.4*	*7.1*	*46%*	*.330*	*1.63*	*5.58*	*6.06*	*0.8*

The Astros finally ran out of patience with Paulino at the end of 2010 and traded him to the Rockies for infielder Clint Barmes. The righty has the raw ability to be a successful starting pitcher, drawing upon a fastball that sits at 95 mph and reaches 98 with heavy boring action, a hard slider, a hammer curveball, and a serviceable changeup. However, his control has long been lacking, and so has his command, as he leaves too many pitches over the heart of the plate. Perhaps a change of scenery will serve Paulino well after his spending his entire 10-year career with the Astros, but the odds are against him as he steps into baseball's toughest pitching environment in Denver.

Wandy Rodriguez

Born: **1/18/1979** Age: **32**
Bats: **S** Throws: **L** Height: **5' 11"** Weight: **160**
Breakout: **12%** Improve: **54%** Collapse: **18%**
Attrition: **12%** MLB: **97%**

Comparables:
Camilo Pascual, Mark Langston, Mike Mussina (66)

YEAR	TEAM	LVL	AGE	W	L	SV	G	GS	IP	H	HR	BB	SO	EqBB9	EqSO9	GB%	BABIP	WHIP	ERA	FRA	WARP
2008	HOU	MLB	29	9	7	0	25	25	137^{1}	136	14	44	131	2.9	8.6	41%	.310	1.35	3.54	4.19	2.4
2009	HOU	MLB	30	14	12	0	33	33	205^{2}	192	21	63	193	2.8	8.4	47%	.302	1.26	3.02	3.57	4.6
2010	HOU	MLB	31	11	12	0	32	32	195	183	16	68	178	3.1	8.2	49%	.304	1.33	3.60	4.31	2.2
2011	*HOU*	*MLB*	*32*	*12*	*9*	*0*	*30*	*30*	*181*	*175*	*19*	*61*	*155*	*3.0*	*7.7*	*46%*	*.302*	*1.30*	*3.87*	*4.21*	*3.5*

Rodriguez certainly doesn't look like a major-league pitcher, and it's easy to wonder if a stiff breeze might knock the lithe lefty off the mound. Yet despite not being blessed with size or plus velocity, Rodriguez knows how to get hitters out, particularly with the aid of an outstanding slow curveball that makes his 89-mph fastball play up. Rodriguez has always been a willing learner, picking up a cutter from Andy Pettitte when the veteran lefty played for the Astros in 2006 and then figuring out how to add sinking action to his changeup last season. Rodriguez struggled early in 2010, but after refining his changeup, he posted a 2.03 ERA in his final 18 starts and will attempt to extend his run of good pitching to this season.

Polin Trinidad

Born: **11/19/1984** Age: **26**
Bats: **L** Throws: **L** Height: **6' 3"** Weight: **195**
Breakout: **10%** Improve: **17%** Collapse: **7%**
Attrition: **15%** MLB: **26%**

Comparables:
Elizardo Ramirez, Wilton Lopez, Mike Ekstrom (78)

YEAR	TEAM	LVL	AGE	W	L	SV	G	GS	IP	H	HR	BB	SO	EqBB9	EqSO9	GB%	BABIP	WHIP	ERA	FRA	WARP
2008	SLM	A+	23	4	2	0	10	10	62	46	2	11	34	1.6	4.9	47%	.228	0.94	2.32	3.29	1.6
2008	CCH	AA	23	6	5	0	18	18	107^{1}	109	13	21	75	1.8	6.3	41%	.287	1.25	3.61	3.25	3.0
2009	CCH	AA	24	7	5	1	13	12	82^{2}	87	7	10	53	1.1	5.8	40%	.304	1.19	2.94	3.41	1.6
2009	ROU	AAA	24	6	5	0	13	12	87^{1}	90	18	25	59	2.6	6.1	41%	.262	1.33	4.54	4.68	0.8
2010	CCH	AA	25	1	3	0	5	4	31^{1}	42	2	8	19	2.3	5.5	51%	.342	1.61	4.02	3.78	0.5
2010	ROU	AAA	25	3	8	0	23	20	118^{1}	144	13	32	74	2.4	5.6	37%	.320	1.55	5.02	5.26	0.9
2011	*HOU*	*MLB*	*26*	*7*	*10*	*0*	*23*	*23*	*141*	*167*	*22*	*43*	*75*	*2.7*	*4.7*	*42%*	*.305*	*1.48*	*5.29*	*5.75*	*0.2*

Trinidad compensates for middling stuff with good control, walking just 2.5 batters per nine innings at Triple-A over the last two seasons. A sinker/slider type whose fastball usually doesn't break 90 mph, he features a good feel for his changeup, but doesn't induce enough grounders to succeed without whiffs. While Trinidad's inability to miss bats would probably expose him in a starting role at the big-league level, he has a shot to fashion a career in middle relief.

Henry Villar

Born: **5/24/1987** Age: **24**
Bats: **R** Throws: **R** Height: **5' 11"** Weight: **170**
Breakout: **0%** Improve: **3%** Collapse: **0%**
Attrition: **1%** MLB: **3%**

Comparables:
Tex Clevenger, Jarrod Washburn, Kirk Saarloos (85)

YEAR	TEAM	LVL	AGE	W	L	SV	G	GS	IP	H	HR	BB	SO	EqBB9	EqSO9	GB%	BABIP	WHIP	ERA	FRA	WARP
2008	GRV	Rk	21	3	6	0	13	13	65^{1}	69	6	12	65	1.7	9.0	52%	.344	1.33	4.41	3.72	1.9
2009	LEX	A	22	3	4	5	43	3	90	80	6	18	109	1.8	10.9	51%	.319	1.12	2.60	3.33	1.6
2010	CCH	AA	23	4	7	5	36	11	102	95	11	42	68	3.7	6.0	51%	.261	1.36	4.15	5.77	0.3
2010	HOU	MLB	23	0	0	0	8	0	6	5	0	3	3	4.5	4.5	50%	.250	1.50	4.50	7.03	-0.5
2011	*HOU*	*MLB*	*24*	*3*	*3*	*0*	*28*	*7*	*70*	*79*	*10*	*32*	*45*	*4.0*	*5.7*	*46%*	*.302*	*1.56*	*5.38*	*5.85*	*-0.4*

Many scouts feel Villar might be better suited for the bullpen than the rotation, but the Astros have held him in high enough esteem to have hidden him on the 40-man roster for the past two winters. His sinker/slider combination has held up as a starter in the minor leagues and might help him get by in the back of a major-league rotation. However, his long-term future seems to lie in relief, since he's saddled with a below-average changeup and the dubious durability suggested by his slight frame.

Wesley Wright

Born: **1/28/1985** Age: **26**
Bats: **R** Throws: **L** Height: **5' 11"** Weight: **160**
Breakout: **3%** Improve: **9%** Collapse: **7%**
Attrition: **4%** MLB: **17%**

Comparables:
Greg Harris, Travis Phelps, Ron Piche (81)

YEAR	TEAM	LVL	AGE	W	L	SV	G	GS	IP	H	HR	BB	SO	EqBB9	EqSO9	GB%	BABIP	WHIP	ERA	FRA	WARP
2008	HOU	MLB	23	4	3	1	71	0	55^{2}	45	8	34	57	5.5	9.2	43%	.252	1.49	5.01	6.30	-0.8
2009	HOU	MLB	24	3	4	0	49	0	44^{2}	53	9	25	47	5.0	9.5	44%	.358	1.75	5.44	5.23	-0.2
2010	ROU	AAA	25	4	1	0	15	14	69^{2}	76	8	33	41	4.3	5.3	46%	.301	1.63	4.65	5.77	0.3
2010	HOU	MLB	25	1	2	0	14	4	33	37	6	13	29	3.5	7.9	45%	.320	1.61	5.73	7.03	-0.5
2011	*HOU*	*MLB*	*26*	*4*	*3*	*0*	*47*	*7*	*71*	*72*	*10*	*38*	*58*	*4.8*	*7.2*	*45%*	*.301*	*1.54*	*5.01*	*5.44*	*-0.1*

The Astros snagged Wright from the Dodgers in the 2007 Rule 5 draft and have been waiting patiently for him to blossom into either a starting pitcher or a shutdown reliever. The southpaw took a step backward last season, losing velocity on a fastball that averaged 88 mph (down from 91 in 2009), and his slider and curveball also lacked their previous sharpness. The culprit could have been a case of biceps tendinitis that eventually landed him on the disabled list in August. When healthy, Wright has the pitches, smarts, and work ethic to be successful. At some point soon, those elements need to be combined into an effective pitcher; otherwise, Wright risks running out of chances with the Astros.

LINEOUTS

HITTERS

PLAYER	TEAM	LVL	AGE	PA	R	2B	3B	HR	RBI	BB	SO	SB-CS	AVG/OBP/SLG	TAv	BABIP	BRR	FRAA	WARP
CF J. Austin*	LNC	A+	19	587	83	25	13	10	59	39	126	54-20	.261/.314/.414	.252	.315	4.8	CF -6	1.1
CF D. DeShields Jr.	GRV	Rk	17	73	10	6	1	0	8	5	18	5-1	.313/.356/.433	.293	.420	1.2	CF -1	0.6
C B. Esposito	ROU	AAA	31	164	11	5	0	2	18	5	31	0-0	.225/.263/.298	.190	.262	-1.9	C 0, P 0	-0.7
	HOU	MLB	31	3	0	0	0	0	0	0	1	0-0	.000/.000/.000	.015	.000	0.0	C 0	-0.1
3B J. Florentino	CCH	AA	26	348	29	17	3	4	36	27	55	0-0	.256/.310/.367	.245	.294	0.0	3B -2, SS -1	0.2
INF A. Hernandez#	COH	AAA	27	187	13	4	0	1	17	12	23	2-4	.234/.278/.275	.214	.258	-0.6	SS 0, 2B 2	-0.1
	CLE	MLB	27	63	5	3	0	0	2	2	9	1-0	.246/.270/.295	.200	.289	-0.7	SS -1, 2B 0	-0.2
	HOU	MLB	27	56	6	2	0	0	1	8	10	2-0	.188/.304/.229	.202	.237	1.2	2B -1, SS 2	0.1
UT M. Kvasnicka	TCV	A-	21	292	31	10	1	5	36	27	48	2-1	.234/.305/.337	.248	.265	0.0	RF -3, 3B -3	-0.4
SS J. Mier	LEX	A	19	573	83	31	1	2	53	63	107	15-7	.235/.323/.314	.249	.288	1.8	SS 5	2.2
SS O. Navarro	ROU	AAA	25	333	41	24	1	6	37	34	67	2-3	.271/.361/.424	.264	.330	0.3	2B 3, SS -5	1.3
	HOU	MLB	25	25	2	0	0	0	0	5	4	0-0	.050/.240/.050	.172	.062	-2.0	SS 0	-0.3
CF T. Steele	CCH	AA	23	252	24	9	3	2	18	10	67	9-4	.228/.258/.315	.219	.306	0.1	CF 6, LF 0	0.2
OF C. Sullivan*	HOU	MLB	30	71	6	1	1	0	4	6	18	0-0	.188/.254/.234	.177	.255	0.4	LF 0, RF 0	-0.4
1B J. Van Ostrand	CCH	AA	25	335	22	17	0	3	44	18	62	1-3	.244/.284/.327	.220	.291	0.0	1B 0, LF 0	-1.3
SS J. Villar	LWD	A	19	420	61	18	4	2	36	26	103	38-13	.272/.332/.358	.254	.352	7.0	SS 0	2.0
	LNC	A+	19	143	18	6	2	3	19	12	50	7-2	.225/.294/.372	.233	.338	-1.0	SS -2	-0.2

Jay Austin has outstanding hand-eye coordination and bat speed, but needs to reduce his strikeouts significantly to reach his high ceiling. ⊘ The first of the Astros' two first-round draft picks last year and the eighth overall selection, **Delino DeShields Jr.** will try to overcome an off-season DUI and follow in the footsteps of his father. Fittingly, the younger DeShields was converted from a center fielder into a second baseman in instructional league at the end of last season. His game is similar to that of his dad, a career .268/.352/.377 hitter, based more on speed and line drives than power. Whether that makes for an early draft pick is still open to debate, as few teams pegged him as higher than a late-first round talent. ⊘ Strong defensive skills behind the plate have kept **Brian Esposito** in professional baseball for 12 years, but he has appeared in just three major-league games, two of which came with the Astros late last season. ⊘ **Jhon Florentino**'s most distinguishing feature is the unique spelling of his first name. ⊘ Diminutive Dominican utilityman **Anderson Hernandez** struggled to post solid numbers between Cleveland and Houston. He's in for another season of shuttling between Triple-A and the majors, not really contributing anything anywhere. ⊘ The Astros drafted **Michael Kvasnicka** in the 2010 supplemental first round because of his bat—they'll figure out his position as they go along. Kvasnicka was primarily a catcher in college, but played some third base and right field in his professional debut. He would give the Astros more bang for the $936,000 bonus they paid him if he could stay behind the plate, and some scouts believe that his mobility and soft hands will allow him to do so. ⊘ **Jiovanni Mier**, the Astros' first-round draft pick in 2009, is an above-average defensive shortstop who runs well but has a lot to learn about hitting. ⊘ **Oswaldo Navarro** resurfaced in the major leagues last season four years after making his debut with the Mariners, but that was more a function of the Astros' injuries than a sign of any progress on his part. ⊘ **T. J. Steele** has the whole toolshed, as the scouts like to say, but that's not going to do him any good unless he figures out how to draw a walk or hit a ball over a fence. Fortunately, he can fall back on a name made for daytime television. ⊘ **Cory Sullivan** is a Quad-A player who is stretched as a major-league regular but could spend another season or two in the bigs as a fifth outfielder if he happens to land in the right place at the right time. ⊘ **James Van Ostrand** is a big Canadian with a nice line-drive stroke, but he doesn't profile as a major-league first baseman. Unfortunately, suspect glove work and a lack of speed preclude him from playing any other position. ⊘ One of three players acquired from the Phillies in the Roy Oswalt trade last July, **Jonathan Villar** is a good defensive shortstop and a bit of a hot dog; his career will be short-circuited if he does not develop some plate discipline.

PITCHERS

PLAYER	TEAM	LVL	AGE	W	L	SV	IP	H	HR	BB	SO	EqBB9	EqSO9	GB%	BABIP	WHIP	ERA	FRA	WARP
J. Banks	ROU	AAA	27	9	12	0	171^{2}	177	25	37	72	1.9	3.8	42%	.263	1.27	4.04	4.89	1.6
	HOU	MLB	27	0	1	0	4	8	1	4	1	9.0	2.3	42%	.389	3.00	13.50	12.71	-0.2
Y. Bazardo	ROU	AAA	25	4	5	1	88^{1}	97	12	26	58	2.7	5.9	47%	.302	1.41	3.87	5.18	0.2
T. Bushue	LEX	A	19	7	8	0	133^{2}	129	18	48	114	3.2	7.7	39%	.294	1.36	4.11	4.59	1.5
D. Carpenter	PMB	A+	24	5	3	20	53^{1}	45	3	15	50	2.5	8.5	43%	.286	1.19	2.36	3.67	0.6
C. Daigle	ROU	AAA	29	2	3	8	44	54	6	13	35	2.7	7.2	47%	.343	1.55	4.91	5.44	-0.1
	HOU	MLB	29	1	1	0	10^{1}	25	3	6	6	5.2	5.2	31%	.458	3.00	11.32	8.40	-0.5
J. De Leon	TCV	A-	22	2	1	6	28	26	0	12	29	3.9	9.3	46%	.329	1.39	0.64	0.99	1.1
	CCH	AA	23	0	2	0	23	29	3	22	23	8.6	9.0	50%	.366	2.35	7.04	7.02	-0.5
G. Majewski	ROU	AAA	30	4	5	2	53^{1}	69	7	18	40	3.1	6.8	53%	.356	1.71	6.24	6.06	-0.5
	HOU	MLB	30	0	0	0	2	5	1	1	1	4.5	4.5	55%	.400	3.00	22.50	17.05	-0.1
C. Sampson	HOU	MLB	32	1	0	0	30^{1}	43	7	8	16	2.4	4.7	54%	.336	1.71	5.93	6.89	-0.8
R. Seaton	LNC	A+	20	6	13	0	146^{1}	198	22	45	85	2.8	5.2	45%	.339	1.72	6.64	6.20	-0.6
B. Thompson	ROU	AAA	28	1	1	0	23^{1}	41	3	4	12	1.6	4.7	49%	.396	1.95	8.87	8.69	-0.9
	KCA	MLB	28	0	4	0	19^{2}	25	4	4	10	1.8	4.6	47%	.300	1.53	6.41	7.59	-0.6
V. Velasquez	GRV	Rk	18	2	2	0	29^{1}	24	4	5	25	1.5	7.7	45%	.241	1.07	3.07	3.82	2.5

Josh Banks is the type of pitcher a team stashes away on its Triple-A roster as an insurance policy that it hopes it never has to cash. Itinerant ground-baller **Yorman Bazardo** failed to sniff the big leagues for the first time since 2006. He'll attempt to get his next glimpse of the majors in Minnesota after receiving a minor-league deal and a ticket to spring training from the Twins. **Tanner Bushue** had a somewhat disappointing first full professional season in 2010, but he offers plenty to like, including a fastball that reaches 94 mph and a power curveball. **David Carpenter** was acquired from the Cardinals last August in a trade for Pedro Feliz and has more upside than most 25-year-old relievers who have yet to pitch above A-ball. He didn't begin pitching until 2008, after starting his professional career as a catcher. **Casey Daigle** will forever be remembered as the husband of legendary Olympic softball pitcher Jennie Finch, which certainly isn't a bad thing. Strong-armed **Jorge De Leon** was converted from a shortstop into a reliever in spring training last year and was impressive enough to be protected on the 40-man roster in November. **Arcenio Leon** is not be confused with former talk-show host Arsenio Hall, but his mid-90s fastball does leave scouts saying, "Hit me with the digits." Leon also comes equipped with a swing-and-miss slider, but his chances of getting to the major leagues hinge on his learning to throw strikes consistently. **Chia-Jen Lo**'s expected quick ascent through the Astros' farm system was slowed in 2010 by a partially torn ulnar collateral ligament in his elbow that did not require surgery but effectively ruined his season. It's hard to believe that **Gary Majewski** made the U.S. pitching staff in the inaugural World Baseball Classic in 2006, in light of the 120 1/3 mostly ineffective innings he has managed in the majors since then. As a hometown kid, **Chris Sampson** earned the affections of Astros fans, but that didn't save him from being designated for assignment after he struggled with shoulder problems and posted a combined 12.44 ERA in July and August. Although **Ross Seaton** had a brutal 2010, his stuff is good and at least some of his poor performance can be traced to pitching at Lancaster, where runs are scored at a higher pace than anywhere else in pro ball. **Brad Thompson** doesn't have hard stuff, but he induces grounders and knows where almost every pitch he throws is headed—often the bleachers. The Royals cut him loose in June, and the Astros followed suit in August. **Vincent Velasquez**, the Astros' second-round pick last year, made a strong professional debut before undergoing September Tommy John surgery that will keep him out of action in 2011.

MANAGER: BRAD MILLS

YEAR	TEAM	W-L	Pythag +/-	Avg PC	100+ P	120+ P	QS	BQS	REL	REL w Zero R	IBB	Subs	PH	PH Avg	PH HR	SB2	CS2	SB3	CS3	SAC Att	SAC %	POS SAC	Squeeze	Swing	In Play
2010	HOU	76-86	9	100.1	92	5	91	4	506	343	39	71	278	.224	3	90	32	10	4	104	72.1%	28	7	116	84

Mills was hired to replace Cecil Cooper prior to last season as much for his personality as his tactical skills. Mills, who spent the previous six seasons as the Red Sox's bench coach, is upbeat and has good people skills, much like Terry Francona, his former boss and best friend. The Astros needed a change of atmosphere after two years of the aloof Cooper, and Mills brought that to a team that got younger once veterans Roy Oswalt and Lance Berkman were traded in late July. The Astros went 36-27 from July 27 on and outperformed their Pythagenport record by 7.9 wins. Owner Drayton McLane was so impressed that he picked up Mills' option for 2012 and added an option year to his contract for 2013. From a strategic standpoint, Mills mostly managed by the numbers, with the exception that he allowed his starting pitchers quite a bit of leeway: the Astros had an NL-high 41 starts of at least 110 pitches.

Kansas City Royals

Dayton Moore's admonitions to Kansas City fans to "trust The Process" have become easy fodder for detractors of the Royals' general manager, and it's easy to see why. As devotees of a team that has managed just one winning season since 1994 and hasn't outscored its opponents over a 162-game schedule since 1991, Royals fans have become accustomed to hollow promises of future glory. Moore has done little at the major-league level to change that attitude, having helped the Royals to just one season of 70 or more wins since taking over as general manager in May 2006. Royals fans can be forgiven if they believe that Moore's Royals peaked at a 75-win fourth-place finish in 2008, given that they won 10 fewer games in 2009 and fell back into the American League Central cellar last year with a record two games worse than the post-fire-sale Indians.

ROYALS PROSPECTUS

2010 W-L: 67-95, 5th in AL Central

Pythag	.396	27th	**Ballpark:** Kauffman Stadium (3-yr. PF: 101). Fountains and waterfalls can't wash away on-field failure
RS/G	4.2	20th	
RA/G	5.2	2nd	
TAv	.265	21st	**2010:** All eyes are on Northwest Arkansas as the Royals finish fifth
BRR	-14.2	29th	
FRA	5.15	29th	**2011:** The stockings are hung by the chimney with care, in hopes that top prospects soon would be there
DER	-11.1	24th	
DL	676	12th	
B-Age	28.9	15th	**Action Items:** Not blocking the youth movement, getting their Greinke's worth
P-Age	27.5	9th	
Salary	$71.4	21st	
M$/MW	$3.34	23rd	

It might have been hard for the Kansas City faithful in 2010 to see past the major-league squad's league-worst pitching and fielding and a lineup that regularly featured Jason Kendall (.256/.318/.297) and Yuniesky Betancourt (.259/.288/.405)—both of whom Moore *totally* acquired on purpose—but somewhere in the outer reaches of the organization, out in Wilmington, North Carolina, and in Northwest Arkansas, The Process was finally, tantalizingly yielding results.

To credit Moore for those first stirrings is to presume that the point of The Process was to tank enough seasons to thoroughly restock the farm system with elite domestic talent via top picks and big spending in the amateur draft; if there was any more to The Process, it must still be in processing. Still, there are few better ways for a moribund franchise to alter its fortunes than via the draft. You need look no further than the Tampa Bay Rays, a team that didn't win more than 70 games in a season in its first decade of existence. But, thanks in large part to several strong drafts and top-four picks that produced the likes of Evan Longoria, B. J. Upton, and three-fifths of Tampa's starting rotation, the Rays have now won baseball's toughest division in two of the last three years.

While the major-league team was busy securing the fifth overall pick in the 2011 draft, the potential core of a winning 2012 Royals team began to coalesce on the team's High-A and Double-A affiliates. Third baseman Mike Moustakas, the second overall pick in the 2007 draft, rebounded from a miserable season at High-A Wilmington in 2009 to crush in his Double-A debut, earning a midseason promotion to Triple-A, where he continued to hit for power and will open the 2011 season with an eye toward claiming the major-league third-base job by season's end. First baseman Eric Hosmer, the third overall pick in the 2008 draft, followed a similar path at a level lower, finishing the season by hitting .313/.365/.615 with 13 homers in his first 50 games at Double-A.

Completing a potential homegrown infield were second baseman Johnny Giavotella, the team's second-round pick in 2008, who hit .322/.395/.460 in his Double-A debut, and 2010 first-round pick Christian Colon, a shortstop who began his professional career at High-A Wilmington hitting a respectable .278/.326/.380. Joining Colon in Wilmington was 2009 third-round pick Wil Myers, a 19-year-old catcher who hit .315/.429/.506 in his full-season debut and .346/.453/.512 in 58 games for High-A Wilmington. Myers may move to right field before reaching the majors, but his bat projects to carry that position, giving the Royals a devastating heart-of-the-order trio, with the righty Myers hitting between lefties Moustakas and Hosmer as soon as late 2012.

On the mound, the Royals have a quartet of left-handed rotation prospects, all of whom are expected to start the 2011 season at Double-A Northwest Arkansas and who could collectively progress to the majors as a ready-made rotation for 2012. Leading that group is 2008 fifth-round pick John Lamb, who dominated the Carolina League as a 19-year-old in 2010 and ranked above Hosmer and Myers and behind only Moustakas on Kevin Goldstein's November ranking of the Royals' top prospects. Lamb is joined by 21-year-old Mike Montgomery, who was taken in 2008's first supplemental round as compensation for departed reliever David Riske, and looks to carry on the fine tradition of Royals pitchers who share his surname, albeit in a different role than Jeff's and hopefully with more longevity than Monty. The team's third-round pick in 2007, 22-year-old Danny Duffy, had a brief crisis of purpose last year that prompted a bizarre spring training retirement, but he returned two months into the season, pitched his way back up through the system, and finished with seven strong starts in his Double-A debut. Chris Dwyer, a 23-year-old who was drafted out of Clemson with the team's fourth-round pick in 2009 and is thus the lone college product of the four, rounds out the quartet.

That's nine players, comprising a full infield, a power and patience offensive engine, and most of a starting rotation. Five of the prospects—Moustakas, Hosmer, Myers, Lamb, and Montgomery—were acquired in the last four drafts and remain on track to make their major-league debuts by the end of the 2012 season with a very good chance to drastically alter the future of the franchise. To that bounty, Moore added another potential front-of-the-rotation arm and Joakim Soria's potential successor as closer in righties Jake Odorizzi and Jeremy Jeffress, respectively, the two key players acquired from the Brewers in December's Zack Greinke trade.

Despite the farm's fertility, a Royals renaissance is far from assured. A lot can go wrong between minor-league prospectdom and major-league stardom, even for players as close to the majors as these. Royals fans hardly need to be reminded of that as they watch former can't-miss-third-base prospect Alex Gordon, once touted as the next George Brett, struggle to prove he belongs in the majors as a light-hitting left fielder at age 27 in his fifth major-league season. Indeed, that Gordon's failures have come on Moore's watch (Gordon was drafted with the second overall pick in Allard Baird's final draft in 2005, but made his major-league debut during Moore's first full season in 2007) surely gives those salivating over the 2011 Northwest Arkansas team some pause. It is one thing to have the talent; it's another to develop it properly. That's not to lay Gordon's failures at Moore's feet—Greinke and Billy Butler have come along nicely on Moore's watch—but to sound a note of caution that even "sure things" can miss the mark.

A greater concern regarding Moore and the ascending prospects is his ability to build a team around them. The suggestion that Moore intentionally tanked the last several seasons to produce superior draft picks is an obvious bit of hyperbole, but had Moore—like *Major League's* fictitious Indians GM Charlie Donovan before him—been under orders to assemble the worst possible team, he wouldn't have needed to do much differently. If the last few years have represented Moore's best effort at constructing a major-league roster, it's fair to wonder whether that influx of talent in 2012 would be enough to overcome his lack of judgment.

Simply employing Jason Kendall as a starting catcher at this point in his career should be a fireable offense for any general manager. Kendall hit .261/.336/.321 from 2005 to 2009 and .244/.329/.315 in his two seasons with the Brewers in 2008 and 2009. Moore not only signed him to start, but also gave him a multiyear, multimillion-dollar contract, then nontendered John Buck and let Miguel Olivo leave as a free agent, only to watch both become All-Stars in 2010. (And while we didn't exactly see that All-Star thing coming, last year's Miguel Olivo comment successfully first-guessed that particularly disastrous sequence of decisions.) Pathetically, Kendall, after hitting .256/.318/.297 in his first season in Kansas City, remains the incumbent at the position. Elsewhere, big righty Dan Cortes may never amount to anything, but trading a well-regarded pitching prospect to make Yuniesky Betancourt your starting shortstop is the sort of move that hurts at both the major- and the minor-league levels. And while Moore had the good sense to ship Betancourt to Milwaukee as part of the Greinke trade, the shortstop he got back—good-field/no-hit Alcides Escobar—may not prove to be a meaningful upgrade.

Worse yet, Moore has become predictable. Once Jeff Francoeur hit free agency, it was just assumed that the sabermetric whipping boy, who was drafted by the Braves during Moore's time in Atlanta's front office, would land in Kansas City, and lo and behold, he did, via a $2.5 million one-year deal, after which Moore dealt his 2011 outfield another blow by signing the execrable Melky Cabrera, who lacks even Francoeur's utility as a right-handed platoon bat and defensive replacement. Grabbing Soria in the Rule 5 draft was a masterstroke, but that happened way back in December 2006, and most of what Moore has done since has had a small or negative impact. Even his big-splash signing of Gil Meche, a deal that looked like a surprising success in the first two seasons of Meche's five-year contract, has lost its luster in light of the right-hander's 5.29 ERA in just 190 2/3 innings over the last two seasons and subsequent retirement. (Fingers can be pointed at former Royals manager Trey Hillman for Meche's collapse, but then it was Meche's fragility that made that deal look so disastrous to begin with.)

Prior to the Greinke deal, Moore hadn't pulled off a single big-impact trade in what is still his only experience as a major-league general manager, though how little he has had to barter with has certainly played a role. And while Moore got a good return for his ace, particularly given that Greinke's going public with his demand for a trade undermined his GM's leverage, the two best players he received out of the four who came back from Milwaukee are, tellingly, the two with the least major-league experience. Lorenzo Cain might indeed prove to be a solid everyday center fielder, something the Royals system was not about to produce on its own, and Escobar might yet develop into a viable major league shortstop. Unfortunately, those possibilities are as speculative as the success of the projected 2012 Royals, and the remaining potential of the 25-year-old Cain and 24-year-old Escobar is considerably less than that of Odorizzi, Jeffress, and the Royals' younger homegrown prospects. As the coming wave of Royals prospects approaches, Moore needs to get better at identifying and acquiring valuable *major-league* talent.

Moore's next-best opportunity for such an acquisition might be via a trade of Soria. Soria's current contract has options that could take him through 2014 at reasonable salaries, but Jeffress, who pitched well in a major-league cup of coffee in September, could be ready to replace him before then, and Soria is a much sought-after closer who could bring a solid return. Butler seems more likely to remain in the powder blues. He would work just fine as a full-time designated hitter should Hosmer force him into such a role, and he won't be a free agent until after the 2013 season. Facing arbitration for the first time this offseason, Butler could yet be signed to an extension that would make him part of the incipient Royals renaissance.

That gives those hypothetical 2012 Royals yet another middle-of-the-order hitter and an ace closer (be it Soria or Jeffress), and there are more relief arms on the way in diminutive lefty Tim Collins, acquired from the Braves in the Kyle Farnsworth/Rich Ankiel deadline dump; 2009 fifth-round pick Louis Coleman; and lefty Everett Teaford, who was just added to the 40-man roster in November. However, even with Cain and Escobar in the mix, the next competitive Royals team could use some outfielders, some backup options in the middle infield, and perhaps a catcher, given Myers' potential inability to stick behind the plate. Moreover, no team can ever have enough pitching prospects, given their high bust rate. Moore addressed most of those needs with the Greinke trade, putting catching talent high on the list for a potential Soria swap. In the short term, however, with Greinke gone and the cream of the pitching prospects slated to start the year in Triple-A, the rotation needs more help than what Vin Mazarro (acquired from the A's for David DeJesus in an anticlimactic trade) and perhaps even free-agent acquisition Jeff Francis can provide.

Indeed, in contrast to the division-rival Indians, who are rebuilding on a similar pace with a lesser collection of top talent but a deeper overall farm system, the Royals don't have a lot of Plan Bs. The potential for the coming crop of prospects to be competitive in 2012 and a contender soon after is great, but so is the potential for disappointment should that opportunity be squandered, be it by the young talent's Gordon-like collapse or by Moore's failure to reinforce the core with a proper supporting cast. Believe it or not, all of that makes this a very exciting time to be a Royals fan, though whether that will still be true after the denouement remains to be seen.

HITTERS

Mike Aviles **2B**

Born: **3/13/1981** Age: **30**
Bats: R Throws: R Height: **5' 9"** Weight: **195**
Breakout: **2%** Improve: **40%** Collapse: **4%**
Attrition: **11%** MLB: **86%**

Comparables:
Luis Maza, Jay Payton, Clint Barmes (70)

YEAR	TEAM	LVL	AGE	PA	R	2B	3B	HR	RBI	BB	SO	SB	CS	AVG_OBP_SLG	TAv	BABIP	BRR	FRAA	WARP
2008	OMA	AAA	27	227	42	21	6	10	42	11	23	3	0	.336/.370/.631	.326	.341	-0.9	2B 7, SS 6	3.4
2008	KCA	MLB	27	441	68	27	4	10	51	18	58	8	3	.325/.354/.480	.290	.357	4.0	SS 5, 2B -1	3.6
2009	KCA	MLB	28	127	10	3	1	1	8	4	26	1	0	.183/.205/.250	.167	.219	-0.6	SS 4, 3B -1	-0.5
2010	OMA	AAA	29	75	8	3	1	1	8	4	10	0	0	.271/.320/.386	.239	.305	0.5	SS 0, 2B 0	0.1
2010	KCA	MLB	29	448	63	16	3	8	32	20	49	14	5	.304/.335/.413	.268	.327	1.3	2B 5, SS 1	1.9
2011	*KCA*	*MLB*	*30*	*437*	*51*	*21*	*2*	*10*	*51*	*23*	*59*	*8*	*3*	*.278/.316/.413*	*.255*	*.301*	*-0.2*	*SS 2, 2B 2*	*1.5*

Aviles returned from a 2009 lost to Tommy John surgery to become one of the Royals' most productive hitters, which sounds more like the setup to a joke than it does an endorsement of Aviles. Unfortunately, the statement is more serious than Royals fans care to remember, as Aviles ranked fifth on the team in True Runs, behind the departed Scott Podsednik and the injured David DeJesus and directly ahead of second-half Giant Jose Guillen. His power didn't return, but Aviles continued to put the ball in play often, the key to his success going forward. He is never going to draw walks consistently, but he rarely whiffs and is one of the few Royals who deserves to wear a glove, giving the team plenty of reasons to find a spot for him in the lineup. Unfortunately, Kansas City will play him at third, where neither his glove nor his bat profiles as well as it does at second.

Yuniesky Betancourt SS

Born: **1/31/1982** Age: **29**
Bats: **R** Throws: **R** Height: **5' 10"** Weight: **190**
Breakout: **2%** Improve: **42%** Collapse: **3%**
Attrition: **10%** MLB: **100%**

Comparables:
Carlos Baerga, Alvin Dark, Jack Wilson (73)

YEAR	TEAM	LVL	AGE	PA	R	2B	3B	HR	RBI	BB	SO	SB	CS	AVG/OBP/SLG	TAv	BABIP	BRR	FRAA	WARP
2008	SEA	MLB	26	590	66	36	3	7	51	17	42	4	4	.279/.297/.392	.243	.285	-2.3	SS -20	-0.9
2009	KCA	MLB	27	263	26	10	5	4	27	11	26	0	2	.240/.266/.370	.218	.248	-0.6	SS -5	-0.7
2009	SEA	MLB	27	245	15	10	1	2	22	10	18	3	1	.250/.269/.330	.220	.251	-1.7	SS -8	-1.0
2010	KCA	MLB	28	588	60	29	2	16	78	23	64	2	3	.259/.286/.405	.249	.265	2.3	SS 6	2.3
2011	*MIL*	*MLB*	*29*	*569*	*60*	*29*	*3*	*9*	*61*	*23*	*49*	*5*	*3*	*.263/.287/.378*	*.233*	*.268*	*-0.6*	*SS -7, 2B 0*	*-0.1*

Betancourt's "improved" 2010 offense still left him with an on-base percentage well under .300, and a career-high in homers has more to do with the right-hander's getting out of Safeco for a full season than it does with any real improvement. Betancourt's defense may have undergone a revival, but we'd need more evidence to state that conclusively—for now, all we know is that he made more plays. He is never going to hit well enough to help a lineup, except in relative terms: last year, he outhit Alcides Escobar, the shortstop he will replace in Milwaukee, and he out-fielded him as well. The problem is that Betancourt is the mediocre thing that he is, whereas Escobar could conceivably get better. Alas, that's the price one pays for a Greinke-level pitcher.

Wilson Betemit 3B

Born: **11/2/1981** Age: **29**
Bats: **S** Throws: **R** Height: **6' 2"** Weight: **155**
Breakout: **6%** Improve: **38%** Collapse: **4%**
Attrition: **9%** MLB: **76%**

Comparables:
Phil Nevin, Bill Hall, Ben Oglivie (66)

YEAR	TEAM	LVL	AGE	PA	R	2B	3B	HR	RBI	BB	SO	SB	CS	AVG/OBP/SLG	TAv	BABIP	BRR	FRAA	WARP
2008	NYA	MLB	26	198	24	13	0	6	25	6	56	0	1	.265/.288/.429	.250	.341	-0.9	1B 0, 3B 0	0.2
2009	CHR	AAA	27	286	36	19	0	11	49	21	73	2	0	.241/.294/.441	.246	.287	1.8	3B 9, 1B 3	1.5
2009	CHA	MLB	27	50	2	5	0	0	3	5	13	0	0	.200/.280/.311	.202	.281	-0.6	1B 1, 3B -2	-0.4
2010	GIG	—	28	65	8	6	0	2	15	6	13	0	0	.281/.338/.491	—	.318	0.0	—	—
2010	OMA	AAA	28	135	9	6	2	2	17	17	23	1	1	.265/.358/.407	.265	.304	-0.7	SS -2, 1B 2	0.4
2010	KCA	MLB	28	315	36	20	0	13	43	36	74	0	0	.297/.378/.511	.320	.361	-1.5	3B -5, 1B -1	1.7
2011	*KCA*	*MLB*	*29*	*342*	*41*	*18*	*0*	*12*	*41*	*35*	*85*	*1*	*0*	*.246/.322/.422*	*.259*	*.298*	*0.0*	*3B -1, 1B 0*	*0.5*

After signing a minor-league deal prior to last season, Betemit became one of the Royals' most productive hitters. It was all due to the switch-hitter's performance against southpaws. A career .230/.275/.362 hitter against lefties heading into 2010, Betemit crushed them to the tune of a .312/.398/.532 line last year. It's a small sample (88 plate appearances) and therefore hard to believe—he didn't hit nearly as well in Omaha before getting the call in late May, and hit a combined .240/.302/.396 in September and October in the majors—but as the player picking up the majority of starts in a platoon, Betemit could provide plenty of pop against righties. The Royals may still be left wishing that they had cashed in their chips rather than attempting to rebottle lightning.

Gregor Blanco CF

Born: **12/12/1983** Age: **27**
Bats: **L** Throws: **L** Height: **5' 11"** Weight: **170**
Breakout: **4%** Improve: **39%** Collapse: **4%**
Attrition: **7%** MLB: **64%**

Comparables:
Richie Ashburn, Kenny Lofton, Freddy Guzman (79)

YEAR	TEAM	LVL	AGE	PA	R	2B	3B	HR	RBI	BB	SO	SB	CS	AVG/OBP/SLG	TAv	BABIP	BRR	FRAA	WARP
2008	ATL	MLB	24	519	52	14	4	1	38	74	99	13	5	.251/.362/.309	.259	.316	5.8	LF -7, CF -3	0.8
2009	GWN	AAA	25	397	54	9	1	2	30	50	70	10	3	.228/.320/.279	.226	.270	5.2	CF -9, LF 0	-0.7
2009	ATL	MLB	25	48	5	0	1	0	1	4	9	2	0	.186/.250/.233	.207	.229	-0.1	CF 0, RF 0	-0.2
2010	LAG	—	26	114	13	3	0	1	6	21	17	5	2	.236/.387/.303	—	.270	0.0	—	—
2010	GWN	AAA	26	187	26	8	0	1	11	23	28	9	1	.286/.382/.357	.268	.321	2.8	CF -4, RF 1	0.6
2010	ATL	MLB	26	66	9	1	1	0	3	8	15	1	2	.310/.394/.362	.275	.419	0.5	CF 0, LF 0	0.3
2010	*KCA*	*MLB*	*26*	*203*	*22*	*8*	*3*	*1*	*11*	*21*	*35*	*10*	*2*	*.274/.345/.369*	*.263*	*.329*	*0.6*	*CF -8, RF 0*	*-0.3*

The 26-year-old Blanco barely played in Atlanta the past two seasons after a poor rookie showing in 2008, but the Royals gave him a shot after acquiring him in the Kyle Farnsworth/Rick Ankiel swap. Blanco is an outfielder who hits like a middle infielder. He is best suited for the role of a fifth man who spends most of his time coming in for defensive purposes. Blanco can take a base on balls with ease, and his wheels let him leg out triples, but opposing outfielders could shift toward the infield against him as they do for the kids who can't hit in Little League, and they would be rewarded more often than not.

Billy Butler 1B

Born: **4/18/1986** Age: **25**
Bats: **R** Throws: **R** Height: **6' 1"** Weight: **240**
Breakout: **4%** Improve: **40%** Collapse: **7%**
Attrition: **18%** MLB: **84%**

Comparables:
Conor Jackson, Gaby Sanchez, Wally Joyner (65)

YEAR	TEAM	LVL	AGE	PA	R	2B	3B	HR	RBI	BB	SO	SB	CS	AVG/OBP/SLG	TAv	BABIP	BRR	FRAA	WARP
2008	OMA	AAA	22	115	18	6	1	5	13	14	7	0	0	.337/.417/.564	.325	.326	0.6	1B -3	0.6
2008	KCA	MLB	22	478	51	22	0	11	55	33	57	0	1	.275/.324/.400	.250	.294	-3.6	1B -4	-0.8
2009	KCA	MLB	23	672	79	51	1	21	93	58	103	1	0	.301/.362/.492	.296	.332	-2.8	1B -3	2.4
2010	KCA	MLB	24	678	82	45	0	15	78	69	78	0	0	.318/.388/.469	.302	.341	-4.4	1B 0	2.9
2011	*KCA*	*MLB*	*25*	*638*	*84*	*38*	*0*	*18*	*79*	*63*	*82*	*1*	*0*	*.291/.362/.455*	*.287*	*.310*	*0.0*	*1B -2*	*1.9*

Butler finished the 2010 season ninth in the American League in True Runs, and while he is more of a designated hitter than a first baseman, that kind of offensive output isn't something to dismiss just because he can't pick it in the field. Butler isn't the most prolific homer hitter; it's all about doubles. He has hit nearly 100 two-baggers over the past two seasons and tied Ben Grieve for third in the single-season record for grounding into double plays in 2010 (first place, non–Jim Rice division). Keeping company with Grieve, who also did this at age 24, would be disconcerting, but Cal Ripken tied for third in his age-24 season as well, with Carl Yastrzemski not far behind.

Christian Colon **SS**

Born: **5/14/1989** Age: **22**
Bats: R Throws: R Height: **6' 1"** Weight: **180**
Breakout: **0%** Improve: **1%** Collapse: **1%**
Attrition: **1%** MLB: **3%**

Comparables:
Asdrubal Cabrera, Wil Cordero, Barry Larkin (81)

YEAR	TEAM	LVL	AGE	PA	R	2B	3B	HR	RBI	BB	SO	SB	CS	AVG/OBP/SLG	TAv	BABIP	BRR	FRAA	WARP
2010	WIL	A+	21	271	38	12	2	3	30	13	33	2	4	.278/.326/.380	.239	.301	-0.6	SS 5	0.9
2011	*KCA*	*MLB*	*22*	*265*	*28*	*12*	*1*	*4*	*27*	*12*	*43*	*1*	*1*	*.252/.290/.365*	*.230*	*.282*	*-0.1*	*SS 5*	*0.6*

The Royals had the fourth pick in the 2010 draft, which is kind of like being the fourth person in line at Best Buy on Black Friday with only three HDTVs left in the store. Once Bryce Harper, Jameson Taillon, and Manny Machado were off the board, the Royals had the best of what was left, and instead of spending big money on risk, they went the safe route with Colon. As a contact-oriented hitter with gap power, Colon is no doubt going to hit, but there are questions about whether he will hit at a star level. With fantastic instincts, soft hands, silky-smooth actions, and a solid arm, Colon can make every play he gets to at shortstop, but as a below-average runner, he leaves questions about his ability to stay on the left side of the infield. His potential to be the kind of player you normally hope for with the fourth overall pick is subject to debate, but he's also the rare talent who could begin his first full year at Double-A and be in the big leagues the following season.

David DeJesus **RF**

Born: **12/20/1979** Age: **31**
Bats: L Throws: L Height: **6' 0"** Weight: **175**
Breakout: **0%** Improve: **46%** Collapse: **2%**
Attrition: **6%** MLB: **99%**

Comparables:
Robin Yount, Orlando Hudson, Kenny Lofton (74)

YEAR	TEAM	LVL	AGE	PA	R	2B	3B	HR	RBI	BB	SO	SB	CS	AVG/OBP/SLG	TAv	BABIP	BRR	FRAA	WARP
2008	KCA	MLB	28	577	70	25	7	12	73	46	71	11	8	.307/.364/.452	.282	.332	-2.4	CF 0, LF 9	3.0
2009	KCA	MLB	29	627	74	28	9	13	71	51	87	4	9	.281/.345/.434	.272	.308	0.4	LF 13, CF 2	3.6
2010	KCA	MLB	30	394	46	23	3	5	37	34	47	3	3	.318/.381/.443	.296	.352	-2.6	RF -1, CF 0	1.7
2011	*OAK*	*MLB*	*31*	*573*	*73*	*29*	*4*	*11*	*66*	*50*	*71*	*7*	*5*	*.290/.356/.433*	*.277*	*.311*	*-1.0*	*LF 8, CF -1*	*2.5*

DeJesus was in the midst of his most productive season when a torn a ligament in his thumb cut his year short. This was a shame not just because of what the Royals lost on the field, but because they had been shopping DeJesus leading up to the trade deadline. They missed him once he was gone, as he finished fourth on the team in True Runs despite playing in just 91 games. Given his solid glove, it's easy to see why the A's added him to their outfield collection of swift defenders who can hit a bit and draw some walks. Although Oakland-Alameda County Coliseum is no picnic for hitters, getting out of Kansas City should help DeJesus in the home-run department—his home isolated power was .095 this year (.149 on the road) due to Kauffman's being a difficult place for left-handers to go deep, and it's not as if he can afford to give up much in terms of the long ball to begin with.

Jarrod Dyson **CF**

Born: **8/15/1984** Age: **26**
Bats: L Throws: R Height: **5' 9"** Weight: **160**
Breakout: **0%** Improve: **16%** Collapse: **2%**
Attrition: **9%** MLB: **28%**

Comparables:
Joey Gathright, Nyjer Morgan, Michael Bourn (76)

YEAR	TEAM	LVL	AGE	PA	R	2B	3B	HR	RBI	BB	SO	SB	CS	AVG/OBP/SLG	TAv	BABIP	BRR	FRAA	WARP
2008	WIL	A+	23	331	40	8	0	0	24	32	60	39	9	.260/.329/.288	.259	.316	3.6	LF 6, CF 1	1.7
2009	BUR	A	24	75	14	2	1	0	5	5	14	9	4	.343/.387/.403	.312	.418	-0.3	CF 3	0.9
2009	NWA	AA	24	283	38	7	4	0	14	27	54	37	6	.258/.322/.319	.254	.317	2.4	CF 1, LF -2	0.8
2010	SJU	—	25	72	9	0	1	0	0	8	9	8	1	.190/.282/.222	—	.218	0.0	—	—
2010	WIL	A+	25	52	7	6	2	0	9	1	9	5	1	.327/.327/.531	.288	.381	0.7	CF 4	0.7
2010	OMA	AAA	25	219	33	10	1	1	19	16	32	13	3	.272/.327/.349	.248	.308	-0.2	CF 10	1.3
2010	KCA	MLB	25	65	11	4	2	1	5	6	16	9	1	.210/.277/.404	.256	.262	-0.4	CF 3	0.4
2011	*KCA*	*MLB*	*26*	*381*	*38*	*15*	*2*	*2*	*30*	*27*	*78*	*31*	*7*	*.245/.296/.318*	*.222*	*.299*	*1.0*	*CF 2, LF 0*	*-0.2*

Dyson came up in September and ran all over the place, stealing nine bases in 18 games and needing just three weeks to take the team lead in highlight-reel catches. Despite all of that excitement, the Royals signed free-agent Melky Cabrera to be the 2011 center fielder. Given both Dyson's and Cabrera's lack of positives, this is a Hobson's choice for the Royals: even if Cabrera plays down to expectations and Dyson eventually claims the job, it's not going to take the Royals long to learn that as exhilarating as speed is, a productive player needs to do other things over the long haul, like hit for some power and not make so many outs. Those are skills that Dyson didn't display in the minors, and there is no reason to think that he's going to start displaying them now just because he's so darn fun to watch.

Josh Fields **3B**
Born: **12/14/1982** Age: **28**
Bats: R Throws: R Height: **6' 1"** Weight: **215**
Breakout: **3%** Improve: **25%** Collapse: **2%**
Attrition: **8%** MLB: **53%**
Comparables:
David Freese, Dave Hollins, Mark Saccomanno (75)

YEAR	TEAM	LVL	AGE	PA	R	2B	3B	HR	RBI	BB	SO	SB	CS	AVG/OBP/SLG	TAv	BABIP	BRR	FRAA	WARP
2008	CHR	AAA	25	318	41	15	3	10	35	37	98	8	2	.246/.340/.431	.252	.341	-3.1	3B -3	0.0
2008	CHA	MLB	25	35	3	1	0	0	2	3	17	0	0	.156/.229/.188	.161	.333	0.4	3B 0	-0.2
2009	CHR	AAA	26	114	15	5	0	5	13	13	22	1	2	.265/.351/.469	.278	.288	-2.4	3B -1	0.2
2009	CHA	MLB	26	268	29	5	2	7	30	25	76	2	3	.222/.298/.347	.232	.291	-0.3	3B 2, 1B -1	0.0
2010	KCA	MLB	27	50	5	0	0	3	6	1	9	0	0	.306/.320/.490	.281	.324	0.4	3B 0	0.3
2011	*PIT*	*MLB*	*28*	*415*	*50*	*16*	*1*	*15*	*49*	*43*	*114*	*7*	*3*	*.247/.325/.423*	*.260*	*.310*	*-0.4*	*3B -2, 1B 0*	*0.7*

Fields was part of the Mark Teahen deal that also brought Chris Getz to the Royals. This swap of disappointments didn't do much for Kansas City in 2010, with Fields barely playing, due to early-season hip surgery that kept him out until September. He hit when he was on the field, but that was a sample small enough to be meaningless. As of the winter meetings, Ned Yost was suggesting that Mike Aviles would get first crack at third base, and with Betemit around to take what playing time is left over, the Royals felt free to nontender Fields. He signed a minors contract with baseball's last-chance saloon, the Pittsburgh Pirates, and will try to grab a bench spot. As he is already 28 but still not established in the major leagues, it seems ever more certain that Fields' best days as an athlete are not to come but lie somewhere behind him on an Oklahoma State football field.

Chris Getz **2B**
Born: **8/30/1983** Age: **27**
Bats: L Throws: R Height: **6' 0"** Weight: **185**
Breakout: **3%** Improve: **30%** Collapse: **7%**
Attrition: **13%** MLB: **56%**
Comparables:
Kevin Frandsen, Alejandro Machado, Dave Cash (79)

YEAR	TEAM	LVL	AGE	PA	R	2B	3B	HR	RBI	BB	SO	SB	CS	AVG/OBP/SLG	TAv	BABIP	BRR	FRAA	WARP
2008	CHR	AAA	24	457	60	24	1	11	52	41	53	11	4	.302/.363/.448	.276	.318	1.2	2B 11, SS -4	3.0
2008	CHA	MLB	24	7	2	0	0	0	1	0	1	1	1	.286/.286/.286	.218	.333	0.0	2B 1	0.1
2009	CHA	MLB	25	415	49	18	4	2	31	30	54	25	2	.261/.323/.347	.246	.297	3.7	2B 9	1.6
2010	KCA	MLB	26	248	23	9	0	0	18	19	28	15	2	.237/.298/.277	.223	.266	2.1	2B -9, 3B -1	-1.1
2011	*KCA*	*MLB*	*27*	*383*	*42*	*17*	*1*	*5*	*34*	*33*	*48*	*16*	*4*	*.259/.327/.358*	*.247*	*.283*	*0.4*	*2B 0, SS -1*	*0.4*

Getz has a career line of .252/.315/.320 in 670 plate appearances, which is a perfect representation of replacement-level production. Picturing a Getz/Yuniesky Betancourt double-play combination is enough to make a sane baseball fan's head explode, but the Royals pulled the plug on that nightmare in favor of Mike Aviles at the keystone, much to the dismay of those in the business of writing jokes about the team. The scrappy Getz is limited to second base and is at his best when he never touches a bat, so using him to fill the utility role makes little sense—not that a little thing like a lack of usefulness has ever stopped the Royals from handing out playing time before.

Johnny Giavotella **2B**
Born: **7/10/1987** Age: **23**
Bats: R Throws: R Height: **5' 8"** Weight: **185**
Breakout: **6%** Improve: **20%** Collapse: **1%**
Attrition: **19%** MLB: **33%**
Comparables:
Luis Valbuena, Blake DeWitt, Travis Denker (73)

YEAR	TEAM	LVL	AGE	PA	R	2B	3B	HR	RBI	BB	SO	SB	CS	AVG/OBP/SLG	TAv	BABIP	BRR	FRAA	WARP
2008	BUR	A	20	310	50	18	2	4	26	25	34	10	7	.299/.352/.421	.298	.321	1.2	2B -2	2.0
2009	WIL	A+	21	561	84	24	8	6	52	66	54	26	9	.258/.344/.380	.280	.271	5.0	2B -7	2.4
2010	NWA	AA	22	597	92	35	5	9	65	61	67	13	7	.322/.395/.460	.298	.349	-0.9	2B 0	3.8
2011	*KCA*	*MLB*	*23*	*515*	*59*	*24*	*2*	*7*	*51*	*45*	*71*	*11*	*4*	*.272/.332/.383*	*.254*	*.300*	*-0.4*	*2B 2*	*1.0*

The stocky five-foot-eight frame of this second-round selection in 2008 doesn't resemble that of your standard high pick, and because he's a second baseman, the unfair comparisons to Dustin Pedroia are inevitable. Pedroia is as special they get, but Giavotella can really hit, consistently putting the barrel of the bat on the ball while smacking doubles all over the field. He's not a runner and he's not a good second baseman, but there are plenty of scouts out there who think he can be at least average, if not better, at the position in terms of overall value.

Alex Gordon **LF**
Born: **2/10/1984** Age: **27**
Bats: L Throws: R Height: **6' 1"** Weight: **220**
Breakout: **2%** Improve: **47%** Collapse: **6%**
Attrition: **12%** MLB: **93%**
Comparables:
Carlos Quentin, Steve Kemp, Joe Charboneau (78)

YEAR	TEAM	LVL	AGE	PA	R	2B	3B	HR	RBI	BB	SO	SB	CS	AVG/OBP/SLG	TAv	BABIP	BRR	FRAA	WARP
2008	KCA	MLB	24	571	72	35	1	16	59	66	120	9	2	.260/.350/.432	.281	.308	0.2	3B -3	2.7
2009	OMA	AAA	25	85	17	4	1	2	10	13	16	0	0	.313/.435/.493	.332	.373	1.5	3B 4	1.3
2009	KCA	MLB	25	189	28	6	0	6	22	21	43	5	0	.232/.323/.378	.250	.274	3.3	3B 4	1.1
2010	OMA	AAA	26	322	59	20	3	14	44	51	72	7	2	.315/.442/.577	.338	.386	0.0	LF 4, RF -2	3.4
2010	KCA	MLB	26	281	34	10	0	8	20	34	62	1	5	.215/.313/.355	.254	.251	-3.2	LF 4, 3B -2	0.1
2011	*KCA*	*MLB*	*27*	*528*	*66*	*25*	*1*	*17*	*59*	*68*	*117*	*8*	*3*	*.246/.352/.420*	*.272*	*.290*	*-0.4*	*3B 0, LF 1*	*1.9*

The curious case of Alex Gordon remains as confounding as ever. He was once the subject of George Brett dreams, but the older Gordon gets, and the more productive his bat should be, the worse his seasons turn out. Last year was no exception:

Kansas City sent him to Omaha to become a left fielder, and the Royals took their time bringing him back despite his impressive work at the plate against PCL competition. Gordon tanked upon return to the majors, hitting just .211/.311/.360 in 62 games. To summarize, the Royals moved a quality-fielding third baseman who couldn't hit well enough for the position to the outfield, where his bat has an even smaller chance of playing well and his defense can no longer shine through, making him dimensionless rather than one-dimensional. It turns out that alchemy works in baseball, but only in reverse.

Eric Hosmer 1B

Born: **10/24/1989** Age: **21**
Bats: L Throws: L Height: **6' 4"** Weight: **215**
Breakout: **2%** Improve: **11%** Collapse: **2%**
Attrition: **10%** MLB: **24%**

Comparables:
Daric Barton, Fernando Martinez, Adam Jones (69)

YEAR	TEAM	LVL	AGE	PA	R	2B	3B	HR	RBI	BB	SO	SB	CS	AVG/OBP/SLG	TAv	BABIP	BRR	FRAA	WARP
2009	BUR	A	19	327	31	17	2	5	49	44	68	3	2	.254/.352/.382	.268	.314	-1.2	1B 4	0.8
2009	WIL	A+	19	107	9	2	2	1	10	9	22	0	0	.206/.280/.299	.227	.257	-1.1	1B 2	-0.3
2010	WIL	A+	20	375	48	29	6	7	51	44	39	11	1	.354/.429/.545	.346	.382	-4.9	1B -3	2.8
2010	NWA	AA	20	211	39	14	3	13	35	15	27	3	1	.313/.365/.615	.326	.310	0.6	1B 4	2.3
2011	*KCA*	*MLB*	*21*	*363*	*45*	*19*	*2*	*11*	*46*	*32*	*66*	*2*	*1*	*.270/.333/.448*	*.273*	*.300*	*0.0*	*1B -9*	*-0.2*

As the third overall pick in the 2008 draft and one of the best high-school hitters in years, Hosmer was one of the biggest disappointments in all of 2009 Prospectland. Post-season LASIK surgery seemed like a lame excuse at the time, but it might have turned out to be—literally—just what the doctor ordered. Hosmer hit for a high average all year, and once he escaped the cavernous park at Wilmington, his power showed up in the Texas League. Once again, he's looking like a potential stud, and he could be ready as soon as 2012. He might be a good-enough athlete to give left field a shot, but even if he can't cut it there, moving Billy Butler to designated hitter to make room for Hosmer's bat wouldn't be the worst thing in the world.

Kila Ka'aihue 1B

Born: **3/29/1984** Age: **27**
Bats: L Throws: R Height: **6' 3"** Weight: **233**
Breakout: **9%** Improve: **45%** Collapse: **5%**
Attrition: **23%** MLB: **80%**

Comparables:
Joey Votto, Josh Whitesell, Adrian Gonzalez (71)

YEAR	TEAM	LVL	AGE	PA	R	2B	3B	HR	RBI	BB	SO	SB	CS	AVG/OBP/SLG	TAv	BABIP	BRR	FRAA	WARP
2008	NWA	AA	24	376	64	11	0	26	79	80	41	3	2	.314/.463/.624	.344	.284	-2.8	1B -6	2.8
2008	OMA	AAA	24	139	27	4	0	11	21	24	26	0	0	.316/.439/.640	.366	.325	0.6	1B 2	2.0
2008	KCA	MLB	24	24	4	0	0	1	1	3	2	0	0	.286/.375/.429	.291	.278	0.3	1B 0	0.1
2009	OMA	AAA	25	555	83	27	1	17	57	102	85	0	1	.252/.391/.433	.298	.271	-2.5	1B -6	1.8
2010	OMA	AAA	26	416	67	16	1	24	78	88	69	2	0	.319/.463/.598	.364	.338	0.0	1B 1	5.1
2010	KCA	MLB	26	206	22	6	1	8	25	24	39	0	1	.217/.306/.394	.255	.230	0.3	1B 0	0.1
2011	*KCA*	*MLB*	*27*	*567*	*80*	*21*	*0*	*27*	*73*	*101*	*100*	*1*	*0*	*.260/.392/.482*	*.304*	*.272*	*-0.1*	*1B -16*	*1.3*

The Ghostface Kila got his first real shot at the majors in August, and considering those two months of playing time, it's difficult to tell what kind of Ka'aihue will show up in 2011. He was as bad as a player can get in August, hitting .167/.239/.274, but in September, things turned around completely: the Hawaiian mashed to the tune of a .274/.361/.548 line with six homers. Ka'aihue is clearly done with Triple-A after destroying the level for the second time in three years, so the Royals need to play him in the majors to see if he can establish himself as something more than a Quadruple-A threat. His exceptional plate patience has carried over into his big-league career, but given how few doubles he hits, his productivity is going to be based largely on how often he clears the fences.

Jason Kendall C

Born: **6/26/1974** Age: **37**
Bats: R Throws: R Height: **6' 0"** Weight: **180**
Breakout: **0%** Improve: **20%** Collapse: **15%**
Attrition: **33%** MLB: **78%**

Comparables:
Paul Lo Duca, Johnny Temple, Dick Groat (68)

YEAR	TEAM	LVL	AGE	PA	R	2B	3B	HR	RBI	BB	SO	SB	CS	AVG/OBP/SLG	TAv	BABIP	BRR	FRAA	WARP
2008	MIL	MLB	34	587	46	30	2	2	49	50	45	8	3	.246/.324/.324	.239	.262	0.0	C 6	1.8
2009	MIL	MLB	35	526	47	19	2	2	43	46	58	7	2	.241/.327/.305	.237	.266	-1.6	C 0	0.8
2010	KCA	MLB	36	490	39	18	0	0	37	37	45	12	7	.256/.314/.297	.222	.276	-0.8	C -1	0.0
2011	*KCA*	*MLB*	*37*	*549*	*54*	*22*	*0*	*2*	*36*	*47*	*53*	*9*	*4*	*.238/.313/.297*	*.225*	*.256*	*-0.5*	*C 1*	*0.3*

The Royals may know how to target players to draft and develop, but they're lost when it comes to the majors. Kendall is the finest example of their myopia. Prior to signing him, the Royals let two catchers (John Buck and Miguel Olivo) go and ignored their capable reserve receiver, Brayan Pena, for the more expensive, less productive veteran. The new starter had only seven days off in the first four months of the season and played through a rotator cuff injury that eventually required surgery. Manager Ned Yost is hopeful that his catcher will be ready by Opening Day, but how will Yost be able to tell whether Kendall is still hurting, or just continuing to be Jason Kendall?

David Lough **OF**

Born: **1/20/1986** Age: **25**
Bats: **L** Throws: **L** Height: **5' 11"** Weight: **180**
Breakout: **4%** Improve: **27%** Collapse: **7%**
Attrition: **30%** MLB: **52%**

Comparables:
Robert Andino, Shin-Soo Choo, Danny Richar (69)

YEAR	TEAM	LVL	AGE	PA	R	2B	3B	HR	RBI	BB	SO	SB	CS	AVG/OBP/SLG	TAv	BABIP	BRR	FRAA	WARP
2008	BUR	A	22	543	76	21	11	16	62	35	70	12	11	.268/.324/.455	.276	.279	-1.2	CF 2, LF 1	2.4
2009	WIL	A+	23	250	28	15	2	5	30	12	34	6	4	.320/.360/.473	.291	.344	1.8	RF 0, LF 1	1.4
2009	NWA	AA	23	253	41	13	2	9	31	12	30	13	4	.331/.368/.517	.329	.347	-2.5	LF -2, CF -2	2.1
2010	OMA	AAA	24	532	65	15	12	11	58	40	72	14	5	.280/.346/.437	.271	.295	0.1	LF 3, CF -1	2.3
2011	*KCA*	*MLB*	*25*	*534*	*60*	*21*	*4*	*13*	*61*	*30*	*90*	*10*	*4*	*.255/.299/.401*	*.245*	*.278*	*-0.3*	*LF -1, CF -4*	*-0.3*

Lough failed to build on his 2009 breakout season, shifting the focus from all of the things he can do to all of the abilities he lacks. He's a contact hitter with gap power and above-average speed, but does nothing at an impact level. He probably won't hit like an everyday corner outfielder, and he's the kind of center fielder who can handle the position in a pinch but falls short in a full-time gig. Lough could carve out a nice career as a fourth outfielder and occasional starter, but—strange as this sounds—he might not be good enough for the Royals teams of the future.

Mitch Maier **CF**

Born: **6/30/1982** Age: **29**
Bats: **L** Throws: **R** Height: **6' 2"** Weight: **210**
Breakout: **0%** Improve: **37%** Collapse: **6%**
Attrition: **15%** MLB: **80%**

Comparables:
Joe Pepitone, Bernie Williams, Al Cowens (76)

YEAR	TEAM	LVL	AGE	PA	R	2B	3B	HR	RBI	BB	SO	SB	CS	AVG/OBP/SLG	TAv	BABIP	BRR	FRAA	WARP
2008	OMA	AAA	26	383	57	24	1	9	41	29	42	12	3	.316/.363/.470	.290	.331	0.2	CF 17	4.0
2008	KCA	MLB	26	97	9	1	1	0	9	2	18	0	2	.286/.309/.319	.217	.347	-0.2	CF 2, RF 0	-0.1
2009	OMA	AAA	27	60	8	3	0	2	10	8	8	1	1	.314/.400/.490	.305	.333	-0.4	CF 2, RF 1	0.6
2009	KCA	MLB	27	397	42	15	3	3	31	43	76	9	2	.243/.328/.331	.241	.295	-0.3	CF 3, RF 4	0.8
2010	KCA	MLB	28	421	41	15	6	5	39	41	68	3	2	.263/.330/.375	.270	.303	-4.5	CF 5, RF -2	1.0
2011	*KCA*	*MLB*	*29*	*501*	*56*	*21*	*2*	*8*	*48*	*47*	*84*	*8*	*3*	*.260/.328/.374*	*.249*	*.296*	*-0.3*	*CF 4, RF 0*	*1.0*

Maier is a quality defender in center field, but his performance at the plate can't keep pace with his glove work. Replacement-level hitting mixed with above-average defense is not a recipe for success; it sounds more like the skill set of a fifth outfielder. But Maier logged even more plate appearances in 2010 than he had the year prior, when he was shown to be stretched in an everyday role. He has an odd career split, with more power against his fellow lefties than right-handers, but neither line is capable of exciting anyone besides the opposing pitcher. Maier will be 29 in late June, so he isn't going to get any better; the team's rather desperate signings of Jeff Francoeur and Melky Cabrera was a tacit acknowledgment of this reality.

Lucas May **C**

Born: **10/24/1984** Age: **26**
Bats: **R** Throws: **R** Height: **5' 11"** Weight: **195**
Breakout: **7%** Improve: **16%** Collapse: **6%**
Attrition: **22%** MLB: **43%**

Comparables:
Jeff Mathis, Nick Hundley, Chris Pettit (76)

YEAR	TEAM	LVL	AGE	PA	R	2B	3B	HR	RBI	BB	SO	SB	CS	AVG/OBP/SLG	TAv	BABIP	BRR	FRAA	WARP
2008	JAX	AA	23	441	54	27	1	13	54	32	112	6	1	.230/.293/.403	.251	.278	0.4	C 0	1.3
2009	CHT	AA	24	277	32	18	1	6	32	31	58	3	1	.306/.390/.468	.295	.373	0.5	C 1	2.2
2010	ABQ	AAA	25	285	47	13	3	11	45	22	60	4	2	.296/.352/.496	.275	.346	0.0	C -1	1.6
2010	OMA	AAA	25	105	14	7	0	5	13	12	19	0	0	.275/.362/.516	.328	.294	0.0	C 0	1.2
2010	KCA	MLB	25	39	3	1	0	0	6	0	10	0	1	.189/.205/.216	.152	.250	0.2	C 0	-0.2
2011	*KCA*	*MLB*	*26*	*383*	*44*	*18*	*1*	*11*	*44*	*30*	*93*	*2*	*1*	*.246/.309/.404*	*.250*	*.298*	*-0.1*	*C -1*	*1.0*

For now, May might be the best option to displace Jason Kendall at catcher, but your cat would be better than Kendall, and yes, we're talking about the cross-eyed one with the extra toes. As a former shortstop and outfielder, May is an excellent athlete for a backstop and boasts good raw power for the position, but it comes with a loopy swing, plenty of strikeouts, very rough receiving skills, and a slow release that holds back an otherwise strong arm. Still, Kendall presents a very low bar, hence May—or Mr. Poozums. Sure, Mr. Poozums can't throw, but he has a very small strike zone and wants to be paid in fish. On the other hand, given declining ocean stocks, nowadays it's more expensive to pay a player in tuna than it is in cash.

Mike Moustakas **3B**

Born: **9/11/1988** Age: **22**
Bats: **L** Throws: **R** Height: **5' 11"** Weight: **230**
Breakout: **4%** Improve: **27%** Collapse: **1%**
Attrition: **18%** MLB: **41%**

Comparables:
Pablo Sandoval, Orlando Cepeda, Billy Butler (58)

YEAR	TEAM	LVL	AGE	PA	R	2B	3B	HR	RBI	BB	SO	SB	CS	AVG/OBP/SLG	TAv	BABIP	BRR	FRAA	WARP
2008	BUR	A	19	549	77	25	3	22	71	43	86	8	4	.272/.337/.468	.293	.289	-0.2	3B 9, SS 4	4.9
2009	WIL	A+	20	530	66	32	2	16	86	32	90	10	6	.250/.296/.421	.272	.274	1.9	3B 0	2.4
2010	NWA	AA	21	298	58	25	0	21	76	26	42	0	1	.347/.413/.687	.365	.342	-0.6	3B 7	4.5
2010	OMA	AAA	21	236	36	16	0	15	48	8	25	2	0	.293/.314/.564	.290	.271	-0.8	3B 1	1.6
2011	*KCA*	*MLB*	*22*	*548*	*67*	*30*	*0*	*25*	*79*	*29*	*99*	*2*	*1*	*.261/.300/.470*	*.263*	*.273*	*-0.1*	*3B 3, SS 1*	*2.1*

Always possessed of one of the fastest bats in the minors, Moustakas finally began to exhibit his plus-plus power consistently in 2010. Despite missing the first part of the season with an oblique strain and playing in only 118 games, he tied for the minor-league lead with 36 home runs. That's special enough, but Moustakas can hit more than homers—he's the rare batter who is more of a hitter with power than a power hitter, as evidenced by a mere 67 strikeouts. Other than a cannon arm, his bat is his ticket to the majors; with 230 pounds on a sub-six-foot frame, he's a wide-bodied, slow-footed defender, but that's not such a big deal for a future cleanup hitter.

Wil Myers C

Born: **12/10/1990** Age: **20**
Bats: **R** Throws: **R** Height: **6' 3"** Weight: **190**
Breakout: **0%** Improve: **2%** Collapse: **1%**
Attrition: **1%** MLB: **5%**

Comparables:
Fernando Martinez, Tony Conigliaro, Al Kaline (66)

YEAR	TEAM	LVL	AGE	PA	R	2B	3B	HR	RBI	BB	SO	SB	CS	AVG/OBP/SLG	TAv	BABIP	BRR	FRAA	WARP
2009	IDA	Rk	18	80	18	7	1	4	14	9	15	2	0	.426/.488/.735	.408	.490	-0.2	C 1	1.5
2010	BUR	A	19	294	42	19	1	10	45	48	55	10	3	.289/.408/.500	.318	.335	-2.7	C 0	2.4
2010	WIL	A+	19	247	28	18	2	4	38	37	39	2	3	.346/.453/.512	.353	.411	-0.3	C 0	2.9
2011	*KCA*	*MLB*	*20*	*313*	*38*	*16*	*1*	*9*	*35*	*37*	*70*	*2*	*1*	*.254/.345/.416*	*.270*	*.306*	*-0.1*	*C 0*	*1.1*

A 2009 third-round pick who signed for a $2 million bonus, Myers made his full-season debut with unmitigated success, at least at the plate if not behind it. He showcased the ability to hit for average with developing power and arguably the best approach in the system, all at the tender age of 19. The question now is where he will play. Myers has all the tools to succeed as a catcher, but he's a downright poor receiver who was charged with 20 passed balls in 75 games behind the plate, and the number would have been higher had not some kind official scorers taken pity on him. Myers' bat is so far ahead of his glove that a move to right field could be in order, but his offensive skill set would make him a star anywhere.

Brayan Pena C

Born: **1/7/1982** Age: **29**
Bats: **S** Throws: **R** Height: **5' 11"** Weight: **220**
Breakout: **1%** Improve: **21%** Collapse: **7%**
Attrition: **9%** MLB: **54%**

Comparables:
Edwin Bellorin, Humberto Quintero, Shane Costa (74)

YEAR	TEAM	LVL	AGE	PA	R	2B	3B	HR	RBI	BB	SO	SB	CS	AVG/OBP/SLG	TAv	BABIP	BRR	FRAA	WARP
2008	OMA	AAA	26	266	33	17	1	6	31	26	17	7	3	.303/.372/.462	.293	.302	-1.5	C -1, 3B -1	1.6
2008	ATL	MLB	26	14	3	1	0	0	0	1	2	0	0	.308/.357/.385	.262	.364	-0.1	—	0.1
2009	OMA	AAA	27	98	11	6	1	4	18	4	9	2	1	.307/.347/.534	.284	.295	-0.4	LF -1, C 0	0.3
2009	KCA	MLB	27	183	17	10	0	6	18	12	18	0	0	.273/.312/.442	.258	.265	0.3	C 0	0.5
2010	KCA	MLB	28	174	11	10	0	1	19	12	27	2	0	.253/.305/.335	.230	.293	-0.4	C 1	0.2
2011	*KCA*	*MLB*	*29*	*304*	*35*	*16*	*0*	*6*	*33*	*21*	*36*	*3*	*2*	*.268/.320/.396*	*.252*	*.282*	*-0.2*	*C -1, LF 0*	*0.6*

Pena has an unmerited reputation as a poor defensive catcher. He has thrown out 31 percent of opposing baserunners in his career, including 29 percent in 2010, and while he has had trouble blocking wild pitches, it doesn't make him unplayable. He's at least as good a defensive option behind the plate as Jason Kendall, who was signed to take the majority of playing time there over Pena. If you had to put money on one of the two putting together an average offensive campaign in 2011, well, let's just say that the Royals' chances of being world champions this year are better than Kendall's chances of outhitting Pena.

Derrick Robinson OF

Born: **9/28/1987** Age: **23**
Bats: **S** Throws: **L** Height: **5' 11"** Weight: **180**
Breakout: **4%** Improve: **12%** Collapse: **1%**
Attrition: **12%** MLB: **25%**

Comparables:
Richie Ashburn, Luis Hernandez, Gerardo Parra (72)

YEAR	TEAM	LVL	AGE	PA	R	2B	3B	HR	RBI	BB	SO	SB	CS	AVG/OBP/SLG	TAv	BABIP	BRR	FRAA	WARP
2008	WIL	A+	20	556	69	22	8	0	34	51	97	62	17	.245/.315/.322	.239	.300	8.3	CF 4	1.4
2009	WIL	A+	21	571	72	19	5	5	47	35	90	69	23	.239/.285/.324	.224	.274	2.1	CF 7	0.4
2010	NWA	AA	22	570	74	26	8	2	48	45	86	50	17	.286/.345/.380	.250	.333	-1.1	CF 9, LF 0	1.8
2011	*KCA*	*MLB*	*23*	*589*	*55*	*22*	*3*	*4*	*47*	*34*	*114*	*47*	*13*	*.232/.273/.307*	*.207*	*.278*	*0.5*	*CF -7, LF 0*	*-2.1*

Every system has that Robinson-esque player, the center fielder with top-of-the-line speed whom you hope can learn how to play baseball. In 2010, Robinson began to do just that, hitting more than 40 points above his career average in his first exposure to Double-A pitching, thanks in part to a career-low strikeout rate. Robinson showed plenty of progress, but he still needs to make more; with a substandard walk rate, he doesn't fit at the top of the order, and his power is nonexistent. Though he had a good season, all Robinson really did was prove that he's ready for Triple-A.

PITCHERS

Brian Bannister

Born: **2/28/1981** Age: **30**
Bats: R Throws: R Height: **6' 2"** Weight: **202**
Breakout: **11%** Improve: **37%** Collapse: **22%**
Attrition: **7%** MLB: **97%**

Comparables:
Matt Morris, Mark Clark, Mark Redman (78)

YEAR	TEAM	LVL	AGE	W	L	SV	G	GS	IP	H	HR	BB	SO	EqBB9	EqSO9	GB%	BABIP	WHIP	ERA	FRA	WARP
2008	KCA	MLB	27	9	16	0	32	33	182^{2}	215	29	58	113	2.9	5.6	38%	.309	1.53	5.76	6.11	-0.4
2009	KCA	MLB	28	7	12	0	26	28	154	161	15	50	98	2.9	5.7	52%	.291	1.40	4.73	5.69	0.4
2010	KCA	MLB	29	7	12	0	24	23	127^{2}	158	23	50	77	3.5	5.4	44%	.316	1.65	6.34	6.35	-1.0
2011	*KCA*	*MLB*	*30*	*9*	*10*	*0*	*27*	*27*	*149*	*171*	*20*	*47*	*86*	*2.8*	*5.2*	*44%*	*.307*	*1.46*	*4.92*	*5.35*	*1.4*

Bannister is a favorite of the stat-head crowd, since he understands advanced statistical concepts and applies them in order to maximize his success on the mound. Unfortunately, that knowledge didn't help in 2010. He again proved susceptible to the long ball, which ruined his overall performance. Bannister's struggles occur when he allows baserunners: with men on from 2008 through 2010, opposing batters have hit .314/.357/.520, against .267/.334/.407 with the bases empty. That second line is a little worse than the league average, but the first is one reason why Bannister has failed to strand a league-average percentage of baserunners since 2007. The team's weak defense has damaged Bannister because of his dependence on getting outs on balls in play, and he'll need help from his defense wherever he goes. This season, his destination will be Japan, as Bannister's formidable intellect determined that he stood to gain both on the field and in the bank from a stint with the Yomiuri Giants.

Jesse Chavez

Born: **8/21/1983** Age: **27**
Bats: R Throws: R Height: **6' 2"** Weight: **175**
Breakout: **2%** Improve: **4%** Collapse: **0%**
Attrition: **0%** MLB: **8%**

Comparables:
Mauro Zarate, Oscar Villarreal, Jay Ritchie (79)

YEAR	TEAM	LVL	AGE	W	L	SV	G	GS	IP	H	HR	BB	SO	EqBB9	EqSO9	GB%	BABIP	WHIP	ERA	FRA	WARP
2008	IND	AAA	24	2	6	14	51	0	68^{2}	58	8	22	70	2.9	9.2	43%	.272	1.17	3.80	5.17	1.0
2008	PIT	MLB	24	0	1	0	15	0	15	20	2	9	16	5.4	9.6	47%	.383	1.93	6.60	6.18	-0.2
2009	PIT	MLB	25	1	4	0	73	0	67^{1}	69	11	22	47	2.9	6.3	39%	.283	1.37	4.14	4.75	0.1
2010	ATL	MLB	26	3	2	0	28	0	36^{2}	40	6	12	29	2.9	7.1	31%	.298	1.45	5.89	5.52	-0.3
2010	KCA	MLB	26	2	3	0	23	0	26	29	5	11	16	3.8	5.5	41%	.279	1.54	5.88	7.23	-0.7
2011	*KCA*	*MLB*	*27*	*3*	*1*	*2*	*63*	*0*	*73*	*81*	*10*	*27*	*54*	*3.3*	*6.6*	*42%*	*.310*	*1.46*	*4.81*	*5.23*	*-0.4*

One of the more baffling things Bobby Cox did in his final year as manager was go to Chavez in relief 28 times before the trade deadline. Chavez was much worse than his ERA in 2009, when he posted a replacement-level WXRL over a full season's worth of innings. He was Atlanta's worst reliever, partly a by-product of the Braves' strong pen, partly a reflection of the fact that Chavez is not a good pitcher. He has a mid-90s fastball that nets a below-average rate of whiffs, and neither his change nor slider is good enough to compensate for that lack of swings and misses. The deal that brought Chavez as part of the return for Rick Ankiel and Kyle Farnsworth was nevertheless worthwhile, as it netted prospect Tim Collins for a couple of nonentities; having to use Chavez was merely one additional cost, the spoonful of medicine that helped the sugar go down.

Bruce Chen

Born: **6/19/1977** Age: **34**
Bats: L Throws: L Height: **6' 2"** Weight: **210**
Breakout: **18%** Improve: **39%** Collapse: **26%**
Attrition: **13%** MLB: **91%**

Comparables:
Hank Aguirre, Orlando Hernandez, Jerry Koosman (75)

YEAR	TEAM	LVL	AGE	W	L	SV	G	GS	IP	H	HR	BB	SO	EqBB9	EqSO9	GB%	BABIP	WHIP	ERA	FRA	WARP
2009	OMA	AAA	32	4	2	0	14	13	82	57	8	23	69	2.5	7.6	37%	.224	1.02	3.40	4.62	0.9
2009	KCA	MLB	32	1	6	0	17	9	62^{1}	74	12	25	45	3.6	6.5	32%	.321	1.65	5.78	5.78	0.1
2010	OMA	AAA	33	0	1	0	3	4	20^{2}	13	0	5	20	2.2	8.7	45%	.255	0.87	1.31	2.32	0.8
2010	KCA	MLB	33	12	7	1	33	25	140^{1}	136	17	57	98	3.7	6.3	35%	.275	1.40	4.17	3.0	0.4
2011	*KCA*	*MLB*	*34*	*6*	*6*	*0*	*23*	*17*	*107^{2}*	*112*	*15*	*39*	*77*	*3.3*	*6.5*	*40%*	*.296*	*1.41*	*4.55*	*4.94*	*1.3*

Chen somehow posted a 4.17 ERA despite pitching in front of one of the most porous defenses in the land, and he did so with peripherals that indicate that his ERA should have been closer to five. Chen throws a multitude of pitches, but none of them is better than average, and most of them are fringe-average and unable to induce whiffs. The key to his season was not allowing home runs at his normal rate, but this suggests nothing but a transient flirtation with effectiveness: he remains a severe fly-ball pitcher who doesn't consistently induce pop-ups, and in light of his iffy control and inability to miss bats, it's clear that the homers will be back before long. The Royals agreed to fork over $2 million to enjoy the regression ride this season.

Louis Coleman

Born: **4/4/1986** Age: **25**
Bats: R Throws: R Height: **6' 4"** Weight: **195**
Breakout: **8%** Improve: **21%** Collapse: **13%**
Attrition: **20%** MLB: **44%**

Comparables:
Ian Kennedy, Sergio Romo, Clay Zavada (76)

YEAR	TEAM	LVL	AGE	W	L	SV	G	GS	IP	H	HR	BB	SO	EqBB9	EqSO9	GB%	BABIP	WHIP	ERA	FRA	WARP
2010	NWA	AA	24	2	1	6	21	1	51^{2}	31	5	14	55	2.4	9.6	35%	.213	0.91	2.09	3.17	0.6
2010	OMA	AAA	24	5	1	1	21	0	40^{1}	31	2	11	48	2.5	10.7	36%	.296	1.17	1.79	1.82	1.7
2011	*KCA*	*MLB*	*25*	*1*	*1*	*0*	*27*	*0*	*54^{2}*	*47*	*5*	*18*	*53*	*3.0*	*8.8*	*42%*	*.292*	*1.20*	*3.27*	*3.56*	*0.8*

Coleman was seen as a cost-conscious senior sign when he was nabbed in the fifth round of the 2009 draft, but he has already reached Triple-A with a 2.06 career minor-league ERA and looks nearly major-league ready. With excellent control of a 91-95 mph fastball and a plus slider, Coleman's overall numbers are excellent, but his splits can be a cause for concern. A low three-quarters arm slot makes him deadly against righties, who hit just .146 against him, but left-handers get a much longer look at the ball and can more easily find their timing. To have a career, Coleman just needs to be effective enough against southpaws to avoid ROOGY status (if there is such a thing), and so far he has succeeded.

Tim Collins

Born: **8/29/1989** Age: **21**
Bats: **L** Throws: **L** Height: **5' 7"** Weight: **155**
Breakout: **7%** Improve: **15%** Collapse: **5%**
Attrition: **0%** MLB: **23%**

Comparables:
Byung-Hyun Kim, Pedro Martinez, Francisco Rodriguez (53)

YEAR	TEAM	LVL	AGE	W	L	SV	G	GS	IP	H	HR	BB	SO	EqBB9	EqSO9	GB%	BABIP	WHIP	ERA	FRA	WARP
2008	LNS	A	18	4	2	14	40	0	69^{1}	36	3	32	99	4.2	12.9	53%	.246	1.01	1.56	2.26	1.9
2009	DUN	A+	19	7	4	3	40	0	64^{2}	47	2	28	99	3.9	13.8	44%	.326	1.21	2.09	2.26	1.9
2010	NHP	AA	20	1	0	9	35	0	43	27	4	16	73	3.3	15.3	38%	.295	1.00	2.51	2.12	1.1
2010	OMA	AAA	20	2	1	4	15	0	20^{1}	9	0	8	21	3.5	9.3	36%	.180	0.84	1.33	3.0	0.4
2011	*KCA*	*MLB*	*21*	*2*	*1*	*2*	*37*	*0*	*53*	*42*	*5*	*28*	*68*	*4.6*	*11.4*	*43%*	*.304*	*1.30*	*3.29*	*3.57*	*0.8*

Nobody was going to draft Collins out of high school, and he received no college offers, but J. P. Ricciardi signed him out of a tryout camp in his hometown. The southpaw put up silly numbers at the lower levels, but few could believe that a five-foot-five (and that might be kind) pitcher would ever be a match for big-league hitters. The fact that he switched teams twice in 2010 only highlights his appeal; now that he's proven himself at every level, he stands on the precipice of the majors. His ultraquick arm action seems like the creation of special effects or camera tricks, and his ability to sit in the low 90s and touch 94 despite utilizing such short levers amazes all who see him in person. Collins also has a solid curve, a plus change, and a natural delivery that hides the ball. He's no longer a novelty act, and he's about to get some important late-inning outs for the Royals.

Aaron Crow

Born: **11/11/1986** Age: **24**
Bats: **R** Throws: **R** Height: **6' 3"** Weight: **190**
Breakout: **20%** Improve: **47%** Collapse: **8%**
Attrition: **11%** MLB: **72%**

Comparables:
Arnie Portocarrero, Bill Parsons, Junichi Tazawa (56)

YEAR	TEAM	LVL	AGE	W	L	SV	G	GS	IP	H	HR	BB	SO	EqBB9	EqSO9	GB%	BABIP	WHIP	ERA	FRA	WARP
2010	WIL	A+	23	2	3	0	7	7	44	51	6	6	53	1.2	10.8	54%	.378	1.32	5.93	6.31	-0.3
2010	NWA	AA	23	7	7	0	22	26	119^{1}	130	13	59	90	4.4	6.8	64%	.315	1.63	5.58	6.76	-1.0
2011	*KCA*	*MLB*	*24*	*9*	*12*	*0*	*28*	*28*	160^{1}	*184*	*23*	*72*	*113*	*4.1*	*6.3*	*50%*	*.319*	*1.59*	*5.47*	*5.95*	*0.5*

No organization can have a perfect season down on the farm, and Crow represented one of Kansas City's few low notes in 2010. After choosing not to sign with the Nationals out of the 2008 draft, Crow got $3 million from the Royals the following year, but the layoff left considerable rust. Scouts see plenty of stuff in his arm, which still reaches the low to mid-90s with a sinking fastball, and his slider still features plenty of break, but an inability to throw strikes as he fought with his mechanics turned Crow into a one-pitch guy at times last year, with predictable results. He shouldn't be written off, but a move to the bullpen could be in order.

Kyle Davies

Born: **9/9/1983** Age: **27**
Bats: **R** Throws: **R** Height: **6' 2"** Weight: **205**
Breakout: **19%** Improve: **50%** Collapse: **19%**
Attrition: **13%** MLB: **99%**

Comparables:
Billy Hoeft, Ben McDonald, Brett Tomko (80)

YEAR	TEAM	LVL	AGE	W	L	SV	G	GS	IP	H	HR	BB	SO	EqBB9	EqSO9	GB%	BABIP	WHIP	ERA	FRA	WARP
2008	OMA	AAA	24	6	2	0	11	11	57^{2}	47	4	21	38	3.3	5.9	49%	.254	1.20	2.03	4.75	0.8
2008	KCA	MLB	24	9	7	0	21	21	113	121	10	43	71	3.4	5.7	40%	.308	1.47	4.06	4.52	1.7
2009	OMA	AAA	25	4	2	0	8	9	46^{1}	47	3	14	44	2.7	8.5	45%	.328	1.32	2.14	3.69	0.9
2009	KCA	MLB	25	8	9	0	22	27	123	122	18	66	86	4.8	6.3	44%	.286	1.56	5.27	5.70	0.4
2010	KCA	MLB	26	8	12	0	32	35	183^{2}	206	20	80	126	3.9	6.2	41%	.316	1.57	5.34	5.46	0.2
2011	*KCA*	*MLB*	*27*	*9*	*11*	*0*	*28*	*28*	153^{2}	*166*	*18*	*66*	*105*	*3.9*	*6.2*	*43%*	*.311*	*1.51*	*4.85*	*5.27*	*1.5*

Davies shaved almost a full point off his walk rate, but that improvement still left him much worse than average in the free-pass department. He also struck out relatively few hitters, as his changeup was the lone offering that gave them any trouble. Like Brian Bannister, Davies suffered from the Royals' propensity for letting baserunners score; he stranded just 67 percent of the men he put on base, no small handicap considering he averaged 1.6 of them per inning. With a full season of Betemit at third, Alex Gordon in left, chubby Melky Cabrera in center, and David DeJesus in Oakland, Kansas City's defense isn't going to help Davies any more in 2011 than it did in 2010.

Danny Duffy

Born: **12/21/1988** Age: **22**
Bats: **L** Throws: **L** Height: **6' 3"** Weight: **195**
Breakout: **5%** Improve: **6%** Collapse: **1%**
Attrition: **5%** MLB: **10%**

Comparables:
Fabio Castro, Jaime Garcia, Scott Sanderson (79)

YEAR	TEAM	LVL	AGE	W	L	SV	G	GS	IP	H	HR	BB	SO	EqBB9	EqSO9	GB%	BABIP	WHIP	ERA	FRA	WARP
2008	BUR	A	19	8	4	0	17	18	81^{2}	56	4	25	102	2.8	11.2	37%	.274	1.04	2.09	2.51	3.1
2009	WIL	A+	20	9	4	0	25	29	132^{2}	111	6	43	132	2.9	9.0	46%	.294	1.17	2.85	2.79	4.2
2010	NWA	AA	21	6	2	0	9	10	50^{1}	50	3	13	56	2.3	10.0	47%	.353	1.27	2.50	2.58	2.1
2011	*KCA*	*MLB*	*22*	*6*	*5*	*0*	*15*	*15*	*75^{2}*	*76*	*8*	*35*	*68*	*4.1*	*8.1*	*42%*	*.313*	*1.46*	*4.41*	*4.79*	*1.3*

Beginning in spring training, when he retired to "reassess his priorities," Duffy had a strange year. When he returned to the game in June after determining that baseball was still ranked somewhere on his to-do list, he showed off the best stuff of his young career, pitching well as high as Double-A. With a fastball that gets into the mid-90s to go with a good changeup, and a good-enough breaking ball, Duffy has the ability to be a big-league starter. Now he has to prove that his stuff can hold up over the course of a full workload; in his three full years as a pro, he's logged just over 270 innings. We have plenty to learn about both his stuff and his commitment, but the pieces of an excellent player are there.

Chris Dwyer

Born: **4/10/1988** Age: **23**
Bats: **R** Throws: **L** Height: **6' 3"** Weight: **210**
Breakout: **2%** Improve: **6%** Collapse: **4%**
Attrition: **8%** MLB: **13%**

Comparables:
Antonio Bastardo, Fernando Hernandez Jr., Jaime Garcia (82)

YEAR	TEAM	LVL	AGE	W	L	SV	G	GS	IP	H	HR	BB	SO	EqBB9	EqSO9	GB%	BABIP	WHIP	ERA	FRA	WARP
2010	WIL	A+	22	6	3	0	15	17	84^{1}	79	3	33	93	3.5	9.9	47%	.328	1.35	2.77	3.49	2.0
2011	*KCA*	*MLB*	*23*	*4*	*4*	*0*	*11*	*11*	*53*	*55*	*6*	*29*	*47*	*4.8*	*7.8*	*44%*	*.316*	*1.56*	*4.82*	*5.24*	*0.7*

Yet another success story from the Royals' amateur draft spending spree, Dwyer was awarded $1.45 million as a fourth-round pick in 2009, solely on the strength of his being a southpaw with impressive velocity. He spent his full-season debut evolving from a thrower into a pitcher by adding an impressive power curveball to his arsenal. In a system loaded with elite portsiders, Dwyer's arm strength ranks with any of them, but he falls well behind them in terms of polish, as the big radar-gun readings only come with considerable effort and occasional control issues. Dwyer needs more time in the oven than do the other morsels in the Double-A Northwest Arkansas rotation last year, but the result should be just as tasty.

Zack Greinke

Born: **10/21/1983** Age: **27**
Bats: **R** Throws: **R** Height: **6' 2"** Weight: **200**
Breakout: **12%** Improve: **41%** Collapse: **30%**
Attrition: **5%** MLB: **97%**

Comparables:
Bert Blyleven, Kevin Millwood, Steve Carlton (69)

YEAR	TEAM	LVL	AGE	W	L	SV	G	GS	IP	H	HR	BB	SO	EqBB9	EqSO9	GB%	BABIP	WHIP	ERA	FRA	WARP
2008	KCA	MLB	24	13	10	0	32	33	202^{1}	202	21	56	183	2.5	8.1	43%	.308	1.29	3.47	3.69	4.7
2009	KCA	MLB	25	16	8	0	33	34	229^{1}	195	11	51	242	2.0	9.5	41%	.303	1.09	2.12	3.07	7.40
2010	KCA	MLB	26	10	14	0	33	35	220	219	18	55	181	2.3	7.4	47%	.306	1.28	4.17	4.67	1.8
2011	*MIL*	*MLB*	*27*	*11*	*7*	*0*	*27*	*27*	*179*	*173*	*17*	*48*	*166*	*2.4*	*8.3*	*44%*	*.310*	*1.23*	*3.52*	*3.83*	*4.6*

If you weren't yet convinced that ERA is a poor indicator of pitcher success, file this into evidence: Zack Greinke and Bruce Chen finished with identical ERAs last season. Greinke struck out more hitters, walked far fewer, and didn't give up many home runs. His 2010 was disappointing when measured against his Cy Young–winning 2009 campaign, but that shouldn't have come as a complete surprise, as the baseball gods had allowed him a year in which he would be impervious to the ill effects of the Kansas City defense. He stranded just 65 percent of his baserunners last year, the result of a recipe that called for just a pinch of Greinke with eight cups of Royal Blue. The more Greinke-centric difference came in the strikeout department: every pitch in his arsenal missed bats in 2009, but his cutter, two-seamer, and changeup all induced a below-average rate of whiffs in 2010, and his slider lost some effectiveness thanks to poorer command. He was in the strike zone more often, but while his control was intact, his command took a hit. Greinke is one of the best pitchers in the game even without that exceptional command, so don't be too disappointed if he can't replicate his Greg Maddux impression. Moving to Milwaukee—one of the few teams with even poorer defensive numbers than the Royals—won't help Greinke, but the switch to the senior circuit and the light-hitting NL Central will make his job easier.

Luke Hochevar

Born: **9/15/1983** Age: **27**
Bats: **R** Throws: **R** Height: **6' 5"** Weight: **205**
Breakout: **17%** Improve: **43%** Collapse: **16%**
Attrition: **25%** MLB: **76%**

Comparables:
Juan Gutierrez, Scott Olsen, Bob Rush (77)

YEAR	TEAM	LVL	AGE	W	L	SV	G	GS	IP	H	HR	BB	SO	EqBB9	EqSO9	GB%	BABIP	WHIP	ERA	FRA	WARP
2008	KCA	MLB	24	6	12	0	22	25	129	143	12	47	72	3.3	5.0	52%	.305	1.51	5.51	5.91	0.0
2009	OMA	AAA	25	5	1	0	8	8	48	41	2	12	36	2.3	6.8	63%	.285	1.10	1.50	3.26	1.3
2009	KCA	MLB	25	7	13	0	25	27	143	167	23	46	106	2.9	6.7	48%	.321	1.55	6.55	6.27	-0.3
2010	KCA	MLB	26	6	6	0	18	18	103	110	9	37	76	3.2	6.6	46%	.312	1.47	4.81	5.29	0.3
2011	*KCA*	*MLB*	*27*	*8*	*8*	*0*	*22*	*22*	*126*	*139*	*15*	*42*	*87*	*3.0*	*6.2*	*48%*	*.313*	*1.43*	*4.82*	*5.24*	*1.3*

Outside of allowing fewer long balls, Hochevar was basically the same pitcher he had been in 2009, but this time around, his ERA came closer to reflecting his underlying performance. A right-elbow strain paused his season from mid-June until September, which qualified as a blow to the Royals' rotation, given Hochevar's status as their second-best starter. Outside of designated ace Zack Greinke, he was the lone member of the rotation who could aspire to have an average day, which is why Ned Yost let Hochevar work through his struggles in innings where Trey Hillman might have yanked him. The most positive indicator from Hochevar's 2010 was a spike in velocity to nearly 93 mph—that extra gas may be just what he needs to help keep the ball in the park.

Gregory Holland

Born: **11/20/1985** Age: **25**
Bats: R Throws: R Height: **5' 11"** Weight: **190**
Breakout: **14%** Improve: **30%** Collapse: **27%**
Attrition: **11%** MLB: **63%**

Comparables:
Mike Jackson, Jeff Reardon, Steve Bedrosian (61)

YEAR	TEAM	LVL	AGE	W	L	SV	G	GS	IP	H	HR	BB	SO	EqBB9	EqSO9	GB%	BABIP	WHIP	ERA	FRA	WARP
2008	WIL	A+	22	4	5	4	33	7	86^1	71	4	36	98	3.8	10.2	42%	.299	1.25	3.34	3.84	1.5
2009	NWA	AA	23	3	2	8	29	0	45^1	46	2	19	49	3.8	9.7	48%	.355	1.43	3.18	3.05	0.8
2010	OMA	AAA	24	3	3	3	35	0	54^2	37	3	30	57	4.9	9.4	46%	.248	1.23	3.62	5.20	0.0
2010	KCA	MLB	24	0	1	0	15	0	18^2	23	3	8	23	3.9	11.1	36%	.377	1.66	6.75	6.10	-0.2
2011	*KCA*	*MLB*	*25*	*2*	*1*	*1*	*38*	*0*	*60^1*	*60*	*6*	*31*	*54*	*4.7*	*8.1*	*44%*	*.314*	*1.52*	*4.51*	*4.90*	*-0.1*

While he looks like Andre the Giant compared to Tiny Tim Collins, Holland still fits firmly in the little-guy/big-arm category. Under six feet tall and without a wide body, Holland still parks his fastball at 95-96 mph and chases it with a slider in the upper 80s. He doesn't make it look easy and has all the accessories of a max-effort delivery—control issues and injury concerns—but the ability to miss bats at the big-league level made him a uniquely valuable addition to the Royals' bullpen at the end of last season. He has earned another look.

Dusty Hughes

Born: **6/29/1982** Age: **29**
Bats: L Throws: L Height: **5' 10"** Weight: **185**
Breakout: **6%** Improve: **11%** Collapse: **4%**
Attrition: **3%** MLB: **24%**

Comparables:
Tom Candiotti, Bob Ojeda, Tom Sturdivant (82)

YEAR	TEAM	LVL	AGE	W	L	SV	G	GS	IP	H	HR	BB	SO	EqBB9	EqSO9	GB%	BABIP	WHIP	ERA	FRA	WARP
2008	NWA	AA	26	5	2	3	20	4	52^2	47	3	16	43	2.7	7.3	37%	.299	1.20	2.91	2.90	1.8
2008	OMA	AAA	26	3	2	0	12	11	55^1	65	8	25	36	4.1	5.9	36%	.324	1.63	5.04	4.32	1.0
2009	OMA	AAA	27	3	3	1	34	11	87^1	79	6	41	76	4.2	7.8	40%	.297	1.40	3.50	3.20	2.1
2009	KCA	MLB	27	0	2	0	8	1	14	13	2	7	15	4.5	9.6	47%	.306	1.57	4.50	5.68	0.0
2010	KCA	MLB	28	1	3	0	57	0	56^1	59	3	24	34	3.8	5.4	36%	.301	1.56	3.83	4.64	0.1
2011	*KCA*	*MLB*	*29*	*5*	*4*	*0*	*39*	*10*	*90^1*	*98*	*10*	*41*	*60*	*4.1*	*6.0*	*41%*	*.310*	*1.54*	*4.98*	*5.41*	*0.3*

Hughes was one of three relievers whom the Royals employed in low-leverage situations, and with good reason, as he featured a 1.4 strikeout-to-walk ratio and a fastball that saw more entries in the 80s than a retirement home. Hughes is left-handed, which means that he'll have a job in 2011 after posting a 3.83 ERA, even if it was undeserved. You could do worse than Hughes at the back of a bullpen, since he is capable of getting left-handers out. Using numerous inferior relief options throughout the season, the Royals tried to prove that Hughes wasn't so bad; the strategy made for a fairly convincing argument in his favor.

Philip Humber

Born: **12/21/1982** Age: **28**
Bats: R Throws: R Height: **6' 4"** Weight: **210**
Breakout: **16%** Improve: **28%** Collapse: **3%**
Attrition: **17%** MLB: **34%**

Comparables:
Joe Martinez, Jason Vargas, Francisley Bueno (77)

YEAR	TEAM	LVL	AGE	W	L	SV	G	GS	IP	H	HR	BB	SO	EqBB9	EqSO9	GB%	BABIP	WHIP	ERA	FRA	WARP
2008	ROC	AAA	25	10	8	0	31	29	136^1	145	21	49	106	3.2	7.0	38%	.302	1.47	4.49	5.12	1.5
2008	MIN	MLB	25	0	0	0	5	0	11^2	11	4	5	6	3.9	4.6	50%	.206	1.46	4.63	6.87	-0.2
2009	ROC	AAA	26	7	9	0	23	23	119^2	135	15	45	87	3.4	6.5	39%	.313	1.57	5.11	5.73	0.1
2009	MIN	MLB	26	0	0	0	8	0	9	17	1	9	9	9.0	9.0	50%	.516	2.89	8.00	3.10	0.2
2010	OMA	AAA	27	5	6	0	21	22	118^2	131	17	20	80	1.5	6.1	48%	.297	1.32	4.40	5.48	0.4
2010	KCA	MLB	27	2	1	0	8	1	21^2	22	1	7	16	2.9	6.6	44%	.304	1.38	4.15	4.03	0.2
2011	*OAK*	*MLB*	*28*	*7*	*8*	*0*	*29*	*20*	*125^1*	*135*	*18*	*45*	*81*	*3.2*	*5.8*	*43%*	*.299*	*1.44*	*4.81*	*5.23*	*0.5*

Humber's prospect status has dried up, but he spent most of the season as a starter for Omaha anyway. From the glass-half-full perspective, Humber could be another Kyle Davies. On the half-empty side, he may find a home in the bullpen, which is where the Royals primarily used him in 2010. With his pitch selection, the move makes sense—he's heavy on the fastballs and curves, with an occasional changeup tossed in for effect. Leaving Humber to rot in Triple-A once more would be a waste, since he has proven his adequacy (if little more) there four times already. He rode the waiver merry-go-round after being designated for assignment in December, ending up with the White Sox by way of Oakland.

John Lamb

Born: **7/10/1990** Age: **20**
Bats: L Throws: L Height: **6' 3"** Weight: **195**
Breakout: **5%** Improve: **9%** Collapse: **1%**
Attrition: **2%** MLB: **15%**

Comparables:
Mike Witt, Bert Blyleven, Jim Palmer (69)

YEAR	TEAM	LVL	AGE	W	L	SV	G	GS	IP	H	HR	BB	SO	EqBB9	EqSO9	GB%	BABIP	WHIP	ERA	FRA	WARP
2009	BNC	Rk	18	2	2	0	6	7	27^{1}	24	4	9	25	3.0	8.2	47%	.267	1.28	3.95	6.05	1.7
2009	IDA	Rk	18	3	1	0	8	9	41^{1}	33	4	11	46	2.4	10.0	43%	.282	1.09	3.70	4.22	1.57
2010	BUR	A	19	2	3	0	8	10	40	26	2	17	43	3.8	9.7	38%	.253	1.15	1.58	2.77	1.4
2010	WIL	A+	19	6	3	0	13	13	74^{2}	59	1	15	90	1.8	10.8	50%	.315	1.03	1.45	2.02	3.3
2010	NWA	AA	19	2	1	0	9	9	41^{2}	42	3	17	34	3.7	7.3	45%	.310	1.49	4.97	5.62	0.4
2011	*KCA*	*MLB*	*20*	*7*	*8*	*0*	*20*	*20*	*102*	*105*	*12*	*49*	*82*	*4.3*	*7.2*	*43%*	*.306*	*1.50*	*4.81*	*5.23*	*1.2*

A tribute to old-school scouting, Lamb was one of the better high-school pitchers in the country entering his senior year, but a fractured elbow suffered in a car accident prevented him from playing. When other teams wrote him off, the Royals stayed in touch to gauge his signability, subsequently selecting him in the fifth round of the 2008 draft and doling out a six-figure bonus. Two years later, he's arguably the top pitching prospect in a system filled with them. There is no weakness to his game, as his fastball sits at 92-94 mph, his changeup is already a plus big-league offering, his curveball should get there soon, and he can throw all three offerings for strikes at any point in the count. Polished well beyond his 20 years, he may just possibly reach the big leagues before he's able to have a celebratory drink without breaking the law.

Victor Marte

Born: **11/8/1980** Age: **30**
Bats: R Throws: R Height: **6' 2"** Weight: **255**
Breakout: **1%** Improve: **1%** Collapse: **0%**
Attrition: **0%** MLB: **2%**

Comparables:
Jason Jennings, Kevin Barry, Alay Soler (76)

YEAR	TEAM	LVL	AGE	W	L	SV	G	GS	IP	H	HR	BB	SO	EqBB9	EqSO9	GB%	BABIP	WHIP	ERA	FRA	WARP
2009	NWA	AA	28	2	1	4	13	0	22	15	1	5	17	2.0	7.0	41%	.226	0.95	2.05	4.50	0.1
2009	OMA	AAA	28	1	4	4	26	0	42^{1}	35	0	20	36	4.3	7.7	50%	.280	1.32	2.13	3.54	0.8
2009	KCA	MLB	28	0	0	0	8	0	12	13	2	12	7	9.0	5.3	49%	.297	2.08	8.25	8.88	-0.4
2010	OMA	AAA	29	4	1	3	25	0	40^{2}	40	3	15	29	3.4	6.5	43%	.289	1.37	3.32	4.89	0.1
2010	KCA	MLB	29	3	0	0	22	0	27^{2}	38	8	15	19	4.9	6.2	44%	.323	1.99	9.76	9.22	-1.1
2011	*KCA*	*MLB*	*30*	*2*	*1*	*1*	*46*	*0*	*71*	*79*	*9*	*33*	*48*	*4.1*	*6.0*	*45%*	*.310*	*1.55*	*5.04*	*5.48*	*-0.6*

If you will forgive an obviously tautological statement, it is difficult for a reliever to have a good strand rate if his every baserunner scores. Marte learned that lesson the hard way, posting an ERA in the same region of the stratosphere reached by some of the balls launched off the bats of his opponents. This may be hard to believe, but Marte is another Royals reliever who strikes out a below-average number of hitters and hands out too many walks for his own good. At least Ned Yost knew what he was dealing with in Marte's case and used this human piñata stuffed with home-run-flavored candy in low-leverage scenarios.

Gil Meche

Born: **9/8/1978** Age: **32**
Bats: R Throws: R Height: **6' 3"** Weight: **200**
Breakout: **9%** Improve: **44%** Collapse: **22%**
Attrition: **12%** MLB: **98%**

Comparables:
Erik Hanson, Sonny Siebert, Kevin Gross (76)

YEAR	TEAM	LVL	AGE	W	L	SV	G	GS	IP	H	HR	BB	SO	EqBB9	EqSO9	GB%	BABIP	WHIP	ERA	FRA	WARP
2008	KCA	MLB	29	14	11	0	34	34	210^{1}	204	19	73	183	3.1	7.8	40%	.303	1.32	3.98	4.10	3.9
2009	KCA	MLB	30	6	10	0	23	23	129	144	17	58	95	4.0	6.6	49%	.311	1.59	5.09	5.60	0.6
2010	KCA	MLB	31	0	5	0	20	9	61^{2}	65	9	38	41	5.5	6.0	45%	.293	1.70	5.69	6.39	-0.5
2011	*KCA*	*MLB*	*32*	*10*	*10*	*0*	*29*	*29*	*164*	*173*	*19*	*67*	*121*	*3.7*	*6.6*	*44%*	*.308*	*1.46*	*4.57*	*4.97*	*2.2*

It is far more fun to pretend that Trey Hillman was fired due to the restraining order that Meche took out after the manager repeatedly attempted to murder what remained of his arm than it is to acknowledge that he was done in by mere incompetence. The damage done to Meche during the Dead Arm Days of 2009 did not heal, and he spent most of last season either absent from the mound or getting shelled. When he returned from a shoulder-related 60-day DL stint in September, Meche pitched in relief and showed some promise in that role, recording 7.6 strikeouts per nine innings pitched and a 2.8 K/BB with a fastball that sat at 93. At $12 million, he would make for a pricey bullpen arm in 2011, but an expensive and effective reliever would be preferable to a third straight year of disappointing, injury-riddled rotation work at the same price tag. However, any further discussion of his role was rendered moot by his decision to leave that hefty paycheck on the table and walk away from the game for good over the winter.

Mike Montgomery

Born: **7/1/1989** Age: **21**
Bats: L Throws: L Height: **6' 5"** Weight: **180**
Breakout: **1%** Improve: **4%** Collapse: **0%**
Attrition: **1%** MLB: **4%**

Comparables:
Shairon Martis, Don Kaiser, Mike Witt (78)

YEAR	TEAM	LVL	AGE	W	L	SV	G	GS	IP	H	HR	BB	SO	EqBB9	EqSO9	GB%	BABIP	WHIP	ERA	FRA	WARP
2008	ROY	Rk	18	2	1	0	12	12	42^{2}	31	2	12	34	2.5	7.2	63%	.257	1.03	1.69	2.62	1.9
2009	BUR	A	19	2	3	0	12	12	58	42	1	24	52	3.7	8.1	59%	.268	1.17	2.17	3.15	1.6
2009	WIL	A+	19	4	1	0	10	11	57^{2}	41	0	15	52	2.3	8.1	46%	.249	1.02	1.87	1.79	2.5
2010	WIL	A+	20	2	0	0	4	4	24^{2}	14	0	4	33	1.5	12.3	60%	.264	0.74	1.09	2.59	0.9
2010	NWA	AA	20	5	4	0	13	13	59^{2}	56	4	26	48	4.0	7.3	49%	.301	1.45	3.47	4.43	1.4
2011	*KCA*	*MLB*	*21*	*6*	*6*	*0*	*16*	*16*	*77*	*80*	*8*	*37*	*54*	*4.3*	*6.3*	*48%*	*.301*	*1.50*	*4.63*	*5.03*	*1.2*

Early in the 2010 season, it looked as though Montgomery might be making a name for himself as one of the best pitching prospects in the game, allowing just three runs in his first four starts at High-A Wilmington with nearly twice as many strikeouts as baserunners allowed. He didn't miss a step following a promotion to Double-A, but missed two months with a sore arm and scuffled upon his return. Montgomery is a highly athletic and almost shockingly coordinated six-foot-five lefty with a plus fastball and even better curve, and everything seemed to be back by the end of the season. Like Duffy, he still has a workload hurdle to cross, as he's yet to throw more than 110 innings in a season, but as far as stuff goes, there are no chinks in his armor.

Sean O'Sullivan

Born: **9/1/1987** Age: **23**
Bats: R Throws: R Height: **6' 2"** Weight: **230**
Breakout: **11%** Improve: **19%** Collapse: **6%**
Attrition: **6%** MLB: **30%**

Comparables:
Carl Pavano, Joe Kennedy, Matt Harrison (74)

YEAR	TEAM	LVL	AGE	W	L	SV	G	GS	IP	H	HR	BB	SO	EqBB9	EqSO9	GB%	BABIP	WHIP	ERA	FRA	WARP
2008	RCU	A+	20	16	8	0	28	26	158	167	8	50	111	2.8	6.3	51%	.311	1.44	4.56	5.43	0.4
2009	SLC	AAA	21	6	4	0	14	14	69	74	9	20	48	2.6	6.3	39%	.294	1.41	5.35	6.18	-0.1
2009	ANA	MLB	21	4	2	0	12	10	51^{2}	60	12	16	29	2.8	5.1	37%	.286	1.49	5.92	6.13	0.0
2010	SLC	AAA	22	5	5	0	15	15	85	95	8	31	58	3.3	6.1	44%	.326	1.52	4.76	5.18	0.7
2010	ANA	MLB	22	1	0	0	5	1	13	7	1	4	6	2.8	4.2	44%	.158	0.85	2.08	5.79	-0.1
2010	KCA	MLB	22	3	6	0	14	13	70^{2}	83	14	27	37	3.4	4.7	41%	.288	1.57	6.11	5.93	-0.3
2011	*KCA*	*MLB*	*23*	*8*	*10*	*0*	*25*	*25*	*135*	*158*	*19*	*51*	*70*	*3.4*	*4.7*	*44%*	*.306*	*1.54*	*5.36*	*5.82*	*0.6*

The most positive thing you can say about O'Sullivan is that he will be only 23 years old in 2011. The problem is that his youth doesn't mean much, since there isn't a lot of room for growth in this right-hander. O'Sullivan relies entirely on his command, as none of his primary offerings—a 90-mph four-seamer, a sinker, and a change—works as a true out pitch. Major-league hitters have had their way with him in his 135 career big-league innings, as the pitch sequencing that worked so well for him in the minors isn't cutting it now. His rate of home runs allowed per nine innings is higher than his strikeout-to-walk ratio, so a moderate improvement won't make him very good, even by Kansas City standards.

Joakim Soria

Born: **5/18/1984** Age: **27**
Bats: R Throws: R Height: **6' 2"** Weight: **170**
Breakout: **22%** Improve: **40%** Collapse: **25%**
Attrition: **5%** MLB: **85%**

Comparables:
Huston Street, Ugueth Urbina, Kerry Ligtenberg (66)

YEAR	TEAM	LVL	AGE	W	L	SV	G	GS	IP	H	HR	BB	SO	EqBB9	EqSO9	GB%	BABIP	WHIP	ERA	FRA	WARP
2008	KCA	MLB	24	2	3	42	63	0	67^{1}	39	5	19	66	2.5	8.8	46%	.207	0.95	1.60	3.21	1.2
2009	KCA	MLB	25	3	2	30	47	0	53	44	5	16	69	2.7	11.7	39%	.300	1.17	2.21	1.89	1.7
2010	KCA	MLB	26	1	2	43	66	0	65^{2}	53	4	16	71	2.2	9.7	48%	.277	1.08	1.78	1.47	2.3
2011	*KCA*	*MLB*	*27*	*3*	*1*	*26*	*52*	*0*	*54*	*46*	*5*	*15*	*59*	*2.5*	*9.7*	*45%*	*.296*	*1.11*	*2.73*	*2.97*	*1.2*

Soria's stint as a strikeout machine in 2009 ended after just the one season, but in its place came a 10 percent increase in ground-ball rate. Soria has excellent control and still strikes out over a batter per inning, so the additional grounders represent just another weapon for a reliever who was already on the very short list of closers that can be counted on from year to year. Barring an undisclosed ailment, Soria's main flaw was not of his own making: he had four appearances of more than an inning all season, and all of them came in April. A reliever this great in a bullpen this awful—Soria accounted for 88 percent of the team's WXRL by himself—should be pitching more often than he does.

Robinson Tejeda

Born: **3/24/1982** Age: **29**
Bats: R Throws: R Height: **6' 3"** Weight: **188**
Breakout: **15%** Improve: **30%** Collapse: **20%**
Attrition: **13%** MLB: **72%**

Comparables:
Ramon Ramirez, Mark Davis, Billy Sadler (73)

YEAR	TEAM	LVL	AGE	W	L	SV	G	GS	IP	H	HR	BB	SO	EqBB9	EqSO9	GB%	BABIP	WHIP	ERA	FRA	WARP
2008	OKL	AAA	26	1	1	1	10	4	33	20	2	10	39	2.7	10.6	33%	.237	0.94	1.91	2.89	0.9
2008	KCA	MLB	26	2	2	0	25	1	39^{1}	22	3	20	41	4.6	9.4	34%	.204	1.09	3.43	2.54	0.8
2008	TEX	MLB	26	0	0	0	4	0	6	5	1	5	4	7.5	6.0	25%	.211	1.67	9.00	4.23	0.8
2009	KCA	MLB	27	4	2	0	35	6	73^{2}	43	4	49	87	6.0	10.6	36%	.231	1.29	3.54	4.72	0.0
2010	KCA	MLB	28	3	5	0	54	0	61	55	5	26	56	3.8	8.3	31%	.292	1.33	3.54	5.13	-0.1
2011	*KCA*	*MLB*	*29*	*5*	*3*	*0*	*55*	*6*	*98^{2}*	*89*	*10*	*53*	*92*	*4.9*	*8.4*	*40%*	*.295*	*1.45*	*4.16*	*4.52*	*0.8*

Tejeda is the closest thing the Royals have to a real set-up man, and though his last two seasons' ERAs were the same, there was much more to love about his 2010 campaign. He took a little heat off his fastball and used it far more often with better location, which cut his walk rate. The improved control came at the expense of his punchouts, but after he handed out over six free passes per nine in 2009, things needed to improve. Tejeda still isn't a great eighth-inning option—in light of his control problems, he's probably better suited for middle relief and lower-leverage situations—but the Royals have no one on hand to replace him.

Kanekoa Texeira

Born: **2/6/1986** Age: **25**
Bats: R Throws: R Height: **6' 2"** Weight: **190**
Breakout: **0%** Improve: **1%** Collapse: **0%**
Attrition: **0%** MLB: **1%**

Comparables:
Cesar Jimenez, Anibal Sanchez, Keith Atherton (83)

YEAR	TEAM	LVL	AGE	W	L	SV	G	GS	IP	H	HR	BB	SO	EqBB9	EqSO9	GB%	BABIP	WHIP	ERA	FRA	WARP
2008	WNS	A+	22	3	1	20	36	0	382	28	0	14	36	3.3	8.4	63%	.255	1.09	0.93	2.89	0.9
2008	BIR	AA	22	3	2	1	15	0	221	18	2	7	24	2.8	9.7	62%	.291	1.21	2.02	2.54	0.8
2009	TRN	AA	23	9	6	2	41	6	1011	90	7	43	88	3.8	7.8	63%	.284	1.33	2.84	4.23	0.8
2010	SEA	MLB	24	0	1	0	16	0	18^2	22	0	10	14	4.8	6.8	48%	.355	1.77	5.30	5.13	-0.1
2010	KCA	MLB	24	1	0	0	27	0	42^2	51	3	15	19	3.2	4.0	56%	.318	1.59	4.64	4.72	0.0
2011	*KCA*	*MLB*	*25*	*2*	*1*	*2*	*41*	*0*	*58*	*65*	*6*	*27*	*39*	*4.2*	*6.0*	*51%*	*.317*	*1.57*	*4.98*	*5.42*	*-0.4*

The Mariners selected Texeira, a Maui native who just turned 25, from the Yankees in the major-league phase of the Rule 5 draft, and the Royals in turn claimed him off waivers from Seattle in early June. Texeira pitched in low-leverage situations more than any other oft-used reliever on the staff, and whatever strikeout ability he showed in his limited time in the Pacific Northwest vanished in Kansas City. While Texeira was probably just trying to fit in with the rest of the KC middle relievers by cutting all of those pesky strikeouts from his appearances, he'll need to get them back if he wants to stick in the majors for more than Rule 5 purposes. His lone interesting pitch heading into the year was his slider, but he quit using that in favor of more fastballs after joining the Royals. Don't hold your breath waiting for those whiffs.

Blake Wood

Born: **8/8/1985** Age: **25**
Bats: R Throws: R Height: **6' 5"** Weight: **230**
Breakout: **0%** Improve: **2%** Collapse: **0%**
Attrition: **1%** MLB: **3%**

Comparables:
Jason Vargas, Edgar Gonzalez, Jo-Jo Reyes (86)

YEAR	TEAM	LVL	AGE	W	L	SV	G	GS	IP	H	HR	BB	SO	EqBB9	EqSO9	GB%	BABIP	WHIP	ERA	FRA	WARP
2008	WIL	A+	22	3	2	0	10	10	57^1	32	3	15	63	2.4	9.9	45%	.225	0.86	2.67	4.19	0.7
2008	NWA	AA	22	5	7	0	18	18	86^2	96	7	32	76	3.3	7.9	49%	.341	1.56	5.29	5.42	0.7
2009	NWA	AA	23	2	8	0	17	13	78^2	92	8	28	49	3.2	5.6	54%	.337	1.58	5.83	5.72	-0.1
2010	KCA	MLB	24	1	3	0	51	0	49^2	54	6	22	31	4.0	5.6	51%	.300	1.55	5.07	2.61	-0.4
2011	*KCA*	*MLB*	*25*	*4*	*5*	*0*	*34*	*10*	*77*	*88*	*10*	*34*	*50*	*4.0*	*5.9*	*46%*	*.317*	*1.58*	*5.32*	*5.78*	*0.0*

Wood's strikeout rates don't scream "95-mph gas," but he boasts impressive velocity nonetheless. He hurls his heater for strikes at an average rate and gets few misses with it, but he does use it to pick up a lot of ground balls (1.5 grounders per fly ball) and groundouts (22 percent). Wood throws a fastball/slider combo almost exclusively, with an occasional changeup thrown in. If his slider were more consistent, he would be able to punch out more hitters and employ it more often, but its suspect nature is part of the reason for his having ended up in the pen after bouncing between dominating and dominated as a starter in the minors. There is reason to hope that he'll become a useful reliever, but his future hinges on that slider.

LINEOUTS

HITTERS

PLAYER	TEAM	LVL	AGE	PA	R	2B	3B	HR	RBI	BB	SO	SB-CS	AVG/OBP/SLG	TAv	BABIP	BRR	FRAA	WARP
3B C. Cuthbert	ROY	Rk	17	76	14	3	2	1	5	6	19	1-1	.265/.342/.412	.260	.354	0.4	3B -6	0.1
	IDA	Rk	17	64	10	4	1	2	10	3	16	1-0	.233/.281/.433	.262	.286	-0.5	3B -4	-0.1
CF B. Eibner	DNP		22	—	—	—	—	—	—	—	—	—			—			—
OF N. Francis	WIL	A+	24	361	55	24	3	16	61	19	85	8-4	.284/.328/.516	.299	.333	2.2	RF 2, CF 0	2.4
INF E. Lucas	OMA	AAA	28	415	52	20	1	13	50	52	68	7-1	.307/.398/.480	.304	.341	0.0	SS -3, 3B 2	2.7
RF J. Miller	OMA	AAA	25	350	45	24	2	18	56	35	113	2-3	.267/.340/.531	.298	.355	-0.9	CF 2, RF 2	2.4
	KCA	MLB	25	60	5	3	0	1	4	4	23	1-0	.236/.300/.346	.242	.387	0.0	RF -1, LF 0	-0.1
OF J. Parraz	OMA	AAA	25	501	58	27	1	11	61	39	78	8-5	.266/.350/.410	.252	.294	0.0	RF 4	0.7
C S. Perez	WIL	A+	20	396	35	21	1	7	53	18	38	1-1	.290/.322/.411	.265	.300	-3.5	C 1	1.4
C M. Pina	NWA	AA	23	302	39	16	0	7	44	24	37	0-0	.259/.319/.398	.232	.267	-2.7	C -1	0.1
	OMA	AAA	23	60	5	2	0	2	5	3	7	0-0	.218/.267/.364	.207	.213	-0.4	C 0	-0.1
1B C. Robinson*	NWA	AA	25	548	90	41	5	29	98	58	86	4-3	.335/.410/.625	.347	.355	-2.1	1B 1, LF 0	5.6
1B S. Thorman*	OMA	AAA	28	532	78	31	2	22	85	48	75	6-4	.280/.348/.491	.292	.292	-0.7	1B -6, 3B 0	1.7

Jeff Bianchi missed the entire 2010 season recovering from Tommy John surgery; he could still have enough value as a right-side only infielder. ⊘ A seven-figure bonus baby out of Nicaragua, third baseman **Cheslor Cuthbert** impressed with both his bat and his glove during his stateside debut. He would be better known if the system weren't so stacked. ⊘ Though 2010 second-round pick **Brett Eibner** has pro potential on the mound, the Royals paid $1.25 million for one of the most impressive, though unproven, power/speed combinations in the draft. ⚾ Outfielder **Nick Francis** came back from a 50-game drug suspension and showed impressive power at High-A Wilmington. For some, he profiles as a future bench player. ⚾ Dartmouth product **Ed Lucas** put up big numbers at Triple-A in his seventh year as a pro, but the Royals had no room for a player in his late 20s, and the Braves scooped him up on waivers. ⚾ Always toolsy, outfielder **Jai Miller** finally got an extended look in the big leagues, but after 23 whiffs in 55 at-bats, he was cut free to go elsewhere—elsewhere, in this case, being Oakland. ⚾ An impressive athlete who never seems to put it all together, outfielder **Jordan Parraz** will frustrate the Yankees in 2011, his third organization of the 2010-2011 offseason. ⚾ One of the better sleepers in the system, catcher **Salvador Perez** is a defensive stalwart who started to show some signs of life with the bat in 2010. ⚾ An excellent defender behind the plate, backstop **Manny Pina** has yet to show much with the bat. ⚾ Although he took home the Texas League triple crown in 2010, **Clint Robinson** is a slow first baseman whom scouts have trouble envisioning as a successful big-league player. ⚾ One of those Triple-A slugging first basemen good for 20 meaningless home runs a year, **Scott Thorman** will take his services to Detroit—or should we say Toledo—in 2011.

PITCHERS

PLAYER	TEAM	LVL	AGE	W	L	SV	IP	H	HR	BB	SO	EqBB9	EqSO9	GB%	BABIP	WHIP	ERA	FRA	WARP
H. Barrera	NWA	AA	24	3	1	1	25	17	1	7	25	2.5	9.0	47%	.250	1.04	1.80	2.61	0.7
B. Bullington	OMA	AAA	29	8	2	0	102	86	8	28	73	2.5	6.4	51%	.264	1.19	2.82	4.30	1.5
	KCA	MLB	29	1	4	0	42^2	51	6	17	29	3.6	6.1	47%	.321	1.69	6.12	5.59	-0.1
R. Colon	KCA	MLB	30	0	0	0	2	5	0	2	1	9.0	4.5	60%	.500	4.00	18.00	8.46	-0.1
J. Cruz	KCA	MLB	31	0	0	0	5^1	9	0	4	7	6.8	11.8	35%	.529	2.44	3.38	-0.74	0.3
G. Hernandez	OMA	AAA	24	10	6	0	144^2	139	31	56	114	3.5	7.1	33%	.263	1.40	4.91	4.64	1.7
P. Keating	WIL	A+	23	2	0	5	30^1	18	2	10	41	3.0	12.3	47%	.254	0.96	1.19	1.95	1.2
	NWA	AA	23	1	1	10	40^2	33	3	19	60	4.3	13.4	49%	.341	1.29	3.10	2.92	0.7
A. Lerew	OMA	AAA	27	9	4	0	123^2	121	4	44	74	3.2	5.4	51%	.293	1.38	2.55	2.54	4.7
	KCA	MLB	27	1	4	0	26^1	34	9	9	18	3.1	6.2	43%	.305	1.71	8.54	8.25	-0.6
T. Melville	WIL	A+	20	2	12	0	112^1	101	10	54	90	4.3	7.2	43%	.281	1.44	4.97	7.16	-1.6
L. Mendoza	OMA	AAA	26	10	9	0	131^2	145	13	32	59	2.2	4.0	51%	.295	1.40	4.10	4.65	1.6
	KCA	MLB	26	0	1	0	4	10	4	3	1	6.8	2.3	38%	.353	3.25	22.50	20.73	-0.7
E. Osuna*	NWA	AA	22	6	2	0	94^2	99	11	11	64	1.1	6.1	40%	.292	1.18	2.95	4.38	1.5
	OMA	AAA	22	1	3	0	29	43	12	16	19	5.0	5.9	32%	.313	2.10	9.31	9.87	-0.9
J. Parrish*	KCA	MLB	32	1	1	0	6	4	2	5	4	7.5	6.0	47%	.133	1.50	3.00	6.51	-0.1
J. Rupe	OMA	AAA	27	2	4	10	52^1	49	5	23	49	4.0	8.5	66%	.297	1.48	2.92	4.51	0.3
	KCA	MLB	27	1	1	0	9^2	14	1	7	8	6.5	7.4	53%	.394	2.17	5.59	5.03	0.0
T. Sample	BUR	A	21	6	10	0	121	105	8	95	115	7.1	8.6	48%	.287	1.72	4.69	5.39	0.6
W. Smith*	RCU	A+	20	2	2	0	37^1	36	4	13	31	3.2	7.5	47%	.296	1.32	4.58	6.01	-0.2
	WIL	A+	20	4	1	0	54^2	48	6	4	51	0.7	8.5	53%	.278	0.98	2.80	3.82	1.0
E. Teaford*	NWA	AA	26	14	3	0	99	91	7	32	113	2.9	10.3	46%	.323	1.27	3.36	3.04	3.4
Y. Ventura	ROY	Rk	19	4	2	0	52^2	49	3	17	58	2.9	10.0	53%	.313	1.32	3.25	3.90	3.7
R. Yambati	ROY	Rk	19	8	2	0	66^1	65	0	12	64	1.6	8.7	64%	.325	1.26	2.71	3.24	5.6

Former big-league outfielder **Brian Anderson** is trying to make it back as a pitcher. He didn't show enough with the Royals to earn a roster spot, but the Yankees are going to give him a look this spring. ⚾ Cuban defector **Noel Arguelles** has yet to throw a pitch in anger since signing with the Royals in December 2009 due to shoulder problems, but retains a spot on the 40-man. ⚾ Righty **Henry Barrera** was sitting in the mid-90s and touching 97 at the end of the year, for which he earned himself an addition to the 40-man roster. ⚾ Selected first overall in the 2002 draft by the Pirates, **Bryan Bullington** set a career high in innings pitched and even toppled the Yankees for his first major-league victory with eight shutout frames in August. Glory is fleeting: after the Royals designated him for assignment, Bullington signed with the Hiroshima Carp. ⚾ **Roman Colon**, another Brave turned Royal, pitched all of four innings for the organization before deciding to take his meager talents to South Korea. ⚾ **Juan Cruz** appeared in five games before the Royals cut him. He underwent surgery to remove a shoulder cyst a month later. He never lost the habit of walking any hitter willing to wait him out, but his strikeout stuff appeared to be back in the short time he pitched, imparting hope that he can fill out the back of a bullpen in 2011. ⚾ Once seen as a potential big-league starter, former Mets and Marlins prospect **Gaby Hernandez** has stalled at the upper levels of the minors, watching his ERA rise along with his weight. ⚾ Some mechanical changes led to a huge jump in velocity for 2009 20th-round-pick

Patrick Keating, who touched 98 mph last year and struck out nearly 13 per nine. **Anthony Lerew**'s career homer rates are spit-take worthy, as he has given up 2.6 per nine in his 61 1/3 innings in the majors. The extreme fly-ball pitcher watched his air balls turn into taters at a faster pace than that of Jose Bautista in 2010. While other Royals pitchers have gone abroad to keep their careers going, Lerew may need to find a planet with stronger gravity. Viewed as an equal to all the big-name left-handed prospects entering the year, **Tim Melville** struggled with mechanics and control at High-A and fell well behind the pack. **Luis Mendoza** throws a fastball that he complements with a second fastball. In the minors, Mendoza was a starter who struck out just *four* batters per nine. Such was the state of the Kansas City pen that he was called up anyway, but his four- and two-seamer combination made things easy on hitters in the bigs; he allowed a home run for each inning he pitched. Skinny left-hander **Edgar Osuna** is fun to watch, thanks to a good breaking ball and nearly supernatural control, but with a fastball that sits in the mid- to upper 80s, he doesn't have much of a future. If only this comment could be about the John Parrish who played Jax Briggs in the *Mortal Kombat* movies, instead of **John Parrish** the professional pitcher—or Maxfield Parrish, or even Homer Parrish, the amputee sailor played so touchingly by real-life veteran Harold Russell in *The Best Years of Our Lives*. Then we could talk about real achievement instead of a veteran southpaw who has never conquered his control. If science proved that a fastball to the head was the quickest way to dispatch zombies during an apocalyptic outbreak of the undead, and **Josh Rupe** were the only professional pitcher around, the living would be doomed: his chances of hitting any of those shambling targets would be slim, given that he can't hit a static one consistently. Righty **Tyler Sample** is a six-foot-seven beast of a human with a very high ceiling, but he won't reach it if he keeps walking the ballpark. A tall left-hander who came from the Angels in the Alberto Callaspo deal, **Will Smith** treats walks as if they are punishable by jail time. That's a good thing, as his stuff is quite hittable. Rail-thin lefty **Everett Teaford** isn't nearly as good as his stats would suggest, but his ability to throw strikes and mix a deep arsenal of average pitches landed him on the 40-man. Despite a small frame, teenage Dominican **Yordano Ventura** was one of the more impressive arms in the Arizona complex league, but he's still a long way from being dubbed Ace Ventura. Ventura's fellow Dominican **Robinson Yambati** showed mid-90s heat and projection in Arizona last summer, earning himself a chance to make his performance hold up in a full-season league. These tropical twins are still far away from the majors, but could be far better known by the time our 2012 edition rolls around.

MANAGER: TREY HILLMAN/NED YOST

YEAR	TEAM	W-L	Pythag +/-	Avg PC	100+ P	120+ P	QS	BQS	REL	REL w Zero R	IBB	Subs	PH	PH Avg	PH HR	SB2	CS2	SB3	CS3	SAC Att	SAC %	POS SAC	Squeeze	Swing	In Play
2008	T.H.	75-87	4	98.2	73	2	76	2	438	277	15	52	71	.270	1	58	32	21	6	57	56.1%	28	0	122	97
2008	N.Y.	83-67	2	96.6	54	6	80	4	398	252	30	23	217	.208	7	85	27	20	7	68	67.6%	17	3	137	108
2009	T.H.	65-97	0	97.6	74	4	70	8	425	212	28	53	90	.207	2	79	27	8	1	64	59.4%	37	3	118	95
2010	T.H.	12-23	0	97.8	14	1	17	2	109	54	3	5	12	.182	0	25	8	4	1	26	57.7%	15	1	36	26
2010	N.Y.	55-72	4	96.7	60	1	51	6	332	206	25	6	56	.244	2	73	35	12	4	46	65.2%	25	2	102	78

Once again, Trey Hillman couldn't get anything going in Kansas City and was fired in mid-May, leaving behind an awful bullpen, a lineup that wasn't scoring any runs, and a rotation with roughly 1½ dependable arms in it. This last deficiency was partly his own doing, thanks to the damage he caused Gil Meche in 2009 by ratcheting up the righty's pitch counts during a dead-arm period. Ned Yost inherited Hillman's leavings, and though the team still performed poorly, there were areas in which he represented an improvement. Yost let Luke Hochevar pitch through his struggles—how else was he supposed to learn?—but had a quick hook when it was necessary, unlike his predecessor. His very worst relievers pitched in the least important situations, excepting Jesse Chavez, who was called upon to retire a multitude of batters better left for more effective options. Yost rarely used subs, which wasn't out of character for him; such reticence made sense, given the lack of depth on the Royals' bench for much of the season.

Los Angeles Angels

The 2010 season might wind up being remembered as the one in which the AL West got the Rally Monkey off its back. After winning five division titles in six years, the Angels finished under .500 for the first time since 2003 and just the third time in manager Mike Scioscia's 11-year tenure. With the emergence of the Rangers not only as contenders but also as potential division powerhouses thanks to new ownership, a lucrative television deal, and a burgeoning farm system, the Halos have suddenly found themselves back on their heels, with no guarantee of restoring their former standing atop the junior circuit's short stack.

The 2009 season had marked a transition of sorts for the Angels. While they had maintained their supremacy in the AL West, the team had won in a markedly different manner than it had in the past, breaking from a brand of baseball that privileged contact skills, batting average, baserunning, and late-inning dominance over power and patience. That squad set a franchise record with 883 runs scored, the league's second-highest total, but it allowed 761 runs, more than any Angels club since 2000, Scioscia's inaugural campaign. Free-agent departures following the season accelerated the transition, as top-of-the-lineup spark plug Chone Figgins, top power hitter Vlad Guerrero, and longtime ace John Lackey—all key components in the team's 2004-2009 run of success—left for greener pastures. While none of that trio performed so well in their new digs that general manager Tony Reagins and company should have regretted their departures, their replacements' 2010 performances were uneven at best.

This particularly applied to the offense, which slumped to just 681 runs, ninth in the league and the franchise's lowest full-season total since 1992; the team's True Average fell from .283 to .265, 10th in the league. Quite simply, the hits stopped falling in, as the Halos' batting average on balls in play dipped from .322 in 2009 to .281 last year. Relative to the league average, that was a 36-point drop, a mortal blow for a team so short of secondary hitting skills that it ranked ninth in isolated power and 12th in walks. Compounding the problem, the Angels suddenly became much more reliant on the long ball to score, plating 37.7 percent of their runs on homers, the league's fourth-highest rate and the franchise's highest since 2000. They lost ground on the basepaths, too; after eight straight years among the league's top three teams in stolen bases, they dipped to seventh, and dropped from 1.3 Equivalent Baserunning Runs in 2009 to -3.5 last year.

ANGELS PROSPECTUS

2010 W-L: 80-82, 3rd in AL West

Pythag	.486	19th
RS/G	4.20	19th
RA/G	4.33	16th
TAv	.265	20th
BRR	-3.5	22nd
FRA	4.29	12th
DER	-5.19	19th
DL	828	22nd
B-Age	29.8	24th
P-Age	28.0	15th
Salary	$105.0	8th
M$/MW	$3.02	21st

Ballpark: Angel Stadium (3-yr. PF: 94). The AL's second-oldest park hasn't had a rainout since 1995, but outfield rock formation draws Druids at each solstice

2010: Fallen Angels miss the playoffs for the first time post-Salmon

2011: The Halos are far from heavenly, but they don't roll over for the Rangers

Action Items: Restocking the system, adding patience and power, anointing the next closer

The biggest blow beyond the losses of Figgins (who had enjoyed a career year in 2009 but struggled for most of 2010 as a Mariner) and Guerrero (who suffered through his worst season as an Angel, only to reinvigorate his career in Texas) was that of Kendry Morales. After breaking out with a 34-homer season in 2009, the first baseman remained a middle-of-the-lineup force through the first two months of 2010, but his season ended in bizarre fashion when he broke his leg during the celebration at home plate following a walk-off grand slam against the Mariners on May 29. The already-sputtering offense dipped from 4.4 runs per game to that point to 4.1 the rest of the way.

At first it appeared that the Angels might actually make lemonade from their first-base lemon, as the team surged in the immediate aftermath of Morales' injury, winning nine out of 10 to take over first place in the AL West on June 7; alas, that was the last day that they held the top spot all season. Once Jeff Mathis returned from a DL stint in mid-June, Mike Napoli took over the bulk of the first-base duties, but he couldn't replicate Morales' production. A thumper who had hit .273/.359/.527 with 40 homers in 706 plate appearances in 2008-2009, Napoli had come up short on playing time because he was never Scioscia's favorite defensive catcher, so the move to first had the makings of a solid solution. Unfortunately, Napoli's plate discipline deserted him, and while he set career highs for homers (26) and plate appearances (510), he hit just .238/.316/.468 for the year.

Across the diamond, the situation was even worse. Brandon Wood, a former top prospect who had cooled his heels for the better part of three seasons in Triple-A, took over third base from Figgins but was unfathomably awful at the plate. He hit .146/.174/.208 in 243 plate appearances, and his .121 TAv was the second-lowest of any player ever to receive 200 plate appearances. To cover for his slide, the team swapped two pitchers to Kansas City in late July for Alberto Callaspo, who couldn't mimic even his thin 2010 performance in Kansas City, let alone his torrid 2009. Middle infielders Howie Kendrick, Erick Aybar, and Maicer Izturis all dipped considerably as well, which was particularly problematic, given that they accounted for a majority of the plate appearances in the lineup's top two spots. In all, the Halos' infield dropped from a robust .289/.352/.443 in 2009 to a miserable .243/.293/.368 in 2010.

The outfield was only somewhat more productive. Torii Hunter stayed healthy and handled a midseason shift from center field to right with minimal fuss, but new center fielder Peter Bourjos (.227 TAv) didn't hit enough to inspire much confidence. Bobby Abreu saw both his average and his OBP dip 38 points below their 2009 levels, to their lowest ebb since 1997. Juan Rivera's slugging percentage fell 69 points. Former Yankee Hideki Matsui, who signed a one-year, $6 million deal to replace Guerrero and wound up seeing time in the outfield for the first time since 2008, was actually the team's most productive hitter, turning in a .303 TAv.

As for the pitching, the rotation actually improved slightly over 2009. Jered Weaver found so much success with a newly integrated two-seam fastball that he led the AL in strikeouts (233), ranked third with a 6.3 Support Neutral Lineup-adjusted Value Above Replacement (SNLVAR) and fifth in ERA (3.01), and set a career high for innings pitched (224.1). Ervin Santana continued his trend toward even-year success, rebounding from an injury-plagued 2009 to shave more than a run off his ERA and place 22nd in SNLVAR. Free agent Joel Pineiro returned to the AL after resurrecting his career in St. Louis, generated plenty of grounders, and posted a 3.84 ERA in 23 starts, though he missed nearly two months with an oblique strain. Dan Haren, who was acquired from the Diamondbacks for a four-player package that included Joe Saunders and 2009 supplemental first-round pick Tyler Skaggs, put up a 2.87 ERA and a .611 SNWP (Support-Neutral Winning Percentage) after arriving in late July. The trade proved to be a major coup, not only in terms of netting a frontline pitcher for less-than-frontline talent, but also in offsetting the unhappiness wrought by Scott Kazmir. The lefty Kazmir was both awful (5.94 ERA, .418 SNWP) and expensive ($8 million) amid shoulder woes and is guaranteed only to cost considerably more in 2011 ($12 million).

Meanwhile, the bullpen was merely mediocre. In his second season as the Halos' closer, Brian Fuentes showed definitively that he was no Francisco Rodriguez: among the 29 pitchers with at least 20 saves, his 4.14 Fair Run Average ranked 24th. He was dealt to Minnesota late in the year, while fill-in Fernando Rodney (3.98 FRA) was hardly an improvement in the first year of his two-year, $11 million deal. Kevin Jepsen had a strong year in a set-up role, but the other relievers whom Scioscia called upon—Scot Shields, Jason Bulger, and the *other* Francisco Rodriguez—finished within a whisker of replacement level.

The team entered the offseason geared to spend significant money to upgrade via the free-agent market, ready to cash checks they had to tear up after pulling their eight-year, $160 million offer to Mark Teixeira in December 2008 and letting the Class of 2009 depart. Unfortunately, money alone can't solve the Angels' problems: the goal of both shoring up the lineup and improving a defense that has spent just one of the last four years in the upper half of the AL Defensive Efficiency rankings is a difficult one to achieve, as so few players embody both qualities.

The return of Morales should help the starting nine considerably, but the offense is still heavy with slappy hitters short on secondary skills, and the Angels should be wary about sinking too much money into multiyear deals for the arbitration-eligible Kendrick and Aybar, neither of whom is much of an asset; better to spend money on a long-term deal for Weaver, who's in his second year of arb eligibility. Beyond that, the team shelled out another multiyear contract to a proven reliever (Scott Downs) despite being burned in recent years by similar deals given to Fuentes, Rodney, and Justin Speier.

Both the lineup and the bullpen might receive some help from the farm system. Catcher Hank Conger, whose season at Triple-A drew mixed reviews on both sides of the ball, stayed healthy and made a positive impression on Scioscia; Conger could find himself taking over a share of the catching duties if Napoli is dealt or the team tires of Mathis's inability to hit big-league pitching. Triple-A first baseman Mark Trumbo, whose 36 homers at Salt Lake City tied for the minor-league lead, could earn time at DH or an outfield corner, though a major free-agent signing would more likely bump Abreu, a nightmarishly bad outfielder, to the DH role and keep Trumbo in the minors. Beyond that, any substantial help on the offensive side is years away, resting primarily on the eventual arrival of 2009 first-rounder Mike Trout, who has rapidly emerged as one of the top minor-league hitting prospects but is still just 19 and coming off half a season of High-A ball.

In the bullpen, power-armed 2006 12th-round pick Jordan Walden could figure in the team's late-game arsenal. Recurrent arm woes forced Walden to shift to relief last year, and he earned a September call-up, where he made a splash with 23 strikeouts in 15.1 innings. Since getting out of the starting business for good after the 2006 season, the veteran left-hander Downs has pitched 236 2/3 innings with a 2.36 ERA while holding left-handers to .201/.274/.297 averages and doing quite well against right-handers as well (.238/.307/.329). Although Downs has rarely been asked to finish games, Scioscia could conceivably give him a try at the spotlight role, given Rodney's weak grip on the closer's position.

Another free-agent addition who might inherit some save opportunities should Rodney falter—almost any member of the pen, including Walden and Jepsen, could—is the ex-Mets left-hander Hisanori Takahashi. A major-league sophomore at 36, the Japanese import closed for the Mets and converted eight of eight save opportunities after former Angel Francisco Rodriguez punched out his own thumb ligament. Takahashi did not allow a home run to a left-handed batter last year in 115 at-bats, though that feat may not be easily repeated without the support of canyonesque Citi Field.

Alas, any hope of a significant near-term boost for the rotation was dashed by the implosion of Trevor Reckling in his half-season at Salt Lake City, leaving the uninspiring likes of Matt Palmer and Trevor Bell as the only on-hand alternatives to Kazmir—at least until 2008 second-rounder Tyler Chatwood, who split his season between High-A and Double-A, gets more seasoning.

Indeed, the minor-league system is only beginning to rebound from a multiyear slide born of successful graduations, flops, trades, tragedy (the death of Nick Adenhart), and a couple of years without first-round picks. After landing five of the first 48 picks in the 2009 draft—including Trout and Skaggs—the Halos similarly ran the table in 2010, signing all five picks they made among the first 40. In doing so, they loaded up on high-school talent, most notably switch-hitting third baseman Kaleb Cowart, who signed for an over-slot $2.3 million bonus, and righty Cam Bedrosian, considered to have one of the best curveballs of any prepster in the draft.

It will take at least a couple years before the current talent in the system can substantially augment the big-league roster, so in the meantime, the Angels will have to continue flexing their financial muscle to keep pace with the Rangers. Fortunately, they're fairly well positioned to do so. After ranking sixth in payroll in both 2008 and 2009 (by both Opening Day and year-end measures), the Angels dropped to eighth in Opening Day payroll in 2010, but that was more sleight of hand than anything else; not included in their $105.0 million figure were the salaries of the released Speier ($5.25 million) and the traded Gary Matthews Jr. ($10.9 million). The team drew 3.25 million fans in 2010, ranking second in the AL behind the Yankees for the seventh straight season, and remains less than halfway through its 10-year, $500 million television deal. Having shed substantial salaries over the past two years, owner Arte Moreno can more easily justify opening his wallet for high-end talent.

While the Rangers are quite reasonably the hip pick to succeed the Angels as the AL West's perennial top threat, the Halos aren't likely to cede their ground quietly. They are on a stronger footing financially than the upstart Texans and have the resources on hand to treat their 2010 as a bump in the road rather than the beginning of the end of their run of success.

HITTERS

Bobby Abreu **RF**

Born: **3/11/1974** Age: **37**
Bats: L Throws: R Height: **6' 0"** Weight: **200**
Breakout: **0%** Improve: **29%** Collapse: **6%**
Attrition: **15%** MLB: **100%**

Comparables:
Raul Ibanez, Don Baylor, Carl Furillo (67)

YEAR	TEAM	LVL	AGE	PA	R	2B	3B	HR	RBI	BB	SO	SB	CS	AVG_OBP_SLG	TAv	BABIP	BRR	FRAA	WARP
2008	NYA	MLB	34	684	100	39	4	20	100	73	109	22	11	.296/.371/.471	.299	.333	2.2	RF -9	3.1
2009	ANA	MLB	35	667	97	29	3	15	103	94	113	30	8	.293/.390/.435	.298	.338	-0.5	RF 0, LF 0	3.4
2010	ANA	MLB	36	667	88	41	1	20	78	87	132	24	10	.255/.352/.435	.297	.296	-4.3	RF -8, LF -5	1.8
2011	*ANA*	*MLB*	*37*	*681*	*86*	*36*	*2*	*18*	*75*	*89*	*124*	*25*	*9*	*.267/.363/.425*	*.280*	*.308*	*-0.6*	*RF -5, LF -1*	*1.6*

Abreu punched yet another ticket to the 20/20 club—the ninth such season of his career, leaving himself only one short of joint record-holders Bobby Bonds and Barry Bonds—but it came at the price of the worst full-season batting average and on-base percentage of his career. The decline was almost entirely BABIP-driven; were Abreu a younger man, we'd probably dismiss the drop-off as a one-year blip, but the outfielder's advancing age increases the odds that his depressed BABIP reflected an erosion of skills, rather than a shift in luck. Still, his highest doubles total since 2006 and a home-run/fly-ball percentage that remained robust by his recent standards suggest that there's still some pop in his bat, and his usual allotment of steals revealed a continued spring in his step. Even if Abreu's BABIP doesn't rebound, he should merit his $9 million for a second straight season. He needs just 433 plate appearances—a mark he's never come close to missing—to put the Angels on the hook for an identical amount in 2012.

Alexi Amarista 2B
Born: **4/6/1989** Age: **22**
Bats: S Throws: R Height: **5' 8"** Weight: **150**
Breakout: **1%** Improve: **5%** Collapse: **2%**
Attrition: **7%** MLB: **16%**
Comparables:
Tony Abreu, Jerry Remy, Jimmy Rollins (65)

YEAR	TEAM	LVL	AGE	PA	R	2B	3B	HR	RBI	BB	SO	SB	CS	AVG_OBP_SLG	TAv	BABIP	BRR	FRAA	WARP
2008	ANG	Rk	19	236	46	6	4	2	21	29	20	22	14	.332/.411/.431	.309	.353	2.7	CF 0, 2B 1	2.3
2009	CDR	A	20	557	84	39	10	4	49	50	61	38	20	.319/.377/.468	.332	.341	0.1	2B 16	6.9
2010	RCU	A+	21	323	39	19	6	4	39	19	42	17	10	.303/.349/.448	.306	.337	-1.9	2B 10	3.1
2010	ARK	AA	21	213	25	2	1	1	20	13	15	4	1	.288/.332/.325	.257	.297	0.6	2B 0	0.5
2010	SLC	AAA	21	70	13	6	3	0	9	1	4	4	2	.400/.412/.585	.340	.406	0.3	2B -1, SS 0	0.7
2011	*ANA*	*MLB*	*22*	*473*	*54*	*23*	*5*	*5*	*51*	*26*	*67*	*18*	*8*	*.280/.317/.392*	*.250*	*.311*	*-1.1*	*2B 9, CF -1*	*1.2*

Amarista backed up his 2009 Midwest League batting title by rocketing through the Angels' system last season, finishing just one level away from escaping the minor leagues' gravitational pull. The diminutive second sacker could have used more development time at Double-A, where his power production cratered. Instead, the Angels aggressively promoted him to Salt Lake, where he quieted fears that he wasn't ready by tearing up the league in a small sample. Amarista's successful season wasn't without its negative indicators, as the Venezuelan's strikeout-to-walk ratio rose from 1.2 to 1.9. Given at least one more full season in the minors to consolidate his offensive approach and further refine his already impressive glove work, Amarista could be ready to complete his accession to Anaheim. Labeling him the heir to Maicer Izturis might be selling him short.

Erick Aybar SS
Born: **1/14/1984** Age: **27**
Bats: S Throws: R Height: **5' 10"** Weight: **170**
Breakout: **2%** Improve: **43%** Collapse: **5%**
Attrition: **11%** MLB: **83%**
Comparables:
Bert Campaneris, Jason Bartlett, Rafael Furcal (73)

YEAR	TEAM	LVL	AGE	PA	R	2B	3B	HR	RBI	BB	SO	SB	CS	AVG_OBP_SLG	TAv	BABIP	BRR	FRAA	WARP
2008	ANA	MLB	24	375	53	18	5	3	39	14	45	7	2	.278/.307/.384	.249	.302	4.1	SS 6, 2B 0	2.0
2009	ANA	MLB	25	556	70	23	9	5	58	30	54	14	7	.312/.345/.423	.272	.329	2.1	SS -6	2.4
2010	ANA	MLB	26	589	69	18	4	5	29	35	81	22	8	.253/.301/.330	.240	.282	5.8	SS -3	1.3
2011	*ANA*	*MLB*	*27*	*429*	*48*	*18*	*4*	*6*	*45*	*25*	*51*	*14*	*6*	*.276/.317/.386*	*.249*	*.295*	*-0.5*	*SS -2*	*0.8*

In last year's book, we predicted an offensive decline for Aybar, and the Dominican obliged by suffering his worst season at the plate since 2007, complete with BABIP correction. As a roughly average defensive shortstop, Aybar might be a bit stretched as an everyday player, even given the woeful state of league-wide offense at that position these days; only the Orioles and Brewers settled for less lumber from their regular shortstops this season. Still, Aybar isn't as bad as his 2010 line would indicate, but he will be hard-pressed to recreate his 2009. The smart money would bet on his making like a baseball version of Goldilocks and settling on the middle ground in his final pre-arbitration season.

Peter Bourjos CF
Born: **3/31/1987** Age: **24**
Bats: R Throws: R Height: **6' 1"** Weight: **180**
Breakout: **3%** Improve: **37%** Collapse: **8%**
Attrition: **25%** MLB: **67%**
Comparables:
Jason Pridie, Michael Bourn, Brett Gardner (66)

YEAR	TEAM	LVL	AGE	PA	R	2B	3B	HR	RBI	BB	SO	SB	CS	AVG_OBP_SLG	TAv	BABIP	BRR	FRAA	WARP
2008	RCU	A+	21	545	83	29	10	9	51	19	96	50	10	.295/.323/.444	.280	.341	7.0	CF -4, LF 0	3.0
2009	ARK	AA	22	504	72	16	14	6	51	49	77	32	12	.281/.347/.423	.296	.317	2.9	CF 9	4.3
2010	SLC	AAA	23	455	85	13	12	13	52	24	78	27	5	.314/.364/.498	.299	.355	7.0	CF 4, LF 1	4.4
2010	ANA	MLB	23	193	19	6	4	6	15	6	40	10	3	.204/.233/.381	.227	.223	1.2	CF 3	0.3
2011	*ANA*	*MLB*	*24*	*560*	*64*	*23*	*8*	*12*	*66*	*28*	*111*	*29*	*7*	*.264/.303/.411*	*.252*	*.307*	*0.7*	*CF -4, LF 0*	*0.7*

All the tools in the world might not put Bourjos' bat back together; an anemic offensive performance like the one he mustered in the majors while serving as the Angels' ninth-place hitter from August on could only be redeemed by a truly superlative showing on defense. Fortunately, Bourjos delivered on that side of the ball, racking up some of the highest runs saved totals detected by defensive metrics among all center fielders, despite starting only 49 games at the position. The size of the sample renders those numbers somewhat suspect, but fielding stats have always loved his work in the minors, and scouts see no reason to disagree. As long as Mike Scioscia doesn't mistake the speedy Bourjos for a leadoff batter, as the manager did during the final week of 2010, the Angels can lug his lumber while crossing their fingers that his next positive WARP score won't come at the cost of a negative VORP.

Alberto Callaspo **3B**

Born: **4/19/1983** Age: **28**
Bats: **S** Throws: **R** Height: **5' 10"** Weight: **175**
Breakout: **1%** Improve: **50%** Collapse: **8%**
Attrition: **6%** MLB: **95%**

Comparables:
Skip Schumaker, Johnny Ray, Bobby Avila (69)

YEAR	TEAM	LVL	AGE	PA	R	2B	3B	HR	RBI	BB	SO	SB	CS	AVG_OBP_SLG	TAv	BABIP	BRR	FRAA	WARP
2008	KCA	MLB	25	234	25	8	3	0	16	19	14	2	1	.305/.359/.371	.269	.323	-1.5	2B -2, SS 1	0.6
2009	KCA	MLB	26	634	79	41	8	11	73	52	51	2	1	.300/.357/.457	.284	.312	0.7	2B -2, 3B -2	2.7
2010	KCA	MLB	27	373	41	19	2	8	43	19	29	3	1	.275/.308/.410	.262	.278	-0.8	3B 0, 2B -2	0.7
2010	ANA	MLB	27	228	22	8	0	2	13	12	13	2	2	.249/.290/.315	.226	.255	1.7	3B 6, 2B 0	0.6
2011	*ANA*	*MLB*	*28*	*505*	*62*	*26*	*4*	*9*	*58*	*38*	*38*	*3*	*2*	*.292/.344/.425*	*.271*	*.298*	*-0.2*	*2B -2, 3B 1*	*1.7*

As *Baseball Prospectus* author emeritus Rany Jazayerli has observed, Callaspo makes a good counterpoint to the argument that Dayton Moore has been lost when making major-league transactions. The Royals acquired Callaspo after 2007 for the dead weight of Billy Buckner and extracted a few wins' worth of production from him at approximately the major-league minimum before flipping him to the Angels, who'd pushed the button in the box marked "Break glass in case of Brandon Wood." Callaspo—who began his career in the Angels system before being traded to the Diamondbacks for Jason Bulger—didn't improve much on Wood's anemic line down the stretch, but his team can expect a more representative performance spurred by a BABIP bounce-back in 2011.

Hank Conger **C**

Born: **1/29/1988** Age: **23**
Bats: **S** Throws: **R** Height: **6' 1"** Weight: **220**
Breakout: **1%** Improve: **17%** Collapse: **6%**
Attrition: **19%** MLB: **39%**

Comparables:
Daric Barton, Joe Torre, James Loney (75)

YEAR	TEAM	LVL	AGE	PA	R	2B	3B	HR	RBI	BB	SO	SB	CS	AVG_OBP_SLG	TAv	BABIP	BRR	FRAA	WARP
2008	RCU	A+	20	318	47	20	2	13	75	14	55	2	1	.303/.333/.517	.302	.326	-1.9	C 0	1.6
2009	ARK	AA	21	524	61	20	3	11	68	55	68	4	2	.295/.366/.424	.296	.320	-1.3	C -2	3.2
2010	SLC	AAA	22	452	56	26	2	11	49	55	58	0	2	.300/.385/.463	.294	.321	-2.1	C -2	2.9
2010	ANA	MLB	22	34	2	1	1	0	5	5	9	0	0	.172/.294/.276	.221	.250	0.0	C 0	0.0
2011	*ANA*	*MLB*	*23*	*452*	*56*	*22*	*2*	*12*	*54*	*40*	*78*	*0*	*0*	*.279/.340/.432*	*.272*	*.313*	*0.0*	*C -2*	*1.5*

After launching a three-run homer in the Futures Game with the eyes of the baseball world upon him, Conger didn't show much else besides a willingness to take a walk in his September audition, but the returns were far more rosy at Triple-A. The formerly fragile catcher stayed healthy for a second consecutive season, and while the apparent improvement in his offensive performance was inflated by his promotion to the hitter-friendly PCL, Conger more than maintained his production relative to the league at the higher level. Conger has made strides behind the plate, where his inaccurate arm lags behind his receiving skills: he led Pacific League catchers with 13 errors, but wasn't charged with a single passed ball. After a miserable 36 at-bats, Conger was banished from winter ball, but he won't follow in Brandon Wood's offensive footsteps any further than that. He's not a masher in the class of Buster Posey or Carlos Santana, but he'll hit enough to erase the memories of Jeff Mathis' offensive ineptitude, as long as Mike Scioscia can overlook the occasional airmailed throw.

Kevin Frandsen **UT**

Born: **5/24/1982** Age: **29**
Bats: **R** Throws: **R** Height: **6' 0"** Weight: **175**
Breakout: **2%** Improve: **24%** Collapse: **6%**
Attrition: **12%** MLB: **65%**

Comparables:
Brent Abernathy, Jeff King, Chris Sabo (74)

YEAR	TEAM	LVL	AGE	PA	R	2B	3B	HR	RBI	BB	SO	SB	CS	AVG_OBP_SLG	TAv	BABIP	BRR	FRAA	WARP
2008	SFN	MLB	26	1	0	0	0	0	0	0	0	0	0	.000/.000/.000	-0.004	.000	0.0	—	—
2009	FRE	AAA	27	474	67	18	2	13	55	23	34	3	4	.295/.348/.438	.269	.291	3.1	SS 1, 2B 5	3.0
2009	SFN	MLB	27	54	3	2	0	0	1	3	4	0	0	.140/.204/.180	.148	.152	0.4	2B -1, SS 0	-0.5
2010	PAW	AAA	28	71	9	3	0	2	4	5	3	2	0	.258/.343/.403	.238	.241	0.0	SS -1, 2B -1	0.1
2010	SLC	AAA	28	155	25	9	1	1	12	7	19	2	1	.277/.353/.380	.248	.311	0.0	3B 2, 2B -2	0.3
2010	ANA	MLB	28	173	22	11	0	0	14	9	10	2	0	.250/.289/.319	.241	.261	-0.6	3B -1, 1B 0	0.0
2011	*ANA*	*MLB*	*29*	*333*	*38*	*16*	*1*	*7*	*35*	*19*	*31*	*3*	*1*	*.261/.318/.388*	*.252*	*.267*	*-0.2*	*SS 0, 3B 1*	*0.7*

Claimed off waivers shortly after his release by the Red Sox in late April, Frandsen benefited from both Maicer Izturis' injury-plagued campaign and the disappearing act pulled off by Brandon Wood's bat. It's unclear whether the Angels benefited from Frandsen, since the former Giant put forth a performance befitting his role as a replacement player. The 28-year-old exhibited some versatility by playing four positions and was hitting .352/.392/.462 before jamming his thumb while scrambling back to the second-base bag on June 26. Though a correction was in store regardless, Frandsen's .116/.164/.130 performance thereafter might lead you to believe that something wasn't right. The righty failed to reach base in his final 28 plate appearances, wiping away much of the value he'd accrued early on. Unimpressed, the Angels nontendered him, and he signed with San Diego.

Torii Hunter **CF**

Born: **7/18/1975** Age: **35**
Bats: R Throws: R Height: **6' 2"** Weight: **205**
Breakout: **0%** Improve: **20%** Collapse: **8%**
Attrition: **10%** MLB: **94%**

Comparables:
Albert Belle, Carl Furillo, Felipe Alou (69)

YEAR	TEAM	LVL	AGE	PA	R	2B	3B	HR	RBI	BB	SO	SB	CS	AVG_OBP_SLG	TAv	BABIP	BRR	FRAA	WARP
2008	ANA	MLB	32	608	85	37	2	21	78	50	108	19	5	.278/.344/.466	.291	.312	1.7	CF 4	4.1
2009	ANA	MLB	33	506	74	26	1	22	90	47	92	18	4	.299/.366/.508	.305	.330	-1.4	CF 5	4.0
2010	ANA	MLB	34	646	76	36	0	23	90	61	106	9	12	.281/.355/.464	.307	.307	-4.0	CF -1, RF 5	4.4
2011	*ANA*	*MLB*	*35*	*607*	*79*	*32*	*1*	*24*	*82*	*54*	*106*	*15*	*7*	*.278/.345/.471*	*.286*	*.303*	*-1.0*	*CF 0, RF 1*	*3.0*

Hunter managed to stave off significant decline for another season, compensating for slight drop-offs on both sides of the ball by avoiding an extended absence like the five-week DL stint he suffered in 2009. His games played and plate appearances approached career highs, and his triple-slash stats hovered at or above their career rates, always a positive indicator for a player in his mid-30s. As a percentage basestealer, Hunter has rarely been much better than break-even, but this year he just plain broke, succeeding in only nine of his 21 attempts; that costly performance accounted for the bulk of the 24th-worst BRR in MLB. The five-year, $90 million deal that Tony Reagins handed Hunter after the 2007 season wasn't well received (except by Hunter), but three-fifths of the way through, the center fielder has more or less earned his paychecks. Advancing age may change that equation, but Hunter has already done enough to vault his contract out of Gary Matthews territory.

Maicer Izturis **INF**

Born: **9/12/1980** Age: **30**
Bats: S Throws: R Height: **5' 8"** Weight: **155**
Breakout: **1%** Improve: **27%** Collapse: **9%**
Attrition: **7%** MLB: **85%**

Comparables:
Don Wert, Len Dykstra, Don Buford (66)

YEAR	TEAM	LVL	AGE	PA	R	2B	3B	HR	RBI	BB	SO	SB	CS	AVG_OBP_SLG	TAv	BABIP	BRR	FRAA	WARP
2008	ANA	MLB	27	321	43	14	2	3	37	26	27	11	2	.269/.327/.362	.250	.284	0.2	SS 4, 2B 0	1.1
2009	ANA	MLB	28	437	75	22	3	8	65	35	41	13	5	.300/.357/.434	.290	.310	0.5	2B -2, SS -3	2.0
2010	ANA	MLB	29	238	27	13	1	3	27	21	27	7	3	.250/.319/.363	.262	.270	-1.3	3B 0, 2B -2	0.5
2011	*ANA*	*MLB*	*30*	*374*	*46*	*19*	*2*	*7*	*40*	*34*	*37*	*10*	*4*	*.282/.347/.410*	*.268*	*.296*	*-0.3*	*2B -1, SS 0*	*1.2*

That Izturis has never held down a starting job owes as much to his health as to his performance when on the field; he has now made DL trips in five of the last six seasons, qualifying as a repeat offender during three of them. Last year, he made two separate trips for shoulder complaints and another for forearm stiffness, tossing in a day-to-day hamstring issue for good measure. When healthy, he's still the envy of most teams' infield bench-men. Still, you'd like your utility guy to be the one replacing injured players, not the one requiring a replacement.

Howie Kendrick **2B**

Born: **7/12/1983** Age: **27**
Bats: R Throws: R Height: **5' 10"** Weight: **195**
Breakout: **3%** Improve: **51%** Collapse: **4%**
Attrition: **12%** MLB: **93%**

Comparables:
Carlos Baerga, Aaron Hill, Pete Rose (74)

YEAR	TEAM	LVL	AGE	PA	R	2B	3B	HR	RBI	BB	SO	SB	CS	AVG_OBP_SLG	TAv	BABIP	BRR	FRAA	WARP
2008	ANA	MLB	24	361	44	26	2	3	37	12	58	11	4	.306/.332/.421	.266	.356	3.3	2B 9	2.3
2009	SLC	AAA	25	87	11	6	1	2	11	7	12	4	2	.346/.414/.526	.320	.391	1.4	2B 5	1.3
2009	ANA	MLB	25	400	61	21	3	10	61	20	71	11	4	.291/.333/.444	.289	.336	1.0	2B 4	2.6
2010	ANA	MLB	26	658	67	41	4	10	75	28	94	14	4	.279/.312/.408	.268	.311	-3.2	2B -11, 1B 0	0.6
2011	*ANA*	*MLB*	*27*	*499*	*62*	*30*	*3*	*11*	*63*	*24*	*77*	*12*	*4*	*.294/.332/.443*	*.272*	*.328*	*-0.3*	*2B 1, 1B 0*	*1.8*

In three of our last four annuals, Kendrick's player comments have mentioned his purported predisposition toward batting titles. With that sentence, we've run the tally to four-for-five, but Kendrick hasn't come any closer to achieving that elusive goal, and he's past the age at which we can confidently predict a great leap forward. For the first time, Kendrick made contact on an above-average percentage of his swings, and he's one fluky-BABIP season away from delivering on his promise. Unfortunately, his walk-deprived offense isn't much to write home about when hit-luck goes against him, and his glove won't make him a star. On the plus side, last season was Kendrick's first without a minor-league layover of some duration, which constitutes a meager kind of progress.

Jeff Mathis **C**

Born: **3/31/1983** Age: **28**
Bats: R Throws: R Height: **6' 0"** Weight: **180**
Breakout: **3%** Improve: **30%** Collapse: **8%**
Attrition: **23%** MLB: **83%**

Comparables:
Randy Hundley, Todd Hundley, Terry Steinbach (79)

YEAR	TEAM	LVL	AGE	PA	R	2B	3B	HR	RBI	BB	SO	SB	CS	AVG_OBP_SLG	TAv	BABIP	BRR	FRAA	WARP
2008	ANA	MLB	25	328	35	8	0	9	42	30	90	2	2	.194/.268/.318	.216	.235	-1.7	C 2	-0.1
2009	ANA	MLB	26	272	26	8	0	5	28	22	73	2	3	.211/.279/.308	.214	.268	-1.5	C 2	-0.1
2010	ANA	MLB	27	218	19	6	1	3	18	6	59	3	0	.195/.216/.278	.189	.248	0.4	C 1	-0.5
2011	*ANA*	*MLB*	*28*	*359*	*36*	*14*	*1*	*8*	*34*	*26*	*89*	*3*	*1*	*.223/.279/.347*	*.222*	*.274*	*-0.2*	*C 2*	*0.2*

After terrorizing the Yankees in the 2009 ALCS, Mathis started the season with a 10-game hitting streak, complete with a pretty .324/.351/.500 line. Angered by the career .200 hitter's attempt to make a mockery of the game, the baseball gods directed a Kevin Jepsen delivery into Mathis's wrist, fracturing a bone and knocking the catcher out of commission for two months. Upon his return, Mathis hit .170/.191/.234, which translates to a .185 TAv, the worst offensive performance by anyone in the majors not named Brandon Wood. While it might be tempting to blame a weakened wrist for his woeful batting, Mathis's bona fides as a sub-replacement-level batter were well established before 2010; the cast only delayed the inevitable. With Mike Napoli pressed into service as a first baseman, Mathis's leash behind the plate was plenty long when he was healthy, but the contrast between his bat and Hank Conger's may be too stark for even Mike Scioscia to ignore.

Hideki Matsui **DH**

Born: **6/12/1974** Age: **37**
Bats: **L** Throws: **R** Height: **6' 2"** Weight: **210**
Breakout: **0%** Improve: **22%** Collapse: **11%**
Attrition: **20%** MLB: **89%**

Comparables:
Raul Ibanez, Ellis Burks, Moises Alou (74)

YEAR	TEAM	LVL	AGE	PA	R	2B	3B	HR	RBI	BB	SO	SB	CS	AVG_OBP_SLG	TAv	BABIP	BRR	FRAA	WARP
2008	NYA	MLB	34	378	44	17	0	9	45	38	47	0	0	.294/.370/.424	.281	.320	-1.4	LF 2, RF -1	1.2
2009	NYA	MLB	35	528	74	21	1	28	90	64	75	0	1	.274/.366/.509	.308	.273	0.6	—	3.1
2010	ANA	MLB	36	558	61	24	1	21	84	67	98	0	1	.274/.358/.459	.303	.303	-2.0	LF -4	2.2
2011	*OAK*	*MLB*	*37*	*465*	*61*	*20*	*1*	*18*	*60*	*55*	*70*	*1*	*0*	*.272/.358/.462*	*.288*	*.284*	*-0.1*	*LF 0, RF 0*	*1.6*

The Yankees chose to part ways with Matsui's creaky knees after 2009, electing to cast their lot with Nick Johnson and his Elijah Price–like medical history. Though their thinking seemed fairly sound at the time, they'd probably like to take a mulligan on that decision, as the one who got away turned in his most durable performance since 2005, while losing little offensively after accounting for his move to a less hitter-friendly park (though he needed a .309/.402/.553 second half to get there). In his age-36 season, the Halos' primary DH even mustered 19 outfield appearances, as if to show Brian Cashman that he could in the wake of his former GM's comments to the contrary. Matsui wasn't especially selective by Yankees standards, but his 10.9-percent UBB rate ranked behind that of only fellow pinstriped expat Bobby Abreu on the more impatient Angels. The hitter-friendly confines of Yankee Stadium will seem even further away this season, as Matsui moves to the vast open spaces of Oakland-Alameda County Coliseum, where he'll serve as the Athletics' primary DH.

Kendry Morales **1B**

Born: **6/20/1983** Age: **28**
Bats: **S** Throws: **R** Height: **6' 1"** Weight: **220**
Breakout: **3%** Improve: **41%** Collapse: **6%**
Attrition: **12%** MLB: **80%**

Comparables:
Orlando Cepeda, Adrian Gonzalez, Micah Hoffpauir (76)

YEAR	TEAM	LVL	AGE	PA	R	2B	3B	HR	RBI	BB	SO	SB	CS	AVG_OBP_SLG	TAv	BABIP	BRR	FRAA	WARP
2008	SLC	AAA	25	340	46	19	0	15	64	19	43	1	3	.341/.376/.543	.308	.355	-1.2	1B -2, RF -1	1.6
2008	ANA	MLB	25	66	6	2	0	3	8	4	7	0	1	.213/.273/.393	.235	.196	-1.4	RF 2, 1B 1	0.0
2009	ANA	MLB	26	622	86	43	2	34	108	46	117	3	7	.306/.355/.569	.315	.329	-4.7	1B 0	3.5
2010	ANA	MLB	27	211	29	5	0	11	39	12	31	0	1	.290/.346/.487	.312	.296	2.1	1B 1	1.5
2011	*ANA*	*MLB*	*28*	*429*	*60*	*23*	*1*	*20*	*66*	*29*	*68*	*2*	*2*	*.301/.351/.520*	*.299*	*.318*	*-0.4*	*1B -2, RF 0*	*1.7*

Morales suffered one of the stranger injuries of the 2010 season when he broke his leg jumping on home plate after hitting a 10th-inning grand slam to win a May 29 contest, marking perhaps the first incidence of a "cart-off" home run in major-league history. The baseball equivalent of a midcoitus coronary isn't a bad way to go, but Morales and his teammates still probably felt that he'd been taken before his time. Leading up to his demise, Morales had been struggling terribly against southpaws, and an increasingly ground-ball-oriented stroke had prevented him from duplicating his 2009 power output. Nonetheless, the Angels struggled to fill the void left by his departure and eagerly await a healthy age-28 season.

Mike Napoli **1B**

Born: **10/31/1981** Age: **29**
Bats: **R** Throws: **R** Height: **6' 0"** Weight: **205**
Breakout: **2%** Improve: **41%** Collapse: **2%**
Attrition: **11%** MLB: **89%**

Comparables:
Jonny Gomes, Albert Belle, Ryan Ludwick (69)

YEAR	TEAM	LVL	AGE	PA	R	2B	3B	HR	RBI	BB	SO	SB	CS	AVG_OBP_SLG	TAv	BABIP	BRR	FRAA	WARP
2008	ANA	MLB	26	274	39	9	1	20	49	35	70	7	3	.273/.372/.586	.343	.292	-3.0	C 0	3.2
2009	ANA	MLB	27	432	60	22	1	20	56	40	103	3	3	.272/.350/.492	.307	.321	-0.9	C -1	3.5
2010	ANA	MLB	28	510	60	24	1	26	68	42	137	4	2	.238/.316/.468	.286	.279	0.2	1B 5, C -1	2.9
2011	*ANA*	*MLB*	*29*	*378*	*50*	*17*	*1*	*19*	*54*	*39*	*96*	*5*	*2*	*.257/.344/.490*	*.289*	*.299*	*-0.3*	*C 0, 1B 1*	*2.3*

Mike Scioscia has never been comfortable with Napoli behind the plate, but the extended absence of Kendry Morales allowed Scioscia to hide the defensively challenged backstop's bat elsewhere on the diamond. That was good news for Napoli, who found himself with more playing time than he ever knew existed, but nothing more than a stopgap solution to a hairy situation for the Angels, since Napoli's bat seems special only in the offense-deprived context of catcher. This is particularly true in that Mickey Hatcher's lessons seem to be getting to him—his walk rate is now little more than half of what it was when he came up, and to make matters worse, he hasn't hit righties much since 2008. Traded to Toronto, he'll finally play every day as the DH while providing insurance at catcher and first base.

Juan Rivera **LF**

Born: **7/3/1978** Age: **32**
Bats: R Throws: R Height: **6' 2"** Weight: **225**
Breakout: **0%** Improve: **25%** Collapse: **12%**
Attrition: **7%** MLB: **81%**

Comparables:
Kevin McReynolds, Ed Kranepool, Kevin Mench (71)

YEAR	TEAM	LVL	AGE	PA	R	2B	3B	HR	RBI	BB	SO	SB	CS	AVG_OBP_SLG	TAv	BABIP	BRR	FRAA	WARP
2008	ANA	MLB	29	280	37	13	0	12	45	16	33	1	1	.246/.282/.438	.247	.233	1.8	LF -2, RF -2	-0.1
2009	ANA	MLB	30	572	75	24	1	25	88	36	57	0	1	.287/.332/.478	.286	.281	-4.8	LF -4, RF -1	1.6
2010	ANA	MLB	31	455	54	20	0	15	52	33	58	2	2	.252/.312/.409	.273	.261	-2.0	LF 4, RF 2	1.8
2011	*ANA*	*MLB*	*32*	*386*	*48*	*18*	*0*	*15*	*51*	*27*	*46*	*2*	*1*	*.273/.325/.456*	*.274*	*.275*	*-0.1*	*LF 1, RF 0*	*1.2*

In retrospect, the late-2004 trade that brought Rivera and Maicer Izturis to Anaheim in exchange for Jose Guillen has worked out well for the Halos. Both players have made significant contributions to the Angels' (mostly) winning ways, though neither would fit anyone's notion of an ideal starter. The arrival of Peter Bourjos put a crimp in Rivera's playing time. But he should recover some of it with the Blue Jays, who acquired him in the Vernon Wells deal.

Andrew Romine **SS**

Born: **12/24/1985** Age: **25**
Bats: S Throws: R Height: **6' 1"** Weight: **190**
Breakout: **0%** Improve: **11%** Collapse: **7%**
Attrition: **24%** MLB: **30%**

Comparables:
Brent Lillibridge, Chin-lung Hu, Hernan Iribarren (76)

YEAR	TEAM	LVL	AGE	PA	R	2B	3B	HR	RBI	BB	SO	SB	CS	AVG_OBP_SLG	TAv	BABIP	BRR	FRAA	WARP
2008	CDR	A	22	543	79	21	4	2	34	55	76	62	18	.260/.339/.336	.252	.294	3.7	SS 4	2.4
2009	RCU	A+	23	555	68	13	9	1	36	51	83	26	11	.278/.341/.349	.269	.318	4.0	SS 7	3.7
2010	ARK	AA	24	454	55	15	4	3	34	50	66	21	9	.282/.370/.366	.275	.319	0.0	SS 12	3.5
2010	ANA	MLB	24	12	0	0	0	0	0	0	4	0	0	.091/.083/.091	.057	.125	0.2	SS 0	-0.2
2011	*ANA*	*MLB*	*25*	*530*	*55*	*18*	*4*	*5*	*44*	*44*	*92*	*26*	*9*	*.252/.310/.336*	*.233*	*.293*	*-0.6*	*SS 10*	*1.4*

Romine leapfrogged Triple-A to make his debut in the majors—where he was reportedly impressed by the quality of the clubhouse bathrooms—when an injury stack overcame the Angels' infield in late September. Although it owed much to the dire condition of the major-league roster, Romine's promotion can still be construed as a reward for a job well done, as the shortstop posted the best on-base percentage of his career at Double-A Arkansas. Judging by the two bases he stole with brother Austin behind the plate in an AFL game, he's quite a competitive fellow; as an above-average fielder with some bat-handling ability (in a "little things" sense) and a willingness to take a walk, Romine probably has a future as a utility infielder, although a major-league homer might prove too much to ask.

Freddy Sandoval **3B**

Born: **8/16/1982** Age: **28**
Bats: S Throws: R Height: **6' 1"** Weight: **200**
Breakout: **1%** Improve: **17%** Collapse: **4%**
Attrition: **8%** MLB: **39%**

Comparables:
Craig Stansberry, Greg Dobbs, Brian Buscher (76)

YEAR	TEAM	LVL	AGE	PA	R	2B	3B	HR	RBI	BB	SO	SB	CS	AVG_OBP_SLG	TAv	BABIP	BRR	FRAA	WARP
2008	SLC	AAA	25	587	92	45	2	15	88	47	74	6	3	.335/.387/.514	.297	.360	1.0	3B 14, 2B -8	4.5
2008	ANA	MLB	25	7	0	0	0	0	0	1	0	0	0	.167/.286/.167	.180	.167	0.0	3B 0, 1B 0	0.0
2009	SLC	AAA	26	303	46	16	5	6	46	26	39	12	3	.300/.360/.458	.283	.332	-0.9	3B -3, 1B 0	1.1
2009	ANA	MLB	26	11	1	1	0	0	0	0	3	0	0	.182/.182/.273	.144	.250	0.1	2B 1, 3B 1	0.0
2010	SLC	AAA	27	95	13	1	1	0	10	12	12	0	0	.210/.326/.247	.238	.246	2.0	3B 1	0.4
2011	*ANA*	*MLB*	*28*	*344*	*43*	*18*	*2*	*7*	*39*	*29*	*52*	*4*	*2*	*.285/.348/.426*	*.273*	*.318*	*-0.1*	*3B 2, 1B -1*	*1.1*

If Baseball-Reference lists "pinch runner" as one of your primary positions, either you haven't gotten much playing time or you're Herb Washington (or both). Sandoval falls into the former camp, which reflects an inability to stay healthy as much as a failure to perform when in the lineup. In 2009, a sprained wrist cost him a chance to fill in for Howie Kendrick, and a strained elbow rendered him unavailable when Maicer Izturis went down last season. When he did play, he didn't hit, a trend that continued in Mexican winter ball. A change of scenery wouldn't hurt, but neither would less time on the trainer's table.

Jean Segura **2B**

Born: **3/17/1990** Age: **21**
Bats: R Throws: L Height: **5' 11"** Weight: **155**
Breakout: **0%** Improve: **0%** Collapse: **1%**
Attrition: **1%** MLB: **2%**

Comparables:
Rennie Stennett, Asdrubal Cabrera, Lou Whitaker (72)

YEAR	TEAM	LVL	AGE	PA	R	2B	3B	HR	RBI	BB	SO	SB	CS	AVG_OBP_SLG	TAv	BABIP	BRR	FRAA	WARP
2009	ORM	Rk	19	177	33	10	4	3	21	11	11	11	3	.346/.390/.512	.352	.353	4.0	2B 10	3.5
2010	CDR	A	20	581	89	24	12	10	79	45	72	50	10	.313/.365/.464	.293	.334	5.3	2B 26	6.4
2011	*ANA*	*MLB*	*21*	*275*	*31*	*13*	*3*	*5*	*31*	*14*	*46*	*7*	*2*	*.271/.303/.397*	*.245*	*.305*	*0.1*	*2B 11, RF 0*	*1.3*

After exceeding expectations last season, Segura now merits a sizeable blip on the prospect radar. The formerly fragile Dominican stayed healthy all season, showcasing superior contact skills, gap power (with potential for more as he packs on the pounds), and the plus-plus speed that enabled him to reach the half-century mark in stolen bases. When Mike Trout was promoted to High-A in mid-July, Segura inherited not only his leadoff spot in the lineup, but perhaps his status as the Midwest League's most exciting position player, and he responded with a .338/.390/.545 second half.

Mike Trout **CF**

Born: **8/7/1991** Age: **19**
Bats: R Throws: R Height: **6' 1"** Weight: **217**
Breakout: **1%** Improve: **8%** Collapse: **0%**
Attrition: **3%** MLB: **11%**

Comparables:
Justin Upton, Cesar Cedeno, Mickey Mantle (54)

YEAR	TEAM	LVL	AGE	PA	R	2B	3B	HR	RBI	BB	SO	SB	CS	AVG_OBP_SLG	TAv	BABIP	BRR	FRAA	WARP
2009	ANG	Rk	17	187	29	7	7	1	25	18	28	13	2	.360/.412/.506	.359	.414	3.9	CF 0, RF 1	3.0
2010	CDR	A	18	368	76	19	7	6	39	46	52	45	9	.362/.454/.526	.349	.416	6.6	CF -3, LF 1	4.8
2010	RCU	A+	18	233	30	9	2	4	19	27	33	11	6	.306/.388/.434	.323	.335	2.3	CF -4, LF 1	2.5
2011	*ANA*	*MLB*	*19*	*428*	*50*	*20*	*4*	*8*	*46*	*36*	*88*	*19*	*4*	*.270/.331/.402*	*.263*	*.324*	*0.5*	*CF -15, LF 0*	*-0.2*

Trout's debut couldn't have gone much better. The teen sensation laid waste to the Midwest League before being promoted to High-A following a two-hit performance as the Futures Game's youngest player, hustling his way to the top of prospect lists with the same speed he displayed on the field. The 25th overall pick in the 2009 draft has been clocked in the 3.9 range to first, which would make him one of the fastest right-handers in the majors if he debuted today. By the time he arrives in "The Show," the center fielder may have slowed slightly, but he'll probably have compensated by heaping additional home runs atop his ample helpings of doubles and triples. All that running doesn't prevent him from taking plenty of walks, making Trout a player about whom talent evaluators of all persuasions can dream. Several teams have already seen major-league returns from their more mature 2009 first-round draftees, but few clubs have more reason to be satisfied with their pick than the Angels.

Mark Trumbo **1B**

Born: **1/16/1986** Age: **25**
Bats: R Throws: R Height: **6' 4"** Weight: **220**
Breakout: **4%** Improve: **28%** Collapse: **3%**
Attrition: **24%** MLB: **55%**

Comparables:
Joey Votto, Brandon Allen, Jesus Guzman (75)

YEAR	TEAM	LVL	AGE	PA	R	2B	3B	HR	RBI	BB	SO	SB	CS	AVG_OBP_SLG	TAv	BABIP	BRR	FRAA	WARP
2008	RCU	A+	22	438	70	28	2	26	68	26	67	7	3	.283/.329/.553	.304	.282	1.8	1B 2	2.8
2008	ARK	AA	22	134	13	7	1	6	25	7	29	1	2	.276/.306/.496	.266	.304	-3.0	1B 3	0.2
2009	ARK	AA	23	581	54	35	3	15	88	37	100	6	3	.291/.332/.452	.287	.327	-4.0	1B -3, RF 1	1.5
2010	SLC	AAA	24	595	103	29	5	36	122	58	126	3	4	.301/.368/.577	.313	.332	0.0	1B 0, RF 6	4.6
2010	ANA	MLB	24	16	1	0	0	0	2	1	8	0	0	.067/.125/.067	.076	.143	0.5	1B 0, RF 0	-0.2
2011	*ANA*	*MLB*	*25*	*597*	*77*	*29*	*3*	*27*	*88*	*38*	*131*	*4*	*2*	*.276/.320/.488*	*.277*	*.310*	*-0.2*	*1B -17, RF 1*	*0.0*

Trumbo did enough at Triple-A to take home some hardware as the organizational player of the year. Perhaps that title would impress a prospective trade partner, but our translations weren't smitten with his work. On the surface, his season was a rousing success: despite his graduation to a higher level of competition, all of Trumbo's rate stats improved, and his home-run total more than doubled, from middling to minor-league–leading. The righty continued to mash in Venezuela, but any attempt to forecast how his numbers would hold up in Anaheim must ding him hard for the forgiving hitting environment of Salt Lake. Clearly, Trumbo is capable of more than he showed in his first 16 major-league plate appearances, but his performance is probably not enough for him to hold down a spot at the game's premier offensive position. At 25, the strapping first baseman may not have much more room for growth, and he won't displace Kendry Morales. If Trumbo does have a major-league future, it may lie in the outfield, where he spent 22 Triple-A games.

Reggie Willits **OF**

Born: **5/30/1981** Age: **30**
Bats: S Throws: R Height: **5' 11"** Weight: **185**
Breakout: **1%** Improve: **24%** Collapse: **7%**
Attrition: **17%** MLB: **60%**

Comparables:
Jim Delsing, Chris Burke, Tommy Watkins (76)

YEAR	TEAM	LVL	AGE	PA	R	2B	3B	HR	RBI	BB	SO	SB	CS	AVG_OBP_SLG	TAv	BABIP	BRR	FRAA	WARP
2008	ANA	MLB	27	136	14	4	0	0	7	21	26	2	1	.194/.309/.232	.215	.236	0.5	LF -1, RF -3	-0.7
2009	SLC	AAA	28	280	40	10	1	1	27	34	44	11	4	.261/.346/.325	.238	.302	4.4	CF 2, LF 3	0.7
2009	ANA	MLB	28	92	12	2	0	0	6	5	17	5	1	.213/.239/.238	.175	.243	2.1	LF -5, RF 0	-0.8
2010	ANA	MLB	29	182	18	7	0	0	8	19	26	2	4	.258/.335/.302	.252	.302	-0.3	LF 1, CF 0	0.3
2011	*ANA*	*MLB*	*30*	*352*	*39*	*14*	*1*	*2*	*26*	*44*	*58*	*12*	*5*	*.255/.345/.331*	*.246*	*.297*	*-0.6*	*CF 0, LF 1*	*0.2*

For a time, Willits was a poor man's Brett Gardner, before a Brett Gardner for the wealthy man hit the market. The switch-hitter's offensive contributions in his fractional 2006 and full 2007 were BABIP-driven and powerless—after nearly a thousand major-league plate appearances, he still has yet to go yard—but the speedy outfielder seemed like the type of player who might be able to sustain BABIPs in the mid-.300s, and his selectivity made him an on-base threat from both sides of the plate. However, the Oklahoman's success has proven to be short-lived. Perhaps realizing that Willits couldn't make them pay, opposing pitchers started throwing a significantly higher percentage of pitches into his strike zone after 2007, cutting into his walk rate. Meanwhile, the slap-hitter started elevating—always a bad sign for players whose flies tend not to leave the yard—and his reduced ground-ball percentage produced a corresponding decrease in BABIP. Since Willits lacks the superior defensive ability and baserunning acumen that one might expect of a player with his skill set, he has languished below replacement level in his sporadic post-2007 work.

Bobby Wilson **C**

Born: **4/8/1983** Age: **28**
Bats: R Throws: R Height: **6' 0"** Weight: **220**
Breakout: **3%** Improve: **22%** Collapse: **11%**
Attrition: **20%** MLB: **57%**

Comparables:
John Baker, J.R. House, Ryan Budde (75)

YEAR	TEAM	LVL	AGE	PA	R	2B	3B	HR	RBI	BB	SO	SB	CS	AVG_OBP_SLG	TAv	BABIP	BRR	FRAA	WARP
2008	SLC	AAA	25	298	33	20	0	4	45	29	45	0	0	.312/.383/.435	.292	.356	-4.3	C 0, 1B 0	1.9
2008	ANA	MLB	25	7	0	0	0	0	1	1	3	0	0	.167/.286/.167	.187	.333	-0.3	C 0	-0.1
2009	SLC	AAA	26	381	38	19	1	8	55	22	56	0	0	.271/.312/.398	.240	.299	-0.6	C 3, 1B 2	0.9
2009	ANA	MLB	26	6	0	1	0	0	0	0	1	0	0	.200/.167/.400	.130	.200	0.0	C 0, 1B 0	0.0
2010	ANA	MLB	27	106	12	6	0	4	15	8	23	0	0	.229/.283/.417	.255	.254	0.8	C -1, 1B 0	0.4
2011	*ANA*	*MLB*	*28*	*273*	*32*	*14*	*0*	*7*	*32*	*21*	*49*	*0*	*0*	*.266/.321/.415*	*.257*	*.298*	*0.0*	*C 0, 1B 0*	*0.9*

In a season that saw serious injuries to Kendry Morales and Jeff Mathis, Wilson escaped the itinerant benchwarmer role that he'd played in 2009, graduating to the more lucrative gig of backup catcher, which allowed him to ride the pine while regularly drawing major-league paychecks. Wilson could outhit Mathis while playing capable defense, but he doesn't possess any skills spectacular enough to unseat the incumbent; in his first career start, Mark Teixeira sent him to the DL with a bad case of home-plate collision, as if to remind him of his lot in life. Consistent with reports of questionable bat speed, Wilson struggled to hit the hard stuff, but punished pitchers for attempting to sneak anything with a bend in it by him. Only 27, he'll be likely to spend the next decade paying dues to the International Brotherhood of Backup Catchers.

Brandon Wood **3B**

Born: **3/2/1985** Age: **26**
Bats: R Throws: R Height: **6' 3"** Weight: **185**
Breakout: **1%** Improve: **19%** Collapse: **4%**
Attrition: **24%** MLB: **47%**

Comparables:
Scott Moore, Andy Marte, Matthew Brown (76)

YEAR	TEAM	LVL	AGE	PA	R	2B	3B	HR	RBI	BB	SO	SB	CS	AVG_OBP_SLG	TAv	BABIP	BRR	FRAA	WARP
2008	SLC	AAA	23	448	82	21	2	31	84	45	104	6	5	.296/.375/.595	.303	.328	2.6	SS -13, 3B 1	2.9
2008	ANA	MLB	23	157	12	4	0	5	13	4	43	4	0	.200/.223/.327	.199	.240	-0.1	SS -5, 3B 0	-0.9
2009	SLC	AAA	24	428	65	28	4	22	72	36	80	1	1	.293/.353/.557	.299	.316	-2.4	3B -7, SS -9	1.1
2009	ANA	MLB	24	46	5	1	0	1	3	3	19	0	0	.195/.261/.293	.197	.318	-1.4	3B -2, 1B 0	-0.5
2010	SLC	AAA	25	54	4	0	0	1	2	3	17	0	0	.196/.241/.255	.179	.273	0.1	3B -1, 1B 0	-0.4
2010	ANA	MLB	25	243	20	2	0	4	14	6	71	1	0	.146/.169/.208	.151	.181	1.8	3B -4, SS 0	-2.0
2011	*ANA*	*MLB*	*26*	*475*	*56*	*19*	*2*	*21*	*63*	*34*	*123*	*3*	*1*	*.246/.300/.442*	*.257*	*.288*	*-0.1*	*SS -6, 3B -4*	*0.4*

Since 1954, the only position player to post a seasonal TAv lower than Brandon Wood's .121 in a minimum of 200 plate appearances is Tony Pena Jr., who managed a .117 mark in 2008. Pena's pitcher-like batting line prefigured a move to the mound midway through the following season, but Wood will have to locate his missing lumber if he hopes to make good in the majors. The 2005 minor-league home-run champ has accumulated less than a full season's worth of at-bats in the bigs as he enters his age-26 season, but he's done little to earn more, walking only infrequently and managing a medley of weak flies on the rare occasions that he's made contact. Wood is Angels property through 2014, but after being displaced by Alberto Callaspo at the deadline, he's more likely to become trade fodder or a nontender candidate than the team's infielder of the future, despite his prospect pedigree.

PITCHERS

Trevor Bell

Born: **10/12/1986** Age: **24**
Bats: L Throws: R Height: **6' 2"** Weight: **185**
Breakout: **2%** Improve: **9%** Collapse: **4%**
Attrition: **6%** MLB: **16%**

Comparables:
Rafael Rodriguez, Alfredo Figaro, Anthony Ortega (79)

YEAR	TEAM	LVL	AGE	W	L	SV	G	GS	IP	H	HR	BB	SO	EqBB9	EqSO9	GB%	BABIP	WHIP	ERA	FRA	WARP
2008	RCU	A+	21	6	8	0	36	12	100^1	106	8	39	80	3.5	7.2	58%	.316	1.49	4.22	4.83	0.7
2009	ARK	AA	22	4	3	0	11	11	68^2	54	1	20	51	2.6	6.7	52%	.256	1.11	2.23	3.12	1.4
2009	SLC	AAA	22	3	4	0	11	11	71^1	67	5	15	38	1.9	4.8	52%	.274	1.18	3.16	3.21	2.0
2009	ANA	MLB	22	1	2	0	8	4	20^1	40	3	11	14	4.9	6.2	39%	.451	2.51	9.74	7.05	-0.2
2010	SLC	AAA	23	2	0	0	6	6	30	30	3	6	19	1.8	5.7	43%	.278	1.27	3.00	2.98	1.1
2010	ANA	MLB	23	2	5	0	25	7	61	77	2	21	45	3.1	6.6	45%	.368	1.62	4.72	3.89	0.8
2011	*ANA*	*MLB*	*24*	*6*	*6*	*0*	*31*	*15*	*109*	*126*	*11*	*42*	*60*	*3.4*	*4.9*	*48%*	*.314*	*1.53*	*4.96*	*5.40*	*0.1*

Bell's second exposure to the majors left fewer scars than the first, but while he's unlikely ever to be burned as badly as he was by his scalding 2009 cup of coffee, the odds are against a complete recovery. At 24, he's probably a finished, fringy product, saddled with a low-90s fastball that garners few swings and misses, and control and ground-ball ability that aren't quite good enough to overcome that handicap. With over 80 major-league innings under his belt, the southpaw from North Hollywood sports a .397 BABIP. His defenders may very well get to more balls in the future, but if the lefty's repertoire doesn't start to look less hittable, the Angels will continue to get their Bell rung.

Jason Bulger

Born: **12/6/1978** Age: **32**
Bats: R Throws: R Height: **6' 4"** Weight: **215**
Breakout: **25%** Improve: **38%** Collapse: **15%**
Attrition: **8%** MLB: **70%**

Comparables:
Mike Gonzalez, Lee Smith, George Sherrill (71)

YEAR	TEAM	LVL	AGE	W	L	SV	G	GS	IP	H	HR	BB	SO	EqBB9	EqSO9	GB%	BABIP	WHIP	ERA	FRA	WARP
2008	SLC	AAA	29	4	0	16	37	0	43	25	0	22	75	4.6	15.7	58%	.333	1.12	0.63	0.40	1.9
2008	ANA	MLB	29	0	0	0	14	0	16	15	3	9	20	5.1	11.3	33%	.308	1.63	7.31	7.64	-0.5
2009	ANA	MLB	30	6	1	1	64	0	65^{2}	46	7	30	68	4.1	9.3	45%	.250	1.17	3.56	4.23	0.7
2010	ANA	MLB	31	0	0	0	25	0	24	25	3	15	25	5.6	9.4	38%	.333	1.75	4.88	4.99	0.0
2011	*ANA*	*MLB*	*32*	*3*	*1*	*2*	*48*	*0*	*49*	*40*	*4*	*27*	*58*	*4.8*	*10.5*	*45%*	*.298*	*1.33*	*3.47*	*3.78*	*0.4*

A montage of snapshots from Bulger's career might best be set to the Eagles' "Wasted Time." For a variety of reasons, certain prospects are forced to toil in the minors long after they've shown that they have little left to prove there, watching as their limited windows of opportunity close. For pitchers, whose ability to perform at a high level can disappear in an instant, those years in purgatory are even more poignant. It took a 0.63 ERA in 2008, his fourth Triple-A season, to earn a then-30-year-old Bulger the extended major-league audition for which he'd been waiting. The righty didn't disappoint in 2009, but his successful campaign ended on an ominous note, as shoulder soreness nearly rendered him unavailable for the playoffs. Last season, the problem recurred, limiting him to three appearances after mid-June. He managed to maintain his strikeout rate when available, but surrendered some control and velocity, which he failed to recover after a long midseason layoff. His ERA would have looked much better sans a disastrous third of an inning in his first outing back, but even so, he wasn't the pitcher that Mike Scioscia had gradually come to trust.

Bobby Cassevah

Born: **9/11/1985** Age: **25**
Bats: R Throws: R Height: **6' 3"** Weight: **195**
Breakout: **0%** Improve: **0%** Collapse: **0%**
Attrition: **0%** MLB: **0%**

Comparables:
Jesus Delgado, Sean Burnett, Marty Bystrom (82)

YEAR	TEAM	LVL	AGE	W	L	SV	G	GS	IP	H	HR	BB	SO	EqBB9	EqSO9	GB%	BABIP	WHIP	ERA	FRA	WARP
2008	RCU	A+	22	2	3	1	44	0	71^{1}	67	1	40	52	5.0	6.6	64%	.300	1.57	3.79	4.82	0.2
2009	ARK	AA	23	3	7	4	57	0	73^{1}	64	2	37	45	4.5	5.5	72%	.273	1.43	3.68	5.43	-0.6
2010	SLC	AAA	24	3	4	5	45	0	59	69	7	25	38	3.8	5.8	74%	.318	1.66	4.27	5.33	-0.0
2010	ANA	MLB	24	1	2	0	16	0	20	23	0	8	8	3.6	3.6	60%	.299	1.60	3.15	3.58	0.3
2011	*ANA*	*MLB*	*25*	*2*	*1*	*1*	*44*	*0*	*60^{1}*	*66*	*6*	*34*	*31*	*5.1*	*4.6*	*56%*	*.302*	*1.66*	*5.31*	*5.77*	*-1.0*

Lefties crushed Cassevah to the tune of a 963 OPS in their 51 major-league plate appearances against him last season, working five walks (one of them intentional) against only one strikeout. On their own, 51 PAs don't constitute a trend, but susceptibility to southpaws has always been Cassevah's bugaboo. The sinkerballer kept the ball down both before and after batters made contact, leading all Angels with at least 20 innings in ground-ball rate (meaning that he managed to best even a Dave Duncan–ized Joel Pineiro in that category). Cassevah limited righties to a 463 OPS, and he's capable of succeeding for multiple innings at a time if deployed correctly. Facing more lefties than righties, as he did last season, doesn't qualify as "correctly," but teams are wise to his weakness and will often be willing to pinch-hit against him in order to gain the platoon advantage, as they did five times in 2010.

Tyler Chatwood

Born: **12/16/1989** Age: **21**
Bats: R Throws: R Height: **6' 0"** Weight: **185**
Breakout: **9%** Improve: **17%** Collapse: **5%**
Attrition: **7%** MLB: **31%**

Comparables:
Jim Palmer, Dan Petry, Camilo Pascual (66)

YEAR	TEAM	LVL	AGE	W	L	SV	G	GS	IP	H	HR	BB	SO	EqBB9	EqSO9	GB%	BABIP	WHIP	ERA	FRA	WARP
2008	ANG	Rk	18	1	2	0	11	11	38	25	1	36	48	8.5	11.4	59%	.296	1.61	3.08	3.98	1.2
2009	CDR	A	19	8	7	0	24	24	116^{1}	99	3	66	106	5.1	8.2	50%	.306	1.44	4.02	5.25	0.5
2010	RCU	A+	20	8	3	0	14	13	81^{1}	71	6	36	70	4.0	7.8	64%	.294	1.34	1.77	2.26	3.1
2010	ARK	AA	20	4	6	0	12	12	68^{1}	72	3	27	36	3.6	4.8	53%	.303	1.48	3.82	4.95	-0.0
2011	*ANA*	*MLB*	*21*	*6*	*9*	*0*	*19*	*19*	*96*	*107*	*10*	*64*	*58*	*5.9*	*5.4*	*49%*	*.309*	*1.76*	*5.74*	*6.24*	*-0.3*

Chatwood posted eye-popping numbers in the hitter-friendly California League, earning a June promotion. The undersized lefty was the youngest of the Double-A Arkansas Travelers, and it showed in his peripherals, if not his ERA, as his strikeout rate plummeted (though his ground-ball rate remained strong). The native Californian can pump his heavy fastball in the mid-90s and already boasts a plus curve, exhibiting impressive polish for his age. Chatwood was rewarded with a start at Salt Lake to end his season and might well begin 2011 there, if the Angels adhere to their pattern of aggressive pitching promotions with their 2010 organizational pitcher of the year.

Dan Haren

Born: **9/17/1980** Age: **30**
Bats: **R** Throws: **R** Height: **6' 5"** Weight: **220**
Breakout: **5%** Improve: **35%** Collapse: **20%**
Attrition: **6%** MLB: **94%**

Comparables:
Johan Santana, Don Drysdale, Fergie Jenkins (63)

YEAR	TEAM	LVL	AGE	W	L	SV	G	GS	IP	H	HR	BB	SO	EqBB9	EqSO9	GB%	BABIP	WHIP	ERA	FRA	WARP
2008	ARI	MLB	27	16	8	0	33	33	216	204	19	40	206	1.7	8.6	44%	.303	1.16	3.33	3.58	5.6
2009	ARI	MLB	28	14	10	0	33	33	229^1	192	27	38	223	1.5	8.8	44%	.267	1.02	3.14	3.87	4.6
2010	ARI	MLB	29	7	8	0	21	21	141	161	23	29	141	1.9	9.0	42%	.336	1.37	4.60	4.57	1.6
2010	ANA	MLB	29	5	4	0	14	14	94	84	8	25	75	2.4	7.2	41%	.274	1.18	2.87	3.09	2.2
2011	*ANA*	*MLB*	*30*	*15*	*8*	*0*	*34*	*34*	*228*	*215*	*24*	*48*	*200*	*1.9*	*7.9*	*44%*	*.293*	*1.15*	*3.19*	*3.47*	*5.6*

As a deadline deal designed to deliver the buyer to October, the Haren trade failed to achieve its intended effect, but to call it a flop would be to fail to recognize that from the Angels' perspective, the swap was only tangentially about 2010. They locked up a durable top-of-the-rotation talent at a reasonable rate through 2013 and did so without surrendering anything but disposable parts to a trade partner in desperate need of financial relief. Perhaps we'd be flattering ourselves if we speculated that Tony Reagins had scoped Haren's SIERA before pulling the trigger on the transaction, but the defense-independent metric did predict the pitcher's posttrade performance much more accurately than his pretrade ERA. The SoCal native rewarded the Angels' faith in his peripherals by finishing strong for the first time since 2005, despite logging a career-high 235 frames and running his streak of consecutive seasons with at least 216 innings pitched to six.

Kevin Jepsen

Born: **7/26/1984** Age: **26**
Bats: **R** Throws: **R** Height: **6' 3"** Weight: **215**
Breakout: **7%** Improve: **13%** Collapse: **6%**
Attrition: **7%** MLB: **23%**

Comparables:
Warner Madrigal, Macay McBride, Bob Veale (79)

YEAR	TEAM	LVL	AGE	W	L	SV	G	GS	IP	H	HR	BB	SO	EqBB9	EqSO9	GB%	BABIP	WHIP	ERA	FRA	WARP
2008	ARK	AA	23	2	1	11	25	0	31^2	22	0	18	35	5.1	9.9	65%	.282	1.26	1.42	2.78	0.8
2008	SLC	AAA	23	1	3	2	15	0	23	17	3	12	21	4.7	8.2	63%	.237	1.26	2.35	6.17	-0.2
2008	ANA	MLB	23	0	1	0	9	0	8^1	8	0	4	7	4.3	7.6	44%	.320	1.44	4.32	5.29	0.0
2009	ANA	MLB	24	6	4	1	54	0	54^2	63	2	19	48	3.1	7.9	56%	.363	1.50	4.94	4.81	0.2
2010	ANA	MLB	25	2	4	0	68	0	59	54	2	29	61	4.4	9.3	56%	.327	1.44	3.97	4.02	0.5
2011	*ANA*	*MLB*	*26*	*3*	*1*	*1*	*54*	*0*	*60*	*60*	*5*	*33*	*53*	*4.9*	*7.9*	*50%*	*.316*	*1.52*	*4.29*	*4.66*	*-0.2*

Jepsen's impressive second half of 2009 carried over into 2010, as the hard-throwing, ground-ball-inducing right-hander posted an ERA more in line with his defense-independent performance than he had during his rookie season. His 2.5 WXRL trailed only that of Brian Fuentes in the Angels' pen, though he didn't sniff a save all season, as Mike Scioscia chose to anoint the inferior (but experienced!) Fernando Rodney as closer after Fuentes' midseason departure. Jepsen maintained the elevated strikeout rate he achieved after adding an effective cutter to his repertoire in July 2009, though his walk rate took a step back toward its frightening minor-league levels. If he can make his 2009 walk rate and his 2010 strikeout rate coincide, he has the potential to serve as the successor to Scot Shields for the next decade. If Rodney shows signs of faltering in his walk year, Jepsen could find himself thrust into an even more lucrative late-inning role.

Scott Kazmir

Born: **1/24/1984** Age: **27**
Bats: **L** Throws: **L** Height: **6' 0"** Weight: **170**
Breakout: **22%** Improve: **52%** Collapse: **20%**
Attrition: **7%** MLB: **99%**

Comparables:
Melido Perez, Don Sutton, Chan Ho Park (73)

YEAR	TEAM	LVL	AGE	W	L	SV	G	GS	IP	H	HR	BB	SO	EqBB9	EqSO9	GB%	BABIP	WHIP	ERA	FRA	WARP
2008	TBA	MLB	24	12	8	0	27	27	152^1	123	23	70	166	4.1	9.8	31%	.265	1.29	3.49	3.59	3.9
2009	ANA	MLB	25	2	2	0	6	6	36^1	28	1	10	26	2.5	6.4	27%	.257	1.07	1.73	1.72	1.8
2009	TBA	MLB	25	8	7	0	20	20	111	121	15	50	91	4.1	7.4	37%	.309	1.59	5.92	6.20	-0.4
2010	ANA	MLB	26	9	15	0	28	28	150	158	25	79	93	4.7	5.6	40%	.281	1.66	5.94	6.38	-1.6
2011	*ANA*	*MLB*	*27*	*12*	*10*	*0*	*30*	*30*	*166^2*	*157*	*20*	*72*	*144*	*3.9*	*7.8*	*39%*	*.289*	*1.37*	*4.18*	*4.55*	*2.3*

Though he only just concluded his age-26 season, little seems to remain of the "Kid K" who earned two All-Star berths and a strikeout title at a tender age while he was with the Rays. Talented young pitchers don't always go out in a blaze of glory, their career-ending (or career-diminishing) troubles easily pinned to one fateful moment; sometimes they fade away incrementally. Kazmir has always been fragile, and after repeated injuries, the lefty has surrendered a few miles per hour from his fastball, slider, and changeup, losing his ability to miss bats in the process. Worse still, his control regressed to levels that were barely acceptable when he was still striking out over 10 batters per nine; as a result, Kazmir's strikeout-to-walk ratio barely topped one, and his 5.94 ERA was the highest of any pitcher permitted to throw as many as 150 innings last season. As a southpaw with a history of success, Kazmir will keep getting his chances, though he might find them coming in the bullpen before long.

Michael Kohn

Born: **6/26/1986** Age: **25**
Bats: R Throws: R Height: **6' 0"** Weight: **200**
Breakout: **15%** Improve: **25%** Collapse: **11%**
Attrition: **4%** MLB: **55%**

Comparables:
Mark Littell, David Robertson, Joey Devine (70)

YEAR	TEAM	LVL	AGE	W	L	SV	G	GS	IP	H	HR	BB	SO	EqBB9	EqSO9	GB%	BABIP	WHIP	ERA	FRA	WARP
2008	ORM	Rk	22	2	0	0	16	0	23^{1}	11	1	11	44	4.2	17.0	50%	.270	0.94	1.93	3.56	0.5
2009	CDR	A	23	4	1	6	28	0	37	20	1	12	60	2.9	14.6	42%	.292	0.92	2.19	2.36	1.0
2009	RCU	A+	23	2	0	3	22	0	28^{2}	13	0	14	43	4.4	13.5	34%	.255	0.94	0.94	0.52	1.7
2010	SLC	AAA	24	3	2	8	26	0	27^{2}	16	3	17	32	5.6	10.6	32%	.210	1.25	1.95	3.60	0.4
2010	ANA	MLB	24	2	0	1	24	0	21^{1}	17	0	17	20	7.2	8.4	44%	.288	1.59	2.11	1.92	0.8
2011	*ANA*	*MLB*	*25*	*2*	*1*	*3*	*45*	*0*	*51^{1}*	*39*	*4*	*30*	*61*	*5.3*	*10.8*	*42%*	*.289*	*1.33*	*3.17*	*3.45*	*0.6*

Kohn's astronomical strikeout rates lost a tick in his transition to the upper minors, and another after his promotion to Anaheim's bullpen, but they remained robust, especially in light of the fact that he climbed three levels in a single season. Equipped with the fastball and slider accessories that come standard with so many reliever models, in addition to a makeup that earned praise from his manager, Kohn will have to lower his scary walk totals to earn high-leverage outings. The righty's ERA remained so low because he didn't permit a single ball to leave the yard, a feat he's unlikely to repeat, though his five big flies allowed in 135 minor-league innings suggest that he might have some skill in that regard. A catcher until his senior year of college, he's far enough behind on the development curve to retain some potential for improvement.

Fabio Martinez Mesa

Born: **10/29/1989** Age: **21**
Bats: R Throws: R Height: **6' 3"** Weight: **190**
Breakout: **11%** Improve: **14%** Collapse: **6%**
Attrition: **6%** MLB: **21%**

Comparables:
Mitch Williams, Vinegar Bend Mizell, Edwin Correa (60)

YEAR	TEAM	LVL	AGE	W	L	SV	G	GS	IP	H	HR	BB	SO	EqBB9	EqSO9	GB%	BABIP	WHIP	ERA	FRA	WARP
2009	ANG	Rk	19	3	2	0	14	13	60^{2}	45	1	36	92	5.3	13.6	57%	.321	1.37	3.26	4.01	3.2
2010	CDR	A	20	7	3	0	20	19	103^{1}	80	6	76	141	6.6	12.3	48%	.327	1.54	3.92	4.04	2.0
2011	*ANA*	*MLB*	*21*	*6*	*7*	*0*	*17*	*17*	*81*	*74*	*8*	*68*	*85*	*7.5*	*9.4*	*46%*	*.307*	*1.74*	*5.16*	*5.61*	*0.4*

Before last season, Mesa had yet to put his enticing repertoire to the test in a full-season league. That changed in 2010, as the righty took his act to Cedar Rapids, where he showcased the same tantalizing package of unpolished promise that already had scouts talking. Mesa's 12.3 strikeouts per nine paced the Midwest League, but his walk rate showed no sign of improvement, ranking third-worst in the circuit. Like many a young flamethrower, Mesa doesn't always know where his pitches are going, which—given the fact that his fastball touches 97—must be as unsettling for opposing batters as it is for him. Armed with a plus slider and a developing changeup, he has the secondary stuff to succeed. Further development time may allow him to repeat his smooth delivery more often, removing his most glaring impediment to stardom.

Anthony Ortega

Born: **8/24/1985** Age: **25**
Bats: R Throws: R Height: **6' 0"** Weight: **185**
Breakout: **0%** Improve: **0%** Collapse: **0%**
Attrition: **0%** MLB: **0%**

Comparables:
Chris Haney, Adam Pettyjohn, Steve Kline (88)

YEAR	TEAM	LVL	AGE	W	L	SV	G	GS	IP	H	HR	BB	SO	EqBB9	EqSO9	GB%	BABIP	WHIP	ERA	FRA	WARP
2008	ARK	AA	22	9	7	0	22	22	135	124	11	49	83	3.3	5.5	47%	.270	1.33	3.73	4.99	0.6
2008	SLC	AAA	22	5	0	0	6	6	39^{1}	46	2	6	22	1.4	5.0	48%	.314	1.40	2.52	4.68	0.5
2009	ANA	MLB	23	0	2	0	3	3	12^{2}	19	4	6	7	4.3	5.0	47%	.333	1.97	9.24	9.40	-0.3
2011	*ANA*	*MLB*	*25*	*4*	*7*	*0*	*23*	*15*	*91^{1}*	*109*	*15*	*45*	*44*	*4.5*	*4.4*	*45%*	*.305*	*1.69*	*6.15*	*6.69*	*-1.0*

Ortega's ceiling never reached the kind of height that makes scouts and real-estate agents swoon, but the six-foot righty has to stoop to fit under it now. In the wake of a successful 2008 in the rotation, injuries have limited the Dominican to 56 total innings over the last two seasons, spread between Double-A and Triple-A, and the majors, but they haven't exerted the same slimming effect on his ERA: Ortega has allowed 62 runs over that span. On the plus side, only 55 of them were earned. A move to the bullpen hasn't kept him healthy so far, though his arm was sound enough to see some action in the Venezuelan winter league.

Matt Palmer

Born: **3/21/1979** Age: **32**
Bats: R Throws: R Height: **6' 2"** Weight: **200**
Breakout: **10%** Improve: **30%** Collapse: **19%**
Attrition: **12%** MLB: **74%**

Comparables:
Mike Smith, Bill Singer, Kevin Gross (74)

YEAR	TEAM	LVL	AGE	W	L	SV	G	GS	IP	H	HR	BB	SO	EqBB9	EqSO9	GB%	BABIP	WHIP	ERA	FRA	WARP
2008	FRE	AAA	29	6	10	0	26	25	142	138	11	72	143	4.6	9.1	50%	.323	1.55	4.18	4.45	2.5
2008	SFN	MLB	29	0	2	0	3	3	12^{2}	17	1	13	3	9.2	2.1	47%	.333	2.53	8.53	7.78	-0.2
2009	ANA	MLB	30	11	2	0	40	13	121^{1}	105	12	55	69	4.1	5.1	53%	.255	1.35	3.93	4.74	1.0
2010	SLC	AAA	31	2	3	2	13	7	46^{1}	32	4	19	36	3.7	7.0	55%	.228	1.15	2.72	4.91	0.5
2010	ANA	MLB	31	1	2	0	14	1	33^{2}	38	1	20	17	5.3	4.5	51%	.314	1.75	4.54	5.14	0.1
2011	*ANA*	*MLB*	*32*	*7*	*6*	*0*	*38*	*17*	*129^{1}*	*127*	*13*	*62*	*80*	*4.3*	*5.6*	*49%*	*.286*	*1.46*	*4.52*	*4.91*	*0.7*

The greatest danger to a team lies not in crashing at the pad of a replacement player like Palmer when the situation calls for it, but in signing an extended lease. The righty turned in yeoman's work while helping to patch together a fractured rotation in 2009, but the Angels wisely quit, if not while they were ahead, at least before they were behind, asking him to take the ball at the start of only one game last season and limiting him to just over 30 innings overall. The righty was a 30-year-old rookie for a reason: his sinker and cutter barely top 90 on a good day, and neither his harder stuff nor his slow curve induces an above-average rate of whiffs. Palmer has experienced some superficial success in relief, but only accompanied by the sort of unsightly strikeout-to-walk ratios that augur high ERAs to come.

Joel Pineiro

Born: **9/25/1978** Age: **32**
Bats: **R** Throws: **R** Height: **6' 1"** Weight: **180**
Breakout: **9%** Improve: **41%** Collapse: **31%**
Attrition: **13%** MLB: **98%**

Comparables:
Brad Radke, Pat Dobson, Bob Friend (73)

YEAR	TEAM	LVL	AGE	W	L	SV	G	GS	IP	H	HR	BB	SO	EqBB9	EqSO9	GB%	BABIP	WHIP	ERA	FRA	WARP
2008	SLN	MLB	29	7	7	1	26	25	148^2	180	22	35	81	2.1	4.9	49%	.313	1.46	5.15	5.62	0.1
2009	SLN	MLB	30	15	12	0	32	32	214	218	11	27	105	1.1	4.4	61%	.290	1.18	3.45	4.14	2.8
2010	ANA	MLB	31	10	7	0	23	23	152^1	155	15	34	92	2.0	5.4	56%	.285	1.25	3.84	4.11	1.6
2011	*ANA*	*MLB*	*32*	*11*	*8*	*0*	*26*	*26*	*165*	*172*	*15*	*36*	*85*	*1.9*	*4.6*	*53%*	*.293*	*1.26*	*3.76*	*4.09*	*2.8*

Frustrating expectations, Pineiro didn't spontaneously combust after being lured away from Dave Duncan's protective aura by the Angels' two-year offer; in fact, even without accounting for the switch to the tougher league, the old dog with new tricks turned in another successful season, marred only by a strained oblique that limited him to 23 starts. The righty retained most of the ground-ball abilities he picked up in St. Louis, and while his pinpoint control slipped slightly, his strikeout rate recovered enough to overcome that decline. Credit the Angels for perceiving a genuine improvement where other teams feared a mirage, enabling them to lock up Pineiro at a below-market rate.

Trevor Reckling

Born: **5/22/1989** Age: **22**
Bats: **L** Throws: **L** Height: **6' 2"** Weight: **205**
Breakout: **7%** Improve: **10%** Collapse: **6%**
Attrition: **6%** MLB: **25%**

Comparables:
Jim Gott, Jim Palmer, Brett Myers (71)

YEAR	TEAM	LVL	AGE	W	L	SV	G	GS	IP	H	HR	BB	SO	EqBB9	EqSO9	GB%	BABIP	WHIP	ERA	FRA	WARP
2008	CDR	A	19	10	7	0	26	26	152^1	137	8	59	128	3.5	7.6	54%	.297	1.38	3.37	3.14	4.4
2009	ARK	AA	20	8	7	0	23	23	135^1	118	4	75	106	5.0	7.1	50%	.295	1.46	2.93	2.62	4.1
2010	ARK	AA	21	3	6	0	14	14	79	74	4	35	62	4.0	7.1	41%	.298	1.46	4.56	5.08	0.0
2010	SLC	AAA	21	4	7	0	14	14	69^2	99	11	50	46	6.5	6.0	42%	.368	2.25	8.53	7.10	-0.6
2011	*ANA*	*MLB*	*22*	*6*	*9*	*0*	*20*	*20*	*115^2*	*123*	*12*	*68*	*74*	*5.4*	*5.7*	*46%*	*.306*	*1.67*	*5.38*	*5.85*	*-0.1*

Drafted out of high school in 2007, Reckling reached Triple-A shortly after turning 21, an achievement to be proud of. Unfortunately, the quality of his work for Salt Lake was nothing to brag about, as the lefty walked more batters than he struck out, posting an unsightly eight-plus ERA. Reckling returned to Double-A a beaten man, but showed occasional signs of brilliance after his demotion, including a 10-strikeout, one-walk performance against Springfield in late July. The southpaw isn't blessed with a blistering fastball or the high strikeout totals that having one often confers, and his ground-ball rate went backward last season. Though he doesn't possess rotation-topping talent, he retains a plus changeup and curve and remains young enough to rehabilitate his prospect image.

Garrett Richards

Born: **5/27/1988** Age: **23**
Bats: **R** Throws: **R** Height: **6' 3"** Weight: **210**
Breakout: **8%** Improve: **19%** Collapse: **3%**
Attrition: **6%** MLB: **22%**

Comparables:
Jaime Garcia, Derek Holland, Carlos Carrasco (75)

YEAR	TEAM	LVL	AGE	W	L	SV	G	GS	IP	H	HR	BB	SO	EqBB9	EqSO9	GB%	BABIP	WHIP	ERA	FRA	WARP
2009	ORM	Rk	21	3	1	0	8	8	35^1	37	0	4	30	1.0	7.6	51%	.352	1.22	1.53	1.57	3.9
2010	CDR	A	22	8	4	0	19	19	108^1	92	6	34	108	2.8	9.0	59%	.295	1.19	3.41	4.31	1.6
2010	RCU	A+	22	4	1	0	7	7	34^2	38	4	9	41	2.4	10.8	54%	.370	1.40	3.89	4.47	0.5
2011	*ANA*	*MLB*	*23*	*6*	*6*	*0*	*17*	*17*	*88*	*93*	*10*	*39*	*63*	*3.9*	*6.4*	*48%*	*.304*	*1.48*	*4.69*	*5.09*	*0.7*

Richards' control regressed from otherworldly to merely superior in his follow-up to an impressive small-sample postdraft performance in 2009, but his prospect status didn't suffer from his first exposure to full-season leagues, and his peripherals only improved after his late-July promotion to High-A. The righty rides a low- to mid-90s fastball and a plus curve to above-average strikeout and ground-ball stats, without accumulating the high walk totals that often threaten to derail pitchers with otherwise positive attributes. The former supplemental first-rounder has the highest ceiling in the Angels' system and could be knocking on the door to the majors before his 24th birthday.

Fernando Rodney

Born: **3/18/1977** Age: **34**
Bats: **R** Throws: **R** Height: **5' 11"** Weight: **170**
Breakout: **16%** Improve: **39%** Collapse: **28%**
Attrition: **10%** MLB: **84%**

Comparables:
Jesse Orosco, Dennis Cook, Jeff Parrett (76)

YEAR	TEAM	LVL	AGE	W	L	SV	G	GS	IP	H	HR	BB	SO	EqBB9	EqSO9	GB%	BABIP	WHIP	ERA	FRA	WARP
2008	DET	MLB	31	0	6	13	38	0	40^1	34	3	30	49	6.7	10.9	43%	.301	1.66	4.91	4.72	0.1
2009	DET	MLB	32	2	5	37	73	0	75^2	70	8	41	61	4.9	7.3	58%	.284	1.49	4.40	4.82	0.2
2010	ANA	MLB	33	4	3	14	72	0	68	70	4	35	53	4.6	7.0	51%	.314	1.62	4.24	3.98	0.6
2011	*ANA*	*MLB*	*34*	*3*	*1*	*14*	*62*	*0*	*63*	*59*	*5*	*33*	*55*	*4.7*	*7.8*	*48%*	*.294*	*1.45*	*4.16*	*4.52*	*-0.1*

The Angels got what they paid for, as Rodney more or less replicated his 2009 showing in Anaheim last season. The question is why they thought that kind of performance was worth

$5.5 million. It seems as if the organization took one look at his fastball velocity and facial hair and wrote a closer-caliber check, without stopping to consider that Rodney hasn't pitched like someone deserving of either that kind of financial windfall or a team's highest-leverage innings since at least 2007. After letting only one save slip away from Detroit in 2009, Rodney blew a third of his opportunities last season, while posting the lowest strikeout rate of his career. He's likely to get a chance to redeem himself in the late innings, but a flock of younger vultures are circling in the Angels' pen.

Francisco Rodriguez

Born: **2/26/1983** Age: **28**
Bats: **R** Throws: **R** Height: **6' 1"** Weight: **195**
Breakout: **1%** Improve: **1%** Collapse: **0%**
Attrition: **0%** MLB: **1%**
Comparables:
Sean Burnett, Shane Komine, Jake Woods (89)

YEAR	TEAM	LVL	AGE	W	L	SV	G	GS	IP	H	HR	BB	SO	EqBB9	EqSO9	GB%	BABIP	WHIP	ERA	FRA	WARP
2008	ARK	AA	25	6	5	1	54	0	79^{2}	81	10	34	72	3.8	8.1	49%	.302	1.51	3.84	4.84	0.2
2009	SLC	AAA	26	5	4	0	44	1	77^{1}	67	8	40	60	4.7	7.0	47%	.267	1.41	3.96	4.70	0.3
2010	SLC	AAA	27	2	1	0	13	0	22^{1}	19	0	6	19	2.4	7.7	57%	.292	1.13	3.63	5.16	0.0
2010	ANA	MLB	27	1	3	0	43	0	47^{1}	46	5	26	36	4.9	6.8	49%	.291	1.54	4.37	4.72	0.1
2011	*ANA*	*MLB*	*28*	*3*	*1*	*0*	*65*	*0*	91^{1}	*99*	*11*	*49*	*57*	*4.9*	*5.7*	*46%*	*.305*	*1.63*	*5.37*	*5.84*	*-1.6*

To paraphrase an expiring Yoda's last words to Luke Skywalker in *Return of the Jedi*, "There is . . . another . . . Rodriguez." This one works cheap, and while he's not saddled with the rap sheet of the more expensive model, he's living proof that major-league minimum doesn't always buy a devastating slider. As a result, he won't make many Angelinos of Anaheim forget their decamped closer. Baseball isn't a perfect meritocracy, but the former Francisco reached the majors seven years younger for good reason: the Angels have little reason to expect any more from this converted starter than they received in 2010.

Ervin Santana

Born: **1/10/1983** Age: **28**
Bats: **R** Throws: **R** Height: **6' 2"** Weight: **160**
Breakout: **10%** Improve: **37%** Collapse: **23%**
Attrition: **9%** MLB: **95%**
Comparables:
Jack McDowell, Ian Snell, Mike Witt (68)

YEAR	TEAM	LVL	AGE	W	L	SV	G	GS	IP	H	HR	BB	SO	EqBB9	EqSO9	GB%	BABIP	WHIP	ERA	FRA	WARP
2008	ANA	MLB	25	16	7	0	32	32	219	198	23	47	214	1.9	8.8	40%	.289	1.16	3.49	3.54	5.1
2009	ANA	MLB	26	8	8	0	24	23	139^{2}	159	24	47	107	3.0	6.9	40%	.318	1.55	5.03	5.12	0.9
2010	ANA	MLB	27	17	10	0	33	33	222^{2}	221	27	73	169	3.0	6.8	37%	.289	1.37	3.92	4.08	2.6
2011	*ANA*	*MLB*	*28*	*12*	*10*	*0*	*30*	*30*	198^{1}	*195*	*24*	*61*	*160*	*2.8*	*7.3*	*40%*	*.295*	*1.29*	*3.97*	*4.32*	*2.8*

It seemed 2008 was Santana's breakout season, but it may also have been the season that broke him. After starting 2009 on the DL with a sprained medial collateral ligament in his pitching elbow, Santana saw his velocity drop by over two mph, and his strikeout rate plummeted along with it. Whether the elbow remained a problem last season, Santana's velocity and defense-independent performance didn't improve, though his luck turned enough for his ERA to return to respectable levels. If Santana proves perpetually unable to recapture his 2008 form, he'll still constitute a valuable asset to the Angels, but not the enviable top-of-the-rotation talent he appeared to be. Of course, he's hardly the first pitcher (or even the first named Santana) to tantalize for a time before succumbing to wear and tear—just one of the most recent.

Rich Thompson

Born: **7/1/1984** Age: **26**
Bats: **R** Throws: **R** Height: **6' 1"** Weight: **180**
Breakout: **5%** Improve: **6%** Collapse: **5%**
Attrition: **3%** MLB: **14%**
Comparables:
Samuel Gervacio, Luis Perdomo, Jose Arredondo (75)

YEAR	TEAM	LVL	AGE	W	L	SV	G	GS	IP	H	HR	BB	SO	EqBB9	EqSO9	GB%	BABIP	WHIP	ERA	FRA	WARP
2008	ANA	MLB	23	0	0	0	2	0	2	4	0	2	1	9.0	4.5	67%	.444	3.00	22.50	21.10	-0.3
2009	SLC	AAA	24	3	1	0	29	0	43^{1}	41	7	11	51	2.3	10.6	36%	.298	1.25	3.12	4.23	0.3
2009	ANA	MLB	24	0	0	0	13	0	19^{1}	27	6	7	21	3.3	9.8	33%	.368	1.81	5.12	3.57	0.3
2010	SLC	AAA	25	1	1	2	19	0	29^{2}	17	0	10	30	3.1	9.2	41%	.246	0.92	0.61	1.36	1.3
2010	ANA	MLB	25	2	0	0	13	0	19^{2}	12	2	4	15	1.8	6.9	39%	.185	0.81	1.37	2.36	0.4
2011	*ANA*	*MLB*	*26*	*2*	*1*	*0*	*40*	*0*	*57*	*52*	*7*	*21*	*54*	*3.3*	*8.4*	*43%*	*.286*	*1.27*	*3.76*	*4.08*	*0.2*

Thompson's bid to join Grant Balfour and Peter Moylan as a full-fledged member of the Effective Australian Relievers Club fizzled for a fourth straight season, though he came closer to qualifying than ever before. Despite a dominant performance in the PCL, the righty didn't sniff the majors until July, and he spent most of August sidelined by shoulder inflammation and Mrs. Thompson's pregnancy, which prevented him from cracking the 20-inning mark for the first time. When healthy, the Aussie finally pitched to his capabilities, utilizing a David Robertson–esque repertoire (featuring a refined cutter) to put his major-league beanball problems in the rearview mirror, where—if his minor-league history is any indication—they're likely to stay.

Jordan Walden

Born: **11/16/1987** Age: **23**
Bats: **R** Throws: **R** Height: **6' 5"** Weight: **240**
Breakout: **2%** Improve: **4%** Collapse: **2%**
Attrition: **3%** MLB: **8%**

Comparables:
Waldis Joaquin, Sean Gallagher, Jhonny Nunez (80)

YEAR	TEAM	LVL	AGE	W	L	SV	G	GS	IP	H	HR	BB	SO	EqBB9	EqSO9	GB%	BABIP	WHIP	ERA	FRA	WARP
2008	CDR	A	20	4	6	0	18	18	107^{1}	80	3	32	91	2.7	7.6	64%	.259	1.07	2.18	2.54	3.9
2008	RCU	A+	20	5	2	0	9	9	49	42	4	24	50	4.4	9.2	53%	.284	1.39	4.04	4.16	0.7
2009	ARK	AA	21	1	5	0	13	13	60	72	4	29	57	4.4	8.6	45%	.376	1.73	5.25	4.89	0.2
2010	ARK	AA	22	1	1	8	38	0	43	44	2	22	38	4.6	8.0	56%	.339	1.53	3.35	3.28	0.8
2010	ANA	MLB	22	0	1	1	16	0	15^{1}	13	1	7	23	4.1	13.5	63%	.353	1.30	2.35	2.19	0.5
2011	*ANA*	*MLB*	*23*	*5*	*4*	*1*	*45*	*8*	*83^{2}*	*87*	*9*	*44*	*61*	*4.8*	*6.6*	*49%*	*.306*	*1.58*	*4.83*	*5.25*	*-0.1*

Most late-inning relievers are made, not born. Walden is no exception, having initially put himself on the prospect map in the rotation, where he had trouble both repeating his delivery and staying healthy enough to try. As Henry David Thoreau presciently advised in his mid-19th-century scouting report, *Walden*, the strapping youngster needed merely to "simplify, simplify," and the Angels eventually came to agree. In the wake of a 2009 campaign riddled with elbow and forearm problems, Walden made the conversion to relief and experienced middling success in the minors before being promoted to Anaheim's struggling bullpen in late August. Once there, he quickly earned Mike Scioscia's trust, and with the aid of a fastball that averaged near 99 mph, briefly laid claim to the title of baseball's hardest thrower before Aroldis Chapman hit the scene. His role change may have lowered his ceiling, but his 15-inning audition went well enough to generate some serious closer buzz heading into 2011.

Jered Weaver

Born: **10/4/1982** Age: **28**
Bats: **R** Throws: **R** Height: **6' 7"** Weight: **205**
Breakout: **5%** Improve: **37%** Collapse: **20%**
Attrition: **12%** MLB: **94%**

Comparables:
Justin Verlander, Josh Beckett, Shaun Marcum (66)

YEAR	TEAM	LVL	AGE	W	L	SV	G	GS	IP	H	HR	BB	SO	EqBB9	EqSO9	GB%	BABIP	WHIP	ERA	FRA	WARP
2008	ANA	MLB	25	11	10	0	30	30	176^{2}	173	20	54	152	2.8	7.7	34%	.298	1.32	4.33	4.35	2.6
2009	ANA	MLB	26	16	8	0	33	33	211	196	26	66	174	2.8	7.4	32%	.278	1.26	3.75	3.75	4.8
2010	ANA	MLB	27	13	12	0	34	34	224^{1}	187	23	54	233	2.2	9.3	38%	.276	1.07	3.01	3.20	5.2
2011	*ANA*	*MLB*	*28*	*14*	*8*	*0*	*31*	*31*	*197*	*178*	*20*	*55*	*177*	*2.5*	*8.1*	*38%*	*.285*	*1.18*	*3.12*	*3.39*	*5.2*

In *BP2010*, we noted that despite setting career highs in innings pitched, strikeouts, and Support-Neutral Winning Percentage, Weaver still wasn't quite "staff ace material." While once more setting personal records in all three categories last season, the lanky right-hander rendered any such caveats unnecessary. Previously only a tick above average in the strikeout rate department, Weaver brought home the major-league strikeout title in 2010, fanning nearly two more batters per nine innings than he had in 2009. Jeff's younger, better brother began throwing fewer changeups and more curves, but his strikeout ability was most enhanced by his increased usage of a refined two-seamer, which also aided the California native in upping his ground-ball rate (in addition to inducing his usual healthy helping of popups). He was a bit over his head early on, as suggested by his whiffing only 8.4 per nine in the second half. Still, while Weaver may have just woven his career year and hasn't consistently carried his home dominance on the road, he's likely to retain at least some of his 2010 gains, giving the Angels a dependable front-of-the-rotation type to pair with Dan Haren for years to come.

LINEOUTS

HITTERS

PLAYER	TEAM	LVL	AGE	PA	R	2B	3B	HR	RBI	BB	SO	SB-CS	AVG/OBP/SLG	TAv	BABIP	BRR	FRAA	WARP
RF C. Aldridge*	MXC		31	201	30	9	1	7	26	37	47	1-3	.299/.428/.494		.382	0.0		0.0
	SLC	AAA	31	338	53	24	1	13	59	35	83	2-1	.318/.388/.535	.319	.398	-1.1	LF -10, RF 1	1.6
	ANA	MLB	31	13	0	0	1	0	1	0	5	0-0	.077/.077/.231	.148	.125	0.0	RF -1, LF 0	-0.2
CF T. Auer	RCU	A+	24	296	57	6	8	3	27	23	42	40-12	.332/.387/.453	.305	.363	1.9	CF 2, LF 1	2.6
	ARK	AA	24	202	30	8	1	2	8	14	31	13-7	.308/.360/.395	.287	.357	0.9	CF -1, RF 0	0.9
	SLC	AAA	24	53	8	2	3	0	4	3	9	1-1	.255/.327/.426	.240	.308	-0.7	CF -2	-0.2
C R. Budde	SLC	AAA	30	199	24	7	0	1	13	21	58	1-1	.244/.325/.302	.229	.347	1.1	C -1, 3B 2	0.4
	ANA	MLB	30	11	2	1	0	1	3	1	5	0-0	.400/.454/.800	.472	.750	-0.2	C 0	0.2
CF C. Clarke#	ANG	Rk	18	180	26	5	7	3	16	14	55	9-2	.216/.294/.389	.262	.308	0.8	CF -8	0.2
CF T. Evans	SLC	AAA	28	502	80	27	4	15	72	28	100	19-8	.283/.323/.455	.265	.328	3.3	RF -1, CF -6	1.0
	ANA	MLB	28	1	0	0	0	0	0	0	1	0-0	.000/.000/.000	.041	.000	0.0	CF 0	0.0
RF R. Grichuk	CDR	A	18	214	41	19	4	7	36	9	50	4-0	.292/.327/.530	.314	.356	0.1	RF 0	1.5
	ANG	Rk	18	52	7	3	2	4	10	3	9	0-0	.327/.365/.714	.389	.333	-0.9	RF -1	0.6
1B G. Jacobo	RCU	A+	23	583	82	26	7	22	107	24	94	6-9	.296/.333/.492	.300	.318	0.7	1B 2	3.4
3B L. Jimenez	CDR	A	22	184	32	15	5	2	38	11	27	6-2	.292/.332/.476	.290	.329	0.0	3B 5	1.5
	RCU	A+	22	344	52	31	4	12	43	13	43	15-8	.286/.324/.522	.296	.293	0.0	3B 2	2.3
1B P. McAnulty*	ARK	AA	29	176	31	3	1	14	27	24	36	1-2	.331/.426/.649	.378	.350	-1.1	LF 1, 1B 0	2.2
	SLC	AAA	29	305	43	18	1	10	54	27	39	0-1	.302/.361/.484	.287	.319	-2.5	1B -4, 3B -2	0.6
	ANA	MLB	29	24	2	0	0	1	2	2	11	0-0	.136/.208/.273	.181	.200	-0.6	1B -1	-0.3
OF J. Moore*	ARK	AA	23	508	72	14	10	13	61	39	122	24-10	.303/.358/.463	.310	.378	0.7	CF -8, LF 3	3.1
1B R. Quinlan	SLC	AAA	33	144	14	6	0	0	8	15	23	1-0	.258/.333/.305	.219	.311	-0.7	1B -1, 3B -5	-1.1
	ANA	MLB	33	36	3	2	0	0	2	2	6	2-0	.121/.167/.182	.181	.143	0.1	1B -1, RF 0	-0.4
OF M. Ryan*	SLC	AAA	32	338	48	22	4	4	37	24	46	2-0	.277/.324/.414	.254	.307	3.1	LF -1, 1B -1	0.4
	ANA	MLB	32	41	3	4	0	0	2	1	5	0-0	.205/.220/.308	.214	.229	0.2	LF 0, 1B 1	0.0

Before his early-July cameo in Anaheim, **Cory Aldridge**'s last major-league start had seen him flanked by B. J. Surhoff and Bernard Gilkey in the outfield for the 2001 Braves, offering yet another piece of compelling evidence that a series of injuries may have opened a portal to an earlier part of the decade on the Angels' bench. ⊘ **Tyson Auer** tore up the California League and held on to more of that offense than could have been expected at the upper levels. An outstanding runner and defensive center fielder, the undrafted Auer faces his biggest obstacle in Peter Bourjos, who's essentially the same player, only younger and more talented. Don't be surprised if the Angels wake up and smell the trade bait. ⊘ The oldest and least talented of the five catchers on the Angels' 40-man, **Ryan Budde** has spent the last four seasons an injury stack or expanded roster away from Anaheim. Like a noncash Christmas gift from an elderly relative, he comes but once a year and lasts only a few days before being exchanged for something more useful. This year that gift will go to the Blue Jays. ⊘ The third of the Angels' three first-round picks in the 2010 draft, the toolsy **Chevez Clarke** flopped in his first exposure to rookie ball, but showed off the same athleticism that made him a coveted commodity in June. His team will take the long view. ⊘ Two-way high schooler **Kaleb Cowart** became a full-time third baseman after the Angels picked him 18th overall in the 2010 draft, and he signed in time to take a few unproductive rookie-league reps. If things don't work out on offense, he'll always have the option to return to the mound, like Casey Kelly before him. ⊘ **Terry Evans** has flashed intriguing power and speed at times, but 2010 wasn't one of them. At 29, he doesn't have a Triple-A track record that suggests success in the majors. He's lucky to have a Baseball-Reference page, but he earned a non-roster invite from the Giants nonetheless. ⊘ Unfazed by his status as the *other* 2009 first-rounder playing for Cedar Rapids, **Randall Grichuk** proved that his power is real, but his approach still needs work. His strikeout-to-walk ratio improved, but not by enough to qualify as respectable, and a thumb injury precipitated by an ill-advised slide into first prevented further development. ⊘ **Gabe Jacobo**'s smooth moves around the first-base bag earned him recognition as the Angels' Minor League Defensive Player of the Year, but he may not have the bat to support the position. ⊘ **Luis Jimenez** has little but a bat to recommend him; fortunately, his lumber appeared to have survived a 2009 lost to a torn labrum. His quick but wild swing produced doubles in droves, but like Detective John Kimble's group of unruly kindergartners, he lacks discipline. ⊘ Another season of strong minor-league production, another unsuccessful and all-too-brief audition in the majors. Same as it ever was for **Paul McAnulty**. ⊘ A strong park-adjusted performance in Double-A and a sizzling follow-up in the AFL upped **Jeremy Moore**'s prospect luster, but significant caveats remain. The defensively adequate outfielder's power ceiling remains moderate, his plus speed has only gotten him in trouble on the basepaths, and his strikeout-to-walk ratio would make Rod Carew cry. Fringy fourth-outfielder type **Chris Pettit** skipped a season he could ill afford to miss after undergoing surgery to repair a torn labrum in March. **Robb Quinlan**'s playing time has decreased for four straight seasons, as has his productivity. The Angels decided to get off the elevator before it reached the subbasement, and released him in early September, freeing him to sign with Philadelphia. Much like World War II, Kendry Morales' fractured leg offered some aging players on the fringe of irrelevance an extended lease on big-league life. **Michael Ryan** hadn't had a comment in an annual or an at-bat in the majors since 2005, but earned both (quite likely for the last time) thanks to a hot spring training and an injury stack.

PITCHERS

PLAYER	TEAM	LVL	AGE	W	L	SV	IP	H	HR	BB	SO	EqBB9	EqSO9	GB%	BABIP	WHIP	ERA	FRA	WARP
Y. Carmona	ARK	AA	25	4	2	12	55^1	35	2	34	52	5.6	8.5	55%	.241	1.38	2.60	4.52	0.2
G. DeHoyos	SLC	AAA	30	5	1	1	82^1	72	4	33	80	3.6	8.8	45%	.300	1.34	3.06	3.50	1.6
R. Fish*	ARK	AA	22	3	5	2	42^1	69	9	18	48	3.8	10.3	41%	.420	2.21	8.93	7.35	-1.1
S. Geltz	RCU	A+	22	3	1	2	34	20	4	10	51	2.6	13.5	43%	.242	0.97	3.44	3.51	0.4
J. Hellweg	CDR	A	21	2	4	16	43^2	20	2	45	66	9.4	13.8	50%	.214	1.60	4.33	5.39	-0.2
S. Shields	ANA	MLB	34	0	3	0	46	45	6	33	39	6.5	7.6	48%	.285	1.74	5.28	6.17	-0.7
B. Stokes	ANA	MLB	30	0	0	0	16^2	26	4	16	16	8.6	8.6	44%	.415	2.58	8.10	8.30	-0.6
D. Tillman	ORM	Rk	21	2	2	10	32^1	23	0	10	50	2.8	14.0	42%	.333	1.12	1.95	1.65	3.7
L. Van Mil	NBR	AA	25	1	2	0	29^2	40	1	22	21	6.8	6.5	54%	.361	2.19	6.37	6.32	-0.5

The Angels' second pick in the first round of the 2010 draft, **Cameron Bedrosian** wet his feet in rookie ball after signing in July, showing off a mid-90s fastball and flashing commendable curves and changeups. The undersized (but still-growing) 19-year-old has better stuff than his Cy Young award-winning father and might stick as a starter. The Angels chose to protect **Ysmael Carmona** from the Rule 5 draft after the Dominican right-hander showed continued strikeout and ground-ball ability in his third full professional season. In light of his historically prohibitive walk rates, he probably owes his Triple-A audition and 40-man roster spot to a low BABIP in the Texas League. It's easy to see why bullpen whisperer Kevin Towers liked **Gabe DeHoyos**. The Angels signed him as a free agent and sent him to the PCL, where he continued to post excellent numbers with the aid of a hard cutter and a complementary 12-to-6 yakker. He should've gotten a shot by now. The Yankees found lefty **Robert Fish**'s 95-mph fastball alluring enough to select him in the Rule 5 draft despite a near-9.00 ERA at Double-A in his first season as a full-time reliever. Not to be confused with 1980s futility infielder Steve Jeltz, **Steven Geltz** is an undersized reliever who has improved with each promotion. His violent delivery constrains his control, but it results in enough strikeouts that he will earn a major-league look, perhaps as early as this season. Cedar Rapids closer **John Hellweg** walked more than a batter per inning in the Midwest League, but was saved from utter disaster by a profusion of strikeouts and grounders. If he ever gets his long limbs under better control, he could find a home in the majors with a team that doesn't mind taking its pitchers Rauch-sized. **Bobby Mosebach**'s second year in the bullpen didn't go as well as his first, primarily because he didn't spend much time there. Two shoulder-related trips to the DL limited him to a shade over 25 mostly ineffective innings, preventing him from refilling his 2009 cup of coffee. Even **Scot Shields** eventually became fungible. The longest-tenured Angel experienced his second lost season in a row and will probably hang them up with a year left on his deal. **Brian Stokes**' shoulder grew tired of his pitching shortly before the Angels could, costing him most of the season. He has always thrown hard and without much movement, but returned from injury hitting only 92 mph. When the end of his career comes, southpaws will be sad to see him go, but he may have a future throwing to batters in the Home Run Derby. Thanks to a heavy fastball that can touch the mid-90s, the Pioneer League proved to be Orem closer **Daniel Tillman**'s cup of tea after his selection in the second round of the 2010 draft. Another serving of tea for the Tillman could lead to a cup of coffee before long. **Loek Van Mil** stands seven feet above the rubber and has been observed to miss the strike zone by approximately the same margin. He's what a young Randy Johnson might have been, had the youthful Unit been Dutch, right-handed, and unable to strike anyone out.

MANAGER: MIKE SCIOSCIA

YEAR	TEAM	W-L	Pythag +/-	Avg PC	100+ P	120+ P	QS	BQS	REL	REL w Zero R	IBB	Subs	PH	PH Avg	PH HR	SB2	CS2	SB3	CS3	SAC Att	SAC %	POS SAC	Squeeze	Swing	In Play
2008	ANA	100-62	11	99.6	85	0	87	5	383	249	32	46	74	.182	0	109	38	19	8	46	69.6%	32	3	147	113
2009	ANA	97-65	4	97.1	83	1	70	9	434	269	35	48	79	.308	2	124	57	22	5	64	67.2%	41	4	180	134
2010	ANA	80-82	1	102.4	107	3	91	7	410	267	33	33	93	.171	0	90	39	14	10	77	54.5%	41	5	157	126

For only the third time in his 11-year tenure as Angels manager—and the first time since 2003—Scioscia's charges finished under .500, though the Halos did extend their streak of exceeding their Pythagorean record to seven seasons, if only just barely. Attributing super-Pythagorean performance to a manager's influence smacks of oversimplification, but the Angels' tendency to play better than the sum of their parts in recent campaigns had enhanced their longtime skipper's reputation. Their failure to summon a slew of wins from thin air last season may have dimmed his aura slightly, but aspects of their offensive approach invited more serious concerns. The hallmark of Scioscia's managerial style has been aggressive and intelligent baserunning, but the Halos ran themselves into outs at an unprecedented rate in 2010. Not since the skipper's first year on the job had the Angels' performance on the bases placed in the bottom half of teams, but last season, the Angels ranked near the dregs while posting a league-low 66.7 percent stolen-base success rate that resulted in an unsightly -6.0 stolen base runs, the worst showing by any team in the past three seasons. Scioscia also ordered more sacrifice attempts than any AL manager outside of Ron Washington and succeeded at the lowest rate in the league. He remains under contract for eight more years, which speaks to ownership's confidence in his abilities as a leader of men—few employees enjoy that kind of job security in any field, let alone one fraught with attrition rates as high as those endemic to the major-league managing biz—but Scioscia's string-pulling last season did little to strengthen his future Hall of Fame case.

Los Angeles Dodgers

The hours leading up to the December 3 nontender deadline were tense ones for the Dodgers. At stake was the status of 27-year-old homegrown catcher Russell Martin, two-time All-Star and anchor of a squad that had reached the playoffs three times in his first four seasons. As a third-year arbitration-eligible player, Martin stood to receive a substantial raise from his $5.05 million salary, but the Dodgers' most immediate concern was the season-ending injury he'd suffered in early August, a hairline fracture of his pelvis caused by an awkward stumble past home plate. He had yet to resume running, let alone baseball activity, as the deadline drew close.

Martin had been unable to arrest a multiseason decline that owed plenty to overuse at the hands of managers Grady Little and Joe Torre, ex-catchers who should have known better but who played him for more innings than any backstop from 2007 through 2009. Questions about Martin's conditioning and commitment had arisen; the player himself conceded that a hard-partying lifestyle had affected his play. Slimming down, bulking up, and drying out failed to recover his dissipated power.

General manager Ned Colletti nontendered Martin, unable to bridge an $800,000 gap in guaranteed money ($4.2 million and $5 million) accompanied by incentives that could have taken the deal to $6 million and unable to trade him for light-hitting Yankee backup Francisco Cervelli, apparently because the Yanks didn't have enough time to review the medicals. (New York eventually signed him as a free agent, for one year at $4 million, with another $1.4 million in incentives.) Colletti immediately turned to 35-year-old Rod Barajas, who had hit .240/.284/.447 overall in 2010 and was one of several uninspiring veterans the GM had traded for late in the season, signing him for $3.25 million, up from just $1.9 million in base salary and incentives in 2009. Ultimately, the Dodgers' fear of overpaying Martin led to their overpaying Barajas by an even greater margin.

DODGERS PROSPECTUS

2010 W-L: 80-82, 4th in NL West

Pythag	.483	20th
RS/G	4.1	21st
RA/G	4.3	19th
TAv	.267	18th
BRR	8.6	6th
FRA	4.15	8th
DER	-13.7	25th
DL	770	17th
B-Age	30.4	27th
P-Age	28.0	16th
Salary	$95.4	11th
M$/MW	$2.72	17th

Ballpark: Dodger Stadium (3-yr. PF: 97). The NL's second-oldest park survives the removal of the "Mannywood" sign unscathed

2010: First sub-.500 finish since 2005 marked by legal battles and clubhouse quarrels

2011: Starters remain strong as Frank and Jamie hit the singles scene

Action Items: Getting the new skipper some experience, mending fences with Matt Kemp

The existential horror of replacing a young, reasonably valuable player with a limited veteran came on the heels of an unsettling season for the Dodgers. They had overcome a slow start, briefly tasting first place and remaining within striking distance up until the All-Star break; at 49-40, they were two games behind the Padres in the NL West, tied with Colorado for the wild-card lead. Alas, despite a second-half 5-13 start that bumped them down into fourth place, Colletti busily dealt prospects as well as Blake DeWitt and James McDonald around the July 31 deadline for Scott Podsednik, Octavio Dotel, Ted Lilly, and Ryan Theriot. When that didn't solve the problem—and why would it have?—Colletti waived Manny Ramirez, who departed for the White Sox on August 30, thus pulling the plug on the offense. Via a 31-43 second half, the Dodgers finished under .500 for the first time since 2005 and just the second time since 1999. The disappointing play of several of assistant GM Logan White's prized draft picks—most notably Martin, Matt Kemp, and James Loney—in combination with the unavailability of Ramirez (who served three stints on the disabled list prior to his departure), a lack of depth in the rotation, and the collapse of a bullpen that had been the NL's best in 2009 aged Torre beyond his years. In early September, the 70-year-old announced that he'd retire at season's end.

This drama unfolded against the surreal backdrop of the divorce proceedings of owner Frank McCourt and wife Jamie, formerly the team's chief executive officer. News of their separation had broken just before the 2009 NLCS, and tawdry details—affairs with limo drivers and lavish spending that included seven country-club memberships, $150,000 for a five-day-a-week hairstylist, $600,000 paid through the team to two sons who did not have titles—became public over the winter at the same time that the team was tightening its belt. Later, news emerged that the McCourts had kept a 71-year-old Russian physicist and spiritual healer named Vladimir Shpunt on payroll to send positive vibes from his Boston base to "tap into the V energy." Shpunt reportedly received a regular-season stipend plus six-figure bonuses for the Dodgers' playoff appearances, and at least one of the McCourts believed he'd been responsible for such moments as Steve Finley's 2004 division-clinching home run.

Just as bizarre was the McCourts' dispute over a 2004 postnuptial marital property agreement (MPA). Three of the six signed copies of the agreement asserted that the Dodgers were the sole property of Frank, an arrangement apparently set up to allow Jamie to shield assets in her name—seven luxury homes and one parcel of land in Mexico—from the liabilities he incurred in buying the Dodgers. However, three contradictory copies of the agreement excluded the Dodgers as Frank's separate property; Frank's lawyer, Larry Silverstein, testified that those were due to a clerical error and admitted to changing them to match the others without telling Jamie. Jamie, who holds a business degree from MIT and was a practicing family law attorney before she worked for Frank, testified that she had never read the document. Can't anyone here play this game?

On December 7, Judge Scott Gordon threw out the MPA, a decision that makes the team subject to California's community property law, under which both McCourts have equal claim on the team as part of the marital estate. Unless one party can buy out the interests of the other—unlikely, given that Frank was rejected several times in seeking additional financing—the Dodgers could be sold. A similar situation recently occurred in San Diego, where the divorce of owner John Moores forced the sale of the Padres. Frank is certain to litigate the ruling, prolonging this circus.

Despite their standing as the game's fourth-most valuable franchise, one that drew more fans than any other team except the Phillies and Yankees, the Dodgers went cheap in 2010. Their Opening Day payroll of $95.3 million ranked 11th in the majors, $5.1 million less than the year before. That figure concealed about $10 million worth of the offloaded salaries of Juan Pierre and Andruw Jones, but the point stands: it's a low payroll for a large-market team, even one whose farm system had yielded numerous players who played for nonmarket salaries.

Overall, the offense dove from fourth in the league in scoring (4.8 runs per game) to 11th (4.1), and from second in the league in True Average (.272) to eighth (.259). It fell from first in batting average and on-base percentage to 10th and eighth, respectively, and from seventh in slugging percentage to 13th. The biggest blow was the loss of Ramirez, who was as effective on a per-out basis (.328 TAv in 2009, .330 in 2010), but who fell from 431 plate appearances to 232 before departing. The Juan Pierre–led replacements for Ramirez in 2009 had hit .316/.376/.402 in 325 plate appearances. Last season, a motley assortment of Garret Anderson, Reed Johnson, Xavier Paul, Jay Gibbons, Podsednik, et al. hit just .241/.283/.346 in 505 PAs while filling in for the ostensible starter.

As if that weren't crippling enough, the Martin/Kemp/Loney/Andre Ethier quartet—three homegrown players plus Colletti's best trade acquisition—collectively slumped while taking up a much greater portion of the Dodgers' limited payroll. Ethier's performance helped buffer the even deeper offensive slides by Loney and Kemp, not to mention Kemp's declining defensive value and mental mistakes and the loss of Martin's playing time to injury. Ethier aside, the homegrown trio lost more than half of its value. Beyond that, the rebound of Rafael Furcal and solid performances of Jamey Carroll and the pretrade DeWitt offset the decline of Casey Blake, the inevitable crash of Ronnie Belliard, and the departure of Orlando Hudson.

Simultaneously, the rotation slipped despite continued improvement from Clayton Kershaw and rebounds by Chad Billingsley and Hiroki Kuroda. A lack of depth forced a scramble to fill the fourth and fifth spots virtually from the get-go; Vicente Padilla, who slotted into the vacancy created by Randy Wolf's departure, missed half the season due to elbow and neck woes, and while Lilly sparkled after his arrival, the team's fate had already been sealed. At the back of the rotation, where the Dodgers got unusually strong work from assorted fifth starters and fill-ins in 2009—Eric Stults, Jeff Weaver, Padilla, Jon Garland, Eric Milton, and others—the work of John Ely, Carlos Monasterios, Charlie Haeger, Ramon Ortiz (!), and associates was brutal in 2010.

The bullpen slipped further than the rotation, as its collective Fair Run Average ballooned from 3.46 to 4.57. Four of the five key relievers whom Torre rode heavily in 2009—Broxton, Ramon Troncoso, Ronald Belisario, and deadline acquisition George Sherrill—declined significantly. A sixth cog, James McDonald, spent most of the first four months stuck at Triple-A before being traded to Pittsburgh. Happier endings were granted to Hong-Chih Kuo, who sparkled while doubling his innings total in a rare bout of health, and Kenley Jansen, who shot up the organizational ladder after converting from catcher last year and shared closer duties with Kuo down the stretch amid Broxton's slump.

Indeed, Jansen was the rare farmhand who provided any positive contribution in 2010 aside from backup catcher A. J. Ellis, who filled in capably for the injured Brad Ausmus and then Martin. Others who might have contributed fumbled opportunities in Los Angeles or went backward in Triple-A. To be fair, the Dodgers have graduated a horde of homegrown players to the majors in recent years and ridden out the storm with the cream of that crop, including Billingsley and Kemp. The system has been further depleted by win-now trades, unsigned picks, and meager signing bonuses. Many of those traded (Delwyn Young, Andy LaRoche, Tony Abreu, and Josh Bell) have yet to pan out, but 2010 rookie Carlos Santana looked like the antidote to Martin's decline, albeit in an Indians uniform.

Colletti's lack of creativity forced many dead-end veterans who might make an Orioles GM blush into the late-2010 lineup, and given another Opening Day payroll target of $95 million (not including deferrals), his taste for proven mediocrity led not only to Barajas but to aging 32-year-old Giants postseason hero Juan Uribe. Overpaid with a three-year, $21 million deal, he'll slot in at second base, and he could eventually take over third once Blake's deal ends. Three years?

The rotation is in better shape. Kuroda returned via a one-year, $12 million deal that included deferred money. Lilly didn't even reach free agency before agreeing to a three-year, $33 million extension, a deal that compared favorably to Wolf's Brewers pact from a year earlier, given Lilly's added durability and higher strikeout rate. Colletti also secured the return of once-and-future fifth starter Garland, who'd enjoyed a strong park-aided season in San Diego, via a one-year, $5 million deal with a vesting option at 190 innings (a level Garland has reached in each of the past nine seasons), and of Padilla, who has been reasonably effective when healthy as a Dodger, for a utility role in case another starter goes down or Broxton can't rediscover his All-Star form.

As for the skipper, hitting coach Don Mattingly succeeds Torre after losing out on the opportunity to do so in New York three years earlier. Other than a hastily arranged stint in the Arizona Fall League, Mattingly has no managerial experience, which became painfully apparent during a July 21 game, when he was forced to remove Broxton. The new skipper had to do so because he returned to the mound after having stepped only a few feet away. To be fair, Major League Baseball admitted that the umpires had ruled incorrectly. At least Mattingly has a chance to bridge the generation gap that opened up between his predecessor and some of the Dodgers' youngsters, most notably Kemp.

As for the rest of the organization, one of the season's pleasant surprises came when the Dodgers signed first-round pick Zach Lee away from a commitment to play quarterback at Louisiana State with a franchise-record $5.25 million bonus. Many presumed the team would punt its pick, given its financial woes, but in landing a power pitcher with ace potential, the team may have secured the steal of the draft. For all of the organization's woes, its large-market advantages and track record of producing talent may see the Dodgers through this crisis, no matter who owns the team.

HITTERS

Rod Barajas **C**

Born: **9/5/1975** Age: **35**
Bats: R Throws: R Height: **6' 2"** Weight: **229**
Breakout: **0%** Improve: **25%** Collapse: **16%**
Attrition: **24%** MLB: **76%**

Comparables:
Orlando Cepeda, Ramon Hernandez, Dmitri Young (69)

YEAR	TEAM	LVL	AGE	PA	R	2B	3B	HR	RBI	BB	SO	SB	CS	AVG/OBP/SLG	TAv	BABIP	BRR	FRAA	WARP
2008	TOR	MLB	32	377	47	23	0	11	49	17	61	0	0	.249/.294/.410	.251	.271	-3.3	C -1, 1B 0	0.8
2009	TOR	MLB	33	460	44	19	0	19	71	20	76	1	0	.226/.257/.403	.236	.227	-0.4	C -2	0.6
2010	NYN	MLB	34	267	30	11	0	12	34	8	39	0	0	.225/.262/.414	.244	.218	-3.7	C 0	0.3
2010	LAN	MLB	34	72	9	3	0	5	13	5	15	0	0	.297/.361/.578	.346	.311	-1.0	C 0	0.8
2011	*LAN*	*MLB*	*35*	*348*	*39*	*16*	*0*	*13*	*43*	*18*	*57*	*0*	*0*	*.241/.287/.416*	*.243*	*.251*	*0.0*	*C -1, 1B 0*	*0.7*

Unable to convince free agent Bengie Molina to switch coasts and generally oblivious to the concept of on-base percentage, Omar Minaya went the bargain-basement route in signing Barajas to a deal worth $500,000 plus incentives. For a while, it almost worked; Hot Rod bopped 11 homers for the Mets by the end of May, hitting a lopsided .269/.292/.552 complemented by just two unintentional walks. Then came a stretch so arid it made the Sahara Desert seem like a Brazilian rainforest: .168/.229/.228 with one homer and four RBI over the next eight weeks, and 25 days missed due to an oblique strain. Upon returning to health, he was shipped westward to cover for Russell Martin's injury, and the Los Angeles–area native went 3-for-4 with two doubles and a homer in a dream-come-true Dodger debut, adding three more homers in his next seven games before cooling off. In the wake of nontendering Martin, the Dodgers moved to re-sign Barajas; he's cheap production behind the plate, but his dip to 15 percent caught stealing after eight straight years above 33 percent generates concern.

Ronnie Belliard INF

Born: **4/7/1975** Age: **36**
Bats: R Throws: R Height: **5' 8"** Weight: **180**
Breakout: **0%** Improve: **19%** Collapse: **10%**
Attrition: **17%** MLB: **69%**

Comparables:
Ray Durham, Bret Boone, Joe Gordon (66)

YEAR	TEAM	LVL	AGE	PA	R	2B	3B	HR	RBI	BB	SO	SB	CS	AVG/OBP/SLG	TAv	BABIP	BRR	FRAA	WARP
2008	WAS	MLB	33	337	37	22	0	11	46	37	58	3	2	.287/.371/.473	.299	.325	-1.3	2B -5, 3B -4	1.2
2009	LAN	MLB	34	83	15	7	0	5	17	6	16	1	0	.351/.398/.636	.356	.393	0.5	2B -3, 3B -2	0.7
2009	WAS	MLB	34	203	25	7	1	5	22	14	40	2	0	.247/.296/.376	.235	.285	-0.5	2B 2, 1B 1	0.2
2010	LAN	MLB	35	185	24	10	1	2	19	18	35	2	2	.216/.292/.327	.239	.256	0.4	2B -1, 3B -1	-0.3
2011	*LAN*	*MLB*	*36*	*394*	*46*	*21*	*1*	*9*	*43*	*33*	*66*	*3*	*1*	*.259/.320/.402*	*.255*	*.288*	*-0.1*	*2B -2, 3B -2*	*0.2*

Belliard forced his way into the lineup at the expense of Orlando Hudson in late 2009, thanks to a torrid streak that played into Joe Torre's hot-hand obsession. The Dodgers brought him back, but his 2010 $825,000 contract was contingent upon his maintaining his end-of-season weight of 209 pounds. Beaten out by the Blake DeWitt/Jamey Carroll second-base platoon, he made his weight but could barely hit it while filling a bench role; he turned in a particularly abysmal 11-for-66 performance against lefties despite a career spent mostly mashing against them. Once the Dodgers cut him loose in early September, he joined Augustus Gloop and Pablo Sandoval on a "Lost Weekend" fudge binge.

Casey Blake 3B

Born: **8/23/1973** Age: **37**
Bats: R Throws: R Height: **6' 2"** Weight: **200**
Breakout: **0%** Improve: **26%** Collapse: **8%**
Attrition: **21%** MLB: **95%**

Comparables:
Doug Decinces, Ken Boyer, Raul Ibanez (73)

YEAR	TEAM	LVL	AGE	PA	R	2B	3B	HR	RBI	BB	SO	SB	CS	AVG/OBP/SLG	TAv	BABIP	BRR	FRAA	WARP
2008	CLE	MLB	34	368	46	24	0	11	58	33	68	2	0	.289/.364/.465	.296	.333	-2.5	3B -3, 1B -1	1.6
2008	LAN	MLB	34	233	26	12	1	10	23	16	52	1	0	.251/.313/.460	.262	.285	0.9	3B -1, 1B 0	0.7
2009	LAN	MLB	35	565	84	25	6	18	79	63	116	3	4	.280/.363/.468	.297	.326	1.5	3B 5, LF 0	4.3
2010	LAN	MLB	36	571	56	28	1	17	64	48	138	0	4	.248/.319/.407	.268	.303	-0.6	3B -2, 1B 0	1.8
2011	*LAN*	*MLB*	*37*	*572*	*69*	*27*	*2*	*17*	*67*	*53*	*120*	*3*	*2*	*.258/.332/.424*	*.266*	*.300*	*-0.4*	*3B -1, 1B 0*	*1.7*

The body count around Blake continues to mount. Acquired at the cost of Carlos Santana—who'd have come in handy with Russell Martin growing more expensive and less effective—Blake re-signed with the Dodgers after the 2008 season and has since proceeded to chase off Andy LaRoche, Josh Bell, and Blake DeWitt while following a career year at age 35 with significant regression last year. He posted his lowest batting average and on-base percentage since 2005 (and the lowest slugging percentage of his career) as his performance against righties absolutely collapsed (.222/.294/.369), and both his walk rates and his strikeout rates moved significantly in the wrong direction, as did his defense. He was a cipher from July onward (.226/.295/.376) after a respectable showing through the end of June (.272/.348/.440). PITCHf/x data suggest that he wasn't making hay with fastballs the way he had in the previous couple of years—an ominous sign in a player his age—but perhaps senior circuit pitchers have simply developed a book on him. With no credible internal candidates left to take over third, the job remains Blake's heading into the final year of his $17-million deal. Yeesh.

Jamey Carroll SS

Born: **2/18/1974** Age: **37**
Bats: R Throws: R Height: **5' 10"** Weight: **175**
Breakout: **2%** Improve: **32%** Collapse: **10%**
Attrition: **21%** MLB: **82%**

Comparables:
Tony Taylor, Davey Lopes, Barry Larkin (71)

YEAR	TEAM	LVL	AGE	PA	R	2B	3B	HR	RBI	BB	SO	SB	CS	AVG/OBP/SLG	TAv	BABIP	BRR	FRAA	WARP
2008	CLE	MLB	34	402	57	13	4	1	36	34	65	7	3	.277/.346/.346	.266	.324	2.5	2B -1, 3B 4	1.7
2009	CLE	MLB	35	358	52	10	2	2	26	36	63	4	2	.276/.352/.340	.259	.335	4.4	2B -1, 3B 0	1.3
2010	LAN	MLB	36	414	46	15	1	0	23	51	64	12	4	.291/.374/.339	.273	.343	3.1	SS 8, 2B 4	3.3
2011	*LAN*	*MLB*	*37*	*397*	*44*	*15*	*2*	*2*	*31*	*42*	*63*	*8*	*3*	*.267/.344/.342*	*.251*	*.309*	*-0.4*	*2B 2, SS 2*	*1.1*

Dodgers fans had every reason to be concerned when the marquee free agent acquired to boost their offense turned out to be Carroll, who arrived in LA via a two-year, $3.85 million deal, but to his credit, the diminutive utilityman had a nice little season. Penciled in to draw the lion's share of starts at second base against lefties, Carroll actually played more shortstop due to Rafael Furcal's injuries and was surprisingly above average there according to FRAA and other defensive systems. He also filled in at third base and (another "yeesh") left field. Meanwhile, his keen batting eye helped him post a career-best True Average despite the league's second-lowest isolated power among hitters with at least 400 plate appearances. Only Ryan Theriot finished lower; luckily, the Dodgers won't enter 2011 with that tandem at the keystone.

Brian Cavazos-Galvez OF

Born: **5/17/1987** Age: **24**
Bats: R Throws: R Height: **6' 0"** Weight: **215**
Breakout: **2%** Improve: **12%** Collapse: **4%**
Attrition: **14%** MLB: **23%**

Comparables:
Carlos Gonzalez, Jake Fox, Chris Pettit (69)

YEAR	TEAM	LVL	AGE	PA	R	2B	3B	HR	RBI	BB	SO	SB	CS	AVG/OBP/SLG	TAv	BABIP	BRR	FRAA	WARP
2009	OGD	Rk	22	323	59	29	3	18	63	10	43	17	8	.322/.353/.618	.340	.322	-5.8	LF 1, RF 5	2.9
2010	GRL	A	23	514	76	43	4	16	77	12	60	43	13	.318/.343/.520	.312	.336	-3.3	CF -1, LF 2	3.8
2011	*LAN*	*MLB*	*24*	*429*	*50*	*27*	*1*	*16*	*61*	*7*	*80*	*11*	*4*	*.265/.280/.455*	*.253*	*.287*	*-0.3*	*CF -4, LF -2*	*-0.1*

After winning Pioneer League MVP honors in 2009, this 12th-round pick out of the University of New Mexico—which shares the Albuquerque Isotopes' hitter-friendly ballpark—hit just

.283/.320/.457 in the first half, but from the All-Star break onward, Cavazos-Galvez feasted at a .372/.383/.615 clip, with a streak in which he hit in 36 out of 37 games. He led the league in doubles and total bases and ranked second in batting average and third in steals (a big surprise), though as in 2009, he was a bit old for his league. He has a long swing and an overly aggressive approach, but Cavazos-Galvez generates tremendous bat speed, can hit to all fields, and sports a strong arm befitting the son of former Dodger reliever Balvino Galvez. There's talk of pushing him to Double-A due to his age and a logjam of outfield prospects behind him.

Ivan DeJesus **2B**

Born: **5/1/1987** Age: **24**
Bats: **R** Throws: **R** Height: **5' 11"** Weight: **190**
Breakout: **3%** Improve: **4%** Collapse: **9%**
Attrition: **16%** MLB: **19%**

Comparables:
Tony Abreu, Justin Turner, Curtis Thigpen (81)

YEAR	TEAM	LVL	AGE	PA	R	2B	3B	HR	RBI	BB	SO	SB	CS	AVG/OBP/SLG	TAv	BABIP	BRR	FRAA	WARP
2008	JAX	AA	21	560	91	21	2	7	58	76	81	16	2	.324/.412/.423	.301	.366	1.9	SS -8, 2B 8	4.5
2010	PDD	—	23	90	13	6	0	1	10	10	16	0	2	.321/.411/.436	—	.393	0.0	—	—
2010	ABQ	AAA	23	580	89	33	2	7	70	32	81	6	1	.296/.335/.405	.248	.330	0.0	2B -2, SS -2	0.4
2011	*LAN*	*MLB*	*24*	*380*	*43*	*18*	*1*	*5*	*37*	*28*	*63*	*5*	*1*	*.279/.329/.380*	*.252*	*.321*	*0.0*	*2B 0, SS -3*	*0.5*

DeJesus missed virtually all of 2009 due to a broken tibia sustained in a home-plate collision during spring training, and leg pain shut down his winter-ball season. He managed to stay healthy last year, but the organizational favorite saw his stock drop with a mediocre year at Albuquerque. Prior to injury, DeJesus had been hailed for his patient, contact-oriented approach and excellent instincts, but his walk rate fell by more than half. He hit just .251/.288/.330 on the road, and his range and footwork around second base drew criticism, though to be fair, it was his first full season at the keystone. Bypassed for a September promotion, during the AFL season he spent time at third base as well as second and impressed Don Mattingly in the process, but the Juan Uribe signing probably consigns him to another year at Triple-A.

A. J. Ellis **C**

Born: **4/9/1981** Age: **30**
Bats: **R** Throws: **R** Height: **6' 3"** Weight: **230**
Breakout: **3%** Improve: **17%** Collapse: **6%**
Attrition: **9%** MLB: **37%**

Comparables:
Carlos Maldonado, Ryan Jorgensen, Bob Boone (68)

YEAR	TEAM	LVL	AGE	PA	R	2B	3B	HR	RBI	BB	SO	SB	CS	AVG/OBP/SLG	TAv	BABIP	BRR	FRAA	WARP
2008	LVG	AAA	27	337	44	17	4	4	59	50	44	0	2	.321/.433/.456	.301	.364	-2.0	C 0, 1B 0	2.7
2008	LAN	MLB	27	3	1	0	0	0	0	0	2	0	0	.000/.000/.000	-0.006	.000	0.0	C 0	-0.1
2009	ABQ	AAA	28	360	48	13	2	0	39	64	44	2	2	.314/.433/.375	.270	.357	0.7	C 2	2.2
2009	LAN	MLB	28	10	0	0	0	0	1	0	1	0	0	.100/.100/.100	.069	.111	0.0	C 0	-0.2
2010	ABQ	AAA	29	76	11	5	1	0	7	13	12	1	0	.262/.400/.377	.245	.320	0.0	C 1	0.3
2010	LAN	MLB	29	128	6	5	0	0	16	14	18	0	0	.278/.352/.324	.254	.316	-1.7	C 0	0.3
2011	*LAN*	*MLB*	*30*	*301*	*36*	*13*	*2*	*2*	*23*	*43*	*46*	*0*	*0*	*.266/.374/.355*	*.265*	*.310*	*0.0*	*C 1, 1B 0*	*1.4*

This 18th-round pick in 2003 beat the bushes long enough to develop solid on-base skills despite a lack of power, so Ellis's overdue induction into the International Brotherhood of Backup Catchers made for a silver lining when Brad Ausmus and eventually Russell Martin got hurt. He threw out 28 percent of base thieves, dutifully took the walks that came with batting ahead of the pitcher, glaciated around the basepaths, and scored fewer runs per time on base than all but two hitters with at least 100 plate appearances. Even without Martin, the Dodgers need look no further for their starter's caddy, though Ellis will apparently have to battle Dioner Navarro for the "honor" of backing up Rod Barajas.

Andre Ethier **RF**

Born: **4/10/1982** Age: **29**
Bats: **L** Throws: **L** Height: **6' 1"** Weight: **208**
Breakout: **1%** Improve: **45%** Collapse: **0%**
Attrition: **9%** MLB: **100%**

Comparables:
Roger Maris, Tony Oliva, Reggie Smith (77)

YEAR	TEAM	LVL	AGE	PA	R	2B	3B	HR	RBI	BB	SO	SB	CS	AVG/OBP/SLG	TAv	BABIP	BRR	FRAA	WARP
2008	LAN	MLB	26	596	90	38	5	20	77	59	88	6	3	.305/.374/.511	.313	.329	1.1	RF -5, LF -3	3.5
2009	LAN	MLB	27	685	92	42	3	31	106	72	116	6	4	.272/.361/.508	.302	.289	3.4	RF -3	4.0
2010	LAN	MLB	28	585	71	33	1	23	82	59	102	2	1	.292/.364/.493	.309	.322	-0.6	RF -8, 1B 0	2.8
2011	*LAN*	*MLB*	*29*	*582*	*80*	*33*	*3*	*22*	*82*	*61*	*89*	*4*	*2*	*.288/.367/.496*	*.299*	*.307*	*-0.4*	*RF -5, LF 0*	*2.6*

After emerging as a star in 2009, Ethier began the year as though bound for even more dizzying heights. He was hitting .392/.457/.744 through May 14, leading the league in both the Triple Crown and triple-slash stats and looking like an MVP candidate when he fractured the pinkie of his right hand during batting practice. Though he missed just 15 games, he hit a mere .260/.335/.413 the rest of the way, bringing his rate stats right in line with 2009, hardly an embarrassment in the grand scheme, particularly given a top-15 finish in True Average. Ethier continues to struggle against lefties—.222/.299/.348 over the last three years, compared with .315/.392/.565 against righties. It's tough to conceptualize benching your most reliable hitter, but perhaps Don Mattingly will be more amenable to sitting him against southpaws than Joe Torre was.

Rafael Furcal **SS**

Born: **10/24/1977** Age: **33**
Bats: **S** Throws: **R** Height: **5' 10"** Weight: **165**
Breakout: **0%** Improve: **45%** Collapse: **4%**
Attrition: **10%** MLB: **99%**

Comparables:
Julio Lugo, Chone Figgins, Jose Cruz (71)

YEAR	TEAM	LVL	AGE	PA	R	2B	3B	HR	RBI	BB	SO	SB	CS	AVG/OBP/SLG	TAv	BABIP	BRR	FRAA	WARP
2008	LAN	MLB	30	164	34	12	2	5	16	20	17	8	3	.357/.439/.573	.342	.380	3.1	SS -4	1.9
2009	LAN	MLB	31	680	93	28	5	9	47	61	89	12	6	.269/.334/.375	.257	.300	5.6	SS 10	3.9
2010	LAN	MLB	32	428	66	23	7	8	43	40	60	22	4	.300/.365/.460	.302	.335	2.5	SS 8	4.3
2011	*LAN*	*MLB*	*33*	*535*	*66*	*25*	*5*	*9*	*58*	*52*	*66*	*19*	*6*	*.282/.349/.415*	*.271*	*.305*	*-0.1*	*SS 6*	*3.1*

Furcal's roller-coaster ride with the Dodgers continues, complete with sporadic availability and widely variable performances due to back and leg woes. After starting hot, he lost most of May to a hamstring strain, but barely missed a beat and was hitting a searing .316/.380/.492 as late as August 2. Alas, lower back pain in the same area where he had a microdiscectomy two years ago cost him another month, and he hit just .237/.310/.329 after returning in September, yet another factor in the Dodger offense's late-season disappearance. Despite his absences, Furcal's VORP ranked fourth in the majors among shortstops. He'll make $12 million in the final guaranteed year of his deal; with 600 plate appearances, his $12 million option for 2012 will vest, locking in a high salary for a player whose availability offers no guarantees.

Jay Gibbons **LF**

Born: **3/2/1977** Age: **34**
Bats: **L** Throws: **L** Height: **6' 0"** Weight: **200**
Breakout: **0%** Improve: **27%** Collapse: **17%**
Attrition: **23%** MLB: **74%**

Comparables:
Al Oliver, Mike Sweeney, Wes Covington (67)

YEAR	TEAM	LVL	AGE	PA	R	2B	3B	HR	RBI	BB	SO	SB	CS	AVG/OBP/SLG	TAv	BABIP	BRR	FRAA	WARP
2008	NAS	AAA	31	115	14	10	0	5	15	6	18	0	0	.312/.348/.541	.290	.337	-0.8	RF -2, LF 1	0.3
2010	ABQ	AAA	33	376	60	28	1	19	83	19	30	0	0	.347/.375/.594	.306	.334	0.3	1B 2, RF -3	2.2
2010	LAN	MLB	33	80	11	2	0	5	17	4	14	0	1	.280/.312/.507	.289	.281	0.5	LF 1, 1B 0	0.6
2011	*LAN*	*MLB*	*34*	*317*	*40*	*18*	*0*	*12*	*44*	*17*	*44*	*0*	*0*	*.287/.324/.471*	*.275*	*.298*	*0.0*	*LF 1, RF -2*	*0.7*

Cited for using PEDs in the December 2007 Mitchell Report, Gibbons was cut by the Orioles the following spring despite there being two years and nearly $12 million remaining on his contract. His career spiraled downward; after a brief stint in the Brewers' organization and a spring invite from the Marlins, he went where washed-up ballplayers' careers go to die: Newark of the independent Atlantic League. Gibbons made the most of an invitation to the Dodgers' minor-league camp, knocking the stuffing out of the ball in Albuquerque and providing a bit of firepower after replacing Garrett Anderson on the big club's roster in August. Re-signing for $650,000 plus incentives, he could find work as the team's top lefty bat off the bench.

Dee Gordon **SS**

Born: **4/22/1988** Age: **23**
Bats: **L** Throws: **R** Height: **5' 11"** Weight: **150**
Breakout: **3%** Improve: **18%** Collapse: **4%**
Attrition: **20%** MLB: **36%**

Comparables:
Jonathan Herrera, Alcides Escobar, Joaquin Arias (70)

YEAR	TEAM	LVL	AGE	PA	R	2B	3B	HR	RBI	BB	SO	SB	CS	AVG/OBP/SLG	TAv	BABIP	BRR	FRAA	WARP
2008	OGD	Rk	20	274	45	13	3	2	27	16	29	18	5	.331/.369/.430	.275	.360	2.9	SS -7	1.3
2009	GRL	A	21	601	96	17	12	3	35	43	90	73	25	.301/.358/.394	.283	.349	7.0	SS -8	3.6
2010	CHT	AA	22	614	86	17	10	2	39	40	89	53	20	.277/.332/.355	.254	.319	3.8	SS -8	1.6
2011	*LAN*	*MLB*	*23*	*505*	*50*	*18*	*5*	*3*	*44*	*22*	*90*	*33*	*10*	*.255/.288/.333*	*.221*	*.300*	*0.1*	*SS -2*	*-0.3*

The Dodgers' top prospect coming into the season, this son of former major-league reliever Tom "Flash" Gordon was aggressively promoted two levels to Double-A Chattanooga. He didn't light up the Southern League as he did the Midwest League; he led the circuit in steals thanks to true 80 speed, but his rawness—the result of his not taking up the game until his senior year of high school—still showed. He struggled with pitch recognition and patience, walking and whiffing at clips similar to those in 2009 and showing no additional power. In the field, he was prone to lapses owing to a lack of concentration. Still, Gordon hardly embarrassed himself, given the jump in competition, and scouts praise his ability to make consistent contact as well as his tools to be a standout defensive shortstop. He's likely bound for Albuquerque.

Jamie Hoffmann **CF**

Born: **8/20/1984** Age: **26**
Bats: **R** Throws: **R** Height: **6' 3"** Weight: **235**
Breakout: **2%** Improve: **14%** Collapse: **5%**
Attrition: **15%** MLB: **32%**

Comparables:
Nick Stavinoha, Carlos Lee, Daniel Ortmeier (74)

YEAR	TEAM	LVL	AGE	PA	R	2B	3B	HR	RBI	BB	SO	SB	CS	AVG/OBP/SLG	TAv	BABIP	BRR	FRAA	WARP
2008	JAX	AA	23	544	64	20	3	10	71	54	73	28	9	.278/.347/.395	.269	.304	4.5	RF -5, CF -1	1.2
2009	CHT	AA	24	129	25	9	2	2	16	22	18	5	3	.307/.457/.495	.315	.358	0.2	RF 12, CF 0	2.0
2009	ABQ	AAA	24	293	44	14	3	8	48	32	37	10	8	.284/.358/.455	.272	.301	-0.5	RF 0, CF 0	0.9
2009	LAN	MLB	24	24	2	2	0	1	7	0	5	0	0	.182/.167/.409	.167	.167	0.0	RF 1	-0.1
2010	ABQ	AAA	25	608	91	36	3	8	74	43	98	17	7	.310/.369/.431	.258	.359	0.0	CF -4, RF -1	1.1
2011	*LAN*	*MLB*	*26*	*527*	*62*	*25*	*3*	*9*	*55*	*43*	*91*	*18*	*7*	*.270/.334/.395*	*.258*	*.310*	*-0.6*	*RF 0, CF -4*	*0.5*

Selected in the NHL's draft but not baseball's, Hoffmann has always been an organizational favorite due to his work ethic and his defensive play. When the Dodgers didn't protect him last winter, the Nationals plucked him with the first pick of the Rule 5 draft, then flipped him to the Yankees for Brian Bruney. Hoffmann never really had a shot to make the Yanks once Randy Winn signed, and after returning to Albuquerque, he was such a human highlight film in his first season of full-time center-field duty that the berm in Isotopes Park might be renamed Hoffmann's Hill in his honor. Sadly, his power curiously waned despite advantageous hitting conditions, and his plate discipline regressed as well. If he has a big-league future, it's likely to be in a bench role.

Chin-lung Hu **SS**

Born: **2/2/1984** Age: **27**
Bats: **R** Throws: **R** Height: **5' 11"** Weight: **190**
Breakout: **3%** Improve: **22%** Collapse: **7%**
Attrition: **19%** MLB: **52%**

Comparables:
Matt Tolbert, Ronny Cedeno, Rafael Ramirez (78)

YEAR	TEAM	LVL	AGE	PA	R	2B	3B	HR	RBI	BB	SO	SB	CS	AVG/OBP/SLG	TAv	BABIP	BRR	FRAA	WARP
2008	LVG	AAA	24	168	21	5	3	1	15	7	19	2	0	.295/.315/.385	.223	.319	2.1	SS 8	1.0
2008	LAN	MLB	24	129	16	2	2	0	9	11	23	2	0	.181/.248/.233	.193	.221	1.7	SS 1, 2B -3	-0.4
2009	ABQ	AAA	25	544	66	21	5	6	53	25	54	14	5	.294/.324/.393	.239	.308	2.6	SS 5, 2B 0	1.6
2009	LAN	MLB	25	6	2	1	0	0	2	0	2	0	0	.400/.333/.600	.249	.500	0.3	SS 0	0.0
2010	ABQ	AAA	26	223	37	11	1	4	25	8	16	8	1	.317/.339/.438	.251	.318	0.3	SS -2, 2B 0	0.4
2010	LAN	MLB	26	25	2	1	0	0	1	0	5	1	0	.130/.160/.174	.119	.158	-0.2	SS -2	-0.5
2011	*LAN*	*MLB*	*27*	*421*	*47*	*19*	*3*	*6*	*46*	*18*	*52*	*8*	*3*	*.278/.306/.392*	*.245*	*.297*	*0.0*	*SS 2, 2B 0*	*0.9*

Acrobatic fielding and developing gap power placed Hu on our top prospects list back in 2008, but vision problems, injuries, and a failure to hit when auditioning have derailed his big-league career. He was hitting at a decent clip in Albuquerque when he went down in early July with a broken thumb that required surgery and cost him another shot at filling in for Rafael Furcal. Traded to the Mets, he joins their high stack of potential utility players.

Reed Johnson **LF**

Born: **12/8/1976** Age: **34**
Bats: **R** Throws: **R** Height: **5' 10"** Weight: **180**
Breakout: **1%** Improve: **19%** Collapse: **19%**
Attrition: **30%** MLB: **77%**

Comparables:
Marlon Anderson, Jacque Jones, Ryan Freel (75)

YEAR	TEAM	LVL	AGE	PA	R	2B	3B	HR	RBI	BB	SO	SB	CS	AVG/OBP/SLG	TAv	BABIP	BRR	FRAA	WARP
2008	CHN	MLB	31	374	52	21	0	6	50	19	68	5	6	.303/.353/.420	.271	.353	4.5	CF -3, LF 4	1.9
2009	CHN	MLB	32	185	23	10	2	4	22	13	27	2	1	.256/.330/.415	.262	.282	0.8	CF -2, RF -1	0.2
2010	LAN	MLB	33	215	24	11	2	2	15	5	50	2	2	.262/.288/.366	.240	.331	1.1	LF 6, RF 0	0.5
2011	*LAN*	*MLB*	*34*	*327*	*37*	*16*	*2*	*5*	*34*	*18*	*60*	*4*	*2*	*.266/.320/.386*	*.251*	*.308*	*-0.4*	*CF -2, LF 2*	*0.4*

On paper, Johnson seemed like an ideal fourth outfielder for the Dodgers, one with the ability to play left field better than Manny Ramirez, crush lefties to cover for Andre Ethier's inability to do the same, and spot in center when necessary, all for the low price of $800,000. It didn't work out well, however. A lack of at-bats exacerbated Johnson's hacktastic tendencies, and the lower-back woes that have plagued his career wiped out most of his July; he hit just .213/.250/.333 after the All-Star break. Johnson did hit southpaws (.301/.324/.466) but curled into a fetal position against righties in about equal time. Johnson's versatility has value, as does his ability to hit left-handers, but given averages of .214/.268/.306 against right-handers over the last two seasons, Johnson presents a tool of overly limited application for today's pitching-clogged rosters. He'll compete for a bench role with the Cubs.

Matt Kemp **CF**

Born: **9/23/1984** Age: **26**
Bats: **R** Throws: **R** Height: **6' 2"** Weight: **230**
Breakout: **2%** Improve: **51%** Collapse: **2%**
Attrition: **10%** MLB: **92%**

Comparables:
Hunter Pence, Andre Dawson, Ellis Burks (66)

YEAR	TEAM	LVL	AGE	PA	R	2B	3B	HR	RBI	BB	SO	SB	CS	AVG/OBP/SLG	TAv	BABIP	BRR	FRAA	WARP
2008	LAN	MLB	23	657	93	38	5	18	76	46	153	35	11	.290/.339/.459	.285	.360	1.7	CF -3, RF -1	3.0
2009	LAN	MLB	24	667	97	25	7	26	101	52	139	34	8	.297/.352/.490	.301	.345	2.1	CF 7, RF 0	5.5
2010	LAN	MLB	25	668	82	25	6	28	89	53	170	19	15	.249/.310/.450	.275	.295	-0.2	CF -9	1.9
2011	*LAN*	*MLB*	*26*	*610*	*80*	*28*	*5*	*23*	*85*	*48*	*131*	*25*	*10*	*.284/.341/.480*	*.286*	*.330*	*-0.8*	*CF -3, RF 0*	*2.7*

To say that Kemp fell off considerably after his breakout 2009 would be an understatement. He incited the ire of Joe Torre and his staff by giving up at-bats, failing to hustle out of the batter's box, blundering on the basepaths and in the field, and showing a general lack of intensity. Those mental shortcomings found their way into his stat line, particularly via a spiking strikeout rate and a drastic drop in defensive value; a 50-point drop in BABIP didn't help, either, and he posted monthly OBPs under .300 from June onward. For his part, Kemp acknowledged a lack of focus—which perhaps had something to do with his being linked to a hard-partying lifestyle—but still didn't improve. Late in the year, his agent agitated for a trade. The Dodgers don't appear interested in accommodating him, hoping that the regime change will help Kemp resume his star-level play.

James Loney **1B**

Born: **5/7/1984** Age: **27**
Bats: L Throws: L Height: **6' 2"** Weight: **220**
Breakout: **2%** Improve: **33%** Collapse: **7%**
Attrition: **13%** MLB: **90%**

Comparables:
Wally Joyner, Dan Johnson, Ryan Garko (73)

YEAR	TEAM	LVL	AGE	PA	R	2B	3B	HR	RBI	BB	SO	SB	CS	AVG/OBP/SLG	TAv	BABIP	BRR	FRAA	WARP
2008	LAN	MLB	24	651	65	35	6	13	90	45	85	7	4	.289/.338/.434	.268	.315	-0.7	1B -8	0.2
2009	LAN	MLB	25	652	73	25	2	13	90	70	68	7	3	.281/.356/.399	.276	.298	-3.8	1B -4	0.8
2010	LAN	MLB	26	648	67	41	2	10	88	52	95	10	5	.267/.329/.395	.260	.302	1.7	1B -4	0.3
2011	*LAN*	*MLB*	*27*	*618*	*77*	*34*	*3*	*13*	*72*	*55*	*75*	*7*	*3*	*.287/.350/.432*	*.274*	*.307*	*-0.4*	*1B -4*	*0.9*

Since his strong rookie season, Loney has incrementally moved backward relative to his positional competition in terms of True Average, from 27 points above the average first baseman in 2007 to 11 points below in 2008, 16 points below in 2009, and 19 points below last year. At the same time, his salary has risen from $400,000 to $3.1 million last year, his first year of arbitration eligibility. While his fluky home/road splits from 2009 evened out, his performance against lefties returned to the abysmal level (.222/.262/.313 in 187 PAs) it occupied in 2008. He also hit just .211/.285/.331 after the All-Star break, playing no small part in the offense's second-half collapse. If Loney weren't a favorite son of assistant GM Logan White, who drafted him with the 19th pick in 2002, he'd be a priority for replacement.

Russell Martin **C**

Born: **2/15/1983** Age: **28**
Bats: R Throws: R Height: **5' 10"** Weight: **210**
Breakout: **0%** Improve: **45%** Collapse: **5%**
Attrition: **10%** MLB: **97%**

Comparables:
Ted Simmons, Mike Hargrove, Yogi Berra (69)

YEAR	TEAM	LVL	AGE	PA	R	2B	3B	HR	RBI	BB	SO	SB	CS	AVG/OBP/SLG	TAv	BABIP	BRR	FRAA	WARP
2008	LAN	MLB	25	650	87	25	0	13	69	90	83	18	6	.280/.385/.396	.284	.309	2.0	C -1, 3B 1	4.5
2009	LAN	MLB	26	588	62	19	0	7	53	69	80	11	6	.250/.350/.329	.253	.283	3.8	C 0, 3B 0	2.4
2010	LAN	MLB	27	387	45	13	0	5	26	48	61	6	2	.248/.346/.332	.256	.286	0.9	C -1	1.4
2011	*NYA*	*MLB*	*28*	*560*	*66*	*23*	*1*	*9*	*49*	*69*	*75*	*12*	*5*	*.264/.360/.370*	*.263*	*.293*	*-0.5*	*C 0, 3B 0*	*2.3*

Martin spent the winter of 2008-2009 using yoga to improve his flexibility, but when his power dissipated, he chose to bulk up, arriving at camp weighing 231 pounds, 25 heavier than the year before. The weight didn't restore his power; his 2010 was essentially a foreshortened carbon copy of his 2009 campaign, ending in early August by a hairline pelvic fracture. With Martin's salary scheduled to increase from $5.05 million via arbitration, the Dodgers nontendered him. The Yankees signed him to a contract with a base of $4 million that can rise to over $5 million with incentives, and they named him their starting catcher, health permitting. Despite his decline, the Dodgers will miss Martin: his high OBPs and plus defense (39 percent caught stealing, third in the NL) make replacing him a nontrivial matter, particularly given a system devoid of near-ready catching prospects. As for the Yankees, Martin's defense will serve as a nice contrast to Jorge Posada's, but with no reason for pitchers to work around him, the last remaining vestige of his early offense may crumble.

Russell Mitchell **3B**

Born: **2/15/1985** Age: **26**
Bats: R Throws: R Height: **5' 11"** Weight: **205**
Breakout: **3%** Improve: **22%** Collapse: **11%**
Attrition: **25%** MLB: **44%**

Comparables:
Angel Chavez, Steve Pearce, Casey McGehee (75)

YEAR	TEAM	LVL	AGE	PA	R	2B	3B	HR	RBI	BB	SO	SB	CS	AVG/OBP/SLG	TAv	BABIP	BRR	FRAA	WARP
2008	JAX	AA	23	542	65	22	4	16	75	42	95	8	4	.264/.321/.425	.266	.291	-2.4	3B -4, 1B 2	1.0
2009	CHT	AA	24	501	63	30	3	13	63	36	84	4	1	.241/.295/.406	.256	.265	-1.0	1B 1, 2B -2	0.6
2010	ABQ	AAA	25	557	97	38	2	23	87	38	78	1	3	.315/.363/.535	.278	.329	0.0	3B 3, 1B -1	2.9
2010	LAN	MLB	25	43	3	0	0	2	4	0	8	0	0	.143/.140/.286	.137	.121	0.4	3B 0, 1B 0	-0.5
2011	*LAN*	*MLB*	*26*	*542*	*64*	*28*	*2*	*18*	*70*	*31*	*98*	*3*	*1*	*.264/.305/.437*	*.257*	*.289*	*-0.1*	*3B -1, 1B -5*	*0.4*

A 15th-round pick in 2003 out of Cartersville, Georgia, Mitchell rebounded from a couple of subpar years at Double-A and rode some park-driven success at Albuquerque (.355/.395/.622 at home, .272/.330/.440 elsewhere) to a spot on the All-Pacific Coast League team and a September cup of coffee in Los Angeles. With the help of Albuquerque hitting coach John Moses, he moved away from his pull-hitting tendency to use more of the field and added the outfield corners to a repertoire that includes second base as well as first and third. He could compete for a utility role in spring training.

Xavier Paul **LF**

Born: **2/25/1985** Age: **26**
Bats: L Throws: R Height: **6' 0"** Weight: **195**
Breakout: **4%** Improve: **23%** Collapse: **2%**
Attrition: **17%** MLB: **50%**

Comparables:
Chris Pettit, Lou Montanez, Justin Huber (79)

YEAR	TEAM	LVL	AGE	PA	R	2B	3B	HR	RBI	BB	SO	SB	CS	AVG/OBP/SLG	TAv	BABIP	BRR	FRAA	WARP
2008	LVG	AAA	23	506	82	28	5	9	68	43	96	17	7	.316/.372/.463	.281	.371	2.6	CF -6, RF -1	2.3
2009	ABQ	AAA	24	129	13	10	2	2	16	10	22	8	2	.328/.372/.500	.272	.379	-0.8	CF -6, RF -1	-0.2
2009	LAN	MLB	24	16	3	1	0	1	1	2	4	0	1	.214/.312/.500	.315	.222	0.1	RF -1, CF 0	0.0
2010	ABQ	AAA	25	250	46	20	1	12	38	18	41	7	3	.325/.384/.579	.292	.354	0.0	LF 2, CF -3	1.5
2010	LAN	MLB	25	133	16	8	1	0	11	8	24	3	1	.231/.271/.314	.215	.277	1.0	LF -1, RF -1	-0.4
2011	*LAN*	*MLB*	*26*	*345*	*42*	*19*	*2*	*9*	*43*	*25*	*67*	*9*	*4*	*.277/.329/.439*	*.267*	*.319*	*-0.3*	*CF -7, LF 0*	*0.3*

The Dodgers' most advanced outfield prospect coming into the year, Paul is nonetheless a classic tweener with neither the bat nor the glove to hold down a regular job. After missing most of 2009 due to a staph infection in his knee and a broken ankle, he spent 2010 yo-yoing between Albuquerque, where he raked, and Los Angeles, where he did little more than fill space during Manny Ramirez's absences. His late season was painful in more ways than one: he didn't hit enough to be considered a viable alternative once Scott Podsednik arrived (ouch), and he lost out on a September call-up after being shut down in mid-August due to a cervical spine inflammation (double-ouch). Out of options, he'll be part of the cattle call to fill the void in left field.

Jaime Pedroza **2B**

Born: **9/12/1986** Age: **24**
Bats: **S** Throws: **R** Height: **5' 8"** Weight: **167**
Breakout: **2%** Improve: **8%** Collapse: **4%**
Attrition: **12%** MLB: **31%**

Comparables:
Oddibe McDowell, Danny Richar, Asdrubal Cabrera (70)

YEAR	TEAM	LVL	AGE	PA	R	2B	3B	HR	RBI	BB	SO	SB	CS	AVG/OBP/SLG	TAv	BABIP	BRR	FRAA	WARP
2008	SBR	A+	21	535	78	31	7	9	57	33	120	25	11	.290/.336/.441	.292	.356	3.3	SS -26, 2B -4	1.2
2009	GRL	A	22	609	100	33	6	15	78	78	162	36	14	.260/.360/.433	.285	.345	4.6	2B 5, SS -1	3.9
2010	CHT	AA	23	487	53	21	4	7	37	62	101	11	8	.280/.378/.401	.278	.345	-4.7	2B -10	0.7
2011	*LAN*	*MLB*	*24*	*550*	*60*	*25*	*3*	*11*	*55*	*50*	*145*	*15*	*6*	*.242/.309/.374*	*.241*	*.310*	*-0.5*	*2B -1, SS -4*	*-0.2*

After a full-season demotion to Low-A in 2009, Pedroza rebounded with a solid campaign in Double-A. He has improved his plate discipline markedly over the past two years, doubling his walk rate while cutting his strikeouts slightly. Alas, his power hasn't developed, he's not running as much or as well as he has, and his defense at second base doesn't draw raves. Unless Ivan DeJesus Jr. makes the big club, Pedroza could wind up back at Chattanooga to start the year.

Scott Podsednik **LF**

Born: **3/18/1976** Age: **35**
Bats: **L** Throws: **L** Height: **6' 0"** Weight: **170**
Breakout: **0%** Improve: **35%** Collapse: **6%**
Attrition: **22%** MLB: **92%**

Comparables:
Jose Cruz, Manny Mota, Milt Thompson (74)

YEAR	TEAM	LVL	AGE	PA	R	2B	3B	HR	RBI	BB	SO	SB	CS	AVG/OBP/SLG	TAv	BABIP	BRR	FRAA	WARP
2008	COL	MLB	32	181	22	8	1	1	15	16	28	12	4	.253/.320/.333	.232	.296	1.6	CF 1, LF 0	0.2
2009	CHA	MLB	33	587	74	25	6	7	48	39	74	30	13	.304/.349/.412	.264	.336	7.0	LF 7, CF 2	2.9
2010	KCA	MLB	34	435	46	8	6	5	44	29	57	30	12	.310/.345/.400	.266	.337	-1.7	LF 7, CF 1	1.6
2010	LAN	MLB	34	160	17	6	1	1	7	11	26	5	3	.262/.313/.336	.236	.312	2.4	LF 5, CF 0	0.6
2011	*LAN*	*MLB*	*35*	*468*	*52*	*19*	*4*	*5*	*45*	*35*	*67*	*25*	*10*	*.273/.324/.370*	*.248*	*.304*	*-1.1*	*LF 5, CF 0*	*0.8*

Podsednik signed with the Royals in January for a mere $1.75 million and reeled off a carbon copy of his 2009 offensive numbers for the first two-thirds of the season while playing some especially strong defense. With Manny Ramirez serving his third stint on the disabled list and eventually bound for another destination, Ned Colletti traded two prospects for Podsednik, perhaps hoping he was getting a cheaper Juan Pierre. Podzilla spent about six weeks as the starting left fielder but didn't find any of Pierre's magic 2009 pixie dust and was eventually sidelined by plantar fasciitis. How such an injury will affect a player whose value depends upon his speed is an open question given that most who have dealt with that injury have been sluggers. Podsednik declined his side of a $2 million mutual option after the season, an act of hubris out of proportion to his modest skills.

Trayvon Robinson **CF**

Born: **9/1/1987** Age: **23**
Bats: **R** Throws: **R** Height: **5' 11"** Weight: **195**
Breakout: **7%** Improve: **33%** Collapse: **11%**
Attrition: **32%** MLB: **60%**

Comparables:
Aaron Cunningham, Adam Jones, Carlos Gonzalez (73)

YEAR	TEAM	LVL	AGE	PA	R	2B	3B	HR	RBI	BB	SO	SB	CS	AVG/OBP/SLG	TAv	BABIP	BRR	FRAA	WARP
2008	SBR	A+	20	489	67	20	8	4	42	33	104	22	12	.276/.323/.385	.262	.340	3.5	CF 1, LF 0	1.9
2009	SBR	A+	21	529	82	28	9	15	54	50	125	43	18	.306/.374/.500	.324	.385	-2.5	CF 2	4.8
2009	CHT	AA	21	70	8	1	2	2	10	10	18	4	2	.246/.343/.439	.288	.300	0.4	CF -3	0.1
2010	PDD	—	22	92	10	4	0	1	7	16	22	6	1	.250/.389/.347	—	.327	0.0	—	—
2010	CHT	AA	22	523	80	23	5	9	57	73	125	38	15	.300/.404/.438	.310	.389	1.7	CF -9	3.4
2011	*LAN*	*MLB*	*23*	*534*	*63*	*23*	*5*	*11*	*59*	*48*	*136*	*28*	*10*	*.264/.326/.405*	*.258*	*.336*	*-0.6*	*CF -14, LF 0*	*-0.1*

After four years of struggling to convert his tools into baseball skills, this 2005 10th-rounder out of LA's Crenshaw High School broke out in the hitter-friendly California League in 2009. Robinson's power outburst turned out to be a mirage, and he struggled through the first half of 2010 at Double-A trying to prove it wasn't a fluke. He hit .308/.464/.453 during the second half while demonstrating more natural gap power and improved plate discipline, which helped him refine true leadoff skills to mesh with his outstanding speed. That speed allows him to cover some of his misreads and route-running mistakes in center, though he is improving; he may wind up in left field, since his arm is below average. Robinson will probably spend 2011 at Triple-A and could get a shot at joining the Dodgers in 2012.

Kyle Russell **RF**

Born: **6/27/1986** Age: **25**
Bats: **L** Throws: **L** Height: **6' 5"** Weight: **195**
Breakout: **2%** Improve: **22%** Collapse: **4%**
Attrition: **21%** MLB: **58%**

Comparables:
Darryl Strawberry, Mark Reynolds, Ian Stewart (61)

YEAR	TEAM	LVL	AGE	PA	R	2B	3B	HR	RBI	BB	SO	SB	CS	AVG/OBP/SLG	TAv	BABIP	BRR	FRAA	WARP
2008	OGD	Rk	22	260	46	13	5	11	46	27	82	4	0	.279/.365/.534	.281	.376	3.3	RF 0, CF -1	1.3
2009	GRL	A	23	563	90	39	7	26	102	72	180	20	2	.272/.371/.545	.315	.376	3.1	RF 11, CF 0	5.4
2010	SBR	A+	24	239	42	11	4	16	53	32	64	8	3	.354/.448/.692	.407	.443	0.3	RF 3, LF -1	4.2
2010	CHT	AA	24	308	36	23	3	10	28	29	113	3	2	.245/.319/.462	.275	.370	0.4	RF 0, CF 0	1.0
2011	*LAN*	*MLB*	*25*	*463*	*55*	*22*	*3*	*20*	*62*	*44*	*167*	*5*	*1*	*.227/.302/.445*	*.256*	*.317*	*0.1*	*RF -2, CF -1*	*0.3*

For the second straight year, "The Texas Wind Machine" placed in the top four in the entire minors in strikeouts thanks to his long stroke, and once again, he used obscene raw power (he's an 80) and a pull-conscious approach to put up big numbers. A 2008 third-round pick, Russell tore up the hitter-friendly California League in the first two months of the season, but struggled due to contact woes upon his initial promotion to Double-A, hitting .168/.252/.274 with 44 strikeouts in 107 plate appearances before the All-Star break. He found a groove in the second half (.287/.355/.562) despite whiffing 35 percent of the time, and had major problems against lefties (.225/.295/.350, with 39 strikeouts in 88 PAs in Double-A). Athletic, above-average both in the field and on the bases, and equipped with a strong arm, he has the tools to be a stud, but remains a ways off from fulfilling his promise. Not drafted until he was a college senior, Russell has always been old for his leagues and will need to get a move on if he wants to have a career of any substance.

Jerry Sands **1B**

Born: **9/28/1987** Age: **23**
Bats: **R** Throws: **R** Height: **6' 4"** Weight: **225**
Breakout: **2%** Improve: **15%** Collapse: **2%**
Attrition: **10%** MLB: **34%**

Comparables:
Chris Davis, Willie McCovey, Brandon Allen (72)

YEAR	TEAM	LVL	AGE	PA	R	2B	3B	HR	RBI	BB	SO	SB	CS	AVG/OBP/SLG	TAv	BABIP	BRR	FRAA	WARP
2008	DGR	Rk	20	185	29	4	0	10	33	29	43	5	0	.205/.346/.438	.284	.204	1.3	RF 10	1.9
2009	GRL	A	21	123	22	7	2	5	19	15	32	1	0	.260/.358/.510	.284	.319	0.8	1B -1, RF 1	0.5
2009	OGD	Rk	21	185	41	9	2	14	39	22	28	0	1	.350/.427/.687	.393	.355	0.9	CF 1, RF 0	3.2
2010	PDD	—	22	105	13	8	0	3	13	16	19	2	1	.299/.410/.494	—	.348	0.0	—	—
2010	GRL	A	22	288	48	16	3	18	46	40	61	14	2	.333/.432/.646	.367	.382	0.2	1B 4, RF 4	4.6
2010	CHT	AA	22	303	54	12	2	17	47	33	62	4	0	.270/.360/.529	.309	.286	3.0	LF 4, 1B -3	2.1
2011	*LAN*	*MLB*	*23*	*364*	*48*	*15*	*2*	*20*	*54*	*36*	*93*	*3*	*1*	*.254/.330/.495*	*.282*	*.288*	*0.0*	*RF 0, 1B -4*	*1.0*

A 25th-round pick out of tiny Catawba College in North Carolina in 2008, Sands came into the year viewed as a sleeper pick for a breakout season, thanks to his combination of power and consistent contact. Break out Sands did, lighting up the Midwest League leaderboards and earning a midseason promotion to Chattanooga, where he continued to pound the ball. Overall, his 35 homers tied for third in the entire minors, and he earned the organization's minor-league player-of-the-year honors. Despite a long swing with occasionally awkward mechanics, Sands can hit to all fields, and while not particularly athletic, he's a solid defender with decent speed and a strong-enough arm to handle right field. He took grounders at third base during his Arizona Fall League stint to increase his options. The Dodgers haven't yet decided where Sands will begin the new season; if Triple-A, it is easy to envision his getting the call if Loney continues to disappoint.

Blake Smith **RF**

Born: **12/9/1987** Age: **23**
Bats: **L** Throws: **R** Height: **6' 2"** Weight: **225**
Breakout: **0%** Improve: **0%** Collapse: **0%**
Attrition: **0%** MLB: **1%**

Comparables:
Clint Hurdle, Bill Melton, Alex Avila (70)

YEAR	TEAM	LVL	AGE	PA	R	2B	3B	HR	RBI	BB	SO	SB	CS	AVG/OBP/SLG	TAv	BABIP	BRR	FRAA	WARP
2009	OGD	Rk	21	120	14	7	0	1	12	13	38	0	0	.212/.308/.308	.251	.318	-1.5	RF 0	0.0
2010	GRL	A	22	493	77	28	2	19	76	49	135	2	3	.281/.363/.488	.299	.362	2.0	RF 6	3.5
2011	*LAN*	*MLB*	*23*	*328*	*33*	*14*	*1*	*10*	*34*	*25*	*110*	*0*	*0*	*.213/.277/.364*	*.223*	*.292*	*0.0*	*RF -2*	*-0.9*

The Dodgers' 2009 second-round pick was a two-way star at UC Berkeley; many scouts preferred Smith's pitching (92-94 mph fastball and signs of two other plus pitches) but the Dodgers saw a higher upside in his hitting. After Smith's rough 2009 debut led some to second-guess their choice, he put up strong offensive numbers and earned all-star honors in his first full minor-league season. A good athlete with a strong arm and plenty of raw power, he has a long swing that leaves him prone to strikeouts; he tied for second in the Midwestern League in whiffs. He's likely to be bound for High-A Rancho Cucamonga.

Angelo Songco **LF**

Born: **9/9/1988** Age: **22**
Bats: **L** Throws: **R** Height: **6' 0"** Weight: **195**
Breakout: **3%** Improve: **6%** Collapse: **2%**
Attrition: **6%** MLB: **9%**

Comparables:
Brad Harman, Carl Yastrzemski, Mat Gamel (79)

YEAR	TEAM	LVL	AGE	PA	R	2B	3B	HR	RBI	BB	SO	SB	CS	AVG/OBP/SLG	TAv	BABIP	BRR	FRAA	WARP
2009	GRL	A	20	134	8	6	2	1	16	10	28	1	0	.150/.224/.258	.174	.183	0.6	LF -5	-1.3
2009	OGD	Rk	20	158	27	11	1	9	29	10	41	0	1	.306/.361/.583	.317	.368	0.5	LF -1	1.2
2010	GRL	A	21	570	87	30	6	15	71	51	91	6	1	.274/.344/.446	.288	.305	2.8	LF -7	2.3
2011	*LAN*	*MLB*	*22*	*442*	*46*	*21*	*2*	*12*	*50*	*26*	*105*	*0*	*0*	*.231/.277/.384*	*.229*	*.275*	*0.0*	*LF -14*	*-1.9*

The Dodgers' fourth-round pick in 2009 out of Loyola Marymount University had an uneven introduction to pro ball, following a hot start at Ogden with a chilly stint at Great Lakes. Songco fared much better in his return engagement, hitting for power, making consistent contact, and showing reasonable patience. He shows pop to all fields, and both his approach at the plate and his makeup draw praise, but since he's nothing special afield, he'll go only as far as his bat will take him.

Ryan Theriot 2B

Born: **12/7/1979** Age: **31**
Bats: **R** Throws: **R** Height: **5' 11"** Weight: **175**
Breakout: **1%** Improve: **33%** Collapse: **2%**
Attrition: **10%** MLB: **98%**

Comparables:
Steve Sax, Bobby Avila, Jack Wilson (76)

YEAR	TEAM	LVL	AGE	PA	R	2B	3B	HR	RBI	BB	SO	SB	CS	AVG/OBP/SLG	TAv	BABIP	BRR	FRAA	WARP
2008	CHN	MLB	28	661	85	19	4	1	38	73	58	22	13	.307/.384/.359	.261	.337	2.0	SS -10	1.9
2009	CHN	MLB	29	677	81	20	5	7	54	51	93	21	10	.284/.337/.369	.242	.315	1.2	SS 4	1.9
2010	CHN	MLB	30	412	44	10	2	1	21	19	46	16	6	.284/.318/.327	.236	.317	-0.4	2B 0, SS -1	0.0
2010	LAN	MLB	30	228	27	5	0	1	8	22	28	4	3	.242/.316/.283	.240	.269	0.9	2B 0	0.2
2011	*SLN*	*MLB*	*31*	*609*	*69*	*22*	*3*	*6*	*55*	*51*	*67*	*20*	*8*	*.284/.340/.367*	*.254*	*.304*	*-0.8*	*SS -3, 2B 0*	*1.3*

Theriot's baserunning made him such an object of derision in Chicago that back in 2008, the blog *Wrigleyville 23* invented and began tracking a stat—TOOTBLAN, for Thrown Out On The Bases Like A Nincompoop—to factor into his deceptively high on-base percentage. In 2010, he tied for fourth in the league in non-stealing/non–force outs made on the basepaths with nine, but while the overall impact as tracked by Baserunning Runs was negligible, his declines in OBP and slugging were not. Theriot's isolated power was the league's lowest among players with at least 400 plate appearances, and his presence in the Dodgers' lineup after the Lilly/DeWitt trade contributed to a dip to 3.6 runs scored per game from August 1 onward. A second-year arbitration candidate who made $2.6 million in 2010, Theriot was sent to St. Louis prior to the nontender deadline and is slated to be the Cardinals' starting shortstop for 2011.

PITCHERS

Ronald Belisario

Born: **12/31/1982** Age: **28**
Bats: **R** Throws: **R** Height: **6' 3"** Weight: **235**
Breakout: **1%** Improve: **3%** Collapse: **3%**
Attrition: **0%** MLB: **8%**

Comparables:
Paul Wilson, Gene Brabender, Bill Dawley (79)

YEAR	TEAM	LVL	AGE	W	L	SV	G	GS	IP	H	HR	BB	SO	EqBB9	EqSO9	GB%	BABIP	WHIP	ERA	FRA	WARP
2008	ALT	AA	25	4	4	9	38	0	57	63	5	26	36	4.1	5.7	53%	.314	1.61	4.42	5.41	-0.3
2009	LAN	MLB	26	4	3	0	69	0	70^{2}	52	4	29	64	3.7	8.2	57%	.245	1.23	2.04	3.16	1.4
2010	LAN	MLB	27	3	1	2	59	0	55^{1}	52	6	19	38	3.1	6.2	63%	.275	1.34	5.04	5.52	-0.5
2011	*LAN*	*MLB*	*28*	*3*	*1*	*3*	*56*	*0*	*61^{2}*	*62*	*7*	*27*	*41*	*4.0*	*6.0*	*50%*	*.294*	*1.46*	*4.53*	*4.92*	*-0.3*

A fantastic free-talent find in 2009, Belisario was a problem child in 2010, serving two stints on the restricted list for troubles of his own making: an arrest for suspicion of driving under the influence in June 2009 delayed his work visa and cost him time in spring training and April, and just after he settled into a groove, he left the team for five weeks to undergo treatment in a substance-abuse program. On the mound, Belisario's strikeout and home-run rates moved substantially in the wrong directions, though he generated a ton of ground balls, shutting down righties (.246/.299/.351) and pitching much better than his results suggested. Unfortunately, 12 of the 24 runners he bequeathed went on to score. The Dodgers could use a return to his reliable 2009 form, so they will be rooting for the pitcher to get his life in order.

Chad Billingsley

Born: **7/29/1984** Age: **26**
Bats: **R** Throws: **R** Height: **6' 0"** Weight: **244**
Breakout: **10%** Improve: **40%** Collapse: **23%**
Attrition: **8%** MLB: **94%**

Comparables:
Andy Benes, Bob Lee, Len Barker (61)

YEAR	TEAM	LVL	AGE	W	L	SV	G	GS	IP	H	HR	BB	SO	EqBB9	EqSO9	GB%	BABIP	WHIP	ERA	FRA	WARP
2008	LAN	MLB	23	16	10	0	35	32	200^{2}	188	14	80	201	3.6	9.0	50%	.313	1.38	3.14	3.39	4.8
2009	LAN	MLB	24	12	11	0	33	32	196^{1}	173	17	86	179	3.9	8.2	48%	.292	1.35	4.03	4.15	2.5
2010	LAN	MLB	25	12	11	0	31	31	191^{2}	176	8	69	171	3.2	8.0	51%	.301	1.33	3.52	3.20	4.7
2011	*LAN*	*MLB*	*26*	*12*	*8*	*0*	*30*	*30*	*181*	*167*	*13*	*75*	*161*	*3.7*	*8.0*	*48%*	*.302*	*1.33*	*3.60*	*3.92*	*4.0*

Clayton Kershaw has surpassed him as the Dodgers' ace, but that doesn't mean that Billingsley has turned into a disappointment. Devoid of the drama of his previous 18 months—early exits in the 2008 NLCS, a broken leg, an All-Star-caliber first half backed by an injury-laden second, and finally an absence from the 2009 post-season rotation—Billingsley enjoyed a nice rebound in 2010. He trimmed his walk and homer rates substantially; aided by his allowing just one homer in 96 innings after the All-Star break, the latter wound up as the league's second-best. Overall, Billingsley finished 16th among NL ERA qualifiers in Support-Neutral Winning Percentage and 15th in SIERA, and only a June stint on the disabled list for a groin strain and a lack of offensive support (3.7 runs per start) took a bit of shine away. He has two more years under club control; it remains to be seen whether the Dodgers will seize the initiative and lock him up.

Jonathan Broxton

Born: **6/16/1984** Age: **27**
Bats: **R** Throws: **R** Height: **6' 4"** Weight: **240**
Breakout: **22%** Improve: **40%** Collapse: **24%**
Attrition: **16%** MLB: **71%**

Comparables:
Rob Dibble, Lee Smith, Dick Radatz (56)

YEAR	TEAM	LVL	AGE	W	L	SV	G	GS	IP	H	HR	BB	SO	EqBB9	EqSO9	GB%	BABIP	WHIP	ERA	FRA	WARP
2008	LAN	MLB	24	3	5	14	70	0	69	54	2	27	88	3.5	11.5	47%	.315	1.22	3.13	3.44	1.1
2009	LAN	MLB	25	7	2	36	73	0	76	44	4	29	114	3.4	13.5	55%	.263	0.97	2.61	3.19	1.2
2010	LAN	MLB	26	5	6	22	64	0	62^1	64	4	28	73	4.0	10.5	46%	.366	1.51	3.90	3.24	0.8
2011	*LAN*	*MLB*	*27*	*4*	*2*	*22*	*76*	*0*	*75*	*60*	*5*	*30*	*93*	*3.6*	*11.1*	*47%*	*.308*	*1.20*	*2.70*	*2.93*	*1.5*

Despite his 2008 and 2009 post-season failings and Joe Torre's occasional inability to get him into the right games, nothing about Broxton's collapse was particularly foreseeable. He carried an 0.83 ERA and a 9.6 strikeout-to-walk ratio in 32 2/3 innings into the June 27 ESPN Sunday Night game against the Yankees—his fourth appearance in five days—where he yielded four runs and took the loss over the course of 48 excruciating-to-watch pitches. From that point onward, Broxton turned into the hillbilly Armando Benitez, rocked for a 7.58 ERA and knocked out of the closer job thanks to the double whammy of drastically eroded strikeout-to-walk rates (1.09 in 29 2/3 innings) and a .382 batting average on balls in play. Put this together with his decreased velocity (down 2.5 mph from 2009), and it is reasonable to infer that compromised mechanics and an inability to put the ball where he intended—whether due to injury, fatigue, or a Matt Stairs hex—were to blame. The Dodgers have indicated that Broxton will be back to closing this season, and their fortunes will depend on their ability to untangle the problems of one of their most expensive and important players.

Rubby De La Rosa

Born: **3/4/1989** Age: **22**
Bats: **R** Throws: **R** Height: **6' 1"** Weight: **170**
Breakout: **4%** Improve: **4%** Collapse: **1%**
Attrition: **1%** MLB: **5%**

Comparables:
Matt Keough, Don Demola, Jason Marquis (79)

YEAR	TEAM	LVL	AGE	W	L	SV	G	GS	IP	H	HR	BB	SO	EqBB9	EqSO9	GB%	BABIP	WHIP	ERA	FRA	WARP
2010	GRL	A	21	4	1	6	14	5	59^1	49	3	17	55	2.6	8.4	56%	.284	1.20	3.19	3.69	0.9
2010	CHT	AA	21	3	1	0	8	8	51	38	1	21	39	3.7	6.9	60%	.264	1.18	1.41	3.29	1.3
2011	*LAN*	*MLB*	*22*	*2*	*2*	*0*	*12*	*6*	58^1	*59*	*6*	*30*	*40*	*4.7*	*6.2*	*48%*	*.297*	*1.53*	*4.70*	*5.11*	*0.2*

De La Rosa came into the year an unheralded prospect after his first season stateside—in which he'd touched 98 mph—ended with his being sent back to the Dominican Republic for disciplinary reasons. Given a full season in the US, he won the organization's minor-league pitcher of the year award. He lit up radar guns, clocking as high as 102 mph in relief, and in the mid-90s as a starter. Shifted to the rotation in late June, he allowed more than two runs in just one of five starts before moving up to Chattanooga, where inconsistent command and control borne of his gangly delivery eroded his walk and strikeout rates. De La Rosa has a power slider and a changeup to go with his heater, but neither qualifies as a plus offering. The Dodgers believe he'll develop into a starter, but many scouts feel he'll ultimately wind up in the bullpen.

Scott Elbert

Born: **8/13/1985** Age: **25**
Bats: **L** Throws: **L** Height: **6' 1"** Weight: **210**
Breakout: **3%** Improve: **7%** Collapse: **5%**
Attrition: **1%** MLB: **14%**

Comparables:
Antonio Bastardo, Bob Howry, Ken Howell (74)

YEAR	TEAM	LVL	AGE	W	L	SV	G	GS	IP	H	HR	BB	SO	EqBB9	EqSO9	GB%	BABIP	WHIP	ERA	FRA	WARP
2008	JAX	AA	22	4	1	0	25	1	41^1	22	2	20	46	4.4	10.0	31%	.213	1.04	2.40	3.15	1.0
2008	LAN	MLB	22	0	1	0	10	0	6	9	2	4	8	6.0	12.0	50%	.438	2.33	12.00	7.99	-0.1
2009	CHT	AA	23	2	3	0	12	11	62^1	59	5	30	87	4.3	12.6	41%	.362	1.51	3.90	3.52	1.6
2009	ABQ	AAA	23	2	1	0	8	7	33^2	34	2	14	38	3.7	10.1	60%	.352	1.48	3.74	3.85	1.0
2009	LAN	MLB	23	2	0	0	19	0	19^2	19	4	7	21	3.2	9.6	47%	.294	1.32	5.03	5.11	-0.1
2010	ABQ	AAA	24	1	1	0	9	9	43^1	46	4	34	45	7.1	9.4	48%	.339	1.90	4.98	4.82	1.1
2010	LAN	MLB	24	0	0	0	1	0	0^2	1	0	3	0	40.5	0.0	0%	.333	6.00	13.50	5.73	0.0
2011	*LAN*	*MLB*	*25*	*4*	*4*	*0*	*29*	*10*	*71*	*66*	*8*	*43*	*75*	*5.4*	*9.4*	*44%*	*.311*	*1.53*	*4.55*	*4.95*	*0.5*

Perhaps in reward for his patience in yo-yoing between Albuquerque's rotation and LA's bullpen while working his way back from a torn labrum, Elbert earned the Dodgers' Minor League Pitcher of the Year honors for 2009. Alas, his 2010 was a lost campaign. Stuck in Albuquerque with the Dodger blues again, he made little progress, due to an astronomical walk rate, and shortly after returning from a one-appearance cameo in the majors, he left the team to deal with personal issues of a still-unspecified nature. He returned a month later, only to be sidelined by shoulder tendinitis until the Arizona Fall League. The Dodgers' top pick in 2004 has an explosive low- to mid-90s fastball and a power curve, but his tendency to overthrow and to pitch deep into counts compromises both his command and his stamina. Having added a cutter in the AFL while demonstrating improved command, he appears ready to accept his lot as a reliever, a route that could find him in the Dodger pen sooner rather than later.

John Ely

Born: **5/17/1986** Age: **25**
Bats: **R** Throws: **R** Height: **6' 2"** Weight: **200**
Breakout: **11%** Improve: **33%** Collapse: **8%**
Attrition: **13%** MLB: **64%**

Comparables:
Ron Schueler, Mike Moore, Johnny Cueto (74)

YEAR	TEAM	LVL	AGE	W	L	SV	G	GS	IP	H	HR	BB	SO	EqBB9	EqSO9	GB%	BABIP	WHIP	ERA	FRA	WARP
2008	WNS	A+	22	10	12	0	27	27	145^{1}	142	18	46	134	2.8	8.3	52%	.305	1.33	4.71	5.32	1.1
2009	BIR	AA	23	14	2	0	27	27	156^{1}	140	9	50	125	2.9	7.2	53%	.289	1.22	2.82	4.13	2.3
2010	ABQ	AAA	24	5	4	0	13	13	68	70	10	29	56	3.8	7.4	49%	.299	1.50	6.22	6.95	0.0
2010	LAN	MLB	24	4	10	0	18	18	100	105	12	40	76	3.6	6.8	46%	.310	1.47	5.49	5.68	-0.4
2011	*LAN*	*MLB*	*25*	*8*	*9*	*0*	*23*	*23*	*129^{1}*	*141*	*18*	*55*	*89*	*3.8*	*6.2*	*48%*	*.309*	*1.52*	*5.03*	*5.47*	*0.8*

The White Sox's 2007 third-round pick out of Miami-Ohio, this Matthew McConaughey doppelganger was one of two pitchers acquired from Chicago in the Juan Pierre deal. Recalled in late April, he shook off a rough debut to reel off six quality starts in a row without a single homer allowed; at one point, he also went 22 2/3 consecutive innings without a walk. Alas, just as he was anointed a rotation savior, the league caught on; Ely was pummeled for an 8.00 ERA while yielding 2.0 homers per nine innings pitched with a 1.22 strikeout-to-walk ratio over his last 11 starts, a gruesome stretch that included a two-month refresher course at Albuquerque. Short on heat—his fastball averaged 87.4 mph and generated swings and misses just 3.5 percent of the time—Ely does have an excellent changeup to go along with a recently added cutter, but he may not have the stuff to survive in a major-league rotation.

Charlie Haeger

Born: **9/19/1983** Age: **27**
Bats: **R** Throws: **R** Height: **6' 1"** Weight: **200**
Breakout: **21%** Improve: **42%** Collapse: **5%**
Attrition: **7%** MLB: **62%**

Comparables:
Dusty Hughes, Ernie Broglio, Dock Ellis (74)

YEAR	TEAM	LVL	AGE	W	L	SV	G	GS	IP	H	HR	BB	SO	EqBB9	EqSO9	GB%	BABIP	WHIP	ERA	FRA	WARP
2008	CHR	AAA	24	10	13	0	28	25	178	167	13	77	117	3.9	5.9	40%	.280	1.46	4.45	4.96	1.7
2008	SDN	MLB	24	0	0	0	4	0	4^{1}	8	2	5	4	10.4	8.3	29%	.400	3.46	16.62	18.85	-0.5
2009	ABQ	AAA	25	11	6	0	22	22	144^{2}	134	16	58	103	3.6	6.4	42%	.271	1.41	3.55	3.96	3.3
2009	LAN	MLB	25	1	1	0	6	3	19	13	4	7	15	3.3	7.1	49%	.177	1.16	3.32	4.12	0.2
2010	SBR	A+	26	2	3	0	5	5	21	21	2	12	17	5.1	7.3	55%	.306	1.57	5.14	5.28	0.1
2010	ABQ	AAA	26	4	3	0	11	10	53^{2}	45	4	42	41	7.1	6.9	33%	.263	1.65	5.70	7.77	-0.5
2010	LAN	MLB	26	0	4	0	9	6	30	36	4	26	30	7.8	9.0	43%	.356	2.10	8.10	7.96	-0.7
2011	*SEA*	*MLB*	*27*	*10*	*10*	*0*	*28*	*28*	*156*	*151*	*18*	*86*	*103*	*5.0*	*6.0*	*42%*	*.281*	*1.52*	*4.71*	*5.12*	*0.8*

After his brief flash of success in late 2009, the Dodgers gave this knuckleballer a shot at their fifth-starter job out of spring training. Haeger struck out 12 in six innings in his first start, but turned into Haeger the Horrible thereafter, with an 0.82 strikeout-to-walk ratio in his final 24 innings, an imbalance no pitcher can survive. After May 8, he made just two brief cameos with the big club, and while he kept the ball in the park at Albuquerque, his control there was nothing to write home about. Tim Wakefield broke through at age 28 and has enjoyed a lengthy big-league career, so it could still happen for Haeger. He's now the Mariners' R&D curiosity.

Kenley Jansen

Born: **9/30/1987** Age: **23**
Bats: **S** Throws: **R** Height: **6' 6"** Weight: **220**
Breakout: **16%** Improve: **21%** Collapse: **16%**
Attrition: **10%** MLB: **41%**

Comparables:
Chris Perez, Joey Devine, J.R. Richard (60)

YEAR	TEAM	LVL	AGE	W	L	SV	G	GS	IP	H	HR	BB	SO	EqBB9	EqSO9	GB%	BABIP	WHIP	ERA	FRA	WARP
2010	CHT	AA	22	4	0	8	22	0	27	14	0	17	50	5.7	16.7	32%	.318	1.15	1.67	0.75	1.1
2010	LAN	MLB	22	1	0	4	25	0	27	12	0	15	41	5.0	13.7	37%	.231	1.04	0.67	-0.29	2.1
2011	*LAN*	*MLB*	*23*	*2*	*1*	*2*	*34*	*0*	*42^{1}*	*30*	*3*	*24*	*58*	*5.0*	*12.3*	*43%*	*.308*	*1.28*	*2.84*	*3.09*	*0.7*

Formerly a light-hitting but cannon-armed catcher, this native of Curaçao was converted to pitching in 2009 and took to it quickly, turning heads with his heat and impressive control in the Arizona Fall League. He blew hitters away at two stops last year, prompting the Dodgers to recall him in late July despite just 56 2/3 pro innings. With a mid-90s fastball, a two-plane slider, and an occasional changeup, he dominated big-league hitters; righties went 3-for-48 against him, lefties 9-for-44, and by year's end, he was occasionally closing. Obviously, Jansen is a work in progress when it comes to refining his secondary pitches, holding runners, and the like, and it remains to be seen how he will handle adversity, but the Dodgers love his work ethic. He could be part of their late-game bullpen picture out of the gate in 2011.

Clayton Kershaw

Born: **3/19/1988** Age: **23**
Bats: **L** Throws: **L** Height: **6' 3"** Weight: **220**
Breakout: **22%** Improve: **43%** Collapse: **20%**
Attrition: **7%** MLB: **91%**

Comparables:
Yovani Gallardo, Jose Deleon, Joba Chamberlain (67)

YEAR	TEAM	LVL	AGE	W	L	SV	G	GS	IP	H	HR	BB	SO	EqBB9	EqSO9	GB%	BABIP	WHIP	ERA	FRA	WARP
2008	JAX	AA	20	2	3	0	13	11	61^{1}	39	0	19	59	2.8	8.7	47%	.239	0.95	1.91	3.05	1.9
2008	LAN	MLB	20	5	5	0	22	21	107^{2}	109	11	52	100	4.3	8.4	51%	.320	1.50	4.26	4.25	1.8
2009	LAN	MLB	21	8	8	0	31	30	171	119	7	91	185	4.8	9.7	41%	.269	1.23	2.79	2.98	5.1
2010	LAN	MLB	22	13	10	0	32	32	204^{1}	160	13	81	212	3.6	9.3	42%	.275	1.21	2.91	3.27	4.8
2011	*LAN*	*MLB*	*23*	*11*	*7*	*0*	*25*	*25*	*140*	*118*	*10*	*67*	*138*	*4.3*	*8.9*	*44%*	*.290*	*1.32*	*3.28*	*3.56*	*4.0*

In just his second full season, Kershaw took another large step toward fulfilling his destiny as a major-league ace. Continuing the shift away from his curveball as the primary accompaniment to his mid-90s fastball, he increasingly relied on his slider, which shares the same release point and early flight path as its knee-buckling sibling but generates almost three times as many swings and misses and about 50 percent more fouls. The switch helped Kershaw cut the previous year's unintentional walk rate by 44 percent while still whiffing more than one hitter per inning. The combination of improved efficiency and maturity allowed him to trim his pitches per inning by seven percent and average one more inning per start. He would rank fourth in the league in strikeout and hit rate, seventh in home-run rate, and ninth in ERA, all without cracking the game's top 25 in Pitcher Abuse Points. It is staggering to realize that Kershaw is roughly four years younger than Tim Lincecum, Ubaldo Jimenez, Josh Johnson, and Cole Hamels. Dude's gonna earn some hardware sooner or later.

Hong-Chih Kuo

Born: **7/23/1981** Age: **29**
Bats: L Throws: L Height: **6' 0"** Weight: **200**
Breakout: **25%** Improve: **49%** Collapse: **26%**
Attrition: **5%** MLB: **93%**

Comparables:
Duane Ward, Rich Gossage, Robb Nen (74)

YEAR	TEAM	LVL	AGE	W	L	SV	G	GS	IP	H	HR	BB	SO	EqBB9	EqSO9	GB%	BABIP	WHIP	ERA	FRA	WARP
2008	LAN	MLB	26	5	3	1	42	3	80	60	4	21	96	2.4	10.8	47%	.281	1.05	2.14	2.40	2.6
2009	LAN	MLB	27	2	0	0	35	0	30	21	2	13	32	3.9	9.6	48%	.253	1.20	3.00	2.82	0.8
2010	LAN	MLB	28	3	2	12	56	0	60	29	1	18	73	2.7	11.0	38%	.206	0.80	1.20	0.84	2.6
2011	*LAN*	*MLB*	*29*	*4*	*2*	*2*	*65*	*0*	*68*	*54*	*5*	*25*	*76*	*3.3*	*10.0*	*44%*	*.289*	*1.15*	*2.60*	*2.82*	*1.4*

On the heels of a 2009 campaign abbreviated by elbow inflammation—not to mention a track record of four elbow surgeries—Kuo's presence on the disabled list with more elbow soreness at the very beginning of the 2010 season rated as an ominous sign. Thankfully, he came off the DL and quickly resumed his dominant form as a top set-up man, even while all others around him fell apart. By mid-August, Kuo was picking up save opportunities, and he fared well, though the Dodgers' understandable reluctance to pitch him on back-to-back days (they did so just four times) required multiple ninth-inning options. He certainly has the stuff to handle full-time closer duty (righties hit .159/.233/.228 against him in 160 PAs; lefties went 6-for-63 and wept openly), but his health concerns mandate picking his spots with care.

Hiroki Kuroda

Born: **2/10/1975** Age: **36**
Bats: R Throws: R Height: **6' 0"** Weight: **190**
Breakout: **15%** Improve: **37%** Collapse: **29%**
Attrition: **9%** MLB: **98%**

Comparables:
Jim Bunning, Early Wynn, Gaylord Perry (59)

YEAR	TEAM	LVL	AGE	W	L	SV	G	GS	IP	H	HR	BB	SO	EqBB9	EqSO9	GB%	BABIP	WHIP	ERA	FRA	WARP
2008	LAN	MLB	33	9	10	0	31	31	183^{1}	181	13	42	116	2.1	5.7	53%	.281	1.25	3.73	4.30	2.5
2009	LAN	MLB	34	8	7	0	21	20	117^{1}	110	12	24	87	1.8	6.7	53%	.272	1.15	3.76	4.56	1.2
2010	LAN	MLB	35	11	13	0	31	31	196^{1}	180	15	48	159	2.2	7.3	53%	.283	1.19	3.39	3.84	3.2
2011	*LAN*	*MLB*	*36*	*12*	*8*	*0*	*29*	*29*	171^{1}	*172*	*15*	*43*	*117*	*2.2*	*6.1*	*50%*	*.295*	*1.25*	*3.47*	*3.77*	*4.2*

Healthwise, the 2009 season treated Kuroda like how the gorilla treated the suitcase in those American Tourister commercials from 30 years ago, but he survived the pounding to rebound with his strongest stateside season. Relying less on his four-seam fastball and more on his slider and splitter, Kuroda got more swings and misses than ever before; his 10.7 percent swinging-strike rate ranked ninth in the majors, and his strikeout rate rose substantially. He did it without compromising his pinpoint control; his unintentional walk rate and strikeout-to-unintentional-walk ratio were both second in the league behind those of Roy Halladay. With his three-year, $35.3 million deal having expired, the Dodgers re-upped for what they hope will be more of the same via a one-year, $12-million deal that defers $2 million apiece to 2012 and 2013.

Ted Lilly

Born: **1/4/1976** Age: **35**
Bats: L Throws: L Height: **6' 0"** Weight: **185**
Breakout: **18%** Improve: **37%** Collapse: **36%**
Attrition: **7%** MLB: **98%**

Comparables:
Mike Mussina, Jim Bunning, Bert Blyleven (73)

YEAR	TEAM	LVL	AGE	W	L	SV	G	GS	IP	H	HR	BB	SO	EqBB9	EqSO9	GB%	BABIP	WHIP	ERA	FRA	WARP
2008	CHN	MLB	32	17	9	0	34	34	204^{2}	187	32	64	184	2.8	8.1	35%	.270	1.26	4.09	4.25	3.6
2009	CHN	MLB	33	12	9	0	27	27	177	151	22	36	151	1.8	7.7	35%	.261	1.07	3.10	3.58	4.1
2010	CHN	MLB	34	3	8	0	18	18	117	104	19	29	89	2.2	6.8	31%	.249	1.15	3.69	3.87	2.3
2010	LAN	MLB	34	7	4	0	12	12	76^{2}	61	13	15	77	1.8	9.0	33%	.244	1.03	3.52	3.48	1.7
2011	*LAN*	*MLB*	*35*	*13*	*9*	*0*	*32*	*32*	199^{1}	*181*	*28*	*55*	*161*	*2.5*	*7.3*	*37%*	*.272*	*1.18*	*3.51*	*3.82*	*4.6*

Twelve years to the day after being traded to the Expos in a deal for Mark Grudzielanek and Carlos Perez—he'd been a 23rd-round draft pick two years earlier—Lilly returned to the Dodgers in a trade that cost Blake DeWitt and two pitching prospects. With Cliff Lee off the market, Lilly was the best starter available at the deadline, despite a 3-8 record born of weak offensive support (2.7 runs per game). Lilly couldn't revive the Dodgers' playoff hopes on his own, but he made a game effort via 10 quality starts out of 12. Lilly's bad luck on home runs per fly ball after coming over was mitigated by his ability to keep runners off base via a lowered walk rate and an abnormally suppressed BABIP; nine of his 13 homers allowed in Dodgers blue were solo shots. In all, he finished with the league's second-lowest walk rate and second-highest home-run rate. Diminished velocity (87.4 average fastball speed) may be enough of a concern to make Lilly's back-loaded three-year, $33 million deal a risk, but he's a substantial upgrade over Vicente Padilla as the fourth starter.

Josh Lindblom

Born: **6/15/1987** Age: **24**
Bats: **R** Throws: **R** Height: **6' 5"** Weight: **240**
Breakout: **6%** Improve: **11%** Collapse: **9%**
Attrition: **17%** MLB: **27%**

Comparables:
Jo-Jo Reyes, David Huff, Jhonny Nunez (73)

YEAR	TEAM	LVL	AGE	W	L	SV	G	GS	IP	H	HR	BB	SO	EqBB9	EqSO9	GB%	BABIP	WHIP	ERA	FRA	WARP
2008	GRL	A	21	0	0	0	8	8	29	14	2	4	33	1.2	10.2	52%	.179	0.66	1.86	2.88	1.0
2009	CHT	AA	22	3	5	0	14	11	57^{1}	55	4	14	46	2.2	7.2	45%	.293	1.29	4.71	5.49	0.2
2009	ABQ	AAA	22	3	0	1	20	3	39	34	3	12	36	2.8	8.3	46%	.284	1.26	2.54	2.15	1.3
2010	ABQ	AAA	23	3	2	0	40	10	95	143	12	32	84	3.0	8.0	38%	.401	1.92	6.25	5.56	0.5
2011	*LAN*	*MLB*	*24*	*5*	*4*	*0*	*28*	*11*	*75^{2}*	*83*	*9*	*26*	*56*	*3.1*	*6.7*	*43%*	*.318*	*1.44*	*4.72*	*5.13*	*0.5*

A closer at Purdue, this 2008 second-round pick progressed quickly through the system and came into the year with a shot at seeing time in the majors. Sadly, Lindblom was beaten relentlessly at Albuquerque, first as a starter—a role some felt was a stretch to begin with—and then as a reliever. His splits aren't suitable to print in a family publication, but suffice it to say that a closer look suggests a case of *hardluckus extremis* in terms of BABIP and home runs per fly ball; his strikeout and walk rates were acceptable, but his ground-ball percentage declined considerably, and Albuquerque's elevation can be hell on earth for a fly-baller. Lindblom has good stuff—a 92-94 mph fastball with heavy sink, a power curve, and a splitter—but he'll have to retrench.

Ethan Martin

Born: **6/6/1989** Age: **22**
Bats: **R** Throws: **R** Height: **6' 2"** Weight: **195**
Breakout: **14%** Improve: **22%** Collapse: **9%**
Attrition: **19%** MLB: **51%**

Comparables:
Franklin Morales, Jim Palmer, Tom Griffin (63)

YEAR	TEAM	LVL	AGE	W	L	SV	G	GS	IP	H	HR	BB	SO	EqBB9	EqSO9	GB%	BABIP	WHIP	ERA	FRA	WARP
2009	GRL	A	20	6	8	1	27	19	100	85	4	61	120	5.5	10.8	41%	.321	1.56	3.87	4.63	0.9
2010	SBR	A+	21	9	14	0	25	22	113^{1}	120	10	81	105	6.4	8.4	44%	.338	1.84	6.35	6.41	-1.1
2011	*LAN*	*MLB*	*22*	*6*	*9*	*0*	*25*	*20*	*103^{1}*	*108*	*13*	*82*	*80*	*7.1*	*7.0*	*42%*	*.311*	*1.84*	*6.02*	*6.54*	*-0.4*

Martin drew mixed reviews in his 2009 pro debut due to both walk and strikeout rates that ranked in the Midwest League's top three. His 2010 season didn't go as well. While his mid-90s fastball and big-breaking curve impressed early, both wore out their welcome as the season went on; he lost velocity, movement, and command over the course of the year and left too many pitches up in the strike zone. After July 5, he allowed as many runs as innings pitched—or more runs than IP—in seven out of nine starts, and his monthly ERAs after April all topped 5.50. Scouts still love his stuff and his upside, but the Dodgers believe he needs to work on the mental aspects of his game, and may have him repeat the level.

Aaron Miller

Born: **9/18/1987** Age: **23**
Bats: **L** Throws: **L** Height: **6' 3"** Weight: **200**
Breakout: **7%** Improve: **15%** Collapse: **5%**
Attrition: **10%** MLB: **24%**

Comparables:
Marc Rzepczynski, Antonio Bastardo, Josh Outman (77)

YEAR	TEAM	LVL	AGE	W	L	SV	G	GS	IP	H	HR	BB	SO	EqBB9	EqSO9	GB%	BABIP	WHIP	ERA	FRA	WARP
2009	GRL	A	21	3	1	0	7	7	30^{1}	22	3	10	38	3.0	11.3	40%	.292	1.12	2.08	2.32	1.7
2010	SBR	A+	22	6	4	0	19	17	101^{2}	76	6	48	99	4.3	8.8	42%	.261	1.27	2.92	3.63	1.6
2010	CHT	AA	22	1	4	0	6	6	23	28	3	18	22	7.0	8.6	42%	.368	2.00	6.65	6.69	-0.1
2011	*LAN*	*MLB*	*23*	*6*	*6*	*0*	*16*	*16*	*80^{1}*	*79*	*10*	*49*	*66*	*5.5*	*7.4*	*42%*	*.298*	*1.58*	*4.91*	*5.34*	*0.8*

A two-way player at Baylor, Miller caught scouts' eyes as a right fielder, but the Dodgers tabbed him as a pitcher in the supplemental phase of the first round in 2009. The 2010 season was his first full year on the mound, and he started hot at Inland Empire, showing low-90s velocity that touched 95 with good command. Promoted to Chattanooga in late June, he struggled with control and was battered while learning that man cannot live by fastball alone; by August, he was back in the Cal League, and his velocity had tailed off. As you'd expect for a pitcher with relatively few innings under his belt, Miller's secondary stuff—a power slider and a changeup—has a ways to go.

Justin Miller

Born: **8/2/1987** Age: **23**
Bats: **R** Throws: **R** Height: **6' 2"** Weight: **190**
Breakout: **2%** Improve: **4%** Collapse: **1%**
Attrition: **1%** MLB: **7%**

Comparables:
Ray Jarvis, Larry Bearnarth, Jim Umbarger (76)

YEAR	TEAM	LVL	AGE	W	L	SV	G	GS	IP	H	HR	BB	SO	EqBB9	EqSO9	GB%	BABIP	WHIP	ERA	FRA	WARP
2008	GRL	A	20	4	11	0	27	25	140	132	6	74	82	4.8	5.3	64%	.283	1.53	3.99	5.77	-0.6
2009	GRL	A	21	5	7	0	21	21	115	125	7	46	66	3.6	5.2	67%	.306	1.56	4.70	5.98	-0.7
2009	SBR	A+	21	0	7	0	7	7	34^{1}	52	3	18	14	4.7	3.7	63%	.383	2.07	8.13	9.55	-1.2
2010	GRL	A	22	4	0	3	16	0	34^{2}	27	0	14	29	3.7	7.6	70%	.265	1.32	1.30	2.89	0.8
2010	CHT	AA	22	2	2	1	28	0	42^{1}	39	3	24	18	5.1	3.8	63%	.269	1.54	2.76	4.75	0.1
2011	*LAN*	*MLB*	*23*	*3*	*6*	*0*	*28*	*10*	*87*	*109*	*12*	*57*	*25*	*5.9*	*2.6*	*55%*	*.306*	*1.89*	*6.69*	*7.28*	*-1.6*

Not to be confused with the heavily tattooed reliever who saw time with the Dodgers in 2010, this Justin Miller was the team's sixth-round pick in 2007 out of Johnson County (Kan.) Community College. He's an extreme ground-baller who relies on a sinker/slider combo; his sinker can touch 95, but control is a problem. Knocked around at two levels as a starter in 2009, he fared better upon converting to the bullpen, restoring a much-needed measure of self-confidence, but most of his improvement owed to a large and likely unsustainable drop in BABIP. Miller's walk rate actually rose, and his strikeout rate crashed through the floor during his Double-A stint. It will take serious work for him to become more famous than his ink-stained namesake.

Carlos Monasterios

Born: **3/21/1986** Age: **25**
Bats: R Throws: R Height: **6' 2"** Weight: **175**
Breakout: **0%** Improve: **2%** Collapse: **1%**
Attrition: **3%** MLB: **3%**

Comparables:
Alfredo Figaro, Rafael Rodriguez, Adam Pettyjohn (85)

YEAR	TEAM	LVL	AGE	W	L	SV	G	GS	IP	H	HR	BB	SO	EqBB9	EqSO9	GB%	BABIP	WHIP	ERA	FRA	WARP
2008	CLR	A+	22	5	8	0	17	16	94^{1}	109	19	33	66	3.1	6.3	50%	.306	1.54	5.53	6.31	-0.5
2009	CLR	A+	23	5	6	2	35	9	82	71	4	27	71	3.0	7.8	48%	.286	1.26	3.51	5.00	0.1
2010	LAN	MLB	24	3	5	0	32	13	88^{1}	99	15	29	52	3.0	5.3	44%	.285	1.54	4.38	4.84	0.4
2011	*LAN*	*MLB*	*25*	*4*	*5*	*0*	*31*	*11*	90^{2}	*106*	*15*	*41*	*46*	*4.1*	*4.6*	*45%*	*.302*	*1.63*	*5.82*	*6.32*	*-0.8*

A Rule 5 pick plucked away from the Phillies via the Mets, Monasterios had all of 7 1/3 innings above High-A ball under his belt when the Dodgers stashed him in their bullpen. While they nursed him through the season without losing his rights, his presence was a mixed blessing, particularly given the marginalization of homegrown prospects such as Scott Elbert and James McDonald. Monasterios pitched well out of the bullpen (2.06 ERA in 35 innings, 0.8 homers per nine, 8.75 strikeout-to-unintentional walk ratio) but was torched as rotation filler (5.91 ERA in 53.1 innings, 2.0 home runs per nine innings, 1.61 strikeouts to unintentional walks). Despite Monasterios's reliance on a 90-ish sinker/slider combo, he proved quite homer-prone and unable to generate a healthy ground-ball percentage, suggesting the need for a deeper toolbox to survive in the majors.

Vicente Padilla

Born: **9/27/1977** Age: **33**
Bats: R Throws: R Height: **6' 2"** Weight: **200**
Breakout: **11%** Improve: **40%** Collapse: **22%**
Attrition: **17%** MLB: **96%**

Comparables:
Erik Hanson, Kevin Gross, Sonny Siebert (78)

YEAR	TEAM	LVL	AGE	W	L	SV	G	GS	IP	H	HR	BB	SO	EqBB9	EqSO9	GB%	BABIP	WHIP	ERA	FRA	WARP
2008	TEX	MLB	30	14	8	0	29	29	171	185	26	65	127	3.4	6.7	43%	.303	1.55	4.74	5.21	1.4
2009	LAN	MLB	31	4	0	0	8	7	39^{1}	36	4	12	38	2.7	8.7	48%	.305	1.22	3.20	2.79	1.3
2009	TEX	MLB	31	8	6	0	18	18	108	120	12	42	59	3.5	4.9	49%	.305	1.57	4.92	5.21	1.1
2010	LAN	MLB	32	6	5	0	16	16	95	79	14	24	84	2.3	8.0	42%	.250	1.16	4.07	5.00	0.2
2011	*LAN*	*MLB*	*33*	*10*	*9*	*0*	*27*	*27*	156^{2}	*160*	*20*	*55*	*110*	*3.1*	*6.3*	*45%*	*.297*	*1.37*	*4.39*	*4.77*	*2.1*

Mustering his highest average fastball velocity since 2005 (92.4 mph), Padilla had much more success working up in the strike zone than in recent years and posted career bests in both the strikeout and the walk departments. At the same time, he became more fly-ball-oriented and had lousy luck on the home-run-per-fly-ball front. Though he avoided further gunshot wounds, his health was spotty; nerve inflammation in his elbow sidelined him after just four starts and cost him almost two months on the DL, and he started just once after August 15, due to a bulging disc in his neck. Having averaged 25 starts over the past seven years, he's a risk; the Dodgers signed him to fulfill a swingman role, with a $2 million base salary plus incentives.

George Sherrill

Born: **4/18/1977** Age: **34**
Bats: L Throws: L Height: **6' 0"** Weight: **210**
Breakout: **17%** Improve: **36%** Collapse: **28%**
Attrition: **9%** MLB: **83%**

Comparables:
Jim Gott, Paul Shuey, Randy Myers (81)

YEAR	TEAM	LVL	AGE	W	L	SV	G	GS	IP	H	HR	BB	SO	EqBB9	EqSO9	GB%	BABIP	WHIP	ERA	FRA	WARP
2008	BAL	MLB	31	3	5	31	57	0	53^{1}	47	6	33	58	5.6	9.8	34%	.291	1.52	4.72	4.50	0.3
2009	BAL	MLB	32	0	1	20	42	0	41^{1}	34	3	13	39	2.8	8.5	34%	.272	1.19	2.40	3.13	0.8
2009	LAN	MLB	32	1	0	1	30	0	27^{2}	19	1	11	22	3.6	7.2	45%	.234	1.08	0.65	1.63	1.0
2010	LAN	MLB	33	2	2	0	65	0	36^{1}	46	4	24	25	5.9	6.2	43%	.333	1.95	7.18	6.64	-0.8
2011	*ATL*	*MLB*	*34*	*3*	*1*	*7*	*65*	*0*	49^{2}	*47*	*5*	*24*	*44*	*4.3*	*8.1*	*42%*	*.304*	*1.44*	*4.11*	*4.47*	*0.1*

Kids, this is what regression looks like. Sherrill put up unreal numbers over the final two months of the 2009 season after arriving from Baltimore via trade, most notably holding batters to a 7-for-43 performance and a .194 BABIP with men on base. That line swung to .337/.443/.593 with a .357 BABIP in 2010, and Sherrill stunk on ice in just about every other way as well. Perhaps owing to mid-back woes that cost him the second half of May, his fastball velocity sank nearly two mph, taking his strikeout rate down while his walk rate ballooned; three separate times, he went at least five straight appearances without notching a strikeout. Furthermore, even given his minimal innings total, he allowed a greater number of inherited runners to score than did any other MLB pitcher; only Bob Howry had a higher fair run average among relievers with at least 35 innings. Facing his final year of arbitration off a $4.5 million salary, Sherrill was an easy nontender. He signed a one-year deal with Atlanta, which needed another bullpen arm after the retirement of Billy Wagner.

Ramon Troncoso

Born: **2/16/1983** Age: **28**
Bats: R Throws: R Height: **6' 2"** Weight: **200**
Breakout: **7%** Improve: **13%** Collapse: **9%**
Attrition: **9%** MLB: **29%**

Comparables:
Tim Wood, Leo Rosales, Tim Crabtree (79)

YEAR	TEAM	LVL	AGE	W	L	SV	G	GS	IP	H	HR	BB	SO	EqBB9	EqSO9	GB%	BABIP	WHIP	ERA	FRA	WARP
2008	LVG	AAA	25	4	0	0	22	0	30^2	43	1	16	18	4.7	5.3	62%	.378	2.02	4.98	7.49	-0.6
2008	LAN	MLB	25	1	1	0	32	0	38	37	2	12	38	2.8	9.0	62%	.333	1.37	4.26	3.13	0.0
2009	LAN	MLB	26	5	4	6	73	0	82^2	83	3	34	55	3.7	6.0	57%	.305	1.45	2.72	3.59	1.2
2010	ABQ	AAA	27	0	2	1	15	0	22	23	5	11	19	4.5	7.8	59%	.305	1.55	5.73	6.33	-0.2
2010	LAN	MLB	27	2	3	0	52	0	54	55	7	18	34	3.0	5.7	54%	.279	1.41	4.50	5.22	-0.3
2011	*LAN*	*MLB*	*28*	*3*	*1*	*1*	*61*	*0*	*72^2*	*78*	*7*	*30*	*47*	*3.7*	*5.9*	*51%*	*.312*	*1.49*	*4.66*	*5.07*	*-0.5*

Even in emerging as a key bullpen cog in 2009, Troncoso was set up for an overwork-related fall, given that he ranked second in the league in relief innings and tailed off late in the year. Sure enough, Joe Torre went to the whip right out of the gate in 2010, using Troncoso 15 times in the season's first 22 games, and just as surely, the pitcher's performance suffered thereafter—five homers and a 6.64 ERA in 21 2/3 innings over the next two months, followed by the better part of July and August spent at Triple-A before a somewhat improved September return. Even with the time away, Troncoso ranked second in the league behind only George Sherrill in allowing 22 inherited runners to score, and that was with the benefit of substantial BABIP and walk-rate improvements. Meanwhile, his velocity dipped relative to 2009, and his home run/fly ball rate went over the wall. Now he's just another question mark in a bullpen full of them.

Jeff Weaver

Born: **8/22/1976** Age: **34**
Bats: R Throws: R Height: **6' 5"** Weight: **200**
Breakout: **2%** Improve: **16%** Collapse: **12%**
Attrition: **16%** MLB: **37%**

Comparables:
Rodrigo Lopez, Dave Borkowski, Ben McDonald (75)

YEAR	TEAM	LVL	AGE	W	L	SV	G	GS	IP	H	HR	BB	SO	EqBB9	EqSO9	GB%	BABIP	WHIP	ERA	FRA	WARP
2008	BUF	AAA	31	2	2	0	13	4	29^2	38	7	10	22	3.0	6.7	45%	.330	1.62	6.06	5.43	0.2
2008	NAS	AAA	31	2	4	0	9	9	55	64	9	20	37	3.3	6.1	44%	.322	1.56	6.22	6.32	-0.2
2009	LAN	MLB	32	6	4	0	28	7	79	87	7	33	64	3.8	7.3	44%	.325	1.58	3.65	2.93	2.2
2010	LAN	MLB	33	5	1	0	43	0	44^1	48	5	20	26	4.1	5.3	40%	.297	1.56	6.09	6.25	-0.8
2011	*LAN*	*MLB*	*34*	*5*	*5*	*0*	*46*	*10*	*109*	*127*	*15*	*40*	*66*	*3.3*	*5.5*	*44%*	*.315*	*1.53*	*5.32*	*5.79*	*-0.6*

Having returned from the outskirts of oblivion in 2009, Weaver picked up where he left off as the Dodgers' utility pitcher in 2010 and carried a 3.09 ERA through the end of June, despite a DL stint due to lower-back tightness. Unfortunately, he was lit up for a 9.43 ERA the rest of the way while battling knee tendinitis; he did three more weeks on the DL and had three other stretches of at least 10 days without pitching. His slider, which had been his best swing-and-miss offering, turned into a piñata, and he was knocked for a .366 BABIP and 1.9 home runs per nine innings over his final nine appearances. If healthy, Weaver can be useful in a minor role.

Allen Webster

Born: **2/10/1990** Age: **21**
Bats: R Throws: R Height: **6' 3"** Weight: **185**
Breakout: **1%** Improve: **3%** Collapse: **0%**
Attrition: **2%** MLB: **3%**

Comparables:
Steve Trout, Dan Petry, Dick Brodowski (79)

YEAR	TEAM	LVL	AGE	W	L	SV	G	GS	IP	H	HR	BB	SO	EqBB9	EqSO9	GB%	BABIP	WHIP	ERA	FRA	WARP
2009	DOD	Rk	19	0	0	0	12	8	441	30	0	14	53	2.8	10.8	60%	.261	1.08	1.62	3.10	2.4
2009	OGD	Rk	19	2	1	0	5	4	241	27	2	4	21	1.5	7.8	41%	.338	1.36	3.70	4.09	1.0
2010	GRL	A	20	12	11	0	28	29	139	128	7	59	124	3.8	8.0	50%	.297	1.43	2.78	4.00	2.4
2011	*LAN*	*MLB*	*21*	*3*	*4*	*0*	*17*	*8*	*69*	*75*	*8*	*43*	*41*	*5.5*	*5.4*	*46%*	*.299*	*1.69*	*5.61*	*6.10*	*-0.5*

An 18th-round pick out of a North Carolina high school in 2008, the baby-faced Webster is looking like a real find thus far, a highly projectable righty who has advanced by leaps and bounds since joining the Dodger organization. He put together a strong short-season campaign in 2009 and continued to progress as he moved up to full-season ball. Webster has two plus pitches, a sinking low-90s fastball that can reach 94 mph and can create plenty of ground balls, and a changeup that was hailed as the best in the Midwest League; he's got a sharp, late-breaking curveball as well. His command is inconsistent, but he has the stuff to be a midrotation starter.

Chris Withrow

Born: **4/1/1989** Age: **22**
Bats: R Throws: R Height: **6' 3"** Weight: **195**
Breakout: **4%** Improve: **4%** Collapse: **0%**
Attrition: **5%** MLB: **5%**

Comparables:
Pete Schourek, Ryan Tucker, Fabio Castro (79)

YEAR	TEAM	LVL	AGE	W	L	SV	G	GS	IP	H	HR	BB	SO	EqBB9	EqSO9	GB%	BABIP	WHIP	ERA	FRA	WARP
2009	SBR	A+	20	6	6	0	19	16	86^1	80	3	45	105	4.7	11.0	43%	.358	1.51	4.69	4.71	0.5
2009	CHT	AA	20	2	2	0	6	6	27^1	24	2	12	26	4.0	8.6	40%	.301	1.36	3.96	4.41	0.4
2010	CHT	AA	21	4	9	0	27	27	129^2	146	13	69	120	4.8	8.4	41%	.340	1.75	5.97	5.99	-0.2
2011	*LAN*	*MLB*	*22*	*4*	*6*	*0*	*13*	*13*	*62*	*66*	*7*	*38*	*50*	*5.5*	*7.3*	*42%*	*.319*	*1.68*	*5.54*	*6.02*	*0.2*

After two years mostly lost to injuries (elbow tenderness and a severe hand gash sustained snorkeling), this 2007 first-rounder out of an Odessa, Texas, high school enjoyed a breakout season in 2009, one that carried him all the way to Double-A Chattanooga. Alas, the return engagement wasn't so happy, as inconsistent mechanics caused the power righty's velocity and control to suffer. At his best, he has a mid-90s fastball, an above-average curve, and a work-in-progress changeup; he'll need to figure out where he left those to get back on track, but he's still young enough to do so.

LINEOUTS

HITTERS

PLAYER	TEAM	LVL	AGE	PA	R	2B	3B	HR	RBI	BB	SO	SB-CS	AVG/OBP/SLG	TAv	BABIP	BRR	FRAA	WARP
LF G. Anderson*	LAN	MLB	38	162	9	6	1	2	12	5	34	1-0	.182/.204/.273	.179	.215	-0.4	LF -3, RF 1	-1.2
C B. Ausmus	LAN	MLB	41	71	4	2	0	0	2	7	15	0-0	.222/.310/.254	.228	.292	-0.9	C -1	-0.1
3B P. Baez	SBR	A+	22	334	41	10	0	6	42	17	68	4-1	.259/.306/.350	.232	.311	-0.5	3B 0	-0.1
CF J. Baldwin*	DOD	Rk	18	195	25	6	2	2	22	9	60	17-3	.274/.313/.363	.247	.385	0.1	CF 3	0.6
C T. Delmonico	SBR	A+	23	243	25	3	0	3	16	36	35	4-1	.284/.418/.345	.293	.325	0.9	C 0	1.7
CF L. Landry*	OGD	Rk	20	274	46	20	4	4	38	20	36	13-9	.349/.399/.510	.318	.392	-2.0	CF -3	2.4
SS J. Lemmerman	OGD	Rk	21	304	69	24	2	12	47	31	56	5-4	.363/.434/.610	.362	.414	-2.6	SS -12	4.5
1B J. Lindsey	ABQ	AAA	33	447	74	41	4	25	97	19	78	0-0	.353/.400/.657	.306	.385	-2.2	1B 1	2.4
	LAN	MLB	33	13	0	0	0	0	0	0	3	0-0	.083/.154/.083	.054	.111	0.1	1B 0	-0.3
OF T. Oeltjen*	ABQ	AAA	27	226	40	18	5	5	33	23	43	14-5	.347/.416/.563	.312	.418	-0.1	RF -4, LF 0	1.2
	NAS	AAA	27	297	47	24	2	8	38	21	59	13-2	.301/.355/.496	.298	.350	4.1	LF 7, RF -2	2.7
	LAN	MLB	27	30	5	1	1	0	1	4	8	0-0	.217/.333/.348	.234	.294	0.9	CF 0, LF -1	-0.1
SS J. Sellers	SBR	A+	24	109	15	7	0	0	12	9	16	2-0	.260/.324/.333	.257	.301	0.2	SS -4	0.0
	ABQ	AAA	24	344	51	17	1	14	56	40	49	5-3	.285/.371/.497	.274	.286	-0.4	SS 4, 3B -1	2.1
RF S. Van Slyke	SBR	A+	23	209	34	12	2	9	35	17	39	3-1	.307/.368/.534	.327	.345	0.0	RF -3, LF 0	1.5
	CHT	AA	23	242	28	7	3	4	29	18	37	4-2	.235/.300/.350	.229	.263	0.0	RF -2, LF 4	-0.1

Unable to resist a bad idea when he saw it, Ned Colletti brought **Garret Anderson** back to California despite a 2009 stint in Atlanta that had "done" written all over it. Anderson posted the lowest TAv of any NL player with 150 PAs, squandering both a roster spot and an old man's dignity. ⚾ A herniated disc cost **Brad Ausmus** more than half his final season, but Russell Martin's injury afforded him the opportunity to climb to seventh on the all-time games-caught list at 1,938. He's also fourth in games played by an Ivy League alum, behind Eddie Collins, Lou Gehrig, and Fred Tenney, and will forever remain first on the traded-by-Randy-Smith list, with five occurrences. ⚾ **Pedro Baez** has big-time power potential and an above-average arm—enough for him to be selected to two Futures Games—but injuries and a lack of plate discipline have prevented him from converting his tools into skills, and his high error rate keeps his fielding percentages in the Hobsonian .900 range. ⚾ Son of the former major-league starter with the same name, **James Baldwin** was the Dodgers' fourth-round pick in 2010. A three-sport star in high school, he's a six-foot-three switch-hitting center fielder with blazing speed and power potential, but he also has a raw approach at the plate, as evidenced by his unsightly strikeout-to-walk ratio. ⚾ For the second year in a row, an injury (this time a broken wrist) cost 2008 sixth-round pick **Tony Delmonico** significant time. Though he has an advanced approach at the plate, he continues to struggle with his conversion from the middle infield to catching; he allowed 22 passed balls and 72 steals (29 percent caught-stealing rate) in 53 games. ⚾ The Dodgers' third-round pick in 2010 out of Louisiana State University, **Leon Landry** is an athletic center fielder with speed, good defense, solid contact skills, and surprising pop for his size. He made a strong-enough debut at Ogden to rank fourth on *Baseball America*'s Pioneer League prospects list. ⚾ A three-year starting shortstop at Duke, **Jake Lemmerman** was the Dodgers' fifth-round pick in 2010. The knock on Lemmerman in school was his hitting; even after putting up video-game numbers at high-altitude Ogden, he'll have to keep raking because he's more likely a second or third baseman down the road. ⚾ The Dodgers' top human-interest story late in the season was 16-year minor-league masher (219 homers, 1,579 hits) **John Lindsey**. Unfortunately, although Lindsey became the oldest non-Japanese rookie to reach the majors since Alan Zinter in 2002, his moment in the sun was abbreviated when a Daniel Hudson pitch broke his hand, requiring surgery. ⚾ A 10-year minor-league vet, Australian-born **Trent Oeltjen** wound up in the Dodger outfield in September after another year of pounding PCL pitching, then played for the Sydney Blue Sox in the new Australian Baseball League in the winter. No word on his platoon splits versus dingoes and kangaroos. ⚾ A 2005 sixth-round pick by the A's, **Justin Sellers** is an undersized (five-foot-ten) shortstop with a strong defensive reputation and good on-base skills. He showed unprecedented pop at Albuquerque—unprecedented for him, but hardly for that hitter-friendly environment—and could have a future as a utilityman. ⚾ After a breakout year in the hitter-friendly California League in

2009, **Scott Van Slyke**, son of the former Cardinals and Pirates mainstay Andy Van Slyke, couldn't maintain his gains in his first extended taste of the high minors and was returned C.O.D. to Inland Empire, the only stop where he's ever really hit.

PITCHERS

PLAYER	TEAM	LVL	AGE	W	L	SV	IP	H	HR	BB	SO	EqBB9	EqSO9	GB%	BABIP	WHIP	ERA	FRA	WARP
J. Adkins*	CHT	AA	24	3	1	1	45^1	40	6	23	50	4.6	10.0	45%	.296	1.46	4.76	5.82	-0.5
R. Cash	DOD	Rk	18	2	2	0	30	29	0	11	25	3.3	7.5	54%	.312	1.40	3.60	4.11	1.0
N. Eovaldi	SBR	A+	20	3	5	0	85	99	3	33	58	3.5	6.1	50%	.354	1.60	4.45	4.77	0.5
G. Gould	OGD	Rk	18	1	4	0	57^2	68	4	20	52	3.1	8.2	53%	.352	1.56	4.06	6.74	-1.6
J. Guerra	CHT	AA	24	2	0	5	27	24	1	22	27	7.3	9.0	59%	.311	1.74	2.33	2.55	0.7
B. Leach*	CHT	AA	27	7	3	0	65	64	5	29	52	4.0	7.2	45%	.311	1.45	4.57	4.56	0.9
	ABQ	AAA	27	3	2	0	39^2	49	2	24	37	5.5	8.5	50%	.370	1.94	6.35	5.71	0.1
Z. Lee	DNP	—	19	—	—	—	—	—	—	—	—	—	—	—	—	—	—	—	—
J. Link	ABQ	AAA	26	3	2	4	60^2	65	5	21	55	3.1	8.2	56%	.324	1.45	3.71	5.03	0.1
	LAN	MLB	26	0	0	0	82	12	0	4	4	4.2	4.2	55%	.375	1.85	4.15	5.98	-0.1
J. Miller	ABQ	AAA	32	0	1	0	37	29	2	16	37	3.9	9.0	47%	.273	1.22	1.95	2.82	0.9
	LAN	MLB	32	0	0	0	24^1	22	4	8	30	3.0	11.1	44%	.310	1.36	4.44	4.74	0.0
R. Ortiz	LAN	MLB	36	0	1	0	7	10	0	5	6	6.4	7.7	42%	.417	2.14	10.29	6.40	-0.1
T. Schlichting	ABQ	AAA	25	3	0	1	47^1	55	5	13	29	2.5	5.5	54%	.316	1.51	4.75	6.27	-0.4
	LAN	MLB	25	1	0	0	22^2	20	0	10	14	4.0	5.6	53%	.270	1.32	3.57	4.56	0.1
S. Tolleson	OGD	Rk	22	1	1	17	28^2	17	1	5	39	1.6	12.4	64%	.271	0.78	0.63	1.84	3.1
C. Wade	ABQ	AAA	27	3	0	2	29^1	35	4	3	20	0.9	6.2	43%	.313	1.41	4.91	5.75	-0.1

Moving to the bullpen helped six-foot-six lefty **James Adkins**, a supplemental first-rounder in 2007, add a tick to his 88-91 mph fastball and boost his strikeout rate above one per inning, though his walk rate remained problematic. ⚾ The Dodgers' 2010 second-round pick, **Ralston Cash** is a six-foot-four prep righty with a projectable frame and clean mechanics, offering an 89-92 mph fastball with some sink, an above-average curve, and a changeup that has a chance to be above average as well. ⚾ **Nathan Eovaldi**, an 11th-round pick in 2008, has a high ceiling thanks to his mid-90s heat, but poor command and a lack of consistency with his breaking pitches have prevented him from turning it into strikeouts thus far. His future may be in the bullpen if he can't expand his arsenal. ⚾ The Dodgers' second-round pick in 2009 out of Maize High School in southern Kansas, **Garrett Gould** received an over-slot $900,000 bonus. Despite an unorthodox delivery, Gould has good command of his arsenal; his best pitch is a swing-and-miss overhand curve, and he has good movement on his low-90s fastball, though diminished velocity became a concern as the season went on. ⚾ A 2004 fourth-round pick, **Javy Guerra** missed nearly half the season due to injuries. Despite his six-foot stature, he's a hard thrower, but Guerra has been so beset by control problems that he has yet to reach Triple-A. ⚾ Clobbered by lefties in his half-season audition as a LOOGY in 2009, hard-throwing six-foot-five **Brent Leach** struggled with his control both before and after moving down from Triple-A to Double-A to return to starting. ⚾ The cash-strapped Dodgers appeared to waste their top pick in choosing **Zach Lee** in the first round last year, given the bonus it figured to take to shake his commitment to play quarterback at Louisiana State. Successfully wooed with a back-loaded $5.25 million bonus, Lee may prove to be the best surprise of the draft thanks to his excellent command of a 91-93 mph fastball that could gain another tick or two as he grows. He also showed off a lively tailing changeup and an inconsistent, slurvy breaking ball in the Arizona Fall League. ⚾ Acquired from the White Sox in the Juan Pierre deal, **Jon Link** is a 2005 Padres draft pick who is known for his on-and-off relationship with his slider while serving as a minor-league closer. He's tough on righties and gets a good number of ground balls, skills that should give him a shot at carving out a spot in the Dodgers' bullpen. ⚾ Despite a fastball that doesn't top 90 mph, tattooed freak **Justin Miller** missed enough bats during his seven weeks with the Dodgers that it's a mystery as to why he spent most of the year marooned at Triple-A. He'll hope for better luck with the Mariners, who signed him to a minor-league deal. ⚾ So short of pitching were the Dodgers that they broke camp with not one but two Zombie Ortizes. **Russ Ortiz** was the one who had put up a 6.56 ERA in over 300 innings from 2005 to 2009; luckily, he was waxed within two weeks of Opening Day. ⚾ Originally drafted as a third baseman, **Travis Schlichting** got his first real taste of pitching in the majors last year, spending all of July with the Dodgers in the longest of four recalls. Lefties went 6-for-35 against his sinker/slider arsenal, and he generated plenty of grounders, but he got lost in the numbers game. Shoulder pain shut him down in August. ⚾ High-school Tommy John surgery survivor **Shawn Tolleson** scared off scouts with his violent delivery and was seen as an afterthought when drafted in the 30th round out of Baylor, but he dominated as a closer in the Pioneer League, using a cutter as his out pitch. ⚾ A victim of the Curse of Scott Proctor—common among those who pitched their way into Joe Torre's good graces—**Cory Wade** underwent surgery last March to repair fraying of his rotator cuff and labrum. He pitched well at Albuquerque from August onward, but the Dodgers left him off the 40-man roster and he signed a minor-league deal with the Rays.

MANAGER: JOE TORRE

YEAR	TEAM	W-L	Pythag +/-	Avg PC	100+ P	120+ P	QS	BQS	REL	REL w Zero R	IBB	Subs	PH	PH Avg	PH HR	SB2	CS2	SB3	CS3	SAC Att	SAC %	POS SAC	Squeeze	Swing	In Play
2008	LAN	84-78	-3	90.9	47	1	78	3	460	295	58	88	275	.233	2	102	40	24	2	85	75.3%	22	10	143	115
2009	LAN	95-67	-5	93.4	54	2	79	2	526	366	68	32	260	.253	5	104	41	12	7	119	65.5%	32	0	153	125
2010	LAN	80-82	2	95.7	72	2	86	4	474	296	75	66	250	.213	2	83	43	9	4	126	67.5%	32	3	155	111

In his 30th and final year of managing, Joe Torre presided over a team whose second-half collapse owed much to the failings of the same young, homegrown stars who had fueled his success in guiding the Dodgers to the NLCS in his previous two campaigns. He's not the first septuagenarian manager to have trouble bridging the generation gap, but in allowing members of his coaching staff to take public shots at Russell Martin and Matt Kemp, Torre made it easier for his players to tune him out as an old codger despite his long track record as a player's manager. Torre didn't cover himself in glory elsewhere, overworking key members of his bullpen early in the season in typical Torre fashion and often failing to get Jonathan Broxton into the situations that mattered most. Taking over in the wake of his retirement is Don Mattingly, who has never managed at any level; he served 6½ seasons as a coach for Torre, all but one of them as a hitting coach. In the rare moments that he's had the chance to run a team, he's shown his inexperience, making a series of widely ridiculed basic errors. While his strategic preferences may be unknown, as a former star two decades younger than Torre, Mattingly has a better shot at reaching the youngsters; he was particularly vocal about connecting with Kemp in the weeks after his appointment, a move that may help motivate the star-caliber center fielder for 2011 and beyond.

Milwaukee Brewers

In the mythology of ancient Greece, King Sisyphus of Corinth was said to have been extraordinarily clever and successful—so clever, in fact, that he managed in one legend to trick and capture Death itself. The gods were not pleased with him, however, and for this and many other perceived offenses, Sisyphus was eventually punished. His curse was to spend eternity rolling a massive stone up a steep hill, only to see it roll back down, thus dooming him to toil endlessly at a task he could never complete.

While no one is likely to accuse Doug Melvin of sharing the legendary hubris of Sisyphus, the Brewers' GM has recently come to endure a similar punishment. Each season, Milwaukee features a power-packed lineup that finishes among the National League's elite. Each season, the Brewers' pitching staff fails so spectacularly that no amount of offensive fireworks can overcome its weight. And each offseason, Melvin renews his labors to improve the team's run prevention, only to see the stone again roll back downhill during the year, crushing the franchise's playoff ambitions. This has been the case ever since the Brewers rode midseason rental CC Sabathia into the 2008 playoffs. The Brewers allowed the fourth-fewest runs in the senior circuit that year, but the departures of Sabathia, who spurned Milwaukee's nine-figure offer for even larger stacks of Steinbrenner loot, and longtime staff leader Ben Sheets, whose checkered injury history finally ended his Brewers career, have left Melvin scrambling to find enough pitching to lift his still-potent offense back into contention.

BREWERS PROSPECTUS

2010 W-L: 77-85, 3rd in NL Central

Pythag	.467	21st
RS/G	4.6	12th
RA/G	5.0	4th
TAv	.276	8th
BRR	1.8	12th
FRA	4.76	26th
DER	-21.2	29th
DL	780	19th
B-Age	27.5	6th
P-Age	29.2	23rd
Salary	$81.1	18th
M$/MW	$2.50	14th

Ballpark: Miller Park (3-yr. PF: 102). It's very nice for Brewers southpaw sluggers to go trav'ling, but it's oh so nice to come home

2010: And they wonder, still they wonder, who'll stop the runs?

2011: Imported aces prop the playoff window open

Action Items: Finding a shortstop, figuring out Fielder, adjusting to life without a farm system

The only NL teams to allow more runs than Milwaukee last year were Arizona and Pittsburgh, while in 2009, only the Nationals ran out a more inflammable pitching staff. Meanwhile, the Brew Crew finished a respectable third in NL runs scored in 2009 and were fourth last year. According to our Value Over Replacement Player (VORP) metric, which measures the amount of production that a player provides compared with a freely available replacement-level player, the dichotomy between Milwaukee's ability to score and its ability to prevent runs has become historic. During the 2009-2010 seasons, Brewers hitters accumulated a grand total of 497.1 VORP, the third-most in the league, behind the well-financed juggernauts in the Bronx and Boston, while their pitchers earned 73.2 VORP, the second-lowest in the league, ahead of only the hapless Pirates. Milwaukee's hitters have thus contributed 423.9 VORP more than the team's pitchers over the last two years, making them the third-most offense-dominant team since 1954, behind only the 1968-1969 and 1976-1977 Cincinnati Reds (see Table 1).

Table 1. A Puncher's Chance: Hitting-Dominant Teams, 1954-2010

Team	Season	Batter VORP	Pitcher VORP	Difference	Wins	Losses
Reds	1968-9	485.8	21.3	464.5	172	152
Reds	1976-7	705.5	265.7	439.8	190	134
Brewers	2009-10	497.1	73.2	423.9	157	167
Red Sox	1964-5	388.2	-22.2	410.4	134	190
Reds	2004-5	405.9	16.3	389.6	149	175

The Big Red Machine appears on this list, not because of its weak pitching but because of the absurdly productive contributions of Joe Morgan, Johnny Bench, Pete Rose, Tony Perez, et al. In general, however, such structurally lopsided teams are rarely successful, regardless of whether a team's overwhelming strength is scoring or preventing runs. Last year's champion Giants, for example, unsurprisingly led the league with a cumulative 280.2 VORP from their pitchers, but also received a respectable, mid-pack 171.6 VORP from their hitters. For the Brewers to get back into contention, they'll need to find some way to improve their pitching from abysmal to at least mediocre, perhaps even at the expense of some hitting. This is hardly breaking news to anyone who follows the team, or to Doug Melvin, who has tried time and again to do exactly that. Unfortunately, the biggest moves he has made to address this problem over the last few seasons have hurt more than they've helped.

The Milwaukee farm system has been adept at developing batting talent, but delivering the quality, inexpensive pitching that is often the lifeblood of a successful organization is a skill that has eluded them. Current ace starter Yovanni Gallardo is the notable exception, but Manny Parra and his ongoing case study in frustration is far more representative of Milwaukee's inability to produce homegrown pitching. Consequently, Melvin has been active in the free-talent market over the years, grabbing Yankees castoff and current closer John Axford from the scrap heap, as well as other occasionally useful bullpen cogs and rotation filler such as Todd Coffey, Derrick Turnbow, Kameron Loe, Chris Narveson, and Mark DiFelice.

The Brewers have also made a slew of minor trades over the years to acquire the likes of Carlos Villanueva, Salomon Torres, Brian Shouse, and Seth McClung, all of whom have had a few shining (if brief) moments. There have been big in-season trades as well—for closer Francisco Cordero in 2006 and Sabathia in 2008—which have worked out well, but at the cost of young sluggers Matt LaPorta and Nelson Cruz. All of these moves show Melvin to possess an admirable, almost Sisyphean craftiness in filling out his roster and a boldness in acquiring top-level talent at the moments when his team most needs it. However, the most important moves he has made have been in the free-agent market, and it's here that Melvin has managed to undo all of his otherwise good work intended to help wake the Brewers from their pitching nightmare.

Beginning with starter Jeff Suppan prior to the 2007 season, the Brewers have endured a series of free-agent signings that have drained their coffers, reduced their payroll flexibility, and provided little in the way of on-field benefit (see Table 2). Suppan pitched reasonably well in his first Milwaukee season, then became a franchise millstone to the tune of -11.7 VORP for $35.75 million over the next three years of his contract. Relievers David Riske and Eric Gagne were disastrous combinations of injury and ineffectiveness that gifted the Brewers with -1.4 VORP for $22.75 million in the years since their signing prior to 2008. The 2009 season saw the arrival of starter Braden Looper and venerable closer Trevor Hoffman; Looper was a one-and-done calamity, while Hoffman's first magical season earned him a more expensive return engagement that quickly turned sour. Last year's market basket featured Randy Wolf, who pitched reasonably well as the team's second starter, along with Doug Davis and LaTroy Hawkins, who combined for an almost unimaginable -20.0 VORP in 54.1 innings, for the bargain price of $7.5 million.

Taken together, last year's Brewers spent over $42 million on free-agent pitching and received a ghastly -15.6 VORP for their trouble. Thankfully, everyone but Hawkins and Wolf is now off the payroll, but with the Brewers on the hook for at least $20 million over the next two seasons, there's some concern that Wolf may become a Suppan-esque burden as he enters his mid-30s. Overall, Melvin's free-agent spending spree cost the team nearly $100 million over the last four seasons and produced a grand total of 26 VORP. To put that in perspective, Kyle Farnsworth produced 26.1 VORP himself during that same period, whereas Barry Zito put up 80.6 VORP, for about $40 million less. Accidents happen, and to forgive is divine, but with a record like that, it's fair to wonder whether owner Mark Attanasio should consider assigning a new PIN to the club's ATM card before Melvin rushes back to the market.

Given these recent calamitous dips into the free-agent pool, Melvin wisely decided to avoid last winter's questionable starting pitcher market and instead made two impact trades that have radically improved Milwaukee's rotation for at least the next two years. First, the Brewers shipped top prospect Brett Lawrie to the Blue Jays for 29-year-old right-hander Shaun Marcum. Though Marcum's fastball sits in the high 80s, his assortment of off-speed stuff and excellent control was sufficient to induce the fifth-highest percentage

Table 2. Rotten Produce

	2007		2008		2009		2010		Total	
	VORP	$ millions	VORP	$ millions	VORP	$ millions	VORP	$ millions	VORP	$ millions
Jeff Suppan	23.3	6.25	3.1	8.25	-4.9	12.75	-11.6	14.75	9.9	42
David Riske			1.6	4	-1.4	4.25	-0.5	4.5	-0.3	12.75
Eric Gagne			-1.1	10					-1.1	10
Trevor Hoffman					22.6	6	-3.9	7	18.7	13
Braden Looper					-1.6	4.75			-1.6	4.75
Randy Wolf							20.4	8.8	20.4	8.8
Doug Davis							-14.1	4.25	-14.1	4.25
LaTroy Hawkins							-5.9	3.25	-5.9	3.25
Total	23.3	6.25	3.6	22.25	14.7	27.75	-15.6	42.55	26	98.8

of swinging strikes in the American League. Marcum had Tommy John surgery in September of 2008 and missed the entire 2009 season. His control wasn't quite as good prior to his injury, so he doesn't have a long track record of posting strikeout-to-walk ratios of nearly 4 to 1. Moving out of the AL East will certainly help him, however, and he's a cinch to be a huge improvement on the parade of submediocrities that have littered the Brewers' rotation in recent years.

If grabbing Marcum was a solid move, Melvin's next acquisition was a stunner. Slow-developing top picks Mark Rogers (overcoming chronic injuries) and Jeremy Jeffress (overcoming chronic) had lit up Miller Park with electrifying debuts last fall, but neither player showed himself quite ready to step into the big-league rotation, so Melvin again stepped outside the organization and traded for ace starter Zack Greinke. The cost was steep—Jeffress, starting shortstop Alcides Escobar, center fielder Lorenzo Cain, and top pitching prospect Jake Odorizzi in exchange for Greinke and shortstop Yuniesky Betancourt—but adding the former Cy Young winner to a rotation already boasting Gallardo, Marcum, and Wolf gives Milwaukee some pitching depth not seen since the departure of Sabathia and Sheets. With free-talent find Chris Narveson slotted into the fifth spot, Melvin has managed to retool his rotation without having to rely on past disappointments like Parra and without again shelling out millions for questionable veteran talent.

Even more impressively, Melvin was able to build his new rotation while retaining Prince Fielder. Trading the slugging first baseman is an elephant that's long grazed in the corner of Melvin's office, since Fielder is entering his final year under team control and agent Scott Boras is certain to take his client onto the market and out of the Brewers' price range next winter. As Fielder's turn to get sprayed with the money hose has become more imminent, his trade value has dropped, and the organization seems to have decided to take one last shot with him in the lineup rather than deal him for a handful of magic beans.

With Fielder still in the fold, new manager Ron Roenicke can pencil in a potent lineup featuring the rest of the bats that Milwaukee's system graduated during the Aughties. Second baseman Rickie Weeks was finally healthy and productive, leading the team in VORP and setting himself up for either a lucrative extension or a free-agent payday at the end of the year. Corey Hart rediscovered his power stroke in right field and earned an extension of his own. Ryan Braun remains one of the league's best hitters and greatest values, under team control through 2015 at eminently reasonable prices. Even third baseman Casey McGehee showed that his surprising power in 2009 wasn't a complete fluke, and he has become an above-average player.

The rest of the lineup is questionable, but probably no worse than it was last year. Betancourt will take over at shortstop for Escobar, whose rookie season was a massive disappointment both at the plate and in the field. Betancourt at his best will be no better than Escobar at his worst, but the serial out-maker should at least duplicate what the Brewers received from the position last year. Rookie catcher Jonathan Lucroy and George Kottaras have solid on-base skills and should provide more production than a Kendall-class receiver at a fraction of the cost, provided new manager Ron Roenicke avoids giving veteran backstop Wil Nieves too much work. Contact-averse speedster Carlos Gomez is still on hand to man center field along with Chris Dickerson, and while a Gomez/Dickerson platoon wouldn't exactly be two great tastes that taste great together, they can at least run down a lot of fly balls between Braun and Hart.

Despite a less-than-stellar bottom of the order, Milwaukee should still field a lineup capable of bludgeoning opponents into submission. The Brewers will again go as far as their rotation can take them, and the addition of Greinke and Marcum should help the pitching staff make a great leap forward into playoff contention. If his new acquisitions pitch as well as hoped, Doug Melvin can perhaps finally enjoy a respite from his Sisyphean toil—until next winter, that is, when Fielder (and perhaps Weeks) will be gone, Greinke and Marcum will be entering their walk years, and a farm system gutted to help finance this year's run will have little help to provide. If history and/or Greek mythology are any guide, a small-market GM, no matter how clever, can never truly beat gravity—the best he can do is put it off for a while.

HITTERS

Ryan Braun LF

Born: **11/17/1983** Age: **27**
Bats: R Throws: R Height: **6' 2"** Weight: **200**
Breakout: **1%** Improve: **58%** Collapse: **4%**
Attrition: **8%** MLB: **97%**

Comparables:
Hanley Ramirez, David Wright, Duke Snider (63)

YEAR	TEAM	LVL	AGE	PA	R	2B	3B	HR	RBI	BB	SO	SB	CS	AVG/OBP/SLG	TAv	BABIP	BRR	FRAA	WARP
2008	MIL	MLB	24	663	92	39	7	37	106	42	129	14	4	.285/.335/.553	.300	.305	-4.4	LF 3	3.9
2009	MIL	MLB	25	708	113	39	6	32	114	57	121	20	6	.320/.386/.551	.325	.353	0.3	LF -1	5.9
2010	MIL	MLB	26	685	101	45	1	25	103	56	105	14	3	.304/.365/.501	.307	.331	4.4	LF 4	5.1
2011	*MIL*	*MLB*	*27*	*670*	*96*	*38*	*4*	*30*	*105*	*54*	*105*	*16*	*5*	*.303/.364/.531*	*.311*	*.320*	*-0.1*	*LF 4*	*4.8*

Braun won his third consecutive Silver Slugger Award last year, even though his power numbers were somewhat less Braun-y than usual. The Hebrew Hammer didn't manage to knock out his accustomed 30 home runs, and his slugging percentage and isolated power marks have declined as he's hit more and more ground balls in each of the past two seasons. Braun's numbers actually held steady against right-handed pitching, but sank to .271/.341/.445 versus the lefties he has traditionally tortured, so perhaps this year's power outage is a bit of small-sample fluke. In any case, Braun's increased comfort in the outfield has made him a much-improved fielder, helping him match his career-high WARP. Still three years short of earning his first eight-figure paycheck, a healthy Braun is certain to remain one of baseball's most valuable commodities, even if his moniker slowly evolves from *slugger* to *hitter*.

Lorenzo Cain **CF**

Born: **4/13/1986** Age: **25**
Bats: R Throws: R Height: **6' 2"** Weight: **200**
Breakout: **7%** Improve: **34%** Collapse: **9%**
Attrition: **30%** MLB: **57%**

Comparables:
Roger Bernadina, Jacoby Ellsbury, Julio Borbon (76)

YEAR	TEAM	LVL	AGE	PA	R	2B	3B	HR	RBI	BB	SO	SB	CS	AVG/OBP/SLG	TAv	BABIP	BRR	FRAA	WARP
2008	BRV	A+	22	356	50	22	4	7	41	29	68	19	4	.287/.357/.448	.285	.343	1.8	RF 3, CF 0	2.0
2008	HUN	AA	22	172	21	9	5	4	17	19	41	6	2	.277/.360/.486	.286	.349	-0.1	CF -3, RF -1	0.6
2009	WIS	A	23	61	3	4	0	0	3	9	15	0	0	.192/.311/.269	.235	.270	-0.2	CF 1	0.1
2009	HUN	AA	23	160	17	6	0	4	15	10	35	3	3	.214/.275/.338	.220	.250	0.6	CF 2	0.0
2010	HUN	AA	24	280	45	6	6	3	18	34	52	21	2	.324/.409/.434	.307	.400	0.0	CF 3	2.4
2010	NAS	AAA	24	100	13	5	3	0	9	11	17	5	1	.299/.384/.425	.256	.366	0.0	CF 4	0.6
2010	MIL	MLB	24	158	17	11	1	1	13	9	28	7	1	.306/.348/.415	.284	.370	1.5	CF 3, RF 0	1.2
2011	*KCA*	*MLB*	*25*	*440*	*48*	*20*	*3*	*6*	*42*	*37*	*95*	*11*	*4*	*.253/.318/.367*	*.246*	*.310*	*-0.1*	*CF -1, RF 0*	*0.4*

Cain was a man in a hurry last year, bouncing back from a season lost to injury and ineffectiveness to rocket his way to Miller Park for a successful late-season audition in center field. He has always impressed with his range and aggressive outfield play, but his biggest breakthrough came at the plate, where Cain was able to lay off pitches out of the zone, cut down on his strikeouts, and punish pitchers' mistakes. This improved approach helped him get on base and take better advantage of his speed, and while he's not likely to continue posting BABIPs north of .370 or develop much more than occasional power, he has enough skills to be an acceptable starter in center right now. The Royals traded for him as part of the Zack Greinke deal in hopes he can be just that.

Craig Counsell **INF**

Born: **8/21/1970** Age: **40**
Bats: L Throws: R Height: **6' 0"** Weight: **180**
Breakout: **0%** Improve: **17%** Collapse: **10%**
Attrition: **20%** MLB: **60%**

Comparables:
Barry Larkin, Wade Boggs, Jim Eisenreich (69)

YEAR	TEAM	LVL	AGE	PA	R	2B	3B	HR	RBI	BB	SO	SB	CS	AVG/OBP/SLG	TAv	BABIP	BRR	FRAA	WARP
2008	MIL	MLB	37	302	31	14	1	1	14	46	42	3	1	.226/.354/.302	.244	.264	1.4	3B -3, SS 5	1.0
2009	MIL	MLB	38	459	62	22	8	4	39	42	54	3	4	.285/.355/.408	.261	.314	1.7	2B 3, 3B 1	2.2
2010	MIL	MLB	39	230	16	8	0	2	21	21	29	1	1	.250/.317/.319	.240	.277	-0.1	SS 0, 3B 0	0.3
2011	*MIL*	*MLB*	*40*	*351*	*36*	*14*	*2*	*1*	*25*	*36*	*44*	*4*	*2*	*.242/.323/.314*	*.232*	*.270*	*-0.3*	*SS 2, 3B 0*	*0.3*

With youth movements well under way in center field, at shortstop, and behind the plate, the Brewers have decided to bring back their one-man Counsell of Elders to provide stability, leadership, and leather utility. At age 40, he's still a defensive whiz-kid around the infield, draws the occasional walk, won't complain if he has to wait a week between plate appearances, and doesn't mind being the butt of intergenerational jokes involving reading glasses, the use of proper grammar and punctuation while texting, and the awkward butchering of modern slang. In short, Counsell can still help the club, fo shizzle.

Kentrail Davis **OF**

Born: **6/29/1988** Age: **23**
Bats: L Throws: R Height: **5' 9"** Weight: **195**
Breakout: **3%** Improve: **7%** Collapse: **2%**
Attrition: **8%** MLB: **13%**

Comparables:
Luis Valbuena, Chad Curtis, Gregorio Petit (72)

YEAR	TEAM	LVL	AGE	PA	R	2B	3B	HR	RBI	BB	SO	SB	CS	AVG/OBP/SLG	TAv	BABIP	BRR	FRAA	WARP
2010	WIS	A	22	290	44	26	5	3	46	31	36	3	1	.335/.421/.518	.329	.374	-0.7	RF 3, CF 0	2.6
2010	BRV	A+	22	150	20	2	5	0	17	17	28	8	2	.244/.380/.341	.266	.316	0.1	CF -3	0.2
2011	*MIL*	*MLB*	*23*	*418*	*45*	*21*	*4*	*4*	*37*	*36*	*79*	*3*	*1*	*.246/.322/.354*	*.242*	*.296*	*-0.1*	*RF -1, CF -3*	*-0.3*

A 2009 sandwich-round pick out of the University of Tennessee, Davis struggled through an injury-plagued stint in High-A, but thrived after a move down to the Midwest League, hitting doubles in droves and showing a surprisingly advanced approach in his pro debut. A compact, muscular presence at the plate (a polite way of saying "short and stocky"), Davis waits patiently for his pitch, lashes line drives from gap to gap, and uses surprising speed—he's a tick above average on the scouting scale—to turn doubles into triples. He has the raw skills to play center, but isn't instinctive out there, leading some to think that he'll eventually be limited to left field. If so, he will need to develop more power to be a big-leaguer.

Chris Dickerson **CF**

Born: **4/10/1982** Age: **29**
Bats: L Throws: L Height: **6' 3"** Weight: **225**
Breakout: **0%** Improve: **31%** Collapse: **3%**
Attrition: **3%** MLB: **67%**

Comparables:
Luis Terrero, Gabe Gross, Leon Roberts (71)

YEAR	TEAM	LVL	AGE	PA	R	2B	3B	HR	RBI	BB	SO	SB	CS	AVG/OBP/SLG	TAv	BABIP	BRR	FRAA	WARP
2008	LOU	AAA	26	414	65	16	9	11	53	54	102	26	7	.287/.379/.479	.295	.365	4.4	CF 2, RF -3	3.0
2008	CIN	MLB	26	122	20	9	2	6	15	17	35	5	3	.304/.410/.608	.335	.403	2.1	LF 0, CF 0	1.3
2009	CIN	MLB	27	299	30	13	3	2	15	39	66	11	3	.275/.368/.373	.267	.356	-2.3	LF 1, CF 2	1.0
2010	LOU	AAA	28	56	12	5	0	3	7	9	13	6	1	.442/.528/.767	.427	.533	0.1	CF 0, RF 0	1.1
2010	CIN	MLB	28	45	8	1	1	0	0	1	19	3	0	.205/.222/.273	.197	.360	1.0	CF -1, LF 0	-0.1
2010	MIL	MLB	28	60	2	1	1	0	5	5	15	1	0	.212/.267/.269	.199	.275	-1.4	CF 0, RF -1	-0.5
2011	*MIL*	*MLB*	*29*	*335*	*39*	*14*	*3*	*6*	*33*	*41*	*82*	*15*	*4*	*.256/.344/.388*	*.260*	*.326*	*0.1*	*CF -2, LF 0*	*0.5*

The Brewers did well to nab Dickerson in exchange for Jim Edmonds, but as has been the case for most of his career, his new employers aren't quite sure what to do with him. At times you can look at Dickerson and see outfielder heaven—tall, speedy, fluid, range enough for center, a good batting eye, and evident power. Look a little closer, however, and you'll notice his helplessness against southpaws and a strikeout rate that would make Ryan Howard blush. Nonetheless, his glove, left-handedness, and minuscule paycheck make him at least a worthwhile fourth outfielder, while a job-share with righty Carlos Gomez might be a good way to leverage their modest talents.

Alcides Escobar **SS**

Born: **12/16/1986** Age: **24**
Bats: R Throws: R Height: **6' 1"** Weight: **175**
Breakout: **4%** Improve: **39%** Collapse: **8%**
Attrition: **36%** MLB: **74%**

Comparables:
Jacoby Ellsbury, Chin-lung Hu, Paul Molitor (70)

YEAR	TEAM	LVL	AGE	PA	R	2B	3B	HR	RBI	BB	SO	SB	CS	AVG/OBP/SLG	TAv	BABIP	BRR	FRAA	WARP
2008	HUN	AA	21	597	95	24	5	8	76	31	82	34	8	.328/.357/.434	.288	.362	5.0	SS 13	5.8
2008	MIL	MLB	21	4	0	0	0	0	0	0	1	0	0	.500/.500/.500	.345	.667	-0.1	SS 0	0.0
2009	NAS	AAA	22	487	76	24	6	4	34	32	65	42	10	.298/.339/.409	.266	.325	3.2	SS 2, 2B -2	2.4
2009	MIL	MLB	22	134	20	3	1	1	11	4	18	4	2	.304/.328/.368	.245	.339	2.0	SS -1	0.4
2010	MIL	MLB	23	552	57	14	10	4	41	36	70	10	4	.235/.286/.326	.222	.262	1.4	SS 0, RF 0	0.2
2011	*KCA*	*MLB*	*24*	*589*	*64*	*23*	*4*	*7*	*58*	*35*	*82*	*24*	*7*	*.271/.313/.370*	*.242*	*.298*	*0.1*	*SS 3, 2B 0*	*1.4*

Escobar was handed the Brewers' shortstop job in spring training and ran with it, straight through a patch of poison ivy, off a cliff, and into a vat of liquid nitrogen. An acrobatic fielder with great speed, little patience, and a demonstrated ability to hit for average, Escobar's bat never got untracked and regressed as the season moved along—his .154/.214/.231 line after September 1 earned him some time on the bench to think things through. His defense suffered as well, as a propensity for sloppy errors undercut the great range and strong arm that gave fans glimpses of Gold Gloves to come. The Royals acquired him as part of the Zack Greinke trade and hope that a change of scenery will help him unleash his obvious talent both in the field and at the plate. He's sure to be an improvement on Yuniesky Betancourt, and he's likely to better last year's .264 BABIP, but even with an improved batting average, his inability to draw walks will keep him near the bottom of the order.

Prince Fielder **1B**

Born: **5/9/1984** Age: **27**
Bats: L Throws: R Height: **6' 0"** Weight: **260**
Breakout: **4%** Improve: **53%** Collapse: **4%**
Attrition: **13%** MLB: **88%**

Comparables:
Adrian Gonzalez, Mark Teixeira, Barry Bonds (49)

YEAR	TEAM	LVL	AGE	PA	R	2B	3B	HR	RBI	BB	SO	SB	CS	AVG/OBP/SLG	TAv	BABIP	BRR	FRAA	WARP
2008	MIL	MLB	24	694	86	30	2	34	102	84	134	3	2	.276/.372/.507	.297	.298	-3.1	1B -5	2.4
2009	MIL	MLB	25	719	103	35	3	46	141	110	138	2	3	.300/.412/.602	.338	.315	-3.3	1B -12	4.8
2010	MIL	MLB	26	714	94	25	0	32	83	114	138	1	0	.261/.401/.471	.308	.291	-4.5	1B 1	3.5
2011	*MIL*	*MLB*	*27*	*691*	*102*	*29*	*1*	*36*	*103*	*100*	*122*	*3*	*1*	*.279/.394/.528*	*.316*	*.291*	*-0.2*	*1B -4*	*3.9*

Fielder's season was something of a disappointment compared with his 2009 breakthrough, as the big man registered career lows in batting average and slugging percentage and saw his intermittent struggles against southpaws resurface, but his overall TAv and WARP scores were right in line with his recent career. Having taken their lumps for years, pitchers conspired to let other Brewers beat them and avoided throwing the ball over the plate, so Fielder rolled his eyes and accepted a career-high 114 free passes, which kept him among the league leaders in on-base percentage. As baseball awaits the dread spectacle of his Boras-fueled free-agent frenzy at season's end, it's de rigueur to rehash the reasons why Fielder won't deserve the megacontract he seeks: bad defense, slow foot speed, and a rotund physique that may not age well. Of course, his 229 VORP over the last four seasons is the eighth-best in baseball and third-best (behind Albert Pujols and Miguel Cabrera) among first basemen, he's only now entering his age-27 season, and he routinely plays nearly every inning of every game. Just sayin'.

Mat Gamel **4C**

Born: **7/26/1985** Age: **25**
Bats: L Throws: R Height: **6' 0"** Weight: **195**
Breakout: **2%** Improve: **24%** Collapse: **12%**
Attrition: **40%** MLB: **63%**

Comparables:
Matthew Brown, Chase Headley, Scott Moore (75)

YEAR	TEAM	LVL	AGE	PA	R	2B	3B	HR	RBI	BB	SO	SB	CS	AVG/OBP/SLG	TAv	BABIP	BRR	FRAA	WARP
2008	HUN	AA	22	572	96	35	7	19	96	55	111	6	7	.329/.395/.537	.310	.386	2.7	3B -4	4.6
2008	MIL	MLB	22	2	0	1	0	0	0	0	1	0	0	.500/.500/1.000	.475	1.000	0.0	3B 0	—
2009	NAS	AAA	23	320	42	18	1	11	48	38	89	1	0	.278/.366/.473	.291	.363	-0.8	3B -4	1.4
2009	MIL	MLB	23	148	11	6	1	5	20	18	54	1	0	.242/.338/.422	.270	.371	0.3	3B -2	0.3
2010	NAS	AAA	24	359	54	24	0	13	67	38	64	3	1	.309/.387/.511	.302	.347	0.0	3B -9, RF 0	1.7
2010	MIL	MLB	24	17	2	1	0	0	1	1	8	0	0	.200/.294/.267	.208	.429	0.2	3B -1, LF 0	-0.1
2011	*MIL*	*MLB*	*25*	*496*	*60*	*24*	*2*	*14*	*58*	*49*	*125*	*2*	*1*	*.262/.336/.426*	*.264*	*.327*	*-0.1*	*3B -8, RF 0*	*0.7*

Third verse, same as the first. Gamel's season in Nashville proved once more that his lefty bat would be an asset at third, but his glove—or, more accurately, his inaccurate arm—just isn't up to the task. Instead, he has become an inexpensive insurance policy at first base, where his middling power and patience would provide adequate production on the cheap, though with little projection left, he'll never be a star there. Still, there's value in that, and as frustrating as it must be to know you're among the top half-dozen bats in the organization but still can't earn a job, Gamel's chance will come as soon as Fielder is gone.

Ryan Gennett **2B**

Born: **5/1/1990** Age: **21**
Bats: L Throws: R Height: **5' 9"** Weight: **164**
Breakout: **2%** Improve: **10%** Collapse: **2%**
Attrition: **2%** MLB: **21%**

Comparables:
Adrian Beltre, Rod Carew, Asdrubal Cabrera (66)

YEAR	TEAM	LVL	AGE	PA	R	2B	3B	HR	RBI	BB	SO	SB	CS	AVG/OBP/SLG	TAv	BABIP	BRR	FRAA	WARP
2010	WIS	A	20	526	87	39	4	9	55	31	91	14	4	.309/.354/.463	.292	.360	1.8	2B 0, SS 1	3.4
2011	*MIL*	*MLB*	*21*	*520*	*54*	*28*	*2*	*8*	*55*	*19*	*111*	*1*	*1*	*.258/.283/.372*	*.230*	*.311*	*0.0*	*2B 1, SS 0*	*-0.2*

"Scooter" Gennett was the talk of the Midwest League early in the year, as the diminutive second sacker hit everything hard in May and June, but his approach regressed in the second half as he posted a .288/.313/.461 line with only seven walks. A high-energy, dirty-uniform player who hangs in well against lefties, Gennett has terrific hitting skills, good speed, surprising power, a steady glove, and a high baseball IQ. He isn't a Pedroia-style contact hitter—note the high strikeout totals—and the jury is out as to whether his skills and approach will play at higher levels, but his impressive professional debut makes Gennett a for-real prospect.

Carlos Gomez **CF**

Born: **12/4/1985** Age: **25**
Bats: R Throws: R Height: **6' 4"** Weight: **195**
Breakout: **4%** Improve: **46%** Collapse: **3%**
Attrition: **14%** MLB: **72%**

Comparables:
Willie Davis, Bake McBride, Jerry Mumphrey (72)

YEAR	TEAM	LVL	AGE	PA	R	2B	3B	HR	RBI	BB	SO	SB	CS	AVG/OBP/SLG	TAv	BABIP	BRR	FRAA	WARP
2008	MIN	MLB	22	614	78	24	7	7	59	25	142	33	11	.258/.295/.361	.237	.328	-0.1	CF 15	1.7
2009	MIN	MLB	23	349	46	15	5	3	28	22	72	14	7	.229/.281/.337	.224	.278	0.3	CF 14	1.1
2010	MIL	MLB	24	318	37	11	3	5	24	17	72	18	3	.247/.298/.357	.234	.305	3.7	CF -10, LF 0	-0.6
2011	*MIL*	*MLB*	*25*	*411*	*42*	*16*	*3*	*5*	*37*	*25*	*85*	*22*	*7*	*.245/.293/.343*	*.228*	*.294*	*-0.1*	*CF 3, LF 0*	*0.1*

It would be great that the speedy Gomez set a career high in on-base percentage last year, if only the OBP in question weren't .298. Combine that with a low batting average, little power, and strikeouts in almost a quarter of his plate appearances, and no amount of speed or defense will ever make starting Gomez in center field a defensible everyday plan—though the trade of Lorenzo Cain to Kansas City may force the Brewers to do just that. If he could learn to take a few more walks or make a little more contact, he might become an asset, but at age 25, with over 1,400 career plate appearances, Gomez is little more likely to discover a better plate approach than he is a needle in a haystack, a cure for cancer, or the explanation for the *Mary Celeste*'s missing crew.

Corey Hart **RF**

Born: **3/24/1982** Age: **29**
Bats: R Throws: R Height: **6' 6"** Weight: **200**
Breakout: **5%** Improve: **44%** Collapse: **1%**
Attrition: **8%** MLB: **95%**

Comparables:
Alex Rios, Andre Dawson, Gary Matthews (72)

YEAR	TEAM	LVL	AGE	PA	R	2B	3B	HR	RBI	BB	SO	SB	CS	AVG/OBP/SLG	TAv	BABIP	BRR	FRAA	WARP
2008	MIL	MLB	26	657	76	45	6	20	91	27	109	23	7	.268/.298/.459	.264	.290	1.8	RF -3	1.2
2009	MIL	MLB	27	472	64	24	3	12	48	43	92	11	6	.260/.335/.418	.268	.304	2.6	RF -11	0.3
2010	MIL	MLB	28	614	91	34	4	31	102	45	140	7	6	.283/.340/.525	.301	.324	2.0	RF -10	2.6
2011	*MIL*	*MLB*	*29*	*538*	*69*	*29*	*3*	*19*	*74*	*40*	*99*	*14*	*6*	*.277/.334/.473*	*.281*	*.305*	*-0.8*	*RF -4*	*1.4*

For several years, Hart's power bat was seen less frequently than images of the Virgin Mary in burnt toast, but that changed in 2010, when the lanky right fielder launched 30 home runs for the first time in his career. Hart had retooled his approach in 2009 and worked deeper counts, shoring up his plummeting on-base percentage but losing much of the juice in his swing; last year, he didn't just wait for his pitch, but also took a big hack when he saw it. The result was an increase in swinging strikes, but also more fly balls and home runs, all without sacrificing enough walks to sink his OBP. The club rewarded his work with a three-year, $26.5 million extension—a solid investment if

Hart keeps producing at this level into his 30s, but if a few more of those fly balls start dying on the warning track and his bat can no longer overcome his declining glove, it's a move the Brewers may regret.

Joe Inglett **UT**

Born: **6/29/1978** Age: **33**
Bats: **L** Throws: **R** Height: **5' 10"** Weight: **180**
Breakout: **1%** Improve: **25%** Collapse: **6%**
Attrition: **14%** MLB: **84%**

Comparables:
Dave Martinez, Willie Harris, Jorge Orta (72)

YEAR	TEAM	LVL	AGE	PA	R	2B	3B	HR	RBI	BB	SO	SB	CS	AVG/OBP/SLG	TAv	BABIP	BRR	FRAA	WARP
2008	SYR	AAA	30	62	12	2	2	1	6	7	7	1	2	.407/.484/.574	.363	.457	0.8	2B -2, LF 1	0.9
2008	TOR	MLB	30	385	44	15	7	3	39	28	43	9	2	.297/.348/.407	.276	.323	4.8	2B -3, RF -1	1.7
2009	LVG	AAA	31	186	29	14	1	3	25	16	18	4	2	.360/.409/.516	.305	.374	1.0	2B 2, LF 0	1.4
2009	TOR	MLB	31	99	10	4	1	0	6	8	21	3	1	.281/.343/.348	.254	.362	-0.4	LF 1, RF -3	-0.1
2010	MIL	MLB	32	159	17	8	5	1	8	15	33	1	0	.255/.333/.404	.264	.324	0.2	RF -2, LF 0	0.1
2011	*MIL*	*MLB*	*33*	*363*	*41*	*16*	*4*	*2*	*34*	*30*	*54*	*6*	*3*	*.272/.331/.367*	*.248*	*.309*	*-0.4*	*2B -2, LF 0*	*0.1*

The Brewers claimed Inglett on waivers prior to last season and plunked him down at the end of their bench. His lefty bat and ability to grab a glove and stand anywhere on the diamond make him useful for double-switching, pinch-hitting, defensive-replacing, and all the other tactical frippery that senior-circuit managers find so enchanting. Give Inglett 300 plate appearances and you'll regret it, but he's perfectly cast as the lubricant that helps keep the other, more important moving parts sliding smoothly around the diamond. He was nontendered in December, because teams correctly treat lube as a commodity product.

George Kottaras **C**

Born: **5/16/1983** Age: **28**
Bats: **L** Throws: **R** Height: **6' 0"** Weight: **185**
Breakout: **5%** Improve: **34%** Collapse: **10%**
Attrition: **23%** MLB: **76%**

Comparables:
Luke Carlin, Dusty Brown, Ryan Doumit (76)

YEAR	TEAM	LVL	AGE	PA	R	2B	3B	HR	RBI	BB	SO	SB	CS	AVG/OBP/SLG	TAv	BABIP	BRR	FRAA	WARP
2008	PAW	AAA	25	462	63	18	0	22	65	64	110	0	0	.243/.348/.456	.268	.279	-1.1	C -1	1.7
2008	BOS	MLB	25	5	1	1	0	0	0	0	2	0	0	.200/.200/.400	.217	.333	0.6	C 0	0.1
2009	BOS	MLB	26	107	15	11	0	1	10	11	25	0	0	.237/.308/.387	.245	.300	-0.2	C -1, 3B 1	0.3
2010	MIL	MLB	27	250	24	12	1	9	26	33	44	2	0	.203/.304/.396	.259	.207	-4.4	C -1, 1B 0	0.4
2011	*MIL*	*MLB*	*28*	*285*	*33*	*13*	*0*	*9*	*31*	*36*	*60*	*1*	*0*	*.233/.329/.400*	*.258*	*.266*	*0.0*	*C -1, 3B 0*	*0.8*

When Gregg Zaun hurt his shoulder in mid-May, Kottaras took over for his fellow Canuck and promptly flashed an Open for Business sign to opposing runners, who stole 44 bases in 52 attempts and compelled the Brewers to hand the everyday job to rookie Jonathan Lucroy. Last year was the best chance yet for Kottaras, a longtime sabermetric favorite, to parlay his patient lefty bat into a permanent starting gig, but there's far more to hitting than walks and the occasional long fly. Kottaras will enter spring training aiming to convince management that he can do the job defensively. If he can, his offensive ceiling will still be higher than Lucroy's. It's also higher than that of Wil Nieves, against whom Kottaras will suffer the indignity of competing for a roster spot.

Brett Lawrie **2B**

Born: **1/18/1990** Age: **21**
Bats: **R** Throws: **R** Height: **6' 0"** Weight: **213**
Breakout: **3%** Improve: **22%** Collapse: **2%**
Attrition: **19%** MLB: **40%**

Comparables:
Elvis Andrus, Justin Upton, Ruben Sierra (64)

YEAR	TEAM	LVL	AGE	PA	R	2B	3B	HR	RBI	BB	SO	SB	CS	AVG/OBP/SLG	TAv	BABIP	BRR	FRAA	WARP
2009	WIS	A	19	423	48	18	5	13	65	41	70	19	11	.274/.348/.454	.294	.302	5.0	2B -3	2.6
2009	HUN	AA	19	53	6	0	1	0	0	0	14	0	2	.269/.283/.308	.214	.368	0.5	2B 0	-0.1
2010	HUN	AA	20	609	90	36	16	8	63	47	118	30	13	.285/.346/.451	.277	.348	2.6	2B 9	3.6
2011	*TOR*	*MLB*	*21*	*538*	*59*	*26*	*5*	*8*	*56*	*35*	*114*	*19*	*7*	*.256/.305/.380*	*.242*	*.311*	*-0.7*	*2B 4*	*0.6*

Lawrie's season was a mixed bag. His leading the Southern League in hits and total bases at age 20 speaks volumes about his bat; he seems likely to grow into a middle-of-the-order thumper. However, there are still ample questions about his defense, as he has looked sloppy and inconsistent at second base, and many scouts feel that a move to an outfield corner is an inevitability. More distressingly, there are whispers about Lawrie's makeup and effort, exacerbated by his apparent refusal to put in more work in the Arizona Fall League. With just a pinch of seasoning, Lawrie can be an all-star—the only questions remaining are at what position and how soon. Having been traded to the Toronto Blue Jays for pitcher Shaun Marcum, the Canadian native has a clearer path to the majors, with fewer established players in front of him than there were with the Brewers.

Jonathan Lucroy **C**

Born: **6/13/1986** Age: **25**
Bats: **R** Throws: **R** Height: **6' 0"** Weight: **195**
Breakout: **2%** Improve: **20%** Collapse: **12%**
Attrition: **20%** MLB: **52%**

Comparables:
Kurt Suzuki, John Jaso, Rob Johnson (80)

YEAR	TEAM	LVL	AGE	PA	R	2B	3B	HR	RBI	BB	SO	SB	CS	AVG/OBP/SLG	TAv	BABIP	BRR	FRAA	WARP
2008	WVA	A	22	274	45	16	1	10	33	30	39	8	1	.310/.391/.510	.331	.333	1.9	C 0	3.0
2008	BRV	A+	22	272	31	12	1	10	44	28	45	1	2	.292/.364/.479	.294	.316	-1.0	C -1	1.7
2009	HUN	AA	23	506	61	32	2	9	66	78	66	1	1	.267/.379/.418	.289	.293	-3.1	C 1	3.4
2010	NAS	AAA	24	83	8	4	0	2	11	3	14	0	0	.238/.265/.363	.226	.266	-0.3	C -1	-0.1
2010	MIL	MLB	24	297	24	9	0	4	26	18	44	4	2	.253/.300/.329	.226	.287	1.5	C 1	0.5
2011	*MIL*	*MLB*	*25*	*496*	*57*	*23*	*1*	*9*	*50*	*45*	*77*	*2*	*1*	*.264/.328/.384*	*.253*	*.293*	*-0.1*	*C 0*	*1.4*

Lucroy started the season at Double-A but finished it as Milwaukee's everyday catcher after Gregg Zaun's injury and the failure of George Kottaras to control the running game gave him his shot sooner than expected. The Brewers were impressed with his strong arm, improvement behind the dish, and hard work to learn the intricacies of managing a game at the major-league level. He left his bat in Huntsville, however, and often looked overmatched—not surprising when you're suddenly facing Tim Lincecum and Roy Halladay after cleansing the palate with Steve Bray and Jarrett Grube—so he'll need to make adjustments at the plate if he wants to stick. His minor-league career featured plenty of on-base ability and double-digit home-run power, so there's reason to think that he can grow into a solid, if unspectacular, big-league backstop.

Casey McGehee 3B

Born: **10/12/1982** Age: **28**
Bats: R Throws: R Height: **6' 1"** Weight: **195**
Breakout: **2%** Improve: **45%** Collapse: **3%**
Attrition: **9%** MLB: **85%**

Comparables:
Edwin Encarnacion, Jorge Cantu, Brooks Robinson (79)

YEAR	TEAM	LVL	AGE	PA	R	2B	3B	HR	RBI	BB	SO	SB	CS	AVG/OBP/SLG	TAv	BABIP	BRR	FRAA	WARP
2008	IOW	AAA	25	550	68	30	0	12	92	40	89	0	3	.296/.345/.429	.264	.333	-3.0	3B 5, C -1	2.1
2008	CHN	MLB	25	25	1	1	0	0	5	0	8	0	0	.167/.160/.208	.123	.235	0.0	3B 2	-0.1
2009	MIL	MLB	26	394	58	20	1	16	66	34	67	0	2	.301/.360/.499	.288	.330	1.9	3B -4, 2B 0	2.0
2010	MIL	MLB	27	670	70	38	1	23	104	50	102	1	1	.285/.337/.464	.285	.306	-4.0	3B -10, 1B 0	2.1
2011	*MIL*	*MLB*	*28*	*544*	*67*	*28*	*0*	*16*	*67*	*43*	*83*	*1*	*1*	*.280/.336/.437*	*.270*	*.303*	*-0.1*	*3B -3, 2B 0*	*1.7*

Cashing a hard-earned paycheck can bring a satisfying sense of accomplishment, but for pure joy, it's hard to beat finding a C-note blowing down the street. That's essentially what the Brewers have in McGehee, as the former Cub waiver-bait built on his surprising 2009 season to become an above-average starter. McGehee's 62 extra-base hits trailed only David Wright among senior-circuit third basemen, and though his batting average and on-base percentage dropped back to levels more consistent with his minor-league numbers, as long as the power sticks around, he will be an asset despite some surprisingly poor glove work. At 28, he's not due for any great leap forward, but he's still a year removed from arbitration, and if he can maintain this level of production into his 30s, he'll remain a wonderfully value-priced complement to the more expensive stars batting in front of him.

Rickie Weeks 2B

Born: **9/13/1982** Age: **28**
Bats: R Throws: R Height: **6' 0"** Weight: **195**
Breakout: **0%** Improve: **46%** Collapse: **1%**
Attrition: **2%** MLB: **95%**

Comparables:
Kelly Johnson, Ron Gant, Ron Santo (69)

YEAR	TEAM	LVL	AGE	PA	R	2B	3B	HR	RBI	BB	SO	SB	CS	AVG/OBP/SLG	TAv	BABIP	BRR	FRAA	WARP
2008	MIL	MLB	25	560	89	22	7	14	46	66	115	19	5	.234/.341/.398	.268	.276	5.5	2B 0	2.3
2009	MIL	MLB	26	162	28	5	2	9	24	12	39	2	2	.272/.340/.517	.298	.313	-0.8	2B 0	1.0
2010	MIL	MLB	27	754	112	32	4	29	83	76	184	11	4	.269/.366/.464	.297	.332	5.8	2B -3	4.6
2011	*MIL*	*MLB*	*28*	*484*	*62*	*20*	*3*	*16*	*57*	*54*	*104*	*12*	*4*	*.259/.359/.440*	*.283*	*.304*	*-0.1*	*2B -2*	*2.0*

The Brewers have waited years to see what Weeks could do when fully healthy and productive, and last year, he finally gave them everything they expected. Patience and power helped Weeks overcome a flock of strikeouts to lead the team in VORP, placing him among the league's best hitters at the keystone, and while defensive metrics tend to disagree more than partners in a buddy cop movie, the consensus is that his glove is no longer a major liability. His speed wasn't much in evidence last year, although Ron Roenicke's more aggressive offensive approach may set Weeks loose on the basepaths to greater effect. Health, not talent, has always been the question with Weeks and will make for some interesting decisions as the Brewers look to extend him past his year-end date with free agency. If his chronic wrist problems are a thing of the past, he can be a franchise cornerstone; if not, he's an albatross contract in waiting.

Gregg Zaun C

Born: **4/14/1971** Age: **40**
Bats: S Throws: R Height: **5' 10"** Weight: **170**
Breakout: **0%** Improve: **11%** Collapse: **10%**
Attrition: **17%** MLB: **48%**

Comparables:
Ron Fairly, Jim Dwyer, Yogi Berra (65)

YEAR	TEAM	LVL	AGE	PA	R	2B	3B	HR	RBI	BB	SO	SB	CS	AVG/OBP/SLG	TAv	BABIP	BRR	FRAA	WARP
2008	TOR	MLB	37	288	31	12	0	6	30	38	38	2	1	.237/.337/.359	.259	.254	-2.9	C 1	1.0
2009	BAL	MLB	38	197	23	10	0	4	13	27	30	0	0	.244/.355/.375	.267	.276	-2.6	C 0	0.7
2009	TBA	MLB	38	99	11	7	0	4	14	4	18	0	2	.287/.323/.489	.282	.319	-1.3	C -1	0.4
2010	MIL	MLB	39	117	11	7	0	2	14	11	12	0	0	.265/.350/.392	.259	.281	-1.0	C -1	0.3
2011	*MIL*	*MLB*	*40*	*291*	*32*	*14*	*0*	*5*	*26*	*32*	*41*	*1*	*1*	*.237/.325/.358*	*.245*	*.258*	*-0.1*	*C 0*	*0.7*

As a 40-year-old catcher, Zaun is almost exactly what he was as a 30-year-old catcher: a switch-hitter with patience, occasional pop, an unnecessary consonant, and enough perceived defensive deficiencies to deter teams from letting him catch every day. The Brewers brought him in last year to replace Jason Kendall—hardly an intimidating task—but Zaun tore his labrum in May, underwent season-ending surgery in June, and wasn't asked back. If his shoulder is healthy, Zaun can still out-hit half the starting catchers in baseball. He signed a minor-league deal with the Padres and will compete to be their reserve catcher.

PITCHERS

Eric Arnett

Born: **1/25/1988** Age: **23**
Bats: R Throws: R Height: **6' 5"** Weight: **230**
Breakout: **0%** Improve: **1%** Collapse: **0%**
Attrition: **0%** MLB: **1%**

Comparables:
Jerry Reuss, Roy Halladay, Ed Halicki (74)

YEAR	TEAM	LVL	AGE	W	L	SV	G	GS	IP	H	HR	BB	SO	EqBB9	EqSO9	GB%	BABIP	WHIP	ERA	FRA	WARP
2009	HEL	Rk	21	0	4	0	14	9	34^2	33	1	21	35	5.4	9.1	61%	.286	1.64	4.41	8.28	-1.3
2010	WIS	A	22	1	9	1	20	16	84^2	98	14	39	60	4.2	6.4	51%	.300	1.75	6.70	7.76	-1.4
2010	BRR	Rk	22	2	0	0	5	1	20	26	1	8	27	3.6	12.2	64%	.446	1.70	6.75	5.90	-0.3
2011	*MIL*	*MLB*	*23*	*2*	*7*	*0*	*18*	*12*	67^1	*85*	*13*	*45*	*34*	*6.0*	*4.6*	*47%*	*.314*	*1.93*	*7.35*	*7.99*	*-1.1*

The first full pro season of the Brewers' top pick in the 2009 draft was an unmitigated disaster. Arnett was a mess mechanically, had trouble repeating his delivery, lost command of his fastball, and frequently saw his velocity drop into the upper-80s. A demotion to rookie ball didn't fix the problem, leaving Arnett and the Brewers' development staff with a lot of work to do in order to rekindle his prospect flame.

John Axford

Born: **4/1/1983** Age: **28**
Bats: R Throws: R Height: **6' 5"** Weight: **195**
Breakout: **10%** Improve: **17%** Collapse: **11%**
Attrition: **10%** MLB: **29%**

Comparables:
Billy Sadler, Francisco Cruceta, Robinson Tejeda (76)

YEAR	TEAM	LVL	AGE	W	L	SV	G	GS	IP	H	HR	BB	SO	EqBB9	EqSO9	GB%	BABIP	WHIP	ERA	FRA	WARP
2008	BRV	A+	25	5	10	0	26	14	95	86	5	73	89	6.9	8.4	47%	.310	1.73	4.55	5.58	0.1
2009	BRV	A+	26	4	1	0	19	0	27^2	14	0	16	43	5.2	14.0	45%	.275	1.08	1.62	2.86	0.7
2009	NAS	AAA	26	5	0	0	22	0	33	23	2	19	37	5.2	10.1	54%	.263	1.27	3.55	4.80	0.1
2009	MIL	MLB	26	0	0	1	7	0	7^2	5	0	6	9	7.0	10.6	32%	.263	1.43	3.52	4.98	0.0
2010	MIL	MLB	27	8	2	24	50	0	58	42	1	27	76	4.2	11.8	50%	.308	1.21	2.48	2.60	1.1
2011	*MIL*	*MLB*	*28*	*3*	*2*	*2*	*48*	*2*	73^1	*67*	*7*	*51*	*77*	*6.2*	*9.4*	*45%*	*.312*	*1.60*	*4.65*	*5.06*	*-0.0*

Axford has become a fan favorite, more because of his facial-hair experiments and rags-to-riches backstory than his stuff, but his mid-90s fastball and sharp-breaking off-speed pitches are no fluke—they generate more than enough swings and misses to work in the ninth inning. The question with him has always been control. Last year, Axford walked a little over four men per nine innings, while his minor-league stat line suffered from over six free passes per nine. Relievers with walk rates that high tend to lose their grip on the closer reins as managers grow frustrated with their self-inflicted jams. Although it's possible that Axford has developed a newfound ability to find the strike zone and will spend the next half-decade closing games at Miller Park, Brewers fans will just as likely wake up one morning to discover that yesterday's Rollie Fingers has morphed into today's Derrick Turnbow. You've been warned.

Zach Braddock

Born: **8/23/1987** Age: **23**
Bats: L Throws: L Height: **6' 2"** Weight: **235**
Breakout: **4%** Improve: **6%** Collapse: **9%**
Attrition: **3%** MLB: **18%**

Comparables:
Len Barker, Bob Turley, B.J. Ryan (74)

YEAR	TEAM	LVL	AGE	W	L	SV	G	GS	IP	H	HR	BB	SO	EqBB9	EqSO9	GB%	BABIP	WHIP	ERA	FRA	WARP
2008	BRV	A+	20	4	7	0	21	11	65^1	55	7	42	80	5.8	11.0	35%	.302	1.59	5.51	4.59	0.8
2009	BRV	A+	21	1	1	0	14	0	24^2	12	2	4	40	1.5	14.6	37%	.227	0.73	1.09	1.06	1.3
2010	MIL	MLB	22	1	2	0	46	0	33^2	29	1	19	41	5.1	11.0	35%	.318	1.49	2.94	3.26	0.6
2011	*MIL*	*MLB*	*23*	*3*	*1*	*0*	*36*	*2*	*47*	*41*	*5*	*28*	*57*	*5.2*	*10.7*	*41%*	*.304*	*1.43*	*4.14*	*4.50*	*0.4*

Braddock's conversion to relief has worked wonders for his career, transforming him from inconsistent injury risk to major-league bullpen cog in just 18 months. The lefty has always missed bats with his mid-90s heat and wipe-out slider, but after a one-year hiatus, walks again featured prominently on the menu. Lefties managed a mere .151/.270/.170 line against him, though right-handers knocked him around—he'll need to keep his slider down in the zone to avoid being painted with the LOOGY brush. The Brewers hope he can step into a prominent set-up role this year, and if he can knock his walk rate down a little, he'll more than earn his keep.

Dave Bush

Born: **11/9/1979** Age: **31**
Bats: R Throws: R Height: **6' 2"** Weight: **212**
Breakout: **10%** Improve: **37%** Collapse: **26%**
Attrition: **15%** MLB: **98%**

Comparables:
Dave Goltz, Erik Hanson, Frank Viola (76)

YEAR	TEAM	LVL	AGE	W	L	SV	G	GS	IP	H	HR	BB	SO	EqBB9	EqSO9	GB%	BABIP	WHIP	ERA	FRA	WARP
2008	MIL	MLB	28	9	10	0	31	29	185	163	29	48	109	2.3	5.3	42%	.236	1.19	4.18	5.39	0.8
2009	MIL	MLB	29	5	9	0	22	21	114^1	131	19	37	89	2.9	7.0	38%	.322	1.60	6.38	6.34	-0.6
2010	MIL	MLB	30	8	13	0	32	31	174^1	198	28	65	107	3.4	5.5	41%	.295	1.53	4.54	5.21	0.6
2011	*MIL*	*MLB*	*31*	*10*	*13*	*0*	*31*	*31*	*174*	*193*	*29*	*58*	*115*	*3.0*	*5.9*	*42%*	*.298*	*1.43*	*5.18*	*5.64*	*1.3*

The only right-handed starters currently working in the majors with less velocity on their fastballs than Bush are knuckleballers Tim Wakefield and R. A. Dickey and necromancer Livan Hernandez, and with Bush's strikeout and walk rates quickly converging, the Brewers cut ties with the veteran right-hander. They received 870 innings of occasionally good work out of him over the last five years, but recently his spot in the rotation had been more a matter of hope than faith. Milwaukee's often-immobile defense hasn't done him any favors, and perhaps a move to a larger ballpark would reduce his sky-high home-run rate and help him achieve a Moyer-esque late-career revival, but the odds aren't good.

Chris Capuano

Born: **8/19/1978** Age: **32**
Bats: L Throws: L Height: **6' 3"** Weight: **210**
Breakout: **11%** Improve: **31%** Collapse: **23%**
Attrition: **11%** MLB: **77%**

Comparables:
Ken Johnson, Larry Christenson, Ben McDonald (74)

YEAR	TEAM	LVL	AGE	W	L	SV	G	GS	IP	H	HR	BB	SO	EqBB9	EqSO9	GB%	BABIP	WHIP	ERA	FRA	WARP
2010	NAS	AAA	31	1	1	0	4	4	25	21	0	4	16	1.4	5.8	44%	.259	1.04	1.44	1.69	1.2
2010	MIL	MLB	31	4	4	0	24	9	66	65	9	21	54	2.9	7.4	44%	.290	1.32	3.95	3.83	1.1
2011	*MIL*	*MLB*	*32*	*9*	*9*	*0*	*39*	*23*	*121*	*128*	*17*	*38*	*93*	*2.8*	*6.9*	*45%*	*.304*	*1.36*	*4.50*	*4.89*	*2.1*

Capuano's return from his second Tommy John surgery may have supplied one of the season's more uplifting stories, but it was his success on the mound that had the Brewers in negotiations to finance a sequel. During his presurgical heyday, Capuano relied more on command and deception than on pure stuff, using his solid changeup and slider to prevent hitters from timing his upper-80s fastball. Each of those pitches was in vintage form last year, and Capuano's peripherals were parked comfortably in their old neighborhood, contributing to a promising 3.97 SIERA. It was only 66 innings, but Capuano certainly showed enough to be worth a shot in the rotation, with an upside of league-average production. That chance will come with the Mets, who signed the pitcher to a one-year deal.

Todd Coffey

Born: **9/9/1980** Age: **30**
Bats: R Throws: R Height: **6' 5"** Weight: **230**
Breakout: **7%** Improve: **16%** Collapse: **13%**
Attrition: **18%** MLB: **32%**

Comparables:
Claudio Vargas, Chris Capuano, John Candelaria (71)

YEAR	TEAM	LVL	AGE	W	L	SV	G	GS	IP	H	HR	BB	SO	EqBB9	EqSO9	GB%	BABIP	WHIP	ERA	FRA	WARP
2008	LOU	AAA	27	3	3	2	34	0	39^{1}	49	4	15	43	3.4	9.8	56%	.378	1.63	4.35	4.26	0.5
2008	CIN	MLB	27	0	0	0	17	0	19^{1}	25	4	6	8	2.8	3.7	57%	.309	1.66	6.05	6.03	-0.2
2008	MIL	MLB	27	1	0	0	9	0	7^{1}	6	0	2	7	2.5	8.6	65%	.300	1.09	0.00	-0.48	0.5
2009	MIL	MLB	28	4	4	2	78	0	83^{2}	76	8	21	65	2.3	7.0	53%	.285	1.20	2.90	3.33	1.3
2010	MIL	MLB	29	2	4	0	69	0	62^{1}	65	8	23	56	3.3	8.1	49%	.310	1.46	4.76	5.74	-0.7
2011	*MIL*	*MLB*	*30*	*4*	*1*	*0*	*73*	*0*	*74*	*78*	*10*	*26*	*60*	*3.1*	*7.2*	*49%*	*.309*	*1.39*	*4.51*	*4.90*	*-0.1*

Each season, teams have to scrounge up enough arms to throw somewhere in the neighborhood of 700,000 pitches over roughly 43,000 innings. That's a lot of work to be divvied up, and if you can hit 95 on a radar gun and throw an actual slider that can dart out of the way of a hitter's swing, someone is bound to offer you a job. Coffey can do exactly that, and while the up-and-down contours of his standard reliever career happened to hit a downslope just when he was due to become expensive, making him nontender material, he's perfectly capable of providing someone with adequate middle relief. He threw far more sliders last year in a failed bid to end his career-long struggles with lefties, but would be better off in the long run just blowing his fastball by overmatched righties.

Doug Davis

Born: **9/21/1975** Age: **35**
Bats: R Throws: L Height: **6' 4"** Weight: **190**
Breakout: **16%** Improve: **34%** Collapse: **24%**
Attrition: **14%** MLB: **88%**

Comparables:
Marv Grissom, Mike Krukow, Rick Sutcliffe (74)

YEAR	TEAM	LVL	AGE	W	L	SV	G	GS	IP	H	HR	BB	SO	EqBB9	EqSO9	GB%	BABIP	WHIP	ERA	FRA	WARP
2008	ARI	MLB	32	6	8	0	26	26	146	160	13	64	112	3.9	6.9	49%	.322	1.56	4.32	4.54	2.5
2009	ARI	MLB	33	9	14	0	34	34	203^{1}	203	25	103	146	4.6	6.5	45%	.291	1.52	4.12	4.48	2.9
2010	MIL	MLB	34	1	4	0	8	8	38^{1}	55	6	21	34	4.9	8.0	49%	.386	2.06	7.51	6.06	-0.2
2011	*MIL*	*MLB*	*35*	*9*	*12*	*0*	*28*	*28*	*160*	*176*	*21*	*81*	*118*	*4.5*	*6.6*	*46%*	*.315*	*1.61*	*5.33*	*5.79*	*1.0*

Davis is nothing if not a survivor, having scratched out an 11-season career despite thyroid cancer, deficient stuff, and enough men on base to cast a remake of *Gone with the Wind*. Last year, Davis was able to pitch around a case of pericarditis, but couldn't wiggle past the nearly two baserunners per inning he allowed or the elbow woes that ended his season after only eight disastrous starts. Since he's now back on the street at age 35 with a new scar on his elbow, it's unlikely that Davis will still be able to fool major-league hitters with his mid-80s "fastball," cutter, and curve. Then again, it was unlikely for him to have ever done so.

Yovani Gallardo

Born: **2/27/1986** Age: **25**
Bats: R Throws: R Height: **6' 1"** Weight: **210**
Breakout: **20%** Improve: **54%** Collapse: **15%**
Attrition: **7%** MLB: **98%**

Comparables:
Jim Maloney, Mark Prior, Kerry Wood (70)

YEAR	TEAM	LVL	AGE	W	L	SV	G	GS	IP	H	HR	BB	SO	EqBB9	EqSO9	GB%	BABIP	WHIP	ERA	FRA	WARP
2008	MIL	MLB	22	0	0	0	4	4	24	22	3	8	20	3.0	7.5	37%	.288	1.25	1.88	2.35	1.0
2009	MIL	MLB	23	13	12	0	30	30	185^{2}	150	21	94	204	4.6	9.9	47%	.275	1.34	3.73	3.94	3.5
2010	MIL	MLB	24	14	7	0	31	31	185	178	12	75	200	3.6	9.7	45%	.324	1.38	3.84	3.62	4.2
2011	*MIL*	*MLB*	*25*	*10*	*7*	*0*	*25*	*25*	*150^{1}*	*136*	*15*	*65*	*159*	*3.9*	*9.5*	*45%*	*.306*	*1.34*	*3.79*	*4.12*	*3.5*

Baseball's most overlooked ace, Gallardo not only took the bats out of opposing hitters' hands, but also wielded a potent piece of lumber himself, winning last year's Silver Slugger Award after posting a .254/.329/.508 line that was good for a .295 TAv. Gallardo out-slugged Ryan Braun, had a higher TAv than Casey McGehee, and owns a career 677 OPS that surpasses that of Carlos Gomez. He saves his best work for the mound, where his low-90s fastball and four-pitch arsenal keep hitters perpetually off-balance, leading to more than a strikeout per inning and lots of weak contact. Nagging injuries have kept him from reaching 200 innings in a season, but they haven't been arm related—this year's culprit was a strained oblique. At 25 years old, just months older than King Felix, he's already among the top handful of starters in baseball, and if he could stay healthy for a full year, or if the Brewers could field an average defense behind him, he would finally get the recognition he deserves.

LaTroy Hawkins

Born: **12/21/1972** Age: **38**
Bats: **R** Throws: **R** Height: **6' 5"** Weight: **195**
Breakout: **16%** Improve: **17%** Collapse: **12%**
Attrition: **10%** MLB: **38%**

Comparables:
Elmer Dessens, Rick Aguilera, Dick Hall (74)

YEAR	TEAM	LVL	AGE	W	L	SV	G	GS	IP	H	HR	BB	SO	EqBB9	EqSO9	GB%	BABIP	WHIP	ERA	FRA	WARP
2008	HOU	MLB	35	2	0	1	24	0	21	11	0	5	25	2.1	10.7	41%	.225	0.76	0.43	2.44	0.8
2008	NYA	MLB	35	1	1	0	33	0	41	42	3	16	23	3.5	5.0	49%	.300	1.41	5.93	6.45	-0.5
2009	HOU	MLB	36	1	4	11	65	0	63^1	60	7	16	45	2.3	6.4	47%	.280	1.23	2.13	2.62	1.6
2010	MIL	MLB	37	0	3	0	18	0	16	21	2	6	18	3.4	10.1	48%	.413	1.81	8.44	6.96	-0.3
2011	*MIL*	*MLB*	*38*	*3*	*1*	*2*	*51*	*0*	*52*	*55*	*6*	*17*	*37*	*2.9*	*6.3*	*46%*	*.301*	*1.37*	*4.21*	*4.58*	*0.1*

Middle relievers, by definition, rarely merit multiyear, multimillion-dollar contracts. They don't pitch enough, or in enough high-leverage situations, to be worth the money, and the increased performance variance that occurs over such small sample sizes makes them less likely than other players to perform at the same level over consecutive years, especially when they're approaching their 40th trip around the sun. Or, to put it another way, signing Hawkins was a bad idea even if he had stayed healthy and pitched effectively last year, and would still have been a bad idea even if he pitches like Mariano Rivera this year. He won't, though.

Kyle Heckathorn

Born: **6/17/1988** Age: **23**
Bats: **R** Throws: **R** Height: **6' 6"** Weight: **225**
Breakout: **9%** Improve: **10%** Collapse: **1%**
Attrition: **8%** MLB: **11%**

Comparables:
Lucas French, Matt Harrison, Yorman Bazardo (81)

YEAR	TEAM	LVL	AGE	W	L	SV	G	GS	IP	H	HR	BB	SO	EqBB9	EqSO9	GB%	BABIP	WHIP	ERA	FRA	WARP
2009	HEL	Rk	21	0	1	0	6	5	22^1	30	4	4	15	1.6	6.0	54%	.351	1.57	5.64	7.51	-0.2
2010	WIS	A	22	6	6	0	17	13	85	82	2	23	67	2.4	7.1	59%	.299	1.27	2.86	4.67	1.0
2010	BRV	A+	22	4	0	0	8	8	39	40	1	10	23	2.3	5.3	53%	.305	1.28	3.00	3.45	0.9
2011	*MIL*	*MLB*	*23*	*3*	*6*	*0*	*14*	*12*	*67*	*83*	*9*	*30*	*31*	*4.0*	*4.1*	*48%*	*.313*	*1.67*	*5.87*	*6.38*	*0.0*

Heckathorn's full-season debut featured plenty of statistical success and unenthusiastic scouting reports. A big-bodied righty, Heckathorn commanded his live fastball quite well, throwing strikes, minimizing walks, and inducing plenty of ground balls en route to a sub-three ERA. Scouts weren't enamored of his slider and change, however, and his strikeout and hit rates were poor for a college pitcher debuting in A-ball. Heckathorn can become a fourth starter if he keeps throwing strikes and develops his secondary pitches; otherwise, he's a future middle reliever. That may sound like a heapin' helpin' of "meh," but the pitching-starved Brewers will take any help they can get.

Trevor Hoffman

Born: **10/13/1967** Age: **43**
Bats: **R** Throws: **R** Height: **6' 0"** Weight: **205**
Breakout: **3%** Improve: **9%** Collapse: **4%**
Attrition: **8%** MLB: **19%**

Comparables:
Ron Reed, Al Worthington, Diomedes Olivo (71)

YEAR	TEAM	LVL	AGE	W	L	SV	G	GS	IP	H	HR	BB	SO	EqBB9	EqSO9	GB%	BABIP	WHIP	ERA	FRA	WARP
2008	SDN	MLB	40	3	6	30	48	0	45^1	38	8	9	46	1.8	9.1	39%	.256	1.04	3.77	4.26	0.4
2009	MIL	MLB	41	3	2	37	55	0	54	35	2	14	48	2.3	8.0	43%	.228	0.93	1.83	2.45	1.1
2010	MIL	MLB	42	2	7	10	50	0	47^1	49	8	19	30	3.6	5.7	33%	.277	1.44	5.89	6.57	-0.9
2011	*MIL*	*MLB*	*43*	*3*	*1*	*17*	*53*	*0*	*51*	*52*	*7*	*17*	*39*	*2.9*	*6.8*	*43%*	*.291*	*1.33*	*4.08*	*4.43*	*0.2*

Hoffman has been working his magic act for so long, slowing down his changeup to maintain its separation from his similarly slowing fastball, while somehow managing to maintain a ridiculously low home-run rate for a fly-ball pitcher, that it seemed like it might go on forever. Early last year, hitters suddenly seemed able to figure out which was which and started hitting him hard, making Hoffman's magical 2009 seem like the outlier, not his struggles in 2008. Moved out of the closer role, the future Hall of Famer took his demotion with grace, going out of his way to ensure that John Axford felt comfortable at his old desk. Hoffman regained a large measure of effectiveness down the stretch, raising hopes that he could still provide someone with a few effective innings, but realized that everyone's seen the magician's hand, and so the show is over. Next stop, a lively Hall of Fame debate.

Jeremy Jeffress

Born: **9/21/1987** Age: **23**
Bats: R Throws: R Height: **6' 0"** Weight: **195**
Breakout: **2%** Improve: **5%** Collapse: **3%**
Attrition: **2%** MLB: **9%**

Comparables:
Billy McCool, Terrell Wade, Scott Garrelts (75)

YEAR	TEAM	LVL	AGE	W	L	SV	G	GS	IP	H	HR	BB	SO	EqBB9	EqSO9	GB%	BABIP	WHIP	ERA	FRA	WARP
2008	BRV	A+	20	4	6	0	15	14	79^1	65	5	41	102	4.7	11.6	54%	.323	1.40	4.09	4.07	1.5
2009	BRV	A+	21	2	1	0	6	5	33	16	2	22	36	6.0	9.8	66%	.189	1.24	1.91	5.03	0.1
2009	HUN	AA	21	1	3	0	8	8	27^1	26	1	33	34	10.9	11.2	59%	.362	2.20	7.58	9.21	-0.7
2010	MIL	MLB	22	1	0	0	10	0	10	8	0	6	8	5.4	7.2	57%	.286	1.40	2.70	5.19	0.0
2011	*KCA*	*MLB*	*23*	*3*	*3*	*0*	*31*	*6*	*60*	*55*	*6*	*44*	*57*	*6.6*	*8.6*	*49%*	*.302*	*1.65*	*5.03*	*5.47*	*0.0*

Jeffress made a successful return from his second drug suspension, toting his upper-90s fastball—insert obligatory "blowing smoke" pun here—and power curve back to the mound. Moved to the bullpen, Jeffress overpowered minor-league batters, racking up strikeouts by the truckload and keeping his walks temporarily in check before making his Brewers debut in September, and wowing scouts during a successful Arizona Fall League stint. Control will always be an issue, as major-league hitters were able to lay off his curveball and can catch up with any fastball if they know when it's coming. Still, it's easy to picture him working critical late innings with the aid of his overwhelming stuff. The Royals thought enough of his success to make him a key component of the Zack Greinke trade—success that was just a pipe dream a year ago and is still just one misstep from being lost forever.

Kameron Loe

Born: **9/10/1981** Age: **29**
Bats: R Throws: R Height: **6' 8"** Weight: **225**
Breakout: **14%** Improve: **20%** Collapse: **12%**
Attrition: **22%** MLB: **40%**

Comparables:
Sergio Mitre, Darrell Rasner, Gene Conley (79)

YEAR	TEAM	LVL	AGE	W	L	SV	G	GS	IP	H	HR	BB	SO	EqBB9	EqSO9	GB%	BABIP	WHIP	ERA	FRA	WARP
2008	OKL	AAA	26	3	5	1	26	4	58	70	7	20	31	3.1	4.8	56%	.317	1.59	5.59	6.73	-0.6
2008	TEX	MLB	26	1	0	0	14	0	30^2	36	3	8	20	2.3	5.9	52%	.320	1.43	3.52	5.35	-0.1
2010	NAS	AAA	28	4	3	0	10	10	62^2	57	6	19	39	2.7	5.6	60%	.263	1.29	3.16	4.87	0.5
2010	MIL	MLB	28	3	5	0	53	0	58^1	54	6	15	46	2.3	7.1	60%	.281	1.22	2.78	3.64	0.8
2011	*MIL*	*MLB*	*29*	*5*	*4*	*0*	*56*	*7*	*116^1*	*129*	*15*	*42*	*70*	*3.3*	*5.5*	*51%*	*.306*	*1.48*	*4.93*	*5.36*	*-0.1*

Loe signed with the Brewers as organizational depth after spending an unsuccessful year in Japan, and the veteran swingman eventually rewarded his new employers with an eye-opening season in Milwaukee's pen. It was no surprise to see the dedicated sinkerballer generate more than his fair share of two-hoppers, but nobody expected all those punchouts. Loe's swinging-strike rate climbed to nearly 10 percent, by far a career high, as his two-seamer kept darting out of the zone, drawing weak swings, soft contact, and inning-long games of infield patty-cake. When veterans suddenly post a season of bullpen dominance, it's usually a fluke, but Loe's sinker seems to be a new pitch, and if he can keep his strikeout rate at its current level, he'll remain a terrific bullpen find.

Mike McClendon

Born: **4/3/1985** Age: **26**
Bats: R Throws: R Height: **6' 5"** Weight: **215**
Breakout: **1%** Improve: **5%** Collapse: **1%**
Attrition: **7%** MLB: **12%**

Comparables:
Doug Mathis, Greg Burke, Joe Martinez (80)

YEAR	TEAM	LVL	AGE	W	L	SV	G	GS	IP	H	HR	BB	SO	EqBB9	EqSO9	GB%	BABIP	WHIP	ERA	FRA	WARP
2008	BRV	A+	23	7	6	10	47	5	88	103	6	15	61	1.5	6.2	58%	.324	1.40	4.19	4.95	0.4
2009	HUN	AA	24	4	4	3	43	3	86	89	4	21	57	2.2	6.0	52%	.308	1.31	3.24	4.63	0.3
2010	NAS	AAA	25	4	3	2	25	3	55^1	53	1	14	44	2.3	7.2	53%	.319	1.27	2.44	3.06	1.5
2010	MIL	MLB	25	2	0	0	17	0	21	15	2	7	21	3.0	9.0	46%	.241	1.05	3.00	3.06	0.4
2011	*MIL*	*MLB*	*26*	*3*	*2*	*2*	*48*	*3*	*90^1*	*105*	*12*	*30*	*50*	*3.0*	*5.0*	*49%*	*.313*	*1.50*	*5.07*	*5.51*	*-0.4*

McClendon came out of nowhere to throw 21 solid innings in the Milwaukee pen, relying on an upper-80s sinker, slider, and changeup to keep hitters off-balance and induce ground balls. Like Loe, McClendon experienced a sudden increase in his strikeout rate; unlike Loe, he allowed too much contact for it to last. He'll get a long look this spring, but McClendon seems destined to bounce back and forth between the Milwaukee and Nashville bullpens for the next few years—not bad work if you can get it.

Chris Narveson

Born: **12/20/1981** Age: **29**
Bats: L Throws: L Height: **6' 3"** Weight: **205**
Breakout: **11%** Improve: **41%** Collapse: **14%**
Attrition: **15%** MLB: **74%**

Comparables:
Erik Hanson, Mark Gubicza, Chuck Finley (75)

YEAR	TEAM	LVL	AGE	W	L	SV	G	GS	IP	H	HR	BB	SO	EqBB9	EqSO9	GB%	BABIP	WHIP	ERA	FRA	WARP
2008	NAS	AAA	26	6	13	0	28	22	136	140	23	57	125	3.8	8.3	42%	.299	1.48	5.43	5.22	1.0
2009	NAS	AAA	27	4	4	5	26	6	75^1	59	3	26	76	3.1	9.1	51%	.271	1.14	3.71	4.19	1.0
2009	MIL	MLB	27	2	0	0	21	4	47	45	7	16	46	3.1	8.8	33%	.284	1.34	3.83	4.03	0.7
2010	MIL	MLB	28	12	9	0	37	28	167^2	172	21	59	137	3.2	7.4	41%	.301	1.41	4.99	5.01	1.0
2011	*MIL*	*MLB*	*29*	*6*	*6*	*0*	*33*	*15*	*115*	*119*	*17*	*47*	*94*	*3.6*	*7.4*	*43%*	*.302*	*1.44*	*4.74*	*5.16*	*0.9*

Not to be confused with Ned (The Head) Ryerson, Narveson must have felt as if he were living the same bad day over and over during his 10-year minor-league odyssey, but Milwaukee's pitching woes provided him with the chance he needed to break the cycle. He started the year in the pen, but was moved to the rotation in late April, where he won more than he lost and pitched better than his 4.99 ERA would indicate. Narveson pitches backward, using three off-speed pitches to set up his upper-80s fastball, changing eye levels and crossing his fingers that all the resulting fly balls stay in the yard—though part of his success this year stemmed from a higher ground-ball rate. Narveson looks to be a perfectly acceptable fifth starter, and while that's nothing special, it's surprising how hard it can be to find one when you really need one.

Jake Odorizzi

Born: **3/27/1990** Age: **21**
Bats: R Throws: R Height: **6' 2"** Weight: **175**
Breakout: **1%** Improve: **3%** Collapse: **0%**
Attrition: **2%** MLB: **3%**

Comparables:
Tex Clevenger, Bruce Kison, Ken Holtzman (82)

YEAR	TEAM	LVL	AGE	W	L	SV	G	GS	IP	H	HR	BB	SO	EqBB9	EqSO9	GB%	BABIP	WHIP	ERA	FRA	WARP
2008	BRR	Rk	18	1	2	0	11	4	20^{2}	18	2	9	19	3.9	8.3	44%	.258	1.35	3.48	5.10	0.3
2009	HEL	Rk	19	1	4	0	12	10	47	55	3	9	43	1.7	8.2	50%	.356	1.40	4.40	4.94	1.4
2010	WIS	A	20	7	3	1	23	20	120^{2}	99	7	40	135	3.0	10.1	46%	.293	1.23	3.43	4.02	2.5
2011	*MIL*	*MLB*	*21*	*3*	*5*	*0*	*14*	*10*	58^{1}	*63*	*8*	*30*	*43*	*4.7*	*6.7*	*44%*	*.308*	*1.61*	*5.51*	*5.99*	*0.3*

After two years of his careful tinkering in rookie ball, the Brewers finally unleashed Odorizzi on the Midwest League, and the impressive righty cut a wide swath. Armed with a boring low-90s fastball, Odorizzi used impressive command and an improving curveball to carve up Low-A hitters, striking out more than a man per inning and drawing praise from scouts for his athleticism and smooth, repeatable delivery. Odorizzi is one of the few Brewers prospects whose stuff, health, and effectiveness project him toward the front of a rotation, reason enough for the Royals to insist he be sent to Kansas City as part of the Zack Greinke trade.

Manny Parra

Born: **10/30/1982** Age: **28**
Bats: L Throws: L Height: **6' 3"** Weight: **200**
Breakout: **25%** Improve: **59%** Collapse: **14%**
Attrition: **9%** MLB: **92%**

Comparables:
Jorge De La Rosa, Erik Hanson, Sonny Siebert (76)

YEAR	TEAM	LVL	AGE	W	L	SV	G	GS	IP	H	HR	BB	SO	EqBB9	EqSO9	GB%	BABIP	WHIP	ERA	FRA	WARP
2008	MIL	MLB	25	10	8	0	32	29	166	181	18	75	147	4.1	8.0	53%	.327	1.55	4.39	4.18	3.0
2009	NAS	AAA	26	1	2	0	4	4	24^{2}	16	0	13	19	4.7	6.9	57%	.225	1.17	2.91	4.83	0.3
2009	MIL	MLB	26	11	11	0	27	27	140	179	19	77	116	5.0	7.5	51%	.349	1.84	6.36	5.69	0.2
2010	MIL	MLB	27	3	10	0	42	16	122	135	18	63	129	4.6	9.5	48%	.337	1.65	5.02	5.00	0.6
2011	*MIL*	*MLB*	*28*	*8*	*10*	*0*	*25*	*25*	*134*	*147*	*17*	*67*	*118*	*4.5*	*7.9*	*49%*	*.326*	*1.59*	*5.19*	*5.64*	*1.1*

Parra's frustrating career in Milwaukee's rotation supports the old saw that familiarity breeds contempt, and not just because fans and management alike have finally tired of his annual failures. In games he's started, Parra has held hitters to a .253/.340/.368 career line the first time they've seen him, and suffered a .313/.391/.498 shellacking thereafter. Following 16 more disastrous starts last year, the Brewers finally took the hint and moved him to the bullpen, where he provided 40 solid innings. The southpaw has always had terrific stuff and maintained a high strikeout rate, but walks have killed him; in relief, those free passes have started to disappear like so many bad memories. His future should be in the pen, and if his pitches continue to make their way across the plate, he could be a tremendous multi-inning weapon.

Amaury Rivas

Born: **12/20/1985** Age: **25**
Bats: R Throws: R Height: **6' 2"** Weight: **210**
Breakout: **1%** Improve: **1%** Collapse: **0%**
Attrition: **1%** MLB: **1%**

Comparables:
Jesus Delgado, Matt Chico, Jeremy Affeldt (83)

YEAR	TEAM	LVL	AGE	W	L	SV	G	GS	IP	H	HR	BB	SO	EqBB9	EqSO9	GB%	BABIP	WHIP	ERA	FRA	WARP
2008	WVA	A	22	8	3	0	19	15	90	83	11	32	70	3.2	7.0	48%	.269	1.31	3.50	4.91	0.6
2008	BRV	A+	22	1	2	0	7	6	30	35	2	11	20	3.3	6.0	42%	.340	1.53	4.20	4.37	0.5
2009	BRV	A+	23	13	7	0	26	23	133	109	11	43	123	2.9	8.3	53%	.267	1.17	2.98	4.31	1.6
2010	HUN	AA	24	11	6	0	25	25	141^{2}	130	7	55	114	3.5	7.3	52%	.304	1.36	3.37	3.92	2.9
2011	*MIL*	*MLB*	*25*	*5*	*7*	*0*	*17*	*17*	*88*	*97*	*13*	*44*	*56*	*4.5*	*5.7*	*47%*	*.301*	*1.60*	*5.43*	*5.91*	*0.6*

Rivas's high-minors debut was a success, as he moved up to Double-A and kept winning games and putting zeroes on the board, although his hit, walk, and strikeout rates moved in the wrong directions against more advanced hitters. Rivas gets good mileage out of his sinking fastball/changeup combination, but at age 25, he's already as good as he's going to get, which makes him middle-reliever material at best.

Mark Rogers

Born: **1/30/1986** Age: **25**
Bats: R Throws: R Height: **6' 3"** Weight: **220**
Breakout: **2%** Improve: **10%** Collapse: **11%**
Attrition: **8%** MLB: **27%**

Comparables:
Antonio Bastardo, Juan Morillo, Bud Norris (73)

YEAR	TEAM	LVL	AGE	W	L	SV	G	GS	IP	H	HR	BB	SO	EqBB9	EqSO9	GB%	BABIP	WHIP	ERA	FRA	WARP
2009	BRV	A+	23	1	3	0	23	22	64^{2}	46	2	29	67	4.0	9.3	55%	.275	1.19	1.67	3.21	2.1
2010	HUN	AA	24	6	8	0	24	24	111^{2}	86	3	69	111	5.6	9.0	56%	.276	1.45	3.71	5.16	1.0
2010	MIL	MLB	24	0	0	0	4	2	10	2	0	3	11	2.7	9.9	52%	.095	0.60	1.80	4.47	0.1
2011	*MIL*	*MLB*	*25*	*8*	*8*	*0*	*23*	*23*	*85*	*79*	*9*	*57*	*76*	*5.9*	*8.0*	*48%*	*.295*	*1.59*	*4.66*	*5.07*	*1.9*

Milwaukee's top pick in the 2004 draft, Rogers overcame two shoulder surgeries to work his way up to Miller Park last September and give Brewers fans a taste of his immense talent, but he still has work to do. He has the stuff to be a force in the rotation, with a moving fastball that sits comfortably in the mid-

90s, a knee-buckling power curve, and a usable changeup, but control and durability remain big issues. At times he struggles with his mechanics, throwing across his body and losing command, which leads to far more walks than a starting pitcher can survive. Just as importantly, he has yet to build up the stamina to work deep into games or assume a full starter's workload. The Brewers plan to continue building him up slowly, probably in Nashville, and he'll need to iron out his control issues, but after a long and sometimes painful wait, he's almost ready.

Cody Scarpetta

Born: **8/25/1988** Age: **22**
Bats: R Throws: R Height: **6' 3"** Weight: **240**
Breakout: **18%** Improve: **25%** Collapse: **7%**
Attrition: **15%** MLB: **34%**

Comparables:
Stan Williams, Brett Cecil, Carlos Carrasco (65)

YEAR	TEAM	LVL	AGE	W	L	SV	G	GS	IP	H	HR	BB	SO	EqBB9	EqSO9	GB%	BABIP	WHIP	ERA	FRA	WARP
2008	HEL	Rk	19	1	0	0	6	4	20^{2}	18	2	8	31	3.5	13.5	52%	.364	1.35	3.48	4.00	0.4
2009	WIS	A	20	4	11	0	26	20	105	83	5	55	116	4.7	9.9	48%	.292	1.40	3.26	4.45	1.2
2010	BRV	A+	21	7	12	0	27	27	128	120	4	67	142	4.7	10.0	42%	.331	1.55	3.87	3.83	2.5
2011	*MIL*	*MLB*	*22*	*6*	*7*	*0*	*21*	*17*	*85^{1}*	*85*	*10*	*57*	*76*	*6.1*	*8.0*	*43%*	*.309*	*1.67*	*5.30*	*5.76*	*0.7*

A beefy right-hander with low-90s velocity, a big 12-to-6 bender, and a name straight out of *Jeopardy*'s dreaded "Opera" category, Scarpetta has missed both bats and the strike zone in equal measure throughout his pro career. If he can cut down on the free passes, he may wind up with a career in the middle of Milwaukee's rotation; if he can't, he's bullpen-bound like the protagonist of Berlioz's *Faust*.

Carlos Villanueva

Born: **11/28/1983** Age: **27**
Bats: R Throws: R Height: **6' 2"** Weight: **190**
Breakout: **24%** Improve: **47%** Collapse: **25%**
Attrition: **13%** MLB: **87%**

Comparables:
Mike Henneman, Shaun Marcum, Rick Aguilera (77)

YEAR	TEAM	LVL	AGE	W	L	SV	G	GS	IP	H	HR	BB	SO	EqBB9	EqSO9	GB%	BABIP	WHIP	ERA	FRA	WARP
2008	MIL	MLB	24	4	7	1	47	9	108^{1}	112	18	30	93	2.5	7.7	49%	.294	1.34	4.07	4.29	1.4
2009	MIL	MLB	25	4	10	3	64	6	96	102	13	35	83	3.3	7.8	43%	.308	1.45	5.34	4.94	0.2
2010	MIL	MLB	26	2	0	1	50	0	52^{2}	48	7	22	67	3.8	11.4	36%	.313	1.41	4.61	4.62	0.1
2011	*TOR*	*MLB*	*27*	*6*	*3*	*2*	*80*	*5*	*116*	*113*	*18*	*42*	*102*	*3.3*	*7.9*	*44%*	*.292*	*1.33*	*4.31*	*4.68*	*0.7*

Villanueva's season was just plain freaky, featuring early dominance, a rapid decline, a demotion to Triple-A, and the odd spectacle of a career junkballer suddenly whiffing 11.5 batters per nine. Villanueva posted a terrific 2.95 SIERA, but it was his 4.61 ERA that caused the Brewers to lose confidence in him—understandably so, since SIERA doesn't appear anywhere on a major-league scoreboard. The Blue Jays acquired Villanueva in December for a player to be named later. He'll be in the mix for a bullpen job, and if he isn't eclipsed by younger, less subtle talents, there's every reason to expect that he'll do just fine.

Randy Wolf

Born: **8/22/1976** Age: **34**
Bats: L Throws: L Height: **6' 0"** Weight: **194**
Breakout: **17%** Improve: **42%** Collapse: **26%**
Attrition: **7%** MLB: **99%**

Comparables:
Jack Morris, Dave Stewart, Jim Palmer (70)

YEAR	TEAM	LVL	AGE	W	L	SV	G	GS	IP	H	HR	BB	SO	EqBB9	EqSO9	GB%	BABIP	WHIP	ERA	FRA	WARP
2008	HOU	MLB	31	6	2	0	12	12	70^{2}	68	7	24	57	3.1	7.3	41%	.292	1.36	3.57	4.52	1.0
2008	SDN	MLB	31	6	10	0	21	21	119^{2}	123	14	47	105	3.5	7.9	41%	.313	1.49	4.74	5.17	0.3
2009	LAN	MLB	32	11	7	0	34	34	214^{1}	178	24	58	160	2.4	6.7	41%	.251	1.13	3.23	4.14	2.8
2010	MIL	MLB	33	13	12	0	34	34	215^{2}	213	29	87	142	3.6	5.9	41%	.275	1.43	4.17	4.68	1.8
2011	*MIL*	*MLB*	*34*	*10*	*9*	*0*	*26*	*26*	*161*	*163*	*22*	*61*	*116*	*3.4*	*6.5*	*42%*	*.290*	*1.38*	*4.46*	*4.84*	*2.4*

Doug Melvin's most recent expensive rotation patch was disturbingly leaky throughout most of the summer, as Wolf owned a 5.07 ERA at the end of July before a late-season surge got his numbers into more comfortable territory. While Wolf stayed healthy, reached the 200-inning mark, and pitched better than any non-Gallardo Brewers starter has in several years, that's a lot of mediocrity for the money. His walk and strikeout rates reached their worst levels in years, he struggled against lefties, and his 4.80 SIERA doesn't bode well for the next three years of his contract. He's not about to pull a complete Suppan, but there's trouble ahead.

LINEOUTS

HITTERS

PLAYER	TEAM	LVL	AGE	PA	R	2B	3B	HR	RBI	BB	SO	SB-CS	AVG/OBP/SLG	TAv	BABIP	BRR	FRAA	WARP
SS L. Cruz	NAS	AAA	26	518	54	29	3	10	68	15	56	0-0	.281/.309/.414	.244	.295	3.8	SS 3, 3B 1	1.9
	MIL	MLB	26	17	2	0	1	0	1	0	2	0-0	.235/.235/.353	.188	.267	-0.2	SS -1	-0.1
OF K. Davis	WIS	A	22	555	86	26	4	22	72	77	120	17-10	.280/.398/.499	.313	.330	-2.9	LF 10	4.5
3B C. Dykstra	WIS	A	21	420	66	10	5	5	39	55	72	27-8	.312/.416/.411	.297	.375	2.3	3B -5, 1B 0	2.3
2B E. Farris	NAS	AAA	24	249	28	9	1	2	15	9	25	14-2	.274/.311/.348	.227	.292	0.0	2B 2	0.0
OF C. Gindl*	HUN	AA	21	534	61	33	1	9	60	55	78	10-5	.272/.352/.406	.281	.302	-2.1	RF -10, CF 2	1.2
OF B. Katin	NAS	AAA	27	393	65	19	1	26	76	39	91	1-0	.286/.382/.580	.313	.315	0.0	RF -7	2.1
CF E. Komatsu*	BRV	A+	22	573	90	31	6	5	63	68	61	28-9	.323/.413/.442	.323	.354	1.4	CF 0, RF 3	5.0
1B J. Koshansky*	NAS	AAA	28	502	67	21	0	26	79	62	152	3-2	.264/.370/.496	.286	.343	0.0	1B -1	1.7
C M. Maldonado	HUN	AA	23	123	9	6	0	2	12	9	24	0-2	.252/.347/.369	.229	.296	0.0	C 0	0.1
	NAS	AAA	23	201	19	9	0	7	26	14	45	0-1	.253/.309/.425	.251	.278	0.0	C 2	0.9
OF A. Salome	BRV	A+	24	272	28	18	0	6	40	23	45	0-1	.286/.349/.433	.295	.327	0.0	RF 1	1.3
CF A. Stern*	NAS	AAA	30	322	48	18	3	5	29	35	47	7-4	.325/.399/.462	.293	.374	3.2	LF -1, RF 0	2.1
	MIL	MLB	30	8	0	0	0	0	1	0	2	0-0	.000/.000/.000	-0.029	.000	0.0	CF 0, RF 0	-0.2

If you heard the name **Luis Cruz** but didn't know who he was, you might very well guess that he's an anonymous Triple-A shortstop with a sub-.300 OBP who will never hit enough to stick in the majors, and you'd be right. ⊘ Former Cal State Fullerton outfielder **Khris Davis** slugged his way through Low-A and won the Midwest League Home Run Derby, which is unassailably cool, but he'll need to show that he can pick on pitchers his own age before moving up the prospect charts. ⊘ Lenny's son, **Cutter Dykstra**, settled in at the hot corner and was a tough out for Midwest League pitchers, though he's unlikely to develop the power you'd prefer from a third baseman. ⊘ Second baseman **Eric Farris** was hurt much of the year, but put his speed and big-league glove on display in the AFL; he also hit .351, and if the Brewers can teach him to take the occasional walk, they may have something here. ⊘ Vertically challenged outfielder **Caleb Gindl** cut down on his strikeouts but lost his home-run pop in his first taste of Double-A, and with scouts down on his tools, he needs eye-popping numbers to stay on the organization's radar. ⊘ Slugger **Brendan Katin** posted a monster Triple-A season, but has long since been consigned to Quadruple-A purgatory, due to his status as an unathletic blob and a strikeout machine who doesn't adjust ever, even with two strikes. Still, he bleeping destroys left-handed pitching and could be the second coming of Shelley Duncan, for whatever that's worth. ⊘ **Erik Komatsu** comes at you with all-around baseball skills rarely seen in a Manatee, hitting for average with gap power, drawing walks, and playing a solid center field; he could be a nice fourth outfielder one day. ⊘ The Pronk of Triple-A, **Joe Koshansky**, with his patience and impressive raw power, might well provide dirt-cheap production to a team willing to overlook his terrifying strikeout rate. ⊘ **Martin Maldonado** was born with a birthmark on his left butt-cheek—a mark that seemed to resemble a smiling Steve Yeager—and the local shaman quickly pronounced that the gods had blessed his destiny as a backup backstop. Fortunately, he's very good at it, with terrific receiving skills, an excellent arm, and a soupçon of power. The gods being cruel, they withheld the ability to hit for any kind of average. ⊘ Former catcher **Angel Salome** suffered through his wife's difficult pregnancy and his own anxiety issues before asking to play the outfield; everyone should be allowed to follow his own bliss, but it's fair to say that Salome's prospect status was based on his ability to hit as a catcher, not just his ability to hit. ⊘ Doug Melvin and Gord Ash may collect fellow Canadians like pocket lint, but the managers don't give them special treatment, meaning that **Adam Stern**'s career year at Nashville isn't about to move him past Chris Dickerson in Milwaukee's fourth-outfielder picture.

PITCHERS

PLAYER	TEAM	LVL	AGE	W	L	SV	IP	H	HR	BB	SO	EqBB9	EqSO9	GB%	BABIP	WHIP	ERA	FRA	WARP
J. Butler	HUN	AA	25	3	5	0	53^1	56	5	26	36	4.4	6.1	50%	.305	1.64	4.56	4.85	0.6
	NAS	AAA	25	5	1	0	45^2	43	2	20	27	4.0	5.4	49%	.281	1.42	4.53	6.03	0.1
M. Estrada	NAS	AAA	26	1	2	0	40	30	1	11	33	2.5	7.4	42%	.257	1.02	3.15	3.88	0.9
	MIL	MLB	26	0	0	0	11^1	14	3	6	13	4.8	10.3	32%	.314	1.85	9.53	8.20	-0.4
B. Kintzler	HUN	AA	25	1	0	10	221	11	0	1	23	0.4	9.4	60%	.200	0.59	0.40	3.78	0.2
—	NAS	AAA	25	3	0	6	262	19	1	6	21	2.1	7.2	65%	.237	0.99	2.36	5.04	0.1
—	MIL	MLB	25	0	1	0	71	10	2	4	9	4.9	11.0	75%	.444	1.91	7.36	6.43	-0.1
D. Merklinger*	BRV	A+	24	7	6	1	133^2	124	9	41	142	2.8	9.6	46%	.320	1.26	3.64	3.69	2.6
J. Nelson	HEL	Rk	21	2	0	3	26^2	30	2	13	33	4.5	11.3	61%	.354	1.64	3.71	5.05	0.0
W. Peralta	BRV	A+	21	6	3	0	105	102	5	40	75	3.4	6.4	54%	.296	1.41	3.86	4.45	0.8
	HUN	AA	21	2	3	0	42^1	43	5	24	29	5.1	6.2	54%	.297	1.69	3.61	4.43	0.6
D. Riske	MIL	MLB	33	0	0	0	23^1	25	2	8	16	3.1	6.2	31%	.303	1.50	5.01	5.42	-0.2
C. Smith	NAS	AAA	29	4	3	26	48	47	7	21	62	3.9	11.6	48%	.342	1.42	3.56	4.09	0.6
	MIL	MLB	29	0	0	0	31	4	0	1	4	2.7	10.8	56%	.444	1.50	5.40	4.28	0.0
M. Stetter*	NAS	AAA	29	3	2	0	42	46	9	18	52	3.9	11.1	47%	.333	1.62	6.21	5.90	-0.3
	MIL	MLB	29	0	0	0	32	7	1	3	3	7.4	7.4	47%	.429	3.00	14.73	12.67	-0.3
T. Thornburg	HEL	Rk	21	1	0	1	23^1	15	2	11	38	4.3	14.8	48%	.295	1.21	1.93	1.27	4.4

Sinkerballer **Josh Butler** hurt his elbow last March, struggled to get outs in the minors after his return, and has been eclipsed by the more stuff-infused bullpen offerings of Axford, Braddock, and Jeffress. ⊘ After a solid 2009 in Milwaukee's pen, reliever **Mark DiFelice** sat out last year with shoulder problems; now that he's healthy again, the Brewers have invited him to camp to see if his cutter still knows how to ROOGY. ⊘ Former Nats farmhand **Marco Estrada** can torture minor leaguers with his assortment of off-speed junk, but the world's best hitters take him deep too often for him to stick. ⊘ Indie-league find **Brandon Kintzler** induces lots of awkward swings with his fastball/slider combination and has a shot to go north with the big club. ⊘ Former Seton Hall lefty **Dan Merklinger** doesn't have overwhelming stuff, with a fastball that tops out at 90 and a nice curve, but if he can tote his terrific walk and strikeout rates to the upper minors this year, he'll have a future. ⊘ Colossal right-hander **Jimmy Nelson** stampeded through the Pioneer League, leaving a trail of strikeout victims in the wake of his low-90s fastball and effective slider; the Brewers will have to sort out whether he's a starter or a reliever, but so far, there's plenty to like. ⊘ Scouts love **Wily Peralta**'s stuff, but his walk rate is still a concern, and his mid-90s heat and improving slider have yet to generate the strikeouts you'd like from a prospect. ⊘ **David Riske** returned from Tommy John surgery to toss a few dozen nondescript relief innings before earning his release, ending his Brewers tenure with a 5.40 ERA and 66 2/3 innings in the books, and $13 million in his pocket. Not that Riske is to blame—the Brewers didn't put a gun to his head, after all, and signing middle relievers to long-term deals is always, well, risky. ⊘ **Chris Smith** can still baffle the kids in Nashville, where he, his changeup, and his curve will spend the summer as bullpen insurance. ⊘ **Mitch Stetter** was sent down to Nashville last April when the Brewers decided to give Jeff Suppan one last futile spin through the rotation, and since then, the Brewers have moved on to Zach Braddock and Manny Parra as their bullpen lefties. Stetter remains a perfectly serviceable LOOGY, and if the Brewers don't find a use for him, someone else probably will. ⊘ Third-round pick **Tyler Thornburg** is short in stature but long on stuff, with a mid-90s fastball and power curve that wowed 'em in rookie ball; he's someone to watch.

MANAGER: KEN MACHA

YEAR	TEAM	W-L	Pythag +/-	Avg PC	100+ P	120+ P	QS	BQS	REL	REL w Zero R	IBB	Subs	PH	PH Avg	PH HR	SB2	CS2	SB3	CS3	SAC Att	SAC %	POS SAC	Squeeze	Swing	In Play
2009	MIL	80-82	2	93.8	65	2	61	3	512	334	60	47	258	.175	1	51	34	17	3	78	74.4%	15	0	133	100
2010	MIL	77-85	2	97.7	78	5	71	5	495	309	42	25	224	.269	4	70	21	11	3	65	53.8%	16	0	128	101

The Brewers didn't exactly fire Macha at season's end; they merely decided not to exercise the 2011 team option they had tacked onto his contract prior to the season. That may be cold comfort for Macha, who probably would have preferred that Milwaukee provide him with better pitching that winter rather than a semantically kinder way of being canned, but his inability to develop warm relationships with his players probably played as big a role as the Brewers' bad pitching in his eventual demise. To replace him, Milwaukee opted for Angels bench coach Ron Roenicke, hoping he can emulate the swift ascension of Joe Maddon and Bud Black from Mike Scioscia's staff to Manager of the Year award winners. Roenicke is thought of as a tremendous communicator and players' manager, which should be a breath of fresh air in what had become a stultifying Brewers clubhouse. He plans to bring a more aggressive style of play, and if that means more steals and extra bags taken by speedy players, all the better. If that means more sacrifice bunts and hit-and-runs in front of Milwaukee's slugging middle of the order, all the worse. In either case, Roenicke's success will depend on the pitching talent that Melvin can scare up at least as much as on any extra runs the new skipper can squeeze out on the basepaths, or hugs he can wrangle from Ryan Braun.

Minnesota Twins

For the first decade of the millennium, the Twins were the little team that could, the franchise that set an example to which all small-market and medium-market franchises aspired. Consistently competitive, they withstood the loss of superstars such as Johan Santana and Torii Hunter on the strength of strong player development and scouting departments, making regular visits to the postseason on limited budgets. They were the model of stability, preferring to promote from within when vacancies occurred in general managers' and other managers' offices. What's more, they Played the Game the Right Way and Did the Little Things.

Everything changed last season, though. The Twins left the quirkiness of indoor baseball at the Hubert H. Humphrey Metrodome, which had quietly seen its name changed to Mall of America Field just days before the Twins' victory over the Tigers in the epic 2009 American League Central tie-breaker, to play outdoors at beautiful and spacious Target Field.

TWINS PROSPECTUS

2010 W-L: 94-68, 1st in AL Central

Pythag	.571	6th
RS/G	4.8	6th
RA/G	4.1	22nd
TAv	.277	6th
BRR	0.4	15th
FRA	4.21	11th
DER	4.09	13th
DL	839	23rd
B-Age	28.4	10th
P-Age	28.5	20th
Salary	$97.6	10th
M$/MW	$1.93	9th

Ballpark: Target Field (1-yr. PF: 100). The inaugural season went without a hitch, though it wasn't easy on the home-run bats

2010: Minnesota spends like a big-market team, but still succumbs to the Yankees

2011: The improved Sox and Tigers aim to send the Twins to Lake Wobegon

Action Items: A healthy Morneau, securing a different playoff draw

Thanks to a spike in ticket sales and the number of luxury suites in their new facility, the Twins suddenly had money to burn. They spent a significant portion of the additional revenue on players, during both the 2009-2010 offseason and the 2010 season, eventually pushing the payroll to $101 million, a figure once unfathomable for a franchise that owner Carl Pohlad privately hoped would be contracted just 10 years earlier. No longer were the Twins lovable and overachieving underdogs; although they may have retained some fraction of their former reputation, they had a payroll that put them in the company of the game's big spenders.

With big money came big expectations, which the Twins kinda, sorta fulfilled by winning the AL Central handily with 94 victories and becoming the first major league team that year to clinch a post-season berth. However, big expectations quickly led to big disappointment in the playoffs when the Yankees—Minnesota's longtime nemesis—swept the Twins in the American League Division Series. Six months' worth of good work was undone in less than a week.

It was the fifth straight time that the Twins' postseason had ended in the first round at the hands of the Yankees. The difference this time was that Twins fans and the Minneapolis/St. Paul media did not shrug their shoulders and chalk the loss up to the local nine's inability to compete with the free-spending team from America's largest market. General manager Bill Smith took heat for failing to trade for an ace who might have helped the Twins overcome the Bombers. Despite taking the Twins to the postseason six times in his nine years as manager, Ron Gardenhire was criticized for running up a 2-12 career record in the postseason and carrying an embarrassing 16-45 lifetime record against the Yankees in the regular season.

As Stan Lee might have said, with great payroll comes great responsibility, but the Twins needn't fear their new powers. They may be in for gradual attendances decreases as the new-ballpark smell fades from Target Field, but as long as they keep selling out regularly, a $100-million payroll is within their grasp. Spending at that level will create expectations of a World Series title, something Twins fans haven't seen since 1991, a victorious campaign that preceded the eight straight losing seasons from 1993 to 2000 and that led to contraction talk.

Reaching the postseason six times in nine seasons is difficult for even well-heeled franchises. The Yankees (eight), Red Sox (six), and Angels (six) managed the same feat between 2002 and 2010, but with financial advantages heretofore unknown to the Twins. Maintaining Minnesota's sustained run of post-season appearances will be a challenge, but the Twins may prove up to the task. Besides increased revenue, they also enjoy the advantage of playing in the AL Central, where only the White Sox and Tigers are big spenders (though not to the extent of the Yankees or Red Sox), while the small-market Indians and Royals are forced to watch their dollars closely.

The Twins showed their willingness to open their wallet in hopes of staying competitive deep into this decade by allotting major money to their modern-day M&M duo of catcher Joe Mauer and first baseman Justin Morneau. The Twins allayed the worst fears of every living soul in the Upper Midwest when they signed Mauer to an eight-year, $184 million contract extension last February; the deal will take effect this season. It is safe to say that no player means more to his franchise than Mauer, as he is not only the best catcher in the game today, but also a local kid who grew up 15 minutes away from Target Field in St. Paul. Calling him the face of the franchise underestimates his importance to the Twins' organizational anatomy.

Mauer failed to match his 2009 MVP season, but he still accumulated a team-leading 50.5 VORP in 2010 to go with a .313 True Average and 5.2 WARP while being hampered for most of the season by knee soreness. Morneau was on his way to an even better year than his 2006 MVP season before July 7, when he suffered a concussion while trying to break up a double play. Morneau turns 30 next season and has three years and $42 million remaining on his six-year, $80 million contract. Though Denard Span doesn't belong in the superstar neighborhood inhabited by Mauer and Morneau, the center fielder also earned a long term-commitment from the Twins, agreeing to a five-year, $16.5 million pact last March. He rewarded them with a subpar offensive season, but finished first in the majors at his position, with eight Fielding Runs Above Average (FRAA).

While Minnesota has locked up three of the first four hitters in its batting order, it has not identified a flagship pitcher. At the end of 2010, the team had only one starter locked into a multiyear deal—right-hander Nick Blackburn—and he struggled badly enough last year to require a four-start Triple-A tune-up in late July. The only pitcher with the type of talent to assume the ace role is left-hander Francisco Liriano, who was slow to recover from the Tommy John surgery that interrupted his promising 2006 rookie campaign. The southpaw pitched a career-high 191 2/3 innings last season, led the AL by allowing just 0.4 home runs per nine innings, and topped the Twins with a .554 Support Neutral Winning Percentage that just edged out Carl Pavano's (.550). Liriano is just 27 and has the raw talent to match up with almost any pitcher. However, until he puts together at least one dominant full season, it's too soon to call him an ace, or for the Twins to feel comfortable committing ace-type cash for his services.

Target Field played big in its inaugural season; while the Twins hit 90 homers on the road, the Twins and their opponents combined to hit just 116 home runs in Minneapolis. At season's close, Morneau lobbied management to shorten the spacious power alleys that measure 377 to left-center, 411 feet to center field's left corner, 403 feet to center field's right corner, and 365 to right-center. Twins brass has no interest in changing the dimensions, even though Morneau hit just four of his 18 home runs at Target Field last season and Mauer went deep only once at home versus eight times on the road.

Despite the power outage, the Twins thrived at home, posting a 53-28 record and a plus-86 run differential and scoring 4.93 runs per game while allowing only 3.86. On the road, Minnesota mustered only a 41-40 record and a plus-24 run differential, averaging 4.72 runs per game while allowing 4.42. Although half of the 10 Twins hitters who earned at least 300 plate appearances had a better OPS in Minnesota, five of the six Minnesota pitchers who worked a minimum of 100 innings had a lower OPS allowed at home (Tables 1 and 2).

Table 1. Aim for the Target: Twins Batters' Home and Road OPS (min: 300 PAs)

Player	Home	Road
Denard Span	761	602
Michael Cuddyer	786	722
Delmon Young	809	841
Joe Mauer	812	923
Jason Kubel	746	753
Orlando Hudson	739	670
Justin Morneau	914	1205
Jim Thome	1112	958
Danny Valencia	979	658

Table 2. Pitching to the Ballpark: Twins Pitchers' Home and Road OPS Allowed (min: 100 IP)

Player	Home	Road
Carl Pavano	731	706
Francisco Liriano	641	706
Scott Baker	746	839
Nick Blackburn	836	843
Kevin Slowey	713	846
Brian Duensing	638	697

The large dimensions of their home park lessen the need for the Twins to develop or recruit strikeout pitchers, but increase their need for players who are more athletic. After last season, Gardenhire said that he would like to add speed to the lineup to enable his team to leg out more doubles and triples. Having concentrated more on multitool players in recent years in the draft and on the international free-agent market, the team now boasts one of the best crops of prospects in the lower minor leagues.

The Twins have built their success on scouting and player development and continue to emphasize those pursuits despite the increased payroll at the major-league level. The team has become one of the biggest players in the Dominican Republic, even signing a top talent, infielder Miguel Sano, in 2009. Some scouts feel that German outfielder Max Kepler, another Minnesota signee, could be the first European amateur to make a major impact in the major leagues.

However, even with more cash, the Twins say their focus will never be on signing big-name free agents at the major-league level (aside from attempting to retain their own), so even if the Twins can't beat the Yankees in October, they won't be joining them. Gardenhire admitted in the aftermath of last October's collapse that he had put a lot of thought into finding a way to get by the Yankees, but never secured a definitive answer. Though he is not a devotee of statistical analysis, Gardenhire should know that his post-season shortcomings can probably be chalked up to the inherent randomness of the playoff format. All the Twins can do is keep putting themselves in position to get back to the post-season and hope that the law of averages eventually allows them to live up to elevated expectations.

HITTERS

Joe Benson **OF**
Born: **3/5/1988** Age: **23**
Bats: **R** Throws: **R** Height: **6' 2"** Weight: **211**
Breakout: **5%** Improve: **24%** Collapse: **2%**
Attrition: **15%** MLB: **41%**
Comparables:
Adam Jones, Michael Saunders, Jordan Schafer (71)

YEAR	TEAM	LVL	AGE	PA	R	2B	3B	HR	RBI	BB	SO	SB	CS	AVG/OBP/SLG	TAv	BABIP	BRR	FRAA	WARP
2008	BLT	A	20	290	39	16	3	4	27	24	73	17	11	.248/.324/.382	.248	.324	-0.1	CF -2, RF -2	-0.1
2009	FTM	A+	21	327	46	10	3	5	29	46	74	14	7	.285/.410/.403	.304	.370	0.6	RF 3, CF -1	2.4
2010	FTM	A+	22	96	16	11	1	4	13	8	21	5	0	.294/.375/.588	.345	.350	0.7	CF -1, RF 0	1.1
2010	NBR	AA	22	423	65	20	7	23	49	39	115	14	9	.251/.336/.527	.306	.300	2.3	CF -2, RF 1	2.9
2011	*MIN*	*MLB*	*23*	*373*	*43*	*16*	*2*	*14*	*45*	*32*	*110*	*10*	*4*	*.226/.303/.414*	*.253*	*.287*	*-0.5*	*CF -6, RF -1*	*-0.2*

Benson is a five-tool talent who enjoyed a breakout season in 2010, finally turning his considerable skills into on-field production after concentrating on football in high school, where he was a Purdue running back recruit. His raw tools exceed those of anyone else in the system, including the more highly touted Aaron Hicks. Benson possesses plus-plus raw power, above-average speed, and an above-average arm. The tool that has lagged behind is the one that really counts, hitting. Benson takes a big cut, reaping the strikeouts attendant on that approach, and will never hit for a high average. Given his ability to play an excellent center field and hit home runs, it may not matter.

Drew Butera **C**
Born: **8/9/1983** Age: **27**
Bats: **R** Throws: **R** Height: **6' 1"** Weight: **205**
Breakout: **3%** Improve: **15%** Collapse: **8%**
Attrition: **17%** MLB: **31%**
Comparables:
Mike Rabelo, Gustavo Molina, Omir Santos (84)

YEAR	TEAM	LVL	AGE	PA	R	2B	3B	HR	RBI	BB	SO	SB	CS	AVG/OBP/SLG	TAv	BABIP	BRR	FRAA	WARP
2008	NBR	AA	24	351	39	18	1	7	39	35	55	0	1	.219/.305/.354	.236	.238	1.2	C 0, 1B 0	0.7
2009	ROC	AAA	25	333	23	16	1	2	25	22	49	0	1	.211/.261/.292	.203	.236	-1.1	C 1	-0.6
2010	MIN	MLB	26	155	11	6	1	2	13	4	25	0	0	.197/.232/.296	.190	.217	-0.1	C 0	-0.4
2011	*MIN*	*MLB*	*27*	*276*	*26*	*12*	*1*	*5*	*25*	*18*	*50*	*0*	*0*	*.216/.270/.328*	*.213*	*.242*	*0.0*	*C 0, 1B 0*	*-0.2*

Upon making his major-league debut with the Twins last April, Butera became part of the answer to a trivia question: "Along with his dad, Sal, this catcher was part of the only father-son duo to play for the Twins." Like his daddy, Drew is a good-field, no-hit catcher, emphasis on no-hit: Drew's bat is overexposed from the moment he parks his van in the player lot. Despite this, with the trade of Jose Morales to the Rockies, Butera is apparently set to become the primary caddy for Joe Mauer. Pray for health (not Butera's).

Alexi Casilla **MI**
Born: **7/20/1984** Age: **26**
Bats: **S** Throws: **R** Height: **5' 9"** Weight: **160**
Breakout: **3%** Improve: **36%** Collapse: **4%**
Attrition: **18%** MLB: **67%**
Comparables:
Don Blasingame, Jerry Remy, Jonathan Herrera (74)

YEAR	TEAM	LVL	AGE	PA	R	2B	3B	HR	RBI	BB	SO	SB	CS	AVG/OBP/SLG	TAv	BABIP	BRR	FRAA	WARP
2008	ROC	AAA	23	121	11	3	0	0	2	18	18	4	3	.219/.339/.250	.216	.253	0.0	SS -2, 2B -3	-0.6
2008	MIN	MLB	23	437	58	15	0	7	50	31	45	7	2	.281/.323/.374	.252	.287	-0.5	2B -10, SS 0	-0.3
2009	ROC	AAA	24	171	21	3	4	2	17	11	23	9	6	.340/.374/.449	.292	.378	-1.1	2B 1	0.9
2009	MIN	MLB	24	256	23	7	3	0	17	22	36	11	0	.202/.277/.259	.199	.236	1.7	2B -4, SS 0	-1.1
2010	MIN	MLB	25	170	21	7	4	1	20	13	17	6	1	.276/.324/.395	.260	.295	0.4	SS 3, 2B 1	0.8
2011	*MIN*	*MLB*	*26*	*467*	*50*	*15*	*3*	*6*	*41*	*38*	*63*	*18*	*6*	*.256/.316/.347*	*.240*	*.280*	*-0.1*	*2B -4, SS 0*	*-0.2*

Casilla reentered the good graces of Twins management last season after a 2009 in which he had not only been dreadful statistically, but angered his employers with a series of mental lapses and a general lack of hustle. He bounced back with a fine 2010 as a part-time player, convincing the Twins to pencil him in as their starting second baseman this season. Casilla will provide some of the speed with which Ron Gardenhire wants to furnish his lineup in order to take advantage of Target Field's dimensions. Orlando Hudson's rates were almost identical to Casilla's, so if the latter is consistent, the team won't be losing anything, but that's not the same as saying the Twins have solved their long-standing problem at the position.

Michael Cuddyer 1B

Born: 3/27/1979 Age: 32
Bats: R Throws: R Height: 6' 2" Weight: 202
Breakout: 0% Improve: 35% Collapse: 2%
Attrition: 8% MLB: 99%
Comparables:
Eric Byrnes, Bill White, Joe Torre (78)

YEAR	TEAM	LVL	AGE	PA	R	2B	3B	HR	RBI	BB	SO	SB	CS	AVG/OBP/SLG	TAv	BABIP	BRR	FRAA	WARP
2008	MIN	MLB	29	279	32	13	4	3	36	25	40	5	1	.249/.330/.370	.264	.286	1.5	RF -2, 1B -1	0.5
2009	MIN	MLB	30	650	93	34	7	32	94	54	118	6	1	.276/.342/.520	.299	.296	-1.4	RF -15, 1B -5	1.6
2010	MIN	MLB	31	675	93	37	5	14	81	58	93	7	3	.271/.336/.417	.272	.298	2.3	1B -9, RF -2	0.6
2011	*MIN*	*MLB*	*32*	*575*	*71*	*28*	*3*	*19*	*71*	*52*	*98*	*6*	*2*	*.263/.335/.438*	*.273*	*.290*	*0.0*	*RF -6, 1B -4*	*0.5*

Cuddyer's power numbers took a nosedive, but the decline couldn't be blamed on Target Field: he had a 786 OPS at home and a 722 mark on the road, while his 14 home runs were split evenly between locales. Cuddyer's power production has always been maddeningly inconsistent, but an additional factor in his free fall from a 32-homer 2009 was probably a right knee injury that bothered him throughout the season and required surgery in October. Cuddyer should be able to drive more balls this season, and his ability and willingness to play each of the infield bags and both corner outfield spots continues to make him a manager's delight.

Estarlin De Los Santos MI

Born: 1/20/1987 Age: 24
Bats: S Throws: R Height: 5' 10" Weight: 185
Breakout: 1% Improve: 5% Collapse: 2%
Attrition: 10% MLB: 16%
Comparables:
Dick Schofield, Luis Hernandez, Ramiro Pena (78)

YEAR	TEAM	LVL	AGE	PA	R	2B	3B	HR	RBI	BB	SO	SB	CS	AVG/OBP/SLG	TAv	BABIP	BRR	FRAA	WARP
2008	BLT	A	21	269	33	4	3	2	25	19	55	15	8	.242/.294/.309	.217	.289	2.4	SS 0, 2B -1	-0.2
2009	FTM	A+	22	284	33	11	7	1	23	13	49	11	4	.290/.324/.397	.279	.344	0.5	SS 2, 2B -2	1.6
2010	FTM	A+	23	262	25	11	3	0	23	22	55	13	2	.274/.340/.346	.261	.350	0.0	SS -5, 2B -7	-0.3
2010	NBR	AA	23	265	21	11	1	1	17	21	60	6	8	.177/.249/.245	.187	.227	0.0	SS 2, 2B -1	-0.9
2011	*MIN*	*MLB*	*24*	*361*	*32*	*13*	*2*	*3*	*29*	*19*	*89*	*9*	*4*	*.220/.260/.301*	*.200*	*.279*	*-0.4*	*SS 2, 2B -2*	*-1.0*

Double-A often separates the prospects from the pretenders, so it's easy to wonder about De Los Santos's future after he looked overmatched last season following a promotion to the Eastern League. He has a strong arm and the range to play shortstop, but he botches enough routine plays to foster some sentiment in the Twins organization in favor of moving him to second base or center field. Outrighted from the 40-man roster in November, De Los Santos will head back to New Britain for what is likely to be his make-or-break year.

Brian Dinkelman OF

Born: 11/10/1983 Age: 27
Bats: L Throws: R Height: 5' 11" Weight: 195
Breakout: 3% Improve: 8% Collapse: 4%
Attrition: 14% MLB: 23%
Comparables:
Brian Horwitz, Ben Francisco, Angel Chavez (75)

YEAR	TEAM	LVL	AGE	PA	R	2B	3B	HR	RBI	BB	SO	SB	CS	AVG/OBP/SLG	TAv	BABIP	BRR	FRAA	WARP
2008	FTM	A+	24	274	44	18	2	2	19	33	28	10	1	.293/.398/.414	.292	.325	3.6	2B -3, SS -1	1.5
2008	NBR	AA	24	216	26	14	2	2	21	10	24	2	2	.247/.296/.369	.224	.269	0.3	2B -4, SS 0	-0.6
2009	NBR	AA	25	542	62	38	2	8	65	55	73	5	6	.296/.376/.440	.302	.326	2.5	2B -3, LF 3	3.7
2010	ROC	AAA	26	592	58	32	2	8	54	52	99	9	4	.265/.336/.379	.252	.307	-0.4	LF -11, RF -1	-0.1
2011	*MIN*	*MLB*	*27*	*534*	*58*	*28*	*1*	*9*	*52*	*43*	*93*	*5*	*2*	*.247/.312/.367*	*.241*	*.281*	*-0.2*	*2B 0, LF -3*	*-0.3*

Dinkelman was the NAIA Player of the Year in 2006 at McKendree University in Illinois, but he hasn't been able to carry his outstanding college numbers into professional baseball. He began his pro career as a middle infielder, but stiff hands and below-average range forced a move to the outfield. Dinkelman doesn't have the power to be a major-league outfielder and lacks the versatility to make it as a utility infielder. Although he surely wouldn't wish ill unto others, his best hope for a taste of the majors is an injury stack on the big club.

J. J. Hardy SS

Born: 8/19/1982 Age: 28
Bats: R Throws: R Height: 6' 2" Weight: 181
Breakout: 3% Improve: 52% Collapse: 4%
Attrition: 11% MLB: 96%
Comparables:
Alan Trammell, Felipe Lopez, Buddy Bell (77)

YEAR	TEAM	LVL	AGE	PA	R	2B	3B	HR	RBI	BB	SO	SB	CS	AVG/OBP/SLG	TAv	BABIP	BRR	FRAA	WARP
2008	MIL	MLB	25	629	78	31	4	24	74	52	98	2	1	.283/.340/.478	.284	.302	-0.5	SS 8	4.6
2009	NAS	AAA	26	74	7	2	0	4	12	3	9	0	0	.254/.284/.451	.248	.241	-0.5	SS -2	0.0
2009	MIL	MLB	26	465	53	16	2	11	47	43	85	0	1	.230/.301/.358	.232	.259	0.8	SS 4	0.9
2010	MIN	MLB	27	375	44	19	3	6	38	28	54	1	1	.268/.317/.394	.264	.296	0.1	SS 2	1.7
2011	*BAL*	*MLB*	*28*	*466*	*55*	*21*	*2*	*14*	*55*	*40*	*70*	*2*	*1*	*.262/.323/.422*	*.262*	*.280*	*-0.1*	*SS 2*	*2.0*

Hardy has generally been considered a disappointment after failing to recapture the offensive mojo of his 2007 and 2008 seasons, in which he hit a combined 50 home runs. However, his glove is outstanding, and given the sorry state of shortstop offense around the league, even Hardy's bat remains a valuable commodity. At 28, he's still young enough to regain some of his lost power; much of his reduced pop last season could be traced back to a jammed wrist suffered on May 5, which never fully healed. The wrist prevented him from generating much loft in his swing, so he hit more ground balls than ever, finishing with a career-high 1.46 GB/FB ratio. Even so, he recovered sufficiently to hit .304/.363/.442 in the second half. Hardy still qualifies as an asset, if something short of the incipient star he appeared to be two years ago, and a winter of rest could help him regain his power stroke with the Orioles, for whom a December trade installed him as the starter.

Brendan Harris INF

Born: **8/26/1980** Age: **30**
Bats: R Throws: R Height: **6' 1"** Weight: **200**
Breakout: **1%** Improve: **47%** Collapse: **3%**
Attrition: **12%** MLB: **88%**

Comparables:
Puddin Head Jones, Don Money, Todd Zeile (85)

YEAR	TEAM	LVL	AGE	PA	R	2B	3B	HR	RBI	BB	SO	SB	CS	AVG/OBP/SLG	TAv	BABIP	BRR	FRAA	WARP
2008	MIN	MLB	27	490	57	29	3	7	49	39	98	1	1	.265/.322/.394	.256	.316	1.0	SS -2, 2B -1	0.7
2009	MIN	MLB	28	454	43	22	1	6	37	29	79	0	2	.260/.308/.361	.250	.303	1.1	SS 4, 3B -4	0.9
2010	ROC	AAA	29	258	31	14	1	4	29	14	41	1	0	.233/.292/.353	.216	.260	0.3	3B -3, SS -3	-1.0
2010	MIN	MLB	29	120	9	3	0	1	4	9	23	0	0	.157/.233/.213	.179	.188	1.1	3B 0, SS -3	-0.9
2011	*MIN*	*MLB*	*30*	*469*	*50*	*22*	*1*	*9*	*46*	*34*	*89*	*1*	*1*	*.246/.305/.368*	*.240*	*.284*	*-0.1*	*SS -3, 3B -3*	*-0.3*

Harris got off to an awful start in 2010 and, predictably for a player whose calling card is supposed to be his bat, spent most of the year in the minor leagues despite signing a two-year, $3.2 million contract before the season. His fate was sealed when rookie Danny Valencia put a hammerlock on the starting third baseman's job. Harris doesn't have enough power to be a regular at the hot corner, and his poor range makes him problematic in the middle infield. He graduated from the College of William & Mary with a degree in politics and aspirations of becoming a lobbyist; perhaps he successfully lobbied for his inclusion in the trade that sent J. J. Hardy to Baltimore, where Harris will attempt to fill the departed Ty Wigginton's utility shoes while residing just a short drive away from Washington.

Aaron Hicks OF

Born: **10/2/1989** Age: **21**
Bats: S Throws: R Height: **6' 2"** Weight: **185**
Breakout: **1%** Improve: **2%** Collapse: **0%**
Attrition: **5%** MLB: **5%**

Comparables:
Willie Mays, Fernando Martinez, Rick Manning (76)

YEAR	TEAM	LVL	AGE	PA	R	2B	3B	HR	RBI	BB	SO	SB	CS	AVG/OBP/SLG	TAv	BABIP	BRR	FRAA	WARP
2008	TWI	Rk	18	204	32	10	4	4	27	28	32	12	2	.318/.407/.491	.310	.364	2.0	CF 2, LF 0	2.1
2009	BLT	A	19	297	43	15	3	4	29	40	55	10	8	.251/.350/.382	.267	.299	0.4	CF 1	1.2
2010	BLT	A	20	518	85	27	6	8	49	88	112	12	9	.279/.398/.428	.310	.355	2.4	CF 5, RF 5	5.1
2011	*MIN*	*MLB*	*21*	*341*	*37*	*14*	*2*	*6*	*30*	*40*	*87*	*5*	*2*	*.232/.321/.353*	*.242*	*.299*	*-0.3*	*CF -8, RF 0*	*-0.5*

To this point in his career, Minnesota's first-round draft pick in 2008 has shown more tools than results. He's a long-limbed, rangy athlete with above-average raw power, above-average speed, good range in center, and an arm that was capable of throwing in the mid-90s when he pitched in high school. He hasn't hit as well as was expected, but the good news is that he has an approach that leads to plenty of walks. Ironically, his selectivity has often been his undoing, as he tends to fall behind in the count while waiting for the perfect pitch. Scouts still have faith that once he finds the fine line between patience and passivity, he could really take off.

Orlando Hudson 2B

Born: **12/12/1977** Age: **33**
Bats: S Throws: R Height: **6' 0"** Weight: **185**
Breakout: **1%** Improve: **44%** Collapse: **0%**
Attrition: **5%** MLB: **95%**

Comparables:
Roberto Alomar, Mark Ellis, Tadahito Iguchi (78)

YEAR	TEAM	LVL	AGE	PA	R	2B	3B	HR	RBI	BB	SO	SB	CS	AVG/OBP/SLG	TAv	BABIP	BRR	FRAA	WARP
2008	ARI	MLB	30	455	54	29	3	8	41	40	62	4	1	.305/.365/.450	.275	.338	0.6	2B 1	1.9
2009	LAN	MLB	31	631	75	35	6	9	62	62	99	8	1	.283/.352/.417	.272	.322	0.8	2B 6	2.9
2010	MIN	MLB	32	559	81	24	5	6	37	50	87	10	3	.268/.335/.372	.262	.308	2.1	2B 7	2.2
2011	*SDN*	*MLB*	*33*	*579*	*71*	*31*	*4*	*9*	*63*	*55*	*80*	*8*	*3*	*.284/.351/.415*	*.271*	*.313*	*0.0*	*2B 3*	*2.2*

Hudson had the worst offensive season of his nine-year career. He was hitting .284/.358/.402 through the end of August, but his bat took the rest of the year off as he was dealing with some nagging minor injuries. His hitting to that point was entirely consistent with what he's done in his career when he didn't have a friendly home park to take advantage of, so the September slowdown should not be a major point of concern. Petco Park, his new home, will have much more of an impact, as from the left side of the plate he won't be hitting any homers, and from the right side he won't be hitting any doubles. Be prepared for the professional groaners to say that the Padres bought into a player on the downward slope, but Hudson will be who he has been, a strong fielder whose hitting is just good, not great.

Luke Hughes **3B**
Born: **8/2/1984** Age: **26**
Bats: R Throws: R Height: **5' 11"** Weight: **205**
Breakout: **4%** Improve: **14%** Collapse: **2%**
Attrition: **15%** MLB: **34%**
Comparables:
Kevin Melillo, Brett Carroll, Kevin Mitchell (74)

YEAR	TEAM	LVL	AGE	PA	R	2B	3B	HR	RBI	BB	SO	SB	CS	AVG/OBP/SLG	TAv	BABIP	BRR	FRAA	WARP
2008	NBR	AA	23	319	53	15	3	15	40	28	70	4	1	.319/.382/.551	.321	.374	-2.0	3B -11, 2B 1	2.0
2008	ROC	AAA	23	117	17	7	1	3	21	7	30	2	0	.283/.325/.453	.268	.355	0.0	3B -5, 2B 0	0.0
2009	NBR	AA	24	229	22	15	3	6	36	19	38	1	1	.250/.319/.445	.277	.272	-1.7	3B -3, 2B 0	0.5
2009	ROC	AAA	24	157	19	8	2	6	28	18	38	2	0	.259/.344/.481	.292	.309	-2.3	3B 0	0.7
2010	ROC	AAA	25	81	12	8	0	1	7	5	18	2	0	.257/.313/.405	.242	.321	0.0	2B 0, 3B 0	0.0
2010	MIN	MLB	25	7	1	0	0	1	1	0	3	0	1	.286/.286/.714	.353	.333	0.0	3B 0	0.1
2011	*MIN*	*MLB*	*26*	*305*	*36*	*14*	*1*	*11*	*38*	*23*	*74*	*2*	*1*	*.250/.311/.429*	*.258*	*.297*	*0.0*	*3B -4, 2B 1*	*0.3*

Hughes became the fifth player in Twins history to homer in his first major-league at-bat last April 28. However, his 2010 season rapidly headed downhill from there, as he was sent back to Triple-A Rochester two days later and eventually required both hernia and groin surgery in June. The Australian has a chance to fashion a major-league career as a bench player, since he has some pop and can play second and third base as well as the outfield corners.

Jason Kubel **OF**
Born: **5/25/1982** Age: **29**
Bats: L Throws: R Height: **5' 11"** Weight: **200**
Breakout: **1%** Improve: **36%** Collapse: **0%**
Attrition: **12%** MLB: **97%**
Comparables:
Reggie Smith, Bobby Murcer, Jackie Jensen (78)

YEAR	TEAM	LVL	AGE	PA	R	2B	3B	HR	RBI	BB	SO	SB	CS	AVG/OBP/SLG	TAv	BABIP	BRR	FRAA	WARP
2008	MIN	MLB	26	517	76	22	5	20	78	47	91	0	1	.272/.335/.471	.285	.295	-0.9	RF 5, LF -2	2.1
2009	MIN	MLB	27	577	81	35	2	28	103	56	105	1	1	.300/.369/.540	.315	.327	-0.2	RF 1, LF 2	4.1
2010	MIN	MLB	28	582	71	23	3	21	92	56	116	0	1	.249/.323/.427	.272	.280	-0.5	RF -2, LF 0	1.1
2011	*MIN*	*MLB*	*29*	*502*	*64*	*23*	*2*	*21*	*67*	*48*	*96*	*1*	*1*	*.263/.335/.461*	*.276*	*.288*	*-0.1*	*RF 0, LF 0*	*1.4*

The Twins picked up Kubel's $5.1-million option to prevent him from becoming a free agent at the end of last season. That set up a pivotal 2011, since Kubel enjoyed a breakthrough season in 2009 but slid back in 2010. Because a severe knee injury cost him both the 2005 season and his speed, Kubel is one of the worst defensive outfielders in the majors and has to hit to be worth playing. Target Field sapped his power—he homered once every 21 at-bats on the road, not too far off his overall 2008-2009 rate, but managed only one every 31 at home. Kubel is also a career .236/.313/.352 hitter against lefties, so for their money, the Twins are getting an extremely limited package, a no-run, no-field, doesn't-fit-their-ballpark platoon player. His 2009 was probably a one-off affair, so we're deeply in Why Bother? territory.

Dustin Martin **OF**
Born: **4/4/1984** Age: **27**
Bats: L Throws: L Height: **6' 2"** Weight: **215**
Breakout: **1%** Improve: **19%** Collapse: **2%**
Attrition: **15%** MLB: **42%**
Comparables:
Will Venable, Bronson Sardinha, Daniel Ortmeier (75)

YEAR	TEAM	LVL	AGE	PA	R	2B	3B	HR	RBI	BB	SO	SB	CS	AVG/OBP/SLG	TAv	BABIP	BRR	FRAA	WARP
2008	NBR	AA	24	573	68	34	8	10	72	49	125	22	11	.290/.353/.447	.275	.359	-1.5	CF 2, LF 2	2.9
2009	ROC	AAA	25	470	58	16	5	5	53	39	92	26	8	.254/.319/.351	.253	.309	1.1	LF -4, CF -5	0.1
2010	ROC	AAA	26	537	70	24	7	11	67	52	138	12	7	.257/.329/.404	.250	.336	-5.7	RF -2, CF 5	0.1
2011	*MIN*	*MLB*	*27*	*520*	*55*	*21*	*3*	*10*	*50*	*42*	*133*	*15*	*6*	*.240/.302/.362*	*.236*	*.307*	*-0.6*	*CF -4, RF -1*	*-0.8*

We only critique players on their performances, not on their anatomical attributes, so please don't take it amiss when we say that Martin doesn't have a distinguishable tool. He hits for some power, can steal a base, and plays solid defense at all three outfield positions. That certainly doesn't make him a hot prospect, but it does at least gives him a chance to play in the major leagues as a placeholder—beats being a gym teacher every time.

Joe Mauer **C**
Born: **4/19/1983** Age: **28**
Bats: L Throws: R Height: **6' 5"** Weight: **220**
Breakout: **3%** Improve: **48%** Collapse: **3%**
Attrition: **11%** MLB: **98%**
Comparables:
Justin Morneau, Garrett Atkins, John Olerud (67)

YEAR	TEAM	LVL	AGE	PA	R	2B	3B	HR	RBI	BB	SO	SB	CS	AVG/OBP/SLG	TAv	BABIP	BRR	FRAA	WARP
2008	MIN	MLB	25	633	98	31	4	9	85	84	50	1	1	.328/.412/.452	.311	.342	2.7	C -2	6.0
2009	MIN	MLB	26	606	94	30	1	28	96	76	63	4	1	.365/.444/.587	.355	.373	0.9	C -3	7.8
2010	MIN	MLB	27	584	88	43	1	9	75	65	53	1	4	.328/.402/.469	.313	.348	3.9	C -2	5.2
2011	*MIN*	*MLB*	*28*	*585*	*84*	*31*	*1*	*17*	*75*	*72*	*58*	*3*	*2*	*.317/.402/.486*	*.310*	*.329*	*-0.3*	*C -2*	*4.6*

Mauer didn't repeat his fantastic 2009 last season, as his extraordinary (and completely out-of-character) .401 opposite-field ISO dropped to a still-impressive .224. Of course, his MVP campaign was one of the best ever by a catcher, so he will remain terrifically valuable even if he falls short of that lofty level. Indeed, in 2010 Mauer was the best backstop in the game and didn't seem beset by either complacency or pressure after signing an eight-year, $184 million contract extension in spring training that will go into effect this season. However, he did suffer from persistent knee pain and required surgery in the offseason. The injury could be a sign that a heavy workload has begun to take a toll on the big backstop; there have been only a handful of catchers of his stature and only one (Sandy Alomar Jr.) with a career of any length, so we don't know how the position will wear on him.

Jose Morales C

Born: **2/20/1983** Age: **28**
Bats: **S** Throws: **R** Height: **5' 11"** Weight: **190**
Breakout: **6%** Improve: **25%** Collapse: **11%**
Attrition: **26%** MLB: **49%**

Comparables:
J.R. House, Michael Aubrey, Vinny Rottino (75)

YEAR	TEAM	LVL	AGE	PA	R	2B	3B	HR	RBI	BB	SO	SB	CS	AVG/OBP/SLG	TAv	BABIP	BRR	FRAA	WARP
2008	ROC	AAA	25	208	18	8	1	4	15	8	28	0	1	.315/.346/.426	.256	.349	0.6	C 1	0.8
2009	ROC	AAA	26	242	30	13	1	2	26	28	27	1	3	.336/.413/.436	.292	.375	-0.2	C -1	1.5
2009	MIN	MLB	26	134	13	6	0	0	7	14	22	0	0	.311/.381/.361	.271	.378	-1.7	C 0	0.4
2010	ROC	AAA	27	295	30	19	1	3	25	34	63	0	0	.264/.350/.380	.254	.335	0.3	C -1	0.5
2010	MIN	MLB	27	44	3	2	0	0	7	6	14	0	0	.194/.296/.250	.196	.292	-0.4	C 0, 1B 0	-0.2
2011	*COL*	*MLB*	*28*	*331*	*35*	*15*	*0*	*2*	*25*	*32*	*60*	*1*	*0*	*.254/.325/.328*	*.235*	*.306*	*-0.1*	*C -1, 1B 0*	*0.1*

Morales hits line drives from both sides of the plate and is willing to take a walk, but his power is negligible. His subpar defensive contributions make him a less-than-ideal understudy for Joe Mauer, but he was the default choice after Wilson Ramos was dealt to the Nationals. Traded to the Rockies in December, he will get a chance to serve as Chris Iannetta's understudy, a great opportunity, given that Morales has little opportunity to surpass Mauer, whereas Iannetta's backups, *All About Eve* style, inevitably shove him to the sidelines by the final reel.

Justin Morneau 1B

Born: **5/15/1981** Age: **30**
Bats: **L** Throws: **R** Height: **6' 4"** Weight: **205**
Breakout: **3%** Improve: **41%** Collapse: **2%**
Attrition: **6%** MLB: **97%**

Comparables:
Mark Teixeira, Eddie Murray, Glenn Davis (74)

YEAR	TEAM	LVL	AGE	PA	R	2B	3B	HR	RBI	BB	SO	SB	CS	AVG/OBP/SLG	TAv	BABIP	BRR	FRAA	WARP
2008	MIN	MLB	27	712	97	47	4	23	129	76	85	0	1	.300/.374/.499	.310	.312	-2.1	1B -16	2.4
2009	MIN	MLB	28	590	85	31	1	30	100	72	86	0	0	.274/.363/.516	.308	.273	0.3	1B -3	3.1
2010	MIN	MLB	29	348	54	25	1	18	56	50	62	0	0	.345/.437/.618	.373	.385	-2.7	1B -2	3.7
2011	*MIN*	*MLB*	*30*	*596*	*84*	*32*	*1*	*28*	*88*	*69*	*90*	*1*	*0*	*.286/.370/.514*	*.304*	*.295*	*-0.1*	*1B -4*	*2.6*

Morneau was in the midst of the best season of his career when he suffered a concussion on July 7 while breaking up a double play. He never returned to action. That Morneau hadn't made any significant progress in his recovery by season's end was unnerving, especially with memories of Corey Koskie still fresh, but doctors insist that a winter of rest will have him ready for Opening Day. The Twins have somehow weathered his absences well; in 2009, they overcame a seven-game deficit to edge out the Tigers for the AL Central title while Morneau sat out September with a strained back. Morneau didn't deserve the MVP award he won in 2006—he wasn't one of the top 20 position players in the AL as ranked by WARP—but he was well on his way to a more legitimate shot at the award before he was struck down. One of the big stories of early 2011 will be if he can pick up where he left off, assuming the docs are right and he can pick up at all. Here's hoping.

Tsuyoshi Nishioka INF

Born: **7/27/1984** Age: **26**
Bats: **S** Throws: **R** Height: **5' 11"** Weight: **165**
Breakout: **-%** Improve: **-%** Collapse: **-%**
Attrition: **-%** MLB: **-%**

Comparables:

YEAR	TEAM	LVL	AGE	PA	R	2B	3B	HR	RBI	BB	SO	SB	CS	AVG/OBP/SLG	TAv	BABIP	BRR	FRAA	WARP
2011	*MIN*	*MLB*	*26*	–	–	–	–	–	–	–	–	–	–	–	–	–	–	–	–

The Twins flashed their newfound financial muscle by winning the posting battle for Japanese middle-infielder Nishioka, but it may prove to have been a Pyrrhic victory. Nishioka won the Pacific League batting title in 2010 and has three Nippon Pro Baseball gold gloves to his name, but he's coming off an anomalous career year, has little power to speak of, and runs into too many outs on the bases. He heads stateside with worse stats and scouting reports than Kaz Matsui, which doesn't inspire confidence.

Trevor Plouffe SS

Born: **6/15/1986** Age: **25**
Bats: **R** Throws: **R** Height: **6' 2"** Weight: **200**
Breakout: **5%** Improve: **18%** Collapse: **10%**
Attrition: **24%** MLB: **40%**

Comparables:
Will Venable, Ian Desmond, Adam Rosales (79)

YEAR	TEAM	LVL	AGE	PA	R	2B	3B	HR	RBI	BB	SO	SB	CS	AVG/OBP/SLG	TAv	BABIP	BRR	FRAA	WARP
2008	NBR	AA	22	249	32	17	3	3	21	16	43	4	2	.269/.321/.410	.267	.315	1.4	SS -6, 3B -1	0.5
2008	ROC	AAA	22	272	34	17	3	6	39	14	47	1	1	.256/.287/.420	.253	.283	0.1	3B 2, 2B 0	1.0
2009	ROC	AAA	23	477	53	23	5	10	60	34	68	3	6	.260/.310/.407	.252	.281	-0.4	SS 3	1.6
2010	ROC	AAA	24	445	53	22	4	15	49	27	90	5	5	.244/.300/.430	.248	.270	0.0	SS -12, 3B 0	0.0
2010	MIN	MLB	24	44	3	1	0	2	6	0	14	0	0	.146/.136/.317	.154	.143	0.4	SS 0, 2B 0	-0.3
2011	*MIN*	*MLB*	*25*	*489*	*52*	*22*	*2*	*13*	*56*	*28*	*100*	*4*	*2*	*.239/.283/.391*	*.237*	*.271*	*-0.3*	*SS -5, 3B 0*	*0.0*

Plouffe has developed some home-run pop since reaching Triple-A in 2009, but his ceiling is no higher than that of a utility infielder, because he doesn't get on base consistently enough to play on an everyday basis. Thanks to good instincts and positioning, his strong arm enables him to play third base and handle shortstop despite below-average range. Plouffe isn't going to live up to the hype that came with his first-round selection in 2004, but he should be able to fashion some sort of major-league career.

Nick Punto INF

Born: 11/8/1977 Age: 33
Bats: S Throws: R Height: 5' 9" Weight: 170
Breakout: 0% Improve: 36% Collapse: 8%
Attrition: 20% MLB: 87%

Comparables:
Spike Owen, Hector Rodriguez, Len Randle (78)

YEAR	TEAM	LVL	AGE	PA	R	2B	3B	HR	RBI	BB	SO	SB	CS	AVG/OBP/SLG	TAv	BABIP	BRR	FRAA	WARP
2008	MIN	MLB	30	378	42	19	4	2	28	32	58	15	6	.283/.339/.381	.258	.329	-0.7	SS 7, 2B 4	2.2
2009	MIN	MLB	31	440	54	15	1	1	38	61	70	16	3	.228/.327/.284	.227	.264	5.1	2B -5, SS -1	-0.1
2010	MIN	MLB	32	288	23	11	1	1	20	28	50	6	2	.238/.309/.302	.239	.284	-0.6	3B 6, SS -2	0.8
2011	*MIN*	*MLB*	*33*	*436*	*45*	*16*	*2*	*4*	*33*	*47*	*74*	*13*	*4*	*.238/.315/.322*	*.230*	*.274*	*-0.1*	*SS 0, 2B 0*	*0.2*

The ballpark-aided revenue boost that helped the Twins bring in outside help also enabled them to absorb spending $4 million on Punto and seeing little return; sidelined by a hamstring injury, he made just 23 plate appearances after July. Punto is a wonderful guy, a scrappy player who provides flexibility by playing good defense at second and third base as well as shortstop. Still, his modest virtues weren't enough to cause the Twins to make the mistake of overpaying him again, as they declined his $5 million option. The Cardinals signed him to a one-year deal, a good match of player and team needs given their weak infield gloves.

Jason Repko RF

Born: 12/27/1980 Age: 30
Bats: R Throws: R Height: 5' 11" Weight: 175
Breakout: 2% Improve: 32% Collapse: 8%
Attrition: 20% MLB: 87%

Comparables:
Tommy Murphy, Tony Gonzalez, Tim Raines (74)

YEAR	TEAM	LVL	AGE	PA	R	2B	3B	HR	RBI	BB	SO	SB	CS	AVG/OBP/SLG	TAv	BABIP	BRR	FRAA	WARP
2008	LVG	AAA	27	535	89	26	7	12	50	50	108	20	6	.283/.370/.449	.275	.340	5.2	RF 11, CF 1	3.5
2008	LAN	MLB	27	20	0	1	0	0	0	2	9	1	0	.167/.250/.222	.193	.333	0.1	LF 1, RF 0	0.1
2009	ABQ	AAA	28	433	70	20	4	16	47	28	81	24	7	.277/.328/.471	.257	.307	4.1	CF 0, RF 5	1.7
2009	LAN	MLB	28	7	0	0	0	0	1	0	2	1	0	.000/.143/.000	.089	.000	0.5	CF 0, RF 0	-0.1
2010	ROC	AAA	29	263	38	8	2	6	28	30	49	10	3	.281/.368/.412	.271	.330	2.6	CF -4, RF 0	1.0
2010	MIN	MLB	29	146	17	6	0	3	9	13	38	3	2	.228/.322/.347	.255	.299	0.9	RF 5, CF 2	1.0
2011	*MIN*	*MLB*	*30*	*389*	*44*	*14*	*2*	*11*	*41*	*33*	*90*	*12*	*4*	*.242/.316/.390*	*.251*	*.289*	*-0.1*	*CF -1, RF 4*	*0.7*

Repko might win (or at least merit) a Gold Glove if he had the chance to play every day, as his outstanding speed allows him to chase down fly balls from gap to gap and turn in Web Gem–type plays. However, even the greatest of defensive players needs to have at least some success at the plate to earn regular appearances, and Repko gets overpowered by fastballs and hard sliders. On a team with the roster space, he'd be a handy guy to have around to serve as a pinch-runner and late-inning caddy for a poor defensive outfielder, but teams that meet that description are hard to come by in the era of the overcrowded bullpen.

Ben Revere OF

Born: 5/3/1988 Age: 23
Bats: L Throws: R Height: 5' 9" Weight: 175
Breakout: 2% Improve: 14% Collapse: 0%
Attrition: 6% MLB: 26%

Comparables:
Erick Aybar, Jacoby Ellsbury, Richie Ashburn (72)

YEAR	TEAM	LVL	AGE	PA	R	2B	3B	HR	RBI	BB	SO	SB	CS	AVG/OBP/SLG	TAv	BABIP	BRR	FRAA	WARP
2008	BLT	A	20	374	51	17	10	1	43	27	31	44	13	.379/.430/.497	.340	.413	4.7	CF 5, LF -1	4.8
2009	FTM	A+	21	517	75	13	4	2	48	40	34	45	17	.311/.371/.369	.279	.329	5.5	CF 6, LF 2	3.5
2010	NBR	AA	22	406	44	10	4	1	23	32	41	36	13	.305/.371/.363	.279	.336	2.0	CF 3, LF 0	2.3
2010	MIN	MLB	22	30	0	0	0	0	2	2	5	0	1	.179/.233/.179	.148	.217	0.0	CF -1, RF 0	-0.3
2011	*MIN*	*MLB*	*23*	*440*	*48*	*14*	*3*	*4*	*39*	*26*	*56*	*29*	*9*	*.277/.323/.353*	*.244*	*.307*	*0.1*	*CF -4, LF 0*	*0.0*

The Twins raised quite a few eyebrows when they selected Revere in the first round of the 2007 draft, but the pint-sized outfielder made it to the major leagues three years later as a 22-year-old. Revere has a chance to be a dynamic leadoff hitter, as he consistently puts the bat on the ball and has enough power to reach the gaps. However, he could use more time in the minor leagues to improve his walk rate and stolen-base percentage. He should get that opportunity to begin this season, as the Twins are deep in outfielders at the major-league level. Revere doesn't have the home-run power associated with a corner outfielder, so he faces a serious obstacle in the person of Denard Span, who is signed to play center through 2014.

Denard Span CF

Born: 2/27/1984 Age: 27
Bats: L Throws: L Height: 6' 0" Weight: 205
Breakout: 1% Improve: 50% Collapse: 6%
Attrition: 17% MLB: 91%

Comparables:
Jacoby Ellsbury, Carl Crawford, Jim Fregosi (63)

YEAR	TEAM	LVL	AGE	PA	R	2B	3B	HR	RBI	BB	SO	SB	CS	AVG/OBP/SLG	TAv	BABIP	BRR	FRAA	WARP
2008	ROC	AAA	24	184	31	11	1	3	14	26	36	15	8	.340/.429/.481	.312	.420	0.8	CF -4, RF -1	1.1
2008	MIN	MLB	24	411	70	16	7	6	47	50	60	18	7	.294/.380/.432	.297	.330	3.7	RF 9, CF -2	3.2
2009	MIN	MLB	25	676	97	16	10	8	68	70	89	23	10	.311/.385/.415	.289	.345	1.4	CF 0, LF 6	4.1
2010	MIN	MLB	26	705	85	24	10	3	58	60	74	26	4	.264/.326/.348	.251	.289	2.6	CF 8	2.2
2011	*MIN*	*MLB*	*27*	*661*	*80*	*24*	*5*	*11*	*68*	*68*	*88*	*25*	*9*	*.281/.354/.402*	*.269*	*.303*	*-0.4*	*CF 1, RF 1*	*2.4*

Span reached base at a combined .390 clip in 2008 and 2009, sparking the offense from the leadoff slot while also playing outstanding defense. Those contributions prompted the Twins to sign Span to a five-year, $16.5-million contract prior to 2010, and he proceeded to turn in a disappointing year. He became just slightly less selective, and that might have been a sign of lessened concentration: his OBP dropped by 61 points and he developed an alarming habit of getting picked off first base. What remained was solid glove work in center field. It's reasonable to expect an offensive bounce-back as he enters his age-27 season.

Jim Thome **DH**
Born: **8/27/1970** Age: **40**
Bats: L Throws: R Height: **6' 4"** Weight: **220**
Breakout: **1%** Improve: **19%** Collapse: **6%**
Attrition: **17%** MLB: **75%**
Comparables:
Frank Thomas, Jason Giambi, Ted Williams (53)

YEAR	TEAM	LVL	AGE	PA	R	2B	3B	HR	RBI	BB	SO	SB	CS	AVG/OBP/SLG	TAv	BABIP	BRR	FRAA	WARP
2008	CHA	MLB	37	602	94	28	0	34	90	91	147	1	0	.245/.362/.503	.296	.273	1.3	—	2.8
2009	CHA	MLB	38	417	58	15	0	23	74	69	116	0	0	.249/.372/.493	.304	.301	-7.0	—	1.5
2009	LAN	MLB	38	17	0	0	0	0	3	0	7	0	0	.235/.235/.235	.198	.400	0.0	—	—
2010	MIN	MLB	39	340	58	16	2	25	59	60	82	0	0	.283/.412/.627	.362	.310	-3.1	—	3.4
2011	*MIN*	*MLB*	*40*	*508*	*71*	*8*	*0*	*30*	*73*	*82*	*134*	*0*	*0*	*.244/.368/.501*	*.297*	*.279*	*0.0*	*—*	*-2.2*

For a 40-year-old who appeared to be in decline and was signed primarily to serve as a pinch-hitter and occasional DH, Thome had a remarkable 2010. When first baseman Justin Morneau suffered a season-ending concussion on July 7, the ensuing lineup shuffle granted Thome more plate appearances than expected. He responded with one of the greatest performances of his distinguished career, launching 25 home runs in just 340 plate appearances, becoming just the fourth player 39 or older (after Barry Bonds, Ted Williams, and Hank Aaron) to slug .600 or higher. It would be asking the impossible to expect more of the same from Thome this season, but it's clear that he still has some thunder left in his lumber.

Matt Tolbert **INF**
Born: **5/4/1982** Age: **29**
Bats: S Throws: R Height: **6' 0"** Weight: **185**
Breakout: **3%** Improve: **35%** Collapse: **7%**
Attrition: **15%** MLB: **75%**
Comparables:
Luis Rivas, Joe Inglett, Clint Barmes (79)

YEAR	TEAM	LVL	AGE	PA	R	2B	3B	HR	RBI	BB	SO	SB	CS	AVG/OBP/SLG	TAv	BABIP	BRR	FRAA	WARP
2008	NBR	AA	26	57	6	3	0	0	6	1	6	3	3	.250/.263/.304	.207	.280	-0.4	SS 0, 2B 0	-0.1
2008	MIN	MLB	26	123	18	6	3	0	6	7	19	7	1	.283/.317/.389	.247	.330	2.2	3B 1, SS 1	0.7
2009	ROC	AAA	27	251	35	11	6	3	22	14	32	7	4	.288/.331/.424	.261	.323	-0.5	2B -2, LF 2	0.4
2009	MIN	MLB	27	231	24	7	1	2	19	21	37	6	2	.232/.290/.308	.225	.257	1.2	2B 7, 3B 2	0.7
2010	ROC	AAA	28	188	19	9	3	1	11	13	30	6	1	.283/.332/.387	.244	.333	1.7	2B -2, SS 2	0.3
2010	MIN	MLB	28	100	7	4	3	1	18	9	18	1	1	.230/.290/.379	.244	.264	-0.5	2B 1, 3B 2	0.3
2011	*MIN*	*MLB*	*29*	*319*	*34*	*14*	*2*	*4*	*30*	*23*	*55*	*9*	*3*	*.249/.301/.357*	*.233*	*.286*	*-0.3*	*2B 0, 3B 1*	*0.1*

Versatility is Tolbert's calling card. He can play all four infield positions and both outfield corners and can serve as an emergency third catcher. He also plays with an excess of energy, prompting Twins manager Ron Gardenhire to nickname him "The Hummingbird." However, Tolbert's value begins and ends with his defense, since he's not much of a hitter and struggles mightily against big-league breaking pitches. He risks being overexposed if utilized in anything more than a bench role.

Danny Valencia **3B**
Born: **9/19/1984** Age: **26**
Bats: R Throws: R Height: **6' 2"** Weight: **210**
Breakout: **3%** Improve: **23%** Collapse: **13%**
Attrition: **23%** MLB: **50%**
Comparables:
James D'Antona, Jeff Baisley, Puddin Head Jones (80)

YEAR	TEAM	LVL	AGE	PA	R	2B	3B	HR	RBI	BB	SO	SB	CS	AVG/OBP/SLG	TAv	BABIP	BRR	FRAA	WARP
2008	FTM	A+	23	251	35	19	3	5	44	27	43	2	2	.336/.402/.518	.322	.392	-0.2	3B 5, SS 1	2.8
2008	NBR	AA	23	287	40	18	2	10	32	18	70	2	1	.289/.334/.485	.282	.356	1.2	3B 3, 1B -1	1.8
2009	NBR	AA	24	252	44	14	4	7	29	31	40	0	2	.284/.373/.482	.308	.318	0.6	3B -2	1.8
2009	ROC	AAA	24	282	35	24	0	7	41	8	37	0	2	.286/.305/.454	.266	.306	0.4	3B -2	0.8
2010	ROC	AAA	25	202	22	15	0	0	24	14	34	2	0	.292/.347/.373	.250	.355	-0.1	3B -2	0.2
2010	MIN	MLB	25	322	31	18	1	7	40	20	46	2	0	.311/.351/.448	.278	.345	-2.9	3B 4	1.6
2011	*MIN*	*MLB*	*26*	*528*	*63*	*29*	*1*	*13*	*63*	*34*	*100*	*1*	*1*	*.273/.321/.421*	*.260*	*.314*	*-0.1*	*3B 0, 1B 0*	*1.4*

Heading into last season, the Twins' hot corner had been home to nothing but cold lumber since 2006, but Valencia more than held his own as the starting third baseman in his 2010 rookie campaign, playing a significant role in the Twins' divisional victory. The Twinkies' lineup improved immensely when he replaced the offensively challenged Nick Punto at the position, and while the 2006 draftee doesn't project to be a huge home-run hitter, he does possess good gap power and decent plate discipline. He hammers fastballs and got better against breaking pitches as the season wore on. Valencia's range is a tick below average, but he figures to stick at third base because of his strong arm and soft hands. Valencia may not be a perennial all-star, but he should be a major upgrade over the government-surplus cheese the Twins were pushing out there before his arrival.

Delmon Young **LF**
Born: **9/14/1985** Age: **25**
Bats: R Throws: R Height: **6' 3"** Weight: **205**
Breakout: **3%** Improve: **42%** Collapse: **7%**
Attrition: **15%** MLB: **78%**
Comparables:
Adam Lind, Ryan Zimmerman, Jeff Francoeur (72)

YEAR	TEAM	LVL	AGE	PA	R	2B	3B	HR	RBI	BB	SO	SB	CS	AVG/OBP/SLG	TAv	BABIP	BRR	FRAA	WARP
2008	MIN	MLB	22	623	81	28	4	10	69	35	105	14	5	.290/.336/.405	.265	.337	2.1	LF -10	0.7
2009	MIN	MLB	23	416	52	16	2	12	60	12	92	2	5	.284/.308/.425	.252	.338	-1.8	LF -4	-0.2
2010	MIN	MLB	24	613	79	46	1	21	112	28	81	5	4	.298/.333/.493	.299	.312	-2.7	LF -12	2.0
2011	*MIN*	*MLB*	*25*	*566*	*69*	*30*	*1*	*17*	*72*	*26*	*98*	*8*	*4*	*.283/.320/.441*	*.267*	*.315*	*-0.6*	*LF -7*	*0.6*

It seems as though Young should have celebrated his 30th birthday by now, but he didn't turn 25 until the last month of his breakout 2010 season. There were many things to like about Young's year, including an improvement in his power numbers and a reduced strikeout rate. Target Field cut into his power numbers; given his 15 home runs on the road, he might have hit 30 dingers this year had he played in a more forgiving park. However, Young remains a free swinger and an atrocious outfielder whose lack of selectivity means that his value will always be driven by batting average. So while the 2007 Rookie-of-the-Year runner-up may have belatedly left the replacement level behind, it would be premature to christen him a star.

PITCHERS

Scott Baker

Born: **9/19/1981** Age: **29**
Bats: R Throws: R Height: **6' 4"** Weight: **221**
Breakout: **11%** Improve: **38%** Collapse: **22%**
Attrition: **1%** MLB: **93%**
Comparables:
Dave Bush, Gaylord Perry, James Shields (61)

YEAR	TEAM	LVL	AGE	W	L	SV	G	GS	IP	H	HR	BB	SO	EqBB9	EqSO9	GB%	BABIP	WHIP	ERA	FRA	WARP
2008	MIN	MLB	26	11	4	0	28	28	172^{1}	161	20	42	141	2.2	7.4	33%	.284	1.20	3.45	3.26	4.8
2009	MIN	MLB	27	15	9	0	33	33	200	190	28	48	162	2.2	7.3	35%	.277	1.21	4.37	4.6	3.5
2010	MIN	MLB	28	12	9	0	29	29	170^{1}	186	23	43	148	2.3	7.8	37%	.323	1.38	4.49	4.15	2.5
2011	*MIN*	*MLB*	*29*	*12*	*9*	*0*	*30*	*30*	182^{2}	*188*	*20*	*46*	*139*	*2.3*	*6.9*	*38%*	*.306*	*1.28*	*3.88*	*4.22*	*3.6*

The move from the Metrodome to Target Field benefited Baker as much as any Twins pitcher, since he was no longer hurt nearly as much by his habit of occasionally leaving a fastball up and out over the middle of the plate; balls that might have been punished in the Metrodome died in the new park's expansive gaps. His ERA at home was more than a run lower than on the road, in large part due to a home-run rate that was about half what it was in foreign stadia. Baker was bothered last season by elbow tendinitis that required two cortisone shots, and although his fastball maintained its 91-mph average velocity, the pitch did not have the same bite. Fortunately, his curveball has become a weapon as he has matured and experimented with throwing it harder. Arthroscopic elbow surgery on his right elbow will, perhaps, restore the big express to its place in his arsenal.

Nick Blackburn

Born: **2/24/1982** Age: **29**
Bats: R Throws: R Height: **6' 4"** Weight: **250**
Breakout: **8%** Improve: **30%** Collapse: **10%**
Attrition: **5%** MLB: **63%**
Comparables:
Paul Maholm, Joe Blanton, Frank Sullivan (55)

YEAR	TEAM	LVL	AGE	W	L	SV	G	GS	IP	H	HR	BB	SO	EqBB9	EqSO9	GB%	BABIP	WHIP	ERA	FRA	WARP
2008	MIN	MLB	26	11	11	0	33	33	193^{1}	224	23	39	96	1.8	4.5	46%	.306	1.40	4.05	4.76	2.2
2009	MIN	MLB	27	11	11	0	33	33	205^{2}	240	25	41	98	1.8	4.3	48%	.301	1.38	4.03	4.43	3.0
2010	ROC	AAA	28	1	0	0	4	4	21^{2}	19	2	6	13	2.5	5.5	66%	.250	1.18	2.49	3.61	0.6
2010	MIN	MLB	28	10	12	0	28	26	161	194	25	40	68	2.2	3.8	52%	.305	1.48	5.42	5.76	-0.6
2011	*MIN*	*MLB*	*29*	*10*	*11*	*0*	*29*	*29*	*173*	*203*	*20*	*41*	*73*	*2.1*	*3.8*	*48%*	*.305*	*1.40*	*4.64*	*5.05*	*1.8*

Blackburn routinely hits 90 mph with one of the better sinkers in the game. However, he tends to fixate on the sinker so much during the course of some starts that he forgets to mix in his other pitches; in fact, he became so sinker-dependent that he was sent to Triple-A in late July for a four-start tune-up. The trip to the minors helped him gain confidence in his other offerings, particularly a changeup that induced plenty of ground balls and proved to be a nice complement to his primary offering, and in eight starts after returning, his ERA was 2.78. Blackburn had arthroscopic elbow surgery at the end of last season, but it was considered minor and he should be 100 percent by spring training. The Twins have cast their lot with Blackburn, who's inked through 2013, but the jury remains out on the wisdom of having locked him up long term.

Alex Burnett

Born: **7/26/1987** Age: **23**
Bats: R Throws: R Height: **6' 0"** Weight: **210**
Breakout: **3%** Improve: **8%** Collapse: **6%**
Attrition: **2%** MLB: **17%**
Comparables:
Julio Valera, Larry Jaster, Jack Fisher (75)

YEAR	TEAM	LVL	AGE	W	L	SV	G	GS	IP	H	HR	BB	SO	EqBB9	EqSO9	GB%	BABIP	WHIP	ERA	FRA	WARP
2008	FTM	A+	20	8	6	0	28	25	143^{2}	151	12	36	84	2.3	5.3	46%	.295	1.34	3.76	4.93	1.3
2009	FTM	A+	21	2	1	4	18	0	22^{2}	14	0	7	26	2.8	10.3	47%	.246	0.97	1.98	3.28	0.4
2009	NBR	AA	21	1	2	9	40	0	55^{1}	36	2	19	52	3.1	8.5	42%	.241	1.05	1.79	3.30	1.0
2010	MIN	MLB	22	2	2	0	41	0	47^{2}	52	6	23	37	4.3	7.0	48%	.322	1.62	5.29	5.42	-0.2
2011	*MIN*	*MLB*	*23*	*4*	*3*	*2*	*59*	*6*	*102*	*116*	*12*	*45*	*55*	*4.0*	*4.9*	*44%*	*.308*	*1.57*	*5.22*	*5.68*	*-0.6*

Burnett made the jump from Double-A to the major leagues last season after earning a roster spot in spring training, and he experienced some initial success with a fastball that sat at 92 mph and a hard slider. However, when big-league hitters quit chasing the slider out of the strike zone, Burnett became tentative and started throwing fewer strikes. He didn't fare much better after being demoted to Triple-A, which suggests that some additional minor-league learning would not go amiss. Although he lacks closer stuff, he could become a solid set-up man once sufficiently seasoned.

Matt Capps

Born: **9/3/1983** Age: **27**
Bats: **R** Throws: **R** Height: **6' 3"** Weight: **238**
Breakout: **11%** Improve: **26%** Collapse: **15%**
Attrition: **5%** MLB: **58%**

Comparables:
Edward Mujica, Tony Pena, Gene Brabender (66)

YEAR	TEAM	LVL	AGE	W	L	SV	G	GS	IP	H	HR	BB	SO	EqBB9	EqSO9	GB%	BABIP	WHIP	ERA	FRA	WARP
2008	PIT	MLB	24	2	3	21	49	0	53^{2}	47	5	5	39	0.8	6.5	33%	.264	1.01	3.02	3.77	0.6
2009	PIT	MLB	25	4	8	27	57	0	54^{1}	73	10	17	46	2.8	7.6	44%	.360	1.71	5.80	4.72	0.1
2010	MIN	MLB	26	2	0	16	27	0	27	24	1	8	21	2.7	7.0	55%	.303	1.19	2.00	2.72	0.6
2010	WAS	MLB	26	3	3	26	47	0	46	51	5	9	38	1.8	7.4	49%	.313	1.30	2.74	3.25	0.7
2011	*MIN*	*MLB*	*27*	*3*	*1*	*15*	*67*	*0*	*68*	*72*	*7*	*18*	*50*	*2.3*	*6.6*	*44%*	*.307*	*1.30*	*3.89*	*4.22*	*0.4*

A year after a miserable season that led to his being nontendered by the lowly Pirates, Capps distinguished himself as the winning pitcher in the 2010 All-Star Game as a representative of the Nationals, then pitched in the postseason after being dealt to the Twins at the trading deadline. While he can dial his fastball up to 96-97 mph and has a hard slider, Capps is not a classic power reliever, relying more on location than overwhelming stuff; his saves total makes him overvalued in both fantasy baseball and the real world. Capps will shift into a set-up role for the Twins if closer Joe Nathan recovers from Tommy John surgery, and that's really the best fit for him.

Jesse Crain

Born: **7/5/1981** Age: **29**
Bats: **R** Throws: **R** Height: **6' 1"** Weight: **205**
Breakout: **17%** Improve: **43%** Collapse: **31%**
Attrition: **7%** MLB: **95%**

Comparables:
Greg McMichael, Jay Howell, Rick Aguilera (82)

YEAR	TEAM	LVL	AGE	W	L	SV	G	GS	IP	H	HR	BB	SO	EqBB9	EqSO9	GB%	BABIP	WHIP	ERA	FRA	WARP
2008	MIN	MLB	26	5	4	0	66	0	62^{2}	62	6	24	50	3.4	7.2	41%	.300	1.39	3.59	4.02	0.8
2009	MIN	MLB	27	7	4	0	56	0	51^{2}	48	3	27	43	4.7	7.5	46%	.296	1.55	4.70	5.14	0.0
2010	MIN	MLB	28	1	1	1	71	0	68	53	5	27	62	3.6	8.2	41%	.262	1.19	3.04	4.25	0.5
2011	*CHA*	*MLB*	*29*	*3*	*1*	*0*	*60*	*0*	*58*	*55*	*6*	*25*	*51*	*3.9*	*7.8*	*44%*	*.295*	*1.36*	*3.99*	*4.34*	*0.4*

After getting off to a bad start last season, Crain reinvented himself by throwing as many sliders as fastballs. This unconventional strategy paid off, and en route to free agency, he pitched as well as any Minnesota reliever over the final four months of the season, with a 1.96 ERA from June on. Crain's control hasn't been as sharp since he underwent shoulder surgery in 2007, but he'd be closer material if he could regain the ability to throw strikes consistently, as the slider gives him an outstanding complement to his 95-mph fastball. A beneficiary of the gamewide fad of gifting relievers with more job security than their performances deserve, Crain heads to Chicago after agreeing to a three-year deal with the White Sox, where he will probably set up Matt Thornton.

Rob Delaney

Born: **9/8/1984** Age: **26**
Bats: **L** Throws: **R** Height: **6' 3"** Weight: **230**
Breakout: **3%** Improve: **7%** Collapse: **6%**
Attrition: **5%** MLB: **13%**

Comparables:
Shawn Kelley, Edward Mujica, Jose Mijares (74)

YEAR	TEAM	LVL	AGE	W	L	SV	G	GS	IP	H	HR	BB	SO	EqBB9	EqSO9	GB%	BABIP	WHIP	ERA	FRA	WARP
2008	FTM	A+	23	1	2	13	23	0	31^{2}	24	1	4	34	1.1	9.7	43%	.280	0.88	1.42	1.79	1.0
2008	NBR	AA	23	2	1	5	23	0	34^{1}	20	2	7	38	1.8	10.0	27%	.234	0.85	1.05	1.38	1.7
2009	NBR	AA	24	1	1	0	26	0	36	32	1	6	40	1.5	10.0	45%	.330	1.08	2.00	1.86	1.2
2009	ROC	AAA	24	7	3	7	36	0	47^{2}	43	5	15	38	2.8	7.2	31%	.270	1.22	4.53	5.09	-0.1
2010	ROC	AAA	25	7	9	4	61	0	80	82	12	23	92	2.6	10.4	37%	.327	1.33	4.73	5.09	0.2
2010	MIN	MLB	25	0	0	0	1	0	1	2	1	1	0	9.0	0.0	75%	.333	3.00	9.00	11.02	0.0
2011	*MIN*	*MLB*	*26*	*2*	*1*	*2*	*48*	*0*	64^{1}	*65*	*7*	*22*	*55*	*3.0*	*7.7*	*40%*	*.311*	*1.35*	*4.10*	*4.45*	*0.2*

Delaney doesn't light up the radar gun—his fastball tops out at 92 mph—but he has racked up impressive strikeout totals thanks to a biting slider. He delivers from a three-quarters arm angle, which makes him lethal to right-handed hitters, but southpaws see his pitches well enough to give him trouble. If Delaney can find a way to combat lefties, he'll have a chance to be a decent major-league middle reliever; until then, he'll bear the ROOGY cross.

Brian Duensing

Born: **2/22/1983** Age: **28**
Bats: **L** Throws: **L** Height: **5' 11"** Weight: **195**
Breakout: **12%** Improve: **47%** Collapse: **12%**
Attrition: **7%** MLB: **79%**

Comparables:
Bob Friend, Donovan Osborne, Jim O'Toole (72)

YEAR	TEAM	LVL	AGE	W	L	SV	G	GS	IP	H	HR	BB	SO	EqBB9	EqSO9	GB%	BABIP	WHIP	ERA	FRA	WARP
2008	ROC	AAA	25	5	11	0	25	24	138^{2}	150	16	34	77	2.2	5.0	52%	.293	1.36	4.28	4.60	2.0
2009	ROC	AAA	26	4	6	0	13	13	75^{1}	87	2	19	44	2.3	5.3	47%	.335	1.43	4.66	3.90	1.6
2009	MIN	MLB	26	5	2	0	24	9	84	84	7	31	53	3.3	5.7	47%	.291	1.40	3.64	4.12	1.5
2010	MIN	MLB	27	10	3	0	53	13	130^{2}	122	11	35	78	2.4	5.4	54%	.272	1.22	2.62	3.53	2.4
2011	*MIN*	*MLB*	*28*	*8*	*7*	*0*	*40*	*20*	146^{2}	*161*	*14*	*47*	*74*	*2.9*	*4.5*	*48%*	*.304*	*1.42*	*4.37*	*4.75*	*1.6*

Last season, Duensing proved that he was more than just a Quad-A pitcher with the ceiling of a spot starter or long reliever. He moved into the rotation when injuries struck in late July and pitched as well as any Twins starter down the stretch, albeit with the aid of a low BABIP. Regardless of any help he may have had along the way, the team went 9-4 in his 13 starts, although he looked helpless in the decisive third game of the ALDS against the Yankees. Duensing doesn't have overwhelming stuff, featuring a fastball that averages 91 mph to go with a slider, curveball, and changeup, but he throws strikes and never gets rattled. He won't be an ace, but he has proven that he can belongs in a major-league rotation.

Brian Fuentes

Born: **8/9/1975** Age: **35**
Bats: **L** Throws: **L** Height: **6' 4"** Weight: **220**
Breakout: **14%** Improve: **21%** Collapse: **21%**
Attrition: **3%** MLB: **71%**

Comparables:
Lee Smith, Francisco Cordero, Todd Worrell (74)

YEAR	TEAM	LVL	AGE	W	L	SV	G	GS	IP	H	HR	BB	SO	EqBB9	EqSO9	GB%	BABIP	WHIP	ERA	FRA	WARP
2008	COL	MLB	32	1	5	30	66	0	62^{2}	47	3	22	82	3.2	11.8	36%	.297	1.12	2.73	2.80	1.5
2009	ANA	MLB	33	1	5	48	65	0	55	53	6	24	46	3.9	7.5	37%	.292	1.49	3.93	3.55	0.8
2010	ANA	MLB	34	4	1	23	39	0	38^{1}	28	5	18	39	4.2	9.2	25%	.235	1.23	3.52	2.64	0.2
2010	MIN	MLB	34	0	0	1	9	0	9^{2}	3	0	2	8	1.9	7.4	25%	.125	0.62	0.00	4.14	0.3
2011	*MIN*	*MLB*	*35*	*3*	*1*	*25*	*62*	*0*	*58*	*51*	*5*	*24*	*56*	*3.7*	*8.6*	*40%*	*.289*	*1.28*	*3.47*	*3.77*	*0.6*

Fuentes was all but untouchable after the Twins acquired him from the Angels late last August, but Minnesota declined his $9 million club option for this season with the expectation that erstwhile closer Joe Nathan would reassume the role. With another past and potential closer on the roster in Matt Capps, Minnesota is well stocked at the end of the bullpen. Fuentes isn't a classic closer, since his fastball rarely breaks 90 mph, but he spots it well and complements it with a good changeup. He signed a two-year deal with Oakland and will likely pitch in a set-up role this season.

Kyle Gibson

Born: **10/23/1987** Age: **23**
Bats: **R** Throws: **R** Height: **6' 6"** Weight: **210**
Breakout: **11%** Improve: **35%** Collapse: **10%**
Attrition: **19%** MLB: **55%**

Comparables:
Homer Bailey, Brian Matusz, Troy Patton (61)

YEAR	TEAM	LVL	AGE	W	L	SV	G	GS	IP	H	HR	BB	SO	EqBB9	EqSO9	GB%	BABIP	WHIP	ERA	FRA	WARP
2010	FTM	A+	22	4	1	0	7	7	43^{1}	33	2	12	40	2.5	8.4	68%	.274	1.09	1.87	2.77	1.4
2010	NBR	AA	22	7	5	0	16	16	93	91	5	22	77	2.1	7.5	54%	.308	1.26	3.39	4.22	1.1
2011	*MIN*	*MLB*	*23*	*9*	*8*	*0*	*25*	*25*	*143^{2}*	*150*	*13*	*51*	*96*	*3.2*	*6.0*	*49%*	*.307*	*1.40*	*4.24*	*4.61*	*2.3*

The Twins' first-round pick in 2009 from the University of Missouri made such rapid progress last year in his professional debut that there was some sentiment in the organization to call him up to the major leagues with the possibility of placing him on the post-season roster. Instead, Gibson finished the season at Triple-A and was named the organization's minor-league pitcher of the year. He's likely to begin the season back at Rochester, but it's nearly inevitable that he will reach the major leagues at some point this summer on the strength of an intelligent approach to pitching and an impressive three-pitch mix that includes a fastball that reaches 94 mph, an outstanding slider, and an advanced changeup.

Deolis Guerra

Born: **4/17/1989** Age: **22**
Bats: **R** Throws: **R** Height: **6' 5"** Weight: **250**
Breakout: **1%** Improve: **3%** Collapse: **0%**
Attrition: **1%** MLB: **3%**

Comparables:
Sean O'Sullivan, Jeff D'Amico, Tommy Hunter (75)

YEAR	TEAM	LVL	AGE	W	L	SV	G	GS	IP	H	HR	BB	SO	EqBB9	EqSO9	GB%	BABIP	WHIP	ERA	FRA	WARP
2008	FTM	A+	19	11	9	0	26	25	130	138	12	71	71	4.9	4.9	36%	.292	1.65	5.47	5.83	0.1
2009	FTM	A+	20	6	8	0	16	15	86^{1}	95	6	25	57	2.6	5.9	49%	.311	1.45	4.69	5.59	-0.1
2009	NBR	AA	20	6	3	0	12	11	62^{2}	62	4	17	49	2.4	7.0	43%	.304	1.34	5.17	5.51	-0.1
2010	NBR	AA	21	2	10	0	19	19	102^{1}	127	14	37	67	3.3	5.9	41%	.334	1.65	6.24	6.78	-1.4
2010	ROC	AAA	21	0	3	0	5	4	25	35	5	8	18	2.9	6.5	51%	.357	1.76	6.84	6.63	-0.2
2011	*MIN*	*MLB*	*22*	*5*	*11*	*0*	*21*	*21*	*111*	*141*	*16*	*55*	*50*	*4.5*	*4.0*	*42%*	*.321*	*1.77*	*6.47*	*7.03*	*-0.9*

It is axiomatic that you can't trade a star player and get anything like an equal return; the Santana trade is a textbook case, though there are many others. Guerra is the only one of the four prospects acquired from the Mets in the 2008 Johan Santana trade still with the Twins. Although the other three played their way out of the organization, Guerra's failure has been particularly galling because the Twins viewed him as a potential number two starter. Instead, he has struggled mightily as he's risen through the farm system, and his stuff has deteriorated; he rarely hits 94 mph with his fastball anymore, and his curveball has lost its bite.

Matt Guerrier

Born: **8/2/1978** Age: **32**
Bats: **R** Throws: **R** Height: **6' 3"** Weight: **185**
Breakout: **11%** Improve: **30%** Collapse: **25%**
Attrition: **16%** MLB: **78%**

Comparables:
Geoff Geary, LaTroy Hawkins, Mike Timlin (76)

YEAR	TEAM	LVL	AGE	W	L	SV	G	GS	IP	H	HR	BB	SO	EqBB9	EqSO9	GB%	BABIP	WHIP	ERA	FRA	WARP
2008	MIN	MLB	29	6	9	1	76	0	76^{1}	84	12	37	59	4.4	7.0	47%	.305	1.59	5.07	5.46	-0.3
2009	MIN	MLB	30	5	1	1	79	0	76^{1}	58	10	16	47	1.9	5.5	44%	.212	1.02	2.36	4.11	0.9
2010	MIN	MLB	31	5	7	1	74	0	71	56	7	22	42	2.8	5.3	48%	.231	1.14	3.17	4.52	0.2
2011	*LAN*	*MLB*	*32*	*4*	*2*	*0*	*80*	*0*	*77*	*73*	*9*	*25*	*51*	*2.9*	*5.9*	*46%*	*.270*	*1.26*	*3.63*	*3.94*	*0.5*

Guerrier has been one of the most durable relievers in the major leagues over the last four seasons, pitching in at least 73 games each year and accumulating a total of 302 games in that span. He is far from overpowering, with a fastball that sits in the 89-91 range, but he has an outstanding slider and a good curveball and mixes his pitches like a starter. The Twins toyed with the idea of making him the closer last spring when Joe Nathan was lost for the season, but ultimately decided that he would be better suited for the set-up role in which he had already experienced so much success. Over the winter, the Dodgers gambled a three-year, $12 million contract, a foolhardy gesture, given the inherent instability of reliever performances—even reliable ol' Guerrier mixed in a 5.19 ERA one year.

Carlos Gutierrez
Born: **9/22/1986** Age: **24**
Bats: **R** Throws: **R** Height: **6' 3"** Weight: **205**
Breakout: **2%** Improve: **2%** Collapse: **2%**
Attrition: **4%** MLB: **7%**
Comparables:
Anthony Ortega, Yorman Bazardo, Trevor Bell (81)

YEAR	TEAM	LVL	AGE	W	L	SV	G	GS	IP	H	HR	BB	SO	EqBB9	EqSO9	GB%	BABIP	WHIP	ERA	FRA	WARP
2008	FTM	A+	21	4	2	1	18	0	27^{2}	27	0	8	22	2.6	7.2	55%	.314	1.27	2.93	3.66	0.3
2009	FTM	A+	22	2	3	0	11	10	54^{2}	37	1	22	33	3.6	5.4	71%	.220	1.12	1.32	5.21	0.2
2009	NBR	AA	22	1	3	0	24	6	54	66	6	26	33	4.3	5.5	59%	.337	1.78	6.17	6.91	-1.1
2010	NBR	AA	23	5	8	2	32	16	122	136	7	50	81	3.7	6.0	61%	.334	1.57	4.57	5.54	-0.2
2011	*MIN*	*MLB*	*24*	*4*	*5*	*0*	*26*	*11*	*82*	*97*	*8*	*42*	*41*	*4.6*	*4.4*	*52%*	*.317*	*1.68*	*5.59*	*6.07*	*-0.3*

Gutierrez has failed to impress since being a first-round draft pick in 2008, but the Twins haven't done him any favors by flip-flopping on his role, moving him from starting to relief and back again. Finally settled into the bullpen, he has made progress harnessing his stuff in shorter stints. In terms of velocity and movement, his sinker is one of the best in the minor leagues, a 95-mph bowling ball, but his inability to command it has held him back so far. He's the kind of pitcher who looks like a big-league pitcher one night and a candidate for release the next. His inconsistency drives scouts mad; Ron Gardenhire will get a chance to join the Frustrated with Gutierrez Club this spring.

Liam Hendriks
Born: **2/10/1989** Age: **22**
Bats: **R** Throws: **R** Height: **6' 1"** Weight: **190**
Breakout: **8%** Improve: **13%** Collapse: **4%**
Attrition: **2%** MLB: **19%**
Comparables:
Bob Welch, Tom Morgan, Frank Pastore (74)

YEAR	TEAM	LVL	AGE	W	L	SV	G	GS	IP	H	HR	BB	SO	EqBB9	EqSO9	GB%	BABIP	WHIP	ERA	FRA	WARP
2009	BLT	A	20	3	5	0	11	11	66^{2}	73	3	15	62	2.0	8.4	60%	.347	1.35	3.51	4.64	0.6
2010	BLT	A	21	2	1	0	6	6	34	16	0	4	39	1.1	10.3	51%	.203	0.62	1.32	2.42	1.3
2010	FTM	A+	21	6	3	0	13	12	74^{2}	63	2	8	66	1.0	8.0	53%	.284	0.97	1.93	3.07	2.0
2011	*MIN*	*MLB*	*22*	*4*	*4*	*0*	*12*	*12*	*73*	*81*	*7*	*25*	*45*	*3.1*	*5.6*	*48%*	*.314*	*1.45*	*4.50*	*4.89*	*0.9*

No team is busier in Australia than the Twins, and Hendriks is their big prize. He has an array of pitches, a two-seam fastball, a four-seamer, a slider, and a change. The fastball is just average, the slider and the change very good, but what makes him special is his supernatural command. He just missed leading the minor leagues in ERA last season; his 1.74 mark was a shade worse than the 1.73 mustered by Braves prospect Brandon Beachy. Given organizational taste, Hendriks is the perfect Twins pitching prospect and could come quickly.

Francisco Liriano
Born: **10/26/1983** Age: **27**
Bats: **L** Throws: **L** Height: **6' 2"** Weight: **185**
Breakout: **10%** Improve: **40%** Collapse: **33%**
Attrition: **9%** MLB: **98%**
Comparables:
Scott Kazmir, Joe Coleman, Sonny Siebert (68)

YEAR	TEAM	LVL	AGE	W	L	SV	G	GS	IP	H	HR	BB	SO	EqBB9	EqSO9	GB%	BABIP	WHIP	ERA	FRA	WARP
2008	ROC	AAA	24	10	2	0	19	19	118	102	8	31	113	2.4	8.6	43%	.289	1.15	3.28	2.88	4.4
2008	MIN	MLB	24	6	4	0	14	14	76	74	7	32	67	3.8	7.9	42%	.302	1.41	3.91	4.53	1.0
2009	MIN	MLB	25	5	13	0	29	24	136^{2}	147	21	65	122	4.3	8.0	43%	.319	1.60	5.80	6.06	-0.2
2010	MIN	MLB	26	14	10	0	31	31	191^{2}	184	9	58	201	2.7	9.4	56%	.331	1.31	3.62	3.55	4.2
2011	*MIN*	*MLB*	*27*	*11*	*8*	*0*	*28*	*28*	*161*	*156*	*13*	*59*	*149*	*3.3*	*8.3*	*46%*	*.315*	*1.33*	*3.75*	*4.08*	*3.6*

It took a long time, but Liriano finally regained the form he had flashed during a sensational 2006 rookie season that ended abruptly when he underwent Tommy John surgery. Last season, the lefty was back to averaging 94 mph on his heater and occasionally running it to 97, and he also regained the feel for his hard slider to go along with a decent changeup. One result was that his ground-ball rate skyrocketed and he became nigh impossible to hit a home run off of, leading the league with 0.4 allowed per nine. The only negative was that Liriano faded late in the season, an understandable occurrence in light of his having undertaken the heaviest workload of his career. His arm is sound, however, and his combination of grounders and a high strikeout rate makes him a strong pick for a further break out this year.

Ron Mahay
Born: **6/28/1971** Age: **40**
Bats: **L** Throws: **L** Height: **6' 2"** Weight: **185**
Breakout: **3%** Improve: **4%** Collapse: **4%**
Attrition: **6%** MLB: **15%**
Comparables:
Paul Assenmacher, Mike Bielecki, Hector Carrasco (79)

YEAR	TEAM	LVL	AGE	W	L	SV	G	GS	IP	H	HR	BB	SO	EqBB9	EqSO9	GB%	BABIP	WHIP	ERA	FRA	WARP
2008	KCA	MLB	37	5	0	0	57	0	64^{2}	61	6	29	49	4.0	6.8	39%	.285	1.41	3.48	4.06	0.8
2009	KCA	MLB	38	1	1	0	41	0	41^{1}	55	9	19	34	4.1	7.4	41%	.338	1.84	4.79	4.67	0.2
2009	MIN	MLB	38	1	0	0	16	0	9	7	1	3	8	3.0	8.0	41%	.240	1.33	2.00	4.56	0.1
2010	MIN	MLB	39	1	1	0	41	0	34	33	5	8	25	2.1	6.6	44%	.272	1.21	3.44	4.00	0.3
2011	*MIN*	*MLB*	*40*	*3*	*1*	*0*	*63*	*0*	*58*	*62*	*7*	*25*	*42*	*3.9*	*6.5*	*43%*	*.308*	*1.50*	*4.80*	*5.21*	*-0.4*

Mahay didn't sign with the Twins until late May last year, then had his season cut short in late August, when he underwent surgery on his right rotator cuff (nonthrowing shoulder). He became a free agent again at the end of the season and pitched well enough in abbreviated action to get a shot at someone's roster in 2011. His fastball is losing some zip—he rarely broke 90 mph last season—but his slider is still tough on left-handed hitters (.219/.239/.281 last season, .232/.303/.386 lifetime), which should enable him to extend what has been a truly unusual career. Few remember that Mahay made his major-league debut as an outfielder with the Red Sox on May 19, 1995, less than two months after serving as a replacement player during the strike. Sixteen years later, he's still kicking, though he now makes his living on the mound.

Jeff Manship

Born: **1/16/1985** Age: **26**
Bats: **R** Throws: **R** Height: **6' 2"** Weight: **210**
Breakout: **19%** Improve: **32%** Collapse: **11%**
Attrition: **25%** MLB: **56%**

Comparables:
Enrique Gonzalez, Joe Martinez, Mike Ekstrom (77)

YEAR	TEAM	LVL	AGE	W	L	SV	G	GS	IP	H	HR	BB	SO	EqBB9	EqSO9	GB%	BABIP	WHIP	ERA	FRA	WARP
2008	FTM	A+	23	7	3	0	13	13	78^{2}	68	0	20	63	2.3	7.2	56%	.292	1.17	2.86	3.84	1.5
2008	NBR	AA	23	3	6	0	14	14	76^{2}	90	8	24	62	2.8	7.3	53%	.337	1.53	4.46	4.83	0.8
2009	NBR	AA	24	6	4	0	13	13	75^{2}	72	2	20	45	2.4	5.4	54%	.286	1.24	4.28	5.25	0.1
2009	ROC	AAA	24	4	2	0	8	8	50^{1}	53	1	17	30	3.0	5.4	49%	.319	1.41	3.22	3.98	1.0
2009	MIN	MLB	24	1	1	0	11	5	31^{2}	39	4	15	21	4.3	6.0	45%	.333	1.74	5.68	5.50	0.1
2010	ROC	AAA	25	3	8	0	19	18	98^{1}	134	13	22	83	2.0	7.6	50%	.382	1.61	5.13	3.97	2.2
2010	MIN	MLB	25	2	1	0	13	1	29	34	3	6	21	1.9	6.5	47%	.330	1.38	5.28	6.01	-0.3
2011	*MIN*	*MLB*	*26*	*6*	*8*	*0*	*25*	*18*	*115*	*138*	*12*	*41*	*67*	*3.2*	*5.2*	*48%*	*.328*	*1.56*	*5.16*	*5.61*	*0.4*

Manship did little to distinguish himself in the major leagues last season, but he made a name for himself in the transactions column, taking five shuttle trips between Triple-A Rochester and the big club. Sadly, this cost him a chance to see former Yankee Bernie Williams rock the house at the city's annual jazz festival. A four-pitch pitcher with an 89-mph fastball, curveball, slider, and changeup, Manship fits the Twins' mold as a strike thrower and draws high marks for his competitiveness, but his stuff is a little short. He would likely be best utilized as a long reliever and spot starter.

Jose Mijares

Born: **10/29/1984** Age: **26**
Bats: **L** Throws: **L** Height: **6' 0"** Weight: **230**
Breakout: **0%** Improve: **1%** Collapse: **3%**
Attrition: **1%** MLB: **4%**

Comparables:
Macay McBride, Terry Mathews, Tom Niedenfuer (79)

YEAR	TEAM	LVL	AGE	W	L	SV	G	GS	IP	H	HR	BB	SO	EqBB9	EqSO9	GB%	BABIP	WHIP	ERA	FRA	WARP
2008	MIN	MLB	23	0	1	0	10	0	10^{1}	3	0	0	5	0.0	4.4	45%	.103	0.29	0.87	3.16	0.2
2009	MIN	MLB	24	2	2	0	71	0	61^{2}	50	7	23	55	3.4	8.0	39%	.259	1.22	2.34	2.37	1.8
2010	MIN	MLB	25	1	1	0	47	0	32^{2}	34	4	9	28	2.5	7.7	32%	.309	1.35	3.58	3.60	0.5
2011	*MIN*	*MLB*	*26*	*3*	*1*	*0*	*54*	*0*	*55*	*53*	*6*	*25*	*47*	*4.1*	*7.6*	*43%*	*.297*	*1.42*	*4.30*	*4.67*	*0.0*

Mijares has put up good numbers in his relatively short major-league career, but he frustrates the Twins, who feel that he could become a dominant left-handed reliever with the proper effort. They would like to see him gain some maturity, show more focus on the mound, and get into better shape. Mijares' best pitches are his slider and curve, but the Twins expect that he could add velocity to his fastball—which averages 91 mph—if he dropped some weight. Shedding a few pounds might also allow him to repeat his delivery more easily. Mijares is 26, so there is some room for growth; the Twins just hope that it doesn't come at his waistline.

Ryan Mullins

Born: **11/13/1983** Age: **27**
Bats: **L** Throws: **L** Height: **6' 6"** Weight: **180**
Breakout: **6%** Improve: **8%** Collapse: **1%**
Attrition: **6%** MLB: **9%**

Comparables:
Pat Misch, Elizardo Ramirez, David Pauley (79)

YEAR	TEAM	LVL	AGE	W	L	SV	G	GS	IP	H	HR	BB	SO	EqBB9	EqSO9	GB%	BABIP	WHIP	ERA	FRA	WARP
2008	NBR	AA	24	9	9	0	30	24	148^{1}	169	18	59	99	3.6	6.0	47%	.317	1.56	4.31	4.34	2.3
2009	NBR	AA	25	11	11	0	28	27	145	175	13	36	133	2.2	8.3	46%	.360	1.50	4.03	3.78	2.9
2010	ROC	AAA	26	4	7	0	19	16	90	106	14	26	58	2.6	5.8	43%	.311	1.49	4.60	4.80	1.1
2011	*MIN*	*MLB*	*27*	*7*	*11*	*0*	*25*	*25*	*134*	*171*	*18*	*53*	*77*	*3.5*	*5.2*	*45%*	*.335*	*1.66*	*5.91*	*6.42*	*-0.3*

Mullins looks the part of a power pitcher at six-foot-six, but is a finesse type who pitches backward, using his curveball and changeup to set up an ordinary fastball. He also has a deceptive delivery that's a tangle of arms and legs and includes a slight hesitation. While that helped Mullins in the lower levels of the minor leagues, he did not fool hitters in his first taste of Triple-A last season and needs more time at that level, especially after missing the second half of 2010 with a strained back. Mullins might be best served by converting to relief, where he could concentrate on retiring left-handed hitters.

Joe Nathan

Born: **11/22/1974** Age: **36**
Bats: **R** Throws: **R** Height: **6' 4"** Weight: **195**
Breakout: **8%** Improve: **15%** Collapse: **10%**
Attrition: **44%** MLB: **82%**

Comparables:
Billy Wagner, Tom Henke, Francisco Cordero (71)

YEAR	TEAM	LVL	AGE	W	L	SV	G	GS	IP	H	HR	BB	SO	EqBB9	EqSO9	GB%	BABIP	WHIP	ERA	FRA	WARP
2008	MIN	MLB	33	1	2	39	68	0	67^2	43	5	18	74	2.4	9.8	49%	.235	0.93	1.33	2.43	1.8
2009	MIN	MLB	34	2	2	47	70	0	68^2	42	7	22	89	2.9	11.7	42%	.232	0.96	2.10	2.13	1.7
2011	*MIN*	*MLB*	*36*	*4*	*2*	*40*	*69*	*0*	*68*	*50*	*5*	*22*	*80*	*2.9*	*10.5*	*45%*	*.280*	*1.05*	*2.17*	*2.36*	*1.9*

Nathan had two bone chips removed from his elbow after the 2009 season, then started feeling pain early in spring training last year before undergoing Tommy John surgery on March 25. He missed the entire year, but the Twins weathered the loss of a closer who had saved at least 36 games in each of the previous six seasons to win the American League Central handily (although they felt the need to acquire two closers along the way). Nathan's rehabilitation went smoothly throughout the summer, and both he and the Twins are confident that he'll be ready to pitch on Opening Day. But as Minnesota has learned in the cases of Francisco Liriano and Pat Neshek, not all pitchers recover from reconstructive elbow surgery quickly. Playing it safe, the Twins kept their options at closer open by retaining arbitration-eligible Matt Capps.

Pat Neshek

Born: **9/4/1980** Age: **30**
Bats: **S** Throws: **R** Height: **6' 3"** Weight: **205**
Breakout: **9%** Improve: **16%** Collapse: **14%**
Attrition: **6%** MLB: **36%**

Comparables:
Dan Plesac, Hank Aguirre, Marcus McBeth (79)

YEAR	TEAM	LVL	AGE	W	L	SV	G	GS	IP	H	HR	BB	SO	EqBB9	EqSO9	GB%	BABIP	WHIP	ERA	FRA	WARP
2008	MIN	MLB	27	0	1	0	15	0	13^1	12	2	4	15	2.7	10.1	32%	.286	1.20	5.40	5.51	-0.1
2010	ROC	AAA	29	5	1	1	30	0	39^1	40	4	13	25	3.0	5.8	41%	.288	1.43	3.89	4.82	0.2
2010	MIN	MLB	29	0	1	0	11	0	9	7	1	8	9	8.0	9.0	32%	.250	1.78	5.00	5.10	0.0
2011	*MIN*	*MLB*	*30*	*2*	*1*	*0*	*48*	*0*	*54*	*51*	*6*	*22*	*47*	*3.7*	*7.7*	*44%*	*.293*	*1.34*	*3.86*	*4.20*	*0.3*

It's been slow going for Neshek since he had Tommy John surgery after the 2008 season. He missed all of 2009, then suffered a strain of the pulley tendon in the palm of his pitching hand in late April last season. The injury was originally misdiagnosed (prompting Neshek to take to Twitter to complain) and kept him on the disabled list for five weeks. Once the side-arming Neshek returned, he did not have the same velocity on his fastball—his heater averaged only 85 mph, down four mph from his presurgery days—and he was forced to rely on his slider. That led to on-field struggles and a demotion to Triple-A, where he spent the majority of the season. His diminished strikeout rate at the lower levels does not inspire confidence in a 2011 rebound, though the second year back from being TJ'd might see him recover some strength.

Carl Pavano

Born: **1/8/1976** Age: **35**
Bats: **R** Throws: **R** Height: **6' 5"** Weight: **230**
Breakout: **17%** Improve: **34%** Collapse: **17%**
Attrition: **12%** MLB: **74%**

Comparables:
Don Newcombe, Ron Reed, David Wells (64)

YEAR	TEAM	LVL	AGE	W	L	SV	G	GS	IP	H	HR	BB	SO	EqBB9	EqSO9	GB%	BABIP	WHIP	ERA	FRA	WARP
2008	NYA	MLB	32	4	2	0	7	7	34^1	41	5	10	15	2.6	3.9	42%	.300	1.60	5.77	6.09	-0.0
2009	CLE	MLB	33	9	8	0	21	21	125^2	150	19	23	88	1.6	6.3	46%	.327	1.40	5.37	5.38	0.6
2009	MIN	MLB	33	5	4	0	12	12	73^2	85	7	16	59	2.0	7.2	41%	.332	1.41	4.64	4.32	1.3
2010	MIN	MLB	34	17	11	0	32	32	221	227	24	37	117	1.5	4.8	53%	.281	1.22	3.67	4.10	2.9
2011	*MIN*	*MLB*	*35*	*6*	*6*	*0*	*17*	*17*	*102^2*	*114*	*11*	*22*	*59*	*1.9*	*5.2*	*47%*	*.307*	*1.32*	*4.22*	*4.59*	*1.6*

Pavano has done a nice job turning his career around and improving his image since his debacle of a four-year stint with the Yankees from 2005 to 2008. He hasn't missed a start in the last two seasons with the Indians and Twins, even qualifying as a workhorse by averaging 6.5 innings per outing. However, Pavano's strikeout rate of 4.8 batters per nine innings in 2010 was a red flag that turned crimson after dropping to 2.8 during the final month of the season. The mustachioed moundsman's rebound has come about in part because he has honed his changeup into an outstanding pitch, and his control is exemplary, but his inability to punch people out with a 90-mph heater will eventually catch up to him.

Glen Perkins

Born: **3/2/1983** Age: **28**
Bats: **L** Throws: **L** Height: **5' 11"** Weight: **200**
Breakout: **12%** Improve: **45%** Collapse: **11%**
Attrition: **10%** MLB: **78%**

Comparables:
Todd Ritchie, Donovan Osborne, Denny Neagle (77)

YEAR	TEAM	LVL	AGE	W	L	SV	G	GS	IP	H	HR	BB	SO	EqBB9	EqSO9	GB%	BABIP	WHIP	ERA	FRA	WARP
2008	ROC	AAA	25	2	1	0	7	6	33^1	28	2	19	27	5.1	7.3	38%	.260	1.44	2.97	3.69	0.8
2008	MIN	MLB	25	12	4	0	26	26	151	183	25	39	74	2.3	4.4	39%	.304	1.49	4.41	4.86	1.3
2009	MIN	MLB	26	6	7	0	18	17	96^1	120	13	23	45	2.1	4.2	49%	.314	1.49	5.89	6.05	-0.1
2010	ROC	AAA	27	4	9	0	26	24	124	160	14	36	98	2.6	7.1	46%	.352	1.62	5.81	4.29	2.4
2010	MIN	MLB	27	1	1	0	13	1	21^2	29	3	5	14	2.1	5.8	53%	.361	1.75	6.23	5.98	-0.1
2011	*MIN*	*MLB*	*28*	*7*	*10*	*0*	*23*	*23*	*122^2*	*148*	*16*	*40*	*68*	*2.9*	*5.0*	*44%*	*.320*	*1.53*	*5.24*	*5.70*	*0.6*

Perkins clashed publicly with management in 2009, claiming that it had wrongfully downplayed the severity of his elbow injury. He then had an awful spring training and first half of the 2010 season at Triple-A before returning to the major leagues as a reliever late in the season. The real positive of 2010 was that Perkins regained velocity on his fastball (which averaged

92 mph) and improved the bite on his slider. This led to what was, by his standards, a successful September (11 innings, 11 strikeouts, 3.09 ERA). If there is a common thread to Perkins' recent career, it is his inability to fool batters. They have hit .305 against him over the last three seasons and rarely strike out. Because he's left-handed, Perkins will get his share of chances, be they from the Twins or other teams, but barring a continuation of his autumn activities, he's just not a major-league pitcher.

Jon Rauch

Born: **9/27/1978** Age: **32**
Bats: **R** Throws: **R** Height: **6' 11"** Weight: **230**
Breakout: **8%** Improve: **24%** Collapse: **21%**
Attrition: **16%** MLB: **59%**

Comparables:
Chad Qualls, Juan Padilla, Scott Proctor (69)

YEAR	TEAM	LVL	AGE	W	L	SV	G	GS	IP	H	HR	BB	SO	EqBB9	EqSO9	GB%	BABIP	WHIP	ERA	FRA	WARP
2008	ARI	MLB	29	0	6	1	26	0	23^1	27	6	9	22	3.5	8.5	35%	.318	1.54	6.56	7.51	-0.7
2008	WAS	MLB	29	4	2	17	48	0	48^1	42	5	7	44	1.3	8.2	34%	.272	1.01	2.98	4.17	0.4
2009	ARI	MLB	30	2	2	2	58	0	54^1	57	5	17	35	2.8	5.8	38%	.294	1.38	4.14	3.91	0.7
2009	MIN	MLB	30	5	1	0	17	0	15^2	13	1	6	14	3.4	8.0	35%	.286	1.28	1.72	2.56	0.6
2010	MIN	MLB	31	3	1	21	59	0	57^2	61	3	14	46	2.2	7.2	38%	.320	1.32	3.12	2.43	1.3
2011	*MIN*	*MLB*	*32*	*4*	*2*	*8*	*79*	*0*	*75*	*76*	*7*	*23*	*56*	*2.7*	*6.7*	*41%*	*.302*	*1.31*	*3.72*	*4.05*	*0.6*

Rauch was moved into the closer's role when Joe Nathan underwent season-ending Tommy John surgery during spring training, and the tallest player in major-league history acquitted himself quite well during the early part of the season. However, when he began to slip in July, the Twins were quick to trade for Nationals closer Matt Capps and move Rauch to a set-up role, where he scuffled. Rauch isn't a hard thrower despite his size—his fastball tops out at 92 mph—which leaves him better served as a seventh-inning pitcher than one deployed in the ninth inning with a lead.

Anthony Slama

Born: **1/6/1984** Age: **27**
Bats: **R** Throws: **R** Height: **6' 3"** Weight: **205**
Breakout: **19%** Improve: **31%** Collapse: **15%**
Attrition: **14%** MLB: **53%**

Comparables:
Tony Sipp, Joey Devine, Billy Sadler (74)

YEAR	TEAM	LVL	AGE	W	L	SV	G	GS	IP	H	HR	BB	SO	EqBB9	EqSO9	GB%	BABIP	WHIP	ERA	FRA	WARP
2008	FTM	A+	24	4	1	25	51	0	71	43	0	24	110	3.0	13.9	47%	.301	0.99	1.01	1.36	2.5
2009	NBR	AA	25	4	2	25	51	0	65^1	46	5	32	93	4.4	12.8	34%	.297	1.23	2.48	2.54	1.6
2010	ROC	AAA	26	2	2	17	54	0	65^1	41	5	32	74	4.4	10.2	46%	.235	1.14	2.20	3.10	1.4
2010	MIN	MLB	26	0	1	0	5	0	4^2	6	1	5	5	9.6	9.6	27%	.357	2.36	7.71	6.03	0.0
2011	*MIN*	*MLB*	*27*	*3*	*1*	*6*	*49*	*0*	*62*	*51*	*5*	*33*	*70*	*4.8*	*10.2*	*43%*	*.301*	*1.35*	*3.40*	*3.69*	*0.7*

Slama has managed more strikeouts than innings pitched at every level of the minor leagues, but the Twins didn't show much confidence in him last season, allowing the righty just 4 2/3 innings in the major leagues despite injury problems in the big club's bullpen. Slama's fastball sits in the 90-92 mph range, but he does have an exceptional slider that could prove to be a wipeout pitch. The key for Slama is getting ahead in the count by spotting his fastball for strikes, which allows him to use the slider to put hitters away. Since he has nothing left to prove in the minor leagues, the time has come for the Twins to give him a shot in the big-league bullpen to see whether he can Slama the door on major-league hitters.

Kevin Slowey

Born: **5/4/1984** Age: **27**
Bats: **R** Throws: **R** Height: **6' 3"** Weight: **195**
Breakout: **10%** Improve: **35%** Collapse: **35%**
Attrition: **10%** MLB: **89%**

Comparables:
John Smiley, Scott Sanderson, Frank Tanana (65)

YEAR	TEAM	LVL	AGE	W	L	SV	G	GS	IP	H	HR	BB	SO	EqBB9	EqSO9	GB%	BABIP	WHIP	ERA	FRA	WARP
2008	MIN	MLB	24	12	11	0	27	27	160^1	161	22	24	123	1.3	6.9	38%	.290	1.18	3.99	4.95	1.3
2009	MIN	MLB	25	10	3	0	16	16	90^2	113	15	15	75	1.5	7.4	34%	.345	1.47	4.86	3.93	2.0
2010	MIN	MLB	26	13	6	0	30	28	155^2	172	21	29	116	1.7	6.7	29%	.308	1.32	4.45	4.31	1.9
2011	*MIN*	*MLB*	*27*	*11*	*9*	*0*	*27*	*27*	*152*	*162*	*19*	*31*	*110*	*1.8*	*6.5*	*38%*	*.306*	*1.27*	*4.00*	*4.35*	*3.0*

Slowey has been one of the most fortunate starting pitchers in the major leagues over the last two years; the Twins' offense gave him 7.4 runs of support in 2009 and 6.2 last season. That helping hand from his hitters and good control have enabled Slowey to go 23-9 in that span, despite a 4.60 ERA. He has won despite being hampered by injuries, undergoing surgery in 2009 to remove bone chips from his right wrist and battling triceps tendinitis last season. He has also frustrated Twins pitching coach Rick Anderson—a big proponent of attacking the strike zone—by nibbling at the corners of the plate with an unremarkable four-pitch mix that includes a high-80s fastball. The complete picture offers ample evidence that Slowey's record is in for some major regression in 2011.

Anthony Swarzak
Born: **9/10/1985** Age: **25**
Bats: **R** Throws: **R** Height: **6' 4"** Weight: **225**
Breakout: **8%** Improve: **14%** Collapse: **5%**
Attrition: **12%** MLB: **25%**
Comparables:
Matt Chico, Tobi Stoner, Enrique Gonzalez (80)

YEAR	TEAM	LVL	AGE	W	L	SV	G	GS	IP	H	HR	BB	SO	EqBB9	EqSO9	GB%	BABIP	WHIP	ERA	FRA	WARP
2008	NBR	AA	22	3	8	0	20	20	101^{2}	126	12	37	76	3.3	6.7	35%	.341	1.63	5.66	6.67	-0.8
2008	ROC	AAA	22	5	0	0	7	7	45	41	4	14	26	2.8	5.2	45%	.262	1.31	1.80	3.64	1.1
2009	ROC	AAA	23	4	5	0	13	13	79^{2}	79	4	21	45	2.4	5.1	42%	.292	1.29	3.27	4.22	1.4
2009	MIN	MLB	23	3	7	0	12	12	59	76	12	20	34	3.1	5.2	36%	.320	1.66	6.25	6.21	-0.1
2010	ROC	AAA	24	5	12	0	22	22	111^{2}	143	14	38	69	3.1	5.6	36%	.333	1.67	6.21	6.31	-0.2
2011	*MIN*	*MLB*	*25*	*7*	*10*	*0*	*23*	*23*	*124*	*150*	*15*	*48*	*65*	*3.5*	*4.7*	*40%*	*.319*	*1.59*	*5.44*	*5.92*	*0.3*

The luster had already faded from Swarzak's star after he made his major-league debut in 2009 and struggled in most of his 12 starts, but he followed that underwhelming effort with a disastrous season at Triple-A, which got off on the wrong foot—literally—when he was nailed in the foot by a line drive in his first start and missed five weeks. Swarzak has plenty of raw ability and two solid pitches—a heater that reaches 94 mph with good sink and a big 12-to-6 curveball. His command of a changeup comes and goes. Questions about Swarzak's desire to compete have arisen since he was drafted in the second round in 2004; whether or not his disappointing performance should be blamed on psychological shortcomings, his results haven't matched his stuff.

Alex Wimmers
Born: **11/1/1988** Age: **22**
Bats: **L** Throws: **R** Height: **6' 2"** Weight: **195**
Breakout: **–%** Improve: **–%** Collapse: **–%**
Attrition: **–%** MLB: **–%**
Comparables:

YEAR	TEAM	LVL	AGE	W	L	SV	G	GS	IP	H	HR	BB	SO	EqBB9	EqSO9	GB%	BABIP	WHIP	ERA	FRA	WARP
2011	*MIN*	*MLB*	*22*	—	—	—	—	—	—	—	—	—	—	—	—	—	—	—	—	—	—

Wimmers was impressive as he kicked off his professional career with four short starts at the High-A level last summer after the Twins made him the 21st selection in the amateur draft and showered him with $1.332 million reasons to sign. While with the Ohio State Buckeyes last spring, he missed four weeks with a strained hamstring, but that didn't prevent him from qualifying as a first-team All-American for a second straight season. Wimmers draws high marks for mound presence and knowledge of pitching. His arsenal includes a two-seam sinking fastball that reaches 93 mph with good movement, a plus curveball that acts as an out pitch against right-handed hitters, and a changeup used primarily to fool lefties. He could start the season at Double-A and climb the ladder quickly.

LINEOUTS

HITTERS

PLAYER	TEAM	LVL	AGE	PA	R	2B	3B	HR	RBI	BB	SO	SB-CS	AVG/OBP/SLG	TAv	BABIP	BRR	FRAA	WARP
OF O. Arcia	ELZ	Rk	19	283	47	21	7	14	51	19	67	4-4	.375/.424/.672	.409	.464	-2.3	CF -5, RF 3	5.8
INF C. Cates	NBR	AA	25	314	25	5	0	0	13	17	20	4-1	.197/.246/.214	.171	.207	-1.7	SS 6, 2B 3	-1.1
OF M. Dolenc	NBR	AA	25	416	45	17	3	7	50	28	129	15-5	.259/.312/.374	.258	.368	1.7	LF 0, RF -4	0.5
OF M. Kepler-Rozycki*	TWI	Rk	17	153	15	6	1	0	11	13	27	6-1	.286/.346/.343	.271	.354	1.0	RF 3, LF 1	0.7
CF A. Morales	BLT	A	20	247	34	13	7	4	36	24	65	18-7	.289/.381/.474	.301	.390	-1.4	RF -6, CF 0	0.6
	FTM	A+	20	301	35	11	3	1	19	28	75	11-5	.272/.347/.349	.261	.361	3.7	CF 4, RF 15	2.8
1B C. Parmelee*	NBR	AA	22	463	51	25	2	6	44	43	70	3-2	.275/.341/.389	.267	.313	-3.6	1B 9, RF 2	1.5
INF M. Sano	TWI	Rk	17	161	23	14	0	4	19	10	43	2-2	.291/.338/.466	.300	.379	-3.5	3B -3, SS 1	0.8
	DWI	Rk	17	80	11	2	1	3	10	14	17	2-1	.344/.463/.547		.422	0.0		0.0
INF S. Singleton#	NBR	AA	24	564	68	43	4	7	50	39	57	2-5	.267/.325/.410	.265	.281	2.6	2B -6, 3B -2	1.0
OF R. Tosoni*	NBR	AA	23	219	22	8	4	4	24	25	52	3-1	.270/.369/.422	.288	.346	0.6	RF -1, LF 0	0.8

Oswaldo Arcia tore up the rookie-level Appalachian League last season and has the look of a potential star, with power and a cannon of an arm. ⚾ The five-foot-three, 145-pound **Chris Cates** is the smallest player in professional baseball and could lose 25 pounds and try his hand at being a jockey if baseball doesn't work out. ⚾ **Mark Dolenc** has the speed to steal some bases, but that won't matter if he doesn't improve his walk rate and on-base percentage. ⚾ **Max Kepler-Rozycki**, the son of ballet dancers, is a five-tool talent trying to become the first amateur from Germany to reach the major leagues after being signed to a bonus reportedly worth just under $800,000 in 2009. His 2010 numbers don't dazzle you, but it's very early and the Twins were overjoyed with what he did. ⚾ **Angel Morales** is a compact athlete, with plenty of tools and a need to refine them. **Chris Parmelee** has climbed through the system slowly, but showed enough power potential for the Twins to protect him on the 40-man roster at the end of 2010. The Twins signed **Miguel Sano**, a big Dominican infielder, to a $3.15 million bonus in 2009. A strapping young man, he moved from short to third, a position more consonant with his size. Scouts love his bat, and if he doesn't stick at third, it's possible he could carry right field. **Steve Singleton** looked as though he had a chance to turn into a decent prospect during his days in the low minors, when he flashed gap power and on-base skills. However, he has struggled since reaching Double-A, and if he doesn't make significant progress this year, his chances of ever making the majors will be probably close to nil. **Rene Tosoni** injured his right shoulder during last spring training and underwent season-ending surgery to repair a torn labrum in June, but his absence didn't prevent the Twins from putting him on the 40-man roster in November.

PITCHERS

PLAYER	TEAM	LVL	AGE	W	L	SV	IP	H	HR	BB	SO	EqBB9	EqSO9	GB%	BABIP	WHIP	ERA	FRA	WARP
D. Bromberg	NBR	AA	22	5	5	0	99^1	105	4	35	65	3.2	5.9	35%	.315	1.46	3.62	3.01	2.8
	ROC	AAA	22	1	4	0	52	47	9	13	47	2.3	8.1	34%	.259	1.25	3.98	5.23	0.3
B. Bullock	FTM	A+	22	0	4	14	37^1	39	2	19	45	4.6	10.9	50%	.394	1.64	3.62	2.07	1.2
	NBR	AA	22	2	4	13	36^2	34	3	24	60	6.0	14.9	41%	.369	1.69	3.44	2.81	0.8
P. Dean*	ELZ	Rk	21	2	2	0	24^1	17	3	1	32	0.4	12.0	45%	.264	0.75	2.59	2.60	3.8
C. DeVries	NBR	AA	25	1	5	1	68^1	87	10	25	63	3.3	8.3	45%	.362	1.69	5.80	6.42	-1.0
	ROC	AAA	25	0	3	0	23^1	26	2	14	24	5.5	9.4	45%	.348	1.73	5.79	6.36	-0.2
R. Flores*	COL	MLB	34	2	0	0	27^1	22	4	13	18	4.3	5.9	35%	.228	1.32	2.96	4.16	0.2
	MIN	MLB	34	0	0	0	3^2	10	2	2	2	4.9	4.9	42%	.471	3.27	4.91	-0.94	0.2
B. Lanigan	FTM	A+	23	3	1	0	54^1	43	2	7	41	1.2	6.8	49%	.256	1.02	2.15	4.37	0.8
	NBR	AA	23	2	3	0	41^1	54	5	12	17	2.6	3.7	48%	.322	1.65	5.23	5.62	0.0
M. McCardell	NBR	AA	25	3	13	0	150	178	23	46	81	2.8	4.9	37%	.312	1.53	5.28	5.52	-0.2
C. Province	NBR	AA	25	6	6	5	80^2	101	6	32	46	3.6	5.2	58%	.335	1.70	5.58	5.86	-0.6
T. Robertson*	NBR	AA	22	4	13	0	144^2	181	17	57	91	3.6	5.7	47%	.337	1.70	5.41	5.42	0.1
A. Salcedo	FTM	A+	19	1	3	0	27^1	42	3	8	16	2.7	5.3	45%	.402	1.99	6.26	5.31	0.1
	ELZ	Rk	19	4	3	1	66	55	3	10	65	1.4	8.9	56%	.292	1.05	3.27	4.07	4.2
M. Soliman	ELZ	Rk	20	5	2	0	64^2	47	5	21	74	2.9	10.4	44%	.268	1.21	3.48	3.76	5.6

David Bromberg has gained a reputation as a battler on the mound, which isn't surprising for someone who earned a spot on the 40-man last year despite having lingered on the draft board until the 32nd round in 2005. Standing at six-foot-six, **Billy Bullock** makes for a formidable presence on the mound and adds to the intimidation factor with a riding fastball that has been clocked as high as 98 mph, which makes him an appealing short-relief prospect. **Clay Condrey** is a serviceable middle reliever when healthy, with a slider, cutter, and 90-mph fastball. However, "healthy" never described his status during a 2010 season spent entirely on the DL due to a strained flexor tendon, preceded by weakness in his shoulder; neither complaint required surgery, but attempts at rest 'n' rehab failed to pay off. **Pat Dean**, the Twins' third-round draft pick last season, has drawn comparisons to Glen Perkins and clearly fits the typical Twins prospect mold; he pounds the strike zone and posted a 37.0 strikeout-to-walk ratio in 29 1/3 innings in his pro debut. **Cole DeVries** grew up dreaming of pitching for the Twinkies in the Twin Cities suburb of Eden Prairie, and although he was signed as an undrafted free agent in 2006 from the University of Minnesota, his outstanding curveball gives him at least an outside chance of pitching in the big leagues. **Randy Flores** has spent parts of 10 seasons in the major leagues, and the little lefty reliever is likely to get a chance to celebrate 11 happy years of LOOGY-dom this season. **Bobby Lanigan** is the ultimate Twins pitching prospects. He throws a ton of strikes, but his stuff is questionable and had trouble missing bats at Double-A. **Mike McCardell** has found the going tougher as he has reached the higher levels of the minor leagues, as hitters who are more experienced aren't as apt to chase his big curveball when it drops out of the strike zone. **Chris Province** had an awful first season in the Twins' system after being acquired from the Red Sox for Boof Bonser, as he failed to command his sinker/slider combination. The Twins have decided to convert **Tyler Robertson** into a reliever, since he has failed to get a feel for his changeup and was knocked around in his first season at Double-A. **Adrian Salcedo** is a loose-limbed athletic pitcher who projects to add velocity to his 94-mph fastball and improve his already above-average curveball. **Manuel Soliman** had an outstanding stateside debut last season and isn't a pitcher anyone wants to dig in against, since he hit 10 batters in 64 2/3 innings.

MANAGER: RON GARDENHIRE

YEAR	TEAM	W-L	Pythag +/-	Avg PC	100+ P	120+ P	QS	BQS	REL	REL w Zero R	IBB	Subs	PH	PH Avg	PH HR	SB2	CS2	SB3	CS3	SAC Att	SAC %	POS SAC	Squeeze	Swing	In Play
2008	MIN	88-75	-2	91.8	47	1	81	5	485	312	38	25	108	.247	3	86	37	16	5	85	61.2%	47	7	138	118
2009	MIN	87-76	0	92.4	56	1	76	8	477	301	20	49	83	.303	4	74	28	11	2	80	63.7%	46	4	150	127
2010	MIN	94-68	1	93.7	57	1	85	6	465	315	19	43	85	.162	2	60	23	8	5	53	71.7%	33	1	129	101

Ron Gardenhire was no longer the bridesmaid in 2010, at least when it came to the American League Manager of the Year award, which he finally secured after having finished second five times. Yet, despite guiding the Twins to the postseason in six of nine attempts since replacing the retired Tom Kelly, Gardenhire has yet to reach a World Series. His teams have gone 6-21 in October, and the Twins have been eliminated by the Yankees in the American League Division Series in each of their last five post-season appearances. That succession of early exits did not deter ownership from rewarding Gardenhire with a two-year extension at the end of last season—an agreement that will keep him in Minnesota through 2013. One of the more interesting aspects of 2010's 94-win season was Gardenhire's tendency to spurn small ball, abandoning his former reliance on the sacrifice bunt and hit-and-run even though the Twins had moved from the Metrodome to spacious Target Field, which was better suited for that style of play. However, that departure from the past will most likely be transient; Gardenhire was just playing to his team's strengths, and he says he wants to see the Twins make drafting and signing speed players a priority in order to take advantage of their new home. On the pitching side, few managers are more protective of their players' arms than Gardenhire; the Twins had but five starts of at least 110 pitches in 2010.

New York Mets

If you had to script an end to the Omar Minaya era in Queens, you couldn't have outdone reality: Oliver Perez, the $12 million-a-year albatross in the Mets' rotation, pitching for the first time in a month on the last day of the season, promptly walked three straight batters to send the Mets home losers in extra innings. A sarcastic chant of "M-V-P" followed the first out that Perez recorded during the debacle and illustrated how fed up the fan-base was—not just with Perez, but with everything the pitcher and his contract represented.

Perez embodies so much that was wrong with the mindset of the Mets' previous administration under general manager Minaya. The Mets gave Minaya his first genuine GM job, since his mandate as the league-appointed guardian of the dying Montreal Expos had included overseeing a form of organizational euthanasia, as opposed to the involuntary manslaughter he could be convicted of for bringing the Mets' roster to its knees. While he had his successes in New York, there were far more misses, and they all came back to one fundamental and repeated problem.

If serving as a general manager can be equated to shopping, then Minaya proved himself capable of doing two things at least adequately. He could go into a high-end store and whip out his credit card, pointing at all of the shiny Pedro Martinez, Carlos Beltran, and Jason Bay baubles and having them wrapped up for the little Mets fans for Christmas. Minaya deserves some kudos for his salesmanship in convincing these stars to choose New York's other team, but signing them was not a matter of good taste, discernment, or insight—these were often the most obvious candidates for large free-agent contracts, and Minaya bought because the Mets had both the need and the budget.

Minaya also demonstrated the ability to dive into the dumpster behind that store and—after rifling through the garbage of others—occasionally come up with a Jose Valentin, Fernando Tatis, or (most recently) R. A. Dickey, all of whom the Mets could utilize. Sure, they were a little used, and they may have had the stench of failure on them, but when employed correctly, they had their uses. Minaya's bargain-hunting wasn't always successful, and sometimes the pieces he picked up stuck around longer than they should have. Or, they were already past their expiration date and beginning to decompose—Fernando Nieve comes to mind—but the GM had no problem rolling up his sleeve and shoving his arm into the waste basket on the off chance that he might find something useful and free.

METS PROSPECTUS

2010 W-L: 79-83, 4th in NL East

Pythag	.503	17th
RS/G	4.0	24th
RA/G	4.0	23rd
TAv	.261	25th
BRR	11.3	5th
FRA	3.96	3rd
DER	-6.38	20th
DL	616	7th
B-Age	28.1	8th
P-Age	29.4	24th
Salary	$134.4	5th
M$/MW	$4.09	26th

Ballpark: Citi Field (2-yr. PF: 96). With more intelligent roster construction, the Mets and their ballpark wouldn't have to be enemies

2010: Mets finish fourth as Minaya's last stand falls flat

2011: The new regime attempts to clean up Omar's mess

Action Items: Better bargain shopping, waiting for contracts to come off the books, restoring fans' faith

What Minaya could not do was shop intelligently at a store like Target, where someone who is wise with his money can come away with a lot of valuable items on the cheap. Minaya never got a handle on putting the finishing touches on his roster. Instead, he was more likely to come home with a $300 Margaritaville Mixer that the Mets didn't really need, blowing his remaining budget and leaving his to-do list undone. Why spend $300 on something that makes margaritas when you can do that by hand, with just the cost of materials as the expense? Plus, with all of the moving parts in a machine like that, chances are good that it will break in a year and you won't be able to fix it. Oliver Perez was Minaya's margarita machine.

Considering the Mets' strong core, they should have been able to overcome injuries to players like Carlos Delgado and Carlos Beltran over the years, but with the roster's middle and lower tiers perennially talent-deprived, this proved an impossible task. Minaya rarely bought low on anything but a player who filled the back end of the roster; the trade for Delgado and the exchange that netted the Mets Johan Santana were without question the best major moves made during

Minaya's tenure, as in both cases, he gave up little for what he acquired. Excluding those swaps, Minaya's transaction record reads like a litany of overpays for players with whom the team was already familiar (Luis Castillo, Oliver Perez) as well as high-priced free agents who weren't worth the money (Francisco Rodriguez), and let's not even get started on his obsession with unwieldy vesting options like the one that still looms in K-Rod's future. Minaya's overspending on mediocrity gave rise to scenarios wherein a player like Jeff Francoeur could consistently pick up at-bats, simply because he was inexpensive and available. While that may be a useful strategy for dating in high school, it's not the way to build a championship roster.

In addition to wasting dollars, the Mets expended outs by the truckload; those are two finite resources that a team can't afford to give away, especially in tandem. Last season was no exception to this trend, as the Mets awarded 40 percent of their plate appearances to players with True Averages of .250 or worse (.260 is average). That was the National League's highest percentage, earning a place in the company of teams like the Astros, Nationals, and Pirates. Drop the threshold to a .240 TAv, and the Mets shift to third in the NL.

It's not as if the players whom the Mets employed showcased fine defense to make up for their offensive inadequacies: they finished eighth in the National League (and 17th in the majors) in Defensive Efficiency. In a park geared toward run prevention, the Mets employed a team full of players who couldn't field, and paired them with a staff that leaned on pitchers like Perez to succeed. This came on the heels of Minaya's comments to the media that he wanted to focus on pitching and defense to succeed, which suggests that he might have needed a refresher on what makes a player a quality defender or useful pitcher if he isn't a high-priced free agent.

Manager Jerry Manuel was sent packing along with Minaya this past offseason, and while he was no master tactician, he wasn't given enough from upstairs to be able to feign adequacy, either. That doesn't excuse his consistent oddities, such as his obsession with Defined Roles for players. Second basemen batted second in Manuel lineups, even if they were offensively challenged like Castillo and Alex Cora. David Wright struck out too much to bat third in Manuel's mind, so Beltran would have batted third—ergo, when Beltran was out, replacement center fielder Angel Pagan hit third. Frank Catalanotto, who was last seen hitting four years and three teams ago, batted cleanup in between Mike Jacobs' designation for assignment and Ike Davis's call-up, just because he happened to be playing first base that day, and that is where first basemen were expected to hit. Manuel actually called for Luis Castillo to lay down a sacrifice bunt against Joe Mather when the outfielder was on the mound in an extra-innings game in April, a decision wrong on so many levels that it's tempting to set aside a 31st chapter of this book just to talk about it.

Minaya was been replaced by Sandy Alderson, who then hired former general managers J. P. Ricciardi and Paul DePodesta to be his right- and left-hand men in a new-look front office, and Manuel was exchanged for Terry Collins after a long and well-publicized succession of managerial interviews. Alderson is best known for his role as Oakland's GM from 1983 to 1997, a successful stretch that included three pennants and a World Series victory, as well as his mentoring of current A's GM Billy Beane. After a stint as MLB's executive vice president for baseball operations, Alderson returned to a front office in 2005, this time as the CEO of the San Diego Padres and part of a brain trust that included many former general managers working in concert. Ricciardi most recently worked as GM of the Toronto Blue Jays, and while his reign yielded some questionable moves and nary a playoff appearance, the foundation for the exciting Toronto club of today was laid during his time at the helm. DePodesta was Beane's top lieutenant in Oakland before becoming the short-lived GM of the Los Angeles Dodgers. He worked with Alderson in San Diego and is renowned for his statistical and scouting acumen. Collins, a former minor-league shortstop, began his managerial career in 1981 and landed his first big-league managing job with the Astros in 1993. Houston's late-season collapse under Collins in 1996 is sure to be headline fodder for the shell-shocked members of the Mets' beat, given New York's recent history, as has been his loss of the Angels' clubhouse in 1999, but for a while, he'll get bonus points by virtue of being someone other than Manuel.

Before a single decision could be made by the new guys, the Mets were obligated to set aside nearly $120 million in payroll distributed among eight players. There will be much more flexibility for this front office after the coming season, when Beltran, Perez, Jose Reyes and Castillo come off the books; unless his option vests, Rodriguez will vanish then as well. Alderson and Co.'s first series of moves involved cutting costs and nontendering nonvital pieces such as John Maine and Chris Carter. It was announced almost immediately that no long-term contracts would be handed out that might hamper the team's rebuilding efforts, just one more sign that the front office is waiting for next year to engineer a real overhaul.

The new regime's preference is to have youngsters Jenrry Mejia and Ruben Tejada spend a full season in Triple-A rather than rushing them to the majors or again forcing Mejia into the bullpen for short-term gain, rather than letting him linger in the rotation with a view toward further development. This is different than the "accelerated development" program that Minaya had in place for prospects, a system that existed partly as a result of Minaya's problems with filling out the back end of the roster through other means. The Mets don't have much help coming from the farm in 2011, which represents another reason for the organization to wait to see what transpires in 2012 and react from there.

Despite his pronouncements to the contrary, Minaya did not build the team to be successful in Citi Field, a park that severely curtails home-run production. Alderson and DePodesta are both fresh off making the Padres jibe with Petco, building a roster that worked in its environment rather than the one that they may have *wanted* to build, and Alderson has already stated that there are no plans to bring in the fences in Flushing. Having those two executives on hand to oversee the Mets' metamorphosis into a team that can use Citi to its advantage should make fans optimistic about the organization's future, especially since Alderson and DePodesta will have access to something they have rarely had the chance to use along with their baseball acumen: cold, hard cash.

HITTERS

Jason Bay LF

Born: 9/20/1978 Age: 32
Bats: R Throws: R Height: 6' 2" Weight: 200
Breakout: 0% Improve: 35% Collapse: 2%
Attrition: 7% MLB: 97%

Comparables:
Josh Willingham, Ron Gant, J.D. Drew (69)

YEAR	TEAM	LVL	AGE	PA	R	2B	3B	HR	RBI	BB	SO	SB	CS	AVG/OBP/SLG	TAv	BABIP	BRR	FRAA	WARP
2008	BOS	MLB	29	211	39	12	2	9	37	22	51	3	0	.294/.370/.527	.319	.354	-0.1	LF -4	1.3
2008	PIT	MLB	29	459	72	23	2	22	64	59	86	7	0	.282/.375/.519	.318	.307	1.4	LF -5	3.2
2009	BOS	MLB	30	638	104	29	3	36	119	94	162	13	3	.267/.384/.537	.324	.315	1.1	LF 11	6.5
2010	NYN	MLB	31	401	48	20	6	6	47	44	91	10	0	.259/.347/.402	.280	.329	0.9	LF -10	0.7
2011	*NYN*	*MLB*	*32*	*602*	*81*	*28*	*2*	*25*	*80*	*75*	*138*	*10*	*2*	*.267/.363/.477*	*.295*	*.314*	*0.3*	*LF 1*	*3.2*

Bay posted the worst power numbers of his career and saw his season end in late July from a whiplash-induced concussion. That isn't how the Mets' front office envisioned the first of his four seasons with the team, but then it's hard to know what they were thinking, given what a poor fit this defensively challenged fly-ball hitter was for Citi Field to begin with. Signed as a bizarre consolation prize after the team's winter-long pursuit of Bengie Molina failed to reach fruition, Bay couldn't hit the ball out of his new Queens home. But he did quite well there (.277/.371/.459), compared with his lackluster showing on the road (.243/.326/.354). Bay wasn't the first hitter to lose track of his power for part of a season; quite often the juice will come back as inexplicably as it disappeared, but Bay's injury foreclosed that possibility. Off-season reports had Bay well on the way to recovery, and if he can repeat his home production while matching it with something more representative of his career numbers on the road, the Mets may yet reap value from this ill-considered acquisition.

Carlos Beltran CF

Born: 4/24/1977 Age: 34
Bats: S Throws: R Height: 6' 1" Weight: 190
Breakout: 1% Improve: 41% Collapse: 4%
Attrition: 8% MLB: 98%

Comparables:
Bernie Williams, Moises Alou, Luis Gonzalez (76)

YEAR	TEAM	LVL	AGE	PA	R	2B	3B	HR	RBI	BB	SO	SB	CS	AVG/OBP/SLG	TAv	BABIP	BRR	FRAA	WARP
2008	NYN	MLB	31	706	116	40	5	27	112	92	96	25	3	.284/.375/.500	.301	.296	3.7	CF -1	5.2
2009	NYN	MLB	32	357	50	22	1	10	48	47	43	11	1	.325/.415/.500	.327	.352	1.1	CF 2	3.7
2010	SLU	A+	33	57	5	5	0	0	5	7	6	0	0	.367/.439/.469	.337	.409	0.6	CF 1	0.7
2010	NYN	MLB	33	255	21	11	3	7	27	30	39	3	1	.255/.341/.427	.282	.275	-1.5	CF -2	0.9
2011	*NYN*	*MLB*	*34*	*530*	*72*	*28*	*2*	*20*	*71*	*65*	*79*	*14*	*3*	*.283/.370/.482*	*.297*	*.299*	*0.5*	*CF -1*	*3.2*

Beltran's 2010 started late for the same reason his 2009 ended early: a bum knee. The arthroscopic surgery on the arthritic portion of his right knee became controversial, as the Mets claimed that they hadn't given Beltran permission to get the procedure done, despite the fact that it was paid for with workers' compensation paperwork that was signed by the team. After some public posturing by the front office and Beltran's agent, Scott Boras, abated, Beltran returned in time for the second half, and although he didn't hit well on the whole, his .321/.365/.603 September may have been a sign that things were looking up for his health. The Mets will decide in the spring whether Angel Pagan will be the center fielder, or if they want to give Beltran one more shot at his old position, balky joint and all—either way, if September is any indication of how he is feeling at the plate, the Mets won't need to be worried, although his days as a threat on the bases have clearly ended.

Chris Carter OF

Born: 9/16/1982 **Age:** 28
Bats: L **Throws:** L **Height:** 6' 0" **Weight:** 230
Breakout: 1% **Improve:** 25% **Collapse:** 6%
Attrition: 18% **MLB:** 50%

Comparables:
Paul McAnulty, Carlos Quentin, Shane Costa (73)

YEAR	TEAM	LVL	AGE	PA	R	2B	3B	HR	RBI	BB	SO	SB	CS	AVG/OBP/SLG	TAv	BABIP	BRR	FRAA	WARP
2008	PAW	AAA	25	522	65	25	2	24	81	41	84	0	0	.300/.356/.515	.292	.317	-2.3	LF 3	2.7
2008	BOS	MLB	25	20	3	0	0	0	3	2	5	0	0	.333/.400/.333	.270	.462	0.5	LF 0	0.1
2009	PAW	AAA	26	478	50	25	0	16	61	42	63	0	0	.294/.358/.465	.285	.311	-6.3	RF 0, LF -1	1.3
2009	BOS	MLB	26	6	0	0	0	0	1	0	4	0	0	.000/.000/.000	.013	.000	0.0	RF 0	-0.1
2010	BUF	AAA	27	123	17	9	2	6	22	8	8	0	0	.336/.390/.611	.322	.323	0.0	LF 0, RF -1	0.9
2010	NYN	MLB	27	180	18	9	0	4	24	12	17	1	2	.264/.317/.389	.262	.274	0.6	LF -2, RF -1	0.1
2011	*NYN*	*MLB*	*28*	*444*	*56*	*22*	*1*	*16*	*59*	*33*	*66*	*1*	*0*	*.278/.332/.458*	*.273*	*.292*	*-0.1*	*LF -2, RF -1*	*0.8*

There are many players like Carter: unathletic, poor defenders who can crush minor-league pitching. He may be of only limited use, but he does give us the chance to explain part of the difference between the Minaya-led Mets and Theo Epstein's Red Sox, Carter's previous organization. The Mets could have offered Billy Wagner arbitration following the 2009 season. Had they done so, he would have turned into two first-round picks—that of the team that signed him, as well as a sandwich-round selection. Instead, the Mets dealt him in August to the Red Sox for a pair of players to be named later—Carter, and Eddie Lora, who in appearing in this sentence has just received his first and likely only mention in this series. When the Braves signed Wagner over the winter, the Red Sox reaped the benefits, drafting Kolbrin Vitek and Anthony Ranaudo with their new picks. The Mets, by the way, had just one first-round selection and no second-round pick in that draft. Even if trading Wagner was a move ordered by the Wilpons to save money, it was a display of terrible management and one more reason to be enthused about Sandy Alderson's arrival. The prospect of further Quadruple-A antics from Carter doesn't supply the same kind of excitement.

Luis Castillo 2B

Born: 9/12/1975 **Age:** 35
Bats: S **Throws:** R **Height:** 5' 11" **Weight:** 145
Breakout: 0% **Improve:** 35% **Collapse:** 6%
Attrition: 18% **MLB:** 85%

Comparables:
Brett Butler, Larry Bowa, Richie Ashburn (62)

YEAR	TEAM	LVL	AGE	PA	R	2B	3B	HR	RBI	BB	SO	SB	CS	AVG/OBP/SLG	TAv	BABIP	BRR	FRAA	WARP
2008	NYN	MLB	32	359	46	7	1	3	28	50	35	17	2	.245/.348/.305	.237	.260	0.7	2B -6	-0.5
2009	NYN	MLB	33	580	77	12	3	1	40	69	58	20	6	.303/.374/.346	.260	.324	2.2	2B -9	0.8
2010	NYN	MLB	34	299	27	4	2	0	17	39	25	8	3	.235/.324/.267	.227	.247	4.1	2B 6	0.7
2011	*NYN*	*MLB*	*35*	*513*	*57*	*14*	*2*	*3*	*39*	*60*	*49*	*16*	*5*	*.271/.345/.336*	*.249*	*.282*	*-0.1*	*2B -6*	*0.0*

Gilbert and Sullivan's Mikado sings that his "object all sublime" is "to let the punishment fit the crime." Had he wandered out to Citi Field last year, he would have had a hard time bending that goal to fit Omar Minaya, for the four-year contract the GM gave Castillo in November 2007 was simultaneously the crime and its punishment. Castillo crushed any optimism that his 2009 revival may have inspired, fitting in fewer than 300 punchless plate appearances around the foot and heel problems that have robbed him of all useful traits except his extreme selectivity. The Mets have not given up on his becoming the second baseman in 2011, but they are going to make him earn it and have amassed a slew of spring-training rivals to fight for the job.

Ike Davis 1B

Born: 3/22/1987 **Age:** 24
Bats: L **Throws:** L **Height:** 6' 4" **Weight:** 215
Breakout: 5% **Improve:** 26% **Collapse:** 3%
Attrition: 27% **MLB:** 60%

Comparables:
Mike Carp, Joey Votto, Travis Ishikawa (78)

YEAR	TEAM	LVL	AGE	PA	R	2B	3B	HR	RBI	BB	SO	SB	CS	AVG/OBP/SLG	TAv	BABIP	BRR	FRAA	WARP
2008	BRO	A-	21	239	17	15	0	0	17	23	43	0	0	.256/.326/.326	.243	.318	-0.1	1B 3	0.1
2009	SLU	A+	22	255	28	17	3	7	28	31	52	0	2	.288/.376/.486	.312	.348	-0.9	1B 6	2.1
2009	BIN	AA	22	233	30	14	0	13	43	26	60	0	0	.309/.386/.565	.336	.381	0.9	1B 6, RF -1	2.5
2010	NYN	MLB	23	601	73	33	1	19	71	72	138	3	2	.264/.351/.440	.290	.321	-0.8	1B 6	2.7
2011	*NYN*	*MLB*	*24*	*456*	*58*	*24*	*0*	*15*	*56*	*49*	*105*	*1*	*1*	*.267/.343/.444*	*.274*	*.319*	*-0.1*	*1B -1, RF 0*	*0.9*

Davis was just 23 in his first major-league season, but that didn't stop him from topping his 90th-percentile PECOTA forecast. While he didn't have trouble hitting at Citi Field, you could see how much force it took for him to put the ball over the fences there. Davis had to crush the ball to get it out, but he was up to that task—the average distance on his homers was nearly 416 feet. Major-league home-run leader Jose Bautista averaged 403 feet on his homers. Much uncertainty still surrounds what Davis will look like as a finished product: he didn't hit lefties well in the minors but did with the Mets, and he strikes out often, which should prevent his batting average from maintaining much altitude. He does play excellent defense at first, and it's hard to deny his power potential. Adam LaRoche is often brought up as a comparable player, but considering Davis' patience and defense, it might be more accurate to forecast his future as the player people wanted Adam LaRoche to be.

Lucas Duda **LF**
Born: **2/3/1986** Age: **25**
Bats: L Throws: R Height: **6' 5"** Weight: **240**
Breakout: **5%** Improve: **16%** Collapse: **6%**
Attrition: **22%** MLB: **35%**
Comparables:
Kila Ka'aihue, Bryan LaHair, Brad Nelson (70)

YEAR	TEAM	LVL	AGE	PA	R	2B	3B	HR	RBI	BB	SO	SB	CS	AVG/OBP/SLG	TAv	BABIP	BRR	FRAA	WARP
2008	SLU	A+	22	559	58	26	3	11	66	66	129	2	7	.263/.358/.398	.266	.335	-1.0	1B -3, RF 1	0.5
2009	BIN	AA	23	467	49	29	1	9	53	61	91	2	2	.281/.379/.428	.288	.339	-4.9	1B 2, LF -2	1.4
2010	BIN	AA	24	197	30	17	0	6	34	29	27	1	0	.286/.411/.503	.322	.310	0.4	LF 3, 1B 0	1.8
2010	BUF	AAA	24	298	44	23	2	17	53	31	57	0	0	.314/.389/.610	.319	.346	0.3	LF -5, 1B 1	2.1
2010	NYN	MLB	24	92	12	6	0	4	13	6	22	0	0	.202/.261/.417	.251	.220	0.6	LF -3	-0.1
2011	*NYN*	*MLB*	*25*	*531*	*65*	*30*	*0*	*17*	*64*	*54*	*119*	*0*	*0*	*.257/.335/.434*	*.267*	*.302*	*0.0*	*1B -8, LF -4*	*-0.1*

Lucas spoke publicly of confidence problems at the plate soon after his September call-up, but once the Duda learned to abide, he tore up major-league pitching, hitting .314/.345/.647 over his final 55 plate appearances. This was a continuation of the power stroke he had discovered in Buffalo: Duda hit 24 homers in his first three years in the minors, during which time he mustered an isolated-power (ISO) high of only .162, but he clubbed 27 homers across three levels in 2010. He is patient and doesn't strike out too often, but thanks to his short track record and Carlos Beltran's contract, he probably won't see much time in the Mets' crowded outfield in 2011. Duda could use the seasoning in Triple-A, though if you don't think he has a major-league future, well, that's just, like, your opinion, man.

Nick Evans **OF**
Born: **1/30/1986** Age: **25**
Bats: R Throws: R Height: **6' 3"** Weight: **210**
Breakout: **3%** Improve: **23%** Collapse: **4%**
Attrition: **27%** MLB: **53%**
Comparables:
Jesus Guzman, Travis Ishikawa, Justin Huber (80)

YEAR	TEAM	LVL	AGE	PA	R	2B	3B	HR	RBI	BB	SO	SB	CS	AVG/OBP/SLG	TAv	BABIP	BRR	FRAA	WARP
2008	BIN	AA	22	326	52	18	7	14	53	26	64	2	1	.311/.365/.561	.314	.353	-0.5	1B 2, LF 1	2.5
2008	NYN	MLB	22	119	18	10	0	2	9	7	24	0	0	.257/.303/.404	.259	.306	0.2	LF -1, 1B 0	0.1
2009	BIN	AA	23	117	16	9	1	3	9	10	22	2	0	.276/.350/.467	.289	.325	0.7	1B -1, RF 0	0.4
2009	BUF	AAA	23	261	27	12	3	10	30	23	55	0	0	.211/.280/.414	.242	.231	-0.3	LF 2, 1B -2	-0.2
2009	NYN	MLB	23	69	5	5	1	1	7	4	20	0	0	.231/.275/.385	.212	.318	-0.1	LF -1, 1B 0	-0.3
2010	BIN	AA	24	391	62	30	0	17	55	40	65	0	1	.294/.366/.527	.307	.317	0.0	1B 5, 3B 1	2.9
2010	BUF	AAA	24	157	26	14	1	6	25	15	23	0	0	.314/.385/.557	.313	.339	0.0	1B -1, 3B -1	0.9
2010	NYN	MLB	24	37	5	3	0	1	5	1	10	0	0	.306/.324/.472	.273	.400	0.1	LF 0, RF 1	0.2
2011	*NYN*	*MLB*	*25*	*491*	*62*	*30*	*2*	*19*	*69*	*36*	*102*	*1*	*0*	*.273/.325/.474*	*.276*	*.309*	*0.0*	*1B -9, LF -1*	*0.4*

Evans recovered from the step back he took in 2009, mashing at both Double-A and Triple-A and capping off his comeback with a solid expanded-roster run as a pinch-hitter in the majors. In the field, Evans is limited to a corner outfield spot or first base, and the Mets are set at each spot at present. His plate discipline comes and goes, and though he saw 4.1 pitches per plate appearance in the majors, he walked in under three percent of them. It's a small sample, but a look at his minor-league walk rates tells the same inconsistent story.

Wilmer Flores **SS**
Born: **8/6/1991** Age: **19**
Bats: R Throws: R Height: **6' 3"** Weight: **175**
Breakout: **0%** Improve: **1%** Collapse: **1%**
Attrition: **1%** MLB: **3%**
Comparables:
Ted Kazanski, Robin Yount, Al Kaline (60)

YEAR	TEAM	LVL	AGE	PA	R	2B	3B	HR	RBI	BB	SO	SB	CS	AVG/OBP/SLG	TAv	BABIP	BRR	FRAA	WARP
2008	KNG	Rk	16	265	36	12	4	8	41	12	28	2	1	.310/.351/.490	.277	.321	-1.4	SS 6	2.0
2009	SAV	A	17	528	44	20	2	3	36	22	72	3	3	.264/.303/.332	.240	.299	-3.0	SS -7	0.0
2010	SAV	A	18	307	30	18	2	7	44	23	37	2	1	.278/.342/.433	.299	.298	-0.5	SS -1	2.2
2010	SLU	A+	18	290	32	18	1	4	40	9	40	2	4	.300/.324/.415	.258	.336	0.3	SS -3	0.8
2011	*NYN*	*MLB*	*19*	*467*	*44*	*21*	*1*	*8*	*46*	*10*	*94*	*1*	*0*	*.235/.253/.338*	*.205*	*.274*	*0.0*	*SS 2*	*-0.6*

Flores returned to A-ball and made much-needed improvements to both his walk rate and his power numbers, earning the 18-year-old Venezuelan product a promotion to High-A, where his plate discipline regressed but his line held up, thanks to a high contact rate. Flores' offensive prowess must continue to grow, as his body limits him at shortstop—the big righty isn't particularly athletic, granting him the defensive range of a large rock—and he may someday be forced to an outfield corner. Given his youth, he has time for his bat to develop enough to support his body forcing him down the defensive spectrum.

Reese Havens **2B**
Born: **10/20/1986** Age: **24**
Bats: L Throws: R Height: **6' 1"** Weight: **195**
Breakout: **0%** Improve: **2%** Collapse: **0%**
Attrition: **2%** MLB: **5%**
Comparables:
Jeff Clement, Brandon Jones, Danny Putnam (74)

YEAR	TEAM	LVL	AGE	PA	R	2B	3B	HR	RBI	BB	SO	SB	CS	AVG/OBP/SLG	TAv	BABIP	BRR	FRAA	WARP
2008	BRO	A-	21	97	13	6	2	3	11	11	27	3	1	.247/.340/.471	.297	.327	-0.4	SS -2	0.2
2009	SLU	A+	22	430	53	19	1	14	52	55	73	3	2	.247/.360/.422	.279	.271	0.0	SS 9	3.3
2010	SLU	A+	23	65	9	2	1	3	7	8	18	0	1	.281/.369/.509	.301	.361	-0.6	2B 0	0.4
2010	BIN	AA	23	75	12	2	1	6	12	6	15	0	2	.338/.400/.662	.365	.362	-0.9	2B 8	1.6
2011	*NYN*	*MLB*	*24*	*218*	*26*	*9*	*1*	*9*	*27*	*21*	*53*	*1*	*0*	*.238/.315/.429*	*.258*	*.275*	*-0.1*	*SS 2, 2B 1*	*0.9*

Havens continued his career-long romance with the disabled list, a lingering oblique injury limiting his season to portions of May and June. Of course, he hit very well when he was on the field, so he didn't have to compost the whole campaign. Havens moved from shortstop to second base, where his glove looked more like it belonged; if he could stay in the lineup long enough to get a look, he could offer a potential solution to the Mets' keystone woes by 2012. His strikeouts will prevent him from posting high batting averages, but with excess patience and power for a middle infielder, he should get on just fine.

Luis Hernandez 2B

Born: 6/26/1984 Age: 27
Bats: S Throws: R Height: 5' 10" Weight: 180
Breakout: 0% Improve: 17% Collapse: 4%
Attrition: 8% MLB: 44%
Comparables:
Alberto Gonzalez, Luis Rivas, Fernando Cortez (77)

YEAR	TEAM	LVL	AGE	PA	R	2B	3B	HR	RBI	BB	SO	SB	CS	AVG/OBP/SLG	TAv	BABIP	BRR	FRAA	WARP
2008	NOR	AAA	24	216	18	7	0	0	11	8	27	2	2	.185/.213/.220	.167	.210	-0.9	SS -6	-2.0
2008	BAL	MLB	24	91	9	1	0	0	3	7	11	2	0	.241/.286/.253	.193	.260	-1.9	SS -1, 2B 1	-0.5
2009	OMA	AAA	25	223	24	10	0	1	26	16	17	1	3	.303/.345/.369	.252	.314	0.1	SS -1, 2B -3	0.2
2009	KCA	MLB	25	81	2	1	0	0	4	4	18	1	0	.206/.247/.219	.168	.259	-0.4	SS 1, 2B -1	-0.5
2010	BIN	AA	26	249	28	12	4	3	32	16	30	4	4	.298/.343/.427	.263	.323	0.0	SS -3	0.7
2010	BUF	AAA	26	208	25	10	4	0	12	10	31	2	1	.280/.319/.376	.245	.321	0.0	SS -2, 2B 3	0.5
2010	NYN	MLB	26	47	4	1	0	2	6	2	7	1	0	.250/.298/.409	.245	.257	0.2	2B 2, SS 0	0.3
2011	*NYN*	*MLB*	*27*	*401*	*41*	*17*	*2*	*4*	*38*	*18*	*60*	*4*	*2*	*.257/.288/.348*	*.223*	*.286*	*-0.3*	*SS -1, 2B 0*	*-0.2*

It hardly came as a shock that Hernandez was fitted for a Royals uniform in 2009, and it was equally unsurprising when he became a Met in 2010; Dayton Moore and Omar Minaya have had much in common in terms of targeting players for their major-league rosters, with the major differentiator being each GM's respective budget. Hernandez spent most of his season failing to draw walks and playing uninspiring middle-infield defense for the Mets' Double-A and Triple-A affiliates, but on September 18, he did crank a homer off the Braves' Tim Hudson one pitch after breaking a bone in his foot, giving himself the opportunity to limp around the bases, Kirk Gibson style.

Fernando Martinez OF

Born: 10/10/1988 Age: 22
Bats: L Throws: R Height: 6' 1" Weight: 200
Breakout: 0% Improve: 4% Collapse: 0%
Attrition: 2% MLB: 8%
Comparables:
Lastings Milledge, Jordan Schafer, Al Kaline (78)

YEAR	TEAM	LVL	AGE	PA	R	2B	3B	HR	RBI	BB	SO	SB	CS	AVG/OBP/SLG	TAv	BABIP	BRR	FRAA	WARP
2008	BIN	AA	19	385	48	19	4	8	43	27	73	6	2	.287/.340/.432	.257	.339	3.3	CF 3	1.6
2009	BUF	AAA	20	190	24	16	2	8	28	11	33	2	1	.290/.337/.540	.294	.316	0.3	LF 0, RF -2	0.8
2009	NYN	MLB	20	100	11	6	0	1	8	5	14	2	0	.176/.240/.275	.217	.195	0.5	LF -2, CF 0	-0.4
2010	BUF	AAA	21	287	39	16	0	12	33	17	65	1	0	.253/.317/.455	.254	.286	0.0	RF 3, CF -4	0.3
2010	NYN	MLB	21	22	1	0	0	0	2	1	5	0	1	.167/.273/.167	.183	.214	-0.1	LF 0, RF -1	-0.2
2011	*NYN*	*MLB*	*22*	*334*	*39*	*18*	*1*	*11*	*42*	*18*	*72*	*3*	*1*	*.258/.303/.428*	*.255*	*.297*	*-0.1*	*CF -4, RF 0*	*0.0*

Martinez missed a month with a hamstring strain while recovering from surgery on his arthritic right knee, again cutting into his development time. The Dominican lefty has averaged just over 300 plate appearances per season in the minors and was disappointing in his repeat of Triple-A in 2010, as injuries have blunted his tools. He doesn't cover as much ground as he used to in center, and the missed time has prevented him from improving his plate discipline as well. The Mets outfield remains occupied, so Martinez will get another season—or only part of one, if his injury history is any guide—at Triple-A.

Daniel Murphy UT

Born: 1/4/1985 Age: 26
Bats: L Throws: R Height: 6' 3" Weight: 210
Breakout: 0% Improve: 33% Collapse: 3%
Attrition: 5% MLB: 76%
Comparables:
Sean Casey, Paul Konerko, Casey Kotchman (80)

YEAR	TEAM	LVL	AGE	PA	R	2B	3B	HR	RBI	BB	SO	SB	CS	AVG/OBP/SLG	TAv	BABIP	BRR	FRAA	WARP
2008	BIN	AA	23	407	56	26	1	13	67	39	46	14	5	.308/.373/.496	.293	.317	0.2	3B 5, 2B 1	3.2
2008	NYN	MLB	23	151	24	9	3	2	17	18	28	0	2	.313/.397/.473	.305	.382	-2.8	LF 0	0.7
2009	NYN	MLB	24	556	60	38	4	12	63	38	69	4	2	.266/.311/.427	.256	.282	3.0	1B 4, LF 4	1.4
2011	*NYN*	*MLB*	*26*	*393*	*50*	*24*	*1*	*11*	*50*	*30*	*52*	*5*	*2*	*.287/.338/.453*	*.274*	*.305*	*-0.2*	*1B 1, 3B 2*	*1.6*

Murphy is a tweener due to both skill and circumstance. He played third base in the minors but isn't a good glove and is blocked by David Wright in any case; his bat isn't strong enough to carry first base and the position is now held by Ike Davis. And even if left field hadn't been deeded to Jason Bay for an additional three years, Murphy's bat wouldn't play and his outfield routes often involved stopping in midplay to ask for directions to the nearest fly ball. Working his way around the diamond, apparently by process of elimination, Murphy spent time at the keystone in the Dominican Winter League without embarrassing himself and could compete for the job in spring training. Even if he were to win the job with a hot spring, health is a concern—he sprained his knee near the end of spring training and was kayoed shortly after returning to minor-league action in late May by an MCL tear sustained when a baserunner took him out at second base. Murphy's contact-oriented bat suggests he could be a natural pinch-hitter, and that may prove to be his best defensive position as well.

Kirk Nieuwenhuis **CF**

Born: **8/7/1987** Age: **23**
Bats: **L** Throws: **R** Height: **6' 3"** Weight: **210**
Breakout: **3%** Improve: **20%** Collapse: **2%**
Attrition: **23%** MLB: **40%**

Comparables:
Jordan Schafer, Carlos Gonzalez, Colby Rasmus (79)

YEAR	TEAM	LVL	AGE	PA	R	2B	3B	HR	RBI	BB	SO	SB	CS	AVG/OBP/SLG	TAv	BABIP	BRR	FRAA	WARP
2008	BRO	A-	20	319	34	15	5	3	29	29	70	11	7	.277/.348/.396	.275	.355	3.1	CF -4, RF 0	1.2
2009	SLU	A+	21	547	91	35	5	16	71	53	118	16	4	.274/.356/.467	.285	.331	2.0	CF -3, 1B 0	2.6
2010	BIN	AA	22	433	81	35	2	16	60	30	93	13	7	.289/.337/.510	.296	.334	-0.3	CF 17	4.4
2010	BUF	AAA	22	133	10	8	1	2	17	11	39	0	0	.225/.295/.358	.230	.312	0.2	CF -6	-0.6
2011	*NYN*	*MLB*	*23*	*484*	*55*	*28*	*2*	*14*	*59*	*31*	*126*	*9*	*3*	*.252/.300/.417*	*.249*	*.313*	*-0.3*	*CF -7, RF 0*	*0.0*

Nieuwenhuis has rocketed through the Mets' minor-league system since being selected in the third round of the 2008 amateur draft. He spent most of last season in the Eastern League, where he posted a career-high ISO, surrendering some of his walks but also suppressing his strikeouts. Things didn't go as well in Buffalo, where he whiffed nearly 30 percent of the time, but such indiscretions can be excused in an age-22 season. The big lefty doesn't have the range to stick in center, but as long as he preserves his patience and makes better contact in his second exposure to Triple-A and beyond, Captain Kirk's bat can handle a corner.

Angel Pagan **CF**

Born: **7/2/1981** Age: **29**
Bats: **S** Throws: **R** Height: **6' 1"** Weight: **180**
Breakout: **0%** Improve: **48%** Collapse: **4%**
Attrition: **14%** MLB: **87%**

Comparables:
Kenny Lofton, Mitch Webster, Jerry Mumphrey (75)

YEAR	TEAM	LVL	AGE	PA	R	2B	3B	HR	RBI	BB	SO	SB	CS	AVG/OBP/SLG	TAv	BABIP	BRR	FRAA	WARP
2008	NYN	MLB	26	105	12	7	1	0	13	11	18	4	0	.275/.343/.374	.265	.329	2.1	LF -3, CF 1	0.3
2009	NYN	MLB	27	376	54	22	11	6	32	25	56	14	7	.306/.346/.487	.289	.343	3.5	CF -7, LF 3	2.0
2010	NYN	MLB	28	633	80	31	7	11	69	44	97	37	9	.290/.337/.425	.279	.327	8.7	CF 10, RF -1	4.6
2011	*NYN*	*MLB*	*29*	*334*	*41*	*18*	*3*	*7*	*41*	*25*	*51*	*16*	*5*	*.288/.335/.436*	*.269*	*.316*	*0.0*	*CF 1, LF 1*	*1.2*

Pagan retained most of the gains he made in his 2009 breakout season. He continued to represent a greater threat at Citi Field than on the road, thanks to his home park's proclivity to encourage extra-base hits that don't clear the fences; he now boasts a two-year line of .325/.366/.504 in Queens. Pagan slowed down after the All-Star break, so manager Jerry Manuel began to play him less. The logic? Manuel believed that since Pagan had never been a full-time player before, benching him would help him become a full-time player in the future. No, that isn't a joke, or a twist of a quote—Manuel's line of reasoning led him to make both that statement and that decision. Pagan isn't a great defensive center fielder, but he is an improvement over a one-legged Carlos Beltran, so the job should be his to lose in the spring. He isn't as young as his lack of major-league experience might lead you to believe, but he is, in fact, as good at baseball as his stats above suggest.

Jose Reyes **SS**

Born: **6/11/1983** Age: **28**
Bats: **S** Throws: **R** Height: **6' 0"** Weight: **160**
Breakout: **1%** Improve: **52%** Collapse: **0%**
Attrition: **5%** MLB: **99%**

Comparables:
Jimmy Rollins, Shane Victorino, Tony Fernandez (63)

YEAR	TEAM	LVL	AGE	PA	R	2B	3B	HR	RBI	BB	SO	SB	CS	AVG/OBP/SLG	TAv	BABIP	BRR	FRAA	WARP
2008	NYN	MLB	25	763	114	37	19	16	68	66	82	56	15	.297/.355/.475	.290	.314	9.2	SS -2	5.9
2009	NYN	MLB	26	166	18	7	2	2	15	18	19	11	2	.279/.355/.395	.269	.307	-1.5	SS -1	0.5
2010	NYN	MLB	27	603	83	29	10	11	54	31	63	30	10	.282/.318/.428	.270	.298	3.4	SS -6	2.5
2011	*NYN*	*MLB*	*28*	*601*	*77*	*31*	*7*	*14*	*76*	*48*	*61*	*42*	*12*	*.293/.345/.454*	*.278*	*.302*	*0.2*	*SS -5*	*2.8*

Reyes continued to be hounded by a variety of maladies in 2010. He was diagnosed with a thyroid condition that delayed his debut in the spring, then injured his oblique in July. The latter injury was slow to heal, hampering his production until the season ended. His 2010 looked much like his 2007, outside of a walk rate that was half of what he'd achieved three years earlier. The talent pool at shortstop is shallow enough that Reyes doesn't need to walk to outproduce the competition, but to qualify as one of the top players in the league at the position, he will need to bump his on-base percentage back up, especially since he has never been a great defender. Although neither Reyes nor the Mets' brass discussed it publicly, whispers about his uncertain future after 2011 could be heard throughout much of the offseason. As long as his plate discipline has not regressed permanently, he'll be worth keeping.

Ruben Tejada **2B**

Born: **9/1/1989** Age: **21**
Bats: **R** Throws: **R** Height: **5' 11"** Weight: **160**
Breakout: **0%** Improve: **5%** Collapse: **1%**
Attrition: **1%** MLB: **10%**

Comparables:
Robin Yount, Asdrubal Cabrera, Edgar Renteria (72)

YEAR	TEAM	LVL	AGE	PA	R	2B	3B	HR	RBI	BB	SO	SB	CS	AVG/OBP/SLG	TAv	BABIP	BRR	FRAA	WARP
2008	SLU	A+	18	555	55	19	4	2	37	41	77	8	5	.229/.288/.296	.219	.260	1.6	SS 2	0.2
2009	BIN	AA	19	553	59	24	3	5	46	37	59	19	3	.289/.342/.381	.263	.308	0.1	SS -8, 2B -1	1.2
2010	BUF	AAA	20	244	25	11	0	1	16	14	36	1	3	.280/.329/.344	.225	.316	0.5	SS 5, 2B 0	0.6
2010	NYN	MLB	20	255	28	12	0	1	15	22	38	2	2	.213/.298/.282	.219	.242	2.6	2B 1, SS -1	-0.1
2011	*NYN*	*MLB*	*21*	*529*	*53*	*23*	*1*	*5*	*46*	*31*	*81*	*6*	*2*	*.249/.294/.336*	*.224*	*.279*	*-0.2*	*SS 1, 2B 0*	*0.0*

Tejada's 2009 season as a teenager at Double-A raised hopes that he could be a solid utility solution or even a way off the *Luis Castillos of the Caribbean* ride at second base, but his punchless performance in Triple-A and the majors in 2010 temporarily placed those dreams on hold. He didn't turn 21 until after the season and his 8.6 percent walk rate for the Mets was actually his best mark since rookie league, so the only real worry provoked by his season is whether Omar Minaya's impulsive decision to rush him to the bigs to sub for the injured Castillo will do him any permanent harm. New general manager Sandy Alderson wisely wants Tejada to spend a full season at Triple-A, so count him out of the initial battle to topple Minaya's self-inflicted albatross from the keystone.

Josh Thole **C**

Born: **10/28/1986** Age: **24**
Bats: **L** Throws: **R** Height: **6' 1"** Weight: **205**
Breakout: **1%** Improve: **17%** Collapse: **8%**
Attrition: **12%** MLB: **38%**
Comparables:
John Jaso, Ted Simmons, Wade Boggs (76)

YEAR	TEAM	LVL	AGE	PA	R	2B	3B	HR	RBI	BB	SO	SB	CS	AVG/OBP/SLG	TAv	BABIP	BRR	FRAA	WARP
2008	SLU	A+	21	402	49	25	2	5	56	45	38	2	1	.300/.381/.427	.289	.319	-7.8	C -1, 1B -2	1.5
2009	BIN	AA	22	442	48	29	2	1	46	42	34	8	4	.328/.394/.422	.284	.348	-0.8	C 1, 1B 0	2.8
2009	NYN	MLB	22	59	2	2	1	0	9	4	5	1	0	.321/.356/.396	.262	.340	-1.1	C 0	0.1
2010	BUF	AAA	23	191	20	19	1	2	17	22	25	0	0	.267/.353/.430	.268	.298	0.0	C -2	0.9
2010	NYN	MLB	23	227	18	7	1	3	17	24	25	1	0	.277/.357/.366	.262	.305	-0.6	C 2	1.1
2011	*NYN*	*MLB*	*24*	*437*	*52*	*25*	*1*	*5*	*44*	*39*	*51*	*3*	*1*	*.280/.343/.392*	*.260*	*.304*	*-0.1*	*C 0, 1B -1*	*1.5*

Even in a more forgiving setting than Citi Field, Thole wouldn't impress anyone with his power; that just isn't one of his skills. With a free-pass rate of nearly 10 percent in his major-league career and the ability to make consistent contact, he may not need to put the ball over the wall to provide offensive value. His defense behind the plate, once a knock against him, has improved significantly—Thole threw out 44 percent of would-be base thieves in the majors last season, compared with 24 percent over the last three years in the minors, and did a capable job of blocking the plate. He earned the long end of the 2011 starting job with his half-season performance (Ronnie Paulino will be his platoon partner), and he should be one of the better catching options in the league, given the depressing state of the position.

Justin Turner **2B**

Born: **11/23/1984** Age: **26**
Bats: **R** Throws: **R** Height: **5' 11"** Weight: **200**
Breakout: **3%** Improve: **18%** Collapse: **13%**
Attrition: **24%** MLB: **40%**
Comparables:
Jarrett Hoffpauir, Aaron Hill, Matt Downs (78)

YEAR	TEAM	LVL	AGE	PA	R	2B	3B	HR	RBI	BB	SO	SB	CS	AVG/OBP/SLG	TAv	BABIP	BRR	FRAA	WARP
2008	SAR	A+	23	151	23	8	1	0	11	12	19	3	1	.316/.384/.390	.282	.368	1.1	2B -3	0.5
2008	CHT	AA	23	323	45	14	1	8	42	33	54	2	1	.289/.356/.432	.272	.322	1.9	2B -12, 3B 1	0.4
2009	NOR	AAA	24	441	54	28	0	2	43	34	37	9	4	.300/.358/.388	.266	.317	1.4	2B 3, SS -1	1.6
2009	BAL	MLB	24	22	2	0	0	0	3	4	3	0	0	.167/.318/.167	.219	.200	1.1	3B 0, 2B 0	0.1
2010	BUF	AAA	25	348	58	22	1	11	35	24	38	5	3	.333/.390/.516	.302	.346	0.0	2B -3, SS -5	1.8
2010	NOR	AAA	25	95	11	8	0	1	8	9	13	2	0	.250/.319/.381	.247	.278	0.0	2B 6, 3B 0	0.8
2010	BAL	MLB	25	9	0	0	0	0	0	0	3	0	0	.000/.000/.000	-0.009	.000	0.0	2B -1, SS 0	-0.3
2010	NYN	MLB	25	9	1	1	0	0	0	1	0	0	0	.125/.222/.250	.184	.125	0.0	2B -1, 3B 1	-0.1
2011	*NYN*	*MLB*	*26*	*460*	*54*	*25*	*0*	*9*	*50*	*33*	*65*	*4*	*2*	*.278/.332/.404*	*.259*	*.303*	*-0.1*	*2B -2, SS -1*	*0.8*

Turner barely spent any time in the majors with either the Orioles or the Mets, the latter of which grabbed him on waivers from the former club, but he improved on his boring 2009 campaign at Norfolk with a combined .316/.374/.478 line at Triple-A. He isn't the most adept fielder, but the little guy can hit well enough to hold down a spot at second. He's something of a right-handed version of Daniel Murphy, with a contact-oriented bat more geared to singles and doubles than walks and home runs. Turner gives the Mets another entrant in their second base derby after Murphy and Brad Emaus. Failing that, he could be the Jeff Keppinger–style utility player the Mets failed to exploit back when they had the actual Jeff Keppinger.

David Wright **3B**

Born: **12/20/1982** Age: **28**
Bats: **R** Throws: **R** Height: **6' 0"** Weight: **200**
Breakout: **0%** Improve: **54%** Collapse: **1%**
Attrition: **6%** MLB: **98%**
Comparables:
Al Rosen, Dan Uggla, Ron Santo (71)

YEAR	TEAM	LVL	AGE	PA	R	2B	3B	HR	RBI	BB	SO	SB	CS	AVG/OBP/SLG	TAv	BABIP	BRR	FRAA	WARP
2008	NYN	MLB	25	736	115	42	2	33	124	94	118	15	5	.302/.390/.534	.324	.321	0.1	3B -5	6.4
2009	NYN	MLB	26	618	88	39	3	10	72	74	140	27	9	.307/.390/.447	.300	.394	3.2	3B -10	3.7
2010	NYN	MLB	27	670	87	36	3	29	103	69	161	19	11	.283/.354/.503	.305	.335	0.8	3B -1	4.8
2011	*NYN*	*MLB*	*28*	*679*	*96*	*39*	*1*	*27*	*96*	*80*	*134*	*22*	*8*	*.297/.379/.503*	*.306*	*.339*	*-0.6*	*3B -4*	*4.5*

In the way that fans and media relate to him, Wright is the Ted Williams of the Mets, the guy whose fault it is, regardless of whether "it" has anything to do with him or not. He's the guy who has to be traded for the team to improve, because, contradictorily, he's both overrated and the player who will bring the greatest return. Wright bounced back from a rough 2009 in which Citi Field seemed to psych him out, a self-inflicted head game that was compounded by a literal one when Matt Cain bounced a fastball off his head. Wright's ability to make contact hasn't been the same since the injury; he struck out once every 5.1 at-bats before, every 3.6 after. Fortunately, his power rebounded, the third baseman launching 12 long balls at Citi Field, more than he had hit in all parks combined in 2009. While at times he struggles at the plate, thanks to occasionally erratic swing mechanics, and his defense at third lies somewhere between inspired and inconsistent, Wright is one of the most talented players in the game and the cornerstone of the Mets' lineup, even if the locals tend not to realize it.

PITCHERS

Manny Acosta

Born: 5/1/1981 **Age:** 30
Bats: R **Throws:** R **Height:** 6' 4" **Weight:** 170
Breakout: 8% **Improve:** 10% **Collapse:** 7%
Attrition: 9% **MLB:** 23%

Comparables:
Jesse Carlson, Santiago Casilla, Juan Perez (71)

YEAR	TEAM	LVL	AGE	W	L	SV	G	GS	IP	H	HR	BB	SO	EqBB9	EqSO9	GB%	BABIP	WHIP	ERA	FRA	WARP
2008	ATL	MLB	27	3	5	3	46	0	53	48	7	26	31	4.4	5.3	55%	.255	1.42	3.57	5.01	0.0
2009	GWN	AAA	28	1	3	2	18	0	27^{1}	21	4	13	25	4.3	8.2	41%	.239	1.25	2.64	4.42	0.2
2009	ATL	MLB	28	1	1	0	36	0	37^{1}	45	4	19	32	4.6	7.7	43%	.350	1.77	4.34	3.09	0.8
2010	BUF	AAA	29	2	3	5	28	0	36^{1}	28	4	15	36	3.7	9.0	48%	.264	1.22	3.47	4.12	0.4
2010	NYN	MLB	29	3	2	1	41	0	39^{2}	30	4	18	42	4.1	9.5	43%	.280	1.21	2.95	3.41	0.7
2011	*NYN*	*MLB*	*30*	*3*	*1*	*1*	*58*	*0*	*66^{2}*	*61*	*7*	*36*	*55*	*4.9*	*7.4*	*46%*	*.290*	*1.46*	*4.23*	*4.59*	*-0.1*

Acosta has been inconsistent throughout his career; sometimes his stuff dominates the opposition, and at other times the Panamanian can't hit the broad side of his homeland's eponymous canal. As a result, he started the season in Triple-A before heeding a call to the majors, where he struck out 9.5 per nine with a sub-three ERA. Unintentionally walking just 3.9 batters per nine qualified as a major accomplishment for the righty, but as long as he can punch out more than twice as many hitters as he lets trot to first, his power fastball will play as a weapon in relief even if he can't be trusted in high-leverage situations. Fortunately for Acosta, there will be ample middle-relief innings to soak up before the set-up crew takes the mound.

Elmer Dessens

Born: 1/13/1972 **Age:** 39
Bats: R **Throws:** R **Height:** 6' 0" **Weight:** 190
Breakout: 6% **Improve:** 12% **Collapse:** 12%
Attrition: 7% **MLB:** 42%

Comparables:
Lindy McDaniel, Mike Timlin, Jay Howell (79)

YEAR	TEAM	LVL	AGE	W	L	SV	G	GS	IP	H	HR	BB	SO	EqBB9	EqSO9	GB%	BABIP	WHIP	ERA	FRA	WARP
2008	MCD	MEX	36	10	2	0	20	19	105	129	10	17	51	1.5	4.4	62%	.326	1.43	4.03	4.72	2.8
2008	ATL	MLB	36	0	1	0	4	0	4	10	1	4	2	9.0	4.5	45%	.474	3.50	22.50	20.27	-0.5
2009	BUF	AAA	37	3	2	11	27	0	35	26	2	9	28	2.3	7.2	45%	.247	1.00	2.31	3.24	0.8
2009	NYN	MLB	37	0	0	0	28	0	32^{2}	24	5	10	14	2.8	3.9	38%	.192	1.10	3.31	5.48	-0.2
2010	NYN	MLB	38	4	2	0	53	0	47	41	4	16	16	3.1	3.1	44%	.239	1.28	2.30	3.15	1.0
2011	*NYN*	*MLB*	*39*	*3*	*2*	*1*	*29*	*5*	*51^{2}*	*53*	*5*	*18*	*27*	*3.2*	*4.7*	*48%*	*.285*	*1.39*	*4.21*	*4.57*	*0.4*

Dessens posted a 2.30 ERA over 47 relief innings last season, which isn't to say that he pitched well. In employing him, the Mets discovered that in the end, the strikeouts that soft-tossing 39-year-old righties take sometimes equal the walks they make, as Dessens both whiffed and issued free passes to 16 batters, making him the first pitcher with an ERA that low and a K/BB ratio of 1.0 or worse since Roger McDowell pulled off a 2.25 figure in 1993. It took a team effort to apply lipstick to Dessens: he ranked 10th in the NL in Bequeathed Runs Prevented, which reveals how heavily superficial relief stats can depend on having other pitchers clean up leftover baserunners with a minimum of spillage. Since teams can't count on his having that kind of support going forward, it may be time to send Elmer to the baseball glue factory.

R. A. Dickey

Born: 10/29/1974 **Age:** 36
Bats: R **Throws:** R **Height:** 6' 3" **Weight:** 205
Breakout: 10% **Improve:** 31% **Collapse:** 23%
Attrition: 16% **MLB:** 91%

Comparables:
Jarrod Washburn, Jim Perry, David Wells (66)

YEAR	TEAM	LVL	AGE	W	L	SV	G	GS	IP	H	HR	BB	SO	EqBB9	EqSO9	GB%	BABIP	WHIP	ERA	FRA	WARP
2008	TAC	AAA	33	2	5	0	7	7	49^{2}	58	2	8	30	1.4	5.4	48%	.333	1.39	3.44	4.14	0.8
2008	SEA	MLB	33	5	8	0	32	14	112^{1}	124	15	51	58	4.1	4.6	47%	.291	1.58	5.21	5.38	-0.1
2009	ROC	AAA	34	2	1	0	5	5	33^{1}	39	1	9	18	2.4	4.9	48%	.322	1.44	5.14	4.67	0.3
2009	MIN	MLB	34	1	1	0	35	1	64^{1}	74	8	30	42	4.2	5.9	48%	.316	1.68	4.62	4.91	0.2
2010	BUF	AAA	35	4	2	0	8	8	60^{2}	55	3	8	37	1.2	5.5	56%	.272	1.10	2.23	4.07	1.3
2010	NYN	MLB	35	11	9	0	27	26	174^{1}	165	13	42	104	2.2	5.4	56%	.276	1.21	2.84	3.43	3.6
2011	*NYN*	*MLB*	*36*	*8*	*7*	*0*	*37*	*20*	*158*	*167*	*15*	*54*	*81*	*3.1*	*4.6*	*49%*	*.291*	*1.40*	*4.23*	*4.59*	*1.5*

It took years, but Dickey finally turned in a quality season as a starter, thanks to command uncharacteristic for a knuckleballer. Nearly 83 percent of his offerings were knucklers, but unlike Tim Wakefield, Dickey can still throw a pitch that resembles a fastball to complement it. His floater misses some bats, and he wisely restricts the use of his heater to counts that encourage called strikes. Dickey has been able to induce grounders and weak contact when hitters do catch up to his butterfly ball, as his 28 percent ground-out rate with the pitch demonstrates. Since Dickey's effectiveness hinges on his primary pitch's unpredictability, he can't be counted on to dispense free passes at a better-than-average rate, but calling Citi Field home will help him cope with that other bugaboo endemic to the knuckleball genus: the occasional ball sent into orbit. At 36, Dickey may never be as good again, or he could have Niekro-like longevity and pitch well for another five years.

Pedro Feliciano

Born: **8/25/1976** Age: **34**
Bats: **L** Throws: **L** Height: **5' 10"** Weight: **185**
Breakout: **26%** Improve: **47%** Collapse: **22%**
Attrition: **12%** MLB: **86%**

Comparables:
Mike Stanton, Mike Jackson, Steve Farr (80)

YEAR	TEAM	LVL	AGE	W	L	SV	G	GS	IP	H	HR	BB	SO	EqBB9	EqSO9	GB%	BABIP	WHIP	ERA	FRA	WARP
2008	NYN	MLB	31	3	4	2	86	0	53^1	57	7	26	50	4.4	8.4	54%	.331	1.61	4.05	3.42	0.9
2009	NYN	MLB	32	6	4	0	88	0	59^1	51	7	18	59	2.7	8.9	56%	.279	1.16	3.19	3.96	0.7
2010	NYN	MLB	33	3	6	0	92	0	62^2	66	1	30	56	4.3	8.0	57%	.348	1.63	3.30	2.97	1.5
2011	*NYN*	*MLB*	*34*	*5*	*2*	*1*	*93*	*0*	*61*	*58*	*5*	*27*	*52*	*3.9*	*7.7*	*49%*	*.303*	*1.38*	*3.86*	*4.20*	*0.2*

For the fourth year in a row, Feliciano induced twice as many grounders as fly balls and punched out over eight batters per nine. More problematically, he remains susceptible to right-handers (831 OPS against in 2010, 898 from 2008 through 2010) and has tended to tail off in the second half, posting a 4.50 ERA postbreak in 2010 and a 4.73 mark from 2008 to 2010, compared with 2.34 and 2.50 figures, respectively, prior to the midsummer classic. This is unsurprising, given that the Mets handed him the ball 344 times over the past four seasons. His 2008-2010 appearances total of 266 is the most all time, surpassing relief workhorses Mike Marshall and Kent Tekulve, and his four-year total also ranks first ahead of Tekulve and Paul Quantrill. Even though his combined innings total was only 239 1/3, the workload clearly wore him down. He's well suited for LOOGY duty (lefties have hit .214/.282/.297 against him lifetime), but after signing him to a two-year pact in December, the Yankees run the risk of obtaining no more than his post-Mets hangover years.

Dillon Gee

Born: **4/28/1986** Age: **25**
Bats: **R** Throws: **R** Height: **6' 1"** Weight: **200**
Breakout: **20%** Improve: **44%** Collapse: **12%**
Attrition: **16%** MLB: **78%**

Comparables:
Johnny Cueto, Marco Estrada, Garrett Olson (71)

YEAR	TEAM	LVL	AGE	W	L	SV	G	GS	IP	H	HR	BB	SO	EqBB9	EqSO9	GB%	BABIP	WHIP	ERA	FRA	WARP
2008	SLU	A+	22	8	6	0	21	21	127^1	117	6	19	94	1.3	6.6	41%	.291	1.14	3.25	3.69	3.0
2008	BIN	AA	22	2	0	0	4	4	27	18	1	5	20	1.7	6.7	47%	.230	0.89	1.33	3.54	0.7
2009	BUF	AAA	23	1	3	0	9	9	48^1	47	5	16	42	3.0	7.8	39%	.298	1.41	4.10	3.67	1.1
2010	BUF	AAA	24	13	8	0	28	28	161^1	174	23	41	165	2.3	9.2	45%	.332	1.42	4.96	4.76	2.5
2010	NYN	MLB	24	2	2	0	5	5	33	25	2	15	17	4.1	4.6	49%	.226	1.21	2.18	3.81	0.5
2011	*NYN*	*MLB*	*25*	*7*	*6*	*0*	*19*	*19*	*110*	*113*	*13*	*37*	*78*	*3.0*	*6.3*	*43%*	*.295*	*1.35*	*4.22*	*4.59*	*1.6*

Gee's ability to throw nearly 200 innings between two levels reveals how well his labrum rehab went after surgery on a slight tear ended his 2009 season. The right-hander owns four pitches, none of which misses bats any more often than the average, but he led the International League in strikeouts on the strength of his fine control. That approach was less successful in the majors, where he fanned just 17 hitters in his first 33 major league innings, a more telling figure than his shiny ERA. Even so, the rookie's command wandered during his jittery first trial, and Queens has not yet seen the real pitcher, the one who can locate so well that the outside corner of Citi Field's home plate will become known as the Gee Spot. The Mets will take some time to pick through their internal pitching options, but the former 21st-round draft choice should get an ample trial in the rotation to start the season.

Sean Green

Born: **4/20/1979** Age: **32**
Bats: **R** Throws: **R** Height: **6' 6"** Weight: **230**
Breakout: **11%** Improve: **26%** Collapse: **12%**
Attrition: **11%** MLB: **47%**

Comparables:
Jeremy Affeldt, Tyler Yates, Jack Taschner (70)

YEAR	TEAM	LVL	AGE	W	L	SV	G	GS	IP	H	HR	BB	SO	EqBB9	EqSO9	GB%	BABIP	WHIP	ERA	FRA	WARP
2008	SEA	MLB	29	4	5	1	72	0	79	80	3	36	62	4.1	7.1	64%	.307	1.54	4.67	5.58	-0.5
2009	NYN	MLB	30	1	4	1	79	0	69^2	64	5	36	54	4.7	7.0	68%	.278	1.56	4.39	5.18	-0.3
2010	BUF	AAA	31	1	1	0	17	0	21^1	23	1	8	20	3.4	8.5	74%	.367	1.56	4.64	4.65	0.2
2010	NYN	MLB	31	0	0	0	11	0	9^1	7	1	8	12	7.7	11.6	75%	.261	2.04	3.86	6.16	-0.2
2011	*MIL*	*MLB*	*32*	*3*	*1*	*0*	*64*	*0*	*65*	*65*	*6*	*33*	*51*	*4.5*	*7.0*	*54%*	*.307*	*1.50*	*4.62*	*5.02*	*-0.2*

Green averaged over 72 innings per season from 2007 to 2009, but a broken rib limited him to less than half that total split between the majors and minors in 2010. While his sinker, fastball, and slider can all miss bats consistently, all except the sinker are just as likely to miss the strike zone, which keeps him from constituting a major strikeout threat. Fortunately, he's an accomplished worm-killer, which makes him a viable bullpen option. He was hit hard in the minors when he returned from injury, but his peripheral rates checked out fine. Green is best suited for a low-leverage role with occasional cameos as a double-play specialist, which should be his role with the Brewers if he can break into a crowded pen.

Ryota Igarashi

Born: **5/28/1979** Age: **32**
Bats: **R** Throws: **R** Height: **5' 11"** Weight: **200**
Breakout: **16%** Improve: **39%** Collapse: **16%**
Attrition: **19%** MLB: **77%**

Comparables:
Bert Blyleven, Andy Messersmith, Mike Trombley (78)

YEAR	TEAM	LVL	AGE	W	L	SV	G	GS	IP	H	HR	BB	SO	EqBB9	EqSO9	GB%	BABIP	WHIP	ERA	FRA	WARP
2010	NYN	MLB	31	1	1	0	34	0	30^1	29	4	18	25	5.3	7.4	38%	.284	1.55	7.12	7.58	-1.0
2011	*NYN*	*MLB*	*32*	*3*	*1*	*0*	*56*	*0*	*55*	*56*	*6*	*25*	*44*	*4.1*	*7.0*	*44%*	*.301*	*1.45*	*4.37*	*4.75*	*-0.2*

Igarashi's first exposure to the States didn't go smoothly. The righty struggled to keep the ball in the strike zone. He also injured his hamstring and landed on the disabled list, which derailed his season and ultimately consigned him to Triple-A. Igarashi relies on his mid-90s fastball and also picked up misses with his changeup on the rare occasions that he chose to throw one. While his ERA still wasn't great, his second-half numbers represented a small-sample improvement, featuring a whiff per inning and a 2.2 K/BB ratio. He will get a second chance to prove that he belongs in a major-league bullpen in 2011, and a salary of just $1.75 million gives him at least a remote chance of being a bargain.

John Maine

Born: **5/8/1981** Age: **30**
Bats: **R** Throws: **R** Height: **6' 4"** Weight: **193**
Breakout: **8%** Improve: **25%** Collapse: **19%**
Attrition: **17%** MLB: **64%**

Comparables:
Byung-Hyun Kim, Brandon Medders, Juan Rincon (72)

YEAR	TEAM	LVL	AGE	W	L	SV	G	GS	IP	H	HR	BB	SO	EqBB9	EqSO9	GB%	BABIP	WHIP	ERA	FRA	WARP
2008	NYN	MLB	27	10	8	0	25	30	140	122	16	67	122	4.3	7.8	42%	.266	1.38	4.18	5.27	0.8
2009	NYN	MLB	28	7	6	0	15	17	81^1	67	8	38	55	4.2	6.1	37%	.242	1.34	4.43	4.74	0.7
2010	NYN	MLB	29	1	3	0	9	8	39^2	47	8	25	39	5.7	8.8	31%	.336	1.87	6.13	5.79	-0.1
2011	*NYN*	*MLB*	*30*	*9*	*7*	*0*	*23*	*23*	*122*	*112*	*14*	*60*	*97*	*4.4*	*7.2*	*42%*	*.279*	*1.41*	*4.10*	*4.45*	*2.2*

Maine's season was largely lost to injury. He made just nine starts before being removed from a game after one pitch on May 20. While Maine claimed that he was healthy enough to stay in, pitching coach Dan Warthen has gone on record as saying that the righty has not always been truthful about his health. His shoulder went under the knife two months later, ending his season, but he should be available by the start of spring training. He won't be with the Mets, who nontendered him to avoid paying a few million dollars for a pitcher who has never thrown 200 innings. As a fly-ball pitcher, Maine won't fare any better for having left Citi Field.

Jenrry Mejia

Born: **10/11/1989** Age: **21**
Bats: **R** Throws: **R** Height: **6' 0"** Weight: **160**
Breakout: **1%** Improve: **10%** Collapse: **2%**
Attrition: **2%** MLB: **13%**

Comparables:
Rich Harden, Mike Fornieles, Ramon Martinez (72)

YEAR	TEAM	LVL	AGE	W	L	SV	G	GS	IP	H	HR	BB	SO	EqBB9	EqSO9	GB%	BABIP	WHIP	ERA	FRA	WARP
2008	BRO	A-	18	3	2	0	11	11	56^2	42	4	23	52	3.7	8.3	63%	.257	1.16	3.49	5.25	0.2
2009	SLU	A+	19	4	1	0	9	9	50^1	41	0	16	44	2.9	7.9	68%	.279	1.17	1.97	4.11	0.8
2009	BIN	AA	19	0	5	0	10	10	44^1	44	2	23	47	4.7	9.5	63%	.333	1.60	4.47	4.84	0.5
2010	BIN	AA	20	2	0	0	6	6	27^1	19	0	14	26	4.6	8.6	66%	.268	1.22	1.32	2.19	1.2
2010	NYN	MLB	20	0	4	0	33	3	39	46	3	19	22	4.4	5.1	61%	.319	1.74	4.62	3.96	0.5
2011	*NYN*	*MLB*	*21*	*5*	*5*	*0*	*24*	*14*	*77*	*78*	*7*	*42*	*55*	*4.9*	*6.3*	*53%*	*.299*	*1.54*	*4.64*	*5.04*	*0.8*

Mejia held his own in Double-A as a teenager in 2009, striking out 9.5 per nine. His success excited New York's front office, which had enrolled the right-hander in an accelerated development program designed to propel the team's top prospects to the majors at a younger age than usual. Even if implemented properly, the program ran the risk of stunting the development of those involved, and unsurprisingly, Mejia's season became a prime example of how not to bring a young hurler along: the Mets stuck him in the bullpen, forced him to focus almost entirely on his fastball—80 percent of his pitches thrown in relief were heaters, which didn't help his change or bender—and used him for all of 27 2/3 innings in that role before sending him back to the minors, where he should have been to begin with. Mejia returned to the rotation in time to make three starts toward the end of the year, but 2010 did little for his growth as a pitcher. He remains an excellent prospect and will spend this season starting in Triple-A under the aegis of the new administration.

Pat Misch

Born: **8/18/1981** Age: **29**
Bats: **R** Throws: **L** Height: **6' 2"** Weight: **170**
Breakout: **8%** Improve: **35%** Collapse: **16%**
Attrition: **6%** MLB: **72%**

Comparables:
Willie Collazo, Jack Kralick, Brad Radke (70)

YEAR	TEAM	LVL	AGE	W	L	SV	G	GS	IP	H	HR	BB	SO	EqBB9	EqSO9	GB%	BABIP	WHIP	ERA	FRA	WARP
2008	FRE	AAA	26	6	5	0	20	13	87	101	15	27	56	2.8	5.8	47%	.305	1.54	5.38	5.99	-0.0
2008	SFN	MLB	26	0	3	0	15	7	52^1	56	11	15	38	2.6	6.5	45%	.276	1.41	5.68	6.71	-0.4
2009	BUF	AAA	27	1	2	0	6	4	25^1	27	1	4	21	1.4	7.5	56%	.325	1.26	4.27	3.46	0.8
2009	FRE	AAA	27	3	0	1	12	1	27	24	1	4	12	1.3	4.0	56%	.267	1.11	2.00	3.64	0.4
2009	NYN	MLB	27	3	4	0	22	7	59	62	9	19	23	2.9	3.5	42%	.268	1.41	4.12	4.55	0.7
2009	SFN	MLB	27	0	0	0	4	0	3^1	6	0	3	0	8.1	0.0	56%	.375	2.70	10.80	10.60	-0.3
2010	BUF	AAA	28	11	4	0	23	23	150^2	150	11	24	99	1.4	5.9	51%	.291	1.20	3.23	4.43	2.6
2010	NYN	MLB	28	0	4	0	12	6	37^2	43	4	4	23	1.0	5.5	53%	.307	1.27	3.82	4.45	0.3
2011	*NYN*	*MLB*	*29*	*8*	*6*	*0*	*43*	*18*	*140^2*	*151*	*15*	*38*	*76*	*2.5*	*4.9*	*47%*	*.296*	*1.35*	*4.26*	*4.63*	*1.4*

Misch is a finesse lefty who has never met a junk pitch he couldn't add to his extensive repertoire. Since he sets up his mid-80s fastball well with softer breaking stuff, the lukewarm heater generates an above-average number of swings-and-misses and is thrown for strikes surprisingly often, considering its modest velocity. He may not be suited for exclusive use as a starter, and he doesn't strike out enough hitters to merit high-leverage innings out of the bullpen, but it's hard to ask for much more out of a swingman. Misch has more control than a South American junta and gets the most out of his limited stuff; better yet, he isn't even arb-eligible, so the price is still right.

Jonathon Niese

Born: **10/27/1986** Age: **24**
Bats: L Throws: L Height: **6' 4"** Weight: **215**
Breakout: **14%** Improve: **38%** Collapse: **12%**
Attrition: **18%** MLB: **67%**

Comparables:
Ricky Romero, Derek Holland, John Danks (75)

YEAR	TEAM	LVL	AGE	W	L	SV	G	GS	IP	H	HR	BB	SO	EqBB9	EqSO9	GB%	BABIP	WHIP	ERA	FRA	WARP
2008	BIN	AA	21	6	7	0	22	22	124^1	118	5	44	112	3.2	8.1	53%	.316	1.32	3.04	3.29	3.7
2008	NWO	AAA	21	5	1	0	7	7	39^2	34	4	14	32	3.2	7.3	55%	.261	1.26	3.40	3.67	1.0
2008	NYN	MLB	21	1	1	0	3	3	14	20	2	8	11	5.1	7.1	50%	.375	2.00	7.07	5.46	0.1
2009	BUF	AAA	22	5	6	0	16	16	94^1	95	7	26	82	2.5	7.8	56%	.313	1.33	3.82	3.69	2.2
2009	NYN	MLB	22	1	1	0	5	5	25^2	27	1	9	18	3.2	6.3	49%	.317	1.40	4.21	3.66	0.5
2010	NYN	MLB	23	9	10	0	30	30	173^2	192	20	62	148	3.2	7.7	48%	.324	1.51	4.20	4.96	0.6
2011	*NYN*	*MLB*	*24*	*9*	*10*	*0*	*26*	*26*	*147^1*	*158*	*15*	*59*	*107*	*3.6*	*6.5*	*49%*	*.315*	*1.48*	*4.69*	*5.10*	*1.4*

For most of 2010, Niese backed up his bona fides as a midrotation starter. Through his first 148 1/3 innings, the southpaw sported a 2.6 K/BB ratio and averaged one homer allowed every nine frames, which put him over his 90th-percentile PECOTA projection. Weariness set in come September, which brought a shifted arm slot, a flatter curve, and inferior peripherals: Niese walked five batters per nine, allowed 36 hits, and coughed up 1.4 homers per nine over his final 25 1/3 innings. Given that all of this transpired in his age-23 season, he can be forgiven for feeling some fatigue, and the ground-balling lefty will remain an important part of the Mets' rotation as long as end-of-season exhaustion doesn't become a repeated theme.

Bobby Parnell

Born: **9/8/1984** Age: **26**
Bats: R Throws: R Height: **6' 4"** Weight: **200**
Breakout: **6%** Improve: **17%** Collapse: **5%**
Attrition: **21%** MLB: **34%**

Comparables:
Josh Outman, Eulogio De La Cruz, Anibal Sanchez (81)

YEAR	TEAM	LVL	AGE	W	L	SV	G	GS	IP	H	HR	BB	SO	EqBB9	EqSO9	GB%	BABIP	WHIP	ERA	FRA	WARP
2008	BIN	AA	23	10	6	0	24	24	127^2	126	14	57	91	4.0	6.4	51%	.289	1.48	4.30	4.92	1.5
2008	NWO	AAA	23	2	2	0	5	4	20^1	25	0	9	23	4.0	10.2	47%	.403	1.67	6.65	4.90	0.3
2008	NYN	MLB	23	0	0	0	6	0	5	3	0	2	3	3.6	5.4	43%	.214	1.00	5.40	5.14	-0.0
2009	NYN	MLB	24	4	8	1	68	8	88^1	101	8	46	74	4.7	7.5	48%	.331	1.71	5.30	4.75	0.5
2010	BUF	AAA	25	1	1	4	24	0	41^1	36	3	17	42	3.7	9.2	66%	.289	1.31	4.14	5.71	-0.2
2010	NYN	MLB	25	0	1	0	41	0	35	41	1	8	33	2.1	8.5	58%	.374	1.40	2.83	2.50	0.9
2011	*NYN*	*MLB*	*26*	*6*	*6*	*0*	*55*	*13*	*111^2*	*120*	*11*	*55*	*81*	*4.4*	*6.5*	*49%*	*.315*	*1.57*	*4.90*	*5.32*	*0.1*

Mets fans had many reasons to be pleased that Francisco Rodriguez lost his closer job, even if they weren't proud of the fact that the police had to get involved in wresting the gig away. Parnell's upper-90s heat and 4.1 K/BB ratio represented two of those reasons. His lone secondary offering of consequence was his slider, which nearly doubled the league average in terms of missing bats. Control had never been Parnell's forte before 2010, but a high strikeout rate can forgive all manner of sins. Lefties presented a greater problem in 2010 than they had in the past, but he has the youth—and the slider—to make adjustments to prevent that split from reappearing.

Mike Pelfrey

Born: **1/14/1984** Age: **27**
Bats: R Throws: R Height: **6' 7"** Weight: **190**
Breakout: **12%** Improve: **34%** Collapse: **20%**
Attrition: **20%** MLB: **74%**

Comparables:
Fausto Carmona, Jeremy Sowers, Edwin Jackson (69)

YEAR	TEAM	LVL	AGE	W	L	SV	G	GS	IP	H	HR	BB	SO	EqBB9	EqSO9	GB%	BABIP	WHIP	ERA	FRA	WARP
2008	NYN	MLB	24	13	11	0	32	32	200^2	209	12	64	110	2.9	4.9	51%	.302	1.43	3.72	3.39	5.1
2009	NYN	MLB	25	10	12	0	31	31	184^1	213	18	66	107	3.2	5.2	52%	.312	1.55	5.03	4.59	1.9
2010	NYN	MLB	26	15	9	1	34	33	204	213	12	68	113	3.0	5.0	51%	.300	1.41	3.66	3.77	3.4
2011	*NYN*	*MLB*	*27*	*10*	*10*	*0*	*28*	*28*	*171*	*183*	*12*	*65*	*92*	*3.4*	*4.8*	*49%*	*.303*	*1.45*	*4.38*	*4.77*	*2.0*

Pelfrey has three varieties of fastball at his disposal: a pure sinker, a two-seamer, and a four-seamer. Legend has it that the tall right-hander also possesses a changeup, but the only one of his four weapons easily distinguished by its velocity and movement is also the least utilized. None of Pelfrey's pitches is a standout offering; all four miss bats at a league-average rate, although the movement on his sinker and two-seamer does help the righty induce ground balls. Pelfrey is a fan favorite, and due to his youth and sometimes-respectable ERAs, he's considered capable of leading a staff in some quarters, but he's not up to that task. Big Pelf had a 2.82 ERA at Citi Field last year, but a 4.95 ERA on the road, where he allowed twice as many homers in 44 fewer innings while averaging fewer than six frames per start. His struggles in less cavernous parks weren't limited to 2010 and represent something more than an artifact of small sample size, which is the reason why his ceiling is no higher than that of a midrotation starter.

Oliver Perez

Born: **8/15/1981** Age: **29**
Bats: **L** Throws: **L** Height: **6' 3"** Weight: **160**
Breakout: **23%** Improve: **37%** Collapse: **19%**
Attrition: **17%** MLB: **69%**

Comparables:
Darryl Kile, Melido Perez, Ken Kravec (64)

YEAR	TEAM	LVL	AGE	W	L	SV	G	GS	IP	H	HR	BB	SO	EqBB9	EqSO9	GB%	BABIP	WHIP	ERA	FRA	WARP
2008	NYN	MLB	26	10	7	0	34	34	194	167	24	105	180	4.9	8.4	35%	.271	1.46	4.22	4.75	2.0
2009	NYN	MLB	27	3	4	0	14	14	66	69	12	58	62	7.9	8.5	32%	.303	1.98	6.82	7.34	-0.6
2010	NYN	MLB	28	0	5	0	17	7	46^{1}	54	9	42	37	8.2	7.2	36%	.317	2.16	6.80	6.72	-0.7
2011	*NYN*	*MLB*	*29*	*8*	*10*	*0*	*26*	*26*	*137^{1}*	*131*	*19*	*88*	*119*	*5.8*	*7.8*	*39%*	*.289*	*1.60*	*5.13*	*5.58*	*0.7*

Johnny Mercer was wrong: sometimes an immovable object just doesn't give, no matter how much force you apply. Confronted with the problem of a pitcher who was utterly ineffective, the Mets begged Perez to look for himself on a minor-league walkabout. Their entreaties were dashed like waves breaking across a rocky shoal. The problem was that in this case, the shoal was being paid $12 million. A case of patella tendinitis came to their rescue, though the timing of the diagnosis, coming just after Perez's refusal to be sent down, provoked an investigation by the commissioner's office. Too much of an extreme fly-ball pitcher for even Citi Field to contain, Perez still strikes out an above-average number of hitters, an incredible feat for the limited time he spends in the strike zone. Only 29, Perez may yet find his way back to respectability, but such moments have been islands in a sea of annoyingly poor performances (picture the bloated Perez floating face down in a sea of moldy Cool Whip). Perez is due one more check from the Mets, a $12 million monument to Omar Minaya's gullibility.

Francisco Rodriguez

Born: **1/7/1982** Age: **29**
Bats: **R** Throws: **R** Height: **6' 0"** Weight: **175**
Breakout: **21%** Improve: **48%** Collapse: **27%**
Attrition: **9%** MLB: **94%**

Comparables:
John Wetteland, Joe Nathan, Jesse Orosco (71)

YEAR	TEAM	LVL	AGE	W	L	SV	G	GS	IP	H	HR	BB	SO	EqBB9	EqSO9	GB%	BABIP	WHIP	ERA	FRA	WARP
2008	ANA	MLB	26	2	3	62	76	0	68^{1}	54	4	34	77	4.5	10.1	42%	.292	1.32	2.24	2.64	1.6
2009	NYN	MLB	27	3	6	35	70	0	68	51	7	38	73	5.0	9.7	38%	.250	1.32	3.71	4.04	0.5
2010	NYN	MLB	28	4	2	25	53	0	57^{1}	45	3	21	67	3.3	10.5	44%	.294	1.19	2.20	2.07	1.5
2011	*NYN*	*MLB*	*29*	*4*	*2*	*35*	*69*	*0*	*66^{2}*	*53*	*5*	*32*	*74*	*4.3*	*10.0*	*43%*	*.289*	*1.28*	*3.05*	*3.32*	*0.9*

Paying Rodriguez $11.5 million per season, as the Mets did in 2010 and will do again in 2011, isn't a terrible fate. He's an overrated closer, but is capable of coming close to earning that money. Until you get to his option year, that is, a $17.5 million season that automatically vests if Rodriguez finishes 55 games in 2011, at least 100 games combined between 2010 and 2011, or is declared healthy by doctors following the 2011 season. Fortunately for K-Rod, winning a Sensitive Male of the Year award is not one of the qualifiers. A $3.5 million buyout has to be paid if any of the three qualifications are not met. He finished 46 games in 2010, so if the Mets are careful, they can avoid having the option vest. Rodriguez isn't expected to miss any time in 2011 due to his arrest for assault, as his anger management classes fit in around the Mets' schedule.

Johan Santana

Born: **3/13/1979** Age: **32**
Bats: **L** Throws: **L** Height: **6' 0"** Weight: **195**
Breakout: **12%** Improve: **43%** Collapse: **23%**
Attrition: **5%** MLB: **96%**

Comparables:
John Smoltz, Jack Morris, Jim Bunning (71)

YEAR	TEAM	LVL	AGE	W	L	SV	G	GS	IP	H	HR	BB	SO	EqBB9	EqSO9	GB%	BABIP	WHIP	ERA	FRA	WARP
2008	NYN	MLB	29	16	7	0	34	34	234^{1}	206	23	63	206	2.4	7.9	44%	.274	1.17	2.53	2.98	7.0
2009	NYN	MLB	30	13	9	0	25	25	166^{2}	156	20	46	146	2.5	7.9	38%	.280	1.23	3.13	3.48	3.7
2010	NYN	MLB	31	11	9	0	29	29	199	179	16	55	144	2.5	6.5	37%	.272	1.19	2.98	3.08	4.9
2011	*NYN*	*MLB*	*32*	*14*	*7*	*0*	*31*	*31*	*210^{2}*	*188*	*20*	*60*	*169*	*2.6*	*7.2*	*41%*	*.278*	*1.18*	*3.09*	*3.36*	*5.7*

Following a winter where seven-year offers were thrown at Cliff Lee by various teams, it pays to remember what happened to Santana. His third season of a six-year deal ended with shoulder surgery that will keep him out until the second half. He is still owed at least $77.5 million when you take his 2014 buyout into account, and he has a full no-trade clause just to make things that much more difficult. Santana was nowhere near as good as his 2010 ERA suggests: he whiffed a below-average number of hitters and gave up 13 homers on the road, versus just three in the expansive Citi Field. Those missing strikeouts aren't a problem that will vanish, either, as his punchout rates have fallen in each of the last three years, and his fastball now sits around 90 mph. Santana also ran into some trouble with the law, as he dealt with a sexual assault allegation in August. All in all, it just wasn't a banner year for the Mets' ace, and this may be the state of things from now on. PECOTA doesn't know about his injury, so that projection belongs to a parallel-universe Santana.

Hisanori Takahashi

Born: **4/2/1975** Age: **36**
Bats: **L** Throws: **L** Height: **5' 10"** Weight: **170**
Breakout: **14%** Improve: **36%** Collapse: **32%**
Attrition: **9%** MLB: **100%**

Comparables:
Mark Langston, Mike Mussina, Jeff Fassero (47)

YEAR	TEAM	LVL	AGE	W	L	SV	G	GS	IP	H	HR	BB	SO	EqBB9	EqSO9	GB%	BABIP	WHIP	ERA	FRA	WARP
2010	NYN	MLB	35	10	6	8	53	12	122	116	13	43	114	3.2	8.4	40%	.298	1.30	3.61	3.68	2.3
2011	*ANA*	*MLB*	*36*	*7*	*4*	*7*	*54*	*12*	*123^{1}*	*117*	*12*	*44*	*106*	*3.2*	*7.7*	*43%*	*.299*	*1.30*	*3.61*	*3.92*	*1.8*

The Japanese southpaw made his major-league debut this year after the Mets signed him to a one-year, $1 million minor-league deal. That turned out to be an excellent investment, with Takahashi throwing 122 innings between 12 starts and 41 relief appearances. He ranked 10th in the National League in expected wins added over replacement-level pitcher (WXRL) despite just 57 1/3 innings out of the pen, and given the 821 OPS he allowed as a starter, it's a good thing he found a home in the pen. The Angels signed Takahashi and his excellent changeup for two years and $8 million, which, with the way he handled the NL out of the pen, could be a steal of a deal for a team with a middling relief corps.

Raul Valdes

Born: **11/27/1977** Age: **33**
Bats: **L** Throws: **L** Height: **5' 11"** Weight: **190**
Breakout: **16%** Improve: **37%** Collapse: **12%**
Attrition: **10%** MLB: **59%**

Comparables:
Dave LaRoche, Jeff Reardon, Jay Howell (76)

YEAR	TEAM	LVL	AGE	W	L	SV	G	GS	IP	H	HR	BB	SO	EqBB9	EqSO9	GB%	BABIP	WHIP	ERA	FRA	WARP
2010	BUF	AAA	32	2	1	0	9	7	36	34	3	9	36	2.3	9.0	31%	.313	1.22	3.00	2.75	1.4
2010	NYN	MLB	32	3	3	1	37	1	58^{2}	59	7	28	56	4.3	8.6	34%	.310	1.55	4.91	4.09	0.5
2011	*SLN*	*MLB*	*33*	*3*	*2*	*0*	*27*	*5*	*55^{1}*	*57*	*6*	*23*	*44*	*3.8*	*7.2*	*42%*	*.310*	*1.45*	*4.53*	*4.93*	*0.2*

Native Cuban Valdes has pitched winter baseball for the Gigantes del Cibao of the Dominican Winter League the last few years, which earned him an invitation to spring training with the Mets in 2010. The 32-year-old pitched well at Buffalo and was quickly moved up to New York, where he made his major-league debut five years after his defection. The former indie-league hurler threw 58 1/3 innings that included one start, and while his control was never there, he did strike out 8.6 batters per nine. Valdes was one of many Mets to refuse a minor-league assignment following the season, and instead became a free agent. The lefty latched on with the Cardinals, where he may help out of the bullpen.

LINEOUTS

HITTERS

PLAYER	TEAM	LVL	AGE	PA	R	2B	3B	HR	RBI	BB	SO	SB-CS	AVG/OBP/SLG	TAv	BABIP	BRR	FRAA	WARP
2B J. Arias	NYN	MLB	25	33	3	1	0	0	4	2	6	0-0	.200/.242/.233	.204	.240	-0.1	2B -1, SS -1	-0.3
	TEX	MLB	25	101	15	5	1	0	9	2	17	1-0	.276/.287/.347	.233	.329	2.1	2B 0, 1B -1	0.1
C H. Blanco	NYN	MLB	38	144	10	5	0	2	8	11	26	1-0	.215/.271/.300	.213	.248	-1.9	C 0	-0.2
CF D. Ceciliani*	BRO	A-	20	303	56	19	12	2	35	24	56	21-14	.351/.410/.531	.338	.429	0.0	CF 8	4.1
CF M. Den Dekker*	SAV	A	22	114	21	13	0	0	15	9	28	3-0	.346/.404/.471	.325	.474	0.0	CF 0	1.2
OF J. Feliciano*	BUF	AAA	31	371	55	18	1	1	28	21	35	6-5	.339/.385/.408	.281	.369	0.5	RF 13, CF 2	2.8
	NYN	MLB	31	119	12	4	1	0	3	6	12	1-0	.232/.269/.287	.194	.250	1.2	RF 2, CF -1	-0.4
3B M. Hessman	BUF	AAA	32	282	43	20	0	18	58	27	60	0-0	.274/.351/.573	.307	.289	0.5	3B 5, 1B -2	2.4
	NYN	MLB	32	65	6	2	1	1	6	8	23	0-0	.127/.262/.254	.212	.194	-1.5	1B 0, 3B 1	-0.3
3B Z. Lutz	BIN	AA	24	263	42	14	0	17	42	33	63	0-2	.289/.389/.578	.326	.329	-1.8	3B -9	1.5
3B J. Marte	SAV	A	19	366	40	19	4	6	44	30	65	4-5	.264/.333/.401	.291	.312	1.4	3B 1	2.4
C M. Nickeas	BIN	AA	27	318	27	15	0	5	33	49	43	1-1	.283/.403/.396	.297	.323	0.0	C 0, 1B -1	2.5
	NYN	MLB	27	10	0	0	0	0	0	0	5	0-0	.200/.200/.200	.108	.400	0.0	C 0	-0.1
OF J. Pridie*	BUF	AAA	26	177	17	6	1	3	19	12	36	9-3	.281/.328/.384	.241	.341	0.8	CF 4	0.6
OF C. Puello	SAV	A	19	469	80	22	1	1	34	32	82	45-10	.292/.375/.359	.285	.352	6.7	RF 3	2.8
3B A. Rodriguez	KNG	Rk	18	267	44	22	0	13	48	15	43	3-1	.312/.352/.556	.330	.333	0.7	3B -6	3.0
C O. Santos	BIN	AA	29	64	5	3	0	1	8	4	7	0-0	.138/.203/.241	.187	.137	0.5	C -1, 1B 0	-0.2
2B J. Satin	SLU	A+	25	245	27	15	0	5	35	30	50	1-5	.316/.406/.459	.310	.389	-6.0	2B -4, 1B 0	0.8
	BIN	AA	25	332	49	24	1	7	39	36	71	1-0	.308/.395/.472	.302	.384	-3.1	2B -6, 1B -3	0.7
UT F. Tatis	NYN	MLB	35	72	6	4	0	2	6	6	19	0-0	.185/.250/.339	.229	.222	0.2	1B 0, 3B -1	-0.2
2B J. Valdespin*	SLU	A+	22	288	40	16	3	6	33	8	45	13-10	.289/.323/.437	.270	.323	0.3	2B 1, SS -3	0.9
	BIN	AA	22	117	8	8	0	0	8	2	23	4-2	.232/.243/.304	.184	.283	0.5	2B -3	-0.9
OF C. Vaughn	BRO	A-	21	313	45	14	5	14	56	34	63	12-5	.307/.396/.557	.339	.347	0.0	RF -4, CF 1	2.9

If you could add together the OPS percentages of **Joaquin Arias** from his stints in New York and Texas, you would have a great infield asset. Unfortunately, that's not how these things work; back in reality, Arias is a terrible hitter even for a utility infielder, and he's not a particularly effective fielder anywhere on the diamond. ⊘ **Henry Blanco** has never been a good hitter, but the bottom fell out with the Mets. Not all was lost: even at age 38, he had the arm to throw out half of the runners who attempted to steal on him, and he still moves around well enough to block the plate adequately. The Diamondbacks signed him to serve as Miguel Montero's relief. ⊘ **Darrell Ceciliani** is a plus-plus runner who can handle center field. He has a line-drive swing—hence the .430 batting average on balls in play—and while he won't keep his average up that high forever, there is a lot to like about the bat of a 20-year-old speedster who has already flashed some serious extra-base hit potential. ⊘ **Matt Den Dekker** is already 22 and has just one pro season under his belt, but A-ball didn't give him any trouble, and he has the potential to move fast. He is an excellent defender in center and comes equipped with a line-drive swing and a basic understanding of the strike zone. ⊘ **Jesus Feliciano** was enjoying his fourth straight season at Triple-A when the Mets came calling, asking him to make his major-league debut as a 31-year-old outfielder. He puts the ball in play often and plays solid defense in the outfield, which helps to compensate for his lack of patience at the plate. ⊘ **Mike Hessman** is the active minor-league leader with 329 career homers. His career line as a busher rests at .231/.314/.460, thanks to approximately eleventy-billion strikeouts, far too many of which showed up for his short stint with the Mets last season. Hessman understandably balked at another minor-league assignment and headed to Japan. ⊘ **Zach Lutz** is a poor defensive third baseman who has very real power. The question is whether it will translate to higher levels, since he has an uppercut swing that can be exploited by more advanced pitchers. ⊘ **Jefry Marte** was clearly unprepared to tackle Single-A in 2009, but he made progress in his second attempt at the level last year. The third baseman replaced some of his strikeouts with free passes while also regaining some of the power he had lost upon his promotion, thanks to impressive bat speed for an 18-year-old. ⊘ **Mike Nickeas** will never be a hitter, but he has been successful at throwing out runners at the upper levels and sports a career minor-league caught-stealing rate of 30 percent. He finally reached the majors in 2010, after several years on the farm and wrist surgery had caused him to contemplate retirement. ⊘ **Jason Pridie** can field at any of the three outfield positions, but he projects to be an offensive zero in the majors, which limits him to a role as a defensive replacement. Given that the Mets have several bad knees in the same outfield, Pridie could have value if employed judiciously. ⊘ **Cesar Puello** doesn't lack the tools to become a successful outfielder, but he remains a raw work in progress in the low minors. The 19-year-old bumped up his walk rate for the second straight season and cut down on his whiffs, and after an abysmal start to the year, he hit .346/.424/.430 in the second half before a back strain cut his season short in mid-August. A mechanical change that allowed him to attack pitches on the inner part of the plate was responsible for that outburst, making him a breakout candidate for 2011. ⊘ **Aderlin Rodriguez** has as much raw power as anyone in the system, and the fact that it already shows up in games in special, but he's almost assuredly a first baseman in the end, so he better keep slugging. ⊘ One season after putting up a replacement-level line in the majors, **Omir Santos** posted an even uglier performance in the minors. His combined .160/.208/.241 line in abbreviated action was breathtakingly awful, unsalvageable by any caliber of defense. Santos refused his minor-league assignment in November and hooked on with the Tigers, who'll pay for the privilege of hoping not to use him. ⊘ **Josh Satin** has some patience, as evidenced by walk rates exceeding 10 percent at two levels this year, and he hits his share of doubles. A stocky, nonathletic second baseman, Satin was 25 in his first stint at Double-A, and while he has some skills, they may not be enough to push the other second-base options ahead of him out of the way. ⊘ **Fernando Tatis** underwent shoulder surgery to repair his labrum in July, and the procedure may have ended his career. While he struggled in limited duty in 2010, he was a solid and inexpensive asset for the Mets for two seasons prior. ⊘ **Jordany Valdespin** rose through three levels in 2009, and his forward progress continued last season with time spent at both High-A and Double-A. Except for a spot of success in Single-A, Valdespin hasn't shown that he can do much except run fast. An experiment at short didn't go well, with 11 errors in 99 chances. ⊘ **Cory Vaughn** is the son of former major-league slugger Greg Vaughn, and the right-handed outfielder takes after his dad. He has shown above-average power, smacking 14 homers and 19 lesser extra-base hits in his pro debut at Low-A, and he has already flashed advanced plate discipline for a 21-year-old.

PITCHERS

PLAYER	TEAM	LVL	AGE	W	L	SV	IP	H	HR	BB	SO	EqBB9	EqSO9	GB%	BABIP	WHIP	ERA	FRA	WARP
K. Allen	SLU	A+	20	6	8	0	101^1	106	6	54	53	4.8	4.7	56%	.300	1.70	5.24	5.82	-0.1
M. Antonini*	BIN	AA	24	6	9	0	131^1	132	17	26	106	1.8	7.3	33%	.293	1.24	4.32	6.02	-0.3
	BUF	AAA	24	2	3	0	37	45	6	5	25	1.2	6.1	38%	.328	1.43	5.11	4.23	0.6
B. Bruney	WAS	MLB	28	1	2	0	17^2	21	1	20	16	10.2	8.2	47%	.357	2.32	7.64	4.23	-0.6
J. Familia	SLU	A+	20	6	9	0	121	117	7	74	137	5.5	10.2	50%	.341	1.70	5.58	6.03	-0.3
M. Harvey	DNP	—	22	—	—	—	—	—	—	—	—	—	—	—	—	—	—	—	—
B. Holt	SLU	A+	23	2	9	0	65	68	4	56	62	7.8	8.6	35%	.344	2.12	7.48	6.99	-0.6
	BIN	AA	23	1	5	0	30	43	2	23	25	6.9	7.5	40%	.398	2.30	10.20	9.07	-1.0
B. Moore	SAV	A	24	3	4	2	79^2	62	5	11	98	1.3	11.1	49%	.302	0.95	2.49	3.27	1.5
	SLU	A+	24	2	4	0	66	69	4	26	61	3.5	8.3	45%	.330	1.52	3.82	4.85	0.6
F. Nieve	BUF	AAA	27	2	1	0	40	49	3	13	31	2.9	7.0	40%	.357	1.58	5.40	4.56	0.7
	NYN	MLB	27	2	4	0	42	37	10	22	38	4.7	8.1	39%	.241	1.45	6.00	6.24	-0.6
E. Ramirez	SLU	A+	22	4	3	0	73^1	56	0	43	65	5.3	8.0	50%	.269	1.48	4.17	4.14	0.7
A. Rodriguez	SAV	A	22	8	9	0	146	116	5	46	152	2.8	9.4	42%	.282	1.18	3.08	3.83	2.4
T. Stoner	BUF	AAA	25	6	10	0	120^2	158	18	43	83	3.2	6.2	45%	.343	1.71	5.97	5.33	1.1
	NYN	MLB	25	0	1	0	2^1	3	0	1	0	3.9	0.0	60%	.300	1.71	3.86	4.01	0.0
J. Urbina*	MTS	Rk	17	5	3	0	48^1	54	5	14	38	2.6	7.1	40%	.325	1.52	5.03	3.86	3.3

Over 101 innings at High-A, **Kyle Allen** walked more hitters than he struck out, threw 10 wild pitches, and hit 12 batters, which gives him one plunk per 10 innings in his pro career. Allen's heater has slightly above-average velocity with sink, but the lack of refinement in his secondary pitches will be the least of his problems if mechanical issues cause his walk and strikeout rates to stay on their current trajectories. Finesse lefty **Michael Antonini** has fringe stuff but great control. The problem is that many of the pitches he puts into the strike zone end up in the stands: he allowed 1.2 homers per nine on the year, and 1.5 in his first shot at Triple-A. On the plus side, his movie *Blow-Up* is a classic. **Brian Bruney** was an extra in the 1990 Arnold Schwarzenegger flick *Kindergarten Cop*. The White Sox signed him to a minor-league contract, but after the way he pitched for the Nationals and at Buffalo for the Mets last season, he may want to give acting another shot. The beefy right-hander will try to make the White Sox after signing a minor-league deal. **Kelvim Escobar** tore his right shoulder capsule before he threw a pitch for the Mets. He can't be counted on in 2011 after throwing just over 25 innings at all levels combined over the last three years. **Jeurys Familia** is unrefined, but his 95-96 mph fastball is one of the best in the system. His strong arm isn't always accurate and got him into trouble with walks last season, but the 20-year-old flashed strikeout potential at High-A, making the Dominican more promising than his ERA would indicate. **Matthew Harvey** was considered a big-time power-pitching prospect coming out of high school, but he elected to go to college. That decision paid off in dollars as well as sorority girls, as the Mets took him seventh overall in last summer's amateur meat market. Harvey has height and above-average fastball velocity to go along with a plus slider, but in light of the inconsistencies that plagued him at North Carolina and the Cape Cod League, his impact potential remains uncertain. At six-foot-four, **Brad Holt** is built like a power pitcher, but that won't help him unless he remembers where he left the strike zone. His 2010 was a total collapse that saw him walk 79 in 95 innings—and that includes the 65 frames he hurled at High-A after a demotion from Binghamton. **Brandon Moore**'s stuff is just average, but he makes up for low voltage with superior command and sequencing. A team can become too attached to freely available talent that outperforms its humble origins, and the Mets' misplaced affection for **Fernando Nieve** is a prime example. The Mets paid for their limerence last season, with 10 homers and 20 unintentional walks over 42 innings. Moving to Pittsburgh won't improve Neive's numbers unless the Pirates demote him to Triple-A, although Double-A might be a better fit. **Elvin Ramirez** is a tall righty who has no idea where the ball is going when it leaves his hand. Sometimes it crosses the plate for a strike, other times it strikes the hitter, and less frequently it bypasses the catcher's vicinity altogether and doesn't stop until it hits the 7 train. Ramirez is not a ground-ball pitcher, but rarely allows homers; if he could find the strike zone more often—as he did in the Dominican Winter League—he would become an intriguing relief option for Washington, which snagged him in the Rule 5 draft. **Armando Rodriguez** is a lanky Dominican with some arm strength and promise. He has above-average velocity and a slurvy bender, but he lacks a changeup to complement those offerings. The 22-year-old repeated Single-A in 2010 and displayed much better control the second time around. **Tobi Stoner**'s name is better than his fastball. He struck out a below-average number of hitters as a 25-year-old at Triple-A and would have a hard time whiffing twice as many batters as he walked, if he were to stick in the majors, since none of the four pitches he uses regularly is capable of generating consistent swings-and-misses. As he serves a 14-year sentence for attempted murder in his native Venezuela, former reliever Ugueth Urbina can take some pleasure in tracking his son **Juan Urbina**'s attempt to follow in his major-league footsteps. The junior, left-handed, and unincarcerated Urbina's fastball sits at 89 mph, but since he just concluded his age-17 season, he has plenty of time to add velocity. As it was, Urbina whiffed 2.7 times more guys than he walked, and while his debut ERA wasn't pretty, he offers plenty of projection.

MANAGER: JERRY MANUEL

YEAR	TEAM	W-L	Pythag +/–	Avg PC	100+ P	120+ P	QS	BQS	REL	REL w Zero R	IBB	Subs	PH	PH Avg	PH HR	SB2	CS2	SB3	CS3	SAC Att	SAC %	POS SAC	Squeeze	Swing	In Play
2008	NYN	55-38	0	101.4	56	2	49	2	324	212	37	46	164	.245	2	54	16	16	3	64	57.8%	21	0	90	63
2009	NYN	70-92	-1	95.6	80	2	76	5	511	331	60	50	286	.206	5	105	41	17	1	120	73.3%	49	3	156	136
2010	NYN	79-83	-2	98.0	92	4	86	8	489	330	55	38	276	.231	3	117	42	12	2	113	65.5%	37	0	151	112

Manuel evinced a tendency to construct counterproductive lineups in which the substitutes for stars would occupy the same slots as the players they were replacing, despite the Grand Canyon–sized divide in talent between them. As a result, he placed subpar hitters in lineup positions that granted them extra plate appearances, hamstringing the Mets' run-scoring potential. He regularly went without calling on closer Francisco Rodriguez for four or five days at a time, solely because no save situation arose. There was no better example of this than the 20-inning contest between the Cardinals and Mets in April, in which Rodriguez didn't pitch until the 19th frame, because that was the first time a save situation presented itself. Mets fans can safely put those memories behind them, since Terry Collins has taken over as the team's manager on a two-year pact. As the organization's minor-league field coordinator, Collins cleaned up the mess left by his predecessor Tony Bernazard, but Collins hasn't managed at the highest level since stepping away from the Angels amid clubhouse upheaval in 1999 (he subsequently managed in Japan and steered the Chinese WBC squad in 2009). The fourth-oldest manager in the majors carries a Showalter-ian reputation for intensity and adeptness at rebuilding, which would seem to make him a good fit for the Mets. While Collins' track record isn't flawless, he *is* on record as understanding that sometimes, you need to win the game before the ninth inning.

New York Yankees

After the Yankees were unceremoniously dumped out of the post-season derby by the Texas Rangers, general manager Brian Cashman said, "We didn't look old against Minnesota [in the division series], and that was a week before. Texas made us look old."

As the old pun goes, denial is a river in the Bronx. The Yankees looked old long before they were abused by Texas. More than looking old, they *are* old. By weighted-average age, they had the fourth-oldest crew of hitters in the majors, trailing only the Phillies, Red Sox, and White Sox. By the same standard, their pitchers were the second-oldest at 30.4, younger only than the Phillies'.

The graying of the Yankees wasn't a problem for most of the season. On August 28, they commenced an eight-game winning streak, whipping the White Sox, A's, and Blue Jays in succession. At its conclusion on September 4, their record of 86-50 was the best in baseball, and they were on a pace to win over 100 games. They lost to the Blue Jays on the fifth, kept losing after welcoming Buck Showalter's revivified Orioles to Yankee Stadium, went to Texas and got swept, and on and on through the end of the season. The Yankees stumbled to a 9-17 finish. Their record in those 26 games was the second-worst in baseball, topped in futility only by the historically inept Mariners, who were one game worse. In doing so, the Yankees ceded the division lead and home-field advantage in the postseason to the Rays.

The team's collapse during this period was total. The Yankees averaged 5.4 runs per game on offense through September 4. From then on, they averaged only 4.9. The pitchers' collective decline was far worse; whereas they had held opponents to 4.1 runs per game into early September, now they had their pianos tuned to an ugly 5.4 runs per game. To place that number in context, the Royals, who had the league's worst pitching staff, allowed 5.2 runs per game on the season.

When an old team fails to perform, it is of course impossible to say, "Aha! This was the moment when they got old!" Indeed, some of the Yankees' problems can be easily explained away by transient injuries to Mark Teixeira, Nick Swisher, Brett Gardner, and Jorge Posada. Each player was hurt during this period, and his performance suffered accordingly. However, no such excuse could be made for the starting rotation, which completely disintegrated (see Table 1).

YANKEES PROSPECTUS

2010 W-L: 95-67, 2nd in AL East

Pythag	.601	1st
RS/G	5.3	1st
RA/G	4.3	18th
TAv	.284	2nd
BRR	5.1	8th
FRA	4.70	25th
DER	30.5	1st
DL	929	25th
B-Age	30.4	26th
P-Age	30.1	29th
Salary	$206.3	1st
M$/MW	$4.23	28th

Ballpark: Yankee Stadium (2-yr. PF: 104). The Bombers been spending most their lives living in a southpaw's paradise

2010: September and ALCS swoons hint at cracks in the armor

2011: With advancing age comes increasing infirmity, but the core can still contend

Action Items: An effective end to the rotation, the notion that youth must be served, and a Jeter victory lap with actual victory included

The Yankees had an aberrant three games against the Twins, then went right back to what they had been doing. Joe Girardi, in apparent contradiction of his boss, said, "The way we played against Texas is similar to the way we played in the month of September."

Placed in the context of the entire season, September and its aftermath might be mistaken for an ill-timed slump that marred the record of an otherwise excellent team. After all, the club did win 95 games, one of only three 2010 teams to do so. This may very well be correct—no canary in the coal mine here, just a sparrow with a bad cough—but it would be a mistake to disregard it entirely, perhaps even to take it as less than the dire warning it seemed to be. After all, the team's age is indisputable, and there are few Yankees who can be counted upon to be better in 2011 than they were in 2010.

In the offseason, the issue of valuing the Yankees by past performance rather than future potential came to revolve around Derek Jeter, who, rumor had it, was asking for a contract comparable in length to Alex Rodriguez's. That Jeter, who was coming off a season in which he hit a career-worst .270/.340/.370, could not lift a ball off the ground for vast stretches of time and fielded with all the animation of his

Table 1. Meltdown in the Bronx

Starter	Starts	Quality Starts	ERA	Team Record
A. J. Burnett	6	2	5.83	1-5
CC Sabathia	5	3	4.11	2-3
Phil Hughes	4	2	5.04	2-2
Ivan Nova	4	1	6.00	3-1
Andy Pettitte	3	1	6.75	1-2
Dustin Moseley	2	0	6.17	0-2
Javier Vazquez	2	0	10.24	0-2
Totals	26	9	5.71	9-17

future Cooperstown plaque, would expect to be employed through his 42nd birthday seemed to display an amazing lack of self-awareness, given how clear it seems that it's not the best that has yet to come, only the worst.

Jeter got the headlines and ultimately a three-year contract with a player option for year four, but what applies to him also applies to the rest of the Yankees. While not every player is likely to go into a Jeter-style free fall, almost all of the regulars except for Robinson Cano and Brett Gardner are 30 and above, and Gardner's ongoing physical problems and age—though he's only getting started in the majors, he's already 27—mean that what you see is likely what you get where he's concerned. Twenty-one-year-old Jesus Montero may or may not get a chance to play in the coming season, having been momentarily shunted aside for the 28-year-old catcher Russell Martin, who is young only in comparison with the rest of the lineup. The Yankees will benefit defensively by employing Martin as their backstop, but barring Martin's return to his freshman- and sophomore-year form, turning aside Montero's bat means leaving a great many runs on the shelf.

The starting rotation has just one youthful member, Phil Hughes, and as the team's winter pursuit of Cliff Lee demonstrated, the Yankees are adamantly opposed to adding any others. Despite having as many midrotation pitching prospects as any team in the game, despite the passing of George Steinbrenner and his oft-self-defeating impatience with young hurlers, the Yankees would rather spend money on well-seasoned veterans and deflowered nonentities than risk a spot on even the most promising youth. This extends down to the most inconsequential roles on the staff, as demonstrated by the club's re-signing of Sergio Mitre and persistence in treating Dustin Moseley as something more than the replacement-level pitcher he is. Whatever doubts the Yankees have about their own prospects, they would, amazingly, rather accept a 5.00 ERA from another organization's 28-year-old washout than get the same performance from a 23-year-old who makes the major-league minimum and offers a greater possibility of exceeding expectations. David Phelps and Adam Warren are not going to be ace starters, but they could be someone's fourth or fifth starter, whereas Mitre and Moseley are never going to be more than roster-fill.

This obsession with the old played out in particularly painful fashion in the saga of Javier Vazquez. A 12-year veteran, Vazquez had enjoyed several excellent seasons, but also some that were confounding, given that they were so far removed from his peak output. In 2004, the Yankees had seen one of those seasons firsthand, after general manager Brian Cashman dealt Nick Johnson, Juan Rivera, and Randy Choate to the Expos for his services. His prior two seasons showed off his perplexing dual nature: in 2008, he posted a 4.67 ERA for the White Sox, and Kenny Williams couldn't wait to get him out of town; in 2009, with the Braves, his ERA was 2.87. In both seasons, Vazquez threw 200 innings—something he had done every year since 2005—and struck out 200 batters. When the Braves made him available for a relatively low price, Cashman couldn't resist rolling the dice and hoping Vazquez would be more 2009 than 2008, and that 2004 would prove to have been a fluke.

As gambles go, it wasn't the worst the Yankees have ever taken (perhaps Hideki Irabu or Kei Igawa deserves that title), but it had the unfortunate side effect of squeezing the openings in the starting rotation down to one. This put the only two young pitchers being considered for a rotation spot, Joba Chamberlain and Phil Hughes, in competition. It was widely rumored that the team was rooting hard for Hughes, given the way that Chamberlain had seemed to flame out at the end of 2009. The Yankees' preference for Hughes overlooked the fact that the club had contributed to his failures with its perverse handling of his workload. We won't recapitulate that story here—that song being better known than "The Battle Hymn of the Republic"—except to conclude it: the upshot of Chamberlain's rise and fall was that the Yankees took a young starter with electric stuff and turned him into an unexceptional reliever so that they could pay Vazquez $11.5 million to give them a 5.32 ERA.

As it turned out, the Yankees could have used both youngsters in the rotation. Hughes had a very mixed season, but now that he has been given the chance to learn from his failures, there is hope that more consistent work is in the offing. Chamberlain could have used the same opportunity, one unencumbered by "Joba Rules," because the Yankees headed into December with more questions than answers about their rotation. Sabathia was his redoubtable self, at least until a meniscus tear in his right knee apparently began to tell in the postseason. Assuming he can continue to withstand the heavy workloads of the past several years, at least one spot is set. Après le grand homme, le déluge: A. J. Burnett is an unsolvable riddle. Andy Pettitte may have retired by the time you read this, but even if not, last season's interminable injury time-out hints that fragility may be a concern at 39. Whether he's retired or not, there may be portions of the season during which Pettitte is simply not there. Hughes was a home-run machine after mid-May, and Vazquez is gone, having decamped to the Marlins on a free-agent contract.

The Yankees might have had two young pitchers available to pitch for the failing Burnett, whose resurrection is anything but assured, the aging and retirement-inclined Pettitte, and Vazquez. Instead, the team had to avidly pursue another impossibly expensive thirtysomething free agent such as Cliff Lee—a chase that led not to New York, but to Philadelphia—and will perhaps also turn to Ivan Nova, a largely untested hurler. Nova received seven starts in August and September. Moseley and Mitre combined to make 12. The Yankees will never know what Nova might have done in 2011 had he made 19 starts last year.

Fortunately for the Yankees, they do have some certainties that will help keep them in contention in 2011. The defense is quite strong with the exception of Jeter and was almost certainly improved with the addition of Martin. On offense, more of the same from the hitters would make for another high-scoring team. While there is no reason to expect improvement from most of the players—Teixeira should have a better April, at least relative to the last one, and, assuming he avoids injury, a better September as well, and Curtis Granderson's new hitting mechanics might take him back to his 2007-2008 peak—but there's little reason to expect anyone to get dramatically worse, either.

As each year ticks by, that will be less and less true, but for this season, the Yankees seem reasonably safe from a team-wide collapse on offense. The two possible exceptions are Posada and Jeter. In the former case, the defrocked catcher is in the last year of his contract, and if he fails to hit, there is always another bat that can be acquired. As for Jeter, if he does not rebound, both on offense and defense, the celebration of his 3,000th hit will be followed by a long, bitter coda.

No one is predicting the collapse of the Yankees. Given the organization's financial and intellectual resources, that is always a foolish thing to do. Yet, as we have often seen, spending does not necessarily equal championships, and even intelligent men have their selective blind spots, prejudices, and foolish notions. In the Yankees' case, it means that they have again failed to inoculate themselves against the forces of age and entropy that threaten the remains of the 2009 championship team.

HITTERS

David Adams 2B

Born: **5/15/1987** Age: **24**
Bats: **R** Throws: **R** Height: **6' 2"** Weight: **190**
Breakout: **2%** Improve: **7%** Collapse: **0%**
Attrition: **10%** MLB: **13%**

Comparables:
Jeff Fiorentino, Danny Richar, Josh Kroeger (81)

YEAR	TEAM	LVL	AGE	PA	R	2B	3B	HR	RBI	BB	SO	SB	CS	AVG/OBP/SLG	TAv	BABIP	BRR	FRAA	WARP
2008	STA	A-	21	297	45	19	2	4	31	32	57	8	2	.257/.350/.393	.285	.313	4.9	2B 9	2.8
2009	CSC	A	22	304	32	23	2	0	34	35	49	8	4	.290/.385/.394	.280	.352	2.5	2B 1, 3B 6	2.2
2009	TAM	A+	22	265	37	17	6	7	41	26	39	3	4	.281/.358/.498	.302	.307	0.8	2B 7	2.6
2010	TRN	AA	23	173	31	15	3	3	32	18	31	5	2	.309/.393/.507	.343	.373	3.3	2B 3	2.5
2011	*NYA*	*MLB*	*24*	*352*	*38*	*20*	*2*	*4*	*33*	*29*	*74*	*4*	*2*	*.245/.310/.359*	*.238*	*.302*	*-0.2*	*2B 7, 3B 1*	*0.8*

Adams was quite nearly a Mariner, having been included in the aborted Cliff Lee deal. Jack Zduriencik balked at what was then described as a high ankle sprain that Adams had suffered on May 23. This was hardly a reason to dismiss Adams—no one had said that he was never going to get better—but Zduriencik must have felt at least partly justified as two months went by and Adams *didn't* get better. Upon further investigation, the sprain turned out to be a fracture, and Adams' season was at an end. To that point, he had pillaged the Eastern League, all the more impressive because he played his home games in the Trenton Thunder's offense-depressing Ballpark of Azkaban. A solid defender who didn't make an error last year, Adams spent the offseason recovering apace. His next challenge will be keeping up the hitting at Triple-A so he can be included in the next big trade package, lest the immovable object that is Robinson Cano render him a minor-league lifer.

Lance Berkman 1B

Born: **2/10/1976** Age: **35**
Bats: **S** Throws: **L** Height: **6' 1"** Weight: **205**
Breakout: **0%** Improve: **38%** Collapse: **2%**
Attrition: **7%** MLB: **97%**

Comparables:
Jeff Bagwell, Carlos Delgado, Todd Helton (74)

YEAR	TEAM	LVL	AGE	PA	R	2B	3B	HR	RBI	BB	SO	SB	CS	AVG/OBP/SLG	TAv	BABIP	BRR	FRAA	WARP
2008	HOU	MLB	32	665	114	46	4	29	106	99	108	18	4	.312/.420/.567	.330	.341	-0.6	1B 22	7.3
2009	HOU	MLB	33	563	73	31	1	25	80	97	98	7	4	.274/.398/.509	.311	.296	-0.2	1B 10	4.2
2010	HOU	MLB	34	358	39	16	1	13	49	60	70	3	2	.245/.372/.436	.297	.279	-0.8	1B 2	1.6
2010	NYA	MLB	34	123	10	7	0	1	9	17	15	0	0	.255/.358/.349	.252	.289	0.1	1B -2	-0.2
2011	*SLN*	*MLB*	*35*	*608*	*86*	*30*	*1*	*26*	*82*	*94*	*107*	*8*	*3*	*.272/.386/.492*	*.304*	*.294*	*-0.3*	*1B 7*	*3.7*

In two June interleague games against the Yankees, Berkman went a futile 0-for-8. Brian Cashman might have taken this as foreshadowing and saved the team a couple of prospects. Slow to recover from knee surgery, Berkman missed the first two weeks of the season and never did find his stroke. Given his age and general conditioning—the only thing that makes it possible to distinguish Berkman from the Met Life blimp is that only one of them has Snoopy tattooed on the side—he might never find it again. At this late stage of his career, Berkman has become a SHINO (Switch-Hitter In Name Only), needing to be protected from southpaws, and deploying him in the field is to be avoided. He did hit .299/.405/.388 (one home run) in September, and he had something of an excuse for his less-than-limber work in a knee that troubled him all season. The little hot streak, the injury, and his impressive history were enough to convince the Cardinals to offer Berkman a one-year contract, but their apparent intent to make him the everyday left fielder is, to put it mildly, optimistic.

Robinson Cano 2B

Born: **10/22/1982** Age: **28**
Bats: **L** Throws: **R** Height: **6' 0"** Weight: **170**
Breakout: **1%** Improve: **53%** Collapse: **1%**
Attrition: **4%** MLB: **100%**

Comparables:
Adrian Beltre, Magglio Ordonez, Ian Kinsler (68)

YEAR	TEAM	LVL	AGE	PA	R	2B	3B	HR	RBI	BB	SO	SB	CS	AVG/OBP/SLG	TAv	BABIP	BRR	FRAA	WARP
2008	NYA	MLB	25	634	70	35	3	14	72	26	65	2	4	.271/.304/.410	.248	.282	-1.3	2B 10	1.6
2009	NYA	MLB	26	674	104	48	2	25	85	30	63	5	7	.320/.352/.520	.298	.324	2.0	2B 6	4.9
2010	NYA	MLB	27	696	104	41	3	29	109	57	77	3	2	.320/.381/.534	.318	.326	0.5	2B -1	5.5
2011	*NYA*	*MLB*	*28*	*639*	*84*	*39*	*2*	*20*	*87*	*40*	*69*	*5*	*3*	*.300/.346/.476*	*.286*	*.309*	*-0.6*	*2B 3*	*3.2*

Cano arrived as an MVP-level player in 2010, something that seemed impossible just a year ago. For the first time, he managed to avoid long slumps in which he lapsed into bad hitting mechanics and self-defeating impatience; September, his worst month (.294/.346/.412), was disappointing only by the standards he had set earlier in the season. Perhaps the most impressive aspect of Cano's season was that it wasn't all driven by batting average. Though he dropped from .336 in the first half to .299 in the second, he continued to get on base and knock the ball for extra bases. He also was able to maintain his hitting with runners on, something that had been a problem throughout his career. His newfound concentration extended to his work in the field, where he won a deserved Gold Glove, making just three errors along the way. Cano sometimes seems to be having too much fun, but he recognized his shortcomings and put in the time toward fixing them, first working on fielding with former coach Larry Bowa, then on hitting with current coach Kevin Long. Now peaking as a result of his efforts, he should give the Yankees more of the same in the years to come.

Francisco Cervelli C

Born: **3/6/1986** Age: **25**
Bats: **R** Throws: **R** Height: **6' 1"** Weight: **210**
Breakout: **2%** Improve: **10%** Collapse: **6%**
Attrition: **4%** MLB: **41%**

Comparables:
Clay Dalrymple, Red Wilson, Cam Carreon (78)

YEAR	TEAM	LVL	AGE	PA	R	2B	3B	HR	RBI	BB	SO	SB	CS	AVG/OBP/SLG	TAv	BABIP	BRR	FRAA	WARP
2008	TRN	AA	22	88	8	5	0	0	8	11	14	0	0	.315/.432/.384	.266	.390	0.3	C 1	0.5
2008	NYA	MLB	22	5	0	0	0	0	0	0	3	0	0	.000/.000/.000	-0.070	.000	0.0	C 0	-0.2
2009	TRN	AA	23	64	8	1	0	2	7	6	13	0	0	.190/.266/.310	.223	.209	0.7	C 1	0.2
2009	SWB	AAA	23	75	7	5	0	1	7	3	13	0	2	.275/.307/.391	.270	.316	0.1	C 0	0.4
2009	NYA	MLB	23	101	13	4	0	1	11	2	11	0	3	.298/.297/.372	.239	.310	-0.5	C -1	0.1
2010	NYA	MLB	24	317	27	11	3	0	38	33	42	1	1	.271/.350/.335	.254	.305	-2.2	C 1, 3B 0	1.0
2011	*NYA*	*MLB*	*25*	*229*	*25*	*10*	*1*	*2*	*19*	*19*	*37*	*1*	*1*	*.258/.323/.343*	*.241*	*.297*	*-0.1*	*C 0, 3B 0*	*0.5*

In the early going, Cervelli was a BABIP fool, with his every little flare dropping in. All too soon, God stopped playing dice with the universe and the normal laws of chance were reinstated; the dying quails of April and May became the plucky homing pigeons of June, July, and August, each determined not to land until it had nested in someone's glove. Cervelli rediscovered his "ability" to flip balls just over the infield in September, but by then it had become abundantly clear that he didn't have the offensive chops to be taken seriously as Jorge Posada's successor. Cervelli did greatly improve his walk rate, which gave his all-singles game a dimension it didn't have the year before, but it's still not enough for him to be a winning regular. More disturbingly, he had a miserable defensive season. Runners had no problem stealing on him, chalking up an 86 percent success rate, the second-worst showing of the 43 catchers who caught 450 or more innings, and he tied for the American League lead in errors with Jason Kendall, who caught 228 more innings. Cervelli's fielding percentage (when putouts from strikeouts are discounted) of .852 was the lowest of any catcher except Posada, and his 0.46 passed balls and wild pitches per nine innings ranked 26th in the group. If Cervelli's defensive game recovers, he'll have a career as a reserve, and if it doesn't, he won't. Or maybe there will be an expansion draft and he'll be the inaugural catcher for the San Antonio Defenders.

Colin Curtis RF

Born: **2/1/1985** Age: **26**
Bats: **L** Throws: **L** Height: **6' 1"** Weight: **200**
Breakout: **4%** Improve: **8%** Collapse: **3%**
Attrition: **14%** MLB: **23%**

Comparables:
Buck Coats, Trevor Crowe, Justin Turner (81)

YEAR	TEAM	LVL	AGE	PA	R	2B	3B	HR	RBI	BB	SO	SB	CS	AVG/OBP/SLG	TAv	BABIP	BRR	FRAA	WARP
2008	TRN	AA	23	562	68	20	3	10	71	55	86	6	3	.255/.327/.368	.260	.284	2.4	LF 10, CF 1	2.4
2009	TRN	AA	24	240	28	14	4	1	19	20	37	7	0	.268/.342/.385	.286	.316	0.5	LF 0, CF -5	0.7
2009	SWB	AAA	24	279	29	10	0	6	29	24	46	1	2	.235/.301/.347	.236	.262	-0.5	LF 4, CF 8	1.0
2010	SWB	AAA	25	269	28	24	0	5	27	21	38	1	2	.289/.358/.452	.272	.322	0.0	RF 5, CF -2	1.1
2010	NYA	MLB	25	64	7	3	0	1	8	4	15	0	0	.186/.250/.288	.204	.233	-0.3	RF 0, LF -1	-0.3
2011	*NYA*	*MLB*	*26*	*486*	*50*	*24*	*2*	*6*	*43*	*36*	*90*	*3*	*1*	*.239/.298/.342*	*.228*	*.282*	*-0.1*	*LF 1, CF -1*	*-0.5*

Curtis stirred hopes that his mediocre minor-league performances were a thing of the past with a torrid Arizona Fall League performance followed by a 6-for-12, two-homer spring training. It wasn't all illusion. Curtis isn't going to be a regular, and at 26, he's not going to get any better, but his ability to make contact and play all three outfield positions adequately qualifies him for a roster spot, though not so much that it won't always be a fight. Another point in his favor: he was one of the few Yankees to do well—small sample alert!—in a pinch-hitting role, going 4-for-11 with a walk and a home run.

Brett Gardner **LF**

Born: 8/24/1983 Age: 27
Bats: L Throws: L Height: 5' 10" Weight: 180
Breakout: 3% Improve: 46% Collapse: 5%
Attrition: 18% MLB: 82%

Comparables:
Gene Richards, Kenny Lofton, Roy White (71)

YEAR	TEAM	LVL	AGE	PA	R	2B	3B	HR	RBI	BB	SO	SB	CS	AVG/OBP/SLG	TAv	BABIP	BRR	FRAA	WARP
2008	SWB	AAA	24	426	68	12	11	3	32	70	76	37	9	.296/.404/.422	.311	.355	1.8	CF 2, LF 4	4.4
2008	NYA	MLB	24	141	18	5	2	0	16	8	30	13	1	.228/.277/.299	.213	.287	1.3	CF 2, LF -1	-0.1
2009	NYA	MLB	25	283	48	5	6	3	22	26	40	26	5	.267/.336/.372	.260	.299	4.7	CF 4	1.6
2010	NYA	MLB	26	570	97	20	7	5	47	79	102	47	9	.276/.379/.379	.286	.335	7.8	LF 6, CF 1	4.0
2011	*NYA*	*MLB*	*27*	*479*	*55*	*18*	*4*	*3*	*39*	*62*	*85*	*37*	*8*	*.261/.355/.354*	*.259*	*.310*	*1.1*	*CF 1, LF 2*	*1.5*

In the previous edition of this book, we said that due to injury, Gardner's 2009 got a grade of "incomplete." Make it two years in a row. Gardner was a revelation in the early going, hitting .321/.403/.418 with 24 steals through his first 70 games and playing excellent defense in left field. But two injuries in June, a sprained left thumb and a contusion of his right wrist, severely changed the shape of his season. Neither kept him out of the lineup, but the aftereffects showed in .232/.363/.340 rates the rest of the way. Already patient, Gardner stopped swinging. The recorded history of taking pitches goes back only 23 years, but in that time, no hitter saw more pitches per plate appearance than Gardner's 4.62. The truth of what Gardner is probably lies close to his overall 2010 rates. With speed and defense, that player is worth starting if he can just stay healthy, something Gardner has been unable to do. He underwent surgery on the right wrist in December, and the Yankees will have to hope there is no carryover.

Curtis Granderson **CF**

Born: 3/16/1981 Age: 30
Bats: L Throws: R Height: 6' 1" Weight: 185
Breakout: 0% Improve: 38% Collapse: 0%
Attrition: 3% MLB: 98%

Comparables:
Andy Van Slyke, Willie Mays, Orlando Hudson (58)

YEAR	TEAM	LVL	AGE	PA	R	2B	3B	HR	RBI	BB	SO	SB	CS	AVG/OBP/SLG	TAv	BABIP	BRR	FRAA	WARP
2008	DET	MLB	27	629	112	26	13	22	66	71	111	12	4	.280/.364/.494	.305	.315	6.5	CF 2	5.5
2009	DET	MLB	28	710	91	23	8	30	71	72	141	20	6	.249/.325/.453	.278	.273	4.8	CF -1	3.6
2010	NYA	MLB	29	528	76	17	7	24	67	53	116	12	2	.247/.322/.468	.292	.273	3.7	CF 2	3.6
2011	*NYA*	*MLB*	*30*	*652*	*82*	*27*	*8*	*23*	*85*	*66*	*134*	*15*	*4*	*.257/.331/.452*	*.272*	*.291*	*0.2*	*CF 1*	*2.6*

Prior to a mid-August tutoring session with Kevin Long, Granderson was in danger of joining Rondell White and Kenny Lofton in the category of veteran outfielders who seemed like promising Yankees additions but proved not to be. His swing mechanics had begun to resemble Balanchine's famous *Spasmodic Dance of the Terminal Octopus*, with parts flying out in every direction except toward the ball. Long encouraged Granderson to calm things down, and the result was a .261/.356/.564, 14-home-run finish to the season; only Jose Bautista hit more homers over that span. More impressively, Granderson began hitting left-handed pitching consistently. Prior to Long's intervention, he had hit .206/.243/.275 against southpaws, lending credence to the argument that the only thing that had kept Granderson from platoon-player status was the credulity of his managers. While 64 plate appearances shouldn't convince anyone that Granderson no longer needs to be protected from same-side pitching, his .286/.375/.500 rebound constituted so dramatic a change that there will be great disappointment in New York if he does not provide a full season's complement of plate appearances at a similar level this season.

Derek Jeter **SS**

Born: 6/26/1974 Age: 37
Bats: R Throws: R Height: 6' 3" Weight: 175
Breakout: 0% Improve: 27% Collapse: 5%
Attrition: 13% MLB: 95%

Comparables:
Johnny Damon, Randy Winn, Jose Cruz (56)

YEAR	TEAM	LVL	AGE	PA	R	2B	3B	HR	RBI	BB	SO	SB	CS	AVG/OBP/SLG	TAv	BABIP	BRR	FRAA	WARP
2008	NYA	MLB	34	668	89	25	3	11	69	52	85	11	5	.300/.359/.408	.275	.329	1.7	SS -18	2.0
2009	NYA	MLB	35	716	107	27	1	18	66	72	90	30	5	.334/.404/.465	.305	.365	-2.3	SS -16	4.2
2010	NYA	MLB	36	739	112	30	3	10	67	63	106	18	5	.270/.340/.370	.255	.307	2.8	SS -14	1.2
2011	*NYA*	*MLB*	*37*	*710*	*83*	*30*	*2*	*9*	*66*	*63*	*102*	*19*	*6*	*.281/.348/.377*	*.263*	*.317*	*0.1*	*SS -19*	*1.0*

Jeter led the majors in ground-ball percentage. This was not just a mechanical failure, but a seeming inability to drive the ball. Perplexingly, Jeter got off to a great start, hitting .330 in April. By the end of the season, the little September hot streak (.342/.436/.392 in Jeter's final 19 games) that followed his reluctant turn to Kevin Long was the subject of great rejoicing throughout the land—in between, the shortstop had hit only .247/.321/.337, and the cheering for a few paltry singles should have been embarrassing to all involved, given the heights from which Jeter had descended. The same reticence should have been observed by coaches and managers who voted for the

Gold Glove; though Jeter made few errors, he also reached relatively few balls. Even if one makes the optimistic assumption that Jeter can turn his offensive game around, a third rebirth of his glove would be unprecedented. For years, Jeter's bat more than made up for the singles he allowed with his leather. That is still true, but the margin is shrinking and will soon vanish altogether. Despite this, as the offseason commenced, Jeter pushed for a contract of four years and up, which suggests at least one of the following: (A) while Jeter may be the closest thing the modern Yankees have to Joe DiMaggio, he lacks DiMaggio's sense of dignity; (B) never mind winning, it's money that matters; (C) the emperor has no clothes but doesn't know; (D) the emperor has no clothes but doesn't care. The Yankees more or less satisfied him, giving him three years and a player option for a fourth, in the hopes that he will play as no aged shortstop has played before.

Why is it each is the last to find / That his legs are gone—that his eyes are bad, / That the quicker reflexes have left his mind, / That he hasn't the stuff that he one day had, / That lost youth mocks, and he doesn't see / The ghost of the fellow that used to be?

—Grantland Rice, "To Any Athlete"

Corban Joseph 2B

Born: **10/28/1988** Age: **22**
Bats: **L** Throws: **R** Height: **6' 0"** Weight: **168**
Breakout: **3%** Improve: **3%** Collapse: **1%**
Attrition: **3%** MLB: **6%**

Comparables:
Dick McAuliffe, Dalton Jones, Wayne Garrett (74)

YEAR	TEAM	LVL	AGE	PA	R	2B	3B	HR	RBI	BB	SO	SB	CS	AVG/OBP/SLG	TAv	BABIP	BRR	FRAA	WARP
2008	YAN	Rk	19	183	25	15	2	2	18	20	24	2	5	.277/.355/.434	.288	.309	0.0	2B -13	-0.2
2009	CSC	A	20	436	39	17	8	4	57	49	61	8	5	.300/.381/.418	.295	.345	0.7	2B -9, 3B 9	2.7
2010	TAM	A+	21	437	52	27	3	6	52	43	74	5	8	.302/.378/.436	.294	.355	-1.5	2B -8, 3B 3	1.9
2010	TRN	AA	21	130	11	6	4	0	13	15	33	1	0	.216/.305/.342	.256	.293	-1.2	2B 3	0.5
2011	*NYA*	*MLB*	*22*	*392*	*40*	*18*	*3*	*3*	*33*	*32*	*82*	*2*	*1*	*.241/.303/.336*	*.226*	*.298*	*-0.2*	*2B -5, 3B 3*	*-0.6*

This 2008 fourth-rounder out of Franklin, Tennessee, got a taste of the bright lights of Trenton, New Jersey, after David Adams went down. Joseph struggled to hit, then required surgery on his right wrist and was knocked out of both the Eastern League playoffs and winter ball. On the plus side, he didn't get mugged. Joseph has a sweet line-drive swing and a decent respect for the strike zone, but the wrist had better come back quickly, as defense isn't Joseph's calling card. Fortunately, at 22 and with Cano in front of him, he doesn't have to go anywhere quickly.

Austin Kearns LF

Born: **5/20/1980** Age: **31**
Bats: **R** Throws: **R** Height: **6' 3"** Weight: **220**
Breakout: **1%** Improve: **39%** Collapse: **5%**
Attrition: **4%** MLB: **88%**

Comparables:
Jason Lane, Cliff Floyd, Ivan Calderon (79)

YEAR	TEAM	LVL	AGE	PA	R	2B	3B	HR	RBI	BB	SO	SB	CS	AVG/OBP/SLG	TAv	BABIP	BRR	FRAA	WARP
2008	WAS	MLB	28	357	40	10	0	7	32	35	63	2	2	.217/.311/.316	.234	.250	-1.8	RF 5	-0.1
2009	WAS	MLB	29	211	20	6	2	3	17	32	51	1	1	.195/.337/.305	.228	.258	1.1	RF -3, CF -1	-0.6
2010	CLE	MLB	30	342	42	18	1	8	42	34	78	4	1	.272/.354/.419	.277	.341	1.1	LF 4, RF 1	1.9
2010	NYA	MLB	30	119	13	3	0	2	7	12	38	0	0	.235/.345/.324	.260	.355	-0.3	LF 2, RF 0	0.4
2011	*CLE*	*MLB*	*31*	*471*	*55*	*19*	*1*	*11*	*45*	*54*	*99*	*4*	*2*	*.247/.345/.382*	*.261*	*.296*	*-0.2*	*RF 2, LF 2*	*1.1*

Kearns is a player whose skills have very limited application, and that's being generous. A .373 April banished memories of Kearns' .209/.320/.312 rates in his last two seasons with the Nationals and punched his ticket to the Yankees and the pennant race. The Yankees needed a potent right-handed alternative to Gardner and Granderson—someone who was also a good defender. Marcus Thames had the requisite punch, but not the glove. Unfortunately, Kearns makes for a lousy platoon player, as he's the rare right-hander who loses power against left-handed pitching. Since he doesn't hit right-handers well enough to play a corner (.255/.341/.426 career) and doesn't make frequent enough contact to pinch-hit (he struck out in 37 percent of his Yankees at-bats), it's not clear what his best usage is beyond late-inning defensive duty. The Indians, who need a right-handed alternative to a left-leaning outfield, signed him once more, but he really doesn't fit their needs.

Brandon Laird 3B

Born: **9/11/1987** Age: **23**
Bats: **R** Throws: **R** Height: **6' 1"** Weight: **215**
Breakout: **4%** Improve: **20%** Collapse: **5%**
Attrition: **26%** MLB: **44%**

Comparables:
Neil Walker, Alex Gordon, Mat Gamel (73)

YEAR	TEAM	LVL	AGE	PA	R	2B	3B	HR	RBI	BB	SO	SB	CS	AVG/OBP/SLG	TAv	BABIP	BRR	FRAA	WARP
2008	CSC	A	20	506	71	31	1	23	86	40	86	1	0	.273/.334/.498	.315	.287	-0.2	1B 0, 3B 1	3.5
2009	TAM	A+	21	501	53	20	4	13	75	39	75	1	1	.266/.329/.415	.269	.291	0.2	3B -1, 1B 1	1.8
2010	TRN	AA	22	454	73	22	2	23	90	38	84	2	2	.291/.355/.523	.322	.315	0.0	3B 7, 1B 0	4.8
2010	SWB	AAA	22	127	13	6	0	2	12	4	27	0	0	.246/.268/.344	.177	.298	-2.2	3B -2, 1B -1	-1.3
2011	*NYA*	*MLB*	*23*	*539*	*60*	*24*	*2*	*17*	*65*	*31*	*112*	*1*	*0*	*.251/.292/.412*	*.244*	*.284*	*0.0*	*3B 1, 1B -4*	*0.0*

Funny thing, genetics. Two brothers, Gerald and Brandon, products of the same parents and raised in the same environment. Both play baseball, but only one got the power gene. Gerald hit 10 home runs in his first 500 major-league at-bats. Brandon should easily double that in his. Conversely, Gerald easily trumps his younger bro in terms of walks, which is a problem because the elder Laird isn't particularly selective. Brandon makes relatively good contact for a power hitter, but as he rose through the minors in 2010, he completely abandoned even the illusion of selectivity and remained impatient throughout the Triple-A playoffs and the Arizona Fall League. Blocked at the infield corners and no defensive whiz, Laird took outfield AFL reps in an effort to become a viable four-corner sub. It's a good idea, but Laird will have to rediscover the strike zone to be valuable in that role or any other.

Melky Mesa CF

Born: 1/31/1987 **Age:** 24
Bats: R **Throws:** R **Height:** 6' 1" **Weight:** 165
Breakout: 4% **Improve:** 20% **Collapse:** 3%
Attrition: 12% **MLB:** 34%
Comparables:
Felix Pie, Andruw Jones, Junior Felix (68)

YEAR	TEAM	LVL	AGE	PA	R	2B	3B	HR	RBI	BB	SO	SB	CS	AVG/OBP/SLG	TAv	BABIP	BRR	FRAA	WARP
2008	STA	A-	21	128	19	5	2	7	23	4	38	4	1	.221/.250/.467	.256	.256	-1.4	RF -1, CF -2	-0.2
2009	CSC	A	22	564	76	24	7	20	74	51	168	18	6	.225/.309/.423	.267	.293	3.5	RF 6, CF 2	2.4
2010	TAM	A+	23	509	81	21	9	19	74	44	129	31	9	.260/.338/.475	.296	.319	0.0	CF 9, RF -1	4.0
2011	*NYA*	*MLB*	*24*	*392*	*40*	*15*	*3*	*13*	*44*	*25*	*126*	*6*	*2*	*.213/.268/.381*	*.228*	*.280*	*-0.1*	*CF -3, RF -1*	*-0.8*

If only Mesa were a couple of years younger. The outfielder has speed, power, and an excellent arm, but at 24, he is only just beginning to figure out the whole hitting thing and is a long way from projecting as a major leaguer. Still, there is reason for hope. Strikeouts have always been a problem for him, due to a kamikaze approach to hitting. Mesa struggled in the first half, making better contact but hitting less; after the break, he went back to free swinging but had far better success in choosing pitches, hitting .278/.348/.548 with seven triples and 14 home runs in 241 at-bats. Now he must not only carry those results forward, but surmount the impossible hitting environment at Trenton. If he can do that, he might have a career as the kind of guy the Mets call up when all of their starting outfielders get hurt.

Juan Miranda 1B

Born: 4/25/1983 **Age:** 28
Bats: L **Throws:** L **Height:** 6' 0" **Weight:** 220
Breakout: 3% **Improve:** 21% **Collapse:** 6%
Attrition: 21% **MLB:** 44%
Comparables:
Paul McAnulty, Chris Shelton, Ryan Garko (77)

YEAR	TEAM	LVL	AGE	PA	R	2B	3B	HR	RBI	BB	SO	SB	CS	AVG/OBP/SLG	TAv	BABIP	BRR	FRAA	WARP
2008	SWB	AAA	25	417	40	22	0	12	52	55	79	2	1	.287/.384/.449	.284	.336	-4.2	1B 7	1.8
2008	NYA	MLB	25	14	2	1	0	0	1	2	4	0	0	.400/.500/.500	.359	.571	0.3	1B 0	0.2
2009	SWB	AAA	26	502	74	30	2	19	82	55	101	1	0	.290/.369/.498	.298	.333	-0.5	1B 10	3.4
2009	NYA	MLB	26	9	2	0	0	1	3	0	4	0	0	.333/.333/.667	.365	.500	0.0	1B -1	0.0
2010	SWB	AAA	27	340	52	15	1	15	43	33	71	1	0	.285/.371/.495	.276	.325	0.0	1B 2	1.0
2010	NYA	MLB	27	71	7	2	1	3	10	7	12	0	0	.219/.296/.422	.257	.224	-0.8	1B 1	0.1
2011	*ARI*	*MLB*	*28*	*472*	*56*	*20*	*0*	*15*	*53*	*50*	*102*	*0*	*0*	*.243/.327/.408*	*.257*	*.280*	*0.0*	*1B -9*	*-0.7*

Cuban time traveler Miranda (he might have been born in 1983; there is an equal probability that he was born in 1883 and witnessed the Rough Riders rushing Kettle Hill) was finally sprung by the Yankees via a November trade to the Diamondbacks. There, he will try to replace Adam LaRoche's mediocre production as the long half of a first-base platoon, though he will have to beat out Brandon Allen to do it. In 94 major-league plate appearances, Miranda has hit .253/.330/.458, and while that is a very small sample, it might be a fair representation of his upside. The average major-league first baseman is a better hitter than that, making Miranda more of a placeholder than an upgrade.

Jesus Montero C

Born: 11/28/1989 **Age:** 21
Bats: R **Throws:** R **Height:** 6' 4" **Weight:** 225
Breakout: 2% **Improve:** 28% **Collapse:** 1%
Attrition: 9% **MLB:** 42%
Comparables:
Billy Butler, Johnny Bench, Ken Griffey (67)

YEAR	TEAM	LVL	AGE	PA	R	2B	3B	HR	RBI	BB	SO	SB	CS	AVG/OBP/SLG	TAv	BABIP	BRR	FRAA	WARP
2008	CSC	A	18	569	86	34	1	17	87	37	83	2	1	.326/.376/.491	.327	.362	-2.0	C 1	5.2
2009	TAM	A+	19	198	26	15	1	8	37	14	26	0	0	.356/.404/.583	.375	.378	-4.0	C -1	2.3
2009	TRN	AA	19	181	19	10	0	9	33	14	21	0	0	.317/.370/.539	.332	.321	-2.5	C 0	1.6
2010	SWB	AAA	20	504	66	34	3	21	75	46	91	0	0	.289/.353/.517	.289	.319	-5.0	C -2	2.9
2011	*NYA*	*MLB*	*21*	*480*	*61*	*27*	*1*	*16*	*64*	*31*	*88*	*0*	*0*	*.286/.330/.462*	*.276*	*.320*	*0.0*	*C -1*	*2.0*

Montero got off to a slow start at Triple-A, not surprising, given that he was a 20-year-old at the minor leagues' highest level. He finally got hot in mid-June and exploded in the second half, raking to the tune of .351/.396/.684 in 44 games after the break. His defense still receives mixed reviews at best, and opponents expressed their opinions of his throwing by attempting 129 steals in his 105 games, finding success 77 percent of the time. Despite this, the confluence of Montero's ready bat and Jorge Posada's increasingly unready arm and receiving skills had seemed to advance his timetable, but after stating that he would get a chance to win the starting catcher's job and relegate Posada to designated hitter/third catcher status, Cashman blinked, signing good-field and increasingly no-hit Dodgers outcast Russell Martin and anointing him the starter. Barring a torrid spring and/or an injury to Martin, Montero would appear to be headed back to Scranton to try to prove to his general manager that he can be a usable major-league backstop.

Eduardo Nunez **SS**

Born: **6/15/1987** Age: **24**
Bats: **S** Throws: **R** Height: **6' 0"** Weight: **155**
Breakout: **4%** Improve: **15%** Collapse: **6%**
Attrition: **14%** MLB: **31%**

Comparables:
Pedro Lopez, Oswaldo Navarro, Edgar Renteria (75)

YEAR	TEAM	LVL	AGE	PA	R	2B	3B	HR	RBI	BB	SO	SB	CS	AVG/OBP/SLG	TAv	BABIP	BRR	FRAA	WARP
2008	TAM	A+	21	402	45	18	3	6	42	19	48	14	10	.271/.301/.383	.245	.290	-1.8	SS 4	1.2
2009	TRN	AA	22	528	70	26	1	9	55	22	63	19	7	.322/.347/.433	.290	.349	1.1	SS -11	2.6
2010	SWB	AAA	23	506	55	25	3	4	50	32	60	23	5	.289/.340/.381	.248	.321	0.0	SS -5, 3B -4	0.3
2010	NYA	MLB	23	53	12	1	0	1	7	3	2	5	0	.280/.321/.360	.244	.277	0.8	3B -2, SS 2	0.1
2011	*NYA*	*MLB*	*24*	*496*	*52*	*22*	*2*	*4*	*47*	*21*	*69*	*15*	*5*	*.269/.298/.353*	*.230*	*.301*	*-0.4*	*SS -4, 3B -1*	*-0.2*

Nunez inserted himself into the Jeter-successor picture, at least transiently, with a solid-if-unexciting season at Scranton. A contact hitter, Nunez displays the fundamentals at the plate that impress scouts, but his approach doesn't produce extra-base hits or walks, which he will need to keep his production up, given that he's not likely to hit .300 regularly. That said, the average major-league shortstop hit .262/.319/.374 last year, and if that's the new standard, then Nunez might actually be, well, not *more* potent than the new kids on the block, but at least *as* potent. Add to his single-icious hitting style an improved defensive approach that saw him dramatically cut his errors, and you have to admit that Nunez may be the face of an impoverished future. Wake the children: the days of the Holy Trinity are at an end.

Ramiro Pena **INF**

Born: **7/18/1985** Age: **25**
Bats: **S** Throws: **R** Height: **5' 11"** Weight: **165**
Breakout: **0%** Improve: **7%** Collapse: **1%**
Attrition: **1%** MLB: **15%**

Comparables:
Don Wert, Tito Fuentes, Shane Robinson (79)

YEAR	TEAM	LVL	AGE	PA	R	2B	3B	HR	RBI	BB	SO	SB	CS	AVG/OBP/SLG	TAv	BABIP	BRR	FRAA	WARP
2008	TRN	AA	22	506	57	20	7	2	45	41	86	8	6	.266/.322/.357	.263	.311	-0.3	SS -6	1.7
2009	SWB	AAA	23	180	18	9	0	2	9	18	28	5	1	.231/.300/.327	.224	.258	0.7	SS 6, 2B 2	0.6
2009	NYA	MLB	23	121	17	6	1	1	10	5	20	4	1	.287/.314/.383	.251	.337	-0.4	SS -1, 3B 1	0.1
2010	NYA	MLB	24	167	18	1	1	0	18	6	27	7	1	.227/.252/.247	.185	.263	-0.4	3B 5, SS -2	-0.5
2011	*NYA*	*MLB*	*25*	*334*	*32*	*13*	*2*	*2*	*27*	*21*	*61*	*7*	*2*	*.242/.285/.315*	*.215*	*.286*	*-0.1*	*SS 1, 3B 1*	*-0.1*

In the way that outfielder Sammy Byrd became known as "Babe Ruth's Legs" when he became the Bambino's late-inning sub in the 1930s, Pena may yet go down in history as "Derek Jeter's Glove." That is, he will if the Yankees wise up. A solid defender and an asset as a pinch-runner, Pena can't hit—his 27 starts at third base miraculously resulted in a 19-8 team record despite his .183/.214/.204 contribution at the position. The Yankees appear content to keep an empty bat on the roster rather than hoping for more successful Hail Marys at the hot corner, but they would gain more from using Pena as a late-inning substitute for the increasingly statuesque Jeter. Incredibly, Pena was called upon to do this just 14 times last year; this act of deference to the aging Captain calls into question why Pena was on the roster in the first place.

Jorge Posada **C**

Born: **8/17/1971** Age: **39**
Bats: **S** Throws: **R** Height: **6' 2"** Weight: **190**
Breakout: **0%** Improve: **14%** Collapse: **8%**
Attrition: **21%** MLB: **82%**

Comparables:
Jason Giambi, Ken Griffey, Frank Robinson (73)

YEAR	TEAM	LVL	AGE	PA	R	2B	3B	HR	RBI	BB	SO	SB	CS	AVG/OBP/SLG	TAv	BABIP	BRR	FRAA	WARP
2008	NYA	MLB	36	195	18	13	1	3	22	24	38	0	0	.268/.364/.411	.268	.328	-1.7	C 0, 1B 0	0.5
2009	NYA	MLB	37	438	56	25	0	22	81	48	101	1	0	.285/.363/.522	.304	.328	-6.1	C 0, 1B 1	3.1
2010	NYA	MLB	38	451	50	23	1	18	57	59	99	3	1	.248/.357/.454	.293	.287	-5.6	C -1, 1B 0	2.2
2011	*NYA*	*MLB*	*39*	*443*	*55*	*23*	*1*	*14*	*51*	*53*	*95*	*2*	*1*	*.255/.349/.429*	*.274*	*.300*	*0.0*	*C 0, 1B 0*	*2.0*

Riddle me this, Batman: When is a catcher like a defective contraceptive? Answer: When that catcher can no longer catch. The Yankees intend to use Posada as their primary designated hitter in 2011, an acknowledgment that his defensive skills, never great, have dramatically decayed. Posada's throwing has fallen off, and he never could block balls in the dirt—his approach is reminiscent of the old Bob Uecker joke about how the best way to catch a knuckleball is to wait for it to stop rolling and pick it up, except not just with knuckleballs. What is uncertain is whether Posada can hit well enough to carry the position. Having gotten off to a terrific start (.326/.406/.618), Posada was sidelined in mid-May by a hairline fracture in his foot. Ready to hit before he was ready to catch, Posada returned 15 games later as the DH, voiced displeasure with the restriction, and slumped. Eased back into the tools of ignorance, he began to hit again, though never truly got hot. On September 7, Posada took a foul tip off his mask that induced concussion-like symptoms, after which he stopped hitting over the remainder of the season and the postseason. From his resumption of catching until his bell got rung, Posada hit .248/.356/.463. Should he be able to do that again at age 39, the Yankees will have an above-average, though unexceptional, DH. It's not ideal, but in his baseball dotage, Posada has become an odd, ill-fitting part.

Alex Rodriguez **3B**

Born: **7/27/1975** Age: **35**
Bats: **R** Throws: **R** Height: **6' 3"** Weight: **190**
Breakout: **0%** Improve: **31%** Collapse: **4%**
Attrition: **8%** MLB: **97%**

Comparables:
Chipper Jones, Derrek Lee, Jorge Posada (66)

YEAR	TEAM	LVL	AGE	PA	R	2B	3B	HR	RBI	BB	SO	SB	CS	AVG/OBP/SLG	TAv	BABIP	BRR	FRAA	WARP
2008	NYA	MLB	32	594	104	33	0	35	103	65	117	18	3	.302/.392/.573	.332	.328	2.3	3B 8	7.0
2009	NYA	MLB	33	535	79	17	1	30	100	80	97	14	2	.286/.402/.532	.321	.303	1.3	3B 2	5.1
2010	NYA	MLB	34	595	77	29	2	30	125	59	98	4	3	.270/.341/.506	.301	.274	-0.3	3B 6	4.5
2011	*NYA*	*MLB*	*35*	*621*	*87*	*26*	*1*	*32*	*90*	*76*	*115*	*13*	*3*	*.272/.368/.506*	*.304*	*.289*	*0.1*	*3B 2*	*4.4*

Rodriguez is the man you love to hate, and he must wonder why. He might paraphrase "Bob Dylan's 115th Dream" and say, "You know they refused Ted Williams, too," to which the natural rejoinder is the song's next line: "You're not him!" After all, the Splendid Splinter never hit a home run on anything harder than black coffee. Still, grant Rodriguez this: he played the season on one leg (between hip and calf injuries) and pharmaceutically clean and still finished eighth in home runs and second in RBI. In short, if Rodriguez is a diminished player, he's making the most of it. The greatest area of concern is not his bat but his glove; never the world's rangiest third baseman, he saw the injuries reflect themselves in declining mobility. Given that Rodriguez is signed through 2017, or his age-42 season, the longer the Yankees can put off the inevitable move from the hot corner, the better.

Austin Romine **C**

Born: **11/22/1988** Age: **22**
Bats: **R** Throws: **R** Height: **6' 1"** Weight: **195**
Breakout: **6%** Improve: **14%** Collapse: **1%**
Attrition: **14%** MLB: **20%**

Comparables:
Carlos Gonzalez, Brad Harman, Josh Thole (75)

YEAR	TEAM	LVL	AGE	PA	R	2B	3B	HR	RBI	BB	SO	SB	CS	AVG/OBP/SLG	TAv	BABIP	BRR	FRAA	WARP
2008	CSC	A	19	436	66	24	1	10	49	25	56	3	0	.300/.344/.437	.303	.327	-4.2	C 1	2.7
2009	TAM	A+	20	481	61	28	3	13	72	29	78	11	5	.276/.322/.441	.276	.305	-4.1	C -1	1.9
2010	TRN	AA	21	497	61	31	0	10	69	37	94	2	0	.268/.324/.402	.270	.316	-2.4	C -1	2.2
2011	*NYA*	*MLB*	*22*	*488*	*51*	*25*	*1*	*9*	*51*	*23*	*99*	*2*	*1*	*.252/.286/.373*	*.231*	*.297*	*0.0*	*C -1*	*0.0*

The son and brother of major leaguers, Romine is the more defensively advanced of the Yankees' upper-level catching prospects, although his caught-stealing percentage was precisely the same as Montero's—it's possible that Romine's good defensive reviews come only because of the contrast to Montero, not because of his own virtues. Romine's season wasn't impressive at first glance, but he had to contend with the difficult hitting environment at Trenton. Nevertheless, he did wear down over the course of the season, his impatience is a detriment, and he has yet to hit for consistent power. In short, he's still plenty raw, but at 22, that's not unexpected. Given doubts about Montero's ability to stick behind the plate, there is a window of opportunity for Romine, but he probably won't be up to grabbing it without some more time in the minors. With Russell Martin pushing Jesus Montero back to Triple-A, Romine might be forced to return to Trenton to start the season, not necessarily a bad thing in his case.

Kevin Russo **UT**

Born: **7/8/1984** Age: **26**
Bats: **R** Throws: **R** Height: **5' 11"** Weight: **190**
Breakout: **4%** Improve: **9%** Collapse: **6%**
Attrition: **12%** MLB: **18%**

Comparables:
Chris Getz, Alejandro Machado, Sam Fuld (82)

YEAR	TEAM	LVL	AGE	PA	R	2B	3B	HR	RBI	BB	SO	SB	CS	AVG/OBP/SLG	TAv	BABIP	BRR	FRAA	WARP
2008	TRN	AA	23	298	46	17	3	2	33	23	42	8	3	.307/.359/.416	.287	.349	1.2	3B 2, 2B 5	2.4
2009	SWB	AAA	24	406	51	18	2	5	31	42	55	13	7	.326/.394/.431	.290	.365	-3.9	2B -1, 3B 2	2.4
2010	SWB	AAA	25	370	41	16	2	1	24	28	65	9	4	.259/.333/.328	.238	.318	0.0	2B 3, 3B 2	-0.1
2010	NYA	MLB	25	54	5	2	0	0	4	3	9	1	0	.184/.241/.224	.172	.220	0.1	LF -1, 3B -1	-0.5
2011	*NYA*	*MLB*	*26*	*396*	*41*	*17*	*2*	*2*	*31*	*31*	*72*	*8*	*4*	*.251/.312/.323*	*.231*	*.302*	*-0.4*	*2B 3, 3B 1*	*0.0*

When you are trying to build a career as a major-league utility player, it helps to be a shortstop first. Russo is primarily a second baseman whom the Yankees are trying to morph into a multiposition sub. Of course, defensive versatility is only a benefit if it helps you get an above-replacement-level bat into the lineup, especially when your glove plays better in the corners. After consecutive .300-plus seasons in the minors, Russo failed to provide that either at Scranton or with the big-league club—his selectivity, which had improved in 2009, went back to "untenable" in 2010. That small change will cost Russo untold dollars, as it's the difference between his having a steady roster spot and being an anonymous traveler on the 25th-man taxi squad.

Gary Sanchez **C**

Born: **12/2/1992** Age: **18**
Bats: **R** Throws: **R** Height: **6' 2"** Weight: **195**
Breakout: **0%** Improve: **0%** Collapse: **0%**
Attrition: **0%** MLB: **0%**

Comparables:
Danny Murphy, Al Kaline, Walt Streuli (60)

YEAR	TEAM	LVL	AGE	PA	R	2B	3B	HR	RBI	BB	SO	SB	CS	AVG/OBP/SLG	TAv	BABIP	BRR	FRAA	WARP
2010	STA	A-	17	60	8	2	0	2	7	3	16	1	1	.278/.333/.426	.304	.351	0.0	C -1	0.4
2010	YAN	Rk	17	136	25	11	0	6	36	11	28	1	1	.353/.419/.597	.384	.414	-1.5	C 0	2.5
2011	*NYA*	*MLB*	*18*	*229*	*23*	*11*	*0*	*7*	*25*	*12*	*76*	*0*	*0*	*.219/.259/.370*	*224*	*.297*	*0.0*	*C-1*	*-0.2*

It is unwise to get overly excited by any 200 plate appearances, but when the PAs in question are the first of a young player's career and, at just 17, he tears the cover off the ball, one has to take notice. Sanchez was hooked in the Dominican Republic and reeled in by a $3 million bonus that topped anything the Yankees had ever given to a player who couldn't yet drink or vote. The bad news is that Sanchez is one of a fistful of catching prospects in the Yankees' organization. The good news is that he has the tools to compete with any of them. He has a wide-open, power-hitter's swing and the innate power to go with it. He's quite raw defensively, but only in the sense that he's young, as opposed to the "forever raw" Montero sense. The next step will be to see how he adjusts to playing in a full-season league.

Nick Swisher **RF**

Born: 11/25/1980 Age: 30
Bats: S Throws: L Height: 6' 0" Weight: 194
Breakout: 2% Improve: 42% Collapse: 4%
Attrition: 9% MLB: 99%

Comparables:
Roger Maris, Reggie Smith, Eric Chavez (69)

YEAR	TEAM	LVL	AGE	PA	R	2B	3B	HR	RBI	BB	SO	SB	CS	AVG/OBP/SLG	TAv	BABIP	BRR	FRAA	WARP
2008	CHA	MLB	27	588	87	21	1	24	69	82	135	3	3	.219/.332/.411	.261	.248	2.8	CF -3, 1B -5	0.7
2009	NYA	MLB	28	607	89	35	1	29	82	97	126	0	0	.249/.369/.498	.299	.270	-1.9	RF 4, 1B -2	3.3
2010	NYA	MLB	29	634	94	33	3	29	89	58	138	1	2	.289/.358/.512	.311	.333	0.6	RF 11, 1B 0	5.1
2011	*NYA*	*MLB*	*30*	*632*	*82*	*30*	*1*	*25*	*80*	*83*	*137*	*2*	*1*	*.252/.354/.457*	*.282*	*.287*	*-0.2*	*RF 5, CF -1*	*2.7*

Kevin Long, who has been mentioned so often in this chapter that he deserves his own entry, got Swisher to quiet his preswing histrionics, replacing all wasted motion with quietude—put your bat on your shoulder, lift it off your shoulder, swing. As a result, Swisher was quicker to the ball, which meant fewer walks but better contact. Old-style low-average/high-walk Swisher and new-flavor high-average/low-walk Swisher were almost equally productive, but in different ways: the former got on base for others, while the latter was more adept at driving others in. Swisher hit .298/.369/.531 through the end of August, when he began to be troubled by a sore knee. The resultant slump dragged his final numbers down, but shouldn't bolster doubts about the sustainability of Swisher's transformation. From his lessons with Long to his sessions with ex-pitching coach Dave Eiland to improve his outfield throwing mechanics, Swisher's goofball rep obscures his dedication.

Mark Teixeira **1B**

Born: 4/11/1980 Age: 31
Bats: S Throws: R Height: 6' 2" Weight: 215
Breakout: 1% Improve: 44% Collapse: 2%
Attrition: 6% MLB: 100%

Comparables:
Lance Berkman, Paul Konerko, Kevin Youkilis (73)

YEAR	TEAM	LVL	AGE	PA	R	2B	3B	HR	RBI	BB	SO	SB	CS	AVG/OBP/SLG	TAv	BABIP	BRR	FRAA	WARP
2008	ANA	MLB	28	234	41	14	0	13	43	32	23	2	0	.358/.449/.632	.383	.346	-0.1	1B 4	3.5
2008	ATL	MLB	28	451	65	27	0	20	78	65	70	0	0	.284/.390/.512	.311	.300	0.2	1B 6	3.3
2009	NYA	MLB	29	707	105	43	3	39	122	81	114	2	0	.292/.383/.565	.329	.302	-6.0	1B -7	4.3
2010	NYA	MLB	30	712	113	36	0	33	108	93	122	0	1	.256/.365/.481	.306	.268	-0.6	1B 14	5.0
2011	*NYA*	*MLB*	*31*	*682*	*96*	*37*	*1*	*31*	*96*	*88*	*114*	*1*	*0*	*.275/.375/.500*	*.303*	*.291*	*0.0*	*1B 5*	*3.8*

One of these years, Teixeira will put together a full season of production. His penchant for slow starts is well known, but in 2010, he really made a fetish of it (.130/.300/.259 in April). He also slowed in September (.220/.346/.349) due to various injuries. In between, he was the usual Teixeira, batting .290/.384/.560. The fall injuries are transient and understandable, but Teixeira's annual April snooze is an example of the power of mind over body and something the first baseman should have outgrown by now. If he requires a spring training reporting date of January 15 to get enough swings in to feel comfortable from Opening Day on, so be it.

Marcus Thames **DH**

Born: 3/6/1977 Age: 34
Bats: R Throws: R Height: 6' 2" Weight: 205
Breakout: 2% Improve: 20% Collapse: 11%
Attrition: 25% MLB: 82%

Comparables:
Larry Hisle, Preston Wilson, Wally Post (66)

YEAR	TEAM	LVL	AGE	PA	R	2B	3B	HR	RBI	BB	SO	SB	CS	AVG/OBP/SLG	TAv	BABIP	BRR	FRAA	WARP
2008	DET	MLB	31	342	51	12	0	25	56	24	95	0	3	.241/.292/.516	.287	.258	-3.4	LF 5, 1B -2	1.5
2009	TOL	AAA	32	54	6	0	0	2	6	5	14	0	0	.245/.315/.367	.238	.303	0.0	LF -1, RF 0	-0.2
2009	DET	MLB	32	294	37	11	1	13	36	29	72	0	2	.252/.323/.454	.272	.291	-1.2	LF -4, 1B 0	0.2
2010	NYA	MLB	33	237	25	7	0	12	33	19	61	0	0	.288/.350/.491	.296	.345	-0.2	LF -2, RF 1	1.0
2011	*NYA*	*MLB*	*34*	*325*	*39*	*12*	*0*	*16*	*43*	*26*	*84*	*1*	*1*	*.244/.306/.448*	*.263*	*.283*	*-0.1*	*LF -1, RF 0*	*0.4*

Thames, whom Brian Cashman threw away on the putrefying remains of Ruben Sierra back in 2003, was a terrific add for the Yankees. Not only did he do his traditionally fine work against southpaws (.300/.352/.454), but despite career rates of only .234/.291/.474 against right-handers coming into the season, he was actually quite playable against them, hitting .268/.347/.549. This came in handy when injuries forced him into more regular work than had been planned. The only hitch was that Thames had no instincts in the outfield. Anything in front of him is inevitably a hit, as he'd rather let the ball drop in than attempt to make a play. The defense didn't bother the Dodgers enough to stop them from making him part of their left field platoon.

PITCHERS

Manny Banuelos

Born: **3/13/1991** Age: **20**
Bats: L Throws: L Height: **5' 10"** Weight: **155**
Breakout: **1%** Improve: **2%** Collapse: **1%**
Attrition: **0%** MLB: **4%**

Comparables:
Oliver Perez, Ken Holtzman, Scott Kazmir (71)

YEAR	TEAM	LVL	AGE	W	L	SV	G	GS	IP	H	HR	BB	SO	EqBB9	EqSO9	GB%	BABIP	WHIP	ERA	FRA	WARP
2008	YAN	Rk	17	4	1	0	12	3	42	32	3	13	37	2.8	7.9	46%	.248	1.21	2.57	4.50	0.6
2009	CSC	A	18	9	5	0	25	19	108	88	4	28	104	2.3	8.7	46%	.282	1.15	2.67	2.71	3.3
2010	TAM	A+	19	0	3	0	10	10	44^1	38	1	14	62	2.9	12.7	46%	.356	1.20	2.23	2.32	1.8
2010	TRN	AA	19	1	2	0	5	6	27	25	2	15	27	5.0	9.0	63%	.338	1.48	3.00	3.47	0.5
2011	*NYA*	*MLB*	*20*	*4*	*5*	*0*	*17*	*12*	*69*	*71*	*9*	*38*	*56*	*4.9*	*7.2*	*44%*	*.303*	*1.56*	*5.04*	*5.48*	*0.6*

Part of the Yankees' Mexican connection, Banuelos is taller than Danny Herrera, but still qualifies as a little lefty by any reasonable standard. Just as Betances was somehow improved by elbow surgery, Banuelos came away from an appendectomy with better stuff than he went in with. (Don't let this get around, because Little League daddies with dollar signs in their eyes will be signing up their sons for unnecessary surgeries.) Banuelos' secondary pitches have also made great strides, and his change rates as a plus offering. Like all young lefties, he occasionally walks a few too many, but his control is not a big problem. This chapter lists several pitching prospects for whom the Yankees have neither the room nor the inclination to make it. Banuelos might seem like one of the fastest risers on the road to trade bait, but his mature approach, combined with his left-handedness, will make it hard even for these convinced fanciers of veterans to pass him up.

Dellin Betances

Born: **3/23/1988** Age: **23**
Bats: R Throws: R Height: **6' 8"** Weight: **245**
Breakout: **14%** Improve: **15%** Collapse: **0%**
Attrition: **7%** MLB: **15%**

Comparables:
Jose Mijares, John Meloan, Kevin Jepsen (80)

YEAR	TEAM	LVL	AGE	W	L	SV	G	GS	IP	H	HR	BB	SO	EqBB9	EqSO9	GB%	BABIP	WHIP	ERA	FRA	WARP
2008	CSC	A	20	9	4	0	22	22	115^1	87	9	59	135	4.6	10.5	43%	.279	1.36	3.67	4.11	1.6
2009	TAM	A+	21	2	5	0	11	11	44^1	48	2	27	44	5.5	8.9	52%	.351	1.74	5.49	4.73	0.5
2010	TAM	A+	22	8	1	0	14	14	71	43	1	19	88	2.4	11.2	43%	.251	0.92	1.77	3.03	2.1
2010	TRN	AA	22	1	1	0	5	7	25^1	16	5	8	35	2.8	12.4	42%	.212	0.99	3.55	4.01	0.3
2011	*NYA*	*MLB*	*23*	*4*	*5*	*0*	*12*	*12*	*58*	*55*	*8*	*34*	*54*	*5.3*	*8.3*	*43%*	*.298*	*1.54*	*4.83*	*5.25*	*0.9*

The Yankees didn't know what to expect out of Betances after a year lost to poundings and ligament-reinforcement surgery. His injury was a chicken-and-egg problem: did he get hurt because he pitched poorly, or pitch poorly because he got hurt? Normally, the latter would be an easy choice, but Betances, who is built like CC Sabathia's hypertrophic younger brother, doesn't have mechanics so much as a huge analog system of wheels, gears, and pulleys. Oddly, the postsurgical Betances was much more organized on the mound than he had been before. His plus fastball survived the knife, still coming in at 95 and touching 97, and he can follow that with a curve that dives and bites like a teenaged vampire heartthrob. If Betances can keep more sand from getting into the pitching gear and develop a third pitch to complement the first two, Trenton won't hold him long.

Andrew Brackman

Born: **12/4/1985** Age: **25**
Bats: R Throws: R Height: **6' 10"** Weight: **240**
Breakout: **12%** Improve: **16%** Collapse: **10%**
Attrition: **25%** MLB: **36%**

Comparables:
Chris Seddon, Kevin Hart, Billy Buckner (73)

YEAR	TEAM	LVL	AGE	W	L	SV	G	GS	IP	H	HR	BB	SO	EqBB9	EqSO9	GB%	BABIP	WHIP	ERA	FRA	WARP
2009	CSC	A	23	2	12	0	29	19	106^2	106	8	76	103	6.4	8.7	56%	.325	1.80	5.90	5.93	-0.7
2010	TAM	A+	24	5	4	0	12	12	60	67	5	9	56	1.4	8.4	59%	.339	1.35	5.10	5.57	0.1
2010	TRN	AA	24	5	7	0	15	14	80^2	77	3	30	70	3.4	7.9	53%	.314	1.42	3.01	3.80	1.3
2011	*NYA*	*MLB*	*25*	*6*	*10*	*0*	*27*	*21*	*119*	*133*	*17*	*68*	*82*	*5.2*	*6.2*	*48%*	*.311*	*1.69*	*5.89*	*6.41*	*0.1*

Brackman convinced some skeptics last year, but there is still a way to go before he justifies his selection as the Yankees' first-round draft pick in 2007. The towering righty's fastball took a step into the low to mid-90s, and the wildness that had plagued him in 2009 was plumb gone. These are signs of a pitcher coming to grips with his mechanics. His approach induces grounders, which makes some sense, given that his pitches are descending from somewhere north of Asgard, and he allowed few home runs. Brackman's future will remain brackish until he refines a third offering, lest he be restricted to two-pitch relief duty, and of course, he has to show that he can do it again this year.

A. J. Burnett

Born: **1/3/1977** Age: **34**
Bats: R Throws: R Height: **6' 5"** Weight: **205**
Breakout: **24%** Improve: **55%** Collapse: **18%**
Attrition: **6%** MLB: **98%**

Comparables:
Ted Lilly, Chuck Finley, Steve Carlton (68)

YEAR	TEAM	LVL	AGE	W	L	SV	G	GS	IP	H	HR	BB	SO	EqBB9	EqSO9	GB%	BABIP	WHIP	ERA	FRA	WARP
2008	TOR	MLB	31	18	10	0	35	34	221^1	211	19	86	231	3.5	9.4	50%	.314	1.38	4.07	3.63	5.1
2009	NYA	MLB	32	13	9	0	33	33	207	193	25	97	195	4.2	8.5	44%	.296	1.45	4.04	4.37	3.6
2010	NYA	MLB	33	10	15	0	33	33	186^2	204	25	78	145	3.8	7.0	46%	.319	1.61	5.26	5.39	0.7
2011	*NYA*	*MLB*	*34*	*11*	*11*	*0*	*30*	*30*	*186*	*185*	*25*	*78*	*168*	*3.8*	*8.1*	*46%*	*.305*	*1.41*	*4.56*	*4.95*	*2.6*

Dates all good Americans know by heart: July 4, 1776; December 7, 1941; November 22, 1963;

and November 1, 2013, also known, respectively, as Independence Day, Pearl Harbor, the Kennedy assassination, and the approximate day that A. J. Burnett's contract expires, celebrated in the Yankees' front office as Independence Day II. On that date—depending on the status of their other long-term commitments—the Yankees may no longer be able to claim that they host one of baseball's most expensive mediocrities. In last year's edition, we said that Burnett comes out of the pen with either no-hitter stuff or absolutely no feel for his pitches. The latter was the case the majority of the time in 2010, particularly down the stretch, when Burnett's ERA was 6.61. There was no injury and no real pattern to it—Burnett was perfectly capable of interrupting a string of poundings with a couple of strong starts, only to turn around and get thrashed by the Mariners. He is what he is: one of baseball's most perplexing mysteries and an all-time great underachiever. Three years to go.

Joba Chamberlain

Born: **9/23/1985** Age: **25**
Bats: **R** Throws: **R** Height: **6' 2"** Weight: **230**
Breakout: **15%** Improve: **46%** Collapse: **15%**
Attrition: **8%** MLB: **93%**

Comparables:
Len Barker, Jordan Zimmermann, Yovani Gallardo (67)

YEAR	TEAM	LVL	AGE	W	L	SV	G	GS	IP	H	HR	BB	SO	EqBB9	EqSO9	GB%	BABIP	WHIP	ERA	FRA	WARP
2008	NYA	MLB	22	4	3	0	42	12	100^{1}	87	5	39	118	3.5	10.6	52%	.324	1.28	2.60	2.97	3.1
2009	NYA	MLB	23	9	6	0	32	31	157^{1}	167	21	76	133	4.3	7.6	45%	.313	1.62	4.75	4.99	1.9
2010	NYA	MLB	24	3	4	3	73	0	71^{2}	71	6	22	77	2.8	9.7	46%	.327	1.31	4.40	4.30	0.3
2011	*NYA*	*MLB*	*25*	*7*	*5*	*1*	*49*	*14*	*109*	*103*	*12*	*45*	*111*	*3.7*	*9.2*	*46%*	*.311*	*1.36*	*4.00*	*4.34*	*2.0*

What a disappointment. Chamberlain is just another middle guy now, one who popped up in the spotlight eighth-inning role well into the season because no one else claimed the job until Kerry Wood was acquired. Joba still has the stuff to be a top reliever and perhaps even an above-average starter, though he doesn't dial it up to 98 anymore. That Joba has gone from future star to generic righty is entirely attributable to the way the Yankees handled him, shoving him into the bullpen as if he had failed as a starter when that was not the case. In 32 career starts through the end of July 2009, Chamberlain pitched 176 innings with a 3.27 ERA. It was at that point that the Yankees sandbagged him with another counterproductive set of rules. For an encore, they subjected him to a farcical competition with Phil Hughes for a rotation spot in spring training, and voilà, you had a pitcher falling prey to the tyranny of low expectations. The good news, barring a trade to a team that will restore Chamberlain to useful employment, is that he's a good candidate for a rebound: his ERA was much higher than his peripherals would have suggested, due to bad luck on balls in play, and if you don't buy that, then note that he settled down in the second half. In 26.2 innings thrown after the trade deadline, Chamberlain's ERA was 2.36, and opposing hitters were limited to a .200/.245/.350 line.

Chad Gaudin

Born: **3/24/1983** Age: **28**
Bats: **R** Throws: **R** Height: **5' 11"** Weight: **165**
Breakout: **28%** Improve: **54%** Collapse: **16%**
Attrition: **16%** MLB: **95%**

Comparables:
Wade Miller, Pete Richert, Al Downing (76)

YEAR	TEAM	LVL	AGE	W	L	SV	G	GS	IP	H	HR	BB	SO	EqBB9	EqSO9	GB%	BABIP	WHIP	ERA	FRA	WARP
2008	CHN	MLB	25	4	2	0	24	0	27^{1}	29	5	10	27	3.3	8.9	33%	.316	1.43	6.26	6.67	-0.5
2008	OAK	MLB	25	5	3	0	26	6	62^{2}	63	6	17	44	2.4	6.3	42%	.295	1.32	3.59	4.07	0.9
2009	NYA	MLB	26	2	0	0	11	6	42	41	7	20	34	4.3	7.3	44%	.274	1.52	3.43	3.95	0.9
2009	SDN	MLB	26	4	10	0	20	19	105^{1}	105	7	56	105	4.8	9.0	45%	.323	1.58	5.13	4.97	0.5
2010	OAK	MLB	27	0	2	0	12	0	171	27	5	5	20	2.6	10.4	36%	.415	2.02	8.83	7.81	-0.6
2010	NYA	MLB	27	1	2	0	30	0	48	46	11	20	33	3.8	6.2	40%	.250	1.48	4.50	5.74	-0.4
2011	*WAS*	*MLB*	*28*	*6*	*5*	*0*	*48*	*13*	*119*	*122*	*15*	*53*	*98*	*4.0*	*7.4*	*43%*	*.306*	*1.46*	*4.67*	*5.07*	*0.5*

Released by the Yankees at the end of spring training, Gaudin hooked on with the A's, rapidly pitched himself off the team, and rebounded back to the Bronx, the Yankees in the interim having lost their intended jack-of-all-trades pitcher, Alfredo Aceves. Whereas Aceves actually has value in the swingman role, Gaudin is more of a hack of all trades. While his slider once inspired hope of future dominance, now it mainly inspires home runs—had Gaudin's rate of 2.2 home runs per nine innings qualified, it would have easily led the majors. Gaudin needs to find a team with a large park and a pitching coach with a track record of fixing misfit toys, but he signed a minor-league deal with the Washington Nationals instead.

Phil Hughes

Born: **6/24/1986** Age: **25**
Bats: **R** Throws: **R** Height: **6' 5"** Weight: **220**
Breakout: **18%** Improve: **41%** Collapse: **27%**
Attrition: **23%** MLB: **87%**

Comparables:
Scott Elarton, Ian Kennedy, Clay Buchholz (67)

YEAR	TEAM	LVL	AGE	W	L	SV	G	GS	IP	H	HR	BB	SO	EqBB9	EqSO9	GB%	BABIP	WHIP	ERA	FRA	WARP
2008	SWB	AAA	22	1	0	0	6	6	29	34	2	9	31	2.8	9.6	42%	.364	1.55	5.90	3.11	1.4
2008	NYA	MLB	22	0	4	0	8	8	34	43	3	15	23	4.0	6.1	36%	.348	1.74	6.62	6.49	-0.1
2009	NYA	MLB	23	8	3	3	51	7	86	68	8	28	96	2.9	10.0	36%	.280	1.17	3.03	3.13	2.5
2010	NYA	MLB	24	18	8	0	31	29	176^{1}	162	25	58	146	3.0	7.5	36%	.274	1.25	4.19	5.24	0.8
2011	*NYA*	*MLB*	*25*	*8*	*6*	*0*	*34*	*18*	121^{1}	*112*	*16*	*43*	*109*	*3.2*	*8.1*	*40%*	*.288*	*1.27*	*3.74*	*4.06*	*2.8*

In 2010, Hughes faded in and out of view like the *Flying Dutchman*. In his first six starts, he went 5-0 with an ERA of 1.38. Thereafter, he was just another guy, and often not a very good one. In his 25 remaining games, he posted a 4.98 ERA, with opposing batters whacking 1.6 home runs per nine innings pitched. From mid-May on, the majority of his appearances failed to rise to the level of a quality start (six innings, three runs or fewer). The conventional, whistling-in-the-dark wisdom now has it that Hughes has paid his dues and will be more consistent in 2011, but he is still a pitcher with intense fly-ball tendencies (he had the fifth-lowest ratio of grounders to fly balls in the majors, but missed ranking second by a trivial fraction) and one who pitches in a park that plays small. On the road, his ERA was 3.47 and he allowed one home run every 53 at-bats. At home, his ERA was 4.66 and balls crossed the fences at a rate of one every 20 at-bats. Unless he can somehow change that, he's going to continue to struggle.

Boone Logan

Born: **8/13/1984** Age: **26**
Bats: R Throws: L Height: **6' 5"** Weight: **200**
Breakout: **10%** Improve: **19%** Collapse: **15%**
Attrition: **18%** MLB: **37%**

Comparables:
Joe Smith, Mark Lowe, Scott Mathieson (80)

YEAR	TEAM	LVL	AGE	W	L	SV	G	GS	IP	H	HR	BB	SO	EqBB9	EqSO9	GB%	BABIP	WHIP	ERA	FRA	WARP
2008	CHA	MLB	23	2	3	0	55	0	42^{1}	57	7	14	42	3.0	8.9	46%	.376	1.70	5.95	5.76	-0.3
2009	GWN	AAA	24	4	2	2	29	0	35^{2}	26	2	17	39	4.3	9.8	49%	.273	1.37	3.28	3.82	0.5
2009	ATL	MLB	24	1	1	0	20	0	17^{1}	21	1	9	10	4.7	5.2	63%	.328	1.79	5.19	6.25	-0.2
2010	SWB	AAA	25	0	1	0	14	0	21^{1}	18	1	4	23	1.7	9.8	46%	.304	1.14	2.11	1.67	0.8
2010	NYA	MLB	25	2	0	0	51	0	40	34	3	20	38	4.5	8.6	48%	.290	1.38	2.93	3.11	0.8
2011	*NYA*	*MLB*	*26*	*3*	*1*	*0*	*60*	*0*	*57*	*56*	*7*	*26*	*51*	*4.0*	*8.0*	*46%*	*.304*	*1.43*	*4.43*	*4.81*	*0.1*

Acquired from the Braves in the Javier Vazquez deal, Logan was up and down until Damaso Marte was lost for the season, after which Logan became the team's sole bullpen southpaw. He was surprisingly effective. Whereas in 2008 he had allowed lefties to hit .291/.324/.505 in 110 plate appearances, this time around he held them to .190/.286/.215. Beginning in late July, he reeled off 24 consecutive scoreless appearances. This is less impressive than it sounds. Because Logan is, appropriately, a spot-lefty—right-handed hitters own .325/.402/.516 career averages against him—the streak comprised all of 14.2 innings. The LOOGY's life is full of small samples, so take that stretch with a grain of salt; Logan has never been consistent and was still troublingly wild last season.

D. J. Mitchell

Born: **5/13/1987** Age: **24**
Bats: R Throws: R Height: **6' 2"** Weight: **165**
Breakout: **19%** Improve: **44%** Collapse: **13%**
Attrition: **9%** MLB: **74%**

Comparables:
Charles Hudson, Junichi Tazawa, Steve Avery (64)

YEAR	TEAM	LVL	AGE	W	L	SV	G	GS	IP	H	HR	BB	SO	EqBB9	EqSO9	GB%	BABIP	WHIP	ERA	FRA	WARP
2009	CSC	A	22	4	1	0	6	6	37	31	1	6	42	1.5	10.2	63%	.316	1.03	1.95	3.85	0.6
2009	TAM	A+	22	8	6	0	19	18	103^{1}	93	1	38	83	3.3	7.2	68%	.306	1.35	2.88	3.93	2.1
2010	TRN	AA	23	11	4	0	23	22	133	128	11	57	96	3.9	6.5	59%	.291	1.44	4.06	5.08	-0.4
2010	SWB	AAA	23	2	0	0	4	4	22^{2}	27	1	9	20	3.6	7.9	43%	.356	1.59	3.97	4.20	0.4
2011	*NYA*	*MLB*	*24*	*8*	*10*	*0*	*25*	*25*	*141^{1}*	*156*	*18*	*69*	*89*	*4.4*	*5.7*	*53%*	*.308*	*1.59*	*5.27*	*5.73*	*1.0*

Another Yankees pitching prospect knocking on the big-league door, Mitchell is a sinkerball specialist who sits 89-91 mph and, lacking a put-away pitch, just hopes to keep the ball on the ground and in the park. Despite the promotion to Triple-A, Mitchell's second pro season wasn't nearly as impressive as the first—posting a 4.00 ERA for the Thunder takes work; it's like posting a 4.00 at Petco. His strikeout rate predictably dropped, but he was also wild for a pitcher of his approach and gave up a surprising number of long balls. He's effective against right-handed hitters; we'll let you know the next time he retires a left-hander. Barring improvement, not impossible, given how fast the Clemson product has moved through the minors, he's headed for middle relief or the back end of a National League rotation.

Sergio Mitre

Born: **2/16/1981** Age: **30**
Bats: R Throws: R Height: **6' 4"** Weight: **210**
Breakout: **15%** Improve: **32%** Collapse: **16%**
Attrition: **17%** MLB: **60%**

Comparables:
Matt Belisle, Lance Cormier, Chris Jakubauskas (77)

YEAR	TEAM	LVL	AGE	W	L	SV	G	GS	IP	H	HR	BB	SO	EqBB9	EqSO9	GB%	BABIP	WHIP	ERA	FRA	WARP
2009	SWB	AAA	28	3	1	0	7	7	45	40	3	5	35	1.0	7.0	65%	.287	1.07	2.20	3.09	2.1
2009	NYA	MLB	28	3	3	0	12	9	51^{2}	71	10	13	32	2.3	5.6	59%	.333	1.68	6.62	6.02	0.1
2010	NYA	MLB	29	0	3	1	27	3	54	43	7	16	29	2.7	4.8	52%	.226	1.13	3.33	5.17	0.0
2011	*NYA*	*MLB*	*30*	*5*	*5*	*0*	*33*	*12*	*93*	*103*	*13*	*27*	*56*	*2.6*	*5.3*	*50%*	*.300*	*1.39*	*4.67*	*5.07*	*1.0*

Sergio Mitre's Baseball-Reference page is sponsored by some individual or organization that chooses to be identified only as "Mets Rule Yankees Stink." Fortunately for the Yankees, Mitre is neither their first rejoinder to that assertion nor their last. Still, it's not clear why he had to be part of the discussion at all. Thrashed as a spot starter (5.93 ERA), he wasn't half-bad as a reliever, posting a 2.45 ERA and allowing only 27 hits in 40 1/3 innings. However, he was much less a ground-ball pitcher than he had been previously and turned in his usual low strike-out rate, which suggests that his small-sample success won't continue once his BABIP returns to a sustainable level. Girardi showed a proper appreciation for Mitre's stuff by using him at times so lacking in tension that "low-leverage" doesn't really do them justice—they were more "non-leverage" situations. That lack of faith leaves open the question of why he was worth keeping on the roster. Mitre is now 30. The world has been waiting a long time for him to arrive, but as Gertrude Stein might have said, it's possible that there is no there there.

Dustin Moseley

Born: **12/26/1981** Age: **29**
Bats: **R** Throws: **R** Height: **6' 4"** Weight: **190**
Breakout: **2%** Improve: **10%** Collapse: **3%**
Attrition: **5%** MLB: **13%**

Comparables:
Brian Burres, Shane Komine, Jake Woods (78)

YEAR	TEAM	LVL	AGE	W	L	SV	G	GS	IP	H	HR	BB	SO	EqBB9	EqSO9	GB%	BABIP	WHIP	ERA	FRA	WARP
2008	SLC	AAA	26	7	10	0	20	20	116^{2}	150	23	34	83	2.6	6.4	47%	.339	1.62	6.94	7.31	-1.1
2008	ANA	MLB	26	2	4	0	12	10	50^{1}	70	6	20	37	3.6	6.6	49%	.372	1.83	6.62	5.31	0.4
2009	ANA	MLB	27	1	0	0	3	3	14^{2}	20	3	3	8	1.8	4.9	41%	.333	1.57	4.30	4.27	0.3
2010	SWB	AAA	28	4	4	0	12	12	72^{2}	83	6	18	55	2.2	6.9	64%	.333	1.45	4.21	5.32	0.3
2010	NYA	MLB	28	4	4	0	16	9	65^{1}	66	13	27	33	3.7	4.5	51%	.261	1.45	4.96	5.35	0.2
2011	*SDN*	*MLB*	*29*	*7*	*8*	*0*	*21*	*21*	*113^{2}*	*129*	*16*	*41*	*71*	*3.2*	*5.6*	*48%*	*.310*	*1.50*	*5.08*	*5.52*	*0.3*

Moseley is a perfectly acceptable last man on a starving man's pitching staff, albeit a man far better suited to extremely low-leverage relief work than starting assignments. The Yankees are far from starving, with a league-pacing payroll and any number of pitching prospects on the cusp, so it is difficult to understand why they would choose to throw away nine starts on a pitcher with no past, present, or future. They then dragged that same nonentity onto the post-season roster along with Sergio Mitre because when you're competing for a championship, it's really important to have your blow-out pitching needs covered. Conclusion: Moseley possesses photos of Derek Jeter kicking an orphan. Despite the potentially damaging evidence, the Yankees nontendered Moseley in December. The Padres signed him to a one-year, $900,000 contract, perhaps operating under the impression that Petco can change any schmo into Jake Peavy.

Hector Noesi

Born: **1/26/1987** Age: **24**
Bats: **R** Throws: **R** Height: **6' 2"** Weight: **175**
Breakout: **7%** Improve: **11%** Collapse: **0%**
Attrition: **6%** MLB: **13%**

Comparables:
Jose Ascanio, Jose Garcia, Daryl Thompson (69)

YEAR	TEAM	LVL	AGE	W	L	SV	G	GS	IP	H	HR	BB	SO	EqBB9	EqSO9	GB%	BABIP	WHIP	ERA	FRA	WARP
2008	STA	A-	21	1	1	0	5	5	24	20	5	7	31	2.6	11.6	35%	.273	1.17	3.00	3.27	0.7
2008	YAN	Rk	21	2	1	0	9	2	24^{2}	23	2	3	24	1.1	8.7	43%	.309	1.09	3.64	4.30	0.4
2009	CSC	A	22	3	4	0	17	11	75^{2}	62	3	11	78	1.3	9.3	49%	.288	0.96	2.38	2.72	2.2
2009	TAM	A+	22	3	0	0	9	9	41^{1}	34	3	4	40	0.9	8.7	36%	.274	0.94	3.92	5.12	0.2
2010	TAM	A+	23	5	2	0	8	8	43	35	3	6	53	1.3	11.1	42%	.291	1.00	2.72	2.40	1.7
2010	TRN	AA	23	8	4	0	17	16	98^{2}	90	7	18	86	1.6	7.9	38%	.294	1.12	3.10	3.28	2.2
2010	SWB	AAA	23	1	2	0	4	4	22	34	2	4	17	1.6	7.0	37%	.405	1.77	7.36	5.45	0.1
2011	*NYA*	*MLB*	*24*	*4*	*4*	*0*	*15*	*11*	*67*	*75*	*10*	*21*	*50*	*2.8*	*6.7*	*41%*	*.311*	*1.42*	*4.75*	*5.16*	*0.8*

A Tommy John survivor, Noesi passed an important test in 2010 by not only pitching well, but also not breaking down. He has an elegant delivery with a high lift to his knee that is reminiscent of Orlando Hernandez, and exemplary command, having walked just 62 in 353 pro innings (1.6 per nine innings). Note that the higher Noesi rose, the harder the going got. That owes something to the strength of his opponents, but also stemmed in part from his lack of spectacular secondary offerings: his fastball has movement and precision, but his curve and change are just decent. He's unlikely to be an ace in the American League, and it should be interesting to see what advanced hitters in Triple-A or the majors do with a fastball-reliant pitcher who is always around the plate. Still, there's a lot here to like, a fourth-starter type with good stuff who doesn't get himself in trouble by nibbling—which is to say, the anti-A.J.

Ivan Nova

Born: **1/12/1987** Age: **24**
Bats: **R** Throws: **R** Height: **6' 4"** Weight: **210**
Breakout: **7%** Improve: **13%** Collapse: **4%**
Attrition: **15%** MLB: **28%**

Comparables:
Jeff Manship, Tobi Stoner, Yorman Bazardo (79)

YEAR	TEAM	LVL	AGE	W	L	SV	G	GS	IP	H	HR	BB	SO	EqBB9	EqSO9	GB%	BABIP	WHIP	ERA	FRA	WARP
2008	TAM	A+	21	8	13	0	26	24	148^{2}	168	6	46	109	2.8	6.6	52%	.347	1.50	4.36	4.51	1.9
2009	TRN	AA	22	5	4	0	12	12	72^{1}	65	3	31	47	3.9	5.9	65%	.279	1.36	2.37	4.02	0.9
2009	SWB	AAA	22	1	4	0	12	12	67	72	4	28	43	3.8	5.8	49%	.318	1.54	5.10	4.64	0.6
2010	SWB	AAA	23	12	3	0	23	23	145	135	10	48	115	3.0	7.1	53%	.298	1.28	2.86	3.91	3.0
2010	NYA	MLB	23	1	2	0	10	7	42	44	4	17	26	3.6	5.6	51%	.294	1.48	4.50	5.18	0.2
2011	*NYA*	*MLB*	*24*	*6*	*8*	*0*	*20*	*20*	*118*	*136*	*15*	*53*	*66*	*4.0*	*5.0*	*50%*	*.310*	*1.59*	*5.23*	*5.68*	*0.8*

After a few years of being too good to dismiss but not good enough to be exciting, Nova upped his prospect cred last season with a strong showing at Scranton that included some of the strikeouts he needed to boost himself out of the Legion of Future Moseleys. Nova was impressive in the majors, but only to a point—through the first 50 pitches of his starts, he held batters to a .219 average. From then on, he was pounded and rapidly found himself caught on the end of Girardi's hook. Nova's low-90s fastball is effective, but his off-speed stuff has always trailed behind, and he clearly needs another wrinkle to fool the hitters seeing him for the third time in a game. The bullpen looms.

Andy Pettitte

Born: **6/15/1972** Age: **39**
Bats: L Throws: L Height: **6' 5"** Weight: **235**
Breakout: **14%** Improve: **38%** Collapse: **18%**
Attrition: **18%** MLB: **77%**

Comparables:
Jose Contreras, Gaylord Perry, David Wells (56)

YEAR	TEAM	LVL	AGE	W	L	SV	G	GS	IP	H	HR	BB	SO	EqBB9	EqSO9	GB%	BABIP	WHIP	ERA	FRA	WARP
2008	NYA	MLB	36	14	14	0	33	33	204	233	19	55	158	2.4	7.0	52%	.333	1.45	4.54	4.04	4.0
2009	NYA	MLB	37	14	8	0	32	32	194^{2}	193	20	75	148	3.5	6.8	44%	.295	1.40	4.16	4.59	3.0
2010	NYA	MLB	38	11	3	0	21	21	129	123	13	40	101	2.8	7.0	46%	.291	1.29	3.28	3.57	3.1
2011	*NYA*	*MLB*	*39*	*12*	*11*	*0*	*32*	*32*	*193*	*205*	*23*	*66*	*139*	*3.1*	*6.5*	*47%*	*.308*	*1.40*	*4.39*	*4.77*	*3.1*

The Boy bit off a stalk of grass and chewed it. "Going to make a long stay here?" he asked, politely.

"Can't hardly say at present," replied the dragon. "It seems a nice place enough—but I've only been here a short time, and one must look about and reflect and consider before settling down. It's rather a serious thing, settling down." —Kenneth Grahame, *The Reluctant Dragon*

Pettitte, the Reluctant Pitcher, has been contemplating settling down with his family for some time now and may actually do it someday. While he dithers, the Yankees have whiled away each of the last four winters wondering if anyone would be wearing number 46 when spring training rolled around. As good as Pettitte was before a groin injury swept him away for two months, it's probably time for the Yankees to turn off the porch light and flip on the No Vacancy sign. Pettitte will turn 39 in June, and as his lingering injury demonstrates, one risk factor in older pitchers is not just arm injuries but everything injuries—the Yankees even had to juggle their post-season rotation when Pettitte's back and hamstrings acted up. Age can mean not just declining stuff, but declining attendance. Further, Pettitte should be evaluated not on his 18 pre-injury starts, but also on his previous four seasons, all of which offered ERAs in the 4.00s. With pitching prospects falling out of every cabinet and change drawer, the wise course would be to move on a year early rather than a year late and let Pettitte go spend time at home already.

David Phelps

Born: **10/9/1986** Age: **24**
Bats: R Throws: R Height: **6' 3"** Weight: **190**
Breakout: **6%** Improve: **24%** Collapse: **6%**
Attrition: **14%** MLB: **42%**

Comparables:
Troy Patton, Junichi Tazawa, Kevin Mulvey (73)

YEAR	TEAM	LVL	AGE	W	L	SV	G	GS	IP	H	HR	BB	SO	EqBB9	EqSO9	GB%	BABIP	WHIP	ERA	FRA	WARP
2008	STA	A-	21	8	2	0	15	15	72^{2}	67	4	18	52	2.2	6.4	53%	.288	1.18	2.72	5.04	0.6
2009	CSC	A	22	10	3	0	19	19	112^{2}	117	9	25	90	2.0	7.2	54%	.320	1.30	2.80	4.03	1.5
2009	TAM	A+	22	3	1	0	7	7	38^{1}	34	1	6	32	1.4	7.5	60%	.295	1.04	1.17	3.74	1.0
2010	TRN	AA	23	6	0	0	14	14	88^{1}	63	2	23	84	2.3	8.6	49%	.264	1.00	2.04	3.01	2.5
2010	SWB	AAA	23	4	2	0	12	11	70^{1}	76	4	13	57	1.7	7.3	44%	.324	1.28	3.07	4.01	1.5
2011	*NYA*	*MLB*	*24*	*7*	*9*	*0*	*22*	*22*	*122*	*140*	*16*	*45*	*75*	*3.3*	*5.5*	*47%*	*.310*	*1.51*	*5.02*	*5.46*	*1.2*

In the three seasons since the Yankees picked him out of Notre Dame in the 14th round of the 2008 draft, Phelps has known few professional setbacks. His overall record—31-8 with a 2.50 ERA—looks like something on Dizzy Dean's encyclopedia page, except with better peripherals than Dizzy had. He is tall, has good mechanics, features a fastball that sits in the low 90s, and hasn't been touched by minor-league bats, so what's not to like? The devil is in the details: Phelps's fastball is a bit straight and his secondary pitches a bit bland, and so scouts doubt that he can fool hitters for six innings at a stretch. Still, when a tyro hurler is consistently successful like this, it pays to remember that the judgments of scouts are merely informed hypotheses and give the guy a chance to fail. Remember, scouts said the same thing about Tyler Clippard and Ian Kennedy, yet each has found his niche in the big leagues.

Ryan Pope

Born: **5/21/1986** Age: **25**
Bats: R Throws: R Height: **6' 3"** Weight: **190**
Breakout: **6%** Improve: **8%** Collapse: **7%**
Attrition: **15%** MLB: **17%**

Comparables:
Marco Estrada, Mike Ekstrom, Rafael Rodriguez (82)

YEAR	TEAM	LVL	AGE	W	L	SV	G	GS	IP	H	HR	BB	SO	EqBB9	EqSO9	GB%	BABIP	WHIP	ERA	FRA	WARP
2008	TAM	A+	22	7	7	0	20	20	104	114	8	22	72	1.9	6.2	46%	.318	1.35	4.15	4.86	1.0
2009	TRN	AA	23	5	12	0	26	25	141^{1}	155	7	34	106	2.2	6.8	41%	.325	1.39	4.78	5.46	-0.7
2010	TRN	AA	24	4	6	17	46	7	94^{1}	88	10	31	85	3.0	8.1	43%	.291	1.34	4.20	4.74	0.3
2011	*NYA*	*MLB*	*25*	*5*	*6*	*3*	*26*	*14*	*93^{1}*	*110*	*14*	*35*	*56*	*3.4*	*5.4*	*43%*	*.314*	*1.55*	*5.50*	*5.98*	*0.2*

After art-school alum Pope followed up a mediocre 2009 showing at Trenton by giving up 22 runs in 35 innings to kick off 2010, the Yankees shifted him to the pen. Faster than you can say, "By the sweet jowls of Jenks!" a closer was born; Pope pitched 56.1 innings in relief with a 3.49 ERA and a 9.7 strikeout rate, which must have shocked even him. There is now a decent chance that at some point in the next year, Tom Lehrer's "Vatican Rag" will sound forth from Yankee Stadium loudspeakers as the Pinstriped Pontiff jogs toward the infield.

Mariano Rivera

Born: **11/29/1969** Age: **41**
Bats: **R** Throws: **R** Height: **6' 2"** Weight: **170**
Breakout: **12%** Improve: **21%** Collapse: **21%**
Attrition: **7%** MLB: **55%**

Comparables:
Larry Andersen, Dennis Eckersley, Hoyt Wilhelm (52)

YEAR	TEAM	LVL	AGE	W	L	SV	G	GS	IP	H	HR	BB	SO	EqBB9	EqSO9	GB%	BABIP	WHIP	ERA	FRA	WARP
2008	NYA	MLB	38	6	5	39	64	0	70^{2}	41	4	6	77	0.8	9.8	55%	.218	0.69	1.40	1.95	2.3
2009	NYA	MLB	39	3	3	44	66	0	66^{1}	48	7	12	72	1.6	9.8	53%	.249	0.92	1.76	2.34	1.7
2010	NYA	MLB	40	3	3	33	61	0	60	39	2	11	45	1.7	6.8	52%	.222	0.92	1.80	3.11	0.9
2011	*NYA*	*MLB*	*41*	*4*	*2*	*29*	*65*	*0*	*67*	*56*	*6*	*14*	*61*	*1.9*	*8.2*	*49%*	*.274*	*1.05*	*2.57*	*2.79*	*1.6*

Rivera is beyond encomiums, so let us skip past the praise for this obvious first-ballot Hall of Famer—please feel free to infer our genuflections. Obligatory obeisances out of the way, some small chinks did appear in Rivera's armor last year. Yes, he finished his third straight season with an ERA below 2.00. Heck, his ERA for his last 500 games is below 2.00. And sure, he was pretty much unhittable during the regular season, holding opposing hitters to a .183 average and an anorexic average on balls in play. The problem, if you can call it that, is that out of respect for the nagging minor injuries that afflict older pitchers, Joe Girardi handled Rivera gingerly. Of the 14 pitchers who had 30 or more saves last year, Rivera pitched the third-fewest innings; he worked on consecutive days only 14 times, second-fewest in the group; he worked the eighth-smallest percentage of his team's high-leverage plate appearances. Rivera is slowly turning into the world's greatest variation on the LOOGY, the CLOOGY (CLoser Only Occasionally Guy). There is a negative spillover effect on the rest of the staff, but as long as Rivera is both this effective and able to respond to heavier usage in the playoffs, the Yankees can afford to have him be the classic car that never leaves the garage. How much longer that obtains now that Rivera is 41 is anyone's guess—the velocity of his fastball *has* gradually declined—but given the way he has continued to defy expectations, there is no profit in predicting his demise.

David Robertson

Born: **4/9/1985** Age: **26**
Bats: **R** Throws: **R** Height: **5' 11"** Weight: **180**
Breakout: **25%** Improve: **41%** Collapse: **15%**
Attrition: **9%** MLB: **80%**

Comparables:
John Wetteland, Ugueth Urbina, Danny Darwin (69)

YEAR	TEAM	LVL	AGE	W	L	SV	G	GS	IP	H	HR	BB	SO	EqBB9	EqSO9	GB%	BABIP	WHIP	ERA	FRA	WARP
2008	SWB	AAA	23	4	0	1	24	0	39^{1}	22	1	21	57	4.8	13.0	54%	.250	1.14	2.06	3.36	0.9
2008	NYA	MLB	23	4	0	0	25	0	30^{1}	29	3	15	36	4.5	10.7	43%	.338	1.45	5.34	5.23	0.0
2009	NYA	MLB	24	2	1	1	45	0	43^{2}	36	4	23	63	4.7	13.0	36%	.320	1.37	3.30	3.68	0.7
2010	NYA	MLB	25	4	5	1	64	0	61^{1}	59	5	34	71	5.0	10.4	43%	.335	1.57	3.82	3.63	0.6
2011	*NYA*	*MLB*	*26*	*3*	*1*	*0*	*56*	*0*	*72*	*60*	*7*	*37*	*88*	*4.6*	*10.9*	*44%*	*.303*	*1.34*	*3.45*	*3.75*	*1.0*

Despite his ability to get strikeouts, consistency has been a problem for Robertson. On the verge of pitching himself into the important eighth-inning role, he got off to a miserable start, with opposing hitters tagging him for .333/.425/.522 rates through the end of May. He settled down thereafter, despite suffering from intermittent lower back problems throughout the season, posting a 2.58 ERA and holding batters to a .225/.328/.300 line over his final 45.1 innings. The back flared up in late September and presumably was still troubling him when he was thrashed by the Rangers in the ALCS. At 26, Robertson is still on the verge. He's wild, he struggles with men on base, and he can be overpowering. He has value, but also a high frustration quotient.

CC Sabathia

Born: **7/21/1980** Age: **30**
Bats: **L** Throws: **L** Height: **6' 7"** Weight: **250**
Breakout: **7%** Improve: **36%** Collapse: **27%**
Attrition: **18%** MLB: **90%**

Comparables:
Brandon Webb, Dan Haren, Carlos Zambrano (54)

YEAR	TEAM	LVL	AGE	W	L	SV	G	GS	IP	H	HR	BB	SO	EqBB9	EqSO9	GB%	BABIP	WHIP	ERA	FRA	WARP
2008	CLE	MLB	27	6	8	0	18	18	122^{1}	117	13	34	123	2.5	9.0	46%	.311	1.26	3.83	3.87	2.4
2008	MIL	MLB	27	11	2	0	17	17	130^{2}	106	6	25	128	1.7	8.8	53%	.283	1.03	1.65	2.41	5.0
2009	NYA	MLB	28	19	8	0	34	34	230	197	18	67	197	2.6	7.7	45%	.277	1.19	3.37	3.88	5.1
2010	NYA	MLB	29	21	7	0	34	34	237^{2}	209	20	74	197	2.8	7.5	52%	.281	1.22	3.18	3.73	4.7
2011	*NYA*	*MLB*	*30*	*15*	*9*	*0*	*33*	*33*	*232*	*212*	*23*	*64*	*199*	*2.5*	*7.7*	*48%*	*.291*	*1.19*	*3.26*	*3.55*	*6.7*

The hardest-working man in show business, Sabathia is a throwback, both an ace and a workhorse, and in 2010, he did it with a minor meniscus tear in his right knee. It is to be hoped that Sabathia's disappointing post-season performance (11 runs in 16 innings) was the result of the injury and not the fatigue of throwing the third-most innings in the majors (trailing Roy Halladay and Felix Hernandez) on the season and 1,033 innings over the last four (961.2 innings in the regular season, 71.1 in the playoffs). That works out to an average of 258 innings per year. No other pitcher in that span has been close to his overall workload—Halladay is second with 983 overall innings. Sabathia has been handled with reasonable caution, at least by the Yankees; just five of 68 pinstriped starts have crossed the 120-pitch barrier, and of those, none rose higher than 123. As we said in last year's edition, "It's not so much that he's abused as he shows up for every start and works deep into games . . . He's handled it before, and seems a safe bet to do so again, but this could always be the year that he doesn't." That observation still goes for 2011 and will continue to apply, with increasing urgency, up through Sabathia's 300th win and his Hall of Fame induction speech.

Javier Vazquez

Born: **7/25/1976** Age: **34**
Bats: R Throws: R Height: **6' 2"** Weight: **195**
Breakout: **21%** Improve: **51%** Collapse: **22%**
Attrition: **3%** MLB: **98%**

Comparables:
Ted Lilly, Jack Morris, Jim Bunning (67)

YEAR	TEAM	LVL	AGE	W	L	SV	G	GS	IP	H	HR	BB	SO	EqBB9	EqSO9	GB%	BABIP	WHIP	ERA	FRA	WARP
2008	CHA	MLB	31	12	16	0	33	33	208^1	214	25	61	200	2.6	8.6	40%	.316	1.35	4.67	4.64	2.5
2009	ATL	MLB	32	15	10	0	32	32	219^1	181	20	44	238	1.8	9.8	43%	.284	1.04	2.87	3.22	5.7
2010	NYA	MLB	33	10	10	0	31	26	157^1	155	32	65	121	3.7	6.9	36%	.269	1.44	5.32	6.28	-1.1
2011	*FLO*	*MLB*	*34*	*13*	*10*	*0*	*32*	*32*	*201*	*191*	*26*	*62*	*197*	*2.8*	*8.8*	*41%*	*.303*	*1.26*	*3.79*	*4.12*	*4.4*

Though Vazquez was a five-star disappointment in his 2004 turn with the Yankees, Brian Cashman scoffed at assertions that the right-hander was psychologically ill-equipped to pitch for the Yankees. The GM sent three players, including uber-prospect Arodys Vizcaino, and cash to the Braves for the pitcher's services. Upon reaching New York, the right-hander flipped the Kander and Ebb song on its head, showing that he can make it anywhere, but can't make it there. His velocity and command were down from 2009, so he didn't come close to 200 strikeouts after reaching that figure for three consecutive years. Of course, he didn't get the requisite innings to do so, as the Yankees put him in the bullpen only to drag him back to the rotation, having convinced themselves that they had no better options. Vazquez rewarded this strategy for a time, but soon went right back to being a doormat. We are loath to credit the lazy amateur psychoanalysis that sportswriters freely dispense to players whom they don't know with a psychologist's intimacy or insight, but the Marlins' eagerness to sign Vazquez to a one-year deal after such a miserable season suggests that Cashman is alone among fellow GMs in not giving the psychological, anywhere-but-New-York theory credence. The Marlins may well be right, but lost velocity is lost velocity, no matter what tricks the mind plays.

Adam Warren

Born: **8/25/1987** Age: **23**
Bats: R Throws: R Height: **6' 1"** Weight: **200**
Breakout: **19%** Improve: **44%** Collapse: **10%**
Attrition: **5%** MLB: **69%**

Comparables:
Johnny Cueto, Frank Pastore, Kevin Millwood (67)

YEAR	TEAM	LVL	AGE	W	L	SV	G	GS	IP	H	HR	BB	SO	EqBB9	EqSO9	GB%	BABIP	WHIP	ERA	FRA	WARP
2009	STA	A-	21	4	2	0	12	12	56^2	49	1	10	50	1.6	7.9	70%	.302	1.04	1.43	1.96	3.0
2010	TAM	A+	22	7	5	0	15	15	81	72	2	17	67	1.9	7.4	58%	.290	1.17	2.22	2.84	2.6
2010	TRN	AA	22	4	2	0	10	10	54^1	49	2	16	59	2.7	9.8	48%	.309	1.26	3.15	3.48	1.3
2011	*NYA*	*MLB*	*23*	*7*	*7*	*0*	*19*	*19*	100^1	*105*	*11*	*38*	*74*	*3.4*	*6.6*	*50%*	*.306*	*1.42*	*4.44*	*4.83*	*1.8*

Last season, Yankees prospects moved up like an advancing army, all of them plunging forward with one goal in mind: be ready to contribute if by some chance the front office can't fill all 12 spots on the major-league staff with guys 30 or over. Warren made the midseason jump to Double-A and didn't skip a beat, actually upping his strikeout rate while summering on the Delaware Riviera. His season climaxed on August 18, when he struck out 15 Bowie Baysox over the course of pitching seven shutout innings. Like David Phelps, Warren has a startlingly good pro record, with a 2.25 ERA in 192 innings, yet isn't considered a major prospect, because although his fastball is good enough, his secondary pitches don't impress. He has command and a nice ground-ball rate, but those attributes aren't considered adequate to qualify for hot-prospecthood. As with Phelps, he should be considered innocent until found guilty, but baseball rarely works that way.

Kerry Wood

Born: **6/16/1977** Age: **34**
Bats: R Throws: R Height: **6' 5"** Weight: **220**
Breakout: **23%** Improve: **34%** Collapse: **20%**
Attrition: **8%** MLB: **72%**

Comparables:
Brian Fuentes, Francisco Cordero, Lee Smith (74)

YEAR	TEAM	LVL	AGE	W	L	SV	G	GS	IP	H	HR	BB	SO	EqBB9	EqSO9	GB%	BABIP	WHIP	ERA	FRA	WARP
2008	CHN	MLB	31	5	4	34	65	0	66^1	54	3	18	84	2.4	11.4	43%	.311	1.19	3.26	3.34	0.9
2009	CLE	MLB	32	3	3	20	58	0	55	48	7	28	63	4.6	10.3	41%	.293	1.44	4.25	4.40	0.5
2010	CLE	MLB	33	1	4	8	23	0	20	21	3	11	18	5.0	8.1	44%	.305	1.70	6.30	6.63	-0.4
2010	NYA	MLB	33	2	0	0	24	0	26	14	1	18	31	6.2	10.7	36%	.228	1.27	0.69	1.55	0.9
2011	*CHN*	*MLB*	*34*	*2*	*1*	*11*	*47*	*0*	*461*	*41*	*4*	*22*	*49*	*4.4*	*9.5*	*43%*	*.305*	*1.38*	*3.92*	*4.26*	*0.3*

Wood's 1.5 seasons in Cleveland resulted in a 4.80 ERA, inflated in large part by command and control problems that resulted in too many walks and home runs. Brian Cashman's deadline-day acquisition of the right-hander for two very minor prospects was the most basic sort of "Let's see if we can capture some of the old magic" flier. It paid off because the Yankees offered two forms of support that the Indians couldn't: then-pitching coach Dave Eiland was able to suggest revisions to Wood's mechanics that made his stuff—particularly his curve—"crisper" (in Eiland's words), and Wood's posttrade teammates offered superior defensive aid. He still struggled to limit his walks when in pinstripes, but with the curveball biting, he was too hard to hit for it to matter. Despite his success, it is likely too much to expect him to continue to pitch at a high level while walking six batters per nine innings. Wood accepted a below-market contract to return to the Cubs, where he will set up Carlos Marmol for an endgame so wild that Mike Quade had better stock up on nitroglycerin pills.

LINEOUTS

HITTERS

PLAYER	TEAM	LVL	AGE	PA	R	2B	3B	HR	RBI	BB	SO	SB-CS	AVG/OBP/SLG	TAv	BABIP	BRR	FRAA	WARP
OF D. Brewer	TRN	AA	22	580	83	34	3	10	84	53	117	29-10	.270/.346/.407	.282	.326	4.6	RF -5, LF 1	2.8
SS R. Corona#	SWB	AAA	23	428	46	20	5	5	31	36	58	14-1	.238/.306/.354	.242	.266	0.0	2B 18, 3B -1	2.0
SS C. Culver#	STA	A-	17	54	2	1	0	0	0	8	10	1-1	.186/.340/.209	.206	.235	0.0	SS -1	-0.2
	YAN	Rk	17	179	21	7	1	2	18	13	41	6-3	.269/.320/.363	.264	.333	-1.2	SS -4	0.6
2B M. Cusick*	TRN	AA	24	227	17	7	3	3	26	22	31	3-1	.234/.310/.343	.243	.259	-3.0	2B -3, 3B -5	-0.9
	SWB	AAA	24	96	11	6	0	0	9	10	7	0-0	.265/.337/.337	.244	.278	-0.3	3B 1	0.2
OF G. Golson	SWB	AAA	24	454	51	23	5	10	40	25	99	17-4	.263/.313/.414	.248	.315	-2.1	CF 1, RF 2	1.0
	NYA	MLB	24	23	3	2	0	0	2	0	3	0-2	.261/.261/.348	.221	.300	-1.8	RF 3, CF 0	0.1
CF S. Heathcott*	CSC	A	19	351	48	16	3	2	30	42	101	15-10	.258/.359/.352	.271	.375	3.2	CF -8	0.9
DH N. Johnson*	NYA	MLB	31	98	13	4	0	2	8	24	23	0-1	.167/.388/.306	.274	.213	0.2	1B 0	0.2
C C. Moeller	SWB	AAA	35	96	8	6	0	1	9	6	15	0-0	.230/.302/.333	.213	.268	-1.4	C -1, LF 0	-0.3
	NYA	MLB	35	15	2	3	0	0	0	1	4	0-0	.214/.267/.429	.232	.300	-0.5	C 0	0.0
C J. Murphy	CSC	A	19	374	46	15	2	7	54	36	64	4-5	.255/.327/.376	.269	.291	1.3	C 1	1.6
INF J. Snyder*	TRN	AA	24	319	56	13	2	3	27	49	44	2-1	.245/.365/.345	.262	.276	2.1	2B 4, 3B 3	1.9
1B J. Vazquez	SWB	AAA	28	316	47	21	0	18	62	17	95	0-0	.270/.313/.526	.267	.333	-1.9	1B 7, 3B -1	0.9

Former Çape Cod darling **Daniel Brewer** sped through Double-A with a line-drive stroke that cranked out 34 doubles last year. He'll need to mash more than that to profile as a corner outfielder, because although he has wheels, his are suboptimal for center field. Utility infielders who can play a vaguely competent shortstop have some value, so the Yankees retained **Reegie Corona** on their 40-man roster despite a terminally weak bat and the broken right humerus he suffered in July. Teenage shortstop **Cito Culver** was a surprise as the Yankees' 2010 first-rounder; the scouting consensus had him slated for a later round. The Bombers convinced themselves they knew better, but it will be a few years before we have half a clue whether they were right—all Culver's 2010 stats tell us is that he's not Ken Griffey Jr. The Yankees acquired **Matt Cusick** from the Astros for LaTroy Hawkins in 2008 and shipped him to Cleveland as the player to be named for Kerry Wood in October 2010. In between, he hit .242/.314/.326 in 116 games in Double-A and Triple-A. The Yankees acquired former Phillies first-rounder (2004) **Greg Golson** from the Rangers for nonprospect Mitch Hilligoss. Golson shouldn't have been insulted by the price he brought; he has all the skills required to be an outfielder and none required to be a hitter. The Yankees' 2009 first-rounder, **Slade Heathcott**, was challenged with a quick promotion to Low-A Charleston. The speedster showed a willingness to take a walk but was quite raw in most other respects—including whiffing in nearly one-third of his plate appearances—and required labrum surgery on his left shoulder at the end of the season. Brian Cashman approached **Nick Johnson** like a game of "Minesweeper," figuring that every possible injury square on the board had been uncovered. Surprise—Johnson has nothing *but* injury squares. Sidelined from May 8 on by not one but *two* wrist surgeries, Johnson failed to hit even when ostensibly healthy, which suggests that all the downtime and busted parts are starting to catch up to him. When Posada got hurt, the Yankees went for the tried, true, and ineffectual in **Chad Moeller** rather than risk rushing Jesus Montero. Fortunately, they didn't need him for long. **J. R. Murphy** is the fourth in New York's quartet of strong catching prospects. Known for power and defense, he showed less than expected of the former and needs more refinement than expected of the latter. **Justin Snyder** has two things going for him in his quest to become a major-league utility infielder: a left-handed swing and a bit of patience. He also has two bigger things going against him: he can't play short, and he hasn't hit in two years. Plucked from the Mexican League, veteran **Jorge Vazquez** has hit .302/.337/.544 with 31 home runs in 153 stateside games, but has also drawn just 26 walks.

PITCHERS

PLAYER	TEAM	LVL	AGE	W	L	SV	IP	H	HR	BB	SO	EqBB9	EqSO9	GB%	BABIP	WHIP	ERA	FRA	WARP
A. Aceves	NYA	MLB	27	3	0	1	12	10	1	4	2	3.0	1.5	50%	.200	1.25	3.00	4.32	0.1
J. Albaladejo	SWB	AAA	27	4	2	43	63^1	38	3	18	82	2.6	11.7	42%	.245	0.92	1.42	1.80	1.8
	NYA	MLB	27	0	0	0	11^1	9	1	8	8	6.4	6.4	44%	.258	1.68	3.97	4.48	0.0
J. Bleich*	TRN	AA	23	3	2	0	41^1	35	2	28	26	6.1	5.7	54%	.268	1.61	4.79	5.32	0.0
W. De La Rosa*	TRN	AA	25	2	4	0	72^2	82	7	41	56	5.1	7.0	35%	.328	1.75	5.33	5.65	-0.4
S. Garrison*	LEL	A+	23	1	1	0	28^2	28	1	10	13	3.2	4.1	59%	.287	1.38	3.14	4.34	0.2
	POR	AAA	23	1	3	0	22^1	34	5	7	17	2.9	6.9	38%	.382	1.90	8.87	7.10	-0.3
C. Heyer	TAM	A+	24	8	4	0	92	92	1	6	66	0.6	6.5	58%	.310	1.12	3.52	3.91	1.7
G. Kontos	TRN	AA	25	0	2	0	32	30	2	11	28	3.1	7.9	43%	.315	1.28	3.38	3.84	0.4
B. Marshall	CSC	A	20	4	2	0	72	52	2	22	56	2.8	7.0	54%	.240	1.04	2.50	4.43	0.7
D. Marte*	NYA	MLB	35	0	0	0	17^2	10	2	11	12	5.6	6.1	31%	.160	1.25	4.08	5.52	-0.1
L. Pendleton	TRN	AA	26	10	4	0	120^2	95	9	45	111	3.4	8.3	42%	.267	1.20	3.43	4.19	1.4
	SWB	AAA	26	2	1	0	34	29	6	12	22	3.2	5.8	39%	.228	1.21	4.24	5.39	0.1
R. Ring*	SWB	AAA	29	2	1	2	42	35	2	11	39	2.4	8.4	60%	.280	1.21	1.93	2.55	1.3
	NYA	MLB	29	0	0	0	2^1	3	0	2	2	7.7	7.7	75%	.375	2.14	15.43	12.74	-0.2
R. Sanchez	SWB	AAA	26	10	8	0	104^1	88	8	59	96	5.1	8.3	46%	.286	1.42	3.97	5.00	0.9
	NYA	MLB	26	0	0	0	4^1	1	0	3	5	6.2	10.4	33%	.111	0.92	0.00	4.19	0.0
P. Venditte	TAM	A+	25	4	1	6	72^2	49	2	14	85	1.7	10.6	43%	.267	0.90	1.73	2.73	1.9

Had he been healthy, **Alfredo Aceves** would probably have found himself in the starting rotation at several points last season, but a lower-back injury that wouldn't heal shelved him from early May on. Outside the infirmary, he's a valuable, versatile pitcher. Winter reports had him getting better, but improvement was claimed throughout the regular season and was always followed by a setback—he added a broken clavicle in December after falling off a bicycle—so don't believe he's (pardon the expression) back until you see him on a mound. The clavicle could delay his return enough that he will miss Opening Day, so that won't be any time soon. ⊘ **Jonathan Albaladejo** had an excellent year at Triple-A, but the Yankees had seen enough in previous trials and showed little interest in giving him another chance, so he's off to Japan, jiggety-jig. ⊘ **Jeremy Bleich**, the only one of the Yankees' top three picks in the 2008 draft to sign, blew out his labrum, and given the weak results he has showed to this point, he isn't likely to be rejoining us for the rest of his career. ⊘ **Neil Cotts** will try to latch on as a LOOGY after a year recuperating from Tommy John surgery. He always had good stuff, but exhibited less control than the Wild Boy of Aveyron. ⊘ Converted outfielder **Wilkin De La Rosa** impressed the Yankees with 94-mph heat in a breakout 2009 season, but nosediving strikeout rates and skyrocketing walk rates rendered him ineffective in a repeat campaign in Double-A. Dropped from the 40-man, De La Rosa hooked on with the Dodgers, who hope he left his wildness and apparent fondness for injecting more promising prospects with B-12 in Trenton. ⊘ **Jose Rafael DePaula** is a big-money, big-arm kid from the Dominican who can get into the upper 90s, but because of an identity scandal, he's 19 with zero experience, and some still question his true age. ⊘ Plucking **Steve Garrison** off waivers from the Padres has outgoing assistant Kevin Towers' paw prints all over it. New Jersey native Garrison has yet to find success at the upper levels, though a permanent move to the bullpen may help him pick up a couple of ticks on a heater that tops out in the low 90s. ⊘ Strike-zone enthusiast **Craig Heyer** allowed just 0.59 walks per nine in 92 innings pitched; couple that with his extreme ground-ball tendencies (a career mark of nearly two worm-kills per fly), and Heyer should earn multiple chances in the majors. ⊘ **George Kontos** was a middling starting prospect before Tommy John surgery; now he's a middling relief prospect. Kontos has often had problems with fly balls; his stroke of good luck was getting selected by the Padres in the Rule 5 draft, where he might have a chance to pitch in a place where fly balls are no problem at all. ⊘ The recipient of an over-slot bonus in 2008, righty **Brett Marshall** made an impressive return from Tommy John surgery and could shoot up prospect charts with a healthy full year. ⊘ Years ago, Brian Cashman threw **Damaso Marte** away on Enrique Wilson, then spent most of a decade contriving ways to get him back. Be careful what you wish for: shoulder problems have rendered Marte an expensive objet d'art; October labrum surgery means it's likely that he will finish out his contract (his 2012 option can and will be bought out) without making another appearance in a Yankees uniform. ⊘ **Lance Pendleton** was drafted way back in 2005, but Tommy John surgery put him on the slow boat to the majors. He's a bit old to be a prospect and compounds a just-okay strikeout rate with fly-ball tendencies. The Astros selected him in the Rule 5 draft, giving him a shot at a fifth starter's job he almost certainly would not have received from the Yankees. ⊘ Traveling left arm with a brain attached, **Royce Ring** pitched quite well at Scranton, but even when Marte went down, the Yankees showed no interest. Had he pitched well during his September call-up, he might have claimed a post-season roster spot. Alas, 'twas not to be, and given Ring's age and past performance, glory delayed probably means glory denied. In a previous life, **Romulo Sanchez** was a Mississippi River paddlewheel steamboat named the *Belle of Maracay*, and he happily ferried passengers up and down from Davenport to Natchez. Out of options, the fastballer will either make the team or sail on to another port. **Pat Venditte**'s ambidextrous pitching may be novel, but that's no reason for the Yankees to treat him like a novelty. Sure, his stuff isn't great, but he has excellent control and a great strikeout rate, piles up the grounders, and always has a platoon advantage. This ain't Charles Victory Faust; a 1.70 ERA in 174.2 innings deserves some respect, regardless of how it was achieved. If the conventional wisdom is correct and Venditte is a mere sideshow act, let him prove it at the upper levels. The Yankees signed **Luis Vizcaino** to a minor-league contract despite the 36-year-old's year away from the game; perhaps they wanted to apologize for 2007, when Joe Torre had him issue 11 free passes in the DH league.

MANAGER: JOE GIRARDI

YEAR	TEAM	W-L	Pythag +/-	Avg PC	100+ P	120+ P	QS	BQS	REL	REL w Zero R	IBB	Subs	PH	PH Avg	PH HR	SB2	CS2	SB3	CS3	SAC Att	SAC %	POS SAC	Squeeze	Swing	In Play
2008	NYA	89-73	1	90.7	44	0	77	4	474	320	37	55	97	.256	4	107	36	11	3	39	79.5%	29	0	173	136
2009	NYA	103-59	6	96.8	79	4	74	4	461	304	28	58	97	.237	3	99	26	12	1	49	63.3%	28	0	145	108
2010	NYA	95-67	-3	97.3	78	2	77	4	430	284	37	40	114	.153	2	93	26	9	4	48	68.8%	27	0	141	110

Girardi plays things close to the vest, which makes thinking along with his strategy very difficult. Why didn't Andy Pettitte come back out for the seventh inning? Why didn't Jorge Posada pinch-hit for Francisco Cervelli one run down in the eighth? Why didn't Mariano Rivera come out to protect that lead? At these times, Girardi's seeming passivity in the face of strategic opportunities can drive you mad, but after the dust settles, he usually discloses that heretofore unrevealed injuries prevented him from making each glaringly obvious move. Fair enough, Joe, but there were still too many times you sat on your hands, most often in deference to the Great Jeter. Long after it was clear that Jeter was in an intractable slump, Girardi hesitated to remove him from the leadoff spot, perhaps not wanting to face the inevitable media frenzy. Nor did he use his glove-only bench player Ramiro Pena as a late-inning substitute for Jeter. In both instances, Girardi abdicated rather than confront his entitled shortstop. The skipper also insisted that Granderson was not a platoon player, long after it was obvious that he was, stuck with Chan Ho Park beyond all reason, and issued far too many intentional walks for a team that plays in the DH league. Against those failings, you have his insight that Cano was ready to blossom and therefore deserved to be batted higher in the order than he had previously; his willingness to bat a power hitter such as Swisher or Granderson second in the order; and his generally adept handling of Mariano Rivera, which kept the pitcher effective and on the roster despite nagging injuries. He also blew just four—or five percent—of his starters' quality starts by pushing them too far, as compared with such luminaries as Charlie Manuel, Ron Washington, and Ozzie Guillen, all of whom sabotaged over 10 percent, or AL Manager of the Year Ron Gardenhire, who blew seven percent. Girardi is a unique character, an oft-confusing combination of rigidity and flexibility. He's not perfect, but suggestions that he might be fired because the Yankees made an early exit from the playoffs were ludicrous. He's among the best in the game today.

Oakland Athletics

It was a rough season for the Oakland A's. While their Bay Area neighbors, the Giants, drew three million fans, played host to a World Series in their gleaming jewel of a ballpark, and rode the combination of a young, homegrown rotation and one of the game's 10 highest payrolls to an unlikely world championship, the A's soldiered on in the outmoded Oakland-Alameda County Coliseum, where just 1.4 million fans showed up to watch the team with the game's third-lowest payroll. On the field, the A's eked out a .500 record on the strength of their own youthful rotation, but off the field, they made little progress in securing a new playing venue, and there is already concern that they may not keep this current nucleus together long enough to transport it to a new park.

As dire as that juxtaposition with their neighbors to the west may be, the A's did make progress in 2010. Their .500 record and second-place finish marked the first time since 2006 that Oakland had finished with at least an even record, or in the top half of the AL West. They drew more fans than in 2009—albeit fewer than 10,000 more—which was enough to escape the distinction of being the AL's least-watched team. And they finally cleared the six-year, $66 million Eric Chavez contract that had hampered the successors of the 2006 division-winning team, a deal whose final four years produced just 0.5 WARP at a cost of $43 million—nearly 18 percent of their total payroll over that span.

Payroll, attendance, and the stadium issue loom increasingly large in the A's picture, and you can't discuss their progress on the field without understanding what's happening off of it, particularly since it's become such a talking point for general manager Billy Beane and owner Lew Wolff. While 24 of the other 29 teams have moved into a new ballpark over the past 22 years—a construction boom that began with the Blue Jays' SkyDome (now Rogers Centre) back in 1989 and will conclude with the Marlins' Miami Ballpark in 2012—and the rest have undergone substantial baseball-oriented renovations, the A's have been stuck in the old and unimproved multisport Coliseum since leaving Kansas City. At Wolff's behest, the entire upper deck is covered with tarps during baseball games, which reduces the stadium's effective capacity to 35,067—the lowest in the majors—without increasing demand for seats.

ATHLETICS PROSPECTUS

2010 W-L: 81-81, 2nd in AL West

Pythag	.526	14th
RS/G	4.1	23rd
RA/G	3.86	28th
TAv	.267	17th
BRR	-3.7	23rd
FRA	4.05	6th
DER	9.33	8th
DL	1,557	30th
B-Age	27.8	7th
P-Age	25.7	1st
Salary	$55.3	27th
M$/MW	$1.40	4th

Ballpark: The Coliseum (3-yr. PF: 95). The most fair territory in the majors puts a hurt on hitting

2010: Young pitching makes the A's first losers in the AL West

2011: The spirit is Willingham, but despite new OF cornermen and Godzilla, the A's can't overtake the Rangers

Action Items: New home, still more power, and some roster stability

That the Oakland ballclub needs a new park is not in doubt; as Beane remarked after free agent Adrian Beltre ignored his overtures before the 2010 season, "The facility's a hurdle. It's a fact." As with any real estate venture, this one comes down to location, location, location. Prior to 2006, Wolff (a real estate developer, of course, and a fraternity brother of none other than Bud Selig) set his sights on 66th Avenue in Oakland, a site near the Coliseum, but the numerous owners of the land were unwilling to sell and the city was unwilling to intervene. From 2006 to early 2009, Wolff pursued a plan to build the proposed Cisco Field and its surrounding Ballpark Village in Fremont, an East Bay suburb 22 miles south of Oakland. When that fell through due to organized community opposition, Wolff turned his attention to San Jose, 42 miles from Oakland. In March 2009, Selig convened a three-man blue-ribbon committee to report on potential sites. The biggest question was whether San Jose would be on the list, and if so, how much the A's would have to pay the Giants for territorial rights. At this writing in December 2010, with the report still incomplete, the city of San Jose is considering a ballot measure for voters to approve the building of a ballpark, while the city of Oakland has funded an environmental impact report for a waterfront site, Victory Court, which might require half a billion dollars of funding for upgrading freeway access before the cost of a ballpark is considered. Wolff is adamant that Victory Court isn't the solution: "We have exhausted every option in Oakland."

As with any potential relocation, the local politics involved are dizzyingly arcane, but the bottom line is that Giants owner Bill Neukom won't let the A's move without paying a king's ransom. Meanwhile, Selig won't strong-arm him into okaying the move sans said ransom, yet he won't tell Wolff he can't move to San Jose, either, effectively producing a stalemate. In the interim, Wolff is locking the A's into a rather self-defeating cycle, limiting their payroll and attendance as though he can starve them out of town, *Major League* style, while ignoring the fact that the team has drawn reasonably well when they've won; they averaged 2.6 million in attendance during their 1988-1992 heyday, and 2.1 million from 2000 to 2003.

Even on a shoestring budget, the 2010 A's had their merits. Most importantly, they were tops in the AL in run prevention. Even with Brett Anderson, the team's best starter in 2009, limited to just 19 starts due to elbow woes, the rotation led the league in Support Neutral Lineup-adjusted Value Above Replacement (SNLVAR). Trevor Cahill, who was considered a blue-chip prospect on the same level as Anderson going into 2009, blossomed after a so-so rookie season, thanks to a much-improved curveball and an assist from Lady Luck; he wound up tied for third in the league in SNLVAR. Gio Gonzalez improved his control and broke out as well, tying for sixth in the league in SNLVAR. Dallas Braden made headlines by pitching a perfect game and telling Alex Rodriguez to get off his mound. When he pitched, Anderson was as good as any of them, and even the now-departed Vin Mazzaro developed into a serviceable back-end starter. The only downside was former Brewers ace Ben Sheets, who, after missing all of 2009, signed a one-year, $10 million deal—19 percent of the Opening Day payroll—and provided just 20 starts with a 4.53 ERA, worth 0.4 WARP, before re-tearing his flexor tendon. The bullpen was less impressive, dropping from third to 11th in WXRL; Andrew Bailey's otherwise strong follow-up to his Rookie of the Year–winning campaign was curtailed because of injuries, and while Craig Breslow and Jerry Blevins picked up some of the slack, both Michael Wuertz and Brad Ziegler fell off considerably from 2009.

The offense bore little resemblance to the ones that helped the A's thrive during the first half of Beane's tenure, scoring fewer runs than all but one A's team since 1998 and ranking 11th in the league in scoring and True Average. First baseman Daric Barton and designated hitter Jack Cust were the only regulars to slug above .400, and they, along with second baseman Mark Ellis and right fielder Ryan Sweeney—one of a seemingly endless collection of fourth or fifth outfielders pressed into starting—were the only players to post OBPs above the AL average of .327. Coco Crisp cleared both bars, but was held to just 328 plate appearances by injuries, and another reserve, Adam Rosales, slugged exactly .400. To be fair, such figures were depressed by the pitcher-friendly ballpark; of the 11 players with at least 200 plate appearances, seven of them—all but third baseman Kevin Kouzmanoff, catcher Kurt Suzuki, left fielder Gabe Gross, and center fielder Rajai Davisk—had TAvs above the league average of .260, but only three (Cust, Barton, and Crisp) were above .275.

The one area in which the A's offense excelled was on the basepaths—ironic, given the *Moneyball*-era team's notorious disdain for small-ball tactics. With Crisp, center fielder Rajai Davis, and shortstop Cliff Pennington leading the way, the team stole 156 bases, the third-most in the league, and did so at a league-best 80.4 percent clip. The aforementioned trio stole 111 bases at an 85 percent clip.

The 2011 A's should have a bit more muscle. Beane traded hard-throwing reliever Henry Rodriguez and outfielder Corey Brown, their 2007 first-round pick, to the Nationals for Josh Willingham, who hit .268/.389/.459 last season and will man left field. Crisp, whose $5.75 million option was picked up, will return to center field. David DeJesus, who hit .318/.384/.443 with the Royals before a torn ligament in his thumb ended his season in mid-July, will play right field after being acquired from the Royals for Mazzaro and pitcher Justin Marks, their 2009 third-round pick. With Cust nontendered and subsequently lost to the Mariners, the DH spot will be filled by going-on-37-year-old Hideki Matsui, who overcame a slow start to hit .274/.361/.459 with 21 homers for the Angels; he signed a one-year, $4.25 million deal. All three outfielders and Matsui could yield compensation picks if they depart via free agency next year.

Meanwhile, back in the rotation, Beane failed to close a deal for Japanese righty Hisashi Iwakuma after winning negotiating rights; nonetheless, the staff should overcome the loss of Mazzaro, with Josh Outman returning from Tommy John surgery to join a fifth-starter mix that includes Bobby Cramer, Tyson Ross, Brandon McCarthy, and prodigal son Rich Harden, and Brian Fuentes and Grant Balfour acquired to bolster the bullpen. McCarthy's extreme fly-balling ways may play well in the Coliseum, provided he can stay healthy; he has appeared on the 60-day DL three years in a row. Harden, who still hasn't made more than 26 starts since 2004 and who endured a grisly season in Texas amid hip and shoulder woes, returned to Oakland via a one-year, $1.5 million deal with another $1.5 million in incentives; he'll transition to the bullpen if a rotation spot doesn't work out.

Lost in the shuffle, at least for the moment, are the A's top prospects, who provide a litany of retrograde motion: their top tyro, left fielder Chris Carter, had a slow first half in the minors, and while he rallied to hit 31 homers, he began his major-league career by going 0-for-33 in two stints before finding his stroke. Michael Taylor, a center fielder acquired from the Blue Jays for Brett Wallace, hit just .272/.348/.392 at Sacramento amid questions about declining bat speed and didn't receive a much-anticipated September call-up. Pitcher Michael Ynoa needed Tommy John surgery after just nine professional innings. Outfielder Grant Desme opted for the priesthood. On a more positive note, first-round draftee Michael Choice, a center fielder taken with the 10th pick, had a strong professional debut, as did two of Oakland's top three 2009 picks, shortstop Grant Green and catcher Max Stassi, but the system has sunk to the middle of the pack in the wake of so many graduations.

For the moment, the team's fate rests on the rotation. The 2009 A's set a record by giving 147 starts (90.7 percent) to pitchers 25 and under, and the 2010 bunch—which lost Braden from that classification—still handed 63.6 percent to relatively inexperienced arms. Other teams that have followed similar patterns while keeping those rotation cores intact include the 1985-1986 Mets, who won a world championship in the latter year and a division title in 1988; the 1989-1991 Braves, who launched a dynasty with pennants in 1991-1992; the 2002-2003 Marlins, who won a world championship in the second year; the 2003-2004 Tigers, who won a pennant in 2006; and the 2007-2009 (Devil) Rays, who won a pennant in that second year and a division title in the third.

Given the likelihood of a three-year lag between breaking ground on a new stadium and moving into it, the Anderson-Cahill-Gonzalez trio might at best have one year of club control in the new park if the issue is resolved by the first half of 2011. Otherwise, Beane will have to go back to the drawing board and continue the endless churn of top pitchers—a practice that began when he traded Tim Hudson and Mark Mulder in December 2004. The latter begat Dan Haren, whose 2007 trade in turn begat Anderson, not to mention Carter and Carlos Gonzalez, who in turn begat Matt Holliday, whose trade netted Wallace, whose trade netted Taylor, and so on. The A's transaction history may read like something out of the Book of Genesis, but what they require is an ending to their own Book of Exodus. Unless Wolff succeeds in leading them to a new home, it may be some time before they succeed in wandering out of the regular-season desert.

HITTERS

Daric Barton **1B**

Born: **8/16/1985** Age: **25**
Bats: L Throws: R Height: **6' 0"** Weight: **225**
Breakout: **6%** Improve: **34%** Collapse: **4%**
Attrition: **13%** MLB: **73%**
Comparables:
James Loney, Joe Foy, Chris Coghlan (70)

YEAR	TEAM	LVL	AGE	PA	R	2B	3B	HR	RBI	BB	SO	SB	CS	AVG/OBP/SLG	TAv	BABIP	BRR	FRAA	WARP
2008	OAK	MLB	22	523	59	17	5	9	47	65	99	2	1	.227/.323/.348	.250	.265	1.6	1B -2, 3B 0	-0.1
2009	SAC	AAA	23	313	48	21	1	9	48	45	43	1	0	.261/.383/.458	.302	.275	0.8	1B 3	1.9
2009	OAK	MLB	23	192	31	12	1	3	24	26	25	0	2	.269/.370/.413	.292	.294	-2.3	1B 3	0.8
2010	OAK	MLB	24	686	80	33	5	10	57	110	102	7	3	.273/.386/.405	.303	.308	1.7	1B 4	3.8
2011	*OAK*	*MLB*	*25*	*619*	*79*	*32*	*3*	*15*	*67*	*88*	*92*	*4*	*2*	*.264/.370/.421*	*.280*	*.287*	*-0.2*	*1B -3, 3B 0*	*1.3*

Finally healthy, Barton blossomed into the A's most valuable player last season, although recognizing what he brought to the roster required an open mind. The lefty led the AL in walks, which helped him post the league's fifth-highest on-base percentage, but his slugging percentage ranked among the worst by a full-time first baseman. That combination placed Barton in the middle of the first-base pack insofar as offensive production, but when his excellent glove work is considered, he sneaks into the top 10. His underwhelming clout compounded a teamwide lack of power exhibited by the A's, who mustered a measly .124 ISO even away from their pitcher-friendly home park. But Barton is still young, and scouts can envision a future in which he adds .300 hitting to his other skills. If so, the A's will be happy to overlook the lack of long balls.

Corey Brown **OF**

Born: **11/26/1985** Age: **25**
Bats: L Throws: L Height: **6' 1"** Weight: **205**
Breakout: **8%** Improve: **24%** Collapse: **6%**
Attrition: **30%** MLB: **50%**
Comparables:
Brandon Boggs, Mat Gamel, Brandon Moss (70)

YEAR	TEAM	LVL	AGE	PA	R	2B	3B	HR	RBI	BB	SO	SB	CS	AVG/OBP/SLG	TAv	BABIP	BRR	FRAA	WARP
2008	KNC	A	22	351	44	18	2	14	49	41	96	12	0	.270/.356/.483	.304	.340	-1.8	CF 2	2.4
2008	STO	A+	22	214	34	9	0	16	34	17	72	4	1	.260/.322/.551	.289	.324	1.5	CF -3	1.3
2009	MID	AA	23	281	46	20	4	9	43	27	69	5	2	.268/.349/.488	.287	.337	-0.8	CF 5	2.0
2010	MID	AA	24	386	63	14	8	10	49	52	93	19	1	.320/.415/.502	.330	.419	1.1	CF -2, LF 0	3.7
2010	SAC	AAA	24	148	21	4	3	5	20	11	36	3	1	.193/.253/.378	.214	.219	2.2	CF 3, RF 2	0.3
2011	*WAS*	*MLB*	*25*	*488*	*57*	*20*	*3*	*17*	*58*	*46*	*144*	*9*	*2*	*.239/.310/.416*	*.252*	*.309*	*0.3*	*CF -7, RF 0*	*0.2*

Moving from a crowded situation in Oakland to Washington as part of the Josh Willingham deal, Brown has a better opportunity for a big-league chance, but he still has to prove he can hit Triple-A pitching, having failed to do so in 2010. See him on the right day, and he is a potential big-league center fielder with above-average power and speed to go with solid defensive skills. The problem is that he's not an especially good hitter; he has whiffed in over 30 percent of his minor-league at-bats. His ability to make up for a lack of average with his secondary skills will define his future.

Travis Buck **LF**

Born: **11/18/1983** Age: **27**
Bats: L Throws: R Height: **6' 2"** Weight: **205**
Breakout: **0%** Improve: **30%** Collapse: **4%**
Attrition: **5%** MLB: **59%**

Comparables:
Jeff Fiorentino, Jackie Jensen, Gabe Gross (78)

YEAR	TEAM	LVL	AGE	PA	R	2B	3B	HR	RBI	BB	SO	SB	CS	AVG/OBP/SLG	TAv	BABIP	BRR	FRAA	WARP
2008	SAC	AAA	24	197	28	8	2	2	17	25	34	4	1	.296/.396/.402	.284	.361	0.3	CF -6, LF 0	0.7
2008	OAK	MLB	24	172	16	9	1	7	25	11	38	1	0	.226/.291/.432	.260	.250	-2.2	RF 2, LF 0	0.2
2009	SAC	AAA	25	266	37	13	3	5	29	23	44	3	1	.272/.342/.418	.282	.307	-2.6	RF -1	0.6
2009	OAK	MLB	25	115	11	3	0	3	10	10	20	1	1	.219/.287/.333	.245	.244	0.1	RF 2, LF -2	0.0
2010	SAC	AAA	26	141	22	7	2	3	17	11	28	3	2	.298/.364/.463	.280	.347	0.0	RF 2, LF 2	1.0
2010	OAK	MLB	26	48	6	2	0	1	2	4	14	1	0	.167/.250/.286	.206	.214	-1.2	LF -2, RF -1	-0.5
2011	*CLE*	*MLB*	*27*	*344*	*39*	*15*	*2*	*8*	*36*	*31*	*71*	*3*	*1*	*.249/.326/.390*	*.254*	*.294*	*-0.1*	*RF 0, LF -1*	*0.2*

Buck's selection as a supplemental-phase first-rounder and subsequent high-average hitting in the minors have receded over the last three years, as he has been plagued by injuries, counterproductively tinkered with his swing mechanics, and complained publicly about how the organization had treated him. A strong spring, combined with Coco Crisp's season-opening injury, created optimism and landed Buck the starting left-field job, but he was quickly shut down with an oblique strain. Between recovery and rehab time, he was out for nearly four months. Nontendered, he signed a minor-league contract with the Indians and will try to slough off the .215/.284/.377 he's hit since his rookie year in pursuit of a bench job.

Adrian Cardenas **INF**

Born: **10/10/1987** Age: **23**
Bats: L Throws: R Height: **6' 0"** Weight: **205**
Breakout: **6%** Improve: **18%** Collapse: **6%**
Attrition: **22%** MLB: **38%**

Comparables:
Luis Valbuena, Matt Antonelli, Ron Hunt (77)

YEAR	TEAM	LVL	AGE	PA	R	2B	3B	HR	RBI	BB	SO	SB	CS	AVG/OBP/SLG	TAv	BABIP	BRR	FRAA	WARP
2008	CLR	A+	20	293	44	11	6	4	23	28	42	16	0	.307/.369/.441	.290	.347	0.4	2B -7	1.0
2008	STO	A+	20	74	11	1	0	1	10	1	14	1	0	.278/.297/.333	.241	.333	1.6	2B -3, SS 1	0.0
2008	MID	AA	20	102	12	4	0	0	7	15	10	0	1	.279/.392/.326	.245	.316	-0.9	SS 1	0.2
2009	MID	AA	21	373	56	26	2	3	55	38	44	5	4	.326/.389/.446	.292	.359	-1.5	2B 5, 3B -5	2.1
2009	SAC	AAA	21	207	23	15	2	1	24	17	29	3	2	.251/.314/.372	.262	.285	-1.5	2B -5, 3B -1	0.1
2010	MID	AA	22	236	36	15	0	3	32	33	23	4	6	.345/.436/.469	.329	.368	-1.5	3B -7, 2B 2	1.6
2010	SAC	AAA	22	231	30	8	1	1	21	17	28	2	2	.267/.320/.329	.234	.297	-0.9	2B -2, 3B -3	-0.7
2011	*OAK*	*MLB*	*23*	*516*	*61*	*26*	*2*	*6*	*51*	*44*	*77*	*7*	*3*	*.281/.340/.388*	*.259*	*.318*	*-0.4*	*2B -1, 3B -5*	*0.7*

A smart plate approach and a line-drive bat have helped Cardenas get on base at every level, but his Triple-A triple-slash line sat at .228/.285/.281 in early June, and he was demoted to Double-A. Things turned around quickly; his two months in the Texas League look like something off the back of Wade Boggs' baseball card. He returned to Sacramento armed with a newfound confidence and hit .313/.362/.385 the rest of the way. Since the A's picked up Mark Ellis's option, Cardenas will have to prove himself again at Triple-A to get a shot at competing with Jemile Weeks for the starting job in 2012.

Matt Carson **RF**

Born: **7/1/1981** Age: **29**
Bats: R Throws: R Height: **6' 2"** Weight: **200**
Breakout: **1%** Improve: **20%** Collapse: **4%**
Attrition: **13%** MLB: **59%**

Comparables:
Ryan Spilborghs, Luis Terrero, Ray Sadler (74)

YEAR	TEAM	LVL	AGE	PA	R	2B	3B	HR	RBI	BB	SO	SB	CS	AVG/OBP/SLG	TAv	BABIP	BRR	FRAA	WARP
2008	TRN	AA	26	122	17	7	4	5	26	9	20	1	1	.277/.328/.545	.316	.295	-1.1	RF 2, CF 1	1.1
2008	SWB	AAA	26	339	53	10	6	10	38	21	63	10	3	.289/.345/.459	.261	.329	3.2	CF -8, RF 10	1.5
2009	SAC	AAA	27	493	68	29	3	25	77	38	94	15	4	.264/.325/.514	.301	.276	2.2	CF -2, RF 5	4.0
2009	OAK	MLB	27	22	1	0	0	1	5	0	7	0	0	.286/.273/.429	.241	.357	-0.3	RF 0, LF 0	-0.1
2010	SAC	AAA	28	276	53	18	2	13	36	24	58	13	4	.303/.377/.553	.311	.349	5.2	CF -1, LF 1	2.7
2010	OAK	MLB	28	83	7	2	0	4	9	2	23	4	0	.177/.193/.354	.219	.185	-0.8	RF 0, CF 0	-0.2
2011	*OAK*	*MLB*	*29*	*455*	*56*	*22*	*2*	*20*	*64*	*30*	*102*	*12*	*4*	*.256/.310/.465*	*.268*	*.287*	*-0.1*	*CF -4, RF 2*	*1.1*

A minor-league veteran with good power, enough athleticism to play center field in a pinch, and a propensity to strike out, Carson got a look at the end of the year (as did most Oakland farmhands with a pulse). He's a classic Quad-A hitter and a fine insurance policy, but he's already in his late 20s and it's unlikely that he will ever offer enough to merit a long-term spot on a team. Consequently, the A's removed Carson from the 40-man roster after the season, but the club wasted little time in securing his services for Sacramento this year.

Chris Carter LF

Born: 12/18/1986 Age: 24
Bats: R Throws: R Height: 6' 5" Weight: 230
Breakout: 1% Improve: 32% Collapse: 10%
Attrition: 23% MLB: 79%
Comparables:
Chris Davis, Joey Votto, Evan Longoria (63)

YEAR	TEAM	LVL	AGE	PA	R	2B	3B	HR	RBI	BB	SO	SB	CS	AVG/OBP/SLG	TAv	BABIP	BRR	FRAA	WARP
2008	STO	A+	21	596	101	32	4	39	104	77	156	4	0	.259/.361/.569	.322	.290	-1.0	3B -8, 1B 1	4.0
2009	MID	AA	22	593	108	41	2	24	101	82	119	13	5	.337/.435/.576	.338	.395	-2.4	1B -10, RF -1	3.8
2009	SAC	AAA	22	58	7	2	0	4	14	3	14	0	1	.259/.293/.519	.333	.270	-2.4	1B -1, LF 0	0.5
2010	SAC	AAA	23	551	92	29	2	31	94	73	138	1	1	.258/.365/.529	.302	.296	0.0	1B -8, LF 2	2.4
2010	OAK	MLB	23	78	9	1	0	3	7	7	21	1	0	.186/.256/.329	.213	.213	0.0	LF -2	-0.4
2011	*OAK*	*MLB*	*24*	*648*	*89*	*31*	*1*	*35*	*98*	*76*	*172*	*5*	*2*	*.258/.348/.510*	*.295*	*.301*	*-0.1*	*1B -18, 3B -2*	*0.8*

Carter was slow to get started at Triple-A, but slugged 16 home runs over a 48-game span to earn his first taste of the big leagues. His start was disastrous—he introduced himself to A's fans with an 0-for-33 streak, the third-worst beginning to a big-league career for a position player since 1920. Recovering, he hit .333 (13-for-39) with three home runs for the balance of the season. With over 100 bombs in his last three seasons, Carter has more power than anyone else in the organization, including the big-league level. When the 2010 season concluded, he appeared to have a real chance at a big-league job, but those hopes were dashed by the Josh Willingham and Hideki Matsui acquisitions. The A's will spend more than $10 million to block their best offensive prospect this year.

Michael Choice OF

Born: 11/10/1989 Age: 21
Bats: R Throws: R Height: 6' 1" Weight: 215
Breakout: 0% Improve: 2% Collapse: 0%
Attrition: 0% MLB: 2%
Comparables:
Billy Conigliaro, Juan Gonzalez, Tom Brunansky (67)

YEAR	TEAM	LVL	AGE	PA	R	2B	3B	HR	RBI	BB	SO	SB	CS	AVG/OBP/SLG	TAv	BABIP	BRR	FRAA	WARP
2010	VAN	A-	20	121	20	10	2	7	26	15	43	6	1	.284/.388/.627	.362	.415	0.0	CF 0	1.7
2011	*OAK*	*MLB*	*21*	—	—	—	—	—	—	—	—	—	—	—	—	—	—	—	—

The A's were surprised to see Choice still on the board when they found themselves on the clock with the 10th overall pick in the 2010 draft. While he didn't face the stiffest of competition at the University of Texas–Arlington, Choice certainly surpassed any statistical benchmarks, hitting .383/.568/.704 with 16 home runs and 76 walks in 60 games for the Mavericks, and some scouts saw him as the best college position player in the draft. He carries a solid tool box, sporting big-time raw power and enough speed to stick in center for now, although right field will probably be his final destination. Thus far, Choice has proved to be good as advertised, launching seven taters in 102 at-bats while making his pro debut in a pitcher's paradise, but the 43 whiffs were a glaring concern. He's not going to move as fast as most of Oakland's recent college picks, but Choice arguably has a higher ceiling than any of them.

Coco Crisp CF

Born: 11/1/1979 Age: 31
Bats: S Throws: R Height: 6' 0" Weight: 185
Breakout: 0% Improve: 37% Collapse: 3%
Attrition: 10% MLB: 93%
Comparables:
Mitch Webster, Kenny Lofton, Jay Payton (76)

YEAR	TEAM	LVL	AGE	PA	R	2B	3B	HR	RBI	BB	SO	SB	CS	AVG/OBP/SLG	TAv	BABIP	BRR	FRAA	WARP
2008	BOS	MLB	28	409	54	18	3	7	41	35	59	20	7	.283/.337/.407	.268	.309	2.6	CF 0	1.7
2009	KCA	MLB	29	215	30	8	5	3	14	29	23	13	2	.228/.330/.378	.245	.239	4.1	CF 2	0.9
2010	OAK	MLB	30	328	51	14	4	8	38	30	49	32	3	.279/.338/.438	.283	.303	6.1	CF 3	2.4
2011	*OAK*	*MLB*	*31*	*406*	*50*	*19*	*3*	*9*	*47*	*39*	*56*	*25*	*6*	*.276/.340/.425*	*.268*	*.295*	*0.8*	*CF 4*	*1.8*

When not dealing with rib soreness, a sprained ankle, or a couple of busted fingers, Crisp turned in a solid performance for an offensively famished club, his first such offensive performance in several years. The plus defender put up numbers well in line with his career rates and stole a career-high 32 bases in just 35 attempts over less than half a season. Even when he hasn't hit, Crisp has been able to contribute via running and fielding, but to be a viable starter, he needs to bring more with the stick, particularly versus right-handed pitchers, than he has for the past half-decade; 2010 was the first time since 2005 that he had been even an average producer at the plate. Combine uncertainty about hitting with durability issues, and you have a tough player to rely upon. Oakland picked up his very reasonable 2011 option, but the hope is that a healthy Crisp can repeat his 2010 performance and be flipped for some more future-oriented talent.

Jack Cust DH

Born: 1/16/1979 Age: 32
Bats: L Throws: R Height: 6' 1" Weight: 205
Breakout: 3% Improve: 35% Collapse: 3%
Attrition: 6% MLB: 96%
Comparables:
Carlos Pena, Reggie Jackson, Manny Ramirez (66)

YEAR	TEAM	LVL	AGE	PA	R	2B	3B	HR	RBI	BB	SO	SB	CS	AVG/OBP/SLG	TAv	BABIP	BRR	FRAA	WARP
2008	OAK	MLB	29	598	84	19	0	33	77	111	197	0	0	.231/.375/.476	.313	.306	-2.6	LF 2, RF -2	3.8
2009	OAK	MLB	30	612	92	16	0	25	70	93	185	4	1	.240/.356/.417	.287	.319	-0.2	RF -13	1.1
2010	SAC	AAA	31	144	21	6	0	4	19	33	33	0	0	.273/.444/.436	.317	.356	-2.2	LF 1, RF 2	1.1
2010	OAK	MLB	31	425	53	19	0	13	52	68	127	2	2	.272/.395/.438	.318	.387	-2.6	LF 0, RF 3	2.7
2011	*SEA*	*MLB*	*32*	*582*	*78*	*21*	*0*	*25*	*68*	*103*	*172*	*2*	*1*	*.245/.381/.449*	*.293*	*.324*	*-0.1*	*LF -1, RF -2*	*2.2*

Despite inking Cust to a one-year, $2.5 million deal, the A's designated him for assignment before last season began and sent him to Triple-A after he cleared waivers. He stewed on the farm until Eric Chavez broke again, at which point Cust was called up to resume his DH-ing duties. What resulted was quite strange: a roller-coaster season in which he spent about 25 games hitting .300-worth of singles, then another 30 in which he added the power back in, and then . . . nothing—or, nothing except walks—as both the singles and the home runs vanished. The overall result contained enough on-base percentage that Cust was still quite valuable, but so much about the season screams "fluke" that if the power doesn't come back, he's likely to be in trouble. The Mariners snapped him up to serve as their primary DH, a role in which he can't help but constitute a massive improvement, given the nearly record-setting incompetence they experienced at the position last year.

Rajai Davis **CF**

Born: **10/19/1980** Age: **30**
Bats: **R** Throws: **R** Height: **5' 11"** Weight: **197**
Breakout: **1%** Improve: **38%** Collapse: **5%**
Attrition: **13%** MLB: **80%**

Comparables:
Mickey Stanley, Marquis Grissom, Del Unser (74)

YEAR	TEAM	LVL	AGE	PA	R	2B	3B	HR	RBI	BB	SO	SB	CS	AVG/OBP/SLG	TAv	BABIP	BRR	FRAA	WARP
2008	OAK	MLB	27	206	20	5	4	3	17	7	34	25	6	.256/.282/.369	.240	.292	2.9	CF 4, 2B 0	0.8
2008	SFN	MLB	27	19	1	0	0	0	0	1	6	4	0	.056/.105/.056	.055	.083	0.1	CF -1, LF 0	-0.4
2009	OAK	MLB	28	432	62	27	5	3	48	29	70	41	12	.305/.359/.423	.281	.359	7.3	CF 3, RF 0	3.1
2010	OAK	MLB	29	561	65	28	3	5	52	26	78	50	11	.284/.319/.377	.259	.321	5.0	CF -1, LF -3	1.7
2011	*TOR*	*MLB*	*30*	*421*	*46*	*20*	*2*	*3*	*39*	*28*	*63*	*40*	*11*	*.272/.323/.360*	*.245*	*.312*	*0.6*	*CF 2, LF -1*	*0.6*

Davis plays a good center field, runs well enough to rank among the league leaders in stolen bases, and owns a quick line-drive stroke that has helped him hit a composite .293 over the last two years. Unfortunately, he has very little power, and his ultra-aggressive approach prevents him from being effective in a leadoff role. Davis would have been a hot commodity 30 years ago, but teams have gotten smarter. Instead of landing a huge haul when they traded him to Toronto in November, the A's scored only a couple of potential middle relievers. With Vernon Wells in center, Davis will be miscast in a corner while failing to help the Blue Jays' improve their self-defeating impatience.

Josh Donaldson **C**

Born: **12/8/1985** Age: **25**
Bats: **R** Throws: **R** Height: **6' 0"** Weight: **215**
Breakout: **4%** Improve: **18%** Collapse: **13%**
Attrition: **32%** MLB: **50%**

Comparables:
Nick Hundley, Juan Miranda, Jeff Clement (80)

YEAR	TEAM	LVL	AGE	PA	R	2B	3B	HR	RBI	BB	SO	SB	CS	AVG/OBP/SLG	TAv	BABIP	BRR	FRAA	WARP
2008	PEO	A	22	254	27	13	0	6	23	17	41	7	1	.217/.276/.349	.236	.239	2.9	C 1	0.7
2008	STO	A+	22	207	37	13	2	9	39	17	29	0	2	.330/.391/.564	.367	.353	1.1	C 0, 3B 1	4.2
2009	MID	AA	23	541	67	37	1	9	91	80	92	7	2	.270/.377/.415	.290	.318	0.4	C -1, 3B 2	4.2
2010	SAC	AAA	24	348	52	14	1	18	67	45	79	3	1	.238/.336/.476	.260	.255	-3.2	C 2, 3B 0	1.1
2010	OAK	MLB	24	34	1	1	0	1	4	2	12	0	0	.156/.206/.281	.176	.211	0.1	C 0, 1B 0	-0.2
2011	*OAK*	*MLB*	*25*	*494*	*59*	*24*	*1*	*17*	*59*	*52*	*107*	*3*	*1*	*.247/.325/.424*	*.262*	*.283*	*0.0*	*C 0, 3B 0*	*1.8*

Donaldson lacks a place on the A's current depth chart, but he should have a career. His pure hitting skills are questionable, but he needed just 86 games to establish a new career high in home runs, and his plate discipline helps make up for his strikeouts and low batting average. Aside from his strong arm, Donaldson remains rough behind the plate, but the hope is he can turn into an Eli Marrero–type catcher-plus backup. For now, he'll while his days away in sunny Sacramento.

Mark Ellis **2B**

Born: **6/6/1977** Age: **34**
Bats: **R** Throws: **R** Height: **5' 11"** Weight: **180**
Breakout: **0%** Improve: **29%** Collapse: **6%**
Attrition: **17%** MLB: **93%**

Comparables:
Roberto Alomar, Ronnie Belliard, Mark Loretta (79)

YEAR	TEAM	LVL	AGE	PA	R	2B	3B	HR	RBI	BB	SO	SB	CS	AVG/OBP/SLG	TAv	BABIP	BRR	FRAA	WARP
2008	OAK	MLB	31	507	56	20	3	12	41	53	65	14	2	.233/.318/.373	.254	.245	2.3	2B 10	2.1
2009	OAK	MLB	32	410	52	23	0	10	61	23	54	10	3	.263/.302/.403	.246	.277	-2.9	2B 5	0.6
2010	OAK	MLB	33	492	45	24	0	5	49	40	56	7	6	.291/.356/.381	.287	.319	-2.0	2B 4	2.5
2011	*OAK*	*MLB*	*34*	*523*	*61*	*25*	*1*	*12*	*56*	*42*	*68*	*9*	*4*	*.263/.326/.396*	*.256*	*.280*	*-0.3*	*2B 7*	*1.6*

Despite missing more than 30 games for the third consecutive year, thanks to early-season hamstring issues and hitting a career-low five home runs, Ellis produced enough for Oakland to pick up his $6 million 2011 option. Ellis is no Dustin Pedroia–style MVP candidate, but he's coming off a career high in batting average (due in part to just the second over-.300 BABIP of his career), he draws a few walks, and he doesn't mess up defensively, having committed a grand total of 19 errors over the past five years. On a young, inexperienced team, the longest-tenured Athletic provides some much-needed stability, but this is still likely to be his last year in Oakland.

Grant Green SS

Born: 9/27/1987 Age: 23
Bats: R Throws: R Height: 6' 3" Weight: 180
Breakout: 1% Improve: 10% Collapse: 4%
Attrition: 7% MLB: 20%

Comparables:
Alex Rodriguez, Wil Cordero, Ernie Banks (71)

YEAR	TEAM	LVL	AGE	PA	R	2B	3B	HR	RBI	BB	SO	SB	CS	AVG/OBP/SLG	TAv	BABIP	BRR	FRAA	WARP
2010	STO	A+	22	606	107	39	6	20	87	38	117	9	5	.318/.363/.520	.308	.363	1.1	SS -13, 2B 0	4.0
2011	*OAK*	*MLB*	*23*	*326*	*39*	*17*	*1*	*12*	*44*	*15*	*74*	*1*	*1*	*.270/.302/.452*	*.261*	*.313*	*-0.1*	*SS -4*	*0.7*

As good as Green's offensive debut was, his full-season stats might have painted an overly conservative picture of his potential at the plate. The club's first-round pick in 2009, he took a while to find his power with wood. After he slugged just two home runs in his first 57 games, he chalked up 18 in his last 74. As a shortstop with that kind of power, Green would be a massive prospect, but for now, he's a shortstop in name only. He's an average runner, and in order to stick at the position, he would have to make up for his lack of speed by playing the position extremely well in all other respects. Instead, Green led the California League with 37 errors in just 114 games, many of the errors due to throwing problems that sometimes bordered on a case of the yips. Even after he completes a likely transition to second base, he could be a special offensive force for an up-the-middle player.

Gabe Gross OF

Born: 10/21/1979 Age: 31
Bats: L Throws: R Height: 6' 3" Weight: 209
Breakout: 0% Improve: 26% Collapse: 12%
Attrition: 11% MLB: 82%

Comparables:
Leon Roberts, Bubba Trammell, Willie Crawford (80)

YEAR	TEAM	LVL	AGE	PA	R	2B	3B	HR	RBI	BB	SO	SB	CS	AVG/OBP/SLG	TAv	BABIP	BRR	FRAA	WARP
2008	MIL	MLB	28	53	6	3	0	0	2	10	7	2	0	.214/.359/.286	.255	.250	0.3	CF -1, RF 1	0.2
2008	TBA	MLB	28	345	40	13	3	13	38	40	75	2	2	.242/.333/.434	.278	.279	-3.7	RF 4, CF -1	1.1
2009	TBA	MLB	29	326	31	16	1	6	36	42	79	6	3	.227/.325/.355	.250	.292	-2.8	RF -2	-0.3
2010	OAK	MLB	30	244	22	11	1	1	25	17	39	5	1	.239/.287/.311	.235	.280	2.3	RF 0, LF -2	-0.4
2011	*OAK*	*MLB*	*31*	*304*	*35*	*14*	*1*	*8*	*32*	*35*	*61*	*5*	*2*	*.245/.330/.393*	*.258*	*.285*	*-0.1*	*RF 0, LF 0*	*0.3*

Gross has played in the majors for seven years, despite turning in only one truly valuable performance at the plate and being perpetually helpless against lefties. One of the secrets of his longevity—along with his gifted glove in right field—is that he's such a good guy. He's a great clubhouse presence, good with young players, excellent with the media, and a model citizen. As such, he's a case study that should be trotted out by every team or agent with a problem player. Instead of washing out of the big leagues and leading a life of minor-league journeyman and/or having to get a real job, he has spent the better half of a decade in the majors, banking roughly $3.5 million in the process. Oakland let him go after the worst year of his career, and the question now is when his performance will reach the point where his likability won't matter. Having hit .232/.311/.335 in roughly a single season's worth of at-bats over the last two seasons, he might already be there.

Jeremy Hermida LF

Born: 1/30/1984 Age: 27
Bats: L Throws: R Height: 6' 4" Weight: 200
Breakout: 2% Improve: 42% Collapse: 6%
Attrition: 17% MLB: 90%

Comparables:
David Murphy, Gary Matthews, Rico Carty (79)

YEAR	TEAM	LVL	AGE	PA	R	2B	3B	HR	RBI	BB	SO	SB	CS	AVG/OBP/SLG	TAv	BABIP	BRR	FRAA	WARP
2008	FLO	MLB	24	559	73	22	3	17	61	48	138	6	1	.249/.322/.406	.255	.310	0.6	RF 4	1.0
2009	FLO	MLB	25	491	48	14	2	13	47	56	101	5	2	.259/.348/.392	.265	.309	1.7	RF 3, LF -5	0.9
2010	PAW	AAA	26	73	7	1	0	2	12	4	16	0	0	.288/.329/.394	.247	.340	-0.5	LF 1, RF 1	0.1
2010	BOS	MLB	26	171	14	8	0	5	27	12	45	1	0	.203/.257/.348	.235	.248	-0.4	LF 4, RF -1	0.1
2010	OAK	MLB	26	68	5	4	0	1	2	4	13	0	0	.250/.294/.359	.229	.300	-0.6	RF -2, LF 0	-0.3
2011	*OAK*	*MLB*	*27*	*456*	*55*	*21*	*1*	*14*	*53*	*44*	*97*	*4*	*1*	*.260/.334/.423*	*.266*	*.304*	*-0.1*	*RF 0, LF 0*	*1.0*

It's fitting that Hermida finished up with Oakland after being released by the Red Sox in late August, as in many ways, he's become a younger generation's Ben Grieve. Once one of the brightest offensive prospects in the game after slugging over .500 as a 23-year-old in the Marlins' pitcher's park, he has been on the downhill side from there, and there's no good explanation for what went wrong. When asked about the more recent vintage of the outfielder, one scout said, "He doesn't do anything well," and that sums up his situation. He won't be back in Oakland, but the Reds will become the latest organization to give him a chance.

Conor Jackson LF

Born: 5/7/1982 Age: 29
Bats: R Throws: R Height: 6' 2" Weight: 225
Breakout: 0% Improve: 36% Collapse: 8%
Attrition: 15% MLB: 88%

Comparables:
Kevin Mench, Carlos May, Bob Watson (70)

YEAR	TEAM	LVL	AGE	PA	R	2B	3B	HR	RBI	BB	SO	SB	CS	AVG/OBP/SLG	TAv	BABIP	BRR	FRAA	WARP
2008	ARI	MLB	26	612	87	31	6	12	75	59	61	10	2	.300/.376/.446	.287	.319	-1.0	LF 4, 1B -3	2.6
2009	ARI	MLB	27	110	8	4	0	1	14	11	16	5	0	.182/.264/.253	.206	.207	0.3	LF -3, 1B -1	-0.7
2010	ARI	MLB	28	172	19	11	0	1	11	20	18	4	1	.238/.326/.331	.254	.263	1.7	LF 1, 1B -1	0.4
2010	OAK	MLB	28	69	6	2	0	1	5	11	9	2	0	.228/.362/.316	.262	.255	-0.8	LF 0	0.1
2011	*OAK*	*MLB*	*29*	*409*	*51*	*21*	*1*	*9*	*45*	*44*	*43*	*6*	*2*	*.275/.357/.422*	*.278*	*.286*	*0.0*	*LF 1, 1B -2*	*1.3*

Like Hermida, Jackson was once seen as an intriguing young hitter, but his lack of production over the last two years owes more to an inability to stay healthy than a degradation of skills. After missing most of 2009 with a fungal disease known as valley fever, Jackson got off to a slow start last season before moving to Oakland in a trade for power reliever Sam Demel. The A's had their eye on Jackson since hoping he'd fall to them in the 2003 draft, but seven years later, they received a player with a never-ending hamstring issue who saw his season come to a merciful end when a strained abdominal muscle turned into surgery for a sports hernia. He still has a good approach, but his formerly average power has evaporated over the past year, and all that the A's are hoping for going into 2011 is a bench bat/occasional starter who can back up at three positions and draw some walks.

Kevin Kouzmanoff 3B

Born: **7/25/1981** Age: **29**
Bats: **R** Throws: **R** Height: **6' 1"** Weight: **210**
Breakout: **2%** Improve: **39%** Collapse: **4%**
Attrition: **11%** MLB: **95%**
Comparables:
Brooks Robinson, Chad Tracy, Gary Gaetti (78)

YEAR	TEAM	LVL	AGE	PA	R	2B	3B	HR	RBI	BB	SO	SB	CS	AVG/OBP/SLG	TAv	BABIP	BRR	FRAA	WARP
2008	SDN	MLB	26	668	71	31	4	23	84	23	139	0	0	.260/.299/.433	.262	.297	-0.5	3B -12	0.9
2009	SDN	MLB	27	573	50	31	1	18	88	27	106	1	0	.255/.302/.420	.250	.285	-2.8	3B -7	0.2
2010	OAK	MLB	28	586	60	32	1	16	71	24	96	2	1	.247/.283/.396	.253	.270	-4.2	3B -1	0.7
2011	*OAK*	*MLB*	*29*	*561*	*67*	*30*	*1*	*20*	*73*	*29*	*96*	*1*	*1*	*.265/.311/.441*	*.261*	*.287*	*0.0*	*3B -5*	*1.1*

When Kouzmanoff leads your team in home runs, you know you've had a poor year at the plate. That was the case for the A's in 2010, but following the acquisitions of Hideki Matsui and Josh Willingham over the offseason, to have the Kouz leading the team once again would be a massive disappointment. Solid glove work and the ability to hit 15-20 home runs are his only skills; he's very slow on the bases and is an extremely impatient hitter who has logged a pair of sub-.300 on-base percentages in two of his four full seasons to go along with a career batting average of .258. He'll be the first-string third baseman again in 2011, but only because the A's lack a more desirable option.

Jeff Larish UT

Born: **10/11/1982** Age: **28**
Bats: **L** Throws: **R** Height: **6' 2"** Weight: **200**
Breakout: **2%** Improve: **19%** Collapse: **4%**
Attrition: **12%** MLB: **50%**
Comparables:
Matthew Brown, Jack Hannahan, Victor Diaz (75)

YEAR	TEAM	LVL	AGE	PA	R	2B	3B	HR	RBI	BB	SO	SB	CS	AVG/OBP/SLG	TAv	BABIP	BRR	FRAA	WARP
2008	TOL	AAA	25	440	49	20	2	21	64	50	109	0	1	.250/.341/.477	.265	.293	-0.7	1B 6, 3B -2	1.0
2008	DET	MLB	25	111	12	6	0	2	16	7	34	2	2	.260/.306/.375	.247	.368	-0.2	3B 0, 1B -1	0.0
2009	TOL	AAA	26	257	38	13	0	6	26	42	56	2	2	.265/.397/.412	.285	.336	2.3	1B -4, 3B 0	0.7
2009	DET	MLB	26	90	13	3	1	4	7	15	25	0	1	.216/.344/.446	.267	.261	-0.9	1B 2, 3B 0	0.2
2010	TOL	AAA	27	352	43	21	0	15	55	45	84	1	0	.275/.373/.497	.291	.328	0.0	3B -3, 1B -1	1.6
2010	DET	MLB	27	10	0	0	0	0	1	0	4	0	0	.200/.200/.200	.122	.333	0.0	1B 0	-0.2
2010	OAK	MLB	27	65	6	3	0	2	8	7	20	1	0	.175/.277/.333	.227	.229	0.6	LF -3, 1B 0	-0.4
2011	*PHI*	*MLB*	*28*	*451*	*55*	*19*	*1*	*16*	*52*	*55*	*119*	*3*	*1*	*.243/.338/.424*	*.267*	*.300*	*-0.2*	*1B -8, 3B -1*	*-0.1*

Oakland snatched Larish up in early August, when Detroit tried to pass him through waivers. During his brief time with the A's, the failed prospect played a laughably bad third base and a poor outfield, and didn't hit. A big slugger who has consistently done damage against right-handed pitching, Larish suffers defensive limitations that have relegated him to journeyman status, and his journey will continue with the Phillies' Triple-A squad in 2011.

Cliff Pennington SS

Born: **6/15/1984** Age: **27**
Bats: **S** Throws: **R** Height: **5' 11"** Weight: **185**
Breakout: **1%** Improve: **41%** Collapse: **9%**
Attrition: **19%** MLB: **88%**
Comparables:
Jim Gilliam, Chris Speier, Jay Bell (73)

YEAR	TEAM	LVL	AGE	PA	R	2B	3B	HR	RBI	BB	SO	SB	CS	AVG/OBP/SLG	TAv	BABIP	BRR	FRAA	WARP
2008	MID	AA	24	244	42	7	2	0	18	39	36	20	1	.260/.377/.314	.253	.314	3.0	SS 5, 2B -1	1.4
2008	SAC	AAA	24	294	47	9	3	2	16	54	34	11	5	.297/.422/.386	.296	.333	0.4	SS 11, 2B 0	3.4
2008	OAK	MLB	24	117	12	5	0	0	9	13	18	4	1	.242/.333/.293	.244	.286	0.3	2B -1, 3B -1	-0.3
2009	SAC	AAA	25	417	48	22	3	3	40	45	54	27	4	.264/.341/.367	.262	.294	5.6	SS 0, 2B 0	2.2
2009	OAK	MLB	25	229	27	11	3	4	21	19	46	7	5	.279/.341/.418	.275	.340	0.0	SS 0	1.3
2010	OAK	MLB	26	576	64	26	8	6	46	50	96	29	5	.250/.313/.368	.265	.287	3.4	SS 14	4.0
2011	*OAK*	*MLB*	*27*	*623*	*72*	*28*	*4*	*9*	*60*	*67*	*100*	*29*	*7*	*.263/.340/.380*	*.256*	*.297*	*0.6*	*SS 6, 2B -1*	*2.5*

Pennington does not hit for power or make contact with any regularity, but he draws walks at a league-average clip and steals a few bases, which enables him to escape "out machine" territory. Given the sorry state of leaguewide offense at his position, his meager work with the lumber made Pennington the most productive offensive shortstop in the AL last season after accounting for his cavernous home park. His real strength lies in the field. He possesses above-average range to both sides and very good fundamentals. His is one of the more underrated skill sets in the game; there simply aren't nearly 30 legitimate shortstop gloves in the majors, so positional scarcity makes Pennington's value greater than his numbers might suggest. Off-season shoulder surgery will delay the start of his spring training, but he's expected to be ready for Opening Day.

Landon Powell **C**

Born: **3/19/1982** Age: **29**
Bats: **S** Throws: **R** Height: **6' 3"** Weight: **255**
Breakout: **0%** Improve: **13%** Collapse: **13%**
Attrition: **10%** MLB: **61%**

Comparables:
Craig Kusick, Erubiel Durazo, Mark Johnson (69)

YEAR	TEAM	LVL	AGE	PA	R	2B	3B	HR	RBI	BB	SO	SB	CS	AVG/OBP/SLG	TAv	BABIP	BRR	FRAA	WARP
2008	SAC	AAA	26	367	42	11	0	15	53	63	85	0	1	.230/.360/.417	.278	.265	-0.1	C -3	2.0
2009	OAK	MLB	27	155	19	7	0	7	30	14	36	0	0	.229/.297/.429	.256	.255	-3.1	C -1, 1B 0	0.1
2010	SAC	AAA	28	55	6	2	0	1	2	10	9	0	0	.200/.346/.311	.232	.229	-0.3	C 0, 1B 0	-0.1
2010	OAK	MLB	28	129	14	4	0	2	11	15	29	1	0	.214/.302/.304	.223	.265	-0.6	C -1, 1B 0	-0.2
2011	*OAK*	*MLB*	*29*	*233*	*27*	*9*	*0*	*8*	*25*	*30*	*53*	*1*	*0*	*.232/.332/.398*	*.258*	*.270*	*0.0*	*C -1, 1B 0*	*0.7*

While he failed to make the team out of spring training, Powell eventually assumed the job he had earned in 2009, serving as a backup to Kurt Suzuki. It's a role he should be well suited for—he's not much of a pure hitter, but he makes up for his shortcoming at the plate with power and patience, and he can be a good defender, depending on what the scale says. With a figure that fluctuates as much as Oprah's, Powell is good when he's merely big (he'll never be svelte, or anything close), but he's been engaged in a battle of the bulge since his amateur days. All Oakland can do is wait and hope that he hasn't outgrown his catcher's gear when he shows up for spring training.

Adam Rosales **2B**

Born: **5/20/1983** Age: **28**
Bats: **R** Throws: **R** Height: **6' 1"** Weight: **195**
Breakout: **0%** Improve: **28%** Collapse: **4%**
Attrition: **9%** MLB: **68%**

Comparables:
Kelly Johnson, Brandon Phillips, Russ Adams (77)

YEAR	TEAM	LVL	AGE	PA	R	2B	3B	HR	RBI	BB	SO	SB	CS	AVG/OBP/SLG	TAv	BABIP	BRR	FRAA	WARP
2008	LOU	AAA	25	473	70	29	7	11	58	22	82	7	1	.287/.338/.463	.271	.328	1.0	3B 2, SS 3	2.9
2008	CIN	MLB	25	30	0	1	0	0	2	1	4	1	0	.207/.233/.241	.219	.240	0.0	3B -2, 2B 0	-0.2
2009	LOU	AAA	26	125	27	8	2	5	20	12	15	4	0	.349/.408/.596	.337	.359	0.8	3B 0, SS 3	1.6
2009	CIN	MLB	26	266	22	10	1	4	19	26	46	1	2	.213/.301/.317	.226	.243	-0.2	3B -1, 1B 3	0.0
2010	OAK	MLB	27	279	31	8	2	7	31	19	65	2	2	.271/.319/.400	.283	.332	0.0	2B -2, SS 0	1.0
2011	*OAK*	*MLB*	*28*	*392*	*46*	*18*	*2*	*10*	*45*	*30*	*74*	*4*	*1*	*.264/.325/.415*	*.261*	*.301*	*-0.1*	*3B -1, 2B 0*	*0.9*

Rosales always had a reputation as the type who outplays his tools, but his showing with the Reds in 2009 convinced many that he'd hit a wall in the big leagues. Picked up for Aaron Miles before the 2010 season, Rosales proved to be a valuable bench player, seeing time at every infield position and left field. The skills still fail to impress, and his defense is a bit short on the left side, but the combination of versatility and a modicum of hitting ability make him a valuable, versatile player who saves some roster spots.

Eric Sogard **2B**

Born: **5/22/1986** Age: **25**
Bats: **L** Throws: **R** Height: **5' 10"** Weight: **185**
Breakout: **4%** Improve: **31%** Collapse: **8%**
Attrition: **31%** MLB: **67%**

Comparables:
Dustin Pedroia, Chin-lung Hu, Chuck Knoblauch (72)

YEAR	TEAM	LVL	AGE	PA	R	2B	3B	HR	RBI	BB	SO	SB	CS	AVG/OBP/SLG	TAv	BABIP	BRR	FRAA	WARP
2008	LEL	A+	22	622	97	42	3	10	87	79	62	16	7	.308/.394/.453	.322	.330	0.8	2B 7, 3B 0	6.4
2009	SAN	AA	23	530	79	25	3	6	51	58	47	10	6	.293/.366/.400	.298	.307	2.5	2B -1	3.5
2010	SAC	AAA	24	597	82	28	6	5	65	75	68	14	9	.300/.391/.407	.287	.335	1.9	2B 3, SS 3	4.0
2010	OAK	MLB	24	9	0	0	0	0	0	2	1	0	1	.429/.556/.429	.490	.500	-0.8	2B -1	0.1
2011	*OAK*	*MLB*	*25*	*609*	*75*	*29*	*3*	*8*	*60*	*66*	*78*	*10*	*5*	*.286/.360/.397*	*.271*	*.315*	*-0.6*	*2B 3, SS 0*	*2.2*

The Padres hoped that Sogard, a small middle infielder who put up huge numbers at Arizona State, could follow a trajectory similar to that of Dustin Pedroia, a small infielder who put up huge numbers at Arizona State before him. They made Sogard their second-round pick in 2007, and while he didn't fulfill their high hopes, he could still have a career. Arriving along with Kevin Kouzmanoff in the Aaron Cunningham deal, Sogard has proven to be a doubles machine in the minors with more walks than strikeouts, but for now, he's stuck behind Mark Ellis at the big-league level, and there are plenty of second-base prospects nipping at his heels. He's trapped between a rock and a hard place, but while he'll never stage a convincing "laser show," someone will eventually give him a shot.

Kurt Suzuki **C**

Born: **10/4/1983** Age: **27**
Bats: **R** Throws: **R** Height: **6' 0"** Weight: **205**
Breakout: **0%** Improve: **44%** Collapse: **4%**
Attrition: **11%** MLB: **96%**

Comparables:
Russell Martin, Ted Simmons, Dioner Navarro (74)

YEAR	TEAM	LVL	AGE	PA	R	2B	3B	HR	RBI	BB	SO	SB	CS	AVG/OBP/SLG	TAv	BABIP	BRR	FRAA	WARP
2008	OAK	MLB	24	588	54	25	1	7	42	44	69	2	3	.279/.345/.370	.267	.309	-2.6	C -3	2.3
2009	OAK	MLB	25	614	74	37	1	15	88	28	59	8	2	.274/.313/.421	.270	.280	1.2	C 2	3.3
2010	OAK	MLB	26	544	54	18	2	13	71	33	49	3	2	.242/.303/.366	.253	.245	-6.2	C -3	0.8
2011	*OAK*	*MLB*	*27*	*560*	*67*	*27*	*1*	*14*	*63*	*38*	*59*	*4*	*2*	*.271/.329/.413*	*.263*	*.279*	*-0.2*	*C -1*	*2.2*

Suzuki was having a perfectly Suzukian season when he agreed to a four-year extension to buy out his remaining arbitration years and a potential first free-agent year, after which everything went south. It's hard to pinpoint exactly what happened, as Suzuki actually walked more and struck out less after signing, but he also had an alarmingly high pop-fly rate and continued to have problems shutting down the running game. His offensive swoon might have been the result of trying to hit like a third- or fourth-spot batter, a role for which he was spectacularly unsuited, but the A's will grant him a mulligan and hope that his lumber recovers over another full season in a starting role.

Ryan Sweeney RF

Born: **2/20/1985** Age: **26**
Bats: **L** Throws: **L** Height: **6' 4"** Weight: **200**
Breakout: **1%** Improve: **34%** Collapse: **8%**
Attrition: **18%** MLB: **69%**

Comparables:
Buck Coats, David Murphy, Terry Puhl (74)

YEAR	TEAM	LVL	AGE	PA	R	2B	3B	HR	RBI	BB	SO	SB	CS	AVG/OBP/SLG	TAv	BABIP	BRR	FRAA	WARP
2008	OAK	MLB	23	433	53	18	2	5	45	38	67	9	1	.287/.349/.383	.274	.328	1.6	RF 8, CF -3	2.2
2009	OAK	MLB	24	534	68	31	3	6	53	40	67	6	5	.293/.346/.407	.280	.325	5.0	RF 10, CF 2	3.7
2010	OAK	MLB	25	331	41	20	2	1	36	24	41	1	1	.294/.341/.383	.269	.332	1.5	RF -1, CF 0	0.8
2011	*OAK*	*MLB*	*26*	*472*	*58*	*25*	*2*	*8*	*52*	*39*	*64*	*5*	*3*	*.288/.346/.413*	*.269*	*.317*	*-0.4*	*RF 5, CF -1*	*1.6*

Sweeney has been a tease for years: no Oakland player looks better in a uniform, and no player on the team has a prettier swing, but now that he's gotten nearly 1,500 plate appearances, it's time to accept that he can hit for average but has no secondary skills. In other words, he's a nice bench outfielder masquerading as an everyday player, something the A's suffered from a surplus of last season. Oakland is onto the charade, and with the acquisitions of David DeJesus and Josh Willingham, Sweeney will go from being part of the problem to part of the solution in a reduced role.

Michael Taylor OF

Born: **12/19/1985** Age: **25**
Bats: **R** Throws: **R** Height: **6' 6"** Weight: **260**
Breakout: **4%** Improve: **13%** Collapse: **2%**
Attrition: **7%** MLB: **21%**

Comparables:
Jamie Hoffmann, Joel Guzman, John Mayberry (71)

YEAR	TEAM	LVL	AGE	PA	R	2B	3B	HR	RBI	BB	SO	SB	CS	AVG/OBP/SLG	TAv	BABIP	BRR	FRAA	WARP
2008	LWD	A	22	288	40	12	3	10	50	31	43	10	3	.361/.441/.554	.376	.404	-4.4	LF 3, RF 0	3.6
2008	CLR	A+	22	266	36	27	1	9	38	19	46	5	6	.329/.380/.560	.322	.374	-0.6	LF 0, RF -3	1.9
2009	REA	AA	23	363	59	22	4	15	65	35	51	18	4	.333/.408/.569	.320	.357	1.5	LF -7, RF 3	2.5
2009	LEH	AAA	23	128	15	6	1	5	19	13	19	3	1	.282/.359/.491	.306	.292	0.4	LF 9, RF -3	1.4
2010	SAC	AAA	24	524	79	26	6	6	78	51	92	16	5	.272/.348/.392	.254	.325	1.5	RF -3, CF -2	0.0
2011	*OAK*	*MLB*	*25*	*523*	*65*	*27*	*3*	*14*	*65*	*43*	*99*	*12*	*4*	*.278/.339/.442*	*.274*	*.318*	*-0.1*	*LF -3, RF -3*	*0.9*

As he entered the year with a career .312/.383/.515 minor-league triple-slash line, the key piece in 2009's Brett Wallace deal was expected to rake at Sacramento in preparation for a September call-up. Instead, Taylor failed to repeat his Triple-A showing from the previous year and spent the season moldering in the minors. Scouts sometimes wondered if they were watching the same player he'd been during his Phillies days, as Taylor altered his swing mechanics in a vain attempt to break out of his slump. He was never able to find his power, and his formerly lauded contact skills took a dive as well. Twelve months ago, he was penciled in as a 2011 big-league regular, but now he's blocked and headed back to Triple-A.

Steven Tolleson INF

Born: **11/1/1983** Age: **27**
Bats: **R** Throws: **R** Height: **5' 11"** Weight: **185**
Breakout: **2%** Improve: **21%** Collapse: **13%**
Attrition: **21%** MLB: **49%**

Comparables:
Brian Barden, Craig Stansberry, Omar Quintanilla (80)

YEAR	TEAM	LVL	AGE	PA	R	2B	3B	HR	RBI	BB	SO	SB	CS	AVG/OBP/SLG	TAv	BABIP	BRR	FRAA	WARP
2008	NBR	AA	24	397	54	28	1	9	50	44	74	12	6	.300/.378/.466	.295	.352	0.9	2B 4, SS -6	2.6
2009	NBR	AA	25	173	21	10	2	2	13	16	20	6	2	.258/.341/.391	.271	.282	1.6	SS -6, 2B -1	0.0
2009	ROC	AAA	25	394	57	17	1	6	27	36	52	7	6	.270/.338/.375	.249	.299	-1.7	2B -3, LF -3	-0.1
2010	SAC	AAA	26	339	52	17	3	9	43	37	50	8	2	.332/.412/.503	.314	.368	1.7	SS -7, 3B 1	2.9
2010	OAK	MLB	26	53	5	3	0	1	4	4	9	0	0	.286/.340/.408	.300	.333	0.1	SS -3, 3B 0	0.0
2011	*OAK*	*MLB*	*27*	*448*	*54*	*22*	*1*	*10*	*49*	*41*	*76*	*8*	*3*	*.274/.341/.412*	*.265*	*.309*	*-0.3*	*SS -5, 2B 0*	*0.9*

Tolleson has all the makings of a fine utility player, a role that allowed his father, Wayne, to last in the big leagues for a decade. He can play any infield position and has a better bat than his old man (which isn't saying much), but his potential positions seem to be occupied by Adam Rosales. The two are very similar talents, but Rosales had the edge of having already proved himself in the majors, a distinction Tolleson lacks unless you interpret his 2010 cup of coffee generously. Though he won't be able to outlast Rosales, who's less than six months his elder, Tolleson will get his break eventually.

Jemile Weeks 2B

Born: **1/26/1987** Age: **24**
Bats: **S** Throws: **R** Height: **5' 9"** Weight: **170**
Breakout: **0%** Improve: **0%** Collapse: **0%**
Attrition: **0%** MLB: **0%**

Comparables:
Marcus Giles, Tony Abreu, Ruben Gotay (79)

YEAR	TEAM	LVL	AGE	PA	R	2B	3B	HR	RBI	BB	SO	SB	CS	AVG/OBP/SLG	TAv	BABIP	BRR	FRAA	WARP
2008	KNC	A	21	90	11	3	1	1	8	13	12	6	2	.297/.422/.405	.299	.344	-0.2	2B -6	-0.1
2009	STO	A+	22	232	29	9	2	7	31	26	40	5	1	.299/.384/.468	.324	.340	0.0	2B -2	1.8
2009	MID	AA	22	123	10	5	0	2	13	10	16	4	0	.238/.293/.343	.253	.245	1.8	2B 3	0.6
2010	MID	AA	23	312	43	14	7	3	33	28	37	11	6	.267/.335/.403	.256	.290	-0.2	2B 2	0.8
2011	*OAK*	*MLB*	*24*	*279*	*32*	*12*	*2*	*6*	*29*	*23*	*46*	*5*	*2*	*.256/.318/.389*	*.250*	*.286*	*-0.1*	*2B 1*	*0.4*

Weeks would be an excellent prospect if he could just stay on the field. If there's some kind of malady that can affect one's lower half, Weeks has had it, with his biggest issue being seemingly chronic hip problems. He has yet to play more than 80 games in a season since becoming the 12th overall pick in the 2008 draft, but when he plays, it's easy to see the bat speed, refined approach, and outstanding athleticism that led to his selection. He will be the leading candidate to start at the keystone in the big leagues in 2012, but only if he can avoid further trips to the infirmary.

PITCHERS

Brett Anderson

Born: **2/1/1988** Age: **23**
Bats: L Throws: L Height: **6' 4"** Weight: **235**
Breakout: **22%** Improve: **56%** Collapse: **15%**
Attrition: **15%** MLB: **86%**
Comparables:
John Candelaria, Brett Cecil, Don Robinson (65)

YEAR	TEAM	LVL	AGE	W	L	SV	G	GS	IP	H	HR	BB	SO	EqBB9	EqSO9	GB%	BABIP	WHIP	ERA	FRA	WARP
2008	STO	A+	20	9	4	0	14	13	74	68	5	18	80	2.2	9.7	60%	.309	1.22	4.01	3.74	1.1
2008	MID	AA	20	2	1	0	6	7	31	27	3	9	38	2.6	11.0	56%	.324	1.19	2.61	2.96	1.1
2009	OAK	MLB	21	11	11	0	30	32	175^{1}	180	20	44	150	2.3	7.7	52%	.310	1.29	4.00	4.77	1.7
2010	OAK	MLB	22	7	6	0	19	19	112^{1}	112	6	22	75	1.8	6.0	55%	.294	1.26	2.80	2.71	3.4
2011	*OAK*	*MLB*	*23*	*10*	*7*	*0*	*25*	*25*	*138^{1}*	*139*	*13*	*38*	*108*	*2.5*	*7.0*	*50%*	*.308*	*1.28*	*3.69*	*4.01*	*2.8*

Anderson's coming-out party was supposed to be held in 2010, but instead it was delayed by a first half that featured disabled-list stints, aborted comebacks, and returns to the shelf—all these problems that come with elbow tendinitis, the default term for arm ouchies, which doctors can't necessarily find the source of. Once healthy, he was good, but also a very different pitcher from the 2009 version, as he began to mix in a sinker with his four-seam fastball and depended much more on his slider as a secondary offering. The result was more ground balls but fewer strikeouts, which leaves us wondering which version will show up this season. Whiffs are more important than worm-burners when forecasting long-term success, and Anderson seemed a better bet when he was missing more bats. Regardless, he's an above-average big-league starter at an age when most southpaws are still stuck on the farm.

Andrew Bailey

Born: **5/31/1984** Age: **27**
Bats: R Throws: R Height: **6' 3"** Weight: **245**
Breakout: **10%** Improve: **15%** Collapse: **6%**
Attrition: **11%** MLB: **23%**
Comparables:
Brad Kilby, Mike Zagurski, Connor Robertson (73)

YEAR	TEAM	LVL	AGE	W	L	SV	G	GS	IP	H	HR	BB	SO	EqBB9	EqSO9	GB%	BABIP	WHIP	ERA	FRA	WARP
2008	MID	AA	24	5	9	0	37	15	110^{1}	99	13	56	110	4.6	9.0	49%	.287	1.46	4.32	5.45	0.6
2009	OAK	MLB	25	6	3	26	68	0	83^{1}	49	5	25	91	2.7	9.8	42%	.217	0.89	1.84	2.08	2.8
2010	OAK	MLB	26	1	3	25	47	0	49	34	3	13	42	2.4	7.7	39%	.237	0.96	1.47	2.51	1.1
2011	*OAK*	*MLB*	*27*	*5*	*3*	*11*	*52*	*5*	*83^{1}*	*71*	*9*	*37*	*77*	*4.0*	*8.3*	*44%*	*.279*	*1.29*	*3.47*	*3.77*	*1.1*

Bailey's spring training was nearly wiped away by a bout with tennis elbow, but he pitched like the guy who had won the Rookie of the Year award a year earlier before further elbow issues cropped up toward the end of the season. He underwent surgery in September to have loose bodies removed from his balky hinge, but he's expected to be ready for spring training. Bailey doesn't have classic closer velocity (not that his 94-95 mph fastball is chopped liver), but his ability to command and get some movement on his heater allows the pitch to play up to the level of a ninth-inning guy. Yes, he now has one not-so-healthy season on his record, but there's little reason to expect anything other than solid work from him going forward.

Jerry Blevins

Born: **9/6/1983** Age: **27**
Bats: L Throws: L Height: **6' 6"** Weight: **180**
Breakout: **6%** Improve: **16%** Collapse: **10%**
Attrition: **13%** MLB: **32%**
Comparables:
Rafael Perez, Matt Daley, R.J. Swindle (74)

YEAR	TEAM	LVL	AGE	W	L	SV	G	GS	IP	H	HR	BB	SO	EqBB9	EqSO9	GB%	BABIP	WHIP	ERA	FRA	WARP
2008	SAC	AAA	24	2	2	10	28	0	32^{1}	31	3	6	36	1.7	10.0	46%	.308	1.21	2.79	3.01	0.7
2008	OAK	MLB	24	1	3	0	36	0	37^{2}	32	2	13	35	3.1	8.4	43%	.291	1.27	3.11	3.59	0.7
2009	SAC	AAA	25	5	3	2	45	0	63^{1}	65	5	18	62	2.6	8.8	44%	.328	1.37	3.84	3.12	1.2
2009	OAK	MLB	25	0	0	0	20	0	22^{1}	19	2	6	23	2.4	9.3	31%	.288	1.12	4.84	4.68	0.1
2010	OAK	MLB	26	2	1	1	63	0	48^{2}	54	7	18	46	3.3	8.5	39%	.318	1.50	3.70	3.23	1.0
2011	*OAK*	*MLB*	*27*	*3*	*1*	*2*	*60*	*0*	*67*	*64*	*6*	*23*	*63*	*3.0*	*8.5*	*43%*	*.306*	*1.29*	*3.61*	*3.93*	*0.4*

Blevins' numbers look just average as opposed to good, since Bob Geren handed him way too many assignments against right-handers, who crushed him to the tune of .311/.392/.500. The southpaw sports an average-velocity fastball and a solid breaking ball, but his real advantage comes in the form of lankiness and arm angles that give left-handers fits. As a LOOGY, he's aces, but his skills limit him to specialized duty, a fact of life that the A's would do well to recognize.

Boof Bonser

Born: **10/14/1981** Age: **29**
Bats: **R** Throws: **R** Height: **6' 4"** Weight: **260**
Breakout: **0%** Improve: **3%** Collapse: **1%**
Attrition: **3%** MLB: **4%**

Comparables:
Alay Soler, Jeff Juden, Jason Jennings (71)

YEAR	TEAM	LVL	AGE	W	L	SV	G	GS	IP	H	HR	BB	SO	EqBB9	EqSO9	GB%	BABIP	WHIP	ERA	FRA	WARP
2008	MIN	MLB	26	3	7	0	47	12	118^1	139	16	36	97	2.7	7.4	42%	.322	1.49	5.93	6.05	-0.7
2010	PAW	AAA	28	0	2	0	9	8	32^2	37	3	14	25	3.9	7.0	44%	.327	1.65	6.34	5.40	0.2
2010	SAC	AAA	28	2	1	0	5	5	23^2	20	2	11	17	4.3	6.6	51%	.269	1.34	4.56	5.53	0.2
2010	BOS	MLB	28	0	0	0	2	0	2	6	0	2	0	9.0	0.0	55%	.546	4.00	18.00	12.76	-0.1
2010	OAK	MLB	28	1	0	0	13	0	23	27	2	6	17	2.3	6.7	51%	.338	1.43	5.09	4.81	0.0
2011	*NYN*	*MLB*	*29*	*7*	*6*	*0*	*42*	*16*	*112*	*121*	*13*	*43*	*82*	*3.5*	*6.6*	*45%*	*.310*	*1.46*	*4.59*	*4.99*	*0.8*

Either Bonser has never quite recovered from 2009 shoulder surgery, or he was simply never that good in the first place. His fastball, slider, and changeup all rank as average on the scouting scale, which is enough to convince teams that they can reap some value from him, but his pitches are rarely all available on the same night, leaving both his arsenal and his potential limited. Now entering the have-arm-will-travel portion of his baseball journey, he's one of those players who'll get a lifetime pass to Triple-A, where he'll secretly root for an injury stack to grant him another shot at "The Show." After bouncing from Boston to Oakland last year, he hooked on with the Mets.

Dallas Braden

Born: **8/13/1983** Age: **27**
Bats: **L** Throws: **L** Height: **6' 1"** Weight: **185**
Breakout: **12%** Improve: **45%** Collapse: **35%**
Attrition: **2%** MLB: **100%**

Comparables:
John Smiley, Steve Avery, Kevin Millwood (76)

YEAR	TEAM	LVL	AGE	W	L	SV	G	GS	IP	H	HR	BB	SO	EqBB9	EqSO9	GB%	BABIP	WHIP	ERA	FRA	WARP
2008	SAC	AAA	24	3	1	0	11	9	53^1	49	7	11	54	1.9	9.1	46%	.302	1.13	2.36	1.73	2.1
2008	OAK	MLB	24	5	4	0	19	10	71^2	77	8	25	41	3.1	5.1	40%	.307	1.45	4.14	4.22	1.0
2009	OAK	MLB	25	8	9	0	22	22	136^2	144	9	42	81	2.8	5.3	38%	.297	1.38	3.89	4.06	2.3
2010	OAK	MLB	26	11	14	0	30	30	192^2	180	17	43	113	2.0	5.3	42%	.270	1.18	3.50	3.83	2.7
2011	*OAK*	*MLB*	*27*	*9*	*6*	*0*	*21*	*21*	*128*	*126*	*11*	*37*	*86*	*2.6*	*6.1*	*42%*	*.292*	*1.27*	*3.57*	*3.88*	*2.6*

Braden enjoyed one of the more unlikely perfect games in baseball history, as strike throwers who require a considerable amount of defensive assistance aren't supposed to retire 27 in a row. Then again, guys who throw in the mid- to upper 80s and depend heavily on a changeup aren't supposed to post ERAs consistently better than league average, either. As evidenced by his notoriously possessive approach to the mound, Braden is the ultimate battler, a control specialist with the confidence and swagger of someone who throws 10 mph harder. Ultimately, his repertoire makes him an unlikely candidate for long-term success, but his self-confidence can be quite convincing.

Craig Breslow

Born: **8/8/1980** Age: **30**
Bats: **L** Throws: **L** Height: **6' 1"** Weight: **180**
Breakout: **20%** Improve: **43%** Collapse: **21%**
Attrition: **11%** MLB: **87%**

Comparables:
Robb Nen, Dave Righetti, Jason Isringhausen (76)

YEAR	TEAM	LVL	AGE	W	L	SV	G	GS	IP	H	HR	BB	SO	EqBB9	EqSO9	GB%	BABIP	WHIP	ERA	FRA	WARP
2008	CLE	MLB	27	0	0	0	7	0	8^1	10	1	5	7	5.4	7.6	46%	.333	1.80	3.24	3.13	0.2
2008	MIN	MLB	27	0	2	1	42	0	38^2	24	0	14	32	3.3	7.4	44%	.233	0.98	1.63	2.01	1.3
2009	MIN	MLB	28	1	2	0	17	0	14^1	11	3	11	11	6.9	6.9	34%	.211	1.60	6.28	6.33	-0.2
2009	OAK	MLB	28	7	5	0	60	0	55^1	37	5	18	44	2.9	7.2	33%	.216	1.03	2.60	4.75	0.3
2010	OAK	MLB	29	4	4	5	75	0	74^2	53	9	29	71	3.5	8.6	31%	.226	1.10	3.01	3.71	1.0
2011	*OAK*	*MLB*	*30*	*4*	*2*	*1*	*72*	*0*	*67*	*57*	*6*	*28*	*60*	*3.7*	*8.0*	*41%*	*.275*	*1.26*	*3.23*	*3.51*	*0.7*

After bouncing around for much of his early 20s, Breslow has seemingly found a home in Oakland after turning in back-to-back effective years with the Athletics. Since he's an extreme fly-ball pitcher, the Coliseum's extensive fair territory minimizes his mistakes. His combination of a fastball, slider, and command that all come in a tick above average makes him a consistent, dependable arm in a world where those two words are rarely used in conjunction when referring to relievers. A healthier and better-stocked bullpen might shift Breslow back one inning from the eighth to the seventh this season, but he should be just as good if called upon earlier.

Trevor Cahill

Born: **3/1/1988** Age: **23**
Bats: **R** Throws: **R** Height: **6' 4"** Weight: **220**
Breakout: **19%** Improve: **48%** Collapse: **12%**
Attrition: **11%** MLB: **82%**

Comparables:
Larry Dierker, Jim Kaat, Sean Gallagher (68)

YEAR	TEAM	LVL	AGE	W	L	SV	G	GS	IP	H	HR	BB	SO	EqBB9	EqSO9	GB%	BABIP	WHIP	ERA	FRA	WARP
2008	STO	A+	20	5	4	0	14	13	87^1	52	3	31	103	3.2	10.6	64%	.246	1.04	2.78	3.44	2.3
2008	MID	AA	20	6	1	0	7	6	37	24	2	19	33	4.6	8.0	66%	.234	1.24	2.19	4.90	0.4
2009	OAK	MLB	21	10	13	0	32	32	178^2	185	27	72	90	3.6	4.5	49%	.272	1.46	4.58	5.32	0.6
2010	OAK	MLB	22	18	8	0	30	30	196^2	155	19	63	118	2.9	5.4	57%	.236	1.14	2.97	4.06	2.4
2011	*OAK*	*MLB*	*23*	*8*	*6*	*0*	*20*	*20*	*122^2*	*108*	*12*	*50*	*82*	*3.7*	*6.0*	*52%*	*.268*	*1.30*	*3.65*	*3.97*	*2.4*

When asked to explain Cahill's transformation from struggling rookie to All-Star who finished fourth in ERA in the American League with a 2.97 mark, one scout simply responded, "Sinker . . . I don't know what else to say." Of course, he could just as easily have said, "BABIP," since despite inducing more grounders on the strength of his improved sinker, Cahill boasted a .238 BABIP, the lowest among AL pitchers with at least 80 innings pitched. That apparent assist from Lady Luck is the one concern with the A's rotation. Sure, they have an exciting young pitching staff, but in Cahilll and Braden, they own a pair of arms who have outpitched their scouting reports to the point where it's hard not to predict at least some regression. It's not a divination of disaster so much as something to be concerned about.

Bobby Cramer

Born: **10/28/1979** Age: **31**
Bats: **L** Throws: **L** Height: **6' 1"** Weight: **210**
Breakout: **4%** Improve: **11%** Collapse: **5%**
Attrition: **2%** MLB: **21%**

Comparables:
Bobby Korecky, Larry Christenson, Dwight Gooden (76)

YEAR	TEAM	LVL	AGE	W	L	SV	G	GS	IP	H	HR	BB	SO	EqBB9	EqSO9	GB%	BABIP	WHIP	ERA	FRA	WARP
2009	MID	AA	29	3	4	0	12	8	43	48	1	13	39	2.7	8.2	62%	.338	1.47	3.35	3.63	1.0
2010	SAC	AAA	30	2	2	0	7	7	41^{2}	41	0	11	35	2.4	7.6	57%	.320	1.26	1.94	2.21	1.9
2010	QUR	AAA	30	13	3	0	22	20	128	116	6	27	123	1.9	8.6	64%	.308	1.16	2.95	–	–
2010	OAK	MLB	30	2	1	0	4	4	23^{2}	20	5	6	13	2.3	4.9	53%	.217	1.10	3.04	4.55	0.2
2011	*OAK*	*MLB*	*31*	*5*	*4*	*0*	*18*	*11*	75^{1}	*79*	*7*	*26*	*54*	*3.1*	*6.5*	*52%*	*.309*	*1.39*	*4.14*	*4.50*	*0.9*

Cramer is one of the best stories in baseball. The A's signed him out of the indie leagues in 2008 and brought him along to Triple-A in 2009. With no clear place for him to begin the 2010 season, they lent him to the Quintana Roo Tigers of the Mexican League, a plot development out of an essential but yet-to-be-filmed movie that combines elements of *Bull Durham*, *Crazy Heart*, and *The Wrestler*. You didn't see the Nationals lending Stephen Strasburg to the Yazoo City, Mississippi, beer league, but the life of an independent-league salvage job is very different from that of a top prospect. Despite the south-of-the-border side trip, Cramer was called upon to fill a spot in the rotation in August, and about a month shy of his 31st birthday, he found himself in the big leagues for the first time ever. He's of a piece with the rest of the A's rotation as a pitcher who succeeds more with moxie than stuff, living in the upper 80s with a cut fastball that sets up a good curve. He's an underdog contender for the fifth-starter job this spring; if he should fail to get the gig, the A's are well stocked with southpaws in the bullpen, so he will probably head back to Sacramento or—who knows?—even more obscure outposts on the fringes of the baseball map.

Justin Duchscherer

Born: **11/19/1977** Age: **33**
Bats: **R** Throws: **R** Height: **6' 3"** Weight: **164**
Breakout: **6%** Improve: **12%** Collapse: **15%**
Attrition: **9%** MLB: **39%**

Comparables:
Willie Hernandez, Joel Peralta, Geoff Geary (69)

YEAR	TEAM	LVL	AGE	W	L	SV	G	GS	IP	H	HR	BB	SO	EqBB9	EqSO9	GB%	BABIP	WHIP	ERA	FRA	WARP
2008	OAK	MLB	30	10	8	0	22	22	141^{2}	107	11	33	95	2.1	6.0	43%	.235	1.04	2.54	4.07	2.3
2010	OAK	MLB	32	2	1	0	5	5	28	26	3	12	18	3.9	5.8	45%	.281	1.39	2.89	3.99	0.3
2011	*OAK*	*MLB*	*33*	*4*	*2*	*0*	*9*	*9*	*50*	*46*	*5*	*15*	*34*	*2.7*	*6.1*	*44%*	*.278*	*1.22*	*3.34*	*3.63*	*1.2*

A combination of elbow problems and clinical depression cost Duchscherer the entire 2009 season, and his 2010 campaign lasted all of five starts before he succumbed to the third hip surgery of his career. With 186 innings accumulated over the last four years, "dependable" is the last word you might use to describe him, unless it's to say that he's dependably unavailable. Yet, his 2008 season was so good, and the need for arms so desperate, that plenty of teams were kicking his tires as we went to press.

Gio Gonzalez

Born: **9/19/1985** Age: **25**
Bats: **R** Throws: **L** Height: **5' 11"** Weight: **185**
Breakout: **23%** Improve: **52%** Collapse: **16%**
Attrition: **10%** MLB: **100%**

Comparables:
Joe Coleman, Johnny Cueto, Jake Peavy (64)

YEAR	TEAM	LVL	AGE	W	L	SV	G	GS	IP	H	HR	BB	SO	EqBB9	EqSO9	GB%	BABIP	WHIP	ERA	FRA	WARP
2008	SAC	AAA	22	8	7	0	23	22	123	106	12	61	128	4.5	9.4	42%	.293	1.37	4.24	5.05	1.0
2008	OAK	MLB	22	1	4	0	10	7	34	32	9	25	34	6.6	9.0	44%	.250	1.76	7.68	10.06	-1.2
2009	SAC	AAA	23	4	1	0	12	12	61	42	5	34	71	5.0	10.5	45%	.259	1.30	2.51	3.63	1.2
2009	OAK	MLB	23	6	7	0	20	17	98^{2}	113	14	56	109	5.1	9.9	47%	.360	1.72	5.75	5.20	0.5
2010	OAK	MLB	24	15	9	0	33	33	200^{2}	171	15	92	171	4.1	7.7	51%	.274	1.33	3.23	3.64	3.7
2011	*OAK*	*MLB*	*25*	*12*	*9*	*0*	*31*	*31*	165^{2}	*147*	*16*	*83*	*157*	*4.5*	*8.5*	*46%*	*.294*	*1.40*	*3.88*	*4.22*	*3.0*

Because he was involved in three trades for big-leaguers before he reached the majors himself, it seems as if Gonzalez has been around forever, yet his breakout performance came in his age-24 season. With his stuff, he needed only to throw fewer balls outside the strike zone to succeed. He established better command of his curveball while showcasing a much-improved changeup to go with what has always been a well-above-average fastball. Improved control made Gonzalez good, but he had to sacrifice some strikeouts to obtain it; coupling his newfound ability to place the ball where he wants it with his former talent for missing bats could make him an All-Star.

Ian Krol

Born: **5/9/1991** Age: **20**
Bats: **L** Throws: **L** Height: **6' 1"** Weight: **180**
Breakout: **3%** Improve: **5%** Collapse: **1%**
Attrition: **1%** MLB: **6%**

Comparables:
Von McDaniel, Milt Pappas, Dan Petry (73)

YEAR	TEAM	LVL	AGE	W	L	SV	G	GS	IP	H	HR	BB	SO	EqBB9	EqSO9	GB%	BABIP	WHIP	ERA	FRA	WARP
2010	KNC	A	19	9	4	0	24	23	118^{2}	98	5	19	91	1.4	6.9	50%	.263	1.05	2.65	3.35	3.1
2011	*OAK*	*MLB*	*20*	*5*	*5*	*0*	*14*	*14*	*66*	*69*	*7*	*26*	*36*	*3.6*	*5.0*	*45%*	*.289*	*1.44*	*4.53*	*4.93*	*0.8*

Krol was kicked off his high-school team due to an alcohol-related incident, and the A's took a risk by dispensing just under $1 million to steer him away from college. He spent his pro debut making that payout look like a bargain. He will never light up a radar gun, but Krol has above-average velocity for a southpaw, a curveball that flashes plus, and perhaps the best changeup in the Midwest League. Added to his pitching arsenal is the kind of poise and command that many big-leaguers can't match. Krol doesn't have the kind of physical projection you look for in an elite prospect, but he's plenty good as is.

Vin Mazzaro

Born: **9/27/1986** Age: **24**
Bats: **R** Throws: **R** Height: **6' 2"** Weight: **210**
Breakout: **10%** Improve: **36%** Collapse: **13%**
Attrition: **14%** MLB: **77%**

Comparables:
Ricky Romero, Chris Carpenter, Jeff Manship (73)

YEAR	TEAM	LVL	AGE	W	L	SV	G	GS	IP	H	HR	BB	SO	EqBB9	EqSO9	GB%	BABIP	WHIP	ERA	FRA	WARP
2008	MID	AA	21	12	3	0	22	22	137^{1}	115	3	36	104	2.4	6.8	54%	.278	1.18	1.90	3.03	4.6
2008	SAC	AAA	21	3	3	0	6	5	33^{2}	49	3	9	27	2.4	7.2	46%	.393	1.87	6.14	4.50	0.7
2009	SAC	AAA	22	2	2	0	10	9	56^{2}	42	2	17	44	2.7	7.0	60%	.248	1.15	2.38	3.14	1.4
2009	OAK	MLB	22	4	9	0	17	17	91^{1}	120	12	39	59	3.8	5.8	40%	.350	1.78	5.32	5.23	0.5
2010	SAC	AAA	23	3	1	0	7	6	37^{1}	35	2	17	38	4.1	9.2	42%	.317	1.48	3.13	4.06	0.7
2010	OAK	MLB	23	6	8	0	24	18	122^{1}	127	19	50	79	3.7	5.8	46%	.281	1.48	4.27	5.15	0.0
2011	*KCA*	*MLB*	*24*	*9*	*10*	*0*	*26*	*26*	150^{1}	*164*	*17*	*62*	*96*	*3.7*	*5.8*	*47%*	*.309*	*1.51*	*4.93*	*5.36*	*1.3*

Mazzaro is difficult to classify. His best pitch is a sinker that rates well in terms of both velocity and movement, yet his ground-ball rate underwhelms due to a tendency to leave the pitch up in the strike zone on the rare occasions that he gets it in the zone. For now, he's a big guy with good stuff (including a power breaking ball), but he needs a good deal of refinement; success won't be as simple as telling him to throw lower. Mazzaro was dealt to Kansas City in the David DeJesus deal, so he'll have one year to figure things out before the Royals' battalion of pitching prospects threatens to take his job.

Henry Rodriguez

Born: **2/25/1987** Age: **24**
Bats: **R** Throws: **R** Height: **6' 0"** Weight: **220**
Breakout: **4%** Improve: **12%** Collapse: **8%**
Attrition: **3%** MLB: **24%**

Comparables:
Bob Turley, Scott Elbert, Al Leiter (69)

YEAR	TEAM	LVL	AGE	W	L	SV	G	GS	IP	H	HR	BB	SO	EqBB9	EqSO9	GB%	BABIP	WHIP	ERA	FRA	WARP
2008	STO	A+	21	2	3	2	20	17	75	57	5	40	104	4.8	12.5	51%	.310	1.32	3.72	4.24	1.4
2008	MID	AA	21	2	7	0	14	10	41	51	1	44	43	9.7	9.4	57%	.397	2.34	7.46	7.03	-0.3
2009	SAC	AAA	22	2	1	4	39	0	45	38	4	42	73	8.4	14.6	42%	.354	1.78	6.20	5.29	-0.1
2009	OAK	MLB	22	0	0	0	3	0	4	4	0	2	4	4.5	9.0	54%	.308	1.75	2.25	3.50	0.0
2010	SAC	AAA	23	0	2	11	20	0	21^{1}	10	1	9	31	3.8	13.2	48%	.200	0.90	1.69	4.10	0.2
2010	OAK	MLB	23	1	0	0	29	0	27^{2}	25	2	13	33	4.2	10.7	41%	.319	1.41	4.55	3.98	0.3
2011	*WAS*	*MLB*	*24*	*4*	*3*	*1*	*40*	*8*	*71*	*66*	*7*	*53*	*79*	*6.6*	*10.0*	*46%*	*.320*	*1.66*	*4.89*	*5.31*	*0.1*

Aroldis Chapman received a ton of attention for his fastball last year, but the velocity of lesser-known, right-handed Rodriguez is barely a tick behind. The stocky Venezuelan is guaranteed to hit triple digits nearly every time out, but he rarely knows where his heater is headed, and his slider exists in name only. He was nothing short of outstanding while pitching in his native land over the winter, and those performances, along with his tantalizing velocity, made him the key element in the trade that brought Josh Willingham to the West Coast. With the Nationals, Rodriguez will get a shot to win a late-inning job in the spring, and he's just as likely to save 20 games in "The Show" this year as he is to spend at least half the season in Double-A.

Tyson Ross

Born: **4/22/1987** Age: **24**
Bats: **R** Throws: **R** Height: **6' 6"** Weight: **225**
Breakout: **10%** Improve: **14%** Collapse: **5%**
Attrition: **11%** MLB: **24%**

Comparables:
Sean Gallagher, Jhonny Nunez, Glen Perkins (84)

YEAR	TEAM	LVL	AGE	W	L	SV	G	GS	IP	H	HR	BB	SO	EqBB9	EqSO9	GB%	BABIP	WHIP	ERA	FRA	WARP
2009	STO	A+	22	5	6	0	18	18	86^{1}	78	10	33	82	3.4	8.6	56%	.278	1.38	4.17	5.21	0.5
2009	MID	AA	22	5	4	0	9	9	50	40	3	20	31	3.6	5.6	62%	.250	1.22	3.96	4.48	1.0
2010	SAC	AAA	23	2	1	0	6	6	25^{1}	22	1	13	30	4.7	10.8	63%	.362	1.55	3.55	4.13	0.7
2010	OAK	MLB	23	1	4	1	26	2	39^{1}	39	4	20	32	4.6	7.3	55%	.310	1.50	5.49	5.58	-0.3
2011	*OAK*	*MLB*	*24*	*5*	*5*	*0*	*22*	*14*	77^{2}	*74*	*8*	*38*	*60*	*4.4*	*6.9*	*50%*	*.293*	*1.45*	*4.44*	*4.82*	*0.8*

Ross was the biggest surprise of Oakland's 2010 spring training, winning the fifth-starter job despite entering the year with only 33 games of professional experience. His lack of a prior performance record was reflected in an unsightly ERA, but he posted solid peripherals and remains impressive on a scouting level, attacking hitters with a 92-95 mph fastball and a slider, both of which rate as above average. His complex delivery created a multitude of problems, as it not only limited his ability to throw strikes, but also led to some arm difficulties, including an elbow problem that ended his season early. Ross's long-term future probably lies in the bullpen, but his short-term outlook includes more time in the minors to smooth things out.

Ben Sheets

Born: **7/18/1978** Age: **32**
Bats: R Throws: R Height: **6' 1"** Weight: **195**
Breakout: **8%** Improve: **37%** Collapse: **25%**
Attrition: **9%** MLB: **90%**

Comparables:
Sonny Siebert, Shane Reynolds, Larry Jansen (74)

YEAR	TEAM	LVL	AGE	W	L	SV	G	GS	IP	H	HR	BB	SO	EqBB9	EqSO9	GB%	BABIP	WHIP	ERA	FRA	WARP
2008	MIL	MLB	29	13	9	0	31	31	198^{1}	181	17	47	158	2.1	7.2	42%	.278	1.15	3.09	3.44	5.1
2010	OAK	MLB	31	4	9	0	20	20	119^{1}	123	18	43	84	3.2	6.3	45%	.288	1.39	4.53	4.84	0.4
2011	*OAK*	*MLB*	*32*	*10*	*7*	*0*	*23*	*23*	*145^{2}*	*143*	*15*	*43*	*110*	*2.7*	*6.8*	*44%*	*.290*	*1.27*	*3.71*	*4.04*	*2.6*

After Sheets missed all of 2009 recovering from elbow surgery, the A's took a gamble by signing him to a $10 million contract, hoping that he could pitch well enough to help the team win or turn into some prospects at the trade deadline. He wasn't awful, but he didn't look much like vintage Sheets, either, as he lost a tick or two from his fastball and his control declined from great to merely good. Before the A's could decide on his second-half future, Sheets' elbow went pop again in July, requiring major surgery with an estimated rehabilitation time of up to 18 months. His chances of appearing in a future edition of this book are slim.

Michael Wuertz

Born: **12/15/1978** Age: **32**
Bats: R Throws: R Height: **6' 3"** Weight: **205**
Breakout: **26%** Improve: **45%** Collapse: **17%**
Attrition: **8%** MLB: **78%**

Comparables:
Eric Plunk, Lee Smith, Pedro Feliciano (73)

YEAR	TEAM	LVL	AGE	W	L	SV	G	GS	IP	H	HR	BB	SO	EqBB9	EqSO9	GB%	BABIP	WHIP	ERA	FRA	WARP
2008	IOW	AAA	29	0	1	4	17	0	20	13	2	14	29	6.3	13.1	56%	.268	1.35	3.60	5.02	0.0
2008	CHN	MLB	29	1	1	0	45	0	44^{2}	44	4	20	30	4.0	6.0	46%	.296	1.43	3.63	4.77	0.1
2009	OAK	MLB	30	6	1	4	74	0	78^{2}	52	6	23	102	2.6	11.7	47%	.266	0.95	2.75	3.26	1.7
2010	OAK	MLB	31	2	3	6	48	0	39^{2}	35	6	21	40	4.8	9.1	44%	.279	1.41	4.31	4.70	0.1
2011	*OAK*	*MLB*	*32*	*4*	*2*	*3*	*71*	*0*	*69*	*57*	*6*	*30*	*74*	*3.9*	*9.6*	*46%*	*.289*	*1.26*	*3.16*	*3.44*	*0.8*

Wuertz's 2009 ability to pound the strike zone regressed to his career norms in 2010, but he was still a solid middle reliever who lived off a plus slider and even picked up a few saves when Andrew Bailey went down. While shoulder problems delayed the start of his season—throwing sliders more than half the time is about as dangerous for your arm as playing in traffic—until May, he remained especially effective against right-handers and should be able to replicate that performance. Wuertz is not a big star, but was an outstanding find, considering he was traded from the Cubs for a pair of minor leaguers who have already played their way out of Chicago's system.

Brad Ziegler

Born: **10/10/1979** Age: **31**
Bats: R Throws: R Height: **6' 4"** Weight: **200**
Breakout: **5%** Improve: **17%** Collapse: **10%**
Attrition: **6%** MLB: **30%**

Comparables:
Justin Hampson, Bobby Korecky, Vinnie Chulk (76)

YEAR	TEAM	LVL	AGE	W	L	SV	G	GS	IP	H	HR	BB	SO	EqBB9	EqSO9	GB%	BABIP	WHIP	ERA	FRA	WARP
2008	SAC	AAA	28	2	0	8	19	0	24^{1}	15	0	4	20	1.5	7.4	69%	.224	0.78	0.37	2.06	0.9
2008	OAK	MLB	28	3	0	11	47	0	59^{2}	47	2	22	30	3.3	4.5	65%	.259	1.17	1.06	2.03	2.4
2009	OAK	MLB	29	2	4	7	69	0	73^{1}	82	2	28	54	3.4	6.6	62%	.351	1.51	3.19	3.10	1.6
2010	OAK	MLB	30	3	7	0	64	0	60^{2}	54	4	28	41	4.2	6.1	56%	.276	1.40	3.26	4.12	0.5
2011	*OAK*	*MLB*	*31*	*4*	*2*	*5*	*80*	*0*	*91^{2}*	*90*	*6*	*34*	*58*	*3.4*	*5.7*	*53%*	*.300*	*1.36*	*3.80*	*4.13*	*0.3*

While his remarkable scoreless streak as a rookie was an extreme fluke, Ziegler remains an effective ground-ball machine as a right-handed specialist. The only question now is how much that's worth. He's entering his final year before arbitration, and in the minds of many teams, an exclusively righty-on-righty reliever is more luxury than necessity. Sidewinders like Ziegler age well, but because of his late start (he converted to the style late in his career), he's already 31 years old and has little room to grow. Still, it's not a stretch to say that he could celebrate his 40th birthday in the bigs.

LINEOUTS

HITTERS

PLAYER	TEAM	LVL	AGE	PA	R	2B	3B	HR	RBI	BB	SO	SB-CS	AVG/OBP/SLG	TAv	BABIP	BRR	FRAA	WARP
DH E. Chavez*	OAK	MLB	32	123	11	8	0	1	10	8	31	0-0	.234/.276/.333	.240	.301	0.2	1B 0	-0.2
2B C. Crumbliss	KNC	A	23	634	95	30	2	5	56	126	92	24-8	.271/.421/.371	.304	.316	1.7	2B -5, CF 0	4.1
2B A. Iwamura*	IND	AAA	31	203	26	10	1	3	16	38	32	0-2	.264/.404/.393	.280	.310	-2.7	3B 0, 2B 0	0.7
	OAK	MLB	31	36	3	1	0	0	4	5	10	0-0	.129/.250/.161	.195	.190	0.0	3B -4	-0.5
	PIT	MLB	31	193	18	6	1	2	9	26	31	3-1	.182/.290/.267	.219	.209	-0.9	2B -5	-0.8
INF T. Ladendorf	STO	A+	22	525	60	30	4	5	41	35	110	20-4	.274/.326/.385	.263	.340	0.8	2B -3, SS -3	1.0
INF D. McPherson*	SAC	AAA	29	354	49	17	2	22	75	31	101	1-0	.267/.339/.541	.296	.321	-1.5	1B 1, 3B -2	1.7
3B S. Parker*	STO	A+	22	627	102	38	5	21	98	84	105	3-1	.296/.392/.508	.312	.327	-4.0	3B -3, 1B 0	4.5
C A. Recker	SAC	AAA	26	276	36	18	2	10	42	22	62	0-1	.288/.341/.496	.288	.341	0.0	C 2, 1B 0	2.1
C M. Stassi	KNC	A	19	465	54	21	1	13	51	45	141	3-3	.229/.310/.380	.256	.310	-2.3	C 0	1.3
LF M. Watson*	SAC	AAA	31	165	25	12	0	9	26	11	24	0-0	.288/.339/.542	.299	.292	1.0	LF 0, RF 0	1.2
	OAK	MLB	31	33	2	2	0	1	4	3	5	0-0	.200/.273/.367	.247	.208	-1.2	LF -3	-0.4
UT C. Wimberly#	SAC	AAA	26	623	97	14	7	3	57	58	64	56-18	.284/.373/.354	.260	.308	6.6	LF 1, CF -5	1.3

Scouts had a difficult time evaluating 2010 second-round pick **Yordy Cabrera** as a high-school player who was nearly 20 (he moved from the Dominican six years ago). His power isn't questionable, but his ability to stay at shortstop is. **Eric Chavez** somehow stayed healthy for two months, but didn't hit much. In late May, he was placed on the disabled list with neck spasms, and they must have been the most spasmodic spasms in the history of man, as he never returned to the lineup. The A's made the no-brainer decision to decline his $12.5 million option for 2011. Little second baseman **Conner Crumbliss** led the minor leagues with 126 walks in 2010, but he still has to prove that he can hit his way on. After not hitting a lick in 2010, infielder **Akinori Iwamura** is heading back to Japan. The lefty had his uses as recently as 2009, but the indignity of being released by the Pirates is as good a reason as any to spurn the Western Hemisphere. An athletic player picked up from Minnesota in 2009 for Orlando Cabrera, **Tyler Ladendorf** played five positions in 2010; versatility is where his value ultimately lies. Minor-league slugging machine **Dallas McPherson** bashed 22 more home runs in just 84 Triple-A games last year. He'll smack some more in the White Sox system this year. Third baseman **Stephen Parker** impressed with his bat in 2010, but his defense at third base needs considerable work. Catcher **Anthony Recker** has plenty of power and could get some at-bats in the big leagues this year as a backup if the need arises. Signed for $1.5 million out of the 2009 draft, backstop **Max Stassi** is an outstanding defensive catcher with intriguing power, but he has to cut down on the whiffs. In returning to the big leagues for this first time since 2005, outfielder **Matt Watson** made himself a great story, but he's still not very good at baseball, so he might as well let that be the happy ending, if you can call a 6-for-30 performance "happy." Tiny **Corey Wimberly** has outstanding speed, draws some walks, and has less power than those corroded Double-A batteries you threw away last month. He'll explore his utilityman potential with the Pirates, who acquired him in a December trade.

PITCHERS

PLAYER	TEAM	LVL	AGE	W	L	SV	IP	H	HR	BB	SO	EqBB9	EqSO9	GB%	BABIP	WHIP	ERA	FRA	WARP
C. Bowers*	SAC	AAA	32	2	1	0	32	24	1	26	50	7.3	14.1	51%	.338	1.59	3.66	4.67	0.2
	OAK	MLB	32	0	1	0	14	12	4	6	18	3.9	11.6	22%	.242	1.36	4.50	6.73	-0.3
A. Capra*	MID	AA	23	6	13	0	130^{2}	120	9	89	118	6.2	8.2	43%	.302	1.65	4.27	4.88	1.4
F. De Los Santos	MID	AA	24	1	5	0	31^{2}	31	1	16	51	4.6	14.7	51%	.405	1.57	6.54	7.34	-0.8
P. Figueroa*	MID	AA	24	1	6	0	71^{1}	84	6	29	57	3.7	7.2	46%	.347	1.62	5.30	4.80	0.6
S. Haviland	STO	A+	24	9	6	0	150^{1}	156	15	40	166	2.4	10.0	41%	.343	1.42	3.65	4.11	2.6
J. James	OAK	MLB	28	0	0	0	4	7	0	4	5	9.0	11.3	46%	.539	3.00	4.50	7.51	-0.1
B. Kilby*	OAK	MLB	27	0	0	0	8^{1}	7	2	0	8	0.0	8.6	13%	.227	0.84	2.16	3.57	0.1
J. Marks*	KNC	A	22	3	12	0	109^{2}	109	11	41	119	3.4	9.8	51%	.334	1.46	4.92	4.07	1.8
C. Mortensen	SAC	AAA	25	13	6	0	165^{1}	161	20	53	112	2.9	6.1	53%	.281	1.31	4.25	5.86	-0.4
	OAK	MLB	25	0	0	0	6	6	1	2	7	3.0	10.5	35%	.313	1.33	4.50	5.42	-0.0
E. Ramirez	SAC	AAA	29	3	4	0	49^{2}	48	5	23	35	4.2	6.4	37%	.279	1.46	3.62	4.47	0.4
	OAK	MLB	29	1	0	0	11	9	1	10	10	8.2	8.2	47%	.242	1.73	4.91	6.06	-0.2
P. Smyth	STO	A+	23	3	6	28	77^{2}	68	4	21	94	2.4	11.0	52%	.315	1.20	3.01	3.77	0.8
R. Wolf	NOR	AAA	27	0	2	0	38^{1}	29	1	15	26	3.5	6.1	56%	.243	1.15	1.88	3.43	0.7
	OAK	MLB	27	0	0	0	12^{2}	12	1	6	9	4.3	6.4	57%	.282	1.50	4.26	4.38	0.1

Journeyman reliever **Cedrick Bowers** spent a career-high 14 games in the big leagues at age 32 and now has a seeming lock on the all-time record for appearances by a guy named "Cedrick." Due to his weak control, he's unlikely to push it any higher. Left-hander **Anthony Capra** has an impressive fastball/changeup combination, but he needs to throw more strikes. Once a top prospect with one of the better young arms in the game, **Faustino De Los Santos** missed plenty of bats in his return from arm surgery, but also got hit hard at Double-A. After missing all of the 2010 season recovering from Tommy John surgery, **Joey Devine** will try to return to a late-innings role this spring. Lefty **Pedro Figueroa**'s struggles in the Texas League following a breakout 2009 season were explained when he succumbed to Tommy John surgery. The first pitcher drafted out of Harvard since 2003, 2008 33rd-round right-hander **Shawn Haviland** led the organization with 169 strikeouts and projects as a middle reliever. It took eight years for **Justin James** to reach the big leagues; now he'll try to earn an encore with Milwaukee. **Jason Jennings** tried another comeback in 2010 and stayed healthy enough to pitch all of 22 minor-league innings. After impressing in a September 2009 call-up, **Brad Kilby** got bit by the shoulder-injury bug in 2010. A second-round pick in 2009, lefty **Justin Marks** has solid stuff, good control, and therefore a fighter's chance. Angular righty **Clayton Mortensen** has intriguing ground-ball rates, but scouts wonder if he can miss enough bats to survive in the big leagues. The A's cut him loose in January to make room for Grant Balfour. **Josh Outman** missed all of 2010 recovering from elbow surgery. In the past, he has shown rare velocity for a lefty. **Edwar Ramirez** has a phenomenal changeup but nothing to go with it, so we're done saying nice things about him. Reliever **Paul Smyth** dominated the California League with moxie and deception; now he has to prove that his magic act will play at the upper levels. **Ross Wolf** throws a low-90s fastball and a cutter, but that hasn't been enough to establish himself in the big leagues. The biggest signing in Dominican history, **Michael Ynoa** enjoyed a pro career that lasted all of nine innings before his elbow exploded. He got himself a new ligament in late August.

MANAGER: BOB GEREN

YEAR	TEAM	W-L	Pythag +/–	Avg PC	100+ P	120+ P	QS	BQS	REL	REL w Zero R	IBB	Subs	PH	PH Avg	PH HR	SB2	CS2	SB3	CS3	SAC Att	SAC %	POS SAC	Squeeze	Swing	In Play
2008	OAK	75-86	0	93.6	48	0	69	6	441	289	45	54	91	.203	2	84	19	2	2	55	54.5%	27	2	109	74
2009	OAK	75-87	-6	92.7	50	0	62	3	488	316	30	48	76	.153	0	117	42	16	2	46	67.4%	26	0	117	78
2010	OAK	81-81	-5	97.5	75	1	94	5	423	272	29	44	107	.236	3	124	33	32	4	67	64.2%	39	1	132	106

Geren was Mr. Average in virtually every statistical category, so it's safe to say that that he didn't rock the managerial boat. He adapted to a roster that was low on sluggers but high on speeders by allowing his A's to attempt more steals than any full-season managers aside from Joe Maddon and Ozzie Guillen, and his busy runners rewarded him with the highest rate of success exhibited by any team except Cito Gaston's Blue Jays, whose Canadian manners precluded them from seeking more than a league-low number of stolen bags. He also upped his sacrifice and pinch-hit rates in a largely futile effort to maximize his team's offensive potential, although he didn't get sac-happy enough to land in Billy Beane's doghouse. Geren issued fewer intentional passes than did any other skipper save Ron Gardenhire and Ron Washington and wasn't afraid to take the training wheels off his top relievers, tying for the league lead with eight saves of more than three outs. Five of these games were pitched by Andrew Bailey, who had tennis elbow early and went for surgery late, so while Geren deserves credit for shrugging off the conventional wisdom and treating his closer as something sturdier than a hothouse flower, he might have picked the wrong season to try. Nevertheless, he has earned positive reviews from his young players, who have complimented his increasingly flexible and laissez-faire approach to in-game tactics. The A's wasted little time in exercising his option for the 2011 season, which will mark his 12th with the organization.

Philadelphia Phillies

The current Phillies front office, led by Ruben Amaro Jr., has defined itself through a series of unpredictable, splashy, and controversial transactions. It isn't just that the Phillies turned out to be the "mystery team" in the Cliff Lee bidding—after trading him a year earlier—or that they doled out eight figures to a first baseman heading for the wrong side of 30 and whose contract wasn't due to expire for another eighteen months. What has characterized the Phillies over the past two seasons has been a willingness to acquire help in areas of the game where they appear not to need it. The results have so far been very positive, but the long-term viability of the plan depends on the organization's ability to cultivate the talent currently inhabiting the lower levels of its farm system.

The Phillies' 2010 season was characterized by a remarkable turnaround. On July 21, they stood two games above .500, in third place, and seven games out of first. From there, the team finished the season on a 49-19 run that secured the best record in baseball for Philadelphia. What defined the Phils' first-half skid in the minds of fans and commentators alike was a stretch of offensive futility that saw them average just 2.6 runs per game over three weeks in late May and early June. With many of the team's sluggers either ineffective (Shane Victorino) or spending time on the disabled list (Chase Utley, Ryan Howard) in July and August, it would have been easy for the Phillies' front office to make a desperate trade for offensive help.

To illustrate the magnitude of the problem, consider Figure 1, which displays the Phillies' runs scored and runs allowed trends over the course of the entire season (including the playoffs). By the time the nonwaiver trade deadline rolled around on July 31, the team's most glaring problem appeared to be its offense, which had been the league's best as recently as 2009. The club's run prevention was strong at approximately four runs per game, a marked improvement over the previous year.

Rather than seek significant outside help, the Phillies held firm on offense, using freely available talent like Wilson Valdez and Ross Gload to fill temporary holes. Their assumption was that the players who were in a slump would eventually rebound, and the players who were injured would eventually regain their health. It sounds obvious now, with hindsight revealing a successful second half, but it wasn't the most popular set of decisions at the time.

The team's offensive struggles were all the more alarming because the Phillies had seemingly squandered an opportunity to have the most intimidating trio of starters in the league when the team dealt Lee to Seattle in December 2009. That they superficially spun the Lee deal as part of the Halladay trade didn't fool anybody, and it was clear that for only slightly more than they would eventually pay Joe Blanton, the Phillies could have kept Lee along with Halladay and Cole Hamels. Given the choice to place their faith in Blanton and the lineup instead of Lee, the Phillies' offensive struggles loomed large over their midsummer swoon.

What Amaro and the rest of the Phillies' front office did do at the waiver deadline is interesting, not so much because of how it played out over the remainder of the season (which is safely in the books), but because of what it says about their decision-making process. Acquiring Roy Oswalt for J. A. Happ and some second-tier prospects (most notably toolsy lottery ticket Anthony Gose) wasn't so much inspired as it was an uncomplicated, easy call, particularly given that the Astros were willing to include $11 million's worth of Oswalt's salary. Still, the swap did illuminate two important aspects of organizational philosophy.

PHILLIES PROSPECTUS

2010 W-L: 97-65, 1st in NL East

Pythag	.586	3rd
RS/G	4.8	7th
RA/G	4.0	26th
TAv	.279	4th
BRR	-5.5	25th
FRA	4.00	5th
DER	3.40	14th
DL	628	8th
B-Age	31.9	30th
P-Age	30.9	30th
Salary	$141.9	4th
M$/MW	$2.73	18th

Ballpark: Citizens Bank Park (3-yr. PF: 100). The place that made Jayson Werth appear to be worth $126 million

2010: Doc writes a prescription for a third consecutive NLCS trip

2011: Four aces of the apocalypse seal up the NL East

Action Items: Acquiring amateur talent to succeed aging core; making sure to have some division-title bubbly on ice

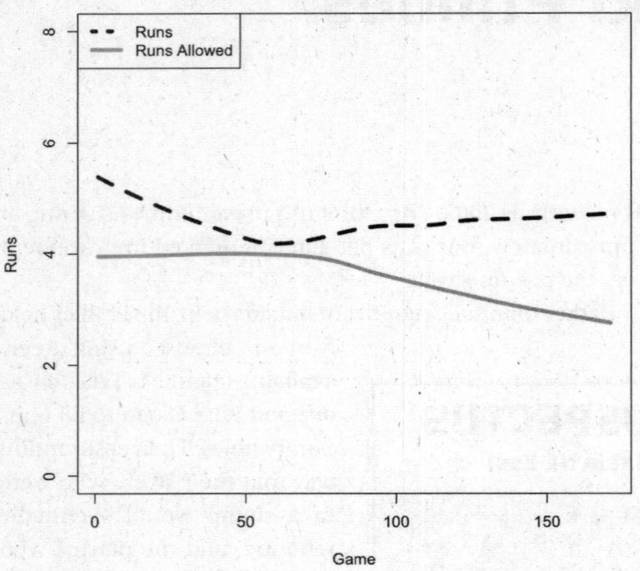

First, the trade reflects an ability to realize that team needs are dynamic. Simply because the offense wasn't performing as well as it had in 2009 didn't mean that the best possible move was to shore up the hitting. Runs are runs, and acquiring Oswalt to replace the starts of J. A. Happ was a perfectly good way to save some. There is more than one way to skin a cat, and the shift in the way that the team went about winning games over the course of the 2010 season was a testament to that observation.

The Oswalt trade also proceeded from an ability to recognize the mistake that had been committed in trading Lee (if not quite as much as did the subsequent decision to fit Lee for a Phillies uniform once again). Just months after shipping Lee away, Amaro reversed course and got the next-best thing. The prospects didn't quite net out, of course, and Oswalt is under contract for another year. But the damage done in the intervening months wasn't nearly enough to keep the Phillies out of the playoffs. Then, after assembling a rotation that was clearly one of the best in baseball, Amaro killed the original zombie by swooping in and signing Lee through at least 2015.

The approach to team building that these moves represent constitutes part of a larger pattern of the Amaro front office: an affinity for ostentatious and decisive deals. The Halladay signing and extension, the Howard extension, the Oswalt deal, the Lee upset—they were all big deals for big-name players designed to put the club over the top in one fell swoop. The primary vice that can hamstring such an approach is an inability to recognize when things have gone awry or a blindness to the need to fix them. Whatever you might think about the individual moves—and there is ample reason to criticize the Howard extension or the Lee trade—it's difficult to argue that subsequent decisions haven't been accurately targeted to address the weaknesses from which the team suffered as a result of its ill-advised prior maneuvers.

For at least the next year, those weaknesses have been largely eliminated. For 2011, the only question mark is how well the team can replace Jayson Werth's production, and there the Phillies already have one of the most promising young hitters in the game lined up. That isn't to say that Domonic Brown will immediately replace Werth's lost contributions—in fact, he's likely to represent a downgrade of approximately three wins—but he will come much cheaper and should provide a long-term solution in right field.

The holes that need to be filled will open in 2012 and beyond, when Oswalt, Jimmy Rollins, Brad Lidge, Raul Ibanez, and Ryan Madson will probably all declare for free agency. Those holes can be filled, and the advance warning the front office has should keep it from getting caught in a bind by any one position or player. It essentially has three windows to find replacements for each: this year's trade deadline, next offseason, and perhaps the 2012 trade deadline. Because this offseason looked very much like a seller's market, not having to brave the free-agent bazaar beyond Lee was a brilliant way to arrange the team's affairs.

This Phillies team's potential unraveling lies beyond 2012, when Howard will start earning $25 million per year, Victorino and Hamels will be free agents, and everyone else on the roster will have grown two years older. In order for the Phillies to remain competitive as their current core begins to fragment or become prohibitively pricey, they'll need their farm system to produce a cohort of talent that stacks up at least decently against the one that has fueled four straight playoff appearances on the backs of Utley, Howard, and Hamels. The organization possesses enough high-ceiling talents in the low minors that the possibility isn't out of the question: some combination of Jonathan Singleton, Jarred Cosart, Brody Colvin, Jesse Biddle, and Jiwan James could pan out on that level if everything breaks the right way. Of course, that's an awful lot to ask for, and counting on prospects to be sure things is no way to run a baseball team. Amplifying these worries, the Phillies surrendered their first-round draft pick by signing Lee. The likely result is that scouting director Chuck LaMar will indulge his past tendencies in the later rounds by drafting—you guessed it—athletes who have yet to manifest their baseball skills in game situations.

For the last two years, the Phillies have engaged in a systematic shift of future success to wins in the present. As each successive year passes, that strategy becomes riskier and riskier, and the day of reckoning approaches. Two consecutive years of dashed playoff hopes have done nothing to alleviate the growing concerns. Still, the plan has had benefits that may accrue even after the current core either departs or declines. The Phillies carry an active streak of 123 home sellouts into the 2011 season, and there is little indication that the streak will conclude next year. Popularity enabled the Phillies to raise ticket prices by an average of $2 to $5 across the board, increasing revenue by several million dollars with little additional overhead. By stacking enough successful seasons together (something largely unfamiliar in Philadelphia), the team has garnered enough goodwill that the momentum could conceivably push it to a level of profitability that would allow the team to devote large amounts of money to talent at all levels. That might be enough to stave off the stagnation that comes from an aging roster and inflated, back-loaded contracts.

It's possible, but the clock is ticking. The Phillies had both the oldest pitching staff and the oldest lineup in baseball last year, as Table 1 demonstrates. This trend was not arrested by the signing of Lee, who is already 32.

Amaro and the Phillies would be well advised to channel their organizational tendency for action and their newfound financial resources towards stockpiling amateur talent. That means being active in the international market, continuing their recent acceptance of paying over-slot for draft picks, and avoiding signing more Type-A free agents, who require draft-pick compensation (at least until such time as a future collective bargaining agreement changes the rules of free agency).

Table 1. Honor Thy Elders: The Five Oldest Major League Staffs and Lineups, 2010

Oldest lineups (average age)	Oldest pitching staffs (average age)
Phillies (31.8)	Phillies (31.1)
Red Sox (30.9)	Yankees (30.4)
White Sox (30.6)	Cardinals (30.2)
Dodgers (30.3)	Braves (30.1)
Yankees (30.3)	Red Sox (29.6)

The Phillies demonstrated in 2010 that old age isn't automatically fatal, but that doesn't meant that it isn't *inevitably* fatal. There is only one way to make a roster younger, and the Phillies need to recognize this before they incur even more significant salary obligations. The farm system has undergone an admirable rebound since it was emptied in the Halladay (and, to a lesser extent, Oswalt) deal, but more must be done if it is to equip the Phillies for the challenges ahead.

HITTERS

Brian Bocock SS

Born: **3/9/1985** Age: **26**
Bats: **R** Throws: **R** Height: **5′ 11″** Weight: **185**
Breakout: **0%** Improve: **2%** Collapse: **2%**
Attrition: **3%** MLB: **6%**
Comparables:
Gregorio Petit, Drew Meyer, Omar Quintanilla (82)

YEAR	TEAM	LVL	AGE	PA	R	2B	3B	HR	RBI	BB	SO	SB	CS	AVG/OBP/SLG	TAv	BABIP	BRR	FRAA	WARP
2008	FRE	AAA	23	141	14	3	0	0	3	14	39	7	3	.163/.248/.187	.161	.230	2.7	SS 11	0.4
2008	SFN	MLB	23	93	4	1	0	0	2	12	29	4	2	.143/.247/.156	.156	.212	1.1	SS 2	-0.4
2009	SJO	A+	24	430	56	25	2	3	48	36	96	6	7	.241/.302/.339	.255	.306	0.0	SS 17	3.1
2009	NRW	AA	24	88	9	1	0	0	3	12	20	2	3	.171/.284/.186	.222	.218	0.5	SS -1	0.0
2010	LEH	AAA	25	439	37	11	3	4	31	49	88	13	6	.226/.313/.303	.222	.276	-0.1	SS -11	-1.0
2010	PHI	MLB	25	5	0	0	0	0	0	0	3	0	0	.000/.000/.000	.019	.000	0.2	SS -1	-0.1
2011	*PHI*	*MLB*	*26*	*406*	*38*	*14*	*1*	*3*	*28*	*39*	*99*	*9*	*4*	*.216/.290/.290*	*.212*	*.280*	*-0.6*	*SS 3*	*-0.2*

Bocock will be 26 on Opening Day and owns a career .228/.304/.309 batting line in nearly 1,800 minor-league plate appearances. It would take an unusual set of circumstances to give him a full season's worth of starts—war, famine, or lockout could do the trick. The smart money might be on zombie apocalypse, since Bocock's thin flesh would be unappealing to the undead (and brains could be considered a PED). Barring a baseball apocalypse, he'll have a future as some organization's warm body, thanks to his strong defensive skills.

Domonic Brown RF

Born: **9/3/1987** Age: **23**
Bats: **L** Throws: **L** Height: **6′ 5″** Weight: **200**
Breakout: **2%** Improve: **30%** Collapse: **1%**
Attrition: **16%** MLB: **56%**
Comparables:
Jay Bruce, Nick Evans, Wladimir Balentien (73)

YEAR	TEAM	LVL	AGE	PA	R	2B	3B	HR	RBI	BB	SO	SB	CS	AVG/OBP/SLG	TAv	BABIP	BRR	FRAA	WARP
2008	LWD	A	20	516	77	23	3	9	54	64	72	22	7	.291/.382/.417	.314	.327	0.0	CF 0, RF 1	4.0
2009	CLR	A+	21	280	41	12	3	11	44	34	48	15	8	.303/.386/.517	.323	.330	-0.3	RF -2, LF 0	2.0
2009	REA	AA	21	162	20	9	4	3	20	14	37	8	1	.279/.346/.456	.283	.355	0.4	RF -7	0.1
2010	REA	AA	22	271	50	16	3	15	47	29	51	12	6	.318/.391/.602	.337	.345	-3.2	RF 6	2.7
2010	LEH	AAA	22	118	15	6	1	5	21	8	23	5	1	.346/.390/.561	.319	.395	1.9	RF -1, LF 0	1.0
2010	PHI	MLB	22	70	8	3	0	2	13	5	24	2	1	.210/.257/.355	.231	.282	0.0	RF 2	0.1
2011	*PHI*	*MLB*	*23*	*477*	*59*	*21*	*3*	*15*	*59*	*42*	*103*	*14*	*5*	*.271/.335/.439*	*.270*	*.319*	*-0.3*	*RF -4, CF -4*	*0.5*

Brown had his best year yet in the minors before being summoned to Philadelphia in late July. He manifested even more of the copious extra-base ability of which he'd long been thought capable, and he showed terrific contact skills. The Phillies' decision to keep him on the major-league bench following his debut was a bit of a head-scratcher, as Brown could have used additional development time against breaking pitches and left-handers. As it was, he rarely saw the light of day in the second half and failed to produce in his intermittent opportunities, making the story of his season *How Green Was My Lehigh Valley*. Brown's long, looping swing will be open to exploitation by major-league pitchers during his initial trips around the league, so the success of his early seasons will hinge on his ability to make adjustments. He'll step in to fill the full-time void left by Jayson Werth and provide yet another power lefty bat in the lineup.

Ben Francisco — OF

Born: **10/23/1981** Age: **29**
Bats: **R** Throws: **R** Height: **6' 1"** Weight: **190**
Breakout: **4%** Improve: **42%** Collapse: **2%**
Attrition: **9%** MLB: **89%**

Comparables:
Bernard Gilkey, Ryan Spilborghs, Scott Hairston (76)

YEAR	TEAM	LVL	AGE	PA	R	2B	3B	HR	RBI	BB	SO	SB	CS	AVG/OBP/SLG	TAv	BABIP	BRR	FRAA	WARP
2008	BUF	AAA	26	104	9	3	1	1	6	11	25	3	0	.228/.308/.315	.215	.299	-0.6	LF -1, RF 1	-0.4
2008	CLE	MLB	26	499	65	32	0	15	54	40	86	4	3	.266/.331/.439	.282	.296	-1.5	LF 6, RF -2	2.1
2009	CLE	MLB	27	355	48	21	1	10	33	33	59	13	3	.250/.332/.422	.275	.274	2.3	LF 3, CF -5	1.2
2009	PHI	MLB	27	104	10	9	0	5	13	5	24	1	4	.278/.317/.526	.301	.319	-1.3	LF 2, CF 1	0.8
2010	PHI	MLB	28	197	24	13	0	6	28	14	35	8	0	.268/.325/.441	.267	.300	-0.6	LF 0, RF 2	0.6
2011	*PHI*	*MLB*	*29*	*437*	*53*	*24*	*1*	*12*	*52*	*38*	*79*	*12*	*4*	*.267/.334/.428*	*.269*	*.300*	*-0.3*	*LF 4, RF -1*	*1.3*

Francisco killed lefties in 2010—the rap sheet reads .284/.344/.557—and yet he received more plate appearances against righties. The distribution of playing time was a mystery, largely because he was one of the team's few threats against the sort of lefty relievers that repeatedly confront the Phillies late in games. There were plenty of situations in which starting Francisco against a left-handed pitcher or pinch-hitting him against a LOOGY was the obvious but unexecuted choice. A platoon of Francisco and Ibanez would be more productive than Ibanez alone.

Freddy Galvis — SS

Born: **11/14/1989** Age: **21**
Bats: **S** Throws: **R** Height: **5' 10"** Weight: **170**
Breakout: **3%** Improve: **7%** Collapse: **0%**
Attrition: **3%** MLB: **10%**

Comparables:
Edgar Renteria, Robin Yount, Mike Caruso (77)

YEAR	TEAM	LVL	AGE	PA	R	2B	3B	HR	RBI	BB	SO	SB	CS	AVG/OBP/SLG	TAv	BABIP	BRR	FRAA	WARP
2008	LWD	A	18	523	59	12	1	3	42	39	58	14	7	.238/.291/.288	.228	.253	-0.2	SS 7	0.9
2009	CLR	A+	19	272	29	8	2	1	15	10	43	6	3	.247/.272/.307	.217	.282	-0.2	SS -3, 3B -1	-0.5
2009	REA	AA	19	63	6	0	0	1	5	2	7	0	1	.197/.222/.246	.193	.208	-0.9	SS -2	-0.5
2010	REA	AA	20	545	58	16	4	5	48	30	89	15	4	.233/.276/.311	.216	.267	5.4	SS 8	0.9
2011	*PHI*	*MLB*	*21*	*476*	*41*	*14*	*2*	*3*	*36*	*19*	*85*	*7*	*3*	*.224/.251/.289*	*.194*	*.260*	*-0.2*	*SS 6, 3B 0*	*-0.8*

Galvis is a dazzling defensive shortstop who has yet to manifest any offensive success, and that goes for the Venezuelan Winter League, too. He'll only have to hit well enough to bat eighth, but even that is looking increasingly like a challenge, as he hasn't shown an aptitude for excelling in *any* of the triple-slash stats. Just 21, he probably has room to grow, and if he can learn to hit like Wilson Valdez, well, you never know. He did hit better in the second half, so having him double up in Double-A would be wise.

Harold Garcia — 2B

Born: **10/25/1986** Age: **24**
Bats: **S** Throws: **R** Height: **5' 11"** Weight: **164**
Breakout: **0%** Improve: **1%** Collapse: **0%**
Attrition: **7%** MLB: **10%**

Comparables:
Danny Richar, Ruben Gotay, Robert Andino (80)

YEAR	TEAM	LVL	AGE	PA	R	2B	3B	HR	RBI	BB	SO	SB	CS	AVG/OBP/SLG	TAv	BABIP	BRR	FRAA	WARP
2008	PHL	Rk	21	210	35	12	5	5	21	20	32	17	2	.299/.400/.511	.304	.333	-1.1	2B 5, 3B -1	1.9
2009	LWD	A	22	502	64	21	5	8	55	29	100	42	12	.291/.347/.414	.283	.347	0.0	2B 13	3.6
2010	CLR	A+	23	204	27	13	3	3	32	12	37	17	6	.335/.397/.492	.311	.399	0.0	2B -2, 3B -1	1.3
2010	REA	AA	23	258	27	9	2	5	32	15	57	12	5	.281/.340/.403	.259	.343	0.0	2B 5, 3B 0	1.1
2011	*PHI*	*MLB*	*24*	*393*	*40*	*16*	*2*	*7*	*38*	*19*	*95*	*14*	*4*	*.238/.288/.355*	*.227*	*.297*	*0.0*	*2B 7, 3B 0*	*0.3*

Garcia is a skinny Venezuelan second baseman who had a very nice year with the stick, posting a combined .305/.365/.441 line. A week after setting the Florida State League hitting-streak record at 37 games, he was called up to Double-A, but he experienced some struggles in Reading, so a repeat engagement is likely in order. Garcia has plus speed, the ability to play either second or third, and a promising bat, although since he's not in the power or patience business, his offensive production is overly tied to batting average. The usual caveats about the limited room for utility types of the nonshortstop persuasion on crowded rosters apply, but if he keeps hitting, the Phillies will find a way to deal.

Ross Gload **UT**

Born: **4/5/1976** Age: **35**
Bats: **L** Throws: **L** Height: **6' 0"** Weight: **185**
Breakout: **0%** Improve: **20%** Collapse: **24%**
Attrition: **40%** MLB: **74%**

Comparables:
Tony Batista, Denny Walling, Dane Iorg (79)

YEAR	TEAM	LVL	AGE	PA	R	2B	3B	HR	RBI	BB	SO	SB	CS	AVG/OBP/SLG	TAv	BABIP	BRR	FRAA	WARP
2008	KCA	MLB	32	418	45	18	1	3	37	23	39	3	4	.273/.316/.348	.236	.294	-2.9	1B -10, LF 1	-1.8
2009	FLO	MLB	33	257	33	10	2	6	29	23	30	0	0	.263/.331/.404	.271	.276	0.4	1B 5, RF 0	1.2
2010	PHI	MLB	34	138	17	8	0	6	22	8	15	1	0	.281/.326/.484	.290	.278	-1.0	1B -1, RF 0	0.4
2011	*PHI*	*MLB*	*35*	*268*	*30*	*12*	*1*	*5*	*28*	*18*	*31*	*2*	*1*	*.269/.320/.389*	*.251*	*.285*	*-0.1*	*1B 0, RF 0*	*0.0*

Gload's true hitting talent lies well below the level of a league-average first baseman, and since there's plenty of left-side swinging to go around in the Phillies' lineup, it's hard to identify the comparative advantage he might bring to the ballclub. Still, when injuries struck, he filled in nicely, which goes to show how certain seemingly inconsequential pickups can look like bright moves in retrospect. Gload is under contract for another year and could get most of his reps off the bench, although Amaro has raised the prospect of his regular participation in a right-field platoon.

Ryan Howard **1B**

Born: **11/19/1979** Age: **31**
Bats: **L** Throws: **L** Height: **6' 4"** Weight: **230**
Breakout: **3%** Improve: **41%** Collapse: **6%**
Attrition: **10%** MLB: **97%**

Comparables:
Carlos Pena, David Ortiz, Travis Hafner (62)

YEAR	TEAM	LVL	AGE	PA	R	2B	3B	HR	RBI	BB	SO	SB	CS	AVG/OBP/SLG	TAv	BABIP	BRR	FRAA	WARP
2008	PHI	MLB	28	700	105	26	4	48	146	81	199	1	1	.251/.339/.543	.295	.285	-4.0	1B 6	3.2
2009	PHI	MLB	29	703	105	37	4	45	141	75	186	8	1	.279/.360/.571	.312	.325	-6.5	1B 11	4.6
2010	PHI	MLB	30	620	88	23	5	31	108	59	157	1	1	.276/.353/.506	.302	.332	-8.0	1B -3	1.9
2011	*PHI*	*MLB*	*31*	*677*	*96*	*27*	*3*	*40*	*107*	*82*	*180*	*3*	*1*	*.268/.360/.532*	*.303*	*.313*	*-0.1*	*1B 2*	*3.5*

Most of the discussion about Howard this year focused on his contract extension, which will pay him $125 million from 2012 through 2016. It's a shame that his future paychecks overshadowed his performance on the field. Outside of August, a month in which he tried to play through an ankle injury, Howard hit .288/.366/.529. He hit better against lefties (.264/.333/.492) than he has over the course of his career (.232/.314/.452) and struck out at his lowest rate yet. On the other hand, he saw fewer pitches than he had in recent years, and his power was down markedly. Will he be worth $25 million six seasons from now? Unlikely, but 2016 is a long way off, and Howard has shown an ability to make adjustments as pitchers have adjusted to him.

Raul Ibanez **LF**

Born: **6/2/1972** Age: **39**
Bats: **L** Throws: **R** Height: **6' 2"** Weight: **210**
Breakout: **0%** Improve: **18%** Collapse: **12%**
Attrition: **19%** MLB: **88%**

Comparables:
Ken Griffey, Carlos Delgado, Dwight Evans (63)

YEAR	TEAM	LVL	AGE	PA	R	2B	3B	HR	RBI	BB	SO	SB	CS	AVG/OBP/SLG	TAv	BABIP	BRR	FRAA	WARP
2008	SEA	MLB	36	707	86	43	3	23	110	64	110	2	4	.293/.358/.479	.306	.322	-0.7	LF 4	4.9
2009	PHI	MLB	37	565	93	32	3	34	93	56	119	4	0	.272/.347/.552	.301	.290	-2.7	LF -7	2.4
2010	PHI	MLB	38	636	75	37	5	16	83	68	108	4	3	.275/.349/.444	.283	.311	-0.2	LF -17, 1B 0	0.9
2011	*PHI*	*MLB*	*39*	*651*	*81*	*34*	*3*	*21*	*80*	*65*	*117*	*4*	*2*	*.266/.338/.440*	*.272*	*.296*	*-0.2*	*LF -7, 1B 0*	*1.2*

Maybe this year everyone can agree to reach a premature conclusion about Ibanez's performance on the basis of an insufficient sample *before* his season kicks off, since previous evaluations were based on just as little evidence. In 2009, he faced supremely idiotic steroid allegations. In 2010, his pre–All Star break line of .243/.326/.397 led some to believe he should be cut from the roster; he hit .309/.375/.494 the rest of the way. Ibanez is the sort of hitter who constantly adjusts his batting stance and watches hours of video in search of something that will work, and thus far, he's generally been able to find it. Consequently, he serves as a useful reminder that while we know most players decline as they age, we can't conclude much about the slope of that decline in individual cases just by looking at a few months of play, especially where late bloomers, already atypical, are concerned.

Jiwan James **CF**

Born: **4/11/1989** Age: **22**
Bats: **S** Throws: **R** Height: **6' 4"** Weight: **180**
Breakout: **0%** Improve: **1%** Collapse: **0%**
Attrition: **0%** MLB: **2%**

Comparables:
Carlos Gomez, Thad Bosley, Ken Hubbs (78)

YEAR	TEAM	LVL	AGE	PA	R	2B	3B	HR	RBI	BB	SO	SB	CS	AVG/OBP/SLG	TAv	BABIP	BRR	FRAA	WARP
2009	WPT	A-	20	134	15	4	3	1	13	11	22	7	4	.264/.336/.372	.281	.316	0.2	CF -7, RF 0	0.0
2010	LWD	A	21	617	85	26	6	5	64	35	132	33	20	.270/.321/.365	.263	.334	-0.4	CF -6	1.4
2011	*PHI*	*MLB*	*22*	*385*	*35*	*15*	*2*	*3*	*31*	*17*	*104*	*8*	*3*	*.228/.264/.307*	*.205*	*.303*	*-0.4*	*CF -16, RF 0*	*-2.6*

In terms of raw speed, James is a 70 runner, but he has yet to figure out how to run the bases. He also has a power hitter's body but has yet to hit for power. That's what happens when you pick the toolsiest *pitcher* left in the 22nd round of the 2007 draft, then turn him into a center fielder. James' tools have impressed scouts, but it will take plenty of patience before he learns how to use them. His potential was fully on display during a 24-game hitting streak (which ended in July), but his overall season line demonstrates how far he has to go.

John Mayberry OF

Born: **12/21/1983** Age: **27**
Bats: **R** Throws: **R** Height: **6' 6"** Weight: **235**
Breakout: **2%** Improve: **19%** Collapse: **2%**
Attrition: **10%** MLB: **31%**

Comparables:
Kevin Mahar, Dave Winfield, Aaron Bates (75)

YEAR	TEAM	LVL	AGE	PA	R	2B	3B	HR	RBI	BB	SO	SB	CS	AVG/OBP/SLG	TAv	BABIP	BRR	FRAA	WARP
2008	FRI	AA	24	90	16	8	0	4	13	4	21	4	1	.268/.322/.512	.280	.310	1.0	RF -5	0.0
2008	OKL	AAA	24	475	49	30	7	16	58	30	85	6	2	.263/.316/.474	.270	.292	-3.2	LF -1, RF -6	0.5
2009	LEH	AAA	25	358	44	20	2	13	43	34	94	6	2	.256/.332/.456	.277	.319	-0.8	RF 1, LF 0	1.3
2009	PHI	MLB	25	60	8	3	0	4	8	2	23	0	0	.211/.250/.474	.234	.267	0.2	LF 2, RF 0	0.1
2010	LEH	AAA	26	547	75	25	1	15	65	39	111	20	3	.267/.328/.412	.260	.313	0.0	RF 2, LF 7	1.8
2010	PHI	MLB	26	13	3	0	0	2	6	1	4	0	1	.333/.385/.833	.425	.333	-1.1	RF -1, CF 0	0.0
2011	*PHI*	*MLB*	*27*	*519*	*59*	*24*	*2*	*16*	*61*	*38*	*125*	*7*	*2*	*.245/.304/.408*	*.250*	*.293*	*-0.2*	*LF 1, RF -2*	*0.2*

It's looking increasingly unlikely that Mayberry will make it as a useful major leaguer. He failed to prove himself for a second straight season in Triple-A, and his virtues as a pinch-hitter are blunted by his having the same strengths as Ben Francisco. Mayberry strikes out often due to his long swing, and he doesn't hit the ball especially far when he gets ahold of it. Since it doesn't cost much to keep him around, Mayberry will go back to Triple-A and hope to make it one day as a backup outfielder.

Placido Polanco 3B

Born: **10/10/1975** Age: **35**
Bats: **R** Throws: **R** Height: **5' 10"** Weight: **168**
Breakout: **0%** Improve: **14%** Collapse: **8%**
Attrition: **17%** MLB: **90%**

Comparables:
Orlando Cabrera, Miguel Tejada, Frank Malzone (69)

YEAR	TEAM	LVL	AGE	PA	R	2B	3B	HR	RBI	BB	SO	SB	CS	AVG/OBP/SLG	TAv	BABIP	BRR	FRAA	WARP
2008	DET	MLB	32	629	91	34	3	8	58	35	43	7	1	.307/.348/.417	.271	.317	3.9	2B -6	2.1
2009	DET	MLB	33	676	82	31	4	10	72	36	46	7	2	.285/.327/.396	.260	.289	0.9	2B 3	2.1
2010	PHI	MLB	34	602	77	27	2	6	52	32	47	5	0	.298/.339/.386	.267	.312	1.6	3B 8, 2B 3	3.3
2011	*PHI*	*MLB*	*35*	*610*	*70*	*28*	*2*	*6*	*59*	*36*	*45*	*5*	*2*	*.291/.336/.379*	*.257*	*.302*	*0.0*	*2B 0, 3B 2*	*1.5*

The large-pated Polanco is a league-average hitter who played very good defense in his first full season at the hot corner. Nowhere do the rules of roster construction decree that your third baseman has to hit for power, and it's especially unnecessary that he do so when pop is provided at so many other spots in the lineup. Some of the offensive production he offered was sapped when he was hit on the elbow by a Tim Hudson fastball in late April; a bone spur ensued and eventually forced Polanco to the DL. He underwent successful surgery to remove the offending material during the offseason and is expected to be ready for spring training. He has an otherwise strong medical track record, so the Phillies can be optimistic about his playing time, if not his ability to draw a walk.

Matt Rizzotti 1B

Born: **12/24/1985** Age: **25**
Bats: **L** Throws: **L** Height: **6' 5"** Weight: **235**
Breakout: **7%** Improve: **15%** Collapse: **6%**
Attrition: **28%** MLB: **38%**

Comparables:
Joe Koshansky, Aaron Bates, Bryan LaHair (79)

YEAR	TEAM	LVL	AGE	PA	R	2B	3B	HR	RBI	BB	SO	SB	CS	AVG/OBP/SLG	TAv	BABIP	BRR	FRAA	WARP
2008	LWD	A	22	437	49	25	2	10	49	65	97	1	1	.268/.380/.430	.311	.336	0.1	1B 4	2.9
2009	CLR	A+	23	404	44	26	1	13	58	48	91	0	0	.263/.351/.454	.288	.316	-1.5	1B -1	1.2
2010	CLR	A+	24	122	18	8	1	1	10	13	22	0	0	.358/.426/.477	.323	.442	0.0	1B -1	0.8
2010	REA	AA	24	310	48	25	0	16	62	40	56	1	1	.361/.452/.635	.370	.412	0.0	1B 0	3.7
2010	LEH	AAA	24	52	0	3	0	0	4	6	14	0	0	.200/.308/.267	.183	.290	0.0	1B -1	-0.4
2011	*PHI*	*MLB*	*25*	*443*	*54*	*23*	*1*	*12*	*50*	*48*	*108*	*0*	*0*	*.260/.341/.421*	*.266*	*.323*	*0.0*	*1B -7*	*-0.1*

For every slugger in his mid-20s on the right-hand side of the defensive spectrum, there comes a season in which he must put up or shut up, move quickly or move on, develop or bust. Rizzotti got the message, hit well at High-A Clearwater, and then switched on the afterburners at Double-A Reading. A product of Manhattan College (a school that gave baseball the seventh-inning stretch but few major leaguers of late), Rizzotti is big, left-handed, and balding, and he's less likely to discover the secret to above-average defense than he is to regrow a thick head of hair (especially if you believe the infomercials). It really is a pity that he's not a righty, since it's difficult to divine his path to the big leagues with the Phillies, even in a bench role. He might need a trade to blossom as a cheap power source a few years down the road.

Jimmy Rollins SS

Born: **11/27/1978** Age: **32**
Bats: **S** Throws: **R** Height: **5' 8"** Weight: **160**
Breakout: **1%** Improve: **43%** Collapse: **0%**
Attrition: **5%** MLB: **100%**

Comparables:
Brian Roberts, Don Buford, Chuck Knoblauch (63)

YEAR	TEAM	LVL	AGE	PA	R	2B	3B	HR	RBI	BB	SO	SB	CS	AVG/OBP/SLG	TAv	BABIP	BRR	FRAA	WARP
2008	PHI	MLB	29	625	76	38	9	11	59	58	55	47	3	.277/.347/.437	.271	.288	7.0	SS 7	4.4
2009	PHI	MLB	30	725	100	43	5	21	77	44	70	31	8	.250/.295/.423	.247	.250	2.7	SS -14	0.8
2010	PHI	MLB	31	394	51	16	3	8	41	40	32	17	1	.243/.320/.374	.263	.246	-0.1	SS -4	1.1
2011	*PHI*	*MLB*	*32*	*660*	*79*	*34*	*6*	*16*	*78*	*55*	*63*	*33*	*6*	*.266/.327/.422*	*.264*	*.270*	*1.7*	*SS -5*	*2.3*

The longest-tenured Phillie's most recent season was worrying for several reasons. Rollins missed nearly three months due to three distinct injuries (calf, foot, and hamstring) and was a marginal offensive asset when he made it into the lineup. His defense remains strong, and he is a heads-up baserunner, but the former NL MVP increasingly looks like a player who will reach base at less than a league-average rate. That makes his only tangible offensive asset his power, which hasn't been much in evidence lately, either. This is the last year of Rollins' contract, and the Phillies' interest in his returning will be almost entirely dictated by his performance in 2011.

Carlos Ruiz C

Born: **1/22/1979** Age: **32**
Bats: **R** Throws: **R** Height: **6' 0"** Weight: **170**
Breakout: **1%** Improve: **29%** Collapse: **2%**
Attrition: **6%** MLB: **86%**

Comparables:
Mike Lieberthal, Jose Vidro, Alan Trammell (72)

YEAR	TEAM	LVL	AGE	PA	R	2B	3B	HR	RBI	BB	SO	SB	CS	AVG/OBP/SLG	TAv	BABIP	BRR	FRAA	WARP
2008	PHI	MLB	29	373	46	14	0	4	31	44	38	1	2	.219/.316/.300	.220	.233	6.5	C 5, 3B 0	1.1
2009	PHI	MLB	30	379	32	26	1	9	43	47	39	3	2	.255/.351/.426	.268	.261	-3.1	C 0	1.6
2010	PHI	MLB	31	433	43	28	1	8	53	55	54	0	1	.302/.400/.447	.305	.336	-5.7	C 1	3.2
2011	*PHI*	*MLB*	*32*	*426*	*52*	*24*	*0*	*7*	*42*	*51*	*51*	*2*	*1*	*.268/.359/.396*	*.268*	*.286*	*-0.2*	*C 1, 3B 0*	*2.1*

Ruiz posted the third-highest TAv by a major-league catcher last season. It's tough to penalize him into a lack of productivity: if you take away his intentional walks, Ruiz still had a .381 OBP, and if you look only at his away stats, his line improves to .330/.419/.489. His signature stroke produces a line-drive double to the gap, and the backstop has walked more than he's struck out for three straight seasons. Even if his BABIP falls back to previous levels, his secondary skills are good enough to give him value. Ruiz had been a good player after coming to the big leagues late, but after turning 30, he morphed into an even better one. As a receiver, he is terrific at blocking the ball and has a strong arm to boot. Under contract for two more seasons, Chooch should continue to be a bargain.

Jonathan Singleton LF

Born: **9/18/1991** Age: **19**
Bats: **L** Throws: **L** Height: **6' 2"** Weight: **215**
Breakout: **0%** Improve: **0%** Collapse: **0%**
Attrition: **1%** MLB: **1%**

Comparables:
Jim Breazeale, Ed Kranepool, Rick Dempsey (68)

YEAR	TEAM	LVL	AGE	PA	R	2B	3B	HR	RBI	BB	SO	SB	CS	AVG/OBP/SLG	TAv	BABIP	BRR	FRAA	WARP
2009	PHL	Rk	17	119	12	9	0	2	12	18	13	1	0	.290/.395/.440	.309	.314	-0.9	1B 2	0.8
2010	LWD	A	18	450	64	25	2	14	77	62	74	9	7	.290/.393/.479	.321	.323	-0.9	1B 7	3.9
2011	*PHI*	*MLB*	*19*	*291*	*32*	*13*	*0*	*7*	*28*	*32*	*68*	*0*	*0*	*.232/.318/.370*	*.246*	*.284*	*0.0*	*1B -8*	*-1.0*

Singleton is a big, left-handed first baseman. At least, he was—he's now a big, left-handed left fielder, after the combination of his largely successful season and the various obstacles to his progression conspired to force a defensive shift. Whether or not his eventual position remains blocked by Ryan Howard, Singleton did his best to force the issue in the first half, as he hit .373/.460/.672 before the break in an assault on Sally League pitching. His second half was as forgettable as his first half was remarkable, but he wasn't the first 18-year-old to experience mixed results. He'll move up a level and hope to show that the true Singleton was the first-half beast and not the second-half bum, all while playing a new position. The Phillies declined to include him in the Oswalt deal, so they clearly have faith in his long-term value.

Mike Sweeney 1B

Born: **7/22/1973** Age: **37**
Bats: **R** Throws: **R** Height: **6' 1"** Weight: **195**
Breakout: **0%** Improve: **16%** Collapse: **20%**
Attrition: **27%** MLB: **59%**

Comparables:
Doug Mientkiewicz, Rocky Nelson, Chris Chambliss (73)

YEAR	TEAM	LVL	AGE	PA	R	2B	3B	HR	RBI	BB	SO	SB	CS	AVG/OBP/SLG	TAv	BABIP	BRR	FRAA	WARP
2008	OAK	MLB	34	136	13	8	0	2	12	7	6	0	0	.286/.331/.397	.276	.286	-0.2	1B -1	0.3
2009	SEA	MLB	35	266	26	15	0	8	34	17	31	0	0	.281/.335/.442	.287	.291	0.8	1B -1	0.9
2010	SEA	MLB	36	110	13	3	0	6	18	9	14	2	0	.263/.327/.475	.299	.250	-0.2	1B 0	0.5
2010	PHI	MLB	36	58	9	2	0	2	8	5	7	1	0	.231/.310/.385	.284	.233	-0.4	1B 1	0.3
2011	*PHI*	*MLB*	*37*	*251*	*29*	*11*	*0*	*7*	*27*	*20*	*32*	*1*	*0*	*.260/.326/.401*	*.259*	*.273*	*0.0*	*1B 0*	*0.2*

Acquired from the Mariners to play first base while Howard was out in August, Sweeney posted a very respectable .280/.357/.480 line in his starts, but struggled when relegated to the bench. On the other hand, he demonstrated that he could play a somewhat convincing first base without immediately getting injured. Sweeney actually has a small reverse platoon split for his career, so his value as a pinch-hitter is lower than it might at first appear. As we near the end of his career, it is fascinating to wonder how history would have regarded this career .297/.366/.486 hitter had he been able to remain a catcher.

Chase Utley 2B

Born: **12/17/1978** Age: **32**
Bats: **L** Throws: **R** Height: **6' 1"** Weight: **170**
Breakout: **1%** Improve: **40%** Collapse: **3%**
Attrition: **6%** MLB: **98%**

Comparables:
Ryne Sandberg, Billy Williams, Carlos Beltran (68)

YEAR	TEAM	LVL	AGE	PA	R	2B	3B	HR	RBI	BB	SO	SB	CS	AVG/OBP/SLG	TAv	BABIP	BRR	FRAA	WARP
2008	PHI	MLB	29	707	113	41	4	33	104	64	104	14	2	.292/.379/.535	.313	.301	-0.1	2B 1, 1B 1	5.7
2009	PHI	MLB	30	687	113	28	4	31	93	88	110	23	0	.282/.397/.508	.317	.300	2.2	2B 8	6.6
2010	PHI	MLB	31	511	75	20	2	16	65	63	63	13	2	.275/.388/.445	.309	.288	1.6	2B 8	4.6
2011	*PHI*	*MLB*	*32*	*656*	*92*	*31*	*3*	*24*	*86*	*74*	*96*	*15*	*3*	*.285/.386/.484*	*.305*	*.302*	*0.7*	*2B 4, 1B 0*	*4.8*

Maybe this is how grown men come to devote several weeks each year trying to convince a small cadre of baseball writers to validate the career of a ballplayer they've never met. Maybe this is how players who were once at the pinnacle of the game get locked out of the Hall of Fame. Consider the flukes of circumstance that have made Utley a perennial MVP bridesmaid; the biomechanics that gave him uncharacteristic yips during the playoffs and the myopia of observers who, for perhaps the only time in the history of baseball, have criminally underrated a tough-as-nails dirty-uniform guy. Might Utley's days of unrecognized glory now give way to injury-plagued thirtysomething seasons? Make no mistake—Utley is still the Phillies' best position player, but his power is starting to seep away and injuries have begun to sap his durability. If he emerges from his peak with fewer than 200 home runs and no MVP awards, will the BBWAA remember that Utley was one of the 10 or so best second basemen of all time? One possible hint: second baseman Joe Gordon *did* win an MVP award, but still had to wait 59 years for his plaque.

Sebastian Valle **C**

Born: **7/24/1990** Age: **20**
Bats: R Throws: L Height: **6' 1"** Weight: **170**
Breakout: **0%** Improve: **0%** Collapse: **0%**
Attrition: **0%** MLB: **0%**

Comparables:
Adrian Beltre, Hank Aaron, Robin Yount (70)

YEAR	TEAM	LVL	AGE	PA	R	2B	3B	HR	RBI	BB	SO	SB	CS	AVG/OBP/SLG	TAv	BABIP	BRR	FRAA	WARP
2008	PHL	Rk	17	185	27	15	0	2	18	12	31	0	0	.281/.341/.407	.264	.331	0.8	C 0	0.8
2009	LWD	A	18	179	16	12	1	1	15	16	37	1	2	.223/.313/.331	.260	.283	-0.8	C 1	0.4
2009	WPT	A-	18	206	25	15	5	6	40	10	41	0	0	.307/.335/.531	.313	.356	-0.5	C 2	2.0
2010	LWD	A	19	485	51	28	1	16	74	27	101	3	2	.255/.298/.430	.255	.290	0.5	C 3	2.1
2011	*PHI*	*MLB*	*20*	*371*	*35*	*18*	*1*	*9*	*39*	*15*	*98*	*0*	*0*	*.218/.250/.351*	*.209*	*.271*	*0.0*	*C 1*	*-0.5*

Valle is a Mexican signee whose best asset is his ability to hit for power. He was extremely streaky in 2010, but he finished the season on a strong note. He will have to gain plate discipline as he develops, but there is time for that, as he was young for A-ball. Reports on his defense—once quite poor—are slowly improving, though his arm will never be a great weapon. He'll get a chance to show that the power is real in High-A Clearwater.

Shane Victorino **CF**

Born: **11/30/1980** Age: **30**
Bats: S Throws: R Height: **5' 9"** Weight: **160**
Breakout: **2%** Improve: **48%** Collapse: **0%**
Attrition: **9%** MLB: **98%**

Comparables:
Chone Figgins, Cesar Tovar, Rafael Furcal (68)

YEAR	TEAM	LVL	AGE	PA	R	2B	3B	HR	RBI	BB	SO	SB	CS	AVG/OBP/SLG	TAv	BABIP	BRR	FRAA	WARP
2008	PHI	MLB	27	627	102	30	8	14	58	45	69	36	11	.293/.349/.447	.280	.311	11.1	CF -4, RF 2	3.8
2009	PHI	MLB	28	694	102	39	13	10	62	60	71	25	8	.292/.356/.445	.280	.313	2.2	CF -17	1.9
2010	PHI	MLB	29	648	84	26	10	18	69	53	79	34	6	.259/.327/.429	.271	.273	4.7	CF 5	3.4
2011	*PHI*	*MLB*	*30*	*595*	*74*	*28*	*6*	*12*	*69*	*51*	*66*	*29*	*8*	*.282/.346/.429*	*.274*	*.296*	*0.4*	*CF -5, RF 0*	*2.0*

This was the first year in the majors in which Victorino failed to improve as a hitter. In the first half, his problem was getting on base. In the second half, it was finding his power stroke. At his best, Victorino gets on base at an above-average clip and hits for enough power to keep pitchers honest. He is tough to beat, in large part because he is a switch-hitter who can drive the ball the other way, but in 2010, he was thwarted by righties, against whom he hit just .233/.305/.376. He'll have to adjust his approach against northpaws to raise his average, and with it, his OBP. That's doubly important because of how dangerous he is on the basepaths: his efforts there were worth more than half a win in 2010.

Jayson Werth **RF**

Born: **5/20/1979** Age: **32**
Bats: R Throws: R Height: **6' 5"** Weight: **190**
Breakout: **0%** Improve: **25%** Collapse: **6%**
Attrition: **10%** MLB: **97%**

Comparables:
Brad Hawpe, Ryan Ludwick, Derrek Lee (70)

YEAR	TEAM	LVL	AGE	PA	R	2B	3B	HR	RBI	BB	SO	SB	CS	AVG/OBP/SLG	TAv	BABIP	BRR	FRAA	WARP
2008	PHI	MLB	29	482	74	16	3	24	67	57	119	20	1	.273/.363/.498	.302	.324	3.0	RF 0, CF 4	3.6
2009	PHI	MLB	30	676	98	26	1	36	99	91	156	20	3	.268/.373/.506	.304	.304	5.4	RF 13, CF 2	5.8
2010	PHI	MLB	31	652	107	46	2	27	85	82	147	13	3	.296/.388/.533	.326	.352	-0.1	RF -2, CF -1	5.0
2011	*WAS*	*MLB*	*32*	*534*	*74*	*25*	*1*	*23*	*73*	*71*	*121*	*13*	*3*	*.271/.372/.487*	*.299*	*.316*	*0.4*	*RF 3, CF 1*	*3.2*

Werth was the Phillies' best hitter in 2010. He had no clear weaknesses and put together the best season of his career. Like many Phillies hitters, his home-run totals have benefited from his stay in Citizens Bank Park. In the last two years, he has launched 39 home runs at home and 24 on the road, but in any park, he remains a strong fielder with a good arm, and he's a smart baserunner in ways that don't always show up on the stat sheet. Seizing the chance to be locked up long into his decline, Werth signed a seven-year, $126 million deal to stay in the NL East, this time with Washington.

PITCHERS

Danys Baez

Born: **9/10/1977** Age: **33**
Bats: **R** Throws: **R** Height: **6' 3"** Weight: **225**
Breakout: **22%** Improve: **29%** Collapse: **19%**
Attrition: **8%** MLB: **62%**

Comparables:
Doug Brocail, Marvin Freeman, Antonio Alfonseca (82)

YEAR	TEAM	LVL	AGE	W	L	SV	G	GS	IP	H	HR	BB	SO	EqBB9	EqSO9	GB%	BABIP	WHIP	ERA	FRA	WARP
2009	BAL	MLB	31	4	6	0	59	0	71^{2}	59	8	22	40	2.8	5.0	61%	.232	1.20	4.02	5.81	-0.4
2010	PHI	MLB	32	3	4	0	51	0	47^{2}	55	6	23	28	4.3	5.3	57%	.314	1.70	5.48	6.05	-0.7
2011	*PHI*	*MLB*	*33*	*3*	*1*	*0*	*57*	*0*	*59*	*61*	*8*	*24*	*32*	*3.6*	*4.9*	*50%*	*.284*	*1.44*	*4.78*	*5.20*	*-0.4*

The notion that a reliever with one thoroughly average year on his record after undergoing Tommy John surgery deserved a guaranteed two-year contract is exactly the kind of thing that makes reasonable fans bang their head against the wall. Baez had terrible peripherals, in large part due to disappearing command of his fastball and a tendency for his breaking ball to hang out over the plate. The result was a finish among the 30 worst relievers in both walk and strikeout rates (minimum 40 innings pitched). There is nothing laudatory about Baez's season except that the next one can't possibly be this bad, even if it's wiped out by another injury.

Antonio Bastardo

Born: **9/21/1985** Age: **25**
Bats: **L** Throws: **L** Height: **5' 11"** Weight: **195**
Breakout: **10%** Improve: **13%** Collapse: **5%**
Attrition: **1%** MLB: **21%**

Comparables:
Dave LaRoche, Cecilio Guante, Bobby Ayala (75)

YEAR	TEAM	LVL	AGE	W	L	SV	G	GS	IP	H	HR	BB	SO	EqBB9	EqSO9	GB%	BABIP	WHIP	ERA	FRA	WARP
2008	CLR	A+	22	2	0	0	5	5	30^{2}	20	2	10	47	2.9	13.8	27%	.300	1.01	1.17	0.75	1.9
2008	REA	AA	22	2	5	0	14	14	67	56	13	37	62	5.0	8.3	32%	.242	1.40	3.76	4.59	1.1
2009	REA	AA	23	2	2	3	11	5	36	22	1	7	41	1.8	10.3	44%	.253	0.86	1.75	2.47	1.5
2009	PHI	MLB	23	2	3	0	6	5	23^{2}	26	4	9	19	3.4	7.2	26%	.306	1.56	6.46	6.52	-0.2
2010	PHI	MLB	24	2	0	0	25	0	18^{2}	19	1	9	26	4.3	12.5	35%	.375	1.61	4.34	3.43	0.3
2011	*PHI*	*MLB*	*25*	*5*	*4*	*0*	*32*	*9*	*66*	*61*	*8*	*31*	*62*	*4.3*	*8.5*	*39%*	*.295*	*1.40*	*4.23*	*4.60*	*0.9*

Despite a season interrupted by elbow problems, Bastardo has made the necessary adjustments to project as a useful bullpen lefty. He has also shown improved command of his two-plane slider, which Bastardo used as an out pitch last season after setting it up with a mid-90s fastball. He also throws a nice changeup that keeps hitters from cheating on the heater. More promisingly, his strong peripherals in both Triple-A and the majors were not the residue of situational use: he had good numbers against both righties and lefties. His improvements have earned him a spot in the bullpen, and a strong showing in spring training could make Bastardo the team's go-to southpaw in 2011.

Jesse Biddle

Born: **10/22/1991** Age: **19**
Bats: **L** Throws: **L** Height: **6' 4"** Weight: **225**
Breakout: **0%** Improve: **0%** Collapse: **0%**
Attrition: **0%** MLB: **0%**

Comparables:
Sandy Koufax, Larry Dierker, Don Drysdale (83)

YEAR	TEAM	LVL	AGE	W	L	SV	G	GS	IP	H	HR	BB	SO	EqBB9	EqSO9	GB%	BABIP	WHIP	ERA	FRA	WARP
2010	PHL	Rk	18	3	1	0	9	9	33^{1}	35	2	9	41	2.4	11.1	44%	.355	1.39	4.32	4.34	1.8
2011	*PHI*	*MLB*	*19*	*4*	*5*	*0*	*11*	*11*	*44^{2}*	*46*	*6*	*27*	*32*	*5.5*	*6.5*	*44%*	*.300*	*1.65*	*5.29*	*5.75*	*0.5*

Philadelphia's Biddle family has deep roots in the nation's history. Nicholas Biddle was president of the Second Bank of the United States. Now, a later Biddle hopes to take the mount at Citizens Bank Park. The Phillies' first-round pick in 2010 signed early and got to work immediately in the rookie- and short-season leagues. A local high-school selection, Biddle impressed scouts with his secondary offerings despite the fact that his prep seasons were interrupted by cold weather. The big lefty throws a low-90s fastball that has potential to add velocity and sink as he develops. His breaking ball also holds the promise of an average pitch. The early returns were promising, but Biddle has a long way to go before he'll be ready for the big leagues. He should open the year with Low-A Lakewood and advance at a moderate pace.

Joe Blanton

Born: **12/11/1980** Age: **30**
Bats: **R** Throws: **R** Height: **6' 3"** Weight: **225**
Breakout: **8%** Improve: **38%** Collapse: **19%**
Attrition: **6%** MLB: **97%**

Comparables:
Dave Bush, Jim Kaat, Don Drysdale (70)

YEAR	TEAM	LVL	AGE	W	L	SV	G	GS	IP	H	HR	BB	SO	EqBB9	EqSO9	GB%	BABIP	WHIP	ERA	FRA	WARP
2008	OAK	MLB	27	5	12	0	20	20	127	145	12	35	62	2.5	4.4	47%	.302	1.43	4.96	5.19	0.3
2008	PHI	MLB	27	4	0	0	13	13	70^{2}	66	10	31	49	3.9	6.2	42%	.264	1.42	4.20	4.88	0.7
2009	PHI	MLB	28	12	8	0	31	31	195^{1}	198	30	59	163	2.7	7.5	42%	.291	1.36	4.05	4.00	3.4
2010	PHI	MLB	29	9	6	0	29	28	175^{2}	206	27	43	134	2.2	6.9	42%	.321	1.43	4.82	4.68	1.4
2011	*PHI*	*MLB*	*30*	*12*	*12*	*0*	*33*	*33*	*202^{2}*	*222*	*28*	*55*	*131*	*2.5*	*5.8*	*44%*	*.302*	*1.37*	*4.46*	*4.85*	*2.7*

When the Phillies traded Cliff Lee and used most of the cash savings to sign Joe Blanton to a three-year, $24 million extension, many observers wept. Lee was a T-bone steak and Blanton was ground beef. The runs weren't lean for Blanton, either, at least in the first half. The innings eater improved his strikeout rate by nearly 50 percent after the All-Star break, and the drop in balls in play mitigated the damage that his high BABIP could wreak. Still, Blanton's rate of hits on balls in play was 30 points higher than both the team's as a whole and his own career average, and his arsenal has not changed significantly over time, so expect improvement. Cheeseburgers may not be as succulent as steak, but they can be equally filling. With Lee back in town, this cheeseburger may be digested in another city, as Blanton was rumored to be heading to all points on the compass as we went to press.

Drew Carpenter

Born: **5/18/1985** Age: **26**
Bats: R Throws: R Height: **6' 3"** Weight: **225**
Breakout: **18%** Improve: **20%** Collapse: **26%**
Attrition: **18%** MLB: **33%**

Comparables:
Tobi Stoner, Enrique Gonzalez, Jason Vargas (78)

YEAR	TEAM	LVL	AGE	W	L	SV	G	GS	IP	H	HR	BB	SO	EqBB9	EqSO9	GB%	BABIP	WHIP	ERA	FRA	WARP
2008	CLR	A+	23	3	3	0	8	8	52^1	44	2	9	32	1.5	5.5	34%	.258	1.03	2.75	2.91	1.7
2008	REA	AA	23	6	8	0	16	16	93^2	114	13	30	69	2.9	6.6	45%	.334	1.57	5.57	6.36	-0.4
2008	PHI	MLB	23	0	0	0	1	0	1	1	0	1	1	9.0	9.0	33%	.333	2.00	0.00	0.91	0.0
2009	LEH	AAA	24	11	6	0	25	26	156	162	18	47	120	2.7	6.9	41%	.307	1.35	3.29	4.19	2.2
2009	PHI	MLB	24	1	0	0	3	1	5^2	11	1	4	5	6.4	7.9	50%	.476	2.82	11.12	17.49	-0.1
2010	LEH	AAA	25	8	11	0	27	27	151	152	18	54	116	3.2	6.9	40%	.296	1.41	4.05	5.73	-0.2
2010	PHI	MLB	25	0	1	0	1	0	3	5	1	0	2	0.0	6.0	42%	.364	1.67	9.00	7.08	-0.1
2011	*PHI*	*MLB*	*26*	*7*	*9*	*0*	*21*	*21*	*126*	*143*	*20*	*49*	*74*	*3.5*	*5.3*	*42%*	*.302*	*1.52*	*5.26*	*5.72*	*0.5*

This is what it looks like when a prospect hits a wall in Triple-A. Carpenter was a second-round selection for the Phillies in 2006, but he has been mediocre since climbing from Clearwater to Lehigh Valley in 2008. In 2010 he took no steps forward, which in reality is a step back for a pitcher without the strikeout stuff to impress the front office. Add to that the fact that he faced an average of three fewer batters per outing and walked an extra batter every third start in comparison to the previous year, and Carpenter's path to the big leagues looks hazy at best.

Brody Colvin

Born: **8/14/1990** Age: **20**
Bats: R Throws: R Height: **6' 3"** Weight: **195**
Breakout: **0%** Improve: **2%** Collapse: **0%**
Attrition: **0%** MLB: **2%**

Comparables:
Lindy McDaniel, Dick Brodowski, Milt Pappas (76)

YEAR	TEAM	LVL	AGE	W	L	SV	G	GS	IP	H	HR	BB	SO	EqBB9	EqSO9	GB%	BABIP	WHIP	ERA	FRA	WARP
2010	LWD	A	19	6	8	0	27	27	138	138	7	42	120	2.7	7.8	52%	.315	1.37	3.39	4.44	1.6
2011	*PHI*	*MLB*	*20*	*4*	*6*	*0*	*14*	*14*	*70^2*	*76*	*9*	*35*	*41*	*4.5*	*5.3*	*46%*	*.296*	*1.57*	*5.19*	*5.64*	*0.5*

The Phillies worked hard to get Colvin in the system; after selecting him in the seventh round of the 2009 draft, they had to pry him away from a firm commitment to pitch for LSU. Going the extra yard (and tossing a $900,000 bonus his way) has started to pay off, as Colvin had the strongest finish of any pitcher in the system. He posted a 2.40 ERA in 45 innings with a 40/11 strikeout-to-walk ratio in his final 10 starts of the season. His big frame could allow him to bump up his low-90s velocity as he develops, and he supplements the fastball with a power downer curve that serves as an out pitch. The biggest knock against Colvin is his delivery, which has a lot of moving parts, but he throws downhill and appeared to drink from the cup of repeatability at season's end. This season, he'll move up to High-A Clearwater, where he'll be a few years younger than the competition. Colvin may take a while to develop, but his upside now seems higher than it did when he was drafted.

Jose Contreras

Born: **12/12/1971** Age: **39**
Bats: R Throws: R Height: **6' 4"** Weight: **224**
Breakout: **11%** Improve: **30%** Collapse: **17%**
Attrition: **8%** MLB: **63%**

Comparables:
Gaylord Perry, Chuck Finley, David Wells (61)

YEAR	TEAM	LVL	AGE	W	L	SV	G	GS	IP	H	HR	BB	SO	EqBB9	EqSO9	GB%	BABIP	WHIP	ERA	FRA	WARP
2008	CHA	MLB	36	7	6	0	20	20	121	130	12	35	70	2.6	5.2	53%	.294	1.39	4.54	4.85	1.3
2009	CHR	AAA	37	3	1	0	5	5	33^1	19	2	16	27	4.3	7.3	49%	.195	1.11	2.43	3.99	0.6
2009	CHA	MLB	37	5	13	0	21	21	114^2	121	11	45	89	3.5	7.0	50%	.304	1.50	5.42	6.57	-0.5
2009	COL	MLB	37	1	0	0	7	2	17	20	2	8	17	4.2	9.0	47%	.367	1.65	1.59	-0.05	1.1
2010	PHI	MLB	38	6	4	4	67	0	56^2	53	5	16	57	2.5	9.1	47%	.318	1.29	3.34	3.58	0.7
2011	*PHI*	*MLB*	*39*	*9*	*8*	*1*	*52*	*21*	*148*	*154*	*17*	*52*	*99*	*3.1*	*6.0*	*48%*	*.297*	*1.39*	*4.36*	*4.74*	*1.8*

The big Cuban righty experienced a second career renaissance, this time in the Philadelphia bullpen. When he signed, there was talk that he might start games, but Contreras showed electric stuff in the late innings and immediately became one of the go-to relievers for tight situations. The result was the highest strikeout-to-walk ratio of his career, thanks to a rejuvenated fastball and a wicked forkball with a unique grip (his thumb never touches the ball). The Phillies liked what they saw and inked Contreras to a two-year, $5.5 million deal in November—nearly the same deal that his countryman, Baez, signed a year earlier. Suffice it to say that Contreras is a better bet.

Jarred Cosart

Born: **5/25/1990** Age: **21**
Bats: **R** Throws: **R** Height: **6' 3"** Weight: **180**
Breakout: **0%** Improve: **0%** Collapse: **0%**
Attrition: **0%** MLB: **0%**

Comparables:
Josh Beckett, Leo Kiely, Andy Rincon (80)

YEAR	TEAM	LVL	AGE	W	L	SV	G	GS	IP	H	HR	BB	SO	EqBB9	EqSO9	GB%	BABIP	WHIP	ERA	FRA	WARP
2009	PHL	Rk	19	2	2	0	7	5	24^{1}	12	0	7	25	2.6	9.3	45%	.203	0.82	2.22	4.15	0.8
2010	LWD	A	20	7	3	0	14	14	71^{1}	60	3	16	77	2.0	9.7	59%	.298	1.14	3.79	4.46	0.7
2011	*PHI*	*MLB*	*21*	*3*	*3*	*0*	*9*	*9*	42^{1}	*41*	*5*	*18*	*32*	*3.8*	*6.7*	*47%*	*.293*	*1.41*	*4.33*	*4.71*	*0.8*

Tall, lanky, and Texan, Cosart did as much to improve his stock in 2010 as anyone in the Phillies system. Before the season began, he was a projectable arm with fewer than 25 pro innings under his belt. By the time he was shut down with a sore elbow (which did not require surgery) in early August, Cosart had done a two-step on his Sally League competition. His stuff is very good now and should only improve; right now, he has a mid-90s fastball, a good curveball, and a developing changeup. Cosart's task will be to refine his secondary offerings and throw plenty of innings. He should open the year with High-A Clearwater with the potential to reach Reading by the end of the season.

Justin De Fratus

Born: **10/21/1987** Age: **23**
Bats: **S** Throws: **R** Height: **6' 4"** Weight: **215**
Breakout: **2%** Improve: **3%** Collapse: **0%**
Attrition: **3%** MLB: **3%**

Comparables:
Jaime Garcia, Cesar Jimenez, Bo McLaughlin (84)

YEAR	TEAM	LVL	AGE	W	L	SV	G	GS	IP	H	HR	BB	SO	EqBB9	EqSO9	GB%	BABIP	WHIP	ERA	FRA	WARP
2008	WPT	A-	20	6	5	0	14	14	83^{1}	87	1	25	74	2.7	8.0	46%	.325	1.37	3.67	3.25	2.1
2009	LWD	A	21	5	6	3	36	12	110	108	3	16	101	1.3	8.3	58%	.324	1.22	2.78	2.15	3.9
2010	CLR	A+	22	2	0	15	29	0	40^{1}	31	1	11	43	2.5	9.7	54%	.294	1.10	1.79	1.70	1.5
2010	REA	AA	22	1	0	6	20	0	24^{2}	17	2	5	28	1.9	10.4	49%	.254	0.91	2.19	3.32	0.4
2011	*PHI*	*MLB*	*23*	*3*	*3*	*3*	*32*	*6*	*70*	*81*	*9*	*27*	*43*	*3.5*	*5.5*	*47%*	*.312*	*1.52*	*5.11*	*5.56*	*-0.2*

De Fratus showed strong results in his first full year as a reliever. The control he exhibited as a starter translated well to the bullpen, and his success carried over to the Arizona Fall League, where he was named a Rising Star and impressed scouts with his effective fastball/slider combo. Most of his mid-90s velocity comes from his lower half; fortunately, his frame looks like the kind that could handle a heavy workload in relief. His ultimate future is definitely as a reliever, but don't cry for his lost potential, as he could be a very good late-inning arm.

Chad Durbin

Born: **12/3/1977** Age: **33**
Bats: **S** Throws: **R** Height: **6' 2"** Weight: **200**
Breakout: **21%** Improve: **35%** Collapse: **21%**
Attrition: **19%** MLB: **85%**

Comparables:
Hank Aguirre, Dick Tidrow, Ernie Johnson (74)

YEAR	TEAM	LVL	AGE	W	L	SV	G	GS	IP	H	HR	BB	SO	EqBB9	EqSO9	GB%	BABIP	WHIP	ERA	FRA	WARP
2008	PHI	MLB	30	5	4	1	71	0	87^{2}	81	5	35	63	3.6	6.5	48%	.296	1.37	2.87	3.44	1.6
2009	PHI	MLB	31	2	2	2	59	0	69^{2}	56	8	47	62	6.1	8.0	40%	.253	1.58	4.39	5.44	-0.4
2010	PHI	MLB	32	4	1	0	64	0	68^{2}	63	7	28	63	3.7	8.3	45%	.296	1.40	3.67	3.62	0.9
2011	*PHI*	*MLB*	*33*	*5*	*2*	*0*	*95*	*0*	*109*	*106*	*14*	*48*	*77*	*4.0*	*6.4*	*45%*	*.283*	*1.41*	*4.43*	*4.81*	*-0.2*

If you ever want to make a persuasive argument that the freely available starters of today can become the useful bullpen stalwarts of tomorrow, you'd be wise to have Chad Durbin's story handy. The Phillies signed and stuck him in the bullpen after he washed out of the Tigers' rotation and was nontendered by Detroit. Much of Durbin's subsequent success has come from his ability to strand runners and from his improved strikeout rates, and his two-seam fastball has enough movement to keep hitters off-balance.

Roy Halladay

Born: **5/14/1977** Age: **34**
Bats: **R** Throws: **R** Height: **6' 6"** Weight: **225**
Breakout: **18%** Improve: **48%** Collapse: **18%**
Attrition: **4%** MLB: **94%**

Comparables:
Hiroki Kuroda, Javier Vazquez, Gaylord Perry (47)

YEAR	TEAM	LVL	AGE	W	L	SV	G	GS	IP	H	HR	BB	SO	EqBB9	EqSO9	GB%	BABIP	WHIP	ERA	FRA	WARP
2008	TOR	MLB	31	20	11	0	34	33	246	220	18	39	206	1.4	7.5	54%	.284	1.10	2.78	3.29	6.4
2009	TOR	MLB	32	17	10	0	32	32	239	234	22	35	208	1.3	7.8	51%	.306	1.15	2.79	2.93	7.7
2010	PHI	MLB	33	21	10	0	33	33	250^{2}	231	24	30	219	1.1	7.9	53%	.290	1.07	2.44	2.66	8.1
2011	*PHI*	*MLB*	*34*	*14*	*8*	*0*	*32*	*32*	*239*	*229*	*24*	*37*	*183*	*1.4*	*6.9*	*51%*	*.294*	*1.11*	*3.05*	*3.32*	*6.8*

Isn't it reassuring to know that some things are still as good as advertised? Halladay's 2010 immediately became one of the greatest pitcher seasons of all time, a dominant regular season studded with a perfect game and a post-season no-hitter. The move to the senior circuit was kind, as Halladay improved in more mundane player-evaluation terms as well. He increased his strikeout-to-walk ratio for the fourth straight season and issued unintentional walks to fewer than three percent of the batters he faced. His new changeup—a split-fingered sweet nothing to the low, outside corner—made him deadlier than ever when he was ahead in the count. Taken literally, Halladay's WARP (the highest of his career) suggests that without him, the Phillies wouldn't have even made the playoffs. He's the rare player who demands agreement among anyone who has ever considered baseball a worthwhile pastime. This is a Hall of Famer at his peak. Watch him every chance you get.

Cole Hamels

Born: **12/27/1983** Age: **27**
Bats: **L** Throws: **L** Height: **6' 3"** Weight: **175**
Breakout: **12%** Improve: **39%** Collapse: **34%**
Attrition: **7%** MLB: **97%**

Comparables:
Ervin Santana, Javier Vazquez, Jack McDowell (64)

YEAR	TEAM	LVL	AGE	W	L	SV	G	GS	IP	H	HR	BB	SO	EqBB9	EqSO9	GB%	BABIP	WHIP	ERA	FRA	WARP
2008	PHI	MLB	24	14	10	0	33	33	227^{1}	193	28	53	196	2.1	7.8	41%	.260	1.09	3.09	3.93	4.4
2009	PHI	MLB	25	10	11	0	32	32	193^{2}	206	24	43	168	2.0	7.8	44%	.317	1.31	4.32	4.26	3.0
2010	PHI	MLB	26	12	11	0	33	33	208^{2}	185	26	60	211	2.6	9.1	47%	.289	1.21	3.06	3.23	5.3
2011	*PHI*	*MLB*	*27*	*13*	*9*	*0*	*31*	*31*	*200*	*186*	*27*	*52*	*177*	*2.3*	*8.0*	*44%*	*.289*	*1.19*	*3.56*	*3.87*	*4.8*

Hamels' 2010 season was a vindication of statistical principles. Prior to the season, the tall lefty might well have had the words DON'T PANIC tattooed in large, friendly letters on his forehead, thanks to stellar peripherals, but that didn't prevent many observers from declaring him an endangered species. Sure enough, his BABIP fell back in line and his ERA was good enough for 12th in the league. Nevertheless, luck rewards those who help themselves, and Hamels' biggest adjustment came via the addition of a cutter—a trick he learned from watching Lee and Halladay. The cutter was especially tough on lefties, and Hamels has begun to double back on his reverse career split (a feature he owes to his primary out pitch, the changeup). With plenty of options against batters from both sides of the plate, Hamels was able to go deeper in games and clean up his own messes. That bodes well for the future, doubly so since he has remained healthy of late.

Austin Hyatt

Born: **5/23/1986** Age: **25**
Bats: **R** Throws: **R** Height: **6' 2"** Weight: **180**
Breakout: **19%** Improve: **46%** Collapse: **20%**
Attrition: **19%** MLB: **82%**

Comparables:
Ramon Ramirez, Gio Gonzalez, Francisco Liriano (63)

YEAR	TEAM	LVL	AGE	W	L	SV	G	GS	IP	H	HR	BB	SO	EqBB9	EqSO9	GB%	BABIP	WHIP	ERA	FRA	WARP
2009	WPT	A-	23	3	0	6	17	5	54^{1}	26	1	12	81	2.0	13.4	33%	.238	0.70	0.66	2.48	1.7
2010	CLR	A+	24	11	5	0	23	21	124^{1}	100	5	35	156	2.5	11.3	38%	.317	1.11	3.04	2.78	4.2
2010	REA	AA	24	0	0	0	4	4	22	21	4	9	25	3.7	10.2	32%	.293	1.41	4.50	4.58	0.2
2011	*PHI*	*MLB*	*25*	*6*	*4*	*0*	*25*	*13*	*98*	*89*	*11*	*40*	*101*	*3.7*	*9.2*	*39%*	*.301*	*1.31*	*3.70*	*4.02*	*2.0*

Hyatt has had more success on the mound than he has in Google's PageRank: the Texas hotel still has him comfortably beat. The Phillies made reservations with the former Alabama Friday night starter in the 15th round of the 2009 draft, and the early results have been encouraging. Hyatt has luxurious control, and his commitment to excellence was recently recognized via the Florida State League Pitcher of the Year honors. The offerings themselves, though, are rather Spartan. Hyatt offers hitters only two views: a fastball and a slider. A third pitch, like the third AAA Diamond, is critical to success in this industry. Hyatt will get an extended stay at Double-A, and his success will dictate his timetable.

Kyle Kendrick

Born: **8/26/1984** Age: **26**
Bats: **R** Throws: **R** Height: **6' 3"** Weight: **190**
Breakout: **11%** Improve: **39%** Collapse: **10%**
Attrition: **2%** MLB: **68%**

Comparables:
Jeff Weaver, Ross Grimsley, Bill Laskey (72)

YEAR	TEAM	LVL	AGE	W	L	SV	G	GS	IP	H	HR	BB	SO	EqBB9	EqSO9	GB%	BABIP	WHIP	ERA	FRA	WARP
2008	PHI	MLB	23	11	9	0	31	30	155^{2}	194	23	57	68	3.3	3.9	46%	.305	1.70	5.49	5.97	-0.1
2009	LEH	AAA	24	9	7	0	24	24	143	133	9	35	62	2.2	3.9	52%	.262	1.21	3.34	4.76	1.1
2009	PHI	MLB	24	3	1	0	9	2	26^{1}	27	1	9	15	3.1	5.1	57%	.302	1.41	3.42	4.45	0.2
2010	PHI	MLB	25	11	10	0	33	31	180^{2}	199	26	49	84	2.4	4.2	45%	.284	1.39	4.73	5.36	0.2
2011	*PHI*	*MLB*	*26*	*10*	*12*	*0*	*31*	*31*	*173^{1}*	*196*	*24*	*53*	*69*	*2.8*	*3.6*	*47%*	*.290*	*1.44*	*4.98*	*5.42*	*1.4*

It wasn't the plan for Kendrick to get this many innings, but it takes quite a mental gymnastics routine to believe that nobody foresaw Jamie Moyer succumbing to injury. Kendrick struck out fewer batters than any other title qualifier, his slider is still a cookie, and he no longer generates a significant number of ground balls. He turned in nine Disaster Starts (more runs than innings pitched) out of 31 in 2010 and did it all while looking like the same pitcher he's always been. He's worth a roster spot only at the league minimum, which gives him one more year to find a way to strike hitters out.

Brad Lidge

Born: **12/23/1976** Age: **34**
Bats: **R** Throws: **R** Height: **6' 5"** Weight: **200**
Breakout: **18%** Improve: **33%** Collapse: **25%**
Attrition: **18%** MLB: **74%**

Comparables:
Joe Nelson, Billy Taylor, Francisco Cordero (72)

YEAR	TEAM	LVL	AGE	W	L	SV	G	GS	IP	H	HR	BB	SO	EqBB9	EqSO9	GB%	BABIP	WHIP	ERA	FRA	WARP
2008	PHI	MLB	31	2	0	41	72	0	69^{1}	50	2	35	92	4.5	11.9	48%	.296	1.24	1.95	1.97	2.2
2009	PHI	MLB	32	0	8	31	67	0	58^{2}	72	11	34	61	5.2	9.4	41%	.355	1.89	7.21	6.56	-0.9
2010	PHI	MLB	33	1	1	27	50	0	45^{2}	32	5	24	52	4.7	10.2	40%	.243	1.25	2.96	3.67	0.5
2011	*PHI*	*MLB*	*34*	*4*	*1*	*15*	*73*	*0*	*67*	*60*	*8*	*34*	*72*	*4.5*	*9.7*	*44%*	*.301*	*1.40*	*4.11*	*4.47*	*0.1*

From a results standpoint, it isn't hard to see why Lidge was miles ahead of his 2009 form last season. The change was patent: the slider was back in a big way. In Lidge's best years, the mid-90s fastball was just a way to set up the breaking ball, not the other way around. For the first time since 2008, Lidge would snap off a slider and the hitters would flinch. His fastball has lost a tick in the interim, so he will have to keep that crisp slider to maintain his results. Given how bad things were two years ago, an old age of unsexy closing isn't the least dignified exit he could have had.

Ryan Madson

Born: **8/28/1980** Age: **30**
Bats: **L** Throws: **R** Height: **6' 6"** Weight: **180**
Breakout: **21%** Improve: **37%** Collapse: **19%**
Attrition: **15%** MLB: **65%**

Comparables:
Steve Hamilton, John Grabow, Juan Rincon (70)

YEAR	TEAM	LVL	AGE	W	L	SV	G	GS	IP	H	HR	BB	SO	EqBB9	EqSO9	GB%	BABIP	WHIP	ERA	FRA	WARP
2008	PHI	MLB	27	4	2	1	76	0	82^{2}	79	6	23	67	2.5	7.3	52%	.300	1.25	3.05	3.37	1.6
2009	PHI	MLB	28	5	5	10	79	0	77^{1}	73	7	22	78	2.6	9.1	48%	.314	1.27	3.26	3.10	1.3
2010	PHI	MLB	29	6	2	5	55	0	53	42	4	13	64	2.2	10.9	51%	.288	1.11	2.55	2.79	1.1
2011	*PHI*	*MLB*	*30*	*4*	*2*	*3*	*85*	*0*	*84*	*81*	*9*	*27*	*75*	*2.8*	*8.0*	*48%*	*.301*	*1.26*	*3.64*	*3.96*	*0.7*

In 2004, the team's inaugural season at CBP and his rookie year, Madson recorded a PhanaVision promo thanking the Phillies for building him a brand new ballpark. Since then, he's become a Broad Street panacea and is now one of the five or so best nonclosing relievers in baseball. Last season was Madson's second year as the Phillies' best reliever, as well as the best of his career, and his changeup remains one of the best pitches in the game. Statistically, he has been at his best in high-leverage situations, but at the same time, his split in save situations is decidedly worse than in nonsave situations. However unlikely it seems, Madson might just be that rare beast: the natural set-up guy.

Scott Mathieson

Born: **2/27/1984** Age: **27**
Bats: **R** Throws: **R** Height: **6' 3"** Weight: **190**
Breakout: **4%** Improve: **8%** Collapse: **6%**
Attrition: **8%** MLB: **15%**

Comparables:
Carlos Guevara, Clay Zavada, Sergio Romo (80)

YEAR	TEAM	LVL	AGE	W	L	SV	G	GS	IP	H	HR	BB	SO	EqBB9	EqSO9	GB%	BABIP	WHIP	ERA	FRA	WARP
2009	REA	AA	25	2	0	1	14	0	21^{1}	15	1	7	18	3.0	7.6	40%	.237	1.03	2.53	3.61	0.3
2010	LEH	AAA	26	3	6	26	54	0	64^{1}	49	8	24	83	3.4	11.7	38%	.285	1.19	2.80	3.88	1.0
2010	PHI	MLB	26	0	0	0	2	0	1^{2}	5	0	2	1	10.8	5.4	56%	.556	4.20	10.80	6.18	0.0
2011	*PHI*	*MLB*	*27*	*3*	*1*	*5*	*51*	*0*	*66*	*60*	*9*	*29*	*64*	*3.9*	*8.7*	*43%*	*.288*	*1.32*	*3.93*	*4.27*	*0.3*

Throw 100 mph? Check. Strike out approximately a third of Triple-A batters faced? Yessir. Close games effectively? Got it. Allow fewer than three runs per nine? No problem, boss. It's hard to imagine what more Mathieson could have done to get a fair shake in the bigs. Apparently, the Phillies want Mathieson to be a relief robot from the future sent to save John Connor, because they brought in Bruce Sutter to teach Mathieson a splitter on top of it all. The thought of his not getting an extended audition in the major-league bullpen in 2011 is too ridiculous to fathom.

Trevor May

Born: **9/23/1989** Age: **21**
Bats: **R** Throws: **R** Height: **6' 5"** Weight: **215**
Breakout: **11%** Improve: **12%** Collapse: **2%**
Attrition: **7%** MLB: **15%**

Comparables:
Neftali Feliz, Vinegar Bend Mizell, Sam McDowell (67)

YEAR	TEAM	LVL	AGE	W	L	SV	G	GS	IP	H	HR	BB	SO	EqBB9	EqSO9	GB%	BABIP	WHIP	ERA	FRA	WARP
2009	LWD	A	19	4	1	0	15	15	77^{1}	58	3	43	95	5.0	11.1	41%	.306	1.33	2.56	2.32	3.1
2010	LWD	A	20	7	3	0	11	11	65	51	3	20	92	2.8	12.7	42%	.331	1.11	2.91	1.98	3.3
2010	CLR	A+	20	5	5	0	16	14	70	53	7	61	90	7.8	11.6	41%	.295	1.70	5.01	4.89	0.6
2011	*PHI*	*MLB*	*21*	*5*	*6*	*0*	*15*	*15*	*76^{2}*	*69*	*9*	*55*	*79*	*6.5*	*9.3*	*41%*	*.302*	*1.63*	*4.85*	*5.27*	*0.9*

May is a tall righty with little sense of the strike zone. He requires plenty of seasoning, as his rough stint at Clearwater demonstrated. Still, he has a live fastball that sits in the low-90s and a demonstrated ability to get hitters out. To hit his spots more often, he will need to find a repeatable delivery, since his follow-through can be quite erratic. After being sent back to A-ball in midseason, May was essentially unhittable. He'll try again in High-A against hitters his own age, and he won't be long for the level if his Lakewood control translates.

Jamie Moyer

Born: **11/18/1962** Age: **48**
Bats: **L** Throws: **L** Height: **6' 0"** Weight: **170**
Breakout: **0%** Improve: **1%** Collapse: **4%**
Attrition: **2%** MLB: **9%**

Comparables:
Phil Niekro, Charlie Hough, Satchel Paige (38)

YEAR	TEAM	LVL	AGE	W	L	SV	G	GS	IP	H	HR	BB	SO	EqBB9	EqSO9	GB%	BABIP	WHIP	ERA	FRA	WARP
2008	PHI	MLB	45	16	7	0	33	33	196^{1}	199	20	62	123	2.8	5.6	45%	.286	1.39	3.71	4.06	3.8
2009	PHI	MLB	46	12	10	0	30	25	162	177	27	43	94	2.4	5.2	42%	.286	1.42	4.89	5.08	0.9
2010	PHI	MLB	47	9	9	0	19	19	111^{2}	103	20	20	63	1.6	5.1	46%	.237	1.16	4.84	6.53	-1.2
2011	*PHI*	*MLB*	*48*	*10*	*12*	*0*	*30*	*30*	*174*	*193*	*31*	*53*	*75*	*2.7*	*3.9*	*44%*	*.277*	*1.41*	*4.96*	*5.39*	*1.4*

Moyer pitched 87 1/3 innings in the major leagues in 1986. Incredibly, he topped that mark in 2010, holding major-league hitters at bay for over 111 frames. His peripherals have hardly slipped in the last decade, and his 2010 walk rate equaled his career-best. Last season, his fastball sat around 80, but he still had a strikeout-to-walk ratio above three. The lefty made seven quality starts in just over half a season before an elbow injury shut him down for the remainder of the year. During a start in the Dominican Winter League, Moyer suffered another elbow injury and underwent Tommy John surgery in December. He says he wants to play again; if he's healthy, some team just may give him a shot for 2012, which would be—wait for it—his age-49 season. The PECOTA is for What-If use only.

Drew Naylor

Born: **5/31/1986** Age: **25**
Bats: **R** Throws: **R** Height: **6' 4"** Weight: **235**
Breakout: **8%** Improve: **13%** Collapse: **6%**
Attrition: **16%** MLB: **22%**

Comparables:
Tobi Stoner, Andrew Carpenter, Mitch Atkins (79)

YEAR	TEAM	LVL	AGE	W	L	SV	G	GS	IP	H	HR	BB	SO	EqBB9	EqSO9	GB%	BABIP	WHIP	ERA	FRA	WARP
2008	LWD	A	22	5	3	0	14	14	87^1	69	8	21	97	2.2	10.0	56%	.275	1.07	2.99	3.84	1.3
2008	CLR	A+	22	3	7	0	13	13	78	86	8	31	59	3.6	6.8	40%	.316	1.53	4.85	4.84	0.7
2009	CLR	A+	23	8	11	0	26	25	158	162	12	37	115	2.1	6.6	44%	.304	1.32	4.22	4.94	0.9
2010	REA	AA	24	12	10	0	27	26	167	173	12	44	113	2.4	6.1	41%	.302	1.37	4.63	4.88	1.3
2011	*PHI*	*MLB*	*25*	*6*	*8*	*0*	*19*	*19*	*116*	*135*	*17*	*46*	*63*	*3.6*	*4.9*	*43%*	*.304*	*1.55*	*5.39*	*5.86*	*0.2*

Australian for inconsistent, Naylor has a fastball that tops out in the low 80s but an effective slow curveball. The large separation in velocity between the curve and his harder stuff has led to some concern that he might be tipping the pitch. It's hard to imagine a major-league role for him without a few extra ticks on the heater, but he has control enough that he could scrape by on the kitchen-sink approach.

Roy Oswalt

Born: **8/29/1977** Age: **33**
Bats: **R** Throws: **R** Height: **6' 0"** Weight: **170**
Breakout: **13%** Improve: **44%** Collapse: **26%**
Attrition: **6%** MLB: **99%**

Comparables:
Warren Spahn, Mike Mussina, Don Sutton (71)

YEAR	TEAM	LVL	AGE	W	L	SV	G	GS	IP	H	HR	BB	SO	EqBB9	EqSO9	GB%	BABIP	WHIP	ERA	FRA	WARP
2008	HOU	MLB	30	17	10	0	32	32	208^2	199	23	47	165	2.0	7.1	51%	.285	1.23	3.54	4.14	3.5
2009	HOU	MLB	31	8	6	0	30	30	181^1	183	19	42	138	2.1	6.8	47%	.298	1.28	4.12	4.09	2.9
2010	HOU	MLB	32	6	12	0	20	20	129	109	13	33	120	2.3	8.4	45%	.273	1.12	3.42	3.80	2.1
2010	PHI	MLB	32	7	1	0	13	12	82^2	53	6	21	73	2.3	7.9	52%	.221	0.93	1.74	2.73	2.5
2011	*PHI*	*MLB*	*33*	*14*	*9*	*0*	*33*	*33*	*209*	*198*	*23*	*52*	*156*	*2.2*	*6.7*	*47%*	*.285*	*1.19*	*3.44*	*3.74*	*5.3*

After an offseason full of questions about his health, Oswalt bounced back and posted one of his finest seasons yet. His stuff—not to mention the degenerative disc in his back—was no worse for the wear. Oswalt posted a 1.74 ERA after his midseason change of address, although his peripherals merely held steady after he bid Houston farewell. At this point, he has a career 3.13 ERA—nearly a fifth of a run better than Halladay's—and 150 wins. He is a year younger than the team's most conspicuous ace and has a strong, if limited, postseason résumé. If he can garner a few more top-line black ink accomplishments (a Cy Young wouldn't hurt), he might just have a shot at the Hall in a dozen years.

Juan Ramirez

Born: **8/16/1988** Age: **22**
Bats: **R** Throws: **R** Height: **6' 3"** Weight: **225**
Breakout: **0%** Improve: **0%** Collapse: **0%**
Attrition: **0%** MLB: **0%**

Comparables:
Tony Brizzolara, Joe Moeller, Kevin Gross (76)

YEAR	TEAM	LVL	AGE	W	L	SV	G	GS	IP	H	HR	BB	SO	EqBB9	EqSO9	GB%	BABIP	WHIP	ERA	FRA	WARP
2008	WIS	A	19	6	9	0	25	22	124	112	9	38	113	2.8	8.2	49%	.293	1.31	3.63	4.31	1.6
2009	HDS	A+	20	8	10	0	28	27	142^1	153	18	53	111	3.4	7.0	45%	.311	1.57	5.12	5.56	1.0
2010	CLR	A+	21	4	3	0	11	11	64^1	63	2	17	55	2.4	7.7	41%	.319	1.37	4.06	3.95	1.2
2010	REA	AA	21	3	4	0	13	13	77^2	89	11	24	60	2.8	7.0	36%	.321	1.49	5.45	4.95	0.5
2011	*PHI*	*MLB*	*22*	*5*	*9*	*0*	*19*	*19*	*102*	*120*	*17*	*51*	*57*	*4.5*	*5.0*	*42%*	*.303*	*1.66*	*6.17*	*6.71*	*-0.5*

A bit of flawed booty received from the Mariners in the Lee trade, a deal no less disastrous for the Phillies getting Lee back via free agency, Ramirez is broken. He's always been a big, projectable pitcher with good stuff and little idea how to use it, and he lacks a strong secondary pitch to match his plus fastball. His season ended with hip-labrum surgery, and while he is expected to be ready by spring training, it might take time to see if he could hack it as a reliever.

J. C. Romero

Born: **6/4/1976** Age: **35**
Bats: **S** Throws: **L** Height: **5' 11"** Weight: **195**
Breakout: **13%** Improve: **28%** Collapse: **18%**
Attrition: **11%** MLB: **65%**

Comparables:
Bruce Ruffin, Paul Shuey, Mike Myers (75)

YEAR	TEAM	LVL	AGE	W	L	SV	G	GS	IP	H	HR	BB	SO	EqBB9	EqSO9	GB%	BABIP	WHIP	ERA	FRA	WARP
2008	PHI	MLB	32	4	4	1	81	0	59	41	5	38	52	5.8	7.9	63%	.232	1.42	2.75	3.80	0.8
2009	PHI	MLB	33	0	0	0	21	0	162	13	2	13	12	7.0	6.5	54%	.250	1.68	2.70	4.23	0.1
2010	PHI	MLB	34	1	0	3	60	0	36^2	30	3	29	28	7.1	6.9	61%	.255	1.75	3.93	4.59	0.1
2011	*PHI*	*MLB*	*35*	*3*	*1*	*1*	*62*	*0*	*45*	*41*	*5*	*31*	*35*	*6.1*	*6.9*	*50%*	*.276*	*1.57*	*4.72*	*5.13*	*-0.3*

Romero should never be allowed to face righties—they have a career .381 OBP against him—but he still has value against lefties. LOOGYs don't have $4-million-per-year value, though, which is why the Phillies declined his option. (They subsequently re-signed him for just over a quarter of that amount.) Romero has barely thrown 50 innings in the last two seasons. Nevertheless, he has long had the ground-ball-aided ability to outperform his strikeout and walk rates; he also hasn't had a BABIP above .265 since 2006.

Vance Worley

Born: **9/25/1987** Age: **23**
Bats: **R** Throws: **R** Height: **6' 2"** Weight: **230**
Breakout: **8%** Improve: **23%** Collapse: **6%**
Attrition: **9%** MLB: **40%**

Comparables:
Don Larsen, Joe Kennedy, Steve Cooke (68)

YEAR	TEAM	LVL	AGE	W	L	SV	G	GS	IP	H	HR	BB	SO	EqBB9	EqSO9	GB%	BABIP	WHIP	ERA	FRA	WARP
2008	LWD	A	20	3	2	0	11	11	61	58	4	7	53	1.0	7.8	56%	.297	1.11	2.66	4.15	0.9
2009	REA	AA	21	7	12	0	27	27	153^1	163	17	49	100	2.9	5.9	43%	.299	1.42	5.34	5.47	0.2
2010	REA	AA	22	9	4	0	19	19	112^2	114	9	36	83	2.9	6.7	47%	.303	1.36	3.20	4.02	2.1
2010	LEH	AAA	22	1	3	0	8	8	45^1	46	3	10	36	2.0	7.2	52%	.314	1.26	3.77	3.12	1.3
2010	PHI	MLB	22	1	1	0	5	2	13	8	1	4	12	2.8	8.3	51%	.206	0.92	1.38	1.72	0.6
2011	*PHI*	*MLB*	*23*	*7*	*8*	*0*	*21*	*21*	*122^1*	*137*	*17*	*44*	*69*	*3.2*	*5.1*	*45%*	*.302*	*1.48*	*5.03*	*5.47*	*0.9*

The bespectacled Worley benefited greatly from a second go-round at Reading, earning himself a pair of major-league starts late in the season. He didn't run out of steam the way he had in 2009, and he pitched well in Triple-A. He won't be better than a fourth starter, but he's a good bet to surpass Kyle Kendrick. Worley's repertoire consists mainly of a fastball, a slider, and a curve, with his changeup serving as more of a show-me pitch. He'll get a crack at the fifth starter's job in camp.

Mike Zagurski

Born: **1/27/1983** Age: **28**
Bats: **L** Throws: **L** Height: **6' 0"** Weight: **225**
Breakout: **11%** Improve: **28%** Collapse: **16%**
Attrition: **11%** MLB: **50%**

Comparables:
Don McMahon, Ken Howell, Mark Worrell (71)

YEAR	TEAM	LVL	AGE	W	L	SV	G	GS	IP	H	HR	BB	SO	EqBB9	EqSO9	GB%	BABIP	WHIP	ERA	FRA	WARP
2009	REA	AA	26	3	4	8	45	0	53	42	7	27	63	4.6	10.7	46%	.267	1.38	3.57	3.94	0.5
2010	LEH	AAA	27	2	3	3	52	0	52^1	44	3	27	71	4.7	12.3	49%	.328	1.40	3.27	3.11	1.4
2010	PHI	MLB	27	0	0	0	8	0	7	8	1	5	11	6.4	14.1	31%	.467	2.14	10.29	9.39	-0.4
2011	*PHI*	*MLB*	*28*	*3*	*1*	*1*	*53*	*0*	*56*	*50*	*6*	*29*	*61*	*4.6*	*9.8*	*45%*	*.304*	*1.40*	*4.09*	*4.44*	*0.1*

Unrecruited out of high school, Zagurski is a corn-fed Nebraskan who finally has a shot at a sustained stint in the big leagues. He's two years removed from Tommy John surgery, and his results at Triple-A were terrific. With Romero back in the fold, Zagurski will battle Antonio Bastardo for the last open spot.

LINEOUTS

HITTERS

PLAYER	TEAM	LVL	AGE	PA	R	2B	3B	HR	RBI	BB	SO	SB-CS	AVG/OBP/SLG	TAv	BABIP	BRR	FRAA	WARP
LF L. Castro	LWD	A	21	556	78	27	9	10	81	34	92	22-13	.257/.305/.406	.271	.287	2.3	LF 3, RF 2	2.3
3B G. Dobbs*	LEH	AAA	31	70	10	3	1	2	9	7	12	2-0	.210/.286/.387	.240	.225	-0.5	RF 0, 3B 0	-0.1
	PHI	MLB	31	176	13	7	0	5	15	12	39	1-1	.196/.250/.331	.209	.225	0.3	3B -6, 1B 0	-1.1
CF T. Gillies*	REA	AA	21	113	15	2	1	2	6	5	24	2-2	.238/.286/.333	.222	.288	0.7	CF 2	0.1
2B C. Hernandez#	WPT	A-	20	287	36	13	2	0	23	26	27	32-6	.325/.390/.392	.303	.359	0.0	2B 0	1.9
RF A. Hewitt	LWD	A	21	465	47	16	3	11	49	13	158	10-6	.202/.243/.327	.214	.287	-2.0	RF 1, LF 0	-1.7
C P. Hoover	LEH	AAA	34	286	23	13	3	2	21	26	65	0-0	.247/.326/.345	.228	.323	0.1	C 0, 1B 0	0.2
	PHI	MLB	34	25	6	2	0	0	2	3	5	0-0	.227/.320/.318	.194	.294	0.1	C 0	-0.1
3B C. Ransom	LEH	AAA	34	443	58	25	1	18	63	40	108	5-2	.261/.333/.467	.272	.311	0.6	3B -13, SS 1	0.7
	PHI	MLB	34	46	6	0	0	2	5	3	11	1-0	.190/.239/.333	.208	.200	0.7	3B -1, 2B 0	-0.1
RF D. Santana	LWD	A	17	202	27	10	0	3	16	29	76	5-6	.182/.322/.297	.249	.307	-1.7	RF -2, LF -1	-0.3
	WPT	A-	17	214	28	9	0	5	20	23	73	4-4	.237/.336/.366	.263	.361	0.0	RF 7	1.0
C D. Sardinha	LEH	AAA	31	242	24	8	0	5	24	13	68	0-0	.207/.261/.311	.204	.270	1.7	C 0	-0.3
	PHI	MLB	31	40	5	2	0	3	8	1	13	0-0	.205/.225/.487	.238	.217	0.0	C 1	0.1
C B. Schneider*	PHI	MLB	33	147	18	4	1	4	15	19	25	0-0	.240/.340/.384	.255	.265	1.2	C -1	0.5
SS W. Valdez	PHI	MLB	32	363	34	16	3	4	35	21	43	7-0	.258/.300/.360	.232	.280	3.6	SS -3, 2B 0	0.3

Leandro Castro isn't big, hasn't shown much power outside the New York-Penn League, and is unlikely to stick in center. His future depends entirely on his light lumber picking up some heft. **Greg Dobbs** hit rock bottom in 2010 and was ineffective no matter where he played. The former ace pinch-hitter has gone 15-for-109 in that role over the last two seasons. His career may be over. Part of the take from the trade that sent Cliff Lee to Seattle, **Tyson Gillies** had a season tarnished by charges of drug possession (later dropped) and poor play, as he proved his 2009 campaign was just another High Desert mirage. **Cesar Hernandez** showed very good contact skills in the New York-Penn League, but his secondary skills are unlikely to develop much further. **Anthony Hewitt**, a 2008 first-rounder, took a big step backward across the board, and he may prove to be the toolsy type who never develops. **Paul Hoover** has always been an underrated president, but that's only because he is so universally disparaged. He's got a strong record in public works and helmed the ship during the worst confluence of economic disasters the United States has ever seen. **Cody Ransom** offers extra-base hits for hire; contact skills sold separately. He's moved on to the Diamondbacks organization. Expectations were high for young Dominican **Domingo Santana** entering the season, but he failed to impress in short-season or Sally League play. He has plenty of opportunities left. Old catchers never die; they just become organizational guys, and **Dane Sardinha** is no exception. **Brian Schneider** had a nice bounce-back year, although most of the difference was due to a few extra singles and a friendlier home park. Schneider is set to earn $1.5 million in 2011, and if he can repeat a league-average batting line, he'll be worth it, though it's worth remembering that aside from short relievers, guys like this represent the most fungible asset in baseball. **Wilson Valdez** is a very good backup, mostly due to his strong defensive play, though he did set career highs in both batting average and slugging percentage—for what that's worth.

PITCHERS

PLAYER	TEAM	LVL	AGE	W	L	SV	IP	H	HR	BB	SO	EqBB9	EqSO9	GB%	BABIP	WHIP	ERA	FRA	WARP
P. Aumont	CLR	A+	21	2	5	1	72^1	74	6	42	77	5.2	9.6	46%	.351	1.69	4.48	4.47	0.9
	REA	AA	21	1	6	0	49^2	55	4	38	38	7.0	7.0	48%	.331	2.01	7.43	7.65	-0.7
M. Cisco	REA	AA	23	4	11	0	91^1	100	10	20	62	2.0	6.1	39%	.303	1.37	4.73	5.00	0.6
S. Escalona*	REA	AA	25	4	8	10	54^1	46	6	22	53	3.7	8.8	55%	.270	1.26	3.81	4.39	0.3
Y. Flande*	REA	AA	24	10	8	0	158^1	178	10	44	84	2.5	4.8	50%	.310	1.47	4.38	4.36	2.4
B. Gordon	LEH	AAA	31	1	3	0	78	73	2	19	86	2.2	9.9	33%	.335	1.19	3.35	4.85	0.4
N. Hernandez*	LWD	A	21	3	1	0	56	38	4	8	52	1.3	8.4	49%	.236	0.86	1.61	1.73	2.6
D. Herndon	PHI	MLB	24	1	3	0	52^1	67	2	17	29	2.9	5.0	58%	.357	1.64	4.30	6.28	-0.9
C. Kissock	CLR	A+	25	6	3	4	54	49	4	8	36	1.3	6.0	55%	.274	1.09	2.17	3.67	0.8
	REA	AA	25	1	0	0	23^1	20	1	4	14	1.6	5.5	47%	.271	1.08	3.86	5.23	-0.1
J. Rodriguez	LWD	A	19	5	1	0	56^1	32	2	22	90	3.5	14.4	42%	.275	0.98	1.44	1.61	3.0
	WPT	A-	19	2	2	0	34	25	2	15	36	4.0	9.5	51%	.256	1.26	2.65	4.59	0.2
J. Sanchez	CLR	A+	22	9	7	0	129^1	109	9	33	84	2.3	5.9	42%	.256	1.13	2.99	5.29	0.5
J. Savery*	LEH	AAA	24	1	12	0	127^1	154	13	51	67	3.6	4.7	47%	.318	1.64	4.66	5.26	0.6
M. Schwimer	REA	AA	24	4	2	9	40	34	5	14	58	3.2	13.1	44%	.319	1.25	3.60	4.08	0.4
	LEH	AAA	24	2	2	0	20	16	1	7	18	3.2	8.1	42%	.259	1.20	1.35	2.37	0.8
M. Stutes	REA	AA	23	3	0	2	35^2	28	2	21	37	5.4	9.5	45%	.283	1.59	3.79	2.66	0.8
	LEH	AAA	23	4	1	1	40^2	29	5	23	42	5.1	9.4	37%	.242	1.32	3.10	3.47	0.9

Part of Amaro's Cliff Lee Folly, **Phillippe Aumont** was converted to starting, promoted, converted back to relieving, and demoted again, all part of a wasted year for a prospect who has yet to find his role. **Michael Cisco** missed about seven weeks due to elbow inflammation and was largely inconsistent when he did pitch. He showed flashes of brilliance, like a one-hit, 10-strikeout masterpiece for Reading, but he gets by mostly on fastball control. **Sergio Escalona** turned 26 in August but has yet to blaze a path to the big-league bullpen and his window may be closing; his best chance at a role may be as a lefty specialist with his new team, the Astros. **Yohan Flande** was treated more like flambé by opposing hitters in 2010. His best offering, a changeup, wasn't good enough to fool Double-A hitters, and none of his pitches rate better than average. The Braves signed him to a minor league deal and invited him to spring training, though it's hard to imagine that his stuff will play any better in their system. A converted outfielder four years into his pitching career, **Brian Gordon** posted an astonishing strikeout rate for a 31-year-old who'd looked as if he was just playing out the string, but couldn't corral a call-up. **Nick Hernandez** relies on pinpoint control to get the job done, so he'll struggle to maintain his success as he climbs the ladder. **David Herndon** was a Rule 5 draftee and therefore had to spend the entire season on the roster or be offered back to the Angels. He pitched almost exclusively in low-leverage situations and was thoroughly unimpressive in that thankless role. It's unclear why a player like Herndon, who lacks both stuff and results, was allowed to soak up a roster spot while Scott Mathieson labored in Triple-A. **Chris Kissock** is a reliever who relies on control and a low-90s fastball with late movement. The eye-popping results that **Julio Rodriguez** had are tough to reconcile with his high-80s fastball, but any uptick in velocity would make him interesting. **Jesus Sanchez** was the catcher in the Bobby Abreu deal; he is now a converted pitcher with good control but no clear out pitch. He signed with the prospect-starved Brewers after being released by the Phillies in December. As a pitcher, **Joe Savery** was one of the most disappointing players in the system. As a first baseman, he's totally untested. If the transition works out, be ready to hear all about it. He hit well in three years at Rice, so it's not completely implausible. ⊘ The gargantuan **Michael Schwimer** has gotten the job done at each stage of the minors, but his velocity is no better than average and is unlikely to improve. ⊘ **Michael Stutes** upped his odds of landing a roster spot by pitching well in his new bullpen role, where his low-90s fastball played up. Poor control is all that holds him back now.

MANAGER: CHARLIE MANUEL

YEAR	TEAM	W-L	Pythag +/-	Avg PC	100+ P	120+ P	QS	BQS	REL	REL w Zero R	IBB	Subs	PH	PH Avg	PH HR	SB2	CS2	SB3	CS3	SAC Att	SAC %	POS SAC	Squeeze	Swing	In Play
2008	PHI	92-70	-2	96.0	62	3	86	6	468	319	64	98	281	.253	9	119	22	17	2	102	69.6%	25	1	131	99
2009	PHI	93-69	0	97.5	86	7	82	4	458	298	31	28	271	.186	9	96	19	21	8	84	65.5%	16	0	140	98
2010	PHI	97-65	1	98.4	87	4	88	13	451	312	42	37	270	.188	8	88	16	20	3	76	57.9%	16	1	126	101

Manuel's press conferences are the highlight of every Phillies postgame. Last year, he featured references to 1980s wrestling icon Ric Flair, warnings to other teams that he would steal their signs if he could, and an age-old reminder that sometimes the bear eats you rather than the other way around. His nuggets of West Virginian wisdom do a nice job of masking the depth of his knowledge of baseball minutiae, making him easy to underestimate. He doesn't mess with his lineup unless he has to—which he did often in 2010, as injuries struck with greater frequency than they had in recent years. His teams have experienced excellent success on the basepaths, and in 2010, the Phillies again boasted the highest stolen-base percentage in baseball. Manuel will be without highly regarded first-base coach Davey Lopes in 2011, so it remains to be seen whether the team's running game will remain among the league's best. Manuel's approach to offense is mostly hands-off, which breeds frustration when the team doesn't score runs, but pays dividends overall. The biggest knock against him last year was his usage of his right-handed fourth outfielder Ben Francisco, who faced more righties than he did lefties.

Pittsburgh Pirates

Over three decades have passed since last they were on top, but the Pirates' dogged pursuit of rock bottom has shown few signs of flagging. It certainly appeared that there was no way that things could get worse after 2001, when the Pirates lost their top three starting pitchers to injury before the regular season began, then proceeded to kick away 100 games in their first year in sparkling new PNC Park, a publicly funded structure that was supposed to spur a franchise renaissance. Then there was the stretch from 2005 to 2009, when the Pirates lost 95, 95, 94, 95, and 99 games. The last of those seasons marked the Pirates' 17th in a row with a losing record, setting the record for most consecutive losing seasons by a major North American professional sports franchise.

PIRATES PROSPECTUS

2010 W-L: 57-105, 6th in NL Central

Pythag	.326	30th
RS/G	3.6	29th
RA/G	5.3	1st
TAv	.253	28th
BRR	-15.8	30th
FRA	5.05	28th
DER	-37.2	30th
DL	659	11th
B-Age	26.1	1st
P-Age	28.2	17th
Salary	$34.9	30th
M$/MW	$2.97	19th

Ballpark: PNC Park (3-yr. PF: 100). Despite the high wall in right, Pedro Alvarez should be glad he was born left-handed

2010: The beginnings of a young core can't save the Bucs from being baseball's worst team

2011: Here comes the fanbase's 19th consecutive nervous breakdown

Action Items: Add pitching, both in the majors and on the farm; nurture young stars; find long-lost dignity

Yet 2010 proved to be an even more humiliating campaign. The Pirates went 57-105, their worst record since the 1952 club finished 42-112. Amazingly, the carnage should have been worse; the Pirates outperformed their Pythagenport record by 4.3 wins last season. Only the Astros won more games than their run differential suggested they should have.

Worst of all, the Pirates became the first National League team in 34 years to win the triple crown of futility by finishing last in the 16-team field in runs scored (3.6 per game), runs allowed (5.4 per game), and Defensive Efficiency (.673). When the 1976 Expos pulled off that feat, there were just 12 teams in the league. The Pirates were just the fourth major-league team since 1954 to bring up the rear in all three categories within its circuit in the same season. Table 1 shows those infamous four, with runs expressed in terms of average marks per game.

Despite being the only pirates outside of a Gilbert and Sullivan musical who give more than they get, the Pirates will go to spring training this year sporting an upbeat attitude (and insofar as we know, without any recourse to mind-altering pharmaceuticals). Part of the expected uplift will be supplied by new manager Clint Hurdle, an outgoing guy who is the opposite of his predecessor, John Russell, the least animated manager in the major leagues. Hurdle led a young Rockies team from the bottom of the NL West to the World Series in 2007, and the Pirates hope he can duplicate that success in Pittsburgh. If nothing else, the gregarious skipper should offer some encouragement to a fanbase that keeps getting the ball pulled away from it as if Pirates ownership and management collectively added up to a Lucy van Pelt–style sadist.

A more substantial reason for positive vibes is that in three years in the general manager's chair, Neal Huntington's administration has gathered what could be the core of a good team. His program of exchanging anything not nailed down for younger players has mostly been a sideshow, producing a few decent prospects and an equal number of clinkers—the exception, and it's not a sure thing, being Jose Tabata—but his team has made its mark in the draft, selecting solid players and proto-stars such as second baseman Neil Walker, third baseman Pedro Alvarez, left fielder Jose Tabata, center fielder Andrew McCutchen, and catcher Tony Sanchez.

The last Pirates player to arrive in the major leagues with more hype than Alvarez was Barry Bonds in 1986. While the third baseman probably won't end his career as the game's all-time home run leader, he is a compelling candidate to become the first Pirate to have a 40-homer season since Willie Stargell in 1973. Tabata was part of Huntington's first major trade in July 2008, coming from the Yankees along with three young pitchers in exchange for Xavier Nady and Damaso Marte. McCutchen and Tabata have the speed and

Table 1. The Not-So-Fantastic Four: Triple Frown "Winners" in the Retrosheet Era

Team	RS	RA	DE	Record
1963 Senators	3.57	5.01	.703	56-106
1973 Rangers	3.82	5.01	.684	57-105
1976 Expos	3.28	4.53	.692	55-107
2010 Pirates	3.62	5.35	.673	57-105

on-base skills to form an outstanding one-two punch at the top of the order.

At 25, Walker is the oldest of the quartet and has emerged as the biggest surprise, even though he was the Pirates' first-round draft pick in 2004 out of Pine-Richland High School in Pittsburgh's northern suburbs. Walker's stock was at its lowest ebb when the 2010 season began, as he was sent to Triple-A Indianapolis for a third straight year and tasked with learning how to serve as a utility player. However, after veteran Akinori Iwamura washed out as the second baseman, Walker was summoned to the major leagues on Memorial Day and put a hammerlock on a starting job.

While McCutchen, Alvarez, Tabata, and Walker give the Pirates a solid lineup foundation, there isn't much immediate help coming from the farm system; catcher Tony Sanchez, middle infielder Chase d'Arnaud, and outfielder Starling Marte aren't likely to arrive until 2012. Consequently, the Pirates' chances of enjoying significant offensive improvement this season hinge heavily on their talented foursome's continued development.

Unfortunately, the Pirates lack equivalent young talent capable of turning their pitching staff around, at least at present. Ross Ohlendorf led the rotation with a 2.3 Support-Neutral Lineup-adjusted Value Above Replacement (SNLVAR) last season, but that mark ranked just 91st among major-league pitchers, and the big right-hander has little upside left at age 28. James McDonald provided 2.0 SNLVAR in 11 starts and 64 innings after being acquired from the Dodgers at the trade deadline, and the Pirates hope the 26-year-old might be ready to blossom as a vital component of their rotation. The pitching staff was so bad last year that set-up reliever Evan Meek was the team's lone representative at the All-Star Game. Meek (2.0), Joel Hanrahan (2.5), and Octavio Dotel (1.1) were the only relievers to add at least one win above replacement level in terms of WXRL, and Dotel's greatest contribution was to be the trade bait that landed McDonald.

The Pirates feel that they can build a bullpen around Hanrahan and Meek, a pair of hard throwers. It's not as if whoever fills out the relief corps will have big shoes to fill, given that the Pirates' 5.2 bullpen WXRL ranked 24th among the 30 major league clubs. The Pirates' best internal hope for a pitching boost last season was right-hander Brad Lincoln, but he managed only a counterproductive -0.6 SNLVAR in nine starts and will need to rehabilitate his image within the organization this season. Though three good-looking starting-pitching prospects finished last season at Double-A in left-handers Rudy Owens and Jeff Locke and right-hander Bryan Morris, none is polished enough to begin the season in the majors.

The strength of the organization lies in the lower levels of the farm system. In a refreshing departure from the past, the Pirates have spent more than $25 million over the past three years to sign draft picks and international free agents, routinely going over slot to lure high-school players with strong college commitments to take the professional route. Ironically, this change of strategy stems from when Frank Coonelly took over as club president prior to the 2008 season, even though he was the man who devised Major League Baseball's slotting system for draft picks while serving as the chief labor lawyer in the central office. The Pirates usually adhered to the slotting system's guidelines until Bob Nutting bought out enough limited partners to gain a controlling interest of the team in 2007, a move that forced out Kevin McClatchy. Nutting has since given Pittsburgh the go-ahead to take big-money risks on teenagers both domestically and abroad.

That strategy has left the Pirates with a number of talented youngsters, particularly pitchers. In fact, the team's top three prospects are all teenagers who entered the organization last year; right-handers Jameson Taillon and Stetson Allie were selected with the team's first two draft picks and Mexican righty Luis Heredia was considered the best pitcher available on the international market. The team paid $11.35 million in bonuses to the trio—$6.5 million to Taillon, $2.6 million to Heredia, and $2.25 million to Allie. By comparison, the Pirates' major-league payroll was $34.9 million at the start of 2010.

In 2009, Pittsburgh drafted and signed left-handers Colton Cain and Zach Dodson and right-hander Zack Von Rosenberg to over-slot bonuses; all three are also among the top prospects in the organization. That leaves the Pirates with the hope that someday soon, the team will be flooded with more talented young pitchers than roster spots, creating depth and trade chips. Of course, that's merely something to dream about—the present isn't quite as bright. And while it is almost unfathomable to think that the Buccos could be as bad as they were last season, nobody saw their 105-loss season coming, either.

When Hurdle was hired after helping the Rangers to the World Series last season in his first year as their hitting coach, it became clear that Nutting was not completely convinced that Huntington had the Pirates on the path back to respectability and beyond. Hurdle received a three-year contract that takes him through 2013, while Huntington is only signed through 2011. Rarely in professional sports does a coach have a longer contract than a GM. When it does happen, it often denotes the executive's tenuous position.

Huntington is clearly next in the fall-guy line now that Russell has been jettisoned. However, it would seem patently unfair not to give Huntington at least five full seasons to prove himself. The gravity of the Pirates' situation when Huntington arrived in Pittsburgh late in the 2007 season cannot be overstated. At the time, the Pirates had only marginal talent on the major league roster and a thin farm system. While the wins have yet to come in Huntington's tenure, the organization is in much better shape. It's fair to say that the team hasn't had this much young talent in the pipeline since former GM Syd Thrift began a rebuilding process in 1986, which led to three straight NL East titles from 1990 to 1992.

The Pirates haven't had a winning season since 1992. The lesson to be learned from that era was it takes time to build a good organization, especially one in a state of decay as advanced as Pittsburgh's. Hurdle may have summed up the team's short-term outlook best during his introductory news conference, when asked about the challenge of trying to turn around a franchise that has become one of professional sports' laughingstocks. "How do you eat an elephant?" Hurdle asked. "One bite at a time." Considering that the average male elephant weighs 11,000 pounds, it would appear that the Pirates still have plenty on which to chew.

HITTERS

Pedro Alvarez 3B

Born: **7/18/1987** Age: **23**
Bats: L Throws: R Height: **6' 3"** Weight: **225**
Breakout: **2%** Improve: **42%** Collapse: **6%**
Attrition: **19%** MLB: **82%**

Comparables:
Evan Longoria, Alex Gordon, Ian Stewart (70)

YEAR	TEAM	LVL	AGE	PA	R	2B	3B	HR	RBI	BB	SO	SB	CS	AVG/OBP/SLG	TAv	BABIP	BRR	FRAA	WARP
2009	LYN	A+	21	284	37	14	1	14	55	37	70	1	1	.247/.342/.486	.301	.282	2.9	3B 2	2.4
2009	ALT	AA	21	258	42	18	0	13	40	34	59	1	0	.333/.419/.590	.350	.401	-2.8	3B 1	2.8
2010	IND	AAA	22	278	42	15	4	13	53	32	68	4	4	.277/.363/.533	.305	.331	-0.3	3B 7	2.8
2010	PIT	MLB	22	386	42	21	1	16	64	37	119	0	0	.257/.326/.461	.275	.341	-1.8	3B 1	1.5
2011	*PIT*	*MLB*	*23*	*600*	*77*	*26*	*2*	*27*	*82*	*64*	*165*	*3*	*1*	*.258/.336/.471*	*.279*	*.317*	*-0.2*	*3B 2*	*2.9*

Alvarez had a tough initial adjustment to the major leagues after being called up last June, suffering from a steady diet of breaking pitches and passivity at the plate. However, he eventually settled in, heating up gradually until exploding in September, when he bopped to the tune of .311/.363/.573 with five home runs in 112 plate appearances. Alvarez's left-handed power stroke is reminiscent of Pirates Hall of Famer Willie Stargell's, and he should mash plenty of home runs over the short porch in right field at PNC Park. Though he can stick it with the bat, Alvarez had a harder time picking it defensively in his rookie year. While he has a good arm and soft hands, his lack of range is likely to precipitate a switch to first base at some point in his career.

John Bowker OF

Born: **7/8/1983** Age: **27**
Bats: L Throws: L Height: **6' 2"** Weight: **190**
Breakout: **0%** Improve: **47%** Collapse: **3%**
Attrition: **19%** MLB: **89%**

Comparables:
Billy Williams, Ryan Spilborghs, Scott Hairston (76)

YEAR	TEAM	LVL	AGE	PA	R	2B	3B	HR	RBI	BB	SO	SB	CS	AVG/OBP/SLG	TAv	BABIP	BRR	FRAA	WARP
2008	FRE	AAA	24	102	13	3	1	2	9	7	23	2	0	.237/.304/.355	.249	.294	-0.9	1B -1, LF 1	0.0
2008	SFN	MLB	24	350	32	14	3	10	43	19	74	1	1	.255/.300/.408	.252	.299	-1.0	1B 2, RF 0	0.2
2009	FRE	AAA	25	450	82	22	4	21	83	74	64	10	6	.342/.451/.596	.366	.362	0.0	RF 2, LF 4	6.2
2009	SFN	MLB	25	73	7	2	2	2	7	4	18	1	0	.194/.247/.373	.217	.229	0.4	LF 2, RF 0	-0.1
2010	FRE	AAA	26	224	36	12	1	14	36	23	37	1	2	.310/.388/.594	.314	.320	-0.4	LF -1, RF 0	1.5
2010	IND	AAA	26	98	10	7	2	4	10	6	20	0	0	.319/.367/.571	.302	.373	-0.8	1B 0, RF 0	0.4
2010	SFN	MLB	26	90	9	3	0	3	8	6	23	0	0	.207/.256/.354	.233	.241	0.4	LF 2, RF -2	0.0
2010	PIT	MLB	26	77	7	5	0	2	13	8	10	0	1	.232/.312/.391	.259	.246	-1.1	RF 0, 1B -1	-0.1
2011	*PIT*	*MLB*	*27*	*483*	*63*	*20*	*2*	*20*	*65*	*49*	*94*	*4*	*2*	*.271/.348/.470*	*.284*	*.300*	*-0.3*	*LF 0, 1B -2*	*1.5*

The Pirates acquired Bowker and Joe Martinez from the Giants for Javier Lopez at last year's trading deadline and made him a September call-up. Though Bowker has raked in Triple-A (.318/.409/.562 in 878 PAs), he has never solved the sticky problem of major league pitching. He finished on a 15-for-46 hot streak after earning only one safety in his first 20 at-bats for the Pirates, but that performance didn't guarantee him a place on next year's team. Bowker's immediate future may hinge on his showing in spring training, since the lefty is out of minor-league options. In his favor, PNC Park seems built for him, since he tends to pull the ball to right field.

Ronny Cedeno **SS**

Born: 2/2/1983 Age: 28
Bats: R Throws: R Height: 6' 0" Weight: 180
Breakout: 6% Improve: 42% Collapse: 10%
Attrition: 12% MLB: 92%

Comparables:
Dave Concepcion, Jason Bartlett, Felipe Lopez (77)

YEAR	TEAM	LVL	AGE	PA	R	2B	3B	HR	RBI	BB	SO	SB	CS	AVG/OBP/SLG	TAv	BABIP	BRR	FRAA	WARP
2008	CHN	MLB	25	236	33	12	0	2	28	18	41	4	1	.269/.326/.352	.255	.322	1.1	2B -1, SS 0	0.5
2009	PIT	MLB	26	170	17	4	1	5	21	9	29	2	0	.258/.300/.394	.241	.280	2.6	SS 1	0.6
2009	SEA	MLB	26	206	15	4	2	5	17	10	50	3	2	.167/.204/.290	.174	.186	2.1	SS 5, 2B -2	-0.7
2010	PIT	MLB	27	502	42	29	3	8	38	23	106	12	3	.256/.289/.383	.244	.309	1.9	SS -6	0.7
2011	*PIT*	*MLB*	*28*	*418*	*45*	*17*	*2*	*9*	*45*	*25*	*81*	*8*	*3*	*.256/.297/.385*	*.239*	*.290*	*-0.2*	*SS -1, 2B -1*	*0.4*

Cedeno has always wowed scouts with his tools, particularly his power and arm, but has consistently disappointed them with his inconsistent play. That was the case again last season. Cedeno had a roller-coaster ride as the Pirates' shortstop, posting monthly OPS marks as low as 256 in June but as high as 919 in July. He was also erratic in the field, interspersing Gold Glove–type plays with botched routine grounders. His 2010 season could vie with his 2008 as the best offensive season of his major league career, which shows just what a miserable hitter Cedeno, a career .245/.284/.356 performer, has been. With no candidate in the system pressing to take up the legacy of Wagner, Vaughan, and Groat (or even Jay Bell, for gosh sakes), the most the Pirates can hope for is that Rule 5 pick Josh Rodriguez can take a few at-bats away from the incumbent, even if his glove isn't good enough to wrest the position away altogether.

Pedro Ciriaco **SS**

Born: 9/27/1985 Age: 25
Bats: R Throws: R Height: 6' 0" Weight: 160
Breakout: 6% Improve: 31% Collapse: 6%
Attrition: 26% MLB: 53%

Comparables:
Anderson Hernandez, Robert Andino, Bert Campaneris (74)

YEAR	TEAM	LVL	AGE	PA	R	2B	3B	HR	RBI	BB	SO	SB	CS	AVG/OBP/SLG	TAv	BABIP	BRR	FRAA	WARP
2008	VIS	A+	22	562	85	26	5	5	61	18	89	40	9	.310/.329/.408	.273	.351	5.4	SS -1, 2B 12	4.3
2009	MOB	AA	23	497	56	15	3	4	54	16	71	38	10	.296/.316/.367	.247	.334	2.1	SS 1, 2B -1	1.3
2010	IND	AAA	24	126	19	9	1	0	6	2	21	5	1	.281/.288/.372	.234	.330	0.0	SS -2	-0.1
2010	RNO	AAA	24	376	44	15	7	6	51	10	53	14	3	.259/.278/.392	.224	.281	0.0	SS 5, 2B -1	0.5
2011	*PIT*	*MLB*	*25*	*519*	*52*	*20*	*3*	*6*	*51*	*11*	*93*	*26*	*7*	*.263/.277/.353*	*.220*	*.305*	*0.5*	*SS 0, 2B 2*	*0.0*

The Pirates seemed genuinely excited when they acquired the speedy and slick-fielding shortstop prospect Ciriaco from the Diamondbacks last year at the trading deadline as part of the Chris Snyder deal, fantasizing that he could blossom into a major-league regular. A month of watching Ciriaco hack away at Indianapolis must have come as a rude awakening, because he can't hit and probably never will. Still, that he never started a game after his September call-up was baffling (he was 3-for-6 in his brief opportunities at bat), since Ronny Cedeno is anything but a sure thing to hold the shortstop job in the long term. Ciriaco almost surely will return to Triple-A to start this season and would be wise to work on developing some plate discipline to help temper his free-swinging ways, but he has so far to go that he could be three times as patient and would still be completely inadequate.

Jeff Clement **1B**

Born: 8/21/1983 Age: 27
Bats: L Throws: R Height: 6' 1" Weight: 210
Breakout: 5% Improve: 28% Collapse: 2%
Attrition: 27% MLB: 53%

Comparables:
Juan Miranda, Matthew Brown, Adrian Gonzalez (80)

YEAR	TEAM	LVL	AGE	PA	R	2B	3B	HR	RBI	BB	SO	SB	CS	AVG/OBP/SLG	TAv	BABIP	BRR	FRAA	WARP
2008	TAC	AAA	24	211	40	17	0	14	43	35	30	0	0	.335/.455/.676	.355	.341	0.1	C 0	2.8
2008	SEA	MLB	24	224	18	10	1	5	23	15	63	0	1	.227/.295/.360	.240	.302	0.6	C 0	0.2
2009	IND	AAA	25	115	16	2	0	7	22	12	27	1	1	.224/.313/.459	.268	.224	0.4	1B -3	0.0
2009	TAC	AAA	25	421	65	33	3	14	68	43	81	1	0	.288/.366/.505	.295	.333	-1.7	C 0, 1B -1	1.8
2010	IND	AAA	26	181	23	15	1	8	33	9	48	1	4	.304/.337/.548	.276	.381	0.0	1B 3, C 0	0.8
2010	PIT	MLB	26	154	11	3	0	7	12	6	37	0	0	.201/.234/.368	.215	.216	-2.2	1B -2	-1.0
2011	*PIT*	*MLB*	*27*	*457*	*57*	*23*	*1*	*19*	*60*	*43*	*104*	*0*	*0*	*.252/.326/.454*	*.268*	*.288*	*0.0*	*1B -3, C 0*	*0.8*

The Pirates were seemingly the only team in baseball that still thought Clement, the third overall pick in the 2005 draft, might still make an impact player in the major leagues when they acquired him from the Mariners as part of a seven-player deal at the 2009 trading deadline. He began last season as the big club's starting first baseman but was sent to Triple-A in June after major-league pitchers refused to grant him clemency for his criminal inability to make contact. After putting on a show in Triple-A, Clement was called back up to the majors on the last day of July and mostly sat, pinch-hitting a pair of home runs before injuring his right knee. He subsequently underwent surgery, and his status for Opening Day is uncertain. Clement has power, but it's tough to be a major-league regular while striking out nearly 30 percent of the time. He'll need to cut down on the whiffs—and how!— just to turn into a useful bench bat.

Chase d'Arnaud **MI**

Born: **1/21/1987** Age: **24**
Bats: **R** Throws: **R** Height: **6' 1"** Weight: **175**
Breakout: **2%** Improve: **12%** Collapse: **3%**
Attrition: **22%** MLB: **35%**

Comparables:
Ronny Cedeno, Eric Patterson, Robert Andino (78)

YEAR	TEAM	LVL	AGE	PA	R	2B	3B	HR	RBI	BB	SO	SB	CS	AVG/OBP/SLG	TAv	BABIP	BRR	FRAA	WARP
2008	SCO	A-	21	183	26	10	5	1	21	11	30	14	2	.286/.333/.423	.284	.338	1.2	SS -7, 3B 3	0.8
2009	WVA	A	22	255	32	14	3	3	31	30	31	17	3	.291/.392/.427	.312	.322	3.6	SS 5	3.0
2009	LYN	A+	22	253	45	19	4	4	26	30	41	14	5	.295/.399/.481	.312	.343	1.9	2B 1, SS -5	2.1
2010	ALT	AA	23	607	91	33	9	6	48	56	102	33	7	.247/.331/.377	.279	.290	0.0	SS -7, 2B -2	2.6
2011	*PIT*	*MLB*	*24*	*446*	*48*	*21*	*3*	*7*	*42*	*37*	*89*	*14*	*4*	*.239/.309/.361*	*.241*	*.283*	*0.3*	*SS -2, 2B 0*	*0.5*

After becoming a breakthrough prospect in 2009 with a strong showing at both Class-A levels (posting combined .293/.398/.454 rates), d'Arnaud caught pneumonia in spring training last March, got off to a horrible start at Double-A, and never seemed to catch up completely. The Pirates say they haven't written d'Arnaud off and will give him a chance to reestablish himself at Altoona. His value was already dinged when the Pirates decided to move him from shortstop to the keystone late last season; the greater offensive expectations associated with his new position will make it more difficult for him to move up the depth charts. He's still a prospect, but just barely.

Argenis Diaz **SS**

Born: **2/12/1987** Age: **24**
Bats: **R** Throws: **R** Height: **6' 0"** Weight: **190**
Breakout: **1%** Improve: **2%** Collapse: **3%**
Attrition: **9%** MLB: **9%**

Comparables:
Gregorio Petit, Brian Bocock, Ramiro Pena (84)

YEAR	TEAM	LVL	AGE	PA	R	2B	3B	HR	RBI	BB	SO	SB	CS	AVG/OBP/SLG	TAv	BABIP	BRR	FRAA	WARP
2008	LNC	A+	21	282	31	9	6	0	29	20	60	3	2	.281/.330/.363	.248	.358	-0.2	SS -5	0.2
2008	PME	AA	21	153	20	8	2	2	23	10	30	0	1	.288/.333/.417	.258	.345	0.8	SS 1	0.8
2009	PME	AA	22	307	21	14	1	0	24	21	60	7	4	.253/.303/.310	.247	.312	-0.1	SS 1	0.8
2009	IND	AAA	22	158	14	1	0	0	8	8	27	1	1	.233/.266/.240	.201	.276	-0.4	SS 4	0.0
2010	IND	AAA	23	304	28	8	1	0	22	19	61	5	1	.248/.302/.285	.207	.306	0.0	SS -3, 2B -2	-1.0
2010	PIT	MLB	23	36	0	1	0	0	2	3	10	0	1	.242/.306/.273	.210	.348	-0.1	SS -3	-0.3
2011	*PIT*	*MLB*	*24*	*412*	*39*	*13*	*2*	*3*	*32*	*23*	*92*	*3*	*2*	*.245/.285/.309*	*.213*	*.307*	*-0.2*	*SS 0, 2B 0*	*-0.4*

Diaz would have a chance to be a star if baseball were a two-platoon sport like football. His range and instincts make him an outstanding defensive shortstop. Alas, Diaz also has to bat in games, and that is where he runs into problems, since he suffers from the lethal combination of no power and no plate discipline. With Pedro Ciriaco around, the Pirates didn't need two players of this model and nontendered Diaz, who subsequently signed a minor-league deal with the Tigers. It's hard to imagine him having any long-term value unless he becomes at least a passable hitter.

Ryan Doumit **C**

Born: **4/3/1981** Age: **30**
Bats: **S** Throws: **R** Height: **6' 0"** Weight: **200**
Breakout: **1%** Improve: **24%** Collapse: **9%**
Attrition: **15%** MLB: **84%**

Comparables:
Del Crandall, Earl Battey, John Baker (77)

YEAR	TEAM	LVL	AGE	PA	R	2B	3B	HR	RBI	BB	SO	SB	CS	AVG/OBP/SLG	TAv	BABIP	BRR	FRAA	WARP
2008	PIT	MLB	27	465	72	34	0	15	69	23	55	2	2	.318/.357/.501	.294	.333	0.0	C 1, 1B 0	3.6
2009	PIT	MLB	28	304	31	16	0	10	38	20	49	4	0	.250/.299/.414	.240	.268	0.0	C 2, RF 0	0.8
2010	PIT	MLB	29	456	42	22	1	13	45	41	87	1	0	.251/.331/.406	.259	.290	-2.9	C 5, RF 0	1.8
2011	*PIT*	*MLB*	*30*	*369*	*45*	*18*	*0*	*12*	*44*	*29*	*63*	*2*	*1*	*.262/.328/.429*	*.264*	*.287*	*-0.1*	*C 2, RF 0*	*1.7*

The Pirates had long hoped that Doumit's defense behind the plate would catch up to his offense. Last season, they finally made the tacit admission that his glove was a lost cause and used him primarily in right field after acquiring catcher Chris Snyder. Doumit's value came mainly from his status as a switch-hitting backstop with pop, but it has sunk considerably in light of the elevated offensive expectations of a corner outfielder. Doumit still has his uses as someone who can be deployed (with varying degrees of ineffectiveness) behind the plate, at first base, and in right field. However, since he is no longer a regular and still has an unpleasant personality, it is certain that the Pirates will refrain from exercising the 2012 and 2013 options on his contract and allow him to become a free agent after this season, if they can't find a trade partner before then.

Brian Friday **MI**

Born: **12/16/1985** Age: **25**
Bats: **R** Throws: **R** Height: **5' 11"** Weight: **190**
Breakout: **4%** Improve: **10%** Collapse: **0%**
Attrition: **16%** MLB: **24%**

Comparables:
Kevin Melillo, Luis Valbuena, Omar Quintanilla (83)

YEAR	TEAM	LVL	AGE	PA	R	2B	3B	HR	RBI	BB	SO	SB	CS	AVG/OBP/SLG	TAv	BABIP	BRR	FRAA	WARP
2008	LYN	A+	22	391	59	20	4	2	29	34	56	16	11	.287/.358/.387	.263	.330	4.2	SS 15	3.4
2009	ALT	AA	23	476	48	22	3	7	46	51	69	7	5	.265/.357/.386	.275	.299	-0.2	SS 1	2.4
2010	IND	AAA	24	337	41	19	5	2	28	39	69	10	7	.257/.347/.378	.262	.320	1.2	2B -4, SS 1	0.9
2011	*PIT*	*MLB*	*25*	*417*	*45*	*18*	*2*	*5*	*36*	*39*	*83*	*8*	*4*	*.243/.317/.348*	*.238*	*.291*	*-0.6*	*SS 5, 2B -1*	*0.8*

The Pirates had hoped their man Friday could blossom into an everyday shortstop when they drafted him out of Rice in the third round of the 2007 draft and cut him a $355,000 check. However, he was moved to second base at Triple-A last season in favor of Argenis Diaz and Pedro Ciriaco. In the wake of his position change, Friday's future occupation looks to be that of a utility infielder. He could have some limited value in that role, since he draws walks and can play adequate defense at both middle infield spots.

Josh Harrison INF

Born: **7/8/1987** Age: **23**
Bats: **R** Throws: **R** Height: **5' 8"** Weight: **175**
Breakout: **2%** Improve: **10%** Collapse: **2%**
Attrition: **10%** MLB: **21%**

Comparables:
Erick Aybar, Tony Abreu, Gregorio Petit (70)

YEAR	TEAM	LVL	AGE	PA	R	2B	3B	HR	RBI	BB	SO	SB	CS	AVG/OBP/SLG	TAv	BABIP	BRR	FRAA	WARP
2008	PEO	A	20	126	15	4	1	1	4	3	11	6	2	.262/.286/.336	.226	.282	2.2	2B 0, RF -1	-0.1
2008	BOI	A-	20	144	27	11	2	1	25	23	12	12	6	.351/.458/.509	.382	.371	0.9	2B 8, LF -1	2.8
2009	PEO	A	21	335	51	17	7	4	33	16	25	16	9	.337/.367/.479	.334	.344	0.5	LF 1, 2B -4	2.9
2009	DAY	A+	21	78	10	3	1	1	9	6	7	10	1	.286/.346/.400	.278	.302	-0.4	LF -1, 3B 1	0.3
2009	LYN	A+	21	155	15	8	1	1	13	1	19	4	1	.270/.277/.362	.217	.285	0.1	3B 1, 2B -3	-0.4
2010	ALT	AA	22	585	74	33	3	4	75	32	52	19	7	.300/.345/.398	.273	.311	3.7	3B -3, 2B 7	3.2
2011	*PIT*	*MLB*	*23*	*491*	*52*	*22*	*3*	*6*	*50*	*19*	*62*	*13*	*5*	*.266/.293/.367*	*.233*	*.287*	*-0.3*	*3B -1, 2B 3*	*-0.1*

The Bucs acquired the diminutive Harrison from the Cubs in the 2009 John Grabow/Tom Gorzelanny trade. He began his 2010 campaign at Double-A. Deciding that his range wasn't up to snuff at the hot corner, the Pirates pushed Harrison to second base, though he saw significant action in left field during the Arizona Fall League. The reality is that while Harrison can hit, he remains a man without a position. Even though he can't play shortstop, after spending this season at Triple-A, Harrison could help off the major league bench in 2012 as a vertically challenged right-handed hitter with gap power.

Gorkys Hernandez CF

Born: **9/7/1987** Age: **23**
Bats: **R** Throws: **R** Height: **6' 0"** Weight: **185**
Breakout: **6%** Improve: **12%** Collapse: **2%**
Attrition: **14%** MLB: **22%**

Comparables:
Greg Golson, Julio Borbon, Jacoby Ellsbury (80)

YEAR	TEAM	LVL	AGE	PA	R	2B	3B	HR	RBI	BB	SO	SB	CS	AVG/OBP/SLG	TAv	BABIP	BRR	FRAA	WARP
2008	MYR	A+	20	467	75	23	6	5	42	48	79	20	4	.264/.345/.387	.265	.310	2.2	CF 22	4.0
2009	ALT	AA	21	374	45	14	2	3	31	24	76	9	8	.262/.310/.340	.244	.323	3.9	CF 2	1.0
2009	MIS	AA	21	228	33	11	2	0	19	15	54	10	8	.316/.360/.387	.280	.421	3.6	CF 3	1.8
2010	ALT	AA	22	415	45	11	4	2	26	33	95	17	3	.266/.333/.334	.249	.344	0.0	CF -6	0.1
2011	*PIT*	*MLB*	*23*	*502*	*50*	*18*	*3*	*5*	*43*	*31*	*121*	*13*	*6*	*.246/.292/.332*	*.223*	*.314*	*-0.7*	*CF -5*	*-1.0*

The Pirates hoped that a second season at Double-A in 2010 would provide Hernandez with the spark the perennial prospect needed to get his career moving. Unfortunately, just when he'd begun to hit well, showing more plate discipline and stealing bases at a higher percentage than he had before, his season ended when he broke a finger attempting to bunt in late July. Hernandez is one of the best defensive center fielders in the minors, but he needs to continue to make progress offensively this season at Triple-A even to think about being a regular in the bigs, something that, with Andrew McCutchen in front of him, would require the third trade of Hernandez's career.

Jason Jaramillo C

Born: **10/9/1982** Age: **28**
Bats: **S** Throws: **R** Height: **6' 0"** Weight: **210**
Breakout: **6%** Improve: **35%** Collapse: **8%**
Attrition: **23%** MLB: **74%**

Comparables:
Omir Santos, Johnny Estrada, David Segui (75)

YEAR	TEAM	LVL	AGE	PA	R	2B	3B	HR	RBI	BB	SO	SB	CS	AVG/OBP/SLG	TAv	BABIP	BRR	FRAA	WARP
2008	LEH	AAA	25	473	48	20	0	8	39	42	82	1	1	.266/.338/.371	.247	.310	-2.4	C -1	1.0
2009	PIT	MLB	26	224	20	14	0	3	26	17	33	1	0	.252/.308/.364	.231	.287	-2.5	C -1	-0.1
2010	IND	AAA	27	96	3	3	0	1	13	5	16	0	0	.239/.281/.307	.205	.274	0.0	C 2	0.0
2010	PIT	MLB	27	97	2	2	0	1	6	8	14	0	0	.149/.227/.207	.157	.164	-0.4	C 0	-0.6
2011	*PIT*	*MLB*	*28*	*294*	*30*	*12*	*0*	*5*	*26*	*24*	*51*	*1*	*0*	*.239/.303/.340*	*.229*	*.273*	*0.0*	*C 0*	*0.3*

Happy-go-lucky optimists, the Pirates were hopeful that Jaramillo would bloom into a starter when they acquired him from the Phillies in a trade for Ronny Paulino during the 2008-2009 offseason. Instead, he's taken on the look of a backup backstop lifer. Jaramillo is above-average defensively with a strong arm but is lacking at the plate, where his propensity for grounding into double plays is compounded by an absence of power. At 28, he is what he is; fortunately, he can make an honest living as what he is for some time.

Garrett Jones 1B

Born: **6/21/1981** Age: **30**
Bats: **L** Throws: **L** Height: **6' 4"** Weight: **225**
Breakout: **5%** Improve: **40%** Collapse: **11%**
Attrition: **15%** MLB: **85%**

Comparables:
Ryan Garko, Lyle Overbay, Eric Karros (75)

YEAR	TEAM	LVL	AGE	PA	R	2B	3B	HR	RBI	BB	SO	SB	CS	AVG/OBP/SLG	TAv	BABIP	BRR	FRAA	WARP
2008	ROC	AAA	27	587	82	33	3	23	92	50	98	9	2	.279/.337/.484	.273	.299	3.3	1B 1, RF -5	1.7
2009	IND	AAA	28	299	44	18	0	12	50	18	47	14	4	.307/.348/.502	.290	.330	2.9	RF 4, LF 1	2.1
2009	PIT	MLB	28	358	45	21	1	21	44	40	76	10	2	.293/.372/.567	.308	.323	-0.9	RF -3, 1B 2	1.9
2010	PIT	MLB	29	654	64	34	1	21	86	53	123	7	3	.247/.306/.414	.256	.274	-3.5	1B 2, RF 0	0.2
2011	*PIT*	*MLB*	*30*	*604*	*74*	*29*	*1*	*23*	*78*	*52*	*116*	*10*	*3*	*.260/.323/.445*	*.265*	*.286*	*-0.1*	*1B -1, RF -2*	*0.7*

There were plenty of reasons to suspect that Jones's surprisingly good rookie season in 2009 would be hard to repeat, one of them being that he had spent parts of five seasons at Triple-A prior to his "breakout." Three home runs in his first two games offered some hope of a better outcome, but sure enough, Jones wasn't the same hitter last season, not least because left-handers neutralized him with a .220/.261/.360 slash line. He opened 2010 playing in right field, but when first baseman Jeff Clement was demoted to Triple-A, Jones returned to the infield to play the cold corner. There is a justified sense that his bubble has burst and that his best use would be coming off the bench as a left-handed bat with some thump. The signing of Lyle Overbay probably places him in that position, assuming he loses a tussle for playing time in right field.

Andy LaRoche 3B

Born: **9/13/1983** Age: **27**
Bats: R Throws: R Height: **6' 1"** Weight: **215**
Breakout: **0%** Improve: **25%** Collapse: **6%**
Attrition: **9%** MLB: **78%**

Comparables:
Puddin Head Jones, Pete O'Brien, Chris Brown (75)

YEAR	TEAM	LVL	AGE	PA	R	2B	3B	HR	RBI	BB	SO	SB	CS	AVG/OBP/SLG	TAv	BABIP	BRR	FRAA	WARP
2008	LVG	AAA	24	166	35	3	0	5	28	37	14	2	1	.293/.452/.439	.323	.287	0.9	3B 3, 2B -1	2.0
2008	LAN	MLB	24	69	7	1	0	2	6	10	7	0	0	.203/.319/.322	.221	.200	0.1	3B -1, 2B -1	-0.2
2008	PIT	MLB	24	183	11	4	0	3	12	14	30	2	0	.152/.224/.232	.169	.164	-0.3	3B 4	-0.8
2009	PIT	MLB	25	590	64	29	5	12	64	50	84	3	1	.258/.327/.401	.249	.282	2.5	3B 7	2.0
2010	PIT	MLB	26	271	27	8	0	4	16	19	43	1	1	.207/.266/.287	.214	.232	0.9	3B 3, 2B 0	-0.1
2011	*PIT*	*MLB*	*27*	*431*	*50*	*16*	*1*	*11*	*44*	*46*	*63*	*3*	*1*	*.249/.332/.387*	*.256*	*.266*	*-0.1*	*3B 3, 2B 0*	*1.3*

LaRoche's disappointing time with the Pirates ended when he was designated for assignment last November. The third baseman was considered one of the best prospects in baseball during his time in the Dodgers' farm system and was the key player whom the Pirates received in the July 2008 three-team trade that sent Jason Bay to the Red Sox and Manny Ramirez to Los Angeles. LaRoche had nearly two full seasons' worth of failed starts at third base to prove himself before he gave way to prospect Pedro Alvarez last June, after a hot April gave way to a "Please don't come to work until you feel better" .168/.221/.237 over the balance of the season. The Pirates even tried to salvage some value from LaRoche by expanding his positional palette, giving him some starts at first and second base and having him take ground balls at shortstop during batting practice. It didn't work out, but some team will probably latch on to the free agent with hopes of restoring some value. He's had streaks of productivity—between September 2009 and April 2010 he hit .320/.381/.516 in 39 games. It's a small sample and not quite a contiguous one, but between that and LaRoche's minor-league record, it's enough to keep alive a faint hope for his future.

Andrew McCutchen CF

Born: **10/10/1986** Age: **24**
Bats: R Throws: R Height: **5' 10"** Weight: **175**
Breakout: **5%** Improve: **49%** Collapse: **6%**
Attrition: **22%** MLB: **90%**

Comparables:
Jacoby Ellsbury, Melky Cabrera, Vada Pinson (62)

YEAR	TEAM	LVL	AGE	PA	R	2B	3B	HR	RBI	BB	SO	SB	CS	AVG/OBP/SLG	TAv	BABIP	BRR	FRAA	WARP
2008	IND	AAA	21	590	75	26	3	9	50	68	87	34	19	.283/.371/.398	.273	.324	3.0	CF 2, LF 0	3.0
2009	IND	AAA	22	219	41	10	8	4	20	17	24	10	2	.303/.361/.493	.297	.329	2.0	CF -3, LF 0	1.3
2009	PIT	MLB	22	493	74	26	9	12	54	54	83	22	5	.286/.365/.471	.289	.328	4.9	CF -12	2.1
2010	PIT	MLB	23	653	95	35	5	16	56	70	89	33	10	.286/.365/.449	.294	.311	4.4	CF -12	3.2
2011	*PIT*	*MLB*	*24*	*649*	*83*	*30*	*5*	*16*	*76*	*70*	*94*	*30*	*10*	*.282/.360/.437*	*.283*	*.309*	*-0.5*	*CF -11, LF 0*	*2.1*

The possibilities seem endless for McCutchen, a young player who possesses both great physical talent and outstanding instincts for the game. He is willing to take a walk, reduced his strikeout rate last season, and has the potential to be a perennial 20-40 man with his power and above-average speed. His defense is a fascinating subject: many scouts feel that he will become a perennial Gold Glove winner with his outstanding range, but various fielding metrics adjudge him a below-average defender. McCutchen detests losing, which is a desirable quality in a player who has already become the face of a franchise trying to overcome a record 18 consecutive losing seasons. It wouldn't hurt if his hunger to win became contagious.

Lastings Milledge OF

Born: **4/5/1985** Age: **26**
Bats: R Throws: R Height: **6' 0"** Weight: **187**
Breakout: **1%** Improve: **42%** Collapse: **6%**
Attrition: **11%** MLB: **81%**

Comparables:
Ben Francisco, Chris Pettit, Shannon Stewart (76)

YEAR	TEAM	LVL	AGE	PA	R	2B	3B	HR	RBI	BB	SO	SB	CS	AVG/OBP/SLG	TAv	BABIP	BRR	FRAA	WARP
2008	WAS	MLB	23	587	65	24	2	14	61	38	96	24	9	.268/.327/.402	.256	.297	0.4	CF -4	1.0
2009	IND	AAA	24	74	7	6	0	0	7	8	10	3	2	.333/.419/.433	.320	.377	0.2	LF 1, CF 0	0.8
2009	SYR	AAA	24	83	11	5	0	0	4	3	16	6	1	.253/.277/.316	.218	.312	0.6	LF 0, CF 3	0.1
2009	PIT	MLB	24	239	20	11	0	4	20	12	37	6	4	.291/.331/.396	.258	.328	-3.6	LF -1	0.0
2009	WAS	MLB	24	26	1	0	0	0	1	1	10	1	0	.167/.231/.167	.145	.286	0.1	CF -1	-0.3
2010	PIT	MLB	25	412	38	21	3	4	34	28	62	5	3	.277/.330/.380	.260	.321	-2.7	LF 3, RF -3	0.4
2011	*PIT*	*MLB*	*26*	*457*	*53*	*20*	*1*	*10*	*49*	*33*	*77*	*13*	*5*	*.269/.330/.398*	*.258*	*.303*	*-0.5*	*CF -1, LF 1*	*0.8*

An early draft of this comment said that Milledge "has flashed jaw-dropping potential on occasion at the major league level." This is one of those rhetorical constructions that is almost impossible to explain in real terms: you've never turned to your buddy in the stands and said something like, "Holy moly, Brad! Did you see Milledge *almost* do that? I'm almost convinced that someday he might *actually* do it!" Yet, the former Mets first-round pick might be the one player who can almost justify such a seemingly nonsensical observation. As Casey Stengel once said of the young Mickey Mantle, Milledge "has it in his body to be great." However, five years into his major-league career, his body is writing checks that his talent can't cash. He looks like a ballplayer, so when he does a ballplayerish thing, your confirmation bias kicks in: he's doing what you *think* he's capable of doing. The problem is it might be another three weeks before he does it again. Nontendered by the Pirates, Milledge will get another job with his flashing, but at 26, he's not young anymore and is likely to be another mediocre half-season away from journeyman fourth outfielder status.

Steve Pearce 1B

Born: **4/13/1983** Age: **28**
Bats: **R** Throws: **R** Height: **5' 11"** Weight: **200**
Breakout: **1%** Improve: **27%** Collapse: **2%**
Attrition: **12%** MLB: **64%**

Comparables:
Matthew Brown, J.R. House, Hank Blalock (76)

YEAR	TEAM	LVL	AGE	PA	R	2B	3B	HR	RBI	BB	SO	SB	CS	AVG/OBP/SLG	TAv	BABIP	BRR	FRAA	WARP
2008	IND	AAA	25	433	47	26	1	12	60	32	75	10	4	.251/.309/.417	.250	.275	-0.7	RF -8, 1B 3	-0.4
2008	PIT	MLB	25	119	6	7	0	4	15	5	22	2	0	.248/.294/.422	.247	.271	-0.7	RF -1, LF 0	-0.1
2009	IND	AAA	26	317	37	18	1	13	54	34	46	3	7	.286/.372/.502	.297	.298	-1.2	1B 4, RF 0	1.7
2009	PIT	MLB	26	186	19	13	1	4	16	21	43	1	0	.206/.296/.370	.231	.254	-0.3	1B 3, RF 0	-0.1
2010	IND	AAA	27	158	25	14	2	3	15	24	27	7	2	.326/.424/.535	.323	.379	1.8	1B -2, RF 1	1.5
2010	PIT	MLB	27	38	5	2	1	0	5	7	6	0	0	.276/.395/.414	.290	.320	0.2	1B 2	0.4
2011	*PIT*	*MLB*	*28*	*466*	*58*	*25*	*1*	*15*	*58*	*46*	*85*	*7*	*3*	*.259/.335/.441*	*.270*	*.287*	*-0.4*	*1B -4, RF -4*	*0.2*

The Pirates' front office was granted a fourth minor-league option for Pearce last winter, meaning that he won't be subjected to waivers if he fails to make the club in spring training and faces the strong possibility of spending the large part of another summer in Indianapolis playing Triple-A ball. Pearce, who underwent season-ending knee surgery last August, will be 28 this season and has nothing left to prove in the International League. He may not be an everyday player, but he can hit for power against left-handers (.304/.372/.552 in 129 major league PAs), which would have made him a good short side of a platoon at first base with Garrett Jones if the Pirates had not decided to sign Lyle Overbay instead.

Alex Presley OF

Born: **7/25/1985** Age: **25**
Bats: **L** Throws: **L** Height: **5' 9"** Weight: **180**
Breakout: **7%** Improve: **30%** Collapse: **5%**
Attrition: **24%** MLB: **44%**

Comparables:
Dave Martinez, Tony Gwynn, Angel Pagan (69)

YEAR	TEAM	LVL	AGE	PA	R	2B	3B	HR	RBI	BB	SO	SB	CS	AVG/OBP/SLG	TAv	BABIP	BRR	FRAA	WARP
2008	LYN	A+	22	325	39	15	1	6	35	29	50	13	6	.258/.320/.380	.260	.285	-2.9	CF 3	0.9
2009	LYN	A+	23	456	51	17	11	4	37	30	87	9	5	.257/.300/.379	.254	.307	-0.7	CF -1, LF 0	0.6
2010	ALT	AA	24	269	42	13	7	6	47	19	33	5	1	.350/.399/.533	.338	.383	-0.6	LF 1, RF 0	2.7
2010	IND	AAA	24	296	44	15	6	6	38	22	42	8	7	.294/.349/.460	.271	.329	4.0	CF -1, LF 1	1.5
2010	PIT	MLB	24	25	2	1	0	0	0	1	8	1	1	.261/.280/.304	.211	.375	-0.3	RF -1, LF -1	-0.4
2011	*PIT*	*MLB*	*25*	*463*	*51*	*19*	*4*	*8*	*49*	*28*	*88*	*9*	*4*	*.261/.302/.383*	*.240*	*.303*	*-0.5*	*CF -8, LF -1*	*-0.8*

No player in the Pirates' farm system improved his stock more in 2010 than Presley, who began the season as a Double-A fourth outfielder, ended it in the major leagues, and was named the organization's minor-league player of the year along the way. Presley will probably be returned to sender and start the season at Triple-A, since he is crowded out by other left-handed-hitting outfielders on the major-league depth chart. While he doesn't have star potential, Presley sprays line drives to all fields and plays decent defense at all three outfield spots. He projects as a major-league fourth outfielder, which is a heckuva lot better than his spot as a fourth outfielder in Altoona last April.

Tony Sanchez C

Born: **5/20/1988** Age: **23**
Bats: **R** Throws: **R** Height: **6' 0"** Weight: **213**
Breakout: **1%** Improve: **3%** Collapse: **3%**
Attrition: **6%** MLB: **17%**

Comparables:
Alex Avila, Jeff Clement, Ed Herrmann (77)

YEAR	TEAM	LVL	AGE	PA	R	2B	3B	HR	RBI	BB	SO	SB	CS	AVG/OBP/SLG	TAv	BABIP	BRR	FRAA	WARP
2009	WVA	A	21	188	29	15	1	7	46	21	34	1	0	.316/.415/.561	.332	.356	-0.1	C -1	1.9
2010	BRA	A+	22	163	16	11	0	1	20	18	25	1	1	.298/.399/.397	.268	.345	-1.2	C 0	0.8
2011	*PIT*	*MLB*	*23*	*236*	*26*	*11*	*0*	*6*	*24*	*21*	*53*	*0*	*0*	*.234/.317/.383*	*.247*	*.279*	*0.0*	*C 0*	*0.5*

Given an outside shot at reaching the big leagues by the end of the year, Sanchez played well in a season limited by injuries, his campaign ending in June, when he suffered a broken jaw after being hit by a pitch. The 2009 first-round pick could be a special player, a catcher who can both hit *and* field, something that will come as quite a novelty to the Pirates after 366 games of Ryan Doumit's unconvincing "Look, Mom! I dressed up as a catcher for Halloween!" routine. He has plus-plus receiving skills and a strong arm that lacks only accuracy. With career minor-league rates of .312/.413/.494 (107 games), Sanchez has shown he is a discriminating hitter, but he doesn't figure to get a lot better from here. So, if the kind of catcher who gets on base at an above-average rate and pops 10 to 12 home runs per year is what you like, then you will like this kind of catcher.

Chris Snyder — C

Born: 2/12/1981 Age: 30
Bats: R Throws: R Height: 6' 3" Weight: 220
Breakout: 2% Improve: 22% Collapse: 7%
Attrition: 13% MLB: 88%

Comparables:
Ed Bailey, Eric Munson, Don Mincher (78)

YEAR	TEAM	LVL	AGE	PA	R	2B	3B	HR	RBI	BB	SO	SB	CS	AVG/OBP/SLG	TAv	BABIP	BRR	FRAA	WARP
2008	ARI	MLB	27	404	48	22	1	16	64	56	101	0	0	.237/.344/.452	.268	.278	-1.0	C 0	2.0
2009	ARI	MLB	28	202	20	7	0	6	22	32	47	0	0	.200/.332/.352	.247	.235	0.0	C 0, 1B 0	0.6
2010	ARI	MLB	29	234	22	8	0	10	32	36	61	0	0	.231/.350/.426	.267	.278	-2.2	C 0	0.9
2010	PIT	MLB	29	142	12	1	0	5	16	16	33	0	0	.169/.268/.298	.207	.184	-2.6	C 1	-0.3
2011	*PIT*	*MLB*	*30*	*321*	*38*	*12*	*0*	*12*	*35*	*44*	*74*	*0*	*0*	*.230/.338/.409*	*.262*	*.263*	*0.0*	*C 0, 1B 0*	*1.4*

Snyder is living, breathing proof that traditional fielding statistics are meaningless. He entered last season with the best fielding percentage of any catcher who had caught at least 500 games in the major leagues, but after the Pirates acquired him from the Diamondbacks in a deadline deal last July, he spent the final two months of the season dropping relays from infielders and pitches from moundsmen. Snyder is not a great offensive player, but he does pack more punch than the average catcher—not that he gave any proof of that in Buccos motley. Nonetheless, the Pirates have cast their lot with him as their starting catcher, shifting Ryan Doumit to right field.

Jose Tabata — LF

Born: 8/12/1988 Age: 22
Bats: R Throws: R Height: 5' 11" Weight: 210
Breakout: 3% Improve: 27% Collapse: 1%
Attrition: 9% MLB: 42%

Comparables:
Elvis Andrus, Rickey Henderson, Dan Driessen (61)

YEAR	TEAM	LVL	AGE	PA	R	2B	3B	HR	RBI	BB	SO	SB	CS	AVG/OBP/SLG	TAv	BABIP	BRR	FRAA	WARP
2008	ALT	AA	19	97	16	6	2	3	13	8	18	8	0	.348/.402/.562	.338	.412	1.2	CF -1	1.1
2008	TRN	AA	19	332	40	9	0	3	36	26	49	10	2	.248/.319/.310	.232	.283	1.5	RF -2	-0.6
2009	ALT	AA	20	254	31	15	1	2	25	20	25	7	6	.303/.370/.404	.289	.332	-0.9	RF 0, CF 0	1.2
2009	IND	AAA	20	148	21	7	1	3	10	10	18	4	2	.276/.331/.410	.261	.296	1.2	RF 1, CF -3	0.2
2010	IND	AAA	21	252	42	13	2	3	19	23	35	25	6	.308/.373/.424	.277	.349	2.6	CF -2, LF 3	1.5
2010	PIT	MLB	21	441	61	21	4	4	35	28	57	19	7	.299/.342/.400	.268	.334	3.2	LF 6, CF -2	1.8
2011	*PIT*	*MLB*	*22*	*507*	*59*	*22*	*2*	*8*	*52*	*36*	*74*	*21*	*7*	*.280/.332/.390*	*.259*	*.312*	*-0.1*	*RF -2, CF -4*	*0.6*

Tabata is not the player the Pirates thought they were getting out of Double-A from the Yankees at the 2008 trading deadline. Scouting reports indicated that he'd grow up to be a masher, but instead, he has turned into an all-around hitter who steals bases at a high percentage and batted second for the Pirates after making his major-league debut last June. Tabata played excellent defense in PNC Park's spacious left field, and the ball still jumps off his bat with enough force to convince some scouts that he will eventually develop the promised pop. As he still lacks the typical corner-outfielder's profile, the theoretical 22-year-old (Tabata's true age can only be ascertained by Doc Brown and his DeLorean) will go as far as his batting average will take him.

Neil Walker — 2B

Born: 9/10/1985 Age: 25
Bats: S Throws: R Height: 6' 3" Weight: 210
Breakout: 5% Improve: 26% Collapse: 11%
Attrition: 26% MLB: 53%

Comparables:
Seth Smith, Freddy Sandoval, Daniel Murphy (71)

YEAR	TEAM	LVL	AGE	PA	R	2B	3B	HR	RBI	BB	SO	SB	CS	AVG/OBP/SLG	TAv	BABIP	BRR	FRAA	WARP
2008	IND	AAA	22	550	69	25	7	16	80	29	102	10	6	.242/.278/.414	.236	.264	2.0	3B 6	1.0
2009	IND	AAA	23	390	38	31	2	14	69	26	60	5	2	.264/.310/.480	.263	.277	1.0	3B -8	0.6
2009	PIT	MLB	23	40	5	1	0	0	0	4	11	1	0	.194/.275/.222	.183	.280	-0.2	3B -1	-0.3
2010	IND	AAA	24	189	25	18	2	6	26	19	31	10	1	.321/.392/.560	.306	.364	0.5	2B 1, LF 3	2.0
2010	PIT	MLB	24	469	57	29	3	12	66	34	83	2	3	.296/.348/.462	.286	.338	-2.7	2B -18, 3B 0	0.4
2011	*PIT*	*MLB*	*25*	*555*	*65*	*30*	*2*	*17*	*69*	*39*	*102*	*9*	*3*	*.258/.311/.427*	*.255*	*.287*	*-0.3*	*3B -3, 2B -4*	*0.5*

Walker made a phoenix-like rise to the Pirates' starting lineup last season, taking over at second base for Akinori Iwamura in late May despite never having played the position before spring training. He went on to have one of the best years of any National League rookie. The Pirates began converting Walker, their first-round draft selection from 2004, into a utility player in spring training both because of generally mediocre hitting results and because he no longer had a future at third base, with Pedro Alvarez set to make the position his long-term domain, but he found a home at the keystone. Walker is, somewhat surprisingly, an above-average offensive player for a second baseman as a switch-hitter with power. What's more, he improved his plate discipline as the 2010 season wore on, a very encouraging sign for a player who had been something of a free swinger throughout his professional career.

Delwyn Young — RF

Born: 6/30/1982 Age: 29
Bats: S Throws: R Height: 5' 8" Weight: 209
Breakout: 0% Improve: 24% Collapse: 3%
Attrition: 4% MLB: 53%

Comparables:
Paul McAnulty, Darnell McDonald, Bob Nieman (71)

YEAR	TEAM	LVL	AGE	PA	R	2B	3B	HR	RBI	BB	SO	SB	CS	AVG/OBP/SLG	TAv	BABIP	BRR	FRAA	WARP
2008	LVG	AAA	26	56	14	5	1	3	10	7	8	0	0	.347/.429/.674	.318	.368	0.4	RF 1, LF 2	0.8
2008	LAN	MLB	26	143	10	9	0	1	7	14	34	0	0	.246/.315/.341	.238	.319	-1.1	LF -1, RF -3	-0.4
2009	PIT	MLB	27	388	40	16	2	7	43	29	90	2	0	.266/.325/.381	.241	.336	-1.9	2B -8, RF 3	-0.6
2010	PIT	MLB	28	207	22	11	1	7	28	13	52	1	0	.236/.285/.414	.253	.284	0.3	RF -5, 3B -2	-0.5
2011	*PIT*	*MLB*	*29*	*386*	*46*	*20*	*1*	*10*	*46*	*30*	*86*	*2*	*1*	*.264/.322/.420*	*.259*	*.315*	*0.0*	*RF -2, 2B -3*	*0.1*

Young put up some big Triple-A numbers while in the Dodgers' organization, but he never matched those marks in nearly two full seasons with the Pirates, who designated him for assignment last November. The free agent has had moments where he showed flashes of his tantalizing talent, like smacking a home run in Stephen Strasburg's otherwise awe-inspiring major league debut last June, but his swing is too inconsistent to make him a good pinch-hitter, and his value as a super-utility player is nil because of his subpar defensive abilities at second base, third base, left field, and right field. He's the classic Quad-A hitter, one likely to spend the rest of his career bouncing between the majors and Triple-A. His next bounce will take him to the Phillies organization.

PITCHERS

Ramon Aguero

Born: **3/10/1988** Age: **23**
Bats: **R** Throws: **R** Height: **6' 4"** Weight: **195**
Breakout: **0%** Improve: **0%** Collapse: **0%**
Attrition: **0%** MLB: **0%**

Comparables:
Ryan Tucker, Joe Kerrigan, Garry Roggenburk (90)

YEAR	TEAM	LVL	AGE	W	L	SV	G	GS	IP	H	HR	BB	SO	EqBB9	EqSO9	GB%	BABIP	WHIP	ERA	FRA	WARP
2008	SCO	A-	20	1	10	0	15	10	49^{1}	64	3	22	35	4.0	6.4	50%	.353	1.87	6.75	7.85	-1.0
2009	WVA	A	21	1	2	0	20	3	49^{2}	58	5	16	40	2.9	7.2	47%	.342	1.65	4.71	5.05	0.1
2009	LYN	A+	21	1	0	0	11	0	21^{2}	20	1	9	22	3.7	9.1	53%	.306	1.47	2.49	2.45	0.7
2011	*PIT*	*MLB*	*23*	*1*	*1*	*0*	*23*	*2*	*46*	*56*	*6*	*27*	*24*	*5.3*	*4.7*	*45%*	*.318*	*1.81*	*6.53*	*7.10*	*-1.0*

Aguero failed to build on his breakthrough 2009 season, suffering a 2010 campaign marred by elbow tendinitis and lower-back stiffness. When he was able to pitch, he didn't get anyone out at Double-A, posting an 8.68 ERA in 18.2 innings with a 17/14 strikeout-to-walk ratio. Thus, the quick rise to the major leagues that had been anticipated by some experts was put on hold. Aguero has become one of the hardest throwers in the system since converting to short relief in 2009, and his fastball now hits 97 with regularity. The 2009 season was also the first in which he was forced to go by his real name and age; he'd previously been known as the more youthful Samuel Vasquez until it was discovered that he had been using someone else's birth certificate, presumably Samuel Vasquez's. What happened to the actual Vasquez? Foul play? Like William Wilson, did Aguero do away with Vasquez only to find he had done away with himself? Was he bribed with a family parcel of land near Hermiston? And what of the woman in white? We shall never know, but Aguero remains one to watch.

Jose Ascanio

Born: **5/2/1985** Age: **26**
Bats: **R** Throws: **R** Height: **6' 0"** Weight: **170**
Breakout: **0%** Improve: **0%** Collapse: **0%**
Attrition: **0%** MLB: **0%**

Comparables:
Jose Garcia, Stan Belinda, Bill Campbell (83)

YEAR	TEAM	LVL	AGE	W	L	SV	G	GS	IP	H	HR	BB	SO	EqBB9	EqSO9	GB%	BABIP	WHIP	ERA	FRA	WARP
2008	IOW	AAA	23	2	1	11	40	0	54^{2}	54	10	23	58	3.8	9.5	42%	.295	1.50	5.10	5.93	-0.3
2008	CHN	MLB	23	0	0	0	6	0	5^{2}	8	1	4	3	6.4	4.8	36%	.333	2.29	7.94	7.39	-0.2
2009	IOW	AAA	24	2	4	0	12	12	51^{1}	47	1	18	47	3.2	8.2	51%	.313	1.38	3.16	4.10	1.1
2009	CHN	MLB	24	0	1	0	14	0	15^{1}	18	1	9	18	5.3	10.6	41%	.395	1.89	3.52	2.63	0.4
2009	PIT	MLB	24	0	1	0	2	0	2^{2}	4	0	0	2	0.0	6.8	50%	.400	1.88	6.75	4.37	0.0
2011	*PIT*	*MLB*	*26*	*3*	*3*	*1*	*33*	*6*	*60*	*61*	*6*	*25*	*50*	*3.8*	*7.5*	*45%*	*.310*	*1.44*	*4.62*	*5.02*	*0.3*

Ascanio had a lost year after undergoing labrum surgery in October 2009, not making his 2010 debut until August, after which he made it through only two minor-league rehab appearances before suffering a hand injury in a home accident, ending his season. Ascanio has pitched a grand total of five times since the Pirates acquired him from the Cubs at the 2009 deadline. Armed with a four-seam fastball that reaches 95 mph and a solid two-seamer, the near-26-year-old Ascanio has a chance to be an effective middle reliever or more—if he can ever get healthy.

Brian Burres

Born: **4/8/1981** Age: **30**
Bats: **L** Throws: **L** Height: **6' 1"** Weight: **182**
Breakout: **17%** Improve: **52%** Collapse: **16%**
Attrition: **6%** MLB: **91%**

Comparables:
Dave Mlicki, Rick Rhoden, Danny Darwin (80)

YEAR	TEAM	LVL	AGE	W	L	SV	G	GS	IP	H	HR	BB	SO	EqBB9	EqSO9	GB%	BABIP	WHIP	ERA	FRA	WARP
2008	BAL	MLB	27	7	10	0	31	22	129^{2}	165	17	50	63	3.5	4.4	37%	.322	1.70	5.97	6.09	-0.2
2009	LVG	AAA	28	6	7	0	19	17	107^{2}	121	11	30	84	2.5	7.0	51%	.320	1.43	4.76	4.91	1.1
2009	TOR	MLB	28	0	2	0	2	2	6^{1}	12	0	5	4	7.1	5.7	50%	.429	2.68	14.21	13.56	-0.3
2010	IND	AAA	29	5	4	0	15	14	82	75	10	34	61	3.7	6.7	46%	.271	1.39	4.28	4.83	1.2
2010	PIT	MLB	29	4	5	0	20	13	79^{1}	87	9	34	45	3.9	5.1	43%	.291	1.60	4.99	5.39	0.1
2011	*PIT*	*MLB*	*30*	*8*	*10*	*0*	*24*	*24*	*135*	*155*	*16*	*57*	*79*	*3.8*	*5.3*	*44%*	*.309*	*1.56*	*5.35*	*5.82*	*0.6*

That Burres spent as much time as he did in the major leagues last season was a sign of the ills that plagued the Pirates' staff. The journeyman didn't pitch well, with awful peripherals and an ugly ERA. Far from overpowering, Burres's fastball rarely surpasses 88 mph. He complements it with a pedestrian curveball, slider, and fastball mix. He is the type of guy a team socks away on its Triple-A roster in case of an apocalypse, a term that fairly describes the 2010 Pirates' pitching staff. The Pirates nontendered Burres in December, content in the knowledge that pitchers with 5.83 career ERAs are more common than ants.

Mike Crotta

Born: **9/24/1984** Age: **26**
Bats: **R** Throws: **R** Height: **6' 6"** Weight: **210**
Breakout: **10%** Improve: **13%** Collapse: **11%**
Attrition: **18%** MLB: **25%**

Comparables:
Cesar Ramos, Craig Stammen, Mike Esposito (73)

YEAR	TEAM	LVL	AGE	W	L	SV	G	GS	IP	H	HR	BB	SO	EqBB9	EqSO9	GB%	BABIP	WHIP	ERA	FRA	WARP
2008	LYN	A+	23	9	10	0	28	28	146^{1}	171	8	25	97	1.5	6.0	64%	.321	1.37	4.68	5.84	0.1
2009	ALT	AA	24	7	8	0	27	27	143^{2}	181	7	33	97	2.1	6.1	59%	.345	1.53	4.76	4.11	2.3
2010	ALT	AA	25	2	0	0	4	4	25^{1}	14	0	3	16	1.1	5.7	65%	.189	0.68	1.78	4.14	0.3
2010	IND	AAA	25	5	10	0	24	24	131^{1}	160	10	37	89	2.5	6.1	58%	.348	1.53	4.93	5.23	1.3
2011	*PIT*	*MLB*	*26*	*6*	*11*	*0*	*23*	*23*	*124*	*166*	*14*	*40*	*51*	*2.9*	*3.7*	*54%*	*.334*	*1.66*	*6.04*	*6.56*	*-0.3*

Crotta has quietly worked his way up through the farm system since becoming the Pirates' 17th-round draft pick in 2006 and is now held in high enough regard by the organization that he was protected on the 40-man roster at the end of last season. Crotta has added some extra zip to his fastball since turning pro and now tops out at 94 mph while sitting at 91-92; he also has a good changeup. He is an extreme pitch-to-contact type with low strikeout and walk percentages, but he compensates by inducing a host of ground balls. Crotta isn't likely to become a star, though he has jockeyed into the hunt for a spot as a fifth starter or middle reliever in the majors. He'll probably begin the season at Triple-A, but he could also be one of the first to get a call if trouble arises in Pittsburgh. But when does *that* ever happen?

Zach Duke

Born: **4/19/1983** Age: **28**
Bats: **L** Throws: **L** Height: **6' 2"** Weight: **212**
Breakout: **14%** Improve: **52%** Collapse: **11%**
Attrition: **7%** MLB: **91%**

Comparables:
Jim Kaat, Bobby J. Jones, Scott Erickson (71)

YEAR	TEAM	LVL	AGE	W	L	SV	G	GS	IP	H	HR	BB	SO	EqBB9	EqSO9	GB%	BABIP	WHIP	ERA	FRA	WARP
2008	PIT	MLB	25	5	14	0	31	31	185	230	19	47	87	2.3	4.2	50%	.315	1.54	4.77	5.27	1.0
2009	PIT	MLB	26	11	16	0	32	32	213	231	23	49	106	2.1	4.5	50%	.293	1.33	4.06	4.50	2.4
2010	PIT	MLB	27	8	15	0	29	29	159	212	25	51	96	2.9	5.4	49%	.338	1.68	5.72	5.22	0.5
2011	*PIT*	*MLB*	*28*	*9*	*13*	*0*	*30*	*30*	*180*	*224*	*21*	*51*	*81*	*2.5*	*4.0*	*48%*	*.320*	*1.52*	*5.36*	*5.83*	*0.6*

Duke's career with the Pirates started with so much promise in 2005, when he was called up from Triple-A in July and posted a 1.81 ERA in 84 1/3 innings. Nonetheless, his stay in Pittsburgh was terminated last November, when he was traded to the Diamondbacks for a player to be named later. Part of the motivation for the deal was that Duke made $4.3 million last season and was eligible for arbitration again. The Pirates' reluctance to hand him a raise for this season was understandable; he was so many shades of awful in 2010 that he could have populated the world's most unappealing box of crayons. He would have had the worst ERA in the major leagues if he had pitched the three additional innings necessary to qualify for the title. Duke threw as high as 93 mph as a rookie, but his stuff has deteriorated—his fastball topped out at 85 in some starts last season, while his curveball looked flat. In his new home, he may see it flattened into the stands even more often than it was last year.

Dana Eveland

Born: **10/29/1983** Age: **27**
Bats: **L** Throws: **L** Height: **6' 1"** Weight: **220**
Breakout: **25%** Improve: **44%** Collapse: **7%**
Attrition: **15%** MLB: **72%**

Comparables:
Enrique Gonzalez, Matt Albers, Jim Kaat (77)

YEAR	TEAM	LVL	AGE	W	L	SV	G	GS	IP	H	HR	BB	SO	EqBB9	EqSO9	GB%	BABIP	WHIP	ERA	FRA	WARP
2008	SAC	AAA	24	3	0	0	3	3	21	23	2	4	21	1.7	9.0	59%	.328	1.29	2.57	3.59	0.5
2008	OAK	MLB	24	9	9	0	29	29	168	172	10	77	118	4.1	6.3	49%	.312	1.55	4.34	4.48	2.0
2009	SAC	AAA	25	8	6	0	21	21	124	133	12	51	92	3.7	6.7	56%	.312	1.52	4.94	2.90	3.5
2009	OAK	MLB	25	2	4	0	13	9	44	70	4	26	22	5.3	4.5	61%	.391	2.18	7.16	6.75	-0.4
2010	IND	AAA	26	0	2	0	11	5	26	41	5	6	26	2.1	9.0	50%	.414	1.81	7.96	7.41	-0.4
2010	TOR	MLB	26	3	4	0	9	9	44^{2}	57	4	27	21	5.4	4.2	53%	.333	1.93	6.45	6.26	-0.2
2010	PIT	MLB	26	0	1	0	3	1	9^{2}	15	0	5	3	4.7	2.8	38%	.385	2.28	8.38	7.14	-0.2
2011	*PIT*	*MLB*	*27*	*7*	*10*	*0*	*23*	*23*	*120*	*140*	*11*	*55*	*76*	*4.1*	*5.7*	*50%*	*.327*	*1.62*	*5.39*	*5.86*	*0.6*

Pirates general manager Neal Huntington is usually a rational guy, but his strangest comment of 2010 came in May, when he acquired Eveland from the Blue Jays. Huntington said he was excited because the Pirates would have contractual control over Eveland—a replacement-level cast-off—for many years to come. It turned out not to matter, as Eveland was outrighted to Triple-A after one start and two relief appearances and never returned to the major leagues. The Dodgers signed him as a minor-league free agent in November and will try to make something out of a guy who throws just 88 mph and has a standard four-pitch mix.

Sean Gallagher

Born: **12/30/1985** Age: **25**
Bats: R Throws: R Height: **6' 2"** Weight: **225**
Breakout: **4%** Improve: **16%** Collapse: **4%**
Attrition: **1%** MLB: **29%**

Comparables:
Len Barker, Gene Brabender, Barry Latman (79)

YEAR	TEAM	LVL	AGE	W	L	SV	G	GS	IP	H	HR	BB	SO	EqBB9	EqSO9	GB%	BABIP	WHIP	ERA	FRA	WARP
2008	IOW	AAA	22	2	2	0	5	5	29	21	2	9	30	2.8	9.3	56%	.250	1.03	3.10	4.77	0.5
2008	CHN	MLB	22	3	4	0	12	10	58^2	58	6	22	49	3.4	7.5	45%	.297	1.43	4.45	4.69	0.7
2008	OAK	MLB	22	2	3	0	11	11	56^2	60	7	36	54	5.7	8.6	28%	.317	1.73	5.88	6.48	-0.5
2009	SAC	AAA	23	1	0	0	5	5	20^2	12	0	6	15	2.6	6.5	52%	.207	0.92	1.74	3.64	0.5
2009	OAK	MLB	23	1	2	0	6	2	14^1	21	1	7	10	4.4	6.3	38%	.392	2.09	8.16	8.86	-0.3
2009	SDN	MLB	23	2	0	0	8	0	5^1	5	0	5	4	8.4	6.8	31%	.313	1.88	0.00	1.74	0.2
2010	SDN	MLB	24	0	0	0	15	0	23^1	24	5	19	21	7.3	8.1	37%	.302	1.93	5.40	5.46	-0.2
2010	PIT	MLB	24	2	1	0	31	0	34^1	38	2	22	22	5.8	5.8	50%	.310	1.78	6.03	7.01	-0.9
2011	*PIT*	*MLB*	*25*	*6*	*6*	*0*	*47*	*14*	104^1	*109*	*10*	*55*	*79*	*4.7*	*6.8*	*43%*	*.309*	*1.57*	*4.97*	*5.40*	*0.5*

Although Gallagher was once considered a top prospect, that ship has not only sailed but also sunk as he has bounced from the Cubs to the Athletics to the Padres to the Pirates over the last two seasons. Just as he approached the six years needed to become a minor-league free agent, the Pirates outrighted him to Triple-A and will retain control of Gallagher this season. While he tinkers in Indy, the righty will need to lower his walk rate and increase his strikeout rate to become an effective major-league pitcher; unfortunately, the same could be said of countless hurlers who will never accomplish either feat. Gallagher has a fastball that reaches 94 mph and a good, hard slider; he just doesn't know where either pitch is going once it leaves his hand.

Joel Hanrahan

Born: **10/6/1981** Age: **29**
Bats: R Throws: R Height: **6' 3"** Weight: **215**
Breakout: **19%** Improve: **34%** Collapse: **15%**
Attrition: **6%** MLB: **63%**

Comparables:
Lee Smith, Bob Johnson, Jim Miller (72)

YEAR	TEAM	LVL	AGE	W	L	SV	G	GS	IP	H	HR	BB	SO	EqBB9	EqSO9	GB%	BABIP	WHIP	ERA	FRA	WARP
2008	WAS	MLB	26	6	3	9	69	0	84^1	73	9	43	93	4.6	9.9	44%	.292	1.39	4.06	4.82	0.2
2009	PIT	MLB	27	0	1	0	33	0	31^1	23	0	20	37	5.7	10.6	28%	.303	1.40	1.72	2.74	0.9
2009	WAS	MLB	27	1	3	5	34	0	32^2	50	3	14	35	3.9	9.6	46%	.431	2.02	7.71	4.61	0.1
2010	PIT	MLB	28	4	1	6	72	0	69^2	58	6	26	100	3.4	12.9	42%	.329	1.26	3.62	3.29	1.3
2011	*PIT*	*MLB*	*29*	*5*	*2*	*5*	*95*	*0*	96^1	*92*	*9*	*48*	*97*	*4.5*	*9.1*	*43%*	*.315*	*1.46*	*4.34*	*4.72*	*-0.0*

Hanrahan had an outstanding season in 2010, consistently blowing hitters away with a fastball that reached 97-98 mph. His performance was especially impressive in light of the end-of-2009 elbow problems that persisted into 2010 and caused him to start the season on the disabled list. Hanrahan also has a plus slider, and the only time he really got into trouble last season was when he would rely more on the breaking ball at the expense of the heater. Hanrahan lost the closer's job twice with the Nationals in 2009, but the change of scenery has suited him well. He enters spring training as the favorite to serve as the stopper, though Evan Meek will be a strong competitor for the role.

Kevin Hart

Born: **11/29/1982** Age: **28**
Bats: R Throws: R Height: **6' 4"** Weight: **215**
Breakout: **0%** Improve: **4%** Collapse: **2%**
Attrition: **5%** MLB: **8%**

Comparables:
Dan Meyer, Wes Littleton, Jonah Bayliss (82)

YEAR	TEAM	LVL	AGE	W	L	SV	G	GS	IP	H	HR	BB	SO	EqBB9	EqSO9	GB%	BABIP	WHIP	ERA	FRA	WARP
2008	IOW	AAA	25	4	2	5	26	10	57^2	38	3	20	63	3.1	9.8	44%	.254	1.07	2.81	3.97	1.1
2008	CHN	MLB	25	2	2	0	21	0	27^2	39	2	18	23	5.9	7.5	59%	.385	2.17	6.51	5.95	-0.3
2009	IOW	AAA	26	3	3	3	22	6	52^1	39	5	20	57	3.4	9.8	44%	.262	1.22	3.10	4.25	0.8
2009	CHN	MLB	26	3	1	0	8	4	27^2	23	3	18	13	5.9	4.2	44%	.238	1.55	2.60	3.73	0.7
2009	PIT	MLB	26	1	8	0	10	10	53^1	74	8	26	39	4.4	6.6	45%	.369	1.91	6.92	7.15	-0.6
2011	*PIT*	*MLB*	*28*	*6*	*7*	*1*	*43*	*16*	*109*	*117*	*14*	*53*	*80*	*4.4*	*6.6*	*45%*	*.308*	*1.55*	*5.22*	*5.67*	*0.3*

Some seasons, a pitcher would have been better off staying in bed. Hart failed to win the fifth starter's job in spring training, then had his 2010 season ended in late April by a torn labrum. The Pirates expect Hart to be ready for the start of the season, but the larger problem is that he is out of minor-league options, which means that the most minor-league time they could buy for him without sneaking him through waivers is a 30-day injury rehabilitation assignment. He's likely to need more than that to get completely back into pitching shape. The Pirates plan to use Hart as a reliever when he does return, which suits him better since his changeup isn't a very good pitch, but he does have two plus offerings in a low-90s fastball and a slider.

Jeff Karstens

Born: **9/24/1982** Age: **28**
Bats: R Throws: R Height: **6' 3"** Weight: **175**
Breakout: **6%** Improve: **28%** Collapse: **6%**
Attrition: **8%** MLB: **51%**

Comparables:
Pat Misch, Esteban Loaiza, Michael O'Connor (74)

YEAR	TEAM	LVL	AGE	W	L	SV	G	GS	IP	H	HR	BB	SO	EqBB9	EqSO9	GB%	BABIP	WHIP	ERA	FRA	WARP
2008	SWB	AAA	25	6	4	0	12	12	68^2	66	8	15	55	2.0	7.2	41%	.290	1.18	3.80	4.47	1.1
2008	PIT	MLB	25	2	6	0	9	9	51^1	56	7	13	23	2.3	4.0	45%	.277	1.34	4.03	5.67	0.2
2009	PIT	MLB	26	4	6	0	39	13	108	115	12	45	52	3.8	4.3	41%	.286	1.50	5.42	5.68	-0.4
2010	PIT	MLB	27	3	10	0	26	19	122^2	146	21	27	72	2.0	5.3	43%	.309	1.42	4.92	4.78	0.8
2011	*PIT*	*MLB*	*28*	*6*	*7*	*0*	*33*	*17*	*123*	*141*	*17*	*38*	*65*	*2.8*	*4.7*	*43%*	*.300*	*1.45*	*4.98*	*5.42*	*0.6*

Karstens has developed into a utility pitcher who can start or work in relief. Still, the Pirates would be wise not to use him extensively in either role, because he gets exposed with overuse and routinely gets bombed after two trips through a lineup. Karstens' fastball tops out at 88 mph, but his strength is his ability to spot it for strikes along with a curveball, slider, and changeup. The original Scary Fly-Ball Guy is a serviceable 12th man on a pitching staff, but is bound to disappoint anyone who thinks he can be much more.

Wil Ledezma

Born: **1/21/1981** Age: **30**
Bats: L Throws: L Height: **6' 3"** Weight: **150**
Breakout: **6%** Improve: **7%** Collapse: **6%**
Attrition: **5%** MLB: **16%**

Comparables:
Santiago Casilla, Chad Fox, Juan Cruz (73)

YEAR	TEAM	LVL	AGE	W	L	SV	G	GS	IP	H	HR	BB	SO	EqBB9	EqSO9	GB%	BABIP	WHIP	ERA	FRA	WARP
2008	ARI	MLB	27	0	0	0	3	0	4	2	0	3	4	6.8	9.0	27%	.200	1.25	0.00	-1.41	0.1
2008	SDN	MLB	27	0	2	0	25	6	54^{1}	49	4	38	49	6.3	8.1	40%	.290	1.66	4.47	4.98	0.2
2009	WAS	MLB	28	0	0	0	5	0	5^{2}	8	1	4	8	6.4	12.7	44%	.412	2.12	9.53	8.47	-0.2
2010	IND	AAA	29	0	1	8	35	0	38^{1}	20	1	19	50	4.5	11.8	40%	.247	1.05	0.94	1.78	1.4
2010	PIT	MLB	29	0	3	0	27	0	19^{2}	25	2	6	22	2.7	10.1	38%	.377	1.63	6.86	4.40	0.1
2011	*PIT*	*MLB*	*30*	*3*	*2*	*1*	*52*	*2*	*71^{1}*	*71*	*6*	*37*	*65*	*4.7*	*8.2*	*43%*	*.315*	*1.51*	*4.46*	*4.85*	*0.1*

The Pirates handled Ledezma quite strangely. Like many teams before them, they fell in love with his arm, the rare left-side appendage that can crank a fastball up to 95 mph. They liked it so much that they signed him to a one-year contract worth $700,000 to avoid arbitration as soon as last season ended. Perhaps the Pirates have found the secret to unlocking Ledezma's potential, as two bad outings last year inflated his ERA and masked a decent season out of the bullpen. Still, $700,000 is an awful lot to risk on a pitcher with a shaky track record for a franchise that literally watches every last penny, all of which makes it doubly odd that they designated him for assignment in late December. He'll head north to Toronto for 2011.

Chris Leroux

Born: **4/14/1984** Age: **27**
Bats: L Throws: R Height: **6' 6"** Weight: **225**
Breakout: **1%** Improve: **5%** Collapse: **0%**
Attrition: **3%** MLB: **5%**

Comparables:
Carmen Pignatiello, Leo Rosales, A.J. Murray (89)

YEAR	TEAM	LVL	AGE	W	L	SV	G	GS	IP	H	HR	BB	SO	EqBB9	EqSO9	GB%	BABIP	WHIP	ERA	FRA	WARP
2008	JUP	A+	24	6	7	1	57	0	74	60	6	26	78	3.2	9.5	45%	.286	1.24	3.53	4.22	0.8
2009	JAX	AA	25	5	3	2	46	0	60	59	0	17	55	2.6	8.3	53%	.333	1.28	2.70	1.85	2.1
2009	FLO	MLB	25	0	0	0	5	0	6^{2}	11	0	4	2	5.4	2.7	52%	.379	2.25	10.80	8.55	-0.2
2010	NWO	AAA	26	0	3	1	21	0	22	26	2	7	20	2.9	8.2	51%	.358	1.59	6.55	5.64	-0.1
2010	FLO	MLB	26	0	0	0	17	0	18	24	1	11	18	5.5	9.0	53%	.426	1.94	7.00	5.86	-0.2
2010	PIT	MLB	26	0	1	0	6	0	4^{2}	4	0	3	4	5.8	7.7	50%	.286	1.50	5.79	6.82	-0.1
2011	*PIT*	*MLB*	*27*	*2*	*1*	*0*	*49*	*0*	*56^{2}*	*63*	*6*	*28*	*41*	*4.5*	*6.4*	*46%*	*.319*	*1.60*	*5.24*	*5.69*	*-0.7*

The Pirates have tried to accumulate as many power arms as possible since Neal Huntington became general manager four years ago, so they jumped at the chance to claim Leroux off waivers from the Marlins late last season. Leroux has a 96-mph fastball and a hard slider, but the former college catcher has yet to establish full command of either pitch. He is going to have to cut down on the walks to be successful in the major leagues, but will get a chance to make the Pirates' wide-open bullpen this spring. The team will also have some roster flexibility, since Leroux has one minor-league option left.

Brad Lincoln

Born: **5/25/1985** Age: **26**
Bats: L Throws: R Height: **6' 0"** Weight: **210**
Breakout: **13%** Improve: **28%** Collapse: **12%**
Attrition: **17%** MLB: **53%**

Comparables:
Glen Perkins, Enrique Gonzalez, Bill Gullickson (74)

YEAR	TEAM	LVL	AGE	W	L	SV	G	GS	IP	H	HR	BB	SO	EqBB9	EqSO9	GB%	BABIP	WHIP	ERA	FRA	WARP
2008	HIC	A	23	5	5	0	11	11	62	72	8	6	46	0.9	6.7	52%	.323	1.29	4.50	4.33	0.9
2008	LYN	A+	23	1	5	0	8	8	41^{2}	42	5	11	29	2.4	6.3	51%	.285	1.29	4.75	5.38	0.3
2009	ALT	AA	24	1	5	0	13	13	75	63	4	18	65	2.2	7.8	46%	.282	1.11	2.28	2.37	2.8
2009	IND	AAA	24	6	2	0	12	12	61^{1}	72	7	10	42	1.5	6.2	35%	.330	1.35	4.70	4.86	0.6
2010	IND	AAA	25	7	5	0	17	17	94	83	9	24	84	2.3	8.0	42%	.280	1.21	4.12	4.88	1.2
2010	PIT	MLB	25	1	4	0	11	9	52^{2}	66	9	15	25	2.6	4.3	39%	.307	1.63	6.66	7.23	-0.9
2011	*PIT*	*MLB*	*26*	*6*	*7*	*0*	*18*	*18*	*98^{2}*	*112*	*13*	*30*	*58*	*2.7*	*5.3*	*43%*	*.305*	*1.44*	*5.05*	*5.49*	*0.8*

Lincoln certainly seemed ready to make the jump to the major leagues when he was called up last June. However, once Pirates pitching coach Joe Kerrigan got hold of him, everything went haywire. Kerrigan inexplicably changed Lincoln's mechanics, and his fastball dropped from 95 mph to 89; he also had a hard time throwing his above-average curveball for strikes. Lincoln was sent back to Triple-A after nine mostly bad starts, and when he was called back in September, he pitched sparingly because of shoulder and neck stiffness. New pitching coach Ray Searage worked with Lincoln in the minor leagues and is hopeful he can get the Pirates' first-round draft selection from 2006 back on track to be remembered for more than just being drafted ahead of Tim Lincecum.

Jeff Locke

Born: **11/20/1987** Age: **23**
Bats: **L** Throws: **L** Height: **6' 2"** Weight: **180**
Breakout: **5%** Improve: **7%** Collapse: **2%**
Attrition: **5%** MLB: **10%**

Comparables:
Anthony Ortega, Troy Patton, Trevor Bell (76)

YEAR	TEAM	LVL	AGE	W	L	SV	G	GS	IP	H	HR	BB	SO	EqBB9	EqSO9	GB%	BABIP	WHIP	ERA	FRA	WARP
2008	ROM	A	20	5	12	0	25	24	139^{2}	150	6	38	113	2.4	7.3	56%	.321	1.37	4.06	3.86	2.4
2009	LYN	A+	21	4	4	0	17	17	81^{2}	98	4	18	56	2.0	6.2	49%	.349	1.43	4.08	4.03	1.6
2009	MYR	A+	21	1	4	0	10	10	45^{2}	47	1	26	43	5.1	8.5	56%	.346	1.71	5.51	4.13	0.8
2010	BRA	A+	22	0	0	0	17	19	85^{1}	81	6	14	82	1.5	8.6	46%	.313	1.20	3.38	3.67	1.3
2010	ALT	AA	22	3	2	0	10	10	57^{2}	57	5	12	56	1.9	8.8	45%	.315	1.28	3.59	2.82	2.2
2011	*PIT*	*MLB*	*23*	*4*	*7*	*0*	*19*	*15*	*97*	*118*	*12*	*41*	*61*	*3.8*	*5.6*	*46%*	*.328*	*1.63*	*5.71*	*6.21*	*-0.2*

Acquired from the Braves in the Nate McLouth deal, Locke spent the early part of his career looking as if he *should* be good, but never quite delivering the results. That changed in 2010, and the key was throwing more strikes. He doesn't have the stuff to blow hitters away, but at the same time, he doesn't have a weakness in his arsenal, either, as his low-90s fastball, curve, and change all rate as average to a tick above. The aim is to have him ready to contribute from the back of a big-league rotation at some point in 2012.

Paul Maholm

Born: **6/25/1982** Age: **29**
Bats: **L** Throws: **L** Height: **6' 2"** Weight: **225**
Breakout: **11%** Improve: **49%** Collapse: **16%**
Attrition: **5%** MLB: **97%**

Comparables:
Andy Pettitte, Jim Kaat, Frank Sullivan (73)

YEAR	TEAM	LVL	AGE	W	L	SV	G	GS	IP	H	HR	BB	SO	EqBB9	EqSO9	GB%	BABIP	WHIP	ERA	FRA	WARP
2008	PIT	MLB	26	9	9	0	31	31	206^{1}	201	21	63	139	2.7	6.1	55%	.290	1.32	3.71	4.28	3.2
2009	PIT	MLB	27	8	9	0	31	31	194^{2}	221	14	60	119	2.8	5.5	53%	.325	1.47	4.44	3.88	3.8
2010	PIT	MLB	28	9	15	0	32	32	185^{1}	228	15	62	102	3.0	5.0	53%	.327	1.61	5.10	5.16	0.8
2011	*PIT*	*MLB*	*29*	*10*	*12*	*0*	*30*	*30*	*188^{2}*	*216*	*17*	*61*	*102*	*2.9*	*4.9*	*51%*	*.317*	*1.47*	*4.88*	*5.31*	*1.5*

Maholm had quietly been a consistent starter for the Pirates for 4½ seasons before everything fell apart for him in the second half of 2010. His fastball often failed to crack 85 mph after usually sitting in the 88-91 range, and he sometimes had trouble commanding his curveball, slider, and changeup. Perhaps Maholm just got beaten down from year after year of losing. It has happened to plenty of other Pirates. Regardless, he will again be asked to serve as one of the key members of a shaky rotation in 2011. On an average team, he would be a fourth starter, but the Pirates need him to play a more prominent role. It would be unrealistic to believe that he'll suddenly morph into an ace, but that's the situation in which the Pirates' thin staff has put them.

Joe Martinez

Born: **2/26/1983** Age: **28**
Bats: **L** Throws: **R** Height: **6' 2"** Weight: **195**
Breakout: **12%** Improve: **21%** Collapse: **3%**
Attrition: **9%** MLB: **28%**

Comparables:
Brian Duensing, Justin Germano, David Pauley (77)

YEAR	TEAM	LVL	AGE	W	L	SV	G	GS	IP	H	HR	BB	SO	EqBB9	EqSO9	GB%	BABIP	WHIP	ERA	FRA	WARP
2008	NRW	AA	25	10	10	0	27	27	148	131	6	37	112	2.3	6.8	58%	.277	1.16	2.37	3.14	4.2
2009	FRE	AAA	26	0	2	0	7	5	35	39	1	8	22	2.1	5.7	59%	.322	1.37	4.89	5.19	0.2
2009	SFN	MLB	26	3	2	0	9	5	30	46	4	12	19	3.6	5.7	55%	.375	1.97	7.50	7.18	-0.4
2010	FRE	AAA	27	5	3	0	14	13	81^{1}	78	6	26	65	2.9	7.2	60%	.300	1.31	3.32	4.22	1.6
2010	IND	AAA	27	1	2	1	7	4	28^{1}	46	6	7	18	2.2	5.8	59%	.385	1.96	5.72	6.83	-0.1
2010	SFN	MLB	27	0	1	0	4	1	11	15	1	6	3	4.9	2.5	58%	.333	2.00	4.91	4.33	0.1
2010	PIT	MLB	27	0	0	0	5	0	82	11	0	3	6	3.1	6.2	55%	.355	1.73	3.12	3.35	0.1
2011	*PIT*	*MLB*	*28*	*7*	*8*	*0*	*30*	*20*	*133*	*157*	*15*	*46*	*75*	*3.1*	*5.1*	*52%*	*.319*	*1.53*	*5.18*	*5.63*	*0.5*

Martinez wasn't even an Average Joe after his acquisition from the Giants at the 2010 trading deadline—he bombed as a starter at Triple-A, then posted poor peripherals while working out of the Pirates' bullpen in September. Martinez has survived in the minors by raining death upon all ground-dwellers, but his fastball rarely hits 90 mph, and he has gained a reputation for lacking competitiveness. All in all, it's not the most encouraging scouting report in the world, which explains why Pittsburgh regifted him to Cleveland in January.

Daniel McCutchen

Born: **9/26/1982** Age: **28**
Bats: **R** Throws: **R** Height: **6' 2"** Weight: **215**
Breakout: **16%** Improve: **33%** Collapse: **14%**
Attrition: **15%** MLB: **55%**

Comparables:
Glen Perkins, Tim Stauffer, Jason Vargas (74)

YEAR	TEAM	LVL	AGE	W	L	SV	G	GS	IP	H	HR	BB	SO	EqBB9	EqSO9	GB%	BABIP	WHIP	ERA	FRA	WARP
2008	TRN	AA	25	4	3	0	9	10	53	43	4	18	52	3.1	8.8	46%	.279	1.17	2.38	2.58	1.8
2008	IND	AAA	25	3	3	0	8	10	48	49	12	7	41	1.3	7.7	38%	.272	1.21	4.69	4.90	0.5
2008	SWB	AAA	25	4	6	0	11	12	70^{1}	73	10	11	58	1.4	7.4	37%	.303	1.21	3.58	4.27	1.0
2009	IND	AAA	26	13	6	0	24	26	142^{2}	145	10	29	110	1.8	6.9	35%	.305	1.24	3.41	3.94	2.7
2009	PIT	MLB	26	1	2	0	6	6	36^{1}	38	6	11	19	2.7	4.7	44%	.271	1.38	4.21	4.77	0.3
2010	IND	AAA	27	4	8	0	13	13	79	71	12	19	39	2.2	4.4	38%	.242	1.22	3.99	4.63	1.2
2010	PIT	MLB	27	2	5	0	28	9	672	83	13	28	38	3.7	5.1	38%	.298	1.67	6.12	5.59	-0.2
2011	*PIT*	*MLB*	*28*	*7*	*8*	*0*	*22*	*22*	*128^{1}*	*142*	*19*	*40*	*72*	*2.8*	*5.1*	*40%*	*.295*	*1.42*	*4.87*	*5.30*	*1.2*

After winning the fifth-starter's job in spring training, McCutchen was on the brink of pitching his way out of the major leagues when he was bombed in his first three starts to the tune of 18 earned runs and five home runs in 11 innings. He shuttled back and forth between the majors and the International League twice after that, but things started to come together for him when he moved to long relief following the second call-up. After that change in role, McCutchen was more aggressive with both his four-seam and two-seam fastballs as well as his curveball, which is his best pitch. This did not save him from being bombed on several occasions. Nonetheless, after swaying on the major-league ledge, McCutchen may have found a niche in middle and long relief.

James McDonald

Born: **10/19/1984** Age: **26**
Bats: **L** Throws: **R** Height: **6' 5"** Weight: **195**
Breakout: **18%** Improve: **39%** Collapse: **16%**
Attrition: **34%** MLB: **65%**

Comparables:
Carlos Torres, Clay Buchholz, Jensen Lewis (76)

YEAR	TEAM	LVL	AGE	W	L	SV	G	GS	IP	H	HR	BB	SO	EqBB9	EqSO9	GB%	BABIP	WHIP	ERA	FRA	WARP
2008	JAX	AA	23	5	3	0	22	22	118^2	98	12	46	113	3.5	8.6	36%	.274	1.26	3.18	2.96	3.8
2008	LVG	AAA	23	2	1	0	5	4	22^1	17	3	7	28	2.8	11.3	32%	.259	1.21	3.63	2.91	0.8
2008	LAN	MLB	23	0	0	0	4	0	6	5	0	1	2	1.5	3.0	19%	.238	1.00	0.00	1.28	0.2
2009	ABQ	AAA	24	1	0	0	6	6	30^1	21	2	14	40	4.2	11.9	26%	.288	1.16	3.27	3.30	1.0
2009	LAN	MLB	24	5	5	0	45	4	63	60	6	34	54	4.9	7.7	46%	.298	1.57	4.00	4.57	0.7
2010	ABQ	AAA	25	6	1	0	12	12	63^1	64	4	24	57	3.4	8.1	46%	.319	1.47	4.41	4.28	1.7
2010	LAN	MLB	25	0	1	0	4	1	72	11	1	5	7	5.9	8.2	27%	.400	2.09	8.22	6.51	-0.2
2010	PIT	MLB	25	4	5	0	11	11	64	59	3	24	61	3.4	8.6	33%	.311	1.30	3.52	3.17	1.7
2011	*PIT*	*MLB*	*26*	*8*	*7*	*0*	*31*	*20*	*125*	*122*	*13*	*57*	*108*	*4.1*	*7.8*	*40%*	*.304*	*1.43*	*4.34*	*4.72*	*1.8*

Red flags were raised when the Dodgers were willing to give McDonald up in a deadline trade for Octavio Dotel last season, particularly since they needed starting pitching themselves and barely gave him a look. McDonald pitched very effectively following the trade, flashing a fastball that routinely sat at 91-93 mph and spiked to 96 while his curveball and changeup also showed plus. The Pirates don't have many sure things on their pitching staff entering this season, but McDonald might qualify as one, and it looks as if general manager Neal Huntington may have pulled off a heist in acquiring him.

Evan Meek

Born: **5/12/1983** Age: **28**
Bats: **R** Throws: **R** Height: **6' 1"** Weight: **190**
Breakout: **14%** Improve: **25%** Collapse: **23%**
Attrition: **7%** MLB: **60%**

Comparables:
Ehren Wassermann, Dave Righetti, Ramon Ramirez (77)

YEAR	TEAM	LVL	AGE	W	L	SV	G	GS	IP	H	HR	BB	SO	EqBB9	EqSO9	GB%	BABIP	WHIP	ERA	FRA	WARP
2008	IND	AAA	25	0	0	2	23	0	41^1	30	2	14	34	3.1	7.4	61%	.239	1.07	2.40	4.27	0.5
2008	PIT	MLB	25	0	1	0	9	0	13	11	3	12	7	8.3	4.8	56%	.211	1.85	6.92	8.10	-0.4
2009	PIT	MLB	26	1	1	0	41	0	47	34	2	29	42	5.6	8.0	52%	.262	1.34	3.45	4.03	0.5
2010	PIT	MLB	27	5	4	4	70	0	80	53	5	31	70	3.5	7.9	57%	.224	1.10	2.14	3.38	1.4
2011	*PIT*	*MLB*	*28*	*3*	*1*	*1*	*58*	*0*	81^2	*76*	*7*	*41*	*63*	*4.6*	*7.0*	*50%*	*.293*	*1.45*	*4.19*	*4.55*	*0.1*

Meek's selection as the Pirates' lone representative to last season's All-Star Game was ridiculed by some in the national media, but he was a deserving selection as one of the best first-half set-up men in the National League. Of course, there's a difference between transient success and sustained dominance, as Meek began to find out during a run of more pedestrian pitching after the All-Star break. His control has improved considerably since his early days in pro ball and was one of the main reasons for his breakthrough last season, along with an elevated ground-ball rate and a substantial assist from the BABIP fairy. The right-hander does have outstanding stuff, featuring a 95-97 mph fastball and a breaking pitch that former Pirates manager John Russell called "a disappearing slider" because it darts so much as it approaches the plate. The Meek may eventually inherit the closer's role, but he is expected to begin this season setting up for Joel Hanrahan. He shouldn't be expected to rise any higher—he has probably already had his career year.

Diego Moreno

Born: **7/21/1986** Age: **24**
Bats: **R** Throws: **R** Height: **6' 1"** Weight: **177**
Breakout: **3%** Improve: **6%** Collapse: **8%**
Attrition: **8%** MLB: **19%**

Comparables:
Samuel Gervacio, Danny Darwin, Sammy Ellis (78)

YEAR	TEAM	LVL	AGE	W	L	SV	G	GS	IP	H	HR	BB	SO	EqBB9	EqSO9	GB%	BABIP	WHIP	ERA	FRA	WARP
2009	WVA	A	22	1	3	5	18	0	45	29	3	14	57	2.8	11.4	40%	.255	1.07	1.80	3.63	0.5
2010	BRA	A+	23	0	0	0	27	0	36^1	14	3	5	54	1.2	13.4	42%	.157	0.55	1.24	2.14	0.9
2011	*PIT*	*MLB*	*24*	*1*	*1*	*0*	*25*	*0*	*43*	*37*	*5*	*17*	*46*	*3.5*	*9.6*	*43%*	*.293*	*1.25*	*3.54*	*3.85*	*0.4*

Moreno got a late start on his professional career, signing as a 20-year-old out of Venezuela in 2006. However, he has put up phenomenal numbers as a reliever in his four professional seasons, the first two of which were spent in the Venezuelan Summer League. Moreno throws a 97-mph fastball and an 85-mph slider and utilizes a three-quarters delivery that is especially tough on right-handers. He did struggle following a late-season promotion to Double-A in 2010, and it will be interesting to see whether that was merely a blip or an indication that higher-level hitters can handle his stuff.

Bryan Morris

Born: **3/28/1987** Age: **24**
Bats: **L** Throws: **R** Height: **6' 3"** Weight: **210**
Breakout: **3%** Improve: **3%** Collapse: **0%**
Attrition: **1%** MLB: **4%**

Comparables:
Ricky Romero, Trevor Bell, Roy Halladay (79)

YEAR	TEAM	LVL	AGE	W	L	SV	G	GS	IP	H	HR	BB	SO	EqBB9	EqSO9	GB%	BABIP	WHIP	ERA	FRA	WARP
2008	GRL	A	21	2	4	0	17	17	81^{2}	74	5	31	72	3.4	7.9	57%	.297	1.31	3.19	3.31	2.1
2009	LYN	A+	22	4	9	0	15	15	72^{2}	87	2	34	32	4.2	4.0	58%	.320	1.66	5.57	5.84	-0.2
2010	BRA	A+	23	0	0	0	8	9	42^{2}	35	0	7	38	1.5	8.0	60%	.280	1.03	0.42	2.18	1.6
2010	ALT	AA	23	6	4	0	19	16	89	87	9	31	84	3.1	8.5	54%	.308	1.39	4.25	4.74	0.8
2011	*PIT*	*MLB*	*24*	*4*	*6*	*0*	*19*	*13*	*88*	*104*	*10*	*45*	*49*	*4.6*	*5.0*	*49%*	*.317*	*1.70*	*5.77*	*6.27*	*-0.2*

Morris reestablished himself as one of the Pirates' better pitching prospects after a rocky 2009 that saw him struggle at the High-A level and receive a two-week suspension from the organization after an argument with an umpire. The right-hander had a much better strikeout rate last season with a heater that sat at 92-93 mph, a very good curveball, and an improving changeup. Fatigue caused Morris to fade later in the season, but he has matured a lot and seems ready to make the jump to Triple-A this year, with a probable call-up to the major leagues looming sometime after the All-Star break. He projects as a number-three starter. Given the current rotation, that would make Morris the team's ace.

Charlie Morton

Born: **11/12/1983** Age: **27**
Bats: **R** Throws: **R** Height: **6' 4"** Weight: **190**
Breakout: **15%** Improve: **45%** Collapse: **12%**
Attrition: **23%** MLB: **64%**

Comparables:
Mike Ekstrom, David Pauley, Marco Estrada (77)

YEAR	TEAM	LVL	AGE	W	L	SV	G	GS	IP	H	HR	BB	SO	EqBB9	EqSO9	GB%	BABIP	WHIP	ERA	FRA	WARP
2008	RIC	AAA	24	5	2	0	13	12	79	51	0	27	72	3.1	8.2	58%	.242	1.01	2.05	3.66	2.1
2008	ATL	MLB	24	4	8	0	16	15	74^{2}	80	9	41	48	4.9	5.8	52%	.290	1.65	6.15	7.16	-0.9
2009	GWN	AAA	25	7	2	0	10	10	64^{2}	52	3	16	55	2.2	7.7	45%	.275	1.08	2.50	2.59	2.3
2009	PIT	MLB	25	5	9	0	18	18	97	102	7	40	62	3.7	5.8	51%	.315	1.52	4.55	4.60	1.3
2010	IND	AAA	26	4	4	0	14	14	80	83	6	30	53	3.4	6.0	56%	.301	1.49	3.83	5.20	0.9
2010	PIT	MLB	26	2	12	0	17	17	79^{2}	112	15	26	59	2.9	6.7	48%	.353	1.82	7.57	7.39	-1.3
2011	*PIT*	*MLB*	*27*	*8*	*9*	*0*	*24*	*24*	*131*	*142*	*14*	*54*	*82*	*3.7*	*5.6*	*49%*	*.306*	*1.50*	*4.90*	*5.33*	*1.3*

With an abominable 1-9 record and a 9.35 ERA through his first 10 starts, Morton was so horrible to begin last season that the Pirates stashed him on the disabled list with the aid of a nebulous claim of shoulder fatigue. The team then had him spend time with a sports psychologist before starting him over at square one in extended spring training. Morton posted a 3.82 ERA at Triple-A, then had a couple of decent starts after being called back up to the major leagues in August. However, his results have never matched up with an arsenal that includes a 94-mph fastball with plenty of life and a plus curveball. The best way to salvage Morton's career seems to be a permanent sabbatical in the bullpen, but the Pirates hard-headedly refuse to give up on the hope that he can become a top-of-the-rotation starter.

Daniel Moskos

Born: **4/28/1986** Age: **25**
Bats: **R** Throws: **L** Height: **6' 1"** Weight: **210**
Breakout: **0%** Improve: **0%** Collapse: **0%**
Attrition: **0%** MLB: **0%**

Comparables:
Jesus Delgado, Anthony Ortega, Dave Campbell (87)

YEAR	TEAM	LVL	AGE	W	L	SV	G	GS	IP	H	HR	BB	SO	EqBB9	EqSO9	GB%	BABIP	WHIP	ERA	FRA	WARP
2008	LYN	A+	22	7	7	0	29	20	110^{1}	124	8	43	78	3.5	6.4	56%	.325	1.57	5.96	6.67	-0.8
2009	ALT	AA	23	11	10	0	27	25	149	159	11	58	77	3.5	4.7	58%	.301	1.50	3.74	4.91	0.7
2010	ALT	AA	24	3	1	21	37	0	41^{1}	26	0	16	43	3.5	9.4	61%	.248	1.09	1.52	2.90	0.8
2011	*PIT*	*MLB*	*25*	*4*	*5*	*2*	*36*	*9*	79^{2}	*94*	*10*	*43*	*41*	*4.8*	*4.6*	*51%*	*.313*	*1.72*	*5.98*	*6.50*	*-0.7*

The most controversial move former Pirates general manager Dave Littlefield made during his ill-starred six years on the job from 2001 to 2007 was his selection of Moskos over Matt Wieters with the fourth overall pick in the 2007 draft. Littlefield insisted that his scouts believed that Moskos could become a shut-down late-game reliever. Although Moskos entered the year with a shiny new "bust" tag all but within reach, he saved his prospect status and maybe his career by moving back to the bullpen. He dominated Double-A with a 95-mph fastball and a wipeout slider, but had trouble throwing strikes when promoted to Triple-A, admitting that he had put too much pressure on himself. Despite this, he could find his way to the majors this year, and while he's not an impact arm, nobody is throwing the word *bust* around anymore, either.

Ross Ohlendorf

Born: **8/8/1982** Age: **28**
Bats: **R** Throws: **R** Height: **6' 4"** Weight: **235**
Breakout: **13%** Improve: **30%** Collapse: **14%**
Attrition: **9%** MLB: **55%**

Comparables:
Tim Stauffer, Jason Vargas, Doc Medich (75)

YEAR	TEAM	LVL	AGE	W	L	SV	G	GS	IP	H	HR	BB	SO	EqBB9	EqSO9	GB%	BABIP	WHIP	ERA	FRA	WARP
2008	IND	AAA	25	4	3	0	7	7	46^{2}	46	7	8	40	1.5	7.7	42%	.296	1.20	3.47	2.96	1.6
2008	SWB	AAA	25	1	1	0	5	5	22^{1}	28	0	5	25	2.0	10.1	57%	.406	1.57	3.63	2.22	1.0
2008	NYA	MLB	25	1	1	0	25	0	40	50	7	19	36	4.3	8.1	48%	.347	1.75	6.30	5.18	0.0
2008	PIT	MLB	25	0	3	0	5	5	22^{2}	36	3	12	13	4.8	5.2	40%	.388	2.12	6.35	5.11	0.2
2009	PIT	MLB	26	11	10	0	29	29	176^{2}	165	25	53	109	2.7	5.6	43%	.264	1.27	3.92	4.57	2.1
2010	PIT	MLB	27	1	11	0	21	21	108^{1}	106	12	44	79	3.7	6.6	35%	.281	1.44	4.07	4.28	1.5
2011	*PIT*	*MLB*	*28*	*8*	*9*	*0*	*24*	*24*	*135*	*148*	*17*	*48*	*86*	*3.2*	*5.7*	*43%*	*.303*	*1.45*	*4.85*	*5.28*	*1.4*

Ohlendorf went *backward* in 2010, landing on the disabled list early with a lower-back strain and missing September with an upper-back strain. When his back wasn't barking, he got little support from his teammates either offensively or defensively. Ohlendorf's fastball is routinely in the 91-93 range, and he has tightened his slider over the years. If he is ever truly to break through, he needs to improve his changeup in order to better counteract left-handed hitters. Ohlendorf is a Princeton graduate and one of the brightest guys in the game; he interned at the U.S. Department of Agriculture during the 2009-2010 offseason. He is also as apt as any other player in the major leagues to purchase a copy of this book, which at the very least could serve as a worthy makeshift plate in his backyard as he attempts to refine his slow stuff.

Rudy Owens

Born: **12/18/1987** Age: **23**
Bats: **L** Throws: **L** Height: **6' 3"** Weight: **215**
Breakout: **11%** Improve: **19%** Collapse: **4%**
Attrition: **12%** MLB: **33%**

Comparables:
Michael Bowden, Jaime Garcia, Britt Burns (69)

YEAR	TEAM	LVL	AGE	W	L	SV	G	GS	IP	H	HR	BB	SO	EqBB9	EqSO9	GB%	BABIP	WHIP	ERA	FRA	WARP
2008	SCO	A-	20	3	6	0	15	13	58	63	2	13	45	2.0	7.0	51%	.324	1.34	4.97	4.76	0.7
2009	WVA	A	21	10	1	0	19	19	100^{2}	71	8	15	91	1.3	8.1	42%	.235	0.94	1.70	1.85	4.7
2009	LYN	A+	21	1	1	0	6	6	23^{1}	29	3	2	22	0.8	8.5	38%	.366	1.37	3.86	2.17	1.5
2010	ALT	AA	22	12	6	0	26	26	150	124	11	23	132	1.4	7.9	48%	.273	1.01	2.46	2.85	4.6
2011	*PIT*	*MLB*	*23*	*6*	*6*	*0*	*17*	*17*	*86*	*92*	*11*	*27*	*56*	*2.8*	*5.9*	*43%*	*.299*	*1.38*	*4.45*	*4.84*	*1.5*

Owens has gone from an obscure 28th-round draft pick who was seemingly headed toward his release from short-season ball in 2008 to the organization's minor-league pitcher of the year for two seasons running. His turnaround came when he began taking the advice of his coaches to pitch off his fastball, which is usually in the 90-92 range but which he commands with the precision of a surgeon, instead of his curveball, which can be erratic. The lefty has also honed his changeup to the point that it now qualifies as a plus pitch. The word *throwback* can be overused in sports, but it's fitting when applied to Owens, who has been known to have his hair permed, eliciting memories of such big-haired pitchers of the 1970s as Randy Jones, Mark Fidrych, and Ross Grimsley. He will start this season at Triple-A, but could reach the big leagues sometime in the second half.

Chris Resop

Born: **11/4/1982** Age: **28**
Bats: **R** Throws: **R** Height: **6' 3"** Weight: **222**
Breakout: **12%** Improve: **24%** Collapse: **13%**
Attrition: **10%** MLB: **43%**

Comparables:
Lee Smith, Ryan Braun, Taylor Tankersley (76)

YEAR	TEAM	LVL	AGE	W	L	SV	G	GS	IP	H	HR	BB	SO	EqBB9	EqSO9	GB%	BABIP	WHIP	ERA	FRA	WARP
2008	ATL	MLB	25	0	1	0	16	0	18^{1}	16	2	10	13	4.9	6.4	51%	.255	1.53	5.89	7.04	-0.4
2010	GWN	AAA	27	6	3	0	15	15	82	53	4	32	91	3.5	10.0	50%	.258	1.06	2.09	3.51	2.2
2010	ATL	MLB	27	0	0	0	1	0	2	5	0	3	2	13.5	9.0	22%	.556	4.00	22.50	14.55	-0.2
2010	PIT	MLB	27	0	0	0	22	0	19	10	1	10	24	4.7	11.4	40%	.214	1.05	1.89	2.94	0.5
2011	*PIT*	*MLB*	*28*	*5*	*3*	*0*	*30*	*9*	*65^{2}*	*59*	*5*	*31*	*59*	*4.3*	*8.1*	*46%*	*.295*	*1.38*	*3.81*	*4.14*	*1.2*

Looking for fresh bodies to fill a depleted bullpen, the Pirates claimed Resop off waivers from the Braves in early August, and he turned out to be quite a find. Resop's fastball sat in the 94-mph range, helping to set up an outstanding curveball that froze right-handed hitters from a three-quarters arm angle. The Pirates don't have many certainties for the bullpen this season, but it's realistic to pencil Resop in just in front of Joel Hanrahan and Evan Meek, who will be the closer and set-up man, albeit not necessarily in that order. There is also an outside chance that the Pirates could look at Resop as a starter, since he dominated the International League in that role during the first half of last season.

Jameson Taillon

Born: **11/18/1991** Age: **19**
Bats: **R** Throws: **R** Height: **6' 3"** Weight: **225**
Breakout: **0%** Improve: **0%** Collapse: **0%**
Attrition: **0%** MLB: **0%**

Comparables:

YEAR	TEAM	LVL	AGE	W	L	SV	G	GS	IP	H	HR	BB	SO	EqBB9	EqSO9	GB%	BABIP	WHIP	ERA	FRA	WARP
2010	DNP	—	19	—	—	—	—	—	—	—	—	—	—	—	—	—	—	—	—	—	—
2011	*PIT*	*MLB*	*19*	—	—	—	—	—	—	—	—	—	—	—	—	—	—	—	—	—	—

The Pirates have changed their draft philosophy of late, often spending seven figures on lower-round picks, but in 2010, they spent huge cash on the second overall pick in the draft, ladling out a club-record $6.5 million to land Taillon. Scouts generally agree he's the best high-school righty to come down the pike in years, with some going as far as to label him the best since Josh Beckett in 1999. He has all the ingredients to be a franchise-changing arm, with a six-foot-seven power-pitcher's build, mid- to upper-90s heat, a curveball that is already above-average, and that aggressive edge that sometimes seems to come naturally simply by being a Texan. All of the warnings that come with teenage arms apply, but the Pirates have not had an arm with this kind of upside in generations.

Donnie Veal

Born: **9/18/1984** Age: **26**
Bats: **L** Throws: **L** Height: **6' 4"** Weight: **235**
Breakout: **3%** Improve: **3%** Collapse: **0%**
Attrition: **1%** MLB: **3%**

Comparables:
Emiliano Fruto, Jeff Nelson, Justin Thomas (86)

YEAR	TEAM	LVL	AGE	W	L	SV	G	GS	IP	H	HR	BB	SO	EqBB9	EqSO9	GB%	BABIP	WHIP	ERA	FRA	WARP
2008	TEN	AA	23	5	10	0	29	29	145^1	150	19	81	123	5.0	7.6	46%	.316	1.62	4.52	4.62	2.3
2009	PIT	MLB	24	1	0	0	19	0	16^1	18	2	20	16	11.0	8.8	43%	.340	2.45	7.16	7.35	-0.4
2010	IND	AAA	25	3	2	0	9	9	49^2	42	3	23	41	4.2	7.5	46%	.277	1.44	4.35	4.75	0.7
2011	*PIT*	*MLB*	*26*	*6*	*8*	*0*	*43*	*17*	*97*	*101*	*12*	*67*	*74*	*6.1*	*6.8*	*44%*	*.302*	*1.71*	*5.64*	*6.13*	*0.1*

Veal appeared to be on his way to conquering his long-standing control problems when he blew out an elbow ligament last season at Triple-A and underwent Tommy John surgery. The southpaw is expected to miss at least the first half of this season and probably won't be fully operational and capable of keeping local systems in line until 2012. He has outstanding raw ability, featuring a 95-mph heater and an above-average curveball, but he has also lost critical development time after spending 2009 in the major leagues as a Rule 5 draft pick, then being limited to 10 starts last season. Veal has the stuff and the work ethic to be a good pitcher, but it's going to be a while before he gets a chance to prove it.

Justin Wilson

Born: **8/18/1987** Age: **23**
Bats: **L** Throws: **L** Height: **6' 2"** Weight: **233**
Breakout: **15%** Improve: **52%** Collapse: **8%**
Attrition: **8%** MLB: **75%**

Comparables:
CC Sabathia, Wayne Simpson, Vin Mazzaro (60)

YEAR	TEAM	LVL	AGE	W	L	SV	G	GS	IP	H	HR	BB	SO	EqBB9	EqSO9	GB%	BABIP	WHIP	ERA	FRA	WARP
2009	LYN	A+	21	6	8	0	26	26	116	118	14	55	94	4.3	7.3	53%	.302	1.55	4.50	3.77	2.8
2010	ALT	AA	22	11	8	0	27	26	142^2	109	4	71	134	4.5	8.5	52%	.273	1.32	3.09	3.11	4.2
2011	*PIT*	*MLB*	*23*	*9*	*10*	*0*	*27*	*27*	*134*	*135*	*14*	*75*	*95*	*5.0*	*6.4*	*47%*	*.297*	*1.57*	*4.89*	*5.31*	*1.7*

A beefy southpaw, Wilson opened eyes in 2010 by limiting Double-A hitters to a .215 batting average, but he has yet to conquer the control problems that have plagued him both as an amateur and a pro. While his fastball is impressive in both velocity and movement, he has trouble throwing it for strikes. This means that it's hard to hit, but batters often let it pass and put him further behind in the count. If he can make just enough improvement to become what scouts like to call "effectively wild," he could find himself in Pittsburgh at some point during the season.

LINEOUTS

HITTERS

PLAYER	TEAM	LVL	AGE	PA	R	2B	3B	HR	RBI	BB	SO	SB-CS	AVG/OBP/SLG	TAv	BABIP	BRR	FRAA	WARP
1B C. Anderson	BRA	A+	23	452	50	27	0	11	63	32	128	2-1	.260/.334/.405	.257	.345	-0.6	1B 1	0.2
1B M. Hague	ALT	AA	24	581	90	30	0	15	86	61	62	3-6	.295/.375/.442	.299	.310	-4.8	1B 10, 3B 0	3.4
C E. Kratz	IND	AAA	30	274	30	22	1	9	41	32	54	1-2	.274/.380/.496	.277	.318	-1.2	C 1, 1B 0	1.6
	PIT	MLB	30	36	2	0	0	0	1	2	9	0-0	.118/.167/.118	.132	.160	-1.5	C 0	-0.4
OF A. Lambo*	ALT	AA	21	102	12	1	0	2	10	9	30	0-0	.275/.353/.352	.287	.390	0.9	LF -1, CF 2	0.7
	CHT	AA	21	198	26	11	2	4	25	15	39	1-1	.271/.323/.420	.274	.321	0.3	LF -2, RF 0	0.5
OF Q. Latimore	BRA	A+	21	528	77	29	2	18	92	31	123	11-0	.268/.337/.446	.275	.317	-0.6	LF -1, CF 2	1.9
CF S. Marte	BRA	A+	21	223	33	17	5	0	31	10	55	14-7	.306/.386/.435	.292	.405	1.9	CF -4, RF 1	1.2
OF B. Moss*	IND	AAA	26	556	73	32	2	22	96	42	118	12-7	.266/.330/.470	.264	.302	-2.9	RF -12, LF 2	0.0
	PIT	MLB	26	27	2	1	0	0	2	1	6	0-0	.154/.185/.192	.121	.200	-0.6	RF -1, LF 0	-0.5
2B J. Negrych*	ALT	AA	25	266	33	11	3	1	35	31	45	2-5	.274/.366/.361	.278	.333	-2.7	LF -2, 2B 0	0.5
	IND	AAA	25	191	26	7	2	3	19	21	34	8-2	.295/.372/.416	.267	.346	1.2	2B -2, 3B -1	0.6
CF J. Van Every*	IND	AAA	30	252	32	9	0	10	29	37	85	3-4	.214/.335/.400	.240	.297	1.8	CF 1, 1B 0	0.6
	BOS	MLB	30	21	5	1	0	1	1	2	9	0-0	.211/.286/.421	.255	.333	-0.9	CF -1, RF 0	-0.2

First baseman **Calvin Anderson** could be this century's "Piano Legs" for his exceedingly top-heavy six-foot-seven frame; it's too bad he can't hit enough for it to matter. ⚾ **Matt Hague** doesn't have enough power to be an everyday first baseman, but his solid walk and strikeout rates, coupled with his ability to play third base and the outfield, could eventually make him a four-corner bench player in the major leagues. ⚾ Drafted in the 29th round way back in 2002, **Erik Kratz** made his major-league debut last July as a 30-year-old in his ninth professional season, but was removed from the 40-man roster in the offseason. He signed a minor-league contract with his hometown Phillies in November. ⚾ The Pirates still believe in former Dodger's prospect **Andrew Lambo**'s bat, but they're in the minority, as scouts generally don't think he will hit enough for a player limited to a corner outfield slot. ⚾ Always one of the better athletes in the system, outfielder **Quincy Latimore** had a semi-breakout year with 19 home runs and 100 RBIs in the Florida State League, but his free-swinging ways will likely catch up to him at Double-A. ⚾ A potential impact defender in center field, **Starling Marte** had his 2010 season interrupted by surgery to repair a broken hamate bone, but the 22-year-old's possibilities are still bright. The potential five-tool player will be summering at Double-A this season. ⚾ **Brandon Moss** got an extended look as the Pirates' right fielder in 2009 and was so disappointing that even a resurgent 2010 at Triple-A couldn't keep him from being dropped from the 40-man roster at the end of the season. The Phillies wasted little time in signing him to a minor-league deal. ⚾ Although he's small and not much of an athlete, the one thing second baseman **Jim Negrych** can do is hit, and the Pirates hope he can get there as he's a semi-hometown hero who set many records during his college days at Pitt. ⚾ **Jonathan Van Every** is a Quad-A player. His 2010 season put the "journey" in "journeyman," as he began and ended the season with the Pirates at Triple-A but was traded to the Red Sox for a short spell in between, receiving a little major-league playing time while the Sox scrambled to find healthy bodies.

PITCHERS

PLAYER	TEAM	LVL	AGE	W	L	SV	IP	H	HR	BB	SO	EqBB9	EqSO9	GB%	BABIP	WHIP	ERA	FRA	WARP
N. Adcock	BRA	A+	22	0	0	0	133^{1}	126	7	35	110	2.4	7.4	52%	.297	1.25	3.51	3.89	1.7
S. Allie	DNP	—	20	—	—	—	—	—	—	—	—	—	—	—	—	—	—	—	—
B. Bass	IND	AAA	28	4	4	2	69	74	3	23	53	3.0	6.9	59%	.333	1.49	3.26	3.97	1.0
	PIT	MLB	28	0	0	0	7^{1}	9	0	10	5	12.3	6.1	58%	.346	2.73	12.27	13.12	-0.5
C. Cain*	SCO	A-	19	1	1	0	34	23	2	14	32	3.7	8.5	32%	.228	1.18	5.03	5.97	-0.1
Z. Dodson*	SCO	A-	19	2	6	0	57^{2}	57	2	27	41	4.2	6.5	43%	.311	1.56	4.84	5.45	0.0
B. Donnelly	PIT	MLB	38	3	1	0	30^{2}	26	6	25	26	7.3	7.6	44%	.238	1.70	5.58	5.90	-0.4
M. Dubee	ALT	AA	24	6	2	5	76^{1}	62	4	19	68	2.2	8.0	52%	.274	1.10	2.24	2.83	1.9
J. Hughes	ALT	AA	24	12	8	0	150^{2}	166	15	41	120	2.5	7.2	58%	.322	1.45	4.42	3.89	2.4
S. Jackson	IND	AAA	28	4	0	0	56^{1}	59	6	19	37	3.0	5.9	53%	.294	1.48	3.51	3.91	0.9
	PIT	MLB	28	0	1	0	11^{1}	17	4	6	7	4.8	5.6	45%	.342	2.03	8.74	8.51	-0.4
C. Jakubauskas	IND	AAA	31	1	4	0	30^{1}	35	2	10	24	3.0	7.2	52%	.337	1.50	4.45	5.23	0.3
	PIT	MLB	31	0	1	0	0^{2}	2	0	0	0	0.0	0.0	0%	.500	3.00	27.00	12.49	-0.0
R. Kelly	WVA	A	22	2	3	4	75	75	9	14	75	1.7	9.0	47%	.306	1.32	4.20	5.29	-0.1
K. McPherson	WVA	A	22	9	9	0	117^{2}	96	14	31	124	2.4	9.5	41%	.265	1.16	3.59	3.81	2.6
C. Park	NYA	MLB	37	2	1	0	35^{1}	40	7	12	29	3.1	7.4	45%	.306	1.50	5.60	6.50	-0.5
	PIT	MLB	37	2	2	0	28^{1}	25	2	7	23	2.2	7.3	56%	.264	1.20	3.49	5.35	-0.2
H. Penn	IND	AAA	25	4	4	0	65^{1}	76	3	23	56	3.2	7.7	59%	.361	1.58	4.68	5.15	0.7
	PIT	MLB	25	0	0	0	2^{1}	8	0	3	0	11.6	0.0	54%	.615	4.71	30.86	17.65	-0.2
J. Thomas*	IND	AAA	26	5	0	4	54^{1}	33	4	10	51	1.7	8.5	39%	.213	0.96	2.48	3.53	1.1
	PIT	MLB	26	0	1	0	13	21	3	5	5	3.5	3.5	33%	.367	2.00	6.23	4.12	0.1
Z. Von Rosenberg	SCO	A-	19	1	6	0	59	60	4	13	39	2.0	5.9	47%	.298	1.27	3.20	3.59	1.2
T. Watson*	ALT	AA	25	6	4	2	111^{1}	82	11	24	105	1.9	8.5	37%	.243	1.00	2.67	3.71	2.0

The Royals selected righty **Nate Adcock** in the Rule 5 draft on the basis of his control of three average pitches, but that's probably not enough to stick, even in Kansas City. ⚾ Another huge arm from the 2010 draft, second round pick **Stetson Allie** has even better raw stuff than Jameson Taillon, often hitting triple digits in high school, but he's wilder than a New Year's Eve party at Diddy's house. ⚾ **Brian Bass** got a couple of shots to pitch out of the Pirates' bullpen last season. He landed an invite to spring training with the Phillies, who are apparently looking to leaven their rotation of the best pitchers in baseball with one of the worst. ⚾ The Pirates went over MLB's recommended slot bonus and signed power lefty **Colton Cain** for $1.125 million as an eighth-round draft choice in 2009. He made a strong debut last season despite back surgery shelving him until June. Off-speed stuff is still in the R&D phase. ⚾ Another high-school pitcher the Pirates went over slot to get, lefty **Zack Dodson** has three solid pitches but seems destined for a little town called fifth-starterville. ⚾ The Pirates released **Brendan Donnelly** last July 25 just before a number of performance bonuses in his contract were set to kick in, and it could be curtains for the age-39 reliever. ⚾ **Michael Dubee**, son of Phillies pitching coach Rich Dubee, is not considered a prospect, but he has consistently gotten batters out in his two years in the Pirates' farm system, which could mean he's some kind of plant. ⚾ The Pirates nabbed the consensus top pitcher on the international amateur free-agent market last summer when they signed 16-year-old Mexican right-hander **Luis Heredia** for a $2.6 million bonus. They see him as a potential top-of-the-rotation starter with a fastball that already sits at 92 mph, but he's far, far away. **Jared Hughes** has bounced between the bullpen and the rotation at Double-A during the last two seasons, and if he has any chance of pitching in the major leagues, it will come as a reliever. His fastball consistently sat at 93 mph last year when used in short stints. The Pirates were enthralled with **Steven Jackson**'s sinker and shuttled him back and forth between Triple-A and the major leagues something like 67 times over the past two seasons, but he became a free agent at the end of 2010 and will seek out another shuttle as fun to ride as the Indy Express. "Ill-fated" is a good way to describe **Chris Jakubauskas**'s brief career with the Pirates, as he was struck in the head by a line drive off the bat of then-Astro Lance Berkman in the first inning of his first start last season on April 24, suffered a concussion, and never returned to the majors. Sent to the A's in return for speedy utility guy Corey Wimberly, right-hander **Ryan Kelly** is a strike-thrower with average stuff, so we get to use terms like "moxie" and "gutsy" in this space. **Kyle McPherson**'s plus changeup and ability to pound the strike zone got him added to the 40-man roster. We'll know more about his ability to get by with more moxie than stuff following a year at the upper levels. Having surpassed Hideo Nomo as the all-time leader in major-league wins by an Asian-American pitcher with 124, **Chan Ho Park** signed with the Orix Buffaloes of Japan. He will be entering his age-39 season at the conclusion of the contract, so a stateside comeback seems unlikely. **Hayden Penn**, who began the season in the major-league bullpen, was starting at Triple-A last June when the Pirates sold his contract to Chiba Lotte of Nippon Professional Baseball. He reenlisted for another tour of duty with the Marines in 2011. **Justin Thomas** used to watch games at PNC Park while playing collegiate ball at nearby Youngstown State, and we can safely assume that when he dreamed of pitching there someday, he performed better than he did as a real-life Pirate last season. **Zack Von Rosenberg**'s professional debut last season was very encouraging following the Pirates' decision to give him an over-slot $1.2 million bonus as their sixth-round draft pick in 2009. He flashed a plus curveball and changeup to go with a 91-mph fastball that should get faster when his six-foot-five frame fills out. **Tony Watson** has both started and relieved in his professional career, but his dominance of left-handed hitters throughout his career suggests that his ultimate major-league role will be as a LOOGY. **Tyler Yates** spent 2010 trying and failing to come back from the second Tommy John surgery of his career. The Pirates re-signed him to a minor-league contract and invited him to spring training in the hopes of getting more of the not-particularly-special pitching he gave them in 2008.

MANAGER: JOHN RUSSELL

YEAR	TEAM	W-L	Pythag +/-	Avg PC	100+ P	120+ P	QS	BQS	REL	REL w Zero R	IBB	Subs	PH	PH Avg	PH HR	SB2	CS2	SB3	CS3	SAC Att	SAC %	POS SAC	Squeeze	Swing	In Play
2008	PIT	67-95	1	92.5	57	1	59	4	497	307	31	21	289	.224	3	52	18	5	1	104	63.5%	36	1	92	72
2009	PIT	62-99	-3	93.3	52	1	82	4	456	293	37	9	247	.267	1	81	29	9	2	90	66.7%	27	0	108	83
2010	PIT	57-105	6	88.5	42	0	67	4	516	313	40	22	275	.213	6	79	35	8	1	94	61.7%	25	2	119	87

Hurdle will initially need to rely more on his people skills than his tactical abilities as he replaces John Russell and tries his hand at turning around a beleaguered franchise. The extroverted Hurdle brings a totally different personality to the clubhouse and will attempt to instill some confidence in a roster that understandably lacks that quality after going 57-105 last year. During his eight seasons as the Rockies' manager from 2002 to 2009, Hurdle led the franchise to its lone World Series appearance. As a strategist, he was most noted for ordering an unusually high number of sacrifice bunts from the hitters at the top of his batting order despite playing his home games in Coors Field, the best hitting environment in the major leagues. Hurdle did cut back on the sacs during the later stages of his mile-high tenure, but it will be telling to see whether he goes back to his bunting ways with Andrew McCutchen and Jose Tabata heading the Pirates' offensive attack. As a manager of pitchers, his most notable act was squeaking into the 2007 playoffs, in large part thanks to a late-season push provided by the then-untried Ubaldo Jimenez and Franklin Morales. The Pirates will require many more such gestures of open-mindedness if they are ever to escape from the morass in which they've been stuck for 18 years.

St. Louis Cardinals

The St. Louis Cardinals are set to enter the 21st century's second decade much as they entered its first: as one of the most successful and respected franchises in baseball. Since the beginning of the 2001 season, the Redbirds have won 904 games, more than any team save the Yankees and Red Sox, and have done so with a payroll that is half-again as small as Boston's and would be considered tip money in the Big Apple. Over the last decade, Cardinals fans have watched their heroes compete in the playoffs seven times, play in two fall classics, and bring home a championship in 2006. It's a record of success that's all the more impressive when you consider that the St. Louis metropolitan area ranks 20th out of the 30 current baseball markets.

While the St. Louis payroll has remained relatively small when compared with the coastal behemoths, having never broken the $100 million mark, the team's continuing ability to draw fans—over 32 million visitors passed through the two Busch Stadiums' turnstiles over the last decade, the third-most in baseball—allowed St. Louis to rank 10th in total outlay for major league salaries. Of the 10 most successful teams in baseball this century, only the Twins and Athletics, small-market franchises frequently stereotyped as belonging to opposite ends of the purported stats/scouts divide but alike in their ability to win on a shoestring, have managed to pay less in salary per regular-season win than the Cardinals (see Table 1). While this is a fairly blunt measure, it speaks well of the Cardinals' abilities to both recognize baseball talent and be willing to spend the necessary cash to acquire and retain it.

Despite the Cardinals' sustained success, there seems to be a general unease among fans about the franchise's future after a sour ending to the 2010 season. The team battled the resurgent Reds into mid-August, but was battered by the dregs of the National League during an ugly 2-8 road trip through Pittsburgh, Washington, and Houston—a circuit that knocked it out of contention.

CARDINALS PROSPECTUS

2010 W-L: 86-76, 2nd in NL Central

Pythag	.563	9th	
RS/G	4.5	14th	
RA/G	4.0	25th	
TAv	.274	10th	
BRR	3.8	9th	
FRA	3.96	4th	
DER	.079	17th	
DL	633	9th	
B-Age	28.5	12th	
P-Age	29.8	28th	
Salary	$93.5	12th	
M$/MW	$2.23	12th	

Ballpark: Busch Stadium (3-yr. PF: 97). If you thought Prince Albert showed spirit in St. Louis, imagine him playing in a palace better-suited to right-handed power

2010: Stars-and-scrubs Redbirds can't hold off the Redlegs

2011: Pujols, Holliday, Carpenter, and Wainwright again give Cards potential

Action Items: Locking up Albert, evening out a top-heavy roster, surviving their own defense

And now, two men who have been instrumental in the team's success since their arrival in 1996, manager Tony La Russa and pitching coach Dave Duncan, have reached federal retirement age, and last year the former purportedly feuded with center fielder Colby Rasmus, leading to whispers that the old man was losing the ability to communicate with his young charges. Yawning voids on the left side of the infield festered all season, as there were no ready fixes in the Cardinals' shallow minor-league system, and GM John Mozeliak raised eyebrows when he tried to spackle over the problem by trading for serial out-maker Pedro Feliz in the heat of a pennant race.

Most unsettling, however, is the contract situation of Albert Pujols. Pujols arrived in St. Louis fully formed as the 2001 NL Rookie of the Year, and since then has won three MVP awards, been runner-up four times, collected two Gold Gloves, and proved he is not only the best player of his generation, but among the most talented of any era. The Cardinals wisely bought out his arbitration years in 2004 and signed him to an eight-year, $111 million contract that turned out to be a bargain, but that deal is set to expire at season's end and the Cardinals hope to work out an extension. It's hard to overestimate Pujols' worth on the open market, especially in light of the five-year, $125 million contract showered on the inferior Ryan Howard last spring, or to know how great a discount he's willing to give the only organization he's known. Owner Bill DeWitt Jr. has shown a willingness to open his checkbook to keep talent, as evidenced by last year's nine-figure deal to retain left fielder Matt Holliday, but there has to be a limit. Unless Phat Albert is willing to accept a deal that's well below his market value, the Cardinals may face a choice between the

Table 1. Ten Winningest Teams of the 21st Century

Team	Wins	Losses	Attendance (millions)	Payroll (millions)	Payroll/Win (millions)	Attd Rank	Payroll Rank	Payroll/Win Rank
NYY	973	644	38.4	$1,783.6	$1.83	1	1	30
BOS	924	695	28.7	$1,249.5	$1.35	8	2	28
STL	904	715	32.7	$875.1	$0.97	3	10	17
LAA	898	722	30.7	$934.5	$1.04	5	6	21
MIN	888	730	22.1	$584.8	$0.66	21	22	4
ATL	888	733	25.4	$929.3	$1.05	12	7	23
PHI	882	737	28.2	$889.7	$1.01	9	9	20
OAK	880	739	19.2	$545.7	$0.62	25	24	3
LAD	856	764	35.0	$1,007.0	$1.18	2	4	26
SFG	850	767	31.4	$835.2	$0.98	4	12	18

completely unfathomable (Pujols in another uniform) and the possibly untenable (a contract so large as to leave little left for complementary parts).

Taken together, that's a long list of things to keep Cardinals fans tossing and turning. Happily for them, none of this is likely to be worth losing much sleep over. The Cards may have looked ugly down the stretch while finishing second last year, but their Pythagorean record based on run differential put them in a virtual dead heat with the Reds—even with all of their lineup problems, the Cardinals played like a 91-win team last year. La Russa and Duncan may be older, but they're hardly over the hill. The manager has always been prone to playing favorites, but this fetish tends to manifest itself in smaller ways, like his odd attachment to a Jason LaRue or a Skip Schumaker. The skipper is way too smart to fail to realize that Rasmus in center field is too valuable a combination of high-octane production and wafer-thin contract to keep on the bench or force out of town, so that seems like a situation that will sort itself out. And Duncan worked his usual mound-whisperer act on Jake Westbrook, who will be back to solidify the back end of the rotation next year, and somehow extracted 13 useful starts from the desiccated remains of Jeff Suppan. Sure, Mozeliak's decision to bring in Feliz was a clunker, but he's the same guy who added Holliday during the 2009 stretch drive in exchange for Brett Wallace, a questionable first-base prospect so completely blocked that the U.S. Army Corps of Engineers couldn't have forced his way onto the Cardinals' roster.

Losing Pujols would be a nightmare, of course, but the Cardinals can take comfort that at least he plays a position at which replacement options are available. As for the fear that paying Pujols a blockbuster salary on top of the money already owed to Holliday will leave the Cardinals unable to populate the rest of their roster, there's reason to think that that grim vision won't come to pass. St. Louis has recently come to be known as a poster child for the "stars and scrubs" approach to roster construction, but just how stars-y and scrubs-y are they, and how likely is it that they could go too far, assembling a collection of talent too hop-heavy to contend?

Certainly, over the last few years the Cardinals have rostered some of the most productive players in the league. Last season, Pujols was second in MLB with 7.8 WARP, while staff ace Adam Wainwright came in tenth with 8.9, and Holliday tied for 14th at 5.4. Taken together, those three earned 19.6 WARP — the highest total in the league for a three-player trio on a single team last year. This is nothing new for the Cardinals, who received more total production from their top three players in WARP than any other team from 2008 through 2010 and have placed in the top 10 every season but one since 2001 (see Table 2).

Table 2. Production from Top 3 Cardinals by Season

YEAR	WARP	Rank	Players
2010	19.6	1	Albert Pujols, Adam Wainwright, Matt Holiday
2009	23.1	1	Albert Pujols, Adam Wainwright, Chris Carpenter
2008	19.6	1	Albert Pujols, Ryan Ludwick, Troy Glaus
2007	12.2	21	Albert Pujols, Adam Wainwright, Chris Duncan
2006	17.2	7	Albert Pujols, Chris Carpenter, Scott Rolen
2005	15.9	4	Albert Pujols, Chris Carpenter, Jim Edmonds
2004	21.4	1	Jim Edmonds, Albert Pujols, Scott Rolen
2003	18.8	2	Albert Pujols, Scott Rolen, Jim Edmonds
2002	15.5	8	Jim Edmonds, Albert Pujols, Edgar Renteria
2001	20.1	3	Darryl Kyle, Matt Morris, Albert Pujols

Over the years, the Cardinals have thrived with unbalanced rosters, and they may very well continue to do so, even with another huge contract on the books should Pujols be re-upped. This competitive model requires inexpensive production from other places, but here again, the Cardinals have players who provide. The "scrub" part of the lineup certainly lived up to its name last year, with the Cardinals posting the worst batting lines in the league at third base (.260/.317/.338) and shortstop (.221/.289/.311), and their leadoff men mustering a league-worst .306 on-base percentage, tied with the always bemusing Dusty Baker's Reds. St. Louis has brought in some veteran spare parts to help improve the offense, but reasonable in-house options also exist. Oft-injured David Freese has the potential to provide excellent patience and power at the hot corner, and if he falters, there's always the possibility that 11th-round find Matt Carpenter could serve up his lunch-menu version of Wade Boggs' game in the bigs. Rookie Daniel Descalso would be a defensive upgrade from Schumaker at second base and might get on base enough to be a table-setter. Newly acquired shortstop Ryan Theriot will provide a bit more offense than the departed Brendan Ryan, though the Cardinals will probably miss Ryan's outstanding glove. Most surprisingly, veteran switch-hitter Lance Berkman has been brought in to play left field, shifting Holliday to right. A former slugger and a former outfielder, Berkman may be able to revive his bat enough to give the lineup a boost, but it's hard to picture him as anything but a statue in the outfield. If his glove proves to be too much of a liability, a right-field platoon of Jon Jay and Allen Craig might not be very exciting but could provide reasonable production at a low cost.

With Albert Pujols taking his accustomed place at first base for at least one more year, a potentially tremendous starting rotation, and a few lineup tweaks to provide more production toward the end of the batting order, the Cardinals look set to compete for the NL Central title in 2011. Despite their difficulties last season, it would be foolish to bet against their ability to extend their long run of success into another decade.

HITTERS

Bryan Anderson **C**

Born: **12/16/1986** Age: **24**
Bats: L Throws: R Height: **6' 1"** Weight: **200**
Breakout: **0%** Improve: **3%** Collapse: **4%**
Attrition: **7%** MLB: **13%**

Comparables:
Jeff Clement, Jose Lobaton, Clint Sammons (78)

YEAR	TEAM	LVL	AGE	PA	R	2B	3B	HR	RBI	BB	SO	SB	CS	AVG_OBP_SLG	TAv	BABIP	BRR	FRAA	WARP
2008	SFD	AA	21	86	12	5	0	2	14	4	12	0	0	.388/.407/.525	.303	.426	-0.9	C 1	0.8
2008	MEM	AAA	21	275	27	13	2	2	27	32	46	2	0	.281/.360/.379	.271	.330	-1.0	C 0	1.4
2009	MEM	AAA	22	174	22	7	3	4	11	10	42	1	0	.245/.293/.399	.261	.308	-0.1	C 0, 1B 0	0.7
2010	MEM	AAA	23	302	39	12	0	12	42	27	54	0	0	.270/.341/.448	.262	.296	0.0	C 0	1.4
2010	SLN	MLB	23	35	1	2	0	0	4	1	7	0	0	.281/.314/.344	.236	.346	0.0	C 0	0.0
2011	*SLN*	*MLB*	*24*	*294*	*34*	*12*	*1*	*8*	*33*	*22*	*63*	*0*	*0*	*.255/.313/.401*	*.248*	*.298*	*0.0*	*C -1, 1B 0*	*0.7*

Defense has always been the question with Anderson, but this year, he not only bounced back from an injury-plagued 2009 to display his usual potent lefty bat, but also impressed the organization with his solid work behind the dish. His collection of skills is superior to those of half of the starting catchers in the league, and in most other organizations, he'd be a shoo-in for at least part-time duty with the big club, but La Russa and Duncan have traditionally preferred top-notch catch-and-throw skills when selecting their Yadi caddies. During the offseason, GM John Mozeliak was said to be looking for a backup backstop who can use his bat for more than pounding in nails. Naturally, the old men in uniform preferred Gerald Laird.

Matt Carpenter **3B**

Born: **11/26/1985** Age: **25**
Bats: L Throws: R Height: **6' 3"** Weight: **200**
Breakout: **2%** Improve: **17%** Collapse: **8%**
Attrition: **16%** MLB: **36%**

Comparables:
Daniel Murphy, Adam Rosales, Jeff Baisley (77)

YEAR	TEAM	LVL	AGE	PA	R	2B	3B	HR	RBI	BB	SO	SB	CS	AVG_OBP_SLG	TAv	BABIP	BRR	FRAA	WARP
2009	QUD	A	23	126	11	6	2	0	10	17	13	2	0	.295/.405/.390	.280	.333	-0.4	3B 3	0.9
2009	PMB	A+	23	128	13	6	1	2	9	10	24	1	0	.219/.281/.342	.235	.253	-1.1	3B 7	0.6
2010	PMB	A+	24	128	17	5	2	1	16	26	14	0	1	.283/.441/.404	.325	.318	-0.8	3B 1	1.3
2010	SFD	AA	24	472	76	26	3	12	53	64	88	11	2	.316/.412/.487	.317	.372	3.1	3B 17	6.2
2011	*SLN*	*MLB*	*25*	*452*	*55*	*21*	*2*	*10*	*48*	*51*	*87*	*4*	*1*	*.264/.349/.407*	*.267*	*.308*	*-0.1*	*3B 12, 1B 0*	*2.7*

An unheralded 13th-round pick in the 2009 draft, Carpenter opened plenty of eyes in his full-season debut, spraying line drives all over the Texas League and earning the organization's position player of the year award. Carpenter has a terrific approach, works deep counts, takes his walks, and uses the whole field, though he's not likely to develop the power most teams look for in a third baseman. His defense improved throughout the year, but he'll never be more than an adequate defender, and as he's now 25, there's no projection left in him. Still, with a good showing at Memphis, he could give the Cardinals a Bill Mueller–style addition to their offense before the year is out.

Adron Chambers **OF**

Born: **10/8/1986** Age: **24**
Bats: L Throws: L Height: **5' 10"** Weight: **185**
Breakout: **3%** Improve: **12%** Collapse: **4%**
Attrition: **15%** MLB: **26%**

Comparables:
Michael Bourn, Brett Gardner, Tony Gwynn (72)

YEAR	TEAM	LVL	AGE	PA	R	2B	3B	HR	RBI	BB	SO	SB	CS	AVG_OBP_SLG	TAv	BABIP	BRR	FRAA	WARP
2008	QUD	A	21	384	56	13	7	3	25	33	66	13	8	.238/.320/.345	.263	.283	-1.1	LF 4, RF 1	1.2
2009	PMB	A+	22	517	66	17	16	1	46	47	96	21	12	.283/.368/.400	.282	.353	0.9	RF 4, CF -1	2.1
2010	SFD	AA	23	292	52	9	5	5	27	31	50	8	4	.282/.376/.417	.281	.332	3.6	CF -5, LF 1	1.2
2010	MEM	AAA	23	83	11	0	1	1	8	9	18	6	1	.290/.390/.362	.281	.365	0.9	LF 0, CF 1	0.5
2011	*SLN*	*MLB*	*24*	*413*	*43*	*15*	*4*	*5*	*36*	*32*	*92*	*10*	*4*	*.234/.304/.339*	*.232*	*.292*	*-0.4*	*CF -5, LF -2*	*-1.0*

One of the organization's most pleasant surprises, Chambers succeeded in his first taste of the high minors. A former college defensive back, he moved up to Double-A and maintained his high on-base percentage, drawing more walks and cutting down on his strikeouts, while seeing some of his triples start to fly over the fence. Chambers needs to take better advantage of his speed, as he's still a little raw in center field and his arm may eventually relegate him to left, but he improved his base-stealing during a stint in the Arizona Fall League. The Cardinals saw enough to stick him on the 40-man roster, and with the team desperate for someone who can hit at the top of the order, he has a chance to break through.

Allen Craig **RF**

Born: **7/18/1984** Age: **26**
Bats: **R** Throws: **R** Height: **6' 2"** Weight: **210**
Breakout: **3%** Improve: **27%** Collapse: **10%**
Attrition: **28%** MLB: **63%**

Comparables:
Adam Lind, Justin Huber, Lou Montanez (76)

YEAR	TEAM	LVL	AGE	PA	R	2B	3B	HR	RBI	BB	SO	SB	CS	AVG_OBP_SLG	TAv	BABIP	BRR	FRAA	WARP
2008	SFD	AA	23	568	84	30	0	22	85	48	87	2	1	.304/.373/.494	.293	.329	2.6	3B 9, LF -2	4.3
2009	MEM	AAA	24	521	78	26	1	26	83	37	95	3	0	.322/.374/.547	.312	.353	-4.4	LF -3, 1B 0	3.1
2010	MEM	AAA	25	350	57	24	2	14	81	34	59	1	0	.320/.389/.549	.313	.351	-3.0	LF 0, 1B 0	2.3
2010	SLN	MLB	25	124	12	7	0	4	18	9	26	0	1	.246/.298/.412	.262	.282	-1.5	RF -2, LF 0	-0.2
2011	*SLN*	*MLB*	*26*	*527*	*69*	*26*	*1*	*22*	*74*	*40*	*106*	*0*	*0*	*.279/.336/.479*	*.283*	*.311*	*0.0*	*LF -3, 3B 1*	*1.6*

Craig has nothing more to prove in the minors; he's 26, and he has a major-league bat and a major-league problem with his glove. He has plummeted down the defensive spectrum from third base, displaying bad hands at first and little range in the outfield, but as his career .321/.380/.548 line in Triple-A shows, all that awkwardness melts away when he's in the batter's box. With Lance Berkman slated to see the majority of time in left, Craig may get some at-bats against lefties to help cover for the starter's platoon issues.

Daniel Descalso **2B**

Born: **10/19/1986** Age: **24**
Bats: **L** Throws: **R** Height: **5' 10"** Weight: **190**
Breakout: **8%** Improve: **22%** Collapse: **10%**
Attrition: **29%** MLB: **47%**

Comparables:
Luis Valbuena, Justin Turner, Chin-lung Hu (81)

YEAR	TEAM	LVL	AGE	PA	R	2B	3B	HR	RBI	BB	SO	SB	CS	AVG_OBP_SLG	TAv	BABIP	BRR	FRAA	WARP
2008	PMB	A+	21	456	57	24	2	8	50	33	53	7	7	.243/.309/.372	.249	.256	1.1	2B -5, SS -4	0.0
2009	SFD	AA	22	324	46	26	5	8	51	31	41	0	1	.323/.395/.531	.322	.354	-0.8	2B 5	3.2
2009	MEM	AAA	22	172	23	4	0	2	17	16	21	3	0	.253/.320/.320	.234	.273	0.9	2B 2, 1B 0	0.2
2010	MEM	AAA	23	531	86	32	3	9	71	47	48	8	4	.282/.350/.421	.272	.291	5.3	2B -1, 1B -2	2.4
2010	SLN	MLB	23	37	6	2	0	0	4	2	6	1	0	.265/.324/.324	.282	.321	0.4	3B 0, SS 0	0.3
2011	*SLN*	*MLB*	*24*	*523*	*60*	*27*	*2*	*10*	*56*	*39*	*75*	*4*	*2*	*.264/.320/.395*	*.253*	*.287*	*-0.2*	*2B 3, SS 0*	*1.1*

Descalso fits the profile of so many Cardinals prospects these days: older than you'd hope with little projection and a mixed set of skills. A contact hitter with gap power, he draws a few walks, though there's some concern that big-league pitchers will knock the bat out of his hands. More importantly, he is solid in the field and would be a huge improvement over Skip Schumaker's cast-iron glove at the keystone. That would make him popular with the pitching staff, who will spend the spring secretly hoping that Descalso appeals to La Russa's unrepentant grinder-love and heads north with the big club.

Pedro Feliz **3B**

Born: **4/27/1977** Age: **34**
Bats: **R** Throws: **R** Height: **6' 1"** Weight: **180**
Breakout: **1%** Improve: **34%** Collapse: **8%**
Attrition: **22%** MLB: **93%**

Comparables:
Joe Randa, Frank Malzone, Buddy Bell (78)

YEAR	TEAM	LVL	AGE	PA	R	2B	3B	HR	RBI	BB	SO	SB	CS	AVG/OBP/SLG	TAv	BABIP	BRR	FRAA	WARP
2008	PHI	MLB	31	463	44	19	2	14	58	33	54	0	0	.249/.300/.402	.245	.254	-2.9	3B 0, SS 0	0.3
2009	PHI	MLB	32	625	62	30	2	12	82	35	68	0	1	.266/.307/.386	.248	.280	-4.0	3B 7, SS 0	1.3
2010	HOU	MLB	33	304	22	12	1	4	31	9	31	1	1	.222/.243/.311	.207	.232	-1.5	3B -5, 1B 3	-1.1
2010	SLN	MLB	33	125	14	0	1	1	9	4	10	0	0	.208/.232/.250	.183	.218	0.4	3B 1	-0.5
2011	*SLN*	*MLB*	*34*	*553*	*59*	*24*	*2*	*14*	*61*	*30*	*64*	*1*	*1*	*.250/.289/.384*	*.238*	*.258*	*-0.1*	*3B 2, 1B 0*	*0.5*

It wasn't shocking when Ed Wade offered Feliz a $4.5 million contract before last season to field grounders and swing through fastballs, since that's what Ed Wade does. Nor was it shocking when Feliz didn't hit a lick for the Astros, since that's what Feliz does. What was shocking was that the Cardinals traded for him in August hoping he could help fill their void at third base, then compounded their mistake by actually letting him play during their subsequent 2-8 road trip to Pittsburgh, Washington, and Houston, a mistake that doomed their playoff ambitions. Feliz has managed to scratch out a 10-year career with an excellent glove and enough home-run power to make the less observant ignore his disastrous on-base percentage, but now that his defense is questionable and his power is gone, there's no longer even a bad reason to give him a starting job.

David Freese 3B

Born: **4/28/1983** Age: **28**
Bats: **R** Throws: **R** Height: **6' 2"** Weight: **220**
Breakout: **3%** Improve: **21%** Collapse: **2%**
Attrition: **7%** MLB: **55%**

Comparables:
James D'Antona, Mark Saccomanno, Mike Morse (74)

YEAR	TEAM	LVL	AGE	PA	R	2B	3B	HR	RBI	BB	SO	SB	CS	AVG/OBP/SLG	TAv	BABIP	BRR	FRAA	WARP
2008	MEM	AAA	25	510	83	29	3	26	91	39	111	5	2	.306/.361/.550	.307	.350	3.4	3B 4	4.8
2009	MEM	AAA	26	225	34	15	0	10	37	22	51	1	0	.300/.369/.525	.304	.355	-4.3	3B -4, 1B -3	0.8
2009	SLN	MLB	26	34	3	2	0	1	7	2	7	0	0	.323/.353/.484	.288	.375	0.2	3B -1, 1B 0	0.1
2010	SLN	MLB	27	270	28	12	1	4	36	21	59	1	1	.296/.356/.404	.273	.368	1.7	3B 2, 1B 0	1.5
2011	*SLN*	*MLB*	*28*	*363*	*46*	*18*	*1*	*14*	*49*	*29*	*83*	*1*	*1*	*.277/.336/.464*	*.277*	*.325*	*-0.1*	*3B -1, 1B 0*	*1.4*

Freese inherited the third-base job last year but couldn't run with it, as a series of lower leg injuries culminating in surgery on both ankles kept him from running much of anywhere. He's back to try again this spring, possibly healthy but definitely a year older—not a good thing for a 28-year-old prospect. Freese has hit everywhere he's been and gets on base, though the prodigious power he showed in the minors has so far melted under the bright lights, and injuries have reduced his range to below-average. The best-case scenario for Freese is that he'll be an inexpensive complement to the millionaires in the middle of the order, but he's not destined for their tax bracket.

Tyler Greene SS

Born: **8/17/1983** Age: **27**
Bats: **R** Throws: **R** Height: **6' 2"** Weight: **190**
Breakout: **4%** Improve: **33%** Collapse: **3%**
Attrition: **23%** MLB: **63%**

Comparables:
Drew T Anderson, Ben Zobrist, Jim Fregosi (72)

YEAR	TEAM	LVL	AGE	PA	R	2B	3B	HR	RBI	BB	SO	SB	CS	AVG/OBP/SLG	TAv	BABIP	BRR	FRAA	WARP
2008	SFD	AA	24	408	62	15	4	16	41	22	99	14	6	.259/.304/.449	.259	.305	2.2	SS 5, 3B 0	2.2
2008	MEM	AAA	24	128	17	7	0	0	7	11	35	6	0	.234/.320/.297	.232	.333	0.9	SS 6	0.8
2009	MEM	AAA	25	388	70	10	5	15	42	38	86	31	3	.291/.366/.482	.296	.344	7.8	SS 8, 3B 1	4.6
2009	SLN	MLB	25	116	9	5	0	2	7	4	32	3	0	.222/.267/.324	.225	.293	1.2	SS 2, 3B -3	0.0
2010	MEM	AAA	26	385	67	21	5	9	34	32	89	12	5	.284/.355/.456	.280	.349	0.0	SS 1	2.5
2010	SLN	MLB	26	122	14	3	1	2	10	13	24	2	0	.221/.328/.327	.255	.266	1.5	SS -2, 2B -1	0.3
2011	*SLN*	*MLB*	*27*	*519*	*59*	*20*	*3*	*15*	*59*	*38*	*134*	*18*	*5*	*.246/.306/.402*	*.249*	*.304*	*0.3*	*SS 5, 3B 0*	*1.8*

Injuries and a hacktastic approach have kept Greene from employing the tools that made him a first-round pick back in 2005, and his prospect clock isn't approaching midnight—it's ticked past into the wee hours. Greene has always had the power, speed, and strong arm to grow into an above-average shortstop, but he's become a soufflé that didn't rise. He hasn't hit during his brief auditions with the big club, and since his defense isn't eye-opening, the Cardinals' lids are growing heavy where he's concerned.

Steven Hill C

Born: **3/14/1985** Age: **26**
Bats: **R** Throws: **R** Height: **5' 11"** Weight: **200**
Breakout: **2%** Improve: **11%** Collapse: **9%**
Attrition: **34%** MLB: **49%**

Comparables:
Matthew Brown, Jake Fox, Steve Pearce (75)

YEAR	TEAM	LVL	AGE	PA	R	2B	3B	HR	RBI	BB	SO	SB	CS	AVG/OBP/SLG	TAv	BABIP	BRR	FRAA	WARP
2008	PMB	A+	23	189	28	11	2	9	34	15	42	0	0	.285/.339/.529	.310	.325	0.0	1B -1, LF 0	1.3
2008	SFD	AA	23	103	13	3	1	5	9	3	31	0	0	.303/.330/.505	.275	.397	-2.4	1B 1, LF -1	0.0
2009	SFD	AA	24	508	62	26	2	19	64	36	106	1	2	.282/.333/.470	.279	.325	-5.4	C 1, LF -4	1.3
2010	SFD	AA	25	406	60	27	1	22	86	38	90	1	0	.280/.352/.543	.302	.313	0.4	C 3, 1B 0	3.4
2010	SLN	MLB	25	3	1	0	0	1	1	0	1	0	0	.333/.333/1.333	.577	.000	0.0	C 0	0.1
2011	*SLN*	*MLB*	*26*	*427*	*52*	*21*	*1*	*20*	*61*	*26*	*111*	*0*	*0*	*.257/.302/.468*	*.264*	*.301*	*0.0*	*C 1, 1B -2*	*0.8*

Hill has some juice in his bat, but calling him a catcher is a little speculative, at least in a Cardinals organization that looks down its nose at even mediocre backstops. He's better behind the plate than, say, Jake Fox or Matt LeCroy, and his power may convince some organization to try him out as an offense-first backup, but it's not likely to be this one—the Cards outrighted Hill in November.

Matt Holliday LF

Born: **1/10/1980** Age: **31**
Bats: **R** Throws: **R** Height: **6' 4"** Weight: **235**
Breakout: **0%** Improve: **32%** Collapse: **5%**
Attrition: **13%** MLB: **100%**

Comparables:
Kevin Youkilis, Mark Teixeira, Carlos Lee (59)

YEAR	TEAM	LVL	AGE	PA	R	2B	3B	HR	RBI	BB	SO	SB	CS	AVG/OBP/SLG	TAv	BABIP	BRR	FRAA	WARP
2008	COL	MLB	28	623	107	38	2	25	88	74	104	28	2	.321/.409/.538	.318	.359	5.4	LF 0	5.4
2009	OAK	MLB	29	400	52	23	1	11	54	46	58	12	3	.286/.378/.454	.304	.315	1.0	LF 4	3.0
2009	SLN	MLB	29	270	42	16	2	13	55	26	43	2	4	.353/.419/.604	.354	.380	2.3	LF -10	2.4
2010	SLN	MLB	30	675	96	45	1	28	103	69	93	9	5	.312/.390/.532	.329	.331	-1.0	LF -2	5.4
2011	*SLN*	*MLB*	*31*	*672*	*100*	*41*	*2*	*29*	*103*	*70*	*102*	*14*	*5*	*.311/.389/.536*	*.320*	*.331*	*-0.3*	*LF -1*	*5.0*

Earning a jaw-dropping free-agent payday is part talent and part timing, so there was some understandable concern that his nine-figure contract was more a matter of his being the least underwhelming veteran hitter in a thin market, but Holliday certainly earned his pay last season. His WARP made the league's 10 Most Wanted list, which speaks to how well he has maintained his defense while proving that his power didn't come just from tapping the Rockies. Age will soon start chipping away at his skills, so he's likely to be overcompensated by the end of his seven-year deal, but so far, the team's Holliday shopping spree has given St. Louis fans the perfect gift.

Jon Jay RF

Born: 3/15/1985 Age: 26
Bats: L Throws: L Height: 5' 11" Weight: 200
Breakout: 3% Improve: 23% Collapse: 9%
Attrition: 25% MLB: 48%
Comparables:
Lastings Milledge, Clete Thomas, Chris Pettit (74)

YEAR	TEAM	LVL	AGE	PA	R	2B	3B	HR	RBI	BB	SO	SB	CS	AVG/OBP/SLG	TAv	BABIP	BRR	FRAA	WARP
2008	SFD	AA	23	427	57	17	3	11	47	39	46	10	7	.306/.372/.457	.303	.317	-0.5	CF 17, LF 0	4.7
2008	MEM	AAA	23	64	8	4	1	1	10	6	10	0	1	.345/.406/.500	.318	.404	0.3	CF 4	1.0
2009	MEM	AAA	24	564	72	23	2	10	54	34	64	20	8	.281/.333/.394	.258	.297	5.6	LF -1, CF 0	1.6
2010	MEM	AAA	25	191	31	16	0	4	32	17	22	13	0	.321/.394/.491	.295	.340	0.0	LF 5, CF 0	1.5
2010	SLN	MLB	25	323	47	19	2	4	27	24	50	2	4	.300/.350/.422	.283	.339	2.7	RF -7, CF 3	1.2
2011	*SLN*	*MLB*	*26*	*523*	*62*	*26*	*2*	*11*	*59*	*37*	*77*	*10*	*5*	*.277/.330/.412*	*.261*	*.301*	*-0.7*	*CF 3, LF 0*	*1.2*

Much like his name, which leads you to suspect that some giggle-inducing moniker has been lopped off the end—possibly "Jingleheimer-Schmidt"—Jay is an incomplete player who isn't quite rangy enough for center or quite powerful enough to start in a corner. What he can do is lash gappers with his attractive lefty swing, provide much better defense than Allen Craig can, and hold the fort until St. Louis acquires a more stylishly equipped outfield alternative. The Cardinals have signed Lance Berkman to man left field, but Jay will be Johnny-on-the-spot should the lumbering first baseman prove too much of a defensive liability to play there every day.

Daryl Jones OF

Born: 6/25/1987 Age: 24
Bats: L Throws: L Height: 6' 0" Weight: 180
Breakout: 7% Improve: 14% Collapse: 3%
Attrition: 18% MLB: 27%
Comparables:
Clete Thomas, Shin-Soo Choo, Jeff Fiorentino (79)

YEAR	TEAM	LVL	AGE	PA	R	2B	3B	HR	RBI	BB	SO	SB	CS	AVG/OBP/SLG	TAv	BABIP	BRR	FRAA	WARP
2008	PMB	A+	21	352	43	11	7	7	35	33	67	18	5	.326/.403/.476	.320	.394	-1.3	LF 3, CF -2	2.9
2008	SFD	AA	21	151	19	6	1	6	14	22	30	6	1	.290/.404/.500	.324	.333	-1.2	LF 4, RF -1	1.4
2009	SFD	AA	22	336	50	14	3	3	29	33	65	7	4	.279/.360/.378	.257	.345	1.7	LF -11, CF -1	-0.5
2010	SFD	AA	23	518	67	17	6	8	48	52	95	15	9	.244/.335/.361	.256	.290	0.0	CF -1, LF -7	0.3
2011	*SLN*	*MLB*	*24*	*454*	*50*	*18*	*3*	*9*	*45*	*37*	*102*	*9*	*3*	*.246/.314/.371*	*.244*	*.300*	*-0.1*	*LF -8, CF -3*	*-0.9*

Treading water is a necessary skill for sailors, lifeguards, and would-be religious figures, but for a baseball prospect, there's little worse. Jones barely kept his head above the elements in his third trip through Double-A, posting numbers similar to those of his disappointing 2009. He has never developed the power stroke scouts believed would eventually appear, and with an iffy arm that limits him defensively, he's not particularly well suited for a bench role. The Cardinals have taken him off the 40-man roster, and now that Jon Jay has motored past him, Jones is running out of time.

Joe Mather 4C

Born: 7/23/1982 Age: 28
Bats: R Throws: R Height: 6' 4" Weight: 195
Breakout: 1% Improve: 18% Collapse: 3%
Attrition: 8% MLB: 36%
Comparables:
Jeff Fiorentino, Gabe Gross, Luke Allen (81)

YEAR	TEAM	LVL	AGE	PA	R	2B	3B	HR	RBI	BB	SO	SB	CS	AVG/OBP/SLG	TAv	BABIP	BRR	FRAA	WARP
2008	MEM	AAA	25	254	45	14	2	17	41	32	36	7	2	.303/.409/.630	.334	.292	0.5	RF -3, CF 0	2.2
2008	SLN	MLB	25	147	20	7	0	8	18	12	32	1	0	.241/.306/.474	.273	.255	0.4	LF 1, RF 0	0.6
2009	SFD	AA	26	65	8	3	0	3	11	5	11	0	2	.207/.277/.414	.226	.200	-1.1	3B -1, RF -2	-0.7
2009	MEM	AAA	26	150	12	6	2	1	14	9	27	7	1	.176/.233/.272	.207	.207	0.0	RF 0, 1B 0	-0.6
2010	MEM	AAA	27	376	55	18	4	10	46	37	74	6	4	.275/.348/.442	.269	.324	0.3	RF -3, CF -2	0.7
2010	SLN	MLB	27	63	5	4	0	0	3	2	11	1	1	.220/.238/.288	.179	.260	-0.1	CF -2, RF -1	-0.8
2011	*ATL*	*MLB*	*28*	*362*	*41*	*15*	*2*	*12*	*42*	*31*	*74*	*6*	*3*	*.239/.308/.407*	*.251*	*.269*	*-0.3*	*RF -4, CF -1*	*-0.3*

A late-blooming four-corner player, Mather suddenly lost much of the impressive power he'd displayed in the last few years, with recurrent wrist injuries the likely culprit. Though he's already 28, the Braves apparently took a cotton to him and claimed him off waivers with the intention of letting him compete for a chunk of Omar Infante's and Matt Diaz's vacated utility time. If only success were a question of mind over Mather, the Braves might have snagged themselves a nice right-handed power threat off the bench, but first their acquisition will have to show that he's still the same player who averaged a home run every 19 at-bats in the minors from 2005 to 2008.

Aaron Miles 2B

Born: 12/15/1976 Age: 34
Bats: S Throws: R Height: 5' 8" Weight: 170
Breakout: 1% Improve: 23% Collapse: 13%
Attrition: 22% MLB: 75%
Comparables:
Bip Roberts, Jeff Frye, Curt Flood (72)

YEAR	TEAM	LVL	AGE	PA	R	2B	3B	HR	RBI	BB	SO	SB	CS	AVG/OBP/SLG	TAv	BABIP	BRR	FRAA	WARP
2008	SLN	MLB	31	407	49	15	2	4	31	23	37	3	3	.318/.351/.400	.265	.338	4.4	2B -4, SS -1	1.3
2009	IOW	AAA	32	91	8	4	0	0	8	2	14	1	2	.253/.264/.299	.210	.293	0.5	2B 2, 3B -1	-0.1
2009	CHN	MLB	32	170	17	7	1	0	5	8	21	3	0	.185/.218/.242	.162	.206	0.9	2B -2, SS -1	-1.5
2010	SFD	AA	33	71	11	4	0	0	13	7	8	0	1	.279/.362/.344	.267	.309	-0.2	2B -2, SS -2	-0.2
2010	SLN	MLB	33	150	14	5	0	0	9	6	14	0	1	.283/.307/.319	.234	.302	0.6	2B 6, 3B -1	0.4
2011	*SLN*	*MLB*	*34*	*362*	*38*	*15*	*1*	*3*	*33*	*21*	*40*	*3*	*1*	*.267/.303/.349*	*.233*	*.286*	*-0.2*	*2B -1, SS -1*	*-0.4*

A fine example of knowing a man by the company he keeps, Miles was traded twice last winter in deals involving Jake Fox, Matt

Spencer, Ronny Morla, Jeff Gray, Adam Rosales, and (wait for it) Willy Taveras, before earning his release from the Reds two weeks into the 2010 season. Since other teams were paying the freight, the Cardinals latched on to Miles as free organizational depth and wound up having to use him more than they would have wished. He can play a number of positions, but not very well, and can hit an empty .270. Now that Miles will cost them actual cash, most GMs should be aware that signing him is approximately 1.6 kilometers from a good idea.

Yadier Molina C

Born: **7/13/1982** Age: **28**
Bats: **R** Throws: **R** Height: **5' 11"** Weight: **225**
Breakout: **0%** Improve: **36%** Collapse: **7%**
Attrition: **12%** MLB: **86%**
Comparables:
Russell Martin, Ramon Hernandez, Ted Simmons (62)

YEAR	TEAM	LVL	AGE	PA	R	2B	3B	HR	RBI	BB	SO	SB	CS	AVG/OBP/SLG	TAv	BABIP	BRR	FRAA	WARP
2008	SLN	MLB	25	485	39	18	0	7	56	32	29	0	2	.304/.346/.392	.254	.308	-5.8	C -1, 1B 1	1.2
2009	SLN	MLB	26	544	45	23	1	6	54	50	39	9	3	.293/.362/.383	.259	.305	-1.9	C 1, 1B 0	2.1
2010	SLN	MLB	27	521	35	19	0	6	62	42	51	8	4	.262/.328/.342	.247	.280	-3.7	C 1, 1B 0	1.2
2011	*SLN*	*MLB*	*28*	*481*	*57*	*21*	*0*	*9*	*48*	*40*	*38*	*5*	*2*	*.281/.343/.391*	*.260*	*.286*	*-0.3*	*C 1, 1B 0*	*2.0*

For the sixth consecutive year, Molina deserved a Gold Glove for his work behind the plate. For the third consecutive year, he actually won it, and given the awesome power of incumbency in Gold Glove voting, it will probably all even out in the end—unless the Cardinals work him to death first. Molina saw action in 136 of the team's first 150 games prior to being shut down with a sore knee, and it doesn't take a leap of faith to think that those two things might be related. He has worked hard to make himself a useful hitter, but his numbers are moving in the wrong direction, and the Cardinals might get more quality out of him if they asked for a little less quantity.

Albert Pujols 1B

Born: **1/16/1980** Age: **31**
Bats: **R** Throws: **R** Height: **6' 3"** Weight: **210**
Breakout: **1%** Improve: **35%** Collapse: **3%**
Attrition: **5%** MLB: **99%**
Comparables:
Mark Teixeira, Lance Berkman, David Ortiz (62)

YEAR	TEAM	LVL	AGE	PA	R	2B	3B	HR	RBI	BB	SO	SB	CS	AVG/OBP/SLG	TAv	BABIP	BRR	FRAA	WARP
2008	SLN	MLB	28	641	101	44	0	37	116	104	54	7	3	.357/.462/.653	.373	.340	-1.2	1B 20, 2B 0	9.7
2009	SLN	MLB	29	700	124	45	1	47	135	115	64	16	4	.328/.443/.659	.366	.299	1.0	1B 26	10.6
2010	SLN	MLB	30	700	115	39	1	42	118	103	76	14	4	.312/.414/.596	.344	.297	2.8	1B 14	7.8
2011	*SLN*	*MLB*	*31*	*671*	*113*	*39*	*0*	*41*	*121*	*103*	*62*	*11*	*4*	*.322/.429/.618*	*.350*	*.299*	*-0.3*	*1B 19, 2B 0*	*8.1*

If you want some perspective on how great Pujols has been and continues to be, take a gander at his .312/.414/.596 stat line, and understand that last year, he posted the lowest batting average of his career, had the lowest on-base percentage since his sophomore season of 2002, and slugged below .600 for just the third time. To balance out that unexpected suckitude, he did lead the NL in home runs, runs scored, and RBIs; won his second Gold Glove and his sixth Silver Slugger; and finished in the top two in MVP voting for the seventh time. Pujols is now on the wrong side of 30, so this year's slight course correction downward may be the start of a slow, inevitable decline, but whatever his next contract pays him, it's hard to imagine that he won't be worth it.

Colby Rasmus CF

Born: **8/11/1986** Age: **24**
Bats: **L** Throws: **L** Height: **6' 2"** Weight: **200**
Breakout: **5%** Improve: **45%** Collapse: **3%**
Attrition: **17%** MLB: **86%**
Comparables:
Ken Griffey, Wladimir Balentien, Reggie Smith (77)

YEAR	TEAM	LVL	AGE	PA	R	2B	3B	HR	RBI	BB	SO	SB	CS	AVG/OBP/SLG	TAv	BABIP	BRR	FRAA	WARP
2008	MEM	AAA	21	387	56	15	0	11	36	49	72	15	3	.251/.344/.396	.262	.283	3.6	CF 8	2.3
2009	SLN	MLB	22	520	72	22	2	16	52	36	95	3	1	.251/.304/.407	.254	.278	2.9	CF 5, LF -1	1.7
2010	SLN	MLB	23	534	85	28	3	23	66	63	148	12	8	.276/.360/.498	.307	.351	2.6	CF -20	2.2
2011	*SLN*	*MLB*	*24*	*486*	*61*	*22*	*2*	*19*	*63*	*50*	*108*	*9*	*4*	*.263/.337/.454*	*.275*	*.303*	*-0.4*	*CF -7, RF 0*	*1.3*

Last year, Rasmus showed us what all the fuss was about, hitting for power, drawing walks, and posting the highest TAv among senior circuit center fielders at the tender age of 23. Rasmus needs to improve on what most eyes and metrics agreed was a sloppy and disappointing season in the field, but he has the tools to be above average out there. More disconcerting are the concerns about his makeup, with last summer's highly publicized rift with manager Tony La Russa and request for a trade reminiscent of previously unexplained periods of lackluster play that some blamed on pouting. Hopefully for Cardinals fans, this was all just a tempest in a teapot and everyone can move on together, since Rasmus possesses talent that is not only extremely valuable, but also particularly well suited to the Cardinals' need for a cheap, slugging lefty bat.

Brendan Ryan SS

Born: **3/26/1982** Age: **29**
Bats: **R** Throws: **R** Height: **6' 2"** Weight: **195**
Breakout: **4%** Improve: **44%** Collapse: **8%**
Attrition: **10%** MLB: **80%**
Comparables:
Jason Bartlett, Mickey Stanley, Carney Lansford (74)

YEAR	TEAM	LVL	AGE	PA	R	2B	3B	HR	RBI	BB	SO	SB	CS	AVG/OBP/SLG	TAv	BABIP	BRR	FRAA	WARP
2008	MEM	AAA	26	88	13	5	0	3	10	4	17	1	0	.238/.273/.412	.236	.254	0.2	2B -3, RF 2	0.0
2008	SLN	MLB	26	218	27	9	0	0	10	16	31	7	2	.244/.303/.289	.230	.284	2.3	SS 0, 2B -4	-0.1
2009	SLN	MLB	27	429	54	19	7	3	37	24	56	14	7	.292/.336/.400	.264	.327	-2.2	SS 28, 2B 0	4.2
2010	SLN	MLB	28	486	50	19	3	2	36	33	60	11	4	.223/.274/.294	.214	.247	1.6	SS 9	0.6
2011	*SEA*	*MLB*	*29*	*454*	*51*	*21*	*3*	*6*	*46*	*31*	*55*	*13*	*5*	*.268/.318/.379*	*.248*	*.287*	*-0.3*	*SS 10, 2B -1*	*1.9*

Ryan spent the year struggling to make solid contact at the plate—his .220 True Average exceeded only those of Pedro Feliz and Cesar Izturis—but to his credit, he never took his difficulties out to the field. He was again spectacular at shortstop, with tremendous range and fine instincts, which led him to post a positive WARP mark despite his offensive travails. At the plate, he continually got under the ball and hit four percent more balls in the air, accounting for much of his precipitous drop in batting average on balls in play. The Mariners acquired him during the offseason as part of their "I'm in the Mood for Glove" roster approach, and since the Cardinals replaced him with Ryan Theriot, a marginally better hitter and much inferior fielder, he'll be missed.

Skip Schumaker 2B

Born: **2/3/1980** Age: **31**
Bats: **L** Throws: **R** Height: **5' 10"** Weight: **175**
Breakout: **0%** Improve: **36%** Collapse: **1%**
Attrition: **4%** MLB: **95%**

Comparables:
Mark Ellis, Bobby Avila, Freddy Sanchez (81)

YEAR	TEAM	LVL	AGE	PA	R	2B	3B	HR	RBI	BB	SO	SB	CS	AVG/OBP/SLG	TAv	BABIP	BRR	FRAA	WARP
2008	SLN	MLB	28	594	86	22	5	8	46	47	60	8	2	.302/.357/.406	.265	.325	3.2	CF -12, LF 5	1.4
2009	SLN	MLB	29	586	85	34	1	4	35	52	69	2	2	.303/.364/.393	.276	.341	0.7	2B -9, LF -1	1.6
2010	SLN	MLB	30	529	66	18	1	5	42	43	64	5	3	.265/.327/.338	.248	.293	0.5	2B 2, RF 3	1.1
2011	*SLN*	*MLB*	*31*	*524*	*62*	*24*	*2*	*8*	*53*	*44*	*61*	*5*	*2*	*.287/.344/.395*	*.263*	*.309*	*-0.3*	*2B -2, CF -2*	*1.0*

La Russa's inspired attempt to cobble together an infield with Schumaker at the keystone stubbed its toe last year, when the former part-time outfielder slumped at the plate and made only mild progress in the field. Like double-play partner Brendan Ryan, Schumaker hit more balls in the air and consequently watched his batting average and on-base percentage drop into the danger zone below which middle infielders without defensive street cred fear to tread. With his defense routinely questioned in many circles, the Cardinals will soon be forced to admit the experiment has not paid off as well as they needed. Still, even if Schumaker is no longer a starter, his adventures in pivot-turning have made him even more perfectly adapted to the utility role he's best suited to fill.

Nick Stavinoha OF

Born: **5/3/1982** Age: **29**
Bats: **R** Throws: **R** Height: **6' 2"** Weight: **225**
Breakout: **0%** Improve: **22%** Collapse: **13%**
Attrition: **11%** MLB: **64%**

Comparables:
Matt Murton, Lou Montanez, Felipe Alou (71)

YEAR	TEAM	LVL	AGE	PA	R	2B	3B	HR	RBI	BB	SO	SB	CS	AVG/OBP/SLG	TAv	BABIP	BRR	FRAA	WARP
2008	MEM	AAA	26	453	67	23	3	16	74	20	50	2	1	.337/.366/.518	.306	.351	-2.0	RF -5, LF -2	2.1
2008	SLN	MLB	26	61	4	1	0	0	4	2	11	0	0	.193/.213/.211	.165	.229	0.6	LF -1, RF -1	-0.6
2009	MEM	AAA	27	295	39	17	2	11	56	25	48	2	0	.282/.353/.490	.292	.302	0.8	1B 2, RF -1	1.4
2009	SLN	MLB	27	91	6	7	0	2	17	2	15	1	0	.230/.242/.379	.216	.250	0.2	LF -4, RF -2	-0.8
2010	MEM	AAA	28	107	19	9	1	6	28	5	16	0	0	.390/.411/.680	.358	.413	0.0	1B 0, RF 1	1.3
2010	SLN	MLB	28	126	11	4	0	2	9	4	28	0	0	.256/.286/.339	.228	.319	0.4	RF -1, LF -1	-0.3
2011	*SLN*	*MLB*	*29*	*374*	*46*	*19*	*1*	*13*	*50*	*19*	*65*	*1*	*0*	*.281/.321/.455*	*.270*	*.309*	*0.0*	*RF -4, LF -2*	*0.2*

Stavinoha is yet another surprisingly old, defensively challenged corner outfielder who would be a first baseman in most organizations—before he's done, Albert Pujols will have forced more defensive conversions than any Cardinal in history, Cardinal Ximenez included. Stavinoha's arsenal contains such diverse elements as fear, surprise, and an almost fanatical devotion to swinging for the fences, but he lacks the glove or patience to be a suitable corner-outfield reserve. St. Louis outrighted him in November.

Randy Winn OF

Born: **6/9/1974** Age: **37**
Bats: **S** Throws: **R** Height: **6' 2"** Weight: **193**
Breakout: **0%** Improve: **33%** Collapse: **13%**
Attrition: **23%** MLB: **94%**

Comparables:
Dusty Baker, Felipe Alou, Garret Anderson (72)

YEAR	TEAM	LVL	AGE	PA	R	2B	3B	HR	RBI	BB	SO	SB	CS	AVG/OBP/SLG	TAv	BABIP	BRR	FRAA	WARP
2008	SFN	MLB	34	667	84	38	2	10	64	59	88	25	2	.306/.363/.426	.283	.339	-1.0	RF 16, LF 1	4.1
2009	SFN	MLB	35	597	65	33	5	2	51	47	93	16	2	.262/.317/.353	.243	.306	3.0	RF 9, LF 2	1.2
2010	NYA	MLB	36	71	6	0	1	1	8	8	15	1	0	.213/.296/.295	.242	.255	1.3	LF -1, RF 1	0.1
2010	SLN	MLB	36	162	16	8	1	3	17	13	22	5	0	.250/.309/.382	.240	.268	1.1	RF 1, CF -2	0.0
2011	*SLN*	*MLB*	*37*	*557*	*63*	*29*	*2*	*8*	*56*	*46*	*79*	*14*	*3*	*.266/.325/.380*	*.251*	*.296*	*0.5*	*RF 8, LF 0*	*1.2*

Have legs, will travel. Winn has reached the Tom Joad period of his career, wandering through New York and St. Louis last year and now looking for work wherever it can be found. Wherever a team needs a defensive replacement in the corner outfield, he'll be there. Wherever there's a team beatin' up a guy, and a manager needs to double-switch, he'll be there. If there's one place where it's been safe to assume that Winn won't be, it's the playoffs: the switch-hitter has never sniffed post-season baseball, a league-pacing streak that continued in 2010 despite his having started the season with the perennially playoff-bound Yankees.

PITCHERS

Mitchell Boggs

Born: **2/15/1984** Age: **27**
Bats: **R** Throws: **R** Height: **6' 4"** Weight: **215**
Breakout: **10%** Improve: **18%** Collapse: **2%**
Attrition: **12%** MLB: **23%**

Comparables:
Tim Stauffer, Glen Perkins, Enrique Gonzalez (81)

YEAR	TEAM	LVL	AGE	W	L	SV	G	GS	IP	H	HR	BB	SO	EqBB9	EqSO9	GB%	BABIP	WHIP	ERA	FRA	WARP
2008	MEM	AAA	24	9	3	0	21	21	125^1	107	11	46	81	3.3	5.8	50%	.261	1.24	3.45	4.35	2.2
2008	SLN	MLB	24	3	2	0	8	6	34	42	5	22	13	5.8	3.4	52%	.303	1.94	7.41	7.93	-0.7
2009	MEM	AAA	25	6	4	0	14	14	76^1	90	8	32	58	3.8	6.8	45%	.336	1.65	4.84	4.56	0.8
2009	SLN	MLB	25	2	3	0	16	9	58	71	3	33	46	5.1	7.1	55%	.374	1.86	4.19	2.70	1.9
2010	SLN	MLB	26	2	3	0	61	0	67^1	60	5	27	52	3.6	7.0	54%	.279	1.35	3.61	4.11	0.5
2011	*SLN*	*MLB*	*27*	*7*	*8*	*0*	*43*	*18*	*129*	*144*	*13*	*62*	*79*	*4.3*	*5.5*	*48%*	*.312*	*1.59*	*5.18*	*5.63*	*0.0*

After Boggs continued to have trouble retiring lefties last year, the Cardinals bowed to the inevitable and moved him to the pen, with very encouraging results. He ditched his ineffective changeup and saw increased velocity on both his fastball and his slider, with the former now sitting in the mid-90s. Not everything was disco, however, as he walked more lefties than he struck out, and his future role will depend on how that particular song ends. If he can even out his platoon splits, he can be a solid set-up man; otherwise, he'll find himself on a slow boat to ROOGY-ville.

Chris Carpenter

Born: **4/27/1975** Age: **36**
Bats: **R** Throws: **R** Height: **6' 6"** Weight: **215**
Breakout: **11%** Improve: **27%** Collapse: **27%**
Attrition: **11%** MLB: **79%**

Comparables:
Ron Reed, Koji Uehara, Connie Johnson (57)

YEAR	TEAM	LVL	AGE	W	L	SV	G	GS	IP	H	HR	BB	SO	EqBB9	EqSO9	GB%	BABIP	WHIP	ERA	FRA	WARP
2008	SLN	MLB	33	0	1	0	4	3	15^1	16	0	4	7	2.3	4.1	56%	.308	1.30	1.76	3.38	0.4
2009	SLN	MLB	34	17	4	0	28	28	192^2	156	7	38	144	1.8	6.7	57%	.269	1.04	2.24	2.78	6.0
2010	SLN	MLB	35	16	9	0	35	35	235	214	21	63	179	2.4	6.9	52%	.279	1.23	3.22	4.12	3.0
2011	*SLN*	*MLB*	*36*	*9*	*5*	*0*	*21*	*21*	136^2	*127*	*10*	*36*	*94*	*2.4*	*6.2*	*51%*	*.289*	*1.19*	*3.21*	*3.49*	*3.6*

Carpenter spent last year on the positive side of his career's "dominant/injured" polarity, tallying 200 innings pitched for the first time in four years and again making an argument to be considered the Cardinals' co-ace. Carpenter has traditionally been able to post ERAs far better than his SIERAs, with 2009's 3.36 SIERA far higher than his unrepeatable 2.24 ERA. It was a good predictor of 2010's 3.22 ERA, however, and given his 3.78 SIERA last year, a continued gradual loss of effectiveness can be reasonably expected in 2011. That's nitpicking, though. That another year of health and effectiveness may make his $15 million option in 2012 something to be considered is an eventuality that few would have imagined possible just two years ago.

Ryan Franklin

Born: **3/5/1973** Age: **38**
Bats: **R** Throws: **R** Height: **6' 3"** Weight: **165**
Breakout: **13%** Improve: **22%** Collapse: **17%**
Attrition: **11%** MLB: **50%**

Comparables:
Cory Lidle, Salomon Torres, Lindy McDaniel (64)

YEAR	TEAM	LVL	AGE	W	L	SV	G	GS	IP	H	HR	BB	SO	EqBB9	EqSO9	GB%	BABIP	WHIP	ERA	FRA	WARP
2008	SLN	MLB	35	6	6	17	74	0	78^2	86	10	30	51	3.4	5.8	44%	.302	1.51	3.55	3.82	1.0
2009	SLN	MLB	36	4	3	38	62	0	61	49	2	24	44	3.5	6.5	48%	.263	1.21	1.92	2.46	1.6
2010	SLN	MLB	37	6	2	27	59	0	65	57	7	10	42	1.4	5.8	45%	.249	1.09	3.46	4.13	0.4
2011	*SLN*	*MLB*	*38*	*4*	*1*	*20*	*69*	*0*	72^1	*72*	*7*	*23*	*42*	*2.8*	*5.2*	*45%*	*.285*	*1.32*	*3.96*	*4.30*	*0.2*

There's a school of thought that argues that making your best reliever your closer is not the optimal choice, since that arrangement precludes him from being used in high-leverage situations earlier in the game with men on base in favor of pitching with a three-run lead in the ninth. If you buy into that idea, then Ryan Franklin is the closer for you. Last year, he closed out 27 of the 29 leads he was handed despite numbers that would have made him a bad choice to come into a tie game with runners on base but that were perfectly acceptable for pitching a single inning with a lead. Given his suddenly minuscule walk rate, there's no reason he can't be trusted to do it again. Perhaps someday a sportswriter will invent a stat that causes the creation of a "Big Lead Closer" and a "Small Lead Closer," but until that happens, Franklin can proudly wear that big silver "C" by himself.

Jaime Garcia

Born: **7/8/1986** Age: **24**
Bats: **L** Throws: **L** Height: **6' 2"** Weight: **200**
Breakout: **9%** Improve: **33%** Collapse: **10%**
Attrition: **11%** MLB: **62%**

Comparables:
Steve Carlton, Brad Mills, Steve Comer (73)

YEAR	TEAM	LVL	AGE	W	L	SV	G	GS	IP	H	HR	BB	SO	EqBB9	EqSO9	GB%	BABIP	WHIP	ERA	FRA	WARP
2008	SFD	AA	21	3	2	0	6	6	35	26	0	16	41	4.1	10.5	63%	.302	1.26	2.06	2.75	1.3
2008	MEM	AAA	21	4	4	0	13	12	71	74	6	26	59	3.3	7.5	56%	.315	1.45	4.44	4.35	1.4
2008	SLN	MLB	21	1	1	0	10	1	16	14	4	8	8	4.5	4.5	62%	.208	1.44	6.19	8.54	-0.6
2009	MEM	AAA	22	2	0	0	4	4	21	17	5	9	22	3.9	9.4	62%	.245	1.33	3.86	4.46	0.6
2010	SLN	MLB	23	13	8	0	28	28	163^1	151	9	64	132	3.5	7.3	57%	.292	1.33	2.70	3.79	2.9
2011	*SLN*	*MLB*	*24*	*8*	*6*	*0*	*21*	*21*	*117*	*114*	*10*	*50*	*88*	*3.9*	*6.8*	*52%*	*.298*	*1.39*	*3.96*	*4.30*	*2.3*

Garcia's rookie season was a revelation, as the young sinkerballer had frustrated batsmen pounding pitch after pitch into the dirt en route to a 2.70 ERA that ranked fourth-best in the National League. Garcia is adept at changing speeds, abetting his late-breaking heater with a cutter, a changeup, and a slow curve that off-balance hitters merely stare at, hoping it misses the zone. Such a wide menu of options means the chance of one pitch's going bad on a given day is higher than with most pitchers, but it also makes it harder for the league to catch on to what he's doing. His walk rate will become a problem if he can't get the swelling down, but Garcia gives the Cardinals hope that they have found yet another ace to help bandage their rotation.

Blake Hawksworth

Born: **3/1/1983** Age: **28**
Bats: R Throws: R Height: **6' 3"** Weight: **195**
Breakout: **6%** Improve: **12%** Collapse: **2%**
Attrition: **9%** MLB: **15%**

Comparables:
Brian Burres, Kelvin Jimenez, Joe Martinez (81)

YEAR	TEAM	LVL	AGE	W	L	SV	G	GS	IP	H	HR	BB	SO	EqBB9	EqSO9	GB%	BABIP	WHIP	ERA	FRA	WARP
2008	MEM	AAA	25	5	7	0	18	17	88^2	111	12	38	83	3.9	8.4	49%	.364	1.77	5.79	5.73	0.3
2009	MEM	AAA	26	5	4	0	12	13	73	61	3	20	57	2.5	7.0	46%	.262	1.14	3.45	4.33	0.7
2009	SLN	MLB	26	4	0	0	30	0	40	29	2	15	20	3.4	4.5	56%	.221	1.13	2.03	3.64	0.6
2010	SLN	MLB	27	4	8	0	45	8	90^1	113	15	35	61	3.5	6.1	52%	.331	1.66	4.98	4.98	0.1
2011	*LAN*	*MLB*	*28*	*6*	*6*	*0*	*41*	*15*	*115*	*126*	*15*	*46*	*72*	*3.6*	*5.6*	*48%*	*.302*	*1.48*	*4.85*	*5.27*	*0.3*

On September 25, Hawksworth's last outing of the season ended when Sam Fuld lined a shot off the side of his face. The Cardinals reliever got up and walked off under his own power, a "hockey tough" moment befitting a man whose name sounds more like a Canucks defenseman than a reliever and whose grandfather was instrumental in bringing the Winter Olympics to Vancouver. Unfortunately, that play was also a perfect analogy for Hawksworth's season, as National League hitters spent the summer hitting Hawksworth hard and driving him out of the park. The good news is that he improved his strikeout rate, and if he can keep his changeup down and lower his home-run rate—a task that should be rendered easier by his November change of address to Chavez Ravine—he might settle in as a serviceable swingman, but nothing more.

Kyle Lohse

Born: **10/4/1978** Age: **32**
Bats: R Throws: R Height: **6' 2"** Weight: **190**
Breakout: **14%** Improve: **40%** Collapse: **28%**
Attrition: **8%** MLB: **95%**

Comparables:
Pat Dobson, Esteban Loaiza, Larry Jansen (81)

YEAR	TEAM	LVL	AGE	W	L	SV	G	GS	IP	H	HR	BB	SO	EqBB9	EqSO9	GB%	BABIP	WHIP	ERA	FRA	WARP
2008	SLN	MLB	29	15	6	0	33	33	200	211	18	49	119	2.2	5.4	47%	.297	1.32	3.78	4.06	3.4
2009	SLN	MLB	30	6	10	0	23	22	117^2	125	16	36	77	2.8	5.9	46%	.287	1.39	4.74	5.29	0.3
2010	SLN	MLB	31	4	8	0	18	18	92	129	9	35	54	3.4	5.3	44%	.364	1.82	6.55	6.19	-0.8
2011	*SLN*	*MLB*	*32*	*10*	*11*	*0*	*28*	*28*	*156^1*	*177*	*16*	*50*	*89*	*2.9*	*5.1*	*46%*	*.311*	*1.46*	*4.75*	*5.17*	*1.4*

Ever notice how car mechanics often drive the junkiest cars, usually something a little exotic that they took in trade and haven't gotten around to fixing up? Kyle Lohse is Dave Duncan's version of a beat-up Triumph TR-7. Whereas Duncan and the Cardinals have had the good sense to ship out their more mundane rebuilds, giving them a fresh coat of paint and foisting them on an unsuspecting world, Lohse was too interesting to get rid of after his magical 2008 season, and St. Louis rewarded him with a four-year contract. Since then, he has broken down every year—last year, he needed surgery on his forearm—leaving the Cardinals hoping against hope that Lohse can at least function as a fifth starter next year. *Caveat emptor*, indeed.

Lance Lynn

Born: **5/12/1987** Age: **24**
Bats: R Throws: R Height: **6' 5"** Weight: **250**
Breakout: **13%** Improve: **36%** Collapse: **15%**
Attrition: **23%** MLB: **69%**

Comparables:
Brett Cecil, Sean Gallagher, Carlos Carrasco (68)

YEAR	TEAM	LVL	AGE	W	L	SV	G	GS	IP	H	HR	BB	SO	EqBB9	EqSO9	GB%	BABIP	WHIP	ERA	FRA	WARP
2009	SFD	AA	22	11	4	0	22	22	126^1	117	5	51	98	3.6	7.0	49%	.299	1.36	2.92	3.93	2.4
2010	MEM	AAA	23	13	10	0	29	29	164	164	21	62	141	3.4	7.7	44%	.300	1.43	4.77	5.28	1.2
2011	*SLN*	*MLB*	*24*	*8*	*7*	*0*	*21*	*21*	*113*	*114*	*12*	*49*	*89*	*3.9*	*7.1*	*45%*	*.304*	*1.43*	*4.39*	*4.77*	*1.6*

A hulking righty who nonetheless relies more on control and deception than overpowering stuff, Lynn struggled early on at Memphis before something clicked. He struck out more than a man per inning during the second half, capping off his season by striking out 16 batters in a playoff game. Despite the granting of his wish by the strikeouts djinn, Lynn is really just a strike-thrower who has a low-90s fastball and a standard assortment of breaking pitches and whose upside is that of a fourth starter. He'll start the year as rotation insurance but will be just a phone call away, and if he can stick after Kyle Lohse's next unfortunate mishap, he may eventually be able to update his profile from "just a strike-thrower" to "just a multimillionaire."

Mike MacDougal
Born: **3/5/1977** Age: **34**
Bats: **S** Throws: **R** Height: **6' 4"** Weight: **195**
Breakout: **10%** Improve: **23%** Collapse: **16%**
Attrition: **12%** MLB: **57%**
Comparables:
Mike Fetters, Doug Henry, Wade Miller (73)

YEAR	TEAM	LVL	AGE	W	L	SV	G	GS	IP	H	HR	BB	SO	EqBB9	EqSO9	GB%	BABIP	WHIP	ERA	FRA	WARP
2008	CHR	AAA	31	0	4	4	38	2	49^{1}	48	2	30	65	5.5	11.9	57%	.359	1.62	3.47	1.86	1.9
2008	CHA	MLB	31	0	0	0	16	0	17	16	0	12	12	6.4	6.4	48%	.308	1.76	2.12	1.99	0.6
2009	CHA	MLB	32	0	0	0	5	0	4^{1}	7	0	7	3	14.5	6.2	53%	.467	3.23	12.46	9.55	-0.2
2009	WAS	MLB	32	1	1	20	52	0	50	45	3	31	31	5.6	5.6	65%	.275	1.58	3.60	4.84	0.0
2010	SLN	MLB	33	1	1	0	17	0	18^{2}	23	1	12	14	5.8	6.8	53%	.344	1.93	7.23	5.84	-0.2
2011	*SLN*	*MLB*	*34*	*2*	*1*	*2*	*49*	*0*	*53*	*55*	*4*	*32*	*38*	*5.5*	*6.4*	*50%*	*.311*	*1.64*	*4.98*	*5.41*	*-0.6*

If there's been one consistent quality in MacDougal's inconsistent 10-year career, it's that he throws hard. Hard enough to break glass, hard enough to break wrist bones, and hard enough to break hearts when managers fall in love with the sound of his fastball popping the mitt and trust him to get big outs, only to be reminded all over again that the crack of the line drives he allows or the roar of a crowd cheering the runs he walks in are always louder. Released by both the Nationals and the Cardinals last year, he's single again and looking to start a new relationship.

Kyle McClellan
Born: **6/12/1984** Age: **27**
Bats: **R** Throws: **R** Height: **6' 4"** Weight: **205**
Breakout: **11%** Improve: **33%** Collapse: **30%**
Attrition: **15%** MLB: **74%**
Comparables:
Jesse Crain, Jeremy Accardo, Kevin Gregg (76)

YEAR	TEAM	LVL	AGE	W	L	SV	G	GS	IP	H	HR	BB	SO	EqBB9	EqSO9	GB%	BABIP	WHIP	ERA	FRA	WARP
2008	SLN	MLB	24	2	7	1	68	0	75^{2}	79	7	26	59	3.1	7.0	50%	.312	1.44	4.04	4.37	0.5
2009	SLN	MLB	25	4	4	3	66	0	66^{2}	56	4	34	51	4.6	6.9	51%	.264	1.38	3.51	4.24	0.4
2010	SLN	MLB	26	1	4	2	68	0	75^{1}	58	9	23	60	2.7	7.2	52%	.231	1.12	2.27	3.50	0.9
2011	*SLN*	*MLB*	*27*	*3*	*1*	*1*	*53*	*0*	*56*	*53*	*5*	*22*	*41*	*3.5*	*6.5*	*48%*	*.285*	*1.33*	*3.75*	*4.07*	*0.3*

McClellan turned in his best year yet in the Cardinals pen, using his five-pitch, low-velocity arsenal to tally 13.5 Adjusted Runs Prevented, second on the team to fireballer Jason Motte. McClellan has carved out a solid niche in middle relief, and there's been some talk of his competing with Motte for closer duties once Ryan Franklin's contract expires. While Motte has the classic power arsenal, he also tends to get lit up by lefties, whereas McClellan's changeup has so far produced a reverse platoon split. Stay tuned—this could get interesting.

Shelby Miller
Born: **10/10/1990** Age: **20**
Bats: **R** Throws: **R** Height: **6' 3"** Weight: **195**
Breakout: **2%** Improve: **2%** Collapse: **1%**
Attrition: **0%** MLB: **3%**
Comparables:
Terry Forster, Jose Rijo, Billy McCool (67)

YEAR	TEAM	LVL	AGE	W	L	SV	G	GS	IP	H	HR	BB	SO	EqBB9	EqSO9	GB%	BABIP	WHIP	ERA	FRA	WARP
2010	QUD	A	19	7	5	0	24	24	104^{1}	97	7	33	140	2.9	12.1	46%	.352	1.28	3.62	3.69	2.7
2011	*SLN*	*MLB*	*20*	*5*	*4*	*0*	*13*	*13*	55^{2}	*52*	*6*	*26*	*54*	*4.3*	*8.8*	*44%*	*.312*	*1.43*	*4.14*	*4.50*	*1.2*

The Cardinals' top prospect and one of the better minor-league pitchers around, Miller is a Texas high schooler who dominated the Midwest League last year. He has effortless gas that reaches the upper 90s, the kind of fastball that by itself can overpower hitters, along with a curveball and an occasional change. The curve could become a true power offering with tight break, giving Miller definite front-of-the-rotation stuff, and a surprisingly low walk rate for a young power pitcher making his full-season debut bodes well for his future development. He'll move up to High-A this year, though it would be groovy in a Chaucerian sort of way if the Cardinals' rotation could concurrently feature a Carpenter, a Miller, and a Wainwright.

Trever Miller
Born: **5/29/1973** Age: **38**
Bats: **R** Throws: **L** Height: **6' 3"** Weight: **175**
Breakout: **12%** Improve: **23%** Collapse: **17%**
Attrition: **9%** MLB: **48%**
Comparables:
Julio Santana, Scott Eyre, Paul Assenmacher (72)

YEAR	TEAM	LVL	AGE	W	L	SV	G	GS	IP	H	HR	BB	SO	EqBB9	EqSO9	GB%	BABIP	WHIP	ERA	FRA	WARP
2008	TBA	MLB	35	2	0	2	68	0	43^{1}	39	2	20	44	4.2	9.1	32%	.316	1.45	4.15	3.68	0.7
2009	SLN	MLB	36	4	1	0	70	0	43^{2}	31	5	11	46	2.3	9.5	37%	.239	1.01	1.86	2.55	1.2
2010	SLN	MLB	37	0	1	0	57	0	36	30	2	16	22	4.0	5.5	42%	.257	1.33	4.25	4.16	0.2
2011	*SLN*	*MLB*	*38*	*4*	*1*	*1*	*70*	*0*	44^{1}	*40*	*4*	*18*	*38*	*3.7*	*7.7*	*42%*	*.289*	*1.32*	*3.72*	*4.04*	*0.2*

In his own way, Miller has reached the pinnacle of achievement for his particular pitching subspecies. The lefty side-armer has spent two years as a LOOGY in Tony La Russa's pen, which must make him akin to being Sergeant Major of the Army among lefty relievers. LOOGY Sergeant of the Majors, perhaps? In any case, Miller again cut down any and all lefty batters who dared to eyeball him, holding them to a .203/.294/.257 line, and by his appearing in more than 45 games, his contract vested, ensuring that he'd keep his place at the top of the lefty-specialist pyramid for at least another year.

Jason Motte
Born: **6/22/1982** Age: **29**
Bats: R Throws: R Height: **6' 0"** Weight: **195**
Breakout: **17%** Improve: **35%** Collapse: **25%**
Attrition: **8%** MLB: **77%**
Comparables:
Paul Shuey, Jay Howell, Arthur Rhodes (66)

YEAR	TEAM	LVL	AGE	W	L	SV	G	GS	IP	H	HR	BB	SO	EqBB9	EqSO9	GB%	BABIP	WHIP	ERA	FRA	WARP
2008	MEM	AAA	26	4	3	9	63	0	66^2	64	6	26	110	3.5	14.8	36%	.395	1.36	3.24	2.19	2.1
2008	SLN	MLB	26	0	0	1	12	0	11	5	0	3	16	2.5	13.1	48%	.238	0.73	0.82	2.56	0.3
2009	SLN	MLB	27	4	4	0	69	0	56^2	57	10	23	54	3.7	8.6	39%	.303	1.45	4.92	5.22	-0.2
2010	SLN	MLB	28	4	2	2	56	0	52^1	41	5	18	54	3.1	9.3	40%	.275	1.13	2.06	2.60	1.2
2011	*SLN*	*MLB*	*29*	*3*	*1*	*2*	*60*	*0*	*57*	*53*	*6*	*24*	*60*	*3.8*	*9.3*	*42%*	*.309*	*1.34*	*3.72*	*4.04*	*0.3*

Motte bounced back from a subpar 2009 to post impressive numbers last year and stake his claim to the oft-sought but rarely fulfilled "future closer" title. Terrorizing the late innings with his upper-90s fastball and devastating slider, Motte led the club with 18.3 Adjusted Runs Prevented, struck out more than a batter per inning, and hacked a few chunks out of his walk rate. He has yet to find the magic elixir to cure his problems with lefties, however, as portside hitters have abused him to the tune of .292/.384/.466 during his career. If Motte can clean up that particular mess, he might someday earn closer cash.

Adam Ottavino
Born: **11/22/1985** Age: **25**
Bats: R Throws: R Height: **6' 5"** Weight: **230**
Breakout: **7%** Improve: **11%** Collapse: **4%**
Attrition: **10%** MLB: **15%**
Comparables:
Jhonny Nunez, Travis Chick, Jo-Jo Reyes (81)

YEAR	TEAM	LVL	AGE	W	L	SV	G	GS	IP	H	HR	BB	SO	EqBB9	EqSO9	GB%	BABIP	WHIP	ERA	FRA	WARP
2008	SFD	AA	22	3	7	0	24	24	115^1	133	16	52	96	4.1	7.5	47%	.329	1.69	5.23	5.76	0.5
2009	MEM	AAA	23	7	12	0	27	27	144	141	12	82	119	5.1	7.4	45%	.308	1.62	4.75	5.09	0.7
2010	MEM	AAA	24	5	3	0	9	9	47^2	43	5	12	43	2.3	8.2	51%	.286	1.23	3.97	4.28	0.8
2010	SLN	MLB	24	0	2	0	5	3	22^1	37	5	9	12	3.6	4.8	37%	.381	2.06	8.46	6.61	-0.2
2011	*SLN*	*MLB*	*25*	*6*	*9*	*0*	*21*	*21*	*105^1*	*115*	*13*	*56*	*73*	*4.8*	*6.3*	*45%*	*.311*	*1.62*	*5.42*	*5.89*	*0.3*

The hits just keep on coming for Ottavino, unfortunately. The former first-rounder suffered through his third difficult season in a row, bouncing back and forth between promising outings in Memphis and disastrous ones in St. Louis before missing the last half of the season with a strained shoulder. The injury didn't require surgery, and Ottavino should be ready for spring training, but the club took him off the 40-man roster. He still has stuff that can miss bats, with a low-90s fastball, a slider, and a changeup, and he made some progress toward reducing his disturbing walk rate, but his future is likely to involve warming up during games rather than before them.

Brad Penny
Born: **5/24/1978** Age: **33**
Bats: R Throws: R Height: **6' 4"** Weight: **200**
Breakout: **10%** Improve: **41%** Collapse: **23%**
Attrition: **16%** MLB: **80%**
Comparables:
Ken Johnson, Bob Rush, Jim Perry (77)

YEAR	TEAM	LVL	AGE	W	L	SV	G	GS	IP	H	HR	BB	SO	EqBB9	EqSO9	GB%	BABIP	WHIP	ERA	FRA	WARP
2008	LAN	MLB	30	6	9	0	19	17	94^2	112	13	42	51	4.0	4.8	51%	.313	1.66	6.27	6.82	-1.1
2009	BOS	MLB	31	7	8	0	24	24	131^2	160	17	42	89	2.9	6.1	42%	.327	1.57	5.61	5.76	0.5
2009	SFN	MLB	31	4	1	0	6	6	41^2	31	5	9	20	1.9	4.3	54%	.206	0.96	2.59	4.14	0.6
2010	SLN	MLB	32	3	4	0	9	9	55^2	63	4	9	35	1.5	5.7	54%	.326	1.35	3.23	3.97	0.9
2011	*SLN*	*MLB*	*33*	*9*	*9*	*0*	*25*	*25*	*145*	*159*	*14*	*48*	*85*	*2.9*	*5.2*	*47%*	*.309*	*1.42*	*4.44*	*4.82*	*1.8*

It didn't take long for the telltale signs of Duncan tutelage to start appearing in Penny's outings: the lowered walk rate, the drastic increase in ground balls, the completely changed approach, the sub-four ERA. Duncan had Penny throwing more splitters than ever before, and the results sparkled, until Penny sprained his back and spent the remainder of the season almost, but not quite, making it back to the mound. While it's hard to say how much of what he learned from Duncan will travel with him and while health will always be a question, an aura of upside potential, perhaps disproportionate to his actual results, lingers from Penny's rare healthy seasons. His new team, the Tigers, will hope that he follows in the footsteps of previous Duncan project and successful transplant Joel Pineiro.

Dennys Reyes
Born: **4/19/1977** Age: **34**
Bats: R Throws: L Height: **6' 3"** Weight: **246**
Breakout: **0%** Improve: **8%** Collapse: **6%**
Attrition: **2%** MLB: **19%**
Comparables:
Doug Brocail, Danny Cox, Jim Bibby (67)

YEAR	TEAM	LVL	AGE	W	L	SV	G	GS	IP	H	HR	BB	SO	EqBB9	EqSO9	GB%	BABIP	WHIP	ERA	FRA	WARP
2008	MIN	MLB	31	3	0	0	75	0	46^1	40	4	15	39	2.9	7.6	59%	.281	1.23	2.33	2.43	1.4
2009	SLN	MLB	32	0	2	1	75	0	41	35	2	21	33	4.6	7.2	57%	.273	1.44	3.29	4.34	0.3
2010	SLN	MLB	33	3	1	1	59	0	38	34	2	21	25	5.0	5.9	51%	.283	1.50	3.55	4.00	0.4
2011	*SLN*	*MLB*	*34*	*4*	*1*	*1*	*72*	*0*	*43^1*	*41*	*3*	*21*	*31*	*4.4*	*6.5*	*49%*	*.297*	*1.45*	*4.15*	*4.52*	*-0.0*

Wha' happened? Reyes and La Russa were destined to get together, the Mick and Bianca of LOOGY-dom, the ultimate "you complete me" moment of bullpen overspecialization, and Reyes goes and blows it all by suddenly deciding not to retire lefties? After years of complete domination, Reyes couldn't possibly have let same-side hitters torch him to the tune of .307/.409/.453 unless he was somehow trying to pitch his way out of St. Louis, could he? We may never learn the inside scoop, although his apparent inability to pass a physical on the way to a contract with the Phillies gives us a hint almost as broad as Reyes himself.

Fernando Salas
Born: **5/30/1985** Age: **26**
Bats: **R** Throws: **R** Height: **6' 2"** Weight: **200**
Breakout: **4%** Improve: **7%** Collapse: **4%**
Attrition: **7%** MLB: **12%**
Comparables:
Sergio Romo, Casey Fien, Warner Madrigal (75)

YEAR	TEAM	LVL	AGE	W	L	SV	G	GS	IP	H	HR	BB	SO	EqBB9	EqSO9	GB%	BABIP	WHIP	ERA	FRA	WARP
2008	SFD	AA	23	7	3	25	60	0	74	65	12	16	100	1.9	12.2	41%	.312	1.12	3.65	3.85	0.9
2009	MEM	AAA	24	3	2	0	24	0	27	22	4	10	24	3.3	8.0	30%	.243	1.22	3.67	5.78	-0.3
2010	MEM	AAA	25	1	0	19	34	0	35^{2}	26	2	9	44	2.3	11.3	37%	.296	1.02	3.79	3.53	0.6
2010	SLN	MLB	25	0	0	0	27	0	30^{2}	28	4	15	29	4.4	8.5	36%	.282	1.40	3.52	2.85	0.6
2011	*SLN*	*MLB*	*26*	*2*	*1*	*4*	*40*	*0*	*44^{1}*	*41*	*6*	*16*	*41*	*3.3*	*8.3*	*41%*	*.296*	*1.30*	*3.86*	*4.19*	*0.2*

Salas is a former Mexican League product who ping-ponged his way between Memphis and St. Louis last year, a likely sign of things to come. Salas used his fastball/slider/changeup combo to strike out nearly a man per inning in the bigs, but he doesn't fool all of the people all of the time. The gopher ball is his El Guapo, as he has allowed a plethora of home runs during his brief stateside career—a fact likely to keep him from becoming a bullpen cog.

Eduardo Sanchez
Born: **2/16/1989** Age: **22**
Bats: **R** Throws: **R** Height: **5' 11"** Weight: **155**
Breakout: **0%** Improve: **0%** Collapse: **0%**
Attrition: **0%** MLB: **0%**
Comparables:
Scott Kazmir, Antonio Osuna, Ismael Valdez (79)

YEAR	TEAM	LVL	AGE	W	L	SV	G	GS	IP	H	HR	BB	SO	EqBB9	EqSO9	GB%	BABIP	WHIP	ERA	FRA	WARP
2008	QUD	A	19	5	1	1	24	5	56^{2}	40	1	25	55	4.0	8.7	51%	.271	1.29	2.86	3.90	0.8
2009	PMB	A+	20	0	1	3	19	0	25	12	2	5	26	1.8	9.4	53%	.175	0.80	1.08	3.20	0.5
2009	SFD	AA	20	2	0	10	42	0	51	35	5	20	56	3.5	9.9	52%	.254	1.16	2.82	3.57	0.7
2009	SFD	AA	20	2	0	10	41	0	50	32	4	20	56	3.6	10.1	52%	.248	1.12	2.70	3.57	0.7
2010	MEM	AAA	21	0	0	3	26	0	27	19	2	12	31	4.0	10.3	47%	.270	1.22	1.67	2.25	1.0
2011	*SLN*	*MLB*	*22*	*2*	*1*	*2*	*38*	*0*	*46*	*40*	*5*	*25*	*42*	*4.8*	*8.3*	*47%*	*.288*	*1.41*	*4.14*	*4.50*	*0.0*

A rail-thin Venezuelan reliever, Sanchez took another giant step toward his future in the Cardinals' bullpen by continuing to impress during a full year in the high minors. Sanchez lives by his fastball, a heavy mid-90s load that generates plenty of ground balls, and a slider that misses bats. He continues to strike out more than a batter per inning, and while his walk rate climbed during his late-season trip to Triple-A, it's hardly high in a power-reliever-prospect kind of way. Only 22, Sanchez is almost ready to lend another power arm to the Cardinals' pen.

Jeff Suppan
Born: **1/2/1975** Age: **36**
Bats: **R** Throws: **R** Height: **6' 1"** Weight: **200**
Breakout: **16%** Improve: **39%** Collapse: **22%**
Attrition: **20%** MLB: **94%**
Comparables:
Masato Yoshii, Johnny Sain, Jim Lonborg (77)

YEAR	TEAM	LVL	AGE	W	L	SV	G	GS	IP	H	HR	BB	SO	EqBB9	EqSO9	GB%	BABIP	WHIP	ERA	FRA	WARP
2008	MIL	MLB	33	10	10	0	31	31	177^{2}	207	30	67	90	3.4	4.6	46%	.301	1.56	4.96	5.56	0.6
2009	MIL	MLB	34	7	12	0	30	30	161^{2}	200	25	74	80	4.1	4.5	51%	.314	1.76	5.29	5.65	0.3
2010	MIL	MLB	35	0	2	0	15	2	31	50	4	12	18	3.5	5.2	43%	.407	2.03	7.84	7.22	-0.6
2010	SLN	MLB	35	3	6	0	15	13	70^{1}	80	9	25	33	3.2	4.2	44%	.301	1.51	3.84	3.95	1.1
2011	*SLN*	*MLB*	*36*	*9*	*14*	*0*	*32*	*32*	*169*	*207*	*22*	*69*	*77*	*3.7*	*4.1*	*46%*	*.319*	*1.64*	*5.74*	*6.24*	*-0.3*

Last year saw the end of the Milwaukee run of Suppan's one-man show, *Long Contract's Journey into Night*, when, after two disastrous April starts and a halfhearted trip to long relief, he was released in June. Signed by the Cardinals, Duncan's former pupil somehow managed a sub-four ERA over 70 innings despite his diminished stuff and abysmal peripherals. Released at year's end, Suppan probably won't find a seat if Duncan doesn't want him back when the free-agent music stops, because of the "fool me twice, shame on me" clause in the boilerplate of most GM contracts.

Adam Wainwright
Born: **8/30/1981** Age: **29**
Bats: **R** Throws: **R** Height: **6' 7"** Weight: **205**
Breakout: **2%** Improve: **33%** Collapse: **25%**
Attrition: **7%** MLB: **95%**
Comparables:
Cliff Lee, Don Drysdale, Josh Beckett (71)

YEAR	TEAM	LVL	AGE	W	L	SV	G	GS	IP	H	HR	BB	SO	EqBB9	EqSO9	GB%	BABIP	WHIP	ERA	FRA	WARP
2008	SLN	MLB	26	11	3	0	20	20	132	122	12	34	91	2.3	6.2	47%	.272	1.20	3.20	3.84	2.5
2009	SLN	MLB	27	19	8	0	34	34	233	216	17	66	212	2.5	8.2	52%	.296	1.22	2.63	3.06	6.4
2010	SLN	MLB	28	20	11	0	33	33	230^{1}	186	15	56	213	2.2	8.3	54%	.275	1.07	2.42	2.88	6.4
2011	*SLN*	*MLB*	*29*	*12*	*7*	*0*	*27*	*27*	*179*	*165*	*12*	*52*	*142*	*2.6*	*7.1*	*49%*	*.294*	*1.21*	*3.14*	*3.41*	*4.9*

Wainwright came in second to Roy Halladay in last year's Cy Young voting, and although Doc edged him in WARP, remember that these totals are imprecise enough that not only was there relatively little difference between the two, but Wainwright did it for about $11 million less. Wainwright dominates games with his curveball, throwing it almost a third of the time last year, and each time analysts think he's reached his ceiling, he kicks it up a notch. Last season, he improved his strikeout and walk rates, his ERA, his win total, his ground-ball and home-run rates—basically, everything that could get better, did. We mean it this time, though: he can't possibly get better than this.

P. J. Walters

Born: **3/12/1985** Age: **26**
Bats: **R** Throws: **R** Height: **6' 4"** Weight: **200**
Breakout: **13%** Improve: **40%** Collapse: **8%**
Attrition: **25%** MLB: **63%**

Comparables:
Mitch Talbot, Brad Mills, Garrett Olson (75)

YEAR	TEAM	LVL	AGE	W	L	SV	G	GS	IP	H	HR	BB	SO	EqBB9	EqSO9	GB%	BABIP	WHIP	ERA	FRA	WARP
2008	SFD	AA	23	1	2	0	6	6	36	35	5	8	34	2.0	8.5	48%	.300	1.28	3.25	3.81	0.9
2008	MEM	AAA	23	9	4	0	23	23	122	123	17	62	122	4.6	9.0	47%	.314	1.58	4.87	5.30	0.7
2009	MEM	AAA	24	8	10	0	21	20	121	128	6	44	113	3.3	8.4	52%	.333	1.50	4.54	4.29	1.9
2009	SLN	MLB	24	0	0	0	8	1	16	21	6	9	14	5.1	7.9	47%	.294	1.88	9.56	9.87	-0.6
2010	MEM	AAA	25	8	5	0	19	18	108^{2}	106	12	30	106	2.5	8.8	38%	.308	1.33	3.81	4.06	2.2
2010	SLN	MLB	25	2	0	0	7	3	30	32	5	10	22	3.0	6.6	43%	.294	1.40	6.00	6.25	-0.4
2011	*SLN*	*MLB*	*26*	*8*	*8*	*0*	*22*	*22*	*125*	*131*	*15*	*52*	*101*	*3.7*	*7.2*	*45%*	*.308*	*1.45*	*4.61*	*5.01*	*1.4*

Walters has made a living out of putting Triple-A hitters to bed with his wicked changeup, a lullaby that only works if he can get ahead in the count. That second part often requires pinpoint command of his upper-80s fastball, something that you can get away with in the minors but only a Hoffman-esque few can manage against the world's best hitters. Still, Walters has enough other off-speed tricks up his sleeve that he might scratch out a living as a long man.

Jake Westbrook

Born: **9/29/1977** Age: **33**
Bats: **R** Throws: **R** Height: **6' 3"** Weight: **200**
Breakout: **9%** Improve: **37%** Collapse: **30%**
Attrition: **16%** MLB: **88%**

Comparables:
Jim Perry, Bob Rush, Ken Johnson (80)

YEAR	TEAM	LVL	AGE	W	L	SV	G	GS	IP	H	HR	BB	SO	EqBB9	EqSO9	GB%	BABIP	WHIP	ERA	FRA	WARP
2008	CLE	MLB	30	1	2	0	5	5	34^{2}	33	5	7	19	1.8	4.9	58%	.262	1.18	3.12	4.25	0.5
2010	CLE	MLB	32	6	7	0	21	21	127^{2}	133	15	44	73	3.1	5.1	54%	.291	1.43	4.65	4.91	0.6
2010	SLN	MLB	32	4	4	0	12	12	75	70	5	24	55	2.9	6.6	65%	.281	1.28	3.48	2.66	2.4
2011	*SLN*	*MLB*	*33*	*8*	*7*	*0*	*21*	*21*	*126*	*133*	*12*	*44*	*72*	*3.1*	*5.1*	*51%*	*.300*	*1.40*	*4.27*	*4.65*	*1.8*

Westbrook returned to the Indians after nearly two years lost to elbow surgery and struggled with his control early on before a midseason trade to St. Louis righted the ship and earned him a two-year, $16.5 million return engagement. Pitchers recovering from Tommy John surgery often require some time to reestablish their command, so that—if not the move to the easier league—may have been the prime factor behind Westbrook's sudden rejuvenation, but many will attribute it to Dave Duncan. After entering Duncan's orbit, Westbrook saw his walks plummet and his strikeouts soar to the highest rate of his career, and the lifelong sinkerball devotee increased his ground-ball percentage by over 10 percentage points—geologists are concerned that giving Duncan someone like Westbrook to work with on a multiyear basis may cause hitters to start pounding the ball through the earth's core. It looks like a marriage made in heaven, and if Westbrook can stay healthy, he's a great bet to solidify the back of the Cardinals' rotation.

LINEOUTS

HITTERS

PLAYER	TEAM	LVL	AGE	PA	R	2B	3B	HR	RBI	BB	SO	SB-CS	AVG/OBP/SLG	TAv	BABIP	BRR	FRAA	WARP
C T. Cruz	PMB	A+	23	202	21	16	1	1	25	19	33	0-2	.282/.348/.398	.290	.336	-3.4	C 1	1.2
	SFD	AA	23	169	26	10	0	6	20	17	30	0-0	.289/.363/.477	.289	.322	-1.2	C 0, 3B 0	1.0
1B M. Hamilton*	MEM	AAA	25	306	53	20	0	18	60	35	70	0-0	.298/.389/.585	.330	.335	0.0	1B -5, LF -2	2.2
	SLN	MLB	25	15	0	0	0	0	0	1	5	0-0	.143/.200/.143	.145	.222	0.0	1B 1	-0.1
SS P. Kozma	SFD	AA	22	570	69	28	2	13	72	56	111	13-2	.243/.318/.384	.256	.280	0.1	SS 18	3.7
C J. LaRue	SLN	MLB	36	63	4	1	0	2	5	5	7	0-0	.196/.270/.321	.225	.188	-1.5	C 0, 1B 0	-0.1
OF N. Longmire	BAT	A-	21	309	53	11	7	9	55	34	62	12-3	.287/.372/.483	.310	.337	0.0	CF -5	1.9
C M. Pagnozzi	MEM	AAA	27	242	20	11	0	1	21	27	49	0-0	.242/.338/.309	.226	.302	0.0	C -1	0.1
	SLN	MLB	27	44	4	2	0	1	10	2	8	0-0	.359/.386/.487	.299	.406	0.1	C 0	0.3
OF S. Robinson	MEM	AAA	25	97	9	5	0	2	13	7	13	0-0	.279/.320/.407	.240	.293	0.0	CF 0	0.1
C R. Stock*	QUD	A	20	351	32	17	0	1	31	39	56	2-2	.213/.300/.277	.228	.255	-1.7	C 0	0.2

A first-round pick last year, **Zack Cox** was signed at the deadline to a multimillion-dollar big-league deal and made his debut in the AFL. He showed patience and advanced hitting skills that make him an on-base threat with gap power. Scouts don't expect him to become much of a home-run threat; they doubt his ability to be a plus defender at third base and dislike his pudgy physique. Of course, that's a lot of hypothesizing based on a month in the desert. ⊘ Catcher **Tony Cruz** used a strong arm to throw out 53 percent of runners last year and worked his way onto the 40-man roster after an impressive showing in the AFL. ⊘ For the second year running, **Mark Hamilton** put up impressive numbers at Triple-A, but since the Cardinals already have a reasonably solid first baseman, he'll need a trade to have a career. ⊘ Former first-rounder **Peter Kozma** has a plus glove and good power for a shortstop, but he makes far too many outs to be anything more than another flavor of disappointment for the Cardinals' middle infield. ⊘ Veteran backstop **Jason LaRue** suffered a concussion during a brawl with the Reds and will probably retire rather than risk a recurrence from a foul tip off the bean, reminding us again of the physical rigors of catching and the monumental stupidity of baseball fights. ⊘ Fifth-round pick **Nick Longmire** was a pleasant surprise, hitting the ball hard, drawing walks, and playing an instinctive center field; his full-season debut will be closely watched. ⊘ **Matt Pagnozzi** has solid catch-and-throw skills but was released due to his inability to meet the offensive requirements of a Cardinals backup catcher; that doesn't bode well for his future. ⊘ Let's hope diminutive outfielder **Shane Robinson** enjoys the Beale Street blues, since his inability to learn how to work his way on base means he'll spend another summer in Memphis. ⊘ Anyone who shorted **Robert Stock** last spring turned a tidy profit on his 2010, as the catcher's value plummeted after he slugged under .300 in his full-season debut.

PITCHERS

PLAYER	TEAM	LVL	AGE	W	L	SV	IP	H	HR	BB	SO	EqBB9	EqSO9	GB%	BABIP	WHIP	ERA	FRA	WARP
B. Augenstein	RNO	AAA	23	6	8	0	120^{2}	162	12	35	101	2.6	7.6	47%	.372	1.70	6.56	6.09	0.6
J. Gast*	BAT	A-	21	6	0	0	35	27	1	8	36	2.1	9.3	56%	.313	1.03	1.54	3.49	0.9
J. Kelly	QUD	A	22	6	8	1	103^{1}	103	3	45	92	3.9	8.0	66%	.337	1.50	4.62	5.71	-0.0
B. King	SFD	AA	23	4	3	0	68	40	5	48	84	6.4	11.1	45%	.236	1.34	2.91	3.27	1.2
D. Kopp	SFD	AA	24	12	4	0	121	126	9	39	78	2.9	5.8	48%	.311	1.38	3.05	4.09	2.4
	MEM	AAA	24	0	5	0	24	38	4	11	12	4.1	4.5	53%	.382	2.17	8.25	8.61	-0.4
E. MacLane*	MEM	AAA	27	8	7	0	147^{2}	163	21	21	82	1.3	5.0	43%	.295	1.29	4.45	4.55	2.1
	SLN	MLB	27	0	1	0	1	1	1	1	0	9.0	0.0	67%	.000	2.00	9.00	15.02	-0.1
A. Reifer	SFD	AA	24	3	1	17	54	53	2	15	52	2.5	8.7	48%	.325	1.31	2.83	2.34	1.4
F. Samuel	SFD	AA	23	2	0	6	22^{1}	18	3	16	27	6.5	11.0	51%	.283	1.67	3.63	4.88	-0.0

The Cardinals never met a soft-tossing, strike-throwing, ground-balling pitcher they didn't think they could fix, so they claimed **Bryan Augenstein** on waivers to see how much of Duncan's magic elixir he can stomach. ⊘ Sixth-rounder **John Gast** is a poised left-hander with low-90s heat, a solid changeup, and a wicked pickoff move; if he can improve his curveball and succeed in his full-season debut, he could move fast. ⊘ Hard-throwing righty **Joe Kelly** made a successful conversion to the rotation; he pitched better than his results, but needs to work on his secondary pitches or he'll wind up back in the bullpen. ⊘ Power reliever **Blake King** found a spot on the 40-man roster, but he won't be a bullpen asset until he can do a much better job of finding the plate. ⊘ Injuries have robbed **David Kopp** of development time. He doesn't generate much swing-and-miss, but his ability to generate ground balls has earned him a spot on the 40-man roster. ⊘ Velo-challenged lefty **Evan MacLane** is a depth-providing organizational soldier, but if he's thrown into the big-league lines, then you know the pitching situation has grown *Volkssturm*-level desperate. ⊘ The Cardinals stashed **Adam Reifer** on the 40-man roster after the fireballer kicked his walk addiction last year at Double-A; if his newfound control sticks, he'll be a weapon in the late innings. ⊘ This just in: Generalissimo **Francisco Samuel**'s prospect status is still dead and will remain so until he can develop even a scintilla of control to abet his mid-90s fastball.

MANAGER: TONY LA RUSSA

YEAR	TEAM	W-L	Pythag +/-	Avg PC	100+ P	120+ P	QS	BQS	REL	REL w Zero R	IBB	Subs	PH	PH Avg	PH HR	SB2	CS2	SB3	CS3	SAC Att	SAC %	POS SAC	Squeeze	Swing	In Play
2008	SLN	86-76	-1	93.0	52	1	76	9	506	318	21	78	273	.239	6	63	27	9	3	109	65.1%	33	1	150	120
2009	SLN	91-71	-1	94.5	54	4	83	3	480	335	23	91	280	.221	8	65	25	10	4	109	62.4%	33	0	127	103
2010	SLN	86-76	-6	95.2	61	0	90	3	454	295	32	52	289	.229	4	68	36	11	5	98	67.3%	39	1	157	127

It's natural for successful people to view their successes as a justification for all their choices, a trap that is both difficult and necessary to avoid for their success to continue. Few managers have been successful as long as La Russa, and few have been so willing to shed the managerial straitjacket and try new things, but as he nears the end of his career, there is a danger that a stubbornness born of a lifetime of validated decisions will become his undoing. Last season was not one of La Russa's career highlights; his increasing testiness and impatience with players and the media have begun to erode confidence in his leadership, and running out 144 different lineups amplified whispers that the skipper's admirable flexibility has descended into compulsive tinkering. La Russa obviously doesn't care what anyone else thinks; that is not only his right, but also a facet of his personality that has aided his career. However, when it leads to a preference for Jon Jay over Colby Rasmus, or Matt Pagnozzi over Bryan Anderson, it starts to hurt more than it helps. For all his flaws, La Russa remains one of the game's savviest tacticians and most subtle thinkers, and it would be a shame if the end of his distinguished career becomes notable more for bloody-mindedness than brilliance.

San Diego Padres

If anyone foresaw the Padres in competition for a playoff spot in 2010, that person kept awfully quiet about it. Our own forecasting system called for 73 San Diego wins, and PECOTA was far from alone in harboring modest expectations—Las Vegas had the team down for 71.5 wins. As first-year general manager Jed Hoyer said, "They don't build those casinos by losing money." Should we—meaning the population of baseball-following fans as a whole—have anticipated a breakout performance from a Padres team that wasn't eliminated from playoff contention until the final day of the regular season?

The short answer is yes, but the 2010 Padres presented an interesting study in multiple hard-to-illuminate facets of team building and on-field production—hence the club's surprise factor. In a number of ways, they were the team that many fans and media members alike thought the 2010 Mariners were going to be: one whose defense and pitching had primed it for a playoff run.

There was reason to believe that the Padres would improve on their 2009 75-win season—for one thing, that club's second-half roster was far different from the one it fielded from April through June, as 15 players made their major-league debuts and 24 rookies saw action overall. The team replaced dead weight—like the aging and injured Brian Giles—with younger players like Will Venable and Kyle Blanks. Jake Peavy had been turned into four young pitchers from the White Sox, one of whom, Clayton Richard, had earned a 2010 rotation spot with his performance as a Friar. Ryan Webb, a reliever acquired in the Scott Hairston deal, was expected to absorb the innings that came before the trio of Luke Gregerson, Mike Adams, and Heath Bell could close the door on the opposition, and a new three-quarters arm angle developed by pitching coach Darren Balsley helped Webb's strikeout rates match his excellent stuff. Top pitching prospect Mat Latos had experienced snippets of success on the mound and was expected to improve in what figured to be his first full season in the majors. These may not have seemed like reasons to expect a contending Padres team, but the revamped 2009 roster won 37 of its final 62 games after claiming victory in just 38 of its first 100.

PADRES PROSPECTUS

2010 W-L: 90-72, 2nd in NL West

Pythag	.560	10th	**Ballpark:** PETCO Park (3-yr. PF: 93). Any pitcher who understands park factors would take a paycut to play here
RS/G	4.1	22nd	
RA/G	3.6	30th	
TAv	.261	24th	**2010:** Pitching and defense make Padres surprising contenders until season's final day
BRR	2.6	11th	
FRA	3.69	1st	
DER	8.28	9th	**2011:** With Adrian on the East Coast, veteran imports can't prop up an empty offense
DL	820	21st	
B-Age	29.3	20th	
P-Age	26.9	5th	**Action Items:** Rotation depth; letting Maybin be all he can be, for whatever that's worth
Salary	$37.8	29th	
M$/MW	$.671	1st	

It was clear last spring that the Padres' bullpen would feature Bell, Adams, and Gregerson, all of whom were considered quality relievers. Both Adams and Bell were believed capable of closing, and most teams would have been happy to have one of those three, never mind the whole trio. There was more to the pen than just this trio; even the Padres' low-leverage innings were thrown by pitchers who would have been entrusted with more important frames on lesser clubs. All of these pitchers—with the exception of Ernesto Frieri—were on the roster by 2009 or the start of 2010. Expecting this collection of relievers to combine for the fifth-highest WXRL of all time would have been a stretch, but betting on it to be a dominant and reliable force for the Padres should not have been.

San Diego's defense in 2009 was not much better than average on the whole, thanks to the team's poor fielding performance over the first few months of the season. However, during their final 62 games, the Padres played much improved defense, and the tweaks made to the roster following the season—trading Kevin Kouzmanoff to get defensively challenged outfielder Chase Headley back to his natural position of third base, adding the underrated glove of Jerry Hairston Jr. to the fold, and inking Yorvit Torrealba to split time with Nick Hundley—were calculated to separate them from the pack even further.

Better fielding is a plus, but better pitching is important as well. San Diego's strikeout rate jumped from 18.9 percent of plate appearances in 2009 to 21.3 percent in 2010, which meant less reliance on a defense that was now more capable of converting the balls that did come its way into outs. The impending improvement was another development that should have been revealed by pre-season analysis. Chris Young and Peavy combined for 27 starts and 157 2/3 innings in 2009, and 13 other pitchers started games for San Diego during that season year; the only three hurlers to clear the 100-IP mark comprised the less-than-stellar trio of Josh Geer, Chad Gaudin, and Kevin Correia. As a result, the 2009 squad ranked last in the NL in innings pitched by starters. It would have been almost impossible for the Padres to avoid improving their pitching after entering the year stocked with higher-upside arms.

The best-case scenario for 2010 involved the development of Latos into someone capable of fronting a rotation, and mid-rotation-level performance by the rest of the pitchers—Richard, free-agent acquisition Jon Garland, Young, and Correia. With the exception of further development from Latos, things didn't quite work out that way. Richard and Garland pitched as well as could have been expected, with the latter taking advantage of the environment en route to his second-best campaign, but Correia struggled for much of the season, Young was hurt after one start, and his replacement, Wade LeBlanc, failed to put together consistent success in his 25 starts.

A superficially underwhelming offense was the main reason for the Padres' under-the-radar status heading into 2010, and it also explains why they continued to be considered a fluke well into the season. San Diego's run-scoring ability has been masked by the most extreme pitcher's park in the majors, which goes double for left-handed hitters like Venable and Adrian Gonzalez. In reality, the Padres have not been much worse than average offensively—average is roughly where they finished in both 2009 and 2010. A middle-of-the-pack lineup is hardly an insuperable handicap when coupled with elite run prevention—the Padres scored 84 more runs than they allowed over the course of last year, and their final third-order standings were also a significant improvement over pre-season projections. Had Gonzalez been healthy all season and Blanks not missed most of the year due to Tommy John surgery, the lineup would have been better than average. That is the point we should care about when investigating whether we should have seen the Padres' 2010 season coming.

Predicting 90 wins might have been overoptimistic, but the low-70s win totals spit out by forecasting systems and Las Vegas were unreasonably low; a more acceptable answer would have lain somewhere in between. A team expected to field an average or better lineup, an average or better rotation, an above-average defense, and an excellent bullpen should not have been deemed bound for mediocrity, and the Padres proved the naysayers wrong by remaining in the playoff hunt until the season's final day.

With a successful first season at the general managerial reins under his belt, Hoyer faced a number of difficult decisions that would shape the future of the franchise in both the short and the long term. Trading Gonzalez to the Red Sox for top prospects Casey Kelly and Anthony Rizzo, as well as the 19-year-old Reymond Fuentes, was the right thing to do for the future of the organization, since it had already been made clear that Gonzalez would not return at a salary that the Padres could afford. Gonzalez brought back a pair of players who could be major-league regulars as early as 2012 at positions of need for San Diego.

Bell is another trade candidate, and Ryan Ludwick, as long as he hits, could also be moved at the deadline. Considering the team's relatively young core, it makes sense to move the remaining well-compensated veterans for talent that can help the Friars stay competitive in the short term while components of the long-term future continue to flourish on the farm, but the team isn't so lost without Gonzalez that 2011 can just be written off in advance.

The bullpen is now without Webb and Edward Mujica, thanks to a trade with the Marlins that netted Cameron Maybin, but those two arms can be replaced internally by Frieri, who didn't pitch a full season in 2010, and Rule 5 selection George Kontos. Bell, Adams, and Gregerson remain, and even if Bell is dealt early on, the pen will be one of the most productive in the majors. What's more, San Diego may not have to rely on its relief corps as heavily, since Latos will be entering his second full campaign with loosened innings restrictions, and the last two-fifths of the rotation look stronger.

If there was one aspect of the roster to blame for the Padres' inability to remain in first place all of last season, it was the back end of the rotation, as Correia and LeBlanc strained the deep bullpen by averaging 5 1/3 innings per start in August. While the fantastic pen had helped carry a young pitching staff throughout the season by shouldering the load after six innings each time out, the repeated failure of those two hurlers to stay in games helped the club burn its greatest advantage every fifth day. Both pitchers lost their spots when rosters expanded, and the two hurlers who replaced them should make for a deeper, more effective starting five.

Tim Stauffer has bounced between the rotation and the bullpen with middling results, but the former first-round selection turned a corner in 2010, thanks to some adjustments to his approach and his fastball. He will now slot in behind Latos in the rotation. Aaron Harang was inked to replace Jon Garland, and while his stuff has diminished, the move from Great American Ballpark to Petco could extend his effectiveness. Cory Luebke is a left-hander who relies on his command to succeed, and the intelligent pitcher knows how to apply his limited physical gifts to retire big-league hitters. More time in the majors should give him a chance to refine his command even further. If one of the five goes down with an injury, LeBlanc could be useful as a spot starter and Dustin Moseley will also be around, but with Young leaving town and Peavy two years removed from Petco, injuries may constitute a lesser problem than they have in recent seasons.

Losing Gonzalez deals a heavy blow to the offense, but a healthy outfield and more productive middle infield can offset some of that damage. The addition of Maybin should help—at worst, he hits like Gwynn did in 2010, but with even better defensive play, and in the scenario the Padres are hoping for, the 23-year-old finally blossoms at the plate. A full season from an able Ludwick will confer the offensive improvement that it was expected to when the outfielder was acquired at last season's trade deadline. If Ludwick is dealt, Chris Denorfia can slide to left field, bumping the capable Aaron Cunningham to fourth-outfielder status. Trade acquisition Jason Bartlett is no longer an elite defender, but he is an average shortstop at the plate and still wears a capable glove. Signing Orlando Hudson to a two-year deal should yield an upgrade over David Eckstein on both sides of the ball, as Hudson is the superior hitter and at least as good defensively.

In short, the Padres' pen will be a little worse (still great, if not historically significant), the rotation should be improved, the defense better, and the lineup, though missing Gonzalez, should not be much less potent. Applying the math of the 2010 preseason, we would put them in the mid-70s neighborhood for wins (progress!), but we know better than to ignore the Friars' components now. A first-place finish would be asking a bit much, but the choices that the organization's higher-ups have already made point toward a future with more years like 2010 than the darker days prior.

HITTERS

Matt Antonelli 2B

Born: **4/8/1985** Age: **26**
Bats: **R** Throws: **R** Height: **6' 0"** Weight: **200**
Breakout: **0%** Improve: **0%** Collapse: **1%** %
Improve: **1%** MLB: **3%**

Comparables:
Drew Meyer, Phil Gagliano, Tom O'Malley (81)

YEAR	TEAM	LVL	AGE	PA	R	2B	3B	HR	RBI	BB	SO	SB	CS	AVG/OBP/SLG	TAv	BABIP	BRR	FRAA	WARP
2008	POR	AAA	23	540	62	19	4	7	39	76	86	6	4	.215/.335/.322	.240	.248	1.1	2B -10	-0.6
2008	SDN	MLB	23	65	6	2	0	1	3	5	11	0	0	.193/.292/.281	.233	.222	0.7	2B -4	-0.4
2009	POR	AAA	24	219	25	11	2	4	22	26	30	1	1	.196/.297/.339	.233	.210	0.7	2B 0	0.0
2011	*SDN*	*MLB*	*26*	*272*	*29*	*11*	*1*	*5*	*23*	*33*	*45*	*2*	*1*	*.221/.321/.341*	*.242*	*.249*	*-0.1*	*2B -3*	*-0.2*

Antonelli had more doctors' appointments than plate appearances last season, a shame, given that the floundering former prospect performed well in the spring before being shut down. An injury to the hamate bone in his left hand required surgery after the Padres tried the rest-and-rehab route, and setbacks kept him from returning for more than a single game. Antonelli has always had noteworthy strike-zone recognition and some thump for a middle infielder, but has yet to conquer Triple-A and will be 26 in April; time is running out. The Padres nontendered him in December, and he will serve as Triple-A depth for the Nationals this season.

Mike Baxter OF

Born: **12/7/1984** Age: **26**
Bats: **L** Throws: **R** Height: **6' 0"** Weight: **190**
Breakout: **5%** Improve: **30%** Collapse: **7%**
Attrition: **26%** MLB: **60%**

Comparables:
Jeff Salazar, Andre Ethier, Brett Carroll (76)

YEAR	TEAM	LVL	AGE	PA	R	2B	3B	HR	RBI	BB	SO	SB	CS	AVG/OBP/SLG	TAv	BABIP	BRR	FRAA	WARP
2008	LEL	A+	23	105	13	4	1	1	17	10	12	3	0	.239/.324/.337	.243	.262	-0.6	RF 0, 1B 1	0.0
2008	SAN	AA	23	370	41	18	4	8	48	39	41	2	2	.272/.349/.426	.267	.286	2.3	RF 4, 1B 3	1.6
2009	SAN	AA	24	229	38	23	1	4	45	23	42	5	2	.376/.441/.559	.370	.456	1.4	RF 4, LF 0	3.3
2009	POR	AAA	24	345	38	17	4	5	34	38	53	9	5	.277/.362/.409	.280	.321	1.2	RF 5, 1B 2	1.7
2010	POR	AAA	25	552	89	30	10	18	72	58	78	22	10	.301/.382/.517	.311	.326	0.0	RF -3, 1B 0	3.3
2010	SDN	MLB	25	9	0	0	0	0	1	0	2	0	0	.125/.111/.125	.047	.143	0.0	1B 0	-0.2
2011	*SDN*	*MLB*	*26*	*532*	*67*	*30*	*4*	*12*	*64*	*48*	*86*	*11*	*4*	*.279/.346/.438*	*.275*	*.312*	*-0.4*	*RF -2, 1B -3*	*0.9*

Baxter has made a habit of putting up plain-looking lines in his debuts at each level, then mashing in repeat campaigns. The former fourth-rounder had the most productive season of his career in his second stint at Portland despite the park's ill treatment of lefties. The outfielder made his major league debut with the Padres in September and played his lone defensive inning at first base, but don't let that fool you—no stretch of the imagination could make him a replacement for Adrian Gonzalez. Baxter's chances of sticking in the majors as anything but a bench player are slim, and Petco is the worst place imaginable for a lefty without Herculean force behind his swing.

Kyle Blanks LF

Born: **9/11/1986** Age: **24**
Bats: **R** Throws: **R** Height: **6' 6"** Weight: **270**
Breakout: **1%** Improve: **17%** Collapse: **2%**
Attrition: **6%** MLB: **26%**

Comparables:
Kent Hrbek, Joel Guzman, Tyler Flowers (64)

YEAR	TEAM	LVL	AGE	PA	R	2B	3B	HR	RBI	BB	SO	SB	CS	AVG/OBP/SLG	TAv	BABIP	BRR	FRAA	WARP
2008	SAN	AA	21	565	75	23	5	20	107	51	90	5	4	.325/.404/.514	.303	.362	-2.6	1B -1	2.6
2009	POR	AAA	22	280	35	9	1	12	38	39	63	0	0	.283/.393/.485	.333	.335	-1.7	1B 5, LF -2	2.5
2009	SDN	MLB	22	172	24	9	0	10	22	18	55	1	1	.250/.355/.514	.306	.325	-1.0	RF -5, LF 1	0.6
2010	SDN	MLB	23	120	14	6	1	3	15	15	46	1	0	.157/.283/.324	.239	.245	1.9	LF -1, 1B 1	0.1
2011	*SDN*	*MLB*	*24*	*391*	*50*	*17*	*1*	*15*	*49*	*40*	*97*	*2*	*1*	*.258/.346/.449*	*.281*	*.312*	*-0.1*	*1B -7, LF -1*	*0.3*

The hulking Blanks was expected to be the Padres' second-best source of power after Adrian Gonzalez, but instead the outfielder struck out in nearly 40 percent of his plate appearances before Tommy John surgery ended his season. That elbow injury may explain why Blanks looked slow on pitches to the outer third of the plate and performed much worse on pitches down the middle than someone with his skill set should have. Nearly all of his offensive output stemmed from pitches on the inner third of the plate, where the least amount of elbow extension was needed. Blanks is always going to whiff and he does have a tendency to chase, but with a healthy elbow, he should recover something closer to his 2009 form this season.

Everth Cabrera SS

Born: **11/17/1986** Age: **24**
Bats: **S** Throws: **R** Height: **5' 10"** Weight: **175**
Breakout: **1%** Improve: **19%** Collapse: **6%**
Attrition: **23%** MLB: **48%**

Comparables:
Brent Lillibridge, Kurt Stillwell, Eric Patterson (75)

YEAR	TEAM	LVL	AGE	PA	R	2B	3B	HR	RBI	BB	SO	SB	CS	AVG/OBP/SLG	TAv	BABIP	BRR	FRAA	WARP
2008	ASH	A	21	550	76	25	6	6	38	52	104	70	16	.284/.360/.397	.273	.340	4.0	2B 7, SS 5	3.7
2009	SDN	MLB	22	438	58	18	8	2	31	46	88	25	8	.255/.336/.361	.267	.317	2.8	SS 8	3.0
2010	SDN	MLB	23	241	22	6	3	1	22	19	54	10	6	.208/.270/.278	.200	.261	0.6	SS -2, 2B 0	-0.7
2011	*SDN*	*MLB*	*24*	*445*	*49*	*19*	*4*	*4*	*41*	*39*	*91*	*29*	*9*	*.256/.321/.359*	*.244*	*.309*	*-0.1*	*SS 3, 2B 3*	*1.2*

Cabrera looked like a nifty Rule 5 steal in 2009, when he turned in an above-average rookie campaign despite having entered the season with just 29 plate appearances above High-A to his credit. The 2010 season was a different story. A hamstring injury put him on the disabled list twice, and poor production while he was active landed him in Triple-A and on the pine. The Padres aren't sure what they have in Cabrera, but their acquisitions of Jason Bartlett and Orlando Hudson over the winter might indicate which way they're leaning. Fortunately, they don't have to reach a final conclusion just yet. Cabrera's aggressive fielding hasn't worked at short, but his strong arm and quick feet translate well to second, where he appeared for 44 defensive innings in 2010 and the majority of his time in the minors with the Rockies.

Drew Cumberland SS

Born: **1/13/1989** Age: **22**
Bats: **L** Throws: **R** Height: **5' 10"** Weight: **175**
Breakout: **2%** Improve: **3%** Collapse: **1%**
Attrition: **2%** MLB: **6%**

Comparables:
Tony Abreu, Everth Cabrera, Asdrubal Cabrera (78)

YEAR	TEAM	LVL	AGE	PA	R	2B	3B	HR	RBI	BB	SO	SB	CS	AVG/OBP/SLG	TAv	BABIP	BRR	FRAA	WARP
2008	FTW	A	19	227	29	8	1	1	17	17	24	16	4	.286/.348/.350	.269	.319	0.7	SS 1, 2B 0	1.1
2009	FTW	A	20	339	57	18	5	2	40	40	36	19	3	.293/.386/.410	.278	.325	0.7	SS -4, 2B 2	1.6
2010	LEL	A+	21	270	63	15	4	7	35	15	34	20	9	.365/.404/.542	.352	.398	4.2	SS -11, 2B 0	2.8
2010	SAN	AA	21	58	5	3	0	0	6	1	11	1	2	.278/.298/.333	.218	.333	0.0	SS -1, 2B 0	-0.1
2011	*SDN*	*MLB*	*22*	*295*	*34*	*15*	*2*	*4*	*32*	*17*	*44*	*11*	*3*	*.281/.323/.400*	*.257*	*.314*	*-0.1*	*SS -3, 2B 0*	*0.7*

Cumberland's 2009 was cut short by an injury, and his 2010 season suffered the same fate, thanks to a slide into a wall that gashed the outside of his knee. It's not the kind of injury that is expected to cause long-term problems, a good thing, since Cumberland mashed at Lake Elsinore before his promotion to Double-A. He has a good stroke, but he is also very aggressive at the plate—so far his approach has resulted in few walks, but on the plus side, he rarely whiffs, either. Cumberland has the athleticism and the arm to stick at his current position, and while his numbers at Lake Elsinore were helped considerably by the offensive environment, if he stays healthy he should provide enough batting average and speed to make up for his lack of secondary skills and provide the answer the club has been seeking at shortstop for some time now.

Aaron Cunningham OF

Born: **4/24/1986** Age: **25**
Bats: **R** Throws: **R** Height: **5' 11"** Weight: **195**
Breakout: **7%** Improve: **34%** Collapse: **5%**
Attrition: **21%** MLB: **54%**

Comparables:
Clete Thomas, Lastings Milledge, Chris Pettit (71)

YEAR	TEAM	LVL	AGE	PA	R	2B	3B	HR	RBI	BB	SO	SB	CS	AVG/OBP/SLG	TAv	BABIP	BRR	FRAA	WARP
2008	MID	AA	22	401	65	18	6	12	52	38	92	12	4	.317/.382/.507	.308	.386	2.8	CF -8, LF 6	3.1
2008	SAC	AAA	22	89	21	5	0	5	14	11	16	3	1	.382/.461/.645	.386	.429	0.9	RF -2, CF 0	1.2
2008	OAK	MLB	22	87	7	7	1	1	14	6	24	2	0	.250/.310/.400	.252	.346	-0.9	LF 4, RF 1	0.5
2009	SAC	AAA	23	375	62	24	1	11	48	33	74	11	4	.302/.371/.479	.303	.357	1.2	LF 1, RF -9	1.6
2009	OAK	MLB	23	57	6	2	0	1	6	3	16	0	0	.151/.210/.245	.185	.194	-0.4	RF -3, LF -1	-0.8
2010	POR	AAA	24	308	30	17	3	7	45	28	68	2	7	.251/.333/.413	.260	.307	-2.7	LF -5, RF -8	-1.1
2010	SDN	MLB	24	147	17	12	1	1	15	7	28	1	3	.288/.326/.417	.261	.343	-0.1	LF -1, RF 0	0.2
2011	*SDN*	*MLB*	*25*	*489*	*59*	*27*	*2*	*13*	*59*	*37*	*109*	*8*	*4*	*.266/.328/.428*	*.267*	*.320*	*-0.7*	*LF -3, RF -6*	*-0.1*

Cunningham was successful in his first extended stay in the bigs, contributing solid play on both sides of the ball. He's something of an offensive tweener, best suited for a bench role, given that his bat will produce only a moderate average and power for a corner outfielder, yet is simultaneously a good-enough hitter that he's capable of handling periods of everyday work without sabotaging his squad. Cunningham will get a crack at the reserve outfielder's job vacated by Scott Hairston, but the presence of the superior Chris Denorfia on the roster might mean more time at Triple-A.

James Darnell **3B**

Born: **1/19/1987** Age: **24**
Bats: R Throws: R Height: **6' 2"** Weight: **195**
Breakout: **2%** Improve: **19%** Collapse: **5%**
Attrition: **17%** MLB: **42%**

Comparables:
Chase Headley, Gordon Beckham, Pete Ward (76)

YEAR	TEAM	LVL	AGE	PA	R	2B	3B	HR	RBI	BB	SO	SB	CS	AVG/OBP/SLG	TAv	BABIP	BRR	FRAA	WARP
2008	EUG	A-	21	78	9	6	1	2	15	11	12	1	1	.373/.462/.582	.376	.434	0.7	3B -1	1.1
2009	FTW	A	22	283	40	17	2	7	38	57	51	5	5	.329/.466/.518	.351	.398	-2.8	3B -8	2.3
2009	LEL	A+	22	269	40	18	2	13	43	30	38	3	1	.294/.375/.553	.343	.301	-0.8	3B 0	2.9
2010	SAN	AA	23	426	46	21	1	10	50	44	64	2	0	.265/.348/.408	.293	.294	-5.3	3B -8	1.3
2011	*SDN*	*MLB*	*24*	*362*	*47*	*20*	*1*	*11*	*45*	*38*	*64*	*1*	*0*	*.276/.354/.449*	*.283*	*.308*	*0.0*	*3B -5*	*1.2*

Darnell's season at Double-A looks disappointing, but he dealt with a finger injury and played in a park that hindered his offensive output. His strike-zone recognition was as advanced as ever, yielding walks in over 10 percent of his plate appearances and punchouts in just 15 percent, but his .142 ISO was well below its High-A level, and he posted the lowest batting average of his pro career, thanks to a .223/.317/.352 line at home. While his .311/.382/.467 road numbers didn't save his season, they do lend credence to the idea that his progression isn't far off track. Darnell has all the tools to be a solid defender at third, but so far, they haven't come together, a problem that may eventually force a move to the outfield.

Jaff Decker **OF**

Born: **2/23/1990** Age: **21**
Bats: L Throws: L Height: **5' 10"** Weight: **190**
Breakout: **1%** Improve: **3%** Collapse: **0%**
Attrition: **2%** MLB: **11%**

Comparables:
Willie Mays, Carlos May, Curt Blefary (66)

YEAR	TEAM	LVL	AGE	PA	R	2B	3B	HR	RBI	BB	SO	SB	CS	AVG/OBP/SLG	TAv	BABIP	BRR	FRAA	WARP
2008	PDR	Rk	18	216	51	11	2	5	34	55	36	9	1	.352/.523/.541	.388	.432	1.0	CF 0, LF 0	3.7
2009	FTW	A	19	455	78	25	2	16	64	85	92	10	6	.299/.442/.514	.336	.360	-1.8	LF -3	4.0
2010	LEL	A+	20	348	53	14	2	17	58	47	80	5	4	.262/.374/.500	.328	.299	-1.0	LF 6, RF 0	3.4
2011	*SDN*	*MLB*	*21*	*350*	*46*	*15*	*1*	*13*	*42*	*50*	*86*	*1*	*1*	*.250/.364/.447*	*.285*	*.302*	*-0.1*	*LF -5, CF -1*	*0.9*

Jaff Decker's name makes him sound more like the lead character in a series of B-level sci-fi flicks than a baseball player—*Captain Jaff Decker and the Killer Space Aliens from Planet Marzipan*, perhaps—but believe us, the kid can handle a bat. Decker hit .305/.439/.616 after the All-Star break, which saved the 20-year-old's seasonal stats from a disastrous May, but he broke his hand on a hit-by-pitch in mid-August. Decker knows how to draw a walk, but he is going to strike out often as he progresses through the minors. The five-foot-ten outfielder lost a bit of his baby fat this year, but being in better shape didn't help his outfield defense much—his bat will be major league ready before his glove is.

Chris Denorfia **OF**

Born: **7/15/1980** Age: **30**
Bats: R Throws: R Height: **6' 1"** Weight: **185**
Breakout: **1%** Improve: **33%** Collapse: **5%**
Attrition: **11%** MLB: **68%**

Comparables:
Rajai Davis, Ryan Spilborghs, Tommy Murphy (75)

YEAR	TEAM	LVL	AGE	PA	R	2B	3B	HR	RBI	BB	SO	SB	CS	AVG/OBP/SLG	TAv	BABIP	BRR	FRAA	WARP
2008	SAC	AAA	27	204	34	13	1	2	20	12	31	5	4	.302/.338/.413	.305	.346	0.9	CF 0, RF 0	1.8
2008	OAK	MLB	27	71	10	3	0	1	9	6	16	2	0	.290/.352/.387	.270	.362	-3.1	CF 1, LF -2	-0.2
2009	SAC	AAA	28	474	62	18	5	9	49	31	52	15	6	.271/.314/.398	.265	.283	0.8	LF 4, CF -2	2.0
2009	OAK	MLB	28	2	1	0	0	0	1	0	0	0	0	.000/.000/.000	.386	.000	0.2	CF 0, LF 0	0.0
2010	POR	AAA	29	134	17	10	4	2	12	12	18	7	1	.306/.368/.504	.311	.343	0.2	LF -1, RF 4	1.1
2010	SDN	MLB	29	317	41	15	2	9	36	27	51	8	4	.271/.334/.433	.283	.298	1.2	CF 3, LF 0	1.8
2011	*SDN*	*MLB*	*30*	*439*	*54*	*22*	*3*	*10*	*52*	*32*	*61*	*12*	*5*	*.285/.336/.427*	*.269*	*.309*	*-0.4*	*CF -2, LF -1*	*1.2*

Denorfia made the most of his first crack at regular playing time. He finished second among San Diego outfielders in True Runs despite appearing in just 99 games and displayed the range and arm to provide above-average defense in a corner. His shortcomings became clearer when he attempted to serve as a replacement for the injured Tony Gwynn in center—Denorfia would barely catch or would fail to reach balls that Gwynn would have caught with room to spare, and it cost the Padres down the stretch. He's capable of at least average play in a corner, but with Ryan Ludwick in tow for a full season in left and Cameron Maybin joining the team, Denorfia will have to settle for fourth-outfielder status.

Luis Durango CF

Born: **4/23/1986** Age: **25**
Bats: **S** Throws: **R** Height: **5' 9"** Weight: **160**
Breakout: **1%** Improve: **18%** Collapse: **2%**
Attrition: **17%** MLB: **43%**

Comparables:
Joey Gathright, Willy Taveras, Alexi Casilla (64)

YEAR	TEAM	LVL	AGE	PA	R	2B	3B	HR	RBI	BB	SO	SB	CS	AVG/OBP/SLG	TAv	BABIP	BRR	FRAA	WARP
2008	FTW	A	22	389	56	11	3	1	25	49	43	14	7	.305/.391/.365	.288	.342	0.3	CF -2, LF 1	1.6
2008	LEL	A+	22	87	20	4	1	0	10	13	7	1	1	.431/.506/.514	.369	.463	-0.5	LF -4	1.2
2009	SAN	AA	23	560	78	9	2	0	25	81	70	44	17	.281/.377/.309	.277	.314	4.5	LF -5, CF 6	2.6
2009	SDN	MLB	23	14	3	0	0	0	0	2	2	2	1	.546/.571/.546	.409	.600	1.1	LF 0, CF 0	0.3
2010	POR	AAA	24	423	42	5	2	0	24	45	59	35	16	.300/.378/.325	.269	.343	0.0	CF 5, LF 1	2.2
2010	SDN	MLB	24	53	8	0	0	0	4	4	7	5	0	.250/.302/.250	.199	.286	1.1	CF -2	-0.3
2011	*SDN*	*MLB*	*25*	*519*	*57*	*14*	*2*	*3*	*38*	*54*	*76*	*23*	*8*	*.273/.345/.331*	*.248*	*.311*	*-0.3*	*CF -2, LF -4*	*-0.2*

Durango's line at Triple-A Portland appeared to hail from the Deadball Era, but the comparison doesn't quite hold; Deadball players had more power. Of Durango's 18 career MLB hits, 12 of them have been bunt or infield singles; he has 70 speed on the 20-80 scouting scale and seems to teleport from base to base. His swiftness is also on display in the outfield, where he boasts plenty of range in center. Given his ability to bunt, draw a walk, run the bases, and play plus defense, Durango has a future as an NL bench player until someone develops a time machine capable of packing him off to the early 20th century.

David Eckstein 2B

Born: **1/20/1975** Age: **36**
Bats: **R** Throws: **R** Height: **5' 6"** Weight: **170**
Breakout: **2%** Improve: **16%** Collapse: **14%**
Attrition: **26%** MLB: **71%**

Comparables:
Eric Young, Cookie Rojas, Horace Clarke (67)

YEAR	TEAM	LVL	AGE	PA	R	2B	3B	HR	RBI	BB	SO	SB	CS	AVG/OBP/SLG	TAv	BABIP	BRR	FRAA	WARP
2008	ARI	MLB	33	73	5	3	0	1	4	7	5	0	0	.219/.301/.313	.218	.220	0.5	2B 6	0.5
2008	TOR	MLB	33	303	26	18	0	1	23	24	27	2	1	.277/.343/.358	.255	.292	0.3	SS -5, 2B 0	0.5
2009	SDN	MLB	34	568	64	27	2	2	51	39	46	3	1	.260/.315/.334	.237	.273	-2.9	2B -11	-1.3
2010	SDN	MLB	35	492	49	23	0	1	29	27	35	8	1	.267/.313/.326	.241	.279	1.8	2B -5	0.0
2011	*SDN*	*MLB*	*36*	*500*	*54*	*25*	*0*	*3*	*43*	*33*	*33*	*5*	*2*	*.273/.324/.348*	*.242*	*.277*	*0.0*	*2B -3, SS -1*	*-0.1*

Eckstein struck out just five times over the first two months of last season, but his bat fell apart in June, and he hit .254/.307/.293 with 30 punchouts and just 10 extra-base hits (all doubles) the rest of the way. Those numbers bookended a calf injury that cost him around 50 games, and while it was to blame for some of Eckstein's struggles, its effect on his production goes to show how little wiggle room he has when straddling the line between help and hindrance. Escaping Petco will help him on a superficial level, but Eckstein hasn't been an above-average hitter since 2007, even with an assist from park adjustments, and second base is now his lone defensive position.

Logan Forsythe 3B

Born: **1/14/1987** Age: **24**
Bats: **R** Throws: **R** Height: **6' 1"** Weight: **205**
Breakout: **1%** Improve: **4%** Collapse: **1%**
Attrition: **11%** MLB: **14%**

Comparables:
Matt Antonelli, Lou Marson, Xavier Paul (77)

YEAR	TEAM	LVL	AGE	PA	R	2B	3B	HR	RBI	BB	SO	SB	CS	AVG/OBP/SLG	TAv	BABIP	BRR	FRAA	WARP
2009	LEL	A+	22	305	46	13	3	8	30	61	48	6	2	.322/.472/.504	.370	.376	-2.0	3B 0	3.9
2009	SAN	AA	22	290	37	9	3	3	31	41	63	5	0	.279/.383/.377	.295	.359	1.6	3B -2	1.9
2010	SAN	AA	23	472	66	22	1	3	38	75	95	17	5	.253/.377/.337	.294	.325	1.0	2B -3, 3B 1	2.6
2011	*SDN*	*MLB*	*24*	*371*	*44*	*16*	*1*	*5*	*32*	*51*	*79*	*5*	*2*	*.256/.363/.366*	*.266*	*.321*	*0.0*	*3B -2, 2B 0*	*0.9*

Forsythe's power didn't return in his second stint at San Antonio, though that shouldn't be a huge surprise, given how horrific the park plays for right-handers, especially those without much pop to spare. He did earn free passes in 16 percent of his plate appearances this season (while whiffing in 20 percent), which suggests that he may have value even if he never does much slugging, especially considering his sound defensive instincts and strong arm at third base. San Diego may get a better sense of Forsythe's true hitting ability by promoting him to Triple-A Tucson and letting him escape San Antonio, though the latter setting wasn't a bad dry run for the privations of Petco.

Adrian Gonzalez 1B

Born: **5/8/1982** Age: **29**
Bats: **L** Throws: **L** Height: **6' 2"** Weight: **220**
Breakout: **4%** Improve: **46%** Collapse: **3%**
Attrition: **9%** MLB: **95%**

Comparables:
Mark Teixeira, Eddie Murray, Albert Belle (72)

YEAR	TEAM	LVL	AGE	PA	R	2B	3B	HR	RBI	BB	SO	SB	CS	AVG/OBP/SLG	TAv	BABIP	BRR	FRAA	WARP
2008	SDN	MLB	26	700	103	32	1	36	119	74	142	0	0	.279/.361/.510	.300	.308	-2.0	1B 0	3.2
2009	SDN	MLB	27	681	90	27	2	40	99	119	109	1	1	.277/.407/.551	.336	.277	-1.2	1B 10	6.6
2010	SDN	MLB	28	693	86	33	0	31	101	93	114	0	0	.298/.391/.511	.329	.321	-6.6	1B 9	5.4
2011	*BOS*	*MLB*	*29*	*685*	*98*	*29*	*1*	*34*	*100*	*90*	*115*	*1*	*0*	*.283/.379/.513*	*.305*	*.297*	*0.0*	*1B 7*	*4.1*

Even a damaged right shoulder that sapped Gonzalez's power couldn't stop him from having another MVP-caliber campaign. He compensated for the ailment by using a more compact swing and a lighter bat after the injury began to bother him in May. This allowed him to sit back and wait for pitches he could drive to the opposite field—the longer follow-through on a swing intended to pull for power caused prohibitive pain. Using this new approach, Gonzalez hit .350/.429/.541 against southpaws, a huge jump from his .248/.323/.433 line in 2006 through

April 2010. The sample was small, but he may want to consider keeping his compact, opposite-field approach against left-handers in the future. Gonzalez won't be back until mid- to late March after extensive "clean-up" surgery on the aforementioned shoulder, but given how he performed with the injury, his production should be unimpaired once he can swing a bat. When he does return, he'll do so in a Red Sox uniform; Gonzalez was dealt to Boston in December for a trio of prospects and Eric Patterson, since his old team knew it could not afford to match the sums he'd command on the open market. Ditching Petco for Fenway will do even more for his numbers than a fully operational shoulder.

Tony Gwynn **CF**

Born: **10/4/1982** Age: **28**
Bats: **L** Throws: **R** Height: **6' 0"** Weight: **185**
Breakout: **6%** Improve: **39%** Collapse: **2%**
Attrition: **18%** MLB: **71%**

Comparables:
Kenny Lofton, Rajai Davis, Nyjer Morgan (76)

YEAR	TEAM	LVL	AGE	PA	R	2B	3B	HR	RBI	BB	SO	SB	CS	AVG/OBP/SLG	TAv	BABIP	BRR	FRAA	WARP
2008	NAS	AAA	25	412	47	9	3	2	26	29	54	20	6	.275/.325/.331	.228	.311	4.0	CF 5, RF -1	0.6
2008	MIL	MLB	25	49	5	1	0	0	1	4	7	3	1	.190/.265/.214	.201	.216	0.4	CF 1, RF 0	-0.1
2009	NAS	AAA	26	175	34	8	1	1	9	20	21	15	1	.309/.383/.395	.305	.346	5.6	CF -1, LF -1	1.7
2009	SDN	MLB	26	451	59	11	6	2	21	48	65	11	7	.270/.346/.344	.259	.311	2.2	CF 10, RF 4	2.7
2010	SDN	MLB	27	339	30	9	3	3	20	41	50	17	4	.204/.298/.287	.227	.230	0.4	CF -11	-1.2
2011	*LAN*	*MLB*	*28*	*458*	*49*	*15*	*3*	*4*	*37*	*45*	*67*	*19*	*6*	*.256/.327/.338*	*.241*	*.290*	*0.0*	*CF -2, RF 0*	*0.2*

After a glance at the stats above, you may wonder how anyone could have justified giving Thin Gwynn a starting gig in the majors. Gwynn isn't as poor at the plate as his 2010 line indicated, but watch him out in center field, and your question will be answered as soon as a sinking liner heads for his airspace. The biggest hint of how highly the team regarded his defensive talents came late in a game on September 29, when Will Venable—who had made two homer-saving catches in center earlier that night—was bumped to a corner in favor of Gwynn. His injured hamate bone and subsequent DL stint helped to doom the Padres' playoff run by cutting into their late-inning defensive depth. The Padres nontendered him after acquiring another gifted defensive center fielder with a more imposing bat in Cameron Maybin. After leaving his father Tony's team, Gwynn quickly moved to his uncle Chris's, signing with the Dodgers to complement their regular outfield options.

Jedd Gyorko **3B**

Born: **9/23/1988** Age: **22**
Bats: **R** Throws: **R** Height: **5' 10"** Weight: **195**
Breakout: **1%** Improve: **2%** Collapse: **0%**
Attrition: **2%** MLB: **3%**

Comparables:
Eric Chavez, Elliott Maddox, Steve Garvey (78)

YEAR	TEAM	LVL	AGE	PA	R	2B	3B	HR	RBI	BB	SO	SB	CS	AVG/OBP/SLG	TAv	BABIP	BRR	FRAA	WARP
2010	FTW	A	21	183	19	11	0	2	23	19	31	1	0	.284/.366/.389	.277	.341	0.0	3B 2, 2B -1	0.8
2010	EUG	A-	21	115	16	6	0	5	18	9	26	1	1	.330/.383/.528	.362	.400	0.0	3B -2	1.4
2011	*SDN*	*MLB*	*22*	*306*	*34*	*14*	*1*	*7*	*33*	*21*	*70*	*0*	*0*	*.251/.305/.391*	*.233*	*.304*	*0.0*	*3B 1, 2B 0*	*0.0*

If there is one thing that everyone knows about the Padres' 2010 second-round draft selection, it's his ability to hit. Gyorko accumulated twice as many extra-base hits as strikeouts as a junior in 2010 and flashed some pop with wood bats in the Cape Cod League in 2009. The Padres shifted him to third base, where he has the arm to stick but no other strong defensive skills; he played shortstop in college only because the rules stipulated that someone had to and he happened to be West Virginia's most distinguished athlete. Gyorko raked at Low-A before slowing down some in A-ball, but his approach—featuring walks in 10 percent of his plate appearances and a reduced postpromotion strikeout rate—augured well for his first full professional season.

Jason Hagerty **C**

Born: **9/13/1987** Age: **23**
Bats: **R** Throws: **R** Height: **6' 3"** Weight: **220**
Breakout: **4%** Improve: **15%** Collapse: **4%**
Attrition: **19%** MLB: **39%**

Comparables:
Gary Carter, Mike Carp, Matt Tuiasosopo (76)

YEAR	TEAM	LVL	AGE	PA	R	2B	3B	HR	RBI	BB	SO	SB	CS	AVG/OBP/SLG	TAv	BABIP	BRR	FRAA	WARP
2009	EUG	A-	21	203	34	12	0	6	26	26	47	0	0	.225/.335/.399	.286	.273	2.0	C 0, 1B 1	1.4
2010	FTW	A	22	534	74	35	3	14	74	88	104	2	1	.302/.423/.494	.320	.362	-2.8	C 2, 1B 0	5.2
2011	*SDN*	*MLB*	*23*	*379*	*45*	*20*	*0*	*10*	*40*	*46*	*93*	*0*	*0*	*.244/.338/.401*	*.263*	*.304*	*0.0*	*C 0, 1B 0*	*1.3*

Hagerty is a switch-hitting catcher who has shown fairly advanced knowledge of the strike zone and promising power by the standards of his position. He's been a bit old for his levels, turning 22 in A-ball last season, but it's hard not to pay attention to a backstop with a 1110 OPS against southpaws and a respectable 859 mark versus righties. The problem—and given his less-than-aggressive league assignments, you knew there had to be one—is his glove; he spent a lot of time at first base at the University of Miami for a reason. Hagerty will start 2011 at High-A, but his bat will propel his glove to an age-appropriate level soon enough.

Jerry Hairston INF

Born: **5/29/1976** Age: **35**
Bats: R Throws: R Height: **5' 10"** Weight: **175**
Breakout: **1%** Improve: **24%** Collapse: **17%**
Attrition: **33%** MLB: **75%**

Comparables:
Alan Trammell, Shannon Stewart, Tommy Holmes (72)

YEAR	TEAM	LVL	AGE	PA	R	2B	3B	HR	RBI	BB	SO	SB	CS	AVG/OBP/SLG	TAv	BABIP	BRR	FRAA	WARP
2008	LOU	AAA	32	85	11	8	2	4	19	3	9	1	1	.380/.400/.684	.348	.382	-0.3	SS 0, RF 1	1.2
2008	CIN	MLB	32	297	47	20	2	6	36	23	36	15	3	.326/.374/.487	.292	.345	1.9	SS -7, CF -2	1.5
2009	CIN	MLB	33	340	47	18	1	8	27	21	46	7	3	.254/.300/.397	.257	.267	2.9	3B -5, SS -2	0.9
2009	NYA	MLB	33	93	15	5	0	2	12	11	8	0	1	.237/.344/.382	.262	.232	0.0	LF 0, 3B 2	0.4
2010	SDN	MLB	34	476	53	13	2	10	50	31	54	9	6	.244/.296/.354	.241	.253	0.8	SS 5, 2B -2	0.8
2011	*SDN*	*MLB*	*35*	*339*	*39*	*16*	*1*	*8*	*38*	*24*	*38*	*8*	*3*	*.263/.315/.401*	*.253*	*.269*	*-0.4*	*SS 0, 2B 0*	*0.7*

Hairston was signed to give the Padres infield depth that they turned out to need: the utility player racked up 476 plate appearances covering for the injuries of others despite making multiple DL appearances of his own. His line was ugly before adjustments for Petco and his position, but the elder half of Hermanos Hairston was one reason that the Padres excelled defensively even when regular shortstop Everth Cabrera and second baseman David Eckstein were knocked out with injuries. Hairston did all that with a fractured tibia that was thought to be shin splints for much of the year; with a healthy leg, he should again provide necessary depth off the bench on both sides of the ball.

Scott Hairston LF

Born: **5/25/1980** Age: **31**
Bats: R Throws: R Height: **6' 0"** Weight: **188**
Breakout: **3%** Improve: **39%** Collapse: **3%**
Attrition: **10%** MLB: **93%**

Comparables:
Milton Bradley, Bernard Gilkey, Jim Ray Hart (80)

YEAR	TEAM	LVL	AGE	PA	R	2B	3B	HR	RBI	BB	SO	SB	CS	AVG/OBP/SLG	TAv	BABIP	BRR	FRAA	WARP
2008	SDN	MLB	28	362	42	18	3	17	31	28	84	3	1	.249/.309/.479	.285	.278	-0.5	CF 0, LF 1	1.9
2009	OAK	MLB	29	248	23	13	1	7	35	8	38	3	2	.236/.262/.391	.235	.249	-2.7	LF 5, CF 0	0.1
2009	SDN	MLB	29	216	26	14	1	10	29	17	45	8	1	.300/.357/.533	.314	.343	0.4	CF -7, LF 3	1.4
2010	SDN	MLB	30	336	34	10	0	10	36	31	69	6	1	.210/.295/.346	.250	.236	-1.5	LF 0, CF 1	0.3
2011	*SDN*	*MLB*	*31*	*391*	*48*	*20*	*1*	*15*	*51*	*32*	*72*	*6*	*2*	*.258/.324/.449*	*.271*	*.280*	*0.0*	*LF 2, CF -2*	*1.2*

Hairston's first half was in the acceptable-for-Petco range at .241/.322/.392, but a sore left shoulder plagued him more as the year continued, which contributed to a 452 second-half OPS. He made $2.45 million in 2010 and was heading into his final year of arbitration and the Padres, flush with outfielders even before trading for Cameron Maybin, nontendered him to avoid that payout. Hairston is a solid defensive outfielder for someone who was supposed to be a DH, and while he is definitely a stretch in center, he can stick in left. When healthy, Hairston has the wallop to make himself a threat against lefties: he hit .281/.339/.528 against southpaws as a Padre and slugged .463 against right-handers. He joined the Mets as outfield depth.

Chase Headley 3B

Born: **5/9/1984** Age: **27**
Bats: S Throws: R Height: **6' 2"** Weight: **195**
Breakout: **2%** Improve: **52%** Collapse: **1%**
Attrition: **14%** MLB: **91%**

Comparables:
Hank Blalock, Jhonny Peralta, Edwin Encarnacion (78)

YEAR	TEAM	LVL	AGE	PA	R	2B	3B	HR	RBI	BB	SO	SB	CS	AVG/OBP/SLG	TAv	BABIP	BRR	FRAA	WARP
2008	POR	AAA	24	295	49	24	1	13	40	31	65	0	0	.305/.383/.556	.321	.361	-1.7	LF -4, 3B 0	2.0
2008	SDN	MLB	24	368	34	19	2	9	38	30	104	4	1	.269/.337/.420	.275	.364	-1.0	LF -2, 3B 0	1.0
2009	SDN	MLB	25	612	62	31	2	12	64	62	133	10	2	.262/.342/.392	.268	.325	1.4	LF -7, 3B -4	0.9
2010	SDN	MLB	26	674	77	29	3	11	58	56	139	17	5	.264/.326/.375	.267	.323	2.7	3B 0	2.6
2011	*SDN*	*MLB*	*27*	*628*	*79*	*34*	*2*	*16*	*74*	*61*	*131*	*9*	*3*	*.276/.349/.433*	*.275*	*.329*	*-0.1*	*LF -3, 3B -2*	*1.9*

After dealing Kevin Kouzmanoff, the Padres moved Headley back to his natural position of third base. The swap paid dividends defensively: at the hot corner, Headley positions himself well and has quick reflexes, range, and a strong arm to boot—essentially the opposite of his attributes in the outfield. Since he was replaced by superior defenders in left, Headley's change of address resulted in a massive net gain on defense for the Friars. Petco reserves a special hell for left-handers, and Headley has hit only .227/.321/.349 from the left side in his career there, but he remains an above-average and cost-controlled piece of their plans, thanks to a .296/.355/.435 road line and plus defense. Expect another year of quiet production, though he won't be quite as inexpensive after qualifying for Super Two status.

Nick Hundley C

Born: **9/8/1983** Age: **27**
Bats: R Throws: R Height: **6' 1"** Weight: **210**
Breakout: **1%** Improve: **35%** Collapse: **5%**
Attrition: **9%** MLB: **90%**

Comparables:
Terry Steinbach, Johnny Romano, Thurman Munson (78)

YEAR	TEAM	LVL	AGE	PA	R	2B	3B	HR	RBI	BB	SO	SB	CS	AVG/OBP/SLG	TAv	BABIP	BRR	FRAA	WARP
2008	POR	AAA	24	243	32	13	0	12	39	17	44	0	0	.232/.284/.451	.246	.235	0.3	C -1	0.7
2008	SDN	MLB	24	216	21	7	1	5	24	11	52	0	0	.237/.278/.359	.229	.288	0.0	C 0	0.2
2009	SDN	MLB	25	289	23	15	2	8	30	28	76	5	1	.238/.311/.406	.258	.301	-1.5	C 1, LF 0	1.1
2010	SDN	MLB	26	307	33	18	2	8	43	25	66	0	5	.249/.306/.418	.265	.290	-4.1	C -1	0.9
2011	*SDN*	*MLB*	*27*	*358*	*42*	*18*	*1*	*12*	*44*	*29*	*75*	*3*	*2*	*.251/.313/.425*	*.258*	*.288*	*-0.2*	*C 0*	*1.3*

The Padres' 2010 bench coach and former backstop Ted Simmons has said that 1,500 at-bats or 500 games caught are needed before you know whether someone is an everyday catcher or a backup. Hundley remains short of both measures, but he was able to reproduce his above-average production at the plate while improving his work behind it. His throwing action—something Simmons and the 26-year-old receiver worked on all season—looked quicker and smoother, which resulted in his retiring 29 percent of would-be base thieves. With Torrealba having declined his option, Hundley will see additional time in 2011. Better production against right-handers (692 OPS in 2010, 708 career) would net him even more innings behind the plate.

Ryan Ludwick LF

Born: **7/13/1978** Age: **32**
Bats: **R** Throws: **L** Height: **6' 3"** Weight: **203**
Breakout: **1%** Improve: **38%** Collapse: **2%**
Attrition: **11%** MLB: **98%**

Comparables:
George Hendrick, Geoff Jenkins, Shawn Green (76)

YEAR	TEAM	LVL	AGE	PA	R	2B	3B	HR	RBI	BB	SO	SB	CS	AVG/OBP/SLG	TAv	BABIP	BRR	FRAA	WARP
2008	SLN	MLB	29	617	104	40	3	37	113	62	146	4	4	.299/.374/.591	.334	.341	2.5	RF 3, LF 1	6.4
2009	SLN	MLB	30	542	63	20	1	22	97	41	106	4	2	.265/.327/.447	.278	.295	2.2	RF -2, LF 0	1.8
2010	SLN	MLB	31	314	44	20	2	11	43	24	64	0	3	.281/.341/.484	.301	.325	-1.4	RF 5, CF 1	2.2
2010	SDN	MLB	31	239	19	7	0	6	26	24	57	0	1	.211/.301/.330	.234	.257	-0.5	RF 4	0.1
2011	*SDN*	*MLB*	*32*	*545*	*72*	*29*	*1*	*24*	*77*	*47*	*109*	*4*	*2*	*.275/.344/.485*	*.288*	*.305*	*-0.5*	*RF 3, LF 1*	*2.6*

Ludwick didn't produce the way the Padres thought he would when they dealt a pair of prospects for him at the deadline, but both the organization and the outfielder blame his underwhelming returns on a nonhealing calf injury. Ludwick's 631 OPS as a Friar was one of the reasons that the team fell out of first, but the Padres tendered him a contract nonetheless, knowing that a healthy Ludwick can contribute. Petco is *the* pitcher's park, but it's actually a better place for right-handers to hit than the Cardinals' latest incarnation of Busch Stadium (*better* being a relative term, of course). Though he has the glove for right, San Diego will stick Ludwick in left in 2011, where the offensive baseline is lower and his defense won't be wasted as much as Will Venable's would be.

Oscar Salazar UT

Born: **6/27/1978** Age: **33**
Bats: **R** Throws: **R** Height: **5' 11"** Weight: **178**
Breakout: **1%** Improve: **24%** Collapse: **9%**
Attrition: **17%** MLB: **75%**

Comparables:
Jacque Jones, Fernando Tatis, Reed Johnson (69)

YEAR	TEAM	LVL	AGE	PA	R	2B	3B	HR	RBI	BB	SO	SB	CS	AVG/OBP/SLG	TAv	BABIP	BRR	FRAA	WARP
2008	NOR	AAA	30	491	71	42	3	13	85	42	56	8	2	.316/.371/.512	.300	.334	2.4	1B -5, 3B 1	2.5
2008	BAL	MLB	30	95	13	3	0	5	15	12	14	0	1	.281/.368/.500	.311	.281	0.0	1B 0, 3B 0	0.7
2009	NOR	AAA	31	213	31	17	1	10	43	13	27	0	3	.372/.409/.618	.346	.393	-1.8	1B -1, RF -4	1.5
2009	BAL	MLB	31	33	6	0	0	2	6	2	4	0	0	.419/.455/.613	.359	.440	0.2	1B 0, 3B -1	0.4
2009	SDN	MLB	31	121	12	8	2	3	19	12	16	0	0	.269/.339/.463	.272	.289	-0.6	LF -1, 1B 0	0.2
2010	SDN	MLB	32	148	19	4	0	3	19	16	23	1	2	.237/.318/.336	.247	.264	-0.7	LF -2, RF -3	-0.4
2011	*SDN*	*MLB*	*33*	*376*	*49*	*22*	*1*	*12*	*50*	*31*	*52*	*3*	*1*	*.293/.350/.467*	*.286*	*.312*	*-0.2*	*1B -6, LF -1*	*0.6*

Salazar was essentially a replacement-level performer for the Padres. He appeared in our 2001 and 2002 annuals, but vanished again until he showed enough consistent pop to resurface in the 2009 edition, which should give you some idea of how useful he is when he's not slugging. He has shown an odd reverse split over the course of his career, and in 2010, supplied most of his production against his fellow righties, and he's also that oddest of creatures: the utility player who doesn't defend well at any position. Now 32 years old, Salazar won't be arb-eligible until 2012, so he may never make enough money to fund his true calling in life: a chain of health-food-conscious restaurants named Salad Czar's.

Matt Stairs LF

Born: **2/27/1968** Age: **43**
Bats: **L** Throws: **R** Height: **5' 9"** Weight: **175**
Breakout: **2%** Improve: **8%** Collapse: **12%**
Attrition: **23%** MLB: **47%**

Comparables:
Hank Aaron, Stan Musial, Brian Downing (56)

YEAR	TEAM	LVL	AGE	PA	R	2B	3B	HR	RBI	BB	SO	SB	CS	AVG/OBP/SLG	TAv	BABIP	BRR	FRAA	WARP
2008	PHI	MLB	40	19	4	1	0	2	5	1	3	0	0	.294/.316/.706	.318	.231	0.1	RF 0	0.2
2008	TOR	MLB	40	368	44	11	1	11	44	41	87	1	1	.250/.342/.394	.263	.308	0.4	LF -1, RF 0	0.4
2009	PHI	MLB	41	129	20	4	0	5	17	23	30	0	0	.194/.357/.379	.275	.221	-0.2	RF -1, LF 2	0.5
2010	SDN	MLB	42	111	16	6	0	6	16	11	32	2	0	.232/.306/.475	.281	.274	0.6	LF 0, 1B 1	0.5
2011	*WAS*	*MLB*	*43*	*285*	*33*	*11*	*0*	*10*	*31*	*33*	*65*	*1*	*1*	*.228/.323/.396*	*.255*	*.264*	*0.0*	*LF 0, RF 0*	*0.2*

Stairs was signed as a clubhouse presence who could pinch-hit and spell more-capable left fielders on occasion, but he showed up looking more like the shortstop he was drafted as than the beefier corner guy he's been ever since, all thanks to the Nutrisystem diet that he picked up from Charlie Manuel. Whether increased fitness contributed to his offensive resurgence can't be determined, but the svelte Stairs posted a translated slugging percentage of .525, thanks to six bombs in limited opportunities—including one that wrested possession of the all-time pinch-hit homer record from Cliff Johnson. The term *professional hitter* may fit Stairs better than any of his gloves ever have, but that didn't stop him from robbing Scott Rolen of a homer in a critical September matchup. Stairs may keep right on slugging if he gets a chance for the Nationals, with whom he signed a minor-league deal for 2011.

Miguel Tejada SS

Born: **5/25/1974** Age: **37**
Bats: **R** Throws: **R** Height: **5' 10"** Weight: **170**
Breakout: **0%** Improve: **20%** Collapse: **14%**
Attrition: **25%** MLB: **90%**

Comparables:
Melvin Mora, Minnie Minoso, Frank Malzone (66)

YEAR	TEAM	LVL	AGE	PA	R	2B	3B	HR	RBI	BB	SO	SB	CS	AVG/OBP/SLG	TAv	BABIP	BRR	FRAA	WARP
2008	HOU	MLB	34	666	92	38	3	13	66	24	72	7	7	.283/.314/.415	.244	.301	-0.6	SS 1	1.5
2009	HOU	MLB	35	674	83	46	1	14	86	19	48	5	2	.313/.340/.455	.270	.318	-0.3	SS 2	3.4
2010	BAL	MLB	36	428	42	16	0	7	39	15	39	0	0	.269/.308/.362	.238	.282	-0.8	3B 4	0.6
2010	SDN	MLB	36	253	31	10	0	8	32	15	28	2	0	.268/.316/.413	.273	.275	-1.4	SS 0, 3B 0	1.1
2011	*SFN*	*MLB*	*37*	*661*	*76*	*32*	*0*	*15*	*73*	*32*	*64*	*4*	*2*	*.278/.319/.402*	*.255*	*.287*	*-0.2*	*SS -1, 3B 1*	*1.9*

Tejada looked like a player on the verge of forced retirement during his stint with Baltimore, but a trade to the Padres rejuvenated the aging Dominican. San Diego gambled that playing for a contender would bring out a different Tejada, who would run and play hard, and that bet paid off, as he hit well above the average shortstop's production level, and—even more surprisingly—performed adequately in the field as well. The list of productive shortstops at age 37 and up consists of a whole lot of Honus Wagner and Luke Appling with a pinch of Ozzie Smith, but the position has become shallow enough across the league that Tejada's bat might, however diminished, still carry him at shortstop. As a result, the defending champions took a one-year chance on him as a replacement for ring-bearer Juan Uribe.

Yorvit Torrealba C

Born: **7/19/1978** Age: **32**
Bats: **R** Throws: **R** Height: **5' 11"** Weight: **190**
Breakout: **2%** Improve: **29%** Collapse: **17%**
Attrition: **24%** MLB: **85%**

Comparables:
Bo Diaz, Milt May, Greg Olson (77)

YEAR	TEAM	LVL	AGE	PA	R	2B	3B	HR	RBI	BB	SO	SB	CS	AVG/OBP/SLG	TAv	BABIP	BRR	FRAA	WARP
2008	COL	MLB	29	261	19	17	0	6	31	12	44	0	4	.246/.287/.394	.234	.268	-2.6	C -2	0.0
2009	COL	MLB	30	242	27	11	1	2	31	21	42	1	1	.291/.347/.380	.252	.341	0.0	C 0	0.8
2010	SDN	MLB	31	363	31	14	0	7	37	33	67	7	5	.271/.342/.379	.266	.320	2.0	C -1	1.8
2011	*TEX*	*MLB*	*32*	*321*	*35*	*15*	*1*	*5*	*31*	*26*	*56*	*4*	*2*	*.256/.318/.366*	*.244*	*.295*	*-0.4*	*C 0, 1B 0*	*0.8*

You would think that moving from Coors to Petco would have robbed Torrealba of any hint of offensive production, but the dimensions and cool air of his new park didn't keep him from posting his highest home-run-per-fly-ball rate since 2006, as the catcher hit .312/.394/.429 at home. He finished around his 90th-percentile PECOTA projection, a sign that we shouldn't expect him to repeat the act—the backstop's BABIP at Petco was an unsustainable .396. The Padres won't have to worry about Torrealba's regressing on their dime, as he elected to become a free agent and signed with the Rangers, automatically becoming the best all-around player (of a very weak bunch) they have had at the position since Ivan Rodriguez's heyday, albeit one who has never started more than 105 games in a season.

Will Venable RF

Born: **10/29/1982** Age: **28**
Bats: **L** Throws: **L** Height: **6' 2"** Weight: **205**
Breakout: **0%** Improve: **45%** Collapse: **4%**
Attrition: **12%** MLB: **81%**

Comparables:
Del Ennis, Lloyd Moseby, Mark Teahen (73)

YEAR	TEAM	LVL	AGE	PA	R	2B	3B	HR	RBI	BB	SO	SB	CS	AVG/OBP/SLG	TAv	BABIP	BRR	FRAA	WARP
2008	POR	AAA	25	496	70	26	4	14	58	44	103	7	3	.292/.359/.464	.291	.348	0.9	CF -14	1.8
2008	SDN	MLB	25	124	16	4	2	2	10	13	21	1	1	.264/.339/.391	.282	.307	1.3	CF 4	1.1
2009	POR	AAA	26	226	33	10	3	12	30	20	46	1	0	.260/.327/.520	.306	.274	0.1	CF -4	1.3
2009	SDN	MLB	26	324	38	14	2	12	38	25	89	6	1	.256/.321/.440	.268	.325	0.5	RF 3, CF -2	0.8
2010	SDN	MLB	27	445	60	11	7	13	51	45	128	29	7	.245/.324/.408	.270	.324	4.0	RF 5, LF 2	2.7
2011	*SDN*	*MLB*	*28*	*545*	*66*	*23*	*4*	*18*	*67*	*50*	*131*	*16*	*5*	*.257/.328/.435*	*.266*	*.309*	*0.0*	*CF -5, RF 2*	*1.2*

The narrative surrounding the late-blooming Venable has largely concerned his respective merits and shortcomings as a fourth outfielder and a full-time player, respectively. The former Princeton basketball and baseball standout's unadjusted numbers make him look like the former, but as with anyone who plays in Petco, those stats are meaningless unless taken in context. The proper adjustments reveal Venable to be not only deserving of full-time status, but well above average and one of the Padres' key contributors. Throw in quality defense in a corner and more than passable performance in center with range and an accurate arm, and you can see why Venable is an underappreciated piece of the Padres' puzzle. Like any lefty, Venable will never hit well at Petco (.221/.298/.379 at home since 2009), but his road numbers (.277/.348/.463) and defensive contributions more than make up for that unfortunate failing. A late-season change to his batting stance raised his elbow higher off the ground to create a shorter and straighter path to the ball and may mean fewer strikeouts and more hits to come in 2011.

Lance Zawadzki **INF**

Born: **5/26/1985** Age: **26**
Bats: **S** Throws: **R** Height: **5' 11"** Weight: **195**
Breakout: **3%** Improve: **19%** Collapse: **14%**
Attrition: **27%** MLB: **49%**

Comparables:
Omar Quintanilla, Brent Lillibridge, Clete Thomas (77)

YEAR	TEAM	LVL	AGE	PA	R	2B	3B	HR	RBI	BB	SO	SB	CS	AVG/OBP/SLG	TAv	BABIP	BRR	FRAA	WARP
2008	FTW	A	23	518	66	26	5	7	58	54	101	28	3	.273/.351/.399	.275	.332	1.9	SS -5, 2B -2	1.9
2009	LEL	A+	24	164	19	6	2	10	34	18	29	3	1	.276/.360/.552	.342	.283	-0.7	SS 1, 2B 1	1.8
2009	SAN	AA	24	392	59	19	5	5	43	44	74	14	1	.289/.372/.416	.292	.356	1.7	SS 9, 3B 1	3.7
2010	SAN	AA	25	161	21	5	1	4	17	13	34	7	1	.216/.280/.345	.241	.255	1.4	SS 0	0.4
2010	POR	AAA	25	248	34	10	1	1	16	21	57	5	5	.231/.298/.298	.228	.304	1.3	SS -4, 2B 1	-0.3
2010	SDN	MLB	25	42	4	2	0	0	1	5	7	1	0	.200/.286/.257	.214	.233	0.7	2B 0, SS 0	0.1
2011	*KCA*	*MLB*	*26*	*510*	*54*	*21*	*2*	*9*	*48*	*44*	*118*	*12*	*3*	*.236/.302/.353*	*.233*	*.291*	*0.3*	*SS 1, 2B 0*	*0.4*

Zawadzki's 2010 shattered the optimism surrounding his pursuit of a major-league career. He spent an awful month in the majors out of necessity, though he wasn't any better at Double-A or Triple-A in what was holistically an atrocious offensive season. The shortstop's strengths had formerly been his approach, bat speed, and ability to hit for power, but expectations may have been raised too high after a .356 BABIP made his 2009 stint in San Antonio look better than it was. His career still has some life: he has a strong arm and enough range to play up the middle, but he is 26 years old and time is running out for him to develop into even a utility infielder. His failure to hit and "ability" to be tolerable in the field at multiple positions must have summoned fond memories of Willie Bloomquist for the Royals, who claimed Zawadzki off waivers over the winter.

PITCHERS

Mike Adams

Born: **7/29/1978** Age: **32**
Bats: **R** Throws: **R** Height: **6' 5"** Weight: **190**
Breakout: **13%** Improve: **37%** Collapse: **21%**
Attrition: **10%** MLB: **72%**

Comparables:
Scot Shields, Scott Strickland, Juan Salas (69)

YEAR	TEAM	LVL	AGE	W	L	SV	G	GS	IP	H	HR	BB	SO	EqBB9	EqSO9	GB%	BABIP	WHIP	ERA	FRA	WARP
2008	SDN	MLB	29	2	3	0	54	0	65^1	49	7	19	74	2.6	10.2	45%	.264	1.04	2.48	3.18	1.4
2009	SDN	MLB	30	0	0	0	37	0	37	14	1	8	45	1.9	10.9	53%	.159	0.59	0.73	2.85	0.9
2010	SDN	MLB	31	4	1	0	70	0	66^2	48	2	23	73	3.1	9.9	41%	.271	1.07	1.76	2.34	2.0
2011	*SDN*	*MLB*	*32*	*3*	*2*	*0*	*60*	*0*	*63*	*51*	*5*	*23*	*66*	*3.3*	*9.3*	*45%*	*.283*	*1.17*	*2.61*	*2.84*	*1.2*

Over the last three seasons, Adams has held right-handers to a 519 OPS and lefties to a 511 mark. He has struck out 10.2 per nine with a K/BB ratio of almost four over that stretch. This isn't some Petco mirage: Adams has a 2.17 career road ERA with 81 whiffs in 78 2/3 innings for the Friars. His wide assortment of pitches—Adams owns a power slider, a four-seam fastball that averages over 93 mph and a two-seamer that gets ground balls—keeps hitters guessing, even more so because he can command all three. Adams, who was third among nonclosers in WXRL in 2010, must get through four years of arbitration before qualifying for free agency (the first of which came over the winter), so even if Heath Bell is dealt in July (or leaves as a free agent after the season), the Padres can count on continuing to have one of the preeminent relievers in the game as their closer for at least three seasons to come.

Heath Bell

Born: **9/29/1977** Age: **33**
Bats: **R** Throws: **R** Height: **6' 2"** Weight: **244**
Breakout: **17%** Improve: **36%** Collapse: **17%**
Attrition: **7%** MLB: **72%**

Comparables:
Roberto Hernandez, Lee Smith, J.R. Richard (60)

YEAR	TEAM	LVL	AGE	W	L	SV	G	GS	IP	H	HR	BB	SO	EqBB9	EqSO9	GB%	BABIP	WHIP	ERA	FRA	WARP
2008	SDN	MLB	30	6	6	0	74	0	78	66	5	28	71	3.2	8.2	47%	.281	1.24	3.58	3.77	1.2
2009	SDN	MLB	31	6	4	42	68	0	69^2	54	3	24	79	3.1	10.2	47%	.297	1.12	2.71	2.37	1.9
2010	SDN	MLB	32	6	1	47	67	0	70	56	1	28	86	3.6	11.1	45%	.322	1.21	1.93	2.12	2.1
2011	*SDN*	*MLB*	*33*	*4*	*2*	*27*	*74*	*0*	*77*	*61*	*4*	*29*	*83*	*3.4*	*9.7*	*46%*	*.295*	*1.18*	*2.56*	*2.78*	*1.5*

The next ad campaign for Wii Fit won't include Bell's wins above replacement, but it should—he has accumulated over 10 WXRL as the Padres' closer since he shed 25 pounds with the exercise software. Bell threw his mid-90s fastball 70 percent of the time in 2010 and picked up strikes on it nearly as often. His heater set up his wicked bender, which didn't generate a ton of whiffs, but was commanded so well that it landed for a strike more often than not. Both pitches helped him set career highs in strikeouts per nine and post yet another K/BB ratio over three and enabled him to avoid blowing a save from May 29 onward. Bell may not last the season as the Padres' closer, since impending free agency makes him a trade candidate, but he will survive without the warm embrace of Petco: Bell owns a 587 road OPS in his time with San Diego.

Simon Castro

Born: **4/9/1988** Age: **23**
Bats: **R** Throws: **R** Height: **6' 5"** Weight: **210**
Breakout: **7%** Improve: **9%** Collapse: **2%**
Attrition: **5%** MLB: **12%**

Comparables:
Jaime Garcia, Fernando Hernandez Jr., Jhonny Nunez (83)

YEAR	TEAM	LVL	AGE	W	L	SV	G	GS	IP	H	HR	BB	SO	EqBB9	EqSO9	GB%	BABIP	WHIP	ERA	FRA	WARP
2008	EUG	A-	20	2	3	0	15	15	65^1	54	3	29	64	4.0	8.8	49%	.285	1.49	4.00	5.02	0.4
2009	FTW	A	21	10	6	0	28	27	140^1	118	9	37	157	2.4	10.1	43%	.302	1.18	3.34	3.66	3.5
2010	SAN	AA	22	7	6	0	24	23	129^2	107	8	36	107	2.5	7.5	50%	.266	1.15	2.92	3.71	2.3
2011	*SDN*	*MLB*	*23*	*6*	*6*	*0*	*17*	*17*	*87^1*	*84*	*10*	*42*	*65*	*4.3*	*6.7*	*44%*	*.287*	*1.44*	*4.45*	*4.84*	*1.0*

Castro broke out in 2009 in the Midwest League, and his 2010 season was all about refining his already impressive stuff at Double-A. His four-seamer sits 92-94, but can touch 96, and his slider is sharp with late movement, coming in anywhere from the low- to mid-80s. His changeup was a poor offering coming into 2010, and he has a tendency to slow his delivery down when he throws it, which will need to be rectified in Triple-A. Castro is on pace to make his major-league debut in 2011, most likely as a late-season call-up. He could use the extra time in the minors to work on missing more bats and refining his command, but he has midrotation potential and may be a major-league starter by 2012.

Kevin Correia

Born: **8/24/1980** Age: **30**
Bats: **R** Throws: **R** Height: **6' 3"** Weight: **200**
Breakout: **11%** Improve: **37%** Collapse: **22%**
Attrition: **9%** MLB: **91%**

Comparables:
Ben McDonald, Kevin Millwood, Erik Hanson (81)

YEAR	TEAM	LVL	AGE	W	L	SV	G	GS	IP	H	HR	BB	SO	EqBB9	EqSO9	GB%	BABIP	WHIP	ERA	FRA	WARP
2008	SFN	MLB	27	3	8	0	25	19	110	141	15	46	66	3.8	5.4	39%	.330	1.74	6.05	6.00	-0.3
2009	SDN	MLB	28	12	11	0	33	33	198	194	17	64	142	2.9	6.5	46%	.294	1.32	3.91	4.26	2.1
2010	SDN	MLB	29	10	10	0	28	26	145	152	20	64	115	4.0	7.1	50%	.302	1.52	5.40	5.69	-0.9
2011	*PIT*	*MLB*	*30*	*8*	*8*	*0*	*23*	*23*	*127^2*	*135*	*14*	*49*	*86*	*3.5*	*6.1*	*45%*	*.303*	*1.44*	*4.50*	*4.89*	*1.9*

It was a tough season for Correia: he started out strong in April, sustaining the success he had found with the Padres in 2009, but his younger brother's death in a hiking accident in mid-May coincided—understandably—with a drop in his performance. From June on, Correia had a 5.95 ERA, 4.2 walks per nine, and an uncharacteristically high home-run rate. There are reasons to be optimistic about his 2011 season: his 4.27 SIERA was solid and tells us that he should be able to pitch to that level even if he continues to walk more batters than average, and his career high in strikeout rate despite major distractions was laudable, as was his continuing metamorphosis from a fly-ball pitcher into a ground-baller. That last point may not work out with the Pirates' infield defense behind him, but Correia's new deal demands that he brave Pittsburgh for two years regardless.

Ernesto Frieri

Born: **7/19/1985** Age: **25**
Bats: **R** Throws: **R** Height: **6' 2"** Weight: **200**
Breakout: **5%** Improve: **14%** Collapse: **4%**
Attrition: **16%** MLB: **23%**

Comparables:
Antonio Bastardo, Fabio Castro, Fernando Hernandez Jr. (76)

YEAR	TEAM	LVL	AGE	W	L	SV	G	GS	IP	H	HR	BB	SO	EqBB9	EqSO9	GB%	BABIP	WHIP	ERA	FRA	WARP
2008	LEL	A+	22	8	6	0	33	18	123^2	125	14	32	108	2.3	7.9	30%	.306	1.30	4.00	4.28	1.6
2009	SAN	AA	23	10	9	0	27	26	140^1	125	13	62	118	4.0	7.6	35%	.277	1.36	3.59	4.95	0.3
2009	SDN	MLB	23	0	0	0	2	0	2	0	0	1	2	4.5	9.0	0%	.000	0.50	0.00	-1.23	0.1
2010	POR	AAA	24	3	1	17	34	0	37^2	14	2	18	49	4.4	11.9	20%	.164	0.91	1.43	3.13	0.8
2010	SDN	MLB	24	1	1	0	33	0	31^2	18	2	17	41	4.8	11.7	24%	.235	1.11	1.71	1.56	1.2
2011	*SDN*	*MLB*	*25*	*6*	*5*	*2*	*38*	*12*	*94*	*86*	*12*	*48*	*82*	*4.6*	*7.8*	*36%*	*.283*	*1.42*	*4.21*	*4.57*	*0.8*

Frieri came up in mid-July when Mike Adams hit the disabled list, and when Adams returned, Frieri had pitched well enough that it was Ryan Webb who was sent down to Portland instead. The righty is a two-pitch reliever, but he uses them well: his heater averages 93 mph and misses 10 percent more bats than the average fastball, and he complements the pitch with a curve that induces plenty of swings-and-misses. His control could be better, but opponents don't often put the ball in play against him. Since he hasn't had problems with allowing homers, he is something of a Two True Outcomes reliever, which is fine when your K/BB ratio is 2.4 and you're in the back end of a pen. The trade of Webb and Edward Mujica to the Marlins will mean even more of those low-leverage innings for Frieri in 2011.

Jon Garland

Born: **9/27/1979** Age: **31**
Bats: **R** Throws: **R** Height: **6' 6"** Weight: **205**
Breakout: **10%** Improve: **40%** Collapse: **24%**
Attrition: **17%** MLB: **90%**

Comparables:
Jason Marquis, Mark Buehrle, Kyle Lohse (72)

YEAR	TEAM	LVL	AGE	W	L	SV	G	GS	IP	H	HR	BB	SO	EqBB9	EqSO9	GB%	BABIP	WHIP	ERA	FRA	WARP
2008	ANA	MLB	28	14	8	0	32	32	196^2	237	23	59	90	2.7	4.1	50%	.313	1.55	4.90	5.19	0.9
2009	ARI	MLB	29	8	11	0	27	27	167^2	188	19	52	83	2.8	4.5	48%	.298	1.47	4.29	4.98	1.3
2009	LAN	MLB	29	3	2	0	6	6	36^1	37	4	9	26	2.2	6.4	49%	.287	1.27	2.72	3.28	0.9
2010	SDN	MLB	30	14	12	0	33	33	200	176	20	87	136	3.9	6.1	53%	.265	1.35	3.47	4.16	2.2
2011	*LAN*	*MLB*	*31*	*12*	*12*	*0*	*34*	*34*	*205*	*219*	*22*	*70*	*108*	*3.1*	*4.7*	*49%*	*.295*	*1.40*	*4.37*	*4.75*	*2.5*

Taking advantage of Petco's dimensions and the defense behind him allowed Garland to have one of the most productive seasons of his career, but the Dodgers will find out that context is crucial after importing him over the winter. Garland is not a bad pitcher by any means—he can give a team 30-plus starts and around 200 innings of league-average work—but he pitched in front of an infield defense that allowed a .215 BABIP on grounders (the league average was .235) and in a park whose dimensions allowed him to elevate his four-seamer to induce whiffs without fear of the hitter's sending a ball into the bleachers. Garland set a career high in both strikeouts and strikeout rate while obtaining 25 percent of his outs on the ground, so losing the ability to throw caution to the winds is no small thing—removed from his 2010 setting, his 4.45 SIERA is closer to the truth than his 3.47 ERA.

Luke Gregerson

Born: **5/14/1984** Age: **27**
Bats: **L** Throws: **R** Height: **6' 3"** Weight: **200**
Breakout: **31%** Improve: **43%** Collapse: **18%**
Attrition: **9%** MLB: **70%**

Comparables:
Sergio Romo, Hong-Chih Kuo, Clay Zavada (77)

YEAR	TEAM	LVL	AGE	W	L	SV	G	GS	IP	H	HR	BB	SO	EqBB9	EqSO9	GB%	BABIP	WHIP	ERA	FRA	WARP
2008	SFD	AA	24	7	5	9	56	0	74^{1}	62	6	26	77	3.1	9.3	56%	.284	1.22	3.39	3.57	1.3
2009	SDN	MLB	25	2	4	1	72	0	75	62	3	30	93	3.6	11.2	47%	.314	1.27	3.12	3.01	1.7
2010	SDN	MLB	26	4	7	2	80	0	78^{1}	47	8	18	89	2.1	10.2	48%	.216	0.84	3.22	4.66	0.1
2011	*SDN*	*MLB*	*27*	*3*	*1*	*2*	*60*	*0*	*65^{2}*	*52*	*6*	*25*	*69*	*3.4*	*9.5*	*47%*	*.284*	*1.17*	*2.78*	*3.02*	*1.1*

Gregerson, like the other two-thirds of the bullpen's Big Three, was not developed by the Padres, but arrived via trade. The right-hander was the player to be named later in the Cardinals' deal for Khalil Greene and, over the past two years, has become another name in a long list of pitchers that former general manager Kevin Towers and his scouts outright stole. Gregerson has amassed 5.7 WXRL with the Padres, which would have ranked first among noncloser relievers on the Cards over that stretch by almost 2.5 wins. His 84-mph slider is his go-to offering: he throws it nearly 60 percent of the time and generates swings-and-misses on 22 percent of its trips to the plate. While he's more susceptible to southpaws than to right-handers, Gregerson's split isn't worth getting worked up about, given that he has held righties to a .162/.228/.253 line.

Mat Latos

Born: **12/9/1987** Age: **23**
Bats: **R** Throws: **R** Height: **6' 6"** Weight: **225**
Breakout: **18%** Improve: **39%** Collapse: **19%**
Attrition: **16%** MLB: **81%**

Comparables:
Phil Hughes, Yovani Gallardo, Scott Elarton (69)

YEAR	TEAM	LVL	AGE	W	L	SV	G	GS	IP	H	HR	BB	SO	EqBB9	EqSO9	GB%	BABIP	WHIP	ERA	FRA	WARP
2008	FTW	A	20	0	3	0	7	5	24^{2}	24	3	8	23	2.9	8.4	51%	.296	1.34	3.28	4.13	0.5
2009	FTW	A	21	3	0	0	4	2	25^{1}	10	1	3	27	1.1	9.6	45%	.164	0.51	0.36	2.51	0.8
2009	SAN	AA	21	5	1	0	9	9	47	32	0	9	46	1.7	8.8	41%	.256	0.89	1.91	2.87	1.4
2009	SDN	MLB	21	4	5	0	10	10	50^{2}	43	7	23	39	4.1	6.9	39%	.252	1.30	4.62	5.79	-0.3
2010	SDN	MLB	22	14	10	0	31	31	184^{2}	150	16	50	189	2.4	9.2	46%	.273	1.09	2.92	3.13	4.5
2011	*SDN*	*MLB*	*23*	*9*	*5*	*0*	*20*	*20*	*103*	*88*	*10*	*36*	*98*	*3.2*	*8.5*	*44%*	*.284*	*1.20*	*3.02*	*3.28*	*3.2*

Missing out on the playoffs may have been good for Latos, who surpassed his career high in innings pitched by 61 2/3 frames in his age-23 campaign. The Padres were more worried about the number of starts he made than the innings he threw: efficiency was his game, and he averaged fewer than 96 pitches per start. His late-season struggles were attributed to a lack of focus: Latos was visibly upset when he would fall behind, and he had an ERA of 7.19 in his losses with a K/BB ratio of just 2.0, compared with 1.50 and 5.1, respectively, in the rest of his starts. Latos seldom had cause to be flustered—he made a major-league record 15 consecutive starts of at least five innings pitched with two runs or fewer allowed—but his lack of self-control was noticeable enough that team officials and pitching coach Darren Balsley were moved to comment on it multiple times. Latos is as good as his numbers indicate, with a SIERA that wasn't far superior to his ERA, and if his mental approach becomes half as good as his stuff, he will be nigh impossible to beat.

Wade LeBlanc

Born: **8/7/1984** Age: **26**
Bats: **L** Throws: **L** Height: **6' 3"** Weight: **200**
Breakout: **13%** Improve: **39%** Collapse: **19%**
Attrition: **24%** MLB: **77%**

Comparables:
Scott Sanderson, Billy Hoeft, Garrett Olson (74)

YEAR	TEAM	LVL	AGE	W	L	SV	G	GS	IP	H	HR	BB	SO	EqBB9	EqSO9	GB%	BABIP	WHIP	ERA	FRA	WARP
2008	POR	AAA	23	11	9	0	26	25	138^{2}	136	21	42	139	2.7	9.0	37%	.304	1.33	5.32	5.45	0.4
2008	SDN	MLB	23	1	3	0	5	4	21^{1}	29	7	15	14	6.3	5.9	43%	.324	2.06	8.02	7.61	-0.4
2009	POR	AAA	24	4	9	0	24	20	121	109	15	31	95	2.3	7.1	45%	.265	1.17	3.87	3.88	2.1
2009	SDN	MLB	24	3	1	0	9	9	46^{1}	35	6	19	30	3.7	5.8	38%	.215	1.25	3.69	5.11	0.2
2010	SDN	MLB	25	8	12	0	26	25	146	157	24	51	110	3.1	6.8	36%	.304	1.44	4.25	3.98	2.0
2011	*SDN*	*MLB*	*26*	*10*	*8*	*0*	*25*	*25*	*137*	*136*	*20*	*51*	*108*	*3.3*	*7.0*	*41%*	*.288*	*1.36*	*4.22*	*4.58*	*1.9*

LeBlanc lost his job in the rotation after a disastrous August that saw him cough up a .285/.336/.562 opponent batting line and average just over 5 1/3 innings per start. His inability to go deep into games made the bullpen work overtime and helped touch off the chain of events that kept the Padres out of the playoffs. The trouble with LeBlanc is that he has no worthwhile complement to his fantastic changeup. It's impossible to survive on one pitch as a starter and even more difficult when that limitation is combined with an inability to locate a mid-80s four-seam fastball anywhere but the middle of the zone.

Cory Luebke

Born: **3/4/1985** Age: **26**
Bats: **R** Throws: **L** Height: **6' 4"** Weight: **215**
Breakout: **15%** Improve: **22%** Collapse: **10%**
Attrition: **25%** MLB: **43%**

Comparables:
Glen Perkins, David Huff, Jason Vargas (80)

YEAR	TEAM	LVL	AGE	W	L	SV	G	GS	IP	H	HR	BB	SO	EqBB9	EqSO9	GB%	BABIP	WHIP	ERA	FRA	WARP
2008	FTW	A	23	3	3	0	10	10	56	52	6	9	40	1.4	6.4	47%	.291	1.14	2.89	4.08	0.9
2008	LEL	A+	23	3	6	0	17	15	72^{1}	97	8	23	60	2.9	7.5	52%	.374	1.66	6.85	6.66	-0.7
2009	LEL	A+	24	8	2	0	14	14	88^{1}	73	3	17	80	1.7	8.2	57%	.289	1.08	2.34	2.70	2.7
2009	SAN	AA	24	3	2	0	9	9	41^{1}	38	3	15	32	3.3	7.0	43%	.276	1.33	3.70	3.83	0.7
2010	SAN	AA	25	5	1	0	10	8	56^{1}	41	2	12	44	1.9	7.1	46%	.234	0.98	2.40	3.67	0.9
2010	POR	AAA	25	5	0	0	9	9	57^{2}	42	6	17	44	2.7	6.9	41%	.225	1.03	2.97	3.98	0.9
2010	SDN	MLB	25	1	1	0	4	3	17^{2}	17	3	6	18	3.1	9.2	47%	.292	1.36	4.08	3.11	0.4
2011	*SDN*	*MLB*	*26*	*7*	*7*	*0*	*19*	*19*	*107*	*112*	*13*	*41*	*72*	*3.4*	*6.0*	*46%*	*.295*	*1.42*	*4.47*	*4.86*	*1.0*

Luebke began the year with an uncertain future as a starter, but another strong season at Triple-A and a commendable audition at the major league level earned him a 2011 job in San Diego's rotation. His stuff is just average; Luebke hits 89-91 with his four- and two-seamers to go with a slider/changeup combo, both of which are in the low- to mid-80s—but his command of all four pitches is a plus skill, and the southpaw's ability to put the ball wherever he wants makes up for his shortfall in stuff. Luebke needs to work on his sequencing against major-league hitters to keep them from guessing correctly and knocking balls out of the park, but his ground-ball rates and ability to hit the corners make him an intriguing pitcher to watch.

Edward Mujica

Born: **5/10/1984** Age: **27**
Bats: **R** Throws: **R** Height: **6' 2"** Weight: **220**
Breakout: **7%** Improve: **33%** Collapse: **19%**
Attrition: **9%** MLB: **65%**

Comparables:
David Wells, Shawn Kelley, Tom Niedenfuer (66)

YEAR	TEAM	LVL	AGE	W	L	SV	G	GS	IP	H	HR	BB	SO	EqBB9	EqSO9	GB%	BABIP	WHIP	ERA	FRA	WARP
2008	BUF	AAA	24	0	2	4	18	0	26	29	2	10	27	3.5	9.3	39%	.346	1.54	4.15	4.80	0.1
2008	CLE	MLB	24	3	2	0	33	0	38^{2}	46	5	10	27	2.3	6.3	31%	.328	1.47	6.75	6.80	-0.6
2009	SDN	MLB	25	3	5	2	67	4	93^{2}	101	14	20	76	1.9	7.3	40%	.306	1.29	3.94	4.05	1.2
2010	SDN	MLB	26	2	1	0	59	0	69^{2}	59	14	6	72	0.8	9.3	45%	.256	0.93	3.62	4.40	0.3
2011	*FLO*	*MLB*	*27*	*3*	*1*	*1*	*57*	*0*	*69^{2}*	*71*	*9*	*17*	*63*	*2.2*	*8.1*	*42%*	*.311*	*1.26*	*3.97*	*4.31*	*0.3*

Mujica is a polarizing reliever, and the fact that he was dealt to Florida in the Maybin trade suggests which side of the debate the Padres are on. He is dominant in controlling the strike zone, with 8.2 strikeouts per nine against 1.4 walks per nine in his Padre career—his 2010 K/BB ratio was *12.0* as a result of his allowing only six free passes in nearly 70 innings. On the other side of the fence—literally—you have Mujica's serious problem with the long ball. During the 2009-2010 seasons, Mujica was the only pitcher with more homers allowed than unintentional walks and at least 163 1/3 innings pitched (his total over that stretch). He almost never pitches inside, relying on the outside part of the plate and his excellent control to get by, but that tendency allows hitters to cheat and keeps Mujica a fungible middle reliever who no longer has the advantage of Petco's generous dimensions on his side.

Aaron Poreda

Born: **10/1/1986** Age: **24**
Bats: **L** Throws: **L** Height: **6' 6"** Weight: **240**
Breakout: **9%** Improve: **12%** Collapse: **6%**
Attrition: **10%** MLB: **21%**

Comparables:
Donald Veal, Waldis Joaquin, Sean Gallagher (70)

YEAR	TEAM	LVL	AGE	W	L	SV	G	GS	IP	H	HR	BB	SO	EqBB9	EqSO9	GB%	BABIP	WHIP	ERA	FRA	WARP
2008	WNS	A+	21	5	5	0	12	12	73^{1}	67	1	18	46	2.2	5.6	55%	.278	1.19	3.32	3.51	2.0
2008	BIR	AA	21	3	4	0	15	15	87^{2}	81	5	22	72	2.3	7.4	50%	.300	1.21	2.98	2.67	3.3
2009	BIR	AA	22	5	4	0	11	11	64^{1}	47	1	35	69	4.9	9.7	52%	.284	1.37	2.38	2.17	2.6
2009	POR	AAA	22	0	3	0	7	6	32^{2}	28	3	37	30	10.2	8.3	50%	.281	2.08	7.16	7.00	-0.7
2009	CHA	MLB	22	1	0	0	10	0	11	9	0	8	12	6.5	9.8	57%	.321	1.64	2.45	2.88	0.3
2009	SDN	MLB	22	0	0	0	4	0	2^{1}	1	0	5	0	19.3	0.0	43%	.143	2.57	3.86	6.13	-0.0
2010	SAN	AA	23	0	1	0	19	0	25	18	1	26	25	9.4	9.0	62%	.266	1.92	2.52	2.74	0.7
2010	POR	AAA	23	1	1	0	20	1	29	13	0	38	22	11.8	6.8	43%	.181	1.90	4.97	5.70	-0.1
2011	*SDN*	*MLB*	*24*	*5*	*5*	*0*	*30*	*13*	*92*	*83*	*7*	*65*	*71*	*6.3*	*6.9*	*48%*	*.282*	*1.60*	*4.63*	*5.03*	*0.3*

Poreda was one of four arms to come over in the Jake Peavy trade of 2009. Although he was considered the jewel of the deal, he is now the least likely to contribute. His 2010 season makes one ponder the nature of the strike zone—French philosopher René Descartes felt that our senses were fallible and that the nature of reality itself was uncertain. If a hurler can never find the plate, does it, in fact, exist? With 64 free passes, eight hit batsmen, and three wild pitches in 54 innings, the only reality Poreda can be certain of is the one outside the strike zone. His lack of control is extreme enough that a reversal of his strikeout and walk rates would give you Daniel Cabrera; unfortunately, even being Daniel Cabrera isn't enough to hold down a major league roster spot.

Cesar Ramos

Born: **6/22/1984** Age: **27**
Bats: **L** Throws: **L** Height: **6' 2"** Weight: **205**
Breakout: **4%** Improve: **7%** Collapse: **0%**
Attrition: **5%** MLB: **7%**

Comparables:
Enrique Gonzalez, Matt Chico, Mike Ekstrom (85)

YEAR	TEAM	LVL	AGE	W	L	SV	G	GS	IP	H	HR	BB	SO	EqBB9	EqSO9	GB%	BABIP	WHIP	ERA	FRA	WARP
2008	POR	AAA	24	9	11	0	28	27	149^{2}	183	17	57	105	3.4	6.3	46%	.341	1.64	5.29	5.03	1.0
2009	POR	AAA	25	5	6	0	15	15	76^{2}	84	7	31	45	3.6	5.3	56%	.295	1.50	3.99	3.82	1.4
2009	SDN	MLB	25	0	1	0	5	2	14^{2}	19	0	4	10	2.5	6.1	47%	.396	1.57	3.07	0.71	0.8
2010	POR	AAA	26	6	7	0	30	15	96	90	7	43	63	4.0	5.9	48%	.290	1.41	3.28	2.64	3.1
2010	SDN	MLB	26	0	1	0	14	0	81	18	1	4	9	4.3	9.7	41%	.515	2.64	11.88	7.20	-0.3
2011	*TBA*	*MLB*	*27*	*8*	*10*	*0*	*37*	*22*	*130^{1}*	*151*	*16*	*58*	*68*	*4.0*	*4.7*	*47%*	*.309*	*1.60*	*5.37*	*5.83*	*0.0*

Ramos doesn't have a true out pitch, and as a pitch-to-contact guy, he allows his share of balls in play. That was the case in his first 23 innings with the Friars, for whom Ramos has walked 3.1 per nine with a BABIP of .363—small-sample caveats apply, of course, but it's hard not to know that a pitcher with fringe-average stuff and a tendency to seek out contact is going to give up plenty of hits. His ERA was shinier in Portland, but there his K/BB ratio was just 1.5, even worse than his career major-league rate of 1.8. Moving to the American League East as part of the Jason Bartlett trade won't make things any easier for him, but the Rays will give him a chance to be a LOOGY in their new-look pen nonetheless.

Clayton Richard

Born: **9/12/1983** Age: **27**
Bats: **L** Throws: **L** Height: **6' 5"** Weight: **240**
Breakout: **13%** Improve: **38%** Collapse: **9%**
Attrition: **22%** MLB: **73%**

Comparables:
Paul Maholm, Don Newcombe, Dana Eveland (73)

YEAR	TEAM	LVL	AGE	W	L	SV	G	GS	IP	H	HR	BB	SO	EqBB9	EqSO9	GB%	BABIP	WHIP	ERA	FRA	WARP
2008	BIR	AA	24	6	6	0	13	13	83^{2}	66	2	16	53	1.7	5.7	52%	.254	1.03	2.47	3.23	2.2
2008	CHR	AAA	24	6	0	0	7	7	44	33	3	4	33	0.8	6.8	57%	.238	0.86	2.45	3.19	1.4
2008	CHA	MLB	24	2	5	0	13	8	47^{2}	61	5	13	29	2.5	5.5	51%	.333	1.55	6.04	6.17	-0.1
2009	CHA	MLB	25	4	3	0	26	14	89	94	10	37	66	3.7	6.7	49%	.310	1.51	4.65	5.21	0.7
2009	SDN	MLB	25	5	2	0	12	12	64	60	7	34	48	4.8	6.8	53%	.283	1.47	4.08	4.69	0.4
2010	SDN	MLB	26	14	9	0	33	33	201^{2}	206	16	78	153	3.5	6.8	47%	.312	1.43	3.75	3.97	2.6
2011	*SDN*	*MLB*	*27*	*10*	*9*	*0*	*28*	*28*	*160^{1}*	*164*	*15*	*65*	*105*	*3.7*	*5.9*	*48%*	*.301*	*1.43*	*4.25*	*4.62*	*1.9*

Richard has turned out to be the prize of the Jake Peavy trade, crossing the 200-inning threshold for the first time in 2010 while improving his K/BB ratio and preserving his slight ground-ball tendencies as the Padres' third-best starter. The lefty showed some potential to become a better strikeout pitcher, though he needs to be more consistent in throwing his changeup, cutter, and slider for strikes for that to come to fruition. He has a future as an above-average starter regardless—more whiffs would just lift him even higher above sea level. Avoiding Coors Field would also help; Richard gave up 17 runs in 15 1/3 innings pitched there in 2010, tacking half a run onto his seasonal ERA.

Adam Russell

Born: **4/14/1983** Age: **28**
Bats: **R** Throws: **R** Height: **6' 8"** Weight: **250**
Breakout: **1%** Improve: **6%** Collapse: **1%**
Attrition: **6%** MLB: **9%**

Comparables:
Ronald Belisario, Alay Soler, Steven Jackson (83)

YEAR	TEAM	LVL	AGE	W	L	SV	G	GS	IP	H	HR	BB	SO	EqBB9	EqSO9	GB%	BABIP	WHIP	ERA	FRA	WARP
2008	CHR	AAA	25	3	2	0	25	0	37^{1}	28	3	19	28	4.6	6.8	46%	.229	1.29	2.90	5.07	0.1
2008	CHA	MLB	25	4	0	0	22	0	26	30	1	10	22	3.5	7.6	45%	.349	1.62	5.19	4.40	0.2
2009	CHR	AAA	26	2	2	5	34	0	56^{1}	39	5	18	51	2.9	8.2	56%	.236	1.07	3.20	4.60	0.3
2009	SDN	MLB	26	3	1	0	15	0	12^{1}	13	0	11	14	8.0	10.2	44%	.361	1.95	3.65	3.14	0.3
2010	POR	AAA	27	4	9	14	50	0	51^{2}	58	4	32	51	5.6	9.0	45%	.351	1.82	4.88	4.29	0.5
2010	SDN	MLB	27	0	0	0	12	0	15^{2}	14	0	5	18	2.9	10.3	50%	.350	1.21	4.02	4.11	0.1
2011	*TBA*	*MLB*	*28*	*4*	*1*	*2*	*76*	*0*	*97*	*100*	*10*	*50*	*69*	*4.6*	*6.4*	*46%*	*.304*	*1.54*	*4.66*	*5.06*	*-0.6*

Russell started to strike hitters out with his mid-90s fastball in 2009, and he relies heavily on the heater, throwing it 67 percent of the time in his 54 career big-league innings. His command is no better than average, but he has induced plenty of weak contact in the minors to make up for that weakness and has never exhibited any problems with the long ball. Russell was the key piece in the Jason Bartlett deal with the Rays and will fill one of the many holes that free agency poked in the Tampa Bay bullpen this past winter.

Tim Stauffer

Born: **6/2/1982** Age: **29**
Bats: **R** Throws: **R** Height: **6' 1"** Weight: **214**
Breakout: **8%** Improve: **29%** Collapse: **12%**
Attrition: **10%** MLB: **63%**

Comparables:
Mark Redman, Craig Swan, Larry Dierker (76)

YEAR	TEAM	LVL	AGE	W	L	SV	G	GS	IP	H	HR	BB	SO	EqBB9	EqSO9	GB%	BABIP	WHIP	ERA	FRA	WARP
2009	POR	AAA	27	2	1	0	4	4	23	16	1	4	16	1.6	6.3	42%	.221	0.87	2.35	3.51	0.5
2009	SDN	MLB	27	4	7	0	14	14	73	71	8	34	53	4.2	6.5	46%	.292	1.51	3.58	3.84	1.2
2010	SDN	MLB	28	6	5	0	32	7	82^{2}	65	3	24	61	2.6	6.6	56%	.263	1.10	1.85	2.64	2.2
2011	*SDN*	*MLB*	*29*	*7*	*6*	*0*	*41*	*16*	*121*	*123*	*11*	*46*	*78*	*3.4*	*5.8*	*47%*	*.295*	*1.39*	*4.12*	*4.48*	*1.2*

Stauffer succeeded at everything he put his hand to in 2010: out of the bullpen, he amassed 1.1 WXRL in 43 innings; as a starter in September, he posted a 2.10 ERA in 34 1/3 innings pitched against the third-toughest competition of any pitcher in the NL with as many innings; and finally, as a pretend doctor, Stauffer correctly self-diagnosed his need for an appendectomy using the WebMD app on his iPhone. The key to his success was a fastball makeover; in 2009, his four-seamer had more vertical movement and less velocity, but the 2010 version exchanged the vertical for horizontal and added an average of two miles per hour. The result was a career-high ground-ball rate, a 1.8 G/F ratio, and groundouts at double the rate of 2009. Expecting another sub-two ERA would be foolhardy, but Stauffer will be San Diego's second-best starter in 2011.

Joe Thatcher

Born: **4/10/1981** Age: **30**
Bats: **L** Throws: **L** Height: **6' 2"** Weight: **230**
Breakout: **8%** Improve: **19%** Collapse: **17%**
Attrition: **6%** MLB: **47%**

Comparables:
Roberto Hernandez, Lee Smith, Mike Schooler (71)

YEAR	TEAM	LVL	AGE	W	L	SV	G	GS	IP	H	HR	BB	SO	EqBB9	EqSO9	GB%	BABIP	WHIP	ERA	FRA	WARP
2008	POR	AAA	27	5	2	3	37	0	39	38	2	11	44	2.5	10.2	55%	.330	1.31	2.54	2.17	1.5
2008	SDN	MLB	27	0	4	0	25	0	25^{2}	42	4	13	17	4.6	6.0	45%	.404	2.14	8.42	6.16	-0.4
2009	SDN	MLB	28	1	0	0	52	0	45	37	2	18	55	3.6	11.0	44%	.321	1.31	2.80	2.19	1.6
2010	SDN	MLB	29	1	0	0	65	0	35	23	1	7	45	1.8	11.6	44%	.265	0.89	1.29	1.56	1.4
2011	*SDN*	*MLB*	*30*	*4*	*2*	*0*	*74*	*0*	*61^{1}*	*52*	*4*	*22*	*63*	*3.2*	*9.3*	*46%*	*.298*	*1.20*	*2.90*	*3.15*	*0.9*

The source of Thatcher's microscopic ERA last season was an anomalous showing against right-handed hitters. Even without reproducing that performance, Thatcher has value to the Padres due to striking out over 38 percent of the left-handers he has faced in the last two years, a rate that places him fifth in the majors (minimum 100 lefties faced). A left shoulder strain kept him off the mound for most of April, but he still appeared in 65 games and allowed only one run between July 9 and the end of the season. He won't be that unstoppable again unless manager Bud Black hides him from right-handers wherever possible.

Ryan Webb

Born: **2/5/1986** Age: **25**
Bats: **R** Throws: **R** Height: **6' 6"** Weight: **215**
Breakout: **4%** Improve: **8%** Collapse: **0%**
Attrition: **5%** MLB: **10%**

Comparables:
Edgar Gonzalez, Matt Chico, Jason Vargas (83)

YEAR	TEAM	LVL	AGE	W	L	SV	G	GS	IP	H	HR	BB	SO	EqBB9	EqSO9	GB%	BABIP	WHIP	ERA	FRA	WARP
2008	MID	AA	22	9	8	0	25	22	130	165	12	44	94	3.0	6.5	51%	.349	1.62	5.19	5.33	1.0
2009	SAC	AAA	23	7	1	2	31	2	45^{2}	57	3	15	39	3.0	7.7	51%	.375	1.62	4.33	2.92	1.3
2009	SDN	MLB	23	2	1	0	28	0	25^{2}	27	3	11	19	3.9	6.7	58%	.289	1.52	3.86	4.07	0.3
2010	POR	AAA	24	1	0	1	17	0	20^{2}	12	1	5	23	2.2	10.2	65%	.229	0.84	0.87	3.02	0.4
2010	SDN	MLB	24	3	1	0	54	0	59	64	1	19	44	2.9	6.7	62%	.335	1.42	2.90	1.75	2.3
2011	*FLO*	*MLB*	*25*	*5*	*3*	*0*	*68*	*5*	*99*	*120*	*12*	*40*	*71*	*3.6*	*6.4*	*50%*	*.338*	*1.61*	*5.48*	*5.95*	*-0.9*

Webb doesn't whiff many hitters for someone with mid-90s heat and wicked movement on all of his pitches, since his irregular release points prevent him from hitting his spots consistently. Last June and September—months during which Webb combined for 28 punchouts in 28 1/3 innings against just seven walks—offer the clearest picture of his potential, but things haven't always gone so well for the imposing right-hander. When the Marlins dangled Cameron Maybin in exchange for Webb and a mutable Mujica, the Friars did the right thing and sent their replaceable pieces packing. Webb may yet grow into his stuff, which would give the Marlins the dominating bullpen presence they crave.

Chris Young

Born: **5/25/1979** Age: **32**
Bats: **R** Throws: **R** Height: **6' 10"** Weight: **250**
Breakout: **9%** Improve: **23%** Collapse: **11%**
Attrition: **10%** MLB: **51%**

Comparables:
Jaret Wright, Aaron Heilman, Tyler Yates (64)

YEAR	TEAM	LVL	AGE	W	L	SV	G	GS	IP	H	HR	BB	SO	EqBB9	EqSO9	GB%	BABIP	WHIP	ERA	FRA	WARP
2008	SDN	MLB	29	7	6	0	18	18	102^{1}	84	13	48	93	4.2	8.2	24%	.255	1.30	3.96	3.70	2.0
2009	SDN	MLB	30	4	6	0	14	14	76	70	12	40	50	4.7	5.9	33%	.250	1.47	5.21	5.56	-0.1
2010	SDN	MLB	31	2	0	0	4	4	20	10	1	11	15	5.0	6.8	32%	.164	1.05	0.90	1.86	0.9
2011	*SDN*	*MLB*	*32*	*9*	*6*	*0*	*22*	*22*	*112*	*91*	*13*	*55*	*94*	*4.4*	*7.5*	*38%*	*.253*	*1.29*	*3.43*	*3.73*	*2.8*

There was a time when Young was a successful starter despite below-average stuff. From 2006 through 2008, his cumulative SIERA was 4.04 while his actual ERA was 3.44—the difference can be chalked up to Petco Park, as well as Young's tendency to generate shallow fly balls. His velocity has steadily fallen over the years, thanks to repeated injuries: whereas his fastball sat around 88-90 in his glory years, it has been closer to 83-85 ever since, and the difference was apparent in Young's subpar combined SIERA for 2009 and 2010 (5.30). Petco and Will Venable's defense enabled Young to keep runs off the board in his brief 2010 action, but it came as no surprise when the Padres declined his option for 2011. Instead, the Mets snapped him up to spend another year in a park with large dimensions.

LINEOUTS

HITTERS

PLAYER	TEAM	LVL	AGE	PA	R	2B	3B	HR	RBI	BB	SO	SB-CS	AVG/OBP/SLG	TAv	BABIP	BRR	FRAA	WARP
INF C. Figueroa*	LEL	A+	23	578	88	25	3	4	66	81	54	26-9	.303/.408/.392	.307	.328	1.4	2B -6, SS -3	3.7
SS J. Galvez	FTW	A	19	466	64	19	3	10	49	58	121	18-7	.259/.360/.397	.274	.343	1.7	SS -7, 2B -2	1.8
OF J. Gerut*	POR	AAA	32	61	7	4	0	1	11	7	5	0-0	.302/.393/.434	.275	.319	-1.1	RF -3, CF -2	-0.4
	MIL	MLB	32	74	7	4	1	2	8	3	17	0-1	.197/.230/.366	.243	.231	-0.9	CF 0, LF 0	-0.1
	BRR	Rk	32	58	11	5	0	2	11	9	3	0-0	.347/.448/.571	.374	.341	0.3	CF 2, RF 1	1.1
OF C. Hunter*	SAN	AA	22	317	34	14	3	4	38	31	22	9-7	.308/.375/.423	.290	.318	-0.6	CF -2	1.6
	POR	AAA	22	285	42	13	3	3	26	16	22	5-1	.263/.305/.370	.247	.270	1.2	CF 6, LF 0	1.0
OF R. Liriano	FTW	A	19	201	21	11	1	2	20	10	54	11-6	.191/.234/.293	.204	.254	0.1	RF -1, CF 3	-0.5
	LEL	A+	19	55	3	2	0	1	6	5	12	3-0	.220/.291/.320	.269	.270	-0.1	RF 0	0.1
	EUG	A-	19	225	35	13	6	0	12	17	53	17-7	.271/.335/.394	.284	.362	0.0	RF 2, CF -2	1.0
C L. Martinez	SAN	AA	25	410	48	16	1	2	31	49	59	3-2	.282/.368/.349	.286	.331	-1.4	C 1	2.8
OF R. Noel	FTW	A	21	52	3	0	1	0	7	5	8	3-0	.136/.269/.182	.173	.167	-0.9	CF 2	-0.2
	EUG	A-	21	142	22	2	2	1	15	25	24	14-3	.277/.426/.357	.313	.341	0.0	CF 8	1.9
OF W. Pena	POR	AAA	28	159	28	6	0	9	34	15	45	0-1	.324/.390/.556	.328	.416	1.4	1B -1, LF 0	1.4
3B E. Rincon	FTW	A	19	565	72	35	1	13	69	44	95	1-2	.250/.315/.399	.259	.283	0.9	3B -11	0.4
C C. Stewart	POR	AAA	28	309	31	14	2	7	39	30	38	1-0	.248/.337/.395	.256	.260	0.3	C 1, 1B -2	1.1
CF D. Tate	PDR	Rk	19	107	19	5	0	2	10	15	41	7-1	.222/.336/.344	.268	.375	0.6	CF -3, RF -2	0.3
OF B. Tekotte	LEL	A+	23	241	41	17	1	8	27	36	46	22-8	.310/.419/.522	.355	.369	0.4	CF -11	2.0
	SAN	AA	23	301	44	8	7	10	37	26	63	6-9	.250/.324/.444	.282	.288	1.5	CF 1, LF -1	1.7
OF E. Williams*	FTW	A	19	447	53	25	5	5	59	51	131	10-5	.244/.333/.372	.255	.349	1.2	LF -3, CF -2	0.5

Cole Figueroa walked more often than he struck out in 2010, and his on-base percentage exceeded his slugging for the second straight season. Without power to worry pitchers, he will see more strikes as pitchers challenge him at the higher levels, but if he can keep drawing walks, he will remain intriguing. He'll continue his career in the Rays' system after becoming part of the Jason Bartlett swap. ⊘ **Jonathan Galvez** is 19 years old and loaded with tools, but he's a walking disaster at shortstop. He made 40 errors in 103 games last season, and while scouts believe that his tools will translate into quality defense at the position, he has plenty of practice reps ahead of him. His strike-zone recognition is solid for his age, though he is sometimes a little preoccupied with power at the expense of selectivity. ⊘ It looked as if **Jody Gerut** had revived his career in 2008 with a strong year at the plate, but since then, the outfielder has been defense-first, as evidenced by his 643 OPS over the following two seasons. He hit well in Triple-A in 2010, which shouldn't be surprising for a 32-year-old; the Padres are keeping him on mostly for inexpensive depth at the upper levels. ⊘ A modest walk rate not seen since 2007 earned **Cedric Hunter** his first stint at Triple-A, but once he got there, those free passes vanished as quickly as they had appeared. Even at the lower levels, his swing generated mostly singles, and he needs those walks to offset his lack of power. ⊘ **Rymer Liriano** turned 19 in late June, but that didn't stop him from touring three levels of A-ball in 2010. The Dominican remains very raw, and there are times when every pitch he sees doubles as a pitch he likes, but his 2009 rookie-level campaign didn't deceive in suggesting that he would hit. ⊘ **Luis Martinez**'s approach at the plate works (11 percent walk rate against a 14 percent punchout rate), but he lacks power. He has thrown out 34 percent of attempted base thieves in his four years in the minors, including 31 percent at San Antonio in 2010, which makes him a worthy Triple-A catcher with potential as a major-league backup. ⊘ **Rico Noel** is another player with more patience than pop, but he is also a grinder who gets the most out of the tools he does possess. The fifth-round selection is just five-foot-nine and 165 pounds, which limits him to singles power, but he is a plus runner and an asset in center. He will get a second chance to succeed at Single-A in 2011. ⊘ **Wily Mo Pena** split the season between the Mets' and Padres' Triple-A affiliates, and at least while in Portland, he mashed as expected. When asked about a potential Pena call-up in September, general manager Jed Hoyer attempted to answer tactfully by mentioning how highly San Diego valued defensive skill in its outfielders. ⊘ **Edinson Rincon** followed up a strong campaign in the Northwest League with a poor showing at Single-A, where his slash line dropped precipitously across the board. He is very young—he turned 20 in mid-August—so there is time for his raw skills at the plate to translate into something that might make up for his glove. At present, Rincon looks like a DH playing third base. ⊘ **Chris Stewart** has the perfect blend of defense and an inability to hit that will keep him employed as a backup catcher for the better part of the next decade. Run to your bookie, and put money on his being a Red Sox backstop within the next five years. ⊘ **Donovan Tate** has spent more time injured than healthy since signing. Coming out of high school, he had potential as a 30-homer, 30-steal center fielder with quality defense highlighted by a strong arm. Now 20 and with just over 100 professional plate appearances to his name, he is well behind the development curve. **Blake Tekotte** is a little guy with decent speed and some defensive ability in the outfield, but the lefty also has some thump in his swing. A .198 ISO in pitcher-friendly San Antonio following a promotion and strong campaign at High-A is noteworthy, though he is 23 and has to work on getting caught less often on the bases. One of the better athletes in the 2009 draft, **Everett Williams** is a very compact athlete who has been plagued by some sizable holes in his swing. Williams can draw a walk, but he whiffs nearly three times as often—even with a .352 BABIP, his batting average was just .244.

PITCHERS

PLAYER	TEAM	LVL	AGE	W	L	SV	IP	H	HR	BB	SO	EqBB9	EqSO9	GB%	BABIP	WHIP	ERA	FRA	WARP
A. Bass	LEL	A+	22	8	7	0	132^{1}	124	9	20	109	1.4	7.4	54%	.296	1.10	3.13	4.36	1.4
D. Carter	FTW	A	23	1	4	0	38	34	6	24	28	5.7	6.6	48%	.252	1.68	6.63	6.92	-0.3
	EUG	A-	23	1	2	0	61	69	8	18	55	2.7	8.1	44%	.343	1.54	4.72	3.98	1.0
B. Gomes	SAN	AA	25	7	2	1	72^{1}	52	2	25	93	3.1	11.6	43%	.294	1.08	1.87	2.74	1.9
J. Hefner	SAN	AA	24	11	8	0	167^{2}	156	11	51	115	2.7	6.2	42%	.287	1.27	2.95	3.47	3.3
R. Liz	POR	AAA	27	8	8	0	123	128	20	38	109	2.8	8.0	39%	.307	1.42	4.83	4.68	1.2
M. Lollis	FTW	A	19	5	2	0	54^{1}	47	3	13	45	2.2	7.5	46%	.286	1.15	1.66	1.90	2.9
	EUG	A-	19	2	2	0	34^{2}	21	0	8	24	2.1	6.3	53%	.216	0.88	2.86	3.76	0.3
L. Perdomo	POR	AAA	26	4	6	1	82	76	7	34	49	3.7	5.4	52%	.269	1.38	3.40	5.00	0.4
	SDN	MLB	26	0	0	0	1	1	1	0	0	0.0	0.0	50%	.000	1.00	9.00	17.18	-0.2
A. Portillo	EUG	A-	18	2	6	0	62	55	2	40	62	5.8	9.0	54%	.312	1.61	4.79	5.71	-0.5
K. Sampson	EUG	A-	19	3	3	0	43	35	4	17	58	3.6	12.1	50%	.320	1.26	3.56	4.96	0.1
E. Scribner	SAN	AA	24	4	5	16	66	51	6	15	81	2.0	11.0	47%	.289	1.08	2.45	2.82	1.4
M. Watt*	FTW	A	21	6	6	0	125	128	5	37	105	2.7	7.6	48%	.321	1.39	3.67	3.60	3.4

Polished pitcher **Anthony Bass** posted a 3.13 ERA despite stranding just 65 percent of his baserunners. His fastball/changeup/breaking ball combination isn't special, but he can put the ball where he wants to, as evidenced by his 1.4 walks per nine innings at High-A this season. His command imparts back-of-the-rotation potential, though his stuff is just as likely to limit him to middle relief. Acquired in the Jake Peavy trade, **Dexter Carter** profiled well for a role in relief, and he may have become a permanent bullpen occupant after a disastrous 2010 that saw him demoted to Low-A. The right-hander is tall and boasts plus velocity, but he didn't always know where the ball was going last season and couldn't miss bats when he did. **Brandon Gomes** has an impressive track record that has been built almost entirely with his curveball, but there are questions about how successful he can be at the higher levels. It's hard to argue with his K/BB ratios or low, low ERA, but those numbers suggest more dominance than the 26-year-old Double-A reliever can actually offer. The Rays will find out whether he's any good, as the potential sleeper is now their property. **Jeremy Hefner**'s ERA is nifty, but his diminished strikeout rate following a promotion to Double-A was alarming. He doesn't have overpowering stuff—his fastball sits 89-91, and he induces far more fly balls than grounders—and he has made it this far by relying on command. Entering his age-25 season, Hefner is as old as the original Hef's latest bride and needs to regain those misplaced whiffs before more advanced hitters make him pay. **Radhames Liz** finally seems to know where the ball is going when it comes out of his hand, but all too often, that destination turns out to be the bleachers, thanks to its tendency to stay straight and elevated. His improved control offers hope that his above-average velocity could play in relief, but until Liz throws better strikes, homeritis will hold him back. **Matt Lollis** didn't turn 20 until September, but he is already comparable in size to the massive Kyle Blanks. Whereas Blanks is a power-hitting outfielder, Lollis is a power-slinging pitcher: he lives in the mid-90s with his naturally sinking fastball and has an unusually clean delivery for someone of his age and size, all of which translates to 2011 breakout potential. **Luis Perdomo** may have a future as a reliever, thanks to a mid-90s fastball and an 88-mph slider, but he hasn't solved Triple-A yet and will be 27 this year. The Padres re-signed the right-hander shortly after nontendering him in December, which leaves him competing for a spot in a stacked bullpen. **Adys Portillo** has not developed as fast as his $2 million signing bonus may have suggested he would, but he was only 18 in his second pro campaign. His fastball already consistently reaches the 94-95 range, but both his command and his control need work: Portillo's strikeout rate climbed to a batter per inning, but his K/BB ratio at Low-A was just 1.6, and that came with five hit batsmen and 12 wild pitches in 62 innings. **Keyvius Sampson** has a powerful arm that belies his small stature. He was held back in spring training, but dominant when on the mound; the right-hander sits around 95 but can touch 97 with his fastball, which helped him whiff over 12 batters per inning at Low-A. Elbow soreness was a problem. **Evan Scribner** repeated Double-A in 2010 and finished with yet another impressive ERA, but his success has stemmed from polished command rather than pure stuff. The right-hander's velocity is nothing special, but the Padres will have room for him at Triple-A, where he could eventually turn into a major-league-quality middle reliever—there are worse things than pitchers who can consistently hit their spots. If all else fails, he can resort to publishing trade books. The Dodgers drafted **Michael Watt**, but he has pitched for the Padres for the last two years. He has generally started, and while he has made only 16 relief appearances with the Friars, his future lies in the pen. Watt is left-handed, so he will get chances, but his velocity is average and his curve isn't much better, which leaves him in danger of being outshone by brighter-burning bulbs.

MANAGER: BUD BLACK

YEAR	TEAM	W-L	Pythag +/-	Avg PC	100+ P	120+ P	QS	BQS	REL	REL w Zero R	IBB	Subs	PH	PH Avg	PH HR	SB2	CS2	SB3	CS3	SAC Att	SAC %	POS SAC	Squeeze	Swing	In Play
2008	SDN	63-99	-3	91.0	49	3	74	4	490	291	61	31	285	.198	3	34	17	2	0	83	71.1%	18	1	123	93
2009	SDN	75-87	9	91.0	47	1	73	4	527	349	58	43	263	.248	9	72	23	10	5	116	63.8%	38	2	123	90
2010	SDN	90-72	-2	95.0	55	0	85	3	499	364	51	69	278	.206	9	114	47	10	1	114	69.3%	44	2	135	98

Black won National League Manager of the Year honors by virtue of overseeing the club whose prospects for success had been most underrated in the spring, but part of the reason for the Padres' surprising performance was his steady hand at the helm. Black employed a more aggressive approach on the bases last season, and the Friars finished second in the NL in steals after an eighth-place showing in 2009. Ensconced in Petco's low-run environment, the Padres could afford to take more chances on the basepaths, which made his more frequent green lights a welcome development. Black drew upon the team's bench depth in both the infield and the outfield, using more subs than he ever had previously, despite wielding a more talented roster. His bullpen management was also noteworthy: not a single Padres starter reached the 120-pitch threshold, thanks to his willingness to trust a deep and talented collection of relievers in order to avoid unnecessarily taxing his young rotation. Continuing to play the injured Scott Hairston when he had superior outfield options at his disposal was a problem, but that was the lone blemish on an otherwise strong season of skippering.

San Francisco Giants

The 2010 world champion San Francisco Giants offered an important lesson in the value of marginal wins. In 2009, the Giants finished third in their division and were generally regarded as overachieving also-rans who wouldn't accomplish anything until they made major lineup upgrades. In 2010, the team won the first World Series title in San Francisco history and the first for the franchise since the New York Giants went all the way in 1954. The difference between the 2009 and 2010 clubs was four victories. In 2009, the Giants won 88 games. In 2010, they won 92, took the division by two games after beating the runner-up Padres on the final game of the season, then rode their major-league-best pitching staff and some clutch hitting to the title.

GIANTS PROSPECTUS

2010 W-L: 92-70, 1st in NL West

Pythag	.580	4th
RS/G	4.3	17th
RA/G	3.6	29th
TAv	.270	13th
BRR	-1.2	19th
FRA	3.8	2nd
DER	18.6	3rd
DL	685	13th
B-Age	29.8	25th
P-Age	27.6	10th
Salary	$98.6	9th
M$/MW	$2.04	10th

Ballpark: AT&T Park (3-yr. PF: 98). Their home park plays nearly neutral, so the Giants' pitching really *was* this good

2010: Unlikely collection of cast-offs and great pitching Lincecums, sees, and conquers

2011: Regression rears its ugly head, but Giants remain competitive

Action Items: More kung-fu, less Panda; loosening the (Brandon) Belt

Yes, the Giants had a little help in winning the division. The Padres, who stood alone atop the West from June 18 to September 9, collapsed in late August with a 10-game losing streak, then limped to the finish line, going 15-14 the rest of the way. The Dodgers, who won the division in 2009 with 95 wins, fell apart completely, bringing Joe Torre's 15-year playoff streak to a close with just 80 victories. The Rockies, who had won the wild card with 92 wins in 2009 and were a popular pre-season pick, also regressed significantly, winning nine fewer games. Still, in the seven seasons since San Francisco won 100 games and its last division title, National League West champions have averaged just over 89 wins, making the difference between 88 and 92 victories crucial.

The Giants did not make any radical improvements to their team heading into 2010. In fact, their biggest off-season acquisitions were Aubrey Huff, a 33-year-old first baseman coming off a miserable .241/.310/.384 performance, and Mark DeRosa, a 35-year-old left fielder/utilityman recuperating from wrist surgery. Unsurprisingly, the Giants did not look much like a potential champion through the first half of the season. Top pitching prospect Madison Bumgarner, who was expected to serve as the fifth starter out of spring training, arrived in camp still lacking the five miles per hour on his fastball he had misplaced the previous fall and was quickly lit up and sent back to Triple-A. More controversially, top prospect Buster Posey was sent down despite a fine exhibition season in a transparent ploy to manipulate his service time.

The team's Opening Day outfield of DeRosa, Aaron Rowand, and John Bowker soon proved to be a total bust, as had replacement fifth starter Todd Wellemeyer. DeRosa re-injured his wrist in May, which ended his season. Second baseman Freddy Sanchez didn't make his first appearance of the year until after DeRosa's last, due to January shoulder surgery. Pablo Sandoval, who was far and away the team's best hitter in 2009, saw his bat go cold after April, perhaps the result of exhaustion after undergoing an intensive (and largely fruitless) off-season conditioning program. Veteran shortstop Edgar Renteria once again couldn't stay healthy. On July 4, the exact midpoint of their season, the Giants lost for the third time in a four-game set in Colorado and fell 7.5 games out of first place with a 41-40 record.

However, the Giants' fortunes had already begun to improve. Minor-league veteran Andres Torres hit his way into the lineup in May and would prove to be the team's second-most productive hitter per VORP (Value Over Replacement Player), and best fielder over the course of the season. Pat Burrell, who had been released by the Rays, was signed on May 29 and installed in left field a week later, with immediate benefits at the plate. Posey was called up the same day Burrell was signed; the former was moved behind the plate after a month at first base when incumbent catcher Bengie Molina, another early-season disappointment, was traded to Texas. Bumgarner, who had recovered some of his velocity and continued to gain strength as the season progressed, joined the party in late June. Juan Uribe again proved to be a solid replacement for Renteria at shortstop. Sanchez showed no ill effects from his shoulder surgery. Huff, who had been pushed to right field by Posey's arrival, unexpectedly had his best season at age 33, anchoring the lineup. As the pennant race heated up, so did mid-August waiver claim Cody Ross, whose hot bat would help carry the Giants through the postseason and became a temporary solution in right field. Posey put the team on his back in July; from July 5 through the end of the regular season, the Giants played .630 baseball, putting themselves in position to take advantage of the Padres' collapse.

In all, the Giants effectively replaced five of their eight regulars during the season. Of the remaining three, Huff was a new arrival and Sanchez had been a 2009 deadline acquisition who had played just 25 games for the team the previous season. The only Giants to make more than 360 plate appearances for the team in both 2009 and 2010 were Sandoval and Uribe, the latter of whom started both seasons on the bench and the former of whom lost his job to healthy, eventual World Series MVP Renteria during the playoffs.

The result of the turnover was a modest increase in run scoring. The Giants scored just 4.06 runs per game relative to a league average of 4.43 in 2009. Through their first 81 games of 2010, they improved to 4.17 runs per game despite a slight decrease in run scoring around the league (4.33 R/G on the season). In their last 81 games, they averaged 4.43 runs. Put as a percentage of the league average, with the normal range of team performance being plus or minus 20 percent of league average, the Giants went from a scoring rate of 91 percent of average in 2009 to 96 percent in the first half of 2010, to 102 percent in the second half of 2010.

By comparison, the Giants allowed their opponents to score at 84 percent of the league-average rate in 2009 and 83 percent of average in 2010. It's easy to argue that the Giants won with their pitching. They did. Their rotation was tied with that of the Phillies for the regular-season lead in value above replacement, and only the Padres got more value from their pitching staff as a whole, with 40.5 wins above replacement to the Giants' 37.2. However, the difference between the Giants' 2009 and 2010 seasons—what got them those four extra wins that allowed their pitching to carry them to a championship—was their incremental improvement in offense.

Despite the improved offense, which peaked in July at 5.32 runs per game and helped drive the team to a 20-8 record that month, the story down the stretch and in October was the Giants' pitching. The team finished August four games behind the Padres, but in September, its pitching staff allowed just 50 runs (1.92 per game). Allow us to repeat that: during the month of September, a span of 26 games, the Giants' pitching staff allowed, on average, fewer than two runs per game. What's more, a full fifth of the runs the staff allowed on the month were scored in a single 10-inning game in Colorado on September 25. Take out those 10 tallies at altitude, and the Giants allowed just 1.6 runs per game in their other 25 September games. They allowed more than three runs in two other games that month, didn't allow more than four runs in any other contest, and allowed two or fewer runs in 19 of their 26 games.

In the postseason, the Giants' staff allowed a comparatively robust 2.73 runs per game in 15 contests. They crushed the Rangers in the World Series, losing just one game while scoring 5.8 runs per game and outscoring Texas 29 to 12. Note, however, that in the first two rounds combined, the Giants outscored their opponents, the Braves and the Phillies, by a single run, scoring just three runs per game. Those are small samples, but they tell you how the Giants won. Which sets up the obvious question: Can they do it again?

There were very obvious ways for the Giants to upgrade over the winter. Posey's was the only spot in the lineup that couldn't have been improved by obtaining a younger, more consistent, or more productive player, but largely due to the albatross contracts of Zito and Rowand, the team lacked the payroll flexibility to do anything dramatic. The Giants' Opening Day payroll in 2010 was roughly $98.6 million. Team president and CEO Larry Baer was willing to increase payroll following the team's World Series win, but only marginally (there's that word again), and probably by less than $10 million, to roughly $108 million. Entering the offseason, the Giants already had $77 million committed to eight players ($31.5 million of that allotted to Zito and Rowand), eight players eligible for arbitration (with 2010 salaries that added up to about $11.3 million), and Huff, Burrell, and Uribe due to become free agents, leaving holes at first base, shortstop, and left field and less than $20 million with which to fill them.

As it was, general manager Brian Sabean spent more than half of his allowance on re-signing Huff for $10 million per season for the next two years with an option for the same amount in 2013. Sabean had hoped to bring back Uribe, but when the infielder jumped ship to the rival Dodgers for an unwarranted three-year deal, the GM inked Miguel Tejada to a one-year, $6.5 million deal the next day. The GM followed that up with a bargain on Burrell, who grew up a Giants fan and re-signed for a remarkably cheap, incentive-free, one-year, $1 million deal without extensively testing the market. Sabean effectively finished his holiday shopping by December 3, filling his three vacant positions for $17.5 million, and had more or less withdrawn from the market as we went to press.

Despite the lack of a meaningful upgrade, there are many reasons to believe that the 2011 Giants will be better than the 2010 champs. Full seasons from Posey and Bumgarner top that list. Full seasons from Burrell and Torres also look to be positives, as both performed for the Giants in 2010 in a manner consistent with their recent histories, Burrell's with the Phillies, and Torres' in the high minors. There's hope that Sandoval can recapture some portion of his 2009 form, which would be a huge boon to the lineup, that DeRosa will have something positive to contribute, and that ace Tim Lincecum can avoid a rough stretch like the one he suffered last August, when he went 0-5 with a 7.82 ERA.

There is also help on the way from the farm system. The Giants' fifth-round draft pick in 2009, first baseman Brandon Belt, had a spectacular professional debut that concluded with a 956 on-base plus slugging percentage (OPS) in 61 Triple-A plate appearances. Word from scouts is that Belt, who hit .352/.455/.620 with 23 homers and 22 stolen bases across three levels, is for real, and thus lurks as a potential midseason upgrade who could replace whichever player from the group of Huff, Burrell, or Ross is struggling the most (our money's on Ross).

Of course, there are ample possibilities for regression or correction. In the rotation, Zito was awful down the stretch, a grim omen for 2011, and Sanchez benefited from a .255 opponents' batting average on balls in play, which suggests a major correction in store for the coming season, particularly given his lack of improvement elsewhere. Matt Cain has also profited from a low BABIP, though he's done so consistently, suggesting that he could be an exception to the rule. Regression in the bullpen, which ranked third in the majors in WXRL in 2010, is almost a given. Huff's performances have fluctuated so much in recent seasons that it's difficult to imagine that at 34, he won't decline from his career year in 2010. There might also have been more to Burrell's struggles with the Rays than a bad neck and a distaste for designated hitting and American League pitching. And at 33, Torres is likely to find repeating his breakout season harder than his recent minor-league track record would suggest.

Still, there's reason for optimism in the City by the Bay. The Giants aren't a great team, but they are half of a great team, and with Posey, Belt, and some useful veterans, the other half is getting better. That is not necessarily true of the other four teams in the Giants' division. As San Francisco showed last year, being only marginally better than your competition can be good enough.

HITTERS

Ehire Adrianza SS

Born: **8/21/1989** Age: **21**
Bats: **S** Throws: **R** Height: **6' 1"** Weight: **165**
Breakout: **0%** Improve: **3%** Collapse: **1%**
Attrition: **1%** MLB: **5%**

Comparables:
Asdrubal Cabrera, Edgar Renteria, Rance Mulliniks (81)

YEAR	TEAM	LVL	AGE	PA	R	2B	3B	HR	RBI	BB	SO	SB	CS	AVG/OBP/SLG	TAv	BABIP	BRR	FRAA	WARP
2008	GIA	Rk	18	63	13	4	0	1	6	7	4	0	1	.255/.349/.382	.257	.260	1.1	SS 2	0.6
2009	AUG	A	19	448	54	15	3	2	46	42	66	7	1	.258/.328/.327	.252	.294	-0.5	SS 8	2.1
2010	SJO	A+	20	508	70	22	5	3	35	47	87	33	15	.256/.333/.348	.255	.303	1.5	SS 27	4.5
2011	*SFN*	*MLB*	*21*	*354*	*34*	*14*	*2*	*3*	*28*	*27*	*70*	*9*	*3*	*.230/.287/.314*	*.217*	*.275*	*-0.2*	*SS 14*	*1.2*

A classic good-field/no-hit shortstop, the scrawny 21-year-old Venezuelan Adrianza is an outstanding fielder who will steal his share of bases and even draw a few walks, but his utter lack of power and his inability to hit for league-average batting lines in the low minors will limit him to a bench role at best in the majors. His running adds bases to his ledger, but it also adds outs. Factor both these observations into Adrianza's career hitting line, and you get an unsightly .226/.315/.357. Still, his glove is so good that it could make him a major-league bench option in short order.

Brandon Belt 1B

Born: **4/20/1988** Age: **23**
Bats: **L** Throws: **L** Height: **6' 5"** Weight: **195**
Breakout: **2%** Improve: **37%** Collapse: **4%**
Attrition: **26%** MLB: **73%**

Comparables:
Matt Joyce, Mat Gamel, Jeremy Hermida (56)

YEAR	TEAM	LVL	AGE	PA	R	2B	3B	HR	RBI	BB	SO	SB	CS	AVG/OBP/SLG	TAv	BABIP	BRR	FRAA	WARP
2010	SJO	A+	22	333	62	28	4	10	62	58	50	18	7	.383/.492/.628	.396	.439	-1.5	1B 5	5.2
2010	RIC	AA	22	201	26	11	6	9	40	22	34	2	1	.337/.413/.623	.376	.373	-0.7	1B 1, RF 3	2.7
2010	FRE	AAA	22	61	11	4	0	4	10	13	15	2	0	.229/.393/.563	.326	.241	-0.8	RF -2, 1B 1	0.3
2011	*SFN*	*MLB*	*23*	*588*	*80*	*31*	*4*	*21*	*78*	*77*	*117*	*13*	*5*	*.278/.372/.481*	*.295*	*.317*	*-0.3*	*1B -11, RF 0*	*1.4*

We're pretty sure Brandon Belt is a myth. The high-school pitcher was drafted twice before heading to the University of Texas, where hitting became his focus. The Giants drafted him as a first baseman in the fifth round in 2009; made some adjustments to his swing, opening him up and lowering his hands; and set him loose on the California League. Belt was flat-out Ruthian at High-A and Double-A and posted a 956 OPS in 61 plate appearances at Triple-A. Altogether, across the top three levels of the minor leagues, Belt hit .352/.455/620 with 23 homers, 112 RBI, and 22 stolen bases in 30 attempts . . . and his name is Brandon *Belt*. This has to be a prank. If not, Aubrey Huff could well find himself pushed into an outfield corner before the ink dries on his new contract.

Gary Brown CF

Born: **9/28/1988** Age: **22**
Bats: **R** Throws: **R** Height: **6' 0"** Weight: **170**
Breakout: **0%** Improve: **0%** Collapse: **0%**
Attrition: **0%** MLB: **0%**

Comparables:
Shannon Stewart, Adolfo Phillips, Eddie Miller (89)

YEAR	TEAM	LVL	AGE	PA	R	2B	3B	HR	RBI	BB	SO	SB	CS	AVG/OBP/SLG	TAv	BABIP	BRR	FRAA	WARP
2011	*SFN*	*MLB*	*22*	—	—	—	—	—	—	—	—	—	—	—	—	—	—	—	—

The 24th overall pick in last year's draft, Gary Brown went 20 picks later than his Cal State Fullerton companion Christian Colon despite being arguably the fastest player in the draft and a very good defensive center fielder, and despite having a batting average 80 points higher, an on-base percentage (OBP) 38 points higher, and a slugging percentage more than 60 points higher than his teammate's. As you might have surmised from the fact that his 80-point advantage in average bought him only a 38-point lead in OBP, Brown doesn't draw many walks, which has distracted some from what he *can* do. Yes, with just nine walks in 50 games in his final collegiate season, Brown is most definitely a free swinger, but when a coach has a player hitting .438, is it really in the player's best interest to mess with his approach? Much like ground balls for pitchers, walks have unfortunately become a black-and-white issue for parts of the statistical community that regard a hitter who walks as good and one who doesn't as bad. The reality is far more complex—and, oh yeah, Brown is good.

Pat Burrell LF

Born: **10/10/1976** Age: **34**
Bats: **R** Throws: **R** Height: **6' 4"** Weight: **225**
Breakout: **1%** Improve: **35%** Collapse: **0%**
Attrition: **5%** MLB: **92%**

Comparables:
Chili Davis, Ken Singleton, Fred McGriff (71)

YEAR	TEAM	LVL	AGE	PA	R	2B	3B	HR	RBI	BB	SO	SB	CS	AVG/OBP/SLG	TAv	BABIP	BRR	FRAA	WARP
2008	PHI	MLB	31	645	84	33	3	33	86	102	136	0	0	.250/.367/.508	.297	.271	-1.1	LF -14	2.2
2009	TBA	MLB	32	475	47	16	1	14	64	57	119	2	0	.221/.316/.367	.245	.272	0.4	RF 0, LF 0	-0.3
2010	TBA	MLB	33	96	9	5	0	2	13	10	28	0	0	.202/.292/.333	.232	.273	0.9	—	-0.1
2010	SFN	MLB	33	341	44	16	0	18	51	47	77	0	2	.266/.364/.509	.310	.297	-0.3	LF -1	2.1
2011	*SFN*	*MLB*	*34*	*552*	*70*	*23*	*0*	*23*	*66*	*82*	*126*	*1*	*0*	*.239/.353/.441*	*.279*	*.274*	*0.0*	*LF -5, RF 0*	*1.3*

An underappreciated hitter but a brutal fielder, Burrell always seemed like a designated hitter trapped in the wrong league, but rather than bring harmony to the universe, his year-plus as the Rays' DH sounded a sour note, to the tune of a .218/.311/.361 batting line. After Burrell began 2010 in miserable fashion, the Rays cut him loose, but reuniting the erstwhile outfielder with his glove in San Francisco seemed to rejuvenate his bat, and his production as a Giant was almost perfectly in sync with his .257/.367/.485 career line as a Phillie. A herniated disk in his neck in 2009 played a part in his Tampa struggles, but it's interesting to look back and see that Burrell, who played only nine innings over two games in the field for the Rays, hit just .153/.258/.222 in 85 at-bats as an inter-league DH for the Phils. Some players just aren't cut out to ride pine between at-bats. Burrell often rode pine following them, however. He started 58 games the Giants won between the regular and postseasons and finished all but four of them on the bench, where he was relegated in favor of superior defensive options.

Emmanuel Burriss 2B

Born: **1/17/1985** Age: **26**
Bats: **S** Throws: **R** Height: **6' 0"** Weight: **170**
Breakout: **0%** Improve: **25%** Collapse: **5%**
Attrition: **6%** MLB: **58%**

Comparables:
Erick Aybar, Toby Harrah, Dave Cash (78)

YEAR	TEAM	LVL	AGE	PA	R	2B	3B	HR	RBI	BB	SO	SB	CS	AVG/OBP/SLG	TAv	BABIP	BRR	FRAA	WARP
2008	FRE	AAA	23	64	6	1	1	0	6	2	6	2	2	.258/.281/.306	.207	.286	0.1	2B 3, SS -1	0.1
2008	SFN	MLB	23	274	32	6	1	1	18	23	24	13	5	.283/.350/.329	.239	.303	1.7	SS -2, 2B 1	0.3
2009	FRE	AAA	24	77	9	2	1	1	7	3	4	6	2	.268/.312/.366	.228	.269	0.5	2B 1	0.1
2009	SFN	MLB	24	220	17	6	0	0	13	14	34	11	4	.238/.291/.267	.209	.282	2.6	2B -3	-0.7
2010	FRE	AAA	25	305	32	11	2	0	22	19	29	11	5	.282/.334/.337	.235	.303	1.4	SS -3, 2B 0	0.1
2010	SFN	MLB	25	5	2	0	0	0	0	0	1	0	0	.400/.400/.400	.289	.500	0.3	2B -1	0.0
2011	*SFN*	*MLB*	*26*	*317*	*33*	*11*	*1*	*2*	*26*	*21*	*37*	*13*	*5*	*.261/.312/.336*	*.233*	*.284*	*-0.5*	*2B 0, SS 0*	*0.0*

The fifth metatarsal bone that Burriss broke in his left foot in June 2009 cracked again in the Giants' Cactus League opener on March 3, requiring a second surgery that erased the first half of his 2010 season. The latter operation, performed by Carolina Panthers orthopedist Robert Anderson, saw the screw inserted in the initial operation replaced with a larger one and marrow extracted from Burriss's hip sprayed on the fracture as part of a new experimental technique to accelerate healing. Burriss avoided another recurrence after returning to action and almost perfectly replicated his career minor-league batting line in 67 Triple-A games, but that last isn't encouraging, and there are concerns about whether the two foot surgeries will have a lasting negative impact on his speed or mobility in the field, since both seemed diminished after his return.

Mark DeRosa **UT**

Born: **2/2/1975** Age: **36**
Bats: R Throws: R Height: **6' 1"** Weight: **195**
Breakout: **0%** Improve: **26%** Collapse: **11%**
Attrition: **26%** MLB: **91%**

Comparables:
Dusty Baker, Hideki Matsui, David Justice (78)

YEAR	TEAM	LVL	AGE	PA	R	2B	3B	HR	RBI	BB	SO	SB	CS	AVG/OBP/SLG	TAv	BABIP	BRR	FRAA	WARP
2008	CHN	MLB	33	592	106	30	3	21	87	69	106	6	0	.286/.375/.482	.301	.318	3.2	2B 0, RF 6	5.0
2009	CLE	MLB	34	314	47	13	0	13	50	29	63	1	1	.270/.341/.457	.284	.301	-1.2	3B -3, LF -3	0.6
2009	SLN	MLB	34	262	31	10	1	10	28	18	58	2	1	.228/.290/.405	.250	.256	1.3	3B -7, LF 1	0.0
2010	SFN	MLB	35	104	9	3	0	1	10	9	16	0	2	.194/.279/.258	.201	.224	-0.4	LF 1, 2B 0	-0.4
2011	*SFN*	*MLB*	*36*	*490*	*59*	*22*	*1*	*14*	*54*	*48*	*91*	*3*	*2*	*.259/.338/.413*	*.267*	*.293*	*-0.2*	*3B -2, 2B -1*	*1.2*

DeRosa tore a tendon sheath in his left wrist soon after being traded to the Cardinals in 2009, but off-season surgery to repair the problem was, in DeRosa's words, "a failure," as the sheath ruptured again in early May 2010, effectively ending his season. DeRosa hit .288/.363/.453 from Opening Day 2006 through his June 27, 2008, trade to St. Louis, but he is now 36 and hasn't faced major league pitching with a healthy left wrist in about 20 months. Anything the Giants get out of the final year of his two-year deal has to be considered a bonus.

Mike Fontenot **INF**

Born: **6/9/1980** Age: **31**
Bats: L Throws: R Height: **5' 8"** Weight: **160**
Breakout: **0%** Improve: **31%** Collapse: **6%**
Attrition: **12%** MLB: **85%**

Comparables:
Andy Green, Tony Gonzalez, Bip Roberts (70)

YEAR	TEAM	LVL	AGE	PA	R	2B	3B	HR	RBI	BB	SO	SB	CS	AVG/OBP/SLG	TAv	BABIP	BRR	FRAA	WARP
2008	CHN	MLB	28	284	40	22	1	9	40	34	51	2	0	.305/.391/.514	.316	.348	0.8	2B -1, SS 0	2.3
2009	CHN	MLB	29	419	38	22	2	9	43	35	83	4	1	.236/.301/.377	.242	.276	-4.9	2B 1, 3B 1	0.0
2010	CHN	MLB	30	185	14	11	3	1	20	10	28	1	2	.284/.330/.402	.258	.329	-0.7	2B -2, 3B 0	0.2
2010	SFN	MLB	30	76	11	2	0	0	5	5	13	0	2	.282/.329/.310	.242	.345	0.8	2B 1, SS -1	0.2
2011	*SFN*	*MLB*	*31*	*364*	*43*	*19*	*2*	*7*	*40*	*32*	*63*	*4*	*2*	*.268/.333/.405*	*.261*	*.306*	*-0.3*	*2B 0, 3B 0*	*0.9*

Fontenot's 2008 was a BABIP-related fluke in a peak-age season. Since then, he has hit just .260/.320/.385 against righties while largely being benched against his fellow lefties and playing subpar defense at second, short, and third. Most expected the Giants to nontender the 30-year-old arbitration-eligible infielder, but the team inked him instead, perhaps figuring that Freddy Sanchez misses a lot of games and the world is full of utility infielders who can't hit even that well.

Darren Ford **CF**

Born: **10/1/1985** Age: **25**
Bats: R Throws: R Height: **5' 11"** Weight: **195**
Breakout: **5%** Improve: **30%** Collapse: **6%**
Attrition: **28%** MLB: **54%**

Comparables:
Roger Bernadina, Brett Gardner, Michael Bourn (74)

YEAR	TEAM	LVL	AGE	PA	R	2B	3B	HR	RBI	BB	SO	SB	CS	AVG/OBP/SLG	TAv	BABIP	BRR	FRAA	WARP
2008	BRV	A+	22	401	57	13	3	2	27	46	88	48	11	.230/.317/.303	.242	.293	4.6	CF -10, LF 0	-0.2
2008	SJO	A+	22	155	21	4	1	0	7	23	42	14	1	.219/.342/.266	.241	.318	2.5	CF -1	0.3
2009	SJO	A+	23	441	81	17	9	9	50	49	97	35	12	.300/.383/.463	.311	.375	1.6	CF 3	4.0
2010	RIC	AA	24	516	64	20	9	5	40	39	106	37	15	.251/.315/.365	.258	.307	0.0	CF 1	1.4
2011	*SFN*	*MLB*	*25*	*506*	*51*	*19*	*4*	*6*	*44*	*42*	*125*	*30*	*8*	*.231/.294/.333*	*.227*	*.295*	*0.6*	*CF -12, LF 0*	*-1.4*

Acquired from the Brewers in the 2008 deadline deal that sent Ray Durham to Milwaukee, Ford is a speed-and-defense center fielder who can't hit. Take out his 2009 season, which was a BABIP-based fluke, and Ford has hit just .237/.316/.324 in 1,388 plate appearances at High-A and Double-A. He'll draw his walks and can leg out his share of triples, but his power is otherwise negligible, and he strikes out roughly once per game. True, Ford has dropped his strikeout rate in each of the last two seasons, but his walk rate is falling faster, and he's now 25 and won't make his Triple-A debut until April, provided it's not delayed by his current legal troubles—the right-hander had just managed to escape four felony charges (for allegedly being less than truthful about a robbery in his account to police) as we went to press.

Conor Gillaspie **3B**

Born: **7/18/1987** Age: **23**
Bats: L Throws: R Height: **6' 1"** Weight: **200**
Breakout: **4%** Improve: **11%** Collapse: **5%**
Attrition: **12%** MLB: **18%**

Comparables:
Daniel Murphy, Neil Walker, Dalton Jones (75)

YEAR	TEAM	LVL	AGE	PA	R	2B	3B	HR	RBI	BB	SO	SB	CS	AVG/OBP/SLG	TAv	BABIP	BRR	FRAA	WARP
2008	SLO	A-	20	80	4	4	0	0	8	9	13	2	0	.268/.350/.324	.246	.328	-1.4	3B -1	-0.1
2008	SFN	MLB	20	7	1	0	0	0	0	2	0	0	0	.200/.429/.200	.266	.200	0.0	3B 0	0.0
2009	SJO	A+	21	530	62	31	2	4	67	55	68	2	3	.286/.362/.386	.291	.325	-5.9	3B -7	2.1
2010	RIC	AA	22	540	57	25	8	8	67	37	67	0	4	.287/.335/.420	.289	.312	1.0	3B -3	2.8
2011	*SFN*	*MLB*	*23*	*406*	*44*	*19*	*2*	*5*	*40*	*28*	*63*	*0*	*0*	*.263/.312/.370*	*.240*	*.298*	*0.0*	*3B -4*	*-0.1*

Drafted with the compensation-round pick the Giants received when Pedro Feliz signed with the Phillies, Gillaspie is yet another flawed third baseman. In stark contrast to Feliz, he is an unexceptional fielder with little power, but while Gillaspie will hit for a bit more average and is more amenable to ball four, his plate discipline is far from impressive. In fact, his unintentional-walk rate dropped considerably with the leap to Double-A last year, falling from one every 9.7 plate appearances in his first two pro seasons to one every 16.2 PAs last year. That leaves an empty .280 average from a player without any marketable skills.

Jose Guillen **RF**

Born: **5/17/1976** Age: **35**
Bats: **R** Throws: **R** Height: **5' 11"** Weight: **165**
Breakout: **0%** Improve: **22%** Collapse: **12%**
Attrition: **21%** MLB: **84%**

Comparables:
Jacque Jones, Magglio Ordonez, Lou Johnson (74)

YEAR	TEAM	LVL	AGE	PA	R	2B	3B	HR	RBI	BB	SO	SB	CS	AVG/OBP/SLG	TAv	BABIP	BRR	FRAA	WARP
2008	KCA	MLB	32	633	69	42	1	20	97	23	106	2	1	.264/.300/.438	.258	.291	-4.8	RF -2, LF 0	0.2
2009	KCA	MLB	33	312	30	8	0	9	40	22	50	1	0	.242/.314/.367	.245	.265	-0.7	RF -7, LF -2	-0.9
2010	KCA	MLB	34	438	52	17	2	16	62	27	84	1	0	.255/.313/.429	.265	.282	-0.2	RF 1	0.6
2010	SFN	MLB	34	139	10	5	0	3	15	5	29	0	0	.266/.317/.375	.236	.320	-0.9	RF -1	-0.3
2011	*SFN*	*MLB*	*35*	*491*	*56*	*21*	*1*	*15*	*56*	*29*	*90*	*2*	*1*	*.254/.312/.407*	*.255*	*.283*	*0.0*	*RF -3, LF 0*	*0.0*

As part of his attempt to acquire every unwanted outfielder in the majors during the 2010 season, Brian Sabean sent a player to be named later (right-hander Kevin Pucetas) to the Royals for the already-designated-for-assignment Guillen in mid-August. Guillen then spent the rest of the season in right field hitting like Jose Guillen without the power, which is to say, not hitting. He was mercifully whacked by a stiff neck in early October and was left off the Giants' post-season roster. In November, Guillen's history of performance-enhancing drug violations got a little longer when he was connected to a shipment of 50 preloaded syringes of human growth hormone (HGH) intercepted by the U.S. Drug Enforcement Agency. Whether this will prevent the itinerant malcontent from landing with an 11th major-league team remains to be seen, though if that's not a disincentive, the .257/.308/.416 he has hit over the last three seasons should be.

Jesus Guzman **UT**

Born: **6/14/1984** Age: **27**
Bats: **R** Throws: **R** Height: **6' 1"** Weight: **215**
Breakout: **0%** Improve: **27%** Collapse: **6%**
Attrition: **23%** MLB: **52%**

Comparables:
James D'Antona, David Freese, Lou Montanez (76)

YEAR	TEAM	LVL	AGE	PA	R	2B	3B	HR	RBI	BB	SO	SB	CS	AVG/OBP/SLG	TAv	BABIP	BRR	FRAA	WARP
2008	MID	AA	24	376	57	21	2	14	76	33	56	5	2	.364/.418/.560	.331	.403	0.5	3B -1, 2B -7	3.1
2008	SAC	AAA	24	65	5	2	0	2	9	4	13	0	2	.237/.277/.373	.260	.261	-0.9	3B -3	-0.2
2009	FRE	AAA	25	500	75	26	5	16	71	37	82	0	2	.321/.378/.507	.304	.360	-0.7	1B 2, 3B 0	2.8
2009	SFN	MLB	25	20	0	0	0	0	0	0	3	0	0	.250/.250/.250	.151	.294	-0.8	1B 0	-0.2
2010	FRE	AAA	26	492	66	28	1	18	72	38	68	6	4	.321/.376/.510	.298	.342	0.1	3B -6, LF -2	2.3
2011	*SFN*	*MLB*	*27*	*484*	*63*	*23*	*1*	*16*	*64*	*34*	*84*	*3*	*1*	*.296/.346/.464*	*.282*	*.328*	*-0.2*	*3B -4, 1B -4*	*0.9*

At the plate, Guzman's two seasons at Triple-A Fresno were nearly identical across the board and generally in sync with his career minor-league numbers, which suggests that he is what he is. In the field, the Giants have moved Guzman around according to projected need (to first base in 2009, to third and left field last year), which suggests that they don't know what he is. As a contact hitter with power who has played everywhere but catcher and center field, Guzman is an intriguing bench option, but if and when his batting average dips below .300, he may no longer seem quite so interesting. The Giants never gave him a meaningful major-league opportunity, but he'll attempt to earn a bench spot with the Padres this season.

Aubrey Huff **1B**

Born: **12/20/1976** Age: **34**
Bats: **L** Throws: **R** Height: **6' 4"** Weight: **221**
Breakout: **0%** Improve: **37%** Collapse: **3%**
Attrition: **7%** MLB: **96%**

Comparables:
Bob Watson, Lyle Overbay, Paul Konerko (75)

YEAR	TEAM	LVL	AGE	PA	R	2B	3B	HR	RBI	BB	SO	SB	CS	AVG/OBP/SLG	TAv	BABIP	BRR	FRAA	WARP
2008	BAL	MLB	31	661	97	48	2	32	108	53	89	4	0	.304/.360/.552	.314	.310	-3.2	3B 0, 1B -1	4.0
2009	BAL	MLB	32	480	51	24	1	13	72	41	74	0	6	.254/.321/.405	.255	.276	-2.6	1B -6	-0.7
2009	DET	MLB	32	117	11	6	0	2	13	10	13	0	0	.189/.265/.302	.209	.198	-0.8	—	-0.6
2010	SFN	MLB	33	668	100	35	5	26	86	83	91	7	0	.290/.385/.506	.318	.303	0.9	1B 7, RF -2	5.8
2011	*SFN*	*MLB*	*34*	*611*	*79*	*32*	*2*	*21*	*78*	*62*	*86*	*4*	*1*	*.271/.349/.456*	*.281*	*.285*	*-0.2*	*1B 0, 3B 0*	*2.0*

Huff and DeRosa were the Giants' big additions last winter. This inspired little confidence in the team's chances heading into 2010, but Huff followed his worst season at the plate with his best, acquitted himself well at first base and both outfield corners, and was credited with being a leader both in the clubhouse and on the field (though the less said about his "rally thong" the better). Huff did all of that for just $3 million last year and was rewarded with a two-year deal worth $20 million with a $10 million option for 2013. As for what the Giants can expect in those next two years, even with his miserable 2009, Huff has hit .280/.353/.484 over the last three seasons, which is above average even at first base. However, Huff is creeping into his mid-30s and could be pushed by Belt into an outfield corner, where he'd be less likely to repeat his solid performance in the field from 2010. Still, the Giants have had such a hard time fielding productive hitters that it's hard to blame them for holding on to the ones they find, and Huff's contract is hardly a potential albatross.

Travis Ishikawa 1B
Born: **9/24/1983** Age: **27**
Bats: **L** Throws: **L** Height: **6' 3"** Weight: **210**
Breakout: **2%** Improve: **24%** Collapse: **5%**
Attrition: **12%** MLB: **55%**
Comparables:
Mike Ivie, Matt Macri, Jeff Baker (83)

YEAR	TEAM	LVL	AGE	PA	R	2B	3B	HR	RBI	BB	SO	SB	CS	AVG/OBP/SLG	TAv	BABIP	BRR	FRAA	WARP
2008	NRW	AA	24	277	34	16	0	8	48	35	45	10	4	.291/.379/.462	.301	.321	-2.3	1B 5	1.7
2008	FRE	AAA	24	192	35	19	3	16	46	14	36	0	1	.310/.370/.737	.345	.303	-0.3	1B 1	2.0
2008	SFN	MLB	24	104	13	6	0	3	15	9	27	1	0	.274/.337/.432	.283	.354	-0.7	1B 4	0.6
2009	SFN	MLB	25	363	49	10	2	9	39	30	89	2	2	.261/.328/.387	.252	.329	0.5	1B 6	0.6
2010	SFN	MLB	26	173	19	11	0	3	22	13	29	0	0	.266/.318/.392	.253	.305	-3.2	1B 0	-0.2
2011	*SFN*	*MLB*	*27*	*365*	*45*	*18*	*1*	*12*	*45*	*32*	*77*	*3*	*1*	*.262/.330/.436*	*.267*	*.304*	*-0.1*	*1B -1*	*0.4*

Once thought to be the team's first baseman of the future, Ishikawa was downgraded to lefty bench bat in 2010 save for a brief period in July and early August, when Bochy's need for Huff in the outfield allowed Ishikawa to make 23 starts at first. He hit just .224/.258/.310 in those games, but batted .286/.341/.429 when entering a game midstream—still not great, but not bad for a reserve. Less encouragingly, that last line was also (and not coincidentally) nearly an exact match for Ishikawa's line against right-handers on the season. Given that he is limited to first base, he needs to do more in those favorable matchups to be worth carrying into his arbitration years.

Thomas Neal LF
Born: **8/17/1987** Age: **23**
Bats: **R** Throws: **R** Height: **6' 1"** Weight: **225**
Breakout: **4%** Improve: **26%** Collapse: **4%**
Attrition: **24%** MLB: **48%**
Comparables:
Mike Carp, Alex Gordon, Brandon Moss (72)

YEAR	TEAM	LVL	AGE	PA	R	2B	3B	HR	RBI	BB	SO	SB	CS	AVG/OBP/SLG	TAv	BABIP	BRR	FRAA	WARP
2008	AUG	A	20	497	69	25	1	15	81	48	103	3	4	.276/.358/.444	.294	.323	-0.5	1B -3	1.8
2009	SJO	A+	21	559	102	41	4	22	90	65	98	3	0	.337/.431/.579	.346	.385	0.3	LF -2, RF -1	5.9
2010	RIC	AA	22	585	69	40	1	12	69	46	94	11	5	.291/.359/.440	.305	.334	0.0	LF -3, RF 4	3.4
2011	*SFN*	*MLB*	*23*	*548*	*67*	*30*	*1*	*16*	*66*	*44*	*113*	*0*	*0*	*.265/.330/.430*	*.266*	*.307*	*0.0*	*LF -5, 1B -2*	*0.4*

Neal's 2009 California League spike should be taken with the same BABIP-flavored grain of salt as Darren Ford's. Indeed, one can see the real Neal in the similarities between his 2008 and 2010 seasons, and what those seasons reveal is an unathletic left fielder who doesn't hit well enough to get by on his bat alone. The good news is that he is just 23, has already worked his way up to Triple-A, and has the bat speed, hand-eye coordination, and strike-zone judgment to improve on what currently looks like an average bat for his position, though he may never develop real corner-outfield-caliber power.

Francisco Peguero CF
Born: **6/1/1988** Age: **23**
Bats: **R** Throws: **R** Height: **6' 0"** Weight: **190**
Breakout: **3%** Improve: **27%** Collapse: **7%**
Attrition: **23%** MLB: **49%**
Comparables:
Greg Golson, Garry Templeton, Jacoby Ellsbury (69)

YEAR	TEAM	LVL	AGE	PA	R	2B	3B	HR	RBI	BB	SO	SB	CS	AVG/OBP/SLG	TAv	BABIP	BRR	FRAA	WARP
2008	AUG	A	20	194	23	2	4	2	15	12	43	15	1	.261/.309/.350	.274	.331	0.6	RF -1	0.6
2008	SLO	A-	20	220	33	11	4	2	28	9	43	10	3	.307/.345/.431	.267	.373	0.8	RF 0	0.6
2009	AUG	A	21	252	28	12	4	1	34	5	39	15	5	.340/.357/.437	.287	.394	1.5	CF 4	1.9
2009	SLO	A-	21	76	14	3	1	0	12	3	9	7	0	.394/.421/.465	.329	.444	1.7	CF 3, RF 0	1.2
2010	SJO	A+	22	538	78	19	16	10	77	18	88	40	22	.329/.358/.488	.307	.380	0.1	CF -4, RF -6	3.0
2011	*SFN*	*MLB*	*23*	*446*	*48*	*18*	*5*	*6*	*49*	*10*	*95*	*17*	*6*	*.275/.290/.384*	*.239*	*.332*	*-0.3*	*RF -5, CF -4*	*-1.0*

Peguero is fast, a good center fielder, and adept at hitting 'em where they ain't, but he doesn't walk (three of his 18 free passes last year were intentional, which gives him an unintentional walk rate of one every 35 2/3 plate appearances), was successful in just 65 percent of his stolen-base attempts last year, and will have to prove that the power surge he showed with San Jose last year was more than just another California League mirage.

Buster Posey C
Born: **3/27/1987** Age: **24**
Bats: **R** Throws: **R** Height: **6' 1"** Weight: **205**
Breakout: **4%** Improve: **43%** Collapse: **5%**
Attrition: **20%** MLB: **75%**
Comparables:
Andy LaRoche, Joe Torre, Steve Pearce (68)

YEAR	TEAM	LVL	AGE	PA	R	2B	3B	HR	RBI	BB	SO	SB	CS	AVG/OBP/SLG	TAv	BABIP	BRR	FRAA	WARP
2009	SJO	A+	22	346	63	23	0	13	58	45	45	6	0	.326/.428/.540	.357	.349	-3.6	C 1	4.3
2009	FRE	AAA	22	151	21	8	1	5	22	17	23	0	1	.321/.391/.511	.307	.349	-0.6	C -1	1.2
2009	SFN	MLB	22	17	1	0	0	0	0	0	4	0	0	.118/.118/.118	.195	.154	0.0	C 1	0.0
2010	FRE	AAA	23	208	31	13	2	6	32	28	30	1	1	.349/.442/.552	.336	.386	-2.4	C 0, 1B 3	2.5
2010	SFN	MLB	23	443	59	23	2	18	67	30	55	0	2	.305/.357/.505	.305	.316	-0.4	C 0, 1B -1	3.2
2011	*SFN*	*MLB*	*24*	*407*	*56*	*21*	*1*	*15*	*56*	*40*	*59*	*1*	*0*	*.298/.370/.488*	*.300*	*.317*	*0.0*	*C 0, 1B 0*	*2.9*

The Buster Posey era in San Francisco didn't begin until July 1, 2010, the day Bengie Molina was traded to the Rangers. Prior to that, Posey spent two months obliterating Triple-A pitching, then a month in big-league limbo as the Giants' first baseman, putting together a 10-game hitting streak in his first two weeks in the bigs, but otherwise biding his time. Finally installed behind the plate, Posey lived up to all the hype by hitting .469/.511/.815 with seven homers and 23 RBI in his first 21 games of July. He spent the rest of the year cooling off, however, save for a nice home-run burst in

September, hitting .254/.317/.447 the rest of the way. Behind the plate, he threw out 37 percent of opposing basestealers, was charged with just one passed ball in 662 innings, and put down the fingers for a team that won a title with its pitching. His final batting line is a reasonable expectation for his future performance, which—combined with his work behind the plate—should make him a perennial All-Star and a franchise cornerstone.

Edgar Renteria SS

Born: **8/7/1975** Age: **35**
Bats: **R** Throws: **R** Height: **6' 1"** Weight: **172**
Breakout: **0%** Improve: **20%** Collapse: **9%**
Attrition: **22%** MLB: **88%**

Comparables:
Shannon Stewart, Marco Scutaro, Dave Concepcion (75)

YEAR	TEAM	LVL	AGE	PA	R	2B	3B	HR	RBI	BB	SO	SB	CS	AVG/OBP/SLG	TAv	BABIP	BRR	FRAA	WARP
2008	DET	MLB	32	547	69	22	2	10	55	37	64	6	3	.270/.316/.382	.253	.289	-1.8	SS -2	1.4
2009	SFN	MLB	33	510	50	19	1	5	48	39	69	7	2	.250/.304/.328	.219	.278	3.3	SS -2	-0.1
2010	SFN	MLB	34	267	25	11	2	3	22	21	43	3	0	.276/.330/.375	.247	.320	-0.3	SS -3	0.3
2011	*SFN*	*MLB*	*35*	*509*	*58*	*22*	*1*	*8*	*49*	*42*	*69*	*7*	*2*	*.271/.328/.375*	*.252*	*.298*	*0.0*	*SS -3*	*1.2*

Renteria looked like the oldest 33-year-old in baseball in 2010, probably because his actual age is somewhere between 35 and 40—we'll never know unless they cut him open and count the rings. His list of ailments over his two Giants seasons is too extensive to recap here; his three stints on the disabled list in 2010 alone added up to 57 days missed. That doesn't include his various day-to-day issues, including nearly two weeks surrendered to a sore elbow down the stretch. Over the season's final three months, he hit just .224/.281/.334 in 135 PAs and didn't attempt a stolen base. That circumstance made him the Giants' starting shortstop in the World Series, and his ability to come through, winning Series MVP honors, seemed like a nice career bookend to the aging (or aged) infielder off into retirement, but as is too often the case, it merely convinced Renteria that he still has something to offer. He doesn't, but the Reds signed him to a one-year deal just the same.

Ryan Rohlinger INF

Born: **10/7/1983** Age: **27**
Bats: **R** Throws: **R** Height: **6' 1"** Weight: **195**
Breakout: **1%** Improve: **22%** Collapse: **4%**
Attrition: **21%** MLB: **47%**

Comparables:
Brendan Harris, Casey McGehee, Rico Petrocelli (77)

YEAR	TEAM	LVL	AGE	PA	R	2B	3B	HR	RBI	BB	SO	SB	CS	AVG/OBP/SLG	TAv	BABIP	BRR	FRAA	WARP
2008	SJO	A+	24	322	45	16	0	7	46	34	50	5	1	.285/.366/.419	.277	.319	1.2	3B -7	1.0
2008	NRW	AA	24	179	27	12	1	6	19	13	20	1	1	.296/.352/.497	.298	.299	0.4	3B 0	1.3
2008	SFN	MLB	24	33	1	1	1	0	2	1	8	0	1	.094/.121/.188	.093	.125	0.2	3B 0, 2B 0	-0.5
2009	FRE	AAA	25	535	74	37	2	16	78	42	90	4	2	.281/.350/.468	.283	.312	0.4	3B 8, SS 0	3.7
2009	SFN	MLB	25	20	0	1	0	0	4	1	6	0	0	.158/.200/.211	.137	.231	-1.4	3B 1, SS 0	-0.2
2010	FRE	AAA	26	325	46	23	0	8	48	29	59	3	0	.311/.392/.477	.284	.365	0.0	SS 6, 3B 4	3.0
2010	SFN	MLB	26	18	1	0	0	0	1	2	5	0	0	.200/.278/.200	.171	.273	-1.2	3B -1, SS -1	-0.4
2011	*SFN*	*MLB*	*27*	*472*	*57*	*25*	*0*	*14*	*56*	*38*	*94*	*2*	*1*	*.258/.325/.424*	*.263*	*.293*	*-0.1*	*3B 5, SS 1*	*2.0*

A college product, Rohlinger has always been a bit old for his leagues, which makes his solid-but-unspectacular career minor-league batting line (.272/.353/.442) less striking. For that reason, the Giants attempted to diversify the third baseman's defensive portfolio in 2009, giving him some exposure at second base and shortstop. The latter worked well enough that Rohlinger spent the majority of his time at shortstop in 2010, which makes him a rare offense-first utility option for the big club.

Cody Ross RF

Born: **12/23/1980** Age: **30**
Bats: **R** Throws: **L** Height: **5' 11"** Weight: **180**
Breakout: **4%** Improve: **41%** Collapse: **2%**
Attrition: **14%** MLB: **100%**

Comparables:
Xavier Nady, Jim Edmonds, Carl Everett (76)

YEAR	TEAM	LVL	AGE	PA	R	2B	3B	HR	RBI	BB	SO	SB	CS	AVG/OBP/SLG	TAv	BABIP	BRR	FRAA	WARP
2008	FLO	MLB	27	506	59	29	5	22	73	33	116	6	1	.260/.316/.488	.275	.299	0.2	CF 4, RF 2	2.6
2009	FLO	MLB	28	603	73	37	1	24	90	34	121	5	2	.271/.322/.470	.268	.306	-2.8	CF -1, RF 3	1.9
2010	FLO	MLB	29	487	60	24	3	11	58	30	100	9	1	.266/.316/.405	.264	.319	0.6	CF -7, RF 4	1.1
2010	SFN	MLB	29	82	10	4	0	3	7	7	21	0	1	.288/.354/.466	.281	.360	-1.0	CF -2, LF -2	-0.2
2011	*SFN*	*MLB*	*30*	*452*	*56*	*24*	*1*	*16*	*59*	*33*	*93*	*5*	*2*	*.266/.326/.453*	*.271*	*.303*	*-0.1*	*CF -3, RF 2*	*1.4*

Ross's isolated power has dropped in each of the last two seasons, which is a bad trend for a player who just turned 30 and doesn't hit for average, draw walks, steal many bases, hit righties, or have sufficient range for center field. An arbitration victory last February that awarded him a $4.45 million salary for 2010 and a .208/.257/.333 performance in 43 games after July 1 prompted the Marlins to waive him in late August. The Giants immediately picked him up, and a late-September hot streak turned into full-blown post-season heroics as Ross hit .337/.410/.697 with eight homers, including four in three consecutive post-season games. As exciting as that was, Ross will go back to being an overextended (and overcompensated) fourth outfielder in April.

Aaron Rowand CF

Born: 8/29/1977 Age: 33
Bats: R Throws: R Height: 6' 1" Weight: 200
Breakout: 0% Improve: 38% Collapse: 9%
Attrition: 15% MLB: 96%

Comparables:
Torii Hunter, Craig Monroe, Leon Wagner (82)

YEAR	TEAM	LVL	AGE	PA	R	2B	3B	HR	RBI	BB	SO	SB	CS	AVG/OBP/SLG	TAv	BABIP	BRR	FRAA	WARP
2008	SFN	MLB	30	611	57	37	0	13	70	44	126	2	4	.271/.339/.410	.265	.329	-2.1	CF 11	2.9
2009	SFN	MLB	31	546	62	30	2	15	64	30	125	4	1	.261/.319/.419	.258	.318	0.9	CF -2	1.3
2010	SFN	MLB	32	357	42	12	2	11	34	16	74	5	3	.230/.280/.378	.237	.262	1.3	CF 2	0.4
2011	*SFN*	*MLB*	*33*	*529*	*63*	*27*	*1*	*15*	*61*	*34*	*106*	*5*	*2*	*.262/.324/.417*	*.261*	*.303*	*-0.4*	*CF 0*	*1.5*

It would be easy to blame Rowand's worst season on the Vicente Padilla pitch that fractured his cheekbone in two places in late April, but he went 11-for-32 with five extra-base hits in his first week off the DL in early May. After that, his bat went into hiding. Rowand hit .202/.259/.320 over his final 275 regular-season plate appearances, lost his center-field job to Andres Torres in early June, and remained a bench player thereafter. In the postseason, he was an afterthought, making just three starts and reaching base just once in those games. For that, he was paid $12 million, as he will be remunerated in each of the next two seasons. The Giants' outfield alternatives aren't strong enough for them to toss Rowand aside as a sunk cost just yet, but that point is quickly approaching.

Freddy Sanchez 2B

Born: 12/21/1977 Age: 33
Bats: R Throws: R Height: 5' 11" Weight: 185
Breakout: 0% Improve: 29% Collapse: 1%
Attrition: 9% MLB: 93%

Comparables:
Mark Ellis, Ronnie Belliard, Roberto Alomar (78)

YEAR	TEAM	LVL	AGE	PA	R	2B	3B	HR	RBI	BB	SO	SB	CS	AVG/OBP/SLG	TAv	BABIP	BRR	FRAA	WARP
2008	PIT	MLB	30	608	76	26	2	9	52	21	63	0	1	.271/.294/.371	.238	.284	-1.5	2B -6	-0.6
2009	PIT	MLB	31	382	45	28	3	6	34	20	60	5	1	.296/.333/.442	.272	.337	-2.9	2B -9	0.2
2009	SFN	MLB	31	107	11	1	0	1	7	2	16	0	0	.284/.290/.324	.216	.318	0.6	2B 4	0.2
2010	SFN	MLB	32	479	55	22	1	7	47	32	68	3	1	.292/.336/.397	.268	.323	-2.0	2B 1	1.4
2011	*SFN*	*MLB*	*33*	*580*	*69*	*32*	*1*	*9*	*64*	*34*	*72*	*3*	*1*	*.292/.332/.408*	*.261*	*.315*	*-0.1*	*2B -5*	*0.9*

Sanchez's 2010 season was bookended by surgeries on his left shoulder, making him the third man in this chapter to have a body part operated on for the second time in a 12-month span. Sanchez's first surgery, performed two days before Christmas in 2009, delayed the start of his 2010 campaign, but despite the need for doctors to go back in to clean things up this past December, he showed little negative impact from the sore joint during the season. In fact, the only thing that made his year distinct from his previous two was a nice little uptick in his walk rate. Sanchez drew an unintentional walk once every 24 plate appearances in his first five seasons as a major-league starter, but dropped that to a still-poor-but-significantly improved 15.4 PAs last year. It has been a long time since Sanchez hit .344, and his lack of secondary skills means that his value is down to a .290 average and a competent glove. He remains under contract to the Giants for this year, after which his limitations should make him a year-to-year player (unless Omar Minaya gets another job).

Pablo Sandoval 3B

Born: 8/11/1986 Age: 24
Bats: S Throws: R Height: 5' 11" Weight: 245
Breakout: 2% Improve: 54% Collapse: 4%
Attrition: 16% MLB: 86%

Comparables:
Billy Butler, James Loney, Ryan Zimmerman (56)

YEAR	TEAM	LVL	AGE	PA	R	2B	3B	HR	RBI	BB	SO	SB	CS	AVG/OBP/SLG	TAv	BABIP	BRR	FRAA	WARP
2008	SJO	A+	21	301	61	25	2	12	59	23	39	2	1	.359/.412/.597	.374	.384	-0.8	C 0, 1B 2	4.7
2008	NRW	AA	21	184	29	13	0	8	37	8	20	0	1	.337/.364/.549	.313	.345	1.8	C 0, 1B 0	1.9
2008	SFN	MLB	21	154	25	10	1	3	24	4	14	0	0	.345/.357/.490	.295	.356	0.4	1B 1, C 0	1.0
2009	SFN	MLB	22	633	81	44	5	25	90	52	83	5	5	.330/.387/.556	.329	.350	-5.3	3B -4, 1B 0	5.3
2010	SFN	MLB	23	616	62	34	3	13	63	47	81	3	2	.268/.323/.409	.261	.291	-0.5	3B -5, 1B -3	0.9
2011	*SFN*	*MLB*	*24*	*628*	*85*	*38*	*2*	*21*	*88*	*46*	*78*	*4*	*2*	*.307/.358/.491*	*.295*	*.322*	*-0.3*	*3B -4, C 0*	*3.3*

Sandoval wasn't just the lynchpin of the 2009 Giants' offense; he *was* their offense. His 2009 VORP was higher than the next four highest totals on the team *combined*. Heading into that offseason, the Giants had visions of a slimmer, more muscular Sandoval who could stick at third base and hold up better under the 162-game grind. The grueling Operation Panda commenced that November and looked to be a rousing success when Sandoval batted .368/.433/.575 in April, but save for a small surge in late August, things went decisively south. He hit just .250/.303/.378 over the remainder of the season, ultimately coughing up the third-base job because of his bat, not his glove (which remained reasonably solid). By season's end, the Giants were back to square one with regard to the snacktastic Sandoval's conditioning. Not only were the Giants threatening to send him back to Triple-A to start 2011 if he didn't shape up, but the Giant Panda Anti-Defamation League was threatening a media campaign. There were some positive indicators last season: after April, Sandoval still hit .310/.364/.500 at home, and his miserable .196/.246/.268 performance on the road owed at least a little to bad luck on balls in play. He also struggled mightily from the right side of the plate (.227/.284/.305), much as he did as a rookie in 2008. That last means either that the lefty-mashing he did in 2009 was a fluke or that whatever adjustments he made to secure that success could be made again. Sandoval is a project, which is disappointing given how brightly he shined in 2009, but he's still just 24 and well worth the effort, which appeared to be paying off in the weight-loss department as we went to press.

Nate Schierholtz **RF**

Born: **2/15/1984** Age: **27**
Bats: **L** Throws: **R** Height: **6' 2"** Weight: **215**
Breakout: **1%** Improve: **35%** Collapse: **7%**
Attrition: **18%** MLB: **82%**

Comparables:
Travis Buck, Kevin McReynolds, Tommy Davis (73)

YEAR	TEAM	LVL	AGE	PA	R	2B	3B	HR	RBI	BB	SO	SB	CS	AVG/OBP/SLG	TAv	BABIP	BRR	FRAA	WARP
2008	FRE	AAA	24	377	62	22	10	18	73	21	51	9	3	.320/.363/.594	.320	.332	2.8	RF -3	3.1
2008	SFN	MLB	24	81	12	8	1	1	5	3	8	0	1	.320/.370/.493	.301	.349	0.6	RF 1	0.6
2009	SFN	MLB	25	308	33	19	2	5	29	16	58	3	1	.267/.302/.400	.245	.311	-0.7	RF 3	0.3
2010	SFN	MLB	26	252	30	13	3	3	17	20	38	4	5	.242/.310/.366	.245	.277	1.0	RF 2	0.3
2011	*SFN*	*MLB*	*27*	*396*	*49*	*23*	*4*	*10*	*51*	*24*	*61*	*7*	*3*	*.278/.325/.447*	*.269*	*.304*	*-0.4*	*RF -1*	*0.8*

Out of options, Schierholtz spent his first full season in the major leagues serving primarily as a defensive replacement. After May 31, postseason included, he appeared in 104 games but started just 12. He is a fine defender, a viable pinch-runner—provided you don't need him to steal—and performed well as a pinch-hitter last year (9-for-29 with six walks and a third of his hits going for extra bases), but the last stat was in a small sample, and his batting line as a sub looked more like his overall line, which isn't about to earn him a starting job anywhere.

Andres Torres **CF**

Born: **1/26/1978** Age: **33**
Bats: **S** Throws: **R** Height: **5' 10"** Weight: **175**
Breakout: **1%** Improve: **39%** Collapse: **4%**
Attrition: **9%** MLB: **92%**

Comparables:
Amos Otis, Robin Yount, David Dellucci (65)

YEAR	TEAM	LVL	AGE	PA	R	2B	3B	HR	RBI	BB	SO	SB	CS	AVG/OBP/SLG	TAv	BABIP	BRR	FRAA	WARP
2008	IOW	AAA	30	479	91	27	10	11	51	55	103	29	4	.306/.384/.501	.302	.373	8.1	LF 0, CF 2	4.7
2009	SFN	MLB	31	170	28	6	8	6	23	16	45	6	1	.270/.341/.533	.302	.343	1.2	LF 1, CF 6	1.9
2010	SFN	MLB	32	570	84	43	8	16	63	56	128	26	7	.268/.340/.479	.288	.326	8.0	CF 5, RF 3	4.9
2011	*SFN*	*MLB*	*33*	*433*	*53*	*23*	*4*	*12*	*53*	*44*	*104*	*18*	*5*	*.259/.332/.436*	*.267*	*.316*	*0.2*	*CF 4, LF 3*	*2.0*

Torres also spent his first full season in the major leagues in 2010, but he was six years older than Schierholtz and had been bouncing around the minors for 12 years with six organizations (one of them twice). A high-school sprinter in his native Puerto Rico, Torres didn't play baseball until his senior year, was drafted by the Tigers after just three scholastic seasons, and, because of his speed, was tutored to be a slap-hitting leadoff man. It wasn't until he returned to the Tigers organization nearly 10 years later that he changed his approach, doing so after finally taking the attention-deficit disorder medication prescribed for him five years earlier. Adopting a heavier bat and patterning his swing after that of Albert Pujols, Torres completely revamped his approach. A career .257/.352/.321 hitter in the majors and minors combined over the previous nine seasons, Torres has hit .285/.361/.489 in 1,831 plate appearances since. That seems like a large-enough sample to suggest that he can repeat his age-32 breakout season, giving the Giants one of the best center fielders in baseball and Aaron Rowand for a combined $12.5 million.

Juan Uribe **INF**

Born: **7/22/1979** Age: **31**
Bats: **R** Throws: **R** Height: **5' 11"** Weight: **173**
Breakout: **2%** Improve: **31%** Collapse: **4%**
Attrition: **8%** MLB: **95%**

Comparables:
Alex Gonzalez, Rich Aurilia, Vern Stephens (80)

YEAR	TEAM	LVL	AGE	PA	R	2B	3B	HR	RBI	BB	SO	SB	CS	AVG/OBP/SLG	TAv	BABIP	BRR	FRAA	WARP
2008	CHA	MLB	28	353	38	22	1	7	40	22	64	1	3	.247/.292/.386	.248	.282	0.5	3B 8, 2B 0	1.3
2009	SFN	MLB	29	432	50	26	4	16	55	25	82	3	1	.289/.326/.495	.289	.321	2.9	3B 1, SS -1	3.1
2010	SFN	MLB	30	575	65	24	2	24	85	45	92	1	2	.248/.310/.440	.263	.256	-0.4	SS -7, 3B 2	1.8
2011	*LAN*	*MLB*	*31*	*486*	*58*	*23*	*2*	*18*	*64*	*34*	*83*	*3*	*2*	*.259/.309/.444*	*.262*	*.276*	*-0.4*	*SS -2, 3B 2*	*1.7*

Even beyond his pennant-clinching homer, Uribe's two Giants seasons ranked among the top three of his 10-year major league career, which isn't as much of a back-handed compliment as it might seem. A player who can fill in capably at all three infield skill positions while hitting for power and not killing you with outs is valuable, and thanks to an unexpected improvement in his walk rate in 2010, Uribe was that player again last year, despite a 40-point drop in batting average. He drew an unintentional walk once every 20 at-bats in his first eight big-league seasons, but improved that number to one every 14.6 at-bats in 2010 and added 10 free bases via manager's order or hit-by-pitch. Of course, there's no guarantee that Uribe won't revert to his hacktastic ways in 2011 and beyond, and even if he doesn't, the three-year, $21 million contract the Dodgers gave him over the winter was too generous in both dimensions.

Eugenio Velez **UT**

Born: **5/16/1982** Age: **29**
Bats: **S** Throws: **R** Height: **6' 1"** Weight: **160**
Breakout: **1%** Improve: **47%** Collapse: **2%**
Attrition: **13%** MLB: **84%**

Comparables:
Cory Sullivan, Steve Finley, Rudy Law (70)

YEAR	TEAM	LVL	AGE	PA	R	2B	3B	HR	RBI	BB	SO	SB	CS	AVG/OBP/SLG	TAv	BABIP	BRR	FRAA	WARP
2008	FRE	AAA	26	188	25	11	4	5	15	17	32	13	9	.310/.372/.509	.291	.358	-1.6	LF -2, 2B -6	0.0
2008	SFN	MLB	26	292	30	16	7	1	30	14	40	15	6	.262/.298/.382	.239	.301	1.7	2B -9, LF -2	-0.8
2009	FRE	AAA	27	197	30	13	3	3	26	13	26	16	9	.297/.340/.451	.282	.329	1.7	CF 0, 2B -1	1.0
2009	SFN	MLB	27	307	39	13	5	5	31	16	55	11	5	.267/.306/.400	.253	.310	5.4	LF -3, 2B 3	0.8
2010	FRE	AAA	28	352	50	13	5	7	35	24	55	31	16	.302/.353/.439	.279	.340	1.1	CF -2, 2B 3	1.5
2010	SFN	MLB	28	66	7	2	0	2	8	6	9	0	0	.164/.227/.309	.210	.143	0.1	LF 2, CF 0	0.1
2011	*SFN*	*MLB*	*29*	*460*	*53*	*21*	*5*	*7*	*50*	*30*	*78*	*31*	*13*	*.274/.319/.398*	*.253*	*.312*	*-1.4*	*2B -2, LF -2*	*0.0*

Velez didn't offer up any surprises in his age-28 season. His Triple-A batting line was right in line with his career rates, and he didn't hit a lick in his three major-league stints before being nontendered in December. His speed and ability to spot at second or in all three pastures earned him a nonroster look from the Dodgers, but there's not much to see here.

PITCHERS

Jeremy Affeldt

Born: **6/6/1979** Age: **32**
Bats: L Throws: L Height: **6' 4"** Weight: **215**
Breakout **18%** Improve: **37%** Collapse: **24%**
Attrition: **15%** MLB: **74%**

Comparables:
Peter Moylan, Jerry Spradlin, Scott Proctor (77)

YEAR	TEAM	LVL	AGE	W	L	SV	G	GS	IP	H	HR	BB	SO	EqBB9	EqSO9	GB%	BABIP	WHIP	ERA	FRA	WARP
2008	CIN	MLB	29	1	1	0	74	0	78^{1}	78	9	25	80	2.9	9.2	57%	.317	1.35	3.33	3.34	1.5
2009	SFN	MLB	30	2	2	0	74	0	62^{1}	42	3	30	55	4.3	7.9	65%	.250	1.20	1.73	2.95	1.3
2010	SFN	MLB	31	4	3	4	53	0	50	56	4	24	44	4.3	7.9	60%	.340	1.66	4.14	4.39	0.2
2011	*SFN*	*MLB*	*32*	*4*	*2*	*1*	*75*	*0*	*71*	*67*	*6*	*32*	*57*	*4.1*	*7.2*	*52%*	*.297*	*1.40*	*4.03*	*4.39*	*0.1*

Affeldt's spike in ground balls and double plays in 2009 proved to be fluky, though he compensated some in 2010 with a boost in infield pop-ups, which probably helped him survive a 106-point increase in his opponents' batting average on balls in play. In the big picture, Affeldt is actually consistent. He's a good, not great, left-handed set-up man whose even platoon split makes him viable beyond a matchup role, as he showed in two perfect innings in relief of Jonathan Sanchez in the Giants' pennant-clinching victory against the Phillies.

Madison Bumgarner

Born: **8/1/1989** Age: **21**
Bats: R Throws: L Height: **6' 4"** Weight: **215**
Breakout **15%** Improve: **38%** Collapse: **9%**
Attrition: **7%** MLB: **65%**

Comparables:
Don Robinson, Don Drysdale, Bert Blyleven (55)

YEAR	TEAM	LVL	AGE	W	L	SV	G	GS	IP	H	HR	BB	SO	EqBB9	EqSO9	GB%	BABIP	WHIP	ERA	FRA	WARP
2008	AUG	A	18	17	3	0	26	28	155^{2}	118	3	23	180	1.3	10.4	43%	.298	0.94	1.27	1.81	7.0
2009	SJO	A+	19	3	1	0	5	5	24^{1}	20	0	4	23	1.5	8.5	41%	.282	1.07	1.48	2.57	0.9
2009	NRW	AA	19	9	1	0	20	19	107	80	6	30	69	2.5	5.8	44%	.236	1.06	1.93	3.55	2.3
2009	SFN	MLB	19	0	0	0	4	1	10	8	2	3	10	2.7	9.0	59%	.240	1.10	1.80	3.78	0.1
2010	FRE	AAA	20	7	1	0	14	14	82^{2}	88	5	22	59	2.4	6.5	48%	.319	1.36	3.16	3.45	2.3
2010	SFN	MLB	20	7	6	0	18	18	111	119	11	26	86	2.1	7.0	46%	.314	1.35	3.00	3.06	3.2
2011	*SFN*	*MLB*	*21*	*11*	*8*	*0*	*28*	*28*	*156*	*157*	*15*	*48*	*108*	*2.8*	*6.2*	*44%*	*.296*	*1.31*	*3.84*	*4.17*	*3.3*

Bumgarner's season ended in a very different place from where it began. In the spring, five miles per hour that had gone missing from his fastball down the stretch in 2009 hadn't returned, and he was getting lit up. The pitcher later admitted that poor off-season conditioning and uncooperative mechanics had largely been to blame; accordingly, he got stronger as the season progressed, his fastball got faster, and his results got better. It didn't take long; Bumgarner posted a 0.94 ERA in May and was called up at the end of June. Back in the majors, he only once followed a nonquality start with another of the same kind, missing by just one out in that lone case. He was dominant down the stretch, posting a 1.18 ERA in his last six starts and striking out 32 men in 32 innings against four walks and one homer in his last five. For those who weren't paying attention, he announced his arrival with eight shutout innings in his only World Series start.

Matt Cain

Born: **10/1/1984** Age: **26**
Bats: R Throws: R Height: **6' 3"** Weight: **231**
Breakout **13%** Improve: **39%** Collapse: **22%**
Attrition: **12%** MLB: **95%**

Comparables:
Freddy Garcia, Andy Benes, Andy Pettitte (61)

YEAR	TEAM	LVL	AGE	W	L	SV	G	GS	IP	H	HR	BB	SO	EqBB9	EqSO9	GB%	BABIP	WHIP	ERA	FRA	WARP
2008	SFN	MLB	23	8	14	0	34	34	217^{2}	206	19	91	186	3.8	7.7	34%	.297	1.40	3.76	3.89	4.1
2009	SFN	MLB	24	14	8	0	33	33	217^{2}	184	22	73	171	3.0	7.1	41%	.263	1.19	2.89	3.35	5.3
2010	SFN	MLB	25	13	11	0	33	33	223^{1}	181	22	61	177	2.5	7.1	37%	.252	1.10	3.14	4.57	1.6
2011	*SFN*	*MLB*	*26*	*14*	*8*	*0*	*32*	*32*	*211*	*188*	*20*	*74*	*165*	*3.1*	*7.0*	*40%*	*.276*	*1.24*	*3.35*	*3.64*	*5.3*

A model of consistency, Cain was up to his usual tricks in 2010: a flock of fly balls, a low opponents' batting average on balls in play, and the overall performance of a solid second starter. Most encouragingly, Cain dropped his walk rate significantly for the second straight season, putting him more than a walk per nine innings below his 2008 rate and resulting in career-bests in walks and hits per innings pitched (WHIP) and strikeout-to-walk ratio. During the regular season, he matched NL leaders Roy Halladay, Adam Wainwright, and Ubaldo Jimenez with 25 quality starts in 33 turns, and in the postseason, he didn't allow an earned run in 21 1/3 innings across three starts. Not bad for a guy who could be the third-best starter on his team in 2011. Cain represents a sharp divide between two ways of evaluating pitchers: process or results. His BABIP perpetually falls below the league average, nearly 50 points below in 2010. Whether this is something that we simply are unable to measure in Cain's approach, or a statistical oddity that has been cherry-picked because of how unlikely it is, is impossible to tell with the data we have at hand. So Cain's value to his team could be the value represented by his Fair RA, as shown in the preceding chart, or the much greater value his ERA suggests. The Giants, of course, are hoping for the latter.

Santiago Casilla
Born: **6/25/1980** Age: **31**
Bats: **R** Throws: **R** Height: **6' 0"** Weight: **164**
Breakout **16%** Improve: **34%** Collapse: **30%**
Attrition: **12%** MLB: **83%**
Comparables:
Paul Abbott, Stan Belinda, Kerry Ligtenberg (78)

YEAR	TEAM	LVL	AGE	W	L	SV	G	GS	IP	H	HR	BB	SO	EqBB9	EqSO9	GB%	BABIP	WHIP	ERA	FRA	WARP
2008	OAK	MLB	28	2	1	2	51	0	50^{1}	60	5	21	43	3.8	7.7	45%	.348	1.67	3.93	2.69	1.6
2009	OAK	MLB	29	1	2	0	46	0	48^{1}	61	6	25	35	4.7	6.5	51%	.335	1.84	5.96	5.56	-0.2
2010	SFN	MLB	30	7	2	2	52	0	55^{1}	40	2	26	56	4.2	9.1	51%	.277	1.27	1.95	2.73	1.5
2011	*SFN*	*MLB*	*31*	*3*	*1*	*1*	*53*	*0*	55^{1}	*53*	*5*	*25*	*48*	*4.1*	*7.9*	*46%*	*.307*	*1.42*	*4.11*	*4.47*	*0.1*

Released by the A's in December 2009, Casilla caught on with the cross-bay Giants, found a couple extra ticks on his fastball, ditched his rarely used changeup for a very effective curve, and emerged with his best major-league season. The Giants' third-best reliever by WXRL, and Bruce Bochy's preferred righty in the sixth and seventh innings, Casilla enjoyed success that was the result of a strong strikeout rate and a little luck with balls in play and fly balls staying in the park. (Casilla, who is not a ground-ball pitcher, allowed just two homers all year and none in 25 appearances on the road.) Normally, we'd caution against expecting a repeat of a career year like that from a short reliever, but given the change in repertoire, Casilla could hold on to some of his gains.

Alex Hinshaw
Born: **10/31/1982** Age: **28**
Bats: **L** Throws: **L** Height: **6' 4"** Weight: **190**
Breakout **8%** Improve: **13%** Collapse: **14%**
Attrition: **11%** MLB: **29%**
Comparables:
Billy Sadler, Francisco Cruceta, Brad Lidge (74)

YEAR	TEAM	LVL	AGE	W	L	SV	G	GS	IP	H	HR	BB	SO	EqBB9	EqSO9	GB%	BABIP	WHIP	ERA	FRA	WARP
2008	SFN	MLB	25	2	1	0	48	0	39^{2}	31	5	29	47	6.6	10.7	27%	.274	1.59	3.40	3.41	0.8
2009	FRE	AAA	26	1	2	1	46	0	52^{1}	42	3	32	72	5.5	12.4	41%	.307	1.47	3.96	3.16	0.9
2009	SFN	MLB	26	0	0	0	9	0	6	10	2	7	2	10.5	3.0	33%	.364	2.83	12.00	12.71	-0.5
2010	FRE	AAA	27	2	4	0	50	0	56	47	3	40	65	6.4	10.4	43%	.299	1.68	4.66	5.04	0.1
2011	*SFN*	*MLB*	*28*	*3*	*1*	*1*	*56*	*0*	57^{1}	*49*	*5*	*38*	*61*	*6.0*	*9.6*	*42%*	*.298*	*1.52*	*4.33*	*4.70*	*-0.1*

Hinshaw seemed to be harnessing his control in 2008, but he took a significant step backward in 2009 and yet another in 2010, walking 6.4 men per nine innings while also hitting seven batters and uncorking seven wild pitches in just 56 innings at Double-A. Hinshaw has excellent stuff, and lefties get a million chances, but he's now 28, he didn't get a sniff from the major league club last year, and everything is heading in the wrong direction.

Tim Lincecum
Born: **6/15/1984** Age: **27**
Bats: **L** Throws: **R** Height: **5' 11"** Weight: **160**
Breakout **21%** Improve: **46%** Collapse: **26%**
Attrition: **2%** MLB: **100%**
Comparables:
Pedro Martinez, Mario Soto, John Montefusco (59)

YEAR	TEAM	LVL	AGE	W	L	SV	G	GS	IP	H	HR	BB	SO	EqBB9	EqSO9	GB%	BABIP	WHIP	ERA	FRA	WARP
2008	SFN	MLB	24	18	5	0	34	33	227	182	11	84	265	3.3	10.5	44%	.304	1.20	2.62	2.88	7.4
2009	SFN	MLB	25	15	7	0	32	32	225^{1}	168	10	68	261	2.7	10.4	49%	.282	1.07	2.48	2.96	6.5
2010	SFN	MLB	26	16	10	0	33	33	212^{1}	194	18	76	231	3.2	9.8	50%	.310	1.30	3.43	3.48	4.5
2011	*SFN*	*MLB*	*27*	*12*	*6*	*0*	*26*	*26*	*177*	*147*	*12*	*63*	*190*	*3.2*	*9.6*	*47%*	*.298*	*1.18*	*2.74*	*2.98*	*6.0*

Replace Lincecum's five August starts with his five post-season starts, and you get this season line: 20-6, 246 K, 2.78 ERA, 1.15 WHIP, 3.42 strikeout-to-walk ratio, 223 2/3 IP. The only thing different about Lincecum's 2010 season was the little hiccup in August, when he went 0-5 with a 7.82 ERA. Some blame the aberration on Lincecum's curious decision to experiment with his famous mechanics, bringing his hands over his head to start his windup rather than keeping them pinned to his thigh, but he did that only for three starts beginning on July 30, and the first two were solid outings. After being lit up by the Cubs in the third, he went back to his old windup, but struggled for three more starts. Lincecum's windup tweak was less the cause of his struggles than a reaction to them, stemming from a poor July 20 start against the Dodgers. The tweak's failure to really help is of little consequence, given that once he did return to form, he was dominant right through the final game of the World Series, going 9-2 with a 2.18 ERA, 0.91 WHIP, 10.8 K/9, and 5.53 K/BB in 12 starts in September and October. In short, Lincecum will be letting his Freak flag fly over AT&T Park again this year.

Javier Lopez
Born: **7/11/1977** Age: **33**
Bats: **L** Throws: **L** Height: **6' 4"** Weight: **200**
Breakout **11%** Improve: **13%** Collapse: **9%**
Attrition: **4%** MLB: **33%**
Comparables:
Ryan Vogelsong, Ben McDonald, Luke Hudson (76)

YEAR	TEAM	LVL	AGE	W	L	SV	G	GS	IP	H	HR	BB	SO	EqBB9	EqSO9	GB%	BABIP	WHIP	ERA	FRA	WARP
2008	BOS	MLB	30	2	0	0	70	0	59^{1}	53	4	27	38	4.1	5.8	61%	.278	1.38	2.43	3.32	1.2
2009	PAW	AAA	31	1	1	0	38	0	39^{2}	35	2	13	23	2.9	5.2	62%	.275	1.23	3.17	4.02	0.5
2009	BOS	MLB	31	0	2	0	14	0	11^{2}	20	1	9	5	6.9	3.9	50%	.404	2.66	9.26	7.92	-0.3
2010	PIT	MLB	32	2	2	0	50	0	38^{2}	39	2	18	22	4.2	5.1	60%	.303	1.53	2.79	3.87	0.4
2010	SFN	MLB	32	2	0	0	27	0	19	11	0	2	16	0.9	7.6	67%	.216	0.68	1.42	3.00	0.4
2011	*SFN*	*MLB*	*33*	*3*	*1*	*0*	*67*	*0*	*56*	*58*	*5*	*25*	*33*	*3.9*	*5.3*	*51%*	*.298*	*1.45*	*4.38*	*4.77*	*-0.1*

Acquired at the trade deadline for first baseman John Bowker and right-hander Joe Martinez, side-arming LOOGY Lopez became a key member of the Giants' bullpen down the stretch, facing higher-leverage situations than everyone else except closer Brian Wilson and chief set-up man Sergio Romo and handling them with aplomb. Not only did Lopez dominate lefties (.164/.188/.179), but he also kept righties in check, raised his typically below-league-average strikeout rate, and issued just two walks to the 69 hitters he faced as a Giant over the season's final two months. In the postseason, he retired 16 of the 18 men he faced, stranded all four runners he inherited, and earned the win in the pennant-clinching game with a scoreless inning of work against the Phillies. He won't be that good again in 2011, but he should settle back into his pre-2009 form, or roughly what he was doing with the Pirates before the Giants rescued him.

Guillermo Mota

Born: **7/25/1973** Age: **37**
Bats: **R** Throws: **R** Height: **6' 4"** Weight: **205**
Breakout **11%** Improve: **19%** Collapse: **16%**
Attrition: **8%** MLB: **47%**

Comparables:
Elmer Dessens, Aaron Fultz, Kaz Ishii (73)

YEAR	TEAM	LVL	AGE	W	L	SV	G	GS	IP	H	HR	BB	SO	EqBB9	EqSO9	GB%	BABIP	WHIP	ERA	FRA	WARP
2008	MIL	MLB	34	5	6	1	58	0	57	52	7	28	50	4.4	7.9	46%	.283	1.40	4.11	5.03	0.0
2009	LAN	MLB	35	3	4	0	61	0	65^1	53	6	24	39	3.3	5.4	39%	.236	1.26	3.44	4.31	0.5
2010	SFN	MLB	36	1	3	1	56	0	54	49	4	22	38	3.7	6.3	39%	.274	1.31	4.33	5.57	-0.5
2011	*SFN*	*MLB*	*37*	*3*	*1*	*1*	*60*	*0*	*60*	*59*	*7*	*24*	*40*	*3.7*	*6.1*	*43%*	*.287*	*1.39*	*4.12*	*4.48*	*0.0*

Mota is like that old shirt you can't quite bring yourself to toss out. It's ugly, stained, and filled with holes; it doesn't fit right; you can't really wear it anywhere without looking unwashed; and your spouse hates it. But it sufficiently clothes you, you have to wear something when doing laundry or mowing the lawn, and every now and again, you begin to think it would look cool in a thrift-shop-chic kind of way. You're wrong, of course, but you keep putting it on. The Giants brought Mota to camp as a nonroster invitee, got suckered into bringing him north, and were briefly rewarded by a hot start, but things got ugly thereafter and he was a net negative per WXRL. Naturally, the Giants signed him to another minor-league contract, but while Mota is never quite bad enough to get thrown out, they really shouldn't wear him in public.

Ramon Ramirez

Born: **8/31/1981** Age: **29**
Bats: **R** Throws: **R** Height: **5' 11"** Weight: **190**
Breakout **19%** Improve: **48%** Collapse: **27%**
Attrition: **7%** MLB: **95%**

Comparables:
Andy McGaffigan, T.J. Mathews, Dave Righetti (83)

YEAR	TEAM	LVL	AGE	W	L	SV	G	GS	IP	H	HR	BB	SO	EqBB9	EqSO9	GB%	BABIP	WHIP	ERA	FRA	WARP
2008	KCA	MLB	26	3	2	1	71	0	71^2	57	2	31	70	3.9	8.8	49%	.287	1.23	2.64	2.99	1.8
2009	BOS	MLB	27	7	4	0	70	0	69^2	61	7	32	52	4.1	6.7	37%	.262	1.39	2.84	3.19	1.5
2010	BOS	MLB	28	0	3	2	44	0	42^1	39	6	16	31	3.4	6.6	36%	.264	1.30	4.46	4.79	0.0
2010	SFN	MLB	28	1	0	1	25	0	27	13	1	11	15	3.7	5.0	39%	.152	0.89	0.67	0.65	1.6
2011	*SFN*	*MLB*	*29*	*3*	*1*	*1*	*64*	*0*	*64*	*59*	*6*	*28*	*51*	*3.9*	*7.1*	*43%*	*.284*	*1.35*	*3.74*	*4.06*	*0.4*

Ramirez's strikeout rate has declined in each of the last two seasons, but a BABIP heading in the same direction has helped him hold the line in his overall numbers. Still, the net effect is not unlike stretching a rubber band; at some point it will snap back, and that's going to hurt, particularly at arbitration prices. Monthly splits show that Ramirez was more effective as the 2010 season went along, but again, luck on balls in play contributed to his superficial success. His highest single-month mark was .289 in April, and in September, his opponents hit just .077 on balls in play. That last stat is harder to repeat than "toy boat."

Chris Ray

Born: **1/12/1982** Age: **29**
Bats: **R** Throws: **R** Height: **6' 3"** Weight: **200**
Breakout **10%** Improve: **27%** Collapse: **32%**
Attrition: **17%** MLB: **69%**

Comparables:
Duaner Sanchez, Chad Cordero, Alan Benes (82)

YEAR	TEAM	LVL	AGE	W	L	SV	G	GS	IP	H	HR	BB	SO	EqBB9	EqSO9	GB%	BABIP	WHIP	ERA	FRA	WARP
2009	BAL	MLB	27	0	4	0	46	0	43^1	64	8	23	39	4.8	8.1	44%	.392	2.03	7.27	6.28	-0.5
2010	TEX	MLB	28	2	0	1	35	0	31^2	24	4	16	16	4.5	4.5	38%	.206	1.26	3.41	5.68	-0.3
2010	SFN	MLB	28	3	0	1	28	0	24	24	1	9	15	3.4	5.6	45%	.303	1.38	4.13	3.90	0.2
2011	*SFN*	*MLB*	*29*	*2*	*1*	*0*	*47*	*0*	*45*	*47*	*5*	*20*	*34*	*4.0*	*6.7*	*44%*	*.301*	*1.47*	*4.56*	*4.96*	*-0.2*

As recently as the spring of 2009, Ray, then returning from a year lost to Tommy John surgery, was expected to assume his previous role as one of the major leagues' 30 closers, but rust and bad luck stymied him that season. After he was flipped to the Rangers in the Kevin Millwood trade, a far more alarming collapse of his strikeout rate undermined his efforts to reestablish himself. That he was the lone return for Bengie Molina suggests that the Giants held out hope (or that the Rangers realized how little Molina had left in the tank), but their nontender in December underlined Ray's inability to live up to his former promise. Now 29, he'll attempt to forge a career as a journeyman middle reliever.

Sergio Romo

Born: **3/4/1983** Age: **28**
Bats: R Throws: R Height: **5' 11"** Weight: **190**
Breakout **20%** Improve: **43%** Collapse: **21%**
Attrition: **3%** MLB: **82%**

Comparables:
Trevor Hoffman, Robb Nen, Joe Sambito (73)

YEAR	TEAM	LVL	AGE	W	L	SV	G	GS	IP	H	HR	BB	SO	EqBB9	EqSO9	GB%	BABIP	WHIP	ERA	FRA	WARP
2008	NRW	AA	25	1	3	11	24	0	27	22	1	7	30	2.3	10.0	30%	.309	1.15	3.33	3.47	0.5
2008	SFN	MLB	25	3	1	0	29	0	34	16	3	8	33	2.1	8.7	33%	.157	0.79	2.12	4.98	0.0
2009	SFN	MLB	26	5	2	2	45	0	34	30	1	11	41	2.9	10.9	32%	.326	1.24	3.97	3.60	0.5
2010	SFN	MLB	27	5	3	0	68	0	62	46	6	14	70	2.0	10.2	37%	.261	1.03	2.18	2.18	1.8
2011	*SFN*	*MLB*	*28*	*4*	*2*	*2*	*67*	*0*	*66^{2}*	*55*	*6*	*20*	*69*	*2.8*	*9.3*	*41%*	*.286*	*1.13*	*2.85*	*3.10*	*1.2*

Sometimes, you make your own luck. Romo had a favorable BABIP in 2010, but a look at his batted-ball types shows an increase in ground balls and a big spike in infield fly outs, which combined to reduce by a significant margin the number of outfield flies he allowed. Romo also carved a chunk out of his line-drive rate, matching his 12 percent rate from his rookie season in 2008. The changes made his .265 BABIP seem less fluky than it otherwise would have appeared. Owner of the second-most feared beard after Brian Wilson's, the junkballing Romo is establishing himself as one of the best set-up men in the business.

Daniel Runzler

Born: **3/30/1985** Age: **26**
Bats: L Throws: L Height: **6' 4"** Weight: **230**
Breakout **8%** Improve: **10%** Collapse: **8%**
Attrition: **8%** MLB: **20%**

Comparables:
Mike Zagurski, Joel Zumaya, Taylor Tankersley (75)

YEAR	TEAM	LVL	AGE	W	L	SV	G	GS	IP	H	HR	BB	SO	EqBB9	EqSO9	GB%	BABIP	WHIP	ERA	FRA	WARP
2008	AUG	A	23	0	1	0	20	0	24^{2}	25	2	19	26	6.9	9.5	61%	.338	1.86	5.47	6.69	-0.5
2008	SLO	A-	23	0	1	0	27	0	30	19	1	21	43	6.3	12.9	65%	.295	1.37	2.10	3.37	0.5
2009	AUG	A	24	1	1	11	19	0	26^{1}	8	0	13	45	4.4	15.4	78%	.195	0.95	0.68	1.85	0.6
2009	SJO	A+	24	1	0	5	19	0	21^{1}	8	1	4	26	1.7	11.0	59%	.140	0.56	0.85	1.50	0.3
2009	SFN	MLB	24	0	0	0	11	0	8^{2}	6	1	5	11	5.2	11.4	48%	.250	1.38	1.04	1.23	0.3
2010	SFN	MLB	25	3	0	0	41	0	32^{2}	29	1	20	37	5.5	10.2	57%	.329	1.53	3.03	2.78	0.8
2011	*SFN*	*MLB*	*26*	*2*	*1*	*1*	*41*	*0*	*45^{1}*	*38*	*4*	*29*	*47*	*5.7*	*9.3*	*50%*	*.294*	*1.48*	*4.12*	*4.48*	*0.0*

As a hard-throwing lefty with control problems, Runzler is comparable to Hinshaw, except that Runzler's wildness hasn't yet reached the tipping point and he's not particularly well suited to situational work, having posted a fairly even platoon split last year before a dislocated knee cap cost him nearly all of the season's second half. That split has reportedly tempted the Giants to convert Runzler to starting, something he last did in his final collegiate season with University of California, Riverside, with poor results. Not that there's any room for Runzler in the Giants' five-deep rotation—more likely, the goal is to stretch him out for long-relief duty.

Jonathan Sanchez

Born: **11/19/1982** Age: **28**
Bats: L Throws: L Height: **6' 2"** Weight: **165**
Breakout **20%** Improve: **42%** Collapse: **32%**
Attrition: **15%** MLB: **94%**

Comparables:
Melido Perez, Oliver Perez, Chad Gaudin (63)

YEAR	TEAM	LVL	AGE	W	L	SV	G	GS	IP	H	HR	BB	SO	EqBB9	EqSO9	GB%	BABIP	WHIP	ERA	FRA	WARP
2008	SFN	MLB	25	9	12	0	29	29	158	154	14	75	157	4.3	8.9	43%	.317	1.49	5.01	5.01	1.4
2009	SFN	MLB	26	8	12	0	32	29	163^{1}	135	19	88	177	4.8	9.8	42%	.276	1.40	4.24	5.02	0.9
2010	SFN	MLB	27	13	9	0	34	33	193^{1}	142	21	96	205	4.5	9.5	42%	.252	1.28	3.07	3.93	3.0
2011	*SFN*	*MLB*	*28*	*10*	*7*	*0*	*25*	*25*	*137*	*118*	*14*	*69*	*138*	*4.5*	*9.0*	*43%*	*.288*	*1.36*	*3.81*	*4.15*	*3.0*

The Giants had the second-best Park Adjusted Defensive Efficiency in the majors behind that of their World Series opponents, and Sanchez was the biggest beneficiary. Unlike the case with Romo, the only difference between Sanchez's 2009 and 2010 seasons was the performance of his defense, which helped him lead the majors with just 6.6 hits allowed per nine innings, in turn shaving more than a run off his 2009 ERA. As a result, the only progress Sanchez really made in 2010—actually, the only progress he has made in three years as a full-time starter—was adding 30 innings to his previous career high. He's due to regress, but all the external factors—league, park, and defense—and one big internal one, strikeouts, are in his favor, so the readjustment might be mild.

Henry Sosa

Born: **7/28/1985** Age: **25**
Bats: R Throws: R Height: **6' 2"** Weight: **195**
Breakout: **0%** Improve: **0%** Collapse: **0%**
Attrition: **0%** MLB: **0%**

Comparables:
Jesus Delgado, Marco Estrada, Josh Outman (86)

YEAR	TEAM	LVL	AGE	W	L	SV	G	GS	IP	H	HR	BB	SO	EqBB9	EqSO9	GB%	BABIP	WHIP	ERA	FRA	WARP
2008	SJO	A+	22	3	4	0	12	12	56^{1}	62	6	18	58	2.9	9.3	38%	.354	1.46	4.32	3.83	1.2
2009	NRW	AA	23	6	0	0	14	14	72^{1}	61	4	25	44	3.1	5.5	33%	.254	1.20	2.37	4.37	0.7
2010	FRE	AAA	24	7	8	0	36	14	115	113	20	55	83	4.3	6.5	40%	.265	1.48	4.07	4.89	1.1
2011	*SFN*	*MLB*	*25*	*4*	*5*	*0*	*20*	*13*	*77^{1}*	*82*	*12*	*40*	*50*	*4.6*	*5.8*	*41%*	*.293*	*1.58*	*5.35*	*5.82*	*0.1*

The hard-throwing Sosa has never developed the command or secondary pitches necessary to succeed as a starter, something the Giants seemed to realize in his Triple-A debut, finally, mercifully moving him to the bullpen only to return him to the Fresno rotation at the end of the season. Regardless, Sosa's future lies in relief, and the sooner the Giants accept that, the sooner he might contribute to the major-league team.

Zach Wheeler

Born: **5/30/1990** Age: **21**
Bats: **R** Throws: **R** Height: **6' 3"** Weight: **180**
Breakout **1%** Improve: **3%** Collapse: **2%**
Attrition: **1%** MLB: **5%**

Comparables:
Dave Boswell, Matt Anderson, Edwin Correa (73)

YEAR	TEAM	LVL	AGE	W	L	SV	G	GS	IP	H	HR	BB	SO	EqBB9	EqSO9	GB%	BABIP	WHIP	ERA	FRA	WARP
2010	AUG	A	20	3	3	0	21	13	58^{2}	47	0	38	70	5.9	10.8	62%	.320	1.58	3.99	3.92	1.0
2011	*SFN*	*MLB*	*21*	*5*	*5*	*0*	*20*	*13*	*56^{2}*	*52*	*5*	*39*	*52*	*6.2*	*8.2*	*47%*	*.298*	*1.60*	*4.72*	*5.13*	*0.8*

The sixth overall pick in the 2009 draft, Wheeler jumped straight from high school to the full-season Sally League in his professional debut with encouraging results, including 70 strikeouts and no home runs allowed in 58 2/3 innings. At his best, he was fantastic, hitting 96 mph with his fastball and inducing a ton of ground balls, but blister issues limited his innings and some wildness proved that he still has a long way to go.

Brian Wilson

Born: **3/16/1982** Age: **29**
Bats: **R** Throws: **R** Height: **6' 1"** Weight: **205**
Breakout **22%** Improve: **44%** Collapse: **27%**
Attrition: **6%** MLB: **89%**

Comparables:
Duane Ward, Rich Gossage, Mark Davis (76)

YEAR	TEAM	LVL	AGE	W	L	SV	G	GS	IP	H	HR	BB	SO	EqBB9	EqSO9	GB%	BABIP	WHIP	ERA	FRA	WARP
2008	SFN	MLB	26	3	2	41	63	0	62^{1}	62	7	28	67	4.0	9.7	52%	.325	1.49	4.62	4.65	0.2
2009	SFN	MLB	27	5	6	38	68	0	72^{1}	60	3	27	83	3.4	10.3	49%	.302	1.22	2.74	3.32	1.1
2010	SFN	MLB	28	3	3	48	70	0	74^{2}	62	3	26	93	3.1	11.2	49%	.316	1.19	1.81	1.78	2.3
2011	*SFN*	*MLB*	*29*	*3*	*1*	*30*	*64*	*0*	*66*	*57*	*5*	*27*	*69*	*3.7*	*9.4*	*47%*	*.303*	*1.27*	*3.15*	*3.43*	*0.9*

The third-most valuable relief pitcher in the majors last season according to WXRL, Wilson not only converted 91 percent of his major-league-leading 53 save opportunities, but also led the majors in saves of four or more outs (10) and was second to Milwaukee rookie John Axford with six five-out saves. After allowing a game-tying double in his first inning of post-season work, he was nearly flawless, picking up the final five outs of Game Six of the NLCS to clinch the pennant and striking out two in a 1-2-3 ninth inning to wrap up the Giants' first Bay-area championship. That he did all of that with a Mohawk, a bushy beard that he inexplicably dyed jet black (which made it look fake), and a flair for interviews simply made a great season a strangely iconic one.

Barry Zito

Born: **5/13/1978** Age: **33**
Bats: **L** Throws: **L** Height: **6' 4"** Weight: **205**
Breakout **12%** Improve: **47%** Collapse: **21%**
Attrition: **11%** MLB: **97%**

Comparables:
Chuck Finley, Vicente Padilla, Doug Davis (69)

YEAR	TEAM	LVL	AGE	W	L	SV	G	GS	IP	H	HR	BB	SO	EqBB9	EqSO9	GB%	BABIP	WHIP	ERA	FRA	WARP
2008	SFN	MLB	30	10	17	0	32	32	180	186	16	102	120	5.1	6.0	37%	.295	1.62	5.15	5.67	0.2
2009	SFN	MLB	31	10	13	0	33	33	192	179	21	81	154	3.8	7.2	40%	.285	1.40	4.03	4.08	3.0
2010	SFN	MLB	32	9	14	0	34	33	199^{1}	184	20	84	150	3.8	6.8	38%	.279	1.38	4.15	4.56	1.7
2011	*SFN*	*MLB*	*33*	*13*	*12*	*0*	*34*	*34*	*199^{2}*	*195*	*21*	*89*	*134*	*4.0*	*6.1*	*40%*	*.287*	*1.42*	*4.28*	*4.65*	*3.0*

Thanks to the arrival of Bumgarner, Zito had the dubious distinction of becoming the first man paid more than $18 million by a playoff team to be left off that team's playoff roster despite being fully healthy. It's not that Zito was bad. He actually sustained the gains he made in 2009 without much additional help from his defense, which—if Sanchez suffers a likely correction—could get him back up to fourth in the rotation's pecking order in the coming season. However, he was clearly the team's worst starter down the stretch, going 1-8 with a 6.66 ERA and just two quality starts in his final 11 games (one of them a relief loss). But hey, it's just another three years and $64.5 million before the Giants will have his contract off the books!

LINEOUTS

HITTERS

PLAYER	TEAM	LVL	AGE	PA	R	2B	3B	HR	RBI	BB	SO	SB-CS	AVG/OBP/SLG	TAv	BABIP	BRR	FRAA	WARP
OF B. Copeland*	FRE	AAA	26	419	47	16	8	4	41	57	67	23-8	.280/.372/.404	.277	.327	3.3	CF 1, RF 3	2.6
SS B. Crawford*	SJO	A+	23	55	10	2	0	2	9	8	8	2-0	.283/.382/.457	.322	.297	1.3	3B -2, SS -1	0.4
	RIC	AA	23	342	43	12	3	7	22	39	77	4-1	.241/.337/.375	.268	.296	3.1	SS 19	3.6
2B C. Culberson	SJO	A+	21	551	80	28	4	16	71	33	99	25-7	.290/.340/.457	.289	.329	0.5	2B -2	3.0
3B C. Dominguez	AUG	A	23	608	85	32	4	21	101	35	133	14-7	.272/.326/.456	.290	.321	2.1	3B 4	4.2
OF T. Graham	FRE	AAA	26	379	60	23	2	2	34	24	54	35-11	.343/.393/.440	.289	.392	0.0	CF -1, RF 1	1.8
C T. Joseph	AUG	A	18	473	46	22	1	16	68	26	116	0-0	.236/.290/.401	.254	.283	-3.9	C -1, 1B 0	0.6
RF R. Kieschnick*	RIC	AA	23	246	21	8	3	4	23	18	55	2-3	.251/.305/.368	.243	.310	0.5	RF 0	0.0
1B B. Pill	FRE	AAA	25	567	63	34	0	16	84	30	65	7-2	.275/.319/.433	.254	.283	0.0	1B -3, 3B 0	-0.2
RF R. Rodriguez	GIA	Rk	17	133	20	6	0	2	14	5	23	4-2	.301/.323/.398	.268	.343	-0.3	RF 0, LF 0	0.5
C E. Whiteside	SFN	MLB	30	141	17	6	1	4	10	8	35	1-2	.238/.291/.397	.253	.289	-1.8	C 0	0.3

At 27, **Ben Copeland** isn't a prospect, but he'll draw some walks and steal some bases, and he can play all over the outfield, which could make him a compelling bench option. ⊘ UCLA product **Brandon Crawford** is a good-field/no-hit shortstop whose repeat of Double-A in 2010 was interrupted by a broken right hand suffered at midseason. ⊘ Living proof that Mike Stanton was once on the Giants, **Charlie Culberson** was drafted with the compensation pick received when Stanton signed with the Reds. The glove of this former high-school shortstop moved him to third in 2009, and his bat moved him to second in 2010. His offense jumped in the latter season, but that might have been little more than a California League spike. ⊘ **Chris Dominguez** has monster power, but no plate approach. The four-year college player will be 24 heading into his High-A debut this spring, so unless he can do a *Benjamin Button*–style backward-aging bit, time has long since run out. ⊘ Outfielder **Tyler Graham**'s apparent breakthrough in Triple-A at age 26 last year was mostly empty batting average propped up by a .396 BABIP. ⊘ The Giants' second-round pick in 2009, high-school catcher **Tommy Joseph** made his pro debut in the Sally League in 2010 and showed power but little else. He projects as a slugger, but not the sort whose value could survive a move to first base. ⊘ A toolsy right fielder out of Texas Tech, **Roger Kieschnick** was disappointing in his Double-A debut before a back injury ended his season at the beginning of July. ⊘ Nice-guy first baseman **Brett Pill**'s production spike in his Double-A debut in 2009 was encouraging, but his return to his previous level at Triple-A last year made it look like a fluke, which was, like, tough medicine to, uhm, ingest, or something. ⊘ Back problems limited toolsy teenage right fielder **Rafael Rodriguez** in his full-season debut in 2010, and given that he didn't turn 18 until July, the Giants saw no need to force the issue, giving him ample rest and letting him finish the season on a "rehab" assignment in rookie ball, where he hit .342/.360/.443 in August. ⊘ Teenage slugger **Angel Villalona** was a headline signing out of his native Dominican Republic in 2006, but has made very different headlines since: he is due to stand trial for a late 2009 nightclub murder. Villalona hasn't played organized ball since the shooting, but according to his lawyer, he was "out in the street practicing" after posting bail. ⊘ Veteran backstop **Eli Whiteside** didn't get into a single post-season game and will have plenty of time to catch up on his reading as Buster Posey's backup.

PITCHERS

PLAYER	TEAM	LVL	AGE	W	L	SV	IP	H	HR	BB	SO	EqBB9	EqSO9	GB%	BABIP	WHIP	ERA	FRA	WARP
D. Bautista	FRE	AAA	27	3	2	9	22^2	14	1	9	28	3.6	11.4	44%	.255	1.17	3.18	2.25	0.7
	SFN	MLB	27	2	0	0	33^2	25	4	27	44	7.2	11.8	36%	.266	1.63	3.74	3.06	0.7
J. Casilla	AUG	A	21	4	1	14	54^1	40	0	17	41	2.8	6.8	60%	.256	1.11	1.16	2.66	1.4
S. Edlefsen	FRE	AAA	25	7	2	6	64^1	55	6	34	50	4.8	7.0	64%	.272	1.44	2.38	2.20	2.3
E. Hacker	FRE	AAA	27	16	8	0	165^2	181	21	62	129	3.4	7.0	46%	.315	1.56	4.51	4.13	3.4
W. Joaquin	FRE	AAA	23	1	2	2	34^2	44	4	22	33	5.8	8.7	46%	.370	2.02	4.93	5.52	0.1
	SFN	MLB	23	0	0	0	4^2	6	0	7	2	13.5	3.9	65%	.353	3.00	9.64	12.71	-0.5
J. Paterson*	FRE	AAA	24	4	3	2	54^1	55	2	24	49	4.0	8.2	52%	.323	1.52	3.48	4.49	0.4
K. Pucetas	FRE	AAA	25	5	7	0	136	172	17	61	95	4.0	6.3	44%	.351	1.79	5.69	5.45	0.9
D. Quinowski*	SJO	A+	24	3	2	2	42^2	35	2	13	51	2.8	10.9	36%	.303	1.16	2.32	1.81	1.5
J. Stoffel	SJO	A+	21	2	4	25	50^2	55	4	24	66	4.3	11.8	54%	.383	1.61	4.80	4.22	0.3
E. Surkamp*	SJO	A+	22	4	2	0	101^1	79	5	22	108	2.0	9.6	43%	.289	1.06	3.11	3.18	2.8
C. Tanner*	RIC	AA	22	9	9	0	149	150	10	64	79	3.9	4.8	56%	.286	1.48	3.68	5.22	-0.6
R. Verdugo*	AUG	A	23	4	1	1	32	26	0	14	50	3.9	14.1	49%	.377	1.25	2.25	1.81	1.1
—	SJO	A+	23	4	0	0	30^2	15	3	19	44	5.7	13.1	44%	.222	1.13	1.47	2.75	0.9
D. Willis*	ARI	MLB	28	1	1	0	22^1	24	3	27	14	10.9	5.6	47%	.313	2.42	6.85	7.79	-0.3
	DET	MLB	28	1	2	0	43^1	48	3	29	33	6.0	6.9	47%	.336	1.82	4.98	4.30	0.6

The Giants brought 27-year-old fireballing journeyman **Denny Bautista** in as a nonroster invitee to spring training, called him up in May, got the usual abundance of strikeouts and walks over the next three months, then designated him for assignment in August. He signed a minor-league contract with the Mariners and will get a chance to be ridiculously wild in relief. A right-handed reliever who throws a heavy, low-90s sinker from a low-three-quarters arm angle, **Jose Casilla** has allowed just two home runs in 185 2/3 professional innings over five seasons, which gives you some idea about how many ground balls he induces. After climbing from High-A to Triple-A in 2009, righty reliever **Steve Edlefsen** successfully replicated his Triple-A performance last year at age 25, which, thanks to his extreme ground-ball rate, meant good results despite too many walks. A middling right-handed starter in his late 20s, **Eric Hacker** is the sort of innings-munching finesse pitcher that the Twins love, so it wasn't overly surprising when Minnesota jumped on him in early November and gave him a spot on its 40-man roster, though that roster spot seems unlikely to interrupt his ongoing tour of Triple-A ballparks. A lesser version of Henry Sosa, **Waldis Joaquin** is an unrefined hard thrower best suited to the bullpen; he was waived after the season, but rejected a claim by the White Sox and ended up back in the Giants' system. A 10th-round pick out of Oregon State in 2007, **Joe Paterson** (one *t*, please) doesn't have Alex Hinshaw's raw stuff, but he has had the better results of late, which makes it a bit perplexing that while Hinshaw was protected on the Giants' 40-man roster, Paterson was left exposed and taken by the Diamondbacks in the Rule 5 draft. This wily southpaw with a good curve is well-suited to match-up work and has a decent chance to stick in the Snakes' rebuilt bullpen. Righty starter **Kevin Pucetas**'s repeat of Triple-A last year went worse than his 2009 debut at the level. Now 26, he was flipped to the Royals as the player to be named later for Jose Guillen. A 46th-round pick back in 2004, lefty reliever **David Quinowski** lost the 2008 season to Tommy John surgery, but has pitched well since his return, continuing to do so after making the leap to Double-A last year. The Giants' fourth-round pick in 2009, righty **Jason Stoffel** closed for the University of Arizona and filled that role again in his full-season debut at High-A San Jose last year, but he projects as more of a set-up man in the majors. A finesse lefty whose fastball tops out in the upper 80s, **Eric Surkamp** saw his 2010 season come to an end when he hurt his hip fielding a ball in mid-July. He's expected back on time to start the season after surgery. How he handles the jump to Double-A could tell us a lot about his future. Lefty starter **Clayton Tanner**'s peripherals all headed in the wrong direction in his Double-A debut last year, suggesting that the Aussie sinkerballer has gone about as far as his mid-80s fastball and finesse repertoire will take him. Baseball-Reference lists 19 Verdugos who have played in the minor leagues, but none who has reached the majors. Lefty reliever **Ryan Verdugo** is one of three active Verdugos, but he'll have to limit his walks if he wants to be the first to reach "The Show." Once one of the game's most marketable players, **Dontrelle Willis** saw his career completely unravel in 2010 as he passed through four organizations in a seven-month span. After the Tigers finally moved on in May, he walked 27 men in 21 1/3 innings across five starts for the Diamondbacks, made eight minor-league relief appearances in the Giants' organization, then signed a minor-league deal in November with the Reds, who will give Willis a look in relief in spring training. They'd be foolish to expect much.

MANAGER: BRUCE BOCHY

YEAR	TEAM	W-L	Pythag +/-	Avg PC	100+ P	120+ P	QS	BQS	REL	REL w Zero R	IBB	Subs	PH	PH Avg	PH HR	SB2	CS2	SB3	CS3	SAC Att	SAC %	POS SAC	Squeeze	Swing	In Play
2008	SFN	72-90	5	99.9	91	8	80	8	478	287	59	60	273	.239	3	99	41	6	1	97	58.8%	26	3	161	133
2009	SFN	88-74	1	97.6	74	5	81	5	457	292	49	76	231	.250	2	69	27	8	0	101	66.3%	18	0	118	99
2010	SFN	92-70	-3	99.6	79	7	90	5	475	326	58	95	219	.262	6	49	28	6	3	108	70.4%	28	2	118	85

Bochy did a bravura job in coaxing the Giants to their first West Coast championship. Yes, the pitching staff made half of his job easy and allowed him to devote a larger portion of his copious cranium to sorting out his makeshift offense, but even there, he impressed. The Giants blew just five quality starts all season and led the majors in save percentage, thanks in part to Bochy's willingness to turn to his closer for more than three outs, doing so more than any other manager did in the majors last year. The skipper succeeded in extracting the maximum safe mileage from his rotation and relief horses, aware that he lacked attractive mounts in the back end of the pen. Only two Giants made 100 or more starts at a given position in 2010, as Bochy and Sabean mixed and matched, and one of those two, Pablo Sandoval, effectively lost his job in September. Bochy didn't allow his decisions to be dictated by contracts, benching Aaron Rowand in favor of Andres Torres and leaving Barry Zito not just out of the post-season rotation (an obvious call), but off the roster entirely. The manager also made regular use of defensive substitutions as per our Pat Burrell comment earlier in this chapter. The result was his first World Series win and a deserved third-place finish in the NL Manager of the Year voting, more than three decades after his major league debut.

Seattle Mariners

The Mariners limped into the 2008-2009 offseason licking their wounds from a cellar-dwelling performance that left them fully 40 games under .500 and devoid of both on- and off-field leadership after the midseason dismissals of manager John McLaren and general manager Bill Bavasi, whose misguided machinations had birthed the stillborn team. Before that October was over, new management was in place. Under freshly minted GM Jack Zduriencik, the Mariners entered the 21st century, wedding a scouting pedigree to an open (and oddly vocal) appreciation for advanced statistics. Powered by a winter's worth of beer and tacos, the newly installed decision makers quickly put their stamp on the active roster, erasing all but the deepest, Carlos Silva–caliber scars left over from Bavasi's tenure.

MARINERS PROSPECTUS

2010 W-L: 61-101, 4th in AL West

Pythag	.366	29th
RS/G	3.2	30th
RA/G	4.3	17th
TAv	.245	30th
BRR	-9.5	27th
FRA	4.57	20th
DER	15.9	4th
DL	692	14th
B-Age	29.6	23rd
P-Age	27.0	6th
Salary	$86.5	14th
M$/MW	$6.17	30th

Ballpark: Safeco Field (3-yr. PF: 93). Extreme pitcher's park can't excuse the offensive meltdown

2010: Historically inept lineup undoes the progress of 2009

2011: Further failures take no one by surprise

Action Items: Establishing young impact arms and bats, securing fifth starter and overhauling bullpen, scoring more runs than the 1906 White Sox

In Zduriencik's first year on the job, the M's added 24 wins to their 2008 tally, escaping from the AL West basement and winding up eight games over .500. Their turnaround came on the strength of a fielding facelift that saw them improve from 26th place in both unadjusted and park-adjusted defensive efficiency (DE and PADE, respectively) to second in DE and third in PADE in the span of a single season. As impressive as their defensive overhaul was, the Mariners remained a deeply flawed team: in their efforts to import high-quality leather, the M's had neglected to land any lumber. The resultant lineup deforestation fostered an unbalanced approach that ultimately terminated the team's attempt at contention; while rookie manager Don Wakamatsu's crew managed to pace the AL in run prevention, they also brought up the rear in run creation. What's more, his squad was actually outscored by its opponents, posting a 75-87 Pythagorean record that set the faint odor of regression to wafting on the Pacific Northwest wind.

Still, while their Cinderella season didn't result in a storybook ending, the Mariners seemed to have made great strides. Despite an uneven roster, they had improved their on-field fortunes considerably in a short time. Even more importantly, they appeared to have distanced themselves from the previous regime's misguided management style and put a winning process in place. Unfortunately, any optimism that arose as a result proved short-lived: last season, the goodwill generated by the organization's 2009 turnaround evaporated in the wake of another about-face. The Mariners' record backslid to 61-101, an identical mark to the one they had managed in the bad old days of 2008. Along the way, their manager was dismissed, and Zduriencik lost much of his luster. Where did it all go wrong?

Despite the 2009 team's offensive inadequacies, most of Seattle's 2009-2010 offseason moves were geared toward shoring up an already-impressive defense. There's nothing wrong with that strategy in the abstract, given that a run saved adds as much value as a run scored. However, the team's league-worst offensive unit offered greater potential for simple and substantial upgrades than a defense that already bordered on the best in the league, suggesting that Jack Z might have gotten more mileage out of a different approach. Zduriencik allowed Russell Branyan—the club's second-most productive hitter—to walk, importing glove man Casey Kotchman to play first base. He also signed Eric Byrnes and re-upped with Jack Wilson, thereby adding two more plus defenders and offensive zeros to the mix, and inked Franklin Gutierrez and Felix Hernandez, two pillars of his run-prevention strategy, to long-term extensions. The centerpiece of Trader Jack's winter was his successful play for Cliff Lee, whose arrival gave Seattle a third potential ace to go along with Hernandez and the injury-plagued Erik Bedard, who was subsequently re-signed to an incentive-laden deal.

Only two of Zduriencik's moves offered any real hope of

offensive assistance. The GM spirited Chone Figgins away from a division rival with a four-year pact, a move calculated to address his team's on-base percentage (OBP) deficiencies. While Figgins seemed a likely candidate to assist in that regard, the M's bought high on the ex-Angel's career year. The 13.9 percent walk rate that had allowed the diminutive infielder to post a superb .395 OBP was his best by a wide margin, and his recent record revealed two subpar offensive seasons in his previous four. Zduriencik did well to extract Milton Bradley from the Cubs for what seemed like an albatross in Carlos Silva, but while the swap stood to add further on-base ability to a lineup sorely lacking it, Bradley had surrendered his power upon departing from Arlington in 2008, and his combustible personality threatened to jeopardize any potential upgrade offered by his bat. The result was an offense that figured to flirt with league average, if everything went right.

Instead, everything went wrong; in effect, last season's Mariners featured a Murphy's Law lineup. Though the 2009 club was deficient at the dish, last year's model truly cleaned its plate, as any semblance of offense in Seattle went the way of Pogues front-man Shane McGowan's original set of teeth. Not since the 1971 Angels and Padres had a team scored fewer runs in a nonstrike year than the Mariners did while plating just 71 percent of the league-average total last season. Part of that historically low scoring could be chalked up to park effects; Safeco Field was the AL's worst hitter's environment, which made the Mariners' performance at the plate appear even worse than it was. However, even after adjusting for the setting of Seattle's demise, the team's offensive ineptitude attained impressive proportions (Table 1).

Table 1. No Offense, But . . . Worst Offenses from 1954 to 2010, with Performance in Following Seasons

Year	Team	TAv	Next-Season TAv	Difference
1965	NYN	.233	.246	.013
1992	CAL	.234	.250	.016
1999	MIN	.235	.243	.008
1963	NYN	.235	.249	.014
1979	TOR	.236	.239	.003
1983	SEA	.237	.255	.018
1980	SEA	.237	.254	.017
1979	OAK	.237	.258	.021
1969	SDN	.237	.257	.020
1964	HOU	.237	.257	.020
2010	SEA	.238	?	?
2004	ARI	.238	.259	.021
2003	DET	.238	.267	.029
2003	LAN	.238	.263	.025
1999	ANA	.238	.266	.028
1998	TBA	.238	.251	.013
1993	FLO	.238	.252	.014
1976	MON	.238	.258	.020

The Mariners tied for the 11th-worst nonstrike-year offensive performance since 1954, with only a few insignificant points separating them from the record holders. The good news is that these historically awful offenses improved by an average of 18 points in the seasons following their respective nadirs. Unfortunately, while none of these clubs failed to achieve at least a dead-cat bounce, only three managed to recover convincingly enough to turn in average performances. Still, the Mariners should take solace that the situation on the offensive side almost certainly can't get worse. Newly hired hitting coach Chris Chambliss might appear to have an unenviable task in front of him as he inherits the league's least successful collection of bats, but in reality, he couldn't ask for a more fortuitous position. Purely as a result of progression to the mean, he's almost certain to oversee a significant improvement in his first year on the job, for which he's likely to earn no small amount of unmerited praise.

As Jeff Sullivan of the Mariners' blog *Lookout Landing* has observed, the 2010 Mariners collectively posted a lower on-base plus slugging percentage (OPS) than much-maligned archetypical replacement player Willie Bloomquist had during his seven-season stay in Seattle. Even with Bloomquist safely exiled to Kansas City and Cincinnati, the Mariners suffered more than their fair share of subreplacement offensive performances (Table 2).

Table 2. The Replacement-Level Killers: Mariners' TAv by Position

Position	Primary Player	Cumulative Positional TAv	Rank
3B	Jose Lopez	.211	30
C	Adam Moore	.212	29
SS	Josh Wilson	.217	28
DH	Russell Branyan	.220	14 (AL)
1B	Casey Kotchman	.244	27
2B	Chone Figgins	.245	21
CF	Franklin Gutierrez	.255	18
LF	Michael Saunders	.273	15
RF	Ichiro Suzuki	.291	10

Seattle received subreplacement offense at five of nine positions last season. In a few cases, the Mariners' inability to field even a moderately acceptable bat bordered on the absurd. Just when M's fans thought it was safe to go back in the DH slot after Jose Vidro's .235/.273/.346 showing as Seattle's primary DH in 2008, they were forced to endure a combined .194/.269/.340 performance from their team's DH crew last season—a line that looked even worse when the reacquired Branyan failed to do his part to prop up the lineup due to the war declared on him by inanimate objects. Designated hitter wasn't the only position at which Mariners hitters exhibited an astonishing failure to produce: Seattle third basemen, egged on by ringleader Jose Lopez, mustered a miserable .226/.259/.324 performance, qualifying for the sixth-lowest team TAv at the hot corner since 1950. The Mariners' DH efforts were only marginally less embarrassing, ranking as the seventh-worst performance since the inception of that position.

Should Zduriencik have seen his team's offensive waterloo approaching? Although the best-case scenario for his club's performance at the plate fell well short of Murderer's Row, it's hard to hold him responsible for failing to foresee the extent of the carnage. Excluding Ichiro, whom projection systems have systematically underrated; Russell Branyan, who wasn't yet with the team; and Josh Wilson, who wasn't deemed worthy of a PECOTA, every Mariners hitter—Michael Saunders excluded—who ended up with at least 200 plate appearance performed worse than projected (Table 3).

Table 3. The Main Offenders: Mariners Offensive Underperformers

Name	PAs	Projected	Actual	Difference
Chone Figgins	702	.272	.261	-.011
Franklin Gutierrez	629	.263	.259	-.004
Jose Lopez	622	.257	.226	-.031
Casey Kotchman	457	.277	.231	-.046
Michael Saunders	327	.250	.250	.000
Milton Bradley	278	.297	.247	-.050
Adam Moore	218	.240	.186	-.054
Jack Wilson	211	.252	.227	-.025
Rob Johnson	209	.230	.225	-.005

These players were selected for inclusion in this table on the basis of their having received significant playing time, which should bias the results in favor of overperformance, but with the exception of Saunders, who barely managed to meet expectations, the remainder reads like a litany of letdowns. In most cases, the players who failed to make the cut were even greater disappointments: for example, PECOTA foresaw a .267 TAv for Ken Griffey Jr., but his .168 actual performance was abysmal enough to send him nodding off into retirement before he could play his way into this underwhelming group. Though it's fair to hold a team armed with inside knowledge to a higher standard in the prognostication department than a relatively uninformed algorithm, Seattle's offensive underperformance reached levels that would have been extremely difficult to see coming.

Nonetheless, in retrospect, the Mariners' win-now mentality over the 2009-2010 offseason smacks of irrational exuberance. Still, the team's efforts to propel itself over a hump that it hadn't actually approached didn't sabotage the Mariners' future in an insuperable way. Trading a package of prospects for a single-season rent-an-ace was the work of a team that believed itself on the verge of contention, but the acquisition of Lee came with a significant escape clause, in that the lefty represented a prime candidate to be flipped at the deadline if Seattle's season went awry. Indeed, Seattle got more from selling high on Lee at the deadline than they'd surrendered to buy high the previous December. The only major move that probably keeps M's execs up at night was the double-Brandon deal that trailed the Lee trade by a week. Sending starter Brandon Morrow to the Blue Jays for reliever Brandon League was a win-now move in theory, but made little sense at the time, even from a short-term perspective. In light of Morrow's emergence in 2010, the deal stands as a black mark against Zduriencik's otherwise-glowing trade record.

Even aside from the Morrow trade and the team's disappointing performance on the field, the developments of 2010 irrevocably sullied the new regime's formerly spotless reputation. In mid-May, the struggling Griffey was reported—via an anonymous clubhouse source—to have slept through a pinch-hit opportunity, which touched off the growing tensions surrounding the ineffective icon's reduced reps. In the wake of his unscheduled in-game slumber, Wakamatsu lost control of his clubhouse, engaging in a highly visible fracas with Chone Figgins and failing to formulate an effective antidote to his team's sloppy play. The sophomore manager took the fall, but Zduriencik deserved blame for awarding Griffey's dead weight a contract in the first place, since the 40-year-old DH wasn't fit for a role on either a rebuilding team or one built to win immediately. Finally, the acquisition of alleged rapist Josh Lueke in the Cliff Lee trade made the Mariners appear either incompetent or downright duplicitous, and the ensuing fallout cost scouting director Carmen Fusco his job. Without considerable improvement in the way the team conducts its business both on and off the field, Zduriencik might soon follow Fusco out the door.

Given the Mariners' sustained success in the field—their defenders were only slightly less efficient at converting balls in play into outs in 2010 than they'd been the season before—respectability might seem only a revitalized offense away. However, while the pitching-and-defense approach remains well suited for Safeco, the Mariners know better than to fall into the same trap that ensnared them in 2010. This isn't just a team without an offense, but is one that also lacks the pitching depth befitting a contender. Lee's mid-season departure and Bedard's inability to take the mound left the team lacking in the rotation, and only Arizona's unmatched lack of relief obscured the depths of the futility to which Seattle's replacement-level pen—which featured only two reliable options in League and David Aardsma—sunk last season.

This Mariners club isn't ready to compete with the best of the AL West, but unlike last year, no one expects it to, which should give Zduriencik the freedom to set his team on the road to more enduring success. Seattle's system isn't deep, but it does boast a pair of potential near-future impact players in Michael Pineda and Dustin Ackley. The big club features a few recent minor-league graduates—Saunders,

Smoak, and Adam Moore—who haven't yet met their major-league expectations, but stand a decent chance of doing so. The presence of those youngsters alongside the higher-priced veterans locked up elsewhere on the roster leaves little room to maneuver, either in terms of dollars or in roster spots, but perhaps that's for the best, since Seattle would be better served by seeing what it has in-house before dipping more than a toe into another organization's talent pool.

With the core of the team's future newly arrived or on the verge of making the majors, the Mariners can focus on avoiding further abject failure for the time being, while hoping for rapid maturation from their aspiring stars. As the aftermath of 2009 indicated, improvements that seem too good to be true often end up that way; while the next winning Mariners team may not come as such a surprise, it should rest on far firmer foundations.

HITTERS

Dustin Ackley 2B

Born: 2/26/1988 Age: 23
Bats: L Throws: R Height: 6' 1" Weight: 185
Breakout: 6% Improve: 27% Collapse: 6%
Attrition: 23% MLB: 63%

Comparables:
Danny Richar, Matt Antonelli, Roberto Alomar (71)

YEAR	TEAM	LVL	AGE	PA	R	2B	3B	HR	RBI	BB	SO	SB	CS	AVG/OBP/SLG	TAv	BABIP	BRR	FRAA	WARP
2010	WTN	AA	22	350	42	21	4	2	28	55	41	8	2	.263/.389/.384	.292	.300	2.1	2B -7	1.4
2010	TAC	AAA	22	237	37	12	4	5	23	20	38	2	1	.274/.338/.439	.286	.308	1.0	2B -12	0.4
2011	*SEA*	*MLB*	*23*	*617*	*76*	*31*	*5*	*11*	*65*	*67*	*91*	*7*	*3*	*.269/.352/.408*	*.272*	*.300*	*-0.2*	*2B -13*	*0.8*

In his first professional season, Ackley didn't hit much like a second overall pick, but he recovered from a frightening .147/.289/.227 April in time to remind the Mariners of why they'd drafted him. His sweet lefty swing didn't do much damage against same-handed pitchers, but even while struggling to learn a new position, Ackley walked more often than he struck out in the Southern League, offering a glimpse of the discipline and contact skills that have scouts sold on his future as a .300 average/.400 on-base percentage hitter. It's not yet clear what lies in store for Ackley's third slash stat, since he hasn't mustered much power with a wood bat, but he did lead the Arizona Fall League (AFL) in on-base plus slugging percentage (OPS) by a wide margin. Of course, the list of those who slugged in the AFL is long and littered with hitters who never showed much pop elsewhere, but we'll probably see Ackley in Seattle at some point this season.

Josh Bard C

Born: 3/30/1978 Age: 33
Bats: S Throws: R Height: 6' 3" Weight: 215
Breakout: 1% Improve: 37% Collapse: 9%
Attrition: 28% MLB: 82%

Comparables:
Rod Barajas, Del Rice, Joe Oliver (79)

YEAR	TEAM	LVL	AGE	PA	R	2B	3B	HR	RBI	BB	SO	SB	CS	AVG/OBP/SLG	TAv	BABIP	BRR	FRAA	WARP
2008	SDN	MLB	30	198	12	9	0	1	16	18	25	0	0	.202/.278/.270	.205	.229	-0.1	C 1	-0.2
2009	WAS	MLB	31	301	23	18	0	6	31	24	50	0	1	.230/.292/.361	.228	.259	-8.5	C 0	-0.6
2010	TAC	AAA	32	95	8	6	0	3	15	7	18	0	0	.235/.284/.412	.245	.254	-1.8	C -1	0.0
2010	SEA	MLB	32	126	10	7	0	3	10	10	27	0	0	.214/.270/.357	.234	.244	-0.2	C -2	0.0
2011	*SEA*	*MLB*	*33*	*304*	*34*	*16*	*0*	*6*	*31*	*28*	*50*	*0*	*0*	*.244/.312/.375*	*.242*	*.271*	*0.0*	*C -1*	*0.6*

In cooking, a bard is a piece of unpalatable meat that takes some heat to preserve the choicer cuts before being discarded. The baseball Bard serves the same function. The Mariners acquired the veteran backstop to complement the more tender pickings that composed the rest of their catching corps, but they would have been better off had they tossed him on the compost pile before he came to the plate. The switch-hitter continued to pile up outs from both sides of the dish and sports a combined .285 on-base percentage (OBP) since 2007, albeit in mostly unfavorable offensive environments. He missed time with a calf strain and a sore neck, but handled the position when healthy, thwarting a third of attempted steals and greeting balls in the dirt with a Gandalf-esque "You shall not pass." An improved defensive showing helped convince the M's to re-sign Bard, which should save him from the indignity of playing for his fourth team in as many years and make it even more likely that he'll retire before he runs out of organizations.

Milton Bradley LF

Born: 4/15/1978 Age: 33
Bats: S Throws: R Height: 6' 0" Weight: 180
Breakout: 0% Improve: 32% Collapse: 12%
Attrition: 20% MLB: 90%

Comparables:
Wally Moon, Greg Vaughn, Fernando Tatis (71)

YEAR	TEAM	LVL	AGE	PA	R	2B	3B	HR	RBI	BB	SO	SB	CS	AVG/OBP/SLG	TAv	BABIP	BRR	FRAA	WARP
2008	TEX	MLB	30	510	83	32	1	22	77	80	112	5	3	.321/.435/.563	.343	.388	-1.2	RF 0, LF 0	4.7
2009	CHN	MLB	31	473	62	17	1	12	40	66	95	2	3	.257/.376/.397	.274	.308	-3.0	RF -2, CF 0	1.0
2010	SEA	MLB	32	278	28	9	1	8	29	28	75	8	2	.205/.291/.348	.250	.256	2.4	LF 6, RF 0	0.9
2011	*SEA*	*MLB*	*33*	*390*	*51*	*16*	*1*	*14*	*46*	*52*	*84*	*6*	*2*	*.262/.369/.443*	*.287*	*.307*	*-0.2*	*RF -1, LF 1*	*1.5*

Bradley's eruptive talent and disruptive personality (or is it disruptive talent and eruptive personality?) have always been a package deal, forcing teams to tolerate the latter in order to profit from the former. Last season, the Mariners got the usual helping of emotional problems, but little to show for it in the win column, as the switch-hitter turned in a below-average offensive season for the first time since 2002. Two seasons removed from leading the AL in OBP, Bradley suffered the ultimate indignity of reaching base less frequently than Rob Johnson. After enduring failure so acute, it's no wonder that Bradley snapped, leaving the ballpark during a mid-May game after being benched by then-manager Don Wakamatsu for an excessive post-strikeout display of emotion. The next day, Bradley asked his employers for help and began receiving anger management counseling. He may have been in a better frame of mind after returning to the lineup just over two weeks later, but he hit even worse the rest of the way. The injury-prone outfielder offers little defensive value, and unless his bat regains its former clout, he'll find little market for his services, no matter how placid his personality. The Mariner's signing of Jack Cust to DH may prevent Bradley from getting the requisite at-bats for a comeback. In light of the arrival of Jack Cust and his former flare-ups with new manager Eric Wedge, Bradley would be wise to stay on his best behavior in 2011, but got off to an inauspicious start with a January arrest.

Russell Branyan **DH**
Born: **12/19/1975** Age: **35**
Bats: L Throws: R Height: **6′ 3″** Weight: **195**
Breakout: **1%** Improve: **27%** Collapse: **9%**
Attrition: **19%** MLB: **95%**
Comparables:
Dick Allen, Chris Richard, Jim Edmonds (56)

YEAR	TEAM	LVL	AGE	PA	R	2B	3B	HR	RBI	BB	SO	SB	CS	AVG/OBP/SLG	TAv	BABIP	BRR	FRAA	WARP
2008	NAS	AAA	32	179	24	15	0	12	36	25	49	4	1	.359/.453/.693	.361	.467	0.8	3B 9, 1B -1	3.2
2008	MIL	MLB	32	152	25	8	0	12	20	19	42	1	0	.250/.342/.583	.310	.266	0.3	3B 0, 1B -1	1.2
2009	SEA	MLB	33	505	64	21	1	31	76	58	149	2	0	.251/.347/.520	.310	.298	-2.9	1B 2	2.9
2010	CLE	MLB	34	190	24	9	0	10	24	16	49	0	0	.263/.326/.491	.305	.307	-0.9	1B 4	1.3
2010	SEA	MLB	34	238	25	10	0	15	33	30	82	1	0	.215/.319/.483	.297	.266	-1.6	1B 0	0.9
2011	*SEA*	*MLB*	*35*	*353*	*47*	*15*	*0*	*20*	*52*	*41*	*105*	*2*	*0*	*.245/.338/.498*	*.286*	*.294*	*0.0*	*1B 2, 3B 2*	*1.6*

Half a season's worth of designated "hitting" by Milton Bradley, Mike Sweeney, Ken Griffey Jr. & Co. convinced the Mariners to reacquire the one that got away, sending a pair of expendable prospects to Cleveland in exchange for Branyan in late June. Given that Mariners designated hitters managed an almost inconceivable .187/.244/.272 line in 423 non-Branyan plate appearances, the lefty's above-average performance at the plate looked positively Edgar-esque. In addition to his customary bouts with lower back soreness, Branyan found time for multiple furniture-related injuries, succumbing to a hotel table that fell on his toe and suffering a bruised tailbone when his chair slipped out from under him in a pizza parlor. Although he struggled to stay healthy, the reigning king of Three True Outcomes walked, struck out, and went yard even more frequently than he had in his first stint in Safeco, handily leading the team in homers despite appearing in only 57 games as a Mariner. Nonetheless, for the second consecutive offseason, the M's chose to cut him loose.

Mike Carp **1B**
Born: **6/30/1986** Age: **25**
Bats: L Throws: R Height: **6′ 2″** Weight: **215**
Breakout: **4%** Improve: **24%** Collapse: **9%**
Attrition: **31%** MLB: **56%**
Comparables:
Joey Votto, Jake Fox, Gaby Sanchez (81)

YEAR	TEAM	LVL	AGE	PA	R	2B	3B	HR	RBI	BB	SO	SB	CS	AVG/OBP/SLG	TAv	BABIP	BRR	FRAA	WARP
2008	BIN	AA	22	566	67	29	1	17	72	79	88	1	2	.299/.403/.471	.300	.335	-5.3	1B -5, LF -4	1.6
2009	TAC	AAA	23	490	66	25	1	15	64	58	99	0	1	.271/.371/.446	.285	.317	-3.5	1B 8, LF -1	2.0
2009	SEA	MLB	23	65	8	3	1	1	5	8	10	0	0	.315/.415/.463	.325	.364	1.5	1B 3	0.9
2010	TAC	AAA	24	463	67	17	1	29	76	41	93	1	2	.257/.328/.516	.291	.259	-2.0	1B -3, LF 8	2.6
2010	SEA	MLB	24	41	1	2	0	0	0	4	8	0	0	.189/.268/.243	.233	.241	-0.6	1B 0, LF 0	-0.2
2011	*SEA*	*MLB*	*25*	*546*	*70*	*24*	*1*	*22*	*71*	*56*	*113*	*1*	*0*	*.262/.344/.459*	*.281*	*.293*	*0.0*	*1B -9, LF 0*	*0.8*

Several varieties of Carp have been classified as invasive species, but despite the Department of Agriculture's best efforts, one of them periodically manages to wrangle a few starts at first base for Seattle. The lefty traded patience for power at Tacoma last season, but while he nearly doubled his 2009 homer total in fewer at-bats, he still ended up looking like something considerably less than a major-league first baseman. Against lefties, Carp is Casey Kotchman without the glove; the rest of the time, he's the equivalent of a defense-deprived Lyle Overbay.

Johermyn Chavez **OF**
Born: **1/26/1989** Age: **22**
Bats: R Throws: R Height: **6′ 3″** Weight: **220**
Breakout: **1%** Improve: **26%** Collapse: **2%**
Attrition: **13%** MLB: **46%**
Comparables:
Jay Bruce, Justin Upton, Matt Kemp (73)

YEAR	TEAM	LVL	AGE	PA	R	2B	3B	HR	RBI	BB	SO	SB	CS	AVG/OBP/SLG	TAv	BABIP	BRR	FRAA	WARP
2008	LNS	A	19	439	40	20	2	7	39	25	128	9	5	.211/.271/.323	.208	.289	-0.7	LF -6, RF -1	-2.2
2009	LNS	A	20	569	87	22	6	21	89	40	137	10	6	.283/.346/.474	.282	.344	1.1	RF -14, LF 0	0.8
2010	HDS	A+	21	605	109	30	7	32	96	52	131	6	9	.315/.387/.577	.319	.361	-1.7	RF 8, CF 0	5.2
2011	*SEA*	*MLB*	*22*	*530*	*62*	*22*	*3*	*22*	*72*	*29*	*148*	*3*	*1*	*.249/.295/.447*	*.256*	*.303*	*-0.3*	*RF -6, LF -6*	*-0.6*

Like Alex Liddi before him, Chavez will have to head to Double-A to prove that he's more than a High Desert mirage after cracking 32 big flies in the Cal League homer haven. The Venezuelan managed a .352 ISO at home, in contrast to a .173 mark on the road, but his muscular build and pull-oriented approach suggest that he won't need the warm Adelanto air to keep launching balls over the wall. Since

2008, Chavez has maintained relatively robust batting averages and walk rates despite his aggressive approach, but runs into problems—literally—after getting on base: when nine of your 15 steal attempts end in an "out" call, it's probably time to stop going. His speed isn't any better in the field, where he's likely to be limited to left, but he might just have the bat for the job.

Chone Figgins 2B

Born: **1/22/1978** Age: **33**
Bats: **S** Throws: **R** Height: **5' 9"** Weight: **155**
Breakout: **0%** Improve: **41%** Collapse: **2%**
Attrition: **7%** MLB: **99%**

Comparables:
Davey Lopes, Julio Lugo, Rafael Furcal (71)

YEAR	TEAM	LVL	AGE	PA	R	2B	3B	HR	RBI	BB	SO	SB	CS	AVG/OBP/SLG	TAv	BABIP	BRR	FRAA	WARP
2008	ANA	MLB	30	520	71	14	1	1	22	62	80	34	13	.276/.365/.318	.255	.332	1.8	3B 1, 2B 0	1.5
2009	ANA	MLB	31	729	114	30	7	5	54	101	114	42	17	.298/.391/.394	.293	.350	4.0	3B 17, 2B -1	6.4
2010	SEA	MLB	32	702	62	21	2	1	35	74	114	42	15	.259/.332/.306	.246	.304	2.8	2B -17	-0.7
2011	*SEA*	*MLB*	*33*	*633*	*74*	*23*	*3*	*6*	*54*	*74*	*99*	*39*	*14*	*.278/.359/.366*	*.262*	*.319*	*-1.0*	*3B 4, 2B -5*	*1.6*

The Mariners went 1-for-2 on their pre-season positional switcheroo, as Jose Lopez picked up where Adrian Beltre left off at third, but Figgins struggled at the keystone. Seattle's game of musical infield positions seemed curious from the start, given the overwhelming evidence that the glorified utilityman does his best defensive work at the hot corner. After slightly more than 2,200 innings at second and over twice that total at third, Figgins now sports –46.4 Fielding Runs Above Average at the former position and a 43.7 mark at the latter, so it would appear that the M's committed the cardinal sin of messing with a good thing when they tried to transplant their new acquisition, though with Jose Lopez out of the picture, they'll rectify that error this season. On the surface, the ex-Angel's performance at the plate looked like the more unexpected aspect of his season, but after adjusting for park, it becomes clear that his output was hardly unprecedented—since 2004, the diminutive switch-hitter has alternated productive and similarly unproductive years at the plate, as fluctuations in his BABIP have dictated his offensive value.

Nick Franklin SS

Born: **3/2/1991** Age: **20**
Bats: **S** Throws: **R** Height: **6' 1"** Weight: **170**
Breakout: **0%** Improve: **0%** Collapse: **0%**
Attrition: **0%** MLB: **0%**

Comparables:
Adrian Beltre, Hank Aaron, Willie Mays (68)

YEAR	TEAM	LVL	AGE	PA	R	2B	3B	HR	RBI	BB	SO	SB	CS	AVG/OBP/SLG	TAv	BABIP	BRR	FRAA	WARP
2010	CLN	A	19	574	89	22	7	23	65	50	123	25	10	.281/.351/.485	.293	.326	0.5	SS -12, 2B 2	3.1
2011	*SEA*	*MLB*	*20*	*336*	*37*	*14*	*2*	*12*	*41*	*18*	*86*	*3*	*1*	*.244/.286/.414*	*.242*	*.293*	*-0.1*	*SS -5, 2B 1*	*0.1*

In last year's annual, we lauded Franklin's speed and defense, but made no mention of any potential for power, which wasn't thought to reside within the switch-hitter's 170-pound frame until his stupefying 2010 season with the Clinton LumberKings. Franklin set the pace with 23 home runs in the pitcher-friendly Midwest League, where fluky slugging displays are hard to come by, and scouts raved that the power was real. Research by BP alum Bryan Smith has revealed no comparable shortstop seasons in the Midwest League this millennium; since 2000, the only teens to match or exceed Franklin's homer tally there were Prince Fielder and Wily Mo Pena, and most of the few players to rival his rate stats have gone on to star at premium offensive positions in the majors. The 2009 first-rounder struggles against lefties, but should stick as a capable middle infielder, which could make his bat truly special. Stay tuned for fireworks this season, as Franklin takes aim for the fences at High Desert.

Franklin Gutierrez CF

Born: **2/21/1983** Age: **28**
Bats: **R** Throws: **R** Height: **6' 2"** Weight: **180**
Breakout: **3%** Improve: **40%** Collapse: **1%**
Attrition: **7%** MLB: **86%**

Comparables:
Ben Francisco, Roberto Kelly, Bobby Thomson (76)

YEAR	TEAM	LVL	AGE	PA	R	2B	3B	HR	RBI	BB	SO	SB	CS	AVG/OBP/SLG	TAv	BABIP	BRR	FRAA	WARP
2008	CLE	MLB	25	440	54	26	2	8	41	27	87	9	3	.248/.305/.384	.252	.294	1.4	RF 18, CF 1	2.3
2009	SEA	MLB	26	629	85	24	1	18	70	46	122	16	5	.283/.332/.425	.279	.323	5.2	CF 11	4.5
2010	SEA	MLB	27	629	61	25	3	12	64	50	137	25	3	.245/.302/.363	.259	.296	-2.5	CF 2	1.5
2011	*SEA*	*MLB*	*28*	*537*	*64*	*25*	*2*	*15*	*62*	*42*	*107*	*16*	*4*	*.268/.324/.417*	*.261*	*.308*	*0.2*	*CF 3, RF 3*	*1.9*

Gutierrez was a revelation in his first season in Safeco, but after earning the moniker "Death to Flying Things" for his ability to rope in any ball that passed through his extensive airspace in 2009, the swift center fielder fell back to earth himself last season. An expected regression in his historically great defensive numbers made his fielding appear merely very good, instead of otherworldly, although the Gold Glove voters belatedly acknowledged his acumen after he set a major-league record for consecutive defensive chances without an error. Perhaps more disappointing was the offensive stagnation that took root in his age-27 sophomore season in Seattle, as he failed to carry forward the progress he had seemed to make at the plate as he entered his prime. Of course, his 2010 TAv was perfectly in line with his career rate, so his BABIP-aided 2009 now appears to have been the exception. The four-year, $20.5 million extension that Gutierrez received last January in return for his arbitration years and first crack at free agency offered potential for a team-friendly steal, but in retrospect, it looks to have been a fair exchange.

Greg Halman CF

Born: **8/26/1987** Age: **23**
Bats: R Throws: R Height: **6' 4"** Weight: **200**
Breakout: **5%** Improve: **30%** Collapse: **3%**
Attrition: **10%** MLB: **59%**

Comparables:
Mark Reynolds, Jay Bruce, Adam Jones (59)

YEAR	TEAM	LVL	AGE	PA	R	2B	3B	HR	RBI	BB	SO	SB	CS	AVG/OBP/SLG	TAv	BABIP	BRR	FRAA	WARP
2008	HDS	A+	20	282	52	15	3	19	53	16	76	23	1	.268/.319/.572	.285	.301	3.2	CF 3, RF 0	2.1
2008	WTN	AA	20	256	43	14	2	10	30	16	66	8	6	.277/.332/.481	.277	.344	1.1	CF 1	1.5
2009	WTN	AA	21	506	64	17	2	25	72	29	183	9	7	.210/.277/.420	.236	.280	0.8	CF 11, RF 10	2.1
2010	TAC	AAA	22	465	82	21	4	33	80	37	169	15	4	.243/.310/.545	.285	.315	0.0	CF -1, RF 7	3.3
2010	SEA	MLB	22	30	1	1	0	0	3	1	11	1	0	.138/.167/.172	.117	.222	0.0	CF 1, LF 0	-0.3
2011	*SEA*	*MLB*	*23*	*525*	*61*	*20*	*3*	*29*	*77*	*29*	*188*	*12*	*4*	*.228/.277/.463*	*.254*	*.296*	*-0.2*	*CF -5, RF 3*	*0.8*

Eleven of Halman's first 29 major-league at-bats ended in strikeouts. Sure, it's a small sample, but that sounds about right, regardless. The big Dutchman got a chance to make his major-league debut only thanks to a resurgent season in Tacoma, but even a successful Halman campaign comes with the caveat of atrocious plate discipline. His strikeout-to-walk (K/BB) ratio improved from 6.3 to 4.6 in his first exposure to the PCL, but even the latter figure isn't the kind of K/BB you'd want to bring home to your mother. Halman isn't well suited for Safeco, but given the opportunity, he'd hit his fair share of home runs. Unfortunately, the collateral damage would probably be prohibitive, in a Dave-Kingman-comes-to-Seattle kind of way.

Rob Johnson C

Born: **7/22/1983** Age: **27**
Bats: R Throws: R Height: **6' 1"** Weight: **200**
Breakout: **1%** Improve: **19%** Collapse: **5%**
Attrition: **16%** MLB: **41%**

Comparables:
Ryan Hanigan, John Stearns, Jason Jaramillo (77)

YEAR	TEAM	LVL	AGE	PA	R	2B	3B	HR	RBI	BB	SO	SB	CS	AVG/OBP/SLG	TAv	BABIP	BRR	FRAA	WARP
2008	TAC	AAA	24	463	55	30	0	9	49	37	61	7	6	.305/.361/.441	.275	.334	-3.2	C -3, LF -3	1.7
2008	SEA	MLB	24	32	1	0	0	1	2	0	6	0	0	.129/.125/.226	.101	.120	0.0	C 1	-0.4
2009	SEA	MLB	25	290	21	19	2	2	27	26	60	1	1	.213/.286/.326	.219	.265	-2.5	C 0	-0.2
2010	TAC	AAA	26	77	9	7	0	1	8	10	12	0	0	.297/.403/.453	.286	.346	0.0	C 1	0.6
2010	SEA	MLB	26	209	23	10	0	2	13	25	46	1	1	.191/.292/.281	.221	.239	-1.5	C -2	-0.3
2011	*SEA*	*MLB*	*27*	*383*	*43*	*21*	*1*	*6*	*38*	*35*	*67*	*4*	*2*	*.251/.322/.375*	*.248*	*.288*	*-0.4*	*C -1, LF 0*	*0.8*

Aside from a strong throwing arm, there's very little to like about Johnson's on-field abilities; any honest accounting of his positive attributes as a player boils down to "he has a nice personality," a description which only rarely results in a date or a starting gig in the majors. The backstop seems to inspire confidence in his battery-mates, but then again, so do the magnetic bands around their necks, which casts doubt upon their testimony. If anything, comparing the two does a disservice to the necklaces; while neither Johnson nor a piece of performance jewelry can regulate the body's energy flow, only the latter actively impairs performance. The catcher routinely violated the prime directive of his position, leading the league in passed balls despite starting only 57 games—a rather dubious distinction for a guy who's ostensibly in there for his defense—and his poor receiving technique rarely results in borderline strikes. These sins might be at least partly forgiven if Johnson had inflicted equal suffering on opposing pitchers, but even by his position's low standards, his bat was a bust. Belatedly, the Mariners appeared to come to their senses, and demoted Johnson to Triple-A in early August. They did even better over the offseason, pawning him off on the Padres after designating him for assignment. Given Johnson's dubious talents, Jed Hoyer need merely hold a door for Jack Zduriencik at some later date to consider his "future considerations" debt fulfilled.

Casey Kotchman 1B

Born: **2/22/1983** Age: **28**
Bats: L Throws: L Height: **6' 3"** Weight: **210**
Breakout: **0%** Improve: **51%** Collapse: **4%**
Attrition: **6%** MLB: **95%**

Comparables:
Sean Casey, Paul Konerko, David Segui (79)

YEAR	TEAM	LVL	AGE	PA	R	2B	3B	HR	RBI	BB	SO	SB	CS	AVG/OBP/SLG	TAv	BABIP	BRR	FRAA	WARP
2008	ANA	MLB	25	398	48	24	0	12	54	18	23	2	1	.287/.327/.448	.275	.279	-2.3	1B 4	1.1
2008	ATL	MLB	25	175	19	4	1	2	20	18	16	0	0	.237/.331/.316	.235	.252	0.1	1B -6	-0.9
2009	ATL	MLB	26	336	29	20	0	6	41	32	28	0	0	.282/.354/.409	.272	.292	-0.6	1B 0	0.6
2009	BOS	MLB	26	95	9	3	0	1	7	7	14	1	0	.218/.284/.287	.227	.250	-0.1	1B 3	0.1
2010	SEA	MLB	27	457	39	20	1	9	51	35	57	0	0	.217/.280/.336	.227	.230	-3.0	1B -3	-1.7
2011	*SEA*	*MLB*	*28*	*413*	*49*	*22*	*1*	*10*	*46*	*35*	*39*	*1*	*1*	*.267/.334/.413*	*.263*	*.272*	*-0.1*	*1B 0*	*0.4*

Although ideally the Mariners would have received something of value when they sent Bill Hall to Boston last January, they would have been better off had they simply given him away rather than accepting Kotchman in return. Among players who have accrued at least as many plate appearances as a first baseman in a single season as the Mariners' new acquisition did while manning the game's premier offensive position, the lefty's lowly TAv ranked third-worst since 1954, behind only the disco-era stylings of Dan Meyer and Dave Stapleton's disastrous 1983. A low BABIP wasn't kind to Kotchman, but he finished more than a few lucky bounces away from respectability, and his combination of extreme ground-ball hitting and slow-motion speed has never resulted in much success on balls in play. He has generally been regarded as a capable fielder (though FRAA doesn't necessarily see him that way), but he'd have to have been good enough to cover the entire right side of the infield by himself to rescue his season from the replacement-level subbasement.

Ryan Langerhans **OF**

Born: **2/20/1980** Age: **31**
Bats: **L** Throws: **L** Height: **6' 3"** Weight: **195**
Breakout: **1%** Improve: **27%** Collapse: **13%**
Attrition: **17%** MLB: **75%**

Comparables:
Johnny Grubb, Don Lenhardt, Jim Russell (78)

YEAR	TEAM	LVL	AGE	PA	R	2B	3B	HR	RBI	BB	SO	SB	CS	AVG/OBP/SLG	TAv	BABIP	BRR	FRAA	WARP
2008	COH	AAA	28	257	40	16	2	3	31	40	57	12	3	.310/.416/.446	.288	.404	0.3	CF -5, RF -2	1.1
2008	WAS	MLB	28	139	17	5	2	3	12	25	31	2	0	.234/.374/.396	.278	.291	-1.3	LF -3, RF 1	0.2
2009	SYR	AAA	29	242	34	16	0	9	40	30	50	7	6	.278/.368/.488	.299	.318	0.5	LF 0, 1B 1	1.1
2009	SEA	MLB	29	122	12	6	1	3	10	14	28	0	1	.218/.303/.386	.254	.250	-0.6	LF 7, CF 3	0.9
2010	SEA	MLB	30	132	12	2	1	3	4	24	51	4	1	.196/.341/.318	.282	.333	1.8	LF 2, 1B 1	1.0
2011	*SEA*	*MLB*	*31*	*322*	*38*	*14*	*1*	*8*	*32*	*45*	*84*	*8*	*3*	*.239/.346/.390*	*.261*	*.309*	*-0.3*	*LF 2, CF -1*	*0.6*

Langerhans goes almost as long between swings as Jose Lopez goes between takes, which might not be the worst strategy in light of how infrequently he makes contact. Among major leaguers with at least 100 plate appearances last season, Langerhans posted the highest strikeout rate, the second-highest average of pitches seen per plate appearance, the third-highest walk rate, and the fourth-highest percentage of misses per swing. Those statistics stabilize quickly, so they tell us a lot about Langerhans despite the fact that the lefty received fewer than 150 plate appearances for the third consecutive season, though it's fair to speculate about the effects of sporadic play (as well as a bothersome bone spur) on his approach. The outfielder's patience is extreme enough that it borders on being a flaw and not a virtue, but he shows no platoon split to speak of, and his plus defensive ability in the corners and ability to play center in a pinch make him an ideal fourth outfield option.

Alex Liddi **3B**

Born: **8/14/1988** Age: **22**
Bats: **R** Throws: **R** Height: **6' 4"** Weight: **176**
Breakout: **1%** Improve: **32%** Collapse: **3%**
Attrition: **19%** MLB: **59%**

Comparables:
Ian Stewart, Wladimir Balentien, B.J. Upton (65)

YEAR	TEAM	LVL	AGE	PA	R	2B	3B	HR	RBI	BB	SO	SB	CS	AVG/OBP/SLG	TAv	BABIP	BRR	FRAA	WARP
2008	WIS	A	19	496	65	26	4	6	53	42	115	17	5	.244/.312/.360	.247	.313	6.4	3B 1, 1B 0	1.4
2009	HDS	A+	20	565	97	44	5	23	104	53	122	10	6	.345/.409/.594	.323	.409	-1.3	3B -3, 1B 2	5.1
2010	WTN	AA	21	565	78	37	8	15	92	50	145	5	7	.281/.353/.476	.288	.362	0.0	3B 4, 1B 3	3.8
2011	*SEA*	*MLB*	*22*	*552*	*67*	*32*	*4*	*16*	*72*	*39*	*143*	*5*	*2*	*.269/.320/.447*	*.266*	*.337*	*-0.2*	*3B 0, 1B 0*	*1.7*

Liddi left his eye-popping 2009 statistics in the heat of High Desert, but there was plenty to like about his performance after his promotion to Double-A, especially if you ask the ladies, with whom he's quite popular. The first professional position player to be imported from Italy maintained his walk rate at the higher level and preserved enough pop to tie for the Southern League lead with 60 extra-base hits. The imposing righty lacks both an obvious weakness and an obvious strength, which limits his potential to that of an average everyday starter. He's not blocked at third base, but if his defense forces a move across the diamond, his bat will become an obstacle.

Jose Lopez **3B**

Born: **11/24/1983** Age: **27**
Bats: **R** Throws: **R** Height: **6' 2"** Weight: **170**
Breakout: **1%** Improve: **52%** Collapse: **1%**
Attrition: **8%** MLB: **90%**

Comparables:
Buddy Bell, Mike Lansing, Robinson Cano (66)

YEAR	TEAM	LVL	AGE	PA	R	2B	3B	HR	RBI	BB	SO	SB	CS	AVG/OBP/SLG	TAv	BABIP	BRR	FRAA	WARP
2008	SEA	MLB	24	687	80	41	1	17	89	27	67	6	3	.297/.319/.443	.276	.303	-2.9	2B 26, 1B 3	5.2
2009	SEA	MLB	25	653	69	42	0	25	96	24	69	3	3	.272/.302/.463	.270	.268	-0.4	2B -5, 1B -1	1.5
2010	SEA	MLB	26	622	49	29	0	10	58	23	66	3	2	.240/.270/.339	.227	.254	-3.7	3B 20	1.2
2011	*COL*	*MLB*	*27*	*636*	*66*	*30*	*0*	*14*	*67*	*29*	*71*	*4*	*2*	*.250/.285/.372*	*.232*	*.258*	*-0.3*	*2B 4, 3B 5*	*0.6*

Lopez entered the league at age 20, but he seemingly stopped developing around the same time. He has never been an offensive star, but his plate production cratered last season, as a reduced percentage of his fly balls left the park. Although his line-drive rate held steady, the Venezuelan's BABIP took a tumble, which left his league-worst on-base percentage even less acceptable than usual; among qualified players, only A. J. Pierzynski walked less frequently. Any M's fan can recite a litany of Lopez's mental mistakes, many of them involving his bad decisions—and apparent lack of effort, which compounds his poor conditioning—on the basepaths, where he cost Seattle more than any player. In his first tour of duty at the hot corner, the former second sacker led all major-league third basemen in FRAA, which dragged him kicking and screaming above replacement level. Lopez will benefit greatly from a change of scenery after heading to the Rockies in a December swap. The Mariners should also profit from his departure.

Matt Mangini **3B**

Born: **12/21/1985** Age: **25**
Bats: **L** Throws: **R** Height: **6' 4"** Weight: **230**
Breakout: **8%** Improve: **14%** Collapse: **5%**
Attrition: **16%** MLB: **27%**

Comparables:
Chris Johnson, Travis Metcalf, Doug Rader (78)

YEAR	TEAM	LVL	AGE	PA	R	2B	3B	HR	RBI	BB	SO	SB	CS	AVG/OBP/SLG	TAv	BABIP	BRR	FRAA	WARP
2008	HDS	A+	22	214	27	12	0	6	25	23	52	3	1	.265/.374/.431	.272	.339	-0.6	3B -7, 1B 0	0.1
2008	WTN	AA	22	257	22	5	0	2	25	12	64	0	1	.202/.245/.248	.172	.261	2.1	3B -3, 1B 1	-1.7
2009	WTN	AA	23	469	48	18	5	12	67	38	92	10	2	.273/.339/.424	.262	.321	-5.4	3B 2, 1B -1	1.0
2010	TAC	AAA	24	477	73	31	4	18	63	26	96	3	0	.313/.352/.521	.292	.364	4.5	3B 13, 1B -3	4.5
2010	SEA	MLB	24	41	2	0	0	0	1	2	13	0	0	.211/.244/.211	.171	.308	-0.4	3B -1	-0.4
2011	*SEA*	*MLB*	*25*	*492*	*56*	*22*	*2*	*14*	*58*	*28*	*116*	*2*	*1*	*.259/.305/.413*	*.249*	*.312*	*0.0*	*3B -1, 1B -1*	*0.6*

Prior to last season, Mangini appeared to lack both the bat and the glove for third base, jeopardizing the 2007 supplemental first-rounder's future. It's still not clear that he possesses the leather, but his bat came around in a big way. The lefty started hitting for slightly more power toward the end of 2009, and maintained those gains and then some in his first exposure to Triple-A, nearly equaling his home-run total from the previous two seasons—which included a stint at High Desert—combined. The improvement earned him a September call-up, giving him the chance to start seven games at third in Seattle and giving the M's the opportunity to evaluate their asset up close. At six-foot-four, Mangini is heavy on his feet and won't make Mariners fans forget the fielding of Adrian Beltre (or Jose Lopez, for that matter), but his developing bat might make up for a few defensive foibles.

Adam Moore C

Born: **5/8/1984** Age: **27**
Bats: R Throws: R Height: **6' 3"** Weight: **220**
Breakout: **0%** Improve: **19%** Collapse: **9%**
Attrition: **21%** MLB: **45%**

Comparables:
Ronny Paulino, Nick Stavinoha, Nick Hundley (78)

YEAR	TEAM	LVL	AGE	PA	R	2B	3B	HR	RBI	BB	SO	SB	CS	AVG/OBP/SLG	TAv	BABIP	BRR	FRAA	WARP
2008	WTN	AA	24	490	60	34	2	14	71	40	77	0	1	.319/.394/.506	.290	.359	-1.4	C 1	3.4
2009	WTN	AA	25	116	14	5	0	3	13	16	21	0	0	.263/.371/.411	.271	.297	-0.2	C -1	0.5
2009	TAC	AAA	25	368	41	19	0	9	43	26	51	1	1	.294/.345/.429	.267	.324	-2.5	C -1	1.6
2009	SEA	MLB	25	24	4	1	0	1	2	0	7	1	0	.217/.250/.391	.231	.267	-0.2	C 0	0.0
2010	TAC	AAA	26	142	18	8	1	3	15	7	24	1	0	.321/.359/.463	.283	.374	0.0	C 0	0.9
2010	SEA	MLB	26	218	12	6	0	4	15	8	63	0	1	.195/.229/.283	.195	.255	-0.4	C -1	-0.6
2011	*SEA*	*MLB*	*27*	*455*	*53*	*23*	*1*	*12*	*52*	*29*	*91*	*1*	*0*	*.264/.317/.410*	*.255*	*.306*	*0.0*	*C -2*	*1.4*

The big leagues proved to be more than Moore could handle in his rookie season, but his performance in the high minors (a combined .309/.391/.489 in Double-A and .302/.350/.439 in Triple-A, both in roughly a full season's worth of plate appearances) suggests that he's capable of far better. A knee injury and subsequent hamstring strain knocked the righty out of commission from mid-May through early August, and he hit no better after healing. Even his defense seemed to lose something in translation from Tacoma, as the righty threw out only 19 percent of attempted basestealers, roughly half the rate he'd managed in the minors as his technique behind the plate improved over the past two seasons. The good news/bad news for Moore is that he is now blocked by the powerful Miguel Olivo. The latter brings his 2008-2010 .462 slugging percentage to Seattle, but also the .296 OBP he compiled in the same period. Olivo is ill-suited to Safeco, which is tough on right-handed power, and he hit only .211/.276/.322 away from Coors Field. Despite the Mariners' two-year commitment to Olivo, Moore need only bide his time.

Michael Saunders LF

Born: **11/19/1986** Age: **24**
Bats: L Throws: R Height: **6' 4"** Weight: **210**
Breakout: **3%** Improve: **24%** Collapse: **3%**
Attrition: **13%** MLB: **34%**

Comparables:
Justin Maxwell, Travis Buck, Gary Matthews (77)

YEAR	TEAM	LVL	AGE	PA	R	2B	3B	HR	RBI	BB	SO	SB	CS	AVG/OBP/SLG	TAv	BABIP	BRR	FRAA	WARP
2008	WTN	AA	21	289	46	18	3	8	30	30	66	11	6	.290/.367/.484	.304	.354	1.3	CF 1, RF 2	2.5
2008	TAC	AAA	21	105	12	4	1	3	16	9	30	1	2	.242/.305/.400	.256	.317	-2.6	CF 1, LF 1	0.1
2009	TAC	AAA	22	282	58	15	2	13	32	25	48	6	3	.310/.372/.544	.318	.332	3.2	LF 3, CF 3	3.3
2009	SEA	MLB	22	129	12	1	3	0	4	6	40	4	1	.221/.256/.279	.201	.325	0.0	LF 6	0.0
2010	TAC	AAA	23	93	6	1	0	0	5	11	17	4	0	.200/.293/.213	.212	.246	0.7	LF 1, CF -2	-0.1
2010	SEA	MLB	23	327	28	11	2	10	33	35	84	6	3	.211/.294/.367	.255	.258	-1.8	LF 7, CF -1	0.8
2011	*SEA*	*MLB*	*24*	*406*	*48*	*16*	*2*	*13*	*47*	*37*	*96*	*9*	*4*	*.251/.319/.416*	*.259*	*.300*	*-0.4*	*LF 4, CF -1*	*1.0*

Saunders was completely undone at the plate in his debut season, but looked slightly more like a major leaguer in 2010, though the resemblance still wasn't strong enough for the Mariners' taste. Called up after posting an uninspiring 506 OPS in Tacoma through early May, he managed to improve on his subpar strikeout and walk rates from 2009, but his contact problems persisted. The lefty has problems with balls tailing away from him, and rarely makes contact when he chases outside the zone; same-handed pitchers have taken advantage of this tendency, which results in a pronounced platoon split. Saunders' pull-oriented approach only infrequently yields balls in play the other way, most of which are hit weakly and don't meet happy endings. It's hard to hand a player with his recent track record a starting job, but short of an overhaul by new hitting coach Chris Chambliss, the chance to learn from failure on a regular basis might be the outfielder's best hope.

Justin Smoak **1B**

Born: **12/5/1986** Age: **24**
Bats: **S** Throws: **L** Height: **6' 4"** Weight: **220**
Breakout: **7%** Improve: **20%** Collapse: **3%**
Attrition: **22%** MLB: **44%**

Comparables:
Mike Carp, John Olerud, Jason Thompson (77)

YEAR	TEAM	LVL	AGE	PA	R	2B	3B	HR	RBI	BB	SO	SB	CS	AVG/OBP/SLG	TAv	BABIP	BRR	FRAA	WARP
2008	CLN	A	21	62	9	3	0	3	6	5	10	0	0	.304/.355/.518	.315	.318	-0.7	1B 1	0.5
2009	FRI	AA	22	227	30	10	0	6	29	39	35	0	0	.328/.449/.481	.344	.375	-4.1	1B 0	1.7
2009	OKL	AAA	22	237	25	11	0	4	23	35	45	0	0	.244/.363/.360	.255	.293	-2.6	1B 0	-0.2
2010	OKL	AAA	23	66	10	6	0	2	5	16	8	0	0	.300/.470/.540	.339	.325	-0.2	1B 1	0.6
2010	TEX	MLB	23	275	31	10	0	8	34	38	57	1	0	.209/.316/.353	.249	.238	-0.3	1B 5	0.4
2010	TAC	AAA	23	159	23	7	0	7	25	23	32	0	0	.271/.377/.481	.313	.302	-0.8	1B -2	1.0
2010	SEA	MLB	23	122	11	4	0	5	14	8	34	0	0	.239/.287/.407	.248	.293	-0.3	1B -1	-0.2
2011	*SEA*	*MLB*	*24*	*398*	*51*	*17*	*0*	*13*	*45*	*55*	*82*	*0*	*0*	*.258/.361/.431*	*.279*	*.299*	*0.0*	*1B -6*	*0.4*

"Rushed" hardly begins to describe Smoak's blitzkrieg through the Rangers' minor-league system. After the briefest of introductions to A-ball in 2008, he split his first full professional season between Double-A and Triple-A; 15 games into the following campaign, he found himself in the majors. Smoak's initial advances went well, but like the German *Heer*, he eventually became overextended and struggled mightily in Arlington, where he showed good patience but subpar power. After nearly signing off on a package headlined by the Yankees' Jesus Montero, the Mariners accepted Smoak as the centerpiece of the return they received for Cliff Lee, but the switch-hitter's struggles continued in Safeco, prompting a remedial trip to Tacoma. Following his subsequent September promotion, the good-gloved first baseman hit .340/.421/.580 in 14 games, and scouts still consider him capable of MLB stardom. Some of his struggles can be explained by a lowly .255 BABIP posted despite a superior line-drive rate, but perhaps he stood to benefit from some additional time to consolidate his minor-league learning. At 24, Smoak remains the offensive foundation of the Mariners' future.

Ichiro Suzuki **RF**

Born: **10/22/1973** Age: **37**
Bats: **L** Throws: **R** Height: **5' 9"** Weight: **160**
Breakout: **0%** Improve: **23%** Collapse: **5%**
Attrition: **15%** MLB: **91%**

Comparables:
Maury Wills, Lou Brock, Jose Cruz (42)

YEAR	TEAM	LVL	AGE	PA	R	2B	3B	HR	RBI	BB	SO	SB	CS	AVG/OBP/SLG	TAv	BABIP	BRR	FRAA	WARP
2008	SEA	MLB	34	749	103	20	7	6	42	51	65	43	4	.311/.359/.386	.280	.333	10.1	RF -1, CF 7	4.6
2009	SEA	MLB	35	678	88	31	4	11	46	32	71	26	9	.352/.385/.465	.313	.382	3.0	RF 1	5.0
2010	SEA	MLB	36	732	74	30	3	6	43	45	86	42	9	.315/.358/.394	.291	.351	1.4	RF -1	3.3
2011	*SEA*	*MLB*	*37*	*729*	*89*	*28*	*4*	*9*	*76*	*45*	*78*	*35*	*8*	*.311/.353/.406*	*.271*	*.335*	*1.1*	*RF -1, CF 1*	*2.1*

Over 200 hits, powered by an MLB-high infield-hit percentage? Check. Prolific basestealing at a superlative rate of success? Check. Stellar play in the field, distinguished by extreme range, a strong arm, and the quickest release in baseball (sorry, Mrs. Suzuki), as determined by the Fans Scouting Report? Check. Although he's had better performances at the plate, Mariners fans were treated to more of the usual lofty play from Ichiro in 2010, even as his team fell to pieces around him. The lefty's indefinite postponement of a sequel to his first-ever DL trip in 2009 enabled him to reach the 162-game mark for the third time in his career. This severely cut into his quality time with the newly released *Dragon Quest IX*, but ensured at least one constant bright spot in an otherwise languid lineup. Suzuki will be 37 on Opening Day, and while he won't continue to cheat Father Time forever, the next chink to appear in his armor will be the first.

Matt Tuiasosopo **3B**

Born: **5/10/1986** Age: **25**
Bats: **R** Throws: **R** Height: **6' 2"** Weight: **223**
Breakout: **4%** Improve: **18%** Collapse: **10%**
Attrition: **17%** MLB: **40%**

Comparables:
Andy LaRoche, Alex Gordon, Josh Fields (72)

YEAR	TEAM	LVL	AGE	PA	R	2B	3B	HR	RBI	BB	SO	SB	CS	AVG/OBP/SLG	TAv	BABIP	BRR	FRAA	WARP
2008	TAC	AAA	22	500	87	32	2	13	73	47	104	4	0	.281/.364/.453	.277	.340	2.0	3B -9	1.7
2008	SEA	MLB	22	47	1	2	1	0	2	2	16	0	0	.159/.213/.250	.188	.250	-0.1	3B 1	-0.2
2009	TAC	AAA	23	269	43	15	0	11	35	36	83	3	1	.261/.364/.473	.299	.353	-0.3	3B 0, 2B -5	1.4
2009	SEA	MLB	23	25	2	1	0	1	2	2	5	0	0	.227/.280/.409	.246	.235	0.0	2B 1	0.1
2010	TAC	AAA	24	176	26	6	0	5	21	32	35	2	2	.252/.392/.399	.289	.301	2.3	3B 0, LF -1	1.2
2010	SEA	MLB	24	138	11	5	0	4	11	9	49	0	0	.173/.232/.307	.216	.240	0.6	LF -2, 3B 1	-0.4
2011	*SEA*	*MLB*	*25*	*397*	*47*	*18*	*1*	*13*	*44*	*44*	*107*	*2*	*1*	*.244/.334/.411*	*.264*	*.308*	*-0.1*	*3B -2, 2B -1*	*0.8*

In a mere 50 major-league games last season, Tuiasosopo managed to spend time at every infield spot as well as left field, so the answer to the long-standing question of which position he might end up playing in the majors thus far appears to be "most of them." Thanks to the aggressive developmental tendencies of the Bavasi era, Tui has been playing catch-up his whole career, but he has made strides despite the positional mayhem. Compared with the punchless hacker he was at the dawn of his professional career, the righty has become a disciplined slugger; of course, what matters more at this stage of his career isn't how far he's come, but how much further he has left to go. The former football star hasn't hit a lick in the majors, but his contact problems might stem in part from intermittent playing time, given that he walked nearly as often as he struck out at Tacoma in 2010. He'll never be playable in the middle infield, so his future playing time hinges on the unlikely event of his bat's developing enough to carry a corner.

Jack Wilson **SS**

Born: **12/29/1977** Age: **33**
Bats: R Throws: R Height: **5' 10"** Weight: **170**
Breakout: **0%** Improve: **30%** Collapse: **9%**
Attrition: **18%** MLB: **86%**

Comparables:
Marco Scutaro, Angel Berroa, Alex Gonzalez (76)

YEAR	TEAM	LVL	AGE	PA	R	2B	3B	HR	RBI	BB	SO	SB	CS	AVG/OBP/SLG	TAv	BABIP	BRR	FRAA	WARP
2008	PIT	MLB	30	330	24	18	1	1	22	13	27	2	2	.272/.306/.348	.229	.289	-1.1	SS 7	0.8
2009	PIT	MLB	31	286	26	18	1	4	31	15	31	2	1	.267/.301/.387	.244	.284	0.7	SS 5	1.1
2009	SEA	MLB	31	116	11	5	0	1	8	6	17	1	0	.224/.259/.299	.208	.250	-0.4	SS -2	-0.4
2010	SEA	MLB	32	211	16	11	1	0	14	7	35	1	2	.249/.275/.316	.234	.289	-1.4	SS 7	0.7
2011	*SEA*	*MLB*	*33*	*430*	*48*	*23*	*1*	*6*	*46*	*23*	*47*	*4*	*2*	*.275/.313/.389*	*.247*	*.288*	*-0.4*	*SS 7*	*1.6*

Wilson's value has evaporated along with his playing time in recent seasons, as four trips to the DL in the last three years have severely curtailed his out-making activities. The righty missed most of May and June with a hamstring strain, then underwent season-ending surgery in August to repair a fractured fifth metacarpal suffered when he slipped in a restroom. His bathroom blunder didn't come at much cost to the Mariners, since his offensive performance was already in the toilet: only eight major-league batters with a minimum of 200 plate appearances managed to walk less frequently in 2010, and Wilson's strikeout rate reached a level rivaled only by that of his rookie campaign. The good news is that FRAA still considered him a strong defender, though other advanced fielding systems offered a more qualified appraisal of his work in limited opportunities. The Mariners are on the hook for one more season of Wilsonian play, but they've already realized that in this Wilson's case, the Fourteen Points describes the approximate difference between his on-base and slugging percentages. After a walk-deprived walk year, he's likely to discover that "He kept us out of WARP" doesn't work as a re-signing slogan.

Josh Wilson **SS**

Born: 3/26/1981 Age: **30**
Bats: R Throws: R Height: **6' 1"** Weight: **178**
Breakout: **2%** Improve: **24%** Collapse: **6%**
Attrition: **13%** MLB: **83%**

Comparables:
Johnny Logan, Alex Grammas, Chris Burke (80)

YEAR	TEAM	LVL	AGE	PA	R	2B	3B	HR	RBI	BB	SO	SB	CS	AVG/OBP/SLG	TAv	BABIP	BRR	FRAA	WARP
2008	IND	AAA	27	337	28	18	1	5	32	24	48	11	5	.276/.338/.396	.254	.303	-3.3	SS -7, 2B -7	-0.8
2008	PAW	AAA	27	122	16	6	0	2	10	5	23	2	0	.223/.287/.330	.209	.264	0.5	SS -7, 2B -1	-0.9
2009	RNO	AAA	28	61	5	3	1	1	10	7	8	1	1	.260/.344/.420	.255	.273	0.1	SS 1	0.3
2009	TAC	AAA	28	60	10	2	0	1	3	2	6	1	0	.245/.267/.340	.202	.240	0.7	SS 1, 2B 0	0.1
2009	ARI	MLB	28	29	0	1	0	0	2	3	3	0	0	.231/.310/.269	.205	.261	0.1	SS 4, P 0	0.3
2009	SDN	MLB	28	43	2	2	0	0	1	3	9	0	0	.105/.186/.158	.133	.133	-0.4	SS -3, P 0	-0.7
2009	SEA	MLB	28	138	14	8	1	3	10	6	32	1	2	.250/.290/.398	.252	.305	-0.7	SS -3, 3B 1	0.1
2010	TAC	AAA	29	86	7	11	1	0	11	0	15	0	1	.333/.341/.494	.272	.391	0.1	SS -1, 2B 0	0.4
2010	SEA	MLB	29	388	22	14	2	2	25	14	74	5	0	.227/.278/.294	.225	.280	-1.4	SS 14, 3B 0	1.2
2011	*SEA*	*MLB*	*30*	*392*	*41*	*19*	*2*	*6*	*37*	*21*	*72*	*5*	*2*	*.243/.296/.354*	*.229*	*.281*	*-0.2*	*SS 0, 2B -1*	*0.1*

What better way to ensure that Jack Wilson wouldn't be missed during an injury-plagued season than to substitute an equally anemic hitter with the same initials and surname? The younger Wilson is a Triple-A hitter at best, and he hit like one in his most extended exposure yet to major league pitching; his batting line would have looked even worse if he hadn't crept close enough to the plate to draw 12 beanballs, which nearly equaled his paltry walk total. Ever since Willie Bloomquist's departure, the Mariners have lacked a true designated gritter, so perhaps Wilson fills some quota for talent-deprived white guys who play multiple positions. Still, a good glove only goes so far, and Wilson doesn't even have one. As a result, he's miscast as anything but a short-term replacement. The Mariners having added glove-man Brendan Ryan, Wilson may find himself the long-term answer at Tacoma.

PITCHERS

David Aardsma

Born: **12/27/1981** Age: **29**
Bats: R Throws: R Height: **6' 5"** Weight: **200**
Breakout: **21%** Improve: **34%** Collapse: **18%**
Attrition: **11%** MLB: **68%**

Comparables:
Hong-Chih Kuo, Jason Frasor, Jorge Julio (73)

YEAR	TEAM	LVL	AGE	W	L	SV	G	GS	IP	H	HR	BB	SO	EqBB9	EqSO9	GB%	BABIP	WHIP	ERA	FRA	WARP
2008	BOS	MLB	26	4	2	0	47	0	48^{2}	49	4	35	49	6.5	9.1	45%	.333	1.83	5.55	5.35	-0.1
2009	SEA	MLB	27	3	6	38	73	0	71^{1}	49	4	34	80	4.3	10.1	27%	.254	1.16	2.52	3.02	1.5
2010	SEA	MLB	28	0	6	31	53	0	49^{2}	33	5	25	49	4.5	8.9	40%	.231	1.21	3.44	4.24	0.4
2011	*SEA*	*MLB*	*29*	*3*	*1*	*16*	*66*	*0*	*66^{1}*	*53*	*6*	*34*	*69*	*4.6*	*9.4*	*41%*	*.282*	*1.32*	*3.33*	*3.62*	*0.6*

Aardsma's 2009 season was one of those glorious relief campaigns that ends before enough innings have piled up for something to go wrong, leaving player and team alike with the nagging feeling that they might have stolen a march on the baseball gods. Despite posting one of the league's highest fly-ball rates, Aardsma held opposing batters to just four home runs in his first crack at closing, as a succession of deep flies seemed to die on the warning track. Last season, they didn't, and the hard thrower coughed up five long balls despite pitching over 20 fewer innings and allowing flies less frequently. Along with the expected correction in Aardsma's home-run-to-fly-ball rate, his strikeout rate shrunk, and his ERA was saved from further bloating only by one of the league's lowest BABIPs. Fortunately, the righty avoided a substantial regression in his walk rate, which could have put an end to his days at the back end of the bullpen.

Blake Beavan

Born: **1/17/1989** Age: **22**
Bats: R Throws: R Height: **6' 7"** Weight: **250**
Breakout: **15%** Improve: **26%** Collapse: **2%**
Attrition: **14%** MLB: **31%**

Comparables:
Tommy Hunter, Matt Harrison, Sean O'Sullivan (57)

YEAR	TEAM	LVL	AGE	W	L	SV	G	GS	IP	H	HR	BB	SO	EqBB9	EqSO9	GB%	BABIP	WHIP	ERA	FRA	WARP
2008	CLN	A	19	10	6	0	23	23	121^{2}	105	12	20	73	1.5	5.4	49%	.251	1.06	2.37	4.59	1.4
2009	BAK	A+	20	5	4	0	12	12	73^{1}	75	6	16	51	2.0	6.3	54%	.297	1.31	4.30	6.05	-0.3
2009	FRI	AA	20	4	4	0	15	15	89^{2}	113	4	12	34	1.2	3.4	46%	.323	1.41	4.01	4.67	0.7
2009	FRI	AA	20	4	4	0	15	15	89^{2}	113	4	13	34	1.3	3.4	46%	.322	1.42	4.01	4.67	0.7
2010	TAC	AAA	21	2	2	0	7	7	40^{1}	56	6	8	22	1.8	4.9	37%	.352	1.65	6.47	5.86	-0.1
2011	*SEA*	*MLB*	*22*	*9*	*9*	*0*	*25*	*25*	*149^{2}*	*174*	*17*	*39*	*64*	*2.4*	*3.8*	*45%*	*.302*	*1.43*	*4.71*	*5.12*	*0.7*

After experiencing unprecedented success deep in the heart of Texas, the second-best pitcher in the Cliff Lee trade struggled with his new organization. Beavan's story serves as a cautionary tale about the perils of mechanical tinkering; the big righty lost his mid-90s heat after the Rangers altered his messy delivery to ward off injury, but he preserved his prospect status by reinventing himself as a combination control artist and ground-ball machine. Beavan tops out in the low 90s and lacks a reliable strikeout pitch, which makes him dependent on his defense and leaves him vulnerable to BABIP spikes like the one that sabotaged him in Tacoma. He'll never be of much use to a fantasy team, but continued improvement in his changeup could make him a capable back-of-the-rotation starter, and his massive frame portends plenty of innings eaten in the future.

Erik Bedard

Born: **3/6/1979** Age: **32**
Bats: L Throws: L Height: **6' 1"** Weight: **186**
Breakout: **26%** Improve: **53%** Collapse: **14%**
Attrition: **7%** MLB: **92%**

Comparables:
Pedro Feliciano, Jason Frasor, Paul Assenmacher (77)

YEAR	TEAM	LVL	AGE	W	L	SV	G	GS	IP	H	HR	BB	SO	EqBB9	EqSO9	GB%	BABIP	WHIP	ERA	FRA	WARP
2008	SEA	MLB	29	6	4	0	15	15	81	70	9	37	72	4.1	8.0	39%	.271	1.37	3.67	4.88	0.6
2009	SEA	MLB	30	5	3	0	15	15	83	65	8	34	90	3.7	9.8	45%	.269	1.24	2.82	3.68	1.7
2011	*SEA*	*MLB*	*32*	*9*	*5*	*0*	*21*	*21*	*114^{1}*	*96*	*10*	*44*	*115*	*3.4*	*9.1*	*44%*	*.290*	*1.22*	*3.09*	*3.36*	*3.1*

The good-when-healthy act that characterized Bedard's first two tours of duty in the Pacific Northwest raised hopes for his third installment, but the Canadian couldn't complete the trilogy in 2010, as the "when healthy" portion of his season-long sojourn on the 60-day DL comprised all of three minor-league rehab starts in late June and early July. The lefty's shoulder pain recurred just as he stood poised to make his major league debut, and after soliciting three opinions in a vain attempt to find a doctor who would give him good news, he extended his streak of consecutive seasons with a shoulder surgery to three in early August. The latest operation turned up only a bone spur, a far less serious finding than the torn labrum that had sent him under the knife a year earlier, and Bedard insists that he'll be ready to take the mound in spring training. If you believe that, his agent would have had an incentive-laden contract to sell you, but Jack Zduriencik already signed it.

Dan Cortes

Born: **3/4/1987** Age: **24**
Bats: R Throws: R Height: **6' 6"** Weight: **230**
Breakout: **10%** Improve: **14%** Collapse: **6%**
Attrition: **12%** MLB: **22%**

Comparables:
Jhonny Nunez, Donald Veal, Carlos Carrasco (79)

YEAR	TEAM	LVL	AGE	W	L	SV	G	GS	IP	H	HR	BB	SO	EqBB9	EqSO9	GB%	BABIP	WHIP	ERA	FRA	WARP
2008	NWA	AA	21	10	4	0	23	23	116^{2}	103	13	55	109	4.2	8.4	38%	.288	1.42	3.78	4.19	2.4
2009	NWA	AA	22	6	6	0	16	15	80^{1}	77	3	50	57	5.6	6.4	48%	.301	1.63	3.92	4.79	0.7
2009	WTN	AA	22	1	5	0	10	10	54^{2}	51	4	35	55	5.8	9.0	44%	.315	1.59	4.94	5.67	-0.0
2010	WTN	AA	23	6	4	1	25	16	83^{2}	77	4	53	85	5.7	9.2	49%	.308	1.61	5.27	6.01	-0.3
2010	SEA	MLB	23	0	1	0	4	0	5^{1}	3	0	3	6	5.1	10.1	21%	.214	1.13	3.38	5.94	-0.1
2011	*SEA*	*MLB*	*24*	*8*	*8*	*0*	*36*	*20*	*119^{2}*	*119*	*12*	*75*	*93*	*5.6*	*7.0*	*43%*	*.302*	*1.62*	*5.00*	*5.43*	*0.1*

As Seattle's bounty in the Yuniesky Betancourt trade, Cortes could have guaranteed that the Mariners got the better end of the deal just by showing up for work, but he didn't stop there. Instead, he has made himself into an important part of the organization's future. The Royals' top pitching prospect at the time of the exchange (which goes to show how far Kansas City's system has come) fizzled as a starter due to subpar control, but came into his own after a midseason conversion to relief. In short stints, his formerly plus fastball added both a second plus and a few ticks. The tall righty needs to further refine his control and slurvy slider to earn a shot at the late innings, but considering his stuff, it's likely that Cortes the Killer will come dancing across the water of Puget Sound for years to come.

Doug Fister

Born: **2/4/1984** Age: **27**
Bats: L Throws: R Height: **6' 8"** Weight: **195**
Breakout: **13%** Improve: **25%** Collapse: **12%**
Attrition: **26%** MLB: **50%**
Comparables:
Justin Germano, Jeff Karstens, Josh Banks (75)

YEAR	TEAM	LVL	AGE	W	L	SV	G	GS	IP	H	HR	BB	SO	EqBB9	EqSO9	GB%	BABIP	WHIP	ERA	FRA	WARP
2008	WTN	AA	24	6	14	0	31	23	134^{1}	155	12	45	104	3.0	7.0	48%	.333	1.57	5.43	5.23	1.0
2009	TAC	AAA	25	6	4	0	22	17	106^{1}	132	10	11	79	0.9	6.7	46%	.346	1.39	3.81	3.42	2.6
2009	SEA	MLB	25	3	4	0	11	10	61	63	11	15	36	2.2	5.3	41%	.271	1.31	4.13	4.52	0.6
2010	SEA	MLB	26	6	14	0	28	28	171	187	13	32	93	1.7	4.9	47%	.302	1.32	4.11	4.03	1.7
2011	*SEA*	*MLB*	*27*	*9*	*8*	*0*	*23*	*23*	*131^{1}*	*147*	*14*	*33*	*76*	*2.3*	*5.2*	*45%*	*.310*	*1.37*	*4.37*	*4.75*	*1.2*

On May 31, 10 starts into his season, Fister sported a 2.45 ERA, which qualified as a surprising development for a pitcher whose career ERA in the minors stood nearly two runs higher. After missing most of June with shoulder fatigue, he did his best to undo the hot start, posting a 5.24 figure thereafter. It might be tempting to blame the shoulder for derailing what could have been a breakout campaign, but the weary wing doesn't deserve scapegoat status; when Fister hit the disabled list, his batting average on balls in play (BABIP) rested at .236, so his season was likely to go south under any circumstances. When the dust settled, most of Fister's peripherals bore a near-perfect resemblance to his 2009 numbers, and his BABIP—like Fister himself—ended up approximating league average. The colossal lefty's size belies his low velocity, and despite superb control, he's unlikely to advance any further since he lacks a strikeout pitch. Still, he took a more entertaining route to average than most—admit it, he had you going for a minute there.

Luke French

Born: **9/13/1985** Age: **25**
Bats: L Throws: L Height: **6' 4"** Weight: **220**
Breakout: **13%** Improve: **19%** Collapse: **7%**
Attrition: **19%** MLB: **30%**
Comparables:
Tobi Stoner, Yorman Bazardo, Jeff Manship (78)

YEAR	TEAM	LVL	AGE	W	L	SV	G	GS	IP	H	HR	BB	SO	EqBB9	EqSO9	GB%	BABIP	WHIP	ERA	FRA	WARP
2008	ERI	AA	22	9	11	0	27	26	170	195	16	60	88	3.2	4.7	50%	.311	1.54	3.97	4.15	3.3
2009	TOL	AAA	23	4	4	0	13	13	81^{2}	71	6	20	72	2.2	7.9	44%	.284	1.13	2.97	3.46	2.0
2009	DET	MLB	23	1	2	0	7	5	29^{1}	33	2	11	19	3.4	5.8	28%	.310	1.53	3.38	2.78	1.1
2009	SEA	MLB	23	3	3	0	8	7	38	54	9	17	23	4.0	5.4	32%	.349	1.89	6.63	6.58	-0.4
2010	TAC	AAA	24	11	3	0	17	17	113^{1}	109	7	23	63	1.8	5.0	38%	.283	1.21	2.94	3.87	2.1
2010	SEA	MLB	24	5	7	0	16	13	87^{2}	88	13	29	37	3.0	3.8	33%	.260	1.38	4.83	6.21	-1.0
2011	*SEA*	*MLB*	*25*	*9*	*10*	*0*	*27*	*27*	*163*	*182*	*19*	*59*	*82*	*3.2*	*4.5*	*42%*	*.299*	*1.47*	*4.79*	*5.21*	*0.5*

Excluding knuckleballers and ex-Mariners in their age-47 seasons, French's fastball was the fourth-slowest among all pitchers who threw a minimum of 80 innings last season. Plenty of air-oriented, low-velo lefties who might be lost elsewhere can carve out a living in Safeco, but French tests the run-restricting capabilities of even the AL's best pitcher's park. Only his changeup induced anything close to a league-average whiff rate last season, and his strikeout rate simply wouldn't have been survivable had a low BABIP not saved him from further carnage. He's major-league material in the sense that he's spent time in the majors, but not in the sense that he's belonged there.

Felix Hernandez

Born: **4/8/1986** Age: **25**
Bats: R Throws: R Height: **6' 3"** Weight: **225**
Breakout: **15%** Improve: **49%** Collapse: **18%**
Attrition: **3%** MLB: **96%**
Comparables:
Roger Clemens, Don Drysdale, Matt Cain (58)

YEAR	TEAM	LVL	AGE	W	L	SV	G	GS	IP	H	HR	BB	SO	EqBB9	EqSO9	GB%	BABIP	WHIP	ERA	FRA	WARP
2008	SEA	MLB	22	9	11	0	31	31	200^{2}	198	17	80	175	3.6	7.8	52%	.314	1.43	3.45	3.73	4.0
2009	SEA	MLB	23	19	5	0	34	34	238^{2}	200	15	71	217	2.7	8.2	54%	.278	1.17	2.49	3.27	6.0
2010	SEA	MLB	24	13	12	0	34	34	249^{2}	194	17	70	232	2.5	8.4	55%	.263	1.09	2.27	3.20	5.4
2011	*SEA*	*MLB*	*25*	*15*	*7*	*0*	*32*	*32*	*223*	*185*	*15*	*67*	*204*	*2.7*	*8.2*	*51%*	*.285*	*1.13*	*2.64*	*2.87*	*6.8*

Not since Fernando Valenzuela and Dwight Gooden has a pitcher accounted for as many innings before the age of 25 as Hernandez. Of course, you don't get a nickname like "King Felix"—or, for that matter, "El Toro" or "Dr. K"—solely for eating innings; the flavor of those frames counts, too, with extra credit awarded for making opposing hitters gag. Valenzuela won the Cy Young award in his rookie campaign, while Gooden finished second in his introduction to the league before bringing home the hardware in his sophomore season. By those standards, Felix took his sweet time to secure the BBWAA's affections; if Fernando's and Doc's relationships with the voters were love at first (or second) sight, Felix's featured only suggestive glances, heavy petting, and waiting till marriage. It took him six seasons to tie the knot, but slow and steady might yet win the righty the career race: Valenzuela had only one comparable season remaining after his award win, and Gooden never returned to those heights. Although a moundsman's long-term outlook is only as strong as his ligaments and tendons, Hernandez seems perfectly equipped to sustain his success—while lesser pitchers are forced to pick their plus peripherals à la carte, Hernandez orders his *prix fixe*.

Shawn Kelley

Born: **4/26/1984** Age: **27**
Bats: R Throws: R Height: **6' 2"** Weight: **215**
Breakout: **5%** Improve: **11%** Collapse: **11%**
Attrition: **4%** MLB: **25%**
Comparables:
Tom Niedenfuer, Warner Madrigal, Todd Worrell (76)

YEAR	TEAM	LVL	AGE	W	L	SV	G	GS	IP	H	HR	BB	SO	EqBB9	EqSO9	GB%	BABIP	WHIP	ERA	FRA	WARP
2008	WTN	AA	24	3	1	9	29	0	42^2	31	2	17	44	3.6	9.3	50%	.269	1.15	2.11	3.73	0.5
2009	SEA	MLB	25	5	4	0	40	0	46	45	9	9	41	1.8	8.0	33%	.279	1.24	4.50	5.69	-0.3
2010	SEA	MLB	26	3	1	0	22	0	25	26	5	12	26	4.3	9.4	26%	.313	1.56	3.96	4.43	0.1
2011	*SEA*	*MLB*	*27*	*2*	*1*	*1*	*32*	*0*	*39^1*	*36*	*5*	*15*	*36*	*3.5*	*8.3*	*42%*	*.298*	*1.32*	*3.84*	*4.17*	*0.1*

In the season following his largely successful jump from Double-A to the majors, Kelley upped his strikeout rate but lost his control. Sometimes, a lapsed feel for the strike zone suggests the need for a mechanical tweak; at other times, the only prescription is elbow surgery. In Kelley's case, the latter was deemed necessary, and the righty went under the knife in September for what was inaccurately termed a "partial" Tommy John surgery. The 2003 total TJ survivor inhaled his anesthesia resigned to sitting out the entirety of 2011, but since only a moderate sprain was discovered, he reset his sights on a May return. That's good news for the Mariners, who would like to get a look at what his low-90s fastball and 10-mph-slower slider could do over a full season.

Brandon League

Born: **3/16/1983** Age: **28**
Bats: R Throws: R Height: **6' 3"** Weight: **192**
Breakout: **19%** Improve: **35%** Collapse: **29%**
Attrition: **13%** MLB: **76%**
Comparables:
Tim Crabtree, Jeff Robinson, Ehren Wassermann (74)

YEAR	TEAM	LVL	AGE	W	L	SV	G	GS	IP	H	HR	BB	SO	EqBB9	EqSO9	GB%	BABIP	WHIP	ERA	FRA	WARP
2008	SYR	AAA	25	2	3	2	20	0	34^1	36	2	10	32	2.6	8.4	69%	.321	1.40	3.94	5.62	-0.1
2008	TOR	MLB	25	1	2	1	31	0	33	28	2	15	23	4.1	6.3	69%	.265	1.39	2.18	3.42	0.5
2009	TOR	MLB	26	3	6	0	67	0	74^2	72	8	21	76	2.5	9.2	56%	.318	1.34	4.58	4.85	0.3
2010	SEA	MLB	27	9	7	6	70	0	79	67	7	27	56	3.1	6.4	63%	.256	1.22	3.42	4.99	-0.2
2011	*SEA*	*MLB*	*28*	*3*	*1*	*1*	*60*	*0*	*72^2*	*66*	*6*	*26*	*58*	*3.2*	*7.2*	*53%*	*.292*	*1.27*	*3.50*	*3.81*	*0.4*

In 2009, League's splitter was baseball's most unhittable offering, inducing swings and misses on 35 percent of its trips to the plate. Once possessed of such a weapon, few pitchers would seek to minimize its impact, but that's precisely what League did in 2010, at least partly at the Mariners' behest. The team altered his delivery in spring training, ostensibly to protect his arm—which had evinced no obvious signs of strain since 2007—and while the change fostered refinements in his infrequently used slider, it seemed to sap his splitter of some of its ability to generate whiffs. At the same time, the righty restricted the splitter's usage, and explained the discrepancy by labeling it a "last-resort pitch." According to League, the decision to throw it more often in 2009 stemmed from poor two-seamer command, which got him into situations where he "had to get a strikeout." With a return of the two-seamer's accuracy, he scaled back his reliance on the splitter. Pitching to contact seems a rather curious decision in the case of a pitcher equipped for better; strikeouts aren't something that League should spurn until the barbarians are at third base, since missing more bats might prevent them from reaching base in the first place. Although his ERA fell on the strength of a BABIP correction, a move to a more spacious home park, and a two-seamer-induced uptick in ground-ball rate, League's defense-independent performance suggests that his new approach could cost him in the long run.

Josh Lueke

Born: **12/5/1984** Age: **26**
Bats: R Throws: R Height: **6' 5"** Weight: **220**
Breakout: **6%** Improve: **17%** Collapse: **12%**
Attrition: **13%** MLB: **29%**
Comparables:
Mark Worrell, Luke Gregerson, Jason Motte (70)

YEAR	TEAM	LVL	AGE	W	L	SV	G	GS	IP	H	HR	BB	SO	EqBB9	EqSO9	GB%	BABIP	WHIP	ERA	FRA	WARP
2008	BAK	A+	23	2	6	1	35	0	59	65	6	16	72	2.4	11.0	45%	.351	1.44	5.03	4.90	-0.2
2010	TAC	AAA	25	1	0	4	15	0	21^1	17	0	7	21	3.0	8.9	42%	.288	1.13	1.69	1.10	0.8
2011	*SEA*	*MLB*	*26*	*2*	*1*	*2*	*33*	*0*	*45*	*41*	*4*	*17*	*48*	*3.3*	*9.4*	*44%*	*.307*	*1.27*	*3.43*	*3.73*	*0.3*

Lueke's first act as a member of the Mariners organization was to get both his new GM in trouble for acquiring him and his new team's professional scouting director fired. The big righty's criminal past touched off an interstate dispute between Zduriencik, dismissed pitching coach Rick Adair, and Rangers GM Jon Daniels, all of whom appeared to disagree about the extent of Seattle's knowledge concerning Lueke's past prison time in connection with an alleged rape at the time of his inclusion in the Cliff Lee trade. The reliever may never escape the consequences of his deplorable actions entirely, but his on-field future appears bright. Although Lueke's legal problems cost him almost all of 2009, he made up for lost time last season, earning multiple promotions and holding his own in Triple-A. His mid-90s fastball and devastating slider seemed to benefit from his time away from the game, and unless public opinion sends him packing, he'll be recruited for late-inning work before long.

Garrett Olson

Born: **10/18/1983** Age: **27**
Bats: R Throws: L Height: **6' 1"** Weight: **195**
Breakout: **20%** Improve: **42%** Collapse: **16%**
Attrition: **13%** MLB: **76%**

Comparables:
Dusty Hughes, Steve Busby, Erik Hanson (76)

YEAR	TEAM	LVL	AGE	W	L	SV	G	GS	IP	H	HR	BB	SO	EqBB9	EqSO9	GB%	BABIP	WHIP	ERA	FRA	WARP
2008	NOR	AAA	24	1	2	0	7	7	36^1	35	1	16	39	4.0	9.7	44%	.333	1.43	2.98	3.14	1.2
2008	BAL	MLB	24	9	10	0	26	26	132^2	168	17	62	83	4.2	5.6	44%	.335	1.79	6.65	6.33	-0.4
2009	TAC	AAA	25	2	3	0	9	9	47^1	38	2	23	38	4.4	7.2	47%	.271	1.37	4.95	4.99	0.3
2009	SEA	MLB	25	3	5	0	31	11	80^1	79	19	34	47	3.8	5.3	35%	.247	1.46	5.71	7.46	-1.3
2010	TAC	AAA	26	2	5	0	12	6	46^2	36	4	15	50	2.9	9.7	40%	.271	1.15	3.66	4.26	0.8
2010	SEA	MLB	26	0	3	1	35	0	37^2	42	6	15	31	3.6	7.4	39%	.300	1.51	4.54	4.53	0.1
2011	*SEA*	*MLB*	*27*	*9*	*7*	*0*	*51*	*20*	*141*	*139*	*17*	*62*	*108*	*3.9*	*6.9*	*43%*	*.291*	*1.41*	*4.39*	*4.77*	*0.8*

Since posting an ERA close to eight in his 2007 introduction to the majors, Olson has trimmed just over a run from that figure in each successive season. Barring a small-sample fluke, that progression will come to an end this season, since the lefty lacks the stuff to send it any lower. His peripherals played up slightly in relief, but he's neither an asset in regular duty nor tough enough on same-handed betters for situational work, though his 0.97 Leverage score pegged him as the most trusted of the interchangeable mop-up men behind David Aardsma and Brandon League.

David Pauley

Born: **6/17/1983** Age: **28**
Bats: R Throws: R Height: **6' 2"** Weight: **185**
Breakout: **8%** Improve: **39%** Collapse: **10%**
Attrition: **8%** MLB: **57%**

Comparables:
Willie Collazo, Brian Burres, Mark Mulder (75)

YEAR	TEAM	LVL	AGE	W	L	SV	G	GS	IP	H	HR	BB	SO	EqBB9	EqSO9	GB%	BABIP	WHIP	ERA	FRA	WARP
2008	PAW	AAA	25	14	4	0	25	25	147	147	10	41	103	2.5	6.3	52%	.302	1.35	3.55	4.62	2.0
2008	BOS	MLB	25	0	1	0	6	2	12^1	23	2	5	11	3.6	8.0	44%	.438	2.35	11.68	8.96	-0.3
2009	NOR	AAA	26	9	12	0	27	26	152^1	171	15	45	108	2.7	6.4	49%	.322	1.52	4.37	4.49	1.8
2010	TAC	AAA	27	1	6	0	15	14	85^2	82	6	26	56	2.7	5.9	47%	.285	1.33	3.68	4.90	0.7
2010	SEA	MLB	27	4	9	0	19	15	90^2	89	13	30	51	3.0	5.1	50%	.260	1.36	4.07	4.88	0.2
2011	*SEA*	*MLB*	*28*	*10*	*9*	*0*	*26*	*26*	*153^2*	*159*	*17*	*53*	*91*	*3.1*	*5.3*	*48%*	*.293*	*1.39*	*4.35*	*4.73*	*1.4*

The cellar-dwelling Orioles never found room for Pauley in 2009, but Seattle allowed him more than 90 innings last season, which might convey some sense of what it meant to be a Mariners fan in 2010. The soft-tossing righty keeps the ball on the ground, but lacks both a strikeout pitch and the pinpoint control required to survive without one. Strong defense and a pitcher's park kept his performance suitable for viewing by prime-time audiences, but awarding that many starts to a pitcher like Pauley is a clear sign that an organization's plan either has gone wrong or was flawed to begin with. Call it the Pauley Exclusion Principle: any team that devotes a roster spot to David Pauley for large portions of the regular season will find itself excluded from the playoffs.

Michael Pineda

Born: **1/18/1989** Age: **22**
Bats: R Throws: R Height: **6' 5"** Weight: **180**
Breakout: **6%** Improve: **9%** Collapse: **2%**
Attrition: **6%** MLB: **12%**

Comparables:
Jose Garcia, Fabio Castro, Scott Sanderson (73)

YEAR	TEAM	LVL	AGE	W	L	SV	G	GS	IP	H	HR	BB	SO	EqBB9	EqSO9	GB%	BABIP	WHIP	ERA	FRA	WARP
2008	WIS	A	19	8	6	0	26	21	138^1	109	7	35	128	2.3	8.3	49%	.271	1.08	1.95	2.65	4.6
2009	HDS	A+	20	4	2	0	10	8	44^1	29	3	6	48	1.2	9.8	53%	.248	0.93	2.84	4.50	1.0
2010	WTN	AA	21	8	1	0	13	13	77	67	1	17	78	2.0	9.1	45%	.306	1.14	2.22	2.40	3.0
2010	TAC	AAA	21	3	3	0	12	12	62^1	54	9	17	76	2.5	11.0	41%	.290	1.19	4.76	4.56	0.9
2011	*SEA*	*MLB*	*22*	*6*	*4*	*0*	*15*	*15*	*85*	*79*	*8*	*29*	*71*	*3.1*	*7.6*	*44%*	*.293*	*1.28*	*3.59*	*3.90*	*1.7*

Pineda is about as close as pitching prospects come to a sure thing. Seattle's top prospect has drawn Pedro comparisons, and while the odds are against his fulfilling them, he could fall well short and still end up a top-of-the-rotation talent. The Dominican combines the electric arm of many an unpolished prospect with the command and control of a finesse lefty, giving him the lofty strikeout totals of the former to go with the stingy walk rates of the latter. Listed at 180 but far more filled-out, the righty suffered none of the elbow problems that plagued him in 2009 en route to a dominant performance in Double-A, and his flukily high ERA at Tacoma hid a stellar K/BB ratio, aided by improved velocity and conditioning. Pineda is considered close enough to the majors that rumors of his imminent arrival swirled after Cliff Lee went to Texas, but he'll probably spend more time at Triple-A, where he'll seek to make his developing changeup more effective at neutralizing lefties.

Mauricio Robles

Born: **3/5/1989** Age: **22**
Bats: L Throws: L Height: **5' 10"** Weight: **205**
Breakout: **10%** Improve: **25%** Collapse: **14%**
Attrition: **11%** MLB: **52%**

Comparables:
Rick Ankiel, John D'Acquisto, Moe Drabowsky (66)

YEAR	TEAM	LVL	AGE	W	L	SV	G	GS	IP	H	HR	BB	SO	EqBB9	EqSO9	GB%	BABIP	WHIP	ERA	FRA	WARP
2008	WMI	A	19	5	3	0	23	16	91^{1}	54	2	54	79	5.3	7.8	34%	.228	1.23	2.66	2.97	2.8
2009	WMI	A	20	4	4	0	11	11	56^{1}	45	6	27	71	4.3	11.3	43%	.300	1.30	4.64	4.85	0.4
2009	HDS	A+	20	3	2	0	7	6	32^{1}	23	1	19	34	5.3	9.5	52%	.275	1.30	2.79	4.45	0.8
2009	LAK	A+	20	4	2	0	7	7	35	34	3	14	40	3.6	10.3	44%	.341	1.46	3.60	3.00	1.2
2010	WTN	AA	21	6	6	0	22	22	114	102	10	51	120	4.0	9.5	42%	.305	1.39	4.11	4.23	2.0
2010	TAC	AAA	21	3	1	0	5	5	28	19	2	20	34	6.4	10.9	34%	.258	1.39	3.54	4.83	0.3
2011	*SEA*	*MLB*	*22*	*7*	*7*	*0*	*18*	*18*	*94*	*87*	*10*	*60*	*85*	*5.7*	*8.1*	*40%*	*.293*	*1.55*	*4.57*	*4.97*	*0.8*

Billy Wagner–sized southpaw Robles possesses strikeout stuff to rival anyone in the Seattle system. A product of the Jarrod Washburn trade, the Venezuelan has a heater that sits in the mid-90s and can touch 97, but he's more than a one-trick pony, featuring a sharp curve, developing changeup, and brand-new two-seamer, which cuts more than it sinks. The lefty's max-effort delivery and resultant poor control could land him—like Wagner—in a bullpen's late-inning mix, though he's not yet at the end of his rotation rope.

Ryan Rowland-Smith

Born: **1/26/1983** Age: **28**
Bats: L Throws: L Height: **6' 3"** Weight: **205**
Breakout: **19%** Improve: **44%** Collapse: **21%**
Attrition: **20%** MLB: **84%**

Comparables:
Glen Perkins, Mark Gubicza, Mark Redman (78)

YEAR	TEAM	LVL	AGE	W	L	SV	G	GS	IP	H	HR	BB	SO	EqBB9	EqSO9	GB%	BABIP	WHIP	ERA	FRA	WARP
2008	SEA	MLB	25	5	3	2	47	12	118^{1}	114	13	48	77	3.7	5.9	41%	.276	1.39	3.42	4.52	1.0
2009	TAC	AAA	26	5	3	0	10	10	56^{1}	61	5	10	38	1.6	6.1	44%	.308	1.31	4.15	3.67	1.2
2009	SEA	MLB	26	5	4	0	15	15	96^{1}	87	9	27	52	2.5	4.9	40%	.252	1.22	3.74	4.05	1.4
2010	TAC	AAA	27	2	4	0	6	6	37	45	4	5	24	1.2	5.8	40%	.320	1.35	5.11	4.34	0.5
2010	SEA	MLB	27	1	10	0	27	20	109^{1}	141	25	44	49	3.6	4.0	38%	.301	1.76	6.75	7.56	-2.4
2011	*HOU*	*MLB*	*28*	*6*	*7*	*0*	*28*	*17*	*113*	*122*	*15*	*38*	*69*	*3.1*	*5.5*	*42%*	*.296*	*1.42*	*4.78*	*5.20*	*0.7*

Rowland-Smith, who's known as "RRS" or "Hyphen" to linguistically lazy Mariners fans, is—stop us if you've heard this before—another slow-throwing, fly-ball-oriented lefty who relied on Safeco Field to protect him from those big, bad opposing batters. Unlike Jason Vargas—but like Luke French—Rowland-Smith lacks the stuff to succeed even with the aid of Seattle's spacious home park, since despite Bud Selig's tendency to tinker with time-honored institutions of the sport (as long as doing so doesn't detract from the all-important "human element"), it's safe to say that road games are here to stay. Away from Safeco, the southpaw might as well have warmed up to the *1812 Overture*, since his practice pitches gave way to an aerial bombardment the likes of which hasn't been seen since Lima Time. Rowland-Smith allowed an astonishing 19 home runs in 55 innings away from Seattle, and in light of his middling control and plummeting strikeout rate, he wasn't going to be of much use to the Mariners, and perhaps not to anyone else. This hard truth did not prevent the hapless Astros from signing Hyphen to dash into their fifth-starter scrum. Minute Maid Park is a far cry from Safeco in the way it treats fly balls aspiring to become home runs, and even though the stadium features a retractable roof, visitors holding tickets for left-field seating are advised to bring their umbrellas: it's going to be raining souvenirs on the Crawford Boxes.

Ian Snell

Born: **10/30/1981** Age: **29**
Bats: R Throws: R Height: **5' 11"** Weight: **170**
Breakout: **24%** Improve: **49%** Collapse: **22%**
Attrition: **16%** MLB: **99%**

Comparables:
Ron Darling, Don Elston, Marty Pattin (77)

YEAR	TEAM	LVL	AGE	W	L	SV	G	GS	IP	H	HR	BB	SO	EqBB9	EqSO9	GB%	BABIP	WHIP	ERA	FRA	WARP
2008	PIT	MLB	26	7	12	0	31	31	164^{1}	201	18	89	135	4.9	7.4	39%	.351	1.78	5.42	5.17	1.2
2009	IND	AAA	27	2	2	0	6	6	37^{1}	28	0	13	47	3.1	11.3	42%	.315	1.13	0.97	1.74	1.7
2009	PIT	MLB	27	2	8	0	15	15	80^{2}	87	7	44	52	4.9	5.8	43%	.313	1.64	5.24	5.43	0.2
2009	SEA	MLB	27	5	2	0	12	12	64^{1}	61	7	39	37	5.5	5.2	37%	.263	1.57	4.20	5.17	0.3
2010	TAC	AAA	28	3	4	0	9	9	48^{2}	58	6	22	39	4.1	7.3	41%	.342	1.70	6.66	5.87	-0.0
2010	SEA	MLB	28	0	5	0	12	8	46^{1}	60	10	25	26	4.9	5.1	36%	.307	1.86	6.41	6.65	-0.7
2011	*SEA*	*MLB*	*29*	*11*	*12*	*0*	*32*	*32*	*169*	*176*	*18*	*81*	*128*	*4.3*	*6.8*	*42%*	*.308*	*1.51*	*4.73*	*5.14*	*1.0*

Snell suffered from clinical depression in 2009, but it probably didn't take a chemical imbalance to get him down last season; a glance at his six-plus ERA would have sufficed. Every aspect of the undersized righty's game has taken a steep trip downhill since his successful 2006 and 2007 seasons in Pittsburgh: he has surrendered a couple of miles per hour from his average fastball, abdicated much of his ability to induce ground balls, and lost control of the strike zone, with attendant consequences for his unsightly strikeout and walk rates. In his major-league work for the Mariners, Snell struck out 63 batters and walked 64, and he hit his targets only slightly more often after a mid-June demotion to Triple-A. In some cases, a trade only changes the scenery; a minor-league invite to St. Louis will likely achieve little beyond changing it again.

Jason Vargas

Born: **2/2/1983** Age: **28**
Bats: L Throws: L Height: **6' 0"** Weight: **215**
Breakout: **22%** Improve: **53%** Collapse: **18%**
Attrition: **11%** MLB: **96%**

Comparables:
Chris Bosio, Eric Milton, Denny Neagle (76)

YEAR	TEAM	LVL	AGE	W	L	SV	G	GS	IP	H	HR	BB	SO	EqBB9	EqSO9	GB%	BABIP	WHIP	ERA	FRA	WARP
2009	TAC	AAA	26	4	3	0	9	9	51^2	48	3	15	46	2.6	8.0	30%	.319	1.22	3.13	3.01	1.6
2009	SEA	MLB	26	3	6	0	23	14	91^2	98	16	24	54	2.4	5.3	38%	.285	1.36	4.91	5.67	0.1
2010	SEA	MLB	27	9	12	0	31	31	192^2	187	18	54	116	2.5	5.4	37%	.272	1.26	3.78	4.07	2.0
2011	*SEA*	*MLB*	*28*	*10*	*8*	*0*	*26*	*26*	*153*	*155*	*16*	*48*	*99*	*2.8*	*5.8*	*40%*	*.290*	*1.32*	*3.99*	*4.34*	*2.1*

Mariners fans may not have felt Jarrod Washburn's absence last season, since the "soft-tossing, fly-balling southpaw" position was filled capably by Vargas. In a smaller park or in front of a less sure-handed group of defenders, the lefty might not have killed opposing batters quite so softly, but there's something to be said for players who make the most of their surroundings. His 4.85 road ERA serves as a warning of what lies in store if the lefty ever takes his plus changeup and command away from Safeco on a full-time basis.

Anthony Varvaro

Born: **10/31/1984** Age: **26**
Bats: R Throws: R Height: **6' 0"** Weight: **195**
Breakout: **4%** Improve: **6%** Collapse: **2%**
Attrition: **1%** MLB: **12%**

Comparables:
Larry Sherry, Robb Nen, Mac Scarce (80)

YEAR	TEAM	LVL	AGE	W	L	SV	G	GS	IP	H	HR	BB	SO	EqBB9	EqSO9	GB%	BABIP	WHIP	ERA	FRA	WARP
2008	HDS	A+	23	3	9	0	30	24	122^2	154	22	82	113	6.0	8.3	42%	.362	2.03	7.11	6.56	-0.2
2009	WTN	AA	24	4	3	8	36	0	54^1	30	1	44	63	7.3	10.4	40%	.230	1.47	2.82	4.48	0.2
2010	WTN	AA	25	1	3	9	31	0	39^1	27	2	21	46	4.8	10.6	42%	.260	1.23	3.20	4.77	0.0
2010	TAC	AAA	25	0	0	0	19	0	25^2	24	1	14	26	5.0	9.3	47%	.311	1.67	5.26	4.72	0.2
2010	SEA	MLB	25	0	1	0	4	0	4	6	2	6	5	13.5	11.3	46%	.364	3.00	11.25	10.65	-0.3
2011	*SEA*	*MLB*	*26*	*3*	*3*	*1*	*39*	*6*	72^1	*72*	*9*	*54*	*61*	*6.7*	*7.7*	*43%*	*.304*	*1.74*	*5.62*	*6.11*	*-1.1*

The Varvaro who made his major league debut after a September call-up to Seattle sports a different elbow ligament, delivery, and role from the one whose elbow problems dropped him to the 12th round of the 2005 draft. The current model's fastball hits the low-90s with good deception, complemented by a major-league-caliber curve and changeup. He has used that repertoire to excellent effect when it comes to striking out minor-league batters, and the five he rang up in his first four innings of major-league labor offer hope that he might continue to miss bats in the majors. However, he also walked six batters in those four frames, which hints at the dark side of his plus stuff, namely, that he doesn't always know where it's going. Varvaro's mechanics improved to an extent after his 2005 elbow reconstruction, but he remains at risk for re-injury and wildness and should be kept no further than a spot start away from the bullpen at all times. A January waiver claim made him property of Atlanta.

LINEOUTS

HITTERS

PLAYER	TEAM	LVL	AGE	PA	R	2B	3B	HR	RBI	BB	SO	SB-CS	AVG/OBP/SLG	TAv	BABIP	BRR	FRAA	WARP
C E. Alfonzo	TAC	AAA	31	188	23	9	2	9	23	8	48	0-1	.253/.298/.483	.259	.294	-0.5	C 0	0.9
	SEA	MLB	31	41	4	1	0	1	4	0	10	0-0	.220/.220/.317	.193	.267	0.6	C -1	-0.1
RF J. Blash	PUL	Rk	20	128	21	6	1	5	20	13	44	1-1	.266/.362/.477	.292	.393	-0.7	RF 7	1.1
UT T. Hulett*	TAC	AAA	27	76	11	6	0	3	12	7	11	0-2	.318/.387/.545	.309	.333	0.0	SS -3, 3B -2	0.5
	PAW	AAA	27	343	38	21	2	4	29	53	63	6-3	.201/.328/.331	.235	.240	0.0	2B -11, 3B -2	-1.5
SS M. Littlewood#	DNP	—	19	—	—	—	—	—	—	—	—	—	—	—	—	—	—	—
2B G. Noriega#	CLN	A	19	410	47	15	0	2	28	20	108	6-4	.227/.280/.283	.209	.305	0.5	2B 5, SS 8	0.3
OF C. Peguero*	WTN	AA	23	553	86	23	5	23	73	56	178	7-9	.254/.340/.463	.285	.351	0.0	LF 2, RF 7	3.1
OF G. Pimentel*	MRN	Rk	17	194	20	7	6	6	31	5	58	5-1	.250/.276/.451	.268	.331	2.1	LF -3, RF -3	0.6
1B R. Poythress	HDS	A+	22	544	88	33	0	31	130	52	100	3-2	.315/.381/.580	.309	.334	-1.1	1B 1, 3B 0	3.3
C G. Quiroz	WTN	AA	28	263	24	17	1	5	35	21	59	0-2	.282/.347/.427	.275	.351	-4.0	C -1	1.0
	TAC	AAA	28	98	13	5	1	2	11	6	16	0-0	.297/.347/.440	.268	.342	-2.4	C 0	0.3
	SEA	MLB	28	7	1	1	0	0	0	0	1	0-0	.286/.286/.429	.269	.333	0.0	C 0	0.0
1B D. Raben*	CLN	A	22	175	26	8	1	8	23	15	49	0-1	.221/.320/.450	.260	.263	-2.6	1B 0	-0.1
	HDS	A+	22	179	35	10	3	12	43	15	47	0-0	.356/.413/.681	.353	.437	-1.6	LF 0, 1B -1	1.6
2B K. Seager*	HDS	A+	22	643	126	40	3	14	74	71	94	13-12	.345/.419/.503	.316	.388	4.2	2B 0, 3B 2	6.0
SS C. Triunfel	WTN	AA	20	498	51	12	1	7	42	13	54	2-8	.257/.286/.332	.222	.273	-2.3	SS -16, 2B -1	-1.9
SS C. Woodward	TAC	AAA	34	453	49	17	2	6	35	40	73	4-1	.232/.303/.329	.230	.262	1.1	SS 2, 2B -3	0.2
	SEA	MLB	34	22	0	1	0	0	0	3	9	0-0	.158/.273/.210	.188	.300	-0.4	SS -3	-0.4

In accordance with the unwritten rules of Mariners roster construction, **Eliezer Alfonzo** didn't hit a lick. Decent defense and a hint of power make him worth playing, but not above Triple-A. ⚾ **Jabari Blash** is your typical toolshed, and we don't mean that in the slangy sense: he's the size of a small building, and he houses an extensive array of skills. The eighth-rounder impressed in his postdraft debut in the Appy League, but a strikeout rate north of 40 percent revealed his rawness. ⚾ Some long-forgotten sin of his forefathers doomed **Tug Hulett** to wander Willie Bloomquist's former organizations in perpetual search of a roster spot, offering slightly less positional flexibility, but a better bat and an equal allotment of scrappiness. ⚾ As the 67th overall pick in the 2010 amateur draft, **Marcus Littlewood** holds the distinction of being the highest-ever selection from Utah. The big high-school shortstop hasn't yet played a professional game, but the Mariners hope he'll add even loftier accolades to his baseball epitaph before all is said and done. ⚾ **Gabriel Noriega** fell apart at the plate in Low-A after a surprisingly strong Appy League offensive showing in 2009. His glove is still good, but increasingly confined to the keystone. ⚾ On paper, **Carlos Peguero** looks a lot like Greg Halman, only older, slower, and a minor-league level behind. Peguero has proven that his power is more than a Cal League creation; unfortunately, so are the strikeouts. ⚾ **Guillermo Pimentel** was born a week before Brett Favre's first start for the Packers. Although the promising Dominican bonus baby's plate discipline was supposed to be a strength, he and the embattled quarterback struck out in public with roughly equal frequency last season. ⚾ **Rich Poythress** exploded offensively last season, launching 31 long balls after entering the season with only two professional homers to his name. Unfortunately, for a 23-year-old bat-only first-base prospect, that kind of success in High Desert doesn't merit much excitement. ⚾ Thanks to the two hits he managed in his seven September plate appearances, **Guillermo Quiroz** was the only Mariners catcher to finish with a positive VORP. The seven-year major league veteran sports a .192 career TAv, so the 40 plate appearances he has averaged per season sounds about right. ⚾ **Dennis Raben** missed all of 2009 recovering from knee surgery, which put him well behind the developmental curve. The bat-only first baseman did his best to catch up last season, hitting well after a promotion to High-A, but [insert standard High Desert disclaimer here]. Eleven of his 12 homers in the Cal League came at home, where he slugged .906, but he'll have to face the cruel world outside Adelanto eventually. ⚾ **Kyle Seager** might look like another beneficiary of the High Desert sun's bat-augmenting rays, but the righty nearly matched his .345/.427/.504 home performance with a robust .344/.411/.502 road line. At best, he's an average runner and defender, so he'll need to continue to hit beyond the Cal League to solidify his prospect status. ⚾ **Carlos Triunfel** extended his string of unimpressive statistical performances last season, though he can't be written off as a prospect as long as he sticks at short and still qualifies as young for his league. ⚾ Except for a one-year exile in 2008, **Chris Woodward** has spent at least some time in the majors in each of the last 12 seasons, which is saying something for a career .241/.298/.367 hitter with a lower lifetime

WARP than Willie Bloomquist. What it's saying is probably something like, "Chris Woodward has an extensive collection of compromising photos."

PITCHERS

PLAYER	TEAM	LVL	AGE	W	L	SV	IP	H	HR	BB	SO	EqBB9	EqSO9	GB%	BABIP	WHIP	ERA	FRA	WARP
M. Cleto	HDS	A+	21	4	9	0	102^1	125	10	44	83	3.9	7.3	48%	.357	1.72	6.16	6.50	-0.2
R. Feierabend*	HDS	A+	24	0	1	0	27^1	31	5	2	20	0.7	6.6	55%	.313	1.22	5.27	7.52	-0.1
	TAC	AAA	24	4	7	0	88^1	122	8	28	45	2.9	4.6	37%	.357	1.76	5.30	4.67	1.1
J. Fields	WTN	AA	24	1	1	6	28^2	19	0	18	28	5.7	8.9	53%	.253	1.31	3.14	4.79	0.0
Y. Medina	CLN	A	21	5	0	0	36	30	3	12	42	3.0	10.5	47%	.293	1.22	2.50	3.64	1.2
	EVE	A-	21	3	2	0	40^2	49	4	15	48	3.4	10.7	47%	.381	1.64	4.20	5.82	0.0
B. Moran*	CLN	A	21	4	1	3	40^1	34	0	6	48	1.3	10.8	47%	.333	1.00	1.34	1.28	1.8
	HDS	A+	21	2	0	1	25^1	22	0	2	29	0.7	10.4	37%	.328	0.96	1.42	1.20	0.8
J. Nelson	PAW	AAA	35	3	2	1	21^2	18	1	14	21	5.9	8.9	37%	.304	1.56	2.49	3.57	0.4
	BOS	MLB	35	0	0	0	8^1	14	2	6	9	6.5	9.7	37%	.429	2.40	9.72	11.88	-0.5
E. Paredes*	WTN	AA	23	2	1	3	34^2	35	1	16	35	4.2	9.2	44%	.337	1.55	3.63	3.00	0.8
	TAC	AAA	23	0	2	0	20^1	24	1	15	12	6.7	5.4	36%	.329	2.09	6.64	5.44	-0.0
E. Ramirez	CLN	A	20	10	4	1	151^2	142	13	21	117	1.3	7.0	53%	.289	1.16	2.97	4.04	2.7
C. Seddon*	TAC	AAA	26	10	4	0	101	95	7	29	65	2.6	5.8	47%	.279	1.26	3.21	3.99	2.2
	SEA	MLB	26	1	0	0	22^1	21	4	10	16	4.0	6.4	46%	.262	1.39	5.64	4.97	-0.0
B. Sweeney	TAC	AAA	36	2	1	1	28^2	20	1	8	32	2.6	10.2	56%	.268	1.10	2.51	2.37	0.8
	SEA	MLB	36	1	2	0	37	33	5	6	14	1.5	3.4	39%	.228	1.05	3.16	3.23	0.6
A. Vasquez*	CLN	A	23	2	2	0	48^2	31	2	7	45	1.3	8.4	57%	.230	0.83	1.29	2.61	1.7
	HDS	A+	23	7	4	0	85	87	6	12	53	1.3	5.6	50% .294	1.19	2.96	4.00	2.0	
	WTN	AA	23	2	3	0	38	44	2	5	27	1.2	6.4	55%	.341	1.39	2.61	2.99	1.4
S. White	SEA	MLB	29	0	1	0	34^1	45	4	11	15	2.9	3.9	46%	.342	1.63	5.24	5.36	-0.3
T. Wilhelmsen	CLN	A	26	6	1	0	44^1	33	1	15	37	3.1	7.6	46%	.242	1.13	2.23	3.10	1.8
	MRN	Rk	26	0	0	0	22	6	0	3	35	1.2	14.3	54%	.154	0.41	0.41	-0.44	4.2
J. Wright	CLE	MLB	35	1	2	0	21^1	25	1	9	9	3.8	3.8	62%	.312	1.69	5.48	7.63	-0.8
	SEA	MLB	35	0	1	0	37	30	2	16	19	3.9	4.6	65%	.248	1.27	3.41	2.83	1.0

Maikel Cleto is living proof that it's possible to earn a 40-man roster spot with a six-plus ERA, especially if you spend the season at High Desert and flash a blazing—albeit straight—fastball. However, the Dominican righty has little to offset his heater and would be better suited for bullpen work in St. Louis, where he'll continue his career after being swapped for Brendan Ryan in December. ⚾ **Ryan Feierabend** didn't experience the typical post–Tommy John bout with control issues; unfortunately, the low-velocity lefty didn't wake up in the recovery room equipped with Jamie Moyer's UCL, either, so he's not close to a major-league comeback. ⚾ **Josh Fields** qualifies as a cautionary tale about using your first-round pick on a college closer. The righty revamped his mechanics in his second season at Double-A, but his ERA improvement was all BABIP. Although a forearm strain shut him down in June, he recovered in time for a decent showing in the Arizona Fall League. ⚾ Despite a torn labrum that deprived economy-sized southpaw **Cesar Jimenez** of 2009 and much of 2010, a strong comeback in Double-A and the Venezuelan Winter League convinced the M's to add the former major leaguer to the 40-man. ⚾ **Yoervis Medina** has spent all of 5 2/3 innings above A-ball, but that didn't stop the Mariners from deeming him worthy of protection from the Rule 5 draft. The big righty racked up the strikeouts, using a fastball that touched 94 to set up some of the best breaking stuff in the Northwest League. ⚾ **Brian Moran** puts up the kind of K/BB ratios that make stat-geeks swoon, but he relies on deception to play up an average fastball and fringy secondary stuff. His bubble might burst in the high minors, but until it does, the M's will promote him with major-league LOOGY-dom in mind. ⚾ After his June release from the Red Sox, **Joe Nelson** spent a month in Tacoma, where he failed to curb the control problems that have made his fringy stuff unpalatable in the majors. As an advanced practitioner of the Vulcan changeup, he must be aware that his continued presence on a major-league roster would be highly illogical. ⚾ **Edward Paredes** survived a 2009 tour of duty in High Desert with only superficial wounds, but after a mostly successful sojourn in the Southern League, the aspiring situational lefty fell to pieces in the Pacific Coast League last season. ⚾ If anyone in the Mariners' system can overcome his unimposing stature, it's **Erasmo Ramirez**. The compact righty touches the low 90s, but superb control and a talent for keeping hitters grounded are his greatest assets. ⚾ The Mariners scraped the bottom of the bullpen barrel in low-leverage situations, and sometimes what came out was **Chris Seddon**. The soft-tossing converted starter's stuff was hardly a revelation in relief. ⚾ After spending three seasons in Japan, **Brian Sweeney** turned in a deceptively effective performance as a part-time mop-up man for Seattle. Only 117 innings into his major-league career, the righty boasts a respectable 3.38 ERA, but his high-80s fastball and career strikeout rate of 4.2 per nine innings don't argue for a reprise performance. The Snakes claimed him off waivers in November, so he'll try not to get smacked around too much in Arizona's bandbox ballpark. ⚾ Soft-tossing changeup artist **Anthony Vasquez** has the potential to be Jason Vargas with better control and more grounders. After running the Cal League gauntlet unscathed, he's not far from back-of-the-rotation-ready. ⚾ Last season's supplemental first-rounder **Taijuan Walker** earned the nickname "Sky Walker" for his high-school basketball exploits, but found retiring Rookie-ball hitters as easy as bull's-eyeing womp rats back home. He's raw, having pitched in only four games prior to his senior year, but his athleticism, mid-90s heater, and developing curve give him top-of-the-rotation potential. ⚾ **Sean White** wasn't even the best pitcher with a Sean-sounding name in the Seattle bullpen, as he posted abysmal peripherals almost identical to those of 2009, but this time without the cooperative BABIP. The damage was limited only by two trips to Tacoma and a sore forearm that kept him out of action for the season's final month. ⚾ In his first prospect life, towering **Tom Wilhelmsen**'s fondness for marijuana earned him two failed drug tests and a suspension. After six years spent traveling the world and tending bar, the ex-Brewer accepted an offer from the Seattle GM who had drafted him. He pitched well enough in the low minors to merit a spot on the 40-man; the righty still throws smoke, though he's given up inhaling. ⚾ **Jamey Wright** signed as a free agent with three different teams in the span of just over five months, a feat made possible by pitching poorly enough to be released by the first two. A low BABIP gave him a longer lease on life with Seattle, but after 15 major league seasons, the carousel is coming to a halt.

MANAGER: DON WAKAMATSU/ERIC WEDGE

YEAR	TEAM	W-L	Pythag +/-	Avg PC	100+ P	120+ P	QS	BQS	REL	REL w Zero R	IBB	Subs	PH	PH Avg	PH HR	SB2	CS2	SB3	CS3	SAC Att	SAC %	POS SAC	Squeeze	Swing	In Play
2009	SEA	85-77	10	95.8	71	1	77	5	409	268	13	27	58	.216	1	70	24	19	8	80	70.0%	55	6	126	96
2010	SEA	42-70	2	97.1	49	2	62	3	254	147	25	16	49	.214	1	85	22	15	4	57	50.9%	25	5	100	75

While the Mariners' on-field struggles certainly didn't strengthen Wakamatsu's job security, his failure to survive a second season in Seattle ultimately came down to clubhouse unrest. The return of Ken Griffey Jr. gave the sophomore skipper the unenviable task of tiptoeing around an aging icon's ego; since the services of the quadragenarian "Kid" had clearly been retained for reasons other than his on-field value, Wakamatsu was placed in the difficult position of having to choose between burying zombie Griffey on the bench—where the fan favorite was apt to doze off—and compromising his team's chances of victory. Ultimately, Griffey became the roster's forgotten (and increasingly frustrated) man, and his fellow veterans—perhaps having presentiments of their own ignoble end-of-career exits—turned on their manager, openly undermining his authority on the infrequent occasions that he attempted to discipline them for their sloppy play. Despite any merits Wakamatsu might have had on the field—where, it must be noted, he wasn't shy about ordering free passes and unsuccessful sacrifices in his second season—the off-field situation was untenable, and Triple-A manager Daren Brown was called in on an interim basis to bring about a rapprochement. After an idle season following his seven-year run as Indians skipper, Eric Wedge was tabbed to oversee Seattle's return to relevance over the long haul. The conservative manager's Cleveland tenure was marked by Pythagorean underperformance, first-half slumps, and slow hooks, as Wedge often preferred to let his starters work themselves into trouble rather than summon fresh arms in relief, most likely a suboptimal strategy, given the penalty pitchers suffer after multiple trips through the order. His tempestuous relationship with Milton Bradley also bears watching, though the pair insist that they've put their differences behind them.

Tampa Bay Rays

"There's no $7 million closer showing up." Those were the words of Rays owner Stuart Sternberg on December 4, 2009, just prior to the Winter Meetings. Less than a week later, the Rays acquired Rafael Soriano from the Braves in a deal for journeyman Jesse Chavez. For the Braves, it was a straight salary dump; after the team had signed Billy Wagner and Takashi Saito to anchor the back end of their bullpen, they were caught off guard by Soriano's accepting arbitration on his $6.35 million 2009 salary. The Rays agreed to the trade and immediately signed Soriano to a one-year, $7.25 million deal, the culmination of what general manager Andrew Friedman termed "a perfect storm of events" that allowed the team to acquire a Type-A free agent without costing themselves a draft pick. The team now had a front-line reliever to bolster a bullpen that had dipped from first in the league in WXRL in 2008 to 11th in 2009 and had fallen from a 97-win breakthrough and a pennant to 84 wins and a seat on the couch in October.

RAYS PROSPECTUS

2010 W-L: 96-66, 1st in AL East

Pythag	.598	2nd
RS/G	5.0	3rd
RA/G	4.0	24th
TAv	.278	5th
BRR	3.5	10th
FRA	4.18	9th
DER	13.1	6th
DL	511	3rd
B-Age	27.5	5th
P-Age	27.2	7th
Salary	$71.9	19th
M$/MW	$1.31	3rd

Ballpark: Tropicana Field (3-yr. PF: 96). It's no Petco, but Rays pitchers benefit from playing in the division's best pitcher's park

2010: Shrewdly-built team bests high-payroll beasts of the East, but bows out early

2011: Rays weather high-profile departures with talent on hand

Action Items: Restocking the bullpen, adding a bat, having Hellickson make Garza a dim memory... and playing to a full house

Thus the Rays stretched their already-stressed finances to the max, adding a closer who took up 10 percent of their Opening Day payroll to enable one more run at a post-season spot while the franchise's two most expensive players, Carl Crawford and Carlos Pena, were still under contract. The move paid off in spades, as the oft-injured Soriano ranked second in the league with 5.9 WXRL, anchoring a unit that returned to lead the league in that category, 4½ wins ahead of the Yankees and eight wins above the Red Sox—the biggest point of separation between the three AL East rivals. Thanks to that move, the Rays topped the game's toughest division and outplayed its two biggest spenders for the second year out of three.

Such resourcefulness and smarts are what have enabled the Rays to compete with the Beasts of the East, achieving parity with a seeming suddenness after so many years as a doormat. Their 2010 season wasn't quite as remarkable as their 2008, when they emerged from a decade-long history filled with nothing but losing seasons to win the division with a $43.8 million Opening Day payroll; both the Rangers and the Reds reached the 2010 postseason as well after beginning the year with lower payrolls than the Rays' $71.9 million. But after absorbing a 44 percent increase in salaries from 2008 to 2009, the Rays still bested two teams that combined to pay out more than five times as much in salary and draw nearly four times as many fans. After the Rays fell short in the postseason—eliminated in a five-game Division Series matchup with the Rangers—the question is how quickly the Rays can retool, particularly in the face of such a perpetual structural imbalance.

The Rays burst out of the gate with a 17-6 record in April, and after overcoming a brief dip in June, held at least the wild-card spot from July 5 onward. Their playoff chase with the Yankees was both thrilling and banal; the AL East changed hands 13 times from the end of July onward, though the two teams were more or less both assured of playoff spots once season-ending injuries overtook the Red Sox. Leading the charge was the team's pitching staff, anchored by a rotation that was four-fifths homegrown and fronted by David Price, the first overall pick of the 2007 draft and the game's top prospect going into the 2009 season. After a dazzling 2008 cameo and an uneven rookie campaign, Price scrapped his infamous slider, broke out a new curveball, and emerged as one of the AL's top starters, ranking second only to Felix Hernandez in SNLVAR. Matt Garza (the lone outsider of the bunch), Wade Davis (a third-round pick in 2004), and Jeff Niemann (the fourth pick of the 2004 draft) all finished in the league's top 32 in SNLVAR, none of them dominant but all effective. Only former staff ace James Shields turned in a subpar season, allowing more hits and homers than any other AL pitcher, a showing that owed something to predictable pitch sequences. In fact, homers were a persistent problem for the unit, with everyone except Price ranking in the league's top eight in home runs per nine.

The bullpen reflected the resourcefulness of Friedman and company; aside from Soriano, only Dan Wheeler made more than $2.1 million. The Rays' top set-up man was Joaquin Benoit, a former Rangers project who was signed to a minor-league deal after missing all of 2009 due to rotator-cuff surgery; he ranked eighth in WXRL. Right behind him in the rankings was Grant Balfour, who peeled off a year similar in caliber to his 2008 showing. While the team had to cope with the season-long absence of J. P. Howell, LOOGY Randy Choate was largely effective. Ironically, Wheeler finished in the red, WXRL-wise, due to some late-season bombings.

Though the team ranked third in the league in scoring, the merits of the Rays' offense were more difficult to appreciate. Playing in one of the AL's toughest pitchers' parks, the Rays ranked 13th in batting average and gave at least 140 plate appearances to four players who finished below the Mendoza line, including everyday first baseman Pena; meanwhile, Ben Zobrist and B. J. Upton both finished with averages under .250. Yet, the Rays ranked fourth in True Average because they led the league in walks (Zobrist and Pena were both in the top six) and were fourth in isolated power (.156). Anchoring the unit were Evan Longoria, who tied Josh Hamilton for the league lead in Wins Above Replacement Player (WARP) and ranked sixth in TAv, and Crawford, who ranked 11th in the latter.

Providing midseason shots in the arm via promotions from Triple-A Durham were catcher John Jaso and right fielder Matt Joyce; the former covered for disappointing production from Kelly Shoppach and Dioner Navarro, and the latter fit into a potent multiposition platoon involving Zobrist and second baseman Sean Rodriguez. Indeed, the versatility of both Zobrist (who saw time at six positions) and Rodriguez (seven positions) helped Rays hitters gain the platoon advantage against opposing pitchers 63.4 percent of the time, second in the league to the Yankees (68.4 percent) and well above the league average (56.3 percent), a testament to manager Joe Maddon's ingenuity. It didn't hurt the defense, either, given the Rays' top four rankings in both Defensive Efficiency and PADE. The only truly sore spot in the lineup was at DH, where Pat Burrell, Hank Blalock, and Willy Aybar combined to hit .226/.301/.339—a performance bad enough to lead the Rays to purge the expensive Burrell and the free-talent pickup Blalock at midseason and to nontender Aybar after it—before former A's first baseman Dan Johnson stabilized the position late in the year.

Entering 2011, the most immediately pressing question is how the Rays can offset the losses of Crawford and Pena. For the former, they boast a blue-chip prospect in Desmond Jennings, a speeder who's been described as a Crawford clone with more plate discipline and the ability to play center field. After winning Southern League MVP honors in 2009 and ranking seventh among our top 101 prospects, Jennings spent the early part of 2010 struggling with the effects of a wrist sprain, most notably a loss of power, but he recovered well enough by the end of the year to quell any anxieties. Less apparent is what will happen at first base. Johnson, who arrived late in the year and hit a lopsided .198/.343/.414 with several big home runs against division rivals, could figure in the mix, but he's 31, with a career major league line of .243/.343/.419. Zobrist could join the fray as well, a notion that would be less unsettling if the power he suddenly showed in 2009 hadn't just as quickly deserted him in 2010. Elsewhere, Jaso and Shoppach will share the catching duties, with Navarro having been nontendered, and Reid Brignac, who saw time at both second base and shortstop, will inherit the latter position from Jason Bartlett, who was traded to San Diego for four prospects.

The rotation entered the off-season with a major question mark hanging over it as well, but for a different reason, in that another blue-chipper, Jeremy Hellickson, was clearly ready after making a strong showing in a late-season audition when Davis and Niemann hit the DL simultaneously. Carving a spot for him required the trade of another starter, Matt Garza, who was arbitration-eligible for the second time and coming off a $3.35-million paycheck. The rotation's temporary talent overload was a nice problem to have—particularly given the way teams have come to value players under club control—and enabled the Rays to replenish the farm with a number of talented tyros.

Hellickson's ascension to a full-time starting role means that he won't be filling a spot in a bullpen that's been decimated by the free agencies of no less than seven relievers (Soriano, Benoit, Balfour, Wheeler, Choate, Chad Qualls, and the non-tendered Lance Cormier) who threw 78 percent of the team's relief innings and collected 93 percent of their WXRL; Andy Sonnanstine is the only returnee who threw more than 20 innings for them in 2010. Soriano, Wheeler and Balfour are all Type-A's who will net two draft picks apiece with their departures, while Benoit and Choate are Type-B's who will net one. The team plans to eschew free-agent relievers more expensive than Kyle Farnsworth—there really is no $7-million closer coming in this time—and will instead try to replicate the successes they've experienced in hunting down such bargains as the hurlers they're replacing; Balfour, Benoit, Choate, and Cormier all joined the organization via minor-league contracts at various points over the past three years. Righty Mike Ekstrom and lefty R.J. Swindle are two Quad-A relievers who spent most of 2010 at Durham but could figure in the team's 2011 plans, and the team will hope to strike gold again with free-agent import Joel Peralta, who'll be 35 on Opening Day.

Also likely to join the bullpen soon is power lefty Jake McGee, who ranked among BP's top 50 prospects in 2007 and 2008 before undergoing Tommy John surgery in mid-2008; he switched to the bullpen at Durham last summer and made a brief cameo in Tampa Bay. He and Hellickson are the vanguard of the next generation of Rays pitching prospects, a veritable embarrassment of riches. Alex Torres and Alex Cobb both ranked among *Baseball America's* top 20 Southern League (Double-A) prospects, and the same can be said for Matt Moore and Joe Cruz in the Florida State League (High-A), Alex Colome in the Midwest League (A), and Jake Thompson in the New York-Penn League (Low-A).

Chris Archer, the Double-A right-hander who came over in the Garza deal, was ranked as the Cubs' top prospect by *Baseball America* prior to switching allegiances. Hellickson and Moore—a power lefty who led the minors in strikeouts for the second straight year—ranked as the top pitching prospects in their respective leagues. The organization's deliberate one-level-a-year promotion system makes it unlikely that any from that bunch will have an impact in 2011, but suffice it to say that there may be a waiting list to crack the team's rotation that stretches into mid-decade. Alas, the ranks of upper-level position players are thin beyond Jennings, but after the Rays failed to sign their top two 2009 draft picks—both middle infielders—they did choose position players with five of their first six picks in 2010 (all of whom signed), and added a quartet of young bats in the Garza divestiture.

You can't have too much pitching, and if the Rays are to continue going toe-to-toe with the Yankees and Red Sox over the coming years, they will have to tap that surplus talent to fill needs elsewhere on the roster, as they began to do in the Garza deal.In June, Sternberg raised the possibility of a hypothetical sale to a new ownership group not necessarily committed to keeping the team in the area if he couldn't get cooperation from local civic and business leaders in finding a site somewhere besides downtown St. Petersburg—where Tropicana Field sits on a peninsula separated from the population center, with limited access to the mainland—and funding for a new ballpark. On September 27, Price and Longoria, the two faces of the franchise, described as "embarrassing" a turnout of 12,466 for a Monday night game in which the Rays could have clinched a post-season berth. Management quickly went into damage-control mode by giving away some 20,000 unsold tickets to the team's home finale two days later, but another shot had been fired. At this writing, Sternberg has gotten a commitment from the Greater Tampa Chamber of Commerce to spend the next year studying the financing of a new park—which, for all of the ways in which his team has differentiated itself from others with outside-the-box thinking, leaves Sternberg treading a path well-worn by many a major league owner. But in a division where they're the have-nots to the Boston/New York haves, aren't the Rays at least entitled to have their cake and eat it, just like the big boys?

HITTERS

Leslie Anderson OF

Born: **3/30/1982** Age: **29**
Bats: L Throws: L Height: **6' 1"** Weight: **205**
Breakout: **2%** Improve: **24%** Collapse: **2%**
Attrition: **9%** MLB: **42%**

Comparables:
John Gall, Michael Aubrey, Brian Buscher (76)

YEAR	TEAM	LVL	AGE	PA	R	2B	3B	HR	RBI	BB	SO	SB	CS	AVG/OBP/SLG	TAv	BABIP	BRR	FRAA	WARP
2010	PCH	A+	28	89	13	3	0	3	11	4	6	0	1	.262/.303/.405	.270	.253	0.0	LF -3, 1B -1	-0.2
2010	MNT	AA	28	204	24	11	1	6	25	18	28	3	1	.304/.382/.475	.283	.333	0.0	1B 1, LF -3	0.5
2010	DUR	AAA	28	129	14	5	0	2	13	5	20	0	0	.328/.359/.418	.263	.376	0.0	LF -4, 1B 1	-0.1
2011	*TBA*	*MLB*	*29*	*451*	*52*	*22*	*0*	*11*	*52*	*25*	*67*	*0*	*0*	*.273/.317/.410*	*.245*	*.296*	*0.0*	*LF -9, 1B -4*	*-1.3*

A veteran of the Cuban national team who played in the first two World Baseball Classics after starring as a center fielder for Camagüey, Anderson defected to Mexico in September 2009. He signed a four-year, $1.725 million deal with the Rays in April after drawing mixed reviews from scouts, who were concerned with his arm strength, speed, and power. More than a year of inactivity initially caused Anderson to struggle with making quality contact, but he improved as he climbed the ladder, hitting for average if not demonstrating much power or plate discipline. Those shortcomings and his drift to the left of the defensive spectrum suggest that any future he might have in the majors is likely to be as a bench player.

Willy Aybar DH

Born: **3/9/1983** Age: **28**
Bats: S Throws: R Height: **6' 0"** Weight: **175**
Breakout: **1%** Improve: **47%** Collapse: **2%**
Attrition: **10%** MLB: **91%**

Comparables:
Chris Sabo, Bill Mueller, Steve Ontiveros (78)

YEAR	TEAM	LVL	AGE	PA	R	2B	3B	HR	RBI	BB	SO	SB	CS	AVG/OBP/SLG	TAv	BABIP	BRR	FRAA	WARP
2008	TBA	MLB	25	362	34	17	2	10	33	32	44	2	2	.253/.326/.411	.266	.265	-2.3	3B 6, 1B 3	1.5
2009	TBA	MLB	26	336	40	12	0	12	41	34	54	1	0	.253/.330/.416	.272	.269	-0.3	1B 0, 2B -1	1.0
2010	TBA	MLB	27	309	23	13	0	6	43	30	61	0	0	.230/.307/.344	.253	.268	-1.2	3B 0, 1B -1	-0.1
2011	*TBA*	*MLB*	*28*	*384*	*46*	*17*	*0*	*11*	*42*	*37*	*60*	*1*	*1*	*.261/.336/.408*	*.264*	*.283*	*-0.1*	*3B 1, 1B 0*	*0.9*

A modestly useful bench bat in 2008 and 2009, Aybar was less so last year, when he might have carved out more time at DH while Pat Burrell and Hank Blalock struggled. Aybar had contact woes against righties, hitting just .219/.322/.305 and whiffing 23 percent of the time, nearly double his 13 percent career rate. Meanwhile, his power and patience both disappeared against lefties as he hit just .246/.305/.391, well down from .276/.368/.455 from 2006 to 2009. The Rays declined his $2.2 million option and nontendered him. During that same period, all major-league right-handed hitters hit .274/.346/.438 against southpaws, so Aybar hasn't exactly earned his lefty-masher's credential. His additional benefit was positional versatility, something the Rays ceased taking advantage of. As a result, there is really less here than meets the eye.

Rocco Baldelli **RF**

Born: **9/25/1981** Age: **29**
Bats: **R** Throws: **R** Height: **6' 4"** Weight: **190**
Breakout: **0%** Improve: **16%** Collapse: **10%**
Attrition: **4%** MLB: **61%**

Comparables:
Larry Bigbie, Luis Terrero, Prentice Redman (71)

YEAR	TEAM	LVL	AGE	PA	R	2B	3B	HR	RBI	BB	SO	SB	CS	AVG/OBP/SLG	TAv	BABIP	BRR	FRAA	WARP
2008	TBA	MLB	26	90	12	5	0	4	13	7	25	0	0	.263/.344/.475	.304	.333	-3.1	RF -1, LF 0	0.1
2009	BOS	MLB	27	163	23	4	1	7	23	11	37	1	0	.255/.313/.436	.283	.293	-1.7	RF -2, CF -1	0.2
2010	TBA	MLB	28	25	4	1	0	1	5	1	5	1	0	.208/.240/.375	.209	.222	0.4	RF 0	0.0
2011	*TBA*	*MLB*	*29*	*215*	*25*	*10*	*0*	*8*	*27*	*13*	*49*	*2*	*1*	*.256/.308/.430*	*.260*	*.298*	*0.0*	*RF -1, CF 0*	*0.2*

Sidelined by continued fatigue problems, Baldelli returned to the Rays' organization and spent the first half of the year as a special assistant, coaching minor leaguers on baserunning and outfield defense. He mounted a second-half comeback that culminated in his homering on his first swing with the Rays, but the fairy tale was interrupted when cramping related to his channelopathy forced him off the post-season roster after just one game in favor of Willy Aybar, leaving his future in doubt.

Jason Bartlett **SS**

Born: **10/30/1979** Age: **31**
Bats: **R** Throws: **R** Height: **6' 0"** Weight: **180**
Breakout: **1%** Improve: **43%** Collapse: **1%**
Attrition: **8%** MLB: **98%**

Comparables:
Barry Larkin, Rafael Furcal, Ryan Theriot (78)

YEAR	TEAM	LVL	AGE	PA	R	2B	3B	HR	RBI	BB	SO	SB	CS	AVG/OBP/SLG	TAv	BABIP	BRR	FRAA	WARP
2008	TBA	MLB	28	494	48	25	3	1	37	22	69	20	6	.286/.326/.361	.252	.328	1.7	SS 0	1.6
2009	TBA	MLB	29	567	90	29	7	14	66	54	89	30	7	.320/.386/.490	.314	.361	4.5	SS -1	5.6
2010	TBA	MLB	30	532	70	27	3	4	47	45	83	11	6	.254/.318/.350	.257	.291	-2.3	SS 4	1.9
2011	*SDN*	*MLB*	*31*	*560*	*68*	*30*	*3*	*8*	*60*	*45*	*79*	*19*	*6*	*.288/.346/.408*	*.268*	*.319*	*-0.2*	*SS 3*	*2.6*

Bartlett didn't come anywhere close to matching his 2009 offensive breakout, as Old Man Regression robbed him of 65 points of BABIP and more than cut his home-run-per-fly-ball (HR/FB) rate in half; his production was literally back where it should have been, with a True Average that fit perfectly between his 2007 and 2008 campaigns. Bartlett's performance against righties returned to submediocrity (.244/.307/.340) after a one-year spike, and his searing performance against lefties from 2007 to 2009 (.344/.411/.492) fell off considerably as well, to .273/.355/.370. Defensively, he had his best year with the leather as a Ray, better even than the one for which he was credited with anchoring the team's historic turnaround afield in 2008. With Reid Brignac demonstrating his readiness and the league lacking capable shortstops, trading the more expensive Bartlett ($4 million in 2010) was an obvious move for a team looking to cut payroll. The Rays sent him to the Padres for three pitching prospects and infielder Cole Figueroa, returning Bartlett to the team that drafted him in 2001. He won't hit as well as the man he's replacing (Miguel Tejada, now with the Giants), but when the two teams meet, the better defender will be sitting in the Padres' dugout.

Tim Beckham **SS**

Born: **1/27/1990** Age: **21**
Bats: **R** Throws: **R** Height: **6' 0"** Weight: **190**
Breakout: **2%** Improve: **6%** Collapse: **2%**
Attrition: **5%** MLB: **11%**

Comparables:
Bob Bailey, Rod Carew, Roberto Alomar (77)

YEAR	TEAM	LVL	AGE	PA	R	2B	3B	HR	RBI	BB	SO	SB	CS	AVG/OBP/SLG	TAv	BABIP	BRR	FRAA	WARP
2008	PRI	Rk	18	197	30	12	0	2	14	13	43	5	1	.243/.294/.345	.255	.299	0.8	SS -4	0.3
2009	BGR	A	19	537	58	33	4	5	63	34	116	13	10	.275/.328/.389	.265	.347	-0.9	SS -5	1.5
2010	PCH	A+	20	542	68	23	5	5	57	62	119	22	14	.256/.346/.359	.256	.324	3.0	SS -20	0.3
2011	*TBA*	*MLB*	*21*	*429*	*42*	*19*	*2*	*5*	*37*	*29*	*110*	*8*	*4*	*.233/.284/.328*	*.220*	*.303*	*-0.5*	*SS -6*	*-0.7*

Buster Posey, Pedro Alvarez, Brian Matusz, Gordon Beckham, and Ike Davis—those are just five of the most substantial contributors from among the baker's dozen of 2008 first-round picks who have reached the majors thus far while Beckham, the first overall selection of that draft, makes glacial progress through the low minors and falls off prospect lists. Even so, it's too early to write him off, since Beckham was selected out of high school, in contrast to the more polished aforementioned products. Beckham hasn't come close to meeting his power projections, but his on-base skills are showing progress; his OBP was 24 points above the league average, while his slugging percentage was just five points lower, and he hit .285/.370/.352 in the second half after a .212/.308/.370 first—all in a league where he was the sixth-youngest regular. Defensively, he cut his errors and showed more consistency in making plays, but his thickening frame has raised doubts about his future at shortstop.

Reid Brignac MI

Born: **1/16/1986** Age: **25**
Bats: **L** Throws: **R** Height: **6' 3"** Weight: **180**
Breakout: **1%** Improve: **12%** Collapse: **1%**
Attrition: **12%** MLB: **29%**

Comparables:
Davey Johnson, Matt Downs, Andy Marte (77)

YEAR	TEAM	LVL	AGE	PA	R	2B	3B	HR	RBI	BB	SO	SB	CS	AVG/OBP/SLG	TAv	BABIP	BRR	FRAA	WARP
2008	DUR	AAA	22	386	43	26	2	9	43	25	93	5	2	.250/.298/.412	.231	.307	-1.1	SS 5, 2B 0	0.6
2008	TBA	MLB	22	11	1	0	0	0	0	1	5	0	0	.000/.091/.000	.056	.000	0.0	SS 0	-0.2
2009	DUR	AAA	23	453	51	28	2	8	44	27	69	5	5	.282/.325/.417	.250	.315	-0.4	SS 2, 2B -4	1.0
2009	TBA	MLB	23	93	9	8	2	1	6	3	20	2	2	.278/.301/.444	.259	.348	0.3	SS 0, 2B 0	0.3
2010	TBA	MLB	24	326	39	13	1	8	45	20	77	3	3	.256/.307/.385	.261	.317	2.4	2B 6, SS 0	1.7
2011	*TBA*	*MLB*	*25*	*420*	*46*	*22*	*1*	*9*	*46*	*25*	*90*	*5*	*3*	*.257/.302/.390*	*.243*	*.305*	*-0.4*	*SS 1, 2B 0*	*0.8*

The Rays finally carved out significant playing time for Brignac, a 2004 second-round pick who was once hailed as a top prospect but has since seen his stock fall considerably. Brignac backed up both Sean Rodriguez at second and Jason Bartlett at short, making 39 and 36 starts, respectively, as well as pinch-hitting for both and switching between the two positions in-game to increase Joe Maddon's options. Offensively, he was as hacktastic as initially feared; among AL hitters with at least 300 plate appearances, Brignac had the fifth-highest strikeout/unintentional walk (K/UIBB) ratio and swung at more pitches outside the zone (42 percent) than all but Vlad Guerrero. Defensively, he was above-average, more so at second than short, but the latter is where he's now penciled into the Rays' lineup after the trade of Bartlett.

Carl Crawford LF

Born: **8/5/1981** Age: **29**
Bats: **L** Throws: **L** Height: **6' 2"** Weight: **219**
Breakout: **0%** Improve: **45%** Collapse: **3%**
Attrition: **5%** MLB: **96%**

Comparables:
Ralph Garr, Ken Griffey, Ken Boyer (58)

YEAR	TEAM	LVL	AGE	PA	R	2B	3B	HR	RBI	BB	SO	SB	CS	AVG/OBP/SLG	TAv	BABIP	BRR	FRAA	WARP
2008	TBA	MLB	26	482	69	12	10	8	57	30	60	25	7	.273/.317/.400	.270	.297	4.9	LF 12, CF 0	3.0
2009	TBA	MLB	27	672	96	28	8	15	68	51	99	60	16	.305/.363/.452	.296	.341	0.5	LF 12	4.8
2010	TBA	MLB	28	663	111	30	13	19	90	46	104	47	10	.307/.351/.495	.321	.340	4.1	LF 11	6.4
2011	*BOS*	*MLB*	*29*	*617*	*78*	*25*	*7*	*16*	*77*	*43*	*94*	*44*	*11*	*.290/.341/.444*	*.277*	*.318*	*0.9*	*LF 11, CF 0*	*3.3*

It was a bittersweet season for Crawford, who turned in his finest campaign for the Rays in his walk year, thus pricing himself even further beyond their reach. Crawford set career highs in True Average, WARP, home runs, and slugging percentage, and his blazing speed was as evident as ever, as he led the league in triples, ranked third in steals, and fourth in Baserunning Runs (BRR). After a halfhearted game of footsie with the Angels, he signed a seven-year, $142 million deal with the Red Sox in early December. Whatever he loses in turf hits—he hit .305/.345/.460 at the Trop, .289/.330/.430 on the road—he should get back from Fenway Park, whose irregular outfield fences might assist him with the occasional inside-the-park home run. The only negative, if you could call it that, is how the lack of room to run in left field may serve to marginalize his ability to cover ground.

Brad Hawpe RF

Born: **6/22/1979** Age: **32**
Bats: **L** Throws: **L** Height: **6' 3"** Weight: **200**
Breakout: **0%** Improve: **33%** Collapse: **4%**
Attrition: **8%** MLB: **97%**

Comparables:
Roy Sievers, Geoff Jenkins, Jay Buhner (73)

YEAR	TEAM	LVL	AGE	PA	R	2B	3B	HR	RBI	BB	SO	SB	CS	AVG/OBP/SLG	TAv	BABIP	BRR	FRAA	WARP
2008	COL	MLB	29	569	69	24	3	25	85	76	134	2	2	.283/.381/.498	.299	.341	-3.5	RF -27	0.3
2009	COL	MLB	30	588	83	42	3	23	86	79	145	1	3	.285/.384/.519	.295	.356	-4.5	RF -10	1.6
2010	COL	MLB	31	300	24	21	2	7	37	36	68	2	1	.255/.343/.432	.262	.314	0.7	RF -5, 1B 0	0.1
2010	TBA	MLB	31	46	7	0	0	2	7	6	17	0	0	.180/.304/.333	.239	.250	0.7	1B 0, RF 0	0.0
2011	*TBA*	*MLB*	*32*	*544*	*73*	*30*	*1*	*20*	*71*	*71*	*126*	*3*	*2*	*.273/.368/.473*	*.292*	*.327*	*-0.3*	*RF -11, 1B 0*	*1.4*

Hawpe entered the year as the Rockies' starting right fielder, but a quad strain, a drop in production, and a roster laden with younger, cheaper outfielders led the Rox to release him in late August, and he was merely an afterthought with the Rays. It's fair to wonder if the Rockies overreacted, given that Seth Smith, Ryan Spilborghs, and Jay Freakin' Payton hit just .276/.360/.387 in September as the team fell short of the postseason. Hawpe was less a product of Coors Field than most; he hit .286/.378/.513 there during his career with the Rockies, compared with a still-usable .274/.369/.471 on the road, but he was a tremendous liability defensively. Moving to the Padres on a one-year contract, he will be tasked with following Adrian Gonzalez, an unenviable task, given just how hard the ballpark will work against him. Still, he's a .281/.371/.451 in 175 PAs at the park.

John Jaso C

Born: **9/19/1983** Age: **27**
Bats: **L** Throws: **R** Height: **6' 2"** Weight: **205**
Breakout: **1%** Improve: **23%** Collapse: **7%**
Attrition: **10%** MLB: **67%**

Comparables:
Tim McCarver, Jason Jaramillo, Andy LaRoche (72)

YEAR	TEAM	LVL	AGE	PA	R	2B	3B	HR	RBI	BB	SO	SB	CS	AVG/OBP/SLG	TAv	BABIP	BRR	FRAA	WARP
2008	MNT	AA	24	356	51	13	2	7	43	62	33	1	0	.271/.407/.405	.283	.282	-2.9	C -2	1.8
2008	DUR	AAA	24	118	14	7	0	5	24	10	14	1	1	.278/.339/.481	.266	.281	-0.6	C 0	0.5
2008	TBA	MLB	24	10	2	0	0	0	0	0	2	0	0	.200/.200/.200	.121	.250	0.0	C 0	-0.1
2009	DUR	AAA	25	387	42	14	2	5	30	46	49	1	0	.266/.362/.366	.260	.295	-2.9	C 2	1.5
2010	TBA	MLB	26	404	57	18	3	5	44	59	39	4	0	.263/.371/.378	.286	.281	-1.6	C -2, 1B 0	2.1
2011	*TBA*	*MLB*	*27*	*429*	*52*	*18*	*1*	*7*	*40*	*56*	*52*	*2*	*1*	*.265/.363/.385*	*.270*	*.285*	*0.0*	*C -1, 1B 0*	*1.9*

Jaso ranked among the Rays' more pleasant surprises in 2010 as the 2003 12th-rounder took advantage of Kelly Shoppach's injury and Dioner Navarro's ineffectiveness to seize the bulk of the playing time at catcher. Considering that the displaced duo hit just .186/.283/.295, anything Jaso did might have looked good, but Joe Maddon was so impressed by Jaso's on-base skills that the backstop batted leadoff in a team-high 45 games and hit .272/.380/.420 from that spot. He has a history of shoulder woes, and his defense is questionable; he threw out only 24 percent of base thieves last year. He's not much against lefties (.191/.333/.277 in just 58 plate appearances), either, but he'll fit perfectly into the long half of a platoon with Shoppach, an impressive feat, given where he ranked on the depth chart a year ago.

Desmond Jennings OF

Born: **10/30/1986** Age: **24**
Bats: **R** Throws: **R** Height: **6' 2"** Weight: **200**
Breakout: **8%** Improve: **25%** Collapse: **7%**
Attrition: **22%** MLB: **49%**

Comparables:
Jacoby Ellsbury, Julio Borbon, Roger Bernadina (74)

YEAR	TEAM	LVL	AGE	PA	R	2B	3B	HR	RBI	BB	SO	SB	CS	AVG/OBP/SLG	TAv	BABIP	BRR	FRAA	WARP
2008	VRO	A+	21	102	17	5	1	2	6	14	16	5	2	.259/.353/.412	.293	.286	2.7	CF 7	1.6
2009	MNT	AA	22	440	69	25	8	8	45	48	52	37	5	.316/.395/.486	.325	.346	11.2	CF 9, RF 3	6.2
2009	DUR	AAA	22	137	23	6	2	3	17	19	15	15	2	.325/.416/.491	.285	.343	1.9	CF -1, LF 0	1.0
2010	DUR	AAA	23	458	82	25	6	3	36	47	67	37	4	.278/.362/.393	.269	.322	0.0	CF 6, RF 2	2.4
2010	TBA	MLB	23	24	3	1	1	0	2	2	4	2	2	.191/.292/.333	.238	.235	0.0	RF -1, CF 2	0.2
2011	*TBA*	*MLB*	*24*	*395*	*47*	*20*	*3*	*5*	*40*	*38*	*61*	*25*	*6*	*.278/.348/.397*	*.268*	*.317*	*0.6*	*CF 1, RF 0*	*1.5*

The Rays' top position prospect, this 2006 10th-round speedster won Southern League MVP honors in 2009 and came into 2010 hailed as a Carl Crawford clone with more plate discipline and the ability to play center field. Alas, Jennings struggled at Triple-A due to a wrist injury that sidelined him for most of April and sapped his ability to drive the ball, though he did improve from a .245/.343/.319 showing through May to a .289/.364/.416 line through August before making a late-season cameo in Tampa Bay. Jennings is an electrifying player who uses his outstanding speed well both on the basepaths and in the outfield. While he has huge shoes to fill, he should emerge as a top-of-the-lineup threat and show more pop than he did last season. He will take over left field from the departed Crawford, though in the wake of the Damon and Ramirez signings, he finds himself tasked with displacing another veteran.

Dan Johnson 1B

Born: **8/10/1979** Age: **31**
Bats: **L** Throws: **R** Height: **6' 2"** Weight: **220**
Breakout: **1%** Improve: **30%** Collapse: **10%**
Attrition: **14%** MLB: **92%**

Comparables:
Chris Shelton, Albert Belle, Roger Maris (68)

YEAR	TEAM	LVL	AGE	PA	R	2B	3B	HR	RBI	BB	SO	SB	CS	AVG/OBP/SLG	TAv	BABIP	BRR	FRAA	WARP
2008	DUR	AAA	28	486	85	23	0	25	83	84	75	0	1	.307/.424/.556	.318	.319	-2.3	1B 3, 3B 1	3.8
2008	OAK	MLB	28	1	0	0	0	0	0	0	0	0	0	.000/.000/.000	.055	.000	0.0	—	—
2008	TBA	MLB	28	28	3	0	0	2	4	3	7	0	0	.200/.286/.440	.252	.188	0.2	1B 1, LF 1	0.2
2010	DUR	AAA	30	427	66	19	0	30	95	75	71	0	0	.303/.430/.624	.337	.298	-3.1	3B 5, LF -2	4.0
2010	TBA	MLB	30	140	16	3	0	7	23	25	27	1	0	.198/.343/.414	.282	.188	0.1	1B -2, 3B 0	0.2
2011	*TBA*	*MLB*	*31*	*531*	*75*	*20*	*0*	*27*	*73*	*84*	*92*	*0*	*0*	*.264/.382/.497*	*.304*	*.271*	*0.0*	*1B -3, 3B 1*	*2.7*

It's the Great Pumpkin, Charlie Brown! The red-headed Johnson achieved cult status among Rays fans for emerging from obscurity to hit five of his seven home runs down the stretch against the Yankees and Red Sox, two of them game winners. Despite the low batting average, Johnson used his power and plate discipline to plug the Rays' Vortex of Suck at designated hitter, batting .254/.343/.559 in that role from August 1 onward; he was just 7-for-54 while playing the field. Interestingly enough, he started five games at third base after playing there extensively at Triple-A, which could enhance his chances of making the team if he is surpassed in the Rays' desultory competition for the first base job.

Matt Joyce RF

Born: **8/3/1984** Age: **26**
Bats: **L** Throws: **R** Height: **6' 2"** Weight: **185**
Breakout: **1%** Improve: **35%** Collapse: **8%**
Attrition: **20%** MLB: **71%**

Comparables:
Vic Wertz, Jeremy Hermida, Joe Mather (75)

YEAR	TEAM	LVL	AGE	PA	R	2B	3B	HR	RBI	BB	SO	SB	CS	AVG/OBP/SLG	TAv	BABIP	BRR	FRAA	WARP
2008	TOL	AAA	23	227	36	13	2	13	41	24	62	2	3	.270/.352/.550	.297	.325	-0.3	RF 4, CF 1	1.7
2008	DET	MLB	23	277	40	16	3	12	33	31	65	0	2	.252/.339/.492	.298	.293	-0.5	LF 2, RF 1	1.8
2009	DUR	AAA	24	493	73	35	2	16	66	67	98	14	5	.273/.373/.482	.294	.317	-2.5	RF 4, LF 2	3.0
2009	TBA	MLB	24	37	3	1	0	3	7	3	7	1	0	.188/.270/.500	.282	.130	-1.0	CF 0, RF 0	0.0
2010	DUR	AAA	25	115	18	8	0	3	12	22	21	1	3	.293/.435/.478	.316	.353	0.0	RF 1, LF 0	0.9
2010	TBA	MLB	25	261	31	15	3	10	40	40	55	2	2	.241/.360/.477	.305	.273	-0.5	RF 5, LF 0	1.9
2011	*TBA*	*MLB*	*26*	*493*	*66*	*27*	*2*	*19*	*64*	*67*	*109*	*8*	*4*	*.260/.362/.467*	*.288*	*.303*	*-0.4*	*RF 2, LF 1*	*2.3*

Acquired from the Tigers in the Edwin Jackson trade after a solid rookie season, Joyce spent 2009 honing his plate discipline and approach against lefties at Durham. He entered 2010 looking to claim a good chunk of playing time in right field, but an elbow strain and minor-league options kept him on the farm until late June. Despite a slow start, he provided much more punch and patience than fellow right fielders Ben Zobrist and Gabe Kapler; among players with 200 PAs against righties, his .263 isolated power (ISO) against pitchers of that handedness ranked ninth in the AL, and his walk rate ranked fourth among

AL batters with at least 200 PAs overall. He went just 2-for-25 against lefties, though it's hard to believe that he couldn't outhit Gabe Kapler's weak line against southpaws after batting .250/.315/.474 against them at Durham in 2009. In any event, he'll occupy at least the long half of the right-field platoon and could pick up a good bit of the production slack left by the dearly departed Crawford and Pena.

Gabe Kapler RF

Born: **8/31/1975** Age: **35**
Bats: **R** Throws: **R** Height: **6' 2"** Weight: **208**
Breakout: **0%** Improve: **12%** Collapse: **14%**
Attrition: **24%** MLB: **61%**

Comparables:
Lloyd McClendon, Fred Valentine, Steve Souchock (72)

YEAR	TEAM	LVL	AGE	PA	R	2B	3B	HR	RBI	BB	SO	SB	CS	AVG/OBP/SLG	TAv	BABIP	BRR	FRAA	WARP
2008	MIL	MLB	32	245	36	17	2	8	38	13	39	3	1	.301/.339/.498	.293	.332	-1.1	CF 0, LF -1	1.1
2009	TBA	MLB	33	238	25	15	1	8	32	29	39	5	2	.239/.328/.439	.265	.253	-3.3	RF 3, CF 1	0.3
2010	TBA	MLB	34	140	18	4	0	2	14	11	24	1	1	.210/.286/.290	.227	.240	-2.1	RF -1, LF -1	-0.8
2011	*TBA*	*MLB*	*35*	*203*	*23*	*10*	*0*	*5*	*22*	*18*	*34*	*3*	*1*	*.251/.320/.394*	*.254*	*.280*	*-0.1*	*RF 0, CF 0*	*0.1*

Back in 2008 and 2009, when he was still everyone's favorite Jewish bodybuilding fourth outfielder, Kapler creamed lefties at a .304/.379/.577 clip, which made him a handy-enough platoon player. Alas, his performance against southpaws collapsed to .206/.271/.289 in 108 plate appearances last season, and his playing time dried up after going on the DL in June for a hip flexor strain. He started just 10 times in the 40 games he spent on the roster after returning, and went just 8-for-41 before being felled by an ankle sprain due to a collision with Matt Wieters. Kapler will spend this spring—and if he's lucky, the season—in Dodger blue.

Evan Longoria 3B

Born: **10/7/1985** Age: **25**
Bats: **R** Throws: **R** Height: **6' 2"** Weight: **210**
Breakout: **3%** Improve: **52%** Collapse: **4%**
Attrition: **11%** MLB: **100%**

Comparables:
David Wright, Miguel Cabrera, Ryan Zimmerman (73)

YEAR	TEAM	LVL	AGE	PA	R	2B	3B	HR	RBI	BB	SO	SB	CS	AVG/OBP/SLG	TAv	BABIP	BRR	FRAA	WARP
2008	TBA	MLB	22	508	67	31	2	27	85	46	122	7	0	.272/.343/.531	.303	.309	1.2	3B 10, SS 0	4.8
2009	TBA	MLB	23	671	102	44	0	33	113	72	140	9	0	.281/.364/.526	.304	.313	3.7	3B 16	6.8
2010	TBA	MLB	24	661	96	46	5	22	104	72	124	15	5	.294/.372/.507	.318	.336	3.0	3B 8	6.6
2011	*TBA*	*MLB*	*25*	*623*	*86*	*37*	*1*	*27*	*90*	*66*	*125*	*10*	*3*	*.282/.362/.502*	*.300*	*.317*	*0.0*	*3B 10, SS 0*	*5.0*

Despite the drop in home runs, Longoria turned in a season every bit as valuable as his fine 2009—so valuable that he finished in a dead heat with AL MVP winner Josh Hamilton for the league's highest WARP. As in the previous season, he cooled off after a scorching-hot start (.323/.388/.581 through the end of May), but this time, the drop-off was less pronounced, and he remained free of the nagging injuries that hampered him in 2009. Though his fielding was a touch less valuable per all the major metrics, he was still quite strong with the glove. As the Rays bemoan the loss of Crawford, they can take comfort in Longoria's having the game's most team-friendly long-term contract; even with all his club options exercised, he'll make "only" $43 million from 2011 through 2016, his age-30 season.

Ty Morrison CF

Born: **7/22/1990** Age: **20**
Bats: **L** Throws: **R** Height: **6' 2"** Weight: **170**
Breakout: **0%** Improve: **0%** Collapse: **0%**
Attrition: **0%** MLB: **0%**

Comparables:
Thad Bosley, Bill Russell, Oscar Gamble (81)

YEAR	TEAM	LVL	AGE	PA	R	2B	3B	HR	RBI	BB	SO	SB	CS	AVG/OBP/SLG	TAv	BABIP	BRR	FRAA	WARP
2009	PRI	Rk	18	265	34	9	2	3	18	27	61	20	5	.271/.358/.369	.286	.347	1.9	LF -1, CF 7	2.1
2010	BGR	A	19	512	65	21	13	6	56	43	133	58	10	.250/.324/.394	.256	.331	4.2	CF -2, RF 2	1.4
2011	*TBA*	*MLB*	*20*	*267*	*24*	*10*	*2*	*3*	*22*	*16*	*82*	*8*	*2*	*.210/.261/.306*	*.203*	*.292*	*0.2*	*CF -4, LF -2*	*-1.5*

Speedy center fielder Ty Morrison, the Rays' fourth-round pick in 2008, overcame a wretched start to his first year of full-season ball (.129/.156/.161 in April, with a 16/1 strikeout-to-walk ratio), but avoided panic and salvaged his season with a .270/.352/.434 performance the rest of the way. He showed improved plate discipline and made progress in carrying his batting-practice power into games; the Rays think he can add another 15-30 pounds of muscle to his frame and get even stronger as a result. Morrison could stand to strike out less frequently so as to reap the benefits of his blazing speed, but for a teenager, his was hardly a bad season.

Dioner Navarro C

Born: **2/9/1984** Age: **27**
Bats: **S** Throws: **R** Height: **5' 10"** Weight: **190**
Breakout: **1%** Improve: **43%** Collapse: **9%**
Attrition: **17%** MLB: **89%**

Comparables:
Gerald Perry, Smoky Burgess, Ryan Hanigan (73)

YEAR	TEAM	LVL	AGE	PA	R	2B	3B	HR	RBI	BB	SO	SB	CS	AVG/OBP/SLG	TAv	BABIP	BRR	FRAA	WARP
2008	TBA	MLB	24	470	44	27	0	7	54	34	49	0	4	.295/.347/.408	.273	.316	-1.6	C -3	2.2
2009	TBA	MLB	25	410	38	15	0	8	32	18	51	5	2	.218/.256/.322	.208	.226	1.0	C -3	-0.6
2010	DUR	AAA	26	169	19	9	0	2	21	23	25	3	0	.284/.387/.390	.291	.325	0.5	C 0	1.2
2010	TBA	MLB	26	142	12	5	0	1	7	12	20	0	1	.194/.261/.258	.195	.213	-4.1	C 1	-0.6
2011	*LAN*	*MLB*	*27*	*397*	*44*	*18*	*0*	*7*	*39*	*33*	*52*	*3*	*1*	*.253/.315/.371*	*.245*	*.270*	*-0.2*	*C -2*	*0.8*

Off-season surgery to stabilize the ulnar nerve in his nonthrowing elbow did nothing to help Navarro's flagging bat, and his failure to hit dropped him behind both Kelly Shoppach and rookie John Jaso on the depth chart, to the point that Navarro was sent to Triple-A in late June. He didn't return until September and left the Rays in a huff after failing to qualify for the playoff roster, so it was hardly surprising that he was nontendered. Ironically, he signed with the Dodgers after they nontendered Russell Martin, whose rapid development in 2005 pushed Navarro out of town in the first place. In retrospect, it's worth remembering that the brief bout of plate discipline that made Navarro a desirable commodity—a thing of the past, given his career .249/.309/.356 line and seven percent walk rate—owed plenty to his batting seventh or eighth in front of even less desirable hitters, though the same can also be said for A. J. Ellis, with whom Navarro will battle for the right to back up Rod Barajas.

Carlos Pena **1B**

Born: **5/17/1978** Age: **33**
Bats: **L** Throws: **L** Height: **6' 2"** Weight: **210**
Breakout: **2%** Improve: **21%** Collapse: **10%**
Attrition: **11%** MLB: **98%**

Comparables:
Gil Hodges, Lance Berkman, Tony Perez (67)

YEAR	TEAM	LVL	AGE	PA	R	2B	3B	HR	RBI	BB	SO	SB	CS	AVG/OBP/SLG	TAv	BABIP	BRR	FRAA	WARP
2008	TBA	MLB	30	607	76	24	2	31	102	96	166	1	1	.247/.377/.494	.314	.298	-1.8	1B 9	4.4
2009	TBA	MLB	31	570	91	25	2	39	100	87	163	3	3	.227/.356/.537	.315	.250	-0.2	1B -8	2.8
2010	TBA	MLB	32	582	64	18	0	28	84	87	158	5	1	.196/.325/.407	.286	.222	0.6	1B -7	1.3
2011	*CHN*	*MLB*	*33*	*580*	*76*	*20*	*1*	*31*	*76*	*89*	*156*	*3*	*1*	*.223/.351/.466*	*.284*	*.252*	*-0.1*	*1B -2*	*1.6*

When archaeologists dig through the remnants of Western civilization a thousand years from now, the ups and downs of Pena's career will have them scratching their heads as much as those of any other player of the past decade. The slugger's value has dropped in each of the past two seasons due to falling BABIPs; last year, his was the majors' second-lowest BABIP among batting-title qualifiers. Much of the decline stemmed from the defensive shift employed against him, the impact of which has increased as his ground-ball rate has shot from 30 percent of all balls in play to 45 percent; among Rays hitters, only speedsters Carl Crawford and Jason Bartlett directed batted balls earthward with greater frequency. Injuries may have played a part; Pena underwent surgery to repair broken fingers inflicted by a 2009-season-ending hit by pitch, and he missed time in August due to plantar fasciitis. Concerns about payroll led the Rays to let him depart as a free agent. He signed a one-year, $10 million deal with the Cubs and was reunited with hitting coach Rudy Jaramillo, who instructed him as a minor leaguer with the Rangers; the move gave Pena a chance at securing a longer deal with a bounce-back season in the Friendly Confines.

Sean Rodriguez **2B**

Born: **4/26/1985** Age: **26**
Bats: **R** Throws: **R** Height: **6' 1"** Weight: **215**
Breakout: **4%** Improve: **32%** Collapse: **5%**
Attrition: **19%** MLB: **73%**

Comparables:
Josh Fields, David Freese, Justin Ruggiano (71)

YEAR	TEAM	LVL	AGE	PA	R	2B	3B	HR	RBI	BB	SO	SB	CS	AVG/OBP/SLG	TAv	BABIP	BRR	FRAA	WARP
2008	SLC	AAA	23	289	68	19	1	21	52	29	45	4	1	.306/.394/.645	.316	.297	-0.6	2B 6, SS -3	2.8
2008	ANA	MLB	23	187	18	8	1	3	10	14	55	3	1	.204/.273/.317	.208	.277	-0.9	2B -1, SS 2	-0.6
2009	DUR	AAA	24	55	10	2	0	1	10	10	10	3	0	.244/.400/.356	.256	.294	0.9	2B 0, 3B -1	0.1
2009	SLC	AAA	24	435	81	17	6	29	93	51	119	9	2	.299/.398/.616	.331	.359	4.4	2B 21, SS -2	6.5
2009	ANA	MLB	24	29	4	0	0	2	4	3	7	0	0	.200/.276/.440	.238	.177	-0.2	2B -3, LF -1	-0.3
2010	TBA	MLB	25	378	52	19	2	9	40	21	97	13	3	.251/.304/.397	.258	.317	-0.6	2B 5, CF -1	1.3
2011	*TBA*	*MLB*	*26*	*448*	*57*	*20*	*2*	*20*	*61*	*40*	*115*	*9*	*3*	*.256/.333/.467*	*.279*	*.303*	*0.1*	*2B 6, SS 0*	*2.5*

Rodriguez provided the most immediate return in the Scott Kazmir trade, receiving a plurality of the starts at second base (78) and endearing himself to Joe Maddon to the point of spotting at every other defensive position except catcher. After hitting well at just about every minor-league stop, he showed less pop and patience than PECOTA had projected, but enough to qualify as an average bat despite his low walk rate; while he mashed lefties (.292/.375/.442 in 136 PAs), he flailed against righties (.229/.270/.372 in 224 PAs, with a 60/7 K/BB ratio). Defensively, he was an asset at second base and didn't embarrass himself at any of the other positions. He'll probably see more time at the keystone in the wake of Reid Brignac's takeover at shortstop, but you can bet that Maddon will continue to utilize his versatility.

Kelly Shoppach **C**

Born: **4/29/1980** Age: **31**
Bats: **R** Throws: **R** Height: **6' 1"** Weight: **210**
Breakout: **4%** Improve: **25%** Collapse: **10%**
Attrition: **13%** MLB: **81%**

Comparables:
Jim Leyritz, Craig Wilson, David Ross (69)

YEAR	TEAM	LVL	AGE	PA	R	2B	3B	HR	RBI	BB	SO	SB	CS	AVG/OBP/SLG	TAv	BABIP	BRR	FRAA	WARP
2008	CLE	MLB	28	403	69	27	0	21	55	36	133	0	0	.261/.345/.517	.302	.352	2.4	C -1	3.5
2009	CLE	MLB	29	327	33	14	0	12	40	33	98	0	0	.214/.333/.399	.268	.277	-0.6	C -2	1.3
2010	TBA	MLB	30	187	17	8	0	5	17	20	71	0	0	.196/.305/.342	.255	.306	-1.3	C -1	0.4
2011	*TBA*	*MLB*	*31*	*262*	*31*	*12*	*0*	*10*	*30*	*24*	*86*	*0*	*0*	*.230/.320/.412*	*.258*	*.312*	*0.0*	*C -1*	*0.8*

Scheduled to share time at catcher with Dioner Navarro, Shoppach tore the meniscus in his right knee in early April and missed eight weeks. He initially hit well upon returning—.263/.396/.421 through the end of June—albeit in just 49 PAs. That kept him in the majors while Navarro was farmed out, but he hit just .175/.277/.317 the rest of the way, striking out 39 percent of the time. He bopped nicely against lefties (.261/.369/.455 in 103 PAs), but disappeared against righties (.114/.232/.200 in 84 PAs), which should fit him into the short half of a platoon with

John Jaso, but minimizes any aspirations to regular duty. Also not helping: Shoppach threw out just 17 percent of attempted base thieves.

Matthew Sweeney 3B

Born: **4/4/1988** Age: **23**
Bats: **L** Throws: **R** Height: **6' 3"** Weight: **215**
Breakout: **1%** Improve: **7%** Collapse: **1%**
Attrition: **8%** MLB: **14%**

Comparables:
Bill Melton, Jeff Clement, Daniel Murphy (76)

YEAR	TEAM	LVL	AGE	PA	R	2B	3B	HR	RBI	BB	SO	SB	CS	AVG/OBP/SLG	TAv	BABIP	BRR	FRAA	WARP
2009	RCU	A+	21	241	39	17	1	9	44	26	37	2	0	.299/.378/.517	.335	.323	-0.7	3B -6	1.7
2010	PCH	A+	22	140	20	9	0	6	16	16	34	0	0	.264/.345/.488	.289	.310	0.9	3B 2	1.0
2010	MNT	AA	22	180	13	7	0	2	25	12	52	1	0	.196/.263/.276	.206	.273	0.3	3B -6	-1.0
2011	*TBA*	*MLB*	*23*	*308*	*34*	*15*	*0*	*8*	*33*	*24*	*77*	*0*	*0*	*.237/.300/.384*	*.239*	*.291*	*0.0*	*3B -5*	*-0.5*

Sweeney came over from the Angels in the Scott Kazmir deal in late 2009, but he didn't leave his penchant for injuries behind. After missing all of 2008 with an ankle ailment and more than two months of 2009 to a hip injury, he had a solid showing at High-A Charlotte. Unfortunately, he struggled in the transition to Double-A, chasing pitches outside the zone, and he didn't play after July 19 due to an elbow strain. Scouts still love Sweeney's sweet swing, his strength, and his pitch-recognition skills, but the offensive bar for his performance is about to be raised. As the owner of a sub-Hobbsonion .860 career fielding percentage at third base, thanks to limited range and poor footwork, he'll probably shift to first base in 2011; it's just as well, because he's not going to replace the Rays' current hot-corner man in this lifetime.

B. J. Upton CF

Born: **8/21/1984** Age: **26**
Bats: **R** Throws: **R** Height: **6' 3"** Weight: **180**
Breakout: **2%** Improve: **57%** Collapse: **2%**
Attrition: **11%** MLB: **87%**

Comparables:
Chris Young, Larry Doby, Franklin Gutierrez (69)

YEAR	TEAM	LVL	AGE	PA	R	2B	3B	HR	RBI	BB	SO	SB	CS	AVG/OBP/SLG	TAv	BABIP	BRR	FRAA	WARP
2008	TBA	MLB	23	639	85	37	2	9	67	97	133	44	16	.274/.382/.402	.286	.342	0.5	CF 5	4.0
2009	TBA	MLB	24	626	79	33	4	11	55	57	152	42	14	.241/.312/.373	.252	.308	-0.1	CF -2	1.0
2010	TBA	MLB	25	610	88	38	4	18	62	67	164	42	9	.237/.321/.424	.277	.304	5.5	CF 5	3.6
2011	*TBA*	*MLB*	*26*	*625*	*76*	*33*	*2*	*16*	*68*	*73*	*149*	*42*	*13*	*.255/.343/.410*	*.268*	*.318*	*-0.2*	*CF 2*	*2.3*

On the surface, the numbers were dismaying, as Upton's batting average declined for the third straight year, his strikeout rate decreased, and he posted an OBP below the league average, justifying Joe Maddon's decision to keep him batting lower in the lineup than the leadoff position he occupied so regularly until August 2009. Maddon showed an increased willingness to bench him, first for a late-June dugout altercation with Evan Longoria following a perceived lack of defensive effort, then for the way he matched up against certain pitchers. Nonetheless, Upton still outproduced the average center fielder, with his highest homer total and isolated power mark since his 2007 presurgical days. He came on strong over the season's final two months (hitting .255/.333/.480 with 10 homers) and ranked fifth among defenders, though none of this prevented him from disappearing during the playoffs. Still under club control for two more years, Upton remains a vital part of the Rays' future, as two-way center fielders are not to be dismissed lightly, even if they fall short of the superstardom that Upton's 2007 seemed to portend.

Ben Zobrist RF

Born: **5/26/1981** Age: **30**
Bats: **S** Throws: **R** Height: **6' 3"** Weight: **200**
Breakout: **0%** Improve: **36%** Collapse: **2%**
Attrition: **4%** MLB: **94%**

Comparables:
Michael Cuddyer, Gary Matthews, Ryan Spilborghs (78)

YEAR	TEAM	LVL	AGE	PA	R	2B	3B	HR	RBI	BB	SO	SB	CS	AVG/OBP/SLG	TAv	BABIP	BRR	FRAA	WARP
2008	DUR	AAA	27	88	15	3	0	4	13	15	16	4	1	.366/.466/.578	.344	.415	0.6	SS 1, 3B 1	1.3
2008	TBA	MLB	27	227	32	10	2	12	30	25	37	3	0	.253/.339/.505	.296	.252	-0.5	SS -4, LF 1	1.2
2009	TBA	MLB	28	599	91	28	7	27	91	91	104	17	6	.297/.404/.543	.336	.325	2.6	2B 8, RF 4	7.0
2010	TBA	MLB	29	655	77	28	2	10	75	92	107	24	3	.238/.342/.353	.268	.269	-0.5	RF 4, 2B -3	1.7
2011	*TBA*	*MLB*	*30*	*524*	*67*	*23*	*2*	*15*	*59*	*71*	*87*	*15*	*4*	*.265/.364/.430*	*.283*	*.292*	*0.2*	*2B 1, RF 2*	*2.4*

Just as quickly as Zobrist turned into one of the league's top offensive forces (which coincided with his tutoring by swing-doctor Jaime Cevallos), so did his power desert him. Last season, Zobrist's home-run-per-fly-ball (HR/FB) rate fell to about one-third of its 2008-2009 levels, from 17.5 percent to 6.0 percent, and his line-drive rate also fell considerably. After hitting .293/.376/.411 through the end of June, he batted just .180/.315/.291 the rest of the way, finishing under the Mendoza line in each of the final three full months. He did miss a week in late July/early August with a lower-back strain, after which he stopped stealing bases, so there is some suspicion that he was playing hurt, but another school of thought suggests that he didn't adjust to the way the league adjusted to him. Zobrist was still a valuable contributor, thanks to his high walk total (fourth in the league) and above-average defense while switching regularly between right field and second base and spotting at first base, center field, and third base. As he is in the third season of a four-year, $18 million deal that bought out his arbitration years, exactly where Zobrist fits into the Rays' 2011 plans remains unclear at this writing; he could return to a roving starter role, figure prominently on first base, or hold down an outfield role until Jennings is deemed ready.

PITCHERS

Grant Balfour

Born: **12/30/1977** Age: **33**
Bats: **R** Throws: **R** Height: **6' 2"** Weight: **175**
Breakout: **15%** Improve: **36%** Collapse: **34%**
Attrition: **12%** MLB: **86%**

Comparables:
Jason Frasor, Troy Percival, Damaso Marte (63)

YEAR	TEAM	LVL	AGE	W	L	SV	G	GS	IP	H	HR	BB	SO	EqBB9	EqSO9	GB%	BABIP	WHIP	ERA	FRA	WARP
2008	DUR	AAA	30	1	0	8	15	0	23^{2}	5	1	10	39	3.8	14.8	43%	.114	0.63	0.38	0.99	1.2
2008	TBA	MLB	30	6	2	4	51	0	58^{1}	28	3	24	82	3.7	12.7	30%	.217	0.89	1.54	2.19	2.3
2009	TBA	MLB	31	5	4	4	73	0	67^{1}	59	6	33	69	4.4	9.2	37%	.296	1.40	4.95	5.26	0.0
2010	TBA	MLB	32	2	1	0	57	0	55^{1}	43	3	17	56	2.8	9.1	30%	.274	1.08	2.28	2.35	1.5
2011	*TBA*	*MLB*	*33*	*3*	*1*	*2*	*52*	*0*	*56*	*43*	*5*	*26*	*64*	*4.1*	*10.3*	*40%*	*.286*	*1.23*	*2.90*	*3.15*	*0.9*

Balfour avoided ball four with more regularity than he had in 2009 and, in doing so, restored himself as a valuable member of the Rays' pen—so valuable, in fact, that he wound up ninth in the league in WXRL despite missing five weeks due to an intercostal strain suffered in a bout of clubhouse horseplay with pitching coach Jim Hickey. He has the stuff to be a closer; his 10.3 strikeouts per nine innings pitched (K/9) over the last three years ranks 15th among relievers, and despite his Type-A free-agent status, he landed a two-year deal with the A's.

Nick Barnese

Born: **1/11/1989** Age: **22**
Bats: **R** Throws: **R** Height: **6' 2"** Weight: **170**
Breakout: **5%** Improve: **5%** Collapse: **0%**
Attrition: **2%** MLB: **5%**

Comparables:
Rick Baldwin, Tommy John, Leo Kiely (78)

YEAR	TEAM	LVL	AGE	W	L	SV	G	GS	IP	H	HR	BB	SO	EqBB9	EqSO9	GB%	BABIP	WHIP	ERA	FRA	WARP
2008	HUD	A-	19	5	3	0	13	13	66	52	1	24	84	3.3	11.5	53%	.317	1.17	2.45	3.83	1.3
2009	BGR	A	20	6	5	0	15	15	74^{2}	56	3	25	62	3.0	7.5	55%	.247	1.20	2.53	3.36	1.8
2010	PCH	A+	21	8	4	0	21	20	122^{1}	114	5	26	100	1.9	7.4	51%	.299	1.29	3.02	3.43	2.9
2011	*TBA*	*MLB*	*22*	*5*	*5*	*0*	*13*	*13*	*69*	*69*	*8*	*31*	*44*	*4.1*	*5.7*	*47%*	*.286*	*1.45*	*4.66*	*5.07*	*0.7*

A third-round pick in 2007, Barnese used to be mentioned in the same breath as Matt Moore, but while Moore has dominated the low minors, Barnese has yet to make a full season's worth of starts, due to arm woes that have slowed his fastball from 91-93 mph to 89-91. He still has outstanding control, a deceptive delivery, a plus curveball, and an improving changeup, not to mention a frame that's only starting to fill out. Whatever his setbacks, he'll be pitching in Double-A in 2011 at age 22, and although his ceiling isn't equal to that of Moore or even Alex Colome, he's still a capable midrotation prospect.

Joaquin Benoit

Born: **7/26/1977** Age: **33**
Bats: **R** Throws: **R** Height: **6' 3"** Weight: **205**
Breakout: **18%** Improve: **39%** Collapse: **26%**
Attrition: **7%** MLB: **82%**

Comparables:
Lee Smith, Eric Plunk, J.R. Richard (74)

YEAR	TEAM	LVL	AGE	W	L	SV	G	GS	IP	H	HR	BB	SO	EqBB9	EqSO9	GB%	BABIP	WHIP	ERA	FRA	WARP
2008	TEX	MLB	30	3	2	1	44	0	45	40	6	35	43	7.0	8.6	28%	.272	1.67	5.00	5.09	0.0
2010	TBA	MLB	32	1	2	1	63	0	60^{1}	30	6	11	75	1.6	11.2	39%	.192	0.68	1.34	2.67	1.4
2011	*DET*	*MLB*	*33*	*4*	*2*	*1*	*72*	*0*	*71*	*58*	*7*	*28*	*79*	*3.5*	*9.9*	*42%*	*.284*	*1.19*	*2.95*	*3.20*	*1.3*

Signed to a minor-league deal after missing 2009 due to rotator cuff surgery, Benoit was the bullpen find of the year. He spent most of April in the minors, then joined the Rays and blew hitters away, recovering more than two miles per hour of lost velocity and posting the highest K/BB ratio and lowest BABIP of any AL reliever. He didn't surrender a run until his 14th outing of the year, allowed just two out of 23 inherited runners to score, and wound up with the league's third-highest WXRL total among set-up men (eighth-highest overall). Because some teams don't pay attention to the volatile nature of relief performances, the owner of a 4.47 career ERA with two good seasons in the last five years snagged a three-year, $16.5 million deal with Detroit. That's an expensive recipe for heartbreak.

Randy Choate

Born: **9/5/1975** Age: **35**
Bats: **L** Throws: **L** Height: **6' 3"** Weight: **180**
Breakout: **9%** Improve: **11%** Collapse: **5%**
Attrition: **1%** MLB: **19%**

Comparables:
Randy Flores, Scott Atchison, Mike Henneman (77)

YEAR	TEAM	LVL	AGE	W	L	SV	G	GS	IP	H	HR	BB	SO	EqBB9	EqSO9	GB%	BABIP	WHIP	ERA	FRA	WARP
2008	NAS	AAA	32	0	4	1	26	2	39	42	4	20	31	4.6	7.2	70%	.314	1.62	5.08	5.17	0.1
2009	TBA	MLB	33	1	0	5	61	0	36^{1}	28	4	11	28	2.7	6.9	66%	.242	1.07	3.22	5.21	0.0
2010	TBA	MLB	34	4	3	0	85	0	44^{2}	41	3	17	40	3.4	8.1	61%	.307	1.37	4.43	3.45	0.8
2011	*FLO*	*MLB*	*35*	*4*	*1*	*1*	*74*	*0*	*52*	*52*	*5*	*21*	*44*	*3.7*	*7.5*	*51%*	*.314*	*1.42*	*4.20*	*4.56*	*0.1*

Other than leading the AL in appearances, Choate's season wasn't particularly distinguished. Lefties hit just .202/.263/.266 against him in 138 plate appearances, a bit better than his career numbers, and while righties raked him at a .410/.521/.641 clip, it was only 49 PAs, so kudos to Joe Maddon for keeping his LOOGY out of harm's way. Still, Choate was 5.2 runs below average in preventing inherited runners from scoring. Having worked year to year for less than $1 million his entire career, he declined arbitration and netted a two-year, $2.5 million deal from the Marlins.

Alex Cobb

Born: **10/7/1987** Age: **23**
Bats: **R** Throws: **R** Height: **6' 1"** Weight: **180**
Breakout: **7%** Improve: **8%** Collapse: **1%**
Attrition: **3%** MLB: **9%**

Comparables:
Fabio Castro, Daryl Thompson, John Smiley (79)

YEAR	TEAM	LVL	AGE	W	L	SV	G	GS	IP	H	HR	BB	SO	EqBB9	EqSO9	GB%	BABIP	WHIP	ERA	FRA	WARP
2008	CGA	A	20	9	7	0	25	25	139^{2}	113	16	35	97	2.3	6.2	59%	.245	1.17	3.29	4.70	1.2
2009	PCH	A+	21	8	5	0	24	23	124^{2}	116	6	31	107	2.2	7.7	55%	.304	1.25	3.03	3.46	3.3
2010	MNT	AA	22	7	5	0	23	22	119^{2}	120	7	35	128	2.6	9.7	55%	.342	1.33	2.71	3.52	2.9
2011	*TBA*	*MLB*	*23*	*6*	*7*	*0*	*17*	*17*	*92*	*97*	*12*	*40*	*62*	*3.9*	*6.0*	*50%*	*.297*	*1.48*	*4.83*	*5.25*	*0.7*

The Rays' system is seemingly littered with pitching prospects named Alex(ander). This one, a fourth-round pick in 2006, lacks the stuff of Colome or Torres, but has put up impressive numbers, thanks to an ability to pitch backward with a big-breaking curveball, a plus changeup (much improved over last year's model and described as a split-change), and a low-90s fastball with a bit of sink. After beginning the year on the DL with an oblique strain, he recovered to lead the Southern League in strikeout rate and ranked fourth in ERA. The depth of the Rays' rotation puts him on a long waiting list, and while the team believes that he can start in the AL East, he's caught in a numbers game.

Alexander Colome

Born: **12/31/1988** Age: **22**
Bats: **R** Throws: **R** Height: **6' 2"** Weight: **184**
Breakout: **5%** Improve: **6%** Collapse: **1%**
Attrition: **6%** MLB: **9%**

Comparables:
Jim Donohue, Pete Schourek, Dick Lemay (75)

YEAR	TEAM	LVL	AGE	W	L	SV	G	GS	IP	H	HR	BB	SO	EqBB9	EqSO9	GB%	BABIP	WHIP	ERA	FRA	WARP
2008	PRI	Rk	19	0	5	0	12	11	46^{1}	50	5	26	52	5.1	10.1	47%	.349	1.79	6.80	7.42	-0.4
2009	HUD	A-	20	7	4	0	15	15	76	46	0	32	94	3.8	11.1	56%	.267	1.09	1.66	3.40	1.7
2010	BGR	A	21	6	6	0	22	22	114	98	14	45	118	3.6	9.3	48%	.286	1.29	3.95	4.69	1.1
2011	*TBA*	*MLB*	*22*	*5*	*6*	*0*	*15*	*15*	*73*	*73*	*10*	*46*	*60*	*5.6*	*7.4*	*45%*	*.294*	*1.62*	*5.31*	*5.78*	*0.3*

This live-armed Dominican is the nephew of Jesus Colome, but don't hold that against him. He's a bit raw, but he has "big-boy stuff," as one Rays official describes it: an explosive mid-90s fastball, a tight curveball that has the makings of a plus pitch, and a changeup that is showing progress. His introduction to full-season ball was uneven, with a 1.92 ERA and 0.5 home runs allowed per nine innings pitched (HR/9) through his first 10 starts, but he carried a 5.66 ERA and 1.6 HR/9 the rest of the way. Colome lost some time to a clavicle injury, though he did close with a flourish in his High-A debut. The Rays still view Colome as having the upside of a front-line starter, but some see him as bullpen-bound if he can't polish his approach.

Lance Cormier

Born: **8/19/1980** Age: **30**
Bats: **R** Throws: **R** Height: **6' 1"** Weight: **192**
Breakout: **15%** Improve: **42%** Collapse: **24%**
Attrition: **13%** MLB: **80%**

Comparables:
LaTroy Hawkins, Russ Kemmerer, Roger Craig (82)

YEAR	TEAM	LVL	AGE	W	L	SV	G	GS	IP	H	HR	BB	SO	EqBB9	EqSO9	GB%	BABIP	WHIP	ERA	FRA	WARP
2008	BAL	MLB	27	3	3	1	45	1	71^{2}	78	4	34	46	4.3	5.8	59%	.316	1.58	4.02	4.73	0.3
2009	TBA	MLB	28	3	3	2	53	0	77^{1}	75	6	25	36	2.9	4.2	52%	.262	1.31	3.26	4.17	0.9
2010	TBA	MLB	29	4	3	0	60	0	62	68	7	34	30	4.9	4.4	50%	.293	1.65	3.92	3.59	0.9
2011	*TBA*	*MLB*	*30*	*3*	*1*	*0*	*65*	*0*	*93*	*100*	*10*	*41*	*49*	*3.9*	*4.7*	*49%*	*.294*	*1.50*	*4.75*	*5.17*	*-0.7*

Cormier put together another solid year of middle relief for the Rays, using his cutter to overcome his lack of velocity (he almost never breaks 90 mph) and drawing enough ground balls to weather his anemic strikeout rate and unhealthy K/BB imbalance. Oddly enough, Cormier has shown a reverse platoon split over the past three years, holding lefties to a .243/.340/.346 line, but getting chafed by righties at a .295/.345/.441 clip; luckily, he has faced slightly more lefties than righties in that time. In all, his is a dangerous way to make a living, but it's a living nonetheless.

Joe Cruz

Born: **7/20/1988** Age: **22**
Bats: **R** Throws: **R** Height: **6' 4"** Weight: **190**
Breakout: **4%** Improve: **5%** Collapse: **0%**
Attrition: **4%** MLB: **5%**

Comparables:
Nick Adenhart, Trevor Bell, Ryan Tucker (81)

YEAR	TEAM	LVL	AGE	W	L	SV	G	GS	IP	H	HR	BB	SO	EqBB9	EqSO9	GB%	BABIP	WHIP	ERA	FRA	WARP
2008	PRI	Rk	19	1	3	0	13	13	54	61	5	14	62	2.3	10.3	55%	.352	1.43	3.17	3.69	1.5
2009	BGR	A	20	5	8	0	21	21	98	110	5	26	99	2.4	9.1	49%	.356	1.41	4.04	3.85	1.7
2010	PCH	A+	21	13	6	0	25	25	142	137	6	39	131	2.5	8.3	49%	.323	1.28	2.85	3.42	3.7
2011	*TBA*	*MLB*	*22*	*5*	*6*	*0*	*15*	*15*	*74^{1}*	*85*	*9*	*35*	*50*	*4.2*	*6.1*	*45%*	*.322*	*1.62*	*5.42*	*5.89*	*0.2*

This 2007 draft-and-follow enjoyed the benefits of improved defensive support in a breakout season at High-A. Cruz started slowly (4.87 ERA, 2.4 K/BB ratio in the first half), but improved secondary offerings (primarily a slow curveball) and mechanical consistency helped him dominate in the second half (1.91 ERA, 4.4 K/BB). Cruz is a pure power righty who's all arms and legs. He can bring it in the mid-90s, though a rough delivery can cost him significant velocity. Until he develops a plus secondary pitch, his future is more likely in the bullpen, particularly in this pitching-rich organization.

Wade Davis

Born: **9/7/1985** Age: **25**
Bats: R Throws: R Height: **6' 5"** Weight: **220**
Breakout: **17%** Improve: **40%** Collapse: **17%**
Attrition: **34%** MLB: **86%**

Comparables:
Phil Coke, Mitch Talbot, Matt Albers (76)

YEAR	TEAM	LVL	AGE	W	L	SV	G	GS	IP	H	HR	BB	SO	EqBB9	EqSO9	GB%	BABIP	WHIP	ERA	FRA	WARP
2008	MNT	AA	22	9	6	0	19	19	107^{2}	104	7	42	81	3.5	6.8	46%	.307	1.44	3.84	4.15	2.1
2008	DUR	AAA	22	4	2	0	9	9	53	39	5	24	55	4.1	9.3	48%	.256	1.26	2.72	3.99	1.5
2009	DUR	AAA	23	10	8	0	28	28	158^{2}	139	14	60	140	3.4	7.9	41%	.276	1.29	3.40	4.03	3.1
2009	TBA	MLB	23	2	2	0	6	6	36^{1}	33	2	13	36	3.2	8.9	40%	.316	1.27	3.72	4.17	0.7
2010	TBA	MLB	24	12	10	0	29	29	168	165	24	62	113	3.3	6.1	40%	.272	1.38	4.02	4.08	2.4
2011	*TBA*	*MLB*	*25*	*11*	*9*	*0*	*29*	*29*	*163*	*154*	*19*	*72*	*125*	*4.0*	*6.9*	*43%*	*.282*	*1.38*	*4.12*	*4.48*	*2.5*

Davis came into the year hailed as one of the game's top power pitching prospects, a notion enhanced by his late-2009 stint in the majors and the trade of Scott Kazmir to open a spot for him in the Rays' rotation. While he established himself as a major-league starter, Davis was overly reliant on his 91-94 mph fastball and rarely fooled hitters with his secondary offerings—a hazard of pitching to the disciplined hitters in the AL East—so his strikeout rate was lower than expected. Furthermore, he became extremely fly-ball-oriented and homer-prone; only three AL ERA qualifiers had a higher fly-ball percentage (FB%) than his 33.8 percent. He made a strong late-season showing (3.09 ERA, 7.0 K/9, 0.8 HR/9 over eight starts) after a brief DL stint for a shoulder strain, but he'll need to continue honing his repertoire to live up to last pre-season's expectations.

Mike Ekstrom

Born: **8/30/1983** Age: **27**
Bats: R Throws: R Height: **6' 0"** Weight: **185**
Breakout: **2%** Improve: **2%** Collapse: **2%**
Attrition: **2%** MLB: **4%**

Comparables:
Marco Estrada, Dusty Hughes, Eulogio De La Cruz (83)

YEAR	TEAM	LVL	AGE	W	L	SV	G	GS	IP	H	HR	BB	SO	EqBB9	EqSO9	GB%	BABIP	WHIP	ERA	FRA	WARP
2008	SAN	AA	24	11	8	1	41	15	108	137	14	34	101	2.8	8.4	56%	.363	1.66	4.58	5.21	0.2
2008	SDN	MLB	24	0	2	0	8	0	9^{2}	14	2	7	6	6.5	5.6	47%	.375	2.17	7.45	6.45	-0.2
2009	POR	AAA	25	4	2	0	42	1	62^{1}	44	2	16	43	2.3	6.2	61%	.236	0.98	1.73	2.60	2.0
2009	SDN	MLB	25	0	0	0	12	0	18^{1}	21	3	8	19	3.9	9.3	47%	.346	1.64	6.38	5.14	-0.1
2010	DUR	AAA	26	6	1	1	39	1	58	55	5	19	48	2.9	7.4	57%	.298	1.31	2.79	2.63	1.7
2010	TBA	MLB	26	0	1	0	15	0	16^{1}	12	0	9	10	5.0	5.5	38%	.255	1.41	3.31	5.35	-0.1
2011	*TBA*	*MLB*	*27*	*5*	*4*	*0*	*66*	*7*	*115*	*127*	*13*	*46*	*74*	*3.6*	*5.8*	*50%*	*.311*	*1.50*	*4.80*	*5.22*	*-0.3*

A 12th-round pick by San Diego in 2004, Ekstrom reached the Rays via the waiver wire in February. He broke camp with the big club, but was quickly tarred and feathered; the runs he allowed all came in his first four outings. Demoted to accommodate Joaquin Benoit's activation, he pitched sparingly in two other big-league stints. Ekstrom is a ground-ball machine with a good slider if only a so-so sinker. With the Rays' bullpen corps significantly thinned by free agency, he'll get a long look at becoming part of their 2011 crew.

Matt Garza

Born: **11/11/1983** Age: **27**
Bats: R Throws: R Height: **6' 4"** Weight: **185**
Breakout: **8%** Improve: **40%** Collapse: **32%**
Attrition: **12%** MLB: **95%**

Comparables:
Mike Witt, Shaun Marcum, Ervin Santana (73)

YEAR	TEAM	LVL	AGE	W	L	SV	G	GS	IP	H	HR	BB	SO	EqBB9	EqSO9	GB%	BABIP	WHIP	ERA	FRA	WARP
2008	TBA	MLB	24	11	9	0	30	30	184^{2}	170	19	59	128	2.9	6.2	43%	.270	1.27	3.70	4.04	3.4
2009	TBA	MLB	25	8	12	0	32	32	203	177	25	79	189	3.5	8.4	40%	.273	1.32	3.95	4.24	3.5
2010	TBA	MLB	26	15	10	1	33	32	204^{2}	193	28	63	150	2.8	6.6	37%	.272	1.29	3.91	5.06	0.4
2011	*CHN*	*MLB*	*27*	*12*	*10*	*0*	*31*	*31*	*191^{2}*	*187*	*23*	*67*	*154*	*3.1*	*7.2*	*41%*	*.297*	*1.33*	*4.15*	*4.51*	*3.8*

Garza's July 26 no-hitter against the Tigers amply demonstrated his outstanding stuff, but the rest of his season illustrated his erratic nature. He has developed into one of the game's most extreme fly-ballers; among AL ERA qualifiers, only Phil Hughes had a lower ground-ball percentage (GB%), and only two had a higher FB% than his 34.5 percent. As a result, Garza ranked fourth in the league in homers allowed and, at one point, put together an eight-start stretch with 1.9 HR/9 and a 7.29 ERA. He had seven disaster starts (more runs than innings pitched), one shy of the major-league lead shared by A. J. Burnett, Scott Kazmir, and four others. He did pitch somewhat more efficiently than in years past and set a career high for innings, but he's currently walking a fine line between sorrow and success. The Cubs will hope that a move to the NL summons more smiles than tears after surrendering half of their farm system in exchange for the right-hander in January.

Jeremy Hellickson

Born: **4/8/1987** Age: **24**
Bats: **R** Throws: **R** Height: **6' 1"** Weight: **185**
Breakout: **18%** Improve: **38%** Collapse: **13%**
Attrition: **16%** MLB: **67%**

Comparables:
Kris Medlen, Scott Sanderson, Johnny Cueto (67)

YEAR	TEAM	LVL	AGE	W	L	SV	G	GS	IP	H	HR	BB	SO	EqBB9	EqSO9	GB%	BABIP	WHIP	ERA	FRA	WARP
2008	VRO	A+	21	7	1	0	14	16	76^2	64	7	5	83	0.6	9.7	46%	.289	0.95	2.00	2.29	3.2
2008	MNT	AA	21	4	4	0	13	13	75^1	84	15	15	79	1.8	9.4	42%	.350	1.34	3.70	3.53	2.0
2009	MNT	AA	22	3	1	0	11	11	56^2	41	4	14	62	2.2	9.8	34%	.261	1.04	2.22	2.27	2.3
2009	DUR	AAA	22	7	1	0	11	12	69^2	39	7	19	88	2.5	11.4	45%	.211	0.89	2.33	3.22	2.0
2010	DUR	AAA	23	12	3	0	21	21	117^2	103	5	35	123	2.7	9.4	38%	.313	1.24	2.45	2.27	5.3
2010	TBA	MLB	23	4	0	0	10	4	36^1	32	5	8	33	2.0	8.2	38%	.267	1.16	3.47	4.14	0.5
2011	*TBA*	*MLB*	*24*	*9*	*6*	*0*	*21*	*21*	*120^2*	*108*	*14*	*41*	*111*	*3.0*	*8.3*	*41%*	*.287*	*1.24*	*3.55*	*3.86*	*2.8*

Hellickson was left to languish in the International League well after the point when organizations with less pitching depth would have added him to their rotations. Fortunately, he used his time well, adding a two-seamer and a cut fastball to an arsenal that already included a four-seamer that can touch 95 and a changeup that's considered his best pitch. He showed outstanding command, missed bats, and got ground balls, and when the injury bug bit the Rays' rotation in August, he impressed in a four-start audition (2.05 ERA, 25/4 K/BB in 26.1 IP). Concerns about his innings total forced him to the bullpen in September, where he was knocked around. The Rays unloaded Matt Garza over the winter to make room for the more-than-major-league-ready youngster, leaving the American League nowhere to hide from the firepower of this fully armed and operational right-hander.

J. P. Howell

Born: **4/25/1983** Age: **28**
Bats: **L** Throws: **L** Height: **6' 0"** Weight: **175**
Breakout: **23%** Improve: **42%** Collapse: **29%**
Attrition: **7%** MLB: **84%**

Comparables:
Xavier Hernandez, Ray Narleski, Dave Righetti (72)

YEAR	TEAM	LVL	AGE	W	L	SV	G	GS	IP	H	HR	BB	SO	EqBB9	EqSO9	GB%	BABIP	WHIP	ERA	FRA	WARP
2008	TBA	MLB	25	6	1	3	64	0	89^1	62	6	39	92	3.9	9.3	55%	.245	1.18	2.22	3.56	1.7
2009	TBA	MLB	26	7	5	17	69	0	66^2	47	7	33	79	4.5	10.7	49%	.256	1.25	2.84	3.53	1.1
2011	*TBA*	*MLB*	*28*	*5*	*2*	*11*	*103*	*0*	*121^2*	*106*	*13*	*51*	*121*	*3.8*	*9.0*	*48%*	*.291*	*1.29*	*3.62*	*3.93*	*0.9*

A vital cog in the Rays' bullpen in 2008 and 2009, Howell served as a multi-inning reliever, a LOOGY, and a closer at various times while throwing more innings than any other southpaw reliever during that span. He was tough on both righties (.180/.280/.305) and lefties (.224/.320/.307) despite having the platoon advantage only one-third of the time. Sidelined by shoulder weakness in spring training, he underwent surgery in late May to repair a torn labrum and missed the entire season. After learning that he wouldn't be ready to start the 2011 season as initially hoped, the Rays nontendered him, then re-signed him for $1.1 million plus incentives.

Kyle Lobstein

Born: **8/12/1989** Age: **21**
Bats: **L** Throws: **L** Height: **6' 3"** Weight: **200**
Breakout: **6%** Improve: **11%** Collapse: **1%**
Attrition: **4%** MLB: **12%**

Comparables:
Billy Hoeft, Ryan Tucker, Mike McCormick (71)

YEAR	TEAM	LVL	AGE	W	L	SV	G	GS	IP	H	HR	BB	SO	EqBB9	EqSO9	GB%	BABIP	WHIP	ERA	FRA	WARP
2009	HUD	A-	19	3	5	0	14	14	73^1	55	4	23	74	2.8	9.1	51%	.260	1.11	2.58	3.18	1.9
2010	BGR	A	20	9	8	0	27	27	148	140	14	54	128	3.3	7.8	39%	.298	1.33	4.14	4.15	2.2
2011	*TBA*	*MLB*	*21*	*6*	*8*	*0*	*19*	*19*	*101^2*	*109*	*15*	*55*	*62*	*4.9*	*5.5*	*42%*	*.293*	*1.62*	*5.45*	*5.92*	*0.0*

Once considered among the nation's top prep lefties, Lobstein is a 2008 second-round pick whose $1.5 million bonus bought out his commitment to the University of Arizona. After a solid pro debut, he struggled in his introduction to full-season ball. As had happened during his senior year of high school, his velocity dipped from its already-middling 89-91 range into 86-87 territory, though it rebounded later in the season; his strikeout rate jumped from 6.8 per nine to 8.6 per nine from the first half to the second. Lobstein's fastball plays up given a much-improved curve and changeup, and the Rays love his unflappable demeanor and advanced feel for pitching, but he has yet to satisfy us by developing an eephus pitch to go with his name.

Jake McGee

Born: **8/6/1986** Age: **24**
Bats: **L** Throws: **L** Height: **6' 3"** Weight: **190**
Breakout: **4%** Improve: **8%** Collapse: **4%**
Attrition: **11%** MLB: **18%**

Comparables:
Antonio Bastardo, Samuel Gervacio, Fernando Hernandez Jr. (82)

YEAR	TEAM	LVL	AGE	W	L	SV	G	GS	IP	H	HR	BB	SO	EqBB9	EqSO9	GB%	BABIP	WHIP	ERA	FRA	WARP
2008	MNT	AA	21	6	4	0	15	15	77^2	65	6	37	65	4.3	7.5	44%	.273	1.33	3.94	4.52	1.2
2009	PCH	A+	22	0	2	0	11	11	22^1	26	2	9	26	3.6	10.5	48%	.400	1.57	6.46	5.31	0.5
2010	MNT	AA	23	3	7	0	19	19	88^1	81	3	33	100	3.4	10.2	44%	.328	1.31	3.57	3.08	2.8
2010	DUR	AAA	23	1	1	1	13	1	20^1	9	0	4	32	1.8	14.2	47%	.237	0.64	0.44	1.12	0.8
2010	TBA	MLB	23	0	0	0	8	0	5	2	0	3	6	5.4	10.8	55%	.182	1.00	1.80	2.49	0.2
2011	*TBA*	*MLB*	*24*	*9*	*7*	*0*	*32*	*21*	*97^1*	*92*	*9*	*48*	*94*	*4.5*	*8.7*	*44%*	*.309*	*1.44*	*4.16*	*4.52*	*1.8*

After an uneven 2009 return from Tommy John surgery, McGee restored his top-prospect status with a healthy season and reached the majors, thanks to a role change. After starting for the first four months of the season at Montgomery, he shifted to the Durham bullpen, dominated Triple-A hitters, and earned a brief cup of coffee with the Rays. McGee has rare velocity for a southpaw, with a 92-95-mph, late-action fastball that he can pump up to 97 as a reliever. His secondary stuff—a power curve and a changeup—lack polish at this point, and his violent delivery occasionally compromises his command. Given the Rays' plethora of young pitchers, McGee's immediate future lies in the bullpen; he could figure in the Rays' late-game plan at some point in 2011.

Matthew Moore

Born: **6/18/1989** Age: **22**
Bats: L Throws: L Height: **6' 2"** Weight: **205**
Breakout: **11%** Improve: **20%** Collapse: **9%**
Attrition: **11%** MLB: **36%**

Comparables:
Henry Rodriguez, Billy McCool, Jose Deleon (59)

YEAR	TEAM	LVL	AGE	W	L	SV	G	GS	IP	H	HR	BB	SO	EqBB9	EqSO9	GB%	BABIP	WHIP	ERA	FRA	WARP
2008	PRI	Rk	19	2	2	0	12	12	54^{1}	30	0	19	77	3.1	12.8	64%	.248	0.98	1.66	3.71	1.4
2009	BGR	A	20	8	5	0	26	26	123	86	6	70	176	5.1	12.9	48%	.303	1.32	3.15	3.41	2.9
2010	PCH	A+	21	6	11	0	26	26	144^{2}	109	7	61	208	3.8	13.0	46%	.326	1.23	3.36	3.29	4.0
2011	*TBA*	*MLB*	*22*	*6*	*5*	*0*	*16*	*16*	83^{2}	*68*	*8*	*55*	*96*	*5.9*	*10.3*	*45%*	*.298*	*1.48*	*4.08*	*4.44*	*1.5*

Stop us if you've heard this one: Moore is a Rays pitching prospect with the potential to be a front-of-the-rotation starter. For the second straight season, the 2007 eighth-rounder from New Mexico started slowly due to difficulty repeating his delivery; he carried a 6.62 ERA and a 2.2 K/BB ratio through his first 11 starts before tweaks to his mechanics and grip helped him recover his dominant form. From June 8 through the end of the regular season, he was almost untouchable (1.39 ERA, 5.0 K/BB, 5.1 H/9). He led the entire minors in strikeouts for the second consecutive season and cut his walk rate by more than 33 percent; *Baseball America* anointed him the Florida State League's top prospect. Moore's 92-96 mph heater and power curve are both outstanding, and his changeup could be a plus pitch with a bit of polish. He'll start the year in Double-A.

Jeff Niemann

Born: **2/28/1983** Age: **28**
Bats: R Throws: R Height: **6' 9"** Weight: **280**
Breakout: **4%** Improve: **13%** Collapse: **5%**
Attrition: **13%** MLB: **23%**

Comparables:
Boof Bonser, Jason Jennings, Carlos Zambrano (63)

YEAR	TEAM	LVL	AGE	W	L	SV	G	GS	IP	H	HR	BB	SO	EqBB9	EqSO9	GB%	BABIP	WHIP	ERA	FRA	WARP
2008	DUR	AAA	25	9	5	0	24	24	133	101	15	50	128	3.4	8.7	48%	.246	1.17	3.59	4.85	2.2
2008	TBA	MLB	25	2	2	0	5	2	16	18	3	8	14	4.5	7.9	47%	.300	1.69	5.06	5.87	-0.1
2009	TBA	MLB	26	13	6	0	31	30	180^{2}	185	17	59	125	2.9	6.2	42%	.301	1.40	3.94	3.96	3.8
2010	TBA	MLB	27	12	8	0	30	29	174^{1}	159	25	61	131	3.1	6.8	45%	.263	1.30	4.39	4.92	0.6
2011	*TBA*	*MLB*	*28*	*10*	*8*	*0*	*26*	*26*	*150*	*140*	*18*	*58*	*116*	*3.5*	*6.9*	*45%*	*.281*	*1.32*	*3.94*	*4.28*	*2.6*

After establishing himself as a viable major-league starter in 2009, Niemann got off to a strong start in 2010, riding a 3.12 ERA into early August, thanks to low BABIP and walk rates (.252 and 2.7 per nine, respectively). Alas, a shoulder strain cost him three weeks, and he was out of rhythm when he returned, rocked for a 9.82 ERA in seven starts, with both his BABIP and his walk rates rising enough (.320 and 4.6) to confirm that he was out of whack. The constant across those splits was an inflated homer rate; he went from having the league's seventh-best figure in 2009 to its fifth-worst in 2010, joining three other members of the Rays' rotation in the bottom 10. Given that his ground-ball-to-fly-ball ratio actually improved, it's tough to get too bent out of shape; he's the same solid midrotation guy he was coming into the year.

David Price

Born: **8/26/1985** Age: **25**
Bats: L Throws: L Height: **6' 6"** Weight: **225**
Breakout: **26%** Improve: **61%** Collapse: **12%**
Attrition: **15%** MLB: **95%**

Comparables:
Matt Cain, Felix Hernandez, Ubaldo Jimenez (65)

YEAR	TEAM	LVL	AGE	W	L	SV	G	GS	IP	H	HR	BB	SO	EqBB9	EqSO9	GB%	BABIP	WHIP	ERA	FRA	WARP
2008	VRO	A+	22	4	0	0	6	6	34^{2}	28	0	7	37	1.8	9.6	50%	.311	1.01	1.82	1.45	1.9
2008	MNT	AA	22	7	0	0	9	9	57	42	7	16	55	2.5	8.7	58%	.246	1.09	1.89	2.86	2.0
2008	DUR	AAA	22	2	1	0	6	6	29	32	1	13	32	4.0	9.9	54%	.378	1.59	4.03	2.58	1.2
2008	TBA	MLB	22	0	0	0	5	1	14	9	1	4	12	2.6	7.7	53%	.205	1.00	1.93	4.00	0.2
2009	DUR	AAA	23	1	4	0	8	8	34^{1}	28	5	18	35	4.7	9.2	45%	.261	1.37	3.94	5.05	0.4
2009	TBA	MLB	23	10	7	0	23	23	128^{1}	119	17	54	102	3.8	7.2	43%	.268	1.38	4.42	5.74	0.3
2010	TBA	MLB	24	19	6	0	32	31	208^{2}	170	15	79	188	3.4	8.1	45%	.270	1.22	2.72	3.50	4.1
2011	*TBA*	*MLB*	*25*	*12*	*8*	*0*	*28*	*28*	*167*	*145*	*17*	*69*	*147*	*3.7*	*7.9*	*46%*	*.278*	*1.27*	*3.46*	*3.76*	*4.0*

In his first full major-league season, Price advanced leaps and bounds beyond his rookie year, living up to the hype that had made him one of the game's top prospects and establishing himself as one of the league's top lefty starters. With his once-vaunted slider having fizzled in 2009, he broke out a new curveball as his breaking pitch of choice, and he grew more efficient with his pitches and with missing more bats. Integrating a two-seam fastball into his arsenal, he boosted his K/BB ratio, cut his homer rate in half, and wound up third in the league in ERA and fifth in hit rate. He received his due from the AL Cy Young voters, finishing second to Felix Hernandez, and it is not difficult to believe that he'll win his own hardware one of these days.

Chad Qualls

Born: **8/17/1978** Age: **32**
Bats: R Throws: R Height: **6' 5"** Weight: **220**
Breakout: **11%** Improve: **27%** Collapse: **18%**
Attrition: **13%** MLB: **56%**

Comparables:
Jerry Spradlin, Shawn Camp, Chris Capuano (71)

YEAR	TEAM	LVL	AGE	W	L	SV	G	GS	IP	H	HR	BB	SO	EqBB9	EqSO9	GB%	BABIP	WHIP	ERA	FRA	WARP
2008	ARI	MLB	29	4	8	9	77	0	73^{2}	61	4	18	71	2.2	8.7	59%	.279	1.11	2.81	3.85	1.0
2009	ARI	MLB	30	2	2	24	51	0	52	53	5	7	45	1.2	7.8	60%	.304	1.19	3.63	4.17	0.3
2010	ARI	MLB	31	1	4	12	43	0	38	61	5	15	34	3.6	8.1	57%	.415	2.03	8.29	7.84	-1.1
2010	TBA	MLB	31	2	0	0	27	0	21	24	2	6	15	2.6	6.4	55%	.328	1.48	5.57	6.26	-0.3
2011	*SDN*	*MLB*	*32*	*4*	*2*	*12*	*79*	*0*	*71*	*72*	*7*	*22*	*60*	*2.7*	*7.5*	*51%*	*.311*	*1.30*	*3.81*	*4.14*	*0.1*

In the wake of surgery to repair the dislocated left patella that prematurely ended his 2009 campaign, Qualls altered his mechanics and developed bad habits—collapsing his plant leg and falling off to the side of the mound—which caused his sinker to flatten out. He was pummeled so mercilessly in Arizona that he lost his closer job in mid-June, allowing the fantasy owners of the Chad Qualls Support Group to go their separate ways. Believing him a candidate to bounce back, the Rays traded for Qualls at the deadline, but most of his improvement could be passed off as simple regression to the mean. A free agent at this writing, he may revert to form given more time to heal, but it's equally possible that he's one more ex-semi-famous person on his way out of the majors.

Aneury Rodriguez

Born: **12/13/1987** Age: **23**
Bats: R Throws: R Height: **6' 3"** Weight: **180**
Breakout: **6%** Improve: **8%** Collapse: **1%**
Attrition: **6%** MLB: **10%**

Comparables:
Shairon Martis, Esmil Rogers, Troy Patton (77)

YEAR	TEAM	LVL	AGE	W	L	SV	G	GS	IP	H	HR	BB	SO	EqBB9	EqSO9	GB%	BABIP	WHIP	ERA	FRA	WARP
2008	MOD	A+	20	9	11	0	28	28	159	155	13	40	141	2.3	8.0	42%	.309	1.29	3.62	4.38	2.3
2009	MNT	AA	21	9	11	0	27	28	142	122	17	59	111	3.7	7.0	36%	.258	1.36	4.25	4.74	1.2
2010	DUR	AAA	22	6	5	0	27	17	113^{2}	104	10	49	94	3.9	7.5	35%	.281	1.37	3.80	5.91	0.3
2011	*HOU*	*MLB*	*23*	*7*	*10*	*0*	*24*	*24*	*125*	*137*	*19*	*60*	*85*	*4.3*	*6.1*	*39%*	*.300*	*1.56*	*5.29*	*5.75*	*0.5*

Acquired from the Rockies in the Jason Hammel deal, Rodriguez had to make a series of adjustments in 2009 to overcome a horrendous start and survive in Double-A; he did so and was nearly unhittable in the second half. His 2010 featured fewer and less-pronounced peaks and valleys; he held his own at Triple-A, but his stuff—an 88-94 mph fastball, a curve, and a changeup—hasn't really improved in two years and grades out as merely average. With quality pitching prospects out the wazoo, the Rays left him unprotected in the Rule 5 draft for the second year in a row. This time, he was taken by the Astros, and he has a good chance to stick with Houston as a long reliever.

James Shields

Born: **12/20/1981** Age: **29**
Bats: R Throws: R Height: **6' 4"** Weight: **214**
Breakout: **12%** Improve: **46%** Collapse: **18%**
Attrition: **2%** MLB: **94%**

Comparables:
Fergie Jenkins, Frank Viola, Dave Bush (68)

YEAR	TEAM	LVL	AGE	W	L	SV	G	GS	IP	H	HR	BB	SO	EqBB9	EqSO9	GB%	BABIP	WHIP	ERA	FRA	WARP
2008	TBA	MLB	26	14	8	0	33	33	215	208	24	40	160	1.7	6.7	47%	.287	1.21	3.56	4.11	3.5
2009	TBA	MLB	27	11	12	0	33	33	219^{2}	239	29	52	167	2.1	6.8	43%	.308	1.33	4.14	4.53	2.8
2010	TBA	MLB	28	13	15	0	34	33	203^{1}	246	34	51	187	2.3	8.3	42%	.341	1.49	5.13	4.61	1.5
2011	*TBA*	*MLB*	*29*	*13*	*10*	*0*	*33*	*33*	*210*	*215*	*28*	*50*	*171*	*2.1*	*7.3*	*44%*	*.304*	*1.26*	*4.02*	*4.36*	*3.1*

After three seasons as the Rays' top starter, Shields mysteriously morphed into a punching bag last year. Despite a career-best strikeout rate and the league's third-best strikeout-to-unintentional walk ratio (K/UIBB), he allowed more hits and homers than any other AL pitcher. Obviously, a BABIP that shot up 33 points had something to do with inflated ERA, but the underlying issue may have been pitch sequencing, specifically, too many first-pitch fastballs right down Broadway. Opponents hit .438/.439/.843 against Shields in the 125 plate appearances that ended after one pitch; his OPS in such circumstances ranked third among pitchers with at least 50 such PAs (behind only the odd couple of Blake Hawksworth and Tim Lincecum) and was well above the major-league average (.334/.340/.534). Nobody topped his 11 first-pitch homers allowed, and only Brad Bergesen allowed as many extra-base hits. Fortunately, that's a correctable problem, but the bigger question is whether Shields will tackle it with the Rays or elsewhere, given the eventual need to carve out a rotation spot for Jeremy Hellickson.

Andy Sonnanstine

Born: **3/18/1983** Age: **28**
Bats: L Throws: R Height: **6' 3"** Weight: **185**
Breakout: **13%** Improve: **46%** Collapse: **18%**
Attrition: **15%** MLB: **84%**

Comparables:
John Smiley, Pat Misch, Brian Burres (73)

YEAR	TEAM	LVL	AGE	W	L	SV	G	GS	IP	H	HR	BB	SO	EqBB9	EqSO9	GB%	BABIP	WHIP	ERA	FRA	WARP
2008	TBA	MLB	25	13	9	0	32	32	193^{1}	212	21	37	124	1.7	5.8	43%	.302	1.31	4.38	4.74	2.0
2009	DUR	AAA	26	5	3	0	9	9	57^{1}	68	4	9	36	1.4	5.7	37%	.330	1.36	4.40	3.84	1.2
2009	TBA	MLB	26	6	9	0	22	18	99^{2}	131	19	34	60	3.1	5.4	44%	.326	1.68	6.77	7.27	-1.2
2010	TBA	MLB	27	3	1	1	41	4	81	83	11	27	50	3.0	5.6	44%	.277	1.44	4.56	4.79	0.2
2011	*TBA*	*MLB*	*28*	*10*	*9*	*0*	*40*	*24*	*165^{1}*	*177*	*22*	*45*	*105*	*2.4*	*5.7*	*43%*	*.299*	*1.35*	*4.46*	*4.85*	*1.5*

The Rays' glut of high-upside arms has long since bumped Sonnanstine from the rotation, but he has carved out a niche as their utility pitcher, taking the occasional start when the injury bug bites, but mostly working in blowouts and extra-inning games. His 0.55 Leverage score was the second-lowest among those with at least 50 innings of relief work. His huge drop in ERA had more to do with regression on balls in play and his rate of homers allowed per fly ball; his SIERAs show that he was basically the same pitcher from 2009 to 2010. Given his unremarkable stuff, this appears to be his lot, but it certainly beats starting for the Pirates.

Rafael Soriano

Born: **12/19/1979** Age: **31**
Bats: **R** Throws: **R** Height: **6' 1"** Weight: **175**
Breakout: **20%** Improve: **46%** Collapse: **25%**
Attrition: **12%** MLB: **95%**

Comparables:
John Wetteland, Robb Nen, Jason Frasor (73)

YEAR	TEAM	LVL	AGE	W	L	SV	G	GS	IP	H	HR	BB	SO	EqBB9	EqSO9	GB%	BABIP	WHIP	ERA	FRA	WARP
2008	ATL	MLB	28	0	1	3	14	0	14	7	1	9	16	5.8	10.3	23%	.200	1.21	2.57	3.59	0.2
2009	ATL	MLB	29	1	6	27	77	0	75^{2}	53	6	27	102	3.2	12.1	33%	.275	1.07	2.97	3.09	1.1
2010	TBA	MLB	30	3	2	45	64	0	62^{1}	36	4	14	57	2.0	8.2	32%	.199	0.82	1.73	2.80	1.2
2011	*NYA*	*MLB*	*31*	*3*	*1*	*23*	*57*	*0*	*56*	*44*	*6*	*18*	*60*	*3.0*	*9.6*	*40%*	*.271*	*1.11*	*2.74*	*2.98*	*1.3*

After surprising the Braves by accepting arbitration after the 2009 season, Soriano wound up salary-dumped on Tampa Bay in a trade for Jesse Chavez. Soriano more than earned his keep for the Rays, dominating AL hitters and finishing with the league's second-highest WXRL and the majors' second-lowest BABIP and fifth-lowest hit rate among pitchers with at least 50 innings pitched; he also led the AL in saves. While his strikeout rate dropped significantly, his K/BB ratio actually improved, and the extra efficiency didn't hurt, either. His performance priced him out of the Rays' range, and over Brian Cashman's protests, he landed a three-year contract with the Yankees that represented both a substantial raise and a reduction in status.

Alexander Torres

Born: **12/8/1987** Age: **23**
Bats: **L** Throws: **L** Height: **5' 10"** Weight: **175**
Breakout: **12%** Improve: **22%** Collapse: **4%**
Attrition: **5%** MLB: **30%**

Comparables:
Pete Richert, Rich Harden, Mike Paul (70)

YEAR	TEAM	LVL	AGE	W	L	SV	G	GS	IP	H	HR	BB	SO	EqBB9	EqSO9	GB%	BABIP	WHIP	ERA	FRA	WARP
2008	RCU	A+	20	3	2	0	10	10	53	52	1	29	62	4.9	10.5	54%	.370	1.58	3.91	3.51	1.1
2008	ANG	Rk	20	4	0	0	4	4	23^{1}	11	1	10	24	3.9	9.3	67%	.213	0.94	1.55	4.25	0.5
2009	RCU	A+	21	10	3	0	21	19	121^{1}	93	4	63	124	4.7	9.2	64%	.288	1.34	2.75	2.40	4.2
2009	ARK	AA	21	3	1	0	5	5	26	23	0	17	25	5.9	8.7	54%	.329	1.58	2.77	2.43	0.9
2010	MNT	AA	22	11	6	0	27	27	142^{2}	136	9	70	150	4.4	9.5	53%	.335	1.48	3.47	4.17	2.4
2011	*TBA*	*MLB*	*23*	*5*	*6*	*0*	*15*	*15*	79^{1}	*79*	*8*	*52*	*66*	*5.9*	*7.5*	*51%*	*.309*	*1.66*	*5.10*	*5.54*	*0.3*

Acquired in the Scott Kazmir trade, this undersized lefty from Venezuela gets excellent movement on his low-90s fastball and has two above-average secondary offerings (curve and changeup). His unorthodox delivery generates concerns, as he compromises his command by throwing across his body; he led the Southern League in walks and strikeouts and averaged just 5.3 innings per start due to high pitch counts. Still, a high ground-ball rate and the ensuing double plays helped to erase some of those baserunners. His upside is that of a second starter, though if he can't cut the walks, he may wind up as a late-inning reliever. Either way, he'll take the next step at Durham.

Dan Wheeler

Born: **12/10/1977** Age: **33**
Bats: **R** Throws: **R** Height: **6' 3"** Weight: **222**
Breakout: **18%** Improve: **30%** Collapse: **29%**
Attrition: **9%** MLB: **71%**

Comparables:
Bobby Seay, John Candelaria, Doug Brocail (67)

YEAR	TEAM	LVL	AGE	W	L	SV	G	GS	IP	H	HR	BB	SO	EqBB9	EqSO9	GB%	BABIP	WHIP	ERA	FRA	WARP
2008	TBA	MLB	30	5	6	13	70	0	66^{1}	44	10	22	53	3.0	7.2	29%	.190	1.00	3.12	5.25	-0.1
2009	TBA	MLB	31	4	5	2	69	0	57^{2}	41	11	9	45	1.4	7.0	33%	.195	0.87	3.59	5.15	0.0
2010	TBA	MLB	32	2	4	3	64	0	48^{1}	36	7	16	46	3.0	8.6	36%	.232	1.10	3.35	3.90	0.6
2011	*BOS*	*MLB*	*33*	*4*	*2*	*5*	*75*	*0*	63^{1}	*55*	*9*	*20*	*56*	*2.8*	*7.9*	*40%*	*.270*	*1.19*	*3.46*	*3.76*	*0.8*

Either Wheeler ran over Joe Maddon's dog or the Rays' skipper grew wary of the pitcher's extreme fly-ball tendencies, because his innings total was his lowest in eight years despite full health, and his Leverage score (1.16) was much lower than at any other time during his second go-round in Tampa Bay. Obviously, the arrivals of Rafael Soriano, Joaquin Benoit, and even grounder-friendly Chad Qualls (1.27 LEV) had something to do with Wheeler's reduced time in the spotlight, but it was surprising nonetheless. Speaking of leverage, while Wheeler's Type-A free-agent status could have been expected to rob him of his, the Red Sox willingly surrendered their second-round pick (the Rays also nabbed the Sox's first-rounder when Boston signed Crawford) to ink him to a one-year, $3 million deal.

LINEOUTS

HITTERS

PLAYER	TEAM	LVL	AGE	PA	R	2B	3B	HR	RBI	BB	SO	SB-CS	AVG/OBP/SLG	TAv	BABIP	BRR	FRAA	WARP
C L. Bailey	RAY	Rk	19	161	18	8	0	5	14	17	47	0-0	.182/.298/.350	.246	.233	0.1	C 2	0.4
DH H. Blalock*	DUR	AAA	29	121	18	5	0	4	24	10	19	2-0	.349/.405/.505	.314	.391	0.7	3B -1	1.0
	TBA	MLB	29	69	8	3	0	1	7	6	15	1-1	.254/.319/.349	.249	.319	0.0	3B 0, 1B 0	0.0
2B T. Bortnick	BGR	A	22	487	72	32	2	8	45	63	67	39-14	.303/.408/.451	.317	.342	3.1	2B -3, SS 1	4.1
CF T. Glaesmann	PRI	Rk	19	261	41	17	5	4	24	13	70	13-6	.233/.297/.398	.242	.309	2.3	CF -3, RF -2	0.3
UT E. Johnson#	DUR	AAA	26	481	72	24	5	11	56	37	92	30-6	.319/.375/.475	.277	.370	3.5	SS -1, LF 0	2.8
C J. Lobaton#	DUR	AAA	25	271	26	11	0	7	33	27	52	1-0	.261/.337/.394	.251	.304	0.0	C -1	0.8
C J. O'Conner	RAY	Rk	18	187	18	13	0	3	29	18	46	1-0	.211/.301/.348	.238	.267	0.0	C 0	0.1
OF F. Perez	DUR	AAA	27	426	46	11	3	4	32	29	97	24-7	.223/.280/.299	.205	.279	0.0	RF -3, LF 4	-1.4
RF B. Reynolds	HUD	A-	21	232	22	17	4	2	28	12	65	12-2	.223/.290/.370	.242	.310	0.0	RF -4	-0.5
RF J. Sale*	DNP	—	19	—	—	—	—	—	—	—	—	—	—	—	—	—	—	—
RF D. Vettleson*	DNP	—	19	—	—	—	—	—	—	—	—	—	—	—	—	—	—	—

Luke Bailey was considered one of the top catching prospects in the 2009 draft before Tommy John surgery dropped him down to the fourth round. Despite significant contact woes, he showed good power and threw out 31 percent of would-be thieves in his pro debut. So desperate were Rays fans to be rid of the scourge of Pat Burrell that they all but picketed the Trop with "Free **Hank Blalock**" signs when he was tearing up Triple-A pitching early in the season. When they finally got their wish just before Blalock could exercise a May 15 opt-out, they found out that his bat was no more lively than that of the man he replaced. He was released to the stifled yawns of 29 other teams. A 16th-round pick in 2009 out of Coastal Carolina University, **Tyler Bortnick** is more blue-collar than blue-chip, a grinder who has put up strong numbers in his first two professional seasons. In 2010, he moved back to his college position of second base after holding his own at shortstop during his pro debut. A third-round pick in 2009, **Todd Glaesmann** offers five-tool potential, but aside from showing off the organization's best outfield arm, he has struggled to convert those tools into skills thus far in the pros. His long swing has resulted in contact woes, but scouts still think highly of him because of a frame that projects to supply plenty of power. **Elliot Johnson**, whose spring 2008 brawl-triggering slide against the Yankees marked a symbolic turning point for his franchise, is organizational depth, not a prospect. Winning International League MVP honors at Durham was enough to restore him to the 40-man roster in November, preventing him from becoming a free agent. On a team whose returning catchers threw out just 20 percent of opposing base thieves, **Jose Lobaton**'s 32 percent kill rate starts to look pretty good. He's a switch-hitter with some patience and a bit of pop, though it's his defensive skills that the Rays most need. **Justin O'Conner** emerged as the top high-school catcher in the 2010 draft despite not converting to the position until his senior year. The Rays tabbed him with the 31st pick, paid $1.025 million to sign him away from his commitment to Arkansas, and enjoyed the fact that he signed early and made a substantial professional debut, but except for an absolute cannon of an arm, he's still very raw. After bookending a lost 2009 with a dislocated left wrist and labrum surgery in his nonthrowing shoulder, the Rays' poet laureate **Fernando Perez** struggled with shoulder pain in 2010, leading to awful numbers; at least his second-half performance (.272/.327/.340) was a decided improvement on his first (.206/.262/.284). He'll try to avoid backsliding with the Cubs this season. A cousin of Robinson Cano, **Burt Reynolds** is no kind of prospect, but in sharing a name with America's leading box-office star from 1978 to 1982, he provides plenty of entertaining double-takes with every at-bat. **Josh Sale** was hailed as the top prep power hitter in the 2010 draft. The Rays chose him with the 17th pick and closed the deal with a $1.62 million bonus, $261,000 over slot. Scouts love Sale's power, outstanding bat speed, and command of the strike zone and believe he will correct minor flaws in his swing. His defensive skills will eventually point him to left field or first base, but there's little doubt that he can reach the high offensive bar at either position. A supplemental first-rounder taken with the 42nd pick of the 2010 draft and signed to an $845,000 bonus, **Drew Vettleson** is a Seattle-area prepster who gained notoriety as a switch-pitcher in high school. His hitting is what impressed pro scouts, though; he has a quiet swing, great bat speed, plus raw power and an advanced approach at the plate, particularly for a player coming from a colder climate that permits less in-game experience. He's a center fielder now, but below-average speed and an above-average arm point him toward a future in right field.

PITCHERS

PLAYER	TEAM	LVL	AGE	W	L	SV	IP	H	HR	BB	SO	EqBB9	EqSO9	GB%	BABIP	WHIP	ERA	FRA	WARP
D. De La Rosa	MNT	AA	27	9	3	4	73	66	3	26	75	3.2	9.2	54%	.321	1.27	1.97	2.41	2.0
S. Dyer	BGR	A	22	2	3	0	42	34	1	4	34	0.9	7.3	55%	.273	1.05	1.71	2.62	1.4
—	PCH	A+	22	5	8	0	93^2	91	4	24	75	2.3	7.2	56%	.303	1.33	3.17	3.71	1.9
R. Ortiz	BUF	AAA	37	2	3	0	48	43	1	8	32	1.5	6.0	50%	.280	1.10	3.38	3.76	1.3
—	LAN	MLB	37	1	2	0	30	33	5	16	21	4.8	6.3	48%	.301	1.63	6.30	5.36	-0.1
Z. Quate	PCH	A+	22	2	2	25	72^1	51	2	18	90	2.2	11.2	44%	.290	0.97	1.49	1.98	2.4
S. Shuman	BGR	A	22	4	5	14	71^2	50	5	38	111	4.8	14.0	44%	.315	1.28	3.01	3.43	1.2
R. Swindle*	DUR	AAA	26	2	4	2	55	45	6	10	55	1.6	9.0	28%	.271	1.00	2.45	2.85	1.4
D. Thayer	DUR	AAA	29	4	1	3	60	68	3	25	55	3.8	8.3	49%	.349	1.62	3.45	4.07	0.7
—	TBA	MLB	29	0	0	0	2	7	1	0	2	0.0	9.0	45%	.600	3.50	27.00	16.66	-0.2
J. Thompson	HUD	A-	20	2	1	0	40	28	0	6	33	1.4	7.4	46%	.252	0.88	1.35	2.08	1.7

One of the biggest first-round busts in history, ex-shortstop/problem drinker **Matt Bush** drifted to the Rays, where he showed mid-90s velocity in a handful of outings despite battling elbow soreness; his electric arm and off-field progress were enough for the team to protect him on the 40-man roster. ⊘ The Rays signed imposing six-foot-six righty **Dane De La Rosa** after stints in three indie leagues over the past three seasons. A ground-baller with a fastball that can reach 94 and a plus curve, he pitched well enough out of the Montgomery bullpen to make the 40-man roster. ⊘ A sixth-round pick in 2008 out of a Colorado junior college, **Shane Dyer** rebounded from a rough 2009. He has a low-90s fastball and a knuckle-curve that he sometimes relies upon too much; his unorthodox delivery has scouts viewing him as a future reliever. ⊘ Having not pitched in the bigs since 2007 and having last posted an ERA below 5.00 in 2004, **Ramon Ortiz** shocked the world by breaking camp with the Dodgers as one of two Zombie Ortizes (Russ being the other). He lasted until mid-May, then bounced through the Mets' and Rays' organizations in search of fresh brains for nourishment. ⊘ A 14th-round pick in 2009 out of Appalachian State, **Zach Quate** has dominated two levels as a closer; he has good command of a plus slider and an average fastball, both delivered from a three-quarters arm angle. ⊘ **Scott Shuman**, a 19th-round pick out of Auburn, had the Midwest League's highest strikeout rate coming out of the bullpen, thanks to mid- to upper-90s velocity and a plus slider. ⊘ Lefty reliever **R. J. Swindle** is a well-traveled junkballer with a sidearm delivery, a low- to mid-80s fastball, and most famously a 55-mph bloop curve. He has held Triple-A lefties to a .200/.270/.276 line over the past three years and could find a spot in the Rays' bullpen in the wake of J. P. Howell's injury. ⊘ After becoming a mustachioed cult hero in 2009, **Dale Thayer** shaved his facial hair and didn't have as strong a season in 2010, either at Durham or in Tampa Bay, where he was clobbered in his lone appearance. Whether or not the minor-league free agent returns to the Rays, he needs to adorn his upper lip to have any chance at success. ⊘ The Rays' second-round pick in the 2010 draft, **Jake Thompson** is a true power arm with a mid-90s fastball and a hard slider; after an up-and-down career at Long Beach State, he dominated the New York-Penn League, thanks to improved mechanics.

MANAGER: JOE MADDON

YEAR	TEAM	W-L	Pythag +/-	Avg PC	100+ P	120+ P	QS	BQS	REL	REL w Zero R	IBB	Subs	PH	PH Avg	PH HR	SB2	CS2	SB3	CS3	SAC Att	SAC %	POS SAC	Squeeze	Swing	In Play
2008	TBA	97-65	5	96.0	71	0	77	2	448	289	29	50	131	.186	3	113	38	28	10	41	56.1%	20	1	135	94
2009	TBA	84-78	-2	99.4	81	1	72	7	508	323	21	48	138	.160	7	167	49	26	11	45	55.6%	24	9	141	101
2010	TBA	96-66	-2	99.1	91	2	91	5	491	343	34	45	173	.245	5	147	39	25	7	68	57.4%	38	9	152	120

Maddon continues to carve a niche as one of the majors' best and most interesting managers, comfortable with progressive thought yet grounded in traditionalism, renowned both for his rapport with players and for his facility in adhering to the front office's occasionally unorthodox ways. In 2010, he coaxed an offense that ranked 13th in batting average to the league's third-highest run total—from a team playing in a pitchers' park, no less—because of his appreciation of the virtues of OBP. He experimented with catcher John Jaso in the leadoff role despite the backstop's lack of speed, and worked a decent season out of the displaced B. J. Upton. He batted the center fielder lower in the lineup despite some ups and downs, reaping the benefits of Upton's rebound against lefties after an off year. Maddon took advantage of the versatility of Ben Zobrist and Sean Rodriguez to work around minor injuries and slumps elsewhere in the lineup, led the league in pinch-hitters by a wide margin

(173, batting .245/.343/.422), and, along the way, managed to secure the platoon advantage for his hitters 63.4 percent of the time, the league's second-highest clip. He didn't overdo one-run strategies, yet the Rays ranked second in the league in stolen-base opportunities and third in success rate. The presence of Rafael Soriano allowed him to adhere to a traditional closer model with regard to his bullpen, which didn't stop his relief corps from leading the league in WXRL and placing three relievers in the individual top 10. He'll be faced with a very different bullpen in 2011, and indeed a very different team, but his flexibility and patience should continue to work in the Rays' favor.

Texas Rangers

An idea can turn to dust or magic,
depending on the talent that rubs against it.
—WILLIAM BERNBACH

On the evening of October 22, 2010, some 51,404 fans were on their feet and in full voice as Neftali Feliz delivered the finishing blow to the New York Yankees, striking out Alex Rodriguez, the former face of the Rangers' franchise, and sending Texas to its first World Series. Earlier that night, the team of the moment had stood tied with the team of history, locked 1-1 heading into the bottom of the fifth inning in Game Six of the American League Championship Series. With two on and two out, Vladimir Guerrero stepped to the plate and delivered one of the biggest hits in Rangers history, rocketing a double to deep center field, scoring two runs and setting the stage for a celebration that was almost 40 years in the making. A few innings later, the Rangers were completely engulfed by the ecstasy of the moment, regressing to the sandlots and Little League parks where it all started. The team was headed to the biggest stage under the brightest lights, and it was doing so on the back of the youngest general manager ever to lead a team to the World Series, Jon Daniels.

RANGERS PROSPECTUS

2010 W-L: 90-72, 1st in AL West

Pythag	.564	8th
RS/G	4.9	5th
RA/G	4.2	20th
TAv	.272	12th
BRR	-4.8	24th
FRA	4.38	13th
DER	10.3	7th
DL	868	24th
B-Age	28.3	9th
P-Age	27.8	13th
Salary	$55.3	28th
M$/MW	$1.09	2nd

Ballpark: Rangers Ballpark in Arlington (3-yr. PF: 105). It's not the humidity, it's the heat *and* the humidity

2010: Rangers ride well-rounded roster to first World Series

2011: Texas loses Lee, but stays strong after tightening its Beltre

Action Items: Keep trying to get starters to hang in, a la Ryan, stop Hamlet-ing on about Feliz's career path

Five years earlier, on October 4, 2005, Jon Daniels had become the youngest general manager in baseball history, occupying the office at age 28. At the time of his ascension, Daniels was younger than most of the players on the roster, and 21 years junior to gritty manager Buck Showalter. Armed with an Ivy League education rather than a robust résumé of on-field experiences, he might have been a new face for the old crowd, but the plan his front office followed wasn't based on a gimmick or an "exploitable market inefficiency"; rather, it was built on the same simple foundation that had been supported championship teams for a century. Daniels' front office would construct a team that was as strong on the farm as it was in the major leagues; a team that featured power arms that could miss bats, and power bats that could frustrate opposing arms; a team that could maintain positive momentum, regardless of payroll flexibility; a team that would be built for a decade rather than a day: the Texas Rangers wanted to build a dynasty.

Every Rangers fan is painfully aware of some of the early missteps taken by the Daniels regime, most notably trading away building blocks like Adrian Gonzalez and John Danks for pieces that didn't amount to much. Accepting of their early stumbles and looking to get back to the plan, the Rangers began to invest heavily in the Latin American market and in the amateur draft, attempting to acquire superstar-level talent before it reached superstar-level prices. Under the skillful eye of A. J. Preller, senior director of player personnel and Daniels' college buddy, the international reach of the Rangers expanded, with more resources being devoted to the talent-rich environments of the Dominican Republic and Venezuela. However, signing players in the international market was just one component of the overall international equation. Thanks to the scouting department's due diligence, the club was able to target high-ceiling Latin American players as trade bounty, landing such franchise heavyweights as Elvis Andrus and Neftali Feliz from the Braves and future pieces like Engel Beltre from the Red Sox. In addition to the successful trade acquisitions, the Rangers have used their international intuition to sign high-ceiling talent like

Martin Perez, Jurickson Profar, Wilmer Font, and Luis Sardinas, thus ensuring that their farm system stays well fertilized and their flag remains firmly planted in foreign markets.

With an equally strong amateur scouting team in place, the Rangers continued to target high-ceiling domestic talent, often looking to the high-school ranks: since 2006, they have selected five prep arms in the first round. With a surplus of early picks in 2007, the Rangers made huge strides in the farm overhaul, drafting six players who would have direct ties to the 2010 American League championship team, including their Game Four starter, starting first baseman, and defrocked center fielder Julio Borbon, plus first-round picks Michael Main and Blake Beavan, who were included in the packages used to acquire Cliff Lee and Bengie Molina, respectively. After their first two seasons at the helm, the Daniels collective might have produced less-than-stellar results at the major-league level, but they had begun to acquire the foundation for future success.

The pieces were starting to accumulate, but the team still needed an identity. Before the start of the 2008 season, baseball legend Nolan Ryan was installed as team president. While this move was correctly perceived as the opening gambit in Ryan's eventual push for an ownership stake, having him on board gave the team instant credibility after the upstart GM had failed to improve the major-league squad. Ryan's presence turned out to be more than just a placative gesture to the fan-base. He helped create a developmental philosophy that would start in the majors and trickle down to the lowest levels of the professional ladder. His immediate influence was reflected in an uptick in expected pitcher workloads and an improvement in the players' overall conditioning. A directive from the "Express" carried weight, and players were eager to follow Ryan's edicts and to seek his advice and one-on-one instruction whenever it was available. The man who personified peak sustainability as a player was now instructing a team being constructed with peak franchise sustainability in mind. The Rangers had taken another step toward their ultimate goal, but before they could enjoy the forward momentum, they had to brace themselves for a tumultuous 15 months of media speculation and legal battles over the team's controlling interest.

On May 27, 2009, Rangers owner Tom Hicks confirmed that he would be open to selling a majority stake in the team he had purchased for $250 million in 1998. After years of small-market-style ownership (the Rangers have had Opening Day payrolls under $70 million in every season since 2004)—years that were preceded by years of reckless spending on players like Rodriguez—Rangers fans were greeted with the news they had been waiting a decade to hear. Unfortunately, the ownership situation would cast a shadow over the Rangers' baseball operations for the better part of two seasons and overshadow the improving products on the field and in the front office. During a period when the Rangers were suffocating under the weight of their owner's financial quagmire, the front office found a way to sign free agents Rich Harden and Vladimir Guerrero to team-friendly deals and make key in-season trades for top-of-the-rotation starter Lee and ALCS Game Four hero Molina.

The struggle finally came to a close on August 12, 2010, when baseball owners unanimously voted to approve the sale of the Rangers to the Chuck Greenberg/Nolan Ryan–led group, which had won the right to buy the team on August 5, agreeing to pay approximately $590 million ($385 million in cash, and over $200 million in existing debt). A complete accounting of the team's ownership difficulties could reach a Pynchonesque word count, but Rangers fans can rejoice in knowing that the 2010 team will be remembered for its on-field triumphs, rather than its off-field drama, and that a fresh approach to ownership should afford the club an opportunity to shed its small-market budget and obtain large-market talent.

From jump street, the Rangers' big off-season free-agent acquisition, Rich Harden, proved to be more DeLoise than Depp, failing to find any form of mechanical consistency, offering replacement-level production when the team was expecting top-of-the-rotation talent. Opening Day starter Scott Feldman was equally inept, forcing the Rangers to rely on the talents of the unproven members of the rotation, most notably ex-Hiroshima Carp Colby Lewis and converted reliever C. J. Wilson, to keep them in the American League West race. Rising to the challenge, the team gelled as Wilson and Lewis, along with Tommy Hunter, provided cover-to-cover stability, keeping the Rangers in the hunt for the pennant and helping them pull away from the pack by August.

Of course, while the success of Lewis, Wilson, Hunter, and subsequently Lee got the attention, the backbone of the pitching skeleton lived in the shadows; despite the team's intention to build a stable of rotation workhorses, the Rangers' bullpen logged more innings than that of any other American League team, yet had the highest percentage of runners stranded and the second-lowest bullpen ERA in the league. Anchored by 2010 Rookie of the Year Neftali Feliz and mentored by veteran sage Darren Oliver, who was drafted by Texas one month after Feliz was born, the relief corps stood its ground despite the workload, relying on a combination of electricity, youth, finesse, and craftiness to bridge the gap between the starters and the win column.

In keeping with Texas tradition, the team's offensive firepower proved to be a formidable for opposing pitching staffs, as the Rangers led the majors in team batting average and finished in the top five in most other offensive categories. However, the Rangers often relied on small-ball tactics, leading the American League in sacrifice hits. Despite the questionable offensive philosophies deployed by manager

Ron Washington, the middle of the Rangers' batting order was still a force to be reckoned with, led by 2010 American League Most Valuable Player Josh Hamilton, who silenced all his doubters and finally lived up to his nearly boundless potential, and the trio of righties (Guerrero, Nelson Cruz, and Ian Kinsler) that lined the order with impact production. The only persistent hole was catcher, caused by the failure of several prospects; a desperate lunge for Matt Treanor and the subsequent fading Molina patched the position to a degree that doesn't quite deserve to be called adequacy.

Armed with a well-rounded team built to excel in all phases of the game, the Rangers marched into the postseason with a certain ambivalence to the pressures associated with the stage. Not only did the Rangers get to sample the tastes of post-season success, but they proved to the fanbase what the entire organization already believed: that the Rangers were, perhaps for the first time in their tortured organizational history, seriously going about the task of trying to win a championship.

An encore will not be easy. The 2010 Texas Rangers were propelled by upper-percentile performances from players like Lewis, Wilson, and Hamilton, and the unexpected rookie production from prospects like Mitch Moreland, Alexi Ogando, and Michael Kirkman. While it's certainly not a given that the aforementioned players will experience statistical regressions in 2011, it is rather optimistic to assume across-the-board consistency going forward. Consistency in baseball starts and ends with adjustment—how players alter their approach after their current approach is exploited or marginalized by the skill set of another player or team.

On the pitching front, the Rangers are ahead of the adjustment curve, even with the loss of Lee, thanks to the sharp mind and even sharper mustache of pitching coach, Mike Maddux, known for espousing the virtues of efficiency and intelligence over the more cavalier "grip it and rip it" philosophies of some pitching coaches. On the other side of the coin, the Rangers will be welcoming a new hitting coach, Thad Bosley, while saying good-bye to the booming presence of new Pirate manager, Clint Hurdle, a coach who had instant credibility with the players and staff and helped Hamilton make the mechanical adjustment that allowed him to fully exploit his skills. Bosley, a product of the Oakland Athletics' coaching system, hasn't worked as major-league coach since early 2003, and he spent the 2010 season coaching at Southwestern College, an evangelical Christian school in Phoenix. It remains to be seen if Bosley can command the same level of respect as Hurdle.

Regardless of his work history, his friendship with Ron Washington, or the offensive philosophy he decides to implement, Bosley will have his hands full. On the surface, the Rangers look like a team that could have some offensive concerns going into 2011: Hamilton isn't likely to hit .359 again, and Kinsler will turn 29 years old during the season and has been injury-prone. Cruz will turn 31 during the season and has yet to play more than 130 games in a season. Michael Young looked as if he needed Geritol in the second half of 2010. The offensive black hole at catcher isn't likely to improve much even with the addition of Yorvit Torrealba, and the farm system lacks the high-impact minor-league personnel ready to augment the roster.

An African proverb says that tomorrow belongs to the people who prepare for it today. From 2005 until 2010, the Rangers prepared and finally earned nearly the best of all tomorrows. Now it's a new day, and preparation must resume. Daniels and company have done a good enough job that there are surely more tomorrows coming, but it is not certain if the next one that belongs to the Rangers will arrive in 2011.

HITTERS

Elvis Andrus **SS**

Born: **8/26/1988** Age: **22**
Bats: R Throws: R Height: **6' 0"** Weight: **200**
Breakout: **3%** Improve: **31%** Collapse: **0%**
Attrition: **10%** MLB: **56%**

Comparables:
Roberto Alomar, Alcides Escobar, Pete Rose (66)

YEAR	TEAM	LVL	AGE	PA	R	2B	3B	HR	RBI	BB	SO	SB	CS	AVG/OBP/SLG	TAv	BABIP	BRR	FRAA	WARP
2008	FRI	AA	19	535	82	19	2	4	65	38	91	54	16	.295/.348/.367	.253	.348	6.7	SS 27	4.9
2009	TEX	MLB	20	541	72	17	8	6	40	40	77	33	6	.267/.322/.373	.247	.296	4.4	SS 1	1.8
2010	TEX	MLB	21	674	88	15	3	0	35	64	96	32	15	.265/.334/.301	.242	.307	3.5	SS 3	1.9
2011	*TEX*	*MLB*	*22*	*593*	*63*	*21*	*4*	*4*	*49*	*48*	*94*	*34*	*10*	*.265/.322/.340*	*.239*	*.304*	*-0.1*	*SS 7*	*1.6*

Andrus is going to have a very long and very successful major-league career, but 2010 was a bit of a setback for the young Venezuelan, especially at the plate. Penciled in as the leadoff hitter from day one, Elvis looked the part in April and May, hitting for average and getting on base at a very high rate. As the year wore on, however, Andrus saw his walk rate decline, and his ability to square up on a pitch seemed to disappear; his second half at the dish was so poor that he only managed six extra-base hits, slugging an anemic .274. Failing to adjust to major-league pitching after it has adjusted to you shows up in the numbers, and looking at a 643 OPS isn't pleasant. But Andrus played most of his sophomore season at the "Love Me Tender" age of 21, and offensive development can take time. Just be patient.

Engel Beltre CF

Born: **11/1/1989** Age: **21**
Bats: **L** Throws: **L** Height: **6' 2"** Weight: **180**
Breakout: **2%** Improve: **12%** Collapse: **1%**
Attrition: **6%** MLB: **16%**

Comparables:
Alcides Escobar, Rocco Baldelli, Rick Manning (70)

YEAR	TEAM	LVL	AGE	PA	R	2B	3B	HR	RBI	BB	SO	SB	CS	AVG/OBP/SLG	TAv	BABIP	BRR	FRAA	WARP
2008	CLN	A	18	598	87	26	9	8	47	15	105	31	11	.283/.303/.403	.256	.328	-0.5	CF 12, LF 0	2.5
2009	BAK	A+	19	389	44	13	5	3	23	17	77	17	7	.227/.278/.317	.208	.277	5.0	CF 1	-0.3
2010	BAK	A+	20	291	38	11	4	5	35	11	34	10	7	.331/.376/.460	.304	.357	-1.1	CF 4	2.4
2010	FRI	AA	20	198	14	4	4	1	14	10	24	8	2	.254/.301/.337	.241	.281	-0.1	CF 10, LF 0	1.1
2011	*TEX*	*MLB*	*21*	*498*	*46*	*20*	*5*	*5*	*47*	*11*	*100*	*12*	*4*	*.234/.255/.330*	*.206*	*.277*	*-0.4*	*CF -7, LF 0*	*-2.0*

After suffering through a disappointing 2009 campaign that saw him experience an offensive regression so severe that even the most optimistic observers couldn't find developmental positives, five-tool center fielder Engel Beltre started to actualize his tools in 2010, taking major steps forward at the plate and reaching Double-A at age 20. The knock on Beltre continues to be his insatiable desire to swing the bat, something that makes his approach exploitable at the higher levels. As his hit tool continues to mature, with the power soon to follow, a more refined approach at the plate could be the difference between a once-promising prospect who tops out at Double-A and a solid-to-average major-league regular. If all goes according to the best-case scenario, that future could begin as early as 2012.

Andres Blanco 2B

Born: **4/11/1984** Age: **27**
Bats: **S** Throws: **R** Height: **5' 10"** Weight: **155**
Breakout: **2%** Improve: **17%** Collapse: **1%**
Attrition: **3%** MLB: **41%**

Comparables:
Melvin Dorta, Jeff Treadway, Wally Backman (77)

YEAR	TEAM	LVL	AGE	PA	R	2B	3B	HR	RBI	BB	SO	SB	CS	AVG/OBP/SLG	TAv	BABIP	BRR	FRAA	WARP
2008	IOW	AAA	24	330	30	8	2	1	36	15	31	9	3	.285/.318/.336	.218	.302	1.5	SS 2, 3B 1	0.4
2009	IOW	AAA	25	258	30	17	2	6	29	17	28	6	1	.304/.349/.474	.281	.314	2.7	SS 0, 3B 1	1.8
2009	CHN	MLB	25	138	15	8	0	1	12	8	14	0	2	.252/.290/.342	.215	.263	0.0	2B 1, SS 1	-0.1
2010	TEX	MLB	26	185	17	10	1	0	13	11	24	0	2	.277/.324/.349	.243	.313	-1.0	2B 4, SS 0	0.5
2011	*TEX*	*MLB*	*27*	*331*	*34*	*15*	*2*	*3*	*30*	*19*	*43*	*4*	*2*	*.257/.302/.346*	*.228*	*.282*	*-0.3*	*SS 1, 2B 1*	*0.2*

When an ankle injury put Ian Kinsler on the shelf during spring training, the Rangers looked for an in-house replacement—someone who could not only provide solid defense at second base, but also keep pitchers honest at the plate. Realizing that the in-house options were Esteban German and Joaquin Arias, the Rangers smartly acquired Andres Blanco from the Cubs. Known for his glove, Blanco didn't disappoint, forming a solid all-Venezuelan double-play team with Andrus and showing versatility by filling in at shortstop and third base. On offense, the switch-hitter started the season very slowly, struggling to make hard contact from both sides of the plate. After Kinsler's return, Blanco settled into his utility role and eventually found his stroke at the plate, hitting over .300 in the second half of the season. Blanco should be a solid-but-unspectacular utilityman going forward and, with his pre-arbitration price tag, an affordable player to have on the roster.

Julio Borbon CF

Born: **2/20/1986** Age: **25**
Bats: **L** Throws: **L** Height: **6' 0"** Weight: **195**
Breakout: **5%** Improve: **35%** Collapse: **7%**
Attrition: **28%** MLB: **62%**

Comparables:
Josh Anderson, Jacoby Ellsbury, Tony Gwynn (74)

YEAR	TEAM	LVL	AGE	PA	R	2B	3B	HR	RBI	BB	SO	SB	CS	AVG/OBP/SLG	TAv	BABIP	BRR	FRAA	WARP
2008	BAK	A+	22	314	47	20	0	2	36	15	30	36	7	.306/.344/.395	.269	.331	5.4	CF -1	1.6
2008	FRI	AA	22	280	40	12	2	5	22	14	32	17	11	.337/.371/.459	.300	.360	0.3	CF 5	2.7
2009	OKL	AAA	23	457	71	12	7	2	34	33	40	25	7	.307/.361/.386	.271	.328	7.4	CF 2, LF 0	2.6
2009	TEX	MLB	23	179	29	4	0	4	20	15	28	19	4	.312/.363/.414	.280	.344	0.3	LF 1, CF 0	0.8
2010	TEX	MLB	24	468	58	11	4	3	42	19	59	15	7	.276/.303/.340	.237	.307	3.6	CF 4, LF 0	0.9
2011	*TEX*	*MLB*	*25*	*571*	*62*	*21*	*4*	*6*	*54*	*31*	*77*	*29*	*9*	*.275/.312/.362*	*.240*	*.303*	*0.0*	*CF -1, LF 0*	*0.3*

Borbon's first full major-league season was a disappointment. He left his bat at the starting block, putting up a meager on-base plus slugging percentage (OPS) of 464 in April followed by another month of mediocrity in May. He started to put some offense together in June, driving the ball with more authority while continuing to showcase his impressive range in the outfield. However, he fell back to earth and struggled for the rest of the season, managing only five extra-base hits in the second half and losing his roster spot when the postseason arrived. As it stands now, the speedy center fielder needs to find another dimension to his offensive game or run the risk of being typecast as a slasher who won't take a walk, which puts him in a very exploitable box and lowers his ceiling substantially.

Jorge Cantu 3B

Born: **1/30/1982** Age: **29**
Bats: **R** Throws: **R** Height: **6' 1"** Weight: **200**
Breakout: **2%** Improve: **38%** Collapse: **3%**
Attrition: **9%** MLB: **95%**

Comparables:
Brooks Robinson, Joe Crede, Kevin Kouzmanoff (80)

YEAR	TEAM	LVL	AGE	PA	R	2B	3B	HR	RBI	BB	SO	SB	CS	AVG/OBP/SLG	TAv	BABIP	BRR	FRAA	WARP
2008	FLO	MLB	26	685	92	41	0	29	95	40	111	6	2	.277/.327/.481	.278	.293	-0.8	3B -7, 1B 2	2.5
2009	FLO	MLB	27	643	68	42	0	16	100	47	81	3	1	.289/.345/.443	.277	.310	-1.7	1B 2, 3B -10	1.1
2010	FLO	MLB	28	410	41	25	0	10	54	23	76	0	0	.262/.310/.409	.255	.298	-0.8	3B -4, 1B 1	0.5
2010	TEX	MLB	28	105	10	4	1	1	2	6	19	0	0	.235/.276/.327	.214	.279	0.8	1B -1, 3B -2	-0.5
2011	*TEX*	*MLB*	*29*	*531*	*63*	*31*	*0*	*14*	*62*	*37*	*87*	*2*	*1*	*.265/.321/.416*	*.258*	*.294*	*-0.1*	*3B -6, 1B 1*	*0.4*

Handicapped by suspect options at first base and hoping that a change of scenery would spark an offensive resurgence, the Rangers sent two minor-league arms to the Marlins for Cantu in late July. Equipped with only nominal defensive versatility, Cantu offered value via his bat; unfortunately, his offensive prowess stayed in Florida, where he was once considered a slightly above-average hitter. As a 28-year-old with poor defensive skills and diminished bat speed, Cantu spent the offseason testing the free-agent waters, hoping to find a team willing to offer multiple years for mediocrity.

Alex Cora **2B**

Born: **10/18/1975** Age: **35**
Bats: **L** Throws: **R** Height: **6' 0"** Weight: **180**
Breakout: **2%** Improve: **22%** Collapse: **15%**
Attrition: **34%** MLB: **71%**

Comparables:
Duane Kuiper, Mike Kingery, Keith Lockhart (70)

YEAR	TEAM	LVL	AGE	PA	R	2B	3B	HR	RBI	BB	SO	SB	CS	AVG/OBP/SLG	TAv	BABIP	BRR	FRAA	WARP
2008	BOS	MLB	32	179	14	8	2	0	9	16	13	1	1	.270/.369/.349	.265	.291	-0.7	SS -1, 2B 1	0.7
2009	NYN	MLB	33	308	31	11	1	1	18	25	28	8	3	.251/.312/.310	.225	.267	-1.6	SS -4, 2B -1	-0.7
2010	NYN	MLB	34	187	13	6	3	0	20	10	16	4	1	.207/.262/.278	.209	.223	-0.7	2B -9, SS -1	-1.5
2010	TEX	MLB	34	7	0	0	0	0	0	0	0	0	0	.286/.286/.286	.217	.286	-0.5	2B -1, 3B 0	-0.1
2011	*TEX*	*MLB*	*35*	*245*	*24*	*10*	*2*	*1*	*19*	*18*	*24*	*4*	*2*	*.239/.301/.319*	*.222*	*.254*	*-0.1*	*SS -1, 2B -2*	*-0.5*

Cora is, by all accounts, a swell individual who has a future in coaching ahead of him if he so desires. Most Mets fans probably wish he had replaced Jerry Manuel as the skipper at some point during last season, since such a move would have served two distinct yet important purposes, removing Manuel and his managerial lunacy from a position of power while taking Cora's "bat" out of the lineup forever. In fact, even an exchange of roles might have yielded a net improvement. Instead, the Mets released him in August, freeing him to spend a four-game stint with the Rangers, after which he again found himself unemployed. He signed a minor-league deal with the Nats, the last-chance saloon.

Nelson Cruz **RF**

Born: **7/1/1980** Age: **30**
Bats: **R** Throws: **R** Height: **6' 3"** Weight: **175**
Breakout: **1%** Improve: **41%** Collapse: **1%**
Attrition: **5%** MLB: **93%**

Comparables:
Alfonso Soriano, Hank Aaron, Jayson Werth (66)

YEAR	TEAM	LVL	AGE	PA	R	2B	3B	HR	RBI	BB	SO	SB	CS	AVG/OBP/SLG	TAv	BABIP	BRR	FRAA	WARP
2008	OKL	AAA	27	448	93	18	3	37	99	56	87	24	8	.342/.429/.695	.358	.357	3.0	RF -5, CF -1	5.1
2008	TEX	MLB	27	133	19	9	1	7	26	17	28	3	1	.330/.421/.609	.350	.388	-0.9	RF 0	1.4
2009	TEX	MLB	28	515	75	21	1	33	76	49	118	20	4	.260/.332/.524	.289	.278	0.1	RF 19, LF 1	4.2
2010	TEX	MLB	29	445	60	31	3	22	78	38	81	17	4	.318/.373/.576	.327	.347	1.7	RF 16, LF 2	5.3
2011	*TEX*	*MLB*	*30*	*531*	*73*	*26*	*2*	*28*	*82*	*51*	*117*	*17*	*5*	*.275/.346/.516*	*.295*	*.306*	*0.0*	*RF 8, LF 0*	*3.4*

Picking up where his impressive 2009 campaign left off, Cruz continued to develop into one of the top right-handed power bats in the American League. A member of the Rangers' "middle-of-the-order mashers who enjoy annual trips to the disabled list" club, Cruz played in only 108 games, hitting the DL three times with hamstring issues. When on the field, he showed all five tools—an ability to hit for average and superlative power, a solid glove, a rocket arm, and surprising speed. As a first-year arbitration-eligible player, Cruz is due for a substantial step up in base pay; if he can stay healthy, he'll be worth every penny and then some.

Chris Davis **1B**

Born: **3/17/1986** Age: **25**
Bats: **L** Throws: **R** Height: **6' 4"** Weight: **235**
Breakout: **6%** Improve: **34%** Collapse: **3%**
Attrition: **22%** MLB: **72%**

Comparables:
Brandon Allen, Joey Votto, Orlando Cepeda (70)

YEAR	TEAM	LVL	AGE	PA	R	2B	3B	HR	RBI	BB	SO	SB	CS	AVG/OBP/SLG	TAv	BABIP	BRR	FRAA	WARP
2008	FRI	AA	22	202	43	14	0	13	42	13	44	5	1	.333/.376/.618	.336	.374	2.6	1B -4	1.6
2008	OKL	AAA	22	127	25	7	1	10	31	13	29	2	0	.333/.402/.685	.365	.365	-0.6	1B 1	1.6
2008	TEX	MLB	22	317	51	23	2	17	55	20	88	1	2	.285/.331/.549	.299	.351	1.2	1B -1, 3B -7	1.1
2009	OKL	AAA	23	194	27	12	1	6	30	25	39	0	1	.327/.418/.521	.323	.393	-2.2	3B -9, 1B 2	0.7
2009	TEX	MLB	23	419	49	15	1	21	59	24	150	0	0	.238/.284/.443	.249	.324	1.2	1B -5, 3B -4	-0.8
2010	OKL	AAA	24	445	67	31	2	14	80	37	105	3	2	.327/.383/.520	.305	.407	0.0	3B -7, 1B 1	2.5
2010	TEX	MLB	24	136	6	9	0	1	4	15	40	3	0	.192/.279/.292	.205	.275	0.5	1B 2, 3B 0	-0.4
2011	*TEX*	*MLB*	*25*	*615*	*75*	*32*	*2*	*24*	*81*	*48*	*175*	*4*	*1*	*.261/.319/.452*	*.266*	*.333*	*-0.1*	*1B -6, 3B -6*	*0.0*

Once a very promising power bat, Davis looks to be a one-hit wonder, topping the charts back in 2008 by slamming 42 extra-base hits in only 80 games, including 17 jacks. After a disappointing 2009 campaign, Davis was given another opportunity to find his swing and opened the 2010 season as the starting first baseman for the Rangers. Unfortunately, he continued to struggle against major-league pitching, getting the hook after only 15 games and watching the Rangers move on without him. As is customary for newly christened Quad-A players, Davis went on to crush Triple-A pitching and earned another major-league call-up after Justin Smoak was traded to the Mariners. Davis is going to float between the two levels until he either makes the necessary adjustments that will allow him to execute against quality pitching or finds himself doing his best Matt Murton impression across the Pacific.

Jeff Francoeur **RF**

Born: **1/8/1984** Age: **27**
Bats: **R** Throws: **R** Height: **6' 4"** Weight: **220**
Breakout: **0%** Improve: **41%** Collapse: **4%**
Attrition: **17%** MLB: **86%**
Comparables:
Ruben Sierra, Chili Davis, Mark Teahen (68)

YEAR	TEAM	LVL	AGE	PA	R	2B	3B	HR	RBI	BB	SO	SB	CS	AVG/OBP/SLG	TAv	BABIP	BRR	FRAA	WARP
2008	ATL	MLB	24	653	71	33	3	11	71	39	111	0	1	.239/.294/.359	.232	.274	0.6	RF -4	-1.1
2009	ATL	MLB	25	324	32	12	2	5	35	12	46	5	1	.250/.281/.352	.223	.275	1.0	RF 3	-0.4
2009	NYN	MLB	25	308	40	20	2	10	41	11	46	1	3	.311/.338/.498	.289	.336	-0.7	RF -5	0.8
2010	NYN	MLB	26	447	42	16	2	11	54	29	76	8	2	.237/.293/.369	.246	.259	-1.9	RF -8	-0.9
2010	TEX	MLB	26	56	8	2	0	2	11	1	5	0	1	.340/.357/.491	.307	.340	-0.4	RF -1, LF -1	0.1
2011	*KCA*	*MLB*	*27*	*637*	*72*	*30*	*2*	*17*	*72*	*39*	*99*	*6*	*3*	*.259/.311/.402*	*.251*	*.283*	*-0.4*	*RF -4, LF 0*	*-0.1*

Acquired from the Mets at the end of August for utility infielder Joaquin Arias, a player whom the Rangers famously chose over Robinson Cano in the Alex Rodriguez trade, Francoeur made an immediate splash in Texas, posting an 848 OPS in 56 plate appearances. The book on Francoeur is Bible-length; with 845 games played before his 27th birthday, the once-promising prospect displays a vulnerability against right-handed pitching—a weakness that is as well-documented as it is exploitable. Instead of subscribing to his small-sample success and heading to arbitration with Francoeur for another year, the team elected to outright him. When no other club claimed him on waivers, Francoeur refused a Triple-A assignment to become a free agent. He inked a one-year deal with the Royals in December, touching off a firestorm of snark that has yet to subside.

Craig Gentry **CF**

Born: **11/29/1983** Age: **27**
Bats: **R** Throws: **R** Height: **6' 2"** Weight: **190**
Breakout: **1%** Improve: **18%** Collapse: **3%**
Attrition: **11%** MLB: **27%**
Comparables:
Clay Timpner, Chris Roberson, Tony Gwynn (83)

YEAR	TEAM	LVL	AGE	PA	R	2B	3B	HR	RBI	BB	SO	SB	CS	AVG/OBP/SLG	TAv	BABIP	BRR	FRAA	WARP
2008	FRI	AA	24	336	43	17	0	4	33	17	55	16	8	.276/.330/.372	.255	.317	-1.1	CF -9, RF 3	0.0
2008	OKL	AAA	24	69	6	1	0	0	1	9	18	1	0	.203/.304/.220	.215	.286	-0.1	CF 4	0.2
2009	FRI	AA	25	588	100	21	7	8	53	49	64	49	6	.303/.374/.418	.298	.326	7.7	CF -7	3.7
2009	TEX	MLB	25	19	2	1	0	0	1	2	5	0	0	.118/.211/.177	.186	.167	0.6	CF -1, RF 0	-0.1
2010	OKL	AAA	26	301	43	7	4	4	35	29	47	12	5	.309/.393/.413	.289	.357	2.4	CF 7	2.7
2010	TEX	MLB	26	35	3	0	0	0	3	1	11	1	0	.212/.229/.212	.151	.304	0.5	CF -2, LF 0	-0.4
2011	*TEX*	*MLB*	*27*	*436*	*46*	*16*	*3*	*5*	*37*	*31*	*81*	*17*	*4*	*.251/.314/.342*	*.236*	*.298*	*0.4*	*CF -7, RF 0*	*-0.5*

Drafted in the 10th round in 2006, the University of Arkansas product looked to be on the path to minor-league obscurity before finding his offensive groove at Double-A Frisco in 2009, latching on to the 40-man roster and getting into 11 major-league games. Since he was 25 years old at the time, many prognosticators turned a blind eye to the toolsy outfielder, but Gentry's outburst for Frisco was echoed at Triple-A Oklahoma City in 2010, earning him a few more cups of coffee with the major-league squad. Despite disappointing results on the biggest stage, Gentry has the tools to become a productive fourth outfielder with above-average defensive skills in center field and a combination of speed and intelligence that would make him a threat on the bases.

Esteban German **2B**

Born: **1/26/1978** Age: **33**
Bats: **R** Throws: **R** Height: **5' 9"** Weight: **165**
Breakout: **0%** Improve: **35%** Collapse: **10%**
Attrition: **21%** MLB: **92%**
Comparables:
Davey Lopes, Jamey Carroll, Kazuo Matsui (76)

YEAR	TEAM	LVL	AGE	PA	R	2B	3B	HR	RBI	BB	SO	SB	CS	AVG/OBP/SLG	TAv	BABIP	BRR	FRAA	WARP
2008	KCA	MLB	30	242	28	14	3	0	22	18	42	7	3	.245/.298/.338	.229	.293	-0.7	LF 0, 2B 3	-0.1
2009	OKL	AAA	31	472	63	15	5	4	59	65	63	35	9	.319/.417/.414	.303	.361	-2.6	3B 2, LF -4	2.3
2009	TEX	MLB	31	50	8	4	0	0	4	4	7	1	0	.304/.360/.391	.292	.359	1.0	3B -1, 2B 1	0.4
2010	OKL	AAA	32	567	79	27	5	5	55	64	77	50	7	.280/.371/.388	.261	.318	3.9	2B 1, 3B -7	1.1
2010	TEX	MLB	32	16	3	0	0	0	1	3	2	4	1	.231/.375/.231	.245	.273	0.3	2B -1, LF 0	-0.1
2011	*TEX*	*MLB*	*33*	*412*	*45*	*17*	*3*	*2*	*32*	*45*	*70*	*22*	*5*	*.253/.339/.335*	*.246*	*.301*	*0.6*	*3B -3, 2B -1*	*-0.1*

German performed adequately while spending most of the 2010 season with the Oklahoma City Redhawks, reaching base at a high clip and showing off his 32-year-old legs. Predominantly a second baseman and defensively versatile, German can hold his own on the left side of the infield and has logged time in the outfield. With a sharp eye at the plate, speed on the bases, and his several gloves, German has some value in a utility role. However, any exposure beyond the basic scope of utilitymanhood would result in sub-replacement-level results.

Vladimir Guerrero **DH**

Born: **2/9/1975** Age: **36**
Bats: **R** Throws: **R** Height: **6' 3"** Weight: **235**
Breakout: **0%** Improve: **25%** Collapse: **5%**
Attrition: **12%** MLB: **92%**
Comparables:
Dante Bichette, Paul O'Neill, Cliff Floyd (65)

YEAR	TEAM	LVL	AGE	PA	R	2B	3B	HR	RBI	BB	SO	SB	CS	AVG/OBP/SLG	TAv	BABIP	BRR	FRAA	WARP
2008	ANA	MLB	33	600	86	31	3	27	91	51	77	5	3	.303/.365/.521	.303	.311	-1.9	RF -4	2.9
2009	ANA	MLB	34	407	62	16	1	15	50	19	56	2	1	.295/.334/.460	.282	.313	-1.4	RF 0	1.1
2010	TEX	MLB	35	643	88	27	1	29	115	35	60	4	5	.300/.345/.496	.295	.292	-5.1	RF 0, LF 0	2.2
2011	*TEX*	*MLB*	*36*	*596*	*77*	*28*	*1*	*23*	*80*	*42*	*73*	*5*	*3*	*.286/.341/.467*	*.281*	*.293*	*-0.5*	*RF -1, LF 0*	*1.6*

Trying to find a middle-of-the-order hitter on the open market with an ultra-tight budget is often not a rewarding experience. Luckily for Jon Daniels and the Rangers, luring Guerrero to Texas for a 2010 base salary of $5.5 million proved to be a positive move. Already well versed in Ballpark-in-Arlington production, Guerrero used the first half of the season to demonstrate how much he had left in the tank, hitting a robust .319/.364/.554. Unfortunately, his numbers in the second half (.278/.322/.426) told a different story, one that read more like a farewell. Guerrero's future lies somewhere in between the two extremes; he may have another couple years of offensive value before he reaches replacement-level extinction. If the Vladdy experiment turns out to have been a one-year fling, both parties will have come out ahead; the Rangers received cleanup-type production on the cheap, and Guerrero proved that his Cooperstown clock isn't quite ready to begin its countdown.

Josh Hamilton **LF**

Born: **5/21/1981** Age: **30**
Bats: **L** Throws: **L** Height: **6' 4"** Weight: **205**
Breakout: **1%** Improve: **41%** Collapse: **0%**
Attrition: **6%** MLB: **98%**

Comparables:
Ryan Ludwick, Andy Pafko, Ken Griffey (72)

YEAR	TEAM	LVL	AGE	PA	R	2B	3B	HR	RBI	BB	SO	SB	CS	AVG/OBP/SLG	TAv	BABIP	BRR	FRAA	WARP
2008	TEX	MLB	27	704	98	35	5	32	130	64	126	9	1	.305/.371/.530	.311	.333	-0.5	CF -13, RF 1	4.1
2009	TEX	MLB	28	365	43	19	2	10	54	24	79	8	3	.268/.315/.426	.260	.319	2.0	CF -5, RF 2	0.8
2010	TEX	MLB	29	571	95	40	3	32	100	43	95	8	1	.359/.410/.633	.363	.389	-0.3	LF 4, CF -3	6.9
2011	*TEX*	*MLB*	*30*	*515*	*71*	*28*	*2*	*22*	*77*	*43*	*98*	*7*	*2*	*.294/.356/.509*	*.298*	*.326*	*0.0*	*CF -5, LF 1*	*2.6*

After a disappointing 2009 season in which Hamilton struggled to stay healthy and productive on the field while dealing with the fallout from a much-publicized relapse off of it, the former first overall pick in the 1999 draft realized his potential in 2010, winning his first batting title to go along with his first MVP award. Easing into the season, Hamilton didn't put it all together until June, but everything after that was straight out of a video game, including a .384/.448/.650 line in second-half action that was abbreviated by a pair of broken ribs. As a second-year arbitration-eligible player, Hamilton will reach free agency in 2013, so the Rangers will be forced to figure out a multiyear solution sooner rather than later. On the surface, locking up an MVP in his prime seems like a no-brainer, but Josh Hamilton isn't your average 29-year-old, and the risks involved with a long-term deal are substantial even in the best of cases. The Rangers have a true superstar on their hands, a player with the story and the skills to become a legend. They also have a player who struggled with drug and alcohol addiction for four years, doing untold damage to a body that has proved fragile in the bigs. The Rangers can't afford to let Hamilton walk away, but neither can they afford to hitch their hopes to a player with so much uncertainty.

Ian Kinsler **2B**

Born: **6/22/1982** Age: **29**
Bats: **R** Throws: **R** Height: **6' 0"** Weight: **200**
Breakout: **0%** Improve: **48%** Collapse: **2%**
Attrition: **6%** MLB: **99%**

Comparables:
Roberto Alomar, Aaron Hill, Brandon Phillips (73)

YEAR	TEAM	LVL	AGE	PA	R	2B	3B	HR	RBI	BB	SO	SB	CS	AVG/OBP/SLG	TAv	BABIP	BRR	FRAA	WARP
2008	TEX	MLB	26	583	102	41	4	18	71	45	67	26	2	.319/.371/.517	.302	.329	5.2	2B -3	4.1
2009	TEX	MLB	27	640	101	32	4	31	86	59	77	31	5	.253/.325/.488	.282	.240	5.7	2B 14	4.8
2010	TEX	MLB	28	460	73	20	1	9	45	56	57	15	5	.286/.380/.412	.294	.311	0.8	2B 7	3.3
2011	*TEX*	*MLB*	*29*	*562*	*72*	*28*	*2*	*18*	*69*	*57*	*73*	*21*	*5*	*.273/.350/.448*	*.280*	*.283*	*0.7*	*2B 7*	*3.1*

One of these years, Kinsler will play a full season without landing on the disabled list; then again, considering that health is a skill that he hasn't yet shown, maybe he won't. Playing in a career-low 103 games, thanks to a high ankle sprain suffered during spring training and a groin strain in late July, Kinsler was noticeably hampered in 2010, getting on base at a career-high clip but watching his power numbers nosedive. When healthy, he is one of the top all-around second basemen in baseball, so it's easy to imagine what value he would have if he were available for an entire season. Until that time comes, all that Rangers fans can do is hope the options available in his stead have something to offer.

Bengie Molina **C**

Born: **7/20/1974** Age: **36**
Bats: **R** Throws: **R** Height: **5' 11"** Weight: **210**
Breakout: **0%** Improve: **24%** Collapse: **7%**
Attrition: **23%** MLB: **89%**

Comparables:
Yogi Berra, Keith Moreland, Ted Simmons (69)

YEAR	TEAM	LVL	AGE	PA	R	2B	3B	HR	RBI	BB	SO	SB	CS	AVG/OBP/SLG	TAv	BABIP	BRR	FRAA	WARP
2008	SFN	MLB	33	569	53	33	0	16	95	19	38	0	0	.293/.322/.445	.266	.285	-10.3	C -2	1.5
2009	SFN	MLB	34	520	54	25	1	20	80	13	68	0	0	.265/.285/.442	.244	.266	-6.6	C -1	0.6
2010	SFN	MLB	35	221	18	6	0	3	17	14	19	0	0	.257/.312/.332	.229	.269	-0.6	C 0	0.2
2010	TEX	MLB	35	195	12	6	1	2	19	10	15	0	0	.240/.272/.320	.205	.240	-2.9	C 0	-0.6
2011	*TEX*	*MLB*	*36*	*496*	*53*	*22*	*1*	*12*	*54*	*21*	*51*	*0*	*0*	*.255/.290/.383*	*.234*	*.261*	*0.0*	*C -1*	*0.6*

In a move that seemed like a head-scratcher to most Rangers fans, Bengie Molina, the eldest of the famous Squatting Molina Brothers, was acquired from the Giants in early July for former first-round pick Michael Main and reliever Chris Ray. With old legs and a sub-replacement bat, Molina looked like a questionable addition, especially when the Rangers already had a queue of young catchers waiting for major-league at-bats. While the wisdom of the acquisition couldn't be seen on the stat sheet, it may have been found in the intangible comfort of the pitching staff, which seemed to enjoy working with the veteran game-caller and reputed pitcher's catcher despite his diminished arm. Molina went 10-for-31 with two home runs in the first two rounds of the playoffs before disappearing in the playoffs, a possible prelude to his vanishing into retirement.

Mitch Moreland 1B

Born: **9/6/1985** Age: **25**
Bats: **L** Throws: **L** Height: **6' 2"** Weight: **230**
Breakout: **6%** Improve: **26%** Collapse: **12%**
Attrition: **30%** MLB: **55%**
Comparables:
Chris Carter, Seth Smith, Adrian Gonzalez (71)

YEAR	TEAM	LVL	AGE	PA	R	2B	3B	HR	RBI	BB	SO	SB	CS	AVG/OBP/SLG	TAv	BABIP	BRR	FRAA	WARP
2008	CLN	A	22	533	64	37	4	18	99	60	67	2	4	.324/.400/.536	.325	.345	-4.5	1B 3, RF 1	3.9
2009	BAK	A+	23	197	34	19	0	8	26	21	26	1	0	.341/.421/.594	.348	.362	-0.1	1B 2, RF -2	1.9
2009	FRI	AA	23	327	51	19	3	8	59	23	42	1	1	.326/.373/.488	.303	.356	-4.1	RF -7, 1B 0	0.8
2010	OKL	AAA	24	412	52	29	2	12	65	47	63	2	1	.289/.371/.484	.289	.314	-0.6	RF 3, 1B 1	2.4
2010	TEX	MLB	24	173	20	4	0	9	25	25	36	3	1	.255/.364/.469	.303	.275	-0.7	1B -5, RF -1	0.3
2011	*TEX*	*MLB*	*25*	*547*	*68*	*30*	*2*	*16*	*67*	*51*	*98*	*2*	*1*	*.269/.337/.439*	*.269*	*.301*	*-0.1*	*RF -4, 1B -4*	*0.3*

A 17th-round pick in 2007, Moreland was labeled a guy with good power potential coming out of college, but perceptible holes in the inner half of his swing seemed to make him more of an organizational player than a legit prospect. In fact, some saw the stocky left-hander as better suited for the mound work in which he had dabbled while at Mississippi State. Moreland ended the positional debate after the 2008 season, when he put up a 936 OPS in the pitcher-friendly Midwest League. Since then, he has climbed the professional ladder, defying expectations along the way and finally emerging as the Rangers' starting first baseman in late July. Moreland isn't a toolsy player, and he lacks defensive value, but his sound approach at the plate, quick hands, and good raw power give him a chance to defy those initial expectations even further and become a solid regular at the major-league level.

David Murphy LF

Born: **10/18/1981** Age: **29**
Bats: **L** Throws: **L** Height: **6' 4"** Weight: **192**
Breakout: **4%** Improve: **44%** Collapse: **1%**
Attrition: **8%** MLB: **94%**
Comparables:
Moises Alou, Hoot Evers, Ben Francisco (77)

YEAR	TEAM	LVL	AGE	PA	R	2B	3B	HR	RBI	BB	SO	SB	CS	AVG/OBP/SLG	TAv	BABIP	BRR	FRAA	WARP
2008	TEX	MLB	26	454	64	28	3	15	74	31	70	7	2	.275/.319/.465	.271	.293	3.6	LF -6, RF 3	1.5
2009	TEX	MLB	27	494	60	24	1	17	57	49	106	9	4	.269/.336/.447	.279	.309	1.9	LF 1, RF 0	2.0
2010	TEX	MLB	28	471	53	26	2	12	65	45	71	14	2	.291/.355/.449	.298	.325	-4.6	LF 0, RF -3	1.7
2011	*TEX*	*MLB*	*29*	*510*	*62*	*27*	*2*	*13*	*60*	*47*	*91*	*9*	*3*	*.269/.334/.426*	*.267*	*.304*	*0.0*	*LF 1, RF -1*	*1.1*

Since being acquired from the Red Sox for Eric Gagne, Murphy has used his versatility to deliver value, playing all three outfield spots and providing a solid left-handed bat at pre-arbitration prices. Lauded for his defense in the past, he took a step back in 2010—though he has a strong arm and solid athleticism, his routes aren't crisp and he lacks the elite first-step quickness that would augment his range. At the plate, Murphy was strong, especially while hitting .311/.388/.509 in the second half, but he's still plagued by below-average performance against left-handed pitching. Given his defensive deterioration, Murphy looks to be a better fit as a fourth outfielder or perhaps as the lefty bat in a platoon situation.

Jurickson Profar SS

Born: **2/20/1993** Age: **18**
Bats: **S** Throws: **R** Height: **5' 11"** Weight: **165**
Breakout: **0%** Improve: **0%** Collapse: **0%**
Attrition: **0%** MLB: **0%**
Comparables:
Kenny Kuhn, Wayne Causey, Alfredo Griffin (76)

YEAR	TEAM	LVL	AGE	PA	R	2B	3B	HR	RBI	BB	SO	SB	CS	AVG/OBP/SLG	TAv	BABIP	BRR	FRAA	WARP
2010	SPO	A-	17	288	42	19	0	4	23	28	46	8	3	.250/.323/.373	.260	.281	0.0	SS 15	2.6
2011	*TEX*	*MLB*	*18*	—	—	—	—	—	—	—	—	—	—	—	—	—	—	—	—

Viewed as a pitcher by most organizations, Curaçao native Profar saw himself as an everyday shortstop—the next Elvis Andrus, if you will. The Rangers agreed and signed the former Little League World Series star for $1.55 million. The precocious 17-year-old made his professional debut in the Northwest League, where the average player was more than four years his senior, and he has already adjusted to the culture of playing stateside baseball. Profar held his own—a considerable accomplishment—offering a rare combination of polish and projectability. His future tools project to be solid-average to plus across the board, but he doesn't have superstar-level individual grades. Profar will take his well-rounded collection of skills to full-season ball in 2011 with the chance to emerge as a top-tier prospect before the year is out.

Max Ramirez C

Born: **10/11/1984** Age: **26**
Bats: **R** Throws: **R** Height: **5' 11"** Weight: **175**
Breakout: **5%** Improve: **20%** Collapse: **2%**
Attrition: **15%** MLB: **43%**

Comparables:
George Kottaras, Howard Johnson, Jeff Mathis (72)

YEAR	TEAM	LVL	AGE	PA	R	2B	3B	HR	RBI	BB	SO	SB	CS	AVG/OBP/SLG	TAv	BABIP	BRR	FRAA	WARP
2008	FRI	AA	23	289	49	16	2	17	50	37	56	2	2	.354/.450/.646	.363	.401	-3.2	C 0, 1B 1	3.7
2008	OKL	AAA	23	80	13	4	0	5	13	10	28	0	0	.246/.338/.522	.297	.324	-0.4	C -1	0.5
2008	TEX	MLB	23	56	9	1	0	2	9	6	16	0	0	.213/.339/.362	.269	.276	0.3	C 0, 1B 0	0.2
2009	OKL	AAA	24	320	29	13	0	5	43	35	85	1	0	.234/.322/.336	.242	.309	-1.6	C 0	0.1
2010	OKL	AAA	25	226	24	9	0	3	29	27	51	0	0	.286/.373/.381	.270	.359	-1.3	C 0	0.8
2010	TEX	MLB	25	85	8	3	0	2	8	12	22	0	0	.217/.341/.348	.266	.277	-2.3	C 0	0.2
2011	*TEX*	*MLB*	*26*	*357*	*40*	*15*	*0*	*9*	*35*	*39*	*99*	*0*	*0*	*.237/.328/.378*	*.252*	*.312*	*0.0*	*C -1, 1B 0*	*0.7*

You would think that with a first name like Maximiliano, Ramirez would be destined for greatness. Unfortunately, his once-bright offensive future has stalled, and the former prospect's major-league potential is very much in doubt. Always a bat-first backstop, the below-average catcher continued to play below-average defense last season, putting the onus on his rotting lumber to carve out a major-league career. Despite a commendable approach that allows him to draw walks and reach base at a respectable rate, Ramirez struggled to make hard contact, failing to slug over .400 in Triple-A for the second straight season. With declining offensive skills and the defensive chops of a designated hitter, Maximiliano is starting to look more like a minor-league tweener than a realistic major-league option.

Jacob Skole CF

Born: **1/17/1992** Age: **19**
Bats: **L** Throws: **R** Height: **6' 1"** Weight: **190**
Breakout: **0%** Improve: **0%** Collapse: **0%**
Attrition: **2%** MLB: **2%**

Comparables:
Bobby Delgreco, Jay Porter, Claudell Washington (80)

YEAR	TEAM	LVL	AGE	PA	R	2B	3B	HR	RBI	BB	SO	SB	CS	AVG/OBP/SLG	TAv	BABIP	BRR	FRAA	WARP
2010	RNG	Rk	18	66	12	4	0	0	10	10	10	0	0	.286/.394/.357	.319	.348	0.0	CF -1	0.6
2010	SPO	A-	18	228	29	9	2	2	27	23	52	6	4	.254/.327/.348	.248	.325	0.0	CF -3	0.1
2011	*TEX*	*MLB*	*19*	—	—	—	—	—	—	—	—	—	—	—	—	—	—	—	—

With the 15th pick in the 2010 draft, Texas selected toolsy Georgia prepster Skole and quickly signed him for $1.557 million. Due to injury setbacks during his senior season and a commitment to play both football and baseball at Georgia Tech, Skole slipped off the early-round radar and appeared to be a reach when the Rangers called his name with their first selection. However, Skole showcased five-tool potential after signing, playing well in the Complex League and subsequently holding his own for 57 games in the collegiate-player-heavy Northwest League. With all of his focus now on baseball, Skole will test the full-season waters at age 19.

Taylor Teagarden C

Born: **12/21/1983** Age: **27**
Bats: **R** Throws: **R** Height: **6' 1"** Weight: **200**
Breakout: **6%** Improve: **34%** Collapse: **3%**
Attrition: **7%** MLB: **64%**

Comparables:
Rick Wilkins, Bobby Estalella, Dick Dietz (75)

YEAR	TEAM	LVL	AGE	PA	R	2B	3B	HR	RBI	BB	SO	SB	CS	AVG/OBP/SLG	TAv	BABIP	BRR	FRAA	WARP
2008	FRI	AA	24	68	6	2	0	2	6	8	23	1	0	.169/.279/.305	.229	.235	-0.2	C 0	-0.1
2008	OKL	AAA	24	218	26	5	3	7	16	28	59	0	1	.225/.330/.396	.246	.287	-2.0	C 0	0.4
2008	TEX	MLB	24	53	10	5	0	6	17	5	19	0	0	.319/.396/.809	.398	.409	0.9	C 1	1.1
2009	TEX	MLB	25	218	26	13	0	6	24	14	76	0	0	.217/.266/.374	.230	.306	1.0	C -1	0.3
2010	FRI	AA	26	220	24	10	1	3	32	25	75	0	0	.242/.336/.353	.251	.377	0.0	C 0	0.7
2010	TEX	MLB	26	85	10	1	0	4	6	8	34	0	0	.155/.247/.338	.234	.189	0.5	C 0	0.2
2011	*TEX*	*MLB*	*27*	*298*	*30*	*11*	*1*	*9*	*29*	*27*	*105*	*0*	*0*	*.205/.281/.351*	*.223*	*.292*	*0.0*	*C -1*	*0.0*

Early in his professional career, Teagarden was considered an odds-on favorite to emerge as a quality catcher at the major-league level. With enough offensive ability to keep pitchers honest and above-average defensive skills, he appeared headed for a backup role at worst and a Varitek-ian starter kit at best. For Teagarden, 2010 was the year that officially put the lie to that projection. Losing all function at the plate, which no doubt carried over to his work behind it, Teagarden lost his swing mechanics and pitch-recognition skills, which left him vulnerable to quality breaking stuff and unable to touch right-handed pitching. He now looks more like a career minor leaguer than a realistic long-term option at the major-league level.

Matt Treanor C

*Born: **3/3/1976** Age: **35**
Bats: **R** Throws: **R** Height: **6' 2"** Weight: **220**
Breakout: **1%** Improve: **17%** Collapse: **17%**
Attrition: **31%** MLB: **62%**

Comparables:
Pidge Browne, Danny Ardoin, Doc Edwards (72)

YEAR	TEAM	LVL	AGE	PA	R	2B	3B	HR	RBI	BB	SO	SB	CS	AVG/OBP/SLG	TAv	BABIP	BRR	FRAA	WARP
2008	FLO	MLB	32	234	19	7	0	2	23	18	53	1	0	.238/.299/.301	.227	.298	1.1	C 0	0.3
2009	DET	MLB	33	14	0	0	0	0	0	1	4	0	0	.000/.071/.000	-0.033	.000	0.0	C 0	-0.4
2010	TEX	MLB	34	272	23	6	1	5	27	22	43	1	2	.211/.283/.308	.217	.228	-2.7	C -1	-0.4
2011	*TEX*	*MLB*	*35*	*188*	*18*	*6*	*1*	*3*	*14*	*17*	*36*	*1*	*0*	*.220/.297/.313*	*.222*	*.258*	*-0.1*	*C -1*	*0.0*

Acquired from the Brewers for the great Rainer (Ray) Gustavo Olmedo before the start of the season, Treanor was able to use his defensive skill set and baseball intelligence to supplement a position weakened by injury and ineffectiveness. While extremely limited on offense and probably devoid of value going forward—especially for a playoff contender—Treanor served his purpose in 2010, offering a steady hand behind the plate and bringing his wife, volleyball gold medalist Misty May Treanor, to the ballpark on a regular basis. The Rangers re-signed him to a one-year deal to caddy for Yorvit Torrealba and can't ask or expect more than consistency on all fronts, missus included.

Michael Young **3B**

Born: **10/19/1976** Age: **34**
Bats: **R** Throws: **R** Height: **6' 1"** Weight: **190**
Breakout: **2%** Improve: **29%** Collapse: **8%**
Attrition: **12%** MLB: **96%**

Comparables:
Casey Blake, Randy Winn, Pedro Feliz (70)

YEAR	TEAM	LVL	AGE	PA	R	2B	3B	HR	RBI	BB	SO	SB	CS	AVG/OBP/SLG	TAv	BABIP	BRR	FRAA	WARP
2008	TEX	MLB	31	708	102	36	2	12	82	55	109	10	0	.284/.339/.402	.262	.323	2.1	SS 12	4.1
2009	TEX	MLB	32	593	76	36	2	22	68	47	90	8	3	.322/.374/.518	.309	.351	-3.4	3B -18	2.6
2010	TEX	MLB	33	718	99	36	3	21	91	50	115	4	2	.284/.330/.444	.273	.311	2.4	3B -9	2.3
2011	*TEX*	*MLB*	*34*	*692*	*83*	*36*	*2*	*15*	*78*	*52*	*113*	*7*	*2*	*.280/.334/.415*	*.265*	*.317*	*-0.1*	*3B -9, SS 1*	*1.7*

No longer the face of a losing franchise, Young finally got a taste of playoff baseball, but he's not quite the force that he was for the inferior Rangers teams of yore. After a slow start to the season, Young found his bat, hitting for average and power and carrying a .500 slugging percentage into July. Unfortunately, he wilted in the summer, watching his offensive production decline every month until it bottomed out over his final 28 games, during which the six-time All-Star produced a 615 OPS. The addition of Adrian Beltre forces his fading glove off of third base. in favor of DH duty, but Young's leadership may be the only non-replacement-level skill he offers by the time his contract runs its course.

PITCHERS

Omar Beltre

Born: **8/24/1981** Age: **29**
Bats: **R** Throws: **R** Height: **6' 3"** Weight: **190**
Breakout: **5%** Improve: **8%** Collapse: **2%**
Attrition: **2%** MLB: **10%**

Comparables:
Carlos Guevara, Eric Hull, Brett Campbell (81)

YEAR	TEAM	LVL	AGE	W	L	SV	G	GS	IP	H	HR	BB	SO	EqBB9	EqSO9	GB%	BABIP	WHIP	ERA	FRA	WARP
2010	OKL	AAA	28	3	9	2	24	14	85	69	2	38	85	4.0	9.0	54%	.303	1.28	2.65	4.36	1.5
2010	TEX	MLB	28	0	1	0	2	2	7	9	3	7	9	9.0	11.6	30%	.353	2.57	9.00	7.24	-0.1
2011	*TEX*	*MLB*	*29*	*3*	*3*	*0*	*15*	*8*	*50*	*48*	*5*	*25*	*45*	*4.5*	*8.0*	*47%*	*.306*	*1.46*	*4.35*	*4.72*	*0.9*

Like fellow Dominican right-hander Alexi Ogando, Beltre was denied entry to the United States after his 2005 involvement in a human trafficking ring, in connection with which he accepted money to enter into marriage with someone seeking a visa. Unlike Ogando, Beltre spent four seasons pitching in the United States prior to the visa scandal, so his story isn't quite as fantastical, but his 2010 season was equally impressive. Jumping to Triple-A to restart his stateside career, Beltre made 24 appearances, including 14 starts, using his plus fastball with boring action, low-80s slider, and splitter/changeup combo to fan 85 Pacific Coast League hitters in as many innings. Beltre made two spot starts for the Rangers, but lost his command and was hit hard, often elevating his fastball up in the zone. With a deep arsenal and the ability to start or relieve, Beltre should have an expanded role for the 2011 squad.

Scott Feldman

Born: **2/7/1983** Age: **28**
Bats: **L** Throws: **R** Height: **6' 5"** Weight: **210**
Breakout: **16%** Improve: **44%** Collapse: **18%**
Attrition: **16%** MLB: **85%**

Comparables:
Brian Bannister, Ben McDonald, Carl Pavano (75)

YEAR	TEAM	LVL	AGE	W	L	SV	G	GS	IP	H	HR	BB	SO	EqBB9	EqSO9	GB%	BABIP	WHIP	ERA	FRA	WARP
2008	TEX	MLB	25	6	8	0	28	25	151^{1}	161	22	56	74	3.3	4.4	45%	.284	1.50	5.29	6.43	-0.4
2009	TEX	MLB	26	17	8	0	34	31	189^{2}	178	18	65	113	3.1	5.4	48%	.273	1.33	4.03	4.42	3.4
2010	TEX	MLB	27	7	11	0	29	22	141^{1}	181	18	45	75	2.9	4.8	43%	.327	1.63	5.48	5.42	0.4
2011	*TEX*	*MLB*	*28*	*7*	*9*	*0*	*22*	*22*	*125*	*142*	*16*	*46*	*67*	*3.3*	*4.8*	*45%*	*.302*	*1.49*	*5.06*	*5.50*	*1.1*

After a smoke-and-mirrors success story in 2009, the smoke dissipated and the mirrors reflected a replacement-level pitcher in 2010. Feldman watched his cutter take a big step back; it went from an aggressive, ground-ball-inducing offering to a pitch that hung more than it cut and found the fat part of bats more often than it splintered them. Feldman lacks an above-average arsenal, but if he could again harness the power of the cut fastball, he would supply some value at the back of the major-league rotation. If not, his future lies in the bullpen, and considering that $11.5 million is coming his way over the next two seasons, it's hard to imagine the Rangers recouping much value from that.

Neftali Feliz

Born: **5/2/1988** Age: **23**
Bats: **R** Throws: **R** Height: **6' 3"** Weight: **215**
Breakout: **5%** Improve: **12%** Collapse: **9%**
Attrition: **5%** MLB: **23%**

Comparables:
Bill Gullickson, Brian Fisher, Ian Kennedy (72)

YEAR	TEAM	LVL	AGE	W	L	SV	G	GS	IP	H	HR	BB	SO	EqBB9	EqSO9	GB%	BABIP	WHIP	ERA	FRA	WARP
2008	CLN	A	20	6	3	0	17	17	82	55	2	28	106	3.1	11.6	53%	.291	1.09	2.52	3.28	2.3
2008	FRI	AA	20	4	3	0	10	10	45^{1}	34	1	23	47	4.6	9.3	41%	.295	1.30	2.98	3.87	1.3
2009	OKL	AAA	21	4	6	0	25	13	77^{1}	69	2	30	75	3.5	8.7	46%	.315	1.32	3.49	4.09	1.3
2009	TEX	MLB	21	1	0	2	20	0	31	13	2	8	39	2.3	11.3	40%	.169	0.77	1.74	2.60	0.8
2010	TEX	MLB	22	4	3	40	70	0	69^{1}	43	5	18	71	2.3	9.2	36%	.224	0.95	2.73	3.75	0.6
2011	*TEX*	*MLB*	*23*	*5*	*3*	*6*	*33*	*10*	*74^{1}*	*63*	*6*	*33*	*73*	*4.1*	*8.8*	*43%*	*.288*	*1.30*	*3.50*	*3.80*	*1.8*

The debate about Feliz's future role continues to fill up blog posts and comment sections the Internet over, but the Dominican flamethrower has a very bright future with the Rangers, regardless of his duties. After a meteoric rise from Double-A to the majors in 2009, the 22-year-old made the transition from set-up man to closer, breaking the rookie save record along the way. On the back of his 80-grade fastball, Feliz overpowered major-league hitters, missing bats without missing his spots, as evidenced by his acceptable 2.3 walks per nine innings. Shoving a once-promising changeup in his back pocket, Feliz became more of a two-pitch power arm, throwing his heater 80 percent of the time and enlisting a plus curveball as his main secondary offering. Without further development of his changeup or enhanced application of his curveball, Feliz may have a hard time making a smooth transition back into a starting role in the immediate future, which limits his value to the team.

Frank Francisco

Born: **9/11/1979** Age: **31**
Bats: **R** Throws: **R** Height: **6' 2"** Weight: **180**
Breakout: **26%** Improve: **47%** Collapse: **15%**
Attrition: **12%** MLB: **87%**

Comparables:
Jason Frasor, Rafael Soriano, Ugueth Urbina (74)

YEAR	TEAM	LVL	AGE	W	L	SV	G	GS	IP	H	HR	BB	SO	EqBB9	EqSO9	GB%	BABIP	WHIP	ERA	FRA	WARP
2008	TEX	MLB	28	3	5	5	58	0	63^{1}	47	7	26	83	3.7	11.8	34%	.270	1.15	3.13	3.28	1.1
2009	TEX	MLB	29	2	3	25	51	0	49^{1}	40	6	15	57	2.7	10.4	30%	.274	1.14	3.83	3.14	0.8
2010	TEX	MLB	30	6	4	2	56	0	52^{2}	49	5	18	60	3.1	10.3	40%	.321	1.29	3.76	3.65	0.6
2011	*TEX*	*MLB*	*31*	*3*	*1*	*5*	*53*	*0*	*53*	*47*	*6*	*21*	*59*	*3.6*	*9.9*	*41%*	*.301*	*1.27*	*3.44*	*3.74*	*0.7*

Armed with a three-pitch power arsenal, the hefty Francisco spent most of the 2009 season as the Rangers' closer, saving 25 games despite landing on the disabled list three times (twice with shoulder tendinitis). After a rocky start to 2010, he was relegated to a set-up role in favor of young flamethrower Neftali Feliz. Eventually, however, Francisco found his niche in the eighth inning, striking out 10.3 batters per nine innings and forming a potent late-inning one-two punch with his Dominican counterpart. Unfortunately, a rib-cage injury sustained in late August left him on the shelf and off the post-season roster. The Type-A free agent accepted the Rangers' offer of salary arbitration rather than attempt to convince potential suitors that he was worth surrendering a draft pick to sign.

Rich Harden

Born: **11/30/1981** Age: **29**
Bats: **L** Throws: **R** Height: **6' 1"** Weight: **180**
Breakout: **21%** Improve: **38%** Collapse: **27%**
Attrition: **17%** MLB: **94%**

Comparables:
Marshall Bridges, Mark Davis, Mike Stanton (64)

YEAR	TEAM	LVL	AGE	W	L	SV	G	GS	IP	H	HR	BB	SO	EqBB9	EqSO9	GB%	BABIP	WHIP	ERA	FRA	WARP
2008	CHN	MLB	26	5	1	0	12	12	71	39	6	30	89	3.8	11.3	30%	.210	1.00	1.77	2.54	2.8
2008	OAK	MLB	26	5	1	0	13	13	77	57	5	31	92	3.6	10.8	30%	.286	1.16	2.34	2.28	3.1
2009	CHN	MLB	27	9	9	0	26	26	141	122	23	67	171	4.3	10.9	41%	.290	1.38	4.09	4.43	2.2
2010	OKL	AAA	28	0	2	0	5	5	23^{1}	21	3	8	34	3.1	13.2	50%	.327	1.30	3.86	4.33	0.4
2010	TEX	MLB	28	5	5	0	20	18	92	91	18	62	75	6.1	7.3	34%	.274	1.76	5.58	6.06	-0.2
2011	*OAK*	*MLB*	*29*	*8*	*5*	*0*	*18*	*18*	*98*	*82*	*12*	*49*	*106*	*4.4*	*9.7*	*39%*	*.284*	*1.32*	*3.70*	*4.03*	*2.0*

One of the more quotable lines from the movie *Road House*, delivered by the late great Patrick Swayze, was, "Pain don't hurt." Watching Harden pitch in 2010 was a pain that *did* hurt—just ask any Rangers fan. The righty was supposed to be the big splash of the Rangers' offseason, a top-of-the-rotation arm that would supply the final piece of the American League West puzzle. Reality asserted itself during spring training, when his stuff appeared to have lost a tick from previous seasons and his feel for the strike zone had slipped off the grid. Harden's performance did not improve with time, making him one of last winter's more disappointing free-agent signings, and he was designated for assignment before the start of the American League Division Series. In December, he returned to his original team, the A's, for whom he'll serve as a reliever or a back-of-the-rotation arm, which wasn't what he had in mind when last he donned the green and gold.

Matt Harrison

Born: **8/16/1985** Age: **25**
Bats: L Throws: L Height: **6' 4"** Weight: **225**
Breakout: **4%** Improve: **10%** Collapse: **3%**
Attrition: **7%** MLB: **21%**

Comparables:
Matt Chico, Edgar Gonzalez, Ron Reed (80)

YEAR	TEAM	LVL	AGE	W	L	SV	G	GS	IP	H	HR	BB	SO	EqBB9	EqSO9	GB%	BABIP	WHIP	ERA	FRA	WARP
2008	FRI	AA	22	3	2	0	9	9	46	49	3	14	35	2.7	6.8	47%	.311	1.37	3.33	3.91	1.0
2008	OKL	AAA	22	3	1	0	6	6	38	40	3	14	20	3.3	4.7	54%	.303	1.42	3.55	3.52	0.9
2008	TEX	MLB	22	9	3	0	15	15	83^2	100	12	31	42	3.3	4.5	40%	.309	1.59	5.49	6.21	0.0
2009	TEX	MLB	23	4	5	0	11	11	63^1	81	9	23	34	3.3	4.8	48%	.335	1.67	6.11	5.58	0.4
2010	TEX	MLB	24	3	2	2	37	6	78^1	80	10	40	46	4.6	5.3	48%	.270	1.56	4.71	5.54	-0.3
2011	*TEX*	*MLB*	*25*	*6*	*7*	*0*	*35*	*16*	115^2	*139*	*16*	*46*	*60*	*3.6*	*4.7*	*46%*	*.314*	*1.61*	*5.63*	*6.12*	*-0.1*

A big lefty who once carried a midrotation ceiling, Harrison has yet to realize his potential since arriving from Atlanta in the Mark Teixeira fleecing. After an impressive spring training (and an injury to Tommy Hunter), Harrison started the season in the Rangers' rotation, making six starts before shoulder tendinitis sidelined him and his 5.29 ERA until late May. Demoted to the pen, Harrison lost confidence in his arsenal, choosing to nibble and avoid rather than trust in his solid-to-average five-pitch mix and attack the strike zone. Pitchers who have a fondness for baserunners and an aversion to strikeouts don't make ideal roster candidates, and while Harrison still has time to carve out a role, his realistic projection is now closer to middle relief than middle of the rotation.

Derek Holland

Born: **10/9/1986** Age: **24**
Bats: S Throws: L Height: **6' 2"** Weight: **195**
Breakout: **24%** Improve: **53%** Collapse: **9%**
Attrition: **8%** MLB: **82%**

Comparables:
Johnny Cueto, Scott Sanderson, Joe Coleman (77)

YEAR	TEAM	LVL	AGE	W	L	SV	G	GS	IP	H	HR	BB	SO	EqBB9	EqSO9	GB%	BABIP	WHIP	ERA	FRA	WARP
2008	CLN	A	21	7	0	0	17	17	93^2	77	2	29	91	2.8	8.7	52%	.298	1.15	2.40	3.20	2.6
2008	BAK	A+	21	3	1	0	5	5	31	20	1	5	37	1.5	10.7	42%	.271	0.84	3.19	3.67	0.7
2008	FRI	AA	21	3	0	0	4	4	26	14	0	6	29	2.1	10.0	50%	.237	0.77	0.69	3.52	1.0
2009	TEX	MLB	22	8	13	0	33	21	1381	160	26	47	107	3.1	7.0	42%	.314	1.53	6.12	6.34	-0.3
2010	OKL	AAA	23	6	2	0	11	11	62^2	50	5	18	51	2.6	7.4	48%	.253	1.13	1.87	3.13	2.0
2010	TEX	MLB	23	3	4	0	14	10	57^1	55	6	24	54	3.8	8.5	42%	.297	1.45	4.08	4.48	0.7
2011	*TEX*	*MLB*	*24*	*8*	*8*	*0*	*22*	*22*	120^1	*123*	*16*	*47*	*95*	*3.5*	*7.1*	*45%*	*.299*	*1.41*	*4.61*	*5.01*	*1.8*

Last year was supposed to usher in his great leap forward, but instead of breaking out, Holland broke down; a sprained knee in spring training forced him to start the season in the minors, and left-rotator-cuff inflammation kept him out of the major-league rotation from late May until August 18. Despite the injury setbacks, Holland pitched very well in his 11 Triple-A starts and wasn't overwhelmed in his major-league appearances, showing the ability to miss bats and limit damage. The 24-year-old lefty features a plus fastball with solid movement, a sharp slider that is very hard on left-handed batters, a changeup that shows promise but lacks consistency, and a soft, show-me curveball with potential for improvement. Holland's future is still very bright; with health and continued maturation of his arsenal, he could develop into a midrotation starter as early as next season.

Tommy Hunter

Born: **7/3/1986** Age: **24**
Bats: R Throws: R Height: **6' 3"** Weight: **255**
Breakout: **8%** Improve: **27%** Collapse: **12%**
Attrition: **15%** MLB: **48%**

Comparables:
Don Larsen, Don Robinson, Don Newcombe (61)

YEAR	TEAM	LVL	AGE	W	L	SV	G	GS	IP	H	HR	BB	SO	EqBB9	EqSO9	GB%	BABIP	WHIP	ERA	FRA	WARP
2008	BAK	A+	21	5	4	0	9	9	58^1	63	6	8	50	1.2	7.7	50%	.326	1.25	3.55	3.35	1.5
2008	FRI	AA	21	4	2	0	8	8	52^1	52	5	17	28	2.9	4.8	46%	.285	1.38	3.79	4.60	0.5
2008	OKL	AAA	21	4	2	0	8	8	53	55	6	9	28	1.5	4.8	51%	.278	1.21	2.89	4.30	1.1
2008	TEX	MLB	21	0	2	0	3	3	11	23	4	3	9	2.5	7.4	33%	.432	2.45	16.36	13.03	-0.5
2009	FRI	AA	22	1	0	0	5	3	21^2	30	1	4	16	1.7	6.6	57%	.358	1.57	4.98	3.59	0.3
2009	OKL	AAA	22	3	2	0	8	8	49^1	53	5	16	35	2.9	6.4	41%	.316	1.44	3.83	4.68	0.5
2009	TEX	MLB	22	9	6	0	19	19	112	113	13	33	64	2.7	5.1	39%	.276	1.32	4.10	4.84	1.4
2010	OKL	AAA	23	1	2	0	6	6	26^2	28	2	11	14	3.8	4.8	53%	.289	1.49	4.05	4.13	0.5
2010	TEX	MLB	23	13	4	0	23	22	128	126	21	32	68	2.3	4.8	42%	.256	1.26	3.73	4.62	1.5
2011	*TEX*	*MLB*	*24*	*7*	*9*	*0*	*22*	*22*	*132*	*150*	*20*	*41*	*70*	*2.8*	*4.7*	*44%*	*.297*	*1.45*	*5.02*	*5.45*	*1.2*

Drafted in the supplemental first round in 2007, the former University of Alabama product made a successful transition from reliever to back-of-the-rotation starter last season, showing the ability to throw strikes and chew innings. Featuring an effective 12-to-6 curveball and a developing cut fastball that he uses to induce weak contact, Hunter mixes his pitches well and owns an unflappable presence on the mound. Without a plus fastball or true wipeout pitch, he struggles to miss bats, which limits his ceiling, but Hunter has value as a pre-arbitration innings horse who provides stability in the back of a rotation. He's also a former judo champion, so just in case he's reading, we'd probably be wise to close by observing that on second thought, he's a lean, fast-twitch athlete with four plus-plus pitches and a smile that could start a war.

Michael Kirkman

Born: **9/18/1986** Age: **24**
Bats: **L** Throws: **L** Height: **6' 4"** Weight: **195**
Breakout: **6%** Improve: **10%** Collapse: **3%**
Attrition: **11%** MLB: **16%**

Comparables:
Josh Outman, Eulogio De La Cruz, Brad Mills (81)

YEAR	TEAM	LVL	AGE	W	L	SV	G	GS	IP	H	HR	BB	SO	EqBB9	EqSO9	GB%	BABIP	WHIP	ERA	FRA	WARP
2008	CLN	A	21	4	3	0	15	14	74^{1}	78	8	23	58	2.8	7.0	47%	.306	1.40	4.36	4.31	1.0
2009	BAK	A+	22	4	1	0	8	7	48	43	1	18	54	3.4	10.1	44%	.336	1.35	1.88	2.18	1.7
2009	FRI	AA	22	5	7	0	18	18	96^{2}	93	9	43	64	4.0	6.0	46%	.282	1.45	4.19	4.60	0.8
2010	OKL	AAA	23	13	3	0	24	22	131	115	8	68	130	4.7	8.9	41%	.296	1.42	3.09	3.69	3.2
2010	TEX	MLB	23	0	0	0	14	0	16^{1}	9	0	10	16	5.5	8.8	50%	.214	1.16	1.65	3.50	0.2
2011	*TEX*	*MLB*	*24*	*5*	*7*	*0*	*16*	*16*	87^{2}	*95*	*11*	*52*	*63*	*5.3*	*6.4*	*43%*	*.310*	*1.68*	*5.43*	*5.90*	*0.5*

Drafted in the fifth round out of high school in 2005, Kirkman drifted off the prospect map, thanks to a series of injury setbacks and subsequent mechanical complications, but regained his feel for the mound in 2009 and took another step forward in 2010 by cracking the 25-man roster after being named the Pacific Coast League Pitcher of the Year. Pitching out of the major-league pen, Kirkman used his low-90s fastball (which can touch 95) to set up his solid slider, but his changeup was a forgotten pitch, and its development will go a long way toward determining his future role. If he can sharpen his command and find a pitch that will keep right-handers honest, Kirkman can stick in a major-league rotation.

Cliff Lee

Born: **8/30/1978** Age: **32**
Bats: **L** Throws: **L** Height: **6' 3"** Weight: **190**
Breakout: **13%** Improve: **42%** Collapse: **26%**
Attrition: **6%** MLB: **97%**

Comparables:
Roy Oswalt, Johan Santana, Fergie Jenkins (64)

YEAR	TEAM	LVL	AGE	W	L	SV	G	GS	IP	H	HR	BB	SO	EqBB9	EqSO9	GB%	BABIP	WHIP	ERA	FRA	WARP
2008	CLE	MLB	29	22	3	0	31	31	223^{1}	214	12	34	170	1.4	6.9	46%	.302	1.13	2.54	2.69	7.6
2009	CLE	MLB	30	7	9	0	22	22	152	165	10	33	107	2.0	6.3	45%	.318	1.32	3.14	2.99	4.8
2009	PHI	MLB	30	7	4	0	12	12	79^{2}	80	7	10	74	1.1	8.4	40%	.312	1.15	3.39	4.08	1.3
2010	SEA	MLB	31	8	3	0	13	13	103^{2}	92	5	6	89	0.5	7.7	41%	.283	0.95	2.34	2.46	3.2
2010	TEX	MLB	31	4	6	0	15	15	108^{2}	103	11	12	96	1.0	8.0	43%	.292	1.07	3.98	4.53	1.0
2011	*PHI*	*MLB*	*32*	*13*	*7*	*0*	*29*	*29*	211^{2}	*206*	*20*	*38*	*159*	*1.6*	*6.8*	*44%*	*.295*	*1.15*	*3.17*	*3.45*	*5.8*

Lee was acquired from the Seattle Mariners on July 9 in exchange for top prospect Justin Smoak, former first-round pick Blake Beavan, hard-throwing relief prospect Josh Lueke, and minor-league infielder Matt Lawson. As evidenced by the size of the package it took to land him, Lee was the best pitcher ever to wear a Rangers uniform, though his bad back meant that the pitcher the Rangers had traded for was not quite the pitcher they received. Still, his post-season heroics made him a legend in a state where baseball legends begin and end with Nolan Ryan. Armed with an above-average four-pitch mix and pristine control, Lee posted one of the best strikeout-to-walk ratios by a starting pitcher in baseball history, striking out 10.3 hitters for every free pass bestowed. Lee's acquisition gave the Rangers the ace that the franchise had sorely lacked, but he spurned their winter overtures in favor of a five-year stint in Philadelphia, where he'll make up one-quarter of the majors' most imposing rotation. He took what appeared to be a lesser deal than those on the table from the Rangers and Yankees, but the deal is still rather substantial as far as yearly pay-out goes. As for the teams he spurned, Lee may retain ace-level value for a few years, but in the long run, they will be thankful they escaped a six- or seven-year commitment.

Colby Lewis

Born: **8/2/1979** Age: **31**
Bats: **R** Throws: **R** Height: **6' 4"** Weight: **215**
Breakout: **9%** Improve: **41%** Collapse: **21%**
Attrition: **10%** MLB: **89%**

Comparables:
Gil Meche, Roger Clemens, Ben Sheets (65)

YEAR	TEAM	LVL	AGE	W	L	SV	G	GS	IP	H	HR	BB	SO	EqBB9	EqSO9	GB%	BABIP	WHIP	ERA	FRA	WARP
2010	TEX	MLB	30	12	13	0	32	32	201	174	21	65	196	2.9	8.8	39%	.275	1.22	3.72	3.88	3.8
2011	*TEX*	*MLB*	*31*	*11*	*8*	*0*	*26*	*26*	165^{1}	*157*	*19*	*54*	*142*	*2.9*	*7.8*	*42%*	*.292*	*1.28*	*3.78*	*4.11*	*3.8*

Originally drafted by the Rangers in the supplemental first round (38th overall) in 1999, Lewis rejoined Texas in 2010 after taking his act abroad and spending two seasons fine-tuning his command with the Hiroshima Toyo Carp of Japan's Central League. Always armed with quality raw stuff, Lewis emerged from his Far East travels with a much better feel for the mound, making the time-honored transition from thrower to pitcher. Relying heavily on a low-90s fastball and a hard, biting slider, Lewis was able to miss bats and eat innings, two qualities that the Rangers had sorely lacked in their starting rotation. Although he was an affordable gamble at the time of the signing, Lewis's contract now appears criminal, with a 2011 base salary of only $3.25 million; the team also holds a 2012 team option for the same amount. The bargain that the Rangers fished out of the Far East brings to mind the Japanese proverb *Nokorimono ni wa fuku ga aru*, "Luck exists in the leftovers."

Mark Lowe

Born: **6/7/1983** Age: **28**
Bats: **R** Throws: **R** Height: **6' 3"** Weight: **190**
Breakout: **20%** Improve: **27%** Collapse: **19%**
Attrition: **9%** MLB: **51%**

Comparables:
Steve Hamilton, Chad Cordero, Doug Henry (79)

YEAR	TEAM	LVL	AGE	W	L	SV	G	GS	IP	H	HR	BB	SO	EqBB9	EqSO9	GB%	BABIP	WHIP	ERA	FRA	WARP
2008	SEA	MLB	25	1	5	1	57	0	63^{2}	78	6	34	55	4.8	7.8	45%	.353	1.82	5.37	5.33	-0.2
2009	SEA	MLB	26	2	7	3	75	0	80	71	7	29	69	3.3	7.8	41%	.274	1.25	3.26	4.50	0.7
2010	SEA	MLB	27	1	3	0	11	0	10^{1}	11	1	5	7	4.4	6.1	27%	.313	1.55	3.48	4.70	0.0
2010	TEX	MLB	27	0	0	0	3	0	3	7	1	1	5	3.0	15.0	30%	.667	2.67	12.00	6.48	-0.1
2011	*TEX*	*MLB*	*28*	*2*	*1*	*1*	*44*	*0*	*46^{2}*	*48*	*5*	*21*	*39*	*4.0*	*7.5*	*44%*	*.312*	*1.48*	*4.64*	*5.04*	*-0.1*

Drafted out of the University of Texas at Arlington by the Seattle Mariners in 2004, the 27-year-old reliever found himself back in Arlington as part of the Cliff Lee/Justin Smoak trade. Still recovering from back surgery, Lowe logged only three innings of work with Texas during the regular season, but should bring his late-inning, 95-mph fastball-slider arsenal to the 2011 bullpen, where he'll attempt to tap into the promise that his production has yet to reflect.

Doug Mathis

Born: **6/7/1983** Age: **28**
Bats: **R** Throws: **R** Height: **6' 3"** Weight: **220**
Breakout: **6%** Improve: **8%** Collapse: **2%**
Attrition: **6%** MLB: **12%**

Comparables:
Edgar Gonzalez, Brian Bass, Matt Chico (84)

YEAR	TEAM	LVL	AGE	W	L	SV	G	GS	IP	H	HR	BB	SO	EqBB9	EqSO9	GB%	BABIP	WHIP	ERA	FRA	WARP
2008	OKL	AAA	25	5	1	0	10	10	53^{2}	51	7	14	36	2.3	6.0	56%	.268	1.23	3.35	5.54	0.3
2008	TEX	MLB	25	2	1	0	8	4	22^{1}	37	3	14	9	5.6	3.6	43%	.395	2.28	6.85	6.35	-0.1
2009	OKL	AAA	26	4	2	0	11	10	57	64	3	15	38	2.4	6.0	54%	.328	1.42	2.84	4.03	1.0
2009	TEX	MLB	26	0	1	1	24	2	42^{2}	39	4	10	25	2.1	5.3	51%	.267	1.20	3.16	4.43	0.4
2010	OKL	AAA	27	5	7	0	18	15	89	116	7	31	54	3.1	5.5	52%	.353	1.71	5.66	6.25	-0.0
2010	TEX	MLB	27	1	1	0	13	0	22^{1}	30	7	11	10	4.4	4.0	52%	.319	1.84	6.04	6.05	-0.2
2011	*TEX*	*MLB*	*28*	*5*	*8*	*0*	*35*	*16*	*115*	*142*	*16*	*46*	*58*	*3.6*	*4.5*	*49%*	*.320*	*1.63*	*5.78*	*6.28*	*-0.2*

Drafted in the 13th round of the 2005 amateur draft, right-hander Doug Mathis is an organizational arm who has seen time at the major-league level in each of the past three seasons, including a solid run of middle relief in 2009. Getting another look in 2010, Mathis was quickly exposed, allowing a remarkable seven home runs in only 22 innings of relief. Finally souring on his average-to-below-average stuff across the board, the Rangers outrighted Mathis in November. He elected free agency, but will struggle to find a home on a 25-man roster.

Brandon McCarthy

Born: **7/7/1983** Age: **27**
Bats: **R** Throws: **R** Height: **6' 7"** Weight: **190**
Breakout: **8%** Improve: **15%** Collapse: **7%**
Attrition: **11%** MLB: **34%**

Comparables:
Nick Masset, Jesse Chavez, Manuel Corpas (74)

YEAR	TEAM	LVL	AGE	W	L	SV	G	GS	IP	H	HR	BB	SO	EqBB9	EqSO9	GB%	BABIP	WHIP	ERA	FRA	WARP
2008	OKL	AAA	24	1	1	0	5	5	26^{2}	21	2	8	23	2.7	7.8	52%	.253	1.09	3.37	5.04	0.3
2008	TEX	MLB	24	1	1	0	5	5	22	20	3	8	10	3.3	4.1	27%	.239	1.32	3.68	5.49	0.2
2009	OKL	AAA	25	0	1	0	5	5	21^{2}	20	1	9	22	3.7	9.1	46%	.317	1.38	4.15	3.90	0.4
2009	TEX	MLB	25	7	4	0	17	17	97^{1}	96	13	36	65	3.3	6.0	40%	.274	1.39	4.62	5.65	0.4
2010	OKL	AAA	26	4	2	0	11	9	56^{1}	51	8	11	44	1.8	7.1	52%	.257	1.16	3.36	4.95	0.7
2011	*OAK*	*MLB*	*27*	*6*	*5*	*0*	*16*	*16*	*85*	*85*	*10*	*31*	*59*	*3.2*	*6.2*	*44%*	*.288*	*1.35*	*4.08*	*4.43*	*1.3*

Since being acquired from the White Sox for John Danks and Nick Masset—two pitchers who have actually contributed to major-league teams—McCarthy has suffered injury setback after injury setback, spending no time at the major-league level in 2010. With diminished stuff and a history of fragility that's threatening to encroach on Nick Johnson's intellectual property, McCarthy's chances of establishing himself as an above-average major-league starter are as thin and fragile as his six-foot-seven frame. After being outrighted in November, McCarthy elected free agency. A successful stint in the Venezuelan winter league drew interest from several major-league clubs, but McCarthy elected to sign with the A's, for whom he'll compete for a starting spot in a park that should suit his fly-ball tendencies.

Guillermo Moscoso

Born: **11/14/1983** Age: **27**
Bats: **R** Throws: **R** Height: **6' 1"** Weight: **200**
Breakout: **6%** Improve: **10%** Collapse: **5%**
Attrition: **8%** MLB: **21%**

Comparables:
Fernando Nieve, Dusty Hughes, Marco Estrada (78)

YEAR	TEAM	LVL	AGE	W	L	SV	G	GS	IP	H	HR	BB	SO	EqBB9	EqSO9	GB%	BABIP	WHIP	ERA	FRA	WARP
2008	LAK	A+	24	2	3	1	15	6	52	36	4	13	72	2.3	12.5	36%	.281	0.98	2.42	3.67	1.1
2008	ERI	AA	24	3	1	0	6	6	34^{2}	24	4	8	50	2.1	13.0	27%	.274	0.92	3.11	4.03	0.8
2009	FRI	AA	25	3	1	0	9	7	42^{1}	41	1	14	36	3.0	7.7	31%	.305	1.30	4.47	4.45	0.4
2009	OKL	AAA	25	5	4	0	12	11	70	56	2	15	60	1.9	7.7	38%	.274	1.06	2.19	2.95	2.1
2009	TEX	MLB	25	0	0	0	10	0	14	15	1	6	12	3.9	7.7	31%	.318	1.57	3.21	5.43	0.0
2010	OKL	AAA	26	7	7	0	23	22	123^{1}	142	17	49	107	3.6	7.8	36%	.324	1.58	5.18	5.80	0.4
2010	TEX	MLB	26	0	0	0	1	0	0^{2}	2	0	2	2	27.0	27.0	0%	1.000	7.50	27.00	14.83	0.0
2011	*TEX*	*MLB*	*27*	*5*	*6*	*0*	*20*	*14*	*89*	*100*	*13*	*35*	*70*	*3.5*	*7.0*	*38%*	*.317*	*1.51*	*5.12*	*5.57*	*0.6*

Acquired from the Tigers for self-proclaimed five-tool player Gerald Laird, the right-handed Moscoso spent the majority of the season pitching for the Oklahoma City Redhawks in the Pacific Coast League, but did get to enjoy 2/3 of an inning of hot major-league coffee in 2010 after sampling 14 innings of Agent Cooper–approved joe in 2009. Armed with little more than a phantom fastball with average-to-plus velocity and crazy life, Moscoso looks to be a better fit out of the pen, but spent most of his time in Triple-A working in the rotation. If his curveball can find some consistency, Moscoso might be able to stick on a major-league roster, but his future role is at the mercy of his development of secondary pitches.

Dustin Nippert

Born: **5/6/1981** Age: **30**
Bats: R Throws: R Height: **6' 8"** Weight: **217**
Breakout: **2%** Improve: **10%** Collapse: **6%**
Attrition: **6%** MLB: **18%**

Comparables:
Tim Corcoran, Jonah Bayliss, D.J. Houlton (79)

YEAR	TEAM	LVL	AGE	W	L	SV	G	GS	IP	H	HR	BB	SO	EqBB9	EqSO9	GB%	BABIP	WHIP	ERA	FRA	WARP
2008	OKL	AAA	27	6	2	0	12	10	63^1	65	8	16	43	2.3	6.1	44%	.295	1.31	3.98	4.11	1.3
2008	TEX	MLB	27	3	5	0	20	6	71^2	92	10	37	55	4.6	6.9	38%	.345	1.81	6.40	5.65	0.0
2009	TEX	MLB	28	5	3	0	20	10	69^2	64	7	29	54	3.7	7.0	42%	.277	1.39	3.88	4.29	1.2
2010	TEX	MLB	29	4	5	0	38	2	56^2	61	7	34	47	5.4	7.5	34%	.320	1.76	4.29	4.05	0.6
2011	*TEX*	*MLB*	*30*	*5*	*6*	*0*	*31*	*13*	*102^2*	*110*	*14*	*49*	*78*	*4.3*	*6.9*	*42%*	*.309*	*1.55*	*5.07*	*5.51*	*0.5*

A lot can go wrong from a mechanical standpoint when you stand six-foot-eight, and a cursory glance at Nippert's stat line reveals that his mechanical inconsistency contributed to a problematic 5.4 walks per nine innings last season. Despite owning a starter's arsenal that features a plus fastball, quality curve, and better-than-you-think changeup, Nippert was relegated to low-leverage bullpen duty, pushed down the late-inning waiting list by power arms Ogando, Francisco, and Feliz. With more such high-upside arms on their way to Arlington, and—thanks to his Super Two status—an early introduction to the wonders of salary arbitration weighing down his bargain potential, Nippert's Texas tenure ended when he was nontendered in December.

Darren O'Day

Born: **10/22/1982** Age: **28**
Bats: R Throws: R Height: **6' 4"** Weight: **225**
Breakout: **6%** Improve: **15%** Collapse: **18%**
Attrition: **14%** MLB: **38%**

Comparables:
Jesse Crain, Lee Smith, Tom Niedenfuer (71)

YEAR	TEAM	LVL	AGE	W	L	SV	G	GS	IP	H	HR	BB	SO	EqBB9	EqSO9	GB%	BABIP	WHIP	ERA	FRA	WARP
2008	SLC	AAA	25	2	2	7	21	0	33	29	3	7	30	1.9	8.2	41%	.292	1.12	3.55	3.33	0.7
2008	ANA	MLB	25	0	1	0	30	0	43^1	49	2	14	29	2.9	6.0	59%	.324	1.55	4.57	4.06	0.5
2009	NYN	MLB	26	0	0	0	4	0	3	5	0	1	2	3.0	6.0	38%	.385	2.33	0.00	4.96	0.0
2009	TEX	MLB	26	2	1	2	64	0	55^2	36	3	17	54	2.7	8.7	43%	.239	1.02	1.94	2.86	1.4
2010	TEX	MLB	27	6	2	0	72	0	62	43	5	12	45	1.7	6.5	39%	.220	0.97	2.03	2.83	1.4
2011	*TEX*	*MLB*	*28*	*3*	*1*	*1*	*52*	*0*	*55*	*52*	*6*	*17*	*42*	*2.8*	*6.8*	*45%*	*.285*	*1.25*	*3.64*	*3.96*	*0.6*

For the small price of a waiver claim fee, the Rangers were able to steal right-handed side-armer Darren O'Day from the Mets in April 2009. Since Texas acquired the former University of Florida closer, O'Day has been one of the most consistent relievers on the 25-man roster, proving to be more than just a novelty specialist. Working with a heavy mid- to upper-80s fastball and a sweeping slider, O'Day throws strikes from a deceptive release and elicits weak contact from hitters who step in from both sides of the box. Without overpowering stuff, O'Day's margin of error is small, so overexposure or a BABIP regression—which some research suggests might be less likely for him than it would be for a more conventional pitcher—could lead to less happy results.

Alexi Ogando

Born: **10/5/1983** Age: **27**
Bats: R Throws: R Height: **6' 4"** Weight: **185**
Breakout: **21%** Improve: **30%** Collapse: **16%**
Attrition: **10%** MLB: **55%**

Comparables:
Joakim Soria, Sergio Romo, Joey Devine (72)

YEAR	TEAM	LVL	AGE	W	L	SV	G	GS	IP	H	HR	BB	SO	EqBB9	EqSO9	GB%	BABIP	WHIP	ERA	FRA	WARP
2010	TEX	MLB	26	4	1	0	44	0	41^2	31	2	16	39	3.5	8.4	45%	.257	1.15	1.30	1.12	1.8
2011	*TEX*	*MLB*	*27*	*2*	*1*	*0*	*32*	*1*	*38*	*32*	*4*	*15*	*40*	*3.4*	*9.4*	*45%*	*.289*	*1.21*	*3.08*	*3.35*	*0.8*

Selected by the Rangers in the minor-league phase of the Rule 5 draft back in 2005, Ogando was to be a reclamation project—a failed hitter with an electric arm who was bound for the mound at age 22. The odds were long to begin with, but they were about to get even longer: in 2005, both Ogando and fellow Rangers farmhand Omar Beltre were involved with a human trafficking ring, in which organized-crime figures paid minor-league players to engage in marriage-for-visa fraud. Banned from entering the United States as a result, Ogando honed his pitching chops in the Dominican Summer League in hopes of one day returning to U.S. soil. After the ban was lifted and a visa was issued (with no phony marriage required), Ogando embarked on a magical season that saw him ride the promotion train from Double-A to the majors, where he not only saw significant and successful time, but also pitched in the World Series. At his best, Ogando features an upper-90s heater that pairs well with a hard slider, but he also mixes in a changeup that moves like a splitter. With a power arsenal, a good feel for the strike zone, and the intestinal fortitude to handle high-leverage situations, Ogando could slide into Francisco's soon-to-be-vacated eighth-inning role.

Darren Oliver

Born: **10/6/1970** Age: **40**
Bats: **R** Throws: **L** Height: **6' 2"** Weight: **200**
Breakout: **9%** Improve: **17%** Collapse: **17%**
Attrition: **9%** MLB: **42%**

Comparables:
Rudy May, Al Reyes, Larry Andersen (63)

YEAR	TEAM	LVL	AGE	W	L	SV	G	GS	IP	H	HR	BB	SO	EqBB9	EqSO9	GB%	BABIP	WHIP	ERA	FRA	WARP
2008	ANA	MLB	37	7	1	0	54	0	72	67	5	16	48	2.0	6.0	49%	.284	1.21	2.88	3.30	1.4
2009	ANA	MLB	38	5	1	0	63	1	73	61	5	22	65	2.7	8.0	46%	.286	1.21	2.71	3.20	1.5
2010	TEX	MLB	39	1	2	1	64	0	61^2	53	4	15	65	2.2	9.5	49%	.310	1.14	2.48	2.19	1.9
2011	*TEX*	*MLB*	*40*	*3*	*1*	*0*	*62*	*0*	*69^1*	*65*	*7*	*21*	*57*	*2.7*	*7.4*	*46%*	*.293*	*1.24*	*3.51*	*3.81*	*0.9*

Which is more impressive? Dennis Eckersley was a very good starting pitcher who became a great reliever. Oliver was a terrible starter who became a very good reliever. Originally drafted by the Rangers in the third round of the 1988 draft, Oliver had a 5.13 ERA in 229 career starters and a 3.36 ERA in 364 games out of the pen, including 2.70 over the last three seasons. He pitched the majority of the 2010 season at the ripe old age of 39 and looking none the worse for wear, though after an excellent first half, he started to show off some LOOGY limitations, struggling when overexposed to right-handed hitters. Relying heavily on a two-pitch mix (upper-80s fastball, upper-70s slider), Oliver used his command and ability to change speeds to miss a career-best 9.5 bats per nine innings. With his 2011 option already vested, he'll return to the Rangers' pen, again hoping to turn his trademark craftiness into a season of positive value.

Martin Perez

Born: **4/4/1991** Age: **20**
Bats: **L** Throws: **L** Height: **6' 0"** Weight: **178**
Breakout: **7%** Improve: **12%** Collapse: **1%**
Attrition: **1%** MLB: **16%**

Comparables:
Steve Avery, Camilo Pascual, Ken Holtzman (66)

YEAR	TEAM	LVL	AGE	W	L	SV	G	GS	IP	H	HR	BB	SO	EqBB9	EqSO9	GB%	BABIP	WHIP	ERA	FRA	WARP
2008	SPO	A-	17	1	2	0	15	15	61^2	66	3	28	53	4.1	7.7	51%	.330	1.56	3.65	4.00	1.3
2009	HIC	A	18	5	5	1	22	14	93^2	82	3	33	105	3.2	10.1	53%	.317	1.24	2.31	2.78	2.9
2009	FRI	AA	18	1	3	0	5	5	21	29	2	5	14	2.1	6.0	50%	.365	1.62	5.57	4.62	0.2
2010	FRI	AA	19	5	8	0	24	23	99^2	117	12	50	101	4.5	9.2	50%	.352	1.68	5.96	4.82	1.1
2011	*TEX*	*MLB*	*20*	*5*	*9*	*0*	*22*	*19*	*90*	*107*	*13*	*51*	*65*	*5.1*	*6.5*	*46%*	*.328*	*1.75*	*6.04*	*6.56*	*0.1*

As the 19-year-old southpaw Perez started the 2010 season in Double-A, he was dubbed a top-tier talent and one of the best left-handers in the minors by most prognosticators. When the season ended, the Venezuelan was still considered a top prospect, but his stock had fallen, and many of the same people who spoke of his greatness last spring are now singing a different tune. Development takes time, and Perez was still a teenager when he made those starts for the Frisco Roughriders. Despite his inconsistent command, his raw stuff was still good enough to miss more than a bat per inning, and his makeup is off the charts. His arsenal is special: a fastball that sits comfortably at 92-96 with arm-side run, a plus curveball that is a true swing-and-miss offering, and a changeup with good deception and fade (a pitch that some scouts project higher than the curve). Perez will look to put it all together in 2011 and has a good chance to enjoy a major-league cup of coffee at the age of 20.

Zach Phillips

Born: **9/21/1986** Age: **24**
Bats: **L** Throws: **L** Height: **6' 1"** Weight: **200**
Breakout: **0%** Improve: **3%** Collapse: **0%**
Attrition: **2%** MLB: **4%**

Comparables:
Josh Outman, Brad Mills, Bob Buhl (78)

YEAR	TEAM	LVL	AGE	W	L	SV	G	GS	IP	H	HR	BB	SO	EqBB9	EqSO9	GB%	BABIP	WHIP	ERA	FRA	WARP
2008	BAK	A+	21	8	9	0	28	28	144^2	161	10	73	117	4.5	7.3	49%	.333	1.67	5.54	5.34	0.8
2009	BAK	A+	22	2	3	2	16	3	44	19	1	11	46	2.3	9.4	57%	.164	0.68	1.23	2.86	1.2
2009	FRI	AA	22	0	0	2	20	0	33^2	27	1	19	29	5.1	7.7	54%	.255	1.39	1.60	2.50	0.7
2010	OKL	AAA	23	3	2	1	33	1	50^1	50	1	29	40	5.2	7.2	57%	.318	1.60	3.22	2.87	1.6
2011	*TEX*	*MLB*	*24*	*5*	*5*	*1*	*49*	*9*	*110*	*126*	*12*	*64*	*73*	*5.2*	*5.9*	*48%*	*.318*	*1.72*	*5.59*	*6.08*	*-0.6*

A 23rd round draft-and-follow pick in 2004, Phillips relies on a three-pitch mix highlighted by an average-to-plus change-up that plays well off his upper-80s fastball. Refined command will be the key to Phillips' future success, as the southpaw walked 29 Triple-A batters in only 50 innings last year and lacks the raw stuff to get away with many mistakes. Added to the 40-man roster before the 2010 season, he's likely to make his major-league debut in 2011. While he won't necessarily be pigeonholed as a LOOGY, his arsenal does have its limitations, so Phillips might have a better chance of sticking on a major-league roster if he develops into a specialist.

Tanner Scheppers

Born: **1/17/1987** Age: **24**
Bats: **R** Throws: **R** Height: **6' 4"** Weight: **200**
Breakout: **15%** Improve: **36%** Collapse: **10%**
Attrition: **22%** MLB: **61%**

Comparables:
Marc Rzepczynski, Clay Buchholz, Ian Kennedy (71)

YEAR	TEAM	LVL	AGE	W	L	SV	G	GS	IP	H	HR	BB	SO	EqBB9	EqSO9	GB%	BABIP	WHIP	ERA	FRA	WARP
2010	OKL	AAA	23	1	3	4	30	7	69	82	5	30	71	3.9	9.3	42%	.374	1.74	5.48	5.35	0.2
2011	*TEX*	*MLB*	*24*	*4*	*3*	*1*	*39*	*7*	*84*	*81*	*9*	*33*	*80*	*3.6*	*8.5*	*44%*	*.310*	*1.35*	*4.06*	*4.41*	*1.1*

After choosing to go the indie-ball route rather than sign with the Pirates in 2008, Scheppers reentered the 2009 draft and fell to the Rangers with the 44th overall pick. Armed with a plus-plus fastball/curve combo, Scheppers made the transition to professional ball look easy, cruising through his brief Double-A tour and showing major-league-quality late-inning stuff.

With an eye toward developing Scheppers as a starter, the Rangers sent the electric right-hander to Triple-A, where he made seven starts and focused on refining his below-average changeup. If the fastball command tightens up and the changeup can become an average pitch, Scheppers has a chance to be a second starter. The more likely scenario has Scheppers showcasing his power arsenal out of the pen, where his fastball can reach the upper 90s and his curve can make hitters look foolish.

Pedro Strop

Born: **6/13/1985** Age: **26**
Bats: **S** Throws: **R** Height: **6' 0"** Weight: **175**
Breakout: **1%** Improve: **4%** Collapse: **5%**
Attrition: **3%** MLB: **11%**

Comparables:
Luis Perdomo, Wesley Wright, Samuel Gervacio (79)

YEAR	TEAM	LVL	AGE	W	L	SV	G	GS	IP	H	HR	BB	SO	EqBB9	EqSO9	GB%	BABIP	WHIP	ERA	FRA	WARP
2009	FRI	AA	24	5	5	4	36	0	51^{1}	48	1	29	48	5.1	8.4	53%	.315	1.54	4.39	3.40	0.7
2009	TEX	MLB	24	0	0	0	7	0	7	6	0	4	9	5.1	11.6	35%	.353	1.43	7.71	5.05	0.0
2010	OKL	AAA	25	1	2	13	39	0	42^{1}	32	1	14	57	3.0	12.2	54%	.307	1.09	1.91	1.86	1.4
2010	TEX	MLB	25	0	0	0	15	0	10^{2}	17	2	11	11	9.3	9.3	35%	.429	2.72	10.13	6.11	-0.2
2011	*TEX*	*MLB*	*26*	*2*	*1*	*2*	*35*	*0*	*41^{2}*	*40*	*4*	*22*	*41*	*4.9*	*8.9*	*46%*	*.317*	*1.51*	*4.56*	*4.96*	*-0.0*

Strop has electric late-inning stuff, but he hasn't yet shown it in the bigs, regardless of the inning. The converted infielder possesses an exceptional arsenal, including a plus-plus fastball with some life, a biting two-plane slider, and a trap-door splitter, but when placed on the biggest stage, Strop's arsenal becomes diluted and his control disappears. If inexperience or major-league jitters are the culprit, then the solution is simple and the payoff is valuable: let him pitch.

C. J. Wilson

Born: **11/18/1980** Age: **30**
Bats: **L** Throws: **L** Height: **6' 2"** Weight: **200**
Breakout: **8%** Improve: **40%** Collapse: **22%**
Attrition: **6%** MLB: **94%**

Comparables:
Rudy May, Greg McMichael, Erik Bedard (71)

YEAR	TEAM	LVL	AGE	W	L	SV	G	GS	IP	H	HR	BB	SO	EqBB9	EqSO9	GB%	BABIP	WHIP	ERA	FRA	WARP
2008	TEX	MLB	27	2	2	24	50	0	46^{1}	49	8	27	41	5.2	8.0	48%	.302	1.68	6.02	7.14	-0.8
2009	TEX	MLB	28	5	6	14	74	0	73^{2}	66	3	32	84	3.9	10.3	57%	.318	1.41	2.81	2.55	2.0
2010	TEX	MLB	29	15	8	0	33	33	204	161	10	93	170	4.1	7.5	50%	.266	1.29	3.35	4.33	3.0
2011	*TEX*	*MLB*	*30*	*6*	*3*	*9*	*44*	*9*	*90*	*81*	*7*	*42*	*80*	*4.2*	*7.9*	*48%*	*.292*	*1.36*	*3.79*	*4.12*	*1.6*

After appearing in 252 career games out of the bullpen, the mercurial southpaw finally got his long-awaited opportunity to audition for a rotation spot, taking the hill in Surprise, Arizona, in hopes of leaving the set-up role behind him. Drawing upon a strong five-pitch assortment, Wilson made the transition look easy, logging 33 starts for the major-league club and supplying a stabilizing presence on a young, pennant-winning team. Wilson turned 30 in November and will be a free agent after the 2011 season, so the Rangers will soon be faced with a decision regarding his long-term future. If he can sharpen his command and show no ill effects from last season's dramatic workload increase, Wilson looks to be a safe bet to remain a high-value rotation arm.

LINEOUTS

HITTERS

PLAYER	TEAM	LVL	AGE	PA	R	2B	3B	HR	RBI	BB	SO	SB-CS	AVG/OBP/SLG	TAv	BABIP	BRR	FRAA	WARP
RF B. Boggs#	OKL	AAA	27	439	72	25	5	10	50	72	93	3-6	.290/.406/.470	.299	.361	0.0	CF 1, RF 0	2.8
	TEX	MLB	27	8	0	0	0	0	0	1	4	0-0	.000/.125/.000	.030	.000	0.0	RF 0, LF 0	-0.1
C K. Deglan*	SPO	A-	18	90	7	2	0	1	4	7	21	0-0	.159/.222/.220	.162	.197	0.0	C 0	-0.6
OF J. Hoying*	SPO	A-	21	267	47	13	5	10	51	19	70	20-9	.325/.378/.543	.344	.418	0.0	LF -5, RF 0	2.4
CF T. Martinez	RNG	Rk	18	233	43	14	3	1	22	9	25	20-7	.313/.357/.422	.284	.340	1.9	CF 4, LF 0	1.6
1B C. McGuiness*	GRN	A	22	341	41	20	1	12	46	53	59	2-3	.298/.416/.504	.328	.340	-5.8	1B 1	2.2
	BAK	A+	22	147	19	3	0	7	22	24	32	1-1	.250/.381/.450	.313	.280	-2.6	1B 1	0.8
3B M. Olt	SPO	A-	21	310	57	16	1	9	43	40	77	6-0	.293/.390/.464	.316	.378	0.0	3B -4	2.4
SS L. Sardinas#	RNG	Rk	17	119	22	4	0	0	8	7	15	8-2	.311/.363/.350	.272	.337	1.3	SS 1	0.9
OF M. Velazquez	HIC	A	22	310	46	17	1	10	53	26	47	12-4	.270/.342/.449	.274	.290	0.7	CF 6, RF 0	1.9
	BAK	A+	22	207	27	6	1	5	25	12	38	3-1	.270/.333/.392	.277	.315	2.8	RF 2, CF -2	0.9
3B C. Villanueva	RNG	Rk	19	210	30	14	1	2	35	13	42	6-2	.314/.365/.431	.303	.383	-1.2	3B -3	1.4

A casualty of the late-season 40-man crunch, **Brandon Boggs** might have lost his place at the table, but the versatile outfielder with power and patience will return to Triple-A in 2011 with the skill set to force his way back into roster contention. After spending most of last season recovering from knee surgery, outfielder **Endy Chavez** will attempt to make a push for a role on the active roster in 2011, but since the Rangers have better options on the depth chart, it looks like an uphill battle for the 33-year-old Venezuelan. ⚾ Top Canadian prep catcher **Kellin Deglan** was selected with the 22nd overall pick in the 2010 draft and signed for a below-slot $1 million bonus. Inflated with helium, thanks to his performance with Canada's Junior National Team, Deglan was considered a first-round possibility, though many draft experts considered him more of a bargain pick for the cash-strapped Rangers than a player whose talent warranted such a high selection. Despite a rough 22-game run in the advanced Northwest League, Deglan impressed scouts with his tools, showing a strong arm behind the plate and some power potential with his swing. ⚾ Drafted in the 10th round from the University of Toledo, alma mater of the great Phillip Baker Hall, outfielder **Jared Hoying** made the most of his short-season experience, winning the Northwest League's MVP award and showcasing a solid collection of tools and plus baseball instincts. ⚾ Son of former major-league infielder Carlos "Cafe" Martinez, **Teodoro "Cafesito" Martinez** more than held his own in rookie ball, making contact, stealing bases, and flashing plus defensive skills in center field. ⚾ Part of the return from the Red Sox for Jarrod Saltalamacchia, **Christopher McGuiness** started to look like a legit prospect in 2010, showing a solid approach at the plate and some developing power potential to go along with a good glove at first. ⚾ Supplemental first-round selection **Michael Olt** displayed excellent defensive chops at the hot corner and above-average power potential, slugging 26 extra-base hits in 69 games for short-season Spokane. ⚾ You've heard of teams signing Japanese free agents, but Japanese *nondrafted* free agents? **Hirotoshi Onaka** is a short, speedy center fielder who hit .327 with five home runs in a 75-game at International Pacific University, but didn't get called to the pros. *Senren sa reta daigaku no dasha* is, roughly speaking, Japanese for "polished college hitter." We'll see if Onaka is one of those. ⚾ While fellow shortstop Jurickson Profar gets most of the prospect love, slick-fielding Venezuelan **Luis Sardinas** is an equally impressive prospect, showing true actions at the position and a promising hit tool from both sides of the plate. ⚾ San Juan native **Miguel Velazquez** shows five tools, but has yet to put them all together at the full-season level. The 22-year-old right fielder already lost a year of development to off-the-field legal issues in his native Puerto Rico and needs to rebound from a subpar 2010 this season to maintain his prospect status. ⚾ Mexico native **Christian Villanueva** more than held his own in his stateside debut, hitting .314 in the rookie Arizona League while showing off an already-plus glove and strong arm at third.

PITCHERS

PLAYER	TEAM	LVL	AGE	W	L	SV	IP	H	HR	BB	SO	EqBB9	EqSO9	GB%	BABIP	WHIP	ERA	FRA	WARP
Y. Brazoban	DNP	AAA	30	—	—	—	—	—	—	—	—	—	—	—	—	—	—	—	—
F. Castillo	BAK	A+	21	1	3	6	51^{2}	41	2	26	65	4.6	11.4	51%	.317	1.37	1.92	2.33	1.5
M. De Los Santos*	HIC	A	21	2	2	0	38^{1}	27	3	24	62	5.7	14.6	41%	.333	1.36	3.99	3.77	0.9
	SPO	A-	21	2	0	0	32	13	0	20	50	5.6	14.1	47%	.210	1.06	1.41	2.28	1.3
C. Eppley	FRI	AA	24	1	1	9	22^{2}	12	0	9	27	3.6	10.9	79%	.231	0.95	1.19	4.32	0.1
	OKL	AAA	24	2	1	1	28^{2}	32	3	13	31	4.1	9.9	53%	.358	1.60	4.08	4.52	0.2
R. Erlin*	HIC	A	19	6	3	1	114^{2}	89	9	17	125	1.3	9.9	41%	.274	0.96	2.12	2.80	4.0
W. Font	HIC	A	20	4	1	0	29^{2}	35	3	13	33	4.0	10.2	49%	.372	1.68	5.16	5.23	0.2
	BAK	A+	20	1	2	0	49	38	5	32	52	5.9	9.6	40%	.273	1.47	3.86	5.00	0.3
B. Loux	DNP	—	22	—	—	—	—	—	—	—	—	—	—	—	—	—	—	—	—
W. Madrigal	OKL	AAA	26	4	2	2	41	33	5	7	33	1.5	7.2	42%	.239	1.00	3.73	4.16	0.5
C. Rapada*	OKL	AAA	29	1	2	2	59^{1}	32	1	21	61	3.2	9.3	50%	.215	0.96	1.82	3.55	1.1
	TEX	MLB	29	0	0	0	9	6	2	7	5	7.0	5.0	33%	.160	1.44	4.00	5.72	-0.1
R. Ross*	HIC	A	21	8	7	0	94	89	2	20	62	1.9	5.9	65%	.284	1.28	2.59	1.42	4.9
	BAK	A+	21	4	4	0	52	67	4	17	49	2.9	8.5	63%	.375	1.69	5.37	5.26	0.3
R. Tucker	JUP	A+	23	1	3	6	30	35	0	24	18	7.2	5.4	39%	.357	2.07	6.00	5.18	-0.1
	NWO	AAA	23	0	5	0	33^{2}	41	3	17	19	4.6	5.2	47%	.317	1.75	6.15	6.89	-0.2
J. Wieland	HIC	A	20	7	4	0	89	84	4	15	71	1.5	7.2	50%	.303	1.15	3.34	4.40	1.3
	BAK	A+	20	4	3	0	59	67	6	10	62	1.5	9.5	39%	.343	1.34	5.19	4.81	0.3

Advice to fringe pitchers: after missing the better part of three seasons recovering from Tommy John and labrum surgery, don't come to camp looking as though you spent the winter sacked out in your beanbag chair eating bagels 'n' schmaltz. **Yhency Brazoban**'s decision to do so earned him a release and a year out of baseball. He pitched his way back in through the Mexican League and the Metsican organization, decent strikeout rates earning a spring training invite from the Rangers. ⚾ A prototypical late-inning power arm with a mid-90s fastball and a bat-evading hard slider, **Fabio Castillo** was one of the first big international signings for the Rangers back in 2005 and finally harnessed his talent in 2010, earning a deserved promotion to Double-A and pitching capably in the Arizona Fall League. ⊘ After losing traction while coping with a visa issue in 2009, lefty **Miguel De Los Santos** reemerged on the stateside scene, using his potent three-pitch mix to miss 112 bats in only 70 1/3 innings over two levels. ⊘ The 1,293rd overall pick in the 2008 draft, side-arming righty **Cody Eppley** made stops at three levels in 2010 and positioned himself as a situational righty in the mold of Darren O'Day. ⊘ Short in stature but not in stuff, left-hander **Robert Erlin** exploded on the full-season scene in 2010, showing three solid-average to plus pitches, plus command, and makeup mature beyond his 19 years. Despite not possessing a top-of-the-rotation ceiling, Erlin's combination of polish and promise makes him a legit prospect and a player who could reach Double-A as a 20-year-old. ⊘ The Rangers added flamethrowing starter **Wilmer Font** to the 40-man roster this fall, but after going under the knife for Tommy John surgery, Font might see his skill-set better utilized in the pen, where he can terrorize hitters with his mid- to upper-90s smoke (assuming, of course, that he regains his once-touted velocity). ⊘ **Eric Hurley** was sidelined with shoulder- and wrist-related injuries for over two years, but the former first-round pick finally made it back to the mound, flashing a low-90s fastball and a slider for the Surprise Rafters in the Arizona Fall League. ⊘ Armed with a solid starter's arsenal, a six-foot-five frame, and an arm so damaged that the D'Backs decided to rescind their contract offer after drafting him and thereby making him a free agent ripe for recruiting by the Rangers, former sixth overall pick **Barret Loux** hopes to prove to his doubters that pitchers don't need healthy shoulders or elbows to succeed. ⊘ Another former position player turned reliever, **Warner Madrigal** battled injury and command issues in 2010, but still has a major-league fastball despite not experiencing major-league results. ⊘ After a year away from baseball, some of which he spent coaching a sad-sack girls' high-school basketball team in Florida, **Seth McClung** received a split contract from the Rangers, opening another chapter in his ongoing (and often losing) battle to post a strikeout rate higher than his walk rate. ⊘ Pitching professionally for the first time since 2006, former golden boy **Mark Prior** made one relief appearance for the Oklahoma City Redhawks, hoping to end his season on a positive note after four years of setbacks. He can keep reliving that scoreless inning with two strikeouts until he does something better this season in the Yankees' system, where he can aim to be reunited in the majors with his old Cubs pitching coach, Larry Rothschild. ⊘ This 29-year-old side-arming LOOGY with an erratic mid-80s fastball logged all of nine innings in the majors in 2010 . . . yep, that's **Clay Rapada**. Using a solid slider to neutralize lefties, Rapada serves his purpose as a specialist, but he is quickly exposed and easily exploited by right-handed hitters, so his claim to a spot on the 25-man roster is shaky, despite excellent minor-league numbers. ⊘ A former second-round pick with a bowling-ball fastball, diminutive southpaw **Robert Ross** will start the 2011 season in the Frisco rotation, hoping to become the first second-round pick to reach the majors with the Rangers since Nick Regilio, who was drafted in 1999. ⊘ The Rangers signed 35-year-old **Yoshinori Tateyama** to add to their ever-growing roster of side-arming relievers. The Japanese import used a solid three-pitch mix to throw strikes and miss bats for the Hokkaido Nippon Ham Fighters. ⊘ Claimed off waivers from the Florida Marlins, former supplemental first-round pick **Ryan Tucker** will look to join the list of successful reclamation projects to emerge from the Rangers' organization in recent years. ⊘ With solid-to-average stuff across the board and an excellent feel for the mound, former 2008 fourth-rounder **Joseph Wieland** looked sharp during his two-level 2010 odyssey, racking up 5.3 whiffs for every free pass allowed.

MANAGER: RON WASHINGTON

YEAR	TEAM	W-L	Pythag +/-	Avg PC	100+ P	120+ P	QS	BQS	REL	REL w Zero R	IBB	Subs	PH	PH Avg	PH HR	SB2	CS2	SB3	CS3	SAC Att	SAC %	POS SAC	Squeeze	Swing	In Play
2008	TEX	79-83	4	91.3	54	1	52	7	457	261	44	38	117	.250	0	71	23	10	2	62	59.7%	33	0	132	93
2009	TEX	87-75	1	96.7	67	5	66	10	436	283	14	12	48	.119	0	117	31	32	3	55	72.7%	35	4	128	96
2010	TEX	90-72	-2	98.1	86	2	73	10	481	320	24	41	86	.216	1	105	42	16	6	81	65.4%	50	7	133	107

On the morning of March 17, 2010, news broke that Washington had failed a drug test administered the previous summer. According to the reports, he had tested positive for cocaine. With the dawn of a new season freshly upon them, the Rangers' front office decided to channel their inner Tammy Wynette and stand by their man, thus setting the tone for a season that would see Washington fully embrace that theme, standing behind his players for better or worse and guiding the team to its first World Series appearance. His abilities to manage the mood of the clubhouse and prepare his team to take the field are the hallmarks of his skill set, qualities that normally reside in the box of esoterica labeled "intangibles." Still, after the players lined up to support their embattled leader, the apparent importance of Washington's interpersonal skills to his team's fortunes is what made his continued presence palatable to the fan-base. On the flip side, Washington's in-game management doesn't always pass the smell test, as his bullpen management (read "mismanagement") and small-ball tendencies can baffle the mind. Although Washington presided over the most sacrifices of any AL manager, he also issued the fewest free passes of any AL field general save Ron Gardenhire. With an American League pennant flying in Arlington and a locker room willing to follow him once more unto the breach, Washington has, however improbably, secured his position as skipper for the foreseeable future.

Toronto Blue Jays

Organizational philosophies, like modes of production, carry inside them the seeds of their own demise. No general manager is so consistent, stable, and critical that he can remain immune to the dangerous tendency of all ideas to run to self-parody. That J. P. Ricciardi had worked for Billy Beane perhaps accelerated the natural process, since Beane's organizational philosophy was set in stone—or at least 12-point pica in the pages of *Moneyball*—less than two years after Ricciardi took the helm of the Blue Jays. By the time he was fired, Ricciardi's legacy was in tatters: he left baseball's sole remaining Canadian outpost a barren farm system, one whale of a Vernon Wells contract, and a lean stable of scouts in his wake.

By now the story of Alex Anthopoulos's ascendance is familiar: revenge of the scouts and the traditionalists strike back. Certainly, when he took control of the Blue Jays in October 2009, one of Anthopoulos's first moves was to expand the budget for scouting and player development. The new regime added more than three dozen scouts in its first few months. And certainly, Anthopoulos himself had a scouting background, working first for the Expos and then for six years as the scouting coordinator under Ricciardi. Never mind that he was a wunderkind who had spent years learning from a Beane acolyte. Ignore his economics degree from McMaster University—who can keep those Canadian universities straight, anyway? He's a scout!

Some of the team's early moves under new leadership suggested such a change in direction. The Jays claimed utility grinder Mike McCoy in November. They signed the car-jumping speedster Joey Gathright. They signed two ostensible backup catchers: Raul Chavez and John Buck. Those seemed like the kinds of moves a GM with a scouting background would make to bolster multiple levels of an organization.

BLUE JAYS PROSPECTUS

2010 W-L: 85-77, 4th in AL East

Pythag	.517	15th
RS/G	4.7	9th
RA/G	4.5	12th
TAv	.274	11th
BRR	-6.5	26th
FRA	4.53	18th
DER	-1.67	18th
DL	1,069	27th
B-Age	29.3	19th
P-Age	27.3	8th
Salary	$62.2	22nd
M$/MW	$1.43	5th

Ballpark: Rogers Centre (3-yr. PF: 102). The 2010 team's homer-happy approach owed much to the stadium formerly known as the SkyDome

2010: Plenty of fireworks, but scant reason to celebrate

2011: Only realignment could save the Jays from another uphill slog

Action Items: Batters with on-base skills, breaking in Kyle and J.P., a reliable closer

In December came the blockbuster trade of Roy Halladay to the Phillies for a package of Kyle Drabek, Michael Taylor, and Travis d'Arnaud. It was exactly the kind of haul that Ricciardi had rebuffed the summer before, but it immediately gave the Blue Jays three new top-100 prospects and dramatically improved their farm system. Even the trade of Michael Taylor, the sweet-swinging outfielder, for classic OBP butcher Brett Wallace couldn't remove the scouting-flavored aura from the new era.

In a startling move later that month, Anthopoulos fleeced the stat-snob orthodoxy's newest darling to the tune of a front-line starter for a middle reliever, prying Brandon Morrow away from Jack Zduriencik and the Mariners in exchange for competent eighth-inning man Brandon League. It was a brilliant move even if it didn't necessarily comport entirely with the bipolar stats/scouts view of the world. After all, stats people have been shouting for years that pitchers tend to be more valuable as starters, that relievers are fungible and mostly overvalued, and that attempts to convert relievers to rotation work are high-reward—if risky—gambles. Still, many refused to let that apparent incongruity get in the way of a good narrative.

More puzzling, perhaps, was the July deal that sent power-hitting shortstop (and strong defender) Alex Gonzalez to Atlanta for Yunel Escobar—a player whose influence in the clubhouse was far from universally praised—and Jo-Jo Reyes. It was tough to spin this as a traditionalist sort of move, particularly given that Gonzalez was on pace for a career year. But who knows what Toronto's new army of major-league scouts saw in Escobar? Maybe they were convinced that he suffered from a correctable hitch in his swing.

The balance was restored just two weeks later, when Anthopoulos dealt Brett Wallace to the Astros for Anthony Gose, one of the toolsiest—and rawest—prospects in the game. The deal was a bit of a head-scratcher at first, since if the transactions are stepped together, it appears that the Blue Jays traded Michael Taylor for Anthony Gose (with Wallace as an intermediary), a move few would have made last offseason. At the time of the trade, though, Anthopoulos said all the right things to confirm his old-school credentials. He stated that his scouts were unanimous in projecting a high ceiling for the team's newest acquisition. He also noted that the team's persistent interest in Gose dated all the way back to the Halladay deal.

The Blue Jays' biggest move this past offseason was sending their reigning most-valuable pitcher, Shaun Marcum, to Milwaukee for quasi-second baseman Brett Lawrie. Marcum posted the sixth-highest strikeout-to-walk ratio in baseball last year, ahead of Cy Young Award–winner Felix Hernandez and every other starting pitcher in the AL East, but he lacks overpowering stuff. On the other hand, Lawrie's bat is promising and he was young for Double-A last year, but his poor defense will ultimately land him in a corner position. With plenty of cost-controlled starting pitchers in the stable, the Blue Jays cashed in the one who was most likely to be at the peak of his value for a well-regarded hitting prospect—an area in which the Jays have had a rocky track record of late.

The early prowess that Anthopoulos has shown at extracting value was on display early in this offseason, as the Blue Jays traded for Miguel Olivo—on its face, perhaps not the savviest move. They gave up a player to be named later or cash for the catcher on the eve of the deadline for his team option, then immediately declined the option and offered the Type-B free agent arbitration. When Olivo declined the offer and signed with Seattle, the Blue Jays received a first-round sandwich pick as compensation. That's important not only because it allows Anthopoulos another opportunity to unleash his new scout army, but also because the 2011 draft class appears to be one of the strongest in recent memory. But that's the kind of inefficiency-seeking that is the hallmark of the spreadsheet approach. What gives?

By now it should be clear that the Anthopoulos-the-scout narrative makes as little sense as the Ricciardi-the-spreadsheet-jockey one did. Anthopoulos is a whippersnapper of the sort that local ink-stained wretches used to revile, and yet he goes gaga for tools with the rest of them. In short, he's a hybrid—the long-awaited synthesis sent to resolve the dialectic in a way that would satisfy even the dustiest German philosopher. The big question, then, is whether Anthopoulos' arrival marks the end of history or the beginning of an era of success in Toronto.

A much larger constraint than organizational philosophy, a specter that has haunted every decision the Blue Jays have made in the last 15 years, is that big gambles aren't worth it unless they overthrow the dominant class structure of the AL East. The Blue Jays play in a relentlessly difficult environment. If the Rays are a good example, winning in the AL East requires years of stockpiling talent before success becomes a possibility.

But there is some reason for hope. Against teams other than the Red Sox, Yankees, and Rays, the Blue Jays boasted a combined .581 winning percentage last season. That mark would have won four divisions in baseball, and the NL Wild Card to boot. While you can't simply take away a team's games against its top divisional opponents, if the Blue Jays can play a full one-third of their games against the bruisers of the league and still wind up eight games over .500, they can't be far from competing.

Still, however promising the team's 2010 results, they were achieved in some ways that are structurally unsustainable. The Blue Jays experienced a very strange offensive season: they set an all-time record for isolated power, posting a .206 ISO that edged out the 1997 Seattle Mariners' mark of .204. Of course, the way to do that is to hit home runs, and led by Jose Bautista's 54, the Jays launched 257 homers in total. That's not only the third-most that any team has ever sent skyward, but also 48 more dingers than the 2009 team hit.

At the same time, the 2010 Blue Jays had the sixth-worst on-base percentage in team history at .312, which ranked 26th in the majors. The result was an off-kilter offense that relied largely on home runs to put numbers on the scoreboard. *Baseball Prospectus* co-founder Joe Sheehan dubbed the percentage of a team's runs scored on the long ball the "Guillen Number," inspired by White Sox manager Ozzie Guillen, who claimed to be running a small-ball offense but actually got most of his production from the home run. Toronto's Guillen Number not only lapped the field in 2010, but set the pace from a historical perspective as well (see Tables 1 and 2).

Table 1. Doing Guillen Proud: 2010 Leaders in Percentage of Runs Scored on Home Runs

Team	Runs	HR Runs	HR Run Percentage
TOR	755	401	0.5311
ARI	713	293	0.4109
BOS	818	336	0.4108
NYA	859	328	0.3818
ANA	681	257	0.3774
MIL	750	281	0.3747
CHA	752	279	0.3710
CIN	790	292	0.3696
COL	770	282	0.3662
CHN	685	248	0.3620

That kind of fireworks display is fun while it lasts, but it's not a repeatable method of scoring runs, since it's much more likely that the team's unstable isolated power will fall than that its on-base percentage will rise. Much more promising is the array of young starters that the Blue Jays have

Table 2. Doing Guillen Even Prouder: Leaders in Percentage of Runs Scored on Home Runs since 1954

Team	Year	Runs	HR Runs	HR Run Percentage
TOR	2010	401	755	.5311
TEX	2005	413	865	.4775
CHA	2008	385	811	.4747
CIN	1956	365	775	.4710
TEX	2003	389	826	.4709
SEA	1999	400	859	.4657
NYA	1961	385	827	.4655
MIN	1964	343	737	.4654
OAK	1996	399	861	.4634
BAL	1987	336	729	.4609

amassed, even after sending Marcum to Milwaukee. The 2011 rotation will probably feature four former first-round draft picks (Brandon Morrow, Ricky Romero, Brett Cecil, and Kyle Drabek). None of them will earn more than a few million dollars, which suggests that the Blue Jays are about to embark on a multiyear stretch with one of the best bargain rotations in baseball.

In most cases, it's difficult to justify spending any money on a bullpen overhaul unless it is the final piece of the puzzle, but that isn't to say that the team's relief corps couldn't use some tinkering. Two of last year's team's top three relievers by WXRL (Scott Downs, 2.62, and Kevin Gregg, 0.66) departed via free agency. Of those who remain, only Shawn Camp was worth more than a win; the rest of the bullpen was approximately replacement level. Still, the organization has plenty of serviceable arms in the high minors, and it's likely that some combination of Jesse Litsch, Marc Rzepczynski, Brad Mills, and Jo-Jo Reyes could provide cheap, moderately effective innings out of the bullpen and make spot starts as needed.

Given all that, the most pressing need the team has at the major-league level is offense, and lots of it. Unfortunately for the Blue Jays, most of the top hitting talent in the system has already arrived and failed to impress. J. P. Arencibia could give the offense a shot in the arm, but for this team to be successful in the medium term, Adam Lind, Travis Snider, and Aaron Hill will have to play at the tops of their respective games. If Vernon Wells and Jose Bautista decline even a little, that slack will have to be picked up elsewhere. The hiring of John Farrell created a swarm of buzz that Manny Ramirez could be enticed to play for Toronto, and such a move would certainly help replace some of the decline in offensive production next year, but no earth-shaking offensive moves appeared to be forthcoming as we went to press.

Potential contradictions in the team's organizational philosophy may yet become apparent, and the age-old conflict between stats and scouts may yet rage once more in Toronto. But for the time being, and for as long as the current synthesis remains in place, there is reason for hope.

HITTERS

J. P. Arencibia — C

Born: **1/5/1986** Age: **25**
Bats: **R** Throws: **R** Height: **6' 1"** Weight: **210**
Breakout: **1%** Improve: **24%** Collapse: **10%**
Attrition: **30%** MLB: **65%**

Comparables:
Jake Fox, Matthew Brown, Johnny Bench (73)

YEAR	TEAM	LVL	AGE	PA	R	2B	3B	HR	RBI	BB	SO	SB	CS	AVG/OBP/SLG	TAv	BABIP	BRR	FRAA	WARP
2008	DUN	A+	22	262	38	22	0	13	62	11	46	0	0	.315/.344/.560	.307	.340	-1.3	C 0	2.2
2008	NHP	AA	22	275	32	14	0	14	43	7	55	0	0	.282/.302/.496	.267	.305	-0.5	C -1	1.0
2009	LVG	AAA	23	500	67	32	1	21	75	26	114	0	1	.236/.284/.444	.245	.267	-1.0	C -1	1.0
2010	LVG	AAA	24	459	76	36	1	32	85	38	85	0	0	.301/.359/.626	.308	.306	0.0	C -3	4.0
2010	TOR	MLB	24	37	3	1	0	2	4	2	11	0	0	.143/.189/.343	.192	.136	-1.6	C 0	-0.3
2011	*TOR*	*MLB*	*25*	*507*	*62*	*29*	*0*	*23*	*73*	*28*	*115*	*0*	*0*	*.258/.301/.471*	*.265*	*.288*	*0.0*	*C -2*	*1.9*

Arencibia has been Toronto's default "backstop of the future" for several years running. His 2009 campaign represented a serious bump in the road, but he was still young in catcher-development terms. In 2010, Arencibia reestablished his contact skills in his second season in Las Vegas (although park-factor caveats apply). Given that the alternatives behind the dish all suffer from the same malady—namely, that much like the big club as a whole, they're all power and no walks—why not go with the guy who has always had the potential to become an offensive force? Still, Arencibia's plate discipline isn't where it will have to be if he is to avoid a career of one-year contracts playing for second-division teams. If he can hone his approach and pair it with the constant threat of majestic home runs, he'll be something special. Last year was a big step forward, but 2011 is an opportunity to establish himself in Toronto for the foreseeable future.

Jose Bautista RF

Born: **10/19/1980** Age: **30**
Bats: **R** Throws: **R** Height: **6' 0"** Weight: **192**
Breakout: **0%** Improve: **39%** Collapse: **4%**
Attrition: **8%** MLB: **99%**

Comparables:
Nick Swisher, Reggie Smith, Roger Maris (75)

YEAR	TEAM	LVL	AGE	PA	R	2B	3B	HR	RBI	BB	SO	SB	CS	AVG/OBP/SLG	TAv	BABIP	BRR	FRAA	WARP
2008	PIT	MLB	27	363	39	15	0	12	44	38	77	1	1	.242/.320/.405	.254	.274	-0.7	3B 0	0.7
2008	TOR	MLB	27	61	7	2	0	3	10	2	14	0	0	.214/.230/.411	.209	.214	-0.1	3B 1, 1B -1	-0.3
2009	TOR	MLB	28	404	53	13	3	13	40	56	85	4	0	.235/.344/.408	.271	.268	4.7	LF -5, RF 1	1.3
2010	TOR	MLB	29	683	111	35	3	54	124	100	116	9	2	.260/.378/.617	.346	.233	-1.6	RF -15, 3B 2	5.4
2011	*TOR*	*MLB*	*30*	*548*	*73*	*25*	*1*	*25*	*74*	*73*	*102*	*6*	*2*	*.253/.357/.479*	*.289*	*.265*	*-0.1*	*3B -1, RF -5*	*2.0*

The facts in the major-league mystery of one Jose Bautista are as follows:

- Bautista's success in 2010 carried over from a strong September 2009, a month in which he hit .257/.339/.606.
- Bautista nearly tripled his career home-run rate in 2010. He also increased his walk rate and decreased his strikeout rate by one-third apiece.
- Of his major-league-best 54 home runs, 53 were hit to left or left-center. In fact, the further he hit the ball, the more likely he was to pull it. He's not a dead-pull hitter; he's a six-foot-under pull hitter.
- Bautista credits at least some of his success to an adjustment he made at the suggestion of first-base coach Dwayne Murphy to begin his swing earlier. The idea was to turn on, and drive, fastballs.

It's extraordinarily rare for a player to go from utility roster-froth to home-run champion, but that's what Bautista did. He won't hit 50 again, even if he maintains the improved plate discipline (in fact, 50-plus-homer guys with good plate discipline have historically suffered bigger drop-offs than their less-patient counterparts). He has become a very good hitter, but if teams are smart, it could be May before he sees an inside fastball.

John Buck C

Born: **7/7/1980** Age: **30**
Bats: **R** Throws: **R** Height: **6' 3"** Weight: **210**
Breakout: **2%** Improve: **33%** Collapse: **9%**
Attrition: **17%** MLB: **92%**

Comparables:
Ben Broussard, Mike Macfarlane, David Ross (75)

YEAR	TEAM	LVL	AGE	PA	R	2B	3B	HR	RBI	BB	SO	SB	CS	AVG/OBP/SLG	TAv	BABIP	BRR	FRAA	WARP
2008	KCA	MLB	27	418	47	23	1	9	48	38	96	0	3	.224/.304/.365	.237	.275	0.2	C -2	0.6
2009	KCA	MLB	28	202	17	12	4	8	36	13	55	1	1	.247/.297/.484	.266	.304	-1.3	C -1	0.7
2010	TOR	MLB	29	437	56	25	0	20	66	16	111	0	0	.281/.314/.489	.284	.335	1.1	C -1	2.7
2011	*FLO*	*MLB*	*30*	*381*	*45*	*18*	*1*	*16*	*50*	*24*	*87*	*1*	*1*	*.248/.302/.440*	*.257*	*.281*	*-0.1*	*C -1*	*1.2*

Like the manager in your fantasy league who decided it would be funny to roster all three Molina brothers, the Blue Jays have seemingly set out to own every low-on-base, high-slugging backstop in the league. They've had John Buck, Jose Molina, and Rod Barajas. They traded for Miguel Olivo. Their catcher of the future—Arencibia—appears to be headed down the same path. Either the Blue Jays have discovered the deep fungibility of second-tier catchers, or they *really* have a type. Buck walked away as a free agent coming off a strong year, but the Jays have taken the catching equivalent of the Pepsi Challenge and are unlikely to notice the difference. Buck won't experience much separation anxiety, either, having received a three-year, $18 million deal from the Marlins, who bought high on a player who is coming off a career year, is moving to a park that doesn't suit his central skill and power, and is but a sneeze away from seeing his OBP fall back under .300.

Travis d'Arnaud C

Born: **2/10/1989** Age: **22**
Bats: **R** Throws: **R** Height: **6' 2"** Weight: **195**
Breakout: **4%** Improve: **11%** Collapse: **0%**
Attrition: **9%** MLB: **13%**

Comparables:
Alex Avila, Conor Gillaspie, Jarrod Saltalamacchia (78)

YEAR	TEAM	LVL	AGE	PA	R	2B	3B	HR	RBI	BB	SO	SB	CS	AVG/OBP/SLG	TAv	BABIP	BRR	FRAA	WARP
2008	LWD	A	19	70	12	5	0	2	5	5	10	0	0	.297/.357/.469	.328	.327	0.8	C 0	0.9
2008	WPT	A-	19	197	21	13	1	4	25	18	29	1	2	.309/.371/.463	.314	.345	-2.8	C 1	1.7
2009	LWD	A	20	540	71	38	1	13	71	41	75	8	4	.255/.319/.419	.275	.273	-2.3	C -1	2.5
2010	DUN	A+	21	292	36	20	1	6	38	20	63	3	1	.259/.315/.411	.262	.312	0.0	C -1	1.0
2011	*TOR*	*MLB*	*22*	*370*	*38*	*21*	*0*	*7*	*37*	*22*	*77*	*1*	*0*	*.240/.287/.362*	*.228*	*.284*	*0.0*	*C -1*	*0.0*

One of the prospects who arrived in Toronto via the Halladay trade, d'Arnaud faced a season hampered by a back injury. The trouble with back injuries is that they can linger—especially in the case of a catcher. On the other hand, that d'Arnaud struggled with injury means that the periodic excellence he showed this year, not the middling batting line, might reasonably be believed. If healthy, d'Arnaud has the defensive talent and all-around package to unseat Arencibia for the major-league job. If not, he'll be another cautionary tale for the occupational hazards of the catching profession.

Brad Emaus **2B**

Born: **3/28/1986** Age: **25**
Bats: **R** Throws: **R** Height: **6' 0"** Weight: **200**
Breakout: **4%** Improve: **19%** Collapse: **17%**
Attrition: **28%** MLB: **53%**

Comparables:
Freddy Sandoval, Ryan Rohlinger, Casey McGehee (78)

YEAR	TEAM	LVL	AGE	PA	R	2B	3B	HR	RBI	BB	SO	SB	CS	AVG/OBP/SLG	TAv	BABIP	BRR	FRAA	WARP
2008	DUN	A+	22	543	87	34	3	12	71	60	56	12	4	.302/.378/.463	.300	.317	-2.4	2B -5, 3B 4	3.3
2009	NHP	AA	23	581	67	28	2	10	67	59	69	10	3	.253/.336/.376	.258	.271	-2.3	2B 10	2.0
2010	NHP	AA	24	170	21	7	0	5	26	31	19	5	0	.272/.402/.434	.310	.278	0.0	2B 4, 3B 1	1.7
2010	LVG	AAA	24	364	58	25	3	10	49	50	50	8	2	.298/.395/.495	.297	.324	0.0	3B 2, 2B -2	2.5
2011	*NYN*	*MLB*	*25*	*552*	*67*	*29*	*1*	*13*	*61*	*58*	*82*	*5*	*2*	*.267/.341/.414*	*.266*	*.290*	*-0.1*	*2B 4, 3B 1*	*2.1*

Emaus has been cut from big-league spring training on his birthday for two consecutive years and will hope to avoid extending his streak this season by legally changing his date of birth. Should he be thwarted in that pursuit, a move to the Mets as a Rule 5 pick may prove as beneficial. Emaus has terrific plate discipline and enough pop to suggest that some could last in the majors. He has bounced between second and third and could play either passably. A perfect-world scenario is that he'll develop into a gap hitter in the mold of Mark Loretta; the Mets will try him on another gap, their gap at second base, and failing that, a utility role.

Edwin Encarnacion **3B**

Born: **1/7/1983** Age: **28**
Bats: **R** Throws: **R** Height: **6' 1"** Weight: **195**
Breakout: **2%** Improve: **42%** Collapse: **2%**
Attrition: **11%** MLB: **96%**

Comparables:
Chad Tracy, Rico Petrocelli, Jorge Cantu (78)

YEAR	TEAM	LVL	AGE	PA	R	2B	3B	HR	RBI	BB	SO	SB	CS	AVG/OBP/SLG	TAv	BABIP	BRR	FRAA	WARP
2008	CIN	MLB	25	582	75	29	1	26	68	61	102	1	0	.251/.340/.466	.282	.264	-3.9	3B -16	1.1
2009	CIN	MLB	26	165	10	6	1	5	16	24	38	1	1	.209/.333/.374	.247	.250	-1.6	3B -2	-0.1
2009	TOR	MLB	26	173	25	5	1	8	23	13	29	1	0	.240/.306/.442	.267	.242	0.8	3B -3	0.4
2010	TOR	MLB	27	367	49	16	0	21	51	29	60	1	0	.244/.305/.482	.278	.235	1.3	3B -4	1.4
2011	*OAK*	*MLB*	*28*	*497*	*66*	*23*	*1*	*24*	*70*	*48*	*81*	*3*	*1*	*.267/.346/.487*	*.289*	*.275*	*0.0*	*3B -9*	*2.0*

A tools checklist for Encarnacion would look like a game of tic-tac-toe after the first move: only one box marked. He is a miserable defender (according to metrics ranging from the Mesozoic to the futuristic), lacks a good arm at third, does not hit for average, and runs poorly. His plate discipline is league-average in a good year. The thing he can do—the reason he is still a starting major-league third baseman—is hit for power. His isolated power put him in the top 25 among players with at least 300 plate appearances in 2010. Claimed off waivers by the Athletics but nontendered before he got to touch the green and gold, Encarnacion won't have to see his numbers decline in a big ballpark in 2011. Instead, he'll return to Toronto for strict DH duty.

Yunel Escobar **SS**

Born: **11/2/1982** Age: **28**
Bats: **R** Throws: **R** Height: **6' 2"** Weight: **200**
Breakout: **1%** Improve: **58%** Collapse: **3%**
Attrition: **8%** MLB: **97%**

Comparables:
Harvey Kuenn, Alexei Ramirez, Jeff Cirillo (72)

YEAR	TEAM	LVL	AGE	PA	R	2B	3B	HR	RBI	BB	SO	SB	CS	AVG/OBP/SLG	TAv	BABIP	BRR	FRAA	WARP
2008	ATL	MLB	25	587	72	24	2	10	60	59	62	2	5	.288/.361/.401	.269	.306	-2.4	SS 12	3.7
2009	ATL	MLB	26	604	89	26	2	14	76	57	62	5	4	.299/.373/.436	.281	.312	1.6	SS 15	5.1
2010	ATL	MLB	27	301	28	12	0	0	19	37	31	5	1	.238/.332/.284	.233	.267	-0.7	SS 13	1.5
2010	TOR	MLB	27	266	32	7	0	4	16	19	26	1	1	.275/.331/.356	.250	.286	0.1	SS -7	0.1
2011	*TOR*	*MLB*	*28*	*578*	*69*	*24*	*1*	*7*	*54*	*59*	*59*	*6*	*3*	*.286/.360/.383*	*.267*	*.303*	*-0.5*	*SS 8*	*3.2*

Like the twi-night doubleheader and the suicide squeeze, the challenge trade is a dying art. The trade that brought Escobar north of the border wasn't strictly a challenge, since it included Jo-Jo Reyes as well, but it was close. The Braves' motivation for completing the exchange was obvious: Escobar didn't hit a lick in the first half, he was apparently regarded as a clubhouse cancer, and there was a division title at stake. Most of Escobar's power, such as it is, comes from hitting the ball the other way. In 2010, he pulled too many grounders at the expense of putting the ball in the air. Still, it isn't hard to divine the Blue Jays' thinking: Escobar may not offer much of a contribution in the chemistry department, but he'll be 28 next season, owns a career .276 TAv, and plays a good shortstop.

Anthony Gose **CF**

Born: **8/10/1990** Age: **20**
Bats: **L** Throws: **L** Height: **6' 1"** Weight: **190**
Breakout: **1%** Improve: **4%** Collapse: **0%**
Attrition: **2%** MLB: **7%**

Comparables:
Claudell Washington, Elvis Andrus, Roberto Alomar (72)

YEAR	TEAM	LVL	AGE	PA	R	2B	3B	HR	RBI	BB	SO	SB	CS	AVG/OBP/SLG	TAv	BABIP	BRR	FRAA	WARP
2009	LWD	A	18	572	72	24	9	2	52	35	110	76	20	.259/.318/.353	.272	.317	2.9	CF -5, LF -2	1.9
2010	DUN	A+	19	113	21	3	2	3	6	13	29	9	5	.255/.360/.426	.276	.323	1.6	CF 2	0.8
2010	CLR	A+	19	461	67	17	11	4	21	32	103	36	27	.263/.325/.385	.259	.335	0.0	CF 11	2.3
2011	*TOR*	*MLB*	*20*	*396*	*36*	*15*	*3*	*2*	*32*	*20*	*103*	*27*	*11*	*.224/.268/.306*	*.209*	*.295*	*-1.3*	*CF -7, LF 0*	*-1.8*

The Blue Jays had their eyes on Gose as early as the Halladay trade, so when the Phillies sent him to the Astros in a package for Roy Oswalt, the Blue Jays came calling with Brett Wallace in hand. It's hard for one trade to carry the burden of representing an entire organizational change in philosophy, but the Wallace-Gose exchange comes close. Toronto got a player with a ceiling as high as they come but almost no results in exchange for a ready-now, low-ceiling corner infielder. There isn't a tool in the shed that Gose doesn't possess, and he began to realize some of his potential in 2010, showing improved patience and power in a league brimming with players significantly older than he. Nevertheless, the degree of disaster instigated by Gose's reckless baserunning reveals how much he has yet to learn; the lefty would be wise to make like Stanley Ipkiss and exclaim, "Somebody stop me!" upon reaching first base, at least until he learns to identify low-percentage opportunities.

Adeiny Hechavarria SS

Born: **4/15/1989** Age: **22**
Bats: **R** Throws: **R** Height: **5' 11"** Weight: **180**
Breakout: **7%** Improve: **12%** Collapse: **3%**
Attrition: **12%** MLB: **22%**

Comparables:
Robin Yount, Edgar Renteria, Bucky Dent (77)

YEAR	TEAM	LVL	AGE	PA	R	2B	3B	HR	RBI	BB	SO	SB	CS	AVG/OBP/SLG	TAv	BABIP	BRR	FRAA	WARP
2010	DUN	A+	21	167	21	7	3	1	7	5	25	7	0	.193/.217/.292	.199	.221	2.7	SS 7	0.5
2010	NHP	AA	21	273	36	11	1	3	34	12	40	6	3	.273/.305/.360	.252	.306	0.7	SS 6	1.5
2011	*TOR*	*MLB*	*22*	*450*	*44*	*20*	*2*	*4*	*41*	*16*	*81*	*8*	*3*	*.248/.275/.333*	*.217*	*.291*	*0.0*	*SS 11*	*0.8*

The Blue Jays signed the Cuban shortstop Hechavarria to a four-year, $10 million contract in April. He's a slick glove man whose bat just needs to be good enough for the ninth spot in the order. He won't hit well enough to justify batting him any higher than that, but pitchers should be happy to have him playing behind them. He hit better after an aggressive promotion to Double-A that was dictated as much by his spot on the 40-man and seven-figure bonus as it was by his offensive performance. Anthopoulos hoped the signing would make a statement about his regime's willingness to spend for top international talent, and the message was received loud and clear, since the deal was the most the Blue Jays had ever awarded to an amateur by a factor of four.

Aaron Hill 2B

Born: **3/21/1982** Age: **29**
Bats: **R** Throws: **R** Height: **5' 11"** Weight: **195**
Breakout: **1%** Improve: **44%** Collapse: **1%**
Attrition: **7%** MLB: **97%**

Comparables:
Chris Sabo, Ian Kinsler, Edgardo Alfonzo (72)

YEAR	TEAM	LVL	AGE	PA	R	2B	3B	HR	RBI	BB	SO	SB	CS	AVG/OBP/SLG	TAv	BABIP	BRR	FRAA	WARP
2008	TOR	MLB	26	229	19	14	0	2	20	16	31	4	2	.263/.319/.361	.252	.294	1.1	2B -2	0.3
2009	TOR	MLB	27	734	103	37	0	36	108	42	98	6	2	.286/.330/.499	.295	.288	1.1	2B 9	5.3
2010	TOR	MLB	28	580	71	22	0	26	68	41	85	2	2	.205/.271/.394	.247	.195	0.9	2B 4	1.1
2011	*TOR*	*MLB*	*29*	*561*	*67*	*27*	*0*	*19*	*68*	*41*	*78*	*4*	*2*	*.260/.317/.426*	*.261*	*.269*	*-0.2*	*2B 5*	*1.8*

Aaron Hill's seasons are the opposite of *Star Trek* movies: only the odd ones are good, or so it has seemed since his first full season as a starter in 2006. His batting average languished 65 points below his career rate and was dragged down by a .196 BABIP, which was the lowest among batting title qualifiers by a staggering 26 points. Some of his line drives in 2009 turned into fly balls in 2010, and those turned into extra outs. What the Jays got was a combination of bad outcomes and bad approach. At least one of those can be expected to improve naturally next year, but Hill needs to work on staying within his swing and avoiding getting under the ball if he hopes to return to his All-Star form.

Jarrett Hoffpauir 2B

Born: **6/18/1983** Age: **28**
Bats: **R** Throws: **R** Height: **5' 9"** Weight: **190**
Breakout: **2%** Improve: **30%** Collapse: **12%**
Attrition: **13%** MLB: **64%**

Comparables:
Alberto Callaspo, Ryan Roberts, Bobby Avila (69)

YEAR	TEAM	LVL	AGE	PA	R	2B	3B	HR	RBI	BB	SO	SB	CS	AVG/OBP/SLG	TAv	BABIP	BRR	FRAA	WARP
2008	MEM	AAA	25	475	48	31	1	4	45	49	45	2	4	.273/.347/.383	.256	.290	1.4	2B -7	0.4
2009	MEM	AAA	26	402	53	22	3	14	53	35	28	4	1	.291/.353/.486	.298	.280	-1.6	2B -1, SS 2	2.7
2009	SLN	MLB	26	16	1	2	0	0	2	4	2	0	0	.250/.438/.417	.290	.300	-0.1	2B 1, 3B 0	0.2
2010	LVG	AAA	27	500	73	26	6	16	73	58	34	8	3	.295/.376/.494	.291	.285	0.0	2B 5, 3B -1	3.3
2010	TOR	MLB	27	37	1	1	0	0	0	2	5	0	0	.206/.243/.235	.175	.233	0.6	3B 2, 2B 1	0.1
2011	*TOR*	*MLB*	*28*	*481*	*58*	*23*	*2*	*9*	*51*	*48*	*50*	*2*	*1*	*.271/.343/.403*	*.264*	*.281*	*-0.1*	*2B -1, 3B 0*	*1.2*

Two-time waiver casualty Hoffpauir has somewhat more potential than previously indicated. Even after adjusting for park, he showed good power for the second straight season in Triple-A. The knock on Hoffpauir is his defense, which isn't strong at second, and since his bat won't carry him any further down the defensive spectrum, he's likely to be a utility asset at best. The Padres think they can use him, so he was claimed off waivers for the second time in as many offseasons.

Fred Lewis LF

Born: **12/9/1980** Age: **30**
Bats: **L** Throws: **R** Height: **6' 2"** Weight: **190**
Breakout: **0%** Improve: **25%** Collapse: **4%**
Attrition: **3%** MLB: **89%**

Comparables:
Bobby Thomson, Shane Mack, Jeff Salazar (75)

YEAR	TEAM	LVL	AGE	PA	R	2B	3B	HR	RBI	BB	SO	SB	CS	AVG/OBP/SLG	TAv	BABIP	BRR	FRAA	WARP
2008	SFN	MLB	27	521	81	25	11	9	40	51	124	21	7	.282/.351/.440	.277	.365	10.1	LF -6, CF -2	2.2
2009	SFN	MLB	28	336	48	21	3	4	20	36	84	8	4	.258/.348/.390	.271	.348	2.7	LF 3	1.6
2010	TOR	MLB	29	480	70	31	5	8	36	38	104	17	6	.262/.331/.414	.266	.324	-0.2	LF -2, RF 2	1.2
2011	*TOR*	*MLB*	*30*	*449*	*53*	*23*	*4*	*7*	*46*	*46*	*99*	*16*	*6*	*.261/.343/.395*	*.263*	*.326*	*-0.4*	*LF -1, CF 0*	*0.8*

Of all the accolades laid at Brian Sabean's feet in the wake of the Giants' World Series victory, a big chunk was due to the midseason acquisition of Cody Ross. Still, it's worth wondering whether that pickup would have been necessary if the Giants had retained the services of Lewis, a lefty who sports a career OBP of .350 and can play multiple outfield positions. Lewis owns a career TAv of .275; Ross's is .274. Their age differs by a matter of weeks, and Lewis comes much cheaper. Count Lewis's unnoticed improvement this year as another example of the sanitizing effect of success, but remember that the savvy moves that Anthopoulos made in 2010 may never receive the same level of recognition. Even after his successes across the border, Lewis was nontendered.

Adam Lind **DH**

Born: **7/17/1983** Age: **27**
Bats: L Throws: L Height: **6' 2"** Weight: **195**
Breakout: **0%** Improve: **46%** Collapse: **3%**
Attrition: **13%** MLB: **92%**

Comparables:
Chase Headley, Gus Bell, Reggie Smith (73)

YEAR	TEAM	LVL	AGE	PA	R	2B	3B	HR	RBI	BB	SO	SB	CS	AVG/OBP/SLG	TAv	BABIP	BRR	FRAA	WARP
2008	SYR	AAA	24	213	24	17	2	6	50	19	36	1	1	.328/.394/.534	.309	.376	0.3	LF -3, RF 0	1.2
2008	TOR	MLB	24	349	48	16	4	9	40	16	59	2	0	.282/.315/.439	.265	.316	5.6	LF -3	1.0
2009	TOR	MLB	25	654	94	46	0	35	114	58	110	1	1	.305/.370/.562	.323	.323	1.2	LF -8	4.3
2010	TOR	MLB	26	613	61	32	3	23	72	38	144	0	0	.237/.287/.425	.253	.277	-3.3	LF -2, 1B 1	-0.2
2011	*TOR*	*MLB*	*27*	*578*	*72*	*31*	*1*	*21*	*76*	*44*	*115*	*1*	*0*	*.269/.327/.454*	*.270*	*.304*	*-0.1*	*LF -3, 1B 0*	*1.0*

Just as the season began, Lind signed one of those option-laden multiyear deals that are all the rage these days. A 25-year-old who hit 35 home runs in 2009 looked like someone in whom one might invest $7 million four years down the road. After a supremely disappointing season, this is no longer the case. Lind's plate discipline, already marginal, evaporated entirely, his power declined sharply, and at times he looked lost at the plate. He was consistently beaten to the outside part of the plate, and pitchers learned to exploit that weakness. On top of that, with the trade of Brett Wallace to Houston, Lind suddenly had newfound duties as the first baseman of the future. His favorable second-half split and the ability of even dead cats to bounce temper the pessimism to a degree.

Jacob Marisnick **CF**

Born: **3/30/1991** Age: **20**
Bats: R Throws: R Height: **6' 4"** Weight: **200**
Breakout: **0%** Improve: **0%** Collapse: **1%**
Attrition: **1%** MLB: **1%**

Comparables:
Fernando Martinez, Jay Porter, Cecil Espy (79)

YEAR	TEAM	LVL	AGE	PA	R	2B	3B	HR	RBI	BB	SO	SB	CS	AVG/OBP/SLG	TAv	BABIP	BRR	FRAA	WARP
2010	LNS	A	19	143	16	8	2	1	12	9	37	9	2	.220/.298/.339	.223	.297	0.0	CF 7, RF 1	0.8
2010	BLJ	Rk	19	142	17	12	0	3	14	13	18	14	1	.287/.373/.459	.332	.311	0.1	CF 2	2.1
2011	*TOR*	*MLB*	*20*	*321*	*31*	*16*	*1*	*4*	*27*	*23*	*81*	*0*	*0*	*.216/.278/.318*	*.214*	*.279*	*0.0*	*CF -4, LF 0*	*-1.0*

Like Gose, Marisnick is a toolsy center fielder. Unlike Gose, Marisnick is huge. Despite his size, he has above-average speed and good instincts on the basepaths (which is more than Gose can say). His first exposure to the more advanced pitching in the Midwest League did not go particularly well, which underscores that Marisnick is a long-term project who may take several years to develop. If he plays to his potential, the wait will be worth it.

Mike McCoy **INF**

Born: **4/2/1981** Age: **30**
Bats: R Throws: R Height: **5' 9"** Weight: **175**
Breakout: **2%** Improve: **22%** Collapse: **3%**
Attrition: **11%** MLB: **53%**

Comparables:
Luis Maza, Doug Bernier, Andy Green (73)

YEAR	TEAM	LVL	AGE	PA	R	2B	3B	HR	RBI	BB	SO	SB	CS	AVG/OBP/SLG	TAv	BABIP	BRR	FRAA	WARP
2008	CSP	AAA	27	162	32	7	2	4	27	15	20	7	1	.343/.389/.507	.303	.358	3.1	2B -3, SS 2	1.4
2008	NOR	AAA	27	176	25	6	1	2	16	19	27	6	3	.276/.347/.368	.268	.312	1.9	2B 5, SS 0	1.4
2009	CSP	AAA	28	572	102	27	5	2	52	80	70	40	6	.307/.393/.400	.280	.336	12.0	SS 14, 3B 2	5.6
2009	COL	MLB	28	6	0	0	0	0	0	0	2	2	0	.000/.000/.000	.012	.000	-0.1	2B 0, RF 0	-0.1
2010	LVG	AAA	29	259	48	14	1	6	26	37	31	17	2	.310/.411/.469	.288	.326	4.3	SS 12, CF 1	3.5
2010	TOR	MLB	29	90	6	4	0	0	3	8	20	5	1	.195/.267/.244	.201	.258	1.6	2B 4, LF 2	0.5
2011	*TOR*	*MLB*	*30*	*420*	*48*	*18*	*2*	*3*	*34*	*52*	*66*	*21*	*5*	*.266/.354/.352*	*.255*	*.307*	*0.6*	*SS 5, 2B 2*	*1.8*

McCoy has a career 12.4 percent minor-league walk rate, which is a nifty trick, but he backs it up with absolutely no legitimate exercise of power. A couple years spent at hitters' havens in Colorado Springs and Las Vegas may have imparted the impression of doubles power, but that was little more than a park-induced mirage. Still, he's cheap and he if he can tally a few singles, he'll put up an OBP on the north side of .300. He played every position except first base and catcher in 2010, so there are worse ways to burn your last roster spot for a month or so at a time.

John McDonald **INF**

Born: **9/24/1974** Age: **36**
Bats: R Throws: R Height: **5' 11"** Weight: **175**
Breakout: **1%** Improve: **22%** Collapse: **7%**
Attrition: **19%** MLB: **63%**

Comparables:
Bob Johnson, Hank Majeski, Nelson Liriano (75)

YEAR	TEAM	LVL	AGE	PA	R	2B	3B	HR	RBI	BB	SO	SB	CS	AVG/OBP/SLG	TAv	BABIP	BRR	FRAA	WARP
2008	TOR	MLB	33	207	18	8	0	1	18	10	25	3	1	.210/.246/.269	.187	.225	-0.2	SS -8, 3B 0	-1.5
2009	TOR	MLB	34	155	15	7	0	4	13	1	18	0	2	.260/.271/.387	.239	.269	-1.5	SS -1, 3B 0	0.2
2010	TOR	MLB	35	163	24	9	2	6	23	6	26	2	1	.250/.270/.454	.253	.256	2.0	2B -1, SS 0	0.4
2011	*TOR*	*MLB*	*36*	*235*	*23*	*10*	*1*	*3*	*22*	*10*	*34*	*3*	*2*	*.240/.270/.336*	*.214*	*.260*	*-0.2*	*SS -2, 3B 1*	*-0.4*

McDonald proved that even punchless middle infielders are not immune to epidemic-level outbreaks of isolated power like the one that beset Toronto in 2010. Sadly, he can't be expected to maintain an extra-base-hit percentage in the double digits, and his defense isn't what it used to be. It's tough to see his career lasting beyond the end of his current deal, which expires at the end of the season. In the meantime, he probably won't be the worst backup infielder in baseball.

Jose Molina C

Born: **6/3/1975** Age: **36**
Bats: **R** Throws: **R** Height: **6' 2"** Weight: **215**
Breakout: **1%** Improve: **23%** Collapse: **9%**
Attrition: **28%** MLB: **64%**

Comparables:
Chad Moeller, Ron Hassey, Greg Myers (76)

YEAR	TEAM	LVL	AGE	PA	R	2B	3B	HR	RBI	BB	SO	SB	CS	AVG/OBP/SLG	TAv	BABIP	BRR	FRAA	WARP
2008	NYA	MLB	33	297	32	17	0	3	18	12	52	0	0	.216/.256/.313	.195	.246	0.6	C 0, 1B 0	-0.7
2009	NYA	MLB	34	155	15	4	0	1	11	14	28	0	0	.217/.290/.268	.207	.261	-0.5	C 1, 1B 1	-0.1
2010	TOR	MLB	35	183	14	4	0	6	12	9	36	1	0	.246/.301/.377	.241	.276	-2.4	C -1	0.1
2011	*TOR*	*MLB*	*36*	*219*	*21*	*9*	*0*	*2*	*18*	*14*	*43*	*1*	*0*	*.227/.281/.313*	*.212*	*.268*	*0.0*	*C 0, 1B 0*	*-0.2*

The middle Molina rates behind brother Yadier in at least some aspects of fielding his position and is the worst hitter of the three. Asked to serve as the primary backup, Jose had one of the most productive seasons of his career. That may be damning with faint praise, but he was easily worth his $800,000 salary last year. Considering his bat and strong defensive abilities—highlighted by stellar receiving skills—the decision to exercise his $1.2 million option for 2011 was an easy one, and the Blue Jays did so even before his older brother had secured the family's fifth World Series ring.

Lyle Overbay 1B

Born: **1/28/1977** Age: **34**
Bats: **L** Throws: **L** Height: **6' 2"** Weight: **215**
Breakout: **1%** Improve: **34%** Collapse: **1%**
Attrition: **11%** MLB: **94%**

Comparables:
Fred McGriff, Bob Watson, Roy Sievers (83)

YEAR	TEAM	LVL	AGE	PA	R	2B	3B	HR	RBI	BB	SO	SB	CS	AVG/OBP/SLG	TAv	BABIP	BRR	FRAA	WARP
2008	TOR	MLB	31	630	76	32	2	15	69	74	116	1	2	.270/.356/.419	.277	.315	-1.2	1B 8	2.3
2009	TOR	MLB	32	500	58	35	1	16	64	74	95	0	0	.265/.372/.466	.297	.305	-1.8	1B 5	2.5
2010	TOR	MLB	33	608	75	37	2	20	67	67	131	1	0	.243/.329/.433	.277	.285	-2.8	1B -1	1.1
2011	*PIT*	*MLB*	*34*	*574*	*70*	*30*	*1*	*17*	*64*	*69*	*115*	*1*	*1*	*.251/.341/.416*	*.266*	*.290*	*-0.1*	*1B 3*	*1.0*

Five seasons after he was acquired by the Blue Jays in a J. P. Ricciardi OBP binge, Overbay became a 34-year-old free agent. He's coming off a down year in which he was roughly league-average across the board, though somewhat worse than par for the lofty offensive standards of his position. He's no longer an especially strong defender, and most of his value comes from his ability to hit righties. Because he's left-handed, he should get opportunities to platoon or pinch-hit for a few more seasons, but he shouldn't be anyone's first choice as a starter. If he's penciled into your team's Opening Day roster, something has already gone awry. Exhibit A: the Pittsburgh Pirates, who signed Overbay in December to serve as their regular first-sacker.

Carlos Perez C

Born: **10/27/1990** Age: **20**
Bats: **R** Throws: **R** Height: **6' 0"** Weight: **193**
Breakout: **0%** Improve: **0%** Collapse: **0%**
Attrition: **0%** MLB: **0%**

Comparables:
Ted Simmons, Butch Benton, Fred Kendall (80)

YEAR	TEAM	LVL	AGE	PA	R	2B	3B	HR	RBI	BB	SO	SB	CS	AVG/OBP/SLG	TAv	BABIP	BRR	FRAA	WARP
2009	BLJ	Rk	18	163	17	11	3	1	21	16	23	2	5	.291/.362/.433	.315	.331	0.9	C 0	1.5
2010	AUB	A-	19	278	44	11	8	2	41	34	41	7	3	.298/.396/.438	.305	.349	0.0	C 1	2.2
2011	*TOR*	*MLB*	*20*	*209*	*21*	*9*	*1*	*1*	*16*	*19*	*45*	*2*	*1*	*.233/.308/.317*	*.228*	*.294*	*-0.2*	*C 0*	*0.0*

Proving that there's no such thing as too many catching prospects even in a system swarming with them, Perez is young and plenty projectable. Playing in the New York-Penn League, Perez continued to show excellent contact skills, but what stuck out most was his much-improved plate discipline. He'll fill in as he develops as a catcher, so there's reason to think that power will manifest down the road. With Arencibia and d'Arnaud ahead of him, the Blue Jays will have little reason to rush him.

Travis Snider LF

Born: **2/2/1988** Age: **23**
Bats: **L** Throws: **L** Height: **5' 11"** Weight: **245**
Breakout: **1%** Improve: **34%** Collapse: **5%**
Attrition: **13%** MLB: **69%**

Comparables:
Jose Canseco, Barry Bonds, Pablo Sandoval (54)

YEAR	TEAM	LVL	AGE	PA	R	2B	3B	HR	RBI	BB	SO	SB	CS	AVG/OBP/SLG	TAv	BABIP	BRR	FRAA	WARP
2008	DUN	A+	20	66	15	5	0	4	7	5	22	1	0	.279/.333/.557	.301	.371	-0.1	—	0.3
2008	NHP	AA	20	423	65	21	0	17	67	52	116	1	1	.262/.357/.461	.269	.333	1.8	RF -2, LF 3	1.2
2008	SYR	AAA	20	70	9	5	0	2	17	4	16	1	0	.344/.386/.516	.304	.426	-0.3	LF -1, RF -2	0.1
2008	TOR	MLB	20	80	10	6	0	2	13	5	23	0	0	.301/.338/.466	.294	.400	0.2	LF -3, RF -1	0.1
2009	LVG	AAA	21	204	32	13	1	14	40	28	47	2	3	.337/.431/.663	.369	.395	-2.7	LF -9, RF 1	1.7
2009	TOR	MLB	21	275	33	14	1	9	29	29	77	1	1	.242/.327/.421	.271	.312	-1.0	LF -4, RF 0	0.3
2010	NHP	AA	22	85	14	5	0	5	17	2	21	3	1	.296/.306/.543	.273	.333	-1.0	RF -1, LF 1	0.1
2010	TOR	MLB	22	319	36	20	0	14	32	21	79	6	3	.255/.304/.463	.273	.302	-3.7	LF 0, RF -3	0.4
2011	*TOR*	*MLB*	*23*	*513*	*63*	*25*	*1*	*20*	*66*	*46*	*138*	*5*	*2*	*.256/.323/.444*	*.267*	*.317*	*-0.3*	*LF -4, RF -4*	*0.4*

It's easy to forget how young Snider is, since he broke in as a 20-year-old. He lost six weeks of last season to a wrist injury, but nonetheless established a new major-league power plateau. The power has yet to manifest against southpaws, and at the moment, his pop is his lone offensive weapon. The lefty's discipline took a step backward in 2010: he walked just seven times after his return in late July. Still, Snider shouldn't be a victim of his own potential, and he will play a season without outsized expectations for perhaps the first time in his professional career. There is still a good chance that Snider will be the major-league hitter his minor-league performances seemed to portend.

Eric Thames **LF**

Born: **11/10/1986** Age: **24**
Bats: **L** Throws: **R** Height: **6' 0"** Weight: **205**
Breakout: **6%** Improve: **14%** Collapse: **4%**
Attrition: **21%** MLB: **32%**

Comparables:
Brandon Jones, Justin Huber, Brett Carroll (75)

YEAR	TEAM	LVL	AGE	PA	R	2B	3B	HR	RBI	BB	SO	SB	CS	AVG/OBP/SLG	TAv	BABIP	BRR	FRAA	WARP
2009	DUN	A+	22	220	33	15	5	3	38	21	40	1	1	.313/.386/.487	.316	.379	-1.1	LF -5, RF 1	1.0
2010	NHP	AA	23	573	95	25	6	27	104	50	121	8	5	.288/.370/.526	.311	.325	-1.0	LF 2	4.0
2011	*TOR*	*MLB*	*24*	*405*	*48*	*18*	*2*	*13*	*49*	*31*	*96*	*3*	*1*	*.255/.320/.428*	*.261*	*.304*	*-0.1*	*LF -4, RF 0*	*0.3*

It can sometimes take time for college hitters from successful programs to adjust to pro ball as they learn an often-unfamiliar system. After two seasons, Pepperdine product Thames has made adjustments and shown power, patience, and the ability to hit for contact. Sure, he's a left fielder and already 24, but he hit 58 extra-base hits in 2010, the hallmark of a player worth promoting aggressively in an attempt to see what you have. He still has room to grow more patient, as his on-base percentage was supported by an unusual number of hit-by-pitches, and his defense is below average. If Travis Snider lays an egg in the first half, it's not impossible to imagine Thames seeing big-league time.

Vernon Wells **CF**

Born: **12/8/1978** Age: **32**
Bats: **R** Throws: **R** Height: **6' 1"** Weight: **210**
Breakout: **0%** Improve: **44%** Collapse: **3%**
Attrition: **7%** MLB: **98%**

Comparables:
Aaron Rowand, Torii Hunter, Kevin McReynolds (75)

YEAR	TEAM	LVL	AGE	PA	R	2B	3B	HR	RBI	BB	SO	SB	CS	AVG/OBP/SLG	TAv	BABIP	BRR	FRAA	WARP
2008	TOR	MLB	29	466	63	22	1	20	78	29	46	4	2	.300/.343/.497	.295	.294	-0.1	CF -6	2.3
2009	TOR	MLB	30	684	84	37	3	15	66	48	86	17	4	.260/.311/.400	.258	.279	2.4	CF -13	0.7
2010	TOR	MLB	31	646	79	44	3	31	88	50	84	6	4	.273/.331/.515	.297	.272	-0.1	CF -4	3.6
2011	*TOR*	*MLB*	*32*	*626*	*76*	*34*	*2*	*19*	*77*	*49*	*81*	*10*	*4*	*.266/.325/.434*	*.267*	*.277*	*-0.3*	*CF -8*	*1.3*

In 2011, Wells' salary will represent between one-third and one-quarter of Toronto's overall payroll. The outfielder's outrageous contract so colors every impression of Wells that it's become almost impossible to evaluate him as a player in isolation. In 2010, Wells beat expectations and his career averages mostly on the strength of a power surge—his 31 home runs were by far his most since he hit 32 in 2006. Yes, he still doesn't walk much, and he was one of the costlier double-play liabilities in the game. But for the first time in a while, it was possible to think about Vernon Wells as something other than a latter-day Darren Dreifort. The remaining $86 million will be owed by the Angels, so in some senses, Wells' was one of the most successful seasons in Jays' history.

Dewayne Wise **OF**

Born: **2/24/1978** Age: **33**
Bats: **L** Throws: **L** Height: **6' 1"** Weight: **180**
Breakout: **0%** Improve: **22%** Collapse: **11%**
Attrition: **17%** MLB: **78%**

Comparables:
Lee Lacy, Karim Garcia, Reggie Taylor (67)

YEAR	TEAM	LVL	AGE	PA	R	2B	3B	HR	RBI	BB	SO	SB	CS	AVG/OBP/SLG	TAv	BABIP	BRR	FRAA	WARP
2008	CHR	AAA	30	222	39	14	3	9	23	22	32	15	7	.319/.396/.565	.315	.338	-1.1	RF 2, CF -2	1.7
2008	CHA	MLB	30	143	19	4	2	6	18	8	32	9	0	.248/.287/.450	.244	.271	1.0	CF 0, LF 1	0.3
2009	CHA	MLB	31	153	11	8	3	2	11	3	27	4	5	.225/.255/.366	.219	.256	0.5	CF 4, RF -2	-0.2
2010	LEH	AAA	32	146	17	11	5	4	13	8	27	2	2	.270/.315/.511	.269	.311	-1.4	CF 1, LF 1	0.7
2010	TOR	MLB	32	118	14	3	2	3	14	4	29	4	0	.250/.280/.393	.227	.309	1.5	RF -1, CF 2	0.2
2011	*TOR*	*MLB*	*33*	*260*	*29*	*13*	*3*	*6*	*30*	*14*	*54*	*8*	*3*	*.247/.294/.397*	*.241*	*.288*	*-0.3*	*CF 1, RF 0*	*0.1*

Wise is a late-game defensive replacement and nothing more. That he started and finished 23 games—mostly at corners, no less—is just bad baseball. Each of those games was against a right-handed starter, but even against opposite-handed pitchers, Wise sports a career .258 OBP. Grant that the second run of *DeWayne Wise: Major-League Fourth Outfielder (The Musical)* has been dictated in large measure by circumstance and one terrific catch; it is difficult to justify using him as anything other than the 25th man on a roster in moments of dire need. Unwilling to keep him on for even that, Toronto outrighted Wise in November, and the ball-shagger elected to pursue free agency.

PITCHERS

Jeremy Accardo

Born: **12/8/1981** Age: **29**
Bats: **R** Throws: **R** Height: **6' 2"** Weight: **190**
Breakout: **12%** Improve: **24%** Collapse: **10%**
Attrition: **2%** MLB: **39%**

Comparables:
Tim Crabtree, Gary Lucas, Lou Pote (80)

YEAR	TEAM	LVL	AGE	W	L	SV	G	GS	IP	H	HR	BB	SO	EqBB9	EqSO9	GB%	BABIP	WHIP	ERA	FRA	WARP
2008	TOR	MLB	26	0	3	4	16	0	12^{1}	15	1	4	5	2.9	3.6	46%	.311	1.62	6.57	7.22	-0.3
2009	LVG	AAA	27	2	1	13	27	0	30	32	1	8	27	2.4	8.1	57%	.333	1.37	2.70	3.61	0.4
2009	TOR	MLB	27	0	0	1	26	0	24^{2}	23	2	17	18	6.2	6.6	46%	.309	1.70	2.55	2.94	0.6
2010	LVG	AAA	28	3	2	24	42	0	44	52	1	15	26	3.1	5.3	52%	.340	1.55	3.48	4.83	0.1
2010	TOR	MLB	28	0	1	0	5	0	62	12	0	3	3	4.1	4.1	44%	.444	2.40	8.10	4.64	0.0
2011	*BAL*	*MLB*	*29*	*3*	*1*	*5*	*53*	*0*	*52*	*58*	*5*	*21*	*34*	*3.6*	*5.7*	*47%*	*.317*	*1.51*	*4.69*	*5.10*	*-0.2*

One of the downsides of having your Triple-A team play in Las Vegas is that it makes life hard on relievers trying to rehabilitate their once-promising careers. It's been mostly downhill since Accardo's breakout 2007 turn as the Toronto closer, and in two years with the 51s, his peripherals have bottomed out. What's more, his brief appearances in the majors have shown that he has lost both velocity and accuracy from his fastball. Still, he hides the ball reasonably well, so a reemergence as a guy who relies on cutting and splitting his heater even more than he used to doesn't seem implausible. Nevertheless, his days of pitching high-leverage innings (and with the Blue Jays, who nontendered him in December) are over. He'll continue the search for his lost setup-man mojo in Baltimore this season.

Taylor Buchholz

Born: **10/13/1981** Age: **29**
Bats: **R** Throws: **R** Height: **6' 4"** Weight: **220**
Breakout: **2%** Improve: **13%** Collapse: **20%**
Attrition: **14%** MLB: **38%**

Comparables:
Leo Rosales, Rich Bordi, Erik Hiljus (75)

YEAR	TEAM	LVL	AGE	W	L	SV	G	GS	IP	H	HR	BB	SO	EqBB9	EqSO9	GB%	BABIP	WHIP	ERA	FRA	WARP
2008	COL	MLB	26	6	6	1	63	0	66^{1}	45	5	18	56	2.4	7.6	40%	.220	0.98	2.17	4.31	0.5
2010	COL	MLB	28	1	0	0	7	0	10	10	2	6	9	5.4	8.1	36%	.308	1.60	4.50	4.95	0.0
2010	TOR	MLB	28	0	0	0	2	0	2	0	0	0	0	0.0	0.0	50%	.000	0.00	0.00	1.82	0.0
2011	*BOS*	*MLB*	*29*	*4*	*2*	*0*	*81*	*0*	*88^{1}*	*90*	*10*	*31*	*61*	*3.1*	*6.3*	*44%*	*.296*	*1.37*	*4.30*	*4.67*	*0.1*

Buchholz spent most of the season recovering from Tommy John surgery, and by the time he made it back to the majors in late July, there wasn't much room for him in the Colorado bullpen. After three mostly ineffective weeks, Buchholz went back on the DL with back stiffness. The Blue Jays claimed him off waivers in September, but released him soon after, so the Red Sox took a flier. The former starter has proven he can be effective in relief, but the skill in question here is health. A risky option like this is best taken on the cheap. The Mets are all about the cheap, so they signed Buccholz to a one-year deal in January in the hopes that he can rediscover the low-90s fastball that made him valuable to the Rockies back in 2008.

Shawn Camp

Born: **11/18/1975** Age: **35**
Bats: **R** Throws: **R** Height: **6' 1"** Weight: **200**
Breakout: **24%** Improve: **40%** Collapse: **16%**
Attrition: **4%** MLB: **72%**

Comparables:
Mike Timlin, Rick Aguilera, Lindy McDaniel (77)

YEAR	TEAM	LVL	AGE	W	L	SV	G	GS	IP	H	HR	BB	SO	EqBB9	EqSO9	GB%	BABIP	WHIP	ERA	FRA	WARP
2008	TOR	MLB	32	3	1	0	40	0	39^{1}	40	2	11	31	2.5	7.1	56%	.317	1.35	4.12	4.24	0.4
2009	TOR	MLB	33	2	6	1	59	0	79^{2}	73	7	29	58	3.3	6.6	56%	.281	1.33	3.50	4.55	0.6
2010	TOR	MLB	34	4	3	2	70	0	72^{1}	71	8	18	46	2.2	5.7	52%	.284	1.29	3.11	3.88	0.7
2011	*TOR*	*MLB*	*35*	*3*	*1*	*2*	*61*	*0*	*68*	*71*	*9*	*21*	*50*	*2.7*	*6.5*	*49%*	*.303*	*1.33*	*4.26*	*4.64*	*0.2*

Camp's three-quarters almost-sidearm delivery generates plenty of ground balls and makes him especially tough on right-handers. That's good, because he doesn't throw hard and his best pitch is his changeup, which makes him easy to overlook until you glance down at your scorecard and realize that he has thrown two shutout innings of relief—a feat he pulled off seven times in 2010. He's the kind of pitcher who makes the manager's job a little easier in lazy, midsummer games, and as a result, Camp should see plenty of innings in his last arbitration year.

Jesse Carlson

Born: **12/31/1980** Age: **30**
Bats: **L** Throws: **L** Height: **6' 1"** Weight: **160**
Breakout: **5%** Improve: **8%** Collapse: **4%**
Attrition: **2%** MLB: **12%**

Comparables:
Joe Hesketh, Doug Bird, Bill Henry (74)

YEAR	TEAM	LVL	AGE	W	L	SV	G	GS	IP	H	HR	BB	SO	EqBB9	EqSO9	GB%	BABIP	WHIP	ERA	FRA	WARP
2008	TOR	MLB	27	7	2	2	69	0	60	41	6	21	55	3.2	8.3	35%	.230	1.08	2.25	3.63	1.0
2009	TOR	MLB	28	1	6	0	73	0	67^{2}	67	7	22	51	2.9	6.8	38%	.287	1.36	4.66	5.13	0.0
2010	LVG	AAA	29	3	1	4	45	0	51	56	6	11	43	1.9	7.6	43%	.321	1.39	4.24	5.38	-0.1
2010	TOR	MLB	29	0	0	1	20	0	13^{2}	13	3	5	8	3.3	5.3	49%	.238	1.39	4.61	7.17	-0.3
2011	*TOR*	*MLB*	*30*	*4*	*1*	*1*	*71*	*0*	*66^{1}*	*68*	*9*	*21*	*51*	*2.8*	*6.9*	*42%*	*.297*	*1.33*	*4.41*	*4.79*	*0.0*

If you're a lefty who can touch 90 mph and locate a sidearm fastball, you get plenty of opportunities to compete for spots in major-league bullpens. Carlson had a nice year pitching mostly in Triple-A, proving that his command-and-control style coupled with an unusual delivery still make him a decent LOOGY candidate, especially since his historical splits are too small to generate useful information. He earned an August call-up, during which he more or less did his thing: all that comes out of Carlson's hand is junk, but it's usually in the strike zone. That's been enough for countless bullpen arms in the past, so who's to deny Carlson a few more useful years as a situational lefty?

Brett Cecil

Born: **7/2/1986** Age: **24**
Bats: **R** Throws: **L** Height: **6' 1"** Weight: **235**
Breakout: **15%** Improve: **50%** Collapse: **18%**
Attrition: **11%** MLB: **95%**

Comparables:
Don Robinson, Rick Reuschel, Don Newcombe (72)

YEAR	TEAM	LVL	AGE	W	L	SV	G	GS	IP	H	HR	BB	SO	EqBB9	EqSO9	GB%	BABIP	WHIP	ERA	FRA	WARP
2008	NHP	AA	21	6	2	0	18	18	77^{2}	66	4	23	87	2.7	10.1	60%	.302	1.21	2.55	3.03	2.8
2008	SYR	AAA	21	2	3	0	6	6	30^{2}	28	1	16	31	4.7	9.1	68%	.310	1.43	4.10	5.16	0.4
2009	LVG	AAA	22	1	5	0	9	9	49	53	2	19	32	3.5	5.9	61%	.313	1.53	5.69	6.85	-0.4
2009	TOR	MLB	22	7	4	0	18	17	93^{1}	116	17	38	69	3.7	6.7	44%	.338	1.70	5.30	5.01	0.9
2010	TOR	MLB	23	15	7	0	28	28	172^{2}	175	18	54	117	2.8	6.1	44%	.293	1.33	4.22	4.63	1.6
2011	*TOR*	*MLB*	*24*	*9*	*8*	*0*	*24*	*24*	126^{1}	*130*	*16*	*44*	*93*	*3.2*	*6.6*	*48%*	*.302*	*1.38*	*4.47*	*4.86*	*2.1*

Cecil is about as unsexy as cost-effective left-handed starters who were drafted in the first round get. He doesn't throw particularly hard—his fastball only hits the low 90s—racks up few strikeouts, walks more batters than you might like, and induces few ground balls. And yet, from April through July, Cecil held opposing batters to just a .292 on-base percentage. The Blue Jays have been aggressive with the University of Maryland product, and it remains to be seen how he'll weather any aftereffects from the extra innings he's been asked to throw. So far, all indications are that Cecil will settle in as a middle-of-the-rotation guy with a great slider and a good changeup. When he faces lefty-heavy lineups, look out.

Scott Downs

Born: **3/17/1976** Age: **35**
Bats: **L** Throws: **L** Height: **6' 2"** Weight: **190**
Breakout: **25%** Improve: **40%** Collapse: **24%**
Attrition: **10%** MLB: **81%**

Comparables:
Rollie Fingers, Jay Howell, Hideki Okajima (77)

YEAR	TEAM	LVL	AGE	W	L	SV	G	GS	IP	H	HR	BB	SO	EqBB9	EqSO9	GB%	BABIP	WHIP	ERA	FRA	WARP
2008	TOR	MLB	32	0	3	5	66	0	70^{2}	54	3	27	57	3.4	7.3	68%	.256	1.20	1.78	2.82	1.6
2009	TOR	MLB	33	1	3	9	48	0	46^{2}	46	4	13	43	2.5	8.3	57%	.304	1.31	3.09	2.50	1.1
2010	TOR	MLB	34	5	5	0	67	0	61^{1}	47	3	14	48	2.1	7.0	59%	.256	1.06	2.64	3.42	1.0
2011	*ANA*	*MLB*	*35*	*3*	*2*	*4*	*65*	*0*	*64*	*56*	*5*	*21*	*53*	*2.9*	*7.4*	*52%*	*.284*	*1.20*	*3.06*	*3.32*	*0.9*

In over 400 innings as a Blue Jay, Downs posted a 3.13 ERA and 2.8 strikeout-to-unintentional-walk ratio. He racks up ground balls, rarely gives up home runs, and does a fine job keeping runners off the bases (especially recently). As a result, he's been a lock to contribute a win or two to his employer's cause for half a decade now. His parting gift to the Jays will be the compensatory draft pick that the Angels will be forced to hand over after inking the Type-A free agent to a three-year deal. If Fernando Rodney should falter, giving Downs the keys to the ninth inning wouldn't be the worst idea, despite his being of the southpaw persuasion.

Kyle Drabek

Born: **12/8/1987** Age: **23**
Bats: **R** Throws: **R** Height: **6' 1"** Weight: **190**
Breakout: **8%** Improve: **13%** Collapse: **2%**
Attrition: **4%** MLB: **18%**

Comparables:
Fabio Castro, Daryl Thompson, Steve Trachsel (75)

YEAR	TEAM	LVL	AGE	W	L	SV	G	GS	IP	H	HR	BB	SO	EqBB9	EqSO9	GB%	BABIP	WHIP	ERA	FRA	WARP
2008	WPT	A-	20	1	2	0	4	4	20^{1}	11	1	6	10	2.7	4.4	56%	.167	0.89	2.22	5.21	0.1
2009	CLR	A+	21	4	1	0	10	9	61^{2}	49	0	19	74	2.8	10.8	47%	.318	1.13	2.48	3.04	1.7
2009	REA	AA	21	8	2	0	15	14	96^{1}	92	9	31	76	2.9	7.1	43%	.288	1.29	3.64	4.37	1.4
2010	NHP	AA	22	14	9	0	27	27	162	126	12	68	132	3.8	7.3	50%	.255	1.22	2.94	4.36	2.3
2010	TOR	MLB	22	0	3	0	3	3	17	18	2	5	12	2.6	6.4	62%	.320	1.35	4.76	5.05	0.1
2011	*TOR*	*MLB*	*23*	*5*	*6*	*0*	*14*	*14*	*85*	*88*	*12*	*40*	*58*	*4.2*	*6.1*	*46%*	*.292*	*1.50*	*4.94*	*5.37*	*0.8*

The biggest mystery about Drabek has been his inability to strike out minor-league hitters at the high rates one would expect from a presumptive future ace. It's a puzzle, since the consensus top prospect in the Toronto system has a repertoire that features both a mid-90s fastball and a hard breaking ball worthy of a shutdown starter. Even those descriptions undersell the quality of the offerings: the fastball has good movement, and the curveball is a simply beautiful species of spike, a 12-to-6 offering that truly falls off the table. For the package to work, though, Drabek will have to offer up the strikeouts in the majors that he never did in the minors. If there's one thing the Blue Jays showed last year, it was that they could translate stuff into results from first-round pitchers (*see also* "Romero, Ricky," and "Morrow, Brandon"). The fact that performance, and not health, is the biggest concern for Drabek speaks very well of his rehab from Tommy John and augurs well for his fortunes in 2011.

Jason Frasor

Born: **8/9/1977** Age: **33**
Bats: **R** Throws: **R** Height: **5' 10"** Weight: **170**
Breakout: **23%** Improve: **49%** Collapse: **30%**
Attrition: **9%** MLB: **96%**

Comparables:
Skip Lockwood, Jesse Orosco, Tippy Martinez (75)

YEAR	TEAM	LVL	AGE	W	L	SV	G	GS	IP	H	HR	BB	SO	EqBB9	EqSO9	GB%	BABIP	WHIP	ERA	FRA	WARP
2008	TOR	MLB	30	1	2	0	49	0	47^{1}	36	4	32	42	6.1	8.0	39%	.248	1.46	4.18	5.06	0.0
2009	TOR	MLB	31	7	3	11	61	0	57^{2}	43	4	16	56	2.5	8.7	39%	.262	1.06	2.50	2.91	1.2
2010	TOR	MLB	32	3	4	4	69	0	63^{2}	61	4	27	65	3.8	9.2	47%	.318	1.45	3.68	3.89	0.6
2011	*TOR*	*MLB*	*33*	*3*	*1*	*4*	*64*	*0*	*60^{2}*	*54*	*6*	*25*	*58*	*3.7*	*8.6*	*44%*	*.295*	*1.30*	*3.65*	*3.97*	*0.6*

Strapped with Type-A free-agent status, Frasor chose to accept the Jays' arbitration offer prior to last season rather than risk diminished appeal to clubs unwilling to part with draft picks. He was given the chance to make the closer's job his out of spring training, but Cito Gaston lost confidence in him after just a few shaky appearances, and Kevin Gregg handled the duties for most of the year. Frasor throws a hard mid-90s fastball that looks all the quicker for its being launched from his diminutive frame. He complements the heater with a good hard slider. Presumably, Frasor will set up for winter acquisition Octavio Dotel, but it's not hard to imagine the 37-year-old sometime closer fumbling enough leads to throw the job open once again.

Kevin Gregg

Born: **6/20/1978** Age: **33**
Bats: **S** Throws: **R** Height: **6' 6"** Weight: **220**
Breakout: **25%** Improve: **39%** Collapse: **17%**
Attrition: **10%** MLB: **71%**

Comparables:
Joaquin Benoit, Tyler Yates, Jeff Nelson (77)

YEAR	TEAM	LVL	AGE	W	L	SV	G	GS	IP	H	HR	BB	SO	EqBB9	EqSO9	GB%	BABIP	WHIP	ERA	FRA	WARP
2008	FLO	MLB	30	7	8	29	72	0	68^{2}	51	3	37	58	4.8	7.6	47%	.247	1.34	3.41	4.50	0.3
2009	CHN	MLB	31	5	6	23	72	0	68^{2}	60	13	30	71	3.9	9.3	38%	.260	1.35	4.72	5.35	-0.3
2010	TOR	MLB	32	2	6	37	63	0	59	52	4	30	58	4.6	8.8	43%	.298	1.41	3.51	3.45	0.7
2011	*BAL*	*MLB*	*33*	*4*	*2*	*30*	*78*	*0*	*73*	*67*	*8*	*34*	*67*	*4.2*	*8.2*	*44%*	*.290*	*1.38*	*3.98*	*4.32*	*0.4*

Gregg walks too many batters, which will continue to keep him from being an especially effective reliever for as long as he keeps it up. That might not sound like the description of a guy who's been handed ninth-inning assignments for the past four seasons, but there's no special alchemy to the customary final frame, no magic aura surrounding guys with a significant number of career saves or snake oil that allows them to strand runners. There are just pitchers like Gregg, who convert a little bit better than 80 percent of their save opportunities and have career ERAs on the crooked side of four. At a guaranteed $2.75 million, he wasn't a terrible acquisition, and at the same price, he might be worth it again. The best thing the Blue Jays get from Gregg may be their supplemental draft pick, since the pitcher departs as a Type-B free agent.

Shawn Hill

Born: **4/28/1981** Age: **30**
Bats: **R** Throws: **R** Height: **6' 2"** Weight: **185**
Breakout: **10%** Improve: **16%** Collapse: **11%**
Attrition: **7%** MLB: **36%**

Comparables:
Erasmo Ramirez, Brad Halsey, Tim Crabtree (75)

YEAR	TEAM	LVL	AGE	W	L	SV	G	GS	IP	H	HR	BB	SO	EqBB9	EqSO9	GB%	BABIP	WHIP	ERA	FRA	WARP
2008	WAS	MLB	27	1	5	0	12	12	63^{1}	88	5	23	39	3.3	5.5	49%	.364	1.77	5.83	5.81	-0.0
2009	SDN	MLB	28	1	1	0	3	3	12	15	1	3	7	2.3	5.3	33%	.318	1.58	5.25	5.15	0.0
2010	BLJ	Rk	29	3	0	0	4	4	22	18	0	1	21	0.4	8.6	59%	.286	0.86	0.41	1.83	3.5
2010	LVG	AAA	29	2	2	0	5	5	21	16	2	5	9	2.1	3.9	47%	.219	1.00	3.00	5.32	0.2
2010	TOR	MLB	29	1	2	0	4	4	20^{2}	24	1	4	14	1.7	6.1	50%	.324	1.40	2.61	2.62	0.8
2011	*TOR*	*MLB*	*30*	*5*	*5*	*0*	*14*	*14*	*71*	*80*	*8*	*20*	*38*	*2.5*	*4.8*	*46%*	*.302*	*1.40*	*4.62*	*5.02*	*1.1*

In between his two Tommy John surgeries, Hill started a mostly harmless 37 games dotted by moments of brilliance. Healthy now for perhaps the first time in his major-league career, Hill recapitulated the ascent of a prospect in his return. It's tough to question his perseverance or dedication, but it's fair to wonder about the state of the sinker that endowed him with such promise as a young pitcher. He was impressive in limited action as the replacement for the sidelined Brandon Morrow, but it takes time to achieve repeatability with a motion that once caused pain with each pitch. The Blue Jays released Hill in November, making him a free agent hoping to latch on to a new club and get in some innings at any level he can.

Casey Janssen

Born: **9/17/1981** Age: **29**
Bats: **R** Throws: **R** Height: **6' 4"** Weight: **205**
Breakout: **15%** Improve: **35%** Collapse: **17%**
Attrition: **22%** MLB: **62%**

Comparables:
Dale Thayer, Larry Christenson, Justin Hampson (74)

YEAR	TEAM	LVL	AGE	W	L	SV	G	GS	IP	H	HR	BB	SO	EqBB9	EqSO9	GB%	BABIP	WHIP	ERA	FRA	WARP
2009	TOR	MLB	27	2	4	1	21	5	40	59	5	14	24	3.2	5.4	50%	.367	1.88	5.85	3.97	0.8
2010	TOR	MLB	28	5	2	0	56	0	68^{2}	74	8	21	63	2.8	8.3	47%	.327	1.44	3.67	3.74	0.8
2011	*TOR*	*MLB*	*29*	*5*	*4*	*0*	*50*	*9*	*88^{2}*	*94*	*11*	*27*	*61*	*2.7*	*6.2*	*46%*	*.304*	*1.36*	*4.44*	*4.83*	*0.8*

Janssen had a very good season—the kind that deserves to be rewarded. He moved to the bullpen in 2009 and gained comfort there in 2010. Used mostly in the seventh and eighth innings, Janssen dialed up his fastball a tick when pitching in relief. He likes to cut and sink his primary offering, which keeps hitters off-balance long enough to hit them with one of his two nifty breaking balls. With his shoulder injuries in the rearview mirror and his big frame apparently capable of handling a season's workload, Janssen can be leaned on in big situations in 2011.

Rommie Lewis Jr.

Born: **9/2/1982** Age: **28**
Bats: **L** Throws: **L** Height: **6' 5"** Weight: **230**
Breakout: **0%** Improve: **4%** Collapse: **0%**
Attrition: **3%** MLB: **4%**

Comparables:
Mike Gosling, A.J. Murray, Edwin Moreno (85)

YEAR	TEAM	LVL	AGE	W	L	SV	G	GS	IP	H	HR	BB	SO	EqBB9	EqSO9	GB%	BABIP	WHIP	ERA	FRA	WARP
2008	BOW	AA	25	1	6	0	38	5	66	81	4	26	63	3.5	8.6	54%	.387	1.67	3.41	1.97	2.6
2009	NHP	AA	26	2	4	1	26	0	42	35	2	22	45	4.7	9.6	33%	.306	1.40	2.14	1.82	1.7
2009	LVG	AAA	26	2	3	0	19	0	24	23	1	9	20	3.4	7.5	53%	.301	1.42	3.00	2.78	0.6
2010	LVG	AAA	27	1	5	5	24	8	53^1	72	7	22	41	3.7	6.9	59%	.365	1.79	7.59	6.38	-0.1
2010	TOR	MLB	27	0	0	0	14	0	18^2	20	4	8	15	3.9	7.2	37%	.291	1.50	6.75	6.34	-0.3
2011	*TOR*	*MLB*	*28*	*3*	*2*	*1*	*39*	*4*	*65*	*74*	*10*	*29*	*47*	*4.1*	*6.6*	*46%*	*.320*	*1.59*	*5.50*	*5.97*	*-0.5*

Lewis is a big lefty with the sort of fastball/slider repertoire you would expect from a pitcher with his frame. He also throws a curveball, which gives him three decent pitches. A former Orioles prospect, Lewis sat out the 2005 season and took a job as a pizza delivery boy, but returned to a potentially more lucrative profession that also rewards accurate deliveries. His biggest challenge will be harnessing his command, but should he do that, he'll have value, at least against lefties. Placed on the DL with shoulder soreness at the end of 2010, Lewis will try to win a job and a roster spot during spring training.

Jesse Litsch

Born: **3/9/1985** Age: **26**
Bats: **R** Throws: **R** Height: **6' 1"** Weight: **205**
Breakout: **13%** Improve: **38%** Collapse: **14%**
Attrition: **13%** MLB: **76%**

Comparables:
Larry Dierker, Glen Perkins, Jim Barr (77)

YEAR	TEAM	LVL	AGE	W	L	SV	G	GS	IP	H	HR	BB	SO	EqBB9	EqSO9	GB%	BABIP	WHIP	ERA	FRA	WARP
2008	SYR	AAA	23	1	1	0	3	3	20	18	1	4	18	1.8	8.1	64%	.298	1.15	3.60	4.81	0.2
2008	TOR	MLB	23	13	9	0	29	28	176	178	20	39	99	2.0	5.1	49%	.278	1.28	3.58	4.37	2.5
2009	TOR	MLB	24	0	1	0	2	2	9	14	4	1	8	1.0	8.0	38%	.357	1.78	9.00	7.17	-0.1
2010	LVG	AAA	25	0	3	0	4	4	22	34	4	3	13	1.2	5.3	40%	.366	1.82	7.77	7.98	-0.2
2010	TOR	MLB	25	1	5	0	9	9	46^2	53	7	15	16	2.9	3.1	45%	.284	1.50	5.79	6.24	-0.2
2011	*TOR*	*MLB*	*26*	*7*	*8*	*0*	*21*	*21*	*125^1*	*137*	*19*	*33*	*66*	*2.4*	*4.7*	*47%*	*.290*	*1.35*	*4.75*	*5.16*	*1.4*

Litsch returned from Tommy John surgery in June and never quite found his groove. Even so, his stuff looked the same as it ever did, which is to say mostly junky. He throws a good cut fastball and a full complement of off-speed pitches, but relies on the sort of approach that requires him to have good command each time out, and in 2010, he just couldn't do that. Litsch had to go back under the knife in August to repair a hip injury, and his recovery schedule should see him healthy in spring training, where the challenge will be to rediscover his command. However, if Kyle Drabek cracks the rotation, Litsch may be left in the bullpen.

Shaun Marcum

Born: **12/14/1981** Age: **29**
Bats: **R** Throws: **R** Height: **6' 0"** Weight: **180**
Breakout: **13%** Improve: **47%** Collapse: **22%**
Attrition: **11%** MLB: **96%**

Comparables:
Bret Saberhagen, Dick Hughes, Dennis Leonard (73)

YEAR	TEAM	LVL	AGE	W	L	SV	G	GS	IP	H	HR	BB	SO	EqBB9	EqSO9	GB%	BABIP	WHIP	ERA	FRA	WARP
2008	TOR	MLB	26	9	7	0	25	25	151^1	126	21	50	123	3.0	7.3	43%	.246	1.22	3.39	4.59	1.9
2010	TOR	MLB	28	13	8	0	31	31	195^1	181	24	43	165	2.0	7.6	39%	.279	1.18	3.64	3.69	4.1
2011	*MIL*	*MLB*	*29*	*9*	*7*	*0*	*23*	*23*	*134^2*	*128*	*19*	*39*	*113*	*2.6*	*7.6*	*42%*	*.286*	*1.24*	*3.88*	*4.22*	*3.0*

It long looked as if the Blue Jays had an interchangeable-parts approach to the non-Halladay section of their rotation. Litsch, Richmond, Marcum—who could keep them all straight? If these players really were interchangeable, then the Blue Jays would have been wise to turn in all their chips and cash out in Marcums. In contrast to Litsch's and McGowan's recoveries, Marcum's return from Tommy John surgery went swimmingly, and the Opening Day starter set career bests in nearly every relevant category. He slashed his walks, leading to a strikeout-to-walk ratio that was sixth-best in the majors, ahead of King Felix, Tim Lincecum, and Francisco Liriano. Despite his being a righty who doesn't throw hard, Marcum's beguiling mix of slow stuff fooled plenty of AL lineups in 2010. If he doesn't have the most intimidating mound presence, he more than makes up for it in results and value. The Brewers acquired the righty in December to serve as a crucial component of their revamped rotation, sending Brett Lawrie north of the border in return; Marcum should reap the dual benefit of escaping the AL East gauntlet and emigrating to the easier league.

Dustin McGowan

Born: **3/24/1982** Age: **29**
Bats: **R** Throws: **R** Height: **6' 3"** Weight: **220**
Breakout: **14%** Improve: **33%** Collapse: **27%**
Attrition: **18%** MLB: **77%**

Comparables:
Todd Worrell, David Wells, Turk Farrell (75)

YEAR	TEAM	LVL	AGE	W	L	SV	G	GS	IP	H	HR	BB	SO	EqBB9	EqSO9	GB%	BABIP	WHIP	ERA	FRA	WARP
2008	TOR	MLB	26	6	7	0	19	19	111^1	115	9	38	85	3.1	6.9	43%	.315	1.42	4.37	4.75	1.2
2011	*TOR*	*MLB*	*29*	*9*	*8*	*0*	*24*	*24*	*139^2*	*137*	*15*	*53*	*114*	*3.4*	*7.3*	*44%*	*.301*	*1.36*	*4.07*	*4.43*	*2.8*

Of the three young Blue Jays starters who were lost to season-length recoveries from surgery, McGowan threw the hardest before landing on the DL. Now, after two years and as many shoulder surgeries, McGowan's career hangs in the balance. Either labrum surgery or rotator-cuff surgery would be serious enough on its own, but both in two years is downright scary. McGowan is out of big-league options, so he'll most likely start the year on the disabled list. If he wants to pitch again in the majors, he'll have to hope for a quick rehab with overwhelmingly positive results.

Brad Mills

Born: **3/5/1985** Age: **26**
Bats: **L** Throws: **L** Height: **5' 11"** Weight: **185**
Breakout: **13%** Improve: **29%** Collapse: **6%**
Attrition: **5%** MLB: **50%**

Comparables:
Ramon Ramirez, Bob Sebra, Eulogio De La Cruz (75)

YEAR	TEAM	LVL	AGE	W	L	SV	G	GS	IP	H	HR	BB	SO	EqBB9	EqSO9	GB%	BABIP	WHIP	ERA	FRA	WARP
2008	LNS	A	23	6	3	0	15	15	81^1	71	3	28	92	3.1	10.2	53%	.319	1.28	2.55	2.23	3.4
2008	DUN	A+	23	4	0	0	6	6	33^1	25	2	12	35	3.2	9.5	38%	.274	1.11	1.35	2.44	1.7
2008	NHP	AA	23	3	2	0	6	6	32^2	24	2	12	32	3.3	8.8	33%	.262	1.13	1.10	2.79	1.2
2009	LVG	AAA	24	2	8	0	14	14	84^1	83	6	35	72	3.7	7.7	46%	.314	1.45	4.06	4.05	1.7
2009	TOR	MLB	24	0	1	0	2	2	7^2	14	4	6	9	7.0	10.6	15%	.435	2.61	14.09	13.61	-0.4
2010	LVG	AAA	25	8	6	0	20	20	112^1	118	15	43	100	3.5	8.0	43%	.310	1.45	4.97	4.69	1.9
2010	TOR	MLB	25	1	0	0	7	3	22^1	20	2	13	18	5.2	7.3	41%	.281	1.52	5.64	5.85	-0.1
2011	*TOR*	*MLB*	*26*	*6*	*7*	*0*	*17*	*17*	*96*	*101*	*14*	*44*	*77*	*4.1*	*7.1*	*43%*	*.308*	*1.50*	*4.96*	*5.39*	*0.9*

Finesse pitchers are fun to watch because they seem to defy gravity, if not with their pitches, at least with their career arcs. As each step along the development chain erodes their strikeout rate without doing anything flattering to their walk rates, fans can simply hope that these pitchers have socked away enough craftiness to survive the upper levels. Mills is flying close to the sun, to be sure, and Las Vegas is not a forgiving place for a pitcher who gets cute with the strike zone. Nevertheless, he's a lefty and has three pitches he can throw for strikes. His success, as high as it may go, depends entirely on his ability to aggressively command the strike zone by keeping hitters off-balance.

Brandon Morrow

Born: **7/26/1984** Age: **26**
Bats: **R** Throws: **R** Height: **6' 3"** Weight: **190**
Breakout: **26%** Improve: **52%** Collapse: **15%**
Attrition: **16%** MLB: **85%**

Comparables:
Edinson Volquez, J.P. Howell, Steve Bedrosian (71)

YEAR	TEAM	LVL	AGE	W	L	SV	G	GS	IP	H	HR	BB	SO	EqBB9	EqSO9	GB%	BABIP	WHIP	ERA	FRA	WARP
2008	TAC	AAA	23	1	2	0	6	5	23^1	17	2	11	26	4.2	10.0	39%	.254	1.20	5.02	5.31	0.2
2008	SEA	MLB	23	3	4	10	45	5	64^2	40	10	34	75	4.7	10.4	34%	.206	1.14	3.34	4.70	0.4
2009	TAC	AAA	24	5	3	0	10	10	55	50	2	23	40	3.8	6.5	41%	.284	1.35	3.44	3.86	1.1
2009	SEA	MLB	24	2	4	6	26	10	69^2	66	10	44	63	5.7	8.1	36%	.286	1.58	4.26	4.57	0.8
2010	TOR	MLB	25	10	7	0	26	26	146^1	136	11	66	178	4.1	10.9	40%	.343	1.44	4.49	4.21	2.4
2011	*TOR*	*MLB*	*26*	*6*	*4*	*3*	*37*	*12*	*89*	*80*	*10*	*45*	*93*	*4.6*	*9.3*	*41%*	*.301*	*1.40*	*4.12*	*4.48*	*1.5*

Consider that Morrow has really only been a starting pitcher for five years, and even then in an on-again, off-again fashion. Now consider that if Morrow had pitched the additional innings needed to qualify for the ERA title without recording even a single strikeout, he still would have led the majors in strikeouts per nine innings pitched. From June until he was shut down in early September, Morrow threw 89 1/3 innings with 112 strikeouts and just 32 walks. His masterpiece came on August 8 against the Rays, a 17-strikeout shutout that was one Evan Longoria single away from being a no-hitter. There is still uncertainty here—the repertoire beyond the electric fastball and hard slider needs further refinement—but there are few pitchers in the game with higher ceilings than Morrow's.

David Purcey

Born: **4/22/1982** Age: **29**
Bats: **L** Throws: **L** Height: **6' 5"** Weight: **230**
Breakout: **7%** Improve: **15%** Collapse: **7%**
Attrition: **14%** MLB: **29%**

Comparables:
Bill Murphy, Brad Salmon, Dan Meyer (73)

YEAR	TEAM	LVL	AGE	W	L	SV	G	GS	IP	H	HR	BB	SO	EqBB9	EqSO9	GB%	BABIP	WHIP	ERA	FRA	WARP
2008	SYR	AAA	26	8	6	0	19	19	117	97	8	34	121	2.6	9.3	45%	.293	1.15	2.69	2.99	4.1
2008	TOR	MLB	26	3	6	0	12	12	65	67	9	29	58	4.0	8.0	33%	.307	1.54	5.54	5.17	0.5
2009	LVG	AAA	27	9	6	0	24	24	139^1	132	7	78	109	5.0	7.0	43%	.302	1.57	4.46	4.81	1.5
2009	TOR	MLB	27	1	3	0	9	9	48	54	6	29	39	5.4	7.3	33%	.327	1.75	6.19	6.19	-0.1
2010	TOR	MLB	28	1	1	1	33	0	34	26	3	15	32	4.0	8.5	31%	.247	1.21	3.71	3.84	0.4
2011	*TOR*	*MLB*	*29*	*7*	*6*	*0*	*52*	*15*	*123*	*124*	*16*	*63*	*100*	*4.6*	*7.3*	*42%*	*.301*	*1.51*	*4.83*	*5.25*	*0.7*

Purcey got a chance to pitch relatively important innings this season, and he did not disappoint; in fact, the bullpen seems like where his stuff always belonged. He's not a low-stress fireman, however, as he has a tendency to load the bases before working his way out of a jam. Purcey is a big guy with a big fastball and is a former first-round pick to boot, so he shouldn't lack chances to assume the Blue Jays' set-up role in 2011. To take the next step forward, he needs to refine his slider further; it's his only weapon besides the heater, and even in 2010, he couldn't reliably throw it for strikes.

Robert Ray
Born: **1/21/1984** Age: **27**
Bats: R Throws: R Height: **6' 5"** Weight: **195**
Breakout: **0%** Improve: **0%** Collapse: **0%**
Attrition: **0%** MLB: **0%**
Comparables:
Beltran Perez, Kelvin Jimenez, Jake Woods (89)

YEAR	TEAM	LVL	AGE	W	L	SV	G	GS	IP	H	HR	BB	SO	EqBB9	EqSO9	GB%	BABIP	WHIP	ERA	FRA	WARP
2008	DUN	A+	24	5	3	0	13	13	70^{2}	71	6	18	60	2.3	7.6	49%	.310	1.33	4.20	4.23	1.3
2008	NHP	AA	24	8	6	0	16	16	96^{1}	108	6	27	72	2.5	6.7	48%	.330	1.47	3.18	3.48	2.7
2009	TOR	MLB	25	1	2	0	4	4	24^{1}	23	4	6	13	2.2	4.8	50%	.250	1.27	4.44	6.31	-0.1
2010	LVG	AAA	26	6	6	0	18	18	96^{1}	118	13	45	75	4.2	7.0	43%	.354	1.75	5.51	5.86	0.6
2010	TOR	MLB	26	0	0	0	3	0	3^{2}	2	0	5	3	12.3	7.4	20%	.200	1.91	2.45	6.21	-0.1
2011	*TOR*	*MLB*	*27*	*4*	*7*	*0*	*15*	*15*	*80*	*96*	*12*	*35*	*51*	*3.8*	*5.6*	*45%*	*.320*	*1.61*	*5.75*	*6.25*	*0.1*

Ray is all elbows and leg kick when he delivers his sinker/slider combination. He had a bad year at Triple-A, but his frame still offers some reason for optimism. That gangly body may also be to blame for the assorted injury problems that have nagged him over the years. If he's going to have a big-league career, it's increasingly likely that it will come as a long reliever or swingman.

Jo-Jo Reyes
Born: **11/20/1984** Age: **26**
Bats: L Throws: L Height: **6' 2"** Weight: **230**
Breakout: **7%** Improve: **15%** Collapse: **5%**
Attrition: **5%** MLB: **27%**
Comparables:
Jason Vargas, Edgar Gonzalez, Don Robinson (79)

YEAR	TEAM	LVL	AGE	W	L	SV	G	GS	IP	H	HR	BB	SO	EqBB9	EqSO9	GB%	BABIP	WHIP	ERA	FRA	WARP
2008	RIC	AAA	23	1	1	0	8	8	39	31	2	16	38	3.7	8.8	54%	.276	1.26	2.31	3.22	1.3
2008	ATL	MLB	23	3	11	0	23	22	113	134	18	52	78	4.1	6.2	49%	.321	1.67	5.81	6.20	-0.3
2009	GWN	AAA	24	4	2	0	15	14	66	68	6	24	32	3.3	4.4	46%	.284	1.41	2.86	3.35	2.1
2009	ATL	MLB	24	0	2	0	6	5	27	27	4	13	21	4.3	7.0	52%	.288	1.52	7.00	9.32	-0.8
2010	GWN	AAA	25	1	5	0	12	10	47^{1}	57	8	15	50	2.9	9.6	48%	.358	1.53	5.70	5.36	0.4
2010	ATL	MLB	25	0	0	0	1	0	3^{1}	10	2	3	2	8.1	5.4	33%	.500	3.90	24.30	19.02	-0.4
2011	*TOR*	*MLB*	*26*	*8*	*10*	*0*	*25*	*25*	*119*	*130*	*18*	*53*	*81*	*4.0*	*6.1*	*47%*	*.304*	*1.53*	*5.28*	*5.74*	*1.1*

Acquired from the Braves in the Alex Gonzalez trade, Reyes has not yet put it all together in the majors, disappointing the Blue Jays, who undoubtedly hoped that a change of scenery would help him realize his potential as a back-of-the-rotation starter. While he's a reclamation project, at least he's a reclamation project with good stuff. He spent the beginning of 2010 fighting a knee injury, but after Jo-Jo got back, his peripherals were solid. If everything works out, he'll be a cheap lefty who can eat innings—as if the Blue Jays needed another guy like that.

Scott Richmond
Born: **8/30/1979** Age: **31**
Bats: R Throws: R Height: **6' 5"** Weight: **225**
Breakout: **10%** Improve: **26%** Collapse: **18%**
Attrition: **19%** MLB: **67%**
Comparables:
Nate Robertson, Dave Bush, Eric Stults (71)

YEAR	TEAM	LVL	AGE	W	L	SV	G	GS	IP	H	HR	BB	SO	EqBB9	EqSO9	GB%	BABIP	WHIP	ERA	FRA	WARP
2008	NHP	AA	28	5	8	0	16	16	89^{2}	89	14	30	84	3.0	8.4	41%	.290	1.36	4.92	6.44	-0.6
2008	SYR	AAA	28	1	3	0	8	8	48	44	6	13	40	2.4	7.5	44%	.277	1.21	3.56	4.24	0.9
2008	TOR	MLB	28	1	3	0	5	5	27	32	2	2	20	0.7	6.7	37%	.345	1.33	4.00	3.30	0.8
2009	TOR	MLB	29	8	11	0	27	24	138^{2}	147	27	59	117	3.8	7.6	35%	.295	1.49	5.52	5.84	0.1
2010	DUN	A+	30	3	0	0	5	4	21	14	0	6	13	2.6	5.6	62%	.212	0.95	1.29	3.45	0.5
2011	*TOR*	*MLB*	*31*	*7*	*9*	*0*	*21*	*21*	*117^{1}*	*126*	*21*	*43*	*88*	*3.3*	*6.8*	*42%*	*.298*	*1.44*	*5.04*	*5.48*	*1.1*

Richmond spent most of 2010 snake-bitten by a variety of shoulder injuries. When he did pitch, he was mostly up to his old tricks: he showed decent command, and the rest was finesse. His reliance on a fastball/slider complement, combined with the fact that he doesn't throw very hard, means that Richmond may be extra vulnerable against lefties.

Josh Roenicke
Born: **8/4/1982** Age: **28**
Bats: R Throws: R Height: **6' 3"** Weight: **200**
Breakout: **5%** Improve: **7%** Collapse: **3%**
Attrition: **5%** MLB: **13%**
Comparables:
Carlos Guevara, Eric Hull, Jailen Peguero (83)

YEAR	TEAM	LVL	AGE	W	L	SV	G	GS	IP	H	HR	BB	SO	EqBB9	EqSO9	GB%	BABIP	WHIP	ERA	FRA	WARP
2008	CHT	AA	25	4	2	10	22	0	22	21	2	12	28	4.9	11.5	48%	.328	1.50	3.27	4.14	0.2
2008	LOU	AAA	25	2	0	3	37	0	41^{1}	39	4	15	44	3.3	9.6	43%	.318	1.33	3.05	3.26	0.9
2008	CIN	MLB	25	0	0	0	5	0	3	6	0	2	6	6.0	18.0	22%	.667	3.00	9.00	3.38	0.1
2009	LOU	AAA	26	1	0	12	27	0	28	30	0	6	32	1.9	10.3	50%	.366	1.36	2.25	1.85	1.0
2009	CIN	MLB	26	0	0	0	11	0	13^{1}	13	0	4	14	2.7	9.5	47%	.361	1.27	3.38	3.73	0.1
2009	TOR	MLB	26	0	0	0	13	0	17^{2}	19	2	12	19	6.1	9.7	48%	.340	1.81	7.13	7.72	-0.4
2010	LVG	AAA	27	9	1	1	36	0	59^{1}	61	7	25	54	3.8	8.2	49%	.314	1.49	3.64	4.78	0.3
2010	TOR	MLB	27	1	0	0	16	0	19	18	1	13	18	6.2	8.5	55%	.298	1.74	5.68	5.64	-0.2
2011	*TOR*	*MLB*	*28*	*2*	*1*	*2*	*46*	*0*	*55*	*55*	*6*	*26*	*50*	*4.2*	*8.2*	*46%*	*.315*	*1.47*	*4.58*	*4.98*	*-0.1*

Roenicke is no doubt very familiar with the flight route between Las Vegas and Toronto, as he made the trip four times during 2010. He brings to the table nothing that isn't also offered by countless other team-controlled pitchers on the Blue Jays' 40-

man roster, except perhaps for a faster fastball. Roenicke's control is prone to abandoning him, his slider is middling, and he hasn't been able to cash in on the opportunities he's been given. If he washes out with the Blue Jays, perhaps his Uncle Ron will give him a spin in Milwaukee.

Ricky Romero

Born: **11/6/1984** Age: **26**
Bats: R Throws: L Height: **6' 0"** Weight: **210**
Breakout: **16%** Improve: **49%** Collapse: **13%**
Attrition: **9%** MLB: **96%**

Comparables:
Rudy May, Ernie Broglio, Steve Busby (71)

YEAR	TEAM	LVL	AGE	W	L	SV	G	GS	IP	H	HR	BB	SO	EqBB9	EqSO9	GB%	BABIP	WHIP	ERA	FRA	WARP
2008	NHP	AA	23	5	5	0	21	21	121^2	139	9	55	78	4.1	5.8	53%	.332	1.64	4.95	5.30	0.7
2008	SYR	AAA	23	3	3	0	7	7	42^2	42	3	20	38	4.2	8.0	57%	.322	1.50	3.37	3.32	1.3
2009	TOR	MLB	24	13	9	0	29	29	178	192	18	79	141	4.0	7.1	55%	.333	1.58	4.30	3.19	5.5
2010	TOR	MLB	25	14	9	0	32	32	210	189	15	82	174	3.5	7.5	56%	.289	1.33	3.73	4.46	2.3
2011	*TOR*	*MLB*	*26*	*9*	*9*	*0*	*25*	*25*	*155*	*161*	*19*	*68*	*116*	*3.9*	*6.7*	*51%*	*.310*	*1.48*	*4.75*	*5.16*	*1.7*

If you're wondering why bonus babies seem to get chance after chance while their fringier cousins are given margins of a hair's breadth, Romero is a good place to start looking for answers. Drafted sixth overall in 2005, he put up mediocre numbers at almost every stop in the high minors. Thrown into the major-league mix in 2009, he thrived under pressure. Relied on to lead the rotation in 2010, he improved across the board. Sometimes, latent talent takes a while to click, and no one is worrying about Romero's poor minor-league peripherals now. He succeeds on the strength of a good fastball with movement and a changeup that lets him retire righties at least as well as lefties. From there, his durability should carry him to a nice major-league career. Much of it should be with the Blue Jays, too, as they inked him to a five-year, $30 million deal (with a club option for a sixth season) in August.

Marc Rzepczynski

Born: **8/29/1985** Age: **25**
Bats: L Throws: L Height: **6' 1"** Weight: **205**
Breakout: **17%** Improve: **45%** Collapse: **8%**
Attrition: **18%** MLB: **77%**

Comparables:
Brad Mills, Johnny Cueto, Steve Busby (71)

YEAR	TEAM	LVL	AGE	W	L	SV	G	GS	IP	H	HR	BB	SO	EqBB9	EqSO9	GB%	BABIP	WHIP	ERA	FRA	WARP
2008	LNS	A	22	7	7	0	23	23	126^1	104	2	43	130	3.1	9.3	69%	.309	1.23	2.56	2.37	4.9
2009	NHP	AA	23	7	5	0	14	14	76^2	80	1	36	88	4.2	10.3	63%	.367	1.57	2.93	3.78	1.6
2009	TOR	MLB	23	2	4	0	11	11	61^1	51	7	30	60	4.4	8.8	52%	.270	1.34	3.67	4.61	0.9
2010	LVG	AAA	24	5	5	0	12	12	67	81	10	27	61	3.6	8.2	55%	.351	1.67	6.04	5.69	0.6
2010	TOR	MLB	24	4	4	0	14	12	63^2	72	8	30	57	4.2	8.1	53%	.342	1.68	4.95	5.47	0.1
2011	*TOR*	*MLB*	*25*	*7*	*8*	*0*	*20*	*20*	*110*	*116*	*14*	*52*	*96*	*4.2*	*7.8*	*53%*	*.320*	*1.52*	*5.02*	*5.46*	*1.0*

Scrabble, Eyechart, Alphabet—call him what you want, but Rzepczynski has to stop giving so many hitters free passes. It's great that his name is unusual ("Just like it's spelled," he must have told countless teachers), and the strikeouts and ground balls are what got him to where he is. The next step, however, is harnessing his control, and it's as likely to happen next year as never. Rzepczynski enjoyed success in the Arizona Fall League and should get a chance to battle Jesse Litsch and Kyle Drabek for the fifth rotation spot in the spring.

Zach Stewart

Born: **9/28/1986** Age: **24**
Bats: R Throws: R Height: **6' 2"** Weight: **205**
Breakout: **8%** Improve: **20%** Collapse: **5%**
Attrition: **10%** MLB: **32%**

Comparables:
Brad Mills, Josh Outman, Johnny Cueto (75)

YEAR	TEAM	LVL	AGE	W	L	SV	G	GS	IP	H	HR	BB	SO	EqBB9	EqSO9	GB%	BABIP	WHIP	ERA	FRA	WARP
2009	SAR	A+	22	1	1	0	7	7	42^1	47	1	8	32	1.7	6.8	59%	.341	1.32	2.13	3.43	1.0
2009	CAR	AA	22	3	0	0	7	7	37	29	1	10	31	2.4	7.5	54%	.275	1.08	1.46	1.86	1.7
2010	NHP	AA	23	8	3	0	26	26	136^1	131	13	54	106	3.6	7.0	49%	.297	1.40	3.63	4.30	2.2
2011	*TOR*	*MLB*	*24*	*5*	*5*	*1*	*30*	*12*	*88*	*95*	*12*	*39*	*63*	*3.9*	*6.4*	*47%*	*.308*	*1.50*	*4.92*	*5.34*	*0.5*

Converted back to starting after spending much of his career as a reliever, Stewart experienced mixed success while reaching a career high in innings pitched. He mostly relies on a sinker/slider combo, which didn't suffer much in the move back to starting. The limitation for Stewart is his ceiling, as he lacks the stuff of a frontline starter. He lost enough of his command in the conversion that it will take him at least another year in the minors before he is fully stretched out and ready for "The Show."

Brian Tallet

Born: **9/21/1977** Age: **33**
Bats: L Throws: L Height: **6' 7"** Weight: **208**
Breakout: **9%** Improve: **18%** Collapse: **9%**
Attrition: **14%** MLB: **39%**

Comparables:
Kip Wells, Shawn Chacon, Tim Corcoran (75)

YEAR	TEAM	LVL	AGE	W	L	SV	G	GS	IP	H	HR	BB	SO	EqBB9	EqSO9	GB%	BABIP	WHIP	ERA	FRA	WARP
2008	TOR	MLB	30	1	2	0	51	0	56^1	52	4	22	47	3.5	7.5	43%	.289	1.33	2.88	2.89	1.5
2009	TOR	MLB	31	7	9	0	37	25	160^2	169	20	72	120	4.0	6.7	38%	.299	1.54	5.32	5.50	0.7
2010	TOR	MLB	32	2	6	0	34	5	77^1	84	20	38	53	4.4	6.2	36%	.266	1.63	6.28	6.73	-1.3
2011	*SLN*	*MLB*	*33*	*4*	*4*	*0*	*45*	*8*	*90*	*94*	*12*	*42*	*64*	*4.2*	*6.4*	*41%*	*.296*	*1.50*	*4.92*	*5.35*	*-0.2*

Here's an exhaustive list of baseball attributes we can be sure Brian Tallet possesses: tall, left-handed, mutton-choppy. Those features vary in their usefulness in recording outs against major-league hitters, but despite his high-80s fastball, poor peripherals, and uneven facial hair, Tallet hangs on. His platoon splits were uncharacteristically extreme in 2010 (righties hit .320/.415/.617 against him), suggesting that he may not have been hiding the ball well with his three-quarters delivery against batters of opposite handedness. After being outrighted from the 40-man roster in November, Tallet elected to pursue free agency and hooked on with the Cardinals.

LINEOUTS

HITTERS

PLAYER	TEAM	LVL	AGE	PA	R	2B	3B	HR	RBI	BB	SO	SB-CS	AVG/OBP/SLG	TAv	BABIP	BRR	FRAA	WARP
C Y. Gomes	DUN	A+	22	247	37	21	1	9	40	9	64	0-0	.275/.312/.489	.266	.342	0.7	C 0	1.1
INF N. Green	POR	AAA	31	159	17	9	1	2	21	13	33	0-4	.264/.325/.382	.248	.324	0.8	SS -4, 3B 0	-0.1
	ABQ	AAA	31	104	15	9	2	2	10	3	19	1-0	.204/.235/.398	.191	.228	0.7	3B 1, SS -1	-0.4
	LAN	MLB	31	9	0	0	0	0	1	0	2	0-0	.125/.222/.125	.160	.167	0.0	2B 1, SS 0	0.0
	TOR	MLB	31	14	2	0	0	0	1	1	3	0-0	.154/.214/.154	.149	.200	0.0	2B 1, SS 0	-0.1
1B M. Jacobs*	BUF	AAA	29	371	53	23	3	15	57	28	65	1-0	.260/.313/.478	.258	.278	1.6	1B 3	0.7
	LVG	AAA	29	157	26	6	0	6	34	21	21	0-0	.308/.389/.492	.309	.312	1.0	1B -4	0.7
	NYN	MLB	29	28	1	1	0	1	2	3	7	0-0	.208/.286/.375	.250	.235	0.0	1B 0	0.0
C B. Jeroloman*	NHP	AA	25	319	37	16	0	7	33	69	91	0-1	.261/.429/.412	.317	.385	-6.5	C 1	2.6
C A. Jimenez	LNS	A	20	293	35	22	0	4	54	18	56	17-4	.305/.347/.435	.277	.360	0.2	C 0	1.6
LF C. Lubanski*	LVG	AAA	25	402	72	24	6	17	57	40	94	4-1	.293/.361/.538	.292	.348	-0.2	LF -9, RF -1	1.2
CF D. Mastroianni	ZUL	—	24	146	24	5	2	1	18	20	20	11-4	.368/.452/.464	—	.429	0.0	—	0.0
	NHP	AA	24	617	101	25	7	4	46	77	96	46-10	.301/.390/.398	.286	.352	4.8	CF -3	3.6
SS G. Pierre	AUB	A-	18	275	29	12	3	3	22	17	64	8-4	.236/.283/.344	.236	.295	0.0	SS -2	0.1
DH R. Ruiz	TOR	MLB	32	40	3	2	0	1	1	0	11	1-0	.150/.150/.275	.143	.179	0.1	1B 0	-0.4
RF M. Sierra	BLJ	Rk	21	54	4	3	0	1	3	6	10	0-0	.271/.352/.396	.268	.324	0.0	RF 3	0.3

Although frightened Floridians might have mistaken him for an unholy union of Esteban Yan and Jonny Gomes sent to remind Rays fans of the lean years, **Yan Gomes** is a 10th-round pick from 2009 who put up big numbers in the Florida State League, including 21 doubles in 247 plate appearances. He'll need to acquire a walk rate worthy of Gomes (or even better, Yan) if he is to rise further. ⊘ Not even playing in the high-octane offensive environment of the Pacific Coast League could make **Nick Green** look like an asset; pray the day never comes when your team has to rely on him. ⊘ **Mike Jacobs** has power but can't find first base with a map, as illustrated by his cumulative .237/.298/.458 triple-slash line from 2008 to 2010. He's not so good at finding it on defense, either. Jacobs suffered the ultimate indignity in 2010 by failing to hold a job with the Mets (despite batting cleanup on Opening Day) and, after spending the balance of the season in Las Vegas following a July trade, was looking for work as we went to press. ⊘ If you can't find a place in your heart for a catcher with a career 18 percent minor-league walk rate, then **Brian Jeroloman** (and come to think of it, this book) might not be for you. ⊘ **A. J. Jimenez** was enjoying a breakout season until the elbow injury that dropped him to the ninth round of the 2008 draft sidelined him again in August. He's an athletic backstop in a system with plenty of catchers, which means that his future is even more speculative. ⊘ Former Royals first-rounder **Chris Lubanski** got the Las Vegas bump, but our translations throw some cold water on the notion that something has clicked. The Marlins awarded him one more in a long line of chances. ⊘ **Darin Mastroianni** is a speedy center fielder with good plate discipline and very little power; if everything works out, he'll be a poor man's Denard Span. ⊘ **Gustavo Pierre** was raw in the New York-Penn League, showing a strong arm but questionable glove skills—he has the tools but not yet an idea of how to use them consistently in games. ⊘ **Randy Ruiz** hit two home runs in his hometown of the Bronx in 2009, but in 2010, he was released and caught on in Japan. Playing for the Tohoku Rakuten Golden Eagles, he hit 12 home runs in 312 plate appearances. ⊘ Dominican outfielder **Moises Sierra**'s best asset is his throwing arm, but he is getting too old for that alone to be enough to wish on. If he's going to have a big-league career, he has to start hitting, and soon.

PITCHERS

PLAYER	TEAM	LVL	AGE	W	L	SV	IP	H	HR	BB	SO	EqBB9	EqSO9	GB%	BABIP	WHIP	ERA	FRA	WARP
H. Alvarez	DUN	A+	20	8	7	0	112^{1}	137	10	27	78	2.2	6.3	52%	.338	1.53	4.33	4.97	1.0
J. Carreno	DUN	A+	23	9	6	0	137^{2}	147	8	30	173	2.0	11.3	44%	.381	1.38	3.73	3.57	3.5
A. Farina	DUN	A+	23	2	1	2	36^{1}	19	0	11	46	2.7	11.5	53%	.244	0.83	1.24	2.88	0.8
D. Farquhar	NHP	AA	23	4	3	17	76^{2}	50	7	42	79	5.0	9.3	48%	.231	1.31	3.52	4.54	0.3
C. Jenkins	LNS	A	22	5	4	0	79^{1}	87	5	13	64	1.5	7.3	56%	.329	1.28	3.63	3.66	1.8
	DUN	A+	22	2	6	0	62^{1}	73	6	18	42	2.6	6.1	54%	.313	1.47	4.33	5.35	0.4
T. Magnuson	NHP	AA	25	3	0	5	73^{1}	70	1	10	63	1.2	7.8	47%	.325	1.12	2.58	2.23	1.9
D. McGuire	DNP	—	22	—	—	—	—	—	—	—	—	—	—	—	—	—	—	—	—
L. Perez*	NHP	AA	25	5	6	0	73^{1}	67	6	37	49	4.6	6.0	59%	.280	1.48	4.54	5.02	0.5
	LVG	AAA	25	5	5	0	86^{2}	107	5	47	56	4.9	5.8	58%	.345	1.93	6.13	5.11	1.0
M. Valdez	LVG	AAA	27	3	5	0	58	92	5	26	35	4.0	5.4	56%	.395	2.09	7.91	7.68	-1.1
	TOR	MLB	27	0	0	0	11	2	0	3	0	20.3	0.0	67%	.333	3.75	20.25	22.57	-0.1

Henderson Alvarez is the kind of ground-ball pitcher who gets no favors from A-ball defenses, but at least his control has stood by him. ⊘ If you're 23 and stuck in A-ball, the way to get attention is to miss bats. **Joel Carreno** took three or four steps forward in 2010 en route to the Dunedin single-season strikeout record—his gem was a 15-strikeout game in July. If he keeps it up, Carreno and his plus slider could move up quickly. ⊘ Despite his small frame, **Alan Farina** put up eye-popping numbers in relief last season, thanks to a live fastball, and he could be useful out of the major-league bullpen before long. ⊘ **Danny Farquhar** is wild to watch, and not just because of the walks, since he relies on multiple arm angles. He was sent to Oakland in the Rajai Davis deal. ⊘ **Dirk Hayhurst**'s *Bullpen Gospels*, one of the best personal memoirs ever written by a player, debuted last March to near-universal acclaim. Unfortunately, the *New York Times* best-selling author had undergone season-ending shoulder surgery by the time his book hit shelves and didn't throw a pitch all year. Now a free agent, he should be ready for spring training. ⊘ The Blue Jays' first-round pick in 2009, **Chad Jenkins** did not live up to the hype in his debut, and his prospect status took a hit in the process. ⊘ **Trystan Magnuson**, a reliever with good control but average stuff, was shipped to Oakland in the Rajai Davis deal. Magnuson is tall and has a decent fastball, but his ceiling is high enough to accommodate only a middle reliever comfortably. ⊘ Viewed as a relatively safe college arm going into the 2010 draft, **Deck McGuire** has the potential for a solid four-pitch mix that features a plus slider and a low-90s fastball. It's worth wondering, though, what the Blue Jays will do with yet one more durable, midrotation arm. Generally that's the kind of problem you deal with when your hand is forced, but with the 11th pick in the draft and plenty of cost-controlled starters in your stable, why not roll the dice? ⊘ **Luis Perez** fell apart completely in Triple-A, as the combination of the tough Las Vegas environment and poor control set fire to his ERA. ⊘ **Aaron Sanchez** has big upside, but much work remains to be done on his fastball and curve; he's the picture of projectability. ⊘ **Noah Syndergaard** was one of three sandwich-round picks by the Jays in the 2010 draft, and he might end up with the best fastball of any of them. ⊘ Once a promising prospect for the Giants, **Merkin Valdez** had his career derailed by Tommy John surgery and is no longer effective. ⊘ A supplemental first rounder in 2010, **Asher Wojciechowski** has plus fastball velocity and a big frame but little else as of yet.

MANAGER: CITO GASTON/ JOHN FARRELL

YEAR	TEAM	W-L	Pythag +/-	Avg PC	100+ P	120+ P	QS	BQS	REL	REL w Zero R	IBB	Subs	PH	PH Avg	PH HR	SB2	CS2	SB3	CS3	SAC Att	SAC %	POS SAC	Squeeze	Swing	In Play
2008	TOR	51-37	-4	99.9	47	3	47	2	215	153	16	34	36	.333	0	26	4	7	0	44	63.6%	27	0	61	46
2009	TOR	75-87	-9	97.5	84	1	77	9	445	284	26	20	48	.289	2	54	20	19	3	36	66.7%	22	0	112	83
2010	TOR	85-77	1	95.7	64	1	83	4	452	288	34	19	40	.105	1	52	16	6	4	23	69.6%	15	0	108	76

And so the second Cito Gaston era comes to a close. Gaston's final year featured some odd moves, like nearly a month's worth of starts from DeWayne Wise, and some pleasant surprises, like an organization-wide case of isolated power. Gaston officially retired to a consulting role with the team in October, paving the way for Alex Anthopoulos to hire Red Sox pitching coach John Farrell to helm the ship for 2011. Farrell, 48, has no managing experience to speak of, having declined other offers to remain with the Red Sox until Toronto was able to woo him away, but he did spend the last four years learning at the side of Terry Francona, who praised the pitching coach's communication skills and work with young pitchers. Farrell will have ample opportunity to continue with these skills in Toronto. In addition to his coaching duties with Boston, Farrell has served as director of player development for the Indians and as coach at Oklahoma State University; Anthopoulos and the Blue Jays stressed the variety of Farrell's experience as an asset in the dugout.

Washington Nationals

The only kind of dignity which is genuine is that which
is not diminished by the indifference of others.
—DAG HAMMARSKJOLD

The Nationals' slow crawl to real relevance at the major-league level took its first fitful drag upward last year. Their forward progress represented the fruits of new general manager Mike Rizzo's first full season at the helm, the product of tacit planning instead of haphazard stumbling, and it yielded a variety of bittersweet prizes that added up to progress. Let us not mistake that small point from the outset: the Nationals are better off now than they were four years ago, or two or six, for that matter. They have begun to escape the long shadow cast by successive self-inflating, careless stewards that was the franchise's legacy as a ward of the industry, first under Omar Minaya and then the Denethor-like defeatist tendencies of Jim Bowden. The Nationals are finally moving into a period that should allow them to define themselves and where their achievements will serve as something more than a transient résumé refresher for the hired help.

NATIONALS PROSPECTUS

2010 W-L: 69-93, 5th in NL East

Pythag	.443	23rd
RS/G	4.0	25th
RA/G	4.6	10th
TAv	.263	22nd
BRR	-2.9	21st
FRA	4.47	16th
DER	-14.9	28th
DL	1,220	29th
B-Age	29.2	18th
P-Age	28.3	19th
Salary	$61.4	23rd
M$/MW	$2.52	16th

Ballpark: Nationals Park (3-yr. PF: 100). If you squint, you can see the Capitol in between parking lots

2010: Another last-place finish enlivened by Strasburg's debut and Harper's selection

2011: A roster cannot live by Werth alone

Action Items: A painless rehab for Strasburg, someone to pitch until he gets back

The team's tokens of treading the slow path toward contention are not especially mysterious. Start with Stephen Strasburg's first appearance on the major-league stage—only the most anticipated prospect debut since David Clyde's with the Rangers in the 1970s—which was perfectly capped by his striking out 14 Pirates on June 8. Unfortunately, that was followed in short order by Strasburg's elbow surgery, perhaps the most noisily regretted operation since Cubs wunderkind Kerry Wood's journey to the surgeon's table little more than a decade ago. You can pity manager Jim Riggleman his association with both, since the responsibility for neither exigency can be laid at his doorstep. But in the meantime, the surgery has left Strasburg's debut little more than a taster for a 2012 season that should finally see the club open a season with two of the game's best young pitchers in the same rotation. At that time, Strasburg will take his place alongside blue-chip hurler Jordan Zimmermann, who is already back from his own Tommy John procedure on his throwing elbow.

Having selected Strasburg first overall in 2009, the club faced further amateur talent-related drama last season. Circumstance favored the Nats by presenting them with a second, equally obvious talent to take with the top overall choice in the draft in June—teen masher Bryce Harper, almost every bit as worthy of a big-league deal as Strasburg had been. Harper was signed to a record contract for a position player, $9.9 million over five years, in the expectation that his power at the plate will be every bit as game-breaking as Strasburg's should be from the mound. A month after drafting Harper, Rizzo also won the in-season scramble to sign the latest defecting Cuban pitcher, World Baseball Classic star Yunesky Maya, for $8 million over four years.

Beyond the big-name prospect scoreboard, the Nats were making careful progress in the standings, moving up from 100-loss to 90-loss territory. Much of their improvement was the product of significantly better bullpen performance on Riggleman's watch in his first full season. The relief corps' performance swung from -54.3 Adjusted Runs Prevented in 2009 to +43.6 in 2010, almost a 10-win swing by itself, even as the lineup was losing roughly five wins' worth of runs on offense over the same period. Better bullpen performance brought the Nats back from epically hopeless to competitive on the mound, creating more games in which even an offense struggling for mediocrity at least had a small chance of matching scores with the opposition. While that might be an endorsement of the decision to remove the 2009 "interim" tag from Riggleman as the club's in-season replacement of Manny Acta, the bullpen performance is one of the least reliable quantities from year to year. As a result, the basis of the team's improvement might not sound extremely reassuring, but hold that thought.

The other major news, both before last season and echoed during the latest offseason, was the Nats' aggressive pursuit of name free agents, notably ones not already the product of Bowden's short stack of solutions. As a peculiar reflection of Bowden's unique genius, the Nats received the benefit of his unblinking faith in repeating his associations with Jose Guillen, Adam Dunn, and Cristian Guzman, always at steep cost and without much reflection about whether these things made sense. In his first offseason, Rizzo focused on run prevention for his big-ticket shopping, adding veteran right-hander Jason Marquis for $15 million over two years after the latter's career year in Colorado, Hall of Fame–bound catcher Ivan Rodriguez for two years, and cast-off closer Matt Capps. The last offered mutual benefit, with the Nats seeking relief help and Capps getting the chance to prove that he was finally healthy.

In some ways, the game that Rizzo is being allowed to play by the Lerner family, as the owners puts their stamp on the club, is one we've seen before, if not in Expos history, at least featuring a former Expos exec, and up toward the border as well. The club in question was the Detroit Tigers, the last team to log consecutive 100-loss seasons. When Dave Dombrowski brought general manager Randy Smith's reign of error to a deserved end a week into the 2002 season, things were unavoidably going to get worse—the legacy of Smith's mismanagement could not be undone in a single season or over the course of a lone Hot Stove campaign, having already plumbed the depths of 96 losses in 2001. Months after joining the organization as president, Dombrowski canned Smith six games into a 106-loss season, which was followed by the ignominy of 119 losses in 2003. The indignity of those dimensions should sound familiar to Nats fans after 2008-2009.

As we know, the Motor City Kitties dug out of that hole, since in 2006, the Tigers won 95 games and a pennant. Player development in the intervening years between Dombrowski's putsch and the Tigers' trip to the postseason had produced some of the club's key star power. In its first draft in 2002, Dombrowski's crew drafted Curtis Granderson in the third round and Joel Zumaya in the 11th, and they grabbed Justin Verlander with the second overall pick of the 2004 draft. Three key players—or as you might observe, *just* three key players—was more than the sum total of worthwhile Smith-era talent that was still contributing. Brandon Inge and Fernando Rodney were the only noteworthy vestiges left.

So where did the talent that delivered the Tigers' turnaround come from? From a front office that scared up talent in every way it could, snapping up some free talent from waivers and the Rule 5 draft and whatever other ticky-tack means, trading aggressively, but also by doing what might have seemed impossible after a pair of 100-loss humiliations: importing high-priced players. Dombrowski embarked on a series of prestige signings, first inking midmarket free agents Jason Johnson, Rondell White, and Fernando Vina to multimillion-dollar, multiyear deals in December before achieving his real attention-getter in February—signing the seemingly ubiquitous Ivan "Pudge" Rodriguez to a four-year, $40 million contract. Remember, Pudge was leaving the world-champion Marlins and was joining the game's worst team. A year later, Dombrowski landed an even bigger free agent, Magglio Ordonez, for an even larger price tag, a minimum of five years and $75 million that wound up running six years for $90 million, while also paying Troy Percival $12 million for two years. A year after that, the GM ran down Kenny Rogers for $24 million over three years, getting his staff the innings-eater it needed to help make a pennant run.

In almost every case, there's good cause for lament over the expense—few if any of these deals delivered anything like full value. However, as easy it is to criticize the amount paid to these men, or to Dontrelle Willis or Jeremy Bonderman, it's also often the cost of doing business. If you want to feel sorry for Mike Ilitch, feel free, but what Dombrowski achieved with all of that expense was to demonstrate a willingness and an ability to pay top dollar for some of the biggest names on the market. The Tigers' propositions to free agents went from laughable begging from a long-term loser in a dead city into plausible pitches from a team taking itself seriously and committed to upsetting its division's apple cart. For men on the short side of their careers, that combination of possible contention and cash is reliably attractive. To get there, Dombrowski had to make massive commitments—to Pudge and Maggs, in particular—but people noticed, within the organization and outside it. Miguel Cabrera and Verlander signed long-term extensions to stick around, and even today, big-name free agents who could choose anywhere, like Victor Martinez just this past winter, pick Detroit.

How does that experience compare to the Nats' lot under Rizzo so far? One of the biggest achievements on the newly minted GM's watch in 2009 was getting star third baseman Ryan Zimmerman to agree to a five-year, $45 million extension, as uncomplicated an expression of a club's commitment to its future as a sullen, swindled fan-base might require. After the Marquis, Pudge, and Capps outlays before the 2010 season, Rizzo was in a position to be taken even more seriously during his second winter at the helm. Seeking to patch up the front end of a rotation that will one day feature both Strasburg and Zimmermann, and just as Dombrowski reached for something better than Jason Johnson as he settled into his new responsibility, Rizzo pursued two of this winter's biggest free-agent pitchers—obvious ace Cliff Lee, in vain, and strike-throwing Carl Pavano, to an uncertain result as we go to press.

Those unsuccessful pursuits were set against one of the most shocking signings of the winter, as Rizzo landed one of the best position players available, former Phillie Jayson Werth. The terms were nothing short of incredible: seven years and $126 million. The money makes this a deal of a piece with the Tigers' similarly huge commitment to Ordonez back in the day—a massive overpayment for a very good ballplayer, in this case one heading into his age-32 through age-38 seasons, whereas Ordonez was committed through ages 31-36. Werth's potential for enjoying a better thirtysomething decade than his injury-interrupted 20s depends on considerable faith in what he's done in the last several seasons *and* faith in his former status as one of the game's best prospects in the late 1990s—unlikely, but not impossible, with the chance that he becomes something like a latter-day Brian Downing, a source of power, patience, and good defense in an outfield corner.

You can see how Rizzo might have talked himself into the expense, but the odds remain long that Werth will deliver, making this very much like Dombrowski's costly gambles in Detroit. However, here as there, the hope is that the Nats can do as the Tigers did with this kind of marquee signing, using it as leverage to entice other players to jump to a newly competitive club. That might sound surprising in discussing a team still searching for its first winning season since the move to D.C., but the NL doesn't have the AL East axis to contend with—getting into the 88- to 92-win range earns a team in the senior circuit a wild-card spin in most years, and within the NL East, the Phillies' aging offensive core makes winning with the game's current-best rotation an uncertain proposition beyond the next year or two.

For the present, Rizzo's ministrations have mostly been devoted to the run-prevention front, in particular his pitching staff, but defensive improvements might also be en route, especially in the middle infield as the homegrown duo of Danny Espinosa and Ian Desmond settle in, and in the outfield with the addition of Werth and the deletion of the DH-worthy Josh Willingham. The bullpen also boasts a ready replacement for Capps in the club's other 2009 first-round pick, Drew Storen, and getting Henry Rodriguez's triple-digit heat from the A's in the Willingham deal means that the unit might do more than simply secure its gains in 2010.

The club's immediate problem in making sure its bid for contention is something serious instead of speculative depends on delivering a much more potent attack. Harper will help, presumably arriving in the Werth-less corner of the outfield—in 2013. Obtaining an upgrade over Nyjer Morgan would be nice, but good help is hard to find in center field. However, the decision to let Adam Dunn slip away via free agency leaves open the biggest bopper's slot, first base. Perhaps this was a short-term calculation based on the understanding that this winter's market was awash in first-base options, but consider the potential payoff of noisily signing someone like Werth as a prestige pickup: *next* winter, Prince Fielder and Albert Pujols both might hit the market. If the Nats are one of the few clubs still willing to keep slinging nine-figure offers, they won't just *deserve* to be taken seriously; they simply will be.

With the hand they hold currently, the Nats won't win this year, but 2012, with Strasburg back, could very well be the franchise's first winning season. Forecasting nothing better than contention for 2013 might, if anything, reflect undue pessimism concerning what Rizzo and company might do in the meantime. There's plenty of room on the bandwagon, but feel free to climb on board early—two seasons into the Rizzo era, the Nats have come to deserve the attention.

HITTERS

Roger Bernadina **OF**

Born: **6/12/1984** Age: **27**
Bats: L Throws: L Height: **6' 1"** Weight: **190**
Breakout: **0%** Improve: **34%** Collapse: **7%**
Attrition: **18%** MLB: **69%**

Comparables:
Jeff Salazar, Jeff Fiorentino, Travis Buck (78)

YEAR	TEAM	LVL	AGE	PA	R	2B	3B	HR	RBI	BB	SO	SB	CS	AVG/OBP/SLG	TAv	BABIP	BRR	FRAA	WARP
2008	HAR	AA	24	303	47	11	7	5	38	31	64	26	9	.323/.393/.474	.320	.403	4.6	CF 4, RF 1	3.8
2008	COH	AAA	24	215	33	13	3	4	16	16	37	15	2	.351/.391/.513	.304	.401	2.2	CF -4, RF -1	1.4
2008	WAS	MLB	24	86	10	1	1	0	2	9	21	4	3	.211/.291/.250	.202	.286	0.1	CF -3, LF 2	-0.3
2009	WAS	MLB	25	5	1	1	0	0	0	1	1	1	0	.250/.400/.500	.303	.333	0.1	CF 0, RF 0	0.1
2010	SYR	AAA	26	69	8	2	1	2	8	6	5	7	2	.377/.426/.541	.318	.375	-0.3	CF -1, LF 2	0.6
2010	WAS	MLB	26	461	51	18	3	11	47	35	93	16	2	.246/.306/.384	.252	.286	2.0	RF -5, LF -3	-0.4
2011	*WAS*	*MLB*	*27*	*384*	*45*	*16*	*2*	*8*	*41*	*34*	*74*	*18*	*5*	*.266/.330/.399*	*.257*	*.310*	*0.2*	*CF -4, RF -1*	*0.3*

Bernadina is a fourth outfielder hailing from Curaçao, the island that was not named after a liqueur only consumed at five in the morning at frat parties after the kids have already drunk all the butane, brake fluid, and Stroh's. While his 2010 big-league breakthrough represented a nice comeback from a broken ankle, Bernadina's gifts present the classic tweener dilemma—not enough bat to play in a corner, but not enough glove to cut it in center. Any team for which he plays every day surrenders runs on both offense and defense, but he can run and slug a little, and he's a handy enough reserve potentially miscast (again) as a regular after the Willingham trade if he can beat out winter addition Rick Ankiel.

Michael Burgess RF

Born: **10/20/1988** Age: **22**
Bats: **L** Throws: **L** Height: **5' 11"** Weight: **195**
Breakout: **3%** Improve: **15%** Collapse: **1%**
Attrition: **14%** MLB: **31%**

Comparables:
Mat Gamel, Wladimir Balentien, Carlos Gonzalez (70)

YEAR	TEAM	LVL	AGE	PA	R	2B	3B	HR	RBI	BB	SO	SB	CS	AVG/OBP/SLG	TAv	BABIP	BRR	FRAA	WARP
2008	HAG	A	19	460	60	26	4	18	60	46	136	5	1	.249/.335/.469	.284	.325	1.4	RF -6	1.3
2008	POT	A+	19	83	12	3	0	6	19	9	26	0	2	.225/.325/.521	.282	.250	0.0	RF -2	0.2
2009	POT	A+	20	545	63	23	2	19	71	54	135	12	8	.235/.325/.410	.270	.287	-6.2	RF -1, CF 0	0.6
2010	POT	A+	21	442	57	21	4	12	70	47	89	5	2	.262/.351/.430	.285	.310	1.2	RF -11, LF 0	0.9
2010	HAR	AA	21	87	11	5	2	6	15	10	27	0	0	.284/.391/.649	.306	.366	-0.9	RF -5	0.0
2011	*WAS*	*MLB*	*22*	*545*	*60*	*23*	*2*	*19*	*63*	*47*	*157*	*2*	*1*	*.220/.292/.398*	*.240*	*.276*	*-0.1*	*RF -17, CF 0*	*-1.9*

A 2007 supplemental first-rounder out of Tampa's Hillsborough High—the school that gave us Gary Sheffield and Doc Gooden, Elijah Dukes, and Carl Everett—Burgess has been moving slowly enough to earn a Heinz endorsement ever since. The squat right fielder has the strong arm for the slot, but the fear is that he can add weight too easily and might lose his ability to cover ground. The big hope for him has long been that his power would develop, and his season-ending tasting course at Double-A suggests that Burgess is about to pick the pace. Unfortunately, good breaking stuff still ties Burgess up, so a batting average sufficient to boost him into the big-league picture remains in the planning stages.

Ian Desmond SS

Born: **9/20/1985** Age: **25**
Bats: **R** Throws: **R** Height: **6' 2"** Weight: **210**
Breakout: **2%** Improve: **42%** Collapse: **11%**
Attrition: **25%** MLB: **73%**

Comparables:
Troy Tulowitzki, Carney Lansford, Yunel Escobar (74)

YEAR	TEAM	LVL	AGE	PA	R	2B	3B	HR	RBI	BB	SO	SB	CS	AVG/OBP/SLG	TAv	BABIP	BRR	FRAA	WARP
2008	HAR	AA	22	364	42	14	0	12	44	31	78	12	8	.251/.313/.406	.253	.286	1.2	SS 2	1.5
2009	HAR	AA	23	189	29	12	1	6	18	16	40	13	4	.306/.370/.494	.306	.368	-1.0	SS 1	1.5
2009	SYR	AAA	23	205	25	12	2	1	14	20	31	8	1	.354/.420/.461	.312	.413	1.7	SS -2, CF 0	1.8
2009	WAS	MLB	23	89	9	7	2	4	12	5	14	1	0	.281/.315/.561	.292	.288	-0.3	SS -3, 2B 0	0.4
2010	WAS	MLB	24	574	59	27	4	10	65	28	109	17	5	.269/.303/.392	.250	.310	2.6	SS -8, RF 0	1.0
2011	*WAS*	*MLB*	*25*	*473*	*55*	*23*	*2*	*11*	*55*	*32*	*91*	*14*	*5*	*.269/.317/.412*	*.256*	*.308*	*-0.1*	*SS -2, 2B 0*	*1.3*

In the annals of the shortstop position, among the trinity-grade stars and the slappy slick-fielding types, you can find guys who have done a bit of everything, hitting for some power, running a little, striking out a lot, but also dropping down the odd bunt. As an example like Greg Gagne reveals, shortstops can even be starters on championship clubs despite low on-base percentages (OBP). Desmond is stamped out of that mold, which is why his name kept coming up in trade rumors over the winter. He's already too old for his bat to show much more than has already been on display, but he can be an asset while hitting about this well if his fielding improves. Desmond's defense is seen as a problem due to a stack of errors 34 high, but between a strong arm and good lateral range, he has the tools to develop into a quality defender.

Adam Dunn 1B

Born: **11/9/1979** Age: **31**
Bats: **L** Throws: **R** Height: **6' 6"** Weight: **240**
Breakout: **4%** Improve: **38%** Collapse: **7%**
Attrition: **14%** MLB: **96%**

Comparables:
Ryan Howard, David Ortiz, Travis Hafner (60)

YEAR	TEAM	LVL	AGE	PA	R	2B	3B	HR	RBI	BB	SO	SB	CS	AVG/OBP/SLG	TAv	BABIP	BRR	FRAA	WARP
2008	ARI	MLB	28	187	21	9	0	8	26	42	44	1	0	.243/.417/.472	.303	.294	-1.3	RF -4, 1B -2	0.6
2008	CIN	MLB	28	464	62	14	0	32	74	80	120	1	1	.233/.373/.528	.306	.243	-1.0	LF -3	2.7
2009	WAS	MLB	29	668	85	29	0	38	105	116	177	0	1	.267/.398/.529	.319	.324	-3.8	1B -8, LF -7	3.1
2010	WAS	MLB	30	648	92	36	2	38	103	77	199	0	1	.260/.357/.536	.316	.329	-5.3	1B -6	2.9
2011	*CHA*	*MLB*	*31*	*656*	*92*	*28*	*1*	*36*	*95*	*101*	*176*	*2*	*1*	*.251/.372/.506*	*.302*	*.296*	*-0.1*	*1B -4, LF -2*	*2.7*

Dunn liberated himself from D.C. early enough that he wouldn't have to worry about starring in *Hondo 2* and will get his shot at slugging for a contending team for the first time in his career. Moving to Chicago's South Side (for four years and $56 million) to DH couldn't come soon enough; the Donkey may be big at the plate, but despite working on his first-base defense, he throws about as well as Frank Thomas did while moving around with all of Jason Giambi's dead-cat dexterity. But will he fill the bill as a DH as effectively as Jim Thome did back in the day? Dunn hit just as many homers last season as he had in 2009, but he swung much more aggressively than ever before, which produced a career-low unintentional walk rate of 10.5 percent and a career-high swinging-strike rate of 25 percent (compared with the 14 percent major-league average). The concern is that these developments might be symptoms of slowing reflexes, not just a change in approach, but as long as he's slugging for an isolated power in the .270s, questions won't get asked. The Cell will help him; although it's less generous to lefties than to right-handers, it's still a great ballpark in which to bop. Add in Dunn's habit of chewing up strike-throwers and soft-tossers, and you can see how easily he could become known as Adam Twinsbane.

Danny Espinosa MI

Born: **4/25/1987** Age: **24**
Bats: **S** Throws: **R** Height: **6' 0"** Weight: **190**
Breakout: **6%** Improve: **23%** Collapse: **7%**
Attrition: **28%** MLB: **49%**

Comparables:
Xavier Paul, Elliot Johnson, Brett Carroll (78)

YEAR	TEAM	LVL	AGE	PA	R	2B	3B	HR	RBI	BB	SO	SB	CS	AVG/OBP/SLG	TAv	BABIP	BRR	FRAA	WARP
2008	VER	A-	21	87	8	2	0	0	4	17	17	2	2	.328/.460/.359	.319	.412	0.8	SS -1	0.8
2009	POT	A+	22	576	90	31	4	18	72	74	129	29	11	.264/.368/.460	.284	.313	1.3	SS 9	4.4
2010	HAR	AA	23	435	66	16	4	18	54	33	94	20	8	.262/.334/.464	.287	.297	2.8	SS 0	3.0
2010	SYR	AAA	23	108	14	2	1	4	15	8	22	5	3	.295/.349/.463	.271	.329	0.9	SS -3, 2B 1	0.4
2010	WAS	MLB	23	112	16	4	1	6	15	9	30	0	2	.214/.277/.447	.259	.239	1.6	2B 0, SS 2	0.6
2011	*WAS*	*MLB*	*24*	*430*	*50*	*17*	*2*	*15*	*51*	*38*	*107*	*13*	*5*	*.236/.309/.413*	*.253*	*.278*	*-0.5*	*SS 2, 2B 0*	*1.4*

Trailing Desmond by a year, Espinosa's turn for a September breakthrough last season was similarly the product of surprising power for a middle infielder, but Espinosa has even more pop at his disposal, generating tremendous torque in a long fly-ball swing. Desmond's presence moved Espinosa across the bag, ending questions over whether Espinosa's accurate arm and good fundamentals would make up for his range at short; at the keystone, Espinosa should be good, with potential for excellence. If there's a problem, it's that the Nats may well find themselves with two very similar batters producing low OBPs, since Espinosa's walk rate rested at seven percent between the majors and minors last year, and his swing isn't expected to produce big batting averages. Accept those few warts, though, and you've got both another power source up the middle and a quality defender. Espinosa may not star, but he'll be a big part of what makes D.C.'s ballclub better.

Jesus Flores C

Born: **10/26/1984** Age: **26**
Bats: **R** Throws: **R** Height: **6' 1"** Weight: **180**
Breakout: **1%** Improve: **29%** Collapse: **10%**
Attrition: **11%** MLB:**760%**

Comparables:
Terry Steinbach, Bill Sudakis, Randy Bush (78)

YEAR	TEAM	LVL	AGE	PA	R	2B	3B	HR	RBI	BB	SO	SB	CS	AVG/OBP/SLG	TAv	BABIP	BRR	FRAA	WARP
2008	COH	AAA	23	69	8	3	0	1	7	8	20	0	0	.153/.275/.254	.169	.211	0.5	C 0, 1B 0	-0.4
2008	WAS	MLB	23	324	23	18	1	8	59	15	78	0	1	.256/.296/.402	.245	.315	-6.0	C -2	0.1
2009	WAS	MLB	24	106	13	3	2	4	15	11	26	0	0	.301/.368/.505	.301	.369	-1.0	C -1	0.7
2011	*WAS*	*MLB*	*26*	*235*	*27*	*11*	*1*	*6*	*26*	*18*	*55*	*1*	*0*	*.249/.312/.394*	*.244*	*.302*	*0.0*	*C -1*	*0.5*

If you were expecting Flores back in action last season, you may as well have been rooting for a presidential pardon to re-planetize Pluto—it just didn't happen. In Flores' case, the failure to turn back the clock stemmed from repeated mishaps while rehabbing the shoulder that shut him down in 2009. Finally playing again in the Venezuelan winter league, Flores caught semiregularly, but at this stage, his future is in danger of being dwarfed as convincingly as the sun's ninth big circling thingamajig: he needs to prove that he's healthy and durable enough to back up Pudge in Wilson Ramos's place, while Derek Norris moves up the ladder with a 2012 ETA. The Nats are sensibly leaving Flores behind the plate for the time being rather than attempting to dress his bat up in first-base livery in the aftermath of Dunn's departure.

Alberto Gonzalez MI

Born: **4/18/1983** Age: **28**
Bats: **R** Throws: **R** Height: **5' 11"** Weight: **165**
Breakout: **2%** Improve: **32%** Collapse: **3%**
Attrition: **7%** MLB: **63%**

Comparables:
Melvin Dorta, Placido Polanco, Luis Rivas (77)

YEAR	TEAM	LVL	AGE	PA	R	2B	3B	HR	RBI	BB	SO	SB	CS	AVG/OBP/SLG	TAv	BABIP	BRR	FRAA	WARP
2008	SWB	AAA	25	213	23	8	0	4	23	16	30	4	2	.250/.310/.356	.229	.269	0.6	SS -2, 2B 0	0.0
2008	NYA	MLB	25	58	4	2	0	0	1	4	8	0	0	.173/.224/.212	.141	.196	-0.1	SS -1, 3B 0	-0.7
2008	WAS	MLB	25	54	10	6	0	1	9	4	6	0	1	.347/.407/.531	.317	.381	-0.2	SS 0, 3B 0	0.4
2009	SYR	AAA	26	92	5	3	1	0	8	1	8	1	0	.311/.315/.367	.225	.337	0.4	SS -2	-0.2
2009	WAS	MLB	26	316	30	16	3	1	33	14	27	1	1	.265/.298/.351	.228	.280	-1.8	2B -1, SS -4	-0.8
2010	WAS	MLB	27	198	20	8	1	0	5	7	30	0	0	.247/.273/.301	.203	.288	-0.8	3B 6, 2B -1	-0.1
2011	*WAS*	*MLB*	*28*	*380*	*39*	*18*	*2*	*3*	*34*	*21*	*46*	*3*	*1*	*.255/.296/.344*	*.228*	*.279*	*-0.2*	*SS -1, 2B 0*	*0.0*

It's too easy to describe the Attorney General's at-bats as torture, but happily, Riggleman kept him safely reserved for defensive-replacement duties and double-switches last year, generally to get Cristian Guzman off the field. Along with Wil Nieves, Gonzalez is on the short list for least dangerous bench bats available in the free world, ahead of most pitchers, hitting coaches, and a few zombies. You need that projection about as much as you need scabies, which would have a similar effect on your fantasy team.

Bryce Harper OF

Born: **10/16/1992** Age: **18**
Bats: **L** Throws: **R** Height: **6' 3"** Weight: **225**
Breakout: **0%** Improve: **0%** Collapse: **0%**
Attrition: **0%** MLB: **0%**

Comparables:

YEAR	TEAM	LVL	AGE	PA	R	2B	3B	HR	RBI	BB	SO	SB	CS	AVG/OBP/SLG	TAv	BABIP	BRR	FRAA	WARP
2011	*WAS*	*MLB*	*18*	—	—	—	—	—	—	—	—	—	—	—	—	—	—	—	—

A year after the draft offered up Strasburg, it yielded an equally historic hitting talent in Harper, whom the Nats selected first overall as well and then signed for a guaranteed $9.9 million over five years (a record for a drafted position player). Harper's calling card is power that merits an easy 80 on the 20-80 scale. Multiple scouts have stated that they've never seen as much in-game power in a player so young; it's the product of excellent bat speed and hand-eye coordination capable of driving balls to all fields. Whether his aggressive approach produces equally big slugging and strikeout numbers will have to wait for his debut in A-ball this spring, but he cut his teeth with a taxi-squad assignment in the AFL and had no problems with older competition. If there are minor negatives to note in the short term, they can be summed up by the observations that he's still adapting to the outfield and that he's a bit beyond cocky. Only in the long term, however, will we learn what he can do against advanced breaking stuff and whether he'll bulk up and take Adam Dunn's place in every dimension once he reaches his 20s. Those days are still years away; while Harper's every feat on the way up will be followed as attentively as Strasburg's were, his initial ETA may have to wait until 2013; even the most precocious hitters usually need more time than similarly gifted pitchers.

Willie Harris UT

Born: **6/22/1978** Age: **33**
Bats: **L** Throws: **R** Height: **5' 9"** Weight: **175**
Breakout: **1%** Improve: **31%** Collapse: **10%**
Attrition: **16%** MLB: **88%**

Comparables:
Jim Dwyer, Dave Martinez, Jorge Orta (71)

YEAR	TEAM	LVL	AGE	PA	R	2B	3B	HR	RBI	BB	SO	SB	CS	AVG/OBP/SLG	TAv	BABIP	BRR	FRAA	WARP
2008	WAS	MLB	30	424	55	14	4	13	43	50	66	13	3	.251/.342/.417	.269	.271	1.2	LF 8, CF 2	2.3
2009	WAS	MLB	31	393	45	18	6	7	27	57	62	11	4	.235/.361/.393	.271	.267	-1.9	CF 0, LF -3	1.0
2010	WAS	MLB	32	262	25	6	2	10	32	33	60	5	2	.183/.290/.362	.235	.198	1.8	RF 3, LF -2	0.3
2011	*WAS*	*MLB*	*33*	*372*	*43*	*15*	*3*	*9*	*36*	*48*	*66*	*12*	*5*	*.233/.337/.380*	*.256*	*.262*	*-0.5*	*LF 1, CF 1*	*0.9*

As if the Nats' bench hadn't enough problems, Harris, one of its key assets, struggled all season long. While his year was bookended by injury, marked by a knee ailment early and a (literal) head-on collision with an outfield wall in September—perhaps the salient issue was his getting cut back from playing about half the time to receiving just 45 starts last year. That's a tough gig for any hitter, and Harris's power/patience proposition at the plate can get ugly in small doses. He's a useful-enough fielder at second, at third, and in the outfield, and if he's put into a more regular playing-time rotation, he should still be productive, but he'll have to catch a skipper's eye in camp.

Adam Kennedy INF

Born: **1/10/1976** Age: **35**
Bats: **L** Throws: **R** Height: **6' 1"** Weight: **192**
Breakout: **0%** Improve: **34%** Collapse: **12%**
Attrition: **31%** MLB: **82%**

Comparables:
Geoff Blum, Kevin Seitzer, Mike Lamb (75)

YEAR	TEAM	LVL	AGE	PA	R	2B	3B	HR	RBI	BB	SO	SB	CS	AVG/OBP/SLG	TAv	BABIP	BRR	FRAA	WARP
2008	SLN	MLB	32	365	42	17	4	2	36	21	43	7	1	.280/.321/.372	.241	.312	2.8	2B 0, RF 1	0.5
2009	DUR	AAA	33	93	11	4	0	3	9	10	12	2	1	.280/.366/.439	.277	.299	-0.1	2B -3, 3B 0	0.1
2009	OAK	MLB	33	587	65	29	1	11	63	45	86	20	6	.289/.344/.410	.278	.323	-0.3	3B 0, 2B -2	2.4
2010	WAS	MLB	34	389	42	16	1	3	31	37	44	14	2	.249/.327/.328	.252	.273	-1.2	2B 2, 1B 0	0.5
2011	*WAS*	*MLB*	*35*	*448*	*49*	*20*	*1*	*6*	*40*	*38*	*58*	*12*	*4*	*.262/.327/.359*	*.245*	*.288*	*0.0*	*2B -1, 3B -1*	*0.2*

"The Oberkfell Puzzle" is not the latest Swedish mystery; it's the proposition that utilitymen who can't play short or center or catch need to do something else well to merit a spot on the majors. Kennedy suffers from a short supply of tangible talents. He can still catch up with a fastball, spray singles around the park, and steal the odd base, but that makes for a fairly limited set of skills to offer a team. He drifted info Washington as infield insurance after winding up one of last winter's free-agent losers, having failed to earn any security after his bounce-back season in Oakland. Pressed into the lineup after Cristian Guzman was dealt to Texas, he didn't hit, which put him back where he was after failing the Cardinals: adrift and running out of chances.

Steve Lombardozzi 2B

Born: **9/20/1988** Age: **22**
Bats: **S** Throws: **R** Height: **6' 0"** Weight: **170**
Breakout: **3%** Improve: **14%** Collapse: **3%**
Attrition: **6%** MLB: **22%**

Comparables:
Danny Richar, Roberto Alomar, Asdrubal Cabrera (75)

YEAR	TEAM	LVL	AGE	PA	R	2B	3B	HR	RBI	BB	SO	SB	CS	AVG/OBP/SLG	TAv	BABIP	BRR	FRAA	WARP
2008	NAT	Rk	19	184	23	4	1	0	24	21	32	4	1	.283/.359/.322	.263	.333	0.2	2B -3, SS -3	0.0
2009	HAG	A	20	576	90	26	7	3	58	62	80	16	7	.296/.372/.395	.296	.338	3.8	2B 8, SS 0	4.6
2010	POT	A+	21	507	71	30	9	1	38	49	60	20	10	.293/.370/.409	.282	.327	2.8	2B -11	1.6
2010	HAR	AA	21	118	19	5	2	5	11	12	15	4	2	.295/.373/.524	.320	.306	0.1	2B -4	0.8
2011	*WAS*	*MLB*	*22*	*469*	*51*	*21*	*3*	*4*	*42*	*39*	*79*	*8*	*3*	*.258/.316/.355*	*.241*	*.299*	*-0.2*	*2B -2, SS 0*	*0.0*

With Espinosa already in the majors, being a second-base prospect in the Nats' system might seem a dead end, but Lombardozzi merits consideration as a playable prospect in his own right. He's already credited for scrappy glove work around the bag (akin to that of his father, Steve, a starter for the Twins in the 1980s). Offensively, he offers the little-man's game, producing a .370 OBP or better in all three seasons as a pro, running aggressively and dropping down bunts. That fistful of homers in Double-A at season's end was unexpected and not repeated in an AFL assignment. He has SHINO potential (for Switch-Hitter In Name Only), since he did very little damage against lefties last year at either level. Lombardozzi has managed to be overlooked as potential major-league material despite belting 50-plus extra-base hits and stealing more than 20 bases while reaching Double-A in his age-21 season. That's a function of his being limited to second, but if he keeps doing what he's been doing, he'll graduate to low-ceiling prospect, then show up in the majors, and before you know it, start making appearances on the short list for Most Underrated Major Leaguer.

Chris Marrero **1B**

Born: **7/2/1988** Age: **22**
Bats: **R** Throws: **R** Height: **6' 3"** Weight: **210**
Breakout: **4%** Improve: **26%** Collapse: **1%**
Attrition: **24%** MLB: **36%**

Comparables:
Nick Evans, Colby Rasmus, Carlos Gonzalez (81)

YEAR	TEAM	LVL	AGE	PA	R	2B	3B	HR	RBI	BB	SO	SB	CS	AVG/OBP/SLG	TAv	BABIP	BRR	FRAA	WARP
2008	POT	A+	19	289	40	15	2	11	38	25	55	0	0	.250/.325/.453	.261	.275	-0.7	1B -2	0.0
2009	POT	A+	20	469	58	21	2	16	65	42	97	2	3	.287/.360/.464	.295	.337	-2.1	1B -2	1.6
2009	HAR	AA	20	84	9	6	0	1	11	8	18	0	1	.267/.345/.387	.253	.339	-0.4	1B -4	-0.4
2010	HAR	AA	21	578	73	28	0	18	82	43	102	1	3	.294/.350/.450	.283	.333	-1.4	1B 1	1.8
2011	*WAS*	*MLB*	*22*	*473*	*55*	*21*	*1*	*15*	*56*	*31*	*105*	*0*	*0*	*.258/.308/.416*	*.253*	*.302*	*0.0*	*1B -16*	*-1.5*

As long as the organization lacks for an established first baseman, Marrero will get mentioned as a prospect. That appraisal might seem uncharitable to a guy who graduated to Double-A at 21 and hit for some power, but the "good enough" standard for first base is higher than his ceiling. Marrero's power and walk numbers for the position are weak, which might be something you could overlook if he fielded like Keith Hernandez, but between his immobility and stone hands, he's better described as Dunn-like. Marrero might drift into the big-league job for a couple of seasons, but the best-case scenario has him following the Rico Brogna career path, where he falls into the right situation, wins a popularity contest or two, and plays for clubs looking to spend their big money at other positions.

Justin Maxwell **OF**

Born: **11/6/1983** Age: **27**
Bats: **R** Throws: **R** Height: **6' 5"** Weight: **225**
Breakout: **4%** Improve: **32%** Collapse: **7%**
Attrition: **21%** MLB: **52%**

Comparables:
Dale Murphy, Chris Dickerson, Bob Allison (72)

YEAR	TEAM	LVL	AGE	PA	R	2B	3B	HR	RBI	BB	SO	SB	CS	AVG/OBP/SLG	TAv	BABIP	BRR	FRAA	WARP
2008	HAR	AA	24	180	35	6	3	7	28	31	28	13	4	.233/.367/.459	.283	.239	0.6	LF 0, RF 0	0.9
2009	SYR	AAA	25	448	68	10	5	13	42	54	136	35	8	.242/.342/.396	.259	.335	2.8	CF 1, LF 0	1.4
2009	WAS	MLB	25	102	12	4	1	4	9	12	32	6	1	.247/.343/.449	.273	.340	0.7	CF -2, RF 0	0.3
2010	SYR	AAA	26	272	34	17	0	6	21	35	75	16	7	.287/.390/.439	.273	.395	0.0	CF 5, RF 0	1.7
2010	WAS	MLB	26	131	14	6	0	3	12	25	43	5	1	.144/.305/.289	.231	.200	0.7	RF 3, CF 2	0.4
2011	*WAS*	*MLB*	*27*	*408*	*47*	*15*	*2*	*13*	*43*	*51*	*119*	*21*	*6*	*.228/.327/.393*	*.256*	*.298*	*0.3*	*CF -1, RF 1*	*0.8*

Already 27, Maxwell is everything you should want in an everyday center fielder. He's a quality glove afield and a plus baserunner, armed with power in his stroke, strong of arm, and fleet of foot. However, between past problems staying healthy and a swing holey enough to be Swiss, he's in danger of never catching the one big break he needs to get the three or four months and a few hundred at-bats necessary to show what he can do. The Mariners' Franklin Gutierrez got his break, but that took a front office willing to bet on him. As long as Maxwell is planted behind Nyjer Morgan's more obvious and more obviously meager day-to-day scraptitude, it isn't happening for Maxwell in D.C., and the addition of Corey Brown—a younger, similarly injury-prone, and talented outfielder—narrows his window still more.

Tyler Moore **1B**

Born: **1/30/1987** Age: **24**
Bats: **R** Throws: **R** Height: **6' 2"** Weight: **185**
Breakout: **2%** Improve: **10%** Collapse: **4%**
Attrition: **15%** MLB: **27%**

Comparables:
Wladimir Balentien, Adam Lind, Jake Fox (76)

YEAR	TEAM	LVL	AGE	PA	R	2B	3B	HR	RBI	BB	SO	SB	CS	AVG/OBP/SLG	TAv	BABIP	BRR	FRAA	WARP
2008	VER	A-	21	280	17	10	0	6	28	13	66	1	1	.200/.239/.306	.208	.242	-2.1	1B 11	-0.5
2009	HAG	A	22	477	38	30	3	9	87	40	111	2	2	.297/.363/.447	.290	.375	-5.4	1B 0	1.2
2010	POT	A+	23	553	78	43	3	31	111	40	125	0	0	.269/.321/.552	.308	.293	-3.4	1B 11	4.1
2011	*WAS*	*MLB*	*24*	*444*	*49*	*23*	*1*	*16*	*56*	*24*	*119*	*0*	*0*	*.238/.278/.416*	*.240*	*.288*	*0.0*	*1B -9*	*-1.4*

A 2008 16th-rounder out of Mississippi State, Moore was just marking time as an organizational player until he exploded in the second half last season, clubbing the Carolina League at a .348/.404/.716 clip. Because of his lack of strike-zone command, power is really his lone plus tool, but he's a good target at first base capable of scooping errant throws capably enough. Because he's already heading into his age-24 season while making his Double-A debut, he can't afford the slightest slip-up, but if he shows that his second half of last season was no fluke, he'll put himself in the Nats' post-All-Star-break picture if they haven't secured a solid first-sacker in the meantime. Yes, it's possible Tyler Moore is gonna make it after all.

Nyjer Morgan **CF**

Born: **7/2/1980** Age: **30**
Bats: L Throws: L Height: **6' 0"** Weight: **170**
Breakout: **2%** Improve: **42%** Collapse: **5%**
Attrition: **16%** MLB: **84%**

Comparables:
Kenny Lofton, Tike Redman, Gene Richards (78)

YEAR	TEAM	LVL	AGE	PA	R	2B	3B	HR	RBI	BB	SO	SB	CS	AVG/OBP/SLG	TAv	BABIP	BRR	FRAA	WARP
2008	IND	AAA	27	352	54	13	4	1	33	18	47	44	8	.298/.344/.373	.256	.341	4.6	LF 14, CF -1	2.2
2008	PIT	MLB	27	175	26	13	0	0	7	10	32	9	5	.294/.343/.375	.263	.362	-0.7	LF 1, CF 1	0.7
2009	PIT	MLB	28	321	39	6	5	2	27	29	49	18	10	.277/.346/.356	.255	.318	0.3	LF 8, CF 0	1.3
2009	WAS	MLB	28	212	34	9	2	1	12	11	25	24	7	.351/.387/.435	.281	.386	3.2	CF 6	1.9
2010	WAS	MLB	29	577	60	17	7	0	24	40	88	34	17	.253/.310/.314	.235	.294	4.6	CF 2	0.8
2011	*WAS*	*MLB*	*30*	*488*	*54*	*19*	*4*	*3*	*42*	*36*	*71*	*34*	*13*	*.274/.330/.353*	*.246*	*.309*	*-1.0*	*CF 2, LF 6*	*1.1*

With the 2010 season in the books, we can now safely dispense with the argument some statheads advanced that Morgan was roughly as valuable as Adam Dunn. To his credit, Morgan is almost as good as a player can get without a bat in his hands, because he's an excellent baserunner (beyond his basestealing) with the speed to cover the middle pasture from gap to gap, although one of the weakest arms in anybody's outfield gives away more bases than you'd like. The defense has to carry his hitting, however, because he's impatiently slappy and overpowered by quality heat. He has spent his career in exactly the right place, whether in Washington or in Pittsburgh, commensurate with his skills—marking time as a second-division starter, providing some value, and helping the Nats' younger pitchers survive their growing pains. He's not any better than that.

Mike Morse **OF**

Born: **3/22/1982** Age: **29**
Bats: R Throws: R Height: **6' 4"** Weight: **220**
Breakout: **0%** Improve: **12%** Collapse: **9%**
Attrition: **7%** MLB: **48%**

Comparables:
Jon Knott, Joe Borchard, Gabe Gross (77)

YEAR	TEAM	LVL	AGE	PA	R	2B	3B	HR	RBI	BB	SO	SB	CS	AVG/OBP/SLG	TAv	BABIP	BRR	FRAA	WARP
2008	SEA	MLB	26	11	0	1	0	0	0	1	4	0	0	.222/.364/.333	.282	.400	0.4	RF 0	0.1
2009	SYR	AAA	27	183	21	12	3	6	34	15	27	2	1	.339/.404/.558	.318	.379	-1.3	1B -2, 3B -5	0.6
2009	TAC	AAA	27	289	38	14	0	10	52	20	50	0	0	.312/.370/.481	.295	.350	-2.3	SS -6, 2B -3	0.5
2009	WAS	MLB	27	55	6	3	0	3	10	3	16	0	0	.250/.291/.481	.272	.303	-0.2	1B 2, RF 1	0.4
2010	SYR	AAA	28	60	12	2	0	3	8	8	11	0	0	.255/.367/.471	.253	.270	0.0	1B 0, RF 0	0.0
2010	WAS	MLB	28	293	36	12	2	15	41	22	64	0	1	.290/.352/.519	.309	.330	-5.2	RF 2, 1B 1	1.6
2011	*WAS*	*MLB*	*29*	*302*	*39*	*15*	*1*	*11*	*39*	*24*	*60*	*1*	*0*	*.277/.341/.458*	*.279*	*.314*	*-0.1*	*RF 0, 1B -1*	*0.8*

You might wonder where Morse's 2010 season came from, but credit Rizzo and company for snagging something of value in a minor exchange. A decade ago, Morse was a prospect, but he lost major chunks of his career to a PED suspension plus injuries to a knee and shoulder. By feeding the Mariners' need to snort up anything within two aisles of leather goods by exchanging Ryan Langerhans for Morse in 2009, the Nats ensured that they had a playable bat at hand once their fascination with Bernadina inevitably wore off. Morse is an impatient hacker sure to undershoot expectations that he'll keep slugging .500 or live up to "Jayson Werth 2.0" comparisons; in his defense, he was especially aggressive relative to his minor-league track record in his first extended big-league work since 2005, understandable given how long it took him to get back. Between left-field platoon chores with Rick Ankiel and an open casting call at first base as we go to press, he should make an effective enough placeholder however he's employed; by the time the Nats develop alternatives, he'll have earned a stretch deal to man a contender's bench.

Wil Nieves **C**

Born: **9/25/1977** Age: **33**
Bats: R Throws: R Height: **5' 11"** Weight: **190**
Breakout: **7%** Improve: **33%** Collapse: **14%**
Attrition: **21%** MLB: **84%**

Comparables:
Paul Phillips, Guillermo Rodriguez, Charlie Lau (82)

YEAR	TEAM	LVL	AGE	PA	R	2B	3B	HR	RBI	BB	SO	SB	CS	AVG/OBP/SLG	TAv	BABIP	BRR	FRAA	WARP
2008	WAS	MLB	30	197	15	9	1	1	20	13	30	0	1	.260/.300/.339	.228	.294	-1.3	C 1	0.2
2009	WAS	MLB	31	248	19	6	0	1	25	17	45	1	0	.259/.315/.299	.219	.313	-0.1	C 1	0.1
2010	WAS	MLB	32	172	10	8	0	3	16	8	29	0	0	.203/.238/.310	.191	.221	-0.9	C 1	-0.4
2011	*MIL*	*MLB*	*33*	*232*	*22*	*9*	*1*	*2*	*18*	*15*	*36*	*1*	*0*	*.235/.281/.305*	*.210*	*.266*	*0.0*	*C 1*	*-0.1*

Daniel Webster once observed that liberty can't exist without virtue, but he just hadn't anticipated the existence of Nieves, who at long last was set free by the Nats without ever demonstrating any positive quality at the plate or behind it in a three-year term as a backup backstop. With career rates below .300 in every major rate stat and a career True Average barely above .200, Nieves is the worst backup to milk a living out of the tools of ignorance since Alberto Castillo. Somebody had to earn that distinction eventually, but Nieves' dismal work at the dish comes without a strong arm, as evidenced by his mediocre 24 percent major-league caught-stealing rate. He'll take his next potshot at playing time as a Brewers nonroster invitee hoping to serve as the understudy for Jon Lucroy, a role in which he'd continue to be the single least suitable backup this side of Spiro Agnew.

Derek Norris C

Born: **2/14/1989** Age: **22**
Bats: **R** Throws: **R** Height: **6' 0"** Weight: **210**
Breakout: **1%** Improve: **15%** Collapse: **0%**
Attrition: **9%** MLB: **27%**

Comparables:
Curt Blefary, Wladimir Balentien, Jordan Schafer (66)

YEAR	TEAM	LVL	AGE	PA	R	2B	3B	HR	RBI	BB	SO	SB	CS	AVG/OBP/SLG	TAv	BABIP	BRR	FRAA	WARP
2008	VER	A-	19	302	42	12	0	10	38	63	56	11	9	.278/.444/.463	.331	.321	1.1	C 0	3.2
2009	HAG	A	20	540	78	30	0	23	84	90	116	6	3	.286/.413/.513	.330	.337	0.5	C -1	5.5
2010	POT	A+	21	399	67	19	0	12	49	89	94	6	3	.235/.419/.419	.310	.296	0.1	C 2	3.8
2011	*WAS*	*MLB*	*22*	*418*	*52*	*16*	*1*	*14*	*44*	*72*	*111*	*1*	*1*	*.226/.365/.412*	*.276*	*.283*	*-0.1*	*C 0*	*1.9*

The team's top prospect that didn't require a first-overall pick, Norris is one of the best offensive backstopping prospects in any organization. He missed last season's start while recovering from off-season surgery on his wrist, suffered a concussion in May, and never really got on track at the plate until he reached the AFL. Nevertheless, he finished second in the Carolina League in OBP because his command of the zone is simply that exceptional. When healthy, he has power to all fields, and given his relative youth, the chance that he might put it all together in Double-A should propel him to the highest stratosphere in prospect rankings. He has more to prove than health, though, because concerns over his work behind the plate persist, centering on his problems with framing pitches and handling breaking stuff; however, his strong arm killed 51 percent of stolen-base attempts last year.

Eury Perez CF

Born: **5/30/1990** Age: **21**
Bats: **R** Throws: **R** Height: **6' 0"** Weight: **180**
Breakout: **2%** Improve: **7%** Collapse: **1%**
Attrition: **4%** MLB: **9%**

Comparables:
Alcides Escobar, Bill Russell, Carlos Gomez (79)

YEAR	TEAM	LVL	AGE	PA	R	2B	3B	HR	RBI	BB	SO	SB	CS	AVG/OBP/SLG	TAv	BABIP	BRR	FRAA	WARP
2009	NAT	Rk	19	205	38	3	5	3	24	15	20	16	8	.381/.434/.503	.329	.407	2.4	CF 3, RF -1	2.6
2010	HAG	A	20	491	88	17	5	3	42	23	74	64	13	.299/.345/.381	.278	.334	5.1	CF 7, RF -1	3.2
2011	*WAS*	*MLB*	*21*	*347*	*34*	*13*	*2*	*4*	*32*	*14*	*67*	*9*	*3*	*.253/.281/.340*	*.222*	*.295*	*-0.2*	*CF -7, RF -1*	*-1.1*

The path from Hagerstown to D.C. is a lot longer than the route the crow flies, but the player who puts planned obsolescence on Nyjer Morgan's plate is in the Nats' system. A plus runner who already boasts an excellent base-stealing technique, Perez slowly adapted during his full-season debut, finishing hot to put himself on the organization's list of top prospects. His defense still needs work; he must master better routes in center and relies too much on his speed to make in-time course corrections, but he throws better than your standard skittering speedster. He lacks patience and power; the hope is he'll add some of the former as he moves up the chain, but if his defense improves, he has Morgan's example ahead of him for how far you can get by flying instead of walking.

J. P. Ramirez LF

Born: **9/29/1989** Age: **21**
Bats: **L** Throws: **L** Height: **5' 10"** Weight: **185**
Breakout: **0%** Improve: **0%** Collapse: **1%**
Attrition: **1%** MLB: **1%**

Comparables:
Fernando Martinez, Hank Aaron, Bill Mazeroski (75)

YEAR	TEAM	LVL	AGE	PA	R	2B	3B	HR	RBI	BB	SO	SB	CS	AVG/OBP/SLG	TAv	BABIP	BRR	FRAA	WARP
2009	VER	A-	19	314	35	18	6	4	39	14	45	6	9	.264/.306/.407	.284	.300	2.0	LF 4, RF 0	1.9
2010	HAG	A	20	551	74	32	4	16	75	25	83	3	6	.296/.341/.470	.291	.324	-1.9	LF -3	2.0
2011	*WAS*	*MLB*	*21*	*293*	*30*	*14*	*2*	*7*	*33*	*10*	*60*	*1*	*1*	*.245/.273/.381*	*.229*	*.283*	*-0.1*	*LF -4, RF 0*	*-0.8*

While the Nats' 2008 draft might best be remembered for the debacle of not getting Aaron Crow signed, the money they had left over went toward persuading Ramirez, a top Texas prep prospect, to give up a college scholarship and go pro for $1 million. So far, you might still wonder if the money was well spent. In his full-season debut, Ramirez showed all of his positives and negatives to full effect: a smooth, flat swing with plenty of line-drive sock, but not a lot of fence-busting power; the ability to make contact, but not a lot of discretion on what to not hack at; and stumpy, short-armed defense that should peg him for left field, if not Quad-A slugging heroics. There's still plenty of time and a good-enough stroke for Ramirez to advance beyond that, but he'll have to make the most of both.

Wilson Ramos C

Born: **8/10/1987** Age: **23**
Bats: **R** Throws: **R** Height: **6' 0"** Weight: **220**
Breakout: **3%** Improve: **6%** Collapse: **4%**
Attrition: **13%** MLB: **20%**

Comparables:
Alex Avila, Pablo Sandoval, Kurt Suzuki (75)

YEAR	TEAM	LVL	AGE	PA	R	2B	3B	HR	RBI	BB	SO	SB	CS	AVG/OBP/SLG	TAv	BABIP	BRR	FRAA	WARP
2008	FTM	A+	20	500	50	23	2	13	78	37	103	0	1	.288/.346/.434	.265	.343	-7.6	C 0	1.1
2009	NBR	AA	21	214	31	16	0	4	29	6	23	0	0	.317/.341/.454	.301	.341	-0.3	C 2	1.9
2010	ROC	AAA	22	295	25	14	0	5	30	12	49	1	2	.241/.280/.345	.217	.274	-1.2	C -1	-0.5
2010	SYR	AAA	22	82	14	3	1	3	8	3	12	0	0	.316/.341/.494	.277	.344	0.6	C 1	0.6
2010	MIN	MLB	22	28	2	3	0	0	1	0	3	0	0	.296/.321/.407	.259	.333	0.1	C 0	0.1
2010	WAS	MLB	22	54	3	4	0	1	4	2	9	0	0	.269/.296/.404	.247	.310	-1.3	C 0	0.1
2011	*WAS*	*MLB*	*23*	*404*	*44*	*20*	*1*	*9*	*46*	*16*	*74*	*1*	*0*	*.263/.293/.393*	*.240*	*.298*	*0.0*	*C 0*	*0.5*

Some kid should win the golden ticket for the right to caddy for Pudge in 2011 after the Nats subjected themselves to the slug-worthlessness of Wil Nieves, and Ramos might be the winner after getting dealt from the Twins for Matt Capps. He has everything going for him as a defender, since he's a nimble receiver and effective plate-blocker who can deter the running game out of existence by annually gunning down 40-50 percent of attempts. At the least, that could get him a decade's worth of backup gigs in the majors, but his aggressiveness at the plate might relegate him to that role, because limited power and a career walk rate of around five percent handicap his ability to put many runs on the board. If Flores appears in camp ready to catch, Ramos may have to work his receiving wizardry in Syracuse, but he's sure to show up at some point and own some portion of playing time behind the plate in the years to come.

Ivan Rodriguez **C**

Born: **11/30/1971** Age: **39**
Bats: R Throws: R Height: **5' 9"** Weight: **205**
Breakout: **1%** Improve: **23%** Collapse: **20%**
Attrition: **33%** MLB: **78%**
Comparables:
Steve Garvey, George Brett, Gary Gaetti (68)

YEAR	TEAM	LVL	AGE	PA	R	2B	3B	HR	RBI	BB	SO	SB	CS	AVG/OBP/SLG	TAv	BABIP	BRR	FRAA	WARP
2008	DET	MLB	36	328	33	16	3	5	32	19	52	6	1	.295/.335/.417	.258	.336	0.3	C 1	1.5
2008	NYA	MLB	36	101	12	4	0	2	3	4	15	4	0	.219/.257/.323	.194	.241	0.6	C 2	0.0
2009	HOU	MLB	37	344	41	15	2	8	34	13	74	0	2	.251/.279/.382	.223	.298	2.5	C 4	0.8
2009	TEX	MLB	37	104	14	8	0	2	13	5	18	1	0	.245/.279/.388	.227	.279	0.8	C 1	0.2
2010	WAS	MLB	38	421	32	18	1	4	49	16	66	2	3	.266/.292/.347	.222	.305	-3.3	C 3	0.1
2011	*WAS*	*MLB*	*39*	*479*	*48*	*22*	*1*	*7*	*46*	*21*	*84*	*4*	*2*	*.251/.282/.351*	*.224*	*.289*	*-0.3*	*C 3*	*0.5*

Having already set the record for games caught and with a ring and an MVP Award in the trophy case, Pudge has nothing to prove heading into his 21st season. Of course, he isn't the same player he once was, and of course, continuing to play "hurts" his career rate stats. As a result, he won't finish a lifetime .300 hitter, but so what? That's his call to make if he's still good enough to play, and there's sufficient industry-wide need for people who can catch to ensure that he is. He'll get closer to his 3,000th hit this season (he's at 2,817 and counting), but even starting for the Nats, he won't reach that tally until 2012 at the earliest. That's if he decides he wants to become the first career catcher to get to that particular landmark, but if he's still willing, someone will give him the chance.

Josh Willingham **LF**

Born: **2/17/1979** Age: **32**
Bats: R Throws: R Height: **6' 1"** Weight: **200**
Breakout: **0%** Improve: **32%** Collapse: **2%**
Attrition: **8%** MLB: **97%**
Comparables:
Andy Pafko, J.D. Drew, Pedro Guerrero (74)

YEAR	TEAM	LVL	AGE	PA	R	2B	3B	HR	RBI	BB	SO	SB	CS	AVG/OBP/SLG	TAv	BABIP	BRR	FRAA	WARP
2008	FLO	MLB	29	416	54	21	5	15	51	48	82	3	2	.254/.363/.470	.294	.288	-1.9	LF -4	1.6
2009	WAS	MLB	30	502	70	29	0	24	61	61	104	4	3	.260/.367/.497	.306	.289	-0.4	LF 2, RF 1	3.5
2010	WAS	MLB	31	451	55	19	2	16	56	67	85	8	0	.268/.388/.460	.307	.304	2.7	LF -10	2.2
2011	*OAK*	*MLB*	*32*	*516*	*70*	*26*	*2*	*21*	*68*	*65*	*98*	*6*	*2*	*.266/.373/.477*	*.299*	*.295*	*0.0*	*LF -6, RF 0*	*2.3*

If you haven't already figured out that Willingham is older than you thought, it's epiphany time: the guy is entering his age-32 season in his last campaign before free agency. With age comes infirmity, and he hobbled all year on a bad knee before it got worse in August, necessitating his abdication from baseball duties seven weeks before season's end. The knee was at least partly to blame for his ugly fielding stats last season, but the expectation is that he'll be healthy enough to man left field for Oakland—he was traded to the A's for Corey Brown and Henry Rodriguez in a nifty bit of converting two seasons of value into prospects worthy of the name, unlike the junk sent to the Marlins to obtain Willingham and Scott Olsen. Having freed Willi to help address a belated realization that power is closer to a necessity than an option, the A's will have to see if his fly-ball stroke will play well in the Coliseum, still one of the league's toughest home-run parks.

Ryan Zimmerman **3B**

Born: **9/28/1984** Age: **26**
Bats: R Throws: R Height: **6' 3"** Weight: **210**
Breakout: **1%** Improve: **55%** Collapse: **5%**
Attrition: **14%** MLB: **98%**
Comparables:
David Wright, Edwin Encarnacion, Nick Markakis (72)

YEAR	TEAM	LVL	AGE	PA	R	2B	3B	HR	RBI	BB	SO	SB	CS	AVG/OBP/SLG	TAv	BABIP	BRR	FRAA	WARP
2008	WAS	MLB	23	466	52	24	1	14	51	31	71	1	1	.283/.333/.442	.274	.308	1.3	3B 1	2.2
2009	WAS	MLB	24	694	110	37	3	33	106	72	119	2	0	.292/.363/.525	.301	.311	1.2	3B 6	5.6
2010	WAS	MLB	25	603	85	32	0	25	85	69	98	4	1	.307/.388/.511	.317	.334	-1.4	3B -10	3.9
2011	*WAS*	*MLB*	*26*	*639*	*87*	*35*	*1*	*26*	*89*	*66*	*99*	*4*	*1*	*.288/.363/.491*	*.298*	*.307*	*-0.1*	*3B -1*	*4.0*

Our revamped FRAA jibes with local debate over whether Zimmerman's defensive reputation is more than a little overblown. The face of the franchise doesn't need to be Brooks Robinson, though, considering that his development as a hitter has topped expectations; he keeps retaining every improvement he makes along the way, whether mashing righties or drawing more walks. You can't begrudge the Nats their decision to give him a five-year, $45 million deal that runs through 2013, but the challenge for them in the meantime will be to put together a ballclub he'll want to re-sign with, as well as one generating enough local revenue to make the proposition practicable, because MVP-caliber twentysomethings never go out of style on the open market.

PITCHERS

Luis Atilano

Born: **5/10/1985** Age: **26**
Bats: **R** Throws: **R** Height: **6' 2"** Weight: **220**
Breakout: **0%** Improve: **2%** Collapse: **2%**
Attrition: **2%** MLB: **7%**

Comparables:
Mark Clark, Amaury Telemaco, Steve Cooke (83)

YEAR	TEAM	LVL	AGE	W	L	SV	G	GS	IP	H	HR	BB	SO	EqBB9	EqSO9	GB%	BABIP	WHIP	ERA	FRA	WARP
2008	HAG	A	23	0	0	1	7	3	25^{2}	29	1	7	13	2.5	4.6	43%	.308	1.40	3.15	5.20	0.0
2008	POT	A+	23	5	2	0	15	11	62	50	5	14	39	2.0	5.7	53%	.251	1.06	2.32	4.36	1.2
2009	HAR	AA	24	7	8	0	21	20	114^{2}	143	12	27	61	2.1	4.8	56%	.332	1.52	4.16	4.70	0.9
2010	WAS	MLB	25	6	7	0	16	16	85^{2}	96	11	32	40	3.4	4.2	42%	.283	1.52	5.15	5.77	-0.2
2011	*WAS*	*MLB*	*26*	*5*	*8*	*0*	*23*	*18*	105^{1}	*132*	*16*	*37*	*40*	*3.2*	*3.4*	*47%*	*.312*	*1.61*	*5.84*	*6.34*	*-0.3*

Like young red wines, finesse right-handers can be a matter of acquired taste or cost-conscious necessity. Unfortunately, not all of them open up and become something special with age, but you can always admire the effort. For a guy utterly without an effective breaking pitch and velocity that tops out around 90, Atilano did well after he was called up to replace Marquis, battling his way through games on nothing more than location and changing speeds. He can get through big-league lineups once and then starts running into trouble, because his bag of tricks is empty. He does the little things like fielding and holding runners well, but then again, he has to. Shut down two months early to have bone chips removed from his elbow, he should be ready to contend for the fifth slot in camp, but he'll need to add a breaking pitch he can throw for strikes, since he's as good as he can get on moxie alone.

Collin Balester

Born: **6/6/1986** Age: **25**
Bats: **R** Throws: **R** Height: **6' 5"** Weight: **195**
Breakout: **5%** Improve: **13%** Collapse: **4%**
Attrition: **16%** MLB: **22%**

Comparables:
Ryan Feierabend, Marco Estrada, Esmil Rogers (81)

YEAR	TEAM	LVL	AGE	W	L	SV	G	GS	IP	H	HR	BB	SO	EqBB9	EqSO9	GB%	BABIP	WHIP	ERA	FRA	WARP
2008	COH	AAA	22	9	3	0	15	15	78^{2}	79	14	23	64	2.6	7.3	41%	.286	1.35	4.00	4.92	1.1
2008	WAS	MLB	22	3	7	0	15	15	80	92	12	28	50	3.2	5.6	40%	.305	1.58	5.51	5.63	0.2
2009	SYR	AAA	23	7	10	0	20	20	107^{1}	129	5	37	71	3.1	6.0	48%	.349	1.60	4.45	4.42	1.7
2009	WAS	MLB	23	1	4	0	7	7	30^{1}	34	10	14	20	4.2	5.9	35%	.264	1.58	6.82	7.40	-0.4
2010	SYR	AAA	24	3	3	0	35	5	69	74	8	32	52	4.2	6.8	50%	.308	1.58	5.87	7.02	-0.7
2010	WAS	MLB	24	0	1	0	17	0	21	15	2	11	28	4.7	12.0	56%	.283	1.33	2.57	3.17	0.4
2011	*WAS*	*MLB*	*25*	*7*	*8*	*0*	*44*	*18*	*130*	*147*	*18*	*55*	*85*	*3.8*	*5.8*	*45%*	*.309*	*1.55*	*5.35*	*5.81*	*-0.0*

Balester's long-anticipated move to the pen came five starts into 2010 at Syracuse—while putting 51 of 111 batters on base, he got tattooed so frequently Sandra Bullock started to suspect he was seeing her ex-husband. After being relegated to relief work in May, Balester posted a 3.38 ERA and struck out more than 20 percent of the batters he faced, using his heavy low-90s heat to good effect. His raw numbers were similarly happy as he started getting late-season stints in the majors, but they came almost entirely in garbage time. He could be the midgame innings muncher the Nats need, but he'll need to win the job in camp and shine early to keep it.

Miguel Batista

Born: **2/19/1971** Age: **40**
Bats: **R** Throws: **R** Height: **6' 0"** Weight: **160**
Breakout: **8%** Improve: **22%** Collapse: **11%**
Attrition: **18%** MLB: **49%**

Comparables:
Sal Maglie, David Cone, Greg Harris (67)

YEAR	TEAM	LVL	AGE	W	L	SV	G	GS	IP	H	HR	BB	SO	EqBB9	EqSO9	GB%	BABIP	WHIP	ERA	FRA	WARP
2008	SEA	MLB	37	4	14	1	44	20	115	135	19	79	73	6.2	5.7	46%	.306	1.91	6.26	6.81	-1.4
2009	SEA	MLB	38	7	4	1	56	0	71^{1}	79	7	38	52	4.8	6.6	48%	.319	1.67	4.04	4.34	0.7
2010	WAS	MLB	39	1	2	2	58	1	82^{2}	71	9	39	55	4.2	6.0	50%	.256	1.39	3.70	4.77	0.0
2011	*WAS*	*MLB*	*40*	*6*	*5*	*2*	*78*	*10*	*133*	*146*	*16*	*69*	*82*	*4.6*	*5.6*	*47%*	*.304*	*1.61*	*5.28*	*5.74*	*-0.8*

The self-described utility pitcher caught a break when Riggleman landed with the Nats after the manager's interim gig skippering the Mariners in 2008—Batista was on that team, and when the need for a middle-innings sponge on the Nats seemed obvious, familiarity and availability generated opportunity. He was up to bucket duty, although an offhand comment after replacing Stephen Strasburg in one game led to a war of words with the reigning Miss Iowa, which he lost. Or did he? Wherever he lands as a free agent, he'll apparently now need time off to accept an invitation to judge the 2011 Miss Iowa pageant. We know your tricks, Dewey, but since the man has written a couple of books and does considerable charity work, he has managed to lead a more interesting life than most garbage-time heroes.

Sean Burnett

Born: **9/17/1982** Age: **28**
Bats: **L** Throws: **L** Height: **5' 11"** Weight: **190**
Breakout: **12%** Improve: **32%** Collapse: **13%**
Attrition: **5%** MLB: **57%**

Comparables:
Billy Koch, Terry Adams, T.J. Mathews (79)

YEAR	TEAM	LVL	AGE	W	L	SV	G	GS	IP	H	HR	BB	SO	EqBB9	EqSO9	GB%	BABIP	WHIP	ERA	FRA	WARP
2008	PIT	MLB	25	1	1	0	58	0	56^{2}	57	7	34	42	5.4	6.7	50%	.298	1.64	4.92	5.28	-0.2
2009	PIT	MLB	26	1	2	1	38	0	32^{1}	22	3	15	23	4.2	6.4	46%	.214	1.24	3.06	4.82	0.0
2009	WAS	MLB	26	1	1	0	33	0	25^{1}	14	3	13	20	4.6	7.1	59%	.162	1.07	2.84	4.45	0.1
2010	WAS	MLB	27	1	7	3	73	0	63	52	3	20	62	2.9	8.9	56%	.280	1.16	2.14	2.29	1.9
2011	*WAS*	*MLB*	*28*	*4*	*2*	*1*	*83*	*0*	76^{2}	*76*	*8*	*36*	*52*	*4.2*	*6.1*	*48%*	*.289*	*1.45*	*4.37*	*4.75*	*-0.1*

Originally a top starting prospect before injuries struck him down (without making him more powerful than we could possibly imagine), Burnett has enjoyed a rebirth as a reliever—a rebirth that transcends working in a situational role; he can get his fastball a tick or two past 90 and mixes in the odd slider. Unlike Tyler Clippard and his sharp-beaked vulturing, Burnett was the Nats' late-game set-up man who performed effectively wire-to-wire, passing leads first to Matt Capps and then Drew Storen, facing right-handed hitters about 60 percent of the time and holding them to a .182/.253/.234 clip instead of running for cover. He's only under Nats control for two more years, but the difference between a good left-handed reliever and a lefty specialist is large enough that he might bring something tasty in a deadline deal in either of the next two Julys.

Adam Carr

Born: **4/1/1984** Age: **27**
Bats: **R** Throws: **R** Height: **6" 2"** Weight: **220**
Breakout: **0%** Improve: **0%** Collapse: **0%**
Attrition: **0%** MLB: **0%**

Comparables:
Jesus Delgado, Josh Newman, Jim Brosnan (88)

YEAR	TEAM	LVL	AGE	W	L	SV	G	GS	IP	H	HR	BB	SO	EqBB9	EqSO9	GB%	BABIP	WHIP	ERA	FRA	WARP
2008	POT	A+	24	3	4	5	21	0	26^1	29	3	13	31	4.4	10.6	45%	.356	1.67	6.16	6.22	-0.3
2008	HAR	AA	24	3	4	11	30	0	33^2	39	7	22	27	5.9	7.2	36%	.311	1.81	6.94	6.88	-0.6
2009	POT	A+	25	2	6	1	24	11	72^2	84	7	34	32	4.2	4.0	45%	.307	1.69	5.82	6.32	-0.5
2010	HAR	AA	26	6	1	5	36	0	50^1	43	2	14	48	2.5	8.6	48%	.295	1.16	3.04	2.95	1.3
2010	SYR	AAA	26	0	1	9	16	0	21^2	16	1	10	19	4.2	8.1	44%	.250	1.23	2.08	2.47	0.6
2011	*WAS*	*MLB*	*27*	*2*	*2*	*3*	*36*	*3*	*57*	*65*	*8*	*33*	*37*	*5.2*	*5.8*	*43%*	*.309*	*1.71*	*5.85*	*6.36*	*-0.9*

An 18th-rounder from the 2006 draft, Carr only just pitched his way onto the 40-man. Expectations that he would arrive sooner were fueled by mid-90s heat and a wicked low-80s slider with excellent depth. However, command was an issue, not all that surprising when you remember that Carr was a big-bopping first baseman at Oklahoma State. Two seasons of struggling terribly to develop any kind of consistency put him on the spot last year, but he finally started throwing strikes in time to get added to the 40-man roster. He'll still struggle against lefties willing to work him for strikes, but the organization will take progress where it can find it, and he'll be toward the back of a pack pitching for bullpen jobs in camp.

Tyler Clippard

Born: **2/14/1985** Age: **26**
Bats: **R** Throws: **R** Height: **6" 4"** Weight: **170**
Breakout: **11%** Improve: **23%** Collapse: **17%**
Attrition: **22%** MLB: **52%**

Comparables:
Jose Ascanio, Luis Perdomo, Dennis Higgins (71)

YEAR	TEAM	LVL	AGE	W	L	SV	G	GS	IP	H	HR	BB	SO	EqBB9	EqSO9	GB%	BABIP	WHIP	ERA	FRA	WARP
2008	COH	AAA	23	6	13	0	27	27	143	129	15	66	125	4.2	7.9	38%	.284	1.38	4.66	5.03	1.9
2008	WAS	MLB	23	1	1	0	2	2	10^1	12	2	7	8	6.1	7.0	18%	.323	1.84	4.35	2.07	0.4
2009	SYR	AAA	24	4	1	1	24	0	39	20	2	15	42	3.5	9.7	45%	.200	0.90	0.92	3.13	0.8
2009	WAS	MLB	24	4	2	0	41	0	60^1	36	9	32	67	4.8	10.0	32%	.197	1.14	2.69	3.02	1.4
2010	WAS	MLB	25	11	8	1	78	0	91	69	8	41	112	4.1	11.1	29%	.284	1.23	3.07	4.23	0.6
2011	*WAS*	*MLB*	*26*	*6*	*4*	*0*	*67*	*8*	*126*	*111*	*16*	*61*	*118*	*4.4*	*8.4*	*39%*	*.283*	*1.37*	*4.03*	*4.38*	*1.1*

In an album released a month after Clippard was born, the Alan Parsons Project sang, "It's a vulture culture / Never lend a loser a hand," and few newborns can have taken that to heart as well as this future National appears to have. After spending 2009 as the Nats' garbageman, he was pushed into set-up duties and was predictably unreliable yet surprisingly durable. At one point in May, he blew leads in four consecutive appearances—but got three wins because the Nats rallied. Baseball Info Solutions has a stat they appropriately call "BS Wins," a tally of wins that a pitcher gets after blowing the save; can you guess who led baseball with five? Clippard's durability, moving fastball, and improved slider make him useful on a team that needs to get innings wherever it can, but *useful* is not entirely the same thing as *good*.

Ross Detwiler

Born: **3/6/1986** Age: **25**
Bats: **R** Throws: **L** Height: **6" 5"** Weight: **185**
Breakout: **8%** Improve: **20%** Collapse: **4%**
Attrition: **21%** MLB: **28%**

Comparables:
Eulogio De La Cruz, Mike Ekstrom, Marco Estrada (76)

YEAR	TEAM	LVL	AGE	W	L	SV	G	GS	IP	H	HR	BB	SO	EqBB9	EqSO9	GB%	BABIP	WHIP	ERA	FRA	WARP
2008	POT	A+	22	8	8	0	26	26	124	140	8	57	114	4.1	8.3	55%	.354	1.65	4.86	4.28	2.4
2009	HAR	AA	23	0	3	0	6	6	27^1	28	2	10	28	3.3	9.2	49%	.321	1.43	2.97	3.94	0.6
2009	SYR	AAA	23	4	2	0	10	10	49^1	56	2	20	42	3.7	7.7	51%	.346	1.54	3.10	3.20	1.6
2009	WAS	MLB	23	1	6	0	15	14	75^2	87	3	33	43	3.9	5.1	45%	.323	1.61	5.00	4.64	0.9
2010	HAR	AA	24	2	2	0	7	7	32^2	38	1	7	31	2.0	8.7	47%	.366	1.46	2.48	1.98	1.5
2010	WAS	MLB	24	1	3	0	8	5	29^2	34	5	14	17	4.2	5.2	44%	.296	1.65	4.25	5.71	-0.0
2011	*WAS*	*MLB*	*25*	*6*	*8*	*0*	*20*	*20*	*97^1*	*112*	*10*	*45*	*64*	*4.2*	*5.9*	*47%*	*.324*	*1.62*	*5.34*	*5.80*	*0.7*

While the Nats expect to wind up with a stack of first-round heroes starring for them in the years to come, they're just hoping to get a back-end starter out of their 2007 top pick, and they may not even get that. A torn hip labrum in February delayed Detwiler's bid for a starting job until the second half, and his recovery from surgery went slowly. He did eventually show up in "The Show," making sporadic appearances and initially struggling with pain and soreness. For all that, he's still a lefty who throws in the low 90s and mixes in a nice curve and change, and he's only 25. Although a product of the previous regime's drafts, he shouldn't fall out of favor just yet; he has had just two full seasons and he's still big and projectable.

Livan Hernandez

Born: **2/20/1975** Age: **36**
Bats: R Throws: R Height: **6' 2"** Weight: **220**
Breakout: **12%** Improve: **37%** Collapse: **17%**
Attrition: **14%** MLB: **94%**
Comparables:
Tim Belcher, David Wells, Jim Kaat (61)

YEAR	TEAM	LVL	AGE	W	L	SV	G	GS	IP	H	HR	BB	SO	EqBB9	EqSO9	GB%	BABIP	WHIP	ERA	FRA	WARP
2008	MIN	MLB	33	10	8	0	23	23	139^{2}	199	18	29	54	1.9	3.5	46%	.345	1.64	5.48	5.68	0.1
2008	COL	MLB	33	3	3	0	8	8	40^{1}	58	7	14	13	3.1	2.9	47%	.342	1.81	8.03	7.40	-0.4
2009	NYN	MLB	34	7	8	0	23	23	135	164	16	51	75	3.4	5.0	42%	.329	1.60	5.47	4.94	0.7
2009	WAS	MLB	34	2	4	0	8	8	48^{2}	56	3	16	27	3.0	5.0	46%	.317	1.48	5.36	5.17	0.1
2010	WAS	MLB	35	10	12	0	33	33	211^{2}	216	16	64	114	2.7	4.8	40%	.287	1.34	3.66	3.94	3.4
2011	*WAS*	*MLB*	*36*	*11*	*13*	*0*	*33*	*33*	*199*	*242*	*24*	*65*	*93*	*2.9*	*4.2*	*44%*	*.316*	*1.54*	*5.14*	*5.59*	*0.9*

In the 1990s, Hernandez was supposed to break down under a workload that would have left most men on Dr. Jobe's table, never to return. In the Aughties, each successive season seemed like a new bit of borrowed time, the next "last" sighting of the oft-drubbed Livan Hernandez. Deathless as a barrow-wight, Livan just keeps proving that human diversity transcends easy assertions about where any one pitcher's career path is supposed to wind up. Last year, the Nats decided to keep him as a late-activated fifth man, but he handily became their best starter. He seems immune to injury, so his capacity to keep doing this could go for a while yet. Just sit back and enjoy watching a big guy who focuses on upsetting timing and throwing strikes as he works his way through a lineup; he keeps his defense busy, chewing up frames and games until you look up and notice that he's cranked out another 30-start season and given you quality starts in two out of every three opportunities.

Cole Kimball

Born: **8/1/1985** Age: **25**
Bats: R Throws: R Height: **6' 3"** Weight: **225**
Breakout: **2%** Improve: **2%** Collapse: **2%**
Attrition: **2%** MLB: **4%**
Comparables:
Victor Garate, Sergio Escalona, Jason Christiansen (73)

YEAR	TEAM	LVL	AGE	W	L	SV	G	GS	IP	H	HR	BB	SO	EqBB9	EqSO9	GB%	BABIP	WHIP	ERA	FRA	WARP
2008	HAG	A	22	6	8	0	28	27	128^{1}	103	5	83	122	5.8	8.6	42%	.291	1.58	5.05	6.00	-0.4
2009	POT	A+	23	4	5	9	39	0	46^{2}	49	4	28	52	5.4	10.0	42%	.338	1.69	6.36	6.53	-0.7
2010	POT	A+	24	3	0	6	19	0	24^{2}	17	0	8	27	3.0	10.0	43%	.283	1.12	1.82	2.90	0.4
2010	HAR	AA	24	5	1	12	38	0	54	33	4	31	74	5.2	12.3	45%	.240	1.28	2.33	4.57	0.2
2011	*WAS*	*MLB*	*25*	*3*	*4*	*2*	*31*	*8*	*67*	*65*	*8*	*48*	*58*	*6.5*	*7.7*	*42%*	*.302*	*1.70*	*5.44*	*5.91*	*-0.2*

Sometimes, live arms just take time to come around, which seems the case for Kimball. The man's middle name may well be mayhem, because between the walks and strikeouts, wild pitches, hit batsmen, balks, blown saves, and high-90s heat, you can be sure that he'll do *something*, whether it's frightening, exciting, or maddening. Kimball has already slung 60 wild pitches in 352 career innings, not counting two more he tossed in a dominant 12-inning AFL stint. That clinched his landing on the 40-man roster, reflecting his potential for relief greatness.

John Lannan

Born: **9/27/1984** Age: **26**
Bats: L Throws: L Height: **6' 5"** Weight: **200**
Breakout: **14%** Improve: **36%** Collapse: **17%**
Attrition: **16%** MLB: **67%**
Comparables:
Kyle Kendrick, Jeremy Sowers, Aaron Laffey (71)

YEAR	TEAM	LVL	AGE	W	L	SV	G	GS	IP	H	HR	BB	SO	EqBB9	EqSO9	GB%	BABIP	WHIP	ERA	FRA	WARP
2008	WAS	MLB	23	9	15	0	31	31	182	172	23	72	117	3.6	5.8	56%	.266	1.38	3.91	4.88	1.6
2009	WAS	MLB	24	9	13	0	33	33	206^{1}	210	22	68	89	3.0	3.9	54%	.273	1.38	3.88	4.87	1.4
2010	HAR	AA	25	1	4	0	7	7	40^{2}	49	3	10	28	2.2	6.3	54%	.346	1.57	4.20	4.45	0.6
2010	WAS	MLB	25	8	8	0	25	25	143^{1}	175	14	49	71	3.1	4.5	51%	.319	1.59	4.65	4.95	0.7
2011	*WAS*	*MLB*	*26*	*10*	*11*	*0*	*29*	*29*	*171^{2}*	*190*	*20*	*63*	*82*	*3.3*	*4.3*	*51%*	*.297*	*1.47*	*4.86*	*5.28*	*1.4*

It's important to distinguish between ground balls being a good unto themselves and grounders leading to a never-ending drumbeat of base hits. Long the risk Lannan was willing to run, last year he ran it less well, but he was handicapped by elbow inflammation and command problems early, which seemed to contribute to his lowering his arm angle and flattening out his sinker. By the middle of June, he was allowing up to almost two baserunners per inning, which led the Nats to grant him a midseason demotion to get reacquainted with all of the good things he used to do. After his recall, he was the worm-killer of old, giving up 71 hits and just 14 walks in 68 1/3 IP and winning six of 11 starts while logging seven quality starts. Most importantly, his strikeout rate after his return was over 16 percent, which would be a career high if he could keep it up. The elbow seems sound, so if the new infield gels behind him, he makes a fine Comeback Player of the Year candidate.

Jason Marquis

Born: **8/21/1978** Age: **32**
Bats: L Throws: R Height: **6' 1"** Weight: **185**
Breakout: **29%** Improve: **55%** Collapse: **23%**
Attrition: **7%** MLB: **100%**
Comparables:
Rick Rhoden, Mike Moore, Larry Jackson (80)

YEAR	TEAM	LVL	AGE	W	L	SV	G	GS	IP	H	HR	BB	SO	EqBB9	EqSO9	GB%	BABIP	WHIP	ERA	FRA	WARP
2008	CHN	MLB	29	11	9	0	29	28	167	172	15	70	91	3.8	4.9	49%	.283	1.50	4.53	5.21	1.4
2009	COL	MLB	30	15	13	0	33	33	216	218	15	80	115	3.3	4.8	56%	.287	1.40	4.04	4.79	2.6
2010	WAS	MLB	31	2	9	0	13	13	58^{2}	76	9	24	31	3.7	4.8	54%	.328	1.84	6.60	6.06	-0.3
2011	*WAS*	*MLB*	*32*	*10*	*11*	*0*	*29*	*29*	*172*	*187*	*19*	*66*	*86*	*3.5*	*4.5*	*50%*	*.297*	*1.47*	*4.81*	*5.23*	*1.6*

If Lannan succeeds in being recognized as a Comeback Player, it won't be for lack of competition on his own staff. A year before Werth became the game's big prestige signing, the Nats won the race to reward Marquis for his career year as a Rockie, which the organization played up to the hilt. Then Marquis showed up looking nothing like the guy who'd helped pitch Colorado into the playoffs. Working with pitching coach/Billy Martin victim Steve McCatty to "find his release point" while getting clobbered eventually gave way to the confession that he needed to have his elbow opened up to remove bone chips. He came back as quickly as possible, taking additional lumps in August before finally rounding back into shape, logging five quality starts in his last seven. Now healthy for the second (and last) year of his deal, he should resume being that unexciting innings-eating proposition that the Nats signed up for to so much fanfare.

J. D. Martin

Born: **1/2/1983** Age: **28**
Bats: **R** Throws: **R** Height: **6' 4"** Weight: **200**
Breakout: **9%** Improve: **19%** Collapse: **9%**
Attrition: **17%** MLB: **32%**

Comparables:
Juan Mateo, Shawn Hill, Francisley Bueno (78)

YEAR	TEAM	LVL	AGE	W	L	SV	G	GS	IP	H	HR	BB	SO	EqBB9	EqSO9	GB%	BABIP	WHIP	ERA	FRA	WARP
2008	AKR	AA	25	11	3	0	31	8	79^2	73	5	19	71	2.1	8.0	45%	.304	1.20	2.48	3.60	2.0
2009	SYR	AAA	26	8	3	0	16	15	88	75	4	10	63	1.0	6.4	42%	.274	0.99	2.66	4.44	1.2
2009	WAS	MLB	26	5	4	0	15	15	77	85	14	24	37	2.8	4.3	38%	.273	1.49	4.44	4.36	1.1
2010	SYR	AAA	27	2	2	0	7	7	41	40	3	8	25	1.8	5.5	44%	.278	1.20	3.51	5.65	0.2
2010	WAS	MLB	27	1	5	0	9	9	48	56	9	11	31	2.1	5.8	38%	.294	1.42	4.13	4.69	0.4
2011	*WAS*	*MLB*	*28*	*5*	*5*	*0*	*23*	*13*	*86^2*	*94*	*11*	*23*	*50*	*2.4*	*5.2*	*43%*	*.294*	*1.35*	*4.47*	*4.86*	*1.0*

Martin is increasingly becoming one of those guys who, if he didn't have bad luck, wouldn't have any luck at all. After the veteran junkballer was finally given a chance to join the rotation in May once Scott Olsen broke down, Martin made it through two months before a back injury shelved him for the rest of the year. He'll contend with Maya and Atilano for the last slot in the rotation, but his victory would be an admission that the other two aren't ready, not an endorsement of his ability to keep the job over the long term.

Shairon Martis

Born: **3/30/1987** Age: **24**
Bats: **R** Throws: **R** Height: **6' 1"** Weight: **175**
Breakout: **10%** Improve: **26%** Collapse: **5%**
Attrition: **10%** MLB: **50%**

Comparables:
Alfredo Figaro, Roger Erickson, Art Houtteman (72)

YEAR	TEAM	LVL	AGE	W	L	SV	G	GS	IP	H	HR	BB	SO	EqBB9	EqSO9	GB%	BABIP	WHIP	ERA	FRA	WARP
2008	HAR	AA	21	4	4	0	14	14	74^2	73	5	28	57	3.4	6.9	43%	.300	1.35	3.98	4.29	1.3
2008	COH	AAA	21	1	2	0	7	7	41^2	42	2	17	42	3.7	9.1	32%	.333	1.44	3.02	3.13	1.4
2008	WAS	MLB	21	1	3	0	5	4	20^2	18	5	12	23	5.2	10.0	33%	.250	1.45	5.66	7.56	-0.3
2009	SYR	AAA	22	4	4	0	13	13	74^1	90	9	18	40	2.2	4.8	33%	.318	1.47	4.97	6.31	-0.4
2009	WAS	MLB	22	5	3	0	15	15	85^2	83	11	39	34	4.1	3.6	42%	.249	1.47	5.25	6.05	-0.3
2010	SYR	AAA	23	8	7	0	27	27	152	156	14	60	99	3.6	5.9	39%	.293	1.43	4.09	4.46	2.7
2011	*WAS*	*MLB*	*24*	*8*	*10*	*0*	*25*	*25*	*136*	*155*	*17*	*58*	*73*	*3.8*	*4.8*	*40%*	*.302*	*1.55*	*5.16*	*5.61*	*0.8*

For all of the Nats' problems in the rotation, the one thing they refused to revisit was the Shairon Martis experience. Leaving the former WBC ace of Holland in upstate New York wasn't some legally required leftover of patroonship, but a choice to see if he'd turn any particular corner. Unfortunately, Martis was much as he's always been, giving up tons of fly balls without especially sharp control or any one dominant offering. He is durable, knows what he's doing, and holds runners well, but absent a difference-making offering, he's a 24-year-old already smushed up against his ceiling and a tough sell for the 40-man roster.

Yunesky Maya

Born: **8/28/1981** Age: **29**
Bats: **R** Throws: **R** Height: **5' 11"** Weight: **170**
Breakout: **4%** Improve: **18%** Collapse: **12%**
Attrition: **11%** MLB: **45%**

Comparables:
Tom Martin, Tommy Phelps, Donn Pall (80)

YEAR	TEAM	LVL	AGE	W	L	SV	G	GS	IP	H	HR	BB	SO	EqBB9	EqSO9	GB%	BABIP	WHIP	ERA	FRA	WARP
2010	WAS	MLB	28	0	3	0	5	5	26	30	3	11	12	3.8	4.2	34%	.300	1.65	5.88	5.79	-0.1
2011	*WAS*	*MLB*	*29*	*3*	*4*	*0*	*10*	*10*	*47^2*	*52*	*6*	*21*	*27*	*4.0*	*5.1*	*44%*	*.302*	*1.56*	*5.17*	*5.62*	*0.4*

Despite Mark's failure to launch a successful ownership bid, Cubans are the game's most exotic commodity, so when word spread that Castroland's hero from the 2009 World Baseball Classic was defecting late in the fall of 2009, he drew interest well beyond what you might expect from his stuff alone. Maya selected the organization already employing a fellow Cubano, Livan Hernandez, signing for four years and $8 million. As ready as he's ever going to be, he's aggressive in using his off-speed stuff at any point in the count and changing arm slots on a big-breaking curve to play off his slider, while shifting speeds and angles on his straighter stuff, alternating high-80s heat and changeups—all of which sounds entertaining, but it adds up to junk that nobody struggled to hit stateside. Considering he was whipped into action in fairly short order after signing in July, you can give him some benefit of the doubt, but remember that he's a junkballer, not the next Livan or Jose Contreras. Cuban phenoms come and go; if you remember Alay Soler, you might ask yourself *why*—because he was Cuban, and Cubans are . . . well, from someplace verboten, so they have to be special, right?

Garrett Mock

Born: **4/25/1983** Age: **28**
Bats: **R** Throws: **R** Height: **6' 3"** Weight: **240**
Breakout: **1%** Improve: **2%** Collapse: **2%**
Attrition: **0%** MLB: **5%**

Comparables:
Ronald Belisario, Jae Kuk Ryu, Edwin Moreno (81)

YEAR	TEAM	LVL	AGE	W	L	SV	G	GS	IP	H	HR	BB	SO	EqBB9	EqSO9	GB%	BABIP	WHIP	ERA	FRA	WARP
2008	COH	AAA	25	6	3	0	19	17	104^{2}	98	9	25	96	2.1	8.3	46%	.297	1.23	3.01	3.35	3.3
2008	WAS	MLB	25	1	3	0	26	3	41	37	4	23	46	5.0	10.1	45%	.308	1.46	4.17	3.85	0.7
2009	SYR	AAA	26	5	1	2	13	8	51	36	2	13	48	2.3	8.5	46%	.258	1.02	2.65	2.63	1.9
2009	WAS	MLB	26	3	10	0	28	15	91^{1}	114	9	44	72	4.3	7.1	50%	.355	1.74	5.62	5.10	0.5
2010	WAS	MLB	27	0	0	0	1	1	3^{1}	4	2	5	3	13.5	8.1	33%	.222	2.70	5.40	6.73	-0.0
2011	*WAS*	*MLB*	*28*	*6*	*6*	*0*	*31*	*16*	*104*	*113*	*12*	*43*	*78*	*3.8*	*6.7*	*46%*	*.317*	*1.51*	*4.91*	*5.34*	*0.6*

Rarely has a name been so apt, but who's the target of Mock-ery, the faithful who believe in his stuff, or the man himself? He won a rotation job in camp, only to suffer a herniated disk in his season debut and sit out the remainder of the major-league season. Although Mock has been long seen as one of the system's few young starters with upside thanks to a plus sinker, this latest injury is why he'll be 28 without having delivered on his promise. In light of the crowded pictures in both the rotation and the pen, not even a demonstration of health would guarantee him much consideration.

Scott Olsen

Born: **1/12/1984** Age: **27**
Bats: **L** Throws: **L** Height: **6' 4"** Weight: **198**
Breakout: **18%** Improve: **51%** Collapse: **23%**
Attrition: **25%** MLB: **95%**

Comparables:
Rick Aguilera, Erik Hanson, Bob Rush (76)

YEAR	TEAM	LVL	AGE	W	L	SV	G	GS	IP	H	HR	BB	SO	EqBB9	EqSO9	GB%	BABIP	WHIP	ERA	FRA	WARP
2008	FLO	MLB	24	8	11	0	33	33	201^{2}	195	30	69	113	3.1	5.0	39%	.258	1.32	4.20	4.87	2.0
2009	WAS	MLB	25	2	4	0	11	11	62^{2}	83	11	25	42	3.6	6.0	38%	.341	1.72	6.03	5.84	-0.1
2010	WAS	MLB	26	4	8	0	17	15	81	93	10	27	53	3.0	5.9	46%	.313	1.51	5.56	6.11	-0.4
2011	*PIT*	*MLB*	*27*	*9*	*11*	*0*	*27*	*27*	*147*	*170*	*20*	*57*	*91*	*3.5*	*5.6*	*42%*	*.310*	*1.53*	*5.25*	*5.71*	*0.8*

There comes a point where either the excuses run out or you have to become a Pirate, but as a result of last season, Olsen has managed both. He's now four years removed from his first and last good season, with more black ink generated by visits to the DL or off-field distractions than anything achieved on the mound. As the latest fourth starter whom Jim Bowden overrated and was burned by (although Bowden was canned before he got to enjoy the full fruitlessness of Olsen's labors), Olsen offered no upside to reap, no breakout potential. There was just another shoulder-related shutdown, plus a start or two to show off some of his former brilliance buried among another series of beatings. If you notice him at all, note that health is a critical skill that Olsen doesn't possess, note that he hasn't been any good since 2006, and note that the man's gone to Pittsburgh, where careers go to die.

Joel Peralta

Born: **3/23/1976** Age: **35**
Bats: **R** Throws: **R** Height: **5' 11"** Weight: **170**
Breakout: **22%** Improve: **37%** Collapse: **31%**
Attrition: **12%** MLB: **83%**

Comparables:
Mike Stanton, Doug Jones, Tug McGraw (76)

YEAR	TEAM	LVL	AGE	W	L	SV	G	GS	IP	H	HR	BB	SO	EqBB9	EqSO9	GB%	BABIP	WHIP	ERA	FRA	WARP
2008	KCA	MLB	32	1	2	0	40	0	52^{2}	56	15	14	38	2.4	6.5	37%	.265	1.37	5.98	6.77	-1.0
2009	CSP	AAA	33	6	0	4	31	0	36^{2}	31	3	11	32	2.7	7.8	37%	.264	1.14	2.45	3.50	0.5
2009	COL	MLB	33	0	3	0	27	0	24^{2}	27	3	12	22	4.4	8.0	28%	.329	1.70	6.20	6.35	-0.4
2010	SYR	AAA	34	2	0	20	28	0	33^{1}	24	1	7	38	1.9	10.3	40%	.277	0.97	1.08	1.21	1.2
2010	WAS	MLB	34	1	0	0	39	0	49	30	5	9	49	1.7	9.0	29%	.200	0.82	2.02	3.52	0.7
2011	*TBA*	*MLB*	*35*	*3*	*1*	*2*	*62*	*0*	*76*	*70*	*9*	*23*	*64*	*2.7*	*7.5*	*40%*	*.281*	*1.21*	*3.50*	*3.80*	*0.7*

Introduced to the organization as a nonroster invitee, Peralta failed to stick in camp, but earned a June call-up after a 20-for-20 performance in save opportunities closing for the Chiefs. Once he arrived, he was a significantly different pitcher than he'd been in previous major-league incarnations, relying on a changeup as his swing-and-miss offering and setting it up with heat that sat around 90 and a show-me curve. That seems to have made him better armed and better able to face lefties than ever before, and in little more than a half-season, he was the Nats' second-best reliever via WXRL (behind only Burnett). The Rays, as enthusiastic for "bargain" changeup artists as they were when they invested (and missed) on Joe Nelson, decided that he was worth a modest $900,000 guaranteed offer, a cheap risk that will look great if Peralta's refabrication sticks, while being totally disposable if not.

Atahualpa Severino

Born: **11/6/1984** Age: **26**
Bats: **L** Throws: **L** Height: **5' 9"** Weight: **170**
Breakout: **0%** Improve: **1%** Collapse: **0%**
Attrition: **1%** MLB: **1%**

Comparables:
Chuck Seelbach, Eduardo Rodriguez, Mark Brandenburg (78)

YEAR	TEAM	LVL	AGE	W	L	SV	G	GS	IP	H	HR	BB	SO	EqBB9	EqSO9	GB%	BABIP	WHIP	ERA	FRA	WARP
2008	HAG	A	23	4	2	1	15	0	33^{1}	28	2	17	34	4.6	9.2	63%	.295	1.47	4.05	5.54	-0.3
2008	POT	A+	23	0	4	0	26	0	38^{2}	31	2	20	31	4.7	7.2	54%	.264	1.34	3.95	4.75	0.1
2009	POT	A+	24	4	0	13	29	0	46	35	4	14	39	2.7	7.6	59%	.240	1.13	2.54	3.64	0.6
2009	HAR	AA	24	6	0	2	15	0	22^{2}	19	1	14	27	5.6	10.7	47%	.321	1.59	2.78	2.20	0.8
2010	SYR	AAA	25	6	3	1	54	0	67^{1}	60	5	29	46	3.9	6.2	52%	.266	1.40	3.34	3.86	1.1
2011	*WAS*	*MLB*	*26*	*2*	*1*	*1*	*34*	*0*	*52*	*52*	*6*	*28*	*35*	*4.8*	*6.1*	*49%*	*.284*	*1.52*	*4.76*	*5.18*	*-0.3*

A diminutive Dominican named for the last ruling *Sapa Inca* ("unique Inca") before the conquistadores showed up, Severino is a lefty made less ordinary thanks to a fastball that touches 94. Unfortunately, that may be the extent of his effective offerings; his off-speed stuff isn't crisp enough for him to be a can't-miss addition to a bullpen, and between wearing down in the second half and then getting lit up in winter ball, he'll be coming to camp with a couple of questions to answer before he can really start gunning for Doug Slaten's job.

Doug Slaten

Born: **2/4/1980** Age: **31**
Bats: **L** Throws: **L** Height: **6' 5"** Weight: **200**
Breakout: **4%** Improve: **18%** Collapse: **9%**
Attrition: **8%** MLB: **28%**

Comparables:
Juan Rincon, Vinnie Chulk, Justin Miller (80)

YEAR	TEAM	LVL	AGE	W	L	SV	G	GS	IP	H	HR	BB	SO	EqBB9	EqSO9	GB%	BABIP	WHIP	ERA	FRA	WARP
2008	ARI	MLB	28	0	3	0	45	0	32^{1}	33	4	14	20	3.9	5.6	39%	.276	1.58	4.73	5.51	-0.2
2009	RNO	AAA	29	3	2	9	39	0	43^{2}	41	3	15	40	3.1	8.2	54%	.309	1.28	3.09	3.31	0.6
2009	ARI	MLB	29	0	0	0	11	0	6^{1}	10	1	1	4	1.4	5.7	44%	.375	1.74	7.11	6.06	-0.1
2010	WAS	MLB	30	4	1	0	49	0	40^{2}	34	2	19	36	4.2	8.0	47%	.283	1.40	3.10	3.13	0.9
2011	*WAS*	*MLB*	*31*	*3*	*1*	*1*	*54*	*0*	*49*	*48*	*5*	*19*	*40*	*3.5*	*7.3*	*46%*	*.304*	*1.36*	*4.01*	*4.36*	*0.2*

Another unheralded bullpen success, Slaten was a good example of how smart shoppers can avoid paying top dollar for situational excellence. Why bother, when you can make do with low-risk waiver claims? Being an extreme situational specialist can be difficult if you're not hidden away from the opposite-handed as much as possible, and pitching in Bank TBNL Ballpark in Phoenix is a tough assignment for any hurler. Once Slaten was added to the Nats' pen in May, Riggleman used him to good effect, extracting a .151/.235/.151 line against lefties from the big southpaw. That will be impossible to repeat, but Slaten is good at the job and, left in it, should continue to succeed.

Craig Stammen

Born: **3/9/1984** Age: **27**
Bats: **R** Throws: **R** Height: **6' 3"** Weight: **200**
Breakout: **14%** Improve: **29%** Collapse: **7%**
Attrition: **16%** MLB: **41%**

Comparables:
Elizardo Ramirez, Mike Ekstrom, Joe Martinez (79)

YEAR	TEAM	LVL	AGE	W	L	SV	G	GS	IP	H	HR	BB	SO	EqBB9	EqSO9	GB%	BABIP	WHIP	ERA	FRA	WARP
2008	POT	A+	24	4	2	1	15	9	69^{1}	59	6	17	62	2.2	8.1	54%	.275	1.11	2.21	3.45	1.8
2008	HAR	AA	24	3	1	0	6	6	38^{1}	22	1	11	31	2.6	7.3	57%	.208	0.86	1.64	3.75	0.9
2008	COH	AAA	24	1	4	0	9	8	43	62	3	16	35	3.3	7.3	50%	.415	1.86	7.33	5.18	0.5
2009	SYR	AAA	25	4	2	0	7	7	40	33	4	8	14	1.8	3.2	61%	.213	1.02	1.80	4.12	0.7
2009	WAS	MLB	25	4	7	0	19	19	105^{2}	112	14	24	48	2.0	4.1	47%	.273	1.32	5.11	6.01	-0.4
2010	SYR	AAA	26	2	0	0	3	3	20	18	2	3	10	1.4	4.5	54%	.246	1.10	2.25	3.77	0.5
2010	WAS	MLB	26	4	4	0	35	19	128	151	13	41	85	2.9	6.0	51%	.327	1.51	5.13	4.25	1.5
2011	*WAS*	*MLB*	*27*	*8*	*10*	*0*	*25*	*25*	139^{2}	*163*	*18*	*47*	*74*	*3.1*	*4.8*	*49%*	*.310*	*1.50*	*5.16*	*5.61*	*0.8*

Own your fetish, or it will own you. Face it, most everyone in your league probably reads this kind of book or books like it and is thus consulting similar blueprints for success. Everyone in the analysis community loves power in the form of big K rates; Stammen's went from improved to excellent after he was mercifully removed from the rotation. Everyone also loves ground-ball outs, and here again, Stammen went from above-average to inducing twice as many grounders as caught flies. So Stammen might seem poised to be a relief star, right? Perhaps, but remember the basics—he doesn't throw that hard or with that much movement, and he leaves everything out over the plate. If that fulfills your need for grounders and Ks, swell, but you might go for better—the Nats aren't handing him any guarantees, and neither should you.

Drew Storen

Born: **8/1/1987** Age: **23**
Bats: **B** Throws: **R** Height: **6' 2"** Weight: **180**
Breakout: **9%** Improve: **26%** Collapse: **10%**
Attrition: **8%** MLB: **43%**

Comparables:
Josh Beckett, Kris Medlen, Bruce Sutter (71)

YEAR	TEAM	LVL	AGE	W	L	SV	G	GS	IP	H	HR	BB	SO	EqBB9	EqSO9	GB%	BABIP	WHIP	ERA	FRA	WARP
2010	WAS	MLB	22	4	4	5	54	0	55^{1}	48	3	22	52	3.6	8.5	41%	.296	1.32	3.58	3.79	0.6
2011	*WAS*	*MLB*	*23*	*2*	*1*	*1*	*45*	*0*	*51*	*47*	*5*	*19*	*49*	*3.3*	*8.5*	*44%*	*.299*	*1.27*	*3.50*	*3.80*	*0.5*

Drafted nine picks after Strasburg with the thought that he'd also move up fast, the former Stanford relief ace was shutting down big-league hitters less than a year after bidding college good-bye. Not unlike Chad Cordero in being enlisted as a short-order solution, he'll end up closing now, but closer connoisseurs sniff that his stuff is dealt from a set-up man's sheath. Still, he possesses a fastball that sits around 94 and touches 98, and he mixes in curves and sliders to good effect. If he's "merely" very effective in the save-generating role, he'll remind folks that Rizzo and company did more than the obvious in the 2009 draft.

Stephen Strasburg

Born: **7/20/1988** Age: **22**
Bats: **R** Throws: **R** Height: **6' 4"** Weight: **220**
Breakout: **23%** Improve: **45%** Collapse: **23%**
Attrition: **11%** MLB: **87%**

Comparables:
Mark Prior, Yovani Gallardo, Clayton Kershaw (54)

YEAR	TEAM	LVL	AGE	W	L	SV	G	GS	IP	H	HR	BB	SO	EqBB9	EqSO9	GB%	BABIP	WHIP	ERA	FRA	WARP
2010	HAR	AA	21	3	1	0	5	5	22	13	0	6	27	2.5	11.0	66%	.250	0.91	1.64	4.58	0.3
2010	SYR	AAA	21	4	1	0	6	6	33^{1}	18	1	7	38	1.9	10.3	67%	.218	0.76	1.08	2.99	1.2
2010	WAS	MLB	21	5	3	0	12	12	68	56	5	17	92	2.3	12.2	47%	.319	1.07	2.91	2.85	2.1
2011	*WAS*	*MLB*	*22*	*11*	*4*	*0*	*23*	*23*	*122^{2}*	*97*	*9*	*35*	*140*	*2.5*	*10.3*	*48%*	*.296*	*1.08*	*2.42*	*2.63*	*5.1*

Not unlike Mark Prior before him, the most-hyped prospect of this or any other lifetime cut his teeth in the minors, but only to take the edge off his inevitable debut. He did everything as expected, and he wasn't being worked too hard for too long. Between triple-digit heat, sliders that touched 90, and a power curve, he featured an assortment of stuff never seen before, and while there was some inevitable fidgeting over his mechanics, nothing was screaming for a fix. Sometimes, a guy is just going to break, and with the shredding of Strasburg's elbow in August and his subsequent Tommy John surgery, the wunderkind of all wunderkinder got quickly acquainted with the risks of the trade. If he requires a full year to rehabilitate, Strasburg won't be back until August or roster expansion, if then; the focus should be on his stepping back into the rotation to stay come Opening Day 2012. Look at the projection and weep for what might have been.

Jordan Zimmermann

Born: **5/23/1986** Age: **25**
Bats: **R** Throws: **R** Height: **6' 2"** Weight: **220**
Breakout: **2%** Improve: **24%** Collapse: **7%**
Attrition: **5%** MLB: **53%**

Comparables:
Britt Burns, Pete Vuckovich, Willie Adams (73)

YEAR	TEAM	LVL	AGE	W	L	SV	G	GS	IP	H	HR	BB	SO	EqBB9	EqSO9	GB%	BABIP	WHIP	ERA	FRA	WARP
2008	POT	A+	22	3	1	1	5	4	27^{1}	15	1	8	31	2.6	10.2	55%	.237	0.84	1.65	1.85	1.5
2008	HAR	AA	22	7	2	0	20	21	106^{2}	89	9	39	103	3.3	8.7	47%	.281	1.23	3.12	3.61	2.8
2009	WAS	MLB	23	3	5	0	16	16	91^{1}	95	10	29	92	2.9	9.1	45%	.332	1.40	4.63	4.41	1.2
2010	WAS	MLB	24	1	2	0	7	7	31	31	8	10	27	2.9	7.8	49%	.261	1.39	4.94	6.20	-0.2
2011	*WAS*	*MLB*	*25*	*6*	*6*	*0*	*17*	*17*	*86^{1}*	*85*	*11*	*31*	*74*	*3.2*	*7.7*	*46%*	*.301*	*1.35*	*4.27*	*4.65*	*1.6*

Preceding Strasburg in all things—top-prospect status, arrival, injury, and return—Zimmermann is already back from his Tommy John procedure, so his future begins anew this spring. During his brief initial return, he was throwing all four of his pitches for strikes, and his fastball velocity was creeping back toward the mid-90s. As the high-upside prospect in a rotation otherwise stocked with soft-tossing strike-throwers, ground-ballers, and geezers, he'll be the pitcher handled with exceptional care. Assuming that he regains his full touch in camp another four months later, he'll remain what he was before surgery: a blue-chip starting prospect who would rate as the expected ace of most rotations—perhaps all but the same one as Strasburg.

LINEOUTS

HITTERS

PLAYER	TEAM	LVL	AGE	PA	R	2B	3B	HR	RBI	BB	SO	SB-CS	AVG/OBP/SLG	TAv	BABIP	BRR	FRAA	WARP
SS R. Hague	HAG	A	21	176	26	12	5	3	27	14	34	3-2	.327/.386/.522	.340	.398	0.0	SS 4	2.4
OF D. Hood	HAG	A	20	541	56	30	3	5	65	33	119	5-7	.285/.333/.388	.263	.361	1.1	RF -1, LF -6	0.5
INF J. Johnson#	POT	A+	24	113	18	8	0	2	11	17	17	3-1	.309/.407/.457	.315	.351	0.0	3B -2, SS 1	0.8
	HAR	AA	24	258	43	16	2	5	31	29	37	5-5	.287/.375/.444	.313	.321	0.0	SS 1, 2B 3	2.9
C S. Leon#	HAG	A	21	385	48	10	6	2	36	50	79	3-3	.249/.340/.335	.259	.311	-3.3	C 0	1.3
C C. Maldonado	SYR	AAA	31	218	16	8	0	3	27	19	45	2-1	.223/.293/.314	.216	.262	-5.0	C 0	-0.6
	WAS	MLB	31	12	1	0	0	1	3	1	2	0-0	.273/.333/.546	.318	.250	-0.1	C 0	0.1
OF K. Mench	SYR	AAA	32	326	27	16	0	3	40	35	30	3-1	.249/.331/.338	.247	.263	-0.9	RF -1, LF -1	-0.3
	WAS	MLB	32	29	2	0	0	0	1	2	6	0-0	.111/.172/.111	.117	.143	-0.1	LF 0	-0.4
UT P. Orr*	SYR	AAA	31	536	63	32	8	12	45	33	90	25-9	.264/.326/.436	.254	.301	2.4	SS 0, 3B 3	2.7

Rick Hague arrived from Rice as a 2010 third-rounder; after an error-prone debut, he'll move off short, but his bat was once considered first-round material. ⊘ Athletic **Destin Hood** showed good plate coverage in his full-season debut, but is sushi-raw in every other way; he'll be on the slow boat to "The Show" for a while yet. ⊘ After washing out of the Royals organization after six seasons, **Josh Johnson** landed with the Nats and helped two different affiliates reach the playoffs as a high-OBP utilityman. ⊘ With strong-armed **Sandy Leon** gunning down 51 percent of base thieves, the Nats have credible catching talent top to bottom in the system . . . . . . not that such depth doesn't make journeymen like **Carlos Maldonado** an unavoidable evil in any organization. After washing out stateside, **Kevin Mench** sloshed over to the Japanese leagues and flopped there as well; presumably, favors (or Favres) involving indiscretions were involved in the decision to inflict him on the good people of Syracuse. Mining the Nats' system for comment-worthy bodies yields **Pete Orr** instead of real nuggets, but the journeyman can still play six positions and run.

PITCHERS

PLAYER	TEAM	LVL	AGE	W	L	SV	IP	H	HR	BB	SO	EqBB9	EqSO9	GB%	BABIP	WHIP	ERA	FRA	WARP
J. Bergmann	SYR	AAA	28	6	4	0	50^{2}	42	6	19	56	3.4	10.0	44%	.271	1.31	2.84	4.57	0.4
	WAS	MLB	28	0	1	0	21	3	2	1	2	3.9	7.7	25%	.167	1.71	15.43	13.80	-0.2
M. Chico*	HAR	AA	27	1	2	0	26	26	2	7	17	2.4	5.9	46%	.289	1.27	3.12	5.08	0.2
	SYR	AAA	27	6	7	0	115^{2}	120	12	34	69	2.7	5.4	42%	.287	1.34	3.73	3.98	2.7
	WAS	MLB	27	0	0	0	5	6	0	0	3	0.0	5.4	61%	.333	1.40	3.60	4.20	0.1
B. Meyers	HAR	AA	24	1	0	0	30^{2}	23	3	7	35	2.1	10.4	56%	.267	1.03	1.47	2.68	1.1
T. Milone*	HAR	AA	23	12	5	0	158	161	10	23	155	1.3	8.8	44%	.330	1.19	2.85	2.34	6.4
A. Morris	POT	A+	23	5	3	2	72	67	4	27	61	3.4	7.6	62%	.289	1.39	3.88	5.72	0.1
B. Peacock	POT	A+	22	4	9	0	103^{1}	109	11	25	118	2.2	10.3	50%	.343	1.34	4.44	4.82	1.1
	HAR	AA	22	2	2	0	38^{2}	33	5	22	30	5.2	7.1	41%	.257	1.44	4.66	5.17	0.2
T. Roark	FRI	AA	23	10	5	0	105	113	8	33	75	2.8	6.4	45%	.318	1.41	4.20	5.22	0.2
	HAR	AA	23	1	1	0	36	35	5	9	33	2.3	8.3	42%	.297	1.22	2.50	5.10	0.2
R. Tatusko	FRI	AA	25	9	2	0	100	94	2	40	58	3.6	5.2	53%	.293	1.34	2.97	3.77	1.8
	HAR	AA	25	3	1	0	36^{2}	30	2	13	36	3.2	9.0	57%	.289	1.22	1.72	2.70	1.4
A. Thompson*	HAR	AA	23	4	13	0	136^{2}	164	16	53	95	3.5	6.3	48%	.331	1.63	5.80	5.22	0.5
T. Walker	WAS	MLB	34	1	0	0	35^{1}	35	5	8	30	2.0	7.6	42%	.294	1.22	3.57	3.37	0.6
J. Wilkie	SYR	AAA	25	4	4	8	69^{2}	57	2	22	62	2.9	8.1	60%	.288	1.17	2.45	3.30	1.7

Nothing could convince the Nats to bring **Jason Bergmann** back after he pitched his way off the team in April, so he'll be in Boston's camp as a nonroster invitee. Chunky **Matt Chico** finally came all the way back from elbow surgery, but was left with the same mediocre assortment he started out with; he re-signed with the team after being designated for assignment in December and will be auditioning for fifth-man gigs forever more. **A. J. Cole** was a top prep prospect with lofty bonus expectations, but got his money from the Nats as a 2010 fourth-rounder; gifted with good heat, he needs to polish a power curve and a changeup to stick as a starter. While **Juan Jaime** could be a high-impact power arm in the pen, he lost 2010 to Tommy John surgery and was claimed by the Snakes on waivers in November. A big strike-thrower with a nifty slider, **Brad Meyers** missed most of 2010 with complications from pre-season foot surgery, but bears watching as he comes back. USC's **Tom Milone** is a strike-throwing finesse lefty who's likely to be doomed to become only too familiar to International League audiences in the years to come. A 2009 fourth-rounder, **A. J. Morris** has a solid sinker/slider mix that might get him fast-tracked if he makes the jump to the pen. **Brad Peacock** was a hitter in high school, but the Nats saw low-90s heat and converted him to pitching; his primary pitch is string-straight, but he's trying a knuckle-curve and change to mix things up. Part of the payoff for sending Cristian Guzman to Texas, **Tanner Roark** has little going for him beyond command of low-temp heat, all the better to cook slowly with. Last summer's second-rounder **Sammy Solis** changes speeds well, but his breaking stuff needs work. The other Ranger received for Guzman, **Ryan Tatusko** boasts a good-enough sinker to put himself into a fringy swingman role. Despite low-90s velocity with good movement, **Aaron Thompson** struggled terribly after the third inning, going from 4.5 runs allowed per nine innings (RA/9) to 8.7, suggesting a future in the pen, not telemarketing—he's a lefty, after all. Tearing up his shoulder in June kept journeyman **Tyler Walker** from logging even more time midgame in losing causes. Former Yankee **Chien-Ming Wang** didn't heal up from shoulder surgery in time to pitch, but he'll be back with the Nats on an incentive-laden deal to see if he's any closer to resuming his career. If stats tell stories, you'll look at **Josh Wilkie**'s strikeouts and grounders and get worked up; unfortunately, his one good pitch is a plus changeup, which tempers excitement over the GWU product's shot at coming home.

MANAGER: JIM RIGGLEMAN

YEAR	TEAM	W-L	Pythag +/-	Avg PC	100+ P	120+ P	QS	BQS	REL	REL w Zero R	IBB	Subs	PH	PH Avg	PH HR	SB2	CS2	SB3	CS3	SAC Att	SAC %	POS SAC	Squeeze	Swing	In Play
2008	SEA	36-54	-3	93.0	39	0	37	1	272	158	25	37	75	.235	0	32	15	6	2	37	56.8%	19	1	84	75
2009	WAS	33-42	1	87.9	16	1	29	3	250	137	33	38	114	.282	2	32	18	5	2	50	66.0%	14	1	55	46
2010	WAS	69-93	-2	89.5	28	2	65	4	522	341	57	91	264	.202	2	102	39	8	1	123	57.7%	40	1	150	106

Always a competent tactician, Riggleman did well in his first real gig since his days with the Cubs after accepting an assignment as tough as his first job with the Padres in the early 1990s. He remains very much the same skipper in terms of his aggressive use of reserves, selecting bench bats with specific applications in mind, and pinch-running and swapping in defensive replacements with abandon; nobody just sits on a Riggleman roster. While tasked with a generally mediocre collection of pitchers and a metastasizing clutterbuck of injuries he could not have anticipated or avoided, he and pitching coach Steve McCatty rolled with a season's worth of haymakers. Happily, he isn't preprogrammed and platoon-minded with his relief roles—he proved willing to expand Burnett's responsibilities instead of shoe-horning him into situational work, while using Clippard as a true long reliever. It will be interesting to see how he handles first Zimmermann and later Strasburg as they approach full strength after injury, given that Riggleman was Kerry Wood's first skipper. These two times around, the process should go much more smoothly, since he's working with material less damaged.

The Baseball Prospectus Top 101 Prospects

Kevin Goldstein

1. Bryce Harper, OF, Nationals

No player in history has entered his draft year with more hype than Harper, who then added to the challenge by skipping out on his final two high-school seasons to play in a tough junior college conference that uses wooden bats. Merely holding his own there would have thrilled scouts, but instead, he made an assault on the record books by hitting .443/.526/.987 with 31 home runs in 228 at-bats. As for holding his own, he did that and more against the Double-A and Triple-A pitching of the Arizona Fall League just days after his 18th birthday. He now enters 2011 with more hype than any player yet to make an official pro debut, and don't be surprised if he exceeds expectations once again, as he's a once-in-a-lifetime offensive talent.

2. Mike Trout, OF, Angels

Already looking like the steal of the 2009 draft, Trout dropped toward the bottom of the first round because scouts didn't see him play either enough or against top competition in rural New Jersey, but not even the Angels expected him to be this good. With top-of-the-line speed, outstanding hitting skills with developing power, and off-the-charts makeup, he has a good chance to become the player that Grady Sizemore was before the injuries took hold.

3. Jesus Montero, C, Yankees

Having hit .351/.396/.684 after the All-Star break as a 20-year-old in Triple-A, Montero presumably has everything it takes to be a middle-of-the-order force on a championship-level team. The problem remains his defense, as evidenced by the Yankees' signing what's left of Russell Martin to catch in 2011. Between Mark Teixeira's long-term deal and the industry's unwillingness to cast young players into designated-hitter roles, one is left wondering if his break will come with a team other than the Yankees.

4. Domonic Brown, OF, Phillies

It's almost as if Brown's late-July call-up worked against him. He spent the last two months of the year riding the pine for a playoff contender, which made it easy to forget what a remarkable minor-league year he had, batting .327/.391/.589 in 93 games. As he is armed with a classic power/speed combination in right field, it's not fair to expect him to replace Jayson Werth as a rookie, but it won't take him long to flourish from there.

5. Julio Teheran, RHP, Braves

The Braves finally took the reins off Teheran in 2010, and with Steven Strasburg graduating to the majors, he went from highly projectable right-hander to the best pitching prospect in baseball. Long, lean, and with nearly perfect arm action, Teheran already gets into the mid-90s with his fastball, has two plus secondary pitches, and wraps it all up in a package of impressive poise and command. The scariest aspect of his outlook is that scouts think he's going to get even better.

6. Aroldis Chapman, RHP, Reds

The tales of 103-mph fastballs in the minors seemed to be something out of P. T. Barnum's playbook, but then, on calibrated big-league radar guns and PITCHf/x cameras, Chapman went and hit 104. If that's not enough, his nasty slider immediately became one of the best breaking balls among relievers the second he got called up. Chapman is still learning how to harness his stuff and that even a straight and up-the-middle triple-digit fastball can get hit. The Reds need to decide if they should use him now, or go for door number three and try to turn him into a starter.

7. Mike Moustakas, 3B, Royals

One step ahead of the rest of the prospects charging through the Royals' system, Moustakas will be the vanguard of the sizable cavalry that will finally rescue Kansas City baseball. After missing the first part of the season with an oblique strain, he needed just 118 games to tie for the minor-league lead with 36 home runs, but just as impressive was his whiffing only 67 times in 484 at-bats, demonstrating that he's not just a slugger; he's a hitter with power.

8. Jameson Taillon, RHP, Pirates

It's going to be a slow process in Pittsburgh, but Taillon has the best shot at becoming the kind of player who changes the direction of an entire franchise. The second overall pick in the 2010 draft would be better known had he not been overshadowed by Bryce Harper, but some think Taillon was a bit historic himself, perhaps the top high-school righty of the last decade. The Pirates haven't had an ace pitcher for so long that the last one's son is now on this list. Taillon could change that.

9. Jeremy Hellickson, RHP, Rays

Hellickson doesn't have the kind of raw stuff that normally lands a player in the top 10, but he's hardly a finesse pitcher. His fastball, curve, and changeup are all at least a tick above average, but it's what he does with his arsenal that is so special. There are decade-plus veterans who don't have Hellickson's polish, as he varies the movement of his fastball and places all of his offerings in the strike zone with laser-like precision. The Rays will find a way to get him to the big league this year, and some scouts have already broken an unwritten rule by comparing him to a young Greg Maddux.

10. Matt Moore, LHP, Rays

One of the most important metrics for evaluating pitching prospects is the ability to miss bats. By leading the minor league in strikeouts in each of the last two years, Moore has proven that he can do just that. With a low- to mid-90s fastball and plus power breaking ball, Moore has more than twice as many strikeouts as hits allowed, and if he keeps that ratio going as he moves into the upper levels this year, he'll move up this list as well.

11. John Lamb, LHP, Royals

While Lamb ran out of gas after reaching Double-A in his first full season, you can't discount how he carved up the Low-A Midwest and High-A Carolina Leagues. In many ways, he's an unproven, left-handed version of Hellickson with no monster pitch, but like a great bartender, he can pound the strike zone with three above-average offerings that he mixes effectively. The Royals' rotation at Double-A Northwest Arkansas should open the year with four of the Top 101 prospects. Lamb is the best bet to reach the majors first.

12. Eric Hosmer, 1B, Royals

Hosmer has been on a roller coaster, and not one of those jolly, crazy-mouse numbers you get on willingly, but a nightmarish, high-speed inversion model like the one in the Batman comic books, where the Joker puts his hostages in the lead car and then cuts the brakes. He went from being the best high-school hitter in the 2008 draft to the biggest disappointment in 2009 to the most impressive turnaround in 2010—not only did Batman make the save, but Hosmer became the *bat*man. Lasik surgery gets much of the credit for Hosmer's rebound, but it was really the catalyst for a number of changes in his game: he developed from a passive hitter into an aggressively patient one who finally saw his tremendous raw power show up in games when he moved up to Double-A. First-base prospects have to project as middle-of-the-order run producers to be good prospects, and Hosmer easily eclipses that bar.

13. Wil Myers, C, Royals

Seen as a tough sign in the 2009 draft, Myers received $2 million from the Royals as a third-round pick, and now 29 other teams wish they had written the check. In his first full season, Myers proved to be a doubles machine with the best on-base skills in a very loaded system, and scouts universally believe that his above-average power will eventually show up in games as well. If Myers really were a catcher, he would rank higher, but his bat is so far ahead of his glove at this point that a switch to right field is likely to be in his future.

14. Kyle Drabek, RHP, Blue Jays

After holding his own in three big-league starts toward the end of the season, Drabek is close to assuming his projected role at the top of the Blue Jays' rotation. As the son of a former Cy Young winner, Drabek has, not surprisingly, a deep arsenal, including a low-90s sinker, a four-seam fastball that he can run up to 96 mph, and one of the better curveballs in the minors. His 2008 Tommy John surgery proved to be the best thing for him, as it forced him to grow up both as a person and as a pitcher. As Kierkegaard said, life can only be understood backwards, but it must be lived forward.

15. Shelby Miller, RHP, Cardinals

To watch Miller pitch during the 2010 season was to see him evolve from thrower to pitcher over the course of a single season. A classic power arm from Texas, Miller has low- to mid-90s heat, touching 97. He showed enough potential in a frequently plus curve and solid changeup to project as a potential top-of-the-rotation piece in the majors. He is a great pick for a 2011 breakout, as he got better as the year went on, including a 13-strikeout, seven-shutout-inning playoff appearance that was among the best performances of the year anywhere in baseball.

16. Manny Machado, SS, Orioles

The third overall pick in the 2010 draft, Machado earned some unfair comparisons to Alex Rodriguez as a Latino-American high school shortstop at a Miami-based high school. He isn't A-Rod, but he's still a premium player who should hit for average and power and provide quality defense along the way. Like Rodriguez, he's likely to slide over to third base at some point in his career, but the bat should play anywhere.

17. Zach Britton, RHP, Orioles

The Orioles have long had one of the most impressive collections of young arms in the minors, and while Brian Matusz, Jake Arrieta, and Chris Tillman have graduated to the majors, some scouts believe Britton will be as good as, if not better than, any of them. His sinker generates as many swings and misses as it does ground balls, and in 2010, he rounded out his game with a plus slider and solid change. He doesn't need much more time in the minors.

18. Desmond Jennings, OF, Rays

Jennings knew he had a job for 2011 all year, since there was no way that the Rays would retain the services of Carl Crawford, but even allowing for a degree of complacency, his Triple-A season was a bit of a disappointment. Injuries (a word that crops up often with Jennings) were a mitigating factor, but the player who once earned comparisons to the player he's replacing now looks like more of a classic leadoff man who can hit, reach base, and run, albeit without the power that was once projected for him.

19. Chris Sale, LHP, White Sox

Some saw Sale as the top college pitcher in the 2010 draft, so it was a bit of a mystery that he fell into the White Sox's lap with the 13th overall pick. Moved temporarily to the bullpen with the hope that he could help in the big leagues, Sale reached the majors faster than any other draftee in the last seven years and held big-league batters to a .185 batting average, thanks to an upper-90s fastball and plus slider. Knowing where his true value lies, the White Sox will get him back to starting. His stuff will tick down a bit in that role, but he still projects as an All-Star.

20. Freddie Freeman, 1B, Braves

Troy Glaus and Derrek Lee were temporary stopgaps at first base for the Braves, buying time for Freeman to spend a final year in preparation for Opening Day 2011. On a scouting level, Freeman is arguably a better pure hitter than Jason Heyward, although Freeman's power is merely average for the position and his approach can become overly aggressive at times. The floor is Wally Joyner, but the ceiling is Will Clark.

21. Mike Montgomery, LHP, Royals

Before a bout of elbow soreness at midseason, Montgomery was presenting his case as one of the best left-handed starting prospects, if not *the* best one, in the minors. A tall, ultra-athletic lefty with three plus pitches, all that remains for Montgomery to do is prove that he can handle a big-league workload, as he has yet to pitch more than 110 innings in a single season. In most organizations, he'd be a no-brainer number one prospect, but with the Royals, he's just part of the crowd.

22. Brandon Belt, 1B/OF, Giants

Belt was an impressive hitter at Texas, but a lack of power dropped him to the fifth round of the 2009 draft, since he didn't profile especially well at a bat-only position. The Giants closed and lowered Belt's stance, transforming him into the minors' breakout player of the year. He started the season at High-A, finished it at Triple-A, and slugged .352/.455/.620 along the way. The Giants re-signed Aubrey Huff, but that doesn't mean Belt is blocked, as either he or Huff will move to left field when the Giants decide "The Belt's" time has arrived.

23. Jacob Turner, RHP, Tigers

The Tigers are notoriously aggressive with their pitching prospects, and that was certainly the case with Turner, as the 2009 first-round pick found himself at High-A just days after his 19th birthday. He's a classic power arm with well-above-average velocity and the kind of control rarely found in a pitcher so young. His statistics were artificially depressed, especially in the strikeout category, as the team forced him to focus on his curveball and change—in other words, he's even better than he looked. While he's not quite on the Rick Porcello path (one that ascended too quickly), he could reach Double-A while still a teenager.

24. Michael Pineda, RHP, Mariners

Seen as a potential breakout player in 2009, Pineda saw his coming-out party delayed by a year because of elbow problems, but he more than made up for it by routinely sitting in the upper 90s while generating plenty of swings and misses at both Double-A and Triple-A. His secondary stuff and control are still improving, but with just one small step forward in those two departments, he will become a frontline starter.

25. Dustin Ackley, 2B, Mariners

It's not that Ackley is bad; it's just that he wasn't as good as advertised when the Mariners made him the number two overall pick in the 2009 draft and signed him for $6 million. He certainly can hit and draw walks with aplomb and should compete for an OBP title or two in the big leagues, but his transition from the outfield to second base was an extremely bumpy one, and the power potential many saw in college didn't translate to wood bats. The Mariners opened a big-league spot for him by jettisoning Jose Lopez, and Ackley is polished enough at the plate to expect few struggles as a rookie.

26. Mike Minor, LHP, Braves

The Braves took some flak (including from yours truly) for selecting Minor with the seventh overall pick in 2009; though he was among the safest bets available, there were plenty of questions about his ceiling. A funny thing happened in 2010, as what was once an average-velocity fastball became a 92-94 mph bullet that touched 96 and allowed his already-impressive command and secondary offerings to play up.

Minor will probably begin the year at the back of the Atlanta rotation and move up from there.

27. Manny Banuelos, LHP, Yankees

The Yankees had a covey of pitching prospects take a huge step forward in 2010, but each man still has something to prove in terms of track record or workload. Although an emergency appendectomy delayed the start of Banuelos's 2010 season, he quickly made up for lost time by reaching Double-A with a fastball that jumped up to the 92-95 mph range and a killer changeup rarely seen in a teenager. His stuff and polish makes it easy for scouts not to hold his lack of stature against him, and he should reach Yankee Stadium before he's legal to drink, assuming the organization waives the rule that says you have to be 29 before you're allowed to be a Yankee.

28. Jason Kipnis, 2B, Indians

Selected more than 60 picks after Ackley, Kipnis is another outfielder who put up huge numbers in college (Arizona State) and converted to second base in his first full season. Not only did he match or exceed Ackley at the plate, but his defensive transition went much more smoothly. A compact athlete with a knack for hard contact, Kipnis's Double-A numbers would have put him among the Eastern League leaders in several categories had he earned enough playing time, and considering the state of the big-league roster, his path to the majors is clear.

29. Gary Sanchez, C, Yankees

Even for a team that spends liberally in the international market, Sanchez's $3 million bonus was an eye-opener, but he looked to be worth every penny in his pro debut. Despite being just 17 years old, Sanchez looked like a man among boys in his Gulf Coast League debut, already bringing his plus-plus power into game situations. Like a young Jesus Montero, he still has plenty of work to do behind the plate, but also like Montero, his offensive potential is almost frightening to consider.

30. Chris Carter, 1B/LF, Athletics

While Carter gained some unwanted national media for the 0-for-33 streak that began his big-league career, it was consistent with his history of slow starts at new levels, and he slugged .622 once he finally got a hit. In an organization desperate for power, Carter should be the solution, with his ability to slug home runs and work the count making up for a big strikeout rate that will probably prevent him from hitting for much of an average. The off-season acquisitions of Hideki Matsui and Josh Willingham leave him temporarily blocked, but the key word there is *temporarily*.

31. Miguel Sano, 3B, Twins

The Twins have always been among the most aggressive international players in nontraditional locations like Europe and Australia, but they've increased their footprint in Latin America as well, dishing out more than $3 million in 2009 for Sano, the best player on the market. His offensive upside is immense, with tremendous raw power and sound hitting instincts. Signed as a shortstop, he has already grown enough to necessitate a slide over to third, and he has the potential to get even bigger and turn into a right fielder. Since he's projecting as a classic cleanup hitter, it's not going to matter what position he ultimately plays.

32. Dellin Betances, RHP, Yankees

Betances has thrown less than 300 innings since signing for $1 million nearly five years ago. When he returned from Tommy John surgery in 2010, everything about his game took a big step in the right direction; he maintained his mid-90s fastball while showing much-improved command and control to go with a curveball that was nearly unhittable when it was on. With a longer track record, he'd be seen as one of the best pitching prospects in the game. The Yankees' inability to secure veteran pitching in the offseason gives him a rare chance to prove himself worthy of the distinction before the organization can block him again.

33. Martin Perez, LHP, Rangers

The Rangers sent Perez to Double-A as a 19-year-old for two reasons: he had the stuff and polish to survive there, and the promotion kept him away from their High-A squad at Bakersfield, a team notorious for both high-octane offense and a poor playing environment. It proved to be too aggressive an assignment, but even while Perez's ERA approached 6.00, he still struck out more than a batter per inning. He has the maturity to turn the setback into a valuable lesson and the talent to be a front-end starter.

34. Tyler Matzek, LHP, Rockies

While Matzek's pro debut was a disappointment on a numbers level, he still showed the kind of athleticism and stuff to project as a star. With mid-90s heat, two quality breaking balls, and a changeup that already rates as average, he has the ability to be a star-level starting pitcher, but now he needs to learn how to use his natural tools to succeed. While he rarely dominated in games, scouts remain very high on him, but he will have to throw more strikes and gain more consistency with all of his pitches to fulfill their expectations.

35. Jean Segura, 2B, Angels

Segura spent the first half of the season in the shadows of Mike Trout at Low-A Cedar Rapids, but once Trout moved up, the second baseman became the most exciting player in the Midwest League. He has no weaknesses offensively: he can hit, has enough power for plenty of doubles and double-digit home runs, is a well-above-average runner, and knows the value of a walk. He could put up massive numbers in the California League this year.

36. Wilin Rosario, C, Rockies

Had he not suffered a season-ending knee injury that will also delay his 2011 season, Rosario would rank even higher on this list. He's the kind of catcher that scouts dream about, with significantly above-average power and arm strength, and he was finally tapping into those tools when the home-plate collision delayed his progress. Chris Iannetta is getting yet another chance to claim the big-league catching job, but like Inger Stevens' hitchhiker, Rosario should be visible in his rearview mirror by the end of the year.

37. Jose Iglesias, SS, Red Sox

Iglesias came from Cuba with the reputation of a defensive stalwart, and he didn't disappoint. The kind of glove man who has scouts showing up early just to watch him go through drills, Iglesias could conceivably have Gold Glove potential, but it was the bat that surprised, as he held his own at Double-A in his stateside debut, leaving many scouts believing he could hit second in a big-league lineup. If he were forced to hit ninth, he'd still be a star just for the glove, so the offense is just gravy.

38. J. P. Arencibia, C, Blue Jays

Arencibia had long had the kind of tools that excite scouts, but that ability finally showed up in the stat sheet in 2010 with a monster season at Triple-A and then a two-homer game in his big-league debut. With John Buck leaving town, the Jays signed Jose Molina to serve as Arencibia's mentor in 2011; Molina will double as an insurance policy should Arencibia need more time in the oven. The Jays' system is packed with intriguing catching prospects at the lower levels, but for now, none matches Arencibia's potential as a run producer at a position where such things are rare.

39. Stetson Allie, RHP, Pirates

With a classic power pitcher's frame, an upper-90s fastball that has already reached triple-digits, and a plus-plus slider, Allie has as high a ceiling as does any other pitching prospect around, but his track record of throwing strikes consists of a six-week stretch leading up to the draft. Prior to that, most scouts feared he was too much of a risk, considering his price tag, and would be best served by going to college. No player on this list combines freakish upside with considerable bust potential like Allie.

40. Lonnie Chisenhall, 3B, Indians

Equipped with the kind of swing that looks as if it were lifted straight out of an instructional video, Chisenhall has hit at every level, and his path toward the hot-corner job in Cleveland is wide open. He's lined up to assume a spot in the big leagues by Opening Day 2012, if not earlier, but there are fair questions about his star potential. Chisenhall's biggest strength is a lack of weaknesses: he's going to hit, but not compete for batting titles; he's going to have power, but of the 20- to 25-homers-per-year variety. That may not describe an MVP candidate, but it's still a star.

41. Derek Norris, C, Nationals

Norris's 2010 numbers need to be taken with a grain of salt, as a hand injury sapped him of his plus power until the end of year and the Arizona Fall League. He's a walk machine, as evidenced by the .419 on-base percentage that went with his .235 batting average, and while he's below-average defensively, he's good enough to stay behind the plate and be an All-Star at the position.

42. Jarrod Parker, RHP, Diamondbacks

The bad news is that Parker missed the entire 2009 season recovering from Tommy John surgery. The good news is that he looked outstanding when he returned to the mound last fall, and new general manager Kevin Towers is already talking about his being in competition for a rotation spot this spring. The GM may be getting ahead of himself, but Parker's mid-90s heat and plus slider are already back, and if the pitcher can avoid the control pitfalls that affect so many in their first years back from surgery, it shouldn't take long for him to get the big call.

43. Drew Pomeranz, RHP, Indians

As a gargantuan lefty with an above-average fastball and a tremendous curve, Pomeranz was, not surprisingly, a top-five pick in the draft. Now the question is, Which Pomeranz did the Indians get? There were plenty of Friday nights during the spring when he was the best college pitcher in the nation, but there were also a disturbing number of rough outings late, including a nine-walk meltdown in front of every important scout in the game. He could move up 25 spots on this list a year from now, or drop 50.

44. Nick Franklin, SS, Mariners

When the Mariners made Franklin a first-round pick in 2009, it was as a good-field/good-hit shortstop with little power projection due to a five-foot-ten, 165-pound frame. So, of course, he went out and led the Midwest League with 23 home runs in a year in a performance that even surprised the Mariners. No player in the game generates more leverage per pound in his swing than this guy does, and while Franklin's athletic ability might force him to second base in the end, middle infielders with power are always a rare commodity.

45. Jenrry Mejia, RHP, Mets

The Mets rushed Mejia to the big-league bullpen to begin the year, but now that he's back to being groomed as a starter, he remains the top prospect in the system by a wide margin. With mid-90s heat, a plus power breaking ball, and a short but bulky frame that's built for innings, Mejia didn't lose too much development time with his big-league stint, as he'll begin 2011 as a 21-year-old in Triple-A and as a pitcher on the verge of the majors, in a role where he'll have far more value.

46. Billy Hamilton, 2B/SS, Reds

While Hamilton has less power than any other player on the Top 101 list, he knows his role as a leadoff man. A slashing hitter with a rapidly improving approach, Hamilton has truly game-changing speed, with the ability to turn singles into doubles, and doubles into triples, and the ability to steal a base every time he gets on. If he can stick at shortstop, he's elite, but even with a permanent move to second base, he could be the kind of old-school leadoff hitter who made baseball in the 1980s so damn exciting.

47. Brett Jackson, OF, Cubs

Jackson has the tools to do it all: while reaching Double-A in his full-season debut, he compiled 14 triples, 12 home runs (with projection for more), 73 walks, and 30 stolen bases. Throw in good defense in center field, and he looks like an All-Star, but there is still plenty of debate over just how much he'll hit in the end, as his game features plenty of swing-and-miss; he might end up more Mike Cameron than a true impact player.

48. Casey Kelly, RHP, Padres

Like Martin Perez listed above, Kelly was challenged with an assignment to Double-A and had more struggles than successes. The tough lesson of 2010 was that not every strike is a good strike, as he grooved far too many pitches against hitters more advanced. The athleticism and raw stuff to be a number two starter in the big leagues remains, and scouts are still plenty high on him, as evidenced by his being the key ingredient in the deal that netted Adrian Gonzalez for the Red Sox.

49. Grant Green, SS, Athletics

As a shortstop who hit .318 with 39 doubles and 20 home runs, Green is no doubt a special prospect, but two items keep him further down the list than his statistics might appear to warrant. First, numbers in the California League must always be treated with a bit of suspicion, given the liberal offensive environment, and second, there is the defense: Green made 37 errors in just 114 games at shortstop in 2010, struggling with his throws on such a level that at times it seemed as if he had a case of the yips. If he can prove the bat is for real at Double-A this year, a move to second base won't matter, as he will still be an offensive force for a middle infielder.

50. Arodys Vizcaino, RHP, Braves

With Melky Cabrera getting fat and earning a release, Vizcaino is the key piece for the Braves in last year's Javier Vazquez deal. Vizcaino was well on his way to elite status when an elbow injury ended his season early, his last eight starts for Low-A Rome revealing a ridiculous 47-to-2 strikeout-to-walk ratio, thanks to nearly supernatural control of a low- to mid-90s fastball and an excellent curve. If he's healthy, he'll shoot up this list so fast that NORAD will be tracking him.

51. Aaron Hicks, OF, Twins

A source of frustration, Hicks still has the elite-level tools that made him the 14th overall pick in 2008, but even after repeating Low-A last year, he's still not filling up the stat sheet as much as you would expect. Making things even more mysterious is an excellent approach, but his plus raw power has yet to lead to double-digit home runs, and he's still prone to chasing breaking pitches. Hicks is a true five-tool talent and a very good center fielder with a cannon for an arm, but a move up to High-A in 2011 isn't going to do him any favors, as the Florida State League isn't exactly the place for an offensive breakout.

52. Zack Wheeler, RHP, Giants

The Giants' first-round pick in 2009, Wheeler was limited to less than 60 innings, because of blisters, during his full-season debut, so for the most part, this evaluation is based on raw tools—which remain in the special category—rather than performance. His low- to mid-90s fastball already touches 98, and his curveball and changeup project to be solid big-league offerings as well. He gets a mulligan for one year, still has an All-Star-level ceiling, and is an excellent breakout candidate for 2011.

53. Devin Mesoraco, C, Reds

A first-round pick in 2007, Mesoraco had fallen out of favor with scouts by seemingly spending much of his bonus on milkshakes. He was soft and slow with little production to make up for a uniform that bulged in all the wrong places. It's the biggest cliché in the game, but Mesoraco really did show up to spring training in the best shape of his life, and the results were immediate: he went from High-A to Triple-A while hitting .302/.377/.587 with 26 home runs, having entered the season with a career-high of nine. Despite the sudden explosion, scouts believed in what they saw, and he's lined up to take over the Reds' big-league backstopping duties by Opening Day 2012, if not before.

54. Zach Lee, RHP, Dodgers

When the Dodgers selected Lee with their first-round pick, many assumed it was a throwaway selection, as the marital drama in the front office figured to prevent any real spending from happening and Lee was seen as all but unsignable, with a commitment to play quarterback at national powerhouse LSU. Nonetheless, Los Angeles shocked the industry by signing Lee to a club-record package of more than $5 million. Needless to say, the words of Jonathan Kent apply: "One thing I do know, son, and that is you are here for a *reason*. I don't know whose reason, or whatever the reason is . . . But I do know one thing. It's *not* to score touchdowns." Lee is a fantastic athlete and a highly projectable, physical right-hander with the raw ability to shoot up the charts now that he's committed to baseball.

55. Kyle Gibson, RHP, Twins

The Twins took a risk by drafting Gibson in the first round of 2009, because a strained forearm had created enough concern to drop him out of the first ten picks. A year later, those concerns proved to be unfounded, as Gibson reached Triple-A in his first full season and should be in the big leagues at some point during the 2011 season. He's exactly what the Twins look for in a pitcher; he doesn't have overwhelming power stuff, but he throws strikes and kills more snakes than a mongoose on greenies with the grounders that result from his three average pitches. The draft is filled with opportunities to overreact, in terms of moving players both up the board and down it, and Gibson is a lesson as to why staying calm is often the best solution.

56. Craig Kimbrel, RHP, Braves

Missing bats has never been a problem for Kimbrel, but too many walks put him in Bobby Cox's doghouse early in the year. He finally started throwing strikes at the end of the season, and when that happened, his plus-plus fastball/slider combo was all but untouchable. The Braves can't relax, not with Kimbrel having been barely in command of his stuff for geologic time, but if he can hang on to the handle he found in the fall, he's going to be one of the best closers around.

57. Brett Lawrie, 2B, Blue Jays

In his second full season, the 20-year-old Lawrie hit 36 doubles and 16 triples at Double-A while adding 30 stolen bases and flirting with .300 for much of the year. That's a great season, but Lawrie does come with his questions. He is not a second baseman and seems to put little work into his defense, with multiple scouts noting his bad body language and negative demeanor. Toronto is hoping that a move from Milwaukee to his native country will turn around the attitude, as the talent is clearly there.

58. Randall Delgado, RHP, Braves

While he's not as exciting as some of the younger Latin American arms in the Braves' system, Delgado is likely to be the first to get to the big leagues and easily projects as at least a midrotation starter. Using a delivery that resulted in one scout's labeling him a "pie-thrower," Delgado throws both an above-average fastball and an above-average curve, while his changeup is big-league-average. He could end up being a bigger, stronger version of Jair Jurrjens.

59. Jordan Lyles, RHP, Astros

Lyles reached Triple-A as a teenager and is the best position player in Houston's system by a healthy margin. But despite his precocious ability to pitch at the upper levels, he's not the prospect he might seem. He's certainly as polished as a Vatican doorknob, but his ceiling is not that of an elite-level prospect. He'll get to the big leagues at a very young age, but he'll always be the type that gets by more with moxie than with stuff.

60. Brody Colvin, RHP, Phillies

The Phillies spent $900,000 on seventh-round pick Colvin in 2009. He started slow in 2010, compiling a 5.69 ERA in his first ten starts, but was among the South Atlantic League's best pitchers in the second half, with a 2.12 mark in his final 17 trips to the mound. Loaded with projection, Colvin is a broad-shouldered, six-foot-four athlete whose fastball already consistently reaches into the mid-90s , and he showed steady improvement with both his curveball and his changeup. He's a good bet to rank both at the top of the Phillies' prospect list and much higher on this list one year from now.

61. Simon Castro, RHP, Padres

A physical doppelganger of Jose Contreras, Castro scores high in the two most important categories for grading a pitching prospect, velocity and command. He places his 92-96 mph fastball in the strike zone with the precision of a surgeon, and that alone is enough to project him as a solid starting pitcher. He's young enough to improve his inconsistent slider and changeup to a degree that might allow him to be more than that.

62. Ben Revere, OF, Twins

Revere has proven that he can do two things: run and hit for average. He's a career .328 hitter who has never finished under .300 in any season, and his top-of-the-order speed allows him to cover acres of ground in center while stealing plenty of bases. Now scouts wonder if that's enough; though his approach is improving, he still needs more patience, he'll never hit for power, and his arm is a bit of a noodle, and not a robust *pappardelle*, but more of a wearied *capelli d'angelo*. Hitting and running is enough to be good, but something has to change for Revere to be great.

63. Jonathan Singleton, 1B, Phillies

The Phillies expected Singleton to play in a short-season league in 2010, but he was so good in extended spring training that they put him in the Low-A South Atlantic league by May. His OPS approached 1100 after forty games, but it was downhill from there as he fell in love with his plus-plus raw power while confronted with an infield shift, a tactic nearly unheard-of in the minor leagues. Opponents have made adjustments to him, and now it is his turn to do the same, with both strength and patience working in his favor.

64. Jordan Walden, RHP, Angels

With a violent delivery, a poor changeup, and a history of elbow issues, Walden was moved to the Angels' bullpen in 2010, and he quickly matured into a potential closer. By the time he arrived in the big leagues, he was routinely blowing away hitters with a triple-digit fastball, and while he'll set up Fernando Rodney in 2011, he should be ready to close the following year. The progress of his changeup will determine how dominant he becomes.

65. Nick Castellanos, 3B, Tigers

Castellanos had the potential to be a top-ten draft pick in 2010, but a high price tag scared teams away. The Tigers were thrilled to see him still on the board with the 44th overall pick, and his $3.45 million bonus was easier to swallow for a team without a first-round selection. While his other tools are average, Castellanos's bat is what excites scouts, as he projects to hit for both average and power at a star level.

66. Chris Dwyer, LHP, Royals

Dwyer signed for just under $1.5 million as a fourth-round pick in 2009 and reached Double-A in his full-season debut. In a system loaded with star-level southpaws, Dwyer has the most pure arm strength, routinely touching the mid-90s, along with a plus curveball that gives him a second go-to weapon. His is not the prettiest delivery, and his changeup lags behind his other offerings, but he should fit comfortably in the middle of a future Royals rotation.

67. Danny Duffy, LHP, Royals

Duffy's 2010 campaign was certainly interesting, as he began the year by retiring at the age of 21. He returned to the game by June and, within the span of three months, went from Low-A to Double-A while pitching well at each level. His average breaking ball is his worst pitch; his fastball and changeup are both plus, but considering his abrupt hiatus from the game, it's understandable that questions about his commitment persist.

68. Trey McNutt, RHP, Cubs

Arguably the scouting find of the 2009 draft, McNutt received $115,000 from the Cubs as a 32nd-round pick and spent most of 2010 forcing scouts to shake their heads and wonder where he came from. A classic power right-hander, McNutt sat at 94-95 mph for much of the year and was touching 98-99 by August. He also throws a plus slider that provided a second swing-and-miss offering. His command and control, as well as his changeup, need work, but he's already the top pitching prospect in a weak Cubs system.

69. Anthony Rizzo, 1B, Padres

The Padres got both the best pitcher (Casey Kelly) and the best hitter (Rizzo) from the Red Sox system in the Adrian Gonzalez trade, and by signing Brad Hawpe to a one-year deal, they telegraphed their expectations that Rizzo can take over by 2012. He hit for average in the past, but he traded some of that average for a significant power upgrade in 2010, with his strikeouts rising significantly in the process. Having shown that he can sometimes hit for average and at other times hit for power, Rizzo will now attempt to do both in the same season.

70. Chris Archer, RHP, Rays

Archer came over from the Indians prior to the 2009 season as part of the Mark DeRosa deal. In 2010, he stopped being projectable and started to become actualized, limiting hitters to a .200 batting average while striking out more than a batter per inning. With a cutting, low- to mid-90s fastball and a true plus slider, Archer can dominate when he's throwing strikes, but that wasn't always the case in 2010. If he can become a more efficient pitcher in 2011, he'll quickly find himself in the big leagues.

71. Alex White, RHP, Indians

The Tribe's first-round pick in 2009, White pitched well in both the Carolina and the Eastern leagues during his first full season, but scouts still aren't quite sure what he is. He succeeds primarily with a sinker/splitter combination, and while both pitches are of high quality, it's fair to wonder how much of his success is based on his unusual approach and how well he'll do as he moves up with a breaking ball that is merely average, at best. There's a wide variance of opinion about him, and this ranking represents the midpoint.

72. Kenley Jansen, RHP, Dodgers

In 2009, Jansen was a no-hit catcher with one of the best arms in the minors. Conversions like his usually take time, but after striking out more than 15 batters per nine innings in the minors, he has already reached the big leagues. Sitting at 93-97 mph with the kind of slider that normally takes years to develop, Jansen has closer potential, but like most inexperienced young arms, he needs to cut down on the walks.

73. Jake McGee, LHP, Rays

Once one of the best power lefties in the game, McGee was never quite the same after a 2008 Tommy John procedure, but a move to the bullpen midway through the 2010 season changed all that. With Rafael Soriano departing via free agency, McGee is suddenly in the thick of the Rays' closer competition, and with mid-90s heat from the left side, he's a candidate to rack up a surprising save total in 2010.

74. Michael Choice, OF, Athletics

Many saw Choice as the best hitter in the draft from a four-year college, and the A's were thrilled to nab him with the 10th overall pick. His plus-plus power showed up in his pro debut, but so did a disturbing propensity to strike out. He's a good athlete with an outside shot at sticking in center field, but even if he's forced to move to right, his power combined with average speed still makes him exciting.

75. Matt Harvey, RHP, Mets

When Harvey elected not to sign with the Angels as a third-round pick in 2007, many predicted that he could be the top pick by the time 2010 rolled around. While his first two collegiate seasons hurt his stock, he finally found his groove as a junior and ended up going seventh overall. Both his fastball and his slider rate as plus, but he was never consistent on campus, looking like an ace one Friday night and a sloppy mess the next. His delayed signing, combined with a late-season 157-pitch game, meant no pro debut until 2011, but he could be at Double-A by the end of the year.

76. Jeremy Jeffress, RHP, Royals

After being suspended three times for marijuana use, Jeffress was facing a lifetime ban with another transgression, so Milwaukee's decision to add him to the 40-man roster said as much about the fact that union members aren't tested for pot as it did his talent. Always in possession of an upper-90s fastball and plus curve, Jeffress began to harness his stuff with a move to the bullpen in 2010 and was one of the key pieces in the Zack Greinke deal. If he keeps throwing strikes, he's the best bet to assume closing duties in Kansas City once the Royals succumb to the inevitable and trade Joakim Soria.

77. Jake Odorizzi, RHP, Royals

While Odorizzi's was the least-known name in the Zack Greinke package, some insist he'll be the best player in the end. He was certainly among the best pitchers in the Midwest League in 2010, as he filled up the strike zone with a fastball that routinely touched 94-95 mph to set up a plus breaking ball. He has gone from being the best starting prospect in the Brewers' system to just a face in the crowd with the Royals, but he should still be the ace of their High-A Wilmington staff.

78. Jurickson Profar, SS, Rangers

Profar's raw numbers don't blow anyone away, but he was 17 years old in a league normally reserved for recently drafted college players. He not only held his own, but often displayed the most mature game on the field. Polished beyond his years, Profar has a patient approach at the plate and outstanding defensive fundamentals. Other than Bryce Harper, there's not another 18-year-old who's a better bet to reach the majors. The question now is how much star potential he has, since his tools aren't nearly as impressive as his polish.

79. Tanner Scheppers, RHP, Rangers

The Rangers did countless things right in 2010, but Scheppers is one thing they did wrong. The right-hander was on the verge of the big leagues, dominating with a mid- to upper-90s fastball. Texas changed direction with him at midseason, moving him to the rotation and forcing him to work on his changeup. The results were disastrous, and when he went back to relieving, he had trouble replicating his early-season success. The Rangers insist that he'll return to starting in 2011, a decision that leaves many scouts scratching their heads.

80. Matt Dominguez, 3B, Marlins

Dominguez doesn't have great offensive numbers, but any scouting discussion of him begins with the glove: he's the best defensive third baseman in the minor leagues, with true Gold Glove potential. His underwhelming stats are partly excused by his youth, and while he's not going to turn into Scott Rolen, he's not going to be Pedro Feliz, either; Dominguez should have solid power and a decent batting average. With the Marlins' current options at the hot corner lacking in redeeming features, he's suddenly on an accelerated path.

81. Luis Heredia, LHP, Pirates

The Pirates had never been big players in the Latin American market, but that changed in the summer of 2010, when they signed Heredia for $2.6 million, nearly seven times their previous high for an international talent. While all the warnings about 16-year-olds apply, Heredia is a six-foot-six lefty who already can get into the low-90s while showing a feel for spinning a breaking ball and taking something off for a changeup. He'll need plenty of innings and is at least five years away. He could be special, but he's so far from fulfilling that prophecy that we're almost observing him from the wrong end of the telescope.

82. Delino DeShields, OF/2B, Astros

We'll assume that you are a savvy-enough reader to know who this guy's father is (hint: not Darth Vader). Like dad, DeShields is a short, slashing hitter with Barry Allen speed, and, again just like pops, he'll move from the outfield to second base for his full-season debut. Junior is wider and more muscular than senior, leaving some to think that he might manifest a bit of power in the end, but even if he doesn't, he should still be a dynamic threat at the top of the batting order.

83. Tyler Skaggs, LHP, Diamondbacks

At the time of the Dan Haren trade, Skaggs was a Low-A pitcher whom few had heard of, but he was the key to the deal. Not yet a great prospect, he offers plenty of the stuff that dreams are made of, exhibiting excellent control of an 89-92 mph fastball that should tick up as his skinny six-foot-five frame fills out, as well as an advanced curve. If Skaggs fails to live up to those dreams, he will be a solid third or fourth starter, but if reaches the ceiling foreseen for him, he will be a star.

84. Dee Gordon, SS, Dodgers

Another scion of a major-league family, Dee is the progeny of Tom Gordon. Scouts have a lot of trouble wrapping their heads around Gordon. While his tools are as exciting as anyone's, he's also a soon-to-be 23-year-old with the kind of rawness normally reserved for teenagers and sashimi. With top-of-the-line speed and a solid arm, Gordon could be a great shortstop, but his poor fundamentals have led to far too many errors. He will never hit for power, so he needs to develop better leadoff skills. Some scouts think he's too far behind the curve, but others drool on the possibility of what he can be when/as/if he starts getting it.

85. Hank Conger, C, Angels

Conger should provide above-average on-base skills and power, as long as the modifier "for a catcher" is thrown in there. The good news is that his defense has improved to the point that scouts believe he can stay behind the plate and do an acceptable job. As an offense-first catcher, he's in the wrong organization, as Mike Scioscia's death grip on Jeff Mathis shows how much the manager values glove work behind the plate.

86. Yasmani Grandal, C, Reds

The 12th overall pick in the 2010 draft, Grandal had an explosive spring at the plate for Miami, showcasing switch-hitting skills with patience and plenty of power, which earned him a $2 million bonus. Defensively, he's a bit of a mixed bag, with an outstanding arm but questionable receiving skills. The biggest obstacle in Grandal's way is out of his control: at the moment he was drafted, no one else could lay claim to the title of Reds catcher of the future. With Devin Mesoraco's surprising explosion, it has become unexpectedly unclear just who is the legitimate claimant and who is the pretender.

87. Andy Oliver, LHP, Tigers

The Tigers have a fetish for big guys who throw hard. Oliver is just that, and left-handed to boot. Given just under $1.5 million dollars to sign, Oliver spent some time in the big leagues before his first full season was up, although the Tigers' thin collection of pitching talent at the upper levels played a role in that decision as well. Scouts think he can be an above-average starting pitcher if he can find some consistency with his breaking ball and changeup, and there was movement in that direction by the end of the year.

88. Christian Colon, SS, Royals

One of the most liberal spenders in the draft over the last few years, the Royals took a surprisingly conservative approach with the fourth overall pick in the draft by taking a very safe pick with little upside. Colon is an outstanding fundamental player both offensively and defensively, but he's not especially athletic, and as a significantly below-average runner, he will probably need to slide over to second base, where his defensive skills could make him a standout defender with a good batting average and a modicum of secondary skills. He's a big leaguer for sure, and likely to be a good one, but there's little chance of greatness.

89. Ian Krol, LHP, Athletics

Krol was a risky pickup for the A's: he was kicked off his high-school baseball team as a senior because of an alcohol-related incident, and his stuff was down while he was pitching for a travel team in Wisconsin. Last year, that stuff returned and brought a little something extra along with it. Krol isn't a power pitcher, but he does sit in the low-90s with his fastball, his changeup was the best in the Midwest League, and the polish continues from there with the command, control, and pitch sequencing rarely found in young lefties. His ceiling is no higher than that of a number three starter, but he could move quickly.

90. Caleb Cowart, 3B, Angels

Cowart had first-round potential in June as both a third baseman and a pitcher. While scouts generally preferred him on the mound, Cowart wanted to hit. The Angels complied with a $2.3 million bonus. As a position player, he lacks tools; he's a switch-hitter with well-above-average power and an excellent arm, as his pitching career suggests, but he's a below-average athlete and fringy defensively. The Angels are convinced that he'll hit enough to compensate for what's lacking.

91. Eduardo Escobar, SS, White Sox

Escobar has always impressed with his defensive acumen, and he finally showed some progress with the bat in 2010. Whereas he was previously a singles hitter with some average, he has added gap power. That's not enough to move him to the top of a lineup, but it is more than enough to make him an everyday player, especially given how good he is with the glove. The biggest surprise of the Arizona Fall League, where he hit .300/.353/.536, Escobar will move up this list if his power continues to grow.

92. Danny Espinosa, 2B, Nationals

With 40 home runs, 54 stolen bases, and 115 walks over the past two minor-league seasons, Espinosa has plenty of secondary skills, and he cemented his grip on this year's big-league second-base job with six September homers in "The Show." He will need to preserve his power, patience, and speed, because he'll always be a .250-ish hitter with a surplus of strikeouts. Even so, 20-20 second basemen with walks are hard to find. He underwent hand surgery after suffering a winter-ball injury in Puerto Rico, but is expected to be 100 percent come spring.

93. Tony Sanchez, C, Pirates

The Pirates saw Sanchez as having a chance at a big-league look by September 2010, but he had trouble staying healthy, although it's hard to call the June fastball to the face that ended his season after just 59 games an example of fragility. He has solid offensive skills for a catcher, with a patient approach and enough power to project as a nice six-hole hitter, but it's his defensive potential that brings his value up, as well as his off-the-charts makeup. Twelve months later, the Pirates are again hoping he can get to Pittsburgh by September.

94. Christian Yelich, OF, Marlins

The Marlins' first-round pick in June, Yelich was one of the top high-school hitters in the country, and as a Southern California product, he has already proven against high-end competition. While his tools are average aside from his bat, he has one of those intrinsically pretty left-handed swings, and the scouts who are especially high on him believe that he will develop power as his long and skinny frame fills out.

95. A. J. Cole, RHP, Nationals

Bryce Harper wasn't the only big-budget draft signing for the Nationals in 2010, as they paid $2 million for Cole after his price tag dropped him to the fourth round. He certainly fits the bill, as he's got long levers, low- to mid-90s heat, and the kind of frame that could add 25 or 30 more pounds. So much of Cole's future depends on how well his secondary pitches develop. With Stephen Strasburg pitching just enough in the big leagues to lose his prospect eligibility, Cole became the best pitching prospect in the system the moment he signed.

96. Guillermo Pimentel, OF, Mariners

One of the most prominent international signees of 2009, Pimentel looked to be worth every bit of his $2 million bonus once scouts finally got to see him play during the complex-league season in Arizona. While most seven-figure international signees are multitooled talents, Pimentel is known solely for his bat, but his raw power falls into that special category that forgives all sins, handicaps, and omissions. Like many teenage Dominicans, Pimentel needs to stop swinging at every pitch. When he does makes contact, it's like Vulcan smiting his anvil with a hammer forged from the meteor that boiled the ancient seas and rained fiery doom on the dinosaurs, scouring the earth to make way for the tragic kingdom of man.

97. Jaff Decker, OF, Padres

Decker's career batting line of .295/.435/.510 tells you everything you need to know about him as a hitter. He can hit for a high average and boasts solid power, and his extreme plate discipline sweetens the pot. The bad news is that Decker's batting line also tells you everything you need to know about him as a prospect, as he's a short, slow, bulky player limited to left field.

98. Wilmer Flores, SS, Mets

Flores continues to hit for a respectable average and added a bit of power in 2010, but everything looks much better when you notice his birth date, as he has already hit .300 in the Florida State League at 18. In short, he's going to hit, and most project him to have average power. What is not so easily projected is where he's going to play. He's certainly not a shortstop, and his lower half is already thickening up rapidly, like porridge in pants, leaving some to wonder if third base will be too small for him. With each move toward an outfield corner, his bat needs to be that much better.

99. Trayvon Robinson, OF, Dodgers

Robinson is the poster boy for the "Plate discipline really *can* be learned!" movement. Once a raw, free-swinging tools player, Robinson has not only learned a solid approach at the plate, but turned into quite the walker, finishing third in the Southern League with a .404 on-base percentage in 2010. Add gap power, plus speed, and solid defense, and his projection has gone from nice little player to future old-school leadoff hitter.

100. Anthony Ranaudo, RHP, Red Sox

Heading into the college season, Ranaudo was the consensus choice for top collegiate pitcher in the country, but he tried to pitch through some elbow problems and put up an ERA north of seven while rarely showing the kind of stuff that earned him those pre-season accolades. There was no corresponding change in his bonus demands, so he fell out of the first round before the Red Sox took a flyer on him with a supplemental pick. Taking a gig in the Cape Cod League after the selection, Ranaudo proved he was healthy with an 0.00 ERA in 30 innings, then signed for more than $2.5 million. With a low- to mid-90s fastball and plus curve that play up due to the arm angles generated by his six-foot-seven frame, Ranaudo could climb this list like King Kong if his elbow is truly sound.

101. Donavan Tate, OF, Padres

Tate has all the tools in the world; few high-school players in the last several drafts have comparable natural abilities. The son of a former NFL running back, Tate has plus-plus raw power and speed, but he entered the professional ranks as 100 percent athlete/zero percent baseball player. Prospects of that description need at-bats and repetition, but a list of injuries that would cause us to have to add a medical appendix to this volume have limited him to just 25 games since he became the second overall pick in the 2009 draft. Tate could be a superstar in five years, but he could also be racking up 200 strikeouts in Double-A, or out of baseball entirely.

Team Name Codes

CODE	TEAM	LEAGUE	AFFILIATION	NAME
ABE	Aberdeen	NYP	Orioles	IronBirds
ABQ	Albuquerque	PCL	Dodgers	Isotopes
AKR	Akron	EAS	Indians	Aeros
ALT	Altoona	EAS	Pirates	Curve
ANA	Los Angeles	AL	-	Angels
ANG	AZL Angels	AZL	Angels	-
ARI	Arizona	NL	-	Diamondbacks
ARK	Arkansas	TEX	Angels	Travelers
ASH	Asheville	SAL	Rockies	Tourists
AST	GCL Astros	GCL	Astros	-
ATH	AZL Athletics	AZL	Athletics	-
ATL	Atlanta	NL	-	Braves
AUB	Auburn	NYP	Jays	Doubledays
AUG	Augusta	SAL	Giants	GreenJackets
BAK	Bakersfield	CAL	Rangers	Blaze
BAL	Baltimore	AL	-	Orioles
BAT	Batavia	NYP	Cardinals	Muckdogs
BGR	Bowling Green	MID	Rays	Hot Rods
BIL	Billings	PIO	Reds	Mustangs
BIN	Binghamton	EAS	Mets	Mets
BIR	Birmingham	SOU	White Sox	Barons
BLJ	GCL Blue Jays	GCL	Jays	-
BLT	Beloit	MID	Twins	Snappers
BLU	Bluefield	APP	Orioles	Orioles
BNC	Burlington	APP	Royals	Royals
BOI	Boise	NOR	Cubs	Hawks
BOS	Boston	AL	-	Red Sox
BOW	Bowie	EAS	Orioles	Baysox
BRA	GCL Braves	GCL	Braves	-
BRI	Bristol	APP	White Sox	White Sox
BRO	Brooklyn	NYP	Mets	Cyclones
BRR	AZL Brewers	AZL	Brewers	-
BRV	Brevard County	FSL	Brewers	Manatees
BUF	Buffalo	INT	Mets	Bisons
BUR	Burlington	MID	Royals	Bees
CAR	Carolina	SOU	Reds	Mudcats
CAS	Casper	PIO	Rockies	Ghosts
CCH	Corpus Christi	TEX	Astros	Hooks
CDR	Cedar Rapids	MID	Angels	Kernels
CHA	Chicago	AL	-	White Sox
CHN	Chicago	NL	-	Cubs
CHR	Charlotte	INT	White Sox	Knights
CHT	Chattanooga	SOU	Dodgers	Lookouts
CIN	Cincinnati	NL	-	Reds
CLE	Cleveland	AL	-	Indians
CLN	Clinton	MID	Mariners	LumberKings
CLR	Clearwater	FSL	Phillies	Threshers
COH	Columbus	INT	Indians	Clippers
COL	Colorado	NL	-	Rockies
CRD	GCL Cardinals	GCL	Cardinals	-
CSC	Charleston	SAL	Yankees	RiverDogs
CSP	Colorado Springs	PCL	Rockies	Sky Sox
CUB	AZL Cubs	AZL	Cubs	-
DAY	Daytona	FSL	Cubs	Cubs
DEL	Delmarva	SAL	Orioles	Shorebirds
DET	Detroit	AL	-	Tigers
DGR	DSL Rangers	DSL	Rangers	-
DME	DSL Mets	DSL	Mets	-
DNV	Danville	APP	Braves	Braves
DOD	AZL Dodgers	AZL	Dodgers	-
DOD	DSL Dodgers	DSL	Dodgers	Dodgers
DUN	Dunedin	FSL	Jays	Blue Jays
DUR	Durham	INT	Rays	Bulls
DYT	Dayton	MID	Reds	Dragons
ELZ	Elizabethton	APP	Twins	Twins
ERI	Erie	EAS	Tigers	SeaWolves
EUG	Eugene	NOR	Padres	Emeralds
EVE	Everett	NOR	Mariners	AquaSox
FLO	Florida	NL	-	Marlins
FRD	Frederick	CAR	Orioles	Keys
FRE	Fresno	PCL	Giants	Grizzlies
FRI	Frisco	TEX	Rangers	RoughRiders
FTM	Fort Myers	FSL	Twins	Miracle
FTW	Fort Wayne	MID	Padres	TinCaps
GIA	AZL Giants	AZL	Giants	-
GRB	Greensboro	SAL	Marlins	Grasshoppers
GRF	Great Falls	PIO	White Sox	Voyagers
GRL	Great Lakes	MID	Dodgers	Loons
GRN	Greenville	SAL	Red Sox	Drive
GRV	Greeneville	APP	Astros	Astros
GWN	Gwinnett	INT	Braves	Braves
HAG	Hagerstown	SAL	Nationals	Suns
HAR	Harrisburg	EAS	Nationals	Senators
HDS	High Desert	CAL	Mariners	Mavericks
HEL	Helena	PIO	Brewers	Brewers
HIC	Hickory	SAL	Rangers	Crawdads
HOU	Houston	NL	-	Astros
HUD	Hudson Valley	NYP	Rays	Renegades
HUN	Huntsville	SOU	Brewers	Stars
IDA	Idaho Falls	PIO	Royals	Chukars
IND	AZL Indians	AZL	Indians	-
IND	Indianapolis	INT	Pirates	Indians
IOW	Iowa	PCL	Cubs	Cubs
JAM	Jamestown	NYP	Marlins	Jammers
JAX	Jacksonville	SOU	Marlins	Suns
JCY	Johnson City	APP	Cardinals	Cardinals

CODE	TEAM	LEAGUE	AFFILIATION	NAME
JUP	Jupiter	FSL	Marlins	Hammerheads
KAN	Kannapolis	SAL	White Sox	Intimidators
KCA	Kansas City	AL	-	Royals
KIN	Kinston	CAR	Indians	Indians
KNC	Kane County	MID	Athletics	Cougars
KNG	Kingsport	APP	Mets	Mets
LAK	Lakeland	FSL	Tigers	Tigers
LAN	Los Angeles	NL	-	Dodgers
LEH	Lehigh Valley	INT	Phillies	IronPigs
LEL	Lake Elsinore	CAL	Padres	Storm
LEX	Lexington	SAL	Astros	Legends
LKC	Lake County	MID	Indians	Captains
LNC	Lancaster	CAL	Astros	JetHawks
LNS	Lansing	MID	Jays	Lugnuts
LOU	Louisville	INT	Reds	Bats
LOW	Lowell	NYP	Red Sox	Spinners
LVG	Las Vegas	PCL	Jays	51s
LWD	Lakewood	SAL	Phillies	BlueClaws
LYN	Lynchburg	CAR	Reds	Hillcats
MEM	Memphis	PCL	Cardinals	Redbirds
MHV	Mahoning Valley	NYP	Indians	Scrappers
MID	Midland	TEX	Athletics	RockHounds
MIL	Milwaukee	NL	-	Brewers
MIN	Minnesota	AL	-	Twins
MIS	Mississippi	SOU	Braves	Braves
MNT	Montgomery	SOU	Rays	Biscuits
MOB	Mobile	SOU	Diamondbacks	BayBears
MOD	Modesto	CAL	Rockies	Nuts
MRL	GCL Marlins	GCL	Marlins	-
MRN	AZL Mariners	AZL	Mariners	-
MSO	Missoula	PIO	Diamondbacks	Osprey
MTS	GCL Mets	GCL	Mets	-
MYR	Myrtle Beach	CAR	Braves	Pelicans
NAS	Nashville	PCL	Brewers	Sounds
NAT	GCL Nationals	GCL	Nationals	-
NBR	New Britain	EAS	Twins	Rock Cats
NHP	New Hampshire	EAS	Jays	Fisher Cats
NOR	Norfolk	INT	Orioles	Tides
NWA	Northwest Arkansas	TEX	Royals	Naturals
NWO	New Orleans	PCL	Marlins	Zephyrs
NYA	New York	AL	-	Yankees
NYN	New York	NL	-	Mets
OAK	Oakland	AL	-	Athletics
OGD	Ogden	PIO	Dodgers	Raptors
OKL	Oklahoma City	PCL	Rangers	RedHawks
OMA	Omaha	PCL	Royals	Royals
ONE	Connecticut	NYP	Tigers	Tigers
ORI	GCL Orioles	GCL	Orioles	-
ORM	Orem	PIO	Angels	Owlz
PAW	Pawtucket	INT	Red Sox	Red Sox
PCH	Charlotte	FSL	Rays	Stone Crabs
PDR	AZL Padres	AZL	Padres	-
PEO	Peoria	MID	Cubs	Chiefs
PHI	Philadelphia	NL	-	Phillies
PHL	GCL Phillies	GCL	Phillies	-

CODE	TEAM	LEAGUE	AFFILIATION	NAME
PIR	GCL Pirates	GCL	Pirates	-
PIT	Pittsburgh	NL	-	Pirates
PMB	Palm Beach	FSL	Cardinals	Cardinals
PME	Portland	EAS	Red Sox	Sea Dogs
POR	Portland	PCL	Padres	Beavers
POT	Potomac	CAR	Nationals	Nationals
PRI	Princeton	APP	Rays	Rays
PUL	Pulaski	APP	Mariners	Mariners
PZA	Minatitlan	MEX	-	Petroleros
QUD	Quad Cities	MID	Cardinals	River Bandits
RAY	GCL Rays	GCL	Rays	-
RCU	Rancho Cucamonga	CAL	Angels	Quakes
REA	Reading	EAS	Phillies	Phillies
RIC	Richmond	EAS	Giants	Squirrels
RNG	AZL Rangers	AZL	Rangers	-
RNO	Reno	PCL	Diamondbacks	Aces
ROC	Rochester	INT	Twins	Wings
ROM	Rome	SAL	Braves	Braves
ROU	Round Rock	PCL	Astros	Express
ROY	AZL Royals	AZL	Royals	-
RSX	GCL Red Sox	GCL	Red Sox	-
SAC	Sacramento	PCL	Athletics	River Cats
SAN	San Antonio	TEX	Padres	Missions
SAV	Savannah	SAL	Mets	Sand Gnats
SBN	South Bend	MID	Diamondbacks	Silver Hawks
SBR	Inland Empire	CAL	Dodgers	66ers
SCO	State College	NYP	Pirates	Spikes
SDN	San Diego	NL	-	Padres
SEA	Seattle	AL	-	Mariners
SFD	Springfield	TEX	Cardinals	Cardinals
SFN	San Fransisco	NL	-	Giants
SJO	San Jose	CAL	Giants	Giants
SLC	Salt Lake	PCL	Angels	Bees
SLM	Salem	CAR	Red Sox	Red Sox
SLN	St. Louis	NL	-	Cardinals
SLO	Salem-Keizer	NOR	Giants	Volcanoes
SLU	St. Lucie	FSL	Mets	Mets
SPO	Spokane	NOR	Rangers	Indians
STA	Staten Island	NYP	Yankees	Yankees
STO	Stockton	CAL	Athletics	Ports
SWB	Scranton/Wilkes-Barre	INT	Yankees	Yankees
SYR	Syracuse	INT	Nationals	Chiefs
TAC	Tacoma	PCL	Mariners	Rainiers
TAM	Tampa	FSL	Yankees	Yankees
TBA	Tampa Bay	AL	-	Rays
TCV	Tri-City	NYP	Astros	ValleyCats
TEN	Tennessee	SOU	Cubs	Smokies
TEX	Texas	AL	-	Rangers
TGR	GCL Tigers	GCL	Tigers	-
TOL	Toledo	INT	Tigers	Mud Hens
TOR	Toronto	AL	-	Blue Jays
TRI	Tri-City	NOR	Rockies	Devils
TRN	Trenton	EAS	Yankees	Thunder
TUL	Tulsa	TEX	Rockies	Drillers
TWI	GCL Twins	GCL	Twins	-

CODE	TEAM	LEAGUE	AFFILIATION	NAME
VAN	Vancouver	NOR	Athletics	Canadians
VER	Vermont	NYP	Nationals	Lake Monsters
VIS	Visalia	CAL	Diamondbacks	Rawhide
VTB	VSL Rays	VSL	Rays	-
WAS	Washington	NL	-	Nationals
WIL	Wilmington	CAR	Royals	Blue Rocks
WIS	Wisconsin	MID	Brewers	Rattlers
WMI	West Michigan	MID	Tigers	Whitecaps
WNS	Winston-Salem	CAR	White Sox	Dash
WPT	Williamsport	NYP	Phillies	Crosscutters
WTN	West Tenn.	SOU	Mariners	Diamond Jaxx
WVA	West Virginia	SAL	Pirates	Power
YAK	Yakima	NOR	Diamondbacks	Bears
YAN	GCL Yankees	GCL	Yankees	-

PECOTA Leaderboards

BATTERS

Batting Average

RANK	NAME	TEAM	AVG
1	Albert Pujols	SLN	.321
2	Joe Mauer	MIN	.317
T3	Ichiro Suzuki	SEA	.311
T3	Matt Holliday	SLN	.311
5	Hanley Ramirez	FLO	.309
T6	Pablo Sandoval	SFN	.307
T6	Miguel Cabrera	DET	.307
8	Ryan Braun	MIL	.303
9	Joey Votto	CIN	.302
10	Kendry Morales	ANA	.301
T11	Robinson Cano	NYA	.299
T11	Martin Prado	ATL	.299
T13	David Wright	NYN	.296
T13	Dustin Pedroia	BOS	.296
15	Howie Kendrick	ANA	.294
T16	Jose Reyes	NYN	.293
T16	Josh Hamilton	TEX	.293
T16	Magglio Ordonez	DET	.293
19	Freddy Sanchez	SFN	.292
20	Alberto Callaspo	ANA	.291

Home Runs

RANK	NAME	TEAM	HR
1	Albert Pujols	SLN	41
2	Ryan Howard	PHI	40
T3	Prince Fielder	MIL	36
T3	Miguel Cabrera	DET	36
T3	Adam Dunn	CHA	36
6	Adrian Gonzalez	BOS	34
T7	Mark Reynolds	BAL	32
T7	Alex Rodriguez	NYA	32
T9	David Ortiz	BOS	31
T9	Dan Uggla	ATL	31
T9	Carlos Pena	CHN	31
T9	Mark Teixeira	NYA	31
13	Ryan Braun	MIL	30
T14	Joey Votto	CIN	29
T14	Matt Holliday	SLN	29
T16	Paul Konerko	CHA	28
T16	Justin Morneau	MIN	28
T16	Nelson Cruz	TEX	28
T19	Alfonso Soriano	CHN	27
T19	Hanley Ramirez	FLO	27

RBI

RANK	NAME	TEAM	RBI
1	Albert Pujols	SLN	121
2	Miguel Cabrera	DET	109
3	Ryan Howard	PHI	107
4	Ryan Braun	MIL	105
T5	Matt Holliday	SLN	103
T5	Prince Fielder	MIL	103
7	Adrian Gonzalez	BOS	100
8	Hanley Ramirez	FLO	98
T9	Mark Teixeira	NYA	96
T9	David Wright	NYN	96
11	Adam Dunn	CHA	95
T12	Joey Votto	CIN	93
T12	Dan Uggla	ATL	93
T14	Evan Longoria	TBA	90
T14	Alex Rodriguez	NYA	90
16	Ryan Zimmerman	WAS	89
T17	Pablo Sandoval	SFN	88
T17	Carlos Lee	HOU	88
T17	Justin Morneau	MIN	88
T17	Hunter Pence	HOU	88

Runs

RANK	NAME	TEAM	R
1	Albert Pujols	SLN	112
T2	Prince Fielder	MIL	102
T2	Miguel Cabrera	DET	102
4	Matt Holliday	SLN	99
5	Adrian Gonzalez	BOS	98
6	Hanley Ramirez	FLO	97
T7	Mark Teixeira	NYA	96
T7	Ryan Braun	MIL	96
T7	David Wright	NYN	96
T7	Ryan Howard	PHI	96
T11	Adam Dunn	CHA	92
T11	Chase Utley	PHI	92
13	Joey Votto	CIN	91
14	Dan Uggla	ATL	90
15	Ichiro Suzuki	SEA	89
16	Nick Markakis	BAL	88
T17	Alex Rodriguez	NYA	87
T17	Ryan Zimmerman	WAS	87
T19	Bobby Abreu	ANA	86
T19	Evan Longoria	TBA	86

Stolen Bases, Major Leaguers

RANK	NAME	TEAM	SB
1	Juan Pierre	CHA	51
2	Carl Crawford	BOS	44
T3	Jose Reyes	NYN	42
T3	B.J. Upton	TBA	42
T3	Jacoby Ellsbury	BOS	42
6	Michael Bourn	HOU	41
7	Rajai Davis	TOR	40
8	Chone Figgins	SEA	39
9	Brett Gardner	NYA	37
T10	Ichiro Suzuki	SEA	35
T10	Hanley Ramirez	FLO	35
T12	Elvis Andrus	TEX	34
T12	Nyjer Morgan	WAS	34
14	Jimmy Rollins	PHI	33
15	Brian Roberts	BAL	30

Stolen Bases, Minor Leaguers

RANK	NAME	TEAM	SB
1	Derrick Robinson	KCA	47
2	Darin Mastroianni	TOR	37
3	Eric Young	COL	34
4	Devaris Gordon	LAN	33
T5	Drew Stubbs	CIN	32
T5	Corey Wimberly	PIT	32
T7	Matt Young	ATL	31
T7	Jarrod Dyson	KCA	31
T7	Tony Campana	CHN	31
T7	Eugenio Velez	SFN	31

On-base Percentage

RANK	NAME	TEAM	OBP
1	Albert Pujols	SLN	.429
T2	Nick Johnson	NYA	.402
T2	Joe Mauer	MIN	.402
T4	Prince Fielder	MIL	.394
T4	Joey Votto	CIN	.394
6	Chipper Jones	ATL	.392
7	Miguel Cabrera	DET	.390
8	Matt Holliday	SLN	.389
9	Manny Ramirez	CHA	.387
T10	Lance Berkman	SLN	.386
T10	Chase Utley	PHI	.386
T10	Kevin Youkilis	BOS	.386
13	Hanley Ramirez	FLO	.383
14	Jack Cust	SEA	.381
T15	Adrian Gonzalez	BOS	.379
T15	Shin-Soo Choo	CLE	.379
T15	David Wright	NYN	.379
18	Todd Helton	COL	.376
19	Mark Teixeira	NYA	.375
20	Adam Dunn	CHA	.372

Isolated Slugging

RANK	NAME	TEAM	ISO
1	Albert Pujols	SLN	.296
2	Ryan Howard	PHI	.264
3	Adam Dunn	CHA	.255
4	Russell Branyan	SEA	.253
5	Miguel Cabrera	DET	.250
6	Prince Fielder	MIL	.248
7	Carlos Pena	CHN	.243
8	Nelson Cruz	TEX	.240
T9	David Ortiz	BOS	.238
T9	Mark Reynolds	BAL	.238
T11	Alex Rodriguez	NYA	.233
T11	Mike Napoli	ANA	.233
13	Joey Votto	CIN	.231
14	Adrian Gonzalez	BOS	.229
T15	Justin Morneau	MIN	.228
T15	Ryan Braun	MIL	.228
17	Jose Bautista	TOR	.226
T18	Matt Holliday	SLN	.225
T18	Mark Teixeira	NYA	.225
20	Dan Uggla	ATL	.221

True Average

RANK	NAME	TEAM	TAv
1	Albert Pujols	SLN	.344
2	Miguel Cabrera	DET	.320
3	Joey Votto	CIN	.317
4	Prince Fielder	MIL	.316
5	Matt Holliday	SLN	.314
6	Ryan Braun	MIL	.311
7	Hanley Ramirez	FLO	.310
8	Kevin Youkilis	BOS	.309
T9	Joe Mauer	MIN	.306
T9	Alex Rodriguez	NYA	.306
11	Mark Teixeira	NYA	.305
12	Adrian Gonzalez	BOS	.304
T13	Adam Dunn	CHA	.303
T13	Chase Utley	PHI	.303
15	Ryan Howard	PHI	.302
T16	Justin Morneau	MIN	.301
T16	Troy Tulowitzki	COL	.301
T18	Josh Hamilton	TEX	.300
T18	David Wright	NYN	.300
20	Manny Ramirez	CHA	.299

Wins Above Replacement Player, American League

RANK	NAME	TEAM	WARP
T1	Evan Longoria	TBA	4.6
T1	Alex Rodriguez	NYA	4.6
3	Joe Mauer	MIN	4.4
T4	Miguel Cabrera	DET	4.0
T4	Adrian Gonzalez	BOS	4.0
T6	Mark Teixeira	NYA	3.9
T6	Kevin Youkilis	BOS	3.9
8	Nelson Cruz	TEX	3.5

9	Robinson Cano	NYA	3.4
10	Carl Crawford	BOS	3.2

Wins Above Replacement Player, National League

RANK	NAME	TEAM	WARP
1	Albert Pujols	SLN	7.7
2	Ryan Braun	MIL	4.9
3	Hanley Ramirez	FLO	4.8
T4	Chase Utley	PHI	4.7
T4	Troy Tulowitzki	COL	4.7
6	Matt Holliday	SLN	4.6
T7	David Wright	NYN	4.1
T7	Brian McCann	ATL	4.1
T7	Joey Votto	CIN	4.1
10	Prince Fielder	MIL	3.9

Wins Above Replacement Player, Catcher

RANK	NAME	TEAM	WARP
1	Joe Mauer	MIN	4.4
2	Brian McCann	ATL	4.1
3	Geovany Soto	CHN	3.1
4	Victor Martinez	DET	2.7
T5	Russell Martin	NYA	2.4
T5	Chris Iannetta	COL	2.4
7	Matt Wieters	BAL	2.2
8	Jorge Posada	NYA	2.1
9	Carlos Ruiz	PHI	2.0
10	Miguel Montero	ARI	1.7

Wins Above Replacement Player, First Base

RANK	NAME	TEAM	WARP
1	Albert Pujols	SLN	7.7
2	Joey Votto	CIN	4.1
T3	Adrian Gonzalez	BOS	4.0
T3	Miguel Cabrera	DET	4.0
T5	Kevin Youkilis	BOS	3.9
T5	Mark Teixeira	NYA	3.9
T5	Prince Fielder	MIL	3.9
T8	Ryan Howard	PHI	3.4
T8	Lance Berkman	SLN	3.4
10	Adam Dunn	CHA	2.8

Wins Above Replacement Player, Second Base

RANK	NAME	TEAM	WARP
1	Chase Utley	PHI	4.7
2	Robinson Cano	NYA	3.4
3	Ian Kinsler	TEX	3.2
4	Dan Uggla	ATL	3.0
5	Dustin Pedroia	BOS	2.5
6	Kelly Johnson	ARI	2.2
7	Rickie Weeks	MIL	2.0
8	Brandon Phillips	CIN	1.9
9	Aaron Hill	TOR	1.8
10	Carlos Guillen	DET	1.7

Wins Above Replacement Player, Third Base

RANK	NAME	TEAM	WARP
T1	Evan Longoria	TBA	4.6
T1	Alex Rodriguez	NYA	4.6
3	David Wright	NYN	4.1
4	Ryan Zimmerman	WAS	3.8
5	Adrian Beltre	TEX	3.1
6	Pablo Sandoval	SFN	2.9
7	Chipper Jones	ATL	2.8
8	Scott Rolen	CIN	2.5
9	Mark Reynolds	BAL	2.4
10	Ian Stewart	COL	2.3

Wins Above Replacement Player, Shortstop

RANK	NAME	TEAM	WARP
1	Hanley Ramirez	FLO	4.8
2	Troy Tulowitzki	COL	4.7
3	Yunel Escobar	TOR	3.2
4	Rafael Furcal	LAN	2.8
5	Stephen Drew	ARI	2.5
6	Jose Reyes	NYN	2.4
T7	Alexei Ramirez	CHA	2.2
T7	Jimmy Rollins	PHI	2.2
9	Jason Bartlett	SDN	2.0
10	J.J. Hardy	BAL	1.9

Wins Above Replacement Player, Left Field

RANK	NAME	TEAM	WARP
1	Ryan Braun	MIL	4.9
2	Matt Holliday	SLN	4.6
3	Carl Crawford	BOS	3.2
4	Jason Bay	NYN	2.9
5	Josh Hamilton	TEX	2.7
6	Manny Ramirez	CHA	2.5
7	Seth Smith	COL	2.3
T8	Ryan Ludwick	SDN	2.0
T8	Alfonso Soriano	CHN	2.0
10	Alex Gordon	KCA	1.9

Wins Above Replacement Player, Center Field

RANK	NAME	TEAM	WARP
1	Carlos Beltran	NYN	2.9
2	Curtis Granderson	NYA	2.8
3	Torii Hunter	ANA	2.4
4	Matt Kemp	LAN	2.3
T5	Grady Sizemore	CLE	2.1
T5	Adam Jones	BAL	2.1
T5	Denard Span	MIN	2.1
T8	Andrew McCutchen	PIT	2.0
T8	Chris Young	ARI	2.0
10	Shane Victorino	PHI	1.9

Wins Above Replacement Player, Right Field

RANK	NAME	TEAM	WARP
1	Nelson Cruz	TEX	3.5
2	Jayson Werth	WAS	3.1
3	Jay Bruce	CIN	2.9
4	Nick Swisher	NYA	2.8
5	Hunter Pence	HOU	2.7
T6	Carlos Quentin	CHA	2.2
T6	Justin Upton	ARI	2.2
T6	Andre Ethier	LAN	2.2
T9	Ben Zobrist	TBA	2.1
T9	J.D. Drew	BOS	2.1

Wins Above Replacement Player, Rookies

RANK	NAME	TEAM	WARP
1	Matt Carpenter	SLN	2.4
T2	Jesus Montero	NYA	2.1
T2	Tyler Flowers	CHA	2.1
T4	Mike Moustakas	KCA	2.0
T4	Robinson Chirinos	CHN	2.0
6	J.P. Arencibia	TOR	1.9
T7	Mike McCoy	TOR	1.8
T7	Derek Norris	WAS	1.8
T7	Ryan Rohlinger	SFN	1.8
10	Brad Emaus	NYN	1.7

Wins Above Replacement Player, Top Risers

RANK	NAME	TEAM	2010 WARP	2011 PREDICTED	CHANGE
1	Grady Sizemore	CLE	-0.7	2.1	2.8
2	Matt LaPorta	CLE	-2.3	0.2	2.5
T3	Ryan Rohlinger	SFN	-0.4	1.8	2.2
T3	J.P. Arencibia	TOR	-0.3	1.9	2.2
T3	Jason Bay	NYN	0.7	2.9	2.2
T6	Tyler Flowers	CHA	0.0	2.1	2.1
T6	Dan Johnson	TBA	0.2	2.3	2.1
T8	Carlos Beltran	NYN	0.9	2.9	2.0
T8	Pablo Sandoval	SFN	0.9	2.9	2.0
T8	Carlos Santana	CLE	1.9	3.9	2.0
T8	Mike Lowell	BOS	-0.3	1.7	2.0
T8	Chris Iannetta	COL	0.4	2.4	2.0
T8	Lance Berkman	SLN	1.4	3.4	2.0
14	Brandon Wood	ANA	-2.0	-0.1	1.9

Wins Above Replacement Player, Greatest Declines

RANK	NAME	TEAM	2010 WARP	2011 PREDICTED	CHANGE
1	Josh Hamilton	TEX	6.9	2.7	4.2
2	Aubrey Huff	SFN	5.8	1.7	4.1
3	Adrian Beltre	TEX	6.9	3.1	3.8
T4	Austin Jackson	DET	3.6	0.0	3.6
T4	Angel Pagan	NYN	4.6	1.0	3.6
6	Jose Bautista	TOR	5.4	2.0	3.4
7	Carl Crawford	BOS	6.4	3.2	3.2
T8	Andres Torres	SFN	4.9	1.8	3.1
T8	Alexei Ramirez	CHA	5.3	2.2	3.1
T8	Daric Barton	OAK	3.8	0.7	3.1
T11	Alex Gonzalez	ATL	4.1	1.2	2.9
T11	Drew Stubbs	CIN	3.9	1.0	2.9
13	Rickie Weeks	MIL	4.6	2.0	2.6
14	Paul Konerko	CHA	4.7	2.2	2.5
15	Joey Votto	CIN	6.5	4.1	2.4

PITCHERS

Wins

RANK	NAME	TEAM	W
T1	Felix Hernandez	SEA	15
T1	CC Sabathia	NYA	15
T1	Dan Haren	ANA	15
T4	Roy Oswalt	PHI	14
T4	Justin Verlander	DET	14
T4	Johan Santana	NYN	14
T4	Jered Weaver	ANA	14
T4	Matt Cain	SFN	14
T4	Roy Halladay	PHI	14
T10	Ted Lilly	LAN	13
T10	Cole Hamels	PHI	13
T10	Javier Vazquez	FLO	13
T10	Cliff Lee	PHI	13
T10	Bronson Arroyo	CIN	13
T10	James Shields	TBA	13
T10	Barry Zito	SFN	13
T10	Derek Lowe	ATL	13
T18	John Lackey	BOS	12
T18	Ubaldo Jimenez	COL	12
T18	Tim Hudson	ATL	12

Strikeouts

RANK	NAME	TEAM	K
1	Felix Hernandez	SEA	204
2	Dan Haren	ANA	200
3	CC Sabathia	NYA	199
4	Justin Verlander	DET	198
5	Javier Vazquez	FLO	197
6	Tim Lincecum	SFN	190
7	Roy Halladay	PHI	183
T8	Jered Weaver	ANA	177
T8	Cole Hamels	PHI	177
10	Jon Lester	BOS	173
11	James Shields	TBA	171
12	Johan Santana	NYN	169
13	A.J. Burnett	NYA	168
T14	Josh Beckett	BOS	167
T14	Ubaldo Jimenez	COL	167
16	Zack Greinke	MIL	166
17	Matt Cain	SFN	165
T18	Ted Lilly	LAN	161
T18	Chad Billingsley	LAN	161
20	Ervin Santana	ANA	160

Earned Run Average (min. 125 IP)

RANK	NAME	TEAM	ERA
1	Felix Hernandez	SEA	2.64
2	Tim Lincecum	SFN	2.74
3	Roy Halladay	PHI	3.05
4	Johan Santana	NYN	3.09
5	Jered Weaver	ANA	3.12
6	Adam Wainwright	SLN	3.14
7	Cliff Lee	PHI	3.17
8	Dan Haren	ANA	3.19
9	Chris Carpenter	SLN	3.21
10	Jake Peavy	CHA	3.24
11	CC Sabathia	NYA	3.26
T12	Josh Johnson	FLO	3.28
T12	Clayton Kershaw	LAN	3.28
14	Justin Verlander	DET	3.32
15	Matt Cain	SFN	3.35
16	Roy Oswalt	PHI	3.44
17	David Price	TBA	3.46
18	Hiroki Kuroda	LAN	3.47
19	Jon Lester	BOS	3.48
20	Ted Lilly	LAN	3.51

Walks plus Hits per Inning Pitched (min. 125 IP)

RANK	NAME	TEAM	WHIP
1	Roy Halladay	PHI	1.11
2	Felix Hernandez	SEA	1.13
T3	Cliff Lee	PHI	1.15
T3	Dan Haren	ANA	1.15
T5	Johan Santana	NYN	1.18
T5	Tim Lincecum	SFN	1.18
T5	Jered Weaver	ANA	1.18
T5	Ted Lilly	LAN	1.18
T9	Cole Hamels	PHI	1.19
T9	CC Sabathia	NYA	1.19
T9	Roy Oswalt	PHI	1.19
T9	Chris Carpenter	SLN	1.19
T13	Adam Wainwright	SLN	1.21
T13	Jake Peavy	CHA	1.21
15	Zack Greinke	MIL	1.23
T16	Shaun Marcum	MIL	1.24
T16	Matt Cain	SFN	1.24
T18	Hiroki Kuroda	LAN	1.25
T18	Justin Verlander	DET	1.25
20	Javier Vazquez	FLO	1.26

Saves

RANK	NAME	TEAM	SV
1	Joe Nathan	MIN	40
2	Francisco Rodriguez	NYN	35
3	Francisco Cordero	CIN	33
4	Kevin Gregg	BAL	30
4	Brian Wilson	SFN	30
6	Mariano Rivera	NYA	29
6	Jonathan Papelbon	BOS	29
8	Heath Bell	SDN	27
8	Bobby Jenks	BOS	27
10	Joakim Soria	KCA	26
11	Brian Fuentes	MIN	25
12	Rafael Soriano	NYA	23
13	Jonathan Broxton	LAN	22
14	Jose Valverde	DET	20
14	Ryan Franklin	SLN	20
16	Trevor Hoffman	MIL	17
16	Carlos Marmol	CHN	17
18	David Aardsma	SEA	16
19	Brandon Lyon	HOU	15
19	Brad Lidge	PHI	15

Strikeouts per Nine Innings (min. 125 IP)

RANK	NAME	TEAM	SO9
1	Tim Lincecum	SFN	9.6
2	Yovani Gallardo	MIL	9.5
3	Jonathan Sanchez	SFN	9.0
4	Clayton Kershaw	LAN	8.9
5	Max Scherzer	DET	8.8
5	Javier Vazquez	FLO	8.8
5	Edinson Volquez	CIN	8.8
8	Jake Peavy	CHA	8.7
8	Josh Johnson	FLO	8.7
10	Ricky Nolasco	FLO	8.5
10	Jon Lester	BOS	8.5
12	Justin Verlander	DET	8.4
13	Zack Greinke	MIL	8.3
13	Francisco Liriano	MIN	8.3
15	Felix Hernandez	SEA	8.2
16	A.J. Burnett	NYA	8.1
16	Jered Weaver	ANA	8.1
18	Josh Beckett	BOS	8.0
18	Daisuke Matsuzaka	BOS	8.0
18	Cole Hamels	PHI	8.0

Wins Above Replacement Player

RANK	NAME	TEAM	WARP
T1	Felix Hernandez	SEA	6.8
T1	Roy Halladay	PHI	6.8
3	CC Sabathia	NYA	6.7
4	Tim Lincecum	SFN	6.0
5	Cliff Lee	PHI	5.8
6	Dan Haren	ANA	5.6
7	Justin Verlander	DET	5.5
T8	Roy Oswalt	PHI	5.3
T8	Matt Cain	SFN	5.3
10	Jered Weaver	ANA	5.2
11	Jake Peavy	CHA	5.0
12	Adam Wainwright	SLN	4.9
13	Cole Hamels	PHI	4.8
14	Ubaldo Jimenez	COL	4.7
T15	Ted Lilly	LAN	4.6
T15	Jon Lester	BOS	4.6
T15	Zack Greinke	MIL	4.6
18	Javier Vazquez	FLO	4.4
19	Bronson Arroyo	CIN	4.3
20	Brandon Webb	TEX	4.2

Wins Above Replacement Player, Rookies

RANK	NAME	TEAM	WARP
1	Aroldis Chapman	CIN	2.9
2	Jeremy Hellickson	TBA	2.8
3	Kyle Gibson	MIN	2.3
4	Joseph Gardner	CLE	2.1
T5	Mike Minor	ATL	2.0
T5	Sam LeCure	CIN	2.0
T5	Austin Hyatt	PHI	2.0
8	Mark Rogers	MIL	1.9
T9	Adam Warren	NYA	1.8
T9	Elih Villanueva	FLO	1.8

Contributors

Tommy Bennett writes the "Expanded Horizons" column for Baseball Prospectus, which encourages heterodox thinking from a numbers-based perspective. He is fascinated by data visualization and what baseball can teach us about everyday life. Before joining BP, Tommy was the editor of Beyond the Box Score. His writing has been featured in many other print and online publications. He is a law student and lives in Brooklyn.

Cliff Corcoran is a regular contributor to SI.com and a coauthor of "The Pinstriped Bible." This marks his sixth year as a writer or an editor of the Baseball Prospectus annual. He has also contributed to the Baseball Prospectus books *Mind Game* and *It Ain't Over 'Til It's Over* and Bronx Banter's *Lasting Yankee Stadium Memories* and edited Howard Bryant's *Juicing the Game* and Brad Snyder's *Well-Paid Slave*, among others. A stay-at-home dad during regular business hours, he lives in northern New Jersey with a wife, daughter, and dog, all of whom he's pretty sure are out of his league.

Ken Funck contributes his "Changing Speeds" column to BaseballProspectus.com when he isn't busy managing various computer systems for the University of Wisconsin. Ken lives outside Madison (America's greatest small city) with his ever-encouraging wife Stephanie, their children Max and Abby, two cats, two dogs, two kayaks, and a canoe. This is Ken's second year contributing to the annual, and his umpteenth year watching teams other than his beloved Cubs play in the World Series.

Steven Goldman is the editor in chief of Baseball Prospectus. In addition to writing the historical analysis column "You Could Look It Up" and numerous other features for BaseballProspectus.com, he has edited the BP-authored books *Mind Game* and *It Ain't Over 'Til It's Over* and has contributed to *Baseball Between the Numbers*. Steven is also the author of the biography *Forging Genius: The Making of Casey Stengel*. He has contributed to the BP annual since 2005 and has been coeditor of the last five editions. He is the creator of the long-running Pinstripedbible.com for the YES Network, cited by *Sports Illustrated* as "an essential online baseball destination," and has appeared on several of the network's television programs. He was a baseball columnist for the *New York Sun* from 2004 to 2008, and his work has appeared in *Yankees Magazine*, *The Village Voice*, *Commentary*, *American Heritage*, and other publications. In his spare time, he publishes original songs at casualobserver music.net. Steven lives in New Jersey with his wife, two children, and two cats named after famous Republicans.

Kevin Goldstein writes about scouting and player development (for the most part) at Baseball Prospectus. With contacts at every level of the game, he covers the systems from top to bottom for all 30 teams and is one of the most respected names in prospect evaluation. He is also the host and producer of "Up and In: The Baseball Prospectus Podcast" with cohost Jason Parks. When he's not watching or writing about baseball, he's thinking or dreaming about baseball, but he also finds time to be a movie snob and play obscure Japanese video games. He lives among the corn in DeKalb, Illinois, with the love of his life, Margaret, kids Xander and Cameron, as well as cats Pickles and Underpants and Otto The Pit Bull, the official dog of Baseball Prospectus.

Jay Jaffe is the founder of the 10-year-old Futility Infielder Web site (www.futilityinfielder.com), one of the oldest baseball blogs. In addition to covering the annual Hall of Fame ballot for BP, he writes the weekly "Prospectus Hit List" and "Prospectus Hit and Run" during the season. This past summer, he joined Steven Goldman in covering the Yankees at YES Network's "Pinstriped Bible." In recent years, he has contributed to BP's *It Ain't Over 'Til It's Over* and *Mind Game*; Will Carroll's *Juice*; and *Fantasy Baseball Index*. A graduate of Brown University, he once came in third in the famous Milwaukee Brewers sausage race and, in December 2010, was elected to become a member of the Baseball Writers Association of America.

Christina Kahrl is one of the founding five of Baseball Prospectus and its executive editor, as well as a member of the Baseball Writers Association of America. Beyond her regular contributions to BaseballProspectus.com, she has written about baseball and football all over the place, including gigs at *Playboy* and Playboy.com, ESPN.com, and SportsIllustrated.com. Happily settled in Chicago's Rogers Park neighborhood, she volunteers and works with state and local civil rights organizations in her spare time.

Ben Lindbergh is an assistant editor and author of BaseballProspectus.com. A recent graduate of Georgetown University, Ben lives in his native Manhattan with a bookshelf of prior Baseball Prospectus publications and an understanding roommate. When not wearing his BP cap, he works as a baseball analyst for Bloomberg Sports, and he has interned for multiple MLB teams. This is his second year contributing to the annual, and his first helping to assemble the literary sausage as an assistant editor.

Marc Normandin is the Fantasy Baseball editor at BaseballProspectus.com, writes the "Player Profile" column there, and is in his fifth year of contributing to the annual. When not writing for Prospectus, he writes about Boston at RedSoxBeacon.com, contributes to ESPN Insider, and roots for the San Diego Padres from Massachusetts. Marc is the former gaming editor of BlastMagazine.com and the founder of BeyondTheBoxScore.com and sometimes even manages to update his personal, no-particular-topic home page, marcnormandin.com.

Jason Parks is a recent addition to the Baseball Prospectus roster, having spent the past three years covering the Texas Rangers minor league system for Baseball Time in Arlington (BBTiA), while also moonlighting as a scout in Mexico and the New York-Penn League. In addition to his regular writing duties, Jason can be heard on the ever-popular "Up and In: The Baseball Prospectus Podcast," which he cohosts with Kevin Goldstein. A native Texan, Jason now calls Brooklyn his home, living in the Bushwick neighborhood with his lovely wife, Arden, and their three cats.

John Perrotto has been a Baseball Prospectus author since 2007 and served as editor in chief for the Web site during the 2010 season. Among the highlights of his 23-year career covering Major League Baseball are being named Baseball Writer of the Year by sportstalk.com (now ESPN Insider) in 2000, serving on the Baseball Writers Association of America's national board of directors in 2002, serving as an official scorer at the 2006 All-Star Game, winning four Associated Press Sports Editor national awards for baseball writing, and covering 16 World Series and 15 All-Star Games. John is a graduate of Geneva College and lives in Beaver Falls, Pennsylvania, with his wife Brenda.

Eric Seidman is an accountant and statistical analyst from Philadelphia. He authors the "Checking the Numbers" and "Seidnotes" columns for Baseball Prospectus and is the author of *Bridging the Statistical Gap*, a book designed to break down complicated concepts to interested, but intimidated, fans. Eric has also been published in SABR's quarterly newsletter, *By the Numbers*, and *The Baseball Research Journal*. Having completed his MBA, Eric plans to sit for the CPA exam in 2011.

Matt Swartz is the author of the weekly column "Ahead in the Count" for Baseball Prospectus. A government economist, Matt received his Ph.D. in economics from the University of Pennsylvania. In his dissertation, he applied economic theory to the study of dating and marriage as a metaphor for how learning and matching work together. Meanwhile, he married his wife Laura while working on said dissertation, evidence that he knew what he was talking about. Further cementing the case, Matt wrote a supplemental chapter to his dissertation discussing interviewing for jobs and was hired at his current job while writing that chapter. Matt's baseball analysis applies economic insight and statistical methods as well. He and Eric Seidman cocreated SIERA, the luck-neutral ERA estimator. Prior to writing at Baseball Prospectus, Matt wrote for the Phillies' blog The Good Phight and the sabermetric blog Statically Speaking.

Acknowledgments

Tommy Bennett: Sara Sargent, Jeff Zimmerman, R.J. Anderson, Brian Levy.

Cliff Corcoran: Rebecca Lorig, Nancy Boyajy, Gordon and Linda Lorig, Ted Keith, Larry Burke.

Ken Funck: Doug Ross, Ken Spindler, Reid Nichols, Len Kasper.

Christina Kahrl: Nancy Hass, Susan Petrone, David Laurila, Jane Leavy, Bruce Miles, Paul Sullivan, Gordon Wittenmyer, Waltona Manion, Charley Wanamaker, Rick Garcia, Art Johnston, Dalila Fridi, Renee Labrana, Sean Ahmed, Suzy Horn, Bobbie Dittmeier, Jonathan Mayo, Gary Gillette, Brian Borawski, Pam Mazzocco, Jon Scher, Brian Kinsella, Ari Kaplan, Dorothy Seymour Mills, Argentina and Calliope Jane, Jon Coppolella, Ozzie Guillen, Bob Roe, Jeff Neuman, Joe Sheehan, Kim Jones, Kim Ng, Michael Mazzocco, John and Lolita O'Brien, Clyde Kahrl, Allison Kreis, Claudia Perry, Andrea Crain, Cyd Zeigler, Diane Firstman, Douglas Hughes, Leslie Heaphy, Bryant Gumbel, Justine Siegal, Jeff Kaufman, Andromeda Oceane Infiniti, Russell Carleton, John Dewan, Greg Pierce, Marie Taney, John Zajc, Stephanie M. Liscio, Gary Huckabay.

Christina dedicates her work on this book to the late Catherine Mazzocco, a guardian from a cherished childhood, a woman of talent and humor and intelligence, and one of the two best grandmothers a little kid could ever imagine.

Steven Goldman: Fred Allen, Andrew Baharlias, Alex Belth, Mike Ferrin, Clemens Goldman, Eliane Goldman, Reuven Goldman, Sarah Goldman, Dr. Stefanie Goldman, Richard Mohring, Kevin Sullivan.

Kevin Goldstein: Anthony Andro, Jorge Arangure, Ike Barinholtz, Rafael Bello, Rob Biertempfel, Roy Blakely, Kent Bonham, Josh Boyd, Jim Breen, Hank Brockett, Kevin Cabral, Craig Calcaterra, Jim Callis, Steve Canter, Mark Carman, Jay Catalano, James Click, John Coppolella, Jerry Crasnick, Mike Curto, Ken Davidoff, Rocco DeMaro, Nick Devlin, Scot Drucker, Richard Durrett, Dan Evans, Mike Ferrin, Diane Firstman, Adam Fisher, Aaron Fitt, David Forst, Brent Gambill, Sam Geaney, Jeremy Goldstein, Carlos Gomez, Derrick Goold, Tom Gordon, Pedro Grifol, Marcos Grunfeld, Jeff Hem, Jon Heyman, Mike Hindman, Bob Hoffmaster, Toby Hyde, Dave Kaplan, Dan Kaufman, Will Kimmey, Chris Kline, Eric Kubota, Josh Kusnick, Keith Law, Matthew Leach, Zachary Levine, Keith Lieppman, Tim Livingston, Scott Lucas, Kiley McDaniel, Matt Meyers, John Mirabelli, Bill Mitchell, Jon Morosi, Jamey Newburg, Jon Newfry, Mark Newman, Rob Neyer, Margaret Nissen, Josh Norris, Billy Owens, Ned Rice, Phil Rogers, Juan Rodriguez, C. Trent Rosencrans, Amanda Rykoff, Rene Saggiadi, John Sanders, Jon Scher, Jon Shestakofsky, Jesse Spector, Kyle Stark, Ali Thanawalla, Shawn Touney, Rob Warmowski, Josh Yates.

Jay Jaffe: Alex Belth, Chaim Bloom, Nate Brown, Neil deMause, Diane Firstman, Ben Kabak, Steve Kaplowitz, Jonah Keri, Emma Span, Nick Stone, Bruce Taylor, Norm Wamer.

Marc Normandin: Neil deMause, Patrick Sullivan, R.J. Anderson, Dan Scotto, Brandon Warne, Mike Fast, Rob McQuown, Adam Morris, Jeff Sullivan, Jason Wojciechowski, Greg Rybarczyk, Jack Moore, Craig Brown, Richard Wade, Jason Collette, Sagiv Edelman, Sky Kalkman, Jeff Creps, Eric Simon, Chad Finn, Brian MacPherson, Jeff Erickson, Derek VanRiper, Eric Mack, Amanda Comak, Owen Good, Will McDonald, Jorge Arangure, Dan Hayes, Rob Bradford, Dave Brown, Mike Petriello, Michael Jong, Michael Street, Bill Baer, Carson Cistulli, John Burnson, Dan Szymborski, Corey Brock, Matt Klaassen, Aaron Gleeman, Craig Calcaterra, Harry Pavlidis, Dan Turkenkopf, Geoff Young, Kiley McDaniel, John Erhardt, Mike Axisa, Joe Pawlikowski, Ben Kabak, Daniel Moroz.

Jason Parks: Jason Cole, Joey Matschulat, Mike Hindman, Val Kilmer.

Matt Swartz: Laura Swartz, Joel Swartz, Nancy Swartz.

Index